D0180293

Webster's
Comprehensive
Spanish-English
Dictionary

(NEW EDITION)

Webster's
Comprehensive
Spanish-English
Dictionary

NEW EDITION

Created in Cooperation with the Editors of
MERRIAM-WEBSTER

THE
POPULAR
GROUP

Copyright © 2010 by Merriam-Webster, Incorporated

Federal Street Press is a trademark of Federal Street Press,
a Division of Merriam-Webster, Incorporated

All rights reserved. No part of this book covered by the copyrights
hereon may be reproduced or copied in any form or by any means—
graphic, electronic, or mechanical, including photocopying, taping,
or information storage and retrieval systems—without written
permission of the publisher.

This edition published by arrangement with Federal Street Press,
a Division of Merriam-Webster, Incorporated

The Popular Group LLC
1700 Broadway
New York, NY 10019

ISBN 978-1-59027-198-8

Printed in the United States of America

Contents

Índice

Preface

This Spanish-English Dictionary is designed to meet the needs of English and Spanish speakers in a time of ever-expanding communication among the countries of the Western Hemisphere. It is intended for language learners, teachers, office workers, tourists, business travelers—anyone who needs to communicate effectively in the Spanish and English languages as they are spoken and written in the Americas.

This new dictionary provides accurate and up-to-date coverage of current vocabulary in both languages, as well as abundant examples of words used in context to illustrate idiomatic usage. The selection of Spanish words and idioms was based on evidence drawn from a wide variety of modern Latin-American sources and interpreted by trained Merriam-Webster bilingual lexicographers. The English entries were chosen by Merriam-Webster editors from the most recent Merriam-Webster dictionaries, and they represent the current basic vocabulary of American English.

All of this material is presented in a format which is based firmly upon and, in many important ways, is similar to the traditional styling found in the Merriam-Webster monolingual dictionaries. The reader who is familiar with Merriam-Webster dictionaries will immediately recognize this style, with its emphasis on convenience and ease of use, clarity and conciseness of the information presented, precise discrimination of senses, and frequent inclusion of example phrases showing words in actual use. Also included are pronunciations (in the International Phonetic Alphabet) for all English words, full coverage of irregular verbs in both languages, a section on basic Spanish grammar, written in English for the English speaker, and one on English grammar written in Spanish, a section of the most common Spanish and English abbreviations, and a detailed Explanatory Notes section, written in English and Spanish, which answers any questions the reader might have concerning the use of this book.

New to this edition is a section of 100 common English idioms, a restructured chart of numbers showing English and Spanish names side by side, as well as sections covering the nations of the world and the metric system. We believe the user will find this an extraordinarily helpful resource.

Prefacio

Este diccionario está diseñado con el fin de satisfacer las necesidades de lenguaje de angloparlantes e hispanoparlantes en una era de continuo crecimiento en la comunicación entre los países del hemisferio occidental. El diccionario está destinado a los estudiantes de estos idiomas, así como a los maestros, oficinistas, turistas, viajeros de negocios, o a cualquier persona que necesite expresarse claramente y eficazmente en inglés o español tal como se hablan y se escriben en las Américas.

Este diccionario provee una cobertura exacta y actualizada del vocabulario corriente en ambos idiomas, así como abundantes ejemplos de palabras empleadas en contexto para ilustrar su uso idiomático. La selección de vocablos y modismos en español se efectuó a base de una vasta gama de fuentes latinoamericanas modernas y fue interpretada por especialistas en lexicografía bilingüe de Merriam-Webster. Las voces inglesas fueron extraídas de los más recientes diccionarios Merriam-Webster por editores de Merriam-Webster, y representan el vocabulario básico actual del inglés americano.

El material se ha organizado en un formato basado en el estilo tradicional característico de los diccionarios monolingües Merriam-Webster. El lector ya familiarizado con los diccionarios Merriam-Webster reconocerá de inmediato este estilo, con su énfasis en la conveniencia y la facilidad de uso, en la claridad y la concisión de la información presentada, en el preciso discernimiento de los sentidos de cada vocablo, y en la frecuente inclusión de frases ejemplares que ilustran el uso de una palabra. Aparecen también pronunciaciones (compuestas en el Alfabeto Fonético Internacional) para todas las voces inglesas, así como una cobertura plena de verbos irregulares en ambos idiomas, una sección de gramática inglesa básica, tablas de abreviaturas comunes, y una sección de Notas explicativas que contesta en detalle cualquier pregunta que pueda tener el lector tocante al uso de este libro.

Esta edición incluye una sección de cien modismos comunes en inglés, una tabla de números rediseñada para mostrar los nombres en inglés y en español uno al lado del otro, y secciones nuevas sobre las naciones del mundo y el sistema métrico. Creemos que éstas proporcionarán al lector un recurso extraordinariamente útil.

Explanatory Notes

Entries

A boldface letter, word, or phrase appearing flush with the left-hand margin of each column of type is a **main entry** or entry word.

> **cafetalero¹, -ra** *adj* . . .
> **eye-opener** . . . *n* . . .
> **walk out** *vi* . . .

The main entry, together with the material that follows it on the same line and succeeding indented lines, constitutes a **dictionary entry**.

Alphabetical order throughout the book follows the order of the English alphabet, without regard to intervening spaces or hyphens, with one exception: words beginning with the Spanish letter *ñ* follow all entries for the letter *n*.

Homographs (words with the same spelling) having different parts of speech are usually given separate dictionary entries and are distinguished by superscript numerals.

> **hail¹** . . . *vt* . . .
> **hail²** *n* . . .
> **hail³** *interj* . . .
> **madrileño¹, -ña** *adj* . . .
> **madrileño², -ña** *n* . . .

Homographs having the same part of speech are normally included at the same dictionary entry, without regard to their different semantic origins. On the English-to-Spanish side, however, separate entries are made if the homographs have distinct inflected forms or if they have distinct pronunciations.

A pair of **guide words** is printed at the top of each page, indicating the first and last main entries that appear on that page.

When a main entry is followed by the word *or* and another spelling, the two spellings are **variants** and both are standard.

> **jailer** *or* **jailor** . . . *n* . . .
> **quizá** *or* **quizás** *adv* . . .

Occasionally, a variant spelling is used only for a particular sense of a word. In these cases, the variant spelling is listed after the sense number of the sense to which it pertains:

> **electric** . . . *adj* **1** *or* **electrical** . . .

Sometimes the entry word is used interchangeably with a longer phrase containing the entry word. For the purposes of this dictionary, such phrases are considered variants of the headword:

> **bunk²** *n* **1** *or* **bunk bed** . . .
> **angina** *nf* **1** *or* **angina de pecho** : angina . . .

Variant wordings of boldface phrases may also be shown:

> **madera** *nf* . . . **3 madera dura** *or* **madera noble** . . .
> **atención¹** *nf* . . . **2 poner atención** *or* **prestar atención** . . .

A main entry may be followed by one or more derivatives or by a homograph with a different functional label. These are **run-on entries**. Each is introduced by a boldface dash and each has a functional label. They are not defined, however, since their equivalents can be readily derived by adding the corresponding foreign-language suffix to the terms used to define the entry word or, in the case of homographs, simply substituting the appropriate part of speech:

> **illegal** . . . *adj* : ilegal — **illegally** *adv*
> (the Spanish adverb is *ilegalmente*)
> **transferir** . . . *vt* TRASLADAR : to transfer
> — **transferible** *adj* (the English adjective is *transferable*)
> **Bosnian** *n* : bosnio *m*, -nia *f* — **Bosnian** *adj* (the Spanish adjective is *bosnio, -nia*)

On the Spanish side of the book, reflexive verbs are sometimes run on undefined:

> **enrollar** *vt* : to roll up, to coil — **enrollarse** *vr*

The absence of a definition means that *enrollarse* has the simple reflexive meaning "to become rolled up or coiled," "to roll itself up."

A main entry may be followed by one or more phrases containing the entry word or an inflected form of the entry word. These are **bold notes**. Each bold note is defined at its own numbered sense:

> **álamo** *nm* 1 : poplar 2 **álamo temblón**
> : aspen
> **hold**[1] . . . *vi* . . . 4 **to hold to** : . . . 5 **to hold**
> **with** : . . .

If the bold note consists only of the entry word and a single preposition, the entry word is represented by a boldface swung dash ∼.

> **pegar** . . . *vi* . . . 3 ∼ **con** : to match, to
> go with . . .

The same bold note phrase may appear at two or more senses if it has more than one distinct meaning:

> **wear**[1] . . . *vt* . . . 3 **to wear out** : gastar
> <he wore out his shoes . . . > 4 **to wear**
> **out** EXHAUST : agotar, fatigar <to wear
> oneself out . . . > . . .
> **estar** . . . *vi* . . . 15 ∼ **por** : to be in favor
> of 16 ∼ **por** : to be about to <está por
> cerrar . . . > . . .

If the use of the entry word is commonly restricted to one particular phrase, then a bold note may be given as the entry word's only sense:

> **ward**[1] . . . *vt* **to ward off** : . . .

Pronunciation of English Entry Words

The matter between a pair of brackets [ ] following the entry word of an English-to-Spanish entry indicates the **pronunciation**. The symbols used are explained in the chart of Pronunciation Symbols.

The presence of variant pronunciations indicates that not all educated speakers pronounce words the same way. A second-place variant is not to be regarded as less acceptable than the pronunciation that is given first. It may, in fact, be used by as many educated speakers as the first variant, but the requirements of the printed page are such that one must precede the other:

> **tomato** [tə'meɪt̬o, -'mɑ-] . . .

When a compound word has less than a full pronunciation, the missing part is to be supplied from the pronunciation at the entry for the unpronounced element of the compound:

> gamma ray [ˈgæmə] . . .
> ray [ˈreɪ] . . .
> smoke¹ [ˈsmoːk] . . .
> smoke detector [dɪˈtɛktər] . . .

In general, no pronunciation is given for open compounds consisting of two or more English words that are main entries at their own alphabetical place:

> water lily *n* : nenúfar *m*

Only the first entry in a series of numbered homographs is given a pronunciation if their pronunciations are the same:

> dab¹ [ˈdæb] *vt* . . .
> dab² *n* . . .

No pronunciation is shown for principal parts of verbs that are formed by regular suffixation, nor for other derivative words formed by common suffixes.

Pronunciation of Spanish Entry Words

Spanish pronunciation is highly regular, so no pronunciations are given for most Spanish-to-English entries. Exceptions have been made for certain words (such as foreign borrowings) whose Spanish pronunciations are not evident from their spellings:

> pizza [ˈpitsa, ˈpisa] . . .
> footing [ˈfuˌtɪŋ] . . .

Functional Labels

A **functional label** is an italic label indicating a part of speech or some other functional classification of the main entry. It follows the pronunciation if one is given. The eight traditional parts of speech, adjective, adverb, conjunction, interjection, noun, preposition, pronoun, and verb, are indicated as follows:

> daily² *adj* . . .
> vagamente *adv* . . .
> and . . . *conj* . . .
> huy *interj* . . .
> jackal . . . *n* . . .
> para *prep* . . .
> neither³ *pron* . . .
> leer . . . *v* . . .

Verbs that are intransitive are labeled *vi*, and verbs that are transitive are labeled *vt*. Entries for verbs that are both transitive and intransitive are labeled *v;* if such an entry includes irregular verb inflections, it is labeled *v* immediately after the main entry, with the labels *vt* and *vi* serving to introduce transitive and intransitive subdivisions when both are present:

> deliberar *vi* : to deliberate
> necessitate . . . *vt* -tated; -tating : necesi-
> tar, requerir
> satisfy . . . *v* -fied; -fying *vt* . . . — *vi* . . .

Two other labels are used to indicate functional classifications of verbs: *v aux* (auxiliary verb) and *v impers* (impersonal verb).

> may . . . *v aux, past* might . . .
> haber¹ . . . *v aux* 1 : have . . . — *v impers*
> 1 hay : there is, there are . . .

In Spanish-to-English noun entries, italic **gender labels** indicate masculine (*m*), feminine (*f*), or masculine or feminine (*mf*) genders of nouns.

> **magnesio** *nm* . . .
> **galaxia** *nf* . . .
> **turista** *nmf* . . .

If both the masculine and feminine forms are shown for a noun referring to a person, the label is simply *n:*

> **director, -tora** *n* . . .

Spanish noun equivalents of English entry words are also labeled for gender:

> **amnesia** . . . *n* : amnesia *f*
> **earache** . . . *n* : dolor *m* de oído
> **gamekeeper** . . . *n* : guardabosque *mf*

The **plurals** of nouns (inflected forms) are shown in this dictionary when they are irregular, when plural suffixation brings about a change in accentuation or in the spelling of the root word, when an English noun ends in a consonant plus *-o* or in *-ey*, when an English noun ends in *-oo*, when an English noun is a compound that pluralizes any element but the last, when a noun has variant plurals, or whenever the dictionary user might have reasonable doubts regarding the spelling of a plural:

> **tooth** . . . *n, pl* **teeth** . . .
> **garrafón** *nm, pl* **-fones** . . .
> **potato** . . . *n, pl* **-toes** . . .
> **abbey** . . . *n, pl* **-beys** . . .
> **cuckoo**[2] *n, pl* **-oos** . . .
> **brother-in-law** . . . *n, pl* **brothers-in-law** . . .
> **quail**[2] *n, pl* **quail** *or* **quails** . . .
> **hábitat** *nm, pl* **-tats** . . .
> **tahúr** *nm, pl* **tahúres** . . .

Cutback inflected forms are used for most nouns on the English-to-Spanish side, regardless of the number of syllables. On the Spanish-to-English side, cutback inflections are given for nouns that have three or more syllables; plurals for shorter words are written out in full:

> **shampoo**[2] *n, pl* **-poos** . . .
> **calamity** . . . *n, pl* **-ties** . . .
> **mouse** . . . *n, pl* **mice** . . .
> **sartén** *nmf, pl* **sartenes** . . .
> **hámster** *nm, pl* **hámsters** . . .
> **federación** *nf, pl* **-ciones** . . .

If only one gender form has a plural which is irregular, that plural form will be given with the appropriate label:

> **campeón, -ona** *n, mpl* **-ones** : champion

The plurals of nouns are usually not shown when the base word is unchanged by the addition of the regular plural suffix or when the noun is unlikely to occur in the plural:

> **apple** . . . *n* : manzana *f*
> **inglés**[3] *nm* : English (language)

Nouns that are plural in form and that regularly occur in plural constructions are labeled as *npl* (for English nouns), *nmpl* (for Spanish masculine nouns), or *nfpl* (for Spanish feminine nouns):

> **knickers** . . . *npl* . . .

> enseres *nmpl* . . .
> mancuernas *nfpl* . . .

Entry words that are unchanged in the plural are labeled *ns & pl* (for English nouns), *nms & pl* (for Spanish masculine nouns), *nfs & pl* (for Spanish feminine nouns), and *nmfs & pl* (for Spanish gender-variable nouns):

> deer . . . *ns & pl* . . .
> lavaplatos *nms & pl* . . .
> tesis *nfs & pl* . . .
> rompehuelgas *nmfs & pl* . . .

The **principal parts of English verbs** are shown when they are irregular, when suffixation brings about a change in spelling of the root word, when the verb ends in *-ey*, when there are variant inflected forms, or whenever it is believed that the dictionary user might have reasonable doubts about the spelling of an inflected form:

> break¹ . . . *v* broke . . .; broken . . .; break-
>   ing . . .
> drag¹ . . . *v* dragged; dragging . . .
> monkey¹ . . . *vi* -keyed; -keying . . .
> label¹ . . . *vt* -beled *or* -belled; -beling *or*
>   -belling . . .
> imagine . . . *vt* -ined; -ining . . .

Cutback inflected forms are usually used when the verb has two or more syllables:

> multiply . . . *v* -plied; -plying . . .
> bevel¹ . . . *v* -eled *or* -elled; -eling *or*
>   -elling . . .
> forgo *or* forego . . . *vt* -went; -gone;
>   -going . . .
> commit . . . *vt* -mitted; -mitting . . .

The principal parts of an English verb are not shown when the base word is unchanged by suffixation:

> delay¹ . . . *vt*
> pitch¹ . . . *vt*

Entries for **irregular Spanish verbs** are cross-referenced by number to the model conjugations appearing in the Conjugation of Spanish Verbs section:

> abnegarse {49} *vr* . . .
> volver {89} *vi* . . .

Entries for Spanish verbs with regular conjugations are not cross-referenced; however, model conjugations for regular Spanish verbs are included in the Conjugation of Spanish Verbs section.

The **comparative and superlative forms** of English adjective and adverb main entries are shown when suffixation brings about a change in spelling of the root word, when the inflection is irregular, and when there are variant inflected forms:

> wet² *adj* wetter; wettest . . .
> good² *adj* better . . .; best . . .
> evil¹ . . . *adj* eviler *or* eviller; evilest *or*
>   evillest . . .

The superlative forms of adjectives and adverbs of two or more syllables are usually cut back; the superlative is shown in full, however, when it is desirable to indicate the pronunciation of the inflected form:

> early¹ . . . *adv* earlier; -est . . .
> gaudy . . . *adj* gaudier; -est . . .
> secure² *adj* -curer; -est . . .

> *but*
> **young**[1] . . . *adj* **younger** [ˈjʌŋɡər];
> **youngest** [-ɡəst] . . .

At a few entries only the superlative form is shown:

> **mere** *adj, superlative* **merest** . . .

The absence of the comparative form indicates that there is no evidence of its use.

The comparative and superlative forms of adjectives and adverbs are usually not shown when the base word is unchanged by suffixation:

> **quiet**[3] *adj* 1 . . .

Usage

Two types of **usage labels** are used in this dictionary—regional and stylistic. Spanish words that are limited in use to a specific area or areas of Latin America, or to Spain, are given labels indicating the countries in which they are most commonly used:

> **guarachear** *vi Cuba, PRi fam* . . .
> **bucket** . . . *n* : . . . cubeta *f Mex*

The following regional labels are used in this book: *Arg* (Argentina), *Bol* (Bolivia), *CA* (Central America), *Car* (Caribbean), *Chile* (Chile), *Col* (Colombia), *CoRi* (Costa Rica), *Cuba* (Cuba), *DomRep* (Dominican Republic), *Ecua* (Ecuador), *Sal* (El Salvador), *Guat* (Guatemala), *Hond* (Honduras), *Mex* (Mexico), *Nic* (Nicaragua), *Pan* (Panama), *Par* (Paraguay), *Peru* (Peru), *PRi* (Puerto Rico), *Spain* (Spain), *Uru* (Uruguay), *Ven* (Venezuela).

Since this book focuses on the Spanish spoken in Latin America, only the most common regionalisms from Spain have been included in order to allow for more thorough coverage of Latin-American forms.

A number of Spanish words are given a *fam* (familiar) label as well, indicating that these words are suitable for informal contexts but would not normally be used in formal writing or speaking. The stylistic label *usu considered vulgar* is added for a word which is usually considered vulgar or offensive but whose widespread use justifies its inclusion in this book. The label is intended to warn the reader that the word in question may be inappropriate in polite conversation.

Definitions are sometimes preceded by parenthetical **usage notes** that give supplementary semantic information:

> **not** . . . *adv* 1 (*used to form a negative*)
> : no . . .
> **within**[2] *prep* . . . 2 (*in expressions of distance*) : . . . 3 (*in expressions of time*)
> : . . .
> **e**[2] *conj* (*used instead of* y *before words beginning with* i *or* hi) : . . .
> **poder**[1] . . . *v aux* . . . 2 (*expressing possibility*) : . . . 3 (*expressing permission*)
> : . . .

Additional semantic orientation is also sometimes given in the form of parenthetical notes appearing within the definition:

> **calibrate** . . . *vt* . . . : calibrar (armas),
> graduar (termómetros)
> **palco** *nm* : box (in a theater or stadium)

Occasionally a usage note is used in place of a definition. This is usually done when the entry word has no single foreign-language equivalent. This type of usage note will be accompanied by examples of common use:

> shall . . . *v aux* . . . 1 (*used to express a*
> *command*) <you shall do as I say
> : harás lo que te digo> . . .

Definitions are sometimes followed by **verbal illustrations** that show a typical use of the word in context or a common idiomatic usage. These verbal illustrations include a translation and are enclosed in angle brackets:

> lejos *adv* 1 : far away, distant <a lo lejos
> : in the distance, far off> . . .
> make[1] . . . 9 . . . : ganar <to make a living
> : ganarse la vida> . . .

Senses

A boldface colon is used to introduce a definition and boldface numerals separate the senses of a word:

> fable . . . *n* : fábula *f*
> laguna *nf* 1 : lagoon 2 : lacuna, gap

Whenever some information (such as a synonym, a boldface word or phrase, a usage note, a cross-reference, or a label) follows a sense number, it applies only to that specific numbered sense:

> abanico *nm* . . . 2 GAMA : . . .
> tonic[2] *n* . . . 2 *or* tonic water : . . .
> grillo *nm* . . . 2 grillos *nmpl* : . . .
> fairy . . . *n, pl* fairies . . . 2 fairy tale : . . .
> myself . . . *pron* 1 (*used reflexively*) : . . .
> pike . . . *n* . . . 3 → turnpike
> atado[2] *nm* . . . 2 *Arg* : . . .

Cross-references

Three different kinds of **cross-references** are used in this dictionary: synonymous, cognate, and inflectional. In each instance the cross-reference is readily recognized by the boldface arrow following the entry word.

Synonymous and cognate cross-references indicate that a definition at the entry cross-referred to can be substituted for the entry word:

> scapula . . . → shoulder blade
> amuck . . . → amok

An inflectional cross-reference is used to identify the entry word as an inflected form of another word (as a noun or verb):

> fue, etc. → ir, ser
> mice → mouse

Synonyms

At many entries or senses in this book, a **synonym** in small capital letters is provided before the boldface colon and the following defining text. These synonyms are all main entries or bold notes elsewhere in the book. They serve as a helpful guide to the meaning of the entry or sense and also give the reader an additional term that might be substituted in a similar context. On the English-to-Spanish side synonyms are particularly abundant, since special care has been taken to guide the English speaker—by means of synonyms, verbal illustrations, or usage notes—to the meaning of the Spanish terms at each sense of a multisense entry.

Notas explicativas

Entradas

Toda letra, palabra o frase en negrita que aparece al extremo del margen izquierdo de la columna de texto de la que forma parte es una **entrada principal**, o lema.

> **cafetalero**[1], **-ra** *adj* . . .
> **eye-opener** . . . *n* . . .
> **walk out** *vi* . . .

La entrada principal, junto con el texto que la sigue tanto en la misma línea como en las líneas sangradas subsiguientes, constituyen una **entrada del diccionario**. El orden alfabético del diccionario concuerda con el orden del alfabeto inglés, con la excepción de las entradas españolas que comienzan con la letra *ñ-*. Éstas aparecen después de las entradas que comienzan con *n-*. Las entradas principales aparecen alfabéticamente, letra por letra, sin tener en cuenta guiones o espacios intermediarios.

Los homógrafos (palabras que se escriben igual) que pertenecen a distintas categorías gramaticales por lo general aparecen en entradas individuales. A estas entradas se les identifica con un número superíndice:

> **hail**[1] . . . *vt* . . .
> **hail**[2] *n* . . .
> **hail**[3] *interj* . . .
> **madrileño**[1], **-ña** *adj* . . .
> **madrileño**[2], **-ña** *n* . . .

Los homógrafos que se clasifican bajo una misma categoría gramatical aparecen incluidos bajo la misma entrada del diccionario, sin tener en cuenta diferencias de origen semántico. Sin embargo, en la sección Inglés-Español se les asigna a cada uno de estos homógrafos una entrada individual si existe entre ellos alguna diferencia ya sea en la inflexión o en la pronunciación.

En el margen superior de cada página aparecen dos **palabras guía** que indican la primera y última entrada de la página correspondiente.

Cuando una entrada principal aparece seguida de la palabra *or* y otra ortografía, las dos ortografías se consideran **variantes**. Ambas ortografías son estándar, y cualquiera de las dos puede usarse según se prefiera:

> **jailer** *or* **jailor** . . . *n* . . .
> **quizá** *or* **quizás** *adv* . . .

Hay ocasiones en las que una variante ortográfica se emplea únicamente para una de las acepciones de una palabra. En tales casos, la variante ortográfica aparece después del número de la acepción a la cual corresponde:

> **electric** . . . *adj* **1** *or* **electrical** . . .

En otros casos, el lema puede intercambiarse con una frase de la que forma parte. Para los fines de este diccionario, tales frases se consideran como variantes del lema:

> **bunk**[2] *n* **1** *or* **bunk bed** . . .
> **angina** *nf* **1** *or* **angina de pecho** : an-
> gina . . .

Las frases en negrita también pueden, a su vez, presentar variantes:

> **madera** *nf* . . . **3 madera dura** *or* **madera**
> **noble** . . .
> **atención**[1] *nf* . . . **2 poner atención** *or*
> **prestar atención** . . .

Una entrada principal puede ser seguida por uno o más derivados del lema, o de un homógrafo de distinta categoría gramatical. Éstas son **entradas secundarias**. Cada una de estas entradas aparece después de un guión en negrita, y cada una posee su propio calificativo. Tales entradas aparecen sin definición, ya que sus equivalentes en el idioma extranjero pueden derivarse fácilmente al combinar la definición del lema con el sufijo correspondiente, o como sucede con los homógrafos, al sustituir la categoría gramatical por otra. Véase por ejemplo:

> **illegal** . . . *adj* : ilegal — **illegally** *adv* (el
> adverbio español es *ilegalmente*)
> **transferir** . . . *vt* TRASLADAR : to transfer
> — **transferible** *adj* (el adjetivo inglés es
> *transferable*)
> **Bosnian** *n* : bosniom, -nia *f* — **Bosnian**
> *adj* (el adjetivo español es *bosnio, -nia*)

En la sección Español-Inglés, los verbos pronominales aparecen en ocasiones como entradas secundarias, sin definición:

> **enrollar** *vt* : to roll up, to coil — **en-**
> **rollarse** *vr*

La ausencia de la definición en este caso comunica al lector de habla inglesa que el verbo *enrollarse* tiene una función expresamente reflexiva. Esto elimina la necesidad de agregar una definición que resultaría superflua como "to become rolled up or coiled," o "to roll itself up."

Una entrada principal puede aparecer acompañada de una o varias **frases en negrita** (generalmente locuciones o términos compuestos) que contienen ya sea el lema, o una inflexión de éste. Cada una de estas frases se presenta como una de las acepciones numeradas del lema:

> **álamo** *nm* **1** : poplar **2** **álamo temblón**
> : aspen
> **hold**[1] . . . *vi* . . . **4 to hold to** : . . . **5 to hold**
> **with** : . . .

Cuando la frase en negrita consta únicamente de una combinación del lema con una preposición, el lema se representa entonces por medio de una tilde en negrita ~.

> **pegar** . . . *vi* . . . **3** ~ **con** : to match, to
> go with . . .

Si la frase en cuestión tiene más de un sentido, entonces puede aparecer en dos o más acepciones de la misma entrada principal:

> **wear**[1] . . . *vt* . . . **3 to wear out** : gastar <he
> wore out his shoes . . . > **4 to wear out**
> EXHAUST : agotar, fatigar <to wear
> oneself out . . . > . . .
> **estar** . . . *vi* . . . **15** ~ **por** : to be in favor
> of **16** ~ **por** : to be about to <está por
> cerrar . . . > . . .

Si el uso común de una palabra está generalmente limitado a una frase determinada, la frase es presentada como la única acepción del lema:

> **ward**[1] . . . *vt* **to ward off** : . . . .

Pronunciación de los lemas ingleses

El texto que aparece entre corchetes [ ] inmediatamente después de un lema en la sección Inglés-Español indica la **pronunciación** del lema. Para una explicación de los símbolos empleados, véase la tabla titulada Símbolos de pronunciación.

La presencia de variantes de pronunciación indica que no todos los hablantes educados del idioma pronuncian una palabra determinada de igual forma. El hecho de que una variante aparezca después de otra no significa que sea menos apropiada que la que aparece primero. De hecho, la segunda variante puede ser tan común como la primera, pero las restricciones de la página impresa exigen que una preceda a la otra.

>   **tomato** [tə'meɪt̬o, -'mɑ-] . . .

Cuando un término compuesto aparece con sólo una pronunciación parcial, la pronunciación del resto del término puede obtenerse bajo la entrada correspondiente a la palabra cuya pronunciación se ha omitido:

>   **gamma ray** ['gæmə] . . .
>   **ray** ['reɪ] . . .
>   **smoke**[1] ['smoːk] . . .
>   **smoke detector** [dɪ'tɛktər] . . .

En general, no se indica la pronunciación de términos compuestos cuando éstos están formados de dos o más palabras inglesas que aparecen en el diccionario como entradas principales:

>   **water lily** *n* : nenúfar *m*

Solamente la primera entrada en una serie de homógrafos numerados incluye la pronunciación si ésta es la misma para todos los otros homógrafos:

>   **dab**[1] ['dæb] *vt* . . .
>   **dab**[2] *n* . . .

No se indica la pronunciación de las partes principales de los verbos formados por sufijación regular, ni por otros derivados formados por sufijos comunes.

Pronunciación de los lemas españoles

Dada la alta regularidad de la pronunciación del español, no se indica la pronunciación de la mayor parte de las entradas que aparecen en la sección Español-Inglés. Sin embargo, se han hecho excepciones para ciertas palabras (tales como aquéllas que se han adaptado de otras lenguas) cuya pronunciación en español no puede derivarse naturalmente de su ortografía:

>   **pizza** ['pitsɑ, 'pisɑ] *nf* : pizza
>   **footing** ['fuˌtɪŋ] . . .

Calificativos funcionales

Un **calificativo** en itálicas que indica la **categoría gramatical** u otra clasificación funcional del lema aparece inmediatamente después de la pronunciación, o si la pronunciación se ha omitido, después del lema. Las ocho categorías gramaticales tradicionales, el adjetivo, el adverbio, la conjunción, la interjección, el sustantivo, la preposición, el pronombre, y el verbo, se indican como sigue:

>   **daily**[2] *adj* . . .
>   **vagamente** *adv* . . .
>   **and** . . . *conj* . . .

> **huy** *interj* . . .
> **jackal** . . . *n* . . .
> **para** *prep* . . .
> **neither**[3] *pron* . . .
> **leer** . . . *v* . . .

Los verbos intransitivos se identifican con el calificativo *vi*, y los transitivos, *vt*. Las entradas para aquellos verbos que son a la vez transitivos e intransitivos llevan el calificativo *v*. Si una de estas entradas incluye inflexiones irregulares, el calificativo *v* aparece inmediatamente después del lema, y las acepciones transitivas e intransitivas son introducidas con los calificativos *vt* y *vi* respectivamente.

> **deliberar** *vi* : to deliberate
> **necessitate** . . . *vt* -tated; -tating : necesi-
> tar, requerir
> **satisfy** . . . *v* -fied; -fying *vt* . . . — *vi* . . .

Por último, dos otros calificativos se emplean para indicar la clasificación funcional de los verbos: *v aux* (verbo auxiliar) y *v impers* (verbo impersonal).

> **may** . . . *v aux, past* **might** . . .
> **haber**[1] . . . *v aux* **1** : have . . . — *v impers*
> **1 hay** : there is, there are . . .

En toda entrada cuyo lema es un sustantivo español, el **género** de éste se indica con los calificativos *m* (masculino), *f* (femenino), o *mf* (masculino o femenino), que aparecen inmediatamente después del calificativo funcional:

> **magnesio** *nm* . . .
> **galaxia** *nf* . . .
> **turista** *nmf* . . .

Si se dan las formas tanto masculina como femenina de un sustantivo que denota a una persona, se aplica el calificativo *n*.

> **director, -tora** *n* . . .

Todo sustantivo español que aparece como definición de un lema inglés es acompañado de un calificativo de género:

> **amnesia** . . . *n* : amnesia *f*
> **earache** . . . *n* : dolor *m* de oído
> **gamekeeper** . . . *n* : guardabosque *mf*

En este diccionario se indica el **plural** de un sustantivo en los siguientes casos: cuando el plural es irregular, cuando la sufijación del plural produce un cambio en la acentuación o la ortografía del vocablo raíz, cuando un sustantivo inglés termina en una consonante seguida de -o o de -ey, cuando un sustantivo inglés termina en -oo, cuando un sustantivo inglés es un término compuesto del cual el elemento a pluralizar no es el último, cuando un sustantivo tiene variantes en el plural, o cuando podría suscitarse una duda razonable en cuanto a la ortografía del plural:

> **tooth** . . . *n, pl* **teeth** . . .
> **garrafón** *nm, pl* -fones . . .
> **potato** . . . *n, pl* -toes . . .
> **abbey** . . . *n, pl* -beys . . .
> **cuckoo**[2] *n, pl* -oos . . .
> **brother-in-law** . . . *n, pl* **brothers-in-law** . . .
> **quail**[2] *n, pl* **quail** *or* **quails** . . .
> **hábitat** *nm, pl* -tats . . .
> **tahúr** *nm, pl* **tahúres** . . .

En la sección Inglés-Español, la forma plural de la mayor parte de los sustantivos se indica por medio de una inflexión reducida, sin tener en cuenta el número de sílabas que el lema contenga. En la sección Español-Inglés, se dan inflexiones reducidas sólo para aquellos sustantivos que contengan tres o más sílabas, mientras que las formas plurales de sustantivos más breves se presentan enteras:

> shampoo[2] *n, pl* -poos . . .
> calamity . . . *n, pl* -ties . . .
> mouse . . . *n, pl* mice . . .
> sartén *nmf, pl* sartenes . . .
> hámster *nm, pl* hámsters . . .
> federación *nf, pl* -ciones . . .

Si se produce un plural irregular en sólo uno de los géneros, la forma plural se da con el calificativo correspondiente:

> campeón, -ona *n, mpl* -ones : champion

La forma plural de un sustantivo generalmente no aparece si el vocablo raíz permanece inalterado por la adición del sufijo plural regular, o cuando no es probable que el sustantivo se use en el plural:

> apple . . . *n* : manzana *f*
> inglés[3] *nm* : English (language)

Aquellos sustantivos que son plurales en forma y que ocurren regularmente en construcciones plurales son clasificados *npl* (si son sustantivos ingleses), *nmpl* (si son sustantivos masculinos españoles), o *nfpl* (si son sustantivos femeninos españoles):

> knickers . . . *npl* . . .
> enseres *nmpl* . . .
> mancuernas *nfpl* . . .

Toda entrada que permanece inalterada en el plural es clasificada *ns & pl* (sustantivos ingleses), *nms & pl* (sustantivos masculinos españoles), *nfs & pl* (sustantivos femeninos españoles), y *nmfs & pl* (sustantivos españoles de género variable):

> deer . . . *ns & pl* . . .
> lavaplatos *nms & pl* . . .
> tesis *nfs & pl* . . .
> rompehuelgas *nmfs & pl* . . .

En la sección Inglés-Español, las **partes principales de los verbos** se indican en los siguientes casos: cuando el verbo es irregular, cuando la sufijación produce un cambio en la ortografía del vocablo raíz, cuando el verbo termina en *-ey*, cuando una inflexión tiene variantes, o cuando puede suscitarse una duda razonable en cuanto a la ortografía de una inflexión:

> break[1] . . . *v* broke . . . ; broken . . . ; break-
> ing . . .
> drag[1] . . . *v* dragged; dragging . . .
> monkey[1] . . . *vi* -keyed; -keying . . .
> label[1] . . . *vt* -beled *or* -belled; -beling *or*
> -belling . . .
> imagine . . . *vt* -ined; -ining . . .

Si el verbo consta de dos o más sílabas, se da generalmente una forma reducida de la inflexión:

> multiply . . . *v* -plied; -plying . . .
> bevel[1] . . . *v* -eled *or* -elled; -eling *or*
> -elling . . .
> forgo *or* forego . . . *vt* -went; -gone;
> -going . . .
> commit . . . *vt* -mitted; -mitting . . .

Las partes principales de un verbo inglés no aparecen cuando el vocablo raíz permanece inalterado por la sufijación.

> **delay**[1] . . . *vt*
> **pitch**[1] . . . *vt*

En cada entrada correspondiente a un **verbo irregular español** aparece un número entre llaves que remite al lector a los modelos de conjugación que aparecen en la sección titulada Conjugación de verbos españoles:

> **abnegarse** {49} *vr* . . .
> **volver** {89} *vi* . . .

Aunque estas remisiones no aparecen en las entradas que corresponden a los verbos regulares españoles, los modelos de conjugación de estas formas pueden consultarse en la susodicha sección.

Las entradas principales de adjetivos y adverbios ingleses incluyen las **formas comparativas y superlativas** cuando la sufijación produce un cambio en la ortografía del vocablo raíz, cuando la inflexión es de forma irregular, o cuando existen variantes de la inflexión:

> **wet**[2] *adj* **wetter; wettest** . . .
> **good**[2] *adj* **better** . . . ; **best** . . .
> **evil**[1] . . . *adj* **eviler** *or* **eviller; evilest** *or*
> **evillest** . . .

Las formas superlativas de adjetivos y adverbios de dos o más sílabas son presentadas generalmente en forma reducida:

> **early**[1] . . . *adv* **earlier; -est** . . .
> **gaudy** . . . *adj* **gaudier; -est** . . .
> **secure**[2] *adj* **-curer; -est** . . .
> *pero*
> **young**[1] . . . *adj* **younger** [ˈjʌŋgər];
> **youngest** [-gəst] . . .

En algunas entradas aparece únicamente la forma superlativa:

> **mere** *adj, superlative* **merest** . . .

La ausencia de la forma comparativa indica que no existe evidencia suficiente de su uso.

Las formas comparativas y superlativas de los adjetivos y adverbios generalmente no se muestran si la sufijación no altera el vocablo raíz:

> **quiet**[3] *adj* **1** . . .

Uso

En este diccionario se emplean dos tipos de **calificativo de uso**: regional y estilístico. Las palabras españolas cuyo uso se limita a ciertas regiones de Latinoamérica o a España, reciben calificativos que indican los países en que suelen usarse con más frecuencia:

> **guarachear** *vi Cuba, PRi fam* . . .
> **bucket** . . . *n* : . . . **cubeta** *f Mex*

Los siguientes calificativos regionales se han empleado en la redacción de este libro: *Arg* (Argentina), *Bol* (Bolivia), *CA* (Centroamérica), *Car* (el Caribe), *Chile* (Chile), *Col* (Colombia), *CoRi* (Costa Rica), *Cuba* (Cuba), *DomRep* (República Dominicana), *Ecua* (Ecuador), *Sal* (El Salvador), *Guat* (Guatemala), *Hond* (Honduras), *Mex* (México), *Nic* (Nicaragua), *Pan* (Panamá), *Par*

(Paraguay), *Peru* (Perú), *PRi* (Puerto Rico), *Spain* (España), *Uru* (Uruguay), *Ven* (Venezuela).

Dado el foco primordialmente latinoamericano de este diccionario, la mayoría de los regionalismos que contiene provienen de América Latina. Sin embargo, se han incluido también algunos regionalismos comunes de España.

Varios vocablos en español reciben un calificativo de *fam* (familiar), lo cual indica que el uso de tales palabras es apropiado solamente en contextos informales. El calificativo estilístico *usu considered vulgar* se emplea para indicar que el uso de la palabra indicada puede considerarse como vulgar u ofensivo. Se han omitido la mayoría de este tipo de voces, pero hay algunas cuyo uso es tan común que el omitirlas resultaría negligente. El propósito de este calificativo es, pues, de servir de advertencia al lector.

En algunos casos, una acepción puede venir precedida de una **nota parentética** que proporciona al lector información semántica suplementaria:

> **not** . . . *adv* **1** (*used to form a negative*)
> : no . . .
> **within²** *prep* . . . **2** (*in expressions of*
> *distance*) : . . . **3** (*in expressions of time*)
> : . . .
> **e²** *conj* (*used instead of* y *before words*
> *beginning with* i *or* hi) : . . .
> **poder¹** . . . *v aux* . . . **2** (*expressing pos-*
> *sibility*) : . . . **3** (*expressing permis-*
> *sion*) : . . .

Este tipo de orientación semántica puede aparecer también entre paréntesis como parte de la definición:

> **calibrate** . . .*vt* . . . : calibrar (armas),
> graduar (termómetros)
> **palco** *nm* : box (in a theater or stadium)

En algunas ocasiones, una **nota de uso** aparece en lugar de una definición. Esto ocurre sólo cuando el lema carece de equivalente en el idioma extranjero. Estas notas de uso aparecen acompañadas de ejemplos que ilustran el uso común del lema:

> **shall** . . . *v aux* . . . **1** (*used to express a*
> *command*) <you shall do as I say
> : harás lo que te digo> . . .

Varias definiciones vienen acompañadas de **ejemplos de uso**. Estos ejemplos sirven para ilustrar un empleo típico del lema en un contexto dado, o un uso idiomático común de la palabra. Los ejemplos de uso incluyen una traducción, y aparecen entre paréntesis angulares:

> **lejos** *adv* **1** : far away, distant <a lo lejos
> : in the distance, far off> . . .
> **make¹** . . . **9** . . . : ganar <to make a living
> : ganarse la vida> . . .

División de las acepciones

Se presenta una **acepción o definición** por medio de dos puntos en negrita:

> **fable** . . . *n* : fábula *f*

Cuando una entrada principal tiene varias acepciones, éstas se indican con un número arábigo, compuesto también en negrita:

> **laguna** *nf* **1** : lagoon **2** : lacuna, gap

Notas explicativas

Cuando alguna información (como un sinónimo, una palabra o frase en negrita, una nota de uso, una remisión, o un calificativo) aparece después de un número de acepción, ésta se aplica única y específicamente a dicha acepción, y no a otras que puedan aparecer bajo la misma entrada principal:

> abanico *nm* . . . 2 GAMA : . . .
> tonic[2] *n* . . . 2 *or* tonic water : . . .
> grillo *nm* . . . 2 grillos *nmpl* : . . .
> fairy . . . *n, pl* fairies . . . 2 fairy tale : . . .
> myself . . . *pron* 1 (*used reflexively*) : . . .
> pike . . . *n* . . . 3 → turnpike
> atado[2] *nm* . . . 2 *Arg* : . . .

Remisiones

Las **remisiones** empleadas en este diccionario se clasifican en tres categorías: sinónima, cognada, e inflexional. Toda remisión puede identificarse inmediatamente por la flecha en negrita que aparece a continuación del lema.

Las remisiones de tipo sinónimo y cognado indican que la definición correspondiente al lema que precede a la flecha puede encontrarse en la entrada a la cual se remite:

> scapula . . . → shoulder blade
> amuck → amok

Las remisiones de tipo inflexional se utilizan para indicar que el lema que precede a la flecha es meramente una inflexión de la entrada a la cual se remite (generalmente un verbo o un sustantivo):

> fue, etc. → ir, ser
> mice → mouse

Sinónimos

En varias entradas y acepciones del diccionario se encuentra, entre los dos puntos en negrita y el texto de la definición, un **sinónimo** compuesto en mayúsculas pequeñas. Toda palabra empleada como sinónimo tiene su propia entrada en el diccionario, ya sea como entrada principal o como frase en negrita. El propósito de estos sinónimos es de orientar al lector y ayudarlo a elegir la acepción correcta, así como de proveer un término que podría usarse alternativamente en el mismo contexto.

Spanish Grammar

Accentuation

Spanish word stress is generally determined according to the following rules:

- Words ending in a vowel, or in *-n* or *-s,* are stressed on the next to last syllable (*zapato, llaman*).
- Words ending in a consonant other than *-n* or *-s* are stressed on the last syllable (*perdiz, curiosidad*).

Exceptions to these rules have a written accent mark over the stressed vowel (*fácil, hablará, último*). There are also a few words which take accent marks in order to distinguish them from homonyms (*si, sí; que, qué; el, él;* etc.).

Adverbs ending in *-mente* have two stressed syllables since they retain both the stress of the root word and of the *-mente* suffix (*lentamente, difícilmente*). Many compounds also have two stressed syllables (*limpiaparabrisas*).

Punctuation and Capitalization

Questions and exclamations in Spanish are preceded by an inverted question mark ¿ and an inverted exclamation mark ¡, respectively:

¿Cuándo llamó Ana?
Y tú, ¿qué piensas?
¡No hagas eso!
Pero, ¡qué lástima!

In Spanish, unlike English, the following words are not capitalized:

- Names of days, months, and languages (*jueves, octubre, español*).
- Spanish adjectives or nouns derived from proper nouns (*los nicaragüenses, una teoría marxista*).

Articles

1. Definite Article

Spanish has five forms of the definite article: *el* (masculine singular), *la* (feminine singular), *los* (masculine plural), *las* (feminine plural), and *lo* (neuter). The first four agree in gender and number with the nouns they limit (*el carro,* the car; *las tijeras,* the scissors), although the form *el* is used with feminine singular nouns beginning with a stressed *a-* or *ha-* (*el águila, el hambre*).

The neuter article *lo* is used with the masculine singular form of an adjective to express an abstract concept (*lo mejor de este método,* the best thing about this method; *lo meticuloso de su trabajo,* the meticulousness of her work; *lo mismo para mí,* the same for me).

Whenever the masculine article *el* immediately follows the words *de* or *a,* it combines with them to form the contractions *del* and *al,* respectively (*viene del campo, vi al hermano de Roberto*).

The use of *el, la, los,* and *las* in Spanish corresponds largely to the use of *the* in English; some exceptions are noted below.

The definite article is used:

- When referring to something as a class (*los gatos son ágiles,* cats are agile; *me gusta el café,* I like coffee).
- In references to meals and in most expressions of time (*¿comiste el almuerzo?,* did you eat lunch?; *vino el año pasado,* he came last year; *son las dos,* it's two o'clock; *prefiero el verano,* I prefer summer; *la reunión es el lunes,* the meeting is on Monday; but: *hoy es lunes,* today is Monday).

- Before titles (except *don, doña, san, santo, santa, fray,* and *sor*) in third-person references to people (*la señora Rivera llamó,* Mrs. Rivera called; but: *hola, señora Rivera,* hello, Mrs. Rivera).
- In references to body parts and personal possessions (*me duele la cabeza,* my head hurts; *dejó el sombrero,* he left his hat).
- To mean "the one" or "the ones" when the subject is already understood (*la de madera,* the wooden one; *los que vi ayer,* the ones I saw yesterday).

The definite article is omitted:

- Before a noun in apposition, if the noun is not modified (*Caracas, capital de Venezuela;* but: *Pico Bolívar, la montaña más alta de Venezuela*).
- Before a number in a royal title (*Carlos Quinto,* Charles the Fifth).

2. Indefinite Article

The forms of the indefinite article in Spanish are *un* (masculine singular), *una* (feminine singular), *unos* (masculine plural), and *unas* (feminine plural). They agree in number and gender with the nouns they limit (*una mesa,* a table; *unos platos,* some plates), although the form *un* is used with feminine singular nouns beginning with a stressed *a-* or *ha-* (*un ala, un hacha*).

The use of *un, una, unos,* and *unas* in Spanish corresponds largely to the use of *a, an,* and *some* in English, with some exceptions:

- Indefinite articles are generally omitted before nouns identifying someone or something as a member of a class or category (*Paco es profesor/católico,* Paco is a professor/Catholic; *se llama páncreas,* it's called a pancreas).
- They are also often omitted in instances where quantity is understood from context (*vine sin chaqueta,* I came without a jacket; *no tengo carro,* I don't have a car).

Nouns

1. Gender

Nouns in Spanish are either masculine or feminine. A noun's gender can often be determined according to the following guidelines:

- Nouns ending in *-aje, -o,* or *-or* are usually masculine (*el traje, el libro, el sabor*), with some exceptions (*la mano, la foto, la labor,* etc.).
- Nouns ending in *-a, -dad, -ión, -tud,* or *-umbre* are usually feminine (*la alfombra, la capacidad, la excepción, la juventud, la certidumbre*). Exceptions include: *el día, el mapa,* and many learned borrowings ending in *-ma* (*el idioma, el tema*).

Most nouns referring to people or animals agree in gender with the subject (*el hombre, la mujer; el hermano, la hermana; el perro, la perra*). However, some nouns referring to people, including those ending in *-ista,* use the same form for both sexes (*el artista, la artista; el modelo, la modelo;* etc.).

A few names of animals exist in only one gender form (*la jirafa, el sapo,* etc.). In these instances, the adjectives *macho* and *hembra* are sometimes used to distinguish males and females (*una jirafa macho,* a male giraffe).

2. Pluralization

Plurals of Spanish nouns are formed as follows:

- Nouns ending in an unstressed vowel or an accented *-é* are pluralized by adding *-s* (*la vaca, las vacas; el café, los cafés*).
- Nouns ending in a consonant other than *-s,* or in a stressed vowel other than *-é,* are generally pluralized by adding *-es* (*el papel, los papeles; el rubí, los rubíes*). Exceptions include *papá* (*papás*) and *mamá* (*mamás*).

- Nouns with an unstressed final syllable ending in -*s* usually have a zero plural (*la crisis, las crisis; el jueves, los jueves*). Other nouns ending in -*s* add -*es* to form the plural (*el mes, los meses; el país, los países*).
- Nouns ending in -*z* are pluralized by changing the -*z* to -*c* and adding -*es* (*el lápiz, los lápices; la vez, las veces*).
- Many compound nouns have a zero plural (*el paraguas, los paraguas; el aguafiestas, los aguafiestas*).
- The plurals of *cualquiera* and *quienquiera* are *cualesquiera* and *quienesquiera*, respectively.

Adjectives

1. Gender and Number

Most adjectives agree in gender and number with the nouns they modify (un chico *alto,* una chica *alta,* unos chicos *altos,* unas chicas *altas*). Some adjectives, including those ending in -*e* and -*ista* (*fuerte, altruista*) and comparative adjectives ending in -*or* (*mayor, mejor*), vary only for number.

Adjectives whose masculine singular forms end in -*o* generally change the -*o* to -*a* to form the feminine (*pequeño → pequeña*). Masculine adjectives ending in -*án,* -*ón,* or -*dor,* and masculine adjectives of nationality which end in a consonant, usually add -*a* to form the feminine (*holgazán → holgazana; llorón → llorona; trabajador → trabajadora; irlandés → irlandesa*).

Adjectives are pluralized in much the same manner as nouns:

- The plurals of adjectives ending in an unstressed vowel or an accented -*é* are formed by adding an -*s* (un postre *rico,* unos postres *ricos;* una camisa *café,* unas camisas *cafés*).
- Adjectives ending in a consonant, or in a stressed vowel other than -*é*, are generally pluralized by adding -*es* (un niño *cortés,* unos niños *corteses;* una persona *iraní,* unas personas *iraníes*).
- Adjectives ending in -*z* are pluralized by changing the -*z* to -*c* and adding -*es* (una respuesta *sagaz,* unas respuestas *sagaces*).

2. Shortening

- The following masculine singular adjectives drop their final -*o* when they occur before a masculine singular noun: *bueno* (*buen*), *malo* (*mal*), *uno* (*un*), *alguno* (*algún*), *ninguno* (*ningún*), *primero* (*primer*), *tercero* (*tercer*).
- *Grande* shortens to *gran* before any singular noun.
- *Ciento* shortens to *cien* before any noun.
- The title *Santo* shortens to *San* before all masculine names except those beginning with *To-* or *Do-* (*San Juan, Santo Tomás*).

3. Position

Descriptive adjectives generally follow the nouns they modify (*una cosa útil, un actor famoso*). However, adjectives that express an inherent quality often precede the noun (*la blanca nieve*).

Some adjectives change meaning depending on whether they occur before or after the noun: *un pobre niño,* a poor (pitiable) child; *un niño pobre,* a poor (not rich) child; *un gran hombre,* a great man; *un hombre grande,* a big man; *el único libro,* the only book; *el libro único,* the unique book; etc.

4. Comparative and Superlative Forms

The comparative of Spanish adjectives is generally rendered as *más . . . que* (more . . . than) or *menos . . . que* (less . . . than): *soy más alta que él,* I'm taller than he; *son menos inteligentes que tú,* they're less intelligent than you.

The superlative of Spanish adjectives usually follows the formula *definite arti-*

cle + (*noun* +) *más/menos* + adjective: *ella es la estudiante más trabajadora,* she is the hardest-working student; *él es el menos conocido,* he's the least known.

A few Spanish adjectives have irregular comparative and superlative forms:

Adjective	Comparative/Superlative
bueno (good)	**mejor** (better, best)
malo (bad)	**peor** (worse, worst)
grande[1] (big, great), **viejo** (old)	**mayor** (greater, older; greatest, oldest)
pequeño[1] (little), **joven** (young)	**menor** (lesser, younger; least, youngest)
mucho (much), **muchos** (many)	**más** (more, most)
poco (little), **pocos** (few)	**menos** (less, least)

[1]These words have regular comparative and superlative forms when used in reference to physical size: *él es más grande que yo; nuestra casa es la más pequeña.*

ABSOLUTE SUPERLATIVE

The absolute superlative is formed by placing *muy* before the adjective, or by adding the suffix *-ísimo* (*ella es muy simpática* or *ella es simpatiquísima,* she is very nice). The absolute superlative using *-ísimo* is formed according to the following rules:

- Adjectives ending in a consonant other than *-z* simply add the *-ísimo* ending (*fácil → facilísimo*).
- Adjectives ending in *-z* change this consonant to *-c* and add *-ísimo* (*feliz → felicísimo*).
- Adjectives ending in a vowel or diphthong drop the vowel or diphthong and add *-ísimo* (*claro → clarísimo; amplio → amplísimo*).
- Adjectives ending in *-co* or *-go* change these endings to *qu* and *gu*, respectively, and add *-ísimo* (*rico → riquísimo; largo → larguísimo*).
- Adjectives ending in *-ble* change this ending to *-bil* and add *-ísimo* (*notable → notabilísimo*).
- Adjectives containing the stressed diphthong *ie* or *ue* will sometimes change these to *e* and *o*, respectively (*ferviente → fervientísimo* or *ferventísimo; bueno → buenísimo* or *bonísimo*).

Adverbs

Adverbs can be formed by adding the adverbial suffix *-mente* to virtually any adjective (*fácil → fácilmente*). If the adjective varies for gender, the feminine form is used as the basis for forming the adverb (*rápido → rápidamente*).

Pronouns

1. Personal Pronouns

The personal pronouns in Spanish are:

Person	Singular		Plural	
FIRST	yo	I	**nosotros, nosotras**	we
SECOND	tú	you (familiar)	**vosotros**[2]**, vosotras**[2]	you, all of you
	vos[1]	you		
	usted	you (formal)	**ustedes**[3]	you, all of you
THIRD	él	he	**ellos, ellas**	they
	ella	she		
	ello	it (neuter)		

[1]Familiar form used in addition to tú in South and Central America.
[2]Familiar form used in Spain.
[3]Formal form used in Spain; familiar and formal form used in Latin America.

FAMILIAR VS. FORMAL

The second person personal pronouns exist in both familiar and formal forms. The familiar forms are generally used when addressing relatives, friends, and children, although usage varies considerably from region to region; the formal forms are used in other contexts to show courtesy, respect, or emotional distance.

In Spain and in the Caribbean, *tú* is used exclusively as the familiar singular "you." In South and Central America, however, *vos* either competes with *tú* to varying degrees or replaces it entirely. (For a more detailed explanation of *vos* and its corresponding verb forms, refer to the Conjugation of Spanish Verbs section.)

The plural familiar form *vosotros, -as* is used only in Spain, where *ustedes* is reserved for formal contexts. In Latin America, *vosotros, -as* is not used, and *ustedes* serves as the all-purpose plural "you."

It should be noted that while *usted* and *ustedes* are regarded as second person pronouns, they take the third person form of the verb.

USAGE

In Spanish, personal pronouns are generally omitted (*voy al cine,* I'm going to the movies; *¿llamaron?,* did they call?), although they are sometimes used for purposes of emphasis or clarity (*se lo diré yo,* I will tell them; *vino ella, pero él se quedó,* she came, but he stayed behind). The forms *usted* and *ustedes* are usually included out of courtesy (*¿cómo está usted?,* how are you?).

Personal pronouns are not generally used in reference to inanimate objects or living creatures other than humans; in these instances, the pronoun is most often omitted (*¿es nuevo? no, es viejo,* is it new? no, it's old).

The neuter third person pronoun *ello* is reserved for indefinite subjects (as abstract concepts): *todo ello implica . . . ,* all of this implies . . . ; *por si ello fuera poco . . . ,* as if that weren't enough. . . . It most commonly appears in formal writing and speech. In less formal contexts, *ello* is often either omitted or replaced with *esto, eso,* or *aquello.*

2. Prepositional Pronouns

Prepositional pronouns are used as the objects of prepositions (*¿es para mí?,* is it for me?; *se lo dio a ellos,* he gave it to them).

The prepositional pronouns in Spanish are:

Singular		**Plural**	
mí	me	**nosotros, nosotras**	us
ti	you	**vosotros[1], vosotras[1]**	you
usted	you (formal)	**ustedes**	you
él	him	**ellos, ellas**	them
ella	her		
ello	it (neuter)		
sí	yourself, himself, herself, itself, oneself	**sí**	yourselves, themselves

[1]Used primarily in Spain.

When the preposition *con* is followed by *mí, ti,* or *sí,* both words are replaced by *conmigo, contigo,* and *consigo,* respectively (*¿vienes conmigo?,* are you coming with me?; *habló contigo,* he spoke with you; *no lo trajo consigo,* she didn't bring it with her).

3. Object Pronouns

DIRECT OBJECT PRONOUNS

Direct object pronouns represent the primary goal or result of the action of a verb. The direct object pronouns in Spanish are:

Singular		Plural	
me	me	**nos**	us
te	you	**os**[1]	you
le[2]	you, him	**les**[2]	you, them
lo	you, him, it	**los**	you, them
la	you, her, it	**las**	you, them

[1]Used only in Spain.
[2]Used mainly in Spain.

Agreement

The third person forms agree in both gender and number with the nouns they replace or the people they refer to (*pintó las paredes*, she painted the walls → *las pintó*, she painted them; *visitaron al señor Juárez*, they visited Mr. Juárez → *lo visitaron*, they visited him). The remaining forms vary only for number.

Position

Direct object pronouns are normally affixed to the end of an affirmative command, a simple infinitive, or a present participle (*¡hazlo!*, do it!; *es difícil hacerlo*, it's difficult to do it; *haciéndolo, aprenderás*, you'll learn by doing it). With constructions involving an auxiliary verb and an infinitive or present participle, the pronoun may occur either immediately before the construction or suffixed to it (*lo voy a hacer* or *voy a hacerlo*, I'm going to do it; *estoy haciéndolo* or *lo estoy haciendo*, I'm doing it). In all other cases, the pronoun immediately precedes the conjugated verb (*no lo haré*, I won't do it).

Regional Variation

In Spain and in a few areas of Latin America, *le* and *les* are used in place of *lo* and *los* when referring to or addressing people (*le vieron*, they saw him; *les vistió*, she dressed them). In most parts of Latin America, however, *los* and *las* are used for the second person plural in both formal and familiar contexts.

The second person plural familiar form *os* is restricted to Spain.

INDIRECT OBJECT PRONOUNS

Indirect object pronouns represent the secondary goal of the action of a verb (*me dio el regalo*, he gave me the gift; *les dije que no*, I told them no). The indirect object pronouns in Spanish are:

Singular		Plural	
me	(to, for, from) me	**nos**	(to, for, from) us
te	(to, for, from) you	**os**[1]	(to, for, from) you
le	(to, for, from) you, him, her, it	**les**	(to, for, from) you, them
se[2]		**se**[2]	

[1]Used only in Spain.
[2]See explanation below.

Position

Indirect object pronouns follow the same rules as direct object pronouns with regard to their position in relation to verbs. When they occur with direct object pronouns, the indirect object pronoun always precedes (*nos lo dio*, she gave it to us; *estoy trayéndotela*, I'm bringing it to you).

Use of *Se*

When the indirect object pronouns *le* or *les* occur before any direct object pronoun beginning with an *l-*, the indirect object pronouns *le* and *les* convert to *se* (*les mandé la carta*, I sent them the letter → *se la mandé*, I sent it to them; *vamos a comprarle los aretes*, let's buy her the earrings → *vamos a comprárselos*, let's buy them for her).

4. Reflexive Pronouns

Reflexive pronouns are used to refer back to the subject of the verb (*me hice daño,* I hurt myself; *se vistieron,* they got dressed, they dressed themselves; *nos lo compramos,* we bought it for ourselves).

The reflexive pronouns in Spanish are:

Singular		Plural	
me	myself	**nos**	ourselves
te	yourself	**os**[1]	yourselves
se	yourself, himself, herself, itself	**se**	yourselves, themselves

[1]Used only in Spain.

Reflexive pronouns are also used:

- When the verb describes an action performed to one's own body, clothing, etc. (*me quité los zapatos,* I took off my shoes; *se arregló el pelo,* he fixed his hair).
- In the plural, to indicate reciprocal action (*se hablan con frecuencia,* they speak with each other frequently).
- In the third person singular and plural, as an indefinite subject reference (*se dice que es verdad,* they say it's true; *nunca se sabe,* one never knows; *se escribieron miles de páginas,* thousands of pages were written).

It should be noted that many verbs which take reflexive pronouns in Spanish have intransitive equivalents in English (*ducharse,* to shower; *quejarse,* to complain; etc.).

5. Relative Pronouns

Relative pronouns introduce subordinate clauses acting as nouns or modifiers (*el libro que escribió* . . . , the book that he wrote . . . ; *las chicas a quienes conociste* . . . , the girls whom you met . . .). In Spanish, the relative pronouns are:

que (that, which, who, whom)
quien, quienes (who, whom, that, whoever, whomever)
el cual, la cual, los cuales, las cuales (which, who)
el que, la que, los que, las que (which, who, whoever)
lo cual (which)
lo que (what, which, whatever)
cuanto, cuanta, cuantos, cuantas (all those that, all that, whatever, whoever, as much as, as many as)

Relative pronouns are not omitted in Spanish as they often are in English: *el carro que vi ayer,* the car (that) I saw yesterday. When relative pronouns are used with prepositions, the preposition precedes the clause (*la película sobre la cual le hablé,* the film I spoke to you about).

The relative pronoun *que* can be used in reference to both people and things. Unlike other relative pronouns, *que* does not take the personal *a* when used as a direct object referring to a person (*el hombre que llamé,* the man that I called; but: *el hombre a quien llamé,* the man whom I called).

Quien is used only in reference to people. It varies in number with the explicit or implied antecedent (*las mujeres con quienes charlamos* . . . , the women we chatted with; *quien lo hizo pagará,* whoever did it will pay).

El cual and *el que* vary for both number and gender, and are therefore often used in situations where *que* or *quien(es)* might create ambiguity: *nos contó algunas cosas sobre los libros, las cuales eran interesantes,* he told us some things about the books which (the things) were interesting.

Lo cual and *lo que* are used to refer back to a whole clause, or to something indefinite (*dijo que iría, lo cual me alegró,* he said he would go, which made me happy; *pide lo que quieras,* ask for whatever you want).

Cuanto varies for both number and gender with the implied antecedent: *conté a cuantas (personas) pude,* I counted as many (people) as I could. If an indefinite mass quantity is referred to, the masculine singular form is used (*anoté cuanto decía,* I jotted down whatever he said).

Possessives

1. Possessive Adjectives

UNSTRESSED FORMS

Singular		Plural	
mi(s)	my	**nuestro(s), nuestra(s)**	our
tu(s)	your	**vuestro(s)[1], vuestra(s)[1]**	your
su(s)	your, his, her, its	**su(s)**	your, their

[1]Used only in Spain.

STRESSED FORMS

Singular		Plural	
mío(s), mía(s)	my, mine, of mine	**nuestro(s), nuestra(s)**	our, ours, of ours
tuyo(s), tuya(s)	your, yours, of yours	**vuestro(s)[1], vuestra(s)[1]**	your, yours, of yours
suyo(s), suya(s)	your, yours, of yours; his, of his; her, hers, of hers; its, of its	**suyo(s), suya(s)**	your, yours, of yours; their, theirs, of theirs

[1]Used only in Spain.

The unstressed forms of possessive adjectives precede the nouns they modify (*mis zapatos,* my shoes; *nuestra escuela,* our school).

The stressed forms occur after the noun and are often used for purposes of emphasis (*el carro tuyo,* your car; *la pluma es mía,* the pen is mine; *unos amigos nuestros,* some friends of ours).

All possessive adjectives agree with the noun in number. The stressed forms, as well as the unstressed forms *nuestro* and *vuestro,* also vary for gender.

2. Possessive Pronouns

The possessive pronouns have the same forms as the stressed possessive adjectives (see table above). They are always preceded by the definite article, and they agree in number and gender with the nouns they replace (*las llaves mías,* my keys → *las mías,* mine; *los guantes nuestros,* our gloves → *los nuestros,* ours).

Demonstratives

1. Demonstrative Adjectives

The demonstrative adjectives in Spanish are:

Singular		Plural	
este, esta	this	**estos, estas**	these
ese, esa	that	**esos, esas** those	
aquel, aquella	that	**aquellos, aquellas**	those

Demonstrative adjectives agree with the nouns they modify in gender and number (*esta chica, aquellos árboles*). They normally precede the noun, but may occasionally occur after for purposes of emphasis or to express contempt: *en la época aquella de cambio,* in that era of change; *el perro ese ha ladrado toda la noche,* that (awful, annoying, etc.) dog barked all night long.

The forms *aquel, aquella, aquellos,* and *aquellas* are generally used in reference to people and things that are relatively distant from the speaker in space or time: *ese libro,* that book (a few feet away); *aquel libro,* that book (way over there).

2. Demonstrative Pronouns

The demonstrative pronouns in Spanish are orthographically identical to the demonstrative adjectives except that they take an accent mark over the stressed vowel (*éste, ése, aquél,* etc.). In addition, there are three neuter forms— *esto, eso,* and *aquello*—which are used when referring to abstract ideas or unidentified things (*¿te dijo eso?,* he said that to you?; *¿qué es esto?,* what is this?; *tráeme todo aquello,* bring me all that stuff).

Except for the neuter forms, demonstrative pronouns agree in gender and number with the nouns they replace (*esta silla,* this chair → *ésta,* this one; *aquellos vasos,* those glasses → *aquéllos,* those ones).

Gramática inglesa

El adjetivo

El adjetivo inglés es invariable en cuanto a número o género, y suele preceder al sustantivo que modifica:

the tall woman   the tall women
a happy child   happy children

Las **formas comparativas y superlativas del adjetivo** inglés se pueden construir de tres maneras. Cuando el adjetivo positivo consta de una sola sílaba, la construcción más común es de añadir los sufijos *-er* o *-est* al vocablo raíz; si el adjetivo positivo consta de más de dos sílabas, suele entonces combinarse con los adverbios *more*, *most*, *less* o *least*; al adjetivo positivo de dos sílabas puede aplicarse cualquiera de las dos fórmulas; y por último, existen los adjetivos irregulares cuyas formas comparativas y superlativas son únicas.

Positivo	Comparativo	Superlativo
clean	cleaner	cleanest
narrow	narrower	narrowest
meaningful	more/less meaningful	most/least meaningful
good	better	best
bad	worse	worst

El **adjetivo demostrativo** *this* o *that* corresponde al adjetivo español *este* o *ese*. Debe notarse que este tipo de adjetivo es el único que tiene forma plural:

Singular	Plural
this	these
that	those

Un **adjetivo descriptivo** describe o indica una cualidad, clase o condición (a fascinating conversation; a positive attitude; a fast computer).

Un **adjetivo indefinido** se usa para designar personas o cosas no identificadas (some children; other hotels).

El **adjetivo interrogativo** se usa para formular preguntas:

Whose office is this?   **Which** book do you want?

Un **sustantivo** puede usarse para **modificar otro sustantivo**. De esta manera el sustantivo funciona igual que un adjetivo (the Vietnam War; word processing).

Llámase **adjetivo posesivo** a la forma posesiva del pronombre personal:

Singular	Plural
my	our
your	your
his/her/its	their

Where's *my* watch?   Where are *our* coats?
Your cab's here.   *Your* tables are ready.
It was *her* idea.   We paid for *their* tickets.
They read *his* book.   the box and *its* contents

Un **adjetivo predicativo** modifica el sujeto de un verbo copulativo (como *be, become, feel, taste, smell,* o *seem*):

She is *happy* with the outcome.   The milk tastes *sour*.
The student seems *puzzled*.

Un **adjetivo propio** es derivado de un nombre propio y suele escribirse con mayúscula:

Victorian furniture　　　　a *Puerto Rican* product

Un **adjetivo relativo** (tal como *which, that, who, whom, whose, where*) se emplea para introducir una cláusula adjetival o sustantiva:

toward late April, by *which* time the report should be finished
not knowing *whose* advice she should follow

El adverbio

La mayor parte de los adverbios ingleses se forman a partir de un adjetivo al que se le agrega el sufijo *-ly*:

mad*ly*　　　wonderful*ly*

Para formar un adverbio de un adjetivo que termina en *-y*, suele cambiarse primero esta terminación a una *-i*, y luego se añade el sufijo *-ly*:

happ*ily*　　　daint*ily*

La forma adverbial que corresponde a varios adjetivos que terminan en *-ic* recibe el sufijo *-ally*:

basic*ally*　　　numeric*ally*

Si un adjetivo termina en *-ly*, el adverbio que le corresponde suele escribirse de la misma manera:

she called her mother *daily*　　　the show started *early*

Por último, hay adverbios que no terminan en *-ly* (por ejemplo, *again, now,* y *too*).

Al igual que el adjetivo, la mayoría de los adverbios ingleses poseen tres grados de comparación: **positivo, comparativo,** y **superlativo.** Como regla general, a un adverbio monosilábico se le añade el sufijo *-er* cuando es comparativo, y *-est* cuando es superlativo. Si el adverbio consta de tres o más sílabas, las formas comparativas y superlativas se forman al combinarlo con los adverbios *more/most* o *less/least*. Las formas comparativas y superlativas de un adverbio de dos sílabas pueden obtenerse empleando uno u otro de los dos métodos:

Positivo	Comparativo	Superlativo
fast	faster	fastest
easy	easier	easiest
madly	more madly	most madly
happily	more happily	most happily

Finalmente, hay algunos adverbios, tales como *quite* y *very*, que no poseen comparativo.

Adverbios tales como *just* y *only* suelen usarse para poner el énfasis en otras palabras. El énfasis producido puede cambiar según la posición del adverbio en la oración:

He *just* nodded to me as he passed.
　　　Sólo me saludó con la cabeza al pasar.
He nodded to me *just* as he passed.
　　　Me saludó con la cabeza *justamente* cuando me pasó.

Los **adverbios relativos** (tales como *when, where,* y *why*) se utilizan principalmente para introducir preguntas:

When will he return?　　　*Where* have the children gone?
Why did you do it?

El artículo

En inglés existe solamente una forma del **artículo definido**, *the*. Este artículo es invariable en cuanto a género o número.

> *The* boys were expelled.   *The* First Lady dined with *the* ambassador.

El **artículo indefinido** *a* se usa con cualquier sustantivo o abreviatura que comience ya sea con una consonante, o con un *sonido* consonántico:

a door	a hat
a B.A. degree	a one-way street
a union	a U.S. Senator

El artículo *a* se emplea también antes de un sustantivo cuya primera sílaba comienza con *h-*, y esta sílaba no es acentuada o tiene solamente una acentuación moderada (a historian, a heroic attempt, a hilarious performance). Sin embargo, en el inglés hablado, suele más usarse el artículo *an* en estos casos (an historian, an heroic attempt, an hilarious performance). Ambas formas son perfectamente aceptables.

El artículo indefinido *an* se usa con cualquier sustantivo o abreviatura que comience con un sonido vocal, sin tener en cuenta si la primera letra del sustantivo es vocal o consonante (an icicle, an nth degree, an honor, an FBI investigation).

La conjunción

Existen tres tipos principales de conjunciones: la conjunción coordinante, la correlativa, y la subordinante.

Las **conjunciones coordinantes**, tales como *and, because, but, for, or, nor, since, so*, y *yet*, se emplean para unir elementos gramaticales de igual valor. Estos elementos pueden ser palabras, frases, cláusulas subordinadas, cláusulas principales, u oraciones completas. Las conjunciones coordinantes se emplean para unir elementos similares (she ordered pencils, pens, *and* erasers), para excluir o contrastar (he is a brilliant *but* arrogant man), para indicar una alternativa (she can wait here *or* go on ahead), para indicar una razón (the report is useless, *for* its information is no longer current), o para precisar un resultado (his diction is excellent, *so* every word is clear).

Las **conjunciones correlativas** se usan en pares, y sirven para unir alternativas y elementos de igual valor gramatical.

> *Either* you go *or* you stay.   He had *neither* looks *nor* wit.

Las **conjunciones subordinantes** se usan para unir una cláusula subordinada a una cláusula principal. Estas conjunciones pueden emplearse para expresar la causa (*because* she learns quickly, she is doing well in her new job), la condición o concesión (don't call *unless* you are coming), el modo (we'll do it *however* you tell us to), el propósito o resultado (he distributes the mail early *so* that they can read it), el tiempo (she kept meetings to a minimum *when* she was president), el lugar o la circunstancia (*wherever* he goes, he is welcomed with open arms), así como las condiciones o posibilidades alternativas (they were undecided *whether* to go or stay).

El sustantivo

A diferencia del sustantivo español, el sustantivo inglés generalmente carece de género. En algunos sustantivos, el género femenino se identifica por la presencia del sufijo - *ess* (empress, hostess); existen también aquellos sustantivos que sólo se aplican a miembros de uno u otro sexo, por ejemplo: *husband, wife, father, mother, brother, sister*, así como nombres de ciertos animales: *bull, cow, deer, doe*, etc. Sin embargo, la mayoría de los sustantivos ingleses son neutros. Cuando es preciso atribuirle un género a un sustantivo neutro, suele combinarse éste con palabras como *male, female, man, woman*, etc., por ejemplo:

a *male* parrot   *women* writers

Los sustantivos ingleses suelen usarse como **sujetos** (the *office* was quiet), **objetos directos** (he locked the *office*), **objetos de una preposición** (the file is in the *office*), **objetos indirectos** (he gave his *client* the papers), **objetos retenidos** (his client was given the *papers*), **nominativos predicativos** (Mrs. Adams is the managing *partner*), **complementos objetivos** (they made Mrs. Adams managing *partner*), **construcciones apositivas** (Mrs. Adams, the managing *partner,* wrote that memo), y **en trato directo** (*Mrs.* Adams, may I present Mr. Bonkowski).

Los sustantivos desempeñan una función adjetival cuando preceden a otros sustantivos:

olive oil   business management
emergency room

La mayoría de los sustantivos ingleses se pluralizan añadiendo -*s* al final del singular (book, books; cat, cats; dog, dogs; tree, trees).

Cuando el sustantivo singular termina en -*s, -x, -z, -ch,* o -*sh,* su forma plural se obtiene añadiendo -*es* al final (cross, crosses; fox, foxes; fez, fezes; witch, witches; wish, wishes).

Si el sustantivo singular termina en -*y* precedida de una consonante, la -*y* es convertida en -*i* y se le añade la terminación -*es* (fairy, fairies; pony, ponies; guppy, guppies).

No todos los sustantivos ingleses obedecen estas normas. Hay algunos sustantivos (generalmente nombres de animales) que no siempre cambian en el plural (fish, fish o fishes; caribou, caribou o caribous). Por último, hay algunos sustantivos que poseen una forma plural única (foot, feet; mouse, mice; knife, knives).

La forma posesiva del sustantivo singular generalmente se obtiene al añadir un apóstrofe seguido de una -*s* al final:

Jackie's passport   this hat is *Billy's*

Cuando el sustantivo termina en -*s,* suele añadirse únicamente el apóstrofe, como sigue:

the *neighbors's* dog   Mr. *Ross's* briefcase

La preposición

La preposición inglesa se combina generalmente con un sustantivo, un pronombre, o el equivalente de un sustantivo (como una frase o cláusula) para formar una frase con función adjetival, adverbial, o sustantiva. Suele distinguirse dos tipos de preposiciones: la preposición simple, es decir, aquélla que consta de una sola palabra (por ejemplo, *against, from, near, of, on, out,* o *without*), y la compuesta, que consta de más de un elemento (como *according to, by means of,* o *in spite of*).

La preposición se emplea generalmente para unir un sustantivo, un pronombre, o el equivalente de un sustantivo al resto de la oración. Una frase preposicional suele emplearse como adverbio o adjetivo.

She expected resistance *on* his part.   He sat down *beside* her.

Las palabras inglesas *after, before, but, for,* y *since* pueden funcionar como preposiciones así como conjunciones. El papel que desempeñan estas palabras suele determinarse según su posición dentro de la oración. Las conjunciones generalmente sirven para unir dos elementos de igual valor gramatical, mientras que las preposiciones suelen preceder a un sustantivo, un pronombre, o una frase sustantiva.

conjunción: I was a bit concerned *but* not panicky.
                [*but* vincula dos adjetivos]
preposición: I was left with nothing *but* hope.
                [*but* precede a un sustantivo]

conjunción:	The device conserves fuel, *for* it is battery-powered.
	[*for* vincula dos cláusulas]
preposición:	The device conserves fuel *for* residual heating.
	[*for* precede a una frase sustantiva]

Una preposición puede aparecer antes de un sustantivo o un pronombre (*below* the desk, *beside* them), después de un adjetivo (antagonistic *to*, insufficient *in*, symbolic *of*), o después de un elemento verbal con el cual combina para formar una frase con función verbal (take *for*, take *over*, come *across*).

A diferencia de la preposición española, la preposición inglesa puede aparecer al final de una oración, lo cual sucede frecuentemente en el uso común, especialmente si la preposición forma parte de una frase con función verbal.

After Rourke left, Joyce took *over*.   What does this all add up *to*?

El pronombre

Los pronombres pueden poseer las características siguientes: caso (nominativo, posesivo, u objetivo); número (singular o plural); persona (primera, segunda, o tercera), y género (masculino, femenino, o neutro). Los pronombres ingleses se clasifican en siete categorías principales, de las cuales cada una juega un papel específico.

Las palabras *this, that, these* y *those* se consideran como pronombres cuando funcionan como sustantivos. (Se les clasifica como adjetivos demostrativos cuando modifican un sustantivo.) El **pronombre demostrativo** indica a una persona o cosa para distinguirla de otras.

These are the best designs we've seen to date.   *Those* are strong words.

El pronombre demostrativo también se usa para distinguir a una persona o cosa cercana de otra que se encuentre a mayor distancia (*this* is my desk; *that* is yours).

El **pronombre indefinido** se emplea para designar a una persona o cosa cuya identidad se desconoce o no se puede establecer de inmediato. Estos pronombres se usan generalmente como referencias en la tercera persona, y no se distinguen en cuanto a género. A continuación se listan ejemplos de pronombres indefinidos.

all	either	none
another	everybody	no one
any	everyone	one
anybody	everything	other
anyone	few	several
anything	many	some
both	much	somebody
each	neither	someone
each one	nobody	something

Los pronombres indefinidos deben concordar en cuanto a número con los verbos que les corresponden. Los siguientes pronombres son singulares y deben usarse con un verbo conjugado en singular: *another, anything, each one, everything, much, nobody, no one, one, other, someone, something.*

Much is being done.   *No one* wants to go.

Los pronombres indefinidos *both, few, many, several* entre otros son plurales, y por lo tanto deben emplearse con verbos conjugados en plural:

Many were called; *few* were chosen.

Algunos pronombres, tales como *all, any, none,* y *some,* pueden presentar un problema ya que pueden usarse tanto con verbos singulares como plurales. Como regla general, los pronombres que se usan con sustantivos no numerables emplean verbos singulares, mientras que aquéllos que se usan con sustantivos numerables suelen tomar un verbo plural.

con sustantivo no numerable: *All* of the *property* is affected.
    None of the *soup* was spilled.
    Some of the *money* was spent.
con sustantivo numerable: *All* of my *shoes* are black.
    None of the *clerks* were available.
    Some of your *friends* were there.

Los **pronombres interrogativos** *what, which, who, whom,* y *whose,* así como las combinaciones de estos con el sufijo *-ever* (*whatever, whichever,* etc.) se usan para introducir una pregunta:

Who is she?   He asked me *who* she was.
Whoever can that be?   We wondered *whoever* that could be.

El **pronombre personal** refleja la persona, el número, y el género del ser u objeto que representa. La mayoría de los pronombres personales toman una forma distinta para cada uno de estos tres casos.

Persona	Nominativo	Posesivo	Objetivo
PRIMERA			
SINGULAR:	I	my, mine	me
PLURAL:	we	our, ours	us
SEGUNDA			
SINGULAR:	you	your, yours	you
PLURAL:	you	your, yours	you
TERCERA			
SINGULAR:	he	his, his	him
	she	her, hers	her
	it	its, its	it
PLURAL:	they	their, theirs	them

Nótese que los pronombres personales en el caso posesivo no llevan apóstrofe, y no deben confundirse con los homófonos *you're, they're, there's, it's.*

Los **pronombres recíprocos** *each other* y *one another* se emplean para indicar una acción o relación mutua:

They do not quarrel with *one another*.
Lou and Andy saw *each other* at the party.

Un pronombre recíproco puede usarse también en el caso posesivo:

They always borrowed *one another*'s money.
The two companies depend on *each other*'s success.

Los **pronombres reflexivos** se forman al combinar los pronombres personales *him, her, it, my, our, them* y *your* con *-self* o *-selves*. El pronombre reflexivo se usa generalmente para expresar una acción reflexiva, o bien para recalcar el sujeto de una oración, cláusula, o frase.

She dressed *herself*.   He asked *himself* if it was worth it.
I *myself* am not concerned.   They wanted to do it *themselves*.

Los **pronombres relativos** son *that, what, which, who, whom,* y *whose,* así como las combinaciones de éstos con la terminación *-ever*. Estos pronombres se emplean para introducir oraciones subordinadas con función sustantiva o adjetival. El pronombre relativo *who* se usa para referirse a personas y, en ciertas ocasiones, algunos animales. *Which* suele usarse para referirse a animales o cosas, y *that* puede usarse para personas, animales, o cosas.

a man *who* sought success   a woman *whom* we trust
Kentucky Firebolt, *who* won yesterday's horse race
an author *whose* novels are well-known
a movie *which* was a big hit   a dog *which* kept barking
a boy *that* behaves well   a movie *that* was a big hit

a dog *that* kept barking   give it to *whomever* you wish
whoever thought of it   pick *whichever* you want

En ciertas ocasiones el pronombre relativo puede omitirse:

The man [*whom*] I was talking to is the senator.

El verbo

El verbo inglés posee típicamente las siguientes características: inflexión (por ejemplo, *help, helps, helping, helped*), persona (primera, segunda, o tercera), número (singular o plural), tiempo (presente, pasado, futuro), aspecto (categorías temporales distintas a los tiempos simples de presente, pasado y futuro), voz (activa o pasiva), y modo (indicativo, subjuntivo e imperativo).

Los verbos regulares ingleses tienen cuatro **inflexiones** diferentes, las cuales se producen al añadir los sufijos -*s* o -*es*, -*ed*, e -*ing*. La mayoría de los verbos irregulares poseen cuatro o cinco inflexiones (por ejemplo, *see, sees, seeing, saw, seen*); y el verbo *be* tiene ocho (*be, is, am, are, being, was, were, been*).

Los verbos que terminan en una -*e* muda conservan por lo general la -*e* al añadírsele un sufijo que comienza con una consonante (como -*s*), pero esta -*e* desaparece si el sufijo comienza con una vocal (como sucede con -*ed* o -*ing*).

arrange; arranges; arranged; arranging   hope; hopes; hoped; hoping

Sin embargo, algunos de estos verbos conservan la -*e* final para no ser confundidos con otras palabras de ortografía igual, por ejemplo:

dye; dyes; dyed; dyeing   [vs. *dying,* del verbo *die*]
singe; singes; singed; singeing   [vs. *singing,* del verbo *sing*]

Si un verbo consta de una sílaba y termina en una sola consonante a la cual precede una sola vocal, la consonante final se repite en algunas inflexiones:

brag; bragged; bragging   grip; gripped; gripping

Cuando un verbo posee esta misma terminación, pero consta de dos o más sílabas, y la última de éstas es acentuada, se repite también la consonante final:

commit; committed; committing   occur; occurred; occurring

Los verbos que terminan en -*y*, precedida de una consonante, suelen cambiar esta -*y* en -*i* en toda inflexión excepto cuando el sufijo correspondiente es -*ing*.

carry; carried; carrying   study; studied; studying

Cuando un verbo termina en -*c*, se le añade una -*k* en inflexiones cuyos sufijos comienzan con -*e* o -*i*.

mimic; mimics; mimicked; mimicking
traffic; traffics; trafficked; trafficking

Los verbos ingleses exhiben generalmente su **presente simple** o **pasado simple** en una sola palabra, por ejemplo:

I do, I did   we write, we wrote

El **tiempo futuro** suele expresarse al combinar el verbo auxiliar *shall* o *will* con la forma presente simple o presente progresiva del verbo:

I *shall* do it.   We *will* come tomorrow.

Llámase aspecto de un verbo a aquellos tiempos que difieren del presente simple, pasado simple, o futuro simple. A continuación se presentan cuatro de estos tiempos o aspectos: el progresivo, el presente perfecto, el pasado perfecto, y el futuro perfecto.

El **tiempo progresivo** expresa una acción que está teniendo lugar en el presente o en el futuro.

He *is* reading the paper.

El **presente perfecto** se emplea para expresar una acción que ha comenzado en el pasado y que continúa en el presente, o también para expresar una acción que haya tenido lugar en un momento indefinido del pasado.

She *has* written a book.

El **pasado perfecto** expresa una acción que fue llevada a cabo antes de otra acción o evento en el pasado.

She *had* written many books previously.

El futuro perfecto indica una acción que será llevada a cabo antes de una acción o evento en el futuro.

We *will* have finished the project by then.

La **voz (activa o pasiva)** indica si el sujeto de la oración es el que desempeña la acción del verbo o si es el objeto de esta acción:

Voz activa: His colleagues *respected* him.
Voz pasiva: He *was* respected by his colleagues.

En inglés existen tres modos: indicativo, imperativo, y subjuntivo.

El **modo indicativo** se emplea ya sea para indicar un hecho, o para hacer una pregunta:

He *is* here.   *Is* he here?

El **modo imperativo** se usa para expresar una orden o una petición:

Come here.   Please *come* here.

El modo subjuntivo expresa una condición contraria a los hechos. El modo subjuntivo en inglés ha caído en desuso, pero suele aparecer en cláusulas introducidas por *if*, y después del verbo *wish*.

I wish he *were* here.   If she *were* there, she could answer that.

Como en español, el verbo inglés puede ser transitivo o intransitivo. El **verbo transitivo** es el que puede llevar un complemento directo:

She *sold* her car.   *Vendió* su coche.

El **verbo intransitivo** no lleva un complemento directo:

He *talked* all day.   *Habló* todo el día.

Conjugation of Spanish Verbs

Simple Tenses

Tense	Regular Verbs Ending in -AR hablar	
PRESENT INDICATIVE	hablo	hablamos
	hablas	habláis
	habla	hablan
PRESENT SUBJUNCTIVE	hable	hablemos
	hables	habléis
	hable	hablen
PRETERIT INDICATIVE	hablé	hablamos
	hablaste	hablasteis
	habló	hablaron
IMPERFECT INDICATIVE	hablaba	hablábamos
	hablabas	hablabais
	hablaba	hablaban
IMPERFECT SUBJUNCTIVE	hablara	habláramos
	hablaras	hablarais
	hablara	hablaran
	or	
	hablase	hablásemos
	hablases	hablaseis
	hablase	hablasen
FUTURE INDICATIVE	hablaré	hablaremos
	hablarás	hablaréis
	hablará	hablarán
FUTURE SUBJUNCTIVE	hablare	habláremos
	hablares	hablareis
	hablare	hablaren
CONDITIONAL	hablaría	hablaríamos
	hablarías	hablaríais
	hablaría	hablarían
IMPERATIVE	—	hablemos
	habla	hablad
	hable	hablen
PRESENT PARTICIPLE (GERUND)	hablando	
PAST PARTICIPLE	hablado	

Regular Verbs Ending in -ER		Regular Verbs Ending in -IR	
comer		vivir	
como	comemos	vivo	vivimos
comes	coméis	vives	vivís
come	comen	vive	viven
coma	comamos	viva	vivamos
comas	comáis	vivas	viváis
coma	coman	viva	vivan
comí	comimos	viví	vivimos
comiste	comisteis	viviste	vivisteis
comió	comieron	vivió	vivieron
comía	comíamos	vivía	vivíamos
comías	comíais	vivías	vivíais
comía	comían	vivía	vivían
comiera	comiéramos	viviera	viviéramos
comieras	comierais	vivieras	vivierais
comiera	comieran	viviera	vivieran
or		*or*	
comiese	comiésemos	viviese	viviésemos
comieses	comieseis	vivieses	vivieseis
comiese	comiesen	viviese	viviesen
comeré	comeremos	viviré	viviremos
comerás	comeréis	vivirás	viviréis
comerá	comerán	vivirá	vivirán
comiere	comiéremos	viviere	viviéremos
comieres	comiereis	vivieres	viviereis
comiere	comieren	viviere	vivieren
comería	comeríamos	viviría	viviríamos
comerías	comeríais	vivirías	viviríais
comería	comerían	viviría	vivirían
—	comamos	—	vivamos
come	comed	vive	vivid
coma	coman	viva	vivan
comiendo		viviendo	
comido		vivido	

Compound Tenses

1. Perfect Tenses

The perfect tenses are formed with *haber* and the past participle:

PRESENT PERFECT
he hablado, etc. (*indicative*);
haya hablado, etc. (*subjunctive*)

PAST PERFECT
había hablado, etc. (*indicative*);
hubiera hablado, etc. (*subjuntive*)
or
hubiese hablado, etc. (*subjunctive*)

PRETERIT PERFECT
hube hablado, etc. (*indicative*)

FUTURE PERFECT
habré hablado, etc. (*indicative*)

CONDITIONAL PERFECT
habría hablado, etc. (*indicative*)

2. Progressive Tenses

The progressive tenses are formed with *estar* and the present participle:

PRESENT PROGRESSIVE
estoy llamando, etc. (*indicative*);
esté llamando, etc. (*subjunctive*)

IMPERFECT PROGRESSIVE
estaba llamando, etc. (*indicative*);
estuviera llamando, etc. (*subjunctive*)
or
estuviese llamando, etc. (*subjunctive*)

PRETERIT PROGRESSIVE
estuve llamando, etc. (*indicative*)

FUTURE PROGRESSIVE
estaré llamando, etc. (*indicative*)

CONDITIONAL PROGRESSIVE
estaría llamando, etc. (*indicative*)

PRESENT PERFECT PROGRESSIVE
he estado llamando, etc. (*indicative*);
haya estado llamando, etc. (*subjunctive*)

PAST PERFECT PROGRESSIVE
había estado llamando, etc. (*indicative*);
hubiera estado llamando, etc. (*subjunctive*)
or
hubiese estado llamando, etc. (*subjunctive*)

Use of *Vos*

In parts of South and Central America, *vos* often replaces or competes with *tú* as the second person familiar personal pronoun. It is particularly well established in the Río de la Plata region and much of Central America.

The pronoun *vos* often takes a distinct set of verb forms, usually in the present tense and the imperative. These vary widely from region to region; examples of the most common forms are shown below.

INFINITIVE FORM	hablar	comer	vivir
PRESENT INDICATIVE	vos hablás	vos comés	vos vivís
PRESENT SUBJUNCTIVE	vos hablés	vos comás	vos vivás
IMPERATIVE	hablá	comé	viví

In some areas, *vos* may take the *tú* or *vosotros* forms of the verb, while in others (as Uruguay), *tú* is combined with the *vos* verb forms.

Irregular Verbs

The *imperfect subjunctive*, the *future subjunctive*, the *conditional*, and the remaining forms of the *imperative* are not included in the model conjugations list, but can be derived as follows:

The *imperfect subjunctive* and the *future subjunctive* are formed from the third person plural form of the preterit tense by removing the last syllable (-*ron*) and adding the appropriate suffix:

PRETERIT INDICATIVE, THIRD PERSON PLURAL (querer)	quisieron
IMPERFECT SUBJUNCTIVE (querer)	quisiera, quisieras, etc. *or* quisiese, quisieses, etc.
FUTURE SUBJUNCTIVE (querer)	quisiere, quisieres, etc.

The conditional uses the same stem as the future indicative:

FUTURE INDICATIVE (poner)	pondré, pondrás, etc.
CONDITIONAL (poner)	pondría, pondrías, etc.

The third person singular, first person plural, and third person plural forms of the *imperative* are the same as the corresponding forms of the present subjunctive.

The second person plural *(vosotros)* form of the *imperative* is formed by removing the final -*r* of the infinitive form and adding a -*d* (ex.: *oír* → *oíd*).

Model Conjugations of Irregular Verbs

The model conjugations below include the following simple tenses: the *present indicative* (IND), the *present subjunctive* (SUBJ), the *preterit indicative* (PRET), the *imperfect indicative* (IMPF), the *future indicative* (FUT), the second person singular form of the *imperative* (IMPER), the *present participle* or *gerund* (PRP), and the *past participle* (PP). Each set of conjugations is preceded by the corresponding infinitive form of the verb, shown in bold type. Only tenses containing irregularities are listed, and the irregular verb forms within each tense are displayed in bold type.

Each irregular verb entry in the Spanish-English section of this dictionary is cross-referred by number to one of the following model conjugations. These cross-reference numbers are shown in curly braces { } immediately following the entry's functional label.

1 **abolir** *(defective verb)* : *IND* abolimos, abolís *(other forms not used); SUBJ (not used); IMPER (only second person plural is used)*

2 **abrir** : *PP* abierto

3 **actuar** : *IND* actúo, actúas, actúa, actuamos, actuáis, actúan; *SUBJ* actúe, actúes, actúe, actuemos, actuéis, actúen; *IMPER* actúa

4 **adquirir** : *IND* adquiero, adquieres, adquiere, adquirimos, adquirís, adquieren; *SUBJ* adquiera, adquieras, adquiera, adquiramos, adquiráis, adquieran; *IMPER* adquiere

5 **airar** : *IND* aíro, aíras, aíra, airamos, airáis, aíran; *SUBJ* aíre, aíres, aíre, airemos, airéis, aíren; *IMPER* aíra

6 **andar** : *PRET* anduve, anduviste, anduvo, anduvimos, anduvisteis, anduvieron

7 **asir** : *IND* asgo, ases, ase, asimos, asís, asen; *SUBJ* asga, asgas, asga, asgamos, asgáis, asgan

8 **aunar** : *IND* aúno, aúnas, aúna, aunamos, aunáis, aúnan; *SUBJ* aúne, aúnes, aúne, aunemos, aunéis, aúnen; *IMPER* aúna

9 **avergonzar** : *IND* avergüenzo, avergüenzas, avergüenza, avergonzamos, avergonzáis, avergüenzan; *SUBJ* avergüence, avergüences, avergüence, avergoncemos, avergoncéis, avergüencen; *PRET* avergoncé; *IMPER* avergüenza

10 **averiguar** : *SUBJ* averigüe, averigües, averigüe, averigüemos, averigüéis, averigüen; *PRET* averigüé, averiguaste, averiguó, averiguamos, averiguasteis, averiguaron

11 **bendecir** : *IND* bendigo, bendices, bendice, bendecimos, bendecís, bendicen; *SUBJ* bendiga, bendigas, bendiga, bendigamos, bendigáis, bendigan; *PRET* bendije, bendijiste, bendijo, bendijimos, bendijisteis, bendijeron; *IMPER* bendice

12 **caber** : *IND* quepo, cabes, cabe, cabemos, cabéis, caben; *SUBJ* quepa, quepas, quepa, quepamos, quepáis, quepan; *PRET* cupe, cupiste, cupo, cupimos, cupisteis, cupieron; *FUT* cabré, cabrás, cabrá, cabremos, cabréis, cabrán

13 **caer** : *IND* caigo, caes, cae, caemos, caéis, caen; *SUBJ* caiga, caigas, caiga, caigamos, caigáis, caigan; *PRET* caí, caíste, cayó, caímos, caísteis, cayeron; *PRP* cayendo; *PP* caído

14 **cocer** : *IND* cuezo, cueces, cuece, cocemos, cocéis, cuecen; *SUBJ* cueza, cuezas, cueza, cozamos, cozáis, cuezan; *IMPER* cuece

15 **coger** : *IND* cojo, coges, coge, cogemos, cogéis, cogen; *SUBJ* coja, cojas, coja, cojamos, cojáis, cojan

16 **colgar** : *IND* cuelgo, cuelgas, cuelga, colgamos, colgáis, cuelgan; *SUBJ* cuelgue, cuelgues, cuelgue, colguemos, colguéis, cuelguen; *PRET* colgué, colgaste, colgó, colgamos, colgasteis, colgaron; *IMPER* cuelga

17 **concernir** *(defective verb; used only in the third person singular and plural of the present indicative, present subjunctive, and imperfect subjunctive) see 25* **discernir**

18 **conocer** : *IND* conozco, conoces, conoce, conocemos, conocéis, conocen; *SUBJ* conozca, conozcas, conozca, conozcamos, conozcáis, conozcan

19 **contar** : *IND* cuento, cuentas, cuenta, contamos, contáis, cuentan; *SUBJ* cuente, cuentes, cuente, contemos, contéis, cuenten; *IMPER* cuenta

20 **creer** : *PRET* creí, creíste, creyó, creímos, creísteis, creyeron; *PRP* creyendo; *PP* creído

21 **cruzar** : *SUBJ* cruce, cruces, cruce, crucemos, crucéis, crucen; *PRET* crucé, cruzaste, cruzó, cruzamos, cruzasteis, cruzaron

22 **dar** : *IND* doy, das, da, damos, dais, dan; *SUBJ* dé, des, dé, demos, deis, den; *PRET* di, diste, dio, dimos, disteis, dieron

23 **decir** : *IND* digo, dices, dice, decimos, decís, dicen; *SUBJ* diga, digas, diga, digamos, digáis, digan; *PRET* dije, dijiste, dijo, dijimos, dijisteis, dijeron; *FUT* diré, dirás, dirá, diremos, diréis, dirán; *IMPER* di; *PRP* diciendo; *PP* dicho

24 **delinquir** : *IND* delinco, delinques, delinque, delinquimos, delinquís, delinquen; *SUBJ* delinca, delincas, delinca, delincamos, delincáis, delincan

25 **discernir** : *IND* discierno, disciernes, discierne, discernimos, discernís, disciernen; *SUBJ* discierna, disciernas, discierna, discernamos, discernáis, disciernan; *IMPER* discierne

26 **distinguir** : *IND* distingo, distingues, distingue, distinguimos, distinguís, distinguen; *SUBJ* distinga, distingas, distinga, distingamos, distingáis, distingan

27 **dormir** : *IND* duermo, duermes, duerme, dormimos, dormís, duermen; *SUBJ* duerma, duermas, duerma, durmamos, durmáis, duerman; *PRET* dormí, dormiste, durmió, dormimos, dormisteis, durmieron; *IMPER* duerme; *PRP* durmiendo

28 **elegir** : *IND* **elijo, eliges, elige,** elegimos, elegís, **eligen;** *SUBJ* **elija, elijas, elija, elijamos, elijáis, elijan;** *PRET* elegí, elegiste, **eligió,** elegimos, elegisteis, **eligieron;** *IMPER* **elige;** *PRP* **eligiendo**

29 **empezar** : *IND* **empiezo, empiezas, empieza,** empezamos, empezáis, **empiezan;** *SUBJ* **empiece, empieces, empiece,** empecemos, empecéis, **empiecen;** *PRET* **empecé,** empezaste, empezó, empezamos, empezasteis, empezaron; *IMPER* **empieza**

30 **enraizar** : *IND* **enraízo, enraízas, enraíza,** enraizamos, enraizáis, **enraízan;** *SUBJ* **enraíce, enraíces, enraíce,** enraicemos, enraicéis, **enraícen;** *PRET* **enraicé,** enraizaste, enraizó, enraizamos, enraizasteis, enraizaron; *IMPER* **enraíza**

31 **erguir** : *IND* **irgo** *or* **yergo, irgues** *or* **yergues, irgue** *or* **yergue,** erguimos, erguís, **irguen** *or* **yerguen;** *SUBJ* **irga** *or* **yerga, irgas** *or* **yergas, irga** *or* **yerga, irgamos, irgáis, irgan** *or* **yergan;** *PRET* erguí, erguiste, **irguió,** erguimos, erguisteis, **irguieron;** *IMPER* **irgue** *or* **yergue;** *PRP* **irguiendo**

32 **errar** : *IND* **yerro, yerras, yerra,** erramos, erráis, **yerran;** *SUBJ* **yerre, yerres, yerre,** erremos, erréis, **yerren;** *IMPER* **yerra**

33 **escribir** : *PP* **escrito**

34 **estar** : *IND* **estoy, estás, está,** estamos, estáis, **están;** *SUBJ* **esté, estés, esté,** estemos, estéis, **estén;** *PRET* **estuve, estuviste, estuvo, estuvimos, estuvisteis, estuvieron;** *IMPER* **está**

35 **exigir** : *IND* **exijo,** exiges, exige, exigimos, exigís, exigen; *SUBJ* **exija, exijas, exija, exijamos, exijáis, exijan**

36 **forzar** : *IND* **fuerzo, fuerzas, fuerza,** forzamos, forzáis, **fuerzan;** *SUBJ* **fuerce, fuerces, fuerce,** forcemos, forcéis, **fuercen;** *PRET* **forcé,** forzaste, forzó, forzamos, forzasteis, forzaron; *IMPER* **fuerza**

37 **freír** : *IND* **frío, fríes, fríe,** freímos, freís, **fríen;** *SUBJ* **fría, frías, fría, friamos, friáis, frían;** *PRET* freí, freíste, frió, freímos, freísteis, frieron; *IMPER* **fríe;** *PRP* **friendo;** *PP* **frito**

38 **gruñir** : *PRET* gruñí, gruñiste, **gruñó,** gruñimos, gruñisteis, **gruñeron;** *PRP* **gruñendo**

39 **haber** : *IND* **he, has, ha, hemos,** habéis, **han;** *SUBJ* **haya, hayas, haya, hayamos, hayáis, hayan;** *PRET* **hube, hubiste, hubo, hubimos, hubisteis, hubieron;** *FUT* **habré, habrás, habrá, habremos, habréis, habrán;** *IMPER* **he**

40 **hacer** : *IND* **hago,** haces, hace, hacemos, hacéis, hacen; *SUBJ* **haga, hagas, haga, hagamos, hagáis, hagan;** *PRET* **hice, hiciste, hizo, hicimos, hicisteis, hicieron;** *FUT* **haré, harás, hará, haremos, haréis, harán;** *IMPER* **haz;** *PP* **hecho**

41 **huir** : *IND* **huyo, huyes, huye,** huimos, huís, **huyen;** *SUBJ* **huya, huyas, huya, huyamos, huyáis, huyan;** *PRET* huí, huiste, **huyó,** huimos, huisteis, **huyeron;** *IMPER* **huye;** *PRP* **huyendo**

42 **imprimir** : *PP* **impreso**

43 **ir** : *IND* **voy, vas, va, vamos, vais, van;** *SUBJ* **vaya, vayas, vaya, vayamos, vayáis, vayan;** *PRET* **fui, fuiste, fue, fuimos, fuisteis, fueron;** *IMPF* **iba, ibas, iba, íbamos, ibais, iban;** *IMPER* **ve;** *PRP* **yendo;** *PP* **ido**

44 **jugar** : *IND* **juego, juegas, juega,** jugamos, jugáis, **juegan;** *SUBJ* **juegue, juegues, juegue, juguemos, juguéis, jueguen;** *PRET* **jugué,** jugaste, jugó, jugamos, jugasteis, jugaron; *IMPER* **juega**

45 **lucir** : *IND* **luzco,** luces, luce, lucimos, lucís, lucen; *SUBJ* **luzca, luzcas, luzca, luzcamos, luzcáis, luzcan**

46 **morir** : *IND* **muero, mueres, muere,** morimos, morís, **mueren;** *SUBJ* **muera, mueras, muera,** muramos, muráis, **mueran;** *PRET* morí, moriste, **murió,** morimos, moristeis, **murieron;** *IMPER* **muere;** *PRP* **muriendo;** *PP* **muerto**

47 **mover** : *IND* **muevo, mueves, mueve,** movemos, movéis, **mueven;** *SUBJ* **mueva, muevas, mueva,** movamos, továis, **muevan;** *IMPER* **mueve**

48 **nacer** : *IND* **nazco,** naces, nace, nacemos, nacéis, nacen; *SUBJ* **nazca, nazcas, nazca, nazcamos, nazcáis, nazcan**

49 **negar** : *IND* **niego, niegas, niega,** negamos, negáis, **niegan;** *SUBJ* **niegue, niegues, niegue,** neguemos, neguéis, **nieguen;** *PRET* **negué,** negaste, negó, negamos, negasteis, negaron; *IMPER* **niega**

50 **oír** : *IND* **oigo, oyes, oye,** oímos, oís, **oyen;** *SUBJ* **oiga, oigas, oiga, oigamos, oigáis, oigan;** *PRET* oí, oíste, **oyó,** oímos, oísteis, **oyeron;** *IMPER* **oye;** *PRP* **oyendo;** *PP* **oído**

51 **oler** : *IND* **huelo, hueles, huele,** olemos, oléis, **huelen;** *SUBJ* **huela, huelas, huela,** olamos, oláis, **huelan;** *IMPER* **huele**

52 **pagar** : *SUBJ* **pague, pagues, pague, paguemos, paguéis, paguen;** *PRET* **pagué,** pagaste, pagó, pagamos, pagasteis, pagaron

53 **parecer** : *IND* **parezco**, pareces, parece, parecemos, parecéis, parecen; *SUBJ* **parezca, parezcas, parezca, parezcamos, parezcáis, parezcan**

54 **pedir** : *IND* **pido, pides, pide**, pedimos, pedís, **piden**; *SUBJ* **pida, pidas, pida, pidamos, pidáis, pidan**; *PRET* pedí, pediste, **pidió**, pedimos, pedisteis, **pidieron**; *IMPER* **pide**; *PRP* **pidiendo**

55 **pensar** : *IND* **pienso, piensas, piensa**, pensamos, pensáis, **piensan**; *SUBJ* **piense, pienses, piense**, pensemos, penséis, **piensen**; *IMPER* **piensa**

56 **perder** : *IND* **pierdo, pierdes, pierde**, perdemos, perdéis, **pierden**; *SUBJ* **pierda, pierdas, pierda**, perdamos, perdáis, **pierdan**; *IMPER* **pierde**

57 **placer** : *IND* **plazco**, places, place, placemos, placéis, placen; *SUBJ* **plazca, plazcas, plazca, plazcamos, plazcáis, plazcan**; *PRET* plací, placiste, plació *or* **plugo**, placimos, placisteis, placieron *or* **pluguieron**

58 **poder** : *IND* **puedo, puedes, puede**, podemos, podéis, **pueden**; *SUBJ* **pueda, puedas, pueda**, podamos, podáis, **puedan**; *PRET* **pude**, pudiste, **pudo**, pudimos, pudisteis, pudieron; *FUT* **podré, podrás, podrá, podremos, podréis, podrán**; *IMPER* **puede**; *PRP* **pudiendo**

59 **podrir** *or* **pudrir** : *PP* **podrido** *(all other forms based on* pudrir*)*

60 **poner** : *IND* **pongo**, pones, pone, ponemos, ponéis, ponen; *SUBJ* **ponga, pongas, ponga, pongamos, pongáis, pongan**; *PRET* **puse**, pusiste, **puso**, pusimos, pusisteis, pusieron; *FUT* **pondré, pondrás, pondrá, pondremos, pondréis, pondrán**; *IMPER* **pon**; *PP* **puesto**

61 **producir** : *IND* **produzco**, produces, produce, producimos, producís, producen; *SUBJ* **produzca, produzcas, produzca, produzcamos, produzcáis, produzcan**; *PRET* **produje, produjiste, produjo, produjimos, produjisteis, produjeron**

62 **prohibir** : *IND* **prohíbo, prohíbes, prohíbe**, prohibimos, prohibís, **prohíben**; *SUBJ* **prohíba, prohíbas, prohíba**, prohibamos, prohibáis, **prohíban**; *IMPER* **prohíbe**

63 **proveer** : *PRET* proveí, **proveíste, proveyó, proveímos, proveísteis, proveyeron**; *PRP* **proveyendo**; *PP* **provisto**

64 **querer** : *IND* **quiero, quieres, quiere**, queremos, queréis, **quieren**; *SUBJ* **quiera, quieras, quiera**, queramos, queráis, **quieran**; *PRET* **quise**, quisiste, **quiso**, quisimos, quisisteis, quisieron; *FUT* **querré, querrás, querrá, querremos, querréis, querrán**; *IMPER* **quiere**

65 **raer** : *IND* rao *or* **raigo** *or* **rayo**, raes, rae, raemos, raéis, raen; *SUBJ* **raiga** *or* **raya**, **raigas** *or* **rayas**, **raiga** *or* **raya, raigamos** *or* **rayamos, raigáis** *or* **rayáis, raigan** *or* **rayan**; *PRET* raí, **raíste**, **rayó, raímos, raísteis, rayeron**; *PRP* **rayendo**; *PP* **raído**

66 **reír** : *IND* **río, ríes, ríe, reímos**, reís, **ríen**; *SUBJ* **ría, rías, ría, riamos, riáis, rían**; *PRET* reí, **reíste**, rió, **reímos, reísteis**, rieron; *IMPER* **ríe**; *PRP* **riendo**; *PP* **reído**

67 **reñir** : *IND* **riño, riñes, riñe**, reñimos, reñís, **riñen**; *SUBJ* **riña, riñas, riña, riñamos, riñáis, riñan**; *PRET* reñí, reñiste, **riñó**, reñimos, reñisteis, **riñeron**; *IMPER* **riñe**; *PRP* **riñendo**

68 **reunir** : *IND* **reúno, reúnes, reúne**, reunimos, reunís, **reúnen**; *SUBJ* **reúna, reúnas, reúna**, reunamos, reunáis, **reúnan**; *IMPER* **reúne**

69 **roer** : *IND* roo *or* **roigo** *or* **royo**, roes, roe, roemos, roéis, roen; *SUBJ* roa *or* **roiga** *or* **roya**, roas *or* **roigas** *or* **royas**, roa *or* **roiga** *or* **roya**, roamos *or* **roigamos** *or* **royamos**, roáis *or* **roigáis** *or* **royáis**, roan *or* **roigan** *or* **royan**; *PRET* roí, **roíste, royó, roímos, roísteis, royeron**; *PRP* **royendo**; *PP* **roído**

70 **romper** : *PP* **roto**

71 **saber** : *IND* **sé**, sabes, sabe, sabemos, sabéis, saben; *SUBJ* **sepa, sepas, sepa, sepamos, sepáis, sepan**; *PRET* **supe**, supiste, **supo**, supimos, supisteis, supieron; *FUT* **sabré, sabrás, sabrá, sabremos, sabréis, sabrán**

72 **sacar** : *SUBJ* **saque, saques, saque, saquemos, saquéis, saquen**; *PRET* **saqué**, sacaste, sacó, sacamos, sacasteis, sacaron

73 **salir** : *IND* **salgo**, sales, sale, salimos, salís, salen; *SUBJ* **salga, salgas, salga, salgamos, salgáis, salgan**; *FUT* **saldré, saldrás, saldrá, saldremos, saldréis, saldrán**; *IMPER* **sal**

74 **satisfacer** : *IND* **satisfago**, satisfaces, satisface, satisfacemos, satisfacéis, satisfacen; *SUBJ* **satisfaga, satisfagas, satisfaga, satisfagamos, satisfagáis, satisfagan**; *PRET* **satisfice, satisficiste, satisfizo, satisficimos, satificisteis, satisficieron**; *FUT* **satisfaré, satisfarás, satisfará, satisfaremos, satisfaréis, satisfarán**; *IMPER* **satisfaz** *or* satisface; *PP* **satisfecho**

75 **seguir** : *IND* **sigo, sigues, sigue**, seguimos, seguís, **siguen**; *SUBJ* **siga, sigas, siga, sigamos, sigáis, sigan**; *PRET* seguí, seguiste, **siguió**, seguimos, seguisteis, **siguieron**; *IMPER* **sigue**; *PRP* **siguiendo**

76 **sentir** : *IND* **siento, sientes, siente,** sentimos, sentís, **sienten;** *SUBJ* **sienta, sientas, sienta, sintamos, sintáis, sientan;** *PRET* sentí, sentiste, **sintió,** sentimos, sentisteis, **sintieron;** *IMPER* **siente;** *PRP* **sintiendo**

77 **ser** : *IND* **soy, eres, es,** somos, sois, **son;** *SUBJ* **sea, seas, sea, seamos, seáis, sean;** *PRET* **fui, fuiste, fue, fuimos, fuisteis, fueron;** *IMPF* **era, eras, era, éramos, erais, eran;** *IMPER* **sé;** *PRP* **siendo;** *PP* **sido**

78 **soler** *(defective verb; used only in the present, preterit, and imperfect indicative, and the present and imperfect subjunctive) see* 47 **mover**

79 **tañer** : *PRET* **tañí,** tañiste, **tañó,** tañimos, tañisteis, **tañeron;** *PRP* **tañendo**

80 **tener** : *IND* **tengo, tienes, tiene,** tenemos, tenéis, **tienen;** *SUBJ* **tenga, tengas, tenga, tengamos, tengáis, tengan;** *PRET* **tuve, tuviste, tuvo, tuvimos, tuvisteis, tuvieron;** *FUT* **tendré, tendrás, tendrá, tendremos, tendréis, tendrán;** *IMPER* **ten**

81 **traer** : *IND* **traigo,** traes, trae, traemos, traéis, traen; *SUBJ* **traiga, traigas, traiga, traigamos, traigáis, traigan;** *PRET* **traje, trajiste, trajo, trajimos, trajisteis, trajeron;** *PRP* **trayendo;** *PP* **traído**

82 **trocar** : *IND* **trueco, truecas, trueca,** trocamos, trocáis, **truecan;** *SUBJ* **trueque, trueques, trueque, troquemos, troquéis, truequen;** *PRET* **troqué,** trocaste, trocó, trocamos, trocasteis, trocaron; *IMPER* **trueca**

83 **uncir** : *IND* **unzo,** unces, unce, uncimos, uncís, uncen; *SUBJ* **unza, unzas, unza, unzamos, unzáis, unzan**

84 **valer** : *IND* **valgo,** vales, vale, valemos, valéis, valen; *SUBJ* **valga, valgas, valga, valgamos, valgáis, valgan;** *FUT* **valdré, valdrás, valdrá, valdremos, valdréis, valdrán**

85 **variar** : *IND* **varío, varías, varía,** variamos, variáis, **varían;** *SUBJ* **varíe, varíes, varíe,** variemos, variéis, **varíen;** *IMPER* **varía**

86 **vencer** : *IND* **venzo,** vences, vence, vencemos, vencéis, vencen; *SUBJ* **venza, venzas, venza, venzamos, venzáis, venzan**

87 **venir** : *IND* **vengo, vienes, viene,** venimos, venís, **vienen;** *SUBJ* **venga, vengas, venga, vengamos, vengáis, vengan;** *PRET* **vine, viniste, vino, vinimos, vinisteis, vinieron;** *FUT* **vendré, vendrás, vendrá, vendremos, vendréis, vendrán;** *IMPER* **ven;** *PRP* **viniendo**

88 **ver** : *IND* **veo, ves, ve,** vemos, veis, ven; *PRET* **vi,** viste, vio, vimos, visteis, vieron; *IMPER* **ve;** *PRP* **viendo;** *PP* **visto**

89 **volver** : *IND* **vuelvo, vuelves, vuelve,** volvemos, volvéis, **vuelven;** *SUBJ* **vuelva, vuelvas, vuelva,** volvamos, volváis, **vuelvan;** *IMPER* **vuelve;** *PP* **vuelto**

90 **yacer** : *IND* **yazco** *or* **yazgo** *or* **yago,** yaces, yace, yacemos, yacéis, yacen; *SUBJ* **yazca** *or* **yazga** *or* **yaga, yazcas** *or* **yazgas** *or* **yagas, yazca** *or* **yazga** *or* **yaga, yazcamos** *or* **yazgamos** *or* **yagamos, yazcáis** *or* **yazgáis** *or* **yagáis, yazcan** *or* **yazgan** *or* **yagan;** *IMPER* **yace** *or* **yaz**

Los verbos irregulares en inglés

Los verbos regulares en inglés, como *call* o *trust*, siguen un patrón previsible en las formas del pasado y el participio pasado (las cuales se llaman las "partes principales"). Éstas se forman agregando *-ed* al infinitivo. A veces, la adición de esta terminación (o *desinencia*) resulta en una sílaba más (*trusted* ['trʌstəd]) y otras veces no (*called* ['kɔld]).

Un verbo se considera regular incluso cuando al añadir *-ed* hace que la consonante final se dobla (*abet, abetted, abetted*) o la *-e* final se elimina (*die, died, died*).

Un verbo se considera irregular si la forma del pasado o del participio pasado no sigue el patrón normal de agregar *-ed* (*swim, swam, swum*) o si una o ambas de éstas tienen otra grafía además de la que termina en *-ed* (*saw, sawed, sawed* o *sawn*). Muchas veces, esta variante ortográfica se forma sustituyendo la *-ed* por *-t* (*burn, burned* o *burnt*), la cual representa una pronunciación típica.

A continuación se ofrece una lista de algunos verbos irregulares en inglés que muestra las formas del pasado y el participio pasado junto con cualquier variante ortográfica que corresponda.

INFINITIVO	PASADO	PARTICIPIO PASADO
arise	arose	arisen
awake	awoke	awoken
	también awaked	*o* awaked
		también awoke
be	was, were	been
bear	bore	borne
		también born
beat	beat	beaten
		o beat
become	became	become
befall	befell	befallen
begin	began	begun
behold	beheld	beheld
bend	bent	bent
beseech	besought	besought
	o beseeched	*o* beseeched
beset	beset	beset
bet	bet	bet
	también betted	*también* betted
bid	bade	bidden
	o bid	*o* bid
		también bade
bind	bound	bound
bite	bit	bitten
		también bit
bleed	bled	bled
blow	blew	blown
break	broke	broken
breed	bred	bred
bring	brought	brought
build	built	built
burn	burned	burned
	o burnt	*o* burnt
burst	burst	burst
	también bursted	*también* bursted
buy	bought	bought
can (auxiliary verb)	could	—
cast	cast	cast
catch	caught	caught
choose	chose	chosen
cling	clung	clung
come	came	come
cost	cost	cost
creep	crept	crept

cut	cut	cut
deal	dealt	dealt
dig	dug	dug
do	did	done
draw	drew	drawn
dream	dreamed	dreamed
	o dreamt	*o* dreamt
drink	drank	drunk
		o drank
drive	drove	driven
dwell	dwelt	dwelt
	o dwelled	*o* dwelled
eat	ate	eaten
fall	fell	fallen
feed	fed	fed
feel	felt	felt
fight	fought	fought
find	found	found
flee	fled	fled
fling	flung	flung
fly	flew	flown
forbid	forbade	forbidden
	también forbad	
forecast	forecast	forecast
	también forecasted	*también* forecasted
forego	forewent	foregone
foresee	foresaw	foreseen
foretell	foretold	foretold
forget	forgot	forgotten
		o forgot
forgive	forgave	forgiven
forsake	forsook	forsaken
freeze	froze	frozen
get	got	got
		o gotten
give	gave	given
go	went	gone
grind	ground	ground
grow	grew	grown
hang	hung	hung
	también hanged	*también* hanged
have	had	had
hear	heard	heard
hide	hid	hidden
		o hid
hit	hit	hit
hold	held	held
hurt	hurt	hurt
keep	kept	kept
kneel	knelt	knelt
	o kneeled	*o* kneeled
know	knew	known
lay	laid	laid
lead	led	led
lean	leaned	leaned
	también leant	
leap	leapt	leapt
	o leaped	*o* leaped
leave	left	left
lend	lent	lent
let	let	let
lie (to recline)	lay	lain
light	lit	lit
	o lighted	*o* lighted
lose	lost	lost

make	made	made
may	might	—
mean	meant	meant
meet	met	met
mow	mowed	mowed
		o mown
pay	paid	paid
put	put	put
quit	quit	quit
	también quitted	*también* quitted
read	read	read
rend	rent	rent
rid	rid	rid
	también ridded	*también* ridded
ride	rode	ridden
ring (to sound)	rang	rung
rise	rose	risen
run	ran	run
saw	sawed	sawed
		o sawn
say	said	said
see	saw	seen
seek	sought	sought
sell	sold	sold
send	sent	sent
set	set	set
shake	shook	shaken
shall (auxiliary verb)	should	—
shear	sheared	sheared
		o shorn
shed	shed	shed
shine	shone	shone
	o shined	*o* shined
shoot	shot	shot
show	showed	shown
		o showed
shrink	shrank	shrunk
	o shrunk	*o* shrunken
shut	shut	shut
sing	sang	sung
	o sung	
sink	sank	sunk
	o sunk	
sit	sat	sat
slay	slew	slain
sleep	slept	slept
slide	slid	slid
sling	slung	slung
smell	smelled	smelled
	o smelt	*o* smelt
sow	sowed	sown
		o sowed
speak	spoke	spoken
speed	sped	sped
	o speeded	*o* speeded
spell	spelled	spelled
spend	spent	spent
spill	spilled	spilled
	también spilt	*también* spilt
spin	spun	spun
spit (to eject saliva)	spit	spit
	o spat	*o* spat
split	split	split
spoil	spoiled	spoiled
	o spoilt	*o* spoilt

spread	spread	spread
spring	sprang	sprung
	o sprung	
stand	stood	stood
steal	stole	stolen
stick	stuck	stuck
sting	stung	stung
stink	stank	stunk
	o stunk	
stride	strode	stridden
strike	struck	struck
		también stricken
swear	swore	sworn
sweep	swept	swept
swell	swelled	swelled
		o swollen
swim	swam	swum
swing	swung	swung
take	took	taken
teach	taught	taught
tear (to rip)	tore	torn
tell	told	told
think	thought	thought
throw	threw	thrown
thrust	thrust	thrust
tread	trod	trodden
		o trod
wake	woke	woken
	también waked	*también* waked
		o woke
waylay	waylaid	waylaid
wear	wore	worn
weave	wove	woven
	o weaved	*o* weaved
wed	wedded	wedded
	también wed	*también* wed
weep	wept	wept
will (auxiliary verb)	would	—
win	won	won
wind (to encircle)	wound	wound
	también winded	*también* winded
withdraw	withdrew	withdrawn
withhold	withheld	withheld
withstand	withstood	withstood
wring	wrung	wrung
write	wrote	written
		también writ

Contracciones en inglés

Los hablantes nativos de inglés frecuentemente acortan (o contraen) nueve palabras comunes en el habla coloquial. Ocho de éstas son verbos: *have, has, had, is, am, are, will,* y *would.* Una es un adverbio: *not.* Estas palabras también se acortan con frecuencia en la escritura informal. La forma acortada de la palabra está unida con la palabra que la precede; cuando la contracción es por escrito, un apóstrofo (') sustituye las letras omitidas.

La tabla siguiente demuestra cómo los ocho verbos son contraídos cuando siguen un pronombre personal.

I have → **I've**	you have → **you've**	she has → **she's**	they have → **they've**
I had → **I'd**	you had → **you'd**	he had → **he'd**	we had → **we'd**
I am → **I'm**	you are → **you're**	it is → **it's**	we are → **we're**
I will → **I'll**	you will → **you'll**	he will → **he'll**	they will → **they'll**
I would → **I'd**	you would → **you'd**	she would → **she'd**	we would → **we'd**

I would have → **I'd have; I would've**
you would have → **you'd have; you would've**
it would have → **it would've; it'd have**
they would have → **they'd have; they would've**

Observe como -*'s* puede sustituir *is* o *has.* (También puede formar el genitivo, como en el ejemplo "Sarah's dog.") La forma contraída -*'d* puede sustituir las palabras *had* o *would.* En preguntas, -*'d* algunas veces sustituye la palabra *did* ("Where'd he go?" "Why'd you do it?").

Las contracciones se forman comúnmente con otros pronombres también: "Who's that?" "What's happening?" "Someone's coming." "Who'd have guessed it?" "That'll be all." "This'll work. " Frecuentemente se forman con sustantivos: "Michael's here." "The coffee's hot." "Time's passing." etc. Y comúnmente se usan con *here* y *there*: "Here's the book." "There'd be plenty of food. "

Las contracciones comúnmente se forman al añadir -*'ve* (*have*) a los verbos modales *would, could, should,* y *might*: "Argentina could've won." "Those should've been better." "I might've known."

Puede contraer el adverbio *not* a -*n't* y combinarlo con los verbos en esta lista:

are → **aren't**	has → **hasn't**	ought → **oughtn't**
can → **can't**	have → **haven't**	should → **shouldn't**
could → **couldn't**	is → **isn't**	was → **wasn't**
did → **didn't**	might → **mightn't**	were → **weren't**
do → **don't**	must → **mustn't**	will → **won't**
does → **doesn't**	need → **needn't**	would → **wouldn't**
had → **hadn't**		

Observe que *will/won't* es el único ejemplo irregular.

La contracción *let's* (*let us*) se utiliza comúnmente incluso en la escritura formal. *Ain't* (*am not, are not, is not, have not, has not*) es común en el habla informal pero nunca se utiliza en la escritura formal. *Y'all* (*you all*) es común en el habla del sur de los Estados Unidos.

Prefijos y sufijos en inglés

El aprendizaje de los prefijos y sufijos comunes en inglés le ayudará a comprender y recordar el significado de muchas palabras inglesas.

PREFIJOS

PREFIJO	SIGNIFICADO	EJEMPLOS
a-, an-	*not, without*	asexual
ante-	*before*	antedate, anteroom
anti-	*against, opposite*	antidote, anticlimax
arch-	*chief, extreme*	archbishop, archenemy
bi-	*two, every other, twice a*	bicycle, bipartisan, biweekly, biannual
co-	*with, together*	coexist, coauthor
counter-	*opposite, against*	counterclockwise, counteract
dis-	*exclude, not*	disbar, disagreeable
ex-	*former*	ex-husband, ex-president
extra-	*outside, beyond*	extracurricular, extraterrestrial
hyper-	*very, too much*	hypercritical, hyperactive, hypertension
hypo-	*under, down, below normal*	hypothermia, hypoallergenic
in-	*not*	incapable, inconsistent
inter-	*between, among*	intermarry, international
mis-	*bad, wrongly*	mistake, mislead
non-	*not*	nonalcoholic, nontoxic
out-	*more than*	outgrow, outnumber
over-	*go beyond, too much, very*	overachieve, overambitious
pre-	*before*	prehistoric, premature
pro-	*favoring, supporting*	pro-American
re-	*again, back*	retell, recall
semi-	*twice a, half, partly, partial*	semiannual, semicircle, semiconsciousness
sub-	*under, division*	subsoil, substandard, subtopic
super-	*more than*	superhighway, superhuman
tri-	*three*	triangle, tricycle
un-	*not, contrary to, reverse, remove*	unable, unethical, unfold, untie
under-	*below, too low or little*	underlying, underpaid

SUFIJOS

SUFIJO	SIGNIFICADO	EJEMPLOS
-able, -ible	*tending to, fit for*	agreeable, collectible
-al	*relating to, action*	fictional, rehearsal
-ant	*one that does, doing or acting*	assistant, coolant, hesitant
-ee	*one who does or receives*	escapee, trainee
-eer	*one who does or makes*	auctioneer, profiteer
-er	*one that has, is, does, or is connected with*	double-decker, foreigner, reporter, prisoner
-ful	*characterized by, amount that fills*	peaceful, helpful, cupful
-fy	*cause to become*	simplify, purify
-ion	*act or process, state or condition*	ignition, perfection
-ish	*almost, approximately*	greenish
-istic, -istical	*relating to, characterized by*	altruistic, egotistical
-itis	*disease, inflammation*	arthritis, bronchitis
-ize	*treat like, become like*	idolize, crystallize
-less	*not having, doing, or becoming*	witless, childless, tireless
-like	*resembling*	apelike, childlike
-ment	*action or process, result, condition*	development, entertainment, excitement
-ness	*condition, quality*	alertness, goodness
-ous	*full of, having or containing*	glamorous, poisonous
-ship	*condition, skill, position, status*	friendship, penmanship, professorship
-ward	*toward*	westward, upward
-y	*characterized by*	dirty, icy, sleepy

Números/Numbers

Números cardinales/Cardinal Numbers

Español/Spanish		Inglés/English
uno	1	one
dos	2	two
tres	3	three
cuatro	4	four
cinco	5	five
seis	6	six
siete	7	seven
ocho	8	eight
nueve	9	nine
diez	10	ten
once	11	eleven
doce	12	twelve
trece	13	thirteen
catorce	14	fourteen
quince	15	fifteen
dieciséis	16	sixteen
diecisiete	17	seventeen
dieciocho	18	eighteen
diecinueve	19	nineteen
veinte	20	twenty
veintiuno	21	twenty-one
veintidós	22	twenty-two
veintitrés	23	twenty-three
veinticuatro	24	twenty-four
veinticinco	25	twenty-five
veintiséis	26	twenty-six
veintisiete	27	twenty-seven
veintiocho	28	twenty-eight
veintinueve	29	twenty-nine
treinta	30	thirty
treinta y uno	31	thirty-one
treinta y dos	32	thirty-two
treinta y tres	33	thirty-three
treinta y cuatro	34	thirty-four
treinta y cinco	35	thirty-five
treinta y seis	36	thirty-six
treinta y siete	37	thirty-seven
treinta y ocho	38	thirty-eight
treinta y nueve	39	thirty-nine
cuarenta	40	forty
cuarenta y uno	41	forty-one
cincuenta	50	fifty
sesenta	60	sixty
setenta	70	seventy
ochenta	80	eighty
noventa	90	ninety
cien	100	hundred
ciento uno	101	hundred one
ciento dos	102	hundred two
doscientos	200	two hundred
trescientos	300	three hundred
cuatrocientos	400	four hundred
quinientos	500	five hundred
seiscientos	600	six hundred
setecientos	700	seven hundred
ochocientos	800	eight hundred
novecientos	900	nine hundred
mil	1,000	thousand

Números ordinales/Ordinal Numbers

Español/Spanish		Inglés/English
primero, -ra	1st	first
segundo, -da	2nd	second
tercero, -ra	3rd	third
cuarto, -ta	4th	fourth
quinto, -ta	5th	fifth
sexto, -ta	6th	sixth
séptimo, -ma	7th	seventh
octavo, -va	8th	eighth
noveno, -na	9th	ninth
décimo, -ma	10th	tenth
undécimo, -ma	11th	eleventh
duodécimo, -ma	12th	twelfth
decimotercero, -ra	13th	thirteenth
decimocuarto, -ta	14th	fourteenth
decimoquinto, -ta	15th	fifteenth
decimosexto, -ta	16th	sixteenth
decimoséptimo, -ma	17th	sevententh
decimoctavo, -va	18th	eighteenth
decimonoveno, -na _or_ decimonono, -na	19th	nineteenth
vigésimo, -ma	20th	twentieth
vigésimoprimero, vigésimaprimera	21st	twenty-first
vigésimosegundo, vigésimasegunda	22nd	twenty-second
trigésimo, -ma	30th	thirtieth
cuadragésimo, -ma	40th	fortieth
quincuagésimo, -ma	50th	fiftieth
sexagésimo, -ma	60th	sixtieth
septuagésimo, -ma	70th	seventieth
octogésimo, -ma	80th	eightieth
nonagésimo, -ma	90th	ninetieth
centésimo, -ma	100th	hundredth
ducentésimo	200th	two hundredth
tricentésimo	300th	three hundredth
cuadringentésimo	400th	four hundredth
quingentésimo	500th	five hundredth
sexcentésimo	600th	six hundredth
septingentésimo	700th	seven hundredth
octingésimo	800th	eight hundredth
noningentésimo	900th	nine hundredth
milésimo	1,000th	one thousandth

Abreviaturas empleadas en este libro/Abbreviations used in this work

	ESPAÑOL/SPANISH	INGLÉS/ENGLISH
adj	adjetivo	adjective
adv	adverbio	adverb
Arg	Argentina	Argentina
Bol	Bolivia	Bolivia
CA	Centroamérica	Central America
Car	Región del Caribe	Caribbean region
Col	Colombia	Colombia
conj	conjunción	conjunction
CoRi	Costa Rica	Costa Rica
DomRep	República Dominicana	Dominican Republic
Ecua	Ecuador	Ecuador
f	femenino	feminine
fam	familiar o coloquial	familiar or colloquial
fpl	femenino plural	feminine plural
Guat	Guatemala	Guatemala
Hond	Honduras	Honduras
interj	interjección	interjection
m	masculino	masculine
Mex	México	Mexico
mf	masculino o femenino	masculine or feminine
mpl	masculino plural	masculine plural
n	sustantivo	noun
nf	sustantivo femenino	feminine noun
nfpl	sustantivo plural femenino	feminine plural noun
nfs & pl	sustantivo plural femenino, invariable en cuanto a número	invariable singular or plural feminine noun
Nic	Nicaragua	Nicaragua
nm	sustantivo masculino	masculine noun
nmf	sustantivo masculino o femenino	masculine or feminine noun
nmfpl	sustantivo plural, invariable en cuanto a género	plural noun invariable for gender
nmfs & pl	sustantivo invariable en cuanto a género y número	noun invariable for both gender and number
nmpl	sustantivo plural masculino	masculine plural noun
nms & pl	sustantivo masculino, invariable en cuanto a número	invariable singular or plural masculine noun
npl	sustantivo plural	plural noun
ns & pl	sustantivo invariable en cuanto a número	noun invariable for plural
Pan	Panamá	Panama
Par	Paraguay	Paraguay
pl	plural	plural
prep	preposición	preposition
PRi	Puerto Rico	Puerto Rico
pron	pronombre	pronoun
Sal	El Salvador	El Salvador
Uru	Uruguay	Uruguay
usu	generalmente	usually
v	verbo	verb
v aux	verbo auxiliar	auxiliary verb
Ven	Venezuela	Venezuela
vi	verbo intransitivo	intransitive verb
v impers	verbo impersonal	impersonal verb
vr	verbo pronominal	reflexive verb
vt	verbo transitivo	transitive verb

Pronunciation Symbols

VOWELS

æ	ask, bat, glad
ɑ	cot, bomb
a	*New England* aunt, *British* ask, glass, *Spanish* casa
e	*Spanish* peso, jefe
ɛ	egg, bet, fed
ə	about, javelin, Alabama
ə	when italicized as in əl, əm, ən, indicates a syllabic pronunciation of the consonant as in bottle, prism, button
i	very, any, thirty, *Spanish* piña
i:	eat, bead, bee
ɪ	id, bid, pit
o	Ohio, yellower, potato, *Spanish* óvalo
o:	oats, own, zone, blow
ɔ	awl, maul, caught, paw
ʊ	sure, should, could
u	*Spanish* uva, culpa
u:	boot, few, coo
ʌ	under, putt, bud
eɪ	eight, wade, bay
aɪ	ice, bite, tie
aʊ	out, gown, plow
ɔɪ	oyster, coil, boy
ər	further, stir
ɒ	*British* bond, god
:	indicates that the preceding vowel is long. Long vowels are almost always diphthongs in English, but not in Spanish.

STRESS MARKS

'	high stress	**pen**manship
ˌ	low stress	penmanˌship

CONSONANTS

b	baby, labor, cab
β	*Spanish* cabo, óvalo
d	day, ready, kid
dʒ	just, badger, fudge
ð	then, either, bathe
f	foe, tough, buff
g	go, bigger, bag
ɣ	*Spanish* tragar, daga
h	hot, aha
j	yes, vineyard
k	cat, keep, lacquer, flock
l	law, hollow, boil
m	mat, hemp, hammer, rim
n	new, tent, tenor, run
ŋ	rung, hang, swinger
ɲ	*Spanish* cabaña, piña
p	pay, lapse, top
r	rope, burn, tar
s	sad, mist, kiss
ʃ	shoe, mission, slush
t	toe, button, mat
ṭ	indicates that some speakers of English pronounce this as a voiced alveolar flap [ɾ], as in later, catty, battle
tʃ	choose, batch
θ	thin, ether, bath
v	vat, never, cave
w	wet, software
x	*German* Bach, *Scots* loch, *Spanish* gente, jefe
z	zoo, easy, buzz
ʒ	jaborandi, azure, beige
h, k, p, t	when italicized indicate sounds which are present in the pronunciation of some speakers of English but absent in that of others, so that *whence* ['hwɛnts] can be pronounced as ['wɛns], ['hwɛns], ['wɛnts], or ['hwɛnts]

Spanish–English
Dictionary

A

a¹ *nf* : first letter of the Spanish alphabet

a² *prep* **1** : to ⟨nos vamos a México : we're going to Mexico⟩ **2** (*used before direct or indirect objects referring to persons*) ⟨¿llamaste a tu papá? : did you call your dad?⟩ ⟨como a usted le guste : as you wish⟩ **3** : in the manner of ⟨papas a la francesa : french fries⟩ **4** : on, by means of ⟨a pie : on foot⟩ **5** : per, each ⟨tres pastillas al día : three pills per day⟩ **6** : at ⟨a las dos : at two o'clock⟩ ⟨al principio : at first⟩ **7** (*with infinitive*) ⟨enséñales a leer : teach them to read⟩ ⟨problemas a resolver : problems to be solved⟩

ábaco *nm* : abacus

abad *nm* : abbot

abadesa *nf* : abbess

abadía *nf* : abbey

abajo *adv* **1** : down ⟨póngalo más abajo : put it further down⟩ ⟨arriba y abajo : up and down⟩ **2** : downstairs **3** : under, beneath ⟨el abajo firmante : the undersigned⟩ **4** : down with ⟨¡abajo la inflación! : down with inflation!⟩ **5** ~ **de** : under, beneath **6 de** ~ : bottom ⟨el cajón de abajo : the bottom drawer⟩ **7 hacia** ~ *or* **para** ~ : downwards **8 cuesta abajo** : downhill **9 río abajo** : downstream

abalanzarse {21} *vr* : to hurl oneself, to rush

abanderado, -da *n* : standard-bearer

abandonado, -da *adj* **1** : abandoned, deserted **2** : neglected **3** : slovenly, unkempt

abandonar *vt* **1** DEJAR : to abandon, to leave **2** : to give up, to quit ⟨abandonaron la búsqueda : they gave up the search⟩ — **abandonarse** *vr* **1** : to neglect oneself **2** ~ **a** : to succumb to, to give oneself over to

abandono *nm* **1** : abandonment **2** : neglect **3** : withdrawal ⟨ganar por abandono : to win by default⟩

abanicar {72} *vt* : to fan — **abanicarse** *vr*

abanico *nm* **1** : fan **2** GAMA : range, gamut

abaratamiento *nm* : price reduction

abaratar *vt* : to lower the price of — **abaratarse** *vr* : to go down in price

abarcar {72} *vt* **1** : to cover, to include, to embrace **2** : to undertake **3** : to monopolize

abaritonado, -da *adj* : baritone

abarrotado, -da *adj* : packed, crammed

abarrotar *vt* : to fill up, to pack

abarrotería *nf CA, Mex* : grocery store

abarrotero, -ra *n Col, Mex* : grocer

abarrotes *nmpl* **1** : groceries, supplies **2 tienda de abarrotes** : general store, grocery store

abastecedor, -dora *n* : supplier

abastecer {53} *vt* : to supply, to stock — **abastecerse** *vr* : to stock up

abastecimiento → abasto

abasto *nm* : supply, supplying ⟨no da abasto : there isn't enough for all⟩

abatido, -da *adj* : dejected, depressed

abatimiento *nm* **1** : drop, reduction **2** : dejection, depression

abatir *vt* **1** DERRIBAR : to demolish, to knock down **2** : to shoot down **3** DEPRIMIR : to depress, to bring low — **abatirse** *vr* **1** DEPRIMIRSE : to get depressed **2** ~ **sobre** : to swoop down on

abdicación *nf, pl* **-ciones** : abdication

abdicar {72} *vt* : to relinquish, to abdicate

abdomen *nm, pl* **-dómenes** : abdomen

abdominal *adj* : abdominal

abecé *nm* : ABC's *pl*

abecedario *nm* ALFABETO : alphabet

abedul *nm* : birch (tree)

abeja *nf* : bee

abejorro *nm* : bumblebee

aberración *nf, pl* **-ciones** : aberration

aberrante *adj* : aberrant, perverse

abertura *nf* **1** : aperture, opening **2** AGUJERO : hole **3** : slit (in a skirt, etc.) **4** GRIETA : crack

abeto *nm* : fir (tree)

abierto¹ *pp* → abrir

abierto², -ta *adj* **1** : open **2** : candid, frank **3** : generous — **abiertamente** *adv*

abigarrado, -da *adj* : multicolored, variegated

abigeato *nm* : rustling (of livestock)

abismal *adj* : abysmal, vast

abismo *nm* : abyss, chasm ⟨al borde del abismo : on the brink of ruin⟩

abjurar *vi* ~ **de** : to abjure — **abjuración** *nf*

ablandamiento *nm* : softening, moderation

ablandar *vt* **1** SUAVIZAR : to soften **2** CALMAR : to soothe, to appease — *vi* : to moderate, to get milder — **ablandarse** *vr* **1** : to become soft, to soften **2** CEDER : to yield, to relent

ablución *nf, pl* **-ciones** : ablution

abnegación *nf, pl* **-ciones** : abnegation, self-denial

abnegado, -da *adj* : self-sacrificing, selfless

abnegarse {49} *vr* : to deny oneself

abobado, -da *adj* **1** : silly, stupid **2** : bewildered

abocarse {72} *vr* **1** DIRIGIRSE : to head, to direct oneself **2** DEDICARSE : to dedicate oneself

abochornar *vt* AVERGONZAR : to embarrass, to shame — **abochornarse** *vr*

abofetear *vt* : to slap

abogacía *nf* : law, legal profession

abogado, -da *n* : lawyer, attorney

abogar {52} *vi* ~ **por** : to plead for, to defend, to advocate

abolengo *nm* LINAJE : lineage, ancestry

abolición *nf, pl* **-ciones** : abolition

abolir {1} *vt* DEROGAR : to abolish, to repeal

abolladura *nf* : dent

abollar *vt* : to dent

abombar *vt* : to warp, to cause to bulge — **abombarse** *vr* : to decompose, to go bad

abominable *adj* ABORRECIBLE : abominable

abominación *nf, pl* **-ciones** : abomination

abominar *vt* ABORRECER : to abominate, to abhor

abonado, -da *n* : subscriber

abonar *vt* **1** : to pay **2** FERTILIZAR : to fertilize — **abonarse** *vr* : to subscribe

abono *nm* **1** : payment, installment **2** FERTILIZANTE : fertilizer **3** : season ticket

abordaje *nm* : boarding

abordar *vt* **1** : to address, to broach **2** : to accost, to waylay **3** : to come on board

aborigen[1] *adj, pl* **-rígenes** : aboriginal, native

aborigen[2] *nmf, pl* **-rígenes** : aborigine, indigenous inhabitant

aborrecer {53} *vt* ABOMINAR, ODIAR : to abhor, to detest, to hate

aborrecible *adj* ABOMINABLE, ODIOSO : abominable, detestable

aborrecimiento *nm* : abhorrence, loathing

abortar *vi* : to have an abortion — *vt* **1** : to abort **2** : to quash, to suppress

abortista *nmf* : abortionist

abortivo, -va *adj* : abortive

aborto *nm* **1** : abortion **2** : miscarriage

abotonar *vt* : to button — **abotonarse** *vr* : to button up

abovedado, -da *adj* : vaulted

abrasador, -dora *adj* : burning, scorching

abrasar *vt* QUEMAR : to burn, to sear, to scorch

abrasivo[1], **-va** *adj* : abrasive

abrasivo[2] *nm* : abrasive

abrazadera *nf* : clamp, brace

abrazar {21} *vt* : to hug, to embrace — **abrazarse** *vr*

abrazo *nm* : hug, embrace

abrebotellas *nms & pl* : bottle opener

abrelatas *nms & pl* : can opener

abrevadero *nm* BEBEDERO : watering trough

abreviación *nf, pl* **-ciones** : abbreviation

abreviar *vt* **1** : to abbreviate **2** : to shorten, to cut short

abreviatura → **abreviación**

abridor *nm* : bottle opener, can opener

abrigado, -da *adj* **1** : sheltered **2** : warm, wrapped up (with clothing)

abrigar {52} *vt* **1** : to shelter, to protect **2** : to keep warm, to dress warmly **3** : to cherish, to harbor ⟨abrigar esper-

anzas : to cherish hopes⟩ — **abrigarse** *vr* : to dress warmly

abrigo *nm* **1** : coat, overcoat **2** : shelter, refuge

abril *nm* : April

abrillantador *nm* : polish

abrillantar *vt* : to polish, to shine

abrir {2} *vt* **1** : to open **2** : to unlock, to undo **3** : to turn on (a tap or faucet) — *vi* : to open, to open up — **abrirse** *vr* **1** : to open up **2** : to clear (of the skies)

abrochar *vt* : to button, to fasten — **abrocharse** *vr* : to fasten, to hook up

abrogación *nf, pl* **-ciones** : abrogation, annulment, repeal

abrogar {52} *vt* : to abrogate, to annul, to repeal

abrojo *nm* : bur (of a plant)

abrumador, -dora *adj* : crushing, overwhelming

abrumar *vt* **1** AGOBIAR : to overwhelm **2** OPRIMIR : to oppress, to burden

abrupto, -ta *adj* **1** : abrupt **2** ESCARPADO : steep — **abruptamente** *adv*

absceso *nm* : abscess

absolución *nf, pl* **-ciones** **1** : absolution **2** : acquittal

absolutismo *nm* : absolutism

absoluto, -ta *adj* **1** : absolute, unconditional **2** en ～ : not at all ⟨no me gustó en absoluto : I did not like it at all⟩ — **absolutamente** *adv*

absolver {89} *vt* **1** : to absolve **2** : to acquit

absorbente *adj* **1** : absorbent **2** : absorbing, engrossing

absorber *vt* **1** : to absorb, to soak up **2** : to occupy, to take up, to engross

absorción *nf, pl* **-ciones** : absorption

absorto, -ta *adj* : absorbed, engrossed

abstemio[1], **-mia** *adj* : abstemious, teetotal

abstemio[2], **-mia** *n* : teetotaler

abstención *nf, pl* **-ciones** : abstention

abstenerse {80} *vr* : to abstain, to refrain

abstinencia *nf* : abstinence

abstracción *nf, pl* **-ciones** : abstraction

abstracto, -ta *adj* : abstract

abstraer {81} *vt* : to abstract — **abstraerse** *vr* : to lose oneself in thought

abstraído, -da *adj* : preoccupied, withdrawn

abstruso, -sa *adj* : abstruse

abstuvo, etc. → **abstenerse**

absuelto *pp* → **absolver**

absurdo[1], **-da** *adj* DISPARATADO, RIDÍCULO : absurd, ridiculous — **absurdamente** *adv*

absurdo[2] *nm* : absurdity

abuchear *vt* : to boo, to jeer

abucheo *nm* : booing, jeering

abuela *nf* **1** : grandmother **2** : old woman **3** ¡tu abuela! *fam* : no way!, forget about it!

abuelo *nm* **1** : grandfather **2** : old man **3** abuelos *nmpl* : grandparents, ancestors

abulia *nf* : apathy, lethargy

abúlico, -ca *adj* : lethargic, apathetic

abultado, -da *adj* : bulging, bulky

abultar *vi* : to bulge — *vt* : to enlarge, to expand

abundancia *nf* : abundance

abundante *adj* : abundant, plentiful — **abundantemente** *adv*

abundar *vi* **1** : to abound, to be plentiful **2** ~ **en** : to be in agreement with

aburrido, -da *adj* **1** : bored, tired, fed up **2** TEDIOSO : boring, tedious

aburrimiento *nm* : boredom, weariness

aburrir *vt* : to bore, to tire — **aburrirse** *vr* : to get bored

abusado, -da *adj Mex fam* : sharp, on the ball

abusador, -dora *n* : abuser

abusar *vi* **1** : to go too far, to do something to excess **2** ~ **de** : to abuse (as drugs) **3** ~ **de** : to take unfair advantage of

abusivo, -va *adj* **1** : abusive **2** : outrageous, excessive

abuso *nm* **1** : abuse **2** : injustice, outrage

abyecto, -ta *adj* : despicable, contemptible

acá *adv* AQUÍ : here, over here ⟨¡ven acá! : come here!⟩

acabado¹, -da *adj* **1** : finished, done, completed **2** : old, worn-out

acabado² *nm* : finish ⟨un acabado brillante : a glossy finish⟩

acabar *vi* **1** TERMINAR : to finish, to end **2** ~ **de** : to have just (done something) ⟨acabo de ver a tu hermano : I just saw your brother⟩ **3** ~ **con** : to put an end to, to stamp out — *vt* TERMINAR : to finish — **acabarse** *vr* TERMINARSE : to come to an end, to run out ⟨se me acabó el dinero : I ran out of money⟩

acacia *nf* : acacia

academia *nf* : academy

académico¹, -ca *adj* : academic, scholastic — **académicamente** *adv*

académico², -ca *n* : academic, academician

acaecer {53} *vt* (*3rd person only*) : to happen, to take place

acalambrarse *vr* : to cramp up, to get a cramp

acallar *vt* : to quiet, to silence

acalorado, -da *adj* : emotional, heated

acaloramiento *nm* **1** : heat **2** : ardor, passion

acalorar *vt* : to heat up, to inflame — **acalorarse** *vr* : to get upset, to get worked up

acampada *nf* : camp, camping ⟨ir de acampada : to go camping⟩

acampar *vi* : to camp

acanalar *vt* **1** : to groove, to furrow **2** : to corrugate

acantilado *nm* : cliff

acanto *nm* : acanthus

acantonar *vt* : to station, to quarter

acaparador, -dora *adj* : greedy, selfish

acaparar *vt* **1** : to stockpile, to hoard **2** : to monopolize

acápite *nm* : paragraph

acariciar *vt* : to caress, to stroke, to pet

ácaro *nm* : mite

acarrear *vt* **1** : to haul, to carry **2** : to bring, to give rise to ⟨los problemas que acarrea : the problems that come along with it⟩

acarreo *nm* : transport, haulage

acartonarse *vr* **1** : to stiffen **2** : to become wizened

acaso *adv* **1** : perhaps, by any chance **2 por si acaso** : just in case

acatamiento *nm* : compliance, observance

acatar *vt* : to comply with, to respect

acaudalado, -da *adj* RICO : wealthy, rich

acaudillar *vt* : to lead, to command

acceder *vi* ~ **a 1** : to accede to, to agree to **2** : to assume (a position) **3** : to gain access to

accesar *vt* : to access (on a computer)

accesibilidad *nf* : accessibility

accesible *adj* ASEQUIBLE : accessible, attainable

acceso *nm* **1** : access **2** : admittance, entrance

accesorio¹, -ria *adj* **1** : accessory **2** : incidental

accesorio² *nm* **1** : accessory **2** : prop (in the theater)

accidentado¹, -da *adj* **1** : eventful, turbulent **2** : rough, uneven **3** : injured

accidentado², -da *n* : accident victim

accidental *adj* : accidental, unintentional — **accidentalmente** *adv*

accidentarse *vr* : to have an accident

accidente *nm* **1** : accident **2** : unevenness **3 accidente geográfico** : geographical feature

acción *nf, pl* **acciones 1** : action **2** ACTO : act, deed **3** : share, stock

accionamiento *nm* : activation

accionar *vt* : to put into motion, to activate — *vi* : to gesticulate

accionario, -ria *adj* : stock ⟨mercado accionario : stock market⟩

accionista *nmf* : stockholder, shareholder

acebo *nm* : holly

acechar *vt* **1** : to watch, to spy on **2** : to stalk, to lie in wait for

acecho *nm* **al acecho** : lying in wait

acedera *nf* : sorrel (herb)

acéfalo, -la *adj* : leaderless

aceitar *vt* : to oil

aceite *nm* **1** : oil **2 aceite de ricino** : castor oil **3 aceite de oliva** : olive oil

aceitera *nf* **1** : cruet (for oil) **2** : oilcan **3** *Mex* : oil refinery

aceitoso, -sa *adj* : oily

aceituna *nf* OLIVA : olive

aceituno *nm* OLIVO : olive tree

aceleración *nf, pl* **-ciones** : acceleration, speeding up

acelerado, -da *adj* : accelerated, speedy

acelerador *nm* : accelerator

aceleramiento *nm* → **aceleración**

acelerar *vt* **1** : to accelerate, to speed up **2** AGILIZAR : to expedite — *vi* : to accelerate (of an automobile) — **acelerarse** *vr* : to hasten, to hurry up

acelga *nf* : chard, Swiss chard

acendrado, -da *adj* : pure, unblemished

acendrar *vt* : to purify, to refine

acento *nm* **1** : accent **2** : stress, emphasis

acentuación *nf, pl* **-ciones** : accentuation

acentuado, -da *adj* : marked, pronounced

acentuar {3} *vt* **1** : to accent **2** : to emphasize, to stress — **acentuarse** *vr* : to become more pronounced

acepción *nf, pl* **-ciones** SIGNIFICADO : sense, meaning

aceptabilidad *nf* : acceptability

aceptable *adj* : acceptable

aceptación *nf, pl* **-ciones** **1** : acceptance **2** APROBACIÓN : approval

aceptar *vt* **1** : to accept **2** : to approve

acequia *nf* **1** : irrigation ditch **2** *Mex* : sewer

acera *nf* : sidewalk

acerado, -da *adj* **1** : made of steel **2** : steely, tough

acerbo, -ba *adj* **1** : harsh, cutting ⟨comentarios acerbos : cutting remarks⟩ **2** : bitter — **acerbamente** *adv*

acerca *prep* ~ **de** : about, concerning

acercamiento *nm* : rapprochement, reconciliation

acercar {72} *vt* APROXIMAR, ARRIMAR : to bring near, to bring closer — **acercarse** *vr* APROXIMARSE, ARRIMARSE : to approach, to draw near

acería *nf* : steel mill

acerico *nm* : pincushion

acero *nm* : steel ⟨acero inoxidable : stainless steel⟩

acérrimo, -ma *adj* **1** : staunch, steadfast **2** : bitter ⟨un acérrimo enemigo : a bitter enemy⟩

acertado, -da *adj* CORRECTO : accurate, correct, on target — **acertadamente** *adv*

acertante[1] *adj* : winning

acertante[2] *nmf* : winner

acertar {55} *vt* : to guess correctly — *vi* **1** ATINAR : to be correct, to be on target **2** ~ **a** : to manage to

acertijo *nm* ADIVINANZA : riddle

acervo *nm* **1** : pile, heap **2** : wealth, heritage ⟨el acervo artístico del instituto : the artistic treasures of the institute⟩

acetato *nm* : acetate

acético, -ca *adj* : acetic ⟨ácido acético : acetic acid⟩

acetileno *nm* : acetylene

acetona *nf* **1** : acetone **2** : nail-polish remover

achacar {72} *vt* : to attribute, to impute ⟨te achaca todos sus problemas : he blames all his problems on you⟩

achacoso, -sa *adj* : frail, sickly

achaparrado, -da *adj* : stunted, scrubby ⟨árboles achaparrados : scrubby trees⟩

achaques *nmpl* : aches and pains

achatar *vt* : to flatten

achicar {72} *vt* **1** REDUCIR : to make smaller, to reduce **2** : to intimidate **3** : to bail out (water) — **achicarse** *vr* : to become intimidated

achicharrar *vt* : to scorch, to burn to a crisp

achicoria *nf* : chicory

achispado, -da *adj fam* : tipsy

achote *or* **achiote** *nm* : annatto seed

achuchón *nm, pl* **-chones** **1** : push, shove **2** *fam* : squeeze, hug **3** *fam* : mild illness

aciago, -ga *adj* : fateful, unlucky

acicalar *vt* **1** PULIR : to polish **2** : to dress up, to adorn — **acicalarse** *vr* : to get dressed up

acicate *nm* **1** : spur **2** INCENTIVO : incentive, stimulus

acidez *nf, pl* **-deces** **1** : acidity **2** : sourness **3 acidez estomacal** : heartburn

acidificar {72} *vt* : to acidify

ácido[1], -da *adj* AGRIO : acid, sour

ácido[2] *nm* : acid

acierto *nm* **1** : correct answer, right choice **2** : accuracy, skill, deftness

acimut *nm* : azimuth

acitronar *vt Mex* : to fry until crisp

aclamación *nf, pl* **-ciones** : acclaim, acclamation

aclamar *vt* : to acclaim, to cheer, to applaud

aclaración *nf, pl* **-ciones** CLARIFICACIÓN : clarification, explanation

aclarar *vt* **1** CLARIFICAR : to clarify, to explain, to resolve **2** : to lighten **3 aclarar la voz** : to clear one's throat — *vi* **1** : to get light, to dawn **2** : to clear up — **aclararse** *vr* : to become clear

aclaratorio, -ria *adj* : explanatory

aclimatar *vt* : to acclimatize — **aclimatarse** *vr* ~ **a** : to get used to — **aclimatación** *nf*

acné *nm* : acne

acobardar *vt* INTIMIDAR : to frighten, to intimidate — **acobardarse** *vr* : to be frightened, to cower

acodarse *vr* ~ **en** : to lean (one's elbows) on

acogedor, -dora *adj* : cozy, warm, friendly

acoger {15} *vt* **1** REFUGIAR : to take in, to shelter **2** : to receive, to welcome — **acogerse** *vr* **1** REFUGIARSE : to take refuge **2** ~ **a** : to resort to, to avail oneself of

acogida *nf* **1** AMPARO, REFUGIO : refuge, protection **2** RECIBIMIENTO : reception, welcome

acolchar *vt* **1** : to pad (a wall, etc.) **2** : to quilt

acólito *nm* **1** MONAGUILLO : altar boy **2** : follower, helper, acolyte

acomedido, -da *adj* : helpful, obliging

acometer *vt* **1** ATACAR : to attack, to assail **2** EMPRENDER : to undertake, to begin — *vi* ~ **contra** : to rush against

acometida *nf* ATAQUE : attack, assault

acomodado, -da *adj* **1** : suitable, appropriate **2** : well-to-do, prosperous

acomodador, -dora *n* : usher, usherette *f*

acomodar *vt* **1** : to accommodate, to make room for **2** : to adjust, to adapt — **acomodarse** *vr* **1** : to settle in **2** ~ **a** : to adapt to

acomodaticio, -cia *adj* : accommodating, obliging

acomodo *nm* **1** : job, position **2** : arrangement, placement **3** : accommodation, lodging

acompañamiento *nm* : accompaniment

acompañante *nmf* **1** COMPAÑERO : companion **2** : accompanist

acompañar *vt* : to accompany, to go with

acompasado, -da *adj* : rhythmic, regular, measured

acomplejado, -da *adj* : full of complexes, neurotic

acondicionado, -da *adj* **1** : equipped, fitted-out **2 bien acondicionado** : in good shape, in a fit state

acondicionador *nm* **1** : conditioner **2 acondicionador de aire** : air conditioner

acondicionar *vt* **1** : to condition **2** : to fit out, to furnish

acongojado, -da *adj* : distressed, upset

acongojarse *vr* : to grieve, to become distressed

aconsejable *adj* : advisable

aconsejar *vt* : to advise, to counsel

acontecer {53} *vt* (*3rd person only*) : to occur, to happen

acontecimiento *nm* SUCESO : event

acopiar *vt* : to gather, to collect, to stockpile

acopio *nm* : collection, stock

acoplamiento *nm* : connection, coupling

acoplar *vt* : to couple, to connect — **acoplarse** *vr* : to fit together

acoquinar *vt* : to intimidate

acorazado¹, -da *adj* BLINDADO : armored

acorazado² *nm* : battleship

acordado, -da *adj* : agreed upon

acordar {19} *vt* **1** : to agree on **2** OTORGAR : to award, to bestow — **acordarse** *vr* RECORDAR : to remember, to recall

acorde¹ *adj* **1** : in agreement, in accordance **2** ~ **con** : in keeping with

acorde² *nm* : chord

acordeón *nm, pl* -**deones** : accordion — **acordeonista** *nmf*

acordonar *vt* **1** : to cordon off **2** : to lace up **3** : to mill (coins)

acorralar *vt* ARRINCONAR : to corner, to hem in, to corral

acortar *vt* : to shorten, to cut short — **acortarse** *vr* **1** : to become shorter **2** : to end early

acosar *vt* PERSEGUIR : to pursue, to hound, to harass

acoso *nm* ASEDIO : harassment ⟨acoso sexual : sexual harassment⟩

acostar {19} *vt* **1** : to lay (something) down **2** : to put to bed — **acostarse** *vr* **1** : to lie down **2** : to go to bed

acostumbrado, -da *adj* **1** HABITUADO : accustomed **2** HABITUAL : usual, customary

acostumbrar *vt* : to accustom — *vi* : to be accustomed, to be in the habit — **acostumbrarse** *vr*

acotación *nf, pl* -**ciones** **1** : marginal note **2** : stage direction

acotado, -da *adj* : enclosed

acotamiento *nm Mex* : shoulder (of a road)

acotar *vt* **1** ANOTAR : to note, to annotate **2** DELIMITAR : to mark off (land), to demarcate

acre¹ *adj* **1** : acrid, pungent **2** MORDAZ : caustic, biting

acre² *nm* : acre

acrecentamiento *nm* : growth, increase

acrecentar {55} *vt* AUMENTAR : to increase, to augment

acreditación *nf, pl* -**ciones** : accreditation

acreditado, -da *adj* **1** : accredited, authorized **2** : reputable

acreditar *vt* **1** : to accredit, to authorize **2** : to credit **3** : to prove, to verify — **acreditarse** *vr* : to gain a reputation

acreedor¹, -dora *adj* : deserving, worthy

acreedor², -dora *n* : creditor

acribillar *vt* **1** : to riddle, to pepper (with bullets, etc.) **2** : to hound, to harass

acrílico *nm* : acrylic

acrimonia *nf* **1** : pungency **2** : acrimony

acrimonioso, -sa *adj* : acrimonious

acriollarse *vr* : to adopt local customs, to go native

acritud *nf* **1** : pungency, bitterness **2** : intensity, sharpness **3** : harshness, asperity

acrobacia *nf* : acrobatics

acróbata *nmf* : acrobat

acrobático, -ca *adj* : acrobatic

acrónimo *nm* : acronym

acta *nf* **1** : document, certificate ⟨acta de nacimiento : birth certificate⟩ **2 actas** *nfpl* : minutes (of a meeting)

actitud *nf* **1** : attitude **2** : posture, position

activación *nf, pl* -**ciones** **1** : activation, stimulation **2** ACELERACIÓN : acceleration, speeding up

activar *vt* **1** : to activate **2** : to stimulate, to energize **3** : to speed up

actividad *nf* : activity

activista *nmf* : activist

activo¹, -va *adj* : active — **activamente** *adv*

activo² *nm* : assets *pl* ⟨activo y pasivo : assets and liabilities⟩

acto *nm* **1** ACCIÓN : act, deed **2** : act (in a play) **3 el acto sexual** : sexual intercourse **4 en el acto** : right away, on the spot **5 acto seguido** : immediately after

actor *nm* ARTISTA : actor

actriz *nf, pl* **actrices** ARTISTA : actress

actuación *nf, pl* **-ciones 1** : performance **2 actuaciones** *nfpl* DILIGENCIAS : proceedings

actual *adj* PRESENTE : present, current

actualidad *nf* **1** : present time ⟨en la actualidad : at present⟩ **2 actualidades** *nfpl* : current affairs

actualización *nf, pl* **-ciones** : updating, modernization

actualizar {21} *vt* : to modernize, to bring up to date

actualmente *adv* : at present, nowadays

actuar {3} *vi* : to act, to perform

actuarial *adj* : actuarial

actuario, -ria *n* : actuary

acuarela *nf* : watercolor

acuario *nm* : aquarium

Acuario *nmf* : Aquarius, Aquarian

acuartelar *vt* : to quarter (troops)

acuático, -ca *adj* : aquatic, water

acuchillar *vt* APUÑALAR : to knife, to stab

acuciante *adj* : pressing, urgent

acucioso, -sa → **acuciante**

acudir *vi* **1** : to go, to come (someplace for a specific purpose) ⟨acudió a la puerta : he went to the door⟩ ⟨acudimos en su ayuda : we came to her aid⟩ **2** : to be present, to show up ⟨acudí a la cita : I showed up for the appointment⟩ **3 ~ a** : to turn to, to have recourse to ⟨hay que acudir al médico : you must consult the doctor⟩

acueducto *nm* : aqueduct

acuerdo *nm* **1** : agreement **2 estar de acuerdo** : to agree **3 de acuerdo con** : in accordance with **4 de ~** : OK, all right

acuicultura *nf* : aquaculture

acullá *adv* : yonder, over there

acumulación *nf, pl* **-ciones** : accumulation

acumulador *nm* : storage battery

acumular *vt* : to accumulate, to amass — **acumularse** *vr* : to build up, to pile up

acumulativo, -va *adj* : cumulative — **acumulativamente** *adv*

acunar *vt* : to rock, to cradle

acuñar *vt* : to coin, to mint

acuoso, -sa *adj* : aqueous, watery

acupuntura *nf* : acupuncture

acurrucarse {72} *vr* : to cuddle, to nestle, to curl up

acusación *nf, pl* **-ciones 1** : accusation, charge **2 la acusación** : the prosecution

acusado¹, -da *adj* : prominent, marked

acusado², -da *n* : defendant

acusador, -dora *n* **1** : accuser **2** FISCAL : prosecutor

acusar *vt* **1** : to accuse, to charge **2** : to reveal, to betray ⟨sus ojos acusaban la desconfianza : his eyes revealed distrust⟩ — **acusarse** *vr* : to confess

acusativo *nm* : objective (in grammar)

acusatorio, -ria *adj* : accusatory

acuse *nm* **acuse de recibo** : acknowledgment of receipt

acústica *nf* : acoustics

acústico, -ca *adj* : acoustic

adagio *nm* **1** REFRÁN : adage, proverb **2** : adagio

adalid *nm* : leader, champion

adaptable *adj* : adaptable — **adaptabilidad** *nf*

adaptación *nf, pl* **-ciones** : adaptation, adjustment

adaptado, -da *adj* : suited, adapted

adaptador *nm* : adapter (in electricity)

adaptar *vt* **1** MODIFICAR : to adapt **2** : to adjust, to fit — **adaptarse** *vr* : to adapt oneself, to conform

adecentar *vt* : to tidy up

adecuación *nf, pl* **-ciones** ADAPTACIÓN : adaptation

adecuadamente *adv* : adequately

adecuado, -da *adj* **1** IDÓNEO : suitable, appropriate **2** : adequate

adecuar {8} *vt* : to adapt, to make suitable — **adecuarse** *vr* **~ a** : to be appropriate for, to fit in with

adefesio *nm* : eyesore, monstrosity

adelantado, -da *adj* **1** : advanced, ahead **2** : fast (of a clock or watch) **3 por ~** : in advance

adelantamiento *nm* **1** : advancement **2** : speeding up

adelantar *vt* **1** : to advance, to move forward **2** : to overtake, to pass **3** : to reveal (information) in advance **4** : to advance, to lend (money) — **adelantarse** *vr* **1** : to advance, to get in front **2 ~ a** : to forestall, to preempt

adelante *adv* **1** : ahead, in front, forward **2 más adelante** : further on, later on **3 ¡adelante!** : come in!

adelanto *nm* **1** : advance, progress **2** : advance payment **3** : earliness ⟨llevamos una hora de adelanto : we're running an hour ahead of time⟩

adelfa *nf* : oleander

adelgazar {21} *vt* : to thin, to reduce — *vi* : to lose weight

ademán *nm, pl* **-manes 1** GESTO : gesture **2 ademanes** *nmpl* : manners

además *adv* **1** : besides, furthermore **2 ~ de** : in addition to, as well as

adenoides *nfpl* : adenoids

adentrarse *vr* **~ en** : to go into, to penetrate

adentro *adv* **1** : inside, within

adentros *nmpl* **decirse para sus adentros** : to say to oneself ⟨me dije para mis adentros que nunca regresaría : I told myself that I'd never go back⟩

adepto¹, -ta *adj* : supportive ⟨ser adepto a : to be a follower of⟩

adepto², -ta *n* PARTIDARIO : follower, supporter

aderezar {21} *vt* **1** SAZONAR : to season, to dress (salad) **2** : to embellish, to adorn

aderezo *nm* **1** : dressing, seasoning **2** : adornment, embellishment

adeudar *vt* **1** : to debit **2** DEBER : to owe

adeudo *nm* **1** DÉBITO : debit **2** *Mex* : debt, indebtedness

adherencia *nf* **1** : adherence, adhesiveness **2** : appendage, accretion

adherente *adj* : adhesive, sticky

adherirse {76} *vr* : to adhere, to stick

adhesión *nf, pl* **-siones 1** : adhesion **2** : attachment, commitment (to a cause, etc.)

adhesivo¹, -va *adj* : adhesive

adhesivo² *nm* : adhesive

adicción *nf, pl* **-ciones** : addiction

adición *nf, pl* **-ciones** : addition

adicional *adj* : additional — **adicionalmente** *adv*

adicionar *vt* : to add

adictivo, -va *adj* : addictive

adicto¹, -ta *adj* **1** : addicted **2** : devoted, dedicated

adicto², -ta *n* **1** : addict **2** PARTIDARIO : supporter, advocate

adiestrador, -dora *n* : trainer

adiestramiento *nm* : training

adiestrar *vt* : to train

adinerado, -da *adj* : moneyed, wealthy

adiós *nm, pl* **adioses 1** DESPEDIDA : farewell, good-bye **2** ¡adiós! : good-bye!

aditamento *nm* : attachment, accessory

aditivo *nm* : additive

adivinación *nf, pl* **-ciones 1** : guess **2** : divination, prediction

adivinanza *nf* ACERTIJO : riddle

adivinar *vt* **1** : to guess **2** : to foretell, to predict

adivino, -na *n* : fortune-teller

adjetivo¹, -va *adj* : adjectival

adjetivo² *nm* : adjective

adjudicación *nf, pl* **-ciones 1** : adjudication **2** : allocation, awarding, granting

adjudicar {72} *vt* **1** : to adjudge, to adjudicate **2** : to assign, to allocate ⟨adjudicar la culpa : to assign the blame⟩ **3** : to award, to grant

adjuntar *vt* : to enclose, to attach

adjunto¹, -ta *adj* : enclosed, attached

adjunto², -ta *n* : deputy, assistant

adjunto³ *nm* : adjunct

administración *nf, pl* **-ciones 1** : administration, management **2** administración de empresas : business administration

administrador, -dora *n* : administrator, manager

administrar *vt* : to administer, to manage, to run

administrativo, -va *adj* : administrative

admirable *adj* : admirable, impressive — **admirablemente** *adv*

admiración *nf, pl* **-ciones** : admiration

admirador, -dora *n* : admirer

admirar *vt* **1** : to admire **2** : to amaze, to astonish — **admirarse** *vr* : to be amazed

admirativo, -va *adj* : admiring

admisibilidad *nf* : admissibility

admisible *adj* : admissible, allowable

admisión *nf, pl* **-siones** : admission, admittance

admitir *vt* **1** : to admit, to let in **2** : to acknowledge, to concede **3** : to allow, to make room for ⟨la ley no admite cambios : the law doesn't allow for changes⟩

admonición *nf, pl* **-ciones** : admonition, warning

admonitorio, -ria *adj* : admonitory

ADN *nm* (ácido desoxirribonucleico) : DNA

adobar *vt* : to marinate

adobe *nm* : adobe

adobo *nm* **1** : marinade, seasoning **2** *Mex* : spicy marinade used for cooking pork

adoctrinamiento *nm* : indoctrination

adoctrinar *vt* : to indoctrinate

adolecer {53} *vi* PADECER : to suffer ⟨adolece de timidez : he suffers from shyness⟩

adolescencia *nf* : adolescence

adolescente¹ *adj* : adolescent, teenage

adolescente² *nmf* : adolescent, teenager

adonde *conj* : where ⟨el lugar adonde vamos es bello : the place where we're going is beautiful⟩

adónde *adv* : where ⟨¿adónde vamos? : where are we going?⟩

adondequiera *adv* : wherever, anywhere ⟨adondequiera que vayas : anywhere you go⟩

adopción *nf, pl* **-ciones** : adoption

adoptar *vt* **1** : to adopt (a measure), to take (a decision) **2** : to adopt (children)

adoptivo, -va *adj* **1** : adopted (children, country) **2** : adoptive (parents)

adoquín *nm, pl* **-quines** : paving stone, cobblestone

adorable *adj* : adorable, lovable

adoración *nf, pl* **-ciones** : adoration, worship

adorador¹, -dora *adj* : adoring, worshipping

adorador², -dora *n* : worshipper

adorar *vt* : to adore, to worship

adormecer {53} *vt* **1** : to make sleepy, to lull to sleep **2** : to numb — **adormecerse** *vr* **1** : to doze off **2** : to go numb

adormecimiento *nm* **1** SUEÑO : drowsiness, sleepiness **2** INSENSIBILIDAD : numbness

adormilarse *vr* : to doze, to drowse

adornar *vt* DECORAR : to decorate, to adorn

adorno *nm* : ornament, decoration

adquirido, -da *adj* **1** : acquired **2** mal adquirido : ill-gotten

adquirir {4} *vt* **1** : to acquire, to gain **2** COMPRAR : to purchase

adquisición *nf, pl* **-ciones 1** : acquisition **2** COMPRA : purchase
adquisitivo, -va *adj* **poder adquisitivo** : purchasing power
adrede *adv* : intentionally, on purpose
adrenalina *nf* : adrenaline
adscribir {33} *vt* : to assign, to appoint — **adscribirse** *vr* ~ **a** : to become a member of
adscripción *nf, pl* **-ciones** : assignment, appointment
adscrito *pp* → **adscribir**
aduana *nf* : customs, customs office
aduanero[1]**, -ra** *adj* : customs
aduanero[2]**, -ra** *n* : customs officer
aducir {61} *vt* : to adduce, to offer as proof
adueñarse *vr* ~ **de** : to take possession of, to take over
adulación *nf, pl* **-ciones** : adulation, flattery
adulador[1]**, -dora** *adj* : flattering
adulador[2]**, -dora** *n* : flatterer, toady
adular *vt* LISONJEAR : to flatter
adulteración *nf, pl* **-ciones** : adulteration
adulterar *vt* : to adulterate
adulterio *nm* : adultery
adúltero[1]**, -ra** *adj* : adulterous
adúltero[2]**, -ra** *n* : adulterer
adultez *nf* : adulthood
adulto, -ta *adj & n* : adult
adusto, -ta *adj* : harsh, severe
advenedizo, -za *n* **1** : upstart, parvenu **2** : newcomer
advenimiento *nm* : advent
adverbio *nm* : adverb — **adverbial** *adj*
adversario[1]**, -ria** *adj* : opposing, contrary
adversario[2]**, -ria** *n* OPOSITOR : adversary, opponent
adversidad *nf* : adversity
adverso, -sa *adj* DESFAVORABLE : adverse, unfavorable — **adversamente** *adv*
advertencia *nf* AVISO : warning
advertir {76} *vt* **1** AVISAR : to warn **2** : to notice, to tell ⟨no advertí que estuviera enojada : I couldn't tell she was angry⟩
Adviento *nm* : Advent
adyacente *adj* : adjacent
aéreo, -rea *adj* **1** : aerial, air **2 correo aéreo** : airmail
aeróbic *nm* : aerobics
aeróbico, -ca *adj* : aerobic
aerobio, -bia *adj* : aerobic
aerodinámica *nf* : aerodynamics
aerodinámico, -ca *adj* : aerodynamic, streamlined
aeródromo *nm* : airfield
aeroespacial *adj* : aerospace
aerolínea *nf* : airline
aeromozo, -za *n* : flight attendant, steward *m*, stewardess *f*
aeronáutica *nf* : aeronautics
aeronáutico, -ca *adj* : aeronautical
aeronave *nf* : aircraft

aeropostal *adj* : airmail
aeropuerto *nm* : airport
aerosol *nm* : aerosol, aerosol spray
aeróstata *nmf* : balloonist
aerotransportado, -da *adj* : airborne
aerotransportar *vt* : to airlift
afabilidad *nf* : affability
afable *adj* : affable — **afablemente** *adv*
afamado, -da *adj* : well-known, famous
afán *nm, pl* **afanes 1** ANHELO : eagerness, desire **2** EMPEÑO : effort, determination
afanador, -dora *n Mex* : cleaning person, cleaner
afanarse *vr* : to toil, to strive
afanosamente *adv* : zealously, industriously, busily
afanoso, -sa *adj* **1** : eager, industrious **2** : arduous, hard
afear *vt* : to make ugly, to disfigure
afección *nf, pl* **-ciones 1** : fondness, affection **2** : illness, complaint
afectación *nf, pl* **-ciones** : affectation
afectado, -da *adj* **1** : affected, mannered **2** : influenced **3** : afflicted **4** : feigned
afectar *vt* **1** : to affect **2** : to upset **3** : to feign, to pretend
afectísimo, -ma *adj* **suyo afectísimo** : yours truly
afectivo, -va *adj* : emotional
afecto[1]**, -ta** *adj* **1** : affected, afflicted **2** : fond, affectionate
afecto[2] *nm* CARIÑO : affection
afectuoso, -sa *adj* CARIÑOSO : affectionate, caring
afeitadora *nf* : shaver, electric razor
afeitar *vt* RASURAR : to shave — **afeitarse** *vr*
afelpado, -da *adj* : plush
afeminado, -da *adj* : effeminate
aferrado, -da *adj* : obstinate, stubborn
aferrarse {55} *vr* : to cling, to hold on
affidávit *nm, pl* **-dávits** : affidavit
afgano, -na *adj & n* : Afghan
AFI *nm* (Alfabeto Fonético Internacional) : IPA
afianzar {21} *vt* **1** : to secure, to strengthen **2** : to guarantee, to vouch for — **afianzarse** *vr* ESTABLECERSE : to establish oneself
afiche *nm* : poster
afición *nf, pl* **-ciones 1** : enthusiasm, penchant, fondness ⟨afición al deporte : love of sports⟩ **2** PASATIEMPO : hobby
aficionado[1]**, -da** *adj* ENTUSIASTA : enthusiastic, keen
aficionado[2]**, -da** *n* **1** ENTUSIASTA : enthusiast, fan **2** : amateur
áfido *nm* : aphid
afiebrado, -da *adj* : feverish
afilado, -da *adj* **1** : sharp **2** : long, pointed ⟨una nariz afilada : a sharp nose⟩
afilador *nm* : sharpener
afilalápices *nms & pl* : pencil sharpener
afilar *vt* : to sharpen
afiliación *nf, pl* **-ciones** : affiliation

afiliado[1], **-da** *adj* : affiliated
afiliado[2], **-da** *n* : member
afiliarse *vr* : to become a member, to join, to affiliate
afín *adj, pl* **afines** 1 PARECIDO : related, similar ⟨la biología y disciplinas afines : biology and related disciplines⟩ 2 PRÓXIMO : adjacent, nearby
afinación *nf, pl* **-ciones** 1 : tune-up 2 : tuning (of an instrument)
afinador, -dora *n* : tuner (of musical instruments)
afinar *vt* 1 : to perfect, to refine 2 : to tune (an instrument) — *vi* : to sing or play in tune
afincarse {72} *vr* : to establish oneself, to settle in
afinidad *nf* : affinity, similarity
afirmación *nf, pl* **-ciones** 1 : statement 2 : affirmation
afirmar *vt* 1 : to state, to affirm 2 REFORZAR : to make firm, to strengthen
afirmativo, -va *adj* : affirmative — **afirmativamente** *adj*
aflicción *nf, pl* **-ciones** DESCONSUELO, PESAR : grief, sorrow
afligido, -da *adj* : grief-stricken, sorrowful
afligir {35} *vt* 1 : to distress, to upset 2 : to afflict — **afligirse** *vr* : to grieve
aflojar *vt* 1 : to loosen, to slacken 2 *fam* : to pay up, to fork over — *vi* : to slacken, to ease up — **aflojarse** *vr* : to become loose, to slacken
afloramiento *nm* : outcropping, emergence
aflorar *vi* : to come to the surface, to emerge
afluencia *nf* 1 : flow, influx 2 : abundance, plenty
afluente *nm* : tributary
afluir {41} *vi* 1 : to flock ⟨la gente afluía a la frontera : people were flocking to the border⟩ 2 : to flow
aforismo *nm* : aphorism
aforo *nm* 1 : appraisal, assessment 2 : maximum capacity (of a theater, highway, etc.)
afortunado, -da *adj* : fortunate, lucky — **afortunadamente** *adv*
afrecho *nm* : bran, mash
afrenta *nf* : affront, insult
afrentar *vt* : to affront, to dishonor, to insult
africano, -na *adj & n* : African
afroamericano, -na *adj & n* : Afro-American
afrodisiaco *or* **afrodisíaco** *nm* : aphrodisiac
afrontamiento *nm* : confrontation
afrontar *vt* : to confront, to face up to
afrutado, -da *adj* : fruity
afuera *adv* 1 : out ⟨¡afuera! : get out!⟩ 2 : outside, outdoors
afueras *nfpl* ALEDAÑOS : outskirts
agachadiza *nf* : snipe (bird)
agachar *vt* : to lower (a part of the body) ⟨agachar la cabeza : to bow one's head⟩

— **agacharse** *vr* : to crouch, to stoop, to bend down
agalla *nf* 1 BRANQUIA : gill 2 **tener agallas** *fam* : to have guts, to have courage
agarradera *nf* ASA, ASIDERO : handle, grip
agarrado, -da *adj fam* : cheap, stingy
agarrar *vt* 1 : to grab, to grasp 2 : to catch, to take — *vi* **agarrar y** *fam* : to do (something) abruptly ⟨el día siguiente agarró y se fue : the next day he up and left⟩ — **agarrarse** *vr* 1 : to hold on, to cling 2 *fam* : to get into a fight ⟨se agarraron a golpes : they came to blows⟩
agarre *nm* : grip, grasp
agarrotarse *vr* 1 : to stiffen up 2 : to seize up
agasajar *vt* : to fête, to wine and dine
agasajo *nm* : lavish attention
ágata *nf* : agate
agave *nm* : agave
agazaparse *vr* 1 AGACHARSE : to crouch 2 : to hide
agencia *nf* : agency, office
agenciar *vt* : to obtain, to procure — **agenciarse** *vr* : to manage, to get by
agenda *nf* 1 : agenda 2 : appointment book
agente *nmf* 1 : agent 2 **agente de viajes** : travel agent 3 **agente de bolsa** : stockbroker 4 **agente de tráfico** : traffic officer
agigantado, -da *adj* GIGANTESCO : gigantic
agigantar *vt* 1 : to increase greatly, to enlarge 2 : to exaggerate
ágil *adj* 1 : agile, nimble 2 : sharp, lively (of a response, etc.) — **ágilmente** *adv*
agilidad *nf* : agility, nimbleness
agilizar {21} *vt* ACELERAR : to expedite, to speed up
agitación *nf, pl* **-ciones** 1 : agitation 2 NERVIOSISMO : nervousness
agitado, -da *adj* 1 : agitated, excited 2 : choppy, rough, turbulent
agitador, -dora *n* PROVOCADOR : agitator
agitar *vt* 1 : to agitate, to shake 2 : to wave, to flap 3 : to stir up — **agitarse** *vr* 1 : to toss about, to flap around 2 : to get upset
aglomeración *nf, pl* **-ciones** 1 : conglomeration, mass 2 GENTÍO : crowd
aglomerar *vt* : to cluster, to amass — **aglomerarse** *vr* : to crowd together
aglutinar *vt* : to bring together, to bind
agnóstico, -ca *adj & n* : agnostic
agobiado, -da *adj* : weary, worn-out, weighted-down
agobiante *adj* 1 : exhausting, overwhelming 2 : stifling, oppressive
agobiar *vt* 1 OPRIMIR : to oppress, to burden 2 ABRUMAR : to overwhelm 3 : to wear out, to exhaust
agonía *nf* : agony, death throes
agonizante *adj* : dying

agonizar {21} *vi* **1** : to be dying **2** : to be in agony **3** : to dim, to fade

agorero, -ra *adj* : ominous

agostar *vt* **1** : to parch **2** : to wither — **agostarse** *vr*

agosto *nm* **1** : August **2 hacer uno su agosto** : to make a fortune, to make a killing

agotado, -da *adj* **1** : exhausted, used up **2** : sold out **3** FATIGADO : worn-out, tired

agotador, -dora *adj* : exhausting

agotamiento *nm* FATIGA : exhaustion

agotar *vt* **1** : to exhaust, to use up **2** : to weary, to wear out — **agotarse** *vr*

agraciado¹, -da *adj* **1** : attractive **2** : fortunate

agraciado², -da *n* : winner

agradable *adj* GRATO, PLACENTERO : pleasant, agreeable — **agradablemente** *adv*

agradar *vi* : to be pleasing ⟨nos agradó mucho el resultado : we were very pleased with the result⟩

agradecer {53} *vt* **1** : to be grateful for **2** : to thank

agradecido, -da *adj* : grateful, thankful

agradecimiento *nm* : gratitude, thankfulness

agrado *nm* **1** GUSTO : taste, liking ⟨no es de su agrado : it's not to his liking⟩ **2** : graciousness, agreeableness **3 con ~** : with pleasure, willingly ⟨lo haré con agrado : I will be happy to do it⟩

agrandar *vt* **1** : to exaggerate **2** : to enlarge — **agrandarse** *vr*

agrario, -ria *adj* : agrarian, agricultural

agravación *nf, pl* **-ciones** : aggravation, worsening

agravante *adj* : aggravating

agravar *vt* **1** : to increase (weight), to make heavier **2** EMPEORAR : to aggravate, to worsen — **agravarse** *vr*

agraviar *vt* INJURIAR, OFENDER : to offend, to insult

agravio *nm* INJURIA : affront, offense, insult

agredir {1} *vt* : to assail, to attack

agregado¹, -da *n* **1** : attaché **2** : assistant professor

agregado² *nm* **1** : aggregate **2** AÑADIDURA : addition, something added

agregar {52} *vt* **1** AÑADIR : to add, to attach **2** : to appoint — **agregarse** *vr* : to join

agresión *nf, pl* **-siones 1** : aggression **2** ATAQUE : attack

agresividad *nf* : aggressiveness, aggression

agresivo, -va *adj* : aggressive — **agresivamente** *adv*

agresor¹, -sora *adj* : hostile, attacking

agresor², -sora *n* **1** : aggressor **2** : assailant, attacker

agreste *adj* **1** CAMPESTRE : rural **2** : wild, untamed

agriar *vt* **1** : to sour, to make sour **2** : to embitter — **agriarse** *vr* : to turn sour

agrícola *adj* : agricultural

agricultor, -tora *n* : farmer, grower

agricultura *nf* : agriculture, farming

agridulce *adj* **1** : bittersweet **2** : sweet-and-sour

agrietar *vt* : to crack — **agrietarse** *vr* **1** : to crack **2** : to chap

agrimensor, -sora *n* : surveyor

agrimensura *nf* : surveying

agrio, agria *adj* **1** ÁCIDO : sour **2** : caustic, acrimonious

agriparse *vr* : to catch the flu

agroindustria *nf* : agribusiness

agronomía *nf* : agronomy

agropecuario, -ria *adj* : pertaining to livestock and agriculture

agrupación *nf, pl* **-ciones** GRUPO : group, association

agrupamiento *nm* : grouping, concentration

agrupar *vt* : to group together

agua *nf* **1** : water **2 agua oxigenada** : hydrogen peroxide **3 aguas negras** *or* **aguas residuales** : sewage **4 como agua para chocolate** *Mex fam* : furious **5 echar aguas** *Mex fam* : to keep an eye out, to be on the lookout

aguacate *nm* : avocado

aguacero *nm* : shower, downpour

aguado, -da *adj* **1** DILUIDO : watered-down, diluted **2** *CA, Col, Mex fam* : soft, flabby **3** *Mex, Peru fam* : dull, boring

aguafiestas *nmfs & pl* : killjoy, stick-in-the-mud, spoilsport

aguafuerte *nm* : etching

aguamanil *nm* : ewer, pitcher

aguanieve *nf* : sleet ⟨caer aguanieve : to be sleeting⟩

aguantar *vt* **1** SOPORTAR : to bear, to tolerate, to withstand **2** : to hold **3 aguantar las ganas** : to resist an urge ⟨no pude aguantar las ganas de reír : I couldn't keep myself from laughing⟩ — *vi* : to hold out, to last — **aguantarse** *vr* **1** : to resign oneself **2** : to restrain oneself

aguante *nm* **1** TOLERANCIA : tolerance, patience **2** RESISTENCIA : endurance, strength

aguar {10} *vt* **1** : to water down, to dilute **2 aguar la fiesta** *fam* : to spoil the party

aguardar *vt* ESPERAR : to wait for, to await — *vi* : to be in store

aguardiente *nm* : clear brandy

aguarrás *nm* : turpentine

agudeza *nf* **1** : keenness, sharpness **2** : shrillness **3** : witticism

agudizar {21} *vt* : to intensify, to heighten

agudo, -da *adj* **1** : acute, sharp **2** : shrill, high-pitched **3** PERSPICAZ : clever, shrewd

agüero *nm* AUGURIO, PRESAGIO : augury, omen

aguijón *nm, pl* **-jones 1** : stinger (of a bee, etc.) **2** : goad

aguijonear *vt* : to goad
águila *nf* **1** : eagle **2 águila o sol** *Mex* : heads or tails
aguileño, -ña *adj* : aquiline
aguilera *nf* : aerie, eagle's nest
aguilón *nm, pl* **-lones** : gable
aguinaldo *nm* **1** : Christmas bonus, year-end bonus **2** *PRi, Ven* : Christmas carol
agüitarse *vr Mex fam* : to have the blues, to feel discouraged
aguja *nf* **1** : needle **2** : steeple, spire
agujerear *vt* : to make a hole in, to pierce
agujero *nm* **1** : hole **2 agujero negro** : black hole (in astronomy)
agujeta *nf* **1** *Mex* : shoelace **2 agujetas** *nfpl* : muscular soreness or stiffness
agusanado, -da *adj* : worm-eaten
aguzar {21} *vt* **1** : to sharpen ⟨aguzar el ingenio : to sharpen one's wits⟩ **2 aguzar el oído** : to prick up one's ears
ah *interj* : oh!
ahí *adv* **1** : there ⟨ahí está : there it is⟩ **2 por ~** : somewhere, thereabouts **3 de ahí que** : with the result that, so that
ahijado, -da *n* : godchild, godson *m*, goddaughter *f*
ahijar {5} *vt* : to adopt (a child)
ahínco *nm* : eagerness, zeal
ahogar {52} *vt* **1** : to drown **2** : to smother **3** : to choke back, to stifle — **ahogarse** *vr*
ahogo *nm* : breathlessness, suffocation
ahondar *vt* : to deepen — *vi* : to elaborate, to go into detail
ahora *adv* **1** : now **2 ahora mismo** : right now **3 hasta ~** : so far **4 por ~** : for the time being
ahorcar {72} *vt* : to hang, to kill by hanging — **ahorcarse** *vr*
ahorita *adv fam* : right now, right away
ahorquillado, -da *adj* : forked
ahorrador, -dora *adj* : thrifty
ahorrar *vt* **1** : to save (money) **2** : to spare, to conserve — *vi* : to save up — **ahorrarse** *vr* : to spare oneself
ahorrativo, -va *adj* : thrifty, frugal
ahorro *nm* : saving ⟨cuenta de ahorros : savings account⟩
ahuecar {72} *vt* **1** : to hollow out **2** : to cup (one's hands) **3** : to plump up, to fluff up
ahuizote *nm Mex fam* : annoying person, pain in the neck
ahumar {8} *vt* : to smoke, to cure
ahuyentar *vt* **1** : to scare away, to chase away **2** : to banish, to dispel ⟨ahuyentar las dudas : to dispel doubts⟩
airado, -da *adj* FURIOSO : angry, irate
airar {5} *vt* : to make angry, to anger
aire *nm* **1** : air **2 aire acondicionado** : air-conditioning **3 darse aires** : to give oneself airs
airear *vt* : to air, to air out — **airearse** *vr* : to get some fresh air
airoso, -sa *adj* **1** : elegant, graceful **2 salir airoso** : to come out winning
aislacionismo *nm* : isolationism

aislacionista *adj & nmf* : isolationist
aislado, -da *adj* : isolated, alone
aislador *nm* : insulator (part)
aislamiento *nm* **1** : isolation **2** : insulation
aislante *nm* : insulator, nonconductor
aislar {5} *vt* **1** : to isolate **2** : to insulate
ajado, -da *adj* **1** : worn, shabby **2** : wrinkled, crumpled
ajar *vt* : to wear out, to spoil
ajardinado, -da *adj* : landscaped
ajedrecista *nmf* : chess player
ajedrez *nm, pl* **-dreces 1** : chess **2** : chess set
ajeno, -na *adj* **1** : alien **2** : of another, of others ⟨propiedad ajena : somebody else's property⟩ **3 ~ a** : foreign to **4 ~ de** : devoid of, free from
ajetreado, -da *adj* : hectic, busy
ajetrearse *vr* : to bustle about, to rush around
ajetreo *nm* : hustle and bustle, fuss
ají *nm, pl* **ajíes** : chili pepper
ajo *nm* : garlic
ajonjolí *nm, pl* **-líes** : sesame
ajuar *nm* : trousseau
ajustable *adj* : adjustable
ajustado, -da *adj* **1** CEÑIDO : tight, tight-fitting **2** : close, tight ⟨una ajustada victoria : a close victory⟩
ajustar *vt* **1** : to adjust, to adapt **2** : to take in (clothing) **3** : to settle, to resolve — **ajustarse** *vr* : to fit, to conform
ajuste *nm* **1** : adjustment **2** : tightening
ajusticiar *vt* EJECUTAR : to execute, to put to death
al *prep* (contraction of a and el) → **a²**
ala *nf* **1** : wing **2** : brim (of a hat)
Alá *nm* : Allah
alabanza *nf* ELOGIO : praise
alabar *vt* : to praise — **alabarse** *vr* : to boast
alabastro *nm* : alabaster
alabear *vt* : to warp — **alabearse** *vr*
alabeo *nm* : warp, warping
alacena *nf* : cupboard, larder
alacrán *nm, pl* **-cranes** ESCORPIÓN : scorpion
alado, -da *adj* : winged
alambique *nm* : still (to distill alcohol)
alambre *nm* **1** : wire **2 alambre de púas** : barbed wire
alameda *nf* **1** : poplar grove **2** : tree-lined avenue
álamo *nm* **1** : poplar **2 álamo temblón** : aspen
alar *nm* : eaves *pl*
alarde *nm* **1** : show, display **2 hacer alarde de** : to make show of, to boast about
alardear *vi* PRESUMIR : to boast, to brag
alargado, -da *adj* : elongated, slender
alargamiento *nm* : lengthening, extension, elongation
alargar {52} *vt* **1** : to extend, to lengthen **2** PROLONGAR : to prolong — **alargarse** *vr*

alarido *nm* : howl, shriek
alarma *nf* : alarm
alarmante *adj* : alarming — **alarmante-
mente** *adv*
alarmar *vt* : to alarm
alazán *nm*, *pl* **-zanes** : sorrel (color or
animal)
alba *nf* AMANECER : dawn, daybreak
albacea *nmf* TESTAMENTARIO : executor, executrix *f*
albahaca *nf* : basil
albanés, -nesa *adj & n*, *mpl* **-neses** : Albanian
albañil *nmf* : bricklayer, mason
albañilería *nf* : bricklaying, masonry
albaricoque *nm* : apricot
albatros *nm* : albatross
albedrío *nm* : will ⟨libre albedrío : free
will⟩
alberca *nf* **1** : reservoir, tank **2** *Mex*
: swimming pool
albergar {52} *vt* ALOJAR : to house, to
lodge, to shelter
albergue *nm* **1** : shelter, refuge **2** : hostel
albino, -na *adj & n* : albino — **albinis-
mo** *nm*
albóndiga *nf* : meatball
albor *nm* **1** : dawning, beginning **2**
BLANCURA : whiteness
alborada *nf* : dawn
alborear *v impers* : to dawn
alborotado, -da *adj* **1** : excited, agitated **2** : rowdy, unruly
alborotador¹, -dora *adj* **1** : noisy, boisterous **2** : rowdy, unruly
alborotador², -dora *n* : agitator, troublemaker, rioter
alborotar *vt* **1** : to excite, to agitate **2**
: to incite, to stir up — **alborotarse** *vr*
1 : to get excited **2** : to riot
alboroto *nm* **1** : disturbance, ruckus **2**
MOTÍN : riot
alborozado, -da *adj* : jubilant
alborozar {21} *vt* : to gladden, to cheer
alborozo *nm* : joy, elation
álbum *nm* : album ⟨álbum de recortes
: scrapbook⟩
albúmina *nf* : albumin
albur *nm* **1** : chance, risk **2** *Mex* : pun
alca *nf* : auk
alcachofa *nf* : artichoke
alcahuete, -ta *n* CHISMOSO : gossip
alcaide *nm* : warden (in a prison)
alcalde, -desa *n* : mayor
alcaldía *nf* **1** : mayoralty **2** AYUN-
TAMIENTO : city hall
álcali *nm* : alkali
alcalino, -na *adj* : alkaline — **alcalin-
idad** *nf*
alcance *nm* **1** : reach **2** : range, scope
alcancía *nf* **1** : piggy bank, money box
2 : collection box (for alms, etc.)
alcanfor *nm* : camphor
alcantarilla *nf* CLOACA : sewer, drain
alcanzar {21} *vt* **1** : to reach **2** : to catch
up with **3** LOGRAR : to achieve, to at-
tain — *vi* **1** DAR : to suffice, to be
enough **2** — **a** : to manage to
alcaparra *nf* : caper
alcapurria *nf PRi* : stuffed fritter made
with taro and green banana
alcaravea *nf* : caraway
alcatraz *nm*, *pl* **-traces** : gannet
alcázar *nm* : fortress, castle
alce¹, etc. → **alzar**
alce² *nm* : moose, European elk
alcoba *nf* : bedroom
alcohol *nm* : alcohol
alcohólico, -ca *adj & n* : alcoholic
alcoholismo *nm* : alcoholism
alcoholizarse {21} *vr* : to become an alcoholic
alcornoque *nm* **1** : cork oak **2** *fam* : idiot, fool
alcurnia *nf* : ancestry, lineage
aldaba *nf* : door knocker
aldea *nf* : village
aldeano¹, -na *adj* : village, rustic
aldeano², -na *n* : villager
aleación *nf*, *pl* **-ciones** : alloy
alear *vt* : to alloy
aleatorio, -ria *adj* : random, fortuitous
— **aleatoriamente** *adv*
alebrestar *vt* : to excite, to make nervous — **alebrestarse** *vr*
aledaño, -ña *adj* : bordering, neighboring
aledaños *nmpl* AFUERAS : outskirts,
surrounding area
alegar {52} *vt* : to assert, to allege — *vi*
DISCUTIR : to argue
alegato *nm* **1** : allegation, claim **2** *Mex*
: argument, summation (in law) **3** : argument, dispute
alegoría *nf* : allegory
alegórico, -ca *adj* : allegorical
alegrar *vt* : to make happy, to cheer up
— **alegrarse** *vr* : to be glad, to rejoice
alegre *adj* **1** : glad, cheerful **2** : colorful, bright **3** *fam* : tipsy
alegremente *adv* : happily, cheerfully
alegría *nf* : joy, cheer, happiness
alejado, -da *adj* : remote
alejamiento *nm* **1** : removal, separation
2 : estrangement
alejar *vt* **1** : to remove, to move away **2**
: to estrange, to alienate — **alejarse** *vr*
1 : to move away, to stray **2** : to drift
apart
alelado, -da *adj* **1** : bewildered, stupe-
fied **2** : foolish, stupid
aleluya *interj* : hallelujah!, alleluia!
alemán¹, -mana *adj & n*, *mpl* **-manes**
: German
alemán² *nm* : German (language)
alentador, -dora *adj* : encouraging
alentar {55} *vt* : to encourage, to inspire
— *vi* : to breathe
alerce *nm* : larch
alérgeno *nm* : allergen
alergia *nf* : allergy
alérgico, -ca *adj* : allergic
alero *nm* **1** : eaves *pl* **2** : forward (in
basketball)

alerón *nm, pl* **-rones** : aileron
alerta[1] *adv* : on the alert
alerta[2] *adj & nf* : alert
alertar *vt* : to alert
aleta *nf* 1 : fin 2 : flipper 3 : small wing
aletargado, -da *adj* : lethargic, sluggish, torpid
aletargarse {52} *vr* : to feel drowsy, to become lethargic
aletear *vi* : to flutter, to flap one's wings
aleteo *nm* : flapping, flutter
alevín *nm, pl* **-vines** 1 : fry, young fish 2 PRINCIPIANTE : beginner
alevosía *nf* 1 : treachery 2 : premeditation
alevoso, -sa *adj* : treacherous
alfabético, -ca *adj* : alphabetical — **alfabéticamente** *adv*
alfabetismo *nm* : literacy
alfabetizado, -da *adj* : literate
alfabetizar {21} *vt* : to alphabetize
alfabeto *nm* : alphabet
alfalfa *nf* : alfalfa
alfanje *nm* : cutlass, scimitar
alfarería *nf* : pottery
alfarero, -ra *n* : potter
alféizar *nm* : sill, windowsill
alfeñique *nm fam* : wimp, weakling
alférez *nmf, pl* **-reces** 1 : second lieutenant 2 : ensign
alfil *nm* : bishop (in chess)
alfiler *nm* 1 : pin 2 BROCHE : brooch
alfiletero *nm* : pincushion
alfombra *nf* : carpet, rug
alfombrado *nm* : carpeting
alfombrar *vt* : to carpet
alfombrilla *nf* : small rug, mat
alforfón *nm, pl* **-fones** : buckwheat
alforja *nf* : saddlebag
alforza *nf* : pleat, tuck
alga *nf* 1 : aquatic plant, alga 2 : seaweed
algarabía *nf* 1 : gibberish, babble 2 : hubbub, uproar
álgebra *nf* : algebra
algebraico, -ca *adj* : algebraic
álgido, -da *adj* 1 : critical, decisive 2 : icy cold
algo[1] *adv* : somewhat, rather ⟨es simpático, pero algo tacaño : he's nice but rather stingy⟩
algo[2] *pron* 1 : something 2 ~ **de** : some, a little ⟨tengo algo de dinero : I've got some money⟩
algodón *nm, pl* **-dones** : cotton
algoritmo *nm* : algorithm
alguacil *nm* : constable
alguien *pron* : somebody, someone
alguno[1]**, -na** *adj* (**algún** *before masculine singular nouns*) 1 : some, any ⟨algún día : someday, one day⟩ 2 (*in negative constructions*) : not any, not at all ⟨no tengo noticia alguna : I have no news at all⟩ 3 **algunas veces** : sometimes
alguno[2]**, -na** *pron* 1 : one, someone, somebody ⟨alguno de ellos : one of them⟩ 2 **algunos, -nas** *pron pl* : some,

a few ⟨algunos quieren trabajar : some want to work⟩
alhaja *nf* : jewel, gem
alhajar *vt* : to adorn with jewels
alharaca *nf* : fuss
alhelí *nm* : wallflower
aliado[1]**, -da** *adj* : allied
aliado[2]**, -da** *n* : ally
alianza *nf* : alliance
aliarse {85} *vr* : to form an alliance, to ally oneself
alias *adv & nm* : alias
alicaído, -da *adj* : depressed, discouraged
alicates *nmpl* PINZAS : pliers
aliciente *nm* 1 INCENTIVO : incentive 2 ATRACCIÓN : attraction
alienación *nf, pl* **-ciones** : alienation, derangement
alienar *vt* ENAJENAR : to alienate
aliento *nm* 1 : breath 2 : courage, strength 3 **dar aliento a** : to encourage
aligerar *vt* 1 : to lighten 2 ACELERAR : to hasten, to quicken
alijo *nm* : cache, consignment (of contraband)
alimaña *nf* : pest, vermin
alimentación *nf, pl* **-ciones** NUTRICIÓN : nutrition, nourishment
alimentar *vt* 1 NUTRIR : to feed, to nourish 2 MANTENER : to support (a family) 3 FOMENTAR : to nurture, to foster — **alimentarse** *vr* ~ **con** : to live on
alimentario, -ria → **alimenticio**
alimenticio, -cia *adj* 1 : nutritional, food, dietary 2 : nutritious, nourishing
alimento *nm* : food, nourishment
aliñar *vt* 1 : to dress (salad) 2 CONDIMENTAR : to season
alineación *nf, pl* **-ciones** 1 : alignment 2 : lineup (in sports)
alineamiento *nm* : alignment
alinear *vt* 1 : to align 2 : to line up — **alinearse** *vr* 1 : to fall in, to line up 2 ~ **con** : to align oneself with
aliño *nm* : seasoning, dressing
alipús *nm, pl* **-puses** *Mex fam* : booze, drink
alisar *vt* : to smooth
aliso *nm* : alder
alistamiento *nm* : enlistment, recruitment
alistar *vt* 1 : to recruit 2 : to make ready — **alistarse** *vr* : to join up, to enlist
aliteración *nf, pl* **-ciones** : alliteration
aliviar *vt* MITIGAR : to relieve, to alleviate, to soothe — **aliviarse** *vr* : to recover, to get better
alivio *nm* : relief
aljaba *nf* : quiver (for arrows)
aljibe *nm* : cistern, well
allá *adv* 1 : there, over there 2 **más allá** : farther away 3 **más allá de** : beyond 4 **allá tú** : that's up to you

allanamiento *nm* 1 : (police) raid 2 **allanamiento de morada** : breaking and entering

allanar *vt* 1 : to raid, to search 2 : to resolve, to solve 3 : to smooth, to level out

allegado¹, -da *adj* : close, intimate

allegado², -da *n* : close friend, relation ⟨parientes y allegados : friends and relations⟩

allegar {52} *vt* : to gather, to collect

allende¹ *adv* : beyond, on the other side

allende² *prep* : beyond ⟨allende las montañas : beyond the mountains⟩

allí *adv* : there, over there ⟨allí mismo : right there⟩ ⟨hasta allí : up to that point⟩

alma *nf* 1 : soul 2 : person, human being 3 **no tener alma** : to be pitiless 4 **tener el alma en un hilo** : to have one's heart in one's mouth

almacén *nm, pl* **-cenes** 1 BODEGA : warehouse, storehouse 2 TIENDA : shop, store 3 **gran almacén** *Spain* : department store

almacenaje → **almacenamiento**

almacenamiento *nm* : storage ⟨almacenamiento de datos : data storage⟩

almacenar *vt* : to store, to put in storage

almacenero, -ra *n* : shopkeeper

almacenista *nm* MAYORISTA : wholesaler

almádena *nf* : sledgehammer

almanaque *nm* : almanac

almeja *nf* : clam

almendra *nf* 1 : almond 2 : kernel

almendro *nm* : almond tree

almiar *nm* : haystack

almíbar *nm* : syrup

almidón *nm, pl* **-dones** : starch

almidonar *vt* : to starch

alminar *nm* MINARETE : minaret

almirante *nm* : admiral

almizcle *nm* : musk

almohada *nf* : pillow

almohadilla *nf* 1 : small pillow, cushion 2 : bag, base (in baseball)

almohadón *nm, pl* **-dones** : bolster, cushion

almohazar {21} *vt* : to curry (a horse)

almoneda *nf* SUBASTA : auction

almorranas *nfpl* HEMORROIDES : hemorrhoids, piles

almorzar {36} *vi* : to have lunch — *vt* : to have for lunch

almuerzo *nm* : lunch

alocado, -da *adj* 1 : crazy 2 : wild, reckless 3 : silly, scatterbrained

alocución *nf, pl* **-ciones** : speech, address

áloe *or* **aloe** *nm* : aloe

alojamiento *nm* : lodging, accommodations *pl*

alojar *vt* ALBERGAR : to house, to lodge — **alojarse** *vr* : to lodge, to room

alondra *nf* : lark, skylark

alpaca *nf* : alpaca

alpinismo *nm* : mountain climbing, mountaineering

alpinista *nmf* : mountain climber

alpino, -na *adj* : Alpine, alpine

alpiste *nm* : birdseed

alquilar *vt* ARRENDAR : to rent, to lease

alquiler *nm* ARRENDAMIENTO : rent, rental

alquimia *nf* : alchemy

alquimista *nmf* : alchemist

alquitrán *nm, pl* **-tranes** BREA : tar

alquitranar *vt* : to tar, to cover with tar

alrededor¹ *adv* 1 : around, about ⟨todo temblaba alrededor : all around things were shaking⟩ 2 ~ **de** : around, approximately ⟨alrededor de quince personas : around fifteen people⟩

alrededor² *prep* ~ **de** : around, about ⟨corrió alrededor de la casa : she ran around the house⟩ ⟨llegaré alrededor de diciembre : I will get there around December⟩

alrededores *nmpl* ALEDAÑOS : surroundings, outskirts

alta *nf* 1 : admission, entry, enrollment 2 **dar de alta** : to release, to discharge (a patient)

altanería *nf* ALTIVEZ, ARROGANCIA : arrogance, haughtiness

altanero, -ra *adj* ALTIVO, ARROGANTE : arrogant, haughty — **altaneramente** *adv*

altar *nm* : altar

altavoz *nm, pl* **-voces** ALTOPARLANTE : loudspeaker

alteración *nf, pl* **-ciones** 1 MODIFICACIÓN : alteration, modification 2 PERTURBACIÓN : disturbance, disruption

alterado, -da *adj* : upset

alterar *vt* 1 MODIFICAR : to alter, to modify 2 PERTURBAR : to disturb, to disrupt — **alterarse** *vr* : to get upset, to get worked up

altercado *nm* DISCUSIÓN, DISPUTA : altercation, argument, dispute

alternador *nm* : alternator

alternancia *nf* : alternation, rotation

alternar *vi* 1 : to alternate 2 : to mix, to socialize — *vt* : to alternate — **alternarse** *vr* : to take turns

alternativa *nf* OPCIÓN : alternative, option

alternativo, -va *adj* 1 : alternating 2 : alternative — **alternativamente** *adv*

alterno, -na *adj* : alternate ⟨corriente alterna : alternating current⟩

alteza *nf* 1 : loftiness, lofty height 2 **Alteza** : Highness

altibajos *nmpl* 1 : unevenness (of terrain) 2 : ups and downs

altímetro *nm* : altimeter

altiplanicie *nf* → **altiplano**

altiplano *nm* : high plateau, upland

altisonante *adj* 1 : pompous, affected (of language) 2 *Mex* : rude, obscene (of language)

altitud *nf* : altitude

altivez *nf, pl* -veces ALTANERÍA, ARROGANCIA : arrogance, haughtiness
altivo, -va *adj* ALTANERO, ARROGANTE : arrogant, haughty
alto[1] *adv* **1** : high **2** : loud, loudly
alto[2], **-ta** *adj* **1** : tall, high **2** : loud ⟨en voz alta : aloud, out loud⟩
alto[3] *nm* **1** ALTURA : height, elevation **2** : stop, halt **3 altos** *nmpl* : upper floors
alto[4] *interj* : halt!, stop!
altoparlante *nm* ALTAVOZ : loudspeaker
altozano *nm* : hillock
altruismo *nm* : altruism
altruista[1] *adj* : altruistic
altruista[2] *nmf* : altruist
altura *nf* **1** : height **2** : altitude **3** : loftiness, nobleness **4 a la altura de** : near, up by ⟨en la avenida San Antonio a la altura de la Calle Tres : on San Antonio Avenue up near Third Street⟩ **5 a estas alturas** : at this point, at this stage of the game
alubia *nf* : kidney bean
alucinación *nf, pl* -ciones : hallucination
alucinante *adj* : hallucinatory
alucinar *vi* : to hallucinate
alucinógeno[1], **-na** *adj* : hallucinogenic
alucinógeno[2] *nm* : hallucinogen
alud *nm* AVALANCHA : avalanche, landslide
aludido, -da *n* **1** : person in question ⟨el aludido : the aforesaid⟩ **2 darse por aludido** : to take it personally
aludir *vi* : to allude, to refer
alumbrado *nm* ILUMINACIÓN : lighting
alumbramiento *nm* **1** : lighting **2** : childbirth
alumbrar *vt* **1** ILUMINAR : to light, to illuminate **2** : to give birth to
alumbre *nm* : alum
aluminio *nm* : aluminum
alumnado *nm* : student body
alumno, -na *n* **1** : pupil, student **2 ex–alumno, -na** : alumnus, alumna *f* **3 ex–alumnos, -nas** *npl* : alumni, alumnae *f*
alusión *nf, pl* -siones : allusion, reference
alusivo, -va *adj* **1** : allusive **2 ~ a** : in reference to, regarding
aluvión *nm, pl* -viones : flood, barrage
alza *nf* SUBIDA : rise ⟨precios en alza : rising prices⟩
alzamiento *nm* LEVANTAMIENTO : uprising, insurrection
alzar {21} *vt* **1** ELEVAR, LEVANTAR : to lift, to raise **2** : to erect — **alzarse** *vr* LEVANTARSE : to rise up
ama *nf* → **amo**
amabilidad *nf* : kindness
amable *adj* : kind, nice — **amablemente** *adv*
amado[1], **-da** *adj* : beloved, darling
amado[2], **-da** *n* : sweetheart, loved one
amaestrar *vt* : to train (animals)
amafiarse *vr Mex fam* : to conspire, to be in cahoots

amagar {52} *vt* **1** : to show signs of (an illness, etc.) **2** : to threaten — *vi* **1** : to be imminent, to threaten **2** : to feint, to dissemble
amago *nm* **1** AMENAZA : threat **2** : sign, hint
amainar *vi* : to abate, to ease up, to die down
amalgama *nf* : amalgam
amalgamar *vt* : to amalgamate, to unite
amamantar *v* : to breast-feed, to nurse, to suckle
amanecer[1] {53} *v impers* **1** : to dawn **2** : to begin to show, to appear **3** : to wake up (in the morning)
amanecer[2] *nm* ALBA : dawn, daybreak
amanerado, -da *adj* : affected, mannered
amansar *vt* **1** : to tame **2** : to soothe, to calm down — **amansarse** *vr*
amante[1] *adj* : loving, fond
amante[2] *nmf* : lover
amañar *vt* : to rig, to fix, to tamper with — **amañarse** *vr* **amañárselas** : to manage
amaño *nm* **1** : skill, dexterity **2** : trick, ruse
amapola *nf* : poppy
amar *vt* : to love — **amarse** *vr*
amargado, -da *adj* : embittered, bitter
amargar {52} *vt* : to make bitter, to embitter — *vi* : to taste bitter
amargo[1], **-ga** *adj* : bitter — **amargamente** *adv*
amargo[2] *nm* : bitterness, tartness
amargura *nf* **1** : bitterness **2** : grief, sorrow
amarilis *nf* : amaryllis
amarillear *vi* : to yellow, to turn yellow
amarillento, -ta *adj* : yellowish
amarillismo *nm* : yellow journalism, sensationalism
amarillo[1], **-lla** *adj* : yellow
amarillo[2] *nm* : yellow
amarra *nf* **1** : mooring, mooring line **2 soltar las amarras de** : to loosen one's grip on
amarrar *vt* **1** : to moor (a boat) **2** ATAR : to fasten, to tie up, to tie down
amartillar *vt* : to cock (a gun)
amasar *vt* **1** : to amass **2** : to knead **3** : to mix, to prepare
amasijo *nm* : jumble, hodgepodge
amasio, -sia *n* : lover, paramour
amateur *adj & nmf* : amateur — **amateurismo** *nm*
amatista *nf* : amethyst
amatorio, -ria *adj* : amatory, sexual ⟨poesía amatoria : love poems⟩
amazona *nf* **1** : Amazon (in mythology) **2** : horsewoman
amazónico, -ca *adj* : amazonian
ambages *nmpl* sin **~** : without hesitation, straight to the point
ámbar *nm* **1** : amber **2 ámbar gris** : ambergris
ambición *nf, pl* -ciones : ambition
ambicionar *vt* : to aspire to, to seek

ambicioso, -sa *adj* : ambitious — **ambiciosamente** *adv*

ambidextro, -tra *adj* : ambidextrous

ambientación *nf, pl* **-ciones** : setting, atmosphere

ambiental *adj* : environmental — **ambientalmente** *adv*

ambientalista *nmf* : environmentalist

ambientar *vt* : to give atmosphere to, to set (in literature and drama) — **ambientarse** *vr* : to adjust, to get one's bearings

ambiente *nm* **1** : atmosphere **2** : environment **3** : surroundings *pl*

ambigüedad *nf* : ambiguity

ambiguo, -gua *adj* : ambiguous

ámbito *nm* : domain, field, area

ambivalencia *nf* : ambivalence

ambivalente *adj* : ambivalent

ambos, -bas *adj & pron* : both

ambulancia *nf* : ambulance

ambulante *adj* **1** : traveling, itinerant **2 vendedor ambulante** : street vendor

ameba *nf* : amoeba

amedrentar *vt* : to frighten, to intimidate — **amedrentarse** *vr*

amén *nm* **1** : amen **2** ~ **de** : in addition to, besides **3 en un decir amén** : in an instant

amenaza *nf* : threat, menace

amenazador, -dora *adj* : threatening, menacing

amenazante → **amenazador**

amenazar {21} *v* : to threaten

amenguar {10} *vt* **1** : to diminish **2** : to belittle, to dishonor

amenidad *nf* : pleasantness, amenity

amenizar {21} *vt* **1** : to make pleasant **2** : to brighten up, to add life to

ameno, -na *adj* : agreeable, pleasant

amento *nm* : catkin

americano, -na *adj & n* : American

amerindio, -dia *adj & n* : Amerindian

ameritar *vt* MERECER : to deserve

ametralladora *nf* : machine gun

amianto *nm* : asbestos

amiba → **ameba**

amigable *adj* : friendly, amicable — **amigablemente** *adv*

amígdala *nf* : tonsil

amigdalitis *nf* : tonsilitis

amigo¹, -ga *adj* : friendly, close

amigo², -ga *n* : friend

amigote *nm* : crony, pal

amilanar *vt* **1** : to frighten **2** : to daunt, to discourage — **amilanarse** *vr* : to lose heart

aminoácido *nm* : amino acid

aminorar *vt* : to reduce, to lessen — *vi* : to diminish

amistad *nf* : friendship

amistoso, -sa *adj* : friendly — **amistosamente** *adv*

amnesia *nf* : amnesia

amnésico, -ca *adj & n* : amnesiac, amnesic

amnistía *nf* : amnesty

amnistiar {85} *vt* : to grant amnesty to

amo, ama *n* **1** : master *m*, mistress *f* **2** : owner, keeper (of an animal) **3 ama de casa** : housewife **4 ama de llaves** : housekeeper

amodorrado, -da *adj* : drowsy

amolar {19} *vt* **1** : to grind, to sharpen **2** : to pester, to annoy

amoldable *adj* : adaptable

amoldar *vt* **1** : to mold **2** : to adapt, to adjust — **amoldarse** *vr*

amonestación *nf, pl* **-ciones** **1** APERCIBIMIENTO : admonition, warning **2 amonestaciones** *nfpl* : banns

amonestar *vt* APERCIBIR : to admonish, to warn

amoníaco *or* **amoniaco** *nm* : ammonia

amontonamiento *nm* : accumulation, piling up

amontonar *vt* **1** APILAR : to pile up, to heap up **2** : to collect, to gather **3** : to hoard — **amontonarse** *vr*

amor *nm* **1** : love **2** : loved one, beloved **3 amor propio** : self-esteem **4 hacer el amor** : to make love

amoral *adj* : amoral

amoratado, -da *adj* : black-and-blue, bruised, livid

amordazar {21} *vt* **1** : to gag, to muzzle **2** : to silence

amorfo, -fa *adj* : shapeless, amorphous

amorío *nm* : love affair, fling

amoroso, -sa *adj* **1** : loving, affectionate **2** : amorous ⟨una mirada amorosa : an amorous glance⟩ **3** : charming, cute — **amorosamente** *adv*

amortiguación *nf* : cushioning, absorption

amortiguador *nm* : shock absorber

amortiguar {10} *vt* : to soften (an impact)

amortizar {21} *vt* : to amortize, to pay off — **amortización** *nf*

amotinado¹, -da *adj* : rebellious, insurgent, mutinous

amotinado², -da *n* : rebel, insurgent, mutineer

amotinamiento *nm* : uprising, rebellion

amotinar *vt* : to incite (to riot), to agitate — **amotinarse** *vr* **1** : to riot, to rebel **2** : to mutiny

amparar *vt* : to safeguard, to protect — **ampararse** *vr* **1** ~ **de** : to take shelter from **2** ~ **en** : to have recourse to

amparo *nm* ACOGIDA, REFUGIO : protection, refuge

amperímetro *nm* : ammeter

amperio *nm* : ampere

ampliable *adj* : expandable, enlargeable, extendible

ampliación *nf, pl* **-ciones** : expansion, extension

ampliar {85} *vt* **1** : to expand, to extend **2** : to widen **3** : to enlarge (photographs) **4** : to elaborate on, to develop (ideas)

amplificador *nm* : amplifier

amplificar {72} *vt* : to amplify — **amplificación** *nf*

amplio, -plia *adj* : broad, wide, ample —
  ampliamente *adj*
amplitud *nf* **1** : breadth, extent **2** : spaciousness
ampolla *nf* **1** : blister **2** : vial, ampoule
ampollar *vt* : to blister — **ampollarse** *vr*
ampolleta *nf* **1** : small vial **2** : hourglass
  3 *Chile* : light bulb
ampulosidad *nf* : pompousness, bombast
ampuloso, -sa *adj* GRANDILOCUENTE
  : pompous, bombastic — **ampulosamente** *adv*
amputar *vt* : to amputate — **amputación** *nf*
amueblar *vt* : to furnish
amuleto *nm* TALISMÁN : amulet, charm
amurallar *vt* : to wall in, to fortify
anacardo *nm* : cashew nut
anaconda *nf* : anaconda
anacrónico, -ca *adj* : anachronistic
anacronismo *nm* : anachronism
ánade *nmf* **1** : duck **2 ánade real** : mallard
anagrama *nm* : anagram
anal *adj* : anal
anales *nmpl* : annals
analfabetismo *nm* : illiteracy
analfabeto, -ta *adj & n* : illiterate
analgésico[1], -ca *adj* : analgesic, painkilling
analgésico[2] *nm* : painkiller, analgesic
análisis *nm* : analysis
analista *nmf* **1** : analyst **2** : annalist
analítico, -ca *adj* : analytical, analytic
  — **analíticamente** *adv*
analizar {21} *vt* : to analyze
analogía *nf* : analogy
analógico, -ca *adj* **1** : analogical **2** : analog ⟨computadora analógica : analog computer⟩
análogo, -ga *adj* : analogous, similar
ananá *or* **ananás** *nm, pl* **-nás** : pineapple
anaquel *nm* REPISA : shelf
anaranjado[1], -da *adj* NARANJA : orange-colored
anaranjado[2] *nm* NARANJA : orange (color)
anarquía *nf* : anarchy
anárquico, -ca *adj* : anarchic
anarquismo *nm* : anarchism
anarquista *adj & nmf* : anarchist
anatema *nm* : anathema
anatomía *nf* : anatomy — **anatomista** *nmf*
anatómico, -ca *adj* : anatomical — **anatómicamente** *adv*
anca *nf* **1** : haunch, hindquarter **2 ancas de rana** : frogs' legs
ancestral *adj* **1** : ancient, traditional **2** : ancestral
ancestro *nm* ASCENDIENTE : ancestor, forefather *m*
ancho[1], -cha *adj* **1** : wide, broad **2** : ample, loose-fitting
ancho[2] *nm* : width, breadth
anchoa *nf* : anchovy

anchura *nf* : width, breadth
ancianidad *nf* SENECTUD : old age
anciano[1], -na *adj* : aged, old, elderly
anciano[2], -na *n* : elderly person
ancla *nf* : anchor
ancladero → **anclaje**
anclaje *nm* : anchorage
anclar *v* FONDEAR : to anchor
andadas *nfpl* **1** : tracks **2 volver a las andadas** : to go back to one's old ways, to backslide
andador[1] *nm* **1** : walker, baby walker **2** *Mex* : walkway
andador[2], -dora *n* : walker, one who walks
andadura *nf* : course, journey ⟨su agotadora andadura al campeonato : his exhausting journey to the championship⟩
andaluz, -luza *adj & n, mpl* **-luces** : Andalusian
andamiaje *nm* **1** : scaffolding **2** ESTRUCTURA : structure, framework
andamio *nm* : scaffold
andanada *nf* **1** : volley, broadside **2 soltar una andanada a** : to reprimand
andanzas *nfpl* : adventures
andar[1] {6} *vi* **1** CAMINAR : to walk **2** IR : to go, to travel **3** FUNCIONAR : to run, to function ⟨el auto anda bien : the car runs well⟩ **4** : to ride ⟨andar a caballo : to ride on horseback⟩ **5** : to be ⟨anda sin dinero : he's broke⟩ — *vt* : to walk, to travel
andar[2] *nm* : walk, gait
andas *nfpl* : stand (for a coffin), bier
andén *nm, pl* **andenes** **1** : (train) platform **2** *CA, Col* : sidewalk
andino, -na *adj* : Andean
andorrano, -na *adj & n* : Andorran
andrajos *nmpl* : rags, tatters
andrajoso, -sa *adj* : ragged, tattered
andrógino, -na *adj* : androgynous
andurriales *nmpl* : remote place
anea *nf* : cattail
anduvo, etc. → **andar**
anécdota *nf* : anecdote
anecdótico, -ca *adj* : anecdotal
anegar {52} *vt* **1** INUNDAR : to flood **2** AHOGAR : to drown **3** : to overwhelm — **anegarse** *vr* : to be flooded
anejo *nm* → **anexo[2]**
anemia *nf* : anemia
anémico, -ca *adj* : anemic
anémona *nf* : anemone
anestesia *nf* : anesthesia
anestesiar *vt* : to anesthetize
anestésico[1], -ca *adj* : anesthetic
anestésico[2] *nm* : anesthetic
anestesista *nmf* : anesthetist
aneurisma *nmf* : aneurysm
anexar *vt* : to annex, to attach
anexión *nf, pl* **-xiones** : annexation
anexo[1], -xa *adj* : attached, joined, annexed
anexo[2] *nm* **1** : annex **2** : supplement (to a book), appendix
anfetamina *nf* : amphetamine

anfibio¹, -bia *adj* : amphibious
anfibio² *nm* : amphibian
anfiteatro *nm* **1** : amphitheater **2** : lecture hall
anfitrión, -triona *n, mpl* **-triones** : host, hostess *f*
ánfora *nf* **1** : amphora **2** *Mex, Peru* : ballot box
ángel *nm* : angel
angelical *adj* : angelic, angelical
angélico, -ca *adj* → **angelical**
angina *nf* **1** *or* **angina de pecho** : angina **2** *Mex* : tonsil
anglicano, -na *adj & n* : Anglican
angloparlante¹ *adj* : English-speaking
angloparlante² *nmf* : English speaker
anglosajón, -jona *adj & n, mpl* **-jones** : Anglo-Saxon
angoleño, -ña *adj & n* : Angolan
angora *nf* : angora
angostar *vt* : to narrow — **angostarse** *vr*
angosto, -ta *adj* : narrow
angostura *nf* : narrowness
anguila *nf* : eel
angular *adj* : angular — **angularidad** *nf*
ángulo *nm* **1** : angle **2** : corner **3 ángulo muerto** : blind spot
anguloso, -sa *adj* : angular, sharp ⟨una cara angulosa : an angular face⟩ — **angulosidad** *nf*
angustia *nf* **1** CONGOJA : anguish, distress **2** : anxiety, worry
angustiar *vt* **1** : to anguish, to distress **2** : to worry — **angustiarse** *vr*
angustioso, -sa *adj* **1** : anguished, distressed **2** : distressing, worrisome
anhelante *adj* : yearning, longing
anhelar *vt* : to yearn for, to crave
anhelo *nm* : longing, yearning
anidar *vi* **1** : to nest **2** : to make one's home, to dwell — *vt* : to shelter
anillo *nm* SORTIJA : ring
ánima *n* ALMA : soul
animación *nf, pl* **-ciones 1** : animation **2** VIVEZA : liveliness
animado, -da *adj* **1** : animated, lively **2** : cheerful — **animadamente** *adv*
animador, -dora *n* **1** : (television) host **2** : cheerleader
animadversión *nf, pl* **-siones** ANIMOSIDAD : animosity, antagonism
animal¹ *adj* **1** : animal **2** ESTÚPIDO : stupid, idiotic **3** : rough, brutish
animal² *nm* : animal
animal³ *nmf* **1** IDIOTA : idiot, fool **2** : brute, beastly person
animar *vt* **1** ALENTAR : to encourage, to inspire **2** : to animate, to enliven **3** : to brighten up, to cheer up — **animarse** *vr*
anímico, -ca *adj* : mental ⟨estado anímico : state of mind⟩
ánimo *nm* **1** ALMA : spirit, soul **2** : mood, spirits *pl* **3** : encouragement **4** PROPÓSITO : intention, purpose ⟨sociedad sin ánimo de lucro : nonprofit organization⟩ **5** : energy, vitality

animosidad *nf* ANIMADVERSIÓN : animosity, ill will
animoso, -sa *adj* : brave, spirited
aniñado, -da *adj* : childlike
aniquilación *nf* → **aniquilamiento**
aniquilamiento *nm* : annihilation, extermination
aniquilar *vt* **1** : to annihilate, to wipe out **2** : to overwhelm, to bring to one's knees — **aniquilarse** *vr*
anís *nm* **1** : anise **2 semilla de anís** : aniseed
aniversario *nm* : anniversary
ano *nm* : anus
anoche *adv* : last night
anochecer¹ {53} *v impers* : to get dark
anochecer² *nm* : dusk, nightfall
anodino, -na *adj* : insipid, dull
ánodo *nm* : anode
anomalía *nf* : anomaly
anómalo, -la *adj* : anomalous
anonadado, -da *adj* : dumbfounded, speechless
anonadar *vt* : to dumbfound, to stun
anonimato *nm* : anonymity
anónimo, -ma *adj* : anonymous — **anónimamente** *adv*
anorexia *nf* : anorexia
anoréxico, -ca *adj* : anorexic
anormal *adj* : abnormal — **anormalmente** *adv*
anormalidad *nf* : abnormality
anotación *nf, pl* **-ciones 1** : annotation, note **2** : scoring (in sports) ⟨lograron una anotación : they managed to score a goal⟩
anotar *vt* **1** : to annotate **2** APUNTAR, ESCRIBIR : to write down, to jot down **3** : to score (in sports) — *vi* : to score
anquilosado, -da *adj* **1** : stiff-jointed **2** : stagnated, stale
anquilosamiento *nm* **1** : stiffness (of joints) **2** : stagnation, paralysis
anquilosarse *vr* **1** : to stagnate **2** : to become stiff or paralyzed
anquilostoma *nm* : hookworm
ánsar *nm* : goose
ansarino *nm* : gosling
ansia *nf* **1** INQUIETUD : apprehensiveness, uneasiness **2** ANGUSTIA : anguish, distress **3** ANHELO : longing, yearning
ansiar {85} *vt* : to long for, to yearn for
ansiedad *nf* : anxiety
ansioso, -sa *adj* **1** : anxious, worried **2** : eager — **ansiosamente** *adv*
antagónico, -ca *adj* : conflicting, opposing
antagonismo *nm* : antagonism
antagonista¹ *adj* : antagonistic
antagonista² *nmf* : antagonist, opponent
antagonizar {21} *vt* : to antagonize
antaño *adv* : yesteryear, long ago
antártico, -ca *adj* **1** : antarctic **2 círculo antártico** : antarctic circle
ante¹ *nm* **1** : elk, moose **2** : suede
ante² *prep* **1** : before, in front of **2** : considering, in view of **3 ante todo** : first and foremost, above all

anteanoche *adv* : the night before last
anteayer *adv* : the day before yesterday
antebrazo *nm* : forearm
antecedente[1] *adj* : previous, prior
antecedente[2] *nm* **1** : precedent **2 antecedentes** *nmpl* : record, background
anteceder *v* : to precede
antecesor, -sora *n* **1** ANTEPASADO : ancestor **2** PREDECESOR : predecessor
antedicho, -cha *adj* : aforesaid, above
antelación *nf, pl* **-ciones 1** : advance notice **2 con** ~ : in advance, beforehand
antemano *adv* **de** ~ : in advance ⟨se lo agradezco de antemano : I thank you in advance⟩
antena *nf* : antenna
antenoche → anteanoche
anteojera *nf* **1** : eyeglass case **2 anteojeras** *nfpl* : blinders
anteojos *nmpl* GAFAS : glasses, eyeglasses
antepasado[1], **-da** *adj* : before last ⟨el domingo antepasado : the Sunday before last⟩
antepasado[2], **-da** *n* ANTECESOR : ancestor
antepecho *nm* **1** : guardrail **2** : ledge, sill
antepenúltimo, -ma *adj* : third from last
anteponer {60} *vt* **1** : to place before ⟨anteponer al interés de la nación el interés de la comunidad : to place the interests of the community before national interest⟩ **2** : to prefer
anteproyecto *nm* **1** : draft, proposal **2 anteproyecto de ley** : bill
antera *nf* : anther
anterior *adj* **1** : previous **2** : earlier ⟨tiempos anteriores : earlier times⟩ **3** : anterior, forward, front
anterioridad *nf* **1** : priority **2 con** ~ : beforehand, in advance
anteriormente *adv* : previously, beforehand
antes *adv* **1** : before, earlier **2** : formerly, previously **3** : rather, sooner ⟨antes prefiero morir : I'd rather die⟩ **4** ~ **de** : before, previous to ⟨antes de hoy : before today⟩ **5 antes que** : before ⟨antes que llegue Luis : before Luis arrives⟩ **6 cuanto antes** : as soon as possible **7 antes bien** : on the contrary
antesala *nf* **1** : anteroom, waiting room, lobby **2** : prelude, prologue
antiaborto, -ta *adj* : antiabortion
antiácido *nm* : antacid
antiadherente *adj* : nonstick
antiaéreo, -rea *adj* : antiaircraft
antiamericano, -na *adj* : anti-American
antibalas *adj* : bulletproof
antibiótico[1], **-ca** *adj* : antibiotic
antibiótico[2] *nm* : antibiotic
antichoque *adj* : shockproof
anticipación *nf, pl* **-ciones 1** : expectation, anticipation **2 con** ~ : in advance

anticipado, -da *adj* **1** : advance, early **2 por** ~ : in advance
anticipar *vt* **1** : to anticipate, to forestall, to deal with in advance **2** : to pay in advance — **anticiparse** *vr* **1** : to be early **2** ADELANTARSE : to get ahead
anticipo *nm* **1** : advance (payment) **2** : foretaste, preview
anticlerical *adj* : anticlerical
anticlimático, -ca *adj* : anticlimactic
anticlímax *nm* : anticlimax
anticomunismo *nm* : anticommunism
anticomunista *adj & nmf* : anticommunist
anticoncepción *nf, pl* **-ciones** : birth control, contraception
anticonceptivo *nm* : contraceptive
anticongelante *nm* : antifreeze
anticuado, -da *adj* : antiquated, outdated
anticuario[1], **-ria** *adj* : antique, antiquarian
anticuario[2], **-ria** *n* : antiquarian, antiquary
anticuario[3] *nm* : antique shop
anticuerpo *nm* : antibody
antidemocrático, -ca *adj* : antidemocratic
antideportivo, -va *adj* : unsportsmanlike
antidepresivo *nm* : antidepressant
antídoto *nm* : antidote
antidrogas *adj* : antidrug
antier → anteayer
antiestético, -ca *adj* : unsightly, unattractive
antifascista *adj & nmf* : antifascist
antifaz *nm, pl* **-faces** : mask
antifeminista *adj & nmf* : antifeminist
antífona *nf* : anthem
antígeno *nm* : antigen
antigualla *nf* **1** : antique **2** : relic, old thing
antiguamente *adv* **1** : formerly, once **2** : long ago
antigüedad *nf* **1** : antiquity **2** : seniority **3** : age ⟨con siglos de antigüedad : centuries-old⟩ **4 antigüedades** *nfpl* : antiques
antiguo, -gua *adj* **1** : ancient, old **2** : former **3** : old-fashioned ⟨a la antigua : in the old-fashioned way⟩ **4 Antiguo Testamento** : Old Testament
antihigiénico, -ca *adj* INSALUBRE : unhygienic, unsanitary
antihistamínico *nm* : antihistamine
antiimperialismo *nm* : anti-imperialism
antiimperialista *adj & nmf* : anti-imperialist
antiinflacionario, -ria *adj* : anti-inflationary
antiinflamatorio, -ria *adj* : anti-inflammatory
antillano[1], **-na** *adj* CARIBEÑO : Caribbean, West Indian
antillano[2], **-na** *n* : West Indian
antílope *nm* : antelope
antimilitarismo *nm* : antimilitarism

antimilitarista *adj & nmf* : antimilitarist
antimonio *nm* : antimony
antimonopolista *adj* : antimonopoly, antitrust
antinatural *adj* : unnatural, perverse
antipatía *nf* : aversion, dislike
antipático, -ca *adj* : obnoxious, unpleasant
antipatriótico, -ca *adj* : unpatriotic
antirrábico, -ca *adj* : antirabies ⟨vacuna antirrábica : rabies vaccine⟩
antirreglamentario, -ria *adj* 1 : unlawful, illegal 2 : foul (in sports)
antirrevolucionario, -ria *adj & n* : antirevolutionary
antirrobo, -ba *adj* : antitheft
antisemita *adj* : anti-Semitic
antisemitismo *nm* : anti-Semitism
antiséptico¹, -ca *adj* : antiseptic
antiséptico² *nm* : antiseptic
antisocial *adj* : antisocial
antitabaco *adj* : antismoking
antiterrorista *adj* : antiterrorist
antítesis *nf* : antithesis
antitoxina *nf* : antitoxin
antitranspirante *nm* : antiperspirant
antojadizo, -za *adj* CAPRICHOSO : capricious
antojarse *vr* 1 APETECER : to be appealing, to be desirable ⟨se me antoja un helado : I feel like having ice cream⟩ 2 : to seem, to appear ⟨los árboles se antojaban fantasmas : the trees seemed like ghosts⟩
antojitos *nmpl Mex* : traditional Mexican snack foods
antojo *nm* 1 CAPRICHO : whim 2 : craving
antología *nf* 1 : anthology 2 de ~ *fam* : fantastic, incredible
antónimo *nm* : antonym
antonomasia *nf* por ~ : par excellence
antorcha *nf* : torch
antracita *nf* : anthracite
antro *nm* 1 : cave, den 2 : dive, seedy nightclub
antropofagia *nf* CANIBALISMO : cannibalism
antropófago¹, -ga *adj* : cannibalistic
antropófago², -ga *n* CANÍBAL : cannibal
antropoide *adj & nmf* : anthropoid
antropología *nf* : anthropology
antropológico, -ca *adj* : anthropological
antropólogo, -ga *n* : anthropologist
anual *adj* : annual, yearly — **anualmente** *adv*
anualidad *nf* : annuity
anuario *nm* : yearbook, annual
anudar *vt* : to knot, to tie in a knot — **anudarse** *vr*
anuencia *nf* : consent
anulación *nf, pl* **-ciones** : annulment, nullification
anular *vt* : to annul, to cancel
anunciador, -dora *n* → **anunciante**
anunciante *nmf* : advertiser
anunciar *vt* 1 : to announce 2 : to advertise

anuncio *nm* 1 : announcement 2 : advertisement, commercial
anzuelo *nm* 1 : fishhook 2 **morder el anzuelo** : to take the bait
añadido *nm* : addition
añadidura *nf* 1 : additive, addition 2 **por ~** : in addition, furthermore
añadir *vt* 1 AGREGAR : to add 2 AUMENTAR : to increase
añejar *vt* : to age, to ripen
añejo, -ja *adj* 1 : aged, vintage 2 : age-old, musty, stale
añicos *nmpl* : smithereens, bits ⟨hacer(se) añicos : to shatter⟩
añil *nm* 1 : indigo 2 : bluing
año *nm* 1 : year ⟨en el año 1990 : in (the year) 1990⟩ ⟨tiene diez años : she is ten years old⟩ 2 : grade ⟨cuarto año : fourth grade⟩ 3 **año bisiesto** : leap year 4 **año luz** : light-year 5 **Año Nuevo** : New Year
añoranza *nf* : longing, yearning
añorar *vt* 1 DESEAR : to long for 2 : to grieve for, to miss — *vi* : to mourn, to grieve
añoso, -sa *adj* : aged, old
aorta *nf* : aorta
apabullante *adj* : overwhelming, crushing
apabullar *vt* : to overwhelm
apacentar {55} *vt* : to pasture, to put to pasture
apache *adj & nmf* : Apache
apachurrado, -da *adj fam* : depressed, down
apachurrar *vt* : to crush, to squash
apacible *adj* : gentle, mild, calm — **apaciblemente** *adv*
apaciguador, -dora *adj* : calming
apaciguamiento *nm* : appeasement
apaciguar {10} *vt* APLACAR : to appease, to pacify — **apaciguarse** *vr* : to calm down
apadrinar *vt* 1 : to be a godparent to 2 : to sponsor, to support
apagado, -da *adj* 1 : off, out ⟨la luz está apagada : the light is off⟩ 2 : dull, subdued
apagador *nm Mex* : switch
apagar {52} *vt* 1 : to turn off, to shut off 2 : to extinguish, to put out — **apagarse** *vr* 1 : to go out, to fade 2 : to wane, to die down
apagón *nm, pl* **-gones** : blackout (of power)
apalancamiento *nm* : leverage
apalancar {72} *vt* 1 : to jack up 2 : to pry open
apalear *vt* : to beat up, to thrash
apantallar *vt Mex* : to dazzle, to impress
apañar *vt* 1 : to seize, to grasp 2 : to repair, to mend — **apañarse** *vr* : to manage, to get along
apaño *nm fam* 1 : patch 2 HABILIDAD : skill, knack
apapachar *vt Mex fam* : to cuddle, to caress — **apapacharse** *vr*

aparador *nm* **1** : sideboard, cupboard **2** ESCAPARATE, VITRINA : shop window
aparato *nm* **1** : machine, appliance, apparatus ⟨aparato auditivo : hearing aid⟩ ⟨aparato de televisión : television set⟩ **2** : system ⟨aparato digestivo : digestive system⟩ **3** : display, ostentation ⟨sin aparato : without ceremony⟩ **4**
aparatos *nmpl* : braces (for the teeth)
aparatoso, -sa *adj* **1** : ostentatious **2** : spectacular
aparcamiento *nm Spain* **1** : parking **2** : parking lot
aparcar {72} *v Spain* : to park
aparcero, -ra *n* : sharecropper
aparear *vt* **1** : to mate (animals) **2** : to match up — **aparearse** *vr* : to mate
aparecer {53} *vi* **1** : to appear **2** PRESENTARSE : to show up **3** : to turn up, to be found — **aparecerse** *vr* : to appear
aparejado, -da *adj* **1 ir aparejado con** : to go hand in hand with **2 llevar aparejado** : to entail
aparejar *vt* **1** PREPARAR : to prepare, to make ready **2** : to harness (a horse) **3** : to fit out (a ship)
aparejo *nm* **1** : equipment, gear **2** : harness, saddle **3** : rig, rigging (of a ship)
aparentar *vt* **1** : to seem, to appear ⟨no aparentas tu edad : you don't look your age⟩ **2** FINGIR : to feign, to pretend
aparente *adj* **1** : apparent **2** : showy, striking — **aparentemente** *adv*
aparición *nf, pl* **-ciones 1** : appearance **2** PUBLICACIÓN : publication, release **3** FANTASMA : apparition, vision
apariencia *nf* **1** ASPECTO : appearance, look **2 en ∼** : seemingly, apparently
apartado *nm* **1** : section, paragraph **2**
apartado postal : post office box
apartamento *nm* DEPARTAMENTO : apartment
apartar *vt* **1** ALEJAR : to move away, to put at a distance **2** : to put aside, to set aside, to separate — **apartarse** *vr* **1** : to step aside, to move away **2** DESVIARSE : to stray
aparte[1] *adv* **1** : apart, aside ⟨modestia aparte : if I say so myself⟩ **2** : separately **3 ∼ de** : apart from, besides
aparte[2] *adj* : separate, special
aparte[3] *nm* : aside (in theater)
apartheid *nm* : apartheid
apasionado, -da *adj* : passionate, enthusiastic — **apasionadamente** *adv*
apasionante *adj* : fascinating, exciting
apasionar *vt* : to enthuse, to excite — **apasionarse** *vr*
apatía *nf* : apathy
apático, -ca *adj* : apathetic
apearse *vr* **1** DESMONTAR : to dismount **2** : to get out of or off (a vehicle)
apedrear *vt* : to stone, to throw stones at
apegado, -da *adj* : attached, close, devoted ⟨es muy apegado a su familia : he is very devoted to his family⟩

apegarse {52} *vr* **∼ a** : to become attached to, to grow fond of
apego *nm* AFICIÓN : attachment, fondness, inclination
apelación *nf, pl* **-ciones** : appeal (in court)
apelar *vi* **1** : to appeal **2 ∼ a** : to resort to
apelativo *nm* APELLIDO : last name, surname
apellidarse *vr* : to have for a last name ⟨¿cómo se apellida? : what is your last name?⟩
apellido *nm* : last name, surname
apelotonar *vt* : to roll into a ball, to bundle up
apenar *vt* : to aggrieve, to sadden — **apenarse** *vr* **1** : to be saddened **2** : to become embarrassed
apenas[1] *adv* : hardly, scarcely
apenas[2] *conj* : as soon as
apéndice *nm* **1** : appendix **2** : appendage
apendicectomía *nf* : appendectomy
apendicitis *nf* : appendicitis
apercibimiento *nm* **1** : preparation **2** AMONESTACIÓN : warning
apercibir *vt* **1** DISPONER : to prepare, to make ready **2** AMONESTAR : to warn **3** OBSERVAR : to observe, to perceive — **apercibirse** *vr* **1** : to get ready **2 ∼ de** : to notice
aperitivo *nm* **1** : appetizer **2** : aperitif
apero *nm* : tool, implement
apertura *nf* **1** : opening, aperture **2** : commencement, beginning **3** : openness
apesadumbrar *vt* : to distress, to sadden — **apesadumbrarse** *vr* : to be weighed down
apestar *vt* **1** : to infect with the plague **2** : to corrupt — *vi* : to stink
apestoso, -sa *adj* : stinking, foul
apetecer {53} *vt* **1** : to crave, to long for ⟨apeteció la fama : he longed for fame⟩ **2** : to appeal to ⟨me apetece un bistec : I feel like having a steak⟩ ⟨¿cuándo te apetece ir? : when do you want to go?⟩ — *vi* : to be appealing
apetecible *adj* : appetizing, appealing
apetito *nm* : appetite
apetitoso, -sa *adj* : appetizing
apiario *nm* : apiary
ápice *nm* **1** : apex, summit **2** PIZCA : bit, smidgen
apicultor, -tora *n* : beekeeper
apicultura *nf* : beekeeping
apilar *vt* AMONTONAR : to heap up, to pile up — **apilarse** *vr*
apiñado, -da *adj* : jammed, crowded
apiñar *vt* : to pack, to cram — **apiñarse** *vr* : to crowd together, to huddle
apio *nm* : celery
apisonadora *nf* : steamroller
apisonar *vt* : to pack down, to tamp
aplacamiento *nm* : appeasement
aplacar {72} *vt* APACIGUAR : to appease, to placate — **aplacarse** *vr* : to calm down

aplanadora *nf* : steamroller
aplanar *vt* : to flatten, to level
aplastante *adj* : crushing, overwhelming
aplastar *vt* : to crush, to squash
aplaudir *v* : to applaud
aplauso *nm* **1** : applause, clapping **2** : praise, acclaim
aplazamiento *nm* : postponement
aplazar {21} *vt* : to postpone, to defer
aplicable *adj* : applicable — **aplicabilidad** *nf*
aplicación *nf, pl* **-ciones 1** : application **2** : diligence, dedication
aplicado, -da *adj* : diligent, industrious
aplicador *nm* : applicator
aplicar {72} *vt* : to apply — **aplicarse** *vr* : to apply oneself
aplique *or* **apliqué** *nm* : appliqué
aplomar *vt* : to plumb, to make vertical
aplomo *nm* : aplomb, composure
apocado, -da *adj* : timid
apocalipsis *nms & pl* : apocalypse ⟨el Libro del Apocalipsis : the Book of Revelation⟩
apocalíptico, -ca *adj* : apocalyptic
apocamiento *nm* : timidity
apocarse {72} *vr* **1** : to shy away, to be intimidated **2** : to humble oneself, to sell oneself short
apócrifo, -fa *adj* : apocryphal
apodar *vt* : to nickname, to call — **apodarse** *vr*
apoderado, -da *n* : proxy, agent
apoderar *vt* : to authorize, to empower — **apoderarse** *vr* ~ **de** : to seize, to take over
apodo *nm* SOBRENOMBRE : nickname
apogeo *nm* : acme, peak, zenith
apología *nf* : defense, apology
apoplejía *nf* : apoplexy, stroke
apoplético, -ca *adj* : apoplectic
aporrear *vt* : to bang on, to beat, to bludgeon
aportación *nf, pl* **-ciones** : contribution
aportar *vt* CONTRIBUIR : to contribute, to provide
aporte *nm* → **aportación**
apostador, -dora *n* : bettor, better
apostar {19} *v* : to bet, to wager ⟨apuesto que no viene : I bet he's not coming⟩
apostasía *nf* : apostasy
apóstata *nmf* : apostate
apostilla *nf* : note
apostillar *vt* : to annotate
apóstol *nm* : apostle
apostólico, -ca *adj* : apostolic
apóstrofe *nmf* : apostrophe
apostura *nf* : elegance, gracefulness
apoyacabezas *nms & pl* : headrest
apoyapiés *nms & pl* : footrest
apoyar *vt* **1** : to support, to back **2** : to lean, to rest — **apoyarse** *vr* **1** ~ **en** : to lean on **2** ~ **en** : to be based on, to rest on
apoyo *nm* : support, backing
apreciable *adj* : appreciable, substantial, considerable

apreciación *nf, pl* **-ciones 1** : appreciation **2** : appraisal, evaluation
apreciar *vt* **1** ESTIMAR : to appreciate, to value **2** EVALUAR : to appraise, to assess — **apreciarse** *vr* : to appreciate, to increase in value
aprecio *nm* **1** ESTIMO : esteem, appreciation **2** EVALUACIÓN : appraisal, assessment
aprehender *vt* **1** : to apprehend, to capture **2** : to conceive of, to grasp
aprehensión *nf, pl* **-siones** : apprehension, capture, arrest
apremiante *adj* : pressing, urgent
apremiar *vt* INSTAR : to pressure, to urge — *vi* URGIR : to be urgent ⟨el tiempo apremia : time is of the essence⟩
apremio *nm* : pressure, urgency
aprender *v* : to learn — **aprenderse** *vr*
aprendiz, -diza *n, mpl* **-dices** : apprentice, trainee
aprendizaje *nm* : apprenticeship
aprensión *nf, pl* **-siones** : apprehension, dread
aprensivo, -va *adj* : apprehensive, worried
apresamiento *nm* : seizure, capture
apresar *vt* : to capture, to seize
aprestar *vt* : to make ready, to prepare — **aprestarse** *vr* : to get ready
apresuradamente *adv* **1** : hurriedly **2** : hastily, too fast
apresurado, -da *adj* : hurried, in a rush
apresuramiento *nm* : hurry, haste
apresurar *vt* : to quicken, to speed up — **apresurarse** *vr* : to hurry up, to make haste
apretado, -da *adj* **1** : tight **2** *fam* : cheap, tightfisted — **apretadamente** *adv*
apretar {55} *vt* **1** : to press, to push (a button) **2** : to tighten **3** : to squeeze — *vi* **1** : to press, to push **2** : to fit tightly, to be too tight ⟨los zapatos me aprietan : my shoes are tight⟩
apretón *nm, pl* **-tones 1** : squeeze **2 apretón de manos** : handshake
apretujar *vt* : to squash, to squeeze — **apretujarse** *vr*
aprieto *nm* APURO : predicament, difficulty ⟨estar en un aprieto : to be in a fix⟩
aprisa *adv* : quickly, hurriedly
aprisionar *vt* **1** : to imprison **2** : to trap, to box in
aprobación *nf, pl* **-ciones** : approval, endorsement
aprobar {19} *vt* **1** : to approve of **2** : to pass (a law, an exam) — *vi* : to pass (in school)
aprobatorio, -ria *adj* : approving
apropiación *nf, pl* **-ciones** : appropriation
apropiado, -da *adj* : appropriate, proper, suitable — **apropiadamente** *adv*
apropiarse *vr* ~ **de** : to take possession of, to appropriate
aprovechable *adj* : usable

aprovechado[1], **-da** *adj* **1** : diligent, hardworking **2** : pushy, opportunistic

aprovechado[2], **-da** *n* : pushy person, opportunist

aprovechamiento *nm* : use, exploitation

aprovechar *vt* : to take advantage of, to make good use of — *vi* **1** : to be of use **2** : to progress, to improve — **aprovecharse** *vr* ~ **de** : to take advantage of, to exploit

aprovisionamiento *nm* : provisions *pl*, supplies *pl*

aprovisionar *vt* : to provide, to supply (with provisions)

aproximación *nf, pl* **-ciones 1** : approximation, estimate **2** : rapprochement

aproximado, -da *adj* : approximate, estimated — **aproximadamente** *adv*

aproximar *vt* ACERCAR, ARRIMAR : to approximate, to bring closer — **aproximarse** *vr* ACERCARSE, ARRIMARSE : to approach, to move closer

aptitud *nf* : aptitude, capability

apto, -ta *adj* **1** : suitable, suited, fit **2** HÁBIL : capable, competent

apuesta *nf* : bet, wager

apuesto, -ta *adj* : elegant, good-looking

apuntador, -dora *n* : prompter

apuntalar *vt* : to prop up, to shore up

apuntar *vt* **1** : to aim, to point **2** ANOTAR : to write down, to jot down **3** INDICAR, SEÑALAR : to point to, to point out **4** : to prompt (in the theater) — *vi* **1** : to take aim **2** : to become evident — **apuntarse** *vr* **1** : to sign up, to enroll **2** : to score

apunte *nm* : note

apuñalar *vt* : to stab

apuradamente *adv* **1** : with difficulty **2** : hurriedly, hastily

apurado, -da *adj* **1** APRESURADO : rushed, pressured **2** : poor, needy **3** : difficult, awkward **4** : embarrassed

apurar *vt* **1** APRESURAR : to hurry, to rush **2** : to use up, to exhaust **3** : to trouble — **apurarse** *vr* **1** APRESURARSE : to hurry up **2** PREOCUPARSE : to worry

apuro *nm* **1** APRIETO : predicament, jam **2** : rush, hurry **3** : embarrassment

aquejar *vt* : to afflict

aquel, aquella *adj, mpl* **aquellos** : that, those

aquél, aquélla *pron, mpl* **aquéllos 1** : that (one), those (ones) **2** : the former

aquello *pron* (*neuter*) : that, that matter, that business ⟨aquello fue algo serio : that was something serious⟩

aquí *adv* **1** : here **2** : now ⟨de aquí en adelante : from now on⟩ **3 por** ~ : around here, hereabouts

aquiescencia *nf* : acquiescence, approval

aquietar *vt* : to allay, to calm — **aquietarse** *vr* : to calm down

aquilatar *vt* **1** : to assay **2** : to assess, to size up

ara *nf* **1** : altar **2 en aras de** : in the interests of, for the sake of

árabe[1] *adj & nmf* : Arab, Arabian

árabe[2] *nm* : Arabic (language)

arabesco *nm* : arabesque — **arabesco, -ca** *adj*

arábigo, -ga *adj* **1** : Arabic, Arabian **2 número arábigo** : Arabic numeral

arable *adj* : arable

arado *nm* : plow

aragonés, -nesa *adj & n, mpl* **-neses** : Aragonese

arancel *nm* : tariff, duty

arándano *nm* : blueberry

arandela *nf* : washer (for a faucet, etc.)

araña *nf* **1** : spider **2** : chandelier

arañar *v* : to scratch, to claw

arañazo *nm* : scratch

arar *v* : to plow

arbitraje *nm* **1** : arbitration **2** : refereeing (in sports)

arbitrar *v* **1** : to arbitrate **2** : to referee, to umpire

arbitrariedad *nf* **1** : arbitrariness **2** INJUSTICIA : injustice, wrong

arbitrario, -ria *adj* **1** : arbitrary **2** : unfair, unjust — **arbitrariamente** *adv*

arbitrio *nm* **1** ALBEDRÍO : will **2** JUICIO : judgment

árbitro, -tra *n* **1** : arbitrator, arbiter **2** : referee, umpire

árbol *nm* **1** : tree **2 árbol genealógico** : family tree

arbolado[1], **-da** *adj* : wooded

arbolado[2] *nm* : woodland

arboleda *nf* : grove, wood

arbóreo, -rea *adj* : arboreal

arbusto *nm* : shrub, bush, hedge

arca *nf* **1** : ark **2** : coffer, chest

arcada *nf* **1** : arcade, series of arches **2 arcadas** *nfpl* : retching ⟨hacer arcadas : to retch⟩

arcaico, -ca *adj* : archaic

arcángel *nm* : archangel

arcano, -na *adj* : arcane

arce *nm* : maple tree

arcén *nm, pl* **arcenes** : hard shoulder, berm

archidiócesis *nfs & pl* : archdiocese

archipiélago *nm* : archipelago

archivador *nm* : filing cabinet

archivar *vt* **1** : to file **2** : to archive

archivero, -ra *n* : archivist

archivista *nmf* : archivist

archivo *nm* **1** : file **2** : archive, archives *pl*

arcilla *nf* : clay

arco *nm* **1** : arch, archway **2** : bow (in archery) **3** : arc **4** : wicket (in croquet) **5** PORTERÍA : goal, goalposts *pl* **6 arco iris** : rainbow

arder *vi* **1** : to burn ⟨el bosque está ardiendo : the forest is in flames⟩ ⟨arder de ira : to burn with anger, to be seething⟩ **2** : to smart, to sting, to burn ⟨le ardía el estómago : he had heartburn⟩

ardid *nm* : scheme, ruse

ardiente *adj* **1** : burning **2** : ardent, passionate — **ardientemente** *adv*

ardilla *nf* **1** : squirrel **2** *or* **ardilla listada** : chipmunk

ardor *nm* **1** : heat **2** : passion, ardor

ardoroso, -sa *adj* : heated, impassioned

arduo, -dua *adj* : arduous, grueling — **arduamente** *adv*

área *nf* : area

arena *nf* **1** : sand ⟨arena movediza : quicksand⟩ **2** : arena

arenga *nf* : harangue, lecture

arengar {52} *vt* : to harangue, to lecture

arenilla *nf* **1** : fine sand **2 arenillas** *nfpl* : kidney stones

arenisca *nf* : sandstone

arenoso, -sa *adj* : sandy, gritty

arenque *nm* : herring

arepa *nf* : cornmeal bread

arete *nm* : earring

argamasa *nf* : mortar (cement)

argelino, -na *adj & n* : Algerian

argentino, -na *adj & n* : Argentinian, Argentine

argolla *nf* : hoop, ring

argón *nm* : argon

argot *nm* : slang

argucia *nf* : sophistry, subtlety

argüir {41} *vi* : to argue — *vt* **1** ARGUMENTAR : to contend, to argue **2** INFERIR : to deduce **3** PROBAR : to prove

argumentación *nf, pl* **-ciones** : line of reasoning, argument

argumentar *vt* : to argue, to contend

argumento *nm* **1** : argument, reasoning **2** : plot, story line

aria *nf* : aria

aridez *nf, pl* **-deces** : aridity, dryness

árido, -da *adj* : arid, dry

Aries *nmf* : Aries

ariete *nm* : battering ram

arisco, -ca *adj* : surly, sullen, unsociable

arista *nf* **1** : ridge, edge **2** : beard (of a plant) **3 aristas** *nfpl* : rough edges, complications, problems

aristocracia *nf* : aristocracy

aristócrata *nmf* : aristocrat

aristocrático, -ca *adj* : aristocratic

aritmética *nf* : arithmetic

aritmético, -ca *adj* : arithmetic, arithmetical — **aritméticamente** *adv*

arlequín *nm, pl* **-quines** : harlequin

arma *nf* **1** : weapon **2 armas** *nfpl* : armed forces **3 arma de fuego** : firearm

armada *nf* : navy, fleet

armadillo *nm* : armadillo

armado, -da *adj* **1** : armed **2** : assembled, put together **3** *PRi* : obstinate, stubborn

armador, -dora *n* : shipowner

armadura *nf* **1** : armor **2** ARMAZÓN : skeleton, framework

armamento *nm* : armament, arms *pl*, weaponry

armar *vt* **1** : to assemble, to put together **2** : to create, to cause ⟨armar un escándalo : to cause a scene⟩ **3** : to arm — **armarse** *vr* **armarse de valor** : to steel oneself

armario *nm* **1** CLÓSET, ROPERO : closet **2** ALACENA : cupboard

armatoste *nm fam* : monstrosity, contraption

armazón *nmf, pl* **-zones 1** ESQUELETO : framework, skeleton ⟨armazón de acero : steel framework⟩ **2** : frames *pl* (of eyeglasses)

armenio, -nia *adj & n* : Armenian

armería *nf* **1** : armory **2** : arms museum **3** : gunsmith's shop **4** : gunsmith's craft

armiño *nm* : ermine

armisticio *nm* : armistice

armonía *nf* : harmony

armónica *nf* : harmonica

armónico, -ca *adj* **1** : harmonic **2** : harmonious — **armónicamente** *adv*

armonioso, -sa *adj* : harmonious — **armoniosamente** *adv*

armonizar {21} *vt* **1** : to harmonize **2** : to reconcile — *vi* : to harmonize, to blend together

arnés *nm, pl* **arneses** : harness

aro *nm* **1** : hoop **2** : napkin ring **3** *Arg, Chile, Uru* : earring

aroma *nm* : aroma, scent

aromático, -ca *adj* : aromatic

arpa *nf* : harp

arpegio *nm* : arpeggio

arpía *nf* : shrew, harpy

arpillera *nf* : burlap

arpista *nmf* : harpist

arpón *nm, pl* **arpones** : harpoon — **arponear** *vt*

arquear *vt* : to arch, to bend — **arquearse** *vr* : to bend, to bow

arqueología *nf* : archaeology

arqueológico, -ca *adj* : archaeological

arqueólogo, -ga *n* : archaeologist

arquero, -ra *n* **1** : archer **2** PORTERO : goalkeeper, goalie

arquetípico, -ca *adj* : archetypal

arquetipo *nm* : archetype

arquitecto, -ta *n* : architect

arquitectónico, -ca *adj* : architectural — **aquitectónicamente** *adv*

arquitectura *nf* : architecture

arrabal *nm* **1** : slum **2 arrabales** *nmpl* : outskirts, outlying area

arracada *nf* : hoop earring

arracimarse *vr* : to cluster together

arraigado, -da *adj* : deep-seated, ingrained

arraigar {52} *vi* : to take root, to become established — **arraigarse** *vr*

arraigo *nm* : roots *pl* ⟨con mucho arraigo : deep-rooted⟩

arrancar {72} *vt* **1** : to pull out, to tear out **2** : to pick, to pluck (a flower) **3** : to start (an engine) **4** : to boot (a computer) — *vi* **1** : to start an engine **2** : to get going — **arrancarse** *vr* : to pull out, to pull off

arrancón *nm, pl* **-cones** *Mex* **1** : sudden loud start (of a car) **2 carrera de arrancones** : drag race

arranque *nm* **1** : starter (of a car) **2** ARREBATO : outburst, fit **3 punto de arranque** : beginning, starting point

arrasar *vt* **1** : to level, to smooth **2** : to devastate, to destroy **3** : to fill to the brim

arrastrar *vt* **1** : to drag, to tow **2** : to draw, to attract — *vi* : to hang down, to trail — **arrastrarse** *vr* **1** : to crawl **2** : to grovel

arrastre *nm* **1** : dragging **2** : pull, attraction **3 red de arrastre** : dragnet, trawling net

arrayán *nm, pl* **-yanes 1** MIRTO : myrtle **2 arrayán brabántico** : bayberry, wax myrtle

arrear *vt* : to urge on, to drive — *vi* : to hurry along

arrebatado, -da *adj* **1** PRECIPITADO : impetuous, hotheaded, rash **2** : flushed, blushing

arrebatar *vt* **1** : to snatch, to seize **2** CAUTIVAR : to captivate — **arrebatarse** *vr* : to get carried away (with anger, etc.)

arrebato *nm* ARRANQUE : fit, outburst

arreciar *vi* : to intensify, to worsen

arrecife *nm* : reef

arreglado, -da *adj* **1** : fixed, repaired **2** : settled, sorted out **3** : neat, tidy **4** : smart, dressed-up

arreglar *vt* **1** COMPONER : to repair, to fix **2** : to tidy up ⟨arregla tu cuarto : pick up your room⟩ **3** : to solve, to work out ⟨quiero arreglar este asunto : I want to settle this matter⟩ — **arreglarse** *vr* **1** : to get dressed (up) ⟨arreglarse el pelo : to get one's hair done⟩ **2 arreglárselas** *fam* : to get by, to manage

arreglo *nm* **1** : repair **2** : arrangement **3** : agreement, understanding

arrellanarse *vr* : to settle (in a chair)

arremangarse {52} *vr* : to roll up one's sleeves

arremeter *vi* EMBESTIR : to attack, to charge

arremetida *nf* EMBESTIDA : attack, onslaught

arremolinarse *vr* **1** : to crowd around, to mill about **2** : to swirl (about)

arrendador, -dora *n* **1** : landlord, landlady *f* **2** : tenant, lessee

arrendajo *nm* : jay

arrendamiento *nm* **1** ALQUILER : rental, leasing **2 contrato de arrendamiento** : lease

arrendar {55} *vt* ALQUILAR : to rent, to lease

arrendatario, -ria *n* : tenant, lessee, renter

arreos *nmpl* GUARNICIONES : tack, harness, trappings

arrepentido, -da *adj* : repentant, remorseful

arrepentimiento *nm* : regret, remorse, repentance

arrepentirse {76} *vr* **1** : to regret, to be sorry **2** : to repent

arrestar *vt* DETENER : to arrest, to detain

arresto *nm* **1** DETENCIÓN : arrest **2 arrestos** *nmpl* : boldness, daring

arriar {85} *vt* **1** : to lower (a flag, etc.) **2** : to slacken (a rope, etc.)

arriate *nm Mex, Spain* : bed (for plants), border

arriba *adv* **1** : up, upwards **2** : above, overhead **3** : upstairs **4 ~ de** : more than **5 de arriba abajo** : from top to bottom, from head to foot

arribar *vi* **1** : to arrive **2** : to dock, to put into port

arribista *nmf* : parvenu, upstart

arribo *nm* : arrival

arriendo *nm* ARRENDAMIENTO : rent, rental

arriero, -ra *n* : mule driver, muleteer

arriesgado, -da *adj* **1** : risky **2** : bold, daring

arriesgar {52} *vt* : to risk, to venture — **arriesgarse** *vr* : to take a chance

arrimado, -da *n Mex fam* : sponger, freeloader

arrimar *vt* ACERCAR, APROXIMAR : to bring closer, to draw near — **arrimarse** *vr* ACERCARSE, APROXIMARSE : to approach, to get close

arrinconar *vt* **1** ACORRALAR : to corner, to box in **2** : to push aside, to abandon

arroba *nf* : arroba (Spanish unit of measurement)

arrobamiento *nm* : rapture, ecstasy

arrobar *vt* : to enrapture, to enchant — **arrobarse** *vr*

arrocero[1], **-ra** *adj* : rice

arrocero[2], **-ra** *n* : rice grower

arrodillarse *vr* : to kneel (down)

arrogancia *nf* ALTANERÍA, ALTIVEZ : arrogance, haughtiness

arrogante *adj* ALTANERO, ALTIVO : arrogant, haughty

arrogarse {52} *vr* : to usurp, to arrogate

arrojado, -da *adj* : daring, fearless

arrojar *vt* **1** : to hurl, to cast, to throw **2** : to give off, to spew out **3** : to yield, to produce **4** *fam* : to vomit — **arrojarse** *vr* PRECIPITARSE : to throw oneself, to leap

arrojo *nm* : boldness, fearlessness

arrollador, -dora *adj* : sweeping, overwhelming

arrollar *vt* **1** : to sweep away, to carry away **2** : to crush, to overwhelm **3** : to run over (with a vehicle)

arropar *vt* : to clothe, to cover (up) — **arroparse** *vr*

arrostrar *vt* : to confront, to face (up to)

arroyo *nm* **1** RIACHUELO : brook, creek, stream **2** : gutter

arroz *nm, pl* **arroces** : rice

arrozal *nm* : rice field, rice paddy

arruga *nf* : wrinkle, fold, crease

arrugado, -da *adj* : wrinkled, creased, lined

arrugar {52} *vt* : to wrinkle, to crease, to pucker — **arrugarse** *vr*

arruinar *vt* : to ruin, to wreck — **arruinarse** *vr* **1** : to be ruined **2** : to fall into ruin, to go bankrupt

arrullar *vt* : to lull to sleep — *vi* : to coo

arrullo *nm* **1** : lullaby **2** : coo (of a dove)

arrumaco *nm fam* : kissing, cuddling

arrumbar *vt* **1** : to lay aside, to put away **2** : to floor, to leave speechless

arsenal *nm* : arsenal

arsénico *nm* : arsenic

arte *nmf* (*usually m in singular, f in plural*) **1** : art ⟨artes y oficios : arts and crafts⟩ ⟨bellas artes : fine arts⟩ **2** HABILIDAD : skill **3** : cunning, cleverness

artefacto *nm* **1** : artifact **2** DISPOSITIVO : device

artemisa *nf* : sagebrush

arteria *nf* : artery — **arterial** *adj*

arteriosclerosis *nf* : arteriosclerosis, hardening of the arteries

artero, -ra *adj* : wily, crafty

artesanal *adj* : pertaining to crafts or craftsmanship, handmade

artesanía *nf* **1** : craftsmanship **2** : handicrafts *pl*

artesano, -na *n* : artisan, craftsman *m*, craftsperson

artesiano, -na *adj* : artesian ⟨pozo artesiano : artesian well⟩

ártico, -ca *adj* : arctic

articulación *nf, pl* **-ciones 1** : articulation, pronunciation **2** COYUNTURA : joint

articular *vt* **1** : to articulate, to utter **2** : to connect with a joint **3** : to coordinate, to orchestrate

articulista *nmf* : columnist

artículo *nm* **1** : article, thing **2** : item, feature, report **3 artículo de comercio** : commodity **4 artículos de primera necesidad** : essentials **5 artículos de tocador** : toiletries

artífice *nmf* **1** ARTESANO : artisan **2** : mastermind, architect

artificial *adj* **1** : artificial, man-made **2** : feigned, false — **artificialmente** *adv*

artificio *nm* **1** HABILIDAD : skill **2** APARATO : device, appliance **3** ARDID : artifice, ruse

artificioso, -sa *adj* **1** : skillful **2** : cunning, deceptive

artillería *nf* : artillery

artillero, -ra *n* : artilleryman *m*, gunner

artilugio *nm* : gadget, contraption

artimaña *nf* : ruse, trick

artista *nmf* **1** : artist **2** ACTOR, ACTRIZ : actor, actress *f*

artístico, -ca *adj* : artistic — **artísticamente** *adv*

artrítico, -ca *adj* : arthritic

artritis *nfs & pl* : arthritis

artrópodo *nm* : arthropod

arveja *nf* GUISANTE : pea

arzobispado *nm* : archbishopric

arzobispo *nm* : archbishop

as *nm* : ace

asa *nf* AGARRADERA, ASIDERO : handle, grip

asado¹, -da *adj* : roasted, grilled, broiled

asado² *nm* **1** : roast **2** : barbecued meat **3** : barbecue, cookout

asador *nm* : spit, rotisserie

asaduras *nfpl* : entrails, offal

asalariado¹, -da *adj* : wage-earning, salaried

asalariado², -da *n* : wage earner

asaltante *nmf* **1** : mugger, robber **2** : assailant

asaltar *vt* **1** : to assault **2** : to mug, to rob **3 asaltar al poder** : to seize power

asalto *nm* **1** : assault **2** : mugging, robbery **3** : round (in boxing) **4 asalto al poder** : coup d'etat

asamblea *nf* : assembly, meeting

asambleísta *nmf* : assemblyman *m*, assemblywoman *f*

asar *vt* : to roast, to grill — **asarse** *vr fam* : to roast, to be dying from heat

asbesto *nm* : asbestos

ascendencia *nf* **1** : ancestry, descent **2** **~ sobre** : influence over

ascendente *adj* : ascending, upward ⟨un curso ascendente : an upward trend⟩

ascender {56} *vt* **1** : to ascend, to rise up **2** : to be promoted ⟨ascendió a gerente : she was promoted to manager⟩ **3** **~ a** : to amount to, to reach ⟨las deudas ascienden a 20 millones de pesos : the debt amounts to 20 million pesos⟩ — *vt* : to promote

ascendiente¹ *nmf* ANCESTRO : ancestor

ascendiente² *nm* INFLUENCIA : influence, ascendancy

ascensión *nf, pl* **-siones 1** : ascent, rise **2 Fiesta de la Ascensión** : Ascension Day

ascenso *nm* **1** : ascent, rise **2** : promotion

ascensor *nm* ELEVADOR : elevator

asceta *nmf* : ascetic

ascético, -ca *adj* : ascetic

ascetismo *nm* : asceticism

asco *nm* **1** : disgust ⟨¡qué asco! : that's disgusting!, how revolting!⟩ **2 darle asco (a alguien)** : to sicken, to revolt **3 estar hecho un asco** : to be filthy **4 hacerle ascos a** : to turn up one's nose at

ascua *nf* **1** BRASA : ember **2 estar en ascuas** *fam* : to be on edge

asear *vt* **1** : to wash, to clean **2** : to tidy up — **asearse** *vr*

asechanza *nf* : snare, trap

asechar *vt* : to set a trap for

asediar *vt* **1** SITIAR : to besiege **2** ACOSAR : to harass

asedio *nm* **1** : siege **2** ACOSO : harassment

asegurador¹, -dora *adj* **1** : insuring, assuring **2** : pertaining to insurance

asegurador[2], **-dora** *n* : insurer, underwriter

aseguradora *nf* : insurance company

asegurar *vt* **1** : to assure **2** : to secure **3** : to insure — **asegurarse** *vr* **1** CERCIORARSE : to make sure **2** : to take out insurance, to insure oneself

asemejar *vt* **1** : to make similar ⟨ese bigote te asemeja a tu abuelo : that mustache makes you look like your grandfather⟩ **2** *Mex* : to be similar to, to resemble — **asemejarse** *vr* ~ **a** : to look like, to resemble

asentaderas *nfpl fam* : bottom, buttocks *pl*

asentado, -da *adj* : settled, established

asentamiento *nm* : settlement

asentar {55} *vt* **1** : to lay down, to set down, to place **2** : to settle, to establish **3** *Mex* : to state, to affirm — **asentarse** *vr* **1** : to settle **2** ESTABLECERSE : to settle down, to establish oneself

asentimiento *nm* : assent, consent

asentir {76} *vt* : to consent, to agree

aseo *nm* : cleanliness

aséptico, -ca *adj* : aseptic, germ-free

asequible *adj* ACCESIBLE : accessible, attainable

aserción *nf* → **aserto**

aserradero *nm* : sawmill

aserrar {55} *vt* : to saw

aserrín *nm, pl* **-rrines** : sawdust

aserto *nm* : assertion, affirmation

asesinar *vt* **1** : to murder **2** : to assassinate

asesinato *nm* **1** : murder **2** : assassination

asesino[1], **-na** *adj* : murderous, homicidal

asesino[2], **-na** *n* **1** : murderer, killer **2** : assassin

asesor, -sora *n* : advisor, consultant

asesoramiento *nm* : advice, counsel

asesorar *vt* : to advise, to counsel — **asesorarse** *vr* ~ **de** : to consult

asesoría *nf* **1** : consulting, advising **2** : consultant's office

asestar {55} *vt* **1** : to aim, to point (a weapon) **2** : to deliver, to deal (a blow)

aseveración *nf, pl* **-ciones** : assertion, statement

aseverar *vt* : to assert, to state

asexual *adj* : asexual — **asexualmente** *adv*

asfaltado[1], **-da** *adj* : asphalted, paved

asfaltado[2] *nm* PAVIMENTO : pavement, asphalt

asfaltar *vt* : to pave, to blacktop

asfalto *nm* : asphalt

asfixia *nf* : asphyxia, asphyxiation, suffocation

asfixiar *vt* : to asphyxiate, to suffocate, to smother — **asfixiarse** *vr*

asga, etc. → **asir**

así[1] *adv* **1** : like this, like that **2** : so, thus ⟨así sea : so be it⟩ **3** ~ **de** : so, about so ⟨una caja así de grande : a box about so big⟩ **4 así que** : so, therefore

5 ~ **como** : as well as **6 así así** : so-so, fair

así[2] *adj* : such, such a ⟨un talento así es inestimable : a talent like that is priceless⟩

así[3] *conj* AUNQUE : even if, even though ⟨no irá, así le paguen : he won't go, even if they pay him⟩

asiático[1], **-ca** *adj* : Asian, Asiatic

asiático[2], **-ca** *n* : Asian

asidero *nm* **1** AGARRADERA, ASA : grip, handle **2** AGARRE : grip, hold

asiduamente *adv* : regularly, frequently

asiduidad *nf* **1** : assiduousness **2** : regularity, frequency

asiduo, -dua *adj* **1** : assiduous **2** : frequent, regular

asiento *nm* **1** : seat, chair ⟨asiento trasero : back seat⟩ **2** : location, site

asignación *nf, pl* **-ciones** **1** : allocation **2** : appointment, designation **3** : allowance, pay **4** *PRi* : homework, assignment

asignar *vt* **1** : to assign, to allocate **2** : to appoint

asignatura *nf* MATERIA : subject, course

asilado, -da *n* : exile, refugee

asilo *nm* : asylum, refuge, shelter

asimetría *nf* : asymmetry

asimétrico, -ca *adj* : asymmetrical, asymmetric

asimilación *nf, pl* **-ciones** : assimilation

asimilar *vt* : to assimilate — **asimilarse** *vr* ~ **a** : to be similar to, to resemble

asimismo *adv* **1** IGUALMENTE : similarly, likewise **2** TAMBIÉN : as well, also

asir {7} *vt* : to seize, to grasp — **asirse** *vr* ~ **a** : to cling to

asistencia *nf* **1** : attendance **2** : assistance **3** : assist (in sports)

asistente[1] *adj* : attending, in attendance

asistente[2] *nmf* **1** : assistant **2 los asistentes** : those present, those in attendance

asistir *vi* : to attend, to be present ⟨asistir a clase : to attend class⟩ — *vt* : to aid, to assist

asma *nf* : asthma

asmático, -ca *adj* : asthmatic

asno *nm* BURRO : ass, donkey

asociación *nf, pl* **-ciones** **1** : association, relationship **2** : society, group, association

asociado[1], **-da** *adj* : associate, associated

asociado[2], **-da** *n* : associate, partner

asociar *vt* **1** : to associate, to connect **2** : to pool (resources) **3** : to take into partnership — **asociarse** *vr* **1** : to become partners **2** ~ **a** : to join, to become a member of

asolar {19} *vt* : to devastate, to destroy

asoleado, -da *adj* : sunny

asolear *vt* : to put in the sun — **asolearse** *vr* : to sunbathe

asomar *vt* : to show, to stick out — *vi* : to appear, to become visible — **aso-**

marse *vr* **1** : to show, to appear **2** : to lean out, to look out ⟨se asomó por la ventana : he leaned out the window⟩

asombrar *vt* MARAVILLAR : to amaze, to astonish — **asombrarse** *vr* : to marvel, to be amazed

asombro *nm* : amazement, astonishment

asombroso, -sa *adj* : amazing, astonishing — **asombrosamente** *adv*

asomo *nm* : hint, trace **2 ni por asomo** : by no means

aspa *nf* : blade (of a fan or propeller)

aspaviento *nm* : exaggerated movement, fuss, flounce

aspecto *nm* **1** : aspect **2** APARIENCIA : appearance, look

aspereza *nf* RUDEZA : roughness, coarseness

áspero, -ra *adj* : rough, coarse, abrasive — **ásperamente** *adv*

aspersión *nf, pl* **-siones** : sprinkling

aspersor *nm* : sprinkler

aspiración *nf, pl* **-ciones** **1** : inhalation, breathing in **2** ANHELO : aspiration, desire

aspiradora *nf* : vacuum cleaner

aspirante *nmf* : applicant, candidate

aspirar *vi* ~ **a** : to aspire to — *vt* : to inhale, to breathe in

aspirina *nf* : aspirin

asquear *vt* : to sicken, to disgust

asquerosidad *nf* : filth, foulness

asqueroso, -sa *adj* : disgusting, sickening, repulsive — **asquerosamente** *adv*

asta *nf* **1** : flagpole ⟨a media asta : at half-mast⟩ **2** : horn, antler **3** : shaft (of a weapon)

ástaco *nm* : crayfish

astado, -da *adj* : horned

aster *nm* : aster

asterisco *nm* : asterisk

asteroide *nm* : asteroid

astigmatismo *nm* : astigmatism

astil *nm* : shaft (of an arrow or feather)

astilla *nf* **1** : splinter, chip **2 de tal palo, tal astilla** : like father, like son

astillar *vt* : to splinter — **astillarse** *vr*

astillero *nm* : dry dock, shipyard

astral *adj* : astral

astringente *adj & nm* : astringent — **astringencia** *nf*

astro *nm* **1** : heavenly body **2** : star

astrología *nf* : astrology

astrológico, -ca *adj* : astrological

astrólogo, -ga *n* : astrologer

astronauta *nmf* : astronaut

astronáutica *nf* : astronautics

astronáutico, -ca *adj* : astronautic, astronautical

astronave *nf* : spaceship

astronomía *nf* : astronomy

astronómico, -ca *adj* : astronomical — **astronómicamente** *adv*

astrónomo, -ma *n* : astronomer

astroso, -sa *adj* DESALIÑADO : slovenly, untidy

astucia *nf* **1** : astuteness, shrewdness **2** : cunning, guile

astuto, -ta *adj* **1** : astute, shrewd **2** : crafty, tricky — **astutamente** *adv*

asueto *nm* : time off, break

asumir *vt* **1** : to assume, to take on ⟨asumir el cargo : to take office⟩ **2** SUPONER : to assume, to suppose

asunción *nf, pl* **-ciones** : assumption

asunto *nm* **1** CUESTIÓN, TEMA : affair, matter, subject **2 asuntos** *nmpl* : affairs, business

asustadizo, -za *adj* : nervous, jumpy, skittish

asustado, -da *adj* : frightened, afraid

asustar *vt* ESPANTAR : to scare, to frighten — **asustarse** *vr*

atacante *nmf* : assailant, attacker

atacar {72} *v* : to attack

atado¹, -da *adj* : shy, inhibited

atado² ** *nm* **1 : bundle, bunch **2** *Arg* : pack (of cigarettes)

atadura *nf* LIGADURA : tie, bond

atajar *vt* **1** IMPEDIR : to block, to stop **2** INTERRUMPIR : to interrupt, to cut off **3** CONTENER : to hold back, to restrain — *vi* ~ **por** : to take a shortcut through

atajo *nm* : shortcut

atalaya *nf* **1** : watchtower **2** : vantage point

atañer {79} *vt* ~ **a** (*3rd person only*) : to concern, to have to do with ⟨eso no me atañe : that does not concern me⟩

ataque *nm* **1** : attack, assault **2** : fit ⟨ataque de risa : fit of laughter⟩ **3 ataque de nervios** : nervous breakdown **4 ataque cardíaco** *or* **ataque al corazón** : heart attack

atar *vt* AMARRAR : to tie, to tie up, to tie down — **atarse** *vr*

atarantado, -da *adj fam* **1** : restless **2** : dazed, stunned

atarantar *vt fam* : to daze, to stun

atarazana *nf* : shipyard

atardecer¹ {53} *v impers* : to get dark

atardecer² *nm* : late afternoon, dusk

atareado, -da *adj* : busy, overworked

atascar {72} *vt* ATORAR : to block, to clog, to stop up **2** : to hinder — **atascarse** *vr* **1** : to become obstructed **2** : to get bogged down **3** PARARSE : to stall

atasco *nm* **1** : blockage **2** EMBOTELLAMIENTO : traffic jam

ataúd *nm* : coffin, casket

ataviar {85} *vt* : to dress, to clothe — **ataviarse** *vr* : to dress up

atavío *nm* ATUENDO : dress, attire

ateísmo *nm* : atheism

atemorizar {21} *vt* : to frighten, to intimidate — **atemorizarse** *vr*

atemperar *vt* : to temper, to moderate

atención¹ *nf, pl* **-ciones** **1** : attention **2 poner atención** *or* **prestar atención** : to pay attention **3 llamar la atención** : to attract attention **4 en atención a** : in view of

atención² *interj* **1** : attention! **2** : watch out!

atender {56} *vt* **1** : to help, to wait on **2** : to look after, to take care of **3** : to heed, to listen to — *vi* : to pay attention

atenerse {80} *vr* : to abide ⟨tendrás que atenerte a las reglas : you will have to abide by the rules⟩

atentado *nm* : attack, assault

atentamente *adv* **1** : attentively, carefully **2** (*used in correspondence*) : sincerely, sincerely yours

atentar {55} *vi* ~ **contra** : to make an attempt on, to threaten ⟨atentaron contra su vida : they made an attempt on his life⟩

atento, -ta *adj* **1** : attentive, mindful **2** CORTÉS : courteous

atenuación *nf, pl* **-ciones** **1** : lessening **2** : understatement

atenuante[1] *adj* : extenuating, mitigating

atenuante[2] *nmf* : extenuating circumstance, excuse

atenuar {3} *vt* **1** MITIGAR : to extenuate, to mitigate **2** : to dim (light), to tone down (colors) **3** : to minimize, to lessen

ateo[1]**, atea** *adj* : atheistic

ateo[2]**, atea** *n* : atheist

aterciopelado, -da *adj* : velvety, downy

aterido, -da *adj* : freezing, frozen

aterrador, -dora *adj* : terrifying

aterrar {55} *vt* : to terrify, to frighten

aterrizaje *nm* : landing (of a plane)

aterrizar {21} *vt* : to land, to touch down

aterrorizar {21} *vt* **1** : to terrify **2** : to terrorize — **aterrorizarse** *vr* : to be terrified

atesorar *vt* : to hoard, to amass

atestado, -da *adj* : crowded, packed

atestar {55} *vt* **1** ATIBORRAR : to crowd, to pack **2** : to witness, to testify to — *vi* : to testify

atestiguar {10} *vt* : to testify to, to bear witness to — *vi* DECLARAR : to testify

atiborrar *vt* : to pack, to crowd — **atiborrarse** *vr* : to stuff oneself

ático *nm* **1** : penthouse **2** BUHARDILLA, DESVÁN : attic

atigrado, -da *adj* : tabby (of cats), striped (of fur)

atildado, -da *adj* : smart, neat, dapper

atildar *vt* **1** : to put a tilde over **2** : to clean up, to smarten up — **atildarse** *vr* : to get spruced up

atinar *vi* ACERTAR : to be accurate, to be on target

atingencia *nf* : bearing, relevance

atípico, -ca *adj* : atypical

atiplado, -da *adj* : shrill, high-pitched

atirantar *vt* : to make taut, to tighten

atisbar *vt* **1** : to spy on, to watch **2** : to catch a glimpse of, to make out

atisbo *nm* : glimpse, sign, hint

atizador *nm* : poker (for a fire)

atizar {21} *vt* **1** : to poke, to stir, to stoke (a fire) **2** : to stir up, to rouse **3** *fam* : to give, to land (a blow)

atlántico, -ca *adj* : Atlantic

atlas *nm* : atlas

atleta *nmf* : athlete

atlético, -ca *adj* : athletic

atletismo *nm* : athletics

atmósfera *nf* : atmosphere

atmosférico, -ca *adj* : atmospheric

atole *nm Mex* **1** : thick hot beverage prepared with corn flour **2 darle atole con el dedo (a alguien)** : to string (someone) along

atollarse *vr* : to get stuck, to get bogged down

atolón *nm, pl* **-lones** : atoll

atolondrado, -da *adj* **1** ATURDIDO : bewildered, dazed **2** DESPISTADO : scatterbrained, absentminded

atómico, -ca *adj* : atomic

atomizador *nm* : atomizer

atomizar {21} *vt* FRAGMENTAR : to fragment, to break into bits

átomo *nm* : atom

atónito, -ta *adj* : astonished, amazed

atontar *vt* **1** : to stupefy **2** : to bewilder, to confuse

atorar *vt* ATASCAR : to block, to clog — **atorarse** *vr* **1** ATASCARSE : to get stuck **2** ATRAGANTARSE : to choke

atormentador, -dora *n* : tormenter

atormentar *vt* : to torment, to torture — **atormentarse** *vr* : to torment oneself, to agonize

atornillar *vt* : to screw (in, on, down)

atorrante *nmf Arg* : bum, loafer

atosigar {52} *vt* : to harass, to annoy

atracadero *nm* : dock, pier

atracador, -dora *n* : robber, mugger

atracar {72} *vt* : to dock, to land — *vt* : to hold up, to rob, to mug — **atracarse** *vr fam* ~ **de** : to gorge oneself with

atracción *nf, pl* **-ciones** : attraction

atraco *nm* : holdup, robbery

atractivo[1]**, -va** *adj* : attractive

atractivo[2] *nm* : attraction, appeal, charm

atraer {81} *vt* : to attract — **atraerse** *vr* **1** : to attract (each other) **2** GANARSE : to gain, to win

atragantarse *vr* : to choke (on food)

atrancar {72} *vt* : to block, to bar — **atrancarse** *vr*

atrapada *nf* : catch

atrapar *vt* : to trap, to capture

atrás *adv* **1** DETRÁS : back, behind ⟨se quedó atrás : he stayed behind⟩ **2** ANTES : ago ⟨mucho tiempo atrás : long ago⟩ **3 para** ~ *or* **hacia** ~ : backwards, toward the rear **4** ~ **de** : in back of, behind

atrasado, -da *adj* **1** : late, overdue **2** : backward **3** : old-fashioned **4** : slow (of a clock or watch)

atrasar *vt* : to delay, to put off — *vi* : to lose time — **atrasarse** *vr* : to fall behind

atraso *nm* **1** RETRASO : lateness, delay ⟨llegó con 20 minutos de atraso : he was 20 minutes late⟩ **2** : backwardness **3 atrasos** *nmpl* : arrears

atravesar {55} *vt* **1** CRUZAR : to cross, to go across **2** : to pierce **3** : to lay across **4** : to go through (a situation or crisis) — **atravesarse** *vr* **1** : to be in the way ⟨se me atravesó : it blocked my path⟩ **2** : to interfere, to meddle

atrayente *adj* : attractive

atreverse *vr* **1** : to dare **2** : to be insolent

atrevido, -da *adj* **1** : bold, daring **2** : insolent

atrevimiento *nm* **1** : daring, boldness **2** : insolence

atribución *nf, pl* **-ciones** : attribution

atribuible *adj* IMPUTABLE : attributable, ascribable

atribuir {41} *vt* **1** : to attribute, to ascribe **2** : to grant, to confer — **atribuirse** *vr* : to take credit for

atribular *vt* : to afflict, to trouble — **atribularse** *vr*

atributo *nm* : attribute

atril *nm* : lectern, stand

atrincherar *vt* : to entrench — **atrincherarse** *vr* **1** : to dig in, to entrench oneself **2** ~ **en** : to hide behind

atrio *nm* **1** : atrium **2** : portico

atrocidad *nf* : atrocity

atrofia *nf* : atrophy

atrofiar *v* : to atrophy

atronador, -dora *adj* : thunderous, deafening

atropellado, -da *adj* **1** : rash, hasty **2** : brusque, abrupt

atropellamiento → **atropello**

atropellar *vt* **1** : to knock down, to run over **2** : to violate, to abuse — **atropellarse** *vr* : to rush through (a task), to trip over one's words

atropello *nm* : abuse, violation, outrage

atroz *adj, pl* **atroces** : atrocious, appalling — **atrozmente** *adv*

atuendo *nm* ATAVÍO : attire, costume

atufar *vt* : to vex, to irritate — **atufarse** *vr* **1** : to get angry **2** : to smell bad, to stink

atún *nm, pl* **atunes** : tuna fish, tuna

aturdimiento *nm* : bewilderment, confusion

aturdir *vt* **1** : to stun, to shock **2** : to bewilder, to confuse, to stupefy

atuvo, etc. → **atenerse**

audacia *nf* OSADÍA : boldness, audacity

audaz *adj, pl* **audaces** : bold, audacious, daring — **audazmente** *adv*

audible *adj* : audible

audición *nf, pl* **-ciones** **1** : hearing **2** : audition

audiencia *nf* : audience

audífono *nm* **1** : hearing aid **2** **audífonos** *nmpl* : headphones, earphones

audio *nm* : audio

audiovisual *adj* : audiovisual

auditar *vt* : to audit

auditivo, -va *adj* : auditory, hearing, aural ⟨aparato auditivo : hearing aid⟩

auditor, -tora *n* : auditor

auditoría *nf* : audit

auditorio *nm* **1** : auditorium **2** : audience

auge *nm* **1** : peak, height **2** : boom, upturn

augur *nm* : augur

augurar *vt* : to predict, to foretell

augurio *nm* AGÜERO, PRESAGIO : augury, omen

augusto, -ta *adj* : august

aula *nf* : classroom

aullar {8} *vt* : to howl, to wail

aullido *nm* : howl, wail

aumentar *vt* ACRECENTAR : to increase, to raise — *vi* : to rise, to increase, to grow

aumento *nm* INCREMENTO : increase, rise

aun *adv* **1** : even ⟨ni aun en coche llegaría a tiempo : I wouldn't arrive on time even if I drove⟩ **2 aun así** : even so **3 aun más** : even more

aún *adv* **1** TODAVÍA : still, yet ⟨¿aún no ha llegado el correo? : the mail still hasn't come?⟩ **2 más aún** : furthermore

aunar {8} *vt* : to join, to combine — **aunarse** *vr* : to unite

aunque *conj* **1** : though, although, even if, even though **2 aunque sea** : at least

aura *nf* **1** : aura **2** : turkey buzzard

áureo, -rea *adj* : golden

aureola *nf* **1** : halo **2** : aura (of power, fame, etc.)

aurícula *nf* : auricle

auricular *nm* : telephone receiver

aurora *nf* **1** : dawn **2 aurora boreal** : aurora borealis

ausencia *nf* : absence

ausentarse *vr* **1** : to leave, to go away **2** ~ **de** : to stay away from

ausente[1] *adj* : absent, missing

ausente[2] *nmf* **1** : absentee **2** : missing person

auspiciar *vt* **1** PATROCINAR : to sponsor **2** FOMENTAR : to foster, to promote

auspicios *nmpl* : sponsorship, auspices

austeridad *nf* : austerity

austero, -ra *adj* : austere

austral[1] *adj* : southern

austral[2] *nm* : former monetary unit of Argentina

australiano, -na *adj & n* : Australian

austriaco *or* **austríaco, -ca** *adj & n* : Austrian

autenticar {72} *vt* : to authenticate — **autenticación** *nf*

autenticidad *nf* : authenticity

auténtico, -ca *adj* : authentic — **auténticamente** *adv*

autentificar {72} *vt* : to authenticate — **autentificación** *nf*

autismo *nm* : autism

autista *adj* : autistic

auto *nm* : auto, car

autoayuda *nf* : self-help

autobiografía *nf* : autobiography

autobiográfico, -ca *adj* : autobiographical

autobús *nm, pl* **-buses** : bus

autocompasión *nf* : self-pity
autocontrol *nm* : self-control
autocracia *nf* : autocracy
autócrata *nmf* : autocrat
autocrático, -ca *adj* : autocratic
autóctono, -na *adj* : indigenous, native ⟨arte autóctono : indigenous art⟩
autodefensa *nf* : self-defense
autodestrucción *nf* : self-destruction — **autodestructivo, -va** *adj*
autodeterminación *nf* : self-determination
autodidacta[1] *adj* : self-taught
autodidacta[2] *nmf* : self-taught person, autodidact
autodidacto[1], **-ta** *adj* → **autodidacta**[1]
autodidacto[2], **-ta** *n* → **autodidacta**[2]
autodisciplina *nf* : self-discipline
autoestima *nf* : self-esteem
autogobierno *nm* : self-government
autografiar *vt* : to autograph
autógrafo *nm* : autograph
autoinfligido, -da *adj* : self-inflicted
automación → **automatización**
autómata *nm* : automaton
automático, -ca *adj* : automatic — **automáticamente** *adv*
automatización *nf* : automation
automatizar {21} *vt* : to automate
automotor, -tora *adj* 1 : self-propelled 2 : automotive, car
automotriz[1] *adj, pl* **-trices** : automotive, car
automotriz[2] *nf, pl* **-trices** : automaker
automóvil *nm* : automobile
automovilista *nmf* : motorist
automovilístico, -ca *adj* : automobile, car ⟨accidente automovilístico : automobile accident⟩
autonombrado, -da *adj* : self-appointed
autonomía *nf* : autonomy
autónomo, -ma *adj* : autonomous — **autónomamente** *adv*
autopista *nf* : expressway, highway
autoproclamado, -da *adj* : self-proclaimed, self-appointed
autopropulsado, -da *adj* : self-propelled
autopsia *nf* : autopsy
autor, -tora *n* 1 : author 2 : perpetrator
autoría *nf* : authorship
autoridad *nf* : authority
autoritario, -ria *adj* : authoritarian
autorización *nf, pl* **-ciones** : authorization
autorizado, -da *adj* 1 : authorized 2 : authoritative
autorizar {21} *vt* : to authorize, to approve
autorretrato *nm* : self-portrait
autoservicio *nm* 1 : self-service restaurant 2 SUPERMERCADO : supermarket
autostop *nm* 1 : hitchhiking 2 **hacer autostop** : to hitchhike
autostopista *nmf* : hitchhiker
autosuficiencia *nf* : self-sufficiency — **autosuficiente** *adj*
auxiliar[1] *vt* : to aid, to assist

auxiliar[2] *adj* : assistant, auxiliary
auxiliar[3] *nmf* 1 : assistant, helper 2 **auxiliar de vuelo** : flight attendant
auxilio *nm* 1 : aid, assistance 2 **primeros auxilios** : first aid
aval *nm* : guarantee, endorsement
avalancha *nf* ALUD : avalanche
avalar *vt* : to guarantee, to endorse
avaluar {3} *vt* : to evaluate, to appraise
avalúo *nm* : appraisal, evaluation
avance *nm* ADELANTO : advance
avanzado, -da *adj* 1 : advanced 2 : progressive
avanzar {21} *v* : to advance, to move forward
avaricia *nf* CODICIA : greed, avarice
avaricioso, -sa *adj* : avaricious, greedy
avaro[1], **-ra** *adj* : miserly, greedy
avaro[2], **-ra** *n* : miser
avasallador, -dora *adj* : overwhelming
avasallamiento *nm* : subjugation, domination
avasallar *vt* : to overpower, to subjugate
ave *nf* 1 : bird 2 **aves de corral** : poultry 3 **ave rapaz** *or* **ave de presa** : bird of prey
avecinarse *vr* : to approach, to come near
avecindarse *vr* : to settle, to take up residence
avellana *nf* : hazelnut, filbert
avellano *nm* : hazel
avena *nf* 1 : oat, oats *pl* 2 : oatmeal
avenencia *nf* : agreement, pact
avenida *nf* : avenue
avenir {87} *vt* 1 : to reconcile, to harmonize — **avenirse** *vr* 1 : to agree, to come to terms 2 : to get along
aventajado, -da *adj* : outstanding
aventajar *vt* 1 : to be ahead of, to lead 2 : to surpass, to outdo
aventar {55} *vt* 1 : to fan 2 : to winnow 3 *Col, Mex* : to throw, to toss — **aventarse** *vr* 1 *Col, Mex* : to hurl oneself 2 *Mex fam* : to dare, to take a chance
aventón *nm, pl* **-tones** *Col, Mex fam* : ride, lift
aventura *nf* 1 : adventure 2 RIESGO : venture, risk 3 : love affair
aventurado, -da *adj* : hazardous, risky
aventurar *vt* : to venture, to risk — **aventurarse** *vr* : to take a risk
aventurero[1], **-ra** *adj* : adventurous
aventurero[2], **-ra** *n* : adventurer
avergonzado, -da *adj* 1 : ashamed 2 : embarrassed
avergonzar {9} *vt* APENAR : to shame, to embarrass — **avergonzarse** *vr* APENARSE : to be ashamed, to be embarrassed
avería *nf* 1 : damage 2 : breakdown, malfunction
averiado, -da *adj* 1 : damaged, faulty 2 : broken down
averiar {85} *vt* : to damage — **averiarse** *vr* : to break down
averiguación *nf, pl* **-ciones** : investigation, inquiry

averiguar {10} *vt* **1** : to find out, to ascertain **2** : to investigate

aversión *nf, pl* **-siones** : aversion, dislike

avestruz *nm, pl* **-truces** : ostrich

avezado, -da *adj* : seasoned, experienced

aviación *nf, pl* **-ciones** : aviation

aviador, -dora *n* : aviator, flyer

aviar {85} *vt* **1** : to prepare, to make ready **2** : to tidy up **3** : to equip, to supply

avicultor, -tora *n* : poultry farmer

avicultura *nf* : poultry farming

avidez *nf, pl* **-deces** : eagerness

ávido, -da *adj* : eager, avid — **ávidamente** *adv*

avieso, -sa *adj* **1** : twisted, distorted **2** : wicked, depraved

avinagrado, -da *adj* : vinegary, sour

avío *nm* **1** : preparation, provision **2** : loan (for agriculture or mining) **3** **avíos** *nmpl* : gear, equipment

avión *nm, pl* **aviones** : airplane

avioneta *nf* : light airplane

avisar *vt* **1** : to notify, to inform **2** : to advise, to warn

aviso *nm* **1** : notice **2** : advertisement, ad **3** ADVERTENCIA : warning **4 estar sobre aviso** : to be on the alert

avispa *nf* : wasp

avispado, -da *adj fam* : clever, sharp

avispero *nm* : wasps' nest

avispón *nm, pl* **-pones** : hornet

avistar *vt* : to sight, to catch sight of

avituallar *vt* : to suppy with food, to provision

avivar *vt* **1** : to enliven, to brighten **2** : to strengthen, to intensify

avizorar *vt* **1** ACECHAR : to spy on, to watch **2** : to observe, to perceive ⟨se avizoran dificultades : difficulties are expected⟩

axila *nf* : underarm, armpit

axioma *nm* : axiom

axiomático, -ca *adj* : axiomatic

ay *interj* **1** : oh! **2** : ouch!, ow!

ayer[1] *adv* : yesterday

ayer[2] *nm* ANTAÑO : yesteryear, days gone by

ayote *nm CA, Mex* : squash, pumpkin

ayuda *nf* **1** : help, assistance **2 ayuda de cámara** : valet

ayudante *nmf* : helper, assistant

ayudar *vt* : to help, to assist — **ayudarse** *vr* **~ de** : to make use of

ayunar *vi* : to fast

ayunas *nfpl* **en ~** : fasting ⟨este medicamento ha de tomarse en ayunas : this medication should be taken on an empty stomach⟩

ayuno *nm* : fast

ayuntamiento *nm* **1** : town hall, city hall **2** : town or city council

azabache *nm* : jet ⟨negro azabache : jet black⟩

azada *nf* : hoe

azafata *nf* **1** : stewardess *f* **2** : hostess *f* (on a TV show)

azafrán *nm, pl* **-franes** **1** : saffron **2** : crocus

azahar *nm* : orange blossom

azalea *nf* : azalea

azar *nm* **1** : chance ⟨juegos de azar : games of chance⟩ **2** : accident, misfortune **3 al azar** : at random, randomly

azaroso, -sa *adj* **1** : perilous, hazardous **2** : turbulent, eventful

azimut *nm* : azimuth

azogue *nm* : mercury, quicksilver

azorar *vt* **1** : to alarm, to startle **2** : to fluster, to embarrass — **azorarse** *vr* : to get embarrassed

azotar *vt* **1** : to whip, to flog **2** : to lash, to batter **3** : to devastate, to afflict

azote *nm* **1** LÁTIGO : whip, lash **2** *fam* : spanking, licking **3** : calamity, scourge

azotea *nf* : flat roof, terraced roof

azteca *adj & nmf* : Aztec

azúcar *nmf* : sugar — **azucarar** *vt*

azucarado, -da *adj* : sweetened, sugary

azucarera *nf* : sugar bowl

azucarero, -ra *adj* : sugar ⟨industria azucarera : sugar industry⟩

azucena *nf* : white lily

azuela *nf* : adze

azufre *nm* : sulphur — **azufroso, -sa** *adj*

azul *adj & nm* : blue

azulado, -da *adj* : bluish

azulejo *nm* : ceramic tile, floor tile

azuloso, -sa *adj* : bluish

azulete *nm* : bluing

azur[1] *adj* CELESTE : azure

azur[2] *n* CELESTE : azure, sky blue

azuzar {21} *vt* : to incite, to egg on

B

b *nf* : second letter of the Spanish alphabet

baba *nf* **1** : spittle, saliva **2** : dribble, drool (of a baby) **3** : slime, ooze

babear *vi* **1** : to drool, to slobber **2** : to ooze

babel *nmf* : babel, chaos, bedlam

babero *nm* : bib

babor *nm* : port, port side

babosa *nf* : slug (mollusk)

babosada *nf CA, Mex* : silly act or remark

baboso, -sa *adj* **1** : drooling, slobbering **2** : slimy **3** *CA, Mex fam* : silly, dumb

babucha *nf* : slipper

babuino *nm* : baboon

bacalao *nm* : cod (fish)

bache *nm* **1** : pothole **2** *PRi* : deep puddle **3** : bad period, rough time ⟨bache económico : economic slump⟩
bachiller *nmf* : high school graduate
bachillerato *nm* : high school diploma
bacilo *nm* : bacillus
bacon *nm Spain* : bacon
bacteria *nf* : bacterium
bacteriano, -na *adj* : bacterial
bacteriología *nf* : bacteriology
bacteriológico, -ca *adj* : bacteriologic, bacteriological
bacteriólogo, -ga *n* : bacteriologist
báculo *nm* **1** : staff, stick **2** : comfort, support
badajo *nm* : clapper (of a bell)
badén *nm, pl* **badenes 1** : (paved) ford, channel **2** : dip, ditch (in a road) **3** : speed bump
bádminton *nm* : badminton
bafle *or* **baffle** *nm* **1** : baffle **2** : speaker, loudspeaker
bagaje *nm* **1** EQUIPAJE : baggage, luggage **2** : background ⟨bagaje cultural : cultural baggage⟩
bagatela *nf* : trifle, trinket
bagre *nm* : catfish
bahía *nf* : bay
bailar *vt* : to dance — *vi* **1** : to dance **2** : to spin **3** : to be loose, to be too big
bailarín¹, -rina *adj, mpl* **-rines 1** : dancing **2** : fond of dancing
bailarín², -rina *n, mpl* **-rines 1** : dancer **2** : ballet dancer, ballerina *f*
baile *nm* **1** : dance **2** : dance party, ball **3 llevarse al baile a** *Mex fam* : to take for a ride, to take advantage of
baja *nf* **1** DESCENSO : fall, drop **2** : slump, recession **3** : loss, casualty **4 dar de baja** : to discharge, to dismiss **5 darse de baja** : to withdraw, to drop out
bajada *nf* **1** : descent **2** : dip, slope **3** : decrease, drop
bajar *vt* **1** DESCENDER : to lower, to let down, to take down **2** REDUCIR : to reduce (prices) **3** INCLINAR : to lower, to bow (the head) **4** : to go down, to descend **5 bajar de categoría** : to downgrade — *vi* **1** : to drop, to fall **2** : to come down, to go down **3** : to ebb (of tides) — **bajarse** *vr* ~ **de** : to get off, to get out of (a vehicle)
bajeza *nf* **1** : low or despicable act **2** : baseness
bajío *nm* **1** : lowland **2** : shoal, sandbank, shallows
bajista *nmf* : bass player, bassist
bajo¹ *adv* **1** : down, low **2** : softly, quietly ⟨habla más bajo : speak more softly⟩
bajo², -ja *adj* **1** : low **2** : short (of stature) **3** : soft, faint, deep (of sounds) **4** : lower ⟨el bajo Amazonas : the lower Amazon⟩ **5** : lowered ⟨con la mirada baja : with lowered eyes⟩ **6** : base, vile **7 los bajos fondos** : the underworld

bajo³ *nm* **1** : bass (musical instrument) **2** : first floor, ground floor **3** : hemline
bajo⁴ *prep* : under, beneath, below
bajón *nm, pl* **bajones** : sharp drop, slump
bajorrelieve *nm* : bas-relief
bala *nf* **1** : bullet **2** : bale
balacera *nf* TIROTEO : shoot-out, gunfight
balada *nf* : ballad
balance *nm* **1** : balance **2** : balance sheet
balancear *vt* **1** : to balance **2** : to swing (one's arms, etc.) **3** : to rock (a boat) — **balancearse** *vr* **1** OSCILAR : to swing, to sway, to rock **2** VACILAR : to hesitate, to vacillate
balanceo *nm* **1** : swaying, rocking **2** : vacillation
balancín *nm, pl* **-cines 1** : rocking chair **2** SUBIBAJA : seesaw
balandra *nf* : sloop
balanza *nf* BÁSCULA : scales *pl,* balance
balar *vi* : to bleat
balaustrada *nf* : balustrade
balaustre *nm* : baluster
balazo *nm* **1** TIRO : shot, gunshot **2** : bullet wound
balboa *nf* : balboa (monetary unit of Panama)
balbucear *vi* **1** : to mutter, to stammer **2** : to prattle, to babble ⟨los niños están balbuceando : the children are prattling away⟩
balbuceo *nm* : mumbling, stammering
balbucir → **balbucear**
balcánico, -ca *adj* : Balkan
balcón *nm, pl* **balcones** : balcony
balde *nm* **1** CUBO : bucket, pail **2 en** ~ : in vain, to no avail
baldío¹, -día *adj* **1** : fallow, uncultivated **2** : useless, vain
baldío² *nm* **1** : wasteland **2** *Mex* : vacant lot
baldosa *nf* LOSETA : floor tile
balear *vt* : to shoot, to shoot at
balero *nm* **1** *Mex* : ball bearing **2** *Mex, PRi* : cup-and-ball toy
balido *nm* : bleat
balín *nm, pl* **balines** : pellet
balística *nf* : ballistics
balístico, -ca *adj* : ballistic
baliza *nf* **1** : buoy **2** : beacon (for aircraft)
ballena *nf* : whale
ballenero¹, -ra *adj* : whaling
ballenero², -ra *n* : whaler
ballenero³ *nm* : whaleboat, whaler
ballesta *nf* **1** : crossbow **2** : spring (of an automobile)
ballet *nm* : ballet
balneario *nm* : spa, bathing resort
balompié *nm* FUTBOL : soccer
balón *nm, pl* **balones** : ball
baloncesto *nm* BASQUETBOL : basketball
balsa *nf* **1** : raft **2** : balsa **3** : pond, pool
balsámico, -ca *adj* : soothing

bálsamo *nm* : balsam, balm
báltico, -ca *adj* : Baltic
baluarte *nm* BASTIÓN : bulwark, bastion
bambolear *vi* **1** : to sway, to swing **2** : to wobble — **bambolearse** *vr*
bamboleo *nm* **1** : swaying, swinging **2** : wobbling
bambú *nm, pl* **bambúes** *or* **bambús** : bamboo
banal *adj* : banal, trivial
banalidad *nf* : banality
banana *nf* : banana
bananero¹, -ra *adj* : banana
bananero² *nm* : banana tree
banano *nm* **1** : banana tree **2** *CA, Col* : banana
banca *nf* **1** : banking **2** BANCO : bench
bancada *nf* **1** : group, faction **2** : workbench
bancal *nm* **1** : terrace (in agriculture) **2** : plot (of land)
bancario, -ria *adj* : bank, banking
bancarrota *nf* QUIEBRA : bankruptcy
banco *nm* **1** : bank ⟨banco central : central bank⟩ ⟨banco de datos : data bank⟩ ⟨banco de arena : sandbank⟩ ⟨banco de sangre : blood bank⟩ **2** BANCA : stool, bench **3** : pew **4** : school (of fish)
banda *nf* **1** : band, strip **2** *Mex* : belt ⟨banda transportadora : conveyor belt⟩ **3** : band (of musicians) **4** : gang (of persons), flock (of birds) **5 banda de rodadura** : tread (of a tire, etc.) **6 banda sonora** *or* **banda de sonido** : sound track
bandada *nf* : flock (of birds), school (of fish)
bandazo *nm* : swerving, lurch
bandearse *vr* : to look after oneself, to cope
bandeja *nf* : tray, platter
bandera *nf* : flag, banner
banderazo *nm* : starting signal (in sports)
banderilla *nf* : banderilla, dart (in bullfighting)
banderín *nm, pl* **-rines** : pennant, small flag
bandidaje *nm* : banditry
bandido, -da *n* BANDOLERO : bandit, outlaw
bando *nm* **1** FACCIÓN : faction, side **2** EDICTO : proclamation
bandolerismo *nm* : banditry
bandolero, -ra *n* BANDIDO : bandit, outlaw
bangladesí *adj & nmf* : Bangladeshi
banjo *nm* : banjo
banquero, -ra *n* : banker
banqueta *nf* **1** : footstool, stool, bench **2** *Mex* : sidewalk
banquete *nm* : banquet
banquetear *v* : to feast
banquillo *nm* **1** : bench (in sports) **2** : dock, defendant's seat
bañadera *nf* → **bañera**

bañar *vt* **1** : to bathe, to wash **2** : to immerse, to dip **3** : to coat, to cover ⟨bañado en lágrimas : bathed in tears⟩ — **bañarse** *vr* **1** : to take a bath, to bathe **2** : to go for a swim
bañera *nf* TINA : bathtub
bañista *nmf* : bather
baño *nm* **1** : bath **2** : swim, dip **3** : bathroom **4 baño María** : double boiler
baqueta *nf* **1** : ramrod **2 baquetas** *nfpl* : drumsticks
bar *nm* : bar, tavern
baraja *nf* : deck of cards
barajar *vt* **1** : to shuffle (cards) **2** : to consider, to toy with
baranda *nf* : rail, railing
barandal *nm* **1** : rail, railing **2** : bannister, handrail
barandilla *nf Spain* : bannister, handrail, railing
barata *nf* **1** *Mex* : sale, bargain **2** *Chile* : cockroach
baratija *nf* : bauble, trinket
baratillo *nm* : rummage sale, flea market
barato¹ *adv* : cheap, cheaply ⟨te lo vendo barato : I'll sell it to you cheap⟩
barato², -ta *adj* : cheap, inexpensive
baratura *nf* **1** : cheapness **2** : cheap thing
barba *nf* **1** : beard, stubble **2** : chin
barbacoa *nf* : barbecue
bárbaramente *adv* : barbarously
barbaridad *nf* **1** : barbarity, atrocity **2 ¡qué barbaridad!** : that's outrageous!
barbarie *nf* : barbarism, savagery
bárbaro¹ *adv fam* : wildly ⟨anoche lo pasamos bárbaro : we had a wild time last night⟩
bárbaro², -ra *adj* **1** : barbarous, wild, uncivilized **2** *fam* : great, fantastic
bárbaro³, -ra *n* : barbarian
barbecho *nm* : fallow land ⟨dejar en barbecho : to leave fallow⟩
barbero, -ra *n* : barber
barbilla *nf* MENTÓN : chin
barbitúrico *nm* : barbiturate
barbudo¹, -da *adj* : bearded
barbudo² *nm* : bearded man
barca *nf* **1** : boat **2 barca de pasaje** : ferryboat
barcaza *nf* : barge
barcia *nf* : chaff
barco *nm* **1** BARCA : boat **2** BUQUE, NAVE : ship
bardo *nm* : bard
bario *nm* : barium
barítono *nm* : baritone
barlovento *nm* : windward
barman *nm* : bartender
barniz *nm, pl* **barnices** **1** LACA : varnish, lacquer **2** : glaze (on ceramics, etc.)
barnizar {21} *vt* **1** : to varnish **2** : to glaze
barométrico, -ca *adj* : barometric
barómetro *nm* : barometer
barón *nm, pl* **barones** : baron

baronesa *nf* : baroness
baronet *nm* : baronet
barquero, -ra : boatman *m*, boatwoman *f*
barquillo *nm* : wafer, thin cookie or cracker
barra *nf* : bar
barraca *nf* **1** CABAÑA, CHOZA : hut, cabin **2** : booth, stall
barracuda *nf* : barracuda
barranca *nf* **1** : hillside, slope **2** → **barranco**
barranco *nm* : ravine, gorge
barredora *nf* : street sweeper (machine)
barrena *nf* **1** TALADRO : drill, auger, gimlet **2** : tailspin
barrenar *vt* **1** : to drill **2** : to undermine
barrendero, -ra *n* : sweeper, street cleaner
barrer *v* : to sweep — **barrerse** *vr* : to slide (in sports)
barrera *nf* OBSTÁCULO : barrier, obstacle ⟨barrera de sonido : sound barrier⟩
barreta *nf* : crowbar
barriada *nf* **1** : district, quarter **2** : slums *pl*
barrica *nf* BARRIL, TONEL : barrel, cask, keg
barricada *nf* : barricade
barrida *nf* **1** : sweep **2** : slide (in sports)
barrido *nm* : sweeping
barriga *nf* PANZA : belly, paunch
barrigón, -gona *adj, mpl* **-gones** *fam* : potbellied, paunchy
barril *nm* **1** BARRICA : barrel, keg **2 cerveza de barril** : draft beer
barrio *nm* **1** : neighborhood, district **2 barrios bajos** : slums *pl*
barro *nm* **1** LODO : mud **2** ARCILLA : clay **3** ESPINILLA, GRANO : pimple, blackhead
barroco, -ca *adj* : baroque
barroso, -sa *adj* ENLODADO : muddy
barrote *nm* : bar (on a window)
barrunto *nm* **1** SOSPECHA : suspicion **2** INDICIO : sign, indication, hint
bártulos *nmpl* : things, belongings ⟨liar los bártulos : to pack one's things⟩
barullo *nm* BULLA : racket, ruckus
basa *nf* : base, pedestal
basalto *nm* : basalt
basar *vt* FUNDAR : to base — **basarse** *vr* FUNDARSE ~ **en** : to be based on
báscula *nf* BALANZA : balance, scales *pl*
base *nf* **1** : base, bottom **2** : base (in baseball) **3** FUNDAMENTO : basis, foundation **4 base de datos** : database **5 a base de** : based on, by means of **6 en base a** : based on, on the basis of
básico, -ca *adj* FUNDAMENTAL : basic — **básicamente** *adv*
basílica *nf* : basilica
basquetbol or **básquetbol** *nm* BALONCESTO : basketball
basset *nm* : basset hound
bastante¹ *adv* **1** : enough, sufficiently ⟨he trabajado bastante : I have worked enough⟩ **2** : fairly, rather, quite ⟨lle-

garon bastante temprano : they arrived quite early⟩
bastante² *adj* : enough, sufficient
bastante³ *pron* : enough ⟨hemos visto bastante : we have seen enough⟩
bastar *vi* : to be enough, to suffice
bastardilla *nf* CURSIVA : italic type, italics *pl*
bastardo, -da *adj & n* : bastard
bastidor *nm* **1** : framework, frame **2** : wing (in theater) ⟨entre bastidores : backstage, behind the scenes⟩
bastilla *nf* : hem
bastión *nf, pl* **bastiones** BALUARTE : bastion, bulwark
basto, -ta *adj* : coarse, rough
bastón *nm, pl* **bastones 1** : cane, walking stick **2** : baton **3 bastón de mando** : staff (of authority)
basura *nf* DESECHOS : garbage, waste, refuse
basurero¹, -ra *n* : garbage collector
basurero² *nm Mex* : garbage can
bata *nf* **1** : bathrobe, housecoat **2** : smock, coverall, lab coat
batalla *nf* **1** : battle **2** : fight, struggle **3 de** ~ : ordinary, everyday ⟨mis zapatos de batalla : my everyday shoes⟩
batallar *vi* LIDIAR, LUCHAR : to battle, to fight
batallón *nm, pl* **-llones** : battalion
batata *nf* : yam, sweet potato
batazo *nm* HIT : hit (in baseball)
bate *nm* : baseball bat
batea *nf* **1** : tray, pan **2** : flat-bottomed boat, punt
bateador, -dora *n* : batter, hitter
batear *vi* : to bat — *vt* : to hit
bateo *nm* : batting (in baseball)
batería *nf* **1** PILA : battery **2** : drum kit, drums *pl* **3 batería de cocina** : kitchen utensils *pl*
baterista *nmf* : drummer
batido *nm* LICUADO : milk shake
batidor *nm* : eggbeater, whisk, mixer
batidora *nf* : (electric) mixer
batir *vt* **1** GOLPEAR : to beat, to hit **2** VENCER : to defeat **3** REVOLVER : to mix, to beat **4** : to break (a record) — **batirse** *vr* : to fight
batista *nf* : batiste, cambric
batuta *nf* **1** : baton **2 llevar la batuta** : to be the leader, to call the tune
baúl *nm* : trunk, chest
bautismal *adj* : baptismal
bautismo *nm* : baptism, christening
bautista *adj & nmf* : Baptist
bautizar {21} *vt* : to baptize, to christen
bautizo → **bautismo**
bávaro, -ra *adj & n* : Bavarian
baya *nf* **1** : berry **2 baya de saúco** : elderberry
bayeta *nf* : cleaning cloth
bayoneta *nf* : bayonet
baza *nf* **1** : trick (in card games) **2 meter baza en** : to butt in on
bazar *nm* : bazaar
bazo *nm* : spleen

bazofia *nf* **1** : table scraps *pl* **2** : slop, swill **3** : hogwash, rubbish
bazuca *nf* : bazooka
beagle *nm* : beagle
beatificar {72} *vt* : to beatify — **beatificación** *nf*
beatífico, -ca *adj* : beatific
beatitud *nf* : beatitude
beato, -ta *adj* **1** : blessed **2** : pious, devout **3** : sanctimonious, overly devout
bebé *nm* : baby
bebedero *nm* **1** ABREVADERO : watering trough **2** *Mex* : drinking fountain
bebedor, -dora *n* : drinker
beber *v* TOMAR : to drink
bebida *nf* : drink, beverage
beca *nf* : grant, scholarship
becado, -da *n* : scholar, scholarship holder
becerro, -rra *n* : calf
begonia *nf* : begonia
beige *adj & nm* : beige
beisbol *or* **béisbol** *nm* : baseball
beisbolista *nmf* : baseball player
beldad *nf* BELLEZA, HERMOSURA : beauty
belén *nf, pl* **belenes** NACIMIENTO : Nativity scene
belga *adj & nmf* : Belgian
beliceño, -ña *adj & n* : Belizean
belicista[1] *adj* : militaristic
belicista[2] *nmf* : warmonger
bélico, -ca *adj* GUERRERO : war, fighting ⟨esfuerzos bélicos : war efforts⟩
belicosidad *nf* : bellicosity
belicoso, -sa *adj* **1** : warlike, martial **2** : aggressive, belligerent
beligerancia *nf* : belligerence
beligerante *adj & nmf* : belligerent
bellaco[1], -ca *adj* : sly, cunning
bellaco[2], -ca *n* : rogue, scoundrel
belleza *nf* BELDAD, HERMOSURA : beauty
bello, -lla *adj* **1** HERMOSO : beautiful **2 bellas artes** : fine arts
bellota *nf* : acorn
bemol *nm* : flat (in music) — **bemol** *adj*
benceno *nm* : benzene
bendecir {11} *vt* **1** CONSAGRAR : to bless, to consecrate **2** ALABAR : to praise, to extol **3 bendecir la mesa** : to say grace
bendición *nf, pl* **-ciones** : benediction, blessing
bendiga, bendijo etc. → **bendecir**
bendito, -ta *adj* **1** : blessed, holy **2** : fortunate **3** : silly, simple-minded
benedictino, -na *adj & n* : Benedictine
benefactor[1], -tora *adj* : beneficent
benefactor[2], -tora *n* : benefactor, benefactress *f*
beneficencia *nf* : beneficence, charity
beneficiar *vt* : to benefit, to be of assistance to — **beneficiarse** *vr* : to benefit, to profit
beneficiario, -ria *n* : beneficiary
beneficio *nm* **1** GANANCIA, PROVECHO : gain, profit **2** : benefit

beneficioso, -sa *adj* PROVECHOSO : beneficial
benéfico, -ca *adj* : charitable, beneficent
benemérito, -ta *adj* : meritorious, worthy
beneplácito *nm* : approval, consent
benevolencia *nf* BONDAD : benevolence, kindness
benévolo, -la *adj* BONDADOSO : benevolent, kind, good
bengala *nf* **luz de bengala 1** : flare (signal) **2** : sparkler
bengalí[1] *adj & nmf* : Bengali
bengalí[2] *nm* : Bengali (language)
benignidad *nf* : mildness, kindness
benigno, -na *adj* : benign, mild
beninés, -nesa *adj & n* : Beninese
benjamín, -mina *n, mpl* **-mines** : youngest child
beodo[1], -da *adj* : drunk, inebriated
beodo[2], -da *n* : drunkard
berberecho *nm* : cockle
berbiquí *nm* : brace (in carpentry)
berenjena *nf* : eggplant
bergantín *nm, pl* **-tines** : brig (ship)
berilo *nm* : beryl
bermudas *nfpl* : Bermuda shorts
berrear *vi* **1** : to bellow, to low **2** : to bawl, to howl
berrido *nm* **1** : bellowing **2** : howl, scream
berrinche *nm fam* : tantrum, conniption
berro *nm* : watercress
berza *nf* : cabbage
besar *vt* : to kiss
beso *nm* : kiss
bestia[1] *adj* **1** : ignorant, stupid **2** : boorish, rude
bestia[2] *nf* : beast, animal
bestia[3] *nmf* **1** IGNORANTE : ignoramus **2** : brute
bestial *adj* **1** : bestial, beastly **2** *fam* : huge, enormous ⟨hace un frío bestial : it's terribly cold⟩ **3** *fam* : great, fantastic
besuquear *vt fam* : to cover with kisses — **besuquearse** *vr fam* : to neck, to smooch
betabel *nm Mex* : beet
betún *nm, pl* **betunes 1** : shoe polish **2** *Mex* : icing
bianual *adj* : biannual
biatlón *nm, pl* **-lones** : biathlon
biberón *nm, pl* **-rones** : baby's bottle
biblia *nf* **1** : bible **2 la Biblia** : the Bible
bíblico, -ca *adj* : biblical
bibliografía *nf* : bibliography
bibliográfico, -ca *adj* : bibliographic, bibliographical
bibliógrafo, -fa *n* : bibliographer
biblioteca *nf* : library
bibliotecario, -ria *n* : librarian
bicameral *adj* : bicameral
bicarbonato *nm* **1** : bicarbonate **2 bicarbonato de soda** : sodium bicarbonate, baking soda
bicentenario *nm* : bicentennial

bíceps *nms & pl* : biceps
bicho *nm* : small animal, bug, insect
bici *nf fam* : bike
bicicleta *nf* : bicycle
bicolor *adj* : two-tone
bicúspide *adj* : bicuspid
bidón *nm, pl* **bidones** : large can, (oil) drum
bien¹ *adv* **1** : well ⟨¿dormiste bien? : did you sleep well?⟩ **2** CORRECTAMENTE : correctly, properly, right ⟨hay que hacerlo bien : it must be done correctly⟩ **3** : very, quite ⟨el libro era bien divertido : the book was very amusing⟩ **4** : easily ⟨bien puede acabarlo en un día : he can easily finish it in a day⟩ **5** : willingly, readily ⟨bien lo aceptaré : I'll gladly accept it⟩ **6 bien que** : although **7 más bien** : rather
bien² *adj* **1** : well, OK, all right ⟨¿te sientes bien? : are you feeling all right?⟩ **2** : pleasant, agreeable ⟨las flores huelen bien : the flowers smell very nice⟩ **3** : satisfactory **4** : correct, right
bien³ *nm* **1** : good ⟨el bien y el mal : good and evil⟩ **2 bienes** *nmpl* : property, goods, possessions
bienal *adj & nf* : biennial — **bienalmente** *adv*
bienaventurado, -da *adj* **1** : blessed **2** : fortunate, happy
bienaventuranzas *nfpl* : Beatitudes
bienestar *nm* **1** : welfare, well-being **2** CONFORT : comfort
bienhechor¹, -chora *adj* : beneficent, benevolent
bienhechor², -chora *n* : benefactor, benefactress *f*
bienintencionado, -da *adj* : well-meaning
bienvenida *nf* **1** : welcome **2 dar la bienvenida a** : to welcome
bienvenido, -da *adj* : welcome
bies *nm* : bias (in sewing)
bife *nm Arg, Chile, Uru* : steak
bífido, -da *adj* : forked
bifocal *adj* : bifocal
bifocales *nmpl* : bifocals
bifurcación *nf, pl* **-ciones** : fork (in a river or road)
bifurcarse {72} *vr* : to fork
bigamia *nf* : bigamy
bígamo, -ma *n* : bigamist
bigote *nm* **1** : mustache **2** : whisker (of an animal)
bigotudo, -da *adj* : mustached, having a big mustache
bikini *nm* : bikini
bilateral *adj* : bilateral — **bilateralmente** *adv*
bilingüe *adj* : bilingual
bilioso, -sa *adj* **1** : bilious **2** : irritable
bilis *nf* : bile
billar *nm* : pool, billiards
billete *nm* **1** : bill ⟨un billete de cinco dólares : a five-dollar bill⟩ **2** BOLETO : ticket ⟨billete de ida y vuelta : round-trip ticket⟩

billetera *nf* : billfold, wallet
billón *nm, pl* **billones** **1** : billion (Great Britain) **2** : trillion (U.S.A.)
bimestral *adj* : bimonthly — **bimestralmente** *adv*
bimotor *adj* : twin-engined
binacional *adj* : binational
binario, -ria *adj* : binary
bingo *nm* : bingo
binocular *adj* : binocular
binoculares *nmpl* : binoculars
binomio *nm* **1** : binomial **2** PAREJA : pair, duo
biodegradable *adj* : biodegradable
biodegradarse *vr* : to biodegrade
biodiversidad *nf* : biodiversity
biofísica *nf* : biophysics
biofísico¹, -ca *adj* : biophysical
biofísico², -ca *n* : biophysicist
biografía *nf* : biography
biográfico, -ca *adj* : biographical
biógrafo, -fa *n* : biographer
biología *nf* : biology
biológico, -ca *adj* : biological, biologic — **biológicamente** *adv*
biólogo, -ga *n* : biologist
biombo *nm* MAMPARA : folding screen, room divider
biomecánica *nf* : biomechanics
biopsia *nf* : biopsy
bioquímica *nf* : biochemistry
bioquímico¹, -ca *adj* : biochemical
bioquímico², -ca *n* : biochemist
biosfera *or* **biósfera** *nf* : biosphere
biotecnología *nf* : biotechnology
biótico, -ca *adj* : biotic
bipartidismo *nm* : two-party system
bipartidista *adj* : bipartisan
bípedo *nm* : biped
birlar *vt fam* : to swipe, to pinch
birmano, -na *adj & n* : Burmese
bis¹ *adv* **1** : twice, again (in music) **2** : a, A ⟨artículo 47 bis : Article 47A⟩ ⟨calle Bolívar, número 70 bis : Bolívar Street, number 70A⟩
bis² *nm* : encore
bisabuelo, -la *n* : great-grandfather *m*, great-grandmother *f*, great-grandparent
bisagra *nf* : hinge
bisecar {72} *vt* : bisect — **bisección** *nf*
bisel *nm* : bevel
biselar *vt* : to bevel
bisexual *adj* : bisexual
bisiesto *adj* **año bisiesto** : leap year
bismuto *nm* : bismuth
bisnieto, -ta *n* : great-grandson *m*, great-granddaughter *f*, great-grandchild
bisonte *nm* : bison, buffalo
bisoñé *nm* : hairpiece, toupee
bisoño¹, -ña *adj* : inexperienced, green
bisoño², -ña *n* : rookie, greenhorn
bistec *nm* : steak, beefsteak
bisturí *nm* ESCALPELO : scalpel
bisutería *nf* : costume jewelry
bit *nm* : bit (unit of information)
bivalvo *nm* : bivalve
bizarría *nf* **1** : courage, gallantry **2** : generosity

bizarro, -rra *adj* **1** VALIENTE : courageous, valiant **2** GENEROSO : generous
bizco, -ca *adj* : cross-eyed
bizcocho *nm* **1** : sponge cake **2** : biscuit **3** *Mex* : breadstick
bizquera *nf* : crossed eyes, squint
blanco¹, -ca *adj* : white
blanco², -ca *n* : white person
blanco³ *nm* **1** : white **2** : target, bull's-eye ⟨dar en el blanco : to hit the target, to hit the nail on the head⟩ **3** : blank space, blank ⟨un cheque en blanco : a blank check⟩
blancura *nf* : whiteness
blancuzco, -ca *adj* **1** : whitish, off-white **2** PÁLIDO : pale
blandir {1} *vt* : to wave, to brandish
blando, -da *adj* **1** SUAVE : soft, tender **2** : weak (in character) **3** : lenient
blandura *nf* **1** : softness, tenderness **2** : leniency
blanqueador *nm* : bleach, whitener
blanquear *vt* **1** : to whiten, to bleach **2** : to shut out (in sports) **3** : to launder (money) — *vi* : to turn white
blanquillo *nm* *CA, Mex* : egg
blasfemar *vi* : to blaspheme
blasfemia *nf* : blasphemy
blasfemo, -ma *adj* : blasphemous
blazer *nm* : blazer
bledo *nm* **no me importa un bledo** *fam* : I couldn't care less, I don't give a damn
blindado, -da *adj* ACORAZADO : armored
blindaje *nm* **1** : armor, armor plating **2** : shield (for cables, machinery, etc.)
bloc *nm, pl* **blocs** : writing pad, pad of paper
blof *nm* *Col, Mex* : bluff
blofear *vi* *Col, Mex* : to bluff
blondo, -da *adj* : blond, flaxen
bloque *nm* **1** : block **2** GRUPO : bloc ⟨el bloque comunista : the Communist bloc⟩
bloquear *vt* **1** OBSTRUIR : to block, to obstruct **2** : to blockade
bloqueo *nm* **1** OBSTRUCCIÓN : blockage, obstruction **2** : blockade
blusa *nf* : blouse
blusón *nm, pl* **blusones** : loose shirt, smock
boa *nf* : boa
boato *nm* : ostentation, show
bobada *nf* **1** : stupid remark or action **2 decir bobadas** : to talk nonsense
bobalicón, -cona *adj, mpl* **-cones** *fam* : silly, stupid
bobina *nf* CARRETE : bobbin, reel
bobo¹, -ba *adj* : silly, stupid
bobo², -ba *n* : fool, simpleton
boca *nf* **1** : mouth **2 boca arriba** : face up, on one's back **3 boca abajo** : face down, prone **4 boca de riego** : hydrant **5 en boca de** : according to
bocacalle *nf* : entrance to a street ⟨gire a la última bocacalle : take the last turning⟩
bocadillo *nm* *Spain* : sandwich

bocado *nm* **1** : bite, mouthful **2** FRENO : bit (of a bridle)
bocajarro *nm* **a ~** : point-blank, directly
bocallave *nf* : keyhole
bocanada *nf* **1** : swig, swallow **2** : puff, mouthful (of smoke) **3** : gust (of air) **4** : stream (of people)
boceto *nm* : sketch, outline
bochinche *nm fam* : ruckus, uproar
bochorno *nm* **1** VERGÜENZA : embarrassment **2** : hot and humid weather **3** : hot flash
bochornoso, -sa *adj* **1** EMBARAZOSO : embarrassing **2** : hot and muggy
bocina *nf* **1** : horn, trumpet **2** : automobile horn **3** : mouthpiece (of a telephone) **4** *Mex* : loudspeaker
bocinazo *nm* : honk (of a horn)
bocio *nm* : goiter
bocón, -cona *n, mpl* **bocones** *fam* : blabbermouth, loudmouth
boda *nf* : wedding
bodega *nf* **1** : wine cellar **2** *Chile, Col, Mex* : storeroom, warehouse **3** (*in various countries*) : grocery store
bofetada *nf* CACHETADA : slap on the face
bofetear *vt* CACHETEAR : to slap
bofetón *nm* → **bofetada**
bofo, -fa *adj* : flabby
boga *nf* : fashion, vogue ⟨estar en boga : to be in style⟩
bogotano¹, -na *adj* : of or from Bogotá
bogotano², -na *n* : person from Bogotá
bohemio, -mia *adj & n* : bohemian, Bohemian
boicot *nm, pl* **boicots** : boycott
boicotear *vt* : to boycott
boina *nf* : beret
boiserie *nf* : wood paneling, wainscoting
boj *nm, pl* **bojes** : box (plant), boxwood
bola *nf* **1** : ball ⟨bola de nieve : snowball⟩ **2** *fam* : lie, fib **3** *Mex fam* : bunch, group ⟨una bola de rateros : a bunch of thieves⟩ **4** *Mex* : uproar, tumult
bolear *vt* *Mex* : to polish (shoes)
bolera *nf* : bowling alley
bolero *nm* : bolero
boleta *nf* **1** : ballot **2** : ticket **3** : receipt
boletería *nf* TAQUILLA : box office, ticket office
boletín *nm, pl* **-tines** **1** : bulletin **2** : journal, review **3 boletín de prensa** : press release
boleto *nm* BILLETE : ticket
boliche *nm* **1** BOLOS : bowling **2** *Arg* : bar, tavern
bólido *nm* **1** : race car **2** METEORO : meteor
bolígrafo *nm* : ballpoint pen
bolillo *nm* **1** : bobbin **2** *Mex* : roll, bun
bolívar *nm* : bolivar (monetary unit of Venezuela)
boliviano¹, -na *adj & n* : Bolivian
boliviano² *nm* : boliviano (monetary unit of Bolivia)

bollo *nm* : bun, sweet roll
bolo *nm* : bowling pin, tenpin
bolos *nmpl* BOLICHE : bowling
bolsa *nf* **1** : bag, sack **2** *Mex* : pocketbook, purse **3** *Mex* : pocket **4 la Bolsa** : the stock market, the stock exchange **5 bolsa de trabajo** : employment agency
bolsear *vi Mex* : to pick pockets
bolsillo *nm* **1** : pocket **2 dinero de bolsillo** : pocket change, loose change
bolso *nm* : pocketbook, handbag
bomba *nf* **1** : bomb **2** : bubble **3** : pump ⟨bomba de gasolina : gas pump⟩
bombachos *nmpl* : baggy pants, bloomers
bombardear *vt* **1** : to bomb **2** : to bombard
bombardeo *nm* **1** : bombing, shelling **2** : bombardment
bombardero *nm* : bomber (airplane)
bombástico, -ca *adj* : bombastic
bombear *vt* : to pump
bombero, -ra *n* : firefighter, fireman *m*
bombilla *nf* : lightbulb
bombillo *nm CA, Col, Ven* : lightbulb
bombo *nm* **1** : bass drum **2** *fam* : exaggerated praise, hype ⟨con bombos y platillos : with great fanfare⟩
bombón *nm, pl* **bombones 1** : bonbon, chocolate **2** *Mex* : marshmallow
bonachón[1], **-chona** *adj, mpl* **-chones** *fam* : good-natured, kindhearted
bonachón[2], **-chona** *n, mpl* **-chones** *fam* BUENAZO : kindhearted person
bonaerense[1] *adj* : of or from Buenos Aires
bonaerense[2] *nmf* : person from Buenos Aires
bonanza *nf* **1** PROSPERIDAD : prosperity ⟨bonanza económica : economic boom⟩ **2** : calm weather **3** : rich ore deposit, bonanza
bondad *nf* BENEVOLENCIA : goodness, kindness ⟨tener la bondad de hacer algo : to be kind enough to do something⟩
bondadoso, -sa *adj* BENÉVOLO : kind, kindly, good — **bondadosamente** *adv*
bonete *nm* : cap, mortarboard
boniato *nm* : sweet potato
bonificación *nf, pl* **-ciones 1** : discount **2** : bonus, extra
bonito[1] *adv* : nicely, well ⟨¡qué bonito canta tu hermana! : your sister sings wonderfully!⟩
bonito[2], **-ta** *adj* LINDO : pretty, lovely ⟨tiene un apartamento bonito : she has a nice apartment⟩
bonito[3] *nm* : bonito (tuna)
bono *nm* **1** : bond ⟨bono bancario : bank bond⟩ **2** : voucher
boqueada *nf* : gasp ⟨dar la última boqueada : to give one's last gasp⟩
boquear *vi* **1** : to gasp **2** : to be dying
boquete *nm* : gap, opening, breach
boquiabierto, -ta *adj* : open-mouthed, speechless, agape

boquilla *nf* : mouthpiece (of a musical instrument)
borbollar *vi* : to bubble
borbotar *or* **borbotear** *vi* : to boil, to bubble, to gurgle
borboteo *nm* : bubbling, gurgling
borda *nf* : gunwale
bordado *nm* : embroidery, needlework
bordar *v* : to embroider
borde *nm* **1** : border, edge **2 al borde de** : on the verge of ⟨estoy al borde de la locura : I'm about to go crazy⟩
bordear *vt* **1** : to border, to skirt ⟨el Río Este bordea Manhattan : the East River borders Manhattan⟩ **2** : to border on ⟨bordea la irrealidad : it borders on unreality⟩ **3** : to line ⟨una calle bordeada de árboles : a street lined with trees⟩
bordillo *nm* : curb
bordo *nm* **a ~** : aboard, on board
boreal *adj* : northern
borgoña *nf* : burgundy
bórico, -ca *adj* : boric ⟨ácido bórico : boric acid⟩
boricua *adj & nmf fam* : Puerto Rican
borinqueño, -ña → **boricua**
borla *nf* **1** : pom-pom, tassel **2** : powder puff
boro *nm* : boron
borrachera *nf* : drunkenness ⟨agarró una borrachera : he got drunk⟩
borrachín, -china *n, mpl* **-chines** *fam* : lush, drunk
borracho[1], **-cha** *adj* EBRIO : drunk, intoxicated
borracho[2], **-cha** *n* : drunk, drunkard
borrador *nm* **1** : rough copy, first draft ⟨en borrador : in the rough⟩ **2** : eraser
borrar *vt* : to erase, to blot out — **borrarse** *vr* **1** : to fade, to fade away **2** : to resign, to drop out **3** *Mex fam* : to split, to leave ⟨me borro : I'm out of here⟩
borrascoso, -sa *adj* : gusty, blustery
borrego, -ga *n* **1** : lamb, sheep **2** : simpleton, fool
borrico → **burro**
borrón *nm, pl* **borrones** : smudge, blot ⟨borrón y cuenta nueva : let's start on a clean slate, let's start over again⟩
borronear *vt* : to smudge, to blot
borroso, -sa *adj* **1** : blurry, smudgy **2** CONFUSO : unclear, confused
boscoso, -sa *adj* : wooded
bosnio, -nia *adj & n* : Bosnian
bosque *nm* : woods, forest
bosquecillo *nm* : grove, copse, thicket
bosquejar *vt* ESBOZAR : to outline, to sketch
bosquejo *nm* **1** TRAZADO : outline, sketch **2** : draft
bostezar {21} *vi* : to yawn
bostezo *nm* : yawn
bota *nf* **1** : boot **2** : wineskin
botana *nf Mex* : snack, appetizer
botanear *vi Mex* : to have a snack
botánica *nf* : botany

botánico[1], **-ca** *adj* : botanical
botánico[2], **-ca** *n* : botanist
botar *vt* **1** ARROJAR : to throw, to fling, to hurl **2** TIRAR : to throw out, to throw away **3** : to launch (a ship)
bote *nm* **1** : small boat ⟨bote de remos : rowboat⟩ **2** : can, jar **3** : jump, bounce **4** *Mex fam* : jail
botella *nf* : bottle
botica *nf* FARMACIA : drugstore, pharmacy
boticario, -ria *n* FARMACÉUTICO : pharmacist, druggist
botín *nm, pl* **botines 1** : baby's bootee **2** : ankle boot **3** : booty, plunder
botiquín *nm, pl* **-quines 1** : medicine cabinet **2** : first-aid kit
botón *nm, pl* **botones 1** : button **2** : bud **3** INSIGNIA : badge
botones *nmfs & pl* : bellhop
botulismo *nm* : botulism
boulevard [ˌbuleˈvar] → **bulevar**
bouquet *nm* **1** : fragrance, bouquet (of wine) **2** RAMILLETE : bouquet (of flowers)
boutique *nf* : boutique
bóveda *nf* **1** : vault, dome **2** CRIPTA : crypt
bovino, -na *adj* : bovine
box *nm, pl* **boxes 1** : pit (in auto racing) **2** *Mex* : boxing
boxeador, -dora *n* : boxer
boxear *vi* : to box
boxeo *nm* : boxing
boya *nf* : buoy
boyante *adj* **1** : buoyant **2** : prosperous, thriving
bozal *nm* **1** : muzzle **2** : halter (for a horse)
bracear *vi* **1** : to wave one's arms **2** : to make strokes (in swimming)
bracero, -ra *n* : migrant worker, day laborer
braguero *nm* : truss (in medicine)
bragueta *nf* : fly, pants zipper
braille *adj & nm* : braille
bramante *nm* : twine, string
bramar *vi* **1** RUGIR : to roar, to bellow **2** : to howl (of the wind)
bramido *nm* : bellowing, roar
brandy *nm* : brandy
branquia *nf* AGALLA : gill
brasa *nf* ASCUA : ember, live coal
brasero *nm* : brazier
brasier *nm Col, Mex* : brassiere, bra
brasileño, -ña *adj & n* : Brazilian
bravata *nf* **1** JACTANCIA : boast, bravado **2** AMENAZA : threat
bravo, -va *adj* **1** FEROZ : ferocious, fierce ⟨un perro bravo : a ferocious dog⟩ **2** EXCELENTE : excellent, great ⟨¡bravo! : bravo!, well done!⟩ **3** : rough, rugged, wild **4** : annoyed, angry
bravucón, -cona *n, mpl* **-cones** : bully
bravuconadas *nfpl* : bravado
bravura *nf* **1** FEROCIDAD : fierceness, ferocity **2** VALENTÍA : bravery

braza *nf* **1** : breaststroke **2** : fathom (unit of length)
brazada *nf* : stroke (in swimming)
brazalete *nm* PULSERA : bracelet, bangle
brazo *nm* **1** : arm **2 brazo derecho** : right-hand man **3 brazos** *nmpl* : hands, laborers
brea *nf* ALQUITRÁN : tar, pitch
brebaje *nm* : potion, brew
brecha *nf* **1** : gap, breach ⟨estar siempre en la brecha : to be always there when needed, to stay in the thick of things⟩ **2** : gash
brécol *nm* : broccoli
brega *nf* **1** LUCHA : struggle, fight **2** : hard work
bregar {52} *vi* **1** LUCHAR : to struggle **2** : to toil, to work hard **3** ~ **con** : to deal with
brete *nm* : jam, tight spot
breve *adj* **1** CORTO : brief, short **2 en** ~ : shortly, in short — **brevemente** *adv*
brevedad *nf* : brevity, shortness
breviario *nm* : breviary
brezal *nm* : heath, moor
brezo *nm* : heather
bribón, -bona *n, mpl* **bribones** : rascal, scamp
bricolaje *or* **bricolage** *nm* : do-it-yourself
brida *nf* : bridle
brigada *nf* **1** : brigade **2** : gang, team, squad
brigadier *nm* : brigadier
brillante[1] *adj* : brilliant, bright — **brillantemente** *adv*
brillante[2] *nm* DIAMANTE : diamond
brillantez *nf* : brilliance, brightness
brillar *vi* : to shine, to sparkle
brillo *nm* **1** LUSTRE : luster, shine **2** : brilliance
brilloso, -sa *adj* LUSTROSO : lustrous, shiny
brincar {72} *vi* **1** SALTAR : to jump around, to leap about **2** : to frolic, to gambol
brinco *nm* **1** SALTO : jump, leap, skip **2 pegar un brinco** : to give a start, to jump
brindar *vi* : to drink a toast ⟨brindó por los vencedores : he toasted the victors⟩ — *vt* OFRECER, PROPORCIONAR : to offer, to provide — **brindarse** *vr* : to offer one's assistance, to volunteer
brindis *nm* : toast, drink ⟨hacer un brindis : to drink a toast⟩
brinque, etc. → **brincar**
brío *nm* **1** : force, determination **2** : spirit, verve
brioso, -sa *adj* : spirited, lively
briqueta *nf* : briquette
brisa *nf* : breeze
británico[1], **-ca** *adj* : British
británico[2], **-ca** *n* **1** : British person **2 los británicos** : the British
brizna *nf* **1** : strand, thread **2** : blade (of grass)

broca *nf* : drill bit
brocado *nm* : brocade
brocha *nf* : paintbrush
broche *nm* **1** ALFILER : brooch **2** : fastener, clasp **3 broche de oro** : finishing touch
brocheta *nf* : skewer
brócoli *nm* : broccoli
broma *nf* **1** CHISTE : joke, prank **2** : fun, merriment **3 en ~** : in jest, jokingly
bromear *vi* : to joke, to fool around ⟨sólo estaba bromeando : I was only kidding⟩
bromista[1] *adj* : fun-loving, joking
bromista[2] *nmf* : joker, prankster
bromo *nm* : bromine
bronca *nf fam* : fight, quarrel, fuss
bronce *nm* : bronze
bronceado[1], **-da** *adj* **1** : tanned, suntanned **2** : bronze
bronceado[2] *nm* **1** : suntan, tan **2** : bronzing
broncearse *vr* : to get a suntan
bronco, -ca *adj* **1** : harsh, rough **2** : untamed, wild
bronquial *adj* : bronchial
bronquio *nm* : bronchial tube, bronchus
bronquitis *nf* : bronchitis
broqueta *nf* : skewer
brotar *vi* **1** : to bud, to sprout **2** : to spring up, to stream, to gush forth **3** : to break out, to appear
brote *nm* **1** : outbreak **2** : sprout, bud, shoot
broza *nf* **1** : brushwood **2** MALEZA : scrub, undergrowth
brujería *nf* HECHICERÍA : witchcraft, sorcery
brujo[1], **-ja** *adj* : bewitching
brujo[2], **-ja** *n* : warlock *m*, witch *f*, sorcerer
brújula *nf* : compass
bruma *nf* : haze, mist
brumoso, -sa *adj* : hazy, misty
bruñir {38} *vt* : to burnish, to polish (metals)
brusco, -ca *adj* **1** SÚBITO : sudden, abrupt **2** : curt, brusque — **bruscamente** *adv*
brusquedad *nf* **1** : abruptness, suddenness **2** : brusqueness
brutal *adj* **1** : brutal **2** *fam* : incredible, terrific — **brutalmente** *adv*
brutalidad *nf* CRUELDAD : brutality
brutalizar {21} *vt* : to brutalize, to maltreat
bruto[1], **-ta** *adj* **1** : gross ⟨peso bruto : gross weight⟩ ⟨ingresos brutos : gross income⟩ **2** : unrefined ⟨petróleo bruto : crude oil⟩ **3** : brutish, stupid
bruto[2], **-ta** *n* **1** : brute **2** : dunce, blockhead
bubónico, -ca *adj* : bubonic
bucal *adj* : oral
bucanero *nm* : buccaneer, pirate
buccino *nm* : whelk
buceador, -dora *n* : diver, scuba diver

bucear *vi* **1** : to dive, to swim underwater **2** : to explore, to delve
buceo *nm* **1** : diving, scuba diving **2** : exploration, searching
buche *nm* **1** : crop (of a bird) **2** *fam* : belly, gut **3** : mouthful ⟨hacer buches : to rinse one's mouth⟩
bucle *nm* **1** : curl, ringlet **2** : loop
bucólico, -ca *adj* : bucolic
budín *nm, pl* **budines** : pudding
budismo *nm* : Buddhism
budista *adj & nmf* : Buddhist
buen *adj* → **bueno**[1]
buenamente *adv* **1** : easily **2** : willingly
buenaventura *nf* **1** : good luck **2** : fortune, future ⟨le dijo la buenaventura : she told his fortune⟩
buenazo, -za *n fam* BONACHÓN : kindhearted person
bueno[1], **-na** *adj* (**buen** *before masculine singular nouns*) **1** : good ⟨una buena idea : a good idea⟩ **2** BONDADOSO : nice, kind **3** APROPIADO : proper, appropriate **4** SANO : well, healthy **5** : considerable, goodly ⟨una buena cantidad : a lot⟩ **6 buenos días** : hello, good day **7 buenas tardes** : good afternoon **8 buenas noches** : good evening, good night
bueno[2] *interj* **1** : OK!, all right! **2** *Mex* : hello! (on the telephone)
buey *nm* : ox, steer
búfalo *nm* **1** : buffalo **2 búfalo de agua** : water buffalo
bufanda *nf* : scarf, muffler
bufar *vi* : to snort
bufet *or* **bufé** *nm* : buffet-style meal
bufete *nm* **1** : law firm, law office **2** : writing desk
bufido *nm* : snort
bufo, -fa *adj* : comic
bufón, -fona *n, mpl* **bufones** : clown, buffoon, jester
bufonada *nf* **1** : jest, buffoonery **2** : sarcasm
buhardilla *nf* **1** ÁTICO, DESVÁN : attic **2** : dormer window
búho *nm* **1** : owl **2** *fam* : hermit, recluse
buhonero, -ra *n* MERCACHIFLE : peddler
buitre *nm* : vulture
bujía *nf* : spark plug
bula *nf* : papal bull
bulbo *nm* : bulb
bulboso, -sa *adj* : bulbous
bulevar *nm* : boulevard
búlgaro, -ra *adj & n* : Bulgarian
bulla *nf* BARULLO : racket, rowdiness
bullicio *nm* **1** : ruckus, uproar **2** : hustle and bustle
bullicioso, -sa *adj* : noisy, busy, turbulent
bullir {38} *vi* **1** HERVIR : to boil **2** MOVERSE : to stir, to bustle about
bulto *nm* **1** : package, bundle **2** : piece of luggage, bag **3** : size, bulk, volume **4** : form, shape **5** : lump (on the body), swelling, bulge

bumerán *nm, pl* **-ranes** : boomerang
búnker *nm, pl* **búnkers** : bunker
búnquer → **búnker**
buñuelo *nm* : fried pastry
buque *nm* BARCO : ship, vessel
burbuja *nf* : bubble, blister (on a surface)
burbujear *vi* **1** : to bubble **2** : to fizz
burbujeo *nm* : bubbling
burdel *nm* : brothel, whorehouse
burdo, -da *adj* **1** : coarse, rough **2** : crude, clumsy ⟨una burda mentira : a clumsy lie⟩ — **burdamente** *adj*
burgués, -guesa *adj & n, mpl* **burgueses** : bourgeois
burguesía *nf* : bourgeoisie, middle class
burla *nf* **1** : mockery, ridicule **2** : joke, trick **3 hacer burla de** : to make fun of, to mock
burlar *vt* ENGAÑAR : to trick, to deceive — **burlarse** *vr* ∼ **de** : to make fun of, to ridicule
burlesco, -ca *adj* : burlesque, comic
burlón[1], -lona *adj, mpl* **burlones** : joking, mocking
burlón[2], -lona *n, mpl* **burlones** : joker
burocracia *nf* : bureaucracy
burócrata *nmf* : bureaucrat
burocrático, -ca *adj* : bureaucratic
burrada *nf fam* : stupid act, nonsense
burrito *nm* : burrito
burro[1], -rra *adj fam* : dumb, stupid

burro[2], -rra *n* **1** ASNO : donkey, ass **2** *fam* : dunce, poor student
burro[3] *nm* **1** : sawhorse **2** *Mex* : ironing board **3** *Mex* : stepladder
bursátil *adj* : stock-market
bursitis *nf* : bursitis
burundés, -desa *adj & n* : Burundian
bus *nm* : bus
busca *nf* : search
buscador, -dora *n* : hunter (for treasure, etc.), prospector
buscapersonas *nms & pl* : beeper, pager
buscapleitos *nmfs & pl* : troublemaker
buscar {72} *vt* **1** : to look for, to seek **2** : to pick up, to collect **3** : to provoke — *vi* : to look, to search ⟨buscó en los bolsillos : he searched through his pockets⟩
buscavidas *nmf & pl* **1** : busybody **2** : go-getter
busque, etc. → **buscar**
búsqueda *nf* : search
busto *nm* : bust
butaca *nf* **1** SILLÓN : armchair **2** : seat (in a theatre) **3** *Mex* : pupil's desk
butano *nm* : butane
buzo[1], -za *adj Mex fam* : smart, astute ⟨ponte buzo! : get with it!, get on the ball!⟩
buzo[2] *nm* : diver, scuba diver
buzón *nm, pl* **buzones** : mailbox
byte *nm* : byte

C

c *nf* : third letter of the Spanish alphabet
cabal *adj* **1** : exact, correct **2** : complete **3** : upright, honest
cabales *nmpl* **no estar en sus cabales** : not to be in one's right mind
cabalgar {52} *vi* : to ride (on horseback)
cabalgata *nf* : cavalcade, procession
cabalidad *nf* **a** ∼ : thoroughly, conscientiously
caballa *nf* : mackerel
caballada *nf* **1** : herd of horses **2** *fam* : nonsense, stupidity, outrageousness
caballar *adj* EQUINO : horse, equine
caballeresco, -ca *adj* : gallant, chivalrous
caballería *nf* **1** : cavalry **2** : horse, mount **3** : knighthood, chivalry
caballeriza *nf* : stable
caballero[1] → **caballeroso**
caballero[2] *nm* **1** : gentleman **2** : knight
caballerosidad *nf* : chivalry, gallantry
caballeroso, -sa *adj* : gentlemanly, chivalrous
caballete *nm* **1** : ridge **2** : easel **3** : trestle (for a table, etc.) **4** : bridge (of the nose) **5** : sawhorse
caballista *nmf* : horseman *m*, horsewoman *f*
caballito *nm* **1** : rocking horse **2 caballito de mar** : seahorse **3 caballitos** *nmpl* : merry-go-round

caballo *nm* **1** : horse **2** : knight (in chess) **3 caballo de fuerza** *or* **caballo de vapor** : horsepower
cabalmente *adv* : fully, exactly
cabaña *nf* CHOZA : cabin, hut
cabaret *nm, pl* **-rets** : nightclub, cabaret
cabecear *vt* : to head (in soccer) — *vi* **1** : to nod one's head **2** : to lurch, to pitch
cabecera *nf* **1** : headboard **2** : head ⟨cabecera de la mesa : head of the table⟩ **3** : heading, headline **4** : headwaters *pl* **5 médico de cabecera** : family doctor **6 cabecera municipal** *CA, Mex* : downtown area
cabecilla *nmf* : ringleader, kingpin
cabellera *nf* : head of hair, mane
cabello *nm* : hair
cabelludo, -da *adj* **1** : hairy **2 cuero cabelludo** : scalp
caber {12} *vi* **1** : to fit, to go ⟨no sé si cabremos todos en el coche : I don't know if we'll all fit in the car⟩ **2** : to be possible ⟨no cabe duda alguna : there's no doubt about it⟩ ⟨cabe que llegue mañana : he may come tomorrow⟩
cabestrillo *nm* : sling ⟨llevo el brazo en cabestrillo : my arm is in a sling⟩
cabestro *nm* : halter (for an animal)
cabeza *nf* **1** : head **2 cabeza hueca** : scatterbrain **3 de** ∼ : head first **4 dolor de cabeza** : headache

cabezada *nf* **1** : butt, blow with the head **2** : nod ⟨echar una cabezada : to take a nap, to doze off⟩

cabezal *nm* : bolster

cabezazo *nm* : butt, blow with the head

cabezón, -zona *adj, mpl* **-zones** *fam* **1** : having a big head **2** : pigheaded, stubborn

cabida *nf* **1** : room, space, capacity **2 dar cabida a** : to accommodate, to hold

cabildear *vi* : to lobby

cabildeo *nm* : lobbying

cabildero, -ra *n* : lobbyist

cabildo *nm* AYUNTAMIENTO **1** : town or city hall **2** : town or city council

cabina *nf* **1** : cabin **2** : booth **3** : cab (of a truck), cockpit (of an airplane)

cabizbajo, -ja *adj* : dejected, downcast

cable *nm* : cable

cableado *nm* : wiring

cabo *nm* **1** : end ⟨al cabo de dos semanas : at the end of two weeks⟩ **2** : stub, end piece **3** : corporal **4** : cape, headland ⟨el Cabo Cañaveral : Cape Canaveral⟩ **5 al fin y al cabo** : after all, in the end **6 llevar a cabo** : to carry out, to do

caboverdiano, -na *adj & n* : Cape Verdean

cabrá, etc. → caber

cabra *nf* : goat

cabrestante *nm* : windlass

cabrío, -ría *adj* : goat, caprine

cabriola *nf* **1** : skip, jump **2 hacer cabriolas** : to prance

cabriolar *vi* : to prance

cabrito *nm* : kid, baby goat

cabús *nm, pl* **cabuses** *Mex* : caboose

cacahuate *or* **cacahuete** *nm* : peanut

cacalote *nm Mex* : crow

cacao *nm* : cacao, cocoa bean

cacarear *vi* : to crow, to cackle, to cluck — *vt fam* : to boast about, to crow about ⟨cacarear un huevo : to brag about an accomplishment⟩

cacareo *nm* **1** : clucking (of a hen), crowing (of a rooster) **2** : boasting

cacatúa *nf* : cockatoo

cace, etc. → cazar

cacería *nf* **1** CAZA : hunt, hunting **2** : hunting party

cacerola *nf* : pan, saucepan

cacha *nf* : butt (of a gun)

cachar *vt fam* : to catch

cacharro *nm* **1** *fam* : thing, piece of junk **2** *fam* : jalopy **3 cacharros** *nmpl* : pots and pans

cache *nm* : cache, cache memory

caché *nm* : cachet

cachear *vt* : to search, to frisk

cachemir *nm* : cashmere

cachetada *nf* BOFETADA : slap on the face

cachete *nm* : cheek

cachetear *vt* BOFETEAR : to slap

cachiporra *nf* : bludgeon, club, blackjack

cachirul *nm Mex fam* : cheating ⟨hacer cachirul : to cheat⟩

cachivache *nm fam* : thing ⟨mete tus cachivaches en el maletero : put your stuff in the trunk⟩

cacho *nm fam* : piece, bit

cachorro, -rra *n* **1** : cub **2** PERRITO : puppy

cachucha *nf Mex* : cap, baseball cap

cacique *nm* **1** : chief (of a tribe) **2** : boss (in politics)

cacofonía *nf* : cacophony

cacofónico, -ca *adj* : cacophonous

cacto *nm* : cactus

cactus → cacto

cada *adj* **1** : each ⟨cuestan diez pesos cada una : they cost ten pesos each⟩ **2** : every ⟨cada vez : every time⟩ **3** : such, some ⟨sales con cada historia : you come up with such crazy stories⟩ **4 cada vez más** : more and more, increasingly **5 cada vez menos** : less and less

cadalso *nm* : scaffold, gallows

cadáver *nm* : corpse, cadaver

cadavérico, -ca *adj* **1** : cadaverous **2** PÁLIDO : deathly pale

caddie *or* **caddy** *nmf, pl* **caddies** : caddy

cadena *nf* **1** : chain **2** : network, channel **3 cadena de montaje** : assembly line **4 cadena perpetua** : life sentence

cadencia *nf* : cadence, rhythm

cadencioso, -sa *adj* : rhythmic, rhythmical

cadera *nf* : hip

cadete *nmf* : cadet

cadmio *nm* : cadmium

caducar {72} *vi* : to expire

caducidad *nf* : expiration

caduco, -ca *adj* **1** : outdated, obsolete **2** : deciduous

caer {13} *vi* **1** : to fall, to drop **2** : to collapse **3** : to hang (down) **4 caer bien** *fam* : to be pleasant, to be likeable ⟨me caes bien : I like you⟩ **5 caer mal** *or* **caer gordo** *fam* : to be unpleasant, to be unlikeable — **caerse** *vr* : to fall down

café[1] *adj* : brown ⟨ojos cafés : brown eyes⟩

café[2] *nm* **1** : coffee **2** : café

cafeína *nf* : caffeine

cafetal *nm* : coffee plantation

cafetalero[1], **-ra** *adj* : coffee ⟨cosecha cafetalera : coffee harvest⟩

cafetalero[2], **-ra** *n* : coffee grower

cafetera *nf* : coffeepot, coffeemaker

cafetería *nf* **1** : coffee shop, café **2** : lunchroom, cafeteria

cafetero[1], **-ra** *adj* : coffee-producing

cafetero[2], **-ra** *n* : coffee grower

caficultura *nf Mex* : coffee industry

caguama *nf* **1** : large Caribbean turtle **2** *Mex* : large bottle of beer

caída *nf* **1** BAJA, DESCENSO : fall, drop **2** : collapse, downfall

caiga, etc. → caer

caimán *nm, pl* **caimanes** : alligator, caiman

caimito *nm* : star apple
caja *nf* **1** : box, case **2** : cash register, checkout counter **3** : bed (of a truck) **4** *fam* : coffin **5 caja fuerte** *or* **caja de caudales** : safe **6 caja de seguridad** : safe-deposit box **7 caja torácica** : rib cage
cajero, -ra *n* **1** : cashier **2** : teller **3 cajero automático** : automated teller machine, ATM
cajeta *nf Mex* : a sweet caramel-flavored spread
cajetilla *nf* : pack (of cigarettes)
cajón *nm, pl* **cajones 1** : drawer, till **2** : crate, case **3 cajón de estacionamiento** *Mex* : parking space
cajuela *nf Mex* : trunk (of a car)
cal *nf* : lime, quicklime
cala *nf* : cove, inlet
calabacín *nm, pl* **-cines** : zucchini
calabacita *nf Mex* : zucchini
calabaza *nf* **1** : pumpkin, squash **2** : gourd **3 dar calabazas a** : to give the brush-off to, to jilt
calabozo *nm* **1** : prison **2** : jail cell
calado[1], -da *adj* **1** : drenched **2** : open-worked
calado[2] *nm* **1** : draft (of a ship) **2** : open-work
calafatear *vt* : to caulk
calamar *nm* **1** : squid **2 calamares** *nmpl* : calamari
calambre *nm* **1** ESPASMO : cramp **2** : electric shock, jolt
calamidad *nf* DESASTRE : calamity, disaster
calamina *nf* : calamine
calamitoso, -sa *adj* : calamitous, disastrous
calaña *nf* : ilk, kind, sort ⟨una persona de mala calaña : a bad sort⟩
calar *vt* **1** : to soak through **2** : to pierce, to penetrate — *vi* : to catch on — **calarse** *vr* : to get drenched
calavera[1] *nf* **1** : skull **2** *Mex* : taillight
calavera[2] *nm* : rake, rogue
calcar {72} *vt* **1** : to trace **2** : to copy, to imitate
calce, etc. → **calzar**
calceta *nf* : knee-high stocking
calcetería *nf* : hosiery
calcetín *nm, pl* **-tines** : sock
calcificar {72} *v* : to calcify — **calcificarse** *vr*
calcinar *vt* : to char, to burn
calcio *nm* : calcium
calco *nm* **1** : transfer, tracing **2** : copy, image
calcomanía *nf* : decal, transfer
calculador, -dora *adj* : calculating
calculadora *nf* : calculator
calcular *vt* **1** : to calculate, to estimate **2** : to plan, to scheme
cálculo *nm* **1** : calculation, estimation **2** : calculus **3** : plan, scheme **4 cálculo biliar** : gallstone **5 hoja de cálculo** : spreadsheet
caldas *nfpl* : hot springs

caldear *vt* : to heat, to warm — **caldearse** *vr* **1** : to heat up **2** : to become heated, to get tense
caldera *nf* **1** : cauldron **2** : boiler
caldo *nm* **1** CONSOMÉ : broth, stock **2** : consommé
caldo de cultivo : culture medium, breeding ground
caldoso, -sa *adj* : watery
calefacción *nf, pl* **-ciones** : heating, heat
calefactor *nm* : heater
caleidoscopio → **calidoscopio**
calendario *nm* **1** : calendar **2** : timetable, schedule
caléndula *nf* : marigold
calentador *nm* : heater
calentamiento *nm* **1** : heating, warming **2** : warm-up (in sports)
calentar {55} *vt* **1** : to heat, to warm **2** *fam* : to annoy, to anger **3** *fam* : to excite, to turn on — **calentarse** *vr* **1** : to get warm, to heat up **2** : to warm up (in sports) **3** *fam* : to become sexually aroused **4** *fam* : to get mad
calentura *nf* **1** FIEBRE : temperature, fever **2** : cold sore
calibrador *nm* : gauge, calipers *pl*
calibrar *vt* : to calibrate — **calibración** *nf*
calibre *nm* **1** : caliber, gauge **2** : importance, excellence **3** : kind, sort ⟨un problema de grueso calibre : a serious problem⟩
calidad *nf* **1** : quality, grade **2** : position, status **3 en calidad de** : as, in the capacity of
cálido, -da *adj* **1** : hot ⟨un clima cálido : a hot climate⟩ **2** : warm ⟨una cálida bienvenida : a warm welcome⟩
calidoscopio *nm* : kaleidoscope
caliente *adj* **1** : hot, warm ⟨mantenerse caliente : to stay warm⟩ **2** : heated, fiery ⟨una disputa caliente : a heated argument⟩ **3** *fam* : sexually excited, horny
califa *nm* : caliph
calificación *nf, pl* **-ciones 1** NOTA : grade (for a course) **2** : rating, score **3** CLASIFICACIÓN : qualification, qualifying ⟨ronda de calificación : qualifying round⟩
calificar {72} *vt* **1** : to grade **2** : to describe, to rate ⟨la calificaron de buena alumna : they described her as a good student⟩ **3** : to qualify, to modify (in grammar)
calificativo[1], -va *adj* : qualifying
calificativo[2] *nm* : qualifier, epithet
caligrafía *nf* **1** ESCRITURA : handwriting **2** : calligraphy
calipso *nm* : calypso
calistenia *nf* : calisthenics
cáliz *nm, pl* **cálices 1** : chalice, goblet **2** : calyx
caliza *nf* : limestone
callado, -da *adj* : quiet, silent — **calladamente** *adv*
callar *vi* : to keep quiet, to be silent — *vt* **1** : to silence, to hush ⟨¡calla a los

niños! : keep the children quiet!〉 **2** : to keep secret — **callarse** *vr* : to remain silent 〈¡cállate! : be quiet!, shut up!〉

calle *nf* : street, road

callejear *vi* : to wander about the streets, to hang out

callejero, -ra *adj* : street 〈perro callejero : stray dog〉

callejón *nm, pl* **-jones 1** : alley **2 callejón sin salida** : dead-end street

callo *nm* **1** : callus, corn **2 callos** *nmpl* : tripe

calloso, -sa *adj* : callous

calma *nf* : calm, quiet

calmante¹ *adj* : calming, soothing

calmante² *nm* : tranquilizer, sedative

calmar *vt* TRANQUILIZAR : to calm, to soothe — **calmarse** *vr* : to calm down

calmo, -ma *adj* TRANQUILO : calm, tranquil

calmoso, -sa *adj* **1** TRANQUILO : calm, quiet **2** LENTO : slow, sluggish

calor *nm* **1** : heat 〈hace calor : it's hot outside〉 〈tener calor : to feel hot〉 **2** : warmth, affection **3** : ardor, passion

caloría *nf* : calorie

calórico, -ca *adj* : caloric

calorífico, -ca *adj* : caloric

calque, etc. → **calcar**

calumnia *nf* : slander, libel — **calumnioso, -sa** *adj*

calumniar *vt* : to slander, to libel

caluroso, -sa *adj* **1** : hot **2** : warm, enthusiastic

calva *nf* : bald spot, bald head

calvario *nm* **1** : Calvary **2** : Stations of the Cross *pl* **3 vivir un calvario** : to suffer great adversity

calvicie *nf* : baldness

calvo¹, -va *adj* : bald

calvo², -va *n* : bald person

calza *nf* : block, wedge

calzada *nf* : roadway, avenue

calzado *nm* : footwear

calzador *nm* : shoehorn

calzar {21} *vt* **1** : to wear (shoes) 〈¿de cuál calza? : what is your shoe size?〉 〈siempre calzaban tenis : they always wore sneakers〉 **2** : to provide with shoes

calzo *nm* : chock, wedge

calzoncillos *nmpl* : underpants, briefs

calzones *nmpl* : underpants, panties

cama *nf* **1** : bed **2 cama elástica** : trampoline

camada *nf* : litter, brood

camafeo *nm* : cameo

camaleón *nm, pl* **-leones** : chameleon

cámara *nf* **1** : camera **2** : chamber, room **3** : house (in government) **4** : inner tube

camarada *nmf* **1** : comrade, companion **2** : colleague

camaradería *nf* : camaraderie

camarero, -ra *n* **1** MESERO : waiter, waitress *f* **2** : bellhop *m*, chambermaid *f* (in a hotel) **3** : steward *m*, stewardess *f* (on a ship, etc.)

camarilla *nf* : political clique

camarógrafo, -fa *n* : cameraman *m*, camerawoman *f*

camarón *nm, pl* **-rones 1** : shrimp **2** : prawn

camarote *nm* : cabin, stateroom

camastro *nm* : small hard bed, pallet

cambalache *nm fam* : swap

cambiante *adj* **1** : changing **2** VARIABLE : changeable, variable

cambiar *vt* **1** ALTERAR, MODIFICAR : to change **2** : to exchange, to trade — *vi* **1** : to change **2 cambiar de velocidad** : to shift gears — **cambiarse** *vr* **1** : to change (clothing) **2** MUDARSE : to move (to a new address)

cambio *nm* **1** : change, alteration **2** : exchange **3** : change (money) **4 en cambio** : instead **5 en cambio** : however, on the other hand

cambista *nmf* : exchange broker

camboyano, -na *adj & n* : Cambodian

cambur *nm Ven* : banana

camelia *nf* : camellia

camello *nm* : camel

camellón *nm, pl* **-llones** *Mex* : traffic island

camerino *nm* : dressing room

camerunés, -nesa *adj, mpl* **-neses** : Cameroonian

camilla *nf* : stretcher

camillero, -ra *n* : orderly (in a hospital)

caminante *nmf* : wayfarer, walker

caminar *vi* ANDAR : to walk, to move — *vt* : to walk, to cover (a distance)

caminata *nf* : hike, long walk

camino *nm* **1** : path, road **2** : journey 〈ponerse en camino : to set off〉 **3** : way 〈a medio camino : halfway there〉

camión *nm, pl* **camiones 1** : truck **2** *Mex* : bus

camionero, -ra *n* **1** : truck driver **2** *Mex* : bus driver

camioneta *nf* : light truck, van

camisa *nf* **1** : shirt **2 camisa de fuerza** : straitjacket

camiseta *nf* **1** : T-shirt **2** : undershirt

camisón *nm, pl* **-sones** : nightshirt, nightgown

camorra *nf fam* : fight, trouble 〈buscar camorra : to pick a fight〉

camote *nm* **1** : root vegetable similar to the sweet potato **2 hacerse camote** *Mex fam* : to get mixed up

campal *adj* : pitched, fierce 〈batalla campal : pitched battle〉

campamento *nm* : camp

campana *nf* : bell

campanada *nf* TAÑIDO : stroke (of a bell), peal

campanario *nm* : bell tower, belfry

campanilla *nf* **1** : small bell, handbell **2** : uvula

campante *adj* : nonchalant, smug 〈seguir tan campante : to go on as if nothing had happened〉

campaña *nf* **1** CAMPO : countryside, country **2** : campaign **3 tienda de campaña** : tent

campañol *nm* : vole

campechana *nf Mex* : puff pastry

campechanía *nf* : geniality

campechano, -na *adj* : open, cordial, friendly

campeón, -peona *n, mpl* **-peones** : champion

campeonato *nm* : championship

cámper *nm* : camper (vehicle)

campero, -ra *adj* : country, rural

campesino, -na *n* : peasant, farm laborer

campestre *adj* : rural, rustic

camping *nm* **1** : camping **2** : campsite

campiña *nf* CAMPO : countryside, country

campista *nmf* : camper

campo *nm* **1** CAMPAÑA : countryside, country **2** : field ⟨campo de aviación : airfield⟩ ⟨su campo de responsabilidad : her field of responsibility⟩

camposanto *nm* : graveyard, cemetery

campus *nms & pl* : campus

camuflaje *nm* : camouflage

camuflajear *vt* : to camouflage

camuflar → **camuflajear**

can *nm* : hound, dog

cana *nf* **1** : gray hair **2 salirle canas** : to go gray, to get gray hair **3 echar una cana al aire** : to let one's hair down

canadiense *adj & nmf* : Canadian

canal[1] *nm* **1** : canal **2** : channel

canal[2] *nmf* : gutter, groove

canalé *nm* : rib, ribbing (in fabric)

canaleta *nf* : gutter

canalete *nm* : paddle

canalizar {21} *vt* : to channel

canalla[1] *adj fam* : low, rotten

canalla[2] *nmf fam* : bastard, swine

canapé *nm* **1** : hors d'oeuvre, canapé **2** SOFÁ : couch, sofa

canario[1], **-ria** *adj* : of or from the Canary Islands

canario[2], **-ria** *n* : Canarian, Canary Islander

canario[3] *nm* : canary

canasta *nf* **1** : basket **2** : canasta (card game)

cancel *nm* **1** : sliding door **2** : partition

cancelación *nf, pl* **-ciones 1** : cancellation **2** : payment in full

cancelar *vt* **1** : to cancel **2** : to pay off, to settle

cáncer *nm* : cancer

Cáncer *nmf* : Cancer

cancerígeno[1], **-na** *adj* : carcinogenic

cancerígeno[2] *nm* : carcinogen

canceroso, -sa *adj* : cancerous

cancha *nf* : court, field (for sports)

canciller *nm* : chancellor

cancillería *nf* : chancellery, ministry

canción *nf, pl* **canciones 1** : song **2 canción de cuna** : lullaby

cancionero[1] *nm* : songbook

cancionero[2], **-ra** *n Mex* : songster, songstress *f*

candado *nm* : padlock

candela *nf* **1** : flame, fire **2** : candle

candelabro *nm* : candelabra

candelero *nm* **1** : candlestick **2 estar en el candelero** : to be the center of attention

candente *adj* : red-hot

candidato, -ta *n* : candidate, applicant

candidatura *nf* : candidacy

candidez *nf* **1** : simplicity **2** INGENUIDAD : naïveté, ingenuousness

cándido, -da *adj* **1** : simple, unassuming **2** INGENUO : naive, ingenuous

candil *nm* : oil lamp

candilejas *nfpl* : footlights

candor *nm* : naïveté, innocence

candoroso, -sa *adj* : naive, innocent

canela *nf* : cinnamon

canesú *nm* : yoke (of clothing)

cangrejo *nm* JAIBA : crab

canguro *nm* **1** : kangaroo **2 hacer de canguro** *Spain* : to baby-sit

caníbal[1] *adj* : cannibalistic

caníbal[2] *nmf* ANTROPÓFAGO : cannibal

canibalismo *nm* ANTROPOFAGIA : cannibalism

canibalizar {21} *vt* : to cannibalize

canica *nf* : marble ⟨jugar a las canicas : to play marbles⟩

caniche *nm* : poodle

canijo, -ja *adj* **1** *fam* : puny, weak **2** *Mex fam* : tough, hard ⟨un examen muy canijo : a very tough exam⟩

canilla *nf* **1** : shin, shinbone **2** *Arg, Uru* : faucet

canino[1], **-na** *adj* : canine

canino[2] *nm* **1** COLMILLO : canine (tooth) **2** : dog, canine

canje *nm* INTERCAMBIO : exchange, trade

canjear *vt* INTERCAMBIAR : to exchange, to trade

cannabis *nm* : cannabis

cano, -na *adj* : gray ⟨un hombre de pelo cano : a gray-haired man⟩

canoa *nf* : canoe

canon *nm, pl* **cánones** : canon

canónico, -ca *adj* **1** : canonical **2 derecho canónico** : canon law

canónigo *nm* : canon (of a church)

canonizar {21} *vt* : to canonize — **canonización** *nf*

canoso, -sa → **cano**

cansado, -da *adj* **1** : tired ⟨estar cansado : to be tired⟩ **2** : tiresome, wearying ⟨ser cansado : to be tiring⟩

cansancio *nm* FATIGA : fatigue, weariness

cansar *vt* FATIGAR : to wear out, to tire — *vi* : to be tiresome — **cansarse** *vr* **1** : to wear oneself out **2** : to get bored

cansino, -na *adj* : slow, weary, lethargic

cantaleta *nf fam* : nagging ⟨la misma cantaleta : the same old story⟩

cantalupo *nm* : cantaloupe

cantante *nmf* : singer

cantar[1] *v* : to sing

cantar[2] *nm* : song, ballad
cántaro *nm* 1 : pitcher, jug 2 **llover a cántaros** *fam* : to rain cats and dogs
cantata *nf* : cantata
cantera *nf* : quarry ⟨cantera de piedra : stone quarry⟩
cántico *nm* : canticle, chant
cantidad[1] *adv fam* : really ⟨ese carro me costó cantidad : that car cost me plenty⟩
cantidad[2] *nf* 1 : quantity 2 : sum, amount (of money) 3 *fam* : a lot, a great many ⟨había cantidad de niños en el parque : there were tons of kids in the park⟩
cantimplora *nf* : canteen, water bottle
cantina *nf* 1 : tavern, bar 2 : canteen, mess, dining quarters *pl*
cantinero, -ra *n* : bartender
canto *nm* 1 : singing 2 : chant ⟨canto gregoriano : Gregorian chant⟩ 3 : song (of a bird) 4 : edge, end ⟨de canto : on end, sideways⟩ 5 **canto rodado** : boulder
cantón *nm, pl* **cantones** 1 : canton 2 *Mex fam* : place, home
cantonés[1], **-nesa** *adj & n, mpl* **-neses** : Cantonese
cantonés[2] *nm, pl* **-neses** : Cantonese (language)
cantor[1], **-tora** *adj* 1 : singing 2 **pájaro cantor** : songbird
cantor[2], **-tora** *n* 1 : singer 2 : cantor
caña *nf* 1 : cane ⟨caña de azúcar : sugarcane⟩ 2 : reed 3 **caña de pescar** : fishing rod 4 **caña del timón** : tiller (of a boat)
cañada *nf* : ravine, gully
cáñamo *nm* : hemp
cañaveral *nm* : sugarcane field
cañería *nf* TUBERÍA : pipes *pl*, piping
caño *nm* 1 : pipe 2 : spout 3 : channel (for navigation)
cañón *nm, pl* **cañones** 1 : cannon 2 : barrel (of a gun) 3 : canyon
cañonear *vt* : to shell, to bombard
cañoneo *nm* : shelling, bombardment
cañonero *nm* : gunboat
caoba *nf* : mahogany
caolín *nm* : kaolin
caos *nm* : chaos
caótico, -ca *adj* : chaotic
capa *nf* 1 : cape, cloak 2 : coating 3 : layer, stratum 4 : (social) class, stratum
capacidad *nf* 1 : capacity 2 : capability, ability
capacitación *nf, pl* **-ciones** : training
capacitar *vt* : to train, to qualify
caparazón *nm, pl* **-zones** : shell, carapace
capataz *nmf, pl* **-taces** : foreman *m*, forewoman *f*
capaz *adj, pl* **capaces** 1 APTO : capable, able 2 COMPETENTE : competent 3 : spacious ⟨capaz para : with room for⟩
capcioso, -sa *adj* : cunning, deceptive ⟨pregunta capciosa : trick question⟩

capea *nf* : amateur bullfight
capear *vt* 1 : to make a pass with the cape (in bullfighting) 2 : to dodge, to weather ⟨capear el temporal : to ride out the storm⟩
capellán *nm, pl* **-llanes** : chaplain
capilar *nm* : capillary — **capilar** *adj*
capilla *nf* : chapel
capirotada *nf Mex* : traditional bread pudding
capirotazo *nm* : flip, flick
capital[1] *adj* 1 : capital 2 : chief, principal
capital[2] *nm* : capital ⟨capital de riesgo : venture capital⟩
capital[3] *nf* : capital, capital city
capitalino[1], **-na** *adj* : of or from a capital city
capitalino[2], **-na** *n* : inhabitant of a capital city
capitalismo *nm* : capitalism
capitalista *adj & nmf* : capitalist
capitalizar {21} *vt* : to capitalize — **capitalización** *nf*
capitán, -tana *n, mpl* **-tanes** : captain
capitanear *vt* : to captain, to command
capitanía *nf* : captaincy
capitel *nm* : capital (of a column)
capitolio *nm* : capitol
capitulación *nf, pl* **-ciones** : capitulation
capitular *vi* : to capitulate, to surrender
capítulo *nm* 1 : chapter, section 2 : matter, subject
capó *nm* : hood (of a car)
capón *nm, pl* **capones** : capon
caporal *nm* 1 : chief, leader 2 : foreman (on a ranch)
capota *nf* : top (of a convertible)
capote *nm* 1 : cloak, overcoat 2 : bullfighter's cape 3 *Mex* COFRE : hood (of a car)
capricho *nm* ANTOJO : whim, caprice
caprichoso, -sa *adj* ANTOJADIZO : capricious, fickle
Capricornio *nmf* : Capricorn
cápsula *nf* : capsule
captar *vt* 1 : to catch, to grasp 2 : to gain, to attract 3 : to harness, to collect (waters)
captor, -tora *n* : captor
captura *nf* : capture, seizure
capturar *vt* : to capture, to seize
capucha *nf* : hood, cowl
capuchina *nf* : nasturtium
capuchino *nm* 1 : Capuchin (monk) 2 : capuchin (monkey) 3 : cappuccino
capullo *nm* 1 : cocoon 2 : bud (of a flower)
caqui *adj & nm* : khaki
cara *nf* 1 : face 2 ASPECTO : look, appearance ⟨¡qué buena cara tiene ese pastel! : that cake looks delicious!⟩ 3 *fam* : nerve, gall 4 ~ **a** *or* **de cara a** : facing 5 **de cara a** : in view of, in the light of
carabina *nf* : carbine
caracol *nm* 1 : snail 2 CONCHA : conch, seashell 3 : cochlea 4 : ringlet

caracola *nf* : conch

carácter *nm, pl* caracteres 1 ÍNDOLE : character, kind, nature 2 TEMPERAMENTO : disposition, temperament 3 : letter, symbol ⟨caracteres chinos : Chinese characters⟩

característica *nf* RASGO : trait, feature, characteristic

característico, -ca *adj* : characteristic — característicamente *adv*

caracterizar {21} *vt* : to characterize — caracterización *nf*

caramba *interj* 1 (*expressing annoyance*) : darn!, heck! 2 (*expressing disgust or surprise*) : jeez!

carámbano *nm* : icicle

carambola *nf* 1 : carom 2 : ruse, trick ⟨por carambola : by a lucky chance⟩

caramelo *nm* 1 : caramel 2 DULCE : candy

caramillo *nm* 1 : pipe, small flute 2 : heap, pile

caraqueño¹, -ña *adj* : of or from Caracas

caraqueño², -ña *n* : person from Caracas

carátula *nf* 1 : title page 2 : cover, dust jacket 3 CARETA : mask 4 *Mex* : face, dial (of a clock or watch)

caravana *nf* 1 : caravan 2 : convoy, motorcade 3 REMOLQUE : trailer

caray → caramba

carbohidrato *nm* : carbohydrate

carbón *nm, pl* carbones 1 : coal 2 : charcoal

carbonatado, -da *adj* : carbonated

carbonato *nm* : carbonate

carboncillo *nm* : charcoal

carbonera *nf* : coal cellar, coal bunker (on a ship)

carbonero, -ra *adj* : coal

carbonizar {21} *vt* : to carbonize, to char

carbono *nm* : carbon

carbunco *or* carbunclo *nm* : carbuncle

carburador *nm* : carburetor

carburante *nm* : fuel

carca *nmf fam* : old fogy

carcacha *nf fam* : jalopy, wreck

carcaj *nm* : quiver (for arrows)

carcajada *nf* : loud laugh, guffaw ⟨reírse a carcajadas : to roar with laughter⟩

carcajearse *vr* : to roar with laughter, to be in stitches

cárcel *nf* PRISIÓN : jail, prison

carcelero, -ra *n* : jailer

carcinogénico, -ca *adj* : carcinogenic

carcinógeno *nm* CANCERÍGENO : carcinogen

carcinoma *nm* : carcinoma

carcomer *vt* : to eat away at, to consume

carcomido, -da *adj* 1 : worm-eaten 2 : decayed, rotten

cardán *nm, pl* cardanes : universal joint

cardar *vt* : to card, to comb

cardenal *nm* 1 : cardinal (in religion) 2 : bruise

cardíaco *or* cardiaco, -ca *adj* : cardiac, heart

cárdigan *nm, pl* -gans : cardigan

cardinal *adj* : cardinal

cardiología *nf* : cardiology

cardiólogo, -ga *n* : cardiologist

cardiovascular *adj* : cardiovascular

cardo *nm* : thistle

cardumen *nm* : school of fish

carear *vt* : to bring face-to-face

carecer {53} *vi* ∼ de : to lack ⟨el cheque carecía de fondos : the check lacked funds⟩

carencia *nf* 1 FALTA : lack 2 ESCASEZ : shortage 3 DEFICIENCIA : deficiency

carente *adj* ∼ de : lacking (in)

carero, -ra *adj fam* : pricey

carestía *nf* 1 : rise in cost ⟨la carestía de la vida : the high cost of living⟩ 2 : dearth, scarcity

careta *nf* MÁSCARA : mask

carey *nm* 1 : hawksbill turtle, sea turtle 2 : tortoiseshell

carga *nf* 1 : loading 2 : freight, load, cargo 3 : burden, responsibility 4 : charge ⟨carga eléctrica : electrical charge⟩ 5 : attack, charge

cargado, -da *adj* 1 : loaded 2 : bogged down, weighted down 3 : close, stuffy 4 : charged ⟨cargado de tensión : charged with tension⟩ 5 FUERTE : strong ⟨café cargado : strong coffee⟩ 6 cargado de hombros : stoop-shouldered

cargador¹, -dora *n* : longshoreman *m*, longshorewoman *f*

cargador² *nm* 1 : magazine (for a firearm) 2 : charger (for batteries)

cargamento *nm* : cargo, load

cargar {52} *vt* 1 : to carry 2 : to load, to fill 3 : to charge — *vi* 1 : to load 2 : to rest (in architecture) 3 ∼ sobre : to fall upon

cargo *nm* 1 : burden, load 2 : charge ⟨a cargo de : in charge of⟩ 3 : position, office

cargue, etc. → cargar

carguero¹, -ra *adj* : freight, cargo ⟨tren carguero : freight train⟩

carguero² *nm* : freighter, cargo ship

cariarse *vr* : to decay (of teeth)

caribe *adj* : Caribbean ⟨el mar Caribe : the Caribbean Sea⟩

caribeño, -ña *adj* : Caribbean

caribú *nm* : caribou

caricatura *nf* 1 : caricature 2 : cartoon

caricaturista *nmf* : caricaturist, cartoonist

caricaturizar {21} *vt* : to caricature

caricia *nf* 1 : caress 2 hacer caricias : to pet, to stroke

caridad *nf* 1 : charity 2 LIMOSNA : alms *pl*

caries *nfs & pl* : cavity (in a tooth)

carillón *nm, pl* -llones 1 : carillon 2 : glockenspiel

cariño *nm* AFECTO : affection, love

cariñoso, -sa *adj* AFECTUOSO : affectionate, loving — cariñosamente *adv*

carioca¹ *adj* : of or from Rio de Janeiro

carioca[2] *nmf* : person from Rio de Janeiro

carisma *nf* : charisma

carismático, -ca *adj* : charismatic

carita *adj Mex fam* : cute (said of a man) ⟨tu primo se cree muy carita : your cousin thinks he's gorgeous⟩

caritativo, -va *adj* : charitable

cariz *nm, pl* **carices** : appearance, aspect

carmesí *adj & nm* : crimson

carmín *nm, pl* **carmines** 1 : carmine 2 **carmín de labios** : lipstick

carnada *nf* CEBO : bait

carnal *adj* 1 : carnal 2 **primo carnal** : first cousin

carnaval *nm* : carnival

carnaza *nf* : bait

carne *nf* 1 : meat ⟨carne molida : ground beef⟩ 2 : flesh ⟨carne de gallina : goose bumps⟩

carné → **carnet**

carnero *nm* 1 : ram, sheep 2 : mutton

carnet *nm* 1 : identification card, ID 2 : membership card 3 **carnet de conducir** *Spain* : driver's license

carnicería *nf* 1 : butcher shop 2 MATANZA : slaughter, carnage

carnicero, -ra *n* : butcher

carnívoro[1], **-ra** *adj* : carnivorous

carnívoro[2] *nm* : carnivore

carnoso, -sa *adj* : fleshy, meaty

caro[1] *adv* : dearly, a lot ⟨pagué caro : I paid a high price⟩

caro[2], **-ra** *adj* 1 : expensive, dear 2 QUERIDO : dear, beloved

carpa *nf* 1 : carp 2 : big top (of a circus) 3 : tent

carpelo *nm* : carpel

carpeta *nf* : folder, binder, portfolio (of drawings, etc.)

carpetazo *nm* **dar carpetazo a** : to shelve, to defer

carpintería *nf* 1 : carpentry 2 : carpenter's workshop

carpintero, -ra *n* : carpenter

carraspear *vi* : to clear one's throat

carraspera *nf* : hoarseness ⟨tener carraspera : to have a frog in one's throat⟩

carrera *nf* 1 : run, running ⟨a la carrera : at full speed⟩ ⟨de carrera : hastily⟩ 2 : race 3 : course of study 4 : career, profession 5 : run (in baseball)

carreta *nf* : cart, wagon

carrete *nm* 1 BOBINA : reel, spool 2 : roll of film

carretel → **carrete**

carretera *nf* : highway, road ⟨carretera de peaje : turnpike⟩

carretero, -ra *adj* : highway ⟨el sistema carretero nacional : the national highway system⟩

carretilla *nf* 1 : wheelbarrow 2 **carretilla elevadora** : forklift

carril *nm* 1 : lane ⟨carretera de doble carril : two-lane highway⟩ 2 : rail (on a railroad track)

carrillo *nm* : cheek, jowl

carrito *nm* : cart ⟨carrito de compras : shopping cart⟩

carrizo *nm* JUNCO : reed

carro *nm* 1 COCHE : car 2 : cart 3 *Chile, Mex* : coach (of a train) 4 **carro alegórico** : float (in a parade)

carrocería *nf* : bodywork, body (of a vehicle)

carroña *nf* : carrion

carroñero, -ra *n* : scavenger (animal)

carroza *nf* 1 : carriage 2 : float (in a parade)

carruaje *nm* : carriage

carrusel *nm* 1 : merry-go-round 2 : carousel ⟨carrusel de equipaje : luggage carousel⟩

carta *nf* 1 : letter 2 NAIPE : playing card 3 : charter, constitution 4 MENÚ : menu 5 : map, chart 6 **tomar cartas en** : to intervene in

cártamo *nm* : safflower

cartearse *vr* ESCRIBIRSE : to write to one another, to correspond

cartel *nm* : sign, poster

cártel *or* **cartel** *nm* : cartel

cartelera *nf* 1 : billboard 2 : marquee

cartera *nf* 1 BILLETERA : wallet, billfold 2 BOLSO : pocketbook, purse 3 : portfolio ⟨cartera de acciones : stock portfolio⟩

carterista *nmf* : pickpocket

cartero, -ra *n* : letter carrier, mailman *m*

cartilaginoso, -sa *adj* : cartilaginous, gristly

cartílago *nm* : cartilage

cartilla *nf* 1 : primer, reader 2 : booklet ⟨cartilla de ahorros : bankbook⟩

cartografía *nf* : cartography

cartógrafo, -fa *n* : cartographer

cartón *nm, pl* **cartones** 1 : cardboard ⟨cartón madera : fiberboard⟩ 2 : carton

cartucho *nm* : cartridge

cartulina *nf* : poster board, cardboard

carúncula *nf* : wattle (of a bird)

casa *nf* 1 : house, building 2 HOGAR : home 3 : household, family 4 : company, firm 5 **echar la casa por la ventana** : to spare no expense

casaca *nf* : jacket

casado[1], **-da** *adj* : married

casado[2], **-da** *n* : married person

casamentero, -ra *n* : matchmaker

casamiento *nm* 1 : marriage 2 BODA : wedding

casar *vt* : to marry — *vi* : to go together, to match up — **casarse** *vr* 1 : to get married 2 **~ con** : to marry

casateniente *nmf Mex* : landlord, landlady *f*

cascabel[1] *nm* : small bell

cascabel[2] *nf* : rattlesnake

cascada *nf* CATARATA, SALTO : waterfall, cascade

cascajo *nm* 1 : pebble, rock fragment 2 *fam* : piece of junk

cascanueces *nms & pl* : nutcracker

cascar {72} *vt* : to crack (a shell) — **cascarse** *vr* : to crack, to chip

cáscara *nf* 1 : skin, peel, rind, husk 2 : shell (of a nut or egg)

cascarón *nm, pl* **-rones** 1 : eggshell 2 *Mex* : shell filled with confetti

cascarrabias *nmfs & pl fam* : grouch, crab

casco *nm* 1 : helmet 2 : hull 3 : hoof 4 : fragment, shard 5 : center (of a town) 6 *Mex* : empty bottle 7 **cascos** *nmpl* : headphones

caserío *nm* 1 : country house 2 : hamlet

casero¹, -ra *adj* 1 : domestic, household 2 : homemade

casero², -ra *n* DUEÑO : landlord *m*, landlady *f*

caseta *nf* : booth, stand, stall ⟨caseta telefónica : telephone booth⟩

casete → **cassette**

casi *adv* 1 : almost, nearly, virtually 2 (*in negative phrases*) : hardly ⟨casi nunca : hardly ever⟩

casilla *nf* 1 : booth 2 : pigeonhole 3 : box (on a form)

casino *nm* 1 : casino 2 : (social) club

caso *nm* 1 : case 2 **en caso de** : in case of, in the event of 3 **hacer caso de** : to pay attention to, to notice 4 **hacer caso omiso de** : to ignore, to take no notice of 5 **no venir al caso** : to be beside the point

caspa *nf* : dandruff

casque, etc. → **cascar**

casquete *nm* 1 : skullcap 2 **casquete glaciar** : ice cap 3 **casquete corto** *Mex* : crew cut

casquillo *nm* : case, casing (of a bullet)

cassette *nmf* : cassette

casta *nf* 1 : caste 2 : lineage, stock ⟨de casta : thoroughbred, purebred⟩ 3 **sacar la casta** *Mex* : to come out ahead

castaña *nf* : chestnut

castañetear *vi* : to chatter (of teeth)

castaño¹, -ña *adj* : chestnut, brown

castaño² *nm* 1 : chestnut tree 2 : chestnut, brown

castañuela *nf* : castanet

castellano¹, -na *adj & n* : Castilian

castellano² *nm* ESPAÑOL : Spanish, Castilian (language)

castidad *nf* : chastity

castigar {52} *vt* : to punish

castigo *nm* : punishment

castillo *nm* 1 : castle 2 **castillo de proa** : forecastle

casto, -ta *adj* : chaste, pure — **castamente** *adv*

castor *nm* : beaver

castración *nf, pl* **-ciones** : castration

castrar *vt* 1 : to castrate, to spay, to neuter, to geld 2 DEBILITAR : to weaken, to debilitate

castrense *adj* : military

casual *adj* 1 FORTUITO : fortuitous, accidental 2 *Mex* : casual (of clothing)

casualidad *nf* 1 : chance 2 **por** ~ **or de** ~ : by chance, by any chance

casualmente *adv* : accidentally, by chance

casucha *or* **casuca** *nf* : shanty, hovel

cataclismo *nm* : cataclysm

catacumbas *nfpl* : catacombs

catador, -dora *n* : wine taster

catalán¹, -lana *adj & n, mpl* **-lanes** : Catalan

catalán² *nm* : Catalan (language)

catálisis *nf* : catalysis

catalítico, -ca *adj* : catalytic

catalizador *nm* 1 : catalyst 2 : catalytic converter

catalogar {52} *vt* : to catalog, to classify

catálogo *nm* : catalog

catamarán *nm, pl* **-ranes** : catamaran

cataplasma *nf* : poultice

catapulta *nf* : catapult

catapultar *vt* : to catapult

catar *vt* 1 : to taste, to sample 2 : to look at, to examine

catarata *nf* 1 CASCADA, SALTO : waterfall 2 : cataract

catarro *nm* RESFRIADO : cold, catarrh

catarsis *nf* : catharsis

catártico, -ca *adj* : cathartic

catástrofe *nf* DESASTRE : catastrophe, disaster

catastrófico, -ca *adj* DESASTROSO : catastrophic, disastrous

catcher *nmf* : catcher (in baseball)

catecismo *nm* : catechism

cátedra *nf* 1 : chair, professorship 2 : subject, class 3 **libertad de cátedra** : academic freedom

catedral *nf* : cathedral

catedrático, -ca *n* PROFESOR : professor

categoría *nf* 1 CLASE : category 2 RANGO : rank, standing 3 **categoría gramatical** : part of speech 4 **de** ~ : first-rate, outstanding

categórico, -ca *adj* : categorical, unequivocal — **categóricamente** *adv*

catéter *nm* : catheter

cátodo *nm* : cathode

catolicismo *nm* : Catholicism

católico, -ca *adj & n* : Catholic

catorce *adj & nm* : fourteen

catorceavo *nm* : fourteenth

catre *nm* : cot

catsup *nm* : ketchup

caucásico, -ca *adj & n* : Caucasian

cauce *nm* 1 LECHO : riverbed 2 : means *pl*, channel

caucho *nm* 1 GOMA : rubber 2 : rubber tree 3 *Ven* : tire

caución *nf, pl* **cauciones** FIANZA : bail, security

caudal *nm* 1 : volume of water 2 RIQUEZA : capital, wealth 3 ABUNDANCIA : abundance

caudillaje *nm* : leadership

caudillo *nm* : leader, commander

causa *nf* **1** MOTIVO : cause, reason, motive ⟨a causa de : because of⟩ **2** IDEAL : cause ⟨morir por una causa : to die for a cause⟩ **3** : lawsuit
causal[1] *adj* : causal
causal[2] *nm* : cause, grounds *pl*
causalidad *nf* : causality
causante[1] *adj* ~ **de** : causing, responsible for
causante[2] *nmf Mex* : taxpayer
causar *vt* **1** : to cause **2** : to provoke, to arouse ⟨eso me causa gracia : that strikes me as being funny⟩
cáustico, -ca *adj* : caustic
cautela *nf* : caution, prudence
cautelar *adj* : precautionary, preventive
cauteloso, -sa *adj* : cautious, prudent — **cautelosamente** *adv*
cauterizar {21} *vt* : to cauterize
cautivador, -dora *adj* : captivating
cautivar *vt* HECHIZAR : to captivate, to charm
cautiverio *nm* : captivity
cautivo, -va *adj & n* : captive
cauto, -ta *adj* : cautious, careful
cavar *vt* : to dig — *vi* ~ **en** : to delve into, to probe
caverna *nf* : cavern, cave
cavernoso, -sa *adj* **1** : cavernous **2** : deep, resounding
caviar *nm* : caviar
cavidad *nf* : cavity
cavilar *vi* : to ponder, to deliberate
cayado *nm* : crook, staff, crosier
cayena *nf* : cayenne pepper
cayó, etc. → **caer**
caza[1] *nf* **1** CACERÍA : hunt, hunting **2** : game
caza[2] *nm* : fighter plane
cazador, -dora *n* **1** : hunter **2 cazador furtivo** : poacher
cazar {21} *vt* **1** : to hunt **2** : to catch, to bag **3** *fam* : to land (a job, a spouse) — *vi* : to go hunting
cazatalentos *nmfs & pl* : talent scout
cazo *nm* **1** : saucepan, pot **2** CUCHARÓN : ladle
cazuela *nf* **1** : pan, saucepan **2** : casserole
cazurro, -ra *adj* : sullen, surly
CD *nm* : CD, compact disk
cebada *nf* : barley
cebar *vt* **1** : to bait **2** : to feed, to fatten **3** : to prime (a pump, etc.) — **cebarse** *vr* ~ **en** : to take it out on
cebo *nm* **1** CARNADA : bait **2** : feed **3** : primer (for firearms)
cebolla *nf* : onion
cebolleta *nf* : scallion, green onion
cebollino *nm* **1** : chive **2** : scallion
cebra *nf* : zebra
cebú *nm, pl* **cebús** *or* **cebúes** : zebu (cattle)
cecear *vi* : to lisp
ceceo *nm* : lisp
cecina *nf* : dried beef, beef jerky
cedazo *nm* : sieve

ceder *vi* **1** : to yield, to give way **2** : to diminish, to abate **3** : to give in, to relent — *vt* : to cede, to hand over
cedro *nm* : cedar
cédula *nf* : document, certificate
céfiro *nm* : zephyr
cegador, -dora *adj* : blinding
cegar {49} *vt* **1** : to blind **2** : to block, to stop up — *vi* : to be blinded, to go blind
cegatón, -tona *adj, mpl* **-tones** *fam* : blind as a bat
ceguera *nf* : blindness
ceiba *nf* : ceiba, silk-cotton tree
ceja *nf* **1** : eyebrow ⟨fruncir las cejas : to knit one's brows⟩ **2** : flange, rim
cejar *vi* : to give in, to back down
celada *nf* : trap, ambush
celador, -dora *n* GUARDIA : guard, warden
celda *nf* : cell (of a jail)
celebración *nf, pl* **-ciones** : celebration
celebrado, -da *adj* CÉLEBRE, FAMOSO : famous, celebrated
celebrante *nmf* OFICIANTE : celebrant
celebrar *vt* **1** FESTEJAR : to celebrate **2** : to hold (a meeting) **3** : to say (Mass) **4** : to welcome, to be happy about — *vi* : to be glad — **celebrarse** *vr* **1** : to be celebrated, to fall **2** : to be held, to take place
célebre *adj* CELEBRADO, FAMOSO : celebrated, famous
celebridad *nf* **1** : celebrity **2** FAMA : fame, renown
celeridad *nf* : celerity, swiftness
celeste[1] *adj* **1** : celestial **2** : sky blue, azure
celeste[2] *nm* : sky blue
celestial *adj* : heavenly, celestial
celibato *nm* : celibacy
célibe *adj & nmf* : celibate
cello *nm* : cello
celo *nm* **1** : zeal, fervor **2** : heat (of females), rut (of males) **3 celos** *nmpl* : jealousy ⟨tenerle celos a alguien : to be jealous of someone⟩
celofán *nm, pl* **-fanes** : cellophane
celosía *nf* **1** : lattice window **2** : latticework, trellis
celoso, -sa *adj* **1** : jealous **2** : zealous — **celosamente** *adv*
celta[1] *adj* : Celtic
celta[2] *nmf* : Celt
célula *nf* : cell
celular *adj* : cellular
celuloide *nm* **1** : celluloid **2** : film, cinema
celulosa *nf* : cellulose
cementar *vt* : to cement
cementerio *nm* : cemetery
cemento *nm* : cement
cena *nf* : supper, dinner
cenador *nm* : arbor
cenagal *nm* : bog, quagmire
cenagoso, -sa *adj* : swampy
cenar *vi* : to have dinner, to have supper — *vt* : to have for dinner or supper

cencerro · cerrar

⟨anoche cenamos tamales : we had tamales for supper last night⟩
cencerro *nm* : cowbell
cenicero *nm* : ashtray
ceniciento, -ta *adj* : ashen
cenit *nm* : zenith, peak
ceniza *nf* **1** : ash **2 cenizas** *nfpl* : ashes (of a deceased person)
cenizo, -za *n* : jinx
cenote *nm Mex* : natural deposit of spring water
censar *vt* : to take a census of
censo *nm* : census
censor, -sora *n* : censor, critic
censura *nf* **1** : censorship **2** : censure, criticism
censurable *adj* : reprehensible, blameworthy
censurar *vt* **1** : to censor **2** : to censure, to criticize
centauro *nm* : centaur
centavo *nm* **1** : cent (in English-speaking countries) **2** : unit of currency in various Latin-American countries
centella *nf* **1** : lightning flash **2** : spark
centellear *vi* **1** : to twinkle **2** : to gleam, to sparkle
centelleo *nm* : twinkling, sparkle
centenar *nm* **1** : hundred **2 a centenares** : by the hundreds
centenario¹, -ria *adj & n* : centenarian
centenario² *nm* : centennial
centeno *nm* : rye
centésimo¹, -ma *adj* : hundredth
centésimo² *nm* : hundredth
centígrado *adj* : centigrade, Celsius
centigramo *nm* : centigram
centímetro *nm* : centimeter
centinela *nmf* : sentinel, sentry
central¹ *adj* **1** : central **2 PRINCIPAL** : main, principal
central² *nf* **1** : main office, headquarters **2 central camionera** *Mex* : bus terminal
centralita *nf* : switchboard
centralizar {21} *vt* : to centralize — **centralización** *nf*
centrar *vt* **1** : to center **2** : to focus — **centrarse** *vr* ~ **en** : to focus on, to concentrate on
céntrico, -ca *adj* : central
centrífugo, -ga *adj* : centrifugal
centrípeto, -ta *adj* : centripetal
centro¹ *nmf* : center (in sports)
centro² *nm* **1 MEDIO** : center ⟨centro de atención : center of attention⟩ ⟨centro de gravedad : center of gravity⟩ **2** : downtown **3 centro de mesa** : centerpiece
centroamericano, -na *adj & n* : Central American
ceñido, -da *adj* **AJUSTADO** : tight, tight-fitting
ceñir {67} *vt* **1** : to encircle, to surround **2** : to hug, to cling to ⟨me ciñe demasiado : it's too tight on me⟩ — **ceñirse** *vr* ~ **a** : to restrict oneself to, to stick to

ceño *nm* **1** : frown, scowl **2 fruncir el ceño** : to frown, to knit one's brows
cepa *nf* **1** : stump (of a tree) **2** : stock (of a vine) **3 LINAJE** : ancestry, stock
cepillar *vt* **1** : to brush **2** : to plane (wood) — **cepillarse** *vr*
cepillo *nm* **1** : brush ⟨cepillo de dientes : toothbrush⟩ **2** : plane (for woodworking)
cepo *nm* : trap (for animals)
cera *nf* **1** : wax ⟨cera de abejas : beeswax⟩ **2** : polish
cerámica *nf* **1** : ceramics *pl* **2** : pottery
cerámico, -ca *adj* : ceramic
ceramista *nmf* **ALFARERO** : potter
cerca¹ *adv* **1** : close, near, nearby **2** ~ **de** : nearly, almost
cerca² *nf* **1** : fence **2** : (stone) wall
cercado *nm* : enclosure
cercanía *nf* **1 PROXIMIDAD** : proximity, closeness **2 cercanías** *nfpl* : outskirts, suburbs
cercano, -na *adj* : near, close
cercar {72} *vt* **1** : to fence in, to enclose **2** : to surround
cercenar *vt* **1** : to cut off, to amputate **2** : to diminish, to curtail
cerceta *nf* : teal (duck)
cerciorarse *vr* **ASEGURARSE** ~ **de** : to make sure of, to verify
cerco *nm* **1** : siege **2** : cordon, circle **3** : fence
cerda *nf* **1** : bristle **2** : sow
cerdo *nm* **1** : pig, hog **2 carne de cerdo** : pork
cereal *nm* : cereal — **cereal** *adj*
cerebelo *nm* : cerebellum
cerebral *adj* : cerebral
cerebro *nm* : brain
ceremonia *nf* : ceremony — **ceremonial** *adj*
ceremonioso, -sa *adj* : ceremonious
cereza *nf* : cherry
cerezo *nm* : cherry tree
cerilla *nf* **1** : match **2** : earwax
cerillo *nm* (*in various countries*) : match
cerner {56} *vt* : to sift — **cernerse** *vr* **1** : to hover **2** ~ **sobre** : to loom over, to threaten
cernidor *nm* : sieve
cernir → **cerner**
cero *nm* : zero
ceroso, -sa *adj* : waxy
cerque, etc. → **cercar**
cerquita *adv fam* : very close, very near
cerrado, -da *adj* **1** : closed, shut **2** : thick, broad ⟨tiene un acento cerrado : she has a thick accent⟩ **3** : cloudy, overcast **4** : quiet, reserved **5** : dense, stupid
cerradura *nf* : lock
cerrajería *nf* : locksmith's shop
cerrajero, -ra *n* : locksmith
cerrar {55} *vt* **1** : to close, to shut **2** : to turn off **3** : to bring to an end — *vi* **1** : to close up, to lock up **2** : to close down — **cerrarse** *vr* **1** : to close **2** : to fasten, to button up **3** : to conclude, to end

cerrazón *nf, pl* **-zones** : obstinacy, stubbornness

cerro *nm* COLINA, LOMA : hill

cerrojo *nm* PESTILLO : bolt, latch

certamen *nm, pl* **-támenes** : competition, contest

certero, -ra *adj* : accurate, precise — **certeramente** *adv*

certeza *nf* : certainty

certidumbre *nf* : certainty

certificable *adj* : certifiable

certificación *nf, pl* **-ciones** : certification

certificado¹, -da *adj* 1 : certified 2 : registered (of mail)

certificado² *nm* 1 : certificate 2 : registered letter

certificar {72} *vt* 1 : to certify 2 : to register (mail)

cervato *nm* : fawn

cervecera *nf* : brewery

cervecería *nf* 1 : brewery 2 : beer hall, bar

cerveza *nf* : beer ⟨cerveza de barril : draft beer⟩

cervical *adj* : cervical

cerviz *nf, pl* **cervices** : nape of the neck, cervix

cesación *nf, pl* **-ciones** : cessation, suspension

cesante *adj* : laid off, unemployed

cesantía *nf* : unemployment

cesar *vi* : to cease, to stop — *vt* : to dismiss, to lay off

cesárea *nf* : cesarean, C-section

cese *nm* 1 : cessation, stop ⟨cese del fuego : cease-fire⟩ 2 : dismissal

cesio *nm* : cesium

cesión *nf, pl* **cesiones** : transfer, assignment ⟨cesión de bienes : transfer of property⟩

césped *nm* : lawn, grass

cesta *nf* 1 : basket 2 : jai alai racket

cesto *nm* 1 : hamper 2 : basket (in basketball) 3 **cesto de (la) basura** : wastebasket

cetrería *nf* : falconry

cetrino, -na *adj* : sallow

cetro *nm* : scepter

chabacano¹, -na *adj* : tacky, tasteless

chabacano² *nm Mex* : apricot

chacal *nm* : jackal

cháchara *nf fam* 1 : small talk, chatter 2 **chácharas** *nfpl* : trinkets, junk

chacharear *vi fam* : to chatter, to gab

chacra *nf Arg, Chile, Peru* : small farm

chadiano, -na *adj & n* : Chadian

chal *nm* MANTÓN : shawl

chalado¹, -da *adj fam* : crazy, nuts

chalado², -da *n* : nut, crazy person

chalán *nm, pl* **chalanes** *Mex* : barge

chalé → chalet

chaleco *nm* : vest

chalet *nm Spain* : house

chalupa *nf* 1 : small boat 2 *Mex* : small stuffed tortilla

chamaco, -ca *n Mex fam* : kid, boy *m*, girl *f*

chamarra *nf* 1 : sheepskin jacket 2 : poncho, blanket

chamba *nf Mex, Peru fam* : job, work

chambear *vi Mex, Peru fam* : to work

chamo, -ma *n Ven fam* 1 : kid, boy *m*, girl *f* 2 : buddy, pal

champaña *or* **champán** *nm* : champagne

champiñón *nm, pl* **-ñones** : mushroom

champú *nm, pl* **-pus** *or* **-púes** : shampoo

champurrado *nm Mex* : hot chocolate thickened with cornstarch

chamuco *nm Mex fam* : devil

chamuscar {72} *vt* : to singe, to scorch — **chamuscarse** *vr*

chamusquina *nf* : scorch

chance *nm* OPORTUNIDAD : chance, opportunity

chancho¹, -cha *adj fam* : dirty, filthy, gross

chancho², -cha *n* 1 : pig, hog 2 *fam* : slob

chanchullero, -ra *adj fam* : shady, crooked

chanchullo *nm fam* : shady deal, scam

chancla *nf* 1 : thong sandal, slipper 2 : old shoe

chancleta → chancla

chanclo *nm* 1 : clog 2 **chanclos** *nmpl* : overshoes, galoshes, rubbers

chancro *nm* : chancre

changarro *nm Mex* : small shop, stall

chango, -ga *n Mex* : monkey

chantaje *nm* : blackmail

chantajear *vt* : to blackmail

chantajista *nmf* : blackmailer

chanza *nf* 1 : joke, jest 2 *Mex fam* : chance, opportunity

chapa *nf* 1 : sheet, panel, veneer 2 : lock 3 : badge

chapado, -da *adj* 1 : plated 2 **chapado a la antigua** : old-fashioned

chapar *vt* 1 : to veneer 2 : to plate (metals)

chaparrón *nm, pl* **-rrones** 1 : downpour 2 : great quantity, torrent

chapeado, -da *adj Col, Mex* : flushed

chapopote *nm Mex* : tar, blacktop

chapotear *vi* : to splash about

chapucero¹, -ra *adj* 1 : crude, shoddy 2 *Mex fam* : dishonest

chapucero², -ra *n* 1 : sloppy worker, bungler 2 *Mex fam* : cheat, swindler

chapulín *nm, pl* **-lines** *CA, Mex* : grasshopper, locust

chapuza *nf* 1 : botched job 2 *Mex fam* : fraud, trick ⟨hacer chapuzas : to cheat⟩

chapuzón *nm, pl* **-zones** : dip, swim ⟨darse un chapuzón : to go for a quick dip⟩

chaqueta *nf* : jacket

charada *nf* : charades (game)

charango *nm* : traditional Andean stringed instrument

charca *nf* : pond, pool

charco *nm* : puddle, pool

charcutería *nf* : delicatessen
charla *nf* : chat, talk
charlar *vi* : to chat, to talk
charlatán[1], **-tana** *adj* : talkative, chatty
charlatán[2], **-tana** *n, mpl* **-tanes** 1 : chatterbox 2 FARSANTE : charlatan, phony
charlatanear *vi* : to chatter away
charol *nm* 1 : lacquer, varnish 2 : patent leather 3 : tray
charola *nf Bol, Mex, Peru* : tray
charreada *nf Mex* : charro show, rodeo
charretera *nf* : epaulet
charro[1], **-rra** *adj* 1 : gaudy, tacky 2 *Mex* : pertaining to charros
charro[2], **-rra** *n Mex* : charro (Mexican cowboy or cowgirl)
chascarrillo *nm fam* : joke, funny story
chasco *nm* 1 BROMA : trick, joke 2 DECEPCIÓN, DESILUSIÓN : disillusionment, disappointment
chasis *or* **chasís** *nm* : chassis
chasquear *vt* 1 : to click (the tongue, fingers, etc.) 2 : to snap (a whip)
chasquido *nm* 1 : click (of the tongue or fingers) 2 : snap, crack
chatarra *nf* : scrap metal
chato, -ta *adj* 1 : pug-nosed 2 : flat
chauvinismo *nm* : chauvinism
chauvinista[1] *adj* : chauvinistic
chauvinista[2] *nmf* : chauvinist
chaval, -vala *n fam* : kid, boy *m*, girl *f*
chavo[1], **-va** *adj Mex fam* : young
chavo[2], **-va** *n Mex fam* : kid, boy *m*, girl *f*
chavo[3] *nm fam* : cent, buck ⟨no tengo un chavo : I'm broke⟩
chayote *nm* : chayote (plant, fruit)
checar {72} *vt Mex* : to check, to verify
checo[1], **-ca** *adj & n* : Czech
checo[2] *nm* : Czech (language)
checoslovaco, -ca *adj & n* : Czechoslovakian
chef *nm* : chef
chelín *nm, pl* **chelines** : shilling
cheque[1], etc. → **checar**
cheque[2] *nm* 1 : check 2 **cheque de viajero** : traveler's check
chequear *vt* 1 : to check, to verify 2 : to check in (baggage)
chequeo *nm* 1 INSPECCIÓN : check, inspection 2 : checkup, examination
chequera *nf* : checkbook
chévere *adj fam* : great, fantastic
chic *adj & nm* : chic
chica → **chico**
chicano, -na *adj & n* : Chicano *m*, Chicana *f*
chicha *nf* : fermented alcoholic beverage made from corn
chícharo *nm* : pea
chicharra *nf* 1 CIGARRA : cicada 2 : buzzer
chicharrón *nm, pl* **-rrones** 1 : pork rind 2 **darle chicharrón a** *Mex fam* : to get rid of
chichón *nm, pl* **chichones** : bump, swelling

chicle *nm* : chewing gum
chicloso *nm Mex* : taffy
chico[1], **-ca** *adj* 1 : little, small 2 : young
chico[2], **-ca** *n* 1 : child, boy *m*, girl *f* 2 : young man *m*, young woman *f*
chicote *nm* LÁTIGO : whip, lash
chiffon → **chifón**
chiflado[1], **-da** *adj fam* : nuts, crazy
chiflado[2], **-da** *n fam* : crazy person, lunatic
chiflar *vi* 1 : to whistle — *vt* : to whistle at, to boo — **chiflarse** *vr fam* ~ **por** : to be crazy about
chiflido *nm* : whistle, whistling
chiflón *nm, pl* **chiflones** : draft (of air)
chifón *nm, pl* **chifones** : chiffon
chilango[1], **-ga** *adj Mex fam* : of or from Mexico City
chilango[2], **-ga** *n Mex fam* : person from Mexico City
chilaquiles *nmpl Mex* : shredded tortillas in sauce
chile *nm* : chili pepper
chileno, -na *adj & n* : Chilean
chillar *vi* 1 : to squeal, to screech 2 : to scream, to yell 3 : to be gaudy, to clash
chillido *nm* 1 : scream, shout 2 : squeal, screech, cry (of an animal)
chillo *nm PRi* : red snapper
chillón, -llona *adj, mpl* **chillones** 1 : piercing, shrill 2 : loud, gaudy
chilpayate *nmf Mex fam* : child, little kid
chimenea *nf* 1 : chimney 2 : fireplace
chimichurri *nm Arg* : traditional hot sauce
chimpancé *nm* : chimpanzee
china *nf* 1 : pebble, small stone 2 *PRi* : orange
chinchar *vt fam* : to annoy, to pester — **chincharse** *vr fam* : to put up with something, to grin and bear it
chinchayote *nm Mex* : chayote root
chinche[1] *nf* 1 : bedbug 2 *Ven* : ladybug 3 : thumbtack
chinche[2] *nmf fam* : nuisance, pain in the neck
chinchilla *nf* : chinchilla
chino[1], **-na** *adj* 1 : Chinese 2 *Mex* : curly, kinky
chino[2], **-na** *n* : Chinese person
chino[3] *nm* : Chinese (language)
chip *nm, pl* **chips** : chip ⟨chip de memoria : memory chip⟩
chipote *nm Mex fam* : bump (on the head)
chipotle *nm Mex* : type of chili pepper
chipriota *adj & nmf* : Cypriot
chiquear *vt Mex* : to spoil, to indulge
chiquero *nm* POCILGA : pigpen, pigsty
chiquillada *nf* : childish prank
chiquillo[1], **-lla** *adj* : very young, little
chiquillo[2], **-lla** *n* : kid, youngster
chiquito[1], **-ta** *adj* : tiny
chiquito[2], **-ta** *n* : little one, baby
chiribita *nf* 1 : spark 2 **chiribitas** *nfpl* : spots before the eyes
chiribitil *nm* 1 DESVÁN : attic, garret 2 : cubbyhole

chirigota *nf fam* : joke
chirimía *nf* : traditional reed pipe
chirimoya *nf* : cherimoya, custard apple
chiripa *nf* **1** : fluke **2 de ~** : by sheer luck
chirivía *nf* : parsnip
chirona *nf fam* : slammer, jail
chirriar {85} *vi* **1** : to squeak, to creak **2** : to screech — **chirriante** *adj*
chirrido *nm* **1** : squeak, squeaking **2** : screech, screeching
chirrión *nm, pl* **chirriones** *Mex* : whip, lash
chisme *nm* **1** : gossip, tale **2** *Spain fam* : gadget, thingamajig
chismear *vi* : to gossip
chismoso[1], **-sa** *adj* : gossipy, gossiping
chismoso[2], **-sa** *n* **1** : gossiper, gossip **2** *Mex fam* : tattletale
chispa[1] *adj* **1** *Mex fam* : lively, vivacious ⟨un perrito chispa : a frisky puppy⟩ **2** *Spain fam* : tipsy
chispa[2] *nf* **1** : spark **2 echar chispas** : to be furious
chispeante *adj* : sparkling, scintillating
chispear *vi* **1** : to give off sparks **2** : to sparkle
chisporrotear *vi* : to crackle, to sizzle
chiste *nm* **1** : joke, funny story **2 tener chiste** : to be funny **3 tener su chiste** *Mex* : to be tricky
chistoso[1], **-sa** *adj* **1** : funny, humorous **2** : witty
chistoso[2], **-sa** *n* : wit, joker
chivas *nfpl Mex fam* : stuff, odds and ends
chivo[1], **-va** *n* **1** : kid, young goat **2 chivo expiatorio** : scapegoat
chivo[2] *nm* **1** : billy goat **2** : fit of anger
chocante *adj* **1** : shocking **2** : unpleasant, rude
chocar {72} *vi* **1** : to crash, to collide **2** : to clash, to conflict **3** : to be shocking ⟨le chocó : he was shocked⟩ **4** *Mex, Ven fam* : to be unpleasant or obnoxious ⟨me choca tu jefe : I can't stand your boss⟩ — *vt* **1** : to shake (hands) **2** : to clink glasses
chochear *vi* **1** : to be senile **2 ~ por** : to dote on, to be soft on
chochín *nm, pl* **-chines** : wren
chocho, -cha *adj* **1** : senile **2** : doting
choclo *nm* **1** : ear of corn, corncob **2** : corn **3 meter el choclo** *Mex fam* : to make a mistake
chocolate *nm* **1** : chocolate **2** : hot chocolate, cocoa
chofer *or* **chófer** *nm* **1** : chauffeur **2** : driver
choke *nm* : choke (of an automobile)
chole *interj Mex fam* **¡ya chole!** : enough!, cut it out!
cholo, -la *adj & n* : mestizo
cholla *nf fam* : head
chollo *nm Spain fam* : bargain
chongo *nm* **1** *Mex* : bun (chignon) **2 chongos** *nmpl Mex* : dessert made with fried bread

choque[1]**, etc.** → **chocar**
choque[2] *nm* **1** : crash, collision **2** : clash, conflict **3** : shock
chorizo *nm* : chorizo, sausage
chorrear *vi* **1** : to drip **2** : to pour out, to gush out
chorrito *nm* : squirt, splash
chorro *nm* **1** : flow, stream, jet **2** *Mex fam* : heap, ton
choteado, -da *adj Mex fam* : worn-out, stale ⟨esa canción está bien choteada : that song's been played to death⟩
chotear *vt* : to make fun of
choteo *nm* : joking around, kidding
chovinismo, chovinista → **chauvinismo, chauvinista**
choza *nf* BARRACA, CABAÑA : hut, shack
chubasco *nm* : downpour, storm
chuchería *nf* : knickknack, trinket
chueco, -ca *adj* **1** : crooked, bent **2** *Chile, Mex fam* : dishonest, shady
chulada *nf Mex, Spain fam* : cute or pretty thing ⟨¡qué chulada de vestido! : what a lovely dress!⟩
chulear *vt Mex fam* : to compliment
chuleta *nf* : cutlet, chop
chulo[1], **-la** *adj* **1** *fam* : cute, pretty **2** *Spain fam* : cocky, arrogant
chulo[2] *nm Spain* : pimp
chupada *nf* **1** : suck, sucking **2** : puff, drag (on a cigarette)
chupado, -da *adj fam* **1** : gaunt, skinny **2** : plastered, drunk
chupaflor *nm* COLIBRÍ : hummingbird
chupamirto *nm Mex* : hummingbird
chupar *vt* **1** : to suck **2** : to absorb **3** : to puff on **4** *fam* : to drink, to guzzle — *vi* : to suckle — **chuparse** *vr* **1** : to waste away **2** *fam* : to put up with **3 ¡chúpate esa!** *fam* : take that!
chupete *nm* **1** : pacifier **2** *Chile, Peru* : lollipop
chupetear *vt* : to suck (at)
chupón *nm, pl* **chupones 1** : sucker (of a plant) **2** : baby bottle, pacifier
churrasco *nm* **1** : steak **2** : barbecued meat
churro *nm* **1** : fried dough **2** *fam* : botch, mess **3** *fam* : attractive person, looker
chusco, -ca *adj* : funny, amusing
chusma *nf* GENTUZA : riffraff, rabble
chutar *vi* : to shoot (in soccer)
chute *nm* : shot (in soccer)
cianuro *nm* : cyanide
cibernética *nf* : cybernetics
cicatriz *nf, pl* **-trices** : scar
cicatrizarse {21} *vr* : to form a scar, to heal
cíclico, -ca *adj* : cyclical
ciclismo *nm* : bicycling
ciclista *nmf* : bicyclist
ciclo *nm* : cycle
ciclomotor *nm* : moped
ciclón *nm, pl* **ciclones** : cyclone
cicuta *nf* : hemlock
cidra *nf* : citron (fruit)
ciega, ciegue etc. → **cegar**

ciego¹, -ga *adj* **1** INVIDENTE : blind **2 a ciegas** : blindly **3 quedarse ciego** : to go blind — **ciegamente** *adv*
ciego², -ga *n* INVIDENTE : blind person
cielo *nm* **1** : sky **2** : heaven **3** : ceiling
ciempiés *nms & pl* : centipede
cien¹ *adj* **1** : a hundred, hundred ⟨las primeras cien páginas : the first hundred pages⟩ **2 cien por cien** *or* **cien por ciento** : a hundred percent, through and through, wholeheartedly
cien² *nm* : one hundred
ciénaga *nf* : swamp, bog
ciencia *nf* **1** : science **2** : learning, knowledge **3 a ciencia cierta** : for a fact, for certain
cieno *nm* : mire, mud, silt
científico¹, -ca *adj* : scientific — **científicamente** *adv*
científico², -ca *n* : scientist
ciento¹ *adj* (*used in compound numbers*) : one hundred ⟨ciento uno : one hundred and one⟩
ciento² *nm* **1** : hundred, group of a hundred **2 por ~** : percent
cierne, etc. → **cerner**
cierra, etc. → **cerrar**
cierre *nm* **1** : closing, closure **2** : fastener, clasp, zipper
cierto, -ta *adj* **1** : true, certain, definite ⟨lo cierto es que ... : the fact is that ... ⟩ **2** : certain, one ⟨cierto día de verano : one summer day⟩ ⟨bajo ciertas circunstancias : under certain circumstances⟩ **3 por ~** : in fact, as a matter of fact — **ciertamente** *adv*
ciervo, -va *n* : deer, stag *m*, hind *f*
cifra *nf* **1** : figure, number **2** : quantity, amount **3** CLAVE : code, cipher
cifrar *vt* **1** : to write in code **2** : to place, to pin ⟨cifró su esperanza en la lotería : he pinned his hopes on the lottery⟩ — **cifrarse** *vr* : to amount ⟨la multa se cifra en millares : the fine amounts to thousands⟩
cigarra *nf* CHICHARRA : cicada
cigarrera *nf* : cigarette case
cigarrillo *nm* : cigarette
cigarro *nm* **1** : cigarette **2** PURO : cigar
cigoto *nm* : zygote
cigüeña *nf* : stork
cilantro *nm* : cilantro, coriander
cilíndrico, -ca *adj* : cylindrical
cilindro *nm* : cylinder
cima *nf* CUMBRE : peak, summit, top
cimarrón, -rrona *adj, mpl* **-rrones** : untamed, wild
címbalo *nm* : cymbal
cimbel *nm* : decoy
cimbrar *vt* : to shake, to rock — **cimbrarse** *vr* : to sway, to swing
cimentar {55} *vt* **1** : to lay the foundation of, to establish **2** : to strengthen, to cement
cimientos *nmpl* : base, foundation(s)
cinc *nm* : zinc
cincel *nm* : chisel

cincelar *vt* **1** : to chisel **2** : to engrave
cincha *nf* : cinch, girth
cinchar *vt* : to cinch (a horse)
cinco *adj & nm* : five
cincuenta *adj & nm* : fifty
cincuentavo¹, -va *adj* : fiftieth
cincuentavo² *nm* : fiftieth (fraction)
cine *nm* **1** : cinema, movies *pl* **2** : movie theater
cineasta *nmf* : filmmaker
cinematográfico, -ca *adj* : movie, film, cinematic ⟨la industria cinematográfica : the film industry⟩
cingalés¹, -lesa *adj & n* : Sinhalese
cingalés² *nm* : Sinhalese (language)
cínico¹, -ca *adj* **1** : cynical **2** : shameless, brazen — **cínicamente** *adv*
cínico², -ca *n* : cynic
cinismo *nm* : cynicism
cinta *nf* **1** : ribbon **2** : tape ⟨cinta métrica : tape measure⟩ **3** : strap, belt ⟨cinta transportadora : conveyor belt⟩
cinto *nm* : strap, belt
cintura *nf* **1** : waist, waistline **2 meter en cintura** *fam* : to bring into line, to discipline
cinturón *nm, pl* **-rones 1** : belt **2 cinturón de seguridad** : seat belt
ciñe, etc. → **ceñir**
ciprés *nm, pl* **cipreses** : cypress
circo *nm* : circus
circón *nm, pl* **circones** : zircon
circonio *nm* : zirconium
circuitería *nf* : circuitry
circuito *nm* : circuit
circulación *nf, pl* **-ciones 1** : circulation **2** : movement **3** : traffic
circular¹ *vi* **1** : to circulate **2** : to move along **3** : to drive
circular² *adj* : circular
circular³ *nf* : circular, flier
circulatorio, -ria *adj* : circulatory
círculo *nm* **1** : circle **2** : club, group
circuncidar *vt* : to circumcise
circuncisión *nf, pl* **-siones** : circumcision
circundar *vt* : to surround — **circundante** *adj*
circunferencia *nf* : circumference
circunflejo, -ja *adj* **acento circunflejo** : circumflex
circunlocución *nf, pl* **-ciones** : circumlocution
circunloquio *nm* → **circunlocución**
circunnavegar {52} *vt* : to circumnavigate — **circunnavegación** *nf*
circunscribir {33} *vt* : to circumscribe, to constrict, to limit — **circunscribirse** *vr*
circunscripción *nf, pl* **-ciones 1** : limitation, restriction **2** : constituency
circunscrito *pp* → **circunscribir**
circunspección *nf, pl* **-ciones** : circumspection, prudence
circunspecto, -ta *adj* : circumspect, prudent
circunstancia *nf* : circumstance
circunstancial *adj* : circumstantial, incidental

circunstante *nmf* **1** : onlooker, bystander **2 los circunstantes** : those present
circunvalación *nf, pl* **-ciones** : surrounding, encircling ⟨carretera de circunvalación : bypass, beltway⟩
circunvecino, -na *adj* : surrounding, neighboring
cirio *nm* : large candle
cirro *nm* : cirrus (cloud)
cirrosis *nf* : cirrhosis
ciruela *nf* **1** : plum **2 ciruela pasa** : prune
cirugía *nf* : surgery
cirujano, -na *n* : surgeon
cisma *nm* : schism, rift
cisne *nm* : swan
cisterna *nf* : cistern, tank
cita *nf* **1** : quote, quotation **2** : appointment, date
citable *adj* : quotable
citación *nf, pl* **-ciones** EMPLAZAMIENTO : summons, subpoena
citadino[1], -na *adj* : of the city, urban
citadino[2], -na *n* : city dweller
citado, -da *adj* : said, aforementioned
citar *vt* **1** : to quote, to cite **2** : to make an appointment with **3** : to summon (to court), to subpoena — **citarse** *vr* ~ **con** : to arrange to meet (someone)
cítara *nf* : zither
citatorio *nm* : subpoena
citoplasma *nm* : cytoplasm
cítrico[1], -ca *adj* : citric
cítrico[2] *nm* : citrus fruit
ciudad *nf* **1** : city, town **2 ciudad universitaria** : college or university campus **3 ciudad perdida** *Mex* : shantytown
ciudadanía *nf* **1** : citizenship **2** : citizenry, citizens *pl*
ciudadano[1], -na *adj* : civic, city
ciudadano[2], -na *n* **1** NACIONAL : citizen **2** HABITANTE : resident, city dweller
ciudadela *nf* : citadel, fortress
cívico, -ca *adj* **1** : civic **2** : public-spirited
civil[1] *adj* **1** : civil **2** : civilian
civil[2] *nmf* : civilian
civilidad *nf* : civility, courtesy
civilización *nf, pl* **-ciones** : civilization
civilizar {21} *vt* : to civilize
civismo *nm* : community spirit, civic-mindedness, civics
cizaña *nf* : discord, rift
clamar *vi* : to clamor, to raise a protest — *vt* : to cry out for
clamor *nm* : clamor, outcry
clamoroso, -sa *adj* : clamorous, resounding, thunderous
clan *nm* : clan
clandestinidad *nf* : secrecy ⟨en la clandestinidad : underground⟩
clandestino, -na *adj* : clandestine, secret
clara *nf* : egg white
claraboya *nf* : skylight
claramente *adv* : clearly

clarear *v impers* **1** : to clear, to clear up **2** : to get light, to dawn — *vi* : to go gray, to turn white
claridad *nf* **1** NITIDEZ : clarity, clearness **2** : brightness, light
clarificación *nf, pl* **-ciones** ACLARACIÓN : clarification, explanation
clarificar {72} *vt* ACLARAR : to clarify, to explain
clarín *nm, pl* **clarines** : bugle
clarinete *nm* : clarinet
clarividencia *nf* **1** : clairvoyance **2** : perspicacity, discernment
clarividente[1] *adj* **1** : clairvoyant **2** : perspicacious, discerning
clarividente[2] *nmf* : clairvoyant
claro[1] *adv* **1** : clearly ⟨habla más claro : speak more clearly⟩ **2** : of course, surely ⟨¡claro!, ¡claro que sí! : absolutely!, of course!⟩ ⟨claro que entendió : of course she understood⟩
claro[2], -ra *adj* **1** : bright, clear **2** : pale, fair, light **3** : clear, evident
claro[3] *nm* **1** : clearing **2 claro de luna** : moonlight
clase *nf* **1** : class **2** ÍNDOLE, TIPO : sort, kind, type
clasicismo *nm* : classicism
clásico[1], -ca *adj* **1** : classic **2** : classical
clásico[2] *nm* : classic
clasificación *nf, pl* **-ciones** **1** : classification, sorting out **2** : rating **3** CALIFICACIÓN : qualification (in competitions)
clasificado, -da *adj* : classified ⟨aviso clasificado : classified ad⟩
clasificar {72} *vt* **1** : to classify, to sort out **2** : to rate, to rank — *vi* CALIFICAR : to qualify (in competitions) — **clasificarse** *vr*
claudicación *nf, pl* **-ciones** : surrender, abandonment of one's principles
claudicar {72} *vi* : to back down, to abandon one's principles
claustro *nm* : cloister
claustrofobia *nf* : claustrophobia
claustrofóbico, -ca *adj* : claustrophobic
cláusula *nf* : clause
clausura *nf* **1** : closure, closing **2** : closing ceremony **3** : cloister
clausurar *vt* **1** : to close, to bring to a close **2** : to close down
clavadista *nmf* : diver
clavado[1], -da *adj* **1** : nailed, fixed, stuck **2** *fam* : punctual, on the dot **3** *fam* : identical ⟨es clavado a su padre : he's the image of his father⟩
clavado[2] *nm* : dive
clavar *vt* **1** : to nail, to hammer **2** HINCAR : to plunge, to stick **3** : to fix (one's eyes) on — **clavarse** *vr* : to stick oneself (with a sharp object)
clave[1] *adj* : key, essential
clave[2] *nf* **1** CIFRA : code **2** : key ⟨la clave del misterio : the key to the mystery⟩ **3** : clef **4** : keystone
clavel *nm* : carnation
clavelito *nm* : pink (flower)

clavicémbalo *nm* : harpsichord
clavícula *nf* : collarbone
clavija *nf* **1** : plug **2** : peg, pin
clavo *nm* **1** : nail ⟨clavo grande : spike⟩ **2** : clove **3 dar en el clavo** : to hit the nail on the head
claxon *nm, pl* **cláxones** : horn (of an automobile)
clemencia *nf* : clemency, mercy
clemente *adj* : merciful
cleptomanía *nf* : kleptomania
cleptómano, -na *n* : kleptomaniac
clerecía *nf* : ministry, ministers *pl*
clerical *adj* : clerical
clérigo, -ga *n* : cleric, member of the clergy
clero *nm* : clergy
cliché *nm* **1** : cliché **2** : stencil **3** : negative (of a photograph)
cliente, -ta *n* : customer, client
clientela *nf* : clientele, customers *pl*
clima *nm* **1** : climate **2** AMBIENTE : atmosphere, ambience
climático, -ca *adj* : climatic
climatización *nf, pl* **-ciones** : air-conditioning
climatizar {21} *vt* : to air-condition — **climatizado, -da** *adj*
clímax *nm* : climax
clínica *nf* : clinic
clínico, -ca *adj* : clinical — **clínicamente** *adv*
clip *nm, pl* **clips 1** : clip **2** : paper clip
clítoris *nms & pl* : clitoris
cloaca *nf* ALCANTARILLA : sewer
clocar {82} *vi* : to cluck
cloche *nm* CA, Car, Col, Ven : clutch (of an automobile)
clon *nm* : clone
cloqué, etc. → clocar
cloquear *vi* : to cluck
clorar *vt* : to chlorinate — **cloración** *nf*
cloro *nm* : chlorine
clorofila *nf* : chlorophyll
cloroformo *nm* : chloroform
cloruro *nm* : chloride
clóset *nm, pl* **clósets 1** : closet **2** : cupboard
club *nm* : club
clueca, clueque etc. → clocar
coa *nf Mex* : hoe
coacción *nf, pl* **-ciones** : coercion, duress
coaccionar *vt* : to coerce
coactivo, -va *adj* : coercive
coagular *v* : to clot, to coagulate — **coagulación** *nf*
coágulo *nm* : clot
coalición *nf, pl* **-ciones** : coalition
coartada *nf* : alibi
coartar *vt* : to restrict, to limit
cobalto *nm* : cobalt
cobarde[1] *adj* : cowardly
cobarde[2] *nmf* : coward
cobardía *nf* : cowardice
cobaya *nf* : guinea pig
cobertizo *nm* : shed, shelter
cobertor *nm* COLCHA : bedspread, quilt

cobertura *nf* **1** : coverage **2** : cover, collateral
cobija *nf* FRAZADA, MANTA : blanket
cobijar *vt* : to shelter — **cobijarse** *vr* : to take shelter
cobra *nf* : cobra
cobrador, -dora *n* **1** : collector **2** : conductor (of a bus or train)
cobrar *vt* **1** : to charge **2** : to collect, to draw, to earn **3** : to acquire, to gain **4** : to recover, to retrieve **5** : to cash (a check) **6** : to claim, to take (a life) **7** : to shoot (game), to bag — *vi* **1** : to be paid **2 llamar por cobrar** *Mex* : to call collect
cobre *nm* : copper
cobrizo, -za *adj* : coppery
cobro *nm* : collection (of money), cashing (of a check)
coca *nf* **1** : coca **2** *fam* : coke, cocaine
cocaína *nf* : cocaine
cocal *nm* : coca plantation
cocción *nf, pl* **cocciones** : cooking
cocear *vi* : to kick (of an animal)
cocer {14} *vt* **1** COCINAR : to cook **2** HERVIR : to boil
cochambre *nmf fam* : filth, grime
cochambroso, -sa *adj* : filthy, grimy
coche *nm* **1** : car, automobile **2** : coach, carriage **3 coche cama** : sleeping car **4 coche fúnebre** : hearse
cochecito *nm* : baby carriage, stroller
cochera *nf* : garage, carport
cochinada *nf fam* **1** : filthy language **2** : disgusting behavior **3** : dirty trick
cochinillo *nm* : suckling pig, piglet
cochino[1], **-na** *adj* **1** : dirty, filthy, disgusting **2** *fam* : rotten, lousy
cochino[2], **-na** *n* : pig, hog
cocido[1], **-da** *adj* **1** : boiled, cooked **2 bien cocido** : well-done
cocido[2] *nm* ESTOFADO, GUISADO : stew
cociente *nm* : quotient
cocimiento *nm* : cooking, baking
cocina *nf* **1** : kitchen **2** : stove **3** : cuisine, cooking
cocinar *v* : to cook
cocinero, -ra *n* : cook, chef
cocineta *nf Mex* : kitchenette
coco *nm* **1** : coconut **2** *fam* : head **3** *fam* : bogeyman
cocoa *nf* : cocoa, hot chocolate
cocodrilo *nm* : crocodile
cocotero *nm* : coconut palm
coctel *or* **cóctel** *nm* **1** : cocktail **2** : cocktail party
coctelera *nf* : cocktail shaker
codazo *nm* **1 darle un codazo a** : to elbow, to nudge **2 abrirse paso a codazos** : to elbow one's way through
codearse *vr* : to rub elbows, to hobnob
códice *nm* : codex, manuscript
codicia *nf* AVARICIA : avarice, covetousness
codiciar *vt* : to covet
codicilo *nm* : codicil
codicioso, -sa *adj* : avaricious, covetous

codificación *nf, pl* **-ciones** **1** : codification **2** : coding, encoding

codificar {72} *vt* **1** : to codify **2** : to code, to encode

código *nm* **1** : code **2** **código postal** : zip code **3** **código morse** : Morse code

codo[1], **-da** *adj Mex* : cheap, stingy

codo[2], **-da** *n Mex* : tightwad, cheapskate

codo[3] *nm* : elbow

codorniz *nf, pl* **-nices** : quail

coeficiente *nm* **1** : coefficient **2** **coeficiente intelectual** : IQ, intelligence quotient

coexistir *vi* : to coexist — **coexistencia** *nf*

cofa *nf* : crow's nest

cofre *nm* **1** BAÚL : trunk, chest **2** *Mex* CAPOTE : hood (of a car)

coger {15} *vt* **1** : to seize, to take hold of **2** : to catch **3** : to pick up **4** : to gather, to pick **5** : to gore — **cogerse** *vr* AGARRARSE : to hold on

cogida *nf* **1** : gathering, harvest **2** : goring

cognición *nf, pl* **-ciones** : cognition

cognitivo, -va *adj* : cognitive

cogollo *nm* **1** : heart (of a vegetable) **2** : bud, bulb **3** : core, crux ⟨el cogollo de la cuestión : the heart of the matter⟩

cogote *nm* : scruff, nape

cohabitar *vi* : to cohabit — **cohabitación** *nf*

cohechar *vt* SOBORNAR : to bribe

cohecho *nm* SOBORNO : bribe, bribery

coherencia *nf* : coherence — **coherente** *adj*

cohesión *nf, pl* **-siones** : cohesion

cohesivo, -va *adj* : cohesive

cohete *nm* : rocket

cohibición *nf, pl* **-ciones** **1** : (legal) restraint **2** INHIBICIÓN : inhibition

cohibido, -da *adj* : inhibited, shy

cohibir {62} *vt* : to inhibit, to make self-conscious — **cohibirse** *vr* : to feel shy or embarrassed

cohorte *nf* : cohort

coima *nf Arg, Chile, Peru* : bribe

coimear *vt Arg, Chile, Peru* : to bribe

coincidencia *nf* : coincidence

coincidente *adj* **1** : coincident **2** ACORDE : coinciding

coincidir *vi* **1** : to coincide **2** : to agree

coito *nm* : sexual intercourse, coitus

coja, etc. → **coger**

cojear *vi* **1** : to limp **2** : to wobble, to rock **3** **cojear del mismo pie** : to be two of a kind

cojera *nf* : limp

cojín *nm, pl* **cojines** : cushion, throw pillow

cojinete *nm* **1** : bearing, bushing **2** **cojinete de bola** : ball bearing

cojo[1], **-ja** *adj* **1** : limping, lame **2** : wobbly **3** : weak, ineffectual

cojo[2], **-ja** *n* : lame person

cojones *nmpl usu considered vulgar* **1** : testicles *pl* **2** : guts *pl*, courage

col *nf* **1** REPOLLO : cabbage **2** **col de Bruselas** : Brussels sprout **3** **col rizada** : kale

cola *nf* **1** RABO : tail ⟨cola de caballo : ponytail⟩ **2** FILA : line (of people) ⟨hacer cola : to wait in line⟩ **3** : cola, drink **4** : train (of a dress) **5** : tails *pl* (of a tuxedo) **6** PEGAMENTO : glue **7** *fam* : buttocks *pl*, rear end

colaboracionista *nmf* : collaborator, traitor

colaborador, -dora *n* **1** : contributor (to a periodical) **2** : collaborator

colaborar *vi* : to collaborate — **colaboración** *nf*

colación *nf, pl* **-ciones** **1** : light meal **2** : comparison, collation ⟨sacar a colación : to bring up, to broach⟩ **3** : conferral (of a degree)

colador *nm* **1** : colander, strainer **2** *PRi* : small coffeepot

colapso *nm* **1** : collapse **2** : standstill

colar {19} *vt* : to strain, to filter — **colarse** *vr* **1** : to sneak in, to cut in line, to gate-crash **2** : to slip up, to make a mistake

colateral[1] *adj* : collateral — **colateralmente** *adv*

colateral[2] *nm* : collateral

colcha *nf* COBERTOR : bedspread, quilt

colchón *nm, pl* **colchones** **1** : mattress **2** : cushion, padding, buffer

colchoneta *nf* : mat (for gymnastic sports)

colear *vi* **1** : to wag its tail **2** **vivito y coleando** *fam* : alive and kicking

colección *nf, pl* **-ciones** : collection

coleccionar *vt* : to collect, to keep a collection of

coleccionista *nmf* : collector

colecta *nf* : collection (of donations)

colectar *vt* : to collect

colectividad *nf* : community, group

colectivo[1], **-va** *adj* : collective — **colectivamente** *adv*

colectivo[2] *nm* **1** : collective **2** *Arg, Bol, Peru* : city bus

colector[1], **-tora** *n* : collector ⟨colector de impuestos : tax collector⟩

colector[2] *nm* **1** : sewer **2** : manifold (of an engine)

colega *nmf* **1** : colleague **2** HOMÓLOGO : counterpart **3** *fam* : buddy

colegiado[1], **-da** *adj* : collegiate

colegiado[2], **-da** *n* **1** ÁRBITRO : referee **2** : member (of a professional association)

colegial[1], **-giala** *adj* **1** : school, collegiate **2** *Mex fam* : green, inexperienced

colegial[2], **-giala** *n* : schoolboy *m*, schoolgirl *f*

colegiatura *nf Mex* : tuition

colegio *nm* **1** : school **2** : college ⟨colegio electoral : electoral college⟩ **3** : professional association

colegir {28} *vt* **1** JUNTAR : to collect, to gather **2** INFERIR : to infer, to deduce

cólera[1] *nm* : cholera

cólera[2] *nf* FURIA, IRA : anger, rage

colérico, -ca *adj* **1** FURIOSO : angry **2** IRRITABLE : irritable

colesterol *nm* : cholesterol

coleta *nf* **1** : ponytail **2** : pigtail

coletazo *nm* : lash, flick (of a tail)

colgado, -da *adj* **1** : hanging, hanged **2** : pending **3 dejar colgado a** : to disappoint, to let down

colgante[1] *adj* : hanging, dangling

colgante[2] *nm* : pendant, charm (on a bracelet)

colgar {16} *vt* **1** : to hang (up), to put up **2** AHORCAR : to hang (someone) **3** : to hang up (a telephone) **4** *fam* : to fail (an exam) — **colgarse** *vr* **1** : to hang, to be suspended **2** AHORCARSE : to hang oneself **3** : to hang up a telephone

colibrí *nm* CHUPAFLOR : hummingbird

cólico *nm* : colic

coliflor *nf* : cauliflower

colilla *nf* : butt (of a cigarette)

colina *nf* CERRO, LOMA : hill

colindante *adj* CONTIGUO : adjacent, neighboring

colindar *vi* : to adjoin, to be adjacent

coliseo *nm* : coliseum

colisión *nf, pl* **-siones** : collision

colisionar *vi* : to collide

collage *nm* : collage

collar *nm* **1** : collar (for an animal) **2** : necklace ⟨collar de perlas : string of pearls⟩

colmado, -da *adj* : heaping

colmar *vt* **1** : to fill to the brim **2** : to fulfill, to satisfy **3** : to heap, to shower ⟨me colmaron de regalos : they showered me with gifts⟩

colmena *nf* : beehive

colmenar *nm* APIARIO : apiary

colmillo *nm* **1** CANINO : canine (tooth), fang **2** : tusk

colmilludo, -da *adj Mex, PRi* : astute, shrewd, crafty

colmo *nm* : height, extreme, limit ⟨el colmo de la locura : the height of folly⟩ ⟨¡eso es el colmo! : that's the last straw!⟩

colocación *nf, pl* **-ciones** **1** : placement, placing **2** : position, job **3** : investment

colocar {72} *vt* **1** PONER : to place, to put **2** : to find a job for **3** : to invest — **colocarse** *vr* **1** SITUARSE : to position oneself **2** : to get a job

colofón *nm, pl* **-fones** **1** : ending, finale **2** : colophon

colofonia *nf* : rosin

colombiano, -na *adj & n* : Colombian

colon *nm* : (intestinal) colon

colón *nm, pl* **colones** : Costa Rican and Salvadoran unit of currency

colonia *nf* **1** : colony **2** : cologne **3** *Mex* : residential area, neighborhood

colonial *adj* : colonial

colonización *nf, pl* **-ciones** : colonization

colonizador[1], **-dora** *adj* : colonizing

colonizador[2], **-dora** *n* : colonizer, colonist

colonizar {21} *vt* : to colonize, to settle

colono, -na *n* **1** : settler, colonist **2** : tenant farmer

coloquial *adj* : colloquial

coloquio *nm* **1** : discussion, talk **2** : conference, symposium

color *nm* **1** : color **2** : paint, dye **3 colores** *nmpl* : colored pencils

coloración *nf, pl* **-ciones** : coloring, coloration

colorado[1], **-da** *adj* **1** ROJO : red **2 ponerse colorado** : to blush **3 chiste colorado** *Mex* : off-color joke

colorado[2] *nm* ROJO : red

colorante *nm* : coloring ⟨colorante de alimentos : food coloring⟩

colorear *vt* : to color — *vi* **1** : to redden **2** : to ripen

colorete *nm* : rouge, blusher

colorido *nm* : color, coloring

colorín *nm, pl* **-rines** **1** : bright color **2** : goldfinch

colosal *adj* : colossal

coloso *nm* : colossus

coludir *vi* : to be in collusion, to conspire

columna *nf* **1** : column **2 columna vertebral** : spine, backbone

columnata *nf* : colonnade

columnista *nmf* : columnist

columpiar *vt* : to push (on a swing) — **columpiarse** *vr* : to swing

columpio *nm* : swing

colusión *nf, pl* **-siones** : collusion

colza *nf* : rape (plant)

coma[1] *nm* : coma

coma[2] *nf* : comma

comadre *nf* **1** : godmother of one's child **2** : mother of one's godchild **3** *fam* : neighbor, female friend **4** *fam* : gossip

comadrear *vi fam* : to gossip

comadreja *nf* : weasel

comadrona *nf* : midwife

comanche *nmf* : Comanche

comandancia *nf* **1** : command headquarters **2** : command

comandante *nmf* **1** : commander, commanding officer **2** : major

comandar *vt* : to command, to lead

comando *nm* **1** : commando **2** : command (for computers)

comarca *nf* REGIÓN : region

comarcal *adj* REGIONAL : regional, local

comatoso, -sa *adj* : comatose

combar *vt* : to bend, to curve — **combarse** *vr* **1** : to bend, to buckle **2** : to warp, to bulge, to sag

combate *nm* **1** : combat **2** : fight, boxing match

combatiente *nmf* : combatant, fighter

combatir *vt* : to combat, to fight against — *vi* : to fight

combatividad *nf* : fighting spirit

combativo, -va *adj* : combative, spirited

combinación *nf, pl* **-ciones** **1** : combination **2** : connection (in travel)

combinar *vt* **1** UNIR : to combine, to mix together **2** : to match, to put together — **combinarse** *vr* : to get together, to conspire

combo *nm* **1** : (musical) band **2** *Chile, Peru* : sledgehammer **3** *Chile, Peru* : punch

combustible[1] *adj* : combustible

combustible[2] *nm* : fuel

combustión *nf, pl* **-tiones** : combustion

comedero *nm* : trough, feeder

comedia *nf* : comedy

comediante *nmf* : actor, actress *f*

comedido, -da *adj* MESURADO : moderate, restrained

comediógrafo, -fa *n* : playwright

comedor *nm* : dining room

comején *nm, pl* **-jenes** : termite

comelón[1], **-lona** *adj, mpl* **-lones** *fam* : gluttonous

comelón[2], **-lona** *n, pl* **-lones** *fam* : big eater, glutton

comensal *nmf* : dinner guest

comentador, -dora *n* → **comentarista**

comentar *vt* **1** : to comment on, to discuss **2** : to mention, to remark

comentario *nm* **1** : comment, remark ⟨sin comentarios : no comment⟩ **2** : commentary

comentarista *nmf* : commentator

comenzar {29} *v* EMPEZAR : to begin, to start

comer[1] *vt* **1** : to eat **2** : to consume, to eat up, to eat into — *vi* **1** : to eat **2** CENAR : to have a meal **3 dar de comer** : to feed — **comerse** *vr* : to eat up

comer[2] *nm* : eating, dining

comercial *adj & nm* : commercial — **comercialmente** *adv*

comercializar {21} *vt* **1** : to commercialize **2** : to market

comerciante *nmf* : merchant, dealer

comerciar *vi* : to do business, to trade

comercio *nm* **1** : commerce, trade **2** NEGOCIO : business, place of business

comestible *adj* : edible

comestibles *nmpl* VÍVERES : groceries, food

cometa[1] *nm* : comet

cometa[2] *nf* : kite

cometer *vt* **1** : to commit **2 cometer un error** : to make a mistake

cometido *nm* : assignment, task

comezón *nf, pl* **-zones** PICAZÓN : itchiness, itching

comible *adj fam* : eatable, edible

comic *or* **cómic** *nm* : comic strip, comic book

comicastro, -tra *n* : second-rate actor, ham

comicidad *nf* HUMOR : humor, wit

comicios *nmpl* : elections, voting

cómico[1], **-ca** *adj* : comic, comical

cómico[2], **-ca** *n* HUMORISTA : comic, comedian, comedienne *f*

comida *nf* **1** : food **2** : meal **3** : dinner **4 comida basura** : junk food **5 comida rápida** : fast food

comidilla *nf* : talk, gossip

comienzo *nm* **1** : start, beginning **2 al comienzo** : at first **3 dar comienzo** : to begin

comillas *nfpl* : quotation marks ⟨entre comillas : in quotes⟩

comilón, -lona → **comelón, -lona**

comilona *nf fam* : feast

comino *nm* **1** : cumin **2 me vale un comino** *fam* : not to matter to someone ⟨no me importa un comino : I couldn't care less⟩

comisaría *nf* : police station

comisario, -ria *n* : commissioner

comisión *nf, pl* **-siones** **1** : commission, committing **2** : committee **3** : percentage, commission ⟨comisión sobre las ventas : sales commission⟩

comisionado[1], **-da** *adj* : commissioned, entrusted

comisionado[2], **-da** *n* → **comisario**

comisionar *vt* : to commission

comité *nm* : committee

comitiva *nf* : retinue, entourage

como[1] *adv* **1** : around, about ⟨cuesta como 500 pesos : it costs around 500 pesos⟩ **2** : kind of, like ⟨tengo como mareos : I'm kind of dizzy⟩

como[2] *conj* **1** : how, as ⟨hazlo como dijiste que lo harías : do it the way you said you would⟩ **2** : since, given that ⟨como estaba lloviendo, no salí : since it was raining, I didn't go out⟩ **3** : if ⟨como lo vuelva a hacer lo arrestarán : if he does that again he'll be arrested⟩ **4 como quiera** : in any way

como[3] *prep* **1** : like, as ⟨ligero como una pluma : light as a feather⟩ **2 así como** : as well as

cómo *adv* : how ⟨¿cómo estás? : how are you?⟩ ⟨¿a cómo están las manzanas? : how much are the apples?⟩ ⟨¿cómo? : excuse me?, what was that?⟩ ⟨¿se puede? ¡cómo no! : may I? please do!⟩

cómoda *nf* : bureau, chest of drawers

comodidad *nf* **1** : comfort **2** : convenience

comodín *nm, pl* **-dines** **1** : joker, wild card **2** : all-purpose word or thing **3** : pretext, excuse

cómodo, -da *adj* **1** CONFORTABLE : comfortable **2** : convenient — **cómodamente** *adv*

comodoro *nm* : commodore

comoquiera *adv* **1** : in any way **2 comoquiera que** : in whatever way, however ⟨comoquiera que sea eso : however that may be⟩

compa *nm fam* : buddy, pal

compactar *vt* : to compact, to compress

compacto, -ta *adj* : compact

compadecer {53} *vt* : to sympathize with, to feel sorry for — **compadecerse** *vr* **1** ~ **de** : to take pity on, to commiserate with **2** ~ **con** : to fit, to accord (with)

compadre *nm* **1** : godfather of one's child **2** : father of one's godchild **3** *fam* : buddy, pal

compaginar *vt* **1** COORDINAR : to combine, to coordinate **2** : to collate

compañerismo *nm* : comradeship, camaraderie

compañero, -ra *n* : companion, mate, partner

compañía *nf* **1** : company ⟨llegó en compañía de su madre : he arrived with his mother⟩ **2** EMPRESA, FIRMA : firm, company

comparable *adj* : comparable

comparación *nf, pl* **-ciones** : comparison

comparado, -da *adj* : comparative ⟨literatura comparada : comparative literature⟩

comparar *vt* : to compare

comparativo¹, -va *adj* : comparative, relative — **comparativamente** *adv*

comparativo² *nm* : comparative degree or form

comparecencia *nf* **1** : appearance (in court) **2 orden de comparecencia** : subpoena, summons

comparecer {53} *vi* : to appear (in court)

compartimiento *or* **compartimento** *nm* : compartment

compartir *vt* : to share

compás *nm, pl* **-pases** **1** : beat, rhythm, time **2** : compass

compasión *nf, pl* **-siones** : compassion, pity

compasivo, -va *adj* : compassionate, sympathetic

compatibilidad *nf* : compatibility

compatible *adj* : compatible

compatriota *nmf* PAISANO : compatriot, fellow countryman

compeler *vt* : to compel

compendiar *vt* : to summarize, to condense

compendio *nm* : summary

compenetración *nf, pl* **-ciones** : rapport, mutual understanding

compenetrarse *vr* **1** : to understand each other **2** ~ **con** : to identify oneself with

compensación *nf, pl* **-ciones** : compensation

compensar *vt* : to compensate for, to make up for — *vi* : to be worth one's while

compensatorio, -ria *adj* : compensatory

competencia *nf* **1** : competition, rivalry **2** : competence

competente *adj* : competent, able — **competentemente** *adv*

competición *nf, pl* **-ciones** : competition

competidor¹, -dora *adj* RIVAL : competing, rival

competidor², -dora *n* RIVAL : competitor, rival

competir {54} *vi* : to compete

competitividad *nf* : competitiveness

competitivo, -va *adj* : competitive — **competitivamente** *adv*

compilar *vt* : to compile — **compilación** *nf*

compinche *nmf fam* **1** : buddy, pal **2** : partner in crime, accomplice

complacencia *nf* : pleasure, satisfaction

complacer {57} *vt* : to please — **complacerse** *vr* ~ **en** : to take pleasure in

complaciente *adj* : obliging, eager to please

complejidad *nf* : complexity

complejo¹, -ja *adj* : complex

complejo² *nm* : complex

complementar *vt* : to complement, to supplement — **complementarse** *vr*

complementario, -ria *adj* : complementary

complemento *nm* **1** : complement, supplement **2** : supplementary pay, allowance

completamente *adv* : completely, totally

completar *vt* TERMINAR : to complete, to finish

completo, -ta *adj* **1** : complete **2** : perfect, absolute **3** : full, detailed

complexión *nf, pl* **-xiones** : (physical) constitution

complicación *nf, pl* **-ciones** : complication

complicado, -da *adj* : complicated

complicar {72} *vt* **1** : to complicate **2** : to involve — **complicarse** *vr*

cómplice *nmf* : accomplice

complicidad *nf* : complicity

complot *nm, pl* **complots** CONFABULACIÓN, CONSPIRACIÓN : conspiracy, plot

componenda *nf* : shady deal, scam

componente *adj & nm* : component, constituent

componer {60} *vt* **1** ARREGLAR : to fix, to repair **2** CONSTITUIR : to make up, to compose **3** : to compose, to write **4** : to set (a bone) — **componerse** *vr* **1** : to improve, to get better **2** ~ **de** : to consist of

comportamiento *nm* CONDUCTA : behavior, conduct

comportarse *vr* : to behave, to conduct oneself

composición *nf, pl* **-ciones** **1** OBRA : composition, work **2** : makeup, arrangement

compositor, -tora *n* : composer, songwriter

compostura *nf* **1** : composure **2** : mending, repair

compra *nf* **1** : purchase **2 ir de compras** : to go shopping **3 orden de compra** : purchase order

comprador, -dora *n* : buyer, shopper
comprar *vt* : to buy, to purchase
compraventa *nf* : buying and selling
comprender *vt* 1 ENTENDER : to comprehend, to understand 2 ABARCAR : to cover, to include — *vi* : to understand ⟨¡ya comprendo! : now I understand!⟩
comprensible *adj* : understandable — **comprensiblemente** *adv*
comprensión *nf, pl* **-siones** 1 : comprehension, understanding, grasp 2 : understanding, sympathy
comprensivo, -va *adj* : understanding
compresa *nf* 1 : compress 2 *or* **compresa higiénica** : sanitary napkin
compresión *nf, pl* **-siones** : compression
compresor *nm* : compressor
comprimido *nm* PÍLDORA, TABLETA : pill, tablet
comprimir *vt* : to compress
comprobable *adj* : verifiable, provable
comprobación *nf, pl* **-ciones** : verification, confirmation
comprobante *nm* 1 : proof ⟨comprobante de identidad : proof of identity⟩ 2 : voucher, receipt ⟨comprobante de ventas : sales slip⟩
comprobar {19} *vt* 1 : to verify, to check 2 : to prove
comprometedor, -dora *adj* : compromising
comprometer *vt* 1 : to compromise 2 : to jeopardize 3 : to commit, to put under obligation — **comprometerse** *vr* 1 : to commit oneself 2 ~ **con** : to get engaged to
comprometido, -da *adj* 1 : compromising, awkward 2 : committed, obliged 3 : engaged (to be married)
compromiso *nm* 1 : obligation, commitment 2 : engagement ⟨anillo de compromiso : engagement ring⟩ 3 : agreement 4 : awkward situation, fix
compuerta *nf* : floodgate
compuesto¹ *pp* → **componer**
compuesto², -ta *adj* 1 : fixed, repaired 2 : compound, composite 3 : decked out, spruced up 4 ~ **de** : made up of, consisting of
compuesto³ *nm* : compound
compulsión *nf, pl* **-siones** : compulsion
compulsivo, -va *adj* 1 : compelling, urgent 2 : compulsive — **compulsivamente** *adv*
compungido, -da *adj* : contrite, remorseful
compungirse {35} *vr* : to feel remorse
compuso, etc. → **componer**
computable *adj* : countable ⟨años computables : years accrued⟩ ⟨ingresos computables : qualifying income⟩
computación *nf, pl* **-ciones** : computing, computers *pl*
computador *nm* → **computadora**
computadora *nf* 1 : computer 2 **computadora portátil** : laptop computer

computar *vt* : to compute, to calculate
computarizar {21} *vt* : to computerize
cómputo *nm* : computation, calculation
comulgar {52} *vi* : to receive Communion
común *adj, pl* **comunes** 1 : common 2 **común y corriente** : ordinary, regular 3 **por lo común** : generally, as a rule
comuna *nf* : commune
comunal *adj* : communal
comunicación *nf, pl* **-ciones** 1 : communication 2 : access, link 3 : message, report
comunicado *nm* 1 : communiqué 2 **comunicado de prensa** : press release
comunicar {72} *vt* 1 : to communicate, to convey 2 : to notify — **comunicarse** *vr* ~ **con** 1 : to contact, to get in touch with 2 : to be connected to
comunicativo, -va *adj* : communicative, talkative
comunidad *nf* : community
comunión *nf, pl* **-niones** 1 : communion, sharing 2 : Communion
comunismo *nm* : communism, Communism
comunista *adj & nmf* : communist
comúnmente *adv* : commonly
con *prep* 1 : with ⟨vengo con mi padre : I'm going with my father⟩ ⟨¿con quién hablas? : who are you speaking to?⟩ 2 : in spite of ⟨con todo : in spite of it all⟩ 3 : to, towards ⟨ella es amable con los niños : she is kind to the children⟩ 4 : by ⟨con llegar temprano : by arriving early⟩ 5 **con (tal) que** : as long as, so long as
conato *nm* : attempt, effort ⟨conato de robo : attempted robbery⟩
cóncavo, -va *adj* : concave
concebible *adj* : conceivable
concebir {54} *vt* 1 : to conceive 2 : to conceive of, to imagine — *vi* : to conceive, to become pregnant
conceder *vt* 1 : to grant, to bestow 2 : to concede, to admit
concejal, -jala *n* : councilman *m*, councilwoman *f*, alderman *m*, alderwoman *f*
concejo *nm* : council ⟨concejo municipal : town council⟩
concentración *nf, pl* **-ciones** : concentration
concentrado *nm* : concentrate
concentrar *vt* : to concentrate — **concentrarse** *vr*
concéntrico, -ca *adj* : concentric
concepción *nf, pl* **-ciones** : conception
concepto *nm* NOCIÓN : concept, idea, opinion
conceptuar {3} *vt* : to regard, to judge
concernir {17} *vi* : to be of concern
concertar {55} *vt* 1 : to arrange, to set up 2 : to agree on, to settle 3 : to harmonize — *vi* : to be in harmony
concesión *nf, pl* **-siones** 1 : concession 2 : awarding, granting
concha *nf* : conch, seashell

conciencia *nf* **1** : conscience **2** : consciousness, awareness
concientizar {21} *vt* : to make aware —
concientizarse *vr* ~ **de** : to realize, to become aware of
concienzudo, -da *adj* : conscientious
concierto *nm* **1** : concert **2** : agreement **3** : concerto
conciliador¹, -dora *adj* : conciliatory
conciliador², -dora *n* : arbitrator, peacemaker
conciliar *vt* : to conciliate, to reconcile — **conciliación** *nf*
conciliatorio, -ria *adj* → **conciliador¹**
concilio *nm* : (church) council
conciso, -sa *adj* : concise — **concisión** *nf*
conciudadano, -na *n* : fellow citizen
cónclave *nm* : conclave, private meeting
concluir {41} *vt* **1** TERMINAR : to conclude, to finish **2** DEDUCIR : to deduce, to infer — *vi* : to end, to conclude
conclusión *nf, pl* **-siones** : conclusion
concluyente *adj* : conclusive
concomitante *adj* : concomitant
concordancia *nf* : agreement, accordance
concordar {19} *vi* : to agree, to coincide — *vt* : to reconcile
concordia *nf* : concord, harmony
concretar *vt* **1** : to pinpoint, to specify **2** : to fulfill, to realize — **concretarse** *vr* : to become real, to take shape
concretizar → **concretar**
concreto¹, -ta *adj* **1** : concrete, actual **2** : definite, specific ⟨en concreto : specifically⟩ — **concretamente** *adv*
concreto² *nm* HORMIGÓN : concrete
concubina *nf* : concubine
concurrencia *nf* **1** : audience, turnout **2** : concurrence
concurrente *adj* : concurrent — **concurrentemente** *adv*
concurrido, -da *adj* : busy, crowded
concurrir *vi* **1** : to converge, to come together **2** : to concur, to agree **3** : to take part, to participate **4** : to attend, to be present ⟨concurrir a una reunión : to attend a meeting⟩ **5** ~ **a** : to contribute to
concursante *nmf* : contestant, competitor
concursar *vt* : to compete in — *vi* : to compete, to participate
concurso *nm* **1** : contest, competition **2** : concurrence, coincidence **3** : crowd, gathering **4** : cooperation, assistance
condado *nm* **1** : county **2** : earldom
conde, -desa *n* : count *m*, earl *m*, countess *f*
condecoración *nf, pl* **-ciones** : decoration, medal
condecorar *vt* : to decorate, to award (a medal)
condena *nf* **1** REPROBACIÓN : disapproval, condemnation **2** SENTENCIA : sentence, conviction

condenable *adj* : reprehensible
condenación *nf, pl* **-ciones** **1** : condemnation **2** : damnation
condenado¹, -da *adj* **1** : fated, doomed **2** : convicted, sentenced **3** *fam* : darn, damned
condenado², -da *n* : convict
condenar *vt* **1** : to condemn **2** : to sentence **3** : to board up, to wall up — **condenarse** *vr* : to be damned
condensación *nf, pl* **-ciones** : condensation
condensar *vt* : to condense
condesa *nf* → **conde**
condescendencia *nf* : condescension
condescender {56} *vi* **1** : to condescend **2** : to agree, to acquiesce
condición *nf, pl* **-ciones** **1** : condition, state **2** : capacity, position **3 condiciones** *nfpl* : conditions, circumstances ⟨condiciones de vida : living conditions⟩
condicional *adj* : conditional — **condicionalmente** *adv*
condicionamiento *nm* : conditioning
condicionar *vt* **1** : to condition, to determine **2** ~ **a** : to be contingent on, to depend on
condimentar *vt* SAZONAR : to season, to spice
condimento *nm* : condiment, seasoning, spice
condiscípulo, -la *n* : classmate
condolencia *nf* : condolence, sympathy
condolerse {47} *vr* : to sympathize
condominio *nm* : condominium, condo
condón *nm, pl* **condones** : condom
cóndor *nm* : condor
conducción *nf, pl* **-ciones** **1** : conduction (of electricity, etc.) **2** DIRECCIÓN : management, direction
conducir {61} *vt* **1** DIRIGIR, GUIAR : to direct, to lead **2** MANEJAR : to drive (a vehicle) — *vi* **1** : to drive a vehicle **2** ~ **a** : to lead to — **conducirse** *vr* PORTARSE : to behave, to conduct oneself
conducta *nf* COMPORTAMIENTO : conduct, behavior
conducto *nm* : conduit, channel, duct
conductor¹, -tora *adj* : conducting, leading
conductor², -tora *n* : driver
conductor³ *nm* : conductor (of electricity, etc.)
conectar *vt* : to connect — *vi* ~ **con** : to link up with, to communicate with
conector *nm* : connector
conejera *nf* : rabbit hutch
conejillo *nm* **conejillo de Indias** : guinea pig
conejo, -ja *n* : rabbit
conexión *nf, pl* **-xiones** : connection
confabulación *nf, pl* **-ciones** COMPLOT, CONSPIRACIÓN : plot, conspiracy
confabularse *vr* : to plot, to conspire
confección *nf, pl* **-ciones** **1** : preparation **2** : tailoring, dressmaking
confeccionar *vt* : to make, to produce, to prepare

confederación *nf, pl* **-ciones** : confederation

confederarse *vr* : to confederate, to form a confederation

conferencia *nf* 1 REUNIÓN : conference, meeting 2 : lecture

conferenciante *nmf* : lecturer

conferencista → **conferenciante**

conferir {76} *vt* : to confer, to bestow

confesar {55} *v* : to confess — **confesarse** *vr* : to go to confession

confesión *nf, pl* **-siones** 1 : confession 2 : creed, denomination

confesionario *nm* : confessional

confesor *nm* : confessor

confeti *nm* : confetti

confiable *adj* : trustworthy, reliable

confiado, -da *adj* 1 : confident, self-confident 2 : trusting — **confiadamente** *adv*

confianza *nf* 1 : trust ⟨de poca confiaza : untrustworthy⟩ 2 : confidence, self-confidence

confianzudo, -da *adj* : forward, presumptuous

confiar {85} *vi* : to have trust, to be trusting — *vt* 1 : to confide 2 : to entrust — **confiarse** *vr* 1 : to be overconfident 2 ~ **a** : to confide in

confidencia *nf* : confidence, secret

confidencial *adj* : confidential — **confidencialmente** *adv*

confidencialidad *nf* : confidentiality

confidente *nmf* 1 : confidant, confidante *f* 2 : informer

configuración *nf, pl* **-ciones** : configuration, shape

configurar *vt* : to shape, to form

confín *nm, pl* **confines** : boundary, limit

confinamiento *nm* : confinement

confinar *vt* 1 : to confine, to limit 2 : to exile — *vi* ~ **con** : to border on

confirmación *nf, pl* **-ciones** : confirmation

confirmar *vt* : to confirm, to substantiate

confiscación *nf, pl* **-ciones** : confiscation

confiscar {72} *vt* DECOMISAR : to confiscate, to seize

confitado, -da *adj* : candied

confite *nm* : comfit, candy

confitería *nf* 1 DULCERÍA : candy store, confectionery 2 : tearoom, café

confitero, -ra *n* : confectioner

confitura *nf* : preserves, jam

conflagración *nf, pl* **-ciones** 1 : conflagration, fire 2 : war

conflictivo, -va *adj* 1 : troubled 2 : controversial

conflicto *nm* : conflict

confluencia *nf* : junction, confluence

confluir {41} *vi* 1 : to converge, to join 2 : to gather, to assemble

conformar *vt* 1 : to form, to create 2 : to constitute, to make up — **conformarse** *vr* 1 RESIGNARSE : to resign oneself 2 : to comply, to conform 3 ~ **con** : to content oneself with, to be satisfied with

conforme[1] *adj* 1 : content, satisfied 2 ~ **a** : in accordance with

conforme[2] *conj* : as ⟨entreguen sus tareas conforme vayan saliendo : hand in your homework as you leave⟩

conformidad *nf* 1 : agreement, consent 2 : resignation

confort *nm* : comfort

confortable *adj* CÓMODO : comfortable

confortar *vt* CONSOLAR : to comfort, to console

confraternidad *nf* : brotherhood, fraternity

confraternización *nf, pl* **-ciones** : fraternization

confraternizar *vi* : to fraternize

confrontación *nf, pl* **-ciones** : confrontation

confrontar *vt* 1 ENCARAR : to confront 2 : to compare 3 : to bring face-to-face — *vi* : to border — **confrontarse** *vr* ~ **con** : to face up to

confundir *vt* : to confuse, to mix up — **confundirse** *vr* : to make a mistake, to be confused ⟨confundirse de número : to get the wrong number⟩

confusión *nf, pl* **-siones** : confusion

confuso, -sa *adj* 1 : confused, mixed-up 2 : obscure, indistinct

congelación *nf, pl* **-ciones** 1 : freezing 2 : frostbite

congelado, -da *adj* HELADO : frozen

congelador *nm* HELADORA : freezer

congelamiento *nm* → **congelación**

congelar *vt* : to freeze — **congelarse** *vr*

congeniar *vi* : to get along (with someone)

congénito, -ta *adj* : congenital

congestión *nf, pl* **-tiones** : congestion

congestionado, -da *adj* : congested

congestionamiento *nm* → **congestión**

congestionarse *vr* 1 : to become flushed 2 : to become congested

conglomerado[1]**, -da** *adj* : conglomerate, mixed

conglomerado[2] *nm* : conglomerate, conglomeration

congoja *nf* ANGUSTIA : anguish, grief

congoleño, -ña *adj & n* : Congolese

congraciarse *vr* : to ingratiate oneself

congratular *vt* FELICITAR : to congratulate

congregación *nf, pl* **-ciones** : congregation, gathering

congregar {52} *vt* : to bring together — **congregarse** *vr* : to congregate, to assemble

congresista *nmf* : congressman *m*, congresswoman *f*

congreso *nm* : congress, conference

congruencia *nf* 1 : congruence 2 COHERENCIA : coherence — **congruente** *adj*

cónico, -ca *adj* : conical, conic

conífera *nf* : conifer

conífero, -ra *adj* : coniferous
conjetura *nf* : conjecture, guess
conjeturar *vt* : to guess, to conjecture
conjugación *nf, pl* **-ciones** : conjugation
conjugar {52} *vt* **1** : to conjugate **2** : to combine
conjunción *nf, pl* **-ciones** : conjunction
conjuntivo, -va *adj* : connective ⟨tejido conjuntivo : connective tissue⟩
conjunto¹, -ta *adj* : joint
conjunto² *nm* **1** : collection, group **2** : ensemble, outfit ⟨conjunto musical : musical ensemble⟩ **3** : whole, entirety ⟨en conjunto : as a whole, altogether⟩
conjurar *vt* **1** : to exorcise **2** : to avert, to ward off — *vi* CONSPIRAR : to conspire, to plot
conjuro *nm* **1** : exorcism **2** : spell
conllevar *vt* **1** : to bear, to suffer **2** IMPLICAR : to entail, to involve
conmemorar *vt* : to commemorate — **conmemoración** *nf*
conmemorativo, -va *adj* : commemorative, memorial
conmigo *pron* : with me ⟨habló conmigo : he talked with me⟩
conminar *vt* AMENAZAR : to threaten, to warn
conmiseración *nf, pl* **-ciones** : pity, commiseration
conmoción *nf, pl* **-ciones** **1** : shock, upheaval **2** *or* **conmoción cerebral** : concussion
conmocionar *vt* : to shake, to shock
conmovedor, -dora *adj* EMOCIONANTE : moving, touching
conmover {47} *vt* **1** EMOCIONAR : to move, to touch **2** : to shake up — **conmoverse** *vr*
conmutador *nm* **1** : switch **2** : switchboard
conmutar *vt* **1** : to commute (a sentence) **2** : to switch, to exchange
connivencia *nf* : connivance
connotación *nf, pl* **-ciones** : connotation
connotar *vt* : to connote, to imply
cono *nm* : cone
conocedor¹, -dora *adj* : knowledgeable
conocedor², -dora *n* : connoisseur, expert
conocer {18} *vt* **1** : to know, to be acquainted with ⟨ya lo conocí : I've already met him⟩ **2** : to meet **3** RECONOCER : to recognize — **conocerse** *vr* **1** : to know each other **2** : to meet **3** : to know oneself
conocido¹, -da *adj* **1** : familiar **2** : well-known, famous
conocido², -da *n* : acquaintance
conocimiento *nm* **1** : knowledge **2** SENTIDO : consciousness
conque *conj* : so, so then, and so ⟨¡ah, conque esas tenemos! : oh, so that's what's going on!⟩
conquista *nf* : conquest
conquistador¹, -dora *adj* : conquering

conquistador², -dora *n* : conqueror
conquistar *vt* : to conquer
consabido, -da *adj* : usual, typical
consagración *nf, pl* **-ciones** : consecration
consagrar *vt* **1** : to consecrate **2** DEDICAR : to dedicate, to devote
consciencia → **conciencia**
consciente *adj* : conscious, aware — **conscientemente** *adv*
conscripción *nf, pl* **-ciones** : conscription, draft
conscripto, -ta *n* : conscript, inductee
consecución *nf, pl* **-ciones** : attainment
consecuencia *nf* **1** : consequence, result ⟨a consecuencia de : as a result of⟩ **2** **en ~** : accordingly
consecuente *adj* : consistent — **consecuentemente** *adv*
consecutivo, -va *adj* : consecutive, successive — **consecutivamente** *adv*
conseguir {75} *vt* **1** : to get, to obtain **2** : to achieve, to attain **3** : to manage to ⟨consiguió acabar el trabajo : she managed to finish the job⟩
consejero, -ra *n* : adviser, counselor
consejo *nm* **1** : advice, counsel **2** : council ⟨consejo de guerra : court-martial⟩
consenso *nm* : consensus
consentido, -da *adj* : spoiled, pampered
consentimiento *nm* : consent, permission
consentir {76} *vt* **1** PERMITIR : to consent to, to allow **2** MIMAR : to pamper, to spoil — *vi* **~ en** : to agree to, to approve of
conserje *nmf* : custodian, janitor, caretaker
conserva *nf* **1** : preserve(s), jam **2 conservas** *nfpl* : canned goods
conservación *nf, pl* **-ciones** : conservation, preservation
conservacionista *nmf* : conservationist
conservador¹, -dora *adj & n* : conservative
conservador² *nm* : preservative
conservadurismo *nf* : conservatism
conservante *nm* : preservative
conservar *vt* **1** : to preserve **2** GUARDAR : to keep, to conserve
conservatorio *nm* : conservatory
considerable *adj* : considerable — **considerablemente** *adv*
consideración *nf, pl* **-ciones** **1** : consideration **2** : respect **3 de ~** : considerable, important
considerado, -da *adj* **1** : considerate, thoughtful **2** : respected
considerar *vt* **1** : to consider, to think over **2** : to judge, to deem **3** : to treat with respect
consigna *nf* **1** ESLOGAN : slogan **2** : assignment, orders *pl* **3** : checkroom
consignación *nf, pl* **-ciones** **1** : consignment **2** ASIGNACIÓN : allocation
consignar *vt* **1** : to consign **2** : to record, to write down **3** : to assign, to allocate

consigo *pron* : with her, with him, with you, with oneself ⟨se llevó las llaves consigo : she took the keys with her⟩

consiguiente *adj* **1** : resulting, consequent **2 por ~** : consequently, as a result

consistencia *nf* : consistency

consistente *adj* **1** : firm, strong, sound **2** : consistent — **consistentemente** *adv*

consistir *vi* **1 ~ en** : to consist of **2 ~ en** : to lie in, to consist in

consola *nf* : console

consolación *nf, pl* **-ciones** : consolation ⟨premio de consolación : consolation prize⟩

consolar {19} *vt* CONFORTAR : to console, to comfort

consolidar *vt* : to consolidate — **consolidación** *nf*

consomé *nm* CALDO : consommé, clear soup

consonancia *nf* **1** : consonance, harmony **2 en consonancia con** : in accordance with

consonante[1] *adj* : consonant, harmonious

consonante[2] *nf* : consonant

consorcio *nm* : consortium

consorte *nmf* : consort, spouse

conspicuo, -cua *adj* : eminent, famous

conspiración *nf, pl* **-ciones** COMPLOT, CONFABULACIÓN : conspiracy, plot

conspirador, -dora *n* : conspirator

conspirar *vi* CONJURAR : to conspire, to plot

constancia *nf* **1** PRUEBA : proof, certainty **2** : record, evidence ⟨que quede constancia : for the record⟩ **3** : perseverance, constancy

constante[1] *adj* : constant — **constantemente** *adv*

constante[2] *nf* : constant

constar *vi* **1** : to be evident, to be on record ⟨que conste : believe me, have no doubt⟩ **2 ~ de** : to consist of

constatación *nf, pl* **-ciones** : confirmation, proof

constatar *vt* **1** : to verify **2** : to state

constelación *nf, pl* **-ciones** : constellation

consternación *nf, pl* **-ciones** : consternation, dismay

consternar *vt* : to dismay, to appall

constipación *nf, pl* **-ciones** : constipation

constipado[1], **-da** *adj* estar constipado : to have a cold

constipado[2] *nm* RESFRIADO : cold

constiparse *vr* : to catch a cold

constitución *nf, pl* **-ciones** : constitution — **constitucional** *adj* — **constitucionalmente** *adv*

constitucionalidad *nf* : constitutionality

constituir {41} *vt* **1** FORMAR : to constitute, to make up, to form **2** FUNDAR : to establish, to set up — **constituirse**

vr **~ en** : to set oneself up as, to become

constitutivo, -va *adj* : constituent, component

constituyente *adj & nmf* : constituent

constreñir {67} *vt* **1** FORZAR, OBLIGAR : to constrain, to oblige **2** LIMITAR : to restrict, to limit

construcción *nf, pl* **-ciones** : construction, building

constructivo, -va *adj* : constructive — **constructivamente** *adv*

constructor, -tora *n* : builder

constructora *nf* : construction company

construir {41} *vt* : to build, to construct

consuelo *nm* : consolation, comfort

consuetudinario, -ria *adj* **1** : customary, habitual **2 derecho consuetudinario** : common law

cónsul *nmf* : consul — **consular** *adj*

consulado *nm* : consulate

consulta *nf* **1** : consultation **2** : inquiry

consultar *vt* : to consult

consultor[1], **-tora** *adj* : consulting ⟨firma consultora : consulting firm⟩

consultor[2], **-tora** *n* : consultant

consultorio *nm* : office (of a doctor or dentist)

consumación *nf, pl* **-ciones** : consummation

consumado, -da *adj* : consummate, perfect

consumar *vt* **1** : to consummate, to complete **2** : to commit, to carry out

consumible *adj* : consumable

consumición *nf, pl* **-ciones** **1** : consumption **2** : drink (in a restaurant)

consumido, -da *adj* : thin, emaciated

consumidor, -dora *n* : consumer

consumir *vt* : to consume — **consumirse** *vr* : to waste away

consumo *nm* : consumption

contabilidad *nf* **1** : accounting, bookkeeping **2** : accountancy

contabilizar {21} *vt* : to enter, to record (in accounting)

contable[1] *adj* : countable

contable[2] *nmf* *Spain* : accountant, bookkeeper

contactar *vt* : to contact — *vi* **~ con** : to get in touch with, to contact

contacto *nm* : contact

contado[1], **-da** *adj* **1** : counted ⟨tenía los días contados : his days were numbered⟩ **2** : rare, scarce ⟨en contadas ocasiones : on rare occasions⟩

contado[2] *nm* al contado : cash ⟨pagar al contado : to pay in cash⟩

contador[1], **-dora** *n* : accountant

contador[2] *nm* : meter ⟨contador de agua : water meter⟩

contaduría *nf* **1** : accounting office **2** CONTABILIDAD : accountancy

contagiar *vt* **1** : to infect **2** : to transmit (a disease) — **contagiarse** *vr* **1** : to be contagious **2** : to become infected

contagio *nm* : contagion, infection

contagioso, -sa *adj* : contagious, catching

contaminación *nf, pl* **-ciones** : contamination, pollution

contaminante *nm* : pollutant, contaminant

contaminar *vt* : to contaminate, to pollute

contar {19} *vt* **1** : to count **2** : to tell **3** : to include — *vi* **1** : to count (up) **2** : to matter, to be of concern ⟨eso no cuenta : that doesn't matter⟩ **3 ~ con** : to rely on, to count on — **contarse** *vr* **~ entre** : to be numbered among

contemplación *nf, pl* **-ciones** : contemplation — **contemplativo, -va** *adj*

contemplar *vt* **1** : to contemplate, to ponder **2** : to gaze at, to look at

contemporáneo, -nea *adj & n* : contemporary

contención *nf, pl* **-ciones** : containment, holding

contencioso, -sa *adj* : contentious

contender {56} *vi* **1** : to contend, to compete **2** : to fight

contendiente *nmf* : contender

contenedor *nm* **1** : container, receptacle **2** : Dumpster™

contener {80} *vt* **1** : to contain, to hold **2** ATAJAR : to restrain, to hold back — **contenerse** *vr* : to restrain oneself

contenido¹, -da *adj* : restrained, reserved

contenido² *nm* : contents *pl*, content

contentar *vt* : to please, to make happy — **contentarse** *vr* : to be satisfied, to be pleased

contento¹, -ta *adj* : contented, glad, happy

contento² *nm* : joy, happiness

contestación *nf, pl* **-ciones 1** : answer, reply **2** : protest

contestar *vt* RESPONDER : to answer — *vi* **1** RESPONDER : to answer, to reply **2** REPLICAR : to answer back

contexto *nm* : context

contienda *nf* **1** : dispute, conflict **2** : contest, competition

contigo *pron* : with you ⟨voy contigo : I'm going with you⟩

contiguo, -gua *adj* COLINDANTE : contiguous, adjacent

continencia *nf* : continence

continente *nm* : continent — **continental** *adj*

contingencia *nf* : contingency, eventuality

contingente *adj & nm* : contingent

continuación *nf, pl* **-ciones 1** : continuation **2 a ~** : next ⟨lo demás sigue a continuación : the rest follows⟩ **3 a continuación de** : after, following

continuar {3} *v* : to continue

continuidad *nf* : continuity

continuo, -nua *adj* : continuous, steady, constant — **continuamente** *adv*

contonearse *vr* : to sway one's hips

contoneo *nm* : swaying, wiggling (of the hips)

contorno *nm* **1** : outline **2 contornos** *nmpl* : outskirts

contorsión *nf, pl* **-siones** : contortion

contra¹ *nf* **1** *fam* : difficulty, snag **2 llevar la contra a** : to oppose, to contradict

contra² *nm* : con ⟨los pros y los contras : the pros and cons⟩

contra³ *prep* : against

contraalmirante *nm* : rear admiral

contraatacar {72} *v* : to counterattack — **contraataque** *nm*

contrabajo *nm* : double bass

contrabalancear *vt* : to counterbalance — **contrabalanza** *nf*

contrabandear *v* : to smuggle

contrabandista *nmf* : smuggler, black marketeer

contrabando *nm* **1** : smuggling **2** : contraband

contracción *nf, pl* **-ciones** : contraction

contracepción *nf, pl* **-ciones** : contraception

contraceptivo *nm* ANTICONCEPTIVO : contraceptive

contrachapado *nm* : plywood

contracorriente *nf* **1** : crosscurrent **2 ir a contracorriente** : to go against the tide

contractual *adj* : contractual

contradecir {11} *vt* DESMENTIR : to contradict — **contradecirse** *vr* DESDECIRSE : to contradict oneself

contradicción *nf, pl* **-ciones** : contradiction

contradictorio, -ria *adj* : contradictory

contraer {81} *vt* **1** : to contract (a disease) **2** : to establish by contract ⟨contraer matrimonio : to get married⟩ **3** : to tighten, to contract — **contraerse** *vr* : to contract, to tighten up

contrafuerte *nm* : buttress

contragolpe *nm* **1** : counterblow **2** : backlash

contrahecho, -cha *adj* : deformed, hunchbacked

contraindicado, -da *adj* : contraindicated — **contraindicación** *nf*

contralor, -lora *n* : comptroller

contralto *nmf* : contralto

contramaestre *nm* **1** : boatswain **2** : foreman

contramandar *vt* : to countermand

contramano *nm* **a ~** : the wrong way (on a street)

contramedida *nf* : countermeasure

contraorden *nf* : countermand

contraparte *nf* **1** : counterpart **2 en ~** : on the other hand

contrapartida *nf* : compensation

contrapelo *nm* **a ~** : in the wrong direction, against the grain

contrapeso *nm* : counterbalance

contraponer {60} *vt* **1** : to counter, to oppose **2** : to contrast, to compare

contraposición *nf, pl* **-ciones** : comparison

contraproducente *adj* : counterproductive

71   contrapunto · cooperador

contrapunto *nm* : counterpoint
contrariar {85} *vt* **1** : to contradict, to oppose **2** : to vex, to annoy
contrariedad *nf* **1** : setback, obstacle **2** : vexation, annoyance
contrario, -ria *adj* **1** : contrary, opposite ⟨al contrario : on the contrary⟩ **2** : conflicting, opposed
contrarrestar *vt* : to counteract
contrarrevolución *nf, pl* **-ciones** : counterrevolution — **contrarrevolucionario, -ria** *adj & n*
contrasentido *nm* : contradiction
contraseña *nf* : password
contrastante *adj* : contrasting
contrastar *vt* **1** : to resist **2** : to check, to confirm — *vi* : to contrast
contraste *nm* : contrast
contratar *vt* **1** : to contract for **2** : to hire, to engage
contratiempo *nm* **1** PERCANCE : mishap, accident **2** DIFICULTAD : setback, difficulty
contratista *nmf* : contractor
contrato *nm* : contract
contravenir {87} *vt* : to contravene, to infringe
contraventana *nf* : shutter
contribución *nf, pl* **-ciones** : contribution
contribuidor, -dora *n* : contributor
contribuir {41} *vt* **1** APORTAR : to contribute **2** : to pay (in taxes) — *vi* **1** : contribute, to help out **2** : to pay taxes
contribuyente[1] *adj* : contributing
contribuyente[2] *nmf* : taxpayer
contrición *nf, pl* **-ciones** : contrition
contrincante *nmf* : rival, opponent
contrito, -ta *adj* : contrite, repentant
control *nm* **1** : control **2** : inspection, check **3** : checkpoint, roadblock
controlador, -dora *n* : controller ⟨controlador aéreo : air traffic controller⟩
controlar *vt* **1** : to control **2** : to monitor, to check
controversia *nf* : controversy
controversial → **controvertido**
controvertido, -da *adj* : controversial
controvertir {76} *vt* : to dispute, to argue about — *vi* : to argue, to debate
contubernio *nm* : conspiracy
contumacia *nf* : obstinacy, stubbornness
contumaz *adj, pl* **-maces** : obstinate, stubbornly disobedient
contundencia *nf* **1** : forcefulness, weight **2** : severity
contundente *adj* **1** : blunt ⟨un objeto contundente : a blunt instrument⟩ **2** : forceful, convincing — **contundentemente** *adv*
contusión *nf, pl* **-siones** : bruise, contusion
contuvo, etc. → **contener**
convalecencia *nf* : convalescence
convalecer {53} *vi* : to convalesce, to recover

convaleciente *adj & nmf* : convalescent
convección *nf, pl* **-ciones** : convection
convencer {86} *vt* : to convince, to persuade — **convencerse** *vr*
convencimiento *nm* : belief, conviction
convención *nf, pl* **-ciones** **1** : convention, conference **2** : pact, agreement **3** : convention, custom
convencional *adj* : conventional — **convencionalmente** *adv*
convencionalismo *nm* : conventionality
conveniencia *nf* **1** : convenience **2** : fitness, suitability, advisability
conveniente *adj* **1** : convenient **2** : suitable, advisable
convenio *nm* PACTO : agreement, pact
convenir {87} *vi* **1** : to be suitable, to be advisable **2** : to agree
convento *nm* **1** : convent **2** : monastery
convergencia *nf* : convergence
convergente *adj* : convergent, converging
converger {15} *vi* **1** : to converge **2** ～ **en** : to concur on
conversación *nf, pl* **-ciones** : conversation
conversador, -dora *n* : conversationalist, talker
conversar *vi* : to converse, to talk
conversión *nf, pl* **-siones** : conversion
converso, -sa *n* : convert
convertible *adj & nm* : convertible
convertidor *nm* : converter
convertir {76} *vt* **1** : to convert **2** : to transform, to change **3** : to exchange (money) — **convertirse** *vr* ～ **en** : to turn into
convexo, -xa *adj* : convex
convicción *nf, pl* **-ciones** : conviction
convicto[1], **-ta** *adj* : convicted
convicto[2], **-ta** *n* : convict, prisoner
convidado, -da *n* : guest
convidar *vt* **1** INVITAR : to invite **2** : to offer
convincente *adj* : convincing — **convincentemente** *adv*
convivencia *nf* **1** : coexistence **2** : cohabitation
convivir *vi* **1** : to coexist **2** : to live together
convocación *nf, pl* **-ciones** : convocation
convocar {72} *vt* : to convoke, to call together
convocatoria *nf* : summons, call
convoy *nm* : convoy
convulsión *nf, pl* **-siones** **1** : convulsion **2** : agitation, upheaval
convulsionar *vt* : to shake, to convulse — **convulsionarse** *vr*
convulsivo, -va *adj* : convulsive
conyugal *adj* : conjugal
cónyuge *nmf* : spouse, partner
coñac *nm* : cognac, brandy
cooperación *nf, pl* **-ciones** : cooperation
cooperador, -dora *adj* : cooperative

cooperar *vi* : to cooperate
cooperativa *nf* : cooperative, co-op
cooperativo, -va *adj* : cooperative
cooptar *vt* : to co-opt
coordenada *nf* : coordinate
coordinación *nf, pl* **-ciones** : coordination
coordinador, -dora *n* : coordinator
coordinar *vt* COMPAGINAR : to coordinate, to combine
copa *nf* **1** : wineglass, goblet **2** : drink ⟨irse de copas : to go out drinking⟩ **3** : cup, trophy
copar *vt* **1** : to take ⟨ya está copado el puesto : the job is already taken⟩ **2** : to fill, to crowd
copartícipe *nmf* : joint partner
copete *nm* **1** : tuft (of hair) **2 estar hasta el copete** : to be completely fed up
copia *nf* **1** : copy **2** : imitation, replica
copiadora *nf* : photocopier
copiar *vt* : to copy
copiloto *nmf* : copilot
copioso, -sa *adj* : copious, abundant
copla *nf* **1** : popular song or ballad **2** : couplet, stanza
copo *nm* **1** : snowflake **2 copos de avena** : rolled oats **3 copos de maíz** : cornflakes
copra *nf* : copra
cópula *nf* : copulation
copular *vi* : to copulate
coque *nm* : coke (fuel)
coqueta *nf* : dressing table
coquetear *vi* : to flirt
coqueteo *nm* : flirting, coquetry
coqueto¹, -ta *adj* : flirtatious, coquettish
coqueto², -ta *n* : flirt
coraje *nm* **1** VALOR : valor, courage **2** IRA : anger ⟨darle coraje a alguien : to make someone angry⟩
corajudo, -da *adj* : brave
coral¹ *nm* **1** : coral **2** : chorale
coral² *nf* : choir
Corán *nm* **el Corán** : the Koran
coraza *nf* **1** : armor, armor plating **2** : shell (of an animal)
corazón *nm, pl* **-zones 1** : heart ⟨de todo corazón : wholeheartedly⟩ ⟨de buen corazón : kindhearted⟩ **2** : core **3** : darling, sweetheart
corazonada *nf* : hunch, impulse
corbata *nf* : tie, necktie
corcel *nm* : steed, charger
corchete *nm* **1** : hook and eye, clasp **2** : square bracket
corcho *nm* : cork
corcholata *nf Mex* : cap, bottle top
corcovear *vi* : to buck
cordel *nm* : cord, string
cordero *nm* : lamb
cordial¹ *adj* : cordial, affable — **cordialmente** *adv*
cordial² *nm* : cordial (liqueur)
cordialidad *nf* : cordiality, warmth
cordillera *nf* : mountain range
córdoba *nf* : Nicaraguan unit of currency

cordón *nm, pl* **cordones 1** : cord ⟨cordón umbilical : umbilical cord⟩ **2** : cordon
cordura *nf* **1** : sanity **2** : prudence, good judgment
coreano¹, -na *adj & n* : Korean
coreano² *nm* : Korean (language)
corear *vt* : to chant, to chorus
coreografía *nf* : choreography
coreografiar {85} *vt* : to choreograph
coreográfico, -ca *adj* : choreographic
coreógrafo, -fa *n* : choreographer
corista *nmf* **1** : chorister **2** : chorus girl *f*
cormorán *nm, pl* **-ranes** : cormorant
cornada *nf* : goring, butt (with the horns)
córnea *nf* : cornea
cornear *vt* : to gore
cornejo *nm* : dogwood (tree)
corneta *nf* : bugle, horn, cornet
cornisa *nf* : cornice
cornudo, -da *adj* : horned
coro *nm* **1** : choir **2** : chorus
corola *nf* : corolla
corolario *nm* : corollary
corona *nf* **1** : crown **2** : wreath, garland **3** : corona (in astronomy)
coronación *nf, pl* **-ciones** : coronation
coronar *vt* **1** : to crown **2** : to reach the top of, to culminate
coronario, -ria *adj* : coronary
coronel, -nela *n* : colonel
coronilla *nf* **1** : crown (of the head) **2 estar hasta la coronilla** : to be completely fed up
corpiño *nm* **1** : bodice **2** *Arg* : brassiere, bra
corporación *nf, pl* **-ciones** : corporation
corporal *adj* : corporal, bodily
corporativo, -va *adj* : corporate
corpóreo, -rea *adj* : corporeal, physical
corpulencia *nf* : corpulence, stoutness, sturdiness
corpulento, -ta *adj* ROBUSTO : robust, stout, sturdy
corpúsculo *nm* : corpuscle
corral *nm* **1** : farmyard **2** : corral, pen, stockyard **3** *or* **corralito** : playpen
correa *nf* : strap, belt
correcaminos *nms & pl* : roadrunner
corrección *nf, pl* **-ciones 1** : correction **2** : correctness, propriety **3** : rebuke, reprimand **4 corrección de pruebas** : proofreading
correccional *nm* REFORMATORIO : reformatory
correctivo, -va *adj* : corrective ⟨lentes correctivos : corrective lenses⟩
correcto, -ta *adj* **1** : correct, right **2** : courteous, polite — **correctamente** *adv*
corrector, -tora *n* : proofreader
corredizo, -za *adj* : sliding ⟨puerta corrediza : sliding door⟩
corredor¹, -dora *n* **1** : runner, racer **2** : agent, broker ⟨corredor de bolsa : stockbroker⟩
corredor² *nm* PASILLO : corridor, hallway

correduría *nf* → **corretaje**

corregir {28} *vt* **1** ENMENDAR : to correct, to emend **2** : to reprimand **3 corregir pruebas** : to proofread — **corregirse** *vr* : to reform, to mend one's ways

correlación *nf, pl* **-ciones** : correlation

correo *nm* **1** : mail ⟨correo aéreo : airmail⟩ **2** : post office

correoso, -sa *adj* : leathery, rough

correr *vi* **1** : to run, to race **2** : to rush **3** : to flow — *vt* **1** : to travel over, to cover **2** : to move, to slide, to roll, to draw (curtains) **3 correr un riesgo** : to run a risk — **correrse** *vr* **1** : to move along **2** : to run, to spill over

correspondencia *nf* **1** : correspondence, mail **2** : equivalence **3** : connection, interchange

corresponder *vi* **1** : to correspond **2** : to pertain, to belong **3** : to be appropriate, to fit **4** : to reciprocate — **corresponderse** *vr* : to write to each other

correspondiente *adj* : corresponding, respective

corresponsal *nmf* : correspondent

corretaje *nm* : brokerage

corretear *vi* **1** VAGAR : to loiter, to wander about **2** : to run around, to scamper about — *vt* : to pursue, to chase

corrida *nf* **1** : run, dash **2** : bullfight

corrido¹, -da *adj* **1** : straight, continuous **2** : worldly, experienced

corrido² *nm* : Mexican narrative folk song

corriente¹ *adj* **1** : common, everyday **2** : current, present **3** *Mex* : cheap, trashy **4 perro corriente** *Mex* : mutt

corriente² *nf* **1** : current ⟨corriente alterna : alternating current⟩ ⟨direct current : corriente continua⟩ **2** : draft **3** TENDENCIA : tendency, trend

corrillo *nm* : small group, clique

corro *nm* : ring, circle (of people)

corroboración *nf, pl* **-ciones** : corroboration

corroborar *vt* : to corroborate

corroer {69} *vt* **1** : to corrode **2** : to erode, to wear away

corromper *vt* **1** : to corrupt **2** : to rot — **corromperse** *vr*

corrompido, -da *adj* CORRUPTO : corrupt, rotten

corrosión *nf, pl* **-siones** : corrosion

corrosivo, -va *adj* : corrosive

corrugar {52} *vt* : to corrugate — **corrugación** *nf*

corrupción *nf, pl* **-ciones** **1** : decay **2** : corruption

corruptela *nf* : corruption, abuse of power

corrupto, -ta *adj* CORROMPIDO : corrupt

corsario *nm* : privateer

corsé *nm* : corset

cortada *nf* : cut, gash

cortador, -dora *n* : cutter

cortadora *nf* : cutter, slicer

cortadura *nf* : cut, slash

cortafuegos *nms & pl* **1** : firebreak **2** : firewall (program)

cortante *adj* : cutting, sharp

cortar *vt* **1** : to cut, to slice, to trim **2** : to cut out, to omit **3** : to cut off, to interrupt **4** : to block, to close off **5** : to curdle (milk) — *vi* **1** : to cut **2** : to break up **3** : to hang up (the telephone) — **cortarse** *vr* **1** : to cut oneself ⟨cortarse el pelo : to cut one's hair⟩ **2** : to be cut off **3** : to sour (of milk)

cortauñas *nms & pl* : nail clippers

corte¹ *nm* **1** : cut, cutting ⟨corte de pelo : haircut⟩ **2** : style, fit

corte² *nf* **1** : court ⟨corte suprema : supreme court⟩ **2 hacer la corte a** : to court, to woo

cortejar *vt* GALANTEAR : to court, to woo

cortejo *nm* **1** GALANTEO : courtship **2** : retinue, entourage

cortés *adj* : courteous, polite — **cortésmente** *adv*

cortesano¹, -na *adj* : courtly

cortesano², -na *n* : courtier

cortesía *nf* **1** : courtesy, politeness **2 de ~** : complimentary, free

corteza *nf* **1** : bark **2** : crust **3** : peel, rind **4** : cortex ⟨corteza cerebral : cerebral cortex⟩

cortijo *nm* : farmhouse

cortina *nf* : curtain

cortisona *nf* : cortisone

corto, -ta *adj* **1** : short (in length or duration) **2** : scarce **3** : timid, shy **4 corto de vista** : nearsighted

cortocircuito *nm* : short circuit

corvejón *nm, pl* **-jones** JARRETE : hock

corvo, -va *adj* : curved, bent

cosa *nf* **1** : thing, object **2** : matter, affair **3 otra cosa** : anything else, something else

cosecha *nf* : harvest, crop

cosechador, -dora *n* : harvester, reaper

cosechadora *nf* : harvester (machine)

cosechar *vt* **1** : to harvest, to reap **2** : to win, to earn, to garner — *vi* : to harvest

coser *vt* **1** : to sew **2** : to stitch up — *vi* : to sew

cosmético¹, -ca *adj* : cosmetic

cosmético² *nm* : cosmetic

cósmico, -ca *adj* : cosmic

cosmonauta *nmf* : cosmonaut

cosmopolita *adj & nmf* : cosmopolitan

cosmos *nm* : cosmos

cosquillas *nfpl* **1** : tickling **2 hacer cosquillas** : to tickle

cosquilleo *nm* : tickling sensation, tingle

cosquilloso, -sa *adj* : ticklish

costa *nf* **1** : coast, shore **2** : cost ⟨a toda costa : at all costs⟩

costado *nm* **1** : side **2 al costado** : alongside

costar {19} *v* : to cost ⟨¿cuánto cuesta? : how much does it cost?⟩

costarricense *adj & nmf* : Costa Rican

costarriqueño, -ña → **costarricense**

coste → **costo**

costear *vt* : to pay for, to finance

costero, -ra *adj* : coastal, coast
costilla *nf* **1** : rib **2** : chop, cutlet **3** *fam* : better half, wife
costo *nm* **1** : cost, price **2 costo de vida** : cost of living
costoso, -sa *adj* : costly, expensive
costra *nf* **1** : crust **2** POSTILLA : scab
costumbre *nf* **1** : custom **2** HÁBITO : habit
costura *nf* **1** : seam **2** : sewing, dressmaking **3 alta costura** : haute couture
costurera *nf* : seamstress *f*
cotejar *vt* : to compare, to collate
cotejo *nm* : comparison, collation
cotidiano, -na *adj* : daily, everyday ⟨la vida cotidiana : daily life⟩
cotización *nf, pl* **-ciones 1** : market price **2** : quote, estimate
cotizado, -da *adj* : in demand, sought after
cotizar {21} *vt* : to quote, to value — **cotizarse** *vr* : to be worth
coto *nm* **1** : enclosure, reserve **2 poner coto a** : to put a stop to
cotorra *nf* **1** : small parrot **2** *fam* : chatterbox, windbag
cotorrear *vi fam* : to chatter, to gab, to blab
cotorreo *nm fam* : chatter, prattle
coyote *nm* **1** : coyote **2** *Mex fam* : smuggler (of illegal immigrants)
coyuntura *nf* **1** ARTICULACIÓN : joint **2** : occasion, moment
coz *nf, pl* **coces** : kick (of an animal)
crac *nm, pl* **cracs** : crash (of the stock market)
cozamos, etc. → **cocer**
craneal *adj* : cranial
cráneo *nf* : cranium, skull — **craneano, -na** *adj*
cráter *nm* : crater
crayón *nm, pl* **-yones** : crayon
creación *nf, pl* **-ciones** : creation
creador¹, -dora *adj* : creative, creating
creador², -dora *n* : creator
crear *vt* **1** : to create, to cause **2** : to originate
creatividad *nf* : creativity
creativo, -va *adj* : creative
crecer {53} *vi* **1** : to grow **2** : to increase
crecida *nf* : flooding, floodwater
crecido, -da *adj* **1** : grown, grown-up **2** : large (of numbers)
creciente *adj* **1** : growing, increasing **2 luna creciente** : waxing moon
crecientemente *adv* : increasingly
crecimiento *nm* **1** : growth **2** : increase
credencial *adj* **cartas credenciales** : credentials
credenciales *nfpl* : documents, documentation, credentials
credibilidad *nf* : credibility
crédito *nm* : credit
credo *nm* : creed, credo
credulidad *nf* : credulity
crédulo, -la *adj* : credulous, gullible
creencia *nf* : belief
creer {20} *v* **1** : to believe **2** : to suppose, to think ⟨creo que sí : I think so⟩

— **creerse** *vr* **1** : to believe, to think **2** : to regard oneself as ⟨se cree guapísimo : he thinks he's so handsome⟩
creíble *adj* : believable, credible
creído, -da *adj* **1** *fam* : conceited **2** : confident, sure
crema *nf* **1** : cream **2 la crema y nata** : the pick of the crop
cremación *nf, pl* **-ciones** : cremation
cremallera *nf* : zipper
cremar *vt* : to cremate
cremoso, -sa *adj* : creamy
crepa *nf Mex* : crepe (pancake)
crepe *or* **crep** *nmf* : crepe (pancake)
crepé *nm* **1** → **crespón 2 papel crepé** : crepe paper
crepitar *vi* : to crackle
crepúsculo *nm* : twilight
crescendo *nm* : crescendo
crespo, -pa *adj* : curly, frizzy
crespón *nm, pl* **crespones** : crepe (fabric)
cresta *nf* **1** : crest **2** : comb (of a rooster)
creta *nf* : chalk (mineral)
cretino, -na *n* : cretin
creyente *nmf* : believer
creyó, etc. → **creer**
crezca, etc. → **crecer**
cría *nf* **1** : breeding, rearing **2** : young **3** : litter
criadero *nm* : hatchery
criado¹, -da *adj* **1** : raised, brought up **2 bien criado** : well-bred
criado², -da *n* : servant, maid *f*
criador, -dora *n* : breeder
crianza *nf* : upbringing, rearing
criar {85} *vt* **1** : to breed **2** : to bring up, to raise
criatura *nf* **1** : baby, child **2** : creature
criba *nf* : sieve, screen
cribar *vt* : to sift
cric *nm, pl* **crics** : jack
crimen *nm, pl* **crímenes** : crime
criminal *adj & nmf* : criminal
crin *nf* **1** : mane **2** : horsehair
criollo¹, -lla *adj* **1** : Creole **2** : native, national ⟨comida criolla : native cuisine⟩
criollo², -lla *n* : Creole
criollo³ *nm* : Creole (language)
cripta *nf* : crypt
críptico, -ca *adj* **1** : cryptic, coded **2** : enigmatic, cryptic
criptón *nm* : krypton
críquet *nm* : cricket (game)
crisálida *nf* : chrysalis, pupa
crisantemo *nm* : chrysanthemum
crisis *nf* **1** : crisis **2 crisis nerviosa** : nervous breakdown
crisma *nf fam* : head ⟨romperle la crisma a alguien : to knock someone's block off⟩
crisol *nm* **1** : crucible **2** : melting pot
crispar *vt* **1** : to cause to contract **2** : to irritate, to set on edge ⟨eso me crispa : that gets on my nerves⟩ — **crisparse** *vr* : to tense up

cristal *nm* **1** VIDRIO : glass, piece of glass **2** : crystal

cristalería *nf* **1** : glassware shop ⟨como chivo en cristalería : like a bull in a china shop⟩ **2** : glassware, crystal

cristalino¹, -na *adj* : crystalline, clear

cristalino² *nm* : lens (of the eye)

cristalizar {21} *vi* : to crystallize — **cristalización** *nf*

cristiandad *nf* : Christendom

cristianismo *nm* : Christianity

cristiano, -na *adj & n* : Christian

Cristo *nm* : Christ

criterio *nm* **1** : criterion **2** : judgment, sense

crítica *nf* **1** : criticism **2** : review, critique

criticar {72} *vt* : to criticize

crítico¹, -ca *adj* : critical — **críticamente** *adv*

crítico², -ca *n* : critic

criticón¹, -cona *adj, mpl* **-cones** *fam* : hypercritical, captious

criticón², -cona *n, mpl* **-cones** *fam* : faultfinder, critic

croar *vi* : to croak

croata *adj & nmf* : Croatian

crocante *adj* : crunchy

croché *or* **crochet** *nm* : crochet

cromático, -ca *adj* : chromatic

cromo *nm* **1** : chromium, chrome **2** : picture card, sports card

cromosoma *nm* : chromosome

crónica *nf* **1** : news report **2** : chronicle, history

crónico, -ca *adj* : chronic

cronista *nmf* **1** : reporter, newscaster **2** HISTORIADOR : chronicler, historian

cronología *nf* : chronology

cronológico, -ca *adj* : chronological — **cronológicamente** *adv*

cronometrador, -dora *n* : timekeeper

cronometrar *vt* : to time, to clock

cronómetro *nm* : chronometer

croquet *nm* : croquet

croqueta *nf* : croquette

croquis *nm* : rough sketch

cruce¹, etc. → **cruzar**

cruce² *nm* **1** : crossing, cross **2** : crossroads, intersection ⟨cruce peatonal : crosswalk⟩

crucero *nm* **1** : cruise **2** : cruiser, warship **3** *Mex* : intersection

crucial *adj* : crucial — **crucialmente** *adv*

crucificar {72} *vt* : to crucify

crucifijo *nm* : crucifix

crucifixión *nf, pl* **-fixiones** : crucifixion

crucigrama *nm* : crossword puzzle

crudo¹, -da *adj* **1** : raw **2** : crude, harsh

crudo² *nm* : crude oil

cruel *adj* : cruel — **cruelmente** *adv*

crueldad *nf* : cruelty

cruento, -ta *adj* : bloody

crujido *nm* **1** : rustling **2** : creaking **3** : crackling (of a fire) **4** : crunching

crujiente *adj* : crunchy, crisp

crujir *vi* **1** : to rustle **2** : to creak, to crack **3** : to crunch

crup *nm* : croup

crustáceo *nm* : crustacean

crutón *nm, pl* **crutones** : crouton

cruz *nf, pl* **cruces** : cross

cruza *nf* : cross (hybrid)

cruzada *nf* : crusade

cruzado¹, -da *adj* : crossed ⟨espadas cruzadas : crossed swords⟩

cruzado² *nm* **1** : crusader **2** : Brazilian unit of currency

cruzar {21} *vt* **1** : to cross **2** : to exchange (words, greetings) **3** : to cross, to interbreed — **cruzarse** *vr* **1** : to intersect **2** : to meet, to pass each other

cuaderno *nm* LIBRETA : notebook

cuadra *nf* **1** : city block **2** : stable

cuadrado¹, -da *adj* : square

cuadrado² *nm* : square ⟨elevar al cuadrado : to square (a number)⟩

cuadragésimo¹ *adj* : fortieth, forty-

cuadragésimo², -ma *n* : fortieth, forty- (in a series)

cuadrante *nm* **1** : quadrant **2** : dial

cuadrar *vi* : to conform, to agree — *vt* : to square — **cuadrarse** *vr* : to stand at attention

cuadriculado *nm* : grid (on a map, etc.)

cuadrilátero *nm* **1** : quadrilateral **2** : ring (in sports)

cuadrilla *nf* : gang, team, group

cuadro *nm* **1** : square ⟨una blusa a cuadros : a checkered blouse⟩ **2** : painting, picture **3** : baseball diamond, infield **4** : panel, board, cadre

cuadrúpedo *nm* : quadruped

cuádruple *adj* : quadruple

cuadruplicar {72} *vt* : to quadruple — **cuadruplicarse** *vr*

cuajada *nf* : curd

cuajar *vi* **1** : to curdle **2** COAGULAR : to clot, to coagulate **3** : to set, to jell **4** : to be accepted ⟨su idea no cuajó : his idea didn't catch on⟩ — *vt* **1** : to curdle **2** ~ **de** : to fill with

cual¹ *prep* : like, as

cual² *pron* **1 el cual, la cual, los cuales, las cuales** : who, whom, which ⟨la razón por la cual lo dije : the reason I said it⟩ **2 lo cual** : which ⟨se rió, lo cual me dio rabia : he laughed, which made me mad⟩ **3 cada cual** : everyone, everybody

cuál¹ *adj* : which, what ⟨¿cuáles libros? : which books?⟩

cuál² *pron* **1** (*in questions*) : which (one), what (one) ⟨¿cuál es el mejor? : which one is the best?⟩ ⟨¿cuál es tu apellido? : what is your last name?⟩ **2 cuál más, cuál menos** : some more, some less

cualidad *nf* : quality, trait

cualitativo, -va *adj* : qualitative — **cualitativamente** *adv*

cualquier *adj* → **cualquiera¹**

cualquiera¹ (**cualquier** *before nouns*) *adj, pl* **cualesquiera 1** : any, whichever ⟨cualquier persona : any person⟩ **2** : everyday, ordinary ⟨un hombre cualquiera : an ordinary man⟩

cualquiera[2] *pron, pl* **cualesquiera** **1** : anyone, anybody, whoever **2** : whatever, whichever

cuán *adv* : how ⟨¡cuán risible fue todo eso! : how funny it all was!⟩

cuando[1] *conj* **1** : when ⟨cuando llegó : when he arrived⟩ **2** : since, if ⟨cuando lo dices : if you say so⟩ **3 cuando más** : at the most **4 de vez en cuando** : from time to time

cuando[2] *prep* : during, at the time of ⟨cuando la guerra : during the war⟩

cuándo *adv & conj* **1** : when ⟨¿cuándo llegará? : when will she arrive?⟩ ⟨no sabemos cuándo será : we don't know when it will be⟩ **2 ¿de cuándo acá?** : since when?, how come?

cuantía *nf* **1** : quantity, extent **2** : significance, import

cuántico, -ca *adj* : quantum ⟨teoría cuántica : quantum theory⟩

cuantioso, -sa *adj* **1** : abundant, considerable **2** : heavy, grave ⟨cuantiosos daños : heavy damage⟩

cuantitativo, -va *adj* : quantitative — **cuantitativamente** *adv*

cuanto[1] *adv* **1** : as much as ⟨come cuanto puedas : eat as much as you can⟩ **2 cuanto antes** : as soon as possible **3 en ~** : as soon as **4 en cuanto a** : as for, as regards

cuanto[2], **-ta** *adj* : as many, whatever ⟨llévate cuantas flores quieras : take as many flowers as you wish⟩

cuanto[3], **-ta** *pron* **1** : as much as, all that, everything ⟨tengo cuanto deseo : I have all that I want⟩ **2 unos cuantos, unas cuantas** : a few

cuánto[1] *adv* : how much, how many ⟨¿a cuánto están las manzanas? : how much are the apples?⟩ ⟨no sé cuánto desean : I don't know how much they want⟩

cuánto[2], **-ta** *adj* : how much, how many ⟨¿cuántos niños tiene? : how many children do you have?⟩

cuánto[3] *pron* : how much, how many ⟨¿cuántos quieren participar? : how many want to take part?⟩ ⟨¿cuánto cuesta? : how much does it cost?⟩

cuarenta *adj & nm* : forty

cuarentavo[1], **-va** *adj* : fortieth

cuarentavo[2] *nm* : fortieth (fraction)

cuarentena *nf* **1** : group of forty **2** : quarantine

Cuaresma *nf* : Lent

cuartear *vt* **1** : to quarter **2** : to divide up — **cuartearse** *vr* AGRIETARSE : to crack, to split

cuartel *nm* **1** : barracks, headquarters **2** : mercy ⟨una guerra sin cuartel : a merciless war⟩

cuartelazo *nm* : coup d'état

cuarteto *nm* : quartet

cuartilla *nf* : sheet (of paper)

cuarto[1], **-ta** *adj* : fourth

cuarto[2], **-ta** *n* : fourth (in a series)

cuarto[3] *nm* **1** : quarter, fourth ⟨cuarto de galón : quart⟩ **2** HABITACIÓN : room

cuarzo *nm* : quartz

cuate, -ta *n Mex* **1** : twin **2** *fam* : buddy, pal

cuatrero, -ra *n* : rustler

cuatrillizo, -za *n* : quadruplet

cuatro *adj & nm* : four

cuatrocientos[1], **-tas** *adj* : four hundred

cuatrocientos[2] *nms & pl* : four hundred

cuba *nf* BARRIL : cask, barrel

cubano, -na *adj & n* : Cuban

cubertería *nf* : flatware, silverware

cubeta *nf* **1** : keg, cask **2** : bulb (of a thermometer) **3** *Mex* : bucket, pail

cúbico, -ca *adj* : cubic, cubed

cubículo *nm* : cubicle

cubierta *nf* **1** : covering **2** FORRO : cover, jacket (of a book) **3** : deck

cubierto[1] *pp* → **cubrir**

cubierto[2] *nm* **1** : cover, shelter ⟨bajo cubierto : under cover⟩ **2** : table setting **3** : utensil, piece of silverware

cubil *nm* : den, lair

cúbito *nm* : ulna

cubo *nm* **1** : cube **2** BALDE : pail, bucket, can ⟨cubo de basura : garbage can⟩ **3** : hub (of a wheel)

cubrecama *nm* COLCHA : bedspread

cubrir {2} *vt* : to cover — **cubrirse** *vr*

cucaracha *nf* : cockroach, roach

cuchara *nf* : spoon

cucharada *nf* : spoonful

cucharilla *or* **cucharita** *nf* : teaspoon

cucharón *nm, pl* **-rones** : ladle

cuchichear *vi* : to whisper

cuchicheo *nm* : whisper

cuchilla *nf* **1** : kitchen knife, cleaver **2** : blade ⟨cuchilla de afeitar : razor blade⟩ **3** : crest, ridge

cuchillada *nf* : stab, knife wound

cuchillo *nm* : knife

cuclillas *nfpl* **en ~** : squatting, crouching

cuco[1], **-ca** *adj fam* : pretty, cute

cuco[2] *nm* : cuckoo

cucurucho *nm* : ice-cream cone

cuece, cueza etc. → **cocer**

cuela, etc. → **colar**

cuelga, cuelgue etc. → **colgar**

cuello *nm* **1** : neck **2** : collar (of a shirt) **3 cuello del útero** : cervix

cuenca *nf* **1** : river basin **2** : eye socket

cuenco *nm* : bowl, basin

cuenta[1], **etc.** → **contar**

cuenta[2] *nf* **1** : calculation, count **2** : account **3** : check, bill **4 darse cuenta** : to realize **5 tener en cuenta** : to bear in mind

cuentagotas *nfs & pl* **1** : dropper **2 con ~** : little by little

cuentista *nmf* **1** : short story writer **2** *fam* : liar, fibber

cuento *nm* **1** : story, tale **2 cuento de hadas** : fairy tale **3 sin ~** : countless

cuerda *nf* **1** : cord, rope, string **2 cuerdas vocales** : vocal cords **3 darle cuerda a** : to wind up (a clock, a toy, etc.)

cuerdo, -da *adj* : sane, sensible
cuerno *nm* 1 : horn, antler 2 : cusp (of the moon) 3 : horn (musical instrument)
cuero *nm* 1 : leather, hide 2 **cuero cabelludo** : scalp
cuerpo *nm* 1 : body 2 : corps
cuervo *nm* : crow, raven
cuesta¹, etc. → **costar**
cuesta² *nf* 1 : slope ⟨cuesta arriba : uphill⟩ 2 **a cuestas** : on one's back
cuestión *nf, pl* **-tiones** ASUNTO, TEMA : matter, affair
cuestionable *adj* : questionable, dubious
cuestionar *vt* : to question
cuestionario *nm* 1 : questionnaire 2 : quiz
cueva *nf* : cave
cuidado *nm* 1 : care 2 : worry, concern 3 **tener cuidado** : to be careful 4 **¡cuidado!** : watch out!, be careful!
cuidador, -dora *n* : caretaker
cuidadoso, -sa *adj* : careful, attentive — **cuidadosamente** *adv*
cuidar *vt* 1 : to take care of, to look after 2 : to pay attention to — *vi* 1 ∼ **de** : to look after 2 **cuidar de que** : to make sure that — **cuidarse** *vr* : to take care of oneself
culata *nf* : butt (of a gun)
culatazo *nf* : kick, recoil
culebra *nf* SERPIENTE : snake
culi *nmf* : coolie
culinario, -ria *adj* : culinary
culminante *adj* **punto culminante** : peak, high point, climax
culminar *vi* : to culminate — **culminación** *nf*
culo *nm* 1 *fam* : backside, behind 2 : bottom (of a glass)
culpa *nf* 1 : fault, blame ⟨echarle la culpa a alguien : to blame someone⟩ 2 : sin
culpabilidad *nf* : guilt
culpable¹ *adj* : guilty
culpable² *nmf* : culprit, guilty party
culpar *vt* : to blame
cultivado, -da *adj* 1 : cultivated, farmed 2 : cultured
cultivador, -dora *n* : cultivator
cultivar *vt* 1 : to cultivate 2 : to foster
cultivo *nm* 1 : cultivation, farming 2 : crop
culto¹, -ta *adj* : cultured, educated
culto² *nm* 1 : worship 2 : cult
cultura *nf* : culture
cultural *adj* : cultural — **culturalmente** *adv*
cumbre *nf* CIMA : top, peak, summit
cumpleaños *nms & pl* : birthday
cumplido¹, -da *adj* 1 : complete, full 2 : courteous, correct
cumplido² *nm* : compliment, courtesy ⟨por cumplido : out of courtesy⟩ ⟨andarse con cumplidos : to stand on ceremony, to be formal⟩
cumplimentar *vt* 1 : to congratulate 2 : to carry out, to perform

cumplimiento *nm* 1 : completion, fulfillment 2 : performance
cumplir *vt* 1 : to accomplish, to carry out 2 : to comply with, to fulfill 3 : to attain, to reach ⟨su hermana cumple los 21 el viernes : her sister will be 21 on Friday⟩ — *vi* 1 : to expire, to fall due 2 : to fulfill one's obligations ⟨cumplir con el deber : to do one's duty⟩ ⟨cumplir con la palabra : to keep one's word⟩ — **cumplirse** *vr* 1 : to come true, to be fulfilled ⟨se cumplieron sus sueños : her dreams came true⟩ 2 : to run out, to expire
cúmulo *nm* 1 MONTÓN : heap, pile 2 : cumulus
cuna *nf* 1 : cradle 2 : birthplace ⟨Puerto Rico es la cuna de la música salsa : Puerto Rico is the birthplace of salsa music⟩
cundir *vi* 1 : to propagate, to spread ⟨cundió el pánico en el vecindario : panic spread throughout the neighborhood⟩ 2 : to progress, to make headway
cuneta *nf* : ditch (in a road), gutter
cuña *nf* : wedge
cuñado, -da *n* : brother-in-law *m*, sister-in-law *f*
cuño *nm* : die (for stamping)
cuota *nf* 1 : fee, dues 2 : quota, share 3 : installment, payment
cupé *nm* : coupe
cupo¹, etc. → **caber**
cupo² *nm* 1 : quota, share 2 : capacity, room
cupón *nm, pl* **cupones** 1 : coupon, voucher 2 **cupón federal** : food stamp
cúpula *nf* : dome, cupola
cura¹ *nm* : priest
cura² *nf* 1 CURACIÓN, TRATAMIENTO : cure, treatment 2 : dressing, bandage
curación *nf, pl* **-ciones** CURA, TRATAMIENTO : cure, treatment
curandero, -ra *nm* 1 : witch doctor 2 : quack, charlatan
curar *vt* 1 : to cure, to heal 2 : to treat, to dress 3 CURTIR : to tan 4 : to cure (meat) — *vi* : to get well, to recover — **curarse** *vr*
curativo, -va *adj* : curative, healing
curiosear *vi* 1 : to snoop, to pry 2 : to browse — *vt* : to look over, to check
curiosidad *nf* 1 : curiosity 2 : curio
curioso, -sa *adj* 1 : curious, inquisitive 2 : strange, unusual, odd — **curiosamente** *adv*
currículo → **currículum**
currículum *nm, pl* **-lums** 1 : résumé, curriculum vitae 2 : curriculum, course of study
curry ['kurri] *nm, pl* **-rries** 1 : curry powder 2 : curry (dish)
cursar *vt* 1 : to attend (school), to take (a course) 2 : to dispatch, to pass on
cursi *adj fam* : affected, pretentious
cursilería *nf* 1 : vulgarity, poor taste 2 : pretentiousness

cursiva *nf* BASTARDILLA : italic type, italics *pl*
curso *nm* **1** : course, direction **2** : school year **3** : course, subject (in school)
cursor *nm* : cursor
curtido, -da *adj* : weather-beaten, leathery (of skin)
curtidor, -dora *n* : tanner
curtiduría *nf* : tannery
curtir *vt* **1** : to tan **2** : to harden, to weather — **curtirse** *vr*
curva *nf* : curve, bend
curvar *vt* : to bend

curvatura *nf* : curvature
curvilíneo, -nea *adj* : curvaceous, shapely
curvo, -va *adj* : curved, bent
cúspide *nf* : zenith, apex, peak
custodia *nf* : custody
custodiar *vt* : to guard, to look after
custodio, -dia *n* : keeper, guardian
cúter *nm* : cutter (boat)
cutícula *nf* : cuticle
cutis *nms & pl* : skin, complexion
cuyo, -ya *adj* **1** : whose, of whom, of which **2 en cuyo caso** : in which case

D

d *nf* : fourth letter of the Spanish alphabet
dable *adj* : feasible, possible
dactilar *adj* **huellas dactilares** : fingerprints
dádiva *nf* : gift, handout
dadivoso, -sa *adj* : generous
dado, -da *adj* **1** : given **2 dado que** : given that, since
dador, -dora *n* : giver, donor
dados *nmpl* : dice
daga *nf* : dagger
dalia *nf* : dahlia
dálmata *nm* : dalmatian
daltónico, -ca *adj* : color-blind
daltonismo *nm* : color blindness
dama *nf* **1** : lady **2 damas** *nfpl* : checkers
damasco *nm* : damask
damisela *nf* : damsel
damnificado, -da *n* : victim (of a disaster)
damnificar {72} *vt* : to damage, to injure
dance, etc. → **danzar**
dandi *nm* : dandy, fop
danés¹, -nesa *adj* : Danish
danés², -nesa *n, mpl* **daneses** : Dane, Danish person
danza *nf* : dance, dancing ⟨danza folklórica : folk dance⟩
danzante, -ta *n* BAILARÍN : dancer
danzar {21} *v* BAILAR : to dance
dañar *vt* **1** : to damage, to spoil **2** : to harm, to hurt — **dañarse** *vr*
dañino, -na *adj* : harmful
daño *nm* **1** : damage **2** : harm, injury **3 hacer daño a** : to harm, to damage **4 daños y perjuicios** : damages
dar {22} *vt* **1** : to give **2** ENTREGAR : to deliver, to hand over **3** : to hit, to strike **4** : to yield, to produce **5** : to perform **6** : to give off, to emit **7 ~ como** or **~ por** : to regard as, to consider — *vi* **1** ALCANZAR : to suffice, to be enough ⟨no me da para dos pasajes : I don't have enough for two fares⟩ **2 ~ a** or **~ sobre** : to overlook, to look out on **3 ~ con** : to run into **4 ~ con** : to hit upon (an idea) **5 dar de sí** : to give, to stretch — **darse** *vr* **1** : to give in, to surrender **2** : to occur, to arise **3** : to grow, to come up **4 ~ con** or **~ contra** : to hit oneself against **5 dárselas de** : to boast about ⟨se las da de muy listo : he thinks he's very smart⟩

dardo *nm* : dart
datar *vt* : to date — *vi* **~ de** : to date from, to date back to
dátil *nm* : date (fruit)
dato *nm* **1** : fact, piece of information **2 datos** *nmpl* : data, information
dé → **dar**
de *prep* **1** : of ⟨la casa de Pepe : Pepe's house⟩ ⟨un niño de tres años : a three-year-old boy⟩ **2** : from ⟨es de Managua : she's from Managua⟩ ⟨salió del edificio : he left the building⟩ **3** : in, at ⟨a las tres de la mañana : at three in the morning⟩ ⟨salen de noche : they go out at night⟩ **4** : than ⟨más de tres : more than three⟩
deambular *vi* : to wander, to roam
debacle *nf* : debacle
debajo *adv* **1** : underneath, below, on the bottom **2 ~ de** : under, underneath **3 por ~** : below, beneath
debate *nm* : debate
debatir *vt* : to debate, to discuss — **debatirse** *vr* : to struggle
debe *nm* : debit column, debit
deber¹ *vt* : to owe — *v aux* **1** : must, have to ⟨debo ir a la oficina : I must go to the office⟩ **2** : should, ought to ⟨deberías buscar trabajo : you ought to look for work⟩ **3** (*expressing probability*) : must ⟨debe ser mexicano : he must be Mexican⟩ — **deberse** *vr* **~ a** : to be due to
deber² *nm* **1** OBLIGACIÓN : duty, obligation **2 deberes** *nmpl, Spain* : homework
debidamente *adv* : properly, duly
debido, -da *adj* **1** : right, proper, due **2 ~ a** : due to, owing to
débil *adj* : weak, feeble — **débilmente** *adv*
debilidad *nf* : weakness, debility, feebleness
debilitamiento *nm* : debilitation, weakening

debilitar *vt* : to debilitate, to weaken — **debilitarse** *vr*
debilucho[1], **-cha** *adj* : weak, frail
debilucho[2], **-cha** *n* : weakling
debitar *vt* : to debit
débito *nm* **1** DEUDA : debt **2** : debit
debut [de'but] *nm, pl* **debuts** : debut
debutante[1] *nmf* : beginner, newcomer
debutante[2] *nf* : debutante *f*
debutar *vi* : to debut, to make a debut
década *nf* DECENIO : decade
decadencia *nf* **1** : decadence **2** : decline
decadente *adj* **1** : decadent **2** : declining
decaer {13} *vi* **1** : to decline, to decay, to deteriorate **2** FLAQUEAR : to weaken, to flag
decaiga, etc. → **decaer**
decano, -na *n* **1** : dean **2** : senior member
decantar *vt* : to decant
decapitar *vt* : to decapitate, to behead
decayó, etc. → **decaer**
decena *nf* : group of ten
decencia *nf* : decency
decenio *nm* DÉCADA : decade
decente *adj* : decent — **decentemente** *adv*
decepción *nf, pl* **-ciones** : disappointment, letdown
decepcionante *adj* : disappointing
decepcionar *vt* : to disappoint, to let down — **decepcionarse** *vr*
deceso *nm* DEFUNCIÓN : death, passing
dechado *nm* **1** : sampler (of embroidery) **2** : model, paragon
decibelio *or* **decibel** *nm* : decibel
decidido, -da *adj* : decisive, determined, resolute — **decididamente** *adv*
decidir *vt* **1** : to decide, to determine ⟨no he decidido nada : I haven't made a decision⟩ **2** : to persuade, to decide ⟨su padre lo decidió a estudiar : his father persuaded him to study⟩ — *vi* : to decide — **decidirse** *vr* : to make up one's mind
decimal *adj* : decimal
décimo, -ma *adj* : tenth — **décimo, -ma** *n*
decimoctavo[1], **-va** *adj* : eighteenth
decimoctavo[2], **-va** *n* : eighteenth (in a series)
decimocuarto[1], **-ta** *adj* : fourteenth
decimocuarto[2], **-ta** *n* : fourteenth (in a series)
decimonoveno[1], **-na** *or* **decimonono, -na** *adj* : nineteenth
decimonoveno[2], **-na** *or* **decimonono, -na** *n* : nineteenth (in a series)
decimoquinto[1], **-ta** *adj* : fifteenth
decimoquinto[2], **-ta** *n* : fifteenth (in a series)
decimoséptimo[1], **-ma** *adj* : seventeenth
decimoséptimo[2], **-ma** *n* : seventeenth (in a series)
decimosexto[1], **-ta** *adj* : sixteenth
decimosexto[2], **-ta** *n* : sixteenth (in a series)

decimotercero[1], **-ra** *adj* : thirteenth
decimotercero[2], **-ra** *n* : thirteenth (in a series)
decir[1] {23} *vt* **1** : to say ⟨dice que no quiere ir : she says she doesn't want to go⟩ **2** : to tell ⟨dime lo que estás pensando : tell me what you're thinking⟩ **3** : to speak, to talk ⟨no digas tonterías : don't talk nonsense⟩ **4** : to call ⟨me dicen Rosy : they call me Rosy⟩ **5 es decir** : that is to say **6 querer decir** : to mean — **decirse** *vr* **1** : to say to oneself **2** : to be said ⟨¿cómo se dice "lápiz" en francés? : how do you say "pencil" in French?⟩
decir[2] *nm* DICHO : saying, expression
decisión *nf, pl* **-siones** : decision, choice
decisivo, -va *adj* : decisive, conclusive — **decisivamente** *adv*
declamar *vi* : to declaim — *vt* : to recite
declaración *nf, pl* **-ciones 1** : declaration, statement **2** TESTIMONIO : deposition, testimony **3 declaración de derechos** : bill of rights **4 declaración jurada** : affidavit
declarado, -da *adj* : professed, open — **declaradamente** *adv*
declarar *vt* : to declare, to state — *vi* ATESTIGUAR : to testify — **declararse** *vr* **1** : to declare oneself, to make a statement **2** : to confess one's love **3** : to plead (in court) ⟨declararse inocente : to plead not guilty⟩
declinación *nf, pl* **-ciones 1** : drop, downward trend **2** : declination **3** : declension (in grammar)
declinar *vt* : to decline, to turn down — *vi* **1** : to draw to a close **2** : to diminish, to decline
declive *nm* **1** DECADENCIA : decline **2** : slope, incline
decodificador *nm* : decoder
decolar *vi Chile, Col, Ecua* : to take off (of an airplane)
decolorar *vt* : to bleach — **decolorarse** *vr* : to fade
decomisar *vt* CONFISCAR : to seize, to confiscate
decomiso *nm* : seizure, confiscation
decoración *nf, pl* **-ciones 1** : decoration **2** : decor **3** : stage set, scenery
decorado *nm* : stage set, scenery
decorador, -dora *n* : decorator
decorar *vt* ADORNAR : to decorate, to adorn
decorativo, -va *adj* : decorative, ornamental
decoro *nm* : decorum, propriety
decoroso, -sa *adj* : decent, proper, respectable
decrecer {53} *vi* : to decrease, to wane, to diminish — **decreciente** *adj*
decrecimiento *nm* : decrease, decline
decrépito, -ta *adj* : decrepit
decretar *vt* : to decree, to order
decreto *nm* : decree
decúbito *nm* : horizontal position ⟨en decúbito prono : prone⟩ ⟨en decúbito supino : supine⟩

dedal *nm* : thimble

dedalera *nf* DIGITAL : foxglove

dedicación *nf, pl* -**ciones** : dedication, devotion

dedicar {72} *vt* CONSAGRAR : to dedicate, to devote — **dedicarse** *vr* ~ **a** : to devote oneself to, to engage in

dedicatoria *nf* : dedication (of a book, song, etc.)

dedo *nm* **1** : finger ⟨dedo meñique : little finger⟩ **2 dedo del pie** : toe

deducción *nf, pl* -**ciones** : deduction

deducible *adj* **1** : deducible, inferable **2** : deductible

deducir {61} *vt* **1** INFERIR : to deduce **2** DESCONTAR : to deduct

defecar {72} *vi* : to defecate — **defecación** *nf*

defecto *nm* **1** : defect, flaw, shortcoming **2 en su defecto** : lacking that, in the absence of that

defectuoso, -sa *adj* : defective, faulty

defender {56} *vt* : to defend, to protect — **defenderse** *vr* **1** : to defend oneself **2** : to get by, to know the basics ⟨su inglés no es perfecto pero se defiende : his English isn't perfect but he gets by⟩

defendible *adj* : defensible, tenable

defensa[1] *nf* : defense

defensa[2] *nmf* : defender, back (in sports)

defensiva *nf* : defensive, defense

defensivo, -va *adj* : defensive — **defensivamente** *adv*

defensor[1], -**sora** *adj* : defending, defense

defensor[2], -**sora** *n* **1** : defender, advocate **2** : defense counsel

defeño, -ña *n* : person from the Federal District (Mexico City)

deferencia *nf* : deference

deficiencia *nf* : deficiency, flaw

deficiente *adj* : deficient

déficit *nm, pl* -**cits** **1** : deficit **2** : shortage, lack

definición *nf, pl* -**ciones** : definition

definido, -da *adj* : definite, well-defined

definir *vt* **1** : to define **2** : to determine

definitivamente *adv* **1** : finally **2** : permanently, for good **3** : definitely, absolutely

definitivo, -va *adj* **1** : definitive, conclusive **2 en definitiva** : all in all, on the whole **3 en definitiva** *Mex* : permanently, for good

deflación *nf, pl* -**ciones** : deflation

deforestación *nf, pl* -**ciones** : deforestation

deformación *nf, pl* -**ciones** **1** : deformation **2** : distortion

deformar *vt* **1** : to deform, to disfigure **2** : to distort — **deformarse** *vr*

deforme *adj* : deformed, misshapen

deformidad *nf* : deformity

defraudación *nf, pl* -**ciones** : fraud

defraudar *vt* **1** ESTAFAR : to defraud, to cheat **2** : to disappoint

defunción *nf, pl* -**ciones** DECESO : death, passing

degeneración *nf, pl* -**ciones** **1** : degeneration **2** : degeneracy, depravity

degenerado, -da *adj* DEPRAVADO : degenerate

degenerar *vi* : to degenerate

degenerativo, -va *adj* : degenerative

degollar {19} *vt* **1** : to slit the throat of, to slaughter **2** DECAPITAR : to behead **3** : to ruin, to destroy

degradación *nf, pl* -**ciones** **1** : degradation **2** : demotion

degradar *vt* **1** : to degrade, to debase **2** : to demote

degustación *nf, pl* -**ciones** : tasting, sampling

degustar *vt* : to taste

deidad *nf* : deity

deificar {72} *vt* : to idolize, to deify

dejado, -da *adj* **1** : slovenly **2** : careless, lazy

dejar *vt* **1** : to leave **2** ABANDONAR : to abandon, to forsake **3** : to let be, to let go **4** PERMITIR : to allow, to permit — *vi* ~ **de** : to stop, to quit ⟨dejar de fumar : to quit smoking⟩ — **dejarse** *vr* **1** : to let oneself be ⟨se deja insultar : he lets himself be insulted⟩ **2** : to forget, to leave ⟨me dejé las llaves en el carro : I left the keys in the car⟩ **3** : to neglect oneself, to let oneself go **4** : to grow ⟨nos estamos dejando el pelo largo : we're growing our hair long⟩

dejo *nm* **1** : aftertaste **2** : touch, hint **3** : (regional) accent

del (*contraction of* **de** *and* **el**) → **de**

delación *nf, pl* -**ciones** : denunciation, betrayal

delantal *nm* **1** : apron **2** : pinafore

delante *adv* **1** ENFRENTE : ahead, in front **2** ~ **de** : before, in front of

delantera *nf* **1** : front, front part, front row ⟨tomar la delantera : to take the lead⟩ **2** : forward line (in sports)

delantero[1], -**ra** *adj* **1** : front, forward **2 tracción delantera** : front-wheel drive

delantero[2], -**ra** *n* : forward (in sports)

delatar *vt* **1** : to betray, to reveal **2** : to denounce, to inform against

delegación *nf, pl* -**ciones** : delegation

delegado, -da *n* : delegate, representative

delegar {52} *vt* : to delegate

deleitar *vt* : to delight, to please — **deleitarse** *vr*

deleite *nm* : delight, pleasure

deletrear *vi* : to spell ⟨¿como se deletrea? : how do you spell it?⟩

deleznable *adj* **1** : brittle, crumbly **2** : slippery **3** : weak, fragile ⟨una excusa deleznable : a weak excuse⟩

delfín *nm, pl* **delfines** **1** : dolphin **2** : dauphin, heir apparent

delgadez *nf* : thinness, skinniness

delgado, -da *adj* **1** FLACO : thin, skinny **2** ESBELTO : slender, slim **3** DELICADO : delicate, fine **4** AGUDO : sharp, clever

deliberación *nf, pl* -**ciones** : deliberation

deliberado, -da *adj* : deliberate, intentional — **deliberadamente** *adv*
deliberar *vi* : to deliberate
deliberativo, -va *adj* : deliberative
delicadeza *nf* **1** : delicacy, fineness **2** : gentleness, softness **3** : tact, discretion, consideration
delicado, -da *adj* **1** : delicate, fine **2** : sensitive, frail **3** : difficult, tricky **4** : fussy, hard to please **5** : tactful, considerate
delicia *nf* : delight
delicioso, -sa *adj* **1** RICO : delicious **2** : delightful
delictivo, -va *adj* : criminal
delictuoso, -sa → **delictivo**
delimitación *nf, pl* **-ciones 1** : demarcation **2** : defining, specifying
delimitar *vt* **1** : to demarcate **2** : to define, to specify
delincuencia *nf* : delinquency, crime
delincuente¹ *adj* : delinquent
delincuente² *nmf* CRIMINAL : delinquent, criminal
delinear *vt* **1** : to delineate, to outline **2** : to draft, to draw up
delinquir {24} *vi* : to break the law
delirante *adj* : delirious
delirar *vi* **1** DESVARIAR : to be delirious **2** : to rave, to talk nonsense
delirio *nm* **1** DESVARÍO : delirium **2** DISPARATE : nonsense, ravings *pl* ⟨delirios de grandeza : delusions of grandeur⟩ **3** FRENESÍ : mania, frenzy ⟨¡fue el delirio! : it was wild!⟩
delito *nm* : crime, offense
delta *nm* : delta
demacrado, -da *adj* : emaciated, gaunt
demagogia *nf* : demagogy
demagógico, -ca *adj* : demagogic, demagogical
demagogo, -ga *n* : demagogue
demanda *nf* **1** : demand ⟨la oferta y la demanda : supply and demand⟩ **2** : petition, request **3** : lawsuit
demandado, -da *n* : defendant
demandante *nmf* : plaintiff
demandar *vt* **1** : to demand **2** REQUERIR : to call for, to require **3** : to sue, to file a lawsuit against
demarcar {72} *vt* : to demarcate — **demarcación** *nf*
demás¹ *adj* : remaining ⟨acabó las demás tareas : she finished the rest of the chores⟩
demás² *pron* **1** lo (la, los, las) demás : the rest, everyone else, everything else ⟨Pepe, Rosa, y los demás : Pepe, Rosa, and everybody else⟩ **2** estar por demás : to be of no use, to be pointless ⟨no estaría por demás : it couldn't hurt, it's worth a try⟩ **3** por demás : extremely **4** por lo demás : otherwise **5** y demás : and so on, et cetera
demasía *nf* en ~ : excessively, in excess
demasiado¹ *adv* **1** : too ⟨vas demasiado aprisa : you're going too fast⟩ **2** : too

much ⟨estoy comiendo demasiado : I'm eating too much⟩
demasiado², **-da** *adj* : too much, too many, excessive
demencia *nf* **1** : dementia **2** LOCURA : madness, insanity
demente¹ *adj* : insane, mad
demente² *nmf* : insane person
demeritar *vt* **1** : to detract from **2** : to discredit
demérito *nm* **1** : fault **2** : discredit, disrepute
democracia *nf* : democracy
demócrata¹ *adj* : democratic
demócrata² *nmf* : democrat
democrático, -ca *adj* : democratic — **democráticamente** *adv*
democratizar {21} *vt* : to democratize, to make democratic
demografía *nf* : demography
demográfico, -ca *adj* : demographic
demoledor, -dora *adj* : devastating
demoler {47} *vt* DERRIBAR, DERRUMBAR : to demolish, to destroy
demolición *nf, pl* **-ciones** : demolition
demonio *nm* DIABLO : devil, demon
demora *nf* : delay
demorar *vt* **1** RETRASAR : to delay **2** TARDAR : to take, to last ⟨la reparación demorará varios días : the repair will take several days⟩ — *vi* : to delay, to linger — **demorarse** *vr* **1** : to be slow, to take a long time **2** : to take too long
demostración *nf, pl* **-ciones** : demonstration
demostrar {19} *vt* : to demonstrate, to show
demostrativo, -va *adj* : demonstrative
demudar *vt* : to change, to alter — **demudarse** *vr* : to change one's expression
denegación *nf, pl* **-ciones** : denial, refusal
denegar {49} *vt* : to deny, to turn down
denigrante *adj* : degrading, humiliating
denigrar *vt* **1** DIFAMAR : to denigrate, to disparage **2** : to degrade, to humiliate
denodado, -da *adj* : bold, dauntless
denominación *nf, pl* **-ciones 1** : name, designation **2** : denomination (of money)
denominador *nm* : denominator
denominar *vt* : to designate, to name
denostar {19} *vt* : to revile
denotar *vt* : to denote, to show
densidad *nf* : density, thickness
denso, -sa *adj* : dense, thick — **densamente** *adv*
dentado, -da *adj* SERRADO : serrated, jagged
dentadura *nf* **1** : teeth *pl* **2** dentadura postiza : dentures *pl*
dental *adj* : dental
dentellada *nf* **1** : bite **2** : tooth mark
dentera *nf* **1** : envy, jealousy **2** dar dentera : to set one's teeth on edge
dentición *nf, pl* **-ciones 1** : teething **2** : dentition, set of teeth

dentífrico *nm* : toothpaste
dentista *nmf* : dentist
dentro *adv* 1 : in, inside 2 : indoors 3
~ **de** : within, inside, in 4 **dentro de
poco** : soon, shortly 5 **dentro de todo**
: all in all, all things considered 6 **por
~** : inwardly, inside
denuedo *nm* : valor, courage
denuesto *nm* : insult
denuncia *nf* 1 : denunciation, condemnation 2 : police report
denunciante *nmf* : accuser (of a crime)
denunciar *vt* 1 : to denounce, to condemn 2 : to report (to the authorities)
deparar *vt* : to have in store for, to provide with ⟨no sabemos lo que nos de-
para el destino : we don't know what
fate has in store for us⟩
departamental *adj* 1 : departmental 2
tienda departamental *Mex* : department store
departamento *nm* 1 : department 2
APARTAMENTO : apartment
departir *vi* : to converse
dependencia *nf* 1 : dependence, dependency ⟨dependencia emocional
: emotional dependence⟩ ⟨dependen-
cia del alcohol : dependence on alco-
hol⟩ 2 : agency, branch office
depender *vi* 1 : to depend 2 ~ **de** : to
depend on 3 ~ **de** : to be subordinate
to
dependiente[1] *adj* : dependent
dependiente[2], **-ta** *n* : clerk, salesperson
deplorable *adj* : deplorable
deplorar *vt* 1 : to deplore 2 LAMENTAR
: to regret
deponer {60} *vt* 1 : to depose, to overthrow 2 : to abandon (an attitude or
stance) 3 **deponer las armas** : to lay
down one's arms — *vi* 1 TESTIFICAR
: to testify, to make a statement 2
EVACUAR : to defecate
deportación *nf, pl* **-ciones** : deportation
deportar *vt* : to deport
deporte *nm* : sport, sports *pl* ⟨hacer deporte : to engage in sports⟩
deportista[1] *adj* 1 : fond of sports 2
: sporty
deportista[2] *nmf* 1 : sports fan 2 : athlete, sportsman *m*, sportswoman *f*
deportividad *nf Spain* : sportsmanship
deportivo, -va *adj* 1 : sports, sporting
⟨artículos deportivos : sporting goods⟩
2 : sporty
deposición *nf, pl* **-ciones** 1 : statement,
testimony 2 : removal from office
depositante *nmf* : depositor
depositar *vt* 1 : to deposit, to place 2
: to store — **depositarse** *vr* : to settle
depósito *nm* 1 : deposit 2 : warehouse,
storehouse
depravación *nf, pl* **-ciones** : depravity
depravado, -da *adj* DEGENERADO : depraved, degenerate
depravar *vt* : to deprave, to corrupt
depreciación *nf, pl* **-ciones** : depreciation

depreciar *vt* : to depreciate, to reduce
the value of — **depreciarse** *vr* : to lose
value
depredación *nf* SAQUEO : depredation,
plunder
depredador[1], **-dora** *adj* : predatory
depredador[2] *nm* 1 : predator 2 SAQUE-
ADOR : plunderer
depresión *nf, pl* **-siones** 1 : depression
2 : hollow, recess 3 : drop, fall 4
: slump, recession
depresivo[1], **-va** *adj* 1 : depressive 2 : depressant
depresivo[2] *nm* : depressant
deprimente *adj* : depressing
deprimir *vt* 1 : to depress 2 : to lower
— **deprimirse** *vr* ABATIRSE : to get depressed
depuesto *pp* → **deponer**
depuración *nf, pl* **-ciones** 1 PURIFI-
CACIÓN : purification 2 PURGA : purge
3 : refinement, polish
depurar *vt* 1 PURIFICAR : to purify 2
PURGAR : to purge
depuso, etc. → **deponer**
derecha *nf* 1 : right 2 : right hand, right
side 3 : right wing, right (in politics)
derechazo *nm* 1 : pass with the cape on
the right hand (in bullfighting) 2 : right
(in boxing) 3 : forehand (in tennis)
derechista[1] *adj* : rightist, right-wing
derechista[2] *nmf* : right-winger
derecho[1] *adv* 1 : straight 2 : upright 3
: directly
derecho[2], **-cha** *adj* 1 : right 2 : right-
hand 3 RECTO : straight, upright, erect
derecho[3] *nm* 1 : right ⟨derechos humanos : human rights⟩ 2 : law ⟨dere-
cho civil : civil law⟩ 3 : right side (of
cloth or clothing)
deriva *nf* 1 : drift 2 **a la deriva** : adrift
derivación *nf, pl* **-ciones** 1 : derivation
2 RAMIFICACIÓN : ramification, consequence
derivar *vi* 1 : to drift 2 ~ **de** : to come
from, to derive from 3 ~ **en** : to result in — *vt* : to steer, to direct ⟨derivó
la discusión hacia la política : he
steered the discussion over to politics⟩
— **derivarse** *vr* : to be derived from, to
arise from
dermatología *nf* : dermatology
dermatológico, -ca *adj* : dermatological
dermatólogo, -ga *n* : dermatologist
derogación *nf, pl* **-ciones** : abolition, repeal
derogar {52} *vt* ABOLIR : to abolish, to
repeal
derramamiento *nm* 1 : spilling, overflowing 2 **derramamiento de sangre**
: bloodshed
derramar *vt* 1 : to spill 2 : to shed (tears,
blood) — **derramarse** *vr* 1 : to spill
over 2 : to scatter
derrame *nm* 1 : spilling, shedding 2
: leakage, overflow 3 : discharge, hemorrhage
derrapar *vi* : to skid

derrape *nm* : skid
derredor *nm* **al derredor** *or* **en derredor** : around, round about
derrengado, -da *adj* **1** : bent, twisted **2** : exhausted
derretir {54} *vt* : to melt, to thaw — **derretirse** *vr* **1** : to melt, to thaw **2** ~ **por** *fam* : to be crazy about
derribar *vt* **1** DEMOLER, DERRUMBAR : to demolish, to knock down **2** : to shoot down, to bring down (an airplane) **3** DERROCAR : to overthrow
derribo *nm* **1** : demolition, razing **2** : shooting down **3** : overthrow
derrocamiento *nm* : overthrow
derrocar {72} *vt* DERRIBAR : to overthrow, to topple
derrochador¹, -dora *adj* : extravagant, wasteful
derrochador², -dora *n* : spendthrift
derrochar *vt* : to waste, to squander
derroche *nm* : extravagance, waste
derrota *nf* **1** : defeat, rout **2** : course (at sea)
derrotar *vt* : to defeat
derrotero *nm* RUTA : course
derrotista *adj & nmf* : defeatist
derruir {41} *vt* : to demolish, to tear down
derrumbamiento *nm* : collapse
derrumbar *vt* **1** DEMOLER, DERRIBAR : to demolish, to knock down **2** DESPEÑAR : to cast down, to topple — **derrumbarse** *vr* DESPLOMARSE : to collapse, to break down
derrumbe *nm* **1** DESPLOME : collapse, fall ⟨el derrumbe del comunismo : the fall of Communism⟩ **2** : landslide
desabastecimiento *nm* : shortage, scarcity
desabasto *nm Mex* : shortage, scarcity
desabrido, -da *adj* : tasteless, bland
desabrigar {52} *vt* **1** : to undress **2** : to uncover **3** : to deprive of shelter
desabrochar *vt* : to unbutton, to undo — **desabrocharse** *vr* : to come undone
desacatar *vt* **1** DESAFIAR : to defy **2** DESOBEDECER : to disobey
desacato *nm* **1** : disrespect **2** : contempt (of court)
desacelerar *vi* : to decelerate, to slow down
desacertado, -da *adj* **1** : mistaken **2** : unwise
desacertar {55} *vi* ERRAR : to err, to be mistaken
desacierto *nm* ERROR : error, mistake
desaconsejable *adj* : inadvisable
desaconsejado, -da *adj* : ill-advised, unwise
desacorde *adj* **1** : conflicting **2** : discordant
desacostumbrado, -da *adj* : unaccustomed, unusual
desacreditar *vt* DESPRESTIGIAR : to discredit, to disgrace
desactivar *vt* : to deactivate, to defuse
desacuerdo *nm* : disagreement
desafiante *adj* : defiant

desafiar {85} *vt* RETAR : to defy, to challenge
desafilado, -da *adj* : blunt
desafinado, -da *adj* : out-of-tune, off-key
desafinarse *vr* : to go out of tune
desafío *nm* **1** RETO : challenge **2** RESISTENCIA : defiance
desafortunado, -da *adj* : unfortunate, unlucky — **desafortunadamente** *adv*
desafuero *nm* ABUSO : injustice, outrage
desagradable *adj* : unpleasant, disagreeable — **desagradablemente** *adv*
desagradar *vi* : to be unpleasant, to be disagreeable
desagradecido, -da *adj* : ungrateful
desagrado *nm* **1** : displeasure **2 con** ~ : reluctantly
desagravio *nm* **1** : apology **2** : amends, reparation
desagregarse {52} *vr* : to break up, to disintegrate
desaguar {10} *vi* : to drain, to empty
desagüe *nm* **1** : drain **2** : drainage
desahogado, -da *adj* **1** : well-off, comfortable **2** : spacious, roomy
desahogar {52} *vt* **1** : to relieve, to ease **2** : to give vent to — **desahogarse** *vr* **1** : to recover, to feel better **2** : to unburden oneself, to let off steam
desahogo *nm* **1** : relief, outlet **2 con** ~ : comfortably
desahuciar *vt* **1** : to deprive of hope **2** : to evict — **desahuciarse** *vr* : to lose all hope
desahucio *nm* : eviction
desairar {5} *vt* : to snub, to rebuff
desaire *nm* : rebuff, snub, slight
desajustar *vt* **1** : to disarrange, to put out of order **2** : to upset (plans)
desajuste *nm* **1** : maladjustment **2** : imbalance **3** : upset, disruption
desalentador, -dora *adj* : discouraging, disheartening
desalentar {55} *vt* DESANIMAR : to discourage, to dishearten — **desalentarse** *vr*
desaliento *nm* : discouragement
desaliñado, -da *adj* : slovenly, untidy
desalmado, -da *adj* : heartless, callous
desalojar *vt* **1** : to remove, to clear **2** EVACUAR : to evacuate, to vacate **3** : to evict
desalojo *nm* **1** : removal, expulsion **2** : evacuation **3** : eviction
desamor *nm* **1** FRIALDAD : indifference **2** ENEMISTAD : dislike, enmity
desamparado, -da *adj* DESVALIDO : helpless, destitute
desamparar *vt* : to abandon, to forsake
desamparo *nm* **1** : abandonment, neglect **2** : helplessness
desamueblado, -da *adj* : unfurnished
desandar {6} *vt* : to go back, to return to the starting point
desangelado, -da *adj* : dull, lifeless
desangrar *vt* : to bleed, to bleed dry — **desangrarse** *vr* **1** : to be bleeding **2** : to bleed to death

desanimar vt DESALENTAR : to discourage, to dishearten — **desanimarse** vr

desánimo nm DESALIENTO : discouragement, dejection

desanudar vt : to untie, to disentangle

desapacible adj : unpleasant, disagreeable

desaparecer {53} vt : to cause to disappear — vi : to disappear, to vanish

desaparecido[1], **-da** adj **1** : late, deceased **2** : missing

desaparecido[2], **-da** n : missing person

desaparición nf, pl **-ciones** : disappearance

desapasionado, -da adj : dispassionate, impartial — **desapasionadamente** adv

desapego nm : coolness, indifference

desapercibido, -da adj **1** : unnoticed **2** DESPREVENIDO : unprepared, off guard

desaprobación nf, pl **-ciones** : disapproval

desaprobar {19} vt REPROBAR : to disapprove of

desaprovechar vt MALGASTAR : to waste, to misuse — vi : to lose ground, to slip back

desarmador nm Mex : screwdriver

desarmar vt **1** : to disarm **2** DESMONTAR : to disassemble, to take apart

desarme nm : disarmament

desarraigado, -da adj : rootless

desarraigar {52} vt : to uproot, to root out

desarreglado, -da adj : untidy, disorganized

desarreglar vt **1** : to mess up **2** : to upset, to disrupt

desarreglo nm **1** : untidiness **2** : disorder, confusion

desarrollar vt : to develop — **desarrollarse** vr : to take place

desarrollo nm : development

desarticulación nf, pl **-ciones 1** : dislocation **2** : breaking up, dismantling

desarticular vt **1** DISLOCAR : to dislocate **2** : to break up, to dismantle

desaseado, -da adj **1** : dirty **2** : messy, untidy

desastre nm CATÁSTROFE : disaster

desastroso, -sa adj : disastrous, catastrophic

desatar vt **1** : to undo, to untie **2** : to unleash **3** : to trigger, to precipitate — **desatarse** vr : to break out, to erupt

desatascar {72} vt : to unblock, to clear

desatención nf, pl **-ciones 1** : absentmindedness, distraction **2** : discourtesy

desatender {56} vt **1** : to disregard **2** : to neglect

desatento, -ta adj **1** DISTRAÍDO : absentminded **2** GROSERO : discourteous, rude

desatinado, -da adj : foolish, silly

desatino nm : folly, mistake

desautorizar {21} vt : to deprive of authority, to discredit

desavenencia nf DISCORDANCIA : disagreement, dispute

desayunar vi : to have breakfast — vt : to have for breakfast

desayuno nm : breakfast

desazón nf, pl **-zones** INQUIETUD : uneasiness, anxiety

desbalance nm : imbalance

desbancar {72} vt : to displace, to oust

desbandada nf : scattering, dispersal

desbarajuste nm DESORDEN : disarray, disorder, mess

desbaratar vt **1** ARRUINAR : to destroy, to ruin **2** DESCOMPONER : to break, to break down — **desbaratarse** vr : to fall apart

desbloquear vt **1** : to open up, to clear, to break through **2** : to free, to release

desbocado, -da adj : unbridled, rampant

desbocarse {72} vr : to run away, to bolt

desbordamiento nm : overflowing

desbordante adj : overflowing, bursting ⟨desbordante de energía : bursting with energy⟩

desbordar vt **1** : to overflow, to spill over **2** : to surpass, to exceed — **desbordarse** vr

descabellado, -da adj : outlandish, ridiculous

descafeinado, -da adj : decaffeinated

descalabrar vt : to hit on the head — **descalabrarse** vr

descalabro nm : setback, misfortune, loss

descalificación nf, pl **-ciones 1** : disqualification **2** : disparaging remark

descalificar {72} vt **1** : to disqualify **2** DESACREDITAR : to discredit — **descalificarse** vr

descalzarse {21} vr : take off one's shoes

descalzo, -za adj : barefoot

descansado, -da adj **1** : rested, refreshed **2** : restful, peaceful

descansar vi : to rest, to relax — vt : to rest ⟨descansar la vista : to rest one's eyes⟩

descansillo nm : landing (of a staircase)

descanso nm **1** : rest, relaxation **2** : break **3** : landing (of a staircase) **4** : intermission

descapotable adj & nm : convertible

descarado, -da adj : brazen, impudent — **descaradamente** adv

descarga nf **1** : discharge **2** : unloading

descargar {52} vt **1** : to discharge **2** : to unload **3** : to release, to free **4** : to take out, to vent (anger, etc.) — **descargarse** vr **1** : to unburden oneself **2** : to quit **3** : to lose power

descargo nm **1** : unloading **2** : defense ⟨testigo de descargo : witness for the defense⟩

descarnado, -da adj : scrawny, gaunt

descaro nm : audacity, nerve

descarriado, -da *adj* : lost, gone astray
descarrilar *vi* : to derail — **descarrilarse** *vr*
descartar *vt* : to rule out, to reject — **descartarse** *vr* : to discard
descascarar *vt* : to peel, to shell, to husk — **descascararse** *vr* : to peel off, to chip
descendencia *nf* **1** : descendants *pl* **2** LINAJE : descent, lineage
descendente *adj* : downward, descending
descender {56} *vt* **1** : to descend, to go down **2** BAJAR : to lower, to take down, to let down — *vi* **1** : to descend, to come down **2** : to drop, to fall **3** ~ **de** : to be a descendant of
descendiente *adj & nm* : descendant
descenso *nm* **1** : descent **2** BAJA, CAÍDA : drop, fall
descentralizar {21} *vt* : to decentralize — **descentralizarse** *vr* — **descentralización** *nf*
descifrable *adj* : decipherable
descifrar *vt* : to decipher, to decode
descodificar {72} *vt* : to decode
descolgar {16} *vt* **1** : to take down, to let down **2** : to pick up, to answer (the telephone)
descollar {19} *vi* SOBRESALIR : to stand out, to be outstanding, to excel
descolorarse *vr* : to fade
descolorido, -da *adj* : discolored, faded
descomponer {60} *vt* **1** : to rot, to decompose **2** DESBARATAR : to break, to break down — **descomponerse** *vr* **1** : to break down **2** : to decompose
descomposición *nf, pl* **-ciones** **1** : breakdown, decomposition **2** : decay
descompresión *nf* : decompression
descompuesto[1] *pp* → **descomponer**
descompuesto[2], **-ta** *adj* **1** : broken down, out of order **2** : rotten, decomposed
descomunal *adj* **1** ENORME : enormous, huge **2** EXTRAORDINARIO : extraordinary
desconcertante *adj* : disconcerting
desconcertar {55} *vt* : to disconcert — **desconcertarse** *vr*
desconchar *vt* : to chip — **desconcharse** *vr* : to chip off, to peel
desconcierto *nm* : uncertainty, confusion
desconectar *vt* **1** : to disconnect, to switch off **2** : to unplug
desconfiado, -da *adj* : distrustful, suspicious
desconfianza *nf* RECELO : distrust, suspicion
desconfiar {85} *vi* ~ **de** : to distrust, to be suspicious of
descongelar *vt* **1** : to thaw **2** : to defrost **3** : to unfreeze (assets — **descongelarse** *vr*
descongestionante *adj & nm* : decongestant

desconocer {18} *vt* **1** IGNORAR : to be unaware of **2** : to fail to recognize
desconocido[1], **-da** *adj* : unknown, unfamiliar
desconocido[2], **-da** *n* EXTRAÑO : stranger
desconocimiento *nm* : ignorance
desconsiderado, -da *adj* : inconsiderate, thoughtless — **desconsideradamente** *adj*
desconsolado, -da *adj* : disconsolate, heartbroken
desconsuelo *nm* AFLICCIÓN : grief, distress, despair
descontaminar *vt* : to decontaminate — **descontaminación** *nf*
descontar {19} *vt* **1** : to discount, to deduct **2** EXCEPTUAR : to except, to exclude
descontento[1], **-ta** *adj* : discontented, dissatisfied
descontento[2] *nm* : discontent, dissatisfaction
descontrol *nm* : lack of control, disorder, chaos
descontrolarse *vr* : to get out of control, to be out of hand
descorazonado, -da *adj* : disheartened, discouraged
descorazonador, -dora *adj* : disheartening, discouraging
descorrer *vt* : to draw back
descortés *adj, pl* **-teses** : discourteous, rude
descortesía *nf* : discourtesy, rudeness
descrédito *nm* DESPRESTIGIO : discredit
descremado, -da *adj* : nonfat, skim
describir {33} *vt* : to describe
descripción *nf, pl* **-ciones** : description
descriptivo, -va *adj* : descriptive
descrito *pp* → **describir**
descuartizar {21} *vt* **1** : to cut up, to quarter **2** : to tear to pieces
descubierto[1] *pp* → **descubrir**
descubierto[2], **-ta** *adj* **1** : exposed, revealed **2** al **descubierto** : out in the open
descubridor, -dora *n* : discoverer, explorer
descubrimiento *nm* : discovery
descubrir {2} *vt* **1** HALLAR : to discover, to find out **2** REVELAR : to uncover, to reveal — **descubrirse** *vr*
descuento *nm* REBAJA : discount
descuidado, -da *adj* **1** : neglectful, careless **2** : neglected, unkempt
descuidar *vt* : to neglect, to overlook — *vi* : to be careless — **descuidarse** *vr* **1** : to be careless, to drop one's guard **2** : to let oneself go
descuido *nm* **1** : carelessness, negligence **2** : slip, oversight
desde *prep* **1** : from **2** : since **3** **desde ahora** : from now on **4** **desde entonces** : since then **5** **desde hace** : for, since (a time) ⟨ha estado nevando desde hace dos días : it's been snowing for

two days⟩ **6 desde luego** : of course
7 desde que : since, ever since **8 desde ya** : right now, immediately
desdecir {11} *vi* **1** ~ **de** : to be unworthy of **2** ~ **de** : to clash with — **desdecirse** *vr* **1** CONTRADECIRSE : to contradict oneself **2** RETRACTARSE : to go back on one's word
desdén *nm, pl* **desdenes** DESPRECIO : disdain, scorn
desdentado, -da *adj* : toothless
desdeñar *vt* DESPRECIAR : to disdain, to scorn, to despise
desdeñoso, -sa *adj* : disdainful, scornful — **desdeñosamente** *adv*
desdibujar *vt* : to blur — **desdibujarse** *vr*
desdicha *nf* **1** : misery **2** : misfortune
desdichado¹, -da *adj* **1** : unfortunate **2** : miserable, unhappy
desdichado², -da *n* : wretch
desdicho *pp* → **desdecir**
desdiga, desdijo etc. → **desdecir**
desdoblar *vt* DESPLEGAR : to unfold
deseable *adj* : desirable
desear *vt* **1** : to wish ⟨te deseo buena suerte : I wish you good luck⟩ **2** QUERER : to want, to desire
desecar {72} *vt* : to dry (flowers, etc.)
desechable *adj* : disposable
desechar *vt* **1** : to discard, to throw away **2** RECHAZAR : to reject
desecho *nm* **1** : reject **2 desechos** *nmpl* RESIDUOS : rubbish, waste
desembarazarse {21} *vr* ~ **de** : to get rid of
desembarcadero *nm* : jetty, landing pier
desembarcar {72} *vi* : to disembark — *vt* : to unload
desembarco *nm* **1** : landing, arrival **2** : unloading
desembarque → **desembarco**
desembocadura *nf* **1** : mouth (of a river) **2** : opening, end (of a street)
desembocar {72} *vi* ~ **en** or ~ **a 1** : to flow into, to join **2** : to lead to, to result in
desembolsar *vt* PAGAR : to disburse, to pay out
desembolso *nm* PAGO : disbursement, payment
desempacar {72} *v* : to unpack
desempate *nm* : tiebreaker, play-off
desempeñar *vt* **1** : to play (a role) **2** : to fulfill, to carry out **3** : to redeem (from a pawnshop) — **desempeñarse** *vr* : to function, to act
desempeño *nm* **1** : fulfillment, carrying out **2** : performance
desempleado¹, -da *adj* : unemployed
desempleado², -da *n* : unemployed person
desempleo *nm* : unemployment
desempolvar *vt* **1** : to dust off **2** : to resurrect, to revive
desencadenar *vt* **1** : to unchain **2** : to trigger, to unleash — **desencadenarse** *vr*

desencajar *vt* **1** : to dislocate **2** : to disconnect, to disengage
desencantar *vt* : to disenchant, to disillusion — **desencantarse** *vr*
desencanto *nm* : disenchantment, disillusionment
desenchufar *vt* : to disconnect, to unplug
desenfadado, -da *adj* **1** : uninhibited, carefree **2** : confident, self-assured
desenfado *nm* **1** DESENVOLTURA : self-assurance, confidence **2** : naturalness, ease
desenfrenadamente *adv* : wildly, with abandon
desenfrenado, -da *adj* : unbridled, unrestrained
desenfreno *nm* : abandon, unrestraint
desenganchar *vt* : to unhitch, to uncouple
desengañar *vt* : to disillusion, to disenchant — **desengañarse** *vr*
desengaño *nm* : disenchantment, disillusionment
desenlace *nm* : ending, outcome
desenlazar {21} *vt* **1** : to untie **2** : to clear up, to resolve
desenmarañar *vt* : to disentangle, to unravel
desenmascarar *vt* : to unmask, to expose
desenredar *vt* : to untangle, to disentangle
desenrollar *vt* : to unroll, to unwind
desentenderse {56} *vr* **1** ~ **de** : to want nothing to do with, to be uninterested in **2** ~ **de** : to pretend ignorance of
desenterrar {55} *vt* **1** EXHUMAR : to exhume **2** : to unearth, to dig up
desentonar *vi* **1** : to clash, to conflict **2** : to be out of tune, to sing off-key
desentrañar *vt* : to get to the bottom of, to unravel
desenvainar *vt* : to draw, to unsheathe (a sword)
desenvoltura *nf* **1** DESENFADO : confidence, self-assurance **2** ELOCUENCIA : eloquence, fluency
desenvolver {89} *vt* : to unwrap, to open — **desenvolverse** *vr* **1** : to unfold, to develop **2** : to manage, to cope
desenvuelto¹ *pp* → **desenvolver**
desenvuelto², -ta *adj* : confident, relaxed, self-assured
deseo *nm* : wish, desire
deseoso, -sa *adj* : eager, anxious
desequilibrar *vt* : to unbalance, to throw off balance — **desequilibrarse** *vr*
desequilibrio *nm* : imbalance
deserción *nf, pl* **-ciones** : desertion, defection
desertar *vi* **1** : to desert, to defect **2** ~ **de** : to abandon, to neglect
desertor, -tora *n* : deserter, defector
desesperación *nf, pl* **-ciones** : desperation, despair

desesperado, -da *adj* : desperate, despairing, hopeless — **desesperadamente** *adv*

desesperanza *nf* : despair, hopelessness

desesperar *vt* : to exasperate — *vi* : to despair, to lose hope — **desesperarse** *vr* : to become exasperated

desestimar *vt* **1** : to reject, to disallow **2** : to have a low opinion of

desfachatez *nf, pl* **-teces** : audacity, nerve, cheek

desfalcador, -dora *n* : embezzler

desfalcar {72} *vt* : to embezzle

desfalco *nm* : embezzlement

desfallecer {53} *vi* **1** : to weaken **2** : to faint

desfallecimiento *nm* **1** : weakness **2** : fainting

desfasado, -da *adj* **1** : out of sync **2** : out of step, behind the times

desfase *nm* : gap, lag ⟨desfase horario : jet lag⟩

desfavorable *adj* : unfavorable, adverse — **desfavorablemente** *adv*

desfavorecido, -da *adj* : underprivileged

desfigurar *vt* **1** : to disfigure, to mar **2** : to distort, to misrepresent

desfiladero *nm* : narrow gorge, defile

desfilar *vi* : to parade, to march

desfile *nm* : parade, procession

desfogar {52} *vt* **1** : to vent **2** *Mex* : to unclog, to unblock — **desfogarse** *vr* : to vent one's feelings, to let off steam

desforestación *nf, pl* **-ciones** : deforestation

desgajar *vt* **1** : to tear off **2** : to break apart — **desgajarse** *vr* : to come apart

desgana *nf* **1** INAPETENCIA : lack of appetite **2** APATÍA : apathy, unwillingness, reluctance

desgano *nm* → **desgana**

desgarbado, -da *adj* : ungainly

desgarrador, -dora *adj* : heartrending, heartbreaking

desgarradura *nf* : tear, rip

desgarrar *vt* **1** : to tear, to rip **2** : to break (one's heart) — **desgarrarse** *vr*

desgarre → **desgarro**

desgarro *nm* : tear

desgarrón *nm, pl* **-rrones** : rip, tear

desgastar *vt* **1** : to use up **2** : to wear away, to wear down

desgaste *nm* : deterioration, wear and tear

desglosar *vt* : to break down, to itemize

desglose *nm* : breakdown, itemization

desgobierno *nm* : anarchy, disorder

desgracia *nf* **1** : misfortune **2** : disgrace **3 por ~** : unfortunately

desgraciadamente *adv* : unfortunately

desgraciado¹, -da *adj* **1** : unfortunate, unlucky **2** : vile, wretched

desgraciado², -da *n* : unfortunate person, wretch

desgranar *vt* : to shuck, to shell

deshabitado, -da *adj* : unoccupied, uninhabited

deshacer {40} *vt* **1** : to destroy, to ruin **2** DESATAR : to undo, to untie **3** : to break apart, to crumble **4** : to dissolve, to melt **5** : to break, to cancel — **deshacerse** *vr* **1** : to fall apart, to come undone **2 ~ de** : to get rid of

deshecho¹ *pp* → **deshacer**

deshecho², -cha *adj* **1** : destroyed, ruined **2** : devastated, shattered **3** : undone, untied

desheredado, -da *adj* MARGINADO : dispossessed, destitute

desheredar *vt* : to disinherit

deshicieron, etc. → **deshacer**

deshidratar *vt* : to dehydrate — **deshidratación** *nf*

deshielo *nm* : thaw, thawing

deshilachar *vt* : to fray — **deshilacharse** *vr*

deshizo → **deshacer**

deshonestidad *nf* : dishonesty

deshonesto, -ta *adj* : dishonest

deshonra *nf* : dishonor, disgrace

deshonrar *vt* : to dishonor, to disgrace

deshonroso, -sa *adj* : dishonorable, disgraceful

deshuesar *vt* **1** : to pit (a fruit, etc.) **2** : to bone, to debone

deshumanizar {21} *vt* : to dehumanize — **deshumanización** *nf*

desidia *nf* **1** APATÍA : apathy, indolence **2** NEGLIGENCIA : negligence, sloppiness

desierto¹, -ta *adj* : deserted, uninhabited

desierto² *nm* : desert

designación *nf, pl* **-ciones** NOMBRAMIENTO : appointment, naming (to an office, etc.)

designar *vt* NOMBRAR : to designate, to appoint, to name

designio *nm* : plan

desigual *adj* **1** : unequal **2** DISPAREJO : uneven

desigualdad *nf* **1** : inequality **2** : unevenness

desilusión *nf, pl* **-siones** DESENCANTO, DESENGAÑO : disillusionment, disenchantment

desilusionar *vt* DESENCANTAR, DESENGAÑAR : to disillusion, to disenchant — **desilusionarse** *vr*

desinfectante *adj & nm* : disinfectant

desinfectar *vt* : to disinfect — **desinfección** *nf*

desinflar *vt* : to deflate — **desinflarse** *vr*

desinhibido, -da *adj* : uninhibited, unrestrained

desintegración *nf, pl* **-ciones** : disintegration

desintegrar *vt* : to disintegrate, to break up — **desintegrarse** *vr*

desinterés *nm* **1** : lack of interest, indifference **2** : unselfishness

desinteresado, -da *adj* GENEROSO : unselfish

desintoxicar {72} *vt* : to detoxify, to detox

desistir *vi* **1** : to desist, to stop **2** ~ **de** : to give up, to relinquish

deslave *nm Mex* : landslide

desleal *adj* INFIEL : disloyal — **deslealmente** *adv*

deslealtad *nf* : disloyalty

desleír {66} *vt* : to dilute, to dissolve

desligar {52} *vt* **1** : to separate, to undo **2** : to free (from an obligation) — **desligarse** *vr* ~ **de** : to extricate oneself from

deslindar *vt* **1** : to mark the limits of, to demarcate **2** : to define, to clarify

deslinde *nm* : demarcation

desliz *nm, pl* **deslices** : error, mistake, slip ⟨desliz de la lengua : slip of the tongue⟩

deslizar {21} *vt* **1** : to slide, to slip **2** : to slip in — **deslizarse** *vr* **1** : to slide, to glide **2** : to slip away

deslucido, -da *adj* **1** : unimpressive, dull **2** : faded, dingy, tarnished

deslucir {45} *vt* **1** : to spoil **2** : to fade, to dull, to tarnish **3** : to discredit

deslumbrar *vt* : to dazzle — **deslumbrante** *adj*

deslustrado, -da *adj* : dull, lusterless

deslustrar *vt* : to tarnish, to dull

deslustre *nm* : tarnish

desmán *nm, pl* **desmanes** **1** : outrage, abuse **2** : misfortune

desmandarse *vr* : to behave badly, to get out of hand

desmantelar *vt* DESMONTAR : to dismantle

desmañado, -da *adj* : clumsy, awkward

desmayado, -da *adj* **1** : fainting, weak **2** : dull, pale

desmayar *vi* : to lose heart, to falter — **desmayarse** *vr* DESVANECERSE : to faint, to swoon

desmayo *nm* **1** : faint, fainting **2 sufrir un desmayo** : to faint

desmedido, -da *adj* DESMESURADO : excessive, undue

desmejorar *vt* : to weaken, to make worse — *vi* : to decline (in health), to get worse

desmembramiento *nm* : dismemberment

desmembrar {55} *vt* **1** : to dismember **2** : to break up

desmemoriado, -da *adj* : absentminded, forgetful

desmentido *nm* : denial

desmentir {76} *vt* **1** NEGAR : to deny, to refute **2** CONTRADECIR : to contradict

desmenuzar {21} *vt* **1** : to break down, to scrutinize **2** : to crumble, to shred — **desmenuzarse** *vr*

desmerecer {53} *vt* : to be unworthy of — *vi* **1** : to decline in value **2** ~ **de** : to compare unfavorably with

desmesurado, -da *adj* DESMEDIDO : excessive, inordinate — **desmesuradamente** *adv*

desmigajar *vt* : to crumble — **desmigajarse** *vr*

desmilitarizado, -da *adj* : demilitarized

desmontar *vt* **1** : to clear, to level off **2** DESMANTELAR : to dismantle, to take apart — *vi* : to dismount

desmonte *nm* : clearing, leveling

desmoralizador, -dora *adj* : demoralizing

desmoralizar {21} *vt* DESALENTAR : to demoralize, to discourage

desmoronamiento *nm* : crumbling, falling apart

desmoronar *vt* : to wear away, to erode — **desmoronarse** *vr* : to crumble, to deteriorate, to fall apart

desmotadora *nf* : gin, cotton gin

desmovilizar {21} *vt* : to demobilize — **desmovilización** *nf*

desnaturalizar {21} *vt* **1** : to denature **2** : to distort, to alter

desnivel *nm* **1** : disparity, difference **2** : unevenness (of a surface)

desnivelado, -da *adj* **1** : uneven **2** : unbalanced

desnudar *vt* **1** : to undress **2** : to strip, to lay bare — **desnudarse** *vr* : to undress, to strip off one's clothing

desnudez *nf, pl* **-deces** : nudity, nakedness

desnudismo → **nudismo**

desnudista → **nudista**

desnudo¹, -da *adj* : nude, naked, bare

desnudo² *nm* : nude

desnutrición *nf, pl* **-ciones** MALNUTRICIÓN : malnutrition, undernourishment

desnutrido, -da *adj* MALNUTRIDO : malnourished, undernourished

desobedecer {53} *v* : to disobey

desobediencia *nf* : disobedience — **desobediente** *adj*

desocupación *nf, pl* **-ciones** : unemployment

desocupado, -da *adj* **1** : vacant, empty **2** : free, unoccupied **3** : unemployed

desocupar *vt* **1** : to empty **2** : to vacate, to move out of — **desocuparse** *vr* : to leave, to quit (a job)

desodorante *adj & nm* : deodorant

desolación *nf, pl* **-ciones** : desolation

desolado, -da *adj* **1** : desolate **2** : devastated, distressed

desolador, -dora *adj* **1** : devastating **2** : bleak, desolate

desollar *vt* : to skin, to flay

desorbitado, -da *adj* **1** : excessive, exorbitant **2 con los ojos desorbitados** : with eyes popping out of one's head

desorden *nm, pl* **desórdenes** **1** DESBARAJUSTE : disorder, mess **2** : disorder, disturbance, upset

desordenado, -da *adj* **1** : untidy, messy **2** : disorderly, unruly

desordenar *vt* : to mess up — **desordenarse** *vr* : to get messed up

desorganización *nf, pl* **-ciones** : disorganization

desorganizar {21} *vt* : to disrupt, to disorganize

desorientación *nf, pl* **-ciones** : disorientation, confusion

desorientar *vt* 1 : to disorient, to mislead, to confuse — **desorientarse** *vr* : to become disoriented, to lose one's way

desovar *vi* : to spawn

despachar *vt* 1 : to complete, to conclude 2 : to deal with, to take care of, to handle 3 : to dispatch, to send off 4 *fam* : to finish off, to kill — **despacharse** *vr fam* : to gulp down, to polish off

despacho *nm* 1 : dispatch, shipment 2 OFICINA : office, study

despacio *adv* LENTAMENTE, LENTO : slowly, slow ⟨¡despacio! : take it easy!, easy does it!⟩

desparasitar *vt* : to worm (an animal), to delouse

desparpajo *nm fam* 1 : self-confidence, nerve 2 *CA* : confusion, muddle

desparramar *vt* 1 : to spill, to splatter 2 : to spread, to scatter

despatarrarse *vr* : to sprawl (out)

despavorido, -da *adj* : terrified, horrified

despecho *nm* 1 : spite 2 **a despecho de** : despite, in spite of

despectivo, -va *adj* 1 : contemptuous, disparaging 2 : derogatory, pejorative

despedazar {21} *vt* : to cut to pieces, to tear apart

despedida *nf* 1 : farewell, good-bye 2 **despedida de soltera** : bridal shower

despedir {54} *vt* 1 : to see off, to show out 2 : to dismiss, to fire 3 EMITIR : to give off, to emit ⟨despedir un olor : to give off an odor⟩ — **despedirse** *vr* : to take one's leave, to say good-bye

despegado, -da *adj* 1 : separated, detached 2 : cold, distant

despegar {52} *vt* : to remove, to detach — *vi* : to take off, to lift off, to blast off

despegue *nm* : takeoff, liftoff

despeinado, -da *adj* : disheveled, tousled ⟨estoy despeinada : my hair's a mess⟩

despeinarse *vr* 1 : to mess up one's hair 2 : to become disheveled ⟨me despeiné : my hair got messed up⟩

despejado, -da *adj* 1 : clear, fair 2 : alert, clear-headed 3 : uncluttered, unobstructed

despejar *vt* 1 : to clear, to free 2 : to clarify — *vi* 1 : to clear up 2 : to punt (in sports)

despeje *nm* 1 : clearing 2 : punt (in sports)

despellejar *vt* : to skin (an animal)

despenalizar {21} *vt* : to legalize — **despenalización** *nf*

despensa *nf* 1 : pantry, larder 2 PROVISIONES : provisions *pl*, supplies *pl*

despeñar *vt* : to hurl down

despepitar *vt* : to seed, to remove the seeds from

desperdiciar *vt* 1 DESAPROVECHAR, MALGASTAR : to waste 2 : to miss, to miss out on

desperdicio *nm* 1 : waste 2 **desperdicios** *nmpl* RESIDUOS : refuse, scraps, rubbish

desperdigar {52} *vt* DISPERSAR : to disperse, to scatter

desperfecto *nm* 1 DEFECTO : flaw, defect 2 : damage

despertador *nm* : alarm clock

despertar {55} *vi* : to awaken, to wake up — *vt* 1 : to arouse, to wake 2 EVOCAR : to elicit, to evoke — **despertarse** *vr* : to wake (oneself) up

despiadado, -da *adj* CRUEL : cruel, merciless, pitiless — **despiadadamente** *adv*

despido *nm* : dismissal, layoff

despierto, -ta *adj* 1 : awake, alert 2 LISTO : clever, sharp ⟨con la mente despierta : with a sharp mind⟩

despilfarrador¹, -dora *adj* : extravagant, wasteful

despilfarrador², -dora *n* : spendthrift, prodigal

despilfarrar *vt* MALGASTAR : to squander, to waste

despilfarro *nm* : extravagance, wastefulness

despintar *vt* : to strip the paint from — **despintarse** *vr* : to fade, to wash off, to peel off

despistado¹, -da *adj* 1 DISTRAÍDO : absentminded, forgetful 2 CONFUSO : confused, bewildered

despistado², -da *n* : scatterbrain, absentminded person

despistar *vt* : to throw off the track, to confuse — **despistarse** *vr*

despiste *nm* 1 : absentmindedness 2 : mistake, slip

desplantador *nm* : garden trowel

desplante *nm* : insolence, rudeness

desplazamiento *nm* 1 : movement, displacement 2 : journey

desplazar {21} *vt* 1 : to replace, to displace 2 TRASLADAR : to move, to shift

desplegar {49} *vt* 1 : to display, to show, to manifest 2 DESDOBLAR : to unfold, to unfurl 3 : to spread (out) 4 : to deploy

despliegue *nm* 1 : display 2 : deployment

desplomarse *vr* 1 : to plummet, to fall 2 DERRUMBARSE : to collapse, to break down

desplome *nm* 1 : fall, drop 2 : collapse

desplumar *vt* : to pluck (a chicken, etc.)

despoblado¹, -da *adj* : uninhabited, deserted

**despoblado² ** *nm* : open country, deserted area

despoblar {19} *vt* : to depopulate

despojar *vt* 1 : to strip, to clear 2 : to divest, to deprive — **despojarse** *vr* 1 **~ de** : to remove (clothing) 2 **~ de** : to relinquish, to renounce

despojos *nmpl* **1** : remains, scraps **2** : plunder, spoils

desportilladura *nf* : chip, nick

desportillar *vt* : to chip — **desportillarse** *vr*

desposeer {20} *vt* : to dispossess

déspota *nmf* : despot, tyrant

despotismo *nm* : despotism — **despótico, -ca** *adj*

despotricar {72} *vi* : to rant and rave, to complain excessively

despreciable *adj* **1** : despicable, contemptible **2** : negligible ⟨nada despreciable : not inconsiderable, significant⟩

despreciar *vt* DESDEÑAR, MENOSPRECIAR : to despise, to scorn, to disdain

despreciativo, -va *adj* : scornful, disdainful

desprecio *nm* DESDÉN, MENOSPRECIO : disdain, contempt, scorn

desprender *vt* **1** SOLTAR : to detach, to loosen, to unfasten **2** EMITIR : to emit, to give off — **desprenderse** *vr* **1** : to come off, to come undone **2** : to be inferred, to follow **3** ∼ **de** : to part with, to get rid of

desprendido, -da *adj* : generous, unselfish, disinterested

desprendimiento *nm* **1** : detachment **2** GENEROSIDAD : generosity **3 desprendimiento de tierras** : landslide

despreocupación *nf, pl* -**ciones** : indifference, lack of concern

despreocupado, -da *adj* : carefree, easygoing, unconcerned

desprestigiar *vt* DESACREDITAR : to discredit, to disgrace — **desprestigiarse** *vr* : to lose prestige

desprestigio *nm* DESCRÉDITO : discredit, disrepute

desprevenido, -da *adj* DESAPERCIBIDO : unprepared, off guard, unsuspecting

desproporción *nf, pl* -**ciones** : disproportion, disparity

desproporcionado, -da : out of proportion

despropósito *nm* : piece of nonsense, absurdity

desprotegido, -da *adj* : unprotected, vulnerable

desprovisto, -ta *adj* ∼ **de** : devoid of, lacking in

después *adv* **1** : afterward, later **2** : then, next **3** ∼ **de** : after, next after ⟨después de comer : after eating⟩ **4 después (de) que** : after ⟨después que lo acabé : after I finished it⟩ **5 después de todo** : after all **6 poco después** : shortly after, soon thereafter

despuntado, -da *adj* : blunt, dull

despuntar *vt* : to blunt — *vi* **1** : to dawn **2** : to sprout **3** : to excel, to stand out

desquiciar *vt* **1** : to unhinge (a door) **2** : to drive crazy — **desquiciarse** *vr* : to go crazy

desquitarse *vr* **1** : to get even, to retaliate **2** ∼ **con** : to take it out on

desquite *nm* : revenge

desregulación *nf, pl* -**ciones** : deregulation

desregular *vt* : to deregulate

desregularización *nf* → **desregulación**

destacadamente *adv* : outstandingly, prominently

destacado, -da *adj* **1** : outstanding, prominent **2** : stationed, posted

destacamento *nm* : detachment (of troops)

destacar {72} *vt* **1** ENFATIZAR, SUBRAYAR : to emphasize, to highlight, to stress **2** : to station, to post — *vi* : to stand out

destajo *nm* **1** : piecework **2 a** ∼ : by the item, by the job

destapador *nm* : bottle opener

destapar *vt* **1** : to open, to take the top off **2** DESCUBRIR : to reveal, to uncover **3** : to unblock, to unclog

destape *nm* : uncovering, revealing

destartalado, -da *adj* : dilapidated, tumbledown

destellar *vi* **1** : to sparkle, to flash, to glint **2** : to twinkle

destello *nm* **1** : flash, sparkle, twinkle **2** : glimmer, hint

destemplado, -da *adj* **1** : out of tune **2** : irritable, out of sorts **3** : unpleasant (of weather)

desteñir {67} *vi* : to run, to fade — **desteñirse** *vr* DESCOLORARSE : to fade

desterrado¹, -da *adj* : banished, exiled

desterrado², -da *n* : exile

desterrar {55} *vt* **1** EXILIAR : to banish, to exile **2** ERRADICAR : to eradicate, to do away with

destetar *vt* : to wean

destiempo *adv* **a** ∼ : at the wrong time

destierro *nm* EXILIO : exile

destilación *nf, pl* -**ciones** : distillation

destilador, -dora *n* : distiller

destilar *vt* **1** : to exude **2** : to distill

destilería *nf* : distillery

destinación *nf, pl* -**ciones** DESTINO : destination

destinado, -da *adj* : destined, bound

destinar *vt* **1** : to appoint, to assign **2** ASIGNAR : to earmark, to allot

destinatario, -ria *n* **1** : addressee **2** : payee

destino *nm* **1** : destiny, fate **2** DESTINACIÓN : destination **3** : use **4** : assignment, post

destitución *nf, pl* -**ciones** : dismissal, removal from office

destituir {41} *vt* : to dismiss, to remove from office

destorcer {14} *vt* : to untwist

destornillador *nm* : screwdriver

destornillar *vt* : to unscrew

destrabar *vt* **1** : to untie, to undo, to ease up **2** : to separate

destreza *nf* HABILIDAD : dexterity, skill

destronar *vt* : to depose, to dethrone

destrozado, -da *adj* **1** : ruined, destroyed **2** : devastated, brokenhearted

destrozar {21} *vt* **1** : to smash, to shatter **2** : to destroy, to wreck — **destrozarse** *vr*

destrozo *nm* **1** DAÑO : damage **2** : havoc, destruction

destrucción *nf, pl* **-ciones** : destruction

destructivo, -va *adj* : destructive

destructor[1], -tora *adj* : destructive

destructor[2] *nm* : destroyer (ship)

destruir {41} *vt* : to destroy — **destruirse** *vr*

desubicado, -da *adj* **1** : out of place **2** : confused, disoriented

desunión *nf, pl* **-niones** : disunity

desunir *vt* : to split, to divide

desusado, -da *adj* **1** INSÓLITO : unusual **2** OBSOLETO : obsolete, disused, antiquated

desuso *nm* : disuse, obsolescence ⟨caer en desuso : to fall into disuse⟩

desvaído, -da *adj* **1** : pale, washed-out **2** : vague, blurred

desvainar *vt* : to shell

desvalido, -da *adj* DESAMPARADO : destitute, helpless

desvalijar *vt* **1** : to ransack **2** : to rob

desvalorización *nf, pl* **-ciones** **1** DEVALUACIÓN : devaluation **2** : depreciation

desvalorizar {21} *vt* : to devalue

desván *nm, pl* **desvanes** ÁTICO, BUHARDILLA : attic

desvanecer {53} *vt* **1** DISIPAR : to make disappear, to dispel **2** : to fade, to blur — **desvanecerse** *vr* **1** : to vanish, to disappear **2** : to fade **3** DESMAYARSE : to faint, to swoon

desvanecimiento *nm* **1** : disappearance **2** DESMAYO : faint **3** : fading

desvariar {85} *vi* **1** DELIRAR : to be delirious **2** : to rave, to talk nonsense

desvarío *nm* DELIRIO : delirium

desvelado, -da *adj* : sleepless

desvelar *vt* **1** : to keep awake **2** REVELAR : to reveal, to disclose — **desvelarse** *vr* **1** : to stay awake **2** : to do one's utmost

desvelo *nm* **1** : sleeplessness **2** **desvelos** *nmpl* : efforts, pains

desvencijado, -da *adj* : dilapidated, rickety

desventaja *nf* : disadvantage, drawback

desventajoso, -sa *adj* : disadvantageous, unfavorable

desventura *nf* INFORTUNIO : misfortune

desventurado, -da *adj* : unfortunate, ill-fated

desvergonzado, -da *adj* : shameless, impudent

desvergüenza *nf* : shamelessness, impudence

desvestir {54} *vt* : to undress — **desvestirse** *vr* : to get undressed

desviación *nf, pl* **-ciones** **1** : deviation, departure **2** : detour, diversion

desviar {85} *vt* **1** : to change the course of, to divert **2** : to turn away, to deflect — **desviarse** *vr* **1** : to branch off **2** APARTARSE : to stray

desvinculación *nf, pl* **-ciones** : dissociation

desvincular *vt* ~ **de** : to separate from, to dissociate from — **desvincularse** *vr*

desvío *nm* **1** : diversion, detour **2** : deviation

desvirtuar {3} *vt* **1** : to impair, to spoil **2** : to detract from **3** : to distort, to misrepresent

detalladamente *adv* : in detail, at great length

detallar *vt* : to detail

detalle *nm* **1** : detail **2 al detalle** : retail

detallista[1] *adj* **1** : meticulous **2** : retail

detallista[2] *nmf* **1** : perfectionist **2** : retailer

detección *nf, pl* **-ciones** : detection

detectar *vt* : to detect — **detectable** *adj*

detective *nmf* : detective

detector *nm* : detector ⟨detector de mentiras : lie detector⟩

detención *nf, pl* **-ciones** **1** ARRESTO : detention, arrest **2** : stop, halt **3** : delay, holdup

detener {80} *vt* **1** ARRESTAR : to arrest, to detain **2** PARAR : to stop, to halt **3** : to keep, to hold back — **detenerse** *vr* **1** : to stop **2** : to delay, to linger

detenidamente *adv* : thoroughly, at length

detenimiento *nm* **con** ~ : carefully, in detail

detentar *vt* : to hold, to retain

detergente *nm* : detergent

deteriorado, -da *adj* : damaged, worn

deteriorar *vt* ESTROPEAR : to damage, to spoil — **deteriorarse** *vr* **1** : to get damaged, to wear out **2** : to deteriorate, to worsen

deterioro *nm* **1** : deterioration, wear **2** : worsening, decline

determinación *nf, pl* **-ciones** **1** : determination, resolve **2 tomar una determinación** : to make a decision

determinado, -da *adj* **1** : certain, particular **2** : determined, resolute

determinante[1] *adj* : determining, deciding

determinante[2] *nm* : determinant

determinar *vt* **1** : to determine **2** : to cause, to bring about — **determinarse** *vr* : to make up one's mind, to decide

detestar *vt* : to detest — **detestable** *adj*

detonación *nf, pl* **-ciones** : detonation

detonador *nm* : detonator

detonante[1] *adj* : detonating, explosive

detonante[2] *nm* **1** → **detonador 2** : catalyst, cause

detonar *vi* : to detonate, to explode

detractor, -tora *n* : detractor, critic

detrás *adv* **1** : behind **2** ~ **de** : in back of **3 por** ~ : from behind

detrimento *nm* : detriment ⟨en detrimento de : to the detriment of⟩

detuvo, etc. → **detener**

deuda *nf* **1** DÉBITO : debt **2 en deuda con** : indebted to

deudo, -da *n* : relative

deudor¹, -dora *adj* : indebted

deudor², -dora *n* : debtor

devaluación *nf, pl* **-ciones** DESVALORIZACIÓN : devaluation

devaluar {3} *vt* : to devalue — **devaluarse** *vr* : to depreciate

devanarse *vr* **devanarse los sesos** : to rack one's brains

devaneo *nm* **1** : flirtation, fling **2** : idle pursuit

devastador, -dora *adj* : devastating

devastar *vt* : to devastate — **devastación** *nf*

devenir {87} *vi* **1** : to come about **2 ～ en** : to become, to turn into

devoción *nf, pl* **-ciones** : devotion

devolución *nf, pl* **-ciones** REEMBOLSO : return, refund

devolver {89} *vt* **1** : to return, to give back **2** REEMBOLSAR : to refund, to pay back **3** : to vomit, to bring up — *vi* : to vomit, to throw up — **devolverse** *vr* : to return, to come back, to go back

devorar *vt* **1** : to devour **2** : to consume

devoto¹, -ta *adj* : devout — **devotamente** *adv*

devoto², -ta *n* : devotee, admirer

di → dar, decir

día *nm* **1** : day ⟨todos los días : every day⟩ **2** : daytime, daylight ⟨de día : by day, in the daytime⟩ ⟨en pleno día : in broad daylight⟩ **3 al día** : up-to-date **4 en su día** : in due time

diabetes *nf* : diabetes

diabético, -ca *adj & n* : diabetic

diablillo *nm* : little devil, imp

diablo *nm* DEMONIO : devil

diablura *nf* **1** : prank **2 diabluras** *nfpl* : mischief

diabólico, -ca *adj* : diabolical, diabolic, devilish

diaconisa *nf* : deaconess

diácono *nm* : deacon

diacrítico, -ca *adj* : diacritic, diacritical

diadema *nf* : diadem, crown

diáfano, -na *adj* : diaphanous

diafragma *nm* : diaphragm

diagnosticar {72} *vt* : to diagnose

diagnóstico¹, -ca *adj* : diagnostic

diagnóstico² *nm* : diagnosis

diagonal *adj & nf* : diagonal — **diagonalmente** *adv*

diagrama *nm* **1** : diagram **2 diagrama de flujo** ORGANIGRAMA : flowchart

dial *nm* : dial (on a radio, etc.)

dialecto *nm* : dialect

dialogar {52} *vi* : to have a talk, to converse

diálogo *nm* : dialogue

diamante *nm* : diamond

diametral *adj* : diametric, diametrical — **diametralmente** *adv*

diámetro *nm* : diameter

diana *nf* **1** : target, bull's-eye **2** *or* **toque de diana** : reveille

diapositiva *nf* : slide, transparency

diario¹ *adv Mex* : every day, daily

diario², -ria *adj* : daily, everyday — **diariamente** *adv*

diario³ *nm* **1** : diary **2** PERIÓDICO : newspaper

diarrea *nf* : diarrhea

diatriba *nf* : diatribe, tirade

dibujante *nmf* **1** : draftsman *m*, draftswoman *f* **2** CARICATURISTA : cartoonist

dibujar *vt* **1** : to draw, to sketch **2** : to portray, to depict

dibujo *nm* **1** : drawing **2** : design, pattern **3 dibujos animados** : (animated) cartoons

dicción *nf, pl* **-ciones** : diction

diccionario *nm* : dictionary

dícese → decir

dicha *nf* **1** SUERTE : good luck **2** FELICIDAD : happiness, joy

dicho¹ *pp* → **decir**

dicho², -cha *adj* : said, aforementioned

dicho³ *nm* DECIR : saying, proverb

dichoso, -sa *adj* **1** : blessed **2** FELIZ : happy **3** AFORTUNADO : fortunate, lucky

diciembre *nm* : December

diciendo → decir

dictado *nm* : dictation

dictador, -dora *n* : dictator

dictadura *nf* : dictatorship

dictamen *nm, pl* **dictámenes 1** : report **2** : judgment, opinion

dictaminar *vt* : to report — *vi* : to give an opinion, to pass judgment

dictar *vt* **1** : to dictate **2** : to pronounce (a judgment) **3** : to give, to deliver ⟨dictar una conferencia : to give a lecture⟩

dictatorial *adj* : dictatorial

didáctico, -ca *adj* : didactic

diecinueve *adj & nm* : nineteen

diecinueveavo¹, -va *adj* : nineteenth

diecinueveavo² *nm* : nineteenth (fraction)

dieciocho *adj & nm* : eighteen

dieciochoavo¹, -va *or* **dieciochavo, -va** *adj* : eighteenth

dieciochoavo² *or* **dieciochavo** *nm* : eighteenth (fraction)

dieciséis *adj & nm* : sixteen

dieciseisavo¹, -va *adj* : sixteenth

dieciseisavo² *nm* : sixteenth (fraction)

diecisiete *adj & nm* : seventeen

diecisieteavo¹, -va *adj* : seventeenth

diecisieteavo² *nm* : seventeenth

diente *nm* **1** : tooth ⟨diente canino : eyetooth, canine tooth⟩ **2** : tusk, fang **3** : prong, tine **4 diente de león** : dandelion

dieron, etc. → dar

diesel ['disɛl] *nm* : diesel

diestra *nf* : right hand

diestramente *adv* : skillfully, adroitly

diestro¹, -tra *adj* **1** : right **2** : skillful, accomplished

diestro² *nm* : bullfighter, matador

dieta *nf* : diet

dietética *nf* : dietetics
dietético, -ca *adj* : dietetic
dietista *nmf* : dietitian
diez *adj & nm, pl* **dieces** : ten
difamación *nf, pl* **-ciones** : defamation, slander
difamar *vt* : to defame, to slander
difamatorio, -ria *adj* : slanderous, defamatory, libelous
diferencia *nf* 1 : difference 2 a **diferencia de** : unlike, in contrast to
diferenciación *nf, pl* **-ciones** : differentiation
diferenciar *vt* : to differentiate between, to distinguish — **diferenciarse** *vr* : to differ
diferendo *nm* : dispute, conflict
diferente *adj* DISTINTO : different — **diferentemente** *adv*
diferir {76} *vt* DILATAR, POSPONER : to postpone, to put off — *vi* : to differ
difícil *adj* : difficult, hard
difícilmente *adv* 1 : with difficulty 2 : hardly
dificultad *nf* : difficulty
dificultar *vt* : to make difficult, to obstruct
dificultoso, -sa *adj* : difficult, hard
difteria *nf* : diphtheria
difundir *vt* 1 : to diffuse, to spread out 2 : to broadcast, to spread
difunto, -ta *adj & n* FALLECIDO : deceased
difusión *nf, pl* **-siones** 1 : spreading 2 : diffusion (of heat, etc.) 3 : broadcast, broadcasting ⟨los medios de difusión : the media⟩
difuso, -sa *adj* : diffuse, widespread
diga, etc. → **decir**
digerir {76} *vt* : to digest — **digerible** *adj*
digestión *nf, pl* **-tiones** : digestion
digestivo, -va *adj* : digestive
digital[1] *adj* : digital — **digitalmente** *adv*
digital[2] *nf* 1 DEDALERA : foxglove 2 : digitalis
dígito *nm* : digit
dignarse *vr* : to deign, to condescend ⟨no se dignó contestar : he didn't deign to answer⟩
dignatario, -ria *n* : dignitary
dignidad *nf* 1 : dignity 2 : dignitary
dignificar {72} *vt* : to dignify
digno, -na *adj* 1 HONORABLE : honorable 2 : worthy — **dignamente** *adv*
digresión *nf, pl* **-ciones** : digression
dije *nm* : charm (on a bracelet)
dijo, etc. → **decir**
dilación *nf, pl* **-ciones** : delay
dilapidar *vt* : to waste, to squander
dilatar *vt* 1 : to dilate, to widen, to expand 2 DIFERIR, POSPONER : to put off, to postpone — **dilatarse** *vr* 1 : to expand (of gases, metals, etc.) 2 *Mex* : to take long, to be long
dilatorio, -ria *adj* : dilatory, delaying
dilema *nm* : dilemma
diletante *nmf* : dilettante

diligencia *nf* 1 : diligence, care 2 : promptness, speed 3 : action, step 4 : task, errand 5 : stagecoach 6 **diligencias** *nfpl* : judicial procedures, formalities
diligente *adj* : diligent — **diligentemente** *adv*
dilucidar *vt* : to elucidate, to clarify
dilución *nf, pl* **-ciones** : dilution
diluir {41} *vt* : to dilute
diluviar *v impers* : to pour (with rain), to pour down
diluvio *nm* 1 : flood 2 : downpour
dimensión *nf, pl* **-siones** : dimension — **dimensional** *adj*
dimensionar *vt* : to measure, to gauge
diminutivo[1]**, -va** *adj* : diminutive
diminutivo[2] *nm* : diminutive
diminuto, -ta *adj* : minute, tiny
dimisión *nf, pl* **-siones** : resignation
dimitir *vi* : to resign, to step down
dimos → **dar**
dinámica *nf* : dynamics
dinámico, -ca *adj* : dynamic — **dinámicamente** *adv*
dinamismo *nm* : energy, vigor
dinamita *nf* : dynamite
dinamitar *vt* : to dynamite
dínamo *or* **dinamo** *nm* : dynamo
dinastía *nf* : dynasty
dineral *nm* : fortune, large sum of money
dinero *nm* : money
dinosaurio *nm* : dinosaur
dintel *nm* : lintel
dio, etc. → **dar**
diocesano, -na *adj* : diocesan
diócesis *nfs & pl* : diocese
dios, diosa *n* : god, goddess *f*
Dios *nm* : God
diploma *nm* : diploma
diplomacia *nf* : diplomacy
diplomado[1]**, -da** *adj* : qualified, trained
diplomado[2] *nm Mex* : seminar
diplomático, -ca *adj* : diplomatic — **diplomáticamente** *adv*
diplomático[2]**, -ca** *n* : diplomat
diptongo *nm* : diphthong
diputación *nf, pl* **-ciones** : deputation, delegation
diputado, -da *n* : delegate, representative
dique *nm* : dike
dirá, etc. → **decir**
dirección *nf, pl* **-ciones** 1 : address 2 : direction 3 : management, leadership 4 : steering (of an automobile)
direccional[1] *adj* : directional
direccional[2] *nf* : directional, turn signal
directa *nf* : high gear
directamente *adv* : straight, directly
directiva *nf* 1 ORDEN : directive 2 DIRECTORIO, JUNTA : board of directors
directivo[1]**, -va** *adj* : executive, managerial
directivo[2]**, -va** *n* : executive, director
directo, -ta *adj* 1 : direct, straight, immediate 2 en ~ : live (in broadcasting)

director, -tora n **1** : director, manager, head **2** : conductor (of an orchestra)
directorial adj : managing, executive
directorio nm **1** : directory **2** DIRECTIVA, JUNTA : board of directors
directriz nf, pl **-trices** : guideline
dirigencia nf : leaders pl, leadership
dirigente[1] adj : directing, leading
dirigente[2] nmf : director, leader
dirigible nm : dirigible, blimp
dirigir {35} vt **1** : to direct, to lead **2** : to address **3** : to aim, to point **4** : to conduct (music) — **dirigirse** vr ~ **a 1** : to go towards **2** : to speak to, to address
dirimir vt **1** : to resolve, to settle **2** : to annul, to dissolve (a marriage)
discapacidad nf MINUSVALÍA : disability, handicap
discapacitado[1], **-da** adj : disabled, handicapped
discapacitado[2], **-da** n : disabled person, handicapped person
discar {72} v : to dial
discernimiento nm : discernment
discernir {25} v : to discern, to distinguish
disciplina nf : discipline
disciplinar vt : to discipline — **disciplinario, -ria** adj
discípulo, -la n : disciple, follower
disc jockey [ˌdiskˈjoke, -ˈdʒo-] nmf : disc jockey
disco nm **1** : phonograph record **2** : disc, disk ⟨disco compacto : compact disc⟩ **3** : discus
díscolo, -la adj : unruly, disobedient
disconforme adj : in disagreement
discontinuidad nf : discontinuity
discontinuo, -nua adj : discontinuous
discordancia nf DESAVENENCIA : conflict, disagreement
discordante adj **1** : discordant **2** : conflicting
discordia nf : discord
discoteca nf **1** : disco, discotheque **2** CA, Mex : record store
discreción nf, pl **-ciones** : discretion
discrecional adj : discretionary
discrepancia nf : discrepancy
discrepar vi **1** : to disagree **2** : to differ
discreto, -ta adj : discreet — **discretamente** adv
discriminación nf, pl **-ciones** : discrimination
discriminar vt **1** : to discriminate against **2** : to distinguish, to differentiate
discriminatorio, -ria adj : discriminatory
disculpa nf **1** : apology **2** : excuse
disculpable adj : excusable
disculpar vt : to excuse, to pardon — **disculparse** vr : to apologize
discurrir vi **1** : to flow **2** : to pass, to go by **3** : to ponder, to reflect
discurso nm **1** ORACIÓN : speech, address **2** : discourse, treatise

discusión nf, pl **-siones 1** : discussion **2** ALTERCADO, DISPUTA : argument
discutible adj : arguable, debatable
discutidor, -dora adj : argumentative
discutir vt **1** : to discuss **2** : to dispute — vi ALTERCAR : to argue, to quarrel
disecar {72} vt **1** : to dissect **2** : to stuff (for preservation)
disección nf, pl **-ciones** : dissection
diseminación nf, pl **-ciones** : dissemination, spreading
diseminar vt : to disseminate, to spread
disensión nf, pl **-siones** : dissension, disagreement
disentería nf : dysentery
disentir {76} vi : to dissent, to disagree
diseñador, -dora n : designer
diseñar vt **1** : to design, to plan **2** : to lay out, to outline
diseño nm : design
disentimiento nm : dissent
disertación nf, pl **-ciones 1** : lecture, talk **2** : dissertation
disertar vi : to lecture, to give a talk
disfraz nm, pl **disfraces 1** : disguise **2** : costume **3** : front, pretense
disfrazar {21} vt **1** : to disguise **2** : to mask, to conceal — **disfrazarse** vr : to wear a costume, to be in disguise
disfrutar vt : to enjoy — vi : to enjoy oneself, to have a good time
disfrute nm : enjoyment
disfunción nf, pl **-ciones** : dysfunction — **disfuncional** adj
disgresión → **digresión**
disgustar vt : to upset, to displease, to make angry — **disgustarse** vr
disgusto nm **1** : annoyance, displeasure **2** : argument, quarrel **3** : trouble, misfortune
disidencia nf : dissidence, dissent
disidente adj & nmf : dissident
disímbolo, -la adj Mex : dissimilar
disímil adj : dissimilar
disimulado, -da adj **1** : concealed, disguised **2** : furtive, sly
disimular vi : to dissemble, to pretend — vt : to conceal, to hide
disimulo nm **1** : dissembling, pretense **2** : slyness, furtiveness **3** : tolerance
disipar vt **1** : to dissipate, to dispel **2** : to squander — **disiparse** vr
diskette [diˈskɛt] nm : floppy disk, diskette
dislocar {72} vt : to dislocate — **dislocación** nf
disminución nf, pl **-ciones** : decrease, drop, fall
disminuir {41} vt REDUCIR : to reduce, to decrease, to lower — vi **1** : to lower **2** : to drop, to fall
disociación nf, pl **-ciones** : dissociation
disociar vt : to dissociate, to separate
disolución nf, pl **-ciones 1** : dissolution, dissolving **2** : breaking up **3** : dissipation
disoluto, -ta adj : dissolute, dissipated

disolver {89} *vt* **1** : to dissolve **2** : to break up — **disolverse** *vr*
disonancia *nf* : dissonance — **disonante** *adj*
dispar *adj* **1** : different, disparate **2** DIVERSO : diverse **3** DESIGUAL : inconsistent
disparado, -da *adj* **salir disparado** *fam* : to take off in a hurry, to rush away
disparar *vi* **1** : to shoot, to fire **2** *Mex fam* : to pay — *vt* **1** : to shoot **2** *Mex fam* : to treat to, to buy — **dispararse** *vr* : to shoot up, to skyrocket
disparatado, -da *adj* ABSURDO, RIDÍCULO : absurd, ridiculous, crazy
disparate *nm* : silliness, stupidity ⟨decir disparates : to talk nonsense⟩
disparejo, -ja *adj* DESIGUAL : uneven
disparidad *nf* : disparity
disparo *nm* TIRO : shot
dispendio *nm* : wastefulness, extravagance
dispendioso, -sa *adj* : wasteful, extravagant
dispensa *nf* : dispensation
dispensable *adj* **1** : dispensable **2** : excusable
dispensar *vt* **1** : to dispense, to give, to grant **2** EXCUSAR : to excuse, to forgive **3** EXIMIR : to exempt
dispensario *nm* **1** : dispensary, clinic **2** *Mex* : dispenser
dispersar *vt* DESPERDIGAR : to disperse, to scatter
dispersión *nf, pl* **-siones** : dispersion
disperso, -sa *adj* : dispersed, scattered
displicencia *nf* : indifference, coldness, disdain
displicente *adj* : indifferent, cold, disdainful
disponer {60} *vt* **1** : to arrange, to lay out **2** : to stipulate, to order **3** : to prepare — *vi* ~ **de** : to have at one's disposal — **disponerse** *vr* ~ **a** : to prepare to, to be about to
disponibilidad *nf* : availability
disponible *adj* : available
disposición *nf, pl* **-ciones** **1** : disposition **2** : aptitude, talent **3** : order, arrangement **4** : willingness, readiness **5 última disposición** : last will and testament
dispositivo *nm* **1** APARATO, MECANISMO : device, mechanism **2** : force, detachment
dispuesto[1] *pp* → **disponer**
dispuesto[2]**, -ta** *adj* PREPARADO : ready, prepared, disposed
dispuso, etc. → **disponer**
disputa *nf* ALTERCADO, DISCUSIÓN : dispute, argument
disputar *vi* : to argue, to contend, to vie — *vt* : to dispute, to question — **disputarse** *vr* : to be in competition for ⟨se disputan la corona : they're fighting for the crown⟩
disquera *nf* : record label, recording company

disquete → **diskette**
disquisición *nf, pl* **-ciones** **1** : formal discourse **2 disquisiciones** *nfpl* : digressions
distancia *nf* : distance
distanciamiento *nm* **1** : distancing **2** : rift, estrangement
distanciar *vt* **1** : to space out **2** : to draw apart — **distanciarse** *vr* : to grow apart, to become estranged
distante *adj* **1** : distant, far-off **2** : aloof
distar *vi* ~ **de** : to be far from ⟨dista de ser perfecto : he is far from perfect⟩
diste → **dar**
distender {56} *vt* : to distend, to stretch
distensión *nf, pl* **-siones** : distension
distinción *nf, pl* **-ciones** : distinction
distinguible *adj* : distinguishable
distinguido, -da *adj* : distinguished, refined
distinguir {26} *vt* **1** : to distinguish **2** : to honor — **distinguirse** *vr*
distintivo, -va *adj* : distinctive, distinguishing
distinto, -ta *adj* **1** DIFERENTE : different **2** CLARO : distinct, clear, evident
distorsión *nf, pl* **-siones** : distortion
distorsionar *vt* : to distort
distracción *nf, pl* **-ciones** **1** : distraction, amusement **2** : forgetfulness **3** : oversight
distraer {81} *vt* **1** : to distract **2** ENTRETENER : to entertain, to amuse — **distraerse** *vr* **1** : to get distracted **2** : to amuse oneself
distraídamente *adv* : absentmindedly
distraído[1] *pp* → **distraer**
distraído[2]**, -da** *adj* **1** : distracted, preoccupied **2** DESPISTADO : absentminded
distribución *nf, pl* **-ciones** : distribution
distribuidor, -dora *n* : distributor
distribuir {41} *vt* : to distribute
distributivo, -va *adj* : distributive
distrital *adj* : district, of the district
distrito *nm* : district
distrofia *nf* : dystrophy ⟨distrofia muscular : muscular dystrophy⟩
disturbio *nm* : disturbance
disuadir *vt* : to dissuade, to discourage
disuasión *nf, pl* **-siones** : dissuasion
disuasivo, -va *adj* : deterrent, discouraging
disuasorio, -ria *adj* : discouraging
disuelto *pp* → **disolver**
disyuntiva *nf* : dilemma
DIU ['diu] *nm* (dispositivo *intrauterino*) : IUD, intrauterine device
diurético[1]**, -ca** *adj* : diuretic
diurético[2] *nm* : diuretic
diurno, -na *adj* : day, daytime
diva *nf* → **divo**
divagar {52} *vi* : to digress
diván *nm, pl* **divanes** : divan
divergencia *nf* : divergence, difference
divergente *adj* : divergent, differing
divergir {35} *vi* **1** : to diverge **2** : to differ, to disagree

diversidad *nf* : diversity, variety
diversificación *nf, pl* **-ciones** : diversification
diversificar {72} *vt* : to diversify
diversión *nf, pl* **-siones** ENTRETENIMIENTO : fun, amusement, diversion
diverso, -sa *adj* : diverse, various
divertido, -da *adj* 1 : amusing, funny 2 : entertaining, enjoyable
divertir {76} *vt* ENTRETENER : to amuse, to entertain — **divertirse** *vr* : to have fun, to have a good time
dividendo *nm* : dividend
dividir *vt* 1 : to divide, to split 2 : to distribute, to share out — **dividirse** *vr*
divieso *nm* : boil
divinidad *nf* : divinity
divino, -na *adj* : divine
divisa *nf* 1 : currency 2 LEMA : motto 3 : emblem, insignia
divisar *vt* : to discern, to make out
divisible *adj* : divisible
división *nf, pl* **-siones** : division
divisionismo *nm* : factionalism
divisivo, -va *adj* : divisive
divisor *nm* : denominator
divisorio, -ria *adj* : dividing
divo, -va *n* 1 : prima donna 2 : celebrity, star
divorciado[1], -da *adj* 1 : divorced 2 : split, divided
divorciado[2], -da *n* : divorcé *m*, divorcée *f*
divorciar *vt* : to divorce — **divorciarse** *vr* : to get a divorce
divorcio *nm* : divorce
divulgación *nf, pl* **-ciones** 1 : spreading, dissemination 2 : popularization
divulgar {52} *vt* 1 : to spread, to circulate 2 REVELAR : to divulge, to reveal 3 : to popularize — **divulgarse** *vr*
dizque *adv* : supposedly, apparently
dobladillar *vt* : to hem
dobladillo *nm* : hem
doblar *vt* 1 : to double 2 PLEGAR : to fold, to bend 3 : to turn ⟨doblar la esquina : to turn the corner⟩ 4 : to dub — *vi* 1 : to turn 2 : to toll, to ring — **doblarse** *vr* 1 : to fold up, to double over 2 : to give in, to yield
doble[1] *adj* : double — **doblemente** *adv*
doble[2] *nm* 1 : double 2 : toll (of a bell), knell
doble[3] *nmf* : stand-in, double
doblegar {52} *vt* 1 : to fold, to crease 2 : to force to yield — **doblegarse** *vr* : to yield, to bow
doblez[1] *nm, pl* **dobleces** : fold, crease
doblez[2] *nm* : duplicity, deceitfulness
doce *adj & nm* : twelve
doceavo[1], -va *adj* : twelfth
doceavo[2] *nm* : twelfth (fraction)
docena *nf* 1 : dozen 2 **docena de fraile** : baker's dozen
docencia *nf* : teaching
docente[1] *adj* : educational, teaching
docente[2] *n* : teacher, lecturer
dócil *adj* : docile — **dócilmente** *adv*

docilidad *nf* : docility
docto, -ta *adj* : learned, erudite
doctor, -tora *n* : doctor
doctorado *nm* : doctorate
doctrina *nf* : doctrine — **doctrinal** *adj*
documentación *nf, pl* **-ciones** : documentation
documental *adj & nm* : documentary
documentar *vt* : to document
documento *nm* : document
dogma *nm* : dogma
dogmático, -ca *adj* : dogmatic
dogmatismo *nm* : dogmatism
dólar *nm* : dollar
dolencia *nf* : ailment, malaise
doler {47} *vi* 1 : to hurt, to ache 2 : to grieve — **dolerse** *vr* 1 : to be distressed 2 : to complain
doliente *nmf* : mourner, bereaved
dolor *nm* 1 : pain, ache ⟨dolor de cabeza : headache⟩ 2 PENA, TRISTEZA : grief, sorrow
dolorido, -da *adj* 1 : sore, aching 2 : hurt, upset
doloroso, -sa *adj* 1 : painful 2 : distressing — **dolorosamente** *adv*
doloso, -sa *adj* : fraudulent — **dolosamente** *adv*
domador, -dora *n* : tamer
domar *vt* : to tame, to break in
domesticado, -da *adj* : domesticated, tame
domesticar {72} *vt* : to domesticate, to tame
doméstico, -ca *adj* : domestic, household
domiciliado, -da *adj* : residing
domiciliario, -ria *adj* 1 : home 2 **arresto domiciliario** : house arrest
domiciliarse *vr* RESIDIR : to reside
domicilio *nm* : home, residence ⟨cambio de domicilio : change of address⟩
dominación *nf, pl* **-ciones** : domination
dominancia *nf* : dominance
dominante *adj* 1 : dominant 2 : domineering
dominar *vt* 1 : to dominate 2 : to master, to be proficient at — *vi* : to predominate, to prevail — **dominarse** *vr* : to control oneself
domingo *nm* : Sunday
dominical *adj* : Sunday ⟨periódico dominical : Sunday newspaper⟩
dominicano, -na *adj & n* : Dominican
dominio *nm* 1 : dominion, power 2 : mastery 3 : domain, field
dominó *nm, pl* **-nós** 1 : domino (tile) 2 : dominoes *pl* (game)
domo *nm* : dome
don[1] *nm* 1 : gift, present 2 : talent
don[2] *nm* 1 : title of courtesy preceding a man's first name 2 **don nadie** : nobody, insignificant person
dona *nf Mex* : doughnut, donut
donación *nf, pl* **-ciones** : donation
donador, -dora *n* : donor
donaire *nm* 1 GARBO : grace, poise 2 : witticism

donante *nf* → donador
donar *vt* : to donate
donativo *nm* : donation
doncella *nf* : maiden, damsel
doncellez *nf* : maidenhood
donde[1] *conj* : where, in which ⟨el pueblo donde vivo : the town where I live⟩
donde[2] *prep* : over by ⟨lo encontré donde la silla : I found it over by the chair⟩
dónde *adv* : where ⟨¿dónde está su casa? : where is your house?⟩
dondequiera *adv* 1 : anywhere, no matter where 2 dondequiera que : wherever, everywhere
doña *nf* : title of courtesy preceding a woman's first name
doquier *adv* por ~ : everywhere, all over
dorado[1], -da *adj* : gold, golden
dorado[2], -da *nm* : gilt
dorar *vt* 1 : to gild 2 : to brown (food)
dormido, -da *adj* 1 : asleep 2 : numb ⟨tiene el pie dormido : her foot's numb, her foot's gone to sleep⟩
dormilón, -lona *n* : sleepyhead, late riser
dormir {27} *vt* : to put to sleep — *vi* : to sleep — dormirse *vr* : to fall asleep
dormitar *vi* : to snooze, to doze
dormitorio *nm* 1 : bedroom 2 : dormitory
dorsal[1] *adj* : dorsal
dorsal[2] *nm* : number (worn in sports)
dorso *nm* 1 : back ⟨el dorso de la mano : the back of the hand⟩ 2 *Mex* : backstroke
dos *adj & nm* : two
doscientos[1], -tas *adj* : two hundred
doscientos[2] *nms & pl* : two hundred
dosel *nm* : canopy
dosificación *nf, pl* -ciones : dosage
dosis *nfs & pl* 1 : dose 2 : amount, quantity
dossier *nm* : dossier
dotación *nf, pl* -ciones 1 : endowment, funding 2 : staff, personnel
dotado, -da *adj* 1 : gifted 2 ~ de : endowed with, equipped with
dotar *vt* 1 : to provide, to equip 2 : to endow
dote *nf* 1 : dowry 2 dotes *nfpl* : talent, gift
doy → dar
draga *nf* : dredge
dragado *nm* : dredging
dragar {52} *vt* : to dredge
dragón *nm, pl* dragones 1 : dragon 2 : snapdragon
drague, etc. → dragar
drama *nm* : drama
dramático, -ca *adj* : dramatic — dramáticamente *adv*
dramatizar {21} *vt* : to dramatize — dramatización *nf*
dramaturgo, -ga *n* : dramatist, playwright

drástico, -ca *adj* : drastic — drásticamente *adv*
drenaje *nm* : drainage
drenar *vt* : to drain
drene *nm Mex* : drain
driblar *vi* : to dribble (in basketball)
drible *nm* : dribble (in basketball)
droga *nf* : drug
drogadicción *nf, pl* -ciones : drug addiction
drogadicto, -ta *n* : drug addict
drogar {52} *vt* : to drug — drogarse *vr* : to take drugs
drogue, etc. → drogar
droguería *nf* FARMACIA : drugstore
dromedario *nm* : dromedary
dual *adj* : dual
dualidad *nf* : duality
dualismo *nm* : dualism
ducha *nf* : shower ⟨darse una ducha : to take a shower⟩
ducharse *vr* : to take a shower
ducho, -cha *adj* : experienced, skilled, expert
dúctil *adj* : ductile
ducto *nm* 1 : duct, shaft 2 : pipeline
duda *nf* : doubt ⟨no cabe duda : there's no doubt about it⟩
dudar *vt* : to doubt — *vi* ~ en : to hesitate to ⟨no dudes en pedirme ayuda : don't hesitate to ask me for help⟩
dudoso, -sa *adj* 1 : doubtful 2 : dubious, questionable — dudosamente *adv*
duele, etc. → doler
duelo *nm* 1 : duel 2 LUTO : mourning
duende *nm* 1 : elf, goblin 2 ENCANTO : magic, charm ⟨una bailarina que tiene duende : a dancer with a certain magic⟩
dueño, -ña *n* 1 : owner, proprietor, proprietress *f* 2 : landlord, landlady *f*
duerme, etc. → dormir
dueto *nm* : duet
dulce[1] *adv* : sweetly, softly
dulce[2] *adj* 1 : sweet 2 : mild, gentle, mellow — dulcemente *adv*
dulce[3] *nm* : candy, sweet
dulcería *nf* : candy store
dulcificante *nm* : sweetener
dulzura *nf* 1 : sweetness 2 : gentleness, mellowness
duna *nf* : dune
dúo *nm* : duo, duet
duodécimo[1], -ma *adj* : twelfth
duodécimo[2], -ma *nm* : twelfth (in a series)
dúplex *nms & pl* : duplex apartment
duplicación *nf, pl* -ciones : duplication, copying
duplicado *nm* : duplicate, copy
duplicar {72} *vt* 1 : to double 2 : to duplicate, to copy
duplicidad *nf* : duplicity
duque *nm* : duke
duquesa *nf* : duchess
durabilidad *nf* : durability
durable → duradero

duración *nf, pl* **-ciones** : duration, length
duradero, -ra *adj* : durable, lasting
duramente *adv* 1 : harshly, severely 2 : hard
durante *prep* : during ⟨durante todo el día : all day long⟩ ⟨trabajó durante tres horas : he worked for three hours⟩
durar *vi* : to last, to endure
durazno *nm* 1 : peach 2 : peach tree

dureza *nf* 1 : hardness, toughness 2 : severity, harshness
durmiente¹ *adj* : sleeping
durmiente² *nmf* : sleeper
durmió, etc. → **dormir**
duro¹ *adv* : hard ⟨trabajé tan duro : I worked so hard⟩
duro², **-ra** *adj* 1 : hard, tough 2 : harsh, severe

E

e¹ *nf* : fifth letter of the Spanish alphabet
e² *conj* (*used instead of* y *before words beginning with* i- *or* hi-) : and
ebanista *nmf* : cabinetmaker
ebanistería *nf* : cabinetmaking
ébano *nm* : ebony
ebriedad *nf* EMBRIAGUEZ : inebriation, drunkenness
ebrio, -bria *adj* EMBRIAGADO : inebriated, drunk
ebullición *nf, pl* **-ciones** : boiling
eccéntrico → **excéntrico**
echar *vt* 1 LANZAR : to throw, to cast, to hurl 2 EXPULSAR : to throw out, to expel 3 EMITIR : to emit, give off 4 BROTAR : to sprout, to put forth 5 DESPEDIR : to fire, to dismiss 6 : to put in, to add 7 **echar a perder** : to spoil, to ruin 8 **echar de menos** : to miss ⟨echan de menos a su madre : they miss their mother⟩ — *vi* 1 : to start off 2 ~ **a** : to begin to — **echarse** *vr* 1 : to throw oneself 2 : to lie down 3 : to put on 4 ~ **a** : to start to 5 **echarse a perder** : to go bad, to spoil 6 **echárselas de** : to pose as
ecléctico, -ca *adj* : eclectic
eclesiástico¹, **-ca** *adj* : ecclesiastical, ecclesiastic
eclesiástico² *nm* CLÉRIGO : cleric, clergyman
eclipsar *vt* 1 : to eclipse 2 : to outshine, to surpass
eclipse *nm* : eclipse
eco *nm* : echo
ecografía *nf* : ultrasound scanning
ecología *nf* : ecology
ecológico, -ca *adj* : ecological — **ecológicamente** *adv*
ecologista *nmf* : ecologist, environmentalist
ecólogo, -ga *n* : ecologist
economía *nf* 1 : economy 2 : economics
económicamente *adv* : financially
económico, -ca *adj* : economic, economical
economista *nmf* : economist
economizar {21} *vt* : to save, to economize on — *vi* : to save up, to be frugal
ecosistema *nm* : ecosystem
ecuación *nf, pl* **-ciones** : equation
ecuador *nm* : equator

ecuánime *adj* 1 : even-tempered 2 : impartial
ecuanimidad *nf* 1 : equanimity 2 : impartiality
ecuatorial *adj* : equatorial
ecuatoriano, -na *adj & n* : Ecuadorian
ecuestre *adj* : equestrian
ecuménico, -ca *adj* : ecumenical
eczema *nm* : eczema
edad *nf* 1 : age ⟨¿qué edad tiene? : how old is she?⟩ 2 ÉPOCA, ERA : epoch, era
edema *nm* : edema
Edén *nm, pl* **Edenes** : Eden, paradise
edición *nf, pl* **-ciones** 1 : edition 2 : publication, publishing
edicto *nm* : edict, proclamation
edificación *nf, pl* **-ciones** 1 : edification 2 : construction, building
edificante *adj* : edifying
edificar {72} *vt* 1 : to edify 2 CONSTRUIR : to build, to construct
edificio *nm* : building, edifice
editar *vt* 1 : to edit 2 PUBLICAR : to publish
editor¹, **-tora** *adj* : publishing ⟨casa editora : publishing house⟩
editor², **-tora** *n* 1 : editor 2 : publisher
editora *nf* : publisher, publishing company
editorial¹ *adj* 1 : publishing 2 : editorial
editorial² *nm* : editorial
editorial³ *nf* : publishing house
editorializar {21} *vi* : to editorialize
edredón *nm, pl* **-dones** COBERTOR, COLCHA : comforter, eiderdown, quilt
educable *adj* : educable, teachable
educación *nf, pl* **-ciones** 1 ENSEÑANZA : education 2 : manners *pl* — **educacional** *adj*
educado, -da *adj* : polite, well-mannered
educador, -dora *n* : educator
educando, -da *n* ALUMNO, PUPILO : pupil, student
educar {72} *vt* 1 : to educate 2 CRIAR : to bring up, to raise 3 : to train — **educarse** *vr* : to be educated
educativo, -va *adj* : educational
efectista *adj* : dramatic, sensational
efectivamente *adv* : really, actually
efectividad *nf* : effectiveness

efectivo¹, -va *adj* **1** : effective **2** : real, actual **3** : permanent, regular (of employment)

efectivo² *nm* : cash

efecto *nm* **1** : effect **2 en ~** : actually, in fact **3 efectos** *nmpl* : goods, property ⟨efectos personales : personal effects⟩

efectuar {3} *vt* : to carry out, to bring about

efervescencia *nf* **1** : effervescence **2** : vivacity, high spirits *pl*

efervescente *adj* **1** : effervescent **2** : vivacious

eficacia *nf* **1** : effectiveness, efficacy **2** : efficiency

eficaz *adj, pl* **-caces 1** : effective **2** EFICIENTE : efficient — **eficazmente** *adv*

eficiencia *nf* : efficiency

eficiente *adj* EFICAZ : efficient — **eficientemente** *adv*

eficientizar {21} *vt Mex* : to streamline, to make more efficient

efigie *nf* : effigy

efímera *nf* : mayfly

efímero, -ra *adj* : ephemeral

efusión *nf, pl* **-siones 1** : effusion **2** : warmth, effusiveness **3 con ~** : effusively

efusivo, -va *adj* : effusive — **efusivamente** *adv*

egipcio, -cia *adj & n* : Egyptian

eglefino *nm* : haddock

ego *nm* : ego

egocéntrico, -ca *adj* : egocentric, self-centered

egoísmo *nm* : selfishness, egoism

egoísta¹ *adj* : selfish, egoistic

egoísta² *nmf* : egoist, selfish person

egotismo *nm* : egotism, conceit

egotista¹ *adj* : egotistic, egotistical, conceited

egotista² *nmf* : egotist, conceited person

egresado, -da *n* : graduate

egresar *vi* : to graduate

egreso *nm* **1** : graduation **2 ingresos y egresos** : income and expenditure

eh *interj* **1** : hey! **2** : eh?, huh?

eje *nm* **1** : axle **2** : axis

ejecución *nf, pl* **-ciones** : execution

ejecutante *nmf* : performer

ejecutar *vt* **1** : to execute, to put to death **2** : to carry out, to perform

ejecutivo, -va *adj & n* : executive

ejecutor, -tora *n* : executor

ejemplar¹ *adj* : exemplary, model

ejemplar² *nm* **1** : copy (of a book, magazine, etc.) **2** : specimen, example

ejemplificar {72} *vt* : to exemplify, to illustrate

ejemplo *nm* **1** : example **2 por ~** : for example **3 dar ejemplo** : to set an example

ejercer {86} *vi* **~ de** : to practice as, to work as — *vt* **1** : to practice **2** : exercise (a right) **3** : to exert

ejercicio *nm* **1** : exercise **2** : practice

ejercitar *vt* **1** : to exercise **2** ADIESTRAR : to drill, to train

ejército *nm* : army

ejidal *adj Mex* : cooperative

ejido *nm* **1** : common land **2** *Mex* : cooperative

ejote *nm Mex* : green bean

el¹ *pron* (*referring to masculine nouns*) **1** : the one ⟨tengo mi libro y el tuyo : I have my book and yours⟩ ⟨de los cantantes me gusta el de México : I prefer the singer from México⟩ **2 el que** : he who, whoever, the one that ⟨el que vino ayer : the one who came yesterday⟩ ⟨el que trabaja duro estará contento : he who works hard will be happy⟩

el², la *art, pl* **los, las** : the ⟨los niños están en la casa : the boys are in the house⟩ ⟨me duele el pie : my foot hurts⟩

él *pron* : he, him ⟨él es mi amigo : he's my friend⟩ ⟨hablaremos con él : we will speak with him⟩

elaboración *nf, pl* **-ciones 1** PRODUCCIÓN : production, making **2** : preparation, devising

elaborado, -da *adj* : elaborate

elaborar *vt* **1** : to make, to produce **2** : to devise, to draw up

elasticidad *nf* : elasticity

elástico¹, -ca *adj* **1** FLEXIBLE : flexible **2** : elastic

elástico² *nm* **1** : elastic (material) **2** : rubber band

elección *nf, pl* **-ciones 1** SELECCIÓN : choice, selection **2** : election

electivo, -va *adj* : elective

electo, -ta *adj* : elect ⟨el presidente electo : the president-elect⟩

elector, -tora *n* : elector, voter

electorado *nm* : electorate

electoral *adj* : electoral, election

electricidad *nf* : electricity

electricista *nmf* : electrician

eléctrico, -ca *adj* : electric, electrical

electrificar {72} *vt* : to electrify — **electrificación** *nf*

electrizar {21} *vt* : to electrify, to thrill — **electrizante** *adj*

electrocardiógrafo *nm* : electrocardiograph

electrocardiograma *nm* : electrocardiogram

electrocutar *vt* : to electrocute — **electrocución** *nf*

electrodo *nm* : electrode

electrodoméstico *nm* : electric appliance

electroimán *nm, pl* **-manes** : electromagnet

electrólisis *nfs & pl* : electrolysis

electrolito *nm* : electrolyte

electromagnético, -ca *adj* : electromagnetic

electromagnetismo *nm* : electromagnetism

electrón *nm, pl* **-trones** : electron

electrónica *nf* : electronics

electrónico, -ca *adj* : electronic — **electrónicamente** *adv*

elefante, -ta *n* : elephant
elegancia *nf* : elegance
elegante *adj* : elegant, smart — **elegantemente** *adv*
elegía *nf* : elegy
elegíaco, -ca *adj* : elegiac
elegibilidad *nf* : eligibility
elegible *adj* : eligible
elegido, -da *adj* **1** : chosen, selected **2** : elected
elegir {28} *vt* **1** ESCOGER, SELECCIONAR : to choose, to select **2** : to elect
elemental *adj* **1** : elementary, basic **2** : fundamental, essential
elemento *nm* : element
elenco *nm* : cast (of actors)
elepé *nm* : long-playing record
elevación *nf, pl* **-ciones** : elevation, height
elevado, -da *adj* **1** : elevated, lofty **2** : high
elevador *nm* ASCENSOR : elevator
elevar *vt* **1** ALZAR : to raise, to lift **2** AUMENTAR : to raise, to increase **3** : to elevate (in a hierarchy), to promote **4** : to present, to submit — **elevarse** *vr* : to rise
elfo *nm* : elf
eliminación *nf, pl* **-ciones** : elimination, removal
eliminar *vt* **1** : to eliminate, to remove **2** : to do in, to kill
elipse *nf* : ellipse
elipsis *nf* : ellipsis
elíptico, -ca *adj* : elliptical, elliptic
elite *or* **élite** *nf* : elite
elixir *or* **elíxir** *nm* : elixir
ella *pron* : she, her ⟨ella es mi amiga : she is my friend⟩ ⟨nos fuimos con ella : we left with her⟩
ello *pron* : it ⟨es por ello que me voy : that's why I'm going⟩
ellos, ellas *pron pl* **1** : they, them **2 de ellos, de ellas** : theirs
elocución *nf, pl* **-ciones** : elocution
elocuencia *nf* : eloquence
elocuente *adj* : eloquent — **elocuentemente** *adv*
elogiar *vt* ENCOMIAR : to praise
elogio *nm* : praise
elote *nm* **1** *Mex* : corn, maize **2** *CA, Mex* : corncob
elucidación *nf, pl* **-ciones** ESCLARECIMIENTO : elucidation
elucidar *vt* ESCLARECER : to elucidate
eludir *vt* EVADIR : to evade, to avoid, to elude
emanación *nf, pl* **-ciones** : emanation
emanar *vi* ~ **de** : to emanate from — *vt* : to exude
emancipar *vt* : to emancipate — **emancipación** *nf*
embadurnar *vt* EMBARRAR : to smear, to daub
embajada *nf* : embassy
embajador, -dora *n* : ambassador
embalaje *nm* : packing, packaging
embalar *vt* EMPAQUETAR : to pack

embaldosar *vt* : to tile, to pave with tiles
embalsamar *vt* : to embalm
embalsar *vt* : to dam, to dam up
embalse *nm* : dam, reservoir
embarazada *adj* ENCINTA, PREÑADA : pregnant, expecting
embarazar {21} *vt* **1** : to obstruct, to hamper **2** PREÑAR : to make pregnant
embarazo *nm* : pregnancy
embarazoso, -sa *adj* : embarrassing, awkward
embarcación *nf, pl* **-ciones** : boat, craft
embarcadero *nm* : wharf, pier, jetty
embarcar {72} *vi* : to embark, to board — *vt* : to load
embarco *nm* : embarkation
embargar {52} *vt* **1** : to seize, to impound **2** : to overwhelm
embargo *nm* **1** : seizure **2** : embargo **3 sin** ~ : however, nevertheless
embarque *nm* **1** : embarkation **2** : shipment
embarrancar {72} *vi* **1** : to run aground **2** : to get bogged down
embarrar *vt* **1** : to cover with mud **2** EMBADURNAR : to smear
embarullar *vt fam* : to muddle, to confuse — **embarullarse** *vr fam* : to get mixed up
embate *nm* **1** : onslaught **2** : battering (of waves or wind)
embaucador, -dora *n* : swindler, deceiver
embaucar {72} *vt* : to trick, to swindle
embeber *vt* : to absorb, to soak up — *vi* : to shrink
embelesado, -da *adj* : spellbound
embelesar *vt* : to enchant, to captivate
embellecer {53} *vt* : to embellish, to beautify
embellecimiento *nm* : beautification, embellishment
embestida *nf* **1** : charge (of a bull) **2** ARREMETIDA : attack, onslaught
embestir {54} *vt* : to hit, to run into, to charge at — *vi* ARREMETER : to charge, to attack
emblanquecer {53} *vt* BLANQUEAR : to bleach, to whiten — **emblanquecerse** *vr* : to turn white
emblema *nm* : emblem
emblemático, -ca *adj* : emblematic
embolia *nf* : embolism
émbolo *nm* : piston
embolsarse *vr* **1** : to pocket (money) **2** : to collect (payment)
emborracharse *vr* EMBRIAGARSE : to get drunk
emborronar *vt* **1** : to blot, to smudge **2** GARABATEAR : to scribble
emboscada *nf* : ambush
emboscar {72} *vt* : to ambush — **emboscarse** *vr* : to lie in ambush
embotadura *nf* : bluntness, dullness
embotar *vt* **1** : to dull, to blunt **2** : to weaken, to enervate
embotellamiento *nm* ATASCO : traffic jam

embotellar *vt* ENVASAR : to bottle
embragar {52} *vi* : to engage the clutch
embrague *nm* : clutch
embravecerse {53} *vr* **1** : to get furious **2** : to get rough ⟨el mar se embraveció : the sea became tempestuous⟩
embriagado, -da *adj* : inebriated, drunk
embriagador, -dora *adj* : intoxicating
embriagarse {52} *vr* EMBORRACHARSE : to get drunk
embriaguez *nf* EBRIEDAD : drunkenness, inebriation
embrión *nm, pl* **embriones** : embryo
embrionario, -ria *adj* : embryonic
embrollo *nm* ENREDO : imbroglio, confusion
embrujar *vt* HECHIZAR : to bewitch
embrujo *nm* : spell, curse
embudo *nm* : funnel
embuste *nm* **1** MENTIRA : lie, fib **2** ENGAÑO : trick, hoax
embustero¹, -ra *adj* : lying, deceitful
embustero², -ra *n* : liar, cheat
embutido *nm* **1** : sausage **2** : inlaid work
embutir *vt* **1** : to cram, to stuff, to jam **2** : to inlay
emergencia *nf* **1** : emergency **2** : emergence
emergente *adj* **1** : emergent **2** : consequent, resultant
emerger {15} *vi* : to emerge, to surface
emético¹, -ca *adj* : emetic
emético² *nm* : emetic
emigración *nf, pl* **-ciones** **1** : emigration **2** : migration
emigrante *adj & nmf* : emigrant
emigrar *vi* **1** : to emigrate **2** : to migrate
eminencia *nf* : eminence
eminente *adj* : eminent, distinguished
eminentemente *adv* : basically, essentially
emisario¹, -ria *n* : emissary
emisario² *nm* : outlet (of a body of water)
emisión *nf, pl* **-siones** **1** : emission **2** : broadcast **3** : issue ⟨emisión de acciones : stock issue⟩
emisor *nm* TRANSMISOR : television or radio transmitter
emisora *nf* : radio station
emitir *vt* **1** : to emit, to give off **2** : to broadcast **3** : to issue **4** : to cast (a vote)
emoción *nf, pl* **-ciones** : emotion — **emocional** *adj* — **emocionalmente** *adv*
emocionado, -da *adj* **1** : moved, affected by emotion **2** ENTUSIASMADO : excited
emocionante *adj* **1** CONMOVEDOR : moving, touching **2** EXCITANTE : exciting, thrilling
emocionar *vt* **1** CONMOVER : to move, to touch **2** : to excite, to thrill — **emocionarse** *vr*
emotivo, -va *adj* : emotional, moving
empacador, -dora *n* : packer

empacar {72} *vt* **1** EMPAQUETAR : to pack **2** : to bale — *vi* : to pack — **empacarse** *vr* **1** : to balk, to refuse to budge **2** *Col, Mex fam* : to eat ravenously, to devour
empachar *vt* **1** ESTORBAR : to obstruct **2** : to give indigestion to **3** DISFRAZAR : to disguise, to mask — **empacharse** *vr* **1** INDIGESTARSE : to get indigestion **2** AVERGONZARSE : to be embarrassed
empacho *nm* **1** INDIGESTIÓN : indigestion **2** VERGÜENZA : embarrassment **3** **no tener empacho en** : to have no qualms about
empadronarse *vr* : to register to vote
empalagar {52} *vt* **1** : to cloy, to surfeit **2** FASTIDIAR : to annoy, to bother
empalagoso, -sa *adj* MELOSO : cloying, excessively sweet
empalar *vt* : to impale
empalizada *nf* : palisade (fence)
empalmar *vt* **1** : to splice, to link **2** : to combine — *vi* : to meet, to converge
empalme *nm* **1** CONEXIÓN : connection, link **2** : junction
empanada *nf* : pie, turnover
empanadilla *nf* : meat or seafood pie
empanar *vt* : to bread
empantanado, -da *adj* : bogged down, delayed
empañar *vt* **1** : to steam up **2** : to tarnish, to sully
empapado, -da *adj* : soggy, sodden
empapar *vt* MOJAR : to soak, to drench — **empaparse** *vr* **1** : to get soaking wet **2 ~ de** : to absorb, to be imbued with
empapelar *vt* : to wallpaper
empaque *nm fam* **1** : presence, bearing **2** : pomposity **3** DESCARO : impudence, nerve
empaquetar *vt* EMBALAR : to pack, to package — **empaquetarse** *vr fam* : to dress up
emparedado *nm* : sandwich
emparedar *vt* : to wall in, to confine
emparejar *vt* **1** : to pair, to match up **2** : to make even — *vi* : to catch up — **emparejarse** *vr* : to pair up
emparentado, -da *adj* : related
emparentar {55} *vi* : to become related by marriage
emparrillado *nm Mex* : gridiron (in football)
empastar *vt* **1** : to fill (a tooth) **2** : to bind (a book)
empaste *nm* : filling (of a tooth)
empatar *vt* : to tie, to connect — *vi* : to result in a draw, to be tied — **empatarse** *vr Ven* : to hook up, to link together
empate *nm* : draw, tie
empatía *nf* : empathy
empecinado, -da *adj* TERCO : stubborn
empecinarse *vr* OBSTINARSE : to be stubborn, to persist
empedernido, -da *adj* INCORREGIBLE : hardened, inveterate
empedrado *nm* : paving, pavement

empedrar {55} *vt* : to pave (with stones)
empeine *nm* : instep
empellón *nm, pl* **-llones** : shove, push
empelotado, -da *adj* **1** *Mex fam* : madly in love **2** *fam* : stark naked
empeñado, -da *adj* : determined, committed
empeñar *vt* **1** : to pawn **2** : to pledge, to give (one's word) — **empeñarse** *vr* **1** : to insist stubbornly **2** : to make an effort
empeño *nm* **1** : pledge, commitment **2** : insistence **3** ESFUERZO : effort, determination **4** : pawning ⟨casa de empeños : pawnshop⟩
empeoramiento *nm* : worsening, deterioration
empeorar *vi* : to deteriorate, to get worse — *vt* : to make worse
empequeñecer {53} *vi* : to diminish, to become smaller — *vt* : to minimize, to make smaller
emperador *nm* : emperor
emperatriz *nf, pl* **-trices** : empress
empero *conj* : however, nevertheless
empezar {29} *v* COMENZAR : to start, to begin
empinado, -da *adj* : steep
empinar *vt* ELEVAR : to lift, to raise — **empinarse** *vr* : to stand on tiptoe
empírico, -ca *adj* : empirical — **empíricamente** *adv*
emplasto *nm* : poultice, dressing
emplazamiento *nm* **1** : location, site **2** CITACIÓN : summons, subpoena
emplazar {21} *vt* **1** CONVOCAR : to convene, to summon **2** : to subpoena **3** UBICAR : to place, to position
empleado, -da *n* : employee
empleador, -dora *n* PATRÓN : employer
emplear *vt* **1** : to employ **2** USAR : to use — **emplearse** *vr* **1** : to get a job **2** : to occupy oneself
empleo *nm* **1** OCUPACIÓN : employment, occupation, job **2** : use, usage
empobrecer {53} *vt* : to impoverish — *vi* : to become poor — **empobrecerse** *vr*
empobrecimiento *nm* : impoverishment
empollar *vi* : to brood eggs — *vt* : to incubate
empolvado, -da *adj* **1** : dusty **2** : powdered, powdery
empolvar *vt* **1** : to cover with dust **2** : to powder — **empolvarse** *vr* **1** : to gather dust **2** : to powder one's face
emporio *nm* **1** : center, capital, empire ⟨un emporio cultural : a cultural center⟩ ⟨un emporio financiero : a financial empire⟩ **2** : department store
empotrado, -da *adj* : built-in ⟨armarios empotrados : built-in cabinets⟩
empotrar *vt* : to build into, to embed
emprendedor, -dora *adj* : enterprising
emprender *vt* : to undertake, to begin

empresa *nf* **1** COMPAÑÍA, FIRMA : company, corporation, firm **2** : undertaking, venture
empresariado *nm* **1** : business world **2** : management, managers *pl*
empresarial *adj* : business, managerial, corporate
empresario, -ria *n* **1** : manager **2** : businessman *m,* businesswoman *f* **3** : impresario
empréstito *nm* : loan
empujar *vi* : to push, to shove — *vt* **1** : to push **2** PRESIONAR : to spur on, to press
empuje *nm* : impetus, drive
empujón *nm, pl* **-jones** : push, shove
empuñadura *nf* MANGO : hilt, handle
empuñar *vt* **1** ASIR : to grasp **2** **empuñar las armas** : to take up arms
emú *nm* : emu
emular *vt* IMITAR : to emulate — **emulación** *nf*
emulsión *nf, pl* **-siones** : emulsion
emulsionante *nm* : emulsifier
emulsionar *vt* : to emulsify
en *prep* **1** : in ⟨en el bolsillo : in one's pocket⟩ ⟨en una semana : in a week⟩ **2** : on ⟨en la mesa : on the table⟩ **3** : at ⟨en casa : at home⟩ ⟨en el trabajo : at work⟩ ⟨en ese momento : at that moment⟩
enagua *nf* : petticoat, slip
enajenación *nf, pl* **-ciones** **1** : transfer (of property) **2** : alienation **3** : absentmindedness
enajenado, -da *adj* : out of one's mind
enajenar *vt* **1** : to transfer (property) **2** : to alienate **3** : to enrapture — **enajenarse** *vr* **1** : to become estranged **2** : to go mad
enaltecer {53} *vt* : to praise, to extol
enamorado¹, -da *adj* : in love
enamorado², -da *n* : lover, sweetheart
enamoramiento *nm* : infatuation, crush
enamorar *vt* : to enamor, to win the love of — **enamorarse** *vr* : to fall in love
enamoriscarse {72} *vr fam* : to have a crush, to be infatuated
enamorizado, -da *adj* : amorous, passionate
enano¹, -na *adj* : tiny, minute
enano², -na *n* : dwarf, midget
enarbolar *vt* **1** : to hoist, to raise **2** : to brandish
enarcar {72} *vt* : to arch, to raise
enardecer {53} *vt* **1** : to arouse (anger, passions) **2** : to stir up, to excite — **enardecerse** *vr*
encabezado *nm Mex* : headline
encabezamiento *nm* **1** : heading **2** : salutation, opening
encabezar {21} *vt* **1** : to head, to lead **2** : to put a heading on
encabritarse *vr* **1** : to rear up **2** *fam* : to get angry
encadenar *vt* **1** : to chain **2** : to connect, to link **3** INMOVILIZAR : to immobilize

encajar *vi* : to fit, to fit together, to fit in — *vt* **1** : to insert, to stick **2** : to take, to cope with ⟨encajó el golpe : he withstood the blow⟩
encaje *nm* **1** : lace **2** : financial reserve
encajonar *vt* **1** : to box, to crate **2** : to cram in
encalar *vt* : to whitewash
encallar *vi* **1** : to run aground **2** : to get stuck
encallecido, -da *adj* : callused
encamar *vt* : to confine to a bed
encaminado, -da *adj* **1** : on the right track **2** ~ **a** : aimed at, designed to
encaminar *vt* **1** : to direct, to channel **2** : to head in the right direction — **encaminarse** *vr* ~ **a** : to head for, to aim at
encandilar *vt* : to dazzle
encanecer {53} *vi* : to gray, to go gray
encantado, -da *adj* **1** : charmed, bewitched **2** : delighted
encantador¹, -dora *adj* : charming, delightful
encantador², -dora *n* : magician
encantamiento *nm* : enchantment, spell
encantar *vt* **1** : to enchant, to bewitch **2** : to charm, to delight ⟨me encanta esta canción : I love this song⟩
encanto *nm* **1** : charm, fascination **2** HECHIZO : spell **3** : delightful person or thing
encañonar *vt* : to point (a gun) at, to hold up
encapotado, -da *adj* : cloudy, overcast
encapotarse *vr* : to cloud over, to become overcast
encaprichado, -da *adj* : infatuated
encaprichamiento *nm* : infatuation
encapuchado, -da *adj* : hooded
encarado, -da *adj* **estar mal encarado** *fam* : to be ugly-looking, to look mean
encaramar *vt* : to raise, to lift up — **encaramarse** *vr* : to perch
encarar *vt* CONFRONTAR : to face, to confront
encarcelación *nf* → **encarcelamiento**
encarcelamiento *nm* : incarceration, imprisonment
encarcelar *vt* : to incarcerate, to imprison
encarecer {53} *vt* **1** : to increase, to raise (price, value) **2** : to beseech, to entreat — **encarecerse** *vr* : to become more expensive
encarecidamente *adv* : insistently, urgently
encarecimiento *nm* : increase, rise (in price)
encargado¹, -da *adj* : in charge
encargado², -da *n* : manager, person in charge
encargar {52} *vt* **1** : to put in charge of **2** : to recommend, to advise **3** : to order, to request — **encargarse** *vr* ~ **de** : to take charge of
encargo *nm* **1** : errand **2** : job assignment **3** : order ⟨hecho de encargo : custom-made, made to order⟩

encariñarse *vr* ~ **con** : to become fond of, to grow attached to
encarnación *nf, pl* **-ciones** : incarnation, embodiment
encarnado¹, -da *adj* **1** : incarnate **2** : flesh-colored **3** : red **4** : ingrown
encarnado² *nm* : red
encarnar *vt* : to incarnate, to embody — **encarnarse** *vr* **encarnarse una uña** : to have an ingrown nail
encarnizado, -da *adj* **1** : bloodshot, inflamed **2** : fierce, bloody
encarnizar {21} *vt* : to enrage, to infuriate — **encarnizarse** *vr* : to be brutal, to attack viciously
encarrilar *vt* : to guide, to put on the right track
encasillar *vt* CLASIFICAR : to classify, to pigeonhole, to categorize
encausar *vt* : to prosecute, to charge
encauzar {21} *vt* : to channel, to guide — **encauzarse** *vr*
encebollado, -da *adj* : cooked with onions
encefalitis *nms & pl* : encephalitis
enceguecedor, -dora *n* : blinding
encendedor *nm* : lighter
encender {56} *vi* : to light — *vt* **1** : to light, to set fire to **2** PRENDER : to switch on **3** : to start (a motor) **4** : to arouse, to kindle — **encenderse** *vr* **1** : to get excited **2** : to blush
encendido¹, -da *adj* **1** : burning **2** : flushed **3** : fiery, passionate
encendido² *nm* : ignition
encerado *nm* **1** : waxing, polishing **2** : blackboard
encerar *vt* : to wax, to polish
encerrar {55} *vt* **1** : to lock up, to shut away **2** : to contain, to include **3** : to involve, to entail
encerrona *nf* **1** TRAMPA : trap, setup **2 prepararle una encerrona a alguien** : to set a trap for someone, to set someone up
encestar *vi* : to make a basket (in basketball)
enchapado *nm* : plating, coating (of metal)
encharcamiento *nm* : flood, flooding
encharcar {72} *vt* : to flood, to swamp — **encharcarse** *vr*
enchilada *nf* : enchilada
enchilar *vt Mex* : to season with chili
enchuecar {72} *vt Chile, Mex fam* : to make crooked, to twist
enchufar *vt* **1** : to plug in **2** : to connect, to fit together
enchufe *nm* **1** : connection **2** : plug, socket
encía *nf* : gum (tissue)
encíclica *nf* : encyclical
enciclopedia *nf* : encyclopedia
enciclopédico, -ca *adj* : encyclopedic
encierro *nm* **1** : confinement **2** : enclosure
encima *adv* **1** : on top, above **2** ADEMÁS : as well, besides **3** ~ **de** : on, on top

of, over **4 por encima de** : above, beyond ⟨por encima de la ley : above the law⟩ **5 echarse encima** : to take upon oneself **6 estar encima de** *fam* : to nag, to criticize **7 quitarse de encima** : to get rid of

encina *nf* : evergreen oak

encinta *adj* EMBARAZADA, PREÑADA : pregnant, expecting

enclaustrado, -da *adj* : cloistered, shut away

enclavado, -da *adj* : buried

enclenque *adj* : weak, sickly

encoger {15} *vt* **1** : to shrink, to make smaller **2** : to intimidate — *vi* : to shrink, to contract — **encogerse** *vr* **1** : to shrink **2** : to be intimidated, to cower, to cringe **3 encogerse de hombros** : to shrug (one's shoulders)

encogido, -da *adj* **1** : shriveled, shrunken **2** TÍMIDO : shy, inhibited

encogimiento *nm* **1** : shrinking, shrinkage **2** TIMIDEZ : shyness

encolar *vt* : to paste, to glue

encolerizar {21} *vt* ENFURECER : to enrage, to infuriate — **encolerizarse** *vr*

encomendar {55} *vt* CONFIAR : to entrust, to commend — **encomendarse** *vr*

encomiable *adj* : commendable, praiseworthy

encomiar *vt* ELOGIAR : to praise, to pay tribute to

encomienda *nf* **1** : charge, mission **2** : royal land grant **3** : parcel

encomio *nm* : praise, eulogy

encomioso, -sa *adj* : eulogistic, laudatory

enconar *vt* **1** : to irritate, to anger **2** : to inflame — **enconarse** *vr* **1** : to become heated **2** : to fester

encono *nm* **1** RENCOR : animosity, rancor **2** : inflammation, infection

encontrado, -da *adj* : contrary, opposing

encontrar {19} *vt* **1** HALLAR : to find **2** : to encounter, to meet — **encontrarse** *vr* **1** REUNIRSE : to meet **2** : to clash, to conflict **3** : to be ⟨su abuelo se encuentra mejor : her grandfather is doing better⟩

encorvar *vt* : to bend, to curve — **encorvarse** *vr* : to hunch over, to stoop

encrespar *vt* **1** : to curl, to ruffle, to ripple **2** : to annoy, to irritate — **encresparse** *vr* **1** : to curl one's hair **2** : to become choppy **3** : to get annoyed

encrucijada *nf* : crossroads

encuadernación *nf, pl* **-ciones** : bookbinding

encuadernar *vt* EMPASTAR : to bind (a book)

encuadrar *vt* **1** ENMARCAR : to frame **2** ENCAJAR : to fit, to insert **3** COMPRENDER : to contain, to include

encubierto *pp* → **encubrir**

encubrimiento *nm* : cover-up

encubrir {2} *vt* : to cover up, to conceal

encuentro *nm* **1** : meeting, encounter **2** : conference, congress

encuerado, -da *adj fam* : naked

encuerar *vt fam* : to undress

encuesta *nf* **1** INVESTIGACIÓN, PESQUISA : inquiry, investigation **2** SONDEO : survey

encuestador, -dora *n* : pollster

encuestar *vt* : to poll, to take a survey of

encumbrado, -da *adj* **1** : lofty, high **2** : eminent, distinguished

encumbrar *vt* **1** : to exalt, to elevate **2** : to extol — **encumbrarse** *vr* : to reach the top

encurtir *vt* ESCABECHAR : to pickle

ende *adv* **por ~** : therefore, consequently

endeble *adj* : feeble, weak

endeblez *nf* : weakness, frailty

endémico, -ca *adj* : endemic

endemoniado, -da *adj* : fiendish, diabolical

endentecer {53} *vi* : to teethe

enderezar {21} *vt* **1** : to straighten (out) **2** : to stand on end, to put upright

endeudado, -da *adj* : in debt, indebted

endeudamiento *nm* : indebtedness

endeudarse *vr* **1** : to go into debt **2** : to feel obliged

endiabladamente *adv* : extremely, diabolically

endiablado, -da *adj* **1** : devilish, diabolical **2** : complicated, difficult

endibia *or* **endivia** *nf* : endive

endilgar {52} *vt fam* : to spring, to foist ⟨me endilgó la responsabilidad : he saddled me with the responsibility⟩

endocrino, -na *adj* : endocrine

endogamia *nf* : inbreeding

endosar *vt* : to endorse

endoso *nm* : endorsement

endulzante *nm* : sweetener

endulzar {21} *vt* **1** : to sweeten **2** : to soften, to mellow — **endulzarse** *vr*

endurecer {53} *vt* : to harden, to toughen — **endurecerse** *vr*

enebro *nm* : juniper

eneldo *nm* : dill

enema *nm* : enema

enemigo, -ga *adj & n* : enemy

enemistad *nf* : enmity, hostility

enemistar *vt* : to make enemies of — **enemistarse** *vr* **con** : to fall out with

energía *nf* : energy

enérgico, -ca *adj* **1** : energetic, vigorous **2** : forceful, emphatic — **enérgicamente** *adv*

energúmeno, -na *n fam* : lunatic, crazy person

enero *nm* : January

enervar *vt* **1** : to enervate **2** *fam* : to annoy, to get on one's nerves — **enervante** *adj*

enésimo, -ma *adj* : umpteenth, nth

enfadar *vt* **1** : to annoy, to make angry **2** *Mex fam* : to bore — **enfadarse** *vr* : to get angry, to get annoyed

enfado *nm* : anger, annoyance
enfadoso, -sa *adj* : irritating, annoying
enfardar *vt* : to bale
énfasis *nms & pl* : emphasis
enfático, -ca *adj* : emphatic — **enfáti-camente** *adv*
enfatizar {21} *vt* DESTACAR, SUBRAYAR : to emphasize
enfermar *vt* : to make sick — *vi* : to fall ill, to get sick — **enfermarse** *vr*
enfermedad *nf* **1** INDISPOSICIÓN : sickness, illness **2** : disease
enfermería *nf* : infirmary
enfermero, -ra *n* : nurse
enfermizo, -za *adj* : sickly
enfermo[1], **-ma** *adj* : sick, ill
enfermo[2], **-ma** *n* **1** : sick person, invalid **2** PACIENTE : patient
enfilar *vt* **1** : to take, to go along ⟨enfiló la carretera de Montevideo : she went up the road to Montevideo⟩ **2** : to line up, to put in a row **3** : to string, to thread **4** : to aim, to direct — *vi* : to make one's way
enflaquecer {53} *vi* : to lose weight, to become thin — *vt* : to emaciate
enfocar {72} *vt* **1** : to focus (on) **2** : to consider, to look at
enfoque *nm* : focus
enfrascamiento *nm* : immersion, absorption
enfrascarse {72} *vr* ~ **en** : to immerse oneself in, to get caught up in
enfrentamiento *nm* : clash, confrontation
enfrentar *vt* : to confront, to face — **enfrentarse** *vr* **1** ~ **con** : to clash with **2** ~ **a** : to face up to
enfrente *adv* **1** DELANTE : in front **2** : opposite
enfriamiento *nm* **1** CATARRO : chill, cold **2** : cooling off, damper
enfriar {85} *vt* **1** : to chill, to cool **2** : to cool down, to dampen — *vi* : to get cold — **enfriarse** *vr* : to get chilled, to catch a cold
enfundar *vt* : to sheathe, to encase
enfurecer {53} *vt* ENCOLERIZAR : to infuriate — **enfurecerse** *vr* : to fly into a rage
enfurecido, -da *adj* : furious, raging
enfurruñarse *vr fam* : to sulk
engalanar *vt* : to decorate, to deck out — **engalanarse** *vr* : to dress up
enganchar *vt* **1** : to hook, to snag **2** : to attach, to hitch up — **engancharse** *vr* **1** : to get snagged, to get hooked **2** : to enlist
enganche *nm* **1** : hook **2** : coupling, hitch **3** *Mex* : down payment
engañar *vt* **1** EMBAUCAR : to trick, to deceive, to mislead **2** : to cheat on, to be unfaithful to — **engañarse** *vr* **1** : to be mistaken **2** : to deceive oneself
engaño *nm* **1** : deception, trick **2** : fake, feint (in sports)
engañoso, -sa *adj* **1** : deceitful **2** : misleading, deceptive

engarrotarse *vr* : to stiffen up, to go numb
engatusamiento *nm* : cajolery
engatusar *vt* : to coax, to cajole
engendrar *vt* **1** : to beget, to father **2** : to give rise to, to engender
engentarse *vr Mex* : to be in a daze
englobar *vt* : to include, to embrace
engomar *vt* : to glue
engordar *vt* : to fatten, to fatten up — *vi* : to gain weight
engorro *nm* : nuisance, bother
engorroso, -sa *adj* : bothersome
engranaje *nm* : gears *pl*, cogs *pl*
engranar *vt* : to mesh, to engage — *vi* : to mesh gears
engrandecer {53} *vt* **1** : to enlarge **2** : to exaggerate **3** : to exalt
engrandecimiento *nm* **1** : enlargement **2** : exaggeration **3** : exaltation
engrane *nm Mex* : cogwheel
engrapadora *nf* : stapler
engrapar *vt* : to staple
engrasar *vt* : to grease, to lubricate
engrase *nm* : greasing, lubrication
engreído, -da *adj* PRESUMIDO, VANIDOSO : vain, conceited, stuck-up
engreimiento *nm* ARROGANCIA : arrogance, conceit
engreír {66} *vt* ENVANECER : to make vain — **engreírse** *vr* : to become conceited
engrosar {19} *vt* : to enlarge, to increase, to swell — *vi* ENGORDAR : to gain weight
engrudo *nm* : paste
engullir {38} *vt* : to gulp down, to gobble up — **engullirse** *vr*
enharinar *vt* : to flour
enhebrar *vt* ENSARTAR : to string, to thread
enhiesto, -ta *adj* **1** : erect, upright **2** : lofty, towering
enhilar *vt* : to thread (a needle, etc.)
enhorabuena *nf* FELICIDADES : congratulations *pl*
enigma *nm* : enigma, mystery
enigmático, -ca *adj* : enigmatic — **enigmáticamente** *adv*
enjabonar *vt* : to soap up, to lather — **enjabonarse** *vr*
enjaezar {21} *vt* : to harness
enjalbegar {52} *vt* : to whitewash
enjambrar *vi* : to swarm
enjambre *nm* **1** : swarm **2** MUCHEDUMBRE : crowd, mob
enjaular *vt* **1** : to cage **2** *fam* : to jail, to lock up
enjuagar {52} *vt* : to rinse — **enjuagarse** *vr* : to rinse out
enjuague *nm* **1** : rinse **2 enjuague bucal** : mouthwash
enjugar {52} *vt* : to wipe away (tears)
enjuiciar *vt* **1** : to indict, to prosecute **2** JUZGAR : to try
enjundioso, -sa *adj* : substantial, weighty
enjuto, -ta *adj* : lean, gaunt

enlace *nm* **1** : bond, link, connection **2** : liaison

enladrillado *nm* : brick paving

enladrillar *vt* : to pave with bricks

enlatar *vt* ENVASAR : to can

enlazar {21} *v* : to join, to link, to fit together

enlistar *vt* : to list — **enlistarse** *vr* : to enlist

enlodado, -da *adj* BARROSO : muddy

enlodar *vt* **1** : to cover with mud **2** : to stain, to sully — **enlodarse** *vr*

enlodazar → enlodar

enloquecedor, -dora *adj* : maddening

enloquecer {53} *vt* ALOCAR : to drive crazy — **enloquecerse** *vr* : to go crazy

enlosado *nm* : flagstone pavement

enlosar *vt* : to pave with flagstone

enlutarse *vr* : to go into mourning

enmaderado *nm* **1** : wood paneling **2** : hardwood floor

enmarañar *vt* **1** : to tangle **2** : to complicate **3** : to confuse, to mix up — **enmarañarse** *vr*

enmarcar {72} *vt* **1** ENCUADRAR : to frame **2** : to provide the setting for

enmascarar *vt* : to mask, to disguise

enmasillar *vt* : to putty, to caulk

enmendar {55} *vt* **1** : to amend **2** CORREGIR : to emend, to correct **3** COMPENSAR : to compensate for — **enmendarse** *vr* : to mend one's ways

enmienda *nf* **1** : amendment **2** : correction, emendation

enmohecerse {53} *vr* **1** : to become moldy **2** OXIDARSE : to rust, to become rusty

enmudecer {53} *vt* : to mute, to silence — *vi* : to fall silent

enmugrar *vt* : to soil, to make dirty — **enmugrarse** *vr* : to get dirty

ennegrecer {53} *vt* : to blacken, to darken — **ennegrecerse** *vr*

ennoblecer {53} *vt* **1** : to ennoble **2** : to embellish

enojadizo, -za *adj* IRRITABLE : irritable, cranky

enojado, -da *adj* **1** : annoyed **2** : angry, mad

enojar *vt* **1** : to anger **2** : to annoy, to upset — **enojarse** *vr*

enojo *nm* **1** CÓLERA : anger **2** : annoyance

enojón, -jona *adj, pl* **-jones** *Chile, Mex fam* : irritable, cranky

enojoso, -sa *adj* FASTIDIOSO, MOLESTOSO : annoying, irritating

enorgullecer {53} *vt* : to make proud — **enorgullecerse** *vr* : to pride oneself

enorme *adj* INMENSO : enormous, huge — **enormemente** *adv*

enormidad *nf* **1** : enormity, seriousness **2** : immensity, hugeness

enraizado, -da *adj* : deep-seated, deeply rooted

enraizar {30} *vi* : to take root

enramada *nf* : arbor, bower

enramar *vt* : to cover with branches

enrarecer {53} *vt* : to rarefy — **enrarecerse** *vr*

enredadera *nf* : climbing plant, vine

enredar *vt* **1** : to tangle up, to entangle **2** : to confuse, to complicate **3** : to involve, to implicate — **enredarse** *vr*

enredo *nm* **1** EMBROLLO : muddle, confusion **2** MARAÑA : tangle

enredoso, -sa *adj* : complicated, tricky

enrejado *nm* **1** : railing **2** : grating, grille **3** : trellis, lattice

enrevesado, -da *adj* : complicated, involved

enriquecer {53} *vt* : to enrich — **enriquecerse** *vr* : to get rich

enriquecido, -da *adj* : enriched

enriquecimiento *nm* : enrichment

enrojecer {53} *vt* : to make red, to redden — **enrojecerse** *vr* : to blush

enrolar *vt* RECLUTAR : to recruit — **enrolarse** *vr* INSCRIBIRSE : to enlist, to sign up

enrollar *vt* : to roll up, to coil — **enrollarse** *vr*

enronquecerse {53} *vr* : to become hoarse

enroscar {72} *vt* TORCER : to twist — **enroscarse** *vr* : to coil, to twine

ensacar {72} *vt* : to bag (up)

ensalada *nf* : salad

ensaladera *nf* : salad bowl

ensalmo *nm* : incantation, spell

ensalzar {21} *vt* **1** : to praise, to extol **2** EXALTAR : to exalt

ensamblaje *nm* : assembly

ensamblar *vt* **1** : to assemble **2** : to join, to fit together

ensanchar *vt* **1** : to widen **2** : to expand, to extend — **ensancharse** *vr*

ensanche *nm* **1** : widening **2** : expansion, development

ensangrentado, -da *adj* : bloody, bloodstained

ensañarse *vr* : to act cruelly, to be merciless

ensartar *vt* **1** ENHEBRAR : to string, to thread **2** : to skewer, to pierce

ensayar *vi* : to rehearse — *vt* **1** : to try out, to test **2** : to assay

ensayista *nmf* : essayist

ensayo *nm* **1** : essay **2** : trial, test **3** : rehearsal **4** : assay (of metals)

enseguida *adv* INMEDIATAMENTE : right away, immediately, at once

ensenada *nf* : cove, inlet

enseña *nf* **1** INSIGNIA : emblem, insignia **2** : standard, banner

enseñanza *nf* **1** EDUCACIÓN : education **2** : teaching

enseñar *vt* **1** : to teach **2** MOSTRAR : to show, to display — **enseñarse** *vr* ∼ **a** : to learn to, to get used to

enseres *nmpl* : equipment, furnishings ⟨*pl* ⟨enseres domésticos : household goods⟩

ensillar *vt* : to saddle (up)

ensimismado, -da *adj* : absorbed, engrossed

ensimismarse *vr* : to lose oneself in thought

ensoberbecerse {53} *vr* : to become haughty

ensombrecer {53} *vt* : to cast a shadow over, to darken — **ensombrecerse** *vr*

ensoñación *nf, pl* **-ciones** : fantasy

ensopar *vt* **1** : to drench **2** : to dunk, to dip

ensordecedor, -dora *adj* : deafening, thunderous

ensordecer {53} *vt* : to deafen — *vi* : to go deaf

ensuciar *vt* : to soil, to dirty — **ensuciarse** *vr*

ensueño *nm* **1** : daydream, revery **2** FANTASÍA : illusion, fantasy

entablar *vt* **1** : to cover with boards **2** : to initiate, to enter into, to start

entallar *vt* AJUSTAR : to tailor, to fit, to take in — *vi* QUEDAR : to fit

ente *nm* **1** : being, entity **2** : body, organization ⟨ente rector : ruling body⟩ **3** *fam* : eccentric, crackpot

enteco, -ca *adj* : gaunt, frail

entenado, -da *n Mex* : stepchild, stepson *m*, stepdaughter *f*

entender[1] {56} *vt* **1** COMPRENDER : to understand **2** OPINAR : to think, to believe **3** : to mean, to intend **4** DEDUCIR : to infer, to deduce — *vi* **1** : to understand ⟨¡ya entiendo! : now I understand!⟩ **2** ~ **de** : to know about, to be good at **3** ~ **en** : to be in charge of — **entenderse** *vr* **1** : to be understood **2** : to get along well, to understand each other **3** ~ **con** : to deal with

entender[2] *nm* **a mi entender** : in my opinion

entendible *adj* : understandable

entendido[1], **-da** *adj* **1** : skilled, expert **2 tener entendido** : to understand, to be under the impression ⟨teníamos entendido que vendrías : we were under the impression you would come⟩ **3 darse por entendido** : to go without saying

entendido[2] *nm* : expert, authority, connoisseur

entendimiento *nm* **1** : intellect, mind **2** : understanding, agreement

enterado, -da *adj* : aware, well-informed ⟨estar enterado de : to be privy to⟩

enteramente *adv* : entirely, completely

enterar *vt* INFORMAR : to inform — **enterarse** *vr* INFORMARSE : to find out, to learn

entereza *nf* **1** INTEGRIDAD : integrity **2** FORTALEZA : fortitude **3** FIRMEZA : resolve

enternecedor, -dora *adj* CONMOVEDOR : touching, moving

enternecer {53} *vt* CONMOVER : to move, to touch

entero[1], **-ra** *adj* **1** : entire, whole **2** : complete, absolute **3** : intact — **enteramente** *adv*

entero[2] *nm* **1** : integer, whole number **2** : point (in finance)

enterramiento *nm* : burial

enterrar {55} *vt* : to bury

entibiar *vt* : to cool (down) — **entibiarse** *vr* : to become lukewarm

entidad *nf* **1** ENTE : entity **2** : body, organization **3** : firm, company **4** : importance, significance

entierro *nm* **1** : burial **2** : funeral

entintar *vt* : to ink

entoldado *nm* : awning

entomología *nf* : entomology

entomólogo, -ga *n* : entomologist

entonación *nf, pl* **-ciones** : intonation

entonar *vi* : to be in tune — *vt* **1** : to intone **2** : to tone up

entonces *adv* **1** : then **2 desde** ~ : since then **3 en aquel entonces** : in those days

entornado, -da *adj* ENTREABIERTO : half-closed, ajar

entornar *vt* ENTREABRIR : to leave ajar

entorno *nm* : surroundings *pl*, environment

entorpecer {53} *vt* **1** : to hinder, to obstruct **2** : to dull — **entorpecerse** *vr* : to dull the senses

entrada *nf* **1** : entrance, entry **2** : ticket, admission **3** : beginning, onset **4** : entrée **5** : cue (in music) **6 entradas** *nfpl* : income ⟨entradas y salidas : income and expenditures⟩ **7 tener entradas** : to have a receding hairline

entrado, -da *adj* **entrado en años** : elderly

entramado *nm* : framework

entrampar *vt* **1** ATRAPAR : to entrap, to ensnare **2** ENGAÑAR : to deceive, to trick

entrante *adj* **1** : next, upcoming ⟨el año entrante : next year⟩ **2** : incoming, new ⟨el presidente entrante : the president elect⟩

entraña *nf* MEOLLO : core, heart, crux **2 entrañas** *nfpl* VÍSCERAS : entrails

entrañable *adj* : close, intimate

entrañar *vt* : to entail, to involve

entrar *vi* **1** : to enter, to go in, to come in **2** : to begin — *vt* **1** : to bring in, to introduce **2** : to access

entre *prep* **1** : between **2** : among

entreabierto[1] *pp* → entreabrir

entreabierto[2], **-ta** *adj* ENTORNADO : half-open, ajar

entreabrir {2} *vt* ENTORNAR : to leave ajar

entreacto *nm* : intermission, interval

entrecano, -na *adj* : grayish, graying

entrecejo *nm* **fruncir el entrecejo** : to knit one's brows

entrecomillar *vt* : to place in quotation marks

entrecortado, -da *adj* **1** : labored, difficult ⟨respiración entrecortada : shortness of breath⟩ **2** : faltering, hesitant ⟨con la voz entrecortada : with a catch in his voice⟩

entrecruzar {21} *vt* ENTRELAZAR : to interweave, to intertwine — **entrecruzarse** *vr*
entredicho *nm* 1 DUDA : doubt, question 2 : prohibition
entrega *nf* 1 : delivery 2 : handing over, surrender 3 : installment ⟨entrega inicial : down payment⟩
entregar {52} *vt* 1 : to deliver 2 DAR : to give, to present 3 : to hand in, to hand over — **entregarse** *vr* 1 : to surrender, to give in 2 : to devote oneself
entrelazar {21} *vt* ENTRECRUZAR : to interweave, to intertwine
entremedias *adv* 1 : in between, halfway 2 : in the meantime
entremés *nm, pl* **-meses** 1 APERITIVO : appetizer, hors d'oeuvre 2 : interlude, short play
entremeterse → entrometerse
entremetido *nm* → entrometido
entremezclar *vt* : to intermingle
entrenador, -dora *n* : trainer, coach
entrenamiento *nm* : training, drill, practice
entrenar *vt* : to train, to drill, to practice — **entrenarse** *vr* : to train, to spar (in boxing)
entreoír {50} *vt* : to hear indistinctly
entrepierna *nf* 1 : inner thigh 2 : crotch 3 : inseam
entrepiso *nm* ENTRESUELO : mezzanine
entresacar {72} *vt* 1 SELECCIONAR : to pick out, to select 2 : to thin out
entresuelo *nm* ENTREPISO : mezzanine
entretanto[1] *adv* : meanwhile
entretanto[2] *nm* **en el entretanto** : in the meantime
entretejer *vt* : to interweave
entretela *nf* : facing (of a garment)
entretener {80} *vt* 1 DIVERTIR : to entertain, to amuse 2 DISTRAER : to distract 3 DEMORAR : to delay, to hold up — **entretenerse** *vr* 1 : to amuse oneself 2 : to dally
entretenido, -da *adj* DIVERTIDO : entertaining, amusing
entretenimiento *nm* 1 : entertainment, pastime 2 DIVERSIÓN : fun, amusement
entrever {88} *vt* 1 : to catch a glimpse of 2 : to make out, to see indistinctly
entreverar *vt* : to mix, to intermingle
entrevero *nm* : confusion, disorder
entrevista *nf* : interview
entrevistador, -dora *n* : interviewer
entrevistar *vt* : to interview — **entrevistarse** *vr* REUNIRSE ～ **con** : to meet with
entristecer {53} *vt* : to sadden
entrometerse *vr* : to interfere, to meddle
entrometido, -da *n* : meddler, busybody
entroncar {72} *vt* RELACIONAR : to establish a relationship between, to connect — *vi* 1 : to be related 2 : to link up, to be connected
entronque *nm* 1 : kinship 2 VÍNCULO : link, connection

entuerto *nm* : wrong, injustice
entumecer {53} *vt* : to make numb, to be numb — **entumecerse** *vr* : to go numb, to fall asleep
entumecido, -da *adj* 1 : numb 2 : stiff (of muscles, joints, etc.)
entumecimiento *nm* : numbness
enturbiar *vt* 1 : to cloud 2 : to confuse — **enturbiarse** *vr*
entusiasmar *vt* : to excite, to fill with enthusiasm — **entusiasmarse** *vr* : to get excited
entusiasmo *nm* : enthusiasm
entusiasta[1] *adj* : enthusiastic
entusiasta[2] *nmf* AFICIONADO : enthusiast
enumerar *vt* : to enumerate — **enumeración** *nf*
enunciación *nf, pl* **-ciones** : enunciation, statement
enunciar *vt* : to enunciate, to state
envainar *vt* : to sheathe
envalentonar *vt* : to make bold, to encourage — **envalentonarse** *vr*
envanecer {53} *vt* ENGREÍR : to make vain — **envanecerse** *vr*
envasar *vt* 1 EMBOTELLAR : to bottle 2 ENLATAR : to can 3 : to pack in a container
envase *nm* 1 : packaging, packing 2 : container 3 LATA : can 4 : empty bottle
envejecer {53} *vt* : to age, to make look old — *vi* : to age, to grow old
envejecido, -da *adj* : aged, old-looking
envejecimiento *nm* : aging
envenenamiento *nm* : poisoning
envenenar *vt* 1 : to poison 2 : to embitter
envergadura *nf* 1 : span, breadth, spread 2 : importance, scope
envés *nm, pl* **enveses** : reverse, opposite side
enviado, -da *n* : envoy, correspondent
enviar {85} *vt* 1 : to send 2 : to ship
envidia *nf* : envy, jealousy
envidiar *vt* : to envy — **envidiable** *adj*
envidioso, -sa *adj* : envious, jealous
envilecer {53} *vt* : to degrade, to debase
envilecimiento *nm* : degradation, debasement
envío *nm* 1 : shipment 2 : remittance
enviudar *vi* : to be widowed, to become a widower
envoltorio *nm* 1 : bundle, package 2 : wrapping, wrapper
envoltura *nf* : wrapper, wrapping
envolver {89} *vt* 1 : to wrap 2 : to envelop, to surround 3 : to entangle, to involve — **envolverse** *vr* 1 : to become involved 2 : to wrap oneself (up)
envuelto *pp* → envolver
enyerbar *vt Mex* : to bewitch
enyesar *vt* 1 : to plaster 2 ESCAYOLAR : to put in a plaster cast
enzima *nf* : enzyme
éon *nm, pl* **eones** : aeon
eperlano *nm* : smelt (fish)

épico, -ca *adj* : epic
epicúreo[1], **-rea** *adj* : epicurean
epicúreo[2], **-rea** *n* : epicure
epidemia *nf* : epidemic
epidémico, -ca *adj* : epidemic
epidermis *nf* : epidermis
epifanía *nf* : feast of the Epiphany (January 6th)
epigrama *nm* : epigram
epilepsia *nf* : epilepsy
epiléptico, -ca *adj & n* : epileptic
epílogo *nm* : epilogue
episcopal *adj* : episcopal
episcopaliano, -na *adj & n* : Episcopalian
episódico, -ca *adj* : episodic
episodio *nm* : episode
epístola *nf* : epistle
epitafio *nm* : epitaph
epíteto *nm* : epithet, name
epítome *nm* : summary, abstract
época *nf* **1** EDAD, ERA, PERÍODO : epoch, age, period **2** : time of year, season **3 de ~** : vintage, antique
epopeya *nf* : epic poem
equidad *nf* JUSTICIA : equity, justice, fairness
equilátero, -ra *adj* : equilateral
equilibrado, -da *adj* : well-balanced
equilibrar *vt* : to balance — **equilibrarse** *vr*
equilibrio *nm* **1** : balance, equilibrium ⟨perder el equilibrio : to lose one's balance⟩ ⟨equilibrio político : balance of power⟩ **2** : poise, aplomb
equilibrista *nmf* ACRÓBATA, FUNÁMBULO : acrobat, tightrope walker
equino, -na *adj* : equine
equinoccio *nm* : equinox
equipaje *nm* BAGAJE : baggage, luggage
equipamiento *nm* : equipping, equipment
equipar *vt* : to equip — **equiparse** *vr*
equiparable *adj* : comparable
equiparar *vt* **1** IGUALAR : to put on a same level, to make equal **2** COMPARAR : to compare
equipo *nm* **1** : team, crew **2** : gear, equipment
equitación *nf, pl* **-ciones** : horseback riding, horsemanship
equitativo, -va *adj* JUSTO : equitable, fair, just — **equitativamente** *adv*
equivalencia *nf* : equivalence
equivalente *adj & nm* : equivalent
equivaler {84} *vi* : to be equivalent
equivocación *nf, pl* **-ciones** ERROR : error, mistake
equivocado, -da *adj* : mistaken, wrong — **equivocadamente** *adv*
equivocar {72} *vt* : to mistake, to confuse — **equivocarse** *vr* : to make a mistake, to be wrong
equívoco[1], **-ca** *adj* AMBIGUO : ambiguous, equivocal
equívoco[2] *nm* : misunderstanding
era[1], etc. → ser
era[2] *nf* EDAD, ÉPOCA : era, age

erario *nm* : public treasury
erección *nf, pl* **-ciones** : erection, raising
eremita *nmf* ERMITAÑO : hermit
ergonomía *nf* : ergonomics
erguido, -da *adj* : erect, upright
erguir {31} *vt* : to raise, to lift up — **erguirse** *vr* : to straighten up
erial *nm* : uncultivated land
erigir {35} *vt* : to build, to erect — **erigirse** *vr* **~ en** : to set oneself up as
erizado, -da *adj* : bristly
erizarse {21} *vr* : to bristle, to stand on end
erizo *nm* **1** : hedgehog **2 erizo de mar** : sea urchin
ermitaño[1], **-ña** *n* EREMITA : hermit, recluse
ermitaño[2] *nm* : hermit crab
erogación *nf, pl* **-ciones** : expenditure
erogar {52} *vt* **1** : to pay out **2** : to distribute
erosión *nf, pl* **-siones** : erosion
erosionar *vt* : to erode
erótico, -ca *adj* : erotic
erotismo *nm* : eroticism
errabundo, -da *adj* ERRANTE, VAGABUNDO : wandering
erradicar {72} *vt* : to eradicate — **erradicación** *nf*
errado, -da *adj* : wrong, mistaken
errante *adj* ERRABUNDO, VAGABUNDO : errant, wandering
errar {32} *vt* FALLAR : to miss — *vi* **1** DESACERTAR : to be wrong, to be mistaken **2** VAGAR : to wander
errata *nf* : misprint, error
errático, -ca *adj* : erratic — **erráticamente** *adv*
erróneo, -nea *adj* EQUIVOCADO : erroneous, wrong — **erróneamente** *adv*
error *nm* EQUIVOCACIÓN : error, mistake
eructar *vi* : to belch, to burp
eructo *nm* : belch, burp
erudición *nf, pl* **-ciones** : erudition, learning
erudito[1], **-ta** *adj* LETRADO : erudite, learned
erudito[2], **-ta** *n* : scholar
erupción *nf, pl* **-ciones** **1** : eruption **2** SARPULLIDO : rash
eruptivo, -va *adj* : eruptive
es → ser
esbelto, -ta *adj* DELGADO : slender, slim
esbirro *nm* : henchman
esbozar {21} *vt* BOSQUEJAR : to sketch, to outline
esbozo *nm* **1** : sketch **2** : rough draft
escabechar *vt* **1** ENCURTIR : to pickle **2** *fam* : to kill, to rub out
escabeche *nm* : brine (for pickling)
escabechina *nf* MASACRE : massacre, bloodbath
escabel *nm* : footstool
escabroso, -sa *adj* **1** : rugged, rough **2** : difficult, tough **3** : risqué
escabullirse {38} *vr* : to slip away, to escape

escala *nf* **1** : scale **2** ESCALERA : ladder **3** : stopover
escalada *nf* : ascent, climb
escalador, -dora *n* ALPINISTA : mountain climber
escalafón *nm, pl* **-fones 1** : list of personnel **2** : salary scale, rank
escalar *vt* : to climb, to scale — *vi* **1** : to go climbing **2** : to escalate
escaldar *vt* : to scald
escalera *nf* **1** : ladder ⟨escalera de tijera : stepladder⟩ **2** : stairs *pl*, staircase **3 escalera mecánica** : escalator
escalfador *nm* : chafing dish
escalfar *vt* : to poach (eggs)
escalinata *nf* : flight of stairs
escalofriante *adj* : horrifying, bloodcurdling
escalofrío *nm* : shiver, chill, shudder
escalón *nm, pl* **-lones 1** : echelon **2** : step, rung
escalonado, -da *adj* GRADUAL : gradual, staggered
escalonar *vt* **1** : to terrace **2** : to stagger, to alternate
escalpelo *nm* BISTURÍ : scalpel
escama *nf* **1** : scale (of fish or reptiles) **2** : flake (of skin)
escamar *vt* **1** : to scale (fish) **2** : to make suspicious
escamocha *nf Mex* : fruit salad
escamoso, -sa *adj* : scaly
escamotear *vt* **1** : to palm, to conceal **2** *fam* : to lift, to swipe **3** : to hide, to cover up
escandalizar {21} *vt* : to shock, to scandalize — *vi* : to make a fuss — **escandalizarse** *vr* : to be shocked
escándalo *nm* **1** : scandal **2** : scene, commotion
escandaloso, -sa *adj* **1** : shocking, scandalous **2** RUIDOSO : noisy, rowdy **3** : flagrant, outrageous — **escandalosamente** *adv*
escandinavo, -va *adj & n* : Scandinavian
escandir *vt* : to scan (poetry)
escanear *vt* : to scan
escáner *nm* : scanner, scan
escaño *nm* **1** : seat (in a legislative body) **2** BANCO : bench
escapada *nf* HUIDA : flight, escape
escapar *vi* HUIR : to escape, to flee, to run away — **escaparse** *vr* : to escape notice, to leak out
escaparate *nm* **1** : shop window **2** : showcase
escapatoria *nf* **1** : loophole, excuse, pretext ⟨no tener escapatoria : to have no way out⟩ **2** ESCAPADA : escape, flight
escape *nm* **1** FUGA : escape **2** : exhaust (from a vehicle)
escapismo *nm* : escapism
escápula *nf* OMÓPLATO : scapula, shoulder blade
escapulario *nm* : scapular
escarabajo *nm* : beetle
escaramuza *nf* **1** : skirmish **2** : scrimmage

escaramuzar {21} *vi* : to skirmish
escarapela *nf* : rosette (ornament)
escarbar *vt* **1** : to dig, to scratch up **2** : to poke, to pick **3** ~ **en** : to investigate, to pry into
escarcha *nf* **1** : frost **2** *Mex, PRi* : glitter
escarchar *vt* **1** : to frost (a cake) **2** : to candy (fruit)
escardar *vt* **1** : to weed, to hoe **2** : to weed out
escariar *vt* : to ream
escarlata *adj & nf* : scarlet
escarlatina *nf* : scarlet fever
escarmentar {55} *vt* : to punish, to teach a lesson to — *vi* : to learn one's lesson
escarmiento *nm* **1** : lesson, warning **2** CASTIGO : punishment
escarnecer {53} *vt* RIDICULIZAR : to ridicule, to mock
escarnio *nm* : ridicule, mockery
escarola *nf* : escarole
escarpa *nf* : escarpment, steep slope
escarpado, -da *adj* : steep, sheer
escarpia *nf* : hook, spike
escasamente *adv* : scarcely, barely
escasear *vi* : to be scarce, to run short
escasez *nf, pl* **-seces** : shortage, scarcity
escaso, -sa *adj* **1** : scarce, scant **2** ~ **de** : short of
escatimar *vt* : to skimp on, to be sparing with ⟨no escatimar esfuerzos : to spare no effort⟩
escayola *nf* **1** : plaster (for casts) **2** : plaster cast
escayolar *vt* : to put in a plaster cast
escena *nf* **1** : scene **2** : stage
escenario *nm* **1** ESCENA : stage **2** : setting, scene ⟨el escenario del crimen : the scene of the crime⟩
escénico, -ca *adj* **1** : scenic **2** : stage
escenificar {72} *vt* : to stage, to dramatize
escepticismo *nm* : skepticism
escéptico[1], -ca *adj* : skeptical
escéptico[2], -ca *n* : skeptic
escindirse *vr* **1** : to split **2** : to break away
escisión *nf, pl* **-siones 1** : split, division **2** : excision
esclarecer {53} *vt* **1** ELUCIDAR : to elucidate, to clarify **2** ILUMINAR : to illuminate, to light up
esclarecimiento *nm* ELUCIDACIÓN : elucidation, clarification
esclavitud *nf* : slavery
esclavización *nf, pl* **-ciones** : enslavement
esclavizar {21} *vt* : to enslave
esclavo, -va *n* : slave
esclerosis *nf* **esclerosis múltiple** : multiple sclerosis
esclusa *nf* : floodgate, lock (of a canal)
escoba *nf* : broom
escobilla *nf* : small broom, brush, whisk broom
escobillón *nm, pl* **-llones** : swab

escocer {14} *vi* ARDER : to smart, to sting — **escocerse** *vr* : to be sore

escocés[1], **-cesa** *adj, mpl* **-ceses** **1** : Scottish **2** : tartan, plaid

escocés[2], **-cesa** *n, mpl* **-ceses** : Scottish person, Scot

escocés[3] *nm* **1** : Scots (language) **2** *pl* **-ceses** : Scotch (whiskey)

escofina *nf* : file, rasp

escoger {15} *vt* ELEGIR, SELECCIONAR : to choose, to select

escogido, -da *adj* : choice, select

escolar[1] *adj* : school

escolar[2] *nmf* : student, pupil

escolaridad *nf* : schooling ⟨escolaridad obligatoria : compulsory education⟩

escolarización *nf, pl* **-ciones** : education, schooling

escollo *nm* **1** : reef **2** OBSTÁCULO : obstacle

escolta *nmf* : escort

escoltar *vt* : to escort, to accompany

escombro *nm* **1** : debris, rubbish **2** **escombros** *nmpl* : ruins, rubble

esconder *vt* OCULTAR : to hide, to conceal

escondidas *nfpl* **1** : hide-and-seek **2** **a ~** : secretly, in secret

escondimiento *nm* : concealment

escondite *nm* **1** ENCONDRIJO : hiding place **2** ESCONDIDAS : hide-and-seek

escondrijo *nm* ESCONDITE : hiding place

escopeta *nf* : shotgun

escoplear *vt* : to chisel (out)

escoplo *nm* : chisel

escora *nf* : list, heeling

escorar *vi* : to list, to heel (of a boat)

escorbuto *nm* : scurvy

escoria *nf* **1** : slag, dross **2** HEZ : dregs *pl*, scum ⟨la escoria de la sociedad : the dregs of society⟩

Escorpio *or* **Escorpión** *nmf* : Scorpio

escorpión *nm, pl* **-piones** ALACRÁN : scorpion

escote *nm* **1** : low neckline **2** **pagar a escote** : to go dutch

escotilla *nf* : hatch, hatchway

escotillón *nf, pl* **-llones** : trapdoor

escozor *nm* : smarting, stinging

escriba *nm* : scribe

escribano, -na *n* **1** : court clerk **2** NOTARIO : notary public

escribir {33} *v* **1** : to write **2** : to spell — **escribirse** *vr* CARTEARSE : to write to one another, to correspond

escrito[1] *pp* → **escribir**

escrito[2], **-ta** *adj* : written

escrito[3] *nm* **1** : written document **2** **escritos** *nmpl* : writings, works

escritor, -tora *n* : writer

escritorio *nm* : desk

escritorzuelo, -la *n* : hack (writer)

escritura *nf* **1** : writing, handwriting **2** : deed **3** **las Escrituras** : the Scriptures

escroto *nm* : scrotum

escrúpulo *nm* : scruple

escrupuloso, -sa *adj* **1** : scrupulous **2** METICULOSO : exact, meticulous — **escrupulosamente** *adv*

escrutador, -dora *adj* : penetrating, searching

escrutar *vt* ESCUDRIÑAR : to scrutinize, to examine closely

escrutinio *nm* : scrutiny

escuadra *nf* **1** : square (instrument) **2** : fleet, squadron

escuadrilla *nf* : squadron, formation, flight

escuadrón *nm, pl* **-drones** : squadron

escuálido, -da *adj* **1** : skinny, scrawny **2** INMUNDO : filthy, squalid

escuchar *vt* **1** : to listen to **2** : to hear — *vi* : to listen — **escucharse** *vr*

escudar *vt* : to shield — **escudarse** *vr* **~ en** : to hide behind

escudero *nm* : squire

escudo *nm* **1** : shield **2** **escudo de armas** : coat of arms

escudriñar *vt* **1** ESCRUTAR : to scrutinize **2** : to inquire into, to investigate

escuela *nf* : school

escueto, -ta *adj* **1** : plain, simple **2** : succinct, concise — **escuetamente** *adv*

escuincle, -cla *n Mex fam* : child, kid

esculcar {72} *vt* : to search

esculpir *vt* **1** : to sculpt **2** : to carve, to engrave — *vi* : to sculpt

escultor, -tora *n* : sculptor

escultórico, -ca *adj* : sculptural

escultura *nf* : sculpture

escultural *adj* : statuesque

escupidera *nf* : spittoon, cuspidor

escupir *v* : to spit

escupitajo *nm* : spit

escurridizo, -za *adj* : slippery, elusive

escurridor *nm* **1** : dish rack **2** : colander

escurrir *vt* **1** : to wring out **2** : to drain — *vi* **1** : to drain **2** : to drip, to dripdry — **escurrirse** *vr* : to slip away

ese, esa *adj, mpl* **esos** : that, those

ése, ésa *pron, mpl* **ésos** : that one, those ones *pl*

esencia *nf* : essence

esencial *adj* : essential — **esencialmente** *adv*

esfera *nf* **1** : sphere **2** : face, dial (of a watch)

esférico[1], **-ca** *adj* : spherical

esférico[2] *nm* : ball (in sports)

esfinge *nf* : sphinx

esforzado, -da *adj* **1** : energetic, vigorous **2** VALIENTE : courageous, brave

esforzar {36} *vt* : to strain — **esforzarse** *vr* : to make an effort

esfuerzo *nm* **1** : effort **2** ÁNIMO, VIGOR : spirit, vigor **3** **sin ~** : effortlessly

esfumar *vt* : to tone down, to soften — **esfumarse** *vr* **1** : to fade away, to vanish **2** *fam* : to take off, to leave

esgrima *nf* : fencing (sport)

esgrimidor, -dora *n* : fencer

esgrimir *vt* **1** : to brandish, to wield **2** : to use, to resort to — *vi* : to fence

esguince *nm* : sprain, strain (of a muscle)

eslabón *nm, pl* **-bones** : link

eslabonar *vt* : to link, to connect, to join

eslavo[1], **-va** *adj* : Slavic

eslavo[2], **-va** *n* : Slav

eslogan *nm, pl* **-lóganes** : slogan

eslovaco, -ca *adj & n* : Slovakian, Slovak

esloveno, -na *adj & nm* : Slovene, Slovenian

esmaltar *vt* : to enamel

esmalte *nm* **1** : enamel **2 esmalte de uñas** : nail polish

esmerado, -da *adj* : careful, painstaking

esmeralda *nf* : emerald

esmerarse *vr* : to take great pains, to do one's utmost

esmeril *nm* : emery

esmero *nm* : meticulousness, great care

esmoquin *nm, pl* **-quins** : tuxedo

esnob[1] *adj, pl* **esnobs** : snobbish

esnob[2] *nmf, pl* **esnobs** : snob

esnobismo *nm* : snobbery, snobbishness

eso *pron* (*neuter*) **1** : that ⟨eso no me gusta : I don't like that⟩ **2 ¡eso es!** : that's it!, that's right! **3 a eso de** : around ⟨a eso de las tres : around three o'clock⟩ **4 en ~** : at that point, just then

esófago *nm* : esophagus

esos → **ese**

ésos → **ése**

esotérico, -ca *adj* : esoteric — **esotéricamente** *adv*

espabilado, -da *adj* : bright, smart

espabilarse *vr* **1** : to awaken **2** : to get a move on **3** : to get smart, to wise up

espacial *adj* **1** : space **2** : spatial

espaciar *vt* DISTANCIAR : to space out, to spread out

espacio *nm* **1** : space, room **2** : period, length (of time) **3 espacio exterior** : outer space

espacioso, -sa *adj* : spacious, roomy

espada[1] *nf* **1** : sword **2 espadas** *nfpl* : spades (in playing cards)

espada[2] *nm* MATADOR, TORERO : bullfighter, matador

espadaña *nf* **1** : belfry **2** : cattail

espadilla *nf* : scull, oar

espagueti *nm or* **espaguetis** *nmpl* : spaghetti

espalda *nf* **1** : back **2 espaldas** *nfpl* : shoulders, back **3 por la espalda** : from behind

espaldarazo *nm* **1** : recognition, support **2** : slap on the back

espaldera *nf* : trellis

espantajo *nm* : scarecrow

espantapájaros *nms & pl* : scarecrow

espantar *vt* ASUSTAR : to scare, to frighten — **espantarse** *vr*

espanto *nm* : fright, fear, horror

espantoso, -sa *adj* **1** : frightening, terrifying **2** : frightful, dreadful

español[1], **-ñola** *adj* : Spanish

español[2], **-ñola** *n* : Spaniard

español[3] *nm* CASTELLANO : Spanish (language)

esparadrapo *nm* : adhesive bandage, Band-Aid™

esparcimiento *nm* **1** DIVERSIÓN, RECREO : entertainment, recreation **2** DESCANSO : relaxation **3** DISEMINACIÓN : dissemination, spreading

esparcir {83} *vt* DISPERSAR : to scatter, to spread — **esparcirse** *vr* **1** : to spread out **2** DESCANSARSE : to take it easy **3** DIVERTIRSE : to amuse oneself

espárrago *nm* : asparagus

espartano, -na *adj* : severe, austere

espasmo *nm* : spasm

espasmódico, -ca *adj* : spasmodic

espástico, -ca *adj* : spastic

espátula *nf* : spatula

especia *nf* : spice

especial *adj & nm* : special

especialidad *nf* : specialty

especialista *nmf* : specialist, expert

especialización *nf, pl* **-ciones** : specialization

especializarse {21} *vr* : to specialize

especialmente *adv* : especially, particularly

especie *nf* **1** : species **2** CLASE, TIPO : type, kind, sort

especificación *nf, pl* **-ciones** : specification

especificar {72} *vt* : to specify

específico, -ca *adj* : specific — **específicamente** *adv*

espécimen *nm, pl* **especímenes** : specimen

especioso, -sa *adj* : specious

espectacular *adj* : spectacular — **espectacularmente** *adv*

espectáculo *nm* **1** : spectacle, sight **2** : show, performance

espectador, -dora *n* : spectator, onlooker

espectro *nm* **1** : ghost, specter **2** : spectrum

especulación *nf, pl* **-ciones** : speculation

especulador, -dora *n* : speculator

especular *vi* : to speculate

especulativo, -va *adj* : speculative

espejismo *nm* **1** : mirage **2** : illusion

espejo *nm* : mirror

espejuelos *nmpl* ANTEOJOS : spectacles, glasses

espeluznante *adj* : hair-raising, terrifying

espera *nf* : wait

esperado, -da *adj* : anticipated

esperanza *nf* : hope, expectation

esperanzado, -da *adj* : hopeful

esperanzador, -dora *adj* : encouraging, promising

esperanzar {21} *vt* : to give hope to

esperar *vt* **1** AGUARDAR : to wait for, to await **2** : to expect **3** : to hope ⟨espero poder trabajar : I hope to be able to work⟩ ⟨espero que sí : I hope so⟩ — *vi*

: to wait — **esperarse** *vr* **1** : to expect, to be hoped ⟨como podría esperarse : as would be expected⟩ **2** : to hold on, to hang on ⟨espérate un momento : hold on a minute⟩
esperma *nmf* : sperm
esperpéntico, -ca *adj* GROTESCO : grotesque
esperpento *nm fam* MAMARRACHO : sight, fright ⟨voy hecha un esperpento : I really look a sight⟩
espesante *nm* : thickener
espesar *vt* : to thicken — **espesarse** *vr*
espeso, -sa *adj* : thick, heavy, dense
espesor *nm* : thickness, density
espesura *nf* **1** : thickness **2** : thicket
espetar *vt* **1** : to blurt out **2** : to skewer
espía *nmf* : spy
espiar {85} *vt* : to spy on, to observe — *vi* : to spy
espiga *nf* **1** : ear (of wheat) **2** : spike (of flowers)
espigado, -da *adj* : willowy, slender
espigar {52} *vt* : to glean, to gather — **espigarse** *vr* : to grow quickly, to shoot up
espigón *nm, pl* **-gones** : breakwater
espina *nf* **1** : thorn **2** : spine ⟨espina dorsal : spinal column⟩ **3** : fish bone
espinaca *nf* **1** : spinach (plant) **2 espinacas** *nfpl* : spinach (food)
espinal *adj* : spinal
espinazo *nm* : backbone
espineta *nf* : spinet
espinilla *nf* **1** BARRO, GRANO : pimple **2** : shin
espino *nm* : hawthorn
espinoso, -sa *adj* **1** : thorny, prickly **2** : bony (of fish) **3** : knotty, difficult
espionaje *nm* : espionage
espiración *nf, pl* **-ciones** : exhalation
espiral *adj & nf* : spiral
espirar *vt* EXHALAR : to breathe out, to give off — *vi* : to exhale
espiritismo *nm* : spiritualism
espiritista *nmf* : spiritualist
espíritu *nm* **1** : spirit **2** ÁNIMO : state of mind, spirits *pl* **3 el Espíritu Santo** : the Holy Ghost
espiritual *adj* : spiritual — **espiritualmente** *adv*
espiritualidad *nf* : spirituality
espita *nf* : spigot, tap
esplendidez *nf, pl* **-deces** ESPLENDOR : magnificence, splendor
espléndido, -da *adj* **1** : splendid, magnificent **2** : generous, lavish — **espléndidamente** *adv*
esplendor *nm* ESPLENDIDEZ : splendor
esplendoroso, -sa *adj* MAGNÍFICO : magnificent, grand
espliego *nm* LAVANDA : lavender
espolear *vt* : to spur on
espoleta *nf* **1** DETONADOR : detonator, fuse **2** : wishbone
espolón *nm, pl* **-lones** : spur (of poultry), fetlock (of a horse)

espolvorear *vt* : to sprinkle, to dust
esponja *nf* **1** : sponge **2 tirar la esponja** : to throw in the towel
esponjado, -da *adj* : spongy
esponjoso, -sa *adj* **1** : spongy **2** : soft, fluffy
esponsales *nmpl* : betrothal, engagement
espontaneidad *nf* : spontaneity
espontáneo, -nea *adj* : spontaneous — **espontáneamente** *adv*
espora *nf* : spore
esporádico, -ca *adj* : sporadic — **esporádicamente** *adv*
esposar *vt* : to handcuff
esposas *nfpl* : handcuffs
esposo, -sa *n* : spouse, wife *f*, husband *m*
esprint *nm* : sprint
esprintar *vi* : to sprint
esprínter *nmf* : sprinter
espuela *nf* : spur
espuerta *nf* : two-handled basket
espulgar {52} *vt* **1** : to delouse **2** : to scrutinize
espuma *nf* **1** : foam **2** : lather **3** : froth, head (on beer)
espumar *vi* : to foam, to froth — *vt* : to skim off
espumoso, -sa *adj* : foamy, frothy
espurio, -ria *adj* : spurious
esputar *v* : to expectorate, to spit
esputo *nm* : spit, sputum
esqueje *nm* : cutting (from a plant)
esquela *nf* **1** : note **2** : notice, announcement
esquelético, -ca *adj* : emaciated, skeletal
esqueleto *nm* **1** : skeleton **2** ARMAZÓN : framework
esquema *nf* BOSQUEJO : outline, sketch, plan
esquemático, -ca *adj* : schematic
esquí *nm* **1** : ski **2 esquí acuático** : water ski, waterskiing
esquiador, -dora *n* : skier
esquiar {85} *vi* : to ski
esquife *nm* : skiff
esquila *nf* **1** CENCERRO : cowbell **2** : shearing
esquilar *vt* TRASQUILAR : to shear
esquimal *adj & nmf* : Eskimo
esquina *nf* : corner
esquinazo *nm* **1** : corner **2 dar esquinazo a** *fam* : to stand up, to give the slip to
esquirla *nf* : splinter (of bone, glass, etc.)
esquirol *nm* ROMPEHUELGAS : strikebreaker, scab
esquisto *nm* : shale
esquivar *vt* **1** EVADIR : to dodge, to evade **2** EVITAR : to avoid
esquivez *nf, pl* **-veces** **1** : aloofness **2** TIMIDEZ : shyness
esquivo, -va *adj* **1** HURAÑO : aloof, unsociable **2** : shy **3** : elusive, evasive
esquizofrenia *nf* : schizophrenia
esquizofrénico, -ca *adj & n* : schizophrenic

esta *adj* → este[1]

ésta → éste

estabilidad *nf* : stability

estabilización *nf, pl* -ciones : stabilization

estabilizador *nm* : stabilizer

estabilizar {21} *vt* : to stabilize — estabilizarse *vr*

estable *adj* : stable, steady

establecer {53} *vt* FUNDAR, INSTITUIR : to establish, to found, to set up — establecerse *vr* INSTALARSE : to settle, to establish oneself

establecimiento *nm* 1 : establishing 2 : establishment, institution, office

establo *nm* : stable

estaca *nf* : stake, picket, post

estacada *nf* 1 : picket fence 2 : stockade

estacar {72} *vt* 1 : to stake out 2 : to fasten down with stakes — estacarse *vr* : to remain rigid

estación *nf, pl* -ciones 1 : station ⟨estación de servicio : service station, gas station⟩ 2 : season

estacional *adj* : seasonal

estacionamiento *nm* 1 : parking 2 : parking lot

estacionar *vt* 1 : to place, to station 2 : to park — estacionarse *vr* 1 : to park 2 : to remain stationary

estacionario, -ria *adj* 1 : stationary 2 : stable

estada *nf* : stay

estadía *nf* ESTANCIA : stay, sojourn

estadio *nm* 1 : stadium 2 : phase, stage

estadista *nmf* : statesman

estadística *nf* 1 : statistic, figure 2 : statistics

estadístico[1], -ca *adj* : statistical — estadísticamente *adv*

estadístico[2], -ca *n* : statistician

estado *nm* 1 : state 2 : status ⟨estado civil : marital status⟩ 3 CONDICIÓN : condition

estadounidense *adj & nmf* AMERICANO, NORTEAMERICANO : American

estafa *nf* : swindle, fraud

estafador, -dora *n* : cheat, swindler

estafar *vt* DEFRAUDAR : to swindle, to defraud

estalactita *nf* : stalactite

estalagmita *nf* : stalagmite

estallar *vi* 1 REVENTAR : to burst, to explode, to erupt 2 : to break out

estallido *nm* 1 EXPLOSIÓN : explosion 2 : report (of a gun) 3 : outbreak, outburst

estambre *nm* 1 : worsted (fabric) 2 : stamen

estampa *nf* 1 ILUSTRACIÓN, IMAGEN : printed image, illustration 2 ASPECTO : appearance, demeanor

estampado[1], -da *adj* : patterned, printed

estampado[2] *nm* : print, pattern

estampar *vt* : to stamp, to print, to engrave

estampida *nf* : stampede

estampilla *nf* 1 : rubber stamp 2 SELLO, TIMBRE : postage stamp

estancado, -da *adj* : stagnant

estancamiento *nm* : stagnation

estancar {72} *vt* 1 : to dam up, to hold back 2 : to bring to a halt, to deadlock — estancarse *vr* 1 : to stagnate 2 : to be brought to a standstill, to be deadlocked

estancia *nf* 1 ESTADÍA : stay, sojourn 2 : ranch, farm

estanciero, -ra *n* : rancher, farmer

estanco, -ca *adj* : watertight

estándar *adj & nm* : standard

estandarización *nf, pl* -ciones : standardization

estandarizar {21} *vt* : to standardize

estandarte *nm* : standard, banner

estanque *nm* 1 : pool, pond 2 : tank, reservoir

estante *nm* REPISA : shelf

estantería *nf* : shelves *pl*, bookcase

estaño *nm* : tin

estaquilla *nf* 1 : peg 2 ESPIGA : spike

estar {34} *v aux* : to be ⟨estoy aprendiendo inglés : I'm learning English⟩ ⟨está terminado : it's finished⟩ — *vi* 1 (*indicating a state or condition*) : to be ⟨está muy alto : he's so tall, he's gotten very tall⟩ ⟨¿ya estás mejor? : are you feeling better now?⟩ ⟨estoy casado : I'm married⟩ 2 (*indicating location*) : to be ⟨están en la mesa : they're on the table⟩ ⟨estamos en la página 2 : we're on page 2⟩ 3 : to be at home ⟨¿está María? : is Maria in?⟩ 4 : to remain ⟨estaré aquí 5 días : I'll be here for 5 days⟩ 5 : to be ready, to be done ⟨estará para las diez : it will be ready by ten o'clock⟩ 6 : to agree ⟨¿estamos? : are we in agreement?⟩ ⟨estoy contigo : I'm with you⟩ 7 ¿cómo estás? : how are you? 8 ¡está bien! : all right!, that's fine! 9 ~ a : to cost 10 ~ a : to be ⟨¿a qué día estamos? : what's today's date?⟩ 11 ~ con : to have ⟨está con fiebre : she has a fever⟩ 12 ~ de : to be ⟨estoy de vacaciones : I'm on vacation⟩ ⟨está de director hoy : he's acting as director today⟩ 13 estar bien (mal) : to be well (sick) 14 ~ para : to be in the mood for 15 ~ por : to be in favor of 16 ~ por : to be about to ⟨está por cerrar : it's on the verge of closing⟩ 17 estar de más : to be unnecessary 18 estar que : to be (in a state or condition) ⟨está que echa chispas : he's hopping mad⟩ — estarse *vr* QUEDARSE : to stay, to remain ⟨¡estáte quieto! : be still!⟩

estarcir {83} *vt* : to stencil

estatal *adj* : state, national

estática *nf* : static

estático, -ca *adj* : static

estatizar {21} *vt* : to nationalize — estatización *nf*

estatua *nf* : statue

estatuilla *nf* : statuette, figurine
estatura *nf* : height, stature ⟨de mediana estatura : of medium height⟩
estatus *nm* : status, prestige
estatutario, -ria *adj* : statutory
estatuto *nm* : statute
este[1], **esta** *adj, mpl* **estos** : this, these
este[2] *adj* : eastern, east
este[3] *nm* **1** ORIENTE : east **2** : east wind **3 el Este** : the East, the Orient
éste, ésta *pron, mpl* **éstos 1** : this one, these ones *pl* **2** : the latter
estela *nf* **1** : wake (of a ship) **2** RASTRO : trail (of dust, smoke, etc.)
estelar *adj* : stellar
estelarizar {21} *vt Mex* : to star in, to be the star of
esténcil *nm* : stencil
estentóreo, -rea *adj* : loud, thundering
estepa *nf* : steppe
éster *nf* : ester
estera *nf* : mat
estercolero *nm* : dunghill
estéreo *adj & nm* : stereo
estereofónico, -ca *adj* : stereophonic
estereotipado, -da *adj* : stereotyped
estereotipar *vt* : to stereotype
estereotipo *nm* : stereotype
estéril *adj* **1** : sterile, germ-free **2** : infertile, barren **3** : futile, vain
esterilidad *nf* **1** : sterility **2** : infertility
esterilizar {21} *vt* **1** : to sterilize, to disinfect **2** : to sterilize (a person), to spay (an animal) — **esterilización** *nf*
esterlina *adj* : sterling
esternón *nm, pl* **-nones** : sternum
estero *nm* : estuary
estertor *nm* : death rattle
estética *nf* : aesthetics
estético, -ca *adj* : aesthetic — **estéticamente** *adv*
estetoscopio *nm* : stethoscope
estibador, -dora *n* : longshoreman, stevedore
estibar *vt* : to load (freight)
estiércol *nm* : dung, manure
estigma *nm* : stigma
estigmatizar {21} *vt* : to stigmatize, to brand
estilarse *vr* : to be in fashion
estilete *nm* : stiletto
estilista *nmf* : stylist
estilizar {21} *vt* : to stylize
estilo *nm* **1** : style **2** : fashion, manner **3** : stylus
estima *nf* ESTIMACIÓN : esteem, regard
estimable *adj* **1** : considerable **2** : estimable, esteemed
estimación *nf, pl* **-ciones 1** ESTIMA : esteem, regard **2** : estimate
estimado, -da *adj* : esteemed, dear ⟨Estimado señor Ortiz : Dear Mr. Ortiz⟩
estimar *vt* **1** APRECIAR : to esteem, to respect **2** EVALUAR : to estimate, to appraise **3** OPINAR : to consider, to deem
estimulación *nf, pl* **-ciones** : stimulation
estimulante[1] *adj* : stimulating
estimulante[2] *nm* : stimulant

estimular *vt* **1** : to stimulate **2** : to encourage
estímulo *nm* **1** : stimulus **2** INCENTIVO : incentive, encouragement
estío *nm* : summertime
estipendio *nm* **1** : salary **2** : stipend, remuneration
estipular *vt* : to stipulate — **estipulación** *nf*
estirado, -da *adj* **1** : stretched, extended **2** PRESUMIDO : stuck-up, conceited
estiramiento *nm* **1** : stretching **2** **estiramiento facial** : face-lift
estirar *vt* : to stretch (out), to extend — **estirarse** *vr*
estirón *nm, pl* **-rones 1** : pull, tug **2 dar un estirón** : to grow quickly, to shoot up
estirpe *nf* LINAJE : lineage, stock
estival *adj* VERANIEGO : summer
esto *pron* (*neuter*) **1** : this ⟨¿qué es esto? : what is this?⟩ **2 en ~** : at this point **3 por ~** : for this reason
estocada *nf* **1** : final thrust (in bullfighting) **2** : thrust, lunge (in fencing)
estofa *nf* CLASE : class, quality ⟨de baja estofa : low-class, poor-quality⟩
estofado *nm* COCIDO, GUISADO : stew
estofar *vt* GUISAR : to stew
estoicismo *nm* : stoicism
estoico[1], **-ca** *adj* : stoic, stoical
estoico[2], **-ca** *n* : stoic
estola *nf* : stole
estomacal *adj* GÁSTRICO : stomach, gastric
estómago *nm* : stomach
estoniano, -na *adj & n* : Estonian
estonio, -nia *adj & n* : Estonian
estopa *nf* **1** : tow (yarn or cloth) **2** : burlap
estopilla *nf* : cheesecloth
estoque *nm* : rapier, sword
estorbar *vt* OBSTRUIR : to obstruct, to hinder — *vi* : to get in the way
estorbo *nm* **1** : obstacle, hindrance **2** : nuisance
estornino *nm* : starling
estornudar *vi* : to sneeze
estornudo *nm* : sneeze
estos *adj* → **este**[1]
éstos → **éste**
estoy → **estar**
estrabismo *nm* : squint
estrado *nm* **1** : dais, platform, bench (of a judge) **2 estrados** *nmpl* : courts of law
estrafalario, -ria *adj* ESTRAMBÓTICO, EXCÉNTRICO : eccentric, bizarre
estragar {52} *vt* DEVASTAR : to ruin, to devastate
estragón *nm* : tarragon
estragos *nmpl* **1** : ravages, destruction, devastation ⟨los estragos de la guerra : the ravages of war⟩ **2 hacer estragos en** *or* **causar estragos entre** : to play havoc with
estrambótico, -ca *adj* ESTRAFALARIO, EXCÉNTRICO : eccentric, bizarre

estrangulamiento *nm* : strangling, strangulation

estrangular *vt* AHOGAR : to strangle — **estrangulación** *nf*

estratagema *nf* ARTIMAÑA : stratagem, ruse

estratega *nmf* : strategist

estrategia *nf* : strategy

estratégico, -ca *adj* : strategic, tactical — **estratégicamente** *adv*

estratificación *nf, pl* **-ciones** : stratification

estratificado, -da *adj* : stratified

estrato *nm* : stratum, layer

estratosfera *nf* : stratosphere

estratosférico, -ca *adj* 1 : stratospheric 2 : astronomical, exorbitant

estrechamiento *nm* 1 : narrowing 2 : narrow point 3 : tightening, strengthening (of relations)

estrechar *vt* 1 : to narrow 2 : to tighten, to strengthen (a bond) 3 : to hug, to embrace 4 **estrechar la mano de** : to shake hands with — **estrecharse** *vr*

estrechez *nf, pl* **-checes** 1 : tightness, narrowness 2 **estrecheces** *nfpl* : financial problems

estrecho¹, -cha *adj* 1 : tight, narrow 2 ÍNTIMO : close — **estrechamente** *adv*

estrecho² *nm* : strait, narrows

estrella *nf* 1 ASTRO : star ⟨estrella fugaz : shooting star⟩ 2 : destiny ⟨tener buena estrella : to be born lucky⟩ 3 : movie star 4 **estrella de mar** : starfish

estrellado, -da *adj* 1 : starry 2 : star-shaped 3 **huevos estrellados** : fried eggs

estrellamiento *nm* : crash, collision

estrellar *vt* : to smash, to crash — **estrellarse** *vr* : to crash, to collide

estrellato *nm* : stardom

estremecedor, -dora *adj* : horrifying

estremecer {53} *vt* : to cause to shake — *vi* : to tremble, to shake — **estremecerse** *vr* : to shudder, to shiver (with emotion)

estremecimiento *nm* : trembling, shaking, shivering

estrenar *vt* 1 : to use for the first time 2 : to premiere, to open — **estrenarse** *vr* : to make one's debut

estreno *nm* DEBUT : debut, premiere

estreñimiento *nm* : constipation

estreñirse {67} *vr* : to be constipated

estrépito *nm* ESTRUENDO : clamor, din

estrepitoso, -sa *adj* : clamorous, noisy — **estrepitosamente** *adv*

estrés *nm, pl* **estreses** : stress

estresante *adj* : stressful

estresar *vt* : to stress, to stress out

estría *nf* : fluting, groove

estribación *nf, pl* **-ciones** 1 : spur, ridge 2 **estribaciones** *nfpl* : foothills

estribar *vi* FUNDARSE ~ **en** : to be due to, to stem from

estribillo *nm* : refrain, chorus

estribo *nm* 1 : stirrup 2 : abutment, buttress 3 **perder los estribos** : to lose one's temper

estribor *nm* : starboard

estricnina *nf* : strychnine

estricto, -ta *adj* SEVERO : strict, severe — **estrictamente** *adv*

estridente *adj* : strident, shrill, loud — **estridentemente** *adv*

estrofa *nf* : stanza, verse

estrógeno *nm* : estrogen

estropajo *nm* : scouring pad

estropear *vt* 1 ARRUINAR : to ruin, to spoil 2 : to break, to damage — **estropearse** *vr* 1 : to spoil, to go bad 2 : to break down

estropicio *nm* DAÑO : damage, breakage

estructura *nf* : structure, framework

estructuración *nf, pl* **-ciones** : structuring, structure

estructural *adj* : structural — **estructuralmente** *adv*

estructurar *vt* : to structure, to organize

estruendo *nm* ESTRÉPITO : racket, din, roar

estruendoso, -sa *adj* : resounding, thunderous

estrujar *vt* APRETAR : to press, to squeeze

estuario *nm* : estuary

estuche *nm* : kit, case

estuco *nm* : stucco

estudiado, -da *adj* : affected, mannered

estudiantado *nm* : student body, students *pl*

estudiante *nmf* : student

estudiantil *adj* : student ⟨la vida estudiantil : student life⟩

estudiar *v* : to study

estudio *nm* 1 : study 2 : studio 3 **estudios** *nmpl* : studies, education

estudioso, -sa *adj* : studious

estufa *nf* 1 : stove, heater 2 *Col, Mex* : cooking stove, range

estupefacción *nf, pl* **-ciones** : stupefaction, astonishment

estupefaciente¹ *adj* : narcotic

estupefaciente² *nm* DROGA, NARCÓTICO : drug, narcotic

estupefacto, -ta *adj* : astonished, stunned

estupendo, -da *adj* MARAVILLOSO : stupendous, marvelous — **estupendamente** *adv*

estupidez *nf, pl* **-deces** 1 : stupidity 2 : nonsense

estúpido¹, -da *adj* : stupid — **estúpidamente** *adj*

estúpido², -da *n* IDIOTA : idiot, fool

estupor *nm* 1 : stupor 2 : amazement

esturión *nm, pl* **-riones** : sturgeon

estuvo, etc. → **estar**

etano *nm* : ethane

etanol *nm* : ethanol

etapa *nf* FASE : stage, phase

etcétera¹ : et cetera, and so on

etcétera² *nmf* : et cetera

éter *nm* : ether

etéreo, -rea *adj* : ethereal, heavenly
eternidad *nf* : eternity
eternizar {21} *vt* PERPETUAR : to make eternal, to perpetuate — **eternizarse** *vr fam* : to take forever
eterno, -na *adj* : eternal, endless — **eternamente** *adv*
ética *nf* : ethics
ético, -ca *adj* : ethical — **éticamente** *adv*
etimología *nf* : etymology
etimológico, -ca *adj* : etymological
etimólogo, -ga *n* : etymologist
etíope *adj & nmf* : Ethiopian
etiqueta *nf* **1** : etiquette **2** : tag, label **3 de ~** : formal, dressy
etiquetar *vt* : to label
étnico, -ca *adj* : ethnic
etnología *nf* : ethnology
etnólogo, -ga *n* : ethnologist
eucalipto *nm* : eucalyptus
Eucaristía *nf* : Eucharist, communion
eucarístico, -ca *adj* : eucharistic
eufemismo *nm* : euphemism
eufemístico, -ca *adj* : euphemistic
eufonía *nf* : euphony
eufónico, -ca *adj* : euphonious
euforia *nf* : euphoria, joyousness
eufórico, -ca *adj* : euphoric, exuberant, joyous — **eufóricamente** *adv*
eunuco *nm* : eunuch
europeo, -pea *adj & n* : European
euskera *nm* : Basque (language)
eutanasia *nf* : euthanasia
evacuación *nf, pl* **-ciones** : evacuation
evacuar *vt* **1** : to evacuate, to vacate **2** : to carry out — *vi* : to have a bowel movement
evadir *vt* ELUDIR : to evade, to avoid — **evadirse** *vr* : to escape, to slip away
evaluación *nf, pl* **-ciones** : assessment, evaluation
evaluador, -dora *n* : assessor
evaluar {3} *vt* : to evaluate, to assess, to appraise
evangélico, -ca *adj* : evangelical — **evangélicamente** *adv*
evangelio *nm* : gospel
evangelismo *nm* : evangelism
evangelista *nm* : evangelist
evangelizador, -dora *n* : evangelist, missionary
evaporación *nf, pl* **-ciones** : evaporation
evaporar *vt* : to evaporate — **evaporarse** *vr* ESFUMARSE : to disappear, to vanish
evasión *nf, pl* **-siones 1** : escape, flight **2** : evasion, dodge
evasiva *nf* : excuse, pretext
evasivo, -va *adj* : evasive
evento *nm* : event
eventual *adj* **1** : possible **2** : temporary ⟨trabajadores eventuales : temporary workers⟩ — **eventualmente** *adv*
eventualidad *nf* : possibility, eventuality
evidencia *nf* **1** : evidence, proof **2 poner en evidencia** : to demonstrate, to make clear

evidenciar *vt* : to demonstrate, to show — **evidenciarse** *vr* : to be evident
evidente *adj* : evident, obvious, clear — **evidentemente** *adv*
eviscerar *vt* : to eviscerate
evitable *adj* : avoidable, preventable
evitar *vt* **1** : to avoid **2** PREVENIR : to prevent **3** ELUDIR : to escape, to elude
evocación *nf, pl* **-ciones** : evocation
evocador, -dora *adj* : evocative
evocar {72} *vt* **1** : to evoke **2** RECORDAR : to recall
evolución *nf, pl* **-ciones 1** : evolution **2** : development, progress
evolucionar *vi* **1** : to evolve **2** : to change, to develop
evolutivo, -va *adj* : evolutionary
exabrupto *nm* : pointed remark
exacción *nf, pl* **-ciones** : levying, exaction
exacerbar *vt* **1** : to exacerbate, to aggravate **2** : to irritate, to exasperate
exactamente *adv* : exactly
exactitud *nf* PRECISIÓN : accuracy, precision, exactitude
exacto, -ta *adj* PRECISO : accurate, precise, exact
exageración *nf, pl* **-ciones** : exaggeration
exagerado, -da *adj* **1** : exaggerated **2** : excessive — **exageradamente** *adv*
exagerar *v* : to exaggerate
exaltación *nf, pl* **-ciones 1** : exaltation **2** : excitement, agitation
exaltado¹, -da *adj* : excitable, hotheaded
exaltado², -da *n* : hothead
exaltar *vt* **1** ENSALZAR : to exalt, to extol **2** : to excite, to agitate — **exaltarse** *vr* ACALORARSE : to get overexcited
ex–alumno → alumno
examen *nm, pl* **exámenes 1** : examination, test **2** : consideration, investigation
examinar *vt* **1** : to examine **2** INSPECCIONAR : to inspect — **examinarse** *vr* : to take an exam
exánime *adj* **1** : lifeless **2** : exhausted
exasperante *adj* : exasperating
exasperar *vt* IRRITAR : to exasperate, to irritate — **exasperación** *nf*
excavación *nf, pl* **-ciones** : excavation
excavadora *nf* : excavator
excavar *v* : to excavate, to dig
excedente¹ *adj* **1** : excessive **2** : excess, surplus
excedente² *nm* : surplus, excess
exceder *vt* : to exceed, to surpass — **excederse** *vr* : to go too far
excelencia *nf* **1** : excellence **2** : excellency ⟨Su Excelencia : His Excellency⟩
excelente *adj* : excellent — **excelentemente** *adv*
excelso, -sa *adj* : lofty, sublime
excentricidad *nf* : eccentricity
excéntrico, -ca *adj & n* : eccentric
excepción *nf, pl* **-ciones** : exception
excepcional *adj* EXTRAORDINARIO : exceptional, extraordinary, rare

excepto *prep* SALVO : except
exceptuar {3} *vt* EXCLUIR : to except, to exclude
excesivo, -va *adj* : excessive — **excesivamente** *adv*
exceso *nm* 1 : excess 2 **excesos** *nmpl* : excesses, abuses 3 **exceso de velocidad** : speeding
excitabilidad *nf* : excitability
excitación *nf, pl* -ciones : excitement
excitante *adj* : exciting
excitar *vt* : to excite, to arouse — **excitarse** *vr*
exclamación *nf, pl* -ciones : exclamation
exclamar *v* : to exclaim
excluir {41} *vt* EXCEPTUAR : to exclude, to leave out
exclusión *nf, pl* -siones : exclusion
exclusividad *nf* 1 : exclusiveness 2 : exclusive rights *pl*
exclusivista *adj & nmf* : exclusivist
exclusivo, -va *adj* : exclusive — **exclusivamente** *adv*
excomulgar {52} *vt* : to excommunicate
excomunión *nf, pl* -niones : excommunication
excreción *nf, pl* -ciones : excretion
excremento *nm* : excrement
excretar *vt* : to excrete
exculpar *vt* : to exonerate, to exculpate — **exculpación** *nf*
excursión *nf, pl* -siones : excursion, outing
excursionista *nmf* 1 : sightseer, tourist 2 : hiker
excusa *nf* 1 PRETEXTO : excuse 2 DISCULPA : apology
excusado *nm Mex* : toilet
excusar *vt* 1 : to excuse 2 : to exempt — **excusarse** *vr* : to apologize, to send one's regrets
execrable *adj* : detestable, abominable
exención *nf, pl* -ciones : exemption
exento, -ta *adj* 1 : exempt, free 2 **exento de impuestos** : tax-exempt
exequias *nfpl* FUNERALES : funeral rites
exhalación *nf, pl* -ciones 1 : exhalation 2 : shooting star ⟨salió como una exhalación : he took off like a shot⟩
exhalar *vt* ESPIRAR : to exhale, to give off
exhaustivo, -va *adj* : exhaustive — **exhaustivamente** *adv*
exhausto, -ta *adj* AGOTADO : exhausted, worn-out
exhibición *nf, pl* -ciones 1 : exhibition, show 2 : showing
exhibir *vt* : to exhibit, to show, to display — **exhibirse** *vr*
exhortación *nf, pl* -ciones : exhortation
exhortar *vt* : to exhort
exhumar *vt* DESENTERRAR : to exhume — **exhumación** *nf*
exigencia *nf* : demand, requirement
exigente *adj* : demanding, exacting
exigir {35} *vt* 1 : to demand, to require 2 : to exact, to levy

exiguo, -gua *adj* : meager
exiliado[1], -da *adj* : exiled, in exile
exiliado[2], -da *n* : exile
exiliar *vt* DESTERRAR : to exile, to banish — **exiliarse** *vr* : to go into exile
exilio *nm* DESTIERRO : exile
eximio, -mia *adj* : distinguished, eminent
eximir *vt* EXONERAR : to exempt
existencia *nf* 1 : existence 2 **existencias** *nfpl* MERCANCÍA : goods, stock
existente *adj* 1 : existing, in existence 2 : in stock
existir *vi* : to exist
éxito *nm* 1 TRIUNFO : success, hit 2 **tener éxito** : to be successful
exitoso, -sa *adj* : successful — **exitosamente** *adv*
éxodo *nm* : exodus
exoneración *nf, pl* -ciones EXENCIÓN : exoneration, exemption
exonerar *vt* 1 EXIMIR : to exempt, to exonerate 2 DESPEDIR : to dismiss
exorbitante *adj* : exorbitant
exorcismo *nm* : exorcism — **exorcista** *nmf*
exorcizar {21} *vt* : to exorcise
exótico, -ca *adj* : exotic
expandir *vt* EXPANSIONAR : to expand — **expandirse** *vr* : to spread
expansión *nf, pl* -siones 1 : expansion, spread 2 DIVERSIÓN : recreation, relaxation
expansionar *vt* EXPANDIR : to expand — **expansionarse** *vr* 1 : to expand 2 DIVERTIRSE : to amuse oneself, to relax
expansivo, -va *adj* : expansive
expatriado, -da *adj & n* : expatriate
expatriarse {85} *vr* 1 EMIGRAR : to emigrate 2 : to go into exile
expectación *nf, pl* -ciones : expectation, anticipation
expectante *adj* : expectant
expectativa *nf* 1 : expectation, hope 2 **expectativas** *nfpl* : prospects
expedición *nf, pl* -ciones : expedition
expediente *nm* 1 : expedient, means 2 ARCHIVO : file, dossier, record
expedir {54} *vt* 1 EMITIR : to issue 2 DESPACHAR : to dispatch, to send
expedito, -ta *adj* 1 : free, clear 2 : quick, easy
expeler *vt* : to expel, to eject
expendedor, -dora *n* : dealer, seller
expendio *nm* TIENDA : store, shop
expensas *nfpl* 1 : expenses, costs 2 **a expensas de** : at the expense of
experiencia *nf* 1 : experience 2 EXPERIMENTO : experiment
experimentación *nf, pl* -ciones : experimentation
experimental *adj* : experimental
experimentar *vi* : to experiment — *vt* 1 : to experiment with, to test out 2 : to experience
experimento *nm* EXPERIENCIA : experiment

experto, -ta *adj & n* : expert
expiación *nf, pl* **-ciones** : expiation, atonement
expiar {85} *vt* : to expiate, to atone for
expiración *nf, pl* **-ciones** VENCIMIENTO : expiration
expirar *vi* **1** FALLECER, MORIR : to pass away, to die **2** : to expire
explanada *nf* : esplanade, promenade
explayar *vt* : to extend — **explayarse** *vr* : to expound, to speak at length
explicable *adj* : explicable, explainable
explicación *nf, pl* **-ciones** : explanation
explicar {72} *vt* : to explain — **explicarse** *vr* : to understand
explicativo, -va *adj* : explanatory
explicitar *vt* : to state explicitly, to specify
explícito, -ta *adj* : explicit — **explícitamente** *adv*
exploración *nf, pl* **-ciones** : exploration
explorador, -dora *n* : explorer, scout
explorar *vt* : to explore — **exploratorio, -ria** *adj*
explosión *nf, pl* **-siones** **1** ESTALLIDO : explosion **2** : outburst ⟨una explosión de ira : an outburst of anger⟩
explosionar *vi* : to explode
explosivo, -va *adj* : explosive
explotación *nf, pl* **-ciones** **1** : exploitation **2** : operation, running
explotar *vt* **1** : to exploit **2** : to operate, to run — *vi* ESTALLAR, REVENTAR : to explode — **explotable** *adj*
exponencial *adj* : exponential — **exponencialmente** *adv*
exponente *nm* : exponent
exponer {60} *vt* **1** : to exhibit, to show, to display **2** : to explain, to present, to set forth **3** : to expose, to risk — *vi* : to exhibit
exportación *nf, pl* **-ciones** **1** : exportation **2 exportaciones** *nfpl* : exports
exportador, -dora *n* : exporter
exportar *vt* : to export — **exportable** *adj*
exposición *nf, pl* **-ciones** **1** EXHIBICIÓN : exposition, exhibition **2** : exposure **3** : presentation, statement
expositor, -tora *n* **1** : exhibitor **2** : exponent
exprés *nms & pl* **1** : express, express train **2** : espresso
expresamente *adv* : expressly, on purpose
expresar *vt* : to express — **expresarse** *vr*
expresión *nf, pl* **-siones** : expression
expresivo, -va *adj* **1** : expressive **2** CARIÑOSO : affectionate — **expresivamente** *adv*
expreso¹, -sa *adj* : express, specific
expreso² *nm* : express train, express
exprimidor *nm* : squeezer, juicer
exprimir *vt* **1** : to squeeze **2** : to exploit
expropiar *vt* : to expropriate, to commandeer — **expropiación** *nf*
expuesto¹ *pp* → **exponer**
expuesto², -ta *adj* **1** : exposed **2** : hazardous, risky

expulsar *vt* : to expel, to eject
expulsión *nf, pl* **-siones** : expulsion
expurgar {52} *vt* : to expurgate
expuso, etc. → **exponer**
exquisitez *nf, pl* **-teces** **1** : exquisiteness, refinement **2** : delicacy, special dish
exquisito, -ta *adj* **1** : exquisite **2** : delicious
extasiarse {85} *vr* : to be in ecstasy, to be enraptured
éxtasis *nms & pl* : ecstasy, rapture
extático, -ca *adj* : ecstatic
extemporáneo, -nea *adj* **1** : unseasonable **2** : untimely
extender {56} *vt* **1** : to spread out, to stretch out **2** : to broaden, to expand ⟨extender la influencia : to broaden one's influence⟩ **3** : to draw up (a document), to write out (a check) — **extenderse** *vr* **1** : to spread **2** : to last
extendido, -da *adj* **1** : outstretched **2** : widespread
extensamente *adv* : extensively, at length
extensible *adj* : extensible, extendable
extensión *nf, pl* **-siones** **1** : extension, stretching **2** : expanse, spread **3** : extent, range **4** : length, duration
extensivo, -va *adj* **1** : extensive **2 hacer extensivo** : to extend
extenso, -sa *adj* **1** : extensive, detailed **2** : spacious, vast
extenuar {3} *vt* : to exhaust, to tire out — **extenuarse** *vr* — **extenuante** *adj*
exterior¹ *adj* **1** : exterior, external **2** : foreign ⟨asuntos exteriores : foreign affairs⟩
exterior² *nm* **1** : outside **2** : abroad
exteriorizar {21} *vt* : to express, to reveal
exteriormente *adv* : outwardly
exterminar *vt* : to exterminate — **exterminación** *nf*
exterminio *nm* : extermination
externar *vt Mex* : to express, to display
externo, -na *adj* : external, outward
extinción *nf, pl* **-ciones** : extinction
extinguidor *nm* : fire extinguisher
extinguir {26} *vt* **1** APAGAR : to extinguish, to put out **2** : to wipe out — **extinguirse** *vr* **1** APAGARSE : to go out, to fade out **2** : to die out, to become extinct
extinto, -ta *adj* : extinct
extintor *nm* : extinguisher
extirpación *n, pl* **-ciones** : removal, excision
extirpar *vt* : to eradicate, to remove, to excise — **extirparse** *vr*
extorsión *nf, pl* **-siones** **1** : extortion **2** : harm, trouble
extorsionar *vt* : to extort
extra¹ *adv* : extra
extra², -ta *adj* **1** : additional, extra **2** : superior, top-quality
extra³ *nmf* : extra (in movies)

extra[4] *nm* : extra expense ⟨paga extra : bonus⟩
extracción *nf, pl* **-ciones** : extraction
extracto *nm* **1** : extract ⟨extracto de vainilla : vanilla extract⟩ **2** : abstract, summary
extractor *nm* : extractor
extracurricular *adj* : extracurricular
extradición *nf, pl* **-ciones** : extradition
extraditar *vt* : to extradite
extraer {81} *vt* : to extract
extraído *pp* → **extraer**
extrajudicial *adj* : out-of-court
extramatrimonial *adj* : extramarital
extranjerizante *adj* : foreign-sounding, foreign-looking
extranjero[1], **-ra** *adj* : foreign
extranjero[2], **-ra** *n* : foreigner
extranjero[3] *nm* : foreign countries *pl* ⟨viajó al extranjero : he traveled abroad⟩ ⟨trabajan en el extranjero : they work overseas⟩
extrañamente *adv* : strangely, oddly
extrañamiento *nm* ASOMBRO : amazement, surprise, wonder
extrañar *vt* : to miss (someone) — **extrañarse** *vr* : to be surprised
extrañeza *nf* **1** : strangeness, oddness **2** : surprise
extraño[1], **-ña** *adj* **1** RARO : strange, odd **2** EXTRANJERO : foreign
extraño[2], **-ña** *n* DESCONOCIDO : stranger
extraoficial *adj* OFICIOSO : unofficial — **extraoficialmente** *adv*
extraordinario, **-ria** *adj* EXCEPCIONAL : extraordinary — **extraordinariamente** *adv*
extrasensorial *adj* : extrasensory ⟨percepción extrasensorial : extrasensory perception⟩
extraterrestre *adj & nmf* : extraterrestrial, alien

extravagancia *nf* : extravagance, outlandishness, flamboyance
extravagante *adj* : extravagant, outrageous, flamboyant
extraviar {85} *vt* **1** : to mislead, to lead astray **2** : to misplace, to lose — **extraviarse** *vr* : to get lost, to go astray
extravío *nm* **1** PÉRDIDA : loss, misplacement **2** : misconduct
extremado, **-da** *adj* : extreme — **extremadamente** *adv*
extremar *vt* : to carry to extremes — **extremarse** *vr* : to do one's utmost
extremidad *nf* **1** : extremity, tip, edge **2 extremidades** *nfpl* : extremities
extremista *adj & nmf* : extremist
extremo[1], **-ma** *adj* **1** : extreme, utmost **2** EXCESIVO : excessive **3 en caso extremo** : as a last resort
extremo[2] *nm* **1** : extreme, end **2 al extremo de** : to the point of **3 en ∼** : in the extreme
extrovertido[1], **-da** *adj* : extroverted, outgoing
extrovertido[2], **-da** *n* : extrovert
extrudir *vt* : to extrude
exuberancia *nf* **1** : exuberance **2** : luxuriance, lushness
exuberante *adj* : exuberant, luxuriant — **exuberantemente** *adv*
exudar *vt* : to exude
exultación *nf, pl* **-ciones** : exultation, elation
exultante *adj* : exultant, elated — **exultantemente** *adv*
exultar *vi* : to exult, to rejoice
eyacular *vi* : to ejaculate — **eyaculación** *nf*
eyección *nf, pl* **-ciones** : ejection, expulsion
eyectar *vt* : to eject, to expel — **eyectarse** *vr*

F

f *nf* : sixth letter of the Spanish alphabet
fábrica *nf* FACTORÍA : factory
fabricación *nf, pl* **-ciones** : manufacture
fabricante *nmf* : manufacturer
fabricar {72} *vt* MANUFACTURAR : to manufacture, to make
fabril *adj* INDUSTRIAL : industrial, manufacturing
fábula *nf* **1** : fable **2** : fabrication, fib
fabuloso, **-sa** *adj* **1** : fabulous, fantastic **2** : mythical, fabled
facción *nf, pl* **facciones 1** : faction **2 facciones** *nfpl* RASGOS : features
faccioso, **-sa** *adj* : factious
faceta *nf* : facet
facha *nf* : appearance, look ⟨estar hecho una facha : to look a sight⟩
fachada *nf* : facade
facial *adj* : facial

fácil *adj* **1** : easy **2** : likely, probable ⟨es fácil que no pase : it probably won't happen⟩
facilidad *nf* **1** : facility, ease **2 facilidades** *nfpl* : facilities, services **3 facilidades** *nfpl* : opportunities
facilitar *vt* **1** : to facilitate **2** : to provide, to supply
fácilmente *adv* : easily, readily
facsímil *or* **facsímile** *nm* **1** : facsimile, copy **2** : fax
facsimilar *adj* : facsimile
factibilidad *nf* : feasibility
factible *adj* : feasible, practicable
facticio, **-cia** *adj* : artificial, factitious
factor[1], **-tora** *n* **1** : agent, factor **2** : baggage clerk
factor[2] *nm* ELEMENTO : factor, element
factoría *nf* FÁBRICA : factory
factótum *nm* : factotum

factura *nf* **1** : making, manufacturing **2** : bill, invoice

facturación *nf, pl* **-ciones 1** : invoicing, billing **2** : check-in

facturar *vt* **1** : to bill, to invoice **2** : to register, to check in

facultad *nf* **1** : faculty, ability ⟨facultades mentales : mental faculties⟩ **2** : authority, power **3** : school (of a university) ⟨facultad de derecho : law school⟩

facultar *vt* : to authorize, to empower

facultativo, -va *adj* **1** OPTATIVO : voluntary, optional **2** : medical ⟨informe facultativo : medical report⟩

faena *nf* : task, job, work ⟨faenas domésticas : housework⟩

faenar *vi* **1** : to work, to labor **2** PESCAR : to fish

fagot *nm* : bassoon

faisán *nm, pl* **faisanes** : pheasant

faja *nf* **1** : sash, belt **2** : girdle **3** : strip (of land)

fajar *vt* **1** : to wrap (a sash or girdle) around **2** : to hit, to thrash — **fajarse** *vr* **1** : to put on a sash or girdle **2** : to come to blows

fajín *nm, pl* **-jines** : sash, belt

fajo *nm* : bundle, sheaf ⟨un fajo de billetes : a wad of cash⟩

falacia *nf* : fallacy

falaz, -laza *adj, mpl* **falaces** FALSO : fallacious, false

falda *nf* **1** : skirt ⟨falda escocesa : kilt⟩ **2** REGAZO : lap (of the body) **3** VERTIENTE : side, slope

faldón *nm, pl* **-dones 1** : tail (of a shirt, etc.) **2** : full skirt **3** **faldón bautismal** : christening gown

falible *adj* : fallible

fálico, -ca *adj* : phallic

falla *nf* **1** : flaw, defect **2** : (geological) fault **3** : fault, failing

fallar *vi* **1** FRACASAR : to fail, to go wrong **2** : to rule (in a court of law) — *vt* **1** ERRAR : to miss (a target) **2** : to pronounce judgment on

fallecer {53} *vi* MORIR : to pass away, to die

fallecido, -da *adj & n* DIFUNTO : deceased

fallecimiento *nm* : demise, death

fallido, -da *adj* : failed, unsuccessful

fallo *nm* **1** SENTENCIA : sentence, judgment, verdict **2** : error, fault

falo *nm* : phallus, penis

falsamente *adv* : falsely

falsear *vt* **1** : to falsify, to fake **2** : to distort — *vi* **1** CEDER : to give way **2** : to be out of tune

falsedad *nf* **1** : falseness, hypocrisy **2** MENTIRA : falsehood, lie

falsete *nm* : falsetto

falsificación *nf, pl* **-ciones 1** : counterfeit, forgery **2** : falsification

falsificador, -dora *n* : counterfeiter, forger

falsificar {72} *vt* **1** : to counterfeit, to forge **2** : to falsify

falso, -sa *adj* **1** FALAZ : false, untrue **2** : counterfeit, forged

falta *nf* **1** CARENCIA : lack ⟨hacer falta : to be lacking, to be needed⟩ **2** DEFECTO : defect, fault, error **3** : offense, misdemeanor **4** : foul (in basketball), fault (in tennis)

faltar *vi* **1** : to be lacking, to be needed ⟨me falta tiempo : I don't have enough time⟩ **2** : to be absent, to be missing **3** QUEDAR : to remain, to be left ⟨faltan pocos días para la fiesta : the party is just a few days away⟩ **4** ¡no faltaba más! : don't mention it!, you're welcome!

falto, -ta *adj* ~ **de** : lacking (in), short of

fama *nf* **1** : fame **2** REPUTACIÓN : reputation **3** **de mala fama** : disreputable

famélico, -ca *adj* HAMBRIENTO : starving, famished

familia *nf* **1** : family **2** **familia política** : in-laws

familiar¹ *adj* **1** CONOCIDO : familiar **2** : familial, family **3** INFORMAL : informal

familiar² *nmf* PARIENTE : relation, relative

familiaridad *nf* **1** : familiarity **2** : informality

familiarizarse {21} *vr* ~ **con** : to familiarize oneself with

famoso¹, -sa *adj* CÉLEBRE : famous

famoso², -sa *n* : celebrity

fanal *nm* **1** : beacon, signal light **2** *Mex* : headlight

fanático, -ca *adj & n* : fanatic

fanatismo *nm* : fanaticism

fandango *nm* : fandango

fanfarria *nf* **1** : (musical) fanfare **2** : pomp, ceremony

fanfarrón¹, -rrona *adj, mpl* **-rrones** *fam* : bragging, boastful

fanfarrón², -rrona *n, mpl* **-rrones** *fam* : braggart

fanfarronada *nf* : boast, bluster

fanfarronear *vi* : to brag, to boast

fango *nm* LODO : mud, mire

fangosidad *nf* : muddiness

fangoso, -sa *adj* LODOSO : muddy

fantasear *vi* : to fantasize, to daydream

fantasía *nf* **1** : fantasy **2** : imagination

fantasioso, -sa *adj* : fanciful

fantasma *nm* : ghost, phantom

fantasmagórico, -ca *adj* : phantasmagoric

fantasmal *adj* : ghostly

fantástico, -ca *adj* **1** : fantastic, imaginary, unreal **2** *fam* : great, fantastic

faquir *nm* : fakir

farándula *nf* : show business, theater

faraón *nm, pl* **faraones** : pharaoh

fardo *nm* **1** : bale **2** : bundle

farfulla *nf* : jabbering

farfullar *v* : to jabber, to gabble

faringe *nf* : pharynx

faríngeo, -gea *adj* : pharyngeal
fariña *nf* : coarse manioc flour
farmacéutico[1], **-ca** *adj* : pharmaceutical
farmacéutico[2], **-ca** *n* : pharmacist
farmacia *nf* : drugstore, pharmacy
fármaco *nm* : medicine, drug
farmacodependencia *nf* : drug addiction
farmacología *nf* : pharmacology
faro *nm* **1** : lighthouse **2** : headlight
farol *nm* **1** : streetlight **2** : lantern, lamp **3** *fam* : bluff **4** *Mex* : headlight
farola *nf* **1** : lamppost **2** : streetlight
farolero, -ra *n fam* : bluffer
farra *nf* : spree, revelry
fárrago *nm* REVOLTIJO : hodgepodge, jumble
farsa *nf* **1** : farce **2** : fake, sham
farsante *nmf* CHARLATÁN : charlatan, fraud, phony
fascículo *nm* : fascicle, part (of a publication)
fascinación *nf, pl* **-ciones** : fascination
fascinante *adj* : fascinating
fascinar *vt* **1** : to fascinate **2** : to charm, to captivate
fascismo *nm* : fascism
fascista *adj & nmf* : fascist
fase *nf* : phase, stage
fastidiar *vt* **1** MOLESTAR : to annoy, to bother, to hassle **2** ABURRIR : to bore — *vi* : to be annoying or bothersome
fastidio *nm* **1** MOLESTIA : annoyance, nuisance, hassle **2** ABURRIMIENTO : boredom
fastidioso, -sa *adj* **1** MOLESTO : annoying, bothersome **2** ABURRIDO : boring
fatal *adj* **1** MORTAL : fatal **2** *fam* : awful, terrible **3** : fateful, unavoidable
fatalidad *nf* **1** : fatality **2** DESGRACIA : misfortune, bad luck
fatalismo *nm* : fatalism
fatalista[1] *adj* : fatalistic
fatalista[2] *nmf* : fatalist
fatalmente *adv* **1** : unavoidably **2** : unfortunately
fatídico, -ca *adj* : fateful, momentous
fatiga *nf* CANSANCIO : fatigue
fatigado, -da *adj* AGOTADO : weary, tired
fatigar {52} *vt* CANSAR : to fatigue, to tire — **fatigarse** *vr* : to wear oneself out
fatigoso, -sa *adj* : fatiguing, tiring
fatuidad *nf* **1** : fatuousness **2** VANIDAD : vanity, conceit
fatuo, -tua *adj* **1** : fatuous **2** PRESUMIDO : vain
fauces *nfpl* : jaws *pl*, maw
faul *nm, pl* **fauls** : foul, foul ball
fauna *nf* : fauna
fausto *nm* : splendor, magnificence
favor *nm* **1** : favor **2 a favor de** : in favor of **3 por** ~ : please
favorable *adj* : favorable — **favorablemente** *adv*
favorecedor, -dora *adj* : becoming, flattering
favorecer {53} *vt* **1** : to favor **2** : to look well on, to suit

favorecido, -da *adj* **1** : flattering **2** : fortunate
favoritismo *nm* : favoritism
favorito, -ta *adj & n* : favorite
fax *nm* : fax, facsimile
fayuca *nf Mex* **1** : contraband **2** : black market
fayuquero *nm Mex* : smuggler, black marketeer
faz *nf* **1** : face, countenance ⟨la faz de la tierra : the face of the earth⟩ **2** : side (of coins, fabric, etc.)
fe *nf* **1** : faith **2** : assurance, testimony ⟨dar fe de : to bear witness to⟩ **3** : intention, will ⟨de buena fe : bona fide, in good faith⟩
fealdad *nf* : ugliness
febrero *nm* : February
febril *adj* : feverish — **febrilmente** *adv*
fecal *adj* : fecal
fecha *nf* **1** : date **2 fecha de caducidad** *or* **fecha de vencimiento** : expiration date **3 fecha límite** : deadline
fechar *vt* : to date, to put a date on
fechoría *nf* : misdeed
fécula *nf* : starch
fecundar *vt* : to fertilize (an egg) — **fecundación** *nf*
fecundidad *nf* **1** : fecundity, fertility **2** : productiveness
fecundo, -da *adj* FÉRTIL : fertile, fecund
federación *nf, pl* **-ciones** : federation
federal *adj* : federal
federalismo *nm* : federalism
federalista *adj & nmf* : federalist
federar *vt* : to federate
fehaciente *adj* : reliable, irrefutable — **fehacientemente** *adv*
feldespato *nm* : feldspar
felicidad *nf* **1** : happiness **2** ¡**felicidades!** : best wishes!, congratulations!, happy birthday!
felicitación *nf, pl* **-ciones** **1** : congratulation ⟨¡felicitaciones! : congratulations!⟩ **2** : greeting card
felicitar *vt* CONGRATULAR : to congratulate — **felicitarse** *vr* ~ **de** : to be glad about
feligrés, -gresa *n, mpl* **-greses** : parishioner
feligresía *nf* : parish
felino, -na *adj & n* : feline
feliz *adj, pl* **felices** **1** : happy **2 Feliz Navidad** : Merry Christmas
felizmente *adv* **1** : happily **2** : fortunately, luckily
felonía *nf* : felony
felpa *nf* **1** : terry cloth **2** : plush
felpudo *nm* : doormat
femenil *adj* : women's, girls' ⟨futbol femenil : women's soccer⟩
femenino, -na *adj* **1** : feminine **2** : women's ⟨derechos femeninos : women's rights⟩ **3** : female
femineidad *nf* : femininity
feminidad *nf* : femininity
feminismo *nm* : feminism
feminista *adj & nmf* : feminist

femoral *adj* : femoral

fémur *nm* : femur, thighbone

fenecer {53} *vi* **1** : to die, to pass away **2** : to come to an end, to cease

fénix *nm* : phoenix

fenomenal *adj* **1** : phenomenal **2** *fam* : fantastic, terrific — **fenomenalmente** *adv*

fenómeno *nm* **1** : phenomenon **2** : prodigy, genius

feo¹ *adv* : badly, bad

feo², **fea** *adj* **1** : ugly **2** : unpleasant, nasty

féretro *nm* ATAÚD : coffin, casket

feria *nf* **1** : fair, market **2** : festival, holiday **3** *Mex* : change (money)

feriado, -da *adj* **día feriado** : public holiday

ferial *nm* : fairground

fermentar *v* : to ferment — **fermentación** *nf*

fermento *nm* : ferment

ferocidad *nf* : ferocity, fierceness

feroz *adj, pl* **feroces** FIERO : ferocious, fierce — **ferozmente** *adv*

férreo, -rrea *adj* **1** : iron **2** : strong, steely ⟨una voluntad férrea : an iron will⟩ **3** : strict, severe **4 vía férrea** : railroad track

ferretería *nf* **1** : hardware store **2** : hardware **3** : foundry, ironworks

férrico, -ca *adj* : ferric

ferrocarril *nm* : railroad, railway

ferrocarrilero → **ferroviario**

ferroso, -sa *adj* : ferrous

ferroviario, -ria *adj* : rail, railroad

ferry *nm, pl* **ferrys** : ferry

fértil *adj* FECUNDO : fertile, fruitful

fertilidad *nf* : fertility

fertilizante¹ *adj* : fertilizing ⟨droga fertilizante : fertility drug⟩

fertilizante² *nm* ABONO : fertilizer

fertilizar *vt* ABONAR : to fertilize — **fertilización** *nf*

ferviente *adj* FERVOROSO : fervent

fervor *nm* : fervor, zeal

fervoroso, -sa *adj* FERVIENTE : fervent, zealous

festejar *vt* **1** CELEBRAR : to celebrate **2** AGASAJAR : to entertain, to wine and dine **3** *Mex fam* : to thrash, to beat

festejo *nm* : celebration, festivity

festín *nm, pl* **festines** : banquet, feast

festinar *vt* : to hasten, to hurry up

festival *nm* : festival

festividad *nf* **1** : festivity **2** : (religious) feast, holiday

festivo, -va *adj* **1** : festive **2 día festivo** : holiday — **festivamente** *adv*

fetal *adj* : fetal

fetiche *nm* : fetish

fétido, -da *adj* : fetid, foul

feto *nm* : fetus

feudal *adj* : feudal — **feudalismo** *nm*

feudo *nm* **1** : fief **2** : domain, territory

fiabilidad *nf* : reliability, trustworthiness

fiable *adj* : trustworthy, reliable

fiado, -da *adj* : on credit

fiador, -dora *n* : bondsman, guarantor

fiambrería *nf* : delicatessen

fiambres *nfpl* : cold cuts

fianza *nf* **1** CAUCIÓN : bail, bond **2** : surety, deposit

fiar {85} *vt* **1** : to sell on credit **2** : to guarantee — **fiarse** *vr* ~ **de** : to place trust in

fiasco *nm* FRACASO : fiasco, failure

fibra *nf* **1** : fiber **2 fibra de vidrio** : fiberglass

fibrilar *vi* : to fibrillate — **fibrilación** *nf*

fibroso, -sa *adj* : fibrous

ficción *nf, pl* **ficciones** **1** : fiction **2** : fabrication, lie

ficha *nf* **1** : index card **2** : file, record **3** : token **4** : domino, checker, counter, poker chip

fichar *vt* **1** : to open a file on **2** : to sign up — *vi* **1** : to punch in, to punch out

fichero *nm* **1** : card file **2** : filing cabinet

ficticio, -cia *adj* : fictitious

fidedigno, -na *adj* FIABLE : reliable, trustworthy

fideicomisario, -ria *n* : trustee

fideicomiso *nm* : trusteeship, trust ⟨guardar en fideicomiso : to hold in trust⟩

fidelidad *nf* : fidelity, faithfulness

fideo *nm* : noodle

fiduciario¹, -ria *adj* : fiduciary

fiduciario², -ria *n* : trustee

fiebre *nf* **1** CALENTURA : fever, temperature ⟨fiebre amarilla : yellow fever⟩ ⟨fiebre palúdica : malaria⟩ **2** : fever, excitement

fiel¹ *adj* **1** : faithful, loyal **2** : accurate — **fielmente** *adv*

fiel² *nm* **1** : pointer (of a scale) **2 los fieles** : the faithful

fieltro *nm* : felt

fiera *nf* **1** : wild animal, beast **2** : fiend, demon ⟨una fiera para el trabajo : a demon for work⟩

fiereza *nf* : fierceness, ferocity

fiero, -ra *adj* FEROZ : fierce, ferocious

fierro *nm* HIERRO : iron

fiesta *nf* **1** : party, fiesta **2** : holiday, feast day

figura *nf* **1** : figure **2** : shape, form **3 figura retórica** : figure of speech

figurado, -da *adj* : figurative — **figuradamente** *adv*

figurar *vi* **1** : to figure, to be included ⟨Rivera figura entre los más grandes pintores de México : Rivera is among Mexico's greatest painters⟩ **2** : to be prominent, to stand out — *vt* : to represent ⟨esta línea figura el horizonte : this line represents the horizon⟩ — **figurarse** *vr* : to imagine, to think ⟨¡figúrate el lío en que se metió! : imagine the mess she got into!⟩

fijación *nf, pl* **-ciones** **1** : fixation, obsession **2** : fixing, establishing **3** : fastening, securing

fijador *nm* **1** : fixative **2** : hair spray

fijamente *adv* : fixedly
fijar *vt* **1** : to fasten, to affix **2** ES-
TABLECER : to establish, to set up **3**
CONCRETAR : to set, to fix ⟨fijar la
fecha : to set the date⟩ — **fijarse** *vr* **1**
: to settle, to become fixed **2** ~ **en** : to
notice, to pay attention to
fijeza *nf* **1** : firmness (of convictions) **2**
: persistence, constancy ⟨mirar con fi-
jeza a : to stare at⟩
fijiano, -na *adj & n* : Fijian
fijo, -ja *adj* **1** : fixed, firm, steady **2** PER-
MANENTE : permanent
fila *nf* **1** HILERA : line, file ⟨ponerse en
fila : to get in line⟩ **2** : rank, row **3 filas** *nfpl* : ranks ⟨cerrar filas : to close
ranks⟩
filamento *nm* : filament
filantropía *nf* : philanthropy
filantrópico, -ca *adj* : philanthropic
filántropo, -pa *n* : philanthropist
filatelia *nf* : philately, stamp collecting
filatelista *nmf* : stamp collector, philat-
elist
fildeador, -dora *n* : fielder
filete *nm* **1** : fillet **2** SOLOMILLO : sirloin **3** : thread (of a screw)
filiación *nf, pl* **-ciones 1** : affiliation,
connection **2** : particulars *pl,* (police)
description
filial¹ *adj* : filial
filial² *nf* : affiliate, subsidiary
filibustero *nm* : freebooter, pirate
filigrana *nf* **1** : filigree **2** : watermark
(on paper)
filipino, -na *adj & n* : Filipino
filmación *nf, pl* **-ciones** : filming, shooting
filmar *vt* : to film, to shoot
filme *or* **film** *nm* PELÍCULA : film, movie
filmina *nf* : slide, transparency
filo *nm* **1** : cutting edge, blade **2** : edge
⟨al filo del escritorio : at the edge of
the desk⟩ ⟨al filo de la medianoche : at
the stroke of midnight⟩
filología *nf* : philology
filólogo, -ga *n* : philologist
filón *nm, pl* **filones 1** : seam, vein (of
minerals) **2** *fam* : successful business,
gold mine
filoso, -sa *adj* : sharp
filosofar *vi* : to philosophize
filosofía *nf* : philosophy
filosófico, -ca *adj* : philosophic, philosophical — **filosóficamente** *adv*
filósofo, -fa *n* : philosopher
filtración *nf* : seepage, leaking
filtrar *v* : to filter — **filtrarse** *vr* : to seep
through, to leak
filtro *nm* : filter
filudo, -da *adj* : sharp
fin *nm* **1** : end **2** : purpose, aim, objective **3 en** ~ : in short **4 fin de semana** : weekend **5 por** ~ : finally, at
last
finado, -da *adj & n* DIFUNTO : deceased
final¹ *adj* : final, ultimate — **finalmente**
adv

final² *nm* : end, conclusion, finale
final³ *nf* : final, play-off
finalidad *nf* **1** : purpose, aim **2** : finality
finalista *nmf* : finalist
finalización *nf* : completion, end
finalizar {21} *v* : to finish, to end
financiación *nf, pl* **-ciones** : financing,
funding
financiamiento *nm* → **financiación**
financiar *vt* : to finance, to fund
financiero¹, -ra *adj* : financial
financiero², -ra *n* : financier
financista *nmf* : financier
finanzas *nfpl* : finances, finance ⟨altas
finanzas : high finance⟩
finca *nf* **1** : farm, ranch **2** : country
house
fineza *nf* FINURA, REFINAMIENTO : refinement
fingido, -da *adj* : false, feigned
fingimiento *nm* : pretense
fingir {35} *v* : to feign, to pretend
finiquitar *vt* **1** : to settle (an account) **2**
: to conclude, to bring to an end
finiquito *nm* : settlement (of an account)
finito, -ta *adj* : finite
finja, etc. → **fingir**
finlandés, -desa *adj & n* : Finnish
fino, -na *adj* **1** : fine, excellent **2** : delicate, slender **3** REFINADO : refined **4**
: sharp, acute ⟨olfato fino : keen sense
of smell⟩ **5** : subtle
finta *nf* : feint
fintar *or* **fintear** *vi* : to feint
finura *nf* **1** : fineness, high quality **2**
FINEZA, REFINAMIENTO : refinement
fiordo *nm* : fjord
fique *nm* : sisal
firma *nf* **1** : signature **2** : signing **3** EM-
PRESA : firm, company
firmamento *nm* : firmament, sky
firmante *nmf* : signer, signatory
firmar *v* : to sign
firme *adj* **1** : firm, resolute **2** : steady,
stable
firmemente *adv* : firmly
firmeza *nf* **1** : firmness, stability **2**
: strength, resolve
firuletes *nmpl* : frills, adornments
fiscal¹ *adj* : fiscal — **fiscalmente** *adv*
fiscal² *nmf* : district attorney, prosecutor
fiscalizar {21} *vt* **1** : to audit, to inspect
2 : to oversee **3** : to criticize
fisco *nm* : national treasury, exchequer
fisgar {52} *vt* HUSMEAR : to pry into, to
snoop on
fisgón, -gona *n, mpl* **fisgones** : snoop,
busybody
fisgonear *vi* : to snoop, to pry
fisgue, etc. → **fisgar**
física *nf* : physics
físico¹, -ca *adj* : physical — **físicamente**
adv
físico², -ca *n* : physicist
físico³ *nm* : physique, figure
fisiología *nf* : physiology

fisiológico, -ca *adj* : physiological, physiologic

fisiólogo, -ga *n* : physiologist

fisión *nf, pl* **fisiones** : fission — **fisionable** *adj*

fisionomía → **fisonomía**

fisioterapeuta *nmf* : physical therapist

fisioterapia *nf* : physical therapy

fisonomía *nf* : physiognomy, features *pl*

fistol *nm Mex* : tie clip

fisura *nf* : fissure, crevasse

fláccido, -da *or* **flácido, -da** *adj* : flaccid, flabby

flaco, -ca *adj* 1 DELGADO : thin, skinny 2 : feeble, weak ⟨una flaca excusa : a feeble excuse⟩

flagelar *vt* : to flagellate — **flagelación** *nf*

flagelo *nm* 1 : scourge, whip 2 : calamity

flagrante *adj* : flagrant, glaring, blatant — **flagrantemente** *adv*

flama *nf* LLAMA : flame

flamante *adj* 1 : bright, brilliant 2 : brand-new

flamear *vi* 1 LLAMEAR : to flame, to blaze 2 ONDEAR : to flap, to flutter

flamenco¹, -ca *adj* 1 : flamenco 2 : Flemish

flamenco², -ca *n* : Fleming, Flemish person

flamenco³ *nm* 1 : Flemish (language) 2 : flamingo 3 : flamenco (music or dance)

flanco *nm* : flank, side

flanquear *vt* : to flank

flaquear *vi* DECAER : to flag, to weaken

flaqueza *nf* 1 DEBILIDAD : frailty, feebleness 2 : thinness 3 : weakness, failing

flato *nm* : gloom, melancholy

flatulento, -ta *adj* : flatulent — **flatulencia** *nf*

flauta *nf* 1 : flute 2 **flauta dulce** : recorder

flautín *nm, pl* **flautines** : piccolo

flautista *nmf* : flute player, flutist

flebitis *nf* : phlebitis

flecha *nf* : arrow

fleco *nm* 1 : bangs *pl* 2 : fringe

flema *nf* : phlegm

flemático, -ca *adj* : phlegmatic, stolid, impassive

flequillo *nm* : bangs *pl*

fletar *vt* 1 : to charter, to hire 2 : to load (freight)

flete *nm* 1 : charter fee 2 : shipping cost 3 : freight, cargo

fletero *nm* : shipper, carrier

flexibilidad *nf* : flexibility

flexibilizar {21} *vt* : to make more flexible

flexible¹ *adj* : flexible

flexible² *nm* 1 : flexible electrical cord 2 : soft hat

flirtear *vi* : to flirt

flojear *vi* 1 DEBILITARSE : to weaken, to flag 2 : to idle, to loaf around

flojedad *nf* : weakness

flojera *nf fam* 1 : lethargy, feeling of weakness 2 : laziness

flojo, -ja *adj* 1 SUELTO : loose, slack 2 : weak, poor ⟨está flojo en las ciencias : he's weak in science⟩ 3 PEREZOSO : lazy

flor *nf* 1 : flower 2 **flor de Pascua** : poinsettia

flora *nf* : flora

floración *nf* : flowering ⟨en plena floración : in full bloom⟩

floral *adj* : floral

floreado, -da *adj* : flowered, flowery

florear *vi* FLORECER : to flower, to bloom — *vt* 1 : to adorn with flowers 2 *Mex* : to flatter, to compliment

florecer {53} *vi* 1 : to bloom, to blossom 2 : to flourish, to thrive

floreciente *adj* 1 : flowering 2 PRÓSPERO : flourishing, thriving

florecimiento *nm* : flowering

floreo *nm* : flourish

florería *nf* : flower shop, florist's

florero¹, -ra *n* : florist

florero² *nm* JARRÓN : vase

floresta *nf* 1 : glade, grove 2 BOSQUE : woods

florido, -da *adj* 1 : full of flowers 2 : florid, flowery ⟨escritos floridos : flowery prose⟩

florista *nmf* : florist

floritura *nf* : frill, embellishment

flota *nf* : fleet

flotabilidad *nf* : buoyancy

flotación *nf, pl* **-ciones** : flotation

flotador *nm* 1 : float 2 : life preserver

flotante *adj* : floating, buoyant

flotar *vi* : to float

flote *nm* a ~ : afloat

flotilla *nf* : flotilla, fleet

fluctuar {3} *vi* 1 : to fluctuate 2 VACILAR : to vacillate — **fluctuación** *nf* — **fluctuante** *adj*

fluidez *nf* 1 : fluency 2 : fluidity

fluido¹, -da *adj* 1 : flowing 2 : fluent 3 : fluid

fluido² *nm* : fluid

fluir {41} *vi* : to flow

flujo *nm* 1 : flow 2 : discharge

flúor *nm* : fluorine

fluoración *nf, pl* **-ciones** : fluoridation

fluorescencia *nf* : fluorescence — **fluorescente** *adj*

fluorizar {21} *vt* : to fluoridate

fluoruro *nm* : fluoride

fluvial *adj* : fluvial, river

fluye, etc. → **fluir**

fobia *nf* : phobia

foca *nf* : seal (animal)

focal *adj* : focal

focha *nf* : coot

foco *nm* 1 : focus 2 : center, pocket 3 : lightbulb 4 : spotlight 5 : headlight

fofo, -fa *adj* 1 ESPONJOSO : soft, spongy 2 : flabby

fogaje *nm* 1 FUEGO : skin eruption, cold sore 2 BOCHORNO : hot and humid weather

fogata *nf* : bonfire
fogón *nm, pl* **fogones** : bonfire
fogonazo *nm* : flash, explosion
fogonero, -ra *n* : stoker (of a furnace), fireman
fogoso, -sa *adj* ARDIENTE : ardent
foguear *vt* : to inure, to accustom
foja *nf* : sheet (of paper)
folículo *nm* : follicle
folio *nm* : folio, leaf
folklore *nm* : folklore
folklórico, -ca *adj* : folk, traditional
follaje *nm* : foliage
folleto *nm* : pamphlet, leaflet, circular
fomentar *vt* **1** : to foment, to stir up **2** PROMOVER : to promote, to foster
fomento *nm* : promotion, encouragement
fonda *nf* **1** POSADA : inn **2** : small restaurant
fondeado, -da *adj fam* : rich, in the money
fondear *vt* **1** : to sound **2** : to sound out, to examine **3** *Mex* : to fund, to finance — *vi* ANCLAR : to anchor — **fondearse** *vr fam* : to get rich
fondeo *nm* **1** : anchoring **2** *Mex* : funding, financing
fondillos *mpl* : seat, bottom (of clothing)
fondo *nm* **1** : bottom **2** : rear, back, end **3** : depth **4** : background **5** : sea bed **6** : fund ⟨fondo de inversiones : investment fund⟩ **7** *Mex* : slip, petticoat **8 fondos** *nmpl* : funds, resources ⟨cheque sin fondos : bounced check⟩ **9 a ~** : thoroughly, in depth **10 en ~** : abreast
fonema *nm* : phoneme
fonética *nf* : phonetics
fonético, -ca *adj* : phonetic
fontanería *nf* PLOMERÍA : plumbing
fontanero, -ra *n* PLOMERO : plumber
footing ['fu,tɪŋ] *nm* : jogging ⟨hacer footing : to jog⟩
foque *nm* : jib
forajido, -da *n* : bandit, fugitive, outlaw
foráneo, -nea *adj* : foreign, strange
forastero, -ra *n* : stranger, outsider
forcejear *vi* : to struggle
forcejeo *nm* : struggle
fórceps *nms & pl* : forceps *pl*
forense *adj* : forensic, legal
forestal *adj* : forest
forja *nf* FRAGUA : forge
forjar *vt* **1** : to forge **2** : to shape, to create ⟨forjar un compromiso : to hammer out a compromise⟩ **3** : to invent, to concoct
forma *nf* **1** : form, shape **2** MANERA, MODO : manner, way **3** : fitness ⟨estar en forma : to be fit, to be in shape⟩ **4 formas** *nfpl* : appearances, conventions
formación *nf, pl* **-ciones** **1** : formation **2** : training ⟨formación profesional : vocational training⟩

formal *adj* **1** : formal **2** : serious, dignified **3** : dependable, reliable
formaldehído *nm* : formaldehyde
formalidad *nf* **1** : formality **2** : seriousness, dignity **3** : dependability, reliability
formalizar {21} *vt* : to formalize, to make official
formalmente *adv* : formally
formar *vt* **1** : to form, to make **2** CONSTITUIR : to constitute, to make up **3** : to train, to educate — **formarse** *vr* DESARROLLARSE : to develop, to take shape **2** EDUCARSE : to be educated
formatear *vt* : to format
formativo, -va *adj* : formative
formato *nm* : format
formidable *adj* **1** : formidable, tremendous **2** *fam* : fantastic, terrific
formón *nm, pl* **formones** : chisel
fórmula *nf* : formula
formulación *nf, pl* **-ciones** : formulation
formular *vt* **1** : to formulate, to draw up **2** : to make, to lodge (a protest or complaint)
formulario *nm* : form ⟨rellenar un formulario : to fill out a form⟩
fornicar {72} *vi* : to fornicate — **fornicación** *nf*
fornido, -da *adj* : well-built, burly, hefty
foro *nm* **1** : forum **2** : public assembly, open discussion
forraje *nm* **1** : forage, fodder **2** : foraging **3** *fam* : hodgepodge
forrajear *vi* : to forage
forrar *vt* **1** : to line (a garment) **2** : to cover (a book)
forro *nm* **1** : lining **2** CUBIERTA : book cover
forsitia *nf* : forsythia
fortachón, -chona *adj, pl* **-chones** *fam* : brawny, strong, tough
fortalecer {53} *vt* : to strengthen, to fortify — **fortalecerse** *vr*
fortalecimiento *nm* **1** : strengthening, fortifying **2** : fortifications
fortaleza *nf* **1** : fortress **2** FUERZA : strength **3** : resolution, fortitude
fortificación *nf, pl* **-ciones** : fortification
fortificar {72} *vt* **1** : to fortify **2** : to strengthen
fortín *nm, pl* **fortines** : small fort
fortuito, -ta *adj* : fortuitous
fortuna *nf* **1** SUERTE : fortune, luck **2** RIQUEZA : wealth, fortune
forzar {36} *vt* **1** OBLIGAR : to force, to compel **2** : to force open **3** : to strain ⟨forzar los ojos : to strain one's eyes⟩
forzosamente *adv* **1** : forcibly, by force **2** : necessarily, inevitably ⟨forzosamente tendrán que pagar : they'll have no choice but to pay⟩
forzoso, -sa *adj* **1** : forced, compulsory **2** : necessary, inevitable
fosa *nf* **1** : ditch, pit ⟨fosa séptica : septic tank⟩ **2** TUMBA : grave **3** : cavity ⟨fosas nasales : nasal cavities, nostrils⟩
fosfato *nm* : phosphate

fosforescencia *nf* : phosphorescence — **fosforescente** *adj*

fósforo *nm* **1** CERILLA : match **2** : phosphorus

fósil¹ *adj* : fossilized, fossil

fósil² *nm* : fossil

fosilizarse {21} *vr* : to fossilize, to become fossilized

foso *nm* **1** FOSA, ZANJA : ditch **2** : pit (of a theater) **3** : moat

foto *nf* : photo, picture

fotocopia *nf* : photocopy — **fotocopiar** *vt*

fotocopiadora *nf* COPIADORA : photocopier

fotoeléctrico, -ca *adj* : photoelectric

fotogénico, -ca *adj* : photogenic

fotografía *nf* **1** : photograph **2** : photography

fotografiar {85} *vt* : to photograph

fotográfico, -ca *adj* : photographic — **fotográficamente** *adv*

fotógrafo, -fa *n* : photographer

fotosíntesis *nf* : photosynthesis

fotosintético, -ca *adj* : photosynthetic

fracasado¹, -da *adj* : unsuccessful, failed

fracasado², -da *n* : failure

fracasar *vi* **1** FALLAR : to fail **2** : to fall through

fracaso *nm* FIASCO : failure

fracción *nf, pl* **fracciones 1** : fraction **2** : part, fragment **3** : faction, splinter group

fraccionamiento *nm* **1** : division, breaking up **2** *Mex* : residential area, housing development

fraccionar *vt* : to divide, to break up

fraccionario, -ria *adj* : fractional

fractura *nf* **1** : fracture **2 fractura complicada** : compound fracture

fracturarse *vr* QUEBRARSE, ROMPERSE : to fracture, to break ⟨fracturarse el brazo : to break one's arm⟩

fragancia *nf* : fragrance, scent

fragante *adj* : fragrant

fragata *nf* : frigate

frágil *adj* **1** : fragile **2** : frail, delicate

fragilidad *nf* **1** : fragility **2** : frailty, delicacy

fragmentar *vt* : to fragment — **fragmentación** *nf*

fragmentario, -ria *adj* : fragmentary, sketchy

fragmento *nm* **1** : fragment, shard **2** : bit, snippet **3** : excerpt, passage

fragor *nm* : clamor, din, roar

fragoroso, -sa *adj* : thunderous, deafening

fragoso, -sa *adj* **1** : rough, uneven **2** : thick, dense

fragua *nf* FORJA : forge

fraguar {10} *vt* **1** : to forge **2** : to conceive, to concoct, to hatch — *vi* : to set, to solidify

fraile *nm* : friar, monk

frambuesa *nf* : raspberry

francamente *adv* **1** : frankly, candidly **2** REALMENTE : really ⟨es francamente admirable : it's really impressive⟩

francés¹, -cesa *adj, mpl* **franceses** : French

francés², -cesa *n, mpl* **franceses** : French person, Frenchman *m*, Frenchwoman *f*

francés³ *nm* : French (language)

franciscano, -na *adj & n* : Franciscan

francmasón, -sona *n, mpl* **-sones** : Freemason — **francmasonería** *nf*

franco¹, -ca *adj* **1** CÁNDIDO : frank, candid **2** PATENTE : clear, obvious **3** : free ⟨franco a bordo : free on board⟩

franco² *nm* : franc

francotirador, -dora *n* : sniper

franela *nf* : flannel

franja *nf* **1** : stripe, band **2** : border, fringe

franquear *vt* **1** : to clear **2** ATRAVESAR : to cross, to go through **3** : to pay the postage on

franqueo *nm* : postage

franqueza *nf* : frankness

franquicia *nf* **1** EXENCIÓN : exemption **2** : franchise

frasco *nm* : small bottle, flask, vial

frase *nf* **1** : phrase **2** ORACIÓN : sentence

frasear *vt* : to phrase

fraternal *adj* : fraternal, brotherly

fraternidad *nf* **1** : brotherhood **2** : fraternity

fraternizar {21} *vi* : to fraternize — **fraternización** *nf*

fraterno, -na *adj* : fraternal, brotherly

fratricida *adj* : fratricidal

fratricidio *nm* : fratricide

fraude *nm* : fraud

fraudulento, -ta *adj* : fraudulent — **fraudulentamente** *adv*

fray *nm* : brother (title of a friar) ⟨Fray Bartolomé : Brother Bartholomew⟩

frazada *nf* COBIJA, MANTA : blanket

frecuencia *nf* : frequency

frecuentar *vt* : to frequent, to haunt

frecuente *adj* : frequent — **frecuentemente** *adv*

fregadera *nf fam* : hassle, pain in the neck

fregadero *nm* : kitchen sink

fregado¹, -da *adj fam* : annoying, bothersome

fregado² *nm* **1** : scrubbing, scouring **2** *fam* : mess, muddle

fregar {49} *vt* **1** : to scrub, to scour, to wash ⟨fregar los trastes : to do the dishes⟩ ⟨fregar el suelo : to scrub the floor⟩ **2** *fam* : to annoy — *vi* **1** : to wash the dishes **2** : to clean, to scrub **3** *fam* : to be annoying

freidera *nf Mex* : frying pan

freír {37} *vt* : to fry — **freírse** *vr*

frenar *vt* **1** : to brake **2** DETENER : to curb, to check — *vi* : to apply the brakes — **frenarse** *vr* : to restrain oneself

frenesí *nm* : frenzy
frenético, -ca *adj* : frantic, frenzied — **frenéticamente** *adv*
freno *nm* **1** : brake **2** : bit (of a bridle) **3** : check, restraint **4 frenos** *nmpl Mex* : braces (for teeth)
frente[1] *nm* **1** : front ⟨al frente de : at the head of⟩ ⟨en frente : in front, opposite⟩ **2** : facade **3** : front line, sphere of activity **4** : front (in meteorology) ⟨frente frío : cold front⟩ **5 hacer frente a** : to face up to, to brave
frente[2] *nf* **1** : forehead, brow **2 frente a frente** : face to face
fresa *nf* **1** : strawberry **2** : drill (in dentistry)
fresco[1], **-ca** *adj* **1** : fresh **2** : cool **3** *fam* : insolent, nervy
fresco[2] *nm* **1** : coolness **2** : fresh air ⟨al fresco : in the open air, outdoors⟩ **3** : fresco
frescor *nm* : cool air ⟨el frescor de la noche : the cool of the evening⟩
frescura *nf* **1** : freshness **2** : coolness **3** : calmness **4** DESCARO : nerve, audacity
fresno *nm* : ash (tree)
freza *nf* : spawn, roe
frezar {21} *vi* DESOVAR : to spawn
friable *adj* : friable
frialdad *nf* **1** : coldness **2** INDIFERENCIA : indifference, unconcern
fríamente *adv* : coldly, indifferently
fricasé *nm* : fricassee
fricción *nf*, *pl* **fricciones 1** : friction **2** : rubbing, massage **3** : discord, disagreement ⟨fricción entre los hermanos : friction between the brothers⟩
friccionar *vt* **1** FROTAR : to rub **2** : to massage
friega[1], **friegue, etc.** → **fregar**
friega[2] *nf* **1** FRICCIÓN : rubdown, massage **2** : annoyance, bother
frigidez *nf* : (sexual) frigidity
frigorífico *nm Spain* : refrigerator
frijol *nm* : bean ⟨frijoles refritos : refried beans⟩
frío[1], **fría** *adj* **1** : cold **2** INDIFERENTE : cool, indifferent
frío[2] *nm* **1** : cold ⟨hace mucho frío esta noche : it's very cold tonight⟩ **2** INDIFERENCIA : coldness, indifference **3 tener frío** : to feel cold ⟨tengo frío : I'm cold⟩ **4 tomar frío** RESFRIARSE : to catch a cold
friolento, -ta *adj* : sensitive to cold
friolera *nf* (*used ironically or humorously*) : trifling amount ⟨una friolera de mil dólares : a mere thousand dollars⟩
friso *nm* : frieze
fritar *vt* : to fry
frito[1] *pp* → **freír**
frito[2], **-ta** *adj* **1** : fried **2** *fam* : worn-out, fed up ⟨tener frito a alguien : to get on someone's nerves⟩ **3** *fam* : fast asleep ⟨se quedó frito en el sofá : she fell asleep on the couch⟩
fritura *nf* **1** : frying **2** : fried food

frivolidad *nf* : frivolity
frívolo, -la *adj* : frivolous — **frívolamente** *adv*
fronda *nf* **1** : frond **2 frondas** *nfpl* : foliage
frondoso, -sa *adj* : leafy, luxuriant
frontal *adj* : frontal, head-on ⟨un choque frontal : a head-on collision⟩
frontalmente *adv* : head-on
frontera *nf* : border, frontier
fronterizo, -za *adj* : border, on the border ⟨estados fronterizos : neighboring states⟩
frontispicio *nm* : frontispiece
frotar *vt* **1** : to rub **2** : to strike (a match) — **frotarse** *vr* : to rub (together)
frote *nm* : rubbing, rub
fructífero, -ra *adj* : fruitful, productive
fructificar {72} *vi* **1** : to bear or produce fruit **2** : to be productive
fructuoso, -sa *adj* : fruitful
frugal *adj* : frugal, thrifty — **frugalmente** *adv*
frugalidad *nf* : frugality
frunce *nm* : gather (in cloth), pucker
fruncido *nm* : gathering, shirring
fruncir {83} *vt* **1** : to gather, to shirr **2 fruncir el ceño** : to knit one's brow, to frown **3 fruncir la boca** : to pucker up, to purse one's lips
frunza, etc. → **fruncir**
frustración *nf*, *pl* **-ciones** : frustration
frustrado, -da *adj* **1** : frustrated **2** : failed, unsuccessful
frustrante *adj* : frustrating
frustrar *vt* : to frustrate, to thwart — **frustrarse** *vr* FRACASAR : to fail, to come to nothing ⟨se frustraron sus esperanzas : his hopes were dashed⟩
fruta *nf* : fruit
frutal[1] *adj* : fruit, fruit-bearing
frutal[2] *nm* : fruit tree
frutilla *nf* : South American strawberry
fruto *nm* **1** : fruit, agricultural product ⟨los frutos de la tierra : the fruits of the earth⟩ **2** : result, consequence ⟨los frutos de su trabajo : the fruits of his labor⟩
fucsia *adj & nm* : fuchsia
fue, etc. → **ir, ser**
fuego *nm* **1** : fire **2** : light ⟨¿tienes fuego? : have you got a light?⟩ **3** : flame, burner (on a stove) **4** : ardor, passion **5** FOGAJE : skin eruption, cold sore **6 fuegos artificiales** *nmpl* : fireworks
fuelle *nm* : bellows
fuente *nf* **1** MANANTIAL : spring **2** : fountain **3** ORIGEN : source ⟨fuentes informativas : sources of information⟩ **4** : platter, serving dish
fuera *adv* **1** : outside, out **2** : abroad, away **3** ~ **de** : outside of, out of, beyond **4** ~ **de** : besides, in addition to ⟨fuera de eso : aside from that⟩ **5 fuera de lugar** : out of place, amiss
fuerce, fuerza etc. → **forzar**

fuero *nm* **1** JURISDICCIÓN : jurisdiction **2** : privilege, exemption **3 fuero interno** : conscience, heart of hearts

fuerte[1] *adv* **1** : strongly, tightly, hard **2** : loudly **3** : abundantly

fuerte[2] *adj* **1** : strong **2** : intense ⟨un fuerte dolor : an intense pain⟩ **3** : loud **4** : extreme, excessive

fuerte[3] *nm* **1** : fort, stronghold **2** : forte, strong point

fuerza *nf* **1** : strength, vigor ⟨fuerza de voluntad : willpower⟩ **2** : force ⟨fuerza bruta : brute force⟩ **3** : power, might ⟨fuerza de brazos : manpower⟩ **4 fuerzas** *nfpl* : forces ⟨fuerzas armadas : armed forces⟩ **5 a fuerza de** : by, by dint of

fuetazo *nm* : lash

fuga *nf* **1** HUIDA : flight, escape **2** : fugue **3** : leak ⟨fuga de gas : gas leak⟩

fugarse {52} *vr* **1** : to escape **2** HUIR : to flee, to run away **3** : to elope

fugaz *adj, pl* **fugaces** : brief, fleeting

fugitivo, -va *adj & n* : fugitive

fulana *nf* : hooker, slut

fulano, -na *n* : so-and-so, what's-his-name, what's-her-name ⟨fulano, mengano, y zutano : Tom, Dick, and Harry⟩ ⟨señora fulana de tal : Mrs. so-and-so⟩

fulcro *nm* : fulcrum

fulgor *nm* : brilliance, splendor

fulgurar *vi* : to shine brightly, to gleam, to glow

fulminante *adj* **1** : fulminating, explosive **2** : devastating, terrible ⟨una mirada fulminante : a withering look⟩

fulminar *vt* **1** : to strike with lightning **2** : to strike down ⟨fulminar a alguien con la mirada : to look daggers at someone⟩

fumador, -dora *n* : smoker

fumar *v* : to smoke

fumble *nm* : fumble (in football)

fumblear *vt* : to fumble (in football)

fumigante *nm* : fumigant

fumigar {52} *vt* : to fumigate — **fumigación** *nf*

funámbulo, -la *n* EQUILIBRISTA : tightrope walker

función *nf, pl* **funciones** **1** : function **2** : duty **3** : performance, show

funcional *adj* : functional — **funcionalmente** *adv*

funcionamiento *nm* **1** : functioning **2 en** ~ : in operation

funcionar *vi* **1** : to function **2** : to run, to work

funcionario, -ria *n* : civil servant, official

funda *nf* **1** : case, cover, sheath **2** : pillowcase

fundación *nf, pl* **-ciones** : foundation, establishment

fundado, -da *adj* : well-founded, justified

fundador, -dora *n* : founder

fundamental *adj* BÁSICO : fundamental, basic — **fundamentalmente** *adv*

fundamentalismo *nm* : fundamentalism

fundamentalista *nmf* : fundamentalist

fundamentar *vt* **1** : to lay the foundations for **2** : to support, to back up **3** : to base, to found

fundamento *nm* : basis, foundation, groundwork

fundar *vt* **1** ESTABLECER, INSTITUIR : to found, to establish **2** BASAR : to base — **fundarse** *vr* ~ **en** : to be based on, to stem from

fundición *nf, pl* **-ciones** **1** : founding, smelting **2** : foundry

fundir *vt* **1** : to melt down, to smelt **2** : to fuse, to merge **3** : to burn out (a lightbulb) — **fundirse** *vr* **1** : to fuse together, to blend, to merge **2** : to melt, to thaw **3** : to fade (in television or movies)

fúnebre *adj* **1** : funeral, funereal **2** LÚGUBRE : gloomy, mournful

funeral[1] *adj* : funeral, funerary

funeral[2] *nm* **1** : funeral **2 funerales** *nmpl* EXEQUIAS : funeral rites

funeraria *nf* **1** : funeral home, funeral parlor **2 director de funeraria** : funeral director, undertaker

funerario, -ria *adj* : funeral

funesto, -ta *adj* : terrible, disastrous ⟨consecuencias funestas : disastrous consequences⟩

fungicida[1] *adj* : fungicidal

fungicida[2] *nm* : fungicide

fungir {35} *vi* : to act, to function ⟨fungir de asesor : to act as a consultant⟩

fungoso, -sa *adj* : fungous

funja, etc. → **fungir**

furgón *nm, pl* **furgones** **1** : van, truck **2** : freight car, boxcar **3 furgón de cola** : caboose

furgoneta *nf* : van

furia *nf* **1** CÓLERA, IRA : fury, rage **2** : violence, fury ⟨la furia de la tormenta : the fury of the storm⟩

furibundo, -da *adj* : furious

furiosamente *adv* : furiously, frantically

furioso, -sa *adj* **1** AIRADO : furious, irate **2** : intense, violent

furor *nm* **1** : fury, rage **2** : violence (of the elements) **3** : passion, frenzy **4** : enthusiasm ⟨hacer furor : to be all the rage⟩

furtivo, -va *adj* : furtive — **furtivamente** *adv*

furúnculo *nm* DIVIESO : boil

fuselaje *nm* : fuselage

fusible *nm* : (electrical) fuse

fusil *nm* : rifle

fusilar *vt* **1** : to shoot, to execute (by firing squad) **2** *fam* : to plagiarize, to pirate

fusilería *nf* **1** : rifles *pl*, rifle fire **2 descarga de fusilería** : fusillade

fusión *nf, pl* **fusiones** **1** : fusion **2** : union, merger

fusionar *vt* **1** : to fuse **2** : to merge, to amalgamate — **fusionarse** *vr*
fusta *nf* : riding crop
fustigar {52} *vt* **1** AZOTAR : to whip, to lash **2** : to upbraid, to berate
futbol *or* **fútbol** *nm* **1** : soccer **2 futbol americano** : football

futbolista *nmf* : soccer player
futesa *nf* **1** : small thing, trifle **2 futesas** *nfpl* : small talk
fútil *adj* : trifling, trivial
futurista *adj* : futuristic
futuro¹, -ra *adj* : future
futuro² *nm* PORVENIR : future

G

g *nf* : seventh letter of the Spanish alphabet
gabán *nm, pl* **gabanes** : topcoat, overcoat
gabardina *nf* **1** : gabardine **2** : trench coat, raincoat
gabarra *nf* : barge
gabinete *nm* **1** : cabinet (in government) **2** : study, office (in the home) **3** : (professional) office
gablete *nm* : gable
gabonés, -nesa *adj & n, mpl* **-neses** : Gabonese
gacela *nf* : gazelle
gaceta *nf* : gazette, newspaper
gachas *nfpl* : porridge
gacho, -cha *adj* **1** : drooping, turned downward **2** *Mex fam* : nasty, awful **3 ir a gachas** *fam* : to go on all fours
gaélico¹, -ca *adj* : Gaelic
gaélico² *nm* : Gaelic (language)
gafas *nfpl* ANTEOJOS : eyeglasses, glasses
gaita *nf* : bagpipes *pl*
gajes *nmpl* **gajes del oficio** : occupational hazards
gajo *nm* **1** : broken branch (of a tree) **2** : cluster, bunch (of fruit) **3** : segment (of citrus fruit)
gala *nf* **1** : gala ⟨vestido de gala : formal dress⟩ ⟨tener algo a gala : to be proud of something⟩ **2 galas** *nfpl* : finery, attire
galáctico, -ca *adj* : galactic
galán *nm, pl* **galanes** **1** : ladies' man, gallant **2** : leading man, hero **3** : boyfriend, suitor
galano, -na *adj* **1** : elegant **2** *Mex* : mottled
galante *adj* : gallant, attentive — **galantemente** *adv*
galantear *vt* **1** CORTEJAR : to court, to woo **2** : to flirt with
galanteo *nm* **1** CORTEJO : courtship **2** : flirtation, flirting
galantería *nf* **1** : gallantry, attentiveness **2** : compliment
galápago *nm* : aquatic turtle
galardón *nm, pl* **-dones** : award, prize
galardonado, -da *adj* : prize-winning
galardonar *vt* : to give an award to
galaxia *nf* : galaxy
galeno *nm fam* : physician, doctor
galeón *nm, pl* **galeones** : galleon
galera *nf* : galley

galería *nf* **1** : gallery, balcony (in a theater) ⟨galería comercial : shopping mall⟩ **2** : corridor, passage
galerón *n, mpl* **-rones** *Mex* : large hall
galés¹, -lesa *adj* : Welsh
galés², -lesa *n, mpl* **galeses** **1** : Welshman *m*, Welshwoman *f* **2 los galeses** : the Welsh
galés³ *nm* : Welsh (language)
galgo *nm* : greyhound
galimatías *nms & pl* : gibberish, nonsense
galio *nm* : gallium
gallardete *nm* : pennant, streamer
gallardía *nf* **1** VALENTÍA : bravery **2** APOSTURA : elegance, gracefulness
gallardo, -da *adj* **1** VALIENTE : brave **2** APUESTO : elegant, graceful
gallear *vi* : to show off, to strut around
gallego¹, -ga *adj* **1** : Galician **2** *fam* : Spanish
gallego², -ga *n* **1** : Galician **2** *fam* : Spaniard
galleta *nf* **1** : cookie **2** : cracker
gallina *nf* **1** : hen **2 gallina de Guinea** : guinea fowl
gallinazo *nm* : vulture, buzzard
gallinero *nm* : chicken coop, henhouse
gallito, -ta *adj fam* : cocky, belligerent
gallo *nm* **1** : rooster, cock **2** *fam* : squeak or crack in the voice **3** *Mex* : serenade **4 gallo de pelea** : gamecock
galo¹, -la *adj* **1** : Gaulish **2** : French
galo², -la *n* : Frenchman *m*, Frenchwoman *f*
galocha *nf* : galosh
galón *nm, pl* **galones** **1** : gallon **2** : stripe (military insignia)
galopada *nf* : gallop
galopante *adj* : galloping ⟨inflación galopante : galloping inflation⟩
galopar *vi* : to gallop
galope *nm* : gallop
galpón *nm, pl* **galpones** : shed, storehouse
galvanizar {21} *vt* : to galvanize — **galvanización** *nf*
gama *nf* **1** : range, spectrum, gamut **2** → **gamo**
gamba *nf* : large shrimp, prawn
gamberro, -rra *n Spain* : hooligan, troublemaker
gambiano, -na *adj & n* : Gambian
gambito *nm* : gambit (in chess)
gameto *nm* : gamete

gamo, -ma *n* : fallow deer
gamuza *nf* **1** : suede **2** : chamois
gana *nf* **1** : desire, inclination **2 de buena gana** : willingly, readily, gladly **3
de mala gana** : reluctantly, halfheartedly **4 tener ganas de** : to feel like, to
be in the mood for ⟨tengo ganas de
bailar : I feel like dancing⟩ **5 ponerle
ganas a algo** : to put effort into something
ganadería *nf* **1** : cattle raising, stock-
breeding **2** : cattle ranch **3** GANADO
: cattle *pl*, livestock
ganadero¹, -ra *adj* : cattle, ranching
ganadero², -ra *n* : rancher, stockbreed-
er
ganado *nm* **1** : cattle *pl*, livestock **2
ganado ovino** : sheep *pl* **3 ganado por-
cino** : swine *pl*
ganador¹, -dora *adj* : winning
ganador², -dora *n* : winner
ganancia *nf* **1** : profit **2 ganancias** *nfpl*
: winnings, gains
ganancioso, -sa *adj* : profitable
ganar *vt* **1** : to win **2** : to gain ⟨ganar
tiempo : to buy time⟩ **3** : to earn ⟨ga-
nar dinero : to make money⟩ **4** : to acquire, to obtain — *vi* **1** : to win **2** : to
profit ⟨salir ganando : to come out
ahead⟩ — **ganarse** *vr* **1** : to gain, to
win ⟨ganarse a alguien : to win someone over⟩ **2** : to earn ⟨ganarse la vida
: to make a living⟩ **3** : to deserve
gancho *nm* **1** : hook **2** : clothes hanger **3** : hairpin, bobby pin **4** *Col* : safety pin
gandul¹ *nm CA, Car, Col* : pigeon pea
gandul², -dula *n fam* : idler, lazybones
gandulear *vi* : to idle, to loaf, to lounge
about
ganga *nf* : bargain
ganglio *nm* **1** : ganglion **2** : gland
gangrena *nf* : gangrene — **gangrenoso,
-sa** *adj*
gángster *nmf, pl* **gángsters** : gangster
gansada *nf* : silly thing, nonsense
ganso, -sa *n* **1** : goose, gander *m* **2** : idiot, fool
gañido *nm* : yelp (of a dog)
gañir {38} *vi* : to yelp
garabatear *v* : to scribble, to scrawl, to
doodle
garabato *nm* **1** : doodle **2 garabatos**
nmpl : scribble, scrawl
garaje *nm* : garage
garante *nmf* : guarantor
garantía *nf* **1** : guarantee, warranty **2**
: security ⟨garantía de trabajo : job se-
curity⟩
garantizar {21} *vt* : to guarantee
garapiña *nf* : pineapple drink
garapiñar *vt* : to candy
garbanzo *nm* : chickpea, garbanzo
garbo *nm* **1** DONAIRE : grace, poise **2**
: jauntiness
garboso, -sa *adj* **1** : graceful **2** : elegant, stylish
garceta *nf* : egret

gardenia *nf* : gardenia
garfio *nm* : hook, gaff, grapnel
gargajo *nm fam* : phlegm
garganta *nf* **1** : throat **2** : neck (of a
person or a bottle) **3** : ravine, narrow
pass
gargantilla *nf* : choker, necklace
gárgara *nf* **1** : gargle, gargling **2 hacer
gárgaras** : to gargle
gargarizar *vi* : to gargle
gárgola *nf* : gargoyle
garita *nf* **1** : cabin, hut **2** : sentry box,
lookout post
garoso, -sa *adj Col, Ven* : gluttonous,
greedy
garra *nf* **1** : claw **2** : hand, paw **3 garras** *nfpl* : claws, clutches ⟨caer en las
garras de alguien : to fall into someone's clutches⟩
garrafa *nf* : decanter, carafe
garrafal *adj* : terrible, monstrous
garrafón *nm, pl* **-fones** : large decanter,
large bottle
garrapata *nf* : tick
garrobo *nm CA* : large lizard, iguana
garrocha *nf* **1** PICA : lance, pike **2** : pole
⟨salto con garrocha : pole vault⟩
garrotazo *nm* : blow (with a club)
garrote *nm* **1** : club, stick **2** *Mex* : brake
garúa *nf* : drizzle
garuar {3} *v impers* LLOVIZNAR : to drizzle
garza *nf* : heron
gas *nm* : gas, vapor, fumes *pl* ⟨gas la-
grimógeno : tear gas⟩
gasa *nf* : gauze
gasear *vt* **1** : to gas **2** : to aerate (a liquid)
gaseosa *nf* REFRESCO : soda, soft drink
gaseoso, -sa *adj* **1** : gaseous **2** : carbonated, fizzy
gasoducto *nm* : gas pipeline
gasolina *nf* : gasoline, gas
gasolinera *nf* : gas station, service station
gastado, -da *adj* **1** : spent **2** : worn,
worn-out
gastador¹, -dora *adj* : extravagant,
spendthrift
gastador², -dora *n* : spendthrift
gastar *vt* **1** : to spend **2** CONSUMIR : to
consume, to use up **3** : to squander, to
waste **4** : to wear ⟨gasta un bigote : he
sports a mustache⟩ — **gastarse** *vr* **1**
: to spend, to expend **2** : to run down,
to wear out
gasto *nm* **1** : expense, expenditure **2**
DETERIORO : wear **3 gastos gen-
erales** *or* **gastos indirectos** : overhead
gástrico, -ca *adj* : gastric
gastritis *nf* : gastritis
gastronomía *nf* : gastronomy
gastronómico, -ca *adj* : gastronomic
gastrónomo, -ma *n* : gourmet
gatas *adv* **andar a gatas** : to crawl, to
go on all fours
gatear *vi* **1** : to crawl **2** : to climb, to
clamber (up)

gatillero *nm Mex* : gunman
gatillo *nm* : trigger
gatito, -ta *n* : kitten
gato[1], -ta *n* : cat
gato[2] *nm* : jack (for an automobile)
gauchada *nf Arg, Uru* : favor, kindness
gaucho *nm* : gaucho
gaveta *nf* 1 CAJÓN : drawer 2 : till
gavilla *nf* 1 : gang, band 2 : sheaf
gaviota *nf* : gull, seagull
gay ['ge, 'gai] *adj* : gay (homosexual)
gaza *nf* : loop
gazapo *nm* 1 : young rabbit 2 : misprint, error
gazmoñería *nf* MOJIGATERÍA : prudery, primness
gazmoño[1], -ña *adj* : prudish, prim
gazmoño[2], -ña *n* MOJIGATO : prude, prig
gaznate *nm* : throat, gullet
gazpacho *nm* : gazpacho
géiser *or* **géyser** *nm* : geyser
gel *nm* : gel
gelatina *nf* : gelatin
gélido, -da *adj* : icy, freezing cold
gelificarse *vr* : to jell
gema *nf* : gem
gemelo[1], -la *adj & n* MELLIZO : twin
gemelo[2] *nm* 1 : cuff link 2 **gemelos** *nmpl* BINOCULARES : binoculars
gemido *nm* : moan, groan, wail
Géminis *nmf* : Gemini
gemir {54} *vi* : to moan, to groan, to wail
gen *or* **gene** *nm* : gene
gendarme *nmf* POLICÍA : police officer, policeman *m*, policewoman *f*
gendarmería *nf* : police
genealogía *nf* : genealogy
genealógico, -ca *adj* : genealogical
generación *nf, pl* **-ciones** 1 : generation ⟨tercera generación : third generation⟩ 2 : generating, creating 3 : class ⟨la generación del '97 : the class of '97⟩
generacional *adj* : generation, generational
generador *nm* : generator
general[1] *adj* 1 : general 2 **en ~** *or* **por lo general** : in general, generally
general[2] *nmf* 1 : general 2 **general de división** : major general
generalidad *nf* 1 : generality, generalization 2 : majority
generalización *nf, pl* **-ciones** 1 : generalization 2 : escalation, spread
generalizado, -da *adj* : generalized, widespread
generalizar {21} *vi* : to generalize — *vt* : to spread, to spread out — **generalizarse** *vr* : to become widespread
generalmente *adv* : usually, generally
generar *vt* : to generate — **generarse** *vr*
genérico, -ca *adj* : generic
género *nm* 1 : genre, class, kind ⟨el género humano : the human race, mankind⟩ 2 : gender (in grammar) 3 **géneros** *nmpl* : goods, commodities
generosidad *nf* : generosity
generoso, -sa *adj* 1 : generous, unselfish 2 : ample — **generosamente** *adv*

genética *nf* : genetics
genético, -ca *adj* : genetic — **genéticamente** *adv*
genetista *nmf* : geneticist
genial *adj* 1 AGRADABLE : genial, pleasant 2 : brilliant ⟨una obra genial : a work of genius⟩ 3 *fam* FORMIDABLE : fantastic, terrific
genialidad *nf* 1 : genius 2 : stroke of genius 3 : eccentricity
genio *nm* 1 : genius 2 : temper, disposition ⟨de mal genio : bad-tempered⟩ 3 : genie
genital *adj* : genital
genitales *nmpl* : genitals, genitalia
genocidio *nm* : genocide
genotipo *nm* : genotype
gente *nf* 1 : people 2 : relatives *pl*, folks *pl* 3 **gente menuda** *fam* : children, kids *pl* 4 **ser buena gente** : to be nice, to be kind
gentil[1] *adj* 1 AMABLE : kind 2 : gentile
gentil[2] *nmf* : gentile
gentileza *nf* 1 AMABILIDAD : kindness 2 CORTESÍA : courtesy
gentilicio, -cia *adj* 1 : national, tribal 2 : family
gentío *nm* MUCHEDUMBRE, MULTITUD : crowd, mob
gentuza *nf* CHUSMA : riffraff, rabble
genuflexión *nf, pl* **-xiones** 1 : genuflection 2 **hacer una genuflexión** : to genuflect
genuino, -na *adj* : genuine — **genuinamente** *adv*
geofísica *nf* : geophysics
geofísico, -ca *adj* : geophysical
geografía *nf* : geography
geográfico, -ca *adj* : geographic, geographical — **geográficamente** *adv*
geógrafo, -fa *n* : geographer
geología *nf* : geology
geológico, -ca *adj* : geologic, geological — **geológicamente** *adv*
geólogo, -ga *n* : geologist
geometría *nf* : geometry
geométrico, -ca *adj* : geometric, geometrical — **geométricamente** *adv*
geopolítica *nf* : geopolitics
geopolítico, -ca *adj* : geopolitical
georgiano, -na *adj & n* : Georgian
geranio *nm* : geranium
gerbo *nm* : gerbil
gerencia *nf* : management, administration
gerencial *adj* : managerial
gerente *nmf* : manager, director
geriatría *nf* : geriatrics
geriátrico, -ca *adj* : geriatric
germanio *nm* : germanium
germano, -na *adj* : Germanic, German
germen *nm, pl* **gérmenes** : germ
germicida *nf* : germicide
germinación *nf, pl* **-ciones** : germination
germinar *vi* : to germinate, to sprout
gerontología *nf* : gerontology
gerundio *nm* : gerund

gesta *nf* : deed, exploit
gestación *nf, pl* **-ciones** : gestation
gesticulación *nf, pl* **-ciones** : gesturing, gesticulation
gesticular *vi* : to gesticulate, to gesture
gestión *nf, pl* **gestiones 1** TRÁMITE : procedure, step **2** ADMINISTRACIÓN : management **3 gestiones** *nfpl* : negotiations
gestionar *vt* **1** : to negotiate, to work towards **2** ADMINISTRAR : to manage, to handle
gesto *nm* **1** ADEMÁN : gesture **2** : facial expression **3** MUECA : grimace
gestor[1], **-tora** *adj* : facilitating, negotiating, managing
gestor[2], **-tora** *n* : facilitator, manager
géyser → **géiser**
ghanés, -nesa *adj & n, mpl* **ghaneses** : Ghanaian
ghetto → **gueto**
giba *nf* **1** : hump (of an animal) **2** : hunchback (of a person)
gibón *nm, pl* **gibones** : gibbon
giboso[1], **-sa** *adj* : hunchbacked, humpbacked
giboso[2], **-sa** *n* : hunchback, humpback
gigabyte *nm* : gigabyte
gigante[1] *adj* : giant, gigantic
gigante[2], **-ta** *n* : giant
gigantesco, -ca *adj* : gigantic, huge
gime, etc. → **gemir**
gimnasia *nf* : gymnastics
gimnasio *nm* : gymnasium, gym
gimnasta *nmf* : gymnast
gimnástico, -ca *adj* : gymnastic
gimotear *vi* LLORIQUEAR : to whine, to whimper
gimoteo *nm* : whimpering
ginebra *nf* : gin
ginecología *nf* : gynecology
ginecológico, -ca *adj* : gynecologic, gynecological
ginecólogo, -ga *n* : gynecologist
ginseng *nm* : ginseng
gira *nf* : tour
giralda *nf* : weather vane
girar *vi* **1** : to turn around, to revolve **2** : to swing around, to swivel — *vt* **1** : to turn, to twist, to rotate **2** : to draft (checks) **3** : to transfer (funds)
girasol *nm* MIRASOL : sunflower
giratorio, -ria *adj* : revolving
giro *nm* **1** VUELTA : turn, rotation **2** : change of direction ⟨giro de 180 grados : U-turn, about-face⟩ **3 giro bancario** : bank draft **4 giro postal** : money order
giroscopio *or* **giróscopo** *nm* : gyroscope
gis *nm Mex* : chalk
gitano, -na *adj & n* : Gypsy
glacial *adj* : glacial, icy — **glacialmente** *adv*
glaciar *nm* : glacier
gladiador *nm* : gladiator
gladiolo *or* **gladíolo** *nm* : gladiolus
glándula *nf* : gland — **glandular** *adj*

glaseado *nm* : glaze, icing
glasear *vt* : to glaze
glaucoma *nm* : glaucoma
glicerina *nf* : glycerin, glycerol
glicinia *nf* : wisteria
global *adj* **1** : global, worldwide **2** : full, comprehensive **3** : total, overall
globalizar {21} *vt* **1** ABARCAR : to include, to encompass **2** : to extend worldwide
globalmente *adv* : globally, as a whole
globo *nm* **1** : globe, sphere **2** : balloon **3 globo ocular** : eyeball
glóbulo *nm* **1** : globule **2** : blood cell, corpuscle
gloria *nf* **1** : glory **2** : fame, renown **3** : delight, enjoyment **4** : star, legend ⟨las glorias del cine : the great names in motion pictures⟩
glorieta *nf* **1** : rotary, traffic circle **2** : bower, arbor
glorificar {72} *vt* ALABAR : to glorify — **glorificación** *nf*
glorioso, -sa *adj* : glorious — **gloriosamente** *adv*
glosa *nf* **1** : gloss **2** : annotation, commentary
glosar *vt* **1** : to gloss **2** : to annotate, to comment on (a text)
glosario *nm* : glossary
glotis *nf* : glottis
glotón[1], **-tona** *adj, mpl* **glotones** : gluttonous
glotón[2], **-tona** *n, mpl* **glotones** : glutton
glotón[3] *nm, pl* **glotones** : wolverine
glotonería *nf* GULA : gluttony
glucosa *nf* : glucose
glutinoso, -sa *adj* : glutinous
gnomo ['nomo] *nm* : gnome
gobernación *nf, pl* **-ciones** : governing, government
gobernador, -dora *n* : governor
gobernante[1] *adj* : ruling, governing
gobernante[2] *nmf* : ruler, leader, governor
gobernar {55} *vt* **1** : to govern, to rule **2** : to steer, to sail (a ship) — *vi* **1** : to govern **2** : to steer
gobierno *nm* : government
goce[1], **etc.** → **gozar**
goce[2] *nm* **1** PLACER : enjoyment, pleasure **2** : use, possession
gol *nm* : goal (in soccer)
golear *vt* : to rout, to score many goals against (in soccer)
goleta *nf* : schooner
golf *nm* : golf
golfista *nmf* : golfer
golfo *nm* : gulf, bay
golondrina *nf* **1** : swallow (bird) **2 golondrina de mar** : tern
golosina *nf* : sweet, snack
goloso, -sa *adj* : fond of sweets ⟨ser goloso : to have a sweet tooth⟩
golpazo *nm* : heavy blow, bang, thump
golpe *nm* **1** : blow ⟨caerle a golpes a alguien : to give someone a beating⟩ **2** : knock **3 de ~** : suddenly **4 de un**

golpe : all at once, in one fell swoop **5**
golpe de estado : coup, coup d'etat **6**
golpe de suerte : stroke of luck
golpeado, -da *adj* **1** : beaten, hit **2** : bruised (of fruit) **3** : dented
golpear *vt* **1** : to beat (up), to hit **2** : to slam, to bang, to strike — *vi* **1** : to knock (at a door) **2** : to beat ⟨la lluvia golpeaba contra el tejado : the rain beat against the roof⟩ — **golpearse** *vr*
golpetear *v* : to knock, to rattle, to tap
golpeteo *nm* : banging, knocking, tapping
goma *nf* **1** : gum ⟨goma de mascar : chewing gum⟩ **2** CAUCHO : rubber ⟨goma espuma : foam rubber⟩ **3** PEGAMENTO : glue **4** : rubber band **5** *Arg* : tire **6** *or* **goma de borrar** : eraser
gomita *nf* : rubber band
gomoso, -sa *adj* : gummy, sticky
góndola *nf* : gondola
gong *nm* : gong
gonorrea *nf* : gonorrhea
gorda *nf Mex* : thick corn tortilla
gordinflón[1], -flona *adj, mpl* **-flones** *fam* : chubby, pudgy
gordinflón[2], -flona *n, mpl* **-flones** *fam* : chubby person
gordo[1], -da *adj* **1** : fat **2** : thick **3** : fatty, greasy, oily **4** : unpleasant ⟨me cae gorda tu tía : I can't stand your aunt⟩
gordo[2], -da *n* : fat person
gordo[3] *nm* **1** GRASA : fat **2** : jackpot
gordura *nf* : fatness, flab
gorgojo *nm* : weevil
gorgotear *vi* : to gurgle, to bubble
gorgoteo *nm* : gurgle
gorila *nm* : gorilla
gorjear *vi* **1** : to chirp, to tweet, to warble **2** : to gurgle
gorjeo *nm* **1** : chirping, warbling **2** : gurgling
gorra *nf* **1** : bonnet **2** : cap **3 de ~** *fam* : for free, at someone else's expense ⟨vivir de gorra : to sponge, to freeload⟩
gorrear *vt fam* : to bum, to scrounge — *vi fam* : to freeload
gorrero, -ra *n fam* : freeloader, sponger
gorrión *nm, pl* **gorriones** : sparrow
gorro *nm* **1** : cap **2 estar hasta el gorro** : to be fed up
gorrón, -rrona *n, mpl* **gorrones** *fam* : freeloader, scrounger
gorronear *vt fam* : to bum, to scrounge — *vi fam* : to freeload
gota *nf* **1** : drop ⟨una gota de sudor : a bead of sweat⟩ ⟨como dos gotas de agua : like two peas in a pod⟩ ⟨sudar la gota gorda : to sweat buckets, to work very hard⟩ **2** : gout
gotear *v* **1** : to drip **2** : to leak — *v impers* LLOVIZNAR : to drizzle
goteo *nm* : drip, dripping
gotera *nf* **1** : leak **2** : stain (from dripping water)
gotero *nm* : (medicine) dropper
gótico, -ca *adj* : Gothic
gourmet *nmf* : gourmet

gozar {21} *vi* **1** : to enjoy oneself, to have a good time **2 ~ de** : to enjoy, to have, to possess ⟨gozar de buena salud : to enjoy good health⟩ **3 ~ con** : to take delight in
gozne *nm* BISAGRA : hinge
gozo *nm* **1** : joy **2** PLACER : enjoyment, pleasure
gozoso, -sa *adj* : joyful
grabación *nf, pl* **-ciones** : recording
grabado *nm* **1** : engraving **2 grabado al aguafuerte** : etching
grabador, -dora *n* : engraver
grabadora *nf* : tape recorder
grabar *vt* **1** : to engrave **2** : to record, to tape — *vi* **grabar al aguafuerte** : to etch — **grabarse** *vr* **grabársele a alguien en la memoria** : to become engraved on someone's mind
gracia *nf* **1** : grace **2** : favor, kindness **3** : humor, wit ⟨su comentario no me hizo gracia : I wasn't amused by his remark⟩ **4 gracias** *nfpl* : thanks ⟨¡gracias! : thank you!⟩ ⟨dar gracias : to give thanks⟩
grácil *adj* **1** : graceful **2** : delicate, slender, fine
gracilidad *nm* : gracefulness
gracioso, -sa *adj* **1** CHISTOSO : funny, amusing **2** : cute, attractive
grada *nf* **1** : harrow **2** PELDAÑO : step, stair **3 gradas** *nfpl* : bleachers, grandstand
gradación *nf, pl* **-ciones** : gradation, scale
gradar *vt* : to harrow, to hoe
gradería *nf* : tiers *pl*, stands *pl*, rows *pl* (in a theater)
gradiente *nf* : gradient, slope
grado *nm* **1** : degree (in meteorology and mathematics) ⟨grado centígrado : degree centigrade⟩ **2** : extent, level, degree ⟨en grado sumo : greatly, to the highest degree⟩ **3** RANGO : rank **4** : year, class (in education) **5 de buen grado** : willingly, readily
graduable *adj* : adjustable
graduación *nf, pl* **-ciones** **1** : graduation (from a school) **2** GRADO : rank **3** : alcohol content, proof
graduado[1], -da *adj* **1** : graduated **2 lentes graduados** : prescription lenses
graduado[2], -da *n* : graduate
gradual *adj* : gradual — **gradualmente** *adv*
graduar {3} *v* **1** : to regulate, to adjust **2** CALIBRAR : to calibrate, to gauge — **graduarse** *vr* : to graduate (from a school)
graffiti *or* **grafiti** *nmpl* : graffiti *pl*
gráfica *nf* → **gráfico[2]**
gráfico[1], -ca *adj* : graphic — **gráficamente** *adv*
gráfico[2] *nm* **1** : graph, chart **2** : graphic (for a computer, etc.) **3 gráfico de barras** : bar graph
grafismo *nm* : graphics *pl*

grafito *nm* : graphite
gragea *nf* **1** : coated pill or tablet **2**
  grageas *nfpl* : sprinkles, jimmies
grajo *nm* : rook (bird)
grama *nf* : grass
gramática *nf* : grammar
gramatical *adj* : grammatical — **gra-
  maticalmente** *adv*
gramo *nm* : gram
gran → **grande**
grana *nf* : scarlet, deep red
granada *nf* **1** : pomegranate **2** : grenade
  ⟨granada de mano : hand grenade⟩
granadero *nm* **1** : grenadier **2**
  granaderos *nmpl Mex* : riot squad
granadino, -na *adj & n* : Grenadian
granado, -da *adj* **1** DISTINGUIDO : distinguished **2** : choice, select
granate *nm* **1** : garnet **2** : deep red, ma-
  roon
grande *adj* (**gran** *before singular nouns*)
  1 : large, big ⟨un libro grande : a big
  book⟩ **2** ALTO : tall **3** NOTABLE : great
  ⟨un gran autor : a great writer⟩ **4** (*indicating intensity*) : great ⟨con gran
  placer : with great pleasure⟩ **5** : old,
  grown-up ⟨hijos grandes : grown chil-
  dren⟩
grandeza *nf* **1** MAGNITUD : greatness,
  size **2** : nobility **3** : generosity, graciousness **4** : grandeur, magnificence
grandilocuencia *nf* : grandiloquence —
  grandilocuente *adj*
grandiosidad *nf* : grandeur
grandioso, -sa *adj* **1** MAGNÍFICO
  : grand, magnificent **2** : grandiose
granel *adv* **1 a ~** : galore, in great quan-
  tities **2 a ~** : in bulk ⟨vender a granel
  : to sell in bulk⟩
granero *nm* : barn, granary
granito *nm* : granite
granizada *nf* : hailstorm
granizar {21} *v impers* : to hail
granizo *nm* : hail
granja *nf* : farm
granjear *vt* : to earn, to win —
  granjearse *vr* : to gain, to earn
granjero, -ra *n* : farmer
grano *nm* **1** PARTÍCULA : grain, particle
  ⟨un grano de arena : a grain of sand⟩
  2 : grain (of rice, etc.), bean (of coffee),
  seed **3** : grain (of wood or rock) **4** BAR-
  RO, ESPINILLA : pimple **5 ir al grano**
  : to get to the point
granuja *nmf* PILLUELO : rascal, urchin
granular[1] *vt* : to granulate — **granularse**
  vr : to break out in spots
granular[2] *adj* : granular, grainy
granza *nf* : chaff
grapa *nf* **1** : staple **2** : clamp
grapadora *nf* ENGRAPADORA : stapler
grapar *vt* ENGRAPAR : to staple
grasa *nf* **1** : grease **2** : fat **3** *Mex* : shoe
  polish
grasiento, -ta *adj* : greasy, oily
graso, -sa *adj* **1** : fatty **2** : greasy, oily
grasoso, -sa *adj* GRASIENTO : greasy,
  oily

gratificación *nf, pl* **-ciones 1** SATISFAC-
  CIÓN : gratification **2** : bonus **3** REC-
  OMPENSA : recompense, reward
gratificar {72} *vt* **1** SATISFACER : to satisfy, to gratify **2** RECOMPENSAR : to reward **3** : to give a bonus to
gratinado, -da *adj* : au gratin
gratis[1] *adv* GRATUITAMENTE : free, for
  free, gratis
gratis[2] *adj* GRATUITO : free, gratis
gratitud *nf* : gratitude
grato, -ta *adj* AGRADABLE, PLACEN-
  TERO : pleasant, agreeable — **grata-
  mente** *adv*
gratuitamente *adv* **1** : gratuitously **2**
  GRATIS : free, for free, gratis
gratuito, -ta *adj* **1** : gratuitous, unwarranted **2** GRATIS : free, gratis
grava *nf* : gravel
gravamen *nm, pl* **-vámenes 1** : burden,
  obligation **2** : (property) tax
gravar *vt* **1** : to burden, to encumber **2**
  : to levy (a tax)
grave *adj* **1** : grave, important **2** : serious, somber **3** : serious (of an illness)
gravedad *nf* **1** : gravity ⟨centro de
  gravedad : center of gravity⟩ **2** : seriousness, severity
gravemente *adv* : gravely, seriously
gravilla *nf* : (fine) gravel
gravitación *nf, pl* **-ciones** : gravitation
gravitacional *adj* : gravitational
gravitar *vi* **1** : to gravitate **2 ~ sobre**
  : to rest on **3 ~ sobre** : to loom over
gravoso, -sa *adj* **1** ONEROSO : burdensome, onerous **2** : costly
graznar *vi* : to caw, to honk, to quack,
  to squawk
graznido *nm* : cawing, honking, quack-
  ing, squawking
gregario, -ria *adj* : gregarious
gregoriano, -na *adj* : Gregorian
gremial *adj* SINDICAL : union, labor
gremio *nm* SINDICATO : union, guild
greña *nf* **1** : mat, tangle **2 greñas** *nfpl*
  MELENAS : shaggy hair, mop
greñudo, -da *n* HIPPIE, MELENUDO
  : longhair, hippie
grey *nf* : congregation, flock
griego[1], **-ga** *adj & n* : Greek
griego[2] *nm* : Greek (language)
grieta *nf* : crack, crevice
grifo *nm* **1** : faucet ⟨agua del grifo : tap
  water⟩ **2** : griffin
grillete *nm* : shackle
grillo *nm* **1** : cricket **2 grillos** *nmpl* : fetters, shackles
grima *nf* **1** : disgust, uneasiness **2 darle grima a alguien** : to get on someone's nerves
gringo, -ga *adj & n* YANQUI : Yankee,
  gringo
gripa *nf Col, Mex* : flu
gripe *nf* : flu
gris *adj* **1** : gray **2** : overcast, cloudy
grisáceo, -cea *adj* : grayish
gritar *v* : to shout, to scream, to cry
gritería *nf* : shouting, clamor

grito *nm* : shout, scream, cry ⟨a grito pelado : at the top of one's voice⟩

groenlandés, -desa *adj & n* : Greenlander

grogui *adj fam* : dazed, groggy

grosella *nf* **1** : currant **2 grosella espinosa** : gooseberry

grosería *nf* **1** : insult, coarse language **2** : rudeness, discourtesy

grosero¹, -ra *adj* **1** : rude, fresh **2** : coarse, vulgar

grosero², -ra *n* : rude person

grosor *nm* : thickness

grosso *adj* **a grosso modo** : roughly, broadly, approximately

grotesco, -ca *adj* : grotesque, hideous

grúa *nf* **1** : crane (machine) **2** : tow truck

gruesa *nf* : gross

grueso¹, -sa *adj* **1** : thick, bulky **2** : heavy, big **3** : heavyset, stout

grueso² *nm* **1** : thickness **2** : main body, mass **3 en ~** : in bulk

grulla *nf* : crane (bird)

grumo *nm* : lump, glob

gruñido *nm* : growl, grunt

gruñir {38} *vi* **1** : to growl, to grunt **2** : to grumble

gruñón¹, -ñona *adj, mpl* **gruñones** *fam* : grumpy, crabby

gruñón², -ñona *n, mpl* **gruñones** *fam* : grumpy person, nag

grupa *nf* : rump, hindquarters *pl*

grupo *nm* : group

gruta *nf* : grotto, cave

guacal *nm Col, Mex, Ven* : crate

guacamayo *nm* : macaw

guacamole *or* **guacamol** *nm* : guacamole

guacamote *nm Mex* : yuca, cassava

guachinango → **huachinango**

guacho, -cha *adj* **1** *Arg, Col, Chile, Peru* : orphaned **2** *Chile, Peru* : odd, unmatched

guadaña *nf* : scythe

guagua *nf* **1** *Arg, Col, Chile, Peru* : baby **2** *Cuba, PRi* : bus

guaira *nf* **1** *CA* : traditional flute **2** *Peru* : smelting furnace

guajiro, -ra *n Cuba* : peasant

guajolote *nm Mex* : turkey

guanábana *nf* : guanabana, soursop (fruit)

guanaco *nm* : guanaco

guandú *nm CA, Car, Col* : pigeon pea

guango, -ga *adj Mex* **1** : loose-fitting, baggy **2** : slack, loose

guano *nm* : guano

guante *nm* **1** : glove ⟨guante de boxeo : boxing glove⟩ **2 arrojarle el guante (a alguien)** : to throw down the gauntlet (to someone)

guantelete *nm* : gauntlet

guapo, -pa *adj* **1** : handsome, good-looking, attractive **2** : elegant, smart **3** *fam* : bold, dashing

guapura *nf fam* : handsomeness, attractiveness, good looks *pl* ⟨¡qué guapura! : what a vision!⟩

guarache → **huarache**

guarachear *vi Cuba, PRi fam* : to go on a spree, to go out on the town

guaraní¹ *adj & nmf* : Guarani

guaraní² *nm* : Guarani (language of Paraguay)

guarda *nmf* **1** GUARDIÁN : security guard **2** : keeper, custodian

guardabarros *nms & pl* : fender, mudguard

guardabosque *nmf* : forest ranger, gamekeeper

guardacostas¹ *nmfs & pl* : coastguardsman

guardacostas² *nms & pl* : coast guard vessel

guardaespaldas *nmfs & pl* : bodyguard

guardafangos *nms & pl* : fender, mudguard

guardameta *nmf* ARQUERO, PORTERO : goalkeeper, goalie

guardapelo *nm* : locket

guardapolvo *nm* **1** : dustcover **2** : duster, housecoat

guardar *vt* **1** : to guard **2** : to maintain, to preserve **3** CONSERVAR : to put away **4** RESERVAR : to save **5** : to keep (a secret or promise) — **guardarse** *vr* **1 ~ de** : to refrain from **2 ~ de** : to guard against, to be careful not to

guardarropa *nm* **1** : cloakroom, checkroom **2** ARMARIO : closet, wardrobe

guardería *nf* : nursery, day-care center

guardia¹ *nf* **1** : guard, defense **2** : guard duty, watch **3 en ~** : on guard

guardia² *nmf* **1** : sentry, guardsman, guard **2** : police officer, policeman *m*, policewoman *f*

guardiamarina *nmf* : midshipman

guardián, -diana *n, mpl* **guardianes** **1** GUARDA : security guard, watchman **2** : guardian, keeper **3 perro guardián** : watchdog

guarecer {53} *vt* : to shelter, to protect — **guarecerse** *vr* : to take shelter

guarida *nf* **1** : den, lair **2** : hideout

guarismo *nm* : figure, numeral

guarnecer {53} *vt* **1** : to adorn **2** : to garnish **3** : to garrison

guarnición *nf, pl* **-ciones** **1** : garnish **2** : garrison **3** : decoration, trimming, setting (of a jewel)

guaro *nm CA* : liquor distilled from sugarcane

guasa *nf fam* **1** : joking, fooling around **2 de ~** : in jest, as a joke

guasón¹, -sona *adj, mpl* **guasones** *fam* : funny, witty

guasón², -sona *n, mpl* **guasones** *fam* : joker, clown

guatemalteco, -ca *adj & n* : Guatemalan

guau *interj* : wow!

guayaba *nf* : guava (fruit)

gubernamental *adj* : governmental

gubernativo, -va → **gubernamental**

gubernatura *nf Mex* : governing body

guepardo *nm* : cheetah

güero, -ra *adj Mex* : blond, fair

guerra *nf* **1** : war ⟨declarar la guerra : to declare war⟩ ⟨guerra sin cuartel : all-out war⟩ **2** : warfare **3** LUCHA : conflict, struggle
guerrear *vi* : to wage war
guerrero¹, -ra *adj* **1** : war, fighting **2** : warlike
guerrero², -ra *n* : warrior
guerrilla *nf* : guerrilla warfare
guerrillero, -ra *adj & n* : guerrilla
gueto *nm* : ghetto
guía¹ *nf* **1** : directory, guidebook **2** ORIENTACIÓN : guidance, direction ⟨la conciencia me sirve como guía : conscience is my guide⟩
guía² *nmf* : guide, leader ⟨guía de turismo : tour guide⟩
guiar {85} *vt* **1** : to guide, to lead **2** CONDUCIR : to manage — **guiarse** *vr* : to be guided by, to go by
guija *nf* : pebble
guijarro *nm* : pebble
guillotina *nf* : guillotine — **guillotinar** *vt*
guinda¹ *adj & nm Mex* : burgundy (color)
guinda² *nf* : morello (cherry)
guineo *nm Car* : banana
guinga *nf* : gingham
guiñada → **guiño**
guiñar *vi* : to wink
guiño *nm* : wink
guión *nm, pl* **guiones 1** : script, screenplay **2** : hyphen, dash **3** ESTANDARTE : standard, banner
guirnalda *nf* : garland
guisa *nf* **1** : manner, fashion **2 a guisa de** : like, by way of **3 de tal guisa** : in such a way

guisado ESTOFADO *nm* : stew
guisante *nm* : pea
guisar *vt* **1** ESTOFAR : to stew **2** *Spain* : to cook
guiso *nm* **1** : stew **2** : casserole
güisqui → **whisky**
guita *nf* : string, twine
guitarra *nf* : guitar
guitarrista *nmf* : guitarist
gula *nf* GLOTONERÍA : gluttony, greed
gusano *nm* **1** LOMBRIZ : worm, earthworm ⟨gusano de seda : silkworm⟩ **2** : caterpillar, maggot, grub
gustar *vt* **1** : to taste **2** : to like ⟨¿gustan pasar? : would you like to come in?⟩ — *vi* **1** : to be pleasing ⟨me gustan los dulces : I like sweets⟩ ⟨a María le gusta Carlos : María is attracted to Carlos⟩ ⟨no me gusta que me griten : I don't like to be yelled at⟩ **2** ~ **de** : to like, to enjoy ⟨no gusta de chismes : she doesn't like gossip⟩ **3 como guste** : as you wish, as you like
gustativo, -va *adj* : taste ⟨papilas gustativas : taste buds⟩
gusto *nm* **1** : flavor, taste **2** : taste, style **3** : pleasure, liking **4** : whim, fancy ⟨a gusto : at will⟩ **5 a** ~ : comfortable, at ease **6 al gusto** : to taste, as one likes **7 mucho gusto** : pleased to meet you
gustosamente *adv* : gladly
gustoso, -sa *adj* **1** : willing, glad ⟨nuestra empresa participará gustosa : our company will be pleased to participate⟩ **2** : zesty, tasty
gutural *adj* : guttural

H

h *nf* : eighth letter of the Spanish alphabet
ha → **haber**
haba *nf* : broad bean
habanero¹, -ra *adj* : of or from Havana
habanero², -ra *n* : native or resident of Havana
haber¹ {39} *v aux* **1** : have, has ⟨no ha llegado el envío : the shipment hasn't arrived⟩ **2** ~ **de** : must ⟨ha de ser tarde : it must be late⟩ — *v impers* **1 hay** : there is, there are ⟨hay dos mensajes : there are two messages⟩ ⟨¿qué hay de nuevo? : what's new?⟩ **2 hay que** : it is necessary ⟨hay que trabajar más rápido : you have to work faster⟩
haber² *nm* **1** : assets *pl* **2** : credit, credit side **3 haberes** *nmpl* : salary, income, remuneration
habichuela *nf* **1** : bean, kidney bean **2** : green bean
hábil *adj* **1** : able, skillful **2** : working ⟨días hábiles : working days⟩
habilidad *nf* CAPACIDAD : ability, skill
habilidoso, -sa *adj* : skillful, clever

habilitación *nf, pl* **-ciones 1** : authorization **2** : furnishing, equipping
habilitar *vt* **1** : to enable, to authorize, to empower **2** : to equip, to furnish
hábilmente *adv* : skillfully, expertly
habitable *adj* : habitable, inhabitable
habitación *nf, pl* **-ciones 1** CUARTO : room **2** DORMITORIO : bedroom **3** : habitation, occupancy
habitante *nmf* : inhabitant, resident
habitar *vt* : to inhabit — *vi* : to reside, to dwell
hábitat *nm, pl* **-tats** : habitat
hábito *nm* **1** : habit, custom **2** : habit (of a monk or nun)
habitual *adj* : habitual, customary — **habitualmente** *adv*
habituar {3} *vt* : to accustom, to habituate — **habituarse** *vr* ~ **a** : to get used to, to grow accustomed to
habla *nf* **1** : speech **2** : language, dialect **3 de** ~ : speaking ⟨de habla inglesa : English-speaking⟩
hablado, -da *adj* **1** : spoken **2 mal hablado** : foulmouthed

hablador¹, -dora *adj* : talkative
hablador², -dora *n* : chatterbox
habladuría *nf* 1 : rumor 2 **habladurías**
nfpl : gossip, scandal
hablante *nmf* : speaker
hablar *vi* 1 : to speak, to talk ⟨hablar en
broma : to be joking⟩ 2 ~ **de** : to mention, to talk about 3 **dar que hablar**
: to make people talk — *vt* 1 : to speak
(a language) 2 : to talk about, to discuss ⟨háblalo con tu jefe : discuss it
with your boss⟩ — **hablarse** *vr* 1 : to
speak to each other, to be on speaking
terms 2 **se habla inglés (etc.)** : English (etc.) spoken
habrá, etc. → **haber**
hacedor, -dora *n* : creator, maker, doer
hacendado, -da *n* : landowner
hacer {40} *vt* 1 : to make 2 : to do, to
perform 3 : to force, to oblige ⟨los hice
esperar : I made them wait⟩ — *vi* : to
act ⟨haces bien : you're doing the right
thing⟩ — *v impers* 1 (*referring to weather*) ⟨hacer frío : to be cold⟩ ⟨hace viento : it's windy⟩ 2 **hace** : ago ⟨hace mucho tiempo : a long time ago, for a long
time⟩ 3 **no le hace** : it doesn't matter,
it makes no difference 4 **hacer falta**
: to be necessary, to be needed — **hacerse** *vr* 1 : to become 2 : to pretend,
to act, to play ⟨hacerse el tonto : to
play dumb⟩ 3 : to seem ⟨el examen se
me hizo difícil : the exam seemed difficult to me⟩ 4 : to get, to grow ⟨se
hace tarde : it's growing late⟩
hacha *nf* : hatchet, ax
hachazo *nm* : blow, chop (with an ax)
hachís *nm* : hashish
hacia *prep* 1 : toward, towards ⟨hacia
abajo : downward⟩ ⟨hacia adelante
: forward⟩ 2 : near, around, about
⟨hacia las seis : about six o'clock⟩
hacienda *nf* 1 : estate, ranch, farm 2
: property 3 : livestock 4 **la Hacienda**
: department of revenue, tax office
hacinar *vt* 1 : to pile up, to stack 2 : to
overcrowd — **hacinarse** *vr* : to crowd
together
hada *nf* : fairy
hado *nm* : destiny, fate
haga, etc. → **hacer**
haitiano, -na *adj & n* : Haitian
hala *interj* Spain 1 (*expressing encouragement or disbelief*) : come on! 2 (*expressing surprise*) : wow! 3 (*expressing
protest*) : hey!
halagador¹, -dora *adj* : flattering
halagador², -dora *n* : flatterer
halagar {52} *vt* : to flatter, to compliment
halago *nm* : flattery, praise
halagüeño, -ña *adj* 1 : flattering 2 : encouraging, promising
halar *vt CA, Car* → **jalar**
halcón *nm, pl* **halcones** : hawk, falcon
halibut *nm, pl* **-buts** : halibut
hálito *nm* 1 : breath 2 : gentle breeze

hallar *vt* 1 ENCONTRAR : to find 2 DE-
SCUBRIR : to discover, to find out —
hallarse *vr* 1 : to be situated, to find
oneself 2 : to feel ⟨no se halla bien : he
doesn't feel comfortable, he feels out
of place⟩
hallazgo *nm* 1 : discovery 2 : find ⟨¡es
un verdadero hallazgo! : it's a real
find!⟩
halo *nm* 1 : halo 2 : aura
halógeno *nm* : halogen
hamaca *nf* : hammock
hambre *nf* 1 : hunger 2 : starvation 3
tener hambre : to be hungry 4 **dar
hambre** : to make hungry
hambriento, -ta *adj* : hungry, starving
hambruna *nf* : famine
hamburguesa *nf* : hamburger
hampa *nf* : criminal underworld
hampón, -pona *n, mpl* **hampones**
: criminal, thug
hámster [ˈxamster] *nm, pl* **hámsters**
: hamster
han → **haber**
handicap *or* **hándicap** [ˈhandiˌkap] *nm,
pl* **-caps** : handicap (in sports)
hangar *nm* : hangar
hará, etc. → **hacer**
haragán¹, -gana *adj, mpl* **-ganes** : lazy,
idle
haragán², -gana *n, mpl* **-ganes** HOL-
GAZÁN : slacker, good-for-nothing
haraganear *vi* : to be lazy, to waste one's
time
haraganería *nf* : laziness
harapiento, -ta *adj* : ragged, tattered
harapos *nmpl* ANDRAJOS : rags, tatters
hardware [ˈhardˌwer] *nm* : computer
hardware
harén *nm, pl* **harenes** : harem
harina *nf* 1 : flour 2 **harina de maíz**
: cornmeal
hartar *vt* 1 : to glut, to satiate 2 FAS-
TIDIAR : to tire, to irritate, to annoy —
hartarse *vr* : to be weary, to get fed up
harto¹ *adv* : most, extremely, very
harto², -ta *adj* 1 : full, satiated 2 : fed
up
hartura *nf* 1 : surfeit 2 : abundance,
plenty
has → **haber**
hasta¹ *adv* : even
hasta² *prep* 1 : until, up until ⟨hasta entonces : until then⟩ ⟨¡hasta luego! : see
you later!⟩ 2 : as far as ⟨nos fuimos
hasta Managua : we went all the way
to Managua⟩ 3 : up to ⟨hasta cierto
punto : up to a certain point⟩ 4 **hasta
que** : until
hastiar {85} *vt* 1 : to make weary, to
bore 2 : to disgust, to sicken — **has-
tiarse** *vr* ~ **de** : to get tired of
hastío *nm* 1 TEDIO : tedium 2 REPUG-
NANCIA : disgust
hato *nm* 1 : flock, herd 2 : bundle (of
possessions)
hawaiano, -na *adj & n* : Hawaiian
hay → **haber¹**

haya[1], etc. → haber
haya[2] *nf* : beech (tree and wood)
hayuco *nm* : beechnut
haz[1] → hacer
haz[2] *nm, pl* **haces 1** FARDO : bundle **2** : beam (of light)
haz[3] *nf, pl* **haces 1** : face **2 haz de la tierra** : surface of the earth
hazaña *nf* PROEZA : feat, exploit
hazmerreír *nm fam* : laughingstock
he[1] {39} → haber
he[2] *v impers* **he aquí** : here is, here are, behold
hebilla *nf* : buckle, clasp
hebra *nf* : strand, thread
hebreo[1], **-brea** *adj & n* : Hebrew
hebreo[2] *nm* : Hebrew (language)
hecatombe *nf* **1** MATANZA : massacre **2** : disaster
heces → hez
hechicería *nf* **1** BRUJERÍA : sorcery, witchcraft **2** : curse, spell
hechicero[1], **-ra** *adj* : bewitching, enchanting
hechicero[2], **-ra** *n* : sorcerer, sorceress *f*
hechizar {21} *vt* **1** EMBRUJAR : to bewitch **2** CAUTIVAR : to charm
hechizo *nm* **1** SORTILEGIO : spell, enchantment **2** ENCANTO : charm, fascination
hecho[1] *pp* → hacer
hecho[2], **-cha** *adj* **1** : made, done **2** : ready-to-wear **3** : complete, finished ⟨hecho y derecho : full-fledged⟩
hecho[3] *nm* **1** : fact **2** : event ⟨hechos históricos : historic events⟩ **3** : act, action **4 de ~** : in fact, in reality
hechura *nf* **1** : style **2** : craftsmanship, workmanship **3** : product, creation
hectárea *nf* : hectare
heder {56} *vi* : to stink, to reek
hediondez *nf, pl* **-deces** : stink, stench
hediondo, **-da** *adj* MALOLIENTE : foul-smelling, stinking
hedor *nm* : stench, stink
hegemonía *nf* **1** : dominance **2** : hegemony (in politics)
helada *nf* : frost (in meteorology)
heladería *nf* : ice-cream parlor, ice-cream stand
helado[1], **-da** *adj* **1** GÉLIDO : icy, freezing cold **2** CONGELADO : frozen
helado[2] *nm* : ice cream
heladora *nf* CONGELADOR : freezer
helar {55} *v* CONGELAR : to freeze — *v impers* : to produce frost ⟨anoche heló : there was frost last night⟩ — **helarse** *vr*
helecho *nm* : fern, bracken
hélice *nf* **1** : spiral, helix **2** : propeller
helicóptero *nm* : helicopter
helio *nm* : helium
helipuerto *nm* : heliport
hembra *adj & nf* : female
hemisférico, **-ca** *adj* : hemispheric, hemispherical
hemisferio *nm* : hemisphere
hemofilia *nf* : hemophilia

hemofílico, **-ca** *adj & n* : hemophiliac
hemoglobina *nf* : hemoglobin
hemorragia *nf* **1** : hemorrhage **2 hemorragia nasal** : nosebleed
hemorroides *nfpl* ALMORRANAS : hemorrhoids, piles
hemos → haber
henchido, **-da** *adj* : swollen, bloated
henchir {54} *vt* **1** : to stuff, to fill **2** : to swell, to swell up — **henchirse** *vr* **1** : to stuff oneself **2** LLENARSE : to fill up, to be full
hender {56} *vt* : to cleave, to split
hendidura *nf* : crack, crevice, fissure
henequén *nm, pl* **-quenes** : sisal hemp
heno *nm* : hay
hepatitis *nf* : hepatitis
heráldica *nf* : heraldry
heráldico, **-ca** *adj* : heraldic
heraldo *nm* : herald
herbario, **-ria** *adj* : herbal
herbicida *nm* : herbicide, weed killer
herbívoro[1], **-ra** *adj* : herbivorous
herbívoro[2] *nm* : herbivore
herbolario, **-ria** *n* : herbalist
hercio *nm* : hertz
hercúleo, **-lea** *adj* : herculean
heredar *vt* : to inherit
heredero, **-ra** *n* : heir, heiress *f*
hereditario, **-ria** *adj* : hereditary
hereje *nmf* : heretic
herejía *nf* : heresy
herencia *nf* **1** : inheritance **2** : heritage **3** : heredity
herético, **-ca** *adj* : heretical
herida *nf* : injury, wound
herido[1], **-da** *adj* **1** : injured, wounded **2** : hurt, offended
herido[2], **-da** *n* : injured person, casualty
herir {76} *vt* **1** : to injure, to wound **2** : to hurt, to offend
hermafrodita *nmf* : hermaphrodite
hermanar *vt* **1** : to unite, to bring together **2** : to match up, to twin (cities)
hermanastro, **-tra** *n* : half brother *m*, half sister *f*
hermandad *nf* **1** FRATERNIDAD : brotherhood ⟨hermandad de mujeres : sisterhood, sorority⟩ **2** : association
hermano, **-na** *n* : sibling, brother *m*, sister *f*
hermético, **-ca** *adj* : hermetic, watertight — **herméticamente** *adv*
hermoso, **-sa** *adj* BELLO : beautiful, lovely — **hermosamente** *adv*
hermosura *nf* BELLEZA : beauty, loveliness
hernia *nf* : hernia
héroe *nm* : hero
heroicidad *nf* : heroism, heroic deed
heroico, **-ca** *adj* : heroic — **heroicamente** *adv*
heroína *nf* **1** : heroine **2** : heroin
heroísmo *nm* : heroism
herpes *nms & pl* **1** : herpes **2** : shingles
herradura *nf* : horseshoe
herraje *nm* : ironwork

herramienta *nf* : tool
herrar {55} *vt* : to shoe (a horse)
herrería *nf* : blacksmith's shop
herrero, -ra *n* : blacksmith
herrumbre *nf* ORÍN : rust
herrumbroso, -sa *adj* OXIDADO : rusty
hertzio *nm* : hertz
hervidero *nm* **1** : mass, swarm **2** : hotbed (of crime, etc.)
hervidor *nm* : kettle
hervir {76} *vi* **1** BULLIR : to boil, to bubble **2** ～ **de** : to teem with, to be swarming with — *vt* : to boil
hervor *nm* **1** : boiling **2** : fervor, ardor
heterogeneidad *nf* : heterogeneity
heterogéneo, -nea *adj* : heterogeneous
heterosexual *adj* & *nmf* : heterosexual
heterosexualidad *nf* : heterosexuality
hexágono *nm* : hexagon — **hexagonal** *adj*
hez *nf, pl* **heces 1** ESCORIA : scum, dregs *pl* **2** : sediment, lees *pl* **3 heces** *nfpl* : feces, excrement
hiato *nm* : hiatus
hibernar *vi* : to hibernate — **hibernación** *nf*
híbrido¹, -da *adj* : hybrid
híbrido² *nm* : hybrid
hicieron, etc. → **hacer**
hidalgo, -ga *n* : nobleman *m*, noblewoman *f*
hidrante *nm* CA, Col : hydrant
hidratar *vt* : to moisturize — **hidratante** *adj*
hidrato *nm* **1** : hydrate **2 hidrato de carbono** : carbohydrate
hidráulico, -ca *adj* : hydraulic
hidroavión *nm, pl* **-viones** : seaplane
hidrocarburo *nm* : hydrocarbon
hidroeléctrico, -ca *adj* : hydroelectric
hidrofobia *nf* RABIA : hydrophobia, rabies
hidrófugo, -ga *adj* : water-repellent
hidrógeno *nm* : hydrogen
hidroplano *nm* : hydroplane
hiede, etc. → **heder**
hiedra *nf* **1** : ivy **2 hiedra venenosa** : poison ivy
hiel *nf* **1** BILIS : bile **2** : bitterness
hiela, etc. → **helar**
hielo *nm* **1** : ice **2** : coldness, reserve ⟨romper el hielo : to break the ice⟩
hiena *nf* : hyena
hiende, etc. → **hender**
hierba *nf* **1** : herb **2** : grass **3 mala hierba** : weed
hierbabuena *nf* : mint, spearmint
hiere, etc. → **herir**
hierra, etc. → **herrar**
hierro *nm* **1** : iron ⟨hierro fundido : cast iron⟩ **2** : branding iron
hierve, etc. → **hervir**
hígado *nm* : liver
higiene *nf* : hygiene
higiénico, -ca *adj* : hygienic — **higiénicamente** *adv*
higienista *nmf* : hygienist
higo *nm* **1** : fig **2 higo chumbo** : prickly pear (fruit)

higrómetro *nm* : hygrometer
higuera *nf* : fig tree
hijastro, -tra *n* : stepson *m*, stepdaughter *f*
hijo, -ja *n* **1** : son *m*, daughter *f* **2 hijos** *nmpl* : children, offspring
híjole *interj* Mex : wow!, good grief!
hilacha *nf* **1** : ravel, loose thread **2 mostrar la hilacha** : to show one's true colors
hilado *nm* **1** : spinning **2** HILO : yarn, thread
hilar *vt* **1** : to spin (thread) **2** : to consider, to string together (ideas) — *vi* **1** : to spin **2 hilar delgado** : to split hairs
hilarante *adj* **1** : humorous, hilarious **2 gas hilarante** : laughing gas
hilaridad *nf* : hilarity
hilera *nf* FILA : file, row, line
hilo *nm* **1** : thread ⟨colgar de un hilo : to hang by a thread⟩ ⟨hilo dental : dental floss⟩ **2** LINO : linen **3** : (electric) wire **4** : theme, thread (of a discourse) **5** : trickle (of water, etc.)
hilvanar *vt* **1** : to baste, to tack **2** : to piece together
himnario *nm* : hymnal
himno *nm* **1** : hymn **2 himno nacional** : national anthem
hincapié *nm* **hacer hincapié en** : to emphasize, to stress
hincar {72} *vt* CLAVAR : to stick, to plunge — **hincarse** *vr* **hincarse de rodillas** : to kneel down, to fall to one's knees
hinchado, -da *adj* **1** : swollen, inflated **2** : pompous, overblown
hinchar *vt* **1** INFLAR : to inflate **2** : to exaggerate — **hincharse** *vr* **1** : to swell up **2** : to become conceited, to swell with pride
hinchazón *nf, pl* **-zones** : swelling
hinche, etc. → **henchir**
hindi *nm* : Hindi
hindú *adj* & *nmf* : Hindu
hinduismo *nm* : Hinduism
hiniesta *nf* : broom (plant)
hinojo *nm* **1** : fennel **2 de hinojos** : on bended knee
hinque, etc. → **hincar**
hipar *vi* : to hiccup
hiperactividad *nf* : hyperactivity
hiperactivo, -va *adj* : hyperactive, overactive
hipérbole *nf* : hyperbole
hiperbólico, -ca *adj* : hyperbolic, exaggerated
hipercrítico, -ca *adj* : hypercritical
hipermetropía *nf* : farsightedness
hipersensibilidad *nf* : hypersensitivity
hipersensible *adj* : hypersensitive
hipertensión *nf, pl* **-siones** : hypertension, high blood pressure
hip-hop [ˌxipˈxop] *nm* : hip-hop (music)
hípico, -ca *adj* : equestrian ⟨concurso hípico : horse show⟩
hipil → **huipil**
hipnosis *nfs* & *pl* : hypnosis

hipnótico, -ca *adj* : hypnotic
hipnotismo *nm* : hypnotism
hipnotizador[1], -dora *adj* 1 : hypnotic 2 : spellbinding, mesmerizing
hipnotizador[2], -dora *n* : hypnotist
hipnotizar {21} *vt* : to hypnotize
hipo *nm* : hiccup, hiccups *pl*
hipocampo *nm* : sea horse
hipocondría *nf* : hypochondria
hipocondríaco, -ca *adj & n* : hypochondriac
hipocresía *nf* : hypocrisy
hipócrita[1] *adj* : hypocritical — hipócritamente *adv*
hipócrita[2] *nmf* : hypocrite
hipodérmico, -ca *adj* aguja hipodérmica : hypodermic needle
hipódromo *nm* : racetrack
hipopótamo *nm* : hippopotamus
hipoteca *nf* : mortgage
hipotecar {72} *vt* 1 : to mortgage 2 : to compromise, to jeopardize
hipotecario, -ria *adj* : mortgage
hipotensión *nf* : low blood pressure
hipotenusa *nf* : hypotenuse
hipótesis *nfs & pl* : hypothesis
hipotético, -ca *adj* : hypothetical — hipotéticamente *adv*
hippie *or* hippy ['hipi] *nmf, pl* hippies [-pis] : hippie
hiriente *adj* : hurtful, offensive
hirió, etc. → herir
hirsuto, -ta *adj* 1 : hirsute, hairy 2 : bristly, wiry
hirviente *adj* : boiling
hirvió, etc. → hervir
hisopo *nm* 1 : hyssop 2 : cotton swab
hispánico, -ca *adj & n* : Hispanic
hispano[1], -na *adj* : Hispanic ⟨de habla hispana : Spanish-speaking⟩
hispano[2], -na *n* : Hispanic (person)
hispanoamericano[1], -na *adj* LATINOAMERICANO : Latin-American
hispanoamericano[2], -na *n* LATINOAMERICANO : Latin American
hispanohablante[1] *adj* : Spanish-speaking
hispanohablante[2] *nmf* : Spanish speaker
histerectomía *nf* : hysterectomy
histeria *nf* 1 : hysteria 2 : hysterics
histérico, -ca *adj* : hysterical — histéricamente *adv*
histerismo *nm* 1 : hysteria 2 : hysterics
historia *nf* 1 : history 2 NARRACIÓN, RELATO : story
historiador, -dora *n* : historian
historial *nm* 1 : record, document 2 CURRÍCULUM : résumé, curriculum vitae
histórico, -ca *adj* 1 : historical 2 : historic, important — históricamente *adv*
historieta *nf* : comic strip
histrionismo *nm* : histrionics, acting
hit ['hit] *nm, pl* hits 1 ÉXITO : hit, popular song 2 : hit (in baseball)
hito *nm* : milestone, landmark

hizo → hacer
hobby ['hɔbi] *nm, pl* hobbies [-bis] : hobby
hocico *nm* : snout, muzzle
hockey ['hoke, -ki] *nm* : hockey
hogar *nm* 1 : home 2 : hearth, fireplace
hogareño, -ña *adj* 1 : home-loving 2 : domestic, homelike
hogaza *nf* : large loaf (of bread)
hoguera *nf* 1 FOGATA : bonfire 2 morir en la hoguera : to burn at the stake
hoja *nf* 1 : leaf, petal, blade (of grass) 2 : sheet (of paper), page (of a book) ⟨hoja de cálculo : spreadsheet⟩ 3 FORMULARIO : form ⟨hoja de pedido : order form⟩ 4 : blade (of a knife) ⟨hoja de afeitar : razor blade⟩
hojalata *nf* : tinplate
hojaldre *nm* : puff pastry
hojarasca *nf* : fallen leaves *pl*
hojear *vt* : to leaf through (a book or magazine)
hojuela *nf* 1 : leaflet, young leaf 2 : flake
hola *interj* : hello!, hi!
holandés[1], -desa *adj, mpl* -deses : Dutch
holandés[2], -desa *n, mpl* -deses : Dutch person, Dutchman *m*, Dutchwoman *f* ⟨los holandeses : the Dutch⟩
holandés[3] *nm* : Dutch (language)
holgadamente *adv* : comfortably, easily ⟨vivir holgadamente : to be well-off⟩
holgado, -da *adj* 1 : loose, baggy 2 : at ease, comfortable
holganza *nf* : leisure, idleness
holgazán[1], -zana *adj, mpl* -zanes : lazy
holgazán[2], -zana *n, mpl* -zanes HARAGÁN : slacker, idler
holgazanear *vi* HARAGANEAR : to laze around, to loaf
holgazanería *nf* PEREZA : idleness, laziness
holgura *nf* 1 : looseness 2 COMODIDAD : comfort, ease
holístico, -ca *adj* : holistic
hollar {19} *vt* : to tread on, to trample
hollín *nm, pl* hollines TIZNE : soot
holocausto *nm* : holocaust
holograma *nm* : hologram
hombre *nm* 1 : man ⟨el hombre : man, mankind⟩ 2 hombre de estado : statesman 3 hombre de negocios : businessman 4 hombre lobo : werewolf
hombrera *nf* 1 : shoulder pad 2 : epaulet
hombría *nf* : manliness
hombro *nm* : shoulder ⟨encogerse de hombros : to shrug one's shoulders⟩
hombruno, -na *adj* : mannish
homenaje *nm* : homage, tribute ⟨rendir homenaje a : to pay tribute to⟩
homenajear *vt* : to pay homage to, to honor
homeopatía *nf* : homeopathy
homicida[1] *adj* : homicidal, murderous
homicida[2] *nmf* ASESINO : murderer
homicidio *nm* ASESINATO : homicide, murder

homilía *nf* : homily, sermon
homófono *nm* : homophone
homogeneidad *nf* : homogeneity
homogeneización *nf* : homogenization
homogeneizar {21} *vt* : to homogenize
homogéneo, -nea *adj* : homogeneous
homógrafo *nm* : homograph
homologación *nf, pl* **-ciones 1** : sanctioning, approval **2** : parity
homologar {52} *vt* **1** : to sanction **2** : to bring into line
homólogo¹, -ga *adj* : homologous, equivalent
homólogo², -ga *n* : counterpart
homónimo¹, -ma *n* TOCAYO : namesake
homónimo² *nm* : homonym
homosexual *adj & nmf* : homosexual
homosexualidad *nf* : homosexuality
honda *nf* : sling
hondo¹ *adv* : deeply
hondo², -da *adj* PROFUNDO : deep ⟨en lo más hondo de : in the depths of⟩ — **hondamente** *adv*
hondonada *nf* **1** : hollow, depression **2** : ravine, gorge
hondura *nf* : depth
hondureño, -ña *adj & n* : Honduran
honestidad *nf* **1** : decency, modesty **2** : honesty, uprightness
honesto, -ta *adj* **1** : decent, virtuous **2** : honest, honorable — **honestamente** *adv*
hongo *nm* **1** : fungus **2** : mushroom
honor *nm* **1** : honor ⟨en honor a la verdad : to be quite honest⟩ **2 honores** *nmpl* : honors ⟨hacer los honores : to do the honors⟩
honorable *adj* HONROSO : honorable — **honorablemente** *adv*
honorario, -ria *adj* : honorary
honorarios *nmpl* : payment, fees (for professional services)
honorífico, -ca *adj* : honorary ⟨mención honorífica : honorable mention⟩
honra *nf* **1** : dignity, self-respect ⟨tener a mucha honra : to take great pride in⟩ **2** : good name, reputation
honradamente *adv* : honestly, decently
honradez *nf, pl* **-deces** : honesty, integrity, probity
honrado, -da *adj* **1** HONESTO : honest, upright **2** : honored
honrar *vt* **1** : to honor **2** : to be a credit to ⟨su generosidad lo honra : his generosity does him credit⟩
honroso, -sa *adj* HONORABLE : honorable — **honrosamente** *adv*
hora *nf* **1** : hour ⟨media hora : half an hour⟩ ⟨a la última hora : at the last minute⟩ ⟨a la hora en punto : on the dot⟩ ⟨horas de oficina : office hours⟩ **2** : time ⟨¿qué hora es? : what time is it?⟩ **3** CITA : appointment
horario *nm* : schedule, timetable, hours *pl* ⟨horario de visita : visiting hours⟩
horca *nf* **1** : gallows *pl* **2** : pitchfork
horcajadas *nfpl* **a ~** : astride, astraddle
horcón *nm, pl* **horcones** : wooden post, prop

horda *nf* : horde
horizontal *adj* : horizontal — **horizontalmente** *adv*
horizonte *nm* : horizon, skyline
horma *nf* **1** : shoe tree **2** : shoemaker's last
hormiga *nf* : ant
hormigón *nm, pl* **-gones** CONCRETO : concrete
hormigonera *nf* : cement mixer
hormigueo *nm* **1** : tingling, pins and needles *pl* **2** : uneasiness
hormiguero *nm* **1** : anthill **2** : swarm (of people)
hormona *nf* : hormone — **hormonal** *adj*
hornacina *nf* : niche, recess
hornada *nf* : batch
hornear *vt* : to bake
hornilla *nf* : burner (of a stove)
horno *nm* **1** : oven ⟨horno crematorio : crematorium⟩ ⟨horno de microondas : microwave oven⟩ **2** : kiln
horóscopo *nm* : horoscope
horqueta *nf* **1** : fork (in a river or road) **2** : crotch (in a tree) **3** : small pitchfork
horquilla *nf* **1** : hairpin, bobby pin **2** : pitchfork
horrendo, -da *adj* : horrendous, horrible
horrible *adj* : horrible, dreadful — **horriblemente** *adv*
horripilante *adj* : horrifying, hair-raising
horripilar *vt* : to horrify, to terrify
horror *nm* : horror, dread
horrorizado, -da *adj* : terrified
horrorizar {21} *vt* : to horrify, to terrify — **horrorizarse** *vr*
horroroso, -sa *adj* **1** : horrifying, terrifying **2** : dreadful, bad
hortaliza *nf* **1** : vegetable **2 hortalizas** *nfpl* : garden produce
hortera *adj* *Spain fam* : tacky, gaudy
hortícola *adj* : horticultural
horticultor, -ra *n* : horticulturist
horticultura *nf* : horticulture
hosco, -ca *adj* : sullen, gloomy
hospedaje *nm* : lodging, accommodations *pl*
hospedar *vt* : to provide with lodging, to put up — **hospedarse** *vr* : to stay, to lodge
hospicio *nm* : orphanage
hospital *nm* : hospital
hospitalario, -ria *adj* : hospitable
hospitalidad *nf* : hospitality
hospitalización *nf, pl* **-ciones** : hospitalization
hospitalizar {21} *vt* : to hospitalize — **hospitalizarse** *vr*
hostería *nf* POSADA : inn
hostia *nf* : host, Eucharist
hostigamiento *nm* : harassment
hostigar {52} *vt* ACOSAR, ASEDIAR : to harass, to pester
hostil *adj* : hostile

hostilidad *nf* **1** : hostility, antagonism **2 hostilidades** *nfpl* : (military) hostilities
hostilizar {21} *vt* : to harass
hotel *nm* : hotel
hotelero[1], **-ra** *adj* : hotel ⟨la industria hotelera : the hotel business⟩
hotelero[2], **-ra** *n* : hotel manager, hotelier
hoy *adv* **1** : today ⟨hoy mismo : right now, this very day⟩ **2** : now, nowadays ⟨de hoy en adelante : from now on⟩
hoyo *nm* AGUJERO : hole
hoyuelo *nm* : dimple
hoz *nf, pl* **hoces** : sickle
hozar {21} *vi* : to root (of a pig)
huachinango *nm Mex* : red snapper
huarache *nm* : huarache sandal
hubo, etc. → **haber**
hueco[1], **-ca** *adj* **1** : hollow, empty **2** : soft, spongy **3** : hollow-sounding, resonant **4** : proud, conceited **5** : superficial
hueco[2] *nm* **1** : hole, hollow, cavity **2** : gap, space **3** : recess, alcove
huele, etc. → **oler**
huelga *nf* **1** PARO : strike **2 hacer huelga** : to strike, to go on strike
huelguista *nmf* : striker
huella[1], **etc.** → **hollar**
huella[2] *nf* **1** : footprint ⟨seguir las huellas de alguien : to follow in someone's footsteps⟩ **2** : mark, impact ⟨dejar huella : to leave one's mark⟩ ⟨sin dejar huella : without a trace⟩ **3 huella digital** *or* **huella dactilar** : fingerprint
huérfano[1], **-na** *adj* **1** : orphan, orphaned **2** : defenseless **3** ~ **de** : lacking, devoid of
huérfano[2], **-na** *n* : orphan
huerta *nf* **1** : large vegetable garden, truck farm **2** : orchard **3** : irrigated land
huerto *nm* **1** : vegetable garden **2** : orchard
hueso *nm* **1** : bone **2** : pit, stone (of a fruit)
huésped[1], **-peda** *n* INVITADO : guest
huésped[2] *nm* : host ⟨organismo huésped : host organism⟩
huestes *nfpl* **1** : followers **2** : troops, army
huesudo, -da *adj* : bony
hueva *nf* : roe, spawn
huevo *nm* : egg ⟨huevos revueltos : scrambled eggs⟩
huida *nf* : flight, escape
huidizo, -za *adj* **1** ESCURRIDIZO : elusive, slippery **2** : shy, evasive
huipil *nm CA, Mex* : traditional sleeveless blouse or dress
huir {41} *vi* **1** ESCAPAR : to escape, to flee **2** ~ **de** : to avoid
huiro *nm Chile, Peru* : seaweed
huizache *nm* : huisache, acacia
hule *nm* **1** : oilcloth, oilskin **2** *Mex* : rubber **3 hule espuma** *Mex* : foam rubber
humanidad *nf* **1** : humanity, mankind

2 : humaneness **3 humanidades** *nfpl* : humanities *pl*
humanismo *nm* : humanism
humanista *nmf* : humanist
humanístico, -ca *adj* : humanistic
humanitario, -ria *adj & n* : humanitarian
humano[1], **-na** *adj* **1** : human **2** BENÉVOLO : humane, benevolent — **humanamente** *adv*
humano[2] *nm* : human being, human
humareda *nf* : cloud of smoke
humeante *adj* **1** : smoky **2** : smoking, steaming
humear *vi* **1** : to smoke **2** : to steam
humectante[1] *adj* : moisturizing
humectante[2] *nm* : moisturizer
humedad *nf* **1** : humidity **2** : dampness, moistness
humedecer {53} *vt* **1** : to humidify **2** : to moisten, to dampen
húmedo, -da *adj* **1** : humid **2** : moist, damp
humidificador *nm* : humidifier
humidificar {72} *vt* : to humidify
humildad *nf* **1** : humility **2** : lowliness
humilde *adj* **1** : humble **2** : lowly ⟨gente humilde : poor people⟩
humildemente *adv* : meekly, humbly
humillación *nf, pl* **-ciones** : humiliation
humillante *adj* : humiliating
humillar *vt* : to humiliate — **humillarse** *vr* : to humble oneself ⟨humillarse a hacer algo : to stoop to doing something⟩
humo *nm* **1** : smoke, steam, fumes **2 humos** *nmpl* : airs *pl*, conceit
humor *nm* **1** : humor **2** : mood, temper ⟨está de buen humor : she's in a good mood⟩
humorada *nf* **1** BROMA : joke, witticism **2** : whim, caprice
humorismo *nm* : humor, wit
humorista *nmf* : humorist, comedian, comedienne *f*
humorístico, -ca *adj* : humorous — **humorísticamente** *adv*
humoso, -sa *adj* : smoky, steamy
humus *nm* : humus
hundido, -da *adj* **1** : sunken **2** : depressed
hundimiento *nm* **1** : sinking **2** : collapse, ruin
hundir *vt* **1** : to sink **2** : to destroy, to ruin — **hundirse** *vr* **1** : to sink down **2** : to cave in **3** : to break down, to go to pieces
húngaro[1], **-ra** *adj & n* : Hungarian
húngaro[2] *nm* : Hungarian (language)
huracán *nm, pl* **-canes** : hurricane
huraño, -ña *adj* **1** : unsociable, aloof **2** : timid, skittish (of an animal)
hurgar {52} *vt* : to poke, to jab, to rake (a fire) — *vi* ~ **en** : to rummage in, to poke through
hurgue, etc. → **hurgar**
hurón *nm, pl* **hurones** : ferret
huronear *vi* : to pry, to snoop

hurra *interj* : hurrah!, hooray!
hurtadillas *nfpl* a ~ : stealthily, on the sly
hurtar *vt* ROBAR : to steal
hurto *nm* 1 : theft, robbery 2 : stolen property, loot
husmear *vt* 1 : to follow the scent of, to track 2 : to sniff out, to pry into — *vi* 1 : to pry, to snoop 2 : to sniff around (of an animal)
huso *nm* 1 : spindle 2 **huso horario** : time zone
huy *interj* : ow!, ouch!
huye, etc. → huir

I

i *nf* : ninth letter of the Spanish alphabet
iba, etc. → ir
ibérico, -ca *adj* : Iberian
ibero, -ra *or* **íbero, -ra** *adj & n* : Iberian
iberoamericano, -na *adj* HISPANOAMERICANO, LATINOAMERICANO : Latin-American
ibis *nfs & pl* : ibis
ice, etc. → izar
iceberg *nm, pl* **icebergs** : iceberg
icono *nm* : icon
iconoclasia *nf* : iconoclasm
iconoclasta *nmf* : iconoclast
ictericia *nf* : jaundice
ida *nf* 1 : going, departure 2 **ida y vuelta** : round-trip 3 **idas y venidas** : comings and goings
idea *nf* 1 : idea, notion 2 : opinion, belief 3 PROPÓSITO : intention
ideal *adj & nm* : ideal — **idealmente** *adv*
idealismo *nm* : idealism
idealista[1] *adj* : idealistic
idealista[2] *nmf* : idealist
idealizar {21} *vt* : to idealize — **idealización** *nf*
idear *vt* : to devise, to think up
ideario *nm* : ideology
ídem *nm* : idem, the same, ditto
idéntico, -ca *adj* : identical, alike — **idénticamente** *adv*
identidad *nf* : identity
identificable *adj* : identifiable
identificación *nf, pl* **-ciones** 1 : identification, identifying 2 : identification document, ID
identificar {72} *vt* : to identify — **identificarse** *vr* 1 : to identify oneself 2 ~ **con** : to identify with
ideología *nf* : ideology — **ideológicamente** *adv*
ideológico, -ca *adj* : ideological
idílico, -ca *adj* : idyllic
idilio *nm* : idyll
idioma *nm* : language ⟨el idioma inglés : the English language⟩
idiomático, -ca *adj* : idiomatic — **idiomáticamente** *adv*
idiosincrasia *nf* : idiosyncrasy
idiosincrásico, -ca *adj* : idiosyncratic
idiota[1] *adj* : idiotic, stupid, foolish
idiota[2] *nmf* : idiot, foolish person
idiotez *nf, pl* **-teces** 1 : idiocy 2 : idiotic act or remark ⟨¡no digas idioteces! : don't talk nonsense!⟩
ido *pp* → ir

idólatra[1] *adj* : idolatrous
idólatra[2] *nmf* : idolater
idolatrar *vt* : to idolize
idolatría *nf* : idolatry
ídolo *nm* : idol
idoneidad *nf* : suitability
idóneo, -nea *adj* ADECUADO : suitable, fitting
iglesia *nf* : church
iglú *nm* : igloo
ignición *nf, pl* **-ciones** : ignition
ignífugo, -ga *adj* : fire-resistant, fireproof
ignominia *nf* : ignominy, disgrace
ignominioso, -sa *adj* : ignominious, shameful
ignorancia *nf* : ignorance
ignorante[1] *adj* : ignorant
ignorante[2] *nmf* : ignorant person, ignoramus
ignorar *vt* 1 : to ignore 2 DESCONOCER : to be unaware of ⟨lo ignoramos por absoluto : we have no idea⟩
ignoto, -ta *adj* : unknown
igual[1] *adv* 1 : in the same way 2 **por** ~ : equally
igual[2] *adj* 1 : equal 2 IDÉNTICO : the same, alike 3 : even, smooth 4 SEMEJANTE : similar 5 CONSTANTE : constant
igual[3] *nmf* : equal, peer
igualación *nf* 1 : equalization 2 : leveling, smoothing 3 : equating (in mathematics)
igualado, -da *adj* 1 : even (of a score) 2 : level 3 *Mex* : disrespectful
igualar *vt* 1 : to equalize 2 : to tie ⟨igualar el marcador : to even the score⟩
igualdad *nf* 1 : equality 2 UNIFORMIDAD : evenness, uniformity
igualmente *adv* 1 : equally 2 ASIMISMO : likewise
iguana *nf* : iguana
ijada *nf* : flank, loin, side
ijar *nm* → ijada
ilegal[1] *adj* : illegal, unlawful — **ilegalmente** *adv*
ilegal[2] *nmf CA, Mex* : illegal alien
ilegalidad *nf* : illegality, unlawfulness
ilegibilidad *nf* : illegibility
ilegible *adj* : illegible — **ilegiblemente** *adv*
ilegitimidad *nf* : illegitimacy
ilegítimo, -ma *adj* : illegitimate, unlawful

ileso, -sa *adj* : uninjured, unharmed
ilícito, -ta *adj* : illicit — **ilícitamente** *adv*
ilimitado, -da *adj* : unlimited
ilógico, -ca *adj* : illogical — **ilógicamente** *adv*
iluminación *nf, pl* **-ciones 1** : illumination **2** ALUMBRADO : lighting
iluminado, -da *adj* : illuminated, lighted
iluminar *vt* **1** : to illuminate, to light (up) **2** : to enlighten
ilusión *nf, pl* **-siones 1** : illusion, delusion **2** ESPERANZA : hope ⟨hacerse ilusiones : to get one's hopes up⟩
ilusionado, -da *adj* ESPERANZADO : hopeful, eager
ilusionar *vt* : to build up hope, to excite — **ilusionarse** *vr* : to get one's hopes up
iluso[1], **-sa** *adj* : naive, gullible
iluso[2], **-sa** *n* SOÑADOR : dreamer, visionary
ilusorio, -ria *adj* ENGAÑOSO : illusory, misleading
ilustración *nf, pl* **-ciones 1** : illustration **2** : erudition, learning ⟨la Ilustración : the Enlightenment⟩
ilustrado, -da *adj* **1** : illustrated **2** DOCTO : learned, erudite
ilustrador, -dora *n* : illustrator
ilustrar *vt* **1** : to illustrate **2** ACLARAR, CLARIFICAR : to explain
ilustrativo, -va *adj* : illustrative
ilustre *adj* : illustrious, eminent
imagen *nf, pl* **imágenes** : image, picture
imaginable *adj* : imaginable, conceivable
imaginación *nf, pl* **-ciones** : imagination
imaginar *vt* : to imagine — **imaginarse** *vr* **1** : to suppose, to imagine **2** : to picture
imaginario, -ria *adj* : imaginary
imaginativo, -va *adj* : imaginative — **imaginativamente** *adv*
imaginería *nf* **1** : imagery **2** : image making (in religion)
imán *nm, pl* **imanes** : magnet
imantar *vt* : to magnetize
imbatible *adj* : unbeatable
imbécil[1] *adj* : stupid, idiotic
imbécil[2] *nmf* **1** : imbecile **2** *fam* : idiot, dope
imborrable *adj* : indelible
imbuir {41} *vt* : to imbue — **imbuirse** *vr*
imitación *nf, pl* **-ciones 1** : imitation **2** : mimicry, impersonation
imitador[1], **-dora** *adj* : imitative
imitador[2], **-dora** *n* **1** : imitator **2** : mimic
imitar *vt* **1** : to imitate, to copy **2** : to mimic, to impersonate
imitativo, -va *adj* → **imitador**[1]
impaciencia *nf* : impatience
impacientar *vt* : to make impatient, to exasperate — **impacientarse** *vr*
impaciente *adj* : impatient — **impacientemente** *adv*
impactado, -da *adj* : shocked, stunned
impactante *adj* **1** : shocking **2** : impressive, powerful

impactar *vt* **1** GOLPEAR : to hit **2** IMPRESIONAR : to impact, to affect — **impactarse** *vr*
impacto *nm* **1** : impact, effect **2** : shock, collision
impagable *adj* **1** : unpayable **2** : priceless
impago *nm* : nonpayment
impalpable *adj* INTANGIBLE : impalpable, intangible
impar[1] *adj* : odd ⟨números impares : odd numbers⟩
impar[2] *nm* : odd number
imparable *adj* : unstoppable
imparcial *adj* : impartial — **imparcialmente** *adv*
imparcialidad *nf* : impartiality
impartir *vt* : to impart, to give
impasible *adj* : impassive, unmoved — **impasiblemente** *adv*
impasse *nm* : impasse
impávido, -da *adj* : undaunted, unperturbed
impecable *adj* INTACHABLE : impeccable, faultless — **impecablemente** *adv*
impedido, -da *adj* : disabled, crippled
impedimento *nm* **1** : impediment, obstacle **2** : disability
impedir {54} *vt* **1** : to prevent, to block **2** : to impede, to hinder
impeler *vt* **1** : to drive, to propel **2** : to impel
impenetrable *adj* : impenetrable — **impenetrabilidad** *nf*
impenitente *adj* : unrepentant, impenitent
impensable *adj* : unthinkable
impensado, -da *adj* : unforeseen, unexpected
imperante *adj* : prevailing
imperar *vi* **1** : to reign, to rule **2** PREDOMINAR : to prevail
imperativo[1], **-va** *adj* : imperative
imperativo[2] *nm* : imperative
imperceptible *adj* : imperceptible — **imperceptiblemente** *adv*
imperdible *nm* *Spain* : safety pin
imperdonable *adj* : unpardonable, unforgivable
imperecedero, -ra *adj* **1** : imperishable **2** INMORTAL : immortal, everlasting
imperfección *nf, pl* **-ciones 1** : imperfection **2** DEFECTO : defect, flaw
imperfecto[1], **-ta** *adj* : imperfect, flawed
imperfecto[2] *nm* : imperfect tense
imperial *adj* : imperial
imperialismo *nm* : imperialism
imperialista *adj & nmf* : imperialist
impericia *nf* : lack of skill, incompetence
imperio *nm* : empire
imperioso, -sa *adj* **1** : imperious **2** : pressing, urgent — **imperiosamente** *adv*
impermeabilizante *adj* : water-repellent
impermeabilizar {21} *vt* : to waterproof
impermeable[1] *adj* **1** : impervious **2** : impermeable, waterproof
impermeable[2] *nm* : raincoat

impersonal *adj* : impersonal — **impersonalmente** *adv*
impertinencia *nf* INSOLENCIA : impertinence, insolence
impertinente *adj* **1** INSOLENTE : impertinent, insolent **2** INOPORTUNO : inappropriate, uncalled-for **3** IRRELEVANTE : irrelevant
imperturbable *adj* : imperturbable, impassive, stolid
ímpetu *nm* **1** : impetus, momentum **2** : vigor, energy **3** : force, violence
impetuoso, -sa *adj* : impetuous, impulsive — **impetuosamente** *adv*
impiedad *nf* : impiety
impío, -pía *adj* : impious, ungodly
implacable *adj* : implacable, relentless — **implacablemente** *adv*
implantación *nf, pl* -ciones **1** : implantation **2** ESTABLECIMIENTO : establishment, introduction
implantado, -da *adj* : well-established
implantar *vt* **1** : to implant **2** ESTABLECER : to establish, to introduce — **implantarse** *vr*
implante *nm* : implant
implementar *vt* : to implement — **implementarse** *vr* — **implementación** *nf*
implemento *nm* : implement, tool
implicación *nf, pl* -ciones : implication
implicar {72} *vt* **1** ENREDAR, ENVOLVER : to involve, to implicate **2** : to imply
implícito, -ta *adj* : implied, implicit — **implícitamente** *adv*
implorar *vt* : to implore
implosión *nf, pl* -siones : implosion — **implosivo, -va** *adj*
implosionar *vi* : to implode
imponderable *adj & nm* : imponderable
imponente *adj* : imposing, impressive
imponer {60} *vt* **1** : to impose **2** : to confer — *vi* : to be impressive, to command respect — **imponerse** *vr* **1** : to take on (a duty) **2** : to assert oneself **3** : to prevail
imponible *adj* : taxable
impopular *adj* : unpopular — **impopularidad** *nf*
importación *nf, pl* -ciones **1** : importation **2 importaciones** *nfpl* : imports
importado, -da *adj* : imported
importador[1], -dora *adj* : importing
importador[2], -dora *n* : importer
importancia *nf* : importance
importante *adj* : important — **importantemente** *adv*
importar *vi* : to matter, to be important ⟨no le importa lo que piensen : she doesn't care what they think⟩ — *vt* : to import
importe *nm* **1** : price, cost **2** : sum, amount
importunar *vt* : to bother, to inconvenience — *vi* : to be inconvenient
importuno, -na *adj* **1** : inopportune, inconvenient **2** : bothersome, annoying
imposibilidad *nf* : impossibility

imposibilitado, -da *adj* **1** : disabled, crippled **2 verse imposibilitado** : to be unable (to do something)
imposibilitar *vt* **1** : to make impossible **2** : to disable, to incapacitate — **imposibilitarse** *vr* : to become disabled
imposible *adj* : impossible
imposición *nf, pl* -ciones **1** : imposition **2** EXIGENCIA : demand, requirement **3** : tax **4** : deposit
impositivo, -va *adj* : tax ⟨tasa impositiva : tax rate⟩
impostor, -tora *n* : impostor
impostura *nf* **1** : fraud, imposture **2** CALUMNIA : slander
impotencia *nf* **1** : impotence, powerlessness **2** : impotence (in medicine)
impotente *adj* **1** : powerless **2** : impotent
impracticable *adj* : impracticable
imprecisión *nf, pl* -siones **1** : imprecision, vagueness **2** : inaccuracy
impreciso, -sa *adj* **1** : imprecise, vague **2** : inaccurate
impredecible *adj* : unpredictable
impregnar *vt* : to impregnate
imprenta *nf* **1** : printing **2** : printing shop, press
imprescindible *adj* : essential, indispensable
impresentable *adj* : unpresentable, unfit
impresión *nf, pl* -siones **1** : print, printing **2** : impression, feeling
impresionable *adj* : impressionable
impresionante *adj* : impressive, incredible, amazing — **impresionantemente** *adv*
impresionar *vt* **1** : to impress, to strike **2** : to affect, to move — *vi* : to make an impression — **impresionarse** *vr* : to be affected, to be removed
impresionismo *nm* : impressionism
impresionista[1] *adj* : impressionist, impressionistic
impresionista[2] *nmf* : impressionist
impreso[1] *pp* → **imprimir**
impreso[2], -sa *adj* : printed
impreso[3] *nm* PUBLICACIÓN : printed matter, publication
impresor, -sora *n* : printer
impresora *nf* : (computer) printer
imprevisible *adj* : unforeseeable
imprevisión *nf, pl* -siones : lack of foresight, thoughtlessness
imprevisto[1], -ta *adj* : unexpected, unforeseen
imprevisto[2] *nm* : unexpected occurrence, contingency
imprimir {42} *vt* **1** : to print **2** : to imprint, to stamp, to impress
improbabilidad *nf* : improbability
improbable *adj* : improbable, unlikely
improcedente *adj* **1** : inadmissible **2** : inappropriate, improper
improductivo, -va *adj* : unproductive
improperio *nm* : affront, insult
impropiedad *nf* : impropriety

impropio, -pia *adj* **1** : improper, incorrect **2** INADECUADO : unsuitable, inappropriate
improvisación *nf, pl* **-ciones** : improvisation, ad-lib
improvisado, -da *adj* : improvised, ad-lib
improvisar *v* : to improvise, to ad-lib
improviso *adj* **de ~** : all of a sudden, unexpectedly
imprudencia *nf* INDISCRECIÓN : imprudence, indiscretion
imprudente *adj* INDISCRETO : imprudent, indiscreet — **imprudentemente** *adv*
impúdico, -ca *adj* : shameless, indecent
impuesto[1] *pp* → **imponer**
impuesto[2] *nm* : tax
impugnar *vt* : to challenge, to contest
impulsar *vt* : to propel, to drive
impulsividad *nf* : impulsiveness
impulsivo, -va *adj* : impulsive — **impulsivamente** *adv*
impulso *nm* **1** : drive, thrust **2** : impulse, urge
impune *adj* : unpunished
impunemente *adv* : with impunity
impunidad *nf* : impunity
impureza *nf* : impurity
impuro, -ra *adj* : impure
impuso, etc. → **imponer**
imputable *adj* ATRIBUIBLE : attributable
imputación *nf, pl* **-ciones 1** : attribution, imputation **2** : accusation
imputar *vt* ATRIBUIR : to impute, to attribute
inacabable *adj* : endless
inacabado, -da *adj* INCONCLUSO : unfinished
inaccesibilidad *nf* : inaccessibility
inaccesible *adj* **1** : inaccessible **2** : unattainable
inacción *nf, pl* **-ciones** : inactivity, inaction
inaceptable *adj* : unacceptable
inactividad *nf* : inactivity, idleness
inactivo, -va *adj* : inactive, idle
inadaptado[1]**, -da** *adj* : maladjusted
inadaptado[2]**, -da** *n* : misfit
inadecuación *nf, pl* **-ciones** : inadequacy
inadecuado, -da *adj* **1** : inadequate **2** IMPROPIO : inappropriate — **inadecuadamente** *adv*
inadmisible *adj* **1** : inadmissible **2** : unacceptable
inadvertencia *nf* : oversight
inadvertidamente *adv* : inadvertently
inadvertido, -da *adj* **1** : unnoticed ⟨pasar inadvertido : to go unnoticed⟩ **2** DESPISTADO, DISTRAÍDO : inattentive, distracted
inagotable *adj* : inexhaustible
inaguantable *adj* INSOPORTABLE : insufferable, unbearable
inalámbrico, -ca *adj* : wireless, cordless
inalcanzable *adj* : unreachable, unattainable

inalienable *adj* : inalienable
inalterable *adj* **1** : unalterable, unchangeable **2** : impassive **3** : colorfast
inamovible *adj* : immovable, fixed
inanición *nf, pl* **-ciones** : starvation
inanimado, -da *adj* : inanimate
inapelable *adj* : indisputable
inapetencia *nf* : lack of appetite
inaplicable *adj* : inapplicable
inapreciable *adj* **1** : imperceptible, negligible **2** : invaluable
inapropiado, -da *adj* : inappropriate, unsuitable
inarticulado, -da *adj* : inarticulate, unintelligible — **inarticuladamente** *adv*
inasequible *adj* : unattainable, inaccessible
inasistencia *nf* AUSENCIA : absence
inatacable *adj* : unassailable, indisputable
inaudible *adj* : inaudible
inaudito, -ta *adj* : unheard-of, unprecedented
inauguración *nf, pl* **-ciones** : inauguration
inaugural *adj* : inaugural, opening
inaugurar *vt* **1** : to inaugurate **2** : to open
inca *adj & nmf* : Inca
incalculable *adj* : incalculable
incalificable *adj* : indescribable
incandescencia *nf* : incandescence — **incandescente** *adj*
incansable *adj* INFATIGABLE : tireless — **incansablemente** *adv*
incapacidad *nf* **1** : inability, incapacity **2** : disability, handicap
incapacitado, -da *adj* **1** : disqualified **2** : disabled, handicapped
incapacitar *vt* **1** : to incapacitate, to disable **2** : to disqualify
incapaz *adj, pl* **-paces 1** : incapable, unable **2** : incompetent, inept
incautación *nf, pl* **-ciones** : seizure, confiscation
incautar *vt* CONFISCAR : to confiscate, to seize — **incautarse** *vr*
incauto, -ta *adj* : unwary, unsuspecting
incendiar *vt* : to set fire to, to burn (down) — **incendiarse** *vr* : to catch fire
incendiario[1]**, -ria** *adj* : incendiary, inflammatory
incendiario[2]**, -ria** *n* : arsonist
incendio *nm* **1** : fire **2 incendio premeditado** : arson
incensario *nm* : censer
incentivar *vt* : to encourage, to stimulate
incentivo *nm* : incentive
incertidumbre *nf* : uncertainty, suspense
incesante *adj* : incessant — **incesantemente** *adv*
incesto *nm* : incest
incestuoso, -sa *adj* : incestuous
incidencia *nf* **1** : incident **2** : effect, impact **3 por ~** : by chance, accidentally

incidental *adj* : incidental
incidentalmente *adv* : by chance
incidente *nm* : incident, occurrence
incidir *vi* **1** ~ **en** : to fall into, to enter into ⟨incidimos en el mismo error : we fell into the same mistake⟩ **2** ~ **en** : to affect, to influence, to have a bearing on
incienso *nm* : incense
incierto, -ta *adj* **1** : uncertain **2** : untrue **3** : unsteady, insecure
incineración *nf, pl* **-ciones 1** : incineration **2** : cremation
incinerador *nm* : incinerator
incinerar *vt* **1** : to incinerate **2** : to cremate
incipiente *adj* : incipient
incisión *nf, pl* **-siones** : incision
incisivo[1], **-va** *adj* : incisive
incisivo[2] *nm* : incisor
inciso *nm* : digression, aside
incitación *nf, pl* **-ciones** : incitement
incitador[1], **-dora** *n* : instigator, agitator
incitador[2], **-dora** *adj* : provocative
incitante *adj* : provocative
incitar *vt* : to incite, to rouse
incivilizado, -da *adj* : uncivilized
inclemencia *nf* : inclemency, severity
inclemente *adj* : inclement
inclinación *nf, pl* **-ciones 1** PROPENSIÓN : inclination, tendency **2** : incline, slope
inclinado, -da *adj* **1** : sloping **2** : inclined, apt
inclinar *vt* : to tilt, to lean, to incline ⟨inclinar la cabeza : to bow one's head⟩ — **inclinarse** *vr* **1** : to lean, to lean over **2** ~ **a** : to be inclined to
incluir {41} *vt* : to include
inclusión *nf, pl* **-siones** : inclusion
inclusive *adv* : inclusively, up to and including
inclusivo, -va *adj* : inclusive
incluso *adv* **1** AUN : even, in fact ⟨es importante e incluso crucial : it is important and even crucial⟩ **2** : inclusively
incógnita *nf* **1** : unknown quantity (in mathematics) **2** : mystery
incógnito, -ta *adj* **1** : unknown **2 de incógnito** : incognito
incoherencia *nf* : incoherence
incoherente *adj* : incoherent — **incoherentemente** *adv*
incoloro, -ra *adj* : colorless
incombustible *adj* : fireproof
incomible *adj* : inedible
incomodar *vt* **1** : to make uncomfortable **2** : to inconvenience — **incomodarse** *vr* : to put oneself out, to take the trouble
incomodidad *nf* **1** : discomfort, awkwardness **2** MOLESTIA : inconvenience, bother
incómodo, -da *adj* **1** : uncomfortable, awkward **2** INCONVENIENTE : inconvenient
incomparable *adj* : incomparable

incompatibilidad *nf* : incompatibility
incompatible *adj* : incompatible, uncongenial
incompetencia *nf* : incompetence
incompetente *adj & nmf* : incompetent
incompleto, -ta *adj* : incomplete
incomprendido, -da *adj* : misunderstood
incomprensible *adj* : incomprehensible
incomprensión *nf, pl* **-siones** : lack of understanding, incomprehension
incomunicación *nf, pl* **-ciones** : lack of communication
incomunicado, -da *adj* **1** : cut off, isolated **2** : in solitary confinement
inconcebible *adj* : inconceivable, unthinkable — **inconcebiblemente** *adv*
inconcluso, -sa *adj* INACABADO : unfinished
incondicional *adj* : unconditional — **incondicionalmente** *adv*
inconexo, -xa *adj* : unconnected, disconnected
inconfesable *adj* : unspeakable, shameful
inconforme *adj & nmf* : nonconformist
inconformidad *nf* : nonconformity
inconformista *adj & nmf* : nonconformist
inconfundible *adj* : unmistakable, obvious — **inconfundiblemente** *adv*
incongruencia *nf* : incongruity
incongruente *adj* : incongruous
inconmensurable *adj* : vast, immeasurable
inconquistable *adj* : unyielding
inconsciencia *nf* **1** : unconsciousness, unawareness **2** : irresponsibility
inconsciente[1] *adj* **1** : unconscious, unaware **2** : reckless, needless — **inconscientemente** *adv*
inconsciente[2] *nm* **el inconsciente** : the unconscious
inconsecuente *adj* : inconsistent — **inconsecuencia** *nf*
inconsiderado, -da *adj* : inconsiderate, thoughtless
inconsistencia *nf* : inconsistency
inconsistente *adj* **1** : weak, flimsy **2** : inconsistent, weak (of an argument)
inconsolable *adj* : inconsolable — **inconsolablemente** *adv*
inconstancia *nf* : inconstancy
inconstante *adj* : inconstant, fickle, changeable
inconstitucional *adj* : unconstitutional
inconstitucionalidad *nf* : unconstitutionality
incontable *adj* INNUMERABLE : countless, innumerable
incontenible *adj* : uncontrollable, unstoppable
incontestable *adj* INCUESTIONABLE, INDISCUTIBLE : irrefutable, indisputable
incontinencia *nf* : incontinence — **incontinente** *adj*
incontrolable *adj* : uncontrollable
incontrolado, -da *adj* : uncontrolled, out of control

incontrovertible *adj* : indisputable
inconveniencia *nf* **1** : inconvenience, trouble **2** : unsuitability, inappropriateness **3** : tactless remark
inconveniente[1] *adj* **1** INCÓMODO : inconvenient **2** INAPROPIADO : improper, unsuitable
inconveniente[2] *nm* : obstacle, problem, snag ⟨no tengo inconveniente en hacerlo : I don't mind doing it⟩
incorporación *nf, pl* **-ciones** : incorporation
incorporar *vt* **1** : to incorporate **2** : to add, to include — **incorporarse** *vr* **1** : to sit up **2** ~ **a** : to join
incorpóreo, -rea *adj* : incorporeal, bodiless
incorrección *n, pl* **-ciones** : impropriety, improper word or action
incorrecto, -ta *adj* : incorrect — **incorrectamente** *adv*
incorregible *adj* : incorrigible — **incorregibilidad** *nf*
incorruptible *adj* : incorruptible
incredulidad *nf* : incredulity, skepticism
incrédulo[1], **-la** *adj* : incredulous, skeptical
incrédulo[2], **-la** *n* : skeptic
increíble *adj* : incredible, unbelievable — **increíblemente** *adv*
incrementar *vt* : to increase — **incrementarse** *vr*
incremento *nm* AUMENTO : increase
incriminar *vt* : to incriminate — **incriminación** *nf*
incriminatorio, -ria *adj* : incriminating, incriminatory
incruento, -ta *adj* : bloodless
incrustación *nf, pl* **-ciones** : inlay
incrustar *vt* **1** : to embed **2** : to inlay — **incrustarse** *vr* : to become embedded
incubación *nf, pl* **-ciones** : incubation
incubadora *nf* : incubator
incubar *v* : to incubate
incuestionable *adj* INCONTESTABLE, INDISCUTIBLE : unquestionable, indisputable — **incuestionablemente** *adv*
inculcar {72} *vt* : to inculcate, to instill
inculpar *vt* ACUSAR : to accuse, to charge
inculto, -ta *adj* **1** : uncultured, ignorant **2** : uncultivated, fallow
incumbencia *nf* : obligation, responsibility
incumbir *vi* (*3rd person only*) ~ **a** : to be incumbent upon, to be of concern to ⟨a mí no me incumbe : it's not my concern⟩
incumplido, -da *adj* : irresponsible, unreliable
incumplimiento *nm* **1** : nonfulfillment, neglect **2 incumplimiento de contrato** : breach of contract
incumplir *vt* : to fail to carry out, to break (a promise, a contract)
incurable *adj* : incurable
incurrir *vi* **1** ~ **en** : to incur ⟨incurrir en gastos : to incur expenses⟩ **2** ~ **en** : to fall into, to commit ⟨incurrió en un error : he made a mistake⟩

incursión *nf, pl* **-siones** : incursion, raid
incursionar *vi* **1** : to raid **2** ~ **en** : to go into, to enter ⟨el actor incursionó en el baile : the actor worked in dance for awhile⟩
indagación *nf, pl* **-ciones** : investigation, inquiry
indagar {52} *vt* : to inquire into, to investigate
indebido, -da *adj* : improper, undue — **indebidamente** *adv*
indecencia *nf* : indecency, obscenity
indecente *adj* : indecent, obscene
indecible *adj* : indescribable, inexpressible
indecisión *nf, pl* **-siones** : indecision
indeciso, -sa *adj* **1** IRRESOLUTO : indecisive **2** : undecided
indeclinable *adj* : unavoidable
indecoro *nm* : impropriety, indecorousness
indecoroso, -sa *adj* : indecorous, unseemly
indefectible *adj* : unfailing, sure
indefendible *adj* : indefensible
indefenso, -sa *adj* : defenseless, helpless
indefinible *adj* : indefinable
indefinido, -da *adj* **1** : undefined, vague **2** INDETERMINADO : indefinite — **indefinidamente** *adv*
indeleble *adj* : indelible — **indeleblemente** *adv*
indelicado, -da *adj* : indelicate, tactless
indemnización *nf, pl* **-ciones** **1** : indemnity **2 indemnización por despido** : severance pay
indemnizar {21} *vt* : to indemnify, to compensate
independencia *nf* : independence
independiente *adj* : independent — **independientemente** *adv*
independizarse {21} *vr* : to become independent, to gain independence
indescifrable *adj* : indecipherable
indescriptible *adj* : indescribable — **indescriptiblemente** *adv*
indeseable *adj & nmf* : undesirable
indestructible *adj* : indestructible
indeterminación *nf, pl* **-ciones** : indeterminacy
indeterminado, -da *adj* **1** INDEFINIDO : indefinite **2** : indeterminate
indexar *vt* INDICIAR : to index (wages, prices, etc.)
indicación *nf, pl* **-ciones** **1** : sign, signal **2** : direction, instruction **3** : suggestion, hint
indicado, -da *adj* **1** APROPIADO : appropriate, suitable **2** : specified, indicated ⟨al día indicado : on the specified day⟩
indicador *nm* **1** : gauge, dial, meter **2** : indicator ⟨indicadores económicos : economic indicators⟩
indicar {72} *vt* **1** SEÑALAR : to indicate **2** ENSEÑAR, MOSTRAR : to show
indicativo[1], **-va** *adj* : indicative
indicativo[2] *nm* : indicative (mood)

índice *nm* **1** : index **2** : index finger, forefinger **3** INDICIO : indication
indiciar *vt* : to index (prices, wages, etc.)
indicio *nm* : indication, sign
indiferencia *nf* : indifference
indiferente *adj* **1** : indifferent, unconcerned **2 ser indiferente** : to be of no concern ⟨me es indiferente : it doesn't matter to me⟩
indígena¹ *adj* : indigenous, native
indígena² *nmf* : native
indigencia *nf* MISERIA : poverty, destitution
indigente *adj & nmf* : indigent
indigestarse *vr* **1** EMPACHARSE : to have indigestion **2** *fam* : to nauseate, to disgust ⟨ese tipo se me indigesta : that guy makes me sick⟩
indigestión *nf, pl* **-tiones** EMPACHO : indigestion
indigesto, -ta *adj* : indigestible, difficult to digest
indignación *nf, pl* **-ciones** : indignation
indignado, -da *adj* : indignant
indignante *adj* : outrageous, infuriating
indignar *vt* : to outrage, to infuriate — **indignarse** *vr*
indignidad *nf* : indignity
indigno, -na *adj* : unworthy
índigo *nm* : indigo
indio¹, -dia *adj* **1** : American Indian, Indian, Amerindian **2** : Indian (from India)
indio², -dia *n* **1** : American Indian **2** : Indian (from India)
indirecta *nf* **1** : hint, innuendo **2 echar indirectas** *or* **lanzar indirectas** : to drop a hint, to insinuate
indirecto, -ta *adj* : indirect — **indirectamente** *adv*
indisciplina *nf* : indiscipline, unruliness
indisciplinado, -da *adj* : undisciplined, unruly
indiscreción *nf, pl* **-ciones** **1** IMPRUDENCIA : indiscretion **2** : tactless remark
indiscreto, -ta *adj* IMPRUDENTE : indiscreet, imprudent — **indiscretamente** *adv*
indiscriminado, -da *adj* : indiscriminate — **indiscriminadamente** *adv*
indiscutible *adj* INCONTESTABLE, INCUESTIONABLE : indisputable, unquestionable — **indiscutiblemente** *adv*
indispensable *adj* : indispensable — **indispensablemente** *adv*
indisponer {60} *vt* **1** : to spoil, to upset **2** : to make ill — **indisponerse** *vr* **1** : to become ill **2** ~ **con** : to fall out with
indisposición *nf, pl* **-ciones** : indisposition, illness
indispuesto, -ta *adj* : unwell, indisposed
indistinguible *adj* : indistinguishable
indistintamente *adv* **1** : indistinctly **2** : indiscriminately
indistinto, -ta *adj* : indistinct, vague, faint

individual *adj* : individual — **individualmente** *adv*
individualidad *nf* : individuality
individualismo *nm* : individualism
individualista¹ *adj* : individualistic
individualista² *nmf* : individualist
individualizar {21} *vt* : to individualize
individuo *nm* : individual, person
indivisible *adj* : indivisible — **indivisibilidad** *nf*
indocumentado, -da *n* : illegal immigrant
índole *nf* **1** : nature, character **2** CLASE, TIPO : sort, kind
indolencia *nf* : indolence, laziness
indolente *adj* : indolent, lazy
indoloro, -ra *adj* : painless
indomable *adj* **1** : indomitable **2** : unruly, unmanageable
indómito, -ta *adj* : indomitable
indonesio, -sia *adj & n* : Indonesian
inducción *nf, pl* **-ciones** : induction
inducir {61} *vt* **1** : to induce, to cause **2** : to infer, to deduce
inductivo, -va *adj* : inductive
indudable *adj* : unquestionable, beyond doubt
indudablemente *adv* : undoubtedly, unquestionably
indulgencia *nf* **1** : indulgence, leniency **2** : indulgence (in religion)
indulgente *adj* : indulgent, lenient
indultar *vt* : to pardon, to reprieve
indulto *nm* : pardon, reprieve
indumentaria *nf* : clothing, attire
industria *nf* : industry
industrial¹ *adj* : industrial
industrial² *nmf* : industrialist, manufacturer
industrialización *nf, pl* **-ciones** : industrialization
industrializar {21} *vt* : to industrialize
industrioso, -sa *adj* : industrious
inédito, -ta *adj* **1** : unpublished **2** : unprecedented
inefable *adj* : ineffable
ineficacia *nf* **1** : inefficiency **2** : ineffectiveness
ineficaz *adj, pl* **-caces** **1** : inefficient **2** : ineffective — **ineficazmente** *adv*
ineficiencia *nf* : inefficiency
ineficiente *adj* : inefficient — **ineficientemente** *adv*
inelegancia *nf* : inelegance — **inelegante** *adj*
inelegible *adj* : ineligible — **inelegibilidad** *nf*
ineludible *adj* : inescapable, unavoidable — **ineludiblemente** *adv*
ineptitud *nf* : ineptitude, incompetence
inepto, -ta *adj* : inept, incompetent
inequidad *nf* : inequity
inequitativo, -va *adj* : inequitable
inequívoco, -ca *adj* : unequivocal, unmistakable — **inequívocamente** *adv*
inercia *nf* **1** : inertia **2** : apathy, passivity **3 por** ~ : out of habit
inerme *adj* : unarmed, defenseless

inerte *adj* : inert
inescrupuloso, -sa *adj* : unscrupulous
inescrutable *adj* : inscrutable
inesperado, -da *adj* : unexpected — **inesperadamente** *adv*
inestabilidad *nf* : instability, unsteadiness
inestable *adj* : unstable, unsteady
inestimable *adj* : inestimable, invaluable
inevitabilidad *nf* : inevitability
inevitable *adj* : inevitable, unavoidable — **inevitablemente** *adv*
inexactitud *nf* : inaccuracy
inexacto, -ta *adj* : inexact, inaccurate
inexcusable *adj* : inexcusable, unforgivable
inexistencia *nf* : lack, nonexistence
inexistente *adj* : nonexistent
inexorable *adj* : inexorable — **inexorablemente** *adv*
inexperiencia *nf* : inexperience
inexperto, -ta *adj* : inexperienced, unskilled
inexplicable *adj* : inexplicable — **inexplicablemente** *adv*
inexplorado, -da *adj* : unexplored
inexpresable *adj* : inexpressible
inexpresivo, -va *adj* : inexpressive, expressionless
inexpugnable *adj* : impregnable
inextinguible *adj* **1** : inextinguishable **2** : unquenchable
inextricable *adj* : inextricable — **inextricablemente** *adv*
infalibilidad *nf* : infallibility
infalible *adj* : infallible — **infaliblemente** *adv*
infame *adj* **1** : infamous **2** : loathsome, vile ⟨tiempo infame : terrible weather⟩
infamia *nf* : infamy, disgrace
infancia *nf* **1** NIÑEZ : infancy, childhood **2** : children *pl* **3** : beginnings *pl*
infante *nm* **1** : infante, prince **2** : infantryman
infantería *nf* : infantry
infantil *adj* **1** : childish, infantile **2** : child's, children's
infantilismo *nm* **1** : infantilism **2** INMADUREZ : childishness
infarto *nm* : heart attack
infatigable *adj* : indefatigable, tireless — **infatigablemente** *adv*
infección *nf, pl* **-ciones** : infection
infeccioso, -sa *adj* : infectious
infectar *vt* : to infect — **infectarse** *vr*
infecto, -ta *adj* **1** : infected **2** : repulsive, sickening
infecundidad *nf* : infertility
infecundo, -da *adj* : infertile, barren
infelicidad *nf* : unhappiness
infeliz[1] *adj, pl* **-lices** **1** : unhappy **2** : hapless, unfortunate, wretched
infeliz[2] *nmf, pl* **-lices** : wretch
inferencia *nf* : inference
inferior[1] *adj* : inferior, lower
inferior[2] *nmf* : inferior, underling
inferioridad *nf* : inferiority

inferir {76} *vt* **1** DEDUCIR : to infer, to deduce **2** : to cause (harm or injury), to inflict
infernal *adj* : infernal, hellish
infestación *n, pl* **-ciones** : infestation
infestar *vt* **1** : to infest **2** : to overrun, to invade
inficción *nf, pl* **-ciones** *Mex* : pollution
infidelidad *nf* : unfaithfulness, infidelity
infiel[1] *adj* : unfaithful, disloyal
infiel[2] *nmf* : infidel, heathen
infierno *nm* **1** : hell **2 el quinto infierno** : the middle of nowhere
infiltrar *vt* : to infiltrate — **infiltrarse** *vr* — **infiltración** *nf*
infinidad *nf* **1** : infinity **2** SINFÍN : great number, huge quantity ⟨una infinidad de veces : countless times⟩
infinitesimal *adj* : infinitesimal
infinitivo *nm* : infinitive
infinito[1] *adv* : infinitely, vastly
infinito[2]**, -ta** *adj* **1** : infinite **2** : limitless, endless **3 hasta lo infinito** : ad infinitum — **infinitamente** *adv*
infinito[3] *nm* : infinity
inflable *adj* : inflatable
inflación *nf, pl* **-ciones** : inflation
inflacionario, -ria *adj* : inflationary
inflacionista → **inflacionario**
inflamable *adj* : flammable
inflamación *nf, pl* **-ciones** : inflammation
inflamar *vt* : to inflame
inflamatorio, -ria *adj* : inflammatory
inflar *vt* HINCHAR : to inflate — **inflarse** *vr* **1** : to swell **2** : to become conceited
inflexibilidad *nf* : inflexibility
inflexible *adj* : inflexible, unyielding
inflexión *nf, pl* **-xiones** : inflection
infligir {35} *vt* : to inflict
influencia *nf* INFLUJO : influence
influenciable *adj* : easily influenced, suggestible
influenciar *vt* : to influence
influenza *nf* : influenza
influir {41} *vt* : to influence — *vi* ~ **en** or ~ **sobre** : to have an influence on, to affect
influjo *nm* INFLUENCIA : influence
influyente *adj* : influential
información *nf, pl* **-ciones** **1** : information **2** INFORME : report, inquiry **3** NOTICIAS : news
informado, -da *adj* : informed ⟨bien informado : well-informed⟩
informador, -dora *n* : informer, informant
informal *adj* **1** : unreliable (of persons) **2** : informal, casual — **informalmente** *adv*
informalidad *nf* : informality
informante *nmf* : informant
informar *vt* ENTERAR : to inform — *vi* : to report — **informarse** *vr* ENTERARSE : to get information, to find out
informática *nf* : computer science, computing

informativo[1], **-va** *adj* : informative
informativo[2] *nm* : news program, news
informatización *nf, pl* **-ciones** : computerization
informatizar {21} *vt* : to computerize
informe[1] *adj* AMORFO : shapeless, formless
informe[2] *nm* **1** : report **2** : reference (for employment) **3 informes** *nmpl* : information, data
infortunado, -da *adj* : unfortunate, unlucky
infortunio *nm* **1** DESGRACIA : misfortune **2** CONTRATIEMPO : mishap
infracción *nf, pl* **-ciones** : violation, offense, infraction
infractor, -tora *n* : offender
infraestructura *nf* : infrastructure
infrahumano, -na *adj* : subhuman
infranqueable *adj* **1** : impassable **2** : insurmountable
infrarrojo, -ja *adj* : infrared
infrecuente *adj* : infrequent
infringir {35} *vt* : to infringe, to breach
infructuoso, -sa *adj* : fruitless — **infructuosamente** *adv*
ínfulas *nfpl* **1** : conceit **2 darse ínfulas** : to put on airs
infundado, -da *adj* : unfounded, baseless
infundio *nm* : false story, lie, tall tale ⟨todo eso son infundios : that's a pack of lies⟩
infundir *vt* **1** : to instill **2 infundir ánimo a** : to encourage **3 infundir miedo a** : to intimidate
infusión *nf, pl* **-siones** : infusion
ingeniar *vt* : to devise, to think up — **ingeniarse** *vr* : to manage, to find a way
ingeniería *nf* : engineering
ingeniero, -ra *n* : engineer
ingenio *nm* **1** : ingenuity **2** CHISPA : wit, wits **3** : device, apparatus **4 ingenio azucarero** : sugar refinery
ingenioso, -sa *adj* **1** : ingenious **2** : clever, witty — **ingeniosamente** *adv*
ingente *adj* : huge, enormous
ingenuidad *nf* : naïveté, ingenuousness
ingenuo[1], **-nua** *adj* CÁNDIDO : naive — **ingenuamente** *adv*
ingenuo[2], **-nua** *n* : naive person
ingerencia → **injerencia**
ingerir {76} *vt* : to ingest, to consume
ingestión *nf, pl* **-tiones** : ingestion
ingle *nf* : groin
inglés[1], **-glesa** *adj, mpl* **ingleses** : English
inglés[2], **-glesa** *n, mpl* **ingleses** : Englishman *m*, Englishwoman *f*
inglés[3] *nm* : English (language)
inglete *nm* : miter joint
ingobernable *adj* : ungovernable, lawless
ingratitud *nf* : ingratitude
ingrato[1], **-ta** *adj* **1** : ungrateful **2** : thankless
ingrato[2], **-ta** *n* : ingrate
ingrediente *nm* : ingredient

ingresar *vt* **1** : to admit ⟨ingresaron a Luis al hospital : Luis was admitted into the hospital⟩ **2** : to deposit — *vi* **1** : to enter, to go in **2** ~ **en** : to join, to enroll in
ingreso *nm* **1** : entrance, entry **2** : admission **3 ingresos** *nmpl* : income, earnings *pl*
íngrimo, -ma *adj* : all alone, all by oneself
inhábil *adj* : unskillful, clumsy
inhabilidad *nf* **1** : unskillfulness **2** : unfitness
inhabilitar *vt* **1** : to disqualify, to bar **2** : to disable
inhabitable *adj* : uninhabitable
inhabituado, -da *adj* ~ **a** : unaccustomed to
inhalador *nm* : inhaler
inhalante *nm* : inhalant
inhalar *vt* : to inhale — **inhalación** *nf*
inherente *adj* : inherent
inhibición *nf, pl* **-ciones** COHIBICIÓN : inhibition
inhibir *vt* : to inhibit — **inhibirse** *vr*
inhóspito, -ta *adj* : inhospitable
inhumación *nf, pl* **-ciones** : interment, burial
inhumanidad *nf* : inhumanity
inhumano, -na *adj* : inhuman, cruel, inhumane
inhumar *vt* : to inter, to bury
iniciación *nf, pl* **-ciones** **1** : initiation **2** : introduction
iniciado, -da *n* : initiate
iniciador[1], **-dora** *adj* : initiatory
iniciador[2], **-dora** *n* : initiator, originator
inicial[1] *adj* : initial, original — **inicialmente** *adv*
inicial[2] *nf* : initial (letter)
iniciar *vt* COMENZAR : to initiate, to begin — **iniciarse** *vr*
iniciativa *nf* : initiative
inicio *nm* COMIENZO : beginning
inicuo, -cua *adj* : iniquitous, wicked
inigualado, -da *adj* : unequaled
inimaginable *adj* : unimaginable
inimitable *adj* : inimitable
ininteligible *adj* : unintelligible
ininterrumpido, -da *adj* : uninterrupted, continuous — **ininterrumpidamente** *adv*
iniquidad *nf* : iniquity, wickedness
injerencia *nf* : interference
injerirse {76} *vr* ENTROMETERSE, INMISCUIRSE : to meddle, to interfere
injertar *vt* : to graft
injerto *nm* : graft ⟨injerto de piel : skin graft⟩
injuria *nf* AGRAVIO : affront, insult
injuriar *vt* INSULTAR : to insult, to revile
injurioso, -sa *adj* : insulting, abusive
injusticia *nf* : injustice, unfairness
injustificable *adj* : unjustifiable
injustificadamente *adv* : unjustifiably, unfairly
injustificado, -da *adj* : unjustified, unwarranted

injusto, -ta *adj* : unfair, unjust — **injustamente** *adv*

inmaculado, -da *adj* : immaculate, spotless

inmadurez *nf, pl* **-reces** : immaturity

inmaduro, -ra *adj* **1** : immature **2** : unripe

inmediaciones *nfpl* : environs, surrounding area

inmediatamente *adv* ENSEGUIDA : immediately

inmediatez *nf, pl* **-teces** : immediacy

inmediato, -ta *adj* **1** : immediate **2** CONTIGUO : adjoining **3 de ~** : immediately, right away **4 ~ a** : next to, close to

inmejorable *adj* : excellent, unbeatable

inmemorial *adj* : immemorial ⟨tiempos inmemoriales : time immemorial⟩

inmensidad *nf* : immensity, vastness

inmenso, -sa *adj* ENORME : immense, huge, vast — **inmensamente** *adv*

inmensurable *adj* : boundless, immeasurable

inmerecido, -da *adj* : undeserved — **inmerecidamente** *adv*

inmersión *nf, pl* **-siones** : immersion

inmerso, -sa *adj* **1** : immersed **2** : involved, absorbed

inmigración *nf, pl* **-ciones** : immigration

inmigrado, -da *adj & n* : immigrant

inmigrante *adj & nmf* : immigrant

inmigrar *vi* : to immigrate

inminencia *nf* : imminence

inminente *adj* : imminent — **inminentemente** *adv*

inmiscuirse {41} *vr* ENTROMETERSE, INJERIRSE : to meddle, to interfere

inmobiliario, -ria *adj* : real estate, property

inmoderación *n, pl* **-ciones** : immoderation, intemperance

inmoderado, -da *adj* : immoderate, excessive — **inmoderamente** *adv*

inmodestia *nf* : immodesty — **inmodesto, -ta** *adj*

inmolar *vt* : to immolate — **inmolación** *nf*

inmoral *adj* : immoral

inmoralidad *nf* : immorality

inmortal *adj & nmf* : immortal

inmortalidad *nf* : immortality

inmortalizar {21} *vt* : to immortalize

inmotivado, -da *adj* **1** : unmotivated **2** : groundless

inmovible *adj* : immovable, fixed

inmóvil *adj* **1** : still, motionless **2** : steadfast

inmovilidad *nf* : immobility

inmovilizar {21} *vt* : to immobilize

inmueble *nm* : building, property

inmundicia *nf* : dirt, filth, trash

inmundo, -da *adj* : dirty, filthy, nasty

inmune *adj* : immune

inmunidad *nf* : immunity

inmunizar {21} *vt* : to immunize — **inmunización** *nf*

inmunología *nf* : immunology

inmunológico, -ca *adj* : immune ⟨sistema inmunológico : immune system⟩

inmutabilidad *nf* : immutability

inmutable *adj* : immutable, unchangeable

innato, -ta *adj* : innate, inborn

innecesario, -ria *adj* : unnecessary — **innecesariamente** *adv*

innegable *adj* : undeniable

innoble *adj* : ignoble — **innoblemente** *adv*

innovación *nf, pl* **-ciones** : innovation

innovador, -dora *adj* : innovative

innovar *vt* : to introduce — *vi* : to innovate

innumerable *adj* INCONTABLE : innumerable, countless

inobjetable *adj* : indisputable, unobjectionable

inocencia *nf* : innocence

inocente[1] *adj* **1** : innocent **2** INGENUO : naive — **inocentemente** *adv*

inocente[2] *nmf* : innocent person

inocentón[1], **-tona** *adj, mpl* **-tones** : naive, gullible

inocentón[2], **-tona** *n, mpl* **-tones** : simpleton, dupe

inocuidad *nf* : harmlessness

inocular *vt* : to inoculate, to vaccinate — **inoculación** *nf*

inocuo, -cua *adj* : innocuous, harmless

inodoro[1], **-ra** *adj* : odorless

inodoro[2] *nm* : toilet

inofensivo, -va *adj* : inoffensive, harmless

inolvidable *adj* : unforgettable

inoperable *adj* : inoperable

inoperante *adj* : ineffective, inoperative

inopinado, -da *adj* : unexpected — **inopinadamente** *adv*

inoportuno, -na *adj* : untimely, inopportune, inappropriate

inorgánico, -ca *adj* : inorganic

inoxidable *adj* **1** : rustproof **2 acero inoxidable** : stainless steel

inquebrantable *adj* : unshakable, unwavering

inquietante *adj* : disturbing, worrisome

inquietar *vt* PREOCUPAR : to disturb, to upset, to worry — **inquietarse** *vr*

inquieto, -ta *adj* **1** : anxious, uneasy, worried **2** : restless

inquietud *nf* **1** : anxiety, uneasiness, worry **2** AGITACIÓN : restlessness

inquilinato *nm* : tenancy

inquilino, -na *n* : tenant, occupant

inquina *nf* **1** : aversion, dislike **2** : ill will ⟨tener inquina a alguien : to have a grudge against someone⟩

inquirir {4} *vi* : to make inquiries — *vt* : to investigate

inquisición *nf, pl* **-ciones** : investigation, inquiry

inquisidor, -dora *adj* : inquisitive

inquisitivo, -va *adj* : inquisitive, curious — **inquisitivamente** *adv*

insaciable *adj* : insatiable

insalubre *adj* **1** : unhealthy **2** ANTIHIGIÉNICO : unsanitary

insalubridad *nf* : unhealthiness
insalvable *adj* : insuperable, insurmountable
insano, -na *adj* 1 LOCO : insane, mad 2 INSALUBRE : unhealthy
insatisfacción *nf, pl* **-ciones** : dissatisfaction
insatisfactorio *nm* : unsatisfactory
insatisfecho, -cha *adj* 1 : dissatisfied 2 : unsatisfied
inscribir {33} *vt* 1 MATRICULAR : to enroll, to register 2 GRABAR : to engrave — **inscribirse** *vr* : to register, to sign up
inscripción *nf, pl* **-ciones** 1 MATRÍCULA : enrollment, registration 2 : inscription
inscrito *pp* → **inscribir**
insecticida¹ *adj* : insecticidal
insecticida² *nm* : insecticide
insecto *nm* : insect
inseguridad *nf* 1 : insecurity 2 : lack of safety 3 : uncertainty
inseguro, -ra *adj* 1 : insecure 2 : unsafe 3 : uncertain
inseminar *vt* : to inseminate — **inseminación** *nf*
insensatez *nf, pl* **-teces** : foolishness, stupidity
insensato¹, -ta *adj* : foolish, senseless
insensato², -ta *n* : fool
insensibilidad *nf* : insensitivity
insensible *adj* : insensitive, unfeeling
inseparable *adj* : inseparable — **inseparablemente** *adv*
inserción *nf, pl* **-ciones** : insertion
insertar *vt* : to insert
inservible *adj* INÚTIL : useless, unusable
insidia *nf* 1 : snare, trap 2 : malice
insidioso, -sa *adj* : insidious
insigne *adj* : noted, famous
insignia *nf* ENSEÑA : insignia, emblem, badge
insignificancia *nf* 1 : insignificance 2 NIMIEDAD : trifle, triviality
insignificante *adj* : insignificant
insincero, -ra *adj* : insincere — **insinceridad** *nf*
insinuación *nf, pl* **-ciones** : insinuation, hint
insinuante *adj* : suggestive
insinuar {3} *vt* : to insinuate, to hint at — **insinuarse** *vr* 1 ~ **a** : to make advances to 2 ~ **en** : to worm one's way into
insipidez *nf, pl* **-deces** : insipidness, blandness
insípido, -da *adj* : insipid, bland
insistencia *nf* : insistence
insistente *adj* : insistent — **insistentemente** *adv*
insistir *v* : to insist
insociable *adj* : unsociable
insolación *nf, pl* **-ciones** : sunstroke
insolencia *nf* IMPERTINENCIA : insolence
insolente *adj* IMPERTINENTE : insolent
insólito, -ta *adj* : rare, unusual

insoluble *adj* : insoluble — **insolubilidad** *nf*
insolvencia *nf* : insolvency, bankruptcy
insolvente *adj* : insolvent, bankrupt
insomne *adj & nmf* : insomniac
insomnio *nm* : insomnia
insondable *adj* : fathomless, deep
insonorizado, -da *adj* : soundproof
insoportable *adj* INAGUANTABLE : unbearable, intolerable
insoslayable *adj* : unavoidable, inescapable
insospechado, -da *adj* : unexpected, unforeseen
insostenible *adj* : untenable
inspección *nf, pl* **-ciones** : inspection
inspeccionar *vt* : to inspect
inspector, -tora *n* : inspector
inspiración *nf, pl* **-ciones** 1 : inspiration 2 INHALACIÓN : inhalation
inspirador, -dora *adj* : inspiring
inspirar *vt* : to inspire — *vi* INHALAR : to inhale
instalación *nf, pl* **-ciones** : installation
instalar *vt* 1 : to install 2 : to instate — **instalarse** *vr* ESTABLECERSE : to settle, to establish oneself
instancia *nf* 1 : petition, request 2 **en última instancia** : as a last resort
instantánea *nf* : snapshot
instantáneo, -nea *adj* : instantaneous — **instantáneamente** *adv*
instante *nm* 1 : instant, moment 2 **al instante** : immediately 3 **a cada instante** : frequently, all the time 4 **por instantes** : constantly, incessantly
instar *vt* APREMIAR : to urge, to press — *vi* URGIR : to be urgent or pressing ⟨insta que vayamos pronto : it is imperative that we leave soon⟩
instauración *nf, pl* **-ciones** : establishment
instaurar *vt* : to establish
instigador, -dora *n* : instigator
instigar {52} *vt* : to instigate, to incite
instintivo, -va *adj* : instinctive — **instintivamente** *adv*
instinto *nm* : instinct
institución *nf, pl* **-ciones** : institution
institucional *adj* : institutional — **institucionalmente** *adv*
institucionalización *nf, pl* **-ciones** : institutionalization
institucionalizar {21} *vt* : to institutionalize
instituir {41} *vt* ESTABLECER, FUNDAR : to institute, to establish, to found
instituto *nm* : institute
institutriz *nf, pl* **-trices** : governess *f*
instrucción *nf, pl* **-ciones** 1 EDUCACIÓN : education 2 **instrucciones** *nfpl* : instructions, directions
instructivo, -va *adj* : instructive, educational
instructor, -tora *n* : instructor
instruir {41} *vt* 1 ADIESTRAR : to instruct, to train 2 ENSEÑAR : to educate, to teach

instrumentación *nf, pl* **-ciones** : orchestration
instrumental *adj* : instrumental
instrumentar *vt* : to orchestrate
instrumentista *nmf* : instrumentalist
instrumento *nm* : instrument
insubordinado, -da *adj* : insubordinate
— **insubordinación** *nf*
insubordinarse *vr* : to rebel
insuficiencia *nf* **1** : insufficiency, inadequacy **2 insuficiencia cardíaca** : heart failure
insuficiente *adj* : insufficient, inadequate — **insuficientemente** *adv*
insufrible *adj* : insufferable
insular *adj* : insular
insularidad *nf* : insularity
insulina *nf* : insulin
insulso, -sa *adj* **1** INSÍPIDO : insipid, bland **2** : dull
insultante *adj* : insulting
insultar *vt* : to insult
insulto *nm* : insult
insumos *nmpl* : supplies ⟨insumos agrícolas : agricultural supplies⟩
insuperable *adj* : insuperable, insurmountable
insurgente *adj & nmf* : insurgent — **insurgencia** *nf*
insurrección *nf, pl* **-ciones** : insurrection, uprising
insustancial *adj* : insubstantial, flimsy
insustituible *adj* : irreplaceable
intachable *adj* : irreproachable, faultless
intacto, -ta *adj* : intact
intangible *adj* IMPALPABLE : intangible, impalpable
integración *nf, pl* **-ciones** : integration
integral *adj* **1** : integral, essential **2 pan integral** : whole grain bread
integrante[1] *adj* : integrating, integral
integrar[2] *nmf* : member
integrar *vt* : to make up, to compose — **integrarse** *vr* : to integrate, to fit in
integridad *nf* **1** RECTITUD : integrity, honesty **2** : wholeness, completeness
integrismo *nm* : fundamentalism
integrista *adj & nmf* : fundamentalist
íntegro, -gra *adj* **1** : honest, upright **2** ENTERO : whole, complete **3** : unabridged
intelecto *nm* : intellect
intelectual *adj & nmf* : intellectual — **intelectualmente** *adv*
intelectualidad *nf* : intelligentsia
inteligencia *nf* : intelligence
inteligente *adj* : intelligent — **inteligentemente** *adv*
inteligible *adj* : intelligible — **inteligibilidad** *nf*
intemperancia *adj* : intemperance, excess
intemperie *nf* **1** : bad weather, elements *pl* **2 a la intemperie** : in the open air, outside
intempestivo, -va *adj* : inopportune, untimely — **intempestivamente** *adv*

intención *nf, pl* **-ciones** : intention, plan
intencionado, -da → **intencional**
intencional *adj* : intentional — **intencionalmente** *adv*
intendencia *nf* : management, administration
intendente *nmf* : quartermaster
intensidad *nf* : intensity
intensificación *nf, pl* **-ciones** : intensification
intensificar {72} *vt* : to intensify — **intensificarse** *vr*
intensivo, -va *adj* : intensive — **intensivamente** *adv*
intenso, -sa *adj* : intense — **intensamente** *adv*
intentar *vt* : to attempt, to try
intento *nm* **1** PROPÓSITO : intent, intention **2** TENTATIVA : attempt, try
interacción *nf, pl* **-ciones** : interaction
interactivo, -va *adj* : interactive
interactuar {3} *vi* : to interact
intercalar *vt* : to intersperse, to insert
intercambiable *adj* : interchangeable
intercambiar *vt* CANJEAR : to exchange, to trade
intercambio *nm* CANJE : exchange, trade
interceder *vi* : to intercede
intercepción *nf, pl* **-ciones** : interception
interceptar *vt* **1** : to intercept, to block **2 interceptar las líneas** : to wiretap
intercesión *nf, pl* **-siones** : intercession
intercomunicación *nf, pl* **-ciones** : intercommunication
interconexión *nf, pl* **-xiones** : interconnection
interconfesional *adj* : interdenominational
interdepartamental *adj* : interdepartmental
interdependencia *nf* : interdependence — **interdependiente** *adj*
interdicción *nf, pl* **-ciones** : interdiction, prohibition
interés *nm, pl* **-reses** : interest
interesado, -da *adj* **1** : interested **2** : selfish, self-seeking
interesante *adj* : interesting
interesar *vt* : to interest — *vi* : to be of interest, to be interesting — **interesarse** *vr*
interestatal *adj* : interstate ⟨autopista interestatal : interstate highway⟩
interestelar *adj* : interstellar
interfase → **interfaz**
interfaz *nf, pl* **-faces** : interface
interferencia *nf* : interference, static
interferir {76} *vi* : to interfere, to meddle — *vt* : to interfere with, to obstruct
intergaláctico, -ca *adj* : intergalactic
intergubernamental *adj* : intergovernmental
interín[1] *or* **ínterin** *adv* : meanwhile
interín[2] *or* **ínterin** *nm, pl* **-rines** : meantime, interim ⟨en el interín : in the meantime⟩

interinamente *adv* : temporarily
interino, -na *adj* : acting, temporary, interim
interior[1] *adj* : interior, inner
interior[2] *nm* **1** : interior, inside **2** : inland region
interiormente *adv* : inwardly
interjección *nf, pl* **-ciones** : interjection
interlocutor, -tora *n* : interlocutor, speaker
interludio *nm* : interlude
intermediario, -ria *adj & n* : intermediary, go-between
intermedio[1], **-dia** *adj* : intermediate
intermedio[2] *nm* **1** : intermission **2 por intermedio de** : by means of
interminable *adj* : interminable, endless — **interminablemente** *adv*
intermisión *nf, pl* **-siones** : intermission, pause
intermitente[1] *adj* **1** : intermittent **2** : flashing, blinking (of a light) — **intermitentemente** *adv*
intermitente[2] *nm* : blinker, turn signal
internacional *adj* : international — **internacionalmente** *adv*
internacionalismo *nm* : internationalism
internacionalizar {21} *vt* : to internationalize
internado *nm* : boarding school
internar *vt* : to commit, to confine — **internarse** *vr* **1** : to penetrate, to advance into **2 ~ en** : to go into, to enter
internista *nmf* : internist
interno[1], **-na** *adj* : internal — **internamente** *adv*
interno[2], **-na** *n* **1** : intern **2** : inmate, internee
interpelación *nf, pl* **-ciones** : appeal, plea
interpelar *vt* : to question (formally)
interpersonal *adj* : interpersonal
interpolar *vt* : to insert, to interpolate
interponer {60} *vt* : to interpose — **interponerse** *vr* : to intervene
interpretación *nf, pl* **-ciones** : interpretation
interpretar *vt* **1** : to interpret **2** : to play, to perform
interpretativo, -va *adj* : interpretive
intérprete *nmf* **1** TRADUCTOR : interpreter **2** : performer
interpuesto *pp* → **interponer**
interracial *adj* : interracial
interrelación *nf, pl* **-ciones** : interrelationship
interrelacionar *vi* : to interrelate
interrogación *nf, pl* **-ciones** **1** : interrogation, questioning **2 signo de interrogación** : question mark
interrogador, -dora *n* : interrogator, questioner
interrogante[1] *adj* : questioning
interrogante[2] *nm* **1** : question mark **2** : query
interrogar {52} *vt* : to interrogate, to question

interrogativo, -va *adj* : interrogative
interrogatorio *nm* : interrogation, questioning
interrumpir *v* : to interrupt
interrupción *nf, pl* **-ciones** : interruption
interruptor *nm* **1** : (electrical) switch **2** : circuit breaker
intersección *nf, pl* **-ciones** : intersection
intersticio *nm* : interstice — **intersticial** *adj*
interuniversitario, -ria *adj* : intercollegiate
interurbano, -na *adj* **1** : intercity **2** : long-distance ⟨llamadas interurbanas : long-distance calls⟩
intervalo *nm* : interval
intervención *nf, pl* **-ciones** **1** : intervention **2** : audit **3 intervención quirúrgica** : operation
intervencionista *adj & nmf* : interventionist
intervenir {87} *vi* **1** : to take part **2** INTERCEDER : to intervene, to intercede — *vt* **1** : to control, to supervise **2** : to audit **3** : to operate on **4** : to tap (a telephone)
interventor, -tora *n* **1** : inspector **2** : auditor, comptroller
intestado, -da *adj* : intestate
intestinal *adj* : intestinal
intestino *nm* : intestine
intimar *vi* **~ con** : to become friendly with — *vt* : to require, to call on
intimidación *nf, pl* **-ciones** : intimidation
intimidad *nf* **1** : intimacy **2** : privacy, private life
intimidar *vt* ACOBARDAR : to intimidate
íntimo, -ma *adj* **1** : intimate, close **2** PRIVADO : private — **íntimamente** *adv*
intitular *vt* : to entitle, to title
intocable *adj* : untouchable
intolerable *adj* : intolerable, unbearable
intolerancia *nf* : intolerance
intolerante[1] *adj* : intolerant
intolerante[2] *nmf* : intolerant person, bigot
intoxicación *nf, pl* **-ciones** : poisoning
intoxicante *nm* : poison
intoxicar {72} *vt* : to poison
intranquilidad *nf* PREOCUPACIÓN : worry, anxiety
intranquilizar {21} *vt* : to upset, to make uneasy — **intranquilizarse** *vr* : to get worried, to be anxious
intranquilo, -la *adj* PREOCUPADO : uneasy, worried
intransigencia *nf* : intransigence
intransigente *adj* : intransigent, unyielding
intransitable *adj* : impassable
intransitivo, -va *adj* : intransitive
intrascendente *adj* : unimportant, insignificant
intratable *adj* **1** : intractable **2** : awkward **3** : unsociable
intravenoso, -sa *adj* : intravenous

intrepidez *nf* : fearlessness
intrépido, -da *adj* : intrepid, fearless
intriga *nf* : intrigue
intrigante *nmf* : schemer
intrigar {52} *v* : to intrigue — **intrigante** *adj*
intrincado, -da *adj* : intricate, involved
intrínseco, -ca *adj* : intrinsic — **intrínsecamente** *adv*
introducción *nf, pl* **-ciones** : introduction
introducir {61} *vt* **1** : to introduce **2** : to bring in **3** : to insert **4** : to input, to enter — **introducirse** *vr* : to penetrate, to get into
introductorio, -ria *adj* : introductory
intromisión *nf, pl* **-siones** : interference, meddling
introspección *nf, pl* **-ciones** : introspection
introspectivo, -va *adj* : introspective
introvertido¹, -da *adj* : introverted
introvertido², -da *n* : introvert
intrusión *nf, pl* **-siones** : intrusion
intruso¹, -sa *adj* : intrusive
intruso², -sa *n* : intruder
intuición *nf, pl* **-ciones** : intuition
intuir {41} *vt* : to intuit, to sense
intuitivo, -va *adj* : intuitive — **intuitivamente** *adv*
inundación *nf, pl* **-ciones** : flood, inundation
inundar *vt* : to flood, to inundate
inusitado, -da *adj* : unusual, uncommon — **inusitadamente** *adv*
inusual *adj* : unusual, uncommon — **inusualmente** *adv*
inútil¹ *adj* INSERVIBLE : useless — **inútilmente** *adv*
inútil² *nmf* : good-for-nothing
inutilidad *nf* : uselessness
inutilizar {21} *vt* **1** : to make useless **2** INCAPACITAR : to disable, to put out of commission
invadir *vt* : to invade
invalidar *vt* : to nullify, to invalidate
invalidez *nf, pl* **-deces** **1** : invalidity **2** : disablement
inválido, -da *adj & n* : invalid
invalorable *adj* : invaluable
invariable *adj* : invariable — **invariablemente** *adv*
invasión *nf, pl* **-siones** : invasion
invasivo, -va *adj* : invasive
invasor¹, -sora *adj* : invading
invasor², -sora *n* : invader
invectiva *nf* : invective, abuse
invencibilidad *nf* : invincibility
invencible *adj* **1** : invincible **2** : insurmountable
invención *nf, pl* **-ciones** **1** INVENTO : invention **2** MENTIRA : fabrication, lie
inventar *vt* **1** : to invent **2** : to fabricate, to make up
inventariar {85} *vt* : to inventory
inventario *nm* : inventory
inventiva *nf* : ingenuity, inventiveness
inventivo, -va *adj* : inventive

invento *nm* INVENCIÓN : invention
inventor, -tora *n* : inventor
invernadero *nm* : greenhouse, hothouse
invernal *adj* : winter, wintry
invernar {55} *vi* **1** : to spend the winter **2** HIBERNAR : to hibernate
inverosímil *adj* : unlikely, far-fetched
inversión *nf, pl* **-siones** **1** : inversion **2** : investment
inversionista *nmf* : investor
inverso¹, -sa *adj* **1** : inverse, inverted **2** CONTRARIO : opposite **3 a la inversa** : on the contrary, vice versa **4 en orden inverso** : in reverse order — **inversamente** *adv*
inverso² *n* : inverse
inversor, -sora *n* : investor
invertebrado¹, -da *adj* : invertebrate
invertebrado² *nm* : invertebrate
invertir {76} *vt* **1** : to invert, to reverse **2** : to invest — *vi* : to make an investment — **invertirse** *vr* : to be reversed
investidura *nf* : investiture, inauguration
investigación *nf, pl* **-ciones** **1** ENCUESTA, INDAGACIÓN : investigation, inquiry **2** : research
investigador¹, -dora *adj* : investigative
investigador², -dora *n* **1** : investigator **2** : researcher
investigar {52} *vt* **1** INDAGAR : to investigate **2** : to research — *vi* ~ **sobre** : to do research into
investir {54} *vt* **1** : to empower **2** : to swear in, to inaugurate
inveterado, -da *adj* : inveterate, deep-seated
invicto, -ta *adj* : undefeated
invidente¹ *adj* CIEGO : blind, sightless
invidente² *nmf* CIEGO : blind person
invierno *nm* : winter, wintertime
inviolable *adj* : inviolable — **inviolabilidad** *nf*
inviolado, -da *adj* : inviolate, pure
invisibilidad *nf* : invisibility
invisible *adj* : invisible — **invisiblemente** *adv*
invitación *nf, pl* **-ciones** : invitation
invitado, -da *n* : guest
invitar *vt* : to invite
invocación *nf, pl* **-ciones** : invocation
invocar {72} *vt* : to invoke, to call on
involucramiento *nm* : involvement
involucrar *vt* : to implicate, to involve — **involucrarse** *vr* : to get involved
involuntario, -ria *adj* : involuntary — **involuntariamente** *adv*
invulnerable *adj* : invulnerable
inyección *nf, pl* **-ciones** : injection, shot
inyectado, -da *adj* **ojos inyectados** : bloodshot eyes
inyectar *vt* : to inject
ion *nm* : ion
iónico, -ca *adj* : ionic
ionizar {21} *vt* : to ionize — **ionización** *nf*
ionosfera *nf* : ionosphere
ir {43} *vi* **1** : to go ⟨ir a pie : to go on foot, to walk⟩ ⟨ir a caballo : to ride

horseback⟩ ⟨ir a casa : to go home⟩ **2**
: to lead, to extend, to stretch ⟨el
camino va de Cali a Bogotá : the road
goes from Cali to Bogotá⟩ **3** FUN-
CIONAR : to work, to function ⟨esta
computadora ya no va : this computer
doesn't work anymore⟩ **4** : to get on,
to get along ⟨¿cómo te va? : how are
you?, how's it going?⟩ ⟨el negocio no
va bien : the business isn't doing well⟩
5 : to suit ⟨ese vestido te va bien : that
dress really suits you⟩ **6** ~ **con** : to be
⟨ir con prisa : to be in a hurry⟩ **7** ~
por : to follow, to go along ⟨fueron por
la costa : they followed the shoreline⟩
8 dejarse ir : to let oneself go **9 ir a
parar** : to end up **10 vamos a ver** : let's
see — *v aux* **1** (*with present participle*)
⟨ir caminando : to walk⟩ ⟨¡voy corriendo! : I'll be right there!⟩ **2** ~ **a** : to
be going to ⟨voy a hacerlo : I'm going
to do it⟩ ⟨el avión va a despegar : the
plane is about to take off⟩ — **irse** *vr* **1**
: to leave, to go ⟨¡vámonos! : let's go!⟩
⟨todo el mundo se fue : everyone left⟩
2 ESCAPARSE : to leak **3** GASTARSE : to
be used up, to be gone
ira *nf* CÓLERA, FURIA : wrath, anger
iracundo, -da *adj* : irate, angry
iraní *adj & nmf* : Iranian
iraquí *adj & nmf* : Iraqi
irascible *adj* : irascible, irritable — **irascibilidad** *nf*
irga, irgue etc. → **erguir**
iridio *nm* : iridium
iridiscencia *nf* : iridescence — **iridiscente** *adj*
iris *nms & pl* **1** : iris **2 arco iris** : rainbow
irlandés[1], **-desa** *adj, mpl* **-deses** : Irish
irlandés[2], **-desa** *n, pl* **-deses** : Irish person, Irishman *m*, Irishwoman *f*
irlandés[3] *nm* : Irish (language)
ironía *nf* : irony
irónico, -ca *adj* : ironic, ironical —
irónicamente *adv*
irracional *adj* : irrational — **irracionalmente** *adv*
irracionalidad *nf* : irrationality
irradiación *nf, pl* **-ciones** : irradiation
irradiar *vt* : to radiate, to irradiate
irrazonable *adj* : unreasonable
irreal *adj* : unreal
irrebatible *adj* : unanswerable, irrefutable
irreconciliable *adj* : irreconcilable
irreconocible *adj* : unrecognizable
irrecuperable *adj* : irrecoverable, irretrievable
irredimible *adj* : irredeemable
irreductible *adj* : unyielding
irreemplazable *adj* : irreplaceable
irreflexión *nf, pl* **-xiones** : thoughtlessness, impetuosity
irreflexivo, -va *adj* : rash, unthinking —
irreflexivamente *adv*
irrefrenable *adj* : uncontrollable, unstoppable ⟨un impulso irrefrenable : an
irresistible urge⟩

irrefutable *adj* : irrefutable
irregular *adj* : irregular — **irregularmente** *adv*
irregularidad *nf* : irregularity
irrelevante *adj* : irrelevant — **irrelevancia** *nf*
irreligioso, -sa *adj* : irreligious
irremediable *adj* : incurable — **irreme-
diablemente** *adv*
irreparable *adj* : irreparable
irreprimible *adj* : irrepressible
irreprochable *adj* : irreproachable
irresistible *adj* : irresistible — **irre-
sistiblemente** *adv*
irresolución *nf, pl* **-ciones** : indecision,
hesitation
irresoluto, -ta *adj* INDECISO : undecided
irrespeto *nm* : disrespect
irrespetuoso, -sa *adj* : disrespectful —
irrespetuosamente *adv*
irresponsabilidad *nf* : irresponsibility
irresponsable *adj* : irresponsible — **irr-
esponsablemente** *adv*
irrestricto, -ta *adj* : unrestricted, unconditional
irreverencia *nf* : disrespect
irreverente *adj* : disrespectful
irreversible *adj* : irreversible
irrevocable *adj* : irrevocable — **irrevo-
cablemente** *adv*
irrigar {52} *vt* : to irrigate — **irrigación**
nf
irrisible *adj* : laughable
irrisión *nf, pl* **-siones** : derision, ridicule
irrisorio, -ria *adj* RISIBLE : ridiculous,
ludicrous
irritabilidad *nf* : irritability
irritable *adj* : irritable
irritación *nf, pl* **-ciones** : irritation
irritante *adj* : irritating
irritar *vt* : to irritate — **irritación** *nf*
irrompible *adj* : unbreakable
irrumpir *vi* ~ **en** : to burst into
irrupción *nf, pl* **-ciones** **1** : irruption **2**
: invasion
isla *nf* : island
islámico, -ca *adj* : Islamic, Muslim
islandés[1], **-desa** *adj, mpl* **-deses** : Icelandic
islandés[2], **-desa** *n, mpl* **-deses** : Icelander
islandés[3] *nm* : Icelandic (language)
isleño, -ña *n* : islander
islote *nm* : islet
isometría *nfs & pl* : isometrics
isométrico, -ca *adj* : isometric
isósceles *adj* : isosceles ⟨triángulo
isósceles : isosceles triangle⟩
isótopo *nm* : isotope
israelí *adj & nmf* : Israeli
istmo *nm* : isthmus
itacate *nm Mex* : pack, provisions *pl*
italiano[1], **-na** *adj & n* : Italian
italiano[2] *nm* : Italian (language)
iterbio *nm* : ytterbium
itinerante *adj* AMBULANTE : traveling,
itinerant
itinerario *nm* : itinerary, route

itrio *nm* : yttrium
izar {21} *vt* : to hoist, to raise ⟨izar la bandera : to raise the flag⟩

izquierda *nf* : left
izquierdista *adj & nmf* : leftist
izquierdo, -da *adj* : left

J

j *nf* : tenth letter of the Spanish alphabet
ja *interj* **1** : ha! **2 ja, ja** : ha-ha!
jabalí *nm* : wild boar
jabalina *nf* : javelin
jabón *nm, pl* **jabones** : soap
jabonar *vt* ENJABONAR : to soap up, to lather — **jabonarse** *vr*
jabonera *nf* : soap dish
jabonoso, -sa *adj* : soapy
jaca *nf* **1** : pony **2** YEGUA : mare
jacal *nm Mex* : shack, hut
jacinto *nm* : hyacinth
jactancia *nf* **1** : boastfulness **2** : boasting, bragging
jactancioso[1], -sa *adj* : boastful
jactancioso[2], -sa *n* : boaster, braggart
jactarse *vr* : to boast, to brag
jade *nm* : jade
jadear *vi* : to pant, to gasp, to puff — **jadeante** *adj*
jadeo *nm* : panting, gasping, puffing
jaez *nm, pl* **jaeces 1** : harness **2** : kind, sort, ilk **3 jaeces** *nmpl* : trappings
jaguar *nm* : jaguar
jai alai *nm* : jai alai
jaiba *nf* CANGREJO : crab
jalapeño *nm Mex* : jalapeño pepper
jalar *vt* **1** : to pull, to tug **2** *fam* : to attract, to draw in ⟨las ideas nuevas lo jalan : new ideas appeal to him⟩ — *vi* **1** : to pull, to pull together **2** *fam* : to hurry up, to get going **3** *Mex fam* : to be in working order ⟨esta máquina no jala : this machine doesn't work⟩
jalbegue *nm* : whitewash
jalea *nf* : jelly
jalear *vt* : to encourage, to urge on
jaleo *nm* **1** *fam* : uproar, ruckus, racket **2** *fam* : confusion, hassle **3** : cheering and clapping (for a dance)
jalón *nm, pl* **jalones 1** : milestone, landmark **2** TIRÓN : pull, tug
jalonar *vt* : to mark, to stake out
jalonear *vt Mex, Peru fam* : to tug at — *vi* **1** *fam* : to pull, to tug **2** *CA fam* : to haggle
jamaica *nf* : hibiscus
jamaicano, -na → jamaiquino
jamaiquino, -na *adj & n* : Jamaican
jamás *adv* **1** NUNCA : never **2 nunca jamás** *or* **jamás de los jamases** : never ever **3 para siempre jamás** : for ever and ever
jamba *nf* : jamb
jamelgo *nm* : nag (horse)
jamón *nm, pl* **jamones** : ham
Januká *nmf* : Hanukkah
japonés[1], -nesa *adj & n, mpl* **-neses** : Japanese

japonés[2] *nm, pl* **-neses** : Japanese (language)
jaque *nm* **1** : check (in chess) ⟨jaque mate : checkmate⟩ **2 tener en jaque** : to intimidate, to bully
jaqueca *nf* : headache, migraine
jarabe *nm* **1** : syrup **2** : Mexican folk dance
jarana *nf* **1** *fam* : revelry, partying, spree **2** *fam* : joking, fooling around **3** : small guitar
jaranear *vi fam* : to go on a spree, to party
jarcia *nf* **1** : rigging **2** : fishing tackle
jardín *nm, pl* **jardines 1** : garden **2 jardín de niños** : kindergarten **3 los jardines** *nmpl* : the outfield
jardinería *nf* : gardening
jardinero, -ra *n* **1** : gardener **2** : outfielder (in baseball)
jarra *nf* **1** : pitcher, jug **2** : stein, mug **3 de jarras** *or* **en jarras** : akimbo
jarrete *nm* **1** : back of the knee **2** CORVEJÓN : hock
jarro *nm* **1** : pitcher, jug **2** : mug
jarrón *nm, pl* **jarrones** FLORERO : vase
jaspe *nm* : jasper
jaspeado, -da *adj* **1** VETEADO : streaked, veined **2** : speckled, mottled
jaula *nf* : cage
jauría *nf* : pack of hounds
javanés, -nesa *adj & n* : Javanese
jazmín *nm, pl* **jazmines** : jasmine
jazz ['jas, 'dʒas] *nm* : jazz
jeans ['jins, 'dʒins] *nmpl* : jeans
jeep ['jip, 'dʒip] *nm, pl* **jeeps** : jeep
jefatura *nf* **1** : leadership **2** : headquarters ⟨jefatura de policía : police headquarters⟩
jefe, -fa *n* **1** : chief, head, leader ⟨jefe de bomberos : fire chief⟩ **2** : boss
Jehová *nm* : Jehovah
jején *nm, pl* **jejenes** : gnat, small mosquito
jengibre *nm* : ginger
jeque *nm* : sheikh, sheik
jerarca *nmf* : leader, chief
jerarquía *nf* **1** : hierarchy **2** RANGO : rank
jerárquico, -ca *adj* : hierarchical
jerbo *nm* : gerbil
jerez *nm, pl* **jereces** : sherry
jerga *nf* **1** : jargon, slang **2** : coarse cloth
jerigonza *nf* GALIMATÍAS : mumbo jumbo, gibberish
jeringa *nf* : syringe
jeringar {52} *vt* **1** : to inject **2** *fam* JOROBAR : to annoy, to pester — *vi fam*

JOROBAR : to be annoying, to be a nuisance
jeringuear → **jeringar**
jeringuilla → **jeringa**
jeroglífico *nm* : hieroglyphic
jersey *nm, pl* **jerseys** 1 : jersey (fabric) 2 *Spain* : sweater
Jesucristo *nm* : Jesus Christ
jesuita *adj & nm* : Jesuit
Jesús *nm* 1 : Jesus 2 ¡**Jesús!** : goodness!, good heavens!
jeta *nf* 1 : snout 2 *fam* : face, mug
jíbaro, -ra *adj* 1 : Jivaro 2 : rustic, rural
jibia *nf* : cuttlefish
jícama *nf* : jicama
jícara *nf Mex* : calabash
jilguero *nm* : European goldfinch
jinete *nmf* : horseman, horsewoman *f*, rider
jinetear *vt* 1 : to ride, to perform (on horseback) 2 DOMAR : to break in (a horse) — *vi* CABALGAR : to ride horseback
jingoísmo [ˌjiŋgoˈizmo, ˌʤiŋ-] *nm* : jingoism
jingoísta *adj* : jingoist, jingoistic
jiote *nm Mex* : rash
jira *nf* : outing, picnic
jirafa *nf* 1 : giraffe 2 : boom microphone
jirón *nm, pl* **jirones** : shred, rag ⟨hecho jirones : in tatters⟩
jitomate *nm Mex* : tomato
jockey [ˈjɔki, ˈʤɔ-] *nmf, pl* **jockeys** [-kis] : jockey
jocosidad *nf* : humor, jocularity
jocoso, -sa *adj* : playful, jocular — **jocosamente** *adv*
jofaina *nf* : washbowl
jogging [ˈjɔgɪn, ˈʤɔ-] *nm* : jogging
jolgorio *nm* : merrymaking, fun
jonrón *nm, pl* **jonrones** : home run
jordano, -na *adj & n* : Jordanian
jornada *nf* 1 : expedition, day's journey 2 **jornada de trabajo** : working day 3 **jornadas** *nfpl* : conference, congress
jornal *nm* 1 : day's pay 2 a ~ : by the day
jornalero, -ra *n* : day laborer
joroba *nf* 1 GIBA : hump 2 *fam* : nuisance, pain in the neck
jorobado¹, -da *adj* GIBOSO : hunchbacked, humpbacked
jorobado², -da *n* GIBOSO : hunchback, humpback
jorobar *vt fam* JERINGAR : to bother, to annoy — *vi fam* JERINGAR : to be annoying, to be a nuisance
jorongo *nm Mex* : full-length poncho
jota *nf* 1 : jot, bit ⟨no entiendo ni jota : I don't understand a word of it⟩ ⟨no se ve ni jota : you can't see a thing⟩ 2 : jack (in playing cards)
joven¹ *adj, pl* **jóvenes** 1 : young 2 : youthful
joven² *nmf, pl* **jóvenes** : young man *m*, young woman *f*, young person

jovial *adj* : jovial, cheerful — **jovialmente** *adv*
jovialidad *nf* : joviality, cheerfulness
joya *nf* 1 : jewel, piece of jewelry 2 : treasure, gem ⟨la nueva empleada es una joya : the new employee is a real gem⟩
joyería *nf* 1 : jewelry store 2 : jewelry 3 **joyería de fantasía** : costume jewelry
joyero, -ra *n* : jeweler
juanete *nm* : bunion
jubilación *nf, pl* **-ciones** 1 : retirement 2 PENSIÓN : pension
jubilado¹, -da *adj* : retired, in retirement
jubilado², -da *nmf* : retired person, retiree
jubilar *vt* 1 : to retire, to pension off 2 *fam* : to get rid of, to discard — **jubilarse** *vr* : to retire
jubileo *nm* : jubilee
júbilo *nm* : jubilation, joy
jubiloso, -sa *adj* : jubilant, joyous
judaico, -ca *adj* : Judaic, Jewish
judaísmo *nm* : Judaism
judía *nf* 1 : bean 2 *or* **judía verde** : green bean, string bean
judicatura *nf* 1 : judiciary, judges *pl* 2 : office of judge
judicial *adj* : judicial — **judicialmente** *adv*
judío¹, -día *adj* : Jewish
judío², -día *n* : Jewish person, Jew
judo [ˈjuðo, ˈʤu-] *nm* : judo
juega, juegue, etc. → **jugar**
juego *nm* 1 : play, playing ⟨poner en juego : to bring into play⟩ 2 : game, sport ⟨juego de cartas : card game⟩ ⟨Juegos Olímpicos : Olympic Games⟩ 3 : gaming, gambling ⟨estar en juego : to be at stake⟩ 4 : set ⟨un juego de llaves : a set of keys⟩ 5 **hacer juego** : to go together, to match 6 **juego de manos** : conjuring trick, sleight of hand
juerga *nf* : partying, binge ⟨irse de juerga : to go on a spree⟩
juerguista *nmf* : reveler, carouser
jueves *nms & pl* : Thursday
juez¹ *nmf, pl* **jueces** 1 : judge 2 ÁRBITRO : umpire, referee
juez², jueza *n* → **juez¹**
jugada *nf* 1 : play, move 2 : trick ⟨hacer una mala jugada : to play a dirty trick⟩
jugador, -dora *n* 1 : player 2 : gambler
jugar {44} *vi* 1 : to play ⟨jugar a la pelota : to play ball⟩ 2 APOSTAR : to gamble, to bet 3 : to joke, to kid — *vt* 1 : to play ⟨jugar un papel : to play a role⟩ ⟨jugar una carta : to play a card⟩ 2 : to bet — **jugarse** *vr* 1 : to risk, to gamble away ⟨jugarse la vida : to risk one's life⟩ 2 **jugarse el todo por el todo** : to risk everything
jugarreta *nf fam* : prank, dirty trick
juglar *nm* : minstrel

jugo *nm* **1** : juice **2** : substance, essence ⟨sacarle el jugo a algo : to get the most out of something⟩

jugosidad *nf* : juiciness, succulence

jugoso, -sa *adj* : juicy

juguete *nm* : toy

juguetear *vi* **1** : to play, to cavort, to frolic **2** : to toy, to fiddle

juguetería *nf* : toy store

juguetón, -tona *adj, mpl* **-tones** : playful — **juguetonamente** *adv*

juicio *nm* **1** : good judgment, reason, sense **2** : opinion ⟨a mi juicio : in my opinion⟩ **3** : trial ⟨llevar a juicio : to take to court⟩

juicioso, -sa *adj* : judicious, wise — **juiciosamente** *adv*

julio *nm* : July

juncia *nf* : sedge

junco *nm* **1** : reed, rush **2** : junk (boat)

jungla *nf* : jungle

junio *nm* : June

junquillo *nm* : jonquil

junta *nf* **1** : board, committee ⟨junta directiva : board of directors⟩ **2** REUNIÓN : meeting, session **3** : junta **4** : joint, gasket

juntamente *adv* **1** : jointly, together ⟨juntamente con : together with⟩ **2** : at the same time

juntar *vt* **1** UNIR : to unite, to combine, to put together **2** REUNIR : to collect, to gather together, to assemble **3** : to close partway ⟨juntar la puerta : to leave the door ajar⟩ — **juntarse** *vr* **1** : to join together **2** : to socialize, to get together

junto, -ta *adj* **1** UNIDO : joined, united **2** : close, adjacent ⟨colgaron los dos retratos juntos : they hung the two paintings side by side⟩ **3** (*used adverbially*) : together ⟨llegamos juntos : we arrived together⟩ **4** ~ **a** : next to, alongside of **5** ~ **con** : together with, along with

juntura *nf* : joint, coupling

Júpiter *nm* : Jupiter

jura *nf* : oath, pledge ⟨jura de bandera : pledge of allegiance⟩

jurado[1] *nm* : jury

jurado[2], **-da** *n* : juror

juramento *nm* **1** : oath ⟨juramento hipocrático : Hippocratic oath⟩ **2** : swearword, oath

jurar *vt* **1** : to swear ⟨jurar lealtad : to swear loyalty⟩ **2** : to take an oath ⟨el alcalde juró su cargo : the mayor took the oath of office⟩ — *vi* : to curse, to swear

jurídico, -ca *adj* : legal

jurisdicción *nf, pl* **-ciones** : jurisdiction

jurisdiccional *adj* : jurisdictional, territorial

jurisprudencia *nf* : jurisprudence, law

jurista *nmf* : jurist

justa *nf* **1** : joust **2** TORNEO : tournament, competition

justamente *adv* **1** PRECISAMENTE : precisely, exactly **2** : justly, fairly

justar *vi* : to joust

justicia *nf* **1** : justice, fairness ⟨hacerle justicia a : to do justice to⟩ ⟨ser de justicia : to be only fair⟩ **2 la justicia** : the law ⟨tomarse la justicia por su mano : to take the law into one's own hands⟩

justiciero, -ra *adj* : righteous, avenging

justificable *adj* : justifiable

justificación *nf, pl* **-ciones** : justification

justificante *nm* **1** : justification **2** : proof, voucher

justificar {72} *vt* **1** : to justify **2** : to excuse, to vindicate

justo[1] *adv* **1** : justly **2** : right, exactly ⟨justo a tiempo : just in time⟩ **3** : tightly

justo[2], **-ta** *adj* **1** : just, fair **2** : right, exact **3** : tight ⟨estos zapatos me quedan muy justos : these shoes are too tight⟩

justo[3], **-ta** *n* : just person ⟨los justos : the just⟩

juvenil *adj* **1** : juvenile, young, youthful **2** ADOLESCENTE : teenage

juventud *nf* **1** : youth **2** : young people

juzgado *nm* TRIBUNAL : court, tribunal

juzgar {52} *vt* **1** : to try, to judge (a case in court) **2** : to pass judgment on **3** CONSIDERAR : to consider, to deem

juzgue, etc. → juzgar

K

k *nf* : eleventh letter of the Spanish alphabet

káiser *nm* : kaiser

kaki → caqui

kaleidoscopio → caleidoscopio

kamikaze *adj & nm* : kamikaze

kampucheano, -na *adj & n* : Kampuchean

kan *nm* : khan

karaoke *nm* : karaoke

karate *or* **kárate** *nm* : karate

kayac *or* **kayak** *nm, pl* **kayacs** *or* **kayaks** : kayak

keniano, -na *adj & n* : Kenyan

kepí *nm* : kepi

kermesse *or* **kermés** [kɛr'mɛs] *nf, pl* **kermesses** *or* **kermeses** [-'meses] : charity fair, bazaar

kerosene *or* **kerosén** *or* **keroseno** *nm* : kerosene, paraffin

kibutz *or* **kibbutz** *nms & pl* : kibbutz

kilo *nm* **1** : kilo, kilogram **2** *fam* : large amount

kilobyte [ˌkiloˈbait] *nm* : kilobyte

kilociclo *nm* : kilocycle

kilogramo *nm* : kilogram

kilohertzio *nm* : kilohertz
kilometraje *nm* : distance in kilometers, mileage
kilométrico, -ca *adj fam* : endless, very long
kilómetro *nm* : kilometer
kilovatio *nm* : kilowatt
kimono *nm* : kimono
kinder ['kɪndɛr] → **kindergarten**
kindergarten [ˌkɪndɛr'gartɛn] *nm, pl* **kindergartens** [-tɛns] : kindergarten, nursery school
kinesiología *nf* : physical therapy

kinesiólogo, -ga *n* : physical therapist
kiosco → **quiosco**
kit *nm, pl* **kits** : kit
kiwi ['kiwi] *nm* **1** : kiwi (bird) **2** : kiwifruit
klaxon → **claxon**
knockout [nɔ'kaut] → **nocaut**
koala *nm* : koala bear
kriptón *nm* : krypton
kurdo[1]**, -da** *adj* : Kurdish
kurdo[2]**, -da** *n* : Kurd
kuwaití [kuˌwai'ti] *adj & nmf* : Kuwaiti

L

l *nf* : twelfth letter of the Spanish alphabet
la[1] *pron* **1** : her, it ⟨llámala hoy : call her today⟩ ⟨sacó la botella y la abrió : he took out the bottle and opened it⟩ **2** (*formal*) : you ⟨no la vi a usted, Señora Díaz : I didn't see you, Mrs. Díaz⟩ **3** : the one ⟨mi casa y la de la puerta roja : my house and the one with the red door⟩ **4 la que** : the one who
la[2] *art* → **el**[2]
laberíntico, -ca *adj* : labyrinthine
laberinto *nm* : labyrinth, maze
labia *nf fam* : gift of gab ⟨tu amigo tiene labia : your friend has a way with words⟩
labial *adj* : labial, lip ⟨lápiz labial : lipstick⟩
labio *nm* **1** : lip **2 labio leporino** : harelip
labor *nf* : work, labor
laborable *adj* **1** : arable **2 día laborable** : workday, business day
laboral *adj* : work, labor ⟨costos laborales : labor costs⟩
laborar *vi* : to work
laboratorio *nm* : laboratory, lab
laboriosidad *nf* : industriousness, diligence
laborioso, -sa *adj* **1** : laborious, hard **2** : industrious, hardworking
labrado[1]**, -da** *adj* **1** : cultivated, tilled **2** : carved, wrought
labrado[2] *nm* : cultivated field
labrador, -dora *n* : farmer
labranza *nf* : farming
labrar *vt* **1** : to carve, to work (metal) **2** : to cultivate, to till **3** : to cause, to bring about
laca *nf* **1** : lacquer, shellac **2** : hair spray **3 laca de uñas** : nail polish
lacayo *nm* : lackey
lace, etc. → **lazar**
lacear *vt* : to lasso
laceración *nf, pl* **-ciones** : laceration
lacerante *adj* : hurtful, wounding
lacerar *vt* **1** : to lacerate, to cut **2** : to hurt, to wound (one's feelings)
lacio, -cia *adj* **1** : limp, lank **2 pelo lacio** : straight hair

lacónico, -ca *adj* : laconic — **lacónicamente** *adv*
lacra *nf* **1** : scar, mark (on the skin) **2** : stigma, blemish
lacrar *vt* : to seal (with wax)
lacrimógeno, -na *adj* **gas lacrimógeno** : tear gas
lacrimoso, -sa *adj* : tearful, moving
lactancia *nf* **1** : lactation **2** : breastfeeding
lactante *nmf* : nursing infant, suckling
lactar *v* : to breast-feed
lácteo, -tea *adj* **1** : dairy **2 Vía Láctea** : Milky Way
láctico, -ca *adj* : lactic
lactosa *nf* : lactose
ladeado, -da *adj* : crooked, tilted, lopsided
ladear *vt* : to tilt, to tip — **ladearse** *vr* : to bend (over)
ladera *nf* : slope, hillside
ladino[1]**, -na** *adj* **1** : cunning, shrewd **2** *CA, Mex* : mestizo
ladino[2]**, -na** *n* **1** : trickster **2** *CA, Mex* : Spanish-speaking Indian **3** *CA, Mex* : mestizo
lado *nm* **1** : side **2 PARTE** : place ⟨miró por todos lados : he looked everywhere⟩ **3 al lado de** : next to, beside **4 de ~** : tilted, sideways ⟨está de lado : it's lying on its side⟩ **5 hacerse a un lado** : to step aside **6 lado a lado** : side by side **7 por otro lado** : on the other hand
ladrar *vi* : to bark
ladrido *nm* : bark (of a dog), barking
ladrillo *nm* **1** : brick **2 AZULEJO** : tile
ladrón, -drona *n, mpl* **ladrones** : robber, thief, burglar
lagartija *nf* : small lizard
lagarto *nm* **1** : lizard **2 lagarto de Indias** : alligator
lago *nm* : lake
lágrima *nf* : tear, teardrop
lagrimear *vi* **1** : to water (of eyes) **2** : to weep easily
laguna *nf* **1** : lagoon **2** : lacuna, gap
laicado *nm* : laity
laico[1]**, -ca** *adj* : lay, secular
laico[2]**, -ca** *n* : layman *m*, laywoman *f*

laja *nf* : slab
lama[1] *nf* : slime, ooze
lama[2] *nm* : lama
lamber *vt* : to lick
lamé *nm* : lamé
lamentable *adj* **1** : unfortunate, lamentable **2** : pitiful, sad
lamentablemente *adv* : unfortunately, regrettably
lamentación *nf, pl* **-ciones** : lamentation, groaning, moaning
lamentar *vt* **1** : to lament **2** : to regret ⟨lo lamento : I'm sorry⟩ — **lamentarse** *vr* : to grumble, to complain
lamento *nm* : lament, groan, cry
lamer *vt* **1** : to lick **2** : to lap against
lamida *nf* : lick
lámina *nf* **1** PLANCHA : sheet, plate **2** : plate, illustration
laminado[1], **-da** *adj* : laminated
laminado[2] *nm* : laminate
laminar *vt* : to laminate — **laminación** *nf*
lámpara *nf* : lamp
lampiño, -ña *adj* : hairless
lamprea *nf* : lamprey
lana *nf* **1** : wool ⟨lana de acero : steel wool⟩ **2** *Mex fam* : money, dough
lance[1], etc. → **lanzar**
lance[2] *nm* **1** INCIDENTE : event, incident **2** RIÑA : quarrel **3** : throw, cast (of a net, etc.) **4** : move, play (in a game), throw (of dice)
lancear *vt* : to spear
lanceta *nf* : lancet
lancha *nf* **1** : small boat, launch **2 lancha motora** : motorboat, speedboat
langosta *nf* **1** : lobster **2** : locust
langostino *nm* : prawn, crayfish
languidecer {53} *vi* : to languish
languidez *nf, pl* **-deces** : languor, listlessness
lánguido, -da *adj* : languid, listless — **lánguidamente** *adv*
lanolina *nf* : lanolin
lanudo, -da *adj* : woolly
lanza *nf* : spear, lance
lanzadera *nf* **1** : shuttle (for weaving) **2 lanzadera espacial** : space shuttle
lanzado, -da *adj* **1** : impulsive, brazen **2** : forward, determined ⟨ir lanzado : to hurtle along⟩
lanzador, -dora *n* : thrower, pitcher
lanzallamas *nms & pl* : flamethrower
lanzamiento *nm* **1** : throw **2** : pitch (in baseball) **3** : launching, launch
lanzar {21} *vt* **1** : to throw, to hurl **2** : to pitch **3** : to launch — **lanzarse** *vr* **1** : to throw oneself (at, into) **2** ∼ **a** : to embark upon, to undertake
laosiano, -na *adj & n* : Laotian
lapicero *nm* **1** : mechanical pencil **2** *CA, Peru* : ballpoint pen
lápida *nf* : marker, tombstone
lapidar *vt* APEDREAR : to stone
lapidario, -ria *adj & n* : lapidary
lápiz *nm, pl* **lápices** **1** : pencil **2 lápiz de labios** *or* **lápiz labial** : lipstick

lapón, -pona *adj & n, mpl* **lapones** : Lapp
lapso *nm* : lapse, space (of time)
lapsus *nms & pl* : error, slip
laptop *nm, pl* **laptops** : laptop
laquear *vt* : to lacquer, to varnish, to shellac
largamente *adv* **1** : at length, extensively **2** : easily, comfortably **3** : generously
largar {52} *vt* **1** SOLTAR : to let loose, to release **2** AFLOJAR : to loosen, to slacken **3** *fam* : to give, to hand over **4** *fam* : to hurl, to let fly (insults, etc.) — **largarse** *vr fam* : to scram, to beat it
largo[1], **-ga** *adj* **1** : long **2 a lo largo** : lengthwise **3 a lo largo de** : along **4 a la larga** : in the long run
largo[2] *nm* : length ⟨tres metros de largo : three meters long⟩
largometraje *nm* : feature film
largue, etc. → **largar**
larguero *nm* : crossbeam
largueza *nf* : generosity, largesse
larguirucho, -cha *adj fam* : lanky
largura *nf* : length
laringe *nf* : larynx
laringitis *nfs & pl* : laryngitis
larva *nf* : larva — **larval** *adj*
las → **el**[2], **los**[1]
lasaña *nf* : lasagna
lasca *nf* : chip, chipping
lascivia *nf* : lasciviousness, lewdness
lascivo, -va *adj* : lascivious, lewd — **lascivamente** *adv*
láser *nm* : laser
lasitud *nf* : lassitude, weariness
laso, -sa *adj* : languid, weary
lástima *nf* **1** : compassion, pity **2** PENA : shame, pity ⟨¡qué lástima! : what a shame!⟩
lastimadura *nf* : injury, wound
lastimar *vt* **1** DAÑAR, HERIR : to hurt, to injure **2** AGRAVIAR : to offend — **lastimarse** *vr* : to hurt oneself
lastimero, -ra *adj* : pitiful, wretched
lastimoso, -sa *adj* **1** : shameful **2** : pitiful, terrible
lastrar *vt* **1** : to ballast **2** : to burden, to encumber
lastre *nm* **1** : burden **2** : ballast
lata *nf* **1** : tinplate **2** : tin can **3** *fam* : pest, bother, nuisance **4 dar lata** *fam* : to bother, to annoy
latencia *nf* : latency
latente *adj* : latent
lateral[1] *adj* **1** : lateral, side **2** : indirect — **lateralmente** *adv*
lateral[2] *nm* : end piece, side
látex *nms & pl* : latex
latido *nm* : beat, throb ⟨latido del corazón : heartbeat⟩
latifundio *nm* : large estate
latigazo *nm* : lash (with a whip)
látigo *nm* AZOTE : whip
latín *nm* : Latin (language)
latino[1], **-na** *adj* **1** : Latin **2** *fam* : Latin-American

latino[2]**, -na** *n fam* : Latin American
latinoamericano[1]**, -na** *adj* HISPANO-
AMERICANO : Latin American
latinoamericano, -na *n* : Latin American
latir *vi* **1** : to beat, to throb **2 latirle a
uno** *Mex fam* : to have a hunch ⟨me
late que no va a venir : I have a feeling
he's not going to come⟩
latitud *nf* **1** : latitude **2** : breadth
lato, -ta *adj* **1** : extended, lengthy **2**
: broad (in meaning)
latón *nm, pl* **latones** : brass
latoso[1]**, -sa** *adj fam* : annoying, bothersome
latoso[2]**, -sa** *n fam* : pest, nuisance
latrocinio *nm* : larceny
laúd *nm* : lute
laudable *adj* : laudable, praiseworthy
laudo *nm* : findings, decision
laureado, -da *adj & n* : laureate
laurear *vt* : to award, to honor
laurel *nm* **1** : laurel **2** : bay leaf **3
dormirse en sus laureles** : to rest on
one's laurels
lava *nf* : lava
lavable *adj* : washable
lavabo *nm* **1** LAVAMANOS : sink, washbowl **2** : lavatory, toilet
lavadero *nm* : laundry room
lavado *nm* **1** : laundry, wash **2** : laun-
dering ⟨lavado de dinero : money laun-
dering⟩
lavadora *nf* : washing machine
lavamanos *nms & pl* LAVABO : sink,
washbowl
lavanda *nf* ESPLIEGO : lavender
lavandería *nf* : laundry (service)
lavandero, -ra *n* : launderer, laundress
f
lavaplatos *nms & pl* **1** : dishwasher **2**
Chile, Col, Mex : kitchen sink
lavar *vt* **1** : to wash, to clean **2** : to launder (money) **3 lavar en seco** : to dry-
clean — **lavarse** *vr* **1** : to wash oneself
2 lavarse las manos de : to wash one's
hands of
lavativa *nf* : enema
lavatorio *nm* : lavatory, washroom
lavavajillas *nms & pl* : dishwasher
laxante *adj & nm* : laxative
laxitud *nf* : laxity, slackness
laxo, -xa *adj* : lax, slack
lazada *nf* : bow, loop
lazar {21} *vt* : to rope, to lasso
lazo *nm* **1** VÍNCULO : link, bond **2** : bow,
ribbon **3** : lasso, lariat
le *pron* **1** : to her, to him, to it ⟨¿qué le
dijiste? : what did you tell him?⟩ **2**
: from her, from him, from it ⟨el ladrón
le robó la cartera : the thief stole his
wallet⟩ **3** : for her, for him, for it ⟨cóm-
prale flores a tu mamá : buy your mom
some flowers⟩ **4** (*formal*) : to you, for
you ⟨le traje un regalo : I brought you
a gift⟩
leal *adj* : loyal, faithful — **lealmente** *adv*
lealtad *nf* : loyalty, allegiance

lebrel *nm* : hound
lección *nf, pl* **lecciones** : lesson
lechada *nf* **1** : whitewash **2** : grout
lechal *adj* : suckling, unweaned
⟨cordero lechal : suckling lamb⟩
leche *nf* **1** : milk ⟨leche en polvo : powdered milk⟩ ⟨leche de magnesia : milk
of magnesia⟩ **2** : milky sap
lechera *nf* **1** : milk jug **2** : dairymaid *f*
lechería *nf* : dairy store
lechero[1]**, -ra** *adj* : dairy
lechero[2]**, -ra** *n* : milkman *m*, milk dealer
lecho *nm* **1** : bed ⟨un lecho de rosas : a
bed of roses⟩ ⟨lecho de muerte
: deathbed⟩ **2** : riverbed **3** : layer, stratum (in geology)
lechón, -chona *n, mpl* **lechones** : suckling pig
lechoso, -sa *adj* : milky
lechuga *nf* : lettuce
lechuza *nf* BÚHO : owl, barn owl
lectivo, -va *adj* : school ⟨año lectivo
: school year⟩
lector[1]**, -tora** *adj* : reading ⟨nivel lector
: reading level⟩
lector[2]**, -tora** *n* : reader
lector[3] *nm* : scanner, reader ⟨lector óptico : optical scanner⟩
lectura *nf* **1** : reading **2** : reading matter
leer {20} *v* : to read
legación *nf, pl* **-ciones** : legation
legado *nm* **1** : legacy, bequest **2** : legate,
emissary
legajo *nm* : dossier, file
legal *adj* : legal, lawful — **legalmente**
adv
legalidad *nf* : legality, lawfulness
legalista *adj* : legalistic
legalizar {21} *vt* : to legalize — **legal-
ización** *nf*
legar {52} *vt* **1** : to bequeath, to hand
down **2** DELEGAR : to delegate
legendario, -ria *adj* : legendary
legible *adj* : legible
legión *nf, pl* **legiones** : legion
legionario, -ria *n* : legionnaire
legislación *nf* **1** : legislation, lawmak-
ing **2** : laws *pl*, legislation
legislador[1]**, -dora** *adj* : legislative
legislador[2]**, -dora** *n* : legislator
legislar *vi* : to legislate
legislativo, -va *adj* : legislative
legislatura *nf* **1** : legislature **2** : term of
office
legitimar *vt* **1** : to legitimize **2** : to authenticate — **legitimación** *nf*
legitimidad *nf* : legitimacy
legítimo, -ma *adj* **1** : legitimate **2** : genuine, authentic — **legítimamente** *adv*
lego[1]**, -ga** *adj* **1** : secular, lay **2** : unin-
formed, ignorant
lego[2]**, -ga** *n* : layperson, layman *m*, laywoman *f*
legua *nf* **1** : league **2 notarse a leguas**
: to be very obvious ⟨se notaba a leguas
: you could tell from a mile away⟩

legue, etc. → **legar**
legumbre *nf* **1** HORTALIZA : vegetable **2** : legume
leíble *adj* : readable
leída *nf* : reading, read ⟨de una leída : in one reading, at one go⟩
leído[1] *pp* → **leer**
leído[2], **-da** *adj* : well-read
lejanía *nf* : remoteness, distance
lejano, -na *adj* : remote, distant, far away
lejía *nf* **1** : lye **2** : bleach
lejos *adv* **1** : far away, distant ⟨a lo lejos : in the distance, far off⟩ ⟨desde lejos : from a distance⟩ **2** : long ago, a long way off ⟨está lejos de los 50 años : he's a long way from 50 years old⟩ **3 de ~** : by far ⟨esta decisión fue de lejos la más fácil : this decision was by far the easiest⟩ **4 ~ de** : far from ⟨lejos de ser reprobado, recibió una nota de B : far from failing, he got a B⟩
lelo, -la *adj* : silly, stupid
lema *nm* : motto, slogan
lencería *nf* : lingerie
lengua *nf* **1** : tongue ⟨morderse la lengua : to bite one's tongue⟩ **2** IDIOMA : language ⟨lengua materna : mother tongue, native language⟩ ⟨lengua muerta : dead language⟩
lenguado *nm* : sole, flounder
lenguaje *nm* **1** : language, speech **2 lenguaje gestual** *or* **lenguaje de gestos** : sign language **3 lenguaje de programación** : programming language
lengüeta *nf* **1** : tongue (of a shoe), tab, flap **2** : reed (of a musical instrument) **3** : barb, point
lengüetada *nf* **beber a lengüetadas** : to lap (up)
lenidad *nf* : leniency
lenitivo, -va *adj* : soothing
lente *nmf* **1** : lens ⟨lentes de contacto : contact lenses⟩ **2 lentes** *nmpl* ANTEOJOS : eyeglasses ⟨lentes de sol : sunglasses⟩
lenteja *nf* : lentil
lentejuela *nf* : sequin, spangle
lentitud *nf* : slowness
lento[1] *adv* DESPACIO : slowly
lento[2], **-ta** *adj* **1** : slow **2** : slow-witted, dull — **lentamente** *adv*
leña *nf* : wood, firewood
leñador, -dora *n* : lumberjack, woodcutter
leñera *nf* : woodshed
leño *nm* : log
leñoso, -sa *adj* : woody
Leo *nmf* : Leo
león, -ona *n, mpl* **leones 1** : lion, lioness *f* **2** (*in various countries*) : puma, cougar
leonado, -da *adj* : tawny
leonino, -na *adj* **1** : leonine **2** : one-sided, unfair
leopardo *nm* : leopard
leotardo *nm* MALLA : leotard, tights *pl*
leperada *nf Mex* : obscenity

lépero, -ra *adj Mex* : vulgar, coarse
lepra *nf* : leprosy
leproso[1], **-sa** *adj* : leprous
leproso[2], **-sa** *n* : leper
lerdo, -da *adj* **1** : clumsy **2** : dull, oafish, slow-witted
les *pron* **1** : to them ⟨dales una propina : give them a tip⟩ **2** : from them ⟨se les privó de su herencia : they were deprived of their inheritance⟩ **3** : for them ⟨les hice sus tareas : I did their homework for them⟩ **4** : to you *pl*, for you *pl* ⟨les compré un regalo : I bought you all a present⟩
lesbiana *nf* : lesbian — **lesbiano, -na** *adj*
lesbianismo *nm* : lesbianism
lesión *nf, pl* **lesiones** HERIDA : lesion, wound, injury ⟨una lesión grave : a serious injury⟩
lesionado, -da *adj* HERIDO : injured, wounded
lesionar *vt* : to injure, to wound — **lesionarse** *vr* : to hurt oneself
lesivo, -va *adj* : harmful, damaging
letal *adj* MORTÍFERO : deadly, lethal — **letalmente** *adv*
letanía *nf* **1** : litany **2** *fam* : spiel, song and dance
letárgico, -ca *adj* : lethargic
letargo *nm* : lethargy, torpor
letón[1], **-tona** *adj & n, mpl* **letones** : Latvian
letón[2] *nm* : Latvian (language)
letra *nf* **1** : letter **2** CALIGRAFÍA : handwriting, lettering **3** : lyrics *pl* **4 al pie de la letra** : word for word, by the book **5 letras** *nfpl* : arts (in education)
letrado[1], **-da** *adj* ERUDITO : learned, erudite
letrado[2], **-da** *n* : attorney-at-law, lawyer
letrero *nm* RÓTULO : sign, notice
letrina *nf* : latrine
letrista *nmf* : lyricist, songwriter
leucemia *nf* : leukemia
leva *nf* : cam
levadizo, -za *adj* **1** : liftable **2 puente levadizo** : drawbridge
levadura *nf* **1** : yeast, leavening **2 levadura en polvo** : baking powder
levantamiento *nm* **1** ALZAMIENTO : uprising **2** : raising, lifting ⟨levantamiento de pesas : weight lifting⟩
levantar *vt* **1** ALZAR : to lift, to raise **2** : to put up, to erect **3** : to call off, to adjourn **4** : to give rise to, to arouse ⟨levantar sospechas : to arouse suspicion⟩ — **levantarse** *vr* **1** : to rise, to stand up **2** : to get out of bed
levar *vt* **levar anclas** : to weigh anchor
leve *adj* **1** : light, slight **2** : trivial, unimportant — **levemente** *adv*
levedad *nf* : lightness
levemente *adv* LIGERAMENTE : lightly, softly
leviatán *nm, pl* **-tanes** : leviathan
léxico[1], **-ca** *adj* : lexical
léxico[2] *nm* : lexicon, glossary
lexicografía *nf* : lexicography

lexicográfico, -ca *adj* : lexicographical, lexicographic
lexicógrafo, -fa *n* : lexicographer
ley *nf* 1 : law ⟨fuera de la ley : outside the law⟩ ⟨la ley de gravedad : the law of gravity⟩ 2 : purity (of metals) ⟨oro de ley : pure gold⟩
leyenda *nf* 1 : legend 2 : caption, inscription
leyó, etc. → leer
liar {85} *vt* 1 ATAR : to bind, to tie (up) 2 : to roll (a cigarette) 3 : to confuse — **liarse** *vr* : to get mixed up
libanés, -nesa *adj & n, mpl* **-neses** : Lebanese
libar *vt* 1 : to suck (nectar) 2 : to sip, to swig (liquor, etc.)
libelo *nm* 1 : libel, lampoon 2 : petition (in court)
libélula *nf* : dragonfly
liberación *nf, pl* **-ciones** : liberation, deliverance ⟨liberación de la mujer : women's liberation⟩
liberado, -da *adj* 1 : liberated ⟨una mujer liberada : a liberated woman⟩ 2 : freed, delivered
liberal *adj & nmf* : liberal
liberalidad *nf* : generosity, liberality
liberalismo *nm* : liberalism
liberalizar {21} *vt* : to liberalize — **liberalización** *nf*
liberar *vt* : to liberate, to free — **liberarse** *vr* : to get free of
liberiano, -na *adj & n* : Liberian
libertad *nf* 1 : freedom, liberty ⟨tomarse la libertad de : to take the liberty of⟩ 2 **libertad bajo fianza** : bail 3 **libertad condicional** : parole
libertador[1], -dora *adj* : liberating
libertador[2], -dora *n* : liberator
libertar *vt* LIBRAR : to set free
libertario, -ria *adj & n* : libertarian
libertinaje *nm* : licentiousness, dissipation
libertino[1], -na *adj* : licentious, dissolute
libertino[2], -na *n* : libertine
libidinoso, -sa *adj* : lustful, lewd
libido *nf* : libido
libio, -bia *adj & n* : Libyan
libra *nf* 1 : pound 2 **libra esterlina** : pound sterling
Libra *nmf* : Libra
libramiento *nm* 1 : liberating, freeing 2 LIBRANZA : order of payment 3 *Mex* : beltway
libranza *nf* : order of payment
librar *vt* 1 LIBERTAR : to deliver, to set free 2 : to wage ⟨librar batalla : to do battle⟩ 3 : to issue ⟨librar una orden : to issue an order⟩ — **librarse** *vr* ~ **de** : to free oneself from, to get out of
libre[1] *adj* 1 : free ⟨un país libre : a free country⟩ ⟨libre de : free from, exempt from⟩ ⟨libre albedrío : free will⟩ 2 DESOCUPADO : vacant 3 **día libre** : day off
libre[2] *nm Mex* : taxi
librea *nf* : livery

librecambio *nm* : free trade
libremente *adv* : freely
librería *nf* : bookstore
librero[1], -ra *n* : bookseller
librero[2] *nm Mex* : bookcase
libresco, -ca *adj* : bookish
libreta *nf* CUADERNO : notebook
libretista *nmf* 1 : librettist 2 : scriptwriter
libreto *nm* : libretto, script
libro *nm* 1 : book ⟨libro de texto : textbook⟩ 2 **libros** *nmpl* : books (in bookkeeping), accounts ⟨llevar los libros : to keep the books⟩
licencia *nf* 1 : permission 2 : leave, leave of absence 3 : permit, license ⟨licencia de conducir : driver's license⟩
licenciado, -da *n* 1 : university graduate 2 ABOGADO : lawyer
licenciar *vt* 1 : to license, to permit, to allow 2 : to discharge 3 : to grant a university degree to — **licenciarse** *vr* : to graduate
licenciatura *nf* 1 : college degree 2 : course of study (at a college or university)
licencioso, -sa *adj* : licentious, lewd
liceo *nm* : secondary school, high school
licitación *nf, pl* **-ciones** : bid, bidding
licitar *vt* : to bid on
lícito, -ta *adj* 1 : lawful, licit 2 JUSTO : just, fair
licor *nm* 1 : liquor 2 : liqueur
licorera *nf* : decanter
licuado *nm* BATIDO : milk shake
licuadora *nf* : blender
licuar {3} *vt* : to liquefy — **licuarse** *vr*
lid *nf* 1 : fight, combat 2 : argument, dispute 3 **lides** *nfpl* : matters, affairs 4 **en buena lid** : fair and square
líder[1] *adj* : leading, foremost
líder[2] *nmf* : leader
liderar *vt* DIRIGIR : to lead, to head
liderato *nm* : leadership, leading
liderazgo → liderato
lidiar *vt* : to fight — *vi* BATALLAR, LUCHAR : to struggle, to battle, to wrestle
liebre *nf* : hare
liendre *nf* : nit
lienzo *nm* 1 : linen 2 : canvas, painting 3 : stretch of wall or fencing
liga *nf* 1 ASOCIACIÓN : league 2 GOMITA : rubber band 3 : garter
ligado, -da *adj* : linked, connected
ligadura *nf* 1 ATADURA : tie, bond 2 : ligature
ligamento *nm* : ligament
ligar {52} *vt* : to bind, to tie (up)
ligeramente *adv* 1 : slightly 2 LEVEMENTE : lightly, gently 3 : casually, flippantly
ligereza *nf* 1 : lightness 2 : flippancy 3 : agility
ligero, -ra *adj* 1 : light, lightweight 2 : slight, minor 3 : agile, quick 4 : lighthearted, superficial
lignito *nm* : lignite

ligue, etc. → **ligar**
lija *nf or* **papel de lija** : sandpaper
lijar *vt* : to sand
lila[1] *adj* : lilac, light purple
lila[2] *nf* : lilac
lima *nf* **1** : lime (fruit) **2** : file ⟨lima de uñas : nail file⟩
limadora *nf* : polisher
limar *vt* **1** : to file **2** : to polish, to put the final touch on **3** : to smooth over ⟨limar las diferencias : to iron out differences⟩
limbo *nm* **1** : limbo **2** : limb (in botany and astronomy)
limeño[1], **-ña** *adj* : of or from Lima, Peru
limeño[2], **-ña** *n* : person from Lima, Peru
limero *nm* : lime tree
limitación *nf, pl* **-ciones 1** : limitation **2** : limit, restriction ⟨sin limitación : unlimited⟩
limitado, -da *adj* **1** RESTRINGIDO : limited **2** : dull, slow-witted
limitar *vt* RESTRINGIR : to limit, to restrict — *vi* ~ **con** : to border on — **limitarse** *vr* ~ **a** : to limit oneself to
límite *nm* **1** : boundary, border **2** : limit ⟨el límite de mi paciencia : the limit of my patience⟩ ⟨límite de velocidad : speed limit⟩ **3 fecha límite** : deadline
limítrofe *adj* LINDANTE, LINDERO : bordering, adjoining
limo *nm* : slime, mud
limón *nm, pl* **limones 1** : lemon **2** : lemon tree **3 limón verde** *Mex* : lime
limonada *nf* : lemonade
limosna *nf* : alms, charity
limosnear *vi* : to beg (for alms)
limosnero, -ra *n* MENDIGO : beggar
limoso, -sa *adj* : slimy
limpiabotas *nmfs & pl* : bootblack
limpiador[1], **-dora** *adj* : cleaning
limpiador[2], **-dora** *n* : cleaning person, cleaner
limpiamente *adv* : cleanly, honestly, fairly
limpiaparabrisas *nms & pl* : windshield wiper
limpiar *vt* **1** : to clean, to cleanse **2** : to clean up, to remove defects **3** *fam* : to clean out (in a game) **4** *fam* : to swipe, to pinch — *vi* : to clean — **limpiarse** *vr*
limpiavidrios *nmfs & pl Mex* : windshield wiper
límpido, -da *adj* : limpid
limpieza *nf* **1** : cleanliness, tidiness **2** : cleaning **3** HONRADEZ : integrity, honesty **4** DESTREZA : skill, dexterity
limpio[1] *adv* : fairly
limpio[2], **-pia** *adj* **1** : clean, neat **2** : honest ⟨un juego limpio : a fair game⟩ **3** : free ⟨limpio de impurezas : pure, free from impurities⟩ **4** : clear, net ⟨ganancia limpia : clear profit⟩
limusina *nf* : limousine
linaje *nm* ABOLENGO : lineage, ancestry
linaza *nf* : linseed
lince *nm* : lynx

linchamiento *nm* : lynching
linchar *vt* : to lynch
lindante *adj* LIMÍTROFE, LINDERO : bordering, adjoining
lindar *vi* **1** ~ **con** : to border, to skirt **2** ~ **con** BORDEAR : to border on, to verge on
linde *nmf* : boundary, limit
lindero[1], **-ra** *adj* LIMÍTROFE, LINDANTE : bordering, adjoining
lindero[2] *nm* : boundary, limit
lindeza *nf* **1** : prettiness **2** : clever remark **3 lindezas** *nfpl, (used ironically)* : insults
lindo[1] *adv* **1** : beautifully, wonderfully ⟨canta lindo tu mujer : your wife sings beautifully⟩ **2 de lo lindo** : a lot, a great deal ⟨los zancudos nos picaban de lo lindo : the mosquitoes were biting away at us⟩
lindo[2], **-da** *adj* **1** BONITO : pretty, lovely **2** MONO : cute
línea *nf* **1** : line ⟨línea divisoria : dividing line⟩ ⟨línea de banda : sideline⟩ **2** : line, course, position ⟨línea de conducta : course of action⟩ ⟨en líneas generales : in general terms, along general lines⟩ **3** : line, service ⟨línea aérea : airline⟩ ⟨línea telefónica : telephone line⟩
lineal *adj* : linear
linfa *nf* : lymph
linfático, -ca *adj* : lymphatic
lingote *nm* : ingot
lingüista *nmf* : linguist
lingüística *nf* : linguistics
lingüístico, -ca *adj* : linguistic
linimento *nm* : liniment
lino *nm* **1** : linen **2** : flax
linóleo *nm* : linoleum
linterna *nf* **1** : lantern **2** : flashlight
lío *nm fam* **1** : confusion, mess **2** : hassle, trouble, jam ⟨meterse en un lío : to get into a jam⟩ **3** : affair, liaison
liofilizar {21} *vt* : to freeze-dry
lioso, -sa *adj fam* **1** : confusing, muddled **2** : troublemaking
liquen *nm* : lichen
liquidación *nf, pl* **-ciones 1** : liquidation **2** : clearance sale **3** : settlement, payment
liquidar *vt* **1** : to liquefy **2** : to liquidate **3** : to settle, to pay off **4** *fam* : to rub out, to kill
liquidez *nf, pl* **-deces** : liquidity
líquido[1], **-da** *adj* **1** : liquid, fluid **2** : net ⟨ingresos líquidos : net income⟩
líquido[2] *nm* **1** : liquid, fluid ⟨líquido de frenos : brake fluid⟩ **2** : ready cash, liquid assets
lira *nf* : lyre
lírica *nf* : lyric poetry
lírico, -ca *adj* : lyric, lyrical
lirio *nm* **1** : iris **2 lirio de los valles** MUGUETE : lily of the valley
lirismo *nm* : lyricism
lirón *nm, pl* **lirones** : dormouse
lisiado[1], **-da** *adj* : disabled, crippled

lisiado², -da *n* : disabled person, cripple
lisiar *vt* : to cripple, to disable — **lisiarse**
vr
liso, -sa *adj* **1** : smooth **2** : flat **3**
: straight ⟨pelo liso : straight hair⟩ **4**
: plain, unadorned ⟨liso y llano : plain
and simple⟩
lisonja *nf* : flattery
lisonjear *vt* ADULAR : to flatter
lista *nf* **1** : list **2** : roster, roll ⟨pasar lista
: to take attendance⟩ **3** : stripe, strip
4 : menu
listado¹, -da *adj* : striped
listado² *nm* : listing
listar *vt* : to list
listeza *nf* : smartness, alertness
listo, -ta *adj* **1** DISPUESTO, PREPARADO
: ready ⟨¿estás listo? : are you ready?⟩
2 : clever, smart
listón *nm, pl* **listones 1** : ribbon **2** : strip
(of wood), lath **3** : high bar (in sports)
lisura *nf* : smoothness
litera *nf* : bunk bed, berth
literal *adj* : literal — **literalmente** *adv*
literario, -ria *adj* : literary
literato, -ta *n* : writer, author
literatura *nf* : literature
litigante *adj & nmf* : litigant
litigar {52} *vi* : to litigate, to be in litigation
litigio *nm* **1** : litigation, lawsuit **2 en ~**
: in dispute
litigioso, -sa *adj* : litigious
litio *nm* : lithium
litografía *nf* **1** : lithography **2** : lithograph
litógrafo, -fa *n* : lithographer
litoral¹ *adj* : coastal
litoral² *nm* : shore, seaboard
litosfera *nf* : lithosphere
litro *nm* : liter
lituano¹, -na *adj & n* : Lithuanian
lituano² *nm* : Lithuanian (language)
liturgia *nf* : liturgy
litúrgico, -ca *adj* : liturgical — **litúrgi-
camente** *adv*
liviandad *nf* LIGEREZA : lightness
liviano, -na *adj* **1** : light, slight **2** IN-
CONSTANTE : fickle
lividez *nf* PALIDEZ : pallor
lívido, -da *adj* **1** AMORATADO : livid **2**
PÁLIDO : pallid, extremely pale
living *nm* : living room
llaga *nf* : sore, wound
llama *nf* **1** : flame **2** : llama
llamada *nf* : call ⟨llamada a larga distancia : long-distance call⟩ ⟨llamada al
orden : call to order⟩
llamado¹, -da *adj* : named, called ⟨una
mujer llamada Rosa : a woman called
Rosa⟩
llamado² → **llamamiento**
llamador *nm* : door knocker
llamamiento *nm* : call, appeal
llamar *vt* **1** : to name, to call **2** : to call,
to summon **3** : to phone, to call up —
llamarse *vr* : to be called, to be named
⟨¿cómo te llamas? : what's your
name?⟩

llamarada *nf* **1** : flare-up, sudden blaze
2 : flushing (of the face)
llamativo, -va *adj* : flashy, showy, striking
llameante *adj* : flaming, blazing
llamear *vi* : to flame, to blaze
llana *nf* **1** : trowel **2** → **llano²**
llanamente *adv* : simply, plainly,
straightforwardly
llaneza *nf* : simplicity, naturalness
llano¹, -na *adj* **1** : even, flat **2** : frank,
open **3** LISO : plain, simple
llano² *nm* : plain
llanta *nf* **1** NEUMÁTICO : tire **2** : rim
llantén *nm, pl* **llantenes** : plantain
(weed)
llanto *nm* : crying, weeping
llanura *nf* : plain, prairie
llave *nf* **1** : key **2** : faucet **3** INTER-
RUPTOR : switch **4** : brace (punctua-
tion mark) **5 llave inglesa** : monkey
wrench
llavero *nm* : key chain, key ring
llegada *nf* : arrival
llegar {52} *vi* **1** : to arrive, to come **2 ~**
a : to arrive at, to reach, to amount to
3 ~ a : to manage to ⟨llegó a terminar
la novela : she managed to finish the
novel⟩ **4 llegar a ser** : to become ⟨llegó
a ser un miembro permanente : he became a permanent member⟩
llegue, etc. → **llegar**
llenar *vt* **1** : to fill, to fill up, to fill in **2**
: to meet, to fulfill ⟨los regalos no
llenaron sus expectativas : the gifts did
not meet her expectations⟩ — **llenarse**
vr : to fill up, to become full
llenito, -ta *adj fam* REGORDETE : chubby, plump
lleno¹, -na *adj* **1** : full, filled **2 de ~**
: completely, fully **3 estar lleno de sí
mismo** : to be full of oneself
lleno² *nm* **1** *fam* : plenty, abundance **2**
: full house, sellout
llevadero, -ra *adj* : bearable
llevar *vt* **1** : to take away, to carry ⟨me
gusta, me lo llevo : I like it, I'll take it⟩
2 : to wear **3** : to take, to lead ⟨lleva-
mos a Pedro al cine : we took Pedro to
the movies⟩ **4 llevar a cabo** : to carry
out **5 llevar adelante** : to carry on, to
keep going — *vi* : to lead ⟨un problema lleva al otro : one problem leads to
another⟩ — *v aux* : to have ⟨llevo mucho tiempo buscándolo : I've been
looking for it for a long time⟩ ⟨lleva
leído medio libro : he's halfway
through the book⟩ — **llevarse** *vr* **1** : to
take away, to carry off **2** : to get along
⟨siempre nos llevábamos bien : we always got along well⟩
llorar *vi* : to cry, to weep — *vt* : to mourn,
to bewail
lloriquear *vi* : to whimper, to whine
lloriqueo *nm* : whimpering, whining
llorón, -rona *n, mpl* **llorones** : crybaby,
whiner
lloroso, -sa *adj* : tearful, sad

llovedizo, -za *adj* : rain ⟨agua llovediza : rainwater⟩

llover {47} *v impers* : to rain ⟨está lloviendo : it's raining⟩ ⟨llover a cántaros : to rain cats and dogs⟩ — *vi* : to rain down, to shower ⟨le llovieron regalos : he was showered with gifts⟩

llovizna *nf* : drizzle, sprinkle

lloviznar *v impers* : to drizzle, to sprinkle

llueve, etc. → **llover**

lluvia *nf* **1** : rain, rainfall **2** : barrage, shower

lluvioso, -sa *adj* : rainy

lo[1] *pron* **1** : him, it ⟨lo vi ayer : I saw him yesterday⟩ ⟨lo entiendo : I understand it⟩ ⟨no lo creo : I don't believe so⟩ **2** (*formal, masculine*) : you ⟨disculpe, señor, no lo oí : excuse me sir, I didn't hear you⟩ **3 lo que** : what, that which ⟨eso es lo que más le gusta : that's what he likes the most⟩

lo[2] *art* **1** : the ⟨lo mejor : the best, the best thing⟩ **2** : how ⟨sé lo bueno que eres : I know how good you are⟩

loa *nf* : praise

loable *adj* : laudable, praiseworthy — **loablemente** *adv*

loar *vt* : to praise, to laud

lobato, -ta *n* : wolf cub

lobby *nm* : lobby, pressure group

lobo, -ba *n* : wolf

lóbrego, -ga *adj* SOMBRÍO : gloomy, dark

lobulado, -da *adj* : lobed

lóbulo *nm* : lobe ⟨lóbulo de la oreja : earlobe⟩

locación *nf, pl* **-ciones 1** : location (in moviemaking) **2** *Mex* : place

local[1] *adj* : local — **localmente** *adv*

local[2] *nm* : premises *pl*

localidad *nf* : town, locality

localización *nf, pl* **-ciones 1** : locating, localization **2** : location

localizar {21} *vt* **1** UBICAR : to locate, to find **2** : to localize — **localizarse** *vr* UBICARSE : to be located ⟨se localiza en el séptimo piso : it is located on the seventh floor⟩

locatario, -ria *n* : tenant

loción *nf, pl* **lociones** : lotion

lócker *nm, pl* **lóckers** : locker

loco[1], **-ca** *adj* **1** DEMENTE : crazy, insane, mad **2 a lo loco** : wildly, recklessly **3 volverse loco** : to go mad

loco[2], **-ca** *n* **1** : crazy person, lunatic **2 hacerse el loco** : to act the fool

locomoción *nf, pl* **-ciones** : locomotion

locomotor, -tora *adj* : locomotive

locomotora *nf* **1** : locomotive **2** : driving force

locuacidad *nf* : loquacity, talkativeness

locuaz *adj, pl* **locuaces** : loquacious, talkative

locución *nf, pl* **-ciones** : locution, phrase ⟨locución adverbial : adverbial phrase⟩

locura *nf* **1** : insanity, madness **2** : crazy thing, folly

locutor, -tora *n* : announcer

lodazal *nm* : bog, quagmire

lodo *nm* BARRO : mud, mire

lodoso, -sa *adj* : muddy

logaritmo *nm* : logarithm

logia *nf* : lodge ⟨logia masónica : Masonic lodge⟩

lógica *nf* : logic

lógico, -ca *adj* : logical — **lógicamente** *adv*

logística *nf* : logistics *pl*

logístico, -ca *adj* : logistic, logistical

logo → **logotipo**

logotipo *nm* : logo

logrado, -da *adj* : successful, well done

lograr *vt* **1** : to get, to obtain **2** : to achieve, to attain — **lograrse** *vr* : to be successful

logro *nm* : achievement, attainment

loma *nf* : hill, hillock

lombriz *nf, pl* **lombrices** : worm ⟨lombriz de tierra : earthworm, night crawler⟩ ⟨lombriz solitaria : tapeworm⟩ ⟨tener lombrices : to have worms⟩

lomo *nm* **1** : back (of an animal) **2** : loin ⟨lomo de cerdo : pork loin⟩ **3** : spine (of a book) **4** : blunt edge (of a knife)

lona *nf* : canvas

loncha *nf* LONJA, REBANADA : slice

lonche *nm* **1** ALMUERZO : lunch **2** *Mex* : submarine sandwich

lonchería *nf Mex* : luncheonette

londinense[1] *adj* : of or from London

londinense[2] *nmf* : Londoner

longaniza *nf* : spicy pork sausage

longevidad *nf* : longevity

longevo, -va *adj* : long-lived

longitud *nf* **1** LARGO : length ⟨longitud de onda : wavelength⟩ **2** : longitude

longitudinal *adj* : longitudinal

lonja *nf* LONCHA, REBANADA : slice

lontananza *nf* : background ⟨en lontananza : in the distance, far away⟩

lord *nm, pl* **lores** (*title in England*) : lord

loro *nm* : parrot

los[1], **las** *pron* **1** : them ⟨hice galletas y se las di a los nuevos vecinos : I made cookies and gave them to the new neighbors⟩ **2** : you ⟨voy a llevarlos a los dos : I am going to take both of you⟩ **3 los que, las que** : those, who, the ones ⟨los que van a cantar deben venir temprano : those who are singing must come early⟩ **4** (*used with* haber) ⟨los hay en varios colores : they come in various colors⟩

los[2] *art* → **el**[2]

losa *nf* : flagstone, paving stone

loseta *nf* BALDOSA : floor tile

lote *nm* **1** : part, share **2** : batch, lot **3** : plot of land, lot

lotería *nf* : lottery

loto *nm* : lotus

loza *nf* **1** : crockery, earthenware **2** : china

lozanía *nf* **1** : healthiness, robustness **2** : luxuriance, lushness

lozano, -na *adj* **1** : robust, healthy-looking ⟨un rostro lozano : a smooth, fresh face⟩ **2** : lush, luxuriant
LSD *nm* : LSD
lubricante[1] *adj* : lubricating
lubricante[2] *nm* : lubricant
lubricar {72} *vt* : to lubricate, to oil — **lubricación** *nf*
lucero *nm* : bright star ⟨lucero del alba : morning star⟩
lucha *nf* **1** : struggle, fight **2** : wrestling
luchador, -dora *n* **1** : fighter **2** : wrestler
luchar *vi* **1** : to fight, to struggle **2** : to wrestle
luchón, -chona *adj, mpl* **luchones** *Mex* : industrious, hardworking
lucidez *nf, pl* **-deces** : lucidity, clarity
lucido, -da *adj* MAGNÍFICO : magnificent, splendid
lúcido, -da *adj* : lucid
luciérnaga *nf* : firefly, glowworm
lucimiento *nm* **1** : brilliance, splendor, sparkle **2** : triumph, success ⟨salir con lucimiento : to succeed with flying colors⟩
lucio *nm* : pike (fish)
lucir {45} *vi* **1** : to shine **2** : to look good, to stand out **3** : to seem, to appear ⟨ahora luce contento : he looks happy now⟩ — *vt* **1** : to wear, to sport **2** : to flaunt, to show off — **lucirse** *vr* **1** : to distinguish oneself, to excel **2** : to show off
lucrarse *vr* : to make a profit
lucrativo, -va *adj* : lucrative, profitable — **lucrativamente** *adv*
lucro *nm* GANANCIA : profit, gain
luctuoso, -sa *adj* : mournful, tragic
luego[1] *adv* **1** DESPUÉS : then, afterwards **2** : later (on) **3 desde ~** : of course **4 ¡hasta luego!** : see you later! **5 luego que** : as soon as **6 luego luego** *Mex fam* : right away, immediately
luego[2] *conj* : therefore ⟨pienso, luego existo : I think, therefore I am⟩
lugar *nm* **1** : place, position ⟨se llevó el primer lugar en su división : she took first place in her division⟩ **2** ESPACIO : space, room **3 dar lugar a** : to give rise to, to lead to **4 en lugar de** : instead of **5 lugar común** : cliché, platitude **6 tener lugar** : to take place
lugareño[1], **-ña** *adj* : village, rural
lugareño[2], **-ña** *n* : villager
lugarteniente *nmf* : lieutenant, deputy
lúgubre *adj* : gloomy, lugubrious
lujo *nm* **1** : luxury **2 de ~** : deluxe
lujoso, -sa *adj* : luxurious
lujuria *nf* : lust, lechery
lujurioso, -sa *adj* : lustful, lecherous
lumbago *nm* : lumbago
lumbar *adj* : lumbar
lumbre *nf* **1** FUEGO : fire **2** : brilliance, splendor **3 poner en la lumbre** : to put on the stove, to warm up
lumbrera *nf* **1** : skylight **2** : vent, port **3** : brilliant person, luminary
luminaria *nf* **1** : altar lamp **2** LUMBRERA : luminary, celebrity
luminiscencia *nf* : luminescence — **luminiscente** *adj*
luminosidad *nf* : luminosity, brightness
luminoso, -sa *adj* : shining, luminous
luna *nf* **1** : moon **2 luna de miel** : honeymoon
lunar[1] *adj* : lunar
lunar[2] *nm* **1** : mole, beauty spot **2** : defect, blemish **3** : polka dot
lunático, -ca *adj & n* : lunatic
lunes *nms & pl* : Monday
luneta *nf* **1** : lens (of eyeglasses) **2** : windshield (of an automobile) **3** : crescent
lupa *nf* : magnifying glass
lúpulo *nm* : hops (plant)
lustrar *vt* : to shine, to polish
lustre *nm* **1** BRILLO : luster, shine **2** : glory, distinction
lustroso, -sa *adj* BRILLOSO : lustrous, shiny
luto *nm* : mourning ⟨estar de luto : to be in mourning⟩
luz *nf, pl* **luces 1** : light **2** : lighting **3** *fam* : electricity **4** : window, opening **5** : light, lamp **6** : span, spread (between supports) **7 a la luz de** : in light of **8 dar a luz** : to give birth **9 traje de luces** : matador's costume
luzca, etc. → **lucir**

M

m *nf* : thirteenth letter of the Spanish alphabet
macabro, -bra *adj* : macabre
macaco[1], **-ca** *adj* : ugly, misshapen
macaco[2], **-ca** *n* : macaque
macadán *nm, pl* **-danes** : macadam
macana *nf* **1** : club, cudgel **2** *fam* : nonsense, silliness **3** *fam* : lie, fib
macanudo, -da *adj fam* : great, fantastic
macarrón *nm, pl* **-rrones 1** : macaroon **2 macarrones** *nmpl* : macaroni
maceta *nf* **1** : flowerpot **2** : mallet **3** *Mex fam* : head
macetero *nm* **1** : plant stand **2** TIESTO : flowerpot, planter
machacar {72} *vt* **1** : to crush, to grind **2** : to beat, to pound — *vi* : to insist, to go on (about)
machacón, -cona *adj, mpl* **-cones** : insistent, tiresome
machete *nm* : machete
machetear *vt* : to hack with a machete — *vi Mex fam* : to plod, to work tirelessly
machismo *nm* **1** : machismo **2** : male chauvinism
machista *nm* : male chauvinist

macho[1] *adj* **1** : male **2** : macho, virile, tough

macho[2] *nm* **1** : male **2** : he-man

machote *nm* **1** *fam* : tough guy, he-man **2** *CA, Mex* : rough draft, model **3** *Mex* : blank form

machucar {72} *vt* **1** : to pound, to beat, to crush **2** : to bruise

machucón *nm, pl* **-cones 1** MORETÓN : bruise **2** : smashing, pounding

macilento, -ta *adj* : gaunt, wan

macis *nm* : mace (spice)

macizo, -za *adj* **1** : solid ⟨oro macizo : solid gold⟩ **2** : strong, strapping **3** : massive

macrocosmo *nm* : macrocosm

mácula *nf* : blemish, stain

madeja *nf* **1** : skein, hank **2** : tangle (of hair)

madera *nf* **1** : wood **2** : lumber, timber **3 madera dura** *or* **madera noble** : hardwood

maderero, -ra *adj* : timber, lumber

madero *nm* : piece of lumber, plank

madrastra *nf* : stepmother

madrazo *nm Mex fam* : punch, blow ⟨se agarraron a madrazos : they beat each other up⟩

madre *nf* **1** : mother **2 madre política** : mother-in-law **3 la Madre Patria** : the mother country (said of Spain)

madrear *vt Mex fam* : to beat up

madreperla *nf* NÁCAR : mother-of-pearl

madreselva *nf* : honeysuckle

madriguera *nf* : burrow, den, lair

madrileño[1], **-ña** *adj* : of or from Madrid

madrileño[2], **-ña** *n* : person from Madrid

madrina *nf* **1** : godmother **2** : bridesmaid **3** : sponsor

madrugada *nf* **1** : early morning, wee hours **2** ALBA : dawn, daybreak

madrugador, -dora *n* : early riser

madrugar {52} *vi* **1** : to get up early **2** : to get a head start

madurar *v* **1** : to ripen **2** : to mature

madurez *nf, pl* **-reces 1** : maturity **2** : ripeness

maduro, -ra *adj* **1** : mature **2** : ripe

maestría *nf* **1** : mastery, skill **2** : master's degree

maestro[1], **-tra** *adj* **1** : masterly, skilled **2** : chief, main **3** : trained ⟨un elefante maestro : a trained elephant⟩

maestro[2], **-tra** *n* **1** : teacher (in grammar school) **2** : expert, master **3** : maestro

Mafia *nf* : Mafia

mafioso, -sa *n* : mafioso, gangster

magdalena *nf* : bun, muffin

magenta *adj & n* : magenta

magia *nf* : magic

mágico, -ca *adj* : magic, magical — **mágicamente** *adv*

magisterio *nm* **1** : teaching **2** : teachers *pl*, teaching profession

magistrado, -da *n* : magistrate, judge

magistral *adj* **1** : masterful, skillful **2** : magisterial

magistralmente *adv* : masterfully, brilliantly

magistratura *nf* : judgeship, magistracy

magma *nm* : magma

magnanimidad *nf* : magnanimity

magnánimo, -ma *adj* GENEROSO : magnanimous — **magnánimamente** *adv*

magnate *nmf* : magnate, tycoon

magnesia *nf* : magnesia

magnesio *nm* : magnesium

magnético, -ca *adj* : magnetic

magnetismo *nm* : magnetism

magnetizar {21} *vt* : to magnetize

magnetófono *nm* : tape recorder

magnetofónico, -ca *adj* **cinta magnetofónica** : magnetic tape

magnificar {72} *vt* **1** : to magnify **2** EXAGERAR : to exaggerate **3** ENSALZAR : to exalt, to extol, to praise highly

magnificencia *nf* : magnificence, splendor

magnífico, -ca *adj* ESPLENDOROSO : magnificent, splendid — **magníficamente** *adv*

magnitud *nf* : magnitude

magnolia *nf* : magnolia (flower)

magnolio *nm* : magnolia (tree)

mago, -ga *n* **1** : magician **2** : wizard (in folk tales, etc.) **3 los Reyes Magos** : the Magi

magro, -gra *adj* **1** : lean (of meat) **2** : meager

maguey *nm* : maguey

magulladura *nf* MORETÓN : bruise

magullar *vt* : to bruise — **magullarse** *vr*

mahometano[1], **-na** *adj* ISLÁMICO : Islamic, Muslim

mahometano[2], **-na** *n* : Muslim

mahonesa → **mayonesa**

maicena *nf* : cornstarch

mainframe [ˈmeinˌfreim] *nm* : mainframe

maíz *nm* : corn, maize

maizal *nm* : cornfield

maja *nf* : pestle

majadería *nf* **1** TONTERÍA : stupidity, foolishness **2** *Mex* LEPERADA : insult, obscenity

majadero[1], **-ra** *adj* **1** : foolish, silly **2** *Mex* LÉPERO : crude, vulgar

majadero[2], **-ra** *n* **1** TONTO : fool **2** *Mex* : rude person, boor

majar *vt* : to crush, to mash

majestad *nf* : majesty ⟨Su Majestad : Your Majesty⟩

majestuosamente *adv* : majestically

majestuosidad *nf* : majesty, grandeur

majestuoso, -sa *adj* : majestic, stately

majo, -ja *adj Spain* **1** : nice, likeable **2** GUAPO : attractive, good-looking

mal[1] *adv* **1** : badly, poorly ⟨baila muy mal : he dances very badly⟩ **2** : wrong, incorrectly ⟨me entendió mal : she misunderstood me⟩ **3** : with difficulty, hardly ⟨mal puedo oírte : I can hardly hear you⟩ **4 de mal en peor** : from bad to worse **5 menos mal** : it could have been worse

mal² *adj* → **malo**
mal³ *nm* **1** : evil, wrong **2** DAÑO : harm, damage **3** DESGRACIA : misfortune **4** ENFERMEDAD : illness, sickness
malabar *adj* **juegos malabares** : juggling
malabarista *nmf* : juggler
malaconsejado, -da *adj* : ill-advised
malacostumbrado, -da *adj* CONSENTIDO : spoiled, pampered
malacostumbrar *vt* : to spoil
malagradecido, -da *adj* INGRATO : ungrateful
malaisio → **malasio**
malaquita *nf* : malachite
malaria *nf* PALUDISMO : malaria
malasio, -sia *adj* & *n* : Malaysian
malauiano, -na *adj* & *n* : Malawian
malaventura *nf* : misadventure, misfortune
malaventurado, -da *adj* MALHADADO : ill-fated, unfortunate
malayo, -ya *adj* & *n* : Malay, Malayan
malbaratar *vt* **1** MALGASTAR : to squander **2** : to undersell
malcriado¹, -da *adj* **1** : ill-bred, ill-mannered **2** : spoiled, pampered
malcriado², -da *n* : spoiled brat
maldad *nf* **1** : evil, wickedness **2** : evil deed
maldecir {11} *vt* : to curse, to damn — *vi* **1** : to curse, to swear **2** ~ **de** : to speak ill of, to slander, to defame
maldición *nf*, *pl* **-ciones** : curse
maldiga, maldijo etc. → **maldecir**
maldito, -ta *adj* **1** : cursed, damned ⟨¡maldita sea! : damn it all!⟩ **2** : wicked
maldoso, -sa *adj Mex* : mischievous
maleable *adj* : malleable
maleante *nmf* : crook, thug
malecón *nm*, *pl* **-cones** : jetty, breakwater
maleducado, -da *adj* : ill-mannered, rude
maleficio *nm* : curse, hex
maléfico, -ca *adj* : evil, harmful
malentender {56} *vt* : to misunderstand
malentendido *nm* : misunderstanding
malestar *nm* **1** : discomfort **2** IRRITACIÓN : annoyance **3** INQUIETUD : uneasiness, unrest
maleta *nf* : suitcase, bag ⟨haz tus maletas : pack your bags⟩
maletero¹, -ra *n* : porter
maletero² *nm* : trunk (of an automobile)
maletín *nm*, *pl* **-tines 1** PORTAFOLIO : briefcase **2** : overnight bag, satchel
malevolencia *nf* : malevolence, wickedness
malévolo, -la *adj* : malevolent, wicked
maleza *nf* **1** : thicket, underbrush **2** : weeds *pl*
malformación *nf*, *pl* **-ciones** : malformation
malgache *adj* & *nmf* : Madagascan
malgastar *vt* : to squander (resources), to waste (time, effort)
malhablado, -da *adj* : foul-mouthed

malhadado, -da *adj* MALAVENTURADO : ill-fated
malhechor, -chora *n* : criminal, delinquent, wrongdoer
malherir {76} *vt* : to injure seriously
malhumor *nm* : bad mood, sullenness
malhumorado, -da *adj* : bad-tempered, cross
malicia *nf* **1** : wickedness, malice **2** : mischief, naughtiness **3** : cunning, craftiness
malicioso, -sa *adj* **1** : malicious **2** PÍCARO : mischievous
malignidad *nf* **1** : malignancy **2** MALDAD : evil
maligno, -na *adj* **1** : malignant ⟨un tumor maligno : a malignant tumor⟩ **2** : evil, harmful, malign
malinchismo *nm Mex* : preference for foreign goods or people — **malinchista** *adj*
malintencionado, -da *adj* : malicious, spiteful
malinterpretar *vt* : to misinterpret
malla *nf* **1** : mesh **2** LEOTARDO : leotard, tights *pl* **3 malla de baño** : bathing suit
mallorquín, -quina *adj* & *n* : Majorcan
malnutrición *nf*, *pl* **-ciones** DESNUTRICIÓN : malnutrition
malnutrido, -da *adj* DESNUTRIDO : malnourished, undernourished
malo¹, -la *adj* (**mal** *before masculine singular nouns*) **1** : bad ⟨mala suerte : bad luck⟩ **2** : wicked, naughty **3** : cheap, poor (quality) **4** : harmful ⟨malo para la salud : bad for one's health⟩ **5** (*using the form* **mal**) : unwell ⟨estar mal del corazón : to have heart trouble⟩ **6 estar de malas** : to be in a bad mood
malo², -la *n* : villain, bad guy (in novels, movies, etc.)
malogrado, -da *adj* : failed, unsuccessful
malograr *vt* **1** : to spoil, to ruin **2** : to waste (an opportunity, time) — **malograrse** *vr* **1** FRACASAR : to fail **2** : to die young
malogro *nm* **1** : untimely death **2** FRACASO : failure
maloliente *adj* HEDIONDO : foul-smelling, smelly
malparado, -da *adj* **salir malparado** *or* **quedar malparado** : to come out of (something) badly, to end up in a bad state
malpensado, -da *adj* : distrustful, suspicious, nasty-minded
malquerencia *nf* AVERSIÓN : ill will, dislike
malquerer {64} *vt* : to dislike
malquiso, etc. → **malquerer**
malsano, -na *adj* : unhealthy
malsonante *adj* : rude, offensive ⟨palabras malsonantes : foul language⟩
malta *nf* : malt
malteada *nf* : malted milk ⟨malteada de chocolate : chocolate malt⟩

maltés, -tesa *adj & n, mpl* **malteses** : Maltese

maltratar *vt* **1** : to mistreat, to abuse **2** : to damage, to spoil

maltrato *nm* : mistreatment, abuse

maltrecho, -cha *adj* : battered, damaged

malucho, -cha *adj fam* : sick, under the weather

malva *adj & nm* : mauve

malvado¹, -da *adj* : evil, wicked

malvado², -da *n* : evildoer, wicked person

malvavisco *nm* : marshmallow

malvender *vt* : to sell at a loss

malversación *nf, pl* **-ciones** : misappropriation (of funds), embezzlement

malversador, -dora *n* : embezzler

malversar *vt* : to embezzle

malvivir *vi* : to live badly, to just scrape by

mamá *nf fam* : mom, mama

mamar *vi* **1** : to suckle **2 darle de mamar a** : to breast-feed — *vt* **1** : to suckle, to nurse **2** : to learn from childhood, to grow up with — **mamarse** *vr fam* : to get drunk

mamario, -ria *adj* : mammary

mamarracho *nm fam* **1** ESPERPENTO : mess, sight **2** : laughingstock, fool **3** : rubbish, junk

mambo *nm* : mambo

mami *nf fam* : mommy

mamífero¹, -ra *adj* : mammalian

mamífero² *nm* : mammal

mamila *nf* **1** : nipple **2** *Mex* : baby bottle, pacifier

mamografía *nf* : mammogram

mamola *nf* : pat, chuck under the chin

mamotreto *nm fam* **1** : huge book, tome **2** ARMATOSTE : hulk, monstrosity

mampara *nf* BIOMBO : screen, room divider

mamparo *nm* : bulkhead

mampostería *nf* : masonry, stonemasonry

mampostero *nm* : mason, stonemason

mamut *nm, pl* **mamuts** : mammoth

maná *nm* : manna

manada *nf* **1** : flock, herd, pack **2** *fam* : horde, mob ⟨llegaron en manada : they came in droves⟩

manantial *nm* **1** FUENTE : spring **2** : source

manar *vi* **1** : to flow **2** : to abound

manatí *nm* : manatee

mancha *nf* **1** : stain, spot, mark ⟨mancha de sangre : bloodstain⟩ **2** : blemish, blot ⟨una mancha en su reputación : a blemish on his reputation⟩ **3** : patch

manchado, -da *adj* : stained

manchar *vt* **1** ENSUCIAR : to stain, to soil **2** DESHONRAR : to sully, to tarnish — **mancharse** *vr* : to get dirty

mancillar *vt* : to sully, to besmirch

manco, -ca *adj* : one-armed, onehanded

mancomunar *vt* : to combine, to pool — **mancomunarse** *vr* : to unite, to join together

mancomunidad *nf* **1** : commonwealth **2** : association, confederation

mancuernas *nfpl* : cuff links

mancuernillas *nf Mex* : cuff links

mandadero, -ra *n* : errand boy *m*, errand girl *f*, messenger

mandado *nm* **1** : order, command **2** : errand ⟨hacer los mandados : to run errands, to go shopping⟩

mandamás *nmf, pl* **-mases** *fam* : boss, bigwig, honcho

mandamiento *nm* **1** : commandment **2** : command, order, warrant ⟨mandamiento judicial : warrant, court order⟩

mandar *vt* **1** ORDENAR : to command, to order **2** ENVIAR : to send ⟨te manda saludos : he sends you his regards⟩ **3** ECHAR : to hurl, to throw **4 ¿mande?** *Mex* : yes?, pardon? — *vi* : to be the boss, to be in charge — **mandarse** *vr Mex* : to take liberties, to take advantage

mandarín *nm* : Mandarin

mandarina *nf* : mandarin orange, tangerine

mandatario, -ria *n* **1** : leader (in politics) ⟨primer mandatario : head of state⟩ **2** : agent (in law)

mandato *nm* **1** : term of office **2** : mandate

mandíbula *nf* **1** : jaw **2** : mandible

mandil *nm* **1** DELANTAL : apron **2** : horse blanket

mandilón *nm, pl* **-lones** *fam* : wimp, coward

mandioca *nf* **1** : manioc, cassava **2** : tapioca

mando *nm* **1** : command, leadership **2** : control (for a device) ⟨mando a distancia : remote control⟩ **3 al mando de** : in charge of **4 al mando de** : under the command of

mandolina *nf* : mandolin

mandón, -dona *adj, mpl* **mandones** : bossy, domineering

mandonear *vt fam* MANGONEAR : to boss around

mandrágora *nf* : mandrake

manecilla *nf* : hand (of a clock), pointer

manejable *adj* **1** : manageable **2** : docile, easily led

manejar *vt* **1** CONDUCIR : to drive (a car) **2** OPERAR : to handle, to operate **3** : to manage **4** : to manipulate (a person) — *vi* : to drive — **manejarse** *vr* **1** COMPORTARSE : to behave **2** : to get along, to manage

manejo *nm* **1** : handling, operation **2** : management

manera *nf* **1** MODO : way, manner, fashion **2 de cualquier manera** *or* **de todas maneras** : anyway, anyhow **3 de manera que** : so, in order that **4 de ninguna manera** : by no means, absolutely not **5 manera de ser** : personality, demeanor

manga *nf* **1** : sleeve **2** MANGUERA : hose
manganeso *nm* : manganese
mangle *nm* : mangrove
mango *nm* **1** : hilt, handle **2** : mango
mangonear *vt fam* : to boss around, to bully — *vi* **1** : to be bossy **2** : to loaf, to fool around
mangosta *nf* : mongoose
manguera *nf* : hose
manguito *nm* **1** : muff **2** : sleeve (of a pipe, etc.), hose (of a car)
maní *nm, pl* **maníes** : peanut
manía *nf* **1** OBSESIÓN : mania, obsession **2** : craze, fad **3** : odd habit, peculiarity **4** : dislike, aversion
maníaco¹, -ca *adj* : maniacal
maníaco², -ca *n* : maniac
maniatar *vt* : to tie the hands of, to manacle
maniático¹, -ca *adj* **1** MANÍACO : maniacal **2** : obsessive **3** : fussy, finicky
maniático², -ca *n* **1** MANÍACO : maniac, lunatic **2** : obsessive person, fanatic **3** : eccentric, crank
manicomio *nm* : insane asylum, madhouse
manicura *nf* : manicure
manicuro, -ra *n* : manicurist
manido, -da *adj* : hackneyed, stale, trite
manifestación *nf, pl* **-ciones 1** : manifestation, sign **2** : demonstration, rally
manifestante *nmf* : demonstrator
manifestar {55} *vt* **1** : to demonstrate, to show **2** : to declare — **manifestarse** *vr* **1** : to be or become evident **2** : to state one's position ⟨se han manifestado a favor del acuerdo : they have declared their support for the agreement⟩ **3** : to demonstrate, to rally
manifiesto¹, -ta *adj* : manifest, evident, clear — **manifiestamente** *adv*
manifiesto² *nm* : manifesto
manija *nf* MANGO : handle
manilla → **manecilla**
manillar *nm* : handlebars *pl*
maniobra *nf* : maneuver, stratagem
maniobrar *v* : to maneuver
manipulación *nf, pl* **-ciones** : manipulation
manipulador¹, -dora *adj* : manipulating, manipulative
manipulador², -dora *n* : manipulator
manipular *vt* **1** : to manipulate **2** MANEJAR : to handle
maniquí¹ *nmf, pl* **-quíes** : mannequin, model
maniquí² *nm, pl* **-quíes** : mannequin, dummy
manirroto¹, -ta *adj* : extravagant
manirroto², -ta *n* : spendthrift
manivela *nf* : crank
manjar *nm* : delicacy, special dish
mano¹ *nf* **1** : hand **2** : coat (of paint or varnish) **3 a** ~ : by hand **4 a** ~ *or* **a la mano** : handy, at hand, nearby **5 darse la mano** : to shake hands **6 de la mano** : hand in hand ⟨la política y la economía van de la mano : politics

and economics go hand in hand⟩ **7 de primera mano** ; firsthand, at firsthand **8 de segunda mano** : secondhand ⟨ropa de segunda mano : secondhand clothing⟩ **9 mano a mano** : one-on-one **10 mano de obra** : labor, manpower **11 mano de mortero** : pestle **12 echar una mano** : to lend a hand **13 mano negra** *Mex fam* : shady dealings *pl*
mano², -na *n Mex fam* : buddy, pal ⟨¡oye, mano! : hey man!⟩
manojo *nm* PUÑADO : handful, bunch
manopla *nf* **1** : mitten, mitt **2** : brass knuckles *pl*
manosear *vt* **1** : to handle or touch excessively **2** ACARICIAR : to fondle, to caress
manotazo *nm* : slap, smack, swipe
manotear *vi* : to wave one's hands, to gesticulate
mansalva *adv* **a** ~ : at close range
mansarda *nf* BUHARDILLA : attic
mansedumbre *nf* **1** : gentleness, meekness **2** : tameness
mansión *nf, pl* **-siones** : mansion
manso, -sa *adj* **1** : gentle, meek **2** : tame — **mansamente** *adv*
manta *nf* **1** COBIJA, FRAZADA : blanket **2** : poncho **3** *Mex* : coarse cotton fabric
manteca *nf* **1** GRASA : lard, fat **2** : butter
mantecoso, -sa *adj* : buttery
mantel *nm* **1** : tablecloth **2** : altar cloth
mantelería *nf* : table linen
mantener {80} *vt* **1** SUSTENTAR : to support, to feed ⟨mantener uno su familia : to support one's family⟩ **2** CONSERVAR : to keep, to preserve **3** CONTINUAR : to keep up, to sustain ⟨mantener una correspondencia : to keep up a correspondence⟩ **4** AFIRMAR : to maintain, to affirm — **mantenerse** *vr* **1** : to support oneself, to subsist **2 mantenerse firme** : to hold one's ground
mantenimiento *nm* **1** : maintenance, upkeep **2** : sustenance, food **3** : preservation
mantequera *nf* **1** : churn **2** : butter dish
mantequería *nf* **1** : creamery, dairy **2** : grocery store
mantequilla *nf* : butter
mantilla *nf* : mantilla
mantis *nf* **mantis religiosa** : praying mantis
manto *nm* **1** : cloak **2** : mantle (in geology)
mantón *nm, pl* **-tones** CHAL : shawl
mantuvo, etc. → **mantener**
manual¹ *adj* **1** : manual ⟨trabajo manual : manual labor⟩ **2** : handy, manageable — **manualmente** *adv*
manual² *nm* : manual, handbook
manualidades *nfpl* : handicrafts (in schools)
manubrio *nm* **1** : handle, crank **2** : handlebars *pl*

manufactura *nf* **1** FABRICACIÓN : manufacture **2** : manufactured item, product **3** FÁBRICA : factory
manufacturar *vt* FABRICAR : to manufacture
manufacturero¹, -ra *adj* : manufacturing
manufacturero², -ra *n* FABRICANTE : manufacturer
manuscrito¹, -ta *adj* : handwritten
manuscrito² *nm* : manuscript
manutención *nf, pl* **-ciones** : maintenance, support
manzana *nf* **1** : apple **2** CUADRA : block (enclosed by streets or buildings) **3** *or* **manzana de Adán** : Adam's apple
manzanal *nm* **1** : apple orchard **2** MANZANO : apple tree
manzanar *nm* : apple orchard
manzanilla *nf* **1** : chamomile **2** : chamomile tea
manzano *nm* : apple tree
maña *nf* **1** : dexterity, skill **2** : cunning, guile **3 mañas** *or* **malas mañas** *nfpl* : bad habits, vices
mañana *nf* **1** : morning **2** : tomorrow
mañanero, -ra *adj* MATUTINO : morning ⟨rocío mañanero : morning dew⟩
mañanitas *nfpl Mex* : birthday serenade
mañoso, -sa *adj* **1** HÁBIL : skillful **2** ASTUTO : cunning, crafty **3** : fussy, finicky
mapa *nm* CARTA : map
mapache *nm* : raccoon
mapamundi *nm* : map of the world
maqueta *nf* : model, mock-up
maquillador, -dora *n* : makeup artist
maquillaje *nm* : makeup
maquillarse *vr* : to put on makeup, to make oneself up
máquina *nf* **1** : machine ⟨máquina de coser : sewing machine⟩ ⟨máquina de escribir : typewriter⟩ **2** LOCOMOTORA : engine, locomotive **3** : machine (in politics) **4 a toda máquina** : at full speed
maquinación *nf, pl* **-ciones** : machination, scheme, plot
maquinal *adj* : mechanical, automatic — **maquinalmente** *adv*
maquinar *vt* : to plot, to scheme
maquinaria *nf* **1** : machinery **2** : mechanism, works *pl*
maquinilla *nf* **1** : small machine or device **2** CA, Car : typewriter
maquinista *nmf* **1** : machinist **2** : railroad engineer
mar *nmf* **1** : sea ⟨un mar agitado : a rough sea⟩ ⟨hacerse a la mar : to set sail⟩ **2 alta mar** : high seas
maraca *nf* : maraca
maraña *nf* **1** : thicket **2** ENREDO : tangle, mess
marasmo *nm* : paralysis, stagnation
maratón *nm, pl* **-tones** : marathon
maravilla *nf* **1** : wonder, marvel ⟨a las mil maravillas : wonderfully, mar-

velously⟩ ⟨hacer maravillas : to work wonders⟩ **2** : marigold
maravillar *vt* ASOMBRAR : to astonish, to amaze — **maravillarse** *vr* : to be amazed, to marvel
maravilloso, -sa *adj* ESTUPENDO : wonderful, marvelous — **maravillosamente** *adv*
marbete *nm* **1** ETIQUETA : label, tag **2** *PRi* : registration sticker (of a car)
marca *nf* **1** : mark **2** : brand, make **3** : trademark ⟨marca registrada : registered trademark⟩ **4** : record (in sports) ⟨batir la marca : to beat the record⟩
marcado, -da *adj* : marked ⟨un marcado contraste : a marked contrast⟩
marcador *nm* **1** TANTEADOR : scoreboard **2** : marker, felt-tipped pen **3 marcador de libros** : bookmark
marcaje *nm* **1** : scoring (in sports) **2** : guarding (in sports)
marcapasos *nms & pl* : pacemaker
marcar {72} *vt* **1** : to mark **2** : to brand (livestock) **3** : to indicate, to show **4** RESALTAR : to emphasize **5** : to dial (a telephone) **6** : to guard (an opponent) **7** ANOTAR : to score (a goal, a point) — *vi* **1** ANOTAR : to score **2** : to dial
marcha *nf* **1** : march **2** : hike, walk ⟨ir de marcha : to go hiking⟩ **3** : pace, speed ⟨a toda marcha : at top speed⟩ **4** : gear (of an automobile) ⟨marcha atrás : reverse, reverse gear⟩ **5 en ~** : in motion, in gear, under way
marchar *vi* **1** IR : to go, to travel **2** ANDAR : to walk **3** FUNCIONAR : to work, to go **4** : to march — **marcharse** *vr* : to leave
marchitar *vi* : to make wither, to wilt — **marchitarse** *vr* **1** : to wither, to shrivel up, to wilt **2** : to languish, to fade away
marchito, -ta *adj* : withered, faded
marcial *adj* : martial, military
marco *nm* **1** : frame, framework **2** : goalposts *pl* **3** AMBIENTE : setting, atmosphere **4** : mark (unit of currency)
marea *nf* : tide
mareado, -da *adj* **1** : dizzy, lightheaded **2** : queasy, nauseous **3** : seasick
marear *vt* **1** : to make sick ⟨los gases me marearon : the fumes made me sick⟩ **2** : to bother, to annoy — **marearse** *vr* **1** : to get sick, to become nauseated **2** : to feel dizzy **3** : to get tipsy
marejada *nf* **1** : surge, swell (of the sea) **2** : undercurrent, ferment, unrest
maremoto *nm* : tidal wave
mareo *nm* **1** : dizzy spell **2** : nausea **3** : seasickness, motion sickness **4** : annoyance, vexation
marfil *nm* : ivory
margarina *nf* : margarine
margarita *nf* **1** : daisy **2** : margarita (cocktail)
margen¹ *nf, pl* **márgenes** : bank (of a river), side (of a street)

margen · masajear

margen² *nm, pl* **márgenes 1** : edge, border **2** : margin ⟨margen de ganancia : profit margin⟩
marginación *nf, pl* **-ciones** : marginalization, exclusion
marginado¹, -da *adj* **1** DESHEREDADO : outcast, alienated, dispossessed **2 clases marginadas** : underclass
marginado², -da *n* : outcast, misfit
marginal *adj* : marginal, fringe
marginalidad *nf* : marginality
marginar *vt* : to ostracize, to exclude
mariachi *nm* : mariachi musician or band
maridaje *nm* : marriage, union
maridar *vt* UNIR : to marry, to unite
marido *nm* ESPOSO : husband
marihuana *or* **mariguana** *or* **marijuana** *nf* : marihuana
marimacho *nmf fam* **1** : mannish woman **2** : tomboy
marimba *nf* : marimba
marina *nf* **1** : coast, coastal area **2** : navy, fleet ⟨marina mercante : merchant marine⟩
marinada *nf* : marinade
marinar *vt* : to marinate
marinero¹, -ra *adj* **1** : seaworthy **2** : sea, marine
marinero² *nm* : sailor
marino¹, -na *adj* : marine, sea
marino² *nm* : sailor, seaman
marioneta *nf* TÍTERE : puppet, marionette
mariposa *nf* **1** : butterfly **2 mariposa nocturna** : moth
mariquita¹ *nf* : ladybug
mariquita² *nm fam* : sissy, wimp
mariscal *nm* **1** : marshal **2 mariscal de campo** : field marshal (in the military), quarterback (in football)
marisco *nm* **1** : shellfish **2 mariscos** *nmpl* : seafood
marisma *nf* : marsh, salt marsh
marital *adj* : marital, married ⟨la vida marital : married life⟩
marítimo, -ma *adj* : maritime, shipping ⟨la industria marítima : the shipping industry⟩
marmita *nf* : (cooking) pot
mármol *nm* : marble
marmóreo, -rea *adj* : marble, marmoreal
marmota *nf* **1** : marmot **2 marmota de América** : woodchuck, groundhog
maroma *nf* **1** : rope **2** : acrobatic stunt **3** *Mex* : somersault
marque, etc. → **marcar**
marqués, -quesa *n, mpl* **marqueses** : marquis *m*, marquess *m*, marquise *f*, marchioness *f*
marquesina *nf* : marquee, canopy
marqueta *nf Mex* : block (of chocolate), lump (of sugar or salt)
marranada *nf* **1** : disgusting thing **2** : dirty trick
marrano¹, -na *adj* : filthy, disgusting
marrano², -na *n* **1** CERDO : pig, hog **2** : dirty pig, slob

marrar *vt* : to miss (a target) — *vi* : to fail, to go wrong
marras *adv* **1** : long ago **2 de ~** : said, aforementioned ⟨el individuo de marras : the individual in question⟩
marrasquino *nm* : maraschino
marrón *adj & nm, pl* **marrones** CASTAÑO : brown
marroquí *adj & nmf, pl* **-quíes** : Moroccan
marsopa *nf* : porpoise
marsupial *nm* : marsupial
marta *nf* **1** : marten **2 marta cebellina** : sable (animal)
Marte *nm* : Mars
martes *nms & pl* : Tuesday
martillar *v* : to hammer
martillazo *nm* : blow with a hammer
martillo *nm* **1** : hammer **2 martillo neumático** : jackhammer
martinete *nm* **1** : heron **2** : pile driver
mártir *nmf* : martyr
martirio *nm* **1** : martyrdom **2** : ordeal, torment
martirizar {21} *vt* **1** : to martyr **2** ATORMENTAR : to torment
marxismo *nm* : Marxism
marxista *adj & nmf* : Marxist
marzo *nm* : March
mas *conj* PERO : but
más¹ *adv* **1** : more ⟨¿hay algo más grande? : is there anything bigger?⟩ **2** : most ⟨Luis es el más alto : Luis is the tallest⟩ **3** : longer ⟨el sabor dura más : the flavor lasts longer⟩ **4** : rather ⟨más querría andar : I would rather walk⟩ **5 a ~** : besides, in addition **6 más allá** : further **7 qué ... más ...** : what ..., what a ... ⟨¡qué día más bonito! : what a beautiful day!⟩
más² *adj* **1** : more ⟨dáme dos kilos más : give me two more kilos⟩ **2** : most ⟨la que ganó más dinero : the one who earned the most money⟩ **3** : else ⟨¿quién más quiere vino? : who else wants wine?⟩
más³ *n* : plus sign
más⁴ *prep* : plus ⟨tres más dos es igual a cinco : three plus two equals five⟩
más⁵ *pron* **1** : more ⟨¿tienes más? : do you have more?⟩ **2 a lo más** : at most **3 de ~** : extra, excess **4 más o menos** : more or less, approximately **5 por más que** : no matter how much ⟨por más que corras no llegarás a tiempo : no matter how fast you run you won't arrive on time⟩
masa *nf* **1** : mass, volume ⟨masa atómica : atomic mass⟩ ⟨producción en masa : mass production⟩ **2** : dough, batter **3 masas** *nfpl* : people, masses ⟨las masas populares : the common people⟩ **4 masa harina** *Mex* : corn flour (for tortillas, etc.)
masacrar *vt* : to massacre
masacre *nf* : massacre
masaje *nm* : massage
masajear *vt* : to massage

masajista *nmf* : masseur *m*, masseuse *f*
mascar {72} *v* MASTICAR : to chew
máscara *nf* **1** CARETA : mask **2** : appearance, pretense **3 máscara antigás** : gas mask
mascarada *nf* : masquerade
mascarilla *nf* **1** : mask (in medicine) ⟨mascarilla de oxígeno : oxygen mask⟩ **2** : facial mask (in cosmetology)
mascota *nf* : mascot
masculinidad *nf* : masculinity
masculino, -na *adj* **1** : masculine, male **2** : manly **3** : masculine (in grammar)
mascullar *v* : to mumble, to mutter
masificado, -da *adj* : overcrowded
masilla *nf* : putty
masivamente *adv* : en masse
masivo, -va *adj* : mass ⟨comunicación masiva : mass communication⟩
masón *nm, pl* **masones** FRANCMASÓN : Mason, Freemason
masonería *nf* FRANCMASONERÍA : Masonry, Freemasonry
masónico, -ca *adj* : Masonic
masoquismo *nm* : masochism
masoquista[1] *adj* : masochistic
masoquista[2] *nmf* : masochist
masque, etc. → **mascar**
masticar {72} *v* MASCAR : to chew, to masticate
mástil *nm* **1** : mast **2** ASTA : flagpole **3** : neck (of a stringed instrument)
mastín *nm, pl* **mastines** : mastiff
mástique *nm* : putty, filler
mastodonte *nm* : mastodon
masturbación *nf, pl* **-ciones** : masturbation
masturbarse *vr* : to masturbate
mata *nf* **1** ARBUSTO : bush, shrub **2** : plant ⟨mata de tomate : tomato plant⟩ **3** : sprig, tuft **4 mata de pelo** : mop of hair
matadero *nm* : slaughterhouse, abattoir
matado, -da *adj Mex* : strenuous, exhausting
matador *nm* TORERO : matador, bullfighter
matamoscas *nms & pl* : flyswatter
matanza *nf* MASACRE : slaughter, butchering
matar *vt* **1** : to kill **2** : to slaughter, to butcher **3** APAGAR : to extinguish, to put out (fire, light) **4** : to tone down (colors) **5** : to pass, to waste (time) **6** : to trump (in card games) — *vi* : to kill — **matarse** *vr* **1** : to be killed **2** SUICIDARSE : to commit suicide **3** *fam* : to exhaust oneself ⟨se mató tratando de terminarlo : he knocked himself out trying to finish it⟩
matasanos *nms & pl fam* : quack
matasellar *vt* : to cancel (a stamp), to postmark
matasellos *nms & pl* : postmark
matatena *nf Mex* : jacks
mate[1] *adj* : matte, dull
mate[2] *nm* **1** : maté **2 jaque mate** : checkmate ⟨darle mate a *or* darle jaque mate a : to checkmate⟩

matemática → **matemáticas**
matemáticas *nfpl* : mathematics, math
matemático[1], **-ca** *adj* : mathematical — **matemáticamente** *adv*
matemático[2], **-ca** *n* : mathematician
materia *nf* **1** : matter ⟨materia gris : gray matter⟩ **2** : material ⟨materia prima : raw material⟩ **3** : (academic) subject **4 en materia de** : on the subject of, concerning
material[1] *adj* **1** : material, physical, real **2 daños materiales** : property damage
material[2] *nm* **1** : material ⟨material de construcción : building material⟩ **2** EQUIPO : equipment, gear
materialismo *nm* : materialism
materialista[1] *adj* : materialistic
materialista[2] *nmf* **1** : materialist **2** *Mex* : truck driver
materializar {21} *vt* : to bring to fruition, to realize — **materializarse** *vr* : to materialize, to come into being
materialmente *adv* **1** : materially, physically ⟨materialmente imposible : physically impossible⟩ **2** : really, absolutely
maternal *adj* : maternal, motherly
maternidad *nf* **1** : maternity, motherhood **2** : maternity hospital, maternity ward
materno, -na *adj* : maternal
matinal *adj* MATUTINO : morning ⟨la pálida luz matinal : the pale morning light⟩
matinée *or* **matiné** *nf* : matinee
matiz *nm, pl* **matices** **1** : hue, shade **2** : nuance
matización *nf, pl* **-ciones** **1** : tinting, toning, shading **2** : clarification (of a statement)
matizar {21} *vt* **1** : to tinge, to tint (colors) **2** : to vary, to modulate (sounds) **3** : to qualify (statements)
matón *nm, pl* **matones** : thug, bully
matorral *nm* **1** : thicket **2** : scrub, scrubland
matraca *nf* **1** : rattle, noisemaker **2 dar la matraca a** : to pester, to nag
matriarca *nf* : matriarch
matriarcado *nm* : matriarchy
matrícula *nf* **1** : list, roll, register **2** INSCRIPCIÓN : registration, enrollment **3** : license plate, registration number
matriculación *nf, pl* **-ciones** : matriculation, registration
matricular *vt* **1** INSCRIBIR : to enroll, to register (a person) **2** : to register (a vehicle) — **matricularse** *vr* : to matriculate
matrimonial *adj* : marital, matrimonial ⟨la vida matrimonial : married life⟩
matrimonio *nm* **1** : marriage, matrimony **2** : married couple
matriz *nf, pl* **matrices** **1** : uterus, womb **2** : original, master copy **3** : main office, headquarters **4** : stub (of a check) **5** : matrix ⟨matriz de puntos : dot matrix⟩

matrona *nf* : matron
matronal *adj* : matronly
matutino[1], **-na** *adj* : morning ⟨la edición matutina : the morning edition⟩
matutino[2] *nm* : morning paper
maullar {8} *vi* : to meow
maullido *nm* : meow
mauritano, -na *adj & n* : Mauritanian
mausoleo *nm* : mausoleum
maxilar *nm* : jaw, jawbone
máxima *nf* : maxim
máxime *adv* ESPECIALMENTE : especially, principally
maximizar {21} *vt* : to maximize
máximo[1], **-ma** *adj* : maximum, greatest, highest
máximo[2] *nm* **1** : maximum **2 al máximo** : to the utmost **3 como ~** : at the most, at the latest
maya[1] *adj & nmf* : Mayan
maya[2] *nmf* : Maya, Mayan
mayo *nm* : May
mayonesa *nf* : mayonnaise
mayor[1] *adj* **1** (*comparative of* **grande**) : bigger, larger, greater, elder, older **2** (*superlative of* **grande**) : biggest, largest, greatest, eldest, oldest **3** : grown-up, mature **4** : main, major **5 mayor de edad** : of (legal) age **6 al por mayor** *or* **por ~** : wholesale
mayor[2] *nmf* **1** : major (in the military) **2** : adult
mayoral *nm* CAPATAZ : foreman, overseer
mayordomo *nm* : butler, majordomo
mayoreo *nm* : wholesale
mayores *nmpl* : grown-ups, elders
mayoría *nf* **1** : majority **2 en su mayoría** : on the whole
mayorista[1] *adj* ALMACENISTA : wholesale
mayorista[2] *nmf* : wholesaler
mayoritariamente *adv* : primarily, chiefly
mayoritario, -ria *adj & n* : majority ⟨un consenso mayoritario : a majority consensus⟩
mayormente *adv* : primarily, chiefly
mayúscula *nf* : capital letter
mayúsculo, -la *adj* **1** : capital, uppercase **2** : huge, terrible ⟨un problema mayúsculo : a huge problem⟩
maza *nf* **1** : mace (weapon) **2** : drumstick **3** *fam* : bore, pest
mazacote *nm* **1** : concrete **2** : lumpy mess (of food) **3** : eyesore, crude work of art
mazapán *nm, pl* **-panes** : marzipan
mazmorra *nf* CALABOZO : dungeon
mazo *nm* **1** : mallet **2** : pestle **3** MANOJO : handful, bunch
mazorca *nf* **1** CHOCLO : cob, ear of corn **2 pelar la mazorca** *Mex fam* : to smile from ear to ear
me *pron* **1** : me ⟨me vieron : they saw me⟩ **2** : to me, for me, from me ⟨dame el libro : give me the book⟩ ⟨me lo compró : he bought it for me⟩ ⟨me robaron la cartera : they stole my pocketbook⟩

3 : myself, to myself, for myself, from myself ⟨me preparé una buena comida : I cooked myself a good dinner⟩ ⟨me equivoqué : I made a mistake⟩
mecánica *nf* : mechanics
mecánico[1], **-ca** *adj* : mechanical — **mecánicamente** *adv*
mecánico[2], **-ca** *n* **1** : mechanic **2** : technician ⟨mecánico dental : dental technician⟩
mecanismo *nm* : mechanism
mecanización *nf, pl* **-ciones** : mechanization
mecanizar {21} *vt* : to mechanize
mecanografía *nf* : typing
mecanografiar {85} *vt* : to type
mecanógrafo, -fa *n* : typist
mecate *nm CA, Mex, Ven* : rope, twine, cord
mecedor *nm* : glider (seat)
mecedora *nf* : rocking chair
mecenas *nmfs & pl* : patron (of the arts), sponsor
mecenazgo *nm* PATROCINIO : sponsorship, patronage
mecer {86} *vt* **1** : to rock **2** COLUMPIAR : to push (on a swing) — **mecerse** *vr* : to rock, to swing, to sway
mecha *nf* **1** : fuse **2** : wick **3 mechas** *nfpl* : highlights (in hair)
mechero *nm* **1** : burner **2** *Spain* : lighter
mechón *nm, pl* **mechones** : lock (of hair)
medalla *nf* : medal, medallion
medallista *nmf* : medalist
medallón *nm, pl* **-llones** **1** : medallion **2** : locket
media *nf* **1** CALCETÍN : sock **2** : average, mean **3 medias** *nfpl* : stockings, hose, tights **4 a medias** : by halves, half and half, halfway ⟨ir a medias : to go halves⟩ ⟨verdad a medias : half-truth⟩
mediación *nf, pl* **-ciones** : mediation
mediado, -da *adj* **1** : half full, half empty, half over **2** : halfway through ⟨mediada la tarea : halfway through the job⟩
mediador, -dora *n* : mediator
mediados *nmpl* **a mediados de** : halfway through, in the middle of ⟨a mediados del mes : towards the middle of the month, mid-month⟩
medialuna *nf* **1** : crescent **2** : croissant, crescent roll
medianamente *adv* : fairly, moderately
medianero, -ra *adj* **1** : dividing **2** : mediating
medianía *nf* **1** : middle position **2** : mediocre person, mediocrity
mediano, -na *adj* **1** : medium, average ⟨la mediana edad : middle age⟩ **2** : mediocre
medianoche *nf* : midnight
mediante *prep* : through, by means of ⟨Dios mediante : God willing⟩
mediar *vi* **1** : to mediate **2** : to be in the middle, to be halfway through **3** : to elapse, to pass ⟨mediaron cinco años entre el inicio de la guerra y el armisti-

cio : five years passed between the start of the war and the armistice⟩ **4** : to be a consideration ⟨media el hecho de que cuesta mucho : one must take into account that it is costly⟩ **5** : to come up, to happen ⟨medió algo urgente : something pressing came up⟩

mediatizar {21} *vt* : to influence, to interfere with

medicación *nf, pl* **-ciones** : medication, treatment

medicamento *nm* : medication, medicine, drug

medicar {72} *vt* : to medicate — **medicarse** *vr* : to take medicine

medicina *nf* : medicine

medicinal *adj* **1** : medicinal **2** : medicated

medicinar *vt* : to give medication to, to dose

medición *nf, pl* **-ciones** : measuring, measurement

médico¹, -ca *adj* : medical ⟨una receta médica : a doctor's prescription⟩

médico², -ca *n* DOCTOR : doctor, physician

medida *nf* **1** : measurement, measure ⟨hecho a medida : custom-made⟩ **2** : measure, step ⟨tomar medidas : to take steps⟩ **3** : moderation, prudence ⟨sin medida : immoderately⟩ **4** : extent, degree ⟨en gran medida : to a great extent⟩

medidor *nm* : meter, gauge

medieval *adj* : medieval — **medievalista** *nmf*

medievo → **medioevo**

medio¹ *adv* **1** : half ⟨está medio dormida : she's half asleep⟩ **2** : rather, kind of ⟨está medio aburrida esta fiesta : this party is rather boring⟩

medio², -dia *adj* **1** : half ⟨una media hora : half an hour⟩ ⟨medio hermano : half brother⟩ ⟨a media luz : in the half-light⟩ ⟨son las tres y media : it's half past three, it's three-thirty⟩ **2** : midway, halfway ⟨a medio camino : halfway there⟩ **3** : middle ⟨la clase media : the middle class⟩ **4** : average ⟨la temperatura media : the average temperature⟩

medio³ *nm* **1** CENTRO : middle, center ⟨en medio de : in the middle of, amid⟩ **2** AMBIENTE : milieu, environment **3** : medium, spiritualist **4** : means *pl*, way ⟨por medio de : by means of⟩ ⟨los medios de comunicación : the media⟩ **5 medios** *nmpl* : means, resources

mediocampista *nmf* : midfielder

mediocre *adj* : mediocre, average

mediocridad *nf* : mediocrity

mediodía *nm* : noon, midday

medioevo *nm* : Middle Ages

medir {54} *vt* **1** : to measure **2** : to weigh, to consider ⟨medir los riesgos : to weigh the risks⟩ — *vi* : to measure — **medirse** *vr* : to be moderate, to exercise restraint

meditabundo, -da *adj* PENSATIVO : pensive, thoughtful

meditación *nf, pl* **-ciones** : meditation, thought

meditar *vi* : to meditate, to think ⟨meditar sobre la vida : to contemplate life⟩ — *vt* **1** : to think over, to consider **2** : to plan, to work out

meditativo, -va *adj* : pensive

mediterráneo, -nea *adj* : Mediterranean

medrar *vi* **1** PROSPERAR : to prosper, to thrive **2** AUMENTAR : to increase, to grow

medro *nm* PROSPERIDAD : prosperity, growth

medroso, -sa *adj* : fainthearted, fearful

médula *nf* **1** : marrow, pith **2 médula espinal** : spinal cord

medular *adj* : fundamental, core ⟨el punto medular : the crux of the matter⟩

medusa *nf* : jellyfish, medusa

megabyte *nm* : megabyte

megáfono *nm* : megaphone

megahercio *nm* : megahertz

megahertzio *nm* : megahertz

megatón *nm, pl* **-tones** : megaton

megavatio *nm* : megawatt

mejicano → **mexicano**

mejilla *nf* : cheek

mejillón *nm, pl* **-llones** : mussel

mejor¹ *adv* **1** : better ⟨Carla cocina mejor que Ana : Carla cooks better than Ann⟩ **2** : best ⟨ella es la que lo hace mejor : she's the one who does it best⟩ **3** : rather ⟨mejor morir que rendirme : I'd rather die than give up⟩ **4** : it's better that . . . ⟨mejor te vas : you'd better go⟩ **5 a lo mejor** : maybe, perhaps

mejor² *adj* **1** (*comparative of* **bueno**) : better ⟨a falta de algo mejor : for lack of something better⟩ **2** (*comparative of* **bien**) : better ⟨está mucho mejor : he's much better⟩ **3** (*superlative of* **bueno**) : best, the better ⟨mi mejor amigo : my best friend⟩ **4** (*superlative of* **bien**) : best, the better ⟨duermo mejor en un clima seco : I sleep best in a dry climate⟩ **5** PREFERIBLE : preferable, better **6 lo mejor** : the best thing, the best part

mejor³ *nmf* (*with definite article*) : the better (one), the best (one)

mejora *nf* : improvement

mejoramiento *nm* : improvement

mejorana *nf* : marjoram

mejorar *vt* : to improve, to make better — *vi* : to improve, to get better — **mejorarse** *vr*

mejoría *nf* : improvement, betterment

mejunje *nm* : concoction, brew

melancolía *nf* : melancholy, sadness

melancólico, -ca *adj* : melancholy, sad

melanoma *nm* : melanoma

melaza *nf* : molasses

melena *nf* **1** : mane **2** : long hair **3 melenas** *nfpl* GREÑAS : shaggy hair, mop

melenudo¹, -da *adj fam* : longhaired
melenudo², -da *n* GREÑUDO : longhair, hippie
melindres *nmpl* **1** : affectation, airs *pl* **2** : finickiness
melindroso¹, -sa *adj* **1** : affected **2** : fussy, finicky
melindroso², -sa *n* : finicky person, fussbudget
melisa *nf* : lemon balm
mella *nf* **1** : dent, nick **2 hacer mella en** : to have an effect on, to make an impression on
mellado, -da *adj* **1** : chipped, dented **2** : gap-toothed
mellar *vt* : to dent, to nick
mellizo, -za *adj & n* GEMELO : twin
melocotón *nm, pl* **-tones** : peach
melodía *nf* : melody, tune
melódico, -ca *adj* : melodic
melodioso, -sa *adj* : melodious
melodrama *nm* : melodrama
melodramático, -ca *adj* : melodramatic
melón *nm, pl* **melones** : melon, cantaloupe
meloso, -sa *adj* **1** : honeyed, sweet **2** EMPALAGOSO : cloying, saccharine
membrana *nf* **1** : membrane **2 membrana interdigital** : web, webbing (of a bird's foot) — **membranoso, -sa** *adj*
membresía *nf* : membership, members *pl*
membrete *nm* : letterhead, heading
membrillo *nm* : quince
membrudo, -da *adj* FORNIDO : muscular, well-built
memez *nf, pl* **memeces** : stupid thing
memo, -ma *adj* : silly, stupid
memorabilia *nf* : memorabilia
memorable *adj* : memorable
memorándum *or* **memorando** *nm, pl* **-dums** *or* **-dos** **1** : memorandum, memo **2** : memo book, appointment book
memoria *nf* **1** : memory ⟨de memoria : by heart⟩ ⟨hacer memoria : to try to remember⟩ ⟨traer a la memoria : to call to mind⟩ **2** RECUERDO : remembrance, memory ⟨su memoria perdurará para siempre : his memory will live forever⟩ **3** : report ⟨memoria annual : annual report⟩ **4 memorias** *nfpl* : memoirs
memorizar {21} *vt* : to memorize — **memorización** *nf*
mena *nf* : ore
menaje *nm* : household goods *pl,* furnishings *pl*
mención *nf, pl* **-ciones** : mention
mencionar *vt* : to mention, to refer to
mendaz *adj, pl* **mendaces** : mendacious, lying
mendicidad *nf* : begging
mendigar {52} *vi* : to beg — *vt* : to beg for
mendigo, -ga *n* LIMOSNERO : beggar
mendrugo *nm* : crust (of bread)

menear *vt* **1** : to shake (one's head) **2** : to sway, to wiggle (one's hips) **3** : to wag (a tail) **4** : to stir (a liquid) — **menearse** *vr* **1** : to wiggle one's hips **2** : to fidget
meneo *nm* **1** : movement **2** : shake, toss **3** : swaying, wagging, wiggling **4** : stir, stirring
menester *nm* **1** : activity, occupation, duties *pl* **2 ser menester** : to be necessary ⟨es menester que vengas : you must come⟩
mengano, -na → **fulano**
mengua *nf* **1** : decrease, decline **2** : lack, want **3** : discredit, dishonor
menguar *vt* : to diminish, to lessen — *vi* **1** : to decline, to decrease **2** : to wane — **menguante** *adj*
meningitis *nf* : meningitis
menisco *nm* : meniscus, cartilage
menjurje → **mejunje**
menopausia *nf* : menopause
menor¹ *adj* **1** (*comparative of* **pequeño**) : smaller, lesser, younger **2** (*superlative of* **pequeño**) : smallest, least, youngest **3** : minor **4 al por menor** : retail **5 ser menor de edad** : to be a minor, to be underage
menor² *nmf* : minor, juvenile
menos¹ *adv* **1** : less ⟨llueve menos en agosto : it rains less in August⟩ **2** : least ⟨el coche menos caro : the least expensive car⟩ **3 ~ de** : less than, fewer than
menos² *adj* **1** : less, fewer ⟨tengo más trabajo y menos tiempo : I have more work and less time⟩ **2** : least, fewest ⟨la clase que tiene menos estudiantes : the class that has the fewest students⟩
menos³ *prep* **1** SALVO, EXCEPTO : except **2** : minus ⟨quince menos cuatro son once : fifteen minus four is eleven⟩
menos⁴ *pron* **1** : less, fewer ⟨no deberías aceptar menos : you shouldn't accept less⟩ **2 al menos** *or* **por lo menos** : at least **3 a menos que** : unless
menoscabar *vt* **1** : to lessen, to diminish **2** : to disgrace, to discredit **3** PERJUDICAR : to harm, to damage
menoscabo *nm* **1** : lessening, diminishing **2** : disgrace, discredit **3** : harm, damage
menospreciar *vt* **1** DESPRECIAR : to scorn, to look down on **2** : to underestimate, to undervalue
menosprecio *nm* DESPRECIO : contempt, scorn
mensaje *nm* : message
mensajero, -ra *n* : messenger
menso, -sa *adj Mex fam* : foolish, stupid
menstrual *adj* : menstrual
menstruar {3} *vi* : to menstruate — **menstruación** *nf*
mensual *adj* : monthly
mensualidad *nf* **1** : monthly payment, installment **2** : monthly salary
mensualmente *adv* : every month, monthly

mensurable *adj* : measurable
menta *nf* **1** : mint, peppermint **2 menta verde** : spearmint
mentado, -da *adj* **1** : aforementioned **2** FAMOSO : renowned, famous
mental *adj* : mental, intellectual — **mentalmente** *adv*
mentalidad *nf* : mentality
mentar {55} *vt* **1** : to mention, to name **2 mentar la madre a** *fam* : to insult, to swear at
mente *nf* : mind ⟨tener en mente : to have in mind⟩
mentecato¹, -ta *adj* : foolish, simple
mentecato², -ta *n* : fool, idiot
mentir {76} *vi* : to lie
mentira *nf* : lie
mentiroso¹, -sa *adj* EMBUSTERO : lying, untruthful
mentiroso², -sa *n* EMBUSTERO : liar
mentís *nm, pl* **mentises** : denial, repudiation ⟨dar el mentís a : to deny, to refute⟩
mentol *nm* : menthol
mentón *nm, pl* **mentones** BARBILLA : chin
mentor *nm* : mentor, counselor
menú *nm, pl* **menús** : menu
menudear *vi* : to occur frequently — *vt* : to do repeatedly
menudencia *nf* **1** : trifle **2 menudencias** *nfpl* : giblets
menudeo *nm* : retail, retailing
menudillos *nmpl* : giblets
menudo¹, -da *adj* **1** : minute, small **2 a ~** FRECUENTEMENTE : often, frequently
menudo² *nm* **1** *Mex* : tripe stew **2 menudos** *nmpl* : giblets
meñique *nm* or **dedo meñique** : little finger, pinkie
meollo *nm* **1** MÉDULA : marrow **2** SESO : brains *pl* **3** ENTRAÑA : essence, core ⟨el meollo del asunto : the heart of the matter⟩
mequetrefe *nm fam* : good-for-nothing
mercachifle *nm* : peddler, hawker
mercadeo *nm* : marketing
mercadería *nf* : merchandise, goods *pl*
mercado *nm* : market ⟨mercado de trabajo *or* mercado laboral : labor market⟩ ⟨mercado de valores *or* mercado bursátil : stock market⟩
mercadotecnia *nf* : marketing
mercancía *nf* : merchandise, goods *pl*
mercante *nmf* : merchant, dealer
mercantil *adj* COMERCIAL : commercial, mercantile
merced *nf* **1** : favor **2 ~ a** : thanks to, due to **3 a merced de** : at the mercy of
mercenario, -ria *adj & n* : mercenary
mercería *nf* : notions store
Mercosur *nm* : economic community consisting of Argentina, Brazil, Paraguay, and Uruguay
mercurio *nm* : mercury
Mercurio *nm* : Mercury (planet)

merecedor, -dora *adj* : deserving, worthy
merecer {53} *vt* : to deserve, to merit — *vi* : to be worthy
merecidamente *adv* : rightfully, deservedly
merecido *nm* : something merited, due ⟨recibieron su merecido : they got their just deserts⟩
merecimiento *nm* : merit, worth
merendar {55} *vi* : to have an afternoon snack — *vt* : to have as an afternoon snack
merendero *nm* **1** : lunchroom, snack bar **2** : picnic area
merengue *nm* **1** : meringue **2** : merengue (dance)
meridiano¹, -na *adj* **1** : midday **2** : crystal clear
meridiano² *nm* : meridian
meridional *adj* SUREÑO : southern
merienda *nf* : afternoon snack, tea
mérito *nm* : merit
meritorio¹, -ria *adj* : deserving, meritorious
meritorio², -ria *n* : intern, trainee
merluza *nf* : hake
merma *nf* **1** : decrease, cut **2** : waste, loss
mermar *vi* : to decrease, to diminish — *vt* : to reduce, to cut down
mermelada *nf* : marmalade, jam
mero¹, -ra *adv Mex fam* **1** : nearly, almost ⟨ya mero me caí : I almost fell⟩ **2** : just, exactly ⟨aquí mero : right here⟩
mero², -ra *adj* **1** : mere, simple **2** *Mex fam* (*used as an intensifier*) : very ⟨en el mero centro : in the very center of town⟩
mero³ *nm* : grouper
merodeador, -dora *n* **1** : marauder **2** : prowler
merodear *vi* **1** : to maraud, to pillage **2** : to prowl around, to skulk
mes *nm* : month
mesa *nf* **1** : table **2** : committee, board
mesada *nf* : allowance, pocket money
mesarse *vr* : to pull at ⟨mesarse los cabellos : to tear one's hair⟩
mesero, -ra *n* CAMARERO : waiter, waitress *f*
meseta *nf* : plateau, tableland
Mesías *nm* : Messiah
mesón *nm, pl* **mesones** : inn
mesonero, -ra *nm* : innkeeper
mestizo¹, -za *adj* **1** : of mixed ancestry **2** HÍBRIDO : hybrid
mestizo², -za *n* : person of mixed ancestry
mesura *nf* **1** MODERACIÓN : moderation, discretion **2** CORTESÍA : courtesy **3** GRAVEDAD : seriousness, dignity
mesurado, -da *adj* COMEDIDO : moderate, restrained
mesurar *vt* : to moderate, to restrain, to temper — **mesurarse** *vr* : to restrain oneself
meta *nf* : goal, objective

metabólico, -ca *adj* : metabolic
metabolismo *nm* : metabolism
metabolizar {21} *vt* : to metabolize
metafísica *nf* : metaphysics
metafísico, -ca *adj* : metaphysical
metáfora *nf* : metaphor
metafórico, -ca *adj* : metaphoric, metaphorical
metal *nm* **1** : metal **2** : brass section (in an orchestra)
metálico, -ca *adj* : metallic, metal
metalistería *nf* : metalworking
metalurgia *nf* : metallurgy
metalúrgico[1], **-ca** *adj* : metallurgical
metalúrgico[2], **-ca** *n* : metallurgist
metamorfosis *nfs & pl* : metamorphosis
metano *nm* : methane
metedura *nf* **metedura de pata** : blunder, faux pas
meteórico, -ca *adj* : meteoric
meteorito *nm* : meteorite
meteoro *nm* : meteor
meteorología *nf* : meteorology
meteorológico, -ca *adj* : meteorologic, meteorological
meteorólogo, -ga *n* : meteorologist
meter *vt* **1** : to put (in) ⟨metieron su dinero en el banco : they put their money in the bank⟩ **2** : to fit, to squeeze ⟨puedes meter dos líneas más en esa página : you can fit two more lines on that page⟩ **3** : to place (in a job) ⟨lo metieron de barrendero : they got him a job as a street sweeper⟩ **4** : to involve ⟨lo metió en un buen lío : she got him in an awful mess⟩ **5** : to make, to cause ⟨meten demasiado ruido : they make too much noise⟩ **6** : to spread (a rumor) **7** : to strike (a blow) **8** : to take up, to take in (clothing) **9 a todo meter** : at top speed — **meterse** *vr* **1** : to get into, to enter **2** *fam* : to meddle ⟨no te metas en lo que no te importa : mind your own business⟩ **3** ~ **con** *fam* : to pick a fight with, to provoke ⟨no te metas conmigo : don't mess with me⟩
metiche[1] *adj Mex fam* : nosy
metiche[2] *nmf Mex fam* : busybody
meticulosidad *nf* : thoroughness, meticulousness
meticuloso, -sa *adj* : meticulous, thorough — **meticulosamente** *adv*
metida *nf* **metida de pata** *fam* : blunder, gaffe, blooper
metódico, -ca *adj* : methodical — **metódicamente** *adv*
metodista *adj & nmf* : Methodist
método *nm* : method
metodología *nf* : methodology
metomentodo *nmf fam* : busybody
metraje *nm* : length (of a film) ⟨de largo metraje : feature-length⟩
metralla *nf* : shrapnel
metralleta *nf* : submachine gun
métrico, -ca *adj* **1** : metric **2 cinta métrica** : tape measure
metro *nm* **1** : meter **2** : subway
metrónomo *nm* : metronome

metrópoli *nf or* **metrópolis** *nfs & pl* : metropolis
metropolitano, -na *adj* : metropolitan
mexicanismo *nm* : Mexican word or expression
mexicano, -na *adj & n* : Mexican
mexicoamericano, -na *adj & n* : Mexican-American
meza, etc. → **mecer**
mezcla *nf* **1** : mixing **2** : mixture, blend **3** : mortar (masonry material)
mezclar *vt* **1** : to mix, to blend **2** : to mix up, to muddle **3** INVOLUCRAR : to involve — **mezclarse** *vr* **1** : to get mixed up (in) **2** : to mix, to mingle (socially)
mezclilla *nf Chile, Mex* : denim ⟨pantalones de mezclilla : jeans⟩
mezcolanza *nf* : jumble, hodgepodge
mezquindad *nf* **1** : meanness, stinginess **2** : petty deed, mean action
mezquino[1], **-na** *adj* **1** : mean, petty **2** : stingy **3** : paltry
mezquino[2] *nm Mex* : wart
mezquita *nf* : mosque
mezquite *nm* : mesquite
mi *adj* : my
mí *pron* **1** : me ⟨es para mí : it's for me⟩ ⟨a mí no me importa : it doesn't matter to me⟩ **2 mí mismo, mí misma** : myself
miasma *nm* : miasma
miau *nm* : meow
mica *nf* : mica
mico *nm* : monkey, long-tailed monkey
micra *nf* : micron
microbio *nm* : microbe, germ
microbiología *nf* : microbiology
microbiológico, -ca *adj* : microbiological
microbús *nm, pl* **-buses** : minibus
microcomputadora *nf* : microcomputer
microcosmos *nms & pl* : microcosm
microficha *nf* : microfiche
microfilm *nm, pl* **-films** : microfilm
micrófono *nm* : microphone
micrómetro *nm* : micrometer
microonda *nf* : microwave
microondas *nms & pl* : microwave, microwave oven
microordenador *nm Spain* : microcomputer
microorganismo *nm* : microorganism
microprocesador *nm* : microprocessor
microscópico, -ca *adj* : microscopic
microscopio *nm* : microscope
mide, etc. → **medir**
miedo *nm* **1** TEMOR : fear ⟨le tiene miedo al perro : he's scared of the dog⟩ ⟨tenían miedo de hablar : they were afraid to speak⟩ **2 dar miedo** : to frighten
miedoso, -sa *adj* TEMEROSO : fearful
miel *nf* : honey
miembro *nm* **1** : member **2** EXTREMIDAD : limb, extremity
mienta, etc. → **mentar**
miente, etc. → **mentir**

mientras[1] *adv* **1** *or* **mientras tanto** : meanwhile, in the meantime **2 mientras más** : the more ⟨mientras más como, más quiero : the more I eat, the more I want⟩

mientras[2] *conj* **1** : while, as ⟨roncaba mientras dormía : he snored while he was sleeping⟩ **2** : as long as ⟨luchará mientras pueda : he will fight as long as he is able⟩ **3 mientras que** : while, whereas ⟨él es alto mientras que ella es muy baja : he is tall, whereas she is very short⟩

miércoles *nms & pl* : Wednesday

miga *nf* **1** : crumb **2 hacer buenas (malas) migas con** : to get along well (poorly) with

migaja *nf* **1** : crumb **2 migajas** *nfpl* SOBRAS : leftovers, scraps

migración *nf, pl* **-ciones** : migration

migrante *nmf* : migrant

migraña *nf* : migraine

migratorio, -ria *adj* : migratory

mijo *nm* : millet

mil[1] *adj* : thousand

mil[2] *nm* : one thousand, a thousand

milagro *nm* : miracle ⟨de milagro : miraculously⟩

milagroso, -sa *adj* : miraculous, marvelous — **milagrosamente** *adv*

milenio *nm* : millennium

milésimo, -ma *adj* : thousandth — **milésimo** *nm*

milicia *nf* **1** : militia **2** : military service

miligramo *nm* : milligram

mililitro *nm* : milliliter

milímetro *nm* : millimeter

militancia *nf* : militancy

militante[1] *adj* : militant

militante[2] *nmf* : militant, activist

militar[1] *vi* **1** : to serve (in the military) **2** : to be active (in politics)

militar[2] *adj* : military

militar[3] *nmf* SOLDADO : soldier

militarismo *nm* : militarism

militarista *adj & nmf* : militarist

militarizar {21} *vt* : to militarize

milla *nf* : mile

millar *nm* : thousand

millón *nm, pl* **millones** : million

millonario, -ria *n* : millionaire

millonésimo[1], **-ma** *adj* : millionth

millonésimo[2] *nm* : millionth

mil millones *nms & pl* : billion

milpa *nf CA, Mex* : cornfield

milpiés *nms & pl* : millipede

mimar *vt* CONSENTIR : to pamper, to spoil

mimbre *nm* : wicker

mimeógrafo *nm* : mimeograph

mímica *nf* **1** : mime, sign language **2** IMITACIÓN : mimicry

mimo *nm* **1** : pampering, indulgence ⟨hacerle mimos a alguien : to pamper someone⟩ **2** : mime

mimoso, -sa *adj* **1** : fussy, finicky **2** : affectionate, clinging

mina *nf* **1** : mine **2** : lead (for pencils)

minar *vt* **1** : to mine **2** DEBILITAR : to undermine

minarete *nm* ALMINAR : minaret

mineral *adj & nm* : mineral

minería *nf* : mining

minero[1], **-ra** *adj* : mining

minero[2], **-ra** *n* : miner, mine worker

miniatura *nf* : miniature

minicomputadora *nf* : minicomputer

minifalda *nf* : miniskirt

minifundio *nm* : small farm

minimizar {21} *vt* : to minimize

mínimo[1], **-ma** *adj* **1** : minimum ⟨salario mínimo : minimum wage⟩ **2** : least, smallest **3** : very small, minute

mínimo[2] *nm* **1** : minimum, least amount **2** : modicum, small amount **3 como ~** : at least

minino, -na *n fam* : pussy, pussycat

miniserie *nf* : miniseries

ministerial *adj* : ministerial

ministerio *nm* : ministry, department

ministro, -tra *n* : minister, secretary ⟨primer ministro : prime minister⟩ ⟨Ministro de Defensa : Secretary of Defense⟩

minivan [ˌminiˈban, -ˈban] *nf, pl* **-vanes** : minivan

minoría *nf* : minority

minorista[1] *adj* : retail

minorista[2] *nmf* : retailer

minoritario, -ria *adj* : minority

mintió, etc. → **mentir**

minuciosamente *adv* **1** : minutely **2** : in great detail **3** : thoroughly, meticulously

minucioso, -sa *adj* **1** : minute **2** DETALLADO : detailed **3** : thorough, meticulous

minué *nm* : minuet

minúsculo, -la *adj* DIMINUTO : tiny, miniscule

minusvalía *nf* : disability, handicap

minusválido[1], **-da** *adj* : handicapped, disabled

minusválido[2], **-da** *n* : handicapped person

minuta *nf* **1** BORRADOR : rough draft **2** : bill, fee

minutero *nm* : minute hand

minuto *nm* : minute

mío[1], **mía** *adj* **1** : my, of mine ⟨¡Dios mío! : my God!, good heavens!⟩ ⟨una amiga mía : a friend of mine⟩ **2** : mine ⟨es mío : it's mine⟩

mío[2], **mía** *pron* (*with definite article*) : mine, my own ⟨tus zapatos son iguales a los míos : your shoes are just like mine⟩

miope *adj* : nearsighted, myopic

miopía *nf* : myopia, nearsightedness

mira *nf* **1** : sight (of a firearm or instrument) **2** : aim, objective ⟨con miras a : with the intention of, with a view to⟩ ⟨de amplias miras : broad-minded⟩ ⟨poner la mira en : to aim at, to aspire to⟩

mirada *nf* **1** : look, glance, gaze **2** EX-PRESIÓN : look, expression ⟨una mirada de sorpresa : a look of surprise⟩

mirado, -da *adj* **1** : cautious, careful **2** : considerate **3 bien mirado** : well thought of **4 mal mirado** : disliked, disapproved of

mirador *nm* : balcony, lookout, vantage point

miramiento *nm* **1** CONSIDERACIÓN : consideration, respect **2 sin miramientos** : without due consideration, carelessly

mirar *vt* **1** : to look at **2** OBSERVAR : to watch **3** REFLEXIONAR : to consider, to think over — *vi* **1** : to look **2** : to face, to overlook **3** ~ **por** : to look after, to look out for — **mirarse** *vr* **1** : to look at oneself **2** : to look at each other

mirasol *nm* GIRASOL : sunflower

miríada *nf* : myriad

mirlo *nm* : blackbird

mirra *nf* : myrrh

mirto *nm* ARRAYÁN : myrtle

misa *nf* : Mass

misantropía *nf* : misanthropy

misantrópico, -ca *adj* : misanthropic

misántropo, -pa *n* : misanthrope

miscelánea *nf* : miscellany

misceláneo, -nea *adj* : miscellaneous

miserable *adj* **1** LASTIMOSO : miserable, wretched **2** : paltry, meager **3** MEZQUINO : stingy, miserly **4** : despicable, vile

miseria *nf* **1** POBREZA : poverty **2** : misery, suffering **3** : pittance, meager amount

misericordia *nf* COMPASIÓN : mercy, compassion

misericordioso, -sa *adj* : merciful

mísero, -ra *adj* **1** : wretched, miserable **2** : stingy **3** : paltry, meager

misil *nm* : missile

misión *nf*, *pl* **misiones** : mission

misionero, -ra *adj & n* : missionary

misiva *nf* : missive, letter

mismísimo, -ma *adj* (*used as an intensifier*) : very, selfsame ⟨el mismísimo día : that very same day⟩

mismo¹ *adv* (*used as an intensifier*) : right, exactly ⟨hazlo ahora mismo : do it right now⟩ ⟨te llamará hoy mismo : he'll definitely call you today⟩

mismo², -ma *adj* **1** : same **2** (*used as an intensifier*) : very ⟨en ese mismo momento : at that very moment⟩ **3** : oneself ⟨lo hizo ella misma : she made it herself⟩ **4 por lo mismo** : for that reason

misoginia *nf* : misogyny

misógino *nm* : misogynist

misterio *nm* : mystery

misterioso, -sa *adj* : mysterious — **misteriosamente** *adv*

misticismo *nm* : mysticism

místico¹, -ca *adj* : mystic, mystical

místico², -ca *n* : mystic

mitad *nf* **1** : half ⟨mitad y mitad : half and half⟩ **2** MEDIO : middle ⟨a mitad de : halfway through⟩ ⟨por la mitad : in half⟩

mítico, -ca *adj* : mythical, mythic

mitigar {52} *vt* ALIVIAR : to mitigate, to alleviate — **mitigación** *nf*

mitin *nm*, *pl* **mítines** : (political) meeting, rally

mito *nm* LEYENDA : myth, legend

mitología *nf* : mythology

mitológico, -ca *adj* : mythological

mitosis *nfs & pl* : mitosis

mitra *nf* : miter (bishop's hat)

mixto, -ta *adj* **1** : mixed, joint **2** : coeducational

mixtura *nf* : mixture, blend

mnemónico, -ca *adj* : mnemonic

mobiliario *nm* : furniture

mocasín *nm*, *pl* **-sines** : moccasin

mocedad *nf* **1** JUVENTUD : youth **2** : youthful prank

mochila *nf* MORRAL : backpack, knapsack

moción *nf*, *pl* **-ciones** **1** MOVIMIENTO : motion, movement **2** : motion (to a court or assembly)

moco *nm* **1** : mucus **2** *fam* : snot ⟨limpiarse los mocos : to wipe one's (runny) nose⟩

mocoso, -sa *n* : kid, brat

moda *nf* **1** : fashion, style **2 a la moda** *or* **de** ~ : in style, fashionable **3 moda pasajera** : fad

modales *nmpl* : manners

modalidad *nf* **1** CLASE : kind, type **2** MANERA : way, manner

modelar *vt* : to model, to mold — **modelarse** *vr* : to model oneself after, to emulate

modelo¹ *adj* : model ⟨una casa modelo : a model home⟩

modelo² *nm* : model, example, pattern

modelo³ *nmf* : model, mannequin

módem *or* **modem** ['moðɛm] *nm* : modem

moderación *nf*, *pl* **-ciones** MESURA : moderation

moderado, -da *adj & n* : moderate — **moderadamente** *adv*

moderador, -dora *n* : moderator, chair

moderar *vt* **1** TEMPERAR : to temper, to moderate **2** : to curb, to reduce ⟨moderar gastos : to curb spending⟩ **3** PRESIDIR : to chair (a meeting) — **moderarse** *vr* **1** : to restrain oneself **2** : to diminish, to calm down

modernidad *nf* **1** : modernity, modernness **2** : modern age

modernismo *nm* : modernism

modernista¹ *adj* : modernist, modernistic

modernista² *nmf* : modernist

modernizar {21} *vt* : to modernize — **modernización** *nf*

moderno, -na *adj* : modern, up-to-date

modestia *nf* : modesty

modesto, -ta *adj* : modest — **modestamente** *adv*
modificación *nf, pl* **-ciones** : alteration
modificador[1], **-dora** *adj* : modifying, moderating
modificador[2] → **modificante**
modificante *nm* : modifier
modificar {72} *vt* ALTERAR : to modify, to alter, to adapt
modismo *nm* : idiom
modista *nmf* 1 : dressmaker 2 : fashion designer
modo *nm* 1 MANERA : way, manner, mode ⟨de un modo u otro : one way or another⟩ ⟨a mi modo de ver : to my way of thinking⟩ 2 : mood (in grammar) 3 : mode (in music) 4 **a modo de** : by way of, in the manner of, like ⟨a modo de ejemplo : by way of example⟩ 5 **de cualquier modo** : in any case, anyway 6 **de modo que** : so, in such a way that 7 **de todos modos** : in any case, anyway 8 **en cierto modo** : in a way, to a certain extent
modorra *nf* : drowsiness, lethargy
modular[1] *v* : to modulate — **modulación** *nf*
modular[2] *adj* : modular
módulo *nm* : module, unit
mofa *nf* 1 : mockery, ridicule 2 **hacer mofa de** : to make fun of, to ridicule
mofarse *vr* ~ **de** : to scoff at, to make fun of
mofeta *nf* ZORRILLO : skunk
mofle *nm CA, Mex* : muffler (of a car)
moflete *nm fam* : fat cheek
mofletudo, -da *adj fam* : fat-cheeked, chubby
mohín *nm, pl* **mohines** : grimace, face
mohino, -na *adj* : gloomy, melancholy
moho *nm* 1 : mold, mildew 2 : rust
mohoso, -sa *adj* 1 : moldy 2 : rusty
moisés *nm, pl* **moiseses** : bassinet, cradle
mojado[1], **-da** *adj* : wet
mojado[2], **-da** *n Mex fam* : illegal immigrant
mojar *vt* 1 : to wet, to moisten 2 : to dunk — **mojarse** *vr* : to get wet
mojigatería *nf* 1 : hypocrisy 2 GAZMOÑERÍA : primness, prudery
mojigato[1], **-ta** *adj* : prudish, prim — **mojigatamente** *adv*
mojigato[2], **-ta** *n* : prude, prig
mojón *nm, pl* **mojones** : boundary stone, marker
molar *nm* MUELA : molar
molcajete *nm Mex* : mortar
molde *nm* 1 : mold, form 2 **letras de molde** : printing, block lettering
moldear *vt* 1 FORMAR : to mold, to shape 2 : to cast
moldura *nf* : molding
mole[1] *nm Mex* 1 : spicy sauce made with chilies and usually chocolate 2 : meat served with mole sauce
mole[2] *nf* : mass, bulk
molécula *nf* : molecule — **molecular** *adj*

moler {47} *vt* 1 : to grind, to crush 2 CANSAR : to exhaust, to wear out
molestar *vt* 1 FASTIDIAR : to annoy, to bother 2 : to disturb, to disrupt — *vi* : to be a nuisance — **molestarse** *vr* ~ **en** : to take the trouble to
molestia *nf* 1 FASTIDIO : annoyance, bother, nuisance 2 : trouble ⟨se tomó la molestia de investigar : she took the trouble to investigate⟩ 3 MALESTAR : discomfort
molesto, -ta *adj* 1 ENOJADO : bothered, annoyed 2 FASTIDIOSO : bothersome, annoying
molestoso, -sa *adj* : bothersome, annoying
molido, -da *adj* 1 MACHACADO : ground, crushed 2 **estar molido** : to be exhausted
molienda *nf* : milling, grinding
molinero, -ra *n* : miller
molinillo *nm* : grinder, mill ⟨molinillo de café : coffee grinder⟩
molino *nm* 1 : mill 2 **molino de viento** : windmill
molla *nf* : soft fleshy part, flesh (of fruit), lean part (of meat)
molleja *nf* : gizzard
molusco *nm* : mollusk
momentáneamente *adv* : momentarily
momentáneo, -nea *adj* 1 : momentary 2 TEMPORARIO : temporary
momento *nm* 1 : moment, instant ⟨espera un momentito : wait just a moment⟩ 2 : time, period of time ⟨momentos difíciles : hard times⟩ 3 : present, moment ⟨los atletas del momento : the athletes of the moment, today's popular athletes⟩ 4 : momentum 5 **al momento** : right away, at once 6 **de** ~ : at the moment, for the moment 7 **de un momento a otro** : any time now 8 **por momentos** : at times
momia *nf* : mummy
monaguillo *nm* ACÓLITO : altar boy
monarca *nmf* : monarch
monarquía *nf* : monarchy
monárquico, -ca *n* : monarchist
monasterio *nm* : monastery
monástico, -ca *adj* : monastic
mondadientes *nms & pl* PALILLO : toothpick
mondar *vt* : to peel
mondongo *nm* ENTRAÑAS : innards *pl*, insides *pl*, guts *pl*
moneda *nf* 1 : coin 2 : money, currency
monedero *nm* : change purse
monetario, -ria *adj* : monetary, financial
mongol, -gola *adj & n* : Mongol, Mongolian
monitor[1], **-tora** *n* : instructor (in sports)
monitor[2] *nm* : monitor ⟨monitor de televisión : television monitor⟩
monitorear *vt* : to monitor
monja *nf* : nun
monje *nm* : monk
mono[1], **-na** *adj fam* : lovely, pretty, cute, darling

mono², **-na** *n* : monkey
monóculo *nm* : monocle
monogamia *nf* : monogamy
monógamo, **-ma** *adj* : monogamous
monografía *nf* : monograph
monograma *nm* : monogram
monolingüe *adj* : monolingual
monolítico, **-ca** *adj* : monolithic
monolito *nm* : monolith
monólogo *nm* : monologue
monomanía *nf* : obsession
monopatín *nm*, *pl* **-tines** 1 : scooter 2 : skateboard
monopolio *nm* : monopoly
monopolizar {21} *vt* : to monopolize — **monopolización** *nf*
monosilábico, **-ca** *adj* : monosyllabic
monosílabo *nm* : monosyllable
monoteísmo *nm* : monotheism
monoteísta¹ *adj* : monotheistic
monoteísta² *nmf* : monotheist
monotonía *nf* 1 : monotony 2 : monotone
monótono, **-na** *adj* : monotonous — **monótonamente** *adv*
monóxido *nm* : monoxide ⟨monóxido de carbono : carbon monoxide⟩
monserga *nf* : gibberish, drivel
monstruo *nm* : monster
monstruosidad *nf* : monstrosity
monstruoso, **-sa** *adj* : monstrous — **monstruosamente** *adv*
monta *nf* 1 : sum, total 2 : importance, value ⟨de poca monta : unimportant, insignificant⟩
montaje *nm* 1 : assembling, assembly 2 : montage
montante *nm* : transom, fanlight
montaña *nf* 1 MONTE : mountain 2 **montaña rusa** : roller coaster
montañero, **-ra** *n* : mountaineer, mountain climber
montañoso, **-sa** *adj* : mountainous
montar *vt* 1 : to mount 2 ESTABLECER : to set up, to establish 3 ARMAR : to assemble, to put together 4 : to edit (a film) 5 : to stage, to put on (a show) 6 : to cock (a gun) 7 **montar en bicicleta** : to get on a bicycle 8 **montar a caballo** CABALGAR : to ride horseback
monte *nm* 1 MONTAÑA : mountain, mount 2 : woodland, scrubland ⟨monte bajo : underbrush⟩ 3 : outskirts (of a town), surrounding country 4 **monte de piedad** : pawnshop
montés *adj*, *pl* **monteses** : wild (of animals or plants)
montículo *nm* 1 : mound, heap 2 : hillock, knoll
monto *nm* : amount, total
montón *nm*, *pl* **-tones** 1 : heap, pile 2 *fam* : ton, load ⟨un montón de preguntas : a ton of questions⟩ ⟨montones de gente : loads of people⟩
montura *nf* 1 : mount (horse) 2 : saddle, tack 3 : setting, mounting (of jewelry) 4 : frame (of glasses)

monumental *adj fam* 1 : tremendous, terrific 2 : massive, huge
monumento *nm* : monument
monzón *nm*, *pl* **monzones** : monsoon
moño *nm* 1 : bun (chignon) 2 LAZO : bow, knot ⟨corbata de moño : bow tie⟩
moquear *vi* : to snivel
moquillo *nm* : distemper
mora *nf* 1 : blackberry 2 : mulberry
morada *nf* RESIDENCIA : dwelling, abode
morado¹, **-da** *adj* : purple
morado² *nm* : purple
morador, **-dora** *n* : dweller, inhabitant
moral¹ *adj* : moral — **moralmente** *adv*
moral² *nf* 1 MORALIDAD : ethics, morality, morals *pl* 2 ÁNIMO : morale, spirits *pl*
moraleja *nf* : moral (of a story)
moralidad *nf* : morality
moralista¹ *adj* : moralistic
moralista² *nmf* : moralist
morar *vi* : to dwell, to reside
moratoria *nf* : moratorium
mórbido, **-da** *adj* : morbid
morboso, **-sa** *adj* : morbid — **morbosidad** *nf*
morcilla *nf* : blood sausage, blood pudding
mordacidad *nf* : bite, sharpness
mordaz *adj* : caustic, scathing
mordaza *nf* 1 : gag 2 : clamp
mordedura *nf* : bite (of an animal)
morder {47} *v* : to bite
mordida *nf* 1 : bite 2 *CA, Mex* : bribe, payoff
mordisco *nm* : bite, nibble
mordisquear *vt* : to nibble (on), to bite
morena *nf* 1 : moraine 2 : moray (eel)
moreno¹, **-na** *adj* 1 : brunette 2 : dark, dark-skinned
moreno², **-na** *n* 1 : brunette 2 : dark-skinned person
moretón *nm*, *pl* **-tones** : bruise
morfina *nf* : morphine
morfología *nf* : morphology
morgue *nf* : morgue
moribundo¹, **-da** *adj* : dying, moribund
moribundo², **-da** *n* : dying person
morillo *nm* : andiron
morir {46} *vi* 1 FALLECER : to die 2 APAGARSE : to die out, to go out
mormón, **-mona** *adj* & *n*, *pl* **mormones** : Mormon
moro¹, **-ra** *adj* : Moorish
moro², **-ra** *n* 1 : Moor 2 : Muslim
morosidad *nf* 1 : delinquency (in payment) 2 : slowness
moroso, **-sa** *adj* 1 : delinquent, in arrears ⟨cuentas morosas : delinquent accounts⟩ 2 : slow, sluggish
morral *nm* MOCHILA : backpack, knapsack
morralla *nf* 1 : small fish 2 : trash, riffraff 3 *Mex* : small change
morriña *nf* : homesickness
morro *nm* HOCICO : snout

morsa *nf* : walrus
morse *nm* : Morse code
mortaja *nf* SUDARIO : shroud
mortal[1] *adj* **1** : mortal **2** FATAL : fatal, deadly — **mortalmente** *adv*
mortal[2] *nmf* : mortal
mortalidad *nf* : mortality
mortandad *nf* **1** : loss of life, death toll **2** : carnage, slaughter
mortero *nm* : mortar (bowl, cannon, or building material)
mortífero, -ra *adj* LETAL : deadly, fatal
mortificación *nf, pl* **-ciones 1** : mortification **2** TORMENTO : anguish, torment
mortificar {72} *vt* **1** : to mortify **2** TORTURAR : to trouble, to torment — **mortificarse** *vr* : to be mortified, to feel embarrassed
mosaico *nm* : mosaic
mosca *nf* **1** : fly **2 mosca común** : housefly
moscada *adj* **nuez moscada** : nutmeg
moscovita *adj & nmf* : Muscovite
mosquearse *vr* **1** : to become suspicious **2** : to take offense
mosquete *nm* : musket
mosquetero *nm* : musketeer
mosquitero *nm* : mosquito net
mosquito *nm* ZANCUDO : mosquito
mostachón *nm, pl* **-chones** : macaroon
mostaza *nf* : mustard
mostrador *nm* : counter (in a store)
mostrar {19} *vt* **1** : to show **2** EXHIBIR : to exhibit, to display — **mostrarse** *vr* : to show oneself, to appear
mota *nf* **1** : fleck, speck **2** : defect, blemish
mote *nm* SOBRENOMBRE : nickname
moteado, -da *adj* : dotted, spotted, dappled
motel *nm* : motel
motín *nm, pl* **motines 1** : riot **2** : rebellion, mutiny
motivación *nf, pl* **-ciones** : motivation — **motivacional** *adj*
motivar *vt* **1** CAUSAR : to cause **2** IMPULSAR : to motivate
motivo *nm* **1** MÓVIL : motive **2** CAUSA : cause, reason **3** TEMA : theme, motif
moto *nf* : motorcycle, motorbike
motocicleta *nf* : motorcycle
motociclismo *nm* : motorcycling
motociclista *nmf* : motorcyclist
motor[1], **-ra** *adj* MOTRIZ : motor
motor[2] *nm* **1** : motor, engine **2** : driving force, cause
motorista *nmf* : motorist
motriz *adj, pl* **motrices** : driving
motu proprio *adv* **de motu proprio** [de 'motu'proprio] : voluntarily, of one's own accord
mousse ['mus] *nmf* : mousse
mover {47} *vt* **1** TRASLADAR : to move, to shift **2** AGITAR : to shake, to nod (the head) **3** ACCIONAR : to power, to drive **4** INDUCIR : to provoke, to cause **5** : to excite, to stir — **moverse** *vr* **1**

: to move, to move over **2** : to hurry, to get a move on **3** : to get moving, to make an effort
movible *adj* : movable
movida *nf* : move (in a game)
móvil[1] *adj* : mobile
móvil[2] *nm* **1** MOTIVO : motive **2** : mobile
movilidad *nf* : mobility
movilizar {21} *vt* : to mobilize — **movilización** *nf*
movimiento *nm* : movement, motion ⟨movimiento del cuerpo : bodily movement⟩ ⟨movimiento sindicalista : labor movement⟩
mozo[1], **-za** *adj* : young, youthful
mozo[2], **-za** *n* **1** JOVEN : young man *m*, young woman *f*, youth **2** : helper, servant **3** *Arg, Chile, Col, Peru* : waiter *m*, waitress *f*
mucamo, -ma *n* : servant, maid *f*
muchacha *nf* : maid
muchacho, -cha *n* **1** : kid, boy *m*, girl *f* **2** JOVEN : young man *m*, young woman *f*
muchedumbre *nf* MULTITUD : crowd, multitude
mucho[1] *adv* **1** : much, a lot ⟨mucho más : much more⟩ ⟨le gusta mucho : he likes it a lot⟩ **2** : long, a long time ⟨tardó mucho en venir : he was a long time getting here⟩ **3 por mucho que** : no matter how much
mucho[2], **-cha** *adj* **1** : a lot of, many, much ⟨mucha gente : a lot of people⟩ ⟨hace mucho tiempo que no lo veo : I haven't seen him in ages⟩ **2 muchas veces** : often
mucho[3], **-cha** *pron* **1** : a lot, many, much ⟨hay mucho que hacer : there is a lot to do⟩ ⟨muchas no vinieron : many didn't come⟩ **2 cuando** ~ *or* **como** ~ : at most **3 con** ~ : by far **4 ni mucho menos** : not at all, far from it
mucílago *nm* : mucilage
mucosidad *nf* : mucus
mucoso, -sa *adj* : mucous, slimy
muda *nf* **1** : change ⟨muda de ropa : change of clothes⟩ **2** : molt, molting
mudanza *nf* **1** CAMBIO : change **2** TRASLADO : move, moving
mudar *v* **1** CAMBIAR : to change **2** : to molt, to shed — **mudarse** *vr* **1** TRASLADARSE : to move (one's residence) **2** : to change (clothes)
mudo[1], **-da** *adj* **1** SILENCIOSO : silent ⟨el cine mudo : silent films⟩ **2** : mute, dumb
mudo[2], **-da** *n* : mute
mueble *nm* **1** : piece of furniture **2 muebles** *nmpl* : furniture, furnishings
mueblería *nf* : furniture store
mueca *nf* : grimace, face
muela *nf* **1** : tooth, molar ⟨dolor de muelas : toothache⟩ ⟨muela de juicio : wisdom tooth⟩ **2** : millstone **3** : whetstone
muele, etc. → moler

muelle[1] *adj* : soft, comfortable, easy
muelle[2] *nm* **1** : wharf, dock **2** RESORTE
: spring
muérdago *nm* : mistletoe
muerde, etc. → **morder**
muere, etc. → **morir**
muerte *nf* : death
muerto[1] *pp* → **morir**
muerto[2], **-ta** *adj* **1** : dead **2** : lifeless, flat,
dull **3** ~ **de** : dying of ⟨estoy muerto
de hambre : I'm dying of hunger⟩
muerto[3], **-ta** *nm* DIFUNTO : dead person,
deceased
muesca *nf* : nick, notch
muestra[1], **etc.** → **mostrar**
muestra[2] *nf* **1** : sample **2** SEÑAL : sign,
show ⟨una muestra de respeto : a show
of respect⟩ **3** EXPOSICIÓN : exhibition,
exposition **4** : pattern, model
mueve, etc. → **mover**
mugido *nm* : moo, lowing, bellow
mugir {35} *vi* : to moo, to low, to bellow
mugre *nf* SUCIEDAD : grime, filth
mugriento, -ta *adj* : filthy
muguete *nm* : lily of the valley
muja, etc. → **mugir**
mujer *nf* **1** : woman **2** ESPOSA : wife
mulato, -ta *adj & n* : mulatto
muleta *nf* : crutch
mullido, -da *adj* **1** : soft, fluffy **2**
: spongy, springy
mulo, -la *n* : mule
multa *nf* : fine
multar *vt* : to fine
multicolor *adj* : multicolored
multicultural *adj* : multicultural
multidisciplinario, -ria *adj* : multidisci-
plinary
multifacético, -ca *adj* : multifaceted
multifamiliar *adj* : multifamily
multilateral *adj* : multilateral
multimedia *nf* : multimedia
multimillonario, -ria *n* : multimillionaire
multinacional *adj* : multinational
múltiple *adj* : multiple
multiplicación *nf, pl* **-ciones** : multiplication
multiplicar {72} *v* **1** : to multiply **2** : to
increase — **multiplicarse** *vr* : to multiply, to reproduce
multiplicidad *nf* : multiplicity
múltiplo *nm* : multiple
multitud *nf* MUCHEDUMBRE : crowd,
multitude
multiuso, -sa *adj* : multipurpose
multivitamínico, -ca *adj* : multivitamin
mundano, -na *adj* : worldly, earthly
mundial *adj* : world, worldwide
mundialmente *adv* : worldwide, all over
the world

mundo *nm* **1** : world **2 todo el mundo**
: everyone, everybody
municiones *nfpl* : ammunition, munitions
municipal *adj* : municipal
municipio *nm* **1** : municipality **2** AYUN-
TAMIENTO : town council
muñeca *nf* **1** : doll **2** MANIQUÍ : mannequin **3** : wrist
muñeco *nm* **1** : doll, boy doll **2** MARI-
ONETA : puppet
muñón *nm, pl* **muñones** : stump (of an
arm or leg)
mural *adj & nm* : mural
muralista *nmf* : muralist
muralla *nf* : rampart, wall
murciélago *nm* : bat (animal)
murga *nf* : band of street musicians
murió, etc. → **morir**
murmullo *nm* **1** : murmur, murmuring
2 : rustling, rustle ⟨el murmullo de las
hojas : the rustling of the leaves⟩
murmurar *vt* **1** : to murmur, to mutter
2 : to whisper (gossip) — *vi* **1** : to murmur **2** CHISMEAR : to gossip
muro *nm* : wall
musa *nf* : muse
musaraña *nf* : shrew
muscular *adj* : muscular
musculatura *nf* : muscles *pl*, musculature
músculo *nm* : muscle
musculoso, -sa *adj* : muscular, brawny
muselina *nf* : muslin
museo *nm* : museum
musgo *nm* : moss
musgoso, -sa *adj* : mossy
música *nf* : music
musical *adj* : musical — **musicalmente**
adv
músico[1], **-ca** *adj* : musical
músico[2], **-ca** *n* : musician
musitar *vt* : to mumble, to murmur
muslo *nm* : thigh
musulmán, -mana *adj & n, mpl* **-manes**
: Muslim
mutación *nf, pl* **-ciones** : mutation
mutante *adj & nm* : mutant
mutar *v* : to mutate
mutilar *vt* : to mutilate — **mutilación** *nf*
mutis *nm* **1** : exit (in theater) **2** : silence
mutual *adj* : mutual
mutuo, -tua *adj* : mutual, reciprocal —
mutuamente *adv*
muy *adv* **1** : very, quite ⟨es muy inteligente : she's very intelligent⟩ ⟨muy
bien : very well, fine⟩ ⟨eso es muy
americano : that's typically American⟩
2 : too ⟨es muy grande para él : it's too
big for him⟩

N

n *nf* : fourteenth letter of the Spanish alphabet

nabo *nm* : turnip

nácar *nm* MADREPERLA : nacre, mother-of-pearl

nacarado, -da *adj* : pearly

nacer {48} *vi* **1** : to be born ⟨nací en Guatemala : I was born in Guatemala⟩ ⟨no nació ayer : he wasn't born yesterday⟩ **2** : to hatch **3** : to bud, to sprout **4** : to rise, to originate **5 nacer para algo** : to be born to be something **6 volver a nacer** : to have a lucky escape

nacido¹, -da *adj* **1** : born **2 recién nacido** : newborn

nacido², -da *n* **1 los nacidos** : those born (at a particular time) **2 recién nacido** : newborn baby

naciente *adj* **1** : newfound, growing **2** : rising ⟨el sol naciente : the rising sun⟩

nacimiento *nm* **1** : birth **2** : source (of a river) **3** : beginning, origin **4** BELÉN : Nativity scene, crèche

nación *nf, pl* **naciones** : nation, country, people (of a country)

nacional¹ *adj* : national

nacional² *nmf* CIUDADANO : national, citizen

nacionalidad *nf* : nationality

nacionalismo *nm* : nationalism

nacionalista¹ *adj* : nationalist, nationalistic

nacionalista² *nmf* : nationalist

nacionalización *nf, pl* **-ciones** **1** : nationalization **2** : naturalization

nacionalizar {21} *vt* **1** : to nationalize **2** : to naturalize (as a citizen) — **nacionalizarse** *vr*

naco, -ca *adj Mex* : trashy, vulgar, common

nada¹ *adv* : not at all, not in the least ⟨no estamos nada cansados : we are not at all tired⟩

nada² *nf* **1** : nothingness **2** : smidgen, bit ⟨una nada le disgusta : the slightest thing upsets him⟩

nada³ *pron* **1** : nothing ⟨no estoy haciendo nada : I'm not doing anything⟩ **2 casi nada** : next to nothing **3 de ~** : you're welcome **4 dentro de nada** : very soon, in no time **5 nada más** : nothing else, nothing more

nadador, -dora *n* : swimmer

nadar *vi* **1** : to swim **2 ~ en** : to be swimming in, to be rolling in — *vt* : to swim

nadería *nf* : small thing, trifle

nadie *pron* : nobody, no one ⟨no vi a nadie : I didn't see anyone⟩

nadir *nm* : nadir

nado *nm* **1** *Mex* : swimming **2 a ~** : swimming ⟨cruzó el río a nado : he swam across the river⟩

nafta *nf* **1** : naphtha **2** (*in various countries*) : gasoline

naftalina *nf* : naphthalene, mothballs *pl*

náhuatl¹ *adj & nmf, pl* **nahuas** : Nahuatl

náhuatl² *nm* : Nahuatl (language)

nailon → nilón

naipe *nm* : playing card

nalga *nf* **1** : buttock **2 nalgas** *nfpl* : buttocks, bottom

nalgada *nf* : smack on the bottom, spanking

namibio, -bia *adj & n* : Namibian

nana *nf* **1** : lullaby **2** *fam* : grandma **3** *CA, Col, Mex, Ven* : nanny

nanay *interj fam* : no way!, not likely!

naranja¹ *adj & nm* : orange (color)

naranja² *nf* : orange (fruit)

naranjal *nm* : orange grove

naranjo *nm* : orange tree

narcisismo *nm* : narcissism

narcisista¹ *adj* : narcissistic

narcisista² *nmf* : narcissist

narciso *nm* : narcissus, daffodil

narcótico¹, -ca *adj* : narcotic

narcótico² *nm* : narcotic

narcotizar {21} *vt* : to drug, to dope

narcotraficante *nmf* : drug trafficker

narcotráfico *nm* : drug trafficking

narigón, -gona *adj, mpl* **-gones** : big-nosed

narigudo → narigón

nariz *nf, pl* **narices** **1** : nose ⟨sonar(se) la nariz : to blow one's nose⟩ **2** : sense of smell

narración *nf, pl* **-ciones** : narration, account

narrador, -dora *n* : narrator

narrar *vt* : to narrate, to tell

narrativa *nf* : narrative, story

narrativo, -va *adj* : narrative

narval *nm* : narwhal

nasa *nf* : creel

nasal *adj* : nasal

nata *nf* **1** : cream ⟨nata batida : whipped cream⟩ **2** : skin (on boiled milk)

natación *nf, pl* **-ciones** : swimming

natal *adj* : native, natal

natalicio *nm* : birthday ⟨el natalicio de George Washington : George Washington's birthday⟩

natalidad *nf* : birthrate

natillas *nfpl* : custard

natividad *nf* : birth, nativity

nativo, -va *adj & n* : native

nato, -ta *adj* : born, natural

natural¹ *adj* **1** : natural **2** : normal ⟨como es natural : naturally, as expected⟩ **3 ~ de** : native of, from **4 de tamaño natural** : life-size

natural² *nm* **1** CARÁCTER : disposition, temperament **2** : native ⟨un natural de Venezuela : a native of Venezuela⟩

naturaleza *nf* **1** : nature ⟨la madre naturaleza : mother nature⟩ **2** ÍNDOLE : nature, disposition, constitution ⟨la naturaleza humana : human nature⟩ **3 naturaleza muerta** : still life

naturalidad *nf* : simplicity, naturalness
naturalismo *nm* : naturalism
naturalista[1] *adj* : naturalistic
naturalista[2] *nmf* : naturalist
naturalización *nf, pl* **-ciones** : naturalization
naturalizar {21} *vt* : to naturalize — **naturalizarse** *vr* NACIONALIZARSE : to become naturalized
naturalmente *adv* 1 : naturally, inherently 2 : of course
naufragar {52} *vi* 1 : to be shipwrecked 2 FRACASAR : to fail, to collapse
naufragio *nm* 1 : shipwreck 2 FRACASO : failure, collapse
náufrago[1], **-ga** *adj* : shipwrecked, castaway
náufrago[2], **-ga** *n* : shipwrecked person, castaway
náusea *nf* 1 : nausea 2 **dar náuseas** : to nauseate, to disgust 3 **náuseas matutinas** : morning sickness
nauseabundo, -da *adj* : nauseating, sickening
náutica *nf* : navigation
náutico, -ca *adj* : nautical
nautilo *nm* : nautilus
navaja *nf* 1 : pocketknife, penknife ⟨navaja de muelle : switchblade⟩ 2 **navaja de afeitar** : straight razor, razor blade
navajo, -ja *adj & n* : Navajo
naval *adj* : naval
nave *nf* 1 : ship ⟨nave capitana : flagship⟩ ⟨nave espacial : spaceship⟩ 2 : nave ⟨nave lateral : aisle⟩ 3 **quemar uno sus naves** : to burn one's bridges
navegabilidad *nf* : navigability
navegable *adj* : navigable
navegación *nf, pl* **-ciones** : navigation
navegante[1] *adj* : sailing, seafaring
navegante[2] *nmf* : navigator
navegar {52} *v* : to navigate, to sail
Navidad *nf* : Christmas, Christmastime ⟨Feliz Navidad : Merry Christmas⟩
navideño, -ña *adj* : Christmas
naviero, -ra *adj* : shipping
náyade *nf* : naiad
nazca, etc. → **nacer**
nazi *adj & nmf* : Nazi
nazismo *nm* : Nazism
nébeda *nf* : catnip
neblina *nf* : light fog, mist
neblinoso, -sa *adj* : misty, foggy
nebulosa *nf* : nebula
nebulosidad *nf* : mistiness, haziness
nebuloso, -sa *adj* 1 : hazy, misty 2 : nebulous, vague
necedad *nf* : stupidity, foolishness ⟨decir necedades : to talk nonsense⟩
necesariamente *adv* : necessarily
necesario, -ria *adj* 1 : necessary 2 **si es necesario** : if need be 3 **hacerse necesario** : to be required
neceser *nm* : toilet kit, vanity case
necesidad *nf* 1 : need, necessity 2 : poverty, want 3 **necesidades** *nfpl* : hardships 4 **hacer sus necesidades** : to relieve oneself

necesitado, -da *adj* : needy
necesitar *vt* 1 : to need 2 : to necessitate, to require — *vi* ~ **de** : to have need of
necio[1], **-cia** *adj* 1 : foolish, silly, dumb 2 *fam* : naughty
necio[2], **-cia** *n* ESTÚPIDO : fool, idiot
necrología *nf* : obituary
necrópolis *nfs & pl* : cemetery
néctar *nm* : nectar
nectarina *nf* : nectarine
neerlandés[1], **-desa** *adj, mpl* **-deses** HOLANDÉS : Dutch
neerlandés[2], **-desa** *n, mpl* **-deses** HOLANDÉS : Dutch person, Dutchman *m*
nefando, -da *adj* : unspeakable, heinous
nefario, -ria *adj* : nefarious
nefasto, -ta *adj* 1 : ill-fated, unlucky 2 : disastrous, terrible
negación *nf, pl* **-ciones** 1 : negation, denial 2 : negative (in grammar)
negar {49} *vt* 1 : to deny 2 REHUSAR : to refuse 3 : to disown — **negarse** *vr* 1 : to refuse 2 : to deny oneself
negativa *nf* 1 : denial 2 : refusal
negativo[1], **-va** *adj* : negative
negativo[2] *nm* : negative (of a photograph)
negligé *nm* : negligee
negligencia *nf* : negligence
negligente *adj* : neglectful, negligent — **negligentemente** *adv*
negociable *adj* : negotiable
negociación *nf, pl* **-ciones** 1 : negotiation 2 **negociación colectiva** : collective bargaining
negociador, -dora *n* : negotiator
negociante *nmf* : businessman *m*, businesswoman *f*
negociar *vt* : to negotiate — *vi* : to deal, to do business
negocio *nm* 1 : business, place of business 2 : deal, transaction 3 **negocios** *nmpl* : commerce, trade, business
negrero, -ra *n* 1 : slave trader 2 *fam* : slave driver, brutal boss
negrita *nf* : boldface (type)
negro[1], **-gra** *adj* 1 : black, dark 2 BRONCEADO : suntanned 3 : gloomy, awful, desperate ⟨la cosa se está poniendo negra : things are looking bad⟩ 4 **mercado negro** : black market
negro[2], **-gra** *n* 1 : dark-skinned person, black person 2 *fam* : darling, dear
negro[3] *nm* : black (color)
negrura *nf* : blackness
negruzco, -ca *adj* : blackish
nene, -na *n* : baby, small child
nenúfar *nm* : water lily
neocelandés → **neozelandés**
neoclasicismo *nm* : neoclassicism
neoclásico, -ca *adj* : neoclassical
neófito, -ta *n* : neophyte, novice
neologismo *nm* : neologism
neón *nm, pl* **neones** : neon
neoyorquino[1], **-na** *adj* : of or from New York

neoyorquino², -na *n* : New Yorker
neozelandés¹, -desa *adj, mpl* **-deses**
: of or from New Zealand
neozelandés², -desa *n, mpl* **-deses**
: New Zealander
nepalés, -lesa *adj & n, mpl* **-leses**
: Nepali
nepotismo *nm* : nepotism
neptunio *nm* : neptunium
Neptuno *nm* : Neptune
nervio *nm* **1** : nerve **2** : tendon, sinew,
gristle (in meat) **3** : energy, drive **4**
: rib (of a vault) **5 nervios** *nmpl*
: nerves ⟨estar mal de los nervios : to
be a bundle of nerves⟩ ⟨ataque de
nervios : nervous breakdown⟩
nerviosamente *adv* : nervously
nerviosidad → **nerviosismo**
nerviosismo *nf* : nervousness, anxiety
nervioso, -sa *adj* **1** : nervous, nerve ⟨sistema nervioso : nervous system⟩ **2**
: high-strung, restless, anxious ⟨ponerse nervioso : to get nervous⟩ **3** : vigorous, energetic
nervudo, -da *adj* : sinewy, wiry
neta *nf Mex fam* : truth ⟨la neta es que
me cae mal : the truth is, I don't like
her⟩
netamente *adv* : clearly, obviously
neto, -ta *adj* **1** : net ⟨peso neto : net
weight⟩ **2** : clear, distinct
neumático¹, -ca *adj* : pneumatic
neumático² *nm* LLANTA : tire
neumonía *nf* PULMONÍA : pneumonia
neural *adj* : neural
neuralgia *nf* : neuralgia
neuritis *nf* : neuritis
neurología *nf* : neurology
neurológico, -ca *adj* : neurological,
neurologic
neurólogo, -ga *n* : neurologist
neurosis *nfs & pl* : neurosis
neurótico, -ca *adj & n* : neurotic
neutral *adj* : neutral
neutralidad *nf* : neutrality
neutralizar {21} *vt* : to neutralize — **neutralización** *nf*
neutro, -tra *adj* **1** : neutral **2** : neuter
neutrón *nm, pl* **neutrones** : neutron
nevada *nf* : snowfall
nevado, -da *adj* **1** : snowcapped **2**
: snow-white
nevar {55} *v impers* : to snow
nevasca *nf* : snowstorm, blizzard
nevera *nf* REFRIGERADOR : refrigerator
nevería *nf Mex* : ice cream parlor
nevisca *nf* : light snowfall, flurry
nevoso, -sa *adj* : snowy
nexo *nm* VÍNCULO : link, connection,
nexus
ni *conj* **1** : neither, nor ⟨afuera no hace
ni frío ni calor : it's neither cold nor
hot outside⟩ **2 ni que** : not even if, not
as if ⟨ni que me pagaran : not even if
they paid me⟩ ⟨ni que fuera (yo) su
madre : it's not as if I were his mother⟩ **3 ni siquiera** : not even ⟨ni siquiera
nos llamaron : they didn't even call us⟩

nicaragüense *adj & nmf* : Nicaraguan
nicho *nm* : niche
nicotina *nf* : nicotine
nido *nm* **1** : nest **2** : hiding place, den
niebla *nf* : fog, mist
niega, niegue etc. → **negar**
nieto, -ta *n* **1** : grandson *m*, granddaughter *f* **2 nietos** *nmpl* : grandchildren
nieva, etc. → **nevar**
nieve *nf* **1** : snow **2** *Cuba, Mex, PRi*
: sherbet
nigeriano, -na *adj & n* : Nigerian
nigua *nf* : sand flea, chigger
nihilismo *nm* : nihilism
nilón *or* **nilon** *nm, pl* **nilones** : nylon
nimbo *nm* **1** : halo **2** : nimbus
nimiedad *nf* INSIGNIFICANCIA : trifle,
triviality
nimio, -mia *adj* INSIGNIFICANTE : insignificant, trivial
ninfa *nf* : nymph
ningunear *vt Mex fam* : to disrespect
ninguno¹, -na (**ningún** *before masculine
singular nouns*) *adj, mpl* **ningunos** : no,
none ⟨no es ninguna tonta : she's no
fool⟩ ⟨no debe hacerse en ningún momento : that should never be done⟩
ninguno², -na *pron* **1** : neither, none
⟨ninguno de los dos ha vuelto aún : neither one has returned yet⟩ **2** : no one,
no other ⟨te quiero más que a ninguna : I love you more than any other⟩
niña *nf* **1** PUPILA : pupil (of the eye) **2**
la niña de los ojos : the apple of one's
eye
niñada *nf* **1** : childishness **2** : trifle, silly thing
niñería → **niñada**
niñero, -ra *n* : baby-sitter, nanny
niñez *nf, pl* **niñeces** INFANCIA : childhood
niño, -ña *n* : child, boy *m*, girl *f*
niobio *nm* : niobium
nipón, -pona *adj & n, mpl* **nipones**
JAPONÉS : Japanese
níquel *nm* : nickel
nitidez *nf, pl* **-deces** CLARIDAD : clarity, vividness, sharpness
nítido, -da *adj* CLARO : clear, vivid, sharp
nitrato *nm* : nitrate
nítrico, -ca *adj* **ácido nítrico** : nitric acid
nitrito *nm* : nitrite
nitrógeno *nm* : nitrogen
nitroglicerina *nf* : nitroglycerin
nivel *nm* **1** : level, height ⟨nivel del mar
: sea level⟩ **2** : level, standard ⟨nivel
de vida : standard of living⟩
nivelar *vt* : to level (out)
nixtamal *nm Mex* : limed corn used for
tortillas
no *adv* **1** : no ⟨¿quieres ir al mercado?
no, voy más tarde : do you want to go
shopping? no, I'm going later⟩ **2** : not
⟨no hagas eso! : don't do that!⟩ ⟨creo
que no : I don't think so⟩ **3** : non- ⟨no
fumador : non-smoker⟩ **4 ¡como no!**
: of course! **5 no bien** : as soon as, no
sooner

nobelio *nm* : nobelium
noble[1] *adj* : noble — **noblemente** *adv*
noble[2] *nmf* : nobleman *m*, noblewoman *f*
nobleza *nf* **1** : nobility **2** HONRADEZ : honesty, integrity
nocaut *nm* : knockout, KO
noche *nf* **1** : night, nighttime, evening **2 buenas noches** : good evening, good night **3 de noche** *or* **por la noche** : at night **4 hacerse de noche** : to get dark
Nochebuena *nf* : Christmas Eve
nochecita *nf* : dusk
Nochevieja *nf* : New Year's Eve
noción *nf, pl* **nociones 1** CONCEPTO : notion, concept **2 nociones** *nfpl* : smattering, rudiments *pl*
nocivo, -va *adj* DAÑINO : harmful, noxious
noctámbulo, -la *n* **1** : sleepwalker **2** : night owl
nocturno[1]**, -na** *adj* : night, nocturnal
nocturno[2] *nm* : nocturne
nodriza *nf* : wet nurse
nódulo *nm* : nodule
nogal *nm* **1** : walnut tree **2** *Mex* : pecan tree **3 nogal americano** : hickory
nómada[1] *adj* : nomadic
nómada[2] *nmf* : nomad
nomás *adv* : only, just ⟨lo hice nomás porque sí : I did it just because⟩ ⟨nomás de recordarlo me enojo : I get angry just remembering it⟩ ⟨nomás faltan dos semanas para Navidad : there are only two weeks left till Christmas⟩
nombradía *nf* RENOMBRE : fame, renown
nombrado, -da *adj* : famous, well-known
nombramiento *nm* : appointment, nomination
nombrar *vt* **1** : to appoint **2** : to mention, to name
nombre *nm* **1** : name ⟨nombre de pluma : pseudonym, pen name⟩ ⟨en nombre : on behalf of⟩ ⟨sin nombre : nameless⟩ **2** : noun ⟨nombre propio : proper noun⟩ **3** : fame, renown
nomenclatura *nf* : nomenclature
nomeolvides *nmfs & pl* : forget-me-not
nómina *nf* : payroll
nominación *nf, pl* **-ciones** : nomination
nominal *adj* : nominal — **nominalmente** *adv*
nominar *vt* : to nominate
nominativo[1]**, -va** *adj* : nominative
nominativo[2] *nm* : nominative (case)
nomo *nm* : gnome
non[1] *adj* IMPAR : odd, not even
non[2] *nm* : odd number
nonagésimo[1]**, -ma** *adj* : ninetieth, ninety-
nonagésimo[2]**, -ma** *n* : ninetieth, ninety- (in a series)
nono, -na *adj* : ninth — **nono** *nm*
nopal *nm* : nopal, cactus
nopalitos *nmpl Mex* : pickled cactus leaves
noquear *vt* : to knock out, to KO

norcoreano, -na *adj & n* : North Korean
nordeste[1] *or* **noreste** *adj* **1** : northeastern **2** : northeasterly
nordeste[2] *or* **noreste** *nm* : northeast
nórdico, -ca *adj & n* **1** ESCANDINAVO : Scandinavian **2** : Norse
noreste → **nordeste**
noria *nf* **1** : waterwheel **2** : Ferris wheel
norirlandés[1]**, -desa** *adj, mpl* **-deses** : Northern Irish
norirlandés[2]**, -desa** *n, mpl* **-deses** : person from Northern Ireland
norma *nf* **1** : rule, regulation **2** : norm, standard
normal *adj* **1** : normal, usual **2** : standard **3 escuela normal** : teacher-training college
normalidad *nf* : normality, normalcy
normalización *nf, pl* **-ciones** *nf* **1** REGULARIZACIÓN : normalization **2** ESTANDARIZACIÓN : standardization
normalizar {21} *vt* **1** REGULARIZAR : to normalize **2** ESTANDARIZAR : to standardize — **normalizarse** *vr* : to return to normal
normalmente *adv* GENERALMENTE : ordinarily, generally
noroeste[1] *adj* **1** : northwestern **2** : northwesterly
noroeste[2] *nm* : northwest
norte[1] *adj* : north, northern
norte[2] *nm* **1** : north **2** : north wind **3** META : aim, objective
norteamericano, -na *adj & n* **1** : North American **2** AMERICANO, ESTADOUNIDENSE : American, native or inhabitant of the United States
norteño[1]**, -ña** *adj* : northern
norteño[2]**, -ña** *n* : Northerner
noruego[1]**, -ga** *adj & n* : Norwegian
noruego[2] *nm* : Norwegian (language)
nos *pron* **1** : us ⟨nos enviaron a la frontera : they sent us to the border⟩ **2** : ourselves ⟨nos divertimos muchísimo : we enjoyed ourselves a great deal⟩ **3** : each other, one another ⟨nos vimos desde lejos : we saw each other from far away⟩ **4** : to us, for us, from us ⟨nos lo dio : he gave it to us⟩ ⟨nos lo compraron : they bought it from us⟩
nosotros, -tras *pron* **1** : we ⟨nosotros llegamos ayer : we arrived yesterday⟩ **2** : us ⟨ven con nosotros : come with us⟩ **3 nosotros mismos** : ourselves ⟨lo arreglamos nosotros mismos : we fixed it ourselves⟩
nostalgia *nf* **1** : nostalgia, longing **2** : homesickness
nostálgico, -ca *adj* **1** : nostalgic **2** : homesick
nota *nf* **1** : note, message **2** : announcement ⟨nota de prensa : press release⟩ **3** : grade, mark (in school) **4** : characteristic, feature, touch **5** : note (in music) **6** : bill, check (in a restaurant)

notable *adj* **1** : notable, noteworthy **2** : outstanding

notación *nf, pl* **-ciones** : notation

notar *vt* **1** : to notice ⟨hacer notar algo : to point out something⟩ **2** : to tell ⟨la diferencia se nota inmediatamente : you can tell the difference right away⟩ — **notarse** *vr* **1** : to be evident, to show **2** : to feel, to seem

notario, -ria *n* : notary, notary public

noticia *nf* **1** : news item, piece of news **2 noticias** *nfpl* : news

noticiero *nm* : news program, newscast

noticioso, -sa *adj* : news ⟨agencia noticiosa : news agency⟩

notificación *nf, pl* **-ciones** : notification

notificar {72} *vt* : to notify, to inform

notoriedad *nf* **1** : knowledge, obviousness **2** : fame, notoriety

notorio, -ria *adj* **1** OBVIO : obvious, evident **2** CONOCIDO : well-known

novato¹, -ta *adj* : inexperienced, new

novato², -ta *n* : beginner, novice

novecientos¹, -tas *adj* : nine hundred

novecientos² *nms & pl* : nine hundred

novedad *nf* **1** : newness, novelty **2** : innovation

novedoso, -sa *adj* : original, novel

novel *adj* NOVATO : inexperienced, new

novela *nf* **1** : novel **2** : soap opera

novelar *vt* : to fictionalize, to make a novel out of

novelesco, -ca *adj* **1** : fictional **2** : fantastic, fabulous

novelista *nmf* : novelist

novena *nf* : novena

noveno, -na *adj* : ninth — **noveno, -na** *n*

noventa *adj & nm* : ninety

noventavo¹, -va *adj* : ninetieth

noventavo² *nm* : ninetieth (fraction)

noviazgo *nm* **1** : courtship, relationship **2** : engagement, betrothal

novicio, -cia *n* **1** : novice (in religion) **2** PRINCIPIANTE : novice, beginner

noviembre *nm* : November

novilla *nf* : heifer

novillada *nf* : bullfight featuring young bulls

novillero, -ra *n* : apprentice bullfighter

novillo *nm* : young bull

novio, -via *n* **1** : boyfriend *m*, girlfriend *f* **2** PROMETIDO : fiancé *m*, fiancée *f* **3** : bridegroom *m*, bride *f*

novocaína *nf* : novocaine

nubarrón *nm, pl* **-rrones** : storm cloud

nube *nf* **1** : cloud ⟨andar en las nubes : to have one's head in the clouds⟩ ⟨por las nubes : sky-high⟩ **2** : cloud (of dust), swarm (of insects, etc.)

nublado¹, -da *adj* **1** NUBOSO : cloudy, overcast **2** : clouded, dim

nublado² *nm* **1** : storm cloud **2** AMENAZA : menace, threat

nublar *vt* **1** : to cloud **2** OSCURECER : to obscure — **nublarse** *vr* : to get cloudy

nubosidad *nf* : cloudiness

nuboso, -sa *adj* NUBLADO : cloudy

nuca *nf* : nape, back of the neck

nuclear *adj* : nuclear

núcleo *nm* **1** : nucleus **2** : center, heart, core

nudillo *nm* : knuckle

nudismo *nm* : nudism

nudista *adj & nmf* : nudist

nudo *nm* **1** : knot ⟨nudo de rizo : square knot⟩ ⟨un nudo en la garganta : a lump in one's throat⟩ **2** : node **3** : junction, hub ⟨nudo de comunicaciones : communication center⟩ **4** : crux, heart (of a problem, etc.)

nudoso, -sa *adj* : knotty, gnarled

nuera *nf* : daughter-in-law

nuestro¹, -tra *adj* : our

nuestro², -tra *pron* (*with definite article*) : ours, our own ⟨el nuestro es más grande : ours is bigger⟩ ⟨es de los nuestros : it's one of ours⟩

nuevamente *adv* : again, anew

nuevas *nfpl* : tidings *pl*

nueve *adj & nm* : nine

nuevecito, -ta *adj* : brand-new

nuevo, -va *adj* **1** : new ⟨una casa nueva : a new house⟩ ⟨¿qué hay de nuevo? : what's new?⟩ **2 de ～** : again, once more **3 Nuevo Testamento** : New Testament

nuez *nf, pl* **nueces 1** : nut **2** : walnut **3** *Mex* : pecan **4 nuez de Adán** : Adam's apple **5 nuez moscada** : nutmeg

nulidad *nf* **1** : nullity **2** : incompetent person ⟨¡es una nulidad! : he's hopeless!⟩

nulo, -la *adj* **1** : null, null and void **2** INEPTO : useless, inept ⟨es nula para la cocina : she's hopeless at cooking⟩

numen *nm* : poetic muse, inspiration

numerable *adj* : countable

numeración *nf, pl* **-ciones 1** : numbering **2** : numbers *pl*, numerals *pl* ⟨numeración romana : Roman numerals⟩

numerador *nm* : numerator

numeral *adj* : numeral

numerar *vt* : to number

numerario, -ria *adj* : long-standing, permanent ⟨profesor numerario : tenured professor⟩

numérico, -ca *adj* : numerical — **numéricamente** *adv*

número *nm* **1** : number ⟨número impar : odd number⟩ ⟨número ordinal : ordinal number⟩ ⟨número arábico : Arabic numeral⟩ ⟨número quebrado : fraction⟩ **2** : issue (of a publication) **3 sin ～** : countless

numeroso, -sa *adj* : numerous

numismática *nf* : numismatics

nunca *adv* **1** : never, ever ⟨nunca es tarde : it's never too late⟩ ⟨no trabaja casi nunca : he hardly ever works⟩ **2 nunca más** : never again **3 nunca jamás** : never ever

nuncio *nm* : harbinger, herald

nupcial *adj* : nuptial, wedding

nupcias *nfpl* : nuptials *pl*, wedding

nutria *nf* **1** : otter **2** : nutria
nutrición *nf, pl* **-ciones** : nutrition, nourishment
nutrido, -da *adj* **1** : nourished ⟨mal nutrido : undernourished, malnourished⟩ **2** : considerable, abundant ⟨de nutrido : full of, abounding in⟩
nutriente *nm* : nutrient
nutrimento *nm* : nutriment
nutrir *vt* **1** ALIMENTAR : to feed, to nourish **2** : to foster, to provide
nutritivo, -va *adj* : nourishing, nutritious

nylon → **nilón**
ñ *nf* : fifteenth letter of the Spanish alphabet
ñame *nm* : yam
ñandú *nm* : rhea
ñapa *nf* : extra amount ⟨de ñapa : for good measure⟩
ñoñear *vi fam* : to whine
ñoño, -ña *adj fam* : whiny, fussy ⟨no seas tan ñoño : don't be such a wimp⟩
ñoquis *nmpl* : gnocchi *pl*
ñu *nm* : gnu, wildebeest

O

o¹ *nf* : sixteenth letter of the Spanish alphabet
o² *conj* (**u** *before words beginning with o-* *or ho-*) **1** : or ⟨¿vienes con nosotros o te quedas? : are you coming with us or staying?⟩ **2** : either ⟨o vienes con nosotros o te quedas : either you come with us or you stay⟩ **3 o sea** : that is to say, in other words
oasis *nms & pl* : oasis
obcecado, -da *adj* **1** : blinded ⟨obcecado por la ira : blinded by rage⟩ **2** : stubborn, obstinate
obcecar {72} *vt* : to blind (by emotions) — **obcecarse** *vr* : to become stubborn
obedecer {53} *vt* : to obey ⟨obedecer órdenes : to obey orders⟩ ⟨obedece a tus padres : obey your parents⟩ — *vi* **1** : to obey **2** ~ **a** : to respond to **3** ~ **a** : to be due to, to result from
obediencia *nf* : obedience
obediente *adj* : obedient — **obedientemente** *adv*
obelisco *nm* : obelisk
obertura *nf* : overture
obesidad *nf* : obesity
obeso, -sa *adj* : obese
óbice *nm* : obstacle, impediment
obispado *nm* DIÓCESIS : bishopric, diocese
obispo *nm* : bishop
obituario *nm* : obituary
objeción *nf, pl* **-ciones** : objection ⟨ponerle objeciones a algo : to object to something⟩
objetar *v* : to object ⟨no tengo nada que objetar : I have no objections⟩
objetividad *nf* : objectivity
objetivo¹, -va *adj* : objective — **objetivamente** *adv*
objetivo² *nm* **1** META : objective, goal, target **2** : lens
objeto *nm* **1** COSA : object, thing **2** OBJETIVO : objective, purpose ⟨con objeto de : in order to, with the aim of⟩ **3 objeto volador no identificado** : unidentified flying object
objetor, -tora *n* : objector ⟨objetor de conciencia : conscientious objector⟩
oblea *nf* **1** : wafer **2 hecho una oblea** *fam* : skinny as a rail

oblicuo, -cua *adj* : oblique — **oblicuamente** *adv*
obligación *nf, pl* **-ciones** **1** DEBER : obligation, duty **2** : bond, debenture
obligado, -da *adj* **1** : obliged **2** : obligatory, compulsory **3** : customary
obligar {52} *vt* : to force, to require, to oblige — **obligarse** *vr* : to commit oneself, to undertake (to do something)
obligatorio, -ria *adj* : mandatory, required, compulsory
obliterar *vt* : to obliterate, to destroy — **obliteración** *nf*
oblongo, -ga *adj* : oblong
obnubilación *nf, pl* **-ciones** : bewilderment, confusion
obnubilar *vt* : to daze, to bewilder
oboe¹ *nm* : oboe
oboe² *nmf* : oboist
obra *nf* **1** : work ⟨obra de arte : work of art⟩ ⟨obra de teatro : play⟩ ⟨obra de consulta : reference work⟩ **2** : deed ⟨una buena obra : a good deed⟩ **3** : construction work **4 obra maestra** : masterpiece **5 obras públicas** : public works **6 por obra de** : thanks to, because of
obrar *vt* : to work, to produce ⟨obrar milagros : to work miracles⟩ — *vi* **1** : to act, to behave ⟨obrar con cautela : to act with caution⟩ **2 obrar en poder de** : to be in possession of
obrero¹, -ra *adj* : working ⟨la clase obrera : the working class⟩
obrero², -ra *n* : worker, laborer
obscenidad *nf* : obscenity
obsceno, -na *adj* : obscene
obscurecer, obscuridad, obscuro → **oscurecer, oscuridad, oscuro**
obsequiar *vt* REGALAR : to give, to present ⟨lo obsequiaron con una placa : they presented him with a plaque⟩
obsequio *nm* REGALO : gift, present
obsequiosidad *nf* : attentiveness, deference
obsequioso, -sa *adj* : obliging, attentive
observable *adj* : observable
observación *nf, pl* **-ciones** **1** : observation, watching **2** : remark, comment
observador¹, -dora *adj* : observant

observador², -dora *n* : observer, watcher
observancia *nf* : observance
observante *adj* : observant ⟨los judíos observantes : observant Jews⟩
observar *vt* **1** : to observe, to watch ⟨estábamos observando a los niños : we were watching the children⟩ **2** NOTAR : to notice **3** ACATAR : to obey, to abide by **4** COMENTAR : to remark, to comment
observatorio *nm* : observatory
obsesión *nf, pl* **-siones** : obsession
obsesionar *vt* : to obsess, to preoccupy excessively — **obsesionarse** *vr*
obsesivo, -va *adj* : obsessive
obseso, -sa *adj* : obsessed
obsolescencia *nf* DESUSO : obsolescence — **obsolescente** *adj*
obsoleto, -ta *adj* DESUSADO : obsolete
obstaculizar {21} *vt* IMPEDIR : to obstruct, to hinder
obstáculo *nm* IMPEDIMENTO : obstacle
obstante¹ *conj* **no obstante** : nevertheless, however
obstante² *prep* **no obstante** : in spite of, despite ⟨mantuvo su inocencia no obstante la evidencia : he maintained his innocence in spite of the evidence⟩
obstar *v impers* ~ **a** *or* ~ **para** : to hinder, to prevent ⟨eso no obsta para que me vaya : that doesn't prevent me from leaving⟩
obstetra *nmf* TOCÓLOGO : obstetrician
obstetricia *nf* : obstetrics
obstétrico, -ca *adj* : obstetric, obstetrical
obstinación *nf, pl* **-ciones 1** TERQUEDAD : obstinacy, stubbornness **2** : perseverance, tenacity
obstinado, -da *adj* **1** TERCO : obstinate, stubborn **2** : persistent — **obstinadamente** *adv*
obstinarse *vr* EMPECINARSE : to be obstinate, to be stubborn
obstrucción *nf, pl* **-ciones** : obstruction, blockage
obstruccionismo *nm* : obstructionism, filibustering
obstruccionista *adj* : obstructionist, filibustering
obstructor, -tora *adj* : obstructive
obstruir {41} *vt* BLOQUEAR : to obstruct, to block, to clog — **obstruirse** *vr*
obtención *nf* : obtaining, procurement
obtener {80} *vt* : to obtain, to secure, to get — **obtenible** *adj*
obturador *nm* : shutter (of a camera)
obtuso, -sa *adj* : obtuse
obtuvo, etc. → **obtener**
obús *nm, pl* **obuses 1** : mortar (weapon) **2** : mortar shell
obviar *vt* : to get around (a difficulty), to avoid
obvio, -via *adj* : obvious — **obviamente** *adv*
oca *nf* : goose

ocasión *nf, pl* **-siones 1** : occasion, time **2** : opportunity, chance **3** : bargain **4 de** ~ : secondhand **5 aviso de ocasión** *Mex* : classified ad
ocasional *adj* **1** : occasional **2** : chance, fortuitous
ocasionalmente *adv* **1** : occasionally **2** : by chance
ocasionar *vt* CAUSAR : to cause, to occasion
ocaso *nm* **1** ANOCHECER : sunset, sundown **2** DECADENCIA : decline, fall
occidental *adj* : western, occidental
occidente *nm* **1** OESTE, PONIENTE : west **2 el Occidente** : the West
oceánico, -ca *adj* : oceanic
océano *nm* : ocean
oceanografía *nf* : oceanography
oceanográfico, -ca *adj* : oceanographic
ocelote *nm* : ocelot
ochenta *adj & nm* : eighty
ochentavo¹, -va *adj* : eightieth
ochentavo² *nm* : eightieth (fraction)
ocho *adj & nm* : eight
ochocientos¹, -tas *adj* : eight hundred
ochocientos² *ms & pl* : eight hundred
ocio *nm* **1** : free time, leisure **2** : idleness
ociosidad *nf* : idleness, inactivity
ocioso, -sa *adj* **1** INACTIVO : idle, inactive **2** INÚTIL : pointless, useless
ocre *nm* : ocher
octágono *nm* : octagon — **octagonal** *adj*
octava *nf* : octave
octavo, -va *adj* : eighth — **octavo, -va** *n*
octeto *nm* **1** : octet **2** : byte
octogésimo¹, -ma *adj* : eightieth, eighty-
octogésimo², -ma *n* : eightieth, eighty- (in a series)
octubre *nm* : October
ocular *adj* **1** : ocular, eye ⟨músculos oculares : eye muscles⟩ **2 testigo ocular** : eyewitness
oculista *nmf* : oculist, ophthalmologist
ocultación *nf, pl* **-ciones** : concealment
ocultar *vt* ESCONDER : to conceal, to hide — **ocultarse** *vr*
oculto, -ta *adj* **1** ESCONDIDO : hidden, concealed **2** : occult
ocupación *nf, pl* **-ciones 1** : occupation, activity **2** : occupancy **3** EMPLEO : employment, job
ocupacional *adj* : occupational, job-related
ocupado, -da *adj* **1** : busy **2** : taken ⟨este asiento está ocupado : this seat is taken⟩ **3** : occupied ⟨territorios ocupados : occupied territories⟩ **4 señal de ocupado** : busy signal
ocupante *nmf* : occupant
ocupar *vt* **1** : to occupy, to take possession of **2** : to hold (a position) **3** : to employ, to keep busy **4** : to fill (space, time) **5** : to inhabit (a dwelling) **6** : to bother, to concern — **ocuparse** *vr* ~ **de 1** : to be concerned with **2** : to take care of

ocurrencia *nf* **1** : occurrence, event **2** : witticism **3** : bright idea
ocurrente *adj* **1** : witty **2** : clever, sharp
ocurrir *vi* : to occur, to happen — **ocurrirse** *vr* ~ **a** : to occur to, to strike ⟨se me ocurrió una mejor idea : a better idea occurred to me⟩
oda *nf* : ode
odiar *vt* ABOMINAR, ABORRECER : to hate
odio *nm* : hate, hatred
odioso, -sa *adj* ABOMINABLE, ABORRECIBLE : hateful, detestable
odisea *nf* : odyssey
odontología *nf* : dentistry, dental surgery
odontólogo, -ga *n* : dentist, dental surgeon
oeste¹ *adj* **1** : west, western ⟨la región oeste : the western region⟩ **2** : westerly
oeste² *nm* **1** : west, West **2** : west wind
ofender *vt* AGRAVIAR : to offend, to insult — *vi* : to offend, to be insulting — **ofenderse** *vr* : to take offense
ofensa *nf* : offense, insult
ofensiva *nf* : offensive ⟨pasar a la ofensiva : to go on the offensive⟩
ofensivo, -va *adj* : offensive, insulting
ofensor, -sora *n* : offender
oferente *nmf* **1** : supplier **2** FUENTE : source ⟨un oferente no identificado : an unidentified source⟩
oferta *nf* **1** : offer **2** : sale, bargain ⟨las camisas están en oferta : the shirts are on sale⟩ **3 oferta y demanda** : supply and demand
ofertar *vt* OFRECER : to offer
oficial¹ *adj* : official — **oficialmente** *adv*
oficial² *nmf* **1** : officer, police officer, commissioned officer (in the military) **2** : skilled worker
oficializar {21} *vt* : to make official
oficiante *nmf* : celebrant
oficiar *vt* **1** : to inform officially **2** : to officiate at, to celebrate (Mass) — *vi* ~ **de** : to act as
oficina *nf* : office
oficinista *nmf* : office worker
oficio *nm* **1** : trade, profession ⟨es electricista de oficio : he's an electrician by trade⟩ **2** : function, role **3** : official communication **4** : experience ⟨tener oficio : to be experienced⟩ **5** : religious ceremony
oficioso, -sa *adj* **1** EXTRAOFICIAL : unofficial **2** : officious — **oficiosamente** *adv*
ofrecer {53} *vt* **1** : to offer **2** : to provide, to give **3** : to present (an appearance, etc.) — **ofrecerse** *vr* **1** : to offer oneself, to volunteer **2** : to open up, to present itself
ofrecimiento *nm* : offer, offering
ofrenda *nf* : offering
oftalmología *nf* : ophthalmology
oftalmólogo, -ga *n* : ophthalmologist
ofuscación *nf*, *pl* **-ciones** : blindness, confusion

ofuscar {72} *vt* **1** : to blind, to dazzle **2** CONFUNDIR : to bewilder, to confuse — **ofuscarse** *vr* ~ **con** : to be blinded by
ogro *nm* : ogre
ohm *nm*, *pl* **ohms** : ohm
ohmio → **ohm**
oídas *nfpl* **de** ~ : by hearsay
oído *nm* **1** : ear ⟨oído interno : inner ear⟩ **2** : hearing ⟨duro de oído : hard of hearing⟩ **3 tocar de oído** : to play by ear
oiga, etc. → **oír**
oír {50} *vi* : to hear — *vt* **1** : to hear **2** ESCUCHAR : to listen to **3** : to pay attention to, to heed **4 ¡oye!** *or* **¡oiga!** : listen!, excuse me!, look here!
ojal *nm* : buttonhole
ojalá *interj* **1** : I hope so!, if only!, God willing! **2** : I hope, I wish, hopefully ⟨¡ojalá que le vaya bien! : I hope things go well for her!⟩ ⟨¡ojalá no llueva! : hopefully it won't rain!⟩
ojeada *nf* : glimpse, glance ⟨echar una ojeada : to have a quick look⟩
ojear *vt* : to eye, to have a look at
ojete *nm* : eyelet
ojiva *nf* : warhead
ojo *nm* **1** : eye **2** : judgment, sharpness ⟨tener buen ojo para : to be a good judge of, to have a good eye for⟩ **3** : hole (in cheese), eye (in a needle), center (of a storm) **4** : span (of a bridge) **5 a ojos vistas** : openly, publicly **6 andar con ojo** : to be careful **7 ojo de agua** *Mex* : spring, source **8 ¡ojo!** : look out!, pay attention!
ola *nf* **1** : wave **2 ola de calor** : heat wave
oleada *nf* : swell, wave ⟨una oleada de protestas : a wave of protests⟩
oleaje *nm* : waves *pl*, surf
óleo *nm* **1** : oil **2** : oil painting
oleoducto *nm* : oil pipeline
oleoso, -sa *adj* : oily
oler {51} *vt* **1** : to smell **2** INQUIRIR : to pry into, to investigate **3** AVERIGUAR : to smell out, to uncover — *vi* **1** : to smell ⟨huele mal : it smells bad⟩ **2** ~ **a** : to smell like, to smell of ⟨huele a pino : it smells like pine⟩ — **olerse** *vr* : to have a hunch, to suspect
olfatear *vt* **1** : to sniff **2** : to sense, to sniff out
olfativo, -va *adj* : olfactory
olfato *nm* **1** : sense of smell **2** : nose, instinct
oligarquía *nf* : oligarchy
olimpiada *or* **olimpíada** *nf* **1** : Olympiad **2** *or* **olympiadas** *nfpl* : Olympics *pl*
olímpico, -ca *adj* : Olympic
olisquear *vt* : to sniff at
oliva *nf* ACEITUNA : olive ⟨aceite de oliva : olive oil⟩
olivo *nm* : olive tree
olla *nf* **1** : pot ⟨olla de presión : pressure cooker⟩ **2 olla podrida** : Spanish stew

olmeca *adj & nmf* : Olmec
olmo *nm* : elm
olor *nm* : smell, odor
oloroso, -sa *adj* : scented, fragrant
olote *nm Mex* : cob, corncob
olvidadizo, -za *adj* : forgetful, absent-minded
olvidar *vt* **1** : to forget, to forget about ⟨olvida lo que pasó : forget about what happened⟩ **2** : to leave behind ⟨olvidé mi chequera en la casa : I left my checkbook at home⟩ — **olvidarse** *vr* : to forget ⟨se me olvidó mi cuaderno : I forgot my notebook⟩ ⟨se le olvidó llamarme : he forgot to call me⟩
olvido *nm* **1** : forgetfulness **2** : oblivion **3** DESCUIDO : oversight
omaní *adj & nmf* : Omani
ombligo *nm* : navel, belly button
ombudsman *nmfs & pl* : ombudsman
omelette *nmf* : omelet
ominoso, -sa *adj* : ominous — **ominosamente** *adv*
omisión *nf, pl* **-siones** : omission, neglect
omiso, -sa *adj* **1** NEGLIGENTE : neglectful **2 hacer caso omiso de** : to ignore
omitir *vt* **1** : to omit, to leave out **2** : to fail to ⟨omitió dar su nombre : he failed to give his name⟩
ómnibus *n, pl* **-bus** *or* **-buses** : bus, coach
omnipotencia *nf* : omnipotence
omnipotente *adj* TODOPODEROSO : omnipotent, almighty
omnipresencia *nf* : ubiquity, omnipresence
omnipresente *adj* : ubiquitous, omnipresent
omnisciente *adj* : omniscient — **omnisciencia** *nf*
omnívoro, -ra *adj* : omnivorous
omóplato *or* **omoplato** *nm* : shoulder blade
once *adj & nm* : eleven
onceavo¹, -va *adj* : eleventh
onceavo² *nm* : eleventh (fraction)
onda *nf* **1** : wave, ripple, undulation ⟨onda sonora : sound wave⟩ **2** : wave (in hair) **3** : scallop (on clothing) **4** *fam* : wavelength, understanding ⟨agarrar la onda : to get the point⟩ ⟨en la onda : on the ball, with it⟩ **5** ¿**qué onda?** *fam* : what's happening?, what's up?
ondear *vi* : to ripple, to undulate, to flutter
ondulación *nf, pl* **-ciones** : undulation
ondulado, -da *adj* **1** : wavy ⟨pelo ondulado : wavy hair⟩ **2** : undulating
ondulante *adj* : undulating
ondular *vt* : to wave (hair) — *vi* : to undulate, to ripple
oneroso, -sa *adj* GRAVOSO : onerous, burdensome
ónix *nm* : onyx
onza *nf* : ounce

opacar {72} *vt* **1** : to make opaque or dull **2** : to outshine, to overshadow
opacidad *nf* **1** : opacity **2** : dullness
opaco, -ca *adj* **1** : opaque **2** : dull
ópalo *nm* : opal
opción *nf, pl* **opciones** **1** ALTERNATIVA : option, choice **2** : right, chance ⟨tener opción a : to be eligible for⟩
opcional *adj* : optional — **opcionalmente** *adv*
ópera *nf* : opera
operación *nf, pl* **-ciones** **1** : operation **2** : transaction, deal
operacional *adj* : operational
operador, -dora *n* **1** : operator **2** : cameraman, projectionist
operante *adj* : operating, working
operar *vt* **1** : to produce, to bring about **2** INTERVENIR : to operate on **3** *Mex* : to operate, to run (a machine) — *vi* **1** : to operate, to function **2** : to deal, to do business — **operarse** *vr* **1** : to come about, to take place **2** : to have an operation
operario, -ria *n* : laborer, worker
operático, -ca → **operístico**
operativo¹, -va *adj* **1** : operating ⟨capacidad operativa : operating capacity⟩ **2** : operative
operativo² *nm* : operation ⟨operativo militar : military operation⟩
opereta *nf* : operetta
operístico, -ca *adj* : operatic
opiato *nm* : opiate
opinable *adj* : arguable
opinar *vi* **1** : to think, to have an opinion **2** : to express an opinion **3 opinar bien de** : to think highly of — *vt* : to think ⟨opinamos lo mismo : we're of the same opinion, we're in agreement⟩
opinión *nf, pl* **-niones** : opinion, belief
opio *nm* : opium
oponente *nmf* : opponent
oponer {60} *vt* **1** CONTRAPONER : to oppose, to place against **2 oponer resistencia** : to resist, to put up a fight — **oponerse** *vr* ~ **a** : to object to, to be against
oporto *nm* : port (wine)
oportunamente *adv* **1** : at the right time, opportunely **2** : appropriately
oportunidad *nf* : opportunity, chance
oportunismo *nm* : opportunism
oportunista¹ *adj* : opportunistic
oportunista² *nmf* : opportunist
oportuno, -na *adj* **1** : opportune, timely **2** : suitable, appropriate
oposición *nf, pl* **-ciones** : opposition
opositor, -tora *n* ADVERSARIO : opponent
oposum *nm* ZARIGÜEYA : opossum
opresión *nf, pl* **-siones** **1** : oppression **2 opresión de pecho** : tightness in the chest
opresivo, -va *adj* : oppressive
opresor¹, -sora *adj* : oppressive
opresor², -sora *n* : oppressor

oprimir *vt* **1** : to oppress **2** : to press, to squeeze ⟨oprima el botón : push the button⟩
oprobio *nm* : opprobrium, shame
optar *vi* **1** ~ **por** : to opt for, to choose **2** ~ **a** : to aspire to, to apply for ⟨dos candidatos optan a la presidencia : two candidates are running for president⟩
optativo, -va *adj* FACULTATIVO : optional
óptica *nf* **1** : optics **2** : optician's shop **3** : viewpoint
óptico¹, -ca *adj* : optical, optic
óptico², -ca *n* : optician
optimismo *nm* : optimism
optimista¹ *adj* : optimistic
optimista² *nmf* : optimist
óptimo, -ma *adj* : optimum, optimal
optometría *nf* : optometry — **optometrista** *nmf*
opuesto¹ *pp* → **oponer**
opuesto² *adj* **1** : opposite, contrary **2** : opposed
opulencia *nf* : opulence — **opulento, -ta** *adj*
opus *nm* : opus
opuso, etc. → **oponer**
ora *conj* : now ⟨los matices eran variados, ora verdes, ora ocres : the hues were varied, now green, now ocher⟩
oración *nf, pl* **-ciones 1** DISCURSO : oration, speech **2** PLEGARIA : prayer **3** FRASE : sentence, clause
oráculo *nm* : oracle
orador, -dora *n* : speaker, orator
oral *adj* : oral — **oralmente** *adv*
órale *interj Mex fam* **1** : sure!, OK! ⟨¿los dos por cinco pesos? ¡órale! : both for five pesos? you've got a deal!⟩ **2** : come on! ⟨¡órale, vámonos! : come on, let's go!⟩
orangután *nm, pl* **-tanes** : orangutan
orar *vi* REZAR : to pray
oratoria *nf* : oratory
oratorio *nm* **1** CAPILLA : oratory, chapel **2** : oratorio
orbe *nm* **1** : orb, sphere **2** GLOBO : globe, world
órbita *nf* **1** : orbit **2** : eye socket **3** ÁMBITO : sphere, field
orbitador *nm* : space shuttle, orbiter
orbital *adj* : orbital
orbitar *v* : to orbit
orden¹ *nm, pl* **órdenes 1** : order ⟨todo está en orden : everything's in order⟩ ⟨por orden cronológico : in chronological order⟩ **2 orden del día** : agenda (at a meeting) **3 orden público** : law and order
orden² *nf, pl* **órdenes 1** : order ⟨una orden religiosa : a religious order⟩ ⟨una orden de tacos : an order of tacos⟩ **2 orden de compra** : purchase order **3 estar a la orden del día** : to be the order of the day, to be prevalent
ordenación *nf, pl* **-ciones 1** : ordination **2** : ordering, organizing
ordenadamente *adv* : in an orderly fashion, neatly

ordenado, -da *adj* : orderly, neat
ordenador *nm Spain* : computer
ordenamiento *nm* **1** : ordering, organizing **2** : code (of laws)
ordenanza¹ *nf* REGLAMENTO : ordinance, regulation
ordenanza² *nm* : orderly (in the armed forces)
ordenar *vt* **1** MANDAR : to order, to command **2** ARREGLAR : to put in order, to arrange **3** : to ordain (a priest)
ordeñar *vt* : to milk
ordeño *nm* : milking
ordinal *nm* : ordinal (number)
ordinariamente *adv* **1** : usually **2** : coarsely
ordinariez *nf* : coarseness, vulgarity
ordinario, -ria *adj* **1** : ordinary **2** : coarse, common, vulgar **3 de ~** : usually
orear *vt* : to air
orégano *nm* : oregano
oreja *nf* : ear
orfanato *nm* : orphanage
orfanatorio *nm Mex* : orphanage
orfebre *nmf* : goldsmith, silversmith
orfebrería *nf* : articles of gold or silver
orfelinato *nm* : orphanage
orgánico, -ca *adj* : organic — **orgánicamente** *adv*
organigrama *nm* : organization chart, flowchart
organismo *nm* **1** : organism **2** : agency, organization
organista *nmf* : organist
organización *nf, pl* **-ciones** : organization
organizador¹, -dora *adj* : organizing
organizador², -dora *n* : organizer
organizar {21} *vt* : to organize, to arrange — **organizarse** *vr* : to get organized
organizativo, -va *adj* : organizational
órgano *nm* : organ
orgasmo *nm* : orgasm
orgía *nf* : orgy
orgullo *nm* : pride
orgulloso, -sa *adj* : proud — **orgullosamente** *adv*
orientación *nf, pl* **-ciones 1** : orientation **2** DIRECCIÓN : direction, course **3** GUÍA : guidance, direction
oriental¹ *adj* **1** : eastern **2** : oriental **3** *Arg, Uru* : Uruguayan
oriental² *nmf* **1** : Easterner **2** : Oriental **3** *Arg, Uru* : Uruguayan
orientar *vt* **1** : to orient, to position **2** : to guide, to direct — **orientarse** *vr* **1** : to orient oneself, to get one's bearings **2** ~ **hacia** : to turn towards, to lean towards
oriente *nm* **1** : east, East **2 el Oriente** : the Orient
orífice *nmf* : goldsmith
orificio *nm* : orifice, opening
origen *nm, pl* **orígenes 1** : origin **2** : lineage, birth **3 dar origen a** : to give rise to **4 en su origen** : originally

original *adj* & *nm* : original — **originalmente** *adv*
originalidad *nf* : originality
originar *vt* : to originate, to give rise to — **originarse** *vr* : to originate, to begin
originario, -ria *adj* ~ **de** : native of
originariamente *adv* : originally
orilla *nf* 1 BORDE : border, edge 2 : bank (of a river) 3 : shore
orillar *vt* 1 : to skirt, to go around 2 : to trim, to edge (cloth) 3 : to settle, to wind up 4 *Mex* : to pull over (a vehicle)
orín *nm* 1 HERRUMBRE : rust 2 **orines** *nmpl* : urine
orina *nf* : urine
orinación *nf* : urination
orinal *nm* : urinal (vessel)
orinar *vi* : to urinate — **orinarse** *vr* : to wet oneself
oriol *nm* OROPÉNDOLA : oriole
oriundo, -da *adj* ~ **de** : native of
orla *nf* : border, edging
orlar *vt* : to edge, to trim
ornamentación *nf, pl* **-ciones** : ornamentation
ornamental *adj* : ornamental
ornamentar *vt* ADORNAR : to ornament, to adorn
ornamento *nm* : ornament, adornment
ornar *vt* : to adorn, to decorate
ornitología *nf* : ornithology
ornitólogo, -ga *n* : ornithologist
ornitorrinco *nm* : platypus
oro *nm* : gold
orondo, -da *adj* 1 : rounded, potbellied (of a container) 2 *fam* : smug, self-satisfied
oropel *nm* : glitz, glitter, tinsel
oropéndola *nf* : oriole
orquesta *nf* : orchestra — **orquestal** *adj*
orquestar *vt* : to orchestrate — **orquestación** *nf*
orquídea *nf* : orchid
ortiga *nf* : nettle
ortodoncia *nf* : orthodontics
ortodoncista *nmf* : orthodontist
ortodoxia *nf* : orthodoxy
ortodoxo, -xa *adj* : orthodox
ortografía *nf* : orthography, spelling
ortográfico, -ca *adj* : orthographic, spelling
ortopedia *nf* : orthopedics
ortopédico, -ca *adj* : orthopedic
ortopedista *nmf* : orthopedist
oruga *nf* 1 : caterpillar 2 : track (of a tank, etc.)
orzuelo *nm* : sty, stye (in the eye)
os *pron pl* (*objective form of* **vosotros**) *Spain* 1 : you, to you 2 : yourselves, to yourselves 3 : each other, to each other
osa *nf* → **oso**
osadía *nf* 1 VALOR : boldness, daring 2 AUDACIA : audacity, nerve
osado, -da *adj* 1 : bold, daring 2 : audacious, impudent — **osadamente** *adv*

osamenta *nf* : skeletal remains *pl*, bones *pl*
osar *vi* : to dare
oscilación *nf, pl* **-ciones** 1 : oscillation 2 : fluctuation 3 : vacillation, wavering
oscilar *vi* 1 BALANCEARSE : to swing, to sway, to oscillate 2 FLUCTUAR : to fluctuate 3 : to vacillate, to waver
oscuramente *adv* : obscurely
oscurecer {53} *vt* 1 : to darken 2 : to obscure, to confuse, to cloud 3 : to cloud — *v impers* : at dusk, at nightfall — *v impers* : to grow dark, to get dark — **oscurecerse** *vr* : to darken, to dim
oscuridad *nf* 1 : darkness 2 : obscurity
oscuro, -ra *adj* 1 : dark 2 : obscure 3 **a oscuras** : in the dark, in darkness
óseo, ósea *adj* : skeletal, bony
ósmosis *or* **osmosis** *nf* : osmosis
oso, osa *n* 1 : bear 2 **Osa Mayor** : Big Dipper 3 **Osa Menor** : Little Dipper 4 **oso blanco** : polar bear 5 **oso hormiguero** : anteater 6 **oso de peluche** : teddy bear
ostensible *adj* : ostensible, apparent — **ostensiblemente** *adv*
ostentación *nf, pl* **-ciones** : ostentation, display
ostentar *vt* 1 : to display, to flaunt 2 POSEER : to have, to hold ⟨ostenta el récord mundial : he holds the world record⟩
ostentoso, -sa *adj* : ostentatious, showy — **ostentosamente** *adv*
osteópata *nmf* : osteopath
osteopatía *n* : osteopathy
osteoporosis *nf* : osteoporosis
ostión *nm, pl* **ostiones** 1 *Mex* : oyster 2 *Chile* : scallop
ostra *nf* : oyster
ostracismo *nm* : ostracism
otear *vt* : to scan, to survey, to look over
otero *nm* : knoll, hillock
otomana *nf* : ottoman (mueble)
otomano, -na *adj* & *n* : Ottoman
otoñal *adj* : autumn, autumnal
otoño *nm* : autumn, fall
otorgamiento *nm* : granting, awarding
otorgar {52} *vt* 1 : to grant, to award 2 : to draw up, to frame (a legal document)
otro¹, otra *adj* 1 : other 2 : another ⟨en otro juego, ellos ganaron : in another game, they won⟩ 3 **otra vez** : again 4 **de otra manera** : otherwise 5 **otra parte** : elsewhere 6 **en otro tiempo** : once, formerly
otro², otra *pron* 1 : another one ⟨dame otro : give me another⟩ 2 : other one ⟨el uno o el otro : one or the other⟩ 3 **los otros, las otras** : the others, the rest ⟨me dio una y se quedó con las otras : he gave me one and kept the rest⟩
ovación *nf, pl* **-ciones** : ovation
ovacionar *vt* : to cheer, to applaud

oval → ovalado
ovalado, -da *adj* : oval
óvalo *nm* : oval
ovárico, -ca *adj* : ovarian
ovario *nm* : ovary
oveja *nf* 1 : sheep, ewe 2 **oveja negra**
: black sheep
overol *nm* : overalls *pl*
ovillar *vt* : to roll into a ball
ovillo *nm* 1 : ball (of yarn) 2 : tangle
ovni *or* OVNI *nm* (*objeto volador no identificado*) : UFO
ovoide *adj* : ovoid, ovoidal
ovulación *nf, pl* -ciones : ovulation
ovular *vi* : to ovulate
óvulo *nm* : ovum

oxidación *nf, pl* -ciones 1 : oxidation
2 : rusting
oxidado, -da *adj* : rusty
oxidar *vt* 1 : to cause to rust 2 : to oxidize — **oxidarse** *vr* : to rust, to become
rusty
óxido *nm* 1 HERRUMBRE, ORÍN : rust 2
: oxide
oxigenar *vt* 1 : to oxygenate 2 : to
bleach (hair)
oxígeno *nm* : oxygen
oxiuro *nm* : pinworm
oye, etc. → oír
oyente *nmf* 1 : listener 2 : auditor, auditing student
ozono *nm* : ozone

P

p *nf* : seventeenth letter of the Spanish
alphabet
pabellón *nm, pl* -llones 1 : pavilion 2
: summerhouse, lodge 3 : flag (of a vessel)
pabilo *nm* MECHA : wick
paca *nf* FARDO : bale
pacana *nf* : pecan
pacer {48} *v* : to graze, to pasture
paces → paz
pachanga *nf fam* : party, bash
paciencia *nf* : patience
paciente *adj & nmf* : patient — **pacientemente** *adv*
pacificación *nf, pl* -ciones : pacification
pacíficamente *adv* : peacefully, peaceably
pacificar {72} *vt* : to pacify, to calm —
pacificarse *vr* : to calm down, to abate
pacífico, -ca *adj* : peaceful, pacific
pacifismo *nm* : pacifism
pacifista *adj & nmf* : pacifist
pacotilla *nf* de ~ : shoddy, trashy
pactar *vt* : to agree on — *vi* : to come to
an agreement
pacto *nm* CONVENIO : pact, agreement
padecer {53} *vt* : to suffer, to endure —
vi ADOLECER ~ **de** : to suffer from
padecimiento *nm* 1 : suffering 2 : ailment, condition
padrastro *nm* 1 : stepfather 2 : hangnail
padre[1] *adj Mex fam* : fantastic, great
padre[2] *nm* 1 : father 2 **padres** *nmpl*
: parents
padrenuestro *nm* : Lord's Prayer, paternoster
padrino *nm* 1 : godfather 2 : best man
3 : sponsor, patron
padrón *nm, pl* padrones : register, roll
⟨padrón municipal : city register⟩
paella *nf* : paella
paga *nf* 1 : payment 2 : pay, wages *pl*
pagadero, -ra *adj* : payable
pagado, -da *adj* 1 : paid 2 **pagado de**
sí mismo : self-satisfied, smug
pagador, -dora *n* : payer

paganismo *nm* : paganism
pagano, -na *adj & n* : pagan
pagar {52} *vt* : to pay, to pay for, to repay — *vi* : to pay
pagaré *nm* VALE : promissory note, IOU
página *nf* : page
pago *nm* 1 : payment 2 **en pago de** : in
return for
pagoda *nf* : pagoda
pague, etc. → pagar
país *nm* 1 NACIÓN : country, nation 2
REGIÓN : region, territory
paisaje *nm* : scenery, landscape
paisano, -na *n* COMPATRIOTA : compatriot, fellow countryman
paja *nf* 1 : straw 2 *fam* : trash, tripe
pajar *nm* : hayloft, haystack
pajarera *nf* : aviary
pájaro *nm* : bird ⟨pájaro cantor : songbird⟩ ⟨pájaro bobo : penguin⟩ ⟨pájaro
carpintero : woodpecker⟩
pajita *nf* : (drinking) straw
pajote *nm* : straw, mulch
pala *nf* 1 : shovel, spade 2 : blade (of
an oar or a rotor) 3 : paddle, racket
palabra *nf* 1 VOCABLO : word 2 PROMESA : word, promise ⟨un hombre de palabra : a man of his word⟩ 3 HABLA
: speech 4 : right to speak ⟨tener la palabra : to have the floor⟩
palabrería *nf* : empty talk
palabrota *nf* : swearword
palacio *nm* 1 : palace, mansion 2 **palacio de justicia** : courthouse
paladar *nm* 1 : palate 2 GUSTO : taste
paladear *vt* SABOREAR : to savor
paladín *nm, pl* -dines : champion, defender
palanca *nf* 1 : lever, crowbar 2 *fam* : leverage, influence 3 **palanca de cambio** *or* **palanca de velocidad** : gearshift
palangana *nf* : washbowl
palanqueta *nf* : jimmy, small crowbar
palco *nm* : box (in a theater or stadium)
palear *vt* 1 : to shovel 2 : to paddle
palenque *nm* 1 ESTACADA : stockade,
palisade 2 : arena, ring

paleontología *nf* : paleontology
paleontólogo, -ga *n* : paleontologist
palestino, -na *adj & n* : Palestinian
palestra *nf* : arena ⟨salir a la palestra : to join the fray⟩
paleta *nf* **1** : palette **2** : trowel **3** : spatula **4** : blade, vane **5** : paddle **6** *CA, Mex* : lollipop, Popsicle
paletilla *nf* : shoulder blade
paliar *vt* MITIGAR : to alleviate, to palliate
paliativo¹, -va *adj* : palliative
paliativo² *nm* : palliative
palidecer {53} *vi* : to turn pale
palidez *nf, pl* **-deces** : paleness, pallor
pálido, -da *adj* : pale
palillo *nm* **1** MONDADIENTES : toothpick **2 palillos** *nmpl* : chopsticks **3 palillo de tambor** : drumstick
paliza *nf* : beating, pummeling ⟨darle una paliza a : to beat, to thrash⟩
palma *nf* **1** : palm (of the hand) **2** : palm (tree or leaf) **3 batir palmas** : to clap, to applaud **4 llevarse la palma** *fam* : to take the cake
palmada *nf* **1** : pat **2** : slap **3** : clap
palmarés *nm* : record (of achievements)
palmario, -ria *adj* MANIFIESTO : clear, manifest
palmeado, -da *adj* : webbed
palmear *vt* : to slap on the back — *vi* : to clap, to applaud
palmera *nf* : palm tree
palmo *nm* **1** : span, small amount **2 palmo a palmo** : bit by bit, inch by inch **3 dejar con un palmo de narices** : to disappoint
palmotear *vi* : to applaud
palmoteo *nm* : clapping, applause
palo *nm* **1** : stick, pole, post **2** : shaft, handle ⟨palo de escoba : broomstick⟩ **3** : mast, spar **4** : wood **5** : blow (with a stick) **6** : suit (of cards)
paloma *nf* **1** : pigeon, dove **2 paloma mensajera** : carrier pigeon
palomilla *nf* : moth
palomitas *nfpl* : popcorn
palpable *adj* : palpable, tangible
palpar *vt* : to feel, to touch
palpitación *nf, pl* **-ciones** : palpitation
palpitar *vi* : to palpitate, to throb — **palpitante** *adj*
palta *nf* : avocado
paludismo *nm* MALARIA : malaria
palurdo, -da *n* : boor, yokel, bumpkin
pampa *nf* : pampa
pampeano, -na *adj* : pampean, pampas
pampero → **pampeano**
pan *nm* **1** : bread **2** : loaf of bread **3** : cake, bar ⟨pan de jabón : bar of soap⟩ **4 pan dulce** *CA, Mex* : traditional pastry **5 pan tostado** : toast **6 ser pan comido** *fam* : to be a piece of cake, to be a cinch
pana *nf* : corduroy
panacea *nf* : panacea
panadería *nf* : bakery, bread shop
panadero, -ra *n* : baker

panal *nm* : honeycomb
panameño, -ña *adj & n* : Panamanian
pancarta *nf* : placard, sign
pancita *nf Mex* : tripe
páncreas *nms & pl* : pancreas
panda *nmf* : panda
pandeado, -da *adj* : warped
pandearse *vr* **1** : to warp **2** : to bulge, to sag
pandemonio *or* **pandemónium** *nm* : pandemonium
pandereta *nf* : tambourine
pandero *nm* : tambourine
pandilla *nf* **1** : group, clique **2** : gang
panecito *nm* : roll, bread roll
panegírico¹, -ca *adj* : eulogistic, panegyrical
panegírico² *nm* : eulogy, panegyric
panel *nm* : panel — **panelista** *nmf*
panera *nf* : bread box
panfleto *nm* : pamphlet
pánico *nm* : panic
panorama *nm* **1** VISTA : panorama, view **2** : scene, situation ⟨el panorama nacional : the national scene⟩ **3** PERSPECTIVA : outlook
panorámico, -ca *adj* : panoramic
panqueque *nm* : pancake
pantaletas *nfpl* : panties
pantalla *nf* **1** : screen, monitor **2** : lampshade **3** : fan
pantalón *nm, pl* **-lones 1** : pants *pl*, trousers *pl* **2 pantalones vaqueros** : jeans **3 pantalones de mezclilla** *Chile, Mex* : jeans **4 pantalones de montar** : jodhpurs
pantano *nm* **1** : swamp, marsh, bayou **2** : reservoir **3** : obstacle, difficulty
pantanoso, -sa *adj* **1** : marshy, swampy **2** : difficult, thorny
panteón *nm, pl* **-teones 1** CEMENTERIO : cemetery **2** : pantheon, mausoleum
pantera *nf* : panther
pantimedias *nfpl Mex* : panty hose
pantomima *nf* : pantomime
pantorrilla *nf* : calf (of the leg)
pantufla *nf* ZAPATILLA : slipper
panza *nf* BARRIGA : belly, paunch
panzón, -zona *adj, mpl* **panzones** : potbellied, paunchy
pañal *nm* : diaper
pañería *nf* **1** : cloth, material **2** : fabric store
pañito *nm* : doily
paño *nm* **1** : cloth **2** : rag, dust cloth **3 paño de cocina** : dishcloth **4 paño higiénico** : sanitary napkin
pañuelo *nm* **1** : handkerchief **2** : scarf
papa¹ *nm* : pope
papa² *nf* **1** : potato **2 papa dulce** : sweet potato **3 papas fritas** : potato chips, french fries **4 papas a la francesa** *Mex* : french fries
papá *nm fam* **1** : dad, pop **2 papás** *nmpl* : parents, folks
papada *nf* **1** : double chin, jowl **2** : dewlap
papagayo *nm* LORO : parrot

papal *adj* : papal
papalote *nm Mex* : kite
papaya *nf* : papaya
papel *nm* **1** : paper, piece of paper **2** : role, part **3 papel de estaño** : tinfoil **4 papel de empapelar** *or* **papel pintado** : wallpaper **5 papel higiénico** : toilet paper **6 papel de lija** : sandpaper
papeleo *nm* : paperwork, red tape
papelera *nf* : wastebasket
papelería *nf* : stationery store
papelero, -ra *adj* : paper
papeleta *nf* **1** : ballot **2** : ticket, slip
paperas *nfpl* : mumps
papi *nm fam* : daddy, papa
papilla *nf* **1** : pap, mash **2 hacer papilla** : to beat to a pulp
papiro *nm* : papyrus
paquete *nm* BULTO : package, parcel
paquistaní *adj & nmf* : Pakistani
par[1] *adj* : even (in number)
par[2] *nm* **1** : pair, couple **2** : equal, peer ⟨sin par : matchless, peerless⟩ **3** : par (in golf) **4** : rafter **5 de par en par** : wide open
par[3] *nf* **1** : par ⟨por encima de la par : above par⟩ **2 a la par que** : at the same time as, as well as ⟨interesante a la par que instructivo : both interesting and informative⟩
para *prep* **1** : for ⟨para ti : for you⟩ ⟨alta para su edad : tall for her age⟩ ⟨una cita para el lunes : an appointment for Monday⟩ **2** : to, towards ⟨para la derecha : to the right⟩ ⟨van para el río : they're heading towards the river⟩ **3** : to, in order to ⟨lo hace para molestarte : he does it to annoy you⟩ **4** : around, by (a time) ⟨para mañana estarán listos : they'll be ready by tomorrow⟩ **5 para adelante** : forwards **6 para atrás** : backwards **7 para que** : so, so that, in order that ⟨te lo digo para que sepas : I'm telling you so you'll know⟩
parabién *nm, pl* **-bienes** : congratulations *pl*
parábola *nf* **1** : parable **2** : parabola
parabrisas *nms & pl* : windshield
paracaídas *nms & pl* : parachute
paracaidista *nmf* **1** : parachutist **2** : paratrooper
parachoques *nms & pl* : bumper
parada *nf* **1** : stop ⟨parada de autobús : bus stop⟩ **2** : catch, save, parry (in sports) **3** DESFILE : parade
paradero *nm* : whereabouts
paradigma *nm* : paradigm
paradisíaco, -ca *or* **paradisiaco, -ca** *adj* : heavenly
parado, -da *adj* **1** : motionless, idle, stopped **2** : standing (up) **3** : confused, bewildered **4 bien (mal) parado** : in good (bad) shape ⟨salió bien parado : it turned out well for him⟩
paradoja *nf* : paradox
paradójico, -ca *adj* : paradoxical
parafernalia *nf* : paraphernalia

parafina *nf* : paraffin
parafrasear *vt* : to paraphrase
paráfrasis *nfs & pl* : paraphrase
paraguas *nms & pl* : umbrella
paraguayo, -ya *adj & n* : Paraguayan
paraíso *nm* **1** : paradise, heaven **2 paraíso fiscal** : tax shelter
paraje *nm* : spot, place
paralelismo *nm* : parallelism, similarity
paralelo[1], **-la** *adj* : parallel
paralelo[2] *nm* : parallel
paralelogramo *nm* : parallelogram
parálisis *nfs & pl* **1** : paralysis **2** : standstill **3 parálisis cerebral** : cerebral palsy
paralítico, -ca *adj & n* : paralytic
paralizar {21} *vt* **1** : to paralyze **2** : to bring to a standstill — **paralizarse** *vr*
parámetro *nm* : parameter
páramo *nm* : barren plateau, moor
parangón *nm, pl* **-gones** **1** : comparison **2 sin ~** : incomparable
paraninfo *nm* : auditorium, assembly hall
paranoia *nf* : paranoia
paranoico, -ca *adj & n* : paranoid
parapeto *nm* : parapet, rampart
parapléjico, -ca *adj & n* : paraplegic
parar *vt* **1** DETENER : to stop **2** : to stand, to prop — *vi* **1** CESAR : to stop **2** : to stay, to put up **3 ir a parar** : to end up, to wind up — **pararse** *vr* **1** : to stop **2** ATASCARSE : to stall (out) **3** : to stand up, to get up
pararrayos *nms & pl* : lightning rod
parasitario, -ria *adj* : parasitic
parasitismo *nm* : parasitism
parásito *nm* : parasite
parasol *nm* SOMBRILLA : parasol
parcela *nf* : parcel, tract of land
parcelar *vt* : to parcel (land)
parchar *vt* : to patch, to patch up
parche *nm* : patch
parcial *adj* : partial — **parcialmente** *adv*
parcialidad *nf* : partiality, bias
parco, -ca *adj* **1** : sparing, frugal **2** : moderate, temperate
pardo, -da *adj* : brownish grey
pardusco → pardo
parecer[1] {53} *vi* **1** : to seem, to look, to appear to be ⟨parece bien fácil : it looks very easy⟩ ⟨así parece : so it seems⟩ ⟨pareces una princesa : you look like a princess⟩ **2** : to think, to have an opinion ⟨me parece que sí : I think so⟩ **3** : to like, to be in agreement ⟨si te parece : if you like, if it's all right with you⟩ — **parecerse** *vr* **~ a** : to resemble
parecer[2] *nm* **1** OPINIÓN : opinion **2** ASPECTO : appearance ⟨al parecer : apparently⟩
parecido[1], **-da** *adj* **1** : similar, alike **2 bien parecido** : good-looking
parecido[2] *nm* : resemblance, similarity
pared *nf* : wall
pareja *nf* **1** : couple, pair **2** : partner, mate

parejo, -ja *adj* **1** : even, smooth, level **2** : equal, similar
parentela *nf* : relations *pl*, kinfolk
parentesco *nm* : relationship, kinship
paréntesis *nms & pl* **1** : parenthesis **2** : digression
parentético, -ca *adj* : parenthetic, parenthetical
paria *nmf* : pariah, outcast
paridad *nf* : parity, equality
pariente *nmf* : relative, relation
parir *vi* : to give birth — *vt* : to give birth to, to bear
parking *nm* : parking lot
parlamentar *vi* : to talk, to parley
parlamentario[1], -ria *adj* : parliamentary
parlamentario[2], -ria *n* : member of parliament
parlamento *nm* **1** : parliament **2** : negotiations *pl*, talks *pl*
parlanchín[1], -china *adj, mpl* **-chines** : chatty, talkative
parlanchín[2], -china *n, mpl* **-chines** : chatterbox
parlante *nm* ALTOPARLANTE : loudspeaker
parlotear *vi fam* : to gab, to chat, to prattle
parloteo *nm fam* : prattle, chatter
paro *nm* **1** HUELGA : strike **2** : stoppage, stopping **3 paro forzoso** : layoff
parodia *nf* : parody
parodiar *vt* : to parody
paroxismo *nm* **1** : fit, paroxysm **2** : peak, height ⟨llevaral paroxismo : to carry to the extreme⟩
parpadear *vi* **1** : to blink **2** : to flicker
parpadeo *nm* **1** : blink, blinking **2** : flickering
párpado *nm* : eyelid
parque *nm* **1** : park **2 parque de atracciones** : amusement park
parquear *vt* : to park — **parquearse** *vr*
parqueo *nm* : parking
parquet *or* **parqué** *nm* : parquet
parquímetro *nm* : parking meter
parra *nf* : vine, grapevine
párrafo *nm* : paragraph
parranda *nf fam* : party, spree
parrilla *nf* **1** : broiler, grill **2** : grate
parrillada *nf* BARBACOA : barbecue
párroco *nm* : parish priest
parroquia *nf* **1** : parish **2** : parish church **3** : customers *pl*, clientele
parroquial *adj* : parochial
parroquiano, -na *nm* **1** : parishioner **2** : customer, patron
parsimonia *nf* **1** : calm **2** : parsimony, thrift
parsimonioso, -sa *adj* **1** : calm, unhurried **2** : parsimonious, thrifty
parte[1] *nm* : report, dispatch
parte[2] *nf* **1** : part, share **2** : part, place ⟨en alguna parte : somewhere⟩ ⟨por todas partes : everywhere⟩ **3** : party (in negotiations, etc.) **4 de parte de** : on behalf of **5 ¿de parte de quién?** : may I ask who's calling? **6 tomar parte** : to take part

partero, -ra *n* : midwife
partición *nf, pl* **-ciones** : division, sharing
participación *nf, pl* **-ciones** **1** : participation **2** : share, interest **3** : announcement, notice
participante *nmf* **1** : participant **2** : competitor, entrant
participar *vi* **1** : to participate, to take part **2 ~ en** : to have a share in — *vt* : to announce, to notify
partícipe *nmf* : participant
participio *nm* : participle
partícula *nf* : particle
particular[1] *adj* **1** : particular, specific **2** : private, personal **3** : special, unique
particular[2] *nm* **1** : matter, detail **2** : individual
particularidad *nf* : characteristic, peculiarity
particularizar {21} *vt* **1** : to distinguish, to characterize **2** : to specify
partida *nf* **1** : departure **2** : item, entry **3** : certificate ⟨partida de nacimiento : birth certificate⟩ **4** : game, match, hand **5** : party, group
partidario, -ria *n* : follower, supporter
partido *nm* **1** : (political) party **2** : game, match ⟨partido de futbol : soccer game⟩ **3** APOYO : support, following **4** PROVECHO : profit, advantage ⟨sacar partido de : to profit from⟩
partir *vt* **1** : to cut, to split **2** : to break, to crack **3** : to share (out), to divide — *vi* **1** : to leave, to depart **2 ~ de** : to start from **3 a partir de** : as of, from ⟨a partir de hoy : as of today⟩ — **partirse** *vr* **1** : to smash, to split open **2** : to chap
partisano, -na *adj & n* : partisan
partitura *nf* : (musical) score
parto *nm* **1** : childbirth, delivery, labor ⟨estar de parto : to be in labor⟩ **2** : product, creation, brainchild
parvulario *nm* : nursery school
párvulo, -la *n* : toddler, preschooler
pasa *nf* **1** : raisin **2 pasa de Corinto** : currant
pasable *adj* : passable, tolerable — **pasablemente** *adv*
pasada *nf* **1** : passage, passing **2** : pass, wipe, coat (of paint) **3 de ~** : in passing **4 mala pasada** : dirty trick
pasadizo *nm* : passageway, corridor
pasado[1], -da *adj* **1** : past ⟨el año pasado : last year⟩ ⟨pasado mañana : the day after tomorrow⟩ ⟨pasadas las siete : after seven o'clock⟩ **2** : stale, bad, overripe **3** : old-fashioned, out-of-date **4** : overripe, slightly spoiled
pasado[2] *nm* : past
pasador *nm* **1** : bolt, latch **2** : barrette **3** *Mex* : bobby pin
pasaje *nm* **1** : ticket (for travel) **2** TARIFA : fare **3** : passageway **4** : passengers *pl*
pasajero[1], -ra *adj* : passing, fleeting
pasajero[2], -ra *n* : passenger

pasamanos *nms & pl* **1** : handrail **2** : bannister
pasante *nmf* : assistant
pasaporte *nm* : passport
pasar *vi* **1** : to pass, to go by, to come by **2** : to come in, to enter ⟨¿se puede pasar? : may we come in?⟩ **3** : to happen ⟨¿qué pasa? : what's happening?, what's going on?⟩ **4** : to manage, to get by **5** : to be over, to end **6** ~ **de** : to exceed, to go beyond **7** ~ **por** : to pretend to be — *vt* **1** : to pass, to give ⟨¿me pasas la sal? : would you pass me the salt?⟩ **2** : to pass (a test) **3** : to go over, to cross **4** : to spend (time) **5** : to tolerate **6** : to go through, to suffer **7** : to show (a movie, etc.) **8** : to overtake, to pass, to surpass **9** : to pass over, to wipe up **10 pasarlo bien** *or* **pasarla bien** : to have a good time **11 pasarlo mal** *or* **pasarla mal** : to have a bad time, to have a hard time **12 pasar por alto** : to overlook, to omit — **pasarse** *vr* **1** : to move, to pass, to go away **2** : to slip one's mind, to forget **3** : to go too far
pasarela *nf* **1** : gangplank **2** : footbridge **3** : runway, catwalk
pasatiempo *nm* : pastime, hobby
Pascua *nf* **1** : Easter **2** : Passover **3** : Christmas **4 Pascuas** *nfpl* : Christmas season
pase *nm* **1** PERMISO : pass, permit **2 pase de abordar** *Mex* : boarding pass
pasear *vi* : to take a walk, to go for a ride — *vt* **1** : to take for a walk **2** : to parade around, to show off — **pasearse** *vr* : to walk around
paseo *nm* **1** : walk, stroll **2** : ride **3** EXCURSIÓN : outing, trip **4** : avenue, walk **5** *or* **paseo marítimo** : boardwalk
pasiflora *nf* : passionflower
pasillo *nm* CORREDOR : hallway, corridor, aisle
pasión *nf, pl* **pasiones** : passion
pasional *adj* : passionate ⟨crimen pasional : crime of passion⟩
pasionaria → pasiflora
pasivo¹, -va *adj* : passive — **pasivamente** *adv*
pasivo² *nm* **1** : liability ⟨activos y pasivos : assets and liabilities⟩ **2** : debit side (of an account)
pasmado, -da *adj* : stunned, flabbergasted
pasmar *vt* : to amaze, to stun — **pasmarse** *vr*
pasmo *nm* **1** : shock, astonishment **2** : wonder, marvel
pasmoso, -sa *adj* : incredible, amazing — **pasmosamente** *adv*
paso¹, -sa *adj* : dried ⟨ciruela pasa : prune⟩
paso² *nm* **1** : passage, passing ⟨de paso : in passing, on the way⟩ **2** : way, path ⟨abrirse paso : to make one's way⟩ **3** : crossing ⟨paso de peatones : crosswalk⟩ ⟨paso a desnivel : underpass⟩ ⟨paso elevado : overpass⟩ **4** : step

⟨paso a paso : step by step⟩ **5** : pace, gait ⟨a buen paso : quickly, at a good rate⟩
pasta *nf* **1** : paste ⟨pasta de dientes *or* pasta dental : toothpaste⟩ **2** : pasta **3** : pastry dough **4 libro en pasta dura** : hardcover book **5 tener pasta de** : to have the makings of
pastar *vi* : to graze — *vt* : to put to pasture
pastel¹ *adj* : pastel
pastel² *nm* **1** : cake ⟨pastel de cumpleaños : birthday cake⟩ **2** : pie, turnover **3** : pastel
pastelería *nf* : pastry shop
pasteurización *nf, pl* **-ciones** : pasteurization
pasteurizar {21} *vt* : to pasteurize
pastilla *nf* **1** COMPRIMIDO, PÍLDORA : pill, tablet **2** : lozenge ⟨pastilla para la tos : cough drop⟩ **3** : cake (of soap), bar (of chocolate)
pastizal *nm* : pasture, grazing land
pasto *nm* **1** : pasture **2** HIERBA : grass, lawn
pastor, -tora *n* **1** : shepherd, shepherdess *f* **2** : minister, pastor
pastoral *adj & nf* : pastoral
pastorear *vt* : to shepherd, to tend
pastorela *nf* **1** : pastoral, pastourelle **2** *Mex* : a traditional Christmas play
pastoso, -sa *adj* **1** : pasty, doughy **2** : smooth, mellow (of sounds)
pata *nf* **1** : paw, leg (of an animal) **2** : foot, leg (of furniture) **3 patas de gallo** : crow's-feet **4 meter la pata** *fam* : to put one's foot in it, to make a blunder
patada *nf* **1** PUNTAPIÉ : kick **2** : stamp (of the foot)
patalear *vi* **1** : to kick **2** : to stamp one's feet
pataleta *nf fam* : tantrum
patán¹ *adj, pl* **patanes** : boorish, crude
patán² *nm, pl* **patanes** : boor, lout
patata *nf Spain* : potato
pateador, -dora *n* : kicker (in sports)
patear *vt* : to kick — *vi* : to stamp one's foot
patentar *vt* : to patent
patente¹ *adj* EVIDENTE : obvious, patent — **patentemente** *adv*
patente² *nf* : patent
paternal *adj* : fatherly, paternal
paternidad *nf* **1** : fatherhood, paternity **2** : parenthood **3** : authorship
paterno, -na *adj* : paternal ⟨abuela paterna : paternal grandmother⟩
patético, -ca *adj* : pathetic, moving
patetismo *nm* : pathos
patíbulo *nm* : gallows, scaffold
patillas *nfpl* : sideburns
patín *nm, pl* **patines** : skate ⟨patín de ruedas : roller skate⟩
patinador, -dora *n* : skater
patinaje *nm* : skating
patinar *vi* **1** : to skate **2** : to skid, to slip **3** *fam* : to slip up, to blunder
patinazo *nm* **1** : skid **2** *fam* : blunder, slipup

patineta *nf* **1** : scooter **2** : skateboard
patinete *nm* : scooter
patio *nm* **1** : courtyard, patio **2 patio de recreo** : playground
patito, -ta *n* : duckling
pato, -ta *n* **1** : duck **2 pato real** : mallard **3 pagar el pato** *fam* : to take the blame
patología *nf* : pathology
patológico, -ca *adj* : pathological
patólogo, -ga *n* : pathologist
patraña *nf* : tall tale, humbug, nonsense
patria *nf* : native land
patriarca *nm* : patriarch — **patriarcal** *adj*
patriarcado *nm* : patriarchy
patrimonio *nm* : patrimony, legacy
patrio, -tria *adj* **1** : native, home ⟨suelo patrio : native soil⟩ **2** : paternal
patriota[1] *adj* : patriotic
patriota[2] *nmf* : patriot
patriotería *nf* : jingoism, chauvinism
patriotero[1], **-ra** *adj* : jingoistic, chauvinistic
patriotero[2], **-ra** *n* : jingoist, chauvinist
patriótico, -ca *adj* : patriotic
patriotismo *nm* : patriotism
patrocinador, -dora *n* : sponsor, patron
patrocinar *vt* : to sponsor
patrocinio *nm* : sponsorship, patronage
patrón[1], **-trona** *n, mpl* **patrones 1** JEFE : boss **2** : patron saint
patrón[2] *nm, pl* **patrones 1** : standard **2** : pattern (in sewing)
patronal *adj* **1** : management, employers' ⟨sindicato patronal : employers' association⟩ **2** : pertaining to a patron saint ⟨fiesta patronal : patron saint's day⟩
patronato *nm* **1** : board, council **2** : foundation, trust
patrono, -na *n* **1** : employer **2** : patron saint
patrulla *nf* **1** : patrol **2** : police car, cruiser
patrullar *v* : to patrol
patrullero *nm* **1** : police car **2** : patrol boat
paulatino, -na *adj* : gradual
paupérrimo, -ma *adj* : destitute, poverty-stricken
pausa *nf* : pause, break
pausado[1] *adv* : slowly, deliberately ⟨habla más pausado : speak more slowly⟩
pausado[2], **-da** *adj* : slow, deliberate — **pausadamente** *adv*
pauta *nf* **1** : rule, guideline **2** : lines *pl* (on paper)
pava *nf Arg, Bol, Chile* : kettle
pavimentar *vt* : to pave
pavimento *nm* : pavement
pavo, -va *n* **1** : turkey **2 pavo real** : peacock **3 comer pavo** : to be a wallflower
pavón *nm, pl* **pavones** : peacock
pavonearse *vr* : to strut, to swagger
pavoneo *nm* : strut, swagger
pavor *nm* TERROR : dread, terror

pavoroso, -sa *adj* ATERRADOR : dreadful, terrifying
payasada *nf* BUFONADA : antic, buffoonery
payasear *vi* : to clown around
payaso, -sa *n* : clown
paz *nf, pl* **paces 1** : peace **2 dejar en paz** : to leave alone **3 hacer las paces** : to make up, to reconcile
pazca, etc. → **pacer**
PC *nmf* : PC, personal computer
peaje *nm* : toll
peatón *nm, pl* **-tones** : pedestrian
peatonal *adj* : pedestrian
peca *nf* : freckle
pecado *nm* : sin
pecador[1], **-dora** *adj* : sinful, sinning
pecador[2], **-dora** *n* : sinner
pecaminoso, -sa *adj* : sinful
pecar {72} *vi* **1** : to sin **2 ~ de** : to be too much (something) ⟨no pecan de amabilidad : they're not overly friendly⟩
pécari *or* **pecarí** *nm* : peccary
pececillo *nm* : small fish
pecera *nf* : fishbowl, fish tank
pecho *nm* **1** : chest **2** SENO : breast, bosom **3** : heart, courage **4 dar el pecho** : to breast-feed **5 tomar a pecho** : to take to heart
pechuga *nf* : breast (of fowl)
pecoso, -sa *adj* : freckled
pectoral *adj* : pectoral
peculado *nm* : embezzlement
peculiar *adj* **1** CARACTERÍSTICO : particular, characteristic **2** RARO : peculiar, uncommon
peculiaridad *nf* : peculiarity
pecuniario, -ria *adj* : pecuniary
pedagogía *nf* : pedagogy
pedagógico, -ca *adj* : pedagogic, pedagogical
pedagogo, -ga *n* : educator, pedagogue
pedal *nm* : pedal
pedalear *vi* : to pedal
pedante[1] *adj* : pedantic
pedante[2] *nmf* : pedant
pedantería *nf* : pedantry
pedazo *nm* TROZO : piece, bit, chunk ⟨caerse a pedazos : to fall to pieces⟩ ⟨hacer pedazos : to tear into shreds, to smash to pieces⟩
pedernal *nm* : flint
pedestal *nm* : pedestal
pedestre *adj* : commonplace, pedestrian
pediatra *nmf* : pediatrician
pediatría *nf* : pediatrics
pediátrico, -ca *adj* : pediatric
pedido *nm* **1** : order (of merchandise) **2** : request
pedigrí *nm* : pedigree
pedir {54} *vt* **1** : to ask for, to request ⟨le pedí un préstamo a Claudia : I asked Claudia for a loan⟩ **2** : to order (food, merchandise) **3 pedir disculpas** *or* **pedir perdón** : to apologize — *vi* **1** : to order **2** : to beg

pedrada *nf* **1** : blow (with a rock or stone) ⟨la ventana se quebró de una pedrada : the window was broken by a rock⟩ **2** *fam* : cutting remark, dig
pedregal *nm* : rocky ground
pedregoso, -sa *adj* : rocky, stony
pedrera *nf* CANTERA : quarry
pedrería *nf* : precious stones *pl*, gems *pl*
pegado, -da *adj* **1** : glued, stuck, stuck together **2** ~ **a** : right next to
pegajoso, -sa *adj* **1** : sticky, gluey **2** : catchy ⟨una tonada pegajosa : a catchy tune⟩
pegamento *nm* : adhesive, glue
pegar {52} *vt* **1** : to glue, to stick, to paste **2** : to attach, to sew on **3** : to infect with, to give ⟨me pegó el resfriado : he gave me his cold⟩ **4** GOLPEAR : to hit, to deal, to strike ⟨me pegaron un puntapié : they gave me a kick⟩ **5** : to give (out with) ⟨pegó un grito : she let out a yell⟩ — *vi* **1** : to adhere, to stick **2** ~ **en** : to hit, to strike (against) **3** ~ **con** : to match, to go with — **pegarse** *vr* **1** GOLPEARSE : to hit oneself, to hit each other **2** : to stick, to take hold **3** : to be contagious **4** *fam* : to tag along, to stick around
pegote *nm* **1** : sticky mess **2** *Mex* : sticker, adhesive label
pegue, etc. → pegar
peinado *nm* : hairstyle, hairdo
peinador, -dora *n* : hairdresser
peinar *vt* : to comb — **peinarse** *vr*
peine *nm* : comb
peineta *nf* : ornamental comb
peladez *nf*, *pl* **-deces** *Mex fam* : obscenity, bad language
pelado, -da *adj* **1** : bald, hairless **2** : peeled **3** : bare, barren **4** : broke, penniless **5** *Mex fam* : coarse, crude
pelador *nm* : peeler
pelagra *nf* : pellagra
pelaje *nm* : coat (of an animal), fur
pelar *vt* **1** : to peel, to shell **2** : to skin **3** : to pluck **4** : to remove hair from **5** *fam* : to clean out (of money) — **pelarse** *vr* **1** : to peel **2** *fam* : to get a haircut **3** *Mex fam* : to split, to leave
peldaño *nm* **1** : step, stair **2** : rung
pelea *nf* **1** LUCHA : fight **2** : quarrel
pelear *vi* **1** LUCHAR : to fight **2** DISPUTAR : to quarrel — **pelearse** *vr*
peleón, -ona *adj*, *mpl* **-ones** *Spain* : quarrelsome, argumentative
peleonero, -ra *adj Mex* : quarrelsome
peletería *nf* **1** : fur shop **2** : fur trade
peletero, -ra *n* : furrier
peliagudo, -da *adj* : tricky, difficult, ticklish
pelícano *nm* : pelican
película *nf* **1** : movie, film **2** : (photographic) film **3** : thin covering, layer
peligrar *vi* : to be in danger
peligro *nm* **1** : danger, peril **2** : risk ⟨correr peligro de : to run the risk of⟩
peligroso, -sa *adj* : dangerous, hazardous

pelirrojo¹, -ja *adj* : red-haired, redheaded
pelirrojo², -ja *n* : redhead
pellejo *nm* **1** : hide, skin **2 salvar el pellejo** : to save one's neck
pellizcar {72} *vt* **1** : to pinch **2** : to nibble on
pellizco *nm* : pinch
pelo *nm* **1** : hair **2** : fur **3** : pile, nap **4 a pelo** : bareback **5 con pelos y señales** : in great detail **6 no tener pelos en la lengua** : to not mince words, to be blunt **7 tomarle el pelo a alguien** : to tease someone, to pull someone's leg
pelón, -lona *adj, mpl* **pelones 1** : bald **2** *fam* : broke **3** *Mex fam* : tough, difficult
pelota *nf* **1** : ball **2** *fam* : head **3 en pelotas** *fam* : naked **4 pelota vasca** : jai alai **5 pasar la pelota** *fam* : to pass the buck
pelotón *nm, pl* **-tones** : squad, detachment
peltre *nm* : pewter
peluca *nf* : wig
peluche *nm* : plush (fabric)
peludo, -da *adj* : hairy, shaggy, bushy
peluquería *nf* **1** : hairdresser's, barber shop **2** : hairdressing
peluquero, -ra *n* : barber, hairdresser
peluquín *nm, pl* **-quines** TUPÉ : hairpiece, toupee
pelusa *nf* : lint, fuzz
pélvico, -ca *adj* : pelvic
pelvis *nfs & pl* : pelvis
pena *nf* **1** CASTIGO : punishment, penalty ⟨pena de muerte : death penalty⟩ **2** AFLICCIÓN : sorrow, grief ⟨morir de pena : to die of a broken heart⟩ ⟨¡qué pena! : what a shame!, how sad!⟩ **3** DOLOR : pain, suffering **4** DIFICULTAD : difficulty, trouble ⟨a duras penas : with great difficulty⟩ **5** VERGÜENZA : shame, embarrassment **6 valer la pena** : to be worthwhile
penacho *nm* **1** : crest, tuft **2** : plume (of feathers)
penal¹ *adj* : penal
penal² *nm* CÁRCEL : prison, penitentiary
penalidad *nf* **1** : hardship **2** : penalty, punishment
penalizar {21} *vt* : to penalize
penalty *nm* : penalty (in sports)
penar *vt* : to punish, to penalize — *vi* : to suffer, to grieve
pendenciero, -ra *adj* : argumentative, quarrelsome
pender *vi* **1** : to hang **2** : to be pending
pendiente¹ *adj* **1** : pending **2 estar pendiente de** : to be watchful of, to be on the lookout for
pendiente² *nm Spain* : earring
pendiente³ *nf* : slope, incline
pendón *nm, pl* **pendones** : banner
péndulo *nm* : pendulum
pene *nm* : penis

penetración *nf, pl* **-ciones 1** : penetration **2** : insight
penetrante *adj* **1** : penetrating, piercing **2** : sharp, acute **3** : deep (of a wound)
penetrar *vi* **1** : to penetrate, to sink in **2** ~ **por** *or* ~ **en** : to pierce, to go in, to enter into ⟨el frío penetra por la ventana : the cold comes right in through the window⟩ — *vt* **1** : to penetrate, to permeate **2** : to pierce ⟨el dolor penetró su corazón : sorrow pierced her heart⟩ **3** : to fathom, to understand
penicilina *nf* : penicillin
península *nf* : peninsula — **peninsular** *adj*
penitencia *nf* : penance, penitence
penitenciaría *nf* : penitentiary
penitente *adj & nmf* : penitent
penol *nm* : yardarm
penoso, -sa *adj* **1** : painful, distressing **2** : difficult, arduous **3** : shy, bashful
pensado, -da *adj* **1 bien pensado** : well thought-out **2 en el momento menos pensado** : when least expected **3 poco pensado** : badly thought-out **4 mal pensado** : evil-minded
pensador, -dora *n* : thinker
pensamiento *nm* **1** : thought **2** : thinking **3** : pansy
pensar {55} *vi* **1** : to think **2** ~ **en** : to think about — *vt* **1** : to think **2** : to think about **3** : to intend, to plan on — **pensarse** *vr* : to think over
pensativo, -va *adj* : pensive, thoughtful
pensión *nf, pl* **pensiones 1** JUBILACIÓN : pension **2** : boarding house **3 pensión alimenticia** : alimony
pensionado, -da *n* → **pensionista**
pensionista *nmf* **1** JUBILADO : pensioner, retiree **2** : boarder, lodger
pentágono *nm* : pentagon — **pentagonal** *adj*
pentagrama *nm* : staff (in music)
penúltimo, -ma *adj* : next to last, penultimate
penumbra *nf* : semidarkness
penuria *nf* **1** ESCASEZ : shortage, scarcity **2** : poverty
peña *nf* : rock, crag
peñasco *nm* : crag, large rock
peñón → **peñasco**
peón *nm, pl* **peones 1** : laborer, peon **2** : pawn (in chess)
peonía *nf* : peony
peor[1] *adv* **1** (*comparative of* **mal**) : worse ⟨se llevan peor que antes : they get along worse than before⟩ **2** (*superlative of* **mal**) : worst ⟨me fue peor que a nadie : I did the worst of all⟩
peor[2] *adj* **1** (*comparative of* **malo**) : worse ⟨es peor que el original : it's worse than the original⟩ **2** (*superlative of* **malo**) : worst ⟨el peor de todos : the worst of all⟩
pepa *nf* : seed, pit (of a fruit)
pepenador, -dora *n CA, Mex* : scavenger
pepenar *vt CA, Mex* : to scavenge, to scrounge

pepinillo *nm* : pickle, gherkin
pepino *nm* : cucumber
pepita *nf* **1** : seed, pip **2** : nugget **3** *Mex* : dried pumpkin seed
peque, etc. → **pecar**
pequeñez *nf, pl* **-ñeces 1** : smallness **2** : trifle, triviality **3 pequeñez de espíritu** : pettiness
pequeño[1]**, -ña** *adj* **1** : small, little ⟨un libro pequeño : a small book⟩ **2** : young **3** BAJO : short
pequeño[2]**, -ña** *n* : child, little one
pera *nf* : pear
peraltar *vt* : to bank (a road)
perca *nf* : perch (fish)
percal *nm* : percale
percance *nm* : mishap, misfortune
percatarse *vr* ~ **de** : to notice, to become aware of
percebe *nm* : barnacle
percepción *nf, pl* **-ciones 1** : perception **2** : idea, notion **3** COBRO : receipt (of payment), collection
perceptible *adj* : perceptible, noticeable — **perceptiblemente** *adv*
percha *nf* **1** : perch **2** : coat hanger **3** : coatrack, coat hook
perchero *nm* : coatrack
percibir *vt* **1** : to perceive, to notice, to sense **2** : to earn, to draw (a salary)
percudido, -da *adj* : grimy
percudir *vt* : to make grimy — **percudirse** *vr*
percusión *nf, pl* **-siones** : percussion
percusor *or* **percutor** *nm* : hammer (of a firearm)
perdedor[1]**, -dora** *adj* : losing
perdedor[2]**, -dora** *n* : loser
perder {56} *vt* **1** : to lose **2** : to miss ⟨perdimos la oportunidad : we missed the opportunity⟩ **3** : to waste (time) — *vi* : to lose — **perderse** *vr* EXTRAVIARSE : to get lost, to stray
perdición *nf, pl* **-ciones** : perdition, damnation
pérdida *nf* **1** : loss **2 pérdida de tiempo** : waste of time
perdidamente *adv* : hopelessly
perdido, -da *adj* **1** : lost **2** : inveterate, incorrigible ⟨es un caso perdido : he's a hopeless case⟩ **3** : in trouble, done for **4 de** ~ *Mex fam* : at least
perdigón *nm, pl* **-gones** : shot, pellet
perdiz *nf, pl* **perdices** : partridge
perdón[1] *nm, pl* **perdones** : forgiveness, pardon
perdón[2] *interj* : excuse me!, sorry!
perdonable *adj* : forgivable
perdonar *vt* **1** DISCULPAR : to forgive, to pardon **2** : to exempt, to excuse
perdurable *adj* : lasting
perdurar *vi* : to last, to endure, to survive
perecedero, -ra *adj* : perishable
perecer {53} *vi* : to perish, to die
peregrinación *nf, pl* **-ciones** : pilgrimage
peregrinaje *nm* → **peregrinación**

peregrino¹, -na *adj* **1** : unusual, odd **2** MIGRATORIO : migratory

peregrino², -na *n* : pilgrim

perejil *nm* : parsley

perenne *adj* : perennial

perentorio, -ria *adj* **1** : peremptory **2** URGENTE : urgent **3** FIJO : fixed, set

pereza *nf* FLOJERA, HOLGAZANERÍA : laziness, idleness

perezoso¹, -sa *adj* FLOJO, HOLGAZÁN : lazy

perezoso² *nm* : sloth (animal)

perfección *nf, pl* -ciones : perfection

perfeccionamiento *nm* : perfecting, refinement

perfeccionar *vt* : to perfect, to refine

perfeccionismo *nm* : perfectionism

perfeccionista *nmf* : perfectionist

perfecto, -ta *adj* : perfect — **perfectamente** *adv*

perfidia *nf* : perfidy, treachery

pérfido, -da *adj* : perfidious

perfil *nm* **1** : profile **2 de** ~ : sideways, from the side **3 perfiles** *nmpl* RASGOS : features, characteristics

perfilar *vt* : to outline, to define — **perfilarse** *vr* **1** : to be outlined, to be silhouetted **2** : to take shape

perforación *nf, pl* -ciones **1** : perforation **2** : drilling

perforadora *nf* **1** : hole punch (for paper) **2** : drill (in mining, etc.)

perforar *vt* **1** : to perforate, to pierce **2** : to drill, to bore

perfumar *vt* : to perfume, to scent — **perfumarse** *vr*

perfume *nm* : perfume, scent

pergamino *nm* : parchment

pérgola *nf* : pergola, arbor

pericia *nf* : skill, expertise

pericial *adj* : expert ⟨testigo pericial : expert witness⟩

perico *nm* COTORRA : small parrot

periferia *nf* : periphery

periférico¹, -ca *adj* : peripheral

periférico² *nm* **1** *CA, Mex* : beltway **2** : peripheral

perilla *nf* **1** : goatee **2** : pommel (on a saddle) **3** *Col, Mex* : knob, handle **4 perilla de la oreja** : earlobe **5 de perillas** *fam* : handy, just right

perímetro *nm* : perimeter

periódico¹, -ca *adj* : periodic — **periódicamente** *adv*

periódico² *nm* DIARIO : newspaper

periodismo *nm* : journalism

periodista *nmf* : journalist

periodístico, -ca *adj* : journalistic, news

período *or* periodo *nm* : period

peripecia *nf* VICISITUD : vicissitude, reversal ⟨las peripecias de su carrera : the ups and downs of her career⟩

periquito *nm* **1** : parakeet **2 periquito australiano** : budgerigar

periscopio *nm* : periscope

perito, -ta *adj & n* : expert

perjudicar {72} *vt* : to harm, to be detrimental to

perjudicial *adj* : harmful, detrimental

perjuicio *nm* **1** : harm, damage **2 en perjuicio de** : to the detriment of

perjurar *vi* : to perjure oneself

perjurio *nm* : perjury

perjuro, -ra *n* : perjurer

perla *nf* **1** : pearl **2 de perlas** *fam* : wonderfully ⟨me viene de perlas : it suits me just fine⟩

permanecer {53} *vi* **1** QUEDARSE : to remain, to stay **2** SEGUIR : to remain, to continue to be

permanencia *nf* **1** : permanence, continuance **2** ESTANCIA : stay

permanente¹ *adj* **1** : permanent **2** : constant — **permanentemente** *adv*

permanente² *nf* : permanent (wave)

permeabilidad *nf* : permeability

permeable *adj* : permeable

permisible *adj* : permissible, allowable

permisividad *nf* : permissiveness

permisivo, -va *adv* : permissive

permiso *nm* **1** : permission **2** : permit, license **3** : leave, furlough **4 con** ~ : excuse me, pardon me

permitir *vt* : to permit, to allow — **permitirse** *vr*

permuta *nf* : exchange

permutar *vt* INTERCAMBIAR : to exchange

pernicioso, -sa *adj* : pernicious, destructive

pernil *nm* **1** : haunch (of an animal) **2** : leg (of meat), ham **3** : trouser leg

perno *nm* : bolt, pin

pernoctar *vi* : to stay overnight, to spend the night

pero¹ *nm* **1** : fault, defect ⟨ponerle peros a : to find fault with⟩ **2** : objection

pero² *conj* : but

perogrullada *nf* : truism, platitude, cliché

peroné *nm* : fibula

perorar *vi* : to deliver a speech

perorata *nf* : oration, long-winded speech

peróxido *nm* : peroxide

perpendicular *adj & nf* : perpendicular

perpetrar *vt* : to perpetrate

perpetuar {3} *vt* ETERNIZAR : to perpetuate

perpetuidad *nf* : perpetuity

perpetuo, -tua *adj* : perpetual — **perpetuamente** *adv*

perplejidad *nf* : perplexity

perplejo, -ja *adj* : perplexed, puzzled

perrada *nf fam* : dirty trick

perrera *nf* : kennel, dog pound

perrero, -ra *n* : dogcatcher

perrito, -ta *n* CACHORRO : puppy, small dog

perro, -rra *n* **1** : dog, bitch *f* **2 perro caliente** : hot dog **3 perro salchicha** : dachshund **4 perro faldero** : lapdog **5 perro cobrador** : retriever

persa¹ *adj & nmf* : Persian

persa² *nm* : Persian (language)

persecución *nf, pl* **-ciones** 1 : pursuit, chase 2 : persecution
perseguidor, -dora *n* 1 : pursuer 2 : persecutor
perseguir {75} *vt* 1 : to pursue, to chase 2 : to persecute 3 : to pester, to annoy
perseverancia *nf* : perseverance
perseverar *vi* : to persevere
persiana *nf* : blind, venetian blind
persignarse *vr* SANTIGUARSE : to cross oneself, to make the sign of the cross
persistir *vi* : to persist — **persistencia** *nf* — **persistente** *adj*
persona *nf* : person
personaje *nm* 1 : character (in drama or literature) 2 : personage, celebrity
personal[1] *adj* : personal — **personalmente** *adv*
personal[2] *nm* : personnel, staff
personalidad *nf* : personality
personalizar {21} *vt* : to personalize
personificar {72} *vi* : to personify — **personificación** *nf*
perspectiva *nf* 1 : perspective, view 2 : prospect, outlook
perspicacia *nf* : shrewdness, perspicacity, insight
perspicaz *adj, pl* **-caces** : shrewd, perspicacious
persuadir *vt* : to persuade — **persuadirse** *vr* : to become convinced
persuasión *nf, pl* **-siones** : persuasion
persuasivo, -va *adj* : persuasive
pertenecer {53} *vi* : to belong
perteneciente *adj* ~ **a** : belonging to
pertenencia *nf* 1 : membership 2 : ownership 3 **pertenencias** *nfpl* : belongings, possessions
pértiga *nf* GARROCHA : pole ⟨salto de pértiga : pole vault⟩
pertinaz *adj, pl* **-naces** 1 OBSTINADO : obstinate 2 PERSISTENTE : persistent
pertinencia *nf* : pertinence, relevance — **pertinente** *adj*
pertrechos *nmpl* : equipment, gear
perturbación *nf, pl* **-ciones** : disturbance, disruption
perturbador, -dora *adj* 1 INQUIETANTE : disturbing, troubling 2 : disruptive
perturbar *vt* 1 : to disturb, to trouble 2 : to disrupt
peruano, -na *adj & n* : Peruvian
perversidad *nf* : perversity, depravity
perversión *nf, pl* **-siones** : perversion
perverso, -sa *adj* : wicked, depraved
pervertido[1]**, -da** *adj* DEPRAVADO : perverted, depraved
pervertido[2]**, -da** *n* : pervert
pervertir {76} *vt* : to pervert, to corrupt
pesa *nf* 1 : weight 2 **levantamiento de pesas** : weightlifting
pesadamente *adv* 1 : heavily 2 : slowly, clumsily
pesadez *nf, pl* **-deces** 1 : heaviness 2 : slowness 3 : tediousness
pesadilla *nf* : nightmare

pesado[1]**, -da** *adj* 1 : heavy 2 : slow 3 : irritating, annoying 4 : tedious, boring 5 : tough, difficult
pesado[2]**, -da** *n fam* : bore, pest
pesadumbre *nf* AFLICCIÓN : grief, sorrow, sadness
pésame *nm* : condolences *pl* ⟨mi más sentido pésame : my heartfelt condolences⟩
pesar[1] *vt* 1 : to weigh 2 EXAMINAR : to consider, to think over — *vi* 1 : to weigh ⟨¿cuánto pesa? : how much does it weigh?⟩ 2 : to be heavy 3 : to weigh heavily, to be a burden ⟨no le pesa : it's not a burden on him⟩ ⟨pesa sobre mi corazón : it weighs upon my heart⟩ 4 INFLUIR : to carry weight, to have bearing 5 (*with personal pronouns*) : to grieve, to sadden ⟨me pesa mucho : I'm very sorry⟩ 6 **pese a** : in spite of, despite
pesar[2] *nm* 1 AFLICCIÓN, PENA : sorrow, grief 2 REMORDIMIENTO : remorse 3 **a pesar de** : in spite of, despite
pesaroso, -sa *adj* 1 : sad, mournful 2 ARREPENTIDO : sorry, regretful
pesca *nf* : fishing
pescadería *nf* : fish market
pescado *nm* : fish (as food)
pescador, -dora *n* : fisherman *m*, fisherwoman *f*
pescar {72} *vt* 1 : to fish for 2 : to catch 3 *fam* : to get a hold of, to land — *vi* : to fish, to go fishing
pescuezo *nm* : neck
pesebre *nm* : manger
pesero *nm Mex* : minibus
peseta *nf* : peseta (Spanish unit of currency)
pesimismo *nm* : pessimism
pesimista[1] *adj* : pessimistic
pesimista[2] *nmf* : pessimist
pésimo, -ma *adj* : dreadful, abominable
peso *nm* 1 : weight, heaviness 2 : burden, responsibility 3 : weight (in sports) 4 BÁSCULA : scales *pl* 5 : peso
pesque, etc. → **pescar**
pesquería *nf* : fishery
pesquero[1]**, -ra** *adj* : fishing ⟨pueblo pesquero : fishing village⟩
pesquero[2] *nm* : fishing boat
pesquisa *nf* INVESTIGACIÓN : inquiry, investigation
pestaña *nf* 1 : eyelash 2 : flange, rim
pestañear *vi* : to blink
pestañeo *nm* : blink
peste *nf* 1 : plague, pestilence 2 : stench, stink 3 : nuisance, pest
pesticida *nm* : pesticide
pestilencia *nf* 1 : stench, foul odor 2 : pestilence
pestilente *adj* 1 : foul, smelly 2 : pestilent
pestillo *nm* CERROJO : bolt, latch
petaca *nf* 1 *Mex* : suitcase 2 **petacas** *nfpl Mex fam* : bottom, behind
pétalo *nm* : petal
petardear *vi* : to backfire

petardeo *nm* : backfiring
petardo *nm* : firecracker
petate *nm Mex* : mat
petición *nf, pl* **-ciones** : petition, request
peticionar *vt* : to petition
peticionario, -ria *n* : petitioner
petirrojo *nm* : robin
peto *nm* : bib (of clothing)
pétreo, -trea *adj* : stone, stony
petrificar {72} *vt* : to petrify
petróleo *nm* : oil, petroleum
petrolero¹, -ra *adj* : oil ⟨industria petrolera : oil industry⟩
petrolero² *nm* : oil tanker
petrolífero, -ra *adj* → **petrolero¹**
petulancia *nf* INSOLENCIA : insolence, petulance
petulante *adj* INSOLENTE : insolent, petulant — **petulantemente** *adv*
petunia *nf* : petunia
peyorativo, -va *adj* : pejorative
pez¹ *nm, pl* **peces** 1 : fish 2 **pez de colores** : goldfish 3 **pez espada** : swordfish 4 **pez gordo** : big shot
pez² *nf, pl* **peces** : pitch, tar
pezón *nm, pl* **pezones** : nipple
pezuña *nf* : hoof ⟨pezuña hendida : cloven hoof⟩
pi *nf* : pi
piadoso, -sa *adj* 1 : compassionate, merciful 2 DEVOTO : pious, devout
pianista *nmf* : pianist, piano player
piano *nm* : piano
piar {85} *vi* : to chirp, to cheep, to tweet
pibe, -ba *n Arg, Uru fam* : kid, child
pica *nf* 1 : pike, lance 2 : goad (in bullfighting) 3 : spade (in playing cards)
picada *nf* 1 : bite, sting (of an insect) 2 : sharp descent
picadillo *nm* 1 : minced meat, hash 2 **hacer picadillo a** : to beat to a pulp
picado, -da *adj* 1 : perforated 2 : minced, chopped 3 : decayed (of teeth) 4 : choppy, rough 5 *fam* : annoyed, miffed
picador *nm* : picador
picadura *nf* 1 : sting, bite 2 : prick, puncture 3 : decay, cavity
picaflor *nm* COLIBRÍ : hummingbird
picana *nf* : goad, prod
picante¹ *adj* 1 : hot, spicy 2 : sharp, cutting 3 : racy, risqué
picante² *nm* 1 : spiciness 2 : hot spices *pl*, hot sauce
picaporte *nm* 1 : latch 2 : door handle 3 ALDABA : door knocker
picar {72} *vt* 1 : to sting, to bite 2 : to peck at 3 : to nibble on 4 : to prick, to puncture, to punch (a ticket) 5 : to grind, to chop 6 : to goad, to incite 7 : to pique, to provoke — *vi* 1 : to itch 2 : to sting 3 : to be spicy 4 : to nibble 5 : to take the bait 6 **~ en** : to dabble in 7 **picar muy alto** : to aim too high — **picarse** *vr* 1 : to get a cavity, to decay 2 : to get annoyed, to take offense
picardía *nf* 1 : cunning, craftiness 2 : prank, dirty trick

picaresco, -ca *adj* 1 : picaresque 2 : rascally, roguish
pícaro¹, -ra *adj* 1 : mischievous 2 : cunning, sly 3 : off-color, risqué
pícaro², -ra *n* 1 : rogue, scoundrel 2 : rascal
picazón *nf, pl* **-zones** COMEZÓN : itch
picea *nf* : spruce (tree)
pichel *nm* : pitcher, jug
pichón, -chona *n, mpl* **pichones** 1 : young pigeon, squab 2 *Mex fam* : novice, greenhorn
picnic *nm* : picnic
pico *nm* 1 : peak 2 : point, spike 3 : beak, bill 4 : pick, pickax 5 **y pico** : and a little, and a bit ⟨las siete y pico : a little after seven⟩ ⟨dos metros y pico : a bit over two meters⟩
picor *nm* : itch, irritation
picoso, -sa *adj Mex* : very hot, spicy
picota *nf* 1 : pillory, stock 2 **poner a alguien en la picota** : to put someone on the spot
picotada *nf* → **picotazo**
picotazo *nm* : peck (of a bird)
picotear *vt* : to peck — *vi* : to nibble, to pick
pictórico, -ca *adj* : pictorial
picudo, -da *adj* 1 : pointy, sharp 2 **~ para** *Mex fam* : clever at, good at
pide, etc. → **pedir**
pie *nm* 1 : foot ⟨a pie : on foot⟩ ⟨de pie : on one's feet, standing⟩ 2 : base, bottom, stem, foot ⟨pie de la cama : foot of the bed⟩ ⟨pie de una lámpara : base of a lamp⟩ ⟨pie de la escalera : bottom of the stairs⟩ ⟨pie de una copa : stem of a glass⟩ 3 : foot (in measurement) ⟨pie cuadrado : square foot⟩ 4 : cue (in theater) 5 **dar pie a** : to give cause for, to give rise to 6 **en pie de igualdad** : on equal footing
piedad *nf* 1 COMPASIÓN : mercy, pity 2 DEVOCIÓN : piety, devotion
piedra *nf* 1 : stone 2 : flint (of a lighter) 3 : hailstone 4 **piedra de afilar** : whetstone, grindstone 5 **piedra angular** : cornerstone 6 **piedra arenisca** : sandstone 7 **piedra caliza** : limestone 8 **piedra imán** : lodestone 9 **piedra de molino** : millstone 10 **piedra de toque** : touchstone
piel *nf* 1 : skin 2 CUERO : leather, hide ⟨piel de venado : deerskin⟩ 3 : fur, pelt 4 CÁSCARA : peel, skin 5 **piel de gallina** : goose bumps *pl* ⟨me pone la piel de gallina : it gives me goose bumps⟩
piélago *nm* **el piélago** : the deep, the ocean
piensa, etc. → **pensar**
pienso *nm* : feed, fodder
pierde, etc. → **perder**
pierna *nf* : leg
pieza *nf* 1 ELEMENTO : piece, part, component ⟨vestido de dos piezas : two-piece dress⟩ ⟨pieza de recambio : spare part⟩ ⟨pieza clave : key element⟩ 2 : piece (in chess) 3 OBRA : piece, work

⟨pieza de teatro : play⟩ **4** : room, bedroom
pifia *nf fam* : goof, blunder
pigargo *nm* : osprey
pigmentación *nf, pl* **-ciones** : pigmentation
pigmento *nm* : pigment
pigmeo, -mea *adj & n* : pygmy, Pygmy
pijama *nm* : pajamas *pl*
pila *nf* **1** BATERÍA : battery ⟨pila de linterna : flashlight battery⟩ **2** MONTÓN : pile, heap **3** : sink, basin, font ⟨pila bautismal : baptismal font⟩ ⟨pila para pájaros : birdbath⟩
pilar *nm* **1** : pillar, column **2** : support, mainstay
píldora *nf* PASTILLA : pill
pillaje *nm* : pillage, plunder
pillar *vt* **1** *fam* : to catch ⟨¡cuidado! ¡nos pillarán! : watch out! they'll catch us!⟩ **2** *fam* : to grasp, to catch on ⟨¿no lo pillas? : don't you get it?⟩
pillo¹, -lla *adj* : cunning, crafty
pillo², -lla *n* **1** : rascal, brat **2** : rogue, scoundrel
pilluelo, -la *n* : urchin
pilón *nm, pl* **pilones 1** PILA : basin **2** : pillar, tower (for cables), pylon (of a bridge) **3** *Mex* : extra, lagniappe
pilotar *vt* : to pilot, to drive
pilote *nm* : pile (stake)
pilotear → **pilotar**
piloto *nm* **1** : pilot, driver **2** : pilot light
piltrafa *nf* **1** : poor quality meat **2** : wretch **3 piltrafas** *nfpl* : food scraps
pimentero *nm* : pepper shaker
pimentón *nm, pl* **-tones 1** : paprika **2** : cayenne pepper
pimienta *nf* **1** : pepper (condiment) **2 pimienta de Jamaica** : allspice
pimiento *nm* : pepper (fruit) ⟨pimiento verde : green pepper⟩
pináculo *nm* **1** : pinnacle (of a building) **2** : peak, acme
pincel *nm* : paintbrush
pincelada *nf* **1** : brushstroke **2 últimas pinceladas** : final touches
pinchar *vt* **1** PICAR : to puncture (a tire) **2** : to prick, to stick **3** : to goad, to tease, to needle — *vi* **1** : to be prickly **2** : to get a flat tire **3** *fam* : to get beaten, to lose out — **pincharse** *vr* : to give oneself an injection
pinchazo *nm* **1** : prick, jab **2** : puncture, flat tire
pingüe *adj* **1** : rich, huge (of profits) **2** : lucrative
pingüino *nm* : penguin
pininos or **pinitos** *nmpl* : first steps ⟨hacer pininos : to take one's first steps, to toddle⟩
pino *nm* : pine, pine tree
pinta *nf* **1** : dot, spot **2** : pint **3** *fam* : aspect, appearance ⟨las peras tienen buena pinta : the pears look good⟩ **4 pintas** *nfpl Mex* : graffiti
pintadas *nfpl* : graffiti

pintar *vt* **1** : to paint **2** : to draw, to mark **3** : to describe, to depict — *vi* **1** : to paint, to draw **2** : to look ⟨no pinta bien : it doesn't look good⟩ **3** *fam* : to count ⟨aquí no pinta nada : he has no say here⟩ — **pintarse** *vr* **1** MAQUILLARSE : to put on makeup **2 pintárselas solo** *fam* : to manage by oneself, to know it all
pintarrajear *vt* : to daub (with paint)
pinto, -ta *adj* : speckled, spotted
pintor, -tora *n* **1** : painter **2 pintor de brocha gorda** : housepainter, dauber
pintoresco, -ca *adj* : picturesque, quaint
pintura *nf* **1** : paint **2** : painting (art, work of art)
pinza *nf* **1** : clothespin **2** : claw, pincer **3** : pleat, dart **4 pinzas** *nfpl* : tweezers **5 pinzas** *nfpl* ALICATES : pliers, pincers
pinzón *nm, pl* **pinzones** : finch
piña *nf* **1** : pineapple **2** : pine cone
piñata *nf* : piñata
piñón *nm, pl* **piñones 1** : pine nut **2** : pinion
pío¹, pía *adj* **1** DEVOTO : pious, devout **2** : piebald, pied, dappled
pío² *nm* : peep, tweet, cheep
piocha *nf* **1** : pickax **2** *Mex* : goatee
piojo *nm* : louse
piojoso, -sa *adj* **1** : lousy **2** : filthy
pionero¹, -ra *adj* : pioneering
pionero², -ra *n* : pioneer
pipa *nf* : pipe (for smoking)
pipián *nm, pl* **pipianes** *Mex* : a spicy sauce or stew
pipiolo, -la *n fam* **1** : greenhorn, novice **2** : kid, youngster
pique¹, etc. → **picar**
pique² *nm* **1** : pique, resentment **2** : rivalry, competition **3 a pique de** : about to, on the verge of **4 irse a pique** : to sink, to founder
piqueta *nf* : pickax
piquete *nm* **1** : picketers *pl*, picket line **2** : squad, detachment **3** *Mex* : prick, jab
piquetear *vt* **1** : to picket **2** *Mex* : to prick, to jab
pira *nf* : pyre
piragua *nf* : canoe — **piragüista** *nmf*
pirámide *nf* : pyramid
piraña *nf* : piranha
pirata¹ *adj* : bootleg, pirated
pirata² *nmf* **1** : pirate **2** : bootlegger **3 pirata aéreo** : hijacker
piratear *vt* **1** : to hijack, to commandeer **2** : to bootleg, to pirate
piratería *nf* : piracy, bootlegging
piromanía *nf* : pyromania
pirómano, -na *n* : pyromaniac
piropo *nm* : flirtatious compliment
pirotecnia *nf* : fireworks *pl*, pyrotechnics *pl*
pirotécnico, -ca *adj* : fireworks, pyrotechnic
pírrico, -ca *adj* : Pyrrhic
pirueta *nf* : pirouette
pirulí *nm* : cone-shaped lollipop

pisada *nf* **1** : footstep **2** HUELLA : footprint

pisapapeles *nms & pl* : paperweight

pisar *vt* **1** : to step on, to set foot in **2** : to walk all over, to mistreat — *vi* : to step, to walk, to tread

piscina *nf* **1** : swimming pool **2** : fish pond

Piscis *nmf* : Pisces

piso *nm* **1** PLANTA : floor, story **2** SUELO : floor **3** *Spain* : apartment

pisotear *vt* **1** : to stamp on, to trample **2** PISAR : to walk all over **3** : to flout, to disregard

pisotón *nm, pl* **-tones** : stamp, step ⟨sufrieron empujones y pisotones : they were pushed and stepped on⟩

pista *nf* **1** RASTRO : trail, track ⟨siguen la pista de los sospechosos : they're on the trail of the suspects⟩ **2** : clue **3** CAMINO : road, trail **4** : track, racetrack **5** : ring, arena, rink **6 pista de aterrizaje** : runway, airstrip **7 pista de baile** : dance floor

pistacho *nm* : pistachio

pistilo *nm* : pistil

pistola *nf* **1** : pistol, handgun **2** : spray gun

pistolera *nf* : holster

pistolero *nm* : gunman

pistón *nm, pl* **pistones** : piston

pita *nf* **1** : agave **2** : pita fiber **3** : twine

pitar *vi* **1** : to blow a whistle **2** : to whistle, to boo **3** : to beep, to honk, to toot — *vt* : to whistle at, to boo

pitido *nm* **1** : whistle, whistling **2** : beep, honk, toot

pito *nm* **1** SILBATO : whistle **2 no me importa un pito** *fam* : I don't give a damn

pitón *nm, pl* **pitones 1** : python **2** : point of a bull's horn

pituitario, -ria *adj* : pituitary

pívot *nmf, pl* **pívots** : center (in basketball)

pivote *nm* : pivot

piyama *nmf* : pajamas *pl*

pizarra *nf* **1** : slate **2** : blackboard **3** : scoreboard

pizarrón *nm, pl* **-rrones** : blackboard, chalkboard

pizca *nf* **1** : pinch ⟨una pizca de canela : a pinch of cinnamon⟩ **2** : speck, trace ⟨ni pizca : not a bit⟩ **3** *Mex* : harvest

pizcar {72} *vt Mex* : to harvest

pizque, etc. → pizcar

pizza ['pitsa, 'pisa] *nf* : pizza

pizzería *nf* : pizzeria, pizza parlor

placa *nf* **1** : sheet, plate **2** : plaque, nameplate **3** : plate (in photography) **4** : badge, insignia **5 placa de matrícula** : license plate, tag **6 placa dental** : plaque, tartar

placebo *nm* : placebo

placenta *nf* : placenta, afterbirth

placentero, -ra *adj* AGRADABLE, GRATO : pleasant, agreeable

placer[1] {57} *vi* GUSTAR : to be pleasing ⟨hazlo como te plazca : do it however you please⟩

placer[2] *nm* **1** : pleasure, enjoyment **2 a ~** : as much as one wants

plácido, -da *adj* TRANQUILO : placid, calm

plaga *nf* **1** : plague, infestation, blight **2** CALAMIDAD : disaster, scourge

plagado, -da *adj* **~ de** : filled with, covered with

plagar {52} *vt* : to plague

plagiar *vt* **1** : to plagiarize **2** SECUESTRAR : to kidnap, to abduct

plagiario, -ria *n* **1** : plagiarist **2** SECUESTRADOR : kidnapper, abductor

plagio *nm* **1** : plagiarism **2** SECUESTRO : kidnapping, abduction

plague, etc. → plagar

plan *nm* **1** : plan, strategy, program ⟨plan de inversiones : investment plan⟩ ⟨plan de estudios : curriculum⟩ **2** PLANO : plan, diagram **3** : attitude, intent, purpose ⟨ponte en plan serio : be serious⟩ ⟨estamos en plan de divertirnos : we're looking to have some fun⟩

plana *nf* **1** : page ⟨noticias en primera plana : front-page news⟩ **2 plana mayor** : staff (in the military)

plancha *nf* **1** : iron, ironing **2** : grill, griddle ⟨a la plancha : grilled⟩ **3** : sheet, plate ⟨plancha para hornear : baking sheet⟩ **4** *fam* : blunder, blooper

planchada *nf* : ironing, pressing

planchado *nm* → planchada

planchar *v* : to iron

planchazo *nm fam* : goof, blunder

plancton *nm* : plankton

planeación *nf* → planeamiento

planeador *nm* : glider (aircraft)

planeamiento *nm* : plan, planning

planear *vt* : to plan — *vi* : to glide (in the air)

planeo *nm* : gliding, soaring

planeta *nm* : planet

planetario[1], **-ria** *adj* **1** : planetary **2** : global, worldwide

planetario[2] *nm* : planetarium

planicie *nf* : plain

planificación *nf* : planning ⟨planificación familiar : family planning⟩

planificar {72} *vt* : to plan

planilla *nf* **1** LISTA : list **2** NÓMINA : payroll **3** TABLA : chart, table **4** *Mex* : slate, ticket (of candidates) **5 planilla de cálculo** *Arg, Chile* : spreadsheet

plano[1], **-na** *adj* : flat, level, plane

plano[2] *nm* **1** PLAN : map, plan **2** : plane (surface) **3** NIVEL : level ⟨en un plano personal : on a personal level⟩ **4** : shot (in photography) **5 de ~** : flatly, outright, directly ⟨se negó de plano : he flatly refused⟩

planta *nf* **1** : plant ⟨planta de interior : houseplant⟩ **2** FÁBRICA : plant, factory **3** PISO : floor, story **4** : staff, employees *pl* **5** : sole (of the foot)

plantación *nf, pl* **-ciones** 1 : plantation 2 : planting

plantado, -da *adj* 1 : planted 2 **dejar plantado** : to stand up (a date), to dump (a lover)

plantar *vt* 1 : to plant, to sow ⟨plantar de flores : to plant with flowers⟩ 2 : to put in, to place 3 *fam* : to plant, to land ⟨plantar un beso : to plant a kiss⟩ 4 *fam* : to leave, to jilt — **plantarse** *vr* 1 : to stand firm 2 *fam* : to arrive, to show up 3 *fam* : to balk

planteamiento *nm* 1 : approach, position ⟨el planteamiento feminista : the feminist viewpoint⟩ 2 : explanation, exposition 3 : proposal, suggestion, plan

plantear *vt* 1 : to set forth, to bring up, to suggest 2 : to establish, to set up 3 : to create, to pose (a problem) — **plantearse** *vr* 1 : to think about 2 : to arise

plantel *nm* 1 : educational institution 2 : staff, team

planteo → **planteamiento**

plantilla *nf* 1 : insole 2 : pattern, template, stencil 3 *Mex, Spain* : staff, roster of employees

plantío *nm* : field (planted with a crop)

plantón *nm, pl* **plantones** 1 : seedling 2 : long wait ⟨darle a alguien un plantón : to stand someone up⟩

plañidero¹, -ra *adj* : mournful

plañidero², -ra *nf* : hired mourner

plañir {38} *v* : to mourn, to lament

plasma *nm* : plasma

plasmar *vt* : to express, to give form to — **plasmarse** *vr*

plasta *nf* : soft mass, lump

plástica *nf* : modeling, sculpture

plasticidad *nf* : plasticity

plástico¹, -ca *adj* : plastic

plástico² *nm* : plastic

plastificar {72} *vt* : to laminate

plata *nf* 1 : silver 2 : money

plataforma *nf* 1 ESTRADO, TARIMA : platform, dais 2 : platform (in politics) 3 : springboard, stepping stone 4 **plataforma continental** : continental shelf 5 **plataforma de lanzamiento** : launchpad 6 **plataforma petrolífera** : oil rig (at sea)

platal *nm* : large sum of money, fortune

platanal *nm* : banana plantation

platanero¹, -ra *adj* : banana, banana-producing

platanero², -n : banana grower

plátano *nm* 1 : banana 2 : plantain 3 **plátano macho** *Mex* : plantain

platea *nf* : orchestra, pit (in a theater)

plateado, -da *adj* 1 : silver, silvery 2 : silver-plated

plática *nf* 1 : talk, lecture 2 : chat, conversation

platicar {72} *vi* : to talk, to chat — *vt Mex* : to tell, to say

platija *nf* : flatfish, flounder

platillo *nm* 1 : saucer ⟨platillo volador : flying saucer⟩ 2 : cymbal 3 *Mex* : dish ⟨platillos típicos : local dishes⟩

platino *nm* : platinum

plato *nm* 1 : plate, dish ⟨lavar los platos : to do the dishes⟩ 2 : serving, helping 3 : course (of a meal) 4 : dish ⟨plato típico : typical dish⟩ 5 : home plate (in baseball) 6 **plato hondo** : soup bowl

plató *nm* : set (in the movies)

platónico, -ca *adj* : platonic

playa *nf* : beach, seashore

playera *nf* 1 : canvas sneaker 2 *CA, Mex* : T-shirt

plaza *nf* 1 : square, plaza 2 : marketplace 3 : room, space, seat (in a vehicle) 4 : post, position 5 **plaza fuerte** : stronghold, fortified city 6 **plaza de toros** : bullring

plazca, etc. → **placer**

plazo *nm* 1 : period, term ⟨un plazo de cinco días : a period of five days⟩ ⟨a largo plazo : long-term⟩ 2 ABONO : installment ⟨pagar a plazos : to pay in installments⟩

pleamar *nf* : high tide

plebe *nf* : common people, masses *pl*

plebeyo¹, -ya *adj* : plebeian

plebeyo², -ya *n* : plebeian, commoner

plegable *adj* : folding, collapsible

plegadizo → **plegable**

plegar {49} *vt* DOBLAR : to fold, to bend — **plegarse** *vr* : to give in, to yield

plegaria *nf* ORACIÓN : prayer

pleito *nm* 1 : lawsuit 2 : fight, argument, dispute

plenamente *adv* COMPLETAMENTE : fully, completely

plenario, -ria *adj* : plenary, full

plenilunio *nm* : full moon

plenipotenciario, -ria *n* : plenipotentiary

plenitud *nf* : fullness, abundance

pleno, -na *adj* COMPLETO ((*often used as an intensifier*)) : full, complete ⟨en pleno uso de sus facultades : in full command of his faculties⟩ ⟨en plena noche : in the middle of the night⟩ ⟨en pleno corazón de la ciudad : right in the heart of the city⟩

plétora *nf* : plethora

pleuresía *nf* : pleurisy

pliega, pliegue etc. → **plegar**

pliego *nm* 1 HOJA : sheet of paper 2 : sealed document

pliegue *nm* 1 DOBLEZ : crease, fold 2 : pleat

plisar *vt* : to pleat

plomada *nf* 1 : plumb line 2 : sinker

plomería *nf* FONTANERÍA : plumbing

plomero, -ra *n* FONTANERO : plumber

plomizo, -za *adj* : leaden

plomo *nm* 1 : lead 2 : plumb line 3 : fuse 4 *fam* : bore, drag 5 **a ~** : plumb, straight

plugo, etc. → **placer**

pluma *nf* 1 : feather 2 : pen 3 **pluma fuente** : fountain pen

plumaje *nm* : plumage
plumero *nm* : feather duster
plumilla *nf* : nib
plumón *nm, pl* **plumones** : down
plumoso, -sa *adj* : feathery, downy
plural *adj & nm* : plural
pluralidad *nf* : plurality
pluralizar {21} *vt* : to pluralize
pluriempleado, -da *adj* : holding more than one job
pluriempleo *nm* : moonlighting
plus *nm* : bonus
plusvalía *nf* : appreciation, capital gain
Plutón *nm* : Pluto
plutocracia *nf* : plutocracy
plutonio *nm* : plutonium
población *nf, pl* **-ciones 1** : population **2** : city, town, village
poblado¹, -da *adj* **1** : inhabited, populated **2** : full, thick ⟨cejas pobladas : bushy eyebrows⟩
poblado² *nm* : village, settlement
poblador, -dora *n* : settler
poblar {19} *vt* **1** : to populate, to inhabit **2** : to settle, to colonize **3** ~ **de** : to stock with, to plant with — **poblarse** *vr* : to fill up, to become crowded
pobre¹ *adj* **1** : poor, impoverished **2** : unfortunate ⟨¡pobre de mí! : poor me!⟩ **3** : weak, deficient ⟨una dieta pobre : a poor diet⟩
pobre² *nmf* : poor person ⟨los pobres : the poor⟩ ⟨¡pobre! : poor thing!⟩
pobremente *adv* : poorly
pobreza *nf* : poverty
pocilga *nf* CHIQUERO : pigsty, pigpen
pocillo *nm* : small coffee cup, demitasse
poción *nf, pl* **pociones** : potion
poco¹ *adv* **1** : little, not much ⟨poco probable : not very likely⟩ ⟨come poco : he doesn't eat much⟩ **2** : a short time, a while ⟨tardaremos poco : we won't be very long⟩ **3 poco antes** : shortly before **4 poco después** : shortly after
poco², -ca *adj* **1** : little, not much, (a) few ⟨tengo poco dinero : I don't have much money⟩ ⟨en no pocas ocasiones : on more than a few occasions⟩ ⟨poca gente : few people⟩ **2 pocas veces** : rarely
poco³, -ca *pron* **1** : little, few ⟨le falta poco para terminar : he's almost finished⟩ ⟨uno de los pocos que quedan : one of the remaining few⟩ **2 un poco** : a little, a bit ⟨un poco de vino : a little wine⟩ ⟨un poco extraño : a bit strange⟩ **3 a** ~ *Mex (used to express disbelief)* ⟨¿a poco no se te hizo difícil? : you mean you didn't find it difficult?⟩ **4 de a poco** : little by little **5 hace poco** : not long ago **6 poco a poco** : little by little **7 dentro de poco** : shortly, in a little while **8 por** ~ : nearly, almost
podar *vt* : to prune, to trim
poder¹ {58} *v aux* **1** : to be able to, can ⟨no puede hablar : he can't speak⟩ **2** *(expressing possibility)* : might, may ⟨puede llover : it may rain at any mo-

ment⟩ ⟨¿cómo puede ser? : how can that be?⟩ **3** *(expressing permission)* : can, may ⟨¿puedo ir a la fiesta? : can I go to the party?⟩ ⟨¿se puede? : may I come in?⟩ — *vi* **1** : to beat, to defeat ⟨cree que le puede a cualquiera : he thinks he can beat anyone⟩ **2** : to be possible ⟨¿crees que vendrán? : do you think they'll come? — maybe⟩ **3** ~ **con** : to cope with, to manage ⟨¡no puedo con estos niños! : I can't handle these children!⟩ **4 no poder más** : to have had enough ⟨no puede más : she can't take anymore⟩ **5 no poder menos que** : to not be able to help ⟨no pudo menos que asombrarse : she couldn't help but be amazed⟩
poder² *nm* **1** : control, power ⟨poder adquisitivo : purchasing power⟩ **2** : authority ⟨el poder legislativo : the legislature⟩ **3** : possession ⟨está en mi poder : it's in my hands⟩ **4** : strength, force ⟨poder militar : military might⟩
poderío *nm* **1** : power **2** : wealth, influence
poderoso, -sa *adj* **1** : powerful **2** : wealthy, influential **3** : effective
podiatría *nf* : podiatry
podio *nm* : podium
pódium → **podio**
podología *nf* : podiatry, chiropody
podólogo, -ga *n* : podiatrist, chiropodist
podrá, etc. → **poder**
podredumbre *nf* **1** : decay, rottenness **2** : corruption
podrido, -da *adj* **1** : rotten, decayed **2** : corrupt
podrir → **pudrir**
poema *nm* : poem
poesía *nf* **1** : poetry **2** POEMA : poem
poeta *nmf* : poet
poético, -ca *adj* : poetic, poetical
pogrom *nm* : pogrom
póker *or* **poker** *nm* : poker (card game)
polaco¹, -ca *adj* : Polish
polaco², -ca *n* : Pole, Polish person
polaco³ *nm* : Polish (language)
polar *adj* : polar
polarizar {21} *vt* : to polarize — **polarizarse** *vr* — **polarización** *nf*
polea *nf* : pulley
polémica *nf* CONTROVERSIA : controversy, polemics
polémico, -ca *adj* CONTROVERTIDO : controversial, polemical
polen *nm, pl* **pólenes** : pollen
policía¹ *nf* : police
policía² *nmf* : police officer, policeman *m*, policewoman *f*
policíaco, -ca *or* **policiaco, -ca** *adj* : police ⟨novela policíaca : detective story⟩
policial *adj* : police
poliéster *nm* : polyester
poligamia *nf* : polygamy
polígamo¹, -ma *adj* : polygamous
polígamo², -ma *n* : polygamist
polígono *nm* : polygon — **poligonal** *adj*

poliinsaturado, -da *adj* : polyunsaturated

polilla *nf* : moth

polimerizar {21} *vt* : to polymerize

polímero *nm* : polymer

polinesio, -sia *adj & n* : Polynesian

polinizar {21} *vt* : to pollinate — **polinización** *nf*

polio *nf* : polio

poliomielitis *nf* : poliomyelitis, polio

polisón *nm, pl* **-sones** : bustle (on clothing)

politécnico, -ca *adj* : polytechnic

politeísmo *nm* : polytheism — **politeísta** *adj & nmf*

política *nf* **1** : politics **2** : policy

políticamente *adv* : politically

político[1], -ca *adj* **1** : political **2** : tactful, politic **3** : by marriage ⟨padre político : father-in-law⟩

político[2], -ca *n* : politician

póliza *nf* : policy ⟨póliza de seguros : insurance policy⟩

polizón *nm, pl* **-zones** : stowaway ⟨viajar de polizón : to stow away⟩

polka *nf* : polka

polla *nf* APUESTA : bet

pollera *nf* **1** : chicken coop **2** : skirt

pollero, -ra *n* **1** : poulterer **2** : poultry farm **3** *Mex fam* COYOTE : smuggler of illegal immigrants

pollito, -ta *n* : chick, young bird, fledgling

pollo, -lla *n* **1** : chicken **2** POLLITO : chick **3** JOVEN : young man *m*, young lady *f*

polluelo *nm* → **pollito**

polo *nm* **1** : pole ⟨el Polo Norte : the North Pole⟩ ⟨polo negativo : negative pole⟩ **2** : polo (sport) **3** : polo shirt **4** : focal point, center **5 polo opuesto** : exact opposite

polución *nf, pl* **-ciones** CONTAMINACIÓN : pollution

polvareda *nf* **1** : cloud of dust **2** : uproar, fuss

polvera *nf* : compact (for face powder)

polvo *nm* **1** : dust **2** : powder **3 polvos** *nmpl* : face powder **4 polvos de hornear** : baking powder **5 hacer polvo** *fam* : to crush, to shatter ⟨vas a hacer polvo el reloj : you're going to destroy your watch⟩

pólvora *nf* **1** : gunpowder **2** : fireworks *pl*

polvoriento, -ta *adj* : dusty, powdery

polvorín *nm, pl* **-rines** : magazine, storehouse (for explosives)

pomada *nf* : ointment, cream

pomelo *nm* : grapefruit

pómez *nf or* **piedra pómez** : pumice

pomo *nm* **1** : pommel (on a sword) **2** : knob, handle **3** : perfume bottle

pompa *nf* **1** : bubble **2** : pomp, splendor **3 pompas fúnebres** : funeral

pompón *nm, pl* **pompones** BORLA : pom-pom

pomposidad *nf* **1** : pomp, splendor **2** : pomposity, ostentation

pomposo, -sa *adj* : pompous — **pomposamente** *adv*

pómulo *nm* : cheekbone

pon → **poner**

ponchadura *nf Mex* : puncture, flat (tire)

ponchar *vt* **1** : to strike out (in baseball) **2** *Mex* : to puncture — **poncharse** *vr* **1** *Col, Ven* : to strike out (in baseball) **2** *Mex* : to blow out (of a tire)

ponche *nm* **1** : punch (drink) **2 ponche de huevo** : eggnog

poncho *nm* : poncho

ponderación *nf, pl* **-ciones** **1** : consideration, deliberation **2** : high praise

ponderar *vt* **1** : to weigh, to consider **2** : to speak highly of

pondrá, etc. → **poner**

ponencia *nf* **1** DISCURSO : paper, presentation, address **2** INFORME : report

ponente *nmf* : speaker, presenter

poner {60} *vt* **1** COLOCAR : to put, to place ⟨pon el libro en la mesa : put the book on the table⟩ **2** AGREGAR, AÑADIR : to put in, to add **3** : to put on (clothes) **4** CONTRIBUIR : to contribute **5** ESCRIBIR : to put in writing ⟨no le puso su nombre : he didn't put his name on it⟩ **6** IMPONER : to set, to impose **7** EXPONER : to put, to expose ⟨lo puso en peligro : she put him in danger⟩ **8** : to prepare, to arrange ⟨poner la mesa : to set the table⟩ **9** : to name ⟨le pusimos Ana : we called her Ana⟩ **10** ESTABLECER : to set up, to establish ⟨puso un restaurante : he opened up a restaurant⟩ **11** INSTALAR : to install, to put in **12** (*with an adjective or adverb*) : to make ⟨siempre lo pones de mal humor : you always put him in a bad mood⟩ **13** : to turn on, to switch on **14** SUPONER : to suppose ⟨pongamos que no viene : supposing he doesn't come⟩ **15** : to lay (eggs) **16** ~ **a** : to start (someone doing something) ⟨lo puse a trabajar : I put him to work⟩ **17** ~ **de** : to place as ⟨la pusieron de directora : they made her director⟩ **18** ~ **en** : to put in (a state or condition) ⟨poner en duda : to call into question⟩ — *vi* **1** : to contribute **2** : to lay eggs — **ponerse** *vr* **1** : to move (into a position) ⟨ponerse de pie : to stand up⟩ **2** : to put on, to wear **3** : to become, to turn ⟨se puso colorado : he turned red⟩ **4** : to set (of the sun or moon)

poni *or* **poney** *nm* : pony

ponga, etc. → **poner**

poniente *nm* **1** OCCIDENTE : west **2** : west wind

ponqué *nm Col, Ven* : cake

pontifical *adj* : pontifical

pontificar {72} *vi* : to pontificate

pontífice *nm* : pontiff, pope

pontón *nm, pl* **pontones** : pontoon

ponzoña *nf* VENENO : poison — **ponzoñoso, -sa** *adj*

popa *nf* **1** : stern **2 a ~** : astern, abaft, aft
popelín *nm, pl* **-lines** : poplin
popelina *nf* : poplin
popote *nm Mex* : (drinking) straw
populachero, -ra *adj* : common, popular, vulgar
populacho *nm* : rabble, masses *pl*
popular *adj* **1** : popular **2** : traditional **3** : colloquial
popularidad *nf* : popularity
popularizar {21} *vt* : to popularize — **popularizarse** *vr*
populista *adj & nmf* : populist — **populismo** *nm*
populoso, -sa *adj* : populous
popurrí *nm* : potpourri
por *prep* **1** : for, during ⟨se quedaron allí por la semana : they stayed there during the week⟩ ⟨por el momento : for now, at the moment⟩ **2** : around, during ⟨por noviembre empieza a nevar : around November it starts to snow⟩ ⟨por la mañana : in the morning⟩ **3** : around (a place) ⟨debe estar por allí : it must be over there⟩ ⟨por todas partes : everywhere⟩ **4** : by, through, along ⟨por la puerta : through the door⟩ ⟨pasé por tu casa : I stopped by your house⟩ ⟨por la costa : along the coast⟩ **5** : for, for the sake of ⟨lo hizo por su madre : he did it for his mother⟩ ⟨¡por Dios! : for heaven's sake!⟩ **6** : because of, on account of ⟨llegué tarde por el tráfico : I arrived late because of the traffic⟩ ⟨dejar por imposible : to give up as impossible⟩ **7** : per ⟨60 millas por hora : 60 miles per hour⟩ ⟨por docena : by the dozen⟩ **8** : for, in exchange for ⟨su hermana habló por él : his sister spoke on his behalf⟩ **9** : by means of ⟨hablar por teléfono : to talk on the phone⟩ ⟨por escrito : in writing⟩ **10** : as for ⟨por mí : as far as I'm concerned⟩ **11** : times ⟨tres por dos son seis : three times two is six⟩ **12** SEGÚN : from, according to ⟨por lo que dices : judging from what you're telling me⟩ **13** : as, for ⟨por ejemplo : for example⟩ **14** : by ⟨hecho por mi abuela : made by my grandmother⟩ ⟨por correo : by mail⟩ **15** : for, in order to ⟨lucha por ganar su respeto : he struggles to win her respect⟩ **16 estar por** : to be about to **17 por ciento** : percent **18 por favor** : please **19 por lo tanto** : therefore, consequently **20 ¿por qué?** : why? **21 por que → porque 22 por . . . que** : no matter how ⟨por mucho que intente : no matter how hard I try⟩ **23 por sí** *or* **por si acaso** : just in case
porcelana *nf* : china, porcelain
porcentaje *nm* : percentage
porche *nm* : porch
porción *nf, pl* **porciones 1** : portion **2** PARTE : part, share **3** RACIÓN : serving, helping

pordiosear *vi* MENDIGAR : beg
pordiosero, -ra *n* MENDIGO : beggar
porfiado, -da *adj* OBSTINADO, TERCO : obstinate, stubborn — **porfiadamente** *adv*
porfiar {85} *vi* : to insist, to persist
pormenor *nm* DETALLE : detail
pormenorizar {21} *vi* : to go into detail — *vt* : to tell in detail
pornografía *nf* : pornography
pornográfico, -ca *adj* : pornographic
poro *nm* : pore
poroso, -sa *adj* : porous — **porosidad** *nf*
poroto *nm Arg, Chile, Uru* : bean
porque *conj* **1** : because **2** *or* **por que** : in order that
porqué *nm* : reason, cause
porquería *nf* **1** SUCIEDAD : dirt, filth **2** : nastiness, vulgarity **3** : worthless thing, trifle **4** : junk food
porra *nf* **1** : nightstick, club **2** *Mex* : cheer, yell ⟨los aficionados le echaban porras : the fans cheered him on⟩
porrazo *nm* **1** : blow, whack **2 de golpe y porrazo** : suddenly
porrista *nmf* **1** : cheerleader **2** : fan, supporter
portaaviones *nms & pl* : aircraft carrier
portada *nf* **1** : title page **2** : cover **3** : facade, front
portador, -dora *n* : carrier, bearer
portafolio *or* **portafolios** *nm, pl* **-lios 1** MALETÍN : briefcase **2** : portfolio (of investments)
portal *nm* **1** : portal, doorway **2** VESTÍBULO : vestibule, hall
portar *vt* **1** : to carry, to bear **2** : to wear — **portarse** *vr* CONDUCIRSE : to behave ⟨pórtate bien : behave yourself⟩
portátil *adj* : portable
portaviandas *nms & pl* : lunch box
portaviones *nm* → **portaaviones**
portavoz *nmf, pl* **-voces** : spokesperson, spokesman *m*, spokeswoman *f*
portazo *nm* : slam (of a door)
porte *nm* **1** ASPECTO : bearing, demeanor **2** TRANSPORTE : transport, carrying ⟨porte pagado : postage paid⟩
portento *nm* MARAVILLA : marvel, wonder
portentoso, -sa *adj* MARAVILLOSO : marvelous, wonderful
porteño, -ña *adj* : of or from Buenos Aires
portería *nf* **1** ARCO : goal, goalposts *pl* **2** : superintendent's office
portero, -ra *n* **1** ARQUERO : goalkeeper, goalie **2** : doorman *m* **3** : janitor, superintendent
pórtico *nm* : portico
portilla *nf* : porthole
portón *nm, pl* **portones 1** : main door **2** : gate
portugués[1], -guesa *adj & n, mpl* **-gueses** : Portuguese
portugués[2] *nm* : Portuguese (language)

porvenir *nm* FUTURO : future
pos *adv* **en pos de** : in pursuit of
posada *nf* **1** : inn **2** *Mex* : Advent celebration
posadero, -ra *n* : innkeeper
posar *vi* : to pose — *vt* : to place, to lay — **posarse** *vr* **1** : to land, to light, to perch **2** : to settle, to rest
posavasos *nms & pl* : coaster (for drinks)
posdata → **postdata**
pose *nf* : pose
poseedor, -dora *n* : possessor, holder
poseer {20} *vt* : to possess, to hold, to have
poseído, -da *adj* : possessed
posesión *nf, pl* **-siones** : possession
posesionarse *vr* ~ **de** : to take possession of, to take over
posesivo[1], **-va** *adj* : possessive
posesivo[2] *nm* : possessive case
posguerra *nf* : postwar period
posibilidad *nf* **1** : possibility **2 posibilidades** *nfpl* : means, income
posibilitar *vt* : to make possible, to permit
posible *adj* : possible — **posiblemente** *adv*
posición *nf, pl* **-ciones 1** : position, place **2** : status, standing **3** : attitude, stance
posicionar *vt* **1** : to position, to place **2** : to establish — **posicionarse** *vr*
positivo[1], **-va** *adj* : positive
positivo[2] *nm* : print (in photography)
poso *nm* **1** : sediment, dregs *pl* **2** : grounds *pl* (of coffee)
posoperatorio, -ria *adj* : postoperative
posponer {60} *vt* **1** : to postpone **2** : to put behind, to subordinate
pospuso, etc. → **posponer**
posta *nf* : relay race
postal[1] *adj* : postal
postal[2] *nf* : postcard
postdata *nf* : postscript
poste *nm* : post, pole ⟨poste de teléfonos : telephone pole⟩
póster *or* **poster** *nm, pl* **pósters** *or* **posters** : poster, placard
postergación *nf, pl* **-ciones** : postponement, deferring
postergar {52} *vt* **1** : to delay, to postpone **2** : to pass over (an employee)
posteridad *nf* : posterity
posterior *adj* **1** ULTERIOR : later, subsequent **2** TRASERO : back, rear
postgrado *nm* : graduate course
postgraduado, -da *n* : graduate student, postgraduate
postigo *nm* **1** CONTRAVENTANA : shutter **2** : small door, wicket gate
postilla *nf* : scab
postizo, -za *adj* : artificial, false ⟨dentadura postiza : dentures⟩
postnatal *adj* : postnatal
postor, -tora *n* : bidder ⟨mejor postor : highest bidder⟩

postración *nf, pl* **-ciones 1** : prostration **2** ABATIMIENTO : depression
postrado, -da *adj* **1** : prostrate **2 postrado en cama** : bedridden
potranco, -ca *n* → **potro**[1]
postrar *vt* DEBILITAR : to debilitate, to weaken — **postrarse** *vr* : to prostrate oneself
postre *nm* : dessert
postrero, -ra *adj* (**postrer** *before masculine singular nouns*) ÚLTIMO : last
postulación *nf, pl* **-ciones 1** : collection **2** : nomination (of a candidate)
postulado *nm* : postulate, assumption
postulante, -ta *n* **1** : postulant **2** : candidate, applicant
postular *vt* **1** : to postulate **2** : to nominate **3** : to propose — **postularse** *vr* : to run, to be a candidate
póstumo, -ma *adj* : posthumous — **póstumamente** *adv*
postura *nf* **1** : posture, position (of the body) **2** ACTITUD, POSICIÓN : position, stance
potable *adj* : drinkable, potable
potaje *nm* : thick vegetable soup, pottage
potasa *nf* : potash
potasio *nm* : potassium
pote *nm* **1** OLLA : pot **2** : jar, container
potencia *nf* **1** : power ⟨potencias extranjeras : foreign powers⟩ ⟨elevado a la tercera potencia : raised to the third power⟩ **2** : capacity, potency
potencial *adj & nm* : potential
potenciar *vt* : to promote, to foster
potenciómetro *nm* : dimmer, dimmer switch
potentado, -da *n* **1** SOBERANO : potentate, sovereign **2** MAGNATE : tycoon, magnate
potente *adj* **1** : powerful, strong **2** : potent, virile
potestad *nf* **1** AUTORIDAD : authority, jurisdiction **2 patria potestad** : custody, guardianship
potrero *nm* **1** : field, pasture **2** : cattle ranch
potro[1], **-tra** *n* : colt *m*, filly *f*
potro[2] *nm* **1** : rack (for torture) **2** : horse (in gymnastics)
pozo *nm* **1** : well ⟨pozo de petróleo : oil well⟩ **2** : deep pool (in a river) **3** : mine shaft **4** *Arg, Par, Uru* : pothole **5 pozo séptico** : cesspool
pozole *nm* *Mex* : spicy stew made with pork and hominy
práctica *nf* **1** : practice, experience **2** EJERCICIO : exercising ⟨la práctica de la medicina : the practice of medicine⟩ **3** APLICACIÓN : application, practice ⟨poner en práctica : to put into practice⟩ **4 prácticas** *nfpl* : training
practicable *adj* : practicable, feasible
prácticamente *adv* : practically
practicante[1] *adj* : practicing ⟨católicos practicantes : practicing Catholics⟩

practicante[2] *nmf* : practicer, practitioner

practicar {72} *vt* **1** : to practice **2** : to perform, to carry out **3** : to exercise (a profession) — *vi* : to practice

práctico, -ca *adj* : practical, useful

pradera *nf* : grassland, prairie

prado *nm* **1** CAMPO : field, meadow **2** : park

pragmático, -ca *adj* : pragmatic — **pragmáticamente** *adv*

pragmatismo *nm* : pragmatism

preámbulo *nm* **1** INTRODUCCIÓN : preamble, introduction **2** RODEO : evasion ⟨gastar preámbulos : to beat around the bush⟩

prebélico, -ca *adj* : antebellum

prebenda *nf* : privilege, perquisite

precalentar {55} *vt* : to preheat

precariedad *nf* : precariousness

precario, -ria *adj* : precarious — **precariamente** *adv*

precaución *nf, pl* **-ciones** **1** : precaution ⟨medidas de precaución : precautionary measures⟩ **2** PRUDENCIA : caution, care ⟨con precaución : cautiously⟩

precautorio, -ria *adj* : precautionary

precaver *vt* PREVENIR : to prevent, to guard against — **precaverse** *vr* PREVENIRSE : to take precautions, to be on guard

precavido, -da *adj* CAUTELOSO : cautious, prudent

precedencia *nf* : precedence, priority

precedente[1] *adj* : preceding, previous

precedente[2] *nm* : precedent

preceder *v* : to precede

precepto *nm* : rule, precept

preciado, -da *adj* : esteemed, prized, valuable

preciarse *vr* **1** JACTARSE : to boast, to brag **2** ~ **de** : to pride oneself on

precinto *nm* : seal

precio *nm* **1** : price **2** : cost, sacrifice ⟨a cualquier precio : whatever the cost⟩

preciosidad *nf* : beautiful thing ⟨este vestido es una preciosidad : this dress is lovely⟩

precioso, -sa *adj* **1** HERMOSO : beautiful, exquisite **2** VALIOSO : precious, valuable

precipicio *nm* **1** : precipice **2** RUINA : ruin

precipitación *nf, pl* **-ciones** **1** PRISA : haste, hurry, rush **2** : precipitation, rain, snow

precipitado, -da *adj* **1** : hasty, sudden **2** : rash — **precipitadamente** *adv*

precipitar *vt* **1** APRESURAR : to hasten, to speed up **2** ARROJAR : to hurl, to throw — **precipitarse** *vr* **1** APRESURARSE : to rush **2** : to act rashly **3** ARROJARSE : to throw oneself

precisamente *adv* JUSTAMENTE : precisely, exactly

precisar *vt* **1** : to specify, to determine exactly **2** NECESITAR : to need, to require — *vi* : to be necessary

precisión *nf, pl* **-siones** **1** EXACTITUD : precision, accuracy **2** CLARIDAD : clarity (of style, etc.) **3** NECESIDAD : necessity ⟨tener precisión de : to have need of⟩

preciso, -sa *adj* **1** EXACTO : precise **2** : very, exact ⟨en ese preciso instante : at that very instant⟩ **3** NECESARIO : necessary

precocidad *nf* : precocity

precocinar *vt* : to precook

preconcebir {54} *vt* : to preconceive

precondición *nf, pl* **-ciones** : precondition

preconizar {21} *vt* **1** : to recommend, to advocate **2** : to extol

precoz *adj, pl* **precoces** **1** : precocious **2** : early, premature — **precozmente** *adv*

precursor, -sora *n* : forerunner, precursor

predecesor, -sora *n* ANTECESOR : predecessor

predecir {11} *vt* : to foretell, to predict

predestinado, -da *adj* : predestined, fated

predestinar *vt* : to predestine — **predestinación** *nf*

predeterminar *vt* : to predetermine

prédica *nf* SERMÓN : sermon

predicado *nm* : predicate

predicador, -dora *n* : preacher

predicar {72} *v* : to preach

predicción *nf, pl* **-ciones** **1** : prediction **2** PRONÓSTICO : forecast ⟨predicción del tiempo : weather forecast⟩

prediga, predijo etc. → **predecir**

predilección *nf, pl* **-ciones** : predilection, preference

predilecto, -ta *adj* : favorite

predio *nm* : property, piece of land

predisponer {60} *vt* **1** : to predispose, to incline **2** : to prejudice, to bias

predisposición *nf, pl* **-ciones** **1** : predisposition, tendency **2** : prejudice, bias

predominante *adj* : predominant — **predominantemente** *adv*

predominar *vi* PREVALECER : to predominate, to prevail

predominio *nm* : predominance, prevalence

preeminente *adj* : preeminent — **preeminencia** *nf*

preescolar *adj & nm* : preschool

preestreno *nm* : preview

prefabricado, -da *adj* : prefabricated

prefacio *nm* : preface

prefecto *nm* : prefect

preferencia *nf* **1** : preference **2** PRIORIDAD : priority **3** **de** ~ : preferably

preferencial *adj* : preferential

preferente *adj* : preferential, special ⟨trato preferente : special treatment⟩

preferentemente *adv* : preferably

preferible *adj* : preferable
preferido, -da *adj & n* : favorite
preferir {76} *vt* : to prefer
prefigurar *vt* : foreshadow, prefigure
prefijo *nm* : prefix
pregonar *vt* **1** : to proclaim, to announce **2** : to hawk (merchandise) **3** : to extol **4** : to reveal, to disclose
pregunta *nf* **1** : question **2 hacer una pregunta** : to ask a question
preguntar *vt* : to ask, to question — *vi* : to ask, to inquire — **preguntarse** *vr* : to wonder
preguntón, -tona *adj, mpl* **-tones** : inquisitive
prehistórico, -ca *adj* : prehistoric
prejuiciado, -da *adj* : prejudiced
prejuicio *nm* : prejudice
prejuzgar {52} *vt* : to prejudge
prelado *nm* : prelate
preliminar *adj & nm* : preliminary
preludio *nm* : prelude
prematrimonial *adj* : premarital
prematuro, -ra *adj* : premature
premeditación *nf, pl* **-ciones** : premeditation
premeditar *vt* : to premeditate, to plan
premenstrual *adj* : premenstrual
premiado, -da *adj* : winning, prizewinning
premiar *vt* **1** : to award a prize to **2** : to reward
premier *nmf* : premier, prime minister
premio *nm* **1** : prize ⟨premio gordo : grand prize, jackpot⟩ **2** : reward **3** : premium
premisa *nf* : premise, basis
premolar *nm* : bicuspid (tooth)
premonición *nf, pl* **-ciones** : premonition
premura *nf* : haste, urgency
prenatal *adj* : prenatal
prenda *nf* **1** : piece of clothing **2** : security, pledge
prendar *vt* **1** : to charm, to captivate **2** : to pawn, to pledge — **prendarse** *vr* ∼ **de** : to fall in love with
prendedor *nm* : brooch, pin
prender *vt* **1** SUJETAR : to pin, to fasten **2** APRESAR : to catch, to apprehend **3** : to light (a cigarette, a match) **4** : to turn on ⟨prende la luz : turn on the light⟩ **5 prender fuego a** : to set fire to — *vi* **1** : to take root **2** : to catch fire **3** : to catch on
prensa *nf* **1** : printing press **2** : press ⟨conferencia de prensa : press conference⟩
prensar *vt* : to press
prensil *adj* : prehensile
preñado, -da *adj* **1** : pregnant **2** ∼ **de** : filled with
preñar *vt* EMBARAZAR : to make pregnant
preñez *nf, pl* **preñeces** : pregnancy
preocupación *nf, pl* **-ciones** INQUIETUD : worry, concern
preocupante *adj* : worrisome

preocupar *vt* INQUIETAR : to worry, to concern — **preocuparse** *vr* APURARSE : to worry, to be concerned
preparación *nf, pl* **-ciones 1** : preparation, readiness **2** : education, training **3** : (medicinal) preparation
preparado¹, -da *adj* **1** : ready, prepared **2** : trained
preparado² *nm* : preparation, mixture
preparar *vt* **1** : to prepare, to make ready **2** : to teach, to train, to coach — **prepararse** *vr*
preparativos *nmpl* : preparations
preparatoria *nf Mex* : high school
preparatorio, -ria *adj* : preparatory
preponderante *adj* : preponderant, predominant — **preponderancia** *nf* —
preponderantemente *adv*
preposición *nf, pl* **-ciones** : preposition — **preposicional** *adj*
prepotente *adj* : arrogant, domineering, overbearing — **prepotencia** *nf*
prerrogativa *nf* : prerogative, privilege
presa *nf* **1** : capture, seizure ⟨hacer presa de : to seize⟩ **2** : catch, prey ⟨presa de : prey to, seized with⟩ **3** : claw, fang **4** DIQUE : dam **5** : morsel, piece (of food)
presagiar *vt* : to presage, to portend
presagio *nm* : omen, portent
presbiterio *nm* : presbytery, sanctuary (of a church)
presbítero *nm* : presbyter
presciencia *nf* : prescience
prescindible *adj* : expendable, dispensable
prescindir *vi* **1** ∼ **de** : to do without, to dispense with **2** DESATENDER : to ignore, to disregard **3** OMITIR : to omit, to skip
prescribir {33} *vt* : to prescribe
prescripción *nf, pl* **-ciones** : prescription
prescrito *pp* → **prescribir**
presencia *nf* **1** : presence **2** ASPECTO : appearance
presenciar *vt* : to be present at, to witness
presentable *adj* : presentable
presentación *nf, pl* **-ciones 1** : presentation **2** : introduction **3** : appearance
presentador, -dora *n* : newscaster, anchorman *m*, anchorwoman *f*
presentar *vt* **1** : to present, to show **2** : to offer, to give **3** : to submit (a document), to launch (a product) **4** : to introduce (a person) — **presentarse** *vr* **1** : to show up, to appear **2** : to arise, to come up **3** : to introduce oneself
presente¹ *adj* **1** : present, in attendance **2** : present, current **3 tener presente** : to keep in mind
presente² *nm* **1** : present (time, tense) **2** : one present ⟨entre los presentes se encontraban ... : those present included ...⟩
presentimiento *nm* : premonition, hunch, feeling

presentir {76} *vt* : to sense, to intuit ⟨presentía lo que iba a pasar : he sensed what was going to happen⟩
preservación *nf, pl* **-ciones** : preservation
preservar *vt* 1 : to preserve 2 : to protect
preservativo *nm* CONDÓN : condom
presidencia *nf* 1 : presidency 2 : chairmanship
presidencial *adj* : presidential
presidente, -ta *n* 1 : president 2 : chair, chairperson 3 : presiding judge
presidiario, -ria *n* : convict, prisoner
presidio *nm* : prison, penitentiary
presidir *vt* 1 MODERAR : to preside over, to chair 2 : to dominate, to rule over
presilla *nf* : eye, loop, fastener
presión *nf, pl* **presiones** 1 : pressure 2 **presión arterial** : blood pressure
presionar *vt* 1 : to pressure 2 : to press, to push — *vi* : to put on the pressure
preso¹, -sa *adj* : imprisoned
preso², -sa *n* : prisoner
prestado, -da *adj* 1 : borrowed, on loan 2 **pedir prestado** : to borrow
prestamista *nmf* : moneylender, pawnbroker
préstamo *nm* : loan
prestar *vt* 1 : to lend, to loan 2 : to render (a service), to give (aid) 3 **prestar atención** : to pay attention 4 **prestar juramento** : to take an oath — **prestarse** *vr* : to lend oneself ⟨se presta a confusiones : it lends itself to confusion⟩
prestatario, -ria *n* : borrower
presteza *nf* : promptness, speed
prestidigitación *nf, pl* **-ciones** : sleight of hand, prestidigitation
prestidigitador, -dora *n* : conjurer, magician
prestigio *nm* : prestige — **prestigioso, -sa** *adj*
presto¹ *adv* : promptly, at once
presto², -ta *adj* 1 : quick, prompt 2 DISPUESTO, PREPARADO : ready
presumido, -da *adj* VANIDOSO : conceited, vain
presumir *vt* SUPONER : to presume, to suppose — *vi* 1 ALARDEAR : to boast, to show off 2 ~ **de** : to consider oneself ⟨presume de inteligente : he thinks he's intelligent⟩
presunción *nf, pl* **-ciones** 1 SUPOSICIÓN : presumption, supposition 2 VANIDAD : conceit, vanity
presunto, -ta *adj* : presumed, supposed, alleged — **presuntamente** *adv*
presuntuoso, -sa *adj* : conceited
presuponer {60} *vt* : to presuppose
presupuestal *adj* : budget, budgetary
presupuestar *vi* : to budget — *vt* : to budget for
presupuestario, -ria *adj* : budget, budgetary
presupuesto *nm* 1 : budget, estimate 2 : assumption, supposition

presurizar {21} *vt* : to pressurize
presuroso, -sa *adj* : hasty, quick
pretencioso, -sa *adj* : pretentious
pretender *vt* 1 INTENTAR : to attempt, to try ⟨pretendo estudiar : I'm trying to study⟩ 2 AFIRMAR : to claim ⟨pretende ser pobre : he claims he's poor⟩ 3 : to seek, to aspire to ⟨¿qué pretendes tú? : what are you after?⟩ 4 CORTEJAR : to court 5 **pretender que** : to expect ⟨¿pretendes que lo crea? : do you expect me to believe you?⟩
pretendiente¹ *nmf* 1 : candidate, applicant 2 : pretender, claimant (to a throne, etc.)
pretendiente² *nm* : suitor
pretensión *nf, pl* **-siones** 1 : intention, hope, plan 2 : pretension ⟨sin pretensiones : unpretentious⟩
pretexto *nm* EXCUSA : pretext, excuse
pretil *nm* : parapet, railing
prevalecer {53} *vi* : to prevail, to triumph
prevaleciente *adj* : prevailing, prevalent
prevalerse {84} *vr* ~ **de** : to avail oneself of, to take advantage of
prevención *nf, pl* **-ciones** 1 : prevention 2 : preparation, readiness 3 : precautionary measure 4 : prejudice, bias
prevenido, -da *adj* 1 PREPARADO : prepared, ready 2 ADVERTIDO : forewarned 3 CAUTELOSO : cautious
prevenir {87} *vt* 1 : to prevent 2 : to warn — **prevenirse** *vr* ~ **contra** *or* ~ **de** : to take precautions against
preventivo, -va *adj* : preventive, precautionary
prever {88} *vt* ANTICIPAR : to foresee, to anticipate
previo, -via *adj* 1 : previous, prior 2 : after, upon ⟨previo pago : after paying, upon payment⟩
previsible *adj* : foreseeable
previsión *nf, pl* **-siones** 1 : foresight 2 : prediction, forecast 3 : precaution
previsor, -sora *adj* : farsighted, prudent
prieto, -ta *adj* 1 : blackish, dark 2 : dark-skinned, swarthy 3 : tight, compressed
prima *nf* 1 : premium 2 : bonus 3 → **primo**
primacía *nf* 1 : precedence, priority 2 : superiority, supremacy
primado *nm* : primate (bishop)
primario, -ria *adj* : primary
primate *nm* : primate
primavera *nf* 1 : spring (season) 2 PRÍMULA : primrose
primaveral *adj* : spring, springlike
primero¹ *adv* 1 : first 2 : rather, sooner
primero², -ra *adj* (**primer** *before masculine singular nouns*) 1 : first 2 : top, leading 3 : fundamental, basic 4 **de primera** : first-rate
primero³, -ra *n* : first
primicia *nf* 1 : first fruits 2 : scoop, exclusive

primigenio, -nia *adj* : original, primary
primitivo, -va *adj* **1** : primitive **2** ORIG-
INAL : original
primo, -ma *n* : cousin
primogénito, -ta *adj & n* : firstborn
primor *nm* **1** : skill, care **2** : beauty, elegance
primordial *adj* **1** : primordial **2** : basic,
fundamental
primoroso, -sa *adj* **1** : exquisite, fine,
delicate **2** : skillful
prímula *nf* : primrose
princesa *nf* : princess
principado *nm* : principality
principal[1] *adj* **1** : main, principal **2**
: foremost, leading
principal[2] *nm* : capital, principal
príncipe *nm* : prince
principesco, -ca *adj* : princely
principiante[1] *adj* : beginning
principiante[2] *nmf* : beginner, novice
principiar *vt* EMPEZAR : to begin
principio *nm* **1** COMIENZO : beginning
2 : principle **3 al principio** : at first **4**
a principios de : at the beginning of ⟨a
principios de agosto : at the beginning
of August⟩ **5 en ~** : in principle
pringar {52} *vt* **1** : to dip (in grease) **2**
: to soil, to spatter (with grease) —
pringarse *vr*
pringoso, -sa *adj* : greasy
pringue[1], etc. → **pringar**
pringue[2] *nm* : grease, drippings *pl*
prior, priora *n* : prior *m*, prioress *f*
priorato *nm* : priory
prioridad *nf* : priority, precedence
prisa *nf* **1** : hurry, rush **2 a ~** *or* **de ~**
: quickly, fast **3 a toda prisa** : as fast
as possible **4 darse prisa** : to hurry **5**
tener prisa : to be in a hurry
prisión *nf, pl* **prisiones 1** CÁRCEL
: prison, jail **2** ENCARCELAMIENTO
: imprisonment
prisionero, -ra *n* : prisoner
prisma *nm* : prism
prismáticos *nmpl* : binoculars
prístino, -na *adj* : pristine
privacidad *nf* : privacy
privación *nf, pl* **-ciones 1** : deprivation
2 : privation, want
privado, -da *adj* : private — **privada-
mente** *adv*
privar *vt* **1** DESPOJAR : to deprive **2** : to
stun, to knock out — **privarse** *vr* : to
deprive oneself
privativo, -va *adj* : exclusive, particular
privilegiado, -da *adj* : privileged
privilegiar *vt* : to grant a privilege to, to
favor
privilegio *nm* : privilege
pro[1] *nm* **1** : pro, advantage ⟨los pros y
contras : the pros and cons⟩ **2 en pro
de** : for, in favor of
pro[2] *prep* : for, in favor of ⟨grupos pro
derechos humanos : groups supporting
human rights⟩
proa *nf* : bow, prow
probabilidad *nf* : probability

probable *adj* : probable, likely
probablemente *adv* : probably
probar {19} *vt* **1** : to demonstrate, to
prove **2** : to test, to try out **3** : to try
on (clothing) **4** : to taste, to sample —
vi : to try — **probarse** *vr* : to try on
(clothing)
probeta *nf* : test tube
probidad *nf* : probity
problema *nm* : problem
problemática *nf* : set of problems ⟨la
problemática que debemos enfrentar
: the problems we must face⟩
probóscide *nf* : proboscis
problemático, -ca *adj* : problematic
procaz *adj, pl* **procaces 1** : insolent, impudent **2** : indecent
procedencia *nf* : origin, source
procedente *adj* **1** : proper, fitting **2 ~
de** : coming from
proceder *vi* **1** AVANZAR : to proceed **2**
: to act, to behave **3** : to be appropriate, to be fitting **4 ~ de** : to originate
from, to come from
procedimiento *nm* : procedure, process
prócer *nmf* : eminent person, leader
procesado, -da *n* : accused, defendant
procesador *nm* : processor ⟨procesador
de textos : word processor⟩
procesamiento *nm* : processing ⟨proce-
samiento de datos : data processing⟩
procesar *vt* **1** : to prosecute, to try **2**
: to process
procesión *nf, pl* **-siones** : procession
proceso *nm* **1** : process **2** : trial, proceedings *pl*
proclama *nf* : proclamation
proclamación *nf, pl* **-ciones** : proclamation
proclamar *vt* : to proclaim — **procla-
marse** *vr*
proclive *adj* **~ a** : inclined to, prone to
proclividad *nf* : proclivity, inclination
procrear *vi* : to procreate — **procreación** *nf*
procurador, -dora *n* ABOGADO : attorney
procurar *vt* **1** INTENTAR : to try, to endeavor **2** CONSEGUIR : to obtain, to
procure **3 procurar hacer** : to manage
to do
prodigar {52} *vt* : to lavish, to be generous with
prodigio *nm* : wonder, marvel
prodigioso, -sa *adj* : prodigious, marvelous
pródigo[1], **-ga** *adj* **1** : generous, lavish **2**
: wasteful, prodigal
pródigo[2], **-ga** *n* : spendthrift, prodigal
producción *nf, pl* **-ciones 1** : production **2 producción en serie** : mass production
producir {61} *vt* **1** : to produce, to make,
to manufacture **2** : to cause, to bring
about **3** : to bear (interest) — **producirse** *vr* : to take place, to occur
productividad *nf* : productivity
productivo, -va *adj* **1** : productive **2** LU-
CRATIVO : profitable

producto *nm* 1 : product 2 : proceeds *pl*, yield
productor, -tora *n* : producer
proeza *nf* HAZAÑA : feat, exploit
profanar *vt* : to profane, to desecrate — **profanación** *nf*
profano¹, -na *adj* 1 : profane 2 : worldly, secular
profano², -na *n* : nonspecialist
profecía *nf* : prophecy
proferir {76} *vt* 1 : to utter 2 : to hurl (insults)
profesar *vt* 1 : to profess, to declare 2 : to practice, to exercise
profesión *nf, pl* **-siones** : profession
profesional *adj & nmf* : professional — **profesionalmente** *adv*
profesionalismo *nm* : professionalism
profesionalizar {21} *vt* : to professionalize
profesionista *nmf Mex* : professional
profesor, -sora *n* 1 MAESTRO : teacher 2 : professor
profesorado *nm* 1 : faculty 2 : teaching profession
profeta *nm* : prophet
profético, -ca *adj* : prophetic
profetisa *nf* : prophetess, prophet
profetizar {21} *vt* : to prophesy
prófugo, -ga *adj & n* : fugitive
profundidad *nf* : depth, profundity
profundizar {21} *vt* 1 : to deepen 2 : to study in depth — *vi* ~ **en** : to go deeply into, to study in depth
profundo, -da *adj* 1 HONDO : deep 2 : profound — **profundamente** *adv*
profusión *nf, pl* **-siones** : abundance, profusion
profuso, -sa *adj* : profuse, abundant, extensive
progenie *nf* : progeny, offspring
progenitor, -tora *n* ANTEPASADO : ancestor, progenitor
progesterona *nf* : progesterone
prognóstico *nm* : prognosis
programa *nm* 1 : program 2 : plan 3 **programa de estudios** : curriculum
programable *adj* : programmable
programación *nf, pl* **-ciones** 1 : programming 2 : planning
programador, -dora *n* : programmer
programar *vt* 1 : to schedule, to plan 2 : to program (a computer, etc.)
progresar *vi* : to progress, to make progress
progresista *adj & nmf* : progressive
progresivo, -va *adj* : progressive, gradual
progreso *nm* : progress
prohibición *nf, pl* **-ciones** : ban, prohibition
prohibir {62} *vt* : to prohibit, to ban, to forbid
prohibitivo, -va *adj* : prohibitive
prohijar {5} *vt* ADOPTAR : to adopt
prójimo *nm* : neighbor, fellow man
prole *nf* : offspring, progeny
proletariado *nm* : proletariat, working class

proletario, -ria *adj & n* : proletarian
proliferar *vi* : to proliferate — **proliferación** *nf*
prolífico, -ca *adj* : prolific
prolijo, -ja *adj* : wordy, long-winded
prólogo *nm* : prologue, preface, foreword
prolongación *nf, pl* **-ciones** : extension, lengthening
prolongar {52} *vt* 1 : to prolong 2 : to extend, to lengthen — **prolongarse** *vr* CONTINUAR : to last, to continue
promediar *vt* 1 : to average 2 : to divide in half — *vi* : to be half over
promedio *nm* 1 : average 2 : middle, midpoint
promesa *nf* : promise
prometedor, -dora *adj* : promising, hopeful
prometer *vt* : to promise — *vi* : to show promise — **prometerse** *vr* COMPROMETERSE : to get engaged
prometido¹, -da *adj* : engaged
prometido², -da *n* NOVIO : fiancé *m*, fiancée *f*
prominente *adj* : prominent — **prominencia** *nf*
promiscuo, -cua *adj* : promiscuous — **promiscuidad** *nf*
promisorio, -ria *adj* 1 : promising 2 : promissory
promoción *nf, pl* **-ciones** 1 : promotion 2 : class, year 3 : play-off (in soccer)
promocionar *vt* : to promote — **promocional** *adj*
promontorio *nm* : promontory, headland
promotor, -tora *n* : promoter
promover {47} *vt* 1 : to promote, to advance 2 FOMENTAR : to foster, to encourage 3 PROVOCAR : to provoke, to cause
promulgación *nf, pl* **-ciones** 1 : enactment 2 : proclamation, enactment
promulgar {52} *vt* 1 : to promulgate, to proclaim 2 : to enact (a law or decree)
prono, -na *adj* : prone
pronombre *nm* : pronoun
pronosticar {72} *vt* : to predict, to forecast
pronóstico *nm* 1 PREDICCIÓN : forecast, prediction 2 : prognosis
prontitud *nf* 1 PRESTEZA : promptness, speed 2 **con** ~ : promptly, quickly
pronto¹ *adv* 1 : quickly, promptly 2 : soon 3 **de** ~ : suddenly 4 **lo más pronto posible** : as soon as possible 5 **tan pronto como** : as soon as
pronto², -ta *adj* 1 RÁPIDO : quick, speedy, prompt 2 PREPARADO : ready
pronunciación *nf, pl* **-ciones** : pronunciation
pronunciado, -da *adj* 1 : pronounced, sharp, steep 2 : marked, noticeable
pronunciamiento *nm* 1 : pronouncement 2 : military uprising
pronunciar *vt* 1 : to pronounce, to say 2 : to give, to deliver (a speech) 3 **pro-**

nunciar un fallo : to pronounce sentence — **pronunciarse** *vr* : to declare oneself
propagación *nf, pl* **-ciones** : propagation, spreading
propaganda *nf* **1** : propaganda **2** PUBLICIDAD : advertising
propagar {52} *vt* **1** : to propagate **2** : to spread, to disseminate — **propagarse** *vr*
propalar *vt* **1** : to divulge **2** : to spread
propano *nm* : propane
propasarse *vr* : to go too far, to overstep one's bounds
propensión *nf, pl* **-siones** INCLINACIÓN : inclination, propensity
propenso, -sa *adj* : prone, susceptible
propiamente *adv* **1** : properly, correctly **2** : exactly, precisely ⟨propiamente dicho : strictly speaking⟩
propiciar *vt* **1** : to propitiate **2** : to favor, to foster
propicio, -cia *adj* : favorable, propitious
propiedad *nf* **1** : property ⟨propiedad privada : private property⟩ **2** : ownership **3** CUALIDAD : property, quality **4** : suitability, appropriateness
propietario[1], -ria *adj* : proprietary
propietario[2], -ria *n* DUEÑO : owner, proprietor
propina *nf* : tip, gratuity
propinar *vt* : to give, to strike ⟨propinar una paliza : to give a beating⟩
propio, -pia *adj* **1** : own ⟨su propia casa : his own house⟩ ⟨sus recursos propios : their own resources⟩ **2** APROPIADO : appropriate, suitable **3** CARACTERÍSTICO : characteristic, typical **4** MISMO : oneself ⟨el propio director : the director himself⟩
proponer {60} *vt* **1** : to propose, to suggest **2** : to nominate — **proponerse** *vr* : to intend, to plan, to set out ⟨lo que se propone lo cumple : he does what he sets out to do⟩
proporción *nf, pl* **-ciones 1** : proportion **2** : ratio (in mathematics) **3 proporciones** *nfpl* : proportions, size ⟨de grandes proporciones : very large⟩
proporcionado, -da *adj* **1** : proportionate **2** : proportioned ⟨bien proporcionado : well-proportioned⟩ — **proporcionadamente** *adv*
proporcional *adj* : proportional — **proporcionalmente** *adv*
proporcionar *vt* **1** : to provide, to give **2** : to proportion, to adapt
proposición *nf, pl* **-ciones** : proposal, proposition
propósito *nm* **1** INTENCIÓN : purpose, intention **2 a** ～ : by the way **3 a** ～ : on purpose, intentionally
propuesta *nf* PROPOSICIÓN : proposal
propulsar *vt* **1** IMPULSAR : to propel, to drive **2** PROMOVER : to promote, to encourage
propulsión *nf, pl* **-siones** : propulsion
propulsor *nm* : propellant

propuso, etc. → **proponer**
prorrata *nf* **1** : share, quota **2 a** ～ : pro rata, proportionately
prórroga *nf* **1** : extension, deferment **2** : overtime (in sports)
prorrogar {52} *vt* **1** : to extend (a deadline) **2** : to postpone
prorrumpir *vi* : to burst forth, to break out ⟨prorrumpí en lágrimas : I burst into tears⟩
prosa *nf* : prose
prosaico, -ca *adj* : prosaic, mundane
proscribir {33} *v* **1** PROHIBIR : to prohibit, to ban, to proscribe **2** DESTERRAR : to banish, to exile
proscripción *nf, pl* **-ciones 1** PROHIBICIÓN : ban, proscription **2** DESTIERRO : banishment
proscrito[1] *pp* → **proscribir**
proscrito[2], -ta *n* **1** DESTERRADO : exile **2** : outlaw
prosecución *nf, pl* **-ciones 1** : continuation **2** : pursuit
proseguir {75} *vt* **1** CONTINUAR : to continue **2** : to pursue (studies, goals) — *vi* : to continue, to go on
prosélito, -ta *n* : proselyte
prospección *nf, pl* **-ciones** : prospecting, exploration
prospectar *vi* : to prospect
prospecto *nm* : prospectus, leaflet, brochure
prosperar *vi* : to prosper, to thrive
prosperidad *nf* : prosperity
próspero, -ra *adj* : prosperous, flourishing
próstata *nf* : prostate
prostitución *nf, pl* **-ciones** : prostitution
prostituir {41} *vt* : to prostitute — **prostituirse** *vr* : to prostitute oneself
prostituto, -ta *n* : prostitute
protagonista *nmf* **1** : protagonist, main character **2** : leader
protagonizar {21} *vt* : to star in
protección *nf, pl* **-ciones** : protection
protector[1], -tora *adj* : protective
protector[2], -tora *n* **1** : protector, guardian **2** : patron
protector[3] *nm* : protector, guard ⟨chaleco protector : chest protector⟩
protectorado *nm* : protectorate
proteger {15} *vt* : to protect, to defend — **protegerse** *vr*
protegido, -da *n* : protégé
proteína *nf* : protein
prótesis *nfs & pl* : prosthesis
protesta *nf* **1** : protest **2** *Mex* : promise, oath
protestante *adj & nmf* : Protestant
protestantismo *nm* : Protestantism
protestar *vi* : to protest, to object — *vt* **1** : to protest, to object to **2** : to declare, to profess
protocolo *nm* : protocol
protón *nm, pl* **protones** : proton
protoplasma *nm* : protoplasm
prototipo *nm* : prototype
protozoario *or* **protozoo** *nm* : protozoan

protuberancia *nf* : protuberance — **protuberante** *adj*
provecho *nm* : benefit, advantage
provechoso, -sa *adj* BENEFICIOSO : beneficial, profitable, useful — **provechosamente** *adv*
proveedor, -dora *n* : provider, supplier
proveer {63} *vt* : to provide, to supply — **proveerse** *vr* ~ **de** : to obtain, to supply oneself with
provenir {87} *vi* ~ **de** : to come from
provenzal[1] *adj* : Provençal
provenzal[2] *nmf* : Provençal
provenzal[3] *nm* : Provençal (language)
proverbio *nm* REFRÁN : proverb — **proverbial** *adj*
providencia *nf* **1** : providence, foresight **2** : Providence, God **3 providencias** *nfpl* : steps, measures
providencial *adj* : providential
provincia *nf* : province — **provincial** *adj*
provinciano, -na *adj* : provincial, unsophisticated
provisión *nf, pl* **-siones** : provision
provisional *adj* : provisional, temporary
provisionalmente *adv* : provisionally, tentatively
provisorio, -ria *adj* : provisional, temporary
provisto *pp* → **proveer**
provocación *nf, pl* **-ciones** : provocation
provocador[1], **-dora** *adj* : provocative, provoking
provocador[2], **-dora** *n* AGITADOR : agitator
provocar {72} *vt* **1** CAUSAR : to provoke, to cause **2** IRRITAR : to provoke, to pique
provocativo, -va *adj* : provocative
proxeneta *nmf* : pimp *m*
próximamente *adv* : shortly, soon
proximidad *nf* **1** : nearness, proximity **2 proximidades** *nfpl* : vicinity
próximo, -ma *adj* **1** : near, close ⟨la Navidad está próxima : Christmas is almost here⟩ **2** SIGUIENTE : next, following ⟨la próxima semana : the following week⟩
proyección *nf, pl* **-ciones 1** : projection **2** : showing, screening (of a film) **3** : range, influence, diffusion
proyectar *vt* **1** : to plan **2** LANZAR : to throw, to hurl **3** : to project, to cast (light or shadow) **4** : to show, to screen (a film)
proyectil *nm* : projectile, missile
proyecto *nm* **1** : plan, project **2 proyecto de ley** : bill
proyector *nm* **1** : projector **2** : spotlight
prudencia *nf* : prudence, care, discretion
prudente *adj* : prudent, sensible, reasonable
prueba[1], **etc.** → **probar**
prueba[2] *nf* **1** : proof, evidence **2** : trial, test **3** : proof (in printing or photography) **4** : event, qualifying round (in sports) **5 a prueba de agua** : waterproof **6 prueba de fuego** : acid test **7 poner a prueba** : to put to the test
prurito *nm* **1** : itching **2** : desire, urge
psicoanálisis *nm* : psychoanalysis — **psicoanalista** *nmf*
psicoanalítico, -ca *adj* : psychoanalytic
psicoanalizar {21} *vt* : to psychoanalyze
psicología *nf* : psychology
psicológico, -ca *adj* : psychological — **psicológicamente** *adv*
psicólogo, -ga *n* : psychologist
psicópata *nmf* : psychopath
psicopático, -ca *adj* : psycopathic
psicosis *nfs & pl* : psychosis
psicosomático, -ca *adj* : psychosomatic
psicoterapeuta *nmf* : psychotherapist
psicoterapia *nf* : psychotherapy
psicótico, -ca *adj & n* : psychotic
psique *nf* : psyche
psiquiatra *nmf* : psychiatrist
psiquiatría *nf* : psychiatry
psiquiátrico[1], **-ca** *adj* : psychiatric
psiquiátrico[2] *nm* : mental hospital
psíquico, -ca *adj* : psychic
psiquis *nfs & pl* : psyche
psoriasis *nf* : psoriasis
ptomaína *nf* : ptomaine
púa *nf* **1** : barb ⟨alambre de púas : barbed wire⟩ **2** : tooth (of a comb) **3** : quill, spine
pubertad *nf* : puberty
pubiano → **púbico**
púbico, -ca *adj* : pubic
publicación *nf, pl* **-ciones** : publication
publicar {72} *vt* **1** : to publish **2** DIVULGAR : to divulge, to disclose
publicidad *nf* **1** : publicity **2** : advertising
publicista *nmf* : publicist
publicitar *vt* **1** : to publicize **2** : to advertise
publicitario, -ria *adj* : advertising, publicity ⟨agencia publicitaria : advertising agency⟩
público[1], **-ca** *adj* : public — **públicamente** *adv*
público[2] *nm* **1** : public **2** : audience, spectators *pl*
puchero *nm* **1** : pot **2** : stew **3** : pout ⟨hacer pucheros : to pout⟩
pucho *nm* **1** : waste, residue **2** : cigarette butt **3 a puchos** : little by little, bit by bit
púdico, -ca *adj* : chaste, modest
pudiente *adj* **1** : powerful **2** : rich, wealthy
pudín *nm, pl* **pudines** BUDÍN : pudding
pudo, etc. → **poder**
pudor *nm* : modesty, reserve
pudoroso, -sa *adj* : modest, reserved, shy
pudrir {59} *vt* **1** : to rot **2** *fam* : to annoy, to upset — **pudrirse** *vr* **1** : to rot **2** : to languish
pueblerino, -na *adj* : provincial, countrified

puebla, etc. → **poblar**
pueblo *nm* **1** NACIÓN : people **2** : common people **3** ALDEA, POBLADO : town, village
puede, etc. → **poder**
puente *nm* **1** : bridge ⟨puente levadizo : drawbridge⟩ **2** : denture, bridge **3 puente aéreo** : airlift
puerco[1], **-ca** *adj* : dirty, filthy
puerco[2], **-ca** *n* **1** CERDO, MARRANO : pig, hog **2** : pig, dirty or greedy person **3 puerco espín** : porcupine
pueril *adj* : childish, puerile
puerro *nm* : leek
puerta *nf* **1** : door, entrance, gate **2 a puerta cerrada** : behind closed doors
puerto *nm* **1** : port, harbor **2** : mountain pass **3 puerto marítimo** : seaport
puertorriqueño, -ña *adj* & *n* : Puerto Rican
pues *conj* **1** : since, because, for ⟨no puedo ir, pues no tengo plata : I can't go, since I don't have any money⟩ ⟨lo hace, pues a él le gusta : he does it because he likes to⟩ **2** (*used interjectionally*) : well, then ⟨pues claro que sí! : well, of course!⟩ ⟨¡pues no voy! : well then, I'm not going!⟩
puesta *nf* **1** : setting ⟨puesta del sol : sunset⟩ **2** : laying (of eggs) **3 puesta a punto** : tune-up **4 puesta en marcha** : start, starting up
puestero, -ra *n* : seller, vendor
puesto[1] *pp* → **poner**
puesto[2], **-ta** *adj* : dressed ⟨bien puesto : well-dressed⟩
puesto[3] *nm* **1** LUGAR, SITIO : place, position **2** : position, job **3** : kiosk, stand, stall **4 puesto que** : since, given that
pugilato *nm* BOXEO : boxing, pugilism
pugilista *nm* BOXEADOR : boxer, pugilist
pugna *nf* **1** CONFLICTO, LUCHA : conflict, struggle **2 en ～** : at odds, in conflict
pugnar *vi* LUCHAR : to fight, to strive, to struggle
pugnaz *adj* : pugnacious
pujante *adj* : mighty, powerful
pujanza *nf* : strength, vigor ⟨pujanza económica : economic strength⟩
pulcritud *nf* **1** : neatness, tidiness **2** ESMERO : meticulousness
pulcro, -cra *adj* **1** : clean, neat **2** : exquisite, delicate, refined
pulga *nf* **1** : flea **2 tener malas pulgas** : to be bad-tempered
pulgada *nf* : inch
pulgar *nm* **1** : thumb **2** : big toe
pulir *vt* **1** : to polish, to shine **2** REFINAR : to refine, to perfect
pulla *nf* **1** : cutting remark, dig, gibe **2** : obscenity
pulmón *nm, pl* **pulmones** : lung
pulmonar *adj* : pulmonary
pulmonía *nf* NEUMONÍA : pneumonia
pulpa *nf* : pulp, flesh
pulpería *nf* : small grocery store

púlpito *nm* : pulpit
pulpo *nm* : octopus
pulsación *nf, pl* **-ciones** **1** : beat, pulsation, throb **2** : keystroke
pulsar *vt* **1** APRETAR : to press, to push **2** : to strike (a key) **3** : to assess — *vi* : to beat, to throb
pulsera *nf* : bracelet
pulso *nm* **1** : pulse ⟨tomarle el pulso a alguien : to take someone's pulse⟩ ⟨tomarle el pulso a la opinión : to sound out opinion⟩ **2** : steadiness (of hand) ⟨dibujo a pulso : freehand sketch⟩
pulular *vi* ABUNDAR : to abound, to swarm ⟨en el río pululan los peces : the river is teeming with fish⟩
pulverizador *nm* **1** : atomizer, spray **2** : spray gun
pulverizar {21} *vt* **1** : to pulverize, to crush **2** : to spray
puma *nf* : cougar, puma
puna *nf* : bleak Andean tableland
punción *nf, pl* **punciones** : puncture
punible *adj* : punishable
punitivo, -va *adj* : punitive
punce, etc. → **punzar**
punta *nf* **1** : tip, end ⟨punta del dedo : fingertip⟩ ⟨en la punta de la lengua : at the tip of one's tongue⟩ **2** : point (of a weapon or pencil) ⟨punta de lanza : spearhead⟩ **3** : point, headland **4** : bunch, lot ⟨una punta de ladrones : a bunch of thieves⟩ **5 a punta de** : by, by dint of
puntada *nf* **1** : stitch (in sewing) **2** PUNZADA : sharp pain, stitch, twinge **3** *Mex* : witticism, quip
puntal *nm* **1** : prop, support **2** : stanchion
puntapié *nm* PATADA : kick
puntazo *nm* CORNADA : wound (from a goring)
puntear *vt* **1** : to pluck (a guitar) **2** : to lead (in sports)
puntería *nf* : aim, marksmanship
puntero *nm* **1** : pointer **2** : leader
puntiagudo, -da *adj* : sharp, pointed
puntilla *nf* **1** : lace edging **2** : dagger (in bullfighting) **3 de puntillas** : on tiptoe
puntilloso, -sa *adj* : punctilious
punto *nm* **1** : dot, point **2** : period (in punctuation) **3** : item, question **4** : spot, place **5** : moment, stage, degree **6** : point (in a score) **7** : stitch **8 en ～** : on the dot, sharp ⟨a las dos en punto : at two o'clock sharp⟩ **9 al punto** : at once **10 a punto fijo** : exactly, certainly **11 dos puntos** : colon **12 hasta cierto punto** : up to a point **13 punto decimal** : decimal point **14 punto de vista** : point of view **15 punto y coma** : semicolon **16 y punto** : period ⟨es el mejor que hay y punto : it's the best there is, period⟩ **17 puntos cardinales** : points of the compass

puntuación *nf, pl* **-ciones 1** : punctuation **2** : scoring, score, grade

puntual *adj* **1** : prompt, punctual **2** : exact, accurate — **puntualmente** *adv*

puntualidad *nf* **1** : promptness, punctuality **2** : exactness, accuracy

puntualizar {21} *vt* **1** : to specify, to state **2** : to point out

puntuar {3} *vt* : to punctuate — *vi* : to score points

punzada *nf* : sharp pain, twinge, stitch

punzante *adj* **1** : sharp **2** CÁUSTICO : biting, caustic

punzar {21} *vt* : to pierce, to puncture

punzón *nm, pl* **punzones 1** : awl **2** : hole punch

puñado *nm* **1** : handful **2 a puñados** : lots of, by the handful

puñal *nm* DAGA : dagger

puñalada *nf* : stab, stab wound

puñetazo *nm* : punch (with the fist)

puño *nm* **1** : fist **2** : handful, fistful **3** : cuff (of a shirt) **4** : handle, hilt

pupila *nf* : pupil (of the eye)

pupilo, -la *n* **1** : pupil, student **2** : ward, charge

pupitre *nm* : writing desk

puré *nm* : purée ⟨puré de papas : mashed potatoes⟩

pureza *nf* : purity

purga *nf* **1** : laxative **2** : purge

purgante *adj & nm* : laxative, purgative

purgar {52} *vt* **1** : to purge, to cleanse **2** : to liquidate (in politics) **3** : to give a laxative to — **purgarse** *vr* **1** : to take a laxative **2** ~ **de** : to purge oneself of

purgatorio *nm* : purgatory

purgue, etc. → **purgar**

purificador *nm* : purifier

purificar {72} *vt* : to purify — **purificación** *nf*

puritano¹, -na *adj* : puritanical, puritan

puritano², -na *n* **1** : Puritan **2** : puritan

puro¹ *adv* : sheer, much ⟨de puro terco : out of sheer stubbornness⟩

puro², -ra *adj* **1** : pure ⟨aire puro : fresh air⟩ **2** : plain, simple, sheer ⟨por pura curiosidad : from sheer curiosity⟩ **3** : only, just ⟨emplean puras mujeres : they only employ women⟩ **4 pura sangre** : Thoroughbred horse

puro³ *nm* : cigar

púrpura *nf* : purple

purpúreo, -rea *adj* : purple

purpurina *nf* : glitter (for decoration)

pus *nm* : pus

pusilánime *adj* COBARDE : pusillanimous, cowardly

puso, etc. → **poner**

pústula *nf* : pustule, pimple

puta *nf* : whore, slut

putrefacción *nf, pl* **-ciones** : putrefaction

putrefacto, -ta *adj* **1** PODRIDO : putrid, rotten **2** : decayed

pútrido, -da *adj* : putrid, rotten

puya *nf* **1** : point (of a lance) **2 lanzar una puya** : to gibe, to taunt

Q

q *nf* : eighteenth letter of the Spanish alphabet

que¹ *conj* **1** : that ⟨dice que está listo : he says that he's ready⟩ ⟨espero que lo haga : I hope that he does it⟩ **2** : than ⟨más que nada : more than anything⟩ **3** (*implying permission or desire*) ⟨¡que entre! : send him in!⟩ ⟨¡que te vaya bien! : I wish you well!⟩ **4** (*indicating a reason or cause*) ⟨¡cuidado, que te caes! : be careful, you're about to fall!⟩ ⟨no provoques al perro, que te va a morder : don't provoke the dog or (else) he'll bite⟩ **5 es que** : the thing is that, I'm afraid that **6 yo que tú** : if I were you

que² *pron* **1** : who, that ⟨la niña que viene : the girl who is coming⟩ **2** : whom, that ⟨los alumnos que enseñé : the students that I taught⟩ **3** : that, which ⟨el carro que me gusta : the car that I like⟩ **4 el (la, lo, las, los) que** → **el¹, la¹, lo¹, los¹**

qué¹ *adv* : how, what ⟨¡qué bonito! : how pretty!⟩

qué² *adj* : what, which ⟨¿qué hora es? : what time is it?⟩

qué³ *pron* : what ⟨¿qué quieres? : what do you want?⟩

quebracho *nm* : quebracho (tree)

quebrada *nf* DESFILADERO : ravine, gorge

quebradizo, -za *adj* FRÁGIL : breakable, delicate, fragile

quebrado¹, -da *adj* **1** : bankrupt **2** : rough, uneven **3** ROTO : broken

quebrado² *nm* : fraction

quebrantamiento *nm* **1** : breaking **2** : deterioration, weakening

quebrantar *vt* **1** : to break, to split, to crack **2** : to weaken **3** : to violate (a law or contract)

quebranto *nm* **1** : break, breaking **2** AFLICCIÓN : affliction, grief **3** PÉRDIDA : loss

quebrar {55} *vt* **1** ROMPER : to break **2** DOBLAR : to bend, to twist — *vi* **1** : to go bankrupt **2** : to fall out, to break up — **quebrarse** *vr*

queda *nf* : curfew

quedar *vi* **1** PERMANECER : to remain, to stay **2** : to be ⟨quedamos contentos con las mejoras : we were pleased with the improvements⟩ **3** : to be situated ⟨queda muy lejos : it's very far, it's too far away⟩ **4** : to be left ⟨quedan sólo dos alternativas : there are only two options left⟩ **5** : to fit, to suit ⟨estos zapatos no me quedan : these shoes don't fit〉 **6 quedar bien (mal)** : to turn out well (badly) **7 ~ en** : to agree, to arrange 〈¿en qué quedamos? : what's the arrangement, then?〉 — **quedarse** *vr* **1** : to stay 〈se quedó en casa : she stayed at home〉 **2** : to keep on 〈se quedó esperando : he kept on waiting〉 **3 quedarse atrás** : to stay behind 〈no quedarse atrás : to be no slouch〉 **4 ~ con** : to remain 〈me quedé con hambre después de comer : I was still hungry after I ate〉

quedo[1] *adv* : softly, quietly

quedo[2], **-da** *adj* : quiet, still

quehacer *nm* **1** : work **2 quehaceres** *nmpl* : chores

queja *nf* : complaint

quejarse *vr* **1** : to complain **2** : to groan, to moan

quejido *nm* **1** : groan, moan **2** : whine, whimper

quejoso, -sa *adj* : complaining, whining

quejumbroso, -sa *adj* : querulous, whining

quema *nf* **1** FUEGO : fire **2** : burning

quemado, -da *adj* **1** : burned, burnt **2** : annoyed **3** : burned-out

quemador *nm* : burner

quemadura *nf* : burn

quemar *vt* : to burn, to set fire to — *vi* : to be burning hot — **quemarse** *vr*

quemarropa *nf a ~* : point-blank

quemazón *nf, pl* **-zones 1** : burning **2** : intense heat **3** : itch **4** : cutting remark

quena *nf* : Peruvian reed flute

quepa, etc. → **caber**

querella *nf* **1** : complaint **2** : lawsuit

querellante *nmf* : plaintiff

querellarse *vr ~* **contra** : to bring suit against, to sue

querer[1] {64} *vt* **1** DESEAR : to want, to desire 〈quiere ser profesor : he wants to be a teacher〉 〈¿cuánto quieres por esta computadora? : how much do you want for this computer?〉 **2** : to love, to like, to be fond of 〈te quiero : I love you〉 **3** (*indicating a request*) 〈¿quieres pasarme la leche? : please pass the milk〉 **4 querer decir** : to mean **5 sin ~** : unintentionally — *vi* : like, want 〈si quieras : if you like〉

querer[2] *nm* : love, affection

querido[1], **-da** *adj* : dear, beloved

querido[2], **-da** *n* : dear, sweetheart

queroseno *nm* : kerosene

querrá, etc. → **querer**

querúbico, -ca *adj* : cherubic

querubín *nm, pl* **-bines** : cherub

quesadilla *nf* : quesadilla

quesería *nf* : cheese shop

queso *nm* : cheese

quetzal *nm* **1** : quetzal (bird) **2** : monetary unit of Guatemala

quicio *nm* **1 estar fuera de quicio** : to be beside oneself **2 sacar de quicio** : to exasperate, to drive crazy

quid *nm* : crux, gist 〈el quid de la cuestión : the crux of the matter〉

quiebra[1], **etc.** → **quebrar**

quiebra[2] *nf* **1** : break, crack **2** BANCARROTA : failure, bankruptcy

quien *pron, pl* **quienes 1** : who, whom 〈no sé quien ganará : I don't know who will win〉 〈las personas con quienes trabajo : the people with whom I work〉 **2** : whoever, whomever 〈quien quiere salir que salga : whoever wants to can leave〉 **3** : anyone, some people 〈hay quienes no están de acuerdo : some people don't agree〉

quién *pron, pl* **quiénes 1** : who, whom 〈¿quién sabe? : who knows?〉 〈¿con quién hablo? : with whom am I speaking?〉 **2 de ~** : whose 〈¿de quién es este libro? : whose book is this?〉

quienquiera *pron, pl* **quienesquiera** : whoever, whomever

quiere, etc. → **querer**

quieto, -ta *adj* **1** : calm, quiet **2** INMÓVIL : still

quietud *nf* **1** : calm, tranquility **2** INMOVILIDAD : stillness

quijada *nf* : jaw, jawbone

quijotesco, -ca *adj* : quixotic

quilate *nm* : karat

quilla *nf* : keel

quimera *nf* : chimera, illusion

quimérico, -ca *adj* : chimeric, fanciful

química *nf* : chemistry

químico[1], **-ca** *adj* : chemical

químico[2], **-ca** *n* : chemist

quimioterapia *nf* : chemotherapy

quimono *nm* : kimono

quince *adj & nm* : fifteen

quinceañero, -ra *n* : fifteen-year-old, teenager

quinceavo[1], **-va** *adj* : fifteenth

quinceavo[2] *nm* : fifteenth (fraction)

quincena *nf* : two week period, fortnight

quincenal *adj* : bimonthly, twice a month

quincuagésimo[1], **-ma** *adj* : fiftieth, fifty-

quincuagésimo[2], **-ma** *n* : fiftieth, fifty- (in a series)

quingombó *nm* : okra

quiniela *nf* : sports lottery

quinientos[1], **-tas** *adj* : five hundred

quinientos[2] *nms & pl* : five hundred

quinina *nf* : quinine

quino *nm* : cinchona

quinqué *nm* : oil lamp

quinquenal *adj* : five-year 〈un plan quinquenal : a five-year plan〉

quinta *nf* : country house, villa

quintaesencia *nf* : quintessence — **quintaesencial** *adj*

quintal *nm* : hundredweight

quinteto *nm* : quintet

quintillizo, -za *n* : quintuplet

quinto, -ta *adj* : fifth — **quinto, -ta** *n*

quíntuplo, -la *adj* : quintuple, five-fold

quiosco *nm* **1** : kiosk **2** : newsstand **3 quiosco de música** : bandstand

quirófano *nm* : operating room

quiromancia *nf* : palmistry
quiropráctica *nf* : chiropractic
quiropráctico, -ca *n* : chiropractor
quirúrgico, -ca *adj* : surgical — **quirúrgicamente** *adv*
quiso, etc. → querer
quisquilloso¹, -sa *adj* : fastidious, fussy
quisquilloso², -sa *n* : fussy person, fussbudget
quiste *nm* : cyst
quitaesmalte *nm* : nail polish remover
quitamanchas *nms & pl* : stain remover

quitanieves *nms & pl* : snowplow
quitar *vt* **1** : to remove, to take away **2** : to take off (clothes) **3** : to get rid of, to relieve — **quitarse** *vr* **1** : to withdraw, to leave **2** : to take off (one's clothes) **3** ~ **de** : to give up (a habit) **4 quitar de encima** : to get rid of
quitasol *nm* : parasol
quiteño¹, -ña *adj* : of or from Quito
quiteño², -ña *n* : person from Quito
quizá *or* **quizás** *adv* : maybe, perhaps
quórum *nm, pl* **quórums** : quorum

R

r *nf* : nineteenth letter of the Spanish alphabet
rábano *nm* **1** : radish **2 rábano picante** : horseradish
rabí *nmf, pl* **rabíes** : rabbi
rabia *nf* **1** HIDROFOBIA : rabies, hydrophobia **2** : rage, anger
rabiar *vi* **1** : to rage, to be furious **2** : to be in great pain **3 a** ~ *fam* : like crazy, like mad
rabieta *nf* BERRINCHE : tantrum
rabino, -na *n* : rabbi
rabioso, -sa *adj* **1** : enraged, furious **2** : rabid
rabo *nm* **1** COLA : tail **2 el rabo del ojo** : the corner of one's eye
racha *nf* **1** : gust of wind **2** : run, series, string ⟨racha perdedora : losing streak⟩
racheado, -da *adj* : gusty, windy
racial *adj* : racial
racimo *nm* : bunch, cluster ⟨un racimo de uvas : a bunch of grapes⟩
raciocinio *nm* : reason, reasoning
ración *nf, pl* **raciones 1** : share, ration **2** PORCIÓN : portion, helping
racional *adj* : rational, reasonable — **racionalmente** *adv*
racionalidad *nf* : rationality
racionalización *nf, pl* **-ciones** : rationalization
racionalizar {21} *vt* **1** : to rationalize **2** : to streamline
racionamiento *nm* : rationing
racionar *vt* : to ration
racismo *nm* : racism
racista *adj & nmf* : racist
radar *nm* : radar
radiación *nf, pl* **-ciones** : radiation, irradiation
radiactividad *nf* : radioactivity
radiactivo, -va *adj* : radioactive
radiador *nm* : radiator
radial *adj* **1** : radial **2** : radio, broadcasting ⟨emisora radial : radio transmitter⟩
radiante *adj* : radiant
radiar *vt* **1** : to radiate **2** : to irradiate **3** : to broadcast (on the radio)
radical¹ *adj* : radical, extreme — **radicalmente** *adv*

radical² *nmf* : radical
radicalismo *nm* : radicalism
radicar {72} *vi* **1** : to be found, to lie **2** ARRAIGAR : to take root — **radicarse** *vr* : to settle, to establish oneself
radio¹ *nm* **1** : radius **2** : radium
radio² *nmf* : radio
radioactividad *nf* : radioactivity
radioactivo, -va *adj* : radioactive
radioaficionado, -da *n* : ham radio operator
radiodifusión *nf, pl* **-siones** : radio broadcasting
radiodifusora *nf* : radio station
radioemisora *nf* : radio station
radiofaro *nm* : radio beacon
radiofónico, -ca *adj* : radio ⟨estación radiofónica pública : public radio station⟩
radiofrecuencia *nf* : radio frequency
radiografía *nf* : X ray (photograph)
radiografiar {85} *vt* : to x-ray
radiología *nf* : radiology
radiólogo, -ga *n* : radiologist
radón *nm* : radon
raer {65} *vt* RASPAR : to scrape, to scrape off
ráfaga *nf* **1** : gust (of wind) **2** : flash, burst ⟨una ráfaga de luz : a flash of light⟩
raid *nm* CA, Mex fam : lift, ride
raído, -da *adj* : worn, shabby
raiga, etc. → raer
raíz *nf, pl* **raíces 1** : root **2** : origin, source **3 a raíz de** : following, as a result of **4 echar raíces** : to take root
raja *nf* **1** : crack, slit **2** : slice, wedge
rajá *nm* : raja
rajadura *nf* : crack, split
rajar *vt* HENDER : to crack, to split — *vi* **1** *fam* : to chatter **2** *fam* : to boast, to brag — **rajarse** *vr* **1** : to crack, to split open *fam* : to back out
rajatabla *adv* **a** ~ : strictly, to the letter
ralea *nf* : kind, sort, ilk ⟨son de la misma valea : they're two of a kind⟩
ralentí *nm* **dejar al ralentí** : to leave (a motor) idling
rallado, -da *adj* **1** : grated **2 pan rallado** : bread crumbs *pl*
rallador *nm* : grater

rallar *vt* : to grate
ralo, -la *adj* : sparse, thin
RAM *nf* : RAM, random-access memory
rama *nf* : branch
ramaje *nm* : branches *pl*
ramal *nm* **1** : branchline **2** : halter, strap
ramera *nf* : harlot, prostitute
ramificación *nf, pl* **-ciones** : ramification
ramificarse {72} *vr* : to branch out, to divide into branches
ramillete *nm* **1** RAMO : bouquet **2** : select group, cluster
ramo *nm* **1** : branch **2** RAMILLETE : bouquet **3** : division (of science or industry) **4 Domingo de Ramos** : Palm Sunday
rampa *nf* : ramp, incline
rana *nf* **1** : frog **2 rana toro** : bullfrog
ranchera *nf Mex* : traditional folk song
ranchería *nf* : settlement
ranchero, -ra *n* : rancher, farmer
rancho *nm* **1** : ranch, farm **2** : hut **3** : settlement, camp **4** : food, mess (for soldiers, etc.)
rancio, -cia *adj* **1** : aged, mellow (of wine) **2** : ancient, old **3** : rancid
rango *nm* **1** : rank, status **2** : high social standing **3** : pomp, splendor
ranúnculo *nm* : buttercup
ranura *nf* : groove, slot
rap *nm* : rap (music)
rapacidad *nf* : rapacity
rapar *vt* **1** : to crop **2** : to shave
rapaz[1] *adj, pl* **rapaces** : rapacious, predatory
rapaz[2], **-paza** *n, mpl* **rapaces** : youngster, child
rape *nm* : close haircut
rapé *nm* : snuff
rapero, -ra *n* : rapper, rap artist
rapidez *nf* : rapidity, speed
rápido[1] *adv* : quickly, fast ⟨¡manejas tan rápido! : you drive so fast!⟩
rápido[2], **-da** *adj* : rapid, quick — **rápidamente** *adv*
rápido[3] *nm* **1** : express train **2 rápidos** *nmpl* : rapids
rapiña *nf* **1** : plunder, pillage **2 ave de rapiña** : bird of prey
raposa *nf* : vixen (fox)
rapsodia *nf* : rhapsody
raptar *vt* SECUESTRAR : to abduct, to kidnap
rapto *nm* **1** SECUESTRO : kidnapping, abduction **2** ARREBATO : fit, outburst
raptor, -tora *n* SECUESTRADOR : kidnapper
raque *nm* : beachcombing
raquero, -ra *n* : beachcomber
raqueta *nf* **1** : racket (in sports) **2** : snowshoe
raquítico, -ca *adj* **1** : scrawny, weak **2** : measly, skimpy
raquitismo *nm* : rickets
raramente *adv* : seldom, rarely
rareza *nf* **1** : rarity **2** : peculiarity, oddity

raro, -ra *adj* **1** EXTRAÑO : odd, strange, peculiar **2** : unusual, rare **3** : exceptional **4 rara vez** : seldom, rarely
ras *nm* **a ras de** : level with
rasar *vt* **1** : to skim, to graze **2** : to level
rascacielos *nms & pl* : skyscraper
rascar {72} *vt* **1** : to scratch **2** : to scrape — **rascarse** *vr* : to scratch an itch
rasgadura *nf* : tear, rip
rasgar {52} *vt* : to rip, to tear — **rasgarse** *vr*
rasgo *nm* **1** : stroke (of a pen) ⟨a grandes rasgos : in broad outlines⟩ **2** CARACTERÍSTICA : trait, characteristic **3** : gesture, deed **4 rasgos** *nmpl* FACCIONES : features
rasgón *nm, pl* **rasgones** : rip, tear
rasgue, etc. → **rasgar**
rasguear *vt* : to strum
rasguñar *vt* **1** : to scratch **2** : to sketch, to outline
rasguño *nm* **1** : scratch **2** : sketch
raso[1], **-sa** *adj* **1** : level, flat **2 soldado raso** : private (in the army) ⟨los soldados rasos : the ranks⟩
raso[2] *nm* : satin
raspadura *nf* **1** : scratching, scraping **2 raspaduras** *nfpl* : scrapings
raspar *vt* **1** : to scrape **2** : to file down, to smooth — *vi* : to be rough
rasque, etc. → **rascar**
rastra *nf* **1** : harrow **2 a rastras** : by dragging, unwillingly
rastrear *vt* **1** : to track, to trace **2** : to comb, to search **3** : to trawl
rastrero, -ra *adj* **1** : creeping, crawling **2** : vile, despicable
rastrillar *vt* : to rake, to harrow
rastrillo *nm* **1** : rake **2 Mex** : razor
rastro *nm* **1** PISTA : trail, track **2** VESTIGIO : trace, sign
rastrojo *nm* : stubble (of plants)
rasuradora *nf Mex, CA* : electric razor, shaver
rasurar *vt* AFEITAR : to shave — **rasurarse** *vr*
rata[1] *nm fam* : pickpocket, thief
rata[2] *nf* **1** : rat **2** *Col, Pan, Peru* : rate, percentage
ratear *vt* : to pilfer, to steal
ratero, -ra *n* : petty thief
ratificación *nf, pl* **-ciones** : ratification
ratificar {72} *vt* **1** : to ratify **2** : to confirm
rato *nm* **1** : while **2 pasar el rato** : to pass the time **3 a cada rato** : all the time, constantly ⟨les sacaba dinero a cada rato : he was always taking money from them⟩ **4 al poco rato** : later, shortly after
ratón[1], **-tona** *n, mpl* **ratones** **1** : mouse **2 ratón de biblioteca** *fam* : bookworm
ratón[2] *nm, pl* **ratones** **1** : (computer) mouse **2** *CoRi* : biceps
ratonera *nf* : mousetrap
raudal *nm* **1** : torrent **2 a raudales** : in abundance

raya¹, etc. → raer
raya² *nf* **1** : line **2** : stripe **3** : skate, ray **4** : part (in the hair) **5** : crease (in clothing)
rayar *vt* **1** ARAÑAR : to scratch **2** : to scrawl on, to mark up ⟨rayaron las paredes : they covered the walls with graffiti⟩ — *vi* **1** : to scratch **2** AMANECER : to dawn, to break ⟨al rayar el alba : at break of day⟩ **3** ~ **con** : to be adjacent to, to be next to **4** ~ **en** : to border on, to verge on ⟨su respuesta raya en lo ridículo : his answer borders on the ridiculous⟩ — **rayarse** *vr*
rayo *nm* **1** : ray, beam ⟨rayo láser : laser beam⟩ ⟨rayo de gamma : gamma ray⟩ ⟨rayo de sol : sunbeam⟩ **2** RELÁMPAGO : lightning bolt **3 rayo X** : X-ray
rayón *nm, pl* **rayones** : rayon
raza *nf* **1** : race ⟨raza humana : human race⟩ **2** : breed, strain **3 de** ~ : thoroughbred, pedigreed
razón *nf, pl* **razones** **1** MOTIVO : reason, motive ⟨en razón de : by reason of, because of⟩ **2** JUSTICIA : rightness, justice ⟨tener razón : to be right⟩ **3** : reasoning, sense ⟨perder la razón : to lose one's mind⟩ **4** : ratio, proportion
razonable *adj* : reasonable — **razonablemente** *adv*
razonado, -da *adj* : itemized, detailed
razonamiento *nm* : reasoning
razonar *v* : to reason, to think
reabastecimiento *nm* : replenishment
reabierto *pp* → reabrir
reabrir {2} *vt* : to reopen — **reabrirse** *vr*
reacción *nf, pl* **-ciones** **1** : reaction **2 motor a reacción** : jet engine
reaccionar *vi* : to react, to respond
reaccionario, -ria *adj & n* : reactionary
reacio, -cia *adj* : resistant, opposed
reacondicionar *vt* : to recondition
reactivación *nf, pl* **-ciones** : reactivation, revival
reactivar *vt* : reactivate, revive
reactor *nm* **1** : reactor ⟨reactor nuclear : nuclear reactor⟩ **2** : jet engine **3** : jet airplane, jet
reafirmar *vt* : to reaffirm, to assert, to strengthen
reajustar *vt* : to readjust, to adjust
reajuste *nm* : readjustment ⟨reajuste de precios : price increase⟩
real *adj* **1** : real, true **2** : royal
realce *nm* **1** : embossing, relief **2 dar realce** : to highlight, to bring out
realeza *nf* : royalty
realidad *nf* **1** : reality **2 en** ~ : in truth, actually
realinear *vt* : to realign
realismo *nm* **1** : realism **2** : royalism
realista¹ *adj* **1** : realistic **2** : realist **3** : royalist
realista² *nmf* **1** : realist **2** : royalist
realización *nf, pl* **-ciones** : execution, realization

realizar {21} *vt* **1** : to carry out, to execute **2** : to produce, to direct (a film or play) **3** : to fulfill, to achieve **4** : to realize (a profit) — **realizarse** *vr* **1** : to come true **2** : to fulfill oneself
realmente *adv* : really, in reality
realzar {21} *vt* **1** : to heighten, to raise **2** : to highlight, to enhance
reanimación *nf, pl* **-ciones** : revival, resuscitation
reanimar *vt* **1** : to revive, to restore **2** : to resuscitate — **reanimarse** *vr* : to come around, to recover
reanudación *nf, pl* **-ciones** : resumption, renewal
reanudar *vt* : to resume, to renew — **reanudarse** *vr* : to resume, to continue
reaparecer {53} *vi* **1** : to reappear **2** : to make a comeback
reaparición *nf, pl* **-ciones** : reappearance
reapertura *nf* : reopening
reata *nf* **1** : rope **2** *Mex* : lasso, lariat **3 de** ~ : single file
reavivar *vt* : to revive, to reawaken
rebaja *nf* **1** : reduction **2** DESCUENTO : discount **3 rebajas** *nfpl* : sale
rebajar *vt* **1** : to reduce, to lower ⟨a precios rebajados : at reduced prices, on sale⟩ **2** : to lessen, to diminish **3** : to humiliate — **rebajarse** *vr* **1** : to humble oneself **2 rebajarse a** : to stoop to
rebanada *nf* : slice
rebanar *vt* : to mop up, to sop up
rebaño *nm* **1** : flock **2** : herd
rebasar *vt* **1** : to surpass, to exceed **2** *Mex* : to pass, to overtake
rebatiña *nf* : scramble, fight (over something)
rebatir *vt* REFUTAR : to refute
rebato *nm* **1** : surprise attack **2 tocar a rebato** : to sound the alarm
rebelarse *vr* : to rebel
rebelde¹ *adj* : rebellious, unruly
rebelde² *nmf* **1** : rebel **2** : defaulter
rebeldía *nf* **1** : rebelliousness **2 en** ~ : in default
rebelión *nf, pl* **-liones** : rebellion
rebobinar *vt* : to rewind
reborde *nm* : border, flange, rim
rebosante *adj* : brimming, overflowing ⟨rebosante de salud : brimming with health⟩
rebosar *vi* **1** : to overflow **2** ~ **de** : to abound in, to be bursting with — *vt* : to radiate
rebotar *vi* **1** : to bounce **2** : to ricochet, to rebound
rebote *nm* **1** : bounce **2** : rebound, ricochet
rebozar {21} *vt* : to coat in batter
rebozo *nm* **1** : shawl, wrap **2 sin** ~ : frankly, openly
rebullir {38} *v* : to move, to stir — **rebullirse** *vr*
rebuscado, -da *adj* : affected, pretentious
rebuscar {72} *vi* : to search thoroughly

rebuznar *vi* : to bray
rebuzno *nm* : bray, braying
recabar *vt* **1** : to gather, to obtain, to collect **2 recabar fondos** : to raise money
recado *nm* **1** : message ⟨mandar recado : to send word⟩ **2** *Spain* : errand
recaer {13} *vi* **1** : to relapse **2** ~ **en** *or* ~ **sobre** : to fall on, to fall to
recaída *nf* : relapse
recaiga, etc. → **recaer**
recalar *vi* : to arrive
recalcar {72} *vt* : to emphasize, to stress
recalcitrante *adj* : recalcitrant
recalentar {55} *vt* **1** : to reheat, to warm up **2** : to overheat
recámara *nf* **1** *Col, Mex, Pan* : bedroom **2** : chamber (of a firearm)
recamarera *nf Mex* : chambermaid
recambio *nm* **1** : spare part **2** : refill (for a pen, etc.)
recapacitar *vi* **1** : to reconsider **2** ~ **en** : to reflect on, to weigh
recapitular *v* : to recapitulate — **recapitulación** *nf*
recargable *adj* : rechargeable
recargado, -da *adj* : overly elaborate or ornate
recargar {52} *vt* **1** : to recharge **2** : to overload
recargo *nm* : surcharge
recatado, -da *adj* MODESTO : modest, demure
recato *nm* PUDOR : modesty
recaudación *nf, pl* **-ciones 1** : collection **2** : earnings *pl*, takings *pl*
recaudador, -dora *n* **recaudador de impuestos** : tax collector
recaudar *vt* : to collect
recaudo *nm* : safe place ⟨a (buen) recaudo : in safe keeping⟩
recayó, etc. → **recaer**
rece, etc. → **rezar**
recelo *nm* : distrust, suspicion
receloso, -sa *adj* : distrustful, suspicious
recepción *nf, pl* **-ciones** : reception
recepcionista *nmf* : receptionist
receptáculo *nm* : receptacle
receptividad *nf* : receptivity, receptiveness
receptivo, -va *adj* : receptive
receptor¹, -tora *adj* : receiving
receptor², -tora *n* **1** : recipient **2** : catcher (in baseball), receiver (in football)
receptor³ *nm* : receiver ⟨receptor de televisión : television set⟩
recesión *nf, pl* **-siones** : recession
recesivo, -va *adj* : recessive
receso *nm* : recess, adjournment
receta *nf* **1** : recipe **2** : prescription
recetar *vt* : to prescribe (medications)
rechazar {21} *vt* **1** : to reject **2** : to turn down, to refuse
rechazo *nm* : rejection, refusal
rechifla *nf* : booing, jeering
rechinar *vi* **1** : to squeak **2** : to grind, to gnash ⟨hacer rechinar los dientes : to grind one's teeth⟩

rechoncho, -cha *adj fam* : chubby, squat
recibidor *nm* : vestibule, entrance hall
recibimiento *nm* : reception, welcome
recibir *vt* **1** : to receive, to get **2** : to welcome — *vi* : to receive visitors — **recibirse** *vr* ~ **de** : to qualify as
recibo *nm* : receipt
reciclable *adj* : recyclable
reciclado → **reciclaje**
reciclaje *nm* **1** : recycling **2** : retraining
reciclar *vt* **1** : to recycle **2** : to retrain
recién *adv* **1** : newly, recently ⟨recién nacido : newborn⟩ ⟨recién casados : newlyweds⟩ ⟨recién llegado : newcomer⟩ **2** : just, only just ⟨recién ahora me acordé : I just now remembered⟩
reciente *adj* : recent — **recientemente** *adv*
recinto *nm* **1** : enclosure **2** : site, premises *pl*
recio¹ *adv* **1** : strongly, hard **2** : loudly, loud
recio², -cia *adj* **1** : severe, harsh **2** : tough, strong
recipiente¹ *nm* : container, receptacle
recipiente² *nmf* : recipient
reciprocar {72} *vi* : to reciprocate
reciprocidad *nf* : reciprocity
recíproco, -ca *adj* : reciprocal, mutual
recitación *nf, pl* **-ciones** : recitation, recital
recital *nm* : recital
recitar *vt* : to recite
reclamación *nf, pl* **-ciones 1** : claim, demand **2** QUEJA : complaint
reclamar *vt* **1** EXIGIR : to demand, to require **2** : to claim — *vi* : to complain
reclamo *nm* **1** : bird call, lure **2** : lure, decoy **3** : inducement, attraction **4** : advertisement **5** : complaint
reclinar *vt* : to rest, to lean — **reclinarse** *vr* : to recline, to lean back
recluir {41} *vt* : to confine, to lock up — **recluirse** *vr* : to shut oneself up, to withdraw
reclusión *nf, pl* **-siones** : imprisonment
recluso, -sa *n* **1** : inmate, prisoner **2** SOLITARIO : recluse
recluta *nmf* : recruit, draftee
reclutamiento *nm* : recruitment, recruiting
reclutar *vt* ENROLAR : to recruit, to enlist
recobrar *vt* : to recover, to regain — **recobrarse** *vr* : to recover, to recuperate
recocer {14} *vt* : to overcook, to cook again
recodo *nm* : bend
recogedor *nm* : dustpan
recoger {15} *vt* **1** : to collect, to gather **2** : to get, to retrieve, to pick up **3** : to clean up, to tidy (up)
recogido, -da *adj* : quiet, secluded
recogimiento *nm* **1** : collecting, gathering **2** : withdrawal **3** : absorption, concentration

recolección *nf, pl* **-ciones** 1 : collection ⟨recolección de basura : trash pickup⟩ 2 : harvest

recolectar *vt* 1 : to gather, to collect 2 : to harvest, to pick

recomendable *adj* : advisable, recommended

recomendación *nf, pl* **-ciones** : recommendation

recomendar {55} *vt* 1 : to recommend 2 ACONSEJAR : to advise

recompensa *nf* : reward, recompense

recompensar *vt* 1 PREMIAR : to reward 2 : to compensate

reconciliación *nf, pl* **-ciones** : reconciliation

reconciliar *vt* : to reconcile — **reconciliarse** *vr*

recóndito, -ta *adj* 1 : remote, isolated 2 : hidden, recondite 3 **en lo más recóndito de** : in the depths of

reconfortar *vt* : to comfort — **reconfortante** *adj*

reconocer {18} *vt* 1 : to recognize 2 : to admit 3 : to examine

reconocible *adj* : recognizable

reconocido, -da *adj* 1 : recognized, accepted 2 : grateful

reconocimiento *nm* 1 : acknowledgment, recognition, avowal 2 : (medical) examination 3 : reconnaissance

reconquista *nf* : reconquest

reconquistar *vt* 1 : to reconquer, to recapture 2 RECUPERAR : to regain, to recover

reconsiderar *vt* : to reconsider — **reconsideración** *nf*

reconstrucción *nf, pl* **-ciones** : reconstruction

reconstruir {41} *vt* : to rebuild, to reconstruct

reconversión *nf, pl* **-siones** : restructuring

reconvertir {76} *vt* 1 : to restructure 2 : to retrain

recopilación *nf, pl* **-ciones** 1 : summary 2 : collection, compilation

recopilar *vt* : to compile, to collect

récord *or* **record** ['rekɔr] *nm, pl* **récords** *or* **records** [-kɔrs] : record ⟨record mundial : world record⟩ — **récord** *or* **record** *adj*

recordar {19} *vt* 1 : to recall, to remember 2 : to remind — *vi* 1 ACORDARSE : to remember 2 DESPERTAR : to wake up

recordatorio¹, -ria *adj* : commemorative

recordatorio² *nm* : reminder

recorrer *vt* 1 : to travel through, to tour 2 : to cover (a distance) 3 : to go over, to look over

recorrido *nm* 1 : journey, trip 2 : path, route, course 3 : round (in golf)

recortar *vt* 1 : to cut, to reduce 2 : to cut out 3 : to trim, to cut off 4 : to outline — **recortarse** *vr* : to stand out ⟨los árboles se recortaban en el horizonte : the trees were silhouetted against the horizon⟩

recorte *nm* 1 : cut, reduction 2 : clipping ⟨recortes de periódicos : newspaper clippings⟩

recostar {19} *vt* : to lean, to rest — **recostarse** *vr* : to lie down, recline

recoveco *nm* 1 VUELTA : bend, turn 2 : nook, corner 3 **recovecos** *nmpl* : intricacies, ins and outs

recreación *nf, pl* **-ciones** 1 : re-creation 2 DIVERSIÓN : recreation, entertainment

recrear *vt* 1 : to re-create 2 : to entertain, to amuse — **recrearse** *vr* : to enjoy oneself

recreativo, -va *adj* : recreational

recreo *nm* 1 DIVERSIÓN : entertainment, amusement 2 : recess, break

recriminación *nf, pl* **-ciones** : reproach, recrimination

recriminar *vt* : to reproach — *vi* : to recriminate — **recriminarse** *vr*

recrudecer {53} *v* : to intensify, to worsen — **recrudecerse** *vr*

rectal *adj* : rectal

rectangular *adj* : rectangular

rectángulo *nm* : rectangle

rectificación *nf, pl* **-ciones** : rectification, correction

rectificar {72} *vt* 1 : to rectify, to correct 2 : to straighten (out)

rectitud *nf* 1 : straightness 2 : honesty, rectitude

recto¹ *adv* : straight

recto², -ta *adj* 1 : straight 2 : upright, honorable 3 : sound

recto³ *nm* : rectum

rector¹, -tora *adj* : governing, managing

rector², -tora *n* : rector

rectoría *nf* : rectory

recubierto *pp* → **recubrir**

recubrir {2} *vt* : to cover, to coat

recuento *nm* : recount, count ⟨un recuento de los votos : a recount of the votes⟩

recuerdo *nm* 1 : memory 2 : souvenir, memento 3 **recuerdos** *nmpl* : regards

recular *vi* 1 : to back up 2 REPLEGARSE : to retreat, to fall back 3 RETRACTARSE : to back down

recuperación *nf, pl* **-ciones** 1 : recovery, recuperation 2 **recuperación de datos** : data retrieval

recuperar *vt* 1 : to recover, to get back, to retrieve 2 : to recuperate 3 : to make up for ⟨recuperar el tiempo perdido : to make up for lost time⟩ — **recuperarse** *vr* ~ **de** : to recover from, to get over

recurrente *adj* : recurrent, recurring

recurrir *vi* 1 ~ **a** : to turn to, to appeal to 2 ~ **a** : to resort to 3 : to appeal (in law)

recurso *nm* 1 : recourse ⟨el último recurso : the last resort⟩ 2 : appeal (in law) 3 **recursos** *nmpl* : resources, means ⟨recursos naturales : natural resources⟩

red *nf* **1** : net, mesh **2** : network, system, chain **3** : trap, snare

redacción *nf, pl* **-ciones 1** : writing, composition **2** : editing

redactar *vt* **1** : to write, to draft **2** : to edit

redactor, -tora *n* : editor

redada *nf* **1** : raid **2** : catch, haul

redefinir *vt* : to redefine — **redefinición** *nf*

redención *nf, pl* **-ciones** : redemption

redentor[1], -tora *adj* : redeeming

redentor[2], -tora *n* : redeemer

redescubierto *pp* → **redescubrir**

redescubrir {2} *vt* : to rediscover

redicho, -cha *adj fam* : affected, pretentious

redil *nm* **1** : sheepfold **2 volver al redil** : to return to the fold

redimir *vt* : to redeem, to deliver (from sin)

rediseñar *vt* : to redesign

redistribuir {41} *vt* : to redistribute — **redistribución** *nf*

rédito *nm* : return, yield

redituar {3} *vt* : to produce, to yield

redoblar *vt* : to redouble, to strengthen — **redoblado, -da** *adj*

redoble *nm* : drum roll

redomado, -da *adj* **1** : sly, crafty **2** : utter, out-and-out

redonda *nf* **1** : region, surrounding area **2 a la redonda** ALREDEDOR : around ⟨de diez millas a la redonda : for ten miles around⟩

redondear *vt* : to round off, to round out

redondel *nm* **1** : ring, circle **2** : bullring, arena

redondez *nf* : roundness

redondo, -da *adj* **1** : round ⟨mesa redonda : round table⟩ **2** : great, perfect ⟨un negocio redondo : an excellent deal⟩ **3** : straightforward, flat ⟨un rechazo redondo : a flat refusal⟩ **4** *Mex* : round-trip **5 en** ~ : around

reducción *nf, pl* **-ciones** : reduction, decrease

reducido, -da *adj* **1** : reduced, limited **2** : small

reducir {61} *vt* **1** DISMINUIR : to reduce, to decrease, to cut **2** : to subdue **3** : to boil down — **reducirse** *vr* ~ **a** : to come down to, to be nothing more than

redundancia *nf* : redundancy

redundante *adj* : redundant

reedición *nf, pl* **-ciones** : reprint

reelegir {28} *vt* : to reelect — **reelección** *nf*

reembolsable *adj* : refundable

reembolsar *vt* **1** : to refund, to reimburse **2** : to repay

reembolso *nm* : refund, reimbursement

reemplazable *adj* : replaceable

reemplazar {21} *vt* : to replace, to substitute

reemplazo *nm* : replacement, substitution

reencarnación *nf, pl* **-ciones** : reincarnation

reencuentro *nm* : reunion

reestablecer {53} *vt* : to reestablish

reestructurar *vt* : to restructure

reexaminar *vt* : to reexamine

refaccionar *vt* : to repair, to renovate

refacciones *nfpl* : repairs, renovations

referencia *nf* **1** : reference **2 hacer referencia a** : to refer to

referendo → **referéndum**

referéndum *nm, pl* **-dums** : referendum

referente *adj* ~ **a** : concerning

réferi *or* **referi** [ˈrɛfɛri] *nmf* : referee

referir {76} *vt* **1** : to relate, to tell **2** : to refer ⟨nos refirió al diccionario : she referred us to the dictionary⟩ — **referirse** *vr* ~ **a** **1** : to refer to **2** ~ **a** : to be concerned, to be in reference to ⟨en lo que se refiere a la educación : as far as education is concerned⟩

refinado[1], -da *adj* : refined

refinado[2] *nm* : refining

refinamiento *nm* **1** : refining **2** FINURA : refinement

refinanciar *vt* : to refinance

refinar *vt* : to refine

refinería *nf* : refinery

reflectante *adj* : reflective, reflecting

reflector[1], -tora *adj* : reflecting

reflector[2] *nm* **1** : spotlight, searchlight **2** : reflector

reflejar *vt* : to reflect — **reflejarse** *vr* : to be reflected ⟨la decepción se refleja en su rostro : the disappointment shows on her face⟩

reflejo *nm* **1** : reflection **2** : reflex **3 reflejos** *nmpl* : highlights, streaks (in hair)

reflexión *nf, pl* **-xiones** : reflection, thought

reflexionar *vi* : to reflect, to think

reflexivo, -va *adj* **1** : reflective, thoughtful **2** : reflexive

reflujo *nm* : ebb, ebb tide

reforma *nf* **1** : reform **2** : alteration, renovation

reformador, -dora *n* : reformer

reformar *vt* **1** : to reform **2** : to change, to alter **3** : to renovate, to repair — **reformarse** *vr* : to mend one's ways

reformatorio *nm* : reformatory

reformular *vt* : to reformulate — **reformulación** *nf*

reforzar {36} *vt* **1** : to reinforce, to strengthen **2** : to encourage, to support

refracción *nf, pl* **-ciones** : refraction

refractar *vt* : to refract — **refractarse** *vr*

refractario, -ria *adj* : refractory, obstinate

refrán *nm, pl* **refranes** ADAGIO : proverb, saying

refregar {49} *vt* : to scrub

refrenar *vt* **1** : to rein in (a horse) **2** : to restrain, to check — **refrenarse** *vr* : to restrain oneself

refrendar *vt* **1** : to countersign, to endorse **2** : to stamp (a passport)

refrescante *adj* : refreshing

refrescar {72} *vt* **1** : to refresh, to cool **2** : to brush up (on) **3 refrescar la memoria** : to refresh one's memory — *vi* : to turn cooler

refresco *nm* : refreshment, soft drink

refriega *nf* : skirmish, scuffle

refrigeración *nf, pl* **-ciones 1** : refrigeration **2** : air-conditioning

refrigerador *nmf* NEVERA : refrigerator

refrigeradora *nf Col, Peru* : refrigerator

refrigerante *nm* : coolant

refrigerar *vt* **1** : to refrigerate **2** : to air-condition

refrigerio *nm* : snack, refreshments *pl*

refrito[1], **-ta** *adj* : refried

refrito[2] *nm* : rehash

refuerzo *nm* : reinforcement, support

refugiado, -da *n* : refugee

refugiar *vt* : to shelter — **refugiarse** *vr* ACOGERSE : to take refuge

refugio *nm* : refuge, shelter

refulgencia *nf* : brilliance, splendor

refulgir {35} *vi* : to shine brightly

refundir *vt* **1** : to recast (metals) **2** : to revise, to rewrite

refunfuñar *vi* : to grumble, to groan

refutar *vt* : to refute — **refutación** *nf*

regadera *nf* **1** : watering can **2** : shower head, shower **3** : sprinkler

regaderazo *nm Mex* : shower

regalar *vt* **1** OBSEQUIAR : to present (as a gift), to give away **2** : to regale, to entertain **3** : to flatter, to make a fuss over — **regalarse** *vr* : to pamper oneself

regalía *nf* : royalty, payment

regaliz *nm, pl* **-lices** : licorice

regalo *nm* **1** OBSEQUIO : gift, present **2** : pleasure, comfort **3** : treat

regañadientes *mpl* **a ~** : reluctantly, unwillingly

regañar *vt* : to scold, to give a talking to — *vi* **1** QUEJARSE : to grumble, to complain **2** REÑIR : to quarrel, to argue

regaño *nm fam* : scolding

regañón, -ñona *adj, mpl* **-ñones** *fam* : grumpy, irritable

regar {49} *vt* **1** : to irrigate **2** : to water **3** : to wash, to hose down **4** : to spill, to scatter

regata *nf* : regatta, yacht race

regate *nm* : dodge, feint

regatear *vt* **1** : to haggle over **2** ESCATIMAR : to skimp on, to be sparing with — *vi* : to bargain, to haggle

regateo *nm* : bargaining, haggling

regatón *nm, pl* **-tones** : ferrule, tip

regazo *nm* : lap (of a person)

regencia *nf* : regency

regenerar *vt* : to regenerate — **regenerarse** *vr* — **regeneración** *nf*

regentar *vt* : to run, to manage

regente *nmf* : regent

regidor, -dora *n* : town councillor

régimen *nm, pl* **regímenes 1** : regime **2** : diet **3** : regimen, rules *pl* ⟨régimen de vida : lifestyle⟩

regimiento *nm* : regiment

regio, -gia *adj* **1** : great, magnificent **2** : regal, royal

región *nf, pl* **regiones** : region, area

regional *adj* : regional — **regionalmente** *adv*

regir {28} *vt* **1** : to rule **2** : to manage, to run **3** : to control, to govern ⟨las costumbres que rigen la conducta : the customs which govern behavior⟩ — *vi* : to apply, to be in force ⟨las leyes rigen en los tres países : the laws apply in all three countries⟩ — **regirse** *vr* **~ por** : to go by, to be guided by

registrador[1], **-dora** *adj* **caja registradora** : cash register

registrador[2], **-dora** *n* : registrar, recorder

registrar *vt* **1** : to register, to record **2** GRABAR : to record, to tape **3** : to search, to examine — **registrarse** *vr* **1** INSCRIBIRSE : to register **2** OCURRIR : to happen, to occur

registro *nm* **1** : register **2** : registration **3** : registry, record office **4** : range (of a voice or musical instrument) **5** : search

regla *nf* **1** NORMA : rule, regulation **2** : ruler ⟨regla de cálculo : slide rule⟩ **3** MENSTRUACIÓN : period, menstruation

reglamentación *nf, pl* **-ciones 1** : regulation **2** : rules *pl*

reglamentar *vt* : to regulate, to set rules for

reglamentario, -ria *adj* : regulation, official ⟨equipo reglamentario : standard equipment⟩

reglamento *nm* : regulations *pl*, rules *pl* ⟨reglamento de tráfico : traffic regulations⟩

regocijar *vt* : to gladden, to delight — **regocijarse** *vr* : to rejoice

regocijo *nm* : delight, rejoicing

regordete, -ta *adj fam* LLENITO : chubby

regresar *vt* DEVOLVER : to give back — *vi* : to return, to come back, to go back

regresión *nf, pl* **-siones** : regression, return

regresivo, -va *adj* : regressive

regreso *nm* **1** : return **2 estar de regreso** : to be back, to be home

reguero *nm* **1** : irrigation ditch **2** : trail, trace **3 propagarse como reguero de pólvora** : to spread like wildfire

regulable *adj* : adjustable

regulación *nf, pl* **-ciones** : regulation, control

regulador[1], **-dora** *adj* : regulating, regulatory

regulador[2] *nm* **1** : regulator, governor **2 regulador de tiro** : damper (in a chimney)

regular[1] *vt* : to regulate, to control

regular[2] *adj* **1** : regular **2** : fair, OK, so-so **3** : medium, average **4 por lo regular** : in general, generally

regularidad *nf* : regularity

regularización *nf, pl* **-ciones** NORMAL-IZACIÓN : normalization
regularizar {21} *vt* NORMALIZAR : to normalize, to make regular
regularmente *adv* : regularly
regusto *nm* : aftertaste
rehabilitar *vt* **1** : to rehabilitate **2** : to reinstate **3** : renovate, to restore — **rehabilitación** *nf*
rehacer {40} *vt* **1** : to redo **2** : to remake, to repair, to renew — **rehacerse** *vr* **1** : to recover **2** ~ **de** : to get over
rehecho *pp* → **rehacer**
rehén *nm, pl* **rehenes** : hostage
rehicieron, etc. → **rehacer**
rehizo → **rehacer**
rehuir {41} *vt* : to avoid, to shun
rehusar {8} *v* : to refuse
reimprimir *vt* : to reprint
reina *nf* : queen
reinado *nm* : reign
reinante *adj* **1** : reigning **2** : prevailing, current
reinar *vi* **1** : to reign **2** : to prevail
reincidencia *nf* : recidivism, relapse
reincidente *nmf* : backslider, recidivist
reincidir *vi* : to backslide, to retrogress
reincorporar *vt* : to reinstate — **reincorporarse** *vr* ~ **a** : to return to, to rejoin
reiniciar *vt* **1** : to resume, to restart **2** : to reboot (a computer)
reino *nm* : kingdom, realm ⟨reino animal : animal kingdom⟩
reinstalar *vt* **1** : to reinstall **2** : to reinstate
reintegración *nf, pl* **-ciones** **1** : reinstatement, reintegration **2** : refund, reimbursement
reintegrar *vt* **1** : to reintegrate, reinstate **2** : to refund, to reimburse — **reintegrarse** *vr* ~ **a** : to return to, to rejoin
reír {66} *vi* : to laugh — *vt* : to laugh at — **reírse** *vr*
reiteración *nf, pl* **-ciones** : reiteration, repetition
reiterado, -da *adj* : repeated ⟨lo explicó en reiteradas ocasiones : he explained it repeatedly⟩ — **reiteradamente** *adv*
reiterar *vt* : to reiterate, to repeat
reiterativo, -va *adj* : repetitive, repetitious
reivindicación *nf, pl* **-ciones** **1** : demand, claim **2** : vindication
reivindicar {72} *vt* **1** : to vindicate **2** : to demand, to claim **3** : to restore
reja *nf* **1** : grille, grating ⟨entre rejas : behind bars⟩ **2** : plowshare
rejilla *nf* : grille, grate, screen
rejuvenecer {53} *vt* : to rejuvenate — *vi* : to be rejuvenated — **rejuvenecerse** *vr*
rejuvenecimiento *nm* : rejuvenation
relación *nf, pl* **-ciones** **1** : relation, connection, relevance **2** : relationship **3** RELATO : account **4** LISTA : list **5** **con relación a** *or* **en relación con** : in re-

lation to, concerning **6** **relaciones-públicas** : public relations
relacionar *vt* : to relate, to connect — **relacionarse** *vr* ~ **con** : to be connected to, to be linked with
relajación *nf, pl* **-ciones** : relaxation
relajado, -da *adj* **1** : relaxed, loose **2** : dissolute, depraved
relajante *adj* : relaxing
relajar *vt* : to relax, to slacken — *vi* : to be relaxing — **relajarse** *vr*
relajo *nm* **1** : commotion, ruckus **2** : joke, laugh ⟨lo hizo de relajo : he did it for a laugh⟩
relamerse *vr* : to smack one's lips, to lick one's chops
relámpago *nm* : flash of lightning
relampaguear *vi* : to flash
relanzar {21} *vt* : to relaunch
relatar *vt* : to relate, to tell
relatividad *nf* : relativity
relativo, -va *adj* **1** : relative **2** **en lo relativo a** : with regard to, concerning — **relativamente** *adv*
relato *nm* **1** : story, tale **2** : account
releer {20} *vt* : to reread
relegar {52} *vt* **1** : to relegate **2** **relegar al olvido** : to consign to oblivion
relevante *adj* : outstanding, important
relevar *vt* **1** : to relieve, to take over from **2** ~ **de** : to exempt from — **relevarse** *vr* : to take turns
relevo *nm* **1** : relief, replacement **2** : relay ⟨carrera de relevos : relay race⟩
relicario *nm* **1** : reliquary **2** : locket
relieve *nm* **1** : relief, projection ⟨mapa en relieve : relief map⟩ ⟨letras en relieve : embossed letters⟩ **2** : prominence, importance **3** **poner en relieve** : to highlight, to emphasize
religión *nf, pl* **-giones** : religion
religiosamente *adv* : religiously, faithfully
religioso[1], **-sa** *adj* : religious
religioso[2], **-sa** *n* : monk *m*, nun *f*
relinchar *vi* : to neigh, to whinny
relincho *nm* : neigh, whinny
reliquia *nf* **1** : relic **2** **reliquia de familia** : family heirloom
rellenar *vt* **1** : to refill **2** : to stuff, to fill **3** : to fill out
relleno[1], **-na** *adj* : stuffed, filled
relleno[2] *nm* : stuffing, filling
reloj *nm* **1** : clock **2** : watch **3** **reloj de arena** : hourglass **4** **reloj de pulsera** : wristwatch **5** **como un reloj** : like clockwork
relojería *nf* **1** : watchmaker's shop **2** : watchmaking, clockmaking
reluciente *adj* : brilliant, shining
relucir {45} *vi* **1** : to glitter, to shine **2** **salir a relucir** : to come to the surface **3** **sacar a relucir** : to bring up, to mention
relumbrante *adj* : dazzling
relumbrar *vi* : to shine brightly
relumbrón *nm, pl* **-brones** **1** : flash, glare **2** **de** ~ : flashy, showy

remachar *vt* **1** : to rivet **2** : to clinch (a nail) **3** : to stress, to drive home — *vi* : to smash, to spike (a ball)
remache *nm* **1** : rivet **2** : smash, spike (in sports)
remanente *nm* **1** : remainder, balance **2** : surplus
remanso *nm* : pool
remar *vi* **1** : to row, to paddle **2** : to struggle, to toil
remarcar {72} *vt* : to emphasize, to stress
rematado, -da *adj* : utter, complete
rematador, -dora *n* : auctioneer
rematar *vt* **1** : to finish off **2** : to auction — *vi* **1** : to shoot **2** : to end
remate *nm* **1** : shot (in sports) **2** : auction **3** : end, conclusion **4 como ~** : to top it off **5 de ~** : completely, utterly
remecer {86} *vt* : to sway, to swing
remedar *vt* **1** IMITAR : to imitate, to copy **2** : to mimic, to ape
remediar *vt* **1** : to remedy, to repair **2** : to help out, to assist **3** EVITAR : to prevent, to avoid
remedio *nm* **1** : remedy, cure **2** : solution **3** : option ⟨no me quedó más remedio : I had no other choice⟩ ⟨no hay remedio : it can't be helped⟩ **4 poner remedio a** : to put a stop to **5 sin ~** : unavoidable, inevitable
remedo *nm* : imitation
rememorar *vi* : to recall ⟨rememorar los viejos tiempos : to reminisce⟩
remendar {55} *vt* **1** : to mend, to patch, to darn **2** : to correct
remero, -ra *n* : rower
remesa *nf* **1** : remittance **2** : shipment
remezón *nm, pl* **-zones** : mild earthquake, tremor
remiendo *nm* **1** : patch **2** : correction
remilgado, -da *adj* **1** : prim, prudish **2** : affected
remilgo *nm* : primness, affectation
reminiscencia *nf* : reminiscence
remisión *nf, pl* **-siones 1** ENVÍO : sending, delivery **2** : remission **3** : reference, cross-reference
remiso, -sa *adj* **1** : lax, remiss **2** : reluctant
remitente[1] *nm* : return address
remitente[2] *nmf* : sender (of a letter, etc.)
remitir *vt* **1** : to send, to remit **2 ~ a** : to refer to, to direct to ⟨nos remitió al diccionario : he referred us to the dictionary⟩ — *vi* : to subside, to let up
remo *nm* **1** : paddle, oar **2** : rowing (sport)
remoción *nf, pl* **-ciones 1** : removal **2** : dismissal
remodelación *nf, pl* **-ciones 1** : remodeling **2** : reorganization, restructuring
remodelar *vt* **1** : to remodel **2** : to restructure
remojar *vt* **1** : to soak, to steep **2** : to dip, to dunk **3** : to celebrate with a drink

remojo *nm* **1** : soaking, steeping **2 poner en remojo** : to soak, to leave soaking
remolacha *nf* : beet
remolcador *nm* : tugboat
remolcar {72} *vt* : to tow, to haul
remolino *nm* **1** : whirlwind **2** : eddy, whirlpool **3** : crowd, throng **4** : cowlick
remolque *nm* **1** : towing, tow **2** : trailer **3 a ~** : in tow
remontar *vt* **1** : to overcome **2** SUBIR : to go up — **remontarse** *vr* **1** : to soar **2 ~ a** : to date from, to go back to
rémora *nf* : obstacle, hindrance
remorder {47} *vt* INQUIETAR : to trouble, to distress
remordimiento *nm* : remorse
remotamente *adv* : remotely, vaguely
remoto, -ta *adj* **1** : remote, unlikely ⟨hay una posibilidad remota : there is a slim possibility⟩ **2** : distant, far-off
remover {47} *vt* **1** : to stir **2** : to move around, to turn over **3** : to stir up **4** : to remove **5** : to dismiss
remozamiento *nm* : renovation
remozar {21} *vt* **1** : to renew, to brighten up **2** : to redo, to renovate
remuneración *nf, pl* **-ciones** : remuneration, pay
remunerar *vt* : to pay, to remunerate
remunerativo, -va *adj* : remunerative
renacer {48} *vi* : to be reborn, to revive
renacimiento *nm* **1** : rebirth, revival **2 el Renacimiento** : the Renaissance
renacuajo *nm* : tadpole, pollywog
renal *adj* : renal, kidney
rencilla *nf* : quarrel
renco, -ca *adj* : lame
rencor *nm* **1** : rancor, enmity, hostility **2 guardar rencor** : to hold a grudge
rencoroso, -sa *adj* : resentful, rancorous
rendición *nf, pl* **-ciones 1** : surrender, submission **2** : yield, return
rendido, -da *adj* **1** : submissive **2** : worn-out, exhausted **3** : devoted
rendija *nf* GRIETA : crack, split
rendimiento *nm* **1** : performance **2** : yield
rendir {54} *vt* **1** : to render, to give ⟨rendir las gracias : to give thanks⟩ ⟨rendir homenaje a : to pay homage to⟩ **2** : to yield **3** CANSAR : to exhaust — *vi* **1** CUNDIR : to progress, to make headway **2** : to last, to go a long way — **rendirse** *vr* : to surrender, to give up
renegado, -da *n* : renegade
renegar {49} *vi* **1 ~ de** : to renounce, to disown, to give up **2 ~ de** : to complain about — *vt* **1** : to deny vigorously **2** : to abhor, to hate
renegociar *vt* : to renegotiate — **renegociación** *nf*
renglón *nm, pl* **renglones 1** : line (of writing) **2** : merchandise, line (of products)

rengo, -ga *adj* : lame
renguear *vi* : to limp
reno *nm* : reindeer
renombrado, -da *adj* : renowned, famous
renombre *nm* NOMBRADÍA : renown, fame
renovable *adj* : renewable
renovación *nf, pl* **-ciones** **1** : renewal ⟨renovación de un contrato : renewal of a contract⟩ **2** : change, renovation
renovar {19} *vt* **1** : to renew, to restore **2** : to renovate
renquear *vi* : to limp, to hobble
renquera *nf* COJERA : limp, lameness
renta *nf* **1** : income **2** : rent **3 impuesto sobre la renta** : income tax
rentable *adj* : profitable
rentar *vt* **1** : to produce, to yield **2** ALQUILAR : to rent
renuencia *nf* : reluctance, unwillingness
renuente *adj* : reluctant, unwilling
renuncia *nf* **1** : resignation **2** : renunciation **3** : waiver
renunciar *vi* **1** : to resign **2** ~ **a** : to renounce, to relinquish ⟨renunció al título : herelinquished the title⟩
reñido, -da *adj* **1** : tough, hard-fought **2** : at odds, on bad terms
reñir {67} *vi* **1** : to argue **2** ~ **con** : to fall out with, to go up against — *vt* : to scold, to reprimand
reo, rea *n* **1** : accused, defendant **2** : offender, culprit
reojo *nm* **de** ~ : out of the corner of one's eye ⟨una mirada de reojo : a sidelong glance⟩
reorganizar {21} *vt* : to reorganize — **reorganización** *nf*
repantigarse {52} *vr* : to slouch, to loll about
reparación *nf, pl* **-ciones** **1** : reparation, amends **2** : repair
reparar *vt* **1** : to repair, to fix, to mend **2** : to make amends for **3** : to correct **4** : to restore, to refresh — *vi* **1** ~ **en** : to observe, to take notice of **2** ~ **en** : to consider, to think about
reparo *nm* **1** : repair, restoration **2** : reservation, qualm ⟨no tuvieron reparos en decírmelo : they didn't hesitate to tell me⟩ **3 poner reparos a** : to find fault with, to object to
repartición *nf, pl* **-ciones** **1** : distribution **2** : department, division
repartidor¹, -dora *adj* : delivery ⟨camión repartidor : delivery truck⟩
repartidor², -dora *n* : delivery person, distributor
repartimiento *nm* → **repartición**
repartir *vt* **1** : to allocate **2** DISTRIBUIR : to distribute, to hand out **3** : to spread
reparto *nm* **1** : allocation **2** : distribution **3** : cast (of characters)
repasar *vt* **1** : to pass by again **2** : to review, to go over **3** : to mend
repaso *nm* **1** : review **2** : mending **3** : checkup, overhaul

repatriar {85} *vt* : to repatriate — **repatriación** *nf*
repavimentar *vt* : to resurface
repelente¹ *adj* : repellent, repulsive
repelente² *nm* : repellent ⟨repelente de insectos : insect repellent⟩
repeler *vt* **1** : to repel, to resist, to repulse **2** : to reject **3** : to disgust ⟨el sabor me repele : I find the taste repulsive⟩
repensar {55} *v* : to rethink, to reconsider
repente *nm* **1** : sudden movement, start ⟨de repente : suddenly⟩ **2** : fit, outburst ⟨un repente de ira : a fit of anger⟩
repentino, -na *adj* : sudden — **repentinamente** *adv*
repercusión *nf, pl* **-siones** : repercussion
repercutir *vi* **1** : to reverberate, to echo **2** ~ **en** : to have effects on, to have repercussions on
repertorio *nm* : repertoire
repetición *nf, pl* **-ciones** **1** : repetition **2** : rerun, repeat
repetidamente *adv* : repeatedly
repetido, -da *adj* **1** : repeated, numerous **2 repetidas veces** : repeatedly, time and again
repetir {54} *vt* **1** : to repeat **2** : to have a second helping of — **repetirse** *vr* **1** : to repeat oneself **2** : to recur
repetitivo, -va *adj* : repetitive, repetitious
repicar {72} *vt* : to ring — *vi* : to ring out, to peal
repique *nm* : ringing, pealing
repisa *nf* : shelf, ledge ⟨repisa de chimenea : mantelpiece⟩ ⟨repisa de ventana : windowsill⟩
replantear *vt* : to redefine, to restate — **replantearse** *vr* : to reconsider
replegar {49} *vt* : to fold — **replegarse** *vr* RETIRARSE : to retreat, to withdraw
repleto, -ta *adj* **1** : replete, full **2** ~ **de** : packed with, crammed with
réplica *nf* **1** : reply **2** : replica, reproduction **3** *Chile, Mex* : aftershock
replicación *nf, pl* **-ciones** : replication
replicar {72} *vi* **1** : to reply, to retort **2** : to argue, to answer back
repliegue *nm* **1** : fold **2** : retreat, withdrawal
repollo *nm* COL : cabbage
reponer {60} *vt* **1** : to replace, to put back **2** : to reinstate **3** : to reply — **reponerse** *vr* : to recover
reportaje *nm* : article, story, report
reportar *vt* **1** : to check, to restrain **2** : to bring, to carry, to yield ⟨me reportó numerosos beneficios : it brought me many benefits⟩ **3** : to report — **reportarse** *vr* **1** CONTENERSE : to control oneself **2** PRESENTARSE : to report, to show up
reporte *nm* : report
reportear *vt* : to report on, to cover

reportero · resentirse

reportero, -ra n 1 : reporter 2 **reportero gráfico** : photojournalist
reposado, -da adj : calm
reposar vi 1 : to rest, to repose 2 : to stand, to settle ⟨deje reposar la masa media hora : let the dough stand for half an hour⟩ 3 : to lie, to be buried — **reposarse** vr : to settle
reposición nf, pl **-ciones** 1 : replacement 2 : reinstatement 3 : revival
repositorio nm : repository
reposo nm : repose, rest
repostar vi 1 : to stock up 2 : to refuel
repostería nf 1 : confectioner's shop 2 : pastry-making
repostero, -ra n : confectioner
repreguntar vt : to cross-examine
repreguntas nfpl : cross-examination
reprender vt : to reprimand, to scold
reprensible adj : reprehensible
represa nf : dam
represalia nf 1 : reprisal, retaliation 2 **tomar represalias** : to retaliate
represar vt : to dam
representación nf, pl **-ciones** 1 : representation 2 : performance 3 **en representación de** : on behalf of
representante nmf 1 : representative 2 : performer
representar vt 1 : to represent, to act for 2 : to perform 3 : to look, to appear as 4 : to symbolize, to stand for 5 : to signify, to mean — **representarse** vr : to imagine, to picture
representativo, -va adj : representative
represión nf, pl **-siones** : repression
represivo, -va adj : repressive
reprimenda nf : reprimand
reprimir vt 1 : to repress 2 : to suppress, to stifle
reprobable adj : reprehensible, culpable
reprobación nf : disapproval
reprobar {19} vt 1 DESAPROBAR : to condemn, to disapprove of 2 : to fail (a course)
reprobatorio, -ria adj : disapproving, admonitory
reprochable adj : reprehensible, reproachable
reprochar vt : to reproach — **reprocharse** vr
reproche nm : reproach
reproducción nf, pl **-ciones** : reproduction
reproducir {61} vt : to reproduce — **reproducirse** vr 1 : to breed, to reproduce 2 : to recur
reproductor, -tora adj : reproductive
reptar vi : to crawl, to slither
reptil[1] adj : reptilian
reptil[2] nm : reptile
república nf : republic
republicanismo nm : republicanism
republicano, -na adj & n : republican
repudiar vt : to repudiate — **repudiación** nf
repudio nm : repudiation
repuesto[1] pp → reponer

repuesto[2] nm 1 : spare part 2 **de ~** : spare ⟨rueda de repuesto : spare wheel⟩
repugnancia nf : repugnance
repugnante adj : repulsive, repugnant, revolting
repugnar vt : to cause repugnance, to disgust — **repugnarse** vr
repujar vt : to emboss
repulsivo, -va adj : repulsive
repuntar vt Arg, Chile : to round up (cattle) — vi : to begin to appear — **repuntarse** vr : to fall out, to quarrel
repuso, etc. → reponer
reputación nf, pl **-ciones** : reputation
reputar vt : to consider, to deem
requerir {76} vt 1 : to require, to call for 2 : to summon, to send for
requesón nm, pl **-sones** : curd cheese, cottage cheese
réquiem nm : requiem
requisa nf 1 : requisition 2 : seizure 3 : inspection
requisar vt 1 : to requisition 2 : to seize 3 INSPECCIONAR : to inspect
requisito nm 1 : requirement 2 **requisito previo** : prerequisite
res nf 1 : beast, animal 2 CA, Mex : beef 3 **reses** nfpl : cattle ⟨60 reses : 60 head of cattle⟩
resabio nm 1 VICIO : bad habit, vice 2 DEJO : aftertaste
resaca nf 1 SOBRESALIR : undertow 2 : hangover
resaltar vi 1 SOBRESALIR : to stand out 2 **hacer resaltar** : to bring out, to highlight — vt : to stress, to emphasize
resarcimiento nm 1 : compensation 2 : reimbursement
resarcir {83} vt : to compensate, to indemnify — **resarcirse** vr **~ de** : to make up for
resbaladizo, -za adj 1 RESBALOSO : slippery 2 : tricky, ticklish, delicate
resbalar vi 1 : to slip, to slide 2 : to slip up, to make a mistake 3 : to skid — **resbalarse** vr
resbalón nm, pl **-lones** : slip
resbaloso, -sa adj : slippery
rescatar vt 1 : to rescue, to save 2 : to recover, to get back
rescate nm 1 : rescue 2 : recovery 3 : ransom
rescindir vt : to rescind, to annul, to cancel
rescisión nf, pl **-siones** : annulment, cancellation
rescoldo nm : embers pl
resecar {72} vt : to make dry, to dry up — **resecarse** vr : to dry up
reseco, -ca adj : dry, dried-up
resentido, -da adj : resentful
resentimiento nm : resentment
resentirse {76} vr 1 : to suffer, to be weakened 2 OFENDERSE : to be upset ⟨se resintió porque la insultaron : she got upset when they insulted her, she resented being insulted⟩ 3 **~ de** : to feel the effects of

reseña *nf* **1** : report, summary, review **2** : description

reseñar *vt* **1** : to review **2** DESCRIBIR : to describe

reserva *nf* **1** : reservation **2** : reserve **3** : confidence, privacy ⟨con la mayor reserva : in strictest confidence⟩ **4 de** ~ : spare, in reserve **5 reservas** *nfpl* : reservations, doubts

reservación *nf, pl* **-ciones** : reservation

reservado, -da *adj* **1** : reserved, reticent **2** : confidential

reservar *vt* : to reserve — **reservarse** *vr* **1** : to save oneself **2** : to conceal, to keep to oneself

reservorio *nm* : reservoir, reserve

resfriado *nm* CATARRO : cold

resfriar {85} *vt* : to cool — **resfriarse** *vr* **1** : to cool off **2** : to catch a cold

resfrío *nm* : cold

resguardar *vt* : to safeguard, to protect — **resguardarse** *vr*

resguardo *nm* **1** : safeguard, protection **2** : receipt, voucher **3** : border guard, coast guard

residencia *nf* **1** : residence **2** : boarding house

residencial *adj* : residential

residente *adj & nmf* : resident

residir *vi* **1** VIVIR : to reside, to dwell **2** ~ **en** : to lie in, to consist of

residual *adj* : residual

residuo *nm* **1** : residue **2** : remainder **3 residuos** *nmpl* : waste ⟨residuos nucleares : nuclear waste⟩

resignación *nf, pl* **-ciones** : resignation

resignar *vt* : to resign — **resignarse** *vr* ~ **a** : to resign oneself to

resina *nf* **1** : resin **2 resina epoxídica** : epoxy

resistencia *nf* **1** : resistance **2** AGUANTE : endurance, strength, stamina

resistente *adj* **1** : resistant **2** : strong, tough

resistir *vt* **1** : to stand, to bear, to tolerate **2** : to withstand — *vi* : to resist ⟨resistió hasta el último minuto : he held out until the last minute⟩ — **resistirse** *vr* ~ **a** : to be resistant to, to be reluctant

resollar {19} *vi* : to breathe heavily, to wheeze

resolución *nf, pl* **-ciones** **1** : resolution, settlement **2** : decision **3** : determination, resolve

resolver {89} *vt* **1** : to resolve, to settle **2** : to decide — **resolverse** *vr* : to make up one's mind

resonancia *nf* **1** : resonance **2** : impact, repercussions *pl*

resonante *adj* **1** : resonant **2** : tremendous, resounding ⟨un éxito resonante : a resounding success⟩

resonar {19} *vi* : to resound, to ring

resoplar *vi* **1** : to puff, to pant **2** : to snort

resoplo *nm* **1** : puffing, panting **2** : snort

resorte *nm* **1** MUELLE : spring **2** : elasticity **3** : influence, means *pl* ⟨tocar resortes : to pull strings⟩

resortera *nf Mex* : slingshot

respaldar *vt* : to back, to support, to endorse — **respaldarse** *vr* : to lean back

respaldo *nm* **1** : back (of an object) **2** : support, backing

respectar *vt* : to concern, to relate to ⟨por lo que a mí respecta : as far as I'm concerned⟩

respectivo, -va *adj* : respective — **respectivamente** *adv*

respecto *nm* **1** ~ **a** : in regard to, concerning **2 al respecto** : on this matter, in this respect

respetable *adj* : respectable — **respetabilidad** *nf*

respetar *vt* : to respect

respeto *nm* **1** : respect, consideration **2 respetos** *nmpl* : respects ⟨presentar sus respetos : to pay one's respects⟩

respetuosidad *nf* : respectfulness

respetuoso, -sa *adj* : respectful — **respetuosamente** *adv*

respingo *nm* : start, jump

respiración *nf, pl* **-ciones** : respiration, breathing

respiradero *nm* : vent, ventilation shaft

respirador *nm* : respirator

respirar *v* : to breathe

respiratorio, -ria *adj* : respiratory

respiro *nm* **1** : breath **2** : respite, break

resplandecer {53} *vi* **1** : to shine **2** : to stand out

resplandeciente *adj* **1** : resplendent, shining **2** : radiant

resplandor *nm* **1** : brightness, brilliance, radiance **2** : flash

responder *vt* : to answer — *vi* **1** : to answer, to reply, to respond **2** ~ **a** : to respond to ⟨responder al tratamiento : to respond to treatment⟩ **3** ~ **de** : to answer for, to vouch for (something) **4** ~ **por** : to vouch for (someone)

responsabilidad *nf* : responsibility

responsable *adj* : responsible — **responsablemente** *adv*

respuesta *nf* : answer, response

resquebrajar *vt* : to split, to crack — **resquebrajarse** *vr*

resquemor *nm* : resentment, bitterness

resquicio *nm* **1** : crack **2** : opportunity, chance **3** : trace ⟨sin un resquicio de remordimiento : without a trace of remorse⟩ **4 resquicio legal** : loophole

resta *nf* SUSTRACCIÓN : subtraction

restablecer {53} *vt* : to reestablish, to restore — **restablecerse** *vr* : to recover

restablecimiento *nm* **1** : reestablishment, restoration **2** : recovery

restallar *vi* : to crack, to crackle, to click

restallido *nm* : crack, crackle

restante *adj* **1** : remaining **2 lo restante, los restantes** : the rest

restañar *vt* : to stanch

restar *vt* **1** : to deduct, to subtract ⟨restar un punto : to deduct a point⟩

2 : to minimize, to play down — *vi* : to remain, to be left

restauración *nf, pl* **-ciones** 1 : restoration 2 : catering, food service

restaurante *nm* : restaurant

restaurar *vt* : to restore

restitución *nf, pl* **-ciones** : restitution, return

restituir {41} *vt* : to return, to restore, to reinstate

resto *nm* 1 : rest, remainder 2 **restos** *nmpl* : remains ⟨restos de comida : leftovers⟩ ⟨restos arqueológicos : archeological ruins⟩ 3 **restos mortales** : mortal remains

restorán *nm, pl* **-ranes** : restaurant

restregadura *nf* : scrub, scrubbing

restregar {49} *vt* 1 : to rub 2 : to scrub — **restregarse** *vr*

restricción *nf, pl* **-ciones** : restriction, limitation

restrictivo, -va *adj* : restrictive

restringido, -da *adj* LIMITADO : limited, restricted

restringir {35} *vt* LIMITAR : to restrict, to limit

restructuración *nf* : restructuring

restructurar *vt* : to restructure

resucitación *nf* : resuscitation ⟨resucitación cardiopulmonar : CPR, cardiopulmonary resuscitation⟩

resucitar *vt* 1 : to resuscitate, to revive, to resurrect 2 : to revitalize

resuello *nm* 1 : puffing, heavy breathing, wheezing 2 : break, breather

resuelto[1] *pp* → **resolver**

resuelto[2], **-ta** *adj* : determined, resolved, resolute

resulta *nf* 1 : consequence, result 2 **a resultas de** *or* **de resultas de** : as a result of

resultado *nm* : result, outcome

resultante *adj & nf* : resultant

resultar *vi* 1 : to work, to work out ⟨mi idea no resultó : my idea didn't work out⟩ 2 : to prove, to turn out to be ⟨resultó bien simpático : he turned out to be very nice⟩ 3 : to lead to, to result in 4 ~ **de** : to be the result of

resumen *nm, pl* **-súmenes** 1 : summary, summation 2 **en** ~ : in summary, in short

resumidero *nm* : drain

resumir *v* : to summarize, to sum up

resurgimiento *nm* : resurgence

resurgir {35} *vi* : to reappear, to revive

resurrección *nf, pl* **-ciones** : resurrection

retablo *nm* 1 : tableau 2 : altarpiece

retador, -dora *n* : challenger (in sports)

retaguardia *nf* : rear guard

retahíla *nf* : string, series ⟨una retahíla de insultos : a volley of insults⟩

retaliación *nf, pl* **-ciones** : retaliation

retama *nf* : broom (plant)

retar *vt* DESAFIAR : to challenge, to defy

retardante *adj* : retardant

retardar *vt* 1 RETRASAR : to delay, to retard 2 : to postpone

retazo *nm* 1 : remnant, scrap 2 : fragment, piece ⟨retazos de su obra : bits and pieces from his writings⟩

retención *nf, pl* **-ciones** 1 : retention 2 : deduction, withholding

retener {80} *vt* 1 : to retain, to keep 2 : to withhold 3 : to detain

retentivo, -va *adj* : retentive

reticencia *nf* 1 : reluctance, reticence 2 : insinuation

reticente *adj* 1 : reluctant, reticent 2 : insinuating, misleading

retina *nf* : retina

retintín *nm, pl* **-tines** 1 : jingle, jangle 2 **con** ~ : sarcastically

retirada *nf* 1 : retreat ⟨batirse en retirada : to withdraw, to beat a retreat⟩ 2 : withdrawal (of funds) 3 : retirement 4 : refuge, haven

retirado, -da *adj* 1 : remote, distant, far off 2 : secluded, quiet

retirar *vt* 1 : to remove, to take away, to recall 2 : to withdraw, to take out — **retirarse** *vr* 1 REPLEGARSE : to retreat, to withdraw 2 JUBILARSE : to retire

retiro *nm* 1 JUBILACIÓN : retirement 2 : withdrawal, retreat 3 : seclusion

reto *nm* DESAFÍO : challenge, dare

retocar {72} *vt* : to touch up

retoñar *vi* : to sprout

retoño *nm* : sprout, shoot

retoque *nm* : retouching

retorcer {14} *vt* 1 : to twist 2 : to wring — **retorcerse** *vr* 1 : to get twisted, to get tangled up 2 : to squirm, to writhe, to wiggle about

retorcijón *nm, pl* **-jones** : cramp, sharp pain

retorcimiento *nm* 1 : twisting, wringing 2 : deviousness

retórica *nf* : rhetoric

retórico, -ca *adj* : rhetorical — **retóricamente** *adv*

retornar *v* : to return

retorno *nm* : return

retozar {21} *vi* : to frolic, to romp

retozo *nm* : frolicking

retozón, -zona *adj, mpl* **-zones** : playful

retracción *nf, pl* **-ciones** : retraction, withdrawal

retractable *adj* : retractable

retractación *nf, pl* **-ciones** : retraction (of a statement, etc.)

retractarse *vr* 1 : to withdraw, to back down 2 ~ **de** : to take back, to retract

retraer {81} *vt* 1 : to bring back 2 : to dissuade — **retraerse** *vr* 1 RETIRARSE : to withdraw, to retire 2 REFUGIARSE : to take refuge

retraído, -da *adj* : withdrawn, retiring, shy

retraimiento *nm* 1 : shyness, timidity 2 : withdrawal

retrasado, -da *adj* 1 : retarded, mentally slow 2 : behind, in arrears 3

: backward (of a country) **4** : slow (of a watch)
retrasar *vt* **1** DEMORAR, RETARDAR : to delay, to hold up **2** : to put off, to postpone — **retrasarse** *vr* **1** : to be late **2** : to fall behind
retraso *nm* **1** ATRASO : delay, lateness **2 retraso mental** : mental retardation
retratar *vt* **1** : to portray, to depict **2** : to photograph **3** : to paint a portrait of
retrato *nm* **1** : depiction, portrayal **2** : portrait, photograph
retrete *nm* : restroom, toilet
retribución *nf, pl* **-ciones 1** : pay, payment **2** : reward
retribuir {41} *vt* **1** : to pay **2** : to reward
retroactivo, -va *adj* : retroactive — **retroactivamente** *adv*
retroalimentación *nf, pl* **-ciones** : feedback
retroceder *vi* **1** : to move back, to turn back **2** : to back off, to back down **3** : to recoil (of a firearm)
retroceso *nm* **1** : backward movement **2** : backing down **3** : setback, relapse **4** : recoil
retrógrado, -da *adj* **1** : reactionary **2** : retrograde
retropropulsión *nf* : jet propulsion
retrospectiva *nf* : retrospective, hindsight
retrospectivo, -va *adj* **1** : retrospective **2 mirada retrospectiva** : backward glance
retrovisor *nm* : rearview mirror
retruécano *nm* : pun, play on words
retumbar *vi* **1** : to boom, to thunder **2** : to resound, to reverberate
retumbo *nm* : booming, thundering, roll
retuvo, etc. → **retener**
reubicar {72} *vt* : to relocate — **reubicación** *nf*
reuma *or* **reúma** *nmf* → **reumatismo**
reumático, -ca *adj* : rheumatic
reumatismo *nm* : rheumatism
reunión *nf, pl* **-niones 1** : meeting **2** : gathering, reunion
reunir {68} *vt* **1** : to unite, to join, to bring together **2** : to have, to possess ⟨reunieron los requisitos necesarios : they fulfilled the necessary requirements⟩ **3** : to gather, to collect, to raise (funds) — **reunirse** *vr* : to meet
reutilizable *adj* : reusable
reutilizar {21} *vt* : to recycle, to reuse
revalidar *vt* **1** : to confirm, to ratify **2** : to defend (a title)
revaluar {3} *vt* : to reevaluate — **revaluación** *n*
revancha *nf* **1** DESQUITE : revenge, requital **2** : rematch
revelación *nf, pl* **-ciones** : revelation
revelado *nm* : developing (of film)
revelador¹, -dora *adj* : revealing
revelador² *nm* : developer
revelar *vt* **1** : to reveal, to disclose **2** : to develop (film)
revendedor, -dora *n* **1** : scalper **2** DETALLISTA : retailer

revender *vt* **1** : to resell **2** : to scalp
reventa *nf* **1** : resale **2** : scalping
reventar {55} *vi* **1** ESTALLAR, EXPLOTAR : to burst, to blow up **2** ~ **de** : to be bursting with — *vt* **1** : to burst **2** *fam* : to annoy, to rile
reventón *nm, pl* **-tones 1** : burst, bursting **2** : blowout, flat tire **3** *Mex fam* : bash, party
reverberar *vi* : to reverberate — **reverberación** *nf*
reverdecer {53} *vi* **1** : to grow green again **2** : to revive
reverencia *nf* **1** : reverence **2** : bow, curtsy
reverenciar *vt* : to revere, to venerate
reverendo¹, -da *adj* **1** : reverend **2** *fam* : total, absolute ⟨es un reverendo imbécil : he is a complete idiot⟩
reverendo², -da *n* : reverend
reverente *adj* : reverent
reversa *nf Col, Mex* : reverse (gear)
reversible *adj* : reversible
reversión *nf, pl* **-siones** : reversion
reverso *nm* **1** : back, other side **2 el reverso de la medalla** : the complete opposite
revertir {76} *vi* **1** : to revert, to go back **2** ~ **en** : to result in, to end up as
revés *nm, pl* **reveses 1** : back, wrong side **2** : setback, reversal **3** : backhand (in sports) **4 al revés** : the other way around, upside down, inside out **5 al revés de** : contrary to
revestimiento *nm* : covering, facing (of a building)
revestir {54} *vt* **1** : to coat, to cover, to surface **2** : to conceal, to disguise **3** : to take on, to assume ⟨la reunión revistió gravedad : the meeting took on a serious note⟩
revisar *vt* **1** : to examine, to inspect, to check **2** : to check over, to overhaul (machinery) **3** : to revise
revisión *nf, pl* **-siones 1** : revision **2** : inspection, check
revisor, -sora *n* **1** : inspector **2** : conductor (on a train)
revista *nf* **1** : magazine, journal **2** : revue **3 pasar revista** : to review, to inspect
revistar *vt* : to review, to inspect
revitalizar {21} *vt* : to revitalize — **revitalización** *nf*
revivir *vi* : to revive, to come alive again — *vt* : to relive
revocación *nf, pl* **-ciones** : revocation, repeal
revocar {72} *vt* **1** : to revoke, to repeal **2** : to plaster (a wall)
revolcar {82} *vt* : to knock over, to knock down — **revolcarse** *vr* : to roll around, to wallow
revolcón *nm, pl* **-cones** *fam* : tumble, fall
revolotear *vi* : to flutter around, to flit
revoloteo *nm* : fluttering, flitting

revoltijo *nm* **1** FÁRRAGO : mess, jumble **2** *Mex* : traditional seafood dish
revoltoso, -sa *adj* : unruly, rebellious
revolución *nf, pl* **-ciones** : revolution
revolucionar *vt* : to revolutionize
revolucionario, -ria *adj & n* : revolutionary
revolver {89} *vt* **1** : to move about, to mix, to shake, to stir **2** : to upset (one's stomach) **3** : to mess up, to rummage through ⟨revolver la casa : to turn the house upside down⟩ — **revolverse** *vr* **1** : to toss and turn **2** VOLVERSE : to turn around
revólver *nm* : revolver
revoque *nm* : plaster
revuelo *nm* **1** : fluttering **2** : commotion, stir
revuelta *nf* : uprising, revolt
revuelto[1] *pp* → **revolver**
revuelto[2], **-ta** *adj* **1** : choppy, rough ⟨mar revuelto : rough sea⟩ **2** : untidy **3 huevos revueltos** : scrambled eggs
rey *nm* : king
reyerta *nf* : brawl, fight
rezagado, -da *n* : straggler, latecomer
rezagar {52} *vt* **1** : to leave behind **2** : to postpone — **rezagarse** *vr* : to fall behind, to lag
rezar {21} *vi* **1** : to pray **2** : to say ⟨como reza el refrán : as the saying goes⟩ **3** ~ **con** : to concern, to have to do with — *vt* : to say, to recite ⟨rezar un Ave María : to say a Hail Mary⟩
rezo *nm* : prayer, praying
rezongar {52} *vi* : to gripe, to grumble
rezumar *v* : to ooze, to leak
ría[1], etc. → **reír**
ría[2] *nf* : estuary
riachuelo *nm* ARROYO : brook, stream
riada *nf* : flood
ribera *nf* : bank, shore
ribete *nm* **1** : border, trim **2** : frill, adornment **3 ribetes** *nmpl* : hint, touch ⟨tiene sus ribetes de genio : there's a touch of genius in him⟩
ribetear *vt* : to border, to edge, to trim
ricamente *adv* : richly, splendidly
rice, etc. → **rizar**
rico[1], **-ca** *adj* **1** : rich, wealthy **2** : fertile **3** : luxurious, valuable **4** : delicious **5** : adorable, lovely **6** : great, wonderful
rico[2], **-ca** *n* : rich person
ridiculez *nf, pl* **-leces** : ridiculousness, absurdity
ridiculizar {21} *vt* : to ridicule
ridículo[1], **-la** *adj* ABSURDO, DISPARATADO : ridiculous, ludicrous — **ridículamente** *adv*
ridículo[2], **-la** *n* **1 hacer el ridículo** : to make a fool of oneself **2 poner en ridículo** : to ridicule
ríe, etc. → **reír**
riega, riegue etc. → **regar**
riego *nm* : irrigation
riel *nm* : rail, track

rienda *nf* **1** : rein **2 dar rienda suelta a** : to give free rein to **3 llevar las riendas** : to be in charge **4 tomar las riendas** : to take control
riesgo *nm* : risk
riesgoso, -sa *adj* : risky
rifa *nf* : raffle
rifar *vt* : to raffle — *vi* : to quarrel, to fight
rifle *nm* : rifle
rige, rija etc. → **regir**
rigidez *nf, pl* **-deces** **1** : rigidity, stiffness ⟨rigidez cadavérica : rigor mortis⟩ **2** : inflexibility
rígido, -da *adj* **1** : rigid, stiff **2** : strict — **rígidamente** *adv*
rigor *nm* **1** : rigor, harshness **2** : precision, meticulousness **3 de** ~ : usual ⟨la respuesta de rigor : the standard reply⟩ **4 de** ~ : essential, obligatory **5 en** ~ : strictly speaking, in reality
riguroso, -sa *adj* : rigorous — **rigurosamente** *adv*
rima *nf* **1** : rhyme **2 rimas** *nfpl* : verse, poetry
rimar *vi* : to rhyme
rimbombante *adj* **1** : grandiose, showy **2** : bombastic, pompous
rímel *or* **rimel** *nm* : mascara
rin *nm Col, Mex* : wheel, rim (of a tire)
rincón *nm, pl* **rincones** : corner, nook
rinde, etc. → **rendir**
rinoceronte *nm* : rhinoceros
riña *nf* **1** : fight, brawl **2** : dispute, quarrel
riñe, etc. → **reñir**
riñón *nm, pl* **riñones** : kidney
río[1] → **reír**
río[2] *nm* **1** : river **2** : torrent, stream ⟨un río de lágrimas : a flood of tears⟩
ripio *nm* **1** : debris, rubble **2** : gravel
riqueza *nf* **1** : wealth, riches *pl* **2** : richness **3 riquezas naturales** : natural resources
risa *nf* **1** : laughter, laugh **2 dar risa** : to make laugh ⟨me dio mucha risa : I found it very funny⟩ **3** *fam* **morirse de la risa** : to die laughing, to crack up
risco *nm* : crag, cliff
risible *adj* IRRISORIO : ludicrous, laughable
risita *nf* : giggle, titter, snicker
risotada *nf* : guffaw
ristra *nf* : string, series *pl*
risueño, -ña *adj* **1** : cheerful, pleasant **2** : promising
rítmico, -ca *adj* : rhythmical, rhythmic — **rítmicamente** *adv*
ritmo *nm* **1** : rhythm **2** : pace, tempo ⟨trabajó a ritmo lento : she worked at a slow pace⟩
rito *nm* : rite, ritual
ritual *adj & nm* : ritual — **ritualmente** *adv*
rival *adj & nmf* COMPETIDOR : rival
rivalidad *nf* : rivalry, competition
rivalizar {21} *vi* ~ **con** : to rival, to compete with

rizado, -da *adj* **1** : curly **2** : ridged **3** : ripply, undulating
rizar {21} *vt* **1** : to curl **2** : to ripple, to ruffle (a surface) **3** : to crumple, to fold — **rizarse** *vr* **1** : to frizz **2** : to ripple
rizo *nm* **1** : curl **2** : loop (in aviation)
robalo *or* **róbalo** *nm* : sea bass
robar *vt* **1** : to steal **2** : to rob, to burglarize **3** SECUESTRAR : to abduct, to kidnap **4** : to captivate — *vi* ~ **en** : to break into
roble *nm* : oak
robo *nm* : robbery, theft
robot *nm, pl* **robots** : robot
robótica *nf* : robotics
robustecer {53} *vt* : to grow stronger, to strengthen
robustez *nf* : sturdiness, robustness
robusto, -ta *adj* : robust, sturdy
roca *nf* : rock, boulder
roce¹, etc. → **rozar**
roce² *nm* **1** : rubbing, chafing **2** : brush, graze, touch **3** : close contact, familiarity **4** : friction, disagreement
rociador *nm* : sprinkler
rociar {85} *vt* : to spray, to sprinkle
rocío *nm* **1** : dew **2** : shower, light rain
rock *or* **rock and roll** *nm* : rock, rock and roll
rocola *nf* : jukebox
rocoso, -sa *adj* : rocky
rodada *nf* : track (of a tire), rut
rodado, -da *adj* **1** : wheeled **2** : dappled (of a horse)
rodadura *nf* : rolling, taxiing
rodaja *nf* : round, slice
rodaje *nm* **1** : filming, shooting **2** : breaking in (of a vehicle)
rodamiento *nm* **1** : bearing ⟨rodamiento de bolas : ball bearings⟩ **2** : rolling
rodante *adj* : rolling
rodar {19} *vi* **1** : to roll, to roll down, to roll along ⟨rodé por la escalera : I tumbled down the stairs⟩ ⟨todo rodaba bien : everthing was going along well⟩ **2** GIRAR : to turn, to go around **3** : to move about, to travel ⟨andábamos rodando por todas partes : we drifted along from place to place⟩ — *vt* **1** : to film, to shoot **2** : to break in (a new vehicle)
rodear *vt* **1** : to surround **2** : to round up (cattle) — *vi* **1** : to go around **2** : to beat around the bush — **rodearse** *vr* ~ **de** : to surround oneself with
rodeo *nm* **1** : rodeo, roundup **2** DESVÍO : detour **3** : evasion ⟨andar con rodeos : to beat around the bush⟩ ⟨sin rodeos : without reservations⟩
rodilla *nf* : knee
rodillo *nm* **1** : roller **2** : rolling pin
rododendro *nm* : rhododendron
roedor¹, -dora *adj* : gnawing
roedor² *nm* : rodent
roer {69} *vt* **1** : to gnaw **2** : to eat away at, to torment
rogar {16} *vt* : to beg, to request — *vi* **1** : to beg, to plead **2** : to pray

roiga, etc. → **roer**
rojez *nf* : redness
rojizo, -za *adj* : reddish
rojo¹, -ja *adj* **1** : red **2 ponerse rojo** : to blush
rojo² *nm* : red
rol *nm* **1** : role **2** : list, roll
rollo *nm* **1** : roll, coil ⟨un rollo de cinta : a roll of tape⟩ ⟨en rollo : rolled up⟩ **2** *fam* : roll of fat **3** *fam* : boring speech, lecture
romance *nm* **1** : Romance language **2** : ballad **3** : romance **4 en buen romance** : simply stated, simply put
romano, -na *adj & n* : Roman
romanticismo *nm* : romanticism
romántico, -ca *adj* : romantic — **románticamente** *adv*
rombo *nm* : rhombus
romería *nf* **1** : pilgrimage, procession **2** : crowd, gathering
romero¹, -ra *n* PEREGRINO : pilgrim
romero² *nm* : rosemary
romo, -ma *adj* : blunt, dull
rompecabezas *nms & pl* : puzzle, riddle
rompehielos *nms & pl* : icebreaker (ship)
rompehuelgas *nmfs & pl* ESQUIROL : strikebreaker, scab
rompenueces *nms & pl* : nutcracker
rompeolas *ns & pl* : breakwater, jetty
romper {70} *vt* **1** : to break, to smash **2** : to rip, to tear **3** : to break off (relations), to break (a contract) **4** : to break through, to break down **5** GASTAR : to wear out — *vi* **1** : to break ⟨al romper del día : at the break of day⟩ **2** ~ **a** : to begin to, to burst out with ⟨romper a llorar : to burst into tears⟩ **3** ~ **con** : to break off with
rompope *nm CA, Mex* : drink similar to eggnog
ron *nm* : rum
roncar {72} *vi* **1** : to snore **2** : to roar
ronco, -ca *adj* **1** : hoarse **2** : husky (of the voice) — **roncamente** *adv*
ronda *nf* **1** : beat, patrol **2** : round (of drinks, of negotiations, of a game)
rondar *vt* **1** : to patrol **2** : to hang around ⟨siempre está rondando la calle : he's always hanging around the street⟩ **3** : to be approximately ⟨debe rondar los cincuenta : he must be about 50⟩ — *vi* **1** : to be on patrol **2** : to prowl around, to roam about
ronque, etc. → **roncar**
ronquera *nf* : hoarseness
ronquido *nm* **1** : snore **2** : roar
ronronear *vi* : to purr
ronroneo *nm* : purr, purring
ronzal *nm* : halter (for an animal)
ronzar {21} *v* : to munch, to crunch
roña *nf* **1** : mange **2** : dirt, filth **3** *fam* : stinginess
roñoso, -sa *adj* **1** : mangy **2** : dirty **3** *fam* : stingy
ropa *nf* **1** : clothes *pl*, clothing **2 ropa interior** : underwear

ropaje *nm* : apparel, garments *pl*, regalia
ropero *nm* ARMARIO, CLÓSET : wardrobe, closet
rosa[1] *adj* : rose-colored, pink
rosa[2] *nm* : rose, pink (color)
rosa[3] *nf* : rose (flower)
rosáceo, -cea *adj* : pinkish
rosado[1], **-da** *adj* **1** : pink **2 vino rosado** : rosé
rosado[2] *nm* : pink (color)
rosal *nm* : rosebush
rosario *nm* **1** : rosary **2** : series ⟨un rosario de islas : a string of islands⟩
rosbif *nm* : roast beef
rosca *nf* **1** : thread (of a screw) ⟨una tapa a rosca : a screw top⟩ **2** : ring, coil
roseta *nf* : rosette
rosquilla *nf* : ring-shaped pastry, doughnut
rostro *nm* : face, countenance
rotación *nf, pl* **-ciones** : rotation
rotar *vt* : to rotate, to turn — *vi* : to turn, to spin
rotativo[1], **-va** *adj* : rotary
rotativo[2] *nm* : newspaper
rotatorio, -ria *adj* → **rotativo**[1]
roto[1] *pp* → **romper**
roto[2], **-ta** *adj* **1** : broken **2** : ripped, torn
rotonda *nf* **1** : traffic circle, rotary **2** : rotunda
rotor *nm* : rotor
rótula *nf* : kneecap
rotular *vt* **1** : to head, to entitle **2** : to label
rótulo *nm* **1** : heading, title **2** : label, sign
rotundo, -da *adj* **1** REDONDO : round **2** : categorical, absolute ⟨un éxito rotundo : a resounding success⟩ — **rotundamente** *adv*
rotura *nf* : break, tear, fracture
roya *nf* : plant rust
roya, etc. → **roer**
rozado, -da *adj* GASTADO : worn
rozadura *nf* **1** : scratch, abrasion **2** : rubbed spot, sore
rozar {21} *vt* **1** : to chafe, to rub against **2** : to border on, to touch on **3** : to graze, to touch lightly — **rozarse** *vr* ~ **con** *fam* : to rub shoulders with
ruandés, -desa *adj & n* : Rwandan
ruano, -na *adj* : roan
rubí *nm, pl* **rubíes** : ruby
rubio, -bia *adj & n* : blond
rublo *nm* : ruble
rubor *nm* **1** : flush, blush **2** : rouge, blusher
ruborizarse {21} *vr* : to blush
rúbrica *nf* : title, heading
rubricar {72} *vt* **1** : to sign with a flourish ⟨firmado y rubricado : signed and sealed⟩ **2** : to endorse, to sanction
rubro *nm* **1** : heading, title **2** : line, area (in business)
rudeza *nf* ASPEREZA : roughness, coarseness

rudimentario, -ria *adj* : rudimentary — **rudimentariamente** *adv*
rudimento *nm* : rudiment, basics *pl*
rudo, -da *adj* **1** : rough, harsh **2** : coarse, unpolished — **rudamente** *adv*
rueda[1], **etc.** → **rodar**
rueda[2] *nf* **1** : wheel **2** RODAJA : round slice **3** : circle, ring **4 rueda de andar** : treadmill **5 rueda de prensa** : press conference **6 ir sobre ruedas** : to go smoothly
ruedita *nf* : caster (on furniture)
ruedo *nm* **1** : bullring, arena **2** : rotation, turn **3** : hem
ruega, ruegue etc. → **rogar**
ruego *nm* : request, appeal, plea
rugido *nm* : roar
rugir {35} *vi* : to roar
ruibarbo *nm* : rhubarb
ruido *nm* : noise, sound
ruidoso, -sa *adj* : loud, noisy — **ruidosamente** *adv*
ruin *adj* **1** : base, despicable **2** : mean, stingy
ruina *nf* **1** : ruin, destruction **2** : downfall, collapse **3 ruinas** *nfpl* : ruins, remains
ruinoso, -sa *adj* **1** : run-down, dilapidated **2** : ruinous, disastrous
ruiseñor *nm* : nightingale
ruja, etc. → **rugir**
ruleta *nf* : roulette
rulo *nm* : curler, roller
rumano, -na *n* : Romanian, Rumanian
rumbo *nm* **1** : direction, course ⟨con rumbo a : bound for, heading for⟩ ⟨perder el rumbo : to go off course, to lose one's bearings⟩ ⟨sin rumbo : aimless, aimlessly⟩ **2** : ostentation, pomp **3** : lavishness, generosity
rumiante *adj & nm* : ruminant
rumiar *vt* : to ponder, to mull over — *vi* **1** : to chew the cud **2** : to ruminate, to ponder
rumor *nm* **1** : rumor **2** : murmur
rumorearse *or* **rumorarse** *vr* : to be rumored ⟨se rumorea que se va : rumor has it that she's leaving⟩
rumoroso, -sa *adj* : murmuring, babbling ⟨un arroyo rumoroso : a babbling brook⟩
rupia *nf* : rupee
ruptura *nf* **1** : break **2** : breaking, breach (of a contract) **3** : breaking off, breakup
rural *adj* : rural
ruso[1], **-sa** *adj & n* : Russian
ruso[2] *nm* : Russian (language)
rústico[1], **-ca** *adj* : rural, rustic
rústico[2], **-ca** *n* : rustic, country dweller
ruta *nf* : route
rutina *nf* : routine, habit
rutinario, -ria *adj* : routine, ordinary ⟨visita rutinaria : routine visit⟩ — **rutinariamente** *adv*

S

s *nf* : twentieth letter of the Spanish alphabet

sábado *nm* **1** : Saturday **2** : Sabbath

sábalo *nm* : shad

sabana *nf* : savanna

sábana *nf* : sheet, bedsheet

sabandija *nf* BICHO : bug, small reptile, pesky creature

sabático, -ca *adj* : sabbatical

sabedor, -dora *adj* : aware, informed

sabelotodo *nmf fam* : know-it-all

saber¹ {71} *vt* **1** : to know **2** : to know how to, to be able to ⟨sabe tocar el violín : she can play the violin⟩ **3** : to learn, to find out **4 a ~** : to wit, namely — *vi* **1** : to know, to suppose **2** : to be informed ⟨supimos del desastre : we heard about the disaster⟩ **3** : to taste ⟨esto no sabe bien : this doesn't taste right⟩ **4 ~ a** : to taste like ⟨sabe a naranja : it tastes like orange⟩ — **saberse** *vr* : to know ⟨ese chiste no me lo sé : I don't know that joke⟩

saber² *nm* : knowledge, learning

sabiamente *adv* : wisely

sabido, -da *adj* : well-known

sabiduría *nf* **1** : wisdom **2** : learning, knowledge

sabiendas *adv* **1 a ~** : knowingly **2 a sabiendas de que** : knowing full well that

sabio¹, **-bia** *adj* **1** PRUDENTE : wise, sensible **2** DOCTO : learned

sabio², **-bia** *n* **1** : wise person **2** : savant, learned person

sable *nm* : saber, cutlass

sabor *nm* **1** : flavor, taste **2 sin ~** : flavorless

saborear *vt* **1** : to taste, to savor **2** : to enjoy, to relish

sabotaje *nm* : sabotage

saboteador, -dora *n* : saboteur

sabotear *vt* : to sabotage

sabrá, etc. → saber

sabroso, -sa *adj* **1** RICO : delicious, tasty **2** AGRADABLE : pleasant, nice, lovely

sabueso *nm* **1** : bloodhound **2** *fam* : detective, sleuth

sacacorchos *nms & pl* : corkscrew

sacapuntas *nms & pl* : pencil sharpener

sacar {72} *vt* **1** : to pull out, to take out ⟨saca el pollo del congelador : take the chicken out of the freezer⟩ **2** : to get, to obtain ⟨saqué un 100 en el examen : I got 100 on the exam⟩ **3** : to get out, to extract ⟨le saqué la información : I got the information from him⟩ **4** : to stick out ⟨sacar la lengua : to stick out one's tongue⟩ **5** : to bring out, to introduce ⟨sacar un libro : to publish a book⟩ ⟨sacaron una moda nueva : they introduced a new style⟩ **6** : to take (photos) **7** : to make (copies) — *vi* **1**

: to kick off (in soccer or football) **2** : to serve (in sports)

sacarina *nf* : saccharin

sacarosa *nf* : sucrose

sacerdocio *nm* : priesthood

sacerdotal *adj* : priestly

sacerdote, -tisa *n* : priest *m*, priestess *f*

saciar *vt* **1** HARTAR : to sate, to satiate **2** SATISFACER : to satisfy

saciedad *nf* : satiety

saco *nm* **1** : bag, sack **2** : sac **3** : jacket, sport coat

sacramento *nm* : sacrament — **sacramental** *adj*

sacrificar {72} *vt* : to sacrifice — **sacrificarse** *vr* : to sacrifice oneself, to make sacrifices

sacrificio *nm* : sacrifice

sacrilegio *nm* : sacrilege

sacrílego, -ga *adj* : sacrilegious

sacristán *nm*, *pl* **-tanes** : sexton, sacristan

sacristía *nf* : sacristy, vestry

sacro, -cra *adj* SAGRADO : sacred ⟨arte sacro : sacred art⟩

sacrosanto, -ta *adj* : sacrosanct

sacudida *nf* **1** : shaking **2** : jerk, jolt, shock **3** : shake-up, upheaval

sacudir *vt* **1** : to shake, to beat **2** : to jerk, to jolt **3** : to dust off **4** CONMOVER : to shake up, to shock — **sacudirse** *vr* : to shake off

sacudón *nm*, *pl* **-dones** : intense jolt or shake-up

sádico¹, **-ca** *adj* : sadistic

sádico², **-ca** *n* : sadist

sadismo *nm* : sadism

safari *nm* : safari

saga *nf* : saga

sagacidad *nf* : sagacity, shrewdness

sagaz *adj*, *pl* **sagaces** PERSPICAZ : shrewd, discerning, sagacious

Sagitario *nmf* : Sagittarius, Sagittarian

sagrado, -da *adj* : sacred, holy

sainete *nm* : comedy sketch, one-act farce ⟨este proceso es un sainete : these proceedings are a farce⟩

sajar *vt* : to lance, to cut open

sal¹ → salir

sal² *nf* **1** : salt **2** *CA, Mex* : misfortune, bad luck

sala *nf* **1** : living room **2** : room, hall ⟨sala de conferencias : lecture hall⟩ ⟨sala de urgencias : emergency room⟩ ⟨sala de baile : ballroom⟩

salado, -da *adj* **1** : salty **2 agua salada** : salt water

salamandra *nf* : salamander

salami *nm* : salami

salar *vt* **1** : to salt **2** : to spoil, to ruin **3** *CoRi, Mex* : to jinx, to bring bad luck

salarial *adj* : salary, salary-related

salario *nm* **1** : salary **2 salario mínimo** : minimum wage

salaz *adj*, *pl* **salaces** : salacious, lecherous

salchicha nf **1** : sausage **2** : frankfurter, wiener

salchichón nf, pl **-chones** : a type of deli meat

salchichonería nf Mex **1** : delicatessen **2** : cold cuts pl

saldar vt : to settle, to pay off ⟨saldar una cuenta : to settle an account⟩

saldo nm **1** : settlement, payment **2** : balance ⟨saldo de cuenta : account balance⟩ **3** : remainder, leftover merchandise

saldrá, etc. → salir

salero nm **1** : saltshaker **2** : wit, charm

salga, etc. → salir

salida nf **1** : exit ⟨salida de emergencia : emergency exit⟩ **2** : leaving, departure **3** SOLUCIÓN : way out, solution **4** : start (of a race) **5** OCURRENCIA : wisecrack, joke **6 salida del sol** : sunrise

saliente[1] adj **1** : departing, outgoing **2** : projecting **3** DESTACADO : salient, prominent

saliente[2] nm **1** : projection, protrusion **2 ventana en saliente** : bay window

salinidad nf : salinity, saltiness

salino, -na adj : saline ⟨solución salina : saline solution⟩

salir {73} vi **1** : to go out, to come out, to get out ⟨salimos todas las noches : we go out every night⟩ ⟨su libro acaba de salir : her book just came out⟩ **2** PARTIR : to leave, to depart **3** APARECER : to appear ⟨salió en todos los diarios : it came out in all the papers⟩ **4** : to project, to stick out **5** : to cost, to come to **6** RESULTAR : to turn out, to prove **7** : to come up, to occur ⟨salga lo que salga : whatever happens⟩ ⟨salió una oportunidad : an opportunity came up⟩ **8 ~ a** : to take after, to look like, to resemble **9 ~ con** : to go out with, to date — **salirse** vr **1** : to escape, to get out, to leak out **2** : to come loose, to come off **3 salirse con la suya** : to get one's own way

saliva nf : saliva

salivar vi : to salivate

salmo nm : psalm

salmón[1] adj : salmon-colored

salmón[2] nm, pl **salmones** : salmon

salmuera nf : brine

salobre adj : brackish, briny

salón nm, pl **salones** **1** : hall, large room ⟨salón de clase : classroom⟩ ⟨salón de baile : ballroom⟩ **2** : salon ⟨salón de belleza : beauty salon⟩ **3** : parlor, sitting room

salpicadera nf Mex : fender

salpicadura nf : spatter, splash

salpicar {72} vt **1** : to spatter, to splash **2** : to sprinkle, to scatter about

salpimentar {55} vt **1** : to season (with salt and pepper) **2** : to spice up

salsa nf **1** : sauce ⟨salsa picante : hot sauce⟩ ⟨salsa inglesa : Worcestershire sauce⟩ ⟨salsa tártara : tartar sauce⟩ **2** : gravy **3** : salsa (music) **4 salsa mexicana** : salsa (sauce)

salsero, -ra n : salsa musician

saltador, -dora n : jumper

saltamontes nms & pl : grasshopper

saltar vi **1** BRINCAR : to jump, to leap **2** : to bounce **3** : to come off, to pop out **4** : to shatter, to break **5** : to explode, to blow up — vt **1** : to jump, to jump over **2** : to skip, to miss — **saltarse** vr OMITIR : to skip, to omit ⟨me salté ese capítulo : I skipped that chapter⟩

saltarín, -rina adj, mpl **-rines** : leaping, hopping ⟨frijol saltarín : jumping bean⟩

salteado, -da adj **1** : sautéed **2** : jumbled up ⟨los episodios se transmitieron salteados : the episodes were broadcast in random order⟩

salteador nm : highwayman

saltear vt **1** SOFREÍR : to sauté **2** : to skip around, to skip over

saltimbanqui nmf : acrobat

salto nm **1** BRINCO : jump, leap, skip **2** : jump, dive (in sports) **3** : gap, omission **4 dar saltos** : to jump up and down **5** or **salto de agua** CATARATA : waterfall

saltón, -tona adj, mpl **saltones** : bulging, protruding

salubre adj : healthful, salubrious

salubridad nf : healthfulness, health

salud nf **1** : health ⟨buena salud : good health⟩ **2 ¡salud!** : bless you! (when someone sneezes) **3 ¡salud!** : cheers!, to your health!

saludable adj **1** SALUBRE : healthful **2** SANO : healthy, well

saludar vt **1** : to greet, to say hello to **2** : to salute — **saludarse** vr

saludo nm **1** : greeting, regards pl **2** : salute

salutación nf, pl **-ciones** : salutation

salva nf **1** : salvo, volley **2 salva de aplausos** : round of applause

salvación nf, pl **-ciones** **1** : salvation **2** RESCATE : rescue

salvado nm : bran

salvador, -dora n **1** : savior, rescuer **2 el Salvador** : the Savior

salvadoreño, -ña adj & n : Salvadoran, El Salvadoran

salvaguardar vt : to safeguard

salvaguardia or **salvaguarda** nf : safeguard, defense

salvajada nf ATROCIDAD : atrocity, act of savagery

salvaje[1] adj **1** : wild ⟨animales salvajes : wild animals⟩ **2** : savage, cruel **3** : primitive, uncivilized

salvaje[2] nmf : savage

salvajismo nm : savagery

salvamento nm **1** : rescuing, lifesaving **2** : salvation **3** : refuge

salvar vt **1** : to save, to rescue **2** : to cover (a distance) **3** : to get around (an obstacle), to overcome (a difficulty) **4**

: to cross, to jump across **5 salvando** : except for, excluding — **salvarse** *vr* 1 : to survive, to escape 2 : to save one's soul

salvavidas[1] *nms & pl* 1 : life preserver 2 **bote salvavidas** : lifeboat

salvavidas[2] *nmf* : lifeguard

salvedad *nf* 1 EXCEPCIÓN : exception 2 : proviso, stipulation

salvia *nf* : sage (plant)

salvo[1], **-va** *adj* 1 : unharmed, sound ⟨sano y salvo : safe and sound⟩ **2 a** ~ : safe from danger

salvo[2] *prep* 1 EXCEPTO : except (for), save ⟨todos asistirán salvo Jaime : all will attend except for Jaime⟩ **2 salvo que** : unless ⟨salvo que llueva : unless it rains⟩

salvoconducto *nm* : safe-conduct

samba *nf* : samba

San *adj* → **santo**[1]

sanar *vt* : to heal, to cure — *vi* : to get well, to recover

sanatorio *nm* 1 : sanatorium 2 : clinic, private hospital

sanción *nf, pl* **sanciones** : sanction

sancionar *vt* 1 : to penalize, to impose a sanction on 2 : to sanction, to approve

sancochar *vt* : to parboil

sandalia *nf* : sandal

sándalo *nm* : sandalwood

sandez *nf, pl* **sandeces** ESTUPIDEZ : nonsense, silly thing to say

sandía *nf* : watermelon

sandwich ['sandwitʃ, 'saŋgwitʃ] *nm, pl* **sandwiches** [-dwitʃes, -gwi-] EMPAREDADO : sandwich

saneamiento *nm* 1 : cleaning up, sanitation 2 : reorganizing, streamlining

sanear *vt* 1 : to clean up, to sanitize 2 : to reorganize, to streamline

sangrante *adj* 1 : bleeding 2 : flagrant, blatant

sangrar *vi* : to bleed — *vt* : to indent (a paragraph, etc.)

sangre *nf* 1 : blood **2 a sangre fría** : in cold blood **3 a sangre y fuego** : by violent force **4 pura sangre** : thoroughbred

sangría *nf* 1 : bloodletting 2 : sangria (wine punch) 3 : drain, draining ⟨una sangría fiscal : a financial drain⟩ 4 : indentation, indenting

sangriento, -ta *adj* 1 : bloody 2 : cruel

sanguijuela *nf* 1 : leech, bloodsucker 2 : sponger, leech

sanguinario, -ria *adj* : bloodthirsty

sanguíneo, -nea *adj* 1 : blood ⟨vaso sanguíneo : blood vessel⟩ 2 : sanguine, ruddy

sanidad *nf* 1 : health 2 : public health, sanitation

sanitario[1], **-ria** *adj* 1 : sanitary 2 : health ⟨centro sanitario : health center⟩

sanitario[2], **-ria** *n* : sanitation worker

sanitario[3] *nm Col, Mex, Ven* : toilet ⟨los sanitarios : the toilets, the restroom⟩

sano, -na *adj* 1 SALUDABLE : healthy 2 : wholesome 3 : whole, intact

santiaguino, -na *adj* : of or from Santiago, Chile

santiamén *nm* **en un santiamén** : in no time at all

santidad *nf* : holiness, sanctity

santificar {72} *vt* : to sanctify, to consecrate, to hallow

santiguarse {10} *vr* PERSIGNARSE : to cross oneself

santo[1], **-ta** *adj* 1 : holy, saintly ⟨el Santo Padre : the Holy Father⟩ ⟨una vida santa : a saintly life⟩ **2 Santo, Santa** (San *before names of masculine saints except those beginning with D or T*) : Saint ⟨Santa Clara : Saint Claire⟩ ⟨Santo Tomás : Saint Thomas⟩ ⟨San Francisco : Saint Francis⟩

santo[2], **-ta** *n* : saint

santo[3] *nm* 1 : saint's day 2 CUMPLEAÑOS : birthday

santuario *nm* : sanctuary

santurrón, -rrona *adj, mpl* **-rrones** : overly pious, sanctimonious — **santurronamente** *adv*

saña *nf* 1 : fury, rage 2 : viciousness ⟨con saña : viciously⟩

sapo *nm* : toad

saque[1], **etc.** → **sacar**

saque[2] *nm* 1 : kickoff (in soccer or football) 2 : serve, service (in sports)

saqueador, -dora *n* DEPREDADOR : plunderer, looter

saquear *vt* : to sack, to plunder, to loot

saqueo *nm* DEPREDACIÓN : sacking, plunder, looting

sarampión *nm* : measles *pl*

sarape *nm CA, Mex* : serape, blanket

sarcasmo *nm* : sarcasm

sarcástico, -ca *adj* : sarcastic

sarcófago *nm* : sarcophagus

sardina *nf* : sardine

sardónico, -ca *adj* : sardonic

sarga *nf* : serge

sargento *nmf* : sergeant

sarna *nf* : mange

sarnoso, -sa *adj* : mangy

sarpullido *nm* ERUPCIÓN : rash

sarro *nm* 1 : deposit, coating 2 : tartar, plaque

sarta *nf* 1 : string, series (of insults, etc.) 2 : string (of pearls, etc.)

sartén *nmf, pl* **sartenes** 1 : frying pan **2 tener la sartén por el mango** : to call the shots, to be in control

sasafrás *nm* : sassafras

sastre, -tra *n* : tailor

sastrería *nf* 1 : tailoring 2 : tailor's shop

Satanás *or* **Satán** *nm* : Satan, the devil

satánico, -ca *adj* : satanic

satélite *nm* : satellite

satín *or* **satén** *nm, pl* **satines** *or* **satenes** : satin

satinado, -da *adj* : satiny, glossy

sátira *nf* : satire

satírico, -ca *adj* : satirical, satiric

satirizar {21} *vt* : to satirize

sátiro *nm* : satyr
satisfacción *nf, pl* **-ciones** : satisfaction
satisfacer {74} *vt* **1** : to satisfy **2** : to fulfill, to meet **3** : to pay, to settle — **satisfacerse** *vr* **1** : to be satisfied **2** : to take revenge
satisfactorio, -ria *adj* : satisfactory — **satisfactoriamente** *adv*
satisfecho, -cha *adj* : satisfied, content, pleased
saturación *nf, pl* **-ciones** : saturation
saturar *vt* **1** : to saturate, to fill up **2** : to satiate, to surfeit
saturnismo *nm* : lead poisoning
Saturno *nm* : Saturn
sauce *nm* : willow
saúco *nm* : elder (tree)
saudí *or* **saudita** *adj & nmf* : Saudi, Saudi Arabian
sauna *nmf* : sauna
savia *nf* : sap
saxofón *nm, pl* **-fones** : saxophone
sazón[1] *nf, pl* **sazones** **1** : flavor, seasoning **2** : ripeness, maturity ⟨en sazón : in season, ripe⟩ **3 a la sazón** : at that time, then
sazón[2] *nmf, pl* **sazones** *Mex* : flavor, seasoning
sazonar *vt* CONDIMENTAR : to season, to spice
scanner *nm* → **escáner**
sé → **saber, ser**
se *pron* **1** : to him, to her, to you, to them ⟨se los daré a ella : I'll give them to her⟩ **2** : each other, one another ⟨se abrazaron : they hugged each other⟩ **3** : himself, herself, itself, yourself, yourselves, themselves ⟨se afeitó antes de salir : he shaved before leaving⟩ **4** (*used in passive constructions*) ⟨se dice que es hermosa : they say she's beautiful⟩ ⟨se habla inglés : English spoken⟩
sea, etc. → **ser**
sebo *nm* **1** : grease, fat **2** : tallow **3** : suet
secado *nm* : drying
secador *nm* : hair dryer
secadora *nf* **1** : dryer, clothes dryer **2** *Mex* : hair dryer
secante *nm* : blotting paper, blotter
secar {72} *v* : to dry — **secarse** *vr* **1** : to get dry **2** : to dry up
sección *nf, pl* **secciones** **1** : section ⟨sección transversal : cross section⟩ **2** : department, division
seco, -ca *adj* **1** : dry **2** DISECADO : dried ⟨fruta seca : dried fruit⟩ **3** : thin, lean **4** : curt, brusque **5** : sharp ⟨un golpe seco : a sharp blow⟩ **6 a secas** : simply, just ⟨se llama Chico, a secas : he's just called Chico⟩ **7 en ~** : abruptly, suddenly ⟨frenar en seco : to make a sudden stop⟩
secoya *nf* : sequoia, redwood
secreción *nf, pl* **-ciones** : secretion
secretar *vt* : to secrete
secretaría *nf* **1** : secretariat, administrative department **2** *Mex* : ministry, cabinet office

secretariado *nm* **1** : secretariat **2** : secretarial profession
secretario, -ria *n* : secretary — **secretarial** *adj*
secreto[1], **-ta** *adj* **1** : secret **2** : secretive — **secretamente** *adv*
secreto[2] *nm* **1** : secret **2** : secrecy
secta *nf* : sect
sectario, -ria *adj & n* : sectarian
sector *nm* : sector
secuaz *nmf, pl* **secuaces** : follower, henchman, underling
secuela *nf* : consequence, sequel ⟨las secuelas de la guerra : the aftermath of the war⟩
secuencia *nf* : sequence
secuestrador, -dora *n* **1** : kidnapper, abductor **2** : hijacker
secuestrar *vt* **1** RAPTAR : to kidnap, to abduct **2** : to hijack, to commandeer **3** CONFISCAR : to confiscate, to seize
secuestro *nm* **1** RAPTO : kidnapping, abduction **2** : hijacking **3** : seizure, confiscation
secular *adj* : secular — **secularismo** *nm* — **secularización** *nf*
secundar *vt* : to support, to second
secundaria *nf* **1** : secondary education, high school **2** *Mex* : junior high school, middle school
secundario, -ria *adj* : secondary
secuoya *nf* : sequoia
sed *nf* **1** : thirst ⟨tener sed : to be thirsty⟩ **2 tener sed de** : to hunger for, to thirst for
seda *nf* : silk
sedación *nf, pl* **-ciones** : sedation
sedal *nm* : fishing line
sedán *nm, pl* **sedanes** : sedan
sedante *adj & nm* CALMANTE : sedative
sedar *vt* : to sedate
sede *nf* **1** : seat, headquarters **2** : venue, site **3 la Santa Sede** : the Holy See
sedentario, -ria *adj* : sedentary
sedición *nf, pl* **-ciones** : sedition — **sedicioso, -sa** *adj*
sediento, -ta *adj* : thirsty, thirsting
sedimentación *nf, pl* **-ciones** : sedimentation
sedimentario, -ria *adj* : sedimentary
sedimento *nm* : sediment
sedoso, -sa *adj* : silky, silken
seducción *nf, pl* **-ciones** : seduction
seducir {61} *vt* **1** : to seduce **2** : to captivate, to charm
seductivo, -va *adj* : seductive
seductor[1], **-tora** *adj* **1** SEDUCTIVO : seductive **2** ENCANTADOR : charming, alluring
seductor[2], **-tora** *n* : seducer
segador, -dora *n* : harvester
segar {49} *vt* **1** : to reap, to harvest, to cut **2** : to sever abruptly ⟨una vida segada por la enfermedad : a life cut short by illness⟩
seglar[1] *adj* LAICO : lay, secular
seglar[2] *nm* LAICO : layperson, layman *m*, laywoman *f*

segmentación *nf, pl* **-ciones** : segmentation

segmentado, -da *adj* : segmented

segmento *nm* : segment

segregar {52} *vt* **1** : to segregate **2** SECRETAR : to secrete

seguida *nf* **en ~** : right away, immediately ⟨vuelvo en seguida : I'll be right back⟩

seguidamente *adv* **1** : next, immediately after **2** : without a break, continuously

seguido¹ *adv* **1** RECTO : straight, straight ahead **2** : often, frequently

seguido², -da *adj* **1** CONSECUTIVO : consecutive, successive ⟨tres días seguidos : three days in a row⟩ **2** : straight, unbroken **3 ~ por** *or* **~ de** : followed by

seguidor, -dora *n* : follower, supporter

seguimiento *nm* **1** : following, pursuit **2** : continuation **3** : tracking, monitoring

seguir {75} *vt* **1** : to follow ⟨el sol sigue la lluvia : sunshine follows the rain⟩ ⟨seguiré tu consejo : I'll follow your advice⟩ ⟨me siguieron con la mirada : they followed me with their eyes⟩ **2** : to go along, to keep on ⟨seguimos toda la carretera panamericana : we continued along the PanAmerican Highway⟩ ⟨siguió hablando : he kept on talking⟩ ⟨seguir el curso : to stay on course⟩ **3** : to take (a course, a treatment) — *vi* **1** : to go on, to keep going ⟨sigue adelante : keep going, carry on⟩ **2** : to remain, to continue to be ⟨¿todavía sigues aquí? : you're still here?⟩ ⟨sigue con vida : she's still alive⟩ **3** : to follow, to come after ⟨la frase que sigue : the following sentence⟩

según¹ *adv* : it depends ⟨según y como : it all depends on⟩

según² *conj* **1** COMO, CONFORME : as, just as ⟨según lo dejé : just as I left it⟩ **2** : depending on how ⟨según se vea : depending on how one sees it⟩

según³ *prep* **1** : according to ⟨según los rumores : according to the rumors⟩ **2** : depending on ⟨según los resultados : depending on the results⟩

segundo¹, -da *adj* : second ⟨el segundo lugar : second place⟩

segundo², -da *n* **1** : second (in a series) **2** : second (person), second-in-command

segundo³ *nm* : second ⟨sesenta segundos : sixty seconds⟩

seguramente *adv* **1** : for sure, surely **2** : probably

seguridad *nf* **1** : safety, security **2** : (financial) security ⟨seguridad social : Social Security⟩ **3** CERTEZA : certainty, assurance ⟨con toda seguridad : with complete certainty⟩ **4** : confidence, self-confidence

seguro¹ *adv* : certainly, definitely ⟨va a llover, seguro : it's going to rain for sure⟩ ⟨¡seguro que sí! : of course!⟩

seguro², -ra *adj* **1** : safe, secure **2** : sure, certain ⟨estoy segura que es él : I'm sure that's him⟩ **3** : reliable, trustworthy **4** : self-assured

seguro³ *nm* **1** : insurance ⟨seguro de vida : life insurance⟩ **2** : fastener, clasp **3** *Mex* : safety pin

seis *adj & nm* : six

seiscientos¹, -tas *adj* : six hundred

seiscientos² *nms & pl* : six hundred

selección *nf, pl* **-ciones** **1** ELECCIÓN : selection, choice **2 selección natural** : natural selection

seleccionar *vt* ELEGIR : to select, to choose

selectivo, -va *adj* : selective — **selectivamente** *adv*

selecto, -ta *adj* **1** : choice, select **2** EXCLUSIVO : exclusive

selenio *nm* : selenium

sellar *vt* **1** : to seal **2** : to stamp

sello *nm* **1** : seal **2** ESTAMPILLA, TIMBRE : postage stamp **3** : hallmark, characteristic

selva *nf* **1** BOSQUE : woods *pl*, forest ⟨selva húmeda : rain forest⟩ **2** JUNGLA : jungle

selvático, -ca *adj* **1** : forest, jungle ⟨sendero selvático : jungle path⟩ **2** : wild

semáforo *nm* **1** : traffic light **2** : stop signal

semana *nf* : week

semanal *adj* : weekly — **semanalmente** *adv*

semanario *nm* : weekly (publication)

semántica *nf* : semantics

semántico, -ca *adj* : semantic

semblante *nm* **1** : countenance, face **2** : appearance, look

semblanza *nf* : biographical sketch, profile

sembrado *nm* : cultivated field

sembrador, -dora *n* : planter, sower

sembradora *nf* : seeder (machine)

sembrar {55} *vt* **1** : to plant, to sow **2** : to scatter, to strew ⟨sembrar el pánico : to spread panic⟩

semejante¹ *adj* **1** PARECIDO : similar, alike **2** TAL : such ⟨nunca he visto cosa semejante : I have never seen such a thing⟩

semejante² *nm* PRÓJIMO : fellowman

semejanza *nf* PARECIDO : similarity, resemblance

semejar *vi* : to resemble, to look like — **semejarse** *vr* : to be similar, to look alike

semen *nm* : semen

semental *nm* : stud (animal) ⟨caballo semental : stallion⟩

semestre *nm* : semester

semicírculo *nm* : semicircle, half circle

semiconductor *nm* : semiconductor

semidiós *nm, pl* **-dioses** : demigod *m*

semifinal *nf* : semifinal

semifinalista¹ *adj* : semifinal

semifinalista² *nmf* : semifinalist

semiformal *adj* : semiformal
semilla *nf* : seed
semillero *nm* **1** : seedbed **2** : hotbed, breeding ground
seminario *nm* **1** : seminary **2** : seminar, graduate course
seminarista *nm* : seminarian
semiprecioso, -sa *adj* : semiprecious
semita[1] *adj* : Semitic
semita[2] *nmf* : Semite
sémola *nf* : semolina
sempiterno, -na *adj* ETERNO : eternal, everlasting
senado *nm* : senate
senador, -dora *n* : senator
sencillamente *adv* : simply, plainly
sencillez *nf* : simplicity
sencillo[1], **-lla** *adj* **1** : simple, easy **2** : plain, unaffected **3** : single
sencillo[2] *nm* **1** : single (recording) **2** : small change (coins) **3** : one-way ticket
senda *nf* CAMINO, SENDERO : path, way
sendero *nm* CAMINO, SENDA : path, way
sendos, -das *adj pl* : each, both ⟨llevaban sendos vestidos nuevos : they were each wearing a new dress⟩
senectud *nf* ANCIANIDAD : old age
senegalés, -lesa *adj & n, mpl* **-leses** : Senegalese
senil *adj* : senile — **senilidad** *nf*
seno *nm* **1** : breast, bosom ⟨los senos : the breasts⟩ ⟨el seno de la familia : the bosom of the family⟩ **2** : sinus **3 seno materno** : womb
sensación *nf, pl* **-ciones 1** IMPRESIÓN : feeling ⟨tener la sensación : to have a feeling⟩ **2** : sensation ⟨causar sensación : to cause a sensation⟩
sensacional *adj* : sensational
sensacionalista *adj* : sensationalistic, lurid
sensatez *nf* **1** : good sense **2 con ~** : sensibly
sensato, -ta *adj* : sensible, sound — **sensatamente** *adv*
sensibilidad *nf* **1** : sensitivity, sensibility **2** SENSACIÓN : feeling
sensibilizar {21} *vt* : to sensitize
sensible *adj* **1** : sensitive **2** APRECIABLE : considerable, significant
sensiblemente *adv* : considerably, significantly
sensiblería *nf* : sentimentality, mush
sensiblero, -ra *adj* : mawkish, sentimental, mushy
sensitivo, -va *adj* **1** : sense ⟨órganos sensitivos : sense organs⟩ **2** : sentient, capable of feeling
sensor *nm* : sensor
sensorial *adj* : sensory
sensual *adj* : sensual, sensuous — **sensualmente** *adv*
sensualidad *nf* : sensuality
sentado, -da *adj* **1** : sitting, seated **2** : established, settled ⟨dar por sentado : to take for granted⟩ ⟨dejar sentado : to make clear⟩ **3** : sensible, steady, judicious

sentar {55} *vt* **1** : to seat, to sit **2** : to establish, to set — *vi* **1** : to suit ⟨ese color te sienta : that color suits you⟩ **2** : to agree with (of food or drink) ⟨las cebollas no me sientan : onions don't agree with me⟩ **3** : to please ⟨le sentó mal el paseo : she didn't enjoy the trip⟩ — **sentarse** *vr* : to sit, to sit down ⟨siéntese, por favor : please have a seat⟩
sentencia *nf* **1** : sentence, judgment **2** : maxim, saying
sentenciar *vt* : to sentence
sentido[1], **-da** *adj* **1** : heartfelt, sincere ⟨mi más sentido pésame : my sincerest condolences⟩ **2** : touchy, sensitive **3** : offended, hurt
sentido[2] *nm* **1** : sense ⟨sentido común : common sense⟩ ⟨los cinco sentidos : the five senses⟩ ⟨sin sentido : senseless⟩ **2** CONOCIMIENTO : consciousness **3** SIGNIFICADO : meaning, sense ⟨doble sentido : double entendre⟩ **4** : direction ⟨calle de sentido único : one-way street⟩
sentimental[1] *adj* **1** : sentimental **2** : love, romantic ⟨vida sentimental : love life⟩
sentimental[2] *nmf* : sentimentalist
sentimentalismo *nm* : sentimentality, sentimentalism
sentimiento *nm* **1** : feeling, emotion **2** PESAR : regret, sorrow
sentir {76} *vt* **1** : to feel, to experience ⟨no siento nada de dolor : I don't feel any pain⟩ ⟨sentía sed : he was feeling thirsty⟩ ⟨sentir amor : to feel love⟩ **2** PERCIBIR : to perceive, to sense ⟨sentir un ruido : to hear a noise⟩ **3** LAMENTAR : to regret, to feel sorry for ⟨lo siento mucho : I'm very sorry⟩ — *vi* **1** : to have feeling, to feel **2 sin ~** : without noticing, inadvertently — **sentirse** *vr* **1** : to feel ⟨¿te sientes mejor? : are you feeling better?⟩ **2** *Chile, Mex* : to take offense
seña *nf* **1** : sign, signal **2 dar señas de** : to show signs of
señal *nf* **1** : signal **2** : sign ⟨señal de tráfico : traffic sign⟩ **3** INDICIO : indication ⟨en señal de : as a token of⟩ **4** VESTIGIO : trace, vestige **5** : scar, mark **6** : deposit, down payment
señalado, -da *adj* : distinguished, notable
señalador *nm* : marker ⟨señalador de libros : bookmark⟩
señalar *vt* **1** INDICAR : to indicate, to show **2** : to mark **3** : to point out, to stress **4** : to fix, to set — **señalarse** *vr* : to distinguish oneself
señor, -ñora *n* **1** : gentleman *m*, man *m*, lady *f*, woman *f*, wife *f* **2** : Sir *m*, Madam *f* ⟨estimados señores : Dear Sirs⟩ **3** : Mr. *m*, Mrs. *f* **4** : lord *m*, lady *f* ⟨el Señor : the Lord⟩
señoría *nf* **1** : lordship **2 Su Señoría** : Your Honor
señorial *adj* : stately, regal

señorío *nm* **1** : manor, estate **2** : dominion, power **3** : elegance, class
señorita *nf* **1** : young lady, young woman **2** : Miss
señuelo *nm* **1** : decoy **2** : bait
sépalo *nm* : sepal
sepa, etc. → **saber**
separación *nf, pl* **-ciones 1** : separation, division **2** : gap, space
separadamente *adv* : separately, apart
separado, -da *adj* **1** : separated **2** : separate ⟨vidas separadas : separate lives⟩ **3 por** ~ : separately
separar *vt* **1** : to separate, to divide **2** : to split up, to pull apart — **separarse** *vr*
sepelio *nm* : interment, burial
sepia[1] *adj & nm* : sepia
sepia[2] *nf* : cuttlefish
septentrional *adj* : northern
séptico, -ca *adj* : septic
septiembre *nm* : September
séptimo[1], **-ma** *adj* : seventh
séptimo[2] *nm* : seventh
septuagésimo[1], **-ma** *adj* : seventieth
septuagésimo[2] *nm* : seventieth
sepulcral *adj* **1** : sepulchral **2** : dismal, gloomy
sepulcro *nm* TUMBA : tomb, sepulchre
sepultar *vt* ENTERRAR : to bury
sepultura *nf* **1** : burial **2** TUMBA : grave, tomb
seque, etc. → **secar**
sequedad *nf* **1** : dryness **2** : brusqueness, curtness
sequía *nf* : drought
séquito *nm* : retinue, entourage
ser[1] {77} *vi* **1** : to be ⟨él es mi hermano : he is my brother⟩ ⟨Camila es linda : Camila is pretty⟩ **2** : to exist, to live ⟨ser, o no ser : to be or not to be⟩ **3** : to take place, to occur ⟨el concierto es el domingo : the concert is on Sunday⟩ **4** (*used with expressions of time, date, season*) ⟨son las diez : it's ten o'clock⟩ ⟨hoy es el 9 : today's the 9th⟩ **5** : to cost, to come to ⟨¿cuánto es? : how much is it?⟩ **6** (*with the future tense*) : to be able to be ⟨¿será posible? : can it be possible?⟩ **7** ~ **de** : to come from ⟨somos de Managua : we're from Managua⟩ **8** ~ **de** : to belong to ⟨ese lápiz es de Juan : that's Juan's pencil⟩ **9 es que** : the thing is that ⟨es que no lo conozco : it's just that I don't know him⟩ **10 ¡sea!** : agreed!, all right! **11 sea...sea** : either...or — *v aux* (*used in passive constructions*) : to be ⟨la cuenta ha sido pagada : the bill has been paid⟩ ⟨él fue asesinado : he was murdered⟩
ser[2] *nm* : being ⟨ser humano : human being⟩
seráfico, -ca *adj* : angelic, seraphic
serbio[1], **-bia** *adj & n* : Serb, Serbian
serbio[2] *nm* : Serbian (language)
serbocroata[1] *adj* : Serbo-Croatian
serbocroata[2] *nm* : Serbo-Croatian (language)

serenar *vt* : to calm, to soothe — **serenarse** *vr* CALMARSE : to calm down
serenata *nf* : serenade
serendipia *nf* : serendipity
serenidad *nf* : serenity, calmness
sereno[1], **-na** *adj* **1** SOSEGADO : serene, calm, composed **2** : fair, clear (of weather) **3** : calm, still (of the sea) — **serenamente** *adv*
sereno[2] *nm* : night watchman
seriado, -da *adj* : serial
serial *nm* : serial (on radio or television)
seriamente *adv* : seriously
serie *nf* **1** : series **2** SERIAL : serial **3 fabricación en serie** : mass production **4 fuera de serie** : extraordinary, amazing
seriedad *nf* **1** : seriousness, earnestness **2** : gravity, importance
serio, -ria *adj* **1** : serious, earnest **2** : reliable, responsible **3** : important **4 en** ~ : seriously, in earnest — **seriamente** *adv*
sermón *nm, pl* **sermones 1** : sermon **2** *fam* : harangue, lecture
sermonear *vt fam* : to harangue, to lecture
serpentear *vi* : to twist, to wind — **serpenteante** *adj*
serpentina *nf* : paper streamer
serpiente *nf* : serpent, snake
serrado, -da *adj* DENTADO : serrated
serranía *nf* : mountainous area
serrano, -na *adj* : from the mountains
serrar {55} *vt* : to saw
serrín *nm, pl* **serrines** : sawdust
serruchar *vt* : to saw up
serrucho *nm* : saw, handsaw
servicentro *nm Peru* : gas station
servicial *adj* : obliging, helpful
servicio *nm* **1** : service **2** SAQUE : serve (in sports) **3 servicios** *nmpl* : restroom
servidor, -dora *n* **1** : servant **2 su seguro servidor** : yours truly (in correspondence)
servidumbre *nf* **1** : servitude **2** : help, servants *pl*
servil *adj* **1** : servile, subservient **2** : menial
servilismo *nm* : servility, subservience
servilleta *nf* : napkin
servir {54} *vt* **1** : to serve, to be of use to **2** : to serve, to wait **3** SURTIR : to fill (an order) — *vi* **1** : to work ⟨mi radio no sirve : my radio isn't working⟩ **2** : to be of use, to be helpful ⟨esa computadora no sirve para nada : that computer's perfectly useless⟩ — **servirse** *vr* **1** : to help oneself to **2** : to be kind enough ⟨sírvase enviarnos un catálogo : please send us a catalog⟩
sésamo *nm* AJONJOLÍ : sesame, sesame seeds *pl*
sesenta *adj & nm* : sixty
sesentavo[1], **-va** *adj* : sixtieth
sesentavo[2] *n* : sixtieth (fraction)
sesgado, -da *adj* **1** : inclined, tilted **2** : slanted, biased

sesgar {52} *vt* **1** : to cut on the bias **2** : to tilt **3** : to bias, to slant
sesgo *nm* : bias
sesgue, etc. → **sesgar**
sesión *nf, pl* **sesiones 1** : session **2** : showing, performance
sesionar *vi* REUNIRSE : to meet, to be in session
seso *nm* **1** : brains, intelligence **2 sesos** *nmpl* : brains (as food)
sesudo, -da *adj* **1** : prudent, sensible **2** : brainy
set *nm, pl* **sets** : set (in tennis)
seta *nf* : mushroom
setecientos[1], **-tas** *adj* : seven hundred
setecientos[2] *nms & pl* : seven hundred
setenta *adj & nm* : seventy
setentavo[1], **-va** *adj* : seventieth
setentavo[2] *nm* : seventieth
setiembre → **septiembre**
seto *nm* **1** : fence, enclosure **2 seto vivo** : hedge
seudónimo *nm* : pseudonym
severidad *nf* **1** : harshness, severity **2** : strictness
severo, -ra *adj* **1** : harsh, severe **2** ESTRICTO : strict — **severamente** *adv*
sexagésimo[1], **-ma** *adj* : sixtieth, sixty-
sexagésimo[2], **-ma** *n* : sixtieth, sixty- (in a series)
sexismo *nm* : sexism — **sexista** *adj & nmf*
sexo *nm* : sex
sextante *nm* : sextant
sexteto *nm* : sextet
sexto, -ta *adj* : sixth — **sexto, -ta** *n*
sexual *adj* : sexual, sex ⟨educación sexual : sex education⟩ — **sexualmente** *adv*
sexualidad *nf* : sexuality
sexy *adj, pl* **sexy** *or* **sexys** : sexy
shock ['ʃɔk, 'tʃɔk] *nm* : shock ⟨estado de shock : state of shock⟩
short *nm, pl* **shorts** : shorts *pl*
show *nm, pl* **shows** : show
si *conj* **1** : if ⟨lo haré si me pagan : I'll do it if they pay me⟩ ⟨si lo supiera te lo diría : if I knew it I would tell you⟩ **2** : whether, if ⟨no importa si funciona o no : it doesn't matter whether it works (or not)⟩ **3** (*expressing desire, protest, or surprise*) ⟨si supiera la verdad : if only I knew the truth⟩ ⟨¡si no quiero! : but I don't want to!⟩ **4 si bien** : although ⟨si bien se ha progresado : although progress has been made⟩ **5 si no** : otherwise, or else ⟨si no, no voy : otherwise I won't go⟩
sí[1] *adv* **1** : yes ⟨sí, gracias : yes, please⟩ ⟨creo que sí : I think so⟩ **2 sí que** : indeed, absolutely ⟨esta vez sí que ganaré : this time I'm sure to win⟩ **3 porque sí** *fam* : because, just because ⟨lo hizo porque sí : she did it just because⟩
sí[2] *nm* : yes ⟨dar el sí : to say yes, to express consent⟩
sí[3] *pron* **1 de por sí** *or* **en sí** : by itself, in itself, per se **2 fuera de sí** : beside

oneself **3 para sí (mismo)** : to himself, to herself, for himself, for herself **4 entre** ~ : among themselves
siamés, -mesa *adj & n, mpl* **siameses** : Siamese
sibilante *adj & nf* : sibilant
siciliano, -na *adj & n* : Sicilian
sico- → **psico-**
sicomoro *or* **sicómoro** *nm* : sycamore
SIDA *or* **sida** *nm* (síndrome de inmunodeficiencia adquirida) : AIDS
siderurgia *nf* : iron and steel industry
siderúrgico, -ca *adj* : steel, iron ⟨la industria siderúrgica : the steel industry⟩
sidra *nf* : hard cider
siega[1], **siegue, etc.** → **segar**
siega[2] *nf* **1** : harvesting **2** : harvest time **3** : harvested crop
siembra[1], **etc.** → **sembrar**
siembra[2] *nf* **1** : sowing **2** : sowing season **3** SEMBRADO : cultivated field
siempre *adv* **1** : always ⟨siempre tienes hambre : you're always hungry⟩ **2** : still ⟨¿siempre te vas? : are you still going?⟩ **3** *Mex* : after all ⟨siempre no fui : I didn't go after all⟩ **4 siempre que** : whenever, every time ⟨siempre que pasa : every time he walks by⟩ **5 para** ~ : forever, for good **6 siempre y cuando** : provided that
sien *nf* : temple (on the forehead)
sienta, etc. → **sentar**
siente, etc. → **sentir**
sierpe *nf* : serpent, snake
sierra[1], **etc.** → **serrar**
sierra[2] *nf* **1** : saw ⟨sierra de vaivén : jigsaw⟩ **2** CORDILLERA : mountain range **3** : mountains *pl* ⟨viven en la sierra : they live in the mountains⟩
siervo, -va *n* **1** : slave **2** : serf
siesta *nf* : nap, siesta
siete *adj & nm* : seven
sífilis *nf* : syphilis
sifón *nm, pl* **sifones** : siphon
siga, sigue etc. → **seguir**
sigilo *nm* : secrecy, stealth
sigiloso, -sa *adj* FURTIVO : furtive, stealthy — **sigilosamente** *adv*
sigla *nf* : acronym, abbreviation
siglo *nm* **1** : century **2** : age ⟨el Siglo de Oro : the Golden Age⟩ ⟨hace siglos que no te veo : I haven't seen you in ages⟩ **3** : world, secular life
signar *vt* : to sign (a treaty or agreement)
signatario, -ria *n* : signatory
significación *nf, pl* **-ciones 1** : significance, importance **2** : signification, meaning
significado *nm* **1** : sense, meaning **2** : significance
significante *adj* : significant
significar {72} *vt* **1** : to mean, to signify **2** : to express, to make known — **significarse** *vr* **1** : to draw attention, to become known **2** : to take a stance
significativo, -va *adj* **1** : significant, important **2** : meaningful — **significativamente** *adv*

signo *nm* **1** : sign ⟨signo de igual : equal sign⟩ ⟨un signo de alegría : a sign of happiness⟩ **2** : (punctuation) mark ⟨signo de interrogación : question mark⟩ ⟨signo de admiración : exclamation point⟩ ⟨signo de intercalación : caret⟩
siguiente *adj* : next, following
sílaba *nf* : syllable
silábico, -ca *adj* : syllabic
silbar *v* : to whistle
silbato *nm* PITO : whistle
silbido *nm* : whistle, whistling
silenciador *nm* **1** : muffler (of an automobile) **2** : silencer
silenciar *vt* **1** : to silence **2** : to muffle
silencio *nm* **1** : silence, quiet ⟨¡silencio! : be quiet!⟩ **2** : rest (in music)
silencioso, -sa *adj* : silent, quiet — **silenciosamente** *adv*
sílice *nf* : silica
silicio *nm* : silicon
silla *nf* **1** : chair **2 silla de ruedas** : wheelchair
sillón *nm, pl* **sillones** : armchair, easy chair
silo *nm* : silo
silueta *nf* **1** : silhouette **2** : figure, shape
silvestre *adj* : wild ⟨flor silvestre : wildflower⟩
silvicultor, -tora *n* : forester
silvicultura *nf* : forestry
sima *nf* ABISMO : chasm, abyss
simbólico, -ca *adj* : symbolic — **simbólicamente** *adj*
simbolismo *nm* : symbolism
simbolizar {21} *vt* : to symbolize
símbolo *nm* : symbol
simetría *nf* : symmetry
simétrico, -ca *adj* : symmetrical, symmetric
simiente *nf* : seed
símil *nm* **1** : simile **2** : analogy, comparison
similar *adj* SEMEJANTE : similar, alike
similitud *nf* : similarity, resemblance
simio *nm* : ape
simpatía *nf* **1** : liking, affection ⟨tomarle simpatía a : to take a liking to⟩ **2** : warmth, friendliness **3** : support, solidarity
simpático, -ca *adj* : nice, friendly, likeable
simpatizante *nf* : sympathizer, supporter
simpatizar {21} *vi* **1** : to get along, to hit it off ⟨simpaticé mucho con él : I really liked him⟩ **2** ~ **con** : to sympathize with, to support
simple¹ *adj* **1** SENCILLO : plain, simple, easy **2** : pure, mere ⟨por simple vanidad : out of pure vanity⟩ **3** : simpleminded, foolish
simple² *n* : fool, simpleton
simplemente *adv* : simply, merely, just
simpleza *nf* **1** : foolishness, simpleness **2** NECEDAD : nonsense
simplicidad *nf* : simplicity

simplificar {72} *vt* : to simplify — **simplificación** *nf*
simplista *adj* : simplistic
simposio *or* **simposium** *nm* : symposium
simulación *nf, pl* **-ciones** : simulation
simulacro *nm* : imitation, sham ⟨simulacro de juicio : mock trial⟩
simular *vt* **1** : to simulate **2** : to feign, to pretend
simultáneo, -nea *adj* : simultaneous — **simultáneamente** *adv*
sin *prep* **1** : without ⟨sin querer : unintentionally⟩ ⟨sin refinar : unrefined⟩ **2** **sin que** : without ⟨lo hicimos sin que él se diera cuenta : we did it without him noticing⟩
sinagoga *nf* : synagogue
sinceridad *nf* : sincerity
sincero, -ra *adj* : sincere, honest, true — **sinceramente** *adv*
síncopa *nf* : syncopation
sincopar *vt* : to syncopate
sincronizar {21} *vt* : to synchronize — **sincronización** *nf*
sindical *adj* GREMIAL : union, labor ⟨representante sindical : union representative⟩
sindicalización *nf, pl* **-ciones** : unionizing, unionization
sindicalizar {21} *vt* : to unionize — **sindicalizarse** *vr* **1** : to form a union **2** : to join a union
sindicar → **sindicalizar**
sindicato *nm* GREMIO : union, guild
síndrome *nm* : syndrome
sinecura *nf* : sinecure
sinfín *nm* : endless number ⟨un sinfín de problemas : no end of problems⟩
sinfonía *nf* : symphony
sinfónica *nf* : symphony orchestra
sinfónico, -ca *adj* : symphonic, symphony
singular¹ *adj* **1** : singular, unique **2** PARTICULAR : peculiar, odd **3** : singular (in grammar) — **singularmente** *adv*
singular² *nm* : singular
singularidad *nf* : uniqueness, singularity
singularizar {21} *vt* : to make unique or distinct — **singularizarse** *vr* : to stand out, to distinguish oneself
siniestrado, -da *adj* : damaged, wrecked ⟨zona siniestrada : disaster zone⟩
siniestro¹, -tra *adj* **1** IZQUIERDO : left, left-hand **2** MALVADO : sinister, evil
siniestro² *nm* : accident, disaster
sinnúmero → **sinfín**
sino *conj* **1** : but, rather ⟨no será hoy, sino mañana : it won't be today, but tomorrow⟩ **2** EXCEPTO : but, except ⟨no hace sino despertar suspicacias : it does nothing but arouse suspicion⟩
sinónimo¹, -ma *adj* : synonymous
sinónimo² *nm* : synonym
sinopsis *nfs & pl* RESUMEN : synopsis, summary
sinrazón *nf, pl* **-zones** : wrong, injustice

sinsabores *nmpl* : woes, troubles
sinsonte *nm* : mockingbird
sintáctico, -ca *adj* : syntactic, syntactical
sintaxis *nfs & pl* : syntax
síntesis *nfs & pl* **1** : synthesis, fusion **2** SINOPSIS : synopsis, summary
sintético, -ca *adj* : synthetic — **sintéticamente** *adv*
sintetizar {21} *vt* **1** : to synthesize **2** RESUMIR : to summarize
sintió, etc. → **sentir**
síntoma *nm* : symptom
sintomático, -ca *adj* : symptomatic
sintonía *nf* **1** : tuning in (of a radio) **2** **en sintonía con** : in tune with, attuned to
sintonizador *nm* : tuner, knob for tuning (of a radio, etc.)
sintonizar {21} *vt* : to tune (in) to — *vi* **1** : to tune in **2 ~ con** : to be in tune with, to empathize with
sinuosidad *nf* : sinuosity
sinuoso, -sa *adj* **1** : winding, sinuous **2** : devious
sinvergüenza[1] *adj* **1** DESCARADO : shameless, brazen, impudent **2** TRAVIESO : naughty
sinvergüenza[2] *nmf* **1** : rogue, scoundrel **2** : brat, rascal
sionista *adj & nmf* : Zionist — **sionismo** *nm*
siqui- → **psiqui-**
siquiera *adv* **1** : at least ⟨dame siquiera un poquito : at least give me a little bit⟩ **2** (*in negative constructions*) : not even ⟨ni siquiera nos saludaron : they didn't even say hello to us⟩
sirena *nf* **1** : mermaid **2** : siren ⟨sirena de niebla : foghorn⟩
sirio, -ria *adj & n* : Syrian
sirope *nm* : syrup
sirve, etc. → **servir**
sirviente, -ta *n* : servant, maid *f*
sisal *nm* : sisal
sisear *vi* : to hiss
siseo *nm* : hiss
sísmico, -ca *adj* : seismic
sismo *nm* **1** TERREMOTO : earthquake **2** TEMBLOR : tremor
sismógrafo *nm* : seismograph
sistema *nm* : system
sistemático, -ca *adj* : systematic — **sistemáticamente** *adv*
sistematizar {21} *vt* : to systematize
sistémico, -ca *adj* : systemic
sitiar *vt* ASEDIAR : to besiege
sitio *nm* **1** LUGAR : place, site ⟨vámonos a otro sitio : let's go somewhere else⟩ **2** ESPACIO : room, space ⟨hacer sitio a : to make room for⟩ **3** : siege ⟨estado de sitio : state of siege⟩ **4** *Mex* : taxi stand
situación *nf, pl* **-ciones** : situation
situado, -da *adj* : situated, placed
situar {3} *vt* UBICAR : to situate, to place, to locate — **situarse** *vr* **1** : to be placed, to be located **2** : to make a place for oneself, to do well

sketch *nm* : sketch, skit
slip *nm* : briefs *pl*, underpants *pl*
smog *nm* : smog
smoking *nm* ESMOQUIN : tuxedo
snob → **esnob**
so *prep* : under ⟨so pena de : under penalty of⟩
sobaco *nm* : armpit
sobado, -da *adj* **1** : worn, shabby **2** : well-worn, hackneyed
sobar *vt* **1** : to finger, to handle **2** : to knead **3** : to rub, to massage **4** *fam* : to beat, to pummel
soberanía *nf* : sovereignty
soberano, -na *adj & n* : sovereign
soberbia *nf* **1** ORGULLO : pride, arrogance **2** MAGNIFICENCIA : magnificence
soberbio, -bia *adj* **1** : proud, arrogant **2** : grand, magnificent
sobornable *adv* : venal, bribable
sobornar *vt* : to bribe
soborno *nm* **1** : bribery **2** : bribe
sobra *nf* **1** : excess, surplus **2 de ~** : extra, to spare **3 sobras** *nfpl* : leftovers, scraps
sobrado, -da *adj* : abundant, excessive, more than enough
sobrante[1] *adj* : remaining, superfluous
sobrante[2] *nm* : remainder, surplus
sobrar *vi* : to be in excess, to be superfluous ⟨más vale que sobre a que falte : it's better to have too much than not enough⟩
sobre[1] *nm* **1** : envelope **2** : packet ⟨un sobre de sazón : a packet of seasoning⟩
sobre[2] *prep* **1** : on, on top of ⟨sobre la mesa : on the table⟩ **2** : over, above **3** : about ⟨¿tiene libros sobre Bolivia? : do you have books on Bolivia?⟩ **4 sobre todo** : especially, above all
sobrealimentar *vt* : to overfeed
sobrecalentar {55} *vt* : to overheat — **sobrecalentarse** *vr*
sobrecama *nmf* : bedspread
sobrecargar {52} *vt* : to overload, to overburden, to weigh down
sobrecoger {15} *vt* **1** : to surprise, to startle **2** : to scare — **sobrecogerse** *vr*
sobrecubierta *nf* : dust jacket
sobredosis *nfs & pl* : overdose
sobreentender {56} *vt* : to infer, to understand
sobreestimar *vt* : to overestimate, to overrate
sobreexcitado, -da *adj* : overexcited
sobreexponer {60} *vt* : to overexpose
sobregirar *vt* : to overdraw
sobregiro *nm* : overdraft
sobrehumano, -na *adj* : superhuman
sobrellevar *vt* : to endure, to bear
sobremanera *adv* : exceedingly
sobremesa *nf* : after-dinner conversation
sobrenatural *adj* : supernatural
sobrenombre *nm* APODO : nickname
sobrentender → **sobreentender**

sobrepasar *vt* : to exceed, to surpass — **sobrepasarse** *vr* PASARSE : to go too far

sobrepelliz *nf, pl* **-pellices** : surplice

sobrepeso *nm* **1** : excess weight **2** : overweight, obesity

sobrepoblación, sobrepoblado → **superpoblación, superpoblado**

sobreponer {60} *vt* **1** SUPERPONER : to superimpose **2** ANTEPONER : to put first, to give priority to — **sobreponerse** *vr* **1** : to pull oneself together **2** ~ **a** : to overcome

sobreprecio *nm* : surcharge

sobreproducción *nf, pl* **-ciones** : overproduction

sobreproducir {61} *vt* : to overproduce

sobreprotector, -tora *adj* : overprotective

sobreproteger {15} *vt* : to overprotect

sobresaliente[1] *adj* **1** : protruding, projecting **2** : outstanding, noteworthy **3** : significant, salient

sobresaliente[2] *nmf* : understudy

sobresalir {73} *vi* **1** : to protrude, to jut out, to project **2** : to stand out, to excel

sobresaltar *vt* : to startle, to frighten — **sobresaltarse** *vr*

sobresalto *nm* : start, fright

sobresueldo *nm* : bonus, additional pay

sobretasa *nf* : surcharge ⟨sobretasa a la gasolina : gas tax⟩

sobretodo *nm* : overcoat

sobrevalorar *or* **sobrevaluar** {3} *vt* : to overvalue, to overrate

sobrevender *vt* : to oversell

sobrevenir {87} *vi* ACAECER : to take place, to come about ⟨podrían sobrevenir complicaciones : complications could occur⟩

sobrevivencia → **supervivencia**

sobreviviente → **superviviente**

sobrevivir *vi* : to survive — *vt* : to outlive, to outlast

sobrevolar {19} *vt* : to fly over, to overfly

sobriedad *nf* : sobriety, moderation

sobrino, -na *n* : nephew *m*, niece *f*

sobrio, -bria *adj* : sober — **sobriamente** *adv*

socarrón, -rrona *adj, mpl* **-rrones 1** : sly, cunning **2** : sarcastic

socavar *vt* : to undermine

sociabilidad *nf* : sociability

sociable *adj* : sociable

social *adj* : social — **socialmente** *adv*

socialista *adj & nmf* : socialist — **socialismo** *nm*

sociedad *nf* **1** : society **2** : company, enterprise **3 sociedad anónima** : incorporated company

socio, -cia *n* **1** : member **2** : partner

socioeconómico, -ca *adj* : socioeconomic

sociología *nf* : sociology

sociológico, -ca *adj* : sociological — **sociológicamente** *adv*

sociólogo, -ga *n* : sociologist

socorrer *vt* : to assist, to come to the aid of

socorrido, -da *adj* ÚTIL : handy, practical

socorrista *nmf* **1** : rescue worker **2** : lifeguard

socorro *nm* AUXILIO **1** : aid, help ⟨equipo de socorro : rescue team⟩ ¡socorro! : help!

soda *nf* : soda, soda water

sodio *nf* : sodium

soez *adj, pl* **soeces** GROSERO : rude, vulgar — **soezmente** *adv*

sofá *nm* : couch, sofa

sofistería *nf* : sophistry — **sofista** *nmf*

sofisticación *nf, pl* **-ciones** : sophistication

sofisticado, -da *adj* : sophisticated

sofocante *adj* : suffocating, stifling

sofocar {72} *vt* **1** AHOGAR : to suffocate, to smother **2** EXTINGUIR : to extinguish, to put out (a fire) **3** APLASTAR : to crush, to put down ⟨sofocar una rebelión : to crush a rebellion⟩ — **sofocarse** *vr* **1** : to suffocate **2** *fam* : to get upset, to get mad

sofreír {66} *vt* : to sauté

sofrito[1], **-ta** *adj* : sautéed

sofrito[2] *nm* : seasoning sauce

softbol *nm* : softball

software *nm* : software

soga *nf* : rope

soja → **soya**

sojuzgar *vt* : to subdue, to conquer, to subjugate

sol *nm* **1** : sun **2** : Peruvian unit of currency

solamente *adv* SÓLO : only, just

solapa *nf* **1** : lapel (of a jacket) **2** : flap (of an envelope)

solapado, -da *adj* : secret, underhanded

solapar *vt* : to cover up, to keep secret — **solaparse** *vr* : to overlap

solar[1] {19} *vt* : to floor, to tile

solar[2] *adj* : solar, sun

solar[3] *nm* **1** TERRENO : lot, piece of land, site **2** *Cuba, Peru* : tenement building

solariego, -ga *adj* : ancestral

solaz *nm, pl* **solaces 1** CONSUELO : solace, comfort **2** DESCANSO : relaxation, recreation

solazarse {21} *vr* : to relax, to enjoy oneself

soldado *nm* **1** : soldier **2 soldado raso** : private, enlisted man

soldador[1], **-dora** *n* : welder

soldador[2] *nm* : soldering iron

soldadura *nf* **1** : welding **2** : soldering, solder

soldar {19} *vt* **1** : to weld **2** : to solder

soleado, -da *adj* : sunny

soledad *nf* : loneliness, solitude

solemne *adj* : solemn — **solemnemente** *adv*

solemnidad *nf* : solemnity

soler {78} *vi* : to be in the habit of, to tend to ⟨solía tomar café por la tarde : she usually drank coffee in the afternoon⟩ ⟨eso suele ocurrir : that frequently happens⟩

solera *nf* **1** : prop, support **2** : tradition

solicitante *nmf* : applicant

solicitar *vt* **1** : to request, to solicit **2** : to apply for ⟨solicitar empleo : to apply for employment⟩

solícito, -ta *adj* : solicitous, attentive, obliging

solicitud *nf* **1** : solicitude, concern **2** : request **3** : application

solidaridad *nf* : solidarity

solidario, -ria *adj* : supportive, united in support ⟨se declararon solidarios con la nueva ley : they declared their support for the new law⟩ ⟨espíritu solidario : spirit of solidarity⟩

solidarizar {21} *vi* : to be in solidarity ⟨solidarizamos con la huelga : we support the strike⟩

solidez *nf* **1** : solidity, firmness **2** : soundness (of an argument, etc.)

solidificar {72} *vt* : to solidify, to make solid — **solidificarse** *vr* — **solidificación** *nf*

sólido[1], -da *adj* **1** : solid, firm **2** : sturdy, well-made **3** : sound, well-founded — **sólidamente** *adv*

sólido[2] *nm* : solid

soliloquio *nm* : soliloquy

solista *nmf* : soloist

solitaria *nf* TENIA : tapeworm

solitario[1], -ria *adj* **1** : lonely **2** : lone, solitary **3** DESIERTO : deserted, lonely ⟨una calle solitaria : a deserted street⟩

solitario[2], -ria *n* : recluse, loner

solitario[3] *nm* : solitaire

sollozar {21} *vi* : to sob

sollozo *nm* : sob

solo[1], -la *adj* **1** : alone, by oneself **2** : lonely **3** ÚNICO : only, sole, unique ⟨hay un solo problema : there's only one problem⟩ **4 a solas** : alone

solo[2] *nm* : solo

sólo *adv* SOLAMENTE : just, only ⟨sólo quieren comer : they just want to eat⟩

solomillo *nm* : sirloin, loin

solsticio *nm* : solstice

soltar {19} *vt* **1** : to let go of, to drop **2** : to release, to set free **3** AFLOJAR : to loosen, to slacken

soltería *nf* : bachelorhood, spinsterhood

soltero[1], -ra *adj* : single, unmarried

soltero[2], -ra *n* **1** : bachelor *m*, single man *m*, single woman *f* **2 apellido de soltera** : maiden name

soltura *nf* **1** : looseness, slackness **2** : fluency (of language) **3** : agility, ease of movement

soluble *adj* : soluble — **solubilidad** *nf*

solución *nf, pl* **-ciones 1** : solution (in a liquid) **2** : answer, solution

solucionar *vt* RESOLVER : to solve, to resolve — **solucionarse** *vr*

solvencia *nf* **1** : solvency **2** : settling, payment (of debts) **3** : reliability ⟨solvencia moral : trustworthiness⟩

solvente[1] *adj* **1** : solvent **2** : reliable, trustworthy

solvente[2] *nm* : solvent

somalí *adj & nmf* : Somalian

sombra *nf* **1** : shadow **2** : shade **3 sombras** *nfpl* : darkness, shadows *pl* **4 sin sombra de duda** : without a shadow of a doubt

sombreado, -da *adj* **1** : shady **2** : shaded, darkened

sombrear *vt* : to shade

sombrerero, -ra *n* : milliner, hatter

sombrero *nm* **1** : hat **2 sin ~** : bareheaded **3 sombrero hongo** : derby

sombrilla *nf* : parasol, umbrella

sombrío, -bría *adj* LÓBREGO : dark, somber, gloomy — **sombríamente** *adv*

someramente *adv* : cursorily, summarily

somero, -ra *adj* : superficial, cursory, shallow

someter *vt* **1** : to subjugate, to conquer **2** : to subordinate **3** : to subject (to treatment or testing) **4** : to submit, to present — **someterse** *vr* **1** : to submit, to yield **2** : to undergo

sometimiento *nm* **1** : submission, subjection **2** : presentation

somnífero[1], -ra *adj* : soporific

somnífero[2] *nm* : sleeping pill

somnolencia *nf* : drowsiness, sleepiness

somnoliento, -ta *adj* : drowsy, sleepy

somorgujo *or* **somormujo** *nm* : loon, grebe

somos → ser[1]

son[1] → ser

son[2] *nm* **1** : sound ⟨al son de la trompeta : at the sound of the trumpet⟩ **2** : news, rumor **3 en son de** : as, in the manner of, by way of ⟨en son de broma : as a joke⟩ ⟨en son de paz : in peace⟩

sonado, -da *adj* : celebrated, famous, much-discussed

sonaja *nf* : rattle

sonajero *nm* : rattle (toy)

sonámbulo, -la *n* : sleepwalker

sonar[1] {19} *vi* **1** : to sound ⟨suena bien : it sounds good⟩ **2** : to ring (bells) **3** : to look or sound familiar ⟨me suena ese nombre : that name rings a bell⟩ **4 ~ a** : to sound like — *vt* **1** : to ring **2** : to blow (a trumpet, a nose) — **sonarse** *vr* : to blow one's nose

sonar[2] *nm* : sonar

sonata *nf* : sonata

sonda *nf* **1** : sounding line **2** : probe **3** CATÉTER : catheter

sondar *vt* **1** : to sound, to probe (in medicine, drilling, etc.) **2** : to probe, to explore (outer space)

sondear *vt* **1** : to sound **2** : to probe **3** : to sound out, to test (opinions, markets)

sondeo *nm* **1** : sounding, probing **2** : drilling **3** ENCUESTA : survey, poll
soneto *nm* : sonnet
sónico, -ca *adj* : sonic
sonido *nm* : sound
sonoridad *nf* : sonority, resonance
sonoro, -ra *adj* **1** : resonant, sonorous, voiced (in linguistics) **2** : resounding, loud **3 banda sonora** : soundtrack
sonreír {66} *vi* : to smile
sonriente *adj* : smiling
sonrisa *nf* : smile
sonrojar *vt* : to cause to blush — **sonrojarse** *vr* : to blush
sonrojo *nm* RUBOR : blush
sonrosado, -da *adj* : rosy, pink
sonsacar {72} *vt* : to wheedle, to extract
sonsonete *nm* **1** : tapping **2** : drone **3** : mocking tone
soñador¹, -dora *adj* : dreamy
soñador², -dora *n* : dreamer
soñar {19} *v* **1** : to dream **2** ~ **con** : to dream about **3 soñar despierto** : to daydream
soñoliento, -ta *adj* : sleepy, drowsy
sopa *nf* **1** : soup **2 estar hecho una sopa** : to be soaked to the bone
sopera *nf* : soup tureen
sopesar *vt* : to weigh, to evaluate
soplar *vi* : to blow — *vt* : to blow on, to blow out, to blow off
soplete *nm* : blowtorch
soplido *nm* : puff
soplo *nm* : puff, gust
soplón, -plona *n, mpl* **soplones** *fam* : tattletale, sneak
sopor *nm* SOMNOLENCIA : drowsiness, sleepiness
soporífero, -ra *adj* : soporific
soportable *adj* : bearable, tolerable
soportar *vt* **1** SOSTENER : to support, to hold up **2** RESISTIR : to withstand, to resist **3** AGUANTAR : to bear, to tolerate
soporte *nm* : base, stand, support
soprano *nmf* : soprano
sor *nf* : Sister (religious title)
sorber *vt* **1** : to sip, to suck in **2** : to absorb, to soak up
sorbete *nm* : sherbet
sorbo *nm* **1** : sip, gulp, swallow **2 beber a sorbos** : to sip
sordera *nf* : deafness
sordidez *nf, pl* **-deces** : sordidness, squalor
sórdido, -da *adj* : sordid, dirty, squalid
sordina *nf* : mute (for a musical instrument)
sordo, -da *adj* **1** : deaf **2** : muted, muffled
sordomudo, -da *n* : deaf-mute
sorgo *nm* : sorghum
soriasis *nfs & pl* : psoriasis
sorna *nf* : sarcasm, mocking tone
sorprendente *adj* : surprising — **sorprendentemente** *adv*
sorprender *vt* : to surprise — **sorprenderse** *vr*

sorpresa *nf* : surprise
sorpresivo, -va *adj* **1** : surprising, surprise **2** IMPREVISTO : sudden, unexpected
sortear *vt* **1** RIFAR : to raffle, to draw lots for **2** : to dodge, to avoid
sorteo *nm* : drawing, raffle
sortija *nf* **1** ANILLO : ring **2** : curl, ringlet
sortilegio *nm* **1** HECHIZO : spell, charm **2** HECHICERÍA : sorcery
SOS *nm* : SOS
sosegado, -da *adj* SERENO : calm, tranquil, serene
sosegar {49} *vt* : to calm, to pacify — **sosegarse** *vr*
sosiego *nm* : tranquillity, serenity, calm
soslayar *vt* ESQUIVAR : to dodge, to evade
soslayo *nm* **de** ~ : obliquely, sideways ⟨mirar de soslayo : to look askance⟩
soso, -sa *adj* **1** INSÍPIDO : bland, flavorless **2** ABURRIDO : dull, boring
sospecha *nf* : suspicion
sospechar *vt* : to suspect — *vi* : to be suspicious
sospechosamente *adv* : suspiciously
sospechoso¹, -sa *adj* : suspicious, suspect
sospechoso², -sa *n* : suspect
sostén *nm, pl* **sostenes 1** APOYO : support **2** : sustenance **3** : brassiere, bra
sostener {80} *vt* **1** : to support, to hold up **2** : to hold ⟨sostenme la puerta : hold the door for me⟩ ⟨sostener una conversación : to hold a conversation⟩ **3** : to sustain, to maintain — **sostenerse** *vr* **1** : to stand, to hold oneself up **2** : to continue, to remain
sostenible *adj* : sustainable, tenable
sostenido¹, -da *adj* **1** : sustained, prolonged **2** : sharp (in music)
**sostenido² ** *nm* : sharp (in music)
sostuvo, etc. → **sostener**
sotana *nf* : cassock
sótano *nm* : basement
sotavento *nm* : lee ⟨a sotavento : leeward⟩
soterrar {55} *vt* **1** : to bury **2** : to conceal, to hide away
soto *nm* : grove, copse
souvenir *nm, pl* **-nirs** RECUERDO : souvenir, memento
soviético, -ca *adj* : Soviet
soy → **ser**
soya *nf* : soy, soybean
spaghetti → **espagueti**
sport [ɛˈspor] *adj* : sport, casual
sprint [ɛˈsprin, -ˈsprint] *nm* : sprint — **sprinter** *nmf*
squash [ɛˈskwaʃ, -ˈskwatʃ] *nm* : squash (sport)
Sr. *nm* : Mr.
Sra. *nf* : Mrs., Ms.
Srta. *or* **Srita.** *nf* : Miss, Ms.
standard → **estándar**
stress → **estrés**
su *adj* **1** : his, her, its, their, one's ⟨su libro : her book⟩ ⟨sus consecuencias

: its consequences⟩ **2** (*formal*) : your
⟨tómese su medicina, señor : take your
medicine, sir⟩
suave *adj* **1** BLANDO : soft **2** LISO
: smooth **3** : gentle, mild **4** *Mex fam*
: great, fantastic
suavemente *adj* : smoothly, gently, softly
suavidad *nf* : softness, smoothness, mellowness
suavizante *nm* : softener, fabric softener
suavizar {21} *vt* **1** : to soften, to smooth
out **2** : to tone down — **suavizarse** *vr*
subacuático, -ca *adj* : underwater
subalterno¹, -na *adj* **1** SUBORDINADO
: subordinate **2** SECUNDARIO : secondary
subalterno², -na *n* SUBORDINADO : subordinate
subarrendar {55} *vt* : to sublet
subasta *nf* : auction
subastador, -dora *n* : auctioneer
subastar *vt* : to auction, to auction off
subcampeón, -peona *n, mpl* **-peones**
: runner-up
subcomité *nm* : subcommittee
subconsciente *adj & nm* : subconscious
— **subconscientemente** *adv*
subcontratar *vt* : to subcontract
subcontratista *nmf* : subcontractor
subcultura *nf* : subculture
subdesarrollado, -da *adj* : underdeveloped
subdirector, -tora *n* : assistant manager
súbdito, -ta *n* : subject (of a monarch)
subdividir *vt* : to subdivide
subdivisión *nf, pl* **-siones** : subdivision
subestimar *vt* : to underestimate, to undervalue
subexponer {60} *vt* : to underexpose
subexposición *nf, pl* **-ciones** : under-
exposure
subgrupo *nm* : subgroup
subibaja *nm* : seesaw
subida *nf* **1** : ascent, climb **2** : rise, increase **3** : slope, hill ⟨ir de subida : to
go uphill⟩
subido, -da *adj* **1** : intense, strong
⟨amarillo subido : bright yellow⟩ **2**
subido de tono : risqué
subir *vt* **1** : to bring up, to take up **2** : to
climb, to go up **3** : to raise — *vi* **1** : to
go up, to come up **2** : to rise, to increase **3** : to be promoted **4** ~ **a** : to
get on, to mount ⟨subir a un tren : to
get on a train⟩ — **subirse** *vr* **1** : to
climb (up) **2** : to pull up (clothing) **3**
subirse a la cabeza : to go to one's
head
súbito, -ta *adj* **1** REPENTINO : sudden
2 de ~ : all of a sudden, suddenly —
súbitamente *adv*
subjetivo, -va *adj* : subjective — **subje-
tivamente** *adv* — **subjetividad** *nf*
subjuntivo¹, -va *adj* : subjunctive
subjuntivo² *nm* : subjunctive
sublevación *nf, pl* **-ciones** ALZAMIEN-
TO : uprising, rebellion

sublevar *vt* : to incite to rebellion —
sublevarse *vr* : to rebel, to rise up
sublimar *vt* : to sublimate — **subli-
mación** *nf*
sublime *adj* : sublime
submarinismo *nm* : scuba diving
submarinista *nmf* : scuba diver
submarino¹, -na *adj* : submarine, undersea
submarino² *nm* : submarine
suboficial *nmf* : noncommissioned officer, petty officer
subordinado, -da *adj & n* : subordinate
subordinar *vt* : to subordinate — **sub-
ordinarse** *vr* — **subordinación** *nf*
subproducto *nm* : by-product
subrayar *vt* **1** : to underline, to underscore **2** ENFATIZAR : to highlight, to
emphasize
subrepticio, -cia *adj* : surreptitious —
subrepticiamente *adv*
subsahariano, -na *adj* : sub-Saharan
subsanar *vt* **1** RECTIFICAR : to rectify,
to correct **2** : to overlook, to excuse **3**
: to make up for
subscribir → **suscribir**
subsecretario, -ria *n* : undersecretary
subsecuente *adj* : subsequent — **sub-
secuentemente** *adv*
subsidiar *vt* : to subsidize
subsidiaria *nf* : subsidiary
subsidio *nm* : subsidy
subsiguiente *adj* : subsequent
subsistencia *nf* **1** : subsistence **2** : sustenance
subsistir *vi* **1** : to subsist, to live **2** : to
endure, to survive
substancia → **sustancia**
subteniente *nmf* : second lieutenant
subterfugio *nm* : subterfuge
subterráneo¹, -nea *adj* : underground,
subterranean
subterráneo² *nm* **1** : underground passage, tunnel **2** *Arg, Uru* : subway
subtítulo *nm* : subtitle, subheading
subtotal *nm* : subtotal
suburbano, -na *adj* : suburban
suburbio *nm* **1** : suburb **2** : slum (outside a city)
subvención *nf, pl* **-ciones** : subsidy,
grant
subvencionar *vt* : to subsidize
subversivo, -va *adj & n* : subversive —
subversión *nf*
subvertir {76} *vt* : to subvert
subyacente *adj* : underlying
subyugar {52} *vt* : to subjugate — **sub-
yugación** *nf*
succión *nf, pl* **succiones** : suction
succionar *vt* : to suck up, to draw in
sucedáneo *nm* : substitute ⟨sucedáneo
de azucar : sugar substitute⟩
suceder *vi* **1** OCURRIR : to happen, to
occur ⟨¿qué sucede? : what's going
on?⟩ ⟨suceda lo que suceda : come
what may⟩ **2** ~ **a** : to follow, to succeed ⟨suceder al trono : to succeed to
the throne⟩ ⟨a la primavera sucede el
verano : summer follows spring⟩

sucesión *nf, pl* **-siones 1** : succession **2** : sequence, series **3** : issue, heirs *pl*
sucesivamente *adv* : successively, consecutively ⟨y así sucesivamente : and so on⟩
sucesivo, -va *adj* : successive ⟨en los días sucesivos : in the days that followed⟩
suceso *nm* **1** : event, happening, occurrence **2** : incident, crime
sucesor, -sora *n* : successor
suciedad *nf* **1** : dirtiness, filthiness **2** MUGRE : dirt, filth
sucinto, -ta *adj* CONCISO : succinct, concise — **sucintamente** *adv*
sucio, -cia *adj* : dirty, filthy
sucre *nm* : Ecuadoran unit of currency
suculento, -ta *adj* : succulent
sucumbir *vi* : to succumb
sucursal *nf* : branch (of a business)
sudadera *nf* : sweatshirt
sudado, -da → **sudoroso**
sudafricano, -na *adj & n* : South African
sudamericano, -na *adj & n* : South American
sudanés, -nesa *adj & n, mpl* **-neses** : Sudanese
sudar *vi* TRANSPIRAR : to sweat, to perspire
sudario *nm* : shroud
sudeste → **sureste**
sudoeste → **suroeste**
sudor *nm* TRANSPIRACIÓN : sweat, perspiration
sudoroso, -sa *adj* : sweaty
sueco¹, -ca *adj* : Swedish
sueco², -ca *n* : Swede
sueco³ *nm* : Swedish (language)
suegro, -gra *n* **1** : father-in-law *m*, mother-in-law *f* **2 suegros** *nmpl* : in-laws
suela *nf* : sole (of a shoe)
suelda, etc. → **soldar**
sueldo *nm* : salary, wage
suele, etc. → **soler**
suelo *nm* **1** : ground ⟨caerse al suelo : to fall down, to hit the ground⟩ **2** : floor, flooring **3** TIERRA : soil, land
suelta, etc. → **soltar**
suelto¹, -ta *adj* : loose, free, unattached
suelto² *nm* : loose change
suena, etc. → **sonar**
sueña, etc. → **soñar**
sueño *nm* **1** : dream **2** : sleep ⟨perder el sueño : to lose sleep⟩ **3** : sleepiness ⟨tener sueño : to be sleepy⟩
suero *nm* **1** : serum **2** : whey
suerte *nf* **1** FORTUNA : luck, fortune ⟨tener suerte : to be lucky⟩ ⟨por suerte : luckily⟩ **2** DESTINO : fate, destiny, lot **3** CLASE, GÉNERO : sort, kind ⟨toda suerte de cosas : all kinds of things⟩
suertudo, -da *adj fam* : lucky
suéter *nm* : sweater
suficiencia *nf* **1** : adequacy, sufficiency **2** : competence, fitness **3** : smugness, self-satisfaction
suficiente *adj* **1** BASTANTE : enough, sufficient ⟨tener suficiente : to have

enough⟩ **2** : suitable, fit **3** : smug, complacent
suficientemente *adv* : sufficiently, enough
sufijo *nm* : suffix
suflé *nm* : soufflé
sufragar {52} *vt* **1** AYUDAR : to help out, to support **2** : to defray (costs) — *vi* : to vote
sufragio *nm* : suffrage, vote
sufrido, -da *adj* **1** : long-suffering, patient **2** : sturdy, serviceable (of clothing)
sufrimiento *nm* : suffering
sufrir *vt* **1** : to suffer ⟨sufrir una pérdida : to suffer a loss⟩ **2** : to tolerate, to put up with ⟨ella no lo puede sufrir : she can't stand him⟩ — *vi* : to suffer
sugerencia *nf* : suggestion
sugerir {76} *vt* **1** PROPONER, RECOMENDAR : to suggest, to recommend, to propose **2** : to suggest, to bring to mind
sugestión *nf, pl* **-tiones** : suggestion, prompting ⟨poder de sugestión : power of suggestion⟩
sugestionable *adj* : suggestible, impressionable
sugestionar *vt* : to influence, to sway —
sugestionarse *vr* ~ **con** : to talk oneself into, to become convinced of
sugestivo, -va *adj* **1** : suggestive **2** : interesting, stimulating
suicida¹ *adj* : suicidal
suicida² *nmf* : suicide victim, suicide
suicidarse *vr* : to commit suicide
suicidio *nm* : suicide
suite *nf* : suite
suizo, -za *adj & n* : Swiss
sujeción *nf, pl* **-ciones 1** : holding, fastening **2** : subjection
sujetador *nm* **1** : fastener **2** : holder ⟨sujetador de tazas : cup holder⟩
sujetalibros *nms & pl* : bookend
sujetapapeles *nms & pl* CLIP : paper clip
sujetar *vt* **1** : to hold on to, to steady, to hold down **2** FIJAR : to fasten, to attach **3** DOMINAR : to subdue, to conquer — **sujetarse** *vr* **1** : to hold on, to hang on **2** ~ **a** : to abide by
sujeto¹, -ta *adj* **1** : secure, fastened **2** ~ **a** : subject to
sujeto² *nm* **1** INDIVIDUO : individual, character **2** : subject (in grammar)
sulfúrico, -ca *adj* : sulfuric
sulfuro *nm* : sulfur
sultán *nm, pl* **sultanes** : sultan
suma *nf* **1** CANTIDAD : sum, quantity **2** : addition
sumamente *adv* : extremely, exceedingly
sumar *vt* **1** : to add, to add up **2** : to add up to, to total — *vi* : to add up — **sumarse** *vr* ~ **a** : to join
sumario¹, -ria *adj* SUCINTO : succinct, summary — **sumariamente** *adv*
sumario² *nm* : summary

sumergir {35} *vt* : to submerge, to immerse, to plunge — **sumergirse** *vr*
sumersión *nf, pl* **-siones** : submersion, immersion
sumidero *nm* : drain, sewer
suministrar *vt* : to supply, to provide
suministro *nm* : supply, provision
sumir *vt* SUMERGIR : to plunge, to immerse, to sink — **sumirse** *vr*
sumisión *nf, pl* **-siones** **1** : submission **2** : submissiveness
sumiso, -sa *adj* : submissive, acquiescent, docile
sumo, -ma *adj* **1** : extreme, great, high ⟨la suma autoridad : the highest authority⟩ **2 a lo sumo** : at the most — **sumamente** *adv*
suntuoso, -sa *adj* : sumptuous, lavish — **suntuosamente** *adv*
supeditar *vt* SUBORDINAR : to subordinate — **supeditación** *nf*
super¹ *or* **súper** *adj fam* : super, great
super² *nm* SUPERMERCADO : market, supermarket
superable *adj* : surmountable
superabundancia *nf* : overabundance, superabundance — **superabundante** *adj*
superar *vt* **1** : to surpass, to exceed **2** : to overcome, to surmount — **superarse** *vr* : to improve oneself
superávit *nm, pl* **-vit** *or* **-vits** : surplus
superchería *nf* : trickery, fraud
supercomputadora *nf* : supercomputer
superestructura *nf* : superstructure
superficial *adj* : superficial — **superficialmente** *adv*
superficialidad *nf* : superficiality
superficie *nf* **1** : surface **2** : area ⟨la superficie de un triángulo : the area of a triangle⟩
superfluidad *nf* : superfluity
superfluo, -flua *adj* : superfluous
superintendente *nmf* : supervisor, superintendent
superior¹ *adj* **1** : superior **2** : upper ⟨nivel superior : upper level⟩ **3** : higher ⟨educación superior : higher education⟩ **4 ~ a** : above, higher than, in excess of
superior² *nm* : superior
superioridad *nf* : superiority
superlativo¹, -va *adj* : superlative
superlativo² *nm* : superlative
supermercado *nm* : supermarket
superpoblación *nf, pl* **-ciones** : overpopulation
superpoblado, -da *adj* : overpopulated
superponer {60} *vt* : to superimpose
superpotencia *nf* : superpower
superproducción → **sobreproducción**
supersónico, -ca *adj* : supersonic
superstición *nf, pl* **-ciones** : superstition
supersticioso, -sa *adj* : superstitious
supervisar *vt* : to supervise, to oversee
supervisión *nf, pl* **-siones** : supervision
supervisor, -sora *n* : supervisor, overseer

supervivencia *nf* : survival
superviviente *nmf* : survivor
supino, -na *adj* : supine
suplantar *vt* : to supplant, to replace
suplemental → **suplementario**
suplementario, -ria *adj* : supplementary, additional, extra
suplemento *nm* : supplement
suplencia *nf* : substitution, replacement
suplente *adj & nmf* : substitute ⟨equipo suplente : replacement team⟩
supletorio, -ria *adj* : extra, additional ⟨teléfono supletorio : extension phone⟩ ⟨cama supletoria : spare bed⟩
súplica *nf* : plea, entreaty
suplicar {72} *vt* IMPLORAR, ROGAR : to entreat, to implore, to supplicate
suplicio *nm* TORMENTO : ordeal, torture
suplir *vt* **1** COMPENSAR : to make up for, to compensate for **2** REEMPLAZAR : to replace, to substitute
supo, etc. → **saber**
suponer {60} *vt* **1** PRESUMIR : to suppose, to assume ⟨supongo que sí : I guess so, I suppose so⟩ ⟨se supone que van a llegar mañana : they're supposed to arrive tomorrow⟩ **2** : to imply, to suggest **3** : to involve, to entail ⟨el éxito supone mucho trabajo : success involves a lot of work⟩
suposición *nf, pl* **-ciones** PRESUNCIÓN : supposition, assumption
supositorio *nm* : suppository
supremacía *nf* : supremacy
supremo, -ma *adj* : supreme
supresión *nf, pl* **-siones** **1** : suppression, elimination **2** : deletion
suprimir *vt* **1** : to suppress, to eliminate **2** : to delete
supuestamente *adv* : supposedly, allegedly
supuesto, -ta *adj* **1** : supposed, alleged **2 por ~** : of course, absolutely
supurar *vi* : to ooze, to discharge
supuso, etc. → **suponer**
sur¹ *adj* : southern, southerly, south
sur² *nm* **1** : south, South **2** : south wind
surafricano, -na → **sudafricano**
suramericano, -na → **sudamericano**
surcar {72} *vt* **1** : to plow (through) **2** : to groove, to score, to furrow
surco *nm* : groove, furrow, rut
sureño¹, -ña *adj* : southern, Southern
sureño², -ña *n* : Southerner
sureste¹ *adj* **1** : southeast, southeastern **2** : southeasterly
sureste² *nm* : southeast, Southeast
surf *nm* : surfing
surfear *vi* : to surf
surfing → **surf**
surfista *nmf* : surfer
surgimiento *nm* : rise, emergence
surgir {35} *vi* : to rise, to arise, to emerge
suroeste¹ *adj* **1** : southwest, southwestern **2** : southwesterly
suroeste² *nm* : southwest, Southwest
surtido¹, -da *adj* **1** : assorted, varied **2** : stocked, provisioned

surtido² *nm* : assortment, selection
surtidor *nm* **1** : jet, spout **2** *Arg, Chile, Spain* : gas pump
surtir *vt* **1** : to supply, to provide ⟨surtir un pedido : to fill an order⟩ **2 surtir efecto** : to have an effect — *vi* : to spout, to spurt up — **surtirse** *vr* : to stock up
susceptible *adj* : susceptible, sensitive — **susceptibilidad** *nf*
suscitar *vt* : to provoke, to give rise to
suscribir {33} *vt* **1** : to sign (a formal document) **2** : to endorse, to sanction — **suscribirse** *vr* ~ **a** : to subscribe to
suscripción *nf, pl* **-ciones 1** : subscription **2** : endorsement, sanction **3** : signing
suscriptor, -tora *n* : subscriber
susodicho, -cha *adj* : aforementioned, aforesaid
suspender *vt* **1** COLGAR : to suspend, to hang **2** : to suspend, to discontinue **3** : to suspend, to dismiss
suspensión *nf, pl* **-siones** : suspension
suspenso *nm* : suspense
suspicacia *nf* : suspicion, mistrust
suspicaz *adj, pl* **-caces** DESCONFIADO : suspicious, wary
suspirar *vi* : to sigh
suspiro *nm* : sigh
surque, etc. → **surcar**
suscrito *pp* → **suscribir**
sustancia *nf* **1** : substance **2 sin** ~ : shallow, lacking substance
sustancial *adj* **1** : substantial **2** ESENCIAL, FUNDAMENTAL : essential, fundamental — **sustancialmente** *adv*
sustancioso, -sa *adj* **1** NUTRITIVO : hearty, nutritious **2** : substantial, solid
sustantivo *nm* : noun

sustentación *nf, pl* **-ciones** SOSTÉN : support
sustentar *vt* **1** : to support, to hold up **2** : to sustain, to nourish **3** : to maintain, to hold (an opinion) — **sustentarse** *vr* : to support oneself
sustento *nm* **1** : means of support, livelihood **2** : sustenance, food
sustitución *nf, pl* **-ciones** : replacement, substitution
sustituir {41} *vt* **1** : to replace, to substitute for **2** : to stand in for
sustituto, -ta *n* : substitute, stand-in
susto *nm* : fright, scare
sustracción *nf, pl* **-ciones 1** RESTA : subtraction **2** : theft
sustraer {81} *vt* **1** : to remove, to take away **2** RESTAR : to subtract **3** : to steal — **sustraerse** *vr* ~ **a** : to avoid, to evade
susurrar *vi* **1** : to whisper **2** : to murmur **3** : to rustle (leaves, etc.) — *vt* : to whisper
susurro *nm* **1** : whisper **2** : murmur **3** : rustle, rustling
sutil *adj* **1** : delicate, thin, fine **2** : subtle
sutileza *nf* **1** : delicacy **2** : subtlety
sutura *nf* : suture
suturar *vt* : to suture
suyo¹, -ya *adj* **1** : his, her, its, theirs ⟨los libros suyos : his books⟩ ⟨un amigo suyo : a friend of hers⟩ ⟨esta casa es suya : this house is theirs⟩ **2** (*formal*) : yours ⟨¿este abrigo es suyo, señor? : is this your coat, sir?⟩
suyo², -ya *pron* **1** : his, hers, theirs ⟨mi guitarra y la suya : my guitar and hers⟩ ⟨ellos trajeron las suyas : they brought theirs, they brought their own⟩ **2** (*formal*) : yours ⟨usted olvidó la suya : you forgot yours⟩
switch *nm* : switch

T

t *nf* : twenty-first letter of the Spanish alphabet
taba *nf* : anklebone
tabacalero¹, -ra *adj* : tobacco ⟨industria tabacalera : tobacco industry⟩
tabacalero², -ra *n* : tobacco grower
tabaco *nm* : tobacco
tábano *nm* : horsefly
taberna *nf* : tavern, bar
tabernáculo *nm* : tabernacle
tabicar {72} *vt* : to wall up
tabique *nm* : thin wall, partition
tabla *nf* **1** : table, list ⟨tabla de multiplicar : multiplication table⟩ **2** : board, plank, slab ⟨tabla de planchar : ironing board⟩ **3** : plot, strip (of land) **4 tablas** *nfpl* : stage, boards *pl*
tablado *nm* **1** : floor **2** : platform, scaffold **3** : stage
tablero *nm* **1** : bulletin board **2** : board (in games) ⟨tablero de ajedrez : chess-

board⟩ ⟨tablero de damas : checkerboard⟩ **3** PIZARRA : blackboard **4** : switchboard **5 tablero de instrumentos** : dashboard, instrument panel
tableta *nf* **1** COMPRIMIDO, PÍLDORA : tablet, pill **2** : bar (of chocolate)
tabletear *vi* : to rattle, to clack
tableteo *nm* : clack, rattling
tablilla *nf* **1** : small board or tablet **2** : bulletin board **3** : splint
tabloide *nm* : tabloid
tablón *nm, pl* **tablones 1** : plank, beam **2 tablón de anuncios** : bulletin board
tabú¹ *adj* : taboo
tabú² *nm, pl* **tabúes** *or* **tabús** : taboo
tabulador *nm* : tabulator
tabular¹ *vt* : to tabulate
tabular² *adj* : tabular
taburete *nm* : footstool, stool
tacañería *nf* : miserliness, stinginess

tacaño · tanto

tacaño¹, -ña adj MEZQUINO : stingy, miserly
tacaño², -ña n : miser, tightwad
tacha nf 1 : flaw, blemish, defect 2 **poner tacha a** : to find fault with 3 **sin ~** : flawless
tachadura nf : erasure, correction
tachar vt 1 : to cross out, to delete 2 **~ de** : to accuse of, to label as ⟨lo tacharon de mentiroso : they accused him of being a liar⟩
tachón nm, pl **tachones** : stud, hobnail
tachonar vt : to stud
tachuela nf : tack, hobnail, stud
tácito, -ta adj : tacit, implicit — **tácitamente** adv
taciturno, -na adj 1 : taciturn 2 : sullen, gloomy
tacle nm : tackle
taclear vt : to tackle (in football)
taco nm 1 : wad, stopper, plug 2 : pad (of paper) 3 : cleat 4 : heel (of a shoe) 5 : cue (in billiards) 6 : light snack, bite 7 : taco
tacón nm, pl **tacones** : heel (of a shoe) ⟨de tacón alto : high-heeled⟩
táctica nf : tactic, tactics pl
táctico¹, -ca adj : tactical
táctico², -ca n : tactician
táctil adj : tactile
tacto nm 1 : touch, touching, feel 2 DELICADEZA : tact
tafetán nm, pl **-tanes** : taffeta
tahúr nm, pl **tahúres** : gambler
tailandés¹, -desa adj & n, pl **-deses** : Thai
tailandés² nm : Thai (language)
taimado, -da adj 1 : crafty, sly 2 Chile : sullen, sulky
tajada nf 1 : slice 2 **sacar tajada** fam : to get one's share
tajante adj 1 : cutting, sharp 2 : decisive, categorical
tajantemente adv : emphatically, categorically
tajar vt : to cut, to slice
tajo nm 1 : cut, slash, gash 2 ESCARPA : steep cliff
tal¹ adv 1 : so, in such a way 2 **tal como** : just as ⟨tal como lo hice : just the way I did it⟩ 3 **con tal que** : provided that, as long as 4 **¿qué tal?** : how are you?, how's it going?
tal² adj 1 : such, such a 2 **tal vez** : maybe, perhaps
tal³ pron 1 : such a one, someone 2 : such a thing, something 3 **tal para cual** : two of a kind
tala nf : felling (of trees)
taladrar vt : to drill
taladro nm : drill, auger ⟨taladro eléctrico : power drill⟩
talante nm 1 HUMOR : mood, disposition 2 VOLUNTAD : will, willingness
talar vt 1 : to cut down, to fell 2 DEVASTAR : to devastate, to destroy
talco nm 1 : talc 2 : talcum powder
talego nm : sack

talento nm : talent, ability
talentoso, -sa adj : talented, gifted
talismán nm, pl **-manes** AMULETO : talisman, charm
talla nf 1 ESTATURA : height 2 : size (in clothing) 3 : stature, status 4 : sculpture, carving
tallar vt 1 : to sculpt, to carve 2 : to measure (someone's height) 3 : to deal (cards)
tallarín nf, pl **-rines** : noodle
talle nm 1 : size 2 : waist, waistline 3 : figure, shape
taller nm 1 : shop, workshop 2 : studio (of an artist)
tallo nm : stalk, stem ⟨tallo de maíz : cornstalk⟩
talón nm, pl **talones** 1 : heel (of the foot) 2 : stub (of a check) 3 **talón de Aquiles** : Achilles' heel
talud nm : slope, incline
tamal nm : tamale
tamaño¹, -ña adj : such a big ⟨¿crees tamaña mentira? : do you believe such a lie?⟩
tamaño² nm 1 : size 2 **de tamaño natural** : life-size
tamarindo nm : tamarind
tambalearse vr 1 : to teeter 2 : to totter, to stagger, to sway — **tambaleante** adj
tambaleo nm : staggering, lurching, swaying
también adv : too, as well, also
tambor nm : drum
tamborilear vi : to drum, to tap
tamborileo nm : tapping, drumming
tamiz nm : sieve
tamizar {21} vt : to sift
tampoco adv : neither, not either ⟨ni yo tampoco : me neither⟩
tampón nm, pl **tampones** 1 : ink pad 2 : tampon
tam–tam nm : tom-tom
tan adv 1 : so, so very ⟨no es tan difícil : it is not that difficult⟩ 2 : as ⟨tan pronto como : as soon as⟩ 3 **tan siquiera** : at least, at the least 4 **tan sólo** : only, merely
tanda nf 1 : turn, shift 2 : batch, lot, series
tándem nm 1 : tandem (bicycle) 2 : duo, pair
tangente adj & nf : tangent — **tangencial** adj
tangible adj : tangible
tango nm : tango
tanino nm : tannin
tanque nm 1 : tank, reservoir 2 : tanker, tank (vehicle)
tanteador nm MARCADOR : scoreboard
tantear vt 1 : to feel, to grope 2 : to size up, to weigh — vi 1 : to keep score 2 : to feel one's way
tanteo nm 1 : estimate, rough calculation 2 : testing, sizing up 3 : scoring
tanto¹ adv 1 : so much ⟨tanto mejor : so much the better⟩ 2 : so long ⟨¿por qué

te tardaste tanto? : why did you take so long?〉

tanto², -ta *adj* **1** : so much, so many, such 〈no hagas tantas preguntas : don't ask so many questions〉〈tiene tanto encanto : he has such charm, he's so charming〉 **2** : as much, as many 〈come tantos dulces como yo : she eats as many sweets as I do〉 **3** : odd, however many 〈cuarenta y tantos años : forty-odd years〉

tanto³ *nm* **1** : certain amount **2** : goal, point (in sports) **3 al tanto** : abreast, in the picture **4 un tanto** : somewhat, rather 〈un tanto cansado : rather tired〉

tanto⁴, -ta *pron* **1** : so much, so many 〈tiene tanto que hacer : she has so much to do〉〈¡no me des tantos! : don't give me so many!〉 **2 entre ~** : meanwhile **3 por lo tanto** : therefore

tañer {79} *vt* **1** : to ring (a bell) **2** : to play (a musical instrument)

tañido *nm* **1** CAMPANADA : ring, peal, toll **2** : sound (of an instrument)

tapa *nf* **1** : cover, top, lid **2** *Spain* : bar snack

tapacubos *nms & pl* : hubcap

tapadera *nf* **1** : cover, lid **2** : front, cover (for an organization or person)

tapar *vt* **1** CUBRIR : to cover, to cover up **2** OBSTRUIR : to block, to obstruct — **taparse** *vr*

tapete *nm* **1** : small rug, mat **2** : table cover **3 poner sobre el tapete** : to bring up for discussion

tapia *nf* : (adobe) wall, garden wall

tapiar *vt* **1** : to wall in **2** : to enclose, to block off

tapicería *nf* **1** : upholstery **2** TAPIZ : tapestry

tapicero, -ra *n* : upholsterer

tapioca *nf* : tapioca

tapir *nm* : tapir

tapiz *nm, pl* **tapices** : tapestry

tapizar {21} *vt* **1** : to upholster **2** : to cover, to carpet

tapón *nm, pl* **tapones 1** : cork **2** : bottle cap **3** : plug, stopper

tapujo *nm* **1** : deceit, pretension **2 sin tapujos** : openly, frankly

taquigrafía *nf* : stenography, shorthand

taquigráfico, -ca *adj* : stenographic

taquígrafo, -fa *n* : stenographer

taquilla *nf* **1** : box office, ticket office **2** : earnings *pl*, take

taquillero, -ra *adj* : box-office, popular 〈un éxito taquillero : a box-office success〉

tarántula *nf* : tarantula

tararear *vt* : to hum

tardanza *nf* : lateness, delay

tardar *vi* **1** : to delay, to take a long time **2** : to be late **3 a más tardar** : at the latest — *vt* DEMORAR : to take (time) 〈tarda una hora : it takes an hour〉

tarde¹ *adv* **1** : late **2 tarde o temprano** : sooner or later

tarde² *nf* **1** : afternoon, evening **2 ¡buenas tardes!** : good afternoon!, good evening! **3 en la tarde** *or* **por la tarde** : in the afternoon, in the evening

tardío, -día *adj* : late, tardy

tardo, -da *adj* : slow

tarea *nf* **1** : task, job **2** : homework

tarifa *nf* **1** : rate 〈tarifas postales : postal rates〉 **2** : fare (for transportation) **3** : price list **4** ARANCEL : duty

tarima *nf* PLATAFORMA : dais, platform, stage

tarjeta *nf* : card 〈tarjeta de crédito : credit card〉〈tarjeta postal : postcard〉

tarro *nm* **1** : jar, pot **2** *Arg, Chile* : can, tin

tarta *nf* **1** : tart **2** : cake

tartaleta *nf* : tart

tartamudear *vi* : to stammer, to stutter

tartamudeo *nm* : stutter, stammer

tartán *nm, pl* **tartanes** : tartan, plaid

tártaro *nm* : tartar

tasa *nf* **1** : rate 〈tasa de desempleo : unemployment rate〉 **2** : tax, fee **3** : appraisal, valuation

tasación *nf, pl* **-ciones** : appraisal, assessment

tasador, -dora *n* : assessor, appraiser

tasar *vt* **1** VALORAR : to appraise, to value **2** : to set the price of **3** : to ration, to limit

tasca *nf* : cheap bar, dive

tatuaje *nm* : tattoo, tattooing

tatuar {3} *vt* : to tattoo

taurino, -na *adj* : bull, bullfighting

Tauro *nmf* : Taurus

tauromaquia *nf* : (art of) bullfighting

taxi *nm, pl* **taxis** : taxi, taxicab

taxidermia *nf* : taxidermy

taxidermista *nmf* : taxidermist

taxímetro *nm* : taximeter

taxista *nmf* : taxi driver

taza *nf* **1** : cup **2** : cupful **3** : (toilet) bowl **4** : basin (of a fountain)

tazón *nm, pl* **tazones 1** : bowl **2** : large cup, mug

te *pron* **1** : you 〈te quiero : I love you〉 **2** : for you, to you, from you 〈me gustaría dártelo : I would like to give it to you〉 **3** : yourself, for yourself, to yourself, from yourself 〈¡cálmate! : calm yourself!〉〈¿te guardaste uno? : did you keep one for yourself?〉 **4** : thee

té *nm* **1** : tea **2** : tea party

tea *nf* : torch

teatral *adj* : theatrical — **teatralmente** *adv*

teatro *nm* **1** : theater **2 hacer teatro** : to put on an act, to exaggerate

teca *nf* : teak

techado *nm* **1** : roof **2 bajo techado** : under cover, indoors

techar *vt* : to roof, to shingle

techo *nm* **1** TEJADO : roof **2** : ceiling **3** : upper limit, ceiling

techumbre *nf* : roofing

tecla *nf* **1** : key (of a musical instrument or a machine) **2 dar en la tecla** : to hit the nail on the head

teclado *nm* : keyboard
teclear *vt* : to type in, to enter
técnica *nf* 1 : technique, skill 2 : technology
técnico[1], -ca *adj* : technical — técnicamente *adv*
técnico[2], -ca *n* : technician, expert, engineer
tecnología *nf* : technology
tecnológico, -ca *adj* : technological — tecnológicamente *adv*
tecolote *nm Mex* : owl
tedio *nm* : tedium, boredom
tedioso, -sa *adj* : tedious, boring — tediosamente *adv*
teja *nf* : tile
tejado *nm* TECHO : roof
tejedor, -dora *n* : weaver
tejer *vt* 1 : to knit, to crochet 2 : to weave 3 FABRICAR : to concoct, to make up, to fabricate
tejido *nm* 1 TELA : fabric, cloth 2 : weave, texture 3 : tissue ⟨tejido muscular : muscle tissue⟩
tejo *nm* 1 : yew 2 : hopscotch (children's game)
tejón *nm, pl* tejones : badger
tela *nf* 1 : fabric, cloth, material 2 tela de araña : spiderweb 3 poner en tela de juicio : to call into question, to doubt
telar *nm* : loom
telaraña *nf* : spiderweb, cobweb
tele *nf fam* : TV, television
telecomunicación *nf, pl* -ciones : telecommunication
teleconferencia *nf* : teleconference
teledifusión *nf, pl* -siones : television broadcasting
teledirigido, -da *adj* : remote-controlled
telefonear *v* : to telephone, to call
telefónico, -ca *adj* : phone, telephone ⟨llamada telefónica : phone call⟩
telefonista *nmf* : telephone operator
teléfono *nm* 1 : telephone 2 llamar por teléfono : to telephone, to make a phone call
telegrafiar {85} *v* : to telegraph
telegráfico, -ca *adj* : telegraphic
telégrafo *nm* : telegraph
telegrama *nm* : telegram
telenovela *nf* : soap opera
telepatía *nf* : telepathy
telepático, -ca *adj* : telepathic — telepáticamente *adv*
telescópico, -ca *adj* : telescopic
telescopio *nm* : telescope
telespectador, -dora *n* : television viewer
telesquí *nm, pl* -squís : ski lift
televidente *nmf* : television viewer
televisar *vt* : to televise
televisión *nf, pl* -siones : television, TV
televisivo, -va *adj* : television ⟨serie televisiva : television series⟩
televisor *nm* : television set
telón *nm, pl* telones 1 : curtain (in theater) 2 telón de fondo : backdrop, background

tema *nm* 1 ASUNTO : theme, topic, subject 2 MOTIVO : motif, central theme
temario *nm* 1 : set of topics (for study) 2 : agenda
temática *nf* : subject matter
temático, -ca *adj* : thematic
temblar {55} *vi* 1 : to tremble, to shake, to shiver ⟨le temblaban las rodillas : his knees were shaking⟩ 2 : to shudder, to be afraid ⟨tiemblo con sólo pensarlo : I shudder to think of it⟩
temblor *nm* 1 : shaking, trembling 2 : tremor, earthquake
tembloroso, -sa *adj* : tremulous, trembling, shaking ⟨con la voz temblorosa : with a shaky voice⟩
temer *vt* : to fear, to dread — *vi* : to be afraid
temerario, -ria *adj* : reckless, rash — temerariamente *adv*
temeridad *nf* 1 : temerity, recklessness, rashness 2 : rash act
temeroso, -sa *adj* MIEDOSO : fearful, frightened
temible *adj* : fearsome, dreadful
temor *nm* MIEDO : fear, dread
témpano *nm* : ice floe
temperamento *nm* : temperament — temperamental *adj*
temperancia *nf* : temperance
temperar *vt* MODERAR : to temper, to moderate — *vi* : to have a change of air
temperatura *nf* : temperature
tempestad *nf* 1 : storm, tempest 2 tempestad de arena : sandstorm
tempestuoso, -sa *adj* : tempestuous, stormy
templado, -da *adj* 1 : temperate, mild 2 : moderate, restrained 3 : warm, lukewarm 4 VALIENTE : courageous, bold
templanza *nf* 1 : temperance, moderation 2 : mildness (of weather)
templar *vt* 1 : to temper (steel) 2 : to restrain, to moderate 3 : to tune (a musical instrument) 4 : to warm up, to cool down — templarse *vr* 1 : to be moderate 2 : to warm up, to cool down
temple *nm* 1 : temper (of steel, etc.) 2 HUMOR : mood ⟨de buen temple : in a good mood⟩ 3 : tuning 4 VALOR : courage
templo *nm* 1 : temple 2 : church, chapel
tempo *nm* : tempo (in music)
temporada *nf* 1 : season, time ⟨temporada de béisbol : baseball season⟩ 2 : period, spell ⟨por temporadas : on and off⟩
temporal[1] *adj* 1 : temporal 2 : temporary
temporal[2] *nm* 1 : storm 2 capear el temporal : to weather the storm
temporalmente *adv* : temporarily
temporario, -ria *adj* : temporary — temporariamente *adv*
temporero[1], -ra *adj* : temporary, seasonal

temporero², -ra *n* : temporary or seasonal worker
temporizador *nm* : timer
tempranero, -ra *adj* **1** : early **2** : early-rising
temprano¹ *adv* : early ⟨lo más temprano posible : as soon as possible⟩
temprano², -na *adj* : early ⟨la parte temprana del siglo : the early part of the century⟩
ten → **tener**
tenacidad *nf* : tenacity, perseverance
tenaz *adj, pl* **tenaces 1** : tenacious, persistent **2** : strong, tough
tenaza *nf, or* **tenazas** *nfpl* **1** : pliers, pincers **2** : tongs **3** : claw (of a crustacean)
tenazmente *adv* : tenaciously
tendedero *nm* : clothesline
tendencia *nf* **1** PROPENSIÓN : tendency, inclination **2** : trend
tendencioso, -sa *adj* : tendentious, biased
tendente → **tendiente**
tender {56} *vt* **1** EXTENDER : to spread out, to lay out **2** : to hang out (clothes) **3** : to lay (cables, etc.) **4** : to set (a trap) — *vi* ~ **a** : to tend to, to have a tendency towards — **tenderse** *vr* : to stretch out, to lie down
tendero, -ra *n* : shopkeeper, storekeeper
tendido *nm* **1** : laying (of cables, etc.) **2** : seats *pl*, section (at a bullfight)
tendiente *adj* ~ **a** : aimed at, designed to
tendón *nm, pl* **tendones** : tendon
tenebrosidad *nf* : darkness, gloom
tendrá, etc. → **tener**
tenebroso, -sa *adj* **1** OSCURO : gloomy, dark **2** SINIESTRO : sinister
tenedor¹, -dora *n* **1** : holder **2 tenedor de libros, tenedora de libros** : bookkeeper
tenedor² *nm* : table fork
tenencia *nf* **1** : possession, holding **2** : tenancy **3** : tenure
tener {80} *vt* **1** : to have ⟨tiene ojos verdes : she has green eyes⟩ ⟨tengo mucho que hacer : I have a lot to do⟩ ⟨tiene veinte años : he's twenty years old⟩ ⟨tiene un metro de largo : it's one meter long⟩ **2** : to hold ⟨ten esto un momento : hold this for a moment⟩ **3** : to feel, to make ⟨tengo frío : I'm cold⟩ ⟨eso nos tiene contentos : that makes us happy⟩ **4** ~ **por** : to think, to consider ⟨me tienes por loco : you think I'm crazy⟩ — *v aux* **1 tener que** : to have to ⟨tengo que salir : I have to leave⟩ ⟨tiene que estar aquí : it has to be here, it must be here⟩ **2** (*with past participle*) ⟨tenía pensado escribirte : I've been thinking of writing to you⟩ — **tenerse** *vr* **1** : to stand up **2** ~ **por** : to consider oneself ⟨me tengo por afortunado : I consider myself lucky⟩
tenería *nf* CURTIDURÍA : tannery
tenga, etc. → **tener**
tenia *nf* SOLITARIA : tapeworm

teniente *nmf* **1** : lieutenant **2 teniente coronel** : lieutenant colonel
tenis *nms & pl* **1** : tennis **2 tenis** *nmpl* : sneakers *pl*
tenista *nmf* : tennis player
tenor *nm* **1** : tenor **2** : tone, sense
tensar *vt* **1** : to tense, to make taut **2** : to draw (a bow) — **tensarse** *vr* : to become tense
tensión *nf, pl* **tensiones 1** : tension, tautness **2** : stress, strain **3 tensión arterial** : blood pressure
tenso, -sa *adj* : tense
tentación *nf, pl* **-ciones** : temptation
tentáculo *nm* : tentacle, feeler
tentador¹, -dora *adj* : tempting
tentador², -dora *n* : tempter, temptress *f*
tentar {55} *vt* **1** TOCAR : to feel, to touch **2** PROBAR : to test, to try **3** ATRAER : to tempt, to entice
tentativa *nf* : attempt, try
tentempié *nm fam* : snack, bite
tenue *adj* **1** : tenuous **2** : faint, weak, dim **3** : light, fine **4** : thin, slender
teñir {67} *vt* **1** : to dye **2** : to stain
teodolito *nm* : theodolite, transit (for surveying)
teología *nf* : theology
teológico, -ca *adj* : theological
teólogo, -ga *n* : theologian
teorema *nm* : theorem
teoría *nf* : theory
teórico¹, -ca *adj* : theoretical — **teóricamente** *adv*
teórico², -ca *n* : theorist
teorizar {21} *vi* : to theorize
tepe *nm* : sod, turf
teponaztle *nm Mex* : traditional drum
tequila *nm* : tequila
terapeuta *nmf* : therapist
terapéutica *nf* : therapeutics
terapéutico, -ca *adj* : therapeutic
terapia *nf* **1** : therapy **2 terapia intensiva** : intensive care
tercer → **tercero**
tercermundista *adj* : third-world
tercero¹, -ra *adj* (**tercer** *before masculine singular nouns*) **1** : third **2 el Tercer Mundo** : the Third World
tercero², -ra *n* : third (in a series)
terceto *nm* **1** : tercet, triplet (in literature) **2** : trio (in music)
terciar *vt* **1** : to place diagonally **2** : to divide into three parts — *vi* **1** : to mediate **2** ~ **en** : to take part in
terciario, -ria *adj* : tertiary
tercio¹, -cia → **tercero**
tercio² *nm* : third ⟨dos tercios : two thirds⟩
terciopelo *nm* : velvet
terco, -ca *adj* OBSTINADO : obstinate, stubborn
tergiversación *nf, pl* **-ciones** : distortion
tergiversar *vt* : to distort, to twist
termal *adj* : thermal, hot
termas *nfpl* : hot springs
térmico, -ca *adj* : thermal, heat ⟨energía térmica : thermal energy⟩

terminación *nf, pl* **-ciones** : termination, conclusion
terminal[1] *adj* : terminal — **terminalmente** *adv*
terminal[2] *nm* (*in some regions f*) : (electric or electronic) terminal
terminal[3] *nf* (*in some regions m*) : terminal, station
terminante *adj* : final, definitive, categorical — **terminantemente** *adv*
terminar *vt* **1** CONCLUIR : to end, to conclude **2** ACABAR : to complete, to finish off — *vi* **1** : to finish **2** : to stop, to end — **terminarse** *vr* **1** : to run out **2** : to come to an end
término *nm* **1** CONCLUSIÓN : end, conclusion **2** : term, expression **3** : period, term of office **4 término medio** : happy medium **5 términos** *nmpl* : terms, specifications ⟨los términos del acuerdo : the terms of the agreement⟩
terminología *nf* : terminology
termita *nf* : termite
termo *nm* : thermos
termodinámica *nf* : thermodynamics
termómetro *nm* : thermometer
termostato *nm* : thermostat
ternera *nf* : veal
ternero, -ra *n* : calf
terno *nm* **1** : set of three **2** : three-piece suit
ternura *nf* : tenderness
terquedad *nf* OBSTINACIÓN : obstinacy, stubbornness
terracota *nf* : terra-cotta
terraplén *nm, pl* **-plenes** : terrace, embankment
terráqueo, -quea *adj* **1** : earth **2 globo terráqueo** : the earth, globe (of the earth)
terrateniente *nmf* : landowner
terraza *nf* **1** : terrace, veranda **2** : balcony (in a theater) **3** : terrace (in agriculture)
terremoto *nm* : earthquake
terrenal *adj* : worldly, earthly
terreno *nm* **1** : terrain **2** SUELO : earth, ground **3** : plot, tract of land **4 perder terreno** : to lose ground **5 preparar el terreno** : to pave the way
terrestre *adj* : terrestrial
terrible *adj* : terrible, horrible — **terriblemente** *adv*
terrier *nmf* : terrier
territorial *adj* : territorial
territorio *nm* : territory
terrón *nm, pl* **terrones 1** : clod (of earth) **2 terrón de azúcar** : lump of sugar
terror *nm* : terror
terrorífico, -ca *adj* : horrific, terrifying
terrorismo *nm* : terrorism
terrorista *adj & nmf* : terrorist
terroso, -sa *adj* : earthy ⟨colores terrosos : earthy colors⟩
terruño *nm* : native land, homeland
terso, -sa *adj* **1** : smooth **2** : glossy, shiny **3** : polished, flowing (of a style)
tersura *nf* **1** : smoothness **2** : shine

tertulia *nf* : gathering, group ⟨tertulia literaria : literary circle⟩
tesauro *nm* : thesaurus
tesis *nfs & pl* : thesis
tesón *nm* : persistence, tenacity
tesonero, -ra *adj* : persistent, tenacious
tesorería *nf* : treasurer's office
tesorero, -ra *n* : treasurer
tesoro *nm* **1** : treasure **2** : thesaurus
test *nm* : test
testaferro *nm* : figurehead
testamentario[1], **-ria** *adj* : testamentary
testamentario[2], **-ria** *n* ALBACEA : executor, executrix *f*
testamento *nm* : testament, will
testar *vi* : to draw up a will
testarudo, -da *adj* : stubborn, pigheaded
testículo *nm* : testicle
testificar {72} *v* : to testify
testigo *nmf* : witness
testimonial *adj* **1** : testimonial **2** : token
testimoniar *vi* : to testify
testimonio *nm* : testimony, statement
teta *nf* : teat
tétano *or* **tétanos** *nm* : tetanus, lockjaw
tetera *nf* **1** : teapot **2** : teakettle
tetilla *nf* **1** : teat **2** : nipple
tetina *nf* : nipple (on a bottle)
tétrico, -ca *adj* : somber, gloomy
textil *adj & nm* : textile
texto *nm* : text
textual *adj* : literal, exact — **textualmente** *adv*
textura *nf* : texture
tez *nf, pl* **teces** : complexion, coloring
ti *pron* **1** : you ⟨es para ti : it's for you⟩ **2 ti mismo, ti misma** : yourself **3** : thee
tía → **tío**
tiamina *nf* : thiamine
tianguis *nm Mex* : open-air market
tibetano[1], **-na** *adj & n* : Tibetan
tibetano[2] *nm* : Tibetan (language)
tibia *nf* : tibia
tibieza *nf* **1** : tepidness **2** : halfheartedness
tibio, -bia *adj* **1** : lukewarm, tepid **2** : cool, unenthusiastic
tiburón *nm, pl* **-rones 1** : shark **2** : raider (in finance)
tic *nm* **1** : click, tick **2 tic nervioso** : tic
tico, -ca *adj & n fam* : Costa Rican
tictac *nm* **1** : ticking, tick-tock **2 hacer tictac** : to tick
tiembla, etc. → **temblar**
tiempo *nm* **1** : time ⟨justo a tiempo : just in time⟩ ⟨perder tiempo : to waste time⟩ ⟨tiempo libre : spare time⟩ **2** : period, age ⟨en los tiempos que corren : nowadays⟩ **3** : season, moment ⟨antes de tiempo : prematurely⟩ **4** : weather ⟨hace buen tiempo : the weather is fine, it's nice outside⟩ **5** : tempo (in music) **6** : half (in sports) **7** : tense (in grammar)
tienda *nf* **1** : store, shop **2 or tienda de campaña** : tent
tiende, etc. → **tender**

tiene, etc. → **tener**
tienta¹, etc. → **tentar**
tienta² *nf* **andar a tientas** : to feel one's way, to grope around
tiernamente *adv* : tenderly
tierno, -na *adj* **1** : affectionate, tender **2** : tender, young
tierra *nf* **1** : land **2** SUELO : ground, earth **3** : country, homeland, soil **4 tierra natal** : native land **5 tierras altas** : highlands **6 la Tierra** : the Earth
tieso, -sa *adj* **1** : stiff, rigid **2** : upright, erect
tiesto *nm* **1** : potsherd **2** MACETA : flowerpot
tiesura *nf* : stiffness, rigidity
tifoidea *nf* : typhoid
tifoideo, -dea *adj* : typhoid ⟨**fiebre tifoidea** : typhoid fever⟩
tifón *nm, pl* **tifones** : typhoon
tifus *nm* : typhus
tigre, -gresa *n* **1** : tiger, tigress *f* **2** : jaguar
tijera *nf* **1** *or* **tijeras** *nfpl* : scissors **2 de ～** : folding ⟨**escalera de tijera** : stepladder⟩
tijereta *nf* : earwig
tijeretada *nf or* **tijeretazo** *nm* : cut, snip
tildar *vt* **～ de** : to brand as, to call ⟨**lo tildaron de traidor** : they branded him as a traitor⟩
tilde *nf* **1** : accent mark **2** : tilde (accent over ñ)
tilo *nm* : linden (tree)
timador, -dora *n* : swindler
timar *vt* : to swindle, to cheat
timbal *nm* **1** : kettledrum **2 timbales** *nmpl* : timpani
timbre *nm* **1** : bell ⟨**tocar el timbre** : to ring the doorbell⟩ **2** : tone, timbre **3** SELLO : seal, stamp **4** *CA, Mex* : postage stamp
timidez *nf* : timidity, shyness
tímido, -da *adj* : timid, shy — **tímidamente** *adv*
timo *nm fam* : swindle, trick, hoax
timón *nm, pl* **timones** : rudder ⟨**estar al timón** : to beat the helm⟩
timonel *nm* : helmsman, coxswain
timorato, -ta *adj* **1** : timorous **2** : sanctimonious
tímpano *nm* **1** : eardrum **2 tímpanos** *nmpl* : timpani, kettledrums
tina *nf* **1** BAÑERA : tub, bathtub **2** : vat
tinaco *nm Mex* : water tank
tinieblas *nfpl* **1** OSCURIDAD : darkness **2** : ignorance
tino *nm* **1** : good judgment, sense **2** : tact, sensitivity, insight
tinta *nf* : ink
tinte *nm* **1** : dye, coloring **2** : overtone ⟨**tintes raciales** : racial overtones⟩
tintero *nm* **1** : inkwell **2 quedarse en el tintero** : to remain unsaid
tintinear *vt* : to jingle, to clink, to tinkle
tintineo *nm* : clink, jingle, tinkle
tinto, -ta *adj* **1** : dyed, stained ⟨**tinto en sangre** : bloodstained⟩ **2** : red (of wine)

tintorería *nf* : dry cleaner (service)
tintura *nf* **1** : dye, tint **2** : tincture ⟨**tintura de yodo** : tincture of iodine⟩
tiña *nf* : ringworm
tiñe, etc. → **teñir**
tío, tía *n* : uncle *m*, aunt *f*
tiovivo *nm* : merry-go-round
tipi *nm* : tepee
típico, -ca *adj* : typical — **típicamente** *adv*
tipificar {72} *vt* **1** : to classify, to categorize **2** : to typify
tiple *nm* : soprano
tipo¹ *nm* **1** CLASE : type, kind, sort **2** : figure, build, appearance **3** : rate ⟨**tipo de interés** : interest rate⟩ **4** : (printing) type, typeface **5** : style, model ⟨**un vestido tipo 60's** : a 60's-style dress⟩
tipo², -pa *n fam* : guy *m*, gal *f*, character
tipografía *nf* : typography, printing
tipográfico, -ca *adj* : typographic, typographical
tipógrafo, -fa *n* : printer, typographer
tique *or* **tiquet** *nm* **1** : ticket **2** : receipt
tira *nf* **1** : strip, strap **2 tira cómica** : comic, comic strip
tirabuzón *nf, pl* **-zones** : corkscrew
tirada *nf* **1** : throw **2** : distance, stretch **3** IMPRESIÓN : printing, issue
tiradero *nm Mex* **1** : dump **2** : mess, clutter
tirador¹ *nm* : handle, knob
tirador², -dora *n* : marksman *m*, markswoman *f*
tiragomas *nms & pl* : slingshot
tiranía *nf* : tyranny
tiránico, -ca *adj* : tyrannical
tiranizar {21} *vt* : to tyrannize
tirano¹, -na *adj* : tyrannical, despotic
tirano², -na *n* : tyrant
tirante¹ *adj* **1** : tense, strained **2** : taut
tirante² *nm* **1** : shoulder strap **2 tirantes** *nmpl* : suspenders
tirantez *nf* **1** : tautness **2** : tension, friction, strain
tirar *vt* **1** : to throw, to hurl, to toss **2** BOTAR : to throw away, to throw out, to waste **3** DERRIBAR : to knock down **4** : to shoot, to fire, to launch **5** : to take (a photo) **6** : to print, to run off — *vi* **1** : to pull, to draw **2** : to shoot **3** : to attract **4** : to get by, to manage ⟨**va tirando** : he's getting along, he's managing⟩ **5 ～ a** : to tend towards, to be rather ⟨**tira a picante** : it's a bit spicy⟩ — **tirarse** *vr* **1** : to throw oneself **2** *fam* : to spend (time)
tiritar *vi* : to shiver, to tremble
tiro *nm* **1** BALAZO, DISPARO : shot, gunshot **2** : shot, kick (in sports) **3** : flue **4** : team (of horses, etc.) **5 a ～** : within range **6 al tiro** : right away **7 tiro de gracia** : coup de grace, death blow
tiroideo, -dea *adj* : thyroid
tiroides *nmf* : thyroid, thyroid gland — **tiroides** *adj*

tirolés, -lesa *adj* : Tyrolean
tirón *nm, pl* **tirones** 1 : pull, tug, yank 2 **de un tirón** : all at once, in one go
tiroteo *nm* 1 : shooting 2 : gunfight, shoot-out
tirria *nf* **tener tirria a** *fam* : to have a grudge against
titánico, -ca *adj* : titanic, huge
titanio *nm* : titanium
títere *nm* : puppet
tití *nm* : marmoset
titilar *vi* : to twinkle, to flicker
titileo *nm* : twinkle, flickering
titiritero, -ra *n* 1 : puppeteer 2 : acrobat
titubear *vi* 1 : to hesitate 2 : to stutter, to stammer — **titubeante** *adj*
titubeo *nm* 1 : hesitation 2 : stammering
titulado, -da *adj* 1 : titled, entitled 2 : qualified
titular[1] *vt* : to title, to entitle — **titularse** *vr* 1 : to be called, to be entitled 2 : to receive a degree
titular[2] *adj* : titular, official
titular[3] *nm* : headline
titular[4] *nmf* 1 : owner, holder 2 : officeholder, incumbent
titularidad *nf* 1 : ownership, title 2 : position, office (with a title) 3 : starting position (in sports)
título *nm* 1 : title 2 : degree, qualification 3 : security, bond 4 **a título de** : by way of, in the capacity of
tiza *nf* : chalk
tiznar *vt* : to blacken (with soot, etc.)
tizne *nm* HOLLÍN : soot
tiznón *nm, pl* **tiznones** : stain, smudge
tlapalería *nf Mex* : hardware store
TNT *nm* (*trinitrotolueno*) : TNT
toalla *nf* : towel
toallita *nf* : washcloth
tobillo *nm* : ankle
tobogán *nm, pl* **-ganes** 1 : toboggan, sled 2 : slide, chute
tocadiscos *nms & pl* : record player, phonograph
tocado[1]**, -da** *adj* 1 : bad, bruised (of fruit) 2 *fam* : touched, not all there
tocado[2] *nm* : headdress
tocador[1] *nm* 1 : dressing table, vanity table 2 **artículos de tocador** : toiletries
tocador[2]**, -dora** *n* : player (of music)
tocante *adj* ∼ **a** : with regard to, regarding
tocar {72} *vt* 1 : to touch, to feel, to handle 2 : to touch on, to refer to 3 : to concern, to affect 4 : to play (a musical instrument) — *vi* 1 : to knock, to ring ⟨tocar a la puerta : to rap on the door⟩ 2 ∼ **en** : to touch on, to border on ⟨eso toca en lo ridículo : that's almost ludicrous⟩ 3 **tocarle a** : to fall to, to be up to, to be one's turn ⟨¿a quién le toca manejar? : whose turn is it to drive?⟩
tocayo, -ya *n* : namesake
tocineta *nf Col, Ven* : bacon
tocino *nm* 1 : bacon 2 : salt pork

tocología *nf* OBSTETRICIA : obstetrics
tocólogo, -ga *n* OBSTETRA : obstetrician
tocón *nm, pl* **tocones** CEPA : stump (of a tree)
todavía *adv* 1 AÚN : still, yet ⟨todavía puedes verlo : you can still see it⟩ 2 : even ⟨todavía más rápido : even faster⟩ 3 **todavía no** : not yet
todo[1]**, -da** *adj* 1 : all, whole, entire ⟨con toda sinceridad : with all sincerity⟩ ⟨toda la comunidad : the whole community⟩ 2 : every, each ⟨a todo nivel : at every level⟩ 3 : maximum ⟨a toda velocidad : at top speed⟩ 4 **todo el mundo** : everyone, everybody
todo[2] *nm* : whole
todo[3]**, -da** *pron* 1 : everything, all, every bit ⟨lo sabe todo : he knows it all⟩ ⟨es todo un soldado : he's every inch a soldier⟩ 2 **todos, -das** *pl* : everybody, everyone, all
todopoderoso, -sa *adj* OMNIPOTENTE : almighty, all-powerful
toga *nf* 1 : toga 2 : gown, robe (for magistrates, etc.)
toldo *nm* : awning, canopy
tolerable *adj* : tolerable — **tolerablemente** *adv*
tolerancia *nf* : tolerance, toleration
tolerante *adj* : tolerant — **tolerantemente** *adv*
tolerar *vt* : to tolerate
tolete *nm* : oarlock
tolva *nf* : hopper (container)
toma *nf* 1 : taking, seizure, capture 2 DOSIS : dose 3 : take, shot 4 **toma de corriente** : wall socket, outlet 5 **toma y daca** : give-and-take
tomar *vt* 1 : to take ⟨tomé el libro : I took the book⟩ ⟨tomar un taxi : to take a taxi⟩ ⟨tomar una foto : to take a photo⟩ ⟨toma dos años : it takes two years⟩ ⟨tomaron medidas drásticas : they took drastic measures⟩ 2 BEBER : to drink 3 CAPTURAR : to capture, to seize 4 **tomar el sol** : to sunbathe 5 **tomar tierra** : to land — *vi* : to drink (alcohol) — **tomarse** *vr* 1 : to take ⟨tomarse la molestia de : to take the trouble to⟩ 2 : to drink, to eat, to have
tomate *nm* : tomato
tomillo *nm* : thyme
tomo *nm* : volume, tome
ton *nm* **sin ton ni son** : without rhyme or reason
tonada *nf* 1 : tune, song 2 : accent
tonalidad *nf* : tonality
tonel *nm* BARRICA : barrel, cask
tonelada *nf* : ton
tonelaje *nm* : tonnage
tónica *nf* 1 : tonic (water) 2 : tonic (in music) 3 : trend, tone ⟨dar la tónica : to set the tone⟩
tónico[1]**, -ca** *adj* : tonic
tónico[2] *nm* : tonic ⟨tónico capilar : hair tonic⟩
tono *nm* 1 : tone ⟨tono muscular : muscle tone⟩ 2 : shade (of colors) 3 : key (in music)

tontamente *adv* : foolishly, stupidly
tontear *vi* **1** : to fool around, to play the fool **2** : to flirt
tontería *nf* **1** : foolishness **2** : stupid remark or action **3 decir tonterías** : to talk nonsense
tonto¹, -ta *adj* **1** : dumb, stupid **2** : silly **3 a tontas y a locas** : without thinking, haphazardly
tonto², -ta *n* : fool, idiot
topacio *nm* : topaz
toparse *vr* ~ **con** : to bump into, to run into, to come across ⟨me topé con algunas dificultades : I ran into some problems⟩
tope *nm* **1** : limit, end ⟨hasta el tope : to the limit, to the brim⟩ **2** : stop, check, buffer ⟨tope de puerta : doorstop⟩ **3** : bump, collision **4** *Mex* : speed bump
tópico¹, -ca *adj* **1** : topical, external **2** : trite, commonplace
tópico² *nm* **1** : topic, subject **2** : cliché, trite expression
topo *nm* **1** : mole (animal) **2** *fam* : clumsy person, blunderer
topografía *nf* : topography
topográfico, -ca *adj* : topographic, topographical
topógrafo, -fa *n* : topographer
toque¹, etc. → **tocar**
toque² *nm* **1** : touch ⟨el último toque : the finishing touch⟩ ⟨un toque de color : a touch of color⟩ **2** : ringing, peal, chime **3** *Mex* : shock, jolt **4 toque de queda** : curfew **5 toque de diana** : reveille
toquetear *vt* : to touch, to handle, to finger
tórax *nm* : thorax
torbellino *nm* : whirlwind
torcedura *nf* **1** : twisting, buckling **2** : sprain
torcer {14} *vt* **1** : to bend, to twist **2** : to sprain **3** : to turn (a corner) **4** : to wring, to wring out **5** : to distort — *vi* : to turn — **torcerse** *vr*
torcido, -da *adj* **1** : twisted, crooked **2** : devious
tordo *nm* ZORZAL : thrush
torear *vt* **1** : to fight (bulls) **2** : to dodge, to sidestep
toreo *nm* : bullfighting
torero, -ra *n* MATADOR : bullfighter, matador
tormenta *nf* **1** : storm ⟨tormenta de nieve : snowstorm⟩ **2** : turmoil, frenzy
tormento *nm* **1** : torment, anguish **2** : torture
tormentoso, -sa *adj* : stormy, turbulent
tornado *nm* : tornado
tornamesa *nmf* : turntable
tornar *vt* **1** : to return, to give back **2** : to make, to render — *vi* : to go back — **tornarse** *vr* : to become, to turn into
tornasol *nm* **1** : reflected light **2** : sunflower **3** : litmus
tornear *vt* : to turn (in carpentry)
torneo *nm* : tournament

tornillo *nm* **1** : screw **2 tornillo de banco** : vise
torniquete *nm* **1** : tourniquet **2** : turnstile
torno *nm* **1** : lathe **2** : winch **3 torno de banco** : vise **4 en torno a** : around, about ⟨en torno a este asunto : about this issue⟩ ⟨en torno suyo : around him⟩
toro *nm* : bull
toronja *nf* : grapefruit
toronjil *nm* : balm, lemon balm
torpe *adj* **1** DESMAÑADO : clumsy, awkward **2** : stupid, dull — **torpemente** *adv*
torpedear *vt* : to torpedo
torpedo *nm* : torpedo
torpeza *nf* **1** : clumsiness, awkwardness **2** : stupidity **3** : blunder
torre *nf* **1** : tower ⟨torre de perforación : oil rig⟩ **2** : turret **3** : rook, castle (in chess)
torrencial *adj* : torrential — **torrencialmente** *adv*
torrente *nm* **1** : torrent **2 torrente sanguíneo** : bloodstream
torreón *nm, pl* **-rreones** : tower (of a castle)
torreta *nf* : turret (of a tank, ship, etc.)
tórrido, -da *adj* : torrid
torsión *nf, pl* **torsiones** : torsion — **torsional** *adj*
torso *nm* : torso, trunk
torta *nf* **1** : torte, cake **2** *Mex* : sandwich
tortazo *nm fam* : blow, wallop
tortilla *nf* **1** : tortilla **2** *or* **tortilla de huevo** : omelet
tórtola *nf* : turtledove
tortuga *nf* **1** : turtle, tortoise **2 tortuga de agua dulce** : terrapin **3 tortuga boba** : loggerhead
tortuoso, -sa *adj* : tortuous, winding
tortura *nf* : torture
torturador, -dora *n* : torturer
torturar *vt* : to torture, to torment
torvo, -va *adj* : grim, stern, baleful
torzamos, etc. → **torcer**
tos *nf* **1** : cough **2 tos ferina** : whooping cough
tosco, -ca *adj* : rough, coarse
toser *vi* : to cough
tosquedad *nf* : crudeness, coarseness, roughness
tostada *nf* **1** : piece of toast **2** : tostada
tostador *nm* **1** : toaster **2** : roaster (for coffee)
tostar {19} *vt* **1** : to toast **2** : to roast (coffee) **3** : to tan — **tostarse** *vr* : to get a tan
tostón *nm, pl* **tostones** *Car* : fried plantain chip
total¹ *adv* : in the end, so ⟨total, que no fui : in short, I didn't go⟩
total² *adj & nm* : total — **totalmente** *adv*
totalidad *nf* : totality, whole
totalitario, -ria *adj & n* : totalitarian
totalitarismo *nm* : totalitarianism

totalizar {21} vt : total, to add up to
tótem nm, pl **tótems** : totem
totopo nm CA, Mex : tortilla chip
totuma nf : calabash
tour ['tur] nm, pl **tours** : tour, excursion
toxicidad nf : toxicity
tóxico[1], **-ca** adj : toxic, poisonous
tóxico[2] nm : poison
toxicomanía nf : drug addiction
toxicómano, -na n : drug addict
toxina nf : toxin
tozudez nf : stubbornness, obstinacy
tozudo, -da adj : stubborn, obstinate —
  tozudamente adv
traba nf **1** : tie, bond **2** : obstacle, hindrance
trabajador[1], **-dora** adj : hardworking
trabajador[2], **-dora** n : worker
trabajar vi **1** : to work ⟨trabaja mucho
  : he works hard⟩ ⟨trabajo de secretaria
  : I work as a secretary⟩ **2** : to strive
  ⟨trabajan por mejores oportunidades
  : they're striving for better opportuni-
  ties⟩ **3** : to act, to perform ⟨trabajar
  en una película : to be in a movie⟩ —
  vt **1** : to work (metal) **2** : to knead **3**
  : to till **4** : to work on ⟨tienes que trabajar el español : you need to work on
  your Spanish⟩
trabajo nm **1** : work, job **2** LABOR
  : labor, work ⟨tengo mucho trabajo : I
  have a lot of work to do⟩ **3** TAREA : task
  4 ESFUERZA : effort **5 costar trabajo**
  : to be difficult **6 tomarse el trabajo**
  : to take the trouble **7 trabajo en
  equipo** : teamwork **8 trabajos** nmpl
  : hardships, difficulties
trabajoso, -sa adj LABORIOSO : laborious — **trabajosamente** adv
trabalenguas nms & pl : tongue twister
trabar vt **1** : to join, to connect **2** : to
  impede, to hold back **3** : to strike up
  (a conversation), to form (a friendship)
  4 : to thicken (sauces) — **trabarse** vr
  1 : to jam **2** : to become entangled **3**
  : to be tongue-tied, to stammer
trabucar {72} vt : to confuse, to mix up
trabuco nm : blunderbuss
tracalero, -ra adj Mex : dishonest, tricky
tracción nf : traction
trace, etc. → **trazar**
tracto nm : tract
tractor nm : tractor
tradición nf, pl **-ciones** : tradition
tradicional adj : traditional — **tradi-
  cionalmente** adv
traducción nf, pl **-ciones** : translation
traducible adj : translatable
traducir {61} vt **1** : to translate **2** : to
  convey, to express — **traducirse** vr ~
  en : to result in
traductor, -tora n : translator
traer {81} vt **1** : to bring ⟨trae una ensalada : bring a salad⟩ **2** CAUSAR : to
  cause, to bring about ⟨el problema
  puede traer graves consecuencias : the
  problem could have serious conse-
  quences⟩ **3** : to carry, to have ⟨todos
  los periódicos traían las mismas noti-

cias : all of the newspapers carried the
  same news⟩ **4** LLEVAR : to wear —
traerse vr **1** : to bring along **2 traérse-
  las** : to be difficult
traficante nmf : dealer, trafficker
traficar {72} vi **1** : to trade, to deal **2** ~
  con : to traffic in
tráfico nm **1** : trade **2** : traffic
tragaluz nf, pl **-luces** : skylight, fanlight
tragar {52} v : to swallow — **tragarse** vr
tragedia nf : tragedy
trágico, -ca adj : tragic — **trágicamente**
  adv
trago nm **1** : swallow, swig **2** : drink,
  liquor **3 trago amargo** : hard time
trague, etc. → **tragar**
traición nf, pl **traiciones 1** : treason **2**
  : betrayal, treachery
traicionar vt : to betray
traicionero, -ra → **traidor**
traidor[1], **-dora** adj : traitorous, treason-
  ous
traidor[2], **-dora** n : traitor
traiga, etc. → **traer**
tráiler or **trailer** nm : trailer
traílla nf **1** : leash **2** : harrow
traje nm **1** : suit **2** : dress **3** : costume
  4 traje de baño : bathing suit
trajín nm, pl **trajines 1** : transport **2** fam
  : hustle and bustle
trajinar vt : to transport, to carry — vi
  : to rush around
trajo, etc. → **traer**
trama nf **1** : plot **2** : weave, weft (fabric)
tramar vt **1** : to plot, to plan **2** : to weave
tramitar vt : to transact, to negotiate, to
  handle
trámite nm : procedure, step
tramo nm **1** : stretch, section **2** : flight
  (of stairs)
trampa nf **1** : trap **2 hacer trampas** : to
  cheat
trampear vt : to cheat
trampero, -ra n : trapper
trampilla nf : trapdoor
trampolín nm, pl **-lines 1** : diving board
  2 : trampoline **3** : springboard ⟨un
  trampolín al éxito : a springboard to
  success⟩
tramposo[1], **-sa** adj : crooked, cheating
tramposo[2], **-sa** n : cheat, swindler
tranca nf **1** : stick, club **2** : bar, crossbar
trancar {72} vt : to bar (a door or window)
trancazo nm GOLPE : blow, hit
trance nm **1** : critical juncture, tough
  time **2** : trance **3 en trance de** : in the
  process of ⟨en trance de extinción : on
  the verge of extinction⟩
tranco nm **1** : stride **2** UMBRAL : threshold
tranque, etc. → **trancar**
tranquilidad nf : tranquility, peace
tranquilizador, -dora adj **1** : soothing **2**
  : reassuring
tranquilizante[1] adj **1** : reassuring **2**
  : tranquilizing

tranquilizante[2] *nm* : tranquilizer
tranquilizar {21} *vt* CALMAR : to calm down, to soothe ⟨tranquilizar la conciencia : to ease the conscience⟩ —
tranquilizarse *vr*
tranquilo, -la *adj* CALMO : calm, tranquil ⟨una vida tranquila : a quiet life⟩ — **tranquilamente** *adv*
transacción *nf, pl* **-ciones** : transaction
transar *vi* TRANSIGIR : to give way, to compromise — *vt* : to buy and sell
transatlántico[1], **-ca** *adj* : transatlantic
transatlántico[2] *nm* : ocean liner
transbordador *nm* 1 : ferry 2 **transbordador espacial** : space shuttle
transbordar *v* : to transfer
transbordo *nm* : transfer
transcendencia → **trascendencia**
transcender → **trascender**
transcribir {33} *vt* : to transcribe
transcrito *pp* → **transcribir**
transcripción *nf, pl* **-ciones** : transcription
transcurrir *vi* : to elapse, to pass
transcurso *nm* : course, progression ⟨en el transcurso de cien años : over the course of a hundred years⟩
transeúnte *nmf* 1 : passerby 2 : transient
transferencia *nf* : transfer, transference
transferir {76} *vt* TRASLADAR : to transfer — **transferible** *adj*
transfigurar *vt* : to transfigure, to transform — **transfiguración** *nf*
transformación *nf, pl* **-ciones** : transformation, conversion
transformador *nm* : transformer
transformar *vt* 1 CONVERTIR : to convert 2 : to transform, to change, to alter — **transformarse** *vr*
transfusión *nf, pl* **-siones** : transfusion
transgredir {1} *vt* : to transgress — **transgresión** *nf*
transgresor, -sora *n* : transgressor
transición *nf, pl* **-ciones** : transition ⟨período de transición : transition period⟩
transido, -da *adj* : overcome, beset ⟨transido de dolor : racked with pain⟩
transigir {35} *vi* 1 : to give in, to compromise 2 ~ **con** : to tolerate, to put up with
transistor *nm* : transistor
transitable *adj* : passable
transitar *vi* : to go, to pass, to travel ⟨transitar por la ciudad : to travel through the city⟩
transitivo, -va *adj* : transitive
tránsito *nm* 1 TRÁFICO : traffic ⟨hora de máximo tránsito : rush hour⟩ 2 : transit, passage, movement 3 : death, passing
transitorio, -ria *adj* 1 : transitory 2 : provisional, temporary — **transitoriamente** *adv*
translúcido, -da *adj* : translucent
translucir → **traslucir**
transmisible *adj* : transmissible

transmisión *nf, pl* **-siones** 1 : transmission, broadcast 2 : transfer 3 : transmission (of an automobile)
transmisor *nm* : transmitter
transmitir *vt* 1 : to transmit, to broadcast 2 : to pass on, to transfer — *vi* : to transmit, to broadcast
transparencia *nf* : transparency
transparentar *vt* : to reveal, to betray — **transparentarse** *vr* 1 : to be transparent 2 : to show through
transparente[1] *adj* : transparent — **transparentemente** *adv*
transparente[2] *nm* : shade, blind
transpiración *nf, pl* **-ciones** SUDOR : perspiration, sweat
transpirado, -da *adj* : sweaty
transpirar *vi* 1 SUDOR : to perspire, to sweat 2 : to transpire
transplantar, transplante → **trasplantar, trasplante**
transponer {60} *vt* 1 : to transpose, to move about 2 TRASPLANTAR : to transplant — **transponerse** *vr* 1 OCULTARSE : to hide 2 PONERSE : to set, to go down (of the sun or moon) 3 DORMITAR : to doze off
transportación *nf, pl* **-ciones** : transportation
transportador *nm* 1 : protractor 2 : conveyor
transportar *vt* 1 : to transport, to carry 2 : to transmit 3 : to transpose (music) — **transportarse** *vr* : to get carried away
transporte *nm* : transport, transportation
transportista *nmf* : hauler, carrier, trucker
transpuso, etc. → **transponer**
transversal *adj* : transverse, cross ⟨corte transversal : cross section⟩
transversalmente *adv* : obliquely
transverso, -sa *adj* : transverse
tranvía *nm* : streetcar, trolley
trapeador *nm* : mop
trapear *vt* : to mop
trapecio *nm* 1 : trapezoid 2 : trapeze
trapezoide *nm* : trapezoid
trapo *nm* 1 : cloth, rag ⟨trapo de polvo : dust cloth⟩ 2 **soltar el trapo** : to burst into tears 3 **trapos** *nmpl fam* : clothes
tráquea *nf* : trachea, windpipe
traquetear *vi* : to clatter, to jolt
traqueteo *nm* 1 : jolting 2 : clattering, clatter
tras *prep* 1 : after ⟨día tras día : day after day⟩ ⟨uno tras otro : one after another⟩ 2 : behind ⟨tras la puerta : behind the door⟩
trasbordar, trasbordo → **transbordar, transbordo**
trascendencia *nf* 1 : importance, significance 2 : transcendence
trascendental *adj* 1 : transcendental 2 : important, momentous
trascendente *adj* 1 : important, significant 2 : transcendent

trascender {56} *vi* **1** : to leak out, to become known **2** : to spread, to have a wide effect **3** ~ **a** : to smell of ⟨la casa trascendía a flores : the house smelled of flowers⟩ **4** ~ **de** : to transcend, to go beyond — *vt* : to transcend

trasero¹, -ra *adj* POSTERIOR : rear, back

trasero² *nm* : buttocks

trasfondo *nm* **1** : background, backdrop **2** : undertone, undercurrent

trasformación → **transformación**

trasgo *nm* : goblin, imp

trasgredir → **transgredir**

trasladar *vt* **1** TRANSFERIR : to transfer, to move **2** POSPONER : to postpone **3** TRADUCIR : to translate **4** COPIAR : to copy, to transcribe — **trasladarse** *vr* MUDARSE : to move, to relocate

traslado *nm* **1** : transfer, move **2** : copy

traslapar *vt* : to overlap — **traslaparse** *vr*

traslapo *nm* : overlap

traslúcido, -da → **translúcido**

traslucir {45} *vi* : to reveal, to show — **traslucirse** *vr* : to show through

trasmano *nm* **a** ~ : out of the way, out of reach

trasmisión, trasmitir → **transmisión, transmitir**

trasnochar *vi* : to stay up all night

trasparencia *nf* **trasparente** → **transparencia, transparente**

traspasar *vt* **1** PERFORAR : to pierce, to go through **2** : to go beyond ⟨traspasar los límites : to overstep the limits⟩ **3** ATRAVESAR : to cross, to go across **4** : to sell, to transfer

traspaso *nm* : transfer, sale

traspié *nm* **1** : stumble **2** : blunder

traspiración → **transpiración**

trasplantar *vt* : to transplant

trasplante *nm* : transplant

trasponer → **transponer**

trasportar → **transportar**

trasquilar *vt* ESQUILAR : to shear

traste *nm* **1** : fret (on a guitar) **2** *CA, Mex, PRi* : kitchen utensil ⟨lavar los trastes : to do the dishes⟩ **3 dar al traste con** : to ruin, to destroy **4 irse al traste** : to fall through

trastornar *vt* : to disturb, to upset, to disrupt — **trastornarse** *vr*

trastorno *nm* **1** : disorder ⟨trastorno mental : mental disorder⟩ **2** : disturbance, upset

trastos *nmpl* **1** : implements, utensils **2** *fam* : pieces of junk, stuff

trasunto *nm* : image, likeness

tratable *adj* **1** : friendly, sociable **2** : treatable

tratado *nm* **1** : treatise **2** : treaty

tratamiento *nm* : treatment

tratante *nmf* : dealer, trader

tratar *vi* **1** ~ **con** : to deal with, to have contact with ⟨no trato mucho con los clientes : I don't have much contact with customers⟩ **2** ~ **de** : to try to ⟨estoy tratando de comer : I am trying to

eat⟩ **3** ~ **de** *or* ~ **sobre** : to be about, to concern ⟨el libro trata de las plantas : the book is about plants⟩ **4** ~ **en** : to deal in ⟨trata en herramientas : he deals in tools⟩ — *vt* **1** : to treat ⟨tratan bien a sus empleados : they treat their employees well⟩ **2** : to handle ⟨trató el tema con delicadeza : he handled the subject tactfully⟩ — **tratarse** *vr* ~ **de** : to be about, to concern

trato *nm* **1** : deal, agreement **2** : relationship, dealings *pl* **3** : treatment ⟨malos tratos : ill-treatment⟩

trauma *nm* : trauma

traumático, -ca *adj* : traumatic — **traumáticamente** *adv*

traumatismo *nm* : injury ⟨traumatismo cervical : whiplash⟩

través *nm* **1 a través de** : across, through **2 al través** : crosswise, across **3 de través** : sideways

travesaño *nm* **1** : crossbar **2** : crossbeam, crosspiece, transom (of a window)

travesía *nf* : voyage, crossing (of the sea)

travesura *nf* **1** : prank, mischievous act **2 travesuras** *nfpl* : mischief

travieso, -sa *adj* : mischievous, naughty — **traviesamente** *adv*

trayecto *nm* **1** : journey **2** : route **3** : trajectory, path

trayectoria *nf* : course, path, trajectory

trayendo → **traer**

traza *nf* **1** DISEÑO : design, plan **2** : appearance

trazado *nm* **1** BOSQUEJO : outline, sketch **2** PLAN : plan, layout

trazar {21} *vt* **1** : to trace **2** : to draw up, to devise **3** : to outline, to sketch

trazo *nm* **1** : stroke, line **2** : sketch, outline

trébol *nm* **1** : clover, shamrock **2** : club (playing card)

trece *adj & nm* : thirteen

treceavo¹, -va *adj* : thirteenth

treceavo² *nm* : thirteenth (fraction)

trecho *nm* **1** : stretch, period ⟨de trecho en trecho : at intervals⟩ **2** : distance, space

tregua *nf* **1** : truce **2** : lull, respite **3 sin** ~ : relentless, unrelenting

treinta *adj & nm* : thirty

treintavo¹, -va *adj* : thirtieth

treintavo² *nm* : thirtieth (fraction)

tremendo, -da *adj* **1** : tremendous, enormous **2** : terrible, dreadful **3** *fam* : great, super

trementina *nf* AGUARRÁS : turpentine

trémulo, -la *adj* **1** : trembling, shaky **2** : flickering

tren *nm* **1** : train **2** : set, assembly ⟨tren de aterrizaje : landing gear⟩ **3** : speed, pace ⟨a todo tren : at top speed⟩

trence, etc. → **trenzar**

trenza *nf* : braid, pigtail

trenzar {21} *vt* : to braid — **trenzarse** *vr* : to get involved

trepador, -dora *adj* : climbing ⟨rosal trepador : rambling rose⟩

trepadora *nf* **1** : climbing plant, climber **2** : nuthatch
trepar *vi* **1** : to climb ⟨trepar a un árbol : to climb up a tree⟩ **2** : to creep, to spread (of a plant)
trepidación *nf, pl* **-ciones** : vibration
trepidante *adj* **1** : vibrating **2** : fast, frantic
trepidar *vi* **1** : to shake, to vibrate **2** : to hesitate, to waver
tres *adj & nm* : three
trescientos[1], **-tas** *adj* : three hundred
trescientos[2] *nms & pl* : three hundred
treta *nf* : trick, ruse
tríada *nf* : triad
triángulo *nm* : triangle — **triangular** *adj*
tribal *adj* : tribal
tribu *nf* : tribe
tribulación *nf, pl* **-ciones** : tribulation
tribuna *nf* **1** : dais, platform **2** : stands *pl*, bleachers *pl*, grandstand
tribunal *nm* : court, tribunal
tributar *vt* : to pay, to render — *vi* : to pay taxes
tributario[1], **-ria** *adj* : tax ⟨evasión tributaria : tax evasion⟩
tributario[2] *nm* : tributary
tributo *nm* **1** : tax **2** : tribute
triciclo *nm* : tricycle
tricolor *adj* : tricolor, tricolored
tridente *nm* : trident
tridimensional *adj* : three-dimensional, 3-D
trienal *adj* : triennial
trifulca *nf fam* : row, ruckus
trigésimo[1], **-ma** *adj* : thirtieth, thirty-
trigésimo[2], **-ma** *n* : thirtieth, thirty- (in a series)
trigo *nm* **1** : wheat **2 trigo rubión** : buckwheat
trigonometría *nf* : trigonometry
trigueño, -ña *adj* **1** : light brown (of hair) **2** MORENO : dark, olive-skinned
trillado, -da *adj* : trite, hackneyed
trilladora *nf* : thresher, threshing machine
trillar *vt* : to thresh
trillizo, -za *n* : triplet
trilogía *nf* : trilogy
trimestral *adj* : quarterly — **trimestralmente** *adv*
trinar *vi* **1** : to thrill **2** : to warble
trinchar *vt* : to carve, to cut up
trinchera *nf* **1** : trench, ditch **2** : trench coat
trineo *nm* : sled, sleigh
trinidad *nf* **la Trinidad** : the Trinity
trino *nm* : trill, warble
trinquete *nm* : ratchet
trío *nm* : trio
tripa *nf* **1** INTESTINO : gut, intestine **2 tripas** *nfpl fam* : belly, tummy, insides *pl* ⟨dolerle a uno las tripas : to have a stomach ache⟩
tripartito, -ta *adj* : tripartite
triple *adj & nm* : triple
triplicado *nm* : triplicate
triplicar {72} *vt* : to triple, to treble

trípode *nm* : tripod
tripulación *nf, pl* **-ciones** : crew
tripulante *nmf* : crew member
tripular *vt* : to man
tris *nm* **estar en un tris de** : to be within an inch of, to be very close to
triste *adj* **1** : sad, gloomy ⟨ponerse triste : to become sad⟩ **2** : desolate, dismal ⟨una perspectiva triste : a dismal outlook⟩ **3** : sorry, sorry-looking ⟨la triste verdad : the sorry truth⟩
tristeza *nf* DOLOR : sadness, grief
tristón, -tona *adj, mpl* **-tones** : melancholy, downhearted
tritón *nm, pl* **tritones** : newt
triturar *vt* : to crush, to grind
triunfal *adj* : triumphal, triumphant — **triunfalmente** *adv*
triunfante *adj* : triumphant, victorious
triunfar *vi* : to triumph, to win
triunfo *nm* **1** : triumph, victory **2** ÉXITO : success **3** : trump (in card games)
triunvirato *nm* : triumvirate
trivial *adj* **1** : trivial **2** : trite, commonplace
trivialidad *nf* : triviality
triza *nf* **1** : shred, bit **2 hacer trizas** : to tear into shreds, to smash to pieces
trocar {82} *vt* **1** CAMBIAR : to exchange, to trade **2** CAMBIAR : to change, to alter, to transform **3** CONFUNDIR : to confuse, to mix up
trocha *nf* : path, trail
troce, etc. → **trozar**
trofeo *nm* : trophy
tromba *nf* **1** : whirlwind **2 tromba de agua** : downpour, cloudburst
trombón *nm, pl* **trombones** **1** : trombone **2** : trombonist — **trombonista** *nmf*
trombosis *nf* : thrombosis
trompa *nf* **1** : trunk (of an elephant), proboscis (of an insect) **2** : horn ⟨trompa de caza : hunting horn⟩ **3** : tube, duct (in the body)
trompada *nf fam* **1** : punch, blow **2** : bump, collision (of persons)
trompeta *nf* : trumpet
trompetista *nmf* : trumpet player, trumpeter
trompo *nm* : spinning top
tronada *nf* : thunderstorm
tronar {19} *vi* **1** : to thunder, to roar **2** : to be furious, to rage **3** CA, Mex fam : to shoot — *v impers* : to thunder ⟨está tronando : it's thundering⟩
tronchar *vt* **1** : to snap, to break off **2** : to cut off (relations)
tronco *nm* **1** : trunk (of a tree) **2** : log **3** : torso
trono *nm* **1** : throne **2** *fam* : toilet
tropa *nf* **1** : troop, soldiers *pl* **2** : crowd, mob **3** : herd (of livestock)
tropel *nm* : mob, swarm
tropezar {29} *vi* **1** : to trip, to stumble **2** : to slip up, to blunder **3 ~ con** : to run into, to bump into **4 ~ con** : to come up against (a problem)

tropezón *nm, pl* **-zones 1** : stumble **2** : mistake, slip
tropical *adj* : tropical
trópico *nm* **1** : tropic ⟨trópico de Cáncer : tropic of Cancer⟩ **2 el trópico** : the tropics
tropiezo *nm* **1** CONTRATIEMPO : snag, setback **2** EQUIVOCACIÓN : mistake, slip
troqué, etc. → **trocar**
troquel *nm* : die (for stamping)
trotamundos *nmf* : globe-trotter
trotar *vi* **1** : to trot **2** : to jog **3** *fam* : to rush about
trote *nm* **1** : trot **2** *fam* : rush, bustle **3 de ~** : durable, for everyday use
trovador, -dora *n* : troubadour
trozar {21} *vt* : to cut up, to dice
trozo *nm* **1** PEDAZO : piece, bit, chunk **2** : passage, extract
trucha *nf* : trout
truco *nm* **1** : trick **2** : knack
truculento, -ta *adj* : horrifying, gruesome
trueca, trueque etc. → **trocar**
truena, etc. → **tronar**
trueno *nm* : thunder
trueque *nm* : barter, exchange
trufa *nf* : truffle
truncar {72} *vt* **1** : to truncate, to cut short **2** : to thwart, to frustrate ⟨truncó sus esperanzas : she shattered their hopes⟩
trunco, -ca *adj* **1** : truncated **2** : unfinished, incomplete
trunque, etc. → **truncar**
tu *adj* **1** : your ⟨tu vestido : your dress⟩ ⟨toma tus vitaminas : take your vitamins⟩ **2** : thy
tú *pron* **1** : you ⟨tú eres mi hijo : you are my son⟩ **2** : thou
tuba *nf* : tuba
tubérculo *nm* : tuber
tuberculosis *nf* : tuberculosis
tuberculoso, -sa *adj* : tuberculous, tubercular
tubería *nf* : pipes *pl*, tubing
tuberoso, -sa *adj* : tuberous
tubo *nm* **1** : tube ⟨tubo de ensayo : test tube⟩ **2** : pipe ⟨tubo de desagüe : drainpipe⟩ **3 tubo digestivo** : alimentary canal
tubular *adj* : tubular
tuerca *nf* : nut ⟨tuercas y tornillos : nuts and bolts⟩
tuerce, etc. → **torcer**
tuerto, -ta *adj* : one-eyed, blind in one eye
tuerza, etc. → **torcer**
tuesta, etc. → **tostar**
tuétano *nm* : marrow
tufo *nm* **1** : fume, vapor **2** *fam* : stench, stink
tugurio *nm* : hovel
tulipán *nm, pl* **-panes** : tulip
tumba *nf* **1** SEPULCRO : tomb **2** FOSA : grave **3** : felling of trees

tumbar *vt* **1** : to knock down **2** : to fell, to cut down — *vi* : to fall down —
tumbarse *vr* ACOSTARSE : to lie down
tumbo *nm* **1** : tumble, fall **2 dar tumbos** : to jolt, to bump around
tumor *nm* : tumor
túmulo *nm* : burial mound
tumulto *nm* **1** ALBOROTO : commotion, tumult **2** MOTÍN : riot **3** MULTITUD : crowd
tumultuoso, -sa *adj* : tumultuous
tuna *nf* : prickly pear (fruit)
tundra *nf* : tundra
tunecino, -na *adj & n* : Tunisian
túnel *nm* : tunnel
tungsteno *nm* : tungsten
túnica *nf* : tunic
tupé *nm* PELUQUÍN : toupee
tupido, -da *adj* **1** DENSO : dense, thick **2** OBSTRUIDO : obstructed, blocked up
turba *nf* **1** : peat **2** : mob, throng
turbación *nf, pl* **-ciones 1** : disturbance **2** : alarm, concern **3** : confusion
turbante *nm* : turban
turbar *vt* **1** : to disturb, to disrupt **2** : to worry, to upset **3** : to confuse
turbina *nf* : turbine
turbio, -bia *adj* **1** : cloudy, murky, turbid **2** : dim, blurred **3** : shady, crooked
turbopropulsor *nm* : turboprop
turborreactor *nm* : turbojet
turbulencia *nf* : turbulence
turbulento, -ta *adj* : turbulent
turco[1]**, -ca** *adj* : Turkish
turco[2]**, -ca** *n* : Turk
turco[3] *nm* : Turkish (language)
turgente *adj* : turgid, swollen
turismo *nm* : tourism, tourist industry
turista *nmf* : tourist, vacationer
turístico, -ca *adj* : tourist, travel
turnar *vi* : to take turns, to alternate
turno *nm* **1** : turn ⟨ya te tocará tu turno : you'll get your turn⟩ **2** : shift, duty ⟨turno de noche : night shift⟩ **3 por turno** : alternately
turón *nm, pl* **turones** : polecat
turquesa *nf* : turquoise
turrón *nm, pl* **turrones** : nougat
tusa *nf* : corn husk
tutear *vt* : to address as *tú*
tutela *nf* **1** : guardianship **2** : tutelage, protection
tuteo *nm* : addressing as *tú*
tutor, -tora *n* **1** : tutor **2** : guardian
tuvo, etc. → **tener**
tuyo[1]**, -ya** *adj* : yours, of yours ⟨un amigo tuyo : a friend of yours⟩ ⟨¿es tuya esta casa? : is this house yours?⟩
tuyo[2]**, -ya** *pron* **1** : yours ⟨ése es el tuyo : that one is yours⟩ ⟨trae la tuya : bring your own⟩ **2 los tuyos** : your relations, your friends ⟨¿vendrán los tuyos? : are your folks coming?⟩
tweed [ˈtwið] *nm* : tweed

U

u¹ *nf* : twenty-second letter of the Spanish alphabet

u² *conj* (*used instead of* o *before words beginning with* o- *or* ho-) : or

ualabí *nm* : wallaby

uapití *nm* : American elk, wapiti

ubicación *nf, pl* **-ciones** : location, position

ubicar {72} *vt* **1** SITUAR : to place, to put, to position **2** LOCALIZAR : to locate, to find — **ubicarse** *vr* **1** LOCALIZARSE : to be placed, to be located **2** SITUARSE : to position oneself

ubicuidad *nf* OMNIPRESENCIA : ubiquity

ubicuo, -cua *adj* OMNIPRESENTE : ubiquitous

ubre *nf* : udder

ucraniano¹, -na *adj & n* : Ukranian

ucraniano² *nm* : Ukranian (language)

Ud., Uds. → **usted**

ufanarse *vr* ~ **de** : to boast about, to pride oneself on

ufano, -na *adj* **1** ORGULLOSO : proud **2** : self-satisfied, smug

ugandés, -desa *adj & n, mpl* **-deses** : Ugandan

ukelele *nm* : ukulele

úlcera *nf* : ulcer — **ulceroso, -sa** *adj*

ulcerar *vt* : to ulcerate — **ulcerarse** *vr* — **ulceración** *nf*

ulceroso, -sa *adj* : ulcerous

ulterior *adj* : later, subsequent — **ulteriormente** *adv*

últimamente *adv* : lately, recently

ultimar *vt* **1** CONCLUIR : to complete, to finish, to finalize **2** MATAR : to kill

ultimátum *nm, pl* **-tums** : ultimatum

último, -ma *adj* **1** : last, final ⟨la última galleta : the last cookie⟩ ⟨en último caso : as a last resort⟩ **2** : last, latest, most recent ⟨su último viaje a España : her last trip to Spain⟩ ⟨en los últimos años : in recent years⟩ **3 por ~** : finally

ultrajar *vt* INSULTAR : to offend, to outrage, to insult

ultraje *nm* INSULTO : outrage, insult

ultramar *nm* **de** ~ *or* **en** ~ : overseas, abroad

ultranza *nf* **1 a** ~ : to the extreme ⟨lo defendió a ultranza : she defended him fiercely⟩ **2 a** ~ : extreme, out-and-out ⟨perfeccionismo a ultranza : rabid perfectionism⟩

ultrarrojo, -ja *adj* : infrared

ultravioleta *adj* : ultraviolet

ulular *vi* **1** : to hoot **2** : to howl, to wail

ululato *nm* : hoot (of an owl), wail (of a person)

umbilical *adj* : umbilical ⟨cordón umbilical : umbilical cord⟩

umbral *nm* : threshold, doorstep

un¹ *adj* → **uno¹**

un², **una** *art, mpl* **unos 1** : a, an **2 unos** *or* **unas** *pl* : some, a few ⟨hace unas semanas : a few weeks ago⟩ **3 unos** *or* **unas** *pl* : about, approximately ⟨unos veinte años antes : about twenty years before⟩

unánime *adj* : unanimous — **unánimemente** *adv*

unanimidad *nf* **1** : unanimity **2 por** ~ : unanimously

unción *nf, pl* **-ciones** : unction

uncir {83} *vt* : to yoke

undécimo¹, -ma *adj* : eleventh

undécimo², -ma *n* : eleventh (in a series)

ungir {35} *vt* : to anoint

ungüento *nm* : ointment, salve

únicamente *adv* : only, solely

unicelular *adj* : unicellular

único¹, -ca *adj* **1** : only, sole **2** : unique, extraordinary

único², -ca *n* : only one ⟨los únicos que vinieron : the only ones who showed up⟩

unicornio *nm* : unicorn

unidad *nf* **1** : unity **2** : unit

unidireccional *adj* : unidirectional

unido, -da *adj* **1** : joined, united **2** : close ⟨unos amigos muy unidos : very close friends⟩

unificar {72} *vt* : to unify — **unificación** *nf*

uniformado, -da *adj* : uniformed

uniformar *vt* ESTANDARIZAR : to standardize, to make uniform

uniforme¹ *adj* : uniform — **uniformemente** *adv*

uniforme² *nm* : uniform

uniformidad *nf* : uniformity

unilateral *adj* : unilateral — **unilateralmente** *adv*

unión *nf, pl* **uniones 1** : union **2** JUNTURA : joint, coupling

unir *vt* **1** JUNTAR : to unite, to join, to link **2** COMBINAR : to combine, to blend — **unirse** *vr* **1** : to join together **2** : to combine, to mix together **3** ~ **a** : to join ⟨se unieron al grupo : they joined the group⟩

unísono *nm* : unison ⟨al unísono : in unison⟩

unitario, -ria *adj* : unitary, unit ⟨precio unitario : unit price⟩

universal *adj* : universal — **universalmente** *adv*

universidad *nf* : university

universitario¹, -ria *adj* : university, college

universitario², -ria *n* : university student, college student

universo *nm* : universe

unja, etc. → **ungir**

uno¹, una *adj* (**un** *before masculine singular nouns*) : one ⟨una silla : one chair⟩ ⟨tiene treinta y un años : he's thirty-one years old⟩ ⟨el tomo uno : volume one⟩

uno² *nm* : one, number one

uno³, una *pron* **1** : one (number) ⟨uno por uno : one by one⟩ ⟨es la una : it's one o'clock⟩ **2** : one (person or thing) ⟨una es mejor que las otras : one (of them) is better than the others⟩ ⟨hacerlo uno mismo : to do it oneself⟩ **3 unos, unas** *pl* : some (ones), some people **4 uno y otro** : both **5 unos y otros** : all of them **6 el uno al otro** : one another, each other ⟨se enseñaron los unos a los otros : they taught each other⟩
untar *vt* **1** : to anoint **2** : to smear, to grease **3** : to bribe
unza, etc. → **uncir**
uña *nf* **1** : fingernail, toenail **2** : claw, hoof, stinger
uranio *nm* : uranium
Urano *nm* : Uranus
urbanidad *nf* : urbanity, courtesy
urbanización *nf, pl* **-ciones** : housing development, residential area
urbanizar {21} *vt* : to develop (an area)
urbano, -na *adj* **1** : urban **2 CORTÉS** : urbane, polite
urbe *nf* : large city, metropolis
urdimbre *nf* : warp (in a loom)
urdu *nm* : Urdu
uretra *nf* : urethra
urgencia *nf* **1** : urgency **2 EMERGENCIA** : emergency
urgente *adj* : urgent — **urgentemente** *adv*
urgir {35} *v impers* : to be urgent, to be pressing ⟨me urge localizarlo : I urgently need to find him⟩ ⟨el tiempo urge : time is running out⟩
urinario¹, -ria *adj* : urinary
urinario² *nm* : urinal (place)
urja, etc. → **urgir**
urna *nf* **1** : urn **2** : ballot box ⟨acudir a las urnas : to go to the polls⟩
urogallo *nm* : grouse (bird)
urraca *nf* **1** : magpie **2 urraca de América** : blue jay

urticaria *nf* : hives
uruguayo, -ya *adj & n* : Uruguayan
usado, -da *adj* **1** : used, secondhand **2** : worn, worn-out
usanza *nf* : custom, usage
usar *vt* **1 EMPLEAR, UTILIZAR** : to use, to make use of **2 CONSUMIR** : to consume, to use (up) **3 LLEVAR** : to wear **4 de usar y tirar** : disposable — **usarse** *vr* **1** : to be used **2** : to be in fashion
uso *nm* **1 EMPLEO, UTILIZACIÓN** : use ⟨de uso personal : for personal use⟩ ⟨hacer uso de : to make use of⟩ **2** : wear ⟨uso y desgaste : wear and tear⟩ **3 USANZA** : custom, usage, habit ⟨al uso de : in the manner of, in the style of⟩
usted *pron* **1** (*formal form of address in most countries; often written as* **Ud.** *or* **Vd.**) : you **2 ustedes** *pl* (*often written as* **Uds.** *or* **Vds.**) : you, all of you
usual *adj* : usual, common, normal ⟨poco usual : not very common⟩ — **usualmente** *adv*
usuario, -ria *n* : user
usura *nf* : usury — **usurario, -ria** *adj*
usurero, -ra *n* : usurer
usurpador, -dora *n* : usurper
usurpar *vt* : to usurp — **usurpación** *nf*
utensilio *nm* : utensil, tool
uterino, -na *adj* : uterine
útero *nm* : uterus, womb
útil *adj* : useful, handy, helpful
útiles *nmpl* : implements, tools
utilidad *nf* **1** : utility, usefulness **2 utilidades** *nfpl* : profits
utilitario, -ria *adj* : utilitarian
utilizable *adj* : usable, fit for use
utilización *nf, pl* **-ciones** : utilization, use
utilizar {21} *vt* : to use, to utilize
útilmente *adv* : usefully
utopía *nf* : utopia
utópico, -ca *adj* : utopian
uva *nf* : grape
uvular *adj* : uvular

V

v *nf* : twenty-third letter of the Spanish alphabet
va → **ir**
vaca *nf* : cow
vacación *nf, pl* **-ciones 1** : vacation ⟨dos semanas de vacaciones : two weeks of vacation⟩ **2 estar de vacaciones** : to be on vacation **3 irse de vacaciones** : to go on vacation
vacacionar *vi Mex* : to vacation
vacacionista *nmf CA, Mex* : vacationer
vacante¹ *adj* : vacant, empty
vacante² *nf* : vacancy (for a job)
vaciado *nm* : cast, casting ⟨vaciado de yeso : plaster cast⟩
vaciar {85} *vt* **1** : to empty, to empty out, to drain **2 AHUECAR** : to hollow out **3**

: to cast (in a mold) — **vi ~ en** : to flow into, to empty into
vacilación *nf, pl* **-ciones** : hesitation, vacillation
vacilante *adj* **1** : hesitant, unsure **2** : shaky, unsteady **3** : flickering
vacilar *vi* **1** : to hesitate, to vacillate, to waver **2** : to be unsteady, to wobble **3** : to flicker **4 fam** : to joke, to fool around
vacío¹, -cía *adj* **1** : vacant **2** : empty **3** : meaningless
vacío² *nm* **1** : emptiness, void **2** : space, gap **3** : vacuum **4 hacerle el vacío a alguien** : to ostracize someone, to give someone the cold shoulder
vacuidad *nf* : vacuity, vacuousness

vacuna *nf* : vaccine
vacunación *nf, pl* **-ciones** INOCU-
LACIÓN : vaccination, inoculation
vacunar *vt* INOCULAR : to vaccinate, to
inoculate
vacuno[1], **-na** *adj* : bovine ⟨ganado vacuno : beef cattle⟩
vacuno[2] *nm* : bovine
vacuo, -cua *adj* : empty, shallow, inane
vadear *vt* : to ford, to wade across
vado *nm* : ford
vagabundear *vi* : to wander, to roam
about
vagabundo[1], **-da** *adj* **1** ERRANTE : wandering **2** : stray
vagabundo[2], **-da** *n* : vagrant, bum,
vagabond
vagamente *adv* : vaguely
vagancia *nf* **1** : vagrancy **2** PEREZA
: laziness, idleness
vagar {52} *vi* ERRAR : to roam, to wander
vagina *nf* : vagina — **vaginal** *adj*
vago[1], **-ga** *adj* **1** : vague **2** PEREZOSO
: lazy, idle
vago[2], **-ga** *n* **1** : idler, loafer **2** VAGA-
BUNDO : vagrant, bum
vagón *nm, pl* **vagones** : car (of a train)
vague, etc. → **vagar**
vaguear *vi* **1** : to loaf, to lounge around
2 VAGAR : to wander
vaguedad *nf* : vagueness
vahído *nm* : dizzy spell
vaho *nm* **1** : breath **2** : vapor, steam (on
glass, etc.)
vaina *nf* **1** : sheath, scabbard **2** : pod
(of a pea or bean) **3** *fam* : nuisance,
bother
vainilla *nf* : vanilla
vaivén *nm, pl* **vaivenes 1** : swinging,
swaying, rocking **2** : change, fluctuation ⟨los vaivenes de la vida : life's ups
and downs⟩
vajilla *nf* : dishes *pl*, set of dishes
valdrá, etc. → **valer**
vale *nm* **1** : voucher **2** PAGARÉ : promissory note, IOU
valedero, -ra *adj* : valid
valentía *nf* : courage, valor
valer {84} *vt* **1** : to be worth ⟨valen una
fortuna : they're worth a fortune⟩ ⟨no
vale protestar : there's no point in
protesting⟩ ⟨valer la pena : to be worth
the trouble⟩ **2** : to cost ⟨¿cuánto vale?
: how much does it cost?⟩ **3** : to earn,
to gain ⟨le valió una reprimenda : it
earned him a reprimand⟩ **4** : to protect, to aid ⟨¡válgame Dios! : God help
me!⟩ **5** : to be equal to — *vi* **1** : to have
value ⟨sus consejos no valen para nada
: his advice is worthless⟩ **2** : to be valid,
to count ⟨eso no vale! : that doesn't
count!⟩ **3 hacerse valer** : to assert oneself **4 más vale** : it's better ⟨más vale
que te vayas : you'd better go⟩ —
valerse *vr* **1** ∼ **de** : to take advantage
of **2 valerse solo** *or* **valerse por sí mismo** : to look after oneself **3** *Mex* : to
be fair ⟨no se vale : it's not fair⟩

valeroso, -sa *adj* : brave, valiant
valet ['balɛt, -'le] *nm* : jack (in playing
cards)
valga, etc. → **valer**
valía *nf* : value, worth
validar *vt* : to validate — **validación** *nf*
validez *nf* : validity
válido, -da *adj* : valid
valiente *adj* **1** : brave, valiant **2** (*used
ironically*) : fine, great ⟨¡valiente ami-
ga! : what a fine friend!⟩ — **valientemente** *adv*
valija *nf* : suitcase, valise
valioso, -sa *adj* PRECIOSO : valuable,
precious
valla *nf* **1** : fence, barricade **2** : hurdle
(in sports) **3** : obstacle, hindrance
vallar *vt* : to fence, to put a fence around
valle *nm* : valley, vale
valor *nm* **1** : value, worth, importance
2 CORAJE : courage, valor **3 valores**
nmpl : values, principles **4 valores**
nmpl : securities, bonds **5 sin** ∼
: worthless
valoración *nf, pl* **-ciones 1** EVALU-
ACIÓN : valuation, appraisal, assessment **2** APRECIACIÓN : appreciation
valorar *vt* **1** EVALUAR : to evaluate, to
appraise, to assess **2** APRECIAR : to value, to appreciate
valorizarse {21} *vr* : to appreciate, to increase in value — **valorización** *nf*
vals *nm* : waltz
valsar *vi* : to waltz
valuación *nf, pl* **-ciones** : valuation, appraisal
valuar {3} *vt* : to value, to appraise, to
assess
válvula *nf* **1** : valve **2 válvula reguladora** : throttle
vamos → **ir**
vampiro *nm* : vampire
van → **ir**
vanadio *nm* : vanadium
vanagloriarse *vr* : to boast, to brag
vanamente *adv* : vainly, in vain
vandalismo *nm* : vandalism
vándalo *nm* : vandal — **vandalismo** *nm*
vanguardia *nf* **1** : vanguard **2** : avante-
garde **3 a la vanguardia** : at the forefront
vanidad *nf* : vanity
vanidoso, -sa *adj* PRESUMIDO : vain,
conceited
vano, -na *adj* **1** INÚTIL : vain, useless **2**
: vain, worthless ⟨vanas promesas
: empty promises⟩ **3 en** ∼ : in vain,
of no avail
vapor *nm* **1** : vapor, steam **2** : steamer,
steamship **3 al vapor** : steamed
vaporizador *nm* : vaporizer
vaporizar {21} *vt* : to vaporize — **vaporizarse** *vr* — **vaporización** *nf*
vaporoso, -sa *adj* **1** : vaporous **2**
: sheer, airy
vapulear *vt* : to beat, to thrash
vaquero[1], **-ra** *adj* : cowboy ⟨pantalón vaquero : jeans⟩

vaquero², **-ra** *n* : cowboy *m*, cowgirl *f*
vaqueros *nmpl* JEANS : jeans
vaquilla *nf* : heifer
vara *nf* **1** : pole, stick, rod **2** : staff (of office) **3** : lance, pike (in bullfighting) **4** : yardstick **5 vara de oro** : goldenrod
varado, -da *adj* **1** : beached, aground **2** : stranded
varar *vt* : to beach (a ship), to strand — *vi* : to run aground
variable *adj* & *nf* : variable — **variabilidad** *nf*
variación *nf*, *pl* **-ciones** : variation
variado, -da *adj* : varied, diverse
variante *adj* & *nf* : variant
varianza *nf* : variance
variar {85} *vt* **1** : to change, to alter **2** : to diversify — *vi* **1** : to vary, to change **2 variar de opinión** : to change one's mind
varicela *nf* : chicken pox
varices *or* **várices** *nfpl* : varicose veins
varicoso, -sa *adj* : varicose
variedad *nf* DIVERSIDAD : variety, diversity
varilla *nf* **1** : rod, bar **2** : spoke (of a wheel) **3** : rib (of an umbrella)
vario, -ria *adj* **1** : varied, diverse **2** : variegated, motley **3** : changeable **4 varios, varias** *pl* : various, several
variopinto, -ta *adj* : diverse, assorted, motley
varita *nf* : wand ⟨varita mágica : magic wand⟩
varón *nm*, *pl* **varones 1** HOMBRE : man, male **2** NIÑO : boy
varonil *adj* **1** : masculine, manly **2** : mannish
vas → **ir**
vasallo *nm* : vassal — **vasallaje** *nm*
vasco¹, -ca *adj* & *n* : Basque
vasco² *nm* : Basque (language)
vascular *adj* : vascular
vasija *nf* : container, vessel
vaso *nm* **1** : glass, tumbler **2** : glassful **3** : vessel ⟨vaso sanguíneo : blood vessel⟩
vástago *nm* **1** : offspring, descendant **2** : shoot (of a plant)
vastedad *nf* : vastness, immensity
vasto, -ta *adj* : vast, immense
vataje *nm* : wattage
vaticinar *vt* : to predict, to foretell
vaticinio *nm* : prediction, prophecy
vatio *nm* : watt
vaya, etc. → **ir**
Vd., Vds. → **usted**
ve, etc. → **ir, ver**
vea, etc. → **ver**
vecinal *adj* : local
vecindad *nf* **1** : neighborhood, vicinity **2 casa de vecindad** : tenement
vecindario *nm* **1** : neighborhood, area **2** : residents *pl*
vecino, -na *n* **1** : neighbor **2** : resident, inhabitant
veda *nf* **1** PROHIBICIÓN : prohibition **2** : closed season (for hunting or fishing)

vedar *vt* **1** : to prohibit, to ban **2** IMPEDIR : to impede, to prevent
vega *nf* : fertile lowland
vegetación *nf*, *pl* **-ciones 1** : vegetation **2 vegetaciones** *nfpl* : adenoids
vegetal *adj* & *nm* : vegetable, plant
vegetar *vi* : to vegetate
vegetarianismo *nm* : vegetarianism
vegetariano, -na *adj* & *n* : vegetarian
vegetativo, -va *adj* : vegetative
vehemente *adj* : vehement — **vehemencia** *nf*
vehículo *nm* : vehicle — **vehicular** *adj*
veía, etc. → **ver**
veinte *adj* & *nm* : twenty
veinteavo¹, -va *adj* : twentieth
veinteavo² *nm* : twentieth (fraction)
veintena *nf* : group of twenty, score ⟨una veintena de participantes : about twenty participants⟩
vejación *nf*, *pl* **-ciones** : ill-treatment, humiliation
vejar *vt* : to mistreat, to ridicule, to harass
vejete *nm* : old fellow, codger
vejez *nf* : old age
vejiga *nf* **1** : bladder **2** AMPOLLA : blister
vela *nf* **1** VIGILIA : wakefulness ⟨pasé la noche en vela : I stayed awake all night⟩ **2** : watch, vigil, wake **3** : candle **4** : sail
velada *nf* : evening party, soirée
velado, -da *adj* **1** : veiled, hidden **2** : blurred **3** : muffled
velador¹, -dora *n* : guard, night watchman
velador² *nm* **1** : candlestick **2** : night table
velar *vt* **1** : to hold a wake over **2** : to watch over, to sit up with **3** : to blur, to expose (a photo) **4** : to veil, to conceal — *vi* **1** : to stay awake **2 ~ por** : to watch over, to look after
velatorio *nm* VELORIO : wake (for the dead)
veleidad *nf* **1** : fickleness **2** : whim, caprice
veleidoso, -sa : fickle, capricious
velero *nm* **1** : sailing ship **2** : sailboat
veleta *nf* : weather vane
vello *nm* **1** : body hair **2** : down, fuzz
vellocino *nm* : fleece
vellón *nm*, *pl* **vellones 1** : fleece, sheepskin **2** PRi : nickel (coin)
vellosidad *nf* : downiness, hairiness
velloso, -sa *adj* : downy, fluffy, hairy
velo *nm* : veil
velocidad *nf* **1** : speed, velocity ⟨velocidad máxima : speed limit⟩ **2** MARCHA : gear (of an automobile)
velocímetro *nm* : speedometer
velocista *nmf* : sprinter
velorio *nm* VELATORIO : wake (for the dead)
velour *nm* : velour, velours
veloz *adj*, *pl* **veloces** : fast, quick, swift — **velozmente** *adv*
ven → **venir**

vena *nf* **1** : vein ⟨vena yugular : jugular vein⟩ **2** : vein, seam, lode **3** : grain (of wood) **4** : style ⟨en vena lírica : in a lyrical vein⟩ **5** : strain, touch ⟨una vena de humor : a touch of humor⟩ **6** : mood
venado *nm* **1** : deer **2** : venison
venal *adj* : venal — **venalidad** *nf*
vencedor, -dora *n* : winner, victor
vencejo *nm* : swift (bird)
vencer {86} *vt* **1** DERROTAR : to vanquish, to defeat **2** SUPERAR : to overcome, to surmount — *vi* **1** GANAR : to win, to triumph **2** CADUCAR : to expire ⟨el plazo vence el jueves : the deadline is Thursday⟩ **3** : to fall due, to mature — **vencerse** *vr* **1** DOMINARSE : to control oneself **2** : to break, to collapse
vencido, -da *adj* **1** : defeated **2** : expired **3** : due, payable **4 darse por vencido** : to give up
vencimiento *nm* **1** : defeat **2** : expiration **3** : maturity (of a loan)
venda *nf* : bandage
vendaje *nm* : bandage, dressing
vendar *vt* **1** : to bandage **2 vendar los ojos** : to blindfold
vendaval *nm* : gale, strong wind
vendedor, -dora *n* : salesperson, salesman *m*, saleswoman *f*
vender *vt* **1** : to sell **2** : to sell out, to betray — **venderse** *vr* **1** : to be sold ⟨se vende : for sale⟩ **2** : to sell out
vendetta *nf* : vendetta
vendible *adj* : salable, marketable
vendimia *nf* : grape harvest
vendrá, etc. → **venir**
veneno *nm* **1** : poison **2** : venom
venenoso, -sa *adj* : poisonous, venomous
venerable *adj* : venerable
veneración *nf, pl* **-ciones** : veneration, reverence
venerar *vt* : to venerate, to revere
venéreo, -rea *adj* : venereal
venero *nm* **1** VENA : seam, lode, vein **2** MANANTIAL : spring **3** FUENTE : origin, source
venezolano, -na *adj & n* : Venezuelan
venga, etc. → **venir**
vengador, -dora *n* : avenger
venganza *nf* : vengeance, revenge
vengar {52} *vt* : to avenge — **vengarse** *vr* : to get even, to revenge oneself
vengativo, -va *adj* : vindictive, vengeful
vengue, etc. → **vengar**
venia *nf* **1** PERMISO : permission, leave **2** PERDÓN : pardon **3** : bow (of the head)
venial *adj* : venial
venida *nf* **1** LLEGADA : arrival, coming **2** REGRESO : return **3 idas y venidas** : comings and goings
venidero, -ra *adj* : coming, future
venir {87} *vi* **1** : to come ⟨lo vi venir : I saw him coming⟩ ⟨¡venga! : come on!⟩ **2** : to arrive ⟨vinieron en coche : they came by car⟩ **3** : to come, to originate ⟨sus zapatos vienen de Italia : her shoes

are from Italy⟩ **4** : to come, to be available ⟨viene envuelto en plástico : it comes wrapped in plastic⟩ **5** : to come back, to return **6** : to affect, to overcome ⟨me vino un vahído : a dizzy spell came over me⟩ **7** : to fit ⟨te viene un poco grande : it's a little big for you⟩ **8** (*with the present participle*) : to have been ⟨viene entrenando diariamente : he's been training daily⟩ **9 ～ a** (*with the infinitive*) : to end up, to turn out ⟨viene a ser lo mismo : it comes out the same⟩ **10 que viene** : coming, next ⟨el año que viene : next year⟩ **11 venir bien** : to be suitable, to be just right — **venirse** *vr* **1** : to come, to arrive **2** : to come back **3 venirse abajo** : to fall apart, to collapse
venta *nf* **1** : sale **2 venta al por menor** *or* **venta al detalle** : retail sales
ventaja *nf* **1** : advantage **2** : lead, head start **3 ventajas** *nfpl* : perks, extras
ventajoso, -sa *adj* **1** : advantageous **2** : profitable — **ventajosamente** *adv*
ventana *nf* **1** : window (of a building) **2 ventana de la nariz** : nostril
ventanal *nm* : large window
ventanilla *nf* **1** : window (of a vehicle or airplane) **2** : ticket window, box office
ventero, -ra *n* : innkeeper
ventilación *nf, pl* **-ciones** : ventilation
ventilador *nm* **1** : ventilator **2** : fan
ventilar *vt* **1** : to ventilate, to air out **2** : to air, to discuss **3** : to make public, to reveal — **ventilarse** *vr* : to get some air
ventisca *nf* : snowstorm, blizzard
ventisquero *nm* : snowdrift
ventosear *vi* : to break wind
ventosidad *nf* : wind, flatulence
ventoso, -sa *adj* : windy
ventrículo *nm* : ventricle
ventrílocuo, -cua *n* : ventriloquist
ventriloquia *nf* : ventriloquism
ventura *nf* **1** : fortune, luck, chance **2** : happiness **3 a la ventura** : at random, as it comes
venturoso, -sa *adj* **1** AFORTUNADO : fortunate, lucky **2** : successful
Venus *nm* : Venus
venza, etc. → **vencer**
ver¹ {88} *vt* **1** : to see ⟨vimos la película : we saw the movie⟩ **2** ENTENDER : to understand ⟨ya lo veo : now I get it⟩ **3** EXAMINAR : to examine, to look into ⟨lo veré : I'll take a look at it⟩ **4** JUZGAR : to see, to judge ⟨a mi manera de ver : to my way of thinking⟩ **5** VISITAR : to meet with, to visit **6** AVERIGUAR : to find out **7 a ver** *or* **vamos a ver** : let's see — *vi* **1** : to see **2** ENTERARSE : to learn, to find out **3** ENTENDER : to understand — **verse** *vr* **1** HALLARSE : to find oneself **2** PARECER : to look, to appear **3** ENCONTRARSE : to see each other, to meet
ver² *nm* **1** : looks *pl*, appearance **2** : opinion ⟨a mi ver : in my view⟩

vera *nf* : side ⟨a la vera del camino : alongside the road⟩
veracidad *nf* : truthfulness, veracity
veranda *nf* : veranda
veraneante *nmf* : summer vacationer
veranear *vi* : to spend the summer
veraniego, -ga *adj* **1** ESTIVAL : summer ⟨el sol veraniego : the summer sun⟩ **2** : summery
verano *nm* : summer
veras *nfpl* **de ~** : really, truly
veraz *adj, pl* **veraces** : truthful, veracious
verbal *adj* : verbal — **verbalmente** *adv*
verbalizar {21} *vt* : to verbalize, to express
verbena *nf* **1** FIESTA : festival, fair **2** : verbena, vervain
verbigracia *adv* : for example
verbo *nm* : verb
verborrea *nf* : verbiage
verbosidad *nf* : verbosity, wordiness
verboso, -sa *adj* : verbose, wordy
verdad *nf* **1** : truth **2 de ~** : really, truly **3 ¿verdad?** : right?, isn't that so?
verdaderamente *adv* : really, truly
verdadero, -dera *adj* **1** REAL, VERÍDICO : true, real **2** AUTÉNTICO : genuine
verde¹ *adj* **1** : green (in color) **2** : green, unripe **3** : inexperienced, green **4** : dirty, risqué
verde² *nm* : green
verdear *vi* : to turn green, to become verdant
verdín *nm, pl* **verdines** : slime, scum
verdor *nm* **1** : greenness **2** : verdure
verdoso, -sa *adj* : greenish
verdugo *nm* **1** : executioner, hangman **2** : tyrant
verdugón *nm, pl* **-gones** : welt, wheal
verdura *nf* : vegetable(s), green(s)
vereda *nf* **1** SENDA : path, trail **2** : sidewalk, pavement
veredicto *nm* : verdict
verga *nf* : spar, yard (of a ship)
vergonzoso, -sa *adj* **1** : disgraceful, shameful **2** : bashful, shy — **vergonzosamente** *adv*
vergüenza *nf* **1** : disgrace, shame **2** : embarrassment **3** : bashfulness, shyness
vericueto *nm* : rough terrain
verídico, -ca *adj* **1** REAL, VERDADERO : true, real **2** VERAZ : truthful
verificación *nf, pl* **-ciones** **1** : verification **2** : testing, checking
verificador, -dora *n* : inspector, tester
verificar {72} *vt* **1** : to verify, to confirm **2** : to test, to check **3** : to carry out, to conduct — **verificarse** *vr* **1** : to take place, to occur **2** : to come true
verja *nf* **1** : rails *pl* (of a fence) **2** : grating, grille **3** : gate
vermut *nm, pl* **vermuts** : vermouth
vernáculo, -la *adj* : vernacular
vernal *adj* : vernal, spring
verosímil *adj* **1** : probable, likely **2** : credible, realistic

verosimilitud *nf* **1** : probability, likeliness **2** : verisimilitude
verraco *nm* : boar
verruga *nf* : wart
versado, -da *adj* **~ en** : versed in, knowledgeable about
versar *vi* **~ sobre** : to deal with, to be about
versátil *adj* **1** : versatile **2** : fickle
versatilidad *nf* **1** : versatility **2** : fickleness
versículo *nm* : verse (in the Bible)
versión *nf, pl* **versiones** **1** : version **2** : translation
verso *nm* : verse
versus *prep* : versus, against
vértebra *nf* : vertebra — **vertebral** *adj*
vertebrado¹, -da *adj* : vertebrate
vertebrado² *nm* : vertebrate
vertedero *nm* **1** : garbage dump **2** DESAGÜE : drain, outlet
verter {56} *vt* **1** : to pour **2** : to spill, to shed **3** : to empty out **4** : to express, to voice **5** : to translate, to render — *vi* : to flow
vertical *adj & nf* : vertical — **verticalmente** *adv*
vértice *nm* : vertex, apex
vertido *nm* : spilling, spill
vertiente *nf* **1** : slope **2** : aspect, side, element
vertiginoso, -sa *adj* : vertiginous — **vertiginosamente** *adv*
vértigo *nm* : vertigo, dizziness
vesícula *nf* **1** : vesicle **2 vesícula biliar** : gallbladder
vesicular *adj* : vesicular
vestíbulo *nm* : vestibule, hall, lobby, foyer
vestido *nm* **1** : dress, costume, clothes *pl* **2** : dress (garment)
vestidor *nm* : dressing room
vestiduras *nfpl* **1** : clothing, raiment, regalia **2** *or* **vestiduras sacerdotales** : vestments
vestigio *nm* : vestige, sign, trace
vestimenta *nf* ROPA : clothing, clothes *pl*
vestir {54} *vt* **1** : to dress, to clothe **2** LLEVAR : to wear **3** ADORNAR : to decorate, to dress up — *vi* **1** : to dress ⟨vestir bien : to dress well⟩ **2** : to look good, to suit the occasion — **vestirse** *vr* **1** : to get dressed **2 ~ de** : to dress up as ⟨se vistieron de soldados : they dressed up as soldiers⟩ **3 ~ de** : to wear, to dress in
vestuario *nm* **1** : wardrobe **2** : dressing room, locker room
veta *nf* **1** : grain (in wood) **2** : vein, seam, lode **3** : trace, streak ⟨una veta de terco : a stubborn streak⟩
vetar *vt* : to veto
veteado, -da *adj* : streaked, veined
veterano, -na *adj & n* : veteran
veterinaria *nf* : veterinary medicine
veterinario¹, -ria *adj* : veterinary
veterinario², -ria *n* : veterinarian

veto *nm* : veto
vetusto, -ta *adj* ANTIGUO : ancient, very old
vez *nf, pl* **veces** 1 : time, occasion ⟨a la vez : at the same time⟩ ⟨a veces : at times, occasionally⟩ ⟨de vez en cuando : from time to time⟩ 2 (*with numbers*) : time ⟨una vez : once⟩ ⟨de una vez : all at once⟩ ⟨de una vez para siempre : once and for all⟩ ⟨dos veces : twice⟩ 3 : turn ⟨a su vez : in turn⟩ ⟨en vez de : instead of⟩ ⟨hacer las veces de : to act as, to stand in for⟩
vía[1] *nf* 1 RUTA, CAMINO : road, route, way ⟨Vía Láctea : Milky Way⟩ 2 MEDIO : means, way ⟨por vía oficial : through official channels⟩ 3 : track, line (of a railroad) 4 : tract, passage ⟨por vía oral : orally⟩ 5 **en vías de** : in the process of ⟨en vías de solución : on the road to a solution⟩ 6 **por ~** : by (in transportation) ⟨por vía aérea : by air, airmail⟩
vía[2] *prep* : via
viable *adj* : viable, feasible — **viabilidad** *nf*
viaducto *nm* : viaduct
viajante *mf* : traveling salesman, traveling saleswoman
viajar *vi* : to travel, to journey
viaje *nm* : trip, journey ⟨viaje de negocios : business trip⟩
viajero[1]**, -ra** *adj* : traveling
viajero[2]**, -ra** *n* 1 : traveler 2 PASAJERO : passenger
vial *adj* : road, traffic
viático *nm* : travel allowance, travel expenses *pl*
víbora *nf* : viper
vibración *nf, pl* **-ciones** : vibration
vibrador *nm* : vibrator
vibrante *adj* 1 : vibrant 2 : vibrating
vibrar *vi* : to vibrate
vibratorio, -ria *adj* : vibratory
vicario, -ria *n* : vicar
vicealmirante *nmf* : vice admiral
vicepresidente, -ta *n* : vice president — **vicepresidencia** *nf*
viceversa *adv* : vice versa, conversely
viciado, -da *adj* : stuffy, close
viciar *vt* 1 : to corrupt 2 : to invalidate 3 FALSEAR : to distort 4 : to pollute, to adulterate
vicio *nm* 1 : vice, depravity 2 : bad habit 3 : defect, blemish
vicioso, -sa *adj* : depraved, corrupt
vicisitud *nf* : vicissitude
víctima *nf* : victim
victimario, -ria *n* ASESINO : killer, murderer
victimizar {21} *vt Arg, Mex* : to victimize
victoria *nf* : victory — **victorioso, -sa** *adj* — **victoriosamente** *adv*
victoriano, -na *adj* : Victorian
vid *nf* : vine, grapevine
vida *nf* 1 : life ⟨la vida cotidiana : everyday life⟩ 2 : life span, lifetime 3 BI-

OGRAFÍA : biography, life 4 : way of life, lifestyle 5 : livelihood ⟨ganarse la vida : to earn one's living⟩ 6 VIVEZA : liveliness 7 **media vida** : half-life
vidente *nmf* 1 : psychic, clairvoyant 2 : sighted person
video *or* **vídeo** *nm* : video
videocasete *or* **videocassette** *nm* : videocassette
videocasetera *or* **videocassettera** *nf* : videocassette recorder, VCR
videocinta *nf* : videotape
videograbar *vt* : to videotape
vidriado *nm* : glaze
vidriar *vt* : to glaze (pottery, tile, etc.)
vidriera *nf* 1 : stained-glass window 2 : glass door or window 3 : store window
vidriero, -ra *n* : glazier
vidrio *nm* 1 : glass, piece of glass 2 : windowpane
vidrioso, -sa *adj* 1 : brittle, fragile 2 : slippery 3 : glassy, glazed (of eyes) 4 : touchy, delicate
vieira *nf* 1 : scallop 2 : scallop shell
viejo[1]**, -ja** *adj* 1 ANCIANO : old, elderly 2 ANTIGUO : former, longstanding ⟨viejas tradiciones : old traditions⟩ ⟨viejos amigos : old friends⟩ 3 GASTADO : old, worn, worn-out
viejo[2]**, -ja** *n* ANCIANO : old man *m*, old woman *f*
viene, etc. → **venir**
viento *nm* 1 : wind 2 **hacer viento** : to be windy 3 **contra viento y marea** : against all odds 4 **viento alisio** : trade wind 5 **viento en popa** : splendidly, successfully
vientre *nm* 1 : abdomen, belly 2 : womb 3 : bowels *pl*
viernes *nms & pl* : Friday
vierte, etc. → **verter**
vietnamita[1] *adj & nmf* : Vietnamese
vietnamita[2] *nm* : Vietnamese (language)
viga *nf* 1 : beam, rafter, girder 2 **viga voladiza** : cantilever
vigencia *nf* 1 : validity 2 : force, effect ⟨entrar en vigencia : to go into effect⟩
vigente *adj* : valid, in force
vigésimo[1]**, -ma** *adj* : twentieth, twenty- ⟨la vigésima segunda edición : the twenty-second edition⟩
vigésimo[2]**, -ma** *n* : twentieth, twenty- (in a series)
vigía *nmf* : lookout
vigilancia *nf* : vigilance, watchfulness ⟨bajo vigilancia : under surveillance⟩
vigilante[1] *adj* : vigilant, watchful
vigilante[2] *nmf* : watchman, guard
vigilar *vt* 1 CUIDAR : to look after, to keep an eye on 2 GUARDAR : to watch over, to guard — *vi* 1 : to be watchful 2 : to keep watch
vigilia *nf* 1 VELA : wakefulness 2 : night work 3 : vigil (in religion)
vigor *nm* 1 : vigor, energy, strength 2 VIGENCIA : force, effect
vigorizante *adj* : invigorating

vigorizar {21} *vt* : to strengthen, to invigorate
vigoroso, -sa *adj* : vigorous — **vigorosamente** *adv*
VIH *nm* (virus de *i*nmunodeficiencia *hu*mana) : HIV
vikingo, -ga *adj & n* : Viking
vil *adj* : vile, despicable
vileza *nf* **1** : vileness **2** : despicable action, villainy
vilipendiar *vt* : to vilify, to revile
villa *nf* **1** : town, village **2** : villa
villancico *nm* : carol, Christmas carol
villano, -na *n* **1** : villain **2** : peasant
vilo *nm* **1 en ～** : in the air **2 en ～** : uncertain, in suspense
vinagre *nm* : vinegar
vinagrera *nf* : cruet (for vinegar)
vinatería *nf* : wine shop
vinculación *nf, pl* **-ciones 1** : linking **2** RELACIÓN : bond, link, connection
vincular *vt* CONECTAR, RELACIONAR : to tie, to link, to connect
vínculo *nm* LAZO : tie, link, bond
vindicación *nf, pl* **-ciones** : vindication
vindicar *vt* **1** : to vindicate **2** : to avenge
vinilo *nm* : vinyl
vino[1], etc. → **venir**
vino[2] *nm* : wine
viña *nf* : vineyard
viñedo *nm* : vineyard
vio, etc. → **ver**
viola *nf* : viola
violación *nf, pl* **-ciones 1** : violation, offense **2** : rape
violador[1]**, -dora** *n* : violator, offender
violador[2] *nm* : rapist
violar *vt* **1** : to rape **2** : to violate (a law or right) **3** PROFANAR : to desecrate
violencia *nf* : violence
violentamente *adv* : by force, violently
violentar *vt* **1** FORZAR : to break open, to force **2** : to distort (words or ideas) — **violentarse** *vr* : to force oneself
violento, -ta *adj* **1** : violent **2** EMBARAZOSO, INCÓMODO : awkward, embarassing
violeta[1] *adj & nm* : violet (color)
violeta[2] *nf* : violet (flower)
violín *nm, pl* **-lines** : violin
violinista *nmf* : violinist
violonchelista *nmf* : cellist
violonchelo *nm* : cello, violoncello
VIP *nmf, pl* **VIPs** : VIP
vira *nf* : welt (of a shoe)
virago *nf* : virago, shrew
viraje *nm* **1** : turn, swerve **2** : change
viral *adj* : viral
virar *vi* : to tack, to turn, to veer
virgen[1] *adj* : virgin ⟨lana virgen : virgin wool⟩
virgen[2] *nmf, pl* **vírgenes** : virgin ⟨la Santísima Virgen : the Blessed Virgin⟩
virginal *adj* : virginal, chaste
virginidad *nf* : virginity
Virgo *nmf* : Virgo
vírico, -ca *adj* : viral
viril *adj* : virile — **virilidad** *nf*

virrey, -rreina *n* : viceroy *m*, vicereine *f*
virtual *adj* : virtual — **virtualmente** *adv*
virtud *nf* **1** : virtue **2 en virtud de** : by virtue of
virtuosismo *nm* : virtuosity
virtuoso[1]**, -sa** *adj* : virtuous — **virtuosamente** *adv*
virtuoso[2]**, -sa** *n* : virtuoso
viruela *nf* **1** : smallpox **2** : pockmark
virulencia *nf* : virulence
virulento, -ta *adj* : virulent
virus *nm* : virus
viruta *nf* : shaving
visa *nf* : visa
visado *nm* *Spain* : visa
visaje *nm* : face, grimace ⟨hacer visajes : to make faces⟩
visceral *adj* : visceral
vísceras *nfpl* : viscera, entrails
visconde, -desa *n* : viscount *m*, viscountess *f*
viscosidad *nf* : viscosity
viscoso, -sa *adj* : viscous
visera *nf* : visor
visibilidad *nf* : visibility
visible *adj* : visible — **visiblemente** *adv*
visión *nf, pl* **visiones 1** : vision, eyesight **2** : view, perspective **3** : vision, illusion ⟨ver visiones : to be seeing things⟩
visionario, -ria *adj & n* : visionary
visita *nf* **1** : visit, call **2** : visitor **3 ir de visita** : to go visiting
visitador, -dora *n* : visitor, frequent caller
visitante[1] *adj* : visiting
visitante[2] *nmf* : visitor
visitar *vt* : to visit
vislumbrar *vt* **1** : to discern, to make out **2** : to begin to see, to have an inkling of
vislumbre *nf* : glimmer, gleam
viso *nm* **1** APARIENCIA : appearance ⟨tener visos de : to seem, to show signs of⟩ **2** DESTELLO : glint, gleam **3** : sheen, iridescence
visón *nm, pl* **visones** : mink
víspera *nf* **1** : eve, day before **2**
vísperas *nfpl* : vespers
vista *nf* **1** VISIÓN : vision, eyesight **2** MIRADA : look, gaze, glance **3** PANORAMA : view, vista, panorama **4** : hearing (in court) **5 a primera vista** : at first sight **6 en vista de** : in view of **7 hacer la vista gorda** : to turn a blind eye **8 ¡hasta la vista!** : so long!, see you! **9 perder de vista** : to lose sight of **10 punto de vista** : point of view
vistazo *nm* : glance, look
viste, etc. → **ver**[1]**, vestir**
visto[1] *pp* → **ver**
visto[2]**, -ta** *adj* **1** : obvious, clear **2** : in view of, considering **3 estar bien visto** : to be approved of **4 estar mal visto** : to be frowned upon **5 por lo visto** : apparently **6 nunca visto** : unheard-of **7 visto que** : since, given that
visto[3] *nm* **visto bueno** : approval

vistoso, -sa *adj* : colorful, bright
visual *adj* : visual — **visualmente** *adv*
visualización *nf, pl* **-ciones** : visualization
visualizar {21} *vt* **1** : to visualize **2** : to display (on a screen)
vital *adj* **1** : vital **2** : lively, dynamic
vitalicio, -cia *adj* : life, lifetime
vitalidad *nf* : vitality
vitamina *nf* : vitamin
vitamínico, -ca *adj* : vitamin ⟨complejos vitamínicos : vitamin compounds⟩
vitorear *vt* : to cheer, to acclaim
vitral *nm* : stained-glass window
vítreo, -rea *adj* : vitreous, glassy
vitrina *nf* **1** : showcase, display case **2** : store window
vitriolo *nm* : vitriol
vituperar *vt* : to condemn, to vituperate against
vituperio *nm* : vituperation, censure
viudez *nf* : widowerhood, widowhood
viudo, -da *n* : widower *m*, widow *f*
vivacidad *nf* VIVEZA : vivacity, liveliness
vivamente *adv* **1** : in a lively manner **2** : vividly **3** : strongly, acutely ⟨lo recomendamos vivamente : we strongly recommend it⟩
vivaque *nm* : bivouac
vivaquear *vi* : to bivouac
vivar *vt* : to cheer
vivaz *adj, pl* **vivaces** **1** : lively, vivacious **2** : clever, sharp **3** : perennial
víveres *nmpl* : provisions, supplies, food
vivero *nm* **1** : nursery (for plants) **2** : hatchery, fish farm
viveza *nf* **1** VIVACIDAD : liveliness **2** BRILLO : vividness, brightness **3** ASTUCIA : cleverness, sharpness
vívido, -da *adj* : vivid, lively
vividor, -dora *n* : sponger, parasite
vivienda *nf* **1** : housing **2** MORADA : dwelling, home
viviente *adj* : living
vivificar {72} *vt* : to vivify, to give life to
vivir[1] *vi* **1** : to live, to be alive **2** SUBSISTIR : to subsist, to make a living **3** RESIDIR : to reside **4** : to spend one's life ⟨vive para trabajar : she lives to work⟩ **5** ~ **de** : to live on — *vt* **1** : to live ⟨vivir su vida : to live one's life⟩ **2** EXPERIMENTAR : to go through, to experience
vivir[2] *nm* **1** : life, lifestyle **2 de mal vivir** : disreputable
vivisección *nf, pl* **-ciones** : vivisection
vivo, -va *adj* **1** : alive **2** INTENSO : vivid, bright, intense **3** ANIMADO : lively, vivacious **4** ASTUTO : sharp, clever **5 en** ~ : live ⟨transmisión en vivo : live broadcast⟩ **6 al rojo vivo** : red-hot
vizconde, -desa *n* : viscount *m*, viscountess *f*
vocablo *nm* PALABRA : word
vocabulario *nm* : vocabulary
vocación *nf, pl* **-ciones** : vocation
vocacional *adj* : vocational
vocal[1] *adj* : vocal

vocal[2] *nmf* : member (of a committee, board, etc.)
vocal[3] *nf* : vowel
vocalista *nmf* CANTANTE : singer, vocalist
vocalizar {21} *vi* : to vocalize
vocear *v* : to shout
vocerío *nm* : clamor, shouting
vocero, -ra *n* PORTAVOZ : spokesperson, spokesman *m*, spokeswoman *f*
vociferante *adj* : vociferous
vociferar *vi* GRITAR : to shout, to yell
vodevil *nm* : vaudeville
vodka *nm* : vodka
voladizo[1]**, -za** *adj* : projecting
voladizo[2] *nm* : projection
volador, -dora *adj* : flying
volando *adv* : quickly, in a hurry
volante[1] *adj* : flying
volante[2] *nm* **1** : steering wheel **2** FOLLETO : flier, circular **3** : shuttlecock **4** : flywheel **5** : balance wheel (of a watch) **6** : ruffle, flounce
volar {19} *vi* **1** : to fly **2** CORRER : to hurry, to rush ⟨el tiempo vuela : time flies⟩ ⟨pasar volando : to fly past⟩ **3** DIVULGARSE : to spread ⟨unos rumores volaban : rumors were spreading around⟩ **4** DESAPARECER : to disappear ⟨el dinero ya voló : the money's already gone⟩ — *vt* **1** : to blow up, to demolish **2** : to irritate
volátil *adj* : volatile — **volatilidad** *nf*
volatilizar {21} *vt* : to volatize — **volatilizarse** *vr*
volcán *nm, pl* **volcanes** : volcano
volcánico, -ca *adj* : volcanic
volcar {82} *vt* **1** : to upset, to knock over, to turn over **2** : to empty out **3** : to make dizzy **4** : to cause a change of mind in **5** : to irritate — *vi* **1** : to overturn, to tip over **2** : to capsize — **volcarse** *vr* **1** : to overturn **2** : to do one's utmost
volea *nf* : volley (in sports)
volear *vi* : to volley (in sports)
voleibol *nm* : volleyball
voleo *nm* **al voleo** : haphazardly, at random
volframio *nm* : wolfram, tungsten
volición *nf, pl* **-ciones** : volition
volqué, etc. → **volcar**
voltaje *nm* : voltage
voltear *vt* **1** : to turn over, to turn upside down **2** : to reverse, to turn inside out **3** : to turn ⟨voltear la cara : to turn one's head⟩ **4** : to knock down — *vi* **1** : to roll over, to do somersaults **2** : to turn ⟨volteó a la izquierda : he turned left⟩ — **voltearse** *vr* **1** : to turn around **2** : to change one's allegiance
voltereta *nf* : somersault, tumble
voltio *nm* : volt
volubilidad *nf* : fickleness, changeableness
voluble *adj* : fickle, changeable
volumen *nm, pl* **-lúmenes** **1** TOMO : volume, book **2** : capacity, size, bulk **3** CANTIDAD : amount ⟨el volumen de

ventas : the volume of sales⟩ **4** : volume, loudness
voluminoso, -sa *adj* : voluminous, massive, bulky
voluntad *nf* **1** : will, volition **2** DESEO
: desire, wish **3** INTENCIÓN : intention
4 a voluntad : at will **5 buena voluntad** : good will **6 mala voluntad** : ill
will **7 fuerza de voluntad** : willpower
voluntario¹, -ria *adj* : voluntary — **vol-
untariamente** *adv*
voluntario², -ria *n* : volunteer
voluntarioso, -sa *adj* **1** : stubborn **2**
: willing, eager
voluptuosidad *nf* : voluptuousness
voluptuoso, -sa *adj* : voluptuous —
voluptuosamente *adv*
voluta *nf* : spiral, column (of smoke)
volver {89} *vi* **1** : to return, to come or
go back ⟨volver a casa : to return
home⟩ **2** : to revert ⟨volver al tema : to
get back to the subject⟩ **3** ∼ **a** : to do
again ⟨volvieron a llamar : they called
again⟩ **4 volver en sí** : to come to, to
regain consciousness — *vt* **1** : to turn,
to turn over, to turn inside out **2** : to
return, to repay, to restore **3** : to cause,
to make ⟨la volvía loca : it was driving
her crazy⟩ — **volverse** *vr* **1** : to become ⟨se volvió deprimido : he became
depressed⟩ **2** : to turn around
vomitar *vi* : to vomit — *vt* **1** : to vomit
2 : to spew out (lava, etc.)
vómito *nm* **1** : vomiting **2** : vomit
voracidad *nf* : voracity
vorágine *nf* : whirlpool, maelstrom
voraz *adj, pl* **voraces** : voracious — **vo-
razmente** *adv*
vórtice *nm* **1** : whirlpool, vortex **2** TOR-
BELLINO : whirlwind
vos *pron* (*in some regions of Latin America*) : you
vosear *vt* : to address as *vos*
vosotros, -tras *pron pl Spain* **1** : you,
yourselves **2** : ye
votación *nf, pl* **-ciones** : vote, voting
votante *nmf* : voter
votar *vi* : to vote — *vt* : to vote for
votivo, -va *adj* : votive
voto *nm* **1** : vote **2** : vow (in religion)
3 votos *nmpl* : good wishes
voy → **ir**
voz *nf, pl* **voces 1** : voice **2** : opinion,
say **3** GRITO : shout, yell **4** : sound **5**
VOCABLO : word, term **6** : rumor **7 a**

voz en cuello : at the top of one's lungs
8 dar voces : to shout **9 en voz alta**
: aloud, in a loud voice **10 en voz baja**
: softly, in a low voice
vudú *nm* : voodoo
vuelco *nm* : upset, overturning ⟨me dio
un vuelco el corazón : my heart
skipped a beat⟩
vuela, etc. → **volar**
vuelca, vuelque etc. → **volcar**
vuelo *nm* **1** : flight, flying ⟨alzar el vuelo : to take flight⟩ **2** : flight (of an aircraft) ⟨vuelo espacial : space flight⟩ **3**
: flare, fullness (of clothing) **4 al vuelo** : on the wing
vuelta *nf* **1** GIRO : turn ⟨se dio la vuelta
: he turned around⟩ **2** REVOLUCIÓN
: circle, revolution ⟨dio la vuelta al
mundo : she went around the world⟩
⟨las ruedas daban vueltas : the wheels
were spinning⟩ **3** : flip, turn ⟨le dio la
vuelta : she flipped it over⟩ **4** : bend,
curve ⟨a la vuelta de la esquina
: around the corner⟩ **5** REGRESO : return ⟨de ida y vuelta : round trip⟩ ⟨a
vuelta de correo : return mail⟩ **6**
: round, lap (in sports or games) **7**
PASEO : walk, drive, ride ⟨dio una
vuelta : he went for a walk⟩ **8** DORSO,
REVÉS : back, other side ⟨a la vuelta
: on the back⟩ **9** : cuff (of pants) **10
darle vueltas** : to think over **11 estar
de vuelta** : to be back
vuelto *pp* → **volver**
vuelve, etc. → **volver**
vuestro¹, -stra *adj Spain* : your, of yours
⟨vuestros coches : your cars⟩ ⟨una
amiga vuestra : a friend of yours⟩
vuestro², -stra *pron Spain,* (*with definite
article*) : yours ⟨la vuestra es más
grande : yours is bigger⟩ ⟨esos son los
vuestros : those are yours⟩
vulcanizar {21} *vt* : to vulcanize
vulgar *adj* **1** : common **2** : vulgar
vulgaridad *nf* : vulgarity
vulgarismo *nm* : vulgarism
vulgarizar {21} *vt* : to vulgarize, to popularize
vulgarmente *adv* : vulgarly, popularly
vulgo *nm* **el vulgo** : the masses, common people
vulnerable *adj* : vulnerable — **vulnerabilidad** *nf*
vulnerar *vt* **1** : to injure, to damage
(one's reputation or honor) **2** : to violate, to break (a law or contract)

W

w *nf* : twenty-fourth letter of the Spanish alphabet
wafle *nm* : waffle
waflera *nf* : waffle iron

wapití *nm* : wapiti, elk
whisky *nm, pl* **whiskys** *or* **whiskies**
: whiskey
wigwam *nm* : wigwam

X

x *nf* : twenty-fifth letter of the Spanish alphabet
xenofobia *nf* : xenophobia
xenófobo¹, -ba *adj* : xenophobic

xenófobo², -ba *n* : xenophobe
xenón *nm* : xenon
xerocopiar *vt* : to photocopy, to xerox
xilófono *nm* : xylophone

Y

y¹ *nf* : twenty-sixth letter of the Spanish alphabet
y² *conj* (**e** *before words beginning with i- or hi-*) **1** : and ⟨mi hermano y yo : my brother and I⟩ ⟨¿y los demás? : and (what about) the others?⟩ **2** (*used in numbers*) ⟨cincuenta y cinco : fifty-five⟩ **3** *fam* : well ⟨y por supuesto : well, of course⟩
ya¹ *adv* **1** : already ⟨ya terminó : she's finished already⟩ **2** : now, right now ⟨¡hazlo ya! : do it now!⟩ ⟨ya mismo : right away⟩ **3** : later, soon ⟨ya iremos : we'll go later on⟩ **4** : no longer, anymore ⟨ya no fuma : he no longer smokes⟩ **5** (*used for emphasis*) ⟨¡ya lo sé! : I know!⟩ ⟨ya lo creo : of course⟩ **6 no ya** : not only ⟨no ya lloran sino gritan : they're not only crying but screaming⟩ **7 ya que** : now that, since ⟨ya que sabe la verdad : now that she knows the truth⟩
ya² *conj* **ya . . . ya** : whether . . . or, first . . . then ⟨ya le gusta, ya no : first he likes it, then he doesn't⟩
yac *nm* : yak
yacer {90} *vi* : to lie ⟨en esta tumba yacen sus abuelos : his grandparents lie in this grave⟩
yacimiento *nm* : bed, deposit ⟨yacimiento petrolífero : oil field⟩
yaga, etc. → **yacer**
yanqui *adj & nmf* : Yankee
yarda *nf* : yard
yate *nm* : yacht
yaz, yazca, yazga etc. → **yacer**
yedra *nf* : ivy
yegua *nf* : mare
yelmo *nm* : helmet
yema *nf* **1** : bud, shoot **2** : yolk (of an egg) **3 yema del dedo** : fingertip
yemenita *adj & nmf* : Yemenite
yen *nm* : yen (currency)
yendo → **ir**

yerba *nf* **1** *or* **yerba mate** : maté **2** → **hierba**
yerga, yergue etc. → **erguir**
yermo¹, -ma *adj* : barren, deserted
yermo² *nm* : wasteland
yerno *nm* : son-in-law
yerra, etc. → **errar**
yerro *nm* : blunder, mistake
yerto, -ta *adj* : rigid, stiff
yesca *nf* : tinder
yeso *nm* **1** : plaster **2** : gypsum
yo¹ *nm* : ego, self
yo² *pron* **1** : I **2** : me ⟨todos menos yo : everyone except me⟩ ⟨tan bajo como yo : as short as me⟩ **3 soy yo** : it is I, it's me
yodado, -da *adj* : iodized
yodo *nm* : iodine
yoduro *nm* : iodide
yoga *nm* : yoga
yogui *nm* : yogi
yogurt *or* **yogur** *nm* : yogurt
yola *nf* : yawl
yoyo *or* **yoyó** *nm* : yo-yo
yuca *nf* **1** : yucca (plant) **2** : cassava, manioc
yucateco¹, -ca *adj* : of or from the Yucatán
yucateco², -ca *n* : person from the Yucatán
yudo → **judo**
yugo *nm* : yoke
yugoslavo, -va *adj & n* : Yugoslavian
yugular *adj* : jugular ⟨vena yugular : jugular vein⟩
yungas *nfpl Bol, Chile, Peru* : warm tropical valleys
yunque *nm* : anvil
yunta *nf* : yoke, team (of oxen)
yuppy *nmf, pl* **yuppies** : yuppie
yute *nm* : jute
yuxtaponer {60} *vt* : to juxtapose — **yuxtaposición** *nf*

Z

z *nf* : twenty-seventh letter of the Spanish alphabet
zacate *nm CA, Mex* **1** : grass, forage **2** : hay
zafacón *nm, pl* **-cones** *Car* : wastebasket
zafar *vt* : to loosen, to untie — **zafarse**

vr **1** : to loosen up, to come undone **2** : to get free of
zafio, -fia *adj* : coarse, crude
zafiro *nm* : sapphire
zaga *nf* **1** : defense (in sports) **2 a la zaga** *or* **en ~** : behind, in the rear
zagual *nm* : paddle (of a canoe)

zaguán *nm, pl* **zaguanes** : front hall, vestibule
zaherir {76} *vt* **1** : to criticize sharply **2** : to wound, to mortify
zahones *nmpl* : chaps
zaino, -na *adj* : chestnut (color)
zalamería *nf* : flattery, sweet talk
zalamero¹, -ra *adj* : flattering, fawning
zalamero², -ra *n* : flatterer
zambiano, -na *adj & nmf* : Zambian
zambullida *nf* : dive, plunge
zambullirse {38} *vr* : to dive, to plunge
zanahoria *nf* : carrot
zancada *nf* : stride, step
zancadilla *nf* **1** : trip, stumble **2** *fam* : trick, ruse
zancos *nmpl* : stilts
zancuda *nf* : wading bird
zancudo *nm* MOSQUITO : mosquito
zángano *nm* : drone, male bee
zanja *nf* : ditch, trench
zanjar *vt* ACLARAR : to settle, to clear up, to resolve
zapallo *nm Arg, Chile, Peru, Uru* : pumpkin
zapapico *nm* : pickax
zapata *nf* : brake shoe
zapatería *nf* **1** : shoemaker's, shoe factory **2** : shoe store
zapatero¹, -ra *adj* : dry, tough, poorly cooked
zapatero², -ra *n* : shoemaker, cobbler
zapatilla *nf* **1** PANTUFLA : slipper **2** *or* **zapatilla de deporte** : sneaker
zapato *nm* : shoe
zar, zarina *n* : czar *m*, czarina *f*
zarandear *vt* **1** : to sift, to sieve **2** : to shake, to jostle, to jiggle
zarapito *nm* : curlew
zarcillo *nm* **1** : earring **2** : tendril (of a plant)
zarigüeya *nf* : opossum
zarista *adj & nmf* : czarist
zarpa *nf* : paw
zarpar *vi* : to set sail, to raise anchor
zarza *nf* : bramble, blackberry bush
zarzamora *nf* **1** : blackberry **2** : bramble, blackberry bush

zarzaparrilla *nf* : sarsaparilla
zepelin *nm, pl* **-lines** : zeppelin
zigoto *nm* : zygote
zigzag *nm, pl* **zigzags** *or* **zigzagues** : zigzag
zigzaguear *vi* : to zigzag
zimbabuense *adj & nmf* : Zimbabwean
zinc *nm* : zinc
zinnia *nf* : zinnia
zíper *nm CA, Mex* : zipper
zircón *nm, pl* **zircones** : zircon
zócalo *nm Mex* : main square
zodíaco *or* **zodiaco** *nm* : zodiac — **zodíacal** *adj*
zombi *or* **zombie** *nmf* : zombie
zona *nf* : zone, district, area
zonzo¹, -za *adj* : stupid, silly
zonzo², -za *n* : idiot, nitwit
zoo *nm* : zoo
zoología *nf* : zoology
zoológico¹, -ca *adj* : zoological
zoológico² *nm* : zoo
zoólogo, -ga *n* : zoologist
zoom *nm* : zoom lens
zopilote *nm CA, Mex* : buzzard
zoquete *nmf fam* : oaf, blockhead
zorrillo *nm* MOFETA : skunk
zorro¹, -rra *adj* : sly, crafty
zorro², -rra *n* **1** : fox, vixen **2** : sly crafty person
zorzal *nm* : thrush
zozobra *nf* : anxiety, worry
zozobrar *vi* : to capsize
zueco *nm* : clog (shoe)
zulú¹ *adj & nmf* : Zulu
zulú² *nm* : Zulu (language)
zumaque *nm* : sumac
zumbar *vi* : to buzz, to hum — *vt fam* **1** : to hit, to thrash **2** : to make fun of
zumbido *nm* : buzzing, humming
zumo *nf* JUGO : juice
zurcir {83} *vt* : to darn, to mend
zurdo¹, -da *adj* : left-handed
zurdo², -da *n* : left-handed person
zurza, etc. → **zurcir**
zutano, -na → **fulano**

English–Spanish Dictionary

A

a¹ ['eɪ] *n, pl* **a's** *or* **as** ['eɪz] : primera letra del alfabeto inglés

a² [ə, 'eɪ] *art* (**an** [ən, 'æn] before vowel or silent *h)* **1** : un *m*, una *f* ⟨a house : una casa⟩ ⟨half an hour : media hora⟩ ⟨what a surprise! : ¡qué sorpresa!⟩ **2** PER : por, a la, al ⟨30 kilometers an hour : 30 kilómetros por hora⟩ ⟨twice a month : dos veces al mes⟩

aardvark ['ɑrd,vɑrk] *n* : oso *m* hormiguero

aback [ə'bæk] *adv* **1** : por sorpresa **2 to be taken aback** : quedarse desconcertado

abacus ['æbəkəs] *n, pl* **abaci** ['æbə,saɪ, -,ki:] *or* **abacuses** : ábaco *m*

abaft [ə'bæft] *adv* : a popa

abalone [,æbə'lo:ni] *n* : abulón *m*, oreja *f* marina

abandon¹ [ə'bændən] *vt* **1** DESERT, FORSAKE : abandonar, desamparar (a alguien), desertar de (algo) **2** GIVE UP, SUSPEND : renunciar a, suspender ⟨he abandoned the search : suspendió la búsqueda⟩ **3** EVACUATE, LEAVE : abandonar, evacuar, dejar ⟨to abandon ship : abandonar el buque⟩ **4 to abandon oneself** : entregarse, abandonarse

abandon² *n* : desenfreno *m* ⟨with wild abandon : desenfrenadamente⟩

abandoned [ə'bændənd] *adj* **1** DESERTED : abandonado **2** UNRESTRAINED : desenfrenado, desinhibido

abandonment [ə'bændənmənt] *n* : abandono *m*, desamparo *m*

abase [ə'beɪs] *vt* **abased; abasing** : degradar, humillar, rebajar

abash [ə'bæʃ] *vt* : avergonzar, abochornar

abashed [ə'bæʃt] *adj* : avergonzado

abate [ə'beɪt] *vi* **abated; abating** : amainar, menguar, disminuir

abattoir ['æbə,twɑr] *n* : matadero *m*

abbess ['æbɪs, -,bɛs, -bəs] *n* : abadesa *f*

abbey ['æbi] *n, pl* **-beys** : abadía *f*

abbot ['æbət] *n* : abad *m*

abbreviate [ə'bri:vi,eɪt] *vt* **-ated; -ating** : abreviar

abbreviation [ə,bri:vi'eɪʃən] *n* : abreviación *f*, abreviatura *f*

ABC's [,eɪ,bi:'si:z] *npl* : abecé *m*

abdicate ['æbdɪ,keɪt] *v* **-cated; -cating** : abdicar

abdication [,æbdɪ'keɪʃən] *n* : abdicación *f*

abdomen ['æbdəmən, æb'do:mən] *n* : abdomen *m*, vientre *m*

abdominal [æb'dɑmənəl] *adj* : abdominal — **abdominally** *adv*

abduct [æb'dʌkt] *vt* : raptar, secuestrar

abduction [æb'dʌkʃən] *n* : rapto *m*, secuestro *m*

abductor [æb'dʌktər] *n* : raptor *m*, -tora *f*; secuestrador *m*, -dora *f*

abed [ə'bɛd] *adv & adj* : en cama

aberrant [æ'bɛrənt, 'æbərənt] *adj* **1** ABNORMAL : anormal, aberrante **2** ATYPICAL : anómalo, atípico

aberration [,æbə'reɪʃən] *n* **1** : aberración *f* **2** DERANGEMENT : perturbación *f* mental

abet [ə'bɛt] *vt* **abetted; abetting** ASSIST : ayudar ⟨to aid and abet : ser cómplice de⟩

abeyance [ə'beɪənts] *n* : desuso *m*, suspensión *f*

abhor [əb'hɔr, æb-] *vt* **-horred; -horring** : abominar, aborrecer

abhorrence [əb'hɔrənts, æb-] *n* : aborrecimiento *m*, odio *m*

abhorrent [əb'hɔrənt, æb-] *adj* : abominable, aborrecible, odioso

abide [ə'baɪd] *v* **abode** [ə'bo:d] *or* **abided; abiding** *vt* STAND : soportar, tolerar ⟨I can't abide them : no los puedo ver⟩ — *vi* **1** ENDURE : quedar, permanecer **2** DWELL : morar, residir **3 to abide by** : atenerse a

ability [ə'bɪləti] *n, pl* **-ties 1** CAPABILITY : aptitud *f*, capacidad *f*, facultad *f* **2** COMPETENCE : competencia *f* **3** TALENT : talento *m*, don *m*, habilidad *f*

abject ['æb,dʒɛkt, æb'-] *adj* **1** WRETCHED : miserable, desdichado **2** HOPELESS : abatido, desesperado **3** SERVILE : servil ⟨abject flattery : halagos serviles⟩ — **abjectly** *adv*

abjure [æb'dʒʊr] *vt* **-jured; -juring** : abjurar de

ablaze [ə'bleɪz] *adj* **1** BURNING : ardiendo, en llamas **2** RADIANT : resplandeciente, radiante

able ['eɪbəl] *adj* **abler; ablest 1** CAPABLE : capaz, hábil **2** COMPETENT : competente

ablution [ə'blu:ʃən] *n* : ablución *f* ⟨to perform one's ablutions : lavarse⟩

ably ['eɪbəli] *adv* : hábilmente, eficientemente

abnormal [æb'nɔrməl] *adj* : anormal — **abnormally** *adv*

abnormality [,æbnər'mæləti, -nɔr-] *n, pl* **-ties** : anormalidad *f*

aboard¹ [ə'bord] *adv* : a bordo

aboard² *prep* : a bordo de

abode¹ → abide

abode² [ə'bo:d] *n* : morada *f*, residencia *f*, vivienda *f*

abolish [ə'bɑlɪʃ] *vt* : abolir, suprimir

abolition [,æbə'lɪʃən] *n* : abolición *f*, supresión *f*

abominable [ə'bɑmənəbəl] *adj* DETESTABLE : abominable, aborrecible, espantoso

abominate [ə'bɑmə,neɪt] *vt* **-nated; -nating** : abominar, aborrecer

abomination [ə,bɑmə'neɪʃən] *n* : abominación *f*

aboriginal [,æbə'rɪdʒənəl] *adj* : aborigen, indígena

aborigine [,æbə'rɪdʒəni] *n* NATIVE : aborigen *mf*, indígena *mf*

abort [ə'bɔrt] *vt* **1** : abortar (en medicina) **2** CALL OFF : suspender, abandonar — *vi* : abortar, hacerse un aborto

abortion [ə'bɔrʃən] *n* : aborto *m*

abortive [ə'bɔrtɪv] *adj* UNSUCCESSFUL : fracasado, frustrado, malogrado

abound [ə'baʊnd] *vi* **to abound in** : abundar en, estar lleno de

about¹ [ə'baʊt] *adv* **1** APPROXIMATELY : aproximadamente, casi, más o menos **2** AROUND : por todas partes, alrededor ⟨the children are running about : los niños están corriendo por todas partes⟩ **3 to be about to** : estar a punto de **4 to be up and about** : estar levantado

about² *prep* **1** AROUND : alrededor de **2** CONCERNING : de, acerca de, sobre ⟨he always talks about politics : siempre habla de política⟩

above¹ [ə'bʌv] *adv* **1** OVERHEAD : por encima, arriba **2** : más arriba ⟨as stated above : como se indica más arriba⟩

above² *adj* : anterior, antedicho ⟨for the above reasons : por las razones antedichas⟩

above³ *prep* **1** OVER : encima de, arriba de, sobre **2** : superior a, por encima de ⟨he's above those things : él está por encima de esas cosas⟩ **3** : más de, superior a ⟨he earns above $50,000 : gana más de $50,000⟩ ⟨a number above 10 : un número superior a 10⟩ **4 above all** : sobre todo

aboveboard¹ [ə'bʌv'bord, -ˌbord] *adv* **open and aboveboard** : sin tapujos

aboveboard² *adj* : legítimo, sincero

abrade [ə'breɪd] *vt* **abraded; abrading 1** ERODE : erosionar, corroer **2** SCRAPE : escoriar, raspar

abrasion [ə'breɪʒən] *n* **1** SCRAPE, SCRATCH : raspadura *f*, rasguño *m* **2** EROSION : erosión *f*

abrasive¹ [ə'breɪsɪv] *adj* **1** ROUGH : abrasivo, áspero **2** BRUSQUE, IRRITATING : brusco, irritante

abrasive² *n* : abrasivo *m*

abreast [ə'brɛst] *adv* **1** : en fondo, al lado ⟨to march three abreast : marchar de tres en fondo⟩ **2 to keep abreast** : mantenerse al día

abridge [ə'brɪdʒ] *vt* **abridged; abridging** : compendiar, resumir

abridgment *or* **abridgement** [ə'brɪdʒmənt] *n* : compendio *m*, resumen *m*

abroad [ə'brɔd] *adv* **1** ABOUT, WIDELY : por todas partes, en todas direcciones ⟨the news spread abroad : la noticia corrió por todas partes⟩ **2** OVERSEAS : en el extranjero, en el exterior

abrogate ['æbrəˌgeɪt] *vt* **-gated; -gating** : abrogar

abrupt [ə'brʌpt] *adj* **1** SUDDEN : abrupto, repentino, súbito **2** BRUSQUE, CURT : brusco, cortante — **abruptly** *adv*

abscess ['æbˌsɛs] *n* : absceso *m*

abscond [æb'skɑnd] *vi* : huir, fugarse

absence ['æbsənts] *n* **1** : ausencia *f* (de una persona) **2** LACK : falta *f*, carencia *f*

absent¹ [æb'sɛnt] *vt* **to absent oneself** : ausentarse

absent² ['æbsənt] *adj* : ausente

absentee [ˌæbsən'tiː] *n* : ausente *mf*

absentminded [ˌæbsənt'maɪndəd] *adj* : distraído, despistado

absentmindedly [ˌæbsənt'maɪndədli] *adv* : distraídamente

absentmindedness [ˌæbsənt'maɪndədnəs] *n* : distracción *f*, despiste *m*

absolute ['æbsəˌluːt, ˌæbsə'luːt] *adj* **1** COMPLETE, PERFECT : completo, pleno, perfecto **2** UNCONDITIONAL : absoluto, incondicional **3** DEFINITE : categórico, definitivo

absolutely ['æbsəˌluːtli, ˌæbsə'luːtli] *adv* **1** COMPLETELY : completamente, absolutamente **2** CERTAINLY : desde luego ⟨do you agree? absolutely! : ¿estás de acuerdo? ¡desde luego!⟩

absolution [ˌæbsə'luːʃən] *n* : absolución *f*

absolutism ['æbsəˌluːˌtɪzəm] *n* : absolutismo *m*

absolve [əb'zɑlv, æb-, -'sɑlv] *vt* **-solved; -solving** : absolver, perdonar

absorb [əb'zɔrb, æb-, -'sɔrb] *vt* **1** : absorber, embeber (un líquido), amortiguar (un golpe, la luz) **2** ENGROSS : absorber **3** ASSIMILATE : asimilar

absorbed [əb'zɔrbd, æb-, -'sɔrbd] *adj* ENGROSSED : absorto, ensimismado

absorbency [əb'zɔrbəntsi, æb-, -'sɔr-] *n* : absorbencia *f*

absorbent [əb'zɔrbənt, æb-, -'sɔr-] *adj* : absorbente

absorbing [əb'zɔrbɪŋ, æb-, -'sɔr-] *adj* : absorbente, fascinante

absorption [əb'zɔrpʃən, æb-, -'sɔrp-] *n* **1** : absorción *f* **2** CONCENTRATION : concentración *f*

abstain [əb'steɪn, æb-] *vi* : abstenerse

abstainer [əb'steɪnər, æb-] *n* : abstemio *m*, -mia *f*

abstemious [æb'stiːmiəs] *adj* : abstemio, sobrio — **abstemiously** *adv*

abstention [əb'stɛntʃən, æb-] *n* : abstención *f*

abstinence ['æbstənənts] *n* : abstinencia *f*

abstract¹ [æb'strækt, 'æbˌ-] *vt* **1** EXTRACT : abstraer, extraer **2** SUMMARIZE : compendiar, resumir

abstract² *adj* : abstracto — **abstractly** [æb'stræktli, 'æbˌ-] *adv*

abstract³ ['æbˌstrækt] *n* : resumen *m*, compendio *m*, sumario *m*

abstraction [æb'strækʃən] *n* **1** : abstracción *f*, idea *f* abstracta **2** ABSENT-MINDEDNESS : distracción *f*

abstruse [əb'struːs, æb-] *adj* : abstruso, recóndito — **abstrusely** *adv*

absurd [əb'sərd, -'zərd] *adj* : absurdo, ridículo, disparatado — **absurdly** *adv*

absurdity [əb'sərdəti, -'zər-] *n, pl* **-ties** 1 : absurdo *m* 2 NONSENSE : disparate *m*, despropósito *m*
abundance [ə'bʌndənts] *n* : abundancia *f*
abundant [ə'bʌndənt] *adj* : abundante, cuantioso, copioso
abundantly [ə'bʌndəntli] *adv* : abundantemente, en abundancia
abuse¹ [ə'bju:z] *vt* **abused; abusing** 1 MISUSE : abusar de 2 MISTREAT : maltratar 3 REVILE : insultar, injuriar, denostar
abuse² [ə'bju:s] *n* 1 MISUSE : abuso *m* 2 MISTREATMENT : abuso *m*, maltrato *m* 3 INSULTS : insultos *mpl*, improperios *mpl* ⟨a string of abuse : una serie de improperios⟩
abuser [ə'bju:zər] *n* : abusador *m*, -dora *f*
abusive [ə'bju:sɪv] *adj* 1 ABUSING : abusivo 2 INSULTING : ofensivo, injurioso, insultante — **abusively** *adv*
abut [ə'bʌt] *v* **abutted; abutting** *vt* : bordear — *vi* **to abut on** : colindar con
abutment [ə'bʌtmənt] *n* 1 BUTTRESS : contrafuerte *m*, estribo *m* 2 CLOSENESS : contigüidad *f*
abysmal [ə'bɪzməl] *adj* 1 DEEP : abismal, insondable 2 TERRIBLE : atroz, desastroso
abysmally [ə'bɪzməli] *adv* : desastrosamente, terriblemente
abyss [ə'bɪs, 'æbɪs] *n* : abismo *m*, sima *f*

acacia [ə'keɪʃə] *n* : acacia *f*
academic¹ [ˌækə'dɛmɪk] *adj* 1 : académico 2 THEORETICAL : teórico — **academically** [-mɪkli] *adv*
academic² *n* : académico *m*, -ca *f*
academician [ˌækədə'mɪʃən] *n* → **academic**
academy [ə'kædəmi] *n, pl* **-mies** : academia *f*
acanthus [ə'kænθəs] *n* : acanto *m*
accede [æk'si:d] *vi* **-ceded; -ceding** 1 AGREE : acceder, consentir 2 ASCEND : subir, acceder ⟨he acceded to the throne : subió al trono⟩
accelerate [ɪk'sɛləˌreɪt, æk-] *v* **-ated; -ating** *vt* : acelerar, apresurar — *vi* : acelerar (dícese de un carro)
acceleration [ɪkˌsɛlə'reɪʃən, æk-] *n* : aceleración *f*
accelerator [ɪk'sɛləˌreɪtər, æk-] *n* : acelerador *m*
accent¹ ['ækˌsɛnt, æk'sɛnt] *vt* : acentuar
accent² ['ækˌsɛnt, -sənt] *n* 1 : acento *m* 2 EMPHASIS, STRESS : énfasis *m*, acento *m*
accentuate [ɪk'sɛntʃuˌeɪt, æk-] *vt* **-ated; -ating** : acentuar, poner énfasis en
accept [ɪk'sɛpt, æk-] *vt* 1 : aceptar 2 ACKNOWLEDGE : admitir, reconocer
acceptability [ɪkˌsɛptə'bɪləti, æk-] *n* : aceptabilidad *f*

acceptable [ɪk'sɛptəbəl, æk-] *adj* : aceptable, admisible — **acceptably** [-bli] *adv*
acceptance [ɪk'sɛptənts, æk-] *n* : aceptación *f*, aprobación *f*
access¹ ['ækˌsɛs] *vt* : obtener acceso a, entrar a
access² *n* : acceso *m*
accessibility [ɪkˌsɛsə'bɪləti] *n, pl* **-ties** : accesibilidad *f*
accessible [ɪk'sɛsəbəl, æk-] *adj* : accesible, asequible
accession [ɪk'sɛʃən, æk-] *n* 1 : ascenso *f*, subida *f* (al trono, etc.) 2 ACQUISITION : adquisición *f*
accessory¹ [ɪk'sɛsəri, æk-] *adj* : auxiliar
accessory² *n, pl* **-ries** 1 : accesorio *m*, complemento *m* 2 ACCOMPLICE : cómplice *mf*
accident ['æksədənt] *n* 1 MISHAP : accidente *m* 2 CHANCE : casualidad *f*
accidental [ˌæksə'dɛntəl] *adj* : accidental, casual, imprevisto, fortuito
accidentally [ˌæksə'dɛntəli, -'dɛntli] *adv* 1 BY CHANCE : por casualidad 2 UNINTENTIONALLY : sin querer, involuntariamente
acclaim¹ [ə'kleɪm] *vt* : aclamar, elogiar
acclaim² *n* : aclamación *f*, elogio *m*
acclamation [ˌæklə'meɪʃən] *n* : aclamación *f*
acclimate ['æklə,meɪt, ə'klaɪmət] → **acclimatize**
acclimatize [ə'klaɪməˌtaɪz] *v* **-tized; -tizing** *vt* 1 : aclimatar 2 **to acclimatize oneself** : aclimatarse
accolade ['ækə,leɪd, -,lɑd] *n* 1 PRAISE : elogio *m* 2 AWARD : galardón *m*
accommodate [ə'kamə,deɪt] *vt* **-dated; -dating** 1 ADAPT : acomodar, adaptar 2 SATISFY : tener·en cuenta, satisfacer 3 HOLD : dar cabida a, tener cabida para
accommodation [əˌkamə'deɪʃən] *n* 1 : adaptación *f*, adecuación *f* 2 **accommodations** *npl* LODGING : alojamiento *m*, hospedaje *m*
accompaniment [ə'kʌmpənəmənt, -'kam-] *n* : acompañamiento *m*
accompanist [ə'kʌmpənɪst, -'kam-] *n* : acompañante *mf*
accompany [ə'kʌmpəni, -'kam-] *vt* **-nied; -nying** : acompañar
accomplice [ə'kampləs, -'kʌm-] *n* : cómplice *mf*
accomplish [ə'kamplɪʃ, -'kʌm-] *vt* : efectuar, realizar, lograr, llevar a cabo
accomplished [ə'kamplɪʃt, -'kʌm-] *adj* : consumado, logrado
accomplishment [ə'kamplɪʃmənt, -'kʌm-] *n* 1 ACHIEVEMENT : logro *m*, éxito *m* 2 SKILL : destreza *f*, habilidad *f*
accord¹ [ə'kɔrd] *vt* GRANT : conceder, otorgar — *vi* **to accord with** : concordar con, conformarse con
accord² *n* 1 AGREEMENT : acuerdo *m*, convenio *m* 2 VOLITION : voluntad *f*

⟨on one's own accord : voluntaria-
mente, de motu proprio⟩
accordance [ə'kɔrdənts] *n* **1** ACCORD
: acuerdo *m*, conformidad *f* **2 in accordance with** : conforme a, según, de
acuerdo con
accordingly [ə'kɔrdɪŋli] *adv* **1** CORRE-
SPONDINGLY : en consecuencia **2** CON-
SEQUENTLY : por consiguiente, por lo
tanto
according to [ə'kɔrdɪŋ] *prep* : según, de
acuerdo con, conforme a
accordion [ə'kɔrdiən] *n* : acordeón *m*
accordionist [ə'kɔrdiənɪst] *n* : acordeonista *mf*
accost [ə'kɔst] *vt* : abordar, dirigirse a
account[1] [ə'kaʊnt] *vt* : considerar, estimar ⟨he accounts himself lucky : se
considera afortunado⟩ — *vi* **to account for** : dar cuenta de, explicar
account[2] *n* **1** : cuenta*f* ⟨savings account
: cuenta de ahorros⟩ **2** EXPLANATION
: versión*f*, explicación*f* **3** REPORT : relato *m*, informe *m* **4** IMPORTANCE : importancia *f* ⟨to be of no account : no
tener importancia⟩ **5 on account of**
BECAUSE OF : a causa de, debido a, por
6 on no account : de ninguna manera
accountability [ə,kaʊntə'bɪləţi] *n* : responsabilidad *f*
accountable [ə'kaʊntəbəl] *adj* : responsable
accountant [ə'kaʊntənt] *n* : contador *m*,
-dora *f*; contable *mf Spain*
accounting [ə'kaʊntɪŋ] *n* : contabilidad
f
accoutrements *or* **accouterments** [ə-
'ku:trəmənts, -'ku:țər-] *npl* **1** EQUIP-
MENT : equipo *m*, avíos *mpl* **2** ACCES-
SORIES : accesorios *mpl* **3** TRAPPINGS
: símbolos *mpl* ⟨the accoutrements of
power : los símbolos del poder⟩
accredit [ə'krɛdət] *vt* : acreditar, autorizar
accreditation [ə,krɛdə'teɪʃən] *n* : acreditación *f*, homologación *f*
accretion [ə'kri:ʃən] *n* **1** : acrecentamiento *m* (proceso) **2** : acreción *f*,
acrecencia *f* (producto)
accrual [ə'kru:əl] *n* : incremento *m*, acumulación *f*
accrue [ə'kru:] *vi* -**crued; -cruing** : acumularse, aumentarse
accumulate [ə'kju:mjə,leɪt] *v* -**lated;
-lating** *vt* : acumular, amontonar — *vi*
: acumularse, amontonarse
accumulation [ə,kju:mjə'leɪʃən] *n* : acumulación *f*, amontonamiento *m*
accuracy ['ækjərəsi] *n* : exactitud*f*, precisión *f*
accurate ['ækjərət] *adj* : exacto, correcto, fiel, preciso — **accurately** *adv*
accusation [,ækjə'zeɪʃən] *n* : acusación
f
accusatory [ə'kju:zə,tori] *adj* : acusatorio
accuse [ə'kju:z] *vt* -**cused; -cusing**
: acusar, delatar, denunciar

accused [ə'kju:zd] *ns & pl* DEFENDANT
: acusado *m*, -da *f*
accuser [ə'kju:zər] *n* : acusador *m*, -dora
f
accustom [ə'kʌstəm] *vt* : acostumbrar,
habituar
ace ['eɪs] *n* : as *m*
acerbic [ə'sərbɪk, æ-] *adj* : acerbo, mordaz
acetate ['æsə,teɪt] *n* : acetato *m*
acetic [ə'si:ţɪk] *adj* : acético
acetone ['æsə,to:n] *n* : acetona *f*
acetylene [ə'sɛţələn, -ţə,li:n] *n* : acetileno *m*
ache[1] ['eɪk] *vi* **ached; aching** **1** : doler
2 to ache for : anhelar, ansiar
ache[2] *n* : dolor *m*
achieve [ə'tʃi:v] *vt* **achieved; achieving**
: lograr, alcanzar, conseguir, realizar
achievement [ə'tʃi:vmənt] *n* : logro *m*,
éxito *m*, realización *f*
acid[1] ['æsəd] *adj* **1** SOUR : ácido, agrio
2 CAUSTIC, SHARP : acerbo, mordaz —
acidly *adv*
acid[2] *n* : ácido *m*
acidic [ə'sɪdɪk, æ-] *adj* : ácido
acidity [ə'sɪdəţi, æ-] *n, pl* -**ties** : acidez *f*
acknowledge [ɪk'nɑlɪdʒ, æk-] *vt* -**edged;
-edging** **1** ADMIT : reconocer, admitir
2 RECOGNIZE : reconocer **3 to acknowledge receipt of** : acusar recibo
de
acknowledgment [ɪk'nɑlɪdʒmənt, æk-] *n*
1 RECOGNITION : reconocimiento *m* **2**
THANKS : agradecimiento *m*
acme ['ækmi] *n* : colmo *m*, apogeo *m*,
cúspide *f*
acne ['ækni] *n* : acné *m*
acolyte ['ækə,laɪt] *n* : acólito *m*
acorn ['eɪ,kɔrn, -kərn] *n* : bellota *f*
acoustic [ə'ku:stɪk] *or* **acoustical**
[-stɪkəl] *adj* : acústico — **acoustically**
adv
acoustics [ə'ku:stɪks] *ns & pl* : acústica
f
acquaint [ə'kweɪnt] *vt* **1** INFORM : enterar, informar **2** FAMILIARIZE : familiarizar **3 to be acquainted with**
: conocer a (una persona), estar al tanto de (un hecho)
acquaintance [ə'kweɪntənts] *n* **1**
KNOWLEDGE : conocimiento *m* **2**
: conocido *m*, -da *f* ⟨friends and ac-
quaintances : amigos y conocidos⟩
acquiesce [,ækwi'ɛs] *vi* -**esced; -escing**
: consentir, conformarse
acquiescence [,ækwi'ɛsənts] *n* : consentimiento *m*, aquiescencia *f*
acquire [ə'kwaɪr] *vt* -**quired; -quiring**
: adquirir, obtener
acquisition [,ækwə'zɪʃən] *n* : adquisición *f*
acquisitive [ə'kwɪzəţɪv] *adj* : adquisitivo, codicioso
acquit [ə'kwɪt] *vt* -**quitted; -quitting** **1**
: absolver, exculpar **2 to acquit one-
self** : comportarse, defenderse
acquittal [ə'kwɪţəl] *n* : absolución *f*, exculpación *f*

acre ['eɪkər] *n* : acre *m*
acreage ['eɪkərɪdʒ] *n* : superficie *f* en acres
acrid ['ækrəd] *adj* **1** BITTER : acre **2** CAUSTIC : acre, mordaz — **acridly** *adv*
acrimonious [,ækrə'moːniəs] *adj* : áspero, cáustico, sarcástico
acrimony ['ækrə,moːni] *n, pl* **-nies** : acrimonia *f*
acrobat ['ækrə,bæt] *n* : acróbata *mf*, saltimbanqui *mf*
acrobatic [,ækrə'bætɪk] *adj* : acrobático
acrobatics [,ækrə'bætɪks] *ns & pl* : acrobacia *f*
acronym ['ækrə,nɪm] *n* : acrónimo *m*
across¹ [ə'krɔs] *adv* **1** CROSSWISE : al través **2** : a través, del otro lado ⟨he's already across : ya está del otro lado⟩ **3** : de ancho ⟨40 feet across : 40 pies de ancho⟩
across² *prep* **1** : al otro lado de ⟨across the street : al otro lado de la calle⟩ **2** : a través de ⟨a log across the road : un tronco a través del camino⟩
acrylic [ə'krɪlɪk] *n* : acrílico *m*
act¹ ['ækt] *vi* **1** PERFORM : actuar, interpretar **2** FEIGN, PRETEND : fingir, simular **3** BEHAVE : comportarse **4** FUNCTION : actuar, servir, funcionar **5** : tomar medidas ⟨he acted to save the business : tomó medidas para salvar el negocio⟩ **6 to act as** : servir de, hacer de
act² *n* **1** DEED : acto *m*, hecho *m*, acción *f* **2** DECREE : ley *f*, decreto *m* **3** : acto *m* (en una obra de teatro), número *m* (en un espectáculo) **4** PRETENSE : fingimiento *m*
action ['ækʃən] *n* **1** DEED : acción *f*, acto *m*, hecho *m* **2** BEHAVIOR : actuación *f*, comportamiento *m* **3** LAWSUIT : demanda *f* **4** MOVEMENT : movimiento *m* **5** COMBAT : combate *m* **6** PLOT : acción *f*, trama *f* **7** MECHANISM : mecanismo *m*
activate ['æktə,veɪt] *vt* **-vated; -vating** : activar
activation [,æktə'veɪʃən] *n* : activación *f*
active ['æktɪv] *adj* **1** MOVING : activo, en movimiento **2** LIVELY : vigoroso, enérgico **3** : en actividad ⟨an active volcano : un volcán en actividad⟩ **4** OPERATIVE : vigente
actively ['æktɪvli] *adv* : activamente, enérgicamente
activist ['æktɪvɪst] *n* : activista *mf* — **activist** *adj*
activity [æk'tɪvəti] *n, pl* **-ties** **1** MOVEMENT : actividad *f*, movimiento *m* **2** VIGOR : vigor *m*, energía *f* **3** OCCUPATION : actividad *f*, ocupación *f*
actor ['æktər] *n* : actor *m*, artista *mf*
actress ['æktrəs] *n* : actriz *f*
actual ['æktʃuəl] *adj* : real, verdadero
actuality [,æktʃu'æləti] *n, pl* **-ties** : realidad *f*

actually ['æktʃuəli, -ʃəli] *adv* : realmente, en realidad
actuary ['æktʃu,ɛri] *n, pl* **-aries** : actuario *m*, -ria *f* de seguros
acumen [ə'kjuːmən] *n* : perspicacia *f*
acupuncture ['ækjuˌpʌŋktʃər] *n* : acupuntura *f*
acute [ə'kjuːt] *adj* **acuter; acutest** **1** SHARP : agudo **2** PERCEPTIVE : perspicaz, sagaz **3** KEEN : fino, muy desarrollado, agudo ⟨an acute sense of smell : un fino olfato⟩ **4** SEVERE : grave **5 acute angle** : ángulo *m* agudo
acutely [ə'kjuːtli] *adv* : intensamente ⟨to be acutely aware : estar perfectamente consciente⟩
acuteness [ə'kjuːtnəs] *n* : agudeza *f*
ad ['æd] → **advertisement**
adage ['ædɪdʒ] *n* : adagio *m*, refrán *m*, dicho *m*
adamant ['ædəmənt, -ˌmænt] *adj* : firme, categórico, inflexible — **adamantly** *adv*
Adam's apple ['ædəmz] *n* : nuez *f* de Adán
adapt [ə'dæpt] *vt* : adaptar, ajustar — *vi* : adaptarse
adaptability [ə,dæptə'bɪləti] *n* : adaptabilidad *f*, flexibilidad *f*
adaptable [ə'dæptəbəl] *adj* : adaptable, amoldable
adaptation [,æ,dæp'teɪʃən, -dəp-] *n* **1** : adaptación *f*, modificación *f* **2** VERSION : versión *f*
adapter [ə'dæptər] *n* : adaptador *m*
add ['æd] *vt* **1** : añadir, agregar ⟨to add a comment : añadir una observación⟩ **2** : sumar ⟨add these numbers : suma estos números⟩ — *vi* : sumar (en total)
adder ['ædər] *n* : víbora *f*
addict¹ [ə'dɪkt] *vt* : causar adicción en
addict² ['ædɪkt] *n* **1** : adicto *m*, -ta *f* **2 drug addict** : drogadicto *m*, -ta *f*; toxicómano *m*, -na *f*
addiction [ə'dɪkʃən] *n* **1** : adicción *f*, dependencia *f* **2 drug addiction** : drogadicción *f*
addictive [ə'dɪktɪv] *adj* : adictivo
addition [ə'dɪʃən] *n* **1** : adición *f*, añadidura *f* **2 in ~** : además, también
additional [ə'dɪʃənəl] *adj* : extra, adicional, de más
additionally [ə'dɪʃənəli] *adv* : además, adicionalmente
additive ['ædətɪv] *n* : aditivo *m*
addle ['ædəl] *vt* **-dled; -dling** : confundir, enturbiar
address¹ [ə'drɛs] *vt* **1** : dirigirse a, pronunciar un discurso ante ⟨to address a jury : dirigirse a un jurado⟩ **2** : dirigir, ponerle la dirección a ⟨to address a letter : dirigir una carta⟩
address² [ə'drɛs, 'æ,drɛs] *n* **1** SPEECH : discurso *m*, alocución *f* **2** : dirección *f* (de una residencia, etc.)
addressee [,æ,drɛ'siː, ə-] *n* : destinatario *m*, -ria *f*

adduce [ə-'duːs, 'djuːs] *vt* **-duced; -duc-ing** : aducir

adenoids ['æd₁nɔɪd, -dən₁ɔɪd] *npl* : adenoides *fpl*

adept [ə'dɛpt] *adj* : experto, hábil — **adeptly** *adv*

adequacy ['ædɪkwəsi] *n, pl* **-cies** : cantidad *f* suficiente

adequate ['ædɪkwət] *adj* **1** SUFFICIENT : adecuado, suficiente **2** ACCEPTABLE, PASSABLE : adecuado, aceptable

adequately ['ædɪkwətli] *adv* : suficientemente, apropiadamente

adhere [æd'hɪr, əd-] *vi* **-hered; -hering 1** STICK : pegarse, adherirse **2 to adhere to** : adherirse a (una política, etc.), cumplir con (una promesa)

adherence [æd'hɪrənts, əd-] *n* : adhesión *f*, adherencia *f*, observancia *f* (de una ley, etc.)

adherent[1] [æd'hɪrənt, əd-] *adj* : adherente, adhesivo, pegajoso

adherent[2] *n* : adepto *m*, -ta *f*; partidario *m*, -ria *f*

adhesion [æd'hiːʒən, əd-] *n* : adhesión *f*

adhesive[1] [æd'hiːsɪv, əd-, -zɪv] *adj* : adhesivo

adhesive[2] *n* : adhesivo *m*, pegamento *m*

adjacent [ə'dʒeɪsənt] *adj* : adyacente, colindante, contiguo

adjective ['ædʒɪktɪv] *n* : adjetivo *m* — **adjectival** [₁ædʒɪk'taɪvəl] *adj*

adjoin [ə'dʒɔɪn] *vt* : lindar con, colindar con

adjoining [ə'dʒɔɪnɪŋ] *adj* : contiguo, colindante

adjourn [ə'dʒərn] *vt* : levantar, suspender ⟨the meeting is adjourned : se levanta la sesión⟩ — *vi* : aplazarse

adjournment [ə'dʒərnmənt] *n* : suspensión *f*, aplazamiento *m*

adjudicate [ə'dʒuːdɪ₁keɪt] *vt* **-cated; -cating** : juzgar, arbitrar

adjudication [ə₁dʒuːdɪ'keɪʃən] *n* **1** JUDGING : arbitrio *m* (judicial) **2** JUDGMENT : fallo *m*

adjunct ['æ₁dʒʌŋkt] *n* : adjunto *m*, complemento *m*

adjust [ə'dʒʌst] *vt* : ajustar, arreglar, regular — *vi* **to adjust to** : adaptarse a

adjustable [ə'dʒʌstəbəl] *adj* : ajustable, regulable, graduable

adjustment [ə'dʒʌstmənt] *n* : ajuste *m*, modificación *f*

ad–lib[1] ['æd'lɪb] *v* **-libbed; -libbing** : improvisar

ad–lib[2] *adj* : improvisado

administer [æd'mɪnəstər, əd-] *vt* : administrar

administration [æd₁mɪnə'streɪʃən, əd-] *n* **1** MANAGING : administración *f*, dirección *f* **2** GOVERNMENT, MANAGEMENT : administración *f*, gobierno *m*

administrative [æd'mɪnə₁streɪtɪv, əd-] *adj* : administrativo — **administratively** *adv*

administrator [æd'mɪnə₁streɪtər, əd-] *n* : administrador *m*, -dora *f*

admirable ['ædmərəbəl] *adj* : admirable, loable — **admirably** *adv*

admiral ['ædmərəl] *n* : almirante *mf*

admiration [₁ædmə'reɪʃən] *n* : admiración *f*

admire [æd'maɪr] *vt* **-mired; -miring** : admirar

admirer [æd'maɪrər] *n* : admirador *m*, -dora *f*

admiring [æd'maɪrɪŋ] *adj* : admirativo, de admiración

admiringly [æd'maɪrɪŋli] *adv* : con admiración

admissible [æd'mɪsəbəl] *adj* : admisible, aceptable

admission [æd'mɪʃən] *n* **1** ADMITTANCE : entrada *f*, admisión *f* **2** ACKNOWLEDGMENT : reconocimiento *m*, admisión *f*

admit [æd'mɪt, əd-] *vt* **-mitted; -mitting 1** : admitir, dejar entrar ⟨the museum admits children : el museo deja entrar a los niños⟩ **2** ACKNOWLEDGE : reconocer, admitir

admittance [æd'mɪtənts, əd-] *n* : admisión *f*, entrada *f*, acceso *m*

admittedly [æd'mɪtədli, əd-] *adv* : la verdad es que, lo cierto es que ⟨admittedly we went too fast : la verdad es que fuimos demasiado de prisa⟩

admonish [æd'manɪʃ, əd-] *vt* : amonestar, reprender

admonition [₁ædmə'nɪʃən] *n* : admonición *f*

ado [ə'duː] *n* **1** FUSS : ruido *m*, alboroto *m* **2** TROUBLE : dificultad *f*, lío *m* **3 without further ado** : sin más preámbulos

adobe [ə'doːbi] *n* : adobe *m*

adolescence [₁ædəl'ɛsənts] *n* : adolescencia *f*

adolescent[1] [₁ædəl'ɛsənt] *adj* : adolescente, de adolescencia

adolescent[2] *n* : adolescente *mf*

adopt [ə'dapt] *vt* : adoptar

adoption [ə'dapʃən] *n* : adopción *f*

adoptive [ə'daptɪv] *adj* : adoptivo

adorable [ə'dorəbəl] *adj* : adorable, encantador

adorably [ə'dorəbli] *adv* : de manera adorable

adoration [₁ædə'reɪʃən] *n* : adoración *f*

adore [ə'dor] *vt* **adored; adoring 1** WORSHIP : adorar **2** LOVE : querer, adorar **3** LIKE : encantarle (algo a uno), gustarle mucho (algo a uno) ⟨I adore your new dress : me encanta tu vestido nuevo⟩

adorn [ə'dorn] *vt* : adornar, ornar, engalanar

adornment [ə'dornmənt] *n* : adorno *m*, decoración *f*

adrenaline [ə'drɛnələn] *n* : adrenalina *f*

adrift [ə'drɪft] *adj & adv* : a la deriva

adroit [ə'drɔɪt] *adj* : diestro, hábil — **adroitly** *adv*

adroitness [ə'drɔɪtnəs] *n* : destreza *f*, habilidad *f*

adult[1] [ə'dʌlt, 'æˌdʌlt] *adj* : adulto
adult[2] *n* : adulto *m*, -ta *f*
adulterate [ə'dʌltəˌreɪt] *vt* **-ated; -ating** : adulterar
adulterous [ə'dʌltərəs] *adj* : adúltero
adultery [ə'dʌltəri] *n, pl* **-teries** : adulterio *m*
adulthood [ə'dʌltˌhʊd]*n* : adultez*f*, edad *f* adulta
advance[1] [æd'vænts, əd-] *v* **-vanced; -vancing** *vt* **1** : avanzar, adelantar ⟨to advance troops : avanzar las tropas⟩ **2** PROMOTE : ascender, promover **3** PROPOSE : proponer, presentar **4** : adelantar, anticipar ⟨they advanced me next month's salary : me adelantaron el sueldo del próximo mes⟩ — *vi* **1** PROCEED : avanzar, adelantarse **2** PROGRESS : progresar
advance[2] *adj* : anticipado ⟨advance notice : previo aviso⟩
advance[3] *n* **1** PROGRESSION : avance *m* **2** PROGRESS : adelanto *m*, mejora *f*, progreso *m* **3** RISE : aumento *m*, alza *f* **4** LOAN : anticipo *m*, préstamo *m* **5** in ~ : por adelantado
advanced [æd'væntst, əd-] *adj* **1** DEVELOPED : avanzado, desarrollado **2** PRECOCIOUS : adelantado, precoz **3** HIGHER : superior
advancement [æd'væntsmənt, əd-] *n* **1** FURTHERANCE : fomento *m*, adelantamiento *m*, progreso *m* **2** PROMOTION : ascenso *m*
advantage [əd'væntɪʤ, æd-] *n* **1** SUPERIORITY : ventaja *f*, superioridad *f* **2** GAIN : provecho *m*, partido *m* **3** to take advantage of : aprovecharse de
advantageous [ˌædˌvænˈteɪʤəs, -vən-] *adj* : ventajoso, provechoso — **advantageously** *adv*
advent ['ædˌvɛnt] *n* **1** Advent : Adviento *m* **2** ARRIVAL : advenimiento *m*, venida *f*
adventure [æd'vɛntʃər, əd-] *n* : aventura *f*
adventurer [æd'vɛntʃərər, əd-] *n* : aventurero *m*, -ra *f*
adventurous [æd'vɛntʃərəs, əd-] *adj* **1** : intrépido, aventurero ⟨an adventurous traveler : un viajero intrépido⟩ **2** RISKY : arriesgado, aventurado
adverb ['ædˌvərb] *n* : adverbio *m* — **adverbial** [æd'vərbiəl] *adj*
adversary ['ædvərˌsɛri] *n, pl* **-saries** : adversario *m*, -ria *f*
adverse [æd'vərs, 'ædˌ] *adj* **1** OPPOSING : opuesto, contrario **2** UNFAVORABLE : adverso, desfavorable — **adversely** *adv*
adversity [æd'vərsəti, əd-]*n, pl* **-ties** : adversidad *f*
advertise ['ædvərˌtaɪz] *v* **-tised; -tising** *vt* : anunciar, hacerle publicidad a — *vi* : hacer publicidad, hacer propaganda
advertisement ['ædvərˌtaɪzmənt; æd'vərtəzmənt] *n* : anuncio *m*

advertiser ['ædvərˌtaɪzər]*n* : anunciante *mf*
advertising ['ædvərˌtaɪzɪŋ] *n* : publicidad *f*, propaganda *f*
advice [æd'vaɪs] *n* : consejo *m*, recomendación *f* ⟨take my advice : sigue mis consejos⟩
advisability [ædˌvaɪzə'bɪləti, əd-] *n* : conveniencia *f*
advisable [æd'vaɪzəbəl, əd-] *adj* : aconsejable, recomendable, conveniente
advise [æd'vaɪz, əd-] *v* **-vised; -vising** *vt* **1** COUNSEL : aconsejar, asesorar **2** RECOMMEND : recomendar **3** INFORM : informar, notificar — *vi* : dar consejo
adviser *or* **advisor** [æd'vaɪzər, əd-] *n* : consejero *m*, -ra *f*; asesor *m*, -sora *f*
advisory [æd'vaɪzəri, əd-] *adj* **1** : consultivo **2 in an advisory capacity** : como asesor
advocacy ['ædvəkəsi] *n* : promoción *f*, apoyo *m*
advocate[1] ['ædvəˌkeɪt]*vt* **-cated; -cating** : recomendar, abogar por, ser partidario de
advocate[2] ['ædvəkət] *n* : defensor *m*, -sora *f*; partidario *m*, -ria *f*
adze ['ædz] *n* : azuela *f*
aeon ['iːən, 'iːˌɑn] *n* : eón *m*, siglo *m*, eternidad *f*
aerate ['ærˌeɪt] *vt* **-ated; -ating** : gasear (un líquido), oxigenar (la sangre)
aerial[1] ['æriəl] *adj* : aéreo
aerial[2] *n* : antena *f*
aerie ['æri, 'ɪri, 'eɪəri] *n* : aguilera *f*
aerobic [ˌær'oːbɪk] *adj* : aerobio, aeróbico ⟨aerobic exercises : ejercicios aeróbicos⟩
aerobics [ˌær'oːbɪks] *ns & pl* : aeróbic *m*
aerodynamic [ˌæroːdaɪ'næmɪk] *adj* : aerodinámico — **aerodynamically** [-mɪkli] *adv*
aerodynamics [ˌæroːdaɪ'næmɪks] *n* : aerodinámica *f*
aeronautical [ˌærə'nɔtɪkəl] *adj* : aeronáutico
aeronautics [ˌærə'nɔtɪks] *n* : aeronáutica *f*
aerosol ['ærəˌsɔl] *n* : aerosol *m*
aerospace[1] ['æroːˌspeɪs] *adj* : aeroespacial
aerospace[2] *n* : espacio *m*
aesthetic [ɛs'θɛtɪk] *adj* : estético — **aesthetically** [-tɪkli] *adv*
aesthetics [ɛs'θɛtɪks] *n* : estética *f*
afar [ə'fɑr] *adv* : lejos, a lo lejos
affability [ˌæfə'bɪləti] *n* : afabilidad *f*
affable ['æfəbəl] *adj* : afable — **affably** *adv*
affair [ə'fær] *n* **1** MATTER : asunto *m*, cuestión *f*, caso *m* **2** EVENT : ocasión *f*, acontecimiento *m* **3** LIAISON : amorío *m*, aventura *f* **4 business affairs** : negocios *mpl* **5 current affairs** : actualidades *fpl*
affect [ə'fɛkt, æ-] *vt* **1** INFLUENCE, TOUCH : afectar, tocar **2** FEIGN : fingir

affectation [ˌæˌfɛk'teɪʃən] n : afectación f

affected [ə'fɛktəd, æ-] adj **1** FEIGNED : afectado, fingido **2** MOVED : conmovido

affecting [ə'fɛktɪŋ, æ-] adj : conmovedor

affection [ə'fɛkʃən] n : afecto m, cariño m

affectionate [ə'fɛkʃənət] adj : afectuoso, cariñoso — **affectionately** adv

affidavit [ˌæfə'deɪvət, 'æfə,-] n : declaración f jurada, affidávit m

affiliate[1] [ə'fɪli,eɪt] v **-ated; -ating** vt : afiliar, asociar ⟨to be affiliated with : estar afiliado a⟩

affiliate[2] [ə'fɪliət] n : afiliado m, -da f (persona), filial f (organización)

affiliation [ə,fɪli'eɪʃən] n : afiliación f, filiación f

affinity [ə'fɪnəti] n, pl **-ties** : afinidad f

affirm [ə'fərm] vt : afirmar, aseverar, declarar

affirmation [ˌæfər'meɪʃən] n : afirmación f, aserto m, declaración f

affirmative[1] [ə'fərmətɪv] adj : afirmativo ⟨affirmative action : acción afirmativa⟩

affirmative[2] n **1** : afirmativa f **2 to answer in the affirmative** : responder afirmativamente, dar una respuesta afirmativa

affix [ə'fɪks] vt : fijar, poner, pegar

afflict [ə'flɪkt] vt **1** : afligir, aquejar **2 to be afflicted with** : padecer de, sufrir de

affliction [ə'flɪkʃən] n **1** TRIBULATION : aflicción f, tribulación f **2** AILMENT : enfermedad f, padecimiento m

affluence ['æ,flu:ənts; æ'flu:-, ə-] n : afluencia f, abundancia f, prosperidad f

affluent ['æ,flu:ənt; æ'flu:-, ə-] adj : próspero, adinerado

afford [ə'ford] vt **1** : tener los recursos para, permitirse el lujo de ⟨I can afford it : puedo permitírmelo, tengo con que comprarlo⟩ **2** PROVIDE : ofrecer, proporcionar, dar

affront[1] [ə'frʌnt] vt : afrentar, insultar, ofender

affront[2] n : afrenta f, insulto m, ofensa f

Afghan ['æf,gæn, -gən] n : afgano m, -na f — **Afghan** adj

afire [ə'faɪr] adj : ardiendo, en llamas

aflame [ə'fleɪm] adj : llameante, en llamas

afloat [ə'flo:t] adv & adj : a flote

afoot [ə'fʊt] adj **1** WALKING : a pie, andando **2** UNDER WAY : en marcha ⟨something suspicious is afoot : algo sospechoso se está tramando⟩

aforementioned [ə'for'mentʃ∫ənd] adj : antedicho, susodicho

aforesaid [ə'for,sɛd] adj : antes mencionado, antedicho

afraid [ə'freɪd] adj **1 to be afraid** : tener miedo **2 to be afraid that** : temerse que ⟨I'm afraid not : me temo que no⟩

afresh [ə'frɛʃ] adv **1** : de nuevo, otra vez **2 to start afresh** : volver a empezar

African ['æfrɪkən] n : africano m, -na f — **African** adj

Afro–American[1] [ˌæfroə'mɛrɪkən] adj : afroamericano m, -na f

Afro–American[2] n : afroamericano

aft ['æft] adv : a popa

after[1] ['æftər] adv **1** AFTERWARD : después **2** BEHIND : detrás, atrás

after[2] adj : posterior, siguiente ⟨in after years : en los años posteriores⟩

after[3] conj : después de, después de que ⟨after we ate : después de que comimos, después de comer⟩

after[4] prep **1** FOLLOWING : después de, tras ⟨after Saturday : después del sábado⟩ ⟨day after day : día tras día⟩ **2** BEHIND : tras de, después de ⟨I ran after the dog : corrí tras del perro⟩ **3** CONCERNING : por ⟨they asked after you : preguntaron por ti⟩ **4 after all** : después de todo

aftereffect ['æftərɪ,fɛkt] n : efecto m secundario

afterlife ['æftər,laɪf] n : vida f venidera, vida f después de la muerte

aftermath ['æftər,mæθ] n : consecuencias fpl, resultados mpl

afternoon [ˌæftər'nu:n] n : tarde f

aftertaste ['æftər,teɪst] n : resabio m, regusto m

afterthought ['æftər,θɔt] n : ocurrencia f tardía, idea f tardía

afterward ['æftərwərd] or **afterwards** [-wərdz] adv : después, luego ⟨soon afterward : poco después⟩

again [ə'gɛn, -'gɪn] adv **1** ANEW, OVER : de nuevo, otra vez **2** BESIDES : además **3 then again** : por otra parte ⟨I may stay, then again I may not : puede ser que me quede, por otra parte, puede que no⟩

against [ə'gɛntst, -'gɪntst] prep **1** TOUCHING : contra ⟨against the wall : contra la pared⟩ **2** OPPOSING : contra, en contra de ⟨I will vote against the proposal : votaré en contra de la propuesta⟩ ⟨against the grain : a contrapelo⟩

agape [ə'geɪp] adj : boquiabierto

agate ['æɡət] n : ágata f

age[1] ['eɪʤ] vi **aged; aging** : envejecer, madurar

age[2] n **1** : edad f ⟨ten years of age : diez años de edad⟩ ⟨to be of age : ser mayor de edad⟩ **2** PERIOD : era f, siglo m, época f **3 old age** : vejez f **4 ages** npl : siglos mpl, eternidad f

aged adj **1** ['eɪʤəd, 'eɪʤd] OLD : anciano, viejo, vetusto **2** ['eɪʤd] (indicating a specified age) ⟨a girl aged 10 : una niña de 10 años de edad⟩

ageless ['eɪʤləs] adj **1** YOUTHFUL : eternamente joven **2** TIMELESS : eterno, perenne

agency ['eɪʤəntsi] n, pl **-cies 1** : agencia f, oficina f ⟨travel agency : agencia

de viajes⟩ **2 through the agency of** : a
través de, por medio de
agenda [ə'ʤndə] *n* : agenda *f*, orden *m*
del día
agent ['eɪʤənt] *n* **1** MEANS : agente *m*,
medio *m*, instrumento *m* **2** REPRE-
SENTATIVE : agente *mf*, representante
mf
aggravate ['ægrə,veɪt] *vt* **-vated; -vating**
1 WORSEN : agravar, empeorar **2** AN-
NOY : irritar, exasperar
aggravation [,ægrə'veɪʃən] *n* **1** WORS-
ENING : empeoramiento *m* **2** ANNOY-
ANCE : molestia *f*, irritación *f*, exasperación *f*
aggregate[1] ['ægrɪ,geɪt] *vt* **-gated; -gat-
ing** : juntar, sumar
aggregate[2] ['ægrɪgət] *adj* : total, global,
conjunto
aggregate[3] ['ægrɪgət] *n* **1** CONGLOM-
ERATE : agregado *m*, conglomerado *m*
2 WHOLE : total *m*, conjunto *m*
aggression [ə'grɛʃən] *n* **1** ATTACK
: agresión *f* **2** AGGRESSIVENESS : agresividad *f*
aggressive [ə'grɛsɪv] *adj* : agresivo —
aggressively *adv*
aggressiveness [ə'grɛsɪvnəs] *n* : agresividad *f*
aggressor [ə'grɛsər] *n* : agresor *m*, -sora
f
aggrieved [ə'gri:vd] *adj* : ofendido, herido
aghast [ə'gæst] *adj* : espantado, aterrado, horrorizado
agile ['æʤəl] *adj* : ágil
agility [ə'ʤɪləti] *n, pl* **-ties** : agilidad *f*
agitate ['æʤə,teɪt] *v* **-tated; -tating** *vt* **1**
SHAKE : agitar **2** UPSET : inquietar,
perturbar — *vi* **to agitate against** : hacer campaña en contra de
agitation [,æʤə'teɪʃən] *n* : agitación *f*,
inquietud *f*
agitator ['æʤə,teɪtər] *n* : agitador *m*,
-dora *f*
agnostic [æg'nɑstɪk] *n* : agnóstico *m*, -ca
f
ago [ə'goː] *adv* : hace ⟨two years ago
: hace dos años⟩ ⟨long ago : hace tiempo, hace mucho tiempo⟩
agog [ə'gɑg] *adj* : ansioso, curioso
agonize ['ægə,naɪz] *vi* **-nized; -nizing**
: tormentarse, angustiarse
agonizing ['ægə,naɪzɪŋ] *adj* : angustioso, terrible — **agonizingly** [-zɪŋli]
adv
agony ['ægəni] *n, pl* **-nies 1** PAIN : dolor *m* **2** ANGUISH : angustia *f*
agrarian [ə'grɛriən] *adj* : agrario
agree [ə'gri:] *v* **agreed; agreeing** *vt* AC-
KNOWLEDGE : estar de acuerdo ⟨he
agreed that I was right : estuvo de
acuerdo en que tenía razón⟩ — *vi* **1**
CONCUR : estar de acuerdo **2** CONSENT
: ponerse de acuerdo **3** TALLY : concordar **4 to agree with** : sentarle bien
(a alguien) ⟨this climate agrees with me
: este clima me sienta bien⟩

agreeable [ə'gri:əbəl] *adj* **1** PLEASING
: agradable, simpático **2** WILLING : dispuesto **3** AGREEING : de acuerdo, conforme
agreeably [ə'gri:əbli] *adv* : agradablemente
agreement [ə'gri:mənt] *n* **1** : acuerdo
m, conformidad *f* ⟨in agreement with
: de acuerdo con⟩ **2** CONTRACT, PACT
: acuerdo *m*, pacto *m*, convenio *m* **3**
CONCORD, HARMONY : concordia *f*
agriculture ['ægrɪ,kʌltʃər] *n* : agricultura
f — **agricultural** [,ægrɪ'kʌltʃərəl] *adj*
aground [ə'graʊnd] *adj* : encallado,
varado
ahead [ə'hɛd] *adv* **1** : al frente, delante,
adelante ⟨he walked ahead : caminó
delante⟩ **2** BEFOREHAND : por adelantado, con antelación **3** LEADING : a
la delantera **4 to get ahead** : adelantar, progresar
ahead of *prep* **1** : al frente de, delante
de, antes de **2 to get ahead of** : adelantarse a
ahoy [ə'hɔɪ] *interj* ship ahoy! : ¡barco a
la vista!
aid[1] ['eɪd] *vt* : ayudar, auxiliar
aid[2] *n* **1** HELP : ayuda *f*, asistencia *f* **2**
ASSISTANT : asistente *mf*
aide ['eɪd] *n* : ayudante *mf*
AIDS ['eɪdz] *n* : SIDA *m*, sida *m*
ail ['eɪl] *vt* : molestar, afligir — *vi* : sufrir,
estar enfermo
aileron ['eɪlə,rɑn] *n* : alerón *m*
ailment ['eɪlmənt] *n* : enfermedad *f*, dolencia *f*, achaque *m*
aim[1] ['eɪm] *vt* **1** : apuntar (un arma), dirigir (una observación) **2** INTEND
: proponerse, querer ⟨he aims to do it
tonight : se propone hacerlo esta
noche⟩ — *vi* **1** POINT : apuntar **2 to
aim at** : aspirar a
aim[2] *n* **1** MARKSMANSHIP : puntería *f* **2**
GOAL : propósito *m*, objetivo *m*, fin *m*
aimless ['eɪmləs] *adj* : sin rumbo, sin objeto
aimlessly ['eɪmləsli] *adv* : sin rumbo, sin
objeto
air[1] ['ær] *vt* **1** : airear, ventilar ⟨to air
out a mattress : airear un colchón⟩ **2**
EXPRESS : airear, manifestar, comunicar **3** BROADCAST : transmitir, emitir
air[2] *n* **1** : aire *m* **2** MELODY : aire *m* **3**
APPEARANCE : aire *m*, aspecto *m* **4 airs**
npl : aires *mpl*, afectación *f* **5 by ∼**
: por avión (dícese de una carta), en
avión (dícese de una persona) **6 to be
on the air** : estar en el aire, estar emi-
tiendo
airborne ['ær,born] *adj* : aerotransportado ⟨airborne troops : tropas aero-
transportadas⟩ **2** FLYING : volando, en
el aire
air–condition [,ærkən'dɪʃən] *vt* : climatizar, condicionar con el aire
air conditioner [,ærkən'dɪʃənər] *n*
: acondicionador *m* de aire

air–conditioning [ˌærkənˈdɪʃənɪŋ] *n* : aire *m* acondicionado

aircraft [ˈærˌkræft] *ns & pl* 1 : avión *m*, aeronave *f* 2 **aircraft carrier** : portaaviones *m*

airfield [ˈærˌfiːld] *n* : aeródromo *m*, campo *m* de aviación

air force *n* : fuerza *f* aérea

airlift [ˈærˌlɪft] *n* : puente *m* aéreo, transporte *m* aéreo

airline [ˈærˌlaɪn] *n* : aerolínea *f*, línea *f* aérea

airliner [ˈærˌlaɪnər] *n* : avión *m* de pasajeros

airmail[1] [ˈærˌmeɪl] *vt* : enviar por vía aérea

airmail[2] *n* : correo *m* aéreo

airman [ˈærmən] *n, pl* **-men** [-mən, -ˌmɛn] 1 AVIATOR : aviador *m*, -dora *f* 2 : soldado *m* de la fuerza aérea

airplane [ˈærˌpleɪn] *n* : avión *m*

airport [ˈærˌport] *n* : aeropuerto *m*

airship [ˈærˌʃɪp] *n* : dirigible *m*, zepelín *m*

airstrip [ˈærˌstrɪp] *n* : pista *f* de aterrizaje

airtight [ˈærˈtaɪt] *adj* : hermético, herméticamente cerrado

airwaves [ˈærˌweɪvz] *npl* : radio *m*, televisión *f*

airy [ˈæri] *adj* **airier** [-iər]; **-est** 1 DELICATE, LIGHT : delicado, ligero 2 BREEZY : aireado, bien ventilado

aisle [ˈaɪl] *n* : pasillo *m*, nave *f* lateral (de una iglesia)

ajar [əˈdʒar] *adj* : entreabierto, entornado

akimbo [əˈkɪmbo] *adj & adv* : en jarras

akin [əˈkɪn] *adj* 1 RELATED : emparentado 2 SIMILAR : semejante, parecido

alabaster [ˈæləˌbæstər] *n* : alabastro *m*

alacrity [əˈlækrəti] *n* : presteza *f*, prontitud *f*

alarm[1] [əˈlarm] *vt* 1 WARN : alarmar, alertar 2 FRIGHTEN : asustar

alarm[2] *n* 1 WARNING : alarma *f*, alerta *f* 2 APPREHENSION, FEAR : aprensión *f*, inquietud *f*, temor *m* 3 **alarm clock** : despertador *m*

alarming [əˈlarmɪŋ] *adj* : alarmante

alas [əˈlæs] *interj* : ¡ay!

Albanian [ælˈbeɪniən] *n* : albanés *m*, -nesa *f* — **Albanian** *adj*

albatross [ˈælbəˌtrɔs] *n, pl* **-tross** or **-trosses** : albatros *m*

albeit [ɔlˈbiːət, æl-] *conj* : aunque

albino [ælˈbaɪno] *n, pl* **-nos** : albino *m*, -na *f*

album [ˈælbəm] *n* : álbum *m*

albumen [ælˈbjuːmən] *n* 1 : clara *f* de huevo 2 → **albumin**

albumin [ælˈbjuːmən] *n* : albúmina *f*

alchemist [ˈælkəmɪst] *n* : alquimista *mf*

alchemy [ˈælkəmi] *n, pl* **-mies** : alquimia *f*

alcohol [ˈælkəˌhɔl] *n* 1 ETHANOL : alcohol *m*, etanol *m* 2 LIQUOR : alcohol *m*, bebidas *fpl* alcohólicas

alcoholic[1] [ˌælkəˈhɔlɪk] *adj* : alcohólico

alcoholic[2] *n* : alcohólico *m*, -ca *f*

alcoholism [ˈælkəhɔˌlɪzəm] *n* : alcoholismo *m*

alcove [ˈælˌkoːv] *n* : nicho *m*, hueco *m*

alderman [ˈɔldərmən] *n, pl* **-men** [-mən, -ˌmɛn] : concejal *mf*

ale [ˈeɪl] *n* : cerveza *f*

alert[1] [əˈlərt] *vt* : alertar, poner sobre aviso

alert[2] *adj* 1 WATCHFUL : alerta, vigilante 2 QUICK : listo, vivo

alert[3] *n* : alerta *f*, alarma *f*

alertly [əˈlərtli] *adv* : con listeza

alertness [əˈlərtnəs] *n* 1 WATCHFULNESS : vigilancia *f* 2 ASTUTENESS : listeza *f*, viveza *f*

alfalfa [ælˈfælfə] *n* : alfalfa *f*

alga [ˈælgə] *n, pl* **-gae** [ˈælˌdʒiː] : alga *f*

algebra [ˈældʒəbrə] *n* : álgebra *m*

algebraic [ˌældʒəˈbreɪk] *adj* : algebraico — **algebraically** [-ɪkli] *adv*

Algerian [ælˈdʒɪriən] *n* : argelino *m*, -na *f* — **Algerian** *adj*

algorithm [ˈælgəˌrɪðəm] *n* : algoritmo *m*

alias[1] [ˈeɪliəs] *adv* : alias

alias[2] *n* : alias *m*

alibi[1] [ˈæləˌbaɪ] *vi* : ofrecer una coartada

alibi[2] *n* 1 : coartada *f* 2 EXCUSE : pretexto *m*, excusa *f*

alien[1] [ˈeɪliən] *adj* 1 STRANGE : ajeno, extraño 2 FOREIGN : extranjero, foráneo 3 EXTRATERRESTRIAL : extraterrestre

alien[2] *n* 1 FOREIGNER : extranjero *m*, -ra *f*; forastero *m*, -ra *f* 2 EXTRATERRESTRIAL : extraterrestre *mf*

alienate [ˈeɪliəˌneɪt] *vt* **-ated; -ating** 1 ESTRANGE : alienar, enajenar 2 **to alienate oneself** : alejarse, distanciarse

alienation [ˌeɪliəˈneɪʃən] *n* : alienación *f*, enajenación *f*

alight [əˈlaɪt] *vi* 1 DISMOUNT : bajarse, apearse 2 LAND : posarse, aterrizar

align [əˈlaɪn] *vt* : alinear

alignment [əˈlaɪnmənt] *n* : alineación *f*, alineamiento *m*

alike[1] [əˈlaɪk] *adv* : igual, del mismo modo

alike[2] *adj* : igual, semejante, parecido

alimentary [ˌæləˈmɛntəri] *adj* 1 : alimenticio 2 **alimentary canal** : tubo *m* digestivo

alimony [ˈæləˌmoːni] *n, pl* **-nies** : pensión *f* alimenticia

alive [əˈlaɪv] *adj* 1 LIVING : vivo, viviente 2 LIVELY : animado, activo 3 ACTIVE : vigente, en uso 4 AWARE : consciente ⟨alive to the danger : consciente del peligro⟩

alkali [ˈælkəˌlaɪ] *n, pl* **-lies** [-ˌlaɪz] or **-lis** [-ˌlaɪz] : álcali *m*

alkaline [ˈælkələn, -ˌlaɪn] *adj* : alcalino

all[1] [ˈɔl] *adv* 1 COMPLETELY : todo, completamente 2 : igual ⟨the score is 14 all : es 14 iguales, están empatados a 14⟩

3 all the better : tanto mejor **4 all the more** : aún más, todavía más

all² *adj* : todo ⟨all the children : todos los niños⟩ ⟨in all likelihood : con toda probabilidad, con la mayor probabilidad⟩

all³ *pron* **1** : todo, -da ⟨they ate it all : lo comieron todo⟩ ⟨that's all : eso es todo⟩ ⟨enough for all : suficiente para todos⟩ **2 all in all** : en general **3 not at all** (*in negative constructions*) : en absoluto, para nada

Allah ['ɑlɑ, ɑ'lɑ] *n* : Alá *m*

all-around [ˌɔlə'raʊnd] *adj* : completo, amplio

allay [ə'leɪ] *vt* **1** ALLEVIATE : aliviar, mitigar **2** CALM : aquietar, calmar

allegation [ˌælɪ'geɪʃən] *n* : alegato *m*, acusación *f*

allege [ə'lɛdʒ] *vt* **-leged; -leging 1** : alegar, afirmar **2 to be alleged** : decirse, pretenderse ⟨she is alleged to be wealthy : se dice que es adinerada⟩

alleged [ə'lɛdʒd, ə'lɛdʒəd] *adj* : presunto, supuesto

allegedly [ə'lɛdʒədli] *adv* : supuestamente, según se alega

allegiance [ə'li:dʒənts] *n* : lealtad *f*, fidelidad *f*

allegorical [ˌælə'gɔrɪkəl] *adj* : alegórico

allegory ['ælə,gori] *n, pl* **-ries** : alegoría *f*

alleluia [ˌɑlə'lu:jə, ˌæ-] → **hallelujah**

allergen ['ælərdʒən] *n* : alérgeno *m*

allergic [ə'lərdʒɪk] *adj* : alérgico

allergy ['ælərdʒi] *n, pl* **-gies** : alergia *f*

alleviate [ə'li:vi,eɪt] *vt* **-ated; -ating** : aliviar, mitigar, paliar

alleviation [ə,li:vi'eɪʃən] *n* : alivio *m*

alley ['æli] *n, pl* **-leys 1** : callejón *m* **2 bowling alley** : bolera *f*

alliance [ə'laɪənts] *n* : alianza *f*, coalición *f*

alligator ['ælə,geɪtər] *n* : caimán *m*

alliteration [ə,lɪtə'reɪʃən] *n* : aliteración *f*

allocate ['ælə,keɪt] *vt* **-cated; -cating** : asignar, adjudicar

allocation [ˌælə'keɪʃən] *n* : asignación *f*, reparto *m*, distribución *f*

allot [ə'lɑt] *vt* **-lotted; -lotting** : repartir, distribuir, asignar

allotment [ə'lɑtmənt] *n* : reparto *m*, asignación *f*, distribución *f*

allow [ə'laʊ] *vt* **1** PERMIT : permitir, dejar **2** ALLOT : conceder, dar **3** ADMIT, CONCEDE : admitir, conceder — *vi* **to allow for** : tener en cuenta

allowable [ə'laʊəbəl] *adj* **1** PERMISSIBLE : permisible, lícito **2** : deducible ⟨allowable expenditure : gasto deducible⟩

allowance [ə'laʊənts] *n* **1** : complemento *m* (para gastos, etc.), mesada *f* (para niños) **2 to make allowance(s)** : tener en cuenta, disculpar

alloy ['æ,lɔɪ] *n* : aleación *f*

all-purpose ['ɔl'pərpəs] *adj* : multiuso ⟨all-purpose flour : harina común⟩

all right¹ *adv* **1** YES : sí, por supuesto **2** WELL : bien ⟨I did all right : me fue bien⟩ **3** DEFINITELY : bien, ciertamente, sin duda ⟨he's sick all right : está bien enfermo⟩

all right² *adj* **1** OK : bien ⟨are you all right? : ¿estás bien?⟩ **2** SATISFACTORY : bien, bueno ⟨your work is all right : tu trabajo es bueno⟩

all-round [ˌɔl'raʊnd] → **all-around**

allspice ['ɔlspaɪs] *n* : pimienta *f* de Jamaica

allude [ə'lu:d] *vi* **-luded; -luding** : aludir, referirse

allure¹ [ə'lʊr] *vt* **-lured; -luring** : cautivar, atraer

allure² *n* : atractivo *m*, encanto *m*

allusion [ə'lu:ʒən] *n* : alusión *f*

ally¹ [ə'laɪ, 'æ,laɪ] *vi* **-lied; -lying** : aliarse

ally² ['æ,laɪ, ə'laɪ] *n* : aliado *m*, -da *f*

almanac ['ɔlmə,næk, 'æl-] *n* : almanaque *m*

almighty [ɔl'maɪti] *adj* : omnipotente, todopoderoso

almond ['ɑmənd, 'ɑl-, 'æ-, 'æl-] *n* : almendra *f*

almost ['ɔl,mo:st, ɔl'mo:st] *adv* : casi, prácticamente

alms ['ɑmz, 'ɑlmz, 'ælmz] *ns & pl* : limosna *f*, caridad *f*

aloe ['ælo:] *n* : áloe *m*

aloft [ə'lɔft] *adv* : en alto, en el aire

alone¹ [ə'lo:n] *adv* : sólo, solamente, únicamente

alone² *adj* : solo ⟨they're alone in the house : están solos en la casa⟩

along¹ [ə'lɔŋ] *adv* **1** FORWARD : adelante ⟨farther along : más adelante⟩ ⟨move along! : ¡circulen, por favor!⟩ **2 to bring along** : traer **3 ~ with** : con, junto con **4 all along** : desde el principio

along² *prep* **1** : por, a lo largo de ⟨along the coast : a lo largo de la costa⟩ **2** : en, en el curso de, por ⟨along the way : en el curso del viaje⟩

alongside¹ [ə,lɔŋ'saɪd] *adv* : al costado, al lado

alongside² *or* **alongside of** *prep* : junto a, al lado de

aloof [ə'lu:f] *adj* : distante, reservado

aloofness [ə'lu:fnəs] *n* : reserva *f*, actitud *f* distante

aloud [ə'laʊd] *adv* : en voz alta

alpaca [æl'pækə] *n* : alpaca *f*

alphabet ['ælfə,bɛt] *n* : alfabeto *m*

alphabetical [ˌælfə'bɛtɪkəl] *or* **alphabetic** [-'bɛtɪk] *adj* : alfabético — **alphabetically** [-tɪkli] *adv*

alphabetize ['ælfəbə,taɪz] *vt* **-ized; -izing** : alfabetizar, poner en orden alfabético

alpine ['æl,paɪn] *adj* : alpino

already [ɔl'rɛdi] *adv* : ya

also ['ɔl,so:] *adv* : también, además

altar ['ɔltər] *n* : altar *m*

alter ['ɔltər] *vt* : alterar, cambiar, modificar

alteration [ˌɔltəˈreɪʃən] *n* : alteración *f*, cambio *m*, modificación *f*

altercation [ˌɔltərˈkeɪʃən] *n* : altercado *m*, disputa *f*

alternate[1] [ˈɔltərˌneɪt] *v* **-nated; -nating** : alternar

alternate[2] [ˈɔltərnət] *adj* **1** : alterno ⟨alternate cycles of inflation and depression : ciclos alternos de inflación y depresión⟩ **2** : uno sí y otro no ⟨he cooks on alternate days : cocina un día sí y otro no⟩

alternate[3] [ˈɔltərnət] *n* : suplente *mf*; sustituto *m*, -ta *f*

alternately [ˈɔltərnətli] *adv* : alternativemente, por turno

alternating current [ˈɔltərˌneɪtɪŋ] *n* : corriente *f* alterna

alternation [ˌɔltərˈneɪʃən] *n* : alternancia *f*, rotación *f*

alternative[1] [ɔlˈtərnətɪv] *adj* : alternativo

alternative[2] *n* : alternativa *f*

alternator [ˈɔltərˌneɪtər] *n* : alternador *m*

although [ɔlˈðoː] *conj* : aunque, a pesar de que

altitude [ˈæltəˌtuːd, -ˌtjuːd] *n* : altitud *f*, altura *f*

alto [ˈælˌtoː] *n, pl* **-tos** : alto *mf*, contralto *mf*

altogether [ˌɔltəˈgɛðər] *adv* **1** COMPLETELY : completamente, totalmente, del todo **2** ON THE WHOLE : en suma, en general

altruism [ˈæltruˌɪzəm] *n* : altruismo *m*

altruistic [ˌæltruˈɪstɪk] *adj* : altruista — **altruistically** [-tɪkli] *adv*

alum [ˈæləm] *n* : alumbre *m*

aluminum [əˈluːmənəm] *n* : aluminio *m*

alumna [əˈlʌmnə] *n, pl* **-nae** [-ˌniː] : exalumna *f*

alumnus [əˈlʌmnəs] *n, pl* **-ni** [-ˌnaɪ] : exalumno *m*

always [ˈɔlwiz, -ˌweɪz] *adv* **1** INVARIABLY : siempre, invariablemente **2** FOREVER : para siempre

am → **be**

amalgam [əˈmælgəm] *n* : amalgama *f*

amalgamate [əˈmælgəˌmeɪt] *vt* **-ated; -ating** : amalgamar, unir, fusionar

amalgamation [əˌmælgəˈmeɪʃən] *n* : fusión *f*, unión *f*

amaryllis [ˌæməˈrɪləs] *n* : amarilis *f*

amass [əˈmæs] *vt* : amasar, acumular

amateur [ˈæmətʃər, -tər, -ˌtur, -ˌtjur] *n* **1** : amateur *mf* **2** BEGINNER : principiante *mf*; aficionado *m*, -da *f*

amateurish [ˈæməˌtʃərɪʃ, -ˌtər-, -ˌtur-, -ˌtjur-] *adj* : amateur, inexperto

amaze [əˈmeɪz] *vt* **amazed; amazing** : asombrar, maravillar, pasmar

amazement [əˈmeɪzmənt] *n* : asombro *m*, sorpresa *f*

amazing [əˈmeɪzɪŋ] *adj* : asombroso, sorprendente — **amazingly** [-zɪŋli] *adv*

Amazon [ˈæməˌzɑn] *n* : amazona *f* (en mitología)

Amazonian [ˌæməˈzoːniən] *adj* : amazónico

ambassador [æmˈbæsədər] *n* : embajador *m*, -dora *f*

amber [ˈæmbər] *n* : ámbar *m*

ambergris [ˈæmbərˌgrɪs, -ˌgriːs] *n* : ámbar *m* gris

ambidextrous [ˌæmbɪˈdɛkstrəs] *adj* : ambidextro — **ambidextrously** *adv*

ambience *or* **ambiance** [ˈæmbiənts, ˈɑmbiˌɑnts] *n* : ambiente *m*, atmósfera *f*

ambiguity [ˌæmbəˈgjuːəti] *n, pl* **-ties** : ambigüedad *f*

ambiguous [æmˈbɪgjuəs] *adj* : ambiguo

ambition [æmˈbɪʃən] *n* : ambición *f*

ambitious [æmˈbɪʃəs] *adj* : ambicioso — **ambitiously** *adv*

ambivalence [æmˈbɪvələnts] *n* : ambivalencia *f*

ambivalent [æmˈbɪvələnt] *adj* : ambivalente

amble[1] [ˈæmbəl] *vi* **-bled; -bling** : ir tranquilamente, pasearse despreocupadamente

amble[2] *n* : paseo *m* tranquilo

ambulance [ˈæmbjələnts] *n* : ambulancia *f*

ambush[1] [ˈæmˌbuʃ] *vt* : emboscar

ambush[2] *n* : emboscada *f*, celada *f*

ameliorate [əˈmiːljəˌreɪt] *v* **-rated; -rating** IMPROVE : mejorar

amelioration [əˌmiːljəˈreɪʃən] *n* : mejora *f*

amen [ˈeɪˈmɛn, ˈɑ-] *interj* : amén

amenable [əˈmiːnəbəl, -ˈmɛ-] *adj* RESPONSIVE : susceptible, receptivo, sensible

amend [əˈmɛnd] *vt* **1** IMPROVE : mejorar, enmendar **2** CORRECT : enmendar, corregir

amendment [əˈmɛndmənt] *n* : enmienda *f*

amends [əˈmɛndz] *ns & pl* : compensación *f*, reparación *f*, desagravio *m*

amenity [əˈmɛnəti, -ˈmiː-] *n, pl* **-ties 1** PLEASANTNESS : lo agradable, amenidad *f* **2 amenities** *npl* : servicios *mpl*, comodidades *fpl*

American [əˈmɛrɪkən] *n* : americano *m*, -na *f* — **American** *adj*

American Indian *n* : indio *m* (americano), india *f* (americana)

amethyst [ˈæməθəst] *n* : amatista *f*

amiability [ˌeɪmiːəˈbɪləti] *n* : amabilidad *f*, afabilidad *f*

amiable [ˈeɪmiːəbəl] *adj* : amable, afable — **amiably** [-bli] *adv*

amicable [ˈæmɪkəbəl] *adj* : amigable, amistoso, cordial — **amicably** [-bli] *adv*

amid [əˈmɪd] *or* **amidst** [əˈmɪdst] *prep* : en medio de, entre

amino acid [əˈmiːno] *n* : aminoácido *m*

amiss[1] [əˈmɪs] *adv* : mal, fuera de lugar ⟨to take amiss : tomar a mal, llevar a mal⟩

amiss[2] *adj* **1** WRONG : malo, inoportuno **2 there's something amiss** : pasa algo, algo anda mal

ammeter [ˈæˌmiːtər] *n* : amperímetro *m*

ammonia [ə'mo:njə] *n* : amoníaco *m*
ammunition [ˌæmjə'nɪʃən] *n* **1** : municiones *fpl* **2** ARGUMENTS : argumentos *mpl*
amnesia [æm'ni:ʒə] *n* : amnesia *f*
amnesty ['æmnəsti] *n, pl* **-ties** : amnistía *f*
amoeba [ə'mi:bə] *n, pl* **-bas** *or* **-bae** [-ˌbi:] : ameba *f*
amoebic [ə'mi:bɪk] *adj* : amébico
amok [ə'mʌk, -'mɑk] *adv* **to run amok** : correr a ciegas, enloquecerse, desbocarse (dícese de la economía, etc.)
among [ə'mʌŋ] *prep* : entre
amoral [eɪ'mɔrəl] *adj* : amoral
amorous ['æmərəs] *adj* **1** PASSIONATE : enamoradizo, apasionado **2** ENAMORED : enamorado **3** LOVING : amoroso, cariñoso
amorously ['æmərəsli] *adv* : con cariño
amorphous [ə'mɔrfəs] *adj* : amorfo, informe
amortize ['æmərˌtaɪz, ə'mɔr-] *vt* **-tized; -tizing** : amortizar
amount[1] [ə'maʊnt] *vi* **to amount to 1** : equivaler a, significar ⟨that amounts to treason : eso equivale a la traición⟩ **2** : ascender (a) ⟨my debts amount to $2000 : mis deudas ascienden a $2000⟩
amount[2] *n* : cantidad *f*, suma *f*
ampere ['æmˌpɪr] *n* : amperio *m*
ampersand ['æmpərˌsænd] *n* : el signo &
amphetamine [æm'fɛtəˌmi:n] *n* : anfetamina *f*
amphibian [æm'fɪbiən] *n* : anfibio *m*
amphibious [æm'fɪbiəs] *adj* : anfibio
amphitheater ['æmfəˌθi:ətər] *n* : anfiteatro *m*
ample ['æmpəl] *adj* **-pler; -plest 1** LARGE, SPACIOUS : amplio, extenso, grande **2** ABUNDANT : abundante, generoso
amplifier ['æmpləˌfaɪər] *n* : amplificador *m*
amplify ['æmpləˌfaɪ] *vt* **-fied; -fying** : amplificar
amply ['æmpli] *adv* : ampliamente, abundantemente, suficientemente
amputate ['æmpjəˌteɪt] *vt* **-tated; -tating** : amputar
amputation [ˌæmpjə'teɪʃən] *n* : amputación *f*
amuck [ə'mʌk] → **amok**
amulet ['æmjələt] *n* : amuleto *m*, talismán *m*
amuse [ə'mju:z] *vt* **amused; amusing 1** ENTERTAIN : entretener, distraer **2** : hacer reír, divertir ⟨the joke amused us : la broma nos hizo reír⟩
amusement [ə'mju:zmənt] *n* **1** ENTERTAINMENT : diversión *f*, entretenimiento *m*, pasatiempo *m* **2** LAUGHTER : risa *f*
an *art* → **a**[2]
anachronism [ə'nækrəˌnɪzəm] *n* : anacronismo *m*
anachronistic [əˌnækrə'nɪstɪk] *adj* : anacrónico

anaconda [ˌænə'kɑndə] *n* : anaconda *f*
anagram ['ænəˌgræm] *n* : anagrama *m*
anal ['eɪnəl] *adj* : anal
analgesic [ˌænəl'ʤi:zɪk, -sɪk] *n* : analgésico *m*
analog ['ænəˌlɔg] *adj* : analógico
analogical [ˌænə'lɑʤɪkəl] *adj* : analógico — **analogically** [-kli] *adv*
analogous [ə'næləgəs] *adj* : análogo
analogy [ə'næləʤi] *n, pl* **-gies** : analogía *f*
analysis [ə'næləsəs] *n, pl* **-yses** [-ˌsi:z] **1** : análisis *m* **2** PSYCHOANALYSIS : psicoanálisis *m*
analyst ['ænəlɪst] *n* **1** : analista *mf* **2** PSYCHOANALYST : psicoanalista *mf*
analytic [ˌænə'lɪtɪk] *or* **analytical** [-tɪkəl] *adj* : analítico — **analytically** [-tɪkli] *adv*
analyze ['ænəˌlaɪz] *vt* **-lyzed; -lyzing** : analizar
anarchic [æ'nɑrkɪk] *adj* : anárquico — **anarchically** [-kɪkli] *adv*
anarchism ['ænərˌkɪzəm, -nɑr-] *n* : anarquismo *m*
anarchist ['ænərkɪst, -nɑr-] *n* : anarquista *mf*
anarchy ['ænərki, -nɑr-] *n* : anarquía *f*
anathema [ə'næθəmə] *n* : anatema *m*
anatomic [ˌænə'tɑmɪk] *or* **anatomical** [-mɪkəl] *adj* : anatómico — **anatomically** [-mɪkli] *adv*
anatomy [ə'nætəmi] *n, pl* **-mies** : anatomía *f*
ancestor ['ænˌsɛstər] *n* : antepasado *m*, -da *f*; antecesor *m*, -sora *f*
ancestral [æn'sɛstrəl] *adj* : ancestral, de los antepasados
ancestry ['ænˌsɛstri] *n* **1** DESCENT : ascendencia *f*, linaje *m*, abolengo *m* **2** ANCESTORS : antepasados *mpl*, -das *fpl*
anchor[1] ['æŋkər] *vt* **1** MOOR : anclar, fondear **2** FASTEN : sujetar, asegurar, fijar
anchor[2] *n* **1** : ancla *f* **2** : presentador *m*, -dora *f* (en televisión)
anchorage ['æŋkərɪʤ] *n* : anclaje *m*
anchovy ['ænˌtʃo:vi, æn'tʃo:-] *n, pl* **-vies** *or* **-vy** : anchoa *f*
ancient ['eɪntʃənt] *adj* **1** : antiguo ⟨ancient history : historia antigua⟩ **2** OLD : viejo
ancients ['eɪntʃənts] *npl* : los antiguos *mpl*
and ['ænd] *conj* **1** : y (**e** *before words beginning with* i- *or* hi-) **2** : con ⟨ham and eggs : huevos con jamón⟩ **3** : a ⟨go and see : ve a ver⟩ **4** : de ⟨try and finish it soon : trata de terminarlo pronto⟩
Andalusian [ˌændə'lu:ʒən] *n* : andaluz *m*, -luza *f* — **Andalusian** *adj*
Andean ['ændiən] *adj* : andino
andiron ['ænˌdaɪərn] *n* : morillo *m*
Andorran [æn'dɔrən] *n* : andorrano *m*, -na *f* — **Andorran** *adj*
androgynous [æn'drɑʤənəs] *adj* : andrógino
anecdotal [ˌænɪk'do:təl] *adj* : anecdótico

anecdote ['ænɪk,do:t] n : anécdota f
anemia [ə'ni:miə] n : anemia f
anemic [ə'ni:mɪk] adj : anémico
anemone [ə'nɛməni] n : anémona f
anesthesia [,ænəs'θi:ʒə] n : anestesia f
anesthetic¹ [,ænəs'θɪɪk] adj : anestésico
anesthetic² n : anestésico m
anesthetist [ə'nɛsθətɪst] n : anestesista mf
anesthetize [ə'nɛsθə,taɪz] vt -tize; -tized : anestesiar
aneurysm ['ænjə,rɪzəm] n : aneurisma mf
anew [ə'nu:, -'nju:] adv : de nuevo, otra vez, nuevamente
angel ['eɪndʒəl] n : ángel m
angelic [æn'dʒɛlɪk] or angelical [-lɪkəl] adj : angélico, angelical — angelically [-lɪkli] adv
anger¹ ['æŋgər] vt : enojar, enfadar
anger² n : enojo m, enfado m, ira f, cólera f, rabia f
angina [æn'dʒaɪnə] n : angina f
angle¹ ['æŋgəl] v angled; angling vt DIRECT, SLANT : orientar, dirigir — vi FISH : pescar (con caña)
angle² n 1 : ángulo m 2 POINT OF VIEW : perspectiva f, punto m de vista
angler ['æŋglər] n : pescador m, -dora f
Anglican ['æŋglɪkən] n : anglicano m, -na f — Anglican adj
Anglo–Saxon¹ [,æŋglo'sæksən] adj : anglosajón
Anglo–Saxon² n : anglosajón m, -jona f
Angolan [æŋ'go:lən, æn-] n : angoleño m, -ña f — Angolan adj
angora [æŋ'gorə, æn-] n : angora f
angrily ['æŋgrəli] adv : furiosamente, con ira
angry ['æŋgri] adj -grier; -est : enojado, enfadado, furioso
anguish ['æŋgwɪʃ] n : angustia f, congoja f
anguished ['æŋgwɪʃt] adj : angustiado, acongojado
angular ['æŋgjələr] adj : angular (dícese de las formas), anguloso (dícese de las caras)
animal ['ænəməl] n 1 : animal m 2 BRUTE : bruto m, -ta f
animate¹ ['ænə,meɪt] vt -mated; -mating : animar
animate² ['ænəmət] adj : animado
animated ['ænə,meɪtəd] adj 1 LIVELY : animado, vivo, vivaz 2 animated cartoon : dibujos mpl animados
animation [,ænə'meɪʃən] n : animación f
animosity [,ænə'masəti] n, pl -ties : animosidad f, animadversión f
anise ['ænəs] n : anís m
aniseed ['ænəs,si:d] n : anís m, semilla f de anís
ankle ['æŋkəl] n : tobillo m
anklebone ['æŋkəl,bo:n] n : taba f
annals ['ænəlz] npl : anales mpl, crónica f
anneal [ə'ni:l] vt 1 TEMPER : templar 2 STRENGTHEN : fortalecer

annex¹ [ə'nɛks, 'æ,nɛks] vt : anexar
annex² ['æ,nɛks, -nɪks] n : anexo m, anejo m
annexation [,æ,nɛk'seɪʃən] n : anexión f
annihilate [ə'naɪə,leɪt] vt -lated; -lating : aniquilar
annihilation [ə,naɪə'leɪʃən] n : aniquilación f, aniquilamiento m
anniversary [,ænə'vərsəri] n, pl -ries : aniversario m
annotate ['ænə,teɪt] vt -tated; -tating : anotar
annotation [,ænə'teɪʃən] n : anotación f
announce [ə'naʊnts] vt -nounced; -nouncing : anunciar
announcement [ə'naʊntsmənt] n : anuncio m
announcer [ə'naʊntsər] n : anunciador m, -dora f; comentarista mf; locutor m, -tora f
annoy [ə'nɔɪ] vt : molestar, fastidiar, irritar
annoyance [ə'nɔɪənts] n 1 IRRITATION : irritación f, fastidio m 2 NUISANCE : molestia f, fastidio m
annoying [ə'nɔɪɪŋ] adj : molesto, fastidioso, engorroso — annoyingly [-ɪŋli] adv
annual¹ ['ænjʊəl] adj : anual — annually adv
annual² n 1 : planta f anual 2 YEARBOOK : anuario m
annuity [ə'nu:əti] n, pl -ties : anualidad f
annul [ə'nʌl] vt anulled; anulling : anular, invalidar
annulment [ə'nʌlmənt] n : anulación f
anode ['æ,no:d] n : ánodo m
anoint [ə'nɔɪnt] vt : ungir
anomalous [ə'namələs] adj : anómalo
anomaly [ə'naməli] n, pl -lies : anomalía f
anonymity [,ænə'nɪməti] n : anonimato m
anonymous [ə'nanəməs] adj : anónimo — anonymously adv
anorexia [,ænə'rɛksiə] n : anorexia f
anorexic [,ænə'rɛksɪk] adj : anoréxico
another¹ [ə'nʌðər] adj : otro
another² pron : otro, otra
answer¹ ['æntsər] vt 1 : contestar (a), responder (a) ⟨to answer the telephone : contestar el teléfono⟩ 2 FULFILL : satisfacer 3 to answer for : ser responsable de, pagar por ⟨she'll answer for that mistake : pagará por ese error⟩ — vi : contestar, responder
answer² n 1 REPLY : respuesta f, contestación f 2 SOLUTION : solución f
answerable ['æntsərəbəl] adj : responsable
ant ['ænt] n : hormiga f
antacid [ænt'æsəd, 'æn,tæ-] n : antiácido m
antagonism [æn'tægə,nɪzəm] n : antagonismo m, hostilidad f
antagonist [æn'tægənɪst] n : antagonista mf

antagonistic [æn͵tægə'nɪstɪk] *adj* : antagonista, hostil
antagonize [æn'tægə͵naɪz] *vt* -nized; -nizing : antagonizar
antarctic [ænt'ɑrktɪk, -'ɑrt̬ɪk] *adj* : antártico
antarctic circle *n* : círculo *m* antártico
anteater ['ænt͵i:t̬ər] *n* : oso *m* hormiguero
antebellum [͵æntɪ'bɛləm] *adj* : prebélico
antecedent[1] [͵æntə'si:dənt] *adj* : antecedente, precedente
antecedent[2] *n* : antecedente *mf*; precursor *m*, -sora *f*
antelope ['ænt̬əl͵o:p] *n, pl* -lope *or* -lopes : antílope *m*
antenna [æn'tɛnə] *n, pl* -nae [-͵ni:, -͵naɪ] *or* -nas : antena *f*
anterior [æn'tɪriər] *adj* : anterior
anthem ['ænθəm] *n* : himno *m* ⟨national anthem : himno nacional⟩
anther ['ænθər] *n* : antera *f*
anthill ['ænt͵hɪl] *n* : hormiguero *m*
anthology [æn'θɑlədʒi] *n, pl* -gies : antología *f*
anthracite ['ænθrə͵saɪt] *n* : antracita *f*
anthropoid[1] ['ænθrə͵pɔɪd] *adj* : antropoide
anthropoid[2] *n* : antropoide *mf*
anthropological [͵ænθrəpə'lɑdʒɪkəl] *adj* : antropológico
anthropologist [͵ænθrə'pɑlədʒɪst] *n* : antropólogo *m*, -ga *f*
anthropology [͵ænθrə'pɑlədʒi] *n* : antropología *f*
antiabortion [͵æntiə'bɔrʃən, ͵æntaɪ-] *adj* : antiaborto
antiaircraft [͵ænti'ær͵kræft, ͵æntaɪ-] *adj* : antiaéreo
anti–American [͵æntiə'mɛrɪkən, ͵æntaɪ-] *adj* : antiamericano
antibiotic[1] [͵æntibaɪ'ɑt̬ɪk, ͵æntaɪ-, -bi-] *adj* : antibiótico
antibiotic[2] *n* : antibiótico *m*
antibody ['ænti͵bɑdi] *n, pl* -bodies : anticuerpo *m*
antic[1] ['æntɪk] *adj* : extravagante, juguetón
antic[2] *n* : payasada *f*, travesura *f*
anticipate [æn'tɪsə͵peɪt] *vt* -pated; -pating 1 FORESEE : anticipar, prever 2 EXPECT : esperar, contar con
anticipation [æn͵tɪsə'peɪʃən] *n* 1 FORESIGHT : previsión *f* 2 EXPECTATION : anticipación *f*, expectación *f*, esperanza *f*
anticipatory [æn'tɪsəpə͵tori] *adj* : en anticipación, en previsión
anticlimactic [͵æntiklaɪ'mæktɪk] *adj* : anticlimático, decepcionante
anticlimax [͵ænti'klaɪ͵mæks] *n* : anticlímax *m*
anticommunism [͵ænti'kɑmjə͵nɪzəm, ͵æntaɪ-] *n* : anticomunismo *m*
anticommunist[1] [͵ænti'kɑmjənɪst, ͵æntaɪ-] *adj* : anticomunista
anticommunist[2] *n* : anticomunista *mf*

antidemocratic [͵ænti͵dɛmə'kræt̬ɪk, ͵æntaɪ-] *adj* : antidemocrático
antidepressant [͵æntidi'prɛsənt] *n* : antidepresivo *m* — antidepressant *adj*
antidote ['ænti͵do:t] *n* : antídoto *m*
antidrug [͵ænti'drʌg, ͵æntaɪ-; 'ænti͵drʌg, 'æntaɪ-] *adj* : antidrogas
antifascist [͵ænti'fæʃɪst, ͵æntaɪ-] *adj* : antifascista
antifeminist [͵ænti'fɛmənɪst, ͵æntaɪ-] *adj* : antifeminista
antifreeze ['ænti͵fri:z] *n* : anticongelante *m*
antigen ['æntɪdʒən, -͵dʒɛn] *n* : antígeno *m*
antihistamine [͵ænti'hɪstə͵mi:n, -mən] *n* : antihistamínico *m*
anti–imperialism [͵æntiɪm'pɪriə͵lɪzəm, ͵æntaɪ-] *n* : antiimperialismo *m*
anti–imperialist [͵æntiɪm'pɪriəlɪst, ͵æntaɪ-] *adj* : antiimperialista
anti–inflammatory [͵æt̬iɪn'flæmətori] *adj* : antiinflamatorio
anti–inflationary [͵æntiɪn'fleɪʃə͵nɛri, ͵æntaɪ-] *adj* : antiinflacionario
antimony ['æntə͵mo:ni] *n* : antimonio *m*
antipathy [æn'tɪpəθi] *n, pl* -thies : antipatía *f*, aversión *f*
antiperspirant [͵ænti'pərspərənt, ͵æntaɪ-] *n* : antitranspirante *m*
antiquarian[1] [͵æntə'kwɛriən] *adj* : antiguo, anticuario ⟨an antiquarian book : un libro antiguo⟩
antiquarian[2] *n* : anticuario *m*, -ria *f*
antiquary ['æntə͵kwɛri] *n* → antiquarian[2]
antiquated ['æntə͵kweɪt̬əd] *adj* : anticuado, pasado de moda
antique[1] [æn'ti:k] *adj* 1 OLD : antiguo, de época ⟨an antique mirror : un espejo antiguo⟩ 2 OLD-FASHIONED : anticuado, pasado de moda
antique[2] *n* : antigüedad *f*
antiquity [æn'tɪkwət̬i] *n, pl* -ties : antigüedad
antirevolutionary [͵ænti͵revə'lu:ʃə͵nɛri, ͵æntaɪ-] *adj* : antirrevolucionario
anti–Semitic [͵æntisə'mɪt̬ɪk, ͵æntaɪ-] *adj* : antisemita
anti–Semitism [͵ænti'sɛmə͵tɪzəm, ͵æntaɪ-] *n* : antisemitismo *m*
antiseptic[1] [͵æntə'sɛptɪk] *adj* : antiséptico — antiseptically [-tɪkli] *adv*
antiseptic[2] *n* : antiséptico *m*
antismoking [͵ænti'smo:kɪŋ, ͵æntaɪ-] *adj* : antitabaco
antisocial [͵ænti'so:ʃəl, ͵æntaɪ-] *adj* 1 : antisocial 2 UNSOCIABLE : poco sociable
antitheft [͵ænti'θɛft, ͵æntaɪ-] *adj* : antirrobo
antithesis [æn'tɪθəsɪs] *n, pl* -eses [-͵si:z] : antítesis *f*
antitoxin [͵ænti'tɑksən, ͵æntaɪ-] *n* : antitoxina *f*
antitrust [͵ænti'trʌst, ͵æntaɪ-] *adj* : antimonopolista
antler ['æntlər] *n* : asta *f*, cuerno *m*

antonym ['æntə,nɪm] *n* : antónimo *m*

anus ['eɪnəs] *n* : ano *m*

anvil ['ænvəl, -vɪl] *n* : yunque *m*

anxiety [æŋk'zaɪəti] *n, pl* -**eties** 1 UN-EASINESS : inquietud *f*, preocupación *f*, ansiedad *f* 2 APPREHENSION : ansiedad *f*, angustia *f*

anxious ['æŋkʃəs] *adj* 1 WORRIED : inquieto, preocupado, ansioso 2 WORRISOME : preocupante, inquietante 3 EAGER : ansioso, deseoso

anxiously ['æŋkʃəsli] *adv* : con inquietud, con ansiedad

any¹ ['ɛni] *adv* 1 : algo ⟨is it any better? : ¿está (algo) mejor?⟩ 2 : para nada ⟨it is not any good : no sirve para nada⟩

any² *adj* 1 : alguno ⟨is there any doubt? : ¿hay alguna duda?⟩ ⟨call me if you have any questions : llámeme si tiene alguna pregunta⟩ 2 : cualquier ⟨I can answer any question : puedo responder a cualquier pregunta⟩ 3 : todo ⟨in any case : en todo caso⟩ 4 : ningún ⟨he would not accept it under any circumstances : no lo aceptaría bajo ninguna circunstancia⟩

any³ *pron* 1 : alguno *m*, -na *f* ⟨are there any left? : ¿queda alguno?⟩ 2 : ninguno *m*, -na *f* ⟨I don't want any : no quiero ninguno⟩

anybody ['ɛni,bʌdi, -,ba-] → **anyone**

anyhow ['ɛni,haʊ] *adv* 1 HAPHAZARDLY : de cualquier manera 2 IN ANY CASE : de todos modos, en todo caso

anymore [,ɛni'mor] *adv* 1 : ya, ya más ⟨he doesn't dance anymore : ya no baila más⟩ 2 : todavía ⟨do they sing anymore? : ¿cantan todavía?⟩

anyone ['ɛni,wʌn] *pron* 1 : alguien ⟨is anyone here? : ¿hay alguien aquí?⟩ ⟨if anyone wants to come : si alguno quiere venir⟩ 2 : cualquiera ⟨anyone can play : cualquiera puede jugar⟩ 3 : nadie ⟨I don't want anyone here : no quiero a nadie aquí⟩

anyplace ['ɛni,pleɪs] → **anywhere**

anything ['ɛni,θɪŋ] *pron* 1 : algo, alguna cosa ⟨do you want anything? : ¿quieres algo?, ¿quieres alguna cosa?⟩ 2 : nada ⟨hardly anything : casi nada⟩ 3 : cualquier cosa ⟨I eat anything : como de todo⟩

anytime ['ɛni,taɪm] *adv* : en cualquier momento, a cualquier hora, cuando sea

anyway ['ɛni,weɪ] → **anyhow**

anywhere ['ɛni,ʰwɛr] *adv* 1 : en algún sitio, en alguna parte ⟨do you see it anywhere? : ¿lo ves en alguna parte?⟩ 2 : en ningún sitio, por ninguna parte ⟨I can't find it anywhere : no puedo encontrarlo por ninguna parte⟩ 3 : en cualquier parte, dondequiera, donde sea ⟨put it anywhere : ponlo dondequiera⟩

aorta [eɪ'ɔrtə] *n, pl* -**tas** *or* -**tae** [-ti, -ˌtaɪ] : aorta *f*

Apache [ə'pætʃi] *n, pl* **Apache** *or* **Apaches** : apache *mf*

apart [ə'pɑrt] *adv* 1 SEPARATELY : aparte, separadamente 2 ASIDE : aparte, a un lado 3 **to fall apart** : deshacerse, hacerse pedazos 4 **to take apart** : desmontar, desmantelar

apartheid [ə'pɑr,teɪt, -,taɪt] *n* : apartheid *m*

apartment [ə'pɑrtmənt] *n* : apartamento *m*, departamento *m*, piso *m* *Spain*

apathetic [,æpə'θɛtɪk] *adj* : apático, indiferente — **apathetically** [-tɪkli] *adv*

apathy ['æpəθi] *n* : apatía *f*, indiferencia *f*

ape¹ ['eɪp] *vt* **aped; aping** : imitar, remedar

ape² *n* : simio *m*; mono *m*, -na *f*

aperitif [ə,pɛrə'ti:f] *n* : aperitivo *m*

aperture ['æpərtʃər, -,tʃʊr] *n* : abertura *f*, rendija *f*, apertura *f* (en fotografía)

apex ['eɪ,pɛks] *n, pl* **apexes** *or* **apices** ['eɪpə,si:z, 'æ-] : ápice *m*, cúspide *f*, cima *f*

aphid ['eɪfɪd, 'æ-] *n* : áfido *m*

aphorism ['æfə,rɪzəm] *n* : aforismo *m*

aphrodisiac [,æfrə'di:zi,æk, -'dɪ-] *n* : afrodisíaco *m*

apiary ['eɪpi,ɛri] *n, pl* -**aries** : apiario *m*, colmenar *m*

apiece [ə'pi:s] *adv* : cada uno

aplenty [ə'plɛnti] *adj* : en abundancia

aplomb [ə'plɑm, -'plʌm] *n* : aplomo *m*

apocalypse [ə'pɑkə,lɪps] *n* : apocalipsis *m*

apocalyptic [ə,pɑkə'lɪptɪk] *adj* : apocalíptico

apocrypha [ə'pɑkrəfə] *n* : textos *mpl* apócrifos

apocryphal [ə'pɑkrəfəl] *adj* : apócrifo

apologetic [ə,pɑlə'dʒɛtɪk] *adj* : lleno de disculpas

apologetically [ə,pɑlə'dʒɛtɪkli] *adv* : disculpándose, con aire de disculpas

apologize [ə'pɑlə,dʒaɪz] *vi* -**gized; -gizing** : disculparse, pedir perdón

apology [ə'pɑlədʒi] *n, pl* -**gies** : disculpa *f*, excusa *f*

apoplectic [,æpə'plɛktɪk] *adj* : apopléctico

apoplexy ['æpə,plɛksi] *n* : apoplejía *f*

apostasy [ə'pɑstəsi] *n, pl* -**sies** : apostasía *f*

apostate [ə'pɑs,teɪt] *n* : apóstata *mf*

apostle [ə'pɑsəl] *n* : apóstol *m*

apostolic [,æpə'stɑlɪk] *adj* : apostólico

apostrophe [ə'pɑstrə,fi:] *n* : apóstrofo *m* (ortográfico)

apothecary [ə'pɑθə,kɛri] *n, pl* -**caries** : boticario *m*, -ria *f*

appall [ə'pɔl] *vt* : consternar, horrorizar

apparatus [,æpə'ræt̬əs, -'reɪ-] *n, pl* -**tuses** *or* -**tus** : aparato *m*, equipo *m*

apparel [ə'pærəl] *n* : atavío *m*, ropa *f*

apparent [ə'pærənt] *adj* 1 VISIBLE : visible 2 OBVIOUS : claro, evidente, manifiesto 3 SEEMING : aparente, ostensible

apparently [ə'pærəntli] *adv* : aparentemente, al parecer

apparition [ˌæpə'rɪʃən] *n* : aparición *f*, visión *f*

appeal¹ [ə'piːl] *vt* : apelar ⟨to appeal a decision : apelar contra una decisión⟩ — *vi* **1 to appeal for** : pedir, solicitar **2 to appeal to** : atraer a ⟨that doesn't appeal to me : eso no me atrae⟩

appeal² *n* **1** : apelación *f* (en derecho) **2** PLEA : ruego *m*, súplica *f* **3** ATTRACTION : atracción *f*, atractivo *m*, interés *m*

appear [ə'pɪr] *vi* **1** : aparecer, aparecerse, presentarse ⟨he suddenly appeared : apareció de repente⟩ **2** COME OUT : aparecer, salir, publicarse **3** : comparecer (ante el tribunal), actuar (en el teatro) **4** SEEM : parecer

appearance [ə'pɪrənts] *n* **1** APPEARING : aparición *f*, presentación *f*, comparecencia *f* (ante un tribunal), publicación *f* (de un libro) **2** LOOK : apariencia *f*, aspecto *m*

appease [ə'piːz] *vt* **-peased; -peasing 1** CALM, PACIFY : aplacar, apaciguar, sosegar **2** SATISFY : satisfacer, mitigar

appeasement [ə'piːzmənt] *n* : aplacamiento *m*, apaciguamiento *m*

append [ə'pɛnd] *vt* : agregar, añadir, adjuntar

appendage [ə'pɛndɪdʒ] *n* **1** ADDITION : apéndice *m*, añadidura *f* **2** LIMB : miembro *m*, extremidad *f*

appendectomy [ˌæpən'dɛktəmi] *n*, *pl* **-mies** : apendicectomía *f*

appendicitis [əˌpɛndə'saɪtəs] *n* : apendicitis *f*

appendix [ə'pɛndɪks] *n*, *pl* **-dixes** *or* **-dices** [-dəˌsiːz] : apéndice *m*

appetite ['æpəˌtaɪt] *n* **1** CRAVING : apetito *m*, deseo *m*, ganas *fpl* **2** PREFERENCE : gusto *m*, preferencia *f* ⟨the cultural appetites of today : los gustos culturales de hoy⟩

appetizer ['æpəˌtaɪzər] *n* : aperitivo *m*, entremés *m*, botana *f Mex*, tapa *f Spain*

appetizing ['æpəˌtaɪzɪŋ] *adj* : apetecible, apetitoso — **appetizingly** [-zɪŋli] *adv*

applaud [ə'plɔd] *v* : aplaudir

applause [ə'plɔz] *n* : aplauso *m*

apple ['æpəl] *n* : manzana *f*

appliance [ə'plaɪənts] *n* **1** : aparato *m* **2 household appliance** : electrodoméstico *m*, aparato *m* electrodoméstico

applicability [ˌæplɪkə'bɪləti, əˌplɪkə-] *n* : aplicabilidad *f*

applicable ['æplɪkəbəl, ə'plɪkə-] *adj* : aplicable, pertinente

applicant ['æplɪkənt] *n* : solicitante *mf*, aspirante *mf*, postulante *mf*; candidato *m*, -ta *f*

application [ˌæplɪ'keɪʃən] *n* **1** USE : aplicación *f*, empleo *m*, uso *m* **2** DILIGENCE : aplicación *f*, diligencia *f*, dedicación *f* **3** REQUEST : solicitud *f*, petición *f*, demanda *f*

applicator ['æpləˌkeɪtər] *n* : aplicador *m*

appliqué¹ [ˌæplə'keɪ] *vt* : decorar con apliques

appliqué² *n* : aplique *m*

apply [ə'plaɪ] *v* **-plied; -plying** *vt* **1** : aplicar (una sustancia, los frenos, el conocimiento) **2 to apply oneself** : dedicarse, aplicarse — *vi* **1** : aplicarse, referirse ⟨the rules apply to everyone : las reglas se aplican a todos⟩ **2 to apply for** : solicitar, pedir

appoint [ə'pɔɪnt] *vt* **1** NAME : nombrar, designar **2** FIX, SET : fijar, señalar, designar ⟨to appoint a date : fijar una fecha⟩ **3** EQUIP : equipar ⟨a well-appointed office : una oficina bien equipada⟩

appointee [əˌpɔɪn'tiː, ˌæ-] *n* : persona *f* designada

appointment [ə'pɔɪntmənt] *n* **1** APPOINTING : nombramiento *m*, designación *f* **2** ENGAGEMENT : cita *f*, hora *f* **3** POST : puesto *m*

apportion [ə'porʃən] *vt* : distribuir, repartir

apportionment [ə'porʃənmənt] *n* : distribución *f*, repartición *f*, reparto *m*

apposite ['æpəzət] *adj* : apropiado, oportuno, pertinente — **appositely** *adv*

appraisal [ə'preɪzəl] *n* : evaluación *f*, valoración *f*, tasación *f*, apreciación *f*

appraise [ə'preɪz] *vt* **-praised; -praising** : evaluar, valorar, tasar, apreciar

appraiser [ə'preɪzər] *n* : tasador *m*, -dora *f*

appreciable [ə'priːʃəbəl, -'prɪʃiə-] *adj* : apreciable, sensible, considerable — **appreciably** [-bli] *adv*

appreciate [ə'priːʃiˌeɪt, -'prɪ-] *v* **-ated; -ating** *vt* **1** VALUE : apreciar, valorar **2** : agradecer ⟨we appreciate his frankness : agradecemos su franqueza⟩ **3** UNDERSTAND : darse cuenta de, entender — *vi* : apreciarse, valorizarse

appreciation [əˌpriːʃi'eɪʃən, -ˌprɪ-] *n* **1** GRATITUDE : agradecimiento *m*, reconocimiento *m* **2** VALUING : apreciación *f*, valoración *f*, estimación *f* ⟨art appreciation : apreciación artística⟩ **3** UNDERSTANDING : comprensión *f*, entendimiento *m*

appreciative [ə'priːʃətɪv, -'prɪ-; ə'priːʃi ˌeɪ-] *adj* **1** : apreciativo ⟨an appreciative audience : un público apreciativo⟩ **2** GRATEFUL : agradecido **3** ADMIRING : de admiración

apprehend [ˌæprɪ'hɛnd] *vt* **1** ARREST : aprehender, detener, arrestar **2** DREAD : temer **3** COMPREHEND : comprender, entender

apprehension [ˌæprɪ'hɛntʃən] *n* **1** ARREST : arresto *m*, detención *f*, aprehensión *f* **2** ANXIETY : aprensión *f*, ansiedad *f*, temor *m* **3** UNDERSTANDING : comprensión *f*, percepción *f*

apprehensive [ˌæprɪ'hɛntsɪv] *adj* : aprensivo, inquieto — **apprehensively** *adv*

apprentice[1] [ə'prɛntɪs] *vt* **-ticed; -ticing** : colocar de aprendiz

apprentice[2] *n* : aprendiz *m*, -diza *f*

apprenticeship [ə'prɛntɪsˌʃɪp] *n* : aprendizaje *f*

apprise [ə'praɪz] *vt* **-prised; -prising** : informar, avisar

approach[1] [ə'proːtʃ] *vt* **1** NEAR : acercarse a **2** APPROXIMATE : aproximarse a **3** : abordar, dirigirse a ⟨I approached my boss with the proposal : me dirigí a mi jefe con la propuesta⟩ **4** TACKLE : abordar, enfocar, considerar — *vi* : acercarse, aproximarse

approach[2] *n* **1** NEARING : acercamiento *m*, aproximación *f* **2** POSITION : enfoque *m*, planteamiento *m* **3** OFFER : propuesta *f*, oferta *f* **4** ACCESS : acceso *m*, vía *f* de acceso

approachable [ə'proːtʃəbəl] *adj* : accesible, asequible

approbation [ˌæprə'beɪʃən] *n* : aprobación *f*

appropriate[1] [ə'proːpriˌeɪt] *vt* **-ated; -ating 1** SEIZE : apropiarse de **2** ALLOCATE : destinar, asignar

appropriate[2] [ə'proːpriət] *adj* : apropiado, adecuado, idóneo — **appropriately** *adv*

appropriateness [ə'proːpriətnəs] *n* : idoneidad *f*, propiedad *f*

appropriation [əˌproːpri'eɪʃən] *n* **1** SEIZURE : apropiación *f* **2** ALLOCATION : asignación *f*

approval [ə'pruːvəl] *n* **1** : aprobación *f*, visto *m* bueno **2 on approval** : a prueba

approve [ə'pruːv] *vt* **-proved; -proving 1** : aprobar, sancionar, darle el visto bueno a **2 to approve of** : consentir en, aprobar ⟨he doesn't approve of smoking : está en contra del tabaco⟩

approximate[1] [ə'praksəˌmeɪt] *vt* **-mated; -mating** : aproximarse a, acercarse a

approximate[2] [ə'praksəmət] *adj* : aproximado

approximately [ə'praksəmətli] *adv* : aproximadamente, más o menos

approximation [əˌpraksə'meɪʃən] *n* : aproximación *f*

appurtenance [ə'pərtənənts] *n* : accesorio *m*

apricot ['æprəˌkat, 'eɪ-] *n* : albaricoque *m*, chabacano *m Mex*

April ['eɪprəl] *n* : abril *m*

apron ['eɪprən] *n* : delantal *m*, mandil *m*

apropos[1] [ˌæprə'poː, 'æprəˌpoː] *adv* : a propósito

apropos[2] *adj* : pertinente, oportuno, acertado

apropos of *prep* : a propósito de

apt ['æpt] *adj* **1** FITTING : apto, apropiado, acertado, oportuno **2** LIABLE : propenso, inclinado **3** CLEVER, QUICK : listo, despierto

aptitude ['æptəˌtuːd, -ˌtjuːd] *n* **1** : aptitud *f*, capacidad *f* ⟨aptitude test : prueba de aptitud⟩ **2** TALENT : talento *m*, facilidad *f*

aptly ['æptli] *adv* : acertadamente

aqua ['ækwə, 'a-] *n* : color *m* aguamarina

aquarium [ə'kwæriəm] *n, pl* **-iums** *or* **-ia** [-iə] : acuario *m*

Aquarius [ə'kwæriəs] *n* : Acuario *mf*

aquatic [ə'kwaṭɪk, -'kwæ-] *adj* : acuático

aqueduct ['ækwəˌdʌkt] *n* : acueducto *m*

aqueous ['eɪkwiəs, 'æ-] *adj* : acuoso

aquiline ['ækwəˌlaɪn, -lən] *adj* : aguileño

Arab[1] ['ærəb] *adj* : árabe

Arab[2] *n* : árabe *mf*

arabesque [ˌærə'bɛsk] *n* : arabesco *m*

Arabian[1] [ə'reɪbiən] *adj* : árabe

Arabian[2] *n* → **Arab**[2]

Arabic[1] ['ærəbɪk] *adj* : árabe

Arabic[2] *n* : árabe *m* (idioma)

arable ['ærəbəl] *adj* : arable, cultivable

arbiter ['arbəṭər] *n* : árbitro *m*, -tra *f*

arbitrary ['arbəˌtreri] *adj* : arbitrario — **arbitrarily** [ˌarbə'trɛrəli] *adv*

arbitrate ['arbəˌtreɪt] *v* **-trated; -trating** : arbitrar

arbitration [ˌarbə'treɪʃən] *n* : arbitraje *m*

arbitrator ['arbəˌtreɪṭər] *n* : árbitro *m*, -tra *f*

arbor ['arbər] *n* : cenador *m*, pérgola *f*

arboreal [ar'boriəl] *adj* : arbóreo

arc[1] ['ark] *vi* **arced; arcing** : formar un arco

arc[2] *n* : arco *m*

arcade [ar'keɪd] *n* **1** ARCHES : arcada *f* **2** MALL : galería *f* comercial

arcane [ar'keɪn] *adj* : arcano, secreto, misterioso

arch[1] ['artʃ] *vt* : arquear, enarcar — *vi* : formar un arco, arquearse

arch[2] *adj* **1** CHIEF : principal **2** MISCHIEVOUS : malicioso, pícaro

arch[3] *n* : arco *m*

archaeological [ˌarkiə'laʤɪkəl] *adj* : arqueológico

archaeologist [ˌarki'aləʤɪst] *n* : arqueólogo *m*, -ga *f*

archaeology *or* **archeology** [ˌarki-'aləʤi] *n* : arqueología *f*

archaic [ar'keɪk] *adj* : arcaico — **archaically** [-ɪkli] *adv*

archangel ['arkˌeɪnʤəl] *n* : arcángel *m*

archbishop [artʃ'bɪʃəp] *n* : arzobispo *m*

archdiocese [artʃ'daɪəsəs, -ˌsiːz, -ˌsiːs] *n* : archidiócesis *f*

archer ['artʃər] *n* : arquero *m*, -ra *f*

archery ['artʃəri] *n* : tiro *m* al arco

archetypal [ˌarkɪ'taɪpəl] *adj* : arquetípico

archetype ['arkɪˌtaɪp] *n* : arquetipo *m*

archipelago [ˌarkə'pɛləˌgoː, ˌartʃ-] *n, pl* **-goes** *or* **-gos** [-goːz] : archipiélago *m*

architect ['arkəˌtɛkt] *n* : arquitecto *m*, -ta *f*

architectural [ˌarkə'tɛktʃərəl] *adj* : arquitectónico — **architecturally** *adv*

architecture ['arkəˌtɛktʃər] *n* : arquitectura *f*

archive ['ar,kaɪv] *n or* **archives** ['ar-ˌkaɪvz] *npl* : archivo *m*

archivist ['ɑrkəvɪst, -ˌkaɪ-] *n* : archivero *m*, -ra *f*; archivista *mf*
archway ['ɑrtʃˌweɪ] *n* : arco *m*, pasadizo *m* abovedado
arctic ['ɑrktɪk, 'ɑrt-] *adj* **1** : ártico ⟨arctic regions : zonas árticas⟩ **2** FRIGID : glacial
arctic circle *n* : círculo *m* ártico
ardent ['ɑrdənt] *adj* **1** PASSIONATE : ardiente, fogoso, apasionado **2** FERVENT : ferviente, fervoroso — **ardently** *adv*
ardor ['ɑrdər] *n* : ardor *m*, pasión *f*, fervor *m*
arduous ['ɑrdʒʊəs] *adj* : arduo, duro, riguroso — **arduously** *adv*
arduousness ['ɑrdʒʊəsnəs] *n* : dureza *f*, rigor *m*
are → **be**
area ['æriə] *n* **1** SURFACE : área *f*, superficie *f* **2** REGION : área *f*, región *f*, zona *f* **3** FIELD : área *f*, terreno *m*, campo *m* (de conocimiento)
area code *n* : código *m* de la zona, prefijo *m* *Spain*
arena [ə'riːnə] *n* **1** : arena *f*, estadio *m* ⟨sports arena : estadio deportivo⟩ **2** : arena *f*, ruedo *m* ⟨the political arena : el ruedo político⟩
Argentine ['ɑrdʒənˌtaɪn, -ˌtiːn] *or* **Argentinean** *or* **Argentinian** [ˌɑrdʒən'tɪniən] *n* : argentino *m*, -na *f* — **Argentine** *or* **Argentinean** *or* **Argentinian** *adj*
argon ['ɑrˌgɑn] *n* : argón *m*
argot ['ɑrgət, -ˌgoː] *n* : argot *m*
arguable ['ɑrgjʊəbəl] *adj* : discutible
argue ['ɑrˌgjuː] *v* -**gued**; -**guing** *vi* **1** REASON : argüir, argumentar, razonar **2** DISPUTE : discutir, pelear(se), alegar — *vt* **1** SUGGEST : sugerir **2** MAINTAIN : alegar, argüir, sostener **3** DISCUSS : discutir, debatir
argument ['ɑrgjəmənt] *n* **1** REASONING : argumento *m*, razonamiento *m* **2** DISCUSSION : discusión *f*, debate *m* **3** QUARREL : pelea *f*, riña *f*, disputa *f*
argumentative [ˌɑrgjə'mɛntətɪv] *adj* : discutidor
argyle ['ɑrˌgaɪl] *n* : diseño *m* de rombos
aria ['ɑriə] *n* : aria *f*
arid ['ærəd] *adj* : árido
aridity [ə'rɪdəti, æ-] *n* : aridez *f*
Aries ['ɛriːz, -iˌiːz] *n* : Aries *mf*
arise [ə'raɪz] *vi* **arose** [ə'roːz]; **arisen** [ə'rɪzən]; **arising 1** ASCEND : ascender, subir, elevarse **2** ORIGINATE : originarse, surgir, presentar **3** GET UP : levantarse
aristocracy [ˌærə'stɑkrəsi] *n, pl* -**cies** : aristocracia *f*
aristocrat [ə'rɪstəˌkræt] *n* : aristócrata *mf*
aristocratic [əˌrɪstə'krætɪk] *adj* : aristocrático, noble
arithmetic[1] [ˌærɪθ'mɛtɪk] *or* **arithmetical** [-tɪkəl] *adj* : aritmético
arithmetic[2] [ə'rɪθməˌtɪk] *n* : aritmética *f*
ark ['ɑrk] *n* : arca *f*

arm[1] ['ɑrm] *vt* : armar — *vi* : armarse
arm[2] *n* **1** : brazo *m* (del cuerpo o de un sillón), manga *f* (de una prenda) **2** BRANCH : rama *f*, sección *f* **3** WEAPON : arma *f* ⟨to take up arms : tomar las armas⟩ **4** → **coat of arms**
armada [ɑr'mɑdə, -'meɪ-] *n* : armada *f*, flota *f*
armadillo [ˌɑrmə'dɪlo] *n, pl* -**los** : armadillo *m*
armament ['ɑrməmənt] *n* : armamento *m*
armchair ['ɑrmˌtʃɛr] *n* : butaca *f*, sillón *m*
armed ['ɑrmd] *adj* **1** : armado ⟨armed robbery : robo a mano armada⟩ **2** **armed forces** : fuerzas *fpl* armadas
Armenian [ɑr'miːniən] *n* : armenio *m*, -nia *f* — **Armenian** *adj*
armistice ['ɑrməstɪs] *n* : armisticio *m*
armor ['ɑrmər] *n* : armadura *f*, coraza *f*
armored ['ɑrmərd] *adj* : blindado, acorazado
armory ['ɑrməri] *n, pl* -**mories** : arsenal *m* (almacén), armería *f* (museo), fábrica *f* de armas
armpit ['ɑrmˌpɪt] *n* : axila *f*, sobaco *m*
army ['ɑrmi] *n, pl* -**mies** **1** : ejército *m* (militar) **2** MULTITUDE : legión *f*, multitud *f*, ejército *m*
aroma [ə'roːmə] *n* : aroma *f*
aromatic [ˌærə'mætɪk] *adj* : aromático
around[1] [ə'raʊnd] *adv* **1** : de circunferencia ⟨a tree three feet around : un árbol de tres pies de circunferencia⟩ **2** : alrededor, a la redonda ⟨for miles around : por millas a la redonda⟩ ⟨all around : por todos lados, todo alrededor⟩ **3** : por ahí ⟨they're somewhere around : deben estar por ahí⟩ **4** APPROXIMATELY : más o menos, aproximadamente ⟨around 5 o'clock : a eso de las 5⟩ **5 to turn around** : darse la vuelta, voltearse
around[2] *prep* **1** SURROUNDING : alrededor de, en torno a **2** THROUGH : por, en ⟨he traveled around Mexico : viajó por México⟩ ⟨around the house : en casa⟩ **3** : a la vuelta de ⟨around the corner : a la vuelta de la esquina⟩ **4** NEAR : alrededor de, cerca de
arousal [ə'raʊzəl] *n* : excitación *f*
arouse [ə'raʊz] *vt* **aroused**; **arousing 1** AWAKE : despertar **2** EXCITE : despertar, suscitar, excitar
arraign [ə'reɪn] *vt* : hacer comparecer (ante un tribunal)
arraignment [ə'reɪnmənt] *n* : orden *m* de comparecencia, acusación *f*
arrange [ə'reɪndʒ] *vt* -**ranged**; -**ranging 1** ORDER : arreglar, poner en orden, disponer **2** SETTLE : arreglar, fijar, concertar **3** ADAPT : arreglar, adaptar
arrangement [ə'reɪndʒmənt] *n* **1** ORDER : arreglo *m*, orden *m* **2** ARRANGING : disposición *f* ⟨floral arrangement : arreglo floral⟩ **3** AGREEMENT : arreglo *m*, acuerdo *m*, convenio *m* **4** arrange-

ments *npl* : preparativos *mpl*, planes *mpl*

array¹ [ə'reɪ] *vt* **1** ORDER : poner en orden, presentar, formar **2** GARB : vestir, ataviar, engalanar

array² *n* **1** ORDER : orden *m*, formación *f* **2** ATTIRE : atavío *m*, galas *mpl* **3** RANGE, SELECTION : selección *f*, serie *f*, gama *f* ⟨an array of problems : una serie de problemas⟩

arrears [ə'rɪrz] *npl* : atrasos *mpl* ⟨to be in arrears : estar atrasado en los pagos⟩

arrest¹ [ə'rest] *vt* **1** APPREHEND : arrestar, detener **2** CHECK, STOP : detener, parar

arrest² *n* **1** APPREHENSION : arresto *m*, detención *f* ⟨under arrest : detenido⟩ **2** STOPPING : paro *m*

arrival [ə'raɪvəl] *n* : llegada *f*, venida *f*, arribo *m*

arrive [ə'raɪv] *vi* -**rived**; -**riving 1** COME : llegar, arribar **2** SUCCEED : triunfar, tener éxito

arrogance ['ærəgənts] *n* : arrogancia *f*, soberbia *f*, altanería *f*, altivez *f*

arrogant ['ærəgənt] *adj* : arrogante, soberbio, altanero, altivo — **arrogantly** *adv*

arrogate ['ærə,geɪt] *vt* -**gated**; -**gating to arrogate to oneself** : arrogarse

arrow ['æro] *n* : flecha *f*

arrowhead ['æro,hɛd] *n* : punta *f* de flecha

arroyo [ə'rɔɪo] *n* : arroyo *m*

arsenal ['arsənəl] *n* : arsenal *m*

arsenic ['arsənɪk] *n* : arsénico *m*

arson ['arsən] *n* : incendio *m* premeditado

arsonist ['arsənɪst] *n* : incendiario *m*, -ria *f*; pirómano *m*, -na *f*

art ['art] *n* **1** : arte *m* **2** SKILL : destreza *f*, habilidad *f*, maña *f* **3 arts** *npl* : letras *fpl* (en la educación) **4 fine arts** : bellas artes *fpl*

arterial [ar'tɪriəl] *adj* : arterial

arteriosclerosis [ar,tɪriosklə'ro:sɪs] *n* : arteriosclerosis *f*

artery ['artəri] *n, pl* -**teries 1** : arteria *f* **2** THOROUGHFARE : carretera *f* principal, arteria *f*

artesian well [ar'ti:ʒən] *n* : pozo *m* artesiano

artful ['artfəl] *adj* **1** INGENIOUS : ingenioso, diestro **2** CRAFTY : astuto, taimado, ladino, artero — **artfully** *adv*

arthritic [ar'θrɪtɪk] *adj* : artrítico

arthritis [ar'θraɪtəs] *n, pl* -**tides** [ar-'θrɪtə,di:z] : artritis *f*

arthropod ['arθrə,pad] *n* : artrópodo *m*

artichoke ['artə,tʃo:k] *n* : alcachofa *f*

article ['artɪkəl] *n* **1** ITEM : artículo *m*, objeto *m* **2** ESSAY : artículo *m* **3** CLAUSE : artículo *m*, cláusula *f* **4** : artículo *m* ⟨definite article : artículo determinado⟩

articulate¹ [ar'tɪkjə,leɪt] *vt* -**lated**; -**lating 1** UTTER : articular, enunciar, expresar **2** CONNECT : articular (en anatomía)

articulate² [ar'tɪkjələt] *adj* **to be articulate** : poder articular palabras, expresarse bien

articulately [ar'tɪkjələtli] *adv* : elocuentemente, con fluidez

articulateness [ar'tɪkjələtnəs] *n* : elocuencia *f*, fluidez *f*

articulation [ar,tɪkjə'leɪʃən] *n* **1** JOINT : articulación *f* **2** UTTERANCE : articulación *f*, declaración *f* **3** ENUNCIATION : articulación *f*, pronunciación *f*

artifact ['artə,fækt] *n* : artefacto *m*

artifice ['artəfəs] *n* : artificio *m*

artificial [,artə'fɪʃəl] *adj* **1** SYNTHETIC : artificial, sintético **2** FEIGNED : artificial, falso, afectado

artificially [,artə'fɪʃəli] *adv* : artificialmente, con afectación

artillery [ar'tɪləri] *n, pl* -**leries** : artillería *f*

artisan ['artəzən, -sən] *n* : artesano *m*, -na *f*

artist ['artɪst] *n* : artista *mf*

artistic [ar'tɪstɪk] *adj* : artístico — **artistically** [-tɪkli] *adv*

artistry ['artəstri] *n* : maestría *f*, arte *m*

artless ['artləs] *adj* : sencillo, natural, ingenuo, cándido — **artlessly** *adv*

artlessness ['artləsnəs] *n* : ingenuidad *f*, candidez *f*

arty ['arti] *adj* **artier; -est** : pretenciosamente artístico

as¹ ['æz] *adv* **1** : tan, tanto ⟨this one's not as difficult : éste no es tan difícil⟩ **2** : como ⟨some trees, as oak and pine : algunos árboles, como el roble y el pino⟩

as² *conj* **1** LIKE : como, igual que **2** WHEN, WHILE : cuando, mientras, a la vez que **3** BECAUSE : porque **4** THOUGH : aunque, por más que ⟨strange as it may appear : por extraño que parezca⟩ **5 as is** : tal como está

as³ *prep* **1** : de ⟨I met her as a child : la conocí de pequeña⟩ **2** LIKE : como ⟨behave as a man : compórtate como un hombre⟩

as⁴ *pron* : que ⟨in the same building as my brother : en el mismo edificio que mi hermano⟩

asbestos [æz'bɛstəs, æs-] *n* : asbesto *m*, amianto *m*

ascend [ə'sɛnd] *vi* : ascender, subir — *vt* : subir, subir a, escalar

ascendancy [ə'sɛndəntsi] *n* : ascendiente *m*, predominio *m*

ascendant¹ [ə'sɛndənt] *adj* **1** RISING : ascendente **2** DOMINANT : superior, dominante

ascendant² *n* **to be in the ascendant** : estar en alza, ir ganando predominio

ascension [ə'sɛntʃən] *n* : ascensión *f*

ascent [ə'sɛnt] *n* **1** RISE : ascensión *f*, subida *f*, ascenso *m* **2** SLOPE : cuesta *f*, pendiente *f*

ascertain [,æsər'teɪn] *vt* : determinar, establecer, averiguar

ascertainable [,æsər'teɪnəbəl] *adj* : determinable, averiguable

ascetic¹ [ə'sɛṭɪk] *adj* : ascético
ascetic² *n* : asceta *mf*
asceticism [ə'sɛṭəˌsɪzəm] *n* : ascetismo *m*
ascribable [ə'skraɪbəbəl] *adj* : atribuible, imputable
ascribe [ə'skraɪb] *vt* **-cribed; -cribing** : atribuir, imputar
aseptic [eɪ'sɛptɪk] *adj* : aséptico
asexual [ˌeɪ'sɛkʃʋəl] *adj* : asexual
as for *prep* CONCERNING : en cuanto a, respecto a, para
ash ['æʃ] *n* **1** : ceniza *f* ⟨to reduce to ashes : reducir a cenizas⟩ **2** : fresno *m* (árbol)
ashamed [ə'ʃeɪmd] *adj* : avergonzado, abochornado, apenado — **ashamedly** [ə'ʃeɪmədli] *adv*
ashen ['æʃən] *adj* : lívido, ceniciento, pálido
ashore [ə'ʃor] *adv* **1** : en tierra **2 to go ashore** : desembarcar
ashtray ['æʃˌtreɪ] *n* : cenicero *m*
Asian¹ ['eɪʒən, -ʃən] *adj* : asiático
Asian² *n* : asiático *m*, -ca *f*
aside [ə'saɪd] *adv* **1** : a un lado ⟨to step aside : hacerse a un lado⟩ **2** : de lado, aparte ⟨jesting aside : bromas aparte⟩ **3 to set aside** : guardar, apartar, reservar
aside from *prep* **1** BESIDES : además de **2** EXCEPT : aparte de, menos
as if *conj* : como si
asinine ['æsənˌaɪn] *adj* : necio, estúpido
ask ['æsk] *vt* **1** : preguntar ⟨ask him if he's coming : pregúntale si viene⟩ **2** REQUEST : pedir, solicitar ⟨to ask a favor : pedir un favor⟩ **3** INVITE : invitar — *vi* **1** INQUIRE : preguntar ⟨I asked about her children : pregunté por sus niños⟩ **2** REQUEST : pedir ⟨we asked for help : pedimos ayuda⟩
askance [ə'skænts] *adv* **1** SIDELONG : de reojo, de soslayo **2** SUSPICIOUSLY : con recelo, con desconfianza
askew [ə'skju:] *adj* : torcido, ladeado
asleep [ə'sli:p] *adj* **1** : dormido, durmiendo **2 to fall asleep** : quedarse dormido
as of *prep* : desde, a partir de
asparagus [ə'spærəgəs] *n* : espárrago *m*
aspect ['æˌspɛkt] *n* : aspecto *m*
aspen ['æspən] *n* : álamo *m* temblón
asperity [æ'spɛrəṭi, ə-] *n*, *pl* **-ties** : aspereza *f*
aspersion [ə'spərʒən] *n* : difamación *f*, calumnia *f*
asphalt ['æsˌfɔlt] *n* : asfalto *m*
asphyxia [æ'sfɪksiə, ə-] *n* : asfixia *f*
asphyxiate [æ'sfɪksiˌeɪt] *v* **-ated; -ating** *vt* : asfixiar — *vi* : asfixiarse
asphyxiation [æˌsfɪksi'eɪʃən] *n* : asfixia *f*
aspirant ['æspərənt, ə'spaɪrənt] *n* : aspirante *mf*, pretendiente *mf*
aspiration [ˌæspə'reɪʃən] *n* **1** DESIRE : aspiración *f*, anhelo *m*, ambición *f* **2** BREATHING : aspiración *f*

aspire [ə'spaɪr] *vi* **-pired; -piring** : aspirar
aspirin ['æsprən, 'æspə-] *n*, *pl* **aspirin** *or* **aspirins** : aspirina *f*
ass ['æs] *n* **1** : asno *m* **2** IDIOT : imbécil *mf*, idiota *mf*
assail [ə'seɪl] *vt* : atacar, asaltar
assailant [ə'seɪlənt] *n* : asaltante *mf*, atacante *mf*
assassin [ə'sæsən] *n* : asesino *m*, -na *f*
assassinate [ə'sæsənˌeɪt] *vt* **-nated; -nating** : asesinar
assassination [əˌsæsən'eɪʃən] *n* : asesinato *m*
assault¹ [ə'sɔlt] *vt* : atacar, asaltar, agredir
assault² *n* : ataque *m*, asalto *m*, agresión *f*
assay¹ [æ'seɪ, 'æˌseɪ] *vt* : ensayar
assay² ['æˌseɪ, æ'seɪ] *n* : ensayo *m*
assemble [ə'sɛmbəl] *v* **-bled; -bling** *vt* **1** GATHER : reunir, recoger, juntar **2** CONSTRUCT : ensamblar, montar, construir — *vi* : reunirse, congregarse
assembly [ə'sɛmbli] *n*, *pl* **-blies 1** MEETING : reunión *f* **2** CONSTRUCTING : ensamblaje *m*, montaje *m*
assemblyman [ə'sɛmblimən] *n*, *pl* **-men** [-mən, -ˌmɛn] : asambleísta *m*
assemblywoman [ə'sɛmbliˌwʋmən] *n*, *pl* **-women** [-ˌwɪmən] : asambleísta *f*
assent¹ [ə'sɛnt] *vi* : asentir, consentir
assent² *n* : asentimiento *m*, aprobación *f*
assert [ə'sərt] *vt* **1** AFFIRM : afirmar, aseverar, mantener **2 to assert oneself** : imponerse, hacerse valer
assertion [ə'sərʃən] *n* : afirmación *f*, aseveración *f*, aserto *m*
assertive [ə'sərṭɪv] *adj* : firme, enérgico
assertiveness [ə'sərṭɪvnəs] *n* : seguridad *f* en sí mismo
assess [ə'sɛs] *vt* **1** IMPOSE : gravar (un impuesto), imponer **2** EVALUATE : evaluar, valorar, aquilatar
assessment [ə'sɛsmənt] *n* : evaluación *f*, valoración *f*
assessor [ə'sɛsər] *n* : evaluador *m*, -dora *f*; tasador *m*, -dora *f*
asset ['æˌsɛt] *n* **1** : ventaja *f*, recurso *m* **2 assets** *npl* : bienes *mpl*, activo *m* ⟨assets and liabilities : activo y pasivo⟩
assiduous [ə'sɪdʒʋəs] *adj* : diligente, aplicado, asiduo — **assiduously** *adv*
assign [ə'saɪn] *vt* **1** APPOINT : designar, nombrar **2** ALLOT : asignar, señalar **3** ATTRIBUTE : atribuir, dar, conceder
assignment [ə'saɪnmənt] *n* **1** TASK : función *f*, tarea *f*, misión *f* **2** HOMEWORK : tarea *f*, asignación *f* *PRi*, deberes *mpl* *Spain* **3** APPOINTMENT : nombramiento *m* **4** ALLOCATION : asignación *f*
assimilate [ə'sɪməˌleɪt] *v* **-lated; -lating** *vt* : asimilar — *vi* : adaptarse, integrarse
assimilation [əˌsɪmə'leɪʃən] *n* : asimilación *f*
assist¹ [ə'sɪst] *vt* : asistir, ayudar
assist² *n* : asistencia *f*, contribución *f*

assistance [ə'sɪstənts] *n* : asistencia *f*, ayuda *f*, auxilio *m*
assistant [ə'sɪstənt] *n* : ayudante *mf*, asistente *mf*
associate¹ [ə'so:ʃi,eɪt, -si-] *v* **-ated; -ating** *vt* **1** CONNECT, RELATE : asociar, relacionar **2 to be associated with** : estar relacionado con, estar vinculado a — *vi* **to associate with** : relacionarse con, frecuentar
associate² [ə'so:ʃiət, -siət] *n* : asociado *m*, -da *f*; colega *mf*; socio *m*, -cia *f*
association [ə,so:ʃi'eɪʃən, -si-] *n* **1** ORGANIZATION : asociación *f*, sociedad *f* **2** RELATIONSHIP : asociación *f*, relación *f*
as soon as *conj* : en cuanto, tan pronto como
assorted [ə'sɔrtəd] *adj* : surtido
assortment [ə'sɔrtmənt] *n* : surtido *m*, variedad *f*, colección *f*
assuage [ə'sweɪdʒ] *vt* **-suaged; -suaging 1** EASE : aliviar, mitigar **2** CALM : calmar, aplacar **3** SATISFY : saciar, satisfacer
assume [ə'su:m] *vt* **-sumed; -suming 1** SUPPOSE : suponer, asumir **2** UNDERTAKE : asumir, encargarse de **3** TAKE ON : adquirir, adoptar, tomar ⟨to assume importance : tomar importancia⟩ **4** FEIGN : adoptar, afectar, simular
assumption [ə'sʌmpʃən] *n* : asunción *f*, presunción *f*
assurance [ə'ʃurənts] *n* **1** CERTAINTY : certidumbre *f*, certeza *f* **2** CONFIDENCE : confianza *f*, aplomo *m*, seguridad *f*
assure [ə'ʃur] *vt* **-sured; -suring** : asegurar, garantizar ⟨I assure you that I'll do it : te aseguro que lo haré⟩
assured [ə'ʃurd] *adj* **1** CERTAIN : seguro, asegurado **2** CONFIDENT : confiado, seguro de sí mismo
aster ['æstər] *n* : aster *m*
asterisk ['æstə,rɪsk] *n* : asterisco *m*
astern [ə'stərn] *adv* **1** BEHIND : detrás, a popa **2** BACKWARDS : hacia atrás
asteroid ['æstə,rɔɪd] *n* : asteroide *m*
asthma ['æzmə] *n* : asma *m*
asthmatic [æz'mætɪk] *adj* : asmático
as though → **as if**
astigmatism [ə'stɪgmə,tɪzəm] *n* : astigmatismo *m*
as to *prep* **1** ABOUT : sobre, acerca de **2** → **according to**
astonish [ə'stɑnɪʃ] *vt* : asombrar, sorprender, pasmar
astonishing [ə'stɑnɪʃɪŋ] *adj* : asombroso, sorprendente, increíble — **astonishingly** *adv*
astonishment [ə'stɑnɪʃmənt] *n* : asombro *m*, estupefacción *f*, sorpresa *f*
astound [ə'staund] *vt* : asombrar, pasmar, dejar estupefacto
astounding [ə'staundɪŋ] *adj* : asombroso, pasmoso — **astoundingly** *adv*
astraddle [ə'strædəl] *adv* : a horcajadas

astral ['æstrəl] *adj* : astral
astray [ə'streɪ] *adv & adj* : perdido, extraviado, descarriado
astride [ə'straɪd] *adv* : a horcajadas
astringency [ə'strɪndʒəntsi] *n* : astringencia *f*
astringent¹ [ə'strɪndʒənt] *adj* : astringente
astringent² *n* : astringente *m*
astrologer [ə'strɑlədʒər] *n* : astrólogo *m*, -ga *f*
astrological [,æstrə'lɑdʒɪkəl] *adj* : astrológico
astrology [ə'strɑlədʒi] *n* : astrología *f*
astronaut ['æstrə,nɔt] *n* : astronauta *mf*
astronautic [,æstrə'nɔtɪk] *or* **astronautical** [-tɪkəl] *adj* : astronáutico
astronautics [,æstrə'nɔtɪks] *ns & pl* : astronáutica *f*
astronomer [ə'strɑnəmər] *n* : astrónomo *m*, -ma *f*
astronomical [,æstrə'nɑmɪkəl] *adj* **1** : astronómico **2** ENORMOUS : astronómico, enorme, gigantesco
astronomy [ə'strɑnəmi] *n, pl* **-mies** : astronomía *f*
astute [ə'stu:t, -'stju:t] *adj* : astuto, sagaz, perspicaz — **astutely** *adv*
astuteness [ə'stu:tnəs, -'stju:t-] *n* : astucia *f*, sagacidad *f*, perspicacia *f*
asunder [ə'sʌndər] *adv* : en dos, en pedazos ⟨to tear asunder : hacer pedazos⟩
as well as¹ *conj* : tanto como
as well as² *prep* BESIDES : además de, aparte de
as yet *adv* : aún, todavía
asylum [ə'saɪləm] *n* **1** REFUGE : refugio *m*, santuario *m*, asilo *m* **2 insane asylum** : manicomio *m*
asymmetrical [,eɪsə'metrɪkəl] *or* **asymmetric** [-'metrɪk] *adj* : asimétrico
asymmetry [,eɪ'sɪmətri] *n* : asimetría *f*
at ['æt] *prep* **1** : en ⟨at the top : en lo alto⟩ ⟨at peace : en paz⟩ ⟨at Ann's house : en casa de Ana⟩ **2** : a ⟨at the rear : al fondo⟩ ⟨at 10 o'clock : a las diez⟩ **3** : por ⟨at last : por fin⟩ ⟨to be surprised at something : sorprenderse por algo⟩ **4** : de ⟨he's laughing at you : está riéndose de ti⟩ **5** : para ⟨you're good at this : eres bueno para esto⟩
at all *adv* : en absoluto, para nada
ate → **eat**
atheism ['eɪθi,ɪzəm] *n* : ateísmo *m*
atheist ['eɪθiɪst] *n* : ateo *m*, atea *f*
atheistic [,eɪθi'ɪstɪk] *adj* : ateo
athlete ['æθ,li:t] *n* : atleta *mf*
athletic [æθ'lɛtɪk] *adj* : atlético
athletics [æθ'lɛtɪks] *ns & pl* : atletismo *m*
Atlantic [ət'læntɪk, æt-] *adj* : atlántico
atlas ['ætləs] *n* : atlas *m*
ATM [,eɪ,ti:'ɛm] *n* : cajero *m* automático
atmosphere ['ætmə,sfɪr] *n* **1** AIR : atmósfera *f*, aire *m* **2** AMBIENCE : ambiente *m*, atmósfera *f*, clima *m*
atmospheric [,ætmə'sfɪrɪk, -'sfɛr-] *adj* : atmosférico — **atmospherically** [-ɪkli] *adv*

atoll ['æˌtɔl, 'eɪ-, -ˌtɑl] *n* : atolón *m*
atom ['ætəm] *n* **1** : átomo *m* **2** SPECK : ápice *m*, pizca *f*
atomic [ə'tɑmɪk] *adj* : atómico
atomic bomb *n* : bomba *f* atómica
atomizer ['ætəˌmaɪzər] *n* : atomizador *m*, pulverizador *m*
atone [ə'to:n] *vt* **atoned; atoning to atone for** : expiar
atonement [ə'to:nmənt] *n* : expiación *f*, desagravio *m*
atop¹ [ə'tɑp] *adj* : encima
atop² *prep* : encima de, sobre
atrium ['eɪtriəm] *n, pl* **atria** [-triə] *or* **atriums 1** : atrio *m* **2** : aurícula *f* (del corazón)
atrocious [ə'tro:ʃəs] *adj* : atroz — **atrociously** *adv*
atrocity [ə'trɑsəti] *n, pl* **-ties** : atrocidad *f*
atrophy¹ ['ætrəfi] *vt* **-phied; -phying** : atrofiar
atrophy² *n, pl* **-phies** : atrofia *f*
attach [ə'tætʃ] *vt* **1** FASTEN : sujetar, atar, amarrar, pegar **2** JOIN : juntar, adjuntar **3** ATTRIBUTE : dar, atribuir ⟨I attached little importance to it : le di poca importancia⟩ **4** SEIZE : embargar **5 to become attached to someone** : encariñarse con alguien
attaché [ˌætə'ʃeɪ, ˌæˌtæ-, ə,tæ-] *n* : agregado *m*, -da *f*
attachment [ə'tætʃmənt] *n* **1** ACCESSORY : accesorio *m* **2** CONNECTION : conexión *f*, acoplamiento *m* **3** FONDNESS : apego *m*, cariño *m*, afición *f*
attack¹ [ə'tæk] *vt* **1** ASSAULT : atacar, asaltar, agredir **2** TACKLE : acometer, combatir, enfrentarse con
attack² *n* **1** : ataque *m*, asalto *m*, acometida *f* ⟨to launch an attack : lanzar un ataque⟩ **2** : ataque *m*, crisis *f* ⟨heart attack : ataque cardíaco, infarto⟩ ⟨attack of nerves : crisis nerviosa⟩
attacker [ə'tækər] *n* : asaltante *mf*
attain [ə'teɪn] *vt* **1** ACHIEVE : lograr, conseguir, alcanzar, realizar **2** REACH : alcanzar, llegar a
attainable [ə'teɪnəbəl] *adj* : alcanzable, realizable, asequible
attainment [ə'teɪnmənt] *n* : logro *m*, consecución *f*, realización *f*
attempt¹ [ə'tɛmpt] *vt* : intentar, tratar de
attempt² *n* : intento *m*, tentativa *f*
attend [ə'tɛnd] *vt* **1** : asistir a ⟨to attend a meeting : asistir a una reunión⟩ **2** : atender, ocuparse de, cuidar ⟨to attend a patient : atender a un paciente⟩ **3** HEED : atender a, hacer caso de **4** ACCOMPANY : acompañar
attendance [ə'tɛndənts] *n* **1** ATTENDING : asistencia *f* **2** TURNOUT : concurrencia *f*
attendant¹ [ə'tɛndənt] *adj* : concomitante, inherente
attendant² *n* : asistente *mf*, acompañante *mf*, guarda *mf*

attention [ə'tɛntʃən] *n* **1** : atención *f* **2 to pay attention** : prestar atención, hacer caso **3 to stand at attention** : estar firme
attentive [ə'tɛntɪv] *adj* : atento — **attentively** *adv*
attentiveness [ə'tɛntɪvnəs] *n* **1** THOUGHTFULNESS : cortesía *f*, consideración *f* **2** CONCENTRATION : atención *f*, concentración *f*
attest [ə'tɛst] *vt* : atestiguar, dar fe de
attestation [ˌæˌts'teɪʃən] *n* : testimonio *m*
attic ['ætɪk] *n* : ático *m*, desván *m*, buhardilla *f*
attire¹ [ə'taɪr] *vt* **-tired; -tiring** : ataviar
attire² *n* : atuendo *m*, atavío *m*
attitude ['ætəˌtu:d, -ˌtju:d] *n* **1** FEELING : actitud *f* **2** POSTURE : postura *f*
attorney [ə'tərni] *n, pl* **-neys** : abogado *m*, -da *f*
attract [ə'trækt] *vt* **1** : atraer **2 to attract attention** : llamar la atención
attraction [ə'trækʃən] *n* : atracción *f*, atractivo *m*
attractive [ə'træktɪv] *adj* : atractivo, atrayente
attractively [ə'træktɪvli] *adv* : de manera atractiva, de buen gusto, hermosamente
attractiveness [ə'træktɪvnəs] *n* : atractivo *m*
attributable [ə'trɪbjuʈəbəl] *adj* : atribuible, imputable
attribute¹ [ə'trɪˌbju:t] *vt* **-tributed; -tributing** : atribuir
attribute² ['ætrəˌbju:t] *n* : atributo *m*, cualidad *f*
attribution [ˌætrə'bju:ʃən] *n* : atribución *f*
attune [ə'tu:n, -'tju:n] *vt* **-tuned; -tuning 1** ADAPT : adaptar, adecuar **2 to be attuned to** : estar en armonía con
atypical [ˌeɪ'tɪpɪkəl] *adj* : atípico
auburn ['ɔbərn] *adj* : castaño rojizo
auction¹ ['ɔkʃən] *vt* : subastar, rematar
auction² *n* : subasta *f*, remate *m*
auctioneer [ˌɔkʃə'nɪr] *n* : subastador *m*, -dora *f*; rematador *m*, -dora *f*
audacious [ɔ'deɪʃəs] *adj* : audaz, atrevido
audacity [ɔ'dæsəti] *n, pl* **-ties** : audacia *f*, atrevimiento *m*, descaro *m*
audible ['ɔdəbəl] *adj* : audible — **audibly** [-bli] *adv*
audience ['ɔdiənts] *n* **1** INTERVIEW : audiencia *f* **2** PUBLIC : audiencia *f*, público *m*, auditorio *m*, espectadores *mpl*
audio¹ ['ɔdiˌo:] *adj* : de sonido, de audio
audio² *n* : audio *m*
audiovisual [ˌɔdio'vɪʒʊəl] *adj* : audiovisual
audit¹ ['ɔdət] *vt* **1** : auditar (finanzas) **2** : asistir como oyente a (una clase o un curso)
audit² *n* : auditoría *f*
audition¹ [ɔ'dɪʃən] *vi* : hacer una audición

audition[2] *n* : audición *f*
auditor ['ɔdətər] *n* **1** : auditor *m*, -tora *f* (de finanzas) **2** STUDENT : oyente *mf*
auditorium [ˌɔdə'toriəm] *n*, *pl* -**riums** or -**ria** [-riə] : auditorio *m*, sala *f*
auditory ['ɔdə,tori] *adj* : auditivo
auger ['ɔgər] *n* : taladro *m*, barrena *f*
augment [ɔg'mɛnt] *vt* : aumentar, incrementar
augmentation [ˌɔgmən'teiʃən] *n* : aumento *m*, incremento *m*
augur[1] ['ɔgər] *vt* : augurar, presagiar — *vi* **to augur well** : ser de buen agüero
augur[2] *n* : augur *m*
augury ['ɔgjuri, -gər-] *n*, *pl* -**ries** : augurio *m*, presagio *m*, agüero *m*
august [ɔ'gʌst] *adj* : augusto
August ['ɔgəst] *n* : agosto *m*
auk ['ɔk] *n* : alca *f*
aunt ['ænt, 'ant] *n* : tía *f*
aura ['ɔrə] *n* : aura *f*
aural ['ɔrəl] *adj* : auditivo
auricle ['ɔrikəl] *n* : aurícula *f*
aurora borealis [ə'rorə,bori'æləs] *n* : aurora *f* boreal
auspices ['ɔspəsəz, -,si:z] *npl* : auspicios *mpl*
auspicious [ɔ'spiʃəs] *adj* : prometedor, propicio, de buen augurio
austere [ɔ'stir] *adj* : austero, severo, adusto — **austerely** *adv*
austerity [ɔ'stɛrəti] *n*, *pl* -**ties** : austeridad *f*
Australian [ɔ'streiljən] *n* : australiano *m*, -na *f* — **Australian** *adj*
Austrian ['ɔstriən] *n* : austriaco *m*, -ca *f* — **Austrian** *adj*
authentic [ə'θɛntik, ɔ-] *adj* : auténtico, genuino — **authentically** [-tikli] *adv*
authenticate [ə'θɛnti,keit, ɔ-] *vt* -**cated; -cating** : autenticar, autentificar
authenticity [ɔ,θɛn'tisəti] *n* : autenticidad *f*
author ['ɔθər] *n* **1** WRITER : escritor *m*, -tora *f*; autor *m*, -tora *f* **2** CREATOR : autor *m*, -tora *f*; creador *m*, -dora *f*; artífice *mf*
authoritarian [ɔ,θɔrə'tɛriən, ə-] *adj* : autoritario
authoritative [ə'θɔrə,teitiv, ɔ-] *adj* **1** RELIABLE : fidedigno, autorizado **2** DICTATORIAL : autoritario, dictatorial, imperioso
authoritatively [ə'θɔrə,teitivli, ɔ-] *adv* **1** RELIABLY : con autoridad **2** DICTATORIALLY : de manera autoritaria
authority [ə'θɔrəti, ɔ-] *n*, *pl* -**ties** **1** EXPERT : autoridad *f*; experto *m*, -ta *f* **2** POWER : autoridad *f*, poder *m* **3** AUTHORIZATION : autorización *f*, licencia *f* **4 the authorities** : las autoridades **5 on good authority** : de buena fuente
authorization [ˌɔθərə'zeiʃən] *n* : autorización *f*
authorize ['ɔθə,raiz] *vt* -**rized; -rizing** : autorizar, facultar
authorship ['ɔθər,ʃip] *n* : autoría *f*
autism ['ɔ,tizəm] *n* : autismo *m*

autistic [ɔ'tistik] *adj* : autista
auto ['ɔto] → **automobile**
autobiographical [ˌɔto,baiə'græfikəl] *adj* : autobiográfico
autobiography [ˌɔtobai'agrəfi] *n*, *pl* -**phies** : autobiografía *f*
autocracy [ɔ'takrəsi] *n*, *pl* -**cies** : autocracia *f*
autocrat ['ɔtə,kræt] *n* : autócrata *mf*
autocratic [ˌɔtə'krætik] *adj* : autocrático — **autocratically** [-tikli] *adv*
autograph[1] ['ɔtə,græf] *vt* : autografiar
autograph[2] *n* : autógrafo *m*
automaker ['ɔto:meikər] *n* : fabricante *mf* de autos, automotriz *f*
automate ['ɔtə,meit] *vt* -**mated; -mating** : automatizar
automatic [ˌɔtə'mætik] *adj* : automático — **automatically** [-tikli] *adv*
automation [ˌɔtə'meiʃən] *n* : automatización *f*
automaton [ɔ'tamə,tan] *n*, *pl* -**atons** or -**ata** [-tə, -,ta] : autómata *m*
automobile [ˌɔtəmo'bi:l, -'mo:,bi:l] *n* : automóvil *m*, auto *m*, carro *m*, coche *m*
automotive [ˌɔtə'mo:tiv] *adj* : automotor
autonomous [ɔ'tanəməs] *adj* : autónomo — **autonomously** *adv*
autonomy [ɔ'tanəmi] *n*, *pl* -**mies** : autonomía *f*
autopsy ['ɔ,tapsi, -təp-] *n*, *pl* -**sies** : autopsia *f*
autumn ['ɔtəm] *n* : otoño *m*
autumnal [ɔ'tʌmnəl] *adj* : otoñal
auxiliary[1] [ɔg'ziljəri, -'ziləri] *adj* : auxiliar
auxiliary[2] *n*, *pl* -**ries** : auxiliar *mf*, ayudante *mf*
avail[1] [ə'veil] *vt* **to avail oneself** : aprovecharse, valerse
avail[2] *n* **1** : provecho *m*, utilidad *f* **2 to no avail** : en vano **3 to be of no avail** : no servir de nada, ser inútil
availability [ə,veilə'biləti] *n*, *pl* -**ties** : disponibilidad *f*
available [ə'veiləbəl] *adj* : disponible
avalanche ['ævə,læntʃ] *n* : avalancha *f*, alud *m*
avarice ['ævərəs] *n* : avaricia *f*, codicia *f*
avaricious [ˌævə'riʃəs] *adj* : avaricioso, codicioso
avenge [ə'vɛndʒ] *vt* **avenged; avenging** : vengar
avenger [ə'vɛndʒər] *n* : vengador *m*, -dora *f*
avenue ['ævə,nu:, -,nju:] *n* **1** : avenida *f* **2** MEANS : vía *f*, camino *m*
average[1] ['ævridʒ, 'ævə-] *vt* -**aged; -aging** **1** : hacer un promedio de ⟨he averages 8 hours a day : hace un promedio de 8 horas diarias⟩ **2** : calcular el promedio de, promediar (en matemáticas)
average[2] *adj* **1** MEAN : medio ⟨the average temperature : la temperatura media⟩ **2** ORDINARY : común, ordinario ⟨the average man : el hombre común⟩

average³ *n* : promedio *m*
averse [ə'vərs] *adj* : reacio, opuesto
aversion [ə'vərʒən] *n* : aversión *f*
avert [ə'vərt] *vt* **1** : apartar, desviar ⟨he averted his eyes from the scene : apartó los ojos de la escena⟩ **2** AVOID, PREVENT : evitar, prevenir
aviary ['eɪvi,eri] *n, pl* **-aries** : pajarera *f*
aviation [,eɪvi'eɪʃən] *n* : aviación *f*
aviator ['eɪvi,eɪtər] *n* : aviador *m*, -dora *f*
avid ['ævɪd] *adj* **1** GREEDY : ávido, codicioso **2** ENTHUSIASTIC : ávido, entusiasta, ferviente — **avidly** *adv*
avocado [,ævə'kɑdo, ,ɑvə-] *n, pl* **-dos** : aguacate *m*, palta *f*
avocation [,ævə'keɪʃən] *n* : pasatiempo *m*, afición *f*
avoid [ə'vɔɪd] *vt* **1** SHUN : evitar, eludir **2** FORGO : evitar, abstenerse de ⟨I always avoided gossip : siempre evitaba los chismes⟩ **3** EVADE : evitar ⟨if I can avoid it : si puedo evitarlo⟩
avoidable [ə'vɔɪdəbəl] *adj* : evitable
avoidance [ə'vɔɪdənts] *n* : el evitar
avoirdupois [,ævərdə'pɔɪz] *n* : sistema *m* inglés de pesos y medidas
avow [ə'vaʊ] *vt* : reconocer, confesar
avowal [ə'vaʊəl] *n* : reconocimiento *m*, confesión *f*
await [ə'weɪt] *vt* : esperar
awake¹ [ə'weɪk] *v* **awoke** [ə'wo:k]; **awoken** [ə'wo:kən] *or* **awaked; awaking** : despertar
awake² *adj* : despierto
awaken [ə'weɪkən] → **awake¹**
award¹ [ə'wɔrd] *vt* : otorgar, conceder, conferir
award² *n* **1** PRIZE : premio *m*, galardón *m* **2** MEDAL : condecoración *f*
aware [ə'wær] *adj* : consciente ⟨to be aware of : darse cuenta de, estar consciente de⟩
awareness [ə'wærnəs] *n* : conciencia *f*, conocimiento *m*
awash [ə'wɔʃ] *adj* : inundado
away¹ [ə'weɪ] *adv* **1** : de aquí ⟨go away! : ¡fuera de aquí!, ¡vete!⟩ **2** : de distancia ⟨10 miles away : 10 millas de distancia, queda a 10 millas⟩ **3 far away** : lejos, a lo lejos **4 right away** : en segui-

da, ahora mismo **5 to be away** : estar ausente, estar de viaje **6 to give away** : regalar (una posesión), revelar (un secreto) **7 to go away** : irse, largarse **8 to put away** : guardar **9 to turn away** : volver la cara
away² *adj* **1** ABSENT : ausente ⟨away for the week : ausente por la semana⟩ **2 away game** : partido *m* que se juega fuera
awe¹ ['ɔ] *vt* **awed; awing** : abrumar, asombrar, impresionar
awe² *n* : asombro *m*
awesome ['ɔsəm] *adj* **1** IMPOSING : imponente, formidable **2** AMAZING : asombroso
awestruck ['ɔ,strʌk] *adj* : asombrado
awful ['ɔfəl] *adj* **1** AWESOME : asombroso **2** DREADFUL : horrible, terrible, atroz **3** ENORMOUS : enorme, tremendo ⟨an awful lot of people : muchísima gente, la mar de gente⟩
awfully ['ɔfəli] *adv* **1** EXTREMELY : terriblemente, extremadamente **2** BADLY : muy mal, espantosamente
awhile [ə'hwaɪl] *adv* : un rato, algún tiempo
awkward ['ɔkwərd] *adj* **1** CLUMSY : torpe, desmañado **2** EMBARRASSING : embarazoso, delicado — **awkwardly** *adv*
awkwardness ['ɔkwərdnəs] *n* **1** CLUMSINESS : torpeza *f* **2** INCONVENIENCE : incomodidad *f*
awl ['ɔl] *n* : punzón *m*
awning ['ɔnɪŋ] *n* : toldo *m*
awry [ə'raɪ] *adj* **1** ASKEW : torcido **2 to go awry** : salir mal, fracasar
ax *or* **axe** ['æks] *n* : hacha *m*
axiom ['æksiəm] *n* : axioma *m*
axiomatic [,æksiə'mætɪk] *adj* : axiomático
axis ['æksɪs] *n, pl* **axes** [-,si:z] : eje *m*
axle ['æksəl] *n* : eje *m*
aye¹ ['aɪ] *adv* : sí
aye² *n* : sí *m*
azalea [ə'zeɪljə] *n* : azalea *f*
azimuth ['æzəməθ] *n* : azimut *m*, acimut *m*
Aztec ['æz,tɛk] *n* : azteca *mf*
azure¹ ['æʒər] *adj* : azur, celeste
azure² *n* : azur *m*

B

b ['bi:] *n, pl* **b's** *or* **bs** ['bi:z] : segunda letra del alfabeto inglés
babble¹ ['bæbəl] *vi* **-bled; -bling 1** PRATTLE : balbucear **2** CHATTER : charlatanear, parlotear *fam* **3** MURMUR : murmurar
babble² *n* : balbuceo *m* (de bebé), parloteo *m* (de adultos), murmullo *m* (de voces, de un arroyo)
babe ['beɪb] *n* → **baby³**
babel ['beɪbəl, 'bæ-] *n* : babel *f*, caos *m*

baboon [bæ'bu:n] *n* : babuino *m*
baby¹ ['beɪbi] *vt* **-bied; -bying** : mimar, consentir
baby² *adj* **1** : de niño ⟨a baby carriage : un cochecito⟩ ⟨baby talk : habla infantil⟩ **2** TINY : pequeño, minúsculo
baby³ *n, pl* **-bies** : bebé *m*; niño *m*, -ña *f*
babyhood ['beɪbi,hʊd] *n* : niñez *f*, primera infancia *f*
babyish ['beɪbiʃ] *adj* : infantil, pueril

baby–sit ['beɪbiˌsɪt] *vi* **-sat** [-ˌsæt]; **-sitting** : cuidar niños, hacer de canguro *Spain*

baby–sitter ['beɪbiˌsɪtər] *n* : niñero *m*, -ra *f*; canguro *mf Spain*

baccalaureate [ˌbækəˈlɔriət] *n* : licenciatura *f*

bachelor ['bætʃələr] *n* **1** : soltero *m* **2** : licenciado *m*, -da *f* ⟨bachelor of arts degree : licenciatura en filosofía y letras⟩

bacillus [bəˈsɪləs] *n, pl* **-li** [-ˌlaɪ] : bacilo *m*

back¹ ['bæk] *vt* **1** *or* **to back up** SUPPORT : apoyar, respaldar **2** *or* **to back up** REVERSE : darle marcha atrás a (un vehículo) **3** : estar detrás de, formar el fondo de ⟨trees back the garden : unos árboles están detrás del jardín⟩ — *vi* **1** *or* **to back up** : retroceder **2 to back away** : echarse atrás **3 to back down** *or* **to back out** : volverse atrás, echarse para atrás

back² *adv* **1** : atrás, hacia atrás, detrás ⟨to move back : moverse atrás⟩ ⟨back and forth : de acá para allá⟩ **2** AGO : atrás, antes, ya ⟨some years back : unos años atrás, ya unos años⟩ ⟨10 months back : hace diez meses⟩ **3** : de vuelta, de regreso ⟨we're back : estamos de vuelta⟩ ⟨she ran back : volvió corriendo⟩ ⟨to call back : llamar de nuevo⟩

back³ *adj* **1** REAR : de atrás, posterior, trasero **2** OVERDUE : atrasado **3 back pay** : atrasos *mpl*

back⁴ *n* **1** : espalda *f* (de un ser humano), lomo *m* (de un animal) **2** : respaldo *m* (de una silla), espalda *f* (de ropa) **3** REVERSE : reverso *m*, dorso *m*, revés *m* **4** REAR : fondo *m*, parte *f* de atrás **5** : defensa *mf* (en deportes)

backache ['bækˌeɪk] *n* : dolor *m* de espalda

backbite ['bækˌbaɪt] *v* **-bit** [-ˌbɪt]; **-bitten** [-ˌbɪtən]; **-biting** *vt* : calumniar, hablar mal de — *vi* : murmurar

backbiter ['bækˌbaɪtər] *n* : calumniador *m*, -dora *f*

backbone ['bækˌbo:n] *n* **1** : columna *f* vertebral **2** FIRMNESS : firmeza *f*, carácter *m*

backdrop ['bækˌdrɑp] *n* : telón *m* de fondo

backer ['bækər] *n* **1** SUPPORTER : partidario *m*, -ria *f* **2** SPONSOR : patrocinador *m*, -dora *f*

backfire¹ ['bækˌfaɪr] *vi* **-fired; -firing 1** : petardear (dícese de un automóvil) **2** FAIL : fallar, salir el tiro por la culata

backfire² *n* : petardeo *m*, explosión *f*

background ['bækˌgraʊnd] *n* **1** : fondo *m* (de un cuadro, etc.), antecedentes *mpl* (de una situación) **2** EXPERIENCE, TRAINING : experiencia *f* profesional, formación *f*

backhand¹ ['bækˌhænd] *adv* : de revés, con el revés

backhand² *n* : revés *m*

backhanded ['bækˌhændəd] *adj* **1** : dado con el revés, de revés **2** INDIRECT : indirecto, ambiguo

backing ['bækɪŋ] *n* **1** SUPPORT : apoyo *m*, respaldo *m* **2** REINFORCEMENT : refuerzo *m* **3** SUPPORTERS : partidarios *mpl*, -rias *fpl*

backlash ['bækˌlæʃ] *n* : reacción *f* violenta

backlog ['bækˌlɔg] *n* : atraso *m*, trabajo *m* acumulado

backpack¹ ['bækˌpæk] *vi* : viajar con mochila

backpack² *n* : mochila *f*

backrest ['bækˌrɛst] *n* : respaldo *m*

backside ['bækˌsaɪd] *n* : trasero *m*

backslide ['bækˌslaɪd] *vi* **-slid** [-ˌslɪd]; **-slid** *or* **-slidden** [-ˌslɪdən]; **-sliding** : recaer, reincidir

backstage [ˌbækˈsteɪdʒ, 'bækˌ-] *adv & adj* : entre bastidores

backtrack ['bækˌtræk] *vi* : dar marcha atrás, volverse atrás

backup ['bækˌʌp] *n* **1** SUPPORT : respaldo *m*, apoyo *m* **2** : copia *f* de seguridad (para computadoras)

backward¹ ['bækwərd] *or* **backwards** [-wərdz] *adv* **1** : hacia atrás **2** : de espaldas ⟨he fell backwards : se cayó de espaldas⟩ **3** : al revés ⟨you're doing it backwards : lo estás haciendo al revés⟩ **4 to bend over backwards** : hacer todo lo posible

backward² *adj* **1** : hacia atrás ⟨a backward glance : una mirada hacia atrás⟩ **2** RETARDED : retrasado **3** SHY : tímido **4** UNDERDEVELOPED : atrasado

backwardness ['bækwərdnəs] *n* : atraso *m* (dícese de una región), retraso *m* (dícese de una persona)

backwoods [ˌbækˈwʊdz] *npl* : monte *m*, región *f* alejada

bacon ['beɪkən] *n* : tocino *m*, tocineta *f Col, Ven*, bacon *m Spain*

bacterial [bækˈtɪriəl] *adj* : bacteriano

bacteriologist [bækˌtɪriˈɑlədʒɪst] *n* : bacteriólogo *m*, -ga *f*

bacteriology [bækˌtɪriˈɑlədʒi] *n* : bacteriología *f*

bacterium [bækˈtɪriəm] *n, pl* **-ria** [-iə] : bacteria *f*

bad¹ ['bæd] *adv* → **badly**

bad² *adj* **1** : malo **2** ROTTEN : podrido **3** SERIOUS, SEVERE : grave **4** DEFECTIVE : defectuoso ⟨a bad check : un cheque sin fondos⟩ **5** HARMFUL : perjudicial **6** CORRUPT, EVIL : malo, corrompido **7** NAUGHTY : travieso **8 from bad to worse** : de mal en peor **9 too bad!** : ¡qué lástima!

bad³ *n* : lo malo ⟨the good and the bad : lo bueno y lo malo⟩

bade → **bid**

badge ['bædʒ] *n* : insignia *f*, botón *m*, chapa *f*

badger¹ ['bædʒər] *vt* : fastidiar, acosar, importunar

badger² *n* : tejón *m*
badly ['bædli] *adv* **1** : mal **2** URGENTLY : mucho, con urgencia **3** SEVERELY : gravemente
badminton ['bæd,mɪntən, -,mɪt-] *n* : bádminton *m*
badness ['bædnəs] *n* : maldad *f*
baffle¹ ['bæfəl] *vi* **-fled; -fling 1** PERPLEX : desconcertar, confundir **2** FRUSTRATE : frustrar
baffle² *n* : deflector *m*, bafle *m* (acústico)
bafflement ['bæfəlmənt] *n* : desconcierto *m*, confusión *f*
bag¹ ['bæg] *v* **bagged; bagging** *vi* SAG : formar bolsas — *vt* **1** : ensacar, poner en una bolsa **2** : cobrar (en la caza), cazar
bag² *n* **1** : bolsa *f*, saco *m* **2** HANDBAG : cartera *f*, bolso *m*, bolsa *f Mex* **3** SUITCASE : maleta *f*, valija *f*
bagatelle [,bægə'tɛl] *n* : bagatela *f*
bagel ['beɪgəl] *n* : rosquilla *f* de pan
baggage ['bægɪʤ] *n* : equipaje *m*
baggy ['bægi] *adj* **-gier; -est** : holgado, ancho
bagpipe ['bæg,paɪp] *n* *or* **bagpipes** ['bæg,paɪps] *npl* : gaita *f*
bail¹ ['beɪl] *vt* **1** : achicar (agua de un bote) **2 to bail out** : poner en libertad (de una cárcel) bajo fianza **3 to bail out** EXTRICATE : sacar de apuros
bail² *n* : fianza *f*, caución *f*
bailiff ['beɪləf] *n* : alguacil *mf*
bailiwick ['beɪli,wɪk] *n* : dominio *m*
bailout ['beɪl,aʊt] *n* : rescate *m* (financiero)
bait¹ ['beɪt] *vt* **1** : cebar (un anzuelo o cepo) **2** HARASS : acosar
bait² *n* : cebo *m*, carnada *f*
bake¹ ['beɪk] *vt* **baked; baking** : hornear, hacer al horno
bake² *n* : fiesta con platos hechos al horno
baker ['beɪkər] *n* : panadero *m*, -ra *f*
baker's dozen *n* : docena *f* de fraile
bakery ['beɪkəri] *n*, *pl* **-ries** : panadería *f*
bakeshop ['beɪk,ʃɑp] *n* : pastelería *f*, panadería *f*
baking powder *n* : levadura *f* en polvo
baking soda → **sodium bicarbonate**
balance¹ ['bælənts] *v* **-anced; -ancing** *vt* **1** : hacer el balance de (una cuenta) ⟨to balance the books : cuadrar las cuentas⟩ **2** EQUALIZE : balancear, equilibrar **3** HARMONIZE : armonizar — *vi* : balancearse
balance² *n* **1** SCALES : balanza *f*, báscula *f* **2** COUNTERBALANCE : contrapeso *m* **3** EQUILIBRIUM : equilibrio *m* **4** REMAINDER : balance *m*, resto *m*
balanced ['bæləntst] *adj* : equilibrado, balanceado
balcony ['bælkəni] *n*, *pl* **-nies 1** : balcón *m*, terraza *f* (de un edificio) **2** : galería *f* (de un teatro)

bald ['bɔld] *adj* **1** : calvo, pelado, pelón **2** PLAIN : simple, puro ⟨the bald truth : la pura verdad⟩
balding ['bɔldɪŋ] *adj* : quedándose calvo
baldly ['bɔldli] *adv* : sin reparos, sin rodeos, francamente
baldness ['bɔldnəs] *n* : calvicie *f*
bale¹ ['beɪl] *vt* **baled; baling** : empacar, hacer balas de
bale² *n* : bala *f*, fardo *m*, paca *f*
baleful ['beɪlfəl] *adj* **1** DEADLY : mortífero **2** SINISTER : siniestro, funesto, torvo ⟨a baleful glance : una mirada torva⟩
balk¹ ['bɔk] *vt* : obstaculizar, impedir — *vi* **1** : plantarse *fam* (dícese de un caballo, etc.) **2 to balk at** : resistirse a, mostrarse reacio a
balk² *n* : obstáculo *m*
Balkan ['bɔlkən] *adj* : balcánico
balky ['bɔki] *adj* **balkier; -est** : reacio, obstinado, terco
ball¹ ['bɔl] *vt* : apelotonar, ovillar
ball² *n* **1** : pelota *f*, bola *f*, balón *m*, ovillo *m* (de lana) **2** : juego *m* con pelota o bola **3** DANCE : baile *m*, baile *m* de etiqueta
ballad ['bæləd] *n* : romance *m*, balada *f*
balladeer [,bælə'dɪr] *n* : cantante *mf* de baladas
ballast¹ ['bæləst] *vt* : lastrar
ballast² *n* : lastre *m*
ball bearing *n* : cojinete *m* de bola
ballerina [,bælə'ri:nə] *n* : bailarina *f*
ballet [bæ'leɪ, 'bæ,leɪ] *n* : ballet *m*
ballistic [bə'lɪstɪk] *adj* : balístico
ballistics [bə'lɪstɪks] *ns & pl* : balística *f*
balloon¹ [bə'lu:n] *vi* **1** : viajar en globo **2** SWELL : hincharse, inflarse
balloon² *n* : globo *m*
balloonist [bə'lu:nɪst] *n* : aeróstata *mf*
ballot¹ ['bælət] *vi* : votar
ballot² *n* **1** : papeleta *f* (de voto) **2** BALLOTING : votación *f* **3** VOTE : voto *m*
ballpoint pen ['bɔl,pɔɪnt] *n* : bolígrafo *m*
ballroom ['bɔl,ru:m, -,rʊm] *n* : sala *f* de baile
ballyhoo ['bæli,hu:] *n* : propaganda *f*, publicidad *f*, bombo *m fam*
balm ['bɑm, 'bɑlm] *n* : bálsamo *m*, ungüento *m*
balmy ['bɑmi, 'bɑl-] *adj* **balmier; -est 1** MILD : templado, agradable **2** SOOTHING : balsámico **3** CRAZY : chiflado *fam*, chalado *fam*
baloney [bə'lo:ni] *n* NONSENSE : tonterías *fpl*, estupideces *fpl*
balsa ['bɔlsə] *n* : balsa *f*
balsam ['bɔlsəm] *n* **1** : bálsamo *m* **2** *or* **balsam fir** : abeto *m* balsámico
Baltic ['bɔltɪk] *adj* : báltico
baluster ['bæləstər] *n* : balaustre *m*
balustrade [,bælə'streɪd] *n* : balaustrada *f*
bamboo [bæm'bu:] *n* : bambú *m*
bamboozle [bæm'bu:zəl] *vt* **-zled; -zling** : engañar, embaucar

ban¹ ['bæn] *vt* **banned; banning** : prohibir, proscribir

ban² *n* : prohibición *f*, proscripción *f*

banal [bə'nɑl, bə'næl, 'beɪnəl] *adj* : banal, trivial

banality [bə'næləti] *n*, *pl* **-ties** : banalidad *f*, trivialidad *f*

banana [bə'nænə] *n* : banano *m*, plátano *m*, banana *f*, cambur *m Ven*, guineo *m Car*

band¹ ['bænd] *vt* **1** BIND : fajar, atar **2 to band together** : unirse, juntarse

band² *n* **1** STRIP : banda *f*, cinta *f* (de un sombrero, etc.) **2** STRIPE : franja *f* **3** : banda *f* (de radiofrecuencia) **4** RING : anillo *m* **5** GROUP : banda *f*, grupo *m*, conjunto *m* ⟨jazz band : conjunto de jazz⟩

bandage¹ ['bændɪdʒ] *vt* **-daged; -daging** : vendar

bandage² *n* : vendaje *m*, venda *f*

bandanna *or* **bandana** [bæn'dænə] *n* : pañuelo *m* (de colores)

bandit ['bændət] *n* : bandido *m*, -da *f*; bandolero *m*, -ra *f*

banditry ['bændətri] *n* : bandolerismo *m*, bandidaje *m*

bandstand ['bænd,stænd] *n* : quiosco *m* de música

bandwagon ['bænd,wægən] *n* **1** : carroza *f* de músicos **2 to jump on the bandwagon** : subirse al carro, seguir la moda

bandy¹ ['bændi] *vt* **-died; -dying 1** EXCHANGE : intercambiar **2 to bandy about** : circular, propagar

bandy² *adj* : arqueado, torcido ⟨bandy-legged : de piernas arqueadas⟩

bane ['beɪn] *n* **1** POISON : veneno *m* **2** RUIN : ruina *f*, pesadilla *f*

baneful ['beɪnfəl] *adj* : nefasto, funesto

bang¹ ['bæŋ] *vt* **1** STRIKE : golpear, darse ⟨he banged his elbow against the door : se dio con el codo en la puerta⟩ **2** SLAM : cerrar (la puerta) con un portazo — *vi* **1** SLAM : cerrarse de un golpe **2 to bang on** : aporrear, golpear ⟨she was banging on the table : aporreaba la mesa⟩

bang² *adv* : directamente, exactamente

bang³ *n* **1** BLOW : golpe *m*, porrazo *m*, trancazo *m* **2** EXPLOSION : explosión *f*, estallido *m* **3** SLAM : portazo *m* **4 bangs** *npl* : flequillo *m*, fleco *m*

Bangladeshi [,bɑŋglə'dɛʃi, ,bæŋ-, ,bʌŋ-, -'deɪ-] *n* : bangladesí *mf* — **Bangladeshi** *adj*

bangle ['bæŋgəl] *n* : brazalete *m*, pulsera *f*

banish ['bænɪʃ] *vt* **1** EXILE : desterrar, exiliar **2** EXPEL : expulsar

banishment ['bænɪʃmənt] *n* **1** EXILE : destierro *m*, exilio *m* **2** EXPULSION : expulsión *f*

banister ['bænəstər] *n* **1** BALUSTER : balaustre *m* **2** HANDRAIL : pasamanos *m*, barandilla *f*, barandal *m*

banjo ['bæn,dʒoː] *n*, *pl* **-jos** : banjo *m*

bank¹ ['bæŋk] *vt* **1** TILT : peraltar (una carretera), ladear (un avión) **2** HEAP : amontonar **3** : cubrir (un fuego) **4** : depositar (dinero en un banco) — *vi* **1** : ladearse (dícese de un avión) **2** : tener una cuenta (en un banco) **3 to bank on** : contar con

bank² *n* **1** MASS : montón *m*, montículo *m*, masa *f* **2** : orilla *f*, ribera *f* (de un río) **3** : peralte *m* (de una carretera) **4** : banco *m* ⟨World Bank : Banco Mundial⟩ ⟨banco de sangre : blood bank⟩

bankbook ['bæŋk,bʊk] *n* : libreta *f* bancaria, libreta *f* de ahorros

banker ['bæŋkər] *n* : banquero *m*, -ra *f*

banking ['bæŋkɪŋ] *n* : banca *f*

bankrupt¹ ['bæŋ,krʌpt] *vt* : hacer quebrar, llevar a la quiebra, arruinar

bankrupt² *adj* **1** : en bancarrota, en quiebra **2 ~ of** LACKING : carente de, falto de

bankrupt³ *n* : fallido *m*, -da *f*; quebrado *m*, -da *f*

bankruptcy ['bæŋ,krʌptsi] *n*, *pl* **-cies** : ruina *f*, quiebra *f*, bancarrota *f*

banner¹ ['bænər] *adj* : excelente

banner² *n* : estandarte *m*, bandera *f*

banns ['bænz] *npl* : amonestaciones *fpl*

banquet¹ ['bæŋkwət] *vi* : celebrar un banquete

banquet² *n* : banquete *m*

banter¹ ['bæntər] *vi* : bromear, hacer bromas

banter² *n* : bromas *fpl*

baptism ['bæp,tɪzəm] *n* : bautismo *m*

baptismal [bæp'tɪzməl] *adj* : bautismal

Baptist ['bæptɪst] *n* : bautista *mf* — **Baptist** *adj*

baptize [bæp'taɪz, 'bæp,taɪz] *vt* **-tized; -tizing** : bautizar

bar¹ ['bɑr] *vt* **barred; barring 1** OBSTRUCT : obstruir, bloquear **2** EXCLUDE : excluir **3** PROHIBIT : prohibir **4** SECURE : atrancar, asegurar ⟨bar the door! : ¡atranca la puerta!⟩

bar² *n* **1** : barra *f*, barrote *m* (de una ventana), tranca *f* (de una puerta) **2** BARRIER : barrera *f*, obstáculo *m* **3** LAW : abogacía *f* **4** STRIPE : franja *f* **5** COUNTER : mostrador *m*, barra *f* **6** TAVERN : bar *m*, taberna *f*

bar³ *prep* **1** : excepto, con excepción de **2 bar none** : sin excepción

barb ['bɑrb] *n* **1** POINT : púa *f*, lengüeta *f* **2** GIBE : pulla *f*

barbarian¹ [bɑr'bæriən] *adj* **1** : bárbaro **2** CRUDE : tosco, bruto

barbarian² *n* : bárbaro *m*, -ra *f*

barbaric [bɑr'bærɪk] *adj* **1** PRIMITIVE : primitivo **2** CRUEL : brutal, cruel

barbarity [bɑr'bærəti] *n*, *pl* **-ties** : barbaridad *f*

barbarous ['bɑrbərəs] *adj* **1** UNCIVILIZED : bárbaro **2** MERCILESS : despiadado, cruel

barbarously ['bɑrbərəsli] *adv* : bárbaramente

barbecue¹ ['bɑrbɪˌkjuː] vt **-cued; -cuing** : asar a la parrilla

barbecue² n : barbacoa f, parrillada f

barbed ['bɑrbd] adj **1** : con púas ⟨barbed wire : alambre de púas⟩ **2** BITING : mordaz

barber ['bɑrbər] n : barbero m, -ra f

barbiturate [bɑr'bɪtʃərət] n : barbitúrico m

bard ['bɑrd] n : bardo m

bare¹ ['bær] vt **bared; baring** : desnudar

bare² adj **1** NAKED : desnudo **2** EXPOSED : descubierto, sin protección **3** EMPTY : desprovisto, vacío **4** MINIMUM : mero, mínimo ⟨the bare necessities : las necesidades mínimas⟩ **5** PLAIN : puro, sencillo

bareback ['bærˌbæk] or **barebacked** [-ˌbækt] adv & adj : a pelo

barefaced ['bærˌfeɪst] adj : descarado

barefoot ['bærˌfʊt] or **barefooted** [-ˌfʊt̬əd] adv & adj : descalzo

bareheaded ['bærˈhɛdəd] adv & adj : sin sombrero, con la cabeza descubierta

barely ['bærli] adv : apenas, por poco

bareness ['bærnəs] n : desnudez f

bargain¹ ['bɑrgən] vi HAGGLE : regatear, negociar — vt BARTER : trocar, cambiar

bargain² n **1** AGREEMENT : acuerdo m, convenio m ⟨to strike a bargain : cerrar un trato⟩ **2** : ganga f ⟨bargain price : precio de ganga⟩

barge¹ ['bɑrdʒ] vi **barged; barging 1** : mover con torpeza **2 to barge in** : entrometerse, interrumpir

barge² n : barcaza f, gabarra f

bar graph n : gráfico m de barras

baritone ['bærəˌtoːn] n : barítono m

barium ['bæriəm] n : bario m

bark¹ ['bɑrk] vi : ladrar — vt or **to bark out** : gritar ⟨to bark out an order : dar una orden a gritos⟩

bark² n **1** : ladrido m (de un perro) **2** : corteza f (de un árbol) **3** or **barque** : tipo de embarcación con velas de proa y popa

barley ['bɑrli] n : cebada f

barn ['bɑrn] n : granero m (para cosechas), establo m (para ganado)

barnacle ['bɑrnɪkəl] n : percebe m

barnyard ['bɑrnˌjɑrd] n : corral m

barometer [bə'rɑmətər] n : barómetro m

barometric [ˌbærə'mɛtrɪk] adj : barométrico

baron ['bærən] n **1** : barón m **2** TYCOON : magnate mf

baroness ['bærənɪs, -nəs, -ˌnɛs] n : baronesa f

baronet [ˌbærə'nɛt, 'bærənət] n : baronet m

baronial [bə'roːniəl] adj **1** : de barón **2** STATELY : señorial, majestuoso

baroque [bə'roːk, -'rɑk] adj : barroco

barracks ['bærəks] ns & pl : cuartel m

barracuda [ˌbærə'kuːdə] n, pl **-da** or **-das** : barracuda f

barrage [bə'rɑʒ, -'rɑdʒ] n **1** : descarga f (de artillería) **2** DELUGE : aluvión m ⟨a barrage of questions : un aluvión de preguntas⟩

barred ['bɑrd] adj : excluido, prohibido

barrel¹ ['bærəl] v **-reled** or **-relled; -reling** or **-relling** vt : embarrilar — vi : ir disparado

barrel² n **1** : barril m, tonel m **2** : cañón m (de un arma de fuego), cilindro m

barren ['bærən] adj **1** STERILE : estéril (dícese de las plantas o la mujer), árido (dícese del suelo) **2** DESERTED : yermo, desierto

barrette [bɑ'rɛt, bə-] n : pasador m, broche m para el cabello

barricade¹ ['bærəˌkeɪd, ˌbærə'-] vt **-caded; -cading** : cerrar con barricadas

barricade² n : barricada f

barrier ['bæriər] n **1** : barrera f **2** OBSTACLE : obstáculo m, impedimento m

barring ['bɑrɪŋ] prep : excepto, salvo, a excepción de

barrio ['bɑrio, 'bær-] n : barrio m

barroom ['bɑrˌruːm, -ˌrʊm] n : bar m

barrow ['bærˌoː] → **wheelbarrow**

bartender ['bɑrˌtɛndər] n : camarero m, -ra f; barman m

barter¹ ['bɑrtər] vt : cambiar, trocar

barter² n : trueque m, permuta f

basalt [bə'sɔlt, 'beɪˌ-] n : basalto m

base¹ ['beɪs] vt **based; basing** : basar, fundamentar, establecer

base² adj **baser; basest 1** : de baja ley (dícese de un metal) **2** CONTEMPTIBLE : vil, despreciable

base³ n, pl **bases** : base f

baseball ['beɪsˌbɔl] n : beisbol m, béisbol m

baseless ['beɪsləs] adj : infundado

basely ['beɪsli] adv : vilmente

basement ['beɪsmənt] n : sótano m

baseness ['beɪsnəs] n : vileza f, bajeza f

bash¹ ['bæʃ] vt : golpear violentamente

bash² n **1** BLOW : golpe m, porrazo m, madrazo m Mex fam **2** PARTY : fiesta f, juerga f fam

bashful ['bæʃfəl] adj : tímido, vergonzoso, penoso

bashfulness ['bæʃfəlnəs] n : timidez f

basic¹ ['beɪsɪk] adj **1** FUNDAMENTAL : básico, fundamental **2** RUDIMENTARY : básico, elemental **3** : básico (en química)

basic² n : fundamento m, rudimento m

basically ['beɪsɪkli] adv : fundamentalmente

basil ['beɪzəl, 'bæzəl] n : albahaca f

basilica [bə'sɪlɪkə] n : basílica f

basin ['beɪsən] n **1** WASHBOWL : palangana f, lavamanos m, lavabo m **2** : cuenca f (de un río)

basis ['beɪsəs] n, pl **bases** [-ˌsiːz] **1** BASE : base f, pilar m **2** FOUNDATION : fundamento m, base f **3 on a weekly basis** : semanalmente

bask ['bæsk] *vi* : disfrutar, deleitarse ⟨to bask in the sun : disfrutar del sol⟩

basket ['bæskət] *n* : cesta *f*, cesto *m*, canasta *f*

basketball ['bæskət,bɔl] *n* : baloncesto *m*, basquetbol *m*

bas–relief [,bɑrɪ'li:f] *n* : bajorrelieve *m*

bass[1] ['bæs] *n*, *pl* **bass** *or* **basses** : róbalo *m* (pesca)

bass[2] ['beɪs] *n* : bajo *m* (tono, voz, cantante)

bass drum *n* : bombo *m*

basset hound ['bæsət,haʊnd] *n* : basset *m*

bassinet [,bæsə'nɛt] *n* : moisés *m*, cuna *f*

bassist ['beɪsɪst] *n* : bajista *mf*

bassoon [bə'su:n, bæ-] *n* : fagot *m*

bass viol ['beɪs'vaɪəl, -,o:l] → **double bass**

bastard[1] ['bæstərd] *adj* : bastardo

bastard[2] *n* : bastardo *m*, -da *f*

bastardize ['bæstər,daɪz] *vt* **-ized; -izing** DEBASE : degradar, envilecer

baste ['beɪst] *vt* **basted; basting** 1 STITCH : hilvanar 2 : bañar (con su jugo durante la cocción)

bastion ['bæstʃən] *n* : bastión *m*, baluarte *m*

bat[1] ['bæt] *vt* **batted; batting** 1 HIT : batear 2 **without batting an eye** : sin pestañear

bat[2] *n* 1 : murciélago *m* (animal) 2 : bate *m* ⟨baseball bat : bate de beisbol⟩

batch ['bætʃ] *n* : hornada *f*, tanda *f*, grupo *m*, cantidad *f*

bate ['beɪt] *vt* **bated; bating** 1 : aminorar, reducir 2 **with bated breath** : con ansiedad, aguantando la respiración

bath ['bæθ, 'baθ] *n*, *pl* **baths** ['bæðz, 'bæθs, 'baðz, 'baθs] 1 BATHING : baño *m* ⟨to take a bath : bañarse⟩ 2 : baño *m* (en fotografía, etc.) 3 BATHROOM : baño *m*, cuarto *m* de baño 4 SPA : balneario *m* 5 LOSS : pérdida *f*

bathe ['beɪð] *vt* **bathed; bathing** *vt* 1 WASH : bañar, lavar 2 SOAK : poner en remojo 3 FLOOD : inundar ⟨to bathe with light : inundar de luz⟩ — *vi* : bañarse, ducharse

bather ['beɪðər] *n* : bañista *mf*

bathrobe ['bæθ,ro:b] *n* : bata *f* (de baño)

bathroom ['bæθ,ru:m, -,rʊm] *n* : baño *m*, cuarto *m* de baño

bathtub ['bæθ,tʌb] *n* : bañera *f*, tina *f* (de baño)

batiste [bə'ti:st] *n* : batista *f*

baton [bə'tɑn] *n* : batuta *f*, bastón *m*

battalion [bə'tæljən] *n* : batallón *m*

batten ['bætən] *vt* **to batten down the hatches** : cerrar las escotillas

batter[1] ['bætər] *vt* 1 BEAT : aporrear, golpear 2 MISTREAT : maltratar

batter[2] *n* 1 : masa *f* para rebozar 2 HITTER : bateador *m*, -dora *f*

battering ram *n* : ariete *m*

battery ['bætəri] *n*, *pl* **-teries** 1 : lesiones *fpl* ⟨assault and battery : agresión con lesiones⟩ 2 ARTILLERY : batería *f* 3 : batería *f*, pila *f* (de electricidad) 4 SERIES : serie *f*

batting ['bætɪŋ] *n* 1 *or* **cotton batting** : algodón *m* en láminas 2 : bateo *m* (en beisbol)

battle[1] ['bætəl] *vi* **-tled; -tling** : luchar, pelear

battle[2] *n* : batalla *f*, lucha *f*, pelea *f*

battle–ax ['bætəl,æks] *n* : hacha *f* de guerra

battlefield ['bætəl,fi:ld] *n* : campo *m* de batalla

battlements ['bætəlmənts] *npl* : almenas *fpl*

battleship ['bætəl,ʃɪp] *n* : acorazado *m*

batty ['bæti] *adj* **-tier; -est** : chiflado *fam*, chalado *fam*

bauble ['bɔbəl] *n* : chuchería *f*, baratija *f*

Bavarian [bə'vɛriən] *n* : bávaro *m*, -ra *f* — **Bavarian** *adj*

bawdiness ['bɔdinəs] *n* : picardía *f*

bawdy ['bɔdi] *adj* **bawdier; -est** : subido de tono, verde, colorado *Mex*

bawl[1] ['bɔl] *vi* : llorar a gritos

bawl[2] *n* : grito *m*, alarido *m*

bawl out *vt* SCOLD : regañar

bay[1] ['beɪ] *vi* HOWL : aullar

bay[2] *adj* : castaño, zaino (dícese de los caballos)

bay[3] *n* 1 : bahía *f* ⟨Bay of Campeche : Bahía de Campeche⟩ 2 *or* **bay horse** : caballo *m* castaño 3 LAUREL : laurel *m* 4 HOWL : aullido *m* 5 : saliente *m* ⟨bay window : ventana en saliente⟩ 6 COMPARTMENT : área *f*, compartimento *m* 7 **at ~** : acorralado

bayberry ['beɪ,bɛri] *n*, *pl* **-ries** : arrayán *m* brabántico

bayonet[1] [,beɪə'nɛt, 'beɪə,nɛt] *vt* **-neted; -neting** : herir *o* matar (con bayoneta)

bayonet[2] *n* : bayoneta *f*

bayou ['baɪ,u:, -,o:] *n* : pantano *m*

bazaar [bə'zɑr] *n* 1 : bazar *m* 2 SALE : venta *f* benéfica

bazooka [bə'zu:kə] *n* : bazuca *f*

BB ['bi:bi] *n* : balín *m*

be ['bi:] *v* **was** ['wəz, 'wɑz]; **were** ['wər]; **been** ['bɪn]; **being; am** ['æm]; **is** ['ɪz]; **are** ['ɑr] *vi* 1 (*expressing equality*) : ser ⟨José is a doctor : José es doctor⟩ ⟨I'm Ann's sister : soy la hermana de Ana⟩ 2 (*expressing quality*) : ser ⟨the tree is tall : el árbol es alto⟩ ⟨you're silly! : ¡eres tonto!⟩ 3 (*expressing origin or possession*) : ser ⟨she's from Managua : es de Managua⟩ ⟨it's mine : es mío⟩ 4 (*expressing location*) : estar ⟨my mother is at home : mi madre está en casa⟩ ⟨the cups are on the table : las tazas están en la mesa⟩ 5 (*expressing existence*) : ser, existir ⟨to be or not to be : ser, o no ser⟩ ⟨I think, therefore I am : pienso, luego existo⟩ 6 (*expressing a state of being*) : estar, tener ⟨how are you? : ¿cómo estás?⟩ ⟨I'm cold : tengo frío⟩ ⟨she's 10 years old : tiene 10 años⟩ ⟨they're both sick : están enfermos los dos⟩ — *v impers* **1** (*indicating time*) : ser ⟨it's eight o'clock : son las ocho⟩ ⟨it's Friday : hoy es viernes⟩ **2** (*indicating a condition*) : hacer, estar ⟨it's sunny : hace sol⟩ ⟨it's very dark outside : está bien oscuro afuera⟩ — *v aux* **1** (*expressing progression*) : estar ⟨what are you doing? —I'm working : ¿qué haces?—estoy trabajando⟩ **2** (*expressing occurrence*) : ser ⟨it was finished yesterday : fue acabado ayer, se acabó ayer⟩ ⟨it was cooked in the oven : se cocinó en el horno⟩ **3** (*expressing possibility*) : poderse ⟨can she be trusted? : ¿se puede confiar en ella?⟩ **4** (*expressing obligation*) : deber ⟨you are to stay here : debes quedarte aquí⟩ ⟨he was to come yesterday : se esperaba que viniese ayer⟩

beach¹ ['biːʧ] *vt* : hacer embarrancar, hacer varar, hacer encallar

beach² *n* : playa *f*

beachcomber ['biːʧˌkoːmər] *n* : raquero *m*, -ra *f*

beachhead ['biːʧˌhɛd] *n* : cabeza *f* de playa

beacon ['biːkən] *n* : faro *m*

bead¹ ['biːd] *vi* : formarse en gotas

bead² *n* **1** : cuenta *f* **2** DROP : gota *f* **3** **beads** *npl* NECKLACE : collar *m*

beady ['biːdi] *adj* **beadier; -est 1** : de forma de cuenta **2 beady eyes** : ojos *mpl* pequeños y brillantes

beagle ['biːɡəl] *n* : beagle *m*

beak ['biːk] *n* : pico *m*

beaker ['biːkər] *n* **1** CUP : taza *f* alta **2** : vaso *m* de precipitados (en un laboratorio)

beam¹ ['biːm] *vi* **1** SHINE : brillar **2** SMILE : sonreír radiantemente — *vt* BROADCAST : transmitir, emitir

beam² *n* **1** : viga *f*, barra *f* **2** RAY : rayo *m*, haz *m* de luz **3** : haz *m* de radiofaro (para guiar pilotos, etc.)

bean ['biːn] *n* **1** : habichuela *f*, frijol *m* **2 broad bean** : haba *f* **3 string bean** : judía *f*

bear¹ ['bær] *v* **bore** ['bor]; **borne** ['born]; **bearing** *vt* **1** CARRY : llevar, portar **2** : dar a luz (a un niño) **3** PRODUCE : dar (frutas, cosechas) **4** ENDURE, SUPPORT : soportar, resistir, aguantar — *vi* **1** TURN : doblar, dar la vuelta ⟨bear right : doble a la derecha⟩ **2 to bear up** : resistir

bear² *n, pl* **bears** *or* **bear** : oso *m*, osa *f*

bearable ['bærəbəl] *adj* : soportable

beard ['bɪrd] *n* **1** : barba *f* **2** : arista *f* (de plantas)

bearded ['bɪrdəd] *adj* : barbudo, de barba

bearer ['bærər] *n* : portador *m*, -dora *f*

bearing ['bærɪŋ] *n* **1** CONDUCT, MANNERS : comportamiento *m*, modales *mpl* **2** SUPPORT : soporte *f* **3** SIGNIFICANCE : relación *f*, importancia *f* ⟨to have no bearing on : no tener nada que ver con⟩ **4** : cojinete *m*, rodamiento *m*

(de una máquina) **5** COURSE, DIRECTION : dirección *f*, rumbo *m* ⟨to get one's bearings : orientarse⟩

beast ['biːst] *n* **1** : bestia *f*, fiera *f* ⟨beast of burden : animal de carga⟩ **2** BRUTE : bruto *m*, -ta *f*; bestia *mf*

beastly ['biːstli] *adj* : detestable, repugnante

beat¹ ['biːt] *v* **beat; beaten** ['biːtən] *or* **beat; beating** *vt* **1** STRIKE : golpear, pegar, darle una paliza (a alguien) **2** DEFEAT : vencer, derrotar **3** AVOID : anticiparse a, evitar ⟨to beat the crowd : evitar el gentío⟩ **4** MASH, WHIP : batir — *vi* THROB : palpitar, latir

beat² *adj* EXHAUSTED : derrengado, muy cansado ⟨I'm beat! : ¡estoy molido!⟩

beat³ *n* **1** : golpe *m*, redoble *m* (de un tambor), latido *m* (del corazón) **2** RHYTHM : ritmo *m*, tiempo *m*

beater ['biːtər] *n* **1** : batidor *m*, -dora *f* **2** EGGBEATER : batidor *m*

beatific [ˌbiːə'tɪfɪk] *adj* : beatífico

beatitude [bi'ætəˌtuːd] *n* **1** : beatitud *f* **2 the Beatitudes** : las bienaventuranzas

beau ['boː] *n, pl* **beaux** *or* **beaus** : pretendiente *m*, galán *m*

beautification [ˌbjuːtəfə'keɪʃən] *n* : embellecimiento *m*

beautiful ['bjuːtɪfəl] *adj* : hermoso, bello, lindo, precioso

beautifully ['bjuːtɪfəli] *adv* **1** ATTRACTIVELY : hermosamente **2** EXCELLENTLY : maravillosamente, excelentemente

beauty ['bjuːti] *n, pl* **-ties** : belleza *f*, hermosura *f*, beldad *f*

beauty shop *or* **beauty salon** *n* : salón *m* de belleza

beaver ['biːvər] *n* : castor *m*

because [bɪ'kʌz, -'kɔz] *conj* : porque

because of *prep* : por, a causa de, debido a

beck ['bɛk] *n* **to be at the beck and call of** : estar a la entera disposición de, estar sometido a la voluntad de

beckon ['bɛkən] *vi* **to beckon to someone** : hacerle señas a alguien

become [bɪ'kʌm] *v* **-came** [-'keɪm]; **-come; -coming** *vi* : hacerse, volverse, ponerse ⟨he became famous : se hizo famoso⟩ ⟨to become sad : ponerse triste⟩ ⟨to become accustomed to : acostumbrarse a⟩ — *vt* **1** BEFIT : ser apropiado para **2** SUIT : favorecer, quedarle bien (a alguien) ⟨that dress becomes you : ese vestido te favorece⟩

becoming [bɪ'kʌmɪŋ] *adj* **1** SUITABLE : apropiado **2** FLATTERING : favorecedor

bed¹ ['bɛd] *v* **bedded; bedding** *vt* : acostar — *vi* : acostarse

bed² *n* **1** : cama *f*, lecho *m* **2** : cauce *m* (de un río), fondo *m* (del mar) **3** : arriate *m* (para plantas) **4** LAYER, STRATUM : estrato *m*, capa *f*

bedbug [ˈbɛdˌbʌg] *n* : chinche *f*
bedclothes [ˈbɛdˌkloːðz, -ˌkloːz] *npl*
: ropa *f* de cama, sábanas *fpl*
bedding [ˈbɛdɪŋ] *n* **1** → **bedclothes 2**
: cama *f* (para animales)
bedeck [bɪˈdɛk] *vt* : adornar, engalanar
bedevil [bɪˈdɛvəl] *vt* **-iled** *or* **-illed; -iling**
or **-illing** : acosar, plagar
bedlam [ˈbɛdləm] *n* : locura *f*, caos *m*,
alboroto *m*
bedraggled [bɪˈdrægəld] *adj* : desaliñado, despeinado
bedridden [ˈbɛdˌrɪdən] *adj* : postrado en
cama
bedrock [ˈbɛdˌrak] *n* : lecho *m* de roca
bedroom [ˈbɛdˌruːm, -ˌrʊm] *n* : dormitorio *m*, habitación *f*, pieza *f*, recámara
f Col, Mex, Pan
bedspread [ˈbɛdˌsprɛd] *n* : cubrecama *m*,
colcha *f*, cobertor *m*
bee [ˈbiː] *n* **1** : abeja *f* (insecto) **2** GATH-
ERING : círculo *m*, reunión *f*
beech [ˈbiːtʃ] *n, pl* **beeches** *or* **beech**
: haya *f*
beechnut [ˈbiːtʃˌnʌt] *n* : hayuco *m*
beef[1] [ˈbiːf] *vt* **to beef up** : fortalecer, reforzar — *vi* COMPLAIN : quejarse
beef[2] *n, pl* **beefs** [ˈbiːfs] *or* **beeves**
[ˈbiːvz] : carne *f* de vaca, carne *f* de res
CA, Mex
beefsteak [ˈbiːfˌsteɪk] *n* : filete *m*, bistec
m
beehive [ˈbiːˌhaɪv] *n* : colmena *f*
beekeeper [ˈbiːˌkiːpər] *n* : apicultor *m*,
-tora *f*
beeline [ˈbiːˌlaɪn] *n* **to make a beeline
for** : ir derecho a, ir directo hacia
been → **be**
beep[1] [ˈbiːp] *v* : pitar
beep[2] *n* : pitido *m*
beeper [ˈbiːpər] *n* : busca *m*, buscapersonas *m*
beer [ˈbɪr] *n* : cerveza *f*
beeswax [ˈbiːzˌwæks] *n* : cera *f* de abejas
beet [ˈbiːt] *n* : remolacha *f*, betabel *m*
Mex
beetle [ˈbiːtəl] *n* : escarabajo *m*
befall [bɪˈfɔl] *v* **-fell** [-ˈfɛl]; **-fallen** [-ˈfɔlən]
vt : sucederle a, acontecerle a — *vi*
: acontecer
befit [bɪˈfɪt] *vt* **-fitted; -fitting** : convenir
a, ser apropiado para
before[1] [bɪˈfor] *adv* **1** : antes ⟨before and
after : antes y después⟩ **2** : anterior
⟨the month before : el mes anterior⟩
before[2] *conj* : antes que ⟨he would die
before surrendering : moriría antes que
rendirse⟩
before[3] *prep* **1** : antes de ⟨before eating
: antes de comer⟩ **2** : delante de, ante
⟨I stood before the house : estaba parada delante de la casa⟩ ⟨before the judge
: ante el juez⟩
beforehand [bɪˈforˌhænd] *adv* : antes,
por adelantado, de antemano, con anticipación
befriend [bɪˈfrɛnd] *vt* : hacerse amigo de

befuddle [bɪˈfʌdəl] *vt* **-dled; -dling** : aturdir, ofuscar, confundir
beg [ˈbɛg] *v* **begged; begging** *vt* : pedir,
mendigar, suplicar ⟨I begged him to go
: le supliqué que fuera⟩ — *vi* : mendigar, pedir limosna
beget [bɪˈgɛt] *vt* **-got** [-ˈgat]; **-gotten**
[-ˈgatən] *or* **-got; -getting** : engendrar
beggar [ˈbɛgər] *n* : mendigo *m*, -ga *f*;
pordiosero *m*, -ra *f*
begin [bɪˈgɪn] *v* **-gan** [-ˈgæn]; **-gun**
[-ˈgʌn]; **-ginning** *vi* : empezar, comenzar, iniciar — *vi* **1** START : empezar,
comenzar, iniciarse **2** ORIGINATE
: nacer, originarse **3 to begin with** : en
primer lugar, para empezar
beginner [bɪˈgɪnər] *n* : principiante *mf*
beginning [bɪˈgɪnɪŋ] *n* : principio *m*,
comienzo *m*
begone [bɪˈgɔn] *interj* : ¡fuera de aquí!
begonia [bɪˈgoːnjə] *n* : begonia *f*
begrudge [bɪˈgrʌdʒ] *vt* **-grudged;
-grudging 1** : dar de mala gana **2** ENVY
: envidiar, resentir
beguile [bɪˈgaɪl] *vt* **-guiled; -guiling 1**
DECEIVE : engañar **2** AMUSE : divertir,
entretener
behalf [bɪˈhæf, -ˈhaf] *n* **1** : favor *m*, beneficio *m*, parte *f* **2 on behalf of** *or* **in
behalf of** : de parte de, en nombre de
behave [bɪˈheɪv] *vi* **-haved; -having**
: comportarse, portarse
behavior [bɪˈheɪvjər] *n* : comportamiento *m*, conducta *f*
behead [bɪˈhɛd] *vt* : decapitar
behest [bɪˈhɛst] *n* **1** : mandato *m*, orden
f **2 at the behest of** : a instancia de
behind[1] [bɪˈhaɪnd] *adv* : atrás, detrás ⟨to
fall behind : quedarse atrás⟩
behind[2] *prep* **1** : atrás de, detrás de, tras
⟨behind the house : detrás de la casa⟩
⟨one behind another : uno tras otro⟩
2 : atrasado con, después de ⟨behind
schedule : atrasado con el trabajo⟩ ⟨I
arrived behind the others : llegué después de los otros⟩ **3** SUPPORTING : en
apoyo de, detrás
behind[3] [bɪˈhaɪnd, ˈbiːˌhaɪnd] *n* : trasero
m
behold [bɪˈhoːld] *vt* **-held; -holding**
: contemplar
beholder [bɪˈhoːldər] *n* : observador *m*,
-dora *f*
behoove [bɪˈhuːv] *vt* **-hooved; -hooving**
: convenirle a, corresponderle a ⟨it be-
hooves us to help him : nos conviene
ayudarlo⟩
beige[1] [ˈbeɪʒ] *adj* : beige
beige[2] *n* : beige *m*
being [ˈbiːɪŋ] *n* **1** EXISTENCE : ser *m*, existencia *f* **2** CREATURE : ser *m*, ente *m*
belabor [bɪˈleɪbər] *vt* **to belabor the
point** : extenderse sobre el tema
belated [bɪˈleɪtəd] *adj* : tardío, retrasado
belch[1] [ˈbɛltʃ] *vi* **1** BURP : eructar **2** EX-
PEL : expulsar, arrojar
belch[2] *n* : eructo *m*

beleaguer [bɪ'li:gər] *vt* **1** BESIEGE : asediar, sitiar **2** HARASS : fastidiar, molestar

belfry ['bɛlfri] *n, pl* **-fries** : campanario *m*

Belgian ['bɛldʒən] *n* : belga *mf* — **Belgian** *adj*

belie [bɪ'laɪ] *vt* **-lied; -lying 1** MISREPRESENT : falsear, ocultar **2** CONTRADICT : contradecir, desmentir

belief [bə'li:f] *n* **1** TRUST : confianza *f* **2** CONVICTION : creencia *f*, convicción *f* **3** FAITH : fe *f*

believable [bə'li:vəbəl] *adj* : verosímil, creíble

believe [bə'li:v] *v* **-lieved; -lieving** : creer

believer [bə'li:vər] *n* **1** : creyente *mf* **2** : partidario *m*, -ria *f*; entusiasta *mf* ⟨she's a great believer in vitamins : ella es una gran partidaria de las vitaminas⟩

belittle [bɪ'lɪt̬əl] *vt* **-littled; -littling 1** DISPARAGE : menospreciar, denigrar, rebajar **2** MINIMIZE : minimizar, quitar importancia a

Belizean [bə'li:ziən] *n* : beliceño *m*, -ña *f* — **Belizean** *adj*

bell¹ ['bɛl] *vt* : ponerle un cascabel a

bell² *n* : campana *f*, cencerro *m* (para una vaca o cabra), cascabel *m* (para un gato), timbre *m* (de teléfono, de la puerta)

belle ['bɛl] *n* : belleza *f*, beldad *f*

bellhop ['bɛl,hɑp] *n* : botones *m*

bellicose ['bɛlɪ,ko:s] *adj* : belicoso *m* —
bellicosity [,bɛlɪ'kɑsət̬i] *n*

belligerence [bə'lɪdʒərənts] *n* : agresividad *f*, beligerancia *f*

belligerent¹ [bə'lɪdʒərənt] *adj* : agresivo, beligerante

belligerent² *n* : beligerante *mf*

bellow¹ ['bɛ,lo:] *vi* : bramar, mugir — *vt* : gritar

bellow² *n* : bramido *m*, grito *m*

bellows ['bɛ,lo:z] *ns & pl* : fuelle *m*

bellwether ['bɛl,wɛðər] *n* : líder *mf*

belly¹ ['bɛli] *vi* **-lied; -lying** SWELL : hincharse, inflarse

belly² *n, pl* **-lies** : abdomen *m*, vientre *m*, barriga *f*, panza *f*

belong [bɪ'lɔŋ] *vi* **1** : pertenecer (a), ser propiedad (de) ⟨it belongs to her : pertenece a ella, es suyo, es de ella⟩ **2** : ser parte (de), ser miembro (de) ⟨he belongs to the club : es miembro del club⟩ **3** : deber estar, ir ⟨your coat belongs in the closet : tu abrigo va en el ropero⟩

belongings [bɪ'lɔŋɪŋz] *npl* : pertenencias *fpl*, efectos *mpl* personales

beloved¹ [bɪ'lʌvəd, -'lʌvd] *adj* : querido, amado

beloved² *n* : amado *m*, -da *f*; enamorado *m*, -da *f*; amor *m*

below¹ [bɪ'lo:] *adv* : abajo

below² *prep* **1** : abajo de, debajo de ⟨below the window : debajo de la ventana⟩ **2** : por debajo de, bajo ⟨below average : por debajo del promedio⟩ ⟨5 degrees below zero : 5 grados bajo cero⟩

belt¹ ['bɛlt] *vt* **1** : ceñir con un cinturón, ponerle un cinturón a **2** THRASH : darle una paliza a, darle un trancazo a

belt² *n* **1** : cinturón *m*, cinto *m* (para el talle) **2** BAND, STRAP : cinta *f*, correa *f*, banda *f Mex* **3** AREA : frente *m*, zona *f*

beltway ['bɛlt,weɪ] *n* : carretera *f* de circunvalación; periférico *m CA, Mex*; libramiento *m Mex*

bemoan [bɪ'mo:n] *vt* : lamentarse de

bemuse [bɪ'mju:z] *vt* **-mused; -musing 1** BEWILDER : confundir, desconcertar **2** ENGROSS : absorber

bench ['bɛntʃ] *n* **1** SEAT : banco *m*, escaño *m*, banca *f* **2** : estrado *m* (de un juez) **3** COURT : tribunal *m*

bend¹ ['bɛnd] *v* **bent** ['bɛnt;]; **bending** *vt* : torcer, doblar, curvar, flexionar — *vi* **1** : torcerse, agacharse ⟨to bend over : inclinarse⟩ **2** TURN : torcer, hacer una curva

bend² *n* **1** TURN : vuelta *f*, recodo *m* **2** CURVE : curva *f*, ángulo *m*, codo *m*

beneath¹ [bɪ'ni:θ] *adv* : bajo, abajo, debajo

beneath² *prep* : bajo de, abajo de, por debajo de

benediction [,bɛnə'dɪkʃən] *n* : bendición *f*

benefactor ['bɛnə,fæktər] *n* : benefactor *m*, -tora *f*

beneficence [bə'nɛfəsənts] *n* : beneficencia *f*

beneficent [bə'nɛfəsənt] *adj* : benéfico, caritativo

beneficial [,bɛnə'fɪʃəl] *adj* : beneficioso, provechoso — **beneficially** *adv*

beneficiary [,bɛnə'fɪʃi,ɛri, -'fɪʃəri] *n, pl* **-ries** : beneficiario *m*, -ria *f*

benefit¹ ['bɛnəfɪt] *vt* : beneficiar — *vi* : beneficiarse

benefit² *n* **1** ADVANTAGE : beneficio *m*, ventaja *f*, provecho *m* **2** AID : asistencia *f*, beneficio *m* **3** : función *f* benéfica (para recaudar fondos)

benevolence [bə'nɛvələnts] *n* : bondad *f*, benevolencia *f*

benevolent [bə'nɛvələnt] *adj* : benévolo, bondadoso — **benevolently** *adv*

Bengali [bɛn'gɔli, bɛŋ-] *n* **1** : bengalí *mf* **2** : bengalí *m* (idioma) — **Bengali** *adj*

benign [bɪ'naɪn] *adj* **1** GENTLE, KIND : benévolo, amable **2** FAVORABLE : propicio, favorable **3** MILD : benigno ⟨a benign tumor : un tumor benigno⟩

Beninese [bə,nɪ'ni:z, -,ni:-, -'ni:s; ,bnɪ'-] *n* : beninés *m*, -nesa *f* — **Beninese** *adj*

bent ['bɛnt] *n* : aptitud *f*, inclinación *f*

benumb [bɪ'nʌm] *vt* : entumecer

benzene ['bɛn,zi:n] *n* : benceno *m*

bequeath [bɪ'kwi:θ, -'kwi:ð] *vt* : legar, dejar en testamento

bequest [bɪ'kwɛst] *n* : legado *m*

berate [bɪ'reɪt] *vt* **-rated; -rating** : reprender, regañar

bereaved¹ [bɪ'ri:vd] *adj* : que está de luto, afligido (por la muerte de alguien)

bereaved² *n* **the bereaved** : los deudos del difunto (o de la difunta)

bereavement [bɪ'ri:vmənt] *n* **1** SORROW ': dolor *m*, pesar *m* **2** LOSS : pérdida *f*

bereft [bɪ'rɛft] *adj* : privado, desprovisto

beret [bə'reɪ] *n* : boina *f*

beriberi [ˌbɛri'bɛri] *n* : beriberi *m*

berm ['bərm] *n* : arcén *m*

berry ['bɛri] *n*, *pl* **-ries** : baya *f*

berserk [bər'sərk, -'zərk] *adj* **1** : enloquecido **2 to go beserk** : volverse loco

berth¹ ['bərθ] *vi* : atracar

berth² *n* **1** DOCK : atracadero *m* **2** ACCOMMODATION : litera *f*, camarote *m* **3** POSITION : trabajo *m*, puesto *m*

beryl ['bɛrəl] *n* : berilo *m*

beseech [bɪ'si:tʃ] *vt* **-seeched** *or* **-sought** [-'sɔt]; **-seeching** : suplicar, implorar, rogar

beset [bɪ'sɛt] *vt* **-set; -setting 1** HARASS : acosar **2** SURROUND : rodear

beside [bɪ'saɪd] *prep* : al lado de, junto a

besides¹ [bɪ'saɪdz] *adv* **1** ALSO : además, también, aparte **2** MOREOVER : además, por otra parte

besides² *prep* **1** : además de, aparte de ⟨six others besides you : seis otros además de ti⟩ **2** EXCEPT : excepto, fuera de, aparte de

besiege [bɪ'si:dʒ] *vt* **-sieged; -sieging** : asediar, sitiar, cercar

besmirch [bɪ'smərtʃ] *vt* : ensuciar, mancillar

best¹ ['bɛst] *vt* : superar, ganar a

best² *adv* (*superlative of* **well**) : mejor ⟨as best I can : lo mejor que puedo⟩

best³ *adj* (*superlative of* **good**) : mejor ⟨my best friend : mi mejor amigo⟩

best⁴ *n* **1 the best** : lo mejor, el mejor, la mejor, los mejores, las mejores **2 at** ∼ : a lo más **3 to do one's best** : hacer todo lo posible

bestial ['bɛstʃəl, 'bi:s-] *adj* **1** : bestial **2** BRUTISH : brutal, salvaje

best man *n* : padrino *m*

bestow [bɪ'sto:] *vt* : conferir, otorgar, conceder

bestowal [bɪ'sto:əl] *n* : concesión *f*, otorgamiento *m*

bet¹ ['bɛt] *v* **bet; betting** *vt* : apostar — *vi* **to bet on** : apostarle a

bet² *n* : apuesta *f*

betoken [bɪ'to:kən] *vt* : denotar, ser indicio de

betray [bɪ'treɪ] *vt* **1** : traicionar ⟨to betray one's country : traicionar uno a su patria⟩ **2** DIVULGE, REVEAL : delatar, revelar ⟨to betray a secret : revelar un secreto⟩

betrayal [bɪ'treɪəl] *n* : traición *f*, delación *f*, revelación *f* ⟨betrayal of trust : abuso de confianza⟩

betrothal [bɪ'tro:ðəl, -'tro-] *n* : esponsales *mpl*, compromiso *m*

betrothed [bɪ'tro:ðd, -'trɔθt] *n* FIANCÉ : prometido *m*, -da *f*

better¹ ['bɛtər] *vt* **1** IMPROVE : mejorar **2** SURPASS : superar

better² *adv* (*comparative of* **well**) **1** : mejor **2** MORE : más ⟨better than 50 miles : más de 50 millas⟩

better³ *adj* (*comparative of* **good**) **1** : mejor ⟨the weather is better today : hace mejor tiempo hoy⟩ ⟨I was sick, but now I'm better : estuve enfermo, pero ahora estoy mejor⟩ **2** : mayor ⟨the better part of a month : la mayor parte de un mes⟩

better⁴ *n* **1** : el mejor, la mejor ⟨the better of the two : el mejor de los dos⟩ **2 to get the better of** : vencer a, quedar por encima de, superar

betterment ['bɛtərmənt] *n* : mejoramiento *m*, mejora *f*

bettor *or* **better** ['bɛtər] *n* : apostador *m*, -dora *f*

between¹ [bɪ'twi:n] *adv* **1** : en medio, por lo medio **2 in** ∼ : intermedio

between² *prep* : entre

bevel¹ ['bɛvəl] *v* **-eled** *or* **-elled; -eling** *or* **-elling** *vt* : biselar — *vi* INCLINE : inclinarse

bevel² *n* : bisel *m*

beverage ['bɛvrɪdʒ, 'bɛvə-] *n* : bebida *f*

bevy ['bɛvi] *n*, *pl* **bevies** : grupo *m* (de personas), bandada *f* (de pájaros)

bewail [bɪ'weɪl] *vt* : lamentarse de, llorar

beware [bɪ'wær] *vi* **to beware of** : tener cuidado con ⟨beware of the dog! : ¡cuidado con el perro!⟩ — *vt* : guardarse de, cuidarse de

bewilder [bɪ'wɪldər] *vt* : desconcertar, dejar perplejo

bewilderment [bɪ'wɪldərmənt] *n* : desconcierto *m*, perplejidad *f*

bewitch [bɪ'wɪtʃ] *vt* **1** : hechizar, embrujar **2** CHARM : cautivar, encantar

bewitchment [bɪ'wɪtʃmənt] *n* : hechizo *m*

beyond¹ [bi'jɑnd] *adv* **1** FARTHER, LATER : más allá, más lejos (en el espacio), más adelante (en el tiempo) **2** MORE : más ⟨$50 and beyond : $50 o más⟩

beyond² *n* **the beyond** : el más allá, lo desconocido

beyond³ *prep* **1** : más allá de ⟨beyond the frontier : más allá de la frontera⟩ **2** : fuera de ⟨beyond one's reach : fuera de su alcance⟩ **3** BESIDES : además de

biannual [ˌbaɪ'ænjuəl] *adj* : bianual — **biannually** *adv*

bias¹ ['baɪəs] *vt* **-ased** *or* **-assed; -asing** *or* **-assing 1** : predisponer, sesgar, influir en, afectar **2 to be biased against** : tener prejuicio contra

bias² *n* **1** : sesgo *m*, bies *m* (en la costura) **2** PREJUDICE : prejuicio *m* **3** TENDENCY : inclinación *f*, tendencia *f*

biased ['baɪəst] *adj* : tendencioso, parcial

bib ['bɪb] *n* **1** : peto *m* **2** : babero *m* (para niños)

Bible ['baɪbəl] *n* : Biblia *f*

biblical ['bɪblɪkəl] *adj* : bíblico

bibliographer [ˌbɪbliˈɑgrəfər] *n* : bibliógrafo *m*, -fa *f*

bibliographic [ˌbɪbliəˈgræfɪk] *adj* : bibliográfico

bibliography [ˌbɪbliˈɑgrəfi] *n*, *pl* **-phies** : bibliografía *f*

bicameral [ˌbaɪˈkæmərəl] *adj* : bicameral

bicarbonate [ˌbaɪˈkɑrbənət, -ˌneɪt] *n* : bicarbonato *m*

bicentennial [ˌbaɪsɛnˈtɛniəl] *n* : bicentenario *m*

biceps [ˈbaɪˌsɛps] *ns & pl* : bíceps *m*

bicker[1] [ˈbɪkər] *vi* : pelear, discutir, reñir

bicker[2] *n* : pelea *f*, riña *f*, discusión *f*

bicuspid [baɪˈkʌspɪd] *n* : premolar *m*, diente *m* bicúspide

bicycle[1] [ˈbaɪsɪkəl, -ˌsɪ-] *vi* **-cled; -cling** : ir en bicicleta

bicycle[2] *n* : bicicleta *f*

bicycling [ˈbaɪsɪkəlɪŋ] *n* : ciclismo *m*

bicyclist [ˈbaɪsɪkəlɪst] *n* : ciclista *mf*

bid[1] [ˈbɪd] *vt* **bade** [ˈbæd, ˈbeɪd] *or* **bid; bidden** [ˈbɪdən] *or* **bid; bidding 1** ORDER : pedir, mandar **2** INVITE : invitar **3** SAY : dar, decir ⟨to bid good evening : dar las buenas noches⟩ ⟨to bid farewell to : decir adiós a⟩ **4** : ofrecer (en una subasta), declarar (en juegos de cartas)

bid[2] *n* **1** OFFER : oferta *f* (en una subasta), declaración *f* (en juegos de cartas) **2** INVITATION : invitación *f* **3** ATTEMPT : intento *m*, tentativa *f*

bidder [ˈbɪdər] *n* : postor *m*, -tora *f*

bide [ˈbaɪd] *v* **bode** [ˈboːd] *or* **bided; biding** *vt* : esperar, aguardar ⟨to bide one's time : esperar el momento oportuno⟩ — *vi* DWELL : morar, vivir

biennial [baɪˈɛniəl] *adj* : bienal — **biennially** *adv*

bier [ˈbɪr] *n* **1** STAND : andas *fpl* **2** COFFIN : ataúd *m*, féretro *m*

bifocals [ˈbaɪˌfoːkəlz] *npl* : lentes *mpl* bifocales, bifocales *mpl*

big [ˈbɪg] *adj* **bigger; biggest 1** LARGE : grande **2** PREGNANT : embarazada **3** IMPORTANT, MAJOR : importante, grande ⟨a big decision : una gran decisión⟩ **4** POPULAR : popular, famoso, conocido

bigamist [ˈbɪgəmɪst] *n* : bígamo *m*, -ma *f*

bigamous [ˈbɪgəməs] *adj* : bígamo

bigamy [ˈbɪgəmi] *n* : bigamia *f*

Big Dipper → **dipper**

bighorn [ˈbɪgˌhɔrn] *n*, *pl* **-horn** *or* **-horns** *or* **bighorn sheep** : oveja *f* salvaje de las montañas

bight [ˈbaɪt] *n* : bahía *f*, ensenada *f*, golfo *m*

bigot [ˈbɪgət] *n* : intolerante *mf*

bigoted [ˈbɪgətəd] *adj* : intolerante, prejuiciado, fanático

bigotry [ˈbɪgətri] *n*, *pl* **-tries** : intolerancia *f*

big shot *n* : pez *m* gordo *fam*, mandamás *mf*

bigwig [ˈbɪgˌwɪg] → **big shot**

bike [ˈbaɪk] *n* **1** : bicicleta *f*, bici *f fam* **2** : motocicleta *f*, moto *f*

bikini [bəˈkiːni] *n* : bikini *m*

bilateral [baɪˈlætərəl] *adj* : bilateral — **bilaterally** *adv*

bile [ˈbaɪl] *n* **1** : bilis *f* **2** IRRITABILITY : mal genio *m*

bilingual [baɪˈlɪŋgwəl] *adj* : bilingüe

bilious [ˈbɪliəs] *adj* **1** : bilioso **2** IRRITABLE : bilioso, colérico

bilk [ˈbɪlk] *vt* : burlar, estafar, defraudar

bill[1] [ˈbɪl] *vt* : pasarle la cuenta a — *vi* : acariciar ⟨to bill and coo : acariciarse⟩

bill[2] *n* **1** LAW : proyecto *m* de ley, ley *f* **2** INVOICE : cuenta *f*, factura *f* **3** POSTER : cartel *m* **4** PROGRAM : programa *m* (del teatro) **5** : billete *m* ⟨a five-dollar bill : un billete de cinco dólares⟩ **6** BEAK : pico *m*

billboard [ˈbɪlˌbɔrd] *n* : cartelera *f*

billet[1] [ˈbɪlət] *vt* : acuartelar, alojar

billet[2] *n* : alojamiento *m*

billfold [ˈbɪlˌfoːld] *n* : billetera *f*, cartera *f*

billiards [ˈbɪljərdz] *n* : billar *m*

billion [ˈbɪljən] *n*, *pl* **billions** *or* **billion** : mil millones *mpl*

billow[1] [ˈbɪlo] *vi* : hincharse, inflarse

billow[2] *n* **1** WAVE : ola *f* **2** CLOUD : nube *f* ⟨a billow of smoke : un nube de humo⟩

billowy [ˈbɪlowi] *adj* : ondulante

billy goat [ˈbɪliˌgoːt] *n* : macho *m* cabrío

bin [ˈbɪn] *n* : cubo *m*, cajón *m*

binary [ˈbaɪnəri, -ˌnɛri] *adj* : binario *m*

bind [ˈbaɪnd] *vt* **bound** [ˈbaʊnd]; **binding 1** TIE : atar, amarrar **2** OBLIGATE : obligar **3** UNITE : aglutinar, ligar, unir **4** BANDAGE : vendar **5** : encuadernar (un libro)

binder [ˈbaɪndər] *n* **1** FOLDER : carpeta *f* **2** : encuadernador *m*, -dora *f* (de libros)

binding [ˈbaɪndɪŋ] *n* **1** : encuadernación *f* (de libros) **2** COVER : cubierta *f*, forro *m*

binge [ˈbɪndʒ] *n* : juerga *f*, parranda *f fam*

bingo [ˈbɪŋˌgoː] *n*, *pl* **-gos** : bingo *m*

binocular [baɪˈnɑkjələr, bə-] *adj* : binocular

binoculars [bəˈnɑkjələrz, baɪ-] *npl* : binoculares *mpl*

biochemical[1] [ˌbaɪoˈkɛmɪkəl] *adj* : bioquímico

biochemical[2] *n* : bioquímico *m*

biochemist [ˌbaɪoˈkɛmɪst] *n* : bioquímico *m*, -ca *f*

biochemistry [ˌbaɪoˈkɛməstri] *n* : bioquímica *f*

biodegradable [ˌbaɪodɪˈgreɪdəbəl] *adj* : biodegradable

biodegradation [ˌbaɪodɛgrəˈdeɪʃən] *n* : biodegradación *f*

biodegrade [ˌbaɪodɪˈgreɪd] *vi* **-graded; -grading** : biodegradarse

biodiversity [ˌbaɪodə'vərsəţi, -daɪ-] *n, pl* **-ties** : bioversidad *f*
biographer [baɪ'ɑgrəfər] *n* : biógrafo *m*, -fa *f*
biographical [ˌbaɪə'græfɪkəl] *adj* : biográfico
biography [baɪ'ɑgrəfi, bi:-] *n, pl* **-phies** : biografía *f*
biologic [ˌbaɪə'lɑʤɪk] *or* **biological** [-ʤɪkəl] *adj* : biológico
biologist [baɪ'ɑləʤɪst] *n* : biólogo *m*, -ga *f*
biology [baɪ'ɑləʤi] *n* : biología *f*
biophysical [ˌbaɪo'fɪzɪkəl] *adj* : biofísico
biophysicist [ˌbaɪo'fɪzəsɪst] *n* : biofísico *m*, -ca *f*
biophysics [ˌbaɪo'fɪzɪks] *ns & pl* : biofísica *f*
biopsy ['baɪˌɑpsi] *n, pl* **-sies** : biopsia *f*
biosphere ['baɪəˌsfɪr] *n* : biosfera *f*, biósfera *f*
biotechnology [ˌbaɪotɛk'nɑləʤi] *n* : biotecnología *f*
biotic [baɪ'ɑtɪk] *adj* : biótico
bipartisan [baɪ'pɑrţəzən, -sən] *adj* : bipartidista, de dos partidas
biped ['baɪˌpɛd] *n* : bípedo *m*
birch ['bərʧ] *n* : abedul *m*
bird ['bərd] *n* : pájaro *m* (pequeño), ave *f* (grande)
birdbath ['bərdˌbæθ, -ˌbɑθ] *n* : pila *f* para pájaros
bird dog *n* : perro *m*, -rra *f* de caza
bird of prey *n* : ave *f* rapaz, ave *f* de presa
birdseed ['bərdˌsi:d] *n* : alpiste *m*
bird's–eye ['bərdzˌaɪ] *adj* **1** : visto desde arriba ⟨bird's-eye view : vista aérea⟩ **2** CURSORY : rápido, somero
birth ['bərθ] *n* **1** : nacimiento *m*, parto *m* **2** ORIGIN : origen *m*, nacimiento *m*
birthday ['bərθˌdeɪ] *n* : cumpleaños *m*, aniversario *m*
birthmark ['bərθˌmɑrk] *n* : mancha *f* de nacimiento
birthplace ['bərθˌpleɪs] *n* : lugar *m* de nacimiento
birthrate ['bərθˌreɪt] *n* : índice *m* de natalidad
birthright ['bərθˌraɪt] *n* : derecho *m* de nacimiento
biscuit ['bɪskət] *n* : bizcocho *m*
bisect ['baɪˌsɛkt, ˌbaɪ'-] *vt* : bisecar
bisexual [ˌbaɪ'sɛkʃʊəl] *adj* : bisexual
bishop ['bɪʃəp] *n* **1** : obispo *m* **2** : alfil *m* (en ajedrez)
bismuth ['bɪzməθ] *n* : bismuto *m*
bison ['baɪzən, -sən] *ns & pl* : bisonte *m*
bistro ['bi:stro, 'bɪs-] *n, pl* **-tros** : bar *m*, restaurante *m* pequeño
bit ['bɪt] *n* **1** FRAGMENT, PIECE : pedazo *m*, trozo *m* ⟨a bit of luck : un poco de suerte⟩ **2** : freno *m*, bocado *m* (de una brida) **3** : broca *f* (de un taladro) **4** : bit *m* (de información)
bitch¹ ['bɪʧ] *vi* COMPLAIN : quejarse, reclamar

bitch² *n* : perra *f*
bite¹ ['baɪt] *v* **bit** ['bɪt]; **bitten** ['bɪtən]; **biting** *vt* **1** : morder **2** STING : picar **3** PUNCTURE : punzar, pinchar **4** GRIP : agarrar — *vi* **1** : morder ⟨that dog bites : ese perro muerde⟩ **2** STING : picar (dícese de un insecto), cortar (dícese del viento) **3** : picar ⟨the fish are biting now : ya están picando los peces⟩ **4** GRAB : agarrarse
bite² *n* **1** BITING : mordisco *m*, dentellada *f* **2** SNACK : bocado *m* ⟨a bite to eat : algo de comer⟩ **3** : picadura *f* (de un insecto), mordedura *f* (de un animal) **4** SHARPNESS : mordacidad *f*, penetración *f*
biting *adj* **1** PENETRATING : cortante, penetrante **2** CAUSTIC : mordaz, sarcástico
bitter ['bɪţər] *adj* **1** ACRID : amargo, acre **2** PENETRATING : cortante, penetrante ⟨bitter cold : frío glacial⟩ **3** HARSH : duro, amargo ⟨to the bitter end : hasta el final⟩ **4** INTENSE, RELENTLESS : intenso, extremo, implacable ⟨bitter hatred : odio implacable⟩
bitterly ['bɪţərli] *adv* : amargamente
bitterness ['bɪţərnəs] *n* : amargura *f*
bittersweet ['bɪţərˌswi:t] *adj* : agridulce
bivalve ['baɪˌvælv] *n* : bivalvo *m* — **bivalve** *adj*
bivouac¹ ['bɪvəˌwæk, 'bɪvˌwæk] *vi* **-ouacked; -ouacking** : acampar, vivaquear
bivouac² *n* : vivaque *m*
bizarre [bə'zɑr] *adj* : extraño, singular, estrafalario, estrambótico — **bizarrely** *adv*
blab ['blæb] *vi* **blabbed; blabbing** : parlotear *fam*, cotorrear *fam*
black¹ ['blæk] *vt* : ennegrecer
black² *adj* **1** : negro (color, raza) **2** SOILED : sucio **3** DARK : oscuro, negro **4** WICKED : malvado, perverso, malo **5** GLOOMY : negro, sombrío, deprimente
black³ *n* **1** : negro *m* (color) **2** : negro *m*, -gra *f* (persona)
black–and–blue [ˌblækən'blu:] *adj* : amoratado
blackball ['blækˌbɔl] *vt* **1** OSTRACIZE : hacerle el vacío a, aislar **2** BOYCOTT : boicotear
blackberry ['blækˌbɛri] *n, pl* **-ries** : mora *f*
blackbird ['blækˌbərd] *n* : mirlo *m*
blackboard ['blækˌbɔrd] *n* : pizarra *f*, pizarrón *m*
blacken ['blækən] *vt* **1** BLACK : ennegrecer **2** DEFAME : deshonrar, difamar, manchar
blackhead ['blækˌhɛd] *n* : espinilla *f*, punto *m* negro
black hole *n* : agujero *m* negro
blackjack ['blækˌʤæk] *n* **1** : cachiporra *f* (arma) **2** : veintiuna *f* (juego de cartas)
blacklist¹ ['blækˌlɪst] *vt* : poner en la lista negra

blacklist² *n* : lista *f* negra
blackmail¹ ['blæk,meɪl] *vt* : chantajear, hacer chantaje a
blackmail² *n* : chantaje *m*
blackmailer ['blæk,meɪlər] *n* : chantajista *mf*
blackout ['blæk,aʊt] *n* 1 : apagón *m* (de poder eléctrico) 2 FAINT : desmayo *m*, desvanecimiento *m*
black out *vt* : dejar sin luz — *vi* FAINT : perder el conocimiento, desmayarse
blacksmith ['blæk,smɪθ] *n* : herrero *m*
blacktop ['blæk,tɑp] *n* : asfalto *m*
bladder ['blædər] *n* : vejiga *f*
blade ['bleɪd] *n* : hoja *f* (de un cuchillo), cuchilla *f* (de un patín), pala *f* (de un remo o una hélice), brizna *f* (de hierba)
blamable ['bleɪməbəl] *adj* : culpable
blame¹ ['bleɪm] *vt* **blamed; blaming** : culpar, echar la culpa a
blame² *n* : culpa *f*
blameless ['bleɪmləs] *adj* : intachable, sin culpa, inocente — **blamelessly** *adv*
blameworthiness ['bleɪm,wərðinəs] *n* : culpa *f*, culpabilidad *f*
blameworthy ['bleɪm,wərði] *adj* : culpable, reprochable, censurable
blanch ['blæntʃ] *vt* WHITEN : blanquear — *vi* PALE : palidecer
bland ['blænd] *adj* : soso, insulso, desabrido ⟨a bland smile : una sonrisa insulsa⟩ ⟨a bland diet : una dieta fácil de digerir⟩
blandishments ['blændɪʃmənts] *npl* : lisonjas *fpl*, halagos *mpl*
blandly ['blændli] *adv* : de manera insulsa
blandness ['blændnəs] *n* : lo insulso, lo desabrido
blank¹ ['blæŋk] *vt* OBLITERATE : borrar
blank² *adj* 1 DAZED : perplejo, desconcertado 2 EXPRESSIONLESS : sin expresión, inexpresivo 3 : en blanco (dícese de un papel), liso (dícese de una pared) 4 EMPTY : vacío, en blanco ⟨a blank stare : una mirada vacía⟩ ⟨his mind went blank : se quedó en blanco⟩
blank³ *n* 1 SPACE : espacio *m* en blanco 2 FORM : formulario *m* 3 CARTRIDGE : cartucho *m* de fogueo 4 *or* **blank key** : llave *f* ciega
blanket¹ [blæŋkət] *vt* : cubrir
blanket² *adj* : global
blanket³ *n* : manta *f*, cobija *f*, frazada *f*
blankly ['blæŋkli] *adv* : sin comprender
blankness ['blæŋknəs] *n* 1 PERPLEXITY : desconcierto *m*, perplejidad *f* 2 EMPTINESS : vacío *m*, vacuidad *f*
blare¹ ['blær] *vi* **blared; blaring** : resonar
blare² *n* : estruendo *m*
blarney ['blɑrni] *n* : labia *f fam*
blasé [blɑ'zeɪ] *adj* : displicente, indiferente
blaspheme [blæs'fi:m, 'blæs,-] *vi* **-phemed; -pheming** : blasfemar
blasphemer [blæs'fi:mər, 'blæs,-] *n* : blasfemo *m*, -ma *f*

blasphemous ['blæsfəməs] *adj* : blasfemo
blasphemy ['blæsfəmi] *n*, *pl* **-mies** : blasfemia *f*
blast¹ ['blæst] *vt* 1 BLOW UP : volar, hacer volar 2 ATTACK : atacar, arremeter contra
blast² *n* 1 GUST : ráfaga *f* 2 EXPLOSION : explosión *f*
blast-off ['blæst,ɔf] *n* : despegue *m*
blast off *vi* : despegar
blatant ['bleɪtənt] *adj* : descarado — **blatantly** ['bleɪtəntli] *adv*
blaze¹ ['bleɪz] *v* **blazed; blazing** *vi* SHINE : arder, brillar, resplandecer — *vt* MARK : marcar, señalar ⟨to blaze a trail : abrir un camino⟩
blaze² *n* 1 FIRE : fuego *m* 2 BRIGHTNESS : resplandor *m*, brillantez *f* 3 OUTBURST : arranque *m* ⟨a blaze of anger : un arranque de cólera⟩ 4 DISPLAY : alarde *m*, llamarada *f* ⟨a blaze of color : un derroche de color⟩
blazer ['bleɪzər] *n* : chaqueta *f* deportiva, blazer *m*
bleach¹ ['bli:tʃ] *vt* : blanquear, decolorar
bleach² *n* : lejía *f*, blanqueador *m*
bleachers ['bli:tʃərz] *ns* & *pl* : gradas *fpl*, tribuna *f* descubierta
bleak ['bli:k] *adj* 1 DESOLATE : inhóspito, sombrío, desolado 2 DEPRESSING : deprimente, triste, sombrío
bleakly ['bli:kli] *adv* : sombríamente
bleakness ['bli:knəs] *n* : lo inhóspito, lo sombrío
blear ['blɪr] *adj* : empañado, nublado
bleary ['blɪri] *adj* 1 : adormilado, fatigado 2 **bleary-eyed** : con los ojos nublados
bleat¹ ['bli:t] *vi* : balar
bleat² *n* : balido *m*
bleed ['bli:d] *v* **bled** ['blɛd]; **bleeding** *vi* 1 : sangrar 2 GRIEVE : sufrir, afligirse 3 EXUDE : exudar (dícese de una planta), correrse (dícese de los colores) — *vt* 1 : sangrar (a una persona), purgar (frenos) 2 **to bleed someone dry** : sacarle todo el dinero a alguien
blemish¹ ['blɛmɪʃ] *vt* : manchar, marcar
blemish² *n* : imperfección *f*, mancha *f*, marca *f*
blend¹ ['blɛnd] *vt* 1 MIX : mezclar 2 COMBINE : combinar, aunar
blend² *n* : mezcla *f*, combinación *f*
blender ['blɛndər] *n* : licuadora *f*
bless ['blɛs] *vt* **blessed** ['blɛst]; **blessing** 1 CONSECRATE : bendecir, consagrar 2 : bendecir ⟨may God bless you! : ¡que Dios te bendiga!⟩ 3 **to bless with** : dotar de 4 **to bless oneself** : santiguarse
blessed ['blɛsəd] *or* **blest** ['blɛst] *adj* : bienaventurado, bendito, dichoso
blessedly ['blɛsədli] *adv* : felizmente, alegremente, afortunadamente
blessing ['blɛsɪŋ] *n* 1 : bendición *f* 2 APPROVAL : aprobación *f*, consentimiento *m*

blew → blow
blight¹ ['blaɪt] *vt* : arruinar, infestar
blight² *n* 1 : añublo *m* 2 PLAGUE : peste *f*, plaga *f* 3 DECAY : deterioro *m*, ruina *f*
blimp ['blɪmp] *n* : dirigible *m*
blind¹ ['blaɪnd] *vt* 1 : cegar, dejar ciego 2 DAZZLE : deslumbrar
blind² *adj* 1 SIGHTLESS : ciego 2 INSENSITIVE : ciego, insensible, sin razón 3 CLOSED : sin salida ⟨blind alley : callejón sin salida⟩
blind³ *n* 1 : persiana *f* (para una ventana) 2 COVER : escondite *m*, escondrijo *m*
blinders ['blaɪndərz] *npl* : anteojeras *fpl*
blindfold¹ ['blaɪnd,fo:ld] *vt* : vendar los ojos
blindfold² *n* : venda *f* (para los ojos)
blinding ['blaɪndɪŋ] *adj* : enceguecedor, cegador ⟨with blinding speed : con una rapidez inusitada⟩
blindly ['blaɪndli] *adv* : a ciegas, ciegamente
blindness ['blaɪndnəs] *n* : ceguera *f*
blink¹ ['blɪŋk] *vi* 1 WINK : pestañear, parpadear 2 : brillar intermitentemente
blink² *n* : pestañeo *m*, parpadeo *m*
blinker ['blɪŋkər] *n* : intermitente *m*, direccional *f*
bliss ['blɪs] *n* 1 HAPPINESS : dicha *f*, felicidad *f* absoluta 2 PARADISE : paraíso *m*
blissful ['blɪsfəl] *adj* : dichoso, feliz — **blissfully** *adv*
blister¹ ['blɪstər] *vi* : ampollarse
blister² *n* : ampolla *f* (en la piel o una superficie), burbuja *f* (en una superficie)
blithe ['blaɪθ, 'blaɪð] *adj* **blither; blithest** 1 CAREFREE : despreocupado 2 CHEERFUL : alegre, risueño — **blithely** *adv*
blitz¹ ['blɪts] *vt* 1 BOMBARD : bombardear 2 : atacar con rapidez
blitz² *n* 1 : bombardeo *m* aéreo 2 CAMPAIGN : ataque *m*, acometida *f*
blizzard ['blɪzərd] *n* : tormenta *f* de nieve, ventisca *f*
bloat ['blo:t] *vi* : hincharse, inflarse
blob ['blab] *n* : gota *f*, mancha *f*, borrón *m*
bloc ['blak] *n* : bloque *m*
block¹ ['blak] *vt* 1 OBSTRUCT : obstruir, bloquear 2 CLOG : atascar, atorar
block² *n* 1 PIECE : bloque *m* ⟨building blocks : cubos de construcción⟩ ⟨auction block : plataforma de subastas⟩ ⟨starting block : taco de salida⟩ 2 OBSTRUCTION : obstrucción *f*, bloqueo *m* 3 : cuadra *f*, manzana *f* (de edificios) ⟨to go around the block : dar la vuelta a la cuadra⟩ 4 BUILDING : edificio *m* (de apartamentos, oficinas, etc.) 5 GROUP, SERIES : serie *f*, grupo *m* ⟨a block of tickets : una serie de entradas⟩ **6 block and tackle** : aparejo *m* de poleas

blockade¹ [bla'keɪd] *vt* **-aded; -ading** : bloquear
blockade² *n* : bloqueo *m*
blockage ['blakɪʤ] *n* : bloqueo *m*, obstrucción *f*
blockhead ['blak,hɛd] *n* : bruto *m*, -ta *f*; estúpido *m*, -da *f*
blond¹ *or* **blonde** ['bland] *adj* : rubio, güero *Mex*, claro (dícese de la madera)
blond² *or* **blonde** *n* : rubio *m*, -bia *f*; güero *m*, -ra *f Mex*
blood ['blʌd] *n* 1 : sangre *f* 2 LIFEBLOOD : vida *f*, alma *f* 3 LINEAGE : linaje *m*, sangre *f*
blood bank *n* : banco *m* de sangre
bloodcurdling ['blʌd,kərdəlɪŋ] *adj* : espeluznante, aterrador
blooded ['blʌdəd] *adj* : de sangre ⟨cold-blooded animal : animal de sangre fría⟩
bloodhound ['blʌd,haʊnd] *n* : sabueso *m*
bloodless ['blʌdləs] *adj* 1 : incruento, sin derramamiento de sangre 2 LIFELESS : desanimado, insípido, sin vida
bloodmobile ['blʌdmo,bi:l] *n* : unidad *f* móvil para donantes de sangre
blood pressure *n* : tensión *f*, presión *f* (arterial)
bloodshed ['blʌd,ʃɛd] *n* : derramamiento *m* de sangre
bloodshot ['blʌd,ʃat] *adj* : inyectado de sangre
bloodstain ['blʌd,steɪn] *n* : mancha *f* de sangre
bloodstained ['blʌd,steɪnd] *adj* : manchado de sangre
bloodstream ['blʌd,stri:m] *n* : torrente *m* sanguíneo, corriente *f* sanguínea
bloodsucker ['blʌd,sʌkər] *n* : sanguijuela *f*
bloodthirsty ['blʌd,θərsti] *adj* : sanguinario
blood vessel *n* : vaso *m* sanguíneo
bloody ['blʌdi] *adj* **bloodier; -est** : ensangrentado, sangriento
bloom¹ ['blu:m] *vi* 1 FLOWER : florecer 2 MATURE : madurar
bloom² *n* 1 FLOWER : flor *f* ⟨to be in bloom : estar en flor⟩ 2 FLOWERING : floración *f* ⟨in full bloom : en plena floración⟩ 3 : rubor *m* (de la tez) ⟨in the bloom of youth : en plena juventud, en la flor de la vida⟩
bloomers ['blu:mərz] *npl* : bombachos *mpl*
blooper ['blu:pər] *n* : metedura *f* de pata *fam*
blossom¹ ['blasəm] *vi* : florecer, dar flor
blossom² *n* : flor *f*
blot¹ ['blat] *vt* **blotted; blotting** 1 SPOT : emborronar, borronear 2 DRY : secar
blot² *n* 1 STAIN : mancha *f*, borrón *m* 2 BLEMISH : mancha *f*, tacha *f*
blotch¹ ['blatʃ] *vt* : emborronar, borronear
blotch² *n* : mancha *f*, borrón *m*
blotchy ['blatʃi] *adj* **blotchier; -est** : lleno de manchas

blotter ['blɑtər] *n* : hoja *f* de papel secante, secante *m*

blouse ['blaʊs, 'blaʊz] *n* : blusa *f*

blow¹ ['blo:] *v* **blew** ['blu:]; **blown** ['blo:n]; **blowing** *vi* **1** : soplar, volar ⟨the wind is blowing hard : el viento está soplando con fuerza⟩ ⟨it blew out the door : voló por la puerta⟩ ⟨the window blew shut : se cerró la ventana⟩ **2** SOUND : sonar ⟨the whistle blew : sonó el silbato⟩ **3 to blow out** : fundirse (dícese de un fusible eléctrico), reventarse (dícese de una llanta) **4 to blow off** : dejar plantado (a alguien), flatar a (una cita, etc.) — *vt* **1** : soplar, echar ⟨to blow smoke : echar humo⟩ **2** SOUND : tocar, sonar **3** SHAPE : soplar, dar forma a ⟨to blow glass : soplar vidrio⟩ **4** BUNGLE : echar a perder

blow² *n* **1** PUFF : soplo *m*, soplido *m* **2** GALE : vendaval *f* **3** HIT, STROKE : golpe *m* **4** CALAMITY : golpe *m*, desastre *m* **5 to come to blows** : llegar a las manos

blower ['blo:ər] *n* FAN : ventilador *m*

blowout ['blo:ˌaʊt] *n* : reventón *m*

blowtorch ['blo:ˌtɔrtʃ] *n* : soplete *m*

blow up *vi* EXPLODE : estallar, hacer explosión — *vt* BLAST : volar, hacer volar

blubber¹ ['blʌbər] *vi* : lloriquear

blubber² *n* : esperma *f* de ballena

bludgeon ['blʌdʒən] *vt* : aporrear

blue¹ ['blu:] *adj* **bluer**; **bluest 1** : azul **2** MELANCHOLY : melancólico, triste

blue² *n* : azul *m*

blueberry ['blu:ˌbɛri] *n, pl* **-ries** : arándano *m*

bluebird ['blu:ˌbərd] *n* : azulejo *m*

blue cheese *n* : queso *m* azul

blueprint ['blu:ˌprɪnt] *n* **1** : plano *m*, proyecto *m*, cianotipo *m* **2** PLAN : anteproyecto *m*, programa *m*

blues ['blu:z] *npl* **1** DEPRESSION : depresión *f*, melancolía *f* **2** : blues *m* ⟨to sing the blues : cantar blues⟩

bluff¹ ['blʌf] *vi* : hacer un farol, blofear *Col, Mex*

bluff² *adj* **1** STEEP : escarpado **2** FRANK : campechano, franco, directo

bluff³ *n* **1** : farol *m*, blof *m Col, Mex* **2** CLIFF : acantilado *m*, risco *m*

bluing *or* **blueing** ['blu:ɪŋ] *n* : añil *m*, azulete *m*

bluish ['blu:ɪʃ] *adj* : azulado

blunder¹ ['blʌndər] *vi* **1** STUMBLE : tropezar, dar traspiés **2** ERR : cometer un error, tropezar, meter la pata *fam*

blunder² *n* : error *m*, fallo *m* garrafal, metedura *f* de pata *fam*

blunderbuss ['blʌndərˌbʌs] *n* : trabuco *m*

blunt¹ ['blʌnt] *vt* : despuntar (aguja o lápiz), desafilar (cuchillo o tijeras), suavizar (crítica)

blunt² *adj* **1** DULL : desafilado, despuntado **2** DIRECT : directo, franco, categórico

bluntly ['blʌntli] *adv* : sin rodeos, francamente, bruscamente

bluntness ['blʌntnəs] *n* **1** DULLNESS : falta *f* de filo, embotadura *f* **2** FRANKNESS : franqueza *f*

blur¹ ['blər] *vt* **blurred**; **blurring** : desdibujar, hacer borroso

blur² *n* **1** SMEAR : mancha *f*, borrón *m* **2** : aspecto *m* borroso ⟨everything was just a blur : todo se volvió borroso⟩

blurb ['blərb] *n* : propaganda *f*, nota *f* publicitaria

blurry ['bləri] *adj* : borroso

blurt ['blərt] *vt* : espetar, decir impulsivamente

blush¹ ['blʌʃ] *vi* : ruborizarse, sonrojarse, hacerse colorado

blush² *n* : rubor *m*, sonrojo *m*

bluster¹ ['blʌstər] *vi* **1** BLOW : soplar con fuerza **2** BOAST : fanfarronear, echar bravatas

bluster² *n* : fanfarronada *f*, bravatas *fpl*

blustery ['blʌstəri] *adj* : borrascoso, tempestuoso

boa ['bo:ə] *n* : boa *f*

boar ['bor] *n* : cerdo *m* macho, verraco *m*

board¹ ['bord] *vt* **1** : embarcarse en, subir a bordo de (una nave o un avión), subir a (un tren o carro) **2** LODGE : hospedar, dar hospedaje con comidas a **3 to board up** : cerrar con tablas

board² *n* **1** PLANK : tabla *f*, tablón *m* **2** : tablero *m* ⟨chessboard : tablero de ajedrez⟩ **3** MEALS : comida *f* ⟨board and lodging : comida y alojamiento⟩ **4** COMMITTEE, COUNCIL : junta *f*, consejo *m*

boarder ['bordər] *n* LODGER : huésped *m*, -peda *f*

boardinghouse ['bordɪŋˌhaʊs] *n* : casa *f* de huéspedes

boarding school *n* : internado *m*

boardwalk ['bordˌwɔk] *n* : paseo *m* marítimo

boast¹ ['bo:st] *vi* : alardear, presumir, jactarse

boast² *n* : jactancia *f*, alarde *m*

boaster ['bo:stər] *n* : presumido *m*, -da *f*; fanfarrón *m*, -rrona *f fam*

boastful ['bo:stfəl] *adj* : jactancioso, fanfarrón *fam*

boastfully ['bo:stfəli] *adv* : de manera jactanciosa

boat¹ ['bo:t] *vt* : transportar en barco, poner a bordo

boat² *n* : barco *m*, embarcación *f*, bote *m*, barca *f*

boatman ['bo:tmən] *n, pl* **-men** [-mən, -ˌmɛn] : barquero *m*

boatswain ['bo:sən] *n* : contramaestre *m*

bob¹ ['bɑb] *v* **bobbed**; **bobbing** *vi* **1** : balancearse, mecerse ⟨to bob up and down : subir y bajar⟩ **2** *or* **to bob up** APPEAR : presentarse, surgir — *vt* **1** : inclinar (la cabeza o el cuerpo) **2** CUT : cortar, recortar ⟨she bobbed her hair : se cortó el pelo⟩

bob² *n* **1** : inclinación *f* (de la cabeza, del cuerpo), sacudida *f* **2** FLOAT : flotador *m*, corcho *m* (de pesca) **3** : pelo *m* corto

bobbin ['babən] *n* : bobina *f*, carrete *m*

bobby pin ['babi͵pɪn] *n* : horquilla *f*

bobcat ['bab͵kæt] *n* : lince *m* rojo

bobolink ['babə͵lɪŋk] *n* : tordo *m* arrocero

bobsled ['bab͵slɛd] *n* : bobsleigh *m*

bobwhite ['bab'hwaɪt] *n* : codorniz *m* (del Nuevo Mundo)

bode¹ ['boːd] *v* **boded; boding** *vt* : presagiar, augurar — *vi* **to bode well** : ser de buen agüero

bode² → **bide**

bodice ['badəs] *n* : corpiño *m*

bodied ['badid] *adj* : de cuerpo ⟨lean-bodied : de cuerpo delgado⟩ ⟨able-bodied : no discapacitado⟩

bodiless ['badiləs, 'badələs] *adj* : incorpóreo

bodily¹ ['badəli] *adv* : en peso ⟨to lift someone bodily : levantar a alguien en peso⟩

bodily² *adj* : corporal, del cuerpo ⟨bodily harm : daños corporales⟩

body ['badi] *n, pl* **bodies** **1** : cuerpo *m*, organismo *m* **2** CORPSE : cadáver *m* **3** PERSON : persona *f*, ser *m* humano **4** : nave *f* (de una iglesia), carrocería (de un automóvil), fuselaje *m* (de un avión), casco *m* (de una nave) **5** COLLECTION, MASS : conjunto *m*, grupo *m*, masa *f* ⟨in a body : todos juntos, en masa⟩ **6** ORGANIZATION : organismo *m*, organización *f*

bodyguard ['badi͵gard] *n* : guardaespaldas *mf*

bog¹ ['bag, 'bɔg] *vt* **bogged; bogging** : empantanar, inundar ⟨to get bogged down : empantanarse⟩

bog² *n* : lodazal *m*, ciénaga *f*, cenagal *m*

bogey ['bugi, 'boː-] *n, pl* **-geys** : terror *m*, coco *m fam*

boggle ['bagəl] *vi* **-gled; -gling** : quedarse atónito, quedarse pasmado ⟨the mind boggles! : ¡es increíble!⟩

boggy ['bagi, 'bɔ-] *adj* **boggier; -est** : cenagoso

bogus ['boːgəs] *adj* : falso, fingido, falaz

bohemian [boː'hiːmiən] *n* : bohemio *m*, -mia *f* — **bohemian** *adj*

boil¹ ['bɔɪl] *v* **1** : hervir **2 to make one's blood boil** : hervirle la sangre a uno — *vt* **1** : hervir, hacer hervir ⟨to boil water : hervir agua⟩ **2** : cocer, hervir ⟨to boil potatoes : cocer papas⟩

boil² *n* **1** BOILING : hervor *m* **2** : furúnculo *m*, divieso *m* (en medicina)

boiler ['bɔɪlər] *n* : caldera *f*

boisterous ['bɔɪstərəs] *adj* : bullicioso, escandaloso — **boisterously** *adv*

bold ['boːld] *adj* **1** COURAGEOUS : valiente **2** INSOLENT : insolente, descarado **3** DARING : atrevido, audaz — **boldly** *adv*

boldface ['boːld͵feɪs] *or* **boldface type** *n* : negrita *f*

boldness ['boːldnəs] *n* **1** COURAGE : valor *m*, coraje *m* **2** INSOLENCE : atrevimiento *m*, insolencia *f*, descaro *m* **3** DARING : audacia *f*

bolero [bə'lɛroː] *n, pl* **-ros** : bolero *m*

Bolivian [bə'lɪviən] *n* : boliviano *m*, -na *f* — **Bolivian** *adj*

boll ['boːl] *n* : cápsula *f* (del algodón)

boll weevil *n* : gorgojo *m* del algodón

bologna [bə'loːni] *n* : salchicha *f* ahumada

bolster¹ ['boːlstər] *vt* **-stered; -stering** : reforzar, reafirmar ⟨to bolster morale : levantar la moral⟩

bolster² *n* : cabezal *m*, almohadón *m*

bolt¹ ['boːlt] *vt* **1** : atornillar, sujetar con pernos ⟨bolted to the floor : sujetado con pernos al suelo⟩ **2** : cerrar con pestillo, echar el cerrojo a ⟨to bolt the door : echar el cerrojo a la puerta⟩ **3 to bolt down** : engullir ⟨she bolted down her dinner : engulló su comida⟩ — *vi* : echar a correr, salir corriendo ⟨he bolted from the room : salió corriendo de la sala⟩

bolt² *n* **1** LATCH : pestillo *m*, cerrojo *m* **2** : tornillo *m*, perno *m* ⟨nuts and bolts : tuercas y tornillos⟩ **3** : rollo *m* ⟨a bolt of cloth : un rollo de tela⟩ **4 lightning bolt** : relámpago *m*, rayo *m*

bomb¹ ['bam] *vt* : bombardear

bomb² *n* : bomba *f*

bombard [bam'bard, bəm-] *vt* : bombardear

bombardier [͵bambə'dɪr] *n* : bombardero *m*, -ra *f*

bombardment [bam'bardmənt] *n* : bombardeo *m*

bombast ['bam͵bæst] *n* : grandilocuencia *f*, ampulosidad *f*

bombastic [bam'bæstɪk] *adj* : grandilocuente, ampuloso, bombástico

bomber ['bamər] *n* : bombardero *m*

bombproof ['bam͵pruːf] *adj* : a prueba de bombas

bombshell ['bam͵ʃɛl] *n* : bomba *f* ⟨a political bombshell : una bomba política⟩

bona fide ['boːnə͵faɪd, 'ba-; ͵boːnə'faɪdi] *adj* **1** : de buena fe ⟨a bona fide offer : una oferta de buena fe⟩ **2** GENUINE : genuino, auténtico

bonanza [bə'nænzə] *n* : bonanza *f*

bonbon ['ban͵ban] *n* : bombón *m*

bond¹ ['band] *vt* **1** INSURE : dar fianza a, asegurar **2** STICK : adherir, pegar — *vi* : adherirse, pegarse

bond² *n* **1** LINK, TIE : vínculo *m*, lazo *m* **2** BAIL : fianza *f*, caución *f* **3** : bono *m* ⟨stocks and bonds : acciones y bonos⟩ **4 bonds** *npl* FETTERS : cadenas *fpl*

bondage ['bandɪdʒ] *n* : esclavitud *f*

bondholder ['band͵hoːldər] *n* : tenedor *m*, -dora *f* de bonos

bondsman ['bandzmən] *n, pl* **-men** [-mən, -͵mn] **1** SLAVE : esclavo *m* **2** SURETY : fiador *m*, -dora *f*

bone¹ ['boːn] *vt* **boned; boning** : deshuesar

bone² *n* : hueso *m*
boneless ['bo:nləs] *adj* : sin huesos, sin espinas
boner ['bo:nər] *n* : metedura *f* de pata, metida *f* de pata
bonfire ['bɑn,faɪr] *n* : hoguera *f*, fogata *f*, fogón *m*
bonito [bə'ni:t̬o] *n, pl* **-tos** *or* **-to** : bonito *m*
bonnet ['bɑnət] *n* : sombrero *m* (de mujer), gorra *f* (de niño)
bonus ['bo:nəs] *n* **1** : prima *f*, bonificación *f* (pagado al empleado) **2** ADVANTAGE, BENEFIT : beneficio *m*, provecho *m*
bony ['bo:ni] *adj* **bonier; -est** : huesudo
boo¹ ['bu:] *vt* : abuchear
boo² *n, pl* **boos** : abucheo *m*
booby ['bu:bi] *n, pl* **-bies** : bobo *m*, -ba *f*; tonto *m*, -ta *f*
book¹ ['bʊk] *vt* : reservar ⟨to book a flight : reservar un vuelo⟩
book² *n* **1** : libro *m* **2 the Book** : la Biblia **3 by the book** : según las reglas
bookcase ['bʊk,keɪs] *n* : estantería *f*, librero *m* Mex
bookend ['bʊk,ɛnd] *n* : sujetalibros *m*
bookie ['bʊki] → **bookmaker**
bookish ['bʊkɪʃ] *adj* : libresco
bookkeeper ['bʊk,ki:pər] *n* : tenedor *m*, -dora *f* de libros; contable *mf Spain*
bookkeeping ['bʊk,ki:pɪŋ] *n* : contabilidad *f*, teneduría *f* de libros
booklet ['bʊklət] *n* : folleto *m*
bookmaker ['bʊk,meɪkər] *n* : corredor *m*, -dora *f* de apuestas
bookmark ['bʊk,mɑrk] *n* : señalador *m* de libros, marcador *m* de libros
bookseller ['bʊk,slər] *n* : librero *m*, -ra *f*
bookshelf ['bʊk,ʃɛlf] *n, pl* **-shelves 1** : estante *m* **2 bookshelves** *npl* : estantería *f*
bookstore ['bʊk,stor] *n* : librería *f*
bookworm ['bʊk,wərm] *n* : ratón *m* de biblioteca *fam*
boom¹ ['bu:m] *vi* **1** THUNDER : tronar, resonar **2** FLOURISH, PROSPER : estar en auge, prosperar
boom² *n* **1** BOOMING : bramido *m*, estruendo *m* **2** FLOURISHING : auge *m* ⟨population boom : auge de población⟩
boomerang ['bu:mə,ræŋ] *n* : bumerán *m*
boon¹ ['bu:n] *adj* **boon companion** : amigo *m*, -ga *f* del alma
boon² *n* : ayuda *f*, beneficio *m*, adelanto *m*
boondocks ['bu:n,dɑks] *npl* : área *f* rural remota, región *f* alejada
boor ['bʊr] *n* : grosero *m*, -ra *f*
boorish ['bʊrɪʃ] *adj* : grosero
boost¹ ['bu:st] *vt* **1** LIFT : levantar, alzar **2** INCREASE : aumentar, incrementar **3** PROMOTE : promover, fomentar, hacer publicidad por

boost² *n* **1** THRUST : impulso *m*, empujón *m* **2** ENCOURAGEMENT : estímulo *m*, aliento *m* **3** INCREASE : aumento *m*, incremento *m*
booster ['bu:stər] *n* **1** SUPPORTER : partidario *m*, -ria *f* **2 booster rocket** : cohete *m* propulsor **3 booster shot** : vacuna *f* de refuerzo
boot¹ ['bu:t] *vt* KICK : dar una patada a, patear
boot² *n* **1** : bota *f*, botín *m* **2** KICK : puntapié *m*, patada *f*
bootee *or* **bootie** ['bu:t̬i] *n* : botita *f*, botín *m*
booth ['bu:θ] *n, pl* **booths** ['bu:ðz, 'bu:θs] : cabina *f* (de teléfono, de votar), caseta *f* (de información), barraca *f* (a una feria)
bootlegger ['bu:t̬,lɛgər] *n* : contrabandista *mf* del alcohol
booty ['bu:t̬i] *n, pl* **-ties** : botín *m*
booze ['bu:z] *n fam* : alcohol *m*
borax ['bor,æks] *n* : bórax *m*
border¹ ['bordər] *vt* **1** EDGE : ribetear, bordear **2** BOUND : limitar con, lindar con — *vi* VERGE : rayar, lindar ⟨that borders on absurdity : eso raya en el absurdo⟩
border² *n* **1** EDGE : borde *m*, orilla *f* **2** TRIM : ribete *m* **3** FRONTIER : frontera *f*
bore¹ ['bor] *vt* **bored; boring 1** PIERCE : taladrar, perforar ⟨to bore metals : taladrar metales⟩ **2** OPEN : hacer, abrir ⟨to bore a tunnel : abrir un túnel⟩ **3** WEARY : aburrir
bore² → **bear¹**
bore³ *n* **1** : pesado *m*, -da *f* (persona aburrida) **2** TEDIOUSNESS : pesadez *f*, lo aburrido **3** DIAMETER : calibre *m*
boredom ['bordəm] *n* : aburrimiento *m*
boring ['borɪŋ] *adj* : aburrido, pesado
born ['born] *adj* **1** : nacido **2** : nato ⟨she's a born singer : es una cantante nata⟩ ⟨he's a born leader : nació para mandar⟩
borne *pp* → **bear¹**
boron ['bor,ɑn] *n* : boro *m*
borough ['bərə] *n* : distrito *m* municipal
borrow ['bɑro] *vt* **1** : pedir prestado, tomar prestado **2** APPROPRIATE : apropiarse de, adoptar
borrower ['bɑrəwər] *n* : prestatario *m*, -ria *f*
Bosnian ['bɑzniən, 'bɔz-] *n* : bosnio *m*, -nia *f* — **Bosnian** *adj*
bosom¹ ['bʊzəm, 'bu:-] *adj* : íntimo
bosom² *n* **1** CHEST : pecho *m* **2** BREAST : pecho *m*, seno *m* **3** CLOSENESS : seno *m* ⟨in the bosom of her family : en el seno de su familia⟩
bosomed ['bʊzəmd, 'bu:-] *adj* : con busto ⟨big-bosomed : con mucho busto⟩
boss¹ ['bɔs] *vt* **1** SUPERVISE : dirigir, supervisar **2 to boss around** : mandonear *fam*, mangonear *fam*
boss² *n* : jefe *m*, -fa *f*; patrón *m*, -trona *f*
bossy ['bɔsi] *adj* **bossier; -est** : mandón *fam*, autoritario, dominante

botanist ['bɑtənɪst] *n* : botánico *m*, -ca *f*
botany ['bɑtəni] *n* : botánica *f* — **botanical** [bə'tænɪkəl] *adj*
botch[1] ['bɑtʃ] *vt* : hacer una chapuza de, estropear
botch[2] *n* : chapuza *f*
both[1] ['boːθ] *adj* : ambos, los dos, las dos ⟨both books : ambos libros, los dos libros⟩
both[2] *conj* : tanto como ⟨both Ann and her mother are tall : tanto Ana como su madre son altas⟩
both[3] *pron* : ambos *m*, -bas *f*; los dos, las dos
bother[1] ['bɑðər] *vt* **1** IRK : preocupar ⟨nothing's bothering me : nada me preocupa⟩ ⟨what's bothering him? : ¿qué le pasa?⟩ **2** PESTER : molestar, fastidiar — *vi* **to bother to** : molestarse en, tomar la molestia de
bother[2] *n* **1** TROUBLE : molestia *f*, problemas *mpl* **2** ANNOYANCE : molestia *f*, fastidio *m*
bothersome ['bɑðərsəm] *adj* : molesto, fastidioso
bottle[1] ['bɑtəl] *vt* **bottled; bottling** : embotellar, envasar
bottle[2] *n* : botella *f*, frasco *m*
bottleneck ['bɑtəl,nɛk] *n* **1** : cuello *m* de botella (en un camino) **2** : embotellamiento *m*, atasco *m* (de tráfico) **3** OBSTACLE : obstáculo *m*
bottom[1] ['bɑtəm] *adj* : más bajo, inferior, de abajo
bottom[2] *n* **1** : fondo *m* (de una caja, de una taza, del mar), pie *m* (de una escalera, una página, una montaña), asiento *m* (de una silla), parte *f* de abajo (de una pila) **2** CAUSE : origen *m*, causa *f* ⟨to get to the bottom of : llegar al fondo de⟩ **3** BUTTOCKS : trasero *m*, nalgas *fpl*
bottomless ['bɑtəmləs] *adj* : sin fondo, sin límites
botulism ['bɑtʃə,lɪzəm] *n* : botulismo *m*
boudoir [bə'dwɑr, buː-; 'buː,-, 'bu-] *n* : tocador *m*
bough ['baʊ] *n* : rama *f*
bought → **buy**[1]
bouillon ['buː,jɑn; 'bʊl,jɑn, -jən] *n* : caldo *m*
boulder ['boːldər] *n* : canto *m* rodado, roca *f* grande
boulevard ['bʊlə,vɑrd, 'buː-] *n* : bulevar *m*, boulevard *m*
bounce[1] ['baʊn̩ts] *v* **bounced; bouncing** *vt* : hacer rebotar — *vi* : rebotar
bounce[2] *n* : rebote *m*
bouncy ['baʊn̩tsi] *adj* **bouncier; -est 1** LIVELY : vivo, exuberante, animado **2** RESILIENT : elástico, flexible **3** : que rebota (dícese de una pelota)
bound[1] ['baʊnd] *vt* : delimitar, rodear — *vi* LEAP : saltar, dar brincos
bound[2] *adj* **1** OBLIGED : obligado **2** : encuadernado, empastado ⟨a book bound in leather : un libro encuadernado en cuero⟩ **3** DETERMINED : decidido, empeñado **4 to be bound to** : ser seguro que, tener que, no caber duda que ⟨it was bound to happen : tenía que suceder⟩ **5 bound for** : con rumbo a ⟨bound for Chicago : con rumbo a Chicago⟩ ⟨to be homeward bound : ir camino a casa⟩
bound[3] *n* **1** LIMIT : límite *m* **2** LEAP : salto *m*, brinco *m*
boundary ['baʊndri, -dəri] *n, pl* **-aries** : límite *m*, línea *f* divisoria, linde *mf*
boundless ['baʊndləs] *adj* : sin límites, infinito
bounteous ['baʊntiəs] *adj* **1** GENEROUS : generoso **2** ABUNDANT : copioso, abundante — **bounteously** *adv*
bountiful ['baʊntɪfəl] *adj* **1** GENEROUS, LIBERAL : munificente, pródigo, generoso **2** ABUNDANT : copioso, abundante
bounty ['baʊnti] *n, pl* **-ties 1** GENEROSITY : generosidad *f*, munificencia *f* **2** REWARD : recompensa *f*
bouquet [boː'keɪ, buː-] *n* **1** : ramo *m*, ramillete *m* **2** FRAGRANCE : bouquet *m*, aroma *m*
bourbon ['bɑrbən, 'bʊr-] *n* : bourbon *m*, whisky *m* americano
bourgeois[1] ['bʊrʒ,wɑ, bʊrʒ'wɑ] *adj* : burgués
bourgeois[2] *n* : burgués *m*, -guesa *f*
bourgeoisie [,bʊrʒ,wɑ'zi] *n* : burguesía *f*
bout ['baʊt] *n* **1** : encuentro *m*, combate *m* (en deportes) **2** ATTACK : ataque *m* (de una enfermedad) **3** PERIOD, SPELL : período *m* (de actividad)
boutique [buː'tiːk] *n* : boutique *f*
bovine[1] ['boː,vaɪn, -,viːn] *adj* : bovino, vacuno
bovine[2] *n* : bovino *m*
bow[1] ['baʊ] *vi* **1** : hacer una reverencia, inclinarse **2** SUBMIT : ceder, resignarse, someterse — *vt* **1** LOWER : inclinar, bajar **2** BEND : doblar
bow[2] ['baʊ] *n* **1** BOWING : reverencia *f*, inclinación *f* **2** : proa *f* (de un barco)
bow[3] ['boː] *vi* CURVE : arquearse, doblarse
bow[4] ['boː] *n* **1** ARCH, CURVE : arco *m*, curva *f* **2** : arco *m* (arma o vara para tocar varios instrumentos de música) **3** : lazo *m*, moño *m* ⟨to tie a bow : hacer un moño⟩
bowels ['baʊəls] *npl* **1** INTESTINES : intestinos *mpl* **2** : entrañas *fpl* ⟨in the bowels of the earth : en las entrañas de la tierra⟩
bower ['baʊər] *n* : enramada *f*
bowl[1] ['boːl] *vi* : jugar a los bolos
bowl[2] *n* : tazón *m*, cuenco *m*
bowler ['boːlər] *n* : jugador *m*, -dora *f* de bolos
bowling ['boːlɪŋ] *n* : bolos *mpl*
box[1] ['bɑks] *vt* **1** PACK : empaquetar, embalar, encajonar **2** SLAP : bofetear, cachetear — *vi* : boxear

box² *n* **1** CONTAINER : caja *f*, cajón *m* **2** COMPARTMENT : compartimento *m*, palco *m* (en el teatro) **3** SLAP : bofetada *f*, cachetada *f* **4** : boj *m* (planta)
boxcar ['baks,kɑr] *n* : vagón *m* de carga, furgón *m*
boxer ['baksər] *n* : boxeador *m*, -dora *f*
boxing ['baksɪŋ] *n* : boxeo *m*
box office *n* : taquilla *f*, boletería *f*
boxwood ['baks,wʊd] *n* : boj *m*
boy ['bɔɪ] *n* **1** : chico *m*, muchacho *m* **2** *or* **little boy** : niño *m*, chico *m* **3** SON : hijo *m*
boycott¹ ['bɔɪ,kɑt] *vt* : boicotear
boycott² *n* : boicot *m*
boyfriend ['bɔɪ,frɛnd] *n* **1** FRIEND : amigo *m* **2** SWEETHEART : novio *m*
boyhood ['bɔɪ,hʊd] *n* : niñez *f*
boyish ['bɔɪʃ] *adj* : de niño, juvenil
bra ['brɑ] → **brassiere**
brace¹ ['breɪs] *v* **braced; bracing** *vt* **1** PROP UP, SUPPORT : apuntalar, apoyar, sostener **2** INVIGORATE : vigorizar **3** REINFORCE : reforzar — *vi* **to brace oneself** PREPARE : prepararse
brace² *n* **1** : berbiquí *m* ⟨brace and bit : berbiquí y barrena⟩ **2** CLAMP, REINFORCEMENT : abrazadera *f*, refuerzo *m* **3** : llave *f* (signo de puntuación)· **4 braces** *npl* : aparatos *mpl* (de ortodoncia), frenos *mpl Mex*
bracelet ['breɪslət] *n* : brazalete *m*, pulsera *f*
bracken ['brækən] *n* : helecho *m*
bracket¹ ['brækət] *vt* **1** SUPPORT : asegurar, apuntalar **2** : poner entre corchetes **3** CATEGORIZE, GROUP : catalogar, agrupar
bracket² *n* **1** SUPPORT : soporte *m* **2** : corchete *m* (marca de puntuación) **3** CATEGORY, CLASS : clase *f*, categoría *f*
brackish ['brækɪʃ] *adj* : salobre
brad ['bræd] *n* : clavo *m* con cabeza pequeña, clavito *m*
brag¹ ['bræg] *vi* **bragged; bragging** : alardear, fanfarronear, jactarse
brag² *n* : alarde *m*, jactancia *f*, fanfarronada *f*
braggart ['brægərt] *n* : fanfarrón *m*, -rrona *f fam*; jactancioso *m*, -sa *f*
braid¹ ['breɪd] *vt* : trenzar
braid² *n* : trenza *f*
braille ['breɪl] *n* : braille *m*
brain¹ ['breɪn] *vt* : romper la crisma a, aplastar el cráneo a
brain² *n* **1** : cerebro *m* **2 brains** *npl* INTELLECT : inteligencia *f*, sesos *mpl*
brainless ['breɪnləs] *adj* : estúpido, tonto
brainstorm ['breɪn,stɔrm] *n* : idea *f* brillante, idea *f* genial
brainy ['breɪni] *adj* **brainier; -est** : inteligente, listo
braise ['breɪz] *vt* **braised; braising** : cocer a fuego lento, estofar
brake¹ ['breɪk] *v* **braked; braking** : frenar
brake² *n* : freno *m*

bramble ['bræmbəl] *n* : zarza *f*, zarzamora *f*
bran ['bræn] *n* : salvado *m*
branch¹ ['bræntʃ] *vi* **1** : echar ramas (dícese de una planta) **2** DIVERGE : ramificarse, separarse
branch² *n* **1** : rama *f* (de una planta) **2** EXTENSION : ramal *m* (de un camino, un ferrocarril, un río), rama *f* (de una familia o un campo de estudiar), sucursal *f* (de una empresa), agencia *f* (del gobierno)
brand¹ ['brænd] *vt* **1** : marcar (ganado) **2** LABEL : tachar, tildar ⟨they branded him as a liar : lo tacharon de mentiroso⟩
brand² *n* **1** : marca *f* (de ganado) **2** STIGMA : estigma *m* **3** MAKE : marca *f* ⟨brand name : marca de fábrica⟩
brandish ['brændɪʃ] *vt* : blandir
brand-new ['brænd'nu:, -'nju:] *adj* : nuevo, flamante
brandy ['brændi] *n, pl* **-dies** : brandy *m*
brash ['bræʃ] *adj* **1** IMPULSIVE : impulsivo, impetuoso **2** BRAZEN : excesivamente desenvuelto, descarado
brass ['bræs] *n* **1** : latón *m* **2** GALL, NERVE : descaro *m*, cara *f fam* **3** OFFICERS : mandamases *mpl fam*
brassiere [brə'zɪr, brɑ-] *n* : sostén *m*, brasier *m Col, Mex*
brassy ['bræsi] *adj* **brassier; -est** : dorado
brat ['bræt] *n* : mocoso *m*, -sa *f*; niño *m* mimado, niña *f* mimada
bravado [brə'vɑdo] *n, pl* **-does** *or* **-dos** : bravuconadas *fpl*, bravatas *fpl*
brave¹ ['breɪv] *vt* **braved; braving** : afrontar, hacer frente a
brave² *adj* **braver; bravest** : valiente, valeroso — **bravely** *adv*
brave³ *n* : guerrero *m* indio
bravery ['breɪvəri] *n* : valor *m*, valentía *f*
bravo ['brɑ,vo] *n, pl* **-vos** : bravo *m*
brawl¹ ['brɔl] *vi* : pelearse, pegarse
brawl² *n* : pelea *f*, reyerta *f*
brawn ['brɔn] *n* : fuerza *f* muscular
brawny ['brɔni] *adj* **brawnier; -est** : musculoso
bray¹ ['breɪ] *vi* : rebuznar
bray² *n* : rebuzno *m*
brazen ['breɪzən] *adj* **1** : de latón **2** BOLD : descarado, directo
brazenly ['breɪzənli] *adv* : descaradamente, insolentemente
brazenness ['breɪzənnəs] *n* : descaro *m*, atrevimiento *m*
brazier ['breɪʒər] *n* : brasero *m*
Brazilian [brə'zɪljən] *n* : brasileño *m*, -ña *f* — **Brazilian** *adj*
Brazil nut [brə'zɪl,nʌt] *n* : nuez *f* de Brasil
breach¹ ['britʃ] *vt* **1** PENETRATE : abrir una brecha en, penetrar **2** VIOLATE : infringir, violar
breach² *n* **1** VIOLATION : infracción *f*, violación *f* ⟨breach of trust : abuso de confianza⟩ **2** GAP, OPENING : brecha *f*

bread¹ ['brɛd] *vt* : empanar
bread² *n* : pan *m*
breadth ['brɛtθ] *n* : ancho *m*, anchura *f*
breadwinner ['brɛd,wɪnər] *n* : sostén *m* de la familia
break¹ ['breɪk] *v* **broke** ['bro:k]; **broken** ['bro:kən]; **breaking** *vt* **1** SMASH : romper, quebrar **2** VIOLATE : infringir, violar, romper **3** SURPASS : batir, superar **4** CRUSH, RUIN : arruinar, deshacer, destrozar ⟨to break one's spirit : quebrantar su espíritu⟩ **5** : dar, comunicar ⟨to break the news : dar las noticias⟩ **6** INTERRUPT : cortar, interrumpir — *vi* **1** : romperse, quebrarse ⟨my calculator broke : se me rompió la calculadora⟩ **2** DISPERSE : dispersarse, despejarse **3** : estallar (dícese de una tormenta), romper (dícese del día) **4** CHANGE : cambiar (dícese del tiempo o de la voz) **5** DECREASE : bajar ⟨my fever broke : me bajó la fiebre⟩ **6** : divulgarse, revelarse ⟨the news broke : la noticia se divulgó⟩ **7 to break into** : forzar, abrir **8 to break out of** : escaparse de **9 to break through** : penetrar
break² *n* **1** : ruptura *f*, rotura *f*, fractura *f* (de un hueso), claro *m* (entre las nubes), cambio *m* (del tiempo) **2** CHANCE : oportunidad *f* ⟨a lucky break : un golpe de suerte⟩ **3** REST : descanso *m* ⟨to take a break : tomar(se) un descanso⟩
breakable ['breɪkəbəl] *adj* : quebradizo, frágil
breakage ['breɪkɪdʒ] *n* **1** BREAKING : rotura *f* **2** DAMAGE : destrozos *mpl*, daños *mpl*
breakdown ['breɪk,daʊn] *n* **1** : avería *f* (de máquinas), interrupción *f* (de comunicaciones), fracaso *m* (de negociaciones) **2** ANALYSIS : análisis *m*, desglose *m* **3** *or* **nervous breakdown** : crisis *f* nerviosa
break down *vi* **1** : estropearse, descomponerse ⟨the machine broke down : la máquina se descompuso⟩ **2** FAIL : fracasar **3** CRY : echarse a llorar — *vt* **1** DESTROY : derribar, echar abajo **2** OVERCOME : vencer (la resistencia), disipar (sospechas) **3** ANALYZE : analizar, descomponer
breaker ['breɪkər] *n* **1** WAVE : ola *f* grande **2** : interruptor *m* automático (de electricidad)
breakfast¹ ['brɛkfəst] *vi* : desayunar
breakfast² *n* : desayuno *m*
breakneck ['breɪk,nɛk] *adj* **at breakneck speed** : a una velocidad vertiginosa
break out *vi* **1** : salirse ⟨she broke out in spots : le salieron granos⟩ **2** ERUPT : estallar (dícese de una guerra, la violencia, etc.) **3** ESCAPE : fugarse, escaparse
breakup ['breɪk,əp] *n* **1** DIVISION : desintegración *f* **2** : ruptura *f*

break up *vt* **1** DIVIDE : dividir **2** : disolver (una muchedumbre, una pelea, etc.) — *vi* **1** BREAK : romperse **2** SEPARATE : deshacerse, separarse ⟨I broke up with him : terminé con él⟩
breast ['brɛst] *n* **1** : pecho *m*, seno *m* (de una mujer) **2** CHEST : pecho *m*
breastbone ['brɛst,bo:n] *n* : esternón *m*
breast-feed ['brɛst,fi:d] *vt* **-fed** [-,fɛd]; **-feeding** : amamantar, darle de mamar (a un niño)
breath ['brɛθ] *n* **1** BREATHING : aliento *m* ⟨to hold one's breath : aguantar la respiración⟩ **2** BREEZE : soplo *m* ⟨a breath of fresh air : un soplo de aire fresco⟩
breathe ['bri:ð] *v* **breathed; breathing** *vi* **1** : respirar **2** LIVE : vivir, respirar — *vt* **1** : respirar, aspirar ⟨to breathe fresh air : respirar el aire fresco⟩ **2** UTTER : decir ⟨I won't breathe a word of this : no diré nada de esto⟩
breathless ['brɛθləs] *adj* : sin aliento, jadeante
breathlessly ['brɛθləsli] *adv* : entrecortadamente, jadeando
breathlessness ['brɛθləsnəs] *n* : dificultad *f* al respirar
breathtaking ['brɛθ,teɪkɪŋ] *adj* IMPRESSIVE : impresionante, imponente
breeches ['brɪtʃəz, 'bri:-] *npl* : pantalones *mpl*, calzones *mpl*, bombachos *mpl*
breed¹ ['bri:d] *v* **bred** ['brɛd]; **breeding** *vt* **1** : criar (animales) **2** ENGENDER : engendrar, producir ⟨familiarity breeds contempt : la confianza hace perder el respeto⟩ **3** RAISE, REAR : criar, educar — *vi* REPRODUCE : reproducirse
breed² *n* **1** : variedad *f* (de plantas), raza *f* (de animales) **2** CLASS : clase *f*, tipo *m*
breeder ['bri:dər] *n* : criador *m*, -dora *f* (de animales); cultivador *m*, -dora *f* (de plantas)
breeze¹ ['bri:z] *vi* **breezed; breezing** : pasar con ligereza ⟨to breeze in : entrar como si nada⟩
breeze² *n* : brisa *f*, soplo *m* (de aire)
breezy ['bri:zi] *adj* **breezier; -est 1** AIRY, WINDY : aireado, ventoso **2** LIVELY : animado, alegre **3** NONCHALANT : despreocupado
brethren → brother
brevity ['brɛvəti] *n, pl* **-ties** : brevedad *f*, concisión *f*
brew¹ ['bru:] *vt* **1** : fabricar, elaborar (cerveza) **2** FOMENT : tramar, maquinar, fomentar — *vi* **1** : fabricar cerveza **2** : amenazar ⟨a storm is brewing : una tormenta amenaza⟩
brew² *n* **1** BEER : cerveza *f* **2** POTION : brebaje *m*
brewer ['bru:ər] *n* : cervecero *m*, -ra *f*
brewery ['bru:əri, 'bruri] *n, pl* **-eries** : cervecería *f*
briar ['braɪər] **→ brier**

bribe¹ ['braɪb] *vt* **bribed; bribing** : sobornar, cohechar, coimear *Arg, Chile, Peru*

bribe² *n* : soborno *m*, cohecho *m*, coima *f Arg, Chile, Peru*, mordida *f CA, Mex*

bribery ['braɪbəri] *n, pl* **-eries** : soborno *m*, cohecho *m*, coima *f*, mordida *f CA, Mex*

bric-a-brac ['brɪkə,bræk] *npl* : baratijas *fpl*, chucherías *fpl*

brick¹ ['brɪk] *vt* **to brick up** : tabicar, tapiar

brick² *n* : ladrillo *m*

bricklayer ['brɪk,leɪər] *n* : albañil *mf*

bricklaying ['brɪk,leɪɪŋ] *n* : albañilería *f*

bridal ['braɪdəl] *adj* : nupcial, de novia

bride ['braɪd] *n* : novia *f*

bridegroom ['braɪd,gruːm] *n* : novio *m*

bridesmaid ['braɪdz,meɪd] *n* : dama *f* de honor

bridge¹ ['brɪdʒ] *vt* **bridged; bridging 1** : tender un puente sobre **2 to bridge the gap** : salvar las diferencias

bridge² *n* **1** : puente *m* **2** : caballete *m* (de la nariz) **3** : puente *m* de mando (de un barco) **4** DENTURE : puente *m* (dental) **5** : bridge *m* (juego de naipes)

bridle¹ ['braɪdəl] *v* **-dled; -dling** *vt* **1** : embridar (un caballo) **2** RESTRAIN : refrenar, dominar, contener — *vi* **to bridle at** : molestarse por, picarse por

bridle² *n* : brida *f*

brief¹ ['briːf] *vt* : dar órdenes a, instruir

brief² *adj* : breve, sucinto, conciso

brief³ *n* **1** : resumen *m*, sumario *m* **2 briefs** *npl* : calzoncillos *mpl*

briefcase ['briːf,keɪs] *n* : portafolio *m*, maletín *m*

briefly ['briːfli] *adv* : brevemente, por poco tiempo ⟨to speak briefly : discursar en pocas palabras⟩

brier ['braɪər] *n* **1** BRAMBLE : zarza *f*, rosal *m* silvestre **2** HEATH : brezo *m* veteado

brig ['brɪg] *n* **1** : bergantín *m* (barco) **2** : calabozo *m* (en un barco)

brigade [brɪ'geɪd] *n* : brigada *f*

brigadier general [,brɪgə'dɪr] *n* : general *m* de brigada

brigand ['brɪgənd] *n* : bandolero *m*, -ra *f*; forajido *m*, -da *f*

bright ['braɪt] *adj* **1** : brillante (dícese del sol, de los ojos), vivo (dícese de un color), claro, fuerte **2** CHEERFUL : alegre, animado ⟨bright and early : muy temprano⟩ **3** INTELLIGENT : listo, inteligente ⟨a bright idea : una idea luminosa⟩

brighten ['braɪtən] *vt* **1** ILLUMINATE : iluminar **2** ENLIVEN : alegrar, animar — *vi* **1** : hacerse más brillante **2 to brighten up** : animarse, alegrarse, mejorar

brightly ['braɪtli] *adv* : vivamente, intensamente, alegremente

brightness ['braɪtnəs] *n* **1** LUMINOSITY : luminosidad *f*, brillantez *f*, resplandor *m*, brillo *m* **2** CHEERFULNESS : alegría *f*, ánimo *m*

brilliance ['brɪljənts] *n* **1** BRIGHTNESS : resplandor *m*, fulgor *m*, brillo *m*, brillantez *f* **2** INTELLIGENCE : inteligencia *f*, brillantez *f*

brilliancy ['brɪljəntsi] → **brilliance**

brilliant ['brɪljənt] *adj* : brillante

brilliantly ['brɪljəntli] *adv* : brillantemente, con brillantez

brim¹ ['brɪm] *vi* **brimmed; brimming 1** *or* **to brim over** : desbordarse, rebosar **2 to brim with tears** : llenarse de lágrimas

brim² *n* **1** : ala *f* (de un sombrero) **2** : borde *m* (de una taza o un vaso)

brimful ['brɪm'fʊl] *adj* : lleno hasta el borde, repleto, rebosante

brimless ['brɪmləs] *adj* : sin ala

brimstone ['brɪm,stoːn] *n* : azufre *m*

brindled ['brɪndəld] *adj* : manchado, pinto

brine ['braɪn] *n* **1** : salmuera *f*, escabeche *m* (para encurtir) **2** OCEAN : océano *m*, mar *m*

bring ['brɪŋ] *vt* **brought** ['brɔt]; **bringing 1** CARRY : traer ⟨bring me some coffee : tráigame un café⟩ **2** PRODUCE : traer, producir, conseguir ⟨his efforts will bring him success : sus esfuerzos le conseguirán el éxito⟩ **3** PERSUADE : convencer, persuadir **4** YIELD : rendir, alcanzar, venderse por ⟨to bring a good price : alcanzar un precio alto⟩ **5 to bring to an end** : terminar (con) **6 to bring to light** : sacar a la luz

bring about *vt* : ocasionar, provocar, determinar

bring forth *vt* PRODUCE : producir

bring out *vt* : sacar, publicar (un libro, etc.)

bring to *vt* REVIVE : resucitar

bring up *vt* **1** REAR : criar **2** MENTION : sacar, mencionar

brininess ['braɪninəs] *n* : salinidad *f*

brink ['brɪŋk] *n* : borde *m*

briny ['braɪni] *adj* **brinier; -est** : salobre

briquette *or* **briquet** [brɪ'kɛt] *n* : briqueta *f*

brisk ['brɪsk] *adj* **1** LIVELY : rápido, enérgico, brioso **2** INVIGORATING : fresco, estimulante

brisket ['brɪskət] *n* : falda *f*

briskly ['brɪskli] *adv* : rápidamente, enérgicamente, con brío

briskness ['brɪsknəs] *n* : brío *m*, rapidez *f*

bristle¹ ['brɪsəl] *vi* **-tled; -tling 1** : erizarse, ponerse de punta **2** : enfurecerse, enojarse ⟨she bristled at the suggestion : se enfureció ante tal sugerencia⟩ **3** : estar plagado, estar repleto ⟨a city bristling with tourists : una ciudad repleta de turistas⟩

bristle² *n* : cerda *f* (de un animal), pelo *m* (de una planta)

bristly ['brɪsəli] *adj* **bristlier; -est** : áspero y erizado

British¹ ['brɪtɪʃ] *adj* : británico

British² *n* **the British** *npl* : los británicos

brittle ['brɪtəl] *adj* -tler; -tlest : frágil, quebradizo
brittleness ['brɪtəlnəs] *n* : fragilidad *f*
broach ['broːʧ] *vt* BRING UP : mencionar, abordar, sacar
broad ['brɔd] *adj* **1** WIDE : ancho **2** SPACIOUS : amplio, extenso **3** FULL : pleno ⟨in broad daylight : en pleno día⟩ **4** OBVIOUS : claro, evidente **5** TOLERANT : tolerante, liberal **6** GENERAL : general **7** ESSENTIAL : principal, esencial ⟨the broad outline : los rasgos esenciales⟩
broadcast¹ ['brɔd,kæst] *vt* -cast; -casting **1** SCATTER : esparcir, diseminar **2** CIRCULATE, SPREAD : divulgar, difundir, propagar **3** TRANSMIT : transmitir, emitir
broadcast² *n* **1** TRANSMISSION : transmisión *f*, emisión *f* **2** PROGRAM : programa *m*, emisión *f*
broadcaster ['brɔd,kæstər] *n* : presentador *m*, -dora *f*; locutor *m*, -tora *f*
broadcloth ['brɔd,klɔθ] *n* : paño *m* fino
broaden ['brɔdən] *vt* : ampliar, ensanchar — *vi* : ampliarse, ensancharse
broadloom ['brɔd,luːm] *adj* : tejido *m* telar ancho
broadly ['brɔdli] *adv* **1** GENERALLY : en general, aproximadamente **2** WIDELY : extensivamente
broad–minded ['brɔd'maɪndəd] *adj* : tolerante, de amplias miras
broad–mindedness [brɔd'maɪndədnəs] *n* : tolerancia *f*
broadside ['brɔd,saɪd] *n* **1** VOLLEY : andanada *f* **2** ATTACK : ataque *m*, invectiva *f*, andanada *f*
brocade [bro'keɪd] *n* : brocado *m*
broccoli ['brɑkəli] *n* : brócoli *m*, brécol *m*
brochure [bro'ʃʊr] *n* : folleto *m*
brogue ['broːg] *n* : acento *m* irlandés
broil¹ ['brɔɪl] *vt* : asar a la parrilla
broil² *n* : asado *m*
broiler ['brɔɪlər] *n* **1** GRILL : parrilla *f* **2** : pollo *m* para asar
broke¹ ['broːk] → **break¹**
broke² *adj* : pelado, arruinado ⟨to go broke : arruinarse, quebrar⟩
broken ['broːkən] *adj* **1** DAMAGED, SHATTERED : roto, quebrado, fracturado **2** IRREGULAR, UNEVEN : accidentado, irregular, recortado **3** VIOLATED : roto, quebrantado **4** INTERRUPTED : interrumpido, descontinuo **5** CRUSHED : abatido, quebrantado ⟨a broken man : un hombre destrozado⟩ **6** IMPERFECT : mal ⟨to speak broken English : hablar el inglés con dificultad⟩
brokenhearted [,broːkən'hɑrtəd] *adj* : descorazonado, desconsolado
broker¹ ['broːkər] *vt* : hacer corretaje de
broker² *n* **1** : agente *mf*; corredor *m*, -dora *f* **2** → **stockbroker**
brokerage ['broːkərɪʤ] *n* : corretaje *m*, agencia *f* de corredores

bromine ['broː,miːn] *n* : bromo *m*
bronchitis [brɑn'kaɪtəs, brɑŋ-] *n* : bronquitis *f*
bronze¹ ['brɑnz] *vt* **bronzed; bronzing** : broncear
bronze² *n* : bronce *m*
brooch ['broːʧ, 'bruːʧ] *n* : broche *m*, prendedor *m*
brood¹ ['bruːd] *vt* **1** INCUBATE : empollar, incubar **2** PONDER : sopesar, considerar — *vi* **1** INCUBATE : empollar **2** REFLECT : rumiar, reflexionar **3** WORRY : ponerse melancólico, inquietarse
brood² *adj* : de cría
brood³ *n* **1** : nidada *f* (de pájaros), camada *f* (de mamíferos)
brooder ['bruːdər] *n* **1** THINKER : pensador *m*, -dora *f* **2** INCUBATOR : incubadora *f*
brook¹ ['brʊk] *vt* TOLERATE : tolerar, admitir
brook² *n* : arroyo *m*
broom ['bruːm, 'brʊm] *n* **1** : retama *f*, hiniesta *f* **2** : escoba *f* (para barrer)
broomstick ['bruːm,stɪk, 'brʊm-] *n* : palo *m* de escoba
broth ['brɔθ] *n, pl* **broths** ['brɔθs, 'brɔðz] : caldo *m*
brothel ['brɑθəl, 'brɔ-] *n* : burdel *m*
brother ['brʌðər] *n, pl* **brothers** *also* **brethren** ['brɔðrən, -ðərn] **1** : hermano *m* **2** KINSMAN : pariente *m*, familiar *m*
brotherhood ['brʌðər,hʊd] *n* **1** FELLOWSHIP : fraternidad *f* **2** ASSOCIATION : hermandad *f*
brother–in–law ['brʌðərɪn,lɔ] *n, pl* **brothers–in–law** : cuñado *m*
brotherly ['brʌðərli] *adj* : fraternal
brought → **bring**
brow ['braʊ] *n* **1** EYEBROW : ceja *f* **2** FOREHEAD : frente *f* **3** : cima *f* ⟨the brow of a hill : la cima de una colina⟩
browbeat ['braʊ,biːt] *vt* -beat; -beaten [-,biːtən] *or* -beat; -beating : intimidar
brown¹ ['braʊn] *vt* **1** : dorar (en cocina) **2** TAN : broncear — *vi* **1** : dorarse (en cocina) **2** TAN : broncearse
brown² *adj* : marrón, café, castaño (dícese del pelo), moreno (dícese de la piel)
brown³ *n* : marrón *m*, café *m*
brownish ['braʊnɪʃ] *adj* : pardo
browse ['braʊz] *vi* **browsed; browsing** **1** GRAZE : pacer **2** LOOK : mirar, echar un vistazo
bruin ['bruːɪn] *n* BEAR : oso *m*
bruise¹ ['bruːz] *vt* **bruised; bruising** **1** : contusionar, machucar, magullar (a una persona) **2** DAMAGE : magullar, dañar (frutas) **3** CRUSH : majar **4** HURT : herir (los sentimientos)
bruise² *n* : moretón *m*, cardenal *m*, magulladura *f* (dícese de frutas)
brunch ['brʌnʧ] *n* : combinación *f* de desayuno y almuerzo
brunet¹ *or* **brunette** [bru'nɛt] *adj* : moreno
brunet² *or* **brunette** *n* : moreno *m*, -na *f*

brunt ['brʌnt] *n* **to bear the brunt of** : llevar el peso de, aguantar el mayor impacto de

brush[1] ['brʌʃ] *vt* **1** : cepillar ⟨to brush one's teeth : cepillarse uno los dientes⟩ **2** SWEEP : barrer, quitar con un cepillo **3** GRAZE : rozar **4 to brush off** DISREGARD : hacer caso omiso de, ignorar — *vi* **to brush up on** : repasar, refrescar, dar un repaso a

brush[2] *n* **1** *or* **brushwood** ['brʌʃ,wʊd] : broza *f* **2** SCRUB, UNDERBRUSH : maleza *f* **3** : cepillo *m*, pincel *m* (de artista), brocha *f* (de pintor) **4** TOUCH : roce *m* **5** SKIRMISH : escaramuza *f*

brush–off ['brʌʃ,ɔf] *n* **to give the brush–off to** : dar calabazas a

brusque ['brʌsk] *adj* : brusco — **brusquely** *adv*

brussels sprout ['brʌsəlz,spraʊt] *n* : col *f* de Bruselas

brutal ['bru:t̬əl] *adj* : brutal, cruel, salvaje — **brutally** *adv*

brutality [bru:'tæləti] *n*, *pl* **-ties** : brutalidad *f*

brutalize ['bru:t̬əl,aɪz] *vt* **-ized; -izing** : brutalizar, maltratar

brute[1] ['bru:t] *adj* : bruto ⟨brute force : fuerza bruta⟩

brute[2] *n* **1** BEAST : bestia *f*, animal *m* **2** : bruto *m*, -ta *f*; bestia *mf* (persona)

brutish ['bru:t̬ɪʃ] *adj* **1** : de animal **2** CRUEL : brutal, salvaje **3** STUPID : bruto, estúpido

bubble[1] ['bʌbəl] *vi* **-bled; -bling** : burbujear ⟨to bubble over with joy : rebosar de alegría⟩

bubble[2] *n* : burbuja *f*

bubbly ['bʌbəli] *adj* **bubblier; -est 1** BUBBLING : burbujeante **2** LIVELY : vivaz, lleno de vida

bubonic plague [bu:'bɑnɪk, 'bju:-] *n* : peste *f* bubónica

buccaneer [,bʌkə'nɪr] *n* : bucanero *m*

buck[1] ['bʌk] *vi* **1** : corcovear (dícese de un caballo o un burro) **2** JOLT : dar sacudidas **3 to buck against** : resistirse a, rebelarse contra **4 to buck up** : animarse, levantar el ánimo — *vt* OPPOSE : oponerse a, ir en contra de

buck[2] *n*, *pl* **buck** *or* **bucks 1** : animal *m* macho, ciervo *m* (macho) **2** DOLLAR : dólar *m* **3 to pass the buck** *fam* : pasar la pelota *fam*

bucket ['bʌkət] *n* : balde *m*, cubo *m*, cubeta *f Mex*

bucketful ['bʌkət,fʊl] *n* : balde *m* lleno

buckle[1] ['bʌkəl] *v* **-led; -ling** *vt* **1** FASTEN : abrochar **2** BEND, TWIST : combar, torcer — *vi* **1** BEND, TWIST : combarse, torcerse, doblarse (dícese de las rodillas) **2 to buckle down** : ponerse a trabajar con esmero **3 to buckle up** : abrocharse

buckle[2] *n* **1** : hebilla *f* **2** TWISTING : torcedura *f*

buckshot ['bʌk,ʃɑt] *n* : perdigón *m*

buckskin ['bʌk,skɪn] *n* : gamuza *f*

bucktooth ['bʌk,tu:θ] *n* : diente *m* saliente, diente *m* salido

buckwheat ['bʌk,ʍwi:t] *n* : trigo *m* rubión, alforfón *m*

bucolic [bju:'kɑlɪk] *adj* : bucólico

bud[1] ['bʌd] *v* **budded; budding** *vt* GRAFT : injertar — *vi* : brotar, hacer brotes

bud[2] *n* : brote *m*, yema *f*, capullo *m* (de una flor)

Buddhism ['bu:,dɪzəm, 'bʊ-] *n* : budismo *m*

Buddhist ['bu:dɪst, 'bʊ-] *n* : budista *mf* — **Buddhist** *adj*

buddy ['bʌdi] *n*, *pl* **-dies** : amigo *m*, -ga *f*; compinche *mf fam*; cuate *m*, -ta *f Mex fam*

budge ['bʌdʒ] *vi* **budged; budging 1** MOVE : moverse, desplazarse **2** YIELD : ceder

budget[1] ['bʌdʒət] *vt* : presupuestar (gastos), asignar (dinero) — *vi* : presupuestar, planear el presupuesto

budget[2] *n* : presupuesto

budgetary ['bʌdʒə,tɛri] *adj* : presupuestario

buff[1] ['bʌf] *vt* POLISH : pulir, sacar brillo a, lustrar

buff[2] *adj* : beige, amarillento

buff[3] *n* **1** : beige *m*, amarillento *m* **2** ENTHUSIAST : aficionado *m*, -da *f*; entusiasta *mf*

buffalo ['bʌfə,lo:] *n*, *pl* **-lo** *or* **-loes 1** : búfalo *m* **2** BISON : bisonte *m*

buffer ['bʌfər] *n* **1** BARRIER : barrera *f* ⟨buffer state : estado tapón⟩ **2** SHOCK ABSORBER : amortiguador *m*

buffet[1] ['bʌfət] *vt* : golpear, zarandear, sacudir

buffet[2] *n* BLOW : golpe *m*

buffet[3] [,bʌ'feɪ, ,bu:-] *n* **1** : bufete *m*, bufé *m* (comida) **2** SIDEBOARD : aparador *m*

buffoon [,bʌ'fu:n] *n* : bufón *m*, -fona *f*; payaso *m*, -sa *f*

buffoonery [,bʌ'fu:nəri] *n*, *pl* **-eries** : bufonada *f*, payasada *f*

bug[1] ['bʌg] *vt* **bugged; bugging 1** PESTER : fastidiar, molestar **2** : ocultar micrófonos en

bug[2] *n* **1** INSECT : bicho *m*, insecto *m* **2** DEFECT : defecto *m*, falla *f*, problema *m* **3** GERM : microbio *m*, virus *m* **4** MICROPHONE : micrófono *m*

bugaboo ['bʌgə,bu:] → **bogey**

bugbear ['bʌg,bær] *n* : pesadilla *f*, coco *m*

buggy ['bʌgi] *n*, *pl* **-gies** : calesa *f* (tirada por caballos), cochecito *m* (para niños)

bugle ['bju:gəl] *n* : clarín *m*, corneta *f*

bugler ['bju:gələr] *n* : corneta *mf*

build[1] ['bɪld] *v* **built** ['bɪlt]; **building** *vt* **1** CONSTRUCT : construir, edificar, ensamblar, levantar **2** DEVELOP : desarrollar, elaborar, forjar **3** INCREASE : incrementar, aumentar — *vi* **to build up** : aumentar, intensificar

build[2] *n* PHYSIQUE : físico *m*, complexión *f*

builder ['bɪldər] *n* : constructor *m*, -tora *f*; contratista *mf*

building ['bɪldɪŋ] *n* **1** EDIFICE : edificio *m* **2** CONSTRUCTION : construcción *f*

built-in ['bɪlt'ɪn] *adj* **1** : empotrado ⟨built-in cabinets : armarios empotrados⟩ **2** INHERENT : incorporado, intrínseco

bulb ['bʌlb] *n* **1** : bulbo *m* (de una planta), cabeza *f* (de ajo), cubeta *f* (de un termómetro) **2** LIGHTBULB : bombilla *f*, foco *m*, bombillo *m* CA, Col, Ven

bulbous ['bʌlbəs] *adj* : bulboso

Bulgarian [bʌl'gæriən, bʊl-] *n* **1** : búlgaro *m*, -ra *f* **2** : búlgaro *m* (idioma) — **Bulgarian** *adj*

bulge¹ ['bʌlʤ] *vi* **bulged; bulging** : abultar, sobresalir

bulge² *n* : bulto *m*, protuberancia *f*

bulk¹ ['bʌlk] *vt* : hinchar — *vi* EXPAND, SWELL : ampliarse, hincharse

bulk² *n* **1** SIZE, VOLUME : volumen *m*, tamaño *m* **2** FIBER : fibra *f* **3** MASS : mole *f* **4 the bulk of** : la mayor parte de **5 in ∼** : en grandes cantidades

bulkhead ['bʌlk‚hɛd] *n* : mamparo *m*

bulky ['bʌlki] *adj* **bulkier; -est** : voluminoso, grande

bull¹ ['bʊl] *adj* : macho

bull² *n* **1** : toro *m*, macho *m* (de ciertas especies) **2** : bula *f* (papal) **3** DECREE : decreto *m*, edicto *m*

bulldog ['bʊl‚dɔg] *n* : bulldog *m*

bulldoze ['bʊl‚do:z] *vt* **-dozed; -dozing 1** LEVEL : nivelar (el terreno), derribar (un edificio) **2** FORCE : forzar ⟨he bulldozed his way through : se abrió paso a codazos⟩

bulldozer ['bʊl‚do:zər] *n* : bulldozer *m*

bullet ['bʊlət] *n* : bala *f*

bulletin ['bʊlətən, -lətən] *n* **1** NOTICE : comunicado *m*, anuncio *m*, boletín *m* **2** NEWSLETTER : boletín *m* (informativo)

bulletin board *n* : tablón *m* de anuncios

bulletproof ['bʊlət‚pru:f] *adj* : antibalas, a prueba de balas

bullfight ['bʊl‚faɪt] *n* : corrida *f* (de toros)

bullfighter ['bʊl‚faɪtər] *n* : torero *m*, -ra *f*; matador *m*

bullfrog ['bʊl‚frɔg] *n* : rana *f* toro

bullheaded ['bʊl'hɛdəd] *adj* : testarudo

bullion ['bʊljən] *n* : oro *m* en lingotes, plata *f* en lingotes

bullock ['bʊlək] *n* **1** STEER : buey *m*, toro *m* castrado **2** : toro *m* joven, novillo *m*

bull's-eye ['bʊlz‚aɪ] *n, pl* **bull's-eyes** : diana *f*, blanco *m*

bully¹ ['bʊli] *vt* **-lied; -lying** : intimidar, amedrentar, mangonear

bully² *n, pl* **-lies** : matón *m*; bravucón *m*, -cona *f*

bulrush ['bʊl‚rʌʃ] *n* : especie *f* de junco

bulwark ['bʊl‚wərk, -‚wɔrk; 'bʌl‚wərk] *n* : baluarte *m*, bastión *f*

bum¹ ['bʌm] *v* **bummed; bumming** *vi* **to bum around** : vagabundear, vagar — *vt* : gorronear *fam*, sablear *fam*

bum² *adj* : inútil, malo ⟨a bum rap : una acusación falsa⟩

bum³ *n* **1** LOAFER : vago *m*, -ga *f* **2** HOBO, TRAMP : vagabundo *m*, -da *f*

bumblebee ['bʌmbəl‚bi:] *n* : abejorro *m*

bump¹ ['bʌmp] *vt* : chocar contra, golpear contra, dar ⟨to bump one's head : darse (un golpe) en la cabeza⟩ — *vi* **to bump into** MEET : encontrarse con, tropezarse con

bump² *n* **1** BULGE : bulto *m*, protuberancia *f* **2** IMPACT : golpe *m*, choque *m* **3** JOLT : sacudida *f*

bumper¹ ['bʌmpər] *adj* : extraordinario, récord ⟨a bumper crop : una cosecha abundante⟩

bumper² *n* : parachoques *mpl*

bumpkin ['bʌmpkən] *n* : palurdo *m*, -da *f*

bumpy ['bʌmpi] *adj* **bumpier; -est** : desigual, lleno de baches (dícese de un camino), agitado (dícese de un vuelo en avión)

bun ['bʌn] *n* : bollo *m*

bunch¹ ['bʌntʃ] *vt* : agrupar, amontonar — *vi* **to bunch up** : amontonarse, agruparse, fruncirse (dícese de una tela)

bunch² *n* : grupo *m*, montón *m*, ramo *m* (de flores)

bundle¹ ['bʌndəl] *vt* **-dled; -dling** : liar, atar

bundle² *n* **1** : fardo *m*, atado *m*, bulto *m*, haz *m* (de palos) **2** PARCEL : paquete *m* **3** LOAD : montón *m* ⟨a bundle of money : un montón de dinero⟩

bungalow ['bʌŋgə‚lo:] *n* : tipo de casa de un solo piso

bungle¹ ['bʌŋgəl] *vt* **-gled; -gling** : echar a perder, malograr

bungle² *n* : chapuza *f*, desatino *m*

bungler ['bʌŋgələr] *n* : chapucero *m*, -ra *f*; inepto *m*, -ta *f*

bunion ['bʌnjən] *n* : juanete *m*

bunk¹ ['bʌŋk] *vi* : dormir (en una litera)

bunk² *n* **1** *or* **bunk bed** : litera *f* **2** NONSENSE : tonterías *fpl*, bobadas *fpl*

bunker ['bʌŋkər] *n* **1** : carbonera *f* (en un barco) **2** SHELTER : búnker *m*

bunny ['bʌni] *n, pl* **-nies** : conejo *m*, -ja *f*

buoy¹ ['bu:i, 'bɔɪ] *vt* **to buoy up 1** : mantener a flote **2** CHEER, HEARTEN : animar, levantar el ánimo a

buoy² *n* : boya *f*

buoyancy ['bɔɪəntsi, 'bu:jən-] *n* **1** : flotabilidad *f* **2** OPTIMISM : confianza *f*, optimismo *m*

buoyant ['bɔɪənt, 'bu:jənt] *adj* : boyante, flotante

bur *or* **burr** ['bər] *n* : abrojo *m* (de una planta)

burden¹ ['bərdən] *vt* : cargar, oprimir

burden² *n* : carga *f*, peso *m*

burdensome ['bərdənsəm] *adj* : oneroso

burdock ['bər‚dɑk] *n* : bardana *f*

bureau ['bjʊro] *n* **1** CHEST OF DRAWERS : cómoda *f* **2** DEPARTMENT : departamento *m* (del gobierno) **3** AGENCY

: agencia *f* ⟨travel bureau : agencia de viajes⟩
bureaucracy [bjʊˈrɑkrəsi] *n, pl* **-cies** : burocracia *f*
bureaucrat [ˈbjʊrəˌkræt] *n* : burócrata *mf*
bureaucratic [ˌbjʊrəˈkrætɪk] *adj* : burocrático
burgeon [ˈbərdʒən] *vi* : florecer, retoñar, crecer
burglar [ˈbərglər] *n* : ladrón *m*, -drona *f*
burglarize [ˈbərgləˌraɪz] *vt* **-ized; -izing** : robar
burglary [ˈbərgləri] *n, pl* **-glaries** : robo *m*
burgle [ˈbərgəl] *vt* **-gled; -gling** : robar
burgundy [ˈbərgəndi] *n, pl* **-dies** : borgoña *m*, vino *m* de Borgoña
burial [ˈbɛriəl] *n* : entierro *m*, sepelio *m*
burlap [ˈbərˌlæp] *n* : arpillera *f*
burlesque[1] [bərˈlɛsk] *vt* **-lesqued; -lesquing** : parodiar
burlesque[2] *n* **1** PARODY : parodia *f* **2** REVUE : revista *f* (musical)
burly [ˈbərli] *adj* **-lier; -liest** : fornido, corpulento, musculoso
Burmese [ˌbərˈmiːz, -ˈmiːs] *n* : birmano *m*, -na *f* — **Burmese** *adj*
burn[1] [ˈbərn] *v* **burned** [ˈbərnd, ˈbərnt] *or* **burnt** [ˈbərnt]; **burning** *vt* **1** : quemar, incendiar ⟨to burn a building : incendiar un edificio⟩ ⟨I burned my hand : me quemé la mano⟩ **2** CONSUME : usar, gastar, consumir — *vi* **1** : arder (dícese de un fuego o un edificio), quemarse (dícese de la comida, etc.) **2** : estar prendido, estar encendido ⟨we left the lights burning : dejamos las luces encendidas⟩ **3 to burn out** : consumirse, apagarse **4 to burn with** : arder de ⟨he was burning with jealousy : ardía de celos⟩
burn[2] *n* : quemadura *f*
burner [ˈbərnər] *n* : quemador *m*
burnish [ˈbərnɪʃ] *vt* : bruñir
burp[1] [ˈbərp] *vi* : eructar — *vt* : hacer eructar
burp[2] *n* : eructo *m*
burr → **bur**
burro [ˈbəro, ˈbʊr-] *n, pl* **-os** : burro *m*
burrow[1] [ˈbəro] *vi* **1** : cavar, hacer una madriguera **2 to burrow into** : hurgar en — *vt* : cavar, excavar
burrow[2] *n* : madriguera *f*, conejera *f* (de un conejo)
bursar [ˈbərsər] *n* : administrador *m*, -dora *f*
bursitis [bərˈsaɪtəs] *n* : bursitis *f*
burst[1] [ˈbərst] *v* **burst; bursting** *vi* **1** : reventarse (dícese de una llanta o un globo), estallar (dícese de obuses o fuegos artificiales), romperse (dícese de un dique) **2 to burst in** : irrumpir en **3 to burst into** : empezar a, echar a ⟨to burst into tears : echarse a llorar⟩ — *vt* : reventar
burst[2] *n* **1** EXPLOSION : estallido *m*, explosión *f*, reventón *m* (de una llanta) **2** OUTBURST : arranque *m* (de actividad,

de velocidad), arrebato *m* (de ira), salva *f* (de aplausos)
Burundian [bʊˈruːndiən, -ˈrʊn-] *n* : burundés *m*, -desa *f* — **Burundian** *adj*
bury [ˈbɛri] *vt* **buried; burying 1** INTER : enterrar, sepultar **2** HIDE : esconder, ocultar **3 to bury oneself in** : enfrascarse en
bus[1] [ˈbʌs] *v* **bused** *or* **bussed** [ˈbʌst]; **busing** *or* **bussing** [ˈbʌsɪŋ] *vt* : transportar en autobús — *vi* : viajar en autobús
bus[2] *n* : autobús *m*, bus *m*, camión *m* *Mex*, colectivo *m* *Arg, Bol, Peru*
busboy [ˈbʌsˌbɔɪ] *n* : ayudante *mf* de camarero
bush [ˈbʊʃ] *n* **1** SHRUB : arbusto *m*, mata *f* **2** THICKET : maleza *f*, matorral *m*
bushel [ˈbʊʃəl] *n* : medida de áridos igual a 35.24 litros
bushing [ˈbʊʃɪŋ] *n* : cojinete *m*
bushy [ˈbʊʃi] *adj* **bushier; -est** : espeso, poblado ⟨bushy eyebrows : cejas pobladas⟩
busily [ˈbɪzəli] *adv* : afanosamente, diligentemente
business [ˈbɪznəs, -nəz] *n* **1** OCCUPATION : ocupación *f*, oficio *m* **2** DUTY, MISSION : misión *f*, deber *m*, responsabilidad *f* **3** ESTABLISHMENT, FIRM : empresa *f*, firma *f*, negocio *m*, comercio *m* **4** COMMERCE : negocios *mpl*, comercio *m* **5** AFFAIR, MATTER : asunto *m*, cuestión *f*, cosa *f* ⟨it's none of your business : no es asunto tuyo⟩
businessman [ˈbɪznəsˌmæn, -nəz-] *n, pl* **-men** [-mən, -ˌmɛn] : empresario *m*, hombre *m* de negocios
businesswoman [ˈbɪznəsˌwʊmən, -nəz-] *n, pl* **-women** [-ˌwɪmən] : empresaria *f*, mujer *f* de negocios
bust[1] [ˈbʌst] *vt* **1** BREAK, SMASH : romper, estropear, destrozar **2** TAME : domar, amansar (un caballo) — *vi* : romperse, estropearse
bust[2] *n* **1** : busto *m* (en la escultura) **2** BREASTS : pecho *m*, senos *mpl*, busto *m*
bustle[1] [ˈbʌsəl] *vi* **-tled; -tling to bustle about** : ir y venir, trajinar, ajetrearse
bustle[2] *n* **1** *or* **hustle and bustle** : bullicio *m*, ajetreo *m* **2** : polisón *m* (en la ropa feminina)
busy[1] [ˈbɪzi] *vt* **busied; busying to busy oneself with** : ocuparse con, ponerse a, entretenerse con
busy[2] *adj* **busier; -est 1** OCCUPIED : ocupado, atareado ⟨he's busy working : está ocupado en su trabajo⟩ ⟨the telephone was busy : el teléfono estaba ocupado⟩ **2** BUSTLING : concurrido, animado ⟨a busy street : una calle concurrida, una calle con mucho tránsito⟩
busybody [ˈbɪziˌbɑdi] *n, pl* **-bodies** : entrometido *m*, -da *f*; metiche *mf fam*; metomentodo *mf*
but[1] [ˈbʌt] *conj* **1** THAT : que ⟨there is no doubt but he is lazy : no cabe duda

que sea perezoso⟩ **2** WITHOUT : sin que **3** NEVERTHELESS : pero, no obstante, sin embargo ⟨I called her but she didn't answer : la llamé pero no contestó⟩ **4** YET : pero ⟨he was poor but proud : era pobre pero orgulloso⟩

but² *prep* EXCEPT : excepto, menos ⟨everyone but Carlos : todos menos Carlos⟩ ⟨the last but one : el penúltimo⟩

butcher¹ ['bʊtʃər] *vt* **1** SLAUGHTER : matar (animales) **2** KILL : matar, asesinar, masacrar **3** BOTCH : estropear, hacer una chapuza

butcher² *n* **1** : carnicero *m*, -ra *f* **2** KILLER : asesino *m*, -na *f* **3** BUNGLER : chapucero *m*, -ra *f*

butler ['bʌtlər] *n* : mayordomo *m*

butt¹ ['bʌt] *vt* **1** : embestir (con los cuernos), darle un cabezazo a **2** ABUT : colindar con, bordear — *vi* **to butt in 1** INTERRUPT : interrumpir **2** MEDDLE : entrometerse, meterse

butt² *n* **1** BUTTING : embestida *f* (de cuernos), cabezazo *m* **2** TARGET : blanco *m* ⟨the butt of their jokes : el blanco de sus bromas⟩ **3** BOTTOM, END : extremo *m*, culata *f* (de un rifle), colilla *f* (de un cigarrillo)

butte ['bjuːt] *n* : colina *f* empinada y aislada

butter¹ ['bʌtər] *vt* **1** : untar con mantequilla **2 to butter up** : halagar

butter² *n* : mantequilla *f*

buttercup ['bʌtər,kʌp] *n* : ranúnculo *m*

butterfat ['bʌtər,fæt] *n* : grasa *f* de la leche

butterfly ['bʌtər,flaɪ] *n, pl* **-flies** : mariposa *f*

buttermilk ['bʌtər,mɪlk] *n* : suero *m* de la leche

butternut ['bʌtər,nʌt] *n* : nogal *m* ceniciento (árbol)

butterscotch ['bʌtər,skatʃ] *n* : caramelo *m* duro hecho con mantequilla

buttery ['bʌtəri] *adj* : mantecoso

buttocks ['bʌtəks, -,taks] *npl* : nalgas *fpl*, trasero *m*

button¹ ['bʌtən] *vt* : abrochar, abotonar — *vi* : abrocharse, abotonarse

button² *n* : botón *m*

buttonhole¹ ['bʌtən,hoːl] *vt* **-holed; -holing** : acorralar

buttonhole² *n* : ojal *m*

buttress¹ ['bʌtrəs] *vt* : apoyar, reforzar

buttress² *n* **1** : contrafuerte *m* (en la arquitectura) **2** SUPPORT : apoyo *m*, sostén *m*

buxom ['bʌksəm] *adj* : con mucho busto, con mucho pecho

buy¹ ['baɪ] *vt* **bought** ['bɔt]; **buying** : comprar

buy² *n* BARGAIN : compra *f*, ganga *f*

buyer ['baɪər] *n* : comprador *m*, -dora *f*

buzz¹ ['bʌz] *vi* : zumbar (dícese de un insecto), sonar (dícese de un teléfono o un despertador)

buzz² *n* **1** : zumbido *m* (de insectos) **2** : murmullo *m*, rumor *m* (de voces)

buzzard ['bʌzərd] *n* VULTURE : buitre *m*, zopilote *m* CA, Mex

buzzer ['bʌzər] *n* : timbre *m*, chicharra *f*

buzzword ['bʌz,wərd] *n* : palabra *f* de moda

by¹ ['baɪ] *adv* **1** NEAR : cerca ⟨he lives close by : vive muy cerca⟩ **2 to stop by** : pasar por casa, hacer una visita **3 to go by** : pasar ⟨they rushed by : pasaron corriendo⟩ **4 to put by** : reservar, poner a un lado **5 by and by** : poco después, dentro de poco **6 by and large** : en general

by² *prep* **1** NEAR : cerca de, al lado de, junto a **2** VIA : por ⟨she left by the door : salió por la puerta⟩ **3** PAST : por, por delante de ⟨they walked by him : pasaron por delante de él⟩ **4** DURING : de, durante ⟨by night : de noche⟩ **5** (*in expressions of time*) : para ⟨we'll be there by ten : estaremos allí para las diez⟩ ⟨by then : para entonces⟩ **6** (*indicating cause or agent*) : por, de, a ⟨built by the Romans : construido por los romanos⟩ ⟨a book by Borges : un libro de Borges⟩ ⟨made by hand : hecho a mano⟩

by and by *adv* : dentro de poco

bygone¹ ['baɪ,gɔn] *adj* : pasado

bygone² *n* **let bygones be bygones** : lo pasado, pasado está

bylaw *or* **byelaw** ['baɪ,lɔ] *n* : norma *f*, reglamento *m*

by-line ['baɪ,laɪn] *n* : data *f*

bypass¹ ['baɪ,pæs] *vt* : evitar

bypass² *n* **1** BELTWAY : carretera *f* de circunvalación **2** DETOUR : desvío *m*

by-product ['baɪ,pradəkt] *n* : subproducto *m*, producto *m* derivado

bystander ['baɪ,stændər] *n* : espectador *m*, -dora *f*

byte ['baɪt] *n* : byte *m*

byway ['baɪ,weɪ] *n* : camino *m* (apartado), carretera *f* secundaria

byword ['baɪ,wərd] *n* **1** PROVERB : proverbio *m*, refrán *m* **2 to be a byword for** : estar sinónimo de

C

c ['si:] *n, pl* **c's** *or* **cs** : tercera letra del alfabeto inglés
cab ['kæb] *n* **1** TAXI : taxi *m* **2** : cabina *f* (de un camión o una locomotora) **3** CARRIAGE : coche *m* de caballos
cabal [kə'bɑl, -'bæl] *n* **1** INTRIGUE, PLOT : conspiración *f*, complot *m*, intriga *f* **2** : grupo *m* de conspiradores
cabaret [ˌkæbə'reɪ] *n* : cabaret *m*
cabbage ['kæbɪʤ] *n* : col *f*, repollo *m*
cabbie *or* **cabby** ['kæbi] *n* : taxista *mf*
cabin ['kæbən] *n* **1** HUT : cabaña *f*, choza *f*, barraca *f* **2** STATEROOM : camarote *m* **3** : cabina *f* (de un automóvil o avión)
cabinet ['kæbnət] *n* **1** CUPBOARD : armario *m* **2** : gabinete *m*, consejo *m* de ministros **3** **medicine cabinet** : botiquín *m*
cabinetmaker ['kæbnətˌmeɪkər] *n* : ebanista *mf*
cabinetmaking ['kæbnətˌmeɪkɪŋ] *n* : ebanistería *f*
cable[1] ['keɪbəl] *vt* **-bled; -bling** : enviar un cable, telegrafiar
cable[2] *n* **1** : cable *m* (para colgar o sostener algo) **2** : cable *m* eléctrico **3** → **cablegram**
cablegram ['keɪbəlˌgræm] *n* : telegrama *m*, cable *m*
caboose [kə'bu:s] *n* : furgón *m* de cola, cabús *m Mex*
cabstand ['kæbˌstænd] *n* : parada *f* de taxis
cacao [kə'kaʊ, -'keɪo] *n, pl* **cacaos** : cacao *m*
cache[1] ['kæʃ] *vt* **cached; caching** : esconder, guardar en un escondrijo
cache[2] *n* **1** : escondite *m*, escondrijo *m* ⟨cache of weapons : escondite de armas⟩ **2** : cache *m* ⟨cache memory : memoria cache⟩
cachet [kæ'ʃeɪ] *n* : caché *m*, prestigio *m*
cackle[1] ['kækəl] *vi* **-led; -ling 1** CLUCK : cacarear **2** : reírse o carcajearse estridentemente ⟨he was cackling with delight : estaba carcajeándose de gusto⟩
cackle[2] *n* **1** : cacareo *m* (de una polla) **2** LAUGH : risa *f* estridente
cacophony [kæ'kɑfəni, -'kɔ-] *n, pl* **-nies** : cacofonía *f*
cactus ['kæktəs] *n, pl* **cacti** [-ˌtaɪ] *or* **-tuses** : cacto *m*, cactus *m*
cadaver [kə'dævər] *n* : cadáver *m*
cadaverous [kə'dævərəs] *adj* : cadavérico
caddie[1] *or* **caddy** ['kædi] *vi* **caddied; caddying** : trabajar de caddie, hacer de caddie
caddie[2] *or* **caddy** *n, pl* **-dies** : caddie *mf*
caddy ['kædi] *n, pl* **-dies** : cajita *f* para té
cadence ['keɪdənts] *n* : cadencia *f*, ritmo *m*
cadenced ['keɪdəntst] *adj* : cadencioso, rítmico

cadet [kə'dɛt] *n* : cadete *mf*
cadmium ['kædmiəm] *n* : cadmio *m*
cadre ['kæˌdreɪ, 'kɑ-, -ˌdri:] *n* : cuadro *m* (de expertos)
café [kæ'feɪ, kə-] *n* : café *m*, cafetería *f*
cafeteria [ˌkæfə'tiriə] *n* : cafetería *f*, restaurante *m* de autoservicio
caffeine [kæ'fi:n] *n* : cafeína *f*
cage[1] ['keɪʤ] *vt* **caged; caging** : enjaular
cage[2] *n* : jaula *f*
cagey ['keɪʤi] *adj* **-gier; -est 1** CAUTIOUS : cauteloso, reservado **2** SHREWD : astuto, vivo — **cagily** [-ʤəli] *adv*
caisson ['keɪˌsɑn, -sən] *n* **1** : cajón *m* de municiones **2** : cajón *m* hidráulico
cajole [kə'ʤo:l] *vt* **-joled; -joling** : engatusar
cajolery [kə'ʤo:ləri] *n* : engatusamiento *m*
cake[1] ['keɪk] *v* **caked; caking** *vt* : cubrir ⟨caked with mud : cubierto de barro⟩ — *vi* : endurecerse
cake[2] *n* **1** : torta *f*, bizcocho *m*, pastel *m* **2** : pastilla *f* (de jabón) **3 to take the cake** : llevarse la palma, ser el colmo
calabash ['kælə,bæʃ] *n* : calabaza *f*
calamari [ˌkɑlə'mɑri] *ns & pl* : calamares *mpl*
calamine ['kælə,maɪn] *n* : calamina *f* ⟨calamine lotion : loción de calamina⟩
calamitous [kə'læmətəs] *adj* : desastroso, catastrófico, calamitoso — **calamitously** *adv*
calamity [kə'læməti] *n, pl* **-ties** : desastre *m*, desgracia *f*, calamidad *f*
calcium ['kælsiəm] *n* : calcio *m*
calcium carbonate ['kɑrbə,neɪt, -nət] *n* : carbonato *m* de calcio
calculable ['kælkjələbəl] *adj* : calculable, computable
calculate ['kælkjə,leɪt] *v* **-lated; -lating** *vt* **1** COMPUTE : calcular, computar **2** ESTIMATE : calcular, creer **3** INTEND : planear, tener la intención de ⟨I calculated on spending $100 : planeaba gastar $100⟩ — *vi* : calcular, hacer cálculos
calculated ['kælkjə,leɪtəd] *adj* **1** ESTIMATED : calculado **2** DELIBERATE : intencional, premeditado, deliberado
calculating ['kælkjə,leɪtɪŋ] *adj* SHREWD : calculador, astuto
calculation [ˌkælkjə'leɪʃən] *n* : cálculo *m*
calculator ['kælkjə,leɪtər] *n* : calculadora *f*
calculus ['kælkjələs] *n, pl* **-li** [-,laɪ] **1** : cálculo *m* ⟨differential calculus : cálculo diferencial⟩ **2** TARTAR : sarro *m* (dental)
caldron ['kɔldrən] → **cauldron**
calendar ['kæləndər] *n* **1** : calendario *m* **2** SCHEDULE : calendario *m*, programa *m*, agenda *f*

calf [ˈkæf, ˈkaf] *n, pl* **calves** [ˈkævz, ˈkavz] **1** : becerro *m*, -rra *f*; ternero *m*, -ra *f* (de vacunos) **2** : cría *f* (de otros mamíferos) **3** : pantorrilla *f* (de la pierna)
calfskin [ˈkæfˌskɪn] *n* : piel *f* de becerro
caliber *or* **calibre** [ˈkæləbər] *n* **1** : calibre *m* ⟨a .38 caliber gun : una pistola de calibre .38⟩ **2** ABILITY : calibre *m*, valor *m*, capacidad *f*
calibrate [ˈkæləˌbreɪt] *vt* **-brated; -brating** : calibrar (armas), graduar (termómetros)
calibration [ˌkæləˈbreɪʃən] *n* : calibrado *m*, calibración *f*
calico [ˈkælɪˌkoː] *n, pl* **-coes** *or* **-cos** **1** : calicó *m*, percal *m* **2** *or* **calico cat** : gato *m* manchado
calipers [ˈkæləpərz] *npl* : calibrador *m*
caliph *or* **calif** [ˈkeɪləf, ˈkæ-] *n* : califa *m*
calisthenics [ˌkæləsˈθɛnɪks] *ns & pl* : calistenia *f*
calk [ˈkɔk] → **caulk**
call[1] [ˈkɔl] *vi* **1** CRY, SHOUT : gritar, vociferar **2** VISIT : hacer (una) visita, visitar **3 to call for** : exigir, requerir, necesitar ⟨it calls for patience : requiere mucha paciencia⟩ — *vt* **1** SUMMON : llamar, convocar **2** TELEPHONE : llamar por teléfono, telefonear **3** NAME : llamar, apodar
call[2] *n* **1** SHOUT : grito *m*, llamada *f* **2** : grito *m* (de un animal), reclamo *m* (de un pájaro) **3** SUMMONS : llamada *f* **4** DEMAND : llamado *m*, petición *f* **5** VISIT : visita *f* **6** DECISION : decisión *f* (en deportes) **7** *or* **telephone call** : llamada *f* (telefónica)
call down *vt* REPRIMAND : reprender, reñir
caller [ˈkɔlər] *n* **1** VISITOR : visita *f* **2** : persona *f* que llama (por teléfono)
calligraphy [kəˈlɪɡrəfi] *n, pl* **-phies** : caligrafía *f*
calling [ˈkɔlɪŋ] *n* : vocación *f*, profesión *f*
calliope [kəˈlaɪəˌpiː, ˈkæliˌoːp] *n* : órgano *m* de vapor
call off *vt* CANCEL : cancelar, suspender
callous[1] [ˈkæləs] *vt* : encallecer
callous[2] *adj* **1** CALLUSED : calloso, encallecido **2** UNFEELING : insensible, desalmado, cruel
callously [ˈkæləsli] *adv* : cruelmente, insensiblemente
callousness [ˈkæləsnəs] *n* : insensibilidad *f*, crueldad *f*
callow [ˈkæloː] *adj* : inexperto, inmaduro
callus [ˈkæləs] *n* : callo *m*
callused [ˈkæləst] *adj* : encallecido, calloso
calm[1] [ˈkam, ˈkalm] *vt* : tranquilizar, calmar, sosegar — *vi* : tranquilizarse, calmarse ⟨calm down! : ¡tranquilízate!⟩
calm[2] *adj* **1** TRANQUIL : calmo, tranquilo, sereno, ecuánime **2** STILL : en calma (dícese del mar), sin viento (dícese del aire)

calm[3] *n* : tranquilidad *f*, calma *f*
calmly [ˈkamli, ˈkalm-] *adv* : con calma, tranquilamente
calmness [ˈkamnəs, ˈkalm-] *n* : calma *f*, tranquilidad *f*
caloric [kəˈlɔrɪk] *adj* : calórico (dícese de los alimentos), calorífico (dícese de la energía)
calorie [ˈkæləri] *n* : caloría *f*
calumniate [kəˈlʌmniˌeɪt] *vt* **-ated; -ating** : calumniar, difamar
calumny [ˈkæləmni] *n, pl* **-nies** : calumnia *f*, difamación *f*
calve [ˈkæv, ˈkav] *vi* **calved; calving** : parir (dícese de los mamíferos)
calves → **calf**
calypso [kəˈlɪpˌsoː] *n, pl* **-sos** : calipso *m*
calyx [ˈkeɪlɪks, ˈkæ-] *n, pl* **-lyxes** *or* **-lyces** [-ləˌsiːz] : cáliz *m*
cam [ˈkæm] *n* : leva *f*
camaraderie [ˌkamˈradəri, ˌkæm-; ˌkaməˈra-] *n* : compañerismo *m*, camaradería *f*
Cambodian [kæmˈboːdiən] *n* : camboyano *m*, -na *f* — **Cambodian** *adj*
came → **come**
camel [ˈkæməl] *n* : camello *m*
camellia [kəˈmiːljə] *n* : camelia *f*
cameo [ˈkæmiˌoː] *n, pl* **-eos** **1** : camafeo *m* **2** *or* **cameo performance** : actuación *f* especial
camera [ˈkæmrə, ˈkæmərə] *n* : cámara *f*, máquina *f* fotográfica
Cameroonian [ˌkæməˈruːniən] *n* : camerunés *m*, -nesa *f*
camouflage[1] [ˈkæməˌflaʒ, -ˌflaʤ] *vt* **-flaged; -flaging** : camuflajear, camuflar
camouflage[2] *n* : camuflaje *m*
camp[1] [ˈkæmp] *vi* : acampar, ir de camping
camp[2] *n* **1** : campamento *m* **2** FACTION : campo *m*, bando *m* ⟨in the same camp : del mismo bando⟩ **3 to pitch camp** : acampar, poner el campamento **4 to break camp** : levantar el campamento
campaign[1] [kæmˈpeɪn] *vi* : hacer (una) campaña
campaign[2] *n* : campaña *f*
campanile [ˌkæmpəˈniːˌli, -ˈniːl] *n, pl* **-niles** *or* **-nili** [-ˈniːˌli] : campanario *m*
camper [ˈkæmpər] *n* **1** : campista *mf* (persona) **2** : cámper *m* (vehículo)
campground [ˈkæmpˌɡraʊnd] *n* : campamento *m*, camping *m*
camphor [ˈkæmpfər] *n* : alcanfor *m*
campsite [ˈkæmpˌsaɪt] *n* : campamento *m*, camping *m*
campus [ˈkæmpəs] *n* : campus *m*, recinto *m* universitario
can[1] [ˈkæn] *v aux, past* **could** [ˈkʊd]; *present s & pl* **can 1** : poder ⟨could you help me? : ¿podría ayudarme?⟩ **2** : saber ⟨she can't drive yet : todavía no sabe manejar⟩ **3** MAY : poder, tener permiso para ⟨can I sit down? : ¿puedo sentarme?⟩ **4** : poder ⟨it can't be! : ¡no

puede ser!⟩ ⟨where can they be? : ¿dónde estarán?⟩

can² [ˈkæn] *vt* **canned; canning 1** : enlatar, envasar ⟨to can tomatoes : enlatar tomates⟩ **2** DISMISS, FIRE : despedir, echar

can³ *n* : lata *f*, envase *m*, cubo *m* ⟨a can of beer : una lata de cerveza⟩ ⟨garbage can : cubo de basura⟩

Canadian [kəˈneɪdiən] *n* : canadiense *mf* — **Canadian** *adj*

canal [kəˈnæl] *n* **1** : canal *m*, tubo *m* ⟨alimentary canal : tubo digestivo⟩ **2** : canal *m* ⟨Panama Canal : Canal de Panamá⟩

canapé [ˈkænəpi, -ˌpeɪ] *n* : canapé *m*

canary [kəˈnɛri] *n*, *pl* **-naries** : canario *m*

cancel [ˈkæntsəl] *vt* **-celed** *or* **-celled; -celing** *or* **-celling** : cancelar

cancellation [ˌkæntsəˈleɪʃən] *n* : cancelación *f*

cancer [ˈkæntsər] *n* : cáncer *m*

Cancer *n* : Cáncer *mf*

cancerous [ˈkæntsərəs] *adj* : canceroso

candelabrum [ˌkændəˈlɑbrəm, -ˈlæ-] *or* **candelabra** [-brə] *n*, *pl* **-bra** *or* **-bras** : candelabro *m*

candid [ˈkændɪd] *adj* **1** FRANK : franco, sincero, abierto **2** : natural, espontáneo (en la fotografía)

candidacy [ˈkændədəsi] *n*, *pl* **-cies** : candidatura *f*

candidate [ˈkændəˌdeɪt, -dət] *n* : candidato *m*, -ta *f*

candidly [ˈkændɪdli] *adv* : con franqueza

candied [ˈkændid] *adj* : confitado

candle [ˈkændəl] *n* : vela *f*, candela *f*, cirio *m* (ceremonial)

candlestick [ˈkændəlˌstɪk] *n* : candelero *m*

candor [ˈkændər] *n* : franqueza *f*

candy [ˈkændi] *n*, *pl* **-dies** : dulce *m*, caramelo *m*

cane¹ [ˈkeɪn] *vt* **caned; caning 1** : tapizar (muebles) con mimbre **2** FLOG : azotar con una vara

cane² *n* **1** : bastón *m* (para andar), vara *f* (para castigar) **2** REED : caña *f*, mimbre *m* (para muebles)

canine¹ [ˈkeɪˌnaɪn] *adj* : canino

canine² *n* **1** DOG : canino *m*; perro *m*, -rra *f* **2** *or* **canine tooth** : colmillo *m*, diente *m* canino

canister [ˈkænəstər] *n* : lata *f*, bote *m*

canker [ˈkæŋkər] *n* : úlcera *f* bucal

cannery [ˈkænəri] *n*, *pl* **-ries** : fábrica *f* de conservas

cannibal [ˈkænəbəl] *n* : caníbal *mf*; antropófago *m*, -ga *f*

cannibalism [ˈkænəbəˌlɪzəm] *n* : canibalismo *m*, antropofagia *f*

cannibalize [ˈkænəbəˌlaɪz] *vt* **-ized; -izing** : canibalizar

cannily [ˈkænəli] *adv* : astutamente, sagazmente

cannon [ˈkænən] *n*, *pl* **-nons** *or* **-non** : cañón *m*

cannot (can not) [ˈkænˌɑt, kəˈnɑt] → **can¹**

canny [ˈkæni] *adj* **-nier; -est** SHREWD : astuto, sagaz

canoe¹ [kəˈnuː] *vt* **-noed; -noeing** : ir en canoa

canoe² *n* : canoa *f*, piragua *f*

canon [ˈkænən] *n* **1** : canon *m* ⟨canon law : derecho canónico⟩ **2** WORKS : canon *m* ⟨the canon of American literature : el canon de la literatura americana⟩ **3** : canónigo *m* (de una catedral) **4** STANDARD : canon *m*, norma *f*

canonical [kəˈnɑnɪkəl] *adj* : canónico

canonize [ˈkænəˌnaɪz] *vt* **-ized; -izing** : canonizar

canopy [ˈkænəpi] *n*, *pl* **-pies** : dosel *m*, toldo *m*

cant¹ [ˈkænt] *vt* TILT : ladear, inclinar — *vi* **1** SLANT : ladearse, inclinarse, escorar (dícese de un barco) **2** : hablar insinceramente

cant² *n* **1** SLANT : plano *m* inclinado **2** JARGON : jerga *f* **3** : palabras *fpl* insinceras

can't [ˈkænt, ˈkant] (*contraction of* **can not**) → **can¹**

cantaloupe [ˈkæntəlˌoːp] *n* : melón *m*, cantalupo *m*

cantankerous [kænˈtæŋkərəs] *adj* : irritable, irascible — **cantankerously** *adv*

cantankerousness [kænˈtæŋkərəsnəs] *n* : irritabilidad *f*, irascibilidad *f*

cantata [kənˈtɑtə] *n* : cantata *f*

canteen [kænˈtiːn] *n* **1** FLASK : cantimplora *f* **2** CAFETERIA : cantina *f*, comedor *m* **3** : club *m* para actividades sociales y recreativas

canter¹ [ˈkæntər] *vi* : ir a medio galope

canter² *n* : medio galope *m*

cantilever [ˈkæntəˌliːvər, -ˌlɛvər] *n* **1** : viga *f* voladiza **2 cantilever bridge** : puente *m* voladizo

canto [ˈkænˌtoː] *n*, *pl* **-tos** : canto *m*

canton [ˈkæntən, -ˌtɑn] *n* : cantón *m*

Cantonese [ˌkæntənˈiːz, -ˈiːs] *n* **1** : cantonés *m*, -nesa *f* **2** : cantonés *m* (idioma) — **Cantonese** *adj*

cantor [ˈkæntər] *n* : solista *mf*

canvas [ˈkænvəs] *n* **1** : lona *f* **2** SAILS : velas *fpl* (de un barco) **3** : lienzo *m*, tela *f* (de pintar) **4** PAINTING : pintura *f*, óleo *m*, cuadro *m*

canvass¹ [ˈkænvəs] *vt* **1** SOLICIT : solicitar votos o pedidos de, hacer campaña entre **2** SOUND OUT : sondear (opiniones, etc.)

canvass² *n* SURVEY : sondeo *m*, encuesta *f*

canyon [ˈkænjən] *n* : cañón *m*

cap¹ [ˈkæp] *vt* **capped; capping 1** COVER : tapar (un recipiente), enfundar (un diente), cubrir (una montaña) **2** CLIMAX : coronar, ser el punto culminante de ⟨to cap it all off : para colmo⟩ **3** LIMIT : limitar, poner un tope a

cap² *n* **1** : gorra *f*, gorro *m*, cachucha *f* Mex ⟨baseball cap : gorra de béisbol⟩

2 COVER, TOP : tapa *f*, tapón *m* (de botellas), corcholata *f Mex* 3 LIMIT : tope *m*, límite *m*
capability [ˌkeɪpəˈbɪləti] *n*, *pl* **-ties** : capacidad *f*, habilidad *f*, competencia *f*
capable [ˈkeɪpəbəl] *adj* : competente, capaz, hábil — **capably** [-bli] *adv*
capacious [kəˈpeɪʃəs] *adj* : amplio, espacioso, de gran capacidad
capacity[1] [kəˈpæsəti] *adj* : completo, total ⟨a capacity crowd : un lleno completo⟩
capacity[2] *n*, *pl* **-ties** 1 ROOM, SPACE : capacidad *f*, cabida *f*, espacio *m* 2 CAPABILITY : habilidad *f*, competencia *f* 3 FUNCTION, ROLE : calidad *f*, función *f* ⟨in his capacity as ambassador : en su calidad de embajador⟩
cape [ˈkeɪp] *n* 1 : capa *f* 2 : cabo *m* ⟨Cape Horn : el Cabo de Hornos⟩
caper[1] [ˈkeɪpər] *vi* : dar saltos, correr y brincar
caper[2] *n* 1 : alcaparra *f* ⟨olives and capers : aceitunas y alcaparras⟩ 2 ANTIC, PRANK : broma *f*, travesura *f* 3 LEAP : brinco *m*, salto *m*
Cape Verdean [ˈkeɪpˈvərdiən] *n* : caboverdiano *m*, -na *f* — **Cape Verdean** *adj*
capful [ˈkæpˌfʊl] *n* : tapa *f*, tapita *f*
capillary[1] [ˈkæpəˌlɛri] *adj* : capilar
capillary[2] *n*, *pl* **-ries** : capilar *m*
capital[1] [ˈkæpətəl] *adj* 1 : capital ⟨capital punishment : pena capital⟩ 2 : mayúsculo (dícese de las letras) 3 : de capital ⟨capital assets : activo fijo⟩ ⟨capital gain : ganancia de capital, plusvalía⟩ 4 EXCELLENT : excelente, estupendo
capital[2] *n* 1 *or* **capital city** : capital *f*, sede *f* del gobierno 2 WEALTH : capital *m* 3 *or* **capital letter** : mayúscula *f* 4 : capitel *m* (de una columna)
capitalism [ˈkæpətəlˌɪzəm] *n* : capitalismo *m*
capitalist[1] [ˈkæpətəlɪst] *or* **capitalistic** [ˌkæpətəlˈɪstɪk] *adj* : capitalista
capitalist[2] *n* : capitalista *mf*
capitalization [ˌkæpətələˈzeɪʃən] *n* : capitalización *f*
capitalize [ˈkæpətəlˌaɪz] *v* **-ized; -izing** *vt* 1 FINANCE : capitalizar, financiar 2 : escribir con mayúscula — *vi* to **capitalize on** : sacar partido de, aprovechar
capitol [ˈkæpətəl] *n* : capitolio *m*
capitulate [kəˈpɪtʃəˌleɪt] *vi* **-lated; -lating** : capitular
capitulation [kəˌpɪtʃəˈleɪʃən] *n* : capitulación *f*
capon [ˈkeɪˌpɑn, -pən] *n* : capón *m*
cappuccino [ˌkɑpəˈtʃiːnoː] *n* : capuchino *m* (café)
caprice [kəˈpriːs] *n* : capricho *m*, antojo *m*
capricious [kəˈprɪʃəs, -ˈpriː-] *adj* : caprichoso — **capriciously** *adv*
Capricorn [ˈkæprɪˌkɔrn] *n* : Capricornio *mf*

capsize [ˈkæpˌsaɪz, kæpˈsaɪz] *v* **-sized; -sizing** *vi* : volcar, volcarse — *vt* : hacer volcar
capstan [ˈkæpstən, -ˌstæn] *n* : cabrestante *m*
capsule [ˈkæpsəl, -ˌsuːl] *n* 1 : cápsula *f* (en la farmacéutica y botánica) 2 **space capsule** : cápsula *f* espacial
captain[1] [ˈkæptən] *vt* : capitanear
captain[2] *n* 1 : capitán *m*, -tana *f* 2 HEADWAITER : jefe *m*, -fa *f* de comedor 3 **captain of industry** : magnate *mf*
caption[1] [ˈkæpʃən] *vt* : ponerle una leyenda a (una ilustración), titular (un artículo), subtitular (una película)
caption[2] *n* 1 HEADING : titular *m*, encabezamiento *m* 2 : leyenda *f* (al pie de una ilustración) 3 SUBTITLE : subtítulo *m*
captivate [ˈkæptəˌveɪt] *vt* **-vated; -vating** CHARM : cautivar, hechizar, encantar
captivating [ˈkæptəˌveɪtɪŋ] *adj* : cautivador, hechicero, encantador
captive[1] [ˈkæptɪv] *adj* : cautivo
captive[2] *n* : cautivo *m*, -va *f*
captivity [kæpˈtɪvəti] *n* : cautiverio *m*
captor [ˈkæptər] *n* : captor *m*, -tora *f*
capture[1] [ˈkæpʃər] *vt* **-tured; -turing** 1 SEIZE : capturar, apresar 2 CATCH : captar ⟨to capture one's interest : captar el interés de uno⟩
capture[2] *n* : captura *f*, apresamiento *m*
car [ˈkɑr] *n* 1 AUTOMOBILE : automóvil *m*, coche *m*, carro *m* 2 : vagón *m*, coche *m* (de un tren) 3 : cabina *f* (de un ascensor)
carafe [kəˈræf, -ˈrɑf] *n* : garrafa *f*
caramel [ˈkɑrməl; ˈkærəməl, -ˌmɛl] *n* 1 : caramelo *m*, azúcar *f* quemada 2 *or* **caramel candy** : caramelo *m*, dulce *m* de leche
carat [ˈkærət] *n* : quilate *m*
caravan [ˈkærəˌvæn] *n* : caravana *f*
caraway [ˈkærəˌweɪ] *n* : alcaravea *f*
carbine [ˈkɑrˌbaɪn, -ˌbiːn] *n* : carabina *f*
carbohydrate [ˌkɑrboˈhaɪˌdreɪt, -drət] *n* : carbohidrato *m*, hidrato *m* de carbono
carbon [ˈkɑrbən] *n* 1 : carbono *m* 2 → **carbon paper** 3 → **carbon copy**
carbonated [ˈkɑrbəˌneɪtəd] *adj* : carbonatado (dícese del agua), gaseoso (dícese de las bebidas)
carbon copy *n* 1 : copia *f* al carbón 2 DUPLICATE : duplicado *m*, copia *f* exacta
carbon paper *n* : papel *m* carbón
carbuncle [ˈkɑrˌbʌŋkəl] *n* : carbunco *m*
carburetor [ˈkɑrbəˌreɪtər, -bjə-] *n* : carburador *m*
carcass [ˈkɑrkəs] *n* : cuerpo *m* (de un animal muerto)
carcinogen [kɑrˈsɪnədʒən, ˈkɑrsənəˌdʒɛn] *n* : carcinógeno *m*, cancerígeno *m*
carcinogenic [ˌkɑrsənoˈdʒɛnɪk] *adj* : carcinogénico
carcinoma [ˌkɑrsəˈnoːmə] *n* : carcinoma *m*

card[1] ['kɑrd] *vt* : cardar (fibras)
card[2] *n* **1** : carta *f*, naipe *m* ⟨to play cards : jugar a las cartas⟩ ⟨a deck of cards : una baraja⟩ **2** : tarjeta *f* ⟨birthday card : tarjeta de cumpleaños⟩ ⟨business card : tarjeta (de visita)⟩
cardboard ['kɑrd,bord] *n* : cartón *m*, cartulina *f*
cardiac ['kɑrdi,æk] *adj* : cardíaco, cardiaco
cardigan ['kɑrdɪgən] *n* : cárdigan *m*, chaqueta *f* de punto
cardinal[1] ['kɑrdənəl] *adj* FUNDAMENTAL : cardinal, fundamental
cardinal[2] *n* : cardenal *m*
cardinal number *n* : número *m* cardinal
cardinal point *n* : punto *m* cardinal
cardiologist [,kɑrdi'alədʒɪst] *n* : cardiólogo *m*, -ga *f*
cardiology [,kɑrdi'alədʒi] *n* : cardiología *f*
cardiovascular [,kɑrdio'væskjələr] *adj* : cardiovascular
care[1] ['kær] *v* **cared; caring** *vi* **1** : importarle a uno ⟨they don't care : no les importa⟩ **2** : preocuparse, inquietarse ⟨she cares about the poor : se preocupa por los pobres⟩ **3 to care for** TEND : cuidar (de), atender, encargarse de **4 to care for** CHERISH : querer, sentir cariño por **5 to care for** LIKE : gustarle (algo a uno) ⟨I don't care for your attitude : tu actitud no me agrada⟩ — *vt* WISH : desear, querer ⟨if you care to go : si deseas ir⟩
care[2] *n* **1** ANXIETY : inquietud *f*, preocupación *f* **2** CAREFULNESS : cuidado *m*, atención *f* ⟨handle with care : manejar con cuidado⟩ **3** CHARGE : cargo *m*, cuidado *m* **4 to take care of** : cuidar (de), atender, encargarse de
careen [kə'ri:n] *vi* **1** SWAY : oscilar, balancearse **2** CAREER : ir a toda velocidad
career[1] [kə'rɪr] *vi* : ir a toda velocidad
career[2] *n* VOCATION : vocación *f*, profesión *f*, carrera *f*
carefree ['kær,fri:, ,kær'-] *adj* : despreocupado
careful ['kærfəl] *adj* **1** CAUTIOUS : cuidadoso, cauteloso **2** PAINSTAKING : cuidadoso, esmerado, meticuloso
carefully ['kærfəli] *adv* : con cuidado, cuidadosamente
carefulness ['kærfəlnəs] *n* **1** CAUTION : cuidado *m*, cautela *f* **2** METICULOUSNESS : esmero *m*, meticulosidad *f*
caregiver ['kær,gɪvər] *n* : persona *f* que cuida a niños o enfermos
careless ['kærləs] *adj* : descuidado, negligente — **carelessly** *adv*
carelessness ['kærləsnəs] *n* : descuido *m*, negligencia *f*
caress[1] [kə'rɛs] *vt* : acariciar
caress[2] *n* : caricia *f*
caret ['kærət] *n* : signo *m* de intercalación
caretaker ['kɛr,teɪkər] *n* : conserje *mf*; velador *m*, -dora *f*

cargo ['kɑr,go:] *n*, *pl* **-goes** *or* **-gos** : cargamento *m*, carga *f*
Caribbean [kærə'bi:ən, kə'rɪbiən] *adj* : caribeño ⟨the Caribbean Sea : el mar Caribe⟩
caribou ['kærə,bu:] *n*, *pl* **-bou** *or* **-bous** : caribú *m*
caricature[1] ['kærɪkə,tʃʊr] *vt* **-tured; -turing** : caricaturizar
caricature[2] *n* : caricatura *f*
caricaturist ['kærɪkə,tʃʊrɪst] *n* : caricaturista *mf*
caries ['kær,i:z] *ns & pl* : caries *f*
carillon ['kærə,lan] *n* : carillón *m*
carmine ['kɑrmən, -,maɪn] *n* : carmín *m*
carnage ['kɑrnɪdʒ] *n* : matanza *f*, carnicería *f*
carnal ['kɑrnəl] *adj* : carnal
carnation [kɑr'neɪʃən] *n* : clavel *m*
carnival ['kɑrnəvəl] *n* : carnaval *m*, feria *f*
carnivore ['kɑrnə,vor] *n* : carnívoro *m*
carnivorous [kɑr'nɪvərəs] *adj* : carnívoro
carol[1] ['kærəl] *vi* **-oled** *or* **-olled; -oling** *or* **-olling** : cantar villancicos
carol[2] *n* : villancico *m*
caroler *or* **caroller** ['kærələr] *n* : persona *f* que canta villancicos
carom[1] ['kærəm] *vi* **1** REBOUND : rebotar ⟨the bullet caromed off the wall : la bala rebotó contra el muro⟩ **2** : hacer carambola (en billar)
carom[2] *n* : carambola *f*
carouse [kə'raʊz] *vt* **-roused; -rousing** : irse de parranda, irse de juerga
carousel *or* **carrousel** [,kærə'sɛl, 'kærə,-] *n* : carrusel *m*, tiovivo *m*
carouser [kə'raʊzər] *n* : juerguista *mf*
carp[1] ['kɑrp] *vi* **1** COMPLAIN : quejarse **2 to carp at** : criticar
carp[2] *n*, *pl* **carp** *or* **carps** : carpa *f*
carpel ['kɑrpəl] *n* : carpelo *m*
carpenter ['kɑrpəntər] *n* : carpintero *m*, -ra *f*
carpentry ['kɑrpəntri] *n* : carpintería *f*
carpet[1] ['kɑrpət] *vt* : alfombrar
carpet[2] *n* : alfombra *f*
carpeting ['kɑrpətɪŋ] *n* : alfombrado *m*
carport ['kɑr,port] *n* : cochera *f*, garaje *m* abierto
carriage ['kærɪdʒ] *n* **1** TRANSPORT : transporte *m* **2** POSTURE : porte *m*, postura *f* **3 horse–drawn carriage** : carruaje *m*, coche *m* **4 baby carriage** : cochecito *m*
carrier ['kæriər] *n* **1** : transportista *mf*, empresa *f* de transportes **2** : portador *m*, -dora *f* (de una enfermedad) **3 aircraft carrier** : portaaviones *m*
carrier pigeon : paloma *f* mensajera
carrion ['kæriən] *n* : carroña *f*
carrot ['kærət] *n* : zanahoria *f*
carry ['kæri] *v* **-ried; -rying** *vt* **1** TRANSPORT : llevar, cargar, transportar (cargamento), conducir (electricidad), portar (un virus) ⟨to carry a bag : cargar una bolsa⟩ ⟨to carry money : llevar dinero encima, traer dinero consi-

go⟩ **2** BEAR : soportar, aguantar, resistir (peso) **3** STOCK : vender, tener en abasto **4** ENTAIL : llevar, implicar, acarrear **5** WIN : ganar (una elección o competición), aprobar (una moción) **6 to carry oneself** : portarse, comportarse ⟨he carried himself honorably : se comportó dignamente⟩ — *vi* : oírse, proyectarse ⟨her voice carries well : su voz se puede oír desde lejos⟩

carryall ['kæri,ɔl] *n* : bolsa *f* de viaje

carry away *vt* **to get carried away** : exaltarse, entusiasmarse

carry on *vt* CONDUCT : realizar, ejercer, mantener ⟨to carry on research : realizar investigaciones⟩ ⟨to carry on a correspondence : mantener una correspondencia⟩ — *vi* **1** : portarse de manera escandalosa o inapropiada ⟨it's embarrassing how he carries on : su manera de comportarse da vergüenza⟩ **2** CONTINUE : seguir, continuar

carry out *vt* **1** PERFORM : llevar a cabo, realizar **2** FULFILL : cumplir

cart¹ ['kɑrt] *vt* : acarrear, llevar

cart² *n* : carreta *f*, carro *m*

cartel [kɑr'tɛl] *n* : cártel *m*

cartilage ['kɑrt̮əlɪʤ] *n* : cartílago *m*

cartilaginous [ˌkɑrt̮əl'æʤənəs] *adj* : cartilaginoso

cartographer [kɑr'tɑgrəfər] *n* : cartógrafo *m*, -fa *f*

cartography [kɑr'tɑgrəfi] *n* : cartografía *f*

carton ['kɑrt̮ən] *n* : caja *f* de cartón

cartoon [kɑr'tu:n] *n* **1** : chiste *m* (gráfico), caricatura *f* ⟨a political cartoon : un chiste político⟩ **2** COMIC STRIP : tira *f* cómica, historieta *f* **3** *or* **animated cartoon** : dibujo *m* animado

cartoonist [kɑr'tu:nɪst] *n* : caricaturista *mf*, dibujante *mf* (de chistes)

cartridge ['kɑrtrɪʤ] *n* : cartucho *m*

carve ['kɑrv] *vt* **carved; carving 1** : tallar (madera), esculpir (piedra), grabar ⟨he carved his name in the bark : grabó su nombre en la corteza⟩ **2** SLICE : cortar, trinchar (carne)

cascade¹ [kæs'keɪd] *vi* **-caded; -cading** : caer en cascada

cascade² *n* : cascada *f*, salto *m* de agua

case¹ ['keɪs] *vt* **cased; casing 1** BOX, PACK : embalar, encajonar **2** INSPECT : observar, inspeccionar (antes de cometer un delito)

case² *n* **1** : caso *m* ⟨an unusual case : un caso insólito⟩ ⟨ablative case : caso ablativo⟩ ⟨a case of the flu : un caso de gripe⟩ **2** BOX : caja *f* **3** CONTAINER : funda *f*, estuche *m* **4 in any case** : de todos modos, en cualquier caso **5 in case** : como precaución ⟨just in case : por si acaso⟩ **6 in case of** : en caso de

casement ['keɪsmənt] *n* : ventana *f* con bisagras

cash¹ ['kæʃ] *vt* : convertir en efectivo, cobrar, cambiar (un cheque)

cash² *n* : efectivo *m*, dinero *m* en efectivo

cashew ['kæ,ʃu:, kə'ʃu:] *n* : anacardo *m*

cashier¹ [kæ'ʃɪr] *vt* : destituir, despedir

cashier² *n* : cajero *m*, -ra *f*

cashmere ['kæʒ,mɪr, 'kæʃ-] *n* : cachemir *m*

casino [kə'si:,no:] *n*, *pl* **-nos** : casino *m*

cask ['kæsk] *n* : tonel *m*, barrica *f*, barril *m*

casket ['kæskət] *n* COFFIN : ataúd *m*, féretro *m*

cassava [kə'sɑvə] *n* : mandioca *f*, yuca *f*

casserole ['kæsə,ro:l] *n* **1** : cazuela *f* **2** : guiso *m*, guisado *m* ⟨tuna casserole : guiso de atún⟩

cassette [kə'sɛt, kæ-] *n* : cassette *mf*

cassock ['kæsək] *n* : sotana *f*

cast¹ ['kæst] *vt* **cast; casting 1** THROW : tirar, echar, arrojar ⟨the die is cast : la suerte está echada⟩ **2** : depositar (un voto) **3** : asignar (papeles en una obra de teatro) **4** MOLD : moldear, fundir, vaciar **5 to cast off** ABANDON : desamparar, abandonar

cast² *n* **1** THROW : lance *m*, lanzamiento *m* **2** APPEARANCE : aspecto *m*, forma *f* **3** : elenco *m*, reparto *m* (de una obra de teatro) **4 plaster cast** : molde *m* de yeso, escayola *f*

castanets [ˌkæstə'nɛts] *npl* : castañuelas *fpl*

castaway¹ ['kæstə,weɪ] *adj* : náufrago

castaway² *n* : náufrago *m*, -ga *f*

caste ['kæst] *n* : casta *f*

caster ['kæstər] *n* : ruedita *f* (de un mueble)

castigate ['kæstə,geɪt] *vt* **-gated; -gating** : castigar severamente, censurar, reprobar

Castilian [kæ'stɪljən] *n* **1** : castellano *m*, -na *f* **2** : castellano *m* (idioma) — **Castilian** *adj*

cast iron *n* : hierro *m* fundido

castle ['kæsəl] *n* **1** : castillo *m* **2** : torre *f* (en ajedrez)

cast–off ['kæst,ɔf] *adj* : desechado

castoff ['kæst,ɔf] *n* : desecho *m*

castrate ['kæs,treɪt] *vt* **-trated; -trating** : castrar

castration [kæ'streɪʃən] *n* : castración *f*

casual ['kæʒʊəl] *adj* **1** FORTUITOUS : casual, fortuito **2** INDIFFERENT : indiferente, despreocupado **3** INFORMAL : informal — **casually** ['kæʒʊəli, 'kæʒəli] *adv*

casualness ['kæʒʊəlnəs] *n* **1** FORTUITOUSNESS : casualidad *f* **2** INDIFFERENCE : indiferencia *f*, despreocupación *f* **3** INFORMALITY : informalidad *f*

casualty ['kæʒʊəlti, 'kæʒəl-] *n*, *pl* **-ties 1** ACCIDENT : accidente *m* serio, desastre *m* **2** VICTIM : víctima *f*; baja *f*; herido *m*, -da *f*

cat ['kæt] *n* : gato *m*, -ta *f*

cataclysm ['kæt̮ə,klɪzəm] *n* : cataclismo *m*

cataclysmal [ˌkætəˈklɪzməl] *or* **cataclysmic** [ˌkætəˈklɪzmɪk] *adj* : catastrófico

catacombs [ˈkætəˌkoːmz] *npl* : catacumbas *fpl*

Catalan [ˈkætələn, -ˌlæn] *n* **1** : catalán *m*, catalana *f* **2** : catalán *m* (idioma) — **Catalan** *adj*

catalog¹ *or* **catalogue** [ˈkætəˌlɔg] *vt* **-loged** *or* **-logued; -loging** *or* **-loguing** : catalogar

catalog² *n* : catálogo *m*

catalyst [ˈkætələst] *n* : catalizador *m*

catalytic [ˌkætəlˈɪtɪk] *adj* : catalítico

catamaran [ˌkætəməˈræn, ˈkætəməˌræn] *n* : catamarán *m*

catapult¹ [ˈkætəˌpʌlt, -ˌpʊlt] *vt* : catapultar

catapult² *n* : catapulta *f*

cataract [ˈkætəˌrækt] *n* : catarata *f*

catarrh [kəˈtɑr] *n* : catarro *m*

catastrophe [kəˈtæstrəˌfiː] *n* : catástrofe *f*

catastrophic [ˌkætəˈstrɑfɪk] *adj* : catastrófico — **catastrophically** [-fɪkli] *adv*

catcall [ˈkætˌkɔl] *n* : rechifla *f*, abucheo *m*

catch¹ [ˈkætʃ, ˈketʃ] *v* **caught** [ˈkɔt]; **catching** *vt* **1** CAPTURE, TRAP : capturar, agarrar, atrapar, coger **2** : agarrar, pillar *fam*, tomar de sorpresa ⟨they caught him red-handed : lo pillaron con las manos en la masa⟩ **3** GRASP : agarrar, captar **4** ENTANGLE : enganchar, enredar **5** : tomar (un tren, etc.) **6** : contagiarse de ⟨to catch a cold : contagiarse de un resfriado, resfriarse⟩ — *vi* **1** GRASP : agarrar **2** HOOK : engancharse **3** IGNITE : prender, agarrar

catch² *n* **1** CATCHING : captura *f*, atrapada *f*, parada *f* (de una pelota) **2** : redada *f* (de pescado), presa *f* (de caza) ⟨he's a good catch : es un buen partido⟩ **3** LATCH : pestillo *m*, pasador *m* **4** DIFFICULTY, TRICK : problema *m*, trampa *f*, truco *m*

catcher [ˈkætʃər, ˈkɛ-] *n* : catcher *mf*; receptor *m*, -tora *f* (en béisbol)

catching [ˈkætʃɪŋ, ˈkɛ-] *adj* : contagioso

catchup [ˈkætʃəp, ˈkɛ-] → **ketchup**

catchword [ˈkætʃˌwərd, ˈketʃ-] *n* : eslogan *m*, lema *m*

catchy [ˈkætʃi, ˈkɛ-] *adj* **catchier; -est** : pegajoso ⟨a catchy song : una canción pegajosa⟩

catechism [ˈkætəˌkɪzəm] *n* : catecismo *m*

categorical [ˌkætəˈgɔrɪkəl] *adj* : categórico, absoluto, rotundo — **categorically** [-kli] *adv*

categorize [ˈkætɪgəˌraɪz] *vt* **-rized; -rizing** : clasificar, catalogar

category [ˈkætəˌgori] *n*, *pl* **-ries** : categoría *f*, género *m*, clase *f*

cater [ˈkeɪtər] *vi* **1** : proveer alimentos (para fiestas, bodas, etc.) **2 to cater to** : atender a ⟨to cater to all tastes : atender a todos los gustos⟩

catercorner¹ [ˈkætiˌkɔrnər, ˈkætə-, ˈkɪti-] *or* **cater–cornered** [-ˌkɔrnərd] *adv* : diagonalmente, en diagonal

catercorner² *or* **cater–cornered** *adj* : diagonal

caterer [ˈkeɪtərər] *n* : proveedor *m*, -dora *f* de comida

caterpillar [ˈkætərˌpɪlər] *n* : oruga *f*

catfish [ˈkætˌfɪʃ] *n* : bagre *m*

catgut [ˈkætˌgʌt] *n* : cuerda *f* de tripa

catharsis [kəˈθɑrsɪs] *n*, *pl* **catharses** [-ˌsiːz] : catarsis *f*

cathartic¹ [kəˈθɑrtɪk] *adj* : catártico

cathartic² *n* : purgante *m*

cathedral [kəˈθiːdrəl] *n* : catedral *f*

catheter [ˈkæθətər] *n* : catéter *m*, sonda *f*

cathode [ˈkæˌθoːd] *n* : cátodo *m*

catholic [ˈkæθəlɪk] *adj* **1** BROAD, UNIVERSAL : liberal, universal **2 Catholic** : católico

Catholic *n* : católico *m*, -ca *f*

Catholicism [kəˈθɑləˌsɪzəm] *n* : catolicismo *m*

catlike [ˈkætˌlaɪk] *adj* : gatuno, felino

catnap¹ [ˈkætˌnæp] *vi* **-napped; -napping** : tomarse una siestecita

catnap² *n* : siesta *f* breve, siestecita *f*

catnip [ˈkætˌnɪp] *n* : nébeda *f*

catsup [ˈketʃəp, ˈkætsəp] → **ketchup**

cattail [ˈkætˌteɪl] *n* : espadaña *f*, anea *f*

cattiness [ˈkætinəs] *n* : malicia *f*

cattle [ˈkætəl] *npl* : ganado *m*, reses *fpl*

cattleman [ˈkætəlmən, -ˌmæn] *n*, *pl* **-men** [-mən, -ˌmen] : ganadero *m*

catty [ˈkæti] *adj* **-tier; -est** : malicioso, malintencionado

catwalk [ˈkætˌwɔk] *n* : pasarela *f*

Caucasian¹ [kɔˈkeɪʒən] *adj* : caucásico

Caucasian² *n* : caucásico *m*, -ca *f*

caucus [ˈkɔkəs] *n* : junta *f* de políticos

caught → **catch**

cauldron [ˈkɔldrən] *n* : caldera *f*

cauliflower [ˈkɑliˌflauər, ˈkɔ-] *n* : coliflor *f*

caulk¹ [ˈkɔk] *vt* : calafatear (un barco), enmasillar (una grieta)

caulk² *n* : masilla *f*

causal [ˈkɔzəl] *adj* : causal

causality [kɔˈzæləti] *n* : causalidad *f*

cause¹ [ˈkɔz] *vt* **caused; causing** : causar, provocar, ocasionar

cause² *n* **1** ORIGIN : causa *f*, origen *m* **2** REASON : causa *f*, razón *f*, motivo *m* **3** LAWSUIT : litigio *m*, pleito *m* **4** MOVEMENT : causa *f*, movimiento *m*

causeless [ˈkɔzləs] *adj* : sin causa

causeway [ˈkɔzˌweɪ] *n* : camino *m* elevado

caustic [ˈkɔstɪk] *adj* **1** CORROSIVE : cáustico, corrosivo **2** BITING : mordaz, sarcástico

cauterize [ˈkɔtəˌraɪz] *vt* **-ized; -izing** : cauterizar

caution¹ [ˈkɔʃən] *vt* : advertir

caution² *n* **1** WARNING : advertencia *f*, aviso *m* **2** CARE, PRUDENCE : precaución *f*, cuidado *m*, cautela *f*

cautionary ['kɔʃə,nɛri] *adv* : admonitorio ⟨cautionary tale : cuento moral⟩
cautious ['kɔʃəs] *adj* : cauteloso, cuidadoso, precavido
cautiously ['kɔʃəsli] *adv* : cautelosamente, con precaución
cautiousness ['kɔʃəsnəs] *n* : cautela *f*, precaución *f*
cavalcade [,kævəl'keɪd, 'kævəl,-] *n* **1** : cabalgata *f* **2** SERIES : serie *f*
cavalier¹ [,kævə'lɪr] *adj* : altivo, desdeñoso — **cavalierly** *adv*
cavalier² *n* : caballero *m*
cavalry ['kævəlri] *n, pl* **-ries** : caballería *f*
cave¹ ['keɪv] *vi* **caved; caving** *or* **to cave in** : derrumbarse
cave² *n* : cueva *f*
cavern ['kævərn] *n* : caverna *f*
cavernous ['kævərnəs] *adj* : cavernoso — **cavernously** *adv*
caviar *or* **caviare** ['kævi,ɑr, 'kɑ-] *n* : caviar *m*
cavity ['kævəṭi] *n, pl* **-ties 1** HOLE : cavidad *f*, hueco *m* **2** CARIES : caries *f*
cavort [kə'vɔrt] *vi* : brincar, hacer cabriolas
caw¹ ['kɔ] *vi* : graznar
caw² *n* : graznido *m*
cayenne pepper [,kaɪ'ɛn, ,keɪ-] *n* : pimienta *f* cayena, pimentón *m*
CD [,si:'di:] *n* : CD *m*, disco *m* compacto
CD-ROM [,si:,di:'ram] *n* : CD-ROM *m*
cease ['si:s] *v* **ceased; ceasing** *vt* : dejar de ⟨they ceased bickering : dejaron de discutir⟩ — *vi* : cesar, pasarse
ceaseless ['si:sləs] *adj* : incesante, continuo
cedar ['si:dər] *n* : cedro *m*
cede ['si:d] *vt* **ceded; ceding** : ceder, conceder
ceiling ['si:lɪŋ] *n* **1** : techo *m*, cielo *m* raso **2** LIMIT : límite *m*, tope *m*
celebrant ['sɛləbrənt] *n* : celebrante *mf*, oficiante *mf*
celebrate ['sɛlə,breɪt] *v* **-brated; -brating** *vt* **1** : celebrar, oficiar ⟨to celebrate Mass : celebrar la misa⟩ **2** : celebrar, festejar ⟨we're celebrating our anniversary : estamos celebrando nuestro aniversario⟩ **3** EXTOL : alabar, ensalzar, exaltar — *vi* : estar de fiesta, divertirse
celebrated ['sɛlə,breɪṭəd] *adj* : célebre, famoso, renombrado
celebration [,sɛlə'breɪʃən] *n* : celebración *f*, festejos *mpl*
celebrity [sə'lɛbrəṭi] *n, pl* **-ties 1** RENOWN : fama *f*, renombre *m*, celebridad *f* **2** PERSONALITY : celebridad *f*, personaje *m*
celery ['sɛləri] *n, pl* **-eries** : apio *m*
celestial [sə'lɛstʃəl, -'lstiəl] *adj* **1** : celeste **2** HEAVENLY : celestial, paradisiaco
celibacy ['sɛləbəsi] *n* : celibato *m*
celibate¹ ['sɛləbət] *adj* : célibe
celibate² *n* : célibe *mf*

cell ['sɛl] *n* **1** : célula *f* (de un organismo) **2** : celda *f* (en una cárcel, etc.) **3** : elemento *m* (de una pila)
cellar ['sɛlər] *n* **1** BASEMENT : sótano *m* **2** : bodega *f* (de vinos)
cellist ['tʃɛlɪst] *n* : violonchelista *mf*
cello ['tʃɛ,lo:] *n, pl* **-los** : violonchelo *m*
cellophane ['sɛlə,feɪn] *n* : celofán *m*
cell phone *n* : teléfono *m* celular
cellular ['sɛljələr] *adj* : celular
celluloid ['sɛljə,lɔɪd] *n* : celuloide
cellulose ['sɛljə,lo:s] *n* : celulosa *f*
Celsius ['sɛlsiəs] *adj* : centígrado ⟨100 degrees Celsius : 100 grados centígrados⟩
Celt ['kɛlt, 'sɛlt] *n* : celta *mf*
Celtic¹ ['kɛltɪk, 'sɛl-] *adj* : celta
Celtic² *n* : celta *m*
cement¹ [sɪ'mɛnt] *vi* : unir o cubrir algo con cemento, cementar
cement² *n* **1** : cemento *m* **2** GLUE : pegamento *m*
cemetery ['sɛmə,tɛri] *n, pl* **-teries** : cementerio *m*, panteón *m*
censer ['sɛntsər] *n* : incensario *m*
censor¹ ['sɛntsər] *vt* : censurar
censor² *n* : censor *m*, -sora *f*
censorious [sɛn'soriəs] *adj* : de censura, crítico
censorship ['sɛntsər,ʃɪp] *n* : censura *f*
censure¹ ['sɛntʃər] *vt* **-sured; -suring** : censurar, criticar, reprobar — **censurable** [-tʃərəbəl] *adj*
censure² *n* : censura *f*, reproche *m* oficial
census ['sɛntsəs] *n* : censo *m*
cent ['sɛnt] *n* : centavo *m*
centaur ['sɛn,tɔr] *n* : centauro *m*
centennial¹ [sɛn'tɛniəl] *adj* : del centenario
centennial² *n* : centenario *m*
center¹ ['sɛntər] *vt* **1** : centrar **2** CONCENTRATE : concentrar, fijar, enfocar — *vi* : centrarse, enfocarse
center² *n* **1** : centro *m* ⟨center of gravity : centro de gravedad⟩ **2** : centro *mf* (en futbol americano), pívot *mf* (en basquetbol)
centerpiece ['sɛntər,pi:s] *n* : centro *m* de mesa
centigrade ['sɛntə,greɪd, 'san-] *adj* : centígrado
centigram ['sɛntə,græm, 'san-] *n* : centigramo *m*
centimeter ['sɛntə,mi:ṭər, 'san-] *n* : centímetro *m*
centipede ['sɛntə,pi:d] *n* : ciempiés *m*
central ['sɛntrəl] *adj* **1** : céntrico, central ⟨in a central location : en un lugar céntrico⟩ **2** MAIN, PRINCIPAL : central, fundamental, principal
Central American¹ *adj* : centroamericano
Central American² *n* : centroamericano *m*, -na *f*
centralization [,sɛntrələ'zeɪʃən] *n* : centralización *f*
centralize ['sɛntrə,laɪz] *vt* **-ized; -izing** : centralizar

centrally ['sɛntrəli] *adv* **1 centrally heated** : con calefacción central **2 centrally located** : céntrico, en un lugar céntrico
centre ['sɛntər] → **center**
centrifugal [sɛn'trɪfjəgəl, -'trɪfɪ-] *adj* : centrífugo
centrifugal force *n* : fuerza *f* centrífuga
century ['sɛntʃəri] *n, pl* **-ries** : siglo *m*
ceramic[1] [sə'ræmɪk] *adj* : de cerámica
ceramic[2] *n* **1** : objeto *m* de cerámica, cerámica *f* **2 ceramics** *npl* : cerámica *f*
cereal[1] ['sɪriəl] *adj* : cereal
cereal[2] *n* : cereal *m*
cerebellum [ˌsɛrə'bɛləm] *n, pl* **-bellums** *or* **-bella** [-'bɛlə] : cerebelo *m*
cerebral [sə'riːbrəl, 'sɛrə-] *adj* : cerebral
cerebral palsy *n* : parálisis *f* cerebral
cerebrum [sə'riːbrəm, 'sɛrə-] *n, pl* **-brums** *or* **-bra** [-brə] : cerebro *m*
ceremonial[1] [ˌsɛrə'moːniəl] *adj* : ceremonial
ceremonial[2] *n* : ceremonial *m*
ceremonious [ˌsɛrə'moːniəs] *adj* **1** FORMAL : ceremonioso, formal **2** CEREMONIAL : ceremonial
ceremony ['sɛrəˌmoːni] *n, pl* **-nies** : ceremonia *f*
cerise [sə'riːs] *n* : rojo *m* cereza
certain[1] ['sərtən] *adj* **1** DEFINITE : cierto, determinado ⟨a certain percentage : un porcentaje determinado⟩ **2** TRUE : cierto, con certeza ⟨I don't know for certain : no sé exactamente⟩ **3** : cierto, alguno ⟨it has a certain charm : tiene cierta gracia⟩ **4** INEVITABLE : seguro, inevitable **5** ASSURED : seguro, asegurado ⟨she's certain to do well : seguro que le irá bien⟩
certain[2] *pron* : ciertos *pl*, algunos *pl* ⟨certain of my friends : algunos de mis amigos⟩
certainly ['sərtənli] *adv* **1** DEFINITELY : ciertamente, seguramente **2** OF COURSE : por supuesto
certainty ['sərtənti] *n, pl* **-ties** : certeza *f*, certidumbre *f*, seguridad *f*
certifiable [ˌsərtə'faɪəbəl] *adj* : certificable
certificate [sər'tɪfɪkət] *n* : certificado *m*, acta *f* ⟨birth certificate : acta de nacimiento⟩
certification [ˌsərtəfə'keɪʃən] *n* : certificación *f*
certify ['sərtəˌfaɪ] *vt* **-fied; -fying 1** VERIFY : certificar, verificar, confirmar **2** ENDORSE : endosar, aprobar oficialmente
certitude ['sərtəˌtuːd, -ˌtjuːd] *n* : certeza *f*, certidumbre *f*
cervical ['sərvɪkəl] *adj* **1** : cervical (dícese del cuello) **2** : del cuello del útero
cervix ['sərvɪks] *n, pl* **-vices** [-və-ˌsiːz] *or* **-vixes 1** NECK : cerviz *f* **2** *or* **uterine cervix** : cuello *m* del útero
cesarean[1] [sɪ'zæriən] *adj* : cesáreo

cesarean[2] *n* : cesárea *f*
cesium ['siːziəm] *n* : cesio *m*
cessation [s'seɪʃən] *n* : cesación *f*, cese *m*
cesspool ['sɛsˌpuːl] *n* : pozo *m* séptico
Chadian ['tʃædiən] *n* : chadiano *m*, -na *f*
— **Chadian** *adj*
chafe ['tʃeɪf] *v* **chafed; chafing** *vi* : enojarse, irritarse — *vt* : rozar
chaff ['tʃæf] *n* **1** : barcia *f*, granzas *fpl* **2 to separate the wheat from the chaff** : separar el grano de la paja
chafing dish ['tʃeɪfɪŋˌdɪʃ] *n* : escalfador *m*
chagrin[1] [ʃə'grɪn] *vt* : desilusionar, avergonzar
chagrin[2] *n* : desilusión *f*, disgusto *m*
chain[1] ['tʃeɪn] *vt* : encadenar
chain[2] *n* **1** : cadena *f* ⟨steel chain : cadena de acero⟩ ⟨restaurant chain : cadena de restaurantes⟩ **2** SERIES : serie *f* ⟨chain of events : serie de eventos⟩ **3 chains** *npl* FETTERS : grillos *mpl*
chair[1] ['tʃer] *vt* : presidir, moderar
chair[2] *n* **1** : silla *f* **2** CHAIRMANSHIP : presidencia *f* **3** → **chairman, chairwoman**
chairman ['tʃermən] *n, pl* **-men** [-mən, -ˌmɛn] : presidente *m*
chairmanship ['tʃermənˌʃɪp] *n* : presidencia *f*
chairwoman ['tʃerˌwumən] *n, pl* **-women** [-ˌwɪmən] : presidenta *f*
chaise longue ['ʃeɪz'lɔŋ] *n, pl* **chaise longues** [-lɔŋ, -'lɔŋz] : chaise longue *f*
chalet [ʃæ'leɪ] *n* : chalet *m*, chalé *m*
chalice ['tʃælɪs] *n* : cáliz *m*
chalk[1] ['tʃɔk] *vt* : escribir con tiza
chalk[2] *n* **1** LIMESTONE : creta *f*, caliza *f* **2** : tiza *f*, gis *m Mex* (para escribir)
chalkboard ['tʃɔkˌbɔrd] → **blackboard**
chalk up *vt* **1** ASCRIBE : atribuir, adscribir **2** SCORE : apuntarse, anotarse (una victoria, etc.)
chalky ['tʃɔki] *adj* **chalkier; -est 1** : calcáreo **2** PALE : pálido **3** POWDERY : polvoriento
challenge[1] ['tʃælɪndʒ] *vt* **-lenged; -lenging 1** DISPUTE : disputar, cuestionar, poner en duda **2** DARE : desafiar, retar **3** STIMULATE : estimular, incentivar
challenge[2] *n* : reto *m*, desafío *m*
challenger ['tʃælɪndʒər] *n* : retador *m*, -dora *f*; contendiente *mf*
chamber ['tʃeɪmbər] *n* **1** ROOM : cámara *f*, sala *f* ⟨the senate chamber : la cámara del senado⟩ **2** : recámara *f* (de un arma de fuego), cámara *f* (de combustión) **3** : cámara *f* ⟨chamber of commerce : cámara de comercio⟩ **4 chambers** *npl or* **judge's chambers** : despacho *m* del juez
chambermaid ['tʃeɪmbərˌmeɪd] *n* : camarera *f*
chamber music *n* : música *f* de cámara
chameleon [kə'miːljən, -liən] *n* : camaleón *m*

chamois [´ʃæmi] *n*, *pl* **chamois** [-mi, -miz] : gamuza *f*

champ¹ [´ʧæmp, ´ʧɑmp] *vi* **1** : masticar ruidosamente **2 to champ at the bit** : impacientarse, comerle a uno la impaciencia

champ² [´ʧæmp] *n* : campeón *m*, -peona *f*

champagne [ʃæm´peɪn] *n* : champaña *m*, champán *m*

champion¹ [´ʧæmpiən] *vt* : defender, luchar por (una causa)

champion² *n* **1** ADVOCATE, DEFENDER : paladín *m*; campeón *m*, -peona *f*; defensor *m*, -sora *f* **2** WINNER : campeón *m*, -peona *f* ⟨world champion : campeón mundial⟩

championship [´ʧæmpiən͵ʃɪp] *n* : campeonato *m*

chance¹ [´ʧænts] *v* **chanced; chancing** *vi* **1** HAPPEN : ocurrir por casualidad **2 to chance upon** : encontrar por casualidad — *vt* RISK : arriesgar

chance² *adj* : fortuito, casual ⟨a chance encounter : un encuentro casual⟩

chance³ *n* **1** FATE, LUCK : azar *m*, suerte *f*, fortuna *f* **2** OPPORTUNITY : oportunidad *f*, ocasión *f* **3** PROBABILITY : probabilidad *f*, posibilidad *f* **4** RISK : riesgo *m* **5** : boleto *m* (de una rifa o lotería) **6 by chance** : por casualidad

chancellor [´ʧæntsələr] *n* **1** : canciller *m* **2** : rector *m*, -tora *f* (de una universidad)

chancre [´ʃæŋkər] *n* : chancro *m*

chancy [´ʧæntsi] *adj* **chancier; -est** : riesgoso, arriesgado

chandelier [͵ʃændə´lɪr] *n* : araña *f* de luces

change¹ [´ʧeɪnʤ] *v* **changed; changing** *vt* **1** ALTER : cambiar, alterar, modificar **2** EXCHANGE : cambiar de, intercambiar ⟨to change places : cambiar de sitio⟩ — *vi* **1** VARY : cambiar, variar, transformarse ⟨you haven't changed : no has cambiado⟩ **2 or to change clothes** : cambiarse (de ropa)

change² *n* **1** ALTERATION : cambio *m* **2** : cambio *m*, vuelto *m* ⟨two dollars change : dos dólares de vuelto⟩ **3** COINS : cambio *m*, monedas *fpl*

changeable [´ʧeɪnʤəbəl] *adj* : cambiante, variable

changeless [´ʧeɪnʤləs] *adj* : invariable, constante

changer [´ʧeɪnʤər] *n* **1** : cambiador *m* ⟨record changer : cambiador de discos⟩ **2 or money changer** : cambista *mf* (de dinero)

channel¹ [´ʧænəl] *vt* **-neled** *or* **-nelled; -neling** *or* **-nelling** : encauzar, canalizar

channel² *n* **1** RIVERBED : cauce *m* **2** STRAIT : canal *m*, estrecho *m* ⟨English Channel : Canal de la Mancha⟩ **3** COURSE, MEANS : vía *f*, conducto *m* ⟨the usual channels : las vías normales⟩ **4** : canal *m* (de televisión)

chant¹ [´ʧænt] *v* : salmodiar, cantar

chant² *n* **1** : salmodia *f* **2 Gregorian chant** : canto *m* gregoriano

Chanukah [´xɑnəkə, ´hɑ-] → **Hanukkah**

chaos [´keɪˌɑs] *n* : caos *m*

chaotic [keɪ´ɑtɪk] *adj* : caótico — **chaotically** [-tɪkli] *adv*

chap¹ [´ʧæp] *vi* **chapped; chapping** : partirse, agrietarse

chap² *n* FELLOW : tipo *m*, hombre *m*

chapel [´ʧæpəl] *n* : capilla *f*

chaperon¹ *or* **chaperone** [´ʃæpə͵roːn] *vt* **-oned; -oning** : ir de chaperón, acompañar

chaperon² *or* **chaperone** *n* : chaperón *m*, -rona *f*; acompañante *mf*

chaplain [´ʧæplɪn] *n* : capellán *m*

chapter [´ʧæptər] *n* **1** : capítulo *m* (de un libro) **2** BRANCH : sección *f*, división *f* (de una organización)

char [´ʧɑr] *vt* **charred; charring 1** BURN : carbonizar **2** SCORCH : chamuscar

character [´kærɪktər] *n* **1** LETTER, SYMBOL : carácter *m* ⟨Chinese characters : caracteres chinos⟩ **2** DISPOSITION : carácter *m*, personalidad *f* ⟨of good character : de buena reputación⟩ **3** : tipo *m*, personaje *m* peculiar ⟨he's quite a character! : ¡él es algo serio!⟩ **4** : personaje *m* (ficticio)

characteristic¹ [͵kærɪktə´rɪstɪk] *adj* : característico, típico — **characteristically** [-tɪkli] *adv*

characteristic² *n* : característica *f*

characterization [͵kærɪktərə´zeɪʃən] *n* : caracterización *f*

characterize [´kærɪktə͵raɪz] *vt* **-ized; -izing** : caracterizar

charades [ʃə´reɪdz] *ns & pl* : charada *f*

charcoal [´ʧɑr͵koːl] *n* : carbón *m*

chard [´ʧɑrd] → **Swiss chard**

charge¹ [´ʧɑrʤ] *v* **charged; charging** *vt* **1** : cargar ⟨to charge the batteries : cargar las pilas⟩ **2** ENTRUST : encomendar, encargar **3** COMMAND : ordenar, mandar **4** ACCUSE : acusar ⟨charged with robbery : acusado de robo⟩ **5** : cargar a una cuenta, comprar a crédito — *vi* **1** : cargar (contra el enemigo) ⟨charge! : ¡a la carga!⟩ **2** : cobrar ⟨they charge too much : cobran demasiado⟩

charge² *n* **1** : carga *f* (eléctrica) **2** BURDEN : carga *f*, peso *m* **3** RESPONSIBILITY : cargo *m*, responsabilidad *f* ⟨to take charge of : hacerse cargo de⟩ **4** ACCUSATION : cargo *m*, acusación *f* **5** COST : costo *m*, cargo *m*, precio *m* **6** ATTACK : carga *f*, ataque *m*

charge card → **credit card**

chargeable [´ʧɑrʤəbəl] *adj* **1** : acusable, perseguible (dícese de un delito) **2 ~ to** : a cargo de (una cuenta)

charger [´ʧɑrʤər] *n* : corcel *m*, caballo *m* (de guerra)

chariot [´ʧæriət] *n* : carro *m* (de guerra)

charisma [kə´rɪzmə] *n* : carisma *m*

charismatic [͵kærəz´mætɪk] *adj* : carismático

charitable ['tʃærətəbəl] *adj* **1** GENER-
OUS : caritativo ⟨a charitable organization : una organización benéfica⟩ **2**
KIND, UNDERSTANDING : generoso,
benévolo, comprensivo — **charitably**
[-bli] *adv*
charitableness ['tʃærətəbəlnəs] *n* : carid-
dad *f*
charity ['tʃærəti] *n, pl* **-ties 1** GENEROS-
ITY : caridad *f* **2** ALMS : caridad *f*,
limosna *f* **3** : organización *f* benéfica,
obra *f* de beneficencia
charlatan ['ʃɑrlətən] *n* : charlatán *m*,
-tana *f*; farsante *mf*
charley horse ['tʃɑrli,hɔrs] *n* : calambre
m
charm¹ ['tʃɑrm] *vt* : encantar, cautivar,
fascinar
charm² *n* **1** AMULET : amuleto *m*, talismán *m* **2** ATTRACTION : encanto *m*,
atractivo *m* ⟨it has a certain charm
: tiene cierto atractivo⟩ **3** : dije *m*, colgante *m* ⟨charm bracelet : pulsera de
dijes⟩
charmer ['tʃɑrmər] *n* : persona *f* encantadora
charming ['tʃɑrmɪŋ] *adj* : encantador,
fascinante
chart¹ ['tʃɑrt] *vt* **1** : trazar un mapa de,
hacer un gráfico de **2** PLAN : trazar,
planear ⟨to chart a course : trazar un
derrotero⟩
chart² *n* **1** MAP : carta *f*, mapa *m* **2** DI-
AGRAM : gráfico *m*, cuadro *m*, tabla *f*
charter¹ ['tʃɑrtər] *vt* **1** : establecer los estatutos de (una organización) **2** RENT
: alquilar, fletar
charter² *n* **1** STATUTES : estatutos *mpl*
2 CONSTITUTION : carta *f*, constitución
f
chartreuse [ʃɑr'truːz, -'truːs] *n* : color *m*
verde-amarillo intenso
chary ['tʃæri] *adj* **charier; -est 1** WARY
: cauteloso, precavido **2** SPARING : parco
chase¹ ['tʃeɪs] *vt* **chased; chasing 1**
PURSUE : perseguir, ir a la caza de **2**
DRIVE : ahuyentar, echar ⟨he chased
the dog from the garden : ahuyentó al
perro del jardín⟩ **3** : grabar (metales)
chase² *n* **1** PURSUIT : persecución *f*,
caza *f* **2 the chase** HUNTING : caza *f*
chaser ['tʃeɪsər] *n* **1** PURSUER : perseguidor *m*, -dora *f* **2** : bebida *f* que se
toma después de un trago de licor
chasm ['kæzəm] *n* : abismo *m*, sima *f*
chassis ['tʃæsi, 'ʃæsi] *n, pl* **chassis** [-siz]
: chasis *m*, armazón *m*
chaste ['tʃeɪst] *adj* **chaster; -est 1** : casto **2** MODEST : modesto, puro **3** AUS-
TERE : austero, sobrio
chastely ['tʃeɪstli] *adv* : castamente
chasten ['tʃeɪsən] *vt* : castigar, sancionar
chasteness ['tʃeɪstnəs] *n* **1** MODESTY
: modestia *f*, castidad *f* **2** AUSTERITY
: sobriedad *f*, austeridad *f*

chastise ['tʃæs,taɪz, tʃæs'-] *vt* **-tised;
-tising 1** REPRIMAND : reprender, corregir, reprobar **2** PUNISH : castigar
chastisement ['tʃæs,taɪzmənt, tʃæs'taɪz-
, 'tʃæstəz-] *n* : castigo *m*, corrección *f*
chastity ['tʃæstəti] *n* : castidad *f*, decencia *f*, modestia *f*
chat¹ ['tʃæt] *vi* **chatted; chatting** : charlar, platicar
chat² *n* : charla *f*, plática *f*
château [ʃæ'toː] *n, pl* **-teaus** [-'toːz] *or*
-teaux [-'toː, -'toːz] : mansión *f*
campestre
chattel ['tʃæt̬əl] *n* : bienes *fpl* muebles,
enseres *mpl*
chatter¹ ['tʃæt̬ər] *vi* **1** : castañetear
(dícese de los dientes) **2** GAB : parlotear
fam, cotorrear *fam*
chatter² *n* **1** CHATTERING : castañeteo
m (de dientes) **2** GABBING : parloteo
m fam, cotorreo *m fam*, cháchara *f fam*
chatterbox ['tʃæt̬ər,bɑks] *n* : parlanchín
m, -china *f*; charlatán *m*, -tana *f*;
hablador *m*, -dora *f*
chatty ['tʃæt̬i] *adj* **chattier; chattiest 1**
TALKATIVE : parlanchín, charlatán **2**
CONVERSATIONAL : familiar, conversador ⟨a chatty letter : una carta llena
de noticias⟩
chauffeur¹ ['ʃoːfər, ʃo'fər] *vi* : trabajar
de chofer privado — *vt* : hacer de
chofer para
chauffeur² *n* : chofer *m* privado
chauvinism ['ʃoːvə,nɪzəm] *n* : chauvinismo *m*, patriotería *f*
chauvinist ['ʃoːvənɪst] *n* : chauvinista
mf; patriotero *m*, -ra *f*
chauvinistic [,ʃoːvə'nɪstɪk] *adj* : chauvinista, patriotero
cheap¹ ['tʃiːp] *adv* : barato ⟨to sell cheap
: vender barato⟩
cheap² *adj* **1** INEXPENSIVE : barato,
económico **2** SHODDY : barato, mal hecho **3** STINGY : tacaño, agarrado *fam*,
codo *Mex*
cheapen ['tʃiːpən] *vt* : degradar, rebajar
cheaply ['tʃiːpli] *adv* : barato, a precio
bajo
cheapness ['tʃiːpnəs] *n* **1** : baratura *f*,
precio *m* bajo **2** STINGINESS : tacañería
f
cheapskate ['tʃiːp,skeɪt] *n* : tacaño *m*,
-ña *f*; codo *m*, -da *f Mex*
cheat¹ ['tʃiːt] *vt* : defraudar, estafar, engañar — *vi* : hacer trampa
cheat² *n* **1** CHEATING : engaño *m*,
fraude *m*, trampa *f* **2** → **cheater**
cheater ['tʃiːtər] *n* : estafador *m*, -dora *f*;
tramposo *m*, -sa *f*
check¹ ['tʃɛk] *vt* **1** HALT : frenar, parar,
detener **2** RESTRAIN : refrenar, contener, reprimir **3** VERIFY : verificar,
comprobar **4** INSPECT : revisar,
chequear, inspeccionar **5** MARK : marcar, señalar **6** : chequear, facturar
(maletas, equipaje) **7** CHECKER : marcar con cuadros **8 to check in** : registrarse en un hotel **9 to check out** : irse
de un hotel

check² *n* **1** HALT : detención *f* súbita, parada *f* **2** RESTRAINT : control *m*, freno *m* **3** INSPECTION : inspección *f*, verificación *f*, chequeo *m* **4** : cheque *m* ⟨to pay by check : pagar con cheque⟩ **5** VOUCHER : resguardo *m*, comprobante *m* **6** BILL : cuenta *f* (en un restaurante) **7** SQUARE : cuadro *m* **8** MARK : marca *f* **9** : jaque *m* (en ajedrez)

checkbook ['tʃɛk,bʊk] *n* : chequera *f*

checker¹ ['tʃɛkər] *vt* : marcar con cuadros

checker² *n* **1** : pieza *f* (en el juego de damas) **2** : verificador *m*, -dora *f* **3** CASHIER : cajero *m*, -ra *f*

checkerboard ['tʃɛkər,bɔrd] *n* : tablero *m* de damas

checkers ['tʃɛkərz] *n* : damas *fpl*

checkmate¹ ['tʃɛk,meɪt] *vt* **-mated; -mating 1** : dar jaque mate a (en ajedrez) **2** THWART : frustrar, arruinar

checkmate² *n* : jaque mate *m*

checkout ['tʃɛk,aʊt] *n or* **checkout counter** : caja *f*

checkpoint ['tʃɛk,pɔɪnt] *n* : puesto *m* de control

checkup ['tʃɛk,ʌp] *n* : examen *m* médico, chequeo *m*

cheddar ['tʃɛdər] *n* : queso *m* Cheddar

cheek ['tʃiːk] *n* **1** : mejilla *f*, cachete *m* **2** IMPUDENCE : insolencia *f*, descaro *m*

cheekbone ['tʃiːk,boːn] *n* : pómulo *m*

cheeky ['tʃiːki] *adj* **cheekier; -est** : descarado, insolente, atrevido

cheep¹ ['tʃiːp] *vi* : piar

cheep² *n* : pío *m*

cheer¹ ['tʃɪr] *vt* **1** ENCOURAGE : alentar, animar **2** GLADDEN : alegrar, levantar el ánimo a **3** ACCLAIM : aclamar, vitorear, echar porras a

cheer² *n* **1** CHEERFULNESS : alegría *f*, buen humor *m*, jovialidad *f* **2** APPLAUSE : aclamación *f*, ovación *f*, aplausos *mpl* ⟨three cheers for the chief! : ¡viva el jefe!⟩ **3 cheers!** : ¡salud!

cheerful ['tʃɪrfəl] *adj* : alegre, de buen humor

cheerfully ['tʃɪrfəli] *adv* : alegremente, jovialmente

cheerfulness ['tʃɪrfəlnəs] *n* : buen humor *m*, alegría *f*

cheerily ['tʃɪrəli] *adv* : alegremente

cheeriness ['tʃɪrinəs] *n* : buen humor *m*, alegría *f*

cheerleader ['tʃɪr,liːdər] *n* : porrista *mf*

cheerless ['tʃɪrləs] *adj* BLEAK : triste, sombrío

cheerlessly ['tʃɪrləsli] *adv* : desanimadamente

cheery ['tʃɪri] *adj* **cheerier; -est** : alegre, de buen humor

cheese ['tʃiːz] *n* : queso *m*

cheesecloth ['tʃiːz,klɔθ] *n* : estopilla *f*

cheesy ['tʃiːzi] *adj* **cheesier; -est 1** : a queso **2** : que contiene queso **3** CHEAP : barato, de mala calidad

cheetah ['tʃiːtʃə] *n* : guepardo *m*

chef ['ʃɛf] *n* : chef *m*

chemical¹ ['kɛmɪkəl] *adj* : químico — **chemically** [-mɪkli] *adv*

chemical² *n* : sustancia *f* química

chemise [ʃə'miːz] *n* **1** : camiseta *f*, prenda *f* interior de una pieza **2** : vestido *m* holgado

chemist ['kɛmɪst] *n* : químico *m*, -ca *f*

chemistry ['kɛmɪstri] *n, pl* **-tries** : química *f*

chemotherapy [,kiːmo'θɛrəpi, ,kɛmo-] *n, pl* **-pies** : quimioterapia *f*

chenille [ʃə'niːl] *n* : felpilla *f*

cherish ['tʃɛrɪʃ] *vt* **1** VALUE : apreciar, valorar **2** HARBOR : abrigar, albergar

cherry ['tʃɛri] *n, pl* **-ries 1** : cereza *f* (fruta) **2** : cerezo *m* (árbol)

cherub ['tʃɛrəb] *n* **1** *pl* **-ubim** ['tʃɛrə,bɪm, 'tʃɛrjə-] ANGEL : ángel *m*, querubín *m* **2** *pl* **-ubs** : niño *m* regordete, niña *f* regordeta

cherubic [tʃə'ruːbɪk] *adj* : querúbico, angelical

chess ['tʃɛs] *n* : ajedrez *m*

chessboard ['tʃɛs,bɔrd] *n* : tablero *m* de ajedrez

chessman ['tʃɛsmən, -,mæn] *n, pl* **-men** [-mən, -,mɛn] : pieza *f* de ajedrez

chest ['tʃɛst] *n* **1** : cofre *m*, baúl *m* **2** : pecho *m* ⟨chest pains : dolores de pecho⟩

chestnut ['tʃɛst,nʌt] *n* **1** : castaña *f* (fruto) **2** : castaño *m* (árbol)

chest of drawers *n* : cómoda *f*

chevron ['ʃɛvrən] *n* : galón *m* (de un oficial militar)

chew¹ ['tʃuː] *vt* : masticar, mascar

chew² *n* : algo que se masca (como tabaco)

chewable ['tʃuːəbəl] *adj* : masticable

chewing gum *n* : goma *f* de mascar, chicle *m*

chewy ['tʃuːi] *adj* **chewier; -est 1** : fibroso (dícese de las carnes o los vegetales) **2** : pegajoso, chicloso (dícese de los dulces)

chic¹ ['ʃiːk] *adj* : chic, elegante, de moda

chic² *n* : chic *m*, elegancia *f*

Chicano [tʃɪ'kɑno] *n* : chicano *m*, -na *f* — **Chicano** *adj*

chick ['tʃɪk] *n* : pollito *m*, -ta *f*; polluelo *m*, -la *f*

chicken ['tʃɪkən] *n* **1** FOWL : pollo *m* **2** COWARD : cobarde *mf*

chickenhearted ['tʃɪkən,hɑrtəd] *n* : miedoso, cobarde

chicken pox *n* : varicela *f*

chickpea ['tʃɪk,piː] *n* : garbanzo *m*

chicle ['tʃɪkəl] *n* : chicle *m* (resina)

chicory ['tʃɪkəri] *n, pl* **-ries 1** : endibia *f* (para ensaladas) **2** : achicoria *f* (aditivo de café)

chide ['tʃaɪd] *vt* **chid** ['tʃɪd] *or* **chided; chid** *or* **chidden** ['tʃɪdən] *or* **chided; chiding** ['tʃaɪdɪŋ] : regañar, reprender

chief¹ ['tʃiːf] *adj* : principal, capital ⟨chief negotiator : negociador en jefe⟩ — **chiefly** *adv*

chief² *n* : jefe *m*, -fa *f*

chieftain ['ʧiːftən] *n* : jefe *m*, -fa *f* (de una tribu)
chiffon [ʃɪ'fɑn, 'ʃɪ,-] *n* : chifón *m*
chigger ['ʧɪɡər] *n* : nigua *f*
chignon ['ʃiːn,jɑn, -,jɔn] *n* : moño *m*, chongo *m* *Mex*
chilblain ['ʧɪl,bleɪn] *n* : sabañón *m*
child ['ʧaɪld] *n, pl* **children** ['ʧɪldrən] **1** BABY, YOUNGSTER : niño *m*, -ña *f*; criatura *f* **2** OFFSPRING : hijo *m*, -ja *f*; progenie *f*
childbearing[1] ['ʧaɪlbɛrɪŋ] *adj* : relativo al parto ⟨of childbearing age : en edad fértil⟩
childbearing[2] → **childbirth**
childbirth ['ʧaɪld,bərθ] *n* : parto *m*
childhood ['ʧaɪld,hʊd] *n* : infancia *f*, niñez *f*
childish ['ʧaɪldɪʃ] *adj* : infantil, inmaduro — **childishly** *adv*
childishness ['ʧaɪldɪʃnəs] *n* : infantilismo *m*, inmadurez *f*
childless ['ʧaɪldləs] *adj* : sin hijos
childlike ['ʧaɪld,laɪk] *adj* : infantil, inocente ⟨a childlike imagination : una imaginación infantil⟩
childproof ['ʧaɪld,pruːf] *adj* : a prueba de niños
Chilean ['ʧɪliən, ʧɪ'leɪən] *n* : chileno *m*, -na *f* — **Chilean** *adj*
chili *or* **chile** *or* **chilli** ['ʧɪli] *n, pl* **chilies** *or* **chiles** *or* **chillies** **1** *or* **chili pepper** : chile *m*, ají *m* **2** : chile *m* con carne
chill[1] ['ʧɪl] *v* : enfriar
chill[2] *adj* : frío, gélido ⟨a chill wind : un viento frío⟩
chill[3] *n* **1** CHILLINESS : fresco *m*, frío *m* **2** SHIVER : escalofrío *m* **3** DAMPER : enfriamiento *m*, frío *m* ⟨to cast a chill over : enfriar⟩
chilliness ['ʧɪlinəs] *n* : frío *m*, fresco *m*
chilly ['ʧɪli] *adj* **chillier; -est** : frío ⟨it's chilly tonight : hace frío esta noche⟩
chime[1] ['ʧaɪm] *v* **chimed; chiming** *vt* : hacer sonar (una campana) — *vi* : sonar una campana, dar campanadas
chime[2] *n* **1** BELLS : juego *m* de campanitas sintonizadas, carillón *m* **2** PEAL : tañido *m*, campanada *f*
chime in *vi* : meterse en una conversación
chimera *or* **chimaera** [kaɪ'mɪrə, kə-] *n* : quimera *f*
chimney ['ʧɪmni] *n, pl* **-neys** : chimenea *f*
chimney sweep *n* : deshollinador *m*, -dora *f*
chimp ['ʧɪmp, 'ʃɪmp] → **chimpanzee**
chimpanzee [,ʧɪm,pæn'ziː, ,ʃɪm-; ʧɪm 'pænzi, ʃɪm-] *n* : chimpancé *m*
chin ['ʧɪn] *n* : barbilla *f*, mentón *m*, barba *f*
china ['ʧaɪnə] *n* **1** PORCELAIN : porcelana *f*, loza *f* **2** CROCKERY, TABLEWARE : loza *f*, vajilla *f*
chinchilla [ʧɪn'ʧɪlə] *n* : chinchilla *f*
Chinese ['ʧaɪ'niːz, -'niːs] *n* **1** : chino *m*, -na *f* **2** : chino *m* (idioma) — **Chinese** *adj*

chink ['ʧɪŋk] *n* : grieta *f*, abertura *f*
chintz ['ʧɪnts] *n* : chintz *m*, chinz *m*
chip[1] ['ʧɪp] *v* **chipped; chipping** *vt* : desportillar, desconchar, astillar (madera) — *vi* : desportillarse, desconcharse, descascararse (dícese de la pintura, etc.)
chip[2] *n* **1** : astilla *f* (de madera o vidrio), lasca *f* (de piedra) ⟨he's a chip off the old block : de tal palo, tal astilla⟩ **2** : bocado *m* pequeño (en rodajas o rebanadas) ⟨tortilla chips : totopos, tortillitas tostadas⟩ **3** : ficha *f* (de póker, etc.) **4** NICK : desportilladura *f*, mella *f* **5** : chip *m* ⟨memory chip : chip de memoria⟩
chip in *v* CONTRIBUTE : contribuir
chipmunk ['ʧɪp,mʌŋk] *n* : ardilla *f* listada
chipper ['ʧɪpər] *adj* : alegre y vivaz
chiropodist [kə'rɑpədɪst, ʃə-] *n* : podólogo *m*, -ga *f*
chiropody [kə'rɑpədi, ʃə-] *n* : podología *f*
chiropractic ['kaɪrə,præktɪk] *n* : quiropráctica *f*
chiropractor ['kaɪrə,præktər] *n* : quiropráctico *m*, -ca *f*
chirp[1] ['ʧərp] *vi* : gorjear (dícese de los pájaros), chirriar (dícese de los grillos)
chirp[2] *n* : gorjeo *m* (de un pájaro), chirrido *m* (de un grillo)
chisel[1] ['ʧɪzəl] *vt* **-eled** *or* **-elled; -eling** *or* **-elling** **1** : cincelar, tallar, labrar **2** CHEAT : estafar, defraudar
chisel[2] *n* : cincel *m* (para piedras y metales), escoplo *m* (para madera), formón *m*
chiseler ['ʧɪzələr] *n* SWINDLER : estafador *m*, -dora *f*; fraude *mf*
chit ['ʧɪt] *n* : resguardo *m*, recibo *m*
chitchat ['ʧɪt,ʧæt] *n* : cotorreo *m*, charla *f*
chivalric [ʃə'vælrɪk] → **chivalrous**
chivalrous ['ʃɪvəlrəs] *adj* **1** KNIGHTLY : caballeresco, relativo a la caballería **2** GENTLEMANLY : caballeroso, honesto, cortés
chivalrousness ['ʃɪvəlrəsnəs] *n* : caballerosidad *f*, cortesía *f*
chivalry ['ʃɪvəlri] *n, pl* **-ries 1** KNIGHTHOOD : caballería *f* **2** CHIVALROUSNESS : caballerosidad *f*, nobleza *f*, cortesía *f*
chive ['ʧaɪv] *n* : cebollino *m*
chloride ['klor,aɪd] *n* : cloruro *m*
chlorinate ['klorə,neɪt] *vt* **-nated; -nating** : clorar
chlorination [,klorə'neɪʃən] *n* : cloración *f*
chlorine ['klor,iːn] *n* : cloro *m*
chloroform ['klorə,fɔrm] *n* : cloroformo *m*
chlorophyll ['klorə,fɪl] *n* : clorofila *f*
chock–full ['ʧak'fʊl, 'ʧʌk-] *adj* : colmado, repleto
chocolate ['ʧakələt, 'ʧɔk-] *n* **1** : chocolate *m* **2** BONBON : bombón *m* **3** : color *m* chocolate, marrón *m*

choice¹ ['ʧɔɪs] *adj* **choicer; -est** : selecto, escogido, de primera calidad
choice² *n* **1** CHOOSING : elección *f*, selección *f* **2** OPTION : elección *f*, opción *f* ⟨I have no choice : no tengo alternativa⟩ **3** PREFERENCE : preferencia *f*, elección *f* **4** VARIETY : surtido *m*, selección *f* ⟨a wide choice : un gran surtido⟩
choir ['kwaɪr] *n* : coro *m*
choirboy ['kwaɪr₁bɔɪ] *n* : niño *m* de coro
choke¹ ['ʧoːk] *v* **choked; choking** *vt* **1** ASPHYXIATE, STRANGLE : sofocar, asfixiar, ahogar, estrangular **2** BLOCK : tapar, obstruir — *vi* **1** SUFFOCATE : asfixiarse, sofocarse, ahogarse, atragantarse (con comida) **2** CLOG : taparse, obstruirse
choke² *n* **1** CHOKING : estrangulación *f* **2** : choke *m* (de un motor)
choker ['ʧoːkər] *n* : gargantilla *f*
cholera ['kɑlərə] *n* : cólera *m*
cholesterol [kə'lɛstə₁rɔl] *n* : colesterol *m*
choose ['ʧuːz] *v* **chose** ['ʧoːz]; **chosen** ['ʧoːzən]; **choosing** *vt* **1** SELECT : escoger, elegir ⟨choose only one : escoja sólo uno⟩ **2** DECIDE : decidir ⟨he chose to leave : decidió irse⟩ **3** PREFER : preferir ⟨which one do you choose? : ¿cuál prefiere?⟩ — *vi* : escoger ⟨much to choose from : mucho de donde escoger⟩
choosy *or* **choosey** ['ʧuːzi] *adj* **choosier; -est** : exigente, remilgado
chop¹ ['ʧɑp] *vt* **chopped; chopping 1** MINCE : picar, cortar, moler (carne) **2** **to chop down** : cortar, talar (un árbol)
chop² *n* **1** CUT : hachazo *m* (con una hacha), tajo *m* (con una cuchilla) **2** BLOW : golpe *m* (penetrante) ⟨karate chop : golpe de karate⟩ **3** : chuleta *f* ⟨pork chops : chuletas de cerdo⟩
chopper ['ʧɑpər] → **helicopter**
choppy ['ʧɑpi] *adj* **choppier; -est 1** : agitado, picado (dícese del mar) **2** DISCONNECTED : incoherente, inconexo
chops ['ʧɑps] *npl* **1** : quijada *f*, mandíbula *f*, boca *f* (de una persona) **2 to lick one's chops** : relamerse
chopsticks ['ʧɑp₁stɪks] *npl* : palillos *mpl*
choral ['korəl] *adj* : coral
chorale [kə'ræl, -'rɑl] *n* **1** : coral *f* (composición musical vocal) **2** CHOIR, CHORUS : coral *f*, coro *m*
chord ['kɔrd] *n* **1** : acorde *m* (en música) **2** : cuerda *f* (en anatomía o geometría)
chore ['ʧor] *n* **1** TASK : tarea *f* rutinaria **2** BOTHER, NUISANCE : lata *f fam*, fastidio *m* **3 chores** *npl* WORK : quehaceres *mpl*, faenas *fpl*
choreograph ['koriə₁græf] *vt* : coreografiar
choreographer [₁kori'ɑgrəfər] *n* : coreógrafo *m*, -fa *f*
choreographic [₁koriə'græfɪk] *adj* : coreográfico
choreography [₁kori'ɑgrəfi] *n, pl* **-phies** : coreografía *f*

chorister ['korəstər] *n* : corista *mf*
chortle¹ ['ʧɔrtəl] *vi* **-tled; -tling** : reírse (con satisfacción o júbilo)
chortle² *n* : risa *f* (de satisfacción o júbilo)
chorus¹ ['korəs] *vt* : corear
chorus² *n* **1** : coro *m* (grupo o composición musical) **2** REFRAIN : coro *m*, estribillo *m*
chose → **choose**
chosen ['ʧoːzən] *adj* : elegido, selecto
chow ['ʧaʊ] *n* **1** FOOD : comida *f* **2** : chow-chow *m* (perro)
chowder ['ʧaʊdər] *n* : sopa *f* de pescado
Christ ['kraɪst] *n* **1** : Cristo *m* **2 for Christ's sake** : ¡por Dios!
christen ['krɪsən] *vt* **1** BAPTIZE : bautizar **2** NAME : bautizar con el nombre de
Christendom ['krɪsəndəm] *n* : cristiandad *f*
christening ['krɪsənɪŋ] *n* : bautismo *m*, bautizo *m*
Christian¹ ['krɪsʧən] *adj* : cristiano
Christian² *n* : cristiano *m*, -na *f*
Christianity [₁krɪsʧi'ænəti, ₁krɪs'ʧæ-] *n* : cristianismo *m*
Christian name *n* : nombre *m* de pila
Christmas ['krɪsməs] *n* : Navidad *f* ⟨Christmas season : las Navidades⟩
chromatic [kro'mætɪk] *adj* : cromático ⟨chromatic scale : escala cromática⟩
chrome ['kro:m] *n* : cromo *m* (metal)
chromium ['kro:miəm] *n* : cromo *m* (elemento)
chromosome ['kro:mə₁so:m, -₁zo:m] *n* : cromosoma *m*
chronic ['krɑnɪk] *adj* : crónico — **chronically** [-nɪkli] *adv*
chronicle¹ ['krɑnɪkəl] *vt* **-cled; -cling** : escribir (una crónica o historia)
chronicle² *n* : crónica *f*, historia *f*
chronicler ['krɑnɪklər] *n* : historiador *m*, -dora *f*; cronista *mf*
chronological [₁krɑnəl'ɑʤɪkəl] *adj* : cronológico — **chronologically** [-kli] *adv*
chronology [krə'nɑləʤi] *n, pl* **-gies** : cronología *f*
chronometer [krə'nɑmətər] *n* : cronómetro *m*
chrysalis ['krɪsələs] *n, pl* **chrysalides** [krɪ'sælə₁diːz] *or* **chrysalises** : crisálida *f*
chrysanthemum [krɪ'sæntθəməm] *n* : crisantemo *m*
chubbiness ['ʧʌbinəs] *n* : gordura *f*
chubby ['ʧʌbi] *adj* **-bier; -est** : gordito, regordete, rechoncho
chuck¹ ['ʧʌk] *vt* **1** TOSS : tirar, lanzar, aventar *Col, Mex* **2 to chuck under the chin** : hacer la mamola
chuck² *n* **1** PAT : mamola *f*, palmada *f* **2** TOSS : lanzamiento *m* **3** *or* **chuck steak** : corte *m* de carne de res
chuckle¹ ['ʧʌkəl] *vi* **-led; -ling** : reírse entre dientes
chuckle² *n* : risita *f*, risa *f* ahogada

chug[1] ['ʧʌg] *vi* **chugged; chugging** : resoplar, traquetear

chug[2] *n* : resoplido *m*, traqueteo *m*

chum[1] ['ʧʌm] *vi* **chummed; chumming** : ser camaradas, ser cuates *Mex fam*

chum[2] *n* : amigo *m*, -ga *f*; camarada *mf*; compinche *mf fam*

chummy ['ʧʌmi] *adj* **-mier; -est** : amistoso ⟨they're very chummy : son muy amigos⟩

chump ['ʧʌmp] *n* : tonto *m*, -ta *f*; idiota *mf*

chunk ['ʧʌnk] *n* **1** PIECE : cacho *m*, pedazo *m*, trozo *m* **2** : cantidad *f* grande ⟨a chunk of money : mucho dinero⟩

chunky ['ʧʌnki] *adj* **chunkier; -est 1** STOCKY : fornido, robusto **2** : que contiene pedazos

church ['ʧərʧ] *n* **1** : iglesia *f* ⟨to go to church : ir a la iglesia⟩ **2** CHRISTIANS : iglesia *f*, conjunto *m* de fieles cristianos **3** DENOMINATION : confesión *f*, secta *f* **4** CONGREGATION : feligreses *mpl*, fieles *mpl*

churchgoer ['ʧərʧ,goːər] *n* : practicante *mf*

churchyard ['ʧərʧ,jɑrd] *n* : cementerio *m* (junto a una iglesia)

churn[1] ['ʧərn] *vt* **1** : batir (crema), hacer (mantequilla) **2** : agitar con fuerza, revolver — *vi* : agitarse, arremolinarse

churn[2] *n* : mantequera *f*

chute ['ʃuːt] *n* : conducto *m* inclinado, vertedero *m* (para basuras)

chutney ['ʧʌtni] *n, pl* **-neys** : chutney *m*

chutzpah ['hʊtspə, 'xʊt-, -,spɑ] *n* : descaro *m*, frescura *f*, cara *f fam*

cicada [sə'keɪdə, -'kɑ-] *n* : cigarra *f*, chicharra *f*

cider ['saɪdər] *n* **1** : jugo *m* (de manzana, etc.) **2 hard cider** : sidra *f*

cigar [sɪ'gɑr] *n* : puro *m*, cigarro *m*

cigarette [,sɪgə'rɛt, 'sɪgə,rɛt] *n* : cigarrillo *m*, cigarro *m*

cilantro [sɪ'lɑntro:, -'læn-] *n* : cilantro *m*

cinch[1] ['sɪnʧ] *vt* **1** : cinchar (un caballo) **2** ASSURE : asegurar

cinch[2] *n* **1** : cincha *f* (para caballos) **2** : algo fácil o seguro ⟨it's a cinch : es bien fácil, es pan comido⟩

cinchona [sɪn'ko:nə] *n* : quino *m*

cinder ['sɪndər] *n* **1** EMBER : brasa *f*, ascua *f* **2 cinders** *npl* ASHES : cenizas *fpl*

cinema ['sɪnəmə] *n* : cine *m*

cinematic [,sɪnə'mætɪk] *adj* : cinematográfico

cinnamon ['sɪnəmən] *n* : canela *f*

cipher ['saɪfər] *n* **1** ZERO : cero *m* **2** CODE : cifra *f*, clave *f*

circa ['sərkə] *prep* : alrededor de, hacia ⟨circa 1800 : hacia el año 1800⟩

circle[1] ['sərkəl] *v* **-cled; -cling** *vt* **1** : encerrar en un círculo, poner un círculo alrededor de **2** : girar alrededor de, dar vueltas a ⟨we circled the building twice : le dimos vueltas al edificio dos veces⟩ — *vi* : dar vueltas

circle[2] *n* **1** : círculo *m* **2** CYCLE : ciclo *m* ⟨to come full circle : volver al punto de partida⟩ **3** GROUP : círculo *m*, grupo *m* (social)

circuit ['sərkət] *n* **1** BOUNDARY : circuito *m*, perímetro *m* (de una zona o un territorio) **2** TOUR : circuito *m*, recorrido *m*, tour *m* **3** : circuito *m* (eléctrico) ⟨a short circuit : un cortocircuito⟩

circuitous [,sər'kju:ətəs] *adj* : sinuoso, tortuoso

circuitry ['sərkətri] *n, pl* **-ries** : sistema *m* de circuitos

circular[1] ['sərkjələr] *adj* ROUND : circular, redondo

circular[2] *n* : circular *f*

circulate ['sərkjə,leɪt] *v* **-lated; -lating** *vi* : circular — *vt* **1** : circular (noticias, etc.) **2** DISSEMINATE : hacer circular, divulgar

circulation [,sərkjə'leɪʃən] *n* : circulación *f*

circulatory ['sərkjələ,tori] *adj* : circulatorio

circumcise ['sərkəm,saɪz] *vt* **-cised; -cising** : circuncidar

circumcision [,sərkəm'sɪʒən, 'sərkəm,-] *n* : circuncisión *f*

circumference [sər'kʌmpfrənts] *n* : circunferencia *f*

circumflex ['sərkəm,flɛks] *n* : acento *m* circunflejo

circumlocution [,sərkəmlo'kju:ʃən] *n* : circunlocución *f*

circumnavigate [,sərkəm'nævə,geɪt] *vt* **-gated; -gating** : circunnavegar

circumscribe ['sərkəm,skraɪb] *vt* **-scribed; -scribing 1** : circunscribir, trazar una figura alrededor de **2** LIMIT : circunscribir, limitar

circumspect ['sərkəm,spɛkt] *adj* : circunspecto, prudente, cauto

circumspection [,sərkəm'spɛkʃən] *n* : circunspección *f*, cautela *f*

circumstance ['sərkəm,stænts] *n* **1** EVENT : circunstancia *f*, acontecimiento *m* **2 circumstances** *npl* SITUATION : circunstancias *fpl*, situación *f* ⟨under the circumstances : dadas las circunstancias⟩ ⟨under no circumstances : de ninguna manera, bajo ningún concepto⟩ **3 circumstances** *npl* : situación *f* económica

circumstantial [,sərkəm'stænʧəl] *adj* : circunstancial

circumvent [,sərkəm'vɛnt] *vt* : evadir, burlar (una ley o regla), sortear (una responsabilidad o dificultad)

circumvention [,sərkəm'vɛnʧən] *n* : evasión *f*

circus ['sərkəs] *n* : circo *m*

cirrhosis [sə'ro:sɪs] *n, pl* **-rhoses** [-'ro:,siːz] : cirrosis *f*

cirrus ['sɪrəs] *n, pl* **-ri** ['sɪr,aɪ] : cirro *m*

cistern ['sɪstərn] *n* : cisterna *f*, aljibe *m*

citadel ['sɪtədəl, -,dɛl] *n* FORTRESS : ciudadela *f*, fortaleza *f*

citation [saɪˈteɪʃən] *n* **1** SUMMONS : emplazamiento *m*, citación *f*, convocatoria *f* (judicial) **2** QUOTATION : cita *f* **3** COMMENDATION : elogio *m*, mención *f* (de honor)

cite [ˈsaɪt] *vt* **cited; citing 1** ARRAIGN, SUBPOENA : emplazar, citar, hacer comparecer (ante un tribunal) **2** QUOTE : citar **3** COMMEND : elogiar, honrar (oficialmente)

citizen [ˈsɪtəzən] *n* : ciudadano *m*, -na *f*

citizenry [ˈsɪtəzənri] *n, pl* **-ries** : ciudadanía *f*, conjunto *m* de ciudadanos

citizenship [ˈsɪtəzənˌʃɪp] *n* : ciudadanía *f* ⟨Nicaraguan citizenship : ciudadanía nicaragüense⟩

citron [ˈsɪtrən] *n* : cidra *f*

citrus [ˈsɪtrəs] *n, pl* **-rus** *or* **-ruses** : cítrico *m*

city [ˈsɪti] *n, pl* **cities** : ciudad *f*

civic [ˈsɪvɪk] *adj* : cívico

civics [ˈsɪvɪks] *ns & pl* : civismo *m*

civil [ˈsɪvəl] *adj* **1** : civil ⟨civil law : derecho civil⟩ **2** POLITE : civil, cortés

civilian [səˈvɪljən] *n* : civil *mf* ⟨soldiers and civilians : soldados y civiles⟩

civility [səˈvɪləti] *n, pl* **-ties** : cortesía *f*, educación *f*

civilization [ˌsɪvələˈzeɪʃən] *n* : civilización *f*

civilize [ˈsɪvəˌlaɪz] *vt* **-lized; -lizing** : civilizar — **civilized** *adj*

civil liberties *npl* : derechos *mpl* civiles

civilly [ˈsɪvəli] *adv* : cortésmente

civil rights *npl* : derechos *mpl* civiles

civil service *n* : administración *f* pública

civil war *n* : guerra *f* civil

clack[1] [ˈklæk] *vi* : tabletear

clack[2] *n* : tableteo *m*

clad [ˈklæd] *adj* **1** CLOTHED : vestido **2** COVERED : cubierto

claim[1] [ˈkleɪm] *vt* **1** DEMAND : reclamar, reivindicar ⟨she claimed her rights : reclamó sus derechos⟩ **2** MAINTAIN : afirmar, sostener ⟨they claim it's theirs : sostienen que es suyo⟩

claim[2] *n* **1** DEMAND : demanda *f*, reclamación *f* **2** DECLARATION : declaración *f*, afirmación *f* **3 to stake a claim** : reclamar, reivindicar

claimant [ˈkleɪmənt] *n* : demandante *mf* (ante un juez), pretendiente *mf* (al trono, etc.)

clairvoyance [klærˈvɔɪənts] *n* : clarividencia *f*

clairvoyant[1] [klærˈvɔɪənt] *adj* : clarividente

clairvoyant[2] *n* : clarividente *mf*

clam [ˈklæm] *n* : almeja *f*

clamber [ˈklæmbər] *vi* : treparse o subirse torpemente

clammy [ˈklæmi] *adj* **-mier; -est** : húmedo y algo frío

clamor[1] [ˈklæmər] *vi* : gritar, clamar

clamor[2] *n* : clamor *m*

clamorous [ˈklæmərəs] *adj* : clamoroso, ruidoso, estrepitoso

clamp[1] [ˈklæmp] *vt* : sujetar con abrazaderas

clamp[2] *n* : abrazadera *f*

clan [ˈklæn] *n* : clan *m*

clandestine [klænˈdɛstɪn] *adj* : clandestino, secreto

clang[1] [ˈklæŋ] *vi* : hacer resonar (dícese de un objeto metálico)

clang[2] *n* : ruido *m* metálico fuerte

clangor [ˈklæŋər, -gər] *n* : estruendo *m* metálico

clank[1] [ˈklæŋk] *vi* : producir un ruido metálico seco

clank[2] *n* : ruido *m* metálico seco

clannish [ˈklænɪʃ] *adj* : exclusivista

clap[1] [ˈklæp] *v* **clapped; clapping** *vt* **1** SLAP, STRIKE : golpear ruidosamente, dar una palmada ⟨to clap one's hands : batir palmas, dar palmadas⟩ **2** APPLAUD : aplaudir — *vi* APPLAUD : aplaudir

clap[2] *n* **1** SLAP : palmada *f*, golpecito *m* **2** NOISE : ruido *m* seco ⟨a clap of thunder : un trueno⟩

clapboard [ˈklæbərd, ˈklæpˌbord] *n* : tabla *f* de madera (para revestir muros)

clapper [ˈklæpər] *n* : badajo *m* (de una campana)

clarification [ˌklærəfəˈkeɪʃən] *n* : clarificación *f*

clarify [ˈklærəˌfaɪ] *vt* **-fied; -fying 1** EXPLAIN : aclarar **2** : clarificar (un líquido)

clarinet [ˌklærəˈnɛt] *n* : clarinete *m*

clarion [ˈklæriən] *adj* : claro y sonoro

clarity [ˈklærəti] *n* : claridad *f*, nitidez *f*

clash[1] [ˈklæʃ] *vi* **1** : sonar, chocarse ⟨the cymbals clashed : los platillos sonaron⟩ **2** : chocar, enfrentarse ⟨the students clashed with the police : los estudiantes se enfrentaron con la policía⟩ **3** CONFLICT : estar en conflicto, oponerse **4** : desentonar (dícese de los colores), coincidir (dícese de los datos)

clash[2] *n* **1** : ruido *m* (producido por un choque) **2** CONFLICT, CONFRONTATION : enfrentamiento *m*, conflicto *m*, choque *m* **3** : desentono *m* (de colores), coincidencia *f* (de datos)

clasp[1] [ˈklæsp] *vt* **1** FASTEN : sujetar, abrochar **2** EMBRACE, GRASP : agarrar, sujetar, abrazar

clasp[2] *n* **1** FASTENING : broche *m*, cierre *m* **2** EMBRACE, SQUEEZE : apretón *m*, abrazo *m*

class[1] [ˈklæs] *vt* : clasificar, catalogar

class[2] *n* **1** KIND, TYPE : clase *f*, tipo *m*, especie *f* **2** : clase *f*, rango *m* social ⟨the working class : la clase obrera⟩ **3** LESSON : clase *f*, curso *m* ⟨English class : clase de inglés⟩ **4** : conjunto *m* de estudiantes, clase *f* ⟨the class of '97 : la promoción del 97⟩

classic[1] [ˈklæsɪk] *adj* : clásico

classic[2] *n* : clásico *m*, obra *f* clásica

classical [ˈklæsɪkəl] *adj* : clásico — **classically** [-kli] *adv*

classicism [ˈklæsəˌsɪzəm] *n* : clasicismo *m*

classification [ˌklæsəfəˈkeɪʃən] *n* : clasificación *f*

classified [ˈklæsəˌfaɪd] *adj* **1** : clasificado ⟨classified ads : avisos clasificados⟩ **2** RESTRICTED : confidencial, secreto ⟨classified documents : documentos secretos⟩

classify [ˈklæsəˌfaɪ] *vt* **-fied; -fying** : clasificar, catalogar

classless [ˈklæsləs] *adj* : sin clases

classmate [ˈklæsˌmeɪt] *n* : compañero *m*, -ra *f* de clase

classroom [ˈklæsˌruːm] *n* : aula *f*, salón *m* de clase

clatter[1] [ˈklæt̬ər] *vi* : traquetear, hacer ruido

clatter[2] *n* : traqueteo *m*, ruido *m*, estrépito *m*

clause [ˈklɔz] *n* : cláusula *f*

claustrophobia [ˌklɔstrəˈfoːbiə] *n* : claustrofobia *f*

claustrophobic [ˌklɔstrəˈfoːbɪk] *adj* : claustrofóbico

clavicle [ˈklævɪkəl] *n* : clavícula *f*

claw[1] [ˈklɔ] *v* : arañar

claw[2] *n* : garra *f*, uña *f* (de un gato), pinza *f* (de un crustáceo)

clay [ˈkleɪ] *n* : arcilla *f*, barro *m*

clayey [ˈkleɪi] *adj* : arcilloso

clean[1] [ˈkliːn] *vt* : limpiar, lavar, asear

clean[2] *adv* : limpio, limpiamente ⟨to play clean : jugar limpio⟩

clean[3] *adj* **1** : limpio **2** UNADULTERATED : puro **3** IRREPROACHABLE : intachable, sin mancha ⟨to have a clean record : no tener antecedentes penales⟩ **4** DECENT : decente **5** COMPLETE : completo, absoluto ⟨a clean break with the past : un corte radical con el pasado⟩

cleaner [ˈkliːnər] *n* **1** : limpiador *m*, -dora *f* **2** : producto *m* de limpieza **3** DRY CLEANER : tintorería *f* (servicio)

cleanliness [ˈklɛnlinəs] *n* : limpieza *f*, aseo *m*

cleanly[1] [ˈkliːnli] *adv* : limpiamente, con limpieza

cleanly[2] [ˈklɛnli] *adj* **-lier; -est** : limpio, pulcro

cleanness [ˈkliːnnəs] *n* : limpieza *f*

cleanse [ˈklɛnz] *vt* **cleansed; cleansing** : limpiar, purificar

cleanser [ˈklɛnzər] *n* : limpiador *m*, purificador *m*

clear[1] [ˈklɪr] *vt* **1** CLARIFY : aclarar, clarificar (un líquido) **2** : despejar (una superficie), desatascar (un tubo), desmontar (una selva) ⟨to clear the table : levantar la mesa⟩ ⟨to clear one's throat : carraspear, aclararse la voz⟩ **3** EXONERATE : absolver, limpiar el nombre de **4** EARN : ganar, sacar (una ganancia de) **5** : pasar sin tocar ⟨he cleared the hurdle : saltó por encima de la valla⟩ **6 to clear up** RESOLVE : aclarar, resolver, esclarecer — *vi* **1**

DISPERSE : irse, despejarse, disiparse **2** : ser compensado (dícese de un cheque) **3 to clear up** : despejar (dícese del tiempo), mejorarse (dícese de una enfermedad)

clear[2] *adv* : claro, claramente

clear[3] *adj* **1** BRIGHT : claro, lúcido **2** FAIR : claro, despejado **3** TRANSPARENT : transparente, translúcido **4** EVIDENT, UNMISTAKABLE : evidente, claro, obvio **5** CERTAIN : seguro **6** UNOBSTRUCTED : despejado, libre

clear[4] *n* **1 in the clear** : inocente, libre de toda sospecha **2 in the clear** SAFE : fuera de peligro

clearance [ˈklɪrənts] *n* **1** CLEARING : despeje *m* **2** SPACE : espacio *m* (libre), margen *m* **3** AUTHORIZATION : autorización *f*, despacho *m* (de la aduana)

clearing [ˈklɪrɪŋ] *n* : claro *m* (de un bosque)

clearly [ˈklɪrli] *adv* **1** DISTINCTLY : claramente, directamente **2** OBVIOUSLY : obviamente, evidentemente

cleat [ˈkliːt] *n* **1** : taco *m* **2 cleats** *npl* : zapatos *mpl* deportivos (con tacos)

cleavage [ˈkliːvɪdʒ] *n* **1** CLEFT : hendidura *f*, raja *f* **2** : escote *m* (del busto)

cleave[1] [ˈkliːv] *vi* **cleaved** *or* **clove** [ˈkloːv]; **cleaving** ADHERE : adherirse, unirse

cleave[2] *vt* **cleaved; cleaving** SPLIT : hender, dividir, partir

cleaver [ˈkliːvər] *n* : cuchilla *f* de carnicero

clef [ˈklɛf] *n* : clave *f*

cleft [ˈklɛft] *n* : hendidura *f*, raja *f*, grieta *f*

clemency [ˈklɛməntsi] *n* : clemencia *f*

clement [ˈklɛmənt] *adj* **1** MERCIFUL : clemente, piadoso **2** MILD : clemente, apacible

clench [ˈklɛntʃ] *vt* **1** CLUTCH : agarrar **2** TIGHTEN : apretar (el puño, los dientes)

clergy [ˈklərdʒi] *n, pl* **-gies** : clero *m*

clergyman [ˈklərdʒimən] *n, pl* **-men** [-mən, -ˌmɛn] : clérigo *m*

cleric [ˈklɛrɪk] *n* : clérigo *m*, -ga *f*

clerical [ˈklɛrɪkəl] *adj* **1** : clerical ⟨a clerical collar : un alzacuello⟩ **2** : de oficina ⟨clerical staff : personal de oficina⟩

clerk[1] [ˈklərk, *Brit* ˈklɑrk] *vi* : trabajar de oficinista, trabajar de dependiente

clerk[2] *n* **1** : funcionario *m*, -ria *f* (de una oficina gubernamental) **2** : oficinista *mf*, empleado *m*, -da *f* de oficina **3** SALESPERSON : dependiente *m*, -ta *f*

clever [ˈklɛvər] *adj* **1** SKILLFUL : ingenioso, hábil **2** SMART : listo, inteligente, astuto

cleverly [ˈklɛvərli] *adv* **1** SKILLFULLY : ingeniosamente, hábilmente **2** INTELLIGENTLY : inteligentemente

cleverness [ˈklɛvərnəs] *n* **1** SKILL : ingenio *m*, habilidad *f* **2** INTELLIGENCE : inteligencia *f*

clew ['klu:] → clue
cliché [kli'ʃeɪ] n : cliché m, tópico m
click¹ ['klɪk] vt 1 : chasquear (los dedos, etc.) ⟨to click one's heels : dar un taconazo⟩ 2 : hacer clic en (un botón, etc.) — vi 1 : hacer clic 2 SNAP : chasquear 3 SUCCEED : tener éxito 4 GET ALONG : congeniar, llevarse bien
click² n : chasquido m (de los dedos, etc.), clic m (de un botón, etc.)
client ['klaɪənt] n : cliente m, -ta f
clientele [ˌklaɪən'tɛl, ˌkli:-] n : clientela f
cliff ['klɪf] n : acantilado m, precipicio m, risco m
climate ['klaɪmət] n : clima m
climatic [klaɪ'mæṭɪk, klə-] adj : climático
climax¹ ['klaɪˌmæks] vi : llegar al punto culminante, culminar — vt : ser el punto culminante de
climax² n : clímax m, punto m culminante
climb¹ ['klaɪm] vt : escalar, trepar a, subir a ⟨to climb a mountain : escalar una montaña⟩ — vi 1 RISE : subir, ascender ⟨prices are climbing : los precios están subiendo⟩ 2 : subirse, treparse ⟨to climb up a tree : treparse a un árbol⟩
climb² n : ascenso m, subida f
climber ['klaɪmər] n 1 : escalador m, -dora f ⟨a mountain climber : un alpinista⟩ 2 : trepadora f (planta)
clinch¹ ['klɪntʃ] vt 1 FASTEN, SECURE : remachar (un clavo), afianzar, abrochar 2 SETTLE : decidir, cerrar ⟨to clinch the title : ganar el título⟩
clinch² n : abrazo m, clinch m (en el boxeo)
clincher ['klɪntʃər] n : argumento m decisivo
cling ['klɪŋ] vi clung ['klʌŋ]; clinging 1 STICK : adherirse, pegarse 2 : aferrarse, agarrarse ⟨he clung to the railing : se aferró a la barandilla⟩
clinic ['klɪnɪk] n : clínica f
clinical ['klɪnɪkəl] adj : clínico — clinically [-kli] adv
clink¹ ['klɪŋk] vi : tintinear
clink² n : tintineo m
clip¹ ['klɪp] vt clipped; clipping 1 CUT : cortar, recortar 2 HIT : golpear, dar un puñetazo a 3 FASTEN : sujetar (con un clip)
clip² n 1 → clippers 2 BLOW : golpe m, puñetazo m 3 PACE : paso m rápido 4 FASTENER : clip m ⟨a paper clip : un sujetapapeles⟩
clipper ['klɪpər] n 1 : clíper m (buque de vela) 2 clippers npl : tijeras fpl ⟨nail clippers : cortauñas⟩
clique ['kli:k, 'klɪk] n : grupo m exclusivo, camarilla f (de políticos)
clitoris ['klɪṭərəs, klɪ'tɔrəs] n, pl clitorides [-'tɔrəˌdi:z] : clítoris m
cloak¹ ['klo:k] vt : encubrir, envolver (en un manto de)

cloak² n : capa f, capote m, manto m ⟨under the cloak of darkness : al amparo de la oscuridad⟩
clobber ['klɑbər] vt : dar una paliza a
clock¹ ['klɑk] vt : cronometrar
clock² n 1 : reloj m (de pared), cronómetro m (en deportes o competencias) 2 around the clock : las veinticuatro horas
clockwise ['klɑkˌwaɪz] adv & adj : en la dirección de las manecillas del reloj
clockwork ['klɑkˌwərk] n : mecanismo m de relojería
clod ['klɑd] n 1 : terrón m 2 OAF : zoquete mf
clog¹ ['klɑg] v clogged; clogging vt 1 HINDER : estorbar, impedir 2 BLOCK : atascar, tapar — vi : atascarse, taparse
clog² n 1 OBSTACLE : traba f, impedimento m, estorbo m 2 : zueco m (zapato)
cloister¹ ['klɔɪstər] vt : enclaustrar
cloister² n : claustro m
clone ['klo:n] n 1 : clon m (de un organismo) 2 COPY : copia f, reproducción f
close¹ ['klo:z] v closed; closing vt : cerrar — vi 1 : cerrarse, cerrar 2 TERMINATE : concluirse, terminar 3 to close in APPROACH : acercarse, aproximarse
close² ['klo:s] adv : cerca, de cerca
close³ adj closer; closest 1 CONFINING : restrictivo, estrecho 2 SECRETIVE : reservado 3 STRICT : estricto, detallado 4 STUFFY : cargado, bochornoso (dícese del tiempo) 5 TIGHT : apretado, entallado, ceñido ⟨it's a close fit : es muy apretado⟩ 6 NEAR : cercano, próximo 7 INTIMATE : íntimo ⟨close friends : amigos íntimos⟩ 8 ACCURATE : fiel, exacto 9 : reñido ⟨a close election : una elección muy reñida⟩
close⁴ ['klo:z] n : fin m, final m, conclusión f
closely ['klo:sli] adv : cerca, de cerca
closeness ['klo:snəs] n 1 NEARNESS : cercanía f, proximidad f 2 INTIMACY : intimidad f
closet¹ ['klɑzət] vt to be closeted with : estar encerrado con
closet² n : armario m, guardarropa f, clóset m
closure ['klo:ʒər] n 1 CLOSING, END : cierre m, clausura f, fin m 2 FASTENER : cierre m
clot¹ ['klɑt] v clotted; clotting vt : coagular, cuajar — vi : cuajarse, coagularse
clot² n : coágulo m
cloth ['klɔθ] n, pl cloths ['klɔðz, 'klɔθs] 1 FABRIC : tela f 2 RAG : trapo m 3 TABLECLOTH : mantel m
clothe ['klo:ð] vt clothed or clad ['klæd]; clothing DRESS : vestir, arropar, ataviar
clothes ['klo:z, 'klo:ðz] npl 1 CLOTHING : ropa f 2 BEDCLOTHES : ropa f de cama
clothespin ['klo:zˌpɪn] n : pinza f (para la ropa)

clothing ['klo:ðɪŋ] *n* : ropa *f*, indumentaria *f*

cloud¹ ['klaʊd] *vt* : nublar, oscurecer — *vi* **to cloud over** : nublarse

cloud² *n* : nube *f*

cloudburst ['klaʊd₁bərst] *n* : chaparrón *m*, aguacero *m*

cloudless ['klaʊdləs] *adj* : despejado, claro

cloudy ['klaʊdi] *adj* **cloudier; -est** : nublado, nuboso

clout¹ ['klaʊt] *vt* : bofetear, dar un tortazo a

clout² *n* **1** BLOW : golpe *m*, tortazo *m* *fam* **2** INFLUENCE : influencia *f*, palanca *f fam*

clove¹ ['klo:v] *n* **1** : diente *m* (de ajo) **2** : clavo *m* (especia)

clove² → **cleave**

cloven hoof ['klo:vən] *n* : pezuña *f* hendida

clover ['klo:vər] *n* : trébol *m*

cloverleaf ['klo:vər₁li:f] *n*, *pl* **-leafs** *or* **-leaves** [-₁li:vz] : intersección *f* en trébol

clown¹ ['klaʊn] *vi* : payasear, bromear ⟨stop clowning around : déjate de payasadas⟩

clown² *n* : payaso *m*, -sa *f*

clownish ['klaʊnɪʃ] *adj* **1** : de payaso **2** BOORISH : grosero — **clownishly** *adv*

cloying ['klɔɪɪŋ] *adj* : empalagoso, meloso

club¹ ['klʌb] *vt* **clubbed; clubbing** : aporrear, dar garrotazos a

club² *n* **1** CUDGEL : garrote *m*, porra *f* **2** : palo *m* ⟨golf club : palo de golf⟩ **3** : trébol *m* (naipe) **4** ASSOCIATION : club *m*

clubfoot ['klʌb₁fʊt] *n*, *pl* **-feet** : pie *m* deforme

clubhouse ['klʌb₁haʊs] *n* : sede *f* de un club

cluck¹ ['klʌk] *vi* : cloquear, cacarear

cluck² *n* : cloqueo *m*, cacareo *m*

clue¹ ['klu:] *vt* **clued; clueing** *or* **cluing** *or* **to clue in** : dar una pista a, informar

clue² *n* : pista *f*, indicio *m*

clump¹ ['klʌmp] *vi* **1** : caminar con pisadas fuertes **2** LUMP : agruparse, aglutinarse — *vt* : amontonar

clump² *n* **1** : grupo *m* (de arbustos o árboles), terrón *m* (de tierra) **2** : pisada *f* fuerte

clumsily ['klʌmzəli] *adv* : torpemente, sin gracia

clumsiness ['klʌmzinəs] *n* : torpeza *f*

clumsy ['klʌmzi] *adj* **-sier; -est 1** AWKWARD : torpe, desmañado **2** TACTLESS : carente de tacto, poco delicado

clung → **cling**

clunky ['klʌŋki] *adj* : torpe, poco elegante

cluster¹ ['klʌstər] *vt* : agrupar, juntar — *vi* : agruparse, apiñarse, arracimarse

cluster² *n* : grupo *m*, conjunto *m*, racimo *m* (de uvas)

clutch¹ ['klʌtʃ] *vt* : agarrar, asir — *vi* **to clutch at** : tratar de agarrar

clutch² *n* **1** GRASP, GRIP : agarre *m*, apretón *m* **2** : embrague *m*, clutch *m* (de una máquina) **3** **clutches** *npl* : garras *fpl* ⟨he fell into their clutches : cayó en sus garras⟩

clutter¹ ['klʌtər] *vt* : atiborrar o atestar de cosas, llenar desordenadamente

clutter² *n* : desorden *m*, revoltijo *m*

coach¹ ['ko:tʃ] *vt* : entrenar (atletas, artistas), preparar (alumnos)

coach² *n* **1** CARRIAGE : coche *m*, carruaje *m*, carroza *f* **2** : vagón *m* de pasajeros (de un tren) **3** BUS : autobús *m*, ómnibus *m* **4** : pasaje *m* aéreo de segunda clase **5** TRAINER : entrenador *m*, -dora *f*

coagulate [ko'ægjə₁leɪt] *v* **-lated; -lating** *vt* : coagular, cuajar — *vi* : coagularse, cuajarse

coal ['ko:l] *n* **1** EMBER : ascua *f*, brasa *f* **2** : carbón *m* ⟨a coal mine : una mina de carbón⟩

coalesce [₁ko:ə'lɛs] *vi* **-alesced; -alescing** : unirse

coalition [₁ko:ə'lɪʃən] *n* : coalición *f*

coarse ['kors] *adj* **coarser; -est 1** : grueso (dícese de la arena o la sal), basto (dícese de las telas), áspero (dícese de la piel) **2** CRUDE, ROUGH : basto, tosco, ordinario **3** VULGAR : grosero — **coarsely** *adv*

coarsen ['korsən] *vt* : hacer áspero o basto — *vi* : volverse áspero o basto

coarseness ['korsnəs] *n* : aspereza *f*, tosquedad *f*

coast¹ ['ko:st] *vi* : deslizarse, rodar sin impulso

coast² *n* : costa *f*, litoral *m*

coastal ['ko:stəl] *adj* : costero

coaster ['ko:stər] *n* : posavasos *m*

coast guard *n* : guardia *f* costera, guardacostas *mpl*

coastline ['ko:st₁laɪn] *n* : costa *f*

coat¹ ['ko:t] *vt* : cubrir, revestir, bañar (en un líquido)

coat² *n* **1** : abrigo *m* ⟨a sport coat : una chaqueta, un saco⟩ **2** : pelaje *m* (de animales) **3** LAYER : capa *f*, mano *f* (de pintura)

coating ['ko:tɪŋ] *n* : capa *f*

coat of arms *n* : escudo *m* de armas

coax ['ko:ks] *vt* : engatusar, persuadir

cob ['kab] → **corncob**

cobalt ['ko:₁bɔlt] *n* : cobalto *m*

cobble ['kabəl] *vt* **cobbled; cobbling 1** : fabricar o remendar (zapatos) **2 to cobble together** : improvisar, hacer apresuradamente

cobbler ['kablər] *n* **1** SHOEMAKER : zapatero *m*, -ra *f* **2 fruit cobbler** : tarta *f* de fruta

cobblestone ['kabəl₁sto:n] *n* : adoquín *m*

cobra ['ko:brə] *n* : cobra *f*

cobweb ['kab₁wɛb] *n* : telaraña *f*

coca ['ko:kə] *n* : coca *f*

cocaine [ko:'keɪn, 'ko:ˌkeɪn] n : cocaína f

cock[1] ['kɑk] vt 1 : ladear ⟨to cock one's head : ladear la cabeza⟩ 2 : montar, amartillar (un arma de fuego)

cock[2] n 1 ROOSTER : gallo m 2 FAUCET : grifo m, llave f 3 : martillo m (de un arma de fuego)

cockatoo ['kɑkəˌtuː] n, pl -toos : cacatúa f

cockeyed ['kɑkˌaɪd] adj 1 ASKEW : ladeado, torcido, chueco 2 ABSURD : disparatado, absurdo

cockfight ['kɑkˌfaɪt] n : pelea f de gallos

cockiness ['kɑkinəs] n : arrogancia f

cockle ['kɑkəl] n : berberecho m

cockpit ['kɑkˌpɪt] n : cabina f

cockroach ['kɑkˌroːtʃ] n : cucaracha f

cocktail ['kɑkˌteɪl] n 1 : coctel m, cóctel m 2 APPETIZER : aperitivo m

cocky ['kɑki] adj cockier; -est : creído, engreído

cocoa ['koːˌkoː] n 1 CACAO : cacao m 2 : cocoa f, chocolate m (bebida)

coconut ['koːkəˌnʌt] n : coco m

cocoon [kə'kuːn] n : capullo m

cod ['kɑd] n, pl cod : bacalao m

coddle ['kɑdəl] vt -dled; -dling : mimar, consentir

code ['koːd] n 1 : código m ⟨civil code : código civil⟩ 2 : código m, clave f ⟨secret code : clave secreta⟩

codeine ['koːˌdiːn] n : codeína f

codex ['koːˌdɛks] n, pl -dexes [-ˌdɛksəz] or -dices [-dəˌsiːz] : códice m

codger ['kɑdʒər] n : viejo m, vejete m

codify ['kɑdəˌfaɪ, 'koː-] vt -fied; -fying : codificar

coeducation [ˌkoːˌɛdʒə'keɪʃən] n : coeducación f, enseñanza f mixta

coeducational [ˌkoːˌɛdʒə'keɪʃənəl] adj : mixto

coefficient [ˌkoːə'fɪʃənt] n : coeficiente m

coerce [ko'ərs] vt -erced; -ercing : coaccionar, forzar, obligar

coercion [ko'ərʒən, -ʃən] n : coacción f

coercive [ko'ərsɪv] adj : coactivo

coexist [ˌkoːɪg'zɪst] vi : coexistir

coexistence [ˌkoːɪg'zɪstənts] n : coexistencia f

coffee ['kɔfi] n : café m

coffeepot ['kɔfiˌpɑt] n : cafetera f

coffee table n : mesa f de centro

coffer ['kɔfər] n : cofre m

coffin ['kɔfən] n : ataúd m, féretro m

cog ['kɑg] n : diente m (de una rueda dentada)

cogent ['koːdʒənt] adj : convincente, persuasivo

cogitate ['kɑdʒəˌteɪt] vi -tated; -tating : reflexionar, meditar, discurrir

cogitation [ˌkɑdʒə'teɪʃən] n : reflexión f, meditación f

cognac ['koːnˌjæk] n : coñac m

cognate ['kɑgˌneɪt] adj : relacionado, afín

cognition [kɑg'nɪʃən] n : cognición f

cognitive ['kɑgnətɪv] adj : cognitivo

cogwheel ['kɑgˌhwiːl] n : rueda f dentada

cohabit [ˌkoː'hæbət] vi : cohabitar

cohere [ko'hɪr] vi -hered; -hering 1 ADHERE : adherirse, pegarse 2 : ser coherente o congruente

coherence [ko'hɪrənts] n : coherencia f, congruencia f

coherent [ko'hɪrənt] adj : coherente, congruente — coherently adv

cohesion [ko'hiːʒən] n : cohesión f

cohesive [ko'hiːsɪv, -zɪv] adj : cohesivo

cohort ['koːˌhɔrt] n 1 : cohorte f (de soldados) 2 COMPANION : compañero m, -ra f; colega mf

coiffure [kwɑ'fjʊr] n : peinado m

coil[1] ['kɔɪl] vt : enrollar — vi : enrollarse, enroscarse

coil[2] n : rollo m (de cuerda, etc.), espiral f (de humo)

coin[1] ['kɔɪn] vt 1 MINT : acuñar (moneda) 2 INVENT : acuñar, crear, inventar ⟨to coin a phrase : como se suele decir⟩

coin[2] n : moneda f

coincide [ˌkoːɪn'saɪd, 'koːɪnˌsaɪd] vi -cided; -ciding : coincidir

coincidence [ko'ɪntsədənts] n : coincidencia f, casualidad f ⟨what a coincidence! : ¡qué casualidad!⟩

coincident [ko'ɪntsədənt] adj : coincidente, concurrente

coincidental [koˌɪntsə'dɛntəl] adj : casual, accidental, fortuito

coitus ['koːətəs] n : coito m

coke ['koːk] n : coque m

colander ['kɑləndər, 'kʌ-] n : colador m

cold[1] ['koːld] adj : frío ⟨it's cold out : hace frío⟩ ⟨a cold reception : una fría recepción⟩ ⟨in cold blood : a sangre fría⟩

cold[2] n 1 : frío m ⟨to feel the cold : sentir frío⟩ 2 : resfriado m, catarro m ⟨to catch a cold : resfriarse⟩

cold-blooded ['koːld'blʌdəd] adj 1 CRUEL : cruel, despiadado 2 : de sangre fría (dícese de los reptiles, etc.)

coldly ['koːldli] adv : fríamente, con frialdad

coldness ['koːldnəs] n : frialdad f (de una persona o una actitud), frío m (de la temperatura)

coleslaw ['koːlˌslɔ] n : ensalada f de col

colic ['kɑlɪk] n : cólico m

coliseum [ˌkɑlə'siːəm] n : coliseo m, arena f

collaborate [kə'læbəˌreɪt] vi -rated; -rating : colaborar

collaboration [kəˌlæbə'reɪʃə n] n : colaboración f

collaborator [kə'læbəˌreɪtər] n 1 COLLEAGUE : colaborador m, -dora f 2 TRAITOR : colaboracionista mf

collage [kə'lɑʒ] n : collage m

collapse[1] [kə'læps] vi -lapsed; -lapsing 1 : derrumbarse, desplomarse, hundirse ⟨the building collapsed : el edificio se derrumbó⟩ **2** FALL : desplomarse, caerse ⟨he collapsed on the bed : se desplomó en la cama⟩ ⟨to collapse with laughter : morirse de risa⟩ **3** FAIL : fracasar, quebrar, arruinarse **4** FOLD : plegarse

collapse² *n* **1** FALL : derrumbe *m*, desplome *m* **2** BREAKDOWN, FAILURE : fracaso *m*, colapso *m* (físico), quiebra *f* (económica)

collapsible [kə'læpsəbəl] *adj* : plegable

collar¹ ['kɑlər] *vt* : agarrar, atrapar

collar² *n* : cuello *m*

collarbone ['kɑlər,bo:n] *n* : clavícula *f*

collate [kə'leɪt; 'kɑ,leɪt, 'ko:-] *vt* -**lated**; -**lating 1** COMPARE : cotejar, comparar **2** : ordenar, recopilar (páginas)

collateral¹ [kə'læţərəl] *adj* : colateral

collateral² *n* : garantía *f*, fianza *f*, prenda *f*

colleague ['kɑ,li:g] *n* : colega *mf*; compañero *m*, -ra *f*

collect¹ [kə'lɛkt] *vt* **1** GATHER : recopilar, reunir, recoger ⟨she collected her thoughts : puso en orden sus ideas⟩ **2** : coleccionar, juntar ⟨to collect stamps : coleccionar timbres⟩ **3** : cobrar (una deuda), recaudar (un impuesto) **4** DRAW : cobrar, percibir (un sueldo, etc.) — *vi* **1** ACCUMULATE : acumularse, juntarse **2** CONGREGATE : congregarse, reunirse

collect² *adv & adj* : por cobrar, a cobro revertido

collectible *or* **collectable** [kə'lɛktəbəl] *adj* : coleccionable

collection [kə'lɛkʃən] *n* **1** COLLECTING : colecta *f* (de contribuciones), cobro *m* (de deudas), recaudación *f* (de impuestos) **2** GROUP : colección *f* (de objetos), grupo *m* (de personas)

collective¹ [kə'lɛktɪv] *adj* : colectivo — **collectively** *adv*

collective² *n* : colectivo *m*

collector [kə'lɛktər] *n* **1** : coleccionista *mf* (de objetos) **2** : cobrador *m*, -dora *f* (de deudas)

college ['kɑlɪʤ] *n* **1** : universidad *f* **2** : colegio *m* (de electores o profesionales)

collegiate [kə'li:ʤət] *adj* : universitario

collide [kə'laɪd] *vi* -**lided**; -**liding** : chocar, colisionar, estrellarse

collie ['kɑli] *n* : collie *mf*

collision [kə'lɪʒən] *n* : choque *m*, colisión *f*

colloquial [kə'lo:kwiəl] *adj* : coloquial

colloquialism [kə'lo:kwiə,lɪzəm] *n* : expresión *f* coloquial

collusion [kə'lu:ʒən] *n* : colusión *f*

cologne [kə'lo:n] *n* : colonia *f*

Colombian [kə'lʌmbiən] *n* : colombiano *m*, -na *f* — **Colombian** *adj*

colon¹ ['ko:lən] *n*, *pl* **colons** *or* **cola** [-lə] : colon *m* (de los intestinos)

colon² *n*, *pl* **colons** : dos puntos *mpl* (signo ortográfico)

colonel ['kərnəl] *n* : coronel *m*

colonial¹ [kə'lo:niəl] *adj* : colonial

colonial² *n* : colono *m*, -na *f*

colonist ['kɑlənɪst] *n* : colono *m*, -na *f*; colonizador *m*, -dora *f*

colonization [,kɑlənə'zeɪʃən] *n* : colonización *f*

colonize ['kɑlə,naɪz] *vt* -**nized**; -**nizing 1** : establecer una colonia en **2** SETTLE : colonizar

colonnade [,kɑlə'neɪd] *n* : columnata *f*

colony ['kɑləni] *n*, *pl* -**nies** : colonia *f*

color¹ ['kʌlər] *vt* **1** : colorear, pintar **2** INFLUENCE : influir en, influenciar — *vi* BLUSH : sonrojarse, ruborizarse

color² *n* **1** : color *m* ⟨primary colors : colores primarios⟩ **2** INTEREST, VIVIDNESS : color *m*, colorido *m* ⟨local color : color local⟩

coloration [kələ'reɪʃən] *n* : coloración *f*

color–blind ['kʌlər,blaɪnd] *adj* : daltónico

color blindness *n* : daltonismo *m*

colored ['kʌlərd] *adj* **1** : de color (dícese de los objetos) **2** : de color, negro (dícese de las personas)

colorfast ['kʌlər,fæst] *adj* : que no se destiñe

colorful ['kʌlərfəl] *adj* **1** : lleno de colorido, de colores vivos **2** PICTURESQUE, STRIKING : pintoresco, llamativo

coloring ['kələrɪŋ] *n* **1** : color *m*, colorido *m* **2 food coloring** : colorante *m*

colorless ['kʌlərləs] *adj* **1** : incoloro, sin color **2** DULL : soso, aburrido

colossal [kə'lɑsəl] *adj* : colosal

colossus [kə'lɑsəs] *n*, *pl* -**si** [-,saɪ] : coloso *m*

colt ['ko:lt] *n* : potro *m*, potranco *m*

column ['kɑləm] *n* : columna *f*

columnist ['kɑləmnɪst, -ləmɪst] *n* : columnista *mf*

coma ['ko:mə] *n* : coma *m*, estado *m* de coma

Comanche [kə'mæntʃi] *n* : comanche *mf* — **Comanche** *adj*

comatose ['ko:mə,to:s, 'kɑ-] *adj* : comatoso, en estado de coma

comb¹ ['ko:m] *vt* **1** : peinar (el pelo) **2** SEARCH : peinar, rastrear, registrar a fondo

comb² *n* **1** : peine *m* **2** : cresta *f* (de un gallo)

combat¹ [kəm'bæt, 'kɑm,bæt] *vt* -**bated** *or* -**batted**; -**bating** *or* -**batting** : combatir, luchar contra

combat² ['kɑm,bæt] *n* : combate *m*, lucha *f*

combatant [kəm'bætənt] *n* : combatiente *mf*

combative [kəm'bæţɪv] *adj* : combativo

combination [,kɑmbə'neɪʃən] *n* : combinación *f*

combine¹ [kəm'baɪn] *v* -**bined**; -**bining** *vt* : combinar, aunar — *vi* : combinarse, mezclarse

combine² ['kɑm,baɪn] *n* **1** ALLIANCE : alianza *f* comercial o política **2** HARVESTER : cosechadora *f*

combustible [kəm'bʌstəbəl] *adj* : inflamable, combustible
combustion [kəm'bʌstʃən] *n* : combustión *f*
come ['kʌm] *vi* came ['keɪm]; **come; coming 1** APPROACH : venir, aproximarse ⟨here they come : acá vienen⟩ **2** ARRIVE : venir, llegar, alcanzar ⟨they came yesterday : vinieron ayer⟩ **3** ORIGINATE : venir, provenir ⟨this wine comes from France : este vino viene de Francia⟩ **4** AMOUNT : llegar, ascender ⟨the investment came to two million : la inversión llegó a dos millones⟩ **5 to come clean** : confesar, desahogar la conciencia **6 to come into** ACQUIRE : adquirir ⟨to come into a fortune : heredar una fortuna⟩ **7 to come off** SUCCEED : tener éxito, ser un éxito **8 to come out** : salir, aparecer, publicarse **9 to come to** REVIVE : recobrar el conocimiento, volver en sí **10 to come to pass** HAPPEN : acontecer **11 to come to terms** : llegar a un acuerdo
comeback ['kʌm,bæk] *n* **1** RETORT : réplica *f*, respuesta *f* **2** RETURN : retorno *m*, regreso *m* ⟨the champion announced his comeback : el campeón anunció su regreso⟩
come back *vi* **1** RETORT : replicar, contestar **2** RETURN : volver ⟨come back here! : ¡vuelve acá!⟩ ⟨that style's coming back : ese estilo está volviendo⟩
comedian [kə'mi:diən] *n* : cómico *m*, -ca *f*; humorista *mf*
comedienne [kə,mi:di'ɛn] *n* : cómica *f*, humorista *f*
comedy ['kɑmədi] *n*, *pl* **-dies** : comedia *f*
comely ['kʌmli] *adj* **-lier; -est** : bello, bonito
comet ['kɑmət] *n* : cometa *m*
comfort[1] ['kʌmpfərt] *vt* **1** CHEER : confortar, alentar **2** CONSOLE : consolar
comfort[2] *n* **1** CONSOLATION : consuelo *m* **2** WELL-BEING : confort *m*, bienestar *m* **3** CONVENIENCE : comodidad *f* ⟨the comforts of home : las comodidades del hogar⟩
comfortable ['kʌmpfərt̬əbəl, 'kʌmpftə-] *adj* : cómodo, confortable — **comfortably** ['kʌmpfərt̬əbli, 'kʌmpftə-] *adv*
comforter ['kʌmpfərt̬ər] *n* QUILT : edredón *m*, cobertor *m*
comic[1] ['kɑmɪk] *adj* : cómico, humorístico
comic[2] *n* **1** COMEDIAN : cómico *m*, -ca *f*; humorista *mf* **2** *or* **comic book** : historieta *f*, cómic *m*
comical ['kɑmɪkəl] *adj* : cómico, gracioso, chistoso
comic strip *n* : tira *f* cómica, historieta *f*
coming ['kʌmɪŋ] *adj* : siguiente, próximo, que viene
comma ['kɑmə] *n* : coma *f*

command[1] [kə'mænd] *vt* **1** ORDER : ordenar, mandar **2** CONTROL, DIRECT : comandar, tener el mando de — *vi* **1** : dar órdenes **2** GOVERN : estar al mando *m*, gobernar
command[2] *n* **1** CONTROL, LEADERSHIP : mando *m*, control *m*, dirección *f* **2** ORDER : orden *f*, mandato *m* **3** MASTERY : maestría *f*, destreza *f*, dominio *m* **4** : tropa *f* asignada a un comandante
commandant ['kɑmən,dɑnt, -,dænt] *n* : comandante *mf*
commandeer [,kɑmən'dɪr] *vt* : piratear, secuestrar (un vehículo, etc.)
commander [kə'mændər] *n* : comandante *mf*
commandment [kə'mændmənt] *n* : mandamiento *m*, orden *f* ⟨the Ten Commandments : los diez mandamientos⟩
commando [kə'mændo:] *n* : comando *m*
commemorate [kə'mɛmə,reɪt] *vt* **-rated; -rating** : conmemorar
commemoration [kə,mɛmə'reɪʃən] *n* : conmemoración *f*
commemorative [kə'mɛmrət̬ɪv, -'mɛmə,reɪt̬ɪv] *adj* : conmemorativo
commence [kə'mɛnts] *v* **-menced; -mencing** *vt* : iniciar, comenzar — *vi* : iniciarse, comenzar
commencement [kə'mɛntsmənt] *n* **1** BEGINNING : inicio *m*, comienzo *m* **2** : ceremonia *f* de graduación
commend [kə'mɛnd] *vt* **1** ENTRUST : encomendar **2** RECOMMEND : recomendar **3** PRAISE : elogiar, alabar
commendable [kə'mɛndəbəl] *adj* : loable, meritorio, encomiable
commendation [,kɑmən'deɪʃən, -,mɛn-] *n* : elogio *m*, encomio *m*
commensurate [kə'mɛntsərət, -'mɛntʃurət] *adj* : proporcionado ⟨commensurate with : en proporción a⟩
comment[1] ['kɑ,mɛnt] *vi* **1** : hacer comentarios **2 to comment on** : comentar, hacer comentarios sobre
comment[2] *n* : comentario *m*, observación *f*
commentary ['kɑmən,tɛri] *n*, *pl* **-taries** : comentario *m*, crónica *f* (deportiva)
commentator ['kɑmən,teɪt̬ər] *n* : comentarista *mf*, cronista *mf* (de deportes)
commerce ['kɑmərs] *n* : comercio *m*
commercial[1] [kə'mərʃəl] *adj* : comercial — **commercially** *adv*
commercial[2] *n* : comercial *m*
commercialize [kə'mərʃə,laɪz] *vt* **-ized; -izing** : comercializar
commiserate [kə'mɪzə,reɪt] *vi* **-ated; -ating** : compadecerse, consolarse
commiseration [kə,mɪzə'reɪʃən] *n* : conmiseración *f*
commission[1] [kə'mɪʃən] *vt* **1** : nombrar (un oficial) **2** : comisionar, encargar ⟨to commission a painting : encargar una pintura⟩

commission² *n* **1** : nombramiento *m* (al grado de oficial) **2** COMMITTEE : comisión *f*, comité *m* **3** COMMITTING : comisión *f*, realización *f* (de un acto) **4** PERCENTAGE : comisión *f* ⟨sales commissions : comisiones de venta⟩
commissioned officer *n* : oficial *mf*
commissioner [kə'mɪʃənər] *n* **1** : comisionado *m*, -da *f*; miembro *m* de una comisión **2** : comisario *m*, -ria *f* (de policía, etc.)
commit [kə'mɪt] *vt* **-mitted; -mitting 1** ENTRUST : encomendar, confiar **2** CONFINE : internar (en un hospital), encarcelar (en una prisión) **3** PERPETRATE : cometer ⟨to commit a crime : cometer un crimen⟩ **4 to commit oneself** : comprometerse
commitment [kə'mɪtmənt] *n* **1** RESPONSIBILITY : compromiso *m*, responsabilidad *f* **2** DEDICATION : dedicación *f*, devoción *f* ⟨commitment to the cause : devoción a la causa⟩
committee [kə'mɪt̬i] *n* : comité *m*
commodious [kə'mo:diəs] *adj* SPACIOUS : amplio, espacioso
commodity [kə'mɑdət̬i] *n, pl* **-ties** : artículo *m* de comercio, mercancía *f*, mercadería *f*
commodore ['kɑmə,dor] *n* : comodoro *m*
common¹ ['kɑmən] *adj* **1** PUBLIC : común, público ⟨the common good : el bien común⟩ **2** SHARED : común ⟨a common interest : un interés común⟩ **3** GENERAL : común, general ⟨it's common knowledge : todo el mundo lo sabe⟩ **4** ORDINARY : ordinario, común y corriente ⟨the common man : el hombre medio, el hombre de la calle⟩
common² *n* **1** : tierra *f* comunal **2 in ～** : en común
common cold *n* : resfriado *m* común
common denominator *n* : denominador *m* común
commoner ['kɑmənər] *n* : plebeyo *m*, -ya *f*
commonly ['kɑmənli] *adv* **1** FREQUENTLY : comúnmente, frecuentemente **2** USUALLY : normalmente
common noun *n* : nombre *m* común
commonplace¹ ['kɑmən,pleɪs] *adj* : común, ordinario
commonplace² *n* : cliché *m*, tópico *m*
common sense *n* : sentido *m* común
commonwealth ['kɑmən,wɛlθ] *n* : entidad *f* política ⟨the British Commonwealth : la Mancomunidad Británica⟩
commotion [kə'mo:ʃən] *n* **1** RUCKUS : alboroto *m*, jaleo *m*, escándalo *m* **2** STIR, UPSET : revuelo *m*, conmoción *f*
communal [kə'mju:nəl] *adj* : comunal
commune¹ [kə'mju:n] *vi* **-muned; -muning** : estar en comunión
commune² ['kɑ,mju:n, kə'mju:n] *n* : comuna *f*

communicable [kə'mju:nɪkəbəl] *adj* CONTAGIOUS : transmisible, contagioso
communicate [kə'mju:nə,keɪt] *v* **-cated; -cating** *vt* **1** CONVEY : comunicar, expresar, hacer saber **2** TRANSMIT : transmitir (una enfermedad), contagiar — *vi* : comunicarse, expresarse
communication [kə,mju:nə'keɪʃən] *n* : comunicación *f*
communicative [kə'mju:nɪ,keɪt̬ɪv, -kət̬ɪv] *adj* : comunicativo
communion [kə'mju:njən] *n* **1** SHARING : comunión *f* **2 Communion** : comunión *f*, eucaristía *f*
communiqué [kə'mju:nə,keɪ, -,mju:nə-'keɪ] *n* : comunicado *m*
communism *or* **Communism** ['kɑmjə-,nɪzəm] *n* : comunismo *m*
communist¹ *or* **Communist** ['kɑmjə-,nɪst] *adj* : comunista ⟨the Communist Party : el Partido Comunista⟩
communist² *or* **Communist** *n* : comunista *mf*
communistic *or* **Communistic** [,kɑmjə-'nɪstɪk] *adj* : comunista
community [kə'mju:nət̬i] *n, pl* **-ties** : comunidad *f*
commute [kə'mju:t] *v* **-muted; -muting** *vt* REDUCE : conmutar, reducir (una sentencia) — *vi* : viajar de la residencia al trabajo
commuter [kə'mju:t̬ər] *n* : persona *f* que viaja diariamente al trabajo
compact¹ [kəm'pækt, 'kɑm,pækt] *vt* : compactar, consolidar, comprimir
compact² [kəm'pækt, 'kɑm,pækt] *adj* **1** DENSE, SOLID : compacto, macizo, denso **2** CONCISE : breve, conciso
compact³ ['kɑm,pækt] *n* **1** AGREEMENT : acuerdo *m*, pacto *m* **2** : polvera *f*, estuche *m* de maquillaje **3** *or* **compact car** : auto *m* compacto
compact disc ['kɑm,pækt'dɪsk] *n* : disco *m* compacto, compact disc *m*
compactly [kəm'pæktli, 'kɑm,pækt-] *adv* **1** DENSELY : densamente, macizamente **2** CONCISELY : concisamente, brevemente
companion [kəm'pænjən] *n* **1** COMRADE : compañero *m*, -ra *f*; acompañante *mf* **2** MATE : pareja *f* (de un zapato, etc.)
companionable [kəm'pænjənəbəl] *adj* : sociable, amigable
companionship [kəm'pænjən,ʃɪp] *n* : compañerismo *m*, camaradería *f*
company ['kʌmpəni] *n, pl* **-nies 1** FIRM : compañía *f*, empresa *f* **2** GROUP : compañía *f* (de actores o soldados) **3** GUESTS : visita *f* ⟨we have company : tenemos visita⟩
comparable ['kɑmpərəbəl] *adj* : comparable, parecido
comparative¹ [kəm'pærət̬ɪv] *adj* RELATIVE : comparativo, relativo — **comparatively** *adv*
comparative² *n* : comparativo *m*

compare¹ [kəm'pær] v -pared; -paring vt : comparar — vi to compare with : poder comparar con, tener comparación con
compare² n : comparación f ⟨beyond compare : sin igual, sin par⟩
comparison [kəm'pærəsən] n : comparación f
compartment [kəm'partmənt] n : compartimento m, compartimiento m
compass ['kʌmpəs, 'kam-] n 1 RANGE, SCOPE : alcance m, extensión f, límites mpl 2 : compás m (para trazar circunferencias) 3 : compás m, brújula f ⟨the points of the compass : los puntos cardinales⟩
compassion [kəm'pæʃən] n : compasión f, piedad f, misericordia f
compassionate [kəm'pæʃənət] adj : compasivo
compatibility [kəm,pæţə'bɪləţi] n : compatibilidad f
compatible [kəm'pæţəbəl] adj : compatible, afín
compatriot [kəm'peɪtriət, -'pæ-] n : compatriota mf; paisano m, -na f
compel [kəm'pɛl] vt -pelled; -pelling : obligar, compeler
compelling [kəm'pɛlɪŋ] adj 1 FORCEFUL : fuerte 2 ENGAGING : absorbente 3 PERSUASIVE : persuasivo, convincente
compendium [kəm'pɛndiəm] n, pl -diums or -dia [-diə] : compendio m
compensate ['kampən,seɪt] v -sated; -sating vi to compensate for : compensar — vt : indemnizar, compensar
compensation [,kampən'seɪʃən] n : compensación f, indemnización f
compensatory [kəm'pɛntsə,tori] adj : compensatorio
compete [kəm'pi:t] vi -peted; -peting : competir, contender, rivalizar
competence ['kampətənts] n : competencia f, aptitud f
competency ['kampətəntsi] → competence
competent ['kampətənt] adj : competente, capaz
competition [,kampə'tɪʃən] n : competencia f, concurso m
competitive [kəm'pɛţəţɪv] adj : competitivo
competitor [kəm'pɛţəţər] n : competidor m, -dora f
compilation [,kampə'leɪʃən] n : recopilación f, compilación f
compile [kəm'paɪl] vt -piled; -piling : compilar, recopilar
complacency [kəm'pleɪsəntsi] n : satisfacción f consigo mismo, suficiencia f
complacent [kəm'pleɪsənt] adj : satisfecho de sí mismo, suficiente
complain [kəm'pleɪn] vi 1 GRIPE : quejarse, regañar, rezongar 2 PROTEST : reclamar, protestar
complaint [kəm'pleɪnt] n 1 GRIPE : queja f 2 AILMENT : afección f, dolencia f

3 ACCUSATION : reclamo m, acusación f
complement¹ ['kamplə,mɛnt] vt : complementar
complement² ['kampləmənt] n : complemento m
complementary [,kamplə'mɛntəri] adj : complementario
complete¹ [kəm'pli:t] vt -pleted; -pleting 1 : completar, hacer entero ⟨this piece completes the collection : esta pieza completa la colección⟩ 2 FINISH : completar, acabar, terminar ⟨she completed her studies : completó sus estudios⟩
complete² adj -pleter; -est 1 WHOLE : completo, entero, íntegro 2 FINISHED : terminado, acabado 3 TOTAL : completo, total, absoluto
completely [kəm'pli:tli] adv : completamente, totalmente
completion [kəm'pli:ʃən] n : finalización f, cumplimiento m
complex¹ [kam'plɛks, kəm-; 'kam,plɛks] adj : complejo, complicado
complex² ['kam,plɛks] n : complejo m
complexion [kəm'plɛkʃən] n : cutis m, tez f ⟨of dark complexion : de tez morena⟩
complexity [kəm'plɛksəţi, kam-] n, pl -ties : complejidad f
compliance [kəm'plaɪənts] n : conformidad f ⟨in compliance with the law : conforme a la ley⟩
compliant [kəm'plaɪənt] adj : dócil, sumiso
complicate ['kamplə,keɪt] vt -cated; -cating : complicar
complicated ['kamplə,keɪţəd] adj : complicado
complication [,kamplə'keɪʃən] n : complicación f
complicity [kəm'plɪsəţi] n, pl -ties : complicidad f
compliment¹ ['kamplə,mɛnt] vt : halagar, florear Mex
compliment² ['kampləmənt] n 1 : halago m, cumplido m 2 compliments npl : saludos mpl ⟨give them my compliments : déles saludos de mi parte⟩
complimentary [,kamplə'mɛntəri] adj 1 FLATTERING : halagador, halagüeño 2 FREE : de cortesía, gratis
comply [kəm'plaɪ] vi -plied; -plying : cumplir, acceder, obedecer
component¹ [kəm'po:nənt, 'kam-,po:-] adj : componente
component² n : componente m, elemento m, pieza f
compose [kəm'po:z] vt -posed; -posing 1 : componer, crear ⟨to compose a melody : componer una melodía⟩ 2 CALM : calmar, serenar ⟨to compose oneself : serenarse⟩ 3 CONSTITUTE : constar, componer ⟨to be composed of : constar de⟩ 4 : componer (un texto a imprimirse)
composer [kəm'po:zər] n : compositor m, -tora f

composite¹ [kɑm'pɑzət, kəm-; 'kɑm-pəzət] *adj* : compuesto (de varias partes)

composite² *n* : compuesto *m*, mezcla *f*

composition [ˌkɑmpə'zɪʃən] *n* **1** MAKE-UP : composición *f* **2** ESSAY : ensayo *m*, trabajo *m*

compost ['kɑm,po:st] *n* : abono *m* vegetal

composure [kəm'po:ʒər] *n* : compostura *f*, serenidad *f*

compound¹ [kɑm'paʊnd, kəm-; 'kɑm-,paʊnd] *vt* **1** COMBINE, COMPOSE : combinar, componer **2** AUGMENT : agravar, aumentar ⟨to compound a problem : agravar un problema⟩

compound² ['kɑm,paʊnd; kɑm'paʊnd, kəm-] *adj* : compuesto ⟨compound interest : interés compuesto⟩

compound³ ['kɑm,paʊnd] *n* **1** MIXTURE : compuesto *m*, mezcla *f* **2** ENCLOSURE : recinto *m* (de residencias, etc.)

compound fracture *n* : fractura *f* complicada

comprehend [ˌkɑmprɪ'hɛnd] *vt* **1** UNDERSTAND : comprender, entender **2** INCLUDE : comprender, incluir, abarcar

comprehensible [ˌkɑmprɪ'hɛntsəbəl] *adj* : comprensible

comprehension [ˌkɑmprɪ'hɛnʃən] *n* : comprensión *f*

comprehensive [ˌkɑmprɪ'hɛntsɪv] *adj* **1** INCLUSIVE : inclusivo, exhaustivo **2** BROAD : extenso, amplio

compress¹ [kəm'prɛs] *vt* : comprimir

compress² ['kɑm,prɛs] *n* : compresa *f*

compression [kəm'prɛʃən] *n* : compresión *f*

compressor [kəm'prɛsər] *n* : compresor *m*

comprise [kəm'praɪz] *vt* **-prised; -prising 1** INCLUDE : comprender, incluir **2** : componerse de, constar de ⟨the installation comprises several buildings : la instalación está compuesta de varios edificios⟩

compromise¹ ['kɑmprə,maɪz] *v* **-mised; -mising** *vi* : transigir, avenirse — *vt* JEOPARDIZE : comprometer, poner en peligro

compromise² *n* : acuerdo *m* mutuo, compromiso *m*

comptroller [kən'tro:lər, 'kɑmp-,tro:-] *n* : contralor *m*, -lora *f*; interventor *m*, -tora *f*

compulsion [kəm'pʌlʃən] *n* **1** COERCION : coacción *f* **2** URGE : compulsión *f*, impulso *m*

compulsive [kəm'pʌlsɪv] *adj* : compulsivo

compulsory [kəm'pʌlsəri] *adj* : obligatorio

compunction [kəm'pʌŋkʃən] *n* **1** QUALM : reparo *m*, escrúpulo *m* **2** REMORSE : remordimiento *m*

computation [ˌkɑmpjʊ'teɪʃən] *n* : cálculo *m*, cómputo *m*

compute [kəm'pju:t] *vt* **-puted; -puting** : computar, calcular

computer [kəm'pju:ʈər] *n* : computadora *f*, computador *m*, ordenador *m Spain*

computerize [kəm'pju:ʈə,raɪz] *vt* **-ized; -izing** : computarizar, informatizar

comrade ['kɑm,ræd] *n* : camarada *mf*; compañero *m*, -ra *f*

con¹ ['kɑn] *vt* **conned; conning** SWINDLE : estafar, timar

con² *adv* : contra

con³ *n* : contra *m* ⟨the pros and cons : los pros y los contras⟩

concave [kɑn'keɪv, 'kɑn,keɪv] *adj* : cóncavo

conceal [kən'si:l] *vt* : esconder, ocultar, disimular

concealment [kən'si:lmənt] *n* : escondimiento *m*, ocultación *f*

concede [kən'si:d] *vt* **-ceded; -ceding 1** ALLOW, GRANT : conceder **2** ADMIT : conceder, reconocer ⟨to concede defeat : reconocer la derrota⟩

conceit [kən'si:t] *n* : engreimiento *m*, presunción *f*

conceited [kən'si:ʈəd] *adj* : presumido, engreído, presuntuoso

conceivable [kən'si:vəbəl] *adj* : concebible, imaginable

conceivably [kən'si:vəbli] *adv* : posiblemente, de manera concebible

conceive [kən'si:v] *v* **-ceived; -ceiving** *vi* : concebir, embarazarse — *vt* IMAGINE : concebir, imaginar

concentrate¹ ['kɑntsən,treɪt] *v* **-trated; -trating** *vt* : concentrar — *vi* : concentrarse

concentrate² *n* : concentrado *m*

concentration [ˌkɑntsən'treɪʃən] *n* : concentración *f*

concentric [kən'sɛntrɪk] *adj* : concéntrico

concept ['kɑn,spt] *n* : concepto *m*, idea *f*

conception [kən'sɛpʃən] *n* **1** : concepción *f* (de un bebé) **2** IDEA : concepto *m*, idea *f*

concern¹ [kən'sərn] *vt* **1** : tratarse de, tener que ver con ⟨the novel concerns a sailor : la novela se trata de un marinero⟩ **2** INVOLVE : concernir, incumbir a, afectar ⟨that does not concern me : eso no me incumbe⟩

concern² *n* **1** AFFAIR : asunto *m* **2** WORRY : inquietud *f*, preocupación *f* **3** BUSINESS : negocio *m*

concerned [kən'sərnd] *adj* **1** ANXIOUS : preocupado, ansioso **2** INTERESTED, INVOLVED : interesado, afectado

concerning [kən'sərnɪŋ] *prep* REGARDING : con respecto a, acerca de, sobre

concert ['kɑn,sərt] *n* **1** AGREEMENT : concierto *m*, acuerdo *m* **2** : concierto *m* (musical)

concerted [kən'sərʈəd] *adj* : concertado, coordinado ⟨to make a concerted effort : coordinar los esfuerzos⟩

concertina [ˌkɑntsər'ti:nə] *n* : concertina *f*

concerto [kən'ʃɛrto:] *n, pl* **-ti** [-ti, -,ti:] *or* **-tos** : concierto *m* ⟨violin concerto : concierto para violín⟩

concession [kən'sɛʃən] *n* : concesión *f*

conch ['kaŋk, 'kanʧ] *n, pl* **conchs** ['kaŋks] *or* **conches** ['kanʧəz] : caracol *m* (animal), caracola *f* (concha)

conciliatory [kən'sɪliə,tori] *adj* : conciliador, conciliatorio

concise [kən'saɪs] *adj* : conciso, breve — **concisely** *adv*

conclave ['kan,kleɪv] *n* : cónclave *m*

conclude [kən'klu:d] *v* **-cluded; -cluding** *vt* **1** END : concluir, finalizar ⟨to conclude a meeting : concluir una reunión⟩ **2** DECIDE : concluir, llegar a la conclusión de — *vi* END : concluir, terminar

conclusion [kən'klu:ʒən] *n* **1** INFERENCE : conclusión *f* **2** END : fin *m*, final *m*

conclusive [kən'klu:sɪv] *adj* : concluyente, decisivo — **conclusively** *adv*

concoct [kən'kakt, kan-] *vt* **1** PREPARE : preparar, confeccionar **2** DEVISE : inventar, tramar

concoction [kən'kakʃən] *n* : invención *f*, mejunje *m*, brebaje *m*

concomitant [kən'kamətənt] *adj* : concomitante

concord ['kan,kord, 'kaŋ-] *n* **1** HARMONY : concordia *f*, armonía *f* **2** AGREEMENT : acuerdo *m*

concordance [kən'kordənts] *n* : concordancia *f*

concourse ['kan,kors] *n* : explanada *f*, salón *m* (para pasajeros)

concrete¹ [kan'kri:t, 'kan,kri:t] *adj* **1** REAL : concreto ⟨concrete objects : objetos concretos⟩ **2** SPECIFIC : determinado, específico **3** : de concreto, de hormigón ⟨concrete walls : paredes de concreto⟩

concrete² ['kan,kri:t, kan'kri:t] *n* : concreto *m*, hormigón *m*

concur [kən'kər] *vi* **concurred; concurring 1** COINCIDE : concurrir, coincidir **2** AGREE : concurrir, estar de acuerdo

concurrent [kən'kərənt] *adj* : concurrente, simultáneo

concussion [kən'kʌʃən] *n* : conmoción *f* cerebral

condemn [kən'dɛm] *vt* **1** CENSURE : condenar, reprobar, censurar **2** : declarar insalubre (alimentos), declarar ruinoso (un edificio) **3** SENTENCE : condenar ⟨condemned to death : condenado a muerte⟩

condemnation [,kan,dɛm'neɪʃən] *n* : condena *f*, reprobación *f*

condensation [,kan,dɛn'seɪʃən, -dən-] *n* : condensación *f*

condense [kən'dɛnts] *v* **-densed; -densing** *vt* **1** ABRIDGE : condensar, resumir **2** : condensar (vapor, etc.) — *vi* : condensarse

condescend [,kandɪ'sɛnd] *vi* **1** DEIGN : condescender, dignarse **2 to condescend to someone** : tratar a alguien con condescendencia

condescension [,kandɪ'sɛnʧən] *n* : condescendencia *f*

condiment ['kandəmənt] *n* : condimento *m*

condition¹ [kən'dɪʃən] *vt* **1** DETERMINE : condicionar, determinar **2** : acondicionar (el pelo o el aire), poner en forma (el cuerpo)

condition² *n* **1** STIPULATION : condición *f*, estipulación *f* ⟨on the condition that : a condición de que⟩ **2** STATE : condición *f*, estado *m* ⟨in poor condition : en malas condiciones⟩ **3 conditions** *npl* : condiciones *fpl*, situación *f* ⟨working conditions : condiciones del trabajo⟩

conditional [kən'dɪʃənəl] *adj* : condicional — **conditionally** *adv*

conditioner [kən'dɪʃənər] *n* : acondicionador *m*

condo ['kando:] → **condominium**

condolence [kən'do:lənts] *n* **1** SYMPATHY : condolencia *f* **2 condolences** *npl* : pésame *m*

condom ['kandəm] *n* : condón *m*

condominium [,kandə'miniəm] *n, pl* **-ums** : condominio *m*

condone [kən'do:n] *vt* **-doned; -doning** : aprobar, perdonar, tolerar

condor ['kandər, -,dor] *n* : cóndor *m*

conducive [kən'du:sɪv, -'dju:-] *adj* : propicio, favorable

conduct¹ [kən'dʌkt] *vt* **1** GUIDE : guiar, conducir ⟨to conduct a tour : guiar una visita⟩ **2** DIRECT : conducir, dirigir ⟨to conduct an orchestra : dirigir una orquesta⟩ **3** CARRY OUT : realizar, llevar a cabo ⟨to conduct an investigation : llevar a cabo una investigación⟩ **4** TRANSMIT : conducir, transmitir (calor, electricidad, etc.) **5 to conduct oneself** BEHAVE : conducirse, comportarse

conduct² ['kan,dʌkt] *n* **1** MANAGEMENT : conducción *f*, dirección *f*, manejo *m* ⟨the conduct of foreign affairs : la conducción de asuntos exteriores⟩ **2** BEHAVIOR : conducta *f*, comportamiento *m*

conduction [kən'dʌkʃən] *n* : conducción *f*

conductivity [,kan,dʌk'tɪvəti] *n, pl* **-ties** : conductividad *f*

conductor [kən'dʌktər] *n* **1** : conductor *m*, -tora *f*; revisor *m*, -sora *f* (en un tren); cobrador *m*, -dora *f* (en un bus); director *m*, -tora *f* (de una orquesta) **2** : conductor *m* (de electricidad, etc.)

conduit ['kan,du:ət, -,dju:-] *n* : conducto *m*, canal *m*, vía *f*

cone ['ko:n] *n* **1** : piña *f* (fruto de las coníferas) **2** : cono *m* (en geometría) **3 ice–cream cone** : cono *m*, barquillo *m*, cucurucho *m*

confection [kən'fɛkʃən] *n* : dulce *m*

confectioner [kən'fɛkʃənər] *n* : confitero *m*, -ra *f*

confederacy [kən'fɛdərəsi] *n, pl* **-cies** : confederación *f*

confederate[1] [kən'fɛdə,reɪt] *v* **-ated; -ating** *vt* : unir, confederar — *vi* : confederarse, aliarse

confederate[2] [kən'fɛdərət] *adj* : confederado

confederate[3] *n* : cómplice *mf*; aliado *m*, -da *f*

confederation [kən,fɛdə'reɪʃən] *n* : confederación *f*, alianza *f*

confer [kən'fər] *v* **-ferred; -ferring** *vt* : conferir, otorgar — *vi* **to confer with** : consultar

conference ['kɑnfrənts, -fərənts] *n* : conferencia *f* ⟨press conference : conferencia de prensa⟩

confess [kən'fɛs] *vt* : confesar — *vi* 1 : confesar ⟨the prisoner confessed : el detenido confesó⟩ 2 : confesarse (en religión)

confession [kən'fɛʃən] *n* : confesión *f*

confessional [kən'fɛʃənəl] *n* : confesionario *m*

confessor [kən'fɛsər] *n* : confesor *m*

confetti [kən'fɛti] *n* : confeti *m*

confidant ['kɑnfə,dɑnt, -,dænt] *n* : confidente *mf*

confide [kən'faɪd] *v* **-fided; -fiding** : confiar

confidence ['kɑnfədənts] *n* 1 TRUST : confianza *f* 2 SELF-ASSURANCE : confianza *f* en sí mismo, seguridad *f* en sí mismo 3 SECRET : confidencia *f*, secreto *m*

confident ['kɑnfədənt] *adj* 1 SURE : seguro 2 SELF-ASSURED : confiado, seguro de sí mismo

confidential [,kɑnfə'dɛntʃəl] *adj* : confidencial — **confidentially** [,kɑnfə-'dɛntʃəli] *adv*

confidently ['kɑnfədəntli] *adv* : con seguridad, con confianza

configuration [kən,fɪgjə'reɪʃən] *n* : configuración *f*

confine [kən'faɪn] *vt* **-fined; -fining** 1 LIMIT : confinar, restringir, limitar 2 IMPRISON : recluir, encarcelar, encerrar

confinement [kən'faɪnmənt] *n* : confinamiento *m*, reclusión *f*, encierro *m*

confines ['kɑn,faɪnz] *npl* : límites *mpl*, confines *mpl*

confirm [kən'fərm] *vt* 1 RATIFY : ratificar 2 VERIFY : confirmar, verificar 3 : confirmar (en religión)

confirmation [,kɑnfər'meɪʃən] *n* : confirmación *f*

confiscate ['kɑnfə,skeɪt] *vt* **-cated; -cating** : confiscar, incautar, decomisar

confiscation [,kɑnfə'skeɪʃən] *n* : confiscación *f*, incautación *f*, decomiso *m*

conflagration [,kɑnflə'greɪʃən] *n* : conflagración *f*

conflict[1] [kən'flɪkt] *vi* : estar en conflicto, oponerse

conflict[2] ['kɑn,flɪkt] *n* : conflicto *m* ⟨to be in conflict : estar en desacuerdo⟩

confluence ['kɑn,flu:ənts, kən'flu:ənts] *n* : confluencia *f*

conform [kən'fɔrm] *vi* 1 ACCORD, COMPLY : ajustarse, adaptarse, conformarse ⟨it conforms with our standards : se ajusta a nuestras normas⟩ 2 CORRESPOND : corresponder, encajar ⟨to conform to the truth : corresponder a la verdad⟩

conformity [kən'fɔrməti] *n, pl* **-ties** : conformidad *f*

confound [kən'faund, kɑn-] *vt* : confundir, desconcertar

confront [kən'frʌnt] *vt* : afrontar, enfrentarse a, encarar

confrontation [,kɑnfrən'teɪʃən] *n* : enfrentamiento *m*, confrontación *f*

confuse [kən'fju:z] *vt* **-fused; -fusing** 1 PUZZLE : confundir, enturbiar 2 COMPLICATE : confundir, enredar, complicar ⟨to confuse the issue : complicar las cosas⟩

confusing [kən'fju:zɪŋ] *adj* : complicado, que confunde

confusion [kən'fju:ʒən] *n* 1 PERPLEXITY : confusión *f* 2 MESS, TURMOIL : confusión *f*, embrollo *m*, lío *m fam*

congeal [kən'dʒi:l] *vi* 1 FREEZE : congelarse 2 COAGULATE, CURDLE : coagularse, cuajarse

congenial [kən'dʒi:niəl] *adj* : agradable, simpático

congenital [kən'dʒɛnətəl] *adj* : congénito

congest [kən'dʒɛst] *vt* 1 : congestionar (en la medicina) 2 OVERCROWD : abarrotar, atestar, congestionar (el tráfico) — *vi* : congestionarse

congestion [kən'dʒɛstʃən] *n* : congestión *f*

conglomerate[1] [kən'glɑmərət] *adj* : conglomerado

conglomerate[2] [kən'glɑmərət] *n* : conglomerado *m*

conglomeration [kən,glɑmə'reɪʃən] *n* : conglomerado *m*, acumulación *f*

Congolese [,kɑŋgə'li:z, -'li:s] *n* : congoleño *m*, -ña *f* — **Congolese** *adj*

congratulate [kən'grædʒə,leɪt, -'grætʃə-] *vt* **-lated; -lating** : felicitar

congratulation [kən,grædʒə'leɪʃən, -,grætʃə-] *n* : felicitación *f* ⟨congratulations! : ¡felicidades!, ¡enhorabuena!⟩

congregate ['kɑŋgrɪ,geɪt] *v* **-gated; -gating** *vt* : congregar, reunir — *vi* : congregarse, reunirse

congregation [,kɑŋgrɪ'geɪʃən] *n* 1 GATHERING : congregación *f*, fieles *mpl* (a un servicio religioso) 2 PARISHIONERS : feligreses *mpl*

congress ['kɑŋgrəs] *n* : congreso *m*

congressional [kən'grɛʃənəl, kɑn-] *adj* : del congreso

congressman ['kɑŋgrəsmən] *n, pl* **-men** [-mən, -,mɛn] : congresista *m*, diputado *m*

congresswoman [ˈkɑŋgrəsˌwʊmən] *n*, *pl* **-women** [-ˌwɪmən] : congresista *f*, diputada *f*

congruence [kənˈgruːənʦ, ˈkɑŋgruənʦ] *n* : congruencia *f*

congruent [kənˈgruːənt, ˈkɑŋgruənt] *adj* : congruente

conic [ˈkɑnɪk] → **conical**

conical [ˈkɑnɪkəl] *adj* : cónico

conifer [ˈkɑnəfər, ˈkoː-] *n* : conífera *f*

coniferous [koːˈnɪfərəs, kə-] *adj* : conífero

conjecture¹ [kənˈʤɛkʧər] *v* **-tured; -turing** : conjeturar

conjecture² *n* : conjetura *f*, presunción *f*

conjugal [ˈkɑnʤɪgəl, kənˈʤuː-] *adj* : conyugal

conjugate [ˈkɑnʤəˌgeɪt] *vt* **-gated; -gating** : conjugar

conjugation [ˌkɑnʤəˈgeɪʃən] *n* : conjugación *f*

conjunction [kənˈʤʌŋkʃən] *n* : conjunción *f* ⟨in conjunction with : en combinación con⟩

conjure [ˈkɑnʤər, ˈkʌn-] *v* **-jured; -juring** *vt* **1** ENTREAT : rogar, suplicar **2 to conjure up** : hacer aparecer (apariciones), evocar (memorias, etc.) — *vi* : practicar la magia

conjurer *or* **conjuror** [ˈkɑnʤərər, ˈkʌn-] *n* : mago *m*, -ga *f*; prestidigitador *m*, -dora *f*

connect [kəˈnɛkt] *vi* : conectar, enlazar, empalmar, comunicarse — *vt* **1** JOIN, LINK : conectar, unir, juntar, vincular **2** RELATE : relacionar, asociar (ideas)

connection [kənˈnɛkʃən] *n* : conexión *f*, enlace *m* ⟨professional connections : relaciones profesionales⟩

connective [kəˈnɛktɪv] *adj* : conectivo, conjuntivo ⟨connective tissue : tejido conjuntivo⟩

connector [kəˈnɛktər] *n* : conector *m*

connivance [kəˈnaɪvənʦ] *n* : connivencia *f*, complicidad *f*

connive [kəˈnaɪv] *vi* **-nived; -niving** CONSPIRE, PLOT : actuar en connivencia, confabularse, conspirar

connoisseur [ˌkɑnəˈsər, -ˈsʊr] *n* : conocedor *m*, -dora *f*; entendido *m*, -da *f*

connotation [ˌkɑnəˈteɪʃən] *n* : connotación *f*

connote [kəˈnoːt] *vt* **-noted; -noting** : connotar

conquer [ˈkɑŋkər] *vt* : conquistar, vencer

conqueror [ˈkɑŋkərər] *n* : conquistador *m*, -dora *f*

conquest [ˈkɑnˌkwɛst, ˈkɑŋ-] *n* : conquista *f*

conscience [ˈkɑnʧənʦ] *n* : conciencia *f*, consciencia *f* ⟨to have a clear conscience : tener la conciencia limpia⟩

conscientious [ˌkɑnʧiˈɛnʧəs] *adj* : concienzudo — **conscientiously** *adv*

conscious [ˈkɑnʧəs] *adj* **1** AWARE : consciente ⟨to become conscious of : darse cuenta de⟩ **2** ALERT, AWAKE : consciente **3** INTENTIONAL : intencional, deliberado

consciously [ˈkɑnʧəsli] *adv* INTENTIONALLY : intencionalmente, deliberadamente, a propósito

consciousness [ˈkɑnʧəsnəs] *n* **1** AWARENESS : conciencia *f*, consciencia *f* **2** : conocimiento *m* ⟨to lose consciousness : perder el conocimiento⟩

conscript¹ [kənˈskrɪpt] *vt* : reclutar, alistar, enrolar

conscript² [ˈkɑnˌskrɪpt] *n* : conscripto *m*, -ta *f*; recluta *mf*

consecrate [ˈkɑnʦəˌkreɪt] *vt* **-crated; -crating** : consagrar

consecration [ˌkɑnʦəˈkreɪʃən] *n* : consagración *f*, dedicación *f*

consecutive [kənˈsɛkətɪv] *adj* : consecutivo, seguido ⟨on five consecutive days : cinco días seguidos⟩

consecutively [kənˈsɛkətɪvli] *adv* : consecutivamente

consensus [kənˈsɛnʦəs] *n* : consenso *m*

consent¹ [kənˈsɛnt] *vi* **1** AGREE : acceder, ponerse de acuerdo **2 to consent to do something** : consentir en hacer algo

consent² *n* : consentimiento *m*, permiso *m* ⟨by common consent : de común acuerdo⟩

consequence [ˈkɑnʦəˌkwɛnʦ, -kwənʦ] *n* **1** RESULT : consecuencia *f*, secuela *f* **2** IMPORTANCE : importancia *f*, trascendencia *f*

consequent [ˈkɑnʦəkwənt, -ˌkwɛnt] *adj* : consiguiente

consequential [ˌkɑnʦəˈkwɛnʧəl] *adj* **1** CONSEQUENT : consiguiente **2** IMPORTANT : importante, trascendente, trascendental

consequently [ˈkɑnʦəkwəntli, -ˌkwɛnt-] *adv* : por consiguiente, por ende, por lo tanto

conservation [ˌkɑnʦərˈveɪʃən] *n* : conservación *f*, protección *f*

conservationist [ˌkɑnʦərˈveɪʃənɪst] *n* : conservacionista *mf*

conservatism [kənˈsərvəˌtɪzəm] *n* : conservadurismo *m*

conservative¹ [kənˈsərvəˌtɪv] *adj* **1** : conservador **2** CAUTIOUS : moderado, cauteloso ⟨a conservative estimate : un cálculo moderado⟩

conservative² *n* : conservador *m*, -dora *f*

conservatory [kənˈsərvəˌtori] *n*, *pl* **-ries** : conservatorio *m*

conserve¹ [kənˈsərv] *vt* **-served; -serving** : conservar, preservar

conserve² [ˈkɑnˌsərv] *n* PRESERVES : confitura *f*

consider [kənˈsɪdər] *vt* **1** CONTEMPLATE : considerar, pensar en ⟨we'd considered attending : habíamos pensado en asistir⟩ **2** : considerar, tener en cuenta ⟨consider the consequences : considera las consecuencias⟩ **3** JUDGE, REGARD : considerar, estimar

considerable [kən'sɪdərəbəl] *adj* : considerable — **considerably** [-bli] *adv*
considerate [kən'sɪdərət] *adj* : considerado, atento
consideration [kən‚sɪdə'reɪʃən] *n* : consideración *f* ⟨to take into consideration : tener en cuenta⟩
considering [kən'sɪdərɪŋ] *prep* : teniendo en cuenta, visto
consign [kən'saɪn] *vt* 1 COMMIT, ENTRUST : confiar, encomendar 2 TRANSFER : consignar, transferir 3 SEND : consignar, enviar (mercancía)
consignment [kən'saɪnmənt] *n* 1 : envío *m*, remesa *f* 2 **on** ~ : en consignación
consist [kən'sɪst] *vi* 1 LIE : consistir ⟨success consists in hard work : el éxito consiste en trabajar duro⟩ 2 : constar, componerse ⟨the set consists of 5 pieces : el juego se compone de 5 piezas⟩
consistency [kən'sɪstəntsi] *n, pl* **-cies** 1 : consistencia *f* (de una mezcla o sustancia) 2 COHERENCE : coherencia *f* 3 UNIFORMITY : regularidad *f*, uniformidad *f*
consistent [kən'sɪstənt] *adj* 1 COMPATIBLE : compatible, coincidente ⟨consistent with policy : coincidente con la política⟩ 2 UNIFORM : uniforme, constante, regular — **consistently** [kən'sɪstəntli] *adv*
consolation [‚kɑntsə'leɪʃə n] *n* 1 : consuelo *m* 2 **consolation prize** : premio *m* de consolación
console¹ [kən'soːl] *vt* **-soled; -soling** : consolar
console² ['kɑn‚soːl] *n* : consola *f*
consolidate [kən'sɑlə‚deɪt] *vt* **-dated; -dating** : consolidar, unir
consolidation [kən‚sɑlə'deɪʃən] *n* : consolidación *f*
consommé [‚kɑntsə'meɪ] *n* : consomé *m*
consonant ['kɑntsənənt] *n* : consonante *m*
consort¹ [kən'sɔrt] *vi* : asociarse, relacionarse, tener trato ⟨to consort with criminals : tener trato con criminales⟩
consort² ['kɑn‚sɔrt] *n* : consorte *mf*
consortium [kən'sɔrʃəm] *n, pl* **-tia** [-ʃə] *or* **-tiums** [-ʃəmz] : consorcio *m*
conspicuous [kən'spɪkjuəs] *adj* 1 OBVIOUS : visible, evidente 2 STRIKING : llamativo
conspicuously [kən'spɪkjuəsli] *adv* : de manera llamativa
conspiracy [kən'spɪrəsi] *n, pl* **-cies** : conspiración *f*, complot *m*, confabulación *f*
conspirator [kən'spɪrətər] *n* : conspirador *m*, -dora *f*
conspire [kən'spaɪr] *vi* **-spired; -spiring** : conspirar, confabularse
constable ['kɑntstəbəl, 'kʌntstə-] *n* : agente *mf* de policía (en un pueblo)
constancy ['kɑntstəntsi] *n, pl* **-cies** : constancia *f*

constant¹ ['kɑntstənt] *adj* 1 FAITHFUL : leal, fiel 2 INVARIABLE : constante, invariable 3 CONTINUAL : constante, continuo
constant² *n* : constante *f*
constantly ['kɑntstəntli] *adv* : constantemente, continuamente
constellation [‚kɑntstə'leɪʃən] *n* : constelación *f*
consternation [‚kɑntstər'neɪʃən] *n* : consternación *f*
constipate ['kɑntstə‚peɪt] *vt* **-pated; -pating** : estreñir
constipation ['kɑntstə'peɪʃən] *n* : estreñimiento *m*, constipación *f* (de vientre)
constituency [kən'stɪtʃuəntsi] *n, pl* **-cies** 1 : distrito *m* electoral 2 : residentes *mpl* de un distrito electoral
constituent¹ [kən'stɪtʃuənt] *adj* 1 COMPONENT : constituyente, componente 2 : constituyente, constitutivo ⟨a constituent assembly : una asamblea constituyente⟩
constituent² *n* 1 COMPONENT : componente *m* 2 ELECTOR, VOTER : elector *m*, -tora *f*; votante *mf*
constitute ['kɑntstə‚tuːt, -‚tjuːt] *vt* **-tuted; -tuting** 1 ESTABLISH : constituir, establecer 2 COMPOSE, FORM : constituir, componer
constitution [‚kɑntstə'tuːʃən, -'tjuː-] *n* : constitución *f*
constitutional [‚kɑntstə'tuːʃənəl, -'tjuː-] *adj* : constitucional
constitutionality [‚kɑntstə‚tuːʃə'næləţi, -‚tjuː-] *n* : constitucionalidad *f*
constrain [kən'streɪn] *vt* 1 COMPEL : constreñir, obligar 2 CONFINE : constreñir, limitar, restringir 3 RESTRAIN : contener, refrenar
constraint [kən'streɪnt] *n* : restricción *f*, limitación *f*
constrict [kən'strɪkt] *vt* : estrechar, apretar, comprimir
constriction [kən'strɪkʃən] *n* : estrechamiento *m*, compresión *f*
construct [kən'strʌkt] *vt* : construir
construction [kən'strʌkʃən] *n* : construcción *f*
constructive [kən'strʌktɪv] *adj* : constructivo
construe [kən'struː] *vt* **-strued; -struing** : interpretar
consul ['kɑntsəl] *n* : cónsul *mf*
consular ['kɑntsələr] *adj* : consular
consulate ['kɑntsələt] *n* : consulado *m*
consult [kən'sʌlt] *vt* : consultar — *vi* **to consult with** : consultar con, solicitar la opinión de
consultant [kən'sʌltənt] *n* : consultor *m*, -tora *f*; asesor *m*, -sora *f*
consultation [‚kɑntsəl'teɪʃən] *n* : consulta *f*
consumable [kən'suːməbəl] *adj* : consumible
consume [kən'suːm] *vt* **-sumed; -suming** : consumir, usar, gastar

consumer [kən'su:mər] *n* : consumidor *m*, -dora *f*

consummate[1] ['kɑntsə,meɪt] *vt* -mated; -mating : consumar

consummate[2] [kən'sʌmət, 'kɑntsə-mət] *adj* : consumado, perfecto

consummation [,kɑntsə'meɪʃən] *n* : consumación *f*

consumption [kən'sʌmpʃən] *n* **1** USE : consumo *m*, uso *m* ⟨consumption of electricity : consumo de electricidad⟩ **2** TUBERCULOSIS : tisis *f*, consunción *f*

contact[1] ['kɑn,tækt, kən'-] *vt* : ponerse en contacto con, contactar (con)

contact[2] ['kɑn,tækt] *n* **1** TOUCHING : contacto *m* ⟨to come into contact with : entrar en contacto con⟩ **2** TOUCH : contacto *m*, comunicación *f* ⟨to lose contact with : perder contacto con⟩ **3** CONNECTION : contacto *m* (en negocios) **4** → **contact lens**

contact lens ['kɑn,tækt'lɛnz] *n* : lente *mf* de contacto, pupilente *m Mex*

contagion [kən'teɪdʒən] *n* : contagio *m*

contagious [kən'teɪdʒəs] *adj* : contagioso

contain [kən'teɪn] *vt* **1** : contener **2 to contain oneself** : contenerse

container [kən'teɪnər] *n* : recipiente *m*, envase *m*

containment [kən'teɪnmənt] *n* : contención *f*

contaminant [kən'tæmənənt] *n* : contaminante *m*

contaminate [kən'tæmə,neɪt] *vt* -nated; -nating : contaminar

contamination [kən,tæmə'neɪʃən] *n* : contaminación *f*

contemplate ['kɑntəm,pleɪt] *v* -plated; -plating *vt* **1** VIEW : contemplar **2** PONDER : contemplar, considerar **3** CONSIDER, PROPOSE : proponerse, proyectar, pensar en ⟨to contemplate a trip : pensar en viajar⟩ — *vi* MEDITATE : meditar

contemplation [,kɑntəm'pleɪʃən] *n* : contemplación *f*

contemplative [kən'templətɪv, 'kɑntəm,pleɪtɪv] *adj* : contemplativo

contemporaneous [kən,tempə'reɪniəs] *adj* → **contemporary**[1]

contemporary[1] [kən'tempə,reri] *adj* : contemporáneo

contemporary[2] *n, pl* -raries : contemporáneo *m*, -nea *f*

contempt [kən'tempt] *n* **1** DISDAIN : desprecio *m*, desdén *m* ⟨to hold in contempt : despreciar⟩ **2** : desacato *m* (ante un tribunal)

contemptible [kən'temptəbəl] *adj* : despreciable, vil

contemptuous [kən'temptʃuəs] *adj* : despectivo, despreciativo, desdeñoso

contemptuously [kən'temptʃuəsli] *adv* : despectivamente, con desprecio

contend [kən'tend] *vi* **1** STRUGGLE : luchar, lidiar, contender ⟨to contend with a problem : lidiar con un proble-

ma⟩ **2** COMPETE : competir ⟨to contend for a position : competir por un puesto⟩ — *vt* **1** ARGUE, MAINTAIN : argüir, sostener, afirmar ⟨he contended that he was right : afirmó que tenía razón⟩ **2** CONTEST : protestar contra (una decisión, etc.), disputar

contender [kən'tendər] *n* : contendiente *mf*; aspirante *mf*; competidor *m*, -dora *f*

content[1] [kən'tent] *vt* SATISFY : contentar, satisfacer

content[2] *adj* : conforme, contento, satisfecho

content[3] *n* CONTENTMENT : contento *m*, satisfacción *f* ⟨to one's heart's content : hasta quedar satisfecho, a más no poder⟩

content[4] ['kɑn,tent] *n* **1** MEANING : contenido *m*, significado *m* **2** PROPORTION : contenido *m*, proporción *f* ⟨fat content : contenido de grasa⟩ **3 contents** *npl* : contenido *m*, sumario *m* (de un libro) ⟨table of contents : índice de materias⟩

contented [kən'tentəd] *adj* : conforme, satisfecho ⟨a contented smile : una sonrisa de satisfacción⟩

contentedly [kən'tentədli] *adv* : con satisfacción

contention [kən'tentʃən] *n* **1** DISPUTE : disputa *f*, discusión *f* **2** COMPETITION : competencia *f*, contienda *f* **3** OPINION : argumento *m*, opinión *f*

contentious [kən'tentʃəs] *adj* : disputador, pugnaz, combativo

contentment [kən'tentmənt] *n* : satisfacción *f*, contento *m*

contest[1] [kən'test] *vt* : disputar, cuestionar, impugnar ⟨to contest a will : impugnar un testamento⟩

contest[2] ['kɑn,test] *n* **1** STRUGGLE : lucha *f*, contienda *f* **2** GAME : concurso *m*, competencia *f*

contestable [kən'testəbəl] *adj* : discutible, cuestionable

contestant [kən'testənt] *n* : concursante *mf*; competidor *m*, -dora *f*

context ['kɑn,tekst] *n* : contexto *m*

contiguous [kən'tɪgjuəs] *adj* : contiguo

continence ['kɑntənənts] *n* : continencia *f*

continent[1] ['kɑntənənt] *adj* : continente

continent[2] *n* : continente *m* — **continental** [,kɑntən'entəl] *adj*

contingency [kən'tɪndʒəntsi] *n, pl* -cies : contingencia *f*, eventualidad *f*

contingent[1] [kən'tɪndʒənt] *adj* **1** POSSIBLE : contingente, eventual **2** ACCIDENTAL : fortuito, accidental **3 to be contingent on** : depender de, estar sujeto a

contingent[2] *n* : contingente *m*

continual [kən'tɪnjuəl] *adj* : continuo, constante — **continually** [kən-'tɪnjuəli, -'tɪnjəli] *adv*

continuance [kən'tɪnjuənts] *n* **1** CONTINUATION : continuación *f* **2** DURA-

TION : duración *f* **3** : aplazamiento *m* (de un proceso)

continuation [kən͵tɪnjuˈeɪʃən] *n* : continuación *f*, prolongación *f*

continue [kənˈtɪnju:] *v* **-tinued; -tinuing** *vi* **1** CARRY ON : continuar, seguir, proseguir ⟨please continue : continúe, por favor⟩ **2** ENDURE, LAST : continuar, prolongarse, durar **3** RESUME : continuar, reanudarse — *vt* **1** : continuar, seguir ⟨she continued writing : continuó escribiendo⟩ **2** RESUME : continuar, reanudar **3** EXTEND, PROLONG : continuar, prolongar

continuity [͵kɑntə-ˈnu:əti, -ˈnju:-] *n, pl* **-ties** : continuidad *f*

continuous [kənˈtɪnjuəs] *adj* : continuo — **continuously** *adv*

contort [kənˈtɔrt] *vt* : torcer, retorcer, contraer (el rostro) — *vi* : contraerse, demudarse

contortion [kənˈtɔrʃən] *n* : contorsión *f*

contour [ˈkɑn͵tʊr] *n* **1** OUTLINE : contorno *m* **2** **contours** *npl* SHAPE : forma *f*, curvas *fpl* **3** **contour map** : mapa *m* topográfico

contraband [ˈkɑntrə͵bænd] *n* : contrabando *m*

contraception [͵kɑntrəˈsɛpʃən] *n* : anticoncepción *f*, contracepción *f*

contraceptive¹ [͵kɑntrəˈsɛptɪv] *adj* : anticonceptivo, contraceptivo

contraceptive² *n* : anticonceptivo *m*, contraceptivo *m*

contract¹ [kənˈtrækt, 1 *usu* ˈkɑn-͵trækt] *vt* **1** : contratar (servicios profesionales) **2** : contraer (una enfermedad, una deuda) **3** TIGHTEN : contraer (un músculo) **4** SHORTEN : contraer (una palabra) — *vi* : contraerse, reducirse

contract² [ˈkɑn͵trækt] *n* : contrato *m*

contraction [kənˈtrækʃən] *n* : contracción *f*

contractor [ˈkɑn͵træktər, kənˈtræk-] *n* : contratista *mf*

contractual [kənˈtræktʃuəl] *adj* : contractual — **contractually** *adv*

contradict [͵kɑntrəˈdɪkt] *vt* : contradecir, desmentir

contradiction [͵kɑntrəˈdɪkʃən] *n* : contradicción *f*

contradictory [͵kɑntrəˈdɪktəri] *adj* : contradictorio

contralto [kənˈtræl͵to:] *n, pl* **-tos** : contralto *m* (voz), contralto *mf* (vocalista)

contraption [kənˈtræpʃən] *n* DEVICE : aparato *m*, artefacto *m*

contrary¹ [ˈkɑn͵trɛri, 2 *often* kən-ˈtrɛri] *adj* **1** OPPOSITE : contrario, opuesto **2** BALKY, STUBBORN : terco, testarudo **3** **contrary to** : al contrario de, en contra de ⟨contrary to the facts : en contra de los hechos⟩

contrary² [ˈkɑn͵trɛri] *n, pl* **-traries** **1** OPPOSITE : lo contrario, lo opuesto **2** **on the contrary** : al contrario, todo lo contrario

contrast¹ [kənˈtræst] *vi* DIFFER : contrastar, diferir — *vt* COMPARE : contrastar, comparar

contrast² [ˈkɑn͵træst] *n* : contraste *m*

contravene [͵kɑntrəˈvi:n] *vt* **-vened; -vening** : contravenir, infringir

contribute [kənˈtrɪbjət] *v* **-uted; -uting** *vt* : contribuir, aportar (dinero, bienes, etc.) — *vi* : contribuir

contribution [͵kɑntrəˈbju:ʃən] *n* : contribución *f*

contributor [kənˈtrɪbjətər] *n* : contribuidor *m*, -dora *f*; colaborador *m*, -dora *f* (en periodismo)

contrite [ˈkɑn͵traɪt, kənˈtraɪt] *adj* REPENTANT : contrito, arrepentido

contrition [kənˈtrɪʃən] *n* : contrición *f*, arrepentimiento *m*

contrivance [kənˈtraɪvənts] *n* **1** DEVICE : aparato *m*, artefacto *m* **2** SCHEME : artimaña *f*, treta *f*, ardid *m*

contrive [kənˈtraɪv] *vt* **-trived; -triving** **1** DEVISE : idear, ingeniar, maquinar **2** MANAGE : lograr, ingeniárselas para ⟨she contrived a way out of the mess : se las ingenió para salir del enredo⟩

control¹ [kənˈtro:l] *vt* **-trolled; -trolling** : controlar, dominar

control² *n* **1** : control *m*, dominio *m*, mando *m* ⟨to be under control : estar bajo control⟩ **2** RESTRAINT : control *m*, limitación *f* ⟨birth control : control natal⟩ **3** : control *m*, dispositivo *m* de mando ⟨remote control : control remoto⟩

controllable [kənˈtro:ləbəl] *adj* : controlable

controller [kənˈtro:lər, ˈkɑn͵-] *n* **1** → **comptroller 2** : controlador *m*, -dora *f* ⟨air traffic controller : controlador aéreo⟩

controversial [͵kɑntrəˈvərʃəl, -siəl] *adj* : controvertido ⟨a controversial decision : una decisión controvertida⟩

controversy [ˈkɑntrə͵vərsi] *n, pl* **-sies** : controversia *f*

controvert [ˈkɑntrə͵vərt, ͵kɑntrəˈ-] *vt* : controvertir, contradecir

contusion [kənˈtu:ʒən, -tju:-] *n* BRUISE : contusión *f*, moretón *m*

conundrum [kəˈnʌndrəm] *n* RIDDLE : acertijo *m*, adivinanza *f*

convalesce [͵kɑnvəˈlɛs] *vi* **-lesced; -lescing** : convalecer

convalescence [͵kɑnvəˈlɛsənts] *n* : convalecencia *f*

convalescent¹ [͵kɑnvəˈlɛsənt] *adj* : convaleciente

convalescent² *n* : convaleciente *mf*

convection [kənˈvɛkʃən] *n* : convección *f*

convene [kənˈvi:n] *v* **-vened; -vening** *vt* : convocar — *vi* : reunirse

convenience [kənˈvi:njənts] *n* **1** : conveniencia *f* ⟨at your convenience : cuando le resulte conveniente⟩ **2** AMENITY : comodidad *f* ⟨modern conveniences : comodidades modernas⟩

convenience store *n* : tienda *f* de conveniencia
convenient [kən'vi:njənt] *adj* : conveniente, cómodo — **conveniently** *adv*
convent ['kɑnvənt, -,vɛnt] *n* : convento *m*
convention [kən'vɛntʃən] *n* **1** PACT : convención *f*, convenio *m*, pacto *m* ⟨the Geneva Convention : la Convención de Ginebra⟩ **2** MEETING : convención *f*, congreso *m* **3** CUSTOM : convención *f*, convencionalismo *m*
conventional [kən'vɛntʃənəl] *adj* : convencional — **conventionally** *adv*
converge [kən'vərdʒ] *vi* **-verged; -verging** : converger, convergir
convergence [kən'vərdʒənts] *n* : convergencia *f*
convergent [kən'vərdʒənt] *adj* : convergente
conversant [kən'vərsənt] *adj* **conversant with** : versado con, experto en
conversation [,kɑnvər'seɪʃən] *n* : conversación *f*
conversational [,kɑnvər'seɪʃənəl] *adj* : familiar ⟨a conversational style : un estilo familiar⟩
converse¹ [kən'vərs] *vi* **-versed; -versing** : conversar
converse² [kən'vərs, 'kɑn,vərs] *adj* : contrario, opuesto, inverso
conversely [kən'vərsli, 'kɑn,vərs-] *adv* : a la inversa
conversion [kən'vərʒən] *n* **1** CHANGE : conversión *f*, transformación *f*, cambio *m* **2** : conversión *f* (a una religión)
convert¹ [kən'vərt] *vt* **1** : convertir (a una religión o un partido) **2** CHANGE : convertir, cambiar — *vi* : convertirse
convert² ['kɑn,vərt] *n* : converso *m*, -sa *f*
converter *or* **convertor** [kən'vərtər] *n* : convertidor *m*
convertible¹ [kən'vərtəbəl] *adj* : convertible
convertible² *n* : convertible *m*, descapotable *m*
convex [kɑn'vɛks, 'kɑn,-, kən'-] *adj* : convexo
convey [kən'veɪ] *vt* **1** TRANSPORT : transportar, conducir **2** TRANSMIT : transmitir, comunicar, expresar (noticias, ideas, etc.)
conveyance [kən'veɪənts] *n* **1** TRANSPORT : transporte *m*, transportación *f* **2** COMMUNICATION : transmisión *f*, comunicación *f* **3** TRANSFER : transferencia *f*, traspaso *m* (de una propiedad)
conveyor [kən'veɪər] *n* : transportador *m*, -dora *f* ⟨conveyor belt : cinta transportadora⟩
convict¹ [kən'vɪkt] *vt* : declarar culpable
convict² ['kɑn,vɪkt] *n* : preso *m*, -sa *f*; presidiario *m*, -ria *f*; recluso *m*, -sa *f*
conviction [kən'vɪkʃən] *n* **1** : condena *f* (de un acusado) **2** BELIEF : convicción *f*, creencia *f*

convince [kən'vɪnts] *vt* **-vinced; -vincing** : convencer
convincing [kən'vɪntsɪŋ] *adj* : convincente, persuasivo
convincingly [kən'vɪntsɪŋli] *adv* : de forma convincente
convivial [kən'vɪvjəl, -'vɪviəl] *adj* : jovial, festivo, alegre
conviviality [kən,vɪvi'æləti] *n, pl* **-ties** : jovialidad *f*
convoke [kən'vo:k] *vt* **-voked; -voking** : convocar
convoluted ['kɑnvə,lu:təd] *adj* : intrincado, complicado
convoy ['kɑn,vɔɪ] *n* : convoy *m*
convulse [kən'vʌls] *v* **-vulsed; -vulsing** *vt* : convulsionar ⟨convulsed with laughter : muerto de risa⟩ — *vi* : sufrir convulsiones
convulsion [kən'vʌlʃən] *n* : convulsión *f*
convulsive [kən'vʌlsɪv] *adj* : convulsivo — **convulsively** *adv*
coo¹ ['ku:] *vi* : arrullar
coo² *n* : arrullo *m* (de una paloma)
cook¹ ['kʊk] *vi* : cocinar — *vt* **1** : preparar (comida) **2 to cook up** CONCOCT : inventar, tramar
cook² *n* : cocinero *m*, -ra *f*
cookbook ['kʊk,bʊk] *n* : libro *m* de cocina
cookery ['kʊkəri] *n, pl* **-eries** : cocina *f*
cookie *or* **cooky** ['kʊki] *n, pl* **-ies** : galleta *f* (dulce)
cooking ['kʊkɪŋ] *n* **1** COOKERY : cocina *f* **2** : cocción *f*, cocimiento *m* ⟨cooking time : tiempo de cocción⟩
cookout ['kʊk,aʊt] *n* : comida *f* al aire libre
cool¹ ['ku:l] *vt* : refrescar, enfriar — *vi* **1** : refrescarse, enfriarse ⟨the pie is cooling : el pastel se está enfriando⟩ **2** : calmarse, tranquilizarse ⟨his anger cooled : su ira se calmó⟩
cool² *adj* **1** : fresco, frío ⟨cool weather : tiempo fresco⟩ **2** CALM : tranquilo, sereno **3** ALOOF : frío, distante
cool³ *n* **1** : fresco *m* ⟨the cool of the evening : el fresco de la tarde⟩ **2** COMPOSURE : calma *f*, serenidad *f*
coolant ['ku:lənt] *n* : refrigerante *m*
cooler ['ku:lər] *n* : nevera *f* portátil
coolie ['ku:li] *n* : culí *m*
coolly ['ku:lli] *adv* **1** CALMLY : con calma, tranquilamente **2** COLDLY : fríamente, con frialdad
coolness ['ku:lnəs] *n* **1** : frescura *f*, frescor *m* ⟨the coolness of the evening : el frescor de la noche⟩ **2** CALMNESS : tranquilidad *f*, serenidad *f* **3** COLDNESS, INDIFFERENCE : frialdad *f*, indiferencia *f*
coop¹ ['ku:p, 'kʊp] *vt or* **to coop up** : encerrar ⟨cooped up in the house : encerrado en la casa⟩
coop² *n* : gallinero *m*
co-op ['ko:,ɑp] *n* → **cooperative²**
cooperate [ko'ɑpə,reɪt] *vi* **-ated; -ating** : cooperar, colaborar

cooperation [ko͵ɑpəˈreɪʃən] *n* : cooperación *f*, colaboración *f*
cooperative[1] [koˈɑpərətɪv, -ˈɑpə͵reɪtɪv] *adj* : cooperativo
cooperative[2] [koˈɑpərətɪv] *n* : cooperativa *f*
co-opt [koˈɑpt] *vt* **1** : nombrar como miembro, cooptar **2** APPROPRIATE : apropiarse de
coordinate[1] [koˈɔrdən͵eɪt] *v* -**nated; -nating** *vt* : coordinar — *vi* : coordinarse, combinar, acordar
coordinate[2] [koˈɔrdənət] *adj* **1** COORDINATED : coordinado **2** EQUAL : igual, semejante
coordinate[3] [koˈɔrdənət] *n* : coordenada *f*
coordination [ko͵ɔrdənˈeɪʃən] *n* : coordinación *f*
coordinator [koˈɔrdən͵eɪtər] *n* : coordinador *m*, -dora *f*
cop [ˈkɑp] → **police officer**
cope [ˈkoːp] *vi* **coped; coping 1** : arreglárselas **2 to cope with** : hacer frente a, poder con ⟨I can't cope with all this! : ¡no puedo con todo esto!⟩
copier [ˈkɑpiər] *n* : copiadora *f*, fotocopiadora *f*
copilot [ˈkoː͵paɪlət] *n* : copiloto *m*
copious [ˈkoːpiəs] *adj* : copioso, abundante — **copiously** *adv*
copiousness [ˈkoːpiəsnəs] *n* : abundancia *f*
copper [ˈkɑpər] *n* : cobre *m*
coppery [ˈkɑpəri] *adj* : cobrizo
copra [ˈkoːprə, ˈkɑ-] *n* : copra *f*
copse [ˈkɑps] *n* THICKET : soto *m*, matorral *m*
copulate [ˈkɑpjə͵leɪt] *vi* -**lated; -lating** : copular
copulation [͵kɑpjəˈleɪʃən] *n* : cópula *f*, relaciones *fpl* sexuales
copy[1] [ˈkɑpi] *vt* **copied; copying 1** DUPLICATE : hacer una copia de, duplicar, reproducir **2** IMITATE : copiar, imitar
copy[2] *n, pl* **copies 1** : copia *f*, duplicado *m* (de un documento), reproducción *f* (de una obra de arte) **2** : ejemplar *m* (de un libro), número *m* (de una revista) **3** TEXT : manuscrito *m*, texto *m*
copyright[1] [ˈkɑpi͵raɪt] *vt* : registrar los derechos de
copyright[2] *n* : derechos *mpl* de autor
coral[1] [ˈkɔrəl] *adj* : de coral ⟨a coral reef : un arrecife de coral⟩
coral[2] *n* : coral *m*
coral snake *n* : serpiente *f* de coral
cord [ˈkɔrd] *n* **1** ROPE, STRING : cuerda *f*, cordón *m*, cordel *m* **2** : cuerda *f*, cordón *m*, médula *f* (en la anatomía) ⟨vocal cords : cuerdas vocales⟩ **3** : cuerda *f* ⟨a cord of firewood : una cuerda de leña⟩ **4** *or* **electric cord** : cable *m* eléctrico
cordial[1] [ˈkɔrdʒəl] *adj* : cordial — **cordially** *adv*
cordial[2] *n* : cordial *m*

cordiality [͵kɔrdʒiˈæləti] *n* : cordialidad *f*
cordless [ˈkɔrdləs] *adj* : inalámbrico
cordon[1] [ˈkɔrdən] *vt* **to cordon off** : acordonar
cordon[2] *n* : cordón *m*
corduroy [ˈkɔrdə͵rɔɪ] *n* **1** : pana *f* **2 corduroys** *npl* : pantalones *mpl* de pana
core[1] [ˈkor] *vt* **cored; coring** : quitar el corazón a (una fruta)
core[2] *n* **1** : corazón *m*, centro *m* (de algunas frutas) **2** CENTER : núcleo *m*, centro *m* **3** ESSENCE : núcleo *m*, meollo *m* ⟨to the core : hasta la médula⟩
coriander [ˈkori͵ændər] *n* : cilantro *m*
cork[1] [ˈkɔrk] *vt* : ponerle un corcho a
cork[2] *n* : corcho *m*
corkscrew [ˈkɔrk͵skruː] *n* : tirabuzón *m*, sacacorchos *m*
cormorant [ˈkɔrmərənt, -͵rænt] *n* : cormorán *m*
corn[1] [ˈkɔrn] *vt* : conservar en salmuera ⟨corned beef : carne en conserva⟩
corn[2] *n* **1** GRAIN : grano *m* **2** : maíz *m*, elote *m* *Mex* ⟨corn tortillas : tortillas de maíz⟩ **3** : callo *m* ⟨corn plaster : emplasto para callos⟩
corncob [ˈkɔrn͵kɑb] *n* : mazorca *f* (de maíz), choclo *m*, elote *m* *CA, Mex*
cornea [ˈkɔrniə] *n* : córnea *f*
corner[1] [ˈkɔrnər] *vt* **1** TRAP : acorralar, arrinconar **2** MONOPOLIZE : monopolizar, acaparar (un mercado) — *vi* : tomar una curva, doblar una esquina (en un automóvil)
corner[2] *n* **1** ANGLE : rincón *m*, esquina *f*, ángulo *m* ⟨the corner of a room : el rincón de una sala⟩ ⟨all corners of the world : todos los rincones del mundo⟩ ⟨to cut corners : atajar, economizar esfuerzos⟩ **2** INTERSECTION : esquina *f* **3** IMPASSE, PREDICAMENT : aprieto *m*, impasse *m* ⟨to be backed into a corner : estar acorralado⟩
cornerstone [ˈkɔrnər͵stoːn] *n* : piedra *f* angular
cornet [kɔrˈnɛt] *n* : corneta *f*
cornfield [ˈkɔrn͵fiːld] *n* : maizal *m*; milpa *f* *CA, Mex*
cornice [ˈkɔrnɪs] *n* : cornisa *f*
cornmeal [ˈkɔrn͵miːl] *n* : harina *f* de maíz
cornstalk [ˈkɔrn͵stɔk] *n* : tallo *m* del maíz
cornstarch [ˈkɔrn͵stɑrtʃ] *n* : maicena *f*, almidón *m* de maíz
cornucopia [͵kɔrnəˈkoːpiə, -njə-] *n* : cornucopia *f*
corolla [kəˈrɑlə] *n* : corola *f*
corollary [ˈkɔrə͵lɛri] *n, pl* -**laries** : corolario *m*
corona [kəˈroːnə] *n* : corona *f* (del sol)
coronary[1] [ˈkɔrə͵nɛri] *adj* : coronario
coronary[2] *n, pl* -**naries 1** : trombosis *f* coronaria **2** HEART ATTACK : infarto *m*, ataque *m* al corazón
coronation [͵kɔrəˈneɪʃən] *n* : coronación *f*

coroner ['kɔrənər] *n* : médico *m* forense
corporal[1] ['kɔrpərəl] *adj* : corporal ⟨corporal punishment : castigos corporales⟩
corporal[2] *n* : cabo *m*
corporate ['kɔrpərət] *adj* : corporativo, empresarial
corporation [ˌkɔrpə'reɪʃən] *n* : sociedad *f* anónima, corporación *f*, empresa *f*
corporeal [kɔr'poriəl] *adj* 1 PHYSICAL : corpóreo 2 MATERIAL : material, tangible — **corporeally** *adv*
corps ['kor] *n, pl* **corps** ['korz] : cuerpo *m* ⟨medical corps : cuerpo médico⟩ ⟨diplomatic corps : cuerpo diplomático⟩
corpse ['kɔrps] *n* : cadáver *m*
corpulence ['kɔrpjələnts] *n* : obesidad *f*, gordura *f*
corpulent ['kɔrpjələnt] *adj* : obeso, gordo
corpuscle ['kɔr,pʌsəl] *n* : corpúsculo *m*, glóbulo *m* (sanguíneo)
corral[1] [kə'ræl] *vt* **-ralled; -ralling** : acorralar, encorralar (ganado)
corral[2] *n* : corral *m*
correct[1] [kə'rɛkt] *vt* 1 RECTIFY : corregir, rectificar 2 REPRIMAND : corregir, reprender
correct[2] *adj* 1 ACCURATE, RIGHT : correcto, exacto ⟨to be correct : estar en lo cierto⟩ 2 PROPER : correcto, apropiado
correction [kə'rɛkʃən] *n* : corrección *f*
corrective [kə'rɛktɪv] *adj* : correctivo
correctly [kə'rɛktli] *adv* : correctamente
correctness [kə'rɛk(t)nəs] *n* 1 ACCURACY : exactitud *f* 2 PROPRIETY : corrección *f*
correlate ['kɔrə,leɪt] *vt* **-lated; -lating** : relacionar, poner en correlación
correlation [ˌkɔrə'leɪʃən] *n* : correlación *f*
correspond [ˌkɔrə'spɑnd] *vi* 1 MATCH : corresponder, concordar, coincidir 2 WRITE : corresponderse, escribirse
correspondence [ˌkɔrə'spɑndənts] *n* : correspondencia *f*
correspondent [ˌkɔrə'spɑndənt] *n* : corresponsal *mf*
corresponding [kɔrə'spɑndɪŋ, kɑr-] *adj* : correspondiente
correspondingly [ˌkɔrə'spɑndɪŋli] *adv* : en consecuencia, de la misma manera
corridor ['kɔrədər, -,dɔr] *n* : corredor *m*, pasillo *m*
corroborate [kə'rɑbə,reɪt] *vt* **-rated; -rating** : corroborar
corroboration [kə,rɑbə'reɪʃən] *n* : corroboración *f*
corrode [kə'ro:d] *v* **-roded; -roding** *vt* : corroer — *vi* : corroerse
corrosion [kə'ro:ʒən] *n* : corrosión *f*
corrosive [kə'ro:sɪv] *adj* : corrosivo
corrugate ['kɔrə,geɪt] *vt* **-gated; -gating** : ondular, acanalar, corrugar

corrugated ['kɔrə,geɪtəd] *adj* : ondulado, acanalado ⟨corrugated cardboard : cartón ondulado⟩
corrupt[1] [kə'rʌpt] *vt* 1 PERVERT : corromper, pervertir, degradar (información) 2 BRIBE : sobornar
corrupt[2] *adj* : corrupto, corrompido
corruptible [kə'rʌptəbəl] *adj* : corruptible
corruption [kə'rʌpʃən] *n* : corrupción *f*
corsage [kɔr'sɑʒ, -'sɑʤ] *n* : ramillete *m* que se lleva como adorno
corset ['kɔrsət] *n* : corsé *m*
cortex ['kɔr,tɛks] *n, pl* **-tices** ['kɔrtə,si:z] *or* **-texes** : corteza *f* ⟨cerebral cortex : corteza cerebral⟩
cortisone ['kɔrtə,so:n, -zo:n] *n* : cortisona *f*
cosmetic[1] [kaz'mɛtɪk] *adj* : cosmético
cosmetic[2] *n* : cosmético *m*
cosmic ['kazmɪk] *adj* 1 : cósmico ⟨cosmic ray : rayo cósmico⟩ 2 VAST : grandioso, inmenso, vasto
cosmonaut ['kazmə,nɔt] *n* : cosmonauta *mf*
cosmopolitan[1] [ˌkazmə'palətən] *adj* : cosmopolita
cosmopolitan[2] *n* : cosmopolita *mf*
cosmos ['kazməs, -,mo:s, -,mas] *n* : cosmos *m*, universo *m*
cost[1] ['kɔst] *v* **cost; costing** *vt* : costar ⟨how much does it cost? : ¿cuánto cuesta?, ¿cuánto vale?⟩ — *vi* : costar ⟨these cost more : éstos cuestan más⟩
cost[2] *n* : costo *m*, precio *m*, coste *m* ⟨cost of living : costo de vida⟩ ⟨victory at all costs : victoria a toda costa⟩
Costa Rican[1] [ˌkɔstə'ri:kən] *adj* : costarricense
Costa Rican[2] *n* : costarricense *mf*
costly ['kɔstli] *adj* : costoso, caro
costume ['kas,tu:m, -,tju:m] *n* 1 : traje *m* ⟨national costume : traje típico⟩ 2 : disfraz *m* ⟨costume party : fiesta de disfraces⟩ 3 OUTFIT : vestimenta *f*, traje *m*, conjunto *m*
cosy ['ko:zi] → **cozy**
cot ['kat] *n* : catre *m*
coterie ['ko:tə,ri, ,ko:tə'-] *n* : tertulia *f*, círculo *m* (social)
cottage ['katɪʤ] *n* : casita *f* (de campo)
cottage cheese *n* : requesón *m*
cotton ['katən] *n* : algodón *m*
cottonmouth ['katən,mauθ] → **moccasin**
cottonseed ['katən,si:d] *n* : semilla *f* de algodón
cotton swab → **swab**
cottontail ['katən,teɪl] *n* : conejo *m* de cola blanca
couch[1] ['kauʧ] *vt* : expresar, formular ⟨couched in strong language : expresado en lenguaje enérgico⟩
couch[2] *n* SOFA : sofá *m*
couch potato *n* : haragán *m*, -gana *f*; vago *m*, -ga *f*
cougar ['ku:gər] *n* : puma *m*
cough[1] ['kɔf] *vi* : toser

cough² *n* : tos *f*
could ['kʊd] → **can**
council ['kaʊntsəl] *n* **1** : concejo *m* ⟨city council : concejo municipal, ayuntamiento⟩ **2** MEETING : concejo *m*, junta *f* **3** BOARD : consejo *m* **4** : concilio *m* (eclesiástico)
councillor *or* **councilor** ['kaʊntsələr] *n* : concejal *m*, -jala *f*
councilman ['kaʊntsəlmən] *n*, *pl* **-men** [-mən, -ˌmɛn] : concejal *m*
councilwoman ['kaʊntsəl,wʊmən] *n*, *pl* **-women** [-ˌwɪmən] : concejala *f*
counsel¹ ['kaʊntsəl] *v* **-seled** *or* **-selled**; **-seling** *or* **-selling** *vt* ADVISE : aconsejar, asesorar, recomendar — *vi* CONSULT : consultar
counsel² *n* **1** ADVICE : consejo *m*, recomendación *f* **2** CONSULTATION : consulta *f* **3** counsel *ns* & *pl* LAWYER : abogado *m*, -da *f*
counselor *or* **counsellor** ['kaʊntsələr] *n* : consejero *m*, -ra *f*; consultor *m*, -tora *f*; asesor *m*, -sora *f*
count¹ ['kaʊnt] *vt* : contar, enumerar — *vi* **1** : contar ⟨to count out loud : contar en voz alta⟩ **2** MATTER : contar, valer, importar ⟨that's what counts : eso es lo que cuenta⟩ **3 to count on** : contar con
count² *n* **1** COMPUTATION : cómputo *m*, recuento *m*, cuenta *f* ⟨to lose count : perder la cuenta⟩ **2** CHARGE : cargo *m* ⟨two counts of robbery : dos cargos de robo⟩ **3** : conde *m* (noble)
countable ['kaʊntəbəl] *adj* : numerable
countdown ['kaʊnt,daʊn] *n* : cuenta *f* atrás
countenance¹ ['kaʊntənənts] *vt* **-nanced; -nancing** : permitir, tolerar
countenance² *n* FACE : semblante *m*, rostro *m*
counter¹ ['kaʊntər] *vt* **1** → **counteract** **2** OPPOSE : oponerse a, resistir — *vi* RETALIATE : responder, contraatacar
counter² *adv* **counter to** : contrario a, en contra de
counter³ *adj* : contrario, opuesto
counter⁴ *n* **1** PIECE : ficha *f* (de un juego) **2** : mostrador *m* (de un negocio), ventanilla *f* (en un banco) **3** : contador *m* (aparato) **4** COUNTERBALANCE : fuerza *f* opuesta, contrapeso *m*
counteract [ˌkaʊntər'ækt] *vt* : contrarrestar
counterattack ['kaʊntərə,tæk] *n* : contraataque *m*
counterbalance¹ [ˌkaʊntər'bælənts] *vt* **-anced; -ancing** : contrapesar
counterbalance² ['kaʊntər,bælənts] *n* : contrapeso *m*
counterclockwise [ˌkaʊntər'klak-,waɪz] *adv* & *adj* : en el sentido opuesto al de las manecillas del reloj
counterfeit¹ ['kaʊntər,fɪt] *vt* **1** : falsificar (dinero) **2** PRETEND : fingir, aparentar
counterfeit² *adj* : falso, inauténtico
counterfeit³ *n* : falsificación *f*

counterfeiter ['kaʊntər,fɪtər] *n* : falsificador *m*, -dora *f*
countermand ['kaʊntər,mænd, ˌkaʊntər'-] *vt* : contramandar
countermeasure ['kaʊntər,mɛʒər] *n* : contramedida *f*
counterpart ['kaʊntər,part] *n* : homólogo *m*, contraparte *f* *Mex*
counterpoint ['kaʊntər,pɔɪnt] *n* : contrapunto *m*
counterproductive [ˌkaʊntərprə'dʌktɪv] *adj* : contraproducente
counterrevolution [ˌkaʊntər,rɛvə-'lu:-ʃən] *n* : contrarrevolución *f*
counterrevolutionary¹ [ˌkaʊntər,rɛvə-'lu:ʃən,ɛri] *adj* : contrarrevolucionario
counterrevolutionary² *n*, *pl* **-ries** : contrarrevolucionario *m*, -ria *f*
countersign ['kaʊntər,saɪn] *n* : contraseña *f*
countess ['kaʊntɪs] *n* : condesa *f*
countless ['kaʊntləs] *adj* : incontable, innumerable
country¹ ['kʌntri] *adj* : campestre, rural
country² *n*, *pl* **-tries 1** NATION : país *m*, nación *f*, patria *f* ⟨country of origin : país de origen⟩ ⟨love of one's country : amor a la patria⟩ **2** : campo *m* ⟨they left the city for the country : se fueron de la ciudad al campo⟩
countryman ['kʌntrimən] *n*, *pl* **-men** [-mən, -ˌmɛn] : compatriota *mf*; paisano *m*, -na *f*
countryside ['kʌntri,saɪd] *n* : campo *m*, campiña *f*
county ['kaʊnti] *n*, *pl* **-ties** : condado *m*
coup ['ku:] *n*, *pl* **coups** ['ku:z] **1** : golpe *m* maestro **2** *or* **coup d'etat** : golpe *m* (de estado), cuartelazo *m*
coupe ['ku:p] *n* : cupé *m*
couple¹ ['kʌpəl] *vt* **-pled; -pling** : acoplar, enganchar, conectar
couple² *n* **1** PAIR : par *m* ⟨a couple of hours : un par de horas, unas dos horas⟩ **2** : pareja *f* ⟨a young couple : una pareja joven⟩
coupling ['kʌplɪŋ] *n* : acoplamiento *m*
coupon ['ku:,pan, 'kju:-] *n* : cupón *m*
courage ['kərɪdʒ] *n* : valor *m*, valentía *f*, coraje *m*
courageous [kə'reɪdʒəs] *adj* : valiente, valeroso
courier ['kʊriər, 'kəriər] *n* : mensajero *m*, -ra *f*
course¹ ['kors] *vi* **coursed; coursing** : correr (a toda velocidad)
course² *n* **1** PROGRESS : curso *m*, transcurso *m* ⟨to run its course : seguir su curso⟩ **2** DIRECTION : rumbo *m* (de un avión), derrota *f*, derrotero *m* (de un barco) **3** PATH, WAY : camino *m*, vía *f* ⟨course of action : línea de conducta⟩ **4** : plato *m* (de una cena) ⟨the main course : el plato principal⟩ **5** : curso *m* (académico) **6 of course** : desde luego, por supuesto ⟨yes, of course! : ¡claro que sí!⟩

court¹ ['kort] *vt* WOO : cortejar, galantear

court² *n* **1** PALACE : palacio *m* **2** RETINUE : corte *f*, séquito *m* **3** COURTYARD : patio *m* **4** : cancha *f* (de tenis, baloncesto, etc.) **5** TRIBUNAL : corte *f*, tribunal *m* ⟨the Supreme Court : la Corte Suprema⟩

courteous ['kərʈiəs] *adj* : cortés, atento, educado — **courteously** *adv*

courtesan ['korʈəzən, 'kər-] *n* : cortesana *f*

courtesy ['kərʈəsi] *n, pl* **-sies** : cortesía *f*

courthouse ['kort,haʊs] *n* : palacio *m* de justicia, juzgado *m*

courtier ['korʈiər, 'kortjər] *n* : cortesano *m*, -na *f*

courtly ['kortli] *adj* **-lier; -est** : distinguido, elegante, cortés

court–martial¹ ['kort,marʃəl] *vt* : someter a consejo de guerra

court–martial² *n, pl* **courts–martial** ['korts,marʃəl] : consejo *m* de guerra

court order *n* : mandamiento *m* judicial

courtroom ['kort,ru:m] *n* : tribunal *m*, corte *f*

courtship ['kort,ʃɪp] *n* : cortejo *m*, noviazgo *m*

courtyard ['kort,jard] *n* : patio *m*

cousin ['kʌzən] *n* : primo *m*, -ma *f*

couture [ku:'tʊr] *n* : industria *f* de la moda ⟨haute couture : alta costura⟩

cove ['ko:v] *n* : ensenada *f*, cala *f*

covenant ['kʌvənənt] *n* : pacto *m*, contrato *m*

cover¹ ['kʌvər] *vt* **1** : cubrir, tapar ⟨cover your head : tápate la cabeza⟩ ⟨covered with mud : cubierto de lodo⟩ **2** HIDE, PROTECT : encubrir, proteger **3** TREAT : tratar **4** INSURE : asegurar, cubrir

cover² *n* **1** SHELTER : cubierta *f*, abrigo *m*, refugio *m* ⟨to take cover : ponerse a cubierto⟩ ⟨under cover of darkness : al amparo de la oscuridad⟩ **2** LID, TOP : cubierta *f*, tapa *f* **3** : cubierta *f* (de un libro), portada *f* (de una revista) **4** **covers** *npl* BEDCLOTHES : ropa *f* de cama, cobijas *fpl*, mantas *fpl*

coverage ['kʌvərɪdʒ] *n* : cobertura *f*

coverlet ['kʌvərlət] *n* : cobertor *m*

covert¹ ['ko:,vərt, 'kʌvərt] *adj* : encubierto, secreto ⟨covert operations : operaciones encubiertas⟩

covert² ['kʌvərt, 'ko:-] *n* THICKET : espesura *f*, maleza *f*

cover–up ['kʌvər,ʌp] *n* : encubrimiento *m* (de algo ilícito)

covet ['kʌvət] *vt* : codiciar

covetous ['kʌvəʈəs] *adj* : codicioso

covey ['kʌvi] *n, pl* **-eys** **1** : bandada *f* pequeña (de codornices, etc.) **2** GROUP : grupo *m*

cow¹ ['kaʊ] *vt* : intimidar, acobardar

cow² *n* : vaca *f*, hembra *f* (de ciertas especies)

coward ['kaʊərd] *n* : cobarde *mf*

cowardice ['kaʊərdɪs] *n* : cobardía *f*

cowardly ['kaʊərdli] *adj* : cobarde

cowboy ['kaʊ,bɔɪ] *n* : vaquero *m*, cowboy *m*

cower ['kaʊər] *vi* : encogerse (de miedo), acobardarse

cowgirl ['kaʊ,gərl] *n* : vaquera *f*

cowherd ['kaʊ,hərd] *n* : vaquero *m*, -ra *f*

cowhide ['kaʊ,haɪd] *n* : cuero *m*, piel *f* de vaca

cowl ['kaʊl] *n* : capucha *f* (de un monje)

cowlick ['kaʊ,lɪk] *n* : remolino *m*

cowpuncher ['kaʊ,pʌnʧər] → **cowboy**

cowslip ['kaʊ,slɪp] *n* : prímula *f*, primavera *f*

coxswain ['kɑksən, -,sweɪn] *n* : timonel *m*

coy ['kɔɪ] *adj* **1** SHY : tímido, cohibido **2** COQUETTISH : coqueto

coyote [kaɪ'o:ʈi, 'kaɪ,o:t] *n, pl* **coyotes** *or* **coyote** : coyote *m*

cozy ['ko:zi] *adj* **-zier; -est** : acogedor, cómodo

CPU [,si:,pi:'ju:] *n* (central processing unit) : CPU *f*

crab ['kræb] *n* : cangrejo *m*, jaiba *f*

crabby ['kræbi] *adj* **-bier; -est** : gruñón, malhumorado

crabgrass ['kræb,græs] *n* : garranchuelo *m*

crack¹ ['kræk] *vi* **1** : chasquear, restallar ⟨the whip cracked : el látigo restalló⟩ **2** SPLIT : rajarse, resquebrajarse, agrietarse **3** : quebrarse (dícese de la voz) — *vt* **1** : restallar, chasquear (un látigo, etc.) **2** SPLIT : rajar, agrietar, resquebrajar **3** BREAK : romper (un huevo), cascar (nueces), forzar (una caja fuerte) **4** SOLVE : resolver, descifrar (un código)

crack² *adj* FIRST-RATE : buenísimo, de primera

crack³ *n* **1** : chasquido *m*, restallido *m*, estallido *m* (de un arma de fuego), crujido *m* (de huesos) ⟨a crack of thunder : un trueno⟩ **2** WISECRACK : chiste *m*, ocurrencia *f*, salida *f* **3** CREVICE : raja *f*, grieta *f*, fisura *f* **4** BLOW : golpe *m* **5** ATTEMPT : intento *m*

crackdown ['kræk,daʊn] *n* : medidas *fpl* enérgicas

crack down *vt* : tomar medidas enérgicas

cracker ['krækər] *n* : galleta *f* (de soda, etc.)

crackle¹ ['krækəl] *vi* **-led; -ling** : crepitar, chisporrotear

crackle² *n* : crujido *m*, chisporroteo *m*

crackpot ['kræk,pɑt] *n* : excéntrico *m*, -ca *f*; chiflado *m*, -da *f*

crack–up ['kræk,ʌp] *n* **1** CRASH : choque *m*, estrellamiento *m* **2** BREAKDOWN : crisis *f* nerviosa

crack up *vt* **1** : estrellar (un vehículo) **2** : hacer reír **3** : elogiar ⟨it isn't all that it's cracked up to be : no es tan bueno como se dice⟩ — *vi* **1** : estrellarse **2** LAUGH : echarse a reír

cradle¹ ['kreɪdəl] vt **-dled; -dling** : acunar, mecer (a un niño)

cradle² n : cuna f

craft ['kræft] n **1** TRADE : oficio m ⟨the craft of carpentry : el oficio de carpintero⟩ **2** CRAFTSMANSHIP, SKILL : arte m, artesanía f, destreza f **3** CRAFTINESS : astucia f, maña f **4** pl usually **craft** BOAT : barco m, embarcación f **5** pl usually **craft** AIRCRAFT : avión m, aeronave f

craftiness ['kræftinəs] n : astucia f, maña f

craftsman ['kræftsmən] n, pl **-men** [-mən, -ˌmɛn] : artesano m, -na f

craftsmanship ['kræftsmənˌʃɪp] n : artesanía f, destreza f

crafty ['kræfti] adj **craftier; -est** : astuto, taimado

crag ['kræg] n : peñasco m

craggy ['krægi] adj **-gier; -est** : peñascoso

cram ['kræm] v **crammed; cramming** vt **1** JAM : embutir, meter **2** STUFF : atiborrar, abarrotar ⟨crammed with people : atiborrado de gente⟩ — vi : estudiar a última hora, memorizar (para un examen)

cramp¹ ['kræmp] vt **1** : dar calambre en **2** RESTRICT : limitar, restringir, entorpecer ⟨to cramp someone's style : cortarle el vuelo a alguien⟩ — vi or **to cramp up** : acalambrarse

cramp² n **1** SPASM : calambre m, espasmo m (de los músculos) **2 cramps** npl : retorcijones mpl ⟨stomach cramps : retorcijones de estómago⟩

cranberry ['krænˌbɛri] n, pl **-berries** : arándano m (rojo y agrio)

crane¹ ['kreɪn] vt **craned; craning** : estirar ⟨to crane one's neck : estirar el cuello⟩

crane² n **1** : grulla f (ave) **2** : grúa f (máquina)

cranial ['kreɪniəl] adj : craneal, craneano

cranium ['kreɪniəm] n, pl **-niums** or **-nia** [-niə] : cráneo m

crank¹ ['kræŋk] vt or **to crank up** : arrancar (con una manivela)

crank² n **1** : manivela f, manubrio m **2** ECCENTRIC : excéntrico m, -ca f

cranky ['kræŋki] adj **crankier; -est** : irritable, malhumorado, enojadizo

cranny ['kræni] n, pl **-nies** : grieta f ⟨every nook and cranny : todos los rincones⟩

crash¹ ['kræʃ] vi **1** SMASH : caerse con estrépito, estrellarse **2** COLLIDE : estrellarse, chocar **3** BOOM, RESOUND : retumbar, resonar — vt **1** SMASH : estrellar **2 to crash a party** : colarse en una fiesta **3 to crash one's car** : tener un accidente

crash² n **1** DIN : estrépito m **2** COLLISION : choque m, colisión f ⟨car crash : accidente automovilístico⟩ **3** FAILURE : quiebra f (de un negocio), crac m (de la bolsa)

crass ['kræs] adj : grosero, de mal gusto

crate¹ ['kreɪt] vt **crated; crating** : empacar en un cajón

crate² n : cajón m (de madera)

crater ['kreɪtər] n : cráter m

cravat [krə'væt] n : corbata f

crave ['kreɪv] vt **craved; craving** : ansiar, apetecer, tener muchas ganas de

craven ['kreɪvən] adj : cobarde, pusilánime

craving ['kreɪvɪŋ] n : ansia f, antojo m, deseo m

crawfish ['krɔˌfɪʃ] → **crayfish**

crawl¹ ['krɔl] vi **1** CREEP : arrastrarse, gatear (dícese de un bebé) **2** TEEM : estar plagado

crawl² n : paso m lento

crayfish ['kreɪˌfɪʃ] n **1** : ástaco m (de agua dulce) **2** : langostino m (de mar)

crayon ['kreɪˌɑn, -ən] n : crayón m

craze ['kreɪz] n : moda f pasajera, manía f

crazed ['kreɪzd] adj : enloquecido

crazily ['kreɪzəli] adv : locamente, erráticamente, insensatamente

craziness ['kreɪzinəs] n : locura f, demencia f

crazy ['kreɪzi] adj **-zier; -est 1** INSANE : loco, demente ⟨to go crazy : volverse loco⟩ **2** ABSURD, FOOLISH : loco, insensato, absurdo **3 like crazy** : como loco **4 to be crazy about** : estar loco por

creak¹ ['kriːk] vi : chirriar, rechinar, crujir

creak² n : chirrido m, crujido m

creaky ['kriːki] adj **creakier; -est** : chirriante, que cruje

cream¹ ['kriːm] vt **1** BEAT, MIX : batir, mezclar (azúcar y mantequilla, etc.) **2** : preparar (alimentos) con crema

cream² n **1** : crema f (de leche) **2** LOTION : crema f, loción f **3** ELITE : crema f, elite f ⟨the cream of the crop : la crema y nata, lo mejor⟩

creamery ['kriːməri] n, pl **-eries** : fábrica f de productos lácteos

creamy ['kriːmi] adj **creamier; -est** : cremoso

crease¹ ['kriːs] vt **creased; creasing 1** : plegar, poner una raya en (pantalones) **2** WRINKLE : arrugar

crease² n : pliegue m, doblez m, raya f (de pantalones)

create [kri'eɪt] vt **-ated; -ating** : crear, hacer

creation [kri'eɪʃən] n : creación f

creative [kri'eɪtɪv] adj : creativo, original ⟨creative people : personas creativas⟩ ⟨a creative work : un obra original⟩

creatively [kri'eɪtɪvli] adv : creativamente, con originalidad

creativity [ˌkriːeɪ'tɪvəti] n : creatividad f

creator [kri'eɪtər] n : creador m, -dora f

creature ['kriːtʃər] n : ser m viviente, criatura f, animal m

credence ['kri:dənts] *n* : crédito *m*
credentials [krɪ'dɛnʃəlz] *npl* : referencias *fpl* oficiales, cartas *fpl* credenciales
credibility [ˌkredə'bɪləti] *n* : credibilidad *f*
credible ['krɛdəbəl] *adj* : creíble
credit[1] ['krɛdɪt] *vt* **1** BELIEVE : creer, dar crédito a **2** : ingresar, abonar ⟨to credit $100 to an account : ingresar $100 en (una) cuenta⟩ **3** ATTRIBUTE : atribuir ⟨they credit the invention to him : a él se le atribuye el invento⟩
credit[2] *n* **1** : saldo *m* positivo, saldo *m* a favor (de una cuenta) **2** : crédito *m* ⟨to buy on credit : comprar a crédito⟩ ⟨credit card : tarjeta de crédito⟩ **3** CREDENCE : crédito *m* ⟨I gave credit to everything he said : di crédito a todo lo que dijo⟩ **4** RECOGNITION : reconocimiento *m* **5** : orgullo *m*, honor *m* ⟨she's a credit to the school : ella es el orgullo de la escuela⟩
creditable ['krɛdɪtəbəl] *adj* : encomiable, loable — **creditably** [-bli] *adv*
credit card *n* : tarjeta de crédito
creditor ['krɛdɪtər] *n* : acreedor *m*, -dora *f*
credo ['kri:do:, 'krei-] *n* : credo *m*
credulity [krɪ'du:ləti, -'dju:-] *n* : credulidad *f*
credulous ['krɛdʒələs] *adj* : crédulo
creed ['kri:d] *n* : credo *m*
creek ['kri:k, 'krɪk] *n* : arroyo *m*, riachuelo *m*
creel ['kri:l] *n* : nasa *f*, cesta *f* (de pescador)
creep[1] ['kri:p] *vi* **crept** ['krɛpt]; **creeping 1** CRAWL : arrastrarse, gatear **2** : moverse lentamente o sigilosamente ⟨he crept out of the house : salió sigilosamente de la casa⟩ **3** SPREAD : trepar (dícese de una planta)
creep[2] *n* **1** CRAWL : paso *m* lento **2** : asqueroso *m*, -sa *f* **3 creeps** *npl* : escalofríos *mpl* ⟨that gives me the creeps : eso me da escalofríos⟩
creeper ['kri:pər] *n* : planta *f* trepadora, trepadora *f*
creepy ['kri:pi] *adj* **1** SPOOKY : espeluznante **2** UNPLEASANT : asqueroso
cremate ['kri:ˌmeɪt] *vt* **-mated; -mating** : cremar
cremation [krɪ'meɪʃən] *n* : cremación *f*
Creole ['kri:ˌo:l] *n* **1** : criollo *m*, criolla *f* **2** : criollo *m* (idioma) — **Creole** *adj*
creosote ['kri:əˌso:t] *n* : creosota *f*
crepe *or* **crêpe** ['kreɪp] *n* **1** : crespón *m* (tela) **2** PANCAKE : crepe *mf*, crepa *f* *Mex*
crescendo [krɪ'ʃɛnˌdo:] *n, pl* **-dos** *or* **-does** : crescendo *m*
crescent ['krɛsənt] *n* : creciente *m*
crest ['krɛst] *n* **1** : cresta *f*, penacho *m* (de una ave) **2** PEAK, TOP : cresta *f* (de una ola), cima *f* (de una colina) **3** : emblema *m* (sobre un escudo de armas)
crestfallen ['krɛstˌfɔlən] *adj* : alicaído, abatido

cretin ['kri:tən] *n* : cretino *m*, -na *f*
crevasse [krɪ'væs] *n* : grieta *f*, fisura *f*
crevice ['krɛvɪs] *n* : grieta *f*, hendidura *f*
crew ['kru:] *n* **1** : tripulación *f* (de una nave) **2** TEAM : equipo *m* (de trabajadores o atletas)
crib ['krɪb] *n* **1** MANGER : pesebre *m* **2** GRANARY : granero *m* **3** : cuna *f* (de un bebé)
crick ['krɪk] *n* : calambre *m*, espasmo *m* muscular
cricket ['krɪkət] *n* **1** : grillo *m* (insecto) **2** : críquet *m* (juego)
crime ['kraɪm] *n* **1** : crimen *m*, delito *m* ⟨to commit a crime : cometer un delito⟩ **2** : crimen *m*, delincuencia *f* ⟨organized crime : crimen organizado⟩
criminal[1] ['krɪmənəl] *adj* : criminal
criminal[2] *n* : criminal *mf*, delincuente *mf*
crimp ['krɪmp] *vt* : ondular, rizar (el pelo), arrugar (una tela, etc.)
crimson ['krɪmzən] *n* : carmesí *m*
cringe ['krɪndʒ] *vi* **cringed; cringing** : encogerse
crinkle[1] ['krɪŋkəl] *v* **-kled; -kling** *vt* : arrugar — *vi* : arrugarse
crinkle[2] *n* : arruga *f*
crinkly ['krɪŋkəli] *adj* : arrugado
cripple[1] ['krɪpəl] *vt* **-pled; -pling 1** DISABLE : lisiar, dejar inválido **2** INCAPACITATE : inutilizar, incapacitar
cripple[2] *n* : lisiado *m*, -da *f*
crisis ['kraɪsɪs] *n, pl* **crises** [-ˌsi:z] : crisis *f*
crisp[1] ['krɪsp] *vt* : tostar, hacer crujiente
crisp[2] *adj* **1** CRUNCHY : crujiente, crocante **2** FIRM, FRESH : firme, fresco ⟨crisp lettuce : lechuga fresca⟩ **3** LIVELY : vivaz, alegre ⟨a crisp tempo : un ritmo alegre⟩ **4** INVIGORATING : fresco, vigorizante ⟨the crisp autumn air : el fresco aire otoñal⟩ — **crisply** *adv*
crisp[3] *n* : postre *m* de fruta (con pedacitos de masa dulce por encima)
crispy ['krɪspi] *adj* **crispier; -est** : crujiente ⟨crispy potato chips : papitas crujientes⟩
crisscross ['krɪsˌkrɔs] *vt* : entrecruzar
criterion [kraɪ'tɪriən] *n, pl* **-ria** [-iə] : criterio *m*
critic ['krɪtɪk] *n* **1** : crítico *m*, -ca *f* (de las artes) **2** FAULTFINDER : detractor *m*, -tora *f*; criticón *m*, -cona *f*
critical ['krɪtɪkəl] *adj* : crítico
critically ['krɪtɪkli] *adv* : críticamente ⟨critically ill : gravemente enfermo⟩
criticism ['krɪtəˌsɪzəm] *n* : crítica *f*
criticize ['krɪtəˌsaɪz] *vt* **-cized; -cizing 1** EVALUATE, JUDGE : criticar, analizar, evaluar **2** CENSURE : criticar, reprobar
critique [krɪ'ti:k] *n* : crítica *f*, evaluación *f*
croak[1] ['kro:k] *vi* : croar
croak[2] *n* : croar *m*, canto *m* (de la rana)
Croatian [kro'eɪʃən] *n* : croata *mf* — **Croatian** *adj*

crochet¹ [kro:'ʃeɪ] *v* : tejer al croché
crochet² *n* : croché *m*, crochet *m*
crock ['krɑk] *n* : vasija *f* de barro
crockery ['krɑkəri] *n* : vajilla *f* (de barro)
crocodile ['krɑkə͵daɪl] *n* : cocodrilo *m*
crocus ['kro:kəs] *n, pl* **-cuses** : azafrán *m*
croissant [krə'sɑnt] *n* : croissant *m*
crone ['kro:n] *n* : vieja *f* arpía, vieja *f* bruja
crony ['kro:ni] *n, pl* **-nies** : amigote *m fam*; compinche *mf fam*
crook¹ ['krʊk] *vt* : doblar (el brazo o el dedo)
crook² *n* **1** STAFF : cayado *m* (de pastor), báculo *m* (de obispo) **2** THIEF : ratero *m*, -ra *f*; ladrón *m*, -drona *f*
crooked ['krʊkəd] *adj* **1** BENT : chueco, torcido **2** DISHONEST : deshonesto
crookedness ['krʊkədnəs] *n* **1** : lo torcido, lo chueco **2** DISHONESTY : falta *f* de honradez
croon ['kru:n] *v* : cantar suavemente
crop¹ ['krɑp] *v* **cropped; cropping** *vt* TRIM : recortar, cortar — *vi* **to crop up** : aparecer, surgir ⟨these problems keep cropping up : estos problemas no cesan de surgir⟩
crop² *n* **1** : buche *m* (de un ave o insecto) **2** WHIP : fusta *f* (de jinete) **3** HARVEST : cosecha *f*, cultivo *m*
croquet [͵kro:'keɪ] *n* : croquet *m*
croquette [͵kro:'kɛt] *n* : croqueta *f*
cross¹ ['krɔs] *vt* **1** : cruzar, atravesar ⟨to cross the street : cruzar la calle⟩ ⟨several canals cross the city : varios canales atraviesan la ciudad⟩ **2** CANCEL : tachar, cancelar ⟨he crossed his name off the list : tachó su nombre de la planilla⟩ **3** INTERBREED : cruzar (en genética)
cross² *adj* **1** : que atraviesa ⟨cross ventilation : ventilación que atraviesa un cuarto⟩ **2** CONTRARY : contrario, opuesto ⟨cross purposes : objetivos opuestos⟩ **3** ANGRY : enojado, de mal humor
cross³ *n* **1** : cruz *f* ⟨the sign of the cross : la señal de la cruz⟩ **2** : cruza *f* (en biología)
crossbones ['krɔs͵bo:nz] *npl* **1** : huesos *mpl* cruzados **2** → **skull**
crossbow ['krɔs͵bo:] *n* : ballesta *f*
crossbreed ['krɔs͵bri:d] *vt* **-bred** [-͵brɛd]; **-breeding** : cruzar
crosscurrent ['krɔs͵kərənt] *n* : contracorriente *f*
cross–examination [͵krɔsɪɡ͵zæmə-'neɪʃən] *n* : repreguntas *fpl*, interrogatorio *m*
cross–examine [͵krɔsɪɡ'zæmən] *vt* **-ined; -ining** : repreguntar
cross–eyed ['krɔs͵aɪd] *adj* : bizco
crossing ['krɔsɪŋ] *n* **1** INTERSECTION : cruce *m*, paso *m* ⟨pedestrian crossing : paso de peatones⟩ **2** VOYAGE : travesía *f* (del mar)

crossly ['krɔsli] *adv* : con enojo, con enfado
cross–reference [͵krɔs'rɛfrənts, -'rɛfə-rənts] *n* : referencia *f*, remisión *f*
crossroads ['krɔs͵ro:dz] *n* : cruce *m*, encrucijada *f*, crucero *m Mex*
cross section *n* **1** SECTION : corte *m* transversal **2** SAMPLE : muestra *f* representativa ⟨a cross section of the population : una muestra representativa de la población⟩
crosswalk ['krɔs͵wɔk] *n* : cruce *m* peatonal, paso *m* de peatones
crossways ['krɔs͵weɪz] → **crosswise**
crosswise¹ ['krɔs͵waɪz] *adv* : transversalmente, diagonalmente
crosswise² *adj* : transversal, diagonal
crossword puzzle ['krɔs͵wərd] *n* : crucigrama *m*
crotch ['krɑtʃ] *n* : entrepierna *f*
crotchety ['krɑtʃəti] *adj* CRANKY : malhumorado, irritable, enojadizo
crouch ['kraʊtʃ] *vi* : agacharse, ponerse de cuclillas
croup ['kru:p] *n* : crup *m*
crouton ['kru:͵tɑn] *n* : crutón *m*
crow¹ ['kro:] *vi* **1** : cacarear, cantar (como un cuervo) **2** BRAG : alardear, presumir
crow² *n* **1** : cuervo *m* (ave) **2** : cantar *m* (del gallo)
crowbar ['kro:͵bɑr] *n* : palanca *f*
crowd¹ ['kraʊd] *vi* : aglomerarse, amontonarse — *vt* : atestar, atiborrar, llenar
crowd² *n* : multitud *f*, muchedumbre *f*, gentío *m*
crown¹ ['kraʊn] *vt* : coronar
crown² *n* : corona *f*
crow's nest *n* : cofa *f*
crucial ['kru:ʃəl] *adj* : crucial, decisivo
crucible ['kru:səbəl] *n* : crisol *m*
crucifix ['kru:sə͵fɪks] *n* : crucifijo *m*
crucifixion [͵kru:sə'fɪkʃən] *n* : crucifixión *f*
crucify ['kru:sə͵faɪ] *vt* **-fied; -fying** : crucificar
crude ['kru:d] *adj* **cruder; -est 1** RAW, UNREFINED : crudo, sin refinar ⟨crude oil : petróleo crudo⟩ **2** VULGAR : grosero, de mal gusto **3** ROUGH : tosco, burdo, rudo
crudely ['kru:dli] *adv* **1** VULGARLY : groseramente **2** ROUGHLY : burdamente, de manera rudimentaria
crudity ['kru:dəti] *n, pl* **-ties 1** VULGARITY : grosería *f* **2** COARSENESS, ROUGHNESS : tosquedad *f*, rudeza *f*
cruel ['kru:əl] *adj* **-eler** *or* **-eller; -elest** *or* **-ellest** : cruel
cruelly ['kru:əli] *adv* : cruelmente
cruelty ['kru:əlti] *n, pl* **-ties** : crueldad *f*
cruet ['kru:ɪt] *n* : vinagrera *f*, aceitera *f*
cruise¹ ['kru:z] *vi* **cruised; cruising 1** : hacer un crucero **2** : navegar o conducir a una velocidad constante ⟨cruising speed : velocidad de crucero⟩
cruise² *n* : crucero *m*

cruiser ['kru:zər] *n* 1 WARSHIP : crucero *m*, buque *m* de guerra 2 : patrulla *f* (de policía)

crumb ['krʌm] *n* : miga *f*, migaja *f*

crumble ['krʌmbəl] *v* -bled; -bling *vt* : desmigajar, desmenuzar — *vi* : desmigajarse, desmoronarse, desmenuzarse

crumbly ['krʌmbli] *adj* : que se desmenuza fácilmente, friable

crumple ['krʌmpəl] *v* -pled; -pling *vt* RUMPLE : arrugar — *vi* 1 WRINKLE : arrugarse 2 COLLAPSE : desplomarse

crunch¹ ['krʌntʃ] *vt* 1 : ronzar (con los dientes) 2 : hacer crujir (con los pies, etc.) — *vi* : crujir

crunch² *n* : crujido *m*

crunchy ['krʌntʃi] *adj* **crunchier; -est** : crujiente

crusade¹ [kru:'seɪd] *vi* -saded; -sading : hacer una campaña (a favor de o contra algo)

crusade² *n* 1 : campaña *f* (de reforma, etc.) 2 **Crusade** : cruzada *f*

crusader [kru:'seɪdər] *n* 1 : cruzado *m* (en la Edad Media) 2 : campeón *m*, -peona *f* (de una causa)

crush¹ ['krʌʃ] *vt* 1 SQUASH : aplastar, apachurrar 2 GRIND, PULVERIZE : triturar, machacar 3 SUPPRESS : aplastar, suprimir

crush² *n* 1 CROWD, MOB : gentío *m*, multitud *f*, aglomeración *f* 2 INFATUATION : enamoramiento *m*

crushing ['krʌʃɪŋ] *adj* : aplastante, abrumador

crust ['krʌst] *n* 1 : corteza *f*, costra *f* (de pan) 2 : tapa *f* de masa, pasta *f* (de un pastel) 3 LAYER : capa *f*, corteza *f* ⟨the earth's crust : la corteza terrestre⟩

crustacean [ˌkrʌs'teɪʃən] *n* : crustáceo *m*

crusty ['krʌsti] *adj* **crustier; -est** 1 : de corteza dura 2 CROSS, GRUMPY : enojado, malhumorado

crutch ['krʌtʃ] *n* : muleta *f*

crux ['krʌks, 'krʊks] *n, pl* **cruxes** : quid *m*, esencia *f*, meollo *m* ⟨the crux of the problem : el quid del problema⟩

cry¹ ['kraɪ] *vi* **cried; crying** 1 SHOUT : gritar ⟨they cried for more : a gritos pidieron más⟩ 2 WEEP : llorar

cry² *n, pl* **cries** 1 SHOUT : grito *m* 2 WEEPING : llanto *m* 3 : chillido *m* (de un animal)

crybaby ['kraɪˌbeɪbi] *n, pl* -bies : llorón *m*, -rona *f*

crypt ['krɪpt] *n* : cripta *f*

cryptic ['krɪptɪk] *adj* : enigmático, críptico

crystal ['krɪstəl] *n* : cristal *m*

crystalline ['krɪstəlɪn] *adj* : cristalino

crystallize ['krɪstəˌlaɪz] *v* -lized; -lizing *vt* : cristalizar, materializar ⟨to crystallize one's thoughts : cristalizar uno sus pensamientos⟩ — *vi* : cristalizarse

cub ['kʌb] *n* : cachorro *m*

Cuban ['kju:bən] *n* : cubano *m*, -na *f* — **Cuban** *adj*

cubbyhole ['kʌbiˌho:l] *n* : chiribitil *m*

cube¹ ['kju:b] *vt* **cubed; cubing** 1 : elevar (un número) al cubo 2 : cortar en cubos

cube² *n* 1 : cubo *m* 2 **ice cube** : cubito *m* de hielo 3 **sugar cube** : terrón *m* de azúcar

cubic ['kju:bɪk] *adj* : cúbico

cubicle ['kju:bɪkəl] *n* : cubículo *m*

cuckoo¹ ['ku:ˌku:, 'kʊ-] *adj* : loco, chiflado

cuckoo² *n, pl* -oos : cuco *m*, cuclillo *m*

cucumber ['kju:ˌkʌmbər] *n* : pepino *m*

cud ['kʌd] *n* **to chew the cud** : rumiar

cuddle ['kʌdəl] *v* -dled; -dling *vi* : abrazarse tiernamente, acurrucarse — *vt* : abrazar

cudgel¹ ['kʌdʒəl] *vt* -geled *or* -gelled; -geling *or* -gelling : apalear, aporrear

cudgel² *n* : garrote *m*, porra *f*

cue¹ ['kju:] *vt* **cued; cuing** *or* **cueing** : darle el pie a, darle la señal a

cue² *n* 1 SIGNAL : señal *f*, pie *m* (en teatro), entrada *f* (en música) 2 : taco *m* (de billar)

cuff¹ ['kʌf] *vt* : bofetear, cachetear

cuff² *n* 1 : puño *m* (de una camisa), vuelta *f* (de pantalones) 2 SLAP : bofetada *f*, cachetada *f* 3 **cuffs** *npl* HANDCUFFS : esposas *fpl*

cuisine [kwɪ'zi:n] *n* : cocina *f* ⟨Mexican cuisine : la cocina mexicana⟩

culinary ['kʌləˌneri, 'kju:lə-] *adj* : culinario

cull ['kʌl] *vt* : seleccionar, entresacar

culminate ['kʌlməˌneɪt] *vi* -nated; -nating : culminar

culmination [ˌkʌlmə'neɪʃən] *n* : culminación *f*, punto *m* culminante

culpable ['kʌlpəbəl] *adj* : culpable

culprit ['kʌlprɪt] *n* : culpable *mf*

cult ['kʌlt] *n* : culto *m*

cultivate ['kʌltəˌveɪt] *vt* -vated; -vating 1 TILL : cultivar, labrar 2 FOSTER : cultivar, fomentar 3 REFINE : cultivar, refinar ⟨to cultivate the mind : cultivar la mente⟩

cultivation [ˌkʌltə'veɪʃən] *n* 1 : cultivo *m* ⟨under cultivation : en cultivo⟩ 2 CULTURE, REFINEMENT : cultura *f*, refinamiento *m*

cultural ['kʌltʃərəl] *adj* : cultural — **culturally** *adv*

culture ['kʌltʃər] *n* 1 CULTIVATION : cultivo *m* 2 REFINEMENT : cultura *f*, educación *f*, refinamiento *m* 3 CIVILIZATION : cultura *f*, civilización *f* ⟨the Incan culture : la cultura inca⟩

cultured ['kʌltʃərd] *adj* 1 EDUCATED, REFINED : culto, educado, refinado 2 : de cultivo, cultivado ⟨cultured pearls : perlas de cultivo⟩

culvert ['kʌlvərt] *n* : alcantarilla *f*

cumbersome ['kʌmbərsəm] *adj* : torpe y pesado, difícil de manejar

cumin ['kʌmən] *n* : comino *m*

cumulative ['kju:mjələtɪv, -ˌleɪtɪv] *adj* : acumulativo

cumulus ['kju:mjələs] *n*, *pl* **-li** [-ˌlaɪ, -ˌli:] : cúmulo *m*

cunning[1] ['kʌnɪŋ] *adj* **1** CRAFTY : astuto, taimado **2** CLEVER : ingenioso, hábil **3** CUTE : mono, gracioso, lindo

cunning[2] *n* **1** SKILL : habilidad *f* **2** CRAFTINESS : astucia *f*, maña *f*

cup[1] ['kʌp] *vt* **cupped; cupping** : ahuecar (las manos)

cup[2] *n* **1** : taza *f* ⟨a cup of coffee : una taza de café⟩ **2** CUPFUL : taza *f* **3** : media pinta *f* (unidad de medida) **4** GOBLET : copa *f* **5** TROPHY : copa *f*, trofeo *m*

cupboard ['kʌbərd] *n* : alacena *f*, armario *m*

cupcake ['kʌpˌkeɪk] *n* : pastelito *m*

cupful ['kʌpˌfʊl] *n* : taza *f*

cupola ['kju:pələ, -ˌlo:] *n* : cúpula *f*

cur ['kər] *n* : perro *m* callejero, perro *m* corriente *Mex*

curate ['kjʊrət] *n* : cura *m*, párroco *m*

curator ['kjʊrˌeɪtər, kjʊ'reɪtər] *n* : conservador *m*, -dora *f* (de un museo); director *m*, -tora *f* (de un zoológico)

curb[1] ['kərb] *vt* : refrenar, restringir, controlar

curb[2] *n* **1** RESTRAINT : freno *m*, control *m* **2** : borde *m* de la acera

curd ['kərd] *n* : cuajada *f*

curdle ['kərdəl] *v* **-dled; -dling** *vi* : cuajarse — *vt* : cuajar ⟨to curdle one's blood : helarle la sangre a uno⟩

cure[1] ['kjʊr] *vt* **cured; curing** **1** HEAL : curar, sanar **2** REMEDY : remediar **3** PROCESS : curar (alimentos, etc.)

cure[2] *n* **1** RECOVERY : curación *f*, recuperación *f* **2** REMEDY : cura *f*, remedio *m*

curfew ['kərˌfju:] *n* : toque *m* de queda

curio ['kjʊriˌo:] *n*, *pl* **-rios** : curiosidad *f*, objeto *m* curioso

curiosity [ˌkjʊri'asəti] *n*, *pl* **-ties** : curiosidad *f*

curious ['kjʊriəs] *adj* **1** INQUISITIVE : curioso **2** STRANGE : curioso, raro

curl[1] ['kərl] *vt* **1** : rizar, ondular (el pelo) **2** COIL : enrollar **3** TWIST : torcer ⟨to curl one's lip : hacer una mueca⟩ — *vi* **1** : rizarse, ondularse **2 to curl up** : acurrucarse (con un libro, etc.)

curl[2] *n* **1** RINGLET : rizo *m* **2** COIL : espiral *f*, rosca *f*

curler ['kərlər] *n* : rulo *m*

curlew ['kərˌlu:, 'kərlˌju:] *n*, *pl* **-lews** *or* **-lew** : zarapito *m*

curly ['kərli] *adj* **curlier; -est** : rizado, crespo

currant ['kərənt] *n* **1** : grosella *f* (fruta) **2** RAISIN : pasa *f* de Corinto

currency ['kərənʦi] *n*, *pl* **-cies** **1** PREVALENCE, USE : uso *m*, aceptación *f*, difusión *f* ⟨to be in currency : estar en uso⟩ **2** MONEY : moneda *f*, dinero *m*

current[1] ['kərənt] *adj* **1** PRESENT : actual ⟨current events : actualidades⟩ **2** PREVALENT : corriente, común — **currently** *adv*

current[2] *n* : corriente *f*

curriculum [kə'rɪkjələm] *n*, *pl* **-la** [-lə] : currículum *m*, currículo *m*, programa *m* de estudio

curriculum vitae ['vi:ˌtaɪ, 'vaɪti] *n*, *pl* **curricula vitae** : currículum *m*, currículo *m*

curry[1] ['kəri] *vt* **-ried; -rying** **1** GROOM : almohazar (un caballo) **2** : condimentar con curry **3 to curry favor** : congraciarse (con alguien)

curry[2] *n*, *pl* **-ries** : curry *m*

curse[1] ['kərs] *v* **cursed; cursing** *vt* **1** DAMN : maldecir **2** INSULT : injuriar, insultar, decir malas palabras a **3** AFFLICT : afligir — *vi* : maldecir, decir malas palabras

curse[2] *n* **1** : maldición *f* ⟨to put a curse on someone : echarle una maldición a alguien⟩ **2** AFFLICTION : maldición *f*, aflicción *f*, cruz *f*

cursor ['kərsər] *n* : cursor *m*

cursory ['kərsəri] *adj* : rápido, superficial, somero

curt ['kərt] *adj* : cortante, brusco, seco — **curtly** *adv*

curtailment [kər'teɪlmənt] *n* : restricción *f*, limitación *f*

curtain ['kərtən] *n* : cortina *f* (de una ventana), telón *m* (en un teatro)

curtness ['kərtnəs] *n* : brusquedad *f*, sequedad *f*

curtsy[1] *or* **curtsey** ['kərtsi] *vt* **-sied** *or* **-seyed; -sying** *or* **-seying** : hacer una reverencia

curtsy[2] *or* **curtsey** *n*, *pl* **-sies** *or* **-seys** : reverencia *f*

curvature ['kərvəˌtʃʊr] *n* : curvatura *f*

curve[1] ['kərv] *v* **curved; curving** *vi* : torcerse, describir una curva — *vt* : encorvar

curve[2] *n* : curva *f*

cushion[1] ['kʊʃən] *vt* **1** : poner cojines o almohadones a **2** SOFTEN : amortiguar, mitigar, suavizar ⟨to cushion a blow : amortiguar un golpe⟩

cushion[2] *n* **1** : cojín *m*, almohadón *m* **2** PROTECTION : colchón *m*, protección *f*

cusp ['kʌsp] *n* : cúspide *f* (de un diente), cuerno *m* (de la luna)

cuspid ['kʌspɪd] *n* : diente *m* canino, colmillo *m*

custard ['kʌstərd] *n* : natillas *fpl*

custodian [ˌkʌ'sto:diən] *n* : custodio *m*, -dia *f*; guardián, -diana *f*

custody ['kʌstədi] *n*, *pl* **-dies** : custodia *f*, cuidado *m* ⟨to be in custody : estar detenido⟩

custom[1] ['kʌstəm] *adj* : a la medida, a la orden

custom[2] *n* **1** : costumbre *f*, tradición *f* **2 customs** *npl* : aduana *f*

customarily [ˌkʌstə'merəli] *adv* : habitualmente, normalmente, de costumbre

customary ['kʌstə,mɛri] *adj* **1** TRADITIONAL : tradicional **2** USUAL : habitual, de costumbre
customer ['kʌstəmər] *n* : cliente *m*, -ta *f*
custom–made ['kʌstəm'meɪd] *adj* : hecho a la medida
cut¹ ['kʌt] *v* **cut; cutting** *vt* **1** : cortar ⟨to cut paper : cortar papel⟩ **2** : cortarse ⟨to cut one's finger : cortarse uno el dedo⟩ **3** TRIM : cortar, recortar ⟨to have one's hair cut : cortarse el pelo⟩ **4** INTERSECT : cruzar, atravesar **5** SHORTEN : acortar, abreviar **6** REDUCE : reducir, rebajar ⟨to cut prices : rebajar los precios⟩ **7 to cut one's teeth** : salirle los dientes a uno — *vi* **1** : cortar, cortarse **2 to cut in** : entrometerse
cut² *n* **1** : corte *m* ⟨a cut of meat : un corte de carne⟩ **2** SLASH : tajo *m*, corte *m*, cortadura *f* **3** REDUCTION : rebaja *f*, reducción *f* ⟨a cut in the rates : una rebaja en las tarifas⟩
cute ['kju:t] *adj* **cuter; -est** : mono *fam*, lindo
cuticle ['kju:tɪkəl] *n* : cutícula *f*
cutlass ['kʌtləs] *n* : alfanje *m*
cutlery ['kʌtləri] *n* : cubiertos *mpl*
cutlet ['kʌtlət] *n* : chuleta *f*
cutter ['kʌtər] *n* **1** : cortadora *f* (implemento) **2** : cortador *m*, -dora *f* (persona) **3** : cúter *m* (embarcación)
cutthroat ['kʌt,θro:t] *adj* : despiadado, desalmado ⟨cutthroat competition : competencia feroz⟩
cutting¹ ['kʌtɪŋ] *adj* **1** : cortante ⟨a cutting wind : un viento cortante⟩ **2** CAUSTIC : mordaz

cutting² *n* : esqueje *m* (de una planta)
cuttlefish ['kʌtəl,fɪʃ] *n, pl* **-fish** *or* **-fishes** : jibia *f*, sepia *f*
cyanide ['saɪə,naɪd, -nɪd] *n* : cianuro *m*
cycle¹ ['saɪkəl] *vi* **-cled; -cling** : andar en bicicleta, ir en bicicleta
cycle² *n* **1** : ciclo *m* ⟨life cycle : ciclo de vida, ciclo vital⟩ **2** BICYCLE : bicicleta *f* **3** MOTORCYCLE : motocicleta *f*
cyclic ['saɪklɪk, 'sɪ-] *or* **cyclical** [-klɪkəl] *adj* : cíclico
cyclist ['saɪklɪst] *n* : ciclista *mf*
cyclone ['saɪ,klo:n] *n* **1** : ciclón *m* **2** TORNADO : tornado *m*
cyclopedia *or* **cyclopaedia** [,saɪklə-'pi:diə] → **encyclopedia**
cylinder ['sɪləndər] *n* : cilindro *m*
cylindrical [sə'lɪndrɪkəl] *adj* : cilíndrico
cymbal ['sɪmbəl] *n* : platillo *m*, címbalo *m*
cynic ['sɪnɪk] *n* : cínico *m*, -ca *f*
cynical ['sɪnɪkəl] *adj* : cínico
cynicism ['sɪnə,sɪzəm] *n* : cinismo *m*
cypress ['saɪprəs] *n* : ciprés *m*
Cypriot ['sɪpriət, -,ɑt] *n* : chipriota *mf* — **Cypriot** *adj*
cyst ['sɪst] *n* : quiste *m*
cytoplasm ['saɪtə,plæzəm] *n* : citoplasma *m*
czar ['zɑr, 'sɑr] *n* : zar *m*
czarina [zɑ'ri:nə, sɑ-] *n* : zarina *f*
Czech ['tʃɛk] *n* **1** : checo *m*, -ca *f* **2** : checo *m* (idioma) — **Czech** *adj*
Czechoslovak [,tʃɛko'slo:,vɑk, -,væk] *or* **Czechoslovakian** [-slo'vɑkiən, -'væk-] *n* : checoslovaco *m*, -ca *f* — **Czechoslovak** *or* **Czechoslovakian** *adj*

D

d ['di:] *n, pl* **d's** *or* **ds** ['di:z] : cuarta letra del alfabeto inglés
dab¹ ['dæb] *vt* **dabbed; dabbing** : darle toques ligeros a, aplicar suavemente
dab² *n* **1** BIT : toque *m*, pizca *f*, poco *m* ⟨a dab of ointment : un toque de ungüento⟩ **2** PAT : toque *m* ligero, golpecito *m*
dabble ['dæbəl] *v* **-bled; -bling** *vt* SPATTER : salpicar — *vi* **1** SPLASH : chapotear **2** TRIFLE : jugar, interesarse superficialmente
dabbler ['dæbələr] *n* : diletante *mf*
dachshund ['dɑks,hʊnt, -,hʊnd; 'dɑksənt, -sənd] *n* : perro *m* salchicha
dad ['dæd] *n* : papá *m fam*
daddy ['dædi] *n, pl* **-dies** : papi *m fam*
daffodil ['dæfə,dɪl] *n* : narciso *m*
daft ['dæft] *adj* : tonto, bobo
dagger ['dægər] *n* : daga *f*, puñal *m*
dahlia ['dæljə, 'dɑl-, 'deɪl-] *n* : dalia *f*
daily¹ ['deɪli] *adv* : a diario, diariamente
daily² *adj* : diario, cotidiano
daily³ *n, pl* **-lies** : diario *m*, periódico *m*
daintily ['deɪntəli] *adv* : delicadamente, con delicadeza

daintiness ['deɪntinəs] *n* : delicadeza *f*, finura *f*
dainty¹ ['deɪnti] *adj* **-tier; -est** **1** DELICATE : delicado **2** FASTIDIOUS : remilgado, melindroso **3** DELICIOUS : exquisito, sabroso
dainty² *n, pl* **-ties** DELICACY : exquisitez *f*, manjar *m*
dairy ['dæri] *n, pl* **-ies** **1** *or* **dairy store** : lechería *f* **2** *or* **dairy farm** : granja *f* lechera
dairymaid ['dæri,meɪd] *n* : lechera *f*
dairyman ['dærimən, -,mæn] *n, pl* **-men** [-mən, -,mɛn] : lechero *m*
dais ['deɪəs] *n* : tarima *f*, estrado *m*
daisy ['deɪzi] *n, pl* **-sies** : margarita *f*
dale ['deɪl] *n* : valle *m*
dally ['dæli] *vi* **-lied; -lying** **1** TRIFLE : juguetear **2** DAWDLE : entretenerse, perder tiempo
dalmatian [dæl'meɪʃən, dɔl-] *n* : dálmata *m*
dam¹ ['dæm] *vt* **dammed; damming** : represar, embalsar
dam² *n* **1** : represa *f*, dique *m* **2** : madre *f* (de animales domésticos)

damage¹ ['dæmɪʤ] *vt* **-aged; -aging**
: dañar (un objeto o una máquina), perjudicar (la salud o una reputación)
damage² *n* **1** : daño *m*, perjuicio *m* **2**
damages *npl* : daños y perjuicios *mpl*
damaging ['dæməʤɪŋ] *adj* : perjudicial
damask ['dæməsk] *n* : damasco *m*
dame ['deɪm] *n* LADY : dama *f*, señora *f*
damn¹ ['dæm] *vt* **1** CONDEMN : condenar **2** CURSE : maldecir
damn² *or* **damned** ['dæmd] *adj* : condenado *fam*, maldito *fam*
damn³ *n* : pito *m*, bledo *m*, comino *m*
⟨it's not worth a damn : no vale un
pito⟩ ⟨I don't give a damn : me importa
un comino⟩
damnable ['dæmnəbəl] *adj* : condenable, detestable
damnation [dæm'neɪʃən] *n* : condenación *f*
damned¹ ['dæmd] *adv* VERY : muy
damned² *adj* **1** → **damnable 2** RE-
MARKABLE : extraordinario
damp¹ ['dæmp] *vt* → **dampen**
damp² *adj* : húmedo
damp³ *n* MOISTURE : humedad *f*
dampen ['dæmpən] *vt* **1** MOISTEN
: humedecer **2** DISCOURAGE : desalentar, desanimar
damper ['dæmpər] *n* **1** : regulador *m* de
tiro (de una chimenea) **2** : sordina *f* (de
un piano) **3 to put a damper on** : desanimar, apagar (el entusiasmo), enfriar
dampness ['dæmpnəs] *n* : humedad *f*
damsel ['dæmzəl] *n* : damisela *f*
dance¹ ['dænts] *v* **danced; dancing**
: bailar
dance² *n* : baile *m*
dancer ['dæntsər] *n* : bailarín *m*, -rina *f*
dandelion ['dændəl,aɪən] *n* : diente *m* de
león
dandruff ['dændrəf] *n* : caspa *f*
dandy¹ ['dændi] *adj* **-dier; -est** : excelente, magnífico, macanudo *fam*
dandy² *n, pl* **-dies 1** FOP : dandi *m* **2**
: algo *m* excelente ⟨this new program
is a dandy : este programa nuevo es
algo excelente⟩
Dane ['deɪn] *n* : danés *m*, -nesa *f*
danger ['deɪnʤər] *n* : peligro *m*
dangerous ['deɪnʤərəs] *adj* : peligroso
dangle ['dæŋgəl] *v* **-gled; -gling** *vi* HANG
: colgar, pender — *vt* **1** SWING : hacer
oscilar **2** PROFFER : ofrecer (como incentivo) **3 to keep someone dangling**
: dejar a alguien en suspenso
Danish¹ ['deɪnɪʃ] *adj* : danés
Danish² *n* : danés *m* (idioma)
dank ['dæŋk] *adj* : frío y húmedo
dapper ['dæpər] *adj* : pulcro, atildado
dappled ['dæpəld] *adj* : moteado ⟨a dappled horse : un caballo rodado⟩
dare¹ ['dær] *v* **dared; daring** *vi* : osar,
atreverse ⟨how dare you! : ¡cómo te
atreves!⟩ — *vt* **1** CHALLENGE : desafiar, retar **2 to dare to do something**
: atreverse a hacer algo, osar hacer algo

dare² *n* : desafío *m*, reto *m*
daredevil ['dær,dɛvəl] *n* : persona *f*
temeraria
daring¹ ['dærɪŋ] *adj* : osado, atrevido,
audaz
daring² *n* : arrojo *m*, coraje *m*, audacia
f
dark ['dɑrk] *adj* **1** : oscuro (dícese del
ambiente o de los colores), moreno
(dícese del pelo o de la piel) **2** SOMBER
: sombrío, triste
darken ['dɑrkən] *vt* **1** DIM : oscurecer **2**
SADDEN : entristecer — *vi* : ensombrecerse, nublarse
darkly ['dɑrkli] *adv* **1** DIMLY : oscuramente **2** GLOOMILY : tristemente **3**
MYSTERIOUSLY : misteriosamente,
enigmáticamente
darkness ['dɑrknəs] *n* : oscuridad *f*,
tinieblas *f*
darling¹ ['dɑrlɪŋ] *adj* **1** BELOVED : querido, amado **2** CHARMING : encantador,
mono *fam*
darling² *n* **1** BELOVED : querido *m*, -da
f; amado *m*, -da *f*; cariño *m*, -ña *f* **2** FA-
VORITE : preferido *m*, -da *f*; favorito *m*,
-ta *f*
darn¹ ['dɑrn] *vt* : zurcir
darn² *n* **1** : zurcido *m* **2** → **damn³**
dart¹ ['dɑrt] *vt* THROW : lanzar, tirar —
vi DASH : lanzarse, precipitarse
dart² *n* **1** : dardo *m* **2 darts** *npl* : juego
m de dardos
dash¹ ['dæʃ] *vt* **1** SMASH : romper, estrellar **2** HURL : arrojar, lanzar **3**
SPLASH : salpicar **4** FRUSTRATE : frustrar **5 to dash off** : hacer (algo) rápidamente — *vi* **1** SMASH : romperse, estrellarse **2** DART : lanzarse, irse
apresuradamente
dash² *n* **1** BURST, SPLASH : arranque *m*,
salpicadura *f* (de aguas) **2** : guión *m*
largo (signo de puntuación) **3** DROP
: gota *f*, pizca *f* **4** VERVE : brío *m* **5**
RACE : carrera *f* ⟨a 100-meter dash
: una carrera de 100 metros⟩ **6 to make**
a dash for it : precipitarse (hacia),
echarse a correr **7** → **dashboard**
dashboard ['dæʃ,bord] *n* : tablero *m* de
instrumentos
dashing ['dæʃɪŋ] *adj* : gallardo, apuesto
data ['deɪtə, 'dæ-, 'dɑ-] *ns & pl* : datos
mpl, información *f*
database ['deɪtə,beɪs, 'dæ-, 'dɑ-] *n* : base
f de datos
date¹ ['deɪt] *v* **dated; dating** *vt* **1** : fechar
(una carta, etc.), datar (un objeto) ⟨it
was dated June 9 : estaba fechada el 9
de junio⟩ **2** : salir con ⟨she's dating my
brother : sale con mi hermano⟩ — *vi*
: datar
date² *n* **1** : fecha *f* ⟨to date : hasta la
fecha⟩ **2** EPOCH, PERIOD : época *f*,
período *m* **3** APPOINTMENT : cita *f* **4**
COMPANION : acompañante *mf* **5** : dátil
m (fruta)
dated ['deɪtəd] *adj* OUT-OF-DATE : anticuado, pasado de moda

datum ['deɪt̬əm, 'dæ-, 'dɑ-] *n, pl* **-ta** [-t̬ə]
or **-tums** : dato *m*
daub¹ ['dɔb] *vt* : embadurnar
daub² *n* : mancha *f*
daughter ['dɔt̬ər] *n* : hija *f*
daughter–in–law ['dɔt̬ərɪn‚lɔ] *n, pl*
daughters–in–law : nuera *f*, hija *f*
política
daunt ['dɔnt] *vt* : amilanar, acobardar,
intimidar
dauntless ['dɔntləs] *adj* : intrépido, impávido
davenport ['dævən‚pɔrt] *n* : sofá *m*
dawdle ['dɔdəl] *vi* **-dled; -dling 1** DAL-
LY : demorarse, entretenerse, perder
tiempo **2** LOITER : vagar, holgazanear,
haraganear
dawn¹ ['dɔn] *vi* **1** : amanecer, alborear,
despuntar ⟨Saturday dawned clear and
bright : el sábado amaneció claro y lu-
minoso⟩ **2 to dawn on** : hacerse obvio
⟨it dawned on me that she was right
: me di cuenta de que tenía razón⟩
dawn² *n* **1** DAYBREAK : amanecer *m*,
alba *f* **2** BEGINNING : albor *m*, comienzo *m* ⟨the dawn of history : los albores
de la historia⟩ **3 from dawn to dusk**
: de sol a sol
day ['deɪ] *n* **1** : día *m* **2** DATE : fecha *f*
3 TIME : día *m*, tiempo *m* ⟨in olden days
: intaño⟩ **4** WORKDAY : jornada *f* laboral
daybreak ['deɪ‚breɪk] *n* : alba *f*, amanecer *m*
day care *n* : servicio *m* de guardería infantil
daydream¹ ['deɪ‚dri:m] *vi* : soñar despierto, fantasear
daydream² *n* : ensueño *m*, ensoñación
f, fantasía *f*
daylight ['deɪ‚laɪt] *n* **1** : luz *f* del día ⟨in
broad daylight : a plena luz del día⟩ **2**
→ **daybreak 3** → **daytime**
daylight saving time *n* : hora *f* de verano
daytime ['deɪ‚taɪm] *n* : horas *fpl* diurnas,
día *m*
daze¹ ['deɪz] *vt* **dazed; dazing 1** STUN
: aturdir **2** DAZZLE : deslumbrar, ofuscar
daze² *n* **1** : aturdimiento *m* **2 in a daze**
: aturdido, atontado
dazzle¹ ['dæzəl] *vt* **-zled; -zling** : deslumbrar, ofuscar
dazzle² *n* : resplandor *m*, brillo *m*
DDT [‚di:‚di:'ti:] *n* : DDT *m*
deacon ['di:kən] *n* : diácono *m*
dead¹ ['dɛd] *adv* **1** ABRUPTLY : repentinamente, súbitamente ⟨to stop dead
: parar en seco⟩ **2** ABSOLUTELY : absolutamente ⟨I'm dead certain : estoy
absolutamente seguro⟩ **3** DIRECTLY
: justo ⟨dead ahead : justo adelante⟩
dead² *adj* **1** LIFELESS : muerto **2** NUMB
: entumecido **3** INDIFFERENT : indiferente, frío **4** INACTIVE : inactivo ⟨a
dead volcano : un volcán inactivo⟩ **5**
: desconectado (dícese del teléfono),

descargado (dícese de una batería) **6**
EXHAUSTED : agotado, derrengado,
muerto **7** OBSOLETE : obsoleto, muerto ⟨a dead language : una lengua muer-
ta⟩ **8** EXACT : exacto ⟨in the dead center : justo en el blanco⟩
dead³ *n* **1 the dead** : los muertos **2 in
the dead of night** : a las altas horas de
la noche **3 in the dead of winter** : en
pleno invierno
deadbeat ['dɛd‚bi:t] *n* **1** LOAFER : vago
m, -ga *f*; holgazán *m*, -zana *f* **2** FREE-
LOADER : gorrón *m*, -rrona *f fam*; gorrero *m*, -ra *f fam*
deaden ['dɛdən] *vt* **1** : atenuar (un
dolor), entorpecer (sensaciones) **2**
DULL : deslustrar **3** DISPIRIT : desanimar **4** MUFFLE : amortiguar, reducir
(sonidos)
dead–end ['dɛd'ɛnd] *adj* **1** : sin salida
⟨dead-end street : calle sin salida⟩ **2**
: sin futuro ⟨a dead-end job : un trabajo sin porvenir⟩
dead end *n* : callejón *m* sin salida
dead heat *n* : empate *m*
deadline ['dɛd‚laɪn] *n* : fecha *f* límite,
fecha *f* tope, plazo *m* (determinado)
deadlock¹ ['dɛd‚lɑk] *vt* : estancar — *vi*
: estancarse, llegar a punto muerto
deadlock² *n* : punto *m* muerto, impasse
m
deadly¹ ['dɛdli] *adv* : extremadamente,
sumamente ⟨deadly serious : muy en
serio⟩
deadly² *adj* **-lier; -est 1** LETHAL : mortal, letal, mortífero **2** ACCURATE : certero, preciso ⟨a deadly aim : una puntería infalible⟩ **3** CAPITAL : capital ⟨the
seven deadly sins : los siete pecados
capitales⟩ **4** DULL : funesto, aburrido
5 EXTREME : extremo, absoluto ⟨a
deadly calm : una calma absoluta⟩
deadpan¹ ['dɛd‚pæn] *adv* : de manera in-
expresiva, sin expresión
deadpan² *adj* : inexpresivo, impasible
deaf ['dɛf] *adj* : sordo
deafen ['dɛfən] *vt* **-ened; -ening** : ensordecer
deafening ['dɛfənɪŋ] *adj* : ensordecedor
deaf–mute ['dɛf'mju:t] *n* : sordomudo
m, -da *f*
deafness ['dɛfnəs] *n* : sordera *f*
deal¹ ['di:l] *v* **dealt; dealing** *vt* **1** AP-
PORTION : repartir ⟨to deal justice
: repartir la justicia⟩ **2** DISTRIBUTE
: repartir, dar (naipes) **3** DELIVER : asestar, propinar ⟨to deal a blow : asestar un golpe⟩ — *vi* **1** : dar, repartir (en
juegos de naipes) **2 to deal in** : comerciar en, traficar con (drogas) **3 to
deal with** CONCERN : tratar de, tener
que ver con ⟨the book deals with
poverty : el libro trata de la pobreza⟩
4 to deal with HANDLE : tratar (con),
encargarse de **5 to deal with** TREAT
: tratar ⟨the judge dealt with him severely : el juez lo trató con severidad⟩
6 to deal with ACCEPT : aceptar (una
situación o desgracia)

deal[2] *n* **1** : reparto *m* (de naipes) **2** AGREEMENT, TRANSACTION : trato *m*, acuerdo *m*, transacción *f* **3** TREATMENT : trato *m* ⟨he got a raw deal : le hicieron una injusticia⟩ **4** BARGAIN : ganga *f*, oferta *f* **5 a good deal** *or* **a great deal** : mucho, una gran cantidad

dealer ['di:lər] *n* : comerciante *mf*, traficante *mf*

dealership ['di:lər,ʃɪp] *n* : concesión *f*

dealings ['di:lɪŋz] *npl* **1** : relaciones *fpl* (personales) **2** TRANSACTIONS : negocios *mpl*, transacciones *fpl*

dean ['di:n] *n* **1** : deán *m* (del clero) **2** : decano *m*, -na *f* (de una facultad o profesión)

dear[1] ['dɪr] *adj* **1** ESTEEMED, LOVED : querido, estimado ⟨a dear friend : un amigo querido⟩ ⟨Dear Sir : Estimado Señor⟩ **2** COSTLY : caro, costoso

dear[2] *n* : querido *m*, -da *f*; amado *m*, -da *f*

dearly ['dɪrli] *adv* **1** : mucho ⟨I love them dearly : los quiero mucho⟩ **2** : caro ⟨to pay dearly : pagar caro⟩

dearth ['dərθ] *n* : escasez *f*, carestía *f*

death ['dɛθ] *n* **1** : muerte *f*, fallecimiento *m* ⟨to be the death of : matar⟩ **2** FATALITY : víctima *f* (mortal); muerto *m*, -ta *f* **3** END : fin *m* ⟨the death of civilization : el fin de la civilización⟩

deathbed ['dɛθ,bɛd] *n* : lecho *m* de muerte

deathblow ['dɛθ,blo:] *n* : golpe *m* mortal

deathless ['dɛθləs] *adj* : eterno, inmortal

deathly ['dɛθli] *adj* : de muerte, sepulcral (dícese del silencio), cadavérico (dícese de la palidez)

debacle [dɪ'bakəl, -'bæ-] *n* : desastre *m*, debacle *m*, fiasco *m*

debar [dɪ'bɑr] *vt* **-barred; -barring** : excluir, prohibir

debase [dɪ'beɪs] *vt* **-based; -basing** : degradar, envilecer

debasement [dɪ'beɪsmənt] *n* : degradación *f*, envilecimiento *m*

debatable [dɪ'beɪt̬əbəl] *adj* : discutible

debate[1] [dɪ'beɪt] *vt* **-bated; -bating** : debatir, discutir

debate[2] *n* : debate *m*, discusión *f*

debauch [dɪ'bɔtʃ] *vt* : pervertir, corromper

debauchery [dɪ'bɔtʃəri] *n*, *pl* **-eries** : libertinaje *m*, disipación *f*, intemperancia *f*

debilitate [dɪ'bɪlə,teɪt] *vt* **-tated; -tating** : debilitar

debility [dɪ'bɪləti] *n*, *pl* **-ties** : debilidad *f*

debit[1] ['dɛbɪt] *vt* : adeudar, cargar, debitar

debit[2] *n* : débito *m*, cargo *m*, debe *m*

debonair [,dɛbə'nær] *adj* : elegante y desenvuelto, apuesto

debris [də'bri:, deɪ-; 'deɪ,bri:] *n*, *pl* **-bris** [-'bri:z, -,bri:z] **1** RUBBLE, RUINS : escombros *mpl*, ruinas *fpl*, restos *mpl* **2** RUBBISH : basura *f*, deshechos *mpl*

debt ['dɛt] *n* **1** : deuda *f* ⟨to pay a debt : saldar una deuda⟩ **2** INDEBTEDNESS : endeudamiento *m*

debtor ['dɛt̬ər] *n* : deudor *m*, -dora *f*

debunk [dɪ'bʌŋk] *vt* DISCREDIT : desacreditar, desprestigiar

debut[1] [deɪ'bju:, 'deɪ,bju:] *vi* : debutar

debut[2] *n* **1** : debut *m* (de un actor), estreno *m* (de una obra) **2** : debut *m*, presentación *f* (en sociedad)

debutante ['dɛbju,tɑnt] *n* : debutante *f*

decade ['dɛ,keɪd, dɛ'keɪd] *n* : década *f*

decadence ['dɛkədənts] *n* : decadencia *f*

decadent ['dɛkədənt] *adj* : decadente

decaf[1] ['di:,kæf] → **decaffeinated**

decaf[2] *n* : café *m* descafeinado

decaffeinated [di'kæfə,neɪt̬əd] *adj* : descafeinado

decal ['di:,kæl, dɪ'kæl] *n* : calcomanía *f*

decamp [dɪ'kæmp] *vi* : irse, largarse *fam*

decant [dɪ'kænt] *vt* : decantar

decanter [dɪ'kæntər] *n* : licorera *f*, garrafa *f*

decapitate [dɪ'kæpə,teɪt] *vt* **-tated; -tating** : decapitar

decay[1] [dɪ'keɪ] *vi* **1** DECOMPOSE : descomponerse, pudrirse **2** DETERIORATE : deteriorarse **3** : cariarse (dícese de los dientes)

decay[2] *n* **1** DECOMPOSITION : descomposición *f* **2** DECLINE, DETERIORATION : decadencia *f*, deterioro *m* **3** : caries *f* (de los dientes)

decease[1] [dɪ'si:s] *vi* **-ceased; -ceasing** : morir, fallecer

decease[2] *n* : fallecimiento *m*, defunción *f*, deceso *m*

deceit [dɪ'si:t] *n* **1** DECEPTION : engaño *m* **2** DISHONESTY : deshonestidad *f*

deceitful [dɪ'si:tfəl] *adj* : falso, embustero, engañoso, mentiroso

deceitfully [dɪ'si:tfəli] *adv* : con engaño, con falsedad

deceitfulness [dɪ'si:tfəlnəs] *n* : falsedad *f*, engaño *m*

deceive [dɪ'si:v] *vt* **-ceived; -ceiving** : engañar, burlar

deceiver [dɪ'si:vər] *n* : impostor *m*, -tora *f*

decelerate [dɪ'sɛlə,reɪt] *vi* **-ated; -ating** : reducir la velocidad, desacelerar

December [dɪ'sɛmbər] *n* : diciembre *m*

decency ['di:səntsi] *n*, *pl* **-cies** : decencia *f*, decoro *m*

decent ['di:sənt] *adj* **1** CORRECT, PROPER : decente, decoroso, correcto **2** CLOTHED : vestido, presentable **3** MODEST : púdico, modesto **4** ADEQUATE : decente, adecuado ⟨decent wages : paga adecuada⟩

decently ['di:səntli] *adv* : decentemente

decentralize [di'sɛntrə,laɪz] *v* **-lized** [-,laɪzd]; **-lizing** [-,laɪzɪŋ] *vt* : descentralizar — *vi* : descentralizarse

deception [dɪ'sɛpʃən] *n* : engaño *m*

deceptive [dɪ'sɛptɪv] *adj* : engañoso, falaz — **deceptively** *adv*
decibel ['dɛsəbəl, -ˌbɛl] *n* : decibelio *m*
decide [dɪ'saɪd] *v* **-cided; -ciding** *vt* 1 CONCLUDE : decidir, llegar a la conclusión de ⟨he decided what to do : decidió qué iba a hacer⟩ 2 DETERMINE : decidir, determinar ⟨one blow decided the fight : un solo golpe determinó la pelea⟩ 3 CONVINCE : decidir ⟨her pleas decided me to help : sus súplicas me decidieron a ayudarla⟩ 4 RESOLVE : resolver — *vi* : decidirse
decided [dɪ'saɪdəd] *adj* 1 UNQUESTIONABLE : indudable 2 RESOLUTE : decidido, resuelto — **decidedly** *adv*
deciduous [dɪ'sɪdʒuəs] *adj* : caduco, de hoja caduca
decimal[1] ['dɛsəməl] *adj* : decimal
decimal[2] *n* : número *m* decimal
decipher [dɪ'saɪfər] *vt* : descifrar — **decipherable** [-əbəl] *adj*
decision [dɪ'sɪʒən] *n* : decisión *f*, determinación *f* ⟨to make a decision : tomar una decisión⟩
decisive [dɪ'saɪsɪv] *adj* 1 DECIDING : decisivo ⟨the decisive vote : el voto decisivo⟩ 2 CONCLUSIVE : decisivo, concluyente, contundente ⟨a decisive victory : una victoria contundente⟩ 3 RESOLUTE : decidido, resuelto, firme
decisively [dɪ'saɪsɪvli] *adv* : con decisión, de manera decisiva
decisiveness [dɪ'saɪsɪvnəs] *n* 1 FORCEFULNESS : contundencia *f* 2 RESOLUTION : firmeza *f*, decisión *f*, determinación *f*
deck[1] ['dɛk] *vt* 1 FLOOR : tumbar, derribar ⟨she decked him with one blow : lo tumbó de un solo golpe⟩ 2 **to deck out** : adornar, engalanar
deck[2] *n* 1 : cubierta *f* (de un barco) 2 *or* **deck of cards** : baraja *f* (de naipes)
declaim [dɪ'kleɪm] *v* : declamar
declaration [ˌdɛklə'reɪʃən] *n* : declaración *f*, pronunciamiento *m* (oficial)
declare [dɪ'klær] *vt* **-clared; -claring** : declarar, manifestar ⟨to declare war : declarar la guerra⟩ ⟨they declared their support : manifestaron su apoyo⟩
decline[1] [dɪ'klaɪn] *v* **-clined; -clining** *vi* 1 DESCEND : descender 2 DETERIORATE : deteriorarse, decaer ⟨her health is declining : su salud se está deteriorando⟩ 3 DECREASE : disminuir, decrecer, decaer 4 REFUSE : rehusar — *vt* 1 INFLECT : declinar 2 REFUSE, TURN DOWN : declinar, rehusar
decline[2] *n* 1 DETERIORATION : decadencia *f*, deterioro *m* 2 DECREASE : disminución *f*, descenso *m* 3 SLOPE : declive *m*, pendiente *f*
decode [dɪ'ko:d] *vt* **-coded; -coding** : descifrar (un mensaje), descodificar (una señal)
decoder [dɪ'ko:dər] *n* : descodificador *m*

decompose [ˌdi:kəm'po:z] *v* **-posed; -posing** *vt* 1 BREAK DOWN : descomponer 2 ROT : descomponer, pudrir — *vi* : descomponerse, pudrirse
decomposition [ˌdi:ˌkɑmpə'zɪʃən] *n* : descomposición *f*
decongestant [ˌdi:kən'dʒɛstənt] *n* : descongestionante *m*
decor *or* **décor** [deɪ'kɔr, 'deɪˌkɔr] *n* : decoración *f*
decorate ['dɛkəˌreɪt] *vt* **-rated; -rating** 1 ADORN : decorar, adornar 2 : condecorar ⟨he was decorated for bravery : lo condecoraron por valor⟩
decoration [ˌdɛkə'reɪʃən] *n* 1 ADORNMENT : decoración *f*, adorno *m* 2 : condecoración *f* (de honor)
decorative ['dɛkərətɪv, -ˌreɪ-] *adj* : decorativo, ornamental, de adorno
decorator ['dɛkəˌreɪtər] *n* : decorador *m*, -dora *f*
decorum [dɪ'korəm] *n* : decoro *m*
decoy[1] ['di:ˌkɔɪ, dɪ'-] *vt* : atraer (con señuelo)
decoy[2] *n* : señuelo *m*, reclamo *m*, cimbel *m*
decrease[1] [dɪ'kri:s] *v* **-creased; -creasing** *vi* : decrecer, disminuir, bajar — *vt* : reducir, disminuir
decrease[2] ['di:ˌkri:s] *n* : disminución *f*, descenso *m*, bajada *f*
decree[1] [dɪ'kri:] *vt* **-creed; -creeing** : decretar
decree[2] *n* : decreto *m*
decrepit [dɪ'krɛpɪt] *adj* 1 FEEBLE : decrépito, débil 2 DILAPIDATED : deteriorado, ruinoso
decry [dɪ'kraɪ] *vt* **-cried; -crying** : censurar, criticar
dedicate ['dɛdɪˌkeɪt] *vt* **-cated; -cating** 1 : dedicar ⟨she dedicated the book to Carlos : le dedicó el libro a Carlos⟩ 2 : consagrar, dedicar ⟨to dedicate one's life : consagrar uno su vida⟩
dedication [ˌdɛdɪ'keɪʃən] *n* 1 DEVOTION : dedicación *f*, devoción *f* 2 : dedicatoria *f* (de un libro, una canción, etc.) 3 CONSECRATION : dedicación *f*
deduce [dɪ'du:s, -'dju:s] *vt* **-duced; -ducing** : deducir, inferir
deduct [dɪ'dʌkt] *vt* : deducir, descontar, restar
deductible [dɪ'dʌktəbəl] *adj* : deducible
deduction [dɪ'dʌkʃən] *n* : deducción *f*
deed[1] ['di:d] *vt* : ceder, transferir
deed[2] *n* 1 ACT : acto *m*, acción *f*, hecho *m* ⟨a good deed : una buena acción⟩ 2 FEAT : hazaña *f*, proeza *f* 3 TITLE : escritura *f*, título *m*
deem ['di:m] *vt* : considerar, juzgar
deep[1] ['di:p] *adv* : hondo, profundamente ⟨to dig deep : cavar hondo⟩
deep[2] *adj* 1 : hondo, profundo ⟨the deep end : la parte honda⟩ ⟨a deep wound : una herida profunda⟩ 2 WIDE : ancho 3 INTENSE : profundo, intenso 4 DARK : intenso, subido ⟨deep red : rojo subido⟩ 5 LOW : profundo ⟨a deep tone

: un tono profundo⟩ **6** ABSORBED : absorto ⟨deep in thought : absorto en la meditación⟩
deep³ *n* **1 the deep** : lo profundo, el piélago **2 the deep of night** : lo más profundo de la noche
deepen ['di:pən] *vt* **1** : ahondar, profundizar **2** INTENSIFY : intensificar — *vi* **1** : hacerse más profundo **2** INTENSIFY : intensificarse
deeply ['di:pli] *adv* : hondo, profundamente ⟨I'm deeply sorry : lo siento sinceramente⟩
deep–seated ['di:p'si:t̬əd] *adj* : profundamente arraigado, enraizado
deer ['dɪr] *ns & pl* : ciervo *m*, venado *m*
deerskin ['dɪr,skɪn] *n* : piel *f* de venado
deface [di'feɪs] *vt* **-faced; -facing** MAR : desfigurar
defacement [di'feɪsmənt] *n* : desfiguración *f*
defamation [,dɛfə'meɪʃən] *n* : difamación *f*
defamatory [di'fæmə,tori] *adj* : difamatorio
defame [di'feɪm] *vt* **-famed; -faming** : difamar, calumniar
default¹ [di'fɔlt, 'di:,fɔlt] *vi* **1** : no cumplir (con una obligación), no pagar **2** : no presentarse (en un tribunal)
default² *n* **1** NEGLECT : omisión *f*, negligencia *f* **2** NONPAYMENT : impago *m*, falta *f* de pago **3 to win by default** : ganar por abandono
defaulter [di'fɔltər] *n* : moroso *m*, -sa *f*; rebelde *mf* (en un tribunal)
defeat¹ [di'fi:t] *vt* **1** FRUSTRATE : frustrar **2** BEAT : vencer, derrotar
defeat² *n* : derrota *f*, rechazo *m* (de legislación), fracaso *m* (de planes, etc.)
defecate ['dɛfɪ,keɪt] *vi* **-cated; -cating** : defecar
defect¹ [di'fɛkt] *vi* : desertar
defect² ['di:,fɛkt, di'fɛkt] *n* : defecto *m*
defection [di'fɛkʃən] *n* : deserción *f*, defección *f*
defective [di'fɛktɪv] *adj* **1** FAULTY : defectuoso **2** DEFICIENT : deficiente
defector [di'fɛktər] *n* : desertor *m*, -tora *f*
defend [di'fɛnd] *vt* : defender
defendant [di'fɛndənt] *n* : acusado *m*, -da *f*; demandado *m*, -da *f*
defender [di'fɛndər] *n* **1** ADVOCATE : defensor *m*, -sora *f* **2** : defensa *mf* (en deportes)
defense [di'fɛnts, 'di:,fɛnts] *n* : defensa *f*
defenseless [di'fɛntsləs] *adj* : indefenso
defensive¹ [di'fɛntsɪv] *adj* : defensivo
defensive² *n* **on the defensive** : a la defensiva
defer [di'fər] *v* **-ferred; -ferring** *vt* POSTPONE : diferir, aplazar, posponer — *vi* **to defer to** : deferir a
deference ['dɛfərənts] *n* : deferencia *f*
deferential [,dɛfə'rɛntʃəl] *adj* : respetuoso
deferment [di'fərmənt] *n* : aplazamiento *m*

defiance [di'faɪənts] *n* : desafío *m*
defiant [di'faɪənt] *adj* : desafiante, insolente
deficiency [di'fɪʃəntsi] *n, pl* **-cies** : deficiencia *f*, carencia *f*
deficient [di'fɪʃənt] *adj* : deficiente, carente
deficit ['dɛfəsɪt] *n* : déficit *m*
defile [di'faɪl] *vt* **-filed; -filing 1** DIRTY : ensuciar, manchar **2** CORRUPT : corromper **3** DESECRATE, PROFANE : profanar **4** DISHONOR : deshonrar
defilement [di'faɪlmənt] *n* **1** DESECRATION : profanación *f* **2** CORRUPTION : corrupción *f* **3** CONTAMINATION : contaminación *f*
define [di'faɪn] *vt* **-fined; -fining 1** BOUND : delimitar, demarcar **2** CLARIFY : aclarar, definir **3** : definir ⟨to define a word : definir una palabra⟩
definite ['dɛfənɪt] *adj* **1** CERTAIN : definido, determinado **2** CLEAR : claro, explícito **3** UNQUESTIONABLE : seguro, incuestionable
definite article *n* : artículo *m* definido
definitely ['dɛfənɪtli] *adv* **1** DOUBTLESSLY : indudablemente, sin duda **2** DEFINITIVELY : definitivamente, seguramente
definition [,dɛfə'nɪʃən] *n* : definición *f*
definitive [di'fɪnət̬ɪv] *adj* **1** CONCLUSIVE : definitivo, decisivo **2** AUTHORITATIVE : de autoridad, autorizado
deflate [di'fleɪt] *v* **-flated; -flating** *vt* **1** : desinflar (una llanta, etc.) **2** REDUCE : rebajar ⟨to deflate one's ego : bajarle los humos a uno⟩ — *vi* : desinflarse
deflation [di'fleɪʃən] *n* **1** : desinflación *f* (de una llanta, etc.) **2** : deflación *f* (económica)
deflect [di'flɛkt] *vt* : desviar — *vi* : desviarse
defoliant [di'fo:liənt] *n* : defoliante *m*
deforestation [di,fɔrə'steɪʃən] *n* : deforestación *f*, desforestación *f*
deform [di'fɔrm] *vt* : deformar
deformation [,di:,fɔr'meɪʃən] *n* : deformación *f*
deformed [di'fɔrmd] *adj* : deforme
deformity [di'fɔrmət̬i] *n, pl* **-ties** : deformidad *f*
defraud [di'frɔd] *vt* : estafar, defraudar
defray [di'freɪ] *vt* : sufragar, costear
defrost [di'frɔst] *vt* : descongelar, deshelar — *vi* : descongelarse, deshelarse
deft ['dɛft] *adj* : hábil, diestro — **deftly** *adv*
defunct [di'fʌŋkt] *adj* **1** DECEASED : difunto, fallecido **2** EXTINCT : extinto, fenecido
defuse [di'fju:z] *vt* : desactivar ⟨to defuse the situation : reducir las tensiones⟩
defy [di'faɪ] *vt* **-fied; -fying 1** CHALLENGE : desafiar, retar **2** DISOBEY : desobedecer **3** RESIST : resistir, hacer imposible, hacer inútil

degenerate · delude

degenerate¹ [dɪ'dʒenə,reɪt] *vi* **-ated; -ating** : degenerar

degenerate² [dɪ'dʒenərət] *adj* : degenerado

degeneration [dɪ,dʒenə'reɪʃən] *n* : degeneración *f*

degenerative [dɪ'dʒenərətɪv] *adj* : degenerative

degradation [,degrə'deɪʃən] *n* : degradación *f*

degrade [dɪ'greɪd] *vt* **-graded; -grading** **1** : degradar, envilecer **2 to degrade oneself** : rebajarse

degrading [dɪ'greɪdɪŋ] *adj* : degradante

degree [dɪ'griː] *n* **1** EXTENT : grado *m* ⟨a third degree burn : una quemadura de tercer grado⟩ **2** : título *m* (de enseñanza superior) **3** : grado *m* (de un círculo, de la temperatura) **4 by degrees** : gradualmente, poco a poco

dehydrate [dɪ'haɪ,dreɪt] *v* **-drated; -drating** *vt* : deshidratar — *vi* : deshidratarse

dehydration [,diːhaɪ'dreɪʃən] *n* : deshidratación *f*

deice [,diː'aɪs] *vt* **-iced; -icing** : deshelar, descongelar

deify ['diːə,faɪ, 'deɪ-] *vt* **-fied; -fying** : deificar

deign ['deɪn] *vi* : dignarse, condescender

deity ['diːəṭi, 'deɪ-] *n, pl* **-ties** **1 the Deity** : Dios *m* **2** GOD, GODDESS : deidad *f*; dios *m*, diosa *f*

dejected [dɪ'dʒektəd] *adj* : abatido, desalentado, desanimado

dejection [dɪ'dʒekʃən] *n* : abatimiento *m*, desaliento *m*, desánimo *m*

delay¹ [dɪ'leɪ] *vt* **1** POSTPONE : posponer, postergar **2** HOLD UP : retrasar, demorar — *vi* : tardar, demorar

delay² *n* **1** LATENESS : tardanza *f* **2** HOLDUP : demora *f*, retraso *m*

delectable [dɪ'lektəbəl] *adj* **1** DELICIOUS : delicioso, exquisito **2** DELIGHTFUL : encantador

delegate¹ ['delɪ,geɪt] *v* **-gated; -gating** : delegar

delegate² ['delɪgət, -,geɪt] *n* : delegado *m*, -da *f*

delegation [,delɪ'geɪʃən] *n* : delegación *f*

delete [dɪ'liːt] *vt* **-leted; -leting** : suprimir, tachar, eliminar

deletion [dɪ'liːʃən] *n* : supresión *f*, tachadura *f*, eliminación *f*

deli ['deli] → **delicatessen**

deliberate¹ [dɪ'lɪbə,reɪt] *v* **-ated; -ating** *vt* : reflexionar sobre, considerar — *vi* : deliberar

deliberate² [dɪ'lɪbərət] *adj* **1** CONSIDERED : reflexionado, premeditado **2** INTENTIONAL : deliberado, intencional **3** SLOW : lento, pausado

deliberately [dɪ'lɪbərətli] *adv* **1** INTENTIONALLY : adrede, a propósito **2** SLOWLY : pausadamente, lentamente

deliberation [dɪ,lɪbə'reɪʃən] *n* **1** CONSIDERATION : deliberación *f*, consideración *f* **2** SLOWNESS : lentitud *f*

delicacy ['delɪkəsi] *n, pl* **-cies** **1** : manjar *m*, exquisitez *f* ⟨caviar is a real delicacy : el caviar es un verdadero manjar⟩ **2** FINENESS : delicadeza *f* **3** FRAGILITY : fragilidad *f*

delicate ['delɪkət] *adj* **1** SUBTLE : delicado ⟨a delicate fragrance : una fragancia delicada⟩ **2** DAINTY : delicado, primoroso, fino **3** FRAGILE : frágil **4** SENSITIVE : delicado ⟨a delicate matter : un asunto delicado⟩

delicately ['delɪkətli] *adv* : delicadamente, con delicadeza

delicatessen [,delɪkə'tesən] *n* : charcutería *f*, fiambrería *f*, salchichonería *f* Mex

delicious [dɪ'lɪʃəs] *adj* : delicioso, exquisito, rico — **deliciously** *adv*

delight¹ [dɪ'laɪt] *vt* : deleitar, encantar — *vi* **to delight in** : deleitarse con, complacerse en

delight² *n* **1** JOY : placer *m*, deleite *m*, gozo *m* **2** : encanto *m* ⟨your garden is a delight : su jardín es un encanto⟩

delightful [dɪ'laɪtfəl] *adj* : delicioso, encantador

delightfully [dɪ'laɪtfəli] *adv* : de manera encantadora, de maravilla

delineate [dɪ'lɪni,eɪt] *vt* **-eated; -eating** : delinear, trazar, bosquejar

delinquency [dɪ'lɪŋkwəntsi] *n, pl* **-cies** : delincuencia *f*

delinquent¹ [dɪ'lɪŋkwənt] *adj* **1** : delincuente **2** OVERDUE : vencido y sin pagar, moroso

delinquent² *n* : delincuente *mf* ⟨juvenile delinquent : delincuente juvenil⟩

delirious [dɪ'lɪriəs] *adj* : delirante ⟨delirious with joy : loco de alegría⟩

delirium [dɪ'lɪriəm] *n* : delirio *m*, desvarío *m*

deliver [dɪ'lɪvər] *vt* **1** FREE : liberar, librar **2** DISTRIBUTE : entregar, repartir **3** : asistir en el parto de (un niño) **4** : pronunciar ⟨to deliver a speech : pronunciar un discurso⟩ **5** PROJECT : despachar, lanzar ⟨he delivered a fast ball : lanzó un pelota rápida⟩ **6** DEAL : propinar, asestar ⟨to deliver a blow : asestar un golpe⟩

deliverance [dɪ'lɪvərənts] *n* : liberación *f*, rescate *m*, salvación *f*

deliverer [dɪ'lɪvərər] *n* RESCUER : libertador *m*, -dora *f*; salvador *m*, -dora *f*

delivery [dɪ'lɪvəri] *n, pl* **-eries** **1** LIBERATION : liberación *f* **2** : entrega *f*, reparto *m* ⟨cash on delivery : entrega contra reembolso⟩ ⟨home delivery : servicio a domicilio⟩ **3** CHILDBIRTH : parto *m*, alumbramiento *m* **4** SPEECH : expresión *f* oral, modo *m* de hablar **5** THROW : lanzamiento *m*

dell ['del] *n* : hondonada *f*, valle *m* pequeño

delta ['deltə] *n* : delta *m*

delude [dɪ'luːd] *vt* **-luded; -luding** **1** : engañar **2 to delude oneself** : engañarse

deluge¹ ['dɛl,ju:ʤ, -,ju:ʒ] *vt* **-uged; -uging 1** FLOOD : inundar **2** OVER-WHELM : abrumar ⟨deluged with requests : abrumado de pedidos⟩

deluge² *n* **1** FLOOD : inundación *f* **2** DOWNPOUR : aguacero *m* **3** BARRAGE : aluvión *m*

delusion [di'lu:ʒən] *n* **1** : ilusión *f* (falsa) **2 delusions of grandeur** : delirios *mpl* de grandeza

deluxe [di'lʌks, -'lʊks] *adj* : de lujo

delve ['dɛlv] *vi* **delved; delving 1** DIG : escarbar **2 to delve into** PROBE : cavar en, ahondar en

demagogue ['dɛmə,gɑg] *n* : demagogo *m*, demagoga *f*

demand¹ [di'mænd] *vt* : demandar, exigir, reclamar

demand² *n* **1** REQUEST : petición *f*, pedido *m*, demanda *f* ⟨by popular demand : a petición del público⟩ **2** CLAIM : reclamación *f*, exigencia *f* **3** MARKET : demanda *f* ⟨supply and demand : la oferta y la demanda⟩

demanding [di'mændɪŋ] *adj* : exigente

demarcation [,di:,mɑr'keɪʃən] *n* : demarcación *f*, deslinde *m*

demean [di'mi:n] *vt* : degradar, rebajar

demeanor [di'mi:nər] *n* : comportamiento *m*, conducta *f*

demented [di'mɛntəd] *adj* : demente, loco

dementia [di'mɛntʃə] *n* : demencia *f*

demerit [di'mɛrət] *n* : demérito *m*

demigod ['dɛmi,gɑd, -,gɔd] *n* : semidiós *m*

demise [dɪ'maɪz] *n* **1** DEATH : fallecimiento *m*, deceso *m* **2** END : hundimiento *m*, desaparición *f* (de una institución, etc.)

demitasse ['dɛmi,tæs, -,tɑs] *n* : taza *f* pequeña (de café)

demobilization [di,mo:bələ'zeɪʃən] *n* : desmovilización *f*

demobilize [di'mo:bə,laɪz] *vt* **-lized; -lizing** : desmovilizar

democracy [di'mɑkrəsi] *n, pl* **-cies** : democracia *f*

democrat ['dɛmə,kræt] *n* : demócrata *mf*

democratic [,dɛmə'krætɪk] *adj* : democrático — **democratically** [-tɪkli] *adv*

demographic [dɛmə'græfɪk] *adj* : demográfico

demolish [di'mɑlɪʃ] *vt* **1** RAZE : demoler, derribar, arrasar **2** DESTROY : destruir, destrozar

demolition [,dɛmə'lɪʃən, ,di:-] *n* : demolición *f*, derribo *m*

demon ['di:mən] *n* : demonio *m*, diablo *m*

demonstrably [di'mɑntstrəbli] *adv* : manifiestamente, claramente

demonstrate ['dɛmən,streɪt] *vt* **-strated; -strating 1** SHOW : demostrar **2** PROVE : probar, demostrar **3** EXPLAIN : explicar, ilustrar

demonstration [,dɛmən'streɪʃən] *n* **1** SHOW : muestra *f*, demostración *f* **2** RALLY : manifestación *f*

demonstrative [di'mɑntstrətɪv] *adj* **1** EFFUSIVE : efusivo, expresivo, demostrativo **2** : demostrativo (en lingüística) ⟨demonstrative pronoun : pronombre demostrativo⟩

demonstrator ['dɛmən,streɪtər] *n* **1** : demostrador *m*, -dora *f* (de productos) **2** PROTESTER : manifestante *mf*

demoralize [di'mɔrə,laɪz] *vt* **-ized; -izing** : desmoralizar

demote [di'mo:t] *vt* **-moted; -moting** : degradar, bajar de categoría

demotion [di'mo:ʃən] *n* : degradación *f*, descenso *m* de categoría

demur [di'mər] *vi* **-murred; -murring 1** OBJECT : oponerse **2 to demur at** : ponerle objeciones a (algo)

demure [di'mjʊr] *adj* : recatado, modesto — **demurely** *adv*

den ['dɛn] *n* **1** LAIR : cubil *m*, madriguera *f* **2** HIDEOUT : guarida *f* **3** STUDY : estudio *m*, gabinete *m*

denature [di'neɪtʃər] *vt* **-tured; -turing** : desnaturalizar

denial [di'naɪəl] *n* **1** REFUSAL : rechazo *m*, denegación *f*, negativa *f* **2** REPUDIATION : negación *f* (de una creencia, etc.), rechazo *m*

denigrate ['dɛni,greɪt] *vt* **-grated; -grating** : denigrar

denim ['dɛnəm] *n* **1** : tela *f* vaquera, mezclilla *f* *Chile, Mex* **2 denims** *npl* → **jeans**

denizen ['dɛnəzən] *n* : habitante *mf*; morador *m*, -dora *f*

denomination [dɪ,nɑmə'neɪʃən] *n* **1** FAITH : confesión *f*, fe *f* **2** VALUE : denominación *f*, valor *m* (de una moneda)

denominator [dɪ'nɑmə,neɪtər] *n* : denominador *m*

denote [di'no:t] *vt* **-noted; -noting 1** INDICATE, MARK : indicar, denotar, señalar **2** MEAN : significar

denouement [,deɪ,nu:'mɑ] *n* : desenlace *m*

denounce [di'naʊnts] *vt* **-nounced; -nouncing 1** CENSURE : denunciar, censurar **2** ACCUSE : denunciar, acusar, delatar

dense ['dɛnts] *adj* **denser; -est 1** THICK : espeso, denso ⟨dense vegetation : vegetación densa⟩ ⟨a dense fog : una niebla espesa⟩ **2** STUPID : estúpido, burro *fam*

densely ['dɛntsli] *adv* **1** THICKLY : densamente **2** STUPIDLY : torpemente

denseness ['dɛntsnəs] *n* **1** → **density 2** STUPIDITY : estupidez *f*

density ['dɛntsəti] *n, pl* **-ties** : densidad *f*

dent¹ ['dɛnt] *vt* : abollar, mellar

dent² *n* : abolladura *f*, mella *f*

dental ['dɛntəl] *adj* : dental

dental floss *n* : hilo *m* dental

dentifrice ['dɛntəfrɪs] *n* : dentífrico *m*, pasta *f* de dientes
dentist ['dɛntɪst] *n* : dentista *mf*
dentistry ['dɛntɪstri] *n* : odontología *f*
dentures ['dɛntʃərz] *npl* : dentadura *f* postiza
denude [di'nu:d, -'nju:d] *vt* -nuded; -nuding STRIP : desnudar, despojar
denunciation [di,nʌntsi'eɪʃən] *n* : denuncia *f*, acusación *f*
deny [di'naɪ] *vt* -nied; -nying **1** REFUTE : desmentir, negar **2** DISOWN, REPUDIATE : negar, renegar de **3** REFUSE : denegar **4 to deny oneself** : privarse, sacrificarse
deodorant [di'o:dərənt] *n* : desodorante *m*
deodorize [di'o:də,raɪz] *vt* -ized; -izing : desodorizar
depart [di'part] *vt* : salirse de — *vi* **1** LEAVE : salir, partir, irse **2** DIE : morir
department [di'partmənt] *n* **1** DIVISION : sección *f* (de una tienda, una organización, etc.), departamento *m* (de una empresa, una universidad, etc.), ministerio *m* (del gobierno) **2** PROVINCE, SPHERE : esfera *f*, campo *m*, competencia *f*
departmental [di,part'mɛntəl, ,di:-] *adj* : departamental
department store *n* : grandes almacenes *mpl*
departure [di'partʃər] *n* **1** LEAVING : salida *f*, partida *f* **2** DEVIATION : desviación *f*
depend [di'pɛnd] *vi* **1** RELY : contar (con), confiar (en) ⟨depend on me! : ¡cuenta conmigo!⟩ **2 to depend on** : depender de ⟨success depends on hard work : el éxito depende de trabajar duro⟩ **3 that depends** : según, eso depende
dependable [di'pɛndəbəl] *adj* : responsable, digno de confianza, fiable
dependence [di'pɛndənts] *n* : dependencia *f*
dependency [di'pɛndəntsi] *n, pl* -cies → dependence **2** : posesión *f* (de una unidad política)
dependent¹ [di'pɛndənt] *adj* : dependiente
dependent² *n* : persona *f* a cargo de alguien
depict [di'pɪkt] *vt* **1** PORTRAY : representar **2** DESCRIBE : describir
depiction [di'pɪkʃən] *n* : representación *f*, descripción *f*
deplete [di'pli:t] *vt* -pleted; -pleting **1** EXHAUST : agotar **2** REDUCE : reducir
depletion [di'pli:ʃən] *n* **1** EXHAUSTION : agotamiento *m* **2** REDUCTION : reducción *f*, disminución *f*
deplorable [di'plorəbəl] *adj* **1** CONTEMPTIBLE : deplorable, despreciable **2** LAMENTABLE : lamentable
deplore [di'plor] *vt* -plored; -ploring **1** REGRET : deplorar, lamentar **2** CONDEMN : condenar, deplorar

deploy [di'plɔɪ] *vt* : desplegar
deployment [di'plɔɪmənt] *n* : despliegue *m*
deport [di'port] *vt* **1** EXPEL : deportar, expulsar (de un país) **2 to deport oneself** BEHAVE : comportarse
deportation [,di:,por'teɪʃən] *n* : deportación *f*
depose [di'po:z] *vt* -posed; -posing : deponer
deposit¹ [di'pazət] *vt* -ited; -iting : depositar
deposit² *n* **1** : depósito *m* (en el banco) **2** DOWN PAYMENT : entrega *f* inicial **3** : depósito *m*, yacimiento *m* (en geología)
deposition [,dɛpə'zɪʃən] *n* TESTIMONY : deposición *f*
depositor [di'pazətər] *n* : depositante *mf*
depository [di'pazə,tori] *n, pl* -ries : almacén *m*, depósito *m*
depot [*in sense 1 usu* 'dɛ,po:, *2 usu* 'di:-] *n* **1** STOREHOUSE : almacén *m*, depósito *m* **2** STATION, TERMINAL : terminal *mf*, estación *f* (de autobuses, ferrocarriles, etc.)
deprave [di'preɪv] *vt* -praved; -praving : depravar, pervertir
depraved [di'preɪvd] *adj* : depravado, degenerado
depravity [di'prævəti] *n, pl* -ties : depravación *f*
depreciate [di'pri:ʃi,eɪt] *v* -ated; -ating *vt* **1** DEVALUE : depreciar, devaluar **2** DISPARAGE : menospreciar, despreciar — *vi* : depreciarse, devaluarse
depreciation [di,pri:ʃi'eɪʃən] *n* : depreciación *f*, devaluación *f*
depress [di'prɛs] *vt* **1** PRESS, PUSH : apretar, presionar, pulsar **2** REDUCE : reducir, hacer bajar (precios, ventas, etc.) **3** SADDEN : deprimir, abatir, entristecer **4** DEVALUE : depreciar
depressant¹ [di'prɛsənt] *adj* : depresivo
depressant² *n* : depresivo *m*
depressed [di'prɛst] *adj* **1** DEJECTED : deprimido, abatido **2** : deprimido, en crisis (dícese de la economía)
depressing [di'prɛsɪŋ] *adj* : deprimente, triste
depression [di'prɛʃən] *n* **1** DESPONDENCY : depresión *f*, abatimiento *m* **2** : depresión (en una superficie) **3** RECESSION : depresión *f* económica, crisis *f*
deprivation [,dɛprə'veɪʃən] *n* : privación *f*
deprive [di'praɪv] *vt* -prived; -priving : privar
depth ['dɛpθ] *n, pl* **depths** ['dɛpθs, 'dɛps] **1** : profundidad *f*, fondo *m* ⟨to study in depth : estudiar a fondo⟩ ⟨in the depths of winter : en pleno invierno⟩
deputize ['dɛpju,taɪz] *vt* -tized; -tizing : nombrar como segundo
deputy ['dɛpjuti] *n, pl* -ties : suplente *mf*; sustituto *m*, -ta *f*
derail [di'reɪl] *v* : descarrilar

derailment [dɪˈreɪlmənt] *n* : descarrilamiento *m*
derange [dɪˈreɪndʒ] *vt* -**ranged; -ranging** **1** DISARRANGE : desarreglar, desordenar **2** DISTURB, UPSET : trastornar, perturbar **3** MADDEN : enloquecer, volver loco
derangement [dɪˈreɪndʒmənt] *n* **1** DISTURBANCE, UPSET : trastorno *m* **2** INSANITY : locura *f*, perturbación *f* mental
derby [ˈdərbi] *n, pl* -**bies** **1** : derby *m* ⟨the Kentucky Derby : el Derby de Kentucky⟩ **2** : sombrero *m* hongo
deregulate [diˈrɛgjʊˌleɪt] *vt* -**lated; -lating** : desregular
deregulation [diˌrɛgjʊˈleɪʃən] *n* : desregulación *f*
derelict[1] [ˈdɛrəˌlɪkt] *adj* **1** ABANDONED : abandonado, en ruinas **2** REMISS : negligente, remiso
derelict[2] *n* **1** : propiedad *f* abandonada **2** VAGRANT : vagabundo *m*, -da *f*
deride [dɪˈraɪd] *vt* -**rided; -riding** : ridiculizar, burlarse de
derision [dɪˈrɪʒən] *n* : escarnio *m*, irrisión *f*, mofa *f*
derisive [dɪˈraɪsɪv] *adj* : burlón
derivation [ˌdɛrəˈveɪʃən] *n* : derivación *f*
derivative[1] [dɪˈrɪvətɪv] *adj* **1** DERIVED : derivado **2** BANAL : carente de originalidad, banal
derivative[2] *n* : derivado *m*
derive [dɪˈraɪv] *v* -**rived; -riving** *vt* **1** OBTAIN : obtener, sacar **2** DEDUCE : deducir, inferir — *vi* : provenir, derivar, proceder
dermatologist [ˌdərməˈtɑlədʒɪst] *n* : dermatólogo *m*, -ga *f*
dermatology [ˌdərməˈtɑlədʒi] *n* : dermatología *f*
derogatory [dɪˈrɑgəˌtori] *adj* : despectivo, despreciativo
derrick [ˈdɛrɪk] *n* **1** CRANE : grúa *f* **2** : torre *f* de perforación (sobre un pozo de petróleo)
descend [dɪˈsɛnd] *vt* : descender, bajar — *vi* **1** : descender, bajar ⟨he descended from the platform : descendió del estrado⟩ **2** DERIVE : descender, provenir **3** STOOP : rebajarse ⟨I descended to his level : me rebajé a su nivel⟩ **4 to descend upon** : caer sobre, invadir
descendant[1] [dɪˈsɛndənt] *adj* : descendente
descendant[2] *n* : descendiente *mf*
descent [dɪˈsɛnt] *n* **1** : bajada *f*, descenso *m* ⟨the descent from the mountain : el descenso de la montaña⟩ **2** ANCESTRY : ascendencia *f*, linaje *f* **3** SLOPE : pendiente *f*, cuesta *f* **4** FALL : caída *f* **5** ATTACK : incursión *f*, ataque *m*
describe [dɪˈskraɪb] *vt* -**scribed; -scribing** : describir
description [dɪˈskrɪpʃən] *n* : descripción *f*

descriptive [dɪˈskrɪptɪv] *adj* : descriptivo ⟨descriptive adjective : adjetivo calificativo⟩
desecrate [ˈdɛsɪˌkreɪt] *vt* -**crated; -crating** : profanar
desecration [ˌdɛsɪˈkreɪʃən] *n* : profanación *f*
desegregate [diˈsɛgrəˌgeɪt] *vt* -**gated; -gating** : eliminar la segregación racial de
desegregation [diˌsɛgrəˈgeɪʃən] *n* : eliminación *f* de la segregación racial
desert[1] [dɪˈzərt] *vt* : abandonar (una persona o un lugar), desertar de (una causa, etc.) — *vi* : desertar
desert[2] [ˈdɛzərt] *adj* : desierto ⟨a desert island : una isla desierta⟩
desert[3] *n* **1** [ˈdɛzərt] : desierto *m* (en geografía) **2** [dɪˈzərt] → **deserts**
deserter [dɪˈzərtər] *n* : desertor *m*, -tora *f*
desertion [dɪˈzərʃən] *n* : abandono *m*, deserción *f* (militar)
deserts [dɪˈzərts] *npl* : merecido *m* ⟨to get one's just deserts : llevarse uno su merecido⟩
deserve [dɪˈzərv] *vt* -**served; -serving** : merecer, ser digno de
deserving [dɪˈzərvɪŋ] *adj* : meritorio ⟨deserving of : digno de⟩
desiccate [ˈdɛsɪˌkeɪt] *vt* -**cated; -cating** : desecar, deshidratar
design[1] [dɪˈzaɪn] *vt* **1** DEVISE : diseñar, concebir, idear **2** PLAN : proyectar **3** SKETCH : trazar, bosquejar
design[2] *n* **1** PLAN, SCHEME : plan *m*, proyecto *m* ⟨by design : a propósito, intencionalmente⟩ **2** SKETCH : diseño *m*, bosquejo *m* **3** PATTERN, STYLE : diseño *m*, estilo *m* **4 designs** *npl* INTENTIONS : propósitos *mpl*, designios *mpl*
designate [ˈdɛzɪgˌneɪt] *vt* -**nated; -nating** **1** INDICATE, SPECIFY : indicar, especificar **2** APPOINT : nombrar, designar
designation [ˌdɛzɪgˈneɪʃən] *n* **1** NAMING : designación *f* **2** NAME : denominación *f*, nombre *m* **3** APPOINTMENT : designación *f*, nombramiento *m*
designer [dɪˈzaɪnər] *n* : diseñador *m*, -dora *f*
desirability [dɪˌzaɪrəˈbɪləti] *n, pl* -**ties** **1** ADVISABILITY : conveniencia *f* **2** ATTRACTIVENESS : atractivo *m*
desirable [dɪˈzaɪrəbəl] *adj* **1** ADVISABLE : conveniente, aconsejable **2** ATTRACTIVE : deseable, atractivo
desire[1] [dɪˈzaɪr] *vt* -**sired; -siring** **1** WANT : desear **2** REQUEST : rogar, solicitar
desire[2] *n* : deseo *m*, anhelo *m*, ansia *m*
desist [dɪˈsɪst, -ˈzɪst] *vi* **to desist from** : desistir de, abstenerse de
desk [ˈdɛsk] *n* : escritorio *m*, pupitre *m* (en la escuela)
desktop [ˈdɛskˌtɑp] *adj* : de escritorio
desolate[1] [ˈdɛsəˌleɪt, -zə-] *vt* -**lated; -lating** : devastar, desolar

desolate² [ˈdɛsələt, -zə-] *adj* **1** BARREN : desolado, desierto, yermo **2** DISCONSOLATE : desconsolado, desolado

desolation [ˌdɛsəˈleɪʃən, -zə-] *n* : desolación *f*

despair¹ [diˈspær] *vi* : desesperar, perder las esperanzas

despair² *n* : desesperación *f*, desesperanza *f*

desperate [ˈdɛspərət] *adj* **1** HOPELESS : desesperado, sin esperanzas **2** RASH : desesperado, precipitado **3** SERIOUS, URGENT : grave, urgente, apremiante ⟨a desperate need : una necesidad apremiante⟩

desperately [ˈdɛspərətli] *adv* : desesperadamente, urgentemente

desperation [ˌdɛspəˈreɪʃən] *n* : desesperación *f*

despicable [diˈspɪkəbəl, ˈdɛspɪ-] *adj* : vil, despreciable, infame

despise [diˈspaɪz] *vt* **-spised; -spising** : despreciar

despite [dəˈspaɪt] *prep* : a pesar de, aún con

despoil [diˈspɔɪl] *vt* : saquear

despondency [diˈspɑndənsi] *n* : desaliento *m*, desánimo *m*, depresión *f*

despondent [diˈspɑndənt] *adj* : desalentado, desanimado

despot [ˈdɛspət, -ˌpɑt] *n* : déspota *mf*; tirano *m*, -na *f*

despotic [dɛsˈpɑtɪk] *adj* : despótico

despotism [ˈdɛspəˌtɪzəm] *n* : despotismo *m*

dessert [diˈzərt] *n* : postre *m*

destination [ˌdɛstəˈneɪʃən] *n* : destino *m*, destinación *f*

destined [ˈdɛstənd] *adj* **1** FATED : predestinado **2** BOUND : destinado, con destino (a), con rumbo (a)

destiny [ˈdɛstəni] *n, pl* **-nies** : destino *m*

destitute [ˈdɛstəˌtuːt, -ˌtjuːt] *adj* **1** LACKING : carente, desprovisto **2** POOR : indigente, en miseria

destitution [ˌdɛstəˈtuːʃən, -ˈtjuː-] *n* : indigencia *f*, miseria *f*

destroy [diˈstrɔɪ] *vt* **1** KILL : matar **2** DEMOLISH : destruir, destrozar

destroyer [diˈstrɔɪər] *n* : destructor *m* (buque)

destructible [diˈstrʌktəbəl] *adj* : destructible

destruction [diˈstrʌkʃən] *n* : destrucción *f*, ruina *f*

destructive · [diˈstrʌktɪv] *adj* : destructor, destructivo

desultory [ˈdɛsəlˌtori] *adj* **1** AIMLESS : sin rumbo, sin objeto **2** DISCONNECTED : inconexo

detach [diˈtætʃ] *vt* : separar, quitar, desprender

detached [diˈtætʃt] *adj* **1** SEPARATE : separado, suelto **2** ALOOF : distante, indiferente **3** IMPARTIAL : imparcial, objetivo

detachment [diˈtætʃmənt] *n* **1** SEPARATION : separación *f* **2** DETAIL : destacamento *m* (de tropas) **3** ALOOFNESS : reserva *f*, indiferencia *f* **4** IMPARTIALITY : imparcialidad *f*

detail¹ [diˈteɪl, ˈdiːˌteɪl] *vt* : detallar, exponer en detalle

detail² *n* **1** : detalle *m*, pormenor *m* **2** : destacamento *m* (de tropas)

detailed [diˈteɪld, ˈdiːˌteɪld] *adj* : detallado, minucioso

detain [diˈteɪn] *vt* **1** HOLD : detener **2** DELAY : entretener, demorar, retrasar

detect [diˈtɛkt] *vt* : detectar, descubrir

detection [diˈtɛkʃən] *n* : descubrimiento *m*

detective [diˈtɛktɪv] *n* : detective *mf* ⟨private detective : detective privado⟩

detector [diˈtɛktər] *n* : detector *m*

detention [diˈtɛnʃən] *n* : detención *m*

deter [diˈtər] *vt* **-terred; -terring** : disuadir, impedir

detergent [diˈtərdʒənt] *n* : detergente *m*

deteriorate [diˈtiriəˌreɪt] *vi* **-rated; -rating** : deteriorarse, empeorar

deterioration [diˌtiriəˈreɪʃən] *n* : deterioro *m*, empeoramiento *m*

determinant¹ [diˈtərmənənt] *adj* : determinante

determinant² *n* **1** : factor *m* determinante **2** : determinante *m* (en matemáticas)

determination [diˌtərməˈneɪʃən] *n* **1** DECISION : determinación *f*, decisión *f* **2** RESOLUTION : resolución *f*, determinación *f* ⟨with grim determination : con una firme resolución⟩

determine [diˈtərmən] *vt* **-mined; -mining 1** ESTABLISH : determinar, establecer **2** SETTLE : decidir **3** FIND OUT : averiguar **4** BRING ABOUT : determinar

determined [diˈtərmənd] *adj* RESOLUTE : decidido, resuelto

deterrent [diˈtərənt] *n* : medida *f* disuasiva

detest [diˈtɛst] *vt* : detestar, odiar, aborrecer

detestable [diˈtɛstəbəl] *adj* : detestable, odioso, aborrecible

dethrone [diˈθroːn] *vt* **-throned; -throning** : destronar

detonate [ˈdɛtənˌeɪt] *v* **-nated; -nating** *vt* : hacer detonar — *vi* : detonar, estallar

detonation [ˌdɛtəˈneɪʃən] *n* : detonación *f*

detour¹ [ˈdiːˌtʊr, diˈtʊr] *vi* : desviarse

detour² *n* : desvío *m*, rodeo *m*

detract [diˈtrækt] *vi* **to detract from** : restarle valor a, quitarle méritos a

detractor [diˈtræktər] *n* : detractor *m*, -tora *f*

detriment [ˈdɛtrəmənt] *n* : detrimento *m*, perjuicio *m*

detrimental [ˌdɛtrəˈmɛntəl] *adj* : perjudicial — **detrimentally** *adv*

devaluation [diˌvæljuˈeɪʃən] *n* : devaluación *f*

devalue [diˈvælˌjuː] *vt* **-ued; -uing** : devaluar, depreciar

devastate ['dɛvə,steɪt] *vt* **-tated; -tating**
: devastar, arrasar, asolar

devastation [,dɛvə'steɪʃən] *n* : devastación *f*, estragos *mpl*

develop [dɪ'vɛləp] *vt* **1** FORM, MAKE
: desarrollar, elaborar, formar **2** : revelar (en fotografía) **3** FOSTER : desarrollar, fomentar **4** EXPLOIT : explotar (recursos), urbanizar (un área) **5** ACQUIRE : adquirir ⟨to develop an interest : adquirir un interés⟩ **6** CONTRACT : contraer (una enfermedad) — *vi* **1** GROW : desarrollarse **2** ARISE : aparecer, surgir

developed [dɪ'vɛləpt] *adj* : avanzado, desarrollado

developer [dɪ'vɛləpər] *n* **1** : inmobiliaria *f*, urbanizadora *f* **2** : revelador *m* (en fotografía)

development [dɪ'vɛləpmənt] *n* **1** : desarrollo *m* ⟨physical development : desarrollo físico⟩ **2** : urbanización *f* (de un área), explotación *f* (de recursos), creación *f* (de inventos) **3** EVENT : acontecimiento *m*, suceso *m* ⟨to await developments : esperar acontecimientos⟩

deviant ['di:viənt] *adj* : desviado, anormal

deviate ['di:vi,eɪt] *v* **-ated; -ating** *vi*
: desviarse, apartarse — *vt* : desviar

deviation [,di:vi'eɪʃən] *n* : desviación *f*

device [dɪ'vaɪs] *n* **1** MECHANISM : dispositivo *m*, aparato *m*, mecanismo *m* **2** EMBLEM : emblema *m*

devil¹ ['dɛvəl] *vt* **-iled** *or* **-illed; -iling** *or* **-illing** **1** : sazonar con picante y especias **2** PESTER : molestar

devil² *n* **1** SATAN : el diablo, Satanás *m* **2** DEMON : diablo *m*, demonio *m* **3** FIEND : persona *f* diabólica; malvado *m*, -da *f*

devilish ['dɛvəlɪʃ] *adj* : diabólico

devilry ['dɛvəlri] *n*, *pl* **-ries** : diabluras *fpl*, travesuras *fpl*

devious ['di:viəs] *adj* **1** CRAFTY : taimado, artero **2** WINDING : tortuoso, sinuoso

devise [dɪ'vaɪz] *vt* **-vised; -vising** **1** INVENT : idear, concebir, inventar **2** PLOT : tramar

devoid [dɪ'vɔɪd] *adj* ∼ **of** : carente de, desprovisto de

devote [dɪ'vo:t] *vt* **-voted; -voting** **1** DEDICATE : consagrar, dedicar ⟨to devote one's life : dedicar uno su vida⟩ **2 to devote oneself** : dedicarse

devoted [dɪ'vo:t̬əd] *adj* **1** FAITHFUL : leal, fiel **2 to be devoted to someone** : tenerle mucho cariño a alguien

devotee [,dɛvə'ti:, -'teɪ] *n* : devoto *m*, -ta *f*

devotion [dɪ'vo:ʃən] *n* **1** DEDICATION : dedicación *f*, devoción *f* **2 devotions** PRAYERS : oraciones *fpl*, devociones *fpl*

devour [dɪ'vauər] *vt* : devorar

devout [dɪ'vaut] *adj* **1** PIOUS : devoto, piadoso **2** EARNEST, SINCERE : sincero, ferviente — **devoutly** *adv*

devoutness [dɪ'vautnəs] *n* : devoción *f*, piedad *f*

dew ['du:, 'dju:] *n* : rocío *m*

dewlap ['du:,læp, 'dju:-] *n* : papada *f*

dew point *n* : punto *m* de condensación

dewy ['du:i, 'dju:i] *adj* **dewier; -est** : cubierto de rocío

dexterity [dɛk'stɛrət̬i] *n*, *pl* **-ties** : destreza *f*, habilidad *f*

dexterous ['dɛkstrəs] *adj* : diestro, hábil

dexterously ['dɛkstrəsli] *adv* : con destreza, con habilidad, hábilmente

dextrose ['dɛk,stro:s] *n* : dextrosa *f*

diabetes [,daɪə'bi:t̬iz] *n* : diabetes *f*

diabetic¹ [,daɪə'bɛt̬ɪk] *adj* : diabético

diabetic² *n* : diabético *m*, -ca *f*

diabolic [,daɪə'bɑlɪk] *or* **diabolical** [-lɪkəl] *adj* : diabólico, satánico

diacritical mark [,daɪə'krɪt̬ɪkəl] *n* : signo *m* diacrítico

diadem ['daɪə,dɛm, -dəm] *n* : diadema *f*

diagnose ['daɪg,no:s, ,daɪg'no:s] *vt* **-nosed; -nosing** : diagnosticar

diagnosis [,daɪg'no:sɪs] *n*, *pl* **-noses** [-'no:,si:z] : diagnóstico *m*

diagnostic [,daɪg'nɑstɪk] *adj* : diagnóstico

diagonal¹ [daɪ'ægənəl] *adj* : diagonal, en diagonal

diagonal² *n* : diagonal *f*

diagonally [daɪ'ægənəli] *adv* : diagonalmente, en diagonal

diagram¹ ['daɪə,græm] *vt* **-gramed** *or* **-grammed; -graming** *or* **-gramming** : hacer un diagrama de

diagram² *n* : diagrama *m*, gráfico *m*, esquema *m*

dial¹ ['daɪl] *v* **dialed** *or* **dialled; dialing** *or* **dialling** : marcar, discar

dial² *n* : esfera *f* (de un reloj), dial *m* (de un radio), disco *m* (de un teléfono)

dialect ['daɪə,lɛkt] *n* : dialecto *m*

dialogue ['daɪə,lɔg] *n* : diálogo *m*

diameter [daɪ'æmət̬ər] *n* : diámetro *m*

diamond ['daɪmənd, 'daɪə-] *n* **1** : diamante *m*, brillante *m* ⟨a diamond necklace : un collar de brillantes⟩ **2** : rombo *m*, forma *f* de rombo **3** : diamante *m* (en naipes) **4** INFIELD : cuadro *m*, diamante *m* (en béisbol)

diaper ['daɪpər, 'daɪə-] *n* : pañal *m*

diaphragm ['daɪə,fræm] *n* : diafragma *m*

diarrhea [,daɪə'ri:ə] *n* : diarrea *f*

diary ['daɪəri] *n*, *pl* **-ries** : diario *m*

diatribe ['daɪə,traɪb] *n* : diatriba *f*

dice¹ ['daɪs] *vt* **diced; dicing** : cortar en cubos

dice² *ns* & *pl* **1** → **die²** **2** : dados *mpl* (juego)

dicker ['dɪkər] *vt* : regatear

dictate¹ ['dɪk,teɪt, dɪk'teɪt] *v* **-tated; -tating** *vt* **1** : dictar ⟨to dictate a letter : dictar una carta⟩ **2** ORDER : mandar, ordenar — *vi* : dar órdenes

dictate² ['dɪkˌteɪt] n 1 : mandato m, orden f 2 **dictates** npl : dictados mpl ⟨the dictates of conscience : los dictados de la conciencia⟩

dictation [dɪk'teɪʃən] n : dictado m

dictator ['dɪkˌteɪʈər] n : dictador m, -dora f

dictatorial [ˌdɪktə'torɪəl] adj : dictatorial — **dictatorially** adv

dictatorship [dɪk'teɪʈərˌʃɪp, 'dɪkˌ-] n : dictadura f

diction ['dɪkʃən] n 1 : lenguaje m, estilo m 2 ENUNCIATION : dicción f, articulación f

dictionary ['dɪkʃəˌnɛri] n, pl -naries : diccionario m

did → **do**

didactic [daɪ'dæktɪk] adj : didáctico

die¹ ['daɪ] vi **died** ['daɪd]; **dying** ['daɪɪŋ] 1 : morir 2 CEASE : morir, morirse ⟨a dying civilization : una civilización moribunda⟩ 3 STOP : apagarse, dejar de funcionar ⟨the motor died : el motor se apagó⟩ 4 **to die down** SUBSIDE : amainar, disminuir 5 **to die out** : extinguirse 6 **to be dying for** or **to be dying to** : morirse por ⟨I'm dying to leave : me muero por irme⟩

die² ['daɪ] n, pl **dice** ['daɪs] : dado m

die³ n, pl **dies** ['daɪz] 1 STAMP : troquel m, cuño m 2 MOLD : matriz f, molde m

diesel ['di:zəl, -səl] n : diesel m

diet¹ ['daɪət] vi : ponerse a régimen, hacer dieta

diet² n : régimen m, dieta f

dietary ['daɪəˌtɛri] adj : alimenticio, dietético

dietitian or **dietician** [ˌdaɪə'tɪʃən] n : dietista mf

differ ['dɪfər] vi **-ferred**; **-ferring** 1 : diferir, diferenciarse 2 VARY : variar 3 DISAGREE : discrepar, diferir, no estar de acuerdo

difference ['dɪfrənts, 'dɪfərənts] n : diferencia f

different ['dɪfrənt, 'dɪfərənt] adj : distinto, diferente

differentiate [ˌdɪfə'rɛnʈʃiˌeɪt] v **-ated**; **-ating** vt 1 : hacer diferente 2 DISTINGUISH : distinguir, diferenciar — vi : distinguir

differentiation [ˌdɪfəˌrɛnʈʃi'eɪʃən] n : diferenciación f

differently ['dɪfrəntli, 'dɪfərənt-] adv : de otra manera, de otro modo, distintamente

difficult ['dɪfɪˌkʌlt] adj : difícil

difficulty ['dɪfɪˌkʌlti] n, pl -ties 1 : dificultad f 2 PROBLEM : problema f, dificultad f

diffidence ['dɪfədənts] n 1 SHYNESS : retraimiento m, timidez f, apocamiento m 2 RETICENCE : reticencia f

diffident ['dɪfədənt] adj 1 SHY : tímido, apocado, inseguro 2 RESERVED : reservado

diffuse¹ [dɪ'fju:z] v **-fused**; **-fusing** vt : difundir, esparcir — vi : difundirse, esparcirse

diffuse² [dɪ'fju:s] adj 1 WORDY : prolijo, verboso 2 WIDESPREAD : difuso

diffusion [dɪ'fju:ʒən] n : difusión f

dig¹ ['dɪg] v **dug** ['dʌg]; **digging** vt 1 : cavar, excavar ⟨to dig a hole : cavar un hoyo⟩ 2 EXTRACT : sacar ⟨to dig up potatoes : sacar papas del suelo⟩ 3 POKE, THRUST : clavar, hincar ⟨he dug me in the ribs : me dio un codazo en las costillas⟩ 4 **to dig up** DISCOVER : descubrir, sacar a luz — vi : cavar, excavar

dig² n 1 POKE : codazo m 2 GIBE : pulla f 3 EXCAVATION : excavación f

digest¹ [daɪ'ʤɛst, dɪ-] vt 1 ASSIMILATE : digerir, asimilar 2 : digerir (comida) 3 SUMMARIZE : compendiar, resumir

digest² ['daɪˌʤɛst] n : compendio m, resumen m

digestible [daɪ'ʤɛstəbəl, dɪ-] adj : digerible

digestion [daɪ'ʤɛstʃən, dɪ-] n : digestión f

digestive [daɪ'ʤɛstɪv, dɪ-] adj : digestivo ⟨the digestive system : el sistema digestivo⟩

digit ['dɪʤət] n 1 NUMERAL : dígito m, número m 2 FINGER, TOE : dedo m

digital ['dɪʤəʈəl] adj : digital — **digitally** adv

dignified ['dɪgnəˌfaɪd] adj : digno, decoroso

dignify ['dɪgnəˌfaɪ] vt **-fied**; **-fying** : significar, honrar

dignitary ['dɪgnəˌtɛri] n, pl -taries : dignatario m, -ria f

dignity ['dɪgnəti] n, pl -ties : dignidad f

digress [daɪ'grɛs, də-] vi : desviarse del tema, divagar

digression [daɪ'grɛʃən, də-] n : digresión f

dike or **dyke** ['daɪk] n : dique m

dilapidated [də'læpəˌdeɪʈəd] adj : ruinoso, desvencijado, destartalado

dilapidation [dəˌlæpə'deɪʃən] n : deterioro m, estado m ruinoso

dilate [daɪ'leɪt, 'daɪˌleɪt] v **-lated**; **-lating** vt : dilatar — vi : dilatarse

dilemma [dɪ'lɛmə] n : dilema m

dilettante ['dɪləˌtɑnt, -ˌtænt] n, pl -tantes [-ˌtɑnts, -ˌtænts] or -tanti [ˌdɪlə'tɑnti, -'tæn-] : diletante mf

diligence ['dɪləʤənts] n : diligencia f, aplicación f

diligent ['dɪləʤənt] adj : diligente ⟨a diligent search : una búsqueda minuciosa⟩ — **diligently** adv

dill ['dɪl] n : eneldo m

dillydally ['dɪliˌdæli] vi **-lied**; **lying** : demorarse, perder tiempo

dilute [daɪ'lu:t, də-] vt **-luted**; **-luting** : diluir, aguar

dilution [daɪ'lu:ʃən, də-] n : dilución f

dim¹ ['dɪm] v **dimmed**; **dimming** vt : atenuar (la luz), nublar (la vista), borrar (la memoria), opacar (una superficie) — *vi* : oscurecerse, apagarse

dim² *adj* **dimmer; dimmest 1** FAINT : oscuro, tenue (dícese de la luz), nublado (dícese de la vista), borrado (dícese de la memoria) **2** DULL : deslustrado **3** STUPID : tonto, torpe

dime [ˈdaɪm] *n* : moneda *f* de diez centavos

dimension [dəˈmɛntʃən, daɪ-] *n* **1** : dimensión *f* **2 dimensions** *npl* EXTENT, SCOPE : dimensiones *fpl*, extensión *f*, medida *f*

diminish [dəˈmɪnɪʃ] *vt* LESSEN : disminuir, reducir, amainar — *vi* DWINDLE, WANE : menguar, reducirse

diminutive [dəˈmɪnjʊt̬ɪv] *adj* : diminutivo, minúsculo

dimly [ˈdɪmli] *adv* : indistintamente, débilmente

dimmer [ˈdɪmər] *n* : potenciómetro *m*, conmutador *m* de luces (en automóviles)

dimness [ˈdɪmnəs] *n* : oscuridad *f*, debilidad *f* (de la vista), imprecisión *f* (de la memoria)

dimple [ˈdɪmpəl] *n* : hoyuelo *m*

din [ˈdɪn] *n* : estrépito *m*, estruendo *m*

dine [ˈdaɪn] *vi* **dined; dining** : cenar

diner [ˈdaɪnər] *n* **1** : comensal *mf* (persona) **2** : vagón *m* restaurante (en un tren) **3** : cafetería *f*, restaurante *m* barato

dinghy [ˈdɪŋi, ˈdɪŋgi, ˈdɪŋki] *n, pl* **-ghies** : bote *m*

dinginess [ˈdɪndʒinəs] *n* **1** DIRTINESS : suciedad *f* **2** SHABBINESS : lo gastado, lo deslucido

dingy [ˈdɪndʒi] *adj* **-gier; -est 1** DIRTY : sucio **2** SHABBY : gastado, deslucido

dinner [ˈdɪnər] *n* : cena *f*, comida *f*

dinosaur [ˈdaɪnəˌsɔr] *n* : dinosaurio *m*

dint [ˈdɪnt] *n* **by dint of** : a fuerza de

diocese [ˈdaɪəsəs, -ˌsiːz, -ˌsiːs] *n, pl* **-ceses** [ˈdaɪəsəsəz] : diócesis *f*

dip¹ [ˈdɪp] *v* **dipped; dipping** *vt* **1** DUNK, PLUNGE : sumergir, mojar, meter **2** LADLE : servir con cucharón **3** LOWER : bajar, arriar (una bandera) — *vi* **1** DESCEND, DROP : bajar en picada, descender **2** SLOPE : bajar, inclinarse

dip² *n* **1** SWIM : chapuzón *m* **2** DROP : descenso *m*, caída *f* **3** SLOPE : cuesta *f*, declive *m* **4** SAUCE : salsa *f*

diphtheria [dɪfˈθɪriə] *n* : difteria *f*

diphthong [ˈdɪfˌθɔŋ] *n* : diptongo *m*

diploma [dəˈploːmə] *n, pl* **-mas** : diploma *m*

diplomacy [dəˈploːməsi] *n* **1** : diplomacia *f* **2** TACT : tacto *m*, discreción *f*

diplomat [ˈdɪpləˌmæt] *n* **1** : diplomático *m*, -ca *f* (en relaciones internacionales) **2** : persona *f* diplomática

diplomatic [ˌdɪpləˈmæt̬ɪk] *adj* : diplomático ⟨diplomatic immunity : inmunidad diplomática⟩

dipper [ˈdɪpər] *n* **1** LADLE : cucharón *m*, cazo *m* **2 Big Dipper** : Osa *f* Mayor **3 Little Dipper** : Osa *f* Menor

dire [ˈdaɪr] *adj* **direr; direst 1** HORRIBLE : espantoso, terrible, horrendo **2** EXTREME : extremo ⟨dire poverty : pobreza extrema⟩

direct¹ [dəˈrɛkt, daɪ-] *vt* **1** ADDRESS : dirigir, mandar **2** AIM, POINT : dirigir **3** GUIDE : indicarle el camino (a alguien), orientar **4** MANAGE : dirigir ⟨to direct a film : dirigir una película⟩ **5** COMMAND : ordenar, mandar

direct² *adv* : directamente

direct³ *adj* **1** STRAIGHT : directo **2** FRANK : franco

direct current *n* : corriente *f* continua

direction [dəˈrɛkʃən, daɪ-] *n* **1** SUPERVISION : dirección *f* **2** INSTRUCTION, ORDER : instrucción *f*, orden *f* **3** COURSE : dirección *f*, rumbo *m* ⟨to change direction : cambiar de dirección⟩ **4 to ask directions** : pedir indicaciones

directional [dəˈrɛkʃənəl, daɪ-] *adj* : direccional

directive [dəˈrɛktɪv, daɪ-] *n* : directiva *f*

directly [dəˈrɛktli, daɪ-] *adv* **1** STRAIGHT : directamente ⟨directly north : directamente al norte⟩ **2** FRANKLY : francamente **3** EXACTLY : exactamente, justo ⟨directly opposite : justo enfrente⟩ **4** IMMEDIATELY : en seguida, inmediatamente

directness [dəˈrɛktnəs, daɪ-] *n* : franqueza *f*

director [dəˈrɛktər, daɪ-] *n* **1** : director *m*, -tora *f* **2 board of directors** : junta *f* directiva, directorio *m*

directory [dəˈrɛktəri, daɪ-] *n, pl* **-ries** : guía *f*, directorio *m* ⟨telephone directory : directorio telefónico⟩

dirge [ˈdərdʒ] *n* : canto *m* fúnebre

dirigible [ˈdɪrədʒəbəl, dəˈrɪdʒə-] *n* : dirigible *m*, zepelín *m*

dirt [ˈdərt] *n* **1** FILTH : suciedad *f*, mugre *f*, porquería *f* **2** SOIL : tierra *f*

dirtiness [ˈdərt̬inəs] *n* : suciedad *f*

dirty¹ [ˈdərt̬i] *vt* **dirtied; dirtying** : ensuciar, manchar

dirty² *adj* **dirtier; -est 1** SOILED, STAINED : sucio, manchado **2** DISHONEST : sucio, deshonesto ⟨a dirty player : un jugador tramposo⟩ ⟨a dirty trick : una mala pasada⟩ **3** INDECENT : indecente, cochino ⟨a dirty joke : un chiste verde⟩

disability [ˌdɪsəˈbɪlət̬i] *n, pl* **-ties** : minusvalía *f*, discapacidad *f*, invalidez *f*

disable [dɪsˈeɪbəl] *vt* **-abled; -abling** : dejar inválido, inutilizar, incapacitar

disabled [dɪsˈeɪbəld] *adj* : minusválido, discapacitado

disabuse [ˌdɪsəˈbjuːz] *vt* **-bused; -busing** : desengañar, sacar del error

disadvantage [ˌdɪsədˈvæntɪdʒ] *n* : desventaja *f*

disadvantageous [ˌdɪsˌædˌvænˈteɪ-dʒəs] *adj* : desventajoso, desfavorable

disagree [ˌdɪsəˈgriː] *vi* **1** DIFFER : discrepar, no coincidir **2** DISSENT : disentir, discrepar, no estar de acuerdo
disagreeable [ˌdɪsəˈgriːəbəl] *adj* : desagradable
disagreement [ˌdɪsəˈgriːmənt] *n* **1** : desacuerdo *m* **2** DISCREPANCY : discrepancia *f* **3** ARGUMENT : discusión *f*, altercado *m*, disputa *f*
disappear [ˌdɪsəˈpɪr] *vi* : desaparecer, desvanecerse ⟨to disappear from view : perderse de vista⟩
disappearance [ˌdɪsəˈpɪrənts] *n* : desaparición *f*
disappoint [ˌdɪsəˈpɔɪnt] *vt* : decepcionar, defraudar, fallar
disappointing [ˌdɪsəˈpɔɪntɪŋ] *adj* : decepcionante
disappointment [ˌdɪsəˈpɔɪntmənt] *n* : decepción *f*, desilusión *f*, chasco *m*
disapproval [ˌdɪsəˈpruːvəl] *n* : desaprobación *f*
disapprove [ˌdɪsəˈpruːv] *vi* **-proved; -proving** : desaprobar, estar en contra
disapprovingly [ˌdɪsəˈpruːvɪŋli] *adv* : con desaprobación
disarm [dɪsˈɑrm] *vt* : desarmar
disarmament [dɪsˈɑrməmənt] *n* : desarme *m* ⟨nuclear disarmament : desarme nuclear⟩
disarrange [ˌdɪsəˈreɪnʤ] *vt* **-ranged; -ranging** : desarreglar, desordenar
disarray [ˌdɪsəˈreɪ] *n* : desorden *m*, confusión *f*, desorganización *f*
disaster [dɪˈzæstər] *n* : desastre *m*, catástrofe *f*
disastrous [dɪˈzæstrəs] *adj* : desastroso
disband [dɪsˈbænd] *vt* : disolver — *vi* : disolverse, dispersarse
disbar [dɪsˈbɑr] *vt* **-barred; -barring** : prohibir de ejercer la abogacía
disbelief [ˌdɪsbɪˈliːf] *n* : incredulidad *f*
disbelieve [ˌdɪsbɪˈliːv] *v* **-lieved; -lieving** : no creer, dudar
disburse [dɪsˈbərs] *vt* **-bursed; -bursing** : desembolsar
disbursement [dɪsˈbərsmənt] *n* : desembolso *m*
disc → **disk**
discard [dɪsˈkɑrd, ˈdɪsˌkɑrd] *vt* : desechar, deshacerse de, botar — *vi* : descartarse (en juegos de naipes)
discern [dɪˈsərn, -ˈzərn] *vt* : discernir, distinguir, percibir
discernible [dɪˈsərnəbəl, -ˈzər-] *adj* : perceptible, visible
discernment [dɪˈsərnmənt, -ˈzərn-] *n* : discernimiento *m*, criterio *m*
discharge¹ [dɪsˈʧɑrʤ, ˈdɪsˌ-] *v* **-charged; -charging 1** UNLOAD : descargar (carga), desembarcar (pasajeros) **2** SHOOT : descargar, disparar **3** FREE : liberar, poner en libertad **4** DISMISS : despedir **5** EMIT : despedir (humo, etc.), descargar (electricidad) **6** : cumplir con (una obligación), saldar (una deuda) — *vi* **1** : descargarse (dícese de una batería) **2** OOZE : supurar

discharge² [ˈdɪsˌʧɑrʤ, dɪsˈ-] *n* **1** EMISSION : descarga *f* (de electricidad), emisión *f* (de gases) **2** DISMISSAL : despido *m* (del empleo), baja *f* (del ejército) **3** SECRETION : secreción *f*
disciple [dɪˈsaɪpəl] *n* : discípulo *m*, -la *f*
discipline¹ [ˈdɪsəplən] *vt* **-plined; -plining 1** PUNISH : castigar, sancionar (a los empleados) **2** CONTROL : disciplinar **3 to discipline oneself** : disciplinarse
discipline² *n* **1** FIELD : disciplina *f*, campo *m* **2** TRAINING : disciplina *f* **3** PUNISHMENT : castigo *m* **4** SELF-CONTROL : dominio *m* de sí mismo
disc jockey *n* : disc jockey *mf*
disclaim [dɪsˈkleɪm] *vt* DENY : negar
disclose [dɪsˈkloːz] *vt* **-closed; -closing** : revelar, poner en evidencia
disclosure [dɪsˈkloːʒər] *n* : revelación *f*
disco [ˈdɪskoː] *n* **1** → **discotheque 2** *or* **disco music** : disco *f*, música *f* disco
discolor [dɪsˈkʌlər] *vt* **1** BLEACH : decolorar **2** FADE : desteñir **3** STAIN : manchar — *vi* : decolorarse, desteñirse
discoloration [dɪsˌkʌləˈreɪʃən] *n* **1** FADING : decoloración *f* **2** STAIN : mancha *f*
discomfort [dɪsˈkʌmfərt] *n* **1** PAIN : molestia *f*, malestar *m* **2** UNEASINESS : inquietud *f*
disconcert [ˌdɪskənˈsərt] *vt* : desconcertar
disconcerting [ˌdɪskənˈsərtɪŋ] *adj* : desconcertante
disconnect [ˌdɪskəˈnɛkt] *vt* : desconectar
disconnected [ˌdɪskəˈnɛktəd] *adj* : inconexo
disconsolate [dɪsˈkɑntsələt] *adj* : desconsolado
discontent [ˌdɪskənˈtɛnt] *n* : descontento *m*
discontented [ˌdɪskənˈtɛntəd] *adj* : descontento
discontinue [ˌdɪskənˈtɪnˌjuː] *vt* **-ued; -uing** : suspender, descontinuar
discontinuity [dɪsˌkɑntəˈnuːəti, -ˈnjuː-] *n, pl* **-ties** : discontinuidad *f*
discontinuous [ˌdɪskənˈtɪnjəwəs] *adj* : discontinuo
discord [ˈdɪsˌkɔrd] *n* **1** STRIFE : discordia *f*, discordancia *f* **2** : disonancia *f* (en música)
discordant [dɪsˈkɔrdənt] *adj* : discordante, discorde — **discordantly** *adv*
discotheque [ˈdɪskəˌtɛk, ˌdɪskəˈtɛk] *n* : discoteca *f*
discount¹ [ˈdɪsˌkaʊnt, dɪsˈ-] *vt* **1** REDUCE : descontar, rebajar (precios) **2** DISREGARD : descartar, ignorar
discount² [ˈdɪsˌkaʊnt] *n* : descuento *m*, rebaja *f*
discourage [dɪsˈkərɪʤ] *vt* **-aged; -aging 1** DISHEARTEN : desalentar, desanimar **2** DISSUADE : disuadir
discouragement [dɪsˈkərɪʤmənt] *n* : desánimo *m*, desaliento *m*

discouraging [dɪs'kərədʒɪŋ] *adj* : desalentador

discourse[1] [dɪs'kors] *vi* -coursed; -coursing : disertar, conversar

discourse[2] ['dɪsˌkors] *n* 1 TALK : conversación *f* 2 SPEECH, TREATISE : discurso *m*, tratado *m*

discourteous [dɪs'kərt̬iəs] *adj* : descortés — **discourteously** *adv*

discourtesy [dɪs'kərt̬əsi] *n, pl* -sies : descortesía *f*

discover [dɪs'kʌvər] *vt* : descubrir

discoverer [dɪs'kʌvərər] *n* : descubridor *m*, -dora *f*

discovery [dɪs'kʌvəri] *n, pl* -ries : descubrimiento *m*

discredit[1] [dɪs'krɛdət] *vt* 1 DISBELIEVE : no creer, dudar 2 : desacreditar, desprestigiar, poner en duda ⟨they discredited his research : desacreditaron sus investigaciones⟩

discredit[2] *n* 1 DISREPUTE : descrédito *m*, desprestigio *m* 2 DOUBT : duda *f*

discreet [dɪs'kri:t] *adj* : discreto — **discreetly** *adv*

discrepancy [dɪs'krɛpəntsi] *n, pl* -cies : discrepancia *f*

discretion [dɪs'krɛʃən] *n* 1 CIRCUMSPECTION : discreción *f*, circunspección *f* 2 JUDGMENT : discernimiento *m*, criterio *m*

discretionary [dɪs'krɛʃəˌnɛri] *adj* : discrecional

discriminate [dɪs'krɪməˌneɪt] *v* -nated; -nating *vt* DISTINGUISH : distinguir, discriminar, diferenciar — *vi* : discriminar ⟨to discriminate against women : discriminar a las mujeres⟩

discrimination [dɪsˌkrɪmə'neɪʃən] *n* 1 PREJUDICE : discriminación *f* 2 DISCERNMENT : discernimiento *m*

discriminatory [dɪs'krɪmənəˌtori] *adj* : discriminatorio

discus ['dɪskəs] *n, pl* -cuses [-kəsəz] : disco *m*

discuss [dɪs'kʌs] *vt* : hablar de, discutir, tratar (de)

discussion [dɪs'kʌʃən] *n* : discusión *f*, debate *m*, conversación *f*

disdain[1] [dɪs'deɪn] *vt* : desdeñar, despreciar ⟨they disdained to reply : no se dignaron a responder⟩

disdain[2] *n* : desdén *m*

disdainful [dɪs'deɪnfəl] *adj* : desdeñoso — **disdainfully** *adv*

disease [dɪ'zi:z] *n* : enfermedad *f*, mal *m*, dolencia *f*

diseased [dɪ'zi:zd] *adj* : enfermo

disembark [ˌdɪsɪm'bark] *v* : desembarcar

disembarkation [dɪsˌɛmˌbar'keɪʃən] *n* : desembarco *m*, desembarque *m*

disembodied [ˌdɪsɪm'badid] *adj* : incorpóreo

disenchant [ˌdɪsɪn'tʃænt] *vt* : desilusionar, desencantar, desengañar

disenchantment [ˌdɪsɪn'tʃæntmənt] *n* : desencanto *m*, desilusión *f*

disengage [ˌdɪsɪn'geɪdʒ] *vt* -gaged; -gaging 1 : soltar, desconectar (un mecanismo) 2 to disengage the clutch : desembragar

disentangle [ˌdɪsɪn'tæŋgəl] *vt* -gled; -gling UNTANGLE : desenredar, desenmarañar

disfavor [dɪs'feɪvər] *n* : desaprobación *f*

disfigure [dɪs'fɪgjər] *vt* -ured; -uring : desfigurar (a una persona), afear (un edificio, un área)

disfigurement [dɪs'fɪgjərmənt] *n* : desfiguración *f*, afeamiento *m*

disfranchise [dɪs'fræn̩ˌtʃaɪz] *vt* -chised; -chising : privar del derecho a votar

disgrace[1] [dɪ'skreɪs] *vt* -graced; -gracing : deshonrar

disgrace[2] *n* 1 DISHONOR : desgracia *f*, deshonra *f* 2 SHAME : vergüenza *f* ⟨he's a disgrace to his family : es una vergüenza para su familia⟩

disgraceful [dɪ'skreɪsfəl] *adj* : vergonzoso, deshonroso, ignominioso

disgracefully [dɪ'skreɪsfəli] *adv* : vergonzosamente

disgruntle [dɪs'grʌntəl] *vt* -tled; -tling : enfadar, contrariar

disguise[1] [dɪ'skaɪz] *vt* -guised; -guising 1 : disfrazar, enmascarar (el aspecto) 2 CONCEAL : encubrir, disimular

disguise[2] *n* : disfraz *m*

disgust[1] [dɪ'skʌst] *vt* : darle asco (a alguien), asquear, repugnar ⟨that disgusts me : eso me da asco⟩

disgust[2] *n* : asco *m*, repugnancia *f*

disgusting [dɪ'skʌstɪŋ] *adj* : asqueroso, repugnante — **disgustingly** *adv*

dish[1] ['dɪʃ] *vt* SERVE : servir

dish[2] *n* 1 : plato *m* ⟨the national dish : el plato nacional⟩ 2 PLATE : plato *m* ⟨to wash the dishes : lavar los platos⟩ 3 serving dish : fuente *f*

dishcloth ['dɪʃˌklɔθ] *n* : paño *m* de cocina (para secar), trapo *m* de fregar (para lavar)

dishearten [dɪs'hartən] *vt* : desanimar, desalentar

dishevel [dɪ'ʃɛvəl] *vt* -eled *or* -elled; -eling *or* -elling : desarreglar, despeinar (el pelo)

disheveled *or* **dishevelled** [dɪ'ʃɛvəld] *adj* : despeinado (dícese del pelo), desarreglado, desaliñado

dishonest [dɪ'sanəst] *adj* : deshonesto, fraudulento — **dishonestly** *adv*

dishonesty [dɪ'sanəsti] *n, pl* -ties : deshonestidad *f*, falta *f* de honradez

dishonor[1] [dɪ'sanər] *vt* : deshonrar

dishonor[2] *n* : deshonra *f*

dishonorable [dɪ'sanərəbəl] *adj* : deshonroso — **dishonorably** [-bli] *adv*

dishrag ['dɪʃˌræg] → **dishcloth**

dishwasher ['dɪʃˌwɔʃər] *n* : lavaplatos *m*, lavavajillas *m*

disillusion [ˌdɪsə'lu:ʒən] *vt* : desilusionar, desencantar, desengañar

disillusionment [ˌdɪsə'lu:ʒənmənt] *n* : desilusión *f*, desencanto *m*

disinclination [dɪsˌɪnkləˈneɪʃən, -ˌɪŋ-] *n* : aversión *f*

disinclined [ˌdɪsɪnˈklaɪnd] *adv* : poco dispuesto

disinfect [ˌdɪsɪnˈfɛkt] *vt* : desinfectar

disinfectant[1] [ˌdɪsɪnˈfɛktənt] *adj* : desinfectante

disinfectant[2] *n* : desinfectante *m*

disinherit [ˌdɪsɪnˈhɛrət] *vt* : desheredar

disintegrate [dɪsˈɪntəˌgreɪt] *v* **-grated; -grating** *vt* : desintegrar, deshacer — *vi* : desintegrarse, deshacerse

disintegration [dɪsˌɪntəˈgreɪʃən] *n* : desintegración *f*

disinterested [dɪsˈɪntərəstəd, -ˌrɛs-] *adj* **1** INDIFFERENT : indiferente **2** IMPARTIAL : imparcial, desinteresado

disinterestedness [dɪsˈɪntərəstədnəs, -ˌrɛs-] *n* : desinterés *m*

disjointed [dɪsˈdʒɔɪntəd] *adj* : inconexo, incoherente

disk *or* **disc** [ˈdɪsk] *n* : disco *m*

disk drive *n* : unidad *f* de disco

diskette [ˌdɪsˈkɛt] *n* : diskette *m*, disquete *m*

dislike[1] [dɪsˈlaɪk] *vt* **-liked; -liking** : tenerle aversión a (algo), tenerle antipatía (a alguien), no gustarle (algo a uno)

dislike[2] *n* : aversión *f*, antipatía *f*

dislocate [ˈdɪsloˌkeɪt, dɪsˈloˑ-] *vt* **-cated; -cating** : dislocar

dislocation [ˌdɪsloˈkeɪʃən] *n* : dislocación *f*

dislodge [dɪsˈlɑdʒ] *vt* **-lodged; -lodging** : sacar, desalojar, desplazar

disloyal [dɪsˈlɔɪəl] *adj* : desleal

disloyalty [dɪsˈlɔɪəlti] *n*, *pl* **-ties** : deslealtad *f*

dismal [ˈdɪzməl] *adj* **1** GLOOMY : sombrío, lúgubre, tétrico **2** DEPRESSING : deprimente, triste

dismantle [dɪsˈmæntəl] *vt* **-tled; -tling** : desmantelar, desmontar, desarmar

dismay[1] [dɪsˈmeɪ] *vt* : consternar

dismay[2] *n* : consternación *f*

dismember [dɪsˈmɛmbər] *vt* : desmembrar

dismiss [dɪsˈmɪs] *vt* **1** : dejar salir, darle permiso (a alguien) para retirarse **2** DISCHARGE : despedir, destituir **3** REJECT : descartar, desechar, rechazar

dismissal [dɪsˈmɪsəl] *n* **1** : permiso *m* para retirarse **2** DISCHARGE : despido *m* (de un empleado), destitución *f* (de un funcionario) **3** REJECTION : rechazo *m*

dismount [dɪsˈmaʊnt] *vi* : desmontar, bajarse, apearse

disobedience [ˌdɪsəˈbiːdiənts] *n* : desobediencia *f* — **disobedient** [-ənt] *adj*

disobey [ˌdɪsəˈbeɪ] *v* : desobedecer

disorder[1] [dɪsˈɔrdər] *vt* : desordenar, desarreglar

disorder[2] *n* **1** DISARRAY : desorden *m* **2** UNREST : disturbios *mpl*, desórdenes *mpl* **3** AILMENT : afección *f*, indisposición *f*, dolencia *f*

disorderly [dɪsˈɔrdərli] *adj* **1** UNTIDY : desordenado, desarreglado **2** UNRULY : indisciplinado, alborotado **3 disorderly conduct** : conducta *f* escandalosa

disorganization [dɪsˌɔrgənəˈzeɪʃən] *n* : desorganización *f*

disorganize [dɪsˈɔrgəˌnaɪz] *vt* **-nized; -nizing** : desorganizar

disorient [dɪsˈɔriˌɛnt] *vt* : desorientar

disown [dɪsˈoːn] *vt* : renegar de, repudiar

disparage [dɪsˈpærɪdʒ] *vt* **-aged; -aging** : menospreciar, denigrar

disparagement [dɪsˈpærɪdʒmənt] *n* : menosprecio *m*

disparate [ˈdɪspərət, dɪsˈpærət] *adj* : dispar, diferente

disparity [dɪsˈpærəti] *n*, *pl* **-ties** : disparidad *f*

dispassionate [dɪsˈpæʃənət] *adj* : desapasionado, imparcial — **dispassionately** *adv*

dispatch[1] [dɪsˈpætʃ] *vt* **1** SEND : despachar, enviar **2** KILL : despachar, matar **3** HANDLE : despachar

dispatch[2] *n* **1** SENDING : envío *m*, despacho *m* **2** MESSAGE : despacho *m*, reportaje *m* (de un periodista), parte *m* (en el ejército) **3** PROMPTNESS : prontitud *f*, rapidez *f*

dispel [dɪsˈpɛl] *vt* **-pelled; -pelling** : disipar, desvanecer

dispensable [dɪˈspɛntsəbəl] *adj* : prescindible

dispensation [ˌdɪspɛnˈseɪʃən] *n* EXEMPTION : exención *m*, dispensa *f*

dispense [dɪsˈpɛnts] *v* **-pensed; -pensing** *vt* **1** DISTRIBUTE : repartir, distribuir, dar **2** ADMINISTER, BESTOW : administrar (justicia), conceder (favores, etc.) **3** : preparar y despachar (medicamentos) — *vi* **to dispense with** : prescindir de

dispenser [dɪsˈpɛntsər] *n* : dispensador *m*, distribuidor *m* automático

dispersal [dɪsˈpərsəl] *n* : dispersión *f*

disperse [dɪsˈpərs] *v* **-persed; -persing** *vt* : dispersar, diseminar — *vi* : dispersarse

dispersion [dɪˈspərʒən] *n* : dispersión *f*

dispirit [dɪˈspɪrət] *vt* : desalentar, desanimar

displace [dɪsˈpleɪs] *vt* **-placed; -placing** **1** : desplazar (un líquido, etc.) **2** REPLACE : reemplazar

displacement [dɪsˈpleɪsmənt] *n* **1** : desplazamiento *m* (de personas) **2** REPLACEMENT : sustitución *f*, reemplazo *m*

display[1] [dɪsˈpleɪ] *vt* : exponer, exhibir, mostrar

display[2] *n* **1** : muestra *f*, exposición *f*, alarde *m* **2** : visualizador *m* (de una computadora)

displease [dɪsˈpliːz] *vt* **-pleased; -pleasing** : desagradar a, disgustar, contrariar

displeasure [dɪs'plɛʒər] *n* : desagrado *m*
disposable [dɪs'po:zəbəl] *adj* **1** : desechable ⟨disposable diapers : pañales desechables⟩ **2** AVAILABLE : disponible
disposal [dɪs'po:zəl] *n* **1** PLACEMENT : disposición *f*, colocación *f* **2** REMOVAL : eliminación *f* **3 to have at one's disposal** : disponer de, tener a su disposición
dispose [dɪs'po:z] *v* **-posed; -posing** *vt* **1** ARRANGE : disponer, colocar **2** INCLINE : predisponer — *vi* **1 to dispose of** DISCARD : desechar, deshacerse de **2 to dispose of** HANDLE : despachar
disposition [ˌdɪspə'zɪʃən] *n* **1** ARRANGEMENT : disposición *f* **2** TENDENCY : predisposición *f*, inclinación *f* **3** TEMPERAMENT : temperamento *m*, carácter *m*
dispossess [ˌdɪspə'zɛs] *vt* : deposeer
disproportion [ˌdɪsprə'porʃən] *n* : desproporción *f*
disproportionate [ˌdɪsprə'porʃənət] *adj* : desproporcionado — **disproportionately** *adv*
disprove [dɪs'pru:v] *vt* **-proved; -proving** : rebatir, refutar
disputable [dɪs'pju:təbəl, 'dɪspjuṭəbəl] *adj* : disputable, discutible
dispute[1] [dɪs'pju:t] *v* **-puted; -puting** *vt* **1** QUESTION : discutir, cuestionar **2** OPPOSE : combatir, resistir — *vi* ARGUE, DEBATE : discutir
dispute[2] *n* **1** DEBATE : debate *m*, discusión *f* **2** QUARREL : disputa *f*, discusión *f*
disqualification [dɪsˌkwɑləfə'keɪʃən] *n* : descalificación *f*
disqualify [dɪs'kwɑlə,faɪ] *vt* **-fied; -fying** : descalificar, inhabilitar
disquiet[1] [dɪs'kwaɪət] *vt* : inquietar
disquiet[2] *n* : ansiedad *f*, inquietud *f*
disregard[1] [ˌdɪsrɪ'gɑrd] *vt* : ignorar, no prestar atención a
disregard[2] *n* : indiferencia *f*
disrepair [ˌdɪsrɪ'pær] *n* : mal estado *m*
disreputable [dɪs'rɛpjuṭəbəl] *adj* : de mala fama (dícese de una persona o un lugar), vergonzoso (dícese de la conducta)
disreputably [dɪs'rɛpjuṭəbli] *adv* : vergonzosamente
disrepute [ˌdɪsrɪ'pju:t] *n* : descrédito *m*, mala fama *f*, deshonra *f*
disrespect [ˌdɪsrɪ'spɛkt] *n* : falta *f* de respeto
disrespectful [ˌdɪsrɪ'spɛktfəl] *adj* : irrespetuoso — **disrespectfully** *adv*
disrobe [dɪs'ro:b] *v* **-robed; -robing** *vt* : desvestir, desnudar — *vi* : desvestirse, desnudarse
disrupt [dɪs'rʌpt] *vt* : trastornar, perturbar
disruption [dɪs'rʌpʃən] *n* : trastorno *m*
disruptive [dɪs'rʌptɪv] *adj* : perjudicial, perturbador — **disruptively** *adv*
dissatisfaction [dɪsˌsæṭəs'fækʃən] *n* : descontento *m*, insatisfacción *f*

dissatisfied [dɪs'sæṭəs,faɪd] *adj* : descontento, insatisfecho
dissatisfy [dɪs'sæṭəs,faɪ] *vt* **-fied; -fying** : no contentar, no satisfacer
dissect [dɪ'sɛkt] *vt* : disecar
dissection [dɪ'sɛkʃən] *n* : disección *f*
dissemble [dɪ'sɛmbəl] *v* **-bled; -bling** *vt* HIDE : ocultar, disimular — *vi* PRETEND : fingir, disimular
disseminate [dɪ'sɛmə,neɪt] *vt* **-nated; -nating** : diseminar, difundir, divulgar
dissemination [dɪˌsɛmə'neɪʃən] *n* : diseminación *f*, difusión *f*
dissension [dɪ'sɛnʧən] *n* : disensión *f*, desacuerdo *m*
dissent[1] [dɪ'sɛnt] *vi* : disentir
dissent[2] *n* : disentimiento *m*, disensión *f*
dissertation [ˌdɪsər'teɪʃən] *n* **1** DISCOURSE : disertación *f*, discurso *m* **2** THESIS : tesis *f*
disservice [dɪs'sərvɪs] *n* : perjuicio *m*
dissident[1] ['dɪsədənt] *adj* : disidente
dissident[2] *n* : disidente *mf*
dissimilar [dɪ'sɪmələr] *adj* : distinto, diferente, disímil
dissipate ['dɪsə,peɪt] *vt* **-pated; -pating** **1** DISPERSE : disipar, dispersar **2** SQUANDER : malgastar, desperdiciar, derrochar, disipar
dissipation [ˌdɪsə'peɪʃən] *n* : disipación *f*, libertinaje *m*
dissociate [dɪ'so:ʃi,eɪt, -si-] *v* **-ated [-ˌeɪṭəd]; -ating [-ˌeɪṭɪŋ]** *vt* : disociar ⟨to disassociate oneself : disociarse⟩ — *vi* : disociarse
dissociation [dɪˌso:ʃi'eɪʃən, -si-] *n* : disociación *f*
dissolute ['dɪsə,lu:t] *adj* : disoluto
dissolution [ˌdɪsə'lu:ʃən] *n* : disolución *f*
dissolve [dɪ'zɑlv] *v* **-solved; -solving** *vt* : disolver — *vi* : disolverse
dissonance ['dɪsənənts] *n* : disonancia *f*
dissuade [dɪ'sweɪd] *vt* **-suaded; -suading** : disuadir
distance[1] ['dɪstənts] *vt* **-tanced [-təntst]; -tancing [-təntsɪŋ] to distance oneself** : distanciarse
distance[2] *n* **1** : distancia *f* ⟨the distance between two points : la distancia entre dos puntos⟩ ⟨in the distance : a lo lejos⟩ **2** RESERVE : actitud *f* distante, reserva *f* ⟨to keep one's distance : guardar las distancias⟩
distant ['dɪstənt] *adj* **1** FAR : distante, lejano **2** REMOTE : distante, lejano, remoto **3** ALOOF : distante, frío
distantly ['dɪstəntli] *adv* **1** LOOSELY : aproximadamente, vagamente **2** COLDLY : fríamente, con frialdad
distaste [dɪs'teɪst] *n* : desagrado *m*, aversión *f*
distasteful [dɪs'teɪstfəl] *adj* : desagradable, de mal gusto
distemper [dɪs'tɛmpər] *n* : moquillo *m*
distend [dɪs'tɛnd] *vt* : dilatar, hinchar — *vi* : dilatarse, hincharse

distill [dɪ'stɪl] *vt* : destilar
distillation [ˌdɪstə'leɪʃən] *n* : destilación *f*
distiller [dɪ'stɪlər] *n* : destilador *m*, -dora *f*
distillery [dɪ'stɪləri] *n, pl* **-ries** [-riz] : destilería *f*
distinct [dɪ'stɪŋkt] *adj* **1** DIFFERENT : distinto, diferente **2** CLEAR, UNMISTAKABLE : marcado, claro, evidente ⟨a distinct possibility : una clara posibilidad⟩
distinction [dɪ'stɪŋkʃən] *n* **1** DIFFERENTIATION : distinción *f* **2** DIFFERENCE : diferencia *f* **3** EXCELLENCE : distinción *f*, excelencia *f* ⟨a writer of distinction : un escritor destacado⟩
distinctive [dɪ'stɪŋktɪv] *adj* : distintivo, característico — **distinctively** *adv*
distinctiveness [dɪ'stɪŋktɪvnəs] *n* : peculiaridad *f*
distinctly [dɪ'stɪŋktli] *adv* : claramente, con claridad
distinguish [dɪs'tɪŋgwɪʃ] *vt* **1** DIFFERENTIATE : distinguir, diferenciar **2** DISCERN : distinguir ⟨he distinguished the sound of the piano : distinguió el sonido del piano⟩ **3 to distinguish oneself** : señalarse, distinguirse — *vi* DISCRIMINATE : distinguir
distinguishable [dɪs'tɪŋgwɪʃəbəl] *adj* : distinguible
distinguished [dɪs'tɪŋgwɪʃt] *adj* : distinguido
distort [dɪ'stɔrt] *vt* **1** MISREPRESENT : distorsionar, tergiversar **2** DEFORM : distorsionar, deformar
distortion [dɪ'stɔrʃən] *n* : distorsión *f*, deformación *f*, tergiversación *f*
distract [dɪ'strækt] *vt* : distraer, entretener
distracted [dɪ'stræktəd] *adj* : distraído
distraction [dɪ'strækʃən] *n* **1** INTERRUPTION : distracción *f*, interrupción *f* **2** CONFUSION : confusión *f* **3** AMUSEMENT : diversión *f*, entretenimiento *m*, distracción *f*
distraught [dɪ'strɔt] *adj* : afligido, turbado
distress[1] [dɪ'strɛs] *vt* : afligir, darle pena (a alguien), hacer sufrir
distress[2] *n* **1** SORROW : dolor *m*, angustia *f*, aflicción *f* **2** PAIN : dolor *m* **3 in ~** : en peligro
distressful [dɪ'strɛsfəl] *adj* : doloroso, penoso
distribute [dɪ'strɪˌbjuːt, -bjʊt] *vt* **-uted; -uting** : distribuir, repartir
distribution [ˌdɪstrə'bjuːʃən] *n* : distribución *f*, reparto *m*
distributive [dɪ'strɪbjʊtɪv] *adj* : distributivo
distributor [dɪ'strɪbjʊtər] *n* : distribuidor *m*, -dora *f*
district ['dɪsˌtrɪkt] *n* **1** REGION : región *f*, zona *f*, barrio *m* (de una ciudad) **2** : distrito *m* (zona política)
distrust[1] [dɪs'trʌst] *vt* : desconfiar de

distrust[2] *n* : desconfianza *f*, recelo *m*
distrustful [dɪs'trʌstfəl] *adj* : desconfiado, receloso, suspicaz
disturb [dɪ'stərb] *vt* **1** BOTHER : molestar, perturbar ⟨sorry to disturb you : perdone la molestia⟩ **2** DISARRANGE : desordenar **3** WORRY : inquietar, preocupar **4 to disturb the peace** : alterar el orden público
disturbance [dɪs'tərbənts] *n* **1** COMMOTION : alboroto *m*, disturbio *m* **2** INTERRUPTION : interrupción *f*
disuse [dɪs'juːs] *n* : desuso *m*
ditch[1] ['dɪtʃ] *vt* **1** : cavar zanjas en **2** DISCARD : deshacerse de, botar
ditch[2] *n* : zanja *f*, fosa *f*, cuneta *f* (en una carretera)
dither ['dɪðər] *n* **to be in a dither** : estar nervioso, ponerse como loco
ditto ['dɪtoː] *n, pl* **-tos** **1** : lo mismo, ídem *m* **2 ditto marks** : comillas *fpl*
ditty ['dɪti] *n, pl* **-ties** : canción *f* corta y simple
diurnal [daɪ'ərnəl] *adj* **1** DAILY : diario, cotidiano **2** : diurno ⟨a diurnal animal : un animal diurno⟩
divan ['daɪˌvæn, dɪ'-] *n* : diván *m*
dive[1] ['daɪv] *vi* **dived** *or* **dove** ['doːv]; **dived; diving 1** PLUNGE : tirarse al agua, zambullirse, dar un clavado **2** SUBMERGE : sumergirse **3** DROP : bajar en picada (dícese de un avión), caer en picada
dive[2] *n* **1** PLUNGE : zambullida *f*, clavado *m* (en el agua) **2** DESCENT : descenso *m* en picada **3** BAR, JOINT : antro *m*
diver ['daɪvər] *n* : saltador *m*, -dora *f*; clavadista *mf*
diverge [də'vərdʒ, daɪ-] *vi* **-verged; -verging 1** SEPARATE : divergir, separarse **2** DIFFER : divergir, discrepar
divergence [də'vərdʒənts, daɪ-] *n* : divergencia *f* — **divergent** [-ənt] *adj*
diverse [daɪ'vərs, də-, 'daɪˌvərs] *adj* : diverso, variado
diversification [daɪˌvərsəfə'keɪʃən, də-] *n* : diversificación *f*
diversify [daɪ'vərsəˌfaɪ, də-] *vt* **-fied; -fying** : diversificar, variar
diversion [daɪ'vərʒən, də-] *n* **1** DEVIATION : desviación *f* **2** AMUSEMENT, DISTRACTION : diversión *f*, distracción *f*, entretenimiento *m*
diversity [daɪ'vərsəti, də-] *n, pl* **-ties** : diversidad *f*
divert [də'vərt, daɪ-] *vt* **1** DEFLECT : desviar **2** DISTRACT : distraer **3** AMUSE : divertir, entretener
divest [daɪ'vɛst, də-] *vt* **1** UNDRESS : desnudar, desvestir **2 to divest of** : despojar de
divide [də'vaɪd] *v* **-vided; -viding** *vt* **1** HALVE : dividir, partir por la mitad **2** SHARE : repartir, dividir **3** : dividir (números) — *vi* : dividirse, dividir (en matemáticas)

dividend ['dɪvə,dɛnd, -dənd] *n* **1** : dividendo *m* (en finanzas) **2** BONUS : beneficio *m*, provecho *m* **3** : dividendo *m* (en matemáticas)

divider [dɪ'vaɪdər] *n* **1** : separador *m* (para ficheros, etc.) **2** *or* **room divider** : mampara *f*, biombo *m*

divination [,dɪvə'neɪʃən] *n* : adivinación *f*

divine[1] [də'vaɪn] *adj* **-viner; -est 1** : divino **2** SUPERB : divino, espléndido — **divinely** *adv*

divine[2] *n* : clérigo *m*, eclesiástico *m*

divinity [də'vɪnəti] *n, pl* **-ties** : divinidad *f*

divisible [dɪ'vɪzəbəl] *adj* : divisible

division [dɪ'vɪʒən] *n* **1** DISTRIBUTION : división *f*, reparto *m* ⟨division of labor : distribución del trabajo⟩ **2** PART : división *f*, sección *f* **3** : división *f* (en matemáticas)

divisive [də'vaɪsɪv] *adj* : divisivo

divisor [dɪ'vaɪzər] *n* : divisor *m*

divorce[1] [də'vors] *v* **-vorced; -vorcing** *vt* : divorciar — *vi* : divorciarse

divorce[2] *n* : divorcio *m*

divorcé [dɪ,vor'seɪ, -'si:; -'vor,-] *n* : divorciado *m*

divorcée [dɪ,vor'seɪ, -'si:; -'vor,-] *n* : divorciada *f*

divulge [də'vʌldʒ, daɪ-] *vt* **-vulged; -vulging** : revelar, divulgar

dizzily ['dɪzəli] *adv* : vertiginosamente

dizziness ['dɪzinəs] *n* : mareo *m*, vahído *m*, vértigo *m*

dizzy ['dɪzi] *adj* **dizzier; -est 1** : mareado ⟨I feel dizzy : estoy mareado⟩ **2** : vertiginoso ⟨a dizzy speed : una velocidad vertiginosa⟩

DNA [,di:,ɛn'eɪ] *n* : ADN *m*

do ['du:] *v* **did** ['dɪd]; **done** ['dʌn]; **doing; does** ['dʌz] *vt* **1** CARRY OUT, PERFORM : hacer, realizar, llevar a cabo ⟨she did her best : hizo todo lo posible⟩ **2** PREPARE : preparar, hacer ⟨do your homework : haz tu tarea⟩ **3** ARRANGE : arreglar, peinar (el pelo) **4 to do in** RUIN : estropear, arruinar **5 to do in** KILL : matar, liquidar *fam* — *vi* **1** : hacer ⟨you did well : hiciste bien⟩ **2** FARE : estar, ir, andar ⟨how are you doing? : ¿cómo estás?, ¿cómo te va?⟩ **3** FINISH : terminar ⟨now I'm done : ya terminé⟩ **4** SERVE : servir, ser suficiente, alcanzar ⟨this will do for now : esto servirá por el momento⟩ **5 to do away with** ABOLISH : abolir, suprimir **6 to do away with** KILL : eliminar, matar **7 to do by** TREAT : tratar ⟨he does well by her : él la trata bien⟩ — *v aux* **1** (*used in interrogative sentences and negative statements*) ⟨do you know her? : ¿la conoces?⟩ ⟨I don't like that : a mí no me gusta eso⟩ **2** (*used for emphasis*) ⟨I do hope you win : espero que vengas⟩ **3** (*used as a substitute verb to avoid repetition*) ⟨do you speak English? yes, I do : ¿habla inglés? sí⟩

docile ['dɑsəl] *adj* : dócil, sumiso

dock[1] ['dɑk] *vt* **1** CUT : cortar **2** : descontar dinero de (un sueldo) — *vi* ANCHOR, LAND : fondear, atracar

dock[2] *n* **1** PIER : atracadero *m* **2** WHARF : muelle *m* **3** : banquillo *m* de los acusados (en un tribunal)

doctor[1] ['dɑktər] *vt* **1** TREAT : tratar, curar **2** ALTER : adulterar, alterar, falsificar (un documento)

doctor[2] *n* **1** : doctor *m*, -tora *f* ⟨Doctor of Philosophy : doctor en filosofía⟩ **2** PHYSICIAN : médico *m*, -ca *f*; doctor *m*, -tora *f*

doctorate ['dɑktərət] *n* : doctorado *m*

doctrine ['dɑktrɪn] *n* : doctrina *f*

document[1] ['dɑkju,mɛnt] *vt* : documentar

document[2] ['dɑkjumənt] *n* : documento *m*

documentary[1] [,dɑkju'mɛntəri] *adj* : documental

documentary[2] *n, pl* **-ries** : documental *m*

documentation [,dɑkjumən'teɪʃən] *n* : documentación *f*

dodge[1] ['dɑdʒ] *v* **dodged; dodging** *vt* : esquivar, eludir, evadir (impuestos) — *vi* : echarse a un lado

dodge[2] *n* **1** RUSE : truco *m*, treta *f*, artimaña *f* **2** EVASION : regate *m*, evasión *f*

dodo ['do:,do:] *n, pl* **-does** *or* **-dos** : dodo *m*

doe ['do:] *n, pl* **does** *or* **doe** : gama *f*, cierva *f*

doer ['du:ər] *n* : hacedor *m*, -dora *f*

does → **do**

doff ['dɑf, 'dɔf] *vt* : quitarse ⟨to doff one's hat : quitarse el sombrero⟩

dog[1] ['dɔg, 'dɑg] *vt* **dogged; dogging** : seguir de cerca, perseguir, acosar ⟨to dog someone's footsteps : seguir los pasos de alguien⟩ ⟨dogged by bad luck : perseguido por la mala suerte⟩

dog[2] *n* : perro *m*, -rra *f*

dogcatcher ['dɔg,kætʃər] *n* : perrero *m*, -ra *f*

dog-eared ['dɔg,ɪrd] *adj* : con las esquinas dobladas

dogged ['dɔgəd] *adj* : tenaz, terco, obstinado

doggy ['dɔgi] *n, pl* **doggies** : perrito *m*, -ta *f*

doghouse ['dɔg,haʊs] *n* : casita *f* de perro

dogma ['dɔgmə] *n* : dogma *m*

dogmatic [dɔg'mætɪk] *adj* : dogmático

dogmatism ['dɔgmə,tɪzəm] *n* : dogmatismo *m*

dogwood ['dɔg,wʊd] *n* : cornejo *m*

doily ['dɔɪli] *n, pl* **-lies** : pañito *m*

doings ['du:ɪŋz] *npl* : eventos *mpl*, actividades *fpl*

doldrums ['do:ldrəmz, 'dɑl-] *npl* **1** : zona *f* de las calmas ecuatoriales **2 to be in the doldrums** : estar abatido (dícese de una persona), estar estancado (dícese de una empresa)

dole ['do:l] *n* **1** ALMS : distribución *f* a los necesitados, limosna *f* **2** : subsidios *mpl* de desempleo

doleful ['do:lfəl] *adj* : triste, lúgubre

dolefully ['do:lfəli] *adv* : con pesar, de manera triste

dole out *vt* **doled out; doling out** : repartir

doll ['dɑl, 'dɔl] *n* : muñeco *m*, -ca *f*

dollar ['dɑlər] *n* : dólar *m*

dolly ['dɑli] *n, pl* **-lies 1** → **doll 2** : plataforma *f* rodante

dolphin ['dɑlfən, 'dɔl-] *n* : delfín *m*

dolt ['do:lt] *n* : imbécil *mf*; tonto *m*, -ta *f*

domain [do'meın, də-] *n* **1** TERRITORY : dominio *m*, territorio *m* **2** FIELD : campo *m*, esfera *f*, ámbito *m* ⟨the domain of art : el ámbito de las artes⟩

dome ['do:m] *n* : cúpula *f*, bóveda *f*

domestic¹ [də'mɛstık] *adj* **1** HOUSEHOLD : doméstico, casero **2** : nacional, interno ⟨domestic policy : política interna⟩ **3** TAME : domesticado

domestic² *n* : empleado *m* doméstico, empleada *f* doméstica

domestically [də'mɛstıkli] *adv* : domésticamente

domesticate [də'mɛstı,keıt] *vt* **-cated; -cating** : domesticar

domicile ['dɑmə,saıl, 'do:-; 'dɑməsıl] *n* : domicilio *m*

dominance ['dɑmənənts] *n* : dominio *m*, dominación *f*

dominant ['dɑmənənt] *adj* : dominante

dominate ['dɑmə,neıt] *v* **-nated; -nating** : dominar

domination [,dɑmə'neıʃən] *n* : dominación *f*

domineer [,dɑmə'nır] *vt* : dominar sobre, avasallar, tiranizar

Dominican [də'mınıkən] *n* : dominicano *m*, -na *f* — **Dominican** *adj*

dominion [də'mınjən] *n* **1** POWER : dominio *m* **2** DOMAIN, TERRITORY : dominio *m*, territorio *m*

domino ['dɑmə,no:] *n, pl* **-noes** *or* **-nos 1** : dominó *m* **2 dominoes** *npl* : dominó *m* (juego)

don ['dɑn] *vt* **donned; donning** : ponerse

donate ['do:,neıt, do:'-] *vt* **-nated; -nating** : donar, hacer un donativo de

donation [do:'neıʃən] *n* : donación *f*, donativo *m*

done¹ ['dʌn] → **do**

done² *adj* **1** FINISHED : terminado, acabado, concluido **2** COOKED : cocinado

donkey ['dɑŋki, 'dʌŋ-] *n, pl* **-keys** : burro *m*, asno *m*

donor ['do:nər] *n* : donante *mf*; donador *m*, -dora *f*

don't ['do:nt] (*contraction* of **do not**) → **do**

doodle¹ ['du:dəl] *v* **-dled; -dling** : garabatear

doodle² *n* : garabato *m*

doom¹ ['du:m] *vt* : condenar

doom² *n* **1** JUDGMENT : sentencia *f*, condena *f* **2** DEATH : muerte *f* **3** FATE : destino *m* **4** RUIN : perdición *f*, ruina *f*

door ['dor] *n* : puerta *f*

doorbell ['dor,bɛl] *n* : timbre *m*

doorknob ['dor,nɑb] *n* : pomo *m*, perilla *f*

doorman ['dormən] *n, pl* **-men** [-mən, -,mɛn] : portero *m*

doormat ['dor,mæt] : felpudo *m*

doorstep ['dor,stɛp] *n* : umbral *m*

doorway ['dor,weı] *n* : entrada *f*, portal *m*

dope¹ ['do:p] *vt* **doped; doping** : drogar, narcotizar

dope² *n* **1** DRUG : droga *f*, estupefaciente *m*, narcótico *m* **2** IDIOT : idiota *mf*; tonto *m*, -ta *f* **3** INFORMATION : información *f*

dormant ['dormənt] *adj* : inactivo, latente

dormer ['dormər] *n* : buhardilla *f*

dormitory ['dormə,tori] *n, pl* **-ries** : dormitorio *m*, residencia *f* de estudiantes

dormouse ['dor,maus] *n* : lirón *m*

dorsal ['dorsəl] *adj* : dorsal — **dorsally** *adv*

dory ['dori] *n, pl* **-ries** : bote *m* de fondo plano

dosage ['do:sıʤ] *n* : dosis *f*

dose¹ ['do:s] *vt* **dosed; dosing** : medicinar

dose² *n* : dosis *f*

dossier ['dɔs,jeı, 'dɑs-] *n* : dossier *m*

dot¹ ['dɑt] *vt* **dotted; dotting 1** : poner el punto sobre (una letra) **2** SCATTER : esparcir, salpicar

dot² *n* : punto *m* ⟨at six on the dot : a las seis en punto⟩ ⟨dots and dashes : puntos y rayas⟩

dote ['do:t] *vi* **doted; doting** : chochear

double¹ ['dʌbəl] *v* **-bled; -bling** *vt* **1** : doblar, duplicar (una cantidad), redoblar (esfuerzos) **2** FOLD : doblar, plegar **3 to double one's fist** : apretar el puño — *vi* **1** : doblarse, duplicarse **2 to double over** : retorcerse

double² *adj* : doble — **doubly** *adv*

double³ *n* : doble *mf*

double bass *n* : contrabajo *m*

double–cross [,dʌbəl'krɔs] *vt* : traicionar

double–crosser [,dʌbəl'krɔsər] *n* : traidor *m*, -dora *f*

double–jointed [,dʌbəl'ʤɔıntəd] *adj* : con articulaciones dobles

double–talk ['dʌbəl,tɔk] *n* : ambigüedades *fpl*, lenguaje *m* con doble sentido

doubt¹ ['daut] *vt* **1** QUESTION : dudar de, cuestionar **2** DISTRUST : desconfiar de **3** : dudar, creer poco probable ⟨I doubt it very much : lo dudo mucho⟩

doubt² *n* **1** UNCERTAINTY : duda *f*, incertidumbre *f* **2** DISTRUST : desconfianza *f* **3** SKEPTICISM : duda *f*, escepticismo *m*

doubtful ['daʊtfəl] *adj* **1** QUESTIONABLE : dudoso **2** UNCERTAIN : dudoso, incierto

doubtfully ['daʊtfəli] *adv* : dudosamente, sin estar convencido

doubtless ['daʊtləs] *or* **doubtlessly** *adv* : sin duda

douche[1] ['duːʃ] *vt* **douched; douching** : irrigar

douche[2] *n* : ducha *f*, irrigación *f*

dough ['doː] *n* : masa *f*

doughnut *or* **donut** ['doː,nʌt] *n* : rosquilla *f*, dona *f Mex*

doughty ['daʊti] *adj* **-tier; -est** : fuerte, valiente

dour ['daʊər, 'dʊr] *adj* **1** STERN : severo, adusto **2** SULLEN : hosco, taciturno — **dourly** *adv*

douse ['daʊs, 'daʊz] *vt* **doused; dousing** **1** DRENCH : empapar, mojar **2** EXTINGUISH : extinguir, apagar

dove[1] ['doːv] → **dive**

dove[2] ['dʌv] *n* : paloma *f*

dovetail ['dʌv,teɪl] *vi* : encajar, enlazar

dowdy ['daʊdi] *adj* **dowdier; -est** : sin gracia, poco elegante

dowel ['daʊəl] *n* : clavija *f*

down[1] ['daʊn] *vt* **1** FELL : tumbar, derribar, abatir **2** DEFEAT : derrotar

down[2] *adv* **1** DOWNWARD : hacia abajo **2 to lie down** : acostarse, echarse **3 to put down (money)** : pagar un depósito (de dinero) **4 to sit down** : sentarse **5 to take down, to write down** : apuntar, anotar

down[3] *adj* **1** DESCENDING : de bajada ⟨the down elevator : el ascensor de bajada⟩ **2** REDUCED : reducido, rebajado ⟨attendance is down : la concurrencia ha disminuido⟩ **3** DOWNCAST : abatido, deprimido

down[4] *n* **1** : plumón *m* **2** : down *m* (en deportes) **3 ups and downs** : altibajos *mpl*

down[5] *prep* **1** : (hacia) abajo ⟨down the mountain : montaña abajo⟩ ⟨I walked down the stairs : bajé por la escalera⟩ **2** ALONG : por, a lo largo de ⟨we ran down the beach : corrimos por la playa⟩ **3** : a través de ⟨down the years : a través de los años⟩

downcast ['daʊn,kæst] *adj* **1** SAD : triste, abatido **2 with downcast eyes** : con los ojos bajos, con los ojos mirando al suelo

downfall ['daʊn,fɔl] *n* : ruina *f*, perdición *f*

downgrade[1] ['daʊn,greɪd] *vt* **-graded; -grading** : bajar de categoría

downgrade[2] *n* : bajada *f*

downhearted ['daʊn,hɑrtəd] *adj* : desanimado, descorazonado

downhill ['daʊn'hɪl] *adv* & *adj* : cuesta abajo

download[1] ['daʊn,loːd] *vt* : descargar (un archivo)

download[2] *n* : descarga *f* (de archivos, etc.)

down payment *n* : entrega *f* inicial

downplay ['daʊn,pleɪ] *vt* : minimizar

downpour ['daʊn,por] *n* : aguacero *m*, chaparrón *m*

downright[1] ['daʊn,raɪt] *adv* THOROUGHLY : absolutamente, completamente

downright[2] *adj* : patente, manifiesto, absoluto ⟨a downright refusal : un rechazo categórico⟩

downside ['daʊn,saɪd] *n* : desventaja *f*

downstairs[1] ['daʊn'stærz] *adv* : abajo

downstairs[2] ['daʊn,stærz] *adj* : del piso de abajo

downstairs[3] ['daʊn'stærz, -,stærz] *n* : planta *f* baja

downstream ['daʊn'striːm] *adv* : río abajo

down-to-earth [,daʊntu'ərth] *adj* : práctico, realista

downtown[1] [,daʊn'taʊn] *adv* : hacia el centro, al centro, en el centro (de la ciudad)

downtown[2] *adj* : del centro (de la ciudad) ⟨downtown Chicago : el centro de Chicago⟩

downtown[3] [,daʊn'taʊn, 'daʊn,taʊn] *n* : centro *m* (de la ciudad)

downtrodden ['daʊn,trɑdən] *adj* : oprimido

downward ['daʊnwərd] *or* **downwards** [-wərdz] *adv* & *adj* : hacia abajo

downwind ['daʊn'wɪnd] *adv* & *adj* : en la dirección del viento

downy ['daʊni] *adj* **downier; -est** **1** : cubierto de plumón, plumoso **2** VELVETY : aterciopelado, velloso

dowry ['daʊri] *n, pl* **-ries** : dote *f*

doze[1] ['doːz] *vi* **dozed; dozing** : dormitar

doze[2] *n* : sueño *m* ligero, cabezada *f*

dozen ['dʌzən] *n, pl* **dozens** *or* **dozen** : docena *f*

drab ['dræb] *adj* **drabber; drabbest** **1** BROWNISH : pardo **2** DULL, LACKLUSTER : monótono, gris, deslustrado

draft[1] ['dræft, 'draft] *vt* **1** CONSCRIPT : reclutar **2** COMPOSE, SKETCH : hacer el borrador de, redactar

draft[2] *adj* **1** : de barril ⟨draft beer : cerveza de barril⟩ **2** : de tiro ⟨draft horses : caballos de tiro⟩

draft[3] *n* **1** HAULAGE : tiro *m* **2** DRINK, GULP : trago *m* **3** OUTLINE, SKETCH : bosquejo *m*, borrador *m*, versión *f* **4** : corriente *f* de aire, chiflón *m*, tiro *m* (de una chimenea) **5** CONSCRIPTION : conscripción *f* **6 bank draft** : giro *m* bancario, letra *f* de cambio

draftee [dræf'tiː] *n* : recluta *mf*

draftsman ['dræftsmən] *n, pl* **-men** [-mən, -,mɛn] : dibujante *mf*

drafty ['dræfti] *adj* **draftier; -est** : con corrientes de aire

drag[1] ['dræg] *v* **dragged; dragging** *vt* **1** HAUL : arrastrar, jalar **2** DREDGE : dragar — *vi* **1** TRAIL : arrastrarse **2** LAG : rezagarse **3** : hacerse pesado, hacerse largo ⟨the day dragged on : el día se hizo largo⟩

drag² *n* **1** RESISTANCE : resistencia *f* (aerodinámica) **2** HINDRANCE : traba *f*, estorbo *m* **3** BORE : pesadez *f*, plomo *m fam*

dragnet ['dræg,nɛt] *n* **1** : red *f* barredera (en pesca) **2** : operativo *m* policial de captura

dragon ['drægən] *n* : dragón *m*

dragonfly ['drægən,flaɪ] *n, pl* **-flies** : libélula *f*

drain¹ ['dreɪn] *vt* **1** EMPTY : vaciar, drenar **2** EXHAUST : agotar, consumir — *vi* **1** : escurrir, escurrirse ⟨the dishes are draining : los platos están escurriéndose⟩ **2** EMPTY : desaguar **3 to drain away** : irse agotando

drain² *n* **1** : desagüe *m* **2** SEWER : alcantarilla *f* **3** GRATING : sumidero *m*, resumidero *m*, rejilla *f* **4** EXHAUSTION : agotamiento *m*, disminución *f* (de energía, etc.) ⟨to be a drain on : agotar, consumir⟩ **5 to throw down the drain** : tirar por la ventana

drainage ['dreɪnɪʤ] *n* : desagüe *m*, drenaje *m*

drainpipe ['dreɪn,paɪp] *n* : tubo *m* de desagüe, caño *m*

drake ['dreɪk] *n* : pato *m* (macho)

drama ['drɑmə, 'dræ-] *n* **1** THEATER : drama *m*, teatro *m* **2** PLAY : obra *f* de teatro, drama *m*

dramatic [drə'mætɪk] *adj* : dramático — **dramatically** [-tɪkli] *adv*

dramatist ['dræmətɪst, 'drɑ-] *n* : dramaturgo *m*, -ga *f*

dramatization [,dræmətə'zeɪʃən, ,drɑ-] *n* : dramatización *f*

dramatize ['dræmə,taɪz, 'drɑ-] *vt* **-tized; -tizing** : dramatizar

drank → **drink**

drape¹ ['dreɪp] *vt* **draped; draping** **1** COVER : cubrir (con tela) **2** HANG : drapear, disponer los pliegues de

drape² *n* **1** HANG : caída *f* **2 drapes** *npl* : cortinas *fpl*

drapery ['dreɪpəri] *n, pl* **-eries** **1** CLOTH : pañería *f*, tela *f* para cortinas **2 draperies** *npl* : cortinas *fpl*

drastic ['dræstɪk] *adj* **1** HARSH, SEVERE : drástico, severo **2** EXTREME : radical, excepcional — **drastically** [-tɪkli] *adv*

draught ['dræft, 'draft] *n* → **draft³**

draughty ['drafti] → **drafty**

draw¹ ['drɔ] *v* **drew** ['dru:]; **drawn** ['drɔn]; **drawing** *vt* **1** PULL : tirar de, jalar, correr (cortinas) **2** ATTRACT : atraer **3** PROVOKE : provocar, suscitar **4** INHALE : aspirar ⟨to draw breath : respirar⟩ **5** EXTRACT : sacar, extraer **6** TAKE : sacar ⟨to draw a number : sacar un número⟩ **7** COLLECT : cobrar, percibir (un sueldo, etc.) **8** BEND : tensar (un arco) **9** TIE : empatar (en deportes) **10** SKETCH : dibujar, trazar **11** FORMULATE : sacar, formular, llegar a ⟨to draw a conclusion : llegar a

una conclusión⟩ **12 to draw out** : hacer hablar (sobre algo), hacer salir de sí mismo **13 to draw up** DRAFT : redactar — *vi* **1** SKETCH : dibujar **2** TUG : tirar, jalar **3 to draw near** : acercarse **4 to draw to a close** : terminar, finalizar **5 to draw up** STOP : parar

draw² *n* **1** DRAWING, RAFFLE : sorteo *m* **2** TIE : empate *m* **3** ATTRACTION : atracción *f* **4** PUFF : chupada *f* (de un cigarrillo, etc.)

drawback ['drɔ,bæk] *n* : desventaja *f*, inconveniente *m*

drawbridge ['drɔ,brɪʤ] *n* : puente *m* levadizo

drawer ['drɔr, 'drɔər] *n* **1** ILLUSTRATOR : dibujante *mf* **2** : gaveta *f*, cajón *m* (en un mueble) **3 drawers** *npl* UNDERPANTS : calzones *mpl*

drawing ['drɔɪŋ] *n* **1** LOTTERY : sorteo *m*, lotería *f* **2** SKETCH : dibujo *m*, bosquejo *m*

drawl¹ ['drɔl] *vi* : hablar arrastrando las palabras

drawl² *n* : habla *f* lenta y con vocales prolongadas

dread¹ ['drɛd] *vt* : tenerle pavor a, temer

dread² *adj* : pavoroso, aterrado

dread³ *n* : pavor *m*, temor *m*

dreadful ['drɛdfəl] *adj* **1** DREAD : pavoroso **2** TERRIBLE : espantoso, atroz, terrible — **dreadfully** *adv*

dream¹ ['dri:m] *v* **dreamed** ['drɛmpt, 'dri:md] *or* **dreamt** ['drɛmpt]; **dreaming** *vi* **1** : soñar ⟨to dream about : soñar con⟩ **2** FANTASIZE : fantasear — *vt* **1** DREAM : soñar **2** IMAGINE : imaginarse **3 to dream up** : inventar, idear

dream² *n* **1** : sueño *m*, ensueño *m* **2 bad dream** NIGHTMARE : pesadilla *f*

dreamer ['dri:mər] *n* : soñador *m*, -dora *f*

dreamlike ['dri:m,laɪk] *adj* : de ensueño

dreamy ['dri:mi] *adj* **dreamier; -est** **1** DISTRACTED : soñador, distraído **2** DREAMLIKE : de ensueño **3** MARVELOUS : maravilloso

drearily ['drɪrəli] *adv* : sombríamente

dreary ['drɪri] *adj* **-rier; -est** : deprimente, lóbrego, sombrío

dredge¹ ['drɛʤ] *vt* **dredged; dredging** **1** DIG : dragar **2** COAT : espolvorear, enharinar

dredge² *n* : draga *f*

dredger ['drɛʤər] *n* : draga *f*

dregs ['drɛgz] *npl* **1** LEES : posos *mpl*, heces *fpl* (de un líquido) **2** : heces *fpl*, escoria *f* ⟨the dregs of society : la escoria de la sociedad⟩

drench ['drɛntʃ] *vt* : empapar, mojar, calar

dress¹ ['drɛs] *vt* **1** CLOTHE : vestir **2** DECORATE : decorar, adornar **3** : preparar (pollo o pescado), aliñar (ensalada) **4** : curar, vendar (una herida) **5** FERTILIZE : abonar (la tierra) — *vi* **1** : vestirse **2 to dress up** : ataviarse, engalanarse, ponerse de etiqueta

dress² *n* **1** APPAREL : indumentaria *f*, ropa *f* **2** : vestido *m*, traje *m* (de mujer)

dresser ['drɛsər] *n* : cómoda *f* con espejo

dressing ['drɛsɪŋ] *n* **1** : vestirse *m* **2** : aderezo *m*, aliño *m* (de ensalada), relleno *m* (de pollo) **3** BANDAGE : vendaje *m*, gasa *f*

dressmaker ['drɛs,meɪkər] *n* : modista *mf*

dressmaking ['drɛs,meɪkɪŋ] *n* : costura *f*

dressy ['drɛsi] *adj* **dressier; -est** : de mucho vestir, elegante

drew → **draw**

dribble¹ ['drɪbəl] *vi* **-bled; -bling 1** DRIP : gotear **2** DROOL : babear **3** : driblar (en basquetbol)

dribble² *n* **1** TRICKLE : goteo *m*, hilo *m* **2** DROOL : baba *f* **3** : drible *m* (en basquetbol)

drier → **dry²**, **dryer**

driest *adj* → **dry²**

drift¹ ['drɪft] *vi* **1** : dejarse llevar por la corriente, ir a la deriva (dícese de un bote), ir sin rumbo (dícese de una persona) **2** ACCUMULATE : amontonarse, acumularse, apilarse

drift² *n* **1** DRIFTING : deriva *f* **2** HEAP, MASS : montón *m* (de arena, etc.), ventisquero *m* (de nieve) **3** MEANING : sentido *m*

drifter ['drɪftər] *n* : vagabundo *m*, -da *f*

driftwood ['drɪft,wʊd] *n* : madera *f* flotante

drill¹ ['drɪl] *vt* **1** BORE : perforar, taladrar **2** INSTRUCT : instruir por repetición — *vi* **1** TRAIN : entrenarse **2 to drill for oil** : perforar en busca de petróleo

drill² *n* **1** : taladro *m*, barrena *f* **2** EXERCISE, PRACTICE : ejercicio *m*, instrucción *f*

drily → **dryly**

drink¹ ['drɪŋk] *v* **drank** ['dræŋk]; **drunk** ['drʌŋk] *or* **drank; drinking** *vt* **1** IMBIBE : beber, tomar **2 to drink up** ABSORB : absorber — *vi* **1** : beber **2** : beber alcohol, tomar

drink² *n* **1** : bebida *f* **2** : bebida *f* alcohólica

drinkable ['drɪŋkəbəl] *adj* : potable

drinker ['drɪŋkər] *n* : bebedor *m*, -dora *f*

drip¹ ['drɪp] *vi* **dripped; dripping** : gotear, chorrear

drip² *n* **1** DROP : gota *f* **2** DRIPPING : goteo *m*

drive¹ ['draɪv] *v* **drove** ['dro:v]; **driven** ['drɪvən]; **driving** *vt* **1** IMPEL : impeler, impulsar **2** OPERATE : guiar, conducir, manejar (un vehículo) **3** COMPEL : obligar, forzar **4** : clavar, hincar ⟨to drive a stake : clavar una estaca⟩ **5** *or* **to drive away** : ahuyentar, echar **6 to drive crazy** : volver loco — *vi* : manejar, conducir ⟨do you know how to drive? : ¿sabes manejar?⟩

drive² *n* **1** RIDE : paseo *m* en coche **2** CAMPAIGN : campaña *f* ⟨fund-raising drive : campaña para recaudar fondos⟩ **3** DRIVEWAY : camino *m* de entrada, entrada *f* **4** TRANSMISSION : transmisión *f* ⟨front-wheel drive : tracción delantera⟩ **5** ENERGY : dinamismo *m*, energía *f* **6** INSTINCT, NEED : instinto *m*, necesidad *f* básica **7** → **disk drive**

drivel ['drɪvəl] *n* : tontería *f*, estupidez *f*

driver ['draɪvər] *n* : conductor *m*, -tora *f*; chofer *m*

driveway ['draɪv,weɪ] *n* : camino *m* de entrada, entrada *f* (para coches)

drizzle¹ ['drɪzəl] *vi* **-zled; -zling** : lloviznar, garuar

drizzle² *n* : llovizna *f*, garúa *f*

droll ['dro:l] *adj* : cómico, gracioso, chistoso — **drolly** *adv*

dromedary ['drɑmə,dɛri] *n*, *pl* **-daries** : dromedario *m*

drone¹ ['dro:n] *vi* **droned; droning 1** BUZZ : zumbar **2** MURMUR : hablar con monotonía, murmurar

drone² *n* **1** : zángano *m* (abeja) **2** FREELOADER : gorrón *m*, -rrona *f* *fam*; parásito *m*, -ta *f* **3** BUZZ, HUM : zumbido *m*, murmullo *m*

drool¹ ['dru:l] *vi* : babear

drool² *n* : baba *f*

droop¹ ['dru:p] *vi* **1** HANG : inclinarse (dícese de la cabeza), encorvarse (dícese de los escombros), marchitarse (dícese de las flores) **2** FLAG : decaer, flaquear ⟨his spirits drooped : se desanimó⟩

droop² *n* : inclinación *f*, caída *f*

drop¹ ['drɑp] *v* **dropped; dropping** *vt* **1** : dejar caer, soltar ⟨she dropped the glass : se le cayó el vaso⟩ ⟨to drop a hint : dejar caer una indirecta⟩ **2** SEND : mandar ⟨drop me a line : mándame unas líneas⟩ **3** ABANDON : abandonar, dejar ⟨to drop the subject : cambiar de tema⟩ **4** LOWER : bajar ⟨he dropped his voice : bajó la voz⟩ **5** OMIT : omitir **6 to drop off** : dejar — *vi* **1** DRIP : gotear **2** FALL : caer(se) **3** DECREASE, DESCEND : bajar, descender ⟨the wind dropped : amainó el viento⟩ **4 to drop back** *or* **to drop behind** : rezagarse, quedarse atrás **5 to drop by** *or* **to drop in** : pasar

drop² *n* **1** : gota *f* (de líquido) **2** DECLINE : caída *f*, bajada *f*, descenso *m* **3** INCLINE : caída *f*, pendiente *f* ⟨a 20-foot drop : una caída de 20 pies⟩ **4** SWEET : pastilla *f*, dulce *m* **5 drops** *npl* : gotas *fpl* (de medicina)

droplet ['drɑplət] *n* : gotita *f*

dropper ['drɑpər] *n* : gotero *m*, cuentagotas *m*

dross ['drɑs, 'drɔs] *n* : escoria *f*

drought ['draʊt] *n* : sequía *f*

drove¹ → **drive**

drove² ['dro:v] *n* : multitud *f*, gentío *m*, manada *f* (de ganado) ⟨in droves : en manada⟩

drown ['draʊn] *vt* **1** : ahogar **2** INUN-DATE : anegar, inundar **3 to drown out** : ahogar — *vi* : ahogarse

drowse[1] ['draʊz] *vi* **drowsed; drowsing** DOZE : dormitar

drowse[2] *n* : sueño *m* ligero, cabezada *f*

drowsiness ['draʊzinəs] *n* : somnolencia *f*, adormecimiento *m*

drowsy ['draʊzi] *adj* **drowsier; -est** : somnoliento, soñoliento

drub ['drʌb] *vt* **drubbed; drubbing 1** BEAT, THRASH : golpear, apalear **2** DEFEAT : derrotar por completo

drudge[1] ['drʌdʒ] *vi* **drudged; drudging** : trabajar como esclavo, trabajar duro

drudge[2] *n* : esclavo *m*, -va *f* del trabajo

drudgery ['drʌdʒəri] *n, pl* **-eries** : trabajo *m* pesado

drug[1] ['drʌg] *vt* **drugged; drugging** : drogar, narcotizar

drug[2] *n* **1** MEDICATION : droga *f*, medicina *f*, medicamento *m* **2** NARCOTIC : narcótico *m*, estupefaciente *m*, droga *f*

druggist ['drʌgɪst] *n* : farmacéutico *m*, -ca *f*

drugstore ['drʌg,stor] *n* : farmacia *f*, botica *f*, droguería *f*

drum[1] ['drʌm] *v* **drummed; drumming** *vt* : meter a fuerza ⟨he drummed it into my head : me lo metió en la cabeza a fuerza⟩ — *vi* : tocar el tambor

drum[2] *n* **1** : tambor *m* **2** : bidón *m* ⟨oil drum : bidón de petróleo⟩

drummer ['drʌmər] *n* : baterista *mf*

drumstick ['drʌm,stɪk] *n* **1** : palillo *m* (de tambor), baqueta *f* **2** : muslo *m* de pollo

drunk[1] *pp* → **drink**[1]

drunk[2] ['drʌŋk] *adj* : borracho, embriagado, ebrio

drunk[3] *n* : borracho *m*, -cha *f*

drunkard ['drʌŋkərd] *n* : borracho *m*, -cha *f*

drunken ['drʌŋkən] *adj* : borracho, ebrio ⟨drunken driver : conductor ebrio⟩ ⟨drunken brawl : pleito de borrachos⟩

drunkenly ['drʌŋkənli] *adv* : como un borracho

drunkenness ['drʌŋkənnəs] *n* : borrachera *f*, embriaguez *f*, ebriedad *f*

dry[1] ['draɪ] *v* **dried; drying** *vt* : secar — *vi* : secarse

dry[2] *adj* **drier; driest 1** : seco **2** THIRSTY : sediento **3** : donde la venta de bebidas alcohólicas está prohibida ⟨a dry county : un condado seco⟩ **4** DULL : aburrido, árido **5** : seco (dícese del vino), brut (dícese de la champaña)

dry–clean ['draɪ,kli:n] *v* : limpiar en seco

dry cleaner *n* : tintorería *f* (servicio)

dry cleaning *n* : limpieza *f* en seco

dryer ['draɪər] *n* **1 hair dryer** : secador *m* **2 clothes dryer** : secadora *f*

dry goods *npl* : artículos *mpl* de confección

dry ice *n* : hielo *m* seco

dryly ['draɪli] *adv* : secamente

dryness ['draɪnəs] *n* : sequedad *f*, aridez *f*

dual ['du:əl, 'dju:-] *adj* : doble

dualism ['du:ə,lɪzəm] *n* : dualismo *m*

dub ['dʌb] *vt* **dubbed; dubbing 1** CALL : apodar **2** : doblar (una película), mezclar (una grabación)

dubious ['du:biəs, 'dju:-] *adj* **1** UNCERTAIN : dudoso, indeciso **2** QUESTIONABLE : sospechoso, dudoso, discutible

dubiously ['du:biəsli, 'dju:-] *adv* **1** UNCERTAINLY : dudosamente, con desconfianza **2** SUSPICIOUSLY : de modo sospechoso, con recelo

duchess ['dʌtʃəs] *n* : duquesa *f*

duck[1] ['dʌk] *vt* **1** LOWER : agachar, bajar (la cabeza) **2** PLUNGE : zambullir **3** EVADE : eludir, evadir — *vi* **to duck down** : agacharse

duck[2] *n, pl* **duck** *or* **ducks** : pato *m*, -ta *f*

duckling ['dʌklɪŋ] *n* : patito *m*, -ta *f*

duct ['dʌkt] *n* : conducto *m*

ductile ['dʌktəl] *adj* : dúctil

dude ['du:d, 'dju:d] *n* **1** DANDY : dandi *m*, dandy *m* **2** GUY : tipo *m*

due[1] ['du:, 'dju:] *adv* : justo a, derecho hacia ⟨due north : derecho hacia el norte⟩

due[2] *adj* **1** PAYABLE : pagadero, sin pagar **2** APPROPRIATE : debido, apropiado ⟨after due consideration : con las debidas consideraciones⟩ **3** EXPECTED : esperado ⟨the train is due soon : esperamos el tren muy pronto, el tren debe llegar pronto⟩ **4 due to** : debido a, por

due[3] *n* **1 to give someone his (her) due** : darle a alguien su merecido **2 dues** *npl* : cuota *f*

duel[1] ['du:əl, 'dju:-] *vi* : batirse en duelo

duel[2] *n* : duelo *m*

duet ['du:ɛt, dju:-] *n* : dúo *m*

due to *prep* : debido a

dug → **dig**

dugout ['dʌg,aʊt] *n* **1** CANOE : piragua *f* **2** SHELTER : refugio *m* subterráneo

duke ['du:k, 'dju:k] *n* : duque *m*

dull[1] ['dʌl] *vt* **1** DIM : opacar, quitar el brillo a, deslustrar **2** BLUNT : embotar (un filo), entorpecer (los sentidos), aliviar (el dolor), amortiguar (sonidos)

dull[2] *adj* **1** STUPID : torpe, lerdo, lento **2** BLUNT : desafilado, despuntado **3** LACKLUSTER : sin brillo, deslustrado **4** BORING : aburrido, soso, pesado — **dully** *adv*

dullness ['dʌlnəs] *n* **1** STUPIDITY : estupidez *f* **2** : embotamiento *m* (de los sentidos) **3** MONOTONY : monotonía *f*, insipidez *f* **4** : falta *f* de brillo **5** BLUNTNESS : falta *f* de filo, embotadura *f*

duly ['du:li, 'dju:-] *adv* PROPERLY : debidamente, a su debido tiempo

dumb ['dʌm] *adj* **1** MUTE : mudo **2** STUPID : estúpido, tonto, bobo — **dumbly** *adv*

dumbbell ['dʌm,bɛl] *n* **1** WEIGHT : pesa *f* **2** : estúpido *m*, -da *f*
dumbfound *or* **dumfound** [,dʌm-'faʊnd] *vt* : dejar atónito, dejar sin habla
dummy ['dʌmi] *n, pl* -mies **1** SHAM : imitación *f*, sustituto *m* **2** PUPPET : muñeco *m* **3** MANNEQUIN : maniquí *m* **4** IDIOT : tonto *m*, -ta *f*; idiota *mf*
dump¹ ['dʌmp] *vt* : descargar, verter
dump² *n* **1** : vertedero *m*, tiradero *m Mex* **2 down in the dumps** : triste, deprimido
dumpling ['dʌmplɪŋ] *n* : bola *f* de masa hervida
dumpy ['dʌmpi] *adj* **dumpier; -est** : rechoncho, regordete
dun¹ ['dʌn] *vt* **dunned; dunning** : apremiar (a un deudor)
dun² *adj* : pardo (color)
dunce ['dʌnts] *n* : estúpido *m*, -da *f*; burro *m*, -rra *f fam*
dune ['duːn, 'djuːn] *n* : duna *f*
dung ['dʌŋ] *n* **1** FECES : excrementos *mpl* **2** MANURE : estiércol *m*
dungaree [,dʌŋgə'riː] *n* **1** DENIM : tela *f* vaquera, mezclilla *f Chile, Mex* **2 dungarees** *npl* : pantalones *mpl* de trabajo hechos de tela vaquera
dungeon ['dʌndʒən] *n* : mazmorra *f*, calabozo *m*
dunk ['dʌŋk] *vt* : mojar, ensopar
duo ['duːoː, 'djuː-] *n, pl* **duos** : dúo *m*, par *m*
dupe¹ ['duːp, djuːp] *vt* **duped; duping** : engañar, embaucar
dupe² *n* : inocentón *m*, -tona *f*; simple *mf*
duplex¹ ['duː,plɛks, 'djuː-] *adj* : doble
duplex² *n* : casa *f* de dos viviendas, dúplex *m*
duplicate¹ ['duːplɪ,keɪt, 'djuː-] *vt* -cated; -cating **1** COPY : duplicar, hacer copias de **2** REPEAT : repetir, reproducir
duplicate² ['duːplɪkət, 'djuː-] *adj* : duplicado ⟨a duplicate invoice : una factura por duplicado⟩
duplicate³ ['duːplɪkət, 'djuː-] *n* : duplicado *m*, copia *f*
duplication [,duːplɪ'keɪʃən, ,djuː-] *n* **1** DUPLICATING : duplicación *f*, repetición *f* (de esfuerzos) **2** DUPLICATE : copia *f*, duplicado *m*
duplicity [dʊ'plɪsəti, ,djuː-] *n, pl* -ties : duplicidad *f*
durability [,dʊrə'bɪləti, ,djʊr-] *n* : durabilidad *f* (de un producto) permanencia *f*
durable ['dʊrəbəl, 'djʊr-] *adj* : duradero
duration [dʊ'reɪʃən, djʊ-] *n* : duración *f*
duress [dʊ'rɛs, djʊ-] *n* : coacción *f*

during ['dʊrɪŋ, 'djʊr-] *prep* : durante
dusk ['dʌsk] *n* : anochecer *m*, crepúsculo *m*
dusky ['dʌski] *adj* **duskier; -est** : oscuro (dícese de los colores)
dust¹ ['dʌst] *vt* **1** : quitar el polvo de **2** SPRINKLE : espolvorear
dust² *n* : polvo *m*
duster ['dʌstər] *n* **1** *or* **dust cloth** : trapo *m* de polvo **2** HOUSECOAT : guardapolvo *m* **3 feather duster** : plumero *m*
dustpan ['dʌst,pæn] *n* : recogedor *m*
dusty ['dʌsti] *adj* **dustier; -est** : cubierto de polvo, polvoriento
Dutch¹ ['dʌtʃ] *adj* : holandés
Dutch² *n* **1** : holandés *m* (idioma) **2 the Dutch** *npl* : los holandeses
Dutch treat *n* : invitación o pago a escote
dutiful ['duːtɪfəl, 'djuː-] *adj* : motivado por sus deberes, responsable
duty ['duːti, 'djuː-] *n, pl* -ties **1** OBLIGATION : deber *m*, obligación *f*, responsabilidad *f* **2** TAX : impuesto *m*, arancel *m*
DVD [,diː,viː'diː] *n* : DVD *m*
dwarf¹ ['dwɔrf] *vt* **1** STUNT : arrestar el crecimiento de **2** : hacer parecer pequeño
dwarf² *n, pl* **dwarfs** ['dwɔrfs] *or* **dwarves** ['dwɔrvz] : enano *m*, -na *f*
dwell ['dwɛl] *vi* **dwelled** *or* **dwelt** ['dwɛlt]; **dwelling 1** RESIDE : residir, morar, vivir **2 to dwell on** : pensar demasiado en, insistir en
dweller ['dwɛlər] *n* : habitante *mf*
dwelling ['dwɛlɪŋ] *n* : morada *f*, vivienda *f*, residencia *f*
dwindle ['dwɪndəl] *vi* -dled; -dling : menguar, reducirse, disminuir
dye¹ ['daɪ] *vt* **dyed; dyeing** : teñir
dye² *n* : tintura *f*, tinte *m*
dying → die
dyke → dike
dynamic [daɪ'næmɪk] *adj* : dinámico
dynamics [daɪ'næmɪks] *npl* : dinámica *f*
dynamite¹ ['daɪnə,maɪt] *vt* -mited; -miting : dinamitar
dynamite² *n* : dinamita *f*
dynamo ['daɪnə,moː] *n, pl* -mos : dínamo *m*, generador *m* de electricidad
dynasty ['daɪnəsti, -,næs-] *n, pl* -ties : dinastía *f*
dysentery ['dɪsən,tɛri] *n, pl* -teries : disentería *f*
dysfunction [dɪs'fʌŋkʃən] *n* : disfunción *f*
dystrophy ['dɪstrəfi] *n, pl* -phies **1** : distrofia *f* **2 → muscular dystrophy**

E

e ['i:] *n, pl* **e's** *or* **es** ['i:z] : quinta letra del alfabeto inglés

each¹ ['i:tʃ] *adv* : cada uno, por persona ⟨they cost $10 each : costaron $10 cada uno⟩

each² *adj* : cada ⟨each student : cada estudiante⟩ ⟨each and every one : todos sin excepción⟩

each³ *pron* **1** : cada uno *m*, cada una *f* ⟨each of us : cada uno de nosotros⟩ **2 each other** : el uno al otro, mutuamente ⟨we are helping each other : nos ayudamos el uno al otro⟩ ⟨they love each other : se aman⟩

eager ['i:gər] *adj* **1** ENTHUSIASTIC : entusiasta, ávido, deseoso **2** ANXIOUS : ansioso, impaciente

eagerly ['i:gərli] *adv* : con entusiasmo, ansiosamente

eagerness ['i:gərnəs] *n* : entusiasmo *m*, deseo *m*, impaciencia *f*

eagle ['i:gəl] *n* : águila *f*

ear ['ɪr] *n* **1** : oído *m*, oreja *f* ⟨inner ear : oído interno⟩ ⟨big ears : orejas grandes⟩ **2 ear of corn** : mazorca *f*, choclo *m*

earache ['ɪr,eɪk] *n* : dolor *m* de oído

eardrum ['ɪr,drʌm] *n* : tímpano *m*

earl ['ərl] *n* : conde *m*

earlobe ['ɪr,lo:b] *n* : lóbulo *m* de la oreja, perilla *f* de la oreja

early¹ ['ərli] *adv* **earlier; -est** : temprano, pronto ⟨he arrived early : llegó temprano⟩ ⟨as early as possible : lo más pronto posible, cuanto antes⟩ ⟨ten minutes early : diez minutos de adelanto⟩

early² *adj* **earlier; -est 1** (*referring to a beginning*) : primero ⟨the early stages : las primeras etapas⟩ ⟨in early May : a principios de mayo⟩ **2** (*referring to antiquity*) : primitivo, antiguo ⟨early man : el hombre primitivo⟩ ⟨early painting : la pintura antigua⟩ **3** (*referring to a designated time*) : temprano, antes de la hora, prematuro ⟨he was early : llegó temprano⟩ ⟨early fruit : frutas tempraneras⟩ ⟨an early death : una muerte prematura⟩

earmark ['ɪr,mɑrk] *vt* : destinar ⟨earmarked funds : fondos destinados⟩

earn ['ərn] *vt* **1** : ganar ⟨to earn money : ganar dinero⟩ **2** DESERVE : ganarse, merecer

earnest¹ ['ərnəst] *adj* : serio, sincero

earnest² *n* **in ~** : en serio, de verdad ⟨we began in earnest : empezamos de verdad⟩

earnestly ['ərnəstli] *adv* **1** SERIOUSLY : con seriedad, en serio **2** FERVENTLY : de todo corazón

earnestness ['ərnəstnəs] *n* : seriedad *f*, sinceridad *f*

earnings ['ərnɪŋz] *npl* : ingresos *mpl*, ganancias *fpl*, utilidades *fpl*

earphone ['ɪr,fo:n] *n* : audífono *m*

earring ['ɪr,rɪŋ] *n* : zarcillo *m*, arete *m*, aro *m Arg, Chile, Uru*, pendiente *m Spain*

earshot ['ɪr,ʃɑt] *n* : alcance *m* del oído

earth ['ərθ] *n* **1** LAND, SOIL : tierra *f*, suelo *m* **2 the Earth** : la Tierra

earthen ['ərθən, -ðən] *adj* : de tierra, de barro

earthenware ['ərθən,wær, -ðən-] *n* : loza *f*, vajillas *fpl* de barro

earthly ['ərθli] *adj* : terrenal, mundano

earthquake ['ərθ,kweɪk] *n* : terremoto *m*, temblor *m*

earthworm ['ərθ,wərm] *n* : lombriz *f* (de tierra)

earthy ['ərθi] *adj* **earthier; -est 1** : terroso ⟨earthy colors : colores terrosos⟩ **2** DOWN-TO-EARTH : realista, práctico, llano **3** COARSE, CRUDE : basto, grosero, tosco ⟨earthy jokes : chistes groseros⟩

earwax ['ɪr,wæks] *n* → **wax²**

earwig ['ɪr,wɪg] *n* : tijereta *f*

ease¹ ['i:z] *v* **eased; easing** *vt* **1** ALLEVIATE : aliviar, calmar, hacer disminuir **2** LOOSEN, RELAX : aflojar (una cuerda), relajar (restricciones), descargar (tensiones) **3** FACILITATE : facilitar — *vi* : calmarse, relajarse

ease² *n* **1** CALM, RELIEF : tranquilidad *f*, comodidad *f*, desahogo *m* **2** FACILITY : facilidad *f* **3 at ~** : relajado, cómodo ⟨to put someone at ease : tranquilizar a alguien⟩

easel ['i:zəl] *n* : caballete *m*

easily ['i:zəli] *adv* **1** : fácilmente, con facilidad **2** UNQUESTIONABLY : con mucho, de lejos

easiness ['i:zinəs] *n* : facilidad *f*, soltura *f*

east¹ ['i:st] *adv* : al este

east² *adj* : este, del este, oriental ⟨east winds : vientos del este⟩

east³ *n* **1** : este *m* **2 the East** : el Oriente

Easter ['i:stər] *n* : Pascua *f* (de Resurrección)

easterly ['i:stərli] *adv & adj* : del este

eastern ['i:stərn] *adj* **1** : Oriental, del Este ⟨Eastern Europe : Europa del Este⟩ **2** : oriental, este

Easterner ['i:stərnər] *n* : habitante *mf* del este

eastward ['i:stwərd] *adv & adj* : hacia el este

easy ['i:zi] *adj* **easier; -est 1** : fácil **2** LENIENT : indulgente

easygoing [,i:zi'go:ɪŋ] *adj* : acomodaticio, tolerante, poco exigente

eat ['i:t] *v* **ate** ['eɪt]; **eaten** ['i:tən]; **eating** *vt* **1** : comer **2** CONSUME : consumir, gastar, devorar ⟨expenses ate up profits : los gastos devoraron las ganancias⟩ **3** CORRODE : corroer — *vi* **1** : comer **2 to eat away at** *or* **to eat into** : comerse **3 to eat out** : comer fuera

eatable¹ ['i:ʈəbəl] *adj* : comestible, comible *fam*
eatable² *n* **1** : algo para comer **2 eatables** *npl* : comestibles *mpl*, alimentos *mpl*
eater ['i:ʈər] *n* : comedor *m*, -dora *f*
eaves ['i:vz] *npl* : alero *m*
eavesdrop ['i:vz‚drɑp] *vi* **-dropped; -dropping** : escuchar a escondidas
eavesdropper ['i:vz‚drɑpər] *n* : persona *f* que escucha a escondidas
ebb¹ ['ɛb] *vi* **1** : bajar, menguar (dícese de la marea) **2** DECLINE : decaer, disminuir
ebb² *n* **1** : reflujo *m* (de una marea) **2** DECLINE : decadencia *f*, declive *m*, disminución *f*
ebony¹ ['ɛbəni] *adj* **1** : de ébano **2** BLACK : de color ébano, negro
ebony² *n, pl* **-nies** : ébano *m*
ebullience [ɪ'bʊljənʦ, -'bʌl-] *n* : efervescencia *f*, vivacidad *f*
ebullient [ɪ'bʊljənt, -'bʌl-] *adj* : efervescente, vivaz
eccentric¹ [ɪk'sɛntrɪk] *adj* **1** : excéntrico ⟨an eccentric wheel : una rueda excéntrica⟩ **2** ODD, SINGULAR : excéntrico, extraño, raro — **eccentrically** [-trɪkli] *adv*
eccentric² *n* : excéntrico *m*, -ca *f*
eccentricity [‚ɪk‚sɛn'trɪsəti] *n, pl* **-ties** : excentricidad *f*
ecclesiastic [ɪ‚kli:zi'æstɪk] *n* : eclesiástico *m*, clérigo *m*
ecclesiastical [ɪ‚kli:zi'æstɪkəl] *or* **ecclesiastic** *adj* : eclesiástico — **ecclesiastically** *adv*
echelon ['ɛʃə‚lɑn] *n* **1** : escalón *m* (de tropas o aviones) **2** LEVEL : nivel *m*, esfera *f*, estrato *m*
echo¹ ['ɛ‚ko:] *v* **echoed; echoing** *vi* : hacer eco, resonar — *vt* : repetir
echo² *n, pl* **echoes** : eco *m*
éclair [eɪ'klær, i-] *n* : pastel *m* relleno de crema
eclectic [ɛ'klɛktɪk, ɪ-] *adj* : ecléctico
eclipse¹ [ɪ'klɪps] *vt* **eclipsed; eclipsing** : eclipsar
eclipse² *n* : eclipse *m*
ecological [‚i:kə'lɑʤɪkəl, ‚ɛkə-] *adj* : ecológico — **ecologically** *adv*
ecologist [i'kɑləʤɪst, ɛ-] *n* : ecólogo *m*, -ga *f*
ecology [i'kɑləʤi, ɛ-] *n, pl* **-gies** : ecología *f*
economic [‚i:kə'nɑmɪk, ‚ɛkə-] *adj* : económico
economical [‚i:kə'nɑmɪkəl, ‚ɛkə-] *adj* : económico — **economically** *adv*
economics [‚i:kə'nɑmɪks, ‚ɛkə-] *n* : economía *f*
economist [i'kɑnəmɪst] *n* : economista *mf*
economize [i'kɑnə‚maɪz] *v* **-mized; -mizing** : economizar, ahorrar
economy [i'kɑnəmi] *n, pl* **-mies 1** : economía *f*, sistema *m* económico **2** THRIFT : economía *f*, ahorro *m*

ecosystem ['i:ko‚sɪstəm] *n* : ecosistema *m*
ecru ['ɛ‚kru:, 'eɪ-] *n* : color *m* crudo
ecstasy ['ɛkstəsi] *n, pl* **-sies** : éxtasis *m*
ecstatic [ɛk'stætɪk, ɪk-] *adj* : extático
ecstatically [ɛk'stætɪkli, ɪk-] *adv* : con éxtasis, con gran entusiasmo
Ecuadoran [‚ɛkwə'dorən] *or* **Ecuadorean** *or* **Ecuadorian** [-'doriən] *n* : ecuatoriano *m*, -na *f* — **Ecuadorean** *or* **Ecuadorian** *adj*
ecumenical [‚ɛkju'mnɪkəl] *adj* : ecuménico
eczema [ɪg'zi:mə, 'ɛgzəmə, 'ɛksə-] *n* : eczema *m*
eddy¹ ['ɛdi] *vi* **eddied; eddying** : arremolinarse, hacer remolinos
eddy² *n, pl* **-dies** : remolino *m*
edema [ɪ'di:mə] *n* : edema *m*
Eden ['i:dən] *n* : Edén *m*
edge¹ ['ɛʤ] *v* **edged; edging** *vt* **1** BORDER : bordear, ribetear, orlar **2** SHARPEN : afilar, aguzar **3** *or* **to edge one's way** : avanzar poco a poco **4 to edge out** : derrotar por muy poco — *vi* ADVANCE : ir avanzando (poco a poco)
edge² *n* **1** : filo *m* (de un cuchillo) **2** BORDER : borde *m*, orilla *f*, margen *m* **3** ADVANTAGE : ventaja *f*
edger ['ɛʤər] *n* : cortabordes *m*
edgewise ['ɛʤ‚waɪz] *adv* SIDEWAYS : de lado, de canto
edginess ['ɛʤinəs] *n* : tensión *f*, nerviosismo *m*
edgy ['ɛʤi] *adj* **edgier; -est** : tenso, nervioso
edible ['ɛdəbəl] *adj* : comestible
edict ['i:‚dɪkt] *n* : edicto *m*, mandato *m*, orden *f*
edification [‚ɛdəfə'keɪʃən] *n* : edificación *f*, instrucción *f*
edifice ['ɛdəfɪs] *n* : edificio *m*
edify ['ɛdə‚faɪ] *vt* **-fied; -fying** : edificar
edit ['ɛdɪt] *vt* **1** : editar, redactar, corregir **2** *or* **to edit out** DELETE : recortar, cortar
edition [ɪ'dɪʃən] *n* : edición *f*
editor ['ɛdɪʈər] *n* : editor *m*, -tora *f*; redactor *m*, -tora *f*
editorial¹ [‚ɛdɪ'toriəl] *adj* **1** : de redacción **2** : editorial ⟨an editorial comment : un comentario editorial⟩
editorial² *n* : editorial *m*
editorship ['ɛdəʈər‚ʃɪp] *n* : dirección *f*
educable ['ɛʤəkəbəl] *adj* : educable
educate ['ɛʤə‚keɪt] *vt* **-cated; -cating 1** TEACH : educar, enseñar **2** INSTRUCT : formar, educar, instruir **3** INFORM : informar, concientizar
education [‚ɛʤə'keɪʃən] *n* : educación *f*
educational [‚ɛʤə'keɪʃənəl] *adj* **1** : docente, de enseñanza ⟨an educational institution : una institución docente⟩ **2** PEDAGOGICAL : pedagógico **3** INSTRUCTIONAL : educativo, instructivo
educator ['ɛʤə‚keɪʈər] *n* : educador *m*, -dora *f*
eel ['i:l] *n* : anguila *f*

eerie ['ɪri] *adj* **-rier; -est 1** SPOOKY : que da miedo, espeluznante **2** GHOSTLY : fantasmagórico

eerily ['ɪrəli] *adv* : de manera extraña y misteriosa

efface [ɪ'feɪs, -] *vt* **-faced; -facing** : borrar

effect[1] [ɪ'fɛkt] *vt* **1** CARRY OUT : efectuar, llevar a cabo **2** ACHIEVE : lograr, realizar

effect[2] *n* **1** RESULT : efecto *m*, resultado *m*, consecuencia *f* ⟨to no effect : sin resultado⟩ **2** MEANING : sentido *m* ⟨something to that effect : algo por el estilo⟩ **3** INFLUENCE : efecto *m*, influencia *f* **4 effects** *npl* BELONGINGS : efectos *mpl*, pertenencias *fpl* **5 to go into effect** : entrar en vigor **6 in** ～ REALLY : en realidad, efectivamente

effective [ɪ'fɛktɪv] *adj* **1** EFFECTUAL : efectivo, eficaz **2** OPERATIVE : vigente — **effectively** *adv*

effectiveness [ɪ'fɛktɪvnəs] *n* : eficacia *f*, efectividad *f*

effectual [ɪ'fɛktʃuəl] *adj* : eficaz, efectivo — **effectually** *adv*

effeminate [ə'fɛmənət] *adj* : afeminado

effervesce [ˌɛfər'vɛs] *vi* **-vesced; -vescing 1** : estar en efervescencia, burbujear (dícese de líquidos) **2** : estar eufórico, estar muy animado (dícese de las personas)

effervescence [ˌɛfər'vɛsənts] *n* **1** : efervescencia *f* **2** LIVELINESS : vivacidad *f*

effervescent [ˌɛfər'vɛsənt] *adj* **1** : efervescente **2** LIVELY, VIVACIOUS : vivaz, animado

effete ['ɛfiːt, ɪ-] *adj* **1** WORN-OUT : desgastado, agotado **2** DECADENT : decadente **3** EFFEMINATE : afeminado

efficacious [ˌɛfə'keɪʃəs] *adj* : eficaz, efectivo

efficacy ['ɛfɪkəsi] *n, pl* **-cies** : eficacia *f*

efficiency [ɪ'fɪʃəntsi] *n, pl* **-cies** : eficiencia *f*

efficient [ɪ'fɪʃənt] *adj* : eficiente — **efficiently** *adv*

effigy ['ɛfədʒi] *n, pl* **-gies** : efigie *f*

effluent ['ɛˌfluːənt, ɛ'fluː-] *n* : efluente *m* — **effluent** *adj*

effort ['ɛfərt] *n* **1** EXERTION : esfuerzo *m* **2** ATTEMPT : tentativa *f*, intento *m* ⟨it's not worth the effort : no vale la pena⟩

effortless ['ɛfərtləs] *adj* : fácil, sin esfuerzo

effortlessly ['ɛfərtləsli] *adv* : sin esfuerzo, fácilmente

effrontery [ɪ'frʌntəri] *n, pl* **-teries** : insolencia *f*, desfachatez *f*, descaro *m*

effusion [ɪ'fjuːʒən, ɛ-] *n* : efusión *f*

effusive [ɪ'fjuːsɪv, ɛ-] *adj* : efusivo — **effusively** *adv*

egg[1] ['ɛg] *vt* **to egg on** : incitar, azuzar, provocar

egg[2] *n* **1** : huevo *m* **2** OVUM : óvulo *m*

eggbeater ['ɛgˌbiːt̬ər] *n* : batidor *m* (de huevos)

eggnog ['ɛgˌnɑg] *n* : ponche *m* de huevo, rompope *m* CA, Mex

eggplant ['ɛgˌplænt] *n* : berenjena *f*

eggshell ['ɛgˌʃl] *n* : cascarón *m*

ego ['iːˌgoː] *n, pl* **egos 1** SELF-ESTEEM : amor *m* propio **2** SELF : ego *m*, yo *m*

egocentric [ˌiːgoː'sɛntrɪk] *adj* : egocéntrico

egoism ['iːgoːˌwɪzəm] *n* : egoísmo *m*

egoist ['iːgoːwɪst] *n* : egoísta *mf*

egoistic [ˌiːgoː'wɪstɪk] *adj* : egoísta

egotism ['iːgəˌtɪzəm] *n* : egotismo *m*

egotist ['iːgətɪst] *n* : egotista *mf*

egotistic [ˌiːgə'tɪstɪk] *or* **egotistical** [-'tɪstɪkəl] *adj* : egotista — **egotistically** *adv*

egregious [ɪ'griːdʒəs] *adj* : atroz, flagrante, mayúsculo — **egregiously** *adv*

egress ['iːˌgrɛs] *n* : salida *f*

egret ['iːgrət, -ˌgrɛt] *n* : garceta *f*

Egyptian [ɪ'dʒɪpʃən] *n* **1** : egipcio *m*, -cia *f* **2** : egipcio *m* (idioma) — **Egyptian** *adj*

eiderdown ['aɪdərˌdaun] *n* **1** : plumón *m* **2** COMFORTER : edredón *m*

eight[1] ['eɪt] *adj* : ocho

eight[2] *n* : ocho *m*

eight hundred[1] *adj* : ochocientos

eight hundred[2] *n* : ochocientos *m*

eighteen[1] [eɪt'tiːn] *adj* : dieciocho

eighteen[2] *n* : dieciocho *m*

eighteenth[1] [eɪt'tiːnθ] *adj* : decimoctavo

eighteenth[2] *n* **1** : decimoctavo *m*, -va *f* (en una serie) **2** : dieciochoavo *m*, dieciochoava parte *f*

eighth[1] ['eɪtθ] *adj* : octavo

eighth[2] *n* **1** : octavo *m*, -va *f* (en una serie) **2** : octavo *m*, octava parte *f*

eightieth[1] ['eɪtiəθ] *adj* : octogésimo

eightieth[2] *n* **1** : octogésimo *m*, -ma *f* (en una serie) **2** : ochentavo *m*, ochentava parte *f*

eighty[1] ['eɪti] *adj* : ochenta

eighty[2] *n, pl* **eighties 1** : ochenta *m* **2 the eighties** : los ochenta *mpl*

either[1] ['iːðər, 'aɪ-] *adj* **1** : cualquiera (de los dos) ⟨we can watch either movie : podemos ver cualquiera de las dos películas⟩ **2** : ninguno de los dos ⟨she wasn't in either room : no estaba en ninguna de las dos salas⟩ **3** EACH : cada ⟨on either side of the street : a cada lado de la calle⟩

either[2] *pron* **1** : cualquiera *mf* (de los dos) ⟨either is fine : cualquiera de los dos está bien⟩ **2** : ninguno *m*, -na *f* (de los dos) ⟨I don't like either : no me gusta ninguno⟩ **3** : algún *m*, alguna *f* ⟨is either of you interested? : ¿está alguno de ustedes (dos) interesado?⟩

either[3] *conj* **1** : o, u ⟨either David or Daniel could go : puede ir (o) David o Daniel⟩ **2** : ni ⟨we won't watch either this movie or the other : no veremos ni esta película ni la otra⟩

ejaculate [i'dʒækjəˌleɪt] *v* **-lated; -lating** *vt* **1** : eyacular **2** EXCLAIM : exclamar — *vi* : eyacular

ejaculation [iˌʤækjəˈleɪʃən] *n* **1** : eyaculación *f* (en fisiología) **2** EXCLAMATION : exclamación *f*
eject [iˈʤɛkt] *vt* : expulsar, expeler
ejection [iˈʤɛkʃən] *n* : expulsión *f*
eke [ˈiːk] *vt* **eked; eking** *or* **to eke out** : ganar a duras penas
elaborate¹ [iˈlæbəˌreɪt] *v* **-rated; -rating** *vt* : elaborar, idear, desarrollar — *vi* **to elaborate on** : ampliar, entrar en detalles
elaborate² [iˈlæbərət] *adj* **1** DETAILED : detallado, minucioso, elaborado **2** COMPLICATED : complicado, intrincado, elaborado — **elaborately** *adv*
elaboration [iˌlæbəˈreɪʃən] *n* : elaboración *f*
elapse [iˈlæps] *vi* **elapsed; elapsing** : transcurrir, pasar
elastic¹ [iˈlæstɪk] *adj* : elástico
elastic² *n* **1** : elástico *m* **2** RUBBER BAND : goma *f*, gomita *f*, elástico *m*, liga *f*
elasticity [iˌlæsˈtɪsəti, ˌiːˌlæs-] *n, pl* **-ties** : elasticidad *f*
elate [iˈleɪt] *vt* **elated; elating** : alborozar, regocijar
elation [iˈleɪʃən] *n* : euforia *f*, júbilo *m*, alborozo *m*
elbow¹ [ˈɛlˌboː] *vt* : darle un codazo a
elbow² *n* : codo *m*
elder¹ [ˈɛldər] *adj* : mayor
elder² *n* **1 to be someone's elder** : ser mayor que alguien **2** : anciano *m*, -na *f* (de un pueblo o una tribu) **3** : miembro *m* del consejo (en varias religiones)
elderberry [ˈɛldərˌbɛri] *n, pl* **-berries** : baya *f* de saúco (fruta), saúco *m* (árbol)
elderly [ˈɛldərli] *adj* : mayor, de edad, anciano
eldest [ˈɛldəst] *adj* : mayor, de más edad
elect¹ [iˈlɛkt] *vt* : elegir
elect² *adj* : electo ⟨the president-elect : el presidente electo⟩
elect³ *npl* **the elect** : los elegidos *mpl*
election [iˈlɛkʃən] *n* : elección *f*
elective¹ [iˈlɛktɪv] *adj* **1** : electivo **2** OPTIONAL : facultativo, optativo
elective² *n* : asignatura *f* electiva
elector [iˈlɛktər] *n* : elector *m*, -tora *f*
electoral [iˈlɛktərəl] *adj* : electoral
electorate [iˈlɛktərət] *n* : electorado *m*
electric [iˈlɛktrɪk] *adj* **1** *or* **electrical** [-trɪkəl] : eléctrico **2** THRILLING : electrizante, emocionante
electrician [iˌlɛkˈtrɪʃən] *n* : electricista *mf*
electricity [iˌlɛkˈtrɪsəti] *n, pl* **-ties** **1** : electricidad *f* **2** CURRENT : corriente *m* eléctrica
electrification [iˌlɛktrəfəˈkeɪʃən] *n* : electrificación *f*
electrify [iˈlɛktrəˌfaɪ] *vt* **-fied; -fying** **1** : electrificar **2** THRILL : electrizar, emocionar
electrocardiogram [iˌlɛktroˈkɑrdiəˌgræm] *n* : electrocardiograma *m*
electrocardiograph [iˌlɛktroˈkɑrdiəˌgræf] *n* : electrocardiógrafo *m*

electrocute [iˈlɛktrəˌkjuːt] *vt* **-cuted; -cuting** : electrocutar
electrocution [iˌlɛktrəˈkjuːʃən] *n* : electrocución *f*
electrode [iˈlɛkˌtroːd] *n* : electrodo *m*
electrolysis [iˌlɛkˈtrɑləsɪs] *n* : electrólisis *f*
electrolyte [iˈlɛktrəˌlaɪt] *n* : electrolito *m*
electromagnet [iˌlɛktroˈmægnət] *n* : electroimán *m*
electromagnetic [iˌlɛktromægˈnɛtɪk] *adj* : electromagnético — **electromagnetically** [-ˌtikli] *adv*
electromagnetism [iˌlɛktroˈmægnəˌtɪzəm] *n* : electromagnetismo *m*
electron [iˈlɛkˌtrɑn] *n* : electrón *m*
electronic [iˌlɛkˈtrɑnɪk] *adj* : electrónico — **electronically** [-nɪkli] *adv*
electronic mail *n* : correo *m* electrónico
electronics [iˌlɛkˈtrɑnɪks] *n* : electrónica *f*
electroplate [iˈlɛktrəˌpleɪt] *vt* **-plated; plating** : galvanizar mediante electrólisis
elegance [ˈɛlɪgənts] *n* : elegancia *f*
elegant [ˈɛlɪgənt] *adj* : elegante — **elegantly** *adv*
elegy [ˈɛləʤi] *n, pl* **-gies** : elegía *f*
element [ˈɛləmənt] *n* **1** COMPONENT : elemento *m*, factor *m* **2** : elemento *m* (en la química) **3** MILIEU : elemento *m*, medio *m* ⟨to be in one's element : estar en su elemento⟩ **4 elements** *npl* RUDIMENTS : elementos *mpl*, rudimentos *mpl*, bases *fpl* **5 the elements** WEATHER : los elementos *mpl*
elemental [ˌɛləˈmɛntəl] *adj* **1** BASIC : elemental, primario **2** : elemental (dícese de los elementos químicos)
elementary [ˌɛləˈmɛntri] *adj* **1** SIMPLE : elemental, simple, fundamental **2** : de enseñanza primaria
elementary school *n* : escuela *f* primaria
elephant [ˈɛləfənt] *n* : elefante *m*, -ta *f*
elevate [ˈɛləˌveɪt] *vt* **-vated; -vating** **1** RAISE : elevar, levantar, alzar **2** EXALT, PROMOTE : elevar, exaltar, ascender **3** ELATE : alborozar, regocijar
elevation [ˌɛləˈveɪʃən] *n* **1** : elevación *f* **2** ALTITUDE : altura *f*, altitud *f* **3** PROMOTION : ascenso *m*
elevator [ˈɛləˌveɪtər] *n* : ascensor *m*, elevador *m*
eleven¹ [ɪˈlɛvən] *adj* : once
eleven² *n* : once *m*
eleventh¹ [ɪlɛvəntθ] *adj* : undécimo
eleventh² *n* **1** : undécimo *m*, -ma *f* (en una serie) **2** : onceavo *m*, onceava parte *f*
elf [ˈɛlf] *n, pl* **elves** [ˈɛlvz] : elfo *m*, geniecillo *m*, duende *m*
elfin [ˈɛlfən] *adj* **1** : de elfo, menudo **2** ENCHANTING, MAGIC : mágico, encantador
elfish [ˈɛlfɪʃ] *adj* **1** : de elfo **2** MISCHIEVOUS : travieso
elicit [ɪˈlɪsət] *vt* : provocar

eligibility [ˌelədʒə'bıləti] *n, pl* **-ties** : elegibilidad *f*
eligible ['elədʒəbəl] *adj* **1** QUALIFIED : elegible **2** SUITABLE : idóneo
eliminate [ı'lımə,neıt] *vt* **-nated; -nating** : eliminar
elimination [ı,lımə'neıʃən] *n* : eliminación *f*
elite [eı'li:t, i-] *n* : elite *f*
elixir [i'lıksər] *n* : elixir *m*
elk ['elk] *n* : alce *m* (de Europa), uapití *m* (de América)
ellipse [ı'lıps, -] *n* : elipse *f*
ellipsis [ı'lıpsəs, -] *n, pl* **-lipses** [-,si:z] **1** : elipsis *f* **2** : puntos *mpl* suspensivos (en la puntuación)
elliptical [ı'lıptıkəl, -] *or* **elliptic** [-tık] *adj* : elíptico
elm ['elm] *n* : olmo *m*
elocution [ˌelə'kju:ʃən] *n* : elocución *f*
elongate [i'lɔŋ,geıt] *vt* **-gated; -gating** : alargar
elongation [ˌi:,lɔŋ'geıʃən] *n* : alargamiento *m*
elope [i'lo:p] *vi* **eloped; eloping** : fugarse
elopement [i'lo:pmənt] *n* : fuga *f*
eloquence ['eləkwənts] *n* : elocuencia *f*
eloquent ['eləkwənt] *adj* : elocuente — **eloquently** *adv*
El Salvadoran [ˌel,sælvə'dorən] *n* : salvadoreño *m*, -ña *f* — **El Salvadoran** *adj*
else¹ ['els] *adv* **1** DIFFERENTLY : de otro modo, de otra manera ⟨how else? : ¿de qué otro modo?⟩ **2** ELSEWHERE : de otro sitio, de otro lugar ⟨where else? : ¿en qué otro sitio?⟩ **3 or else** OTHERWISE : si no, de lo contrario
else² *adj* **1** OTHER : otro ⟨anyone else : cualquier otro⟩ ⟨everyone else : todos los demás⟩ ⟨nobody else : ningún otro, nadie más⟩ ⟨somebody else : otra persona⟩ **2** MORE : más ⟨nothing else : nada más⟩ ⟨what else? : ¿qué más?⟩
elsewhere ['els,hwer] *adv* : en otra parte, en otro sitio, en otro lugar
elucidate [i'lu:sə,deıt] *vt* **-dated; -dating** : dilucidar, elucidar, esclarecer
elucidation [i,lu:sə'deıʃən] *n* : elucidación *f*, esclarecimiento *m*
elude [i'lu:d] *vt* **eluded; eluding** : eludir, evadir
elusive [i'lu:sıv] *adj* **1** EVASIVE : evasivo, esquivo **2** SLIPPERY : huidizo, escurridizo **3** FLEETING, INTANGIBLE : impalpable, fugaz
elusively [i'lu:sıvli] *adv* : de manera esquiva
elves → **elf**
emaciate [i'meıʃi,eıt] *vt* **-ated; -ating** : enflaquecer
emaciation [i,meısi'eıʃən, -ʃi-] *n* : enflaquecimiento *m*, escualidez *f*, delgadez *f* extrema
e-mail ['i:,meıl] *n* : e-mail *m*
emanate ['emə,neıt] *v* **-nated; -nating** *vi* : emanar, provenir, proceder — *vt* : emanar

emanation [ˌemə'neıʃən] *n* : emanación *f*
emancipate [i'mæntsə,peıt] *vt* **-pated; -pating** : emancipar
emancipation [i,mæntsə'peıʃən] *n* : emancipación *f*
emasculate [i'mæskjə,leıt] *vt* **-lated; -lating** **1** CASTRATE : castrar, emascular **2** WEAKEN : debilitar
embalm [ım'bam, em-, -'balm] *vt* : embalsamar
embankment [ım'bæŋkmənt, em-] *n* : terraplén *m*, muro *m* de contención
embargo¹ [ım'bargo, em-] *vt* **-goed; -going** : imponer un embargo sobre
embargo² *n, pl* **-goes** : embargo *m*
embark [ım'bark, em-] *vt* : embarcar — *vi* **1** : embarcarse **2 to embark on** START : emprender, embarcarse en
embarkation [ˌem,bar'keıʃən] *n* : embarque *m*, embarco *m*
embarrass [ım'bærəs, em-] *vt* : avergonzar, abochornar
embarrassing [ım'bærəsıŋ, em-] *adj* : embarazoso, violento
embarrassment [ım'bærəsmənt, em-] *n* : vergüenza *f*, pena *f*
embassy ['embəsi] *n, pl* **-sies** : embajada *f*
embed [ım'bed, em-] *vt* **-bedded; -bedding** : incrustar, empotrar, grabar (en la memoria)
embellish [ım'belıʃ, em-] *vt* : adornar, embellecer
embellishment [ım'belıʃmənt, em-] *n* : adorno *m*
ember ['embər] *n* : ascua *f*, brasa *f*
embezzle [ım'bezəl, em-] *vt* **-zled; -zling** : desfalcar, malversar
embezzlement [ım'bezəlmənt, em-] *n* : desfalco *m*, malversación *f*
embezzler [ım'bezələr, em-] *n* : desfalcador *m*, -dora *f*; malversador *m*, -dora *f*
embitter [ım'bıtər, em-] *vt* : amargar
emblem ['embləm] *n* : emblema *m*, símbolo *m*
emblematic [ˌemblə'mætık] *adj* : emblemático, simbólico
embodiment [ım'badımənt, em-] *n* : encarnación *f*, personificación *f*
embody [ım'badi, em-] *vt* **-bodied; -bodying** : encarnar, personificar
emboss [ım'bas, em-, -'bɔs] *vt* : repujar, grabar en relieve
embrace¹ [ım'breıs, em-] *vt* **-braced; -bracing** **1** HUG : abrazar **2** ADOPT, TAKE ON : adoptar, aceptar **3** INCLUDE : abarcar, incluir
embrace² *n* : abrazo *m*
embroider [ım'brɔıdər, em-] *vt* : bordar (una tela), adornar (una historia)
embroidery [ım'brɔıdəri, em-] *n, pl* **-deries** : bordado *m*
embroil [ım'brɔıl, em-] *vt* : embrollar, enredar
embryo ['embri,o:] *n, pl* **embryos** : embrión *m*

embryonic [ˌɛmbriˈɑnɪk] *adj* : embrionario

emend [iˈmɛnd] *vt* : enmendar, corregir

emendation [ˌiːˌmɛnˈdeɪʃən] *n* : enmienda *f*

emerald¹ [ˈɛmrəld, ˈɛmə-] *adj* : verde esmeralda

emerald² *n* : esmeralda *f*

emerge [iˈmərdʒ] *vi* emerged; emerging : emerger, salir, aparecer, surgir

emergence [iˈmərdʒənts] *n* : aparición *f*, surgimiento *m*

emergency [iˈmərdʒəntsi] *n, pl* -cies : emergencia *f*

emergent [iˈmərdʒənt] *adj* : emergente

emery [ˈɛməri] *n, pl* -eries : esmeril *m*

emetic¹ [iˈmɛtɪk] *adj* : vomitivo, emético

emetic² *n* : vomitivo *m*, emético *m*

emigrant [ˈɛmɪɡrənt] *n* : emigrante *mf*

emigrate [ˈɛməˌɡreɪt] *vi* -grated; -grating : emigrar

emigration [ˌɛməˈɡreɪʃən] *n* : emigración *f*

eminence [ˈɛmənənts] *n* 1 PROMINENCE : eminencia *f*, prestigio *m*, renombre *m* 2 DIGNITARY : eminencia *f*; dignatario *m*, -ria *f* ⟨Your Eminence : Su Eminencia⟩

eminent [ˈɛmənənt] *adj* : eminente, ilustre

eminently [ˈɛmənəntli] *adv* : sumamente

emissary [ˈɛməˌsɛri] *n, pl* -saries : emisario *m*, -ria *f*

emission [iˈmɪʃən] *n* : emisión *f*

emit [iˈmɪt] *vt* emitted; emitting : emitir, despedir, producir

emote [iˈmoːt] *vi* emoted; emoting : exteriorizar las emociones

emotion [iˈmoːʃən] *n* : emoción *f*, sentimiento *m*

emotional [iˈmoːʃənəl] *adj* 1 : emocional, afectivo ⟨an emotional reaction : una reacción emocional⟩ 2 MOVING : emocionante, emotivo, conmovedor

emotionally [iˈmoːʃənəli] *adv* : emocionalmente

empathy [ˈɛmpəθi] *n* : empatía *f*

emperor [ˈɛmpərər] *n* : emperador *m*

emphasis [ˈɛmfəsɪs] *n, pl* -phases [-ˌsiːz] : énfasis *m*, hincapié *m*

emphasize [ˈɛmfəˌsaɪz] *vt* -sized; -sizing : enfatizar, destacar, subrayar, hacer hincapié en

emphatic [ɪmˈfætɪk, ɛm-] *adj* : enfático, enérgico, categórico — emphatically [-ɪkli] *adv*

empire [ˈɛmˌpaɪr] *n* : imperio *m*

empirical [ɪmˈpɪrɪkəl, ɛm-] *adj* : empírico — empirically [-ɪkli] *adv*

employ¹ [ɪmˈplɔɪ, ɛm-] *vt* 1 USE : usar, utilizar 2 HIRE : contratar, emplear 3 OCCUPY : ocupar, dedicar, emplear

employ² [ɪmˈplɔɪ, ɛm-; ˈɪmˌ-, ˈɛmˌ-] *n* 1 : puesto *m*, cargo *m*, ocupación *f* 2 to be in the employ of : estar al servicio de, trabajar para

employee [ɪmˌplɔɪˈiː, ɛm-, -ˈplɔɪˌiː] *n* : empleado *m*, -da *f*

employer [ɪmˈplɔɪər, ɛm-] *n* : patrón *m*, -trona *f*; empleador *m*, -dora *f*

employment [ɪmˈplɔɪmənt, ɛm-] *n* : trabajo *m*, empleo *m*

empower [ɪmˈpaʊər, ɛm-] *vt* : facultar, autorizar, conferirle poder a

empowerment [ɪmˈpaʊərmənt, ɛm-] *n* : autorización *f*

empress [ˈɛmprəs] *n* : emperatriz *f*

emptiness [ˈɛmptinəs] *n* : vacío *m*, vacuidad *f*

empty¹ [ˈɛmpti] *v* -tied; -tying *vt* : vaciar — *vi* : desaguar (dícese de un río)

empty² *adj* emptier; -est 1 : vacío 2 VACANT : desocupado, libre 3 MEANINGLESS : vacío, hueco, vano

empty–handed [ˌɛmptiˈhændəd] *adj* : con las manos vacías

empty–headed [ˌɛmptiˈhɛdəd] *adj* : cabeza hueca, tonto

emu [ˈiːˌmjuː] *n* : emú *m*

emulate [ˈɛmjəˌleɪt] *vt* -lated; -lating : emular

emulation [ˌɛmjəˈleɪʃən] *n* : emulación *f*

emulsifier [ɪˈmʌlsəˌfaɪər] *n* : emulsionante *m*

emulsify [ɪˈmʌlsəˌfaɪ] *vt* -fied; -fying : emulsionar

emulsion [ɪˈmʌlʃən] *n* : emulsión *f*

enable [ɪˈneɪbəl, ɛ-] *vt* -abled; -abling 1 EMPOWER : habilitar, autorizar, facultar 2 PERMIT : hacer posible, posibilitar, permitir

enact [ɪˈnækt, ɛ-] *vt* 1 : promulgar (un ley o decreto) 2 : representar (un papel en el teatro)

enactment [ɪˈnæktmənt, ɛ-] *n* : promulgación *f*

enamel¹ [ɪˈnæməl] *vt* -eled *or* -elled; -eling *or* -elling : esmaltar

enamel² *n* : esmalte *m*

enamor [ɪˈnæmər] *vt* 1 : enamorar 2 to be enamored of : estar enamorado de (una persona), estar entusiasmado con (algo)

encamp [ɪnˈkæmp, ɛn-] *vi* : acampar

encampment [ɪnˈkæmpmənt, ɛn-] *n* : campamento *m*

encase [ɪnˈkeɪs, ɛn-] *vt* -cased; -casing : encerrar, revestir

encephalitis [ɪnˌsfəˈlaɪtəs, ɛn-] *n, pl* -litides [ˈlɪtəˌdiːz] : encefalitis *f*

enchant [ɪnˈtʃænt, ɛn-] *vt* 1 BEWITCH : hechizar, encantar, embrujar 2 CHARM, FASCINATE : cautivar, fascinar, encantar

enchanting [ɪnˈtʃæntɪŋ, ɛn-] *adj* : encantador

enchanter [ɪnˈtʃæntər, ɛn-] *n* SORCERER : mago *m*, encantador *m*

enchantment [ɪnˈtʃæntmənt, ɛn-] *n* 1 SPELL : encanto *m*, hechizo *m* 2 CHARM : encanto *m*

enchantress [ɪnˈtʃæntrəs, ɛn-] *n* 1 SORCERESS : maga *f*, hechicera *f* 2 CHARMER : mujer *f* cautivadora

encircle [ɪnˈsərkəl, ɛn-] *vt* -cled; -cling : rodear, ceñir, cercar

enclose [ɪn'kloːz, ɛn-] *vt* **-closed;
-closing 1** SURROUND : encerrar, cercar, rodear **2** INCLUDE : incluir, adjuntar, acompañar ⟨please find enclosed : le enviamos adjunto⟩
enclosure [ɪn'kloːʒər, ɛn-] *n* **1** ENCLOSING : encierro *m* **2** : cercado *m* (de terreno), recinto *m* ⟨an enclosure for the press : un recinto para la prensa⟩ **3** ADJUNCT : anexo *m* (con una carta), documento *m* adjunto
encode [ɪn'koːd, ɛn-] *vt* : cifrar (mensajes, etc.), codificar (en informática)
encompass [ɪn'kʌmpəs, ɛn-, -'kɑm-] *vt* **1** SURROUND : circundar, rodear **2** INCLUDE : abarcar, comprender
encore ['ɑn₁kor] *n* : bis *m*, repetición *f*
encounter[1] [ɪn'kaʊntər, ɛn-] *vt* **1** MEET : encontrar, encontrarse con, toparse con, tropezar con **2** FIGHT : combatir, luchar contra
encounter[2] *n* : encuentro *m*
encourage [ɪn'kərɪʤ, ɛn-] *vt* **-aged;
-aging 1** HEARTEN, INSPIRE : animar, alentar **2** FOSTER : fomentar, promover
encouragement [ɪn'kərɪʤmənt, ɛn-] *n* : ánimo *m*, aliento *m*
encouraging [ɪn'kərəʤɪŋ, ɛn-] *adj* : alentador, esperanzador
encroach [ɪn'kroːʧ, ɛn-] *vi* **to encroach on** : invadir, abusar (derechos), quitar (tiempo)
encroachment [ɪn'kroːʧmənt, ɛn-] *n* : invasión *f*, usurpación *f*
encrust [ɪn'krʌst, ɛn-] *vt* **1** : recubrir con una costra **2** INLAY : incrustar ⟨encrusted with gems : incrustado de gemas⟩
encumber [ɪn'kʌmbər, ɛn-] *vt* **1** BLOCK : obstruir, estorbar **2** BURDEN : cargar, gravar
encumbrance [ɪn'kʌmbrənts, ɛn-] *n* : estorbo *m*, carga *f*, gravamen *m*
encyclopedia [ɪn₁saɪklə'piːdiə, ɛn-] *n* : enciclopedia *f*
encyclopedic [ɪn₁saɪklə'piːdɪk, ɛn-] *adj* : enciclopédico
end[1] ['ɛnd] *vt* **1** STOP : terminar, poner fin a **2** CONCLUDE : concluir, terminar — *vi* : terminar(se), acabar, concluir(se)
end[2] *n* **1** EXTREMITY : extremo *m*, final *m*, punta *f* **2** CONCLUSION : fin *m*, final *m* **3** AIM : fin *m*
endanger [ɪn'deɪnʤər, ɛn-] *vt* : poner en peligro
endear [ɪn'dɪr, ɛn-] *vt* **to endear oneself to** : ganarse la simpatía de, granjearse el cariño de
endearment [ɪn'dɪrmənt, ɛn-] *n* : expresión *f* de cariño
endeavor[1] [ɪn'dɛvər, ɛn-] *vt* : intentar, esforzarse por ⟨he endeavored to improve his work : intentó por mejorar su trabajo⟩
endeavor[2] *n* : intento *m*, esfuerzo *m*
endemic [ɛn'dɛmɪk, ɪn-] *adj* : endémico

ending ['ɛndɪŋ] *n* **1** CONCLUSION : final *m*, desenlace *m* **2** SUFFIX : sufijo *m*, terminación *f*
endive ['ɛn₁daɪv, ₁ɑn'diːv] *n* : endibia *f*, endivia *f*
endless ['ɛndləs] *adj* **1** INTERMINABLE : interminable, inacabable, sin fin **2** INUMERABLE : innumerable, incontable
endlessly ['ɛndləsli] *adv* : interminablemente, eternamente, sin parar
endocrine ['ɛndəkrən, -₁kraɪn, -₁kriːn] *adj* : endocrino
endorse [ɪn'dors, ɛn-] *vt* **-dorsed;
-dorsing 1** SIGN : endosar, firmar **2** APPROVE : aprobar, sancionar
endorsement [ɪn'dorsmənt, ɛn-] *n* **1** SIGNATURE : endoso *m*, firma *f* **2** APPROVAL : aprobación *f*, aval *m*
endow [ɪn'daʊ, ɛn-] *vt* : dotar
endowment [ɪn'daʊmənt, ɛn-] *n* **1** FUNDING : dotación *f* **2** DONATION : donación *f*, legado *m* **3** ATTRIBUTE, GIFT : atributo *m*, dotes *fpl*
endurable [ɪn'dʊrəbəl, ɛn-, -'djʊr-] *adj* : tolerable, soportable
endurance [ɪn'dʊrənts, ɛn-, -'djʊr-] *n* : resistencia *f*, aguante *m*
endure [ɪn'dʊr, ɛn-, -'djʊr] *v* **-dured;
-during** *vt* **1** BEAR : resistir, soportar, aguantar **2** TOLERATE : tolerar, soportar — *vi* LAST : durar, perdurar
enema ['ɛnəmə] *n* : enema *m*, lavativa *f*
enemy ['ɛnəmi] *n, pl* **-mies** : enemigo *m*, -ga *f*
energetic [₁ɛnər'ʤɛtɪk] *adj* : enérgico, vigoroso — **energetically** [-tɪkli] *adv*
energize ['ɛnər₁ʤaɪz] *vt* **-gized; -gizing
1** ACTIVATE : activar **2** INVIGORATE : vigorizar
energy ['ɛnərʤi] *n, pl* **-gies 1** VITALITY : energía *f*, vitalidad *f* **2** EFFORT : esfuerzo *m*, energías *fpl* **3** POWER : energía *f* ⟨atomic energy : energía atómica⟩
enervate ['ɛnər₁veɪt] *vt* **-vated; -vating** : enervar, debilitar
enfold [ɪn'foːld, ɛn-] *vt* : envolver
enforce [ɪn'fors, ɛn-] *vt* **-forced; -forcing
1** : hacer respetar, hacer cumplir (una ley, etc.) **2** IMPOSE : imponer ⟨to enforce obedience : imponer la obediencia⟩
enforcement [ɪn'forsmənt, ɛn-] *n* : imposición *f*
enfranchise [ɪn'fræn₁ʧaɪz, ɛn-] *vt* **-chised; -chising** : conceder el voto a
enfranchisement [ɪn'fræn₁ʧaɪzmənt, ɛn-] *n* : concesión *f* del voto
engage [ɪn'geɪʤ, ɛn-] *v* **-gaged; -gaging**
vt **1** ATTRACT : captar, atraer, llamar ⟨to engage one's attention : captar la atención⟩ **2** MESH : engranar ⟨to engage the clutch : embragar⟩ **3** COMMIT : comprometer ⟨to get engaged : comprometerse⟩ **4** HIRE : contratar **5** : entablar combate con (un enemigo)

— *vi* **1** PARTICIPATE : participar **2 to engage in combat** : entrar en combate
engagement [ɪnˈgeɪʤmənt, ɛn-] *n* **1** APPOINTMENT : cita *f*, hora *f* **2** BETROTHAL : compromiso *m*
engaging [ɪnˈgeɪʤɪŋ, ɛn-] *adj* : atractivo, encantador, interesante
engender [ɪnˈʤɛndər, ɛn-] *vt* **-dered; -dering** : engendrar
engine [ˈɛnʤən] *n* **1** MOTOR : motor *m* **2** LOCOMOTIVE : locomotora *f*, máquina *f*
engineer[1] [ˌɛnʤəˈnɪr] *vt* **1** : diseñar, construir (un sistema, un mecanismo, etc.) **2** CONTRIVE : maquinar, tramar, fraguar
engineer[2] *n* **1** : ingeniero *m*, -ra *f* **2** : maquinista *mf* (de locomotoras)
engineering [ˌɛnʤəˈnɪrɪŋ] *n* : ingeniería *f*
English[1] [ˈɪŋglɪʃ, ˈɪŋlɪʃ] *adj* : inglés
English[2] *n* **1** : inglés *m* (idioma) **2 the English** : los ingleses
Englishman [ˈɪŋglɪʃmən, ˈɪŋlɪʃ-] *n, pl* **-men** [-mən, -ˌmɛn] : inglés *m*
Englishwoman [ˈɪŋglɪʃˌwʊmən, ˈɪŋlɪʃ-] *n, pl* **-women** [-ˌwɪmən] : inglesa *f*
engrave [ɪnˈgreɪv, ɛn-] *vt* **-graved; -graving** : grabar
engraver [ɪnˈgreɪvər, ɛn-] *n* : grabador *m*, -dora *f*
engraving [ɪnˈgreɪvɪŋ, ɛn-] *n* : grabado *m*
engross [ɪnˈgroːs, ɛn-] *vt* : absorber
engrossed [ɪnˈgroːst, ɛn-] *adj* : absorto
engrossing [ɪnˈgroːsɪŋ, ɛn-] *adj* : fascinante, absorbente
engulf [ɪnˈgʌlf, ɛn-] *vt* : envolver, sepultar
enhance [ɪnˈhænts, ɛn-] *vt* **-hanced; -hancing** : realzar, aumentar, mejorar
enhancement [ɪnˈhæntsmənt, ɛn-] *n* : mejora *f*, realce *m*, aumento *m*
enigma [ɪˈnɪgmə] *n* : enigma *m*
enigmatic [ˌɛnɪgˈmætɪk, ˌiːnɪg-] *adj* : enigmático — **enigmatically** [-t̬ɪkli] *adv*
enjoin [ɪnˈʤɔɪn, ɛn-] *vt* **1** COMMAND : ordenar, imponer **2** FORBID : prohibir, vedar
enjoy [ɪnˈʤɔɪ, ɛn-] *vt* **1** : disfrutar, gozar de ⟨did you enjoy the book? : ¿te gustó el libro?⟩ ⟨to enjoy good health : gozar de buena salud⟩ **2 to enjoy oneself** : divertirse, pasarlo bien
enjoyable [ɪnˈʤɔɪəbəl, ɛn-] *adj* : agradable, placentero, divertido
enjoyment [ɪnˈʤɔɪmənt, ɛn-] *n* : placer *m*, goce *m*, disfrute *m*, deleite *m*
enlarge [ɪnˈlɑrʤ, ɛn-] *v* **-larged; -larging** *vt* : extender, agrandar, ampliar — *vi* **1** : ampliarse **2 to enlarge upon** : extenderse sobre, entrar en detalles sobre
enlargement [ɪnˈlɑrʤmənt, ɛn-] *n* : expansión *f*, ampliación *f* (dícese de fotografías)
enlarger [ɪnˈlɑrʤər, ɛn-] *n* : ampliadora *f*

enlighten [ɪnˈlaɪt̬ən, ɛn-] *vt* : iluminar, aclarar
enlightenment [ɪnˈlaɪt̬ənmənt, ɛn-] *n* **1** : ilustración *f* ⟨the Enlightenment : la Ilustración⟩ **2** CLARIFICATION : aclaración *f*
enlist [ɪnˈlɪst, ɛn-] *vt* **1** ENROLL : alistar, reclutar **2** SECURE : conseguir ⟨to enlist the support of : conseguir el apoyo de⟩ — *vi* : alistarse
enlisted man [ɪnˈlɪstəd, ɛn-] *n* : soldado *m* raso
enlistment [ɪnˈlɪstmənt, ɛn-] *n* : alistamiento *m*, reclutamiento *m*
enliven [ɪnˈlaɪvən, ɛn-] *vt* : animar, alegrar, darle vida a
enmity [ˈɛnmət̬i] *n, pl* **-ties** : enemistad *f*, animadversión *f*
ennoble [ɪˈnoːbəl, ɛ-] *vt* **-bled; -bling** : ennoblecer
ennui [ˌɑnˈwiː] *n* : hastío *m*, tedio *m*, fastidio *m*, aburrimiento *m*
enormity [ɪˈnɔrmət̬i] *n, pl* **-ties 1** ATROCITY : atrocidad *f*, barbaridad *f* **2** IMMENSITY : enormidad *f*, inmensidad *f*
enormous [ɪˈnɔrməs] *adj* : enorme, inmenso, tremendo — **enormously** *adv*
enough[1] [ɪˈnʌf] *adv* **1** : bastante, suficientemente **2 fair enough!** : ¡está bien!, ¡de acuerdo! **3 strangely enough** : por extraño que parezca **4 sure enough** : en efecto, sin duda alguna **5 well enough** : muy bien, bastante bien
enough[2] *adj* : bastante, suficiente ⟨do we have enough chairs? : ¿tenemos suficientes sillas?⟩
enough[3] *pron* : (lo) suficiente, (lo) bastante ⟨enough to eat : lo suficiente para comer⟩ ⟨it's not enough : no basta⟩ ⟨I've had enough! : ¡estoy harto!, ¡está bueno ya!⟩
enquire [ɪnˈkwaɪr, ɛn-] **enquiry** [ˈɪnˌkwaɪri, ˈɛn-, -kwəri; ɪnˈkwaɪri, ɛnˈ-] → **inquire, inquiry**
enrage [ɪnˈreɪʤ, ɛn-] *vt* **-raged; -raging** : enfurecer, encolerizar
enraged [ɪnˈreɪʤd, ɛn-] *adj* : enfurecido, furioso
enrich [ɪnˈrɪtʃ, ɛn-] *vt* : enriquecer
enrichment [ɪnˈrɪtʃmənt, ɛn-] *n* : enriquecimiento *m*
enroll *or* **enrol** [ɪnˈroːl, ɛn-] *v* **-rolled; -rolling** *vt* : matricular, inscribir — *vi* : matricularse, inscribirse
enrollment [ɪnˈroːlmənt, ɛn-] *n* : matrícula *f*, inscripción *f*
en route [ɑˈruːt, ɛnˈraʊt] *adv* : de camino, por el camino
ensconce [ɪnˈskɑnts, ɛn-] *vt* **-sconced; -sconcing** : acomodar, instalar, establecer cómodamente
ensemble [ɑnˈsɑmbəl] *n* : conjunto *m*
enshrine [ɪnˈʃraɪn, ɛn-] *vt* **-shrined; -shrining** : conservar religiosamente, preservar
ensign [ˈɛntsən, ˈɛnˌsaɪn] *n* **1** FLAG : enseña *f*, pabellón *m* **2** : alférez *mf* (de fragata)

enslave [ɪn'sleɪv, ɛn-] *vt* **-slaved; -slaving** : esclavizar

enslavement [ɪn'sleɪvmənt, ɛn-] *n* : esclavización *f*

ensnare [ɪn'snær, ɛn-] *vt* **-snared; -snaring** : atrapar

ensue [ɪn'su:, ɛn-] *vi* **-sued; -suing** : seguir, resultar

ensure [ɪn'ʃʊr, ɛn-] *vt* **-sured; -suring** : asegurar, garantizar

entail [ɪn'teɪl, ɛn-] *vt* : implicar, suponer, conllevar

entangle [ɪn'tæŋgəl, ɛn-] *vt* **-gled; -gling** : enredar

entanglement [ɪn'tæŋgəlmənt, ɛn-] *n* : enredo *m*

enter ['ɛntər] *vt* **1** : entrar en, entrar a **2** BEGIN : entrar en, comenzar, iniciar **3** RECORD : anotar, inscribir, dar entrada a ⟨to enter data : introducir datos⟩ **4** JOIN : entrar en, alistarse en, hacerse socio de — *vi* **1** : entrar **2 to enter into** : entrar en, firmar (un acuerdo), entablar (negociaciones, etc.)

enterprise ['ɛntər,praɪz] *n* **1** UNDERTAKING : empresa *f* **2** BUSINESS : empresa *f*, firma *f* **3** INITIATIVE : iniciativa *f*, empuje *m*

enterprising ['ɛntər,praɪzɪŋ] *adj* : emprendedor

entertain [,ɛntər'teɪn] *vt* **1** : recibir, agasajar ⟨to entertain guests : tener invitados⟩ **2** CONSIDER : considerar, contemplar **3** AMUSE : entretener, divertir

entertainer [,ɛntər'teɪnər] *n* : artista *mf*

entertaining [,ɛntər'teɪnɪŋ] *adj* : entretenido, divertido

entertainment [,ɛntər'teɪnmənt] *n* : entretenimiento *m*, diversión *f*

enthrall *or* **enthral** [ɪn'θrɔl, ɛn-] *vt* **-thralled; -thralling** : cautivar, embelesar

enthuse [ɪn'θuiz, ɛn-] *v* **-thused; -thusing** *vt* **1** EXCITE : entusiasmar **2** : decir con entusiasmo — *vi* **to enthuse over** : hablar con entusiasmo sobre

enthusiasm [ɪn'θu:zi,æzəm, ɛn-, -'θju:-] *n* : entusiasmo *m*

enthusiast [ɪn'θu:zi,æst, ɛn-, -'θju:-, -əst] *n* : entusiasta *mf*; aficionado *m*, -da *f*

enthusiastic [ɪn,θu:zi'æstɪk, ɛn-, -,θju:-] *adj* : entusiasta, aficionado

enthusiastically [ɪn,θu:zi'æstɪkli, ɛn-, -,θju:-] *adv* : con entusiasmo

entice [ɪn'taɪs, ɛn-] *vt* **-ticed; -ticing** : atraer, tentar

enticement [ɪn'taɪsmənt, ɛn-] *n* : tentación *f*, atracción *f*, señuelo *m*

entire [ɪn'taɪr, ɛn-] *adj* : entero, completo

entirely [ɪn'taɪrli, ɛn-] *adv* : completamente, totalmente

entirety [ɪn'taɪrti, ɛn-, -'taɪrəti] *n, pl* **-ties** : totalidad *f*

entitle [ɪn'taɪt̮əl, ɛn-] *vt* **-tled; -tling 1** NAME : titular, intitular **2** : dar derecho a ⟨it entitles you to enter free : le da derecho a entrar gratis⟩ **3 to be entitled to** : tener derecho a

entitlement [ɪn'taɪt̮əlmənt, ɛn-] *n* RIGHT : derecho *m*

entity ['ɛntət̮i] *n, pl* **-ties** : entidad *f*, ente *m*

entomologist [,ɛntə'malədʒɪst] *n* : entomólogo *m*, -ga *f*

entomology [,ɛntə'malədʒi] *n* : entomología *f*

entourage [,antʊ'raʒ] *n* : séquito *m*

entrails ['ɛn,treɪlz, -rəlz] *npl* : entrañas *fpl*, vísceras *fpl*

entrance[1] [ɪn'træn/s, ɛn-] *vt* **-tranced; -trancing** : encantar, embelesar, fascinar

entrance[2] ['ɛntrən/s] *n* **1** ENTERING : entrada *f* ⟨to make an entrance : entrar en escena⟩ **2** ENTRY : entrada *f*, puerta *f* **3** ADMISSION : entrada *f*, ingreso *m* ⟨entrance examination : examen de ingreso⟩

entrant ['ɛntrənt] *n* : candidato *m*, -ta *f* (en un examen); participante *mf* (en un concurso)

entrap [ɪn'træp, ɛn-] *vt* **-trapped; -trapping** : atrapar, entrampar, hacer caer en una trampa

entrapment [ɪn'træpmənt, ɛn-] *n* : captura *f*

entreat [ɪn'tri:t, ɛn-] *vt* : suplicar, rogar

entreaty [ɪn'tri:t̮i, ɛn-] *n, pl* **-treaties** : ruego *m*, súplica *f*

entrée *or* **entree** ['an,treɪ, ,an'-] *n* : plato *m* principal

entrench [ɪn'trɛntʃ, ɛn-] *vt* **1** FORTIFY : atrincherar (una posición militar) **2** : consolidar, afianzar ⟨firmly entrenched in his job : afianzado en su puesto⟩

entrepreneur [,antrəprə'nər, -'njʊr] *n* : empresario *m*, -ria *f*

entrust [ɪn'trʌst, ɛn-] *vt* : confiar, encomendar

entry ['ɛntri] *n, pl* **-tries 1** ENTRANCE : entrada *f* **2** NOTATION : entrada *f*, anotación *f*

entwine [ɪn'twaɪn, ɛn-] *vt* **-twined; -twining** : entrelazar, entretejer, entrecruzar

enumerate [ɪ'nu:mə,reɪt, ɛ-, -'nju:-] *vt* **-ated; -ating 1** LIST : enumerar **2** COUNT : contar, enumerar

enumeration [ɪ,nu:mə'reɪʃən, ɛ-, -,nju:-] *n* : enumeración *f*, lista *f*

enunciate [i'nʌn/si,eɪt, ɛ-] *vt* **-ated; -ating 1** STATE : enunciar, decir **2** PRONOUNCE : articular, pronunciar

enunciation [i,nʌn/si'eɪʃən, ɛ-] *n* **1** STATEMENT : enunciación *f*, declaración *f* **2** ARTICULATION : articulación *f*, pronunciación *f*, dicción *f*

envelop [ɪn'vləp, ɛn-] *vt* : envolver, cubrir

envelope ['ɛnvə,lo:p, 'an-] *n* : sobre *m*

enviable ['ɛnviəbəl] *adj* : envidiable

envious ['ɛnviəs] *adj* : envidioso — **enviously** *adv*

environment [ɪn'vaɪrənmənt, ɛn-, -'vaɪərn-] *n* : medio *m* (ambiente), ambiente *m*, entorno *m*

environmental [ɪn,vaɪrən'mɛntəl, ɛn-, -,vaɪərn-] *adj* : ambiental

environmentalist [ɪn,vaɪrən'mɛntəlɪst, ɛn-, -,vaɪərn-] *n* : ecologista *mf*

environs [ɪn'vaɪrənz, ɛn-, -'vaɪərnz] *npl* : alrededores *mpl*, entorno *m*, inmediaciones *fpl*

envisage [ɪn'vɪzɪdʒ, ɛn-] *vt* **-aged; -aging 1** IMAGINE : imaginarse, concebir **2** FORESEE : prever

envision [ɪn'vɪʒən, ɛn-] *vt* : imaginar

envoy ['ɛn,vɔɪ, 'an-] *n* : enviado *m*, -da *f*

envy¹ ['ɛnvi] *vt* **-vied; -vying** : envidiar

envy² *n, pl* **envies** : envidia *f*

enzyme ['ɛn,zaɪm] *n* : enzima *f*

eon ['iːən, iː,an] → **aeon**

epaulet [,pə'lɛt] *n* : charretera *f*

ephemeral [ɪ'fɛmərəl, -'fiː-] *adj* : efímero, fugaz

epic¹ ['ɛpɪk] *adj* : épico

epic² *n* : poema *m* épico, epopeya *f*

epicure ['ɛpɪ,kjʊr] *n* : epicúreo *m*, -rea *f*; gastrónomo *m*, -ma *f*

epicurean [,ɛpɪkjʊ'riːən, -'kjʊriən] *adj* : epicúreo

epidemic¹ [,ɛpə'dɛmɪk] *adj* : epidémico

epidemic² *n* : epidemia *f*

epidermis [,ɛpə'dərməs] *n* : epidermis *f*

epigram ['ɛpə,græm] *n* : epigrama *m*

epilepsy ['ɛpə,lɛpsi] *n, pl* **-sies** : epilepsia *f*

epileptic¹ [,ɛpə'lɛptɪk] *adj* : epiléptico

epileptic² *n* : epiléptico *m*, -ca *f*

epilogue ['ɛpə,lɔg, -,lag] *n* : epílogo *m*

epiphany [ɪ'pɪfəni] *n, pl* **-nies 1 Epiphany** : Epifanía *f* **2 to have an epiphany** : tener una revelación

episcopal [ɪ'pɪskəpəl] *adj* : episcopal

Episcopalian [ɪ,pɪskə'peɪljən] *n* : episcopalista *mf*; episcopaliano *m*, -na *f*

episode ['ɛpə,soːd] *n* : episodio *m*

episodic [,ɛpə'sadɪk] *adj* : episódico

epistle [ɪ'pɪsəl] *n* : epístola *f*, carta *f*

epitaph ['ɛpə,tæf] *n* : epitafio *m*

epithet ['ɛpə,θɛt, -θət] *n* : epíteto *m*

epitome [ɪ'pɪtəmi] *n* **1** SUMMARY : epítome *m*, resumen *m* **2** EMBODIMENT : personificación *f*

epitomize [ɪ'pɪtə,maɪz] *vt* **-mized; -mizing 1** SUMMARIZE : resumir **2** EMBODY : ser la personificación de, personificar

epoch ['ɛpək, 'ɛ,pak, 'iː,pak] *n* : época *f*, era *f*

epoxy [ɪ'paksi] *n, pl* **epoxies** : resina *f* epoxídica

equable ['ɛkwəbəl, 'iː-] *adj* **1** CALM, STEADY : ecuánime **2** UNIFORM : estable (dícese de la temperatura), constante (dícese del clima), uniforme

equably ['ɛkwəbli, 'iː-] *adv* : con ecuanimidad

equal¹ ['iːkwəl] *vt* **equaled** *or* **equalled; equaling** *or* **equalling 1** : ser igual a

⟨two plus three equals five : dos más tres es igual a cinco⟩ **2** MATCH : igualar

equal² *adj* **1** SAME : igual **2** ADEQUATE : adecuado, capaz

equal³ *n* : igual *mf*

equality [ɪ'kwaləti] *n, pl* **-ties** : igualdad *f*

equalize ['iːkwə,laɪz] *vt* **-ized; -izing** : igualar, equiparar

equally ['iːkwəli] *adv* : igualmente, por igual

equanimity [,iːkwə'nɪməti, ,ɛ-] *n, pl* **-ties** : ecuanimidad *f*

equate [ɪ'kweɪt] *vt* **equated; equating** : equiparar, identificar

equation [ɪ'kweɪʒən] *n* : ecuación *f*

equator [ɪ'kweɪtər] *n* : ecuador *m*

equatorial [,iːkwə'toriəl, ,ɛ-] *adj* : ecuatorial

equestrian¹ [ɪ'kwɛstriən, ɛ-] *adj* : ecuestre

equestrian² *n* : jinete *mf*, caballista *mf*

equilateral [,iːkwə'lætərəl, ,ɛ-] *adj* : equilátero

equilibrium [,iːkwə'lɪbriəm, ,ɛ-] *n, pl* **-riums** *or* **-ria** [-briə] : equilibrio *m*

equine ['iː,kwaɪn, 'ɛ-] *adj* : equino, hípico

equinox ['iːkwə,naks, 'ɛ-] *n* : equinoccio *m*

equip [ɪ'kwɪp] *vt* **equipped; equipping 1** FURNISH : equipar **2** PREPARE : preparar

equipment [ɪ'kwɪpmənt] *n* : equipo *m*

equitable ['ɛkwətəbəl] *adj* : equitativo, justo, imparcial

equity ['ɛkwəti] *n, pl* **-ties 1** FAIRNESS : equidad *f*, imparcialidad *f* **2** VALUE : valor *m* líquido

equivalence [ɪ'kwɪvələnts] *n* : equivalencia *f*

equivalent¹ [ɪ'kwɪvələnt] *adj* : equivalente

equivalent² *n* : equivalente *m*

equivocal [ɪ'kwɪvəkəl] *adj* **1** AMBIGUOUS : equívoco, ambiguo **2** QUESTIONABLE : incierto, dudoso, sospechoso

equivocate [ɪ'kwɪvə,keɪt] *vi* **-cated; -cating** : usar lenguaje equívoco, andarse con evasivas

equivocation [ɪ,kwɪvə'keɪʃən] *n* : evasiva *f*, subterfugio *m*

era ['ɪrə, 'ɛrə, 'iːrə] *n* : era *f*, época *f*

eradicate [ɪ'rædə,keɪt] *vt* **-cated; -cating** : erradicar

erase [ɪ'reɪs] *vt* **erased; erasing** : borrar

eraser [ɪ'reɪsər] *n* : goma *f* de borrar, borrador *m*

erasure [ɪ'reɪʃər] *n* : tachadura *f*

ere¹ ['ɛr] *conj* : antes de que

ere² *prep* **1** : antes de **2 ere long** : dentro de poco

erect¹ [ɪ'rɛkt] *vt* **1** CONSTRUCT : erigir, construir **2** RAISE : levantar **3** ESTABLISH : establecer

erect² *adj* : erguido, derecho, erecto

erection [ɪˈrɛkʃən] *n* **1** : erección *f* (en fisiología) **2** BUILDING : construcción *f*

ergonomics [ˌərɡəˈnɑmɪks] *npl* : ergonomía *f*

ermine [ˈərmən] *n* : armiño *m*

erode [ɪˈroːd] *vt* **eroded; eroding** : erosionar (el suelo), corroer (metales)

erosion [ɪˈroːʒən] *n* : erosión *f*, corrosión *f*

erotic [ɪˈrɑtɪk] *adj* : erótico — **erotically** [-tɪkli] *adv*

eroticism [ɪˈrɑtəˌsɪzəm] *n* : erotismo *m*

err [ˈɛr, ˈər] *vi* : cometer un error, equivocarse, errar

errand [ˈɛrənd] *n* : mandado *m*, encargo *m*, recado *m* *Spain* ⟨an errand of mercy : una misión de caridad⟩

errant [ˈɛrənt] *adj* **1** WANDERING : errante **2** ASTRAY : descarriado

erratic [ɪˈrætɪk] *adj* **1** INCONSISTENT : errático, irregular, inconsistente **2** ECCENTRIC : excéntrico, raro

erratically [ɪˈrætɪkli] *adv* : erráticamente, de manera irregular

erroneous [ɪˈroːniəs, ɛ-] *adj* : erróneo — **erroneously** *adv*

error [ˈɛrər] *n* : error *m*, equivocación *f* ⟨to be in error : estar equivocado⟩

ersatz [ˈɛrˌsɑts, ˈərˌsæts] *adj* : artificial, sustituto

erstwhile [ˈərstˌhwaɪl] *adj* : antiguo

erudite [ˈɛrəˌdaɪt, ˈɛrjʊ-] *adj* : erudito, letrado

erudition [ˌɛrəˈdɪʃən, ˌɛrjʊ-] *n* : erudición *f*

erupt [ɪˈrʌpt] *vi* **1** : hacer erupción (dícese de un volcán o un sarpullido) **2** : estallar (dícese de la cólera o de la violencia)

eruption [ɪˈrʌpʃən] *n* : erupción *f*, estallido *m*

eruptive [ɪˈrʌptɪv] *adj* : eruptivo

escalate [ˈɛskəˌleɪt] *v* **-lated; -lating** *vt* : intensificar (un conflicto), aumentar (precios) — *vi* : intensificarse, aumentarse

escalation [ˌɛskəˈleɪʃən] *n* : intensificación *f*, escalada *f*, aumento *m*, subida *f*

escalator [ˈɛskəˌleɪtər] *n* : escalera *f* mecánica

escapade [ˈɛskəˌpeɪd] *n* : aventura *f*

escape[1] [ɪˈskeɪp, ɛ-] *v* **-caped; -caping** *vt* : escaparse de, librarse de, evitar — *vi* : escaparse, fugarse, huir

escape[2] *n* **1** FLIGHT : fuga *f*, huida *f*, escapada *f* **2** LEAKAGE : escape *m*, fuga *f* **3** : escapatoria *f*, evasión *f* ⟨to have no escape : no tener escapatoria⟩ ⟨escape from reality : evasión de la realidad⟩

escapee [ɪˌskeɪˈpiː, ˌɛ-] *n* : fugitivo *m*, -va *f*

escarole [ˈɛskəˌroːl] *n* : escarola *f*

escarpment [ɪsˈkɑrpmənt, ɛs-] *n* : escarpa *f*, escarpadura *f*

eschew [ɛˈʃuː, ɪsˈtʃuː] *vt* : evitar, rehuir, abstenerse de

escort[1] [ɪˈskɔrt, ɛ-] *vt* **1** : escoltar ⟨to escort a ship : escoltar un barco⟩ **2** ACCOMPANY : acompañar

escort[2] [ˈɛsˌkɔrt] *n* **1** : escolta *f* ⟨armed escort : escolta armada⟩ **2** COMPANION : acompañante *mf*; compañero *m*, -ra *f*

escrow [ˈɛsˌkroː] *n* **in escrow** : en depósito, en custodia de un tercero

Eskimo [ˈɛskəˌmoː] *n* **1** : esquimal *mf* **2** : esquimal *m* (idioma) — **Eskimo** *adj*

esophagus [ɪˈsɑfəɡəs, iː-] *n*, *pl* **-gi** [-ˌɡaɪ, -ˌdʒaɪ] : esófago *m*

esoteric [ˌɛsəˈtɛrɪk] *adj* : esotérico, hermético

especially [ɪˈspɛʃəli] *adv* : especialmente, particularmente

espionage [ˈɛspiəˌnɑʒ, -ˌnɑdʒ] *n* : espionaje *m*

espouse [ɪˈspaʊz, ɛ-] *vt* **espoused; espousing** **1** MARRY : casarse con **2** ADOPT, ADVOCATE : apoyar, adherirse a, adoptar

espresso [ɛˈsprɛˌsoː] *n*, *pl* **-sos** : café *m* exprés

essay[1] [ˈɛseɪ, ˈɛˌseɪ] *vt* : intentar, tratar

essay[2] [ˈɛˌseɪ] *n* **1** COMPOSITION : ensayo *m*, trabajo *m* **2** ATTEMPT : intento *m*

essayist [ˈɛˌseɪɪst] *n* : ensayista *mf*

essence [ˈɛsənts] *n* **1** CORE : esencia *f*, núcleo *m*, meollo *m* ⟨in essence : esencialmente⟩ **2** EXTRACT : esencia *f*, extracto *m* **3** PERFUME : esencia *f*, perfume *m*

essential[1] [ɪˈsɛntʃəl] *adj* : esencial, imprescindible, fundamental — **essentially** *adv*

essential[2] *n* : elemento *m* esencial, lo imprescindible

establish [ɪˈstæblɪʃ, ɛ-] *vt* **1** FOUND : establecer, fundar **2** SET UP : establecer, instaurar, instituir **3** PROVE : demostrar, probar

establishment [ɪˈstæblɪʃmənt, ɛ-] *n* **1** ESTABLISHING : establecimiento *m*, fundación *f*, instauración *f* **2** BUSINESS : negocio *m*, establecimiento *m* **3 the Establishment** : la clase dirigente

estate [ɪˈsteɪt, ɛ-] *n* **1** POSSESSIONS : bienes *mpl*, propiedad *f*, patrimonio *m* **2** PROPERTY : hacienda *f*, finca *f*, propiedad *f*

esteem[1] [ɪˈstiːm, ɛ-] *vt* : estimar, apreciar

esteem[2] *n* : estima *f*, aprecio *m*

ester [ˈɛstər] *n* : éster *m*

esthetic [ɛsˈθɛtɪk] → **aesthetic**

estimable [ˈɛstəməbəl] *adj* : estimable

estimate[1] [ˈɛstəˌmeɪt] *vt* **-mated; -mating** : calcular, estimar

estimate[2] [ˈɛstəmət] *n* **1** : cálculo *m* aproximado ⟨to make an estimate : hacer un cálculo⟩ **2** ASSESSMENT : valoración *f*, estimación *f*

estimation [ˌɛstəˈmeɪʃən] *n* **1** JUDGMENT : juicio *m*, opinión *f* ⟨in my estimation : en mi opinión, según mis cálculos⟩ **2** ESTEEM : estima *f*, aprecio *m*

estimator ['ɛstə,meɪt̬ər] *n* : tasador *m*, -dora *f*

Estonian [ɛ'stoːniən] *n* : estonio *m*, -nia *f* — **Estonian** *adj*

estrange [ɪ'streɪndʒ, ɛ-] *vt* **-tranged; -tranging** : enajenar, apartar, alejar

estrangement [ɪ'streɪndʒmənt, ɛ-] *n* : alejamiento *m*, distanciamiento *m*

estrogen ['ɛstrədʒən] *n* : estrógeno *m*

estrus ['ɛstrəs] *n* : celo *m*

estuary ['ɛstʃu,wɛri] *n, pl* **-aries** : estuario *m*, -ría *f*

et cetera [ɛt'sɛt̬ərə, -'sɛtrə] : etcétera

etch ['ɛtʃ] *v* : grabar al aguafuerte

etching ['ɛtʃɪŋ] *n* : aguafuerte *m*, grabado *m* al aguafuerte

eternal [ɪ'tərnəl, iː-] *adj* **1** EVERLASTING : eterno **2** INTERMINABLE : constante, incesante

eternally [ɪ'tərnəli, iː-] *adv* : eternamente, para siempre

eternity [ɪ'tərnət̬i, iː-] *n, pl* **-ties** : eternidad *f*

ethane ['ɛ,θeɪn] *n* : etano *m*

ethanol ['ɛθə,nɔl, -,noːl] *n* : etanol *m*

ether ['iːθər] *n* : éter *m*

ethereal [ɪ'θɪriəl, iː-] *adj* **1** CELESTIAL : etéreo, celeste **2** DELICATE : delicado

ethical ['ɛθɪkəl] *adj* : ético — **ethically** *adv*

ethics ['ɛθɪks] *ns & pl* **1** : ética *f* **2** MORALITY : ética *f*, moral *f*, moralidad *f*

Ethiopian [,iːθi'oːpiən] *n* : etíope *mf* — **Ethiopian** *adj*

ethnic ['ɛθnɪk] *adj* : étnico

ethnologist [ɛθ'nɑlədʒɪst] *n* : etnólogo *m*, -ga *f*

ethnology [ɛθ'nɑlədʒi] *n* : etnología *f*

etiquette ['ɛt̬ɪkət, -,kɛt] *n* : etiqueta *f*, protocolo *m*

etymological [,ɛt̬əmə'lɑdʒɪkəl] *adj* : etimológico

etymology [,ɛt̬ə'mɑlədʒi] *n, pl* **-gies** : etimología *f*

eucalyptus [,juːkə'lɪptəs] *n, pl* **-ti** [-,taɪ] *or* **-tuses** [-təsəz] : eucalipto *m*

Eucharist ['juːkərɪst] *n* : Eucaristía *f*

eulogize ['juːlə,dʒaɪz] *vt* **-gized; -gizing** : elogiar, encomiar

eulogy ['juːlədʒi] *n, pl* **-gies** : elogio *m*, encomio *m*, panegírico *m*

eunuch ['juːnək] *n* : eunuco *m*

euphemism ['juːfə,mɪzəm] *n* : eufemismo *m*

euphemistic [,juːfə'mɪstɪk] *adj* : eufemístico

euphony ['juːfəni] *n, pl* **-nies** : eufonía *f*

euphoria [jʊ'foriə] *n* : euforia *f*

euphoric [jʊ'forɪk] *adj* : eufórico

European [,jʊrə'piːən] *n* : europeo *m*, europea *f* — **European** *adj*

euthanasia [,juːθə'neɪʒə, -ʒiə] *n* : eutanasia *f*

evacuate [ɪ'vækju,eɪt] *v* **-ated; -ating** *vt* VACATE : evacuar, desalojar — *vi* WITHDRAW : retirarse

evacuation [ɪ,vækjʊ'eɪʃən] *n* : evacuación *f*, desalojo *m*

evade [ɪ'veɪd] *vt* **evaded; evading** : evadir, eludir, esquivar

evaluate [ɪ'vælju,eɪt] *vt* **-ated; -ating** : evaluar, valorar, tasar

evaluation [ɪ,vælju'eɪʃən] *n* : evaluación *f*, valoración *f*, tasación *f*

evangelical [,iː,væn'dʒɛlɪkəl, ,ɛvən-] *adj* : evangélico

evangelist [ɪ'vændʒəlɪst] *n* **1** : evangelista *m* **2** PREACHER : predicador *m*, -dora *f*

evaporate [ɪ'væpə,reɪt] *vi* **-rated; -rating 1** VAPORIZE : evaporarse **2** VANISH : evaporarse, desvanecerse, esfumarse

evaporation [ɪ,væpə'reɪʃən] *n* : evaporación *f*

evasion [ɪ'veɪʒən] *n* : evasión *f*

evasive [ɪ'veɪsɪv] *adj* : evasivo

evasiveness [ɪ'veɪsɪvnəs] *n* : carácter *m* evasivo

eve ['iːv] *n* **1** : víspera *f* ⟨on the eve of the festivities : en vísperas de las festividades⟩ **2** → **evening**

even[1] ['iːvən] *vt* **1** LEVEL : allanar, nivelar, emparejar **2** EQUALIZE : igualar, equilibrar — *vi* **to even out** : nivelarse, emparejarse

even[2] *adv* **1** : hasta, incluso ⟨even a child can do it : hasta un niño puede hacerlo⟩ ⟨he looked content, even happy : se le veía satisfecho, incluso feliz⟩ **2** (*in negative constructions*) : ni siquiera ⟨he didn't even try : ni siquiera lo intentó⟩ **3** (*in comparisons*) : aún, todavía ⟨even better : aún mejor, todavía mejor⟩ **4 even if** : aunque **5 even so** : aun así **6 even though** : aun cuando, a pesar de que

even[3] *adj* **1** SMOOTH : uniforme, liso, parejo **2** FLAT : plano, llano **3** EQUAL : igual, igualado ⟨an even score : un marcador igualado⟩ **4** REGULAR : regular, constante ⟨an even pace : un ritmo constante⟩ **5** EXACT : exacto, justo **6 :** par ⟨even number : número par⟩ **7 to be even** : estar en paz, estar a mano **8 to get even** : desquitarse, vengarse

evening ['iːvnɪŋ] *n* : tarde *f*, noche *f* ⟨in the evening : por la noche⟩

evenly ['iːvənli] *adv* **1** UNIFORMLY : de modo uniforme, de manera constante **2** FAIRLY : igualmente, equitativamente

evenness ['iːvənnəs] *n* : uniformidad *f*, igualdad *f*, regularidad *f*

event [ɪ'vɛnt] *n* **1** : acontecimiento *m*, suceso *m*, prueba *f* (en deportes) **2 in the event that** : en caso de que

eventful [ɪ'vɛntfəl] *adj* : lleno de incidentes, memorable

eventual [ɪ'vɛntʃʊəl] *adj* : final, consiguiente

eventuality [ɪ,vɛntʃʊ'æləti] *n, pl* **-ties** : eventualidad *f*

eventually [ɪ'vɛntʃʊəli] *adv* : al fin, con el tiempo, algún día

ever ['ɛvər] *adv* **1** ALWAYS : siempre ⟨as ever : como siempre⟩ ⟨ever since : desde entonces⟩ **2** (*in questions*) : alguna vez, algún día ⟨have you ever been to Mexico? : ¿has estado en México alguna vez?⟩ **3** (*in negative constructions*) : nunca ⟨doesn't he ever work? : ¿es que nunca trabaja?⟩ ⟨nobody ever helps me : nadie nunca me ayuda⟩ **4** (*in comparisons*) : nunca ⟨better than ever : mejor que nunca⟩ **5** (*as intensifier*) ⟨I'm ever so happy! : ¡estoy tan y tan feliz!⟩ ⟨he looks ever so angry : parece estar muy enojado⟩

evergreen¹ ['ɛvər,gri:n] *adj* : de hoja perenne

evergreen² *n* : planta *f* de hoja perenne

everlasting [,ɛvər'læstɪŋ] *adj* : eterno, perpetuo, imperecedero

evermore [,ɛvər'mor] *adv* : eternamente

every ['ɛvri] *adj* **1** EACH : cada ⟨every time : cada vez⟩ ⟨every other house : cada dos casas⟩ **2** ALL : todo ⟨every month : todos los meses⟩ ⟨every woman : toda mujer, todas las mujeres⟩ **3** COMPLETE : pleno, entero ⟨to have every confidence : tener plena confianza⟩

everybody ['ɛvri,bʌdi, -,bɑ-] *pron* : todos *mpl*, -das *fpl*; todo el mundo

everyday [,ɛvri'deɪ, 'ɛvri,-] *adj* : cotidiano, diario, corriente ⟨everyday clothes : ropa de todos los días⟩

everyone ['ɛvri,wʌn] → **everybody**

everything ['ɛvri,θɪŋ] *pron* : todo

everywhere ['ɛvri,ʍɛr] *adv* : en todas partes, por todas partes, dondequiera ⟨I looked everywhere : busqué en todas partes⟩ ⟨everywhere we go : dondequiera que vayamos⟩

evict [ɪ'vɪkt] *vt* : desalojar, desahuciar

eviction [ɪ'vɪkʃən] *n* : desalojo *m*, desahucio *m*

evidence ['ɛvədənts] *n* **1** INDICATION : indicio *m*, señal *m* ⟨to be in evidence : estar a la vista⟩ **2** PROOF : evidencia *f*, prueba *f* **3** TESTIMONY : testimonio *m*, declaración *f* ⟨to give evidence : declarar como testigo, prestar declaración⟩

evident ['ɛvidənt] *adj* : evidente, patente, manifiesto

evidently ['ɛvidəntli, ,ɛvi'dɛntli] *adv* **1** CLEARLY : claramente, obviamente **2** APPARENTLY : aparentemente, evidentemente, al parecer

evil¹ ['i:vəl, -vɪl] *adj* **eviler** *or* **eviller**; **evilest** *or* **evillest** **1** WICKED : malvado, malo, maligno **2** HARMFUL : nocivo, dañino, pernicioso **3** UNPLEASANT : desagradable ⟨an evil odor : un olor horrible⟩

evil² *n* **1** WICKEDNESS : mal *m*, maldad *f* **2** MISFORTUNE : desgracia *f*, mal *m*

evildoer [,i:vəl'du:ər, ,i:vɪl-] *n* : malvado *m*, -da *f*

evince [ɪ'vɪnts] *vt* **evinced**; **evincing** : mostrar, manifestar, revelar

eviscerate [ɪ'vɪsə,reɪt] *vt* **-ated**; **-ating** : eviscerar, destripar (un pollo, etc.)

evocation [,i:vo'keɪʃən, ,ɛ-] *n* : evocación *f*

evocative [i'vɑkətɪv] *adj* : evocador

evoke [i'vo:k] *vt* **evoked**; **evoking** : evocar, provocar

evolution [,ɛvə'lu:ʃən, ,i:-] *n* : evolución *f*, desarrollo *m*

evolutionary [,ɛvə'lu:ʃə,nɛri, ,i:-] *adj* : evolutivo

evolve [i'vɑlv] *vi* **evolved**; **evolving** : evolucionar, desarrollarse

ewe ['ju:] *n* : oveja *f*

exacerbate [ɪg'zæsər,beɪt] *vt* **-bated**; **-bating** : exacerbar

exact¹ [ɪg'zækt, ɛ-] *vt* : exigir, imponer, arrancar

exact² *adj* : exacto, preciso — **exactly** *adv*

exacting [ɪ'zæktɪŋ, ɛg-] *adj* : exigente, riguroso

exactitude [ɪg'zæktə,tu:d, ɛg-, -,tju:d] *n* : exactitud *f*, precisión *f*

exaggerate [ɪg'zædʒə,reɪt, ɛg-] *v* **-ated**; **-ating** : exagerar

exaggerated [ɪg'zædʒə,reɪtəd, ɛg-] *adj* : exagerado — **exaggeratedly** *adv*

exaggeration [ɪg,zædʒə'reɪʃən, ɛg-] *n* : exageración *f*

exalt [ɪg'zɔlt, ɛg-] *vt* : exaltar, ensalzar, glorificar

exaltation [,ɛg,zɔl'teɪʃən, ,ɛk,sɔl-] *n* : exaltación *f*

exam [ɪg'zæm, ɛg-] → **examination**

examination [ɪg,zæmə'neɪʃən, ɛg-] *n* **1** TEST : examen *m* **2** INSPECTION : inspección *f*, revisión *f* **3** INVESTIGATION : examen *m*, estudio *m*

examine [ɪg'zæmən, ɛg-] *vt* **-ined**; **-ining** **1** TEST : examinar **2** INSPECT : inspeccionar, revisar **3** STUDY : examinar

example [ɪg'zæmpəl, ɛg-] *n* : ejemplo *m* ⟨for example : por ejemplo⟩ ⟨to set an example : dar ejemplo⟩

exasperate [ɪg'zæspə,reɪt, ɛg-] *vt* **-ated**; **-ating** : exasperar, sacar de quicio

exasperation [ɪg,zæspə'reɪʃən, ɛg-] *n* : exasperación *f*

excavate ['ɛkskə,veɪt] *vt* **-vated**; **-vating** : excavar

excavation [,ɛkskə'veɪʃən] *n* : excavación *f*

exceed [ɪk'si:d, ɛk-] *vt* **1** SURPASS : exceder, rebasar, sobrepasar **2** : exceder de, sobrepasar ⟨not exceeding two months : que no exceda de dos meses⟩

exceedingly [ɪk'si:dɪŋli, ɛk-] *adv* : extremadamente, sumamente

excel [ɪk'sɛl, ɛk-] *v* **-celled**; **-celling** *vi* : sobresalir, descollar, lucirse — *vt* : superar

excellence ['ɛksələnts] *n* : excelencia *f*

excellency ['ɛksələntsi] *n*, *pl* **-cies** : excelencia *f* ⟨His Excellency : Su Excelencia⟩

excellent ['ɛksələnt] *adj* : excelente, sobresaliente — **excellently** *adv*

except¹ [ɪkˈsɛpt] *vt* : exceptuar, excluir
except² *conj* : pero, si no fuera por
except³ *prep* : excepto, menos, salvo ⟨everyone except Carlos : todos menos Carlos⟩
exception [ɪkˈsɛpʃən] *n* 1 : excepción *f* 2 **to take exception to** : ofenderse por, objetar a
exceptional [ɪkˈsɛpʃənəl] *adj* : excepcional, extraordinario — **exceptionally** *adv*
excerpt¹ [ɛkˈsɔrpt, ɛgˈzɔrpt, ˈɛk₁-, ˈg₁-] *vt* : escoger, seleccionar
excerpt² [ˈɛk₁sɔrpt, ˈɛg₁zɔrpt] *n* : pasaje *m*, selección *f*
excess¹ [ˈɛk₁sɛs, ɪkˈsɛs] *adj* 1 : excesivo, de sobra 2 **excess baggage** : exceso *m* de equipaje
excess² [ɪkˈsɛs, ˈɛk₁sɛs] *n* 1 SUPERFLUITY : exceso *m*, superfluidad *f* ⟨an excess of energy : un exceso de energía⟩ 2 SURPLUS : excedente *m*, sobrante *m* ⟨in excess of : superior a⟩
excessive [ɪkˈsɛsɪv, ɛk-] *adj* : excesivo, exagerado, desmesurado — **excessively** *adv*
exchange¹ [ɪksˈtʃeɪndʒ, ɛks-; ˈɛks₁tʃeɪndʒ] *vt* -**changed; -changing** : cambiar, intercambiar, canjear
exchange² *n* 1 : cambio *m*, intercambio *m*, canje *m* 2 **stock exchange** : bolsa *f* (de valores)
exchangeable [ɪksˈtʃeɪndʒəbəl, ɛks-] *adj* : canjeable
excise¹ [ɪkˈsaɪz, ɛk-] *vt* -**cised; -cising** : extirpar
excise² [ˈɛk₁saɪz] *n* **excise tax** : impuesto *m* interno, impuesto *m* sobre el consumo
excision [ɪkˈsɪʒən, ɛk-] *n* : extirpación *f*, excisión *f*
excitability [ɪk₁saɪtəˈbɪləti, ɛk-] *n* : excitabilidad *f*
excitable [ɪkˈsaɪtəbəl, ɛk-] *adj* : excitable
excitation [₁ɛk₁saɪˈteɪʃən] *n* : excitación *f*
excite [ɪkˈsaɪt, ɛk-] *vt* -**cited; -citing** 1 AROUSE, STIMULATE : excitar, mover, estimular 2 ANIMATE : entusiasmar, animar 3 EVOKE, PROVOKE : provocar, despertar, suscitar ⟨to excite curiosity : despertar la curiosidad⟩
excited [ɪkˈsaɪtəd, ɛk-] *adj* 1 STIMULATED : excitado, estimulado 2 ENTHUSIASTIC : entusiasmado, emocionado
excitedly [ɪkˈsaɪtədli, ɛk-] *adv* : con excitación, con entusiasmo
excitement [ɪkˈsaɪtmənt, ɛk-] *n* 1 ENTHUSIASM : entusiasmo *m*, emoción *f* 2 AGITATION : agitación *f*, alboroto *m*, conmoción *f* 3 AROUSAL : excitación *f*
exciting [ɪkˈsaɪtɪŋ, ɛk-] *adj* 1 : emocionante 2 AROUSING : excitante
exclaim [ɪksˈkleɪm, ɛk-] *v* : exclamar
exclamation [₁ɛkskləˈmeɪʃən] *n* : exclamación *f*
exclamation point *n* : signo *m* de admiración

exclamatory [ɪksˈklæmə₁tori, ɛks-] *adj* : exclamativo
exclude [ɪksˈkluːd, ɛks-] *vt* -**cluded; -cluding** 1 BAR : excluir, descartar, no admitir 2 EXPEL : expeler, expulsar
exclusion [ɪksˈkluːʒən, ɛks-] *n* : exclusión *f*
exclusive¹ [ɪksˈkluːsɪv, ɛks-] *adj* 1 SOLE : exclusivo, único 2 SELECT : exclusivo, selecto
exclusive² *n* : exclusiva *f*
exclusively [ɪksˈkluːsɪvli, ɛks-] *adv* : exclusivamente, únicamente
exclusiveness [ɪksˈkluːsɪvnəs, ɛks-] *n* : exclusividad *f*
excommunicate [₁ɛkskəˈmjuːnə₁keɪt] *vt* -**cated; -cating** : excomulgar
excommunication [₁ɛkskə₁mjuːnəˈkeɪʃən] *n* : excomunión *f*
excrement [ˈɛkskrəmənt] *n* : excremento *m*
excrete [ɪkˈskriːt, ɛk-] *vt* -**creted; -creting** : excretar
excretion [ɪkˈskriːʃən, ɛk-] *n* : excreción *f*
excruciating [ɪkˈskruːʃi₁eɪtɪŋ, ɛk-] *adj* : insoportable, atroz, terrible — **excruciatingly** *adv*
exculpate [ˈɛkskəl₁peɪt] *vt* -**pated; -pating** : exculpar
excursion [ɪkˈskərʒən, ɛk-] *n* 1 OUTING : excursión *f*, paseo *m* 2 DIGRESSION : digresión *f*
excuse¹ [ɪkˈskjuːz, ɛk-] *vt* -**cused; -cusing** 1 PARDON : disculpar, perdonar ⟨excuse me : con permiso, perdóneme, perdón⟩ 2 EXEMPT : eximir, disculpar 3 JUSTIFY : excusar, justificar
excuse² [ɪkˈskjuːs, ɛk-] *n* 1 JUSTIFICATION : excusa *f*, justificación *f* 2 PRETEXT : pretexto *m* 3 **to make one's excuses to someone** : pedirle disculpas a alguien
execute [ˈɛksɪ₁kjuːt] *vt* -**cuted; -cuting** 1 CARRY OUT : ejecutar, llevar a cabo, desempeñar 2 ENFORCE : ejecutar, cumplir (un testamento, etc.) 3 KILL : ejecutar, ajusticiar
execution [₁ɛksɪˈkjuːʃən] *n* 1 PERFORMANCE : ejecución *f*, desempeño *m* 2 IMPLEMENTATION : cumplimiento *m* 3 : ejecución *f* (por un delito)
executioner [₁ɛksɪˈkjuːʃənər] *n* : verdugo *m*
executive¹ [ɪgˈzɛkjət ɪv, ɛg-] *adj* : ejecutivo
executive² *n* : ejecutivo *m*, -va *f*
executor [ɪgˈzɛkjətər, ɛg-] *n* : albacea *m*, testamentario *m*
executrix [ɪgˈzɛkjə₁trɪks, ɛg-] *n, pl* **executrices** [-₁zɛkjəˈtraɪ₁siːz] *or* **executrixes** [-ˈzɛkjə₁trɪksəz] : albacea *f*, testamentaria *f*
exemplary [ɪgˈzɛmpləri, ɛg-] *adj* : ejemplar
exemplify [ɪgˈzɛmplə₁faɪ, ɛg-] *vt* -**fied; -fying** : ejemplificar, ilustrar, demostrar

exempt[1] [ɪg'zɛmpt, ɛg-] *vt* : eximir, dispensar, exonerar

exempt[2] *adj* : exento, eximido

exemption [ɪg'zɛmpʃən, ɛg-] *n* : exención *f*

exercise[1] ['ɛksər,saɪz] *v* **-cised; -cising** *vt* **1** : ejercitar (el cuerpo) **2** USE : ejercer, hacer uso de — *vi* : hacer ejercicio

exercise[2] *n* **1** : ejercicio *m* **2 exercises** *npl* WORKOUT : ejercicios *mpl* físicos **3 exercises** *npl* CEREMONY : ceremonia *f*

exert [ɪg'zərt, ɛg-] *vt* **1** : ejercer, emplear **2 to exert oneself** : esforzarse

exertion [ɪg'zərʃən, ɛg-] *n* **1** USE : ejercicio *m* (de autoridad, etc.), uso *m* (de fuerza, etc.) **2** EFFORT : esfuerzo *m*, empeño *m*

exhalation [,ɛksə'leɪʃən, ,ɛkshə-] *n* : exhalación *f*, espiración *f*

exhale [ɛks'heɪl] *v* **-haled; -haling** *vt* **1** : exhalar, espirar **2** EMIT : exhalar, despedir, emitir — *vi* : espirar

exhaust[1] [ɪg'zɔst, ɛg-] *vt* **1** DEPLETE : agotar **2** TIRE : cansar, fatigar, agotar **3** EMPTY : vaciar

exhaust[2] *n* **1 exhaust fumes** : gases *mpl* de escape **2 exhaust pipe** : tubo *m* de escape **3 exhaust system** : sistema *m* de escape

exhausted [ɪg'zɔstəd, ɛg-] *adj* : agotado, derrengado

exhausting [ɪg'zɔstɪŋ, ɛg-] *adj* : extenuante, agotador

exhaustion [ɪg'zɔstʃən, ɛg-] *n* : agotamiento *m*

exhaustive [ɪg'zɔstɪv, ɛg-] *adj* : exhaustivo

exhibit[1] [ɪg'zɪbət, ɛg-] *vt* **1** DISPLAY : exhibir, exponer **2** PRODUCE, SHOW : mostrar, presentar

exhibit[2] *n* **1** OBJECT : objeto *m* expuesto **2** EXHIBITION : exposición *f*, exhibición *f* **3** EVIDENCE : prueba *f* instrumental

exhibition [,ɛksə'bɪʃən] *n* **1** : exposición *f*, exhibición *f* **2 to make an exhibition of oneself** : dar el espectáculo, hacer el ridículo

exhibitor [ɪg'zɪbətər] *n* : expositor *m*, -tora *f*

exhilarate [ɪg'zɪlə,reɪt, ɛg-] *vt* **-rated; -rating** : alegrar, levantar el ánimo de

exhilaration [ɪg,zɪlə'reɪʃən, ɛg-] *n* : alegría *f*, regocijo *m*, júbilo *m*

exhort [ɪg'zɔrt, ɛg-] *vt* : exhortar

exhortation [,ɛk,sɔr'teɪʃən, -sər-; ,ɛg-,zɔr-] *n* : exhortación *f*

exhumation [,ɛksju'meɪʃən, -hju-; ,ɛgzu-, -zju-] *n* : exhumación *f*

exhume [ɪg'zu:m, -'zju:m; ɪks'ju:m, -'hju:m] *vt* **-humed; -huming** : exhumar, desenterrar

exigencies ['ɛksɪdʒəntsiz, ɪg'zɪdʒən,si:z] *npl* : exigencias *fpl*

exile[1] ['ɛg,zaɪl, 'ɛk,saɪl] *vt* **exiled; exiling** : exiliar, desterrar

exile[2] *n* **1** BANISHMENT : exilio *m*, destierro *m* **2** OUTCAST : exiliado *m*, -da *f*; desterrado *m*, -da *f*

exist [ɪg'zɪst, ɛg-] *vi* **1** BE : existir **2** LIVE : subsistir, vivir

existence [ɪg'zɪstənts, ɛg-] *n* : existencia *f*

existent [ɪg'zɪstənt, ɛg-] *adj* : existente

existing [ɪg'zɪstɪŋ] *adj* : existente

exit[1] ['ɛgzət, 'ɛksət] *vi* : salir, hacer mutis (en el teatro) — *vt* : salir de

exit[2] *n* **1** DEPARTURE : salida *f*, partida *f* **2** EGRESS : salida *f* ⟨emergency exit : salida de emergencia⟩

exodus ['ɛksədəs] *n* : éxodo *m*

exonerate [ɪg'zɑnə,reɪt, ɛg-] *vt* **-ated; -ating** : exonerar, disculpar, absolver

exoneration [ɪg,zɑnə'reɪʃən, ɛg-] *n* : exoneración *f*

exorbitant [ɪg'zɔrbətənt, ɛg-] *adj* : exorbitante, excesivo

exorcise ['ɛk,sɔr,saɪz, -sər-] *vt* **-cised; -cising** : exorcizar

exorcism ['ɛksər,sɪzəm] *n* : exorcismo *m*

exotic[1] [ɪg'zɑtɪk, ɛg-] *adj* : exótico — **exotically** [-ɪkli] *adv*

exotic[2] *n* : planta *f* exótica

expand [ɪk'spænd, ɛk-] *vt* **1** ENLARGE : expandir, dilatar, aumentar, ampliar **2** EXTEND : extender — *vi* **1** ENLARGE : ampliarse, extenderse **2** : expandirse, dilatarse (dícese de los metales, gases, etc.)

expanse [ɪk'spænts, ɛk-] *n* : extensión *f*

expansion [ɪk'spænʃən, ɛk-] *n* **1** ENLARGEMENT : expansión *f*, ampliación *f* **2** EXPANSE : extensión *f*

expansive [ɪk'spæntsɪv, ɛk-] *adj* **1** : expansivo **2** OUTGOING : expansivo, comunicativo **3** AMPLE : ancho, amplio — **expansively** *adv*

expansiveness [ɪk'spæntsɪvnəs, ɛk-] *n* : expansibilidad *f*

expatriate[1] [ɛks'peɪtri,eɪt] *vt* **-ated; -ating** : expatriar

expatriate[2] [ɛks'peɪtriət, -,eɪt] *adj* : expatriado

expatriate[3] [ɛks'peɪtriət, -,eɪt] *n* : expatriado *m*, -da *f*

expect [ɪk'spkt, ɛk-] *vt* **1** SUPPOSE : suponer, imaginarse **2** ANTICIPATE : esperar **3** COUNT ON, REQUIRE : contar con, esperar — *vi* **to be expecting** : estar embarazada

expectancy [ɪk'spɛktəntsi, ɛk-] *n, pl* **-cies** : expectativa *f*, esperanza *f*

expectant [ɪk'spɛktənt, ɛk-] *adj* **1** ANTICIPATING : expectante **2** EXPECTING : futuro ⟨expectant mother : futura madre⟩

expectantly [ɪk'spɛktəntli, ɛk-] *adv* : con expectación

expectation [,ɛk,spɛk'teɪʃən] *n* **1** ANTICIPATION : expectación *f* **2** EXPECTANCY : expectativa *f*

expedient[1] [ɪk'spi:diənt, ɛk-] *adj* : conveniente, oportuno

expedient[2] *n* : expediente *m*, recurso *m*

expedite ['ɛkspə,daɪt] *vt* **-dited; -diting** **1** FACILITATE : facilitar, dar curso a **2** HASTEN : acelerar

expedition [,ɛkspə'dɪʃən] *n* : expedición *f*

expeditious [,ɛkspə'dɪʃəs] *adj* : pronto, rápido

expel [ɪk'spɛl, ɛk-] *vt* **-pelled; -pelling** : expulsar, expeler

expend [ɪk'spɛnd, ɛk-] *vt* **1** DISBURSE : gastar, desembolsar **2** CONSUME : consumir, agotar

expendable [ɪk'spɛndəbəl, ɛk-] *adj* : prescindible

expenditure [ɪk'spɛndɪtʃər, ɛk-, -,tʃʊr] *n* : gasto *m*

expense [ɪk'spɛnts, ɛk-] *n* **1** COST : gasto *m* **2 expenses** *npl* : gastos *mpl*, expensas *fpl* **3 at the expense of** : a expensas de

expensive [ɪk'spɛntsɪv, ɛk-] *adj* : costoso, caro — **expensively** *adv*

experience[1] [ɪk'spɪriənts, ɛk-] *vt* **-enced; -encing** : experimentar (sentimientos), tener (dificultades), sufrir (una pérdida)

experience[2] *n* : experiencia *f*

experienced [ɪk'spɪriəntst, ɛk-] *adj* : con experiencia, experimentado

experiment[1] [ɪk'spɛrəmənt, ɛk-, -'spɪr-] *vi* : experimentar, hacer experimentos

experiment[2] *n* : experimento *m*

experimental [ɪk,spɛrə'mɛntəl, ɛk-, -,spɪr-] *adj* : experimental — **experimentally** *adv*

experimentation [ɪk,spɛrəmən'teɪʃən, ɛk-, -,spɪr-] *n* : experimentación *f*

expert[1] ['ɛk,spərt, ɪk'spərt] *adj* : experto, de experto, pericial (dícese de un testigo) — **expertly** *adv*

expert[2] ['ɛk,spərt] *n* : experto *m*, -ta *f*; perito *m*, -ta *f*; especialista *mf*

expertise [,ɛkspər'ti:z] *n* : pericia *f*, competencia *f*

expiate ['ɛkspi,eɪt] *vt* **-ated; -ating** : expiar

expiation [,ɛkspi'eɪʃən] *n* : expiación *f*

expiration [,ɛkspə'reɪʃən] *n* **1** EXHALATION : exhalación *f*, espiración *f* **2** DEATH : muerte *f* **3** TERMINATION : vencimiento *m*, caducidad *f*

expire [ɪk'spaɪr, ɛk-] *vi* **-pired; -piring 1** EXHALE : espirar **2** DIE : expirar, morir **3** TERMINATE : caducar, vencer

explain [ɪk'spleɪn, ɛk-] *vt* : explicar

explanation [,ɛksplə'neɪʃən] *n* : explicación *f*

explanatory [ɪk'splænə,tori, ɛk-] *adj* : explicativo, aclaratorio

expletive ['ɛksplətɪv] *n* : improperio *m*, palabrota *f fam*, grosería *f*

explicable [ɛk'splɪkəbəl, 'ɛksplɪ-] *adj* : explicable

explicit [ɪk'splɪsət, ɛk-] *adj* : explícito, claro, categórico, rotundo — **explicitly** *adv*

explicitness [ɪk'splɪsətnəs, ɛk-] *n* : claridad *f*, carácter *m* explícito

explode [ɪk'splo:d, ɛk-] *v* **-ploded; -ploding** *vt* **1** BURST : hacer explosionar, hacer explotar **2** REFUTE : rebatir, refutar, desmentir — *vi* **1** BURST : explotar, estallar, reventar **2** SKYROCKET : dispararse

exploit[1] [ɪk'splɔɪt, ɛk-] *vt* : explotar, aprovecharse de

exploit[2] ['ɛk,splɔɪt] *n* : hazaña *f*, proeza *f*

exploitation [,ɛk,splɔɪ'teɪʃən] *n* : explotación *f*

exploration [,ɛksplə'reɪʃən] *n* : exploración *f*

exploratory [ɪk'splorə,tori, ɛk-] *adj* : exploratorio

explore [ɪk'splor, ɛk-] *vt* **-plored; -ploring** : explorar, investigar, examinar

explorer [ɪk'splorər, ɛk-] *n* : explorador *m*, -dora *f*

explosion [ɪk'splo:ʒən, ɛk-] *n* : explosión *f*, estallido *m*

explosive[1] [ɪk'splo:sɪv, ɛk-] *adj* : explosivo, fulminante — **explosively** *adv*

explosive[2] *n* : explosivo *m*

exponent [ɪk'spo:nənt, 'ɛk,spo:-] *n* **1** : exponente *m* **2** ADVOCATE : defensor *m*, -sora *f*; partidario *m*, -ria *f*

exponential [,ɛkspə'nɛntʃəl] *adj* : exponencial — **exponentially** *adv*

export[1] [ɛk'sport, 'ɛk,sport] *vt* : exportar

export[2] ['ɛk,sport] *n* **1** : artículo *m* de exportación **2** → exportación

exportation [,ɛk,spor'teɪʃən] *n* : exportación *f*

exporter [ɛk'sportər, 'ɛk,spor-] *n* : exportador *m*, -dora *f*

expose [ɪk'spo:z, ɛk-] *vt* **-posed; -posing 1** : exponer (al peligro, a los elementos, a una enfermedad) **2** : exponer (una película a la luz) **3** DISCLOSE : descubrir, revelar, poner en evidencia **4** UNMASK : desenmascarar

exposé *or* **expose** [,ɛkspo'zeɪ] *n* : exposición *f* (de hechos), revelación *f* (de un escándalo)

exposed [ɪk'spo:zd, ɛk-] *adj* : descubierto, sin protección

exposition [,ɛkspə'zɪʃən] *n* : exposición *f*

exposure [ɪk'spo:ʒər, ɛk-] *n* **1** : exposición *f* **2** CONTACT : exposición *f*, experiencia *f*, contacto *m* **3** UNMASKING : desenmascaramiento *m* **4** ORIENTATION : orientación *f* ⟨a room with a northern exposure : una sala orientada al norte⟩

expound [ɪk'spaʊnd, ɛk-] *vt* : exponer, explicar — *vi* : hacer comentarios detallados

express[1] [ɪk'sprɛs, ɛk-] *vt* **1** SAY : expresar, comunicar **2** SHOW : expresar, manifestar, externar *Mex* **3** SQUEEZE : exprimir ⟨to express the juice from a lemon : exprimir el jugo de un limón⟩

express[2] *adv* : por correo exprés, por correo urgente

express³ *adj* **1** EXPLICIT : expreso, manifiesto **2** SPECIFIC : específico ⟨for that express purpose : con ese fin específico⟩ **3** RAPID : expreso, rápido
express⁴ *n* **1** : correo *m* exprés, correo *m* urgente **2** : expreso *m* (tren)
expression [ɪk'sprɛʃən, ɛk-] *n* **1** UTTERANCE : expresión *f* ⟨freedom of expression : libertad de expresión⟩ **2** : expresión *f* (en la matemática) **3** PHRASE : frase *f*, expresión *f* **4** LOOK : expresión *f*, cara *f*, gesto *m* ⟨with a sad expression : con un gesto de tristeza⟩
expressionless [ɪk'sprɛʃənləs, ɛk-] *adj* : inexpresivo
expressive [ɪk'sprɛsɪv, ɛk-] *adj* : expresivo
expressway [ɪk'sprɛs,weɪ, ɛk-] *n* : autopista *f*
expulsion [ɪk'spʌlʃən, ɛk-] *n* : expulsión *f*
expurgate ['ɛkspər,geɪt] *vt* **-gated; -gating** : expurgar
exquisite [ɛk'skwɪzət, 'ɛk,skwɪ-] *adj* **1** FINE : exquisito, delicado, primoroso **2** INTENSE : intenso, extremo
extant ['ɛkstənt, ɛk'stænt] *adj* : existente
extemporaneous [ɛk,stɛmpə'reɪniəs] *adj* : improvisado — **extemporaneously** *adv*
extend [ɪk'stɛnd, ɛk-] *vt* **1** STRETCH : extender, tender **2** PROLONG : prolongar, prorrogar **3** ENLARGE : agrandar, ampliar, aumentar **4** PROFFER : extender, dar, ofrecer — *vi* : extenderse
extended [ɪk'stɛndəd, ɛk-] *adj* LENGTHY : prolongado, largo
extension [ɪk'stɛntʃən, ɛk-] *n* **1** EXTENDING : extensión *f*, ampliación *f*, prórroga *f*, prolongación *f* **2** ANNEX : ampliación *f*, anexo *m* **3** : extensión *f* (de teléfono)
extensive [ɪk'stɛnsɪv, ɛk-] *adj* : extenso, vasto, amplio — **extensively** *adv*
extent [ɪk'stɛnt, ɛk-] *n* **1** SIZE : extensión *f*, magnitud *f* **2** DEGREE, SCOPE : alcance *m*, grado *m* ⟨to a certain extent : hasta cierto punto⟩
extenuate [ɪk'stɛnjə,weɪt, ɛk-] *vt* **-ated; -ating** : atenuar, aminorar, mitigar ⟨extenuating circumstances : circunstancias atenuantes⟩
extenuation [ɪk,stɛnjə'weɪʃən, ɛk-] *n* : atenuación *f*, aminoración *f*
exterior¹ [ɛk'stɪriər] *adj* : exterior
exterior² *n* : exterior *m*
exterminate [ɪk'stərmə,neɪt, ɛk-] *vt* **-nated; -nating** : exterminar
extermination [ɪk,stərmə'neɪʃən, ɛk-] *n* : exterminación *f*, exterminio *m*
exterminator [ɪk'stərmə,neɪtər, ɛk-] *n* : exterminador *m*, -dora *f*
external [ɪk'stərnəl, ɛk-] *adj* : externo, exterior — **externally** *adv*
extinct [ɪk'stɪŋkt, ɛk-] *adj* : extinto
extinction [ɪk'stɪŋkʃən, ɛk-] *n* : extinción *f*
extinguish [ɪk'stɪŋgwɪʃ, ɛk-] *vt* : extinguir, apagar

extinguisher [ɪk'stɪŋgwɪʃər, ɛk-] *n* : extinguidor *m*, extintor *m*
extirpate ['ɛkstər,peɪt] *vt* **-pated; -pating** : extirpar, exterminar
extol [ɪk'sto:l, ɛk-] *vt* **-tolled; -tolling** : exaltar, ensalzar, alabar
extort [ɪk'stɔrt, ɛk-] *vt* : extorsionar
extortion [ɪk'stɔrʃən, ɛk-] *n* : extorsión *f*
extra¹ ['ɛkstrə] *adv* : extra, más, extremadamente, super ⟨extra special : super especial⟩
extra² *adj* **1** ADDITIONAL : adicional, suplementario, de más **2** SUPERIOR : superior
extra³ *n* : extra *m*
extract¹ [ɪk'strækt, ɛk-] *vt* : extraer, sacar
extract² ['ɛk,strækt] *n* **1** EXCERPT : pasaje *m*, selección *f*, trozo *m* **2** : extracto *m* ⟨vanilla extract : extracto de vainilla⟩
extraction [ɪk'strækʃən, ɛk-] *n* : extracción *f*
extractor [ɪk'stræktər, ɛk-] *n* : extractor *m*
extracurricular [,ɛkstrəkə'rɪkjələr] *adj* : extracurricular
extradite ['ɛkstrə,daɪt] *vt* **-dited; -diting** : extraditar
extradition [,ɛkstrə'dɪʃən] *n* : extradición *f*
extramarital [,ɛkstrə'mærətəl] *adj* : extramatrimonial
extraneous [ɛk'streɪniəs] *adj* **1** OUTSIDE : extrínseco, externo **2** SUPERFLUOUS : superfluo, ajeno — **extraneously** *adv*
extraordinary [ɪk'strɔrdən,ɛri, ,ɛkstrə'ɔrd-] *adj* : extraordinario, excepcional — **extraordinarily** [ɪk,strɔrdən'ɛrəli, ,ɛkstrə,ɔrd-] *adv*
extrasensory [,ɛkstrə'sɛntsəri] *adj* : extrasensorial
extraterrestrial¹ [,ɛkstrətə'rɛstriəl] *adj* : extraterrestre
extraterrestrial² *n* : extraterrestre *mf*
extravagance [ɪk'strævɪgənts, ɛk-] *n* **1** EXCESS : exceso *m*, extravagancia *f* **2** WASTEFULNESS : derroche *m*, despilfarro *m* **3** LUXURY : lujo *m*
extravagant [ɪk'strævɪgənt, ɛk-] *adj* **1** EXCESSIVE : excesivo, extravagante **2** WASTEFUL : despilfarrador, derrochador, gastador **3** EXORBITANT : costoso, exorbitante
extravagantly [ɪk'strævɪgəntli, ɛk-] *adv* **1** LAVISHLY : a lo grande **2** EXCESSIVELY : exageradamente, desmesuradamente
extravaganza [ɪk,strævə'gænzə, ɛk-] *n* : gran espectáculo *m*
extreme¹ [ɪk'stri:m, ɛk-] *adj* **1** UTMOST : extremo, sumo ⟨of extreme importance : de suma importancia⟩ **2** INTENSE : intenso, extremado ⟨extreme cold : frío extremado⟩ **3** EXCESSIVE : excesivo, extremo ⟨extreme views : opiniones extremas⟩ ⟨extreme measures : medidas excepcionales, medi-

das drásticas⟩ **4** OUTERMOST : extremo
⟨the extreme north : el norte extremo⟩
extreme² *n* **1** : extremo *m* **2 in the ex-**
treme : en extremo, en sumo grado
extremely [ɪk'stri:mli, ɛk-] *adv* : sumamente, extremadamente, terrible-
mente
extremist [ɪk'stri:mɪst, ɛk-] *n* : extremista *mf* — **extremist** *adj*
extremity [ɪk'strɛməţi, ɛk-] *n, pl* **-ties 1**
EXTREME : extremo *m* **2 extremities**
npl LIMBS : extremidades *fpl*
extricate ['ɛkstrə,keɪt] *vt* **-cated; -cating**
: librar, sacar
extrinsic [ɪk'strɪnzɪk, -'strɪn/sɪk] *adj* : extrínseco
extrovert ['ɛkstrə,vərt] *n* : extrovertido
m, -da *f*
extroverted ['ɛkstrə,vərţəd] *adj* : extrovertido
extrude [ɪk'stru:d, ɛk-] *vt* **-truded;**
-truding : extrudir, expulsar
exuberance [ɪg'zu:bərən/s, ɛg-] *n* **1** JOY-
OUSNESS : euforia *f*, exaltación *f* **2** VIG-
OR : exuberancia *f*, vigor *m*
exuberant [ɪg'zu:bərənt, ɛg-] *adj* **1** JOY-
OUS : eufórico **2** LUSH : exuberante —
exuberantly *adv*
exude [ɪg'zu:d, ɛg-] *vt* **-uded; -uding 1**
OOZE : rezumar, exudar **2** EMANATE
: emanar, irradiar
exult [ɪg'zʌlt, ɛg-] *vi* : exultar, regocijarse
exultant [ɪg'zʌltənt, ɛg-] *adj* : exultante,
jubiloso — **exultantly** *adv*
exultation [,ɛksəl'teɪʃən, ,ɛgzəl-] *n* : exultación *f*, júbilo *m*, alborozo *m*

eye¹ ['aɪ] *vt* **eyed; eyeing** *or* **eying** : mirar, observar
eye² *n* **1** : ojo *m* **2** VISION : visión *f*, vista
f, ojo *m* ⟨a good eye for bargains : un
buen ojo para las gangas⟩ **3** GLANCE
: mirada *f*, ojeada *f* **4** ATTENTION : atención *f* ⟨to catch one's eye : llamar la
atención⟩ **5** POINT OF VIEW : punto *m*
de vista ⟨in the eyes of the law : según
la ley⟩ **6** : ojo *m* (de una aguja, una
papa, una tormenta)
eyeball ['aɪ,bɔl] *n* : globo *m* ocular
eyebrow ['aɪ,braʊ] *n* : ceja *f*
eyedropper ['aɪ,drɑpər] *n* : cuentagotas
f
eyeglasses ['aɪ,glæsəz] *npl* : anteojos
mpl, lentes *mpl*, espejuelos *mpl*, gafas
fpl
eyelash ['aɪ,læʃ] *n* : pestaña *f*
eyelet ['aɪlət] *n* : ojete *m*
eyelid ['aɪ,lɪd] *n* : párpado *m*
eye–opener ['aɪ,o:pənər] *n* : revelación
f, sorpresa *f*
eye–opening ['aɪ,o:pənɪŋ] *adj* : revelador
eyepiece ['aɪ,pi:s] *n* : ocular *m*
eyesight ['aɪ,saɪt] *n* : vista *f*, visión *f*
eyesore ['aɪ,sor] *n* : monstruosidad *f*,
adefesio *m*
eyestrain ['aɪ,streɪn] *n* : fatiga *f* visual,
vista *f* cansada
eyetooth ['aɪ,tu:θ] *n* : colmillo *m*
eyewitness ['aɪ'wɪtnəs] *n* : testigo *mf* ocular, testigo *mf* presencial
eyrie ['aɪri] → **aerie**

F

f ['ɛf] *n, pl* **f's** *or* **fs** ['ɛfs] : sexta letra del
alfabeto inglés
fable ['feɪbəl] *n* : fábula *f*
fabled ['feɪbəld] *adj* : legendario, fabuloso
fabric ['fæbrɪk] *n* **1** MATERIAL : tela *f*,
tejido *m* **2** STRUCTURE : estructura *f*
⟨the fabric of society : la estructura de
la sociedad⟩
fabricate ['fæbrɪ,keɪt] *vt* **-cated; -cating**
1 CONSTRUCT, MANUFACTURE : con-
struir, fabricar **2** INVENT : inventar
(excusas o mentiras)
fabrication [,fæbrɪ'keɪʃən] *n* **1** LIE
: mentira *f*, invención *f* **2** MANUFAC-
TURE : fabricación *f*
fabulous ['fæbjələs] *adj* **1** LEGENDARY
: fabuloso, legendario **2** INCREDIBLE
: increíble, fabuloso ⟨fabulous wealth
: riqueza fabulosa⟩ **3** WONDERFUL
: magnífico, estupendo, fabuloso —
fabulously *adv*
facade [fə'sɑd] *n* : fachada *f*
face¹ ['feɪs] *v* **faced; facing** *vt* **1** LINE
: recubrir (una superficie), forrar
(ropa) **2** CONFRONT : enfrentarse a,
afrontar, hacer frente a ⟨to face the

music : afrontar las consecuencias⟩ ⟨to
face the facts : aceptar la realidad⟩ **3**
: estar de cara a, estar enfrente de ⟨she's
facing her brother : está de cara a su
hermano⟩ **4** OVERLOOK : dar a — *vi*
: mirar (hacia), estar orientado (a)
face² *n* **1** : cara *f*, rostro *m* ⟨he told me
to my face : me lo dijo a la cara⟩ **2** EX-
PRESSION : cara *f*, expresión *f* ⟨to pull
a long face : poner mala cara⟩ **3** GRI-
MACE : mueca *f* ⟨to make faces : hacer muecas⟩ **4** APPEARANCE : fisonomía
f, aspecto *m* ⟨the face of society : la
fisonomía de la sociedad⟩ **5** EFFRON-
TERY : desfachatez *f* **6** PRESTIGE : prestigio *m* ⟨to lose face : desprestigiarse⟩
7 FRONT, SIDE : cara *f* (de una moneda), esfera *f* (de un reloj), fachada *f* (de
un edificio), pared *f* (de una montaña)
8 SURFACE : superficie *f*, faz *f* (de la
tierra), cara *f* (de la luna) **9 in the face**
of DESPITE : en medio de, en visto de,
ante
facedown ['feɪs,daʊn] *adv* : boca abajo
faceless ['feɪsləs] *adj* ANONYMOUS
: anónimo
face–lift ['feɪs,lɪft] *n* **1** : estiramiento *m*

facial **2** RENOVATION : renovación *f*, remozamiento *m*

facet [ˈfæsət] *n* **1** : faceta *f* (de una piedra) **2** ASPECT : faceta *f*, aspecto *m*

facetious [fəˈsiːʃəs] *adj* : gracioso, burlón, bromista

facetiously [fəˈsiːʃəsli] *adv* : en tono de burla

facetiousness [fəˈsiːʃəsnəs] *n* : jocosidad *f*

face-to-face *adv* & *adj* : cara a cara

faceup [ˈfeɪsˌʌp] *adv* : boca arriba

face value *n* : valor *m* nominal

facial¹ [ˈfeɪʃəl] *adj* : de la cara, facial

facial² *n* : tratamiento *m* facial, limpieza *f* de cutis

facile [ˈfæsəl] *adj* SUPERFICIAL : superficial, simplista

facilitate [fəˈsɪləˌteɪt] *vt* **-tated; -tating** : facilitar

facility [fəˈsɪləti] *n, pl* **-ties 1** EASE : facilidad *f* **2** CENTER, COMPLEX : centro *m*, complejo *m* **3 facilities** *npl* AMENITIES : comodidades *fpl*, servicios *mpl*

facing [ˈfeɪsɪŋ] *n* **1** LINING : entretela *f* (de una prenda) **2** : revestimiento *m* (de un edificio)

facsimile [fækˈsɪməli] *n* : facsímile *m*, facsímil *m*

fact [ˈfækt] *n* **1** : hecho *m* ⟨as a matter of fact : de hecho⟩ **2** INFORMATION : información *f*, datos *mpl* ⟨facts and figures : datos y cifras⟩ **3** REALITY : realidad *f* ⟨in fact : en realidad⟩

faction [ˈfækʃən] *n* : facción *m*, bando *m*

factional [ˈfækʃənəl] *adj* : entre facciones

factious [ˈfækʃəs] *adj* : faccioso, contencioso

factitious [fækˈtɪʃəs] *adj* : artificial, facticio

factor [ˈfæktər] *n* : factor *m*

factory [ˈfæktəri] *n, pl* **-ries** : fábrica *f*

factual [ˈfæktʃʊəl] *adj* : basado en hechos, objetivo

factually [ˈfæktʃʊəli] *adv* : en cuanto a los hechos

faculty [ˈfækəlti] *n, pl* **-ties 1** : facultad *f* ⟨the faculty of sight : las facultades visuales, el sentido de la vista⟩ **2** APTITUDE : aptitud *f*, facilidad *f* **3** TEACHERS : cuerpo *m* docente

fad [ˈfæd] *n* : moda *f* pasajera, manía *f*

fade [ˈfeɪd] *v* **faded; fading** *vi* **1** WITHER : debilitarse (dícese de las personas), marchitarse (dícese de las flores y las plantas) **2** DISCOLOR : desteñirse, decolorarse **3** DIM : apagarse (dícese de la luz), perderse (dícese de los sonidos), fundirse (dícese de las imágenes) **4** VANISH : desvanecerse, decaer — *vt* DISCOLOR : desteñir

fag [ˈfæg] *vt* **fagged; fagging** EXHAUST : cansar, fatigar

fagot *or* **faggot** [ˈfægət] *n* : haz *m* de leña

Fahrenheit [ˈfærənˌhaɪt] *adj* : Fahrenheit

fail¹ [ˈfeɪl] *vi* **1** WEAKEN : fallar, deteriorarse **2** STOP : fallar, detenerse ⟨his heart failed : le falló el corazón⟩ **3** : fracasar, fallar ⟨her plan failed : su plan fracasó⟩ ⟨the crops failed : se perdió la cosecha⟩ **4** : quebrar ⟨a business about to fail : una empresa a punto de quebrar⟩ **5 to fail in** : faltar a, no cumplir con ⟨to fail in one's duties : faltar a sus deberes⟩ — *vt* **1** FLUNK : reprobar (un examen) **2** : fallar ⟨words fail me : las palabras me fallan, no encuentro palabras⟩ **3** DISAPPOINT : fallar, decepcionar ⟨don't fail me! : ¡no me falles!⟩

fail² *n* : fracaso *m*

failing [ˈfeɪlɪŋ] *n* : defecto *m*

failure [ˈfeɪljər] *n* **1** : fracaso *m*, malogro *m* ⟨crop failure : pérdida de la cosecha⟩ ⟨heart failure : insuficiencia cardíaca⟩ ⟨engine failure : falla mecánica⟩ **2** BANKRUPTCY : bancarrota *f*, quiebra *f* **3** : fracaso *m* (persona) ⟨he was a failure as a manager : como gerente, fue un fracaso⟩

faint¹ [ˈfeɪnt] *vi* : desmayarse

faint² *adj* **1** COWARDLY, TIMID : cobarde, tímido **2** DIZZY : mareado ⟨faint with hunger : desfallecido de hambre⟩ **3** SLIGHT : leve, ligero, vago ⟨I haven't the faintest idea : no tengo la más mínima idea⟩ **4** INDISTINCT : tenue, indistinto, apenas perceptible

faint³ *n* : desmayo *m*

fainthearted [ˈfeɪntˈhɑrtəd] *adj* : cobarde, pusilánime

faintly [ˈfeɪntli] *adv* : débilmente, ligeramente, levemente

faintness [ˈfeɪntnəs] *n* **1** INDISTINCTNESS : lo débil, falta *f* de claridad **2** FAINTING : desmayo *m*, desfallecimiento *m*

fair¹ [ˈfær] *adj* **1** ATTRACTIVE, BEAUTIFUL : bello, hermoso, atractivo **2** (*relating to weather*) : bueno, despejado ⟨fair weather : tiempo despejado⟩ **3** JUST : justo, imparcial **4** ALLOWABLE : permisible **5** BLOND, LIGHT : rubio (dícese del pelo), blanco (dícese de la tez) **6** ADEQUATE : bastante, adecuado ⟨fair to middling : mediano, regular⟩ **7 fair game** : presa *f* fácil **8 to play fair** : jugar limpio

fair² *n* : feria *f*

fairground [ˈfærˌgraʊnd] *n* : parque *m* de diversiones

fairly [ˈfærli] *adv* **1** IMPARTIALLY : imparcialmente, limpiamente, equitativamente **2** QUITE : bastante **3** MODERATELY : medianamente

fairness [ˈfærnəs] *n* **1** IMPARTIALITY : imparcialidad *f*, justicia *f* **2** LIGHTNESS : blancura *f* (de la piel), lo rubio (del pelo)

fairy [ˈfæri] *n, pl* **fairies 1** : hada *f* **2 fairy tale** : cuento *m* de hadas

fairyland [ˈfæriˌlænd] *n* **1** : país *m* de las hadas **2** : lugar *m* encantador

faith [ˈfeɪθ] *n, pl* **faiths** [ˈfeɪθs, ˈfeɪðz] **1** BELIEF : fe *f* **2** ALLEGIANCE : lealtad *f* **3** CONFIDENCE, TRUST : confianza *f*, fe *f* **4** RELIGION : religión *f*

faithful [ˈfeɪθfəl] *adj* : fiel — **faithfully** *adv*

faithfulness [ˈfeɪθfəlnəs] *n* : fidelidad *f*

faithless [ˈfeɪθləs] *adj* **1** DISLOYAL : desleal **2** : infiel (en la religión) — **faithlessly** *adv*

faithlessness [ˈfeɪθləsnəs] *n* : deslealtad *f*

fake¹ [ˈfeɪk] *v* **faked; faking** *vt* **1** FALSIFY : falsificar, falsear **2** FEIGN : fingir — *vi* **1** PRETEND : fingir **2** : hacer un engaño, hacer una finta (en deportes)

fake² *adj* : falso, fingido, postizo

fake³ *n* **1** IMITATION : imitación *f*, falsificación *f* **2** IMPOSTOR : impostor *m*, -tora *f*; charlatán *m*, -tana *f*; farsante *mf* **3** FEINT : engaño *m*, finta *f* (en deportes)

faker [ˈfeɪkər] *n* : impostor *m*, -tora *f*; charlatán *m*, -tana *f*; farsante *mf*

fakir [fəˈkɪr, ˈfeɪkər] *n* : faquir *m*

falcon [ˈfælkən, ˈfɔl-] *n* : halcón *m*

falconry [ˈfælkənri, ˈfɔl-] *n* : cetrería *f*

fall¹ [ˈfɔl] *vi* **fell** [ˈfɛl]; **fallen** [ˈfɔlən]; **falling 1** : caer, caerse ⟨to fall out of bed : caer de la cama⟩ ⟨to fall down : caerse⟩ **2** HANG : caer **3** DESCEND : caer (dícese de la lluvia o de la noche), bajar (dícese de los precios), descender (dícese de la temperatura) **4** : caer (a un enemigo), rendirse ⟨the city fell : la ciudad se rindió⟩ **5** OCCUR : caer ⟨Christmas falls on a Friday : la Navidad cae en viernes⟩ **6 to fall asleep** : dormirse, quedarse dormido **7 to fall from grace** SIN : perder la gracia **8 to fall sick** : caer enfermo, enfermarse **9 to fall through** : fracasar, caer en la nada **10 to fall to** : tocar a, corresponder a ⟨the task fell to him : le tocó hacerlo⟩

fall² *n* **1** TUMBLE : caída *f* ⟨to break one's fall : frenar uno su caída⟩ ⟨a fall of three feet : una caída de tres pies⟩ **2** FALLING : derrumbe *m* (de rocas), aguacero *m* (de lluvia), nevada *f* (de nieve), bajada *f* (de precios), disminución *f* (de cantidades) **3** AUTUMN : otoño *m* **4** DOWNFALL : caída *f*, ruina *f* **5 falls** *npl* WATERFALL : cascada *f*, catarata *f*

fallacious [fəˈleɪʃəs] *adj* : erróneo, engañoso, falaz

fallacy [ˈfæləsi] *n, pl* **-cies** : falacia *f*

fall back *vi* **1** RETREAT : retirarse, replegarse **2 to fall back on** : recurrir a

fall guy *n* SCAPEGOAT : chivo *m* expiatorio

fallible [ˈfæləbəl] *adj* : falible

fallout [ˈfɔlˌaʊt] *n* **1** : lluvia *f* radioactiva **2** CONSEQUENCES : secuelas *fpl*, consecuencias *fpl*

fallow¹ [ˈfælo] *vt* : barbechar

fallow² *adj* **to lie fallow** : estar en barbecho

fallow³ *n* : barbecho *m*

false [ˈfɔls] *adj* **falser; falsest 1** UNTRUE : falso **2** ERRONEOUS : erróneo, equivocado **3** FAKE : falso, postizo **4** UNFAITHFUL : infiel **5** FRAUDULENT : fraudulento ⟨under false pretenses : por fraude⟩

falsehood [ˈfɔlsˌhʊd] *n* : mentira *f*, falsedad *f*

falsely [ˈfɔlsli] *adv* : falsamente, con falsedad

falseness [ˈfɔlsnəs] *n* : falsedad *f*

falsetto [fɔlˈsetoː] *n, pl* **-tos** : falsete *m*

falsification [ˌfɔlsəfəˈkeɪʃən] *n* : falsificación *f*, falseamiento *m*

falsify [ˈfɔlsəˌfaɪ] *vt* **-fied; fying** : falsificar, falsear

falsity [ˈfɔlsəti] *n, pl* **-ties** : falsedad *f*

falter [ˈfɔltər] *vi* **-tered; -tering 1** TOTTER : tambalearse **2** STAMMER : titubear, tartamudear **3** WAVER : vacilar

faltering [ˈfɔltərɪŋ] *adj* : titubeante, vacilante

fame [ˈfeɪm] *n* : fama *f*

famed [ˈfeɪmd] *adj* : famoso, célebre, afamado

familial [fəˈmɪljəl, -liəl] *adj* : familiar

familiar¹ [fəˈmɪljər] *adj* **1** KNOWN : familiar, conocido ⟨to be familiar with : estar familiarizado con⟩ **2** INFORMAL : familiar, informal **3** INTIMATE : íntimo, de confianza **4** FORWARD : confianzudo, atrevido — **familiarly** *adv*

familiar² *n* : espíritu *m* guardián

familiarity [fəˌmɪliˈærəti, -ˌmɪlˈjær-] *n, pl* **-ties 1** KNOWLEDGE : conocimiento *m*, familiaridad *f* **2** INFORMALITY, INTIMACY : confianza *f*, familiaridad *f* **3** FORWARDNESS : exceso *m* de confianza, descaro *m*

familiarize [fəˈmɪljəˌraɪz] *vt* **-ized; -izing 1** : familiarizar **2 to familiarize oneself** : familiarizarse

family [ˈfæmli, ˈfæmə-] *n, pl* **-lies** : familia *f*

family room *n* : living *m*, sala *f* (informal)

family tree *n* : árbol *m* genealógico

famine [ˈfæmən] *n* : hambre *f*, hambruna *f*

famish [ˈfæmɪʃ] *vi* **to be famished** : estar famélico, estar hambriento, morir de hambre *fam*

famous [ˈfeɪməs] *adj* : famoso

famously [ˈfeɪməsli] *adv* **to get on famously** : llevarse de maravilla

fan¹ [ˈfæn] *vt* **fanned; fanning 1** : abanicar (a una persona), avivar (un fuego) **2** STIMULATE : avivar, estimular

fan² *n* **1** : ventilador *m*, abanico *m* **2** ADMIRER, ENTHUSIAST : aficionado *m*, -da *f*; entusiasta *mf*; admirador *m*, -dora *f*

fanatic¹ [fəˈnætɪk] *or* **fanatical** [-ţɪ-kəl] *adj* : fanático

fanatic² *n* : fanático *m*, -ca *f*

fanaticism [fə'næt̬ə,sɪzəm] *n* : fanatismo *m*

fanciful ['fæntsɪfəl] *adj* **1** CAPRICIOUS : caprichoso, fantástico, extravagante **2** IMAGINATIVE : imaginativo — **fancifully** *adv*

fancy[1] ['fæntsi] *vt* **-cied; -cying 1** IMAGINE : imaginarse, figurarse ⟨fancy that! : ¡figúrate!, ¡imagínate!⟩ **2** CRAVE : apetecer, tener ganas de

fancy[2] *adj* **-cier; -est 1** ELABORATE : elaborado **2** LUXURIOUS : lujoso, elegante — **fancily** ['fæntsəli] *adv*

fancy[3] *n, pl* **-cies 1** LIKING : gusto *m*, afición *f* **2** WHIM : antojo *m*, capricho *m* **3** IMAGINATION : fantasía *f*, imaginación *f*

fandango [fæn'dæŋgo] *n, pl* **-gos** : fandango *m*

fanfare ['fæn,fær] *n* : fanfarria *f*

fang ['fæŋ] *n* : colmillo *m* (de un animal), diente *m* (de una serpiente)

fanlight ['fæn,laɪt] *n* : tragaluz *m*

fantasia [fæn'teɪʒə, -ziə; ,fæntə-'zi:ə] *n* : fantasía *f*

fantasize ['fæntə,saɪz] *vi* **-sized; -sizing** : fantasear

fantastic [fæn'tæstɪk] *adj* **1** UNBELIEVABLE : fantástico, increíble, extraño **2** ENORMOUS : fabuloso, inmenso ⟨fantastic sums : sumas fabulosas⟩ **3** WONDERFUL : estupendo, fantástico, bárbaro *fam*, macanudo *fam* — **fantastically** [-tɪkli] *adv*

fantasy ['fæntəsi] *n, pl* **-sies** : fantasía *f*

far[1] ['fɑr] *adv* **farther** ['fɑrðər] *or* **further** ['fər-]; **farthest** *or* **furthest** [-ðəst] **1** : lejos ⟨far from here : lejos de aquí⟩ ⟨to go far : llegar lejos⟩ ⟨as far as Chicago : hasta Chicago⟩ ⟨far away : a lo lejos⟩ **2** MUCH : muy, mucho ⟨far bigger : mucho más grande⟩ ⟨far superior : muy superior⟩ ⟨it's by far the best : es con mucho el mejor⟩ **3** (*expressing degree or extent*) ⟨the results are far off : salieron muy inexactos los resultados⟩ ⟨to go so far as : decir tanto como⟩ ⟨to go far enough : tener el alcance necesario⟩ **4** (*expressing progress*) ⟨the work is far advanced : el trabajo está muy avanzado⟩ ⟨to take (something) too far : llevar (algo) demasiado lejos⟩ **5 far and wide** : por todas partes **6 far from it!** : ¡todo lo contrario! **7 so far** : hasta ahora, todavía

far[2] *adj* **farther** *or* **further; farthest** *or* **furthest 1** REMOTE : lejano, remoto ⟨the Far East : el Lejano Oriente, el Extremo Oriente⟩ ⟨a far country : un país lejano⟩ **2** LONG : largo ⟨a far journey : un viaje largo⟩ **3** EXTREME : extremo ⟨the far right : la extrema derecha⟩ ⟨at the far end of the room : en el otro extremo de la sala⟩

faraway ['fɑrə,weɪ] *adj* : remoto, lejano

farce ['fɑrs] *n* : farsa *f*

farcical ['fɑrsɪkəl] *adj* : absurdo, ridículo

fare[1] ['fær] *vi* **fared; faring** : ir, salir ⟨how did you fare? : ¿cómo te fue?⟩

fare[2] *n* **1** : pasaje *m*, billete *m*, boleto *m* ⟨half fare : medio pasaje⟩ **2** FOOD : comida *f*

farewell[1] [fær'wɛl] *adj* : de despedida

farewell[2] *n* : despedida *f*

far-fetched ['fɑr'fɛtʃt] *adj* : improbable, exagerado

farina [fə'ri:nə] *n* : harina *f*

farm[1] ['fɑrm] *vt* **1** : cultivar, labrar **2** : criar (animales) — *vi* : ser agricultor

farm[2] *n* : granja *f*, hacienda *f*, finca *f*, estancia *f*

farmer ['fɑrmər] *n* : agricultor *m*, granjero *m*

farmhand ['fɑrm,hænd] *n* : peón *m*

farmhouse ['fɑrm,haʊs] *n* : granja *f*, vivienda *f* del granjero, casa *f* de hacienda

farming ['fɑrmɪŋ] *n* : labranza *f*, cultivo *m*, crianza *f* (de animales)

farmland ['fɑrm,lænd] *n* : tierras *fpl* de labranza

farmyard ['fɑrm,jɑrd] *n* : corral *m*

far-off ['fɑr,ɔf, -'ɔf] *adj* : remoto, distante, lejano

far-reaching ['fɑr'ri:tʃɪŋ] *adj* : de gran alcance

farsighted ['fɑr,saɪt̬əd] *adj* **1** : hipermétrope **2** JUDICIOUS : con visión de futuro, previsor, precavido

farsightedness ['fɑr,saɪt̬ədnəs] *n* **1** : hipermetropía *f* **2** PRUDENCE : previsión *f*

farther[1] ['fɑrðər] *adv* **1** AHEAD : más lejos (en el espacio), más adelante (en el tiempo) **2** MORE : más

farther[2] *adj* : más lejano, más remoto

farthermost ['fɑrðər,mo:st] *adj* : (el) más lejano

farthest[1] ['fɑrðəst] *adv* **1** : lo más lejos ⟨I jumped farthest : salté lo más lejos⟩ **2** : lo más avanzado ⟨he progressed farthest : progresó al punto más avanzado⟩ **3** : más ⟨the farthest developed plan : el plan más desarrollado⟩

farthest[2] *adj* : más lejano

fascicle ['fæsɪkəl] *n* : fascículo *m*

fascinate ['fæsən,eɪt] *vt* **-nated; -nating** : fascinar, cautivar

fascinating ['fæsən,eɪt̬ɪŋ] *adj* : fascinante

fascination [,fæsən'eɪʃən] *n* : fascinación *f*

fascism ['fæʃ,ɪzəm] *n* : fascismo *m*

fascist[1] ['fæʃɪst] *adj* : fascista

fascist[2] *n* : fascista *mf*

fashion[1] ['fæʃən] *vt* : formar, moldear

fashion[2] *n* **1** MANNER : manera *f*, modo *m* **2** CUSTOM : costumbre *f* **3** STYLE : moda *f*

fashionable ['fæʃənəbəl] *adj* : de moda, chic

fashionably ['fæʃənəbli] *adv* : a la moda

fast[1] ['fæst] *vi* : ayunar

fast[2] *adv* **1** SECURELY : firmemente, seguramente ⟨to hold fast : agarrarse bien⟩ 2 RAPIDLY : rápidamente, rápido, de prisa 3 **to run fast** : ir adelantado (dícese de un reloj) 4 SOUNDLY : profundamente ⟨fast asleep : profundamente dormido⟩

fast³ adj 1 SECURE : firme, seguro ⟨to make fast : amarrar (un barco)⟩ 2 FAITHFUL : leal ⟨fast friends : amigos leales⟩ 3 RAPID : rápido, veloz 4 : adelantado ⟨my watch is fast : tengo el reloj adelantado⟩ 5 DEEP : profundo ⟨a fast sleep : un sueño profundo⟩ 6 COLORFAST : inalterable, que no destiñe 7 DISSOLUTE : extravagante, disipado, disoluto

fast⁴ n : ayuno m

fasten ['fæsən] vt 1 ATTACH : sujetar, atar 2 FIX : fijar ⟨to fasten one's eyes on : fijar los ojos en⟩ 3 SECURE : abrochar (ropa o cinturones), atar (cordones), cerrar (una maleta) — vi : abrocharse, cerrar

fastener ['fæsənər] n : cierre m, sujetador m

fastening ['fæsənɪŋ] n : cierre m, sujetador m

fast food n : comida f rápida

fastidious [fæs'tɪdiəs] adj : quisquilloso, exigente — **fastidiously** adv

fat¹ ['fæt] adj **fatter; fattest** 1 OBESE : gordo, obeso 2 THICK : grueso

fat² n : grasa f

fatal ['feɪt̬əl] adj 1 DEADLY : mortal 2 ILL-FATED : malhadado, fatal 3 MOMENTOUS : fatídico

fatalism ['feɪt̬əl,ɪzəm] n : fatalismo m

fatalist ['feɪt̬əlɪst] n : fatalista mf

fatalistic [,feɪt̬əl'ɪstɪk] adj : fatalista

fatality [feɪ'tælət̬i, fə-] n, pl **-ties** : víctima f mortal

fatally ['feɪt̬əli] adv : mortalmente

fate ['feɪt] n 1 DESTINY : destino m 2 END, LOT : final m, suerte f

fated ['feɪt̬əd] adj : predestinado

fateful ['feɪtfəl] adj 1 MOMENTOUS : fatídico, aciago 2 PROPHETIC : profético — **fatefully** adv

father¹ ['faðər] vt : engendrar

father² n 1 : padre m ⟨my father and my mother : mi padre y mi madre⟩ ⟨Father Smith : el padre Smith⟩ 2 **the Father** GOD : el Padre, Dios m

fatherhood ['faðər,hʊd] n : paternidad f

father-in-law ['faðərɪn,lɔ] n, pl **fathers-in-law** : suegro m

fatherland ['faðər,lænd] n : patria f

fatherless ['faðərləs] adj : huérfano de padre, sin padre

fatherly ['faðərli] adj : paternal

fathom¹ ['fæðəm] vt UNDERSTAND : entender, comprender

fathom² n : braza f

fatigue¹ [fə'ti:g] vt **-tigued; -tiguing** : fatigar, cansar

fatigue² n : fatiga f

fatness ['fætnəs] n : gordura f (de una persona o un animal), grosor m (de un objeto)

fatten ['fæt̬ən] vt : engordar, cebar

fatty ['fæt̬i] adj **fattier; -est** : graso, grasoso, adiposo (dícese de los tejidos)

fatuous ['fætʃuəs] adj : necio, fatuo — **fatuously** adv

faucet ['fɔsət] n : llave f, canilla f Arg, Uru, grifo m

fault¹ ['fɔlt] vt : encontrar defectos a

fault² n 1 SHORTCOMING : defecto m, falta f 2 DEFECT : falta f, defecto m, falla f 3 BLAME : culpa f 4 FRACTURE : falla f (geológica)

faultfinder ['fɔlt,faɪndər] n : criticón m, -cona f

faultfinding ['fɔlt,faɪndɪŋ] n : crítica f

faultless ['fɔltləs] adj : sin culpa, sin imperfecciones, impecable

faultlessly ['fɔltləsli] adv : impecablemente, perfectamente

faulty ['fɔlti] adj **faultier; -est** : defectuoso, imperfecto — **faultily** ['fɔltəli] adv

fauna ['fɔnə] n : fauna f

faux ['fo:] adj : de imitación

faux pas [,fo:'pɑ] n, pl **faux pas** [same or -'pɑz] : metedura f de pata fam

favor¹ ['feɪvər] vt 1 SUPPORT : estar a favor de, ser partidario de, apoyar 2 OBLIGE : hacerle un favor a 3 PREFER : preferir 4 RESEMBLE : parecerse a, salir a

favor² n : favor m ⟨in favor of : a favor de⟩ ⟨an error in his favor : un error a su favor⟩

favorable ['feɪvərəbəl] adj : favorable, propicio

favorably ['feɪvərəbli] adv : favorablemente, bien

favorite¹ ['feɪvərət] adj : favorito, preferido

favorite² n : favorito m, -ta f; preferido m, -da f

favoritism ['feɪvərə,tɪzəm] n : favoritismo m

fawn¹ ['fɔn] vi : adular, lisonjear

fawn² n : cervato m

fax ['fæks] n : facsímil m, facsímile m

faze ['feɪz] vt **fazed; fazing** : desconcertar, perturbar

fear¹ ['fɪr] vt : temer, tener miedo de — vi : temer

fear² n : miedo m, temor m ⟨for fear of : por temor a⟩

fearful ['fɪrfəl] adj 1 FRIGHTENING : espantoso, aterrador, horrible 2 FRIGHTENED : temeroso, miedoso

fearfully ['fɪrfəli] adv 1 EXTREMELY : extremadamente, terriblemente 2 TIMIDLY : con temor

fearless ['fɪrləs] adj : intrépido, impávido

fearlessly ['fɪrləsli] adv : sin temor

fearlessness ['fɪrləsnəs] n : intrepidez f, impavidez f

fearsome ['fɪrsəm] adj : aterrador

feasibility [,fi:zə'bɪlət̬i] n : viabilidad f, factibilidad f

feasible ['fi:zəbəl] adj : viable, factible, realizable

feast¹ ['fi:st] *vi* : banquetear — *vt* **1** : agasajar, festejar **2** to feast one's eyes on : regalarse la vista con

feast² *n* **1** BANQUET : banquete *m*, festín *m* **2** FESTIVAL : fiesta *f*

feat ['fi:t] *n* : proeza *f*, hazaña *f*

feather¹ ['fɛðər] *vt* **1** : emplumar **2** to feather one's nest : hacer su agosto

feather² *n* **1** : pluma *f* **2** a feather in one's cap : un triunfo personal

feathered ['fɛðərd] *adj* : con plumas

feathery ['fɛðəri] *adj* **1** DOWNY : plumoso **2** LIGHT : liviano

feature¹ ['fi:tʃər] *v* -tured; -turing *vt* **1** IMAGINE : imaginarse **2** PRESENT : presentar — *vi* : figurar

feature² *n* **1** CHARACTERISTIC : característica *f*, rasgo *m* **2** : largometraje *m* (en el cine), artículo *m* (en un periódico), documental *m* (en la televisión) **3** features *npl* : rasgos *mpl*, facciones *fpl* ⟨delicate features : facciones delicadas⟩

February ['fɛbjuˌri, 'fɛbʊ-, 'fbrʊ-] *n* : febrero *m*

fecal ['fi:kəl] *adj* : fecal

feces ['fi:ˌsi:z] *npl* : heces *fpl*, excrementos *mpl*

feckless ['fɛkləs] *adj* : irresponsable

fecund ['fɛkənd, 'fi:-] *adj* : fecundo

fecundity [fɪ'kʌndəti, fɛ-] *n* : fecundidad *f*

federal ['fɛdrəl, -dərəl] *adj* : federal

federalism ['fɛdrəˌlɪzəm, -dərə-] *n* : federalismo *m*

federalist¹ ['fɛdrəlɪst, -dərə-] *adj* : federalista

federalist² *n* : federalista *mf*

federate ['fɛdəˌreɪt] *vt* -ated; -ating : federar

federation [ˌfɛdə'reɪʃən] *n* : federación *f*

fedora [fɪ'dorə] *n* : sombrero *m* flexible de fieltro

fed up *adj* : harto

fee ['fi:] *n* **1** : honorarios *mpl* (a un médico, un abogado, etc.) **2** entrance fee : entrada *f*

feeble ['fi:bəl] *adj* -bler; -blest **1** WEAK : débil, endeble **2** INEFFECTIVE : flojo, pobre, poco convincente

feebleminded [ˌfi:bəl'maɪndəd] *adj* **1** : débil mental **2** FOOLISH, STUPID : imbécil, tonto

feebleness ['fi:bəlnəs] *n* : debilidad *f*

feebly ['fi:bli] *adv* : débilmente

feed¹ ['fi:d] *v* fed ['fɛd]; feeding *vt* **1** : dar de comer a, nutrir, alimentar (a una persona) **2** : alimentar (un fuego o una máquina), proveer (información), introducir (datos) — *vi* : comer, alimentarse

feed² *n* **1** NOURISHMENT : alimento *m* **2** FODDER : pienso *m*

feedback ['fi:dˌbæk] *n* **1** : realimentación *f* (electrónica) **2** RESPONSE : reacción *f*

feeder ['fi:dər] *n* : comedero *m* (para animales)

feel¹ ['fi:l] *v* felt ['fɛlt]; feeling *vi* **1** : sentirse, encontrarse ⟨I feel tired : me siento cansada⟩ ⟨he feels hungry : tiene hambre⟩ ⟨she feels like a fool : se siente como una idiota⟩ ⟨to feel like doing something : tener ganas de hacer algo⟩ **2** SEEM : parecer ⟨it feels like spring : parece primavera⟩ **3** THINK : parecerse, opinar, pensar ⟨how does he feel about that? : ¿qué opina él de eso?⟩ — *vt* **1** TOUCH : tocar, palpar **2** SENSE : sentir ⟨to feel the cold : sentir el frío⟩ **3** CONSIDER : sentir, creer, considerar ⟨to feel (it) necessary : creer necesario⟩

feel² *n* **1** SENSATION, TOUCH : sensación *f*, tacto *m* **2** ATMOSPHERE : ambiente *m*, atmósfera *f* **3** to have a feel for : tener un talento especial para

feeler ['fi:lər] *n* : antena *f*, tentáculo *m*

feeling ['fi:lɪŋ] *n* **1** SENSATION : sensación *f*, sensibilidad *f* **2** EMOTION : sentimiento *m* **3** OPINION : opinión *f* **4** feelings *npl* SENSIBILITIES : sentimientos *mpl* ⟨to hurt someone's feelings : herir los sentimientos de alguien⟩

feet → foot

feign ['feɪn] *vt* : simular, aparentar, fingir

feint¹ ['feɪnt] *vi* : fintar, fintear

feint² *n* : finta *f*

feldspar ['fɛldˌspɑr] *n* : feldespato *m*

felicitate [fɪ'lɪsəˌteɪt] *vt* -tated; -tating : felicitar, congratular

felicitation [fɪˌlɪsə'teɪʃən] *n* : felicitación *f*

felicitous [fɪ'lɪsətəs] *adj* : acertado, oportuno

feline¹ ['fi:ˌlaɪn] *adj* : felino

feline² *n* : felino *m*, -na *f*

fell¹ ['fɛl] *vt* : talar (un árbol), derribar (a una persona)

fell² → fall

fellow ['fɛˌlo:] *n* **1** COMPANION : compañero *m*, -ra *f*; camarada *mf* **2** ASSOCIATE : socio *m*, -cia *f* **3** MAN : tipo *m*, hombre *m*

fellowman [ˌfɛlo'mæn] *n*, *pl* -men : prójimo *m*, semejante *m*

fellowship ['fɛlo:ˌʃɪp] *n* **1** COMPANIONSHIP : camaradería *f*, compañerismo *m* **2** ASSOCIATION : fraternidad *f* **3** GRANT : beca *f* (de investigación)

felon ['fɛlən] *n* : malhechor *m*, -chora *f*; criminal *mf*

felonious [fə'lo:niəs] *adj* : criminal

felony ['fɛləni] *n*, *pl* -nies : delito *m* grave

felt¹ ['fɛlt] *n* : fieltro *m*

felt² → feel

female¹ ['fi:ˌmeɪl] *adj* : femenino

female² *n* **1** : hembra *f* (de animal) **2** WOMAN : mujer *f*

feminine ['fɛmənən] *adj* : femenino

femininity [ˌfɛmə'nɪnəti] *n* : feminidad *f*, femineidad *f*

feminism ['fɛməˌnɪzəm] *n* : feminismo *m*

feminist¹ ['fɛmənɪst] *adj* : feminista

feminist² *n* : feminista *mf*

femoral ['fɛmərəl] *adj* : femoral
femur ['fi:mər] *n, pl* **femurs** *or* **femora** ['fɛmərə] : fémur *m*
fence[1] ['fɛnʦ] *v* **fenced; fencing** *vt* : vallar, cercar — *vi* : hacer esgrima
fence[2] *n* : cerca *f*, valla *f*, cerco *m*
fencer ['fɛnʦər] *n* : esgrimista *mf*; esgrimidor *m*, -dora *f*
fencing ['fɛnʦɪŋ] *n* **1** : esgrima *m* (deporte) **2** : materiales *mpl* para cercas **3** ENCLOSURE : cercado *m*
fend ['fɛnd] *vt* **to fend off** : rechazar (un enemigo), parar (un golpe), eludir (una pregunta) — *vi* **to fend for oneself** : arreglárselas sólo, valerse por sí mismo
fender ['fɛndər] *n* : guardabarros *mpl*, salpicadera *f Mex*
fennel ['fɛnəl] *n* : hinojo *m*
ferment[1] [fər'mɛnt] *v* : fermentar
ferment[2] ['fər,mɛnt] *n* **1** : fermento *m* (en la química) **2** TURMOIL : agitación *f*, conmoción *f*
fermentation [,fərmən'teɪʃən, -,mɛn-] *n* : fermentación *f*
fern ['fərn] *n* : helecho *m*
ferocious [fə'ro:ʃəs] *adj* : feroz — **ferociously** *adv*
ferociousness [fə'ro:ʃəsnəs] *n* : ferocidad *f*
ferocity [fə'rɑsəti] *n* : ferocidad *f*
ferret[1] ['fɛrət] *vi* SNOOP : hurgar, husmear — *vt* **to ferret out** : descubrir
ferret[2] *n* : hurón *m*
ferric ['fɛrɪk] *or* **ferrous** ['fɛrəs] *adj* : férrico
Ferris wheel ['fɛrɪs] *n* : noria *f*
ferry[1] ['fɛri] *vt* **-ried; -rying** : llevar, transportar
ferry[2] *n, pl* **-ries** : transbordador *m*, ferry *m*
ferryboat ['fɛri,bo:t] *n* : transbordador *m*, ferry *m*
fertile ['fərtəl] *adj* : fértil, fecundo
fertility [fər'tɪləti] *n* : fertilidad *f*
fertilization [,fərtələ'zeɪʃən] *n* : fertilización *f* (del suelo), fecundación (de un huevo)
fertilize ['fərtəl,aɪz] *vt* **-ized; -izing** **1** : fecundar (un huevo) **2** : fertilizar, abonar (el suelo)
fertilizer ['fərtəl,aɪzər] *n* : fertilizante *m*, abono *m*
fervent ['fərvənt] *adj* : ferviente, fervoroso, ardiente — **fervently** *adv*
fervid ['fərvɪd] *adj* : ardiente, apasionado — **fervidly** *adv*
fervor ['fərvər] *n* : fervor *m*, ardor *m*
fester ['fɛstər] *vi* : enconarse, supurar
festival ['fɛstəvəl] *n* : fiesta *f*, festividad *f*, festival *m*
festive ['fɛstɪv] *adj* : festivo — **festively** *adv*
festivity [fɛs'tɪvəti] *n, pl* **-ties** : festividad *f*, celebración *f*
festoon[1] [fɛs'tu:n] *vt* : adornar, engalanar
festoon[2] *n* GARLAND : guirnalda *f*
fetal ['fi:təl] *adj* : fetal

fetch ['fɛʧ] *vt* **1** BRING : traer, recoger, ir a buscar **2** REALIZE : realizar, venderse por ⟨the jewelry fetched $10,000 : las joyas se vendieron por $10,000⟩
fetching ['fɛʧɪŋ] *adj* : atractivo, encantador
fête[1] ['feɪt, 'fɛt] *vt* **fêted; fêting** : festejar, agasajar
fête[2] *n* : fiesta *f*
fetid ['fɛtəd] *adj* : fétido
fetish ['fɛtɪʃ] *n* : fetiche *m*
fetlock ['fɛt,lɑk] *n* : espolón *m*
fetter ['fɛtər] *vt* : encadenar, poner grillos a
fetters ['fɛtərz] *npl* : grillos *mpl*, grilletes *mpl*, cadenas *fpl*
fettle ['fɛtəl] *n* **in fine fettle** : en buena forma, en plena forma
fetus ['fi:təs] *n* : feto *m*
feud[1] ['fju:d] *vi* : pelear, contender
feud[2] *n* : contienda *f*, enemistad *f* (heredada)
feudal ['fju:dəl] *adj* : feudal
feudalism ['fju:dəl,ɪzəm] *n* : feudalismo *m*
fever ['fi:vər] *n* : fiebre *f*, calentura *f*
feverish ['fi:vərɪʃ] *adj* **1** : afiebrado, con fiebre, febril **2** FRANTIC : febril, frenético
few[1] ['fju:] *adj* : pocos ⟨with few exceptions : con pocas excepciones⟩ ⟨a few times : varias veces⟩
few[2] *pron* **1** : pocos ⟨few (of them) were ready : pocos estaban listos⟩ **2 a few** : algunos, unos cuantos **3 few and far between** : contados
fewer ['fju:ər] *pron* : menos ⟨the fewer the better : cuantos menos mejor⟩
fez ['fɛz] *n, pl* **fezzes** : fez *m*
fiancé [,fi:,ɑn'seɪ, ,fi:'ɑn,seɪ] *n* : prometido *m*, novio *m*
fiancée [,fi:,ɑn'seɪ, ,fi:'ɑn,seɪ] *n* : prometida *f*, novia *f*
fiasco [fi'æs,ko:] *n, pl* **-coes** : fiasco *m*, fracaso *m*
fiat ['fi:,ɑt, -,æt, -ət; 'faɪət, -,æt] *n* : decreto *m*, orden *m*
fib[1] ['fɪb] *vi* **fibbed; fibbing** : decir mentirillas
fib[2] *n* : mentirilla *f*, bola *f fam*
fibber ['fɪbər] *n* : mentirosillo *m*, -lla *f*; cuentista *mf fam*
fiber *or* **fibre** ['faɪbər] *n* : fibra *f*
fiberboard ['faɪbər,bord] *n* : cartón *m* madera
fiberglass ['faɪbər,glæs] *n* : fibra *f* de vidrio
fibrillate ['fɪbrə,leɪt, 'faɪ-] *vi* **-lated; -lating** : fibrilar
fibrillation [,fɪbrə'leɪʃən, ,faɪ-] *n* : fibrilación *f*
fibrous ['faɪbrəs] *adj* : fibroso
fibula ['fɪbjələ] *n, pl* **-lae** [-,li:, -,laɪ] *or* **-las** : peroné *m*
fickle ['fɪkəl] *adj* : inconstante, voluble, veleidoso
fickleness ['fɪkəlnəs] *n* : volubilidad *f*, inconstancia *f*, veleidad *f*

fiction ['fɪkʃən] *n* : ficción *f*
fictional ['fɪkʃənəl] *adj* : ficticio
fictitious [fɪk'tɪʃəs] *adj* **1** IMAGINARY : ficticio, imaginario **2** FALSE : falso, ficticio
fiddle[1] ['fɪdəl] *vi* -dled; -dling **1** : tocar el violín **2 to fiddle with** : juguetear con, toquetear
fiddle[2] *n* : violín *m*
fiddler ['fɪdlər, 'fɪdələr] *n* : violinista *mf*
fiddlesticks ['fɪdəl,stɪks] *interj* : ¡tonterías!
fidelity [fə'dɛləti, faɪ-] *n, pl* -ties : fidelidad *f*
fidget[1] ['fɪdʒət] *vi* **1** : moverse, estarse inquieto **2 to fidget with** : juguetear con
fidget[2] *n* **1** : persona *f* inquieta **2 fidgets** *npl* RESTLESSNESS : inquietud *f*
fidgety ['fɪdʒəti] *adj* : inquieto
fiduciary[1] [fə'du:ʃi,ɛri, -'dju:-, -ʃəri] *adj* : fiduciario
fiduciary[2] *n, pl* -ries : fiduciario *m*, -ria *f*
field[1] ['fi:ld] *vt* : interceptar y devolver (una pelota), presentar (un candidato), sortear (una pregunta)
field[2] *adj* : de campaña, de campo ⟨field hospital : hospital de campaña⟩ ⟨field goal : gol de campo⟩ ⟨field trip : viaje de estudio⟩
field[3] *n* **1** : campo *m* (de cosechas, de batalla, de magnetismo) **2** : campo *m*, cancha *f* (en deportes) **3** : campo *m* (de trabajo), esfera *f* (de actividades)
fielder ['fi:ldər] *n* : jugador *m*, -dora *f* de campo; fildeador *m*, -dora *f*
field glasses *n* : binoculares *mpl*, gemelos *mpl*
fiend ['fi:nd] *n* **1** DEMON : demonio *m* **2** EVILDOER : persona *f* maligna; malvado *m*, -da *f* **3** FANATIC : fanático *m*, -ca *f*
fiendish ['fi:ndɪʃ] *adj* : diabólico — **fiendishly** *adv*
fierce ['fɪrs] *adj* **fiercer; -est 1** FEROCIOUS : fiero, feroz **2** HEATED : acalorado **3** INTENSE : intenso, violento, fuerte — **fiercely** *adv*
fierceness ['fɪrsnəs] *n* **1** FEROCITY : ferocidad *f*, fiereza *f* **2** INTENSITY : intensidad *f*, violencia *f*
fieriness ['faɪərinəs] *n* : pasión *f*, ardor *m*
fiery ['faɪəri] *adj* **fierier; -est 1** BURNING : ardiente, llameante **2** GLOWING : encendido **3** PASSIONATE : acalorado, ardiente, fogoso
fiesta [fi'ɛstə] *n* : fiesta *f*
fife ['faɪf] *n* : pífano *m*
fifteen[1] [fɪf'ti:n] *adj* : quince
fifteen[2] *n* : quince *m*
fifteenth[1] [fɪf'ti:nθ] *adj* : decimoquinto
fifteenth[2] *n* **1** : decimoquinto *m*, -ta *f* (en una serie) **2** : quinceavo *m*, quinceava parte *f*
fifth[1] ['fɪfθ] *adj* : quinto

fifth[2] *n* **1** : quinto *m*, -ta *f* (en una serie) **2** : quinto *m*, quinta parte *f* **3** : quinta *f* (en la música)
fiftieth[1] ['fɪftiəθ] *adj* : quincuagésimo
fiftieth[2] *n* **1** : quincuagésimo *m*, -ma *f* (en una serie) **2** : cincuentavo *m*, cincuentava parte *f*
fifty[1] ['fɪfti] *adj* : cincuenta
fifty[2] *n, pl* -ties : cincuenta *m*
fifty-fifty[1] [,fɪfti'fɪfti] *adv* : a medias, mitad y mitad
fifty-fifty[2] *adj* **to have a fifty-fifty chance** : tener un cincuenta por ciento de posibilidades
fig ['fɪg] *n* : higo *m*
fight[1] ['faɪt] *v* **fought** ['fɔt]; **fighting** *vi* : luchar, combatir, pelear — *vt* : luchar contra, combatir contra
fight[2] *n* **1** COMBAT : lucha *f*, pelea *f*, combate *m* **2** MATCH : pelea *f*, combate *m* (en boxeo) **3** QUARREL : disputa *f*, pelea *f*, pleito *m*
fighter ['faɪtər] *n* **1** COMBATANT : luchador *m*, -dora *f*; combatiente *mf* **2** BOXER : boxeador *m*, -dora *f*
figment ['fɪgmənt] *n* **figment of the imagination** : producto *m* de la imaginación
figurative ['fɪgjərətɪv, -gə-] *adj* : figurado, metafórico
figuratively ['fɪgjərətɪvli, -gə-] *adv* : en sentido figurado, de manera metafórica
figure[1] ['fɪgjər, -gər] *v* -ured; -uring *vt* **1** CALCULATE : calcular **2** ESTIMATE : figurarse, calcular ⟨he figured it was possible : se figuró que era posible⟩ — *vi* **1** FEATURE, STAND OUT : figurar, destacar **2 that figures!** : ¡obvio!, ¡no me extraña nada!
figure[2] *n* **1** DIGIT : número *m*, cifra *f* **2** PRICE : precio *m*, cifra *f* **3** PERSONAGE : figura *f*, personaje *m* **4** : figura *f*, tipo *m*, físico *m* ⟨to have a good figure : tener buen tipo, tener un buen físico⟩ **5** DESIGN, OUTLINE : figura *f* **6 figures** *npl* : aritmética *f*
figurehead ['fɪgjər,hɛd, -gər-] *n* : testaferro *m*, líder *mf* sin poder
figure of speech *n* : figura *f* retórica, figura *f* de hablar
figure out *vt* **1** UNDERSTAND : entender **2** RESOLVE : resolver (un problema, etc.)
figurine [,fɪgjə'ri:n] *n* : estatuilla *f*
Fijian ['fi:dʒiən, fɪ'ji:ən] *n* : fijiano *m*, -na *f* — **Fijian** *adj*
filament ['fɪləmənt] *n* : filamento *m*
filbert ['fɪlbərt] *n* : avellana *f*
filch ['fɪlʧ] *vt* : hurtar, birlar *fam*
file[1] ['faɪl] *v* **filed; filing** *vt* **1** CLASSIFY : clasificar **2** : archivar (documentos) **3** SUBMIT : presentar ⟨to file charges : presentar cargos⟩ **4** SMOOTH : limar — *vi* : desfilar, entrar (o salir) en fila
file[2] *n* **1** : lima *f* ⟨nail file : lima de uñas⟩ **2** DOCUMENTS : archivo *m* **3** LINE : fila *f*

filial ['fɪliəl, 'fɪljəl] *adj* : filial
filibuster[1] ['fɪlə,bʌstər] *vi* : practicar el obstruccionismo
filibuster[2] *n* : obstruccionismo *m*
filibusterer ['fɪlə,bʌstərər] *n* : obstruccionista *mf*
filigree ['fɪlə,griː] *n* : filigrana *f*
Filipino [,fɪlə'piːnoː] *n* : filipino *m*, -na *f* — **Filipino** *adj*
fill[1] ['fɪl] *vt* **1** : llenar, ocupar ⟨to fill a cup : llenar una taza⟩ ⟨to fill a room : ocupar una sala⟩ **2** STUFF : rellenar **3** PLUG : tapar, rellenar, empastar (un diente) **4** SATISFY : cumplir con, satisfacer **5** *or* **to fill out** : llenar, re-llenar ⟨to fill out a form : rellenar un formulario⟩
fill[2] *n* **1** FILLING, STUFFING : relleno *m* **2** **to eat one's fill** : comer lo suficiente **3** **to have one's fill of** : estar harto de
filler ['fɪlər] *n* : relleno *m*
fillet[1] ['fɪlət, fɪ'leɪ, 'fɪ,leɪ] *vt* : cortar en filetes
fillet[2] *n* : filete *m*
fill in *vt* INFORM : informar, poner al corriente — *vi* **to fill in for** : reemplazar a
filling ['fɪlɪŋ] *n* **1** : relleno *m* **2** : empaste *m* (de un diente)
filling station → **gas station**
filly ['fɪli] *n, pl* **-lies** : potra *f*, potranca *f*
film[1] ['fɪlm] *vt* : filmar — *vi* : rodar
film[2] *n* **1** COATING : capa *f*, película *f* **2** : película *f* (fotográfica) **3** MOVIE : película *f*, filme *m*
filmmaker ['fɪlm,meɪkər] *n* : cineasta *mf*
filmy ['fɪlmi] *adj* **filmier; -est 1** GAUZY : diáfano, vaporoso **2** : cubierto de una película
filter[1] ['fɪltər] *vt* : filtrar
filter[2] *n* : filtro *m*
filth ['fɪlθ] *n* : mugre *f*, porquería *f*, roña *f*
filthiness ['fɪlθinəs] *n* : suciedad *f*
filthy ['fɪlθi] *adj* **filthier; -est 1** DIRTY : mugriento, sucio **2** OBSCENE : obsceno, indecente
filtration [fɪl'treɪʃən] *n* : filtración *f*
fin ['fɪn] *n* **1** : aleta *f* **2** : alerón *m* (de un automóvil o un avión)
finagle [fə'neɪgəl] *vt* **-gled; -gling** : arreglárselas para conseguir
final[1] ['faɪnəl] *adj* **1** DEFINITIVE : definitivo, final, inapelable **2** ULTIMATE : final **3** LAST : último, final
final[2] *n* **1** : final *f* (en deportes) **2 finals** *npl* : exámenes *mpl* finales
finale [fɪ'næli, -'nɑ-] *n* : final *m* ⟨grand finale : final triunfal⟩
finalist ['faɪnəlɪst] *n* : finalista *mf*
finality [faɪ'næləti, fə-] *n, pl* **-ties** : finalidad *f*
finalize ['faɪnəl,aɪz] *vt* **-ized; -izing** : finalizar
finally ['faɪnəli] *adv* **1** LASTLY : por último, finalmente **2** EVENTUALLY : por fin, al final **3** DEFINITIVELY : definitivamente

finance[1] [fə'nænts, 'faɪ,nænts] *vt* **-nanced; -nancing** : financiar
finance[2] *n* **1** : finanzas *fpl* **2 finances** *npl* RESOURCES : recursos *mpl* financieros
financial [fə'nænʧəl, faɪ-] *adj* : financiero, económico
financially [fə'nænʧəli, faɪ-] *adv* : económicamente
financier [,fɪnən'sɪr, ,faɪ,næn-] *n* : financiero *m*, -ra *f*; financista *mf*
financing [fə'næntsɪŋ, 'faɪ,næntsɪŋ] *n* : financiación *f*, financiamiento *m*
finch ['fɪnʧ] *n* : pinzón *m*
find[1] ['faɪnd] *vt* **found** ['faʊnd]; **finding 1** LOCATE : encontrar, hallar ⟨I can't find it : no lo encuentro⟩ ⟨to find one's way : encontrar el camino, orientarse⟩ **2** DISCOVER, REALIZE : descubrir, darse cuenta de ⟨he found it difficult : descubrió que era difícil⟩ **3** DECLARE : declarar, hallar ⟨they found him guilty : lo declararon culpable⟩
find[2] *n* : hallazgo *m*
finder ['faɪndər] *n* : descubridor *m*, -dora *f*
finding ['faɪndɪŋ] *n* **1** FIND : hallazgo *m* **2 findings** *npl* : conclusiones *fpl*
find out *vt* DISCOVER : descubrir, averiguar — *vi* LEARN : enterarse
fine[1] ['faɪn] *vt* **fined; fining** : multar
fine[2] *adj* **finer; -est 1** PURE : puro (dícese del oro y de la plata) **2** THIN : fino, delgado **3** : fino ⟨fine sand : arena fina⟩ **4** SMALL : pequeño, minúsculo ⟨fine print : letras minúsculas⟩ **5** SUBTLE : sutil, delicado **6** EXCELLENT : excelente, magnífico, selecto **7** FAIR : bueno ⟨it's a fine day : hace buen tiempo⟩ **8** EXQUISITE : exquisito, delicado, fino **9 fine arts** : bellas artes *fpl*
fine[3] *n* : multa *f*
finely ['faɪnli] *adv* **1** EXCELLENTLY : con arte **2** ELEGANTLY : elegantemente **3** PRECISELY : con precisión **4 to chop finely** : picar muy fino, picar en trozos pequeños
fineness ['faɪnnəs] *n* **1** EXCELLENCE : excelencia *f* **2** ELEGANCE : elegancia *f*, refinamiento *m* **3** DELICACY : delicadeza *f*, lo fino **4** PRECISION : precisión *f* **5** SUBTLETY : sutileza *f* **6** PURITY : ley *f* (de oro y plata)
finery ['faɪnəri] *n* : galas *fpl*, adornos *mpl*
finesse[1] [fə'nɛs] *vt* **-nessed; -nessing** : ingeniar
finesse[2] *n* **1** REFINEMENT : refinamiento *m*, finura *f* **2** TACT : delicadeza *f*, tacto *m*, diplomacia *f* **3** CRAFTINESS : astucia *f*
finger[1] ['fɪŋgər] *vt* **1** HANDLE : tocar, toquetear **2** ACCUSE : acusar, delatar
finger[2] *n* : dedo *m*
fingerling ['fɪŋgərlɪŋ] *n* : pez *m* pequeño y joven
fingernail ['fɪŋgər,neɪl] *n* : uña *f*
fingerprint[1] ['fɪŋgər,prɪnt] *vt* : tomar las huellas digitales a

fingerprint[2] *n* : huella *f* digital
fingertip ['fɪŋgər,tɪp] *n* : punta *f* del dedo, yema *f* del dedo
finicky ['fɪnɪki] *adj* : maniático, melindroso, mañoso
finish[1] ['fɪnɪʃ] *vt* **1** COMPLETE : acabar, terminar **2** : aplicar un acabado a (muebles, etc.)
finish[2] *n* **1** END : fin *m*, final *m* **2** REFINEMENT : refinamiento *m* **3** : acabado *m* ⟨a glossy finish : un acabado brillante⟩
finite ['faɪ,naɪt] *adj* : finito
fink ['fɪŋk] *n* : mequetrefe *mf fam*
Finn ['fɪn] *n* : finlandés *m*, -desa *f*
Finnish[1] ['fɪnɪʃ] *adj* : finlandés
Finnish[2] *n* : finlandés *m* (idioma)
fiord [fi'ɔrd] → **fjord**
fir ['fər] *n* : abeto *m*
fire[1] ['faɪr] *vt* **fired; firing 1** IGNITE, KINDLE : encender **2** ENLIVEN : animar, avivar **3** DISMISS : despedir **4** SHOOT : disparar **5** BAKE : cocer (cerámica)
fire[2] *n* **1** : fuego *m* **2** BURNING : incendio *m* ⟨fire alarm : alarma contra incendios⟩ ⟨to be on fire : estar en llamas⟩ **3** ENTHUSIASM : ardor *m*, entusiasmo *m* **4** SHOOTING : disparos *mpl*, fuego *m*
firearm ['faɪr,ɑrm] *n* : arma *f* de fuego
fireball ['faɪr,bɔl] *n* **1** : bola *f* de fuego **2** METEOR : bólido *m*
firebreak ['faɪr,breɪk] *n* : cortafuegos *m*
firebug ['faɪr,bʌg] *n* : pirómano *m*, -na *f*; incendiario *m*, -ria *f*
firecracker ['faɪr,krækər] *n* : petardo *m*
fire escape *n* : escalera *f* de incendios
firefighter ['faɪr,faɪtər] *n* : bombero *m*, -ra *f*
firefly ['faɪr,flaɪ] *n, pl* **-flies** : luciérnaga *f*
fireman ['faɪrmən] *n, pl* **-men** [-mən, -,mɛn] **1** FIREFIGHTER : bombero *m*, -ra *f* **2** STOKER : fogonero *m*, -ra *f*
fireplace ['faɪr,pleɪs] *n* : hogar *m*, chimenea *f*
fireproof[1] ['faɪr,pru:f] *vt* : hacer incombustible
fireproof[2] *adj* : incombustible, ignífugo
fireside[1] ['faɪr,saɪd] *adj* : informal ⟨fireside chat : charla informal⟩
fireside[2] *n* **1** HEARTH : chimenea *f*, hogar *m* **2** HOME : hogar *m*, casa *f*
firewall ['faɪr,wɔl] *n* : cortafuegos *m*
firewood ['faɪr,wʊd] *n* : leña *f*
fireworks ['faɪr,wərks] *npl* : fuegos *mpl* artificiales, pirotecnia *f*
firm[1] ['fərm] *vt or* **to firm up** : endurecer
firm[2] *adj* **1** VIGOROUS : fuerte, vigoroso **2** SOLID, UNYIELDING : firme, duro, sólido **3** UNCHANGING : firme, inalterable **4** RESOLUTE : firme, resuelto
firm[3] *n* : empresa *f*, firma *f*, compañía *f*
firmament ['fərməmənt] *n* : firmamento *m*
firmly ['fərmli] *adv* : firmemente
firmness ['fərmnəs] *n* : firmeza *f*
first[1] ['fərst] *adv* **1** : primero ⟨finish your homework first : primero termina tu

tarea⟩ ⟨first and foremost : ante todo⟩ ⟨first of all : en primer lugar⟩ **2** : por primera vez ⟨I saw it first in Boston : lo vi por primera vez en Boston⟩
first[2] *adj* **1** : primero ⟨the first time : la primera vez⟩ ⟨at first sight : a primera vista⟩ ⟨in the first place : en primer lugar⟩ ⟨the first ten applicants : los diez primeros candidatos⟩ **2** FOREMOST : principal, primero ⟨first tenor : tenor principal⟩
first[3] *n* **1** : primero *m*, -ra *f* **2** *or* **first gear** : primera *f* **3 at** ~ : al principio
first aid *n* : primeros auxilios *mpl*
first–class[1] ['fərst'klæs] *adv* : en primera ⟨to travel first-class : viajar en primera⟩
first–class[2] *adj* : de primera
first class *n* : primera clase *f*
firsthand[1] ['fərst'hænd] *adv* : directamente
firsthand[2] *adj* : de primera mano
first lieutenant *n* : teniente *mf*; teniente primero *m*, teniente primera *f*
firstly ['fərstli] *adv* : primeramente, principalmente, en primer lugar
first–rate[1] ['fərst'reɪt] *adv* : muy bien
first–rate[2] *adj* : de primera, de primera clase
first sergeant *n* : sargento *mf*
firth ['fərθ] *n* : estuario *m*
fiscal ['fɪskəl] *adj* : fiscal — **fiscally** *adv*
fish[1] ['fɪʃ] *vi* **1** : pescar **2 to fish for** SEEK : buscar, rebuscar ⟨to fish for compliments : andar a la caza de cumplidos⟩ — *vt* : pescar
fish[2] *n, pl* **fish** *or* **fishes** : pez *m* (vivo), pescado *m* (para comer)
fisherman ['fɪʃərmən] *n, pl* **-men** [-mən, -,mɛn] : pescador *m*, -dora *f*
fishery ['fɪʃəri] *n, pl* **-eries 1** → **fishing 2** : zona *f* pesquera, pesquería *f*
fishhook ['fɪʃ,hʊk] *n* : anzuelo *m*
fishing ['fɪʃɪŋ] *n* : pesca *f*, industria *f* pesquera
fishing pole *n* : caña *f* de pescar
fish market *n* : pescadería *f*
fishy ['fɪʃi] *adj* **fishier; -est 1** : a pescado ⟨a fishy taste : un sabor a pescado⟩ **2** QUESTIONABLE : dudoso, sospechoso ⟨there's something fishy going on : aquí hay gato encerrado⟩
fission ['fɪʃən, -ʒən] *n* : fisión *f*
fissure ['fɪʃər] *n* : fisura *f*, hendidura *f*
fist ['fɪst] *n* : puño *m*
fistful ['fɪst,fʊl] *n* : puñado *m*
fisticuffs ['fɪstɪ,kʌfs] *npl* : lucha *f* a puñetazos
fit[1] ['fɪt] *v* **fitted; fitting** *vt* **1** MATCH : corresponder a, coincidir con ⟨the punishment fits the crime : el castigo corresponde al crimen⟩ **2** : quedar ⟨the dress doesn't fit me : el vestido no me queda⟩ **3** GO : caber, encajar en ⟨her key fits the lock : su llave encaja en la cerradura⟩ **4** INSERT, INSTALL : poner, colocar **5** ADAPT : adecuar, ajustar, adaptar **6** *or* **to fit out** EQUIP : equipar

— *vi* **1** : quedar, entallar ⟨these pants don't fit : estos pantalones no me quedan⟩ **2** CONFORM : encajar, cuadrar **3 to fit in** : encajar, estar integrado
fit² *adj* **fitter; fittest 1** SUITABLE : adecuado, apropiado, conveniente **2** QUALIFIED : calificado, competente **3** HEALTHY : sano, en forma
fit³ *n* **1** ATTACK : ataque *m*, acceso *m*, arranque *m* **2 to be a good fit** : quedar bien **3 to be a tight fit** : ser muy entallado (de ropa), estar apretado (de espacios)
fitful ['fɪtfəl] *adj* : irregular, intermitente — **fitfully** *adv*
fitness ['fɪtnəs] *n* **1** HEALTH : salud *f*, buena forma *f* (física) **2** SUITABILITY : idoneidad *f*
fitting¹ ['fɪtɪŋ] *adj* : adecuado, apropiado
fitting² *n* : accesorio *m*
five¹ ['faɪv] *adj* : cinco
five² *n* : cinco *m*
five hundred¹ *adj* : quinientos
five hundred² *n* : quinientos *m*
fix¹ ['fɪks] *vt* **1** ATTACH, SECURE : sujetar, asegurar, fijar **2** ESTABLISH : fijar, concretar, establecer **3** REPAIR : arreglar, reparar **4** PREPARE : preparar ⟨to fix dinner : preparar la cena⟩ **5** : arreglar, amañar ⟨to fix a race : arreglar una carrera⟩ **6** RIVET : fijar (los ojos, la mirada, etc.)
fix² *n* **1** PREDICAMENT : aprieto *m*, apuro *m* **2** : posición *f* ⟨to get a fix on : establecer la posición de⟩
fixate ['fɪk,seɪt] *vi* **-ated; -ating** : obsesionarse
fixation [fɪk'seɪʃən] *n* : fijación *f*, obsesión *f*
fixed ['fɪkst] *adj* **1** STATIONARY : estacionario, inmóvil **2** UNCHANGING : fijo, inalterable **3** INTENT : fijo ⟨a fixed stare : una mirada fija⟩ **4 to be comfortably fixed** : estar en posición acomodada
fixedly ['fɪksədli] *adv* : fijamente
fixedness ['fɪksədnəs, 'fɪkst-] *n* : rigidez *f*
fixture ['fɪkstʃər] *n* **1** : parte *f* integrante, elemento *m* fijo **2 fixtures** *npl* : instalaciones *fpl* (de una casa)
fizz¹ ['fɪz] *vi* : burbujear
fizz² *n* : efervescencia *f*, burbujeo *m*
fizzle¹ ['fɪzəl] *vi* **-zled; -zling 1** FIZZ : burbujear **2** FAIL : fracasar
fizzle² *n* : fracaso *m*, fiasco *m*
fjord [fi'ɔrd] *n* : fiordo *m*
flab ['flæb] *n* : gordura *f*
flabbergast ['flæbər,gæst] *vt* : asombrar, pasmar, dejar atónito
flabby ['flæbi] *adj* **-bier; -est** : blando, fofo, aguado *CA, Col, Mex*
flaccid ['flæksəd, 'flæsəd] *adj* : fláccido
flag¹ ['flæg] *vi* **flagged; flagging 1** : hacer señales con banderas **2** WEAKEN : flaquear, desfallecer

flag² *n* : bandera *f*, pabellón *m*, estandarte *m*
flagon ['flægən] *n* : jarra *f* grande
flagpole ['flæg,po:l] *n* : asta *f*, mástil *m*
flagrant ['fleɪgrənt] *adj* : flagrante — **flagrantly** *adv*
flagship ['flæg,ʃɪp] *n* : buque *m* insignia
flagstaff ['flæg,stæf] → **flagpole**
flagstone ['flæg,sto:n] *n* : losa *f*, piedra *f*
flail¹ ['fleɪl] *vt* **1** : trillar (grano) **2** : sacudir, agitar (los brazos)
flail² *n* : mayal *m*
flair ['flær] *n* : don *m*, facilidad *f*
flak ['flæk] *ns & pl* **1** : fuego *m* antiaéreo **2** CRITICISM : críticas *fpl*
flake¹ ['fleɪk] *vi* **flaked; flaking** : desmenuzarse, pelarse (dícese de la piel)
flake² *n* : copo *m* (de nieve), escama *f* (de la piel), astilla *f* (de madera)
flamboyance [flæm'bɔɪənts] *n* : extravagancia *f*, rimbombancia *f*
flamboyant [flæm'bɔɪənt] *adj* : exuberante, extravagante, rimbombante
flame¹ ['fleɪm] *vi* **flamed; flaming 1** BLAZE : arder, llamear **2** GLOW : brillar, encenderse
flame² *n* BLAZE : llama *f* ⟨to burst into flames : estallar en llamas⟩ ⟨to go up in flame : incendiarse⟩
flamethrower ['fleɪm,θro:ər] *n* : lanzallamas *m*
flamingo [flə'mɪŋgo] *n*, *pl* **-gos** : flamenco *m*
flammable ['flæməbəl] *adj* : inflamable, flamable
flange ['flændʒ] *n* : reborde *m*, pestaña *f*
flank¹ ['flæŋk] *vt* **1** : flanquear (para defender o atacar) **2** BORDER, LINE : bordear
flank² *n* : ijada *f* (de un animal), costado *m* (de una persona), falda *f* (de una colina), flanco *m* (de un cuerpo de soldados)
flannel ['flænəl] *n* : franela *f*
flap¹ ['flæp] *v* **flapped; flapping** *vi* **1** : aletear ⟨the bird was flapping (its wings) : el pájaro aleteaba⟩ **2** FLUTTER : ondear, agitarse — *vt* : batir, agitar
flap² *n* **1** FLAPPING : aleteo *m*, aletazo *m* (de alas) **2** : soplada *f* (de un sobre), hoja *f* (de una mesa), faldón *m* (de una chaqueta)
flapjack ['flæp,dʒæk] → **pancake**
flare¹ ['flær] *vi* **flared; flaring 1** FLAME, SHINE : llamear, brillar **2 to flare up** : estallar, explotar (de cólera)
flare² *n* **1** FLASH : destello *m* **2** SIGNAL : (luz *f* de) bengala *f* **3 solar flare** : erupción *f* solar
flash¹ ['flæʃ] *vi* **1** SHINE, SPARKLE : destellar, brillar, relampaguear **2** : pasar como un relámpago ⟨an idea flashed through my mind : una idea me cruzó la mente como un relámpago⟩ — *vt* : despedir, lanzar (una luz), transmitir (un mensaje)

flash² *adj* SUDDEN : repentino
flash³ *n* **1** : destello *m* (de luz), fogonazo *m* (de una explosión) **2 flash of lightning** : relámpago *m* **3 in a flash** : de repente, de un abrir y cerrar los ojos
flashback ['flæʃ,bæk] *n* : flashback *m*
flashiness ['flæʃinəs] *n* : ostentación *f*
flashlight ['flæʃ,laɪt] *n* : linterna *f*
flashy ['flæʃi] *adj* **flashier; -est** : llamativo, ostentoso
flask ['flæsk] *n* : frasco *m*
flat¹ ['flæt] *vt* **flatted; flatting 1** FLATTEN : aplanar, achatar **2** : bajar de tono (en música)
flat² *adv* **1** EXACTLY : exactamente ⟨in ten minutes flat : en diez minutos exactos⟩ **2** : desafinado, demasiado bajo (en la música)
flat³ *adj* **flatter; flattest 1** EVEN, LEVEL : plano, llano **2** SMOOTH : liso **3** DEFINITE : categórico, rotundo, explícito ⟨a flat refusal : una negativa categórica⟩ **4** DULL : aburrido, soso, monótono (dícese la voz) **5** DEFLATED : desinflado, pinchado, ponchado *Mex* **6** : bemol (en música) ⟨to sing flat : cantar desafinado⟩
flat⁴ *n* **1** PLAIN : llano *m*, terreno *m* llano **2** : bemol *m* (en la música) **3** APARTMENT : apartamento *m*, departamento *m* **4** *or* **flat tire** : pinchazo *m*, ponchadura *f Mex*
flatbed ['flæt,bɛd] *n* : camión *m* de plataforma
flatcar ['flæt,kɑr] *n* : vagón *m* abierto
flatfish ['flæt,fɪʃ] *n* : platija *f*
flat-footed ['flæt,fʊtəd, ,flæt'-] *adj* : de pies planos
flatly ['flætli] *adv* DEFINITELY : categóricamente, rotundamente
flatness ['flætnəs] *n* **1** EVENNESS : lo llano, lisura *f*, uniformidad *f* **2** DULLNESS : monotonía *f*
flat-out ['flæt'aʊt] *adj* **1** : frenético, a toda máquina ⟨a flat-out effort : un esfuerzo frenético⟩ **2** CATEGORICAL : descarado, rotundo, categórico
flatten ['flætən] *vt* : aplanar, achatar
flatter ['flætər] *vt* **1** OVERPRAISE : adular **2** COMPLIMENT : halagar **3** : favorecer ⟨the photo flatters you : la foto te favorece⟩
flatterer ['flætərər] *n* : adulador *m*, -dora *f*
flattering ['flætərɪŋ] *adj* **1** COMPLIMENTARY : halagador **2** BECOMING : favorecedor
flattery ['flætəri] *n, pl* **-ries** : halagos *mpl*
flatulence ['flætʃələnts] *n* : flatulencia *f*, ventosidad *f*
flatulent ['flætʃələnt] *adj* : flatulento
flatware ['flæt,wær] *n* : cubertería *f*, cubiertos *mpl*
flaunt¹ ['flɔnt] *vt* : alardear, hacer alarde de
flaunt² *n* : alarde *m*, ostentación *f*
flavor¹ ['fleɪvər] *vt* : dar sabor a, sazonar

flavor² *n* **1** : gusto *m*, sabor *m* **2** FLAVORING : sazón *f*, condimento *m*
flavorful ['fleɪvərfəl] *adj* : sabroso
flavoring ['fleɪvərɪŋ] *n* : condimento *m*, sazón *f*
flavorless ['fleɪvərləs] *adj* : sin sabor
flaw ['flɔ] *n* : falla *f*, defecto *m*, imperfección *f*
flawed ['flɔd] *adj* : imperfecto, con defectos
flawless ['flɔləs] *adj* : impecable, perfecto — **flawlessly** *adv*
flax ['flæks] *n* : lino *m*
flaxen ['flæksən] *adj* : rubio, blondo (dícese del pelo)
flay ['fleɪ] *vt* **1** SKIN : desollar, despellejar **2** VILIFY : criticar con dureza, vilipendiar
flea ['fli:] *n* : pulga *f*
fleck¹ ['flɛk] *vt* : salpicar
fleck² *n* : mota *f*, pinta *f*
fledgling ['flɛdʒlɪŋ] *n* : polluelo *m*, pollito *m*
flee ['fli:] *v* **fled** ['flɛd]; **fleeing** *vi* : huir, escapar(se) — *vt* : huir de
fleece¹ ['fli:s] *vt* **fleeced; fleecing 1** SHEAR : esquilar, trasquilar **2** SWINDLE : estafar, defraudar
fleece² *n* : lana *f*, vellón *m*
fleet¹ ['fli:t] *vi* : moverse con rapidez
fleet² *adj* SWIFT : rápido, veloz
fleet³ *n* : flota *f*
fleet admiral *n* : almirante *mf*
fleeting ['fli:tɪŋ] *adj* : fugaz, breve
flesh ['flɛʃ] *n* **1** : carne *f* (de seres humanos y animales) **2** : pulpa *f* (de frutas)
flesh out *vt* : desarrollar, darle cuerpo a
fleshy ['flɛʃi] *adj* **fleshier; -est** : gordo (dícese de las personas), carnoso (dícese de la fruta)
flew → **fly**
flex ['flɛks] *vt* : doblar, flexionar
flexibility [,flɛksə'bɪləti] *n, pl* **-ties** : flexibilidad *f*, elasticidad *f*
flexible ['flɛksəbəl] *adj* : flexible — **flexibly** [-bli] *adv*
flick¹ ['flɪk] *vt* : dar un capirotazo a (con el dedo) ⟨to flick a switch : darle al interruptor⟩ — *vi* **1** FLIT : revolotear **2 to flick through** : hojear (un libro)
flick² *n* : coletazo *m* (de una cola), capirotazo *m* (de un dedo)
flicker¹ ['flɪkər] *vi* **1** FLUTTER : revolotear, aletear **2** BLINK, TWINKLE : parpadear, titilar
flicker² *n* **1** : parpadeo *m*, titileo *m* **2** HINT, TRACE : indicio *m*, rastro *m* ⟨a flicker of hope : un rayo de esperanza⟩
flier ['flaɪər] *n* **1** AVIATOR : aviador *m*, -dora *f* **2** CIRCULAR : folleto *m* publicitario, circular *f*
flight ['flaɪt] *n* **1** : vuelo *m* (de aves o aviones), trayectoria *f* (de proyectiles) **2** TRIP : vuelo *m* **3** FLOCK, SQUADRON : bandada *f* (de pájaros), escuadrilla *f* (de aviones) **4** ESCAPE : huida *f*, fuga

f **5 flight of fancy** : ilusiones *fpl*, fantasía *f* **6 flight of stairs** : tramo *m*
flight attendant *n* : auxiliar *mf* de vuelo
flightless ['flaɪtləs] *adj* : no volador
flighty ['flaɪti] *adj* **flightier; -est** : caprichoso, frívolo
flimsy [flɪmzi] *adj* **flimsier; -est** **1** LIGHT, THIN : ligero, fino **2** WEAK : endeble, poco sólido **3** IMPLAUSIBLE : pobre, flojo, poco convincente ⟨a flimsy excuse : una excusa floja⟩
flinch ['flɪntʃ] *vi* **1** WINCE : estremecerse **2** RECOIL : recular, retroceder
fling[1] ['flɪŋ] *vt* **flung** ['flʌŋ]; **flinging** **1** THROW : lanzar, tirar, arrojar **2 to fling oneself** : lanzarse, tirarse, precipitarse
fling[2] *n* **1** THROW : lanzamiento *m* **2** ATTEMPT : intento *m* **3** AFFAIR : aventura *f* **4** BINGE : juerga *f*
flint ['flɪnt] *n* : pedernal *m*
flinty ['flɪnti] *adj* **flintier; -est** **1** : de pedernal **2** STERN, UNYIELDING : severo, inflexible
flip[1] ['flɪp] *v* **flipped; flipping** *vt* **1** TOSS : tirar ⟨to flip a coin : echar a cara o cruz⟩ **2** OVERTURN : dar la vuelta a, voltear — *vi* **1** : moverse bruscamente **2 to flip through** : hojear (un libro)
flip[2] *adj* : insolente, descarado
flip[3] *n* **1** FLICK : capirotazo *m*, golpe *m* ligero **2** SOMERSAULT : voltereta *f*
flip-flop ['flɪp,flɑp] *n* **1** REVERSAL : giro *m* radical **2** THONG : chancla *f*, chancleta *f*
flippancy ['flɪpəntsi] *n, pl* **-cies** : ligereza *f*, falta *f* de seriedad
flippant ['flɪpənt] *adj* : ligero, frívolo, poco serio
flipper ['flɪpər] *n* : aleta *f*
flirt[1] ['flərt] *vi* **1** : coquetear, flirtear **2** TRIFLE : jugar ⟨to flirt with death : jugar con la muerte⟩
flirt[2] *n* : coqueto *m*, -ta *f*
flirtation [,flər'teɪʃən] *n* : devaneo *m*, coqueteo *m*
flirtatious [,flər'teɪʃəs] *adj* : insinuante, coqueto
flit ['flɪt] *vi* **flitted; flitting** **1** : revolotear **2 to flit about** : ir y venir rápidamente
float[1] ['floːt] *vi* **1** : flotar **2** WANDER : vagar, errar — *vt* **1** : poner a flote, hacer flotar (un barco) **2** LAUNCH : hacer flotar (una empresa) **3** ISSUE : emitir (acciones en la bolsa)
float[2] *n* **1** : flotador *m*, corcho *m* (para pescar) **2** BUOY : boya *f* **3** : carroza *f* (en un desfile)
floating ['floːtɪŋ] *adj* : flotante
flock[1] ['flɑk] *vi* **1** : moverse en rebaño **2** CONGREGATE : congregarse, reunirse
flock[2] *n* : rebaño *m* (de ovejas), bandada *f* (de pájaros)
floe ['floː] *n* : témpano *m* de hielo
flog ['flɑg] *vt* **flogged; flogging** : azotar, fustigar
flood[1] ['flʌd] *vt* : inundar, anegar

flood[2] *n* **1** INUNDATION : inundación *f* **2** TORRENT : avalancha *f*, diluvio *m*, torrente *m* ⟨a flood of tears : un mar de lágrimas⟩
floodlight ['flʌd,laɪt] *n* : foco *m*
floodwater ['flʌd,wɔtər] *n* : crecida *f*, creciente *f*
floor[1] ['flor] *vt* **1** : solar, poner suelo a (una casa o una sala) **2** KNOCK DOWN : derribar, echar al suelo **3** NONPLUS : desconcertar, confundir, dejar perplejo
floor[2] *n* **1** : suelo *m*, piso *m* ⟨dance floor : pista de baile⟩ **2** STORY : piso *m*, planta *f* ⟨ground floor : planta baja⟩ ⟨second floor : primer piso⟩ **3** : mínimo *m* (de sueldos, precios, etc.)
floorboard ['flor,bord] *n* : tabla *f* del suelo, suelo *m*, piso *m*
flooring ['florɪŋ] *n* : entarimado *m*
flop[1] ['flɑp] *vi* **flopped; flopping** **1** FLAP : golpearse, agitarse **2** COLLAPSE : dejarse caer, desplomarse **3** FAIL : fracasar
flop[2] *n* **1** FAILURE : fracaso *m* **2 to take a flop** : caerse
floppy ['flɑpi] *adj* **-pier; -est** **1** : blando, flexible **2 floppy disk** : diskette *m*, disquete *m*
flora ['florə] *n* : flora *f*
floral ['florəl] *adj* : floral, floreado
florid ['florɪd] *adj* **1** FLOWERY : florido **2** REDDISH : rojizo
florist ['florɪst] *n* : florista *mf*
floss[1] ['flɔs] *vi* : limpiarse los dientes con hilo dental
floss[2] *n* **1** : hilo *m* de seda (de bordar) **2** → **dental floss**
flotation [flo'teɪʃən] *n* : flotación *f*
flotilla [flo'tɪlə] *n* : flotilla *f*
flotsam ['flɑtsəm] *n* **1** : restos *mpl* flotantes (en el mar) **2 flotsam and jetsam** : desechos *mpl*, restos *mpl*
flounce[1] ['flaʊnts] *vi* **flounced; flouncing** : moverse haciendo aspavientos ⟨she flounced into the room : entró en la sala haciendo aspavientos⟩
flounce[2] *n* **1** RUFFLE : volante *m* **2** FLOURISH : aspaviento *m*
flounder[1] ['flaʊndər] *vi* **1** STRUGGLE : forcejear **2** STUMBLE : no saber qué hacer o decir, perder el hilo (en un discurso)
flounder[2] *n, pl* **flounder** *or* **flounders** : platija *f*
flour[1] ['flaʊər] *vt* : enharinar
flour[2] *n* : harina *f*
flourish[1] ['flərɪʃ] *vi* THRIVE : florecer, prosperar, crecer (dícese de las plantas) — *vt* BRANDISH : blandir
flourish[2] *n* : floritura *f*, floreo *m*
flourishing ['flərɪʃɪŋ] *adj* : floreciente, próspero
flout ['flaʊt] *vt* : desacatar, burlarse de
flow[1] ['floː] *vi* **1** COURSE : fluir, manar, correr **2** CIRCULATE : circular, correr ⟨traffic is flowing smoothly : el tránsito está circulando con fluidez⟩

flow² *n* **1** FLOWING : flujo *m*, circulación *f* **2** STREAM : corriente *f*, chorro *m*

flower¹ ['flaʊər] *vi* : florecer, florear

flower² *n* : flor *f*

flowered ['flaʊərd] *adj* : florido, floreado

floweriness ['flaʊərinəs] *n* : floritura *f*

flowering¹ ['flaʊəriŋ] *adj* : floreciente

flowering² *n* : floración *f*, florecimiento *m*

flowerpot ['flaʊər,pɑt] *n* : maceta *f*, tiesto *m*, macetero *m*

flowery ['flaʊəri] *adj* **1** : florido **2** FLOWERED : floreado, de flores

flowing ['floːɪŋ] *adj* : fluido, corriente

flown → **fly**

flu ['fluː] *n* : gripe *f*, gripa *f Col, Mex*

fluctuate ['flʌktʃʊ,eɪt] *vi* **-ated; -ating** : fluctuar

fluctuation [,flʌktʃʊ'eɪʃən] *n* : fluctuación *f*

flue ['fluː] *n* : tiro *m*, salida *f* de humos

fluency ['fluːənsi] *n* : fluidez *f*, soltura *f*

fluent ['fluːənt] *adj* : fluido

fluently ['fluːəntli] *adv* : con soltura, con fluidez

fluff¹ ['flʌf] *vt* **1** : mullir ⟨to fluff up the pillows : mullir las almohadas⟩ **2** BUNGLE : echar a perder, equivocarse

fluff² *n* **1** FUZZ : pelusa *f* **2** DOWN : plumón *m*

fluffy ['flʌfi] *adj* **fluffier; -est 1** DOWNY : lleno de pelusa, velloso **2** SPONGY : esponjoso

fluid¹ ['fluːɪd] *adj* : fluido

fluid² *n* : fluido *m*, líquido *m*

fluidity [flu'ɪdəti] *n* : fluidez *f*

fluid ounce *n* : onza *f* líquida (29.57 mililitros)

fluke ['fluːk] *n* : golpe *m* de suerte, chiripa *f*, casualidad *f*

flung → **fling**

flunk ['flʌŋk] *vt* FAIL : reprobar — *vi* : salir reprobando

fluorescence [,flʊr'ɛsənts, ,flɔr-] *n* : fluorescencia *f*

fluorescent [,flʊr'ɛsənt, ,flɔr-] *adj* : fluorescente

fluoridate ['flɔrə,deɪt, 'flʊr-] *vt* **-dated; -dating** : fluorizar

fluoridation [,flɔrə'deɪʃən, ,flʊr-] *n* : fluorización *f*, fluoración *f*

fluoride ['flɔr,aɪd, 'flʊr-] *n* : fluoruro *m*

fluorine ['flʊr,iːn] *n* : flúor *m*

fluorocarbon [,flɔro'kɑrbən, ,flʊr-] *n* : fluorocarbono *m*

flurry ['flɜri] *n, pl* **-ries 1** GUST : ráfaga *f* **2** SNOWFALL : nevisca *f* **3** BUSTLE : frenesí *m*, bullicio *m* **4** BARRAGE : aluvión *m*, oleada *f* ⟨a flurry of questions : un aluvión de preguntas⟩

flush¹ ['flʌʃ] *vt* **1** : limpiar con agua ⟨to flush the toilet : jalar la cadena⟩ **2** RAISE : hacer salir, levantar (en la caza) — *vi* BLUSH : ruborizarse, sonrojarse

flush² *adv* : al mismo nivel, a ras

flush³ *adj* **1** *or* **flushed** ['flʌʃt] : colorado, rojo, encendido (dícese de la cara) **2** FILLED : lleno a rebosar **3** ABUNDANT : copioso, abundante **4** AFFLUENT : adinerado **5** ALIGNED, SMOOTH : alineado, liso **6 flush against** : pegado a, contra

flush⁴ *n* **1** FLOW, JET : chorro *m*, flujo *m* rápido **2** SURGE : arrebato *m*, arranque *m* ⟨a flush of anger : un arrebato de cólera⟩ **3** BLUSH : rubor *m*, sonrojo *m* **4** GLOW : resplandor *m*, flor *f* ⟨the flush of youth : la flor de la juventud⟩ ⟨in the flush of victory : en la euforia del triunfo⟩

fluster¹ ['flʌstər] *vt* : poner nervioso, aturdir

fluster² *n* : agitación *f*, confusión *f*

flute ['fluːt] *n* : flauta *f*

fluted ['fluːtəd] *adj* **1** GROOVED : estriado, acanalado **2** WAVY : ondulado

fluting ['fluːtɪŋ] *n* : estrías *fpl*

flutist ['fluːtɪst] *n* : flautista *mf*

flutter¹ ['flʌtər] *vi* **1** : revolotear (dícese de un pájaro), ondear (dícese de una bandera), palpitar con fuerza (dícese del corazón) **2 to flutter about** : ir y venir, revolotear — *vt* : sacudir, batir

flutter² *n* **1** FLUTTERING : revoloteo *m*, aleteo *m* **2** COMMOTION, STIR : revuelo *m*, agitación *f*

flux ['flʌks] *n* **1** : flujo *m* (en física y medicina) **2** CHANGE : cambio *m* ⟨to be in a state of flux : estar cambiando continuamente⟩

fly¹ ['flaɪ] *v* **flew** ['fluː]; **flown** ['floːn]; **flying** *vi* **1** : volar (dícese de los pájaros, etc.) **2** TRAVEL : volar (dícese de los aviones), ir en avión (dícese de los pasajeros) **3** FLOAT : flotar, ondear **4** FLEE : huir, escapar **5** RUSH : correr, irse volando **6** PASS : pasar (volando) ⟨how time flies! : ¡cómo pasa el tiempo!⟩ **7 to fly open** : abrir de golpe — *vt* : pilotar (un avión), hacer volar (una cometa)

fly² *n, pl* **flies 1** : mosca *f* ⟨to drop like flies : caer como moscas⟩ **2** : bragueta *f* (de pantalones, etc.)

flyer → **flier**

flying saucer *n* : platillo *m* volador

flypaper ['flaɪ,peɪpər] *n* : papel *m* matamoscas

flyspeck ['flaɪ,spɛk] *n* **1** : excremento *m* de mosca **2** SPECK : motita *f*, puntito *m*

flyswatter ['flaɪ,swɑtər] *n* : matamoscas *m*

flywheel ['flaɪ,ʍiːl] *n* : volante *m*

foal¹ ['foːl] *vi* : parir

foal² *n* : potro *m*, -tra *f*

foam¹ ['foːm] *vi* : hacer espuma

foam² *n* : espuma *f*

foamy ['foːmi] *adj* **foamier; -est** : espumoso

focal ['foːkəl] *adj* **1** : focal, central **2 focal point** : foco *m*, punto *m* de referencia

fo'c'sle ['foːksəl] → **forecastle**

focus¹ ['fo:kəs] v **-cused** or **-cussed;**
-cusing or **-cussing** vt **1** : enfocar (un
instrumento) **2** CONCENTRATE : concentrar, centrar — vi : enfocar, fijar la
vista

focus² n, pl **-ci** ['fo:,saɪ, -,kaɪ] **1** : foco m
⟨to be in focus : estar enfocado⟩ **2** FO-
CUSING : enfoque m **3** CENTER : centro m, foco m

fodder ['fɑdər] n : pienso m, forraje m

foe ['fo:] n : enemigo m, -ga f

fog¹ ['fɔg, 'fɑg] v **fogged; fogging** vt
: empañar — vi **to fog up** : empañarse

fog² n : niebla f, neblina f

foggy ['fɔgi, 'fɑ-] adj **foggier; -est** : nebuloso, brumoso

foghorn ['fɔg,hɔrn, 'fɑg-] n : sirena f de
niebla

fogy ['fo:gi] n, pl **-gies** : carca mf fam,
persona f chapada a la antigua

foible ['fɔɪbəl] n : flaqueza f, debilidad f

foil¹ ['fɔɪl] vt : frustrar, hacer fracasar

foil² n **1** : lámina f de metal, papel m de
aluminio **2** CONTRAST : contraste m,
complemento m **3** SWORD : florete m
(en esgrima)

foist ['fɔɪst] vt : encajar, endilgar fam,
colocar

fold¹ ['fo:ld] vt **1** BEND : doblar, plegar
2 CLASP : cruzar (brazos), enlazar
(manos), plegar (alas) **3** EMBRACE : estrechar, abrazar **4 to fold in** : incorporar ⟨fold in the cream : incorpore la
crema⟩ — vi **1** FAIL : fracasar **2 to fold
up** : doblarse, plegarse

fold² n **1** SHEEPFOLD : redil m (para ovejas) **2** FLOCK : rebaño m ⟨to return to
the fold : volver al redil⟩ **3** CREASE
: pliegue m, doblez m

folder ['fo:ldər] n **1** CIRCULAR : circular f, folleto m **2** BINDER : carpeta f

foliage ['fo:liɪʤ, -lɪʤ] n : follaje m

folio ['fo:li,o:] n, pl **-lios** : folio m

folk¹ ['fo:k] adj : popular, folklórico
⟨folk customs : costumbres populares⟩
⟨folk dance : danza folklórica⟩

folk² n, pl **folk** or **folks 1** PEOPLE : gente
f **2 folks** npl : familia f, padres mpl

folklore ['fo:k,lor] n : folklore m

folklorist ['fo:k,lorist] n : folklorista mf

folksy ['fo:ksi] adj **folksier; -est**
: campechano

follicle ['fɑlɪkəl] n : folículo m

follow ['falo] vt **1** : seguir ⟨follow the
guide : siga al guía⟩ ⟨she followed the
road : siguió el camino, continuó por
el camino⟩ **2** PURSUE : perseguir,
seguir **3** OBEY : seguir, cumplir, observar **4** UNDERSTAND : entender —
vi **1** : seguir **2** UNDERSTAND : entender **3 it follows that . . .** : se deduce
que . . .

follower ['faloər] n : seguidor m, -dora f

following¹ ['faloɪŋ] adj NEXT : siguiente

following² n FOLLOWERS : seguidores
mpl

following³ prep AFTER : después de

follow through vi **to follow through with**
: continuar con, realizar

follow up vt : seguir (una sugerencia,
etc.), investigar (una huella)

folly ['fɑli] n, pl **-lies** : locura f, desatino
m

foment [fo'mɛnt] vt : fomentar

fond ['fɑnd] adj **1** LOVING : cariñoso,
tierno **2** PARTIAL : aficionado **3** FER-
VENT : ferviente, fervoroso

fondle ['fɑndəl] vt **-dled; -dling** : acariciar

fondly ['fɑndli] adv : cariñosamente,
afectuosamente

fondness ['fɑndnəs] n **1** LOVE : cariño
m **2** LIKING : afición f

fondue [fɑn'du:, -'dju:] n : fondue f

font ['fɑnt] n **1** or **baptismal font** : pila
f bautismal **2** FOUNTAIN : fuente f

food ['fu:d] n : comida f, alimento m

food chain n : cadena f alimenticia

foodstuffs ['fu:d,stʌfs] npl : comestibles
mpl

fool¹ ['fu:l] vi **1** JOKE : bromear, hacer
el tonto **2** TOY : jugar, juguetear ⟨don't
fool with the computer : no juegues con
la computadora⟩ **3 to fool around**
: perder el tiempo ⟨he fools around instead of working : pierde el tiempo en
vez de trabajar⟩ — vt DECEIVE : engañar, burlar

fool² n **1** IDIOT : idiota mf; tonto m, -ta
f; bobo m, -ba f **2** JESTER : bufón m,
-fona f

foolhardiness ['fu:l,hɑrdinəs] n : imprudencia f

foolhardy ['fu:l,hɑrdi] adj RASH : imprudente, temerario, precipitado

foolish ['fu:lɪʃ] adj **1** STUPID : insensato,
estúpido **2** SILLY : idiota, tonto

foolishly ['fu:lɪʃli] adv : tontamente

foolishness ['fu:lɪʃnəs] n : insensatez f,
estupidez f, tontería f

foolproof ['fu:l,pru:f] adj : infalible

foot ['fʊt] n, pl **feet** ['fi:t] : pie m

footage ['fʊtɪʤ] n : medida f en pies, metraje m (en el cine)

football ['fʊt,bɔl] n : futbol m americano, fútbol m americano

footbridge ['fʊt,brɪʤ] n : pasarela f,
puente m peatonal

foothills ['fʊt,hɪlz] npl : estribaciones fpl

foothold ['fʊt,ho:ld] n **1** : punto m de
apoyo **2 to gain a foothold** : afianzarse
en una posición

footing ['fʊtɪŋ] n **1** BALANCE : equilibrio m **2** FOOTHOLD : punto m de apoyo
3 BASIS : base f ⟨on an equal footing
: en igualdad⟩

footlights ['fʊt,laɪts] npl : candilejas fpl

footlocker ['fʊt,lɑkər] n : baúl m pequeño, cofre m

footloose ['fʊt,lu:s] adj : libre y sin compromiso

footman ['fʊtmən] n, pl **-men** [-mən,
-,mɛn] : lacayo m

footnote ['fʊt,no:t] n : nota f al pie de la
página

footpath ['fʊt,pæθ] n : sendero m, senda f, vereda f

footprint ['fʊt͵prɪnt] *n* : huella *f*
footrace ['fʊt͵reɪs] *n* : carrera *f* pedestre
footrest ['fʊt͵rest] *n* : apoyapiés *m*, reposapiés *m*
footstep ['fʊt͵step] *n* 1 STEP : paso *m* 2 FOOTPRINT : huella *f*
footstool ['fʊt͵stuːl] *n* : taburete *m*, escabel *m*
footwear ['fʊt͵wær] *n* : calzado *m*
footwork ['fʊt͵wərk] *n* : juego *m* de piernas, juego *m* de pies
fop ['fɑp] *n* : petimetre *m*, dandi *m*
for¹ ['fɔr] *conj* : puesto que, porque
for² *prep* 1 (*indicating purpose*) : para, de ⟨clothes for children : ropa para niños⟩ ⟨it's time for dinner : es la hora de comer⟩ 2 BECAUSE OF : por ⟨for fear of : por miedo de⟩ 3 (*indicating a recipient*) : para, por ⟨a gift for you : un regalo para ti⟩ 4 (*indicating support*) : por ⟨he fought for his country : luchó por su patria⟩ 5 (*indicating a goal*) : por, para ⟨a cure for cancer : una cura para el cáncer⟩ ⟨for your own good : por tu propio bien⟩ 6 (*indicating correspondence or exchange*) : por, para ⟨I bought it for $5 : lo compré por $5⟩ ⟨a lot of trouble for nothing : mucha molestia para nada⟩ 7 AS FOR : para, con respecto a 8 (*indicating duration*) : durante, por ⟨he's going for two years : se va por dos años⟩ ⟨I spoke for ten minutes : hablé (durante) diez minutos⟩ ⟨she has known it for three months : lo sabe desde hace tres meses⟩
forage¹ ['fɔrɪdʒ] *v* **-aged; -aging** *vi* : hurgar (en busca de alimento) — *vt* : buscar (provisiones)
forage² *n* : forraje *m*
foray ['fɔr͵eɪ] *n* : incursión *f*
forbear¹ [fɔr'bær] *vi* **-bore** [-'bor]; **-borne** [-'born]; **-bearing** 1 ABSTAIN : abstenerse 2 : tener paciencia
forbear² → forbear
forbearance [fɔr'bærənts] *n* 1 ABSTAINING : abstención *f* 2 PATIENCE : paciencia *f*
forbid [fər'bɪd] *vt* **-bade** [-'bæd, -'beɪd]; **-bidden** [-'bɪdən]; **-bidding** 1 PROHIBIT : prohibir 2 PREVENT : impedir
forbidding [fər'bɪdɪŋ] *adj* 1 IMPOSING : imponente 2 DISAGREEABLE : desagradable, ingrato 3 GRIM : severo
force¹ ['fɔrs] *vt* **forced; forcing** 1 COMPEL : obligar, forzar 2 : forzar ⟨to force open the window : forzar la ventana⟩ ⟨to force a lock : forzar una cerradura⟩ 3 IMPOSE : imponer, obligar
force² *n* 1 : fuerza *f* 2 **by force** : por la fuerza 3 **in force** : en vigor, en vigencia
forced ['fɔrst] *adj* : forzado, forzoso
forceful ['fɔrsfəl] *adj* : fuerte, energético, contundente
forcefully ['fɔrsfəli] *adv* : con energía, con fuerza
forcefulness ['fɔrsfəlnəs] *n* : contundencia *f*, fuerza *f*

forceps ['fɔrsəps, -͵seps] *ns & pl* : fórceps *m*
forcible ['fɔrsəbəl] *adj* 1 FORCED : forzoso 2 CONVINCING : contundente, convincente — **forcibly** [-bli] *adv*
ford¹ ['fɔrd] *vt* : vadear
ford² *n* : vado *m*
fore¹ ['fɔr] *adv* 1 FORWARD : hacia adelante 2 **fore and aft** : de popa a proa
fore² *adj* 1 FORWARD : delantero, de adelante 2 FORMER : anterior
fore³ *n* 1 : frente *m*, delantera *f* 2 **to come to the fore** : empezar a destacar, saltar a primera plana
fore-and-aft ['fɔrən'æft, -ənd-] *adj* : longitudinal
forearm ['fɔr͵ɑrm] *n* : antebrazo *m*
forebear ['fɔr͵bær] *n* : antepasado *m*, -da *f*
foreboding [for'boːdɪŋ] *n* : premonición *f*, presentimiento *m*
forecast¹ ['fɔr͵kæst] *vt* **-cast; -casting** : pronosticar, predecir
forecast² *n* : predicción *f*, pronóstico *m*
forecastle ['foːksəl] *n* : castillo *m* de proa
foreclose [for'kloːz] *vt* **-closed; -closing** : ejecutar (una hipoteca)
forefather ['fɔr͵fɑðər] *n* : antepasado *m*, ancestro *m*
forefinger ['fɔr͵fɪŋgər] *n* : índice *m*, dedo *m* índice
forefoot ['fɔr͵fʊt] *n* : pata *f* delantera
forefront ['fɔr͵frʌnt] *n* : frente *m*, vanguardia *f* ⟨in the forefront : a la vanguardia⟩
forego [for'goː] *vt* **-went; -gone; -going** 1 PRECEDE : preceder 2 → forgo
foregoing [for'goːɪŋ] *adj* : precedente, anterior
foregone [for'gɔn] *adj* : previsto ⟨a foregone conclusion : un resultado inevitable⟩
foreground ['fɔr͵graʊnd] *n* : primer plano *m*
forehand¹ ['fɔr͵hænd] *adj* : directo, derecho
forehand² *n* : golpe *m* del derecho
forehead ['fɔrəd, 'fɔr͵hed] *n* : frente *f*
foreign ['fɔrən] *adj* 1 : extranjero, exterior ⟨foreign countries : países extranjeros⟩ ⟨foreign trade : comercio exterior⟩ 2 ALIEN : ajeno, extraño ⟨foreign to their nature : ajeno a su carácter⟩ ⟨a foreign body : un cuerpo extraño⟩
foreigner ['fɔrənər] *n* : extranjero *m*, -ra *f*
foreknowledge [for'nɑlɪdʒ] *n* : conocimiento *m* previo
foreleg ['fɔr͵leg] *n* : pata *f* delantera
foreman ['fɔrmən] *n, pl* **-men** [-mən, -͵men] : capataz *mf* ⟨foreman of the jury : presidente del jurado⟩
foremost¹ ['fɔr͵moːst] *adv* : en primer lugar
foremost² *adj* : más importante, principal, grande
forenoon ['fɔr͵nuːn] *n* : mañana *m*

forensic [fə'rɛn̪sɪk] *adj* **1** RHETORICAL : retórico, de argumentación **2** : forense ⟨forensic medicine : medicina forense⟩

foreordain [ˌfoɾoɾ'deɪn] *vt* : predestinar, predeterminar

forequarter ['foɾˌkwɔɾtəɾ] *n* : cuarto *m* delantero

forerunner ['foɾˌrʌnəɾ] *n* : precursor *m*, -sora *f*

foresee [foɾ'siː] *vt* **-saw; -seen; -seeing** : prever

foreseeable [foɾ'siːəbəl] *adj* : previsible ⟨in the foreseeable future : en el futuro inmediato⟩

foreshadow [foɾ'ʃædoː] *vt* : anunciar, prefigurar

foresight ['foɾˌsaɪt] *n* : previsión *f*

foresighted ['foɾˌsaɪt̪əd] *adj* : previsto

forest ['foɾəst] *n* : bosque *m* (en zonas templadas), selva *f* (en zonas tropicales)

forestall [foɾ'stɔl] *vt* **1** PREVENT : prevenir, impedir **2** PREEMPT : adelantarse a

forested ['foɾəst̪əd] *adj* : arbolado

forester ['foɾəstəɾ] *n* : silvicultor *m*, -tora *f*

forestland ['foɾəstˌlænd] *n* : zona *f* boscosa

forest ranger → **ranger**

forestry ['foɾəstri] *n* : silvicultura *f*, ingeniería *f* forestal

foreswear → **forswear**

foretaste[1] ['foɾˌteɪst] *vt* **-tasted; -tasting** : anticipar

foretaste[2] *n* : anticipo *m*

foretell [foɾ'tɛl] *vt* **-told; -telling** : predecir, pronosticar, profetizar

forethought ['foɾˌθɔt] *n* : previsión *f*, reflexión *f* previa

forever [foɾ'ɛvəɾ] *adv* **1** PERPETUALLY : para siempre, eternamente **2** CONTINUALLY : siempre, constantemente

forevermore [foɾˌɛvəɾ'moɾ] *adv* : por siempre jamás

forewarn [foɾ'wɔɾn] *vt* : prevenir, advertir

foreword ['foɾwəɾd] *n* : prólogo *m*

forfeit[1] ['foɾfət] *vt* : perder el derecho a

forfeit[2] *n* **1** FINE, PENALTY : multa *f* **2** : prenda *f* (en un juego)

forge[1] ['foɾʤ] *v* **forged; forging** *vt* **1** : forjar (metal o un plan) **2** COUNTERFEIT : falsificar — *vi* **to forge ahead** : avanzar, seguir adelante

forge[2] *n* : forja *f*

forger ['foɾʤəɾ] *n* : falsificador *m*, -dora *f*

forgery ['foɾʤəri] *n, pl* **-eries** : falsificación *f*

forget [fəɾ'gɛt] *v* **-got** [-'gɑt]; **-gotten** [-'gɑt̪ən] *or* **-got; -getting** *vt* : olvidar — *vi* **to forget about** : olvidarse de, no acordarse de

forgetful [fəɾ'gɛt̪fəl] *adj* : olvidadizo

forget-me-not [fəɾ'gɛtmiˌnɑt] *n* : nomeolvides *mf*

forgettable [fəɾ'gɛt̪əbəl] *adj* : poco memorable

forgivable [fəɾ'gɪvəbəl] *adj* : perdonable

forgive [fəɾ'gɪv] *vt* **-gave** [-'geɪv]; **-given** [-'gɪvən]; **-giving** : perdonar

forgiveness [fəɾ'gɪvnəs] *n* : perdón *m*

forgiving [fəɾ'gɪvɪŋ] *adj* : indulgente, comprensivo, clemente

forgo *or* **forego** [foɾ'goː] *vt* **-went; -gone; -going** : privarse de, renunciar a

fork[1] ['foɾk] *vi* : ramificarse, bifurcarse — *vt* **1** : levantar (con un tenedor, una horca, etc.) **2 to fork over** : desembolsar

fork[2] *n* **1** : tenedor *m* (utensilio de cocina) **2** PITCHFORK : horca *f*, horquilla *f* **3** : bifurcación *f* (de un río o camino), horqueta *f* (de un árbol)

forked ['foɾkt, 'foɾkəd] *adj* : bífido, ahorquillado

forklift ['foɾkˌlɪft] *n* : carretilla *f* elevadora

forlorn [foɾ'loɾn] *adj* **1** DESOLATE : abandonado, desolado, desamparado **2** SAD : triste **3** DESPERATE : desesperado

forlornly [foɾ'loɾnli] *adv* **1** SADLY : con tristeza **2** HALFHEARTEDLY : sin ánimo

form[1] ['foɾm] *vt* **1** FASHION, MAKE : formar **2** DEVELOP : moldear, desarrollar **3** CONSTITUTE : constituir, formar **4** ACQUIRE : adquirir (un hábito), formar (una idea) — *vi* : tomar forma, formarse

form[2] *n* **1** SHAPE : forma *f*, figura *f* **2** MANNER : manera *f*, forma *f* **3** DOCUMENT : formulario *m* **4** : forma *f* ⟨in good form : en buena forma⟩ ⟨true to form : en forma consecuente⟩ **5** MOLD : molde *m* **6** KIND, VARIETY : clase *f*, tipo *m* **7** : forma *f* (en gramática) ⟨plural forms : formas plurales⟩

formal[1] ['foɾməl] *adj* **1** CEREMONIOUS : formal, de etiqueta, ceremonioso **2** OFFICIAL : formal, oficial, de forma

formal[2] *n* **1** BALL : baile *m* formal, baile *m* de etiqueta **2** *or* **formal dress** : traje *m* de etiqueta

formaldehyde [foɾ'mældəˌhaɪd] *n* : formaldehído *m*

formality [foɾ'mæləti] *n, pl* **-ties** : formalidad *f*

formalize ['foɾməˌlaɪz] *vt* **-ized; -izing** : formalizar

formally ['foɾməli] *adv* : formalmente

format[1] ['foɾˌmæt] *vt* **-matted; -matting** : formatear

format[2] *n* : formato *m*

formation [foɾ'meɪʃən] *n* **1** FORMING : formación *f* **2** SHAPE : forma *f* **3 in formation** : en formación

formative ['foɾmətɪv] *adj* : formativo

former ['foɾməɾ] *adj* **1** PREVIOUS : antiguo, anterior ⟨the former president : el antiguo presidente⟩ **2** : primero (de dos)

formerly ['foɾməɾli] *adv* : anteriormente, antes

formidable ['fɔrmədəbəl, fɔr'mɪdə-] adj
: formidable — **formidably** adv
formless ['fɔrmləs] adj : informe, amorfo
formula ['fɔrmjələ] n, pl **-las** or **-lae** [-ˌliː,
-ˌlaɪ] **1** : fórmula f **2 baby formula**
: preparado m para biberón
formulate ['fɔrmjəˌleɪt] vt **-lated; -lating**
: formular, hacer
formulation [ˌfɔrmjə'leɪʃən] n : formulación f
fornicate ['fɔrnəˌkeɪt] vi **-cated; -cating**
: fornicar
fornication [ˌfɔrnə'keɪʃən] n : fornicación f
forsake [fər'seɪk] vt **-sook** [-'sʊk];
-saken [-'seɪkən]; **-saking 1** ABANDON
: abandonar, desamparar **2** RELIN-
QUISH : renunciar a
forswear [fɔr'swær] v **-swore; -sworn;
-swearing** vt RENOUNCE : renunciar a
— vi : perjurar
forsythia [fər'sɪθiə] n : forsitia f
fort ['fɔrt] n **1** STRONGHOLD : fuerte m,
fortaleza f, fortín m **2** BASE : base f militar
forte ['fɔrt, 'fɔrˌteɪ] n : fuerte m
forth ['fɔrθ] adv **1** : adelante ⟨from this
day forth : de hoy en adelante⟩ **2 and
so forth** : etcétera
forthcoming [fɔrθ'kʌmɪŋ, 'fɔrθˌ-] adj **1**
COMING : próximo **2** DIRECT, OPEN
: directo, franco, comunicativo
forthright ['fɔrθˌraɪt] adj : directo, franco — **forthrightly** adv
forthrightness ['fɔrθˌraɪtnəs] n : franqueza f
forthwith [fɔrθ'wɪθ, -'wɪð] adv : inmediatamente, en el acto, enseguida
fortieth¹ ['fɔrtiəθ] adj : cuadragésimo
fortieth² n **1** : cuadragésimo m, -ma f
(en una serie) **2** : cuarentavo m,
cuarentava parte f
fortification [ˌfɔrtəfə'keɪʃən] n : fortificación f
fortify ['fɔrtəˌfaɪ] vt **-fied; -fying** : fortificar
fortitude ['fɔrtəˌtuːd, -ˌtjuːd] n : fortaleza
f, valor m
fortnight ['fɔrtˌnaɪt] n : quince días mpl,
dos semanas fpl
fortnightly¹ ['fɔrtˌnaɪtli] adv : cada
quince días
fortnightly² adj : quincenal
fortress ['fɔrtrəs] n : fortaleza f
fortuitous [fɔr'tuːətəs, -'tjuː-] adj : fortuito, accidental
fortunate ['fɔrtʃənət] adj : afortunado
fortunately ['fɔrtʃənətli] adv : afortunadamente, con suerte
fortune ['fɔrtʃən] n **1** : fortuna f ⟨to seek
one's fortune : buscar uno su fortuna⟩
2 LUCK : suerte f, fortuna f **3** DESTINY,
FUTURE : destino m, buenaventura f **4**
: dineral m, platal m ⟨she spent a fortune : se gastó un dineral⟩
fortune–teller ['fɔrtʃənˌtɛlər] n : adivino
m, -na f

fortune–telling ['fɔrtʃənˌtɛlɪŋ] n : adivinación f
forty¹ ['fɔrti] adj : cuarenta
forty² n, pl **forties** : cuarenta m
forum ['fɔrəm] n, pl **-rums** : foro m
forward¹ ['fɔrwərd] vt **1** PROMOTE : promover, adelantar, fomentar **2** SEND
: remitir, enviar
forward² adv **1** : adelante, hacia adelante ⟨to go forward : irse adelante⟩ **2
from this day forward** : de aquí en adelante
forward³ adj **1** : hacia adelante, delantero **2** BRASH : atrevido, descarado
forward⁴ n : delantero m, -ra f (en deportes)
forwarder ['fɔrwərdər] n : agencia f de
transportes, agente mf expedidor
forwardness ['fɔrwərdnəs] n : atrevimiento m, descaro m
forwards ['fɔrwərdz] adv → **forward²**
fossil¹ ['fɑsəl] adj : fósil
fossil² n : fósil m
fossilize ['fɑsəˌlaɪz] vt **-ized; -izing** : fos-
ilizar — vi : fosilizarse
foster¹ ['fɑstər] vt : promover, fomentar
foster² adj : adoptivo ⟨foster child : niño
adoptivo⟩
fought → **fight**
foul¹ ['faʊl] vi : cometer faltas (en deportes) — vt **1** DIRTY, POLLUTE : contaminar, ensuciar **2** TANGLE : enredar
foul² adv **1** → **foully 2** : contra las reglas
foul³ adj **1** REPULSIVE : asqueroso, repugnante **2** CLOGGED : atascado, obstruido **3** TANGLED : enredado **4** OB-
SCENE : obsceno **5** BAD : malo ⟨foul
weather : mal tiempo⟩ **6** : antirreglamentario (en deportes)
foul⁴ n : falta f, faul m
foully ['faʊli] adv : asquerosamente
foulmouthed ['faʊlˌmæuːðd, -ˌmaʊθt]
adj : malhablado
foulness ['faʊlnəs] n **1** DIRTINESS : suciedad f **2** INCLEMENCY : inclemencia
f **3** OBSCENITY : obscenidad f, grosería
f
foul play n : actos mpl criminales
foul–up ['faʊlˌʌp] n : lío m, confusión f,
desastre m
foul up vt SPOIL : estropear, arruinar —
vi BUNGLE : echar todo a perder
found¹ → **find**
found² ['faʊnd] vt : fundar, establecer
foundation [faʊn'deɪʃən] n **1** FOUND-
ING : fundación f **2** BASIS : fundamento
m, base f **3** INSTITUTION : fundación f
4 : cimientos mpl (de un edificio)
founder¹ ['faʊndər] vi SINK : hundirse,
irse a pique
founder² n : fundador m, -dora f
founding ['faʊndɪŋ] adj : fundador ⟨the
founding fathers : los fundadores⟩
foundling ['faʊndlɪŋ] n : expósito m, -ta
f
foundry ['faʊndri] n, pl **-dries** : fundición f

fount ['faʊnt] *n* SOURCE : fuente *f*, origen *m*
fountain ['faʊntən] *n* **1** SPRING : fuente *f*, manantial *m* **2** SOURCE : fuente *f*, origen *m* **3** JET : chorro *m* (de agua), surtidor *m*
fountain pen *n* : pluma *f* fuente
four[1] ['for] *adj* : cuatro
four[2] *n* **1** : cuatro *m* **2 on all fours** : a gatas
fourfold ['for₁fo:ld, -'fo:ld] *adj* : cuadruple
four hundred[1] *adj* : cuatrocientos
four hundred[2] *n* : cuatrocientos *m*
fourscore ['for'skor] *adj* EIGHTY : ochenta *m*
fourteen[1] [for'ti:n] *adj* : catorce
fourteen[2] *n* : catorce *m*
fourteenth[1] [for'ti:nθ] *adj* : decimocuarto
fourteenth[2] *n* **1** : decimocuarto *m*, -ta *f* (en una serie) **2** : catorceavo *m*, catorceava parte *f*
fourth[1] ['forθ] *adj* : cuarto
fourth[2] *n* **1** : cuarto *m*, -ta *f* (en una serie) **2** : cuarto *m*, cuarta parte *f*
fowl ['faʊl] *n, pl* **fowl** *or* **fowls** **1** BIRD : ave *f* **2** CHICKEN : pollo *m*
fox[1] ['faks] *vt* **1** TRICK : engañar **2** BAFFLE : confundir
fox[2] *n, pl* **foxes** : zorro *m*, -ra *f*
foxglove ['faks₁glʌv] *n* : dedalera *f*, digital *f*
foxhole ['faks₁ho:l] *n* : hoyo *m* para atrincherarse, trinchera *f* individual
foxy ['faksi] *adj* **foxier; -est** SHREWD : astuto
foyer ['fɔɪər, 'fɔɪ₁jeɪ] *n* : vestíbulo *m*
fracas ['freɪkəs, 'fræ-] *n, pl* **-cases** [-kəsəz] : altercado *m*, pelea *f*, reyerta *f*
fraction ['frækʃən] *n* **1** : fracción *f*, quebrado *m* **2** PORTION : porción *f*, parte *f*
fractional ['frækʃənəl] *adj* **1** : fraccionario **2** TINY : minúsculo, mínimo, insignificante
fractious ['frækʃəs] *adj* **1** UNRULY : rebelde **2** IRRITABLE : malhumorado, irritable
fracture[1] ['fræktʃər] *vt* **-tured; -turing** : fracturar
fracture[2] *n* **1** : fractura *f* (de un hueso) **2** CRACK : fisura *f*, grieta *f*, falla *f* (geológica)
fragile ['frædʒəl, -₁dʒaɪl] *adj* : frágil
fragility [frə'dʒɪləti] *n, pl* **-ties** : fragilidad *f*
fragment[1] ['fræg₁mɛnt] *vt* : fragmentar — *vi* : fragmentarse, hacerse añicos
fragment[2] ['frægmənt] *n* : fragmento *m*, trozo *m*, pedazo *m*
fragmentary ['frægmən₁teri] *adj* : fragmentario, incompleto
fragmentation [₁frægmən'teɪʃən, -₁mn-] *n* : fragmentación *f*
fragrance ['freɪgrənts] *n* : fragancia *f*, aroma *m*

fragrant ['freɪgrənt] *adj* : fragante, aromático — **fragrantly** *adv*
frail ['freɪl] *adj* : débil, delicado
frailty ['freɪlti] *n, pl* **-ties** : debilidad *f*, flaqueza *f*
frame[1] ['freɪm] *vt* **framed; framing** **1** FORMULATE : formular, elaborar **2** BORDER : enmarcar, encuadrar **3** INCRIMINATE : incriminar
frame[2] *n* **1** BODY : cuerpo *m* **2** : armazón *f* (de un edificio, un barco, o un avión), bastidor *m* (de un automóvil), cuadro *m* (de una bicicleta), marco *m* (de un cuadro, una ventana, una puerta, etc.) **3 frames** *npl* : armazón *mf*, montura *f* (para anteojos) **4 frame of mind** : estado *m* de ánimo
framework ['freɪm₁wərk] *n* **1** SKELETON, STRUCTURE : armazón *f*, estructura *f* **2** BASIS : marco *m*
franc ['fræŋk] *n* : franco *m*
franchise ['fræn₁tʃaɪz] *n* **1** LICENSE : licencia *f* exclusiva, concesión *f* (en comercio) **2** SUFFRAGE : sufragio *m*
franchisee [₁fræn₁tʃaɪ'zi:, -tʃə-] *n* : concesionario *m*, -ria *f*
Franciscan [fræn'sɪskən] *n* : franciscano *m*, -na *f* — **Franciscan** *adj*
frank[1] ['fræŋk] *vt* : franquear
frank[2] *adj* : franco, sincero, cándido — **frankly** *adv*
frank[3] *n* : franqueo *m* (de correo)
frankfurter ['fræŋkfərtər, -₁fər-] *or* **frankfurt** [-fərt] *n* : salchicha *f* (de Frankfurt, de Viena), perro *m* caliente
frankincense ['fræŋkən₁sɛnts] *n* : incienso *m*
frankness ['fræŋknəs] *n* : franqueza *f*, sinceridad *f*, candidez *f*
frantic ['fræntɪk] *adj* : frenético, desesperado — **frantically** *adv*
fraternal [frə'tərnəl] *adj* : fraterno, fraternal
fraternity [frə'tərnəti] *n, pl* **-ties** : fraternidad *f*
fraternization [₁frætərnə'zeɪʃən] *n* : fraternización *f*, confraternización *f*
fraternize ['frætər₁naɪz] *vi* **-nized; -nizing** : fraternizar, confraternizar
fratricidal [₁frætrə'saɪdəl] *adj* : fratricida
fratricide ['frætrə₁saɪd] *n* : fratricidio *m*
fraud ['frɔd] *n* **1** DECEPTION, SWINDLE : fraude *m*, estafa *f*, engaño *m* **2** IMPOSTOR : impostor *m*, -tora *f*; farsante *mf*
fraudulent ['frɔdʒələnt] *adj* : fraudulento — **fraudulently** *adv*
fraught ['frɔt] *adj* **fraught with** : lleno de, cargado de
fray[1] ['freɪ] *vt* **1** WEAR : desgastar, deshilachar **2** IRRITATE : crispar, irritar (los nervios) — *vi* : desgastarse, deshilacharse
fray[2] *n* : pelea *f* ⟨to join the fray : salir a la palestra⟩ ⟨to return to the fray : volver a la carga⟩

frazzle¹ ['fræzəl] *vt* **-zled; -zling 1** FRAY : desgastar, deshilachar **2** EXHAUST : agotar, fatigar

frazzle² *n* EXHAUSTION : agotamiento *m*

freak ['fri:k] *n* **1** ODDITY : ejemplar *m* anormal, fenómeno *m*, rareza *f* **2** ENTHUSIAST : entusiasta *mf*

freakish ['fri:kɪʃ] *adj* : extraño, estrafalario, raro

freak out *vi* : ponerse como loco — *vt* : darle un ataque (a alguien)

freckle¹ ['frɛkəl] *vi* **-led; -ling** : cubrirse de pecas

freckle² *n* : peca *f*

free¹ ['fri:] *vt* **freed; freeing 1** LIBERATE : libertar, liberar, poner en libertad **2** RELIEVE, RID : librar, eximir **3** RELEASE, UNTIE : desatar, soltar **4** UNCLOG : desatascar, destapar

free² *adv* **1** FREELY : libremente **2** GRATIS : gratuitamente, gratis

free³ *adj* **freer; freest 1** : libre ⟨free as a bird : libre como un pájaro⟩ **2** EXEMPT : libre ⟨tax-free : libre de impuestos⟩ **3** GRATIS : gratuito, gratis **4** VOLUNTARY : espontáneo, voluntario, libre **5** UNOCCUPIED : desocupado, libre **6** LOOSE : suelto

freebooter ['fri:ˌbu:ţər] *n* : pirata *mf*

freeborn ['fri:'bɔrn] *adj* : nacido libre

freedom ['fri:dəm] *n* : libertad *f*

free–for–all ['fri:fərˌɔl] *n* : pelea *f*, batalla *f* campal

freelance¹ ['fri:ˌlænts] *vi* **-lanced; -lancing** : trabajar por cuenta propia

freelance² *adj* : por cuenta propia, independiente

freeload ['fri:ˌlo:d] *vi* : gorronear *fam*, gorrear *fam*

freeloader ['fri:ˌlo:dər] *n* : gorrón *m*, -rrona *f*; gorrero *m*, -ra *f*; vividor *m*, -dora *f*

freely ['fri:li] *adv* **1** FREE : libremente **2** GRATIS : gratis, gratuitamente

freestanding ['fri:'stændɪŋ] *adj* : de pie, no empotrado, independiente

freeway ['fri:ˌweɪ] *n* : autopista *f*

freewill ['fri:ˌwɪl] *adj* : de propia voluntad

free will *n* : libre albedrío *m*, propia voluntad *f*

freeze¹ ['fri:z] *v* **froze** ['fro:z]; **frozen** ['fro:zən]; **freezing** *vi* **1** : congelarse, helarse ⟨the water froze in the lake : el agua se congeló en el lago⟩ ⟨my blood froze : se me heló la sangre⟩ ⟨I'm freezing : me estoy helando⟩ **2** STOP : quedarse inmóvil — *vt* : helar, congelar (líquidos), congelar (alimentos, precios, activos)

freeze² *n* **1** FROST : helada *f* **2** FREEZING : congelación *f*, congelamiento *m*

freeze–dried ['fri:z'draɪd] *adj* : liofilizado

freeze–dry ['fri:z'draɪ] *vt* **-dried; -drying** : liofilizar

freezer ['fri:zər] *n* : congelador *m*

freezing ['fri:zɪŋ] *adj* : helando ⟨it's freezing! : ¡hace un frío espantoso!⟩

freezing point *n* : punto *m* de congelación

freight¹ ['freɪt] *vt* : enviar como carga

freight² *n* **1** SHIPPING, TRANSPORT : transporte *m*, porte *m*, flete *m* **2** GOODS : mercancías *fpl*, carga *f*

freighter ['freɪţər] *n* : carguero *m*, buque *m* de carga

French¹ ['frɛntʃ] *adj* : francés

French² *n* **1** : francés *m* (idioma) **2 the French** *npl* : los franceses

french fries ['frɛntʃˌfraɪz] *npl* : papas *fpl* fritas

Frenchman ['frɛntʃmən] *n, pl* **-men** [-mən, -ˌmɛn] : francés *m*

Frenchwoman ['frɛntʃˌwʊmən] *n, pl* **-women** [-ˌwɪmən] : francesa *f*

frenetic [frɪ'nɛţɪk] *adj* : frenético — **frenetically** [-ţɪkli] *adv*

frenzied ['frɛnzid] *adj* : frenético

frenzy ['frɛnzi] *n, pl* **-zies** : frenesí *m*

frequency ['fri:kwəntsi] *n, pl* **-cies** : frecuencia *f*

frequent¹ [frɪ'kwɛnt, 'fri:kwənt] *vt* : frecuentar

frequent² ['fri:kwənt] *adj* : frecuente — **frequently** *adv*

fresco ['frɛsˌko:] *n, pl* **-coes** : fresco *m*

fresh ['frɛʃ] *adj* **1** : dulce ⟨freshwater : agua dulce⟩ **2** PURE : puro **3** fresco ⟨fresh fruits : frutas frescas⟩ **4** CLEAN, NEW : limpio, nuevo ⟨fresh clothes : ropa limpia⟩ ⟨fresh evidence : evidencia nueva⟩ **5** REFRESHED : fresco, descansado **6** IMPERTINENT : descarado, impertinente

freshen ['frɛʃən] *vt* : refrescar, arreglar — *vi* **to freshen up** : arreglarse, lavarse

freshet ['frɛʃət] *n* : arroyo *m* desbordado

freshly ['frɛʃli] *adv* : recientemente, recién

freshman ['frɛʃmən] *n, pl* **-men** [-mən, -ˌmɛn] : estudiante *mf* de primer año universitario

freshness ['frɛʃnəs] *n* : frescura *f*

freshwater ['frɛʃˌwɔţər] *n* : agua *f* dulce

fret¹ ['frɛt] *vi* **fretted; fretting** : preocuparse, inquietarse

fret² *n* **1** VEXATION : irritación *f*, molestia *f* **2** WORRY : preocupación *f* **3** : traste *m* (de un instrumento musical)

fretful ['frɛtfəl] *adj* : fastidioso, quejoso, neurótico

fretfully ['frɛtfəli] *adv* : ansiosamente, fastidiosamente, inquieto

fretfulness ['frɛtfəlnəs] *n* : inquietud *f*, irritabilidad *f*

friable ['fraɪəbəl] *adj* : friable, pulverizable

friar ['fraɪər] *n* : fraile *m*

fricassee¹ ['frɪkəˌsi:, ˌfrɪkə'si:] *vt* **-seed; -seeing** : cocinar al fricasé

fricassee² *n* : fricasé *m*

friction ['frɪkʃən] *n* **1** RUBBING : fricción *f* **2** CONFLICT : fricción *f*, roce *m*

Friday ['fraɪˌdeɪ, -di] *n* : viernes *m*

fridge ['frɪʤ] → **refrigerator**

friend ['frɛnd] *n* : amigo *m*, -ga *f*
friendless ['frɛndləs] *adj* : sin amigos
friendliness ['frɛndlinəs] *n* : simpatía *f*, amabilidad *f*
friendly ['frɛndli] *adj* **-lier; -est 1** : simpático, amable, de amigo ⟨a friendly child : un niño simpático⟩ ⟨friendly advice : consejo de amigo⟩ **2** : agradable, acogedor ⟨a friendly atmosphere : un ambiente agradable⟩ **3** GOOD-NATURED : amigable, amistoso ⟨friendly competition : competencia amistosa⟩
friendship ['frɛnd͵ʃɪp] *n* : amistad *f*
frieze ['fri:z] *n* : friso *m*
frigate ['frɪgət] *n* : fragata *f*
fright ['fraɪt] *n* : miedo *m*, susto *m*
frighten ['fraɪtən] *vt* : asustar, espantar
frightened ['fraɪtənd] *adj* : asustado, temeroso
frightening ['fraɪtənɪŋ] *adj* : espantoso, aterrador
frightful ['fraɪtfəl] *adj* **1** → frightening **2** TREMENDOUS : espantoso, tremendo
frightfully ['fraɪtfəli] *adv* : terriblemente, tremendamente
frigid ['frɪʤɪd] *adj* : glacial, extremadamente frío
frigidity [frɪ'ʤɪdəṭi] *n* **1** COLDNESS : frialdad *f* **2** : frigidez *f* (sexual)
frill ['frɪl] *n* **1** RUFFLE : volante *m* **2** EMBELLISHMENT : floritura *f*, adorno *m*
frilly ['frɪli] *adj* **frillier; -est 1** RUFFLY : con volantes **2** OVERDONE : recargado
fringe¹ ['frɪnʤ] *vt* **fringed; fringing** : orlar, bordear
fringe² *n* **1** BORDER : fleco *m*, orla *f* **2** EDGE : periferia *f*, margen *m* **3 fringe benefits** : incentivos *mpl*, extras *mpl*
frisk ['frɪsk] *vi* FROLIC : retozar, juguetear — *vt* SEARCH : cachear, registrar
friskiness ['frɪskinəs] *n* : vivacidad *f*
frisky ['frɪski] *adj* **friskier; -est** : retozón, juguetón
fritter¹ ['frɪṭər] *vt* : desperdiciar, malgastar ⟨I frittered away the money : malgasté el dinero⟩
fritter² *n* : buñuelo *m*
frivolity [frɪ'valəṭi] *n*, *pl* **-ties** : frivolidad *f*
frivolous ['frɪvələs] *adj* : frívolo, de poca importancia
frivolously ['frɪvələsli] *adv* : frívolamente, a la ligera
frizz¹ ['frɪz] *vi* : rizarse, encresparse, ponerse chino *Mex*
frizz² *n* : rizos *mpl* muy apretados
frizzy ['frɪzi] *adj* **frizzier; -est** : rizado, crespo, chino *Mex*
fro ['fro:] *adv* **to and fro** : de aquí para allá, de un lado para otro
frock ['frak] *n* DRESS : vestido *m*
frog ['frɔg, 'frag] *n* **1** : rana *f* **2** FASTENER : alamar *m* **3 to have a frog in one's throat** : tener carraspera
frogman ['frɔg͵mæn, 'frag-, -mən] *n*, *pl* **-men** [-mən, -͵mɛn] : hombre *m* rana, submarinista *mf*

frolic¹ ['fralɪk] *vi* **-icked; -icking** : retozar, juguetear
frolic² *n* FUN : diversión *f*
frolicsome ['fralɪksəm] *adj* : juguetón
from ['frʌm, 'fram] *prep* **1** (*indicating a starting point*) : desde, de, a partir de ⟨from Cali to Bogota : de Cali a Bogotá⟩ ⟨where are you from? : ¿de dónde eres?⟩ ⟨from that time onward : desde entonces⟩ ⟨from tomorrow : a partir de mañana⟩ **2** (*indicating a source or sender*) : de ⟨a letter from my friend : una carta de mi amiga⟩ ⟨a quote from Shakespeare : una cita de Shakespeare⟩ **3** (*indicating distance*) : de ⟨10 feet from the entrance : a 10 pies de la entrada⟩ **4** (*indicating a cause*) : de ⟨red from crying : rojos de llorar⟩ ⟨he died from the cold : murió del frío⟩ **5** OFF, OUT OF : de ⟨she took it from the drawer : lo sacó del cajón⟩ **6** (*with adverbs or adverbial phrases*) : de, desde ⟨from above : desde arriba⟩ ⟨from among : de entre⟩
frond ['frand] *n* : fronda *f*, hoja *f*
front¹ ['frʌnt] *vi* **1** FACE : dar, estar orientado ⟨the house fronts north : la casa da al norte⟩ **2** : servir de pantalla ⟨he fronts for his boss : sirve de pantalla para su jefe⟩
front² *adj* : delantero, de adelante, primero ⟨the front row : la primera fila⟩
front³ *n* **1** : frente *m*, parte *f* de adelante, delantera *f* ⟨the front of the class : el frente de la clase⟩ ⟨at the front of the train : en la parte delantera del tren⟩ **2** AREA, ZONE : frente *m*, zona *f* ⟨the Eastern front : el frente oriental⟩ ⟨on the educational front : en el frente de la enseñanza⟩ **3** FACADE : fachada *f* (de un edificio o una persona) **4** : frente *m* (en meteorología)
frontage ['frʌntɪʤ] *n* : fachada *f*, frente *m*
frontal ['frʌntəl] *adj* : frontal, de frente
frontier [͵frʌn'tɪr] *n* : frontera *f*
frontiersman [͵frʌn'tɪrzmən] *n*, *pl* **-men** [-mən, -͵mɛn] : hombre *m* de la frontera
frontispiece ['frʌntəs͵pi:s] *n* : frontispicio *m*
frost¹ ['frɔst] *vt* **1** FREEZE : helar **2** ICE : escarchar (pasteles)
frost² *n* **1** : helada *f* (en meteorología) **2** : escarcha *f* ⟨frost on the window : escarcha en la ventana⟩
frostbite ['frɔst͵baɪt] *n* : congelación *f*
frostbitten ['frɔst͵bɪtən] *adj* : congelado (dícese de una persona), quemado (dícese de una planta)
frosting ['frɔstɪŋ] *n* ICING : glaseado *m*, betún *m* *Mex*
frosty ['frɔsti] *adj* **frostier; -est 1** CHILLY : helado, frío **2** COOL, UNFRIENDLY : frío, glacial
froth ['frɔθ] *n*, *pl* **froths** ['frɔθs, 'frɔðz] : espuma *f*

frothy ['frɔθi] *adj* **frothier; -est** : espumoso

frown[1] ['fraʊn] *vi* **1** : fruncir el ceño, fruncir el entrecejo **2 to frown at** : mirar (algo) con ceño, mirar (a alguien) con ceño

frown[2] *n* : ceño *m* (fruncido)

frowsy *or* **frowzy** ['fraʊzi] *adj* **frowsier** *or* **frowzier; -est** : desaliñado, desaseado

froze → **freeze**

frozen → **freeze**

frugal ['fru:gəl] *adj* : frugal, ahorrativo, parco — **frugally** *adv*

frugality [fru'gæləti] *n* : frugalidad *f*

fruit[1] ['fru:t] *vi* : dar fruto

fruit[2] *n* **1** : fruta *f* (término genérico), fruto *m* (término particular) **2 fruits** *npl* REWARDS : frutos *mpl* ⟨the fruits of his labor : los frutos de su trabajo⟩

fruitcake ['fru:t,keɪk] *n* : pastel *m* de frutas

fruitful ['fru:tfəl] *adj* : fructífero, provechoso

fruition [fru'ɪʃən] *n* **1** : cumplimiento *m*, realización *f* **2 to bring to fruition** : realizar

fruitless ['fru:tləs] *adj* : infructuoso, inútil — **fruitlessly** *adv*

fruity ['fru:ṭi] *adj* **fruitier; -est** : (con sabor) a fruta

frumpy ['frʌmpi] *adj* **frumpier; -est** : anticuado y sin atractivo

frustrate ['frʌs,treɪt] *vt* **-trated; -trating** : frustrar

frustrating ['frʌs,treɪṭɪŋ] *adj* : frustrante — **frustratingly** *adv*

frustration [,frʌs'treɪʃən] *n* : frustración *f*

fry[1] ['fraɪ] *vt* **fried; frying** : freír

fry[2] *n, pl* **fries 1** : fritura *f*, plato *m* frito **2** : fiesta *f* en que se sirven frituras **3** *pl* **fry** : alevín *m* (pez)

frying pan *n* : sartén *mf*

fuchsia ['fju:ʃə] *n* **1** : fucsia *f* (planta) **2** : fucsia *m* (color)

fuddle ['fʌdəl] *vt* **-dled; -dling** : confundir, atontar

fuddy-duddy ['fʌdi,dʌdi] *n, pl* **-dies** : persona *f* chapada a la antigua, carca *mf*

fudge[1] ['fʌdʒ] *vt* **fudged; fudging 1** FALSIFY : amañar, falsificar **2** DODGE : esquivar

fudge[2] *n* : dulce *m* blando de chocolate y leche

fuel[1] ['fju:əl] *vt* **-eled** *or* **-elled; -eling** *or* **-elling 1** : abastecer de combustible **2** STIMULATE : estimular

fuel[2] *n* : combustible *m*, carburante *m* (para motores)

fugitive[1] ['fju:dʒəṭɪv] *adj* **1** RUNAWAY : fugitivo **2** FLEETING : efímero, pasajero, fugaz

fugitive[2] *n* : fugitivo *m*, -va *f*

fugue ['fju:g] *n* : fuga *f*

fulcrum ['fʊlkrəm, 'fʌl-] *n, pl* **-crums** *or* **-cra** [-krə] : fulcro *m*

fulfill *or* **fulfil** [fʊl'fɪl] *vt* **-filled; -filling 1** PERFORM : cumplir con, realizar, llevar a cabo **2** SATISFY : satisfacer

fulfillment [fʊl'fɪlmənt] *n* **1** PERFORMANCE : cumplimiento *m*, ejecución *f* **2** SATISFACTION : satisfacción *f*, realización *f*

full[1] ['fʊl, 'fʌl] *adv* **1** VERY : muy ⟨full well : muy bien, perfectamente⟩ **2** ENTIRELY : completamente ⟨she swung full around : giró completamente⟩ **3** DIRECTLY : de lleno, directamente ⟨he looked me full in the face : me miró directamente a la cara⟩

full[2] *adj* **1** FILLED : lleno **2** COMPLETE : completo, pleno **3** MAXIMUM : todo, pleno ⟨at full speed : a toda velocidad⟩ ⟨in full bloom : en plena flor⟩ **4** PLUMP : redondo, llenito *fam*, regordete *fam* ⟨a full face : una cara redonda⟩ ⟨a full figure : un cuerpo llenito⟩ **5** AMPLE : amplio ⟨a full skirt : una falda amplia⟩

full[3] *n* **1 to pay in full** : pagar en su totalidad **2 to the full** : al máximo

full-fledged ['fʊl'flɛdʒd] *adj* : hecho y derecho

fullness ['fʊlnəs] *n* **1** ABUNDANCE : plenitud *f*, abundancia *f* **2** : amplitud *f* (de una falda)

fully ['fʊli] *adv* **1** COMPLETELY : completamente, totalmente **2** : al menos, por lo menos ⟨fully half of them : al menos la mitad de ellos⟩

fulsome ['fʊlsəm] *adj* : excesivo, exagerado, efusivo

fumble[1] ['fʌmbəl] *v* **-bled; -bling** *vt* **1** : dejar caer, fumblear **2 to fumble one's way** : ir a tientas — *vi* **1** GROPE : hurgar, tantear **2 to fumble with** : manejar con torpeza

fumble[2] *n* : fumble *m* (en futbol americano)

fume[1] ['fju:m] *vi* **fumed; fuming 1** SMOKE : echar humo, humear **2** : estar furioso

fume[2] *n* : gas *m*, humo *m*, vapor *m*

fumigate ['fju:mə,geɪt] *vt* **-gated; -gating** : fumigar

fumigation [,fju:mə'geɪʃən] *n* : fumigación *m*

fun[1] ['fʌn] *adj* : divertido, entretenido

fun[2] *n* **1** AMUSEMENT : diversión *f*, entretenimiento *m* **2** ENJOYMENT : disfrute *m* **3 to have fun** : divertirse **4 to make fun of** : reírse de, burlarse de

function[1] ['fʌŋkʃən] *vi* : funcionar, desempeñarse, servir

function[2] *n* **1** PURPOSE : función *f* **2** GATHERING : reunión *f* social, recepción *f* **3** CEREMONY : ceremonia *f*, acto *m*

functional ['fʌŋkʃənəl] *adj* : funcional — **functionally** *adv*

functionary ['fʌŋkʃə,nɛri] *n, pl* **-aries** : funcionario *m*, -ria *f*

fund[1] ['fʌnd] *vt* : financiar

fund² *n* **1** SUPPLY : reserva *f*, cúmulo *m* **2** : fondo *m* ⟨investment fund : fondo de inversiones⟩ **3 funds** *npl* RESOURCES : fondos *mpl*
fundamental¹ [ˌfʌndəˈmɛntəl] *adj* **1** BASIC : fundamental, básico **2** PRINCIPAL : esencial, principal **3** INNATE : innato, intrínseco
fundamental² *n* : fundamento *m*
fundamentalism [ˌfʌndəˈmɛntəlˌɪzəm] *n* : integrismo *m*, fundamentalismo *m*
fundamentalist [ˌfʌndəˈmɛntəlɪst] *n* : integrista *mf*, fundamentalista *mf* — **fundamentalist** *adj*
fundamentally [ˌfʌndəˈmɛntəli] *adv* : fundamentalmente, básicamente
funding [ˈfʌndɪŋ] *n* : financiación *f*
fund-raiser [ˈfʌndˌreɪzər] *n* : función *f* para recaudar fondos
funeral¹ [ˈfjuːnərəl] *adj* **1** : funeral, funerario, fúnebre ⟨funeral procession : cortejo fúnebre⟩ **2 funeral home** : funeraria *f*
funeral² *n* : funeral *m*, funerales *mpl*
funereal [fjuːˈnɪriəl] *adj* : fúnebre
fungal [ˈfʌŋgəl] *adj* : de hongos, micótico
fungicidal [ˌfʌndʒəˈsaɪdəl, ˌfʌngə-] *adj* : fungicida
fungicide [ˈfʌndʒəˌsaɪd, ˈfʌŋgə-] *n* : fungicida *m*
fungous [ˈfʌŋgəs] *adj* : fungoso
fungus [ˈfʌŋgəs] *n*, *pl* **fungi** [ˈfʌnˌdʒaɪ, ˈfʌŋˌgaɪ] : hongo *m*
funk [ˈfʌŋk] *n* **1** FEAR : miedo *m* **2** DEPRESSION : depresión *f*
funky [ˈfʌŋki] *adj* **funkier; -est** ODD, QUAINT : raro, extraño, original
funnel¹ [ˈfʌnəl] *vt* **-neled; -neling** CHANNEL : canalizar, encauzar
funnel² *n* **1** : embudo *m* **2** SMOKESTACK : chimenea *f* (de un barco o vapor)
funnies [ˈfʌniz] *npl* : tiras *fpl* cómicas
funny [ˈfʌni] *adj* **funnier; -est 1** AMUSING : divertido, cómico **2** STRANGE : extraño, raro
fur¹ [ˈfər] *adj* : de piel
fur² *n* **1** : pelaje *m*, piel *f* **2** : prenda *f* de piel
furbish [ˈfərbɪʃ] *vt* : pulir, limpiar
furious [ˈfjʊriəs] *adj* **1** ANGRY : furioso **2** FRANTIC : violento, frenético, vertiginoso (dícese de la velocidad)
furiously [ˈfjʊriəsli] *adv* **1** ANGRILY : furiosamente **2** FRANTICALLY : frenéticamente
furlong [ˈfərˌlɔŋ] *n* : estadio *m* (201.2 m)
furlough¹ [ˈfərˌloː] *vt* : dar permiso a, dar licencia a
furlough² *n* LEAVE : permiso *m*, licencia *f*
furnace [ˈfərnəs] *n* : horno *m*
furnish [ˈfərnɪʃ] *vt* **1** SUPPLY : proveer, suministrar **2** : amueblar ⟨furnished apartment : departamento amueblado⟩
furnishings [ˈfərnɪʃɪŋz] *npl* **1** ACCESSORIES : accesorios *mpl* **2** FURNITURE : muebles *mpl*, mobiliario *m*

furniture [ˈfərnɪtʃər] *n* : muebles *mpl*, mobiliario *m*
furor [ˈfjʊrˌɔr, -ər] *n* **1** RAGE : furia *f*, rabia *f* **2** UPROAR : escándalo *m*, jaleo *m*, alboroto *m*
furrier [ˈfəriər] *n* : peletero *m*, -ra *f*
furrow¹ [ˈfəroː] *vt* **1** : surcar **2 to furrow one's brow** : fruncir el ceño
furrow² *n* **1** GROOVE : surco *m* **2** WRINKLE : arruga *f*, surco *m*
furry [ˈfəri] *adj* **furrier; -est** : peludo (dícese de un animal), peluche (dícese de un objeto)
further¹ [ˈfərðər] *vt* : promover, fomentar
further² *adv* **1** FARTHER : más lejos, más adelante **2** MOREOVER : además **3** MORE : más ⟨I'll consider it further in the morning : lo consideraré más en la mañana⟩
further³ *adj* **1** FARTHER : más lejano **2** ADDITIONAL : adicional, más
furtherance [ˈfərðərənts] *n* : promoción *f*, fomento *m*, adelantamiento *m*
furthermore [ˈfərðərˌmor] *adv* : además
furthermost [ˈfərðərˌmoːst] *adj* : más lejano, más distante
furthest [ˈfərðəst] → **farthest¹, farthest²**
furtive [ˈfərtɪv] *adj* : furtivo, sigiloso — **furtively** *adv*
furtiveness [ˈfərtɪvnəs] *n* STEALTH : sigilo *m*
fury [ˈfjʊri] *n*, *pl* **-ries 1** RAGE : furia *f*, ira *f* **2** VIOLENCE : furia *f*, furor *m*
fuse¹ [ˈfjuːz] *or* **fuze** *vt* **fused** *or* **fuzed; fusing** *or* **fuzing** : equipar con un fusible
fuse² *v* **fused; fusing** *vt* **1** SMELT : fundir **2** MERGE : fusionar, fundir — *vi* : fundirse, fusionarse
fuse³ *n* : fusible *m*
fuselage [ˈfjuːsəˌlɑʒ, -zə-] *n* : fuselaje *m*
fusillade [ˈfjuːsəˌlɑd, -ˌleɪd, ˌfjuːsəˈ-, -zə-] *n* : descarga *f* de fusilería
fusion [ˈfjuːʒən] *n* : fusión *f*
fuss¹ [ˈfʌs] *vi* **1** WORRY : preocuparse **2 to fuss with** : juguetear con, toquetear **3 to fuss over** : mimar
fuss² *n* **1** COMMOTION : alboroto *m*, escándalo *m* **2** ATTENTION : atenciones *fpl* **3** COMPLAINT : quejas *fpl*
fussbudget [ˈfʌsˌbʌdʒət] *n* : quisquilloso *m*, -sa *f*; melindroso *m*, -sa *f*
fussiness [ˈfʌsinəs] *n* **1** IRRITABILITY : irritabilidad *f* **2** ORNATENESS : lo recargado **3** METICULOUSNESS : meticulosidad *f*
fussy [ˈfʌsi] *adj* **fussier; -est 1** IRRITABLE : irritable, nervioso **2** OVERELABORATE : recargado **3** METICULOUS : meticuloso **4** FASTIDIOUS : quisquilloso, exigente
futile [ˈfjuːtəl, ˈfjuːˌtaɪl] *adj* : inútil, vano
futility [fjuːˈtɪləti] *n*, *pl* **-ties** : inutilidad *f*
future¹ [ˈfjuːtʃər] *adj* : futuro
future² *n* : futuro *m*
futuristic [ˌfjuːtʃəˈrɪstɪk] *adj* : futurista
fuze → **fuse¹**

fuzz ['fʌz] *n* : pelusa *f*
fuzziness ['fʌzinəs] *n* 1 DOWNINESS : vellosidad *f* 2 INDISTINCTNESS : falta *f* de claridad

fuzzy ['fʌzi] *adj* **fuzzier; -est** 1 FLUFFY, FURRY : con pelusa, peludo 2 INDISTINCT : indistinto ⟨a fuzzy image : una imagen borrosa⟩

G

g ['ʤiː] *n, pl* **g's** *or* **gs** ['ʤiːz] : séptima letra del alfabeto inglés
gab[1] ['gæb] *vi* **gabbed; gabbing** : charlar, cotorrear *fam*, parlotear *fam*
gab[2] *n* CHATTER : cotorreo *m fam*, parloteo *m fam*
gabardine ['gæbər,diːn] *n* : gabardina *f*
gabby ['gæbi] *adj* **gabbier; -est** : hablador, parlanchín
gable ['geɪbəl] *n* : hastial *m*, aguilón *m*
Gabonese [,gæbə'niːz, -'niːs] *n* : gabonés *m*, -nesa *f* — **Gabonese** *adj*
gad ['gæd] *vi* **gadded; gadding** WANDER : deambular, vagar, callejear
gadfly ['gæd,flaɪ] *n, pl* **-flies** 1 : tábano *m* (insecto) 2 FAULTFINDER : criticón *m*, -cona *f fam*
gadget ['gæʤət] *n* : artilugio *m*, aparato *m*
gadgetry ['gæʤətri] *n* : artilugios *mpl*, aparatos *mpl*
Gaelic ['geɪlɪk, 'gæ] *n* : gaélico *m* (idioma) — **Gaelic** *adj*
gaff ['gæf] *n* 1 : garfio *m* 2 → **gaffe**
gaffe ['gæf] *n* : metedura *f* de pata *fam*
gag[1] ['gæg] *v* **gagged; gagging** *vt* : amordazar ⟨to tie up and gag : atar y amordazar⟩ — *vi* 1 CHOKE : atragantarse 2 RETCH : hacer arcadas
gag[2] *n* 1 : mordaza *f* (para la boca) 2 JOKE : chiste *m*
gage → **gauge**
gaggle ['gægəl] *n* : bandada *f*, manada *f* (de gansos)
gaiety ['geɪəti] *n, pl* **-eties** 1 MERRYMAKING : juerga *f* 2 MERRIMENT : alegría *f*, regocijo *m*
gaily ['geɪli] *adv* : alegremente
gain[1] ['geɪn] *vt* 1 ACQUIRE, OBTAIN : ganar, obtener, adquirir, conseguir ⟨to gain knowledge : adquirir conocimientos⟩ ⟨to gain a victory : obtener una victoria⟩ 2 REACH : alcanzar, llegar a 3 INCREASE : ganar, aumentar ⟨to gain weight : aumentar de peso⟩ 4 : adelantarse, ganar ⟨the watch gains two minutes a day : el reloj se adelanta dos minutos por día⟩ — *vi* 1 PROFIT : beneficiarse 2 INCREASE : aumentar
gain[2] *n* 1 PROFIT : beneficio *m*, ganancia *f*, lucro *m*, provecho *m* 2 INCREASE : aumento *m*
gainful ['geɪnfəl] *adj* : lucrativo, beneficioso, provechoso ⟨gainful employment : trabajo remunerado⟩
gait ['geɪt] *n* : paso *m*, andar *m*, manera *f* de caminar
gal ['gæl] *n* : muchacha *f*
gala[1] ['geɪlə, 'gæ-, 'gɑ-] *adj* : de gala

gala[2] *n* : gala *f*, fiesta *f*
galactic [gə'læktɪk] *adj* : galáctico
galaxy ['gæləksi] *n, pl* **-axies** : galaxia *f*
gale ['geɪl] *n* 1 WIND : vendaval *f*, viento *m* fuerte 2 **gales of laughter** : carcajadas *fpl*
gall[1] ['gɔl] *vt* 1 CHAFE : rozar 2 IRRITATE, VEX : irritar, molestar
gall[2] *n* 1 BILE : bilis *f*, hiel *f* 2 INSOLENCE : audacia *f*, insolencia *f*, descaro *m* 3 SORE : rozadura *f* (de un caballo) 4 : agalla *f* (de una planta)
gallant ['gælənt] *adj* 1 BRAVE : valiente, gallardo 2 CHIVALROUS, POLITE : galante, cortés
gallantry ['gæləntri] *n, pl* **-ries** : galantería *f*, caballerosidad *f*
gallbladder ['gɔl,blædər] *n* : vesícula *f* biliar
galleon ['gæljən] *n* : galeón *m*
gallery ['gæləri] *n, pl* **-leries** 1 BALCONY : galería *f* (para espectadores) 2 CORRIDOR : pasillo *m*, galería *f*, corredor *m* 3 : galería *f* (para exposiciones)
galley ['gæli] *n, pl* **-leys** : galera *f*
gallium ['gæliəm] *n* : galio *m*
gallivant ['gælə,vænt] *vi* : callejear
gallon ['gælən] *n* : galón *m*
gallop[1] ['gæləp] *vi* : galopar
gallop[2] *n* : galope *m*
gallows ['gæ,loːz] *n, pl* **-lows** *or* **-lowses** [-,loːzəz] : horca *f*
gallstone ['gɔl,stoːn] *n* : cálculo *m* biliar
galore [gə'lor] *adj* : en abundancia ⟨bargains galore : muchísimas gangas⟩
galoshes [gə'lɑʃəz] *npl* : galochas *fpl*, chanclos *mpl*
galvanize ['gælvən,aɪz] *vt* **-nized; -nizing** 1 STIMULATE : estimular, excitar, impulsar 2 : galvanizar (metales)
Gambian ['gæmbiən] *n* : gambiano *m*, -na *f* — **Gambian** *adj*
gambit ['gæmbɪt] *n* 1 : gambito *m* (en ajedrez) 2 STRATAGEM : estratagema *f*, táctica *f*
gamble[1] ['gæmbəl] *v* **-bled; -bling** *vi* : jugar, arriesgarse — *vt* 1 BET, WAGER : apostar, jugarse 2 RISK : arriesgar
gamble[2] *n* 1 BET : apuesta *f* 2 RISK : riesgo *m*
gambler ['gæmbələr] *n* : jugador *m*, -dora *f*
gambling ['gæmbəlɪŋ] *n* : juego *m*
gambol ['gæmbəl] *vi* **-boled** *or* **-bolled; -boling** *or* **-bolling** FROLIC : retozar, juguetear
game[1] ['geɪm] *adj* 1 READY : listo, dispuesto ⟨we're game for anything : es-

tamos listos para lo que sea⟩ **2** LAME
: cojo
game² *n* **1** AMUSEMENT : juego *m*, diversión *f* **2** CONTEST : juego *m*, partido *m*, concurso *m* **3** : caza *f* ⟨big game : caza mayor⟩
gamecock ['geɪm,kɑk] *n* : gallo *m* de pelea
gamekeeper ['geɪm,ki:pər] *n* : guardabosque *mf*
gamely ['geɪmli] *adv* : animosamente
gamma ray ['gæmə] *n* : rayo *m* gamma
gamut ['gæmət] *n* : gama *f*, espectro *m* ⟨to run the gamut : pasar por toda la gama⟩
gamy *or* **gamey** ['geɪmi] *adj* **gamier; -est** : con sabor de animal de caza, fuerte
gander ['gændər] *n* **1** : ganso *m* (animal) **2** GLANCE : mirada *f*, vistazo *m*, ojeada *f*
gang¹ ['gæŋ] *vi* **to gang up** : agruparse, unirse
gang² *n* : banda *f*, pandilla *f*
gangling ['gæŋglɪn] *adj* LANKY : larguirucho *fam*
ganglion ['gæŋgliən] *n*, *pl* **-glia** [-gliə] : ganglio *m*
gangplank ['gæŋ,plæŋk] *n* : pasarela *f*
gangrene ['gæŋ,gri:n, 'gæn-; gæŋ'-, gæn'-] *n* : gangrena *f*
gangrenous ['gæŋgrənəs] *adj* : gangrenoso
gangster ['gæŋstər] *n* : gángster *mf*
gangway ['gæŋ,weɪ] *n* **1** : pasarela *f* **2 gangway!** : ¡abran paso!
gap ['gæp] *n* **1** BREACH, OPENING : espacio *m*, brecha *f*, abertura *f* **2** GORGE : desfiladero *m*, barranco *m* **3** : laguna *f* ⟨a gap in my education : una laguna en mi educación⟩ **4** INTERVAL : pausa *f*, intervalo *m* **5** DISPARITY : brecha *f*, disparidad *f*
gape¹ ['geɪp] *vi* **gaped; gaping 1** OPEN : abrirse, estar abierto **2** STARE : mirar fijamente con la boca abierta, mirar boquiabierto
gape² *n* **1** OPENING : abertura *f*, brecha *f* **2** STARE : mirada *f* boquiabierta
garage¹ [gə'rɑʒ, -'rɑʤ] *vt* **-raged; -raging** : dejar en un garaje
garage² *n* : garaje *m*, cochera *f*
garb¹ ['gɑrb] *vt* : vestir, ataviar
garb² *n* : vestimenta *f*, atuendo *f*
garbage ['gɑrbɪʤ] *n* : basura *f*, desechos *mpl*
garbageman ['gɑrbɪʤmən] *n*, *pl* **-men** [-mən, -,mɛn] : basurero *m*
garble ['gɑrbəl] *vt* **-bled; -bling** : tergiversar, distorsionar
garbled ['gɑrbəld] *adj* : incoherente, incomprensible
garden¹ ['gɑrdən] *vi* : trabajar en el jardín
garden² *n* : jardín *m*
gardener ['gɑrdənər] *n* : jardinero *m*, -ra *f*
gardenia [gɑr'di:njə] *n* : gardenia *f*
gardening ['gɑrdənɪn] *n* : jardinería *f*

gargantuan [gɑr'gæntʃuən] *adj* : gigantesco, colosal
gargle¹ ['gɑrgəl] *vi* **-gled; -gling** : hacer gárgaras, gargarizar
gargle² *n* : gárgara *f*
gargoyle ['gɑr,gɔɪl] *n* : gárgola *f*
garish ['gærɪʃ] *adj* GAUDY : llamativo, chillón, charro — **garishly** *adv*
garland¹ ['gɑrlənd] *vt* : adornar con guirnaldas
garland² *n* : guirnalda *f*
garlic ['gɑrlɪk] *n* : ajo *m*
garment ['gɑrmənt] *n* : prenda *f*
garner ['gɑrnər] *vt* : recoger, cosechar
garnet ['gɑrnət] *n* : granate *m*
garnish¹ ['gɑrnɪʃ] *vt* : aderezar, guarnecer
garnish² *n* : aderezo *m*, guarnición *f*
garret ['gærət] *n* : buhardilla *f*, desván *m*
garrison¹ ['gærəsən] *vt* **1** QUARTER : acuartelar (tropas) **2** OCCUPY : guarnecer, ocupar (con tropas)
garrison² *n* **1** : guarnición *f* (ciudad) **2** FORT : fortaleza *f*, poste *m* militar
garrulous ['gærələs] *adj* : charlatán, parlanchín, garlero *Col fam*
garter ['gɑrtər] *n* : liga *f*
gas¹ ['gæs] *v* **gassed; gassing** *vt* : gasear — *vi* **to gas up** : llenar el tanque con gasolina
gas² *n*, *pl* **gases** ['gæsəz] **1** : gas *m* ⟨tear gas : gas lacrimógeno⟩ **2** GASOLINE : gasolina *f*
gaseous ['gæʃəs, 'gæsiəs] *adj* : gaseoso
gash¹ ['gæʃ] *vt* : hacer un tajo en, cortar
gash² *n* : cuchillada *f*, tajo *m*
gasket ['gæskət] *n* : junta *f*
gas mask *n* : máscara *f* antigás
gasoline ['gæsə,li:n, ,gæsə'-] *n* : gasolina *f*, nafta *f*
gasp¹ ['gæsp] *vi* **1** : boquear ⟨to gasp with surprise : gritar de asombro⟩ **2** PANT : jadear, respirar con dificultad
gasp² *n* **1** : boqueada *f* ⟨a gasp of surprise : un grito sofocado⟩ **2** PANTING : jadeo *m*
gas station *n* : estación *f* de servicio, gasolinera *f*
gastric ['gæstrɪk] *adj* : gástrico ⟨gastric juice : jugo gástrico⟩
gastronomic [,gæstrə'nɑmɪk] *adj* : gastronómico
gastronomy [gæs'trɑnəmi] *n* : gastronomía *f*
gate ['geɪt] *n* : portón *m*, verja *f*, puerta *f*
gatekeeper ['geɪt,ki:pər] *n* : guarda *mf*; guardián *m*, -diana *f*
gateway ['geɪt,weɪ] *n* : puerta *f* (de acceso), entrada *f*
gather ['gæðər] *vt* **1** ASSEMBLE : juntar, recoger, reunir **2** HARVEST : recoger, cosechar **3** : fruncir (una tela) **4** INFER : deducir, suponer
gathering ['gæðərɪn] *n* : reunión *f*
gauche ['goːʃ] *adj* : torpe, falto de tacto

gaudy ['gɔdi] *adj* **gaudier; -est** : chillón, llamativo

gauge¹ ['geɪʤ] *vt* **gauged; gauging 1** MEASURE : medir **2** ESTIMATE, JUDGE : estimar, evaluar, juzgar

gauge² *n* **1** : indicador *m* ⟨pressure gauge : indicador de presión⟩ **2** CALIBER : calibre *m* **3** INDICATION : indicio *m*, muestra *f*

gaunt ['gɔnt] *adj* : demacrado, enjuto, descarnado

gauntlet ['gɔntlət] *n* : guante *m* ⟨to run the gauntlet of : exponerse a⟩

gauze ['gɔz] *n* : gasa *f*

gauzy ['gɔzi] *adj* **gauzier; -est** : diáfano, vaporoso

gave → **give**

gavel ['gævəl] *n* : martillo *m* (de un juez, un subastador, etc.)

gawk ['gɔk] *vi* GAPE : mirar boquiabierto

gawky ['gɔki] *adj* **gawkier; -est** : desmañado, torpe, desgarbado

gay ['geɪ] *adj* **1** MERRY : alegre **2** BRIGHT, COLORFUL : vistoso, vivo **3** HOMOSEXUAL : homosexual

gaze¹ ['geɪz] *vi* **gazed; gazing** : mirar (fijamente)

gaze² *n* : mirada *f* (fija)

gazelle [gə'zɛl] *n* : gacela *f*

gazette [gə'zɛt] *n* : gaceta *f*

gazetteer [ˌgæzə'tɪr] *n* : diccionario *m* geográfico

gear¹ ['gɪr] *vt* ADAPT, ORIENT : adaptar, ajustar, orientar ⟨a book geared to children : un libro adaptado a los niños⟩ — *vi* **to gear up** : prepararse

gear² *n* **1** CLOTHING : ropa *f* **2** BELONGINGS : efectos *mpl* personales **3** EQUIPMENT, TOOLS : equipo *m*, aparejo *m*, herramientas *fpl* ⟨fishing gear : aparejo de pescar⟩ ⟨landing gear : tren de aterrizaje⟩ **4** COGWHEEL : rueda *f* dentada **5** : marcha *f*, velocidad *f* (de un vehículo) ⟨to put in gear : poner en marcha⟩ ⟨to change gear(s) : cambiar de velocidad⟩

gearshift ['gɪrˌʃɪft] *n* : palanca *f* de cambio, palanca *f* de velocidad

geek ['gik] *n fam* : intelectual *mf*

geese → **goose**

Geiger counter ['gaɪgərˌkaʊntər] *n* : contador *m* Geiger

gel ['ʤɛl] *n* : gel *m*

gelatin ['ʤɛlətən] *n* : gelatina *f*

gem ['ʤɛm] *n* : joya *f*, gema *f*, alhaja *f*

Gemini ['ʤɛməˌnaɪ] *n* : Géminis *mf*

gemstone ['ʤɛmˌstoːn] *n* : piedra *f* (semipreciosa o preciosa), gema *f*

gender ['ʤɛndər] *n* **1** SEX : sexo *m* **2** : género *m* (en la gramática)

gene ['ʤiːn] *n* : gen *m*, gene *m*

genealogical [ˌʤiːniə'lɑʤɪkəl] *adj* : genealógico

genealogy [ˌʤiːni'ɑləʤi, ˌʤɛ-, -'æ-] *n, pl* **-gies** : genealogía *f*

genera → **genus**

general¹ ['ʤɛnrəl, 'ʤɛnə-] *adj* : general ⟨in general : en general, por lo general⟩

general² *n* : general *mf*

generality [ˌʤɛnə'ræləti] *n, pl* **-ties** : generalidad *f*

generalization [ˌʤɛnrələ'zeɪʃən, ˌʤɛnərə-] *n* : generalización *f*

generalize ['ʤɛnrəˌlaɪz, 'ʤɛnərə-] *v* **-ized; -izing** : generalizar

generally ['ʤɛnrəli, 'ʤɛnərə-] *adv* : generalmente, por lo general, en general

generate ['ʤɛnəˌreɪt] *vt* **-ated; -ating** : generar, producir

generation [ˌʤɛnə'reɪʃən] *n* : generación *f*

generator ['ʤɛnəˌreɪtər] *n* : generador *m*

generic [ʤə'nɛrɪk] *adj* : genérico

generosity [ˌʤɛnə'rɑsəti] *n, pl* **-ties** : generosidad *f*

generous ['ʤɛnərəs] *adj* **1** OPENHANDED : generoso, dadivoso, desprendido **2** ABUNDANT, AMPLE : abundante, amplio, generoso — **generously** *adv*

genetic [ʤə'nɛtɪk] *adj* : genético — **genetically** [-tɪkli] *adv*

geneticist [ʤə'nɛtəsɪst] *n* : genetista *mf*

genetics [ʤə'nɛtɪks] *n* : genética *f*

genial ['ʤiːniəl] *adj* GRACIOUS : simpático, cordial, afable — **genially** *adv*

geniality [ˌʤiːni'æləti] *n* : simpatía *f*, afabilidad *f*

genie ['ʤiːni] *n* : genio *m*

genital ['ʤɛnətəl] *adj* : genital

genitals ['ʤɛnətəlz] *npl* : genitales *mpl*

genius ['ʤiːnjəs] *n* : genio *m*

genocide ['ʤɛnəˌsaɪd] *n* : genocidio *m*

genre ['ʒɑnrə, 'ʒɑr] *n* : género *m*

genteel [ʤɛn'tiːl] *adj* : cortés, fino, refinado

gentile¹ ['ʤɛnˌtaɪl] *adj* : gentil

gentile² *n* : gentil *mf*

gentility [ʤɛn'tɪləti] *n, pl* **-ties 1** : nobleza *f* (de nacimiento) **2** POLITENESS, REFINEMENT : cortesía *f*, refinamiento *m*

gentle ['ʤɛntəl] *adj* **-tler; -tlest 1** NOBLE : bien nacido, noble **2** DOCILE : dócil, manso **3** KINDLY : bondadoso, amable **4** MILD : suave, apacible ⟨a gentle breeze : una brisa suave⟩ **5** SOFT : suave (dícese de un sonido), ligero (dícese del tacto) **6** MODERATE : moderado, gradual ⟨a gentle slope : una cuesta gradual⟩

gentleman ['ʤɛntəlmən] *n, pl* **-men** [-mən, -ˌmɛn] : caballero *m*, señor *m*

gentlemanly ['ʤɛntəlmənli] *adj* : caballeroso

gentleness ['ʤɛntəlnəs] *n* : delicadeza *f*, suavidad *f*, ternura *f*

gentlewoman ['ʤɛntəlˌwʊmən] *n, pl* **-women** [-ˌwɪmən] : dama *f*, señora *f*

gently ['ʤɛntli] *adv* **1** CAREFULLY, SOFTLY : con cuidado, suavemente, ligeramente **2** KINDLY : amablemente, con delicadeza

gentry ['ʤɛntri] *n, pl* **-tries** : aristocracia *f*

genuflect ['ʤɛnjuˌflɛkt] *vi* : doblar la rodilla, hacer una genuflexión

genuflection [ˌʤɛnjuˈflɛkʃən] *n* : genuflexión *f*

genuine ['ʤɛnjuwən] *adj* **1** AUTHENTIC, REAL : genuino, verdadero, auténtico **2** SINCERE : sincero — **genuinely** *adv*

genus ['ʤiːnəs] *n, pl* **genera** ['ʤɛ-nərə] : género *m*

geographer [ʤiˈɑgrəfər] *n* : geógrafo *m*, -fa *f*

geographical [ˌʤiːəˈgræfɪkəl] *or* **geographic** [-fɪk] *adj* : geográfico — **geographically** [-fɪkli] *adv*

geography [ʤiˈɑgrəfi] *n, pl* **-phies** : geografía *f*

geologic [ˌʤiːəˈlɑʤɪk] *or* **geological** [-ʤɪkəl] *adj* : geológico — **geologically** [-ʤɪkli] *adv*

geologist [ʤiˈɑləʤɪst] *n* : geólogo *m*, -ga *f*

geology [ʤiˈɑləʤi] *n* : geología *f*

geometric [ˌʤiːəˈmɛtrɪk] *or* **geometrical** [-trɪkəl] *adj* : geométrico

geometry [ʤiˈɑmətri] *n, pl* **-tries** : geometría *f*

geopolitical [ˌʤiːopəˈlɪtɪkəl] *adj* : geopolítico

Georgian ['ʤɔrʤən] *n* **1** : georgiano *m* (idioma) **2** : georgiano *m*, -na *f* — **Georgian** *adj*

geranium [ʤəˈreɪniəm] *n* : geranio *m*

gerbil ['ʤərbəl] *n* : jerbo *m*, gerbo *m*

geriatric [ˌʤɛriˈætrɪk] *adj* : geriátrico

geriatrics [ˌʤɛriˈætrɪks] *n* : geriatría *f*

germ ['ʤərm] *n* **1** MICROORGANISM : microbio *m*, germen *m* **2** BEGINNING : germen *m*, principio *m* ⟨the germ of a plan : el germen de un plan⟩

German ['ʤərmən] *n* **1** : alemán *m*, -mana *f* **2** : alemán *m* (idioma) — **German** *adj*

germane [ʤərˈmeɪn] *adj* : relevante, pertinente

Germanic¹ [ʤərˈmænɪk] *adj* : germánico, germano

Germanic² : germánico *m* (idioma)

germanium [ʤərˈmeɪniəm] *n* : germanio *m*

germ cell *n* : célula *f* germen

germicide ['ʤərməˌsaɪd] *n* : germicida *m*

germinate ['ʤərməˌneɪt] *v* **-nated; -nating** *vi* : germinar — *vt* : hacer germinar

germination [ˌʤərməˈneɪʃən] *n* : germinación *f*

gerund ['ʤɛrənd] *n* : gerundio *m*

gestation [ʤɛˈsteɪʃən] *n* : gestación *f*

gesture¹ ['ʤɛstʃər] *vi* **-tured; -turing** : gesticular, hacer gestos

gesture² *n* **1** : gesto *m*, ademán *m* **2** SIGN, TOKEN : gesto *m*, señal *f* ⟨a gesture of friendship : una señal de amistad⟩

get ['gɛt] *v* **got** ['gɑt]; **got** *or* **gotten** ['gɑtən]; **getting** *vt* **1** OBTAIN : conseguir, obtener, adquirir **2** RECEIVE : recibir ⟨to get a letter : recibir una carta⟩ **3** EARN : ganar ⟨he gets $10 an hour : gana $10 por hora⟩ **4** FETCH : traer ⟨get me my book : tráigame el libro⟩ **5** CATCH : tomar (un tren, etc.), agarrar (una pelota, una persona, etc.) **6** CONTRACT : contagiarse de, contraer ⟨she got the measles : le dio el sarampión⟩ **7** PREPARE : preparar (una comida) **8** PERSUADE : persuadir, mandar a hacer ⟨I got him to agree : logré convencerlo⟩ **9** (*to cause to be*) ⟨to get one's hair cut : cortarse el pelo⟩ **10** UNDERSTAND : entender ⟨now I get it! : ¡ya entiendo!⟩ **11 to have got** : tener ⟨I've got a headache : tengo un dolor de cabeza⟩ **12 to have got to** : tener que ⟨you've got to come : tienes que venir⟩ — *vi* **1** BECOME : ponerse, volverse, hacerse ⟨to get angry : ponerse furioso, enojarse⟩ **2** GO, MOVE : ir, avanzar ⟨he didn't get far : no avanzó mucho⟩ **3** ARRIVE : llegar ⟨to get home : llegar a casa⟩ **4 to get to be** : llegar a ser ⟨she got to be the director : llegó a ser directora⟩ **5 to get ahead** : adelantarse, progresar **6 to get along** : llevarse bien (con alguien), congeniar **7 to get by** MANAGE : arreglárselas **8 to get over** OVERCOME : superar, consolarse de **9 to get together** MEET : reunirse **10 to get up** : levantarse

getaway ['gɛtəˌweɪ] *n* ESCAPE : fuga *f*, huida *f*, escapada *f*

geyser ['gaɪzər] *n* : géiser *m*

Ghanaian ['gɑniən, 'gæ-] *n* : ghanés *m*, -nesa *f* — **Ghanaian** *adj*

ghastly ['gæstli] *adj* **-lier; -est** **1** HORRIBLE : horrible, espantoso **2** PALE : pálido, cadavérico

gherkin ['gərkən] *n* : pepinillo *m*

ghetto ['gɛtoː] *n, pl* **-tos** *or* **-toes** : gueto *m*

ghost ['goːst] *n* **1** : fantasma *f*, espectro *m* **2 the Holy Ghost** : el Espíritu Santo

ghostly ['goːstli] *adv* : fantasmal

ghoul ['guːl] *n* **1** : demonio *m* necrófago **2** : persona *f* de gustos macabros

GI [ˌʤiːˈaɪ] *n, pl* **GI's** *or* **GIs** : soldado *m* estadounidense

giant¹ ['ʤaɪənt] *adj* : gigante, gigantesco, enorme

giant² *n* : gigante *m*, -ta *f*

gibberish ['ʤɪbərɪʃ] *n* : galimatías *m*, jerigonza *f*

gibbon ['gɪbən] *n* : gibón *m*

gibe¹ ['ʤaɪb] *vi* **gibed; gibing** : mofarse, burlarse

gibe² *n* : pulla *f*, burla *f*, mofa *f*

giblets ['ʤɪbləts] *npl* : menudos *mpl*, menudencias *fpl*

giddiness ['gɪdinəs] *n* **1** DIZZINESS : vértigo *m*, mareo *m* **2** SILLINESS : frivolidad *f*, estupidez *f*

giddy ['gɪdi] *adj* **-dier; -est 1** DIZZY : mareado, vertiginoso **2** FRIVOLOUS, SILLY : frívolo, tonto

gift ['gɪft] *n* **1** TALENT : don *m*, talento *m*, dotes *fpl* **2** PRESENT : regalo *m*, obsequio *m*

gifted ['gɪftəd] *adj* TALENTED : talentoso

gig ['gɪg] *vi* : trabajo *m* (de duración limitada) ⟨to play a gig : tocar en un concierto⟩

gigabyte ['dʒɪgə,baɪt, 'gɪ-] *n* : gigabyte *m*

gigantic [dʒaɪ'gæntɪk] *adj* : gigantesco, enorme, colosal

giggle¹ ['gɪgəl] *vi* **-gled; -gling** : reírse tontamente

giggle² *n* : risita *f*, risa *f* tonta

gild ['gɪld] *vt* **gilded** *or* **gilt** ['gɪlt]; **gilding** : dorar

gill ['gɪl] *n* : agalla *f*, branquia *f*

gilt¹ ['gɪlt] *adj* : dorado

gilt² *n* : dorado *m*

gimlet ['gɪmlət] *n* **1** : barrena *f* (herramienta) **2** : bebida *f* de vodka o ginebra y limón

gimmick ['gɪmɪk] *n* **1** GADGET : artilugio *m* **2** CATCH : engaño *m*, trampa *f* **3** SCHEME, TRICK : ardid *m*, truco *m*

gin ['dʒɪn] *n* **1** : desmotadora *f* (de algodón) **2** : ginebra *f* (bebida alcohólica)

ginger ['dʒɪndʒər] *n* : jengibre *m*

ginger ale *n* : ginger ale *m*, gaseosa *f* de jengibre

gingerbread ['dʒɪndʒər,brɛd] *n* : pan *m* de jengibre

gingerly ['dʒɪndʒərli] *adv* : con cuidado, cautelosamente

gingham ['gɪŋəm] *n* : guinga *f*

ginseng ['dʒɪn,sɪŋ, -,sɛŋ] *n* : ginseng *m*

giraffe [dʒə'ræf] *n* : jirafa *f*

gird ['gərd] *vt* **girded** *or* **girt** ['gərt]; **girding 1** BIND : ceñir, atar **2** ENCIRCLE : rodear **3 to gird oneself** : prepararse

girder ['gərdər] *n* : viga *f*

girdle¹ ['gərdəl] *vt* **-dled; -dling 1** GIRD : ceñir, atar **2** SURROUND : rodear, circundar

girdle² *n* : faja *f*

girl ['gərl] *n* **1** : chica *f*, muchacha *f* **2** *or* **little girl** : niña *f*, chica *f* **3** SWEETHEART : novia *f* **4** DAUGHTER : hija *f*

girlfriend ['gərl,frɛnd] *n* : novia *f*, amiga *f*

girlhood ['gərl,hʊd] *n* : niñez *f*, juventud *f* (de una muchacha)

girlish ['gərlɪʃ] *adj* : de niña

girth ['gərθ] *n* **1** : circunferencia *f* (de un árbol, etc.), cintura *f* (de una persona) **2** CINCH : cincha *f* (para caballos, etc.)

gist ['dʒɪst] *n* : quid *m*, meollo *m*

give¹ ['gɪv] *v* **gave** ['geɪv]; **given** ['gɪvən]; **giving** *vt* **1** HAND, PRESENT : dar, regalar, obsequiar ⟨give it to me : dámelo⟩ ⟨they gave him a gold watch : le regalaron un reloj de oro⟩ **2** PAY : dar, pagar ⟨I'll give you $10 for this one : te daré $10 por éste⟩ **3** UTTER : dar, pronunciar ⟨to give a shout : dar un grito⟩ ⟨to give a speech : pronunciar un discurso⟩ ⟨to give a verdict : dictar sentencia⟩ **4** PROVIDE : dar ⟨to give one's word : dar uno su palabra⟩ ⟨to give a party : dar una fiesta⟩ **5** CAUSE : dar, causar, ocasionar ⟨to give trouble : causar problemas⟩ ⟨to give someone to understand : darle a entender a alguien⟩ **6** GRANT : dar, otorgar ⟨to give permission : dar permiso⟩ — *vi* **1** : hacer regalos **2** YIELD : ceder, romperse ⟨it gave under the weight of the crowd : cedió bajo el peso de la muchedumbre⟩ **3 to give in** *or* **to give up** SURRENDER : rendirse, entregarse **4 to give out** : agotarse, acabarse ⟨the supplies gave out : las provisiones se agotaron⟩

give² *n* FLEXIBILITY : flexibilidad *f*, elasticidad *f*

giveaway ['gɪvə,weɪ] *n* **1** : revelación *f* involuntaria **2** GIFT : regalo *m*, obsequio *m*

given ['gɪvən] *adj* **1** INCLINED : dado, inclinado ⟨he's given to quarreling : es muy dado a discutir⟩ **2** SPECIFIC : dado, determinado ⟨at a given time : en un momento dado⟩

given name *n* : nombre *m* de pila

give up *vt* : dejar, renunciar a, abandonar ⟨to give up smoking : dejar de fumar⟩

gizzard ['gɪzərd] *n* : molleja *f*

glacial ['gleɪʃəl] *adj* : glacial — **glacially** *adv*

glacier ['gleɪʃər] *n* : glaciar *m*

glad ['glæd] *adj* **gladder; gladdest 1** PLEASED : alegre, contento ⟨she was glad I came : se alegró de que haya venido⟩ ⟨glad to meet you! : ¡mucho gusto!⟩ **2** HAPPY, PLEASING : feliz, agradable ⟨glad tidings : buenas nuevas⟩ **3** WILLING : dispuesto, gustoso ⟨I'll be glad to do it : lo haré con mucho gusto⟩

gladden ['glædən] *vt* : alegrar

glade ['gleɪd] *n* : claro *m*

gladiator ['glædi,eɪtər] *n* : gladiador *m*

gladiolus [,glædi'o:ləs] *n*, *pl* **-li** [-li, -,laɪ] : gladiolo *m*, gladíolo *m*

gladly ['glædli] *adv* : con mucho gusto

gladness ['glædnəs] *n* : alegría *f*, gozo *m*

glamor *or* **glamour** ['glæmər] *n* : atractivo *m*, hechizo *m*, encanto *m*

glamorous ['glæmərəs] *adj* : atractivo, encantador

glance¹ ['glænts] *vi* **glanced; glancing 1** RICOCHET : rebotar ⟨it glanced off the wall : rebotó en la pared⟩ **2 to glance at** : mirar, echar un vistazo a **3 to glance away** : apartar los ojos

glance² *n* : mirada *f*, vistazo *m*, ojeada *f*

gland ['glænd] *n* : glándula *f*

glandular ['glændʒʊlər] *adj* : glandular

glare¹ ['glær] *vi* **glared; glaring 1** SHINE : brillar, relumbrar **2** STARE : mirar con ira, lanzar una mirada feroz

glare² *n* **1** BRIGHTNESS : resplandor *m*, luz *f* deslumbrante **2** : mirada *f* feroz

glaring ['glærɪŋ] *adj* **1** BRIGHT : deslumbrante, brillante **2** FLAGRANT, OBVIOUS : flagrante, manifiesto ⟨a glaring error : un error que salta a la vista⟩

glass ['glæs] *n* **1** : vidrio *m*, cristal *m* ⟨stained glass : vidrio de color⟩ **2** : vaso *m* ⟨a glass of milk : un vaso de leche⟩ **3 glasses** *npl* SPECTACLES : gafas *fpl*, anteojos *mpl*, lentes *mpl*, espejuelos *mpl*

glassblowing ['glæs,bloːɪŋ] *n* : soplado *m* del vidrio

glassful ['glæs,fʊl] *n* : vaso *m*, copa *f*

glassware ['glæs,wær] *n* : cristalería *f*

glassy ['glæsi] *adj* **glassier; -est 1** VITREOUS : vítreo **2** : vidrioso ⟨glassy eyes : ojos vidriosos⟩

glaucoma [glaʊ'koːmə, glɔ-] *n* : glaucoma *m*

glaze¹ ['gleɪz] *vt* **glazed; glazing 1** : ponerle vidrios a (una ventana, etc.) **2** : vidriar (cerámica) **3** : glasear (papel, verduras, etc.)

glaze² *n* : vidriado *m*, glaseado *m*, barniz *m*

glazier ['gleɪʒər] *n* : vidriero *m*, -ra *f*

gleam¹ ['gliːm] *vi* : brillar, destellar, relucir

gleam² *n* **1** LIGHT : luz *f* (oscura) **2** GLINT : destello *m* **3** GLIMMER : rayo *m*, vislumbre *f* ⟨a gleam of hope : un rayo de esperanza⟩

glean ['gliːn] *vt* : recoger, espigar

glee ['gliː] *n* : alegría *f*, júbilo *m*, regocijo *m*

gleeful ['gliːfəl] *adj* : lleno de alegría

glen ['glɛn] *n* : cañada *f*

glib ['glɪb] *adj* **glibber; glibbest 1** : simplista ⟨a glib reply : una respuesta simplista⟩ **2** : con mucha labia (dícese de una persona)

glibly ['glɪbli] *adv* : con mucha labia

glide¹ ['glaɪd] *vi* **glided; gliding** : deslizarse (en una superficie), planear (en el aire)

glide² *n* : planeo *m*

glider ['glaɪdər] *n* **1** : planeador *m* (aeronave) **2** : mecedor *m* (tipo de columpio)

glimmer¹ ['glɪmər] *vi* : brillar con luz trémula

glimmer² *n* **1** : luz *f* trémula, luz *f* tenue **2** GLEAM : rayo *m*, vislumbre *f* ⟨a glimmer of understanding : un rayo de entendimiento⟩

glimpse¹ ['glɪmps] *vt* **glimpsed; glimpsing** : vislumbrar, entrever

glimpse² *n* : mirada *f* breve ⟨to catch a glimpse of : alcanzar a ver, vislumbrar⟩

glint¹ ['glɪnt] *vi* GLEAM, SPARKLE : destellar, fulgurar

glint² *n* **1** SPARKLE : destello *m*, centelleo *m* **2 to have a glint in one's eye** : chispearle los ojos a uno

glisten¹ ['glɪsən] *vi* : brillar, centellear

glisten² *n* : brillo *m*, centelleo *m*

glitch ['glɪtʃ] *n* **1** MALFUNCTION : mal funcionamiento *m* **2** SNAG : problema *m*, complicación *f*

glitter¹ ['glɪtər] *vi* **1** SPARKLE : destellar, relucir, brillar **2** FLASH : relampaguear ⟨his eyes glittered in anger : le relampagueaban los ojos de ira⟩

glitter² *n* **1** BRIGHTNESS : brillo *m* **2** : purpurina *f* (para decoración)

glitz ['glɪts] *n* : oropel *m*

gloat ['gloːt] *vi* **to gloat over** : regodearse en

glob ['glɑb] *n* : plasta *f*, masa *f*, grumo *m*

global ['gloːbəl] *adj* **1** SPHERICAL : esférico **2** WORLDWIDE : global, mundial — **globally** *adv*

globe ['gloːb] *n* **1** SPHERE : esfera *f*, globo *m* **2** EARTH : globo *m*, Tierra *f* **3** : globo *m* terráqueo (modelo de la Tierra)

globe-trotter ['gloːb,trɑtər] *n* : trotamundos *mf*

globular ['glɑbjʊlər] *adj* : globular

globule ['glɑ,bjuːl] *n* : glóbulo *m*

gloom ['gluːm] *n* **1** DARKNESS : penumbra *f*, oscuridad *f* **2** MELANCHOLY : melancolía *f*, tristeza *f*

gloomily ['gluːməli] *adv* : tristemente

gloomy ['gluːmi] *adj* **gloomier; -est 1** DARK : oscuro, tenebroso ⟨gloomy weather : tiempo gris⟩ **2** MELANCHOLY : melancólico **3** PESSIMISTIC : pesimista **4** DEPRESSING : deprimente, lúgubre

glorification [,glorəfə'keɪʃən] *n* : glorificación *f*

glorify ['glorə,faɪ] *vt* **-fied; -fying** : glorificar

glorious ['gloriəs] *adj* **1** ILLUSTRIOUS : glorioso, ilustre **2** MAGNIFICENT : magnífico, espléndido, maravilloso — **gloriously** *adv*

glory¹ ['glori] *vi* **-ried; -rying** EXULT : exultar, regocijarse

glory² *n, pl* **-ries 1** RENOWN : gloria *f*, fama *f*, honor *m* **2** PRAISE : gloria *f* ⟨glory to God : gloria a Dios⟩ **3** MAGNIFICENCE : magnificencia *f*, esplendor *m*, gloria *f* **4 to be in one's glory** : estar uno en su gloria

gloss¹ ['glɔs, 'glɑs] *vt* **1** EXPLAIN : glosar, explicar **2** POLISH : lustrar, pulir **3 to gloss over** : quitarle importancia a, minimizar

gloss² *n* **1** SHINE : lustre *m*, brillo *m* **2** EXPLANATION : glosa *f*, explicación *f* breve **3** → **glossary**

glossary ['glɔsəri, 'glɑ-] *n, pl* **-ries** : glosario *m*

glossy ['glɔsi, 'glɑ-] *adj* **glossier; -est** : brillante, lustroso, satinado (dícese del papel)

glove ['glʌv] *n* : guante *m*

glow¹ ['gloː] *vi* **1** SHINE : brillar, resplandecer **2** BRIM : rebosar ⟨to glow with health : rebosar de salud⟩

glow[2] *n* **1** BRIGHTNESS : resplandor *m*, brillo *m*, luminosidad *f* **2** FEELING : sensación *f* (de bienestar), oleada *f* (de sentimiento) **3** INCANDESCENCE : incandescencia *f*

glower ['glaʊər] *vi* : fruncir el ceño

glowworm ['glo:ˌwərm] *n* : luciérnaga *f*

glucose ['glu:ˌko:s] *n* : glucosa *f*

glue[1] ['glu:] *vt* **glued; gluing** *or* **glueing** : pegar, encolar

glue[2] *n* : pegamento *m*, cola *f*

gluey ['glu:i] *adj* **gluier; -est** : pegajoso

glum ['glʌm] *adj* **glummer; glummest 1** SULLEN : hosco, sombrío **2** DREARY, GLOOMY : sombrío, triste, melancólico

glut[1] ['glʌt] *vt* **glutted; glutting 1** SATIATE : saciar, hartar **2** : inundar (el mercado)

glut[2] *n* : exceso *m*, superabundancia *f*

glutinous ['glu:tənəs] *adj* STICKY : pegajoso, glutinoso

glutton ['glʌtən] *n* : glotón *m*, -tona *f*

gluttonous ['glʌtənəs] *adj* : glotón

gluttony ['glʌtəni] *n, pl* **-tonies** : glotonería *f*, gula *f*

gnarled ['nɑrld] *adj* **1** KNOTTY : nudoso **2** TWISTED : retorcido

gnash ['næʃ] *vt* : hacer rechinar (los dientes)

gnat ['næt] *n* : jején *m*

gnaw ['nɔ] *vt* : roer

gnome ['no:m] *n* : gnomo *m*

gnu ['nu:, 'nju:] *n, pl* **gnu** *or* **gnus** : ñu *m*

go[1] ['go:] *v* **went** ['wɛnt]; **gone** ['gɔn, 'gɑn]; **going; goes** ['go:z] *vi* **1** PROCEED : ir ⟨to go slow : ir despacio⟩ ⟨to go shopping : ir de compras⟩ **2** LEAVE : irse, marcharse, salir ⟨let's go! : ¡vámonos!⟩ ⟨the train went on time : el tren salió a tiempo⟩ **3** DISAPPEAR : desaparecer, pasarse, irse ⟨her fear is gone : se le ha pasado el miedo⟩ ⟨my pen is gone! : ¡mi pluma desapareció!⟩ **4** EXTEND : ir, extenderse, llegar ⟨this road goes to the river : este camino se extiende hasta el río⟩ ⟨to go from top to bottom : ir de arriba abajo⟩ **5** FUNCTION : funcionar, marchar ⟨the car won't go : el coche no funciona⟩ ⟨to get something going : poner algo en marcha⟩ **6** SELL : venderse ⟨it goes for $15 : se vende por $15⟩ **7** PROGRESS : ir, andar, seguir ⟨my exam went well : me fue bien en el examen⟩ ⟨how did the meeting go? : ¿qué tal la reunión?⟩ **8** BECOME : volverse, quedarse ⟨he's going crazy : está volviéndose loco⟩ ⟨the tire went flat : la llanta se desinfló⟩ **9** FIT : caber ⟨it will go through the door : cabe por la puerta⟩ **10 anything goes!** : ¡todo vale! **11 to go** : faltar ⟨only 10 days to go : faltan sólo 10 días⟩ **12 to go back on** : faltar uno a (su promesa) **13 to go bad** SPOIL : estropearse, echarse a perder **14 to go for** : interesarse uno en, gustarle a uno (algo, alguien) ⟨I don't go for that : eso

no me interesa⟩ **15 to go off** EXPLODE : estallar **16 to go with** MATCH : armonizar con, hacer juego con — *v aux* **to be going to** : ir a ⟨I'm going to write a letter : voy a escribir una carta⟩ ⟨it's not going to last : no va a durar⟩

go[2] *n, pl* **goes 1** ATTEMPT : intento *m* ⟨to have a go at : intentar, probar⟩ **2** SUCCESS : éxito *m* **3** ENERGY : energía *f*, empuje *m* ⟨to be on the go : no parar, no descansar⟩

goad[1] ['go:d] *vt* : aguijonear (un animal), incitar (a una persona)

goad[2] *n* : aguijón *m*

goal ['go:l] *n* **1** : gol *m* (en deportes) ⟨to score a goal : anotar un gol⟩ **2** *or* **goalposts** : portería *f* **3** AIM, OBJECTIVE : meta *m*, objetivo *m*

goalie ['go:li] → **goalkeeper**

goalkeeper ['go:lˌki:pər] *n* : portero *m*, -ra *f*; guardameta *mf*; arquero *m*, -ra *f*

goaltender ['go:lˌtɛndər] → **goalkeeper**

goat ['go:t] *n* **1** : cabra *f* (hembra) **2 billy goat** : macho *m* cabrío, chivo *m*

goatee [go:'ti:] *n* : barbita *f* de chivo, piocha *f Mex*

goatskin ['go:tˌskɪn] *n* : piel *f* de cabra

gob ['gɑb] *n* : masa *f*, grumo *m*

gobble ['gɑbəl] *v* **-bled; -bling** *vt* **to gobble up** : tragar, engullir — *vi* : hacer ruidos de pavo

gobbledygook ['gɑbəldiˌgʊk, -ˌgu:k] *n* GIBBERISH : jerigonza *f*

go–between ['go:bɪˌtwi:n] *n* : intermediario *m*, -ria *f*; mediador *m*, -dora *f*

goblet ['gɑblət] *n* : copa *f*

goblin ['gɑblən] *n* : duende *m*, trasgo *m*

god ['gɑd, 'gɔd] *n* **1** : dios *m* **2 God** : Dios *m*

godchild ['gɑdˌtʃaɪld, 'gɔd-] *n, pl* **-children** : ahijado *m*, -da *f*

goddess ['gɑdəs, 'gɔ-] *n* : diosa *f*

godfather ['gɑdˌfɑðər, 'gɔd-] *n* : padrino *m*

godless ['gɑdləs, 'gɔd-] *adj* : ateo

godlike ['gɑdˌlaɪk, 'gɔd-] *adj* : divino

godly ['gɑdli, 'gɔd-] *adj* **-lier; -est 1** DIVINE : divino **2** DEVOUT, PIOUS : piadoso, devoto, beato

godmother ['gɑdˌmʌðər, 'gɔd-] *n* : madrina *f*

godparents ['gɑdˌpærənts, 'gɔd-] *npl* : padrinos *mpl*

godsend ['gɑdˌsɛnd, 'gɔd-] *n* : bendición *f*, regalo *m* divino

goes → **go**

go-getter ['go:ˌgɛtər] *n* : persona *f* ambiciosa, buscavidas *mf fam*

goggle ['gɑgəl] *vi* **-gled; -gling** : mirar con ojos desorbitados

goggles ['gɑgəlz] *npl* : gafas *fpl* (protectoras), anteojos *mpl*

goings-on [ˌgo:ɪŋz'ɑn, -'ɔn] *npl* : sucesos *mpl*, ocurrencias *fpl*

goiter ['gɔɪtər] *n* : bocio *m*

gold ['go:ld] *n* : oro *m*

golden ['go:ldən] *adj* **1** : (hecho) de oro **2** : dorado, de color oro ⟨golden hair

: pelo rubio⟩ **3** FLOURISHING, PROSPEROUS : dorado, próspero ⟨golden years : años dorados⟩ **4** FAVORABLE : favorable, excelente ⟨a golden opportunity : una excelente oportunidad⟩

goldenrod ['go:ldən‚rad] *n* : vara *f* de oro

golden rule *n* : regla *f* de oro

goldfinch ['go:ld‚fɪntʃ] *n* : jilguero *m*

goldfish ['go:ld‚fɪʃ] *n* : pez *m* de colores

goldsmith ['go:ld‚smɪθ] *n* : orífice *mf*, orfebre *mf*

golf[1] ['galf, 'gɔlf] *vi* : jugar (al) golf

golf[2] *n* : golf *m*

golfer ['galfər, 'gɔl-] *n* : golfista *mf*

gondola ['gandələ, gɑn'do:lə] *n* : góndola *f*

gone ['gɔn] *adj* **1** DEAD : muerto **2** PAST : pasado, ido **3** LOST : perdido, desaparecido **4 to be far gone** : estar muy avanzado **5 to be gone on** : estar loco por

goner ['gɔnər] *n* **to be a goner** : estar en las últimas

gong ['gɔŋ, 'gɑŋ] *n* : gong *m*

gonorrhea [‚gɑnə'ri:ə] *n* : gonorrea *f*

good[1] ['gʊd] *adv* **1** (*used as an intensifier*) : bien ⟨a good strong rope : una cuerda bien fuerte⟩ **2** WELL : bien

good[2] *adj* **better** ['bɛtər]; **best** ['bɛst] **1** PLEASANT : bueno, agradable ⟨good news : buenas noticias⟩ ⟨to have a good time : divertirse⟩ **2** BENEFICIAL : bueno, beneficioso ⟨good for a cold : beneficioso para los resfriados⟩ ⟨it's good for you : es bueno para uno⟩ **3** FULL : completo, entero ⟨a good hour : una hora entera⟩ **4** CONSIDERABLE : bueno, bastante ⟨a good many people : muchísima gente, un buen número de gente⟩ **5** ATTRACTIVE, DESIRABLE : bueno, bien ⟨a good salary : un buen sueldo⟩ ⟨to look good : quedar bien⟩ **6** KIND, VIRTUOUS : bueno, amable ⟨she's a good person : es buena gente⟩ ⟨that's good of you! : ¡qué amable!⟩ ⟨good deeds : buenas obras⟩ **7** SKILLED : bueno, hábil ⟨to be good at : tener facilidad para⟩ **8** SOUND : bueno, sensato ⟨good advice : buenos consejos⟩ **9** (*in greetings*) : bueno ⟨good morning : buenos días⟩ ⟨good afternoon (evening) : buenas tardes⟩ ⟨good night : buenas noches⟩

good[3] *n* **1** RIGHT : bien *m* ⟨to do good : hacer el bien⟩ **2** GOODNESS : bondad *f* **3** BENEFIT : bien *m*, provecho *m* ⟨it's for your own good : es por tu propio bien⟩ **4 goods** *npl* PROPERTY : efectos *mpl* personales, posesiones *fpl* **5 goods** *npl* WARES : mercancía *f*, mercadería *f*, artículos *mpl* **6 for ~** : para siempre

good–bye *or* **good–by** [gʊd'baɪ] *n* : adiós *m*

good–for–nothing ['gʊdfər‚nʌθɪŋ] *n* : inútil *mf*; haragán *m*, -gana *f*; holgazán *m*, -zana *f*

Good Friday *n* : Viernes *m* Santo

good–hearted ['gʊd'hɑrtəd] *adj* : bondadoso, benévolo, de buen corazón

good–looking ['gʊd'lʊkɪŋ] *adj* : bello, bonito, guapo

goodly ['gʊdli] *adj* **-lier; -est** : considerable, importante ⟨a goodly number : un número considerable⟩

good–natured ['gʊd'neɪtʃərd] *adj* : amigable, amistoso, bonachón *fam*

goodness ['gʊdnəs] *n* **1** : bondad *f* **2 thank goodness!** : ¡gracias a Dios!, ¡menos mal!

good–tempered ['gʊd'tɛmpərd] *adj* : de buen genio

goodwill [‚gʊd'wɪl] *n* **1** BENEVOLENCE : benevolencia *f*, buena voluntad *f* **2** : buen nombre *m* (de comercios), renombre *m* comercial

goody ['gʊdi] *n, pl* **goodies** : cosa *f* rica para comer, golosina *f*

gooey ['gu:i] *adj* **gooier; gooiest** : pegajoso

goof[1] ['gu:f] *vi* **1 to goof off** : holgazanear **2 to goof around** : hacer tonterías **3 to goof up** BLUNDER : cometer un error

goof[2] *n* **1** : bobo *m*, -ba *f*; tonto *m*, -ta *f* **2** BLUNDER : error *m*, planchazo *m fam*

goofy ['gu:fi] *adj* **goofier; -est** SILLY : tonto, bobo

goose ['gu:s] *n, pl* **geese** ['gi:s] : ganso *m*, -sa *f*; ánsar *m*; oca *f*

gooseberry ['gu:s‚bɛri:, 'gu:z-] *n, pl* **-berries** : grosella *f* espinosa

goose bumps *npl* : carne *f* de gallina

gooseflesh ['gu:s‚flɛʃ] → **goose bumps**

goose pimples → **goose bumps**

gopher ['go:fər] *n* : taltuza *f*

gore[1] ['gor] *vt* **gored; goring** : cornear

gore[2] *n* BLOOD : sangre *f*

gorge[1] ['gɔrdʒ] *vt* **gorged; gorging 1** SATIATE : saciar, hartar **2 to gorge oneself** : hartarse, atiborrarse, atracarse *fam*

gorge[2] *n* RAVINE : desfiladero *m*

gorgeous ['gɔrdʒəs] *adj* : hermoso, espléndido, magnífico

gorilla [gə'rɪlə] *n* : gorila *m*

gory ['gori] *adj* **gorier; -est** BLOODY : sangriento

gosling ['gazlɪŋ, 'gɔz-] *n* : ansarino *m*

gospel ['gaspəl] *n* **1** *or* **Gospel** : evangelio *m* ⟨the four Gospels : los cuatro evangelios⟩ **2 the gospel truth** : el evangelio, la pura verdad

gossamer ['gasəmər, 'gazə-] *adj* : tenue, sutil ⟨gossamer wings : alas tenues⟩

gossip[1] ['gasɪp] *vi* : chismear, contar chismes

gossip[2] *n* **1** : chismoso *m*, -sa *f* (persona) **2** RUMOR : chisme *m*, rumor *m*

gossipy ['gasɪpi] *adj* : chismoso

got → **get**

Gothic ['gaθɪk] *adj* : gótico

gotten → **get**

gouge[1] ['gaʊdʒ] *vt* **gouged; gouging 1** : excavar, escoplear (con una gubia) **2** SWINDLE : estafar, extorsionar

gouge² *n* **1** CHISEL : gubia *f*, formón *m*
2 GROOVE : ranura *f*, hoyo *m* (hecho
por un formón)

goulash ['gu:ˌlɑʃ, -ˌlæʃ] *n* : estofado *m*,
guiso *m* al estilo húngaro

gourd ['gord, 'gʊrd] *n* : calabaza *f*

gourmand ['gʊrˌmɑnd] *n* **1** GLUTTON
: glotón *m*, -tona *f* **2** → **gourmet**

gourmet ['gʊrˌmeɪ, gʊr'meɪ] *n* : gourmet
mf; gastrónomo *m*, -ma *f*

gout ['gaʊt] *n* : gota *f*

govern ['gʌvərn] *vt* **1** RULE : gobernar
2 CONTROL, DETERMINE : determinar,
controlar, guiar **3** RESTRAIN : dominar
(las emociones, etc.) — *vi* : gobernar

governess ['gʌvərnəs] *n* : institutriz *f*

government ['gʌvərmənt] *n* : gobierno
m

governmental [ˌgʌvər'mentəl] *adj* : gubernamental, gubernativo

governor ['gʌvənər, 'gʌvərnər] *n* **1**
: gobernador *m*, - dora *f* (de un estado,
etc.) **2** : regulador *m* (de una máquina)

governorship ['gʌvənərˌʃɪp, 'gʌvərnər-]
n : cargo *m* de gobernador

gown ['gaʊn] *n* **1** : vestido *m* ⟨evening
gown : traje de fiesta⟩ **2** : toga *f* (de
magistrados, clérigos, etc.)

grab¹ ['græb] *v* **grabbed; grabbing** *vt*
SNATCH : agarrar, arrebatar — *vi*
: agarrarse

grab² *n* **1 to make a grab for** : tratar de
agarrar **2 up for grabs** : disponible, libre

grace¹ ['greɪs] *vt* **graced; gracing 1**
HONOR : honrar **2** ADORN : adornar,
embellecer

grace² *n* **1** : gracia *f* ⟨by the grace of
God : por la gracia de Dios⟩ **2** BLESS-
ING : bendición *f* (de la mesa) **3**
RESPITE : plazo *m*, gracia *f* ⟨a five days'
grace (period) : un plazo de cinco días⟩
4 GRACIOUSNESS : gentileza *f*, cortesía
f **5** ELEGANCE : elegancia *f*, gracia *f* **6**
to be in the good graces of : estar en
buenas relaciones con **7 with good
grace** : de buena gana

graceful ['greɪsfəl] *adj* : lleno de gracia,
garboso, grácil

gracefully ['greɪsfəli] *adv* : con gracia,
con garbo

gracefulness ['greɪsfəlnəs] *n* : gracilidad
f, apostura *f*, gallardía *f*

graceless ['greɪsləs] *adj* **1** DISCOURTE-
OUS : descortés **2** CLUMSY, INELEGANT
: torpe, desgarbado, poco elegante

gracious ['greɪʃəs] *adj* : cortés, gentil,
cordial

graciously ['greɪʃəsli] *adv* : gentilmente

graciousness ['greɪʃəsnəs] *n* : gentileza
f

gradation [greɪ'deɪʃən, grə-] *n* : gradación *f*

grade¹ ['greɪd] *vt* **graded; grading 1**
SORT : clasificar **2** LEVEL : nivelar **3**
: calificar (exámenes, alumnos)

grade² *n* **1** QUALITY : categoría *f*, calidad *f* **2** RANK : grado *m*, rango *m* (mil-

itar) **3** YEAR : grado *m*, curso *m*, año
m ⟨sixth grade : el sexto grado⟩ **4**
MARK : nota *f*, calificación *f* (en educación) **5** SLOPE : cuesta *f*, pendiente
f, gradiente *f*

grade school → **elementary school**

gradient ['greɪdiənt] *n* : gradiente *f*

gradual ['grædʒuəl] *adj* : gradual, paulatino

gradually ['grædʒuəli, 'grædʒəli] *adv*
: gradualmente, poco a poco

graduate¹ ['grædʒuˌeɪt] *v* **-ated; -ating** *vi*
: graduarse, licenciarse — *vt* : graduar
⟨a graduated thermometer : un termómetro graduado⟩

graduate² ['grædʒuət] *adj* : de postgrado ⟨graduate course : curso de post-
grado⟩

graduate³ *n* **1** : licenciado *m*, -da *f*; graduado *m*, -da *f* (de la universidad) **2**
: bachiller *mf* (de la escuela secundaria)

graduate student *n* : postgraduado *m*,
-da *f*

graduation [ˌgrædʒu'eɪʃən] *n* : graduación *f*

graffiti [grə'fiːˌti, græ-] *npl* : pintadas *fpl*,
graffiti *mpl*

graft¹ ['græft] *vt* : injertar

graft² *n* **1** : injerto *m* ⟨skin graft : injerto cutáneo⟩ **2** CORRUPTION : sobor-
no *m* (político), ganancia *f* ilegal

grain ['greɪn] *n* **1** : grano *m* ⟨a grain of
corn : un grano de maíz⟩ ⟨like a grain
of sand : como grano de arena⟩ **2** CE-
REALS : cereales *mpl* **3** : veta *f*, vena *f*,
grano *m* (de madera) **4** SPECK, TRACE
: pizca *f*, ápice *m* ⟨a grain of truth : una
pizca de verdad⟩ **5** grano *m* (unidad de
peso)

gram ['græm] *n* : gramo *m*

grammar ['græmər] *n* : gramática *f*

grammar school → **elementary school**

grammatical [grə'mætɪkəl] *adj* : gramatical — **grammatically** [-kli] *adv*

granary ['greɪnəri, 'græ-] *n, pl* **-ries**
: granero *m*

grand ['grænd] *adj* **1** FOREMOST
: grande **2** IMPRESSIVE : impresionante, magnífico ⟨a grand view : una
vista magnífica⟩ **3** LAVISH : grandioso,
suntuoso, lujoso ⟨to live in a grand
manner : vivir a lo grande⟩ **4** FABU-
LOUS : fabuloso, magnífico ⟨to have a
grand time : pasarlo estupendamente,
pasarlo en grande⟩ **5 grand total** : total *m*, suma *f* total

grandchild ['grænd,tʃaɪld] *n, pl* **-chil-
dren** : nieto *m*, -ta *f*

granddaughter ['grænd,dɔtər] *n* : nieta
f

grandeur ['grændʒər] *n* : grandiosidad *f*,
esplendor *m*

grandfather ['grænd,fɑðər] *n* : abuelo *m*

grandiose ['grændi,oːs, ˌgrændi'-] *adj* **1**
IMPOSING : imponente, grandioso **2**
POMPOUS : pomposo, presuntuoso

grandma ['græn,mɑ, -ˌmɔ] *n* : abuelita
f, nana *f*

grandmother ['grænd,mʌðər] *n* : abuela
f

grandpa ['græm,pɑ, -,pɔ] *n* : abuelito *m*

grandparents ['grænd,pærənts] *npl*
: abuelos *mpl*

grandson ['grænd,sʌn] *n* : nieto *m*

grandstand ['grænd,stænd] *n* : tribuna
f

granite ['grænɪt] *n* : granito *m*

grant¹ ['grænt] *vt* **1** ALLOW : conceder
⟨to grant a request : conceder una peti-
ción⟩ **2** BESTOW : conceder, dar, otorgar ⟨to grant a favor : otorgar un fa-
vor⟩ **3** ADMIT : reconocer, admitir ⟨I'll
grant that he's clever : reconozco que
es listo⟩ **4 to take for granted** : dar
(algo) por sentado

grant² *n* **1** GRANTING : concesión *f*,
otorgamiento *m* **2** SCHOLARSHIP : beca
f **3** SUBSIDY : subvención *f*

granular ['grænjʊlər] *adj* : granular

granulated ['grænjʊ,leɪtəd] *adj* : granu-
lado

grape ['greɪp] *n* : uva *f*

grapefruit ['greɪp,fruːt] *n* : toronja *f*,
pomelo *m*

grapevine ['greɪp,vaɪn] *n* **1** : vid *f*, parra *f* **2 through the grapevine** : por
vías secretas ⟨I heard it through the
grapevine : me lo contaron⟩

graph ['græf] *n* : gráfica *f*, gráfico *m*

graphic ['græfɪk] *adj* **1** VIVID : vívido,
gráfico **2 graphic arts** : artes gráficas

graphically ['græfɪkli] *adv* : gráficamente

graphite ['græ,faɪt] *n* : grafito *m*

grapnel ['græpnəl] *n* : rezón *m*

grapple ['græpəl] *v* **-pled; -pling** *vt* GRIP
: agarrar (con un garfio) — *vi* STRUG-
GLE : forcejear, luchar (con un problema, etc.)

grasp¹ ['græsp] *vt* **1** GRIP, SEIZE : agarrar, asir **2** COMPREHEND : entender,
comprender — *vi* **to grasp at**
: aprovechar

grasp² *n* **1** GRIP : agarre *m* **2** CONTROL
: control *m*, garras *fpl* **3** REACH : alcance *m* ⟨within your grasp : a su al-
cance⟩ **4** UNDERSTANDING : comprensión *f*, entendimiento *m*

grass ['græs] *n* **1** : hierba *f* (planta) **2**
PASTURE : pasto *m*, zacate *m CA, Mex*
3 LAWN : césped *m*, pasto *m*

grasshopper ['græs,hɑpər] *n* : saltamontes *m*

grassland ['græs,lænd] *n* : pradera *f*

grassy ['græsi] *adj* **grassier; -est** : cubierto de hierba

grate¹ ['greɪt] *v* **grated; -ing** *vt* **1** : rallar
(en cocina) **2** SCRAPE : rascar **3 to
grate one's teeth** : hacer rechinar los
dientes — *vi* **1** RASP, SQUEAK : chirriar **2** IRRITATE : irritar ⟨to grate on
one's nerves : crisparle los nervios a
uno⟩

grate² *n* **1** : parrilla *f* (para cocinar) **2**
GRATING : reja *f*, rejilla *f*, verja *f* (en
una ventana)

grateful ['greɪtfəl] *adj* : agradecido

gratefully ['greɪtfəli] *adv* : con agradecimiento

gratefulness ['greɪtfəlnəs] *n* : gratitud *f*,
agradecimiento *m*

grater ['greɪtər] *n* : rallador *m*

gratification [,grætəfə'keɪʃən] *n* : gratificación *f*

gratify ['grætə,faɪ] *vt* **-fied; -fying 1**
PLEASE : complacer **2** SATISFY : satisfacer, gratificar

grating ['greɪtɪŋ] *n* : reja *f*, rejilla *f*

gratis¹ ['grætəs, 'greɪ-] *adv* : gratis, gratuitamente

gratis² *adj* : gratis, gratuito

gratitude ['grætə,tuːd, -,tjuːd] *n* : gratitud *f*, agradecimiento *m*

gratuitous [grə'tuːətəs] *adj* : gratuito

gratuity [grə'tuːəti] *n, pl* **-ities** TIP
: propina *f*

grave¹ ['greɪv] *adj* **graver; -est 1** IM-
PORTANT : grave, de mucha gravedad
2 SERIOUS, SOLEMN : grave, serio

grave² *n* : tumba *f*, sepultura *f*

gravel ['grævəl] *n* : grava *f*, gravilla *f*

gravelly ['grævəli] *adj* **1** : de grava **2**
HARSH : áspero (dícese de la voz)

gravely ['greɪvli] *adv* : gravemente

gravestone ['greɪv,stoːn] *n* : lápida *f*

graveyard ['greɪv,jɑrd] *n* CEMETERY
: cementerio *m*, panteón *m*, camposanto *m*

gravitate ['grævə,teɪt] *vi* **-tated; -tating**
: gravitar

gravitation [,grævə'teɪʃən] *n* : gravitación *f*

gravitational [,grævə'teɪʃənəl] *adj*
: gravitacional

gravity ['grævəti] *n, pl* **-ties 1** SERIOUS-
NESS : gravedad *f*, seriedad *f* **2**
: gravedad *f* ⟨the law of gravity : la ley
de la gravedad⟩

gravy ['greɪvi] *n, pl* **-vies** : salsa *f*
(preparada con el jugo de la carne asa-
da)

gray¹ ['greɪ] *vt* : hacer gris — *vi* : encanecer, ponerse gris

gray² *adj* **1** : gris (dícese del color) **2**
: cano, canoso ⟨gray hair : pelo canoso⟩
⟨to go gray : volverse cano⟩ **3** DISMAL,
GLOOMY : gris, triste

gray³ *n* : gris *m*

grayish ['greɪɪʃ] *adj* : grisáceo

graze ['greɪz] *v* **grazed; grazing** *vi* : pastar, pacer — *vt* **1** : pastorear (ganado)
2 BRUSH : rozar **3** SCRATCH : raspar

grease¹ ['griːs, 'griːz] *vt* **greased; greasing** : engrasar, lubricar

grease² ['griːs] *n* : grasa *f*

greasy ['griːsi, -zi] *adj* **greasier; -est 1**
: grasiento **2** OILY : graso, grasoso

great ['greɪt] *adj* **1** LARGE : grande ⟨a
great mountain : una montaña grande⟩
⟨a great crowd : una gran muchedum-
bre⟩ **2** INTENSE : intenso, fuerte,
grande ⟨great pain : gran dolor⟩ **3** EM-
INENT : grande, eminente, distinguido
⟨a great poet : un gran poeta⟩ **4** EX-
CELLENT, TERRIFIC : excelente, estu-

pendo, fabuloso ⟨to have a great time
: pasarlo en grande⟩ **5 a great while**
: mucho tiempo
great–aunt [ˌgreɪtˈænt, -ˈɑnt] *n* : tía *f*
abuela
greater [ˈgreɪtər] (*comparative of* **great**)
: mayor
greatest [ˈgreɪtəst] (*superlative of* **great**)
: el mayor, la mayor
great–grandchild [ˌgreɪtˈgrænd-ˌtʃaɪld]
n, pl **-children** [-ˌtʃɪldrən] : bisnieto *m*,
-ta *f*
great–grandfather [ˌgreɪtˈgrænd-ˌfɑðər]
n : bisabuelo *m*
great–grandmother [ˌgreɪtˈgrænd-
ˌmʌðər] *n* : bisabuela *f*
greatly [ˈgreɪtli] *adv* **1** MUCH : mucho,
sumamente ⟨to be greatly improved
: haber mejorado mucho⟩ **2** VERY
: muy ⟨greatly superior : muy superi-
or⟩
greatness [ˈgreɪtnəs] *n* : grandeza *f*
great–uncle [ˌgreɪtˈʌŋkəl] *n* : tío *m* abuelo
grebe [ˈgriːb] *n* : somorgujo *m*
greed [ˈgriːd] *n* **1** AVARICE : avaricia *f*,
codicia *f* **2** GLUTTONY : glotonería *f*,
gula *f*
greedily [ˈgriːdəli] *adv* : con avaricia,
con gula
greediness [ˈgriːdinəs] → **greed**
greedy [ˈgriːdi] *adj* **greedier; -est** **1**
AVARICIOUS : codicioso, avaricioso **2**
GLUTTONOUS : glotón
Greek [ˈgriːk] *n* **1** : griego *m*, -ga *f* **2**
: griego *m* (idioma) — **Greek** *adj*
green¹ [ˈgriːn] *adj* **1** : verde (dícese del
color) **2** UNRIPE : verde, inmaduro **3**
INEXPERIENCED : verde, novato
green² *n* **1** : verde *m* **2 greens** *npl* VEG-
ETABLES : verduras *fpl*
greenery [ˈgriːnəri] *n, pl* **-eries** : plantas
fpl verdes, vegetación *f*
greenhorn [ˈgriːnˌhorn] *n* : novato *m*, -ta
f
greenhouse [ˈgriːnˌhaʊs] *n* : invernadero *m*
greenhouse effect : efecto *m* invernadero
greenish [ˈgriːnɪʃ] *adj* : verdoso
Greenlander [ˈgriːnləndər, -ˌlæn-] *n*
: groenlandés *m*, -desa *f*
greenness [ˈgriːnnəs] *n* **1** : verdor *m* **2**
INEXPERIENCE : inexperiencia *f*
green thumb *n* **to have a green thumb**
: tener buena mano para las plantas
greet [ˈgriːt] *vt* **1** : saludar ⟨to greet a
friend : saludar a un amigo⟩ **2** : acoger,
recibir ⟨they greeted him with boos : lo
recibieron con abucheos⟩
greeting [ˈgriːtɪŋ] *n* **1** : saludo *m* **2**
greetings *npl* REGARDS : saludos *mpl*,
recuerdos *mpl*
gregarious [grɪˈgæriəs] *adj* : gregario
(dícese de los animales), sociable
(dícese de las personas) — **gregari-
ously** *adv*
gregariousness [grɪˈgæriəsnəs] *n* : sociabilidad *f*

gremlin [ˈgrɛmlən] *n* : duende *m*
grenade [grəˈneɪd] *n* : granada *f*
Grenadian [grəˈneɪdiən] *n* : granadino
m, -na *f* — **Grenadian** *adj*
grew → **grow**
grey → **gray**
greyhound [ˈgreɪˌhaʊnd] *n* : galgo *m*
grid [ˈgrɪd] *n* **1** GRATING : rejilla *f* **2** NET-
WORK : red *f* (de electricidad, etc.) **3**
: cuadriculado *m* (de un mapa)
griddle [ˈgrɪdəl] *n* : plancha *f*
griddle cake → **pancake**
gridiron [ˈgrɪdˌaɪərn] *n* **1** GRILL : parrilla *f* **2** : campo *m* de futbol americano
gridlock [ˈgrɪdˌlɑk] *n* : atasco *m* completo (de una red de calles)
grief [ˈgriːf] *n* **1** SORROW : dolor *m*, pena
f **2** ANNOYANCE, TROUBLE : proble-
mas *mpl*, molestia *f*
grievance [ˈgriːvənts] *n* COMPLAINT
: queja *f*
grieve [ˈgriːv] *v* **grieved; grieving** *vt* DIS-
TRESS : afligir, entristecer, apenar — *vi*
1 : sufrir, afligirse **2 to grieve for** *or* **to
grieve over** : llorar, lamentar
grievous [ˈgriːvəs] *adj* **1** OPPRESSIVE
: gravoso, opresivo, severo **2** GRAVE,
SERIOUS : grave, severo, doloroso
grievously [ˈgriːvəsli] *adv* : gravemente,
de gravedad
grill¹ [ˈgrɪl] *vt* **1** : asar (a la parrilla) **2**
INTERROGATE : interrogar
grill² *n* **1** : parrilla *f* (para cocinar) **2**
: parrillada *f* (comida) **3** RESTAURANT
: grill *m*
grille *or* **grill** [ˈgrɪl] *n* : reja *f*, enrejado *m*
grim [ˈgrɪm] *adj* **grimmer; grimmest** **1**
CRUEL : cruel, feroz **2** STERN : adusto, severo ⟨a grim expression : un gesto
severo⟩ **3** GLOOMY : sombrío, deprimente **4** SINISTER : macabro, siniestro
5 UNYIELDING : inflexible, persistente
⟨with grim determination : con una
voluntad de hierro⟩
grimace¹ [ˈgrɪməs, grɪˈmeɪs] *vi* **-maced;
-macing** : hacer muecas
grimace² *n* : mueca *f*
grime [ˈgraɪm] *n* : mugre *f*, suciedad *f*
grimly [ˈgrɪmli] *adv* **1** STERNLY : severamente **2** RESOLUTELY : inexorablemente
grimy [ˈgraɪmi] *adj* **grimier; -est** : mugriento, sucio
grin¹ [ˈgrɪn] *vi* **grinned; grinning** : sonreír abiertamente
grin² *n* : sonrisa *f* abierta
grind¹ [ˈgraɪnd] *v* **ground** [ˈgraʊnd];
grinding *vt* **1** CRUSH : moler,
machacar, triturar **2** SHARPEN : afilar
3 POLISH : pulir, esmerilar (lentes, es-
pejos) **4 to grind one's teeth** : rechi-
narle los dientes a uno **5 to grind down**
OPPRESS : oprimir, agobiar — *vi* **1**
: funcionar con dificultad, rechinar ⟨to
grind to a halt : pararse poco a poco,
llegar a un punto muerto⟩ **2** STUDY
: estudiar mucho

grind² *n* : trabajo *m* pesado ⟨the daily grind : la rutina diaria⟩

grinder ['graɪndər] *n* : molinillo *m* ⟨coffee grinder : molinillo de café⟩

grindstone ['graɪnd‚stoːn] *n* : piedra *m* de afilar

grip¹ ['grɪp] *vt* **gripped; gripping 1** GRASP : agarrar, asir **2** HOLD, INTEREST : captar el interés de

grip² *n* **1** GRASP : agarre *m*, asidero *m* ⟨to have a firm grip on something : agarrarse bien de algo⟩ **2** CONTROL, HOLD : control *m*, dominio *m* ⟨to lose one's grip on : perder el control de⟩ ⟨inflation tightened its grip on the economy : la inflación se afianzó en su dominio de la economía⟩ **3** UNDERSTANDING : comprensión *f*, entendimiento *m* ⟨to come to grips with : llegar a entender⟩ **4** HANDLE : asidero *m*, empuñadura *f* (de un arma)

gripe¹ ['graɪp] *v* **griped; griping** *vt* IRRITATE, VEX : irritar, fastidiar, molestar — *vi* COMPLAIN : quejarse, rezongar

gripe² *n* : queja *f*

grippe ['grɪp] *n* : influenza *f*, gripe *f*, gripa *f* Col, Mex

grisly ['grɪzli] *adj* **-lier; -est** : horripilante, horroroso, truculento

grist ['grɪst] *n* : molienda *f* ⟨it's all grist for the mill : todo ayuda, todo es provechoso⟩

gristle ['grɪsəl] *n* : cartílago *m*

gristly ['grɪsli] *adj* **-tlier; -est** : cartilaginoso

grit¹ ['grɪt] *vt* **gritted; gritting** : hacer rechinar (los dientes, etc.)

grit² *n* **1** SAND : arena *f* **2** GRAVEL : grava *f* **3** COURAGE : valor *m*, coraje *m* **4** **grits** *npl* : sémola *f* de maíz

gritty ['grɪti] *adj* **-tier; -est 1** : arenoso ⟨a gritty surface : una superficie arenosa⟩ **2** PLUCKY : valiente

grizzled ['grɪzəld] *adj* : entrecano

grizzly bear ['grɪzli] *n* : oso *m* pardo

groan¹ ['groːn] *vi* **1** MOAN : gemir, quejarse **2** CREAK : crujir

groan² *n* **1** MOAN : gemido *m*, quejido *m* **2** CREAK : crujido *m*

grocer ['groːsər] *n* : tendero *m*, -ra *f*

grocery ['groːsəri, -ʃəri] *n, pl* **-ceries 1** *or* **grocery store** : tienda *f* de comestibles, tienda *f* de abarrotes **2** **groceries** *npl* : comestibles *mpl*, abarrotes *mpl*

groggy ['grɑgi] *adj* **-gier; -est** : atontado, grogui, tambaleante

groin ['grɔɪn] *n* : ingle *f*

grommet ['grɑmət, 'grʌ-] *n* : arandela *f*

groom¹ ['gruːm, 'grʊm] *vt* **1** : cepillar, almohazar (un animal) **2** : arreglar, cuidar ⟨well-groomed : bien arreglado⟩ **3** PREPARE : preparar

groom² *n* **1** : mozo *m*, -za *f* de cuadra **2** BRIDEGROOM : novio *m*

groove¹ ['gruːv] *vt* **grooved; grooving** : acanalar, hacer ranuras en, surcar

groove² *n* **1** FURROW, SLOT : ranura *f*, surco *m* **2** RUT : rutina *f*

grope ['groːp] *v* **groped; groping** *vi* : andar a tientas, tantear ⟨he groped for the switch : buscó el interruptor a tientas⟩ — *vt* **to grope one's way** : avanzar a tientas

gross¹ ['groːs] *vt* : tener entrada bruta de, recaudar en bruto

gross² *adj* **1** FLAGRANT : flagrante, grave ⟨a gross error : un error flagrante⟩ ⟨a gross injustice : una injusticia grave⟩ **2** FAT : muy gordo, obeso **3** : bruto ⟨gross national product : producto nacional bruto⟩ **4** COARSE, VULGAR : grosero, basto

gross³ *n* **1** *pl* **gross** : gruesa *f* (12 docenas) **2** *or* **gross income** : ingresos *mpl* brutos

grossly ['groːsli] *adv* **1** EXTREMELY : extremadamente ⟨grossly unfair : totalmente injusto⟩ **2** CRUDELY : groseramente

grotesque [groː'tɛsk] *adj* : grotesco

grotesquely [groː'tɛskli] *adv* : de forma grotesca

grotto ['grɑtoː] *n, pl* **-toes** : gruta *f*

grouch¹ ['graʊʧ] *vi* : refunfuñar, rezongar

grouch² *n* **1** COMPLAINT : queja *f* **2** GRUMBLER : gruñón *m*, -ñona *f*; cascarrabias *mf fam*

grouchy ['graʊʧi] *adj* **grouchier; -est** : malhumorado, gruñón

ground¹ ['graʊnd] *vt* **1** BASE : fundar, basar **2** INSTRUCT : enseñar los conocimientos básicos a ⟨to be well grounded in : ser muy entendido en⟩ **3** : conectar a tierra (un aparato eléctrico) **4** : varar, hacer encallar (un barco) **5** : restringir (un avión o un piloto) a la tierra

ground² *n* **1** EARTH, SOIL : suelo *m*, tierra *f* ⟨to dig (in) the ground : cavar la tierra⟩ ⟨to fall to the ground : caerse al suelo⟩ **2** LAND, TERRAIN : terreno *m* ⟨hilly ground : terreno alto⟩ ⟨to lose ground : perder terreno⟩ **3** BASIS, REASON : razón *f*, motivo *m* ⟨grounds for complaint : motivos de queja⟩ **4** BACKGROUND : fondo *m* **5** FIELD : campo *m*, plaza *f* ⟨parade ground : plaza de armas⟩ **6** : tierra *f* (para electricidad) **7** **grounds** *npl* PREMISES : recinto *m*, terreno *m* **8** **grounds** *npl* DREGS : posos *mpl* (de café)

ground³ → **grind**

groundhog ['graʊnd‚hɔg] *n* : marmota *f* (de América)

groundless ['graʊndləs] *adj* : infundado

groundwork ['graʊnd‚wərk] *n* **1** FOUNDATION : fundamento *m*, base *f* **2** PREPARATION : trabajo *m* preparatorio

group¹ ['gruːp] *vt* : agrupar

group² *n* : grupo *m*, agrupación *f*, conjunto *m*, compañía *f*

grouper ['gruːpər] *n* : mero *m*

grouse¹ ['graʊs] *vi* **groused; grousing** : quejarse, rezongar, refunfuñar

grouse² *n, pl* **grouse** *or* **grouses** : urogallo *m* (ave)

grout ['graʊt] *n* : lechada *f*

grove ['groːv] *n* : bosquecillo *m*, arboleda *f*, soto *m*

grovel ['grɑvəl, 'grʌ-] *vi* **-eled** *or* **-elled; -eling** *or* **-elling 1** CRAWL : arrastrarse **2** : humillarse, postrarse ⟨to grovel before someone : postrarse ante alguien⟩

grow ['groː] *v* **grew** ['gruː]; **grown** ['groːn]; **growing** *vi* **1** : crecer ⟨palm trees grow on the islands : las palmas crecen en las islas⟩ ⟨my hair grows very fast : mi pelo crece muy rápido⟩ **2** DEVELOP, MATURE : desarrollarse, madurar **3** INCREASE : crecer, aumentar **4** BECOME : hacerse, volverse, ponerse ⟨she was growing angry : se estaba poniendo furiosa⟩ ⟨to grow dark : oscurecerse⟩ **5 to grow up** : hacerse mayor ⟨grow up! : ¡no seas niño!⟩ — *vt* **1** CULTIVATE, RAISE : cultivar **2** : dejar crecer ⟨to grow one's hair : dejarse crecer el pelo⟩

grower ['groːər] *n* : cultivador *m*, -dora *f*

growl¹ ['graʊl] *vi* : gruñir (dícese de un animal), refunfuñar (dícese de una persona)

growl² *n* : gruñido *m*

grown-up¹ ['groːnˌəp] *adj* : adulto, mayor

grown-up² *n* : adulto *m*, -ta *f*; persona *f* mayor

growth ['groːθ] *n* **1** : crecimiento *m* ⟨to stunt one's growth : detener el crecimiento⟩ **2** INCREASE : aumento *m*, crecimiento *m*, expansión *f* **3** DEVELOPMENT : desarrollo *m* ⟨economic growth : desarrollo económico⟩ ⟨a five days' growth of beard : una barba de cinco días⟩ **4** LUMP, TUMOR : bulto *m*, tumor *m*

grub¹ ['grʌb] *vi* **grubbed; grubbing 1** DIG : escarbar **2** RUMMAGE : hurgar, buscar **3** DRUDGE : trabajar duro

grub² *n* **1** : larva *f* ⟨beetle grub : larva del escarabajo⟩ **2** DRUDGE : esclavo *m*, -va *f* del trabajo **3** FOOD : comida *f*

grubby ['grʌbi] *adj* **grubbier; -est** : mugriento, sucio

grudge¹ ['grʌdʒ] *vt* **grudged; grudging** : resentir, envidiar

grudge² *n* : rencor *m*, resentimiento *m* ⟨to hold a grudge : guardar rencor⟩

grueling *or* **gruelling** ['gruːlɪŋ, 'gruːə-] *adj* : extenuante, agotador, duro

gruesome ['gruːsəm] *adj* : horripilante, truculento, horroroso

gruff ['grʌf] *adj* **1** BRUSQUE : brusco ⟨a gruff reply : una respuesta brusca⟩ **2** HOARSE : ronco — **gruffly** *adv*

grumble¹ ['grʌmbəl] *vi* **-bled; -bling 1** COMPLAIN : refunfuñar, rezongar, quejarse **2** RUMBLE : hacer un ruido sordo, retumbar (dícese del trueno)

grumble² *n* **1** COMPLAINT : queja *f* **2** RUMBLE : ruido *m* sordo, estruendo *m*

grumbler ['grʌmbələr] *n* : gruñón *m*, -ñona *f*

grumpy ['grʌmpi] *adj* **grumpier; -est** : malhumorado, gruñón

grungy ['grʌndʒi] *adj* : sucio

grunt¹ ['grʌnt] *vi* : gruñir

grunt² *n* : gruñido *m*

guacamole [ˌgwɑkəˈmoːli] *n* : guacamole *m*, guacamol *m*

guarantee¹ [ˌgærənˈtiː] *vt* **-teed; -teeing 1** PROMISE : asegurar, prometer **2** : poner bajo garantía, garantizar (un producto o servicio)

guarantee² *n* **1** PROMISE : garantía *f*, promesa *f* ⟨lifetime guarantee : garantía de por vida⟩ **2** → **guarantor**

guarantor [ˌgærənˈtɔr] *n* : garante *mf*; fiador *m*, -dora *f*

guaranty [ˌgærənˈtiː] → **guarantee**

guard¹ ['gɑrd] *vt* **1** DEFEND, PROTECT : defender, proteger **2** : guardar, vigilar, custodiar ⟨to guard the frontier : vigilar la frontera⟩ ⟨she guarded my secret well : guardó bien mi secreto⟩ — *vi* **to guard against** : protegerse contra, evitar

guard² *n* **1** WATCHMAN : guarda *mf* ⟨security guard : guarda de seguridad⟩ **2** VIGILANCE : guardia *f*, vigilancia *f* ⟨to be on guard : estar en guardia⟩ ⟨to let one's guard down : bajar la guardia⟩ **3** SAFEGUARD : salvaguardia *f*, dispositivo *m* de seguridad (en una máquina) **4** PRECAUTION : precaución *f*, protección *f*

guardhouse ['gɑrdˌhaʊs] *n* : cuartel *m* de la guardia

guardian ['gɑrdiən] *n* **1** PROTECTOR : guardián *m*, -diana *f*; custodio *m*, -dia *f* **2** : tutor *m*, -tora *f* (de un niño)

guardianship ['gɑrdiənˌʃɪp] *n* : custodia *f*, tutela *f*

Guatemalan [ˌgwɑtəˈmɑlən] *n* : guatemalteco *m*, -ca *f* — **Guatemalan** *adj*

guava ['gwɑvə] *n* : guayaba *f*

gubernatorial [ˌguːbənəˈtoriːəl, ˌgjuː-] *adj* : del gobernador

guerrilla *or* **guerilla** [gəˈrɪlə] *n* : guerrillero *m*, -ra *f*

guess¹ ['gɛs] *vt* **1** CONJECTURE : adivinar, conjeturar ⟨guess what happened! : ¡adivina lo que pasó!⟩ **2** SUPPOSE : pensar, creer, suponer ⟨I guess so : supongo que sí⟩ **3** : adivinar correctamente, acertar ⟨to guess the answer : acertar la respuesta⟩ — *vi* : adivinar

guess² *n* : conjetura *f*, suposición *f*

guesswork ['gɛsˌwərk] *n* : suposiciones *fpl*, conjeturas *fpl*

guest ['gɛst] *n* : huésped *mf*; invitado *m*, -da *f*

guffaw¹ [gəˈfɔ] *vi* : reírse a carcajadas, carcajearse *fam*

guffaw² [gəˈfɔ, 'gʌˌfɔ] *n* : carcajada *f*, risotada *f*

guidance ['gaɪdənts] *n* : orientación *f*, consejos *mpl*

guide[1] ['gaɪd] *vt* **guided; guiding 1** DIRECT, LEAD : guiar, dirigir, conducir **2** ADVISE, COUNSEL : aconsejar, orientar

guide[2] *n* : guía *f*

guidebook ['gaɪd,bʊk] *n* : guía *f* (para viajeros)

guideline ['gaɪd,laɪn] *n* : pauta *f*, directriz *f*

guild ['gɪld] *n* : gremio *m*, sindicato *m*, asociación *f*

guile ['gaɪl] *n* : astucia *f*, engaño *m*

guileless ['gaɪlləs] *adj* : inocente, cándido, sin malicia

guillotine[1] ['gɪlə,ti:n, 'gi:jə,-] *vt* **-tined; -tining** : guillotinar

guillotine[2] *n* : guillotina *f*

guilt ['gɪlt] *n* : culpa *f*, culpabilidad *f*

guilty ['gɪlti] *adj* **guiltier; -est** : culpable

guinea fowl ['gɪni] *n* : gallina *f* de Guinea

guinea pig *n* : conejillo *m* de Indias, cobaya *f*

guise ['gaɪz] *n* : apariencia *f*, aspecto *m*, forma *f*

guitar [gə'tɑr, gɪ-] *n* : guitarra *f*

guitarist [gə'tɑrɪst, gɪ-] *n* : guitarrista *mf*

gulch ['gʌltʃ] *n* : barranco *m*, quebrada *f*

gulf ['gʌlf] *n* **1** : golfo *m* ⟨the Gulf of Mexico : el Golfo de México⟩ **2** GAP : brecha *f* ⟨the gulf between generations : la brecha entre las generaciones⟩ **3** CHASM : abismo *m*

gull ['gʌl] *n* : gaviota *f*

gullet ['gʌlət] *n* : garganta *f*

gullible ['gʌlɪbəl] *adj* : crédulo

gully ['gʌli] *n, pl* **-lies** : barranco *m*, hondonada *f*

gulp[1] ['gʌlp] *vt* **1** : engullir, tragar ⟨he gulped down the whiskey : engulló el whisky⟩ **2** SUPPRESS : suprimir, reprimir, tragar ⟨to gulp down a sob : reprimir un sollozo⟩ — *vi* : tragar saliva, tener un nudo en la garganta

gulp[2] *n* : trago *m*

gum ['gʌm] *n* **1** CHEWING GUM : goma *f* de mascar, chicle *m* **2 gums** *npl* : encías *fpl*

gumbo ['gʌm,bo:] *n* : sopa *f* de quingombó

gumdrop ['gʌm,drɑp] *n* : pastilla *f* de goma

gummy ['gʌmi] *adj* **gummier; -est** : gomoso

gumption ['gʌmpʃən] *n* : iniciativa *f*, agallas *fpl fam*

gun[1] ['gʌn] *vt* **gunned; gunning 1** *or* **to gun down** : matar a tiros, asesinar **2** : acelerar (rápidamente) ⟨to gun the engine : acelerar el motor⟩

gun[2] *n* **1** CANNON : cañón *m* **2** FIREARM : arma *f* de fuego **3** SPRAY GUN : pistola *f* **4 to jump the gun** : adelantarse, salir antes de tiempo

gunboat ['gʌn,bo:t] *n* : cañonero *m*

gunfight ['gʌn,faɪt] *n* : tiroteo *m*, balacera *f*

gunfire ['gʌn,faɪr] *n* : disparos *mpl*

gunman ['gʌnmən] *n, pl* **-men** [-mən, -,men] : pistolero *m*, gatillero *m Mex*

gunner ['gʌnər] *n* : artillero *m*, -ra *f*

gunnysack ['gʌni,sæk] *n* : saco *m* de yute

gunpowder ['gʌn,paʊdər] *n* : pólvora *f*

gunshot ['gʌn,ʃɑt] *n* : disparo *m*, tiro *m*, balazo *m*

gunwale ['gʌnəl] *n* : borda *f*

guppy ['gʌpi] *n, pl* **-pies** : lebistes *m*

gurgle[1] ['gərgəl] *vi* **-gled; -gling 1** : borbotar, gorgotear (dícese de un líquido) **2** : gorjear (dícese de un niño)

gurgle[2] *n* **1** : borboteo *m*, gorgoteo *m* (de un líquido) **2** : gorjeo *m* (de un niño)

gush ['gʌʃ] *vi* **1** SPOUT : surgir, salir a chorros, chorrear **2** : hablar con entusiasmo efusivo ⟨she gushed with praise : se deshizo en elogios⟩

gust ['gʌst] *n* : ráfaga *f*, racha *f*

gusto ['gʌs,to:] *n, pl* **gustoes** : entusiasmo *m* ⟨with gusto : con deleite, con ganas⟩

gusty ['gʌsti] *adj* **gustier; -est** : racheado

gut[1] ['gʌt] *vt* **gutted; gutting 1** EVISCERATE : destripar (un pollo, etc.), limpiar (un pescado) **2** : destruir el interior de (un edificio)

gut[2] *n* **1** INTESTINE : intestino *m* **2 guts** *npl* INNARDS : tripas *fpl fam*, entrañas *fpl* **3 guts** *npl* COURAGE : valentía *f*, agallas *fpl*

gutter ['gʌtər] *n* **1** : canal *mf*, canaleta *f* (de un techo) **2** : cuneta *f*, arroyo *m* (de una calle)

guttural ['gʌtərəl] *adj* : gutural

guy ['gaɪ] *n* **1** *or* **guyline** : cuerda *f* tensora, cable *m* **2** FELLOW : tipo *m*, hombre *m*

guzzle ['gʌzəl] *vt* **-zled; -zling** : chupar, tragarse

gym ['dʒɪm] → **gymnasium**

gymnasium [dʒɪm'neɪziəm, -ʒəm] *n, pl* **-siums** *or* **-sia** [-zi:ə, -ʒə] : gimnasio *m*

gymnast ['dʒɪmnəst, -,næst] *n* : gimnasta *mf*

gymnastic [dʒɪm'næstɪk] *adj* : gimnástico

gymnastics [dʒɪm'næstɪks] *ns & pl* : gimnasia *f*

gynecologist [,gaɪnə'kɑlədʒɪst, ,dʒɪnə-] *n* : ginecólogo *m*, -ga *f*

gynecology [,gaɪnə'kɑlədʒi, ,dʒɪnə-] *n* : ginecología *f*

gyp[1] ['dʒɪp] *vt* **gypped; gypping** : estafar, timar

gyp[2] *n* **1** SWINDLER : estafador *m*, -dora *f* **2** FRAUD, SWINDLE : estafa *f*, timo *m fam*

gypsum ['dʒɪpsəm] *n* : yeso *m*

Gypsy ['dʒɪpsi] *n, pl* **-sies** : gitano *m*, -na *f*

gyrate ['dʒaɪ,reɪt] *vi* **-rated; -rating** : girar, rotar

gyration [dʒaɪ'reɪʃən] *n* : giro *m*, rotación *f*

gyroscope ['dʒaɪrə,sko:p] *n* : giroscopio *m*, giróscopo *m*

H

h ['eɪʧ] *n, pl* **h's** *or* **hs** ['eɪʧəz] : octava letra del alfabeto inglés

ha ['hɑ] *interj* : ¡ja!

haberdashery ['hæbər,dæʃəri] *n, pl* **-eries** : tienda *f* de ropa para caballeros

habit ['hæbɪt] *n* **1** CUSTOM : hábito *m*, costumbre *f* **2** : hábito *m* (de un monje o una religiosa) **3** ADDICTION : dependencia *f*, adicción *f*

habitable ['hæbɪtəbəl] *adj* : habitable

habitat ['hæbɪ,tæt] *n* : hábitat *m*

habitation [,hæbɪ'teɪʃən] *n* **1** OCCUPANCY : habitación *f* **2** RESIDENCE : residencia *f*, morada *f*

habit–forming ['hæbɪt,fɔrmɪŋ] *adj* : que crea dependencia

habitual [hə'bɪʧʊəl] *adj* **1** CUSTOMARY : habitual, acostumbrado **2** INVETERATE : incorregible, empedernido — **habitually** *adv*

habituate [hə'bɪʧʊ,eɪt] *vt* **-ated; -ating** : habituar, acostumbrar

hack[1] ['hæk] *vt* : cortar, tajear (a hachazos, etc.) ⟨to hack one's way : abrirse paso⟩ — *vi* **1** : hacer tajos **2** COUGH : toser

hack[2] *n* **1** CHOP : hachazo *m*, tajo *m* **2** HORSE : caballo *m* de alquiler **3** WRITER : escritor *m*, -tora *f* a sueldo; escritorzuelo *m*, -la *f* **4** COUGH : tos *f* seca

hackles ['hækəlz] *npl* **1** : pluma *f* erizada (de un ave), pelo *m* erizado (de un perro, etc.) **2 to get one's hackles up** : ponerse furioso

hackney ['hækni] *n, pl* **-neys** : caballo *m* de silla, caballo *m* de tiro

hackneyed ['hæknid] *adj* TRITE : trillado, gastado

hacksaw ['hæk,sɔ] *n* : sierra *f* para metales

had → **have**

haddock ['hædək] *ns & pl* : eglefino *m*

hadn't ['hædənt] (*contraction* of **had not**) → **have**

haft ['hæft] *n* : mango *m*, empuñadura *f*

hag ['hæg] *n* **1** WITCH : bruja *f*, hechicera *f* **2** CRONE : vieja *f* fea

haggard ['hægərd] *adj* : demacrado, macilento — **haggardly** *adv*

haggle ['hægəl] *vi* **-gled; -gling** : regatear

ha–ha [,hɑ'hɑ, 'hɑ'hɑ] *interj* : ¡ja, ja!

hail[1] ['heɪl] *vt* **1** GREET : saludar **2** SUMMON : llamar ⟨to hail a taxi : llamar un taxi⟩ — *vi* : granizar (en meteorología)

hail[2] *n* **1** : granizo *m* **2** BARRAGE : aluvión *m*, lluvia *f*

hail[3] *interj* : ¡salve!

hailstone ['heɪl,sto:n] *n* : granizo *m*, piedra *f* de granizo

hailstorm ['heɪl,stɔrm] *n* : granizada *f*

hair ['hær] *n* **1** : pelo *m*, cabello *m* ⟨to get one's hair cut : cortarse el pelo⟩ **2** : vello *m* (en las piernas, etc.)

hairbreadth ['hær,brɛdθ] *or* **hairsbreadth** ['hærz-] *n* **by a hairbreadth** : por un pelo

hairbrush ['hær,brʌʃ] *n* : cepillo *m* (para el pelo)

haircut ['hær,kʌt] *n* : corte *m* de pelo

hairdo ['hær,du:] *n, pl* **-dos** : peinado *m*

hairdresser ['hær,drɛsər] *n* : peluquero *m*, -ra *f*

hairiness ['hærinəs] *n* : vellosidad *f*

hairless ['hærləs] *adj* : sin pelo, calvo, pelón

hairline ['hær,laɪn] *n* **1** : línea *f* delgada **2** : nacimiento *m* del pelo ⟨to have a receding hairline : tener entradas⟩

hairpin ['hær,pɪn] *n* : horquilla *f*

hair–raising ['hær,reɪzɪŋ] *adj* : espeluznante

hair spray *n* : laca *f*, fijador *m* (para el pelo)

hairstyle ['hær,staɪl] *n* : peinado *m*

hairy ['hæri] *adj* **hairier; -est** : peludo, velludo

Haitian ['heɪʃən, 'heɪtiən] *n* : haitiano *m*, -na *f* — **Haitian** *adj*

hake ['heɪk] *n* : merluza *f*

hale[1] ['heɪl] *vt* **haled; haling** : arrastrar, halar ⟨to hale to court : arrastrar al tribunal⟩

hale[2] *adj* : saludable, robusto

half[1] ['hæf, 'haf] *adv* : medio, a medias ⟨half cooked : medio cocido⟩

half[2] *adj* : medio, a medias ⟨a half hour : una media hora⟩ ⟨a half truth : una verdad a medias⟩

half[3] *n, pl* **halves** ['hævz, 'havz] **1** : mitad *f* ⟨half of my friends : la mitad de mis amigos⟩ ⟨in half : por la mitad⟩ **2** : tiempo *m* (en deportes)

half brother *n* : medio hermano *m*, hermanastro *m*

halfhearted ['hæf'hɑrtəd] *adj* : sin ánimo, poco entusiasta

halfheartedly ['hæf'hɑrtədli] *adv* : con poco entusiasmo, sin ánimo

half–life ['hæf,laɪf] *n, pl* **half–lives** : media vida *f*

half sister *n* : media hermana *f*, hermanastra *f*

halfway[1] ['hæf'weɪ] *adv* : a medio camino, a mitad de camino

halfway[2] *adj* : medio, intermedio ⟨a halfway point : un punto intermedio⟩

half–wit ['hæf,wɪt] *n* : tonto *m*, -ta *f*; imbécil *mf*

half–witted ['hæf,wɪtəd] *adj* : estúpido

halibut ['hælɪbət] *ns & pl* : halibut *m*

hall ['hɔl] *n* **1** BUILDING : residencia *f* estudiantil, facultad *f* (de una universidad) **2** VESTIBULE : entrada *f*, vestíbulo *m*, zaguán *m* **3** CORRIDOR : corredor *m*, pasillo *m* **4** AUDITORIUM : sala *f*, salón *m* ⟨concert hall : sala de conciertos⟩ **5 city hall** : ayuntamiento *m*

hallelujah [,hælə'lu:jə, ,hɑ-] *interj* : ¡aleluya!

hallmark ['hɔl,mɑrk] *n* : sello *m* (distintivo)

hallow ['hæ,lo:] *vt* : santificar, consagrar

hallowed ['hæ,lo:d, 'hæ,lo:əd, 'hɑ,lo:d] *adj* : sagrado

Halloween [,hælə'wi:n, ,hɑ-] *n* : víspera *f* de Todos los Santos

hallucinate [hæ'lu:sən,eɪt] *vi* **-nated; -nating** : alucinar

hallucination [hə,lu:sən'eɪʃən] *n* : alucinación *f*

hallucinatory [hə'lu:sənə,tori] *adj* : alucinante

hallucinogen [hə'lu:sənədʒən] *n* : alucinógeno *m*

hallucinogenic [hə,lu:sənə'dʒenɪk] *adj* : alucinógeno

hallway ['hɔl,weɪ] *n* **1** ENTRANCE : entrada *f* **2** CORRIDOR : corredor *m*, pasillo *m*

halo ['heɪ,lo:] *n, pl* **-los** *or* **-loes** : aureola *f*, halo *m*

halt[1] ['hɔlt] *vi* : detenerse, pararse — *vt* **1** STOP : detener, parar (a una persona) **2** INTERRUPT : interrumpir (una actividad)

halt[2] *n* **1** : alto *m*, parada *f* **2 to come to a halt** : pararse, detenerse

halter ['hɔltər] *n* **1** : cabestro *m*, ronzal *m* (para un animal) **2** : blusa *f* sin espalda

halting ['hɔltɪŋ] *adj* HESITANT : vacilante, titubeante — **haltingly** *adv*

halve ['hæv, 'hav] *vt* **halved; halving 1** DIVIDE : partir por la mitad **2** REDUCE : reducir a la mitad

halves → **half**

ham ['hæm] *n* **1** : jamón *m* **2** *or* **ham actor** : comicastro *m*, -tra *f* **3** *or* **ham radio operator** : radioaficionado *m*, -da *f* **4 hams** *npl* HAUNCHES : ancas *fpl*

hamburger ['hæm,bərgər] *or* **hamburg** [-,bərg] *n* **1** : carne *f* molida **2** : hamburguesa *f* (emparedado)

hamlet ['hæmlət] *n* VILLAGE : aldea *f*, poblado *m*

hammer[1] ['hæmər] *vt* **1** STRIKE : clavar, golpear **2** NAIL : clavar, martillar **3 to hammer out** NEGOTIATE : elaborar, negociar, llegar a — *vi* : martillar, golpear

hammer[2] *n* **1** : martillo *m* **2** : percusor *m*, percutor *m* (de un arma de fuego)

hammock ['hæmək] *n* : hamaca *f*

hamper[1] ['hæmpər] *vt* : obstaculizar, dificultar

hamper[2] *n* : cesto *m*, canasta *f*

hamster ['hæmpstər] *n* : hámster *m*

hamstring ['hæm,strɪŋ] *vt* **-strung** [-,strʌŋ]; **-stringing 1** : cortarle el tendón del corvejón a (un animal) **2** INCAPACITATE : incapacitar, inutilizar

hand[1] ['hænd] *vt* : pasar, dar, entregar

hand[2] *n* **1** : mano *f* ⟨made by hand : hecho a mano⟩ **2** POINTER : manecilla *f*, aguja *f* (de un reloj o instrumento) **3** SIDE : lado *m* ⟨on the other hand : por otro lado⟩ **4** HANDWRITING : letra *f*, escritura *f* **5** APPLAUSE : aplauso *m* **6** : mano *f*, cartas *fpl* (en juegos de naipes)

7 WORKER : obrero *m*, -ra *f*; trabajador *m*, -dora *f* **8 to ask for someone's hand (in marriage)** : pedir la mano de alguien **9 to lend a hand** : echar una mano

handbag ['hænd,bæg] *n* : cartera *f*, bolso *m*, bolsa *f* *Mex*

handball ['hænd,bɔl] *n* : frontón *m*, pelota *f*

handbill ['hænd,bɪl] *n* : folleto *m*, volante *m*

handbook ['hænd,bʊk] *n* : manual *m*

handcuff ['hænd,kʌf] *vt* : esposar, ponerle esposas (a alguien)

handcuffs ['hænd,kʌfs] *npl* : esposas *fpl*

handful ['hænd,fʊl] *n* : puñado *m*

handgun ['hænd,gʌn] *n* : pistola *f*, revólver *m*

handheld ['hænd,held] *adj* : de mano

handicap[1] ['hændi,kæp] *vt* **-capped; -capping 1** : asignar un handicap a (en deportes) **2** HAMPER : obstaculizar, poner en desventaja

handicap[2] *n* **1** DISABILITY : minusvalía *f*, discapacidad *f* **2** DISADVANTAGE : desventaja *f*, handicap *m* (en deportes)

handicapped ['hændi,kæpt] *adj* DISABLED : minusválido, discapacitado

handicraft ['hændi,kræft] *n* : artesanía *f*

handily ['hændəli] *adv* EASILY : fácilmente, con facilidad

handiwork ['hændi,wərk] *n* **1** WORK : trabajo *m* **2** CRAFTS : artesanías *fpl*

handkerchief ['hæŋkərtʃəf, -,tʃi:f] *n, pl* **-chiefs** : pañuelo *m*

handle[1] ['hændəl] *v* **-dled; -dling** *vt* **1** TOUCH : tocar **2** MANAGE : tratar, manejar, despachar **3** SELL : comerciar con, vender — *vi* : responder, conducirse (dícese de un vehículo)

handle[2] *n* : asa *m*, asidero *m*, mango *m* (de un cuchillo, etc.), pomo *m* (de una puerta), tirador *m* (de un cajón)

handlebars ['hændəl,bɑrz] *npl* : manubrio *m*, manillar *m*

handler ['hændələr] *n* : cuidador *m*, -dora *f*

handling ['hændəlɪŋ] *n* **1** MANAGEMENT : manejo *m* **2** TOUCHING : manoseo *m* **3 shipping and handling** : porte *m*, transporte *m*

handmade ['hænd,meɪd] *adj* : hecho a mano

hand-me-downs ['hændmi,daʊnz] *npl* : ropa *f* usada

handout ['hænd,aʊt] *n* **1** AID : dádiva *f*, limosna *f* **2** LEAFLET : folleto *m*

handpick ['hænd'pɪk] *vt* : seleccionar con cuidado

handrail ['hænd,reɪl] *n* : pasamanos *m*, barandilla *f*, barandal *m*

handsaw ['hænd,sɔ] *n* : serrucho *m*

hands down *adv* **1** EASILY : con facilidad **2** UNQUESTIONABLY : con mucho, de lejos

handshake ['hænd,ʃeɪk] *n* : apretón *m* de manos

handsome ['hæntsəm] *adj* **-somer; -est**
1 ATTRACTIVE : apuesto, guapo, atractivo **2** GENEROUS : generoso **3** SIZ
ABLE : considerable
handsomely ['hæntsəmli] *adv* **1** ELE
GANTLY : elegantemente **2** GENER
OUSLY : con generosidad
handspring ['hænd₁sprɪŋ] *n* : voltereta *f*
handstand ['hænd₁stænd] *n* **to do a**
handstand : pararse de manos
hand-to-hand ['hændtə'hænd] *adj*
: cuerpo a cuerpo
handwriting ['hænd₁raɪtɪŋ] *n* : letra *f*, escritura *f*
handwritten ['hænd₁rɪtən] *adj* : escrito a
mano
handy ['hændi] *adj* **handier; -est 1**
NEARBY : a mano, cercano **2** USEFUL
: útil, práctico **3** DEXTEROUS : hábil
hang[1] ['hæŋ] *v* **hung** ['hʌŋ]**; hanging** *vt*
1 SUSPEND : colgar, tender, suspender
2 *past tense often* **hanged** EXECUTE
: colgar, ahorcar **3 to hang one's head**
: bajar la cabeza — *vi* **1** FALL : caer
(dícese de las telas y la ropa) **2** DAN
GLE : colgar **3** HOVER : flotar, sostenerse en el aire **4** : ser ahorcado **5**
DROOP : inclinarse **6 to hang up** : colgar ⟨he hung up on me : me colgó⟩
hang[2] *n* **1** DRAPE : caída *f* **2 to get the**
hang of something : agarrarle la onda
a algo
hangar ['hæŋər, 'hæŋgər] *n* : hangar *m*
hanger ['hæŋər] *n* : percha *f*, gancho *m*
(para ropa)
hangman ['hæŋmən] *n, pl* **-men** [-mən,
-₁mɛn] : verdugo *m*
hangnail ['hæŋ₁neɪl] *n* : padrastro *m*
hangout ['hæŋ₁aʊt] *n* : lugar *m* popular,
sitio *m* muy frecuentado
hangover ['hæŋ₁oːvər] *n* : resaca *f*
hank ['hæŋk] *n* : madeja *f*
hanker ['hæŋkər] *vi* **to hanker for** : tener ansias de, tener ganas de
hankering ['hæŋkərɪŋ] *n* : ansia *f*, anhelo *m*
hansom ['hæntsəm] *n* : coche *m* de caballos
Hanukkah ['xɑnəkə, 'hɑ-] *n* : Januká,
Hanukkah
haphazard [hæp'hæzərd] *adj* : casual,
fortuito, al azar — **haphazardly** *adv*
hapless ['hæpləs] *adj* UNFORTUNATE
: desafortunado, desventurado — **haplessly** *adv*
happen ['hæpən] *vi* **1** OCCUR : pasar,
ocurrir, suceder, tener lugar **2** BEFALL
: pasar, acontecer ⟨what happened to
her? : ¿qué le ha pasado?⟩ **3** CHANCE
: resultar, ocurrir por casualidad ⟨it
happened that I wasn't home : resulta
que estaba fuera de casa⟩ ⟨he happens
to be right : da la casualidad de que
tiene razón⟩
happening ['hæpənɪŋ] *n* : suceso *m*,
acontecimiento *m*
happiness ['hæpinəs] *n* : felicidad *f*,
dicha *f*

happy ['hæpi] *adj* **-pier; -est 1** JOYFUL
: feliz, contento, alegre **2** FORTUNATE
: afortunado, feliz — **happily** [-pəli] *adv*
happy-go-lucky ['hæpigoː'lʌki] *adj*
: despreocupado
harangue[1] [hə'ræŋ] *vt* **-rangued; -ranguing** : arengar
harangue[2] *n* : arenga *f*
harass [hə'ræs, 'hærəs] *vt* **1** BESIEGE,
HOUND : acosar, asediar, hostigar **2**
ANNOY : molestar
harassment [hə'ræsmənt, 'hærəsmənt]
n : acoso *m*, hostigamiento *m* ⟨sexual
harrassment : acoso sexual⟩
harbinger ['hɑrbɪndʒər] *n* **1** HERALD
: heraldo *m*, precursor *m* **2** OMEN : presagio *m*
harbor[1] ['hɑrbər] *vt* **1** SHELTER : dar
refugio a, albergar **2** CHERISH, KEEP
: abrigar, guardar, albergar ⟨to harbor
doubts : guardar dudas⟩
harbor[2] *n* **1** REFUGE : refugio *m* **2** PORT
: puerto *m*
hard[1] ['hɑrd] *adv* **1** FORCEFULLY
: fuerte, con fuerza ⟨the wind blew
hard : el viento sopló fuerte⟩ **2** STREN
UOUSLY : duro, mucho ⟨to work hard
: trabajar duro⟩ **3 to take something**
hard : tomarse algo muy mal, estar muy
afectado por algo
hard[2] *adj* **1** FIRM, SOLID : duro, firme,
sólido **2** DIFFICULT : difícil, arduo **3**
SEVERE : severo, duro ⟨a hard winter
: un invierno severo⟩ **4** UNFEELING
: insensible, duro **5** DILIGENT : diligente ⟨to be a hard worker : ser muy
trabajador⟩ **6 hard liquor** : bebidas *fpl*
fuertes **7 hard water** : agua *f* dura
hardcover ['hɑrd₁kʌvər] *adj* : de pasta
dura, de tapa dura
hard disk *n* : disco *m* duro
hard drive → hard disk
harden ['hɑrdən] *vt* : endurecer
hardheaded [₁hɑrd'hɛdəd] *adj* **1** STUB
BORN : testarudo, terco **2** REALISTIC
: realista, práctico — **hardheadedly**
adv
hard-hearted [₁hɑrd'hɑrtəd] *adj* : despiadado, insensible — **hard-heartedly** *adv*
hard-heartedness [₁hɑrd'hɑrtədnəs] *n*
: dureza *f* de corazón
hardly ['hɑrdli] *adv* **1** SCARCELY : apenas, casi ⟨I hardly knew her : apenas
la conocía⟩ ⟨hardly ever : casi nunca⟩
2 NOT : difícilmente, poco, no ⟨they
can hardly blame me! : ¡difícilmente
pueden echarme la culpa!⟩ ⟨it's hardly likely : es poco probable⟩
hardness ['hɑrdnəs] *n* **1** FIRMNESS
: dureza *f* **2** DIFFICULTY : dificultad *f*
3 SEVERITY : severidad *f*
hardship ['hɑrd₁ʃɪp] *n* : dificultad *f*, privación *f*
hardware ['hɑrd₁wær] *n* **1** TOOLS : ferretería *f* **2** : hardware *m* (de una computadora)
hardwood ['hɑrd₁wʊd] *n* : madera *f* dura,
madera *f* noble

hardworking ['hard'wərkıŋ] *adj* : trabajador

hardy ['hardi] *adj* **-dier; -est** : fuerte, robusto, resistente (dícese de las plantas) — **hardily** [-dəli] *adv*

hare ['hær] *n, pl* **hare** *or* **hares** : liebre *f*

harebrained ['hær₁breınd] *adj* : estúpido, absurdo, disparatado

harelip ['hær₁lıp] *n* : labio *m* leporino

harem ['hærəm] *n* : harén *m*

hark ['hark] *vi* **1** (*used only in the imperative*) LISTEN : escuchar **2 hark back** RETURN : volver **3 hark back** RECALL : recordar

harlequin ['harlıkən, -kwən] *n* : arlequín *m*

harm[1] ['harm] *vt* : hacerle daño a, perjudicar

harm[2] *n* : daño *m*, perjuicio *m*

harmful ['harmfəl] *adj* : dañino, perjudicial — **harmfully** *adv*

harmless ['harmləs] *adj* : inofensivo, inocuo — **harmlessly** *adv*

harmlessness ['harmləsnəs] *n* : inocuidad *f*

harmonic [har'manık] *adj* : armónico — **harmonically** [-nıkli] *adv*

harmonica [har'manıkə] *n* : armónica *f*

harmonious [har'mo:niəs] *adj* : armonioso — **harmoniously** *adv*

harmonize ['harmə₁naız] *v* **-nized; -nizing** : armonizar

harmony ['harməni] *n, pl* **-nies** : armonía *f*

harness[1] ['harnəs] *vt* **1** : enjaezar (un animal) **2** UTILIZE : utilizar, aprovechar

harness[2] *n* : arreos *mpl*, guarniciones *fpl*, arnés *m*

harp[1] ['harp] *vi* **to harp on** : insistir sobre, machacar sobre

harp[2] *n* : arpa *m*

harpist ['harpıst] *n* : arpista *mf*

harpoon[1] [har'pu:n] *vt* : arponear

harpoon[2] *n* : arpón *m*

harpsichord ['harpsı₁kɔrd] *n* : clavicémbalo *m*

harrow[1] ['hær₁o:] *vt* **1** CULTIVATE : gradar, labrar (la tierra) **2** TORMENT : atormentar

harrow[2] *n* : grada *f*, rastra *f*

harry ['hæri] *vt* **-ried; -rying** HARASS : acosar, hostigar

harsh ['harʃ] *adj* **1** ROUGH : áspero **2** SEVERE : duro, severo **3** : discordante (dícese de los sonidos) — **harshly** *adv*

harshness ['harʃnəs] *n* **1** ROUGHNESS : aspereza *f* **2** SEVERITY : dureza *f*, severidad *f*

harvest[1] ['harvəst] *v* : cosechar

harvest[2] *n* **1** HARVESTING : siega *f*, recolección *f* **2** CROP : cosecha *f*

harvester ['harvəstər] *n* : segador *m*, -dora *f*; cosechadora *f* (máquina)

has → **have**

hash[1] ['hæʃ] *vt* **1** MINCE : picar **2 to hash over** DISCUSS : discutir, repasar

hash[2] *n* **1** : picadillo *m* (comida) **2** JUMBLE : revoltijo *m*, fárrago *m*

hasn't ['hæzənt] (*contraction* of **has not**) → **has**

hasp ['hæsp] *n* : picaporte *m*, pestillo *m*

hassle[1] ['hæsəl] *vt* **-sled; -sling** : fastidiar, molestar

hassle[2] *n* **1** ARGUMENT : discusión *f*, disputa *f*, bronca *f* **2** FIGHT : pelea *f*, riña *f* **3** BOTHER, TROUBLE : problemas *mpl*, lío *m*

hassock ['hæsək] *n* **1** CUSHION : almohadón *m*, cojín *m* **2** FOOTSTOOL : escabel *m*

haste ['heıst] *n* **1** : prisa *f*, apuro *m* **2 to make haste** : darse prisa, apurarse

hasten ['heısən] *vt* : acelerar, precipitar — *vi* : apresurarse, apurarse

hasty ['heısti] *adj* **hastier; -est** **1** HURRIED, QUICK : rápido, apresurado, apurado **2** RASH : precipitado — **hastily** [-təli] *adv*

hat ['hæt] *n* : sombrero *m*

hatch[1] ['hætʃ] *vt* **1** : incubar, empollar (huevos) **2** DEVISE : idear, tramar — *vi* : salir del cascarón

hatch[2] *n* : escotilla *f*

hatchery ['hætʃəri] *n, pl* **-ries** : criadero *m*

hatchet ['hætʃət] *n* : hacha *f*

hatchway ['hætʃ₁weı] *n* : escotilla *f*

hate[1] ['heıt] *vt* **hated; hating** : odiar, aborrecer, detestar

hate[2] *n* : odio *m*

hateful ['heıtfəl] *adj* : odioso, aborrecible, detestable — **hatefully** *adv*

hatred ['heıtrəd] *n* : odio *m*

hatter ['hætər] *n* : sombrerero *m*, -ra *f*

haughtiness ['hotinəs] *n* : altanería *f*, altivez *f*

haughty ['hoti] *adj* **-tier; -est** : altanero, altivo — **haughtily** [-təli] *adv*

haul[1] ['hol] *vt* **1** DRAG, PULL : arrastrar, jalar **2** TRANSPORT : transportar

haul[2] *n* **1** PULL : tirón *m*, jalón *m* **2** CATCH : redada *f* **3** JOURNEY : viaje *m*, trayecto *m* ⟨it's a long haul : es un trayecto largo⟩

haulage ['holıʤ] *n* : transporte *m*, tiro *m*

hauler ['holər] *n* : transportista *mf*

haunch ['hontʃ] *n* **1** HIP : cadera *f* **2 haunches** *npl* HINDQUARTERS : ancas *fpl*, cuartos *mpl* traseros

haunt[1] ['hont] *vt* **1** : aparecer en (dícese de un fantasma) **2** FREQUENT : frecuentar, rondar **3** PREOCCUPY : perseguir, obsesionar

haunt[2] *n* : guarida *f* (de animales o ladrones), lugar *m* predilecto

haunting ['hontıŋ] *adj* : obsesionante, evocador — **hauntingly** *adv*

haute ['o:t] *adj* **1** : de moda, de categoría **2 haute couture** [₁o:tku'tur] : alta costura *f* **3 haute cuisine** [₁o:tkwı'zi:n] : alta cocina *f*

have ['hæv, *in sense 3 as an auxiliary verb usu* 'hæf] *v* **had** ['hæd]; **having; has** ['hæz, *in sense 3 as an auxiliary verb usu* 'hæs] *vt* **1** POSSESS : tener ⟨do you have

change? : ¿tienes cambio?⟩ **2** EXPERI-
ENCE, UNDERGO : tener, experimentar, sufrir ⟨I have a toothache : tengo
un dolor de muelas⟩ **3** INCLUDE : tener, incluir ⟨April has 30 days : abril
tiene 30 días⟩ **4** CONSUME : comer,
tomar **5** RECEIVE : tener, recibir ⟨he
had my permission : tenía mi permiso⟩
6 ALLOW : permitir, dejar ⟨I won't have
it! : ¡no lo permitiré!⟩ **7** HOLD : hacer
⟨to have a party : dar una fiesta⟩ ⟨to
have a meeting : convocar una re-
unión⟩ **8** HOLD : tener ⟨he had me in
his power : me tenía en su poder⟩ **9**
BEAR : tener (niños) **10** (*indicating
causation*) ⟨she had a dress made
: mandó hacer un vestido⟩ ⟨to have
one's hair cut : cortarse el pelo⟩ — *v
aux* **1** : haber ⟨she has been very busy
: ha estado muy ocupada⟩ ⟨I've lived
here three years : hace tres años que
vivo aquí⟩ **2** (*used in tags*) ⟨you've finished, haven't you? : ha terminado,
¿no?⟩ **3 to have to** : deber, tener que
⟨we have to leave : tenemos que salir⟩
haven ['heɪvən] *n* : refugio *m*
havoc ['hævək] *n* **1** DESTRUCTION : estragos *mpl*, destrucción *f* **2** CHAOS,
DISORDER : desorden *m*, caos *m*
Hawaiian[1] [hə'waɪən] *adj* : hawaiano
Hawaiian[2] *n* : hawaiano *m*, -na *f*
hawk[1] ['hɔk] *vt* : pregonar, vender (mercancías) en la calle
hawk[2] *n* : halcón *m*
hawker ['hɔkər] *n* : vendedor *m*, -dora *f*
ambulante
hawthorn ['hɔ,θɔrn] *n* : espino *m*
hay ['heɪ] *n* : heno *m*
hay fever *n* : fiebre *f* del heno
hayloft ['heɪ,lɔft] *n* : pajar *m*
hayseed ['heɪ,si:d] *n* : palurdo *m*, -da *f*
haystack ['heɪ,stæk] *n* : almiar *m*
haywire ['heɪ,waɪr] *adj* : descompuesto,
desbaratado ⟨to go haywire : estro-
pearse⟩
hazard[1] ['hæzərd] *vt* : arriesgar, aventurar
hazard[2] *n* **1** DANGER : peligro *m*, riesgo *m* **2** CHANCE : azar *m*
hazardous ['hæzərdəs] *adj* : arriesgado,
peligroso
haze[1] ['heɪz] *vt* hazed; hazing : abrumar, acosar
haze[2] *n* : bruma *f*, neblina *f*
hazel ['heɪzəl] *n* **1** : avellano *m* (árbol)
2 : color *m* avellana
hazelnut ['heɪzəl,nʌt] *n* : avellana *f*
haziness ['heɪzinəs] *n* **1** MISTINESS
: nebulosidad *f* **2** VAGUENESS
: vaguedad *f*
hazy ['heɪzi] *adj* hazier; -est **1** MISTY
: brumoso, neblinoso, nebuloso **2**
VAGUE : vago, confuso
he ['hi:] *pron* : él
head[1] ['hɛd] *vt* **1** LEAD : encabezar **2**
DIRECT : dirigir — *vi* : dirigirse
head[2] *adj* MAIN : principal ⟨the head office : la oficina central, la sede⟩

head[3] *n* **1** : cabeza *f* ⟨from head to foot
: de pies a cabeza⟩ **2** MIND : mente *f*,
cabeza *f* **3** TIP, TOP : cabeza *f* (de un
clavo, un martillo, etc.), cabecera *f* (de
una mesa o un río), punta *f* (de una
flecha), flor *m* (de un repollo, etc.), encabezamiento *m* (de una carta, etc.),
espuma *f* (de cerveza) **4** DIRECTOR,
LEADER : director *m*, -tora *f*; jefe *m*, -fa
f; cabeza *f* (de una familia) **5** : cara *f*
(de una moneda) ⟨heads or tails : cara
o cruz⟩ **6** : cabeza *f* ⟨500 head of cattle : 500 cabezas de ganado⟩ ⟨$10 a
head : $10 por cabeza⟩ **7 to come to
a head** : llegar a un punto crítico
headache ['hɛd,eɪk] *n* : dolor *m* de
cabeza, jaqueca *f*
headband ['hɛd,bænd] *n* : cinta *f* del
pelo
headdress ['hɛd,drɛs] *n* : tocado *m*
headfirst ['hɛd'fərst] *adv* : de cabeza
headgear ['hɛd,gɪr] *n* : gorro *m*, casco
m, sombrero *m*
heading ['hɛdɪŋ] *n* **1** DIRECTION : dirección *f* **2** TITLE : encabezamiento *m*,
título *m* **3** : membrete *m* (de una carta)
headland ['hɛdlənd, -,lænd] *n* : cabo *m*
headlight ['hɛd,laɪt] *n* : faro *m*, foco *m*,
farol *m Mex*
headline ['hɛd,laɪn] *n* : titular *m*
headlong[1] ['hɛd'lɔŋ] *adv* **1** HEADFIRST
: de cabeza **2** HASTILY : precipitadamente
headlong[2] ['hɛd,lɔŋ] *adj* : precipitado
headmaster ['hɛd,mæstər] *n* : director
m
headmistress ['hɛd,mɪstrəs, -'mɪs-] *n*
: directora *f*
head–on ['hɛd'ɑn, -'ɔn] *adv & adj* : de
frente
headphones ['hɛd,fo:nz] *npl* : audífonos
mpl, cascos *mpl*
headquarters ['hɛd,kwɔrtərz] *ns & pl* **1**
SEAT : oficina *f* central, sede *f* **2** : cuartel *m* general (de los militares)
headrest ['hɛd,rɛst] *n* : apoyacabezas *m*
headship ['hɛd,ʃɪp] *n* : dirección *f*
head start *n* : ventaja *f*
headstone ['hɛd,sto:n] *n* : lápida *f*
headstrong ['hɛd'strɔŋ] *adj* : testarudo,
obstinado, empecinado
headwaiter ['hɛd'weɪtər] *n* : jefe *m*, -fa *f*
de comedor
headwaters ['hɛd,wɔtərz, -,wɑ-] *npl*
: cabecera *f*
headway ['hɛd,weɪ] *n* : progreso *m* ⟨to
make headway against : avanzar con-
tra⟩
heady ['hɛdi] *adj* headier; -est **1** IN-
TOXICATING : embriagador, excitante
2 SHREWD : astuto, sagaz
heal ['hi:l] *vt* : curar, sanar — *vi* **1** : sanar, curarse **2 to heal up** : cicatrizarse
healer ['hi:lər] *n* **1** : curandero *m*, -dera
f **2** : curador *m*, -dora *f* (cosa)
health ['hɛlθ] *n* : salud *f*

healthful ['hɛlθfəl] *adj* : saludable, salubre — **healthfully** *adv*
healthy ['hɛlθi] *adj* **healthier; -est** : sano, bien — **healthily** [-θəli] *adv*
heap¹ ['hiːp] *vt* **1** PILE : amontonar, apilar **2** SHOWER : colmar
heap² *n* : montón *m*, pila *f*
hear ['hɪr] *v* **heard** ['hərd]; **hearing** *vt* **1** : oír ⟨do you hear me? : ¿me oyes?⟩ **2** HEED : oír, prestar atención a **3** LEARN : oír, enterarse de — *vi* **1** : oír ⟨to hear about : oír hablar de⟩ **2 to hear from** : tener noticias de
hearing ['hɪrɪŋ] *n* **1** : oído *m* ⟨hard of hearing : duro de oído⟩ **2** : vista *f* (en un tribunal) **3** ATTENTION : consideración *f*, oportunidad *f* de expresarse **4** EARSHOT : alcance *m* del oído
hearing aid *n* : audífono *m*
hearken ['harkən] *vt* : escuchar
hearsay ['hɪr,seɪ] *n* : rumores *mpl*
hearse ['hərs] *n* : coche *m* fúnebre
heart ['hart] *n* **1** : corazón *m* **2** CENTER, CORE : corazón *m*, centro *m* ⟨the heart of the matter : el meollo del asunto⟩ **3** FEELINGS : corazón *m*, sentimientos *mpl* ⟨a broken heart : un corazón destrozado⟩ ⟨to have a good heart : tener buen corazón⟩ ⟨to take something to heart : tomarse algo a pecho⟩ **4** COURAGE : valor *m*, corazón *m* ⟨to take heart : animarse, cobrar ánimos⟩ **5 hearts** *npl* : corazones *mpl* (en juegos de naipes) **6 by heart** : de memoria
heartache ['hart,eɪk] *n* : pena *f*, angustia *f*
heart attack *n* : infarto *m*, ataque *m* al corazón
heartbeat ['hart,biːt] *n* : latido *m* (del corazón)
heartbreak ['hart,breɪk] *n* : congoja *f*, angustia *f*
heartbreaking ['hart,breɪkɪŋ] *adj* : desgarrador, que parte el corazón
heartbroken ['hart,broːkən] *adj* : desconsolado, destrozado
heartburn ['hart,bərn] *n* : acidez *f* estomacal
hearten ['hartən] *vt* : alentar, animar
heartfelt ['hart,fɛlt] *adj* : sentido
hearth ['harθ] *n* : hogar *m*, chimenea *f*
heartily ['hartəli] *adv* **1** ENTHUSIASTICALLY : de buena gana, con entusiasmo **2** TOTALLY : totalmente, completamente
heartless ['hartləs] *adj* : desalmado, despiadado, cruel
heartsick ['hart,sɪk] *adj* : abatido, desconsolado
heartstrings ['hart,strɪŋz] *npl* : fibras *fpl* del corazón
heartwarming ['hart,wɔrmɪŋ] *adj* : conmovedor, emocionante
hearty ['harti] *adj* **heartier; -est 1** CORDIAL, WARM : cordial, caluroso **2** STRONG : fuerte ⟨to have a hearty appetite : ser de buen comer⟩ **3** SUBSTANTIAL : abundante, sustancioso ⟨a

hearty breakfast : un desayuno abundante⟩
heat¹ ['hiːt] *vt* : calentar
heat² *n* **1** WARMTH : calor *m* **2** HEATING : calefacción *f* **3** EXCITEMENT : calor *m*, entusiasmo *m* ⟨in the heat of the moment : en el calor del momento⟩ **4** ESTRUS : celo *m*
heated ['hiːtəd] *adj* **1** WARMED : calentado **2** IMPASSIONED : acalorado, apasionado
heater ['hiːtər] *n* : calentador *m*, estufa *f*, calefactor *m*
heath ['hiːθ] *n* **1** MOOR : brezal *m*, páramo *m* **2** HEATHER : brezo *m*
heathen¹ ['hiːðən] *adj* : pagano
heathen² *n*, *pl* **-thens** *or* **-then** : pagano *m*, -na *f*; infiel *mf*
heather ['hɛðər] *n* : brezo *m*
heave¹ ['hiːv] *v* **heaved** *or* **hove** ['hoːv]; **heaving** *vt* **1** LIFT, RAISE : levantar con esfuerzo **2** HURL : lanzar, tirar **3 to heave a sigh** : echar un suspiro, suspirar — *vi* **1** : subir y bajar, palpitar (dícese del pecho) **2 to heave up** RISE : levantarse
heave² *n* **1** EFFORT : gran esfuerzo *m* (para levantar algo) **2** THROW : lanzamiento *m*
heaven ['hɛvən] *n* **1** : cielo *m* ⟨for heaven's sake : por Dios⟩ **2 heavens** *npl* SKY : cielo *m* ⟨the heavens opened up : empezó a llover a cántaros⟩
heavenly ['hɛvənli] *adj* **1** : celestial, celeste **2** DELIGHTFUL : divino, encantador
heavily ['hɛvəli] *adv* **1** : pesadamente, con mucho peso **2** LABORIOUSLY : trabajosamente, penosamente **3** : mucho
heaviness ['hɛvinəs] *n* : peso *m*, pesadez *f*
heavy ['hɛvi] *adj* **heavier; -est 1** WEIGHTY : pesado **2** DENSE, THICK : denso, espeso, grueso **3** BURDENSOME : oneroso, gravoso **4** PROFOUND : profundo **5** SLUGGISH : lento, tardo **6** STOUT : corpulento **7** SEVERE : severo, duro, fuerte
heavy-duty ['hɛvi'duːti, -'djuː-] *adj* : muy resistente, fuerte
heavyweight ['hɛvi,weɪt] *n* : peso *m* pesado (en deportes)
Hebrew¹ ['hiː,bruː] *adj* : hebreo
Hebrew² *n* **1** : hebreo *m*, -brea *f* **2** : hebreo *m* (idioma)
heck ['hɛk] *n* : ¡caramba!, ¡caray! ⟨a heck of a lot : un montón⟩ ⟨what the heck is ... ? : ¿que diablos es ... ?⟩
heckle ['hɛkəl] *vt* **-led; -ling** : interrumpir (a un orador)
hectare ['hɛk,tær] *n* : hectárea *f*
hectic ['hɛktɪk] *adj* : agitado, ajetreado — **hectically** [-tɪkli] *adv*
he'd ['hiːd] (*contraction of* **he had** *or* **he would**) → **have, would**
hedge¹ ['hɛdʒ] *v* **hedged; hedging** *vt* **1** : cercar con un seto **2 to hedge one's bet** : cubrirse — *vi* **1** : dar rodeos, con-

testar con evasivas **2 to hedge against**
: cubrirse contra, protegerse contra
hedge² *n* **1** : seto *m* vivo **2** SAFEGUARD
: salvaguardia *f*, protección *f*
hedgehog ['hɛdʒ,hɔg, -hɑg] *n* : erizo *m*
heed¹ ['hi:d] *vt* : prestar atención a, hacer caso de
heed² *n* : atención *f*
heedless ['hi:dləs] *adj* : descuidado, despreocupado, inconsciente ⟨to be
heedless of : hacer caso omiso de⟩ —
heedlessly *adv*
heel¹ ['hi:l] *vi* : inclinarse
heel² *n* : talón *m* (del pie), tacón *m* (de
calzado)
heft ['hɛft] *vt* : sopesar
hefty ['hɛfti] *adj* **heftier; -est** : robusto,
fornido, pesado
hegemony [hɪ'dʒɛməni] *n, pl* **-nies**
: hegemonía *f*
heifer ['hɛfər] *n* : novilla *f*
height ['haɪt] *n* **1** PEAK : cumbre *f*, cima
f, punto *m* alto ⟨at the height of her career : en la cumbre de su carrera⟩ ⟨the
height of stupidity : el colmo de la es-
tupidez⟩ **2** TALLNESS : estatura *f* (de
una persona), altura *f* (de un objeto) **3**
ALTITUDE : altura *f*
heighten ['haɪtən] *vt* **1** : hacer más alto
2 INTENSIFY : aumentar, intensificar
— *vi* : aumentarse, intensificarse
heinous ['heɪnəs] *adj* : atroz, abominable, nefando
heir ['ær] *n* : heredero *m*, -ra *f*
heiress ['ærəs] *n* : heredera *f*
heirloom ['ær,lu:m] *n* : reliquia *f* de familia
held → **hold**
helicopter ['hɛlə,kɑptər] *n* : helicóptero
m
helium ['hi:liəm] *n* : helio *m*
helix ['hi:lɪks] *n, pl* **helices** ['hɛlə,si:z,
'hi:-] *or* **helixes** ['hi:lɪksəz] : hélice *f*
hell ['hɛl] *n* : infierno *m*
he'll ['hi:l, 'hɪl] (*contraction of* **he shall**
or **he will**) → **shall, will**
hellish ['hɛlɪʃ] *adj* : horroroso, infernal
hello [hə'lo:, hɛ-] *interj* : ¡hola!
helm ['hɛlm] *n* **1** : timón *m* **2 to take
the helm** : tomar el mando
helmet ['hɛlmət] *n* : casco *m*
help¹ ['hɛlp] *vt* **1** AID, ASSIST : ayudar,
auxiliar, socorrer, asistir **2** ALLEVIATE
: aliviar **3** SERVE : servir ⟨help yourself! : ¡sírvete!⟩ **4** AVOID : evitar ⟨it
can't be helped : no lo podemos evitar,
no hay más remedio⟩ ⟨I couldn't help
smiling : no pude menos que sonreír⟩
help² *n* **1** ASSISTANCE : ayuda *f* ⟨help!
: ¡socorro!, ¡auxilio!⟩ **2** STAFF : personal *m* (en una oficina), servicio *m*
doméstico
helper ['hɛlpər] *n* : ayudante *mf*
helpful ['hɛlpfəl] *adj* **1** OBLIGING : servicial, amable, atento **2** USEFUL : útil,
práctico — **helpfully** *adv*
helpfulness ['hɛlpfəlnəs] *n* **1** KINDNESS
: bondad *f*, amabilidad *f* **2** USEFULNESS
: utilidad *f*

helping ['hɛlpɪŋ] *n* : porción *f*
helpless ['hɛlpləs] *adj* **1** POWERLESS
: incapaz, impotente **2** DEFENSELESS
: indefenso
helplessly ['hɛlpləsli] *adv* : en vano, inútilmente
helplessness ['hɛlpləsnəs] *n* POWER-
LESSNESS : incapacidad *f*, impotencia *f*
helter-skelter [,hɛltər'skɛltər] *adv* : atropelladamente, precipitadamente
hem¹ ['hɛm] *vt* **hemmed; hemming 1**
: dobladillar **2 to hem in** : encerrar
hem² *n* : dobladillo *m*, bastilla *f*
hemisphere ['hɛmə,sfɪr] *n* : hemisferio
m
hemispheric [,hɛmə'sfɪrɪk, -'sfr-] *or*
hemispherical [-ɪkəl] *adj* : hemisférico
hemlock ['hɛm,lɑk] *n* : cicuta *f*
hemoglobin ['hi:mə,glo:bən] *n* : hemoglobina *f*
hemophilia [,hi:mə'fɪliə] *n* : hemofilia *f*
hemorrhage¹ ['hɛmərɪdʒ] *vi* **-rhaged;
-rhaging** : sufrir una hemorragia
hemorrhage² *n* : hemorragia *f*
hemorrhoids ['hɛmə,rɔɪdz, 'hɛm-,rɔɪdz]
npl : hemorroides *fpl*, almorranas *fpl*
hemp ['hɛmp] *n* : cáñamo *m*
hen ['hɛn] *n* : gallina *f*
hence ['hɛnts] *adv* **1** : de aquí, de ahí
⟨10 years hence : de aquí a 10 años⟩ ⟨a
dog bit me, hence my dislike of animals
: un perro me mordió, de ahí mi aversión a los animales⟩ **2** THEREFORE
: por lo tanto, por consiguiente
henceforth ['hɛnts,forθ, ,hɛnts'-] *adv* : de
ahora en adelante
henchman ['hɛntʃmən] *n, pl* **-men** [-mən,
-,mɛn] : secuaz *mf*, esbirro *m*
henpeck ['hɛn,pɛk] *vt* : dominar (al marido)
hepatitis [,hɛpə'taɪtəs] *n, pl* **-titides**
[-'tɪtə,di:z] : hepatitis *f*
her¹ ['hər] *adj* : su, de ella ⟨her house
: su casa, la casa de ella⟩
her² ['hər, ər] *pron* **1** (*used as direct object*) : la ⟨I saw her yesterday : la vi
ayer⟩ **2** (*used as indirect object*) : le, se
⟨he gave her the book : le dio el libro⟩
⟨he sent it to her : se lo mandó⟩ **3** (*used
as object of a preposition*) : ella ⟨we did
it for her : lo hicimos por ella⟩ ⟨taller
than her : más alto que ella⟩
herald¹ ['hɛrəld] *vt* ANNOUNCE : anunciar, proclamar
herald² *n* **1** MESSENGER : heraldo *m* **2**
HARBINGER : precursor *m*
heraldic [hɛ'rældɪk, hə-] *adj* : heráldico
heraldry ['hɛrəldri] *n, pl* **-ries** : heráldica
f
herb ['ərb, 'hərb] *n* : hierba *f*
herbal ['ərbəl, 'hər-] *adj* : herbario
herbicide ['ərbə,saɪd, 'hər-] *n* : herbicida *m*
herbivore ['ərbə,vor, 'hər-] *n* : herbívoro
m
herbivorous [,ər'bɪvərəs, ,hər-] *adj* : herbívoro
herculean [,hərkjə'li:ən, ,hər'kju:-liən]
adj : herçúleo, sobrehumano

herd¹ ['hərd] *vt* : reunir en manada, conducir en manada — *vi* : ir en manada (dícese de los animales), apiñarse (dícese de la gente)

herd² *n* : manada *f*

herder ['hərdər] → **herdsman**

herdsman ['hərdzmən] *n, pl* **-men** [-mən, -ˌmɛn] : vaquero *m* (de ganado), pastor *m* (de ovejas)

here ['hɪr] *adv* **1** : aquí, acá ⟨come here! : ¡ven acá!⟩ ⟨right here : aquí mismo⟩ **2** NOW : en este momento, ahora, ya ⟨here he comes : ya viene⟩ ⟨here it's three o'clock (already) : ahora son las tres⟩ **3** : en este punto ⟨here we agree : estamos de acuerdo en este punto⟩ **4 here you are!** : ¡toma!

hereabouts ['hɪrəˌbaʊts] *or* **hereabout** [-ˌbaʊt] *adv* : por aquí (cerca)

hereafter¹ [hɪr'æftər] *adv* **1** : de aquí en adelante, a continuación **2** : en el futuro

hereafter² *n* **the hereafter** : el más allá

hereby [hɪr'baɪ] *adv* : por este medio

hereditary [hə'rɛdəˌtɛri] *adj* : hereditario

heredity [hə'rɛdəti] *n* : herencia *f*

herein [hɪr'ɪn] *adv* : aquí

hereof [hɪr'ʌv] *adv* : de aquí

hereon [hɪr'ɑn, -'ɔn] *adv* : sobre esto

heresy ['hɛrəsi] *n, pl* **-sies** : herejía *f*

heretic ['hɛrəˌtɪk] *n* : hereje *mf*

heretical [hə'rɛtɪkəl] *adj* : herético

hereto [hɪr'tuː] *adv* : a esto

heretofore ['hɪrtəˌfor] *adv* HITHERTO : hasta ahora

hereunder [hɪr'ʌndər] *adv* : a continuación, abajo

hereupon [hɪrə'pɑn, -'pɔn] *adv* : con esto, en ese momento

herewith [hɪr'wɪθ] *adv* : adjunto

heritage ['hɛrətɪʤ] *n* : patrimonio *m* (nacional)

hermaphrodite [hər'mæfrəˌdaɪt] *n* : hermafrodita *mf*

hermetic [hər'mɛtɪk] *adj* : hermético — **hermetically** [-tɪkli] *adv*

hermit ['hərmət] *n* : ermitaño *m*, -ña *f*; eremita *mf*

hernia ['hərniə] *n, pl* **-nias** *or* **-niae** [-niˌiː, -niˌaɪ] : hernia *f*

hero ['hiːˌroː, 'hɪrˌoː] *n, pl* **-roes** **1** : héroe *m* **2** PROTAGONIST : protagonista *mf*

heroic [hɪ'roːɪk] *adj* : heroico — **heroically** [-ɪkli] *adv*

heroics [hɪ'roːɪks] *npl* : actos *mpl* heroicos

heroin ['hɛroən] *n* : heroína *f*

heroine ['hɛroən] *n* **1** : heroína *f* **2** PROTAGONIST : protagonista *f*

heroism ['hɛroˌɪzəm] *n* : heroísmo *m*

heron ['hɛrən] *n* : garza *f*

herpes ['hərˌpiːz] *n* : herpes *m*

herring ['hɛrɪŋ] *n, pl* **-ring** *or* **-rings** : arenque *m*

hers ['hərz] *pron* : suyo, -ya; suyos, -yas; de ella ⟨these shoes are hers : estos zapatos son suyos⟩ ⟨hers are bigger : los de ella son más grandes⟩

herself [hər'sɪlf] *pron* **1** (*used reflexively*) : se ⟨she dressed herself : se vistió⟩ **2** (*used emphatically*) : ella misma ⟨she fixed it herself : lo arregló ella misma, lo arregló por sí sola⟩

hertz ['hərts, 'hrts] *ns & pl* : hercio *m*

he's ['hiːz] (*contraction of* he is *or* he has) → be, have

hesitancy ['hɛzətəntsi] *n, pl* **-cies** : vacilación *f*, titubeo *m*, indecisión *f*

hesitant ['hɛzətənt] *adj* : titubeante, vacilante — **hesitantly** *adv*

hesitate ['hɛzəˌteɪt] *vi* **-tated; -tating** : vacilar, titubear

hesitation [ˌhɛzə'teɪʃən] *n* : vacilación *f*, indecisión *f*, titubeo *m*

heterogeneous [ˌhɛtərə'ʤiːniəs, -njəs] *adj* : heterogéneo

heterosexual¹ [ˌhɛtəro'skʃuəl] *adj* : heterosexual

heterosexual² *n* : heterosexual *mf*

heterosexuality [ˌhɛtəroˌskʃu'æləti] *n* : heterosexualidad *f*

hew ['hjuː] *v* **hewed; hewed** *or* **hewn** ['hjuːn]; **hewing** *vt* **1** CUT : cortar, talar (árboles) **2** SHAPE : labrar, tallar — *vi* CONFORM : conformarse, ceñirse

hex¹ ['hɛks] *vt* : hacerle un maleficio (a alguien)

hex² *n* : maleficio *m*

hexagon ['hɛksəˌgɑn] *n* : hexágono *m*

hexagonal [hɛk'sægənəl] *adj* : hexagonal

hey ['heɪ] *interj* : ¡eh!, ¡oye!

heyday ['heɪˌdeɪ] *n* : auge *m*, apogeo *m*

hi ['haɪ] *interj* : ¡hola!

hiatus [haɪ'eɪtəs] *n* **1** : hiato *m* **2** PAUSE : pausa *f*

hibernate ['haɪbərˌneɪt] *vi* **-nated; -nating** : hibernar, invernar

hibernation [ˌhaɪbər'neɪʃən] *n* : hibernación *f*

hiccup¹ ['hɪkəp] *vi* **-cuped; -cuping** : hipar, tener hipo

hiccup² *n* : hipo *m* ⟨to have the hiccups : tener hipo⟩

hick ['hɪk] *n* BUMPKIN : palurdo *m*, -da *f*

hickory ['hɪkəri] *n, pl* **-ries** : nogal *m* americano

hidden¹ ['hɪdən] *adj* : oculto

hide¹ ['haɪd] *v* **hid** ['hɪd]; **hidden** ['hɪdən] *or* **hid**; **hiding** *vt* **1** CONCEAL : esconder **2** : ocultar ⟨to hide one's motives : ocultar unos sus motivos⟩ **3** SCREEN : tapar, no dejar ver — *vi* : esconderse

hide² *n* : piel *f*, cuero *m* ⟨to save one's hide : salvar el pellejo⟩

hide-and-seek ['haɪdənd'siːk] *n* **to play hide-and-seek** : jugar a las escondidas

hidebound ['haɪdˌbaʊnd] *adj* : rígido, conservador

hideous ['hɪdiəs] *adj* : horrible, horroroso, espantoso — **hideously** *adv*

hideout ['haɪdˌaʊt] *n* : guarida *f*, escondrijo *m*

hierarchical [ˌhaɪə'rɑrkɪkəl] *adj* : jerárquico

hierarchy ['haɪə,rɑrki] *n, pl* **-chies** : jerarquía *f*

hieroglyphic [,haɪərə'glɪfɪk] *n* : jeroglífico *m*

hi-fi ['haɪ'faɪ] *n* 1 → **high fidelity** 2 : equipo *m* de alta fidelidad

high¹ ['haɪ] *adv* : alto

high² *adj* 1 TALL : alto ⟨a high wall : una pared alta⟩ 2 ELEVATED : alto, elevado ⟨high prices : precios elevados⟩ ⟨high blood pressure : presión alta⟩ 3 GREAT, IMPORTANT : grande, importante, alto ⟨a high number : un número grande⟩ ⟨high society : alta sociedad⟩ ⟨high hopes : grandes esperanzas⟩ 4 : alto (en música) 5 INTOXICATED : borracho, drogado

high³ *n* 1 : récord *m*, punto *m* máximo ⟨to reach an all-time high : batir el récord⟩ 2 : zona *f* de alta presión (en meteorología) 3 *or* **high gear** : directa *f* 4 **on high** : en las alturas

highbrow ['haɪ,braʊ] *n* : intelectual *mf*

higher ['haɪər] *adj* : superior

high fidelity *n* : alta fidelidad *f*

high–flown ['haɪ'floːn] *adj* : altisonante

high–handed ['haɪ'hændəd] *adj* : arbitrario

highlands ['haɪləndz] *npl* : tierras *fpl* altas, altiplano *m*

highlight¹ ['haɪ,laɪt] *vt* 1 EMPHASIZE : destacar, poner en relieve, subrayar 2 : ser el punto culminante de

highlight² *n* : punto *m* culminante

highly ['haɪli] *adv* 1 VERY : muy, sumamente 2 FAVORABLY : muy bien ⟨to speak highly of : hablar muy bien de⟩ ⟨to think highly of : tener en mucho a⟩

highness ['haɪnəs] *n* 1 HEIGHT : altura *f* 2 **Highness** : Alteza *f* ⟨Your Royal Highness : Su Alteza Real⟩

high–pitched ['haɪ'pɪtʃt] *adj* : agudo

high–rise ['haɪ,raɪz] *adj* : alto, de muchas plantas

high school *n* : escuela *f* superior, escuela *f* secundaria

high seas *npl* : alta mar *f*

high–spirited ['haɪ'spɪrətəd] *adj* : vivaz, muy animado, brioso

high–strung [,haɪ'strʌŋ] *adj* : nervioso, excitable

highway ['haɪ,weɪ] *n* : carretera *f*

highwayman ['haɪ,weɪmən] *n, pl* **-men** [-mən, -,mɛn] : salteador *m* (de caminos), bandido *m*

hijack¹ ['haɪ,dʒæk] *vt* : secuestrar

hijack² *n* : secuestro *m*

hijacker ['haɪ,dʒækər] *n* : secuestrador *m*, -dora *f*

hike¹ ['haɪk] *v* **hiked; hiking** *vi* : hacer una caminata — *vt* RAISE : subir

hike² *n* 1 : caminata *f*, excursión *f* 2 INCREASE : subida *f* (de precios)

hiker ['haɪkər] *n* : excursionista *mf*

hilarious [hɪ'lærɪəs, haɪ'-] *adj* : muy divertido, hilarante

hilarity [hɪ'lærəti, haɪ-] *n* : hilaridad *f*

hill ['hɪl] *n* 1 : colina *f*, cerro *m* 2 SLOPE : cuesta *f*, pendiente *f*

hillbilly ['hɪl,bɪli] *n, pl* **-lies** : palurdo *m*, -da *f* (de las montañas)

hillock ['hɪlək] *n* : loma *f*, altozano *m*, otero *m*

hillside ['hɪl,saɪd] *n* : ladera *f*, cuesta *f*

hilltop ['hɪl,tɑp] *n* : cima *f*, cumbre *f*

hilly ['hɪli] *adj* **hillier; -est** : montañoso, accidentado

hilt ['hɪlt] *n* : puño *m*, empuñadura *f*

him ['hɪm, əm] *pron* 1 (*used as direct object*) : lo ⟨I found him : lo encontré⟩ 2 (*used as indirect object*) : le, se ⟨we gave him a present : le dimos un regalo⟩ ⟨I sent it to him : se lo mandé⟩ 3 (*used as object of a preposition*) : él ⟨she was thinking of him : pensaba en él⟩ ⟨younger than him : más joven que él⟩

himself [hɪm'sɛlf] *pron* 1 (*used reflexively*) : se ⟨he washed himself : se lavó⟩ 2 (*used emphatically*) : él mismo ⟨he did it himself : lo hizo él mismo, lo hizo por sí solo⟩

hind¹ ['haɪnd] *adj* : trasero, posterior ⟨hind legs : patas traseras⟩

hind² *n* : cierva *f*

hinder ['hɪndər] *vt* : dificultar, impedir, estorbar

Hindi ['hɪndi:] *n* : hindi *m*

hindquarters ['haɪnd,kwɔrtərz] *npl* : cuartos *mpl* traseros

hindrance ['hɪndrənts] *n* : estorbo *m*, obstáculo *m*, impedimento *m*

hindsight ['haɪnd,saɪt] *n* : retrospectiva *f* ⟨with the benefit of hindsight : en retrospectiva, con la perspectiva que da la experiencia⟩

Hindu¹ ['hɪn,du:] *adj* : hindú

Hindu² *n* : hindú *mf*

Hinduism ['hɪndu:,ɪzəm] *n* : hinduismo *m*

hinge¹ ['hɪndʒ] *v* **hinged; hinging** *vt* : unir con bisagras — *vi* **to hinge on** : depender de

hinge² *n* : bisagra *f*, gozne *m*

hint¹ ['hɪnt] *vt* : insinuar, dar a entender — *vi* : soltar indirectas

hint² *n* 1 INSINUATION : insinuación *f*, indirecta *f* 2 TIP : consejo *m*, sugerencia *f* 3 TRACE : pizca *f*, indicio *m*

hinterland ['hɪntər,lænd, -lənd] *n* : interior *m* (de un país)

hip ['hɪp] *n* : cadera *f*

hip–hop ['hɪp,hɑp] *n* : hip-hop *m*

hippie ['hɪpi] *n* : hippie *mf*, hippy *mf*

hippopotamus [,hɪpə'pɑtəməs] *n, pl* **-muses** *or* **-mi** [-,maɪ] : hipopótamo *m*

hippo ['hɪpo:] *n, pl* **hippos** → **hippopotamus**

hire¹ ['haɪr] *vt* **hired; hiring** 1 EMPLOY : contratar, emplear 2 RENT : alquilar, arrendar

hire² *n* 1 RENT : alquiler *m* ⟨for hire : se alquila⟩ 2 WAGES : paga *f*, sueldo *m* 3 EMPLOYEE : empleado *m*, -da *f*

his¹ ['hɪz, ɪz] *adj* : su, sus, de él ⟨his hat : su sombrero, el sombrero de él⟩

his² *pron* : suyo, -ya; suyos, suyas; de él ⟨the decision is his : la decisión es suya⟩ ⟨it's his, not hers : es de él, no de ella⟩

Hispanic[1] [hɪ'spænɪk] *adj* : hispano, hispánico

Hispanic[2] *n* : hispano *m*, -na *f*; hispánico *m*, -ca *f*

hiss[1] ['hɪs] *vi* : sisear, silbar — *vt* : decir entre dientes

hiss[2] *n* : siseo *m*, silbido *m*

historian [hɪ'stɔriən] *n* : historiador *m*, -dora *f*

historic [hɪ'stɔrɪk] *or* **historical** [-ɪkəl] *adj* : histórico — **historically** [-ɪkli] *adv*

history ['hɪstəri] *n, pl* **-ries** 1 : historia *f* 2 RECORD : historial *m*

histrionics [ˌhɪstri'ɑnɪks] *ns & pl* : histrionismo *m*

hit[1] ['hɪt] *v* **hit; hitting** *vt* 1 STRIKE : golpear, pegar, batear (una pelota) ⟨he hit the dog : le pegó al perro⟩ 2 : chocar contra, dar con, dar en (el blanco) ⟨the car hit a tree : el coche chocó contra un árbol⟩ 3 AFFECT : afectar ⟨the news hit us hard : la noticia nos afectó mucho⟩ 4 ENCOUNTER : tropezar con, toparse con ⟨to hit a snag : tropezar con un obstáculo⟩ 5 REACH : llegar a, alcanzar ⟨the price hit $10 a pound : el precio alcanzó los $10 dólares por libra⟩ ⟨to hit town : llegar a la ciudad⟩ ⟨to hit the headlines : ser noticia⟩ 6 **to hit on** *or* **to hit upon** : dar con — *vi* : golpear

hit[2] *n* 1 BLOW : golpe *m* 2 : impacto *m* (de un arma) 3 SUCCESS : éxito *m*

hitch[1] ['hɪtʃ] *vt* 1 : mover con sacudidas 2 ATTACH : enganchar, atar, amarrar 3 → hitchhike 4 **to hitch up** : subirse (los pantalones, etc.)

hitch[2] *n* 1 JERK : tirón *m*, jalón *m* 2 OBSTACLE : obstáculo *m*, impedimento *m*, tropiezo *m*

hitchhike ['hɪtʃˌhaɪk] *vi* **-hiked; -hiking** : hacer autostop, ir de aventón *Col, Mex fam*

hitchhiker ['hɪtʃˌhaɪkər] *n* : autostopista *mf*

hither ['hɪðər] *adv* : acá, por aquí

hitherto ['hɪðərˌtuː, ˌhɪðər'-] *adv* : hasta ahora

hitter ['hɪtər] *n* BATTER : bateador *m*, -dora *f*

HIV [ˌɛɪtʃˌaɪ'viː] *n* (*h*uman *i*mmunodeficiency *v*irus) : VIH *m*, virus *m* del sida

hive ['haɪv] *n* 1 : colmena *f* 2 SWARM : enjambre *m* 3 : lugar *m* muy activo ⟨a hive of activity : un hervidero de actividad⟩

hives ['haɪvz] *ns & pl* : urticaria *f*

hoard[1] ['hɔrd] *vt* : acumular, atesorar

hoard[2] *n* : tesoro *m*, reserva *f*, provisión *f*

hoarfrost ['hɔrˌfrɔst] *n* : escarcha *f*

hoarse ['hɔrs] *adj* **hoarser; -est** : ronco — **hoarsely** *adv*

hoarseness ['hɔrsnəs] *n* : ronquera *f*

hoary ['hɔri] *adj* **hoarier; -est** 1 : cano, canoso 2 OLD : vetusto, antiguo

hoax[1] ['hoːks] *vt* : engañar, embaucar, bromear

hoax[2] *n* : engaño *m*, broma *f*

hobble[1] ['hɑbəl] *v* **-bled; -bling** *vi* LIMP : cojear, renguear — *vt* : manear (un animal)

hobble[2] *n* 1 LIMP : cojera *f*, rengo *m* 2 : maniota *f* (para un animal)

hobby ['hɑbi] *n, pl* **-bies** : pasatiempo *m*, afición *f*

hobgoblin ['hɑbˌgɑblən] *n* : duende *m*

hobnail ['hɑbˌneɪl] *n* : tachuela *f*

hobnob ['hɑbˌnɑb] *vi* **-nobbed; -nobbing** : codearse

hobo ['hoːˌboː] *n, pl* **-boes** : vagabundo *m*, -da *f*

hock[1] ['hɑk] *vt* PAWN : empeñar

hock[2] *n* **in hock** : empeñado

hockey ['hɑki] *n* : hockey *m*

hodgepodge ['hɑdʒˌpɑdʒ] *n* : mezcolanza *f*

hoe[1] ['hoː] *vt* **hoed; hoeing** : azadonar

hoe[2] *n* : azada *f*, azadón *m*

hog[1] ['hɔg, 'hɑg] *vt* **hogged; hogging** : acaparar, monopolizar

hog[2] *n* 1 PIG : cerdo *m*, -da *f* 2 GLUTTON : glotón *m*, -tona *f*

hogshead ['hɔgzˌhɛd, 'hɑgz-] *n* : tonel *m*

hoist[1] ['hɔɪst] *vt* : levantar, alzar, izar (una bandera, una vela)

hoist[2] *n* : grúa *f*

hold[1] ['hoːld] *v* **held** ['hɛld]; **holding** *vt* 1 POSSESS : tener ⟨to hold office : ocupar un puesto⟩ 2 RESTRAIN : detener, controlar ⟨to hold one's temper : controlar su mal genio⟩ 3 CLASP, GRASP : agarrar, coger ⟨to hold hands : agarrarse de la mano⟩ 4 : sujetar, mantener fijo ⟨hold this nail for me : sujétame este clavo⟩ 5 CONTAIN : contener, dar cabida a 6 SUPPORT : aguantar, sostener 7 REGARD : considerar, tener ⟨he held me responsible : me consideró responsable⟩ 8 CONDUCT : celebrar (una reunión), realizar (un evento), mantener (una conversación) — *vi* 1 : aguantar, resistir ⟨the rope will hold : la cuerda resistirá⟩ 2 : ser válido, valer ⟨my offer still holds : mi oferta todavía es válida⟩ 3 **to hold forth** : perorar, arengar 4 **to hold to** : mantenerse firme en 5 **to hold with** : estar de acuerdo con

hold[2] *n* 1 GRIP : agarre *m*, llave *f* (en deportes) 2 CONTROL : control *m*, dominio *m* ⟨to get hold of oneself : controlarse⟩ 3 DELAY : demora *f* ⟨to put on hold : suspender temporalmente⟩ 4 : bodega *f* (en un barco o un avión) 5 **to get hold of** : conseguir, localizar

holder ['hoːldər] *n* : poseedor *m*, -dora *f*; titular *mf*

holdings ['hoːldɪŋz] *npl* : propiedades *fpl*

hold out *vi* 1 LAST : aguantar, durar 2 RESIST : resistir

holdup ['hoːldˌʌp] *n* 1 ROBBERY : atraco *m* 2 DELAY : retraso *m*, demora *f*

hold up *vt* 1 ROB : robarle (a alguien), atracar, asaltar 2 DELAY : retrasar

hole ['hoːl] *n* : agujero *m*, hoyo *m*

holiday ['hɑlə,deɪ] *n* **1** : día *m* feriado, fiesta *f* **2** VACATION : vacaciones *fpl*
holiness ['ho:linəs] *n* **1** : santidad *f* **2** His Holiness : Su Santidad
holistic [ho:'lɪstɪk] *adj* : holístico
holler[1] ['hɑlər] *vi* : gritar, chillar
holler[2] *n* : grito *m*, chillido *m*
hollow[1] ['hɑ,lo:] *vt or* to hollow out : ahuecar
hollow[2] *adj* **-lower; -est** **1** : hueco, hundido (dícese de las mejillas, etc.), cavernoso (dícese de un sonido) **2** EMPTY, FALSE : vacío, falso
hollow[3] *n* **1** CAVITY : hueco *m*, depresión *f*, cavidad *f* **2** VALLEY : hondonada *f*, valle *m*
hollowness ['hɑ,lo:nəs] *n* **1** HOLLOW : hueco *m*, cavidad *f* **2** FALSENESS : falsedad *f* **3** EMPTINESS : vacuidad *f*
holly ['hɑli] *n, pl* **-lies** : acebo *m*
hollyhock ['hɑli,hɑk] *n* : malvarrosa *f*
holocaust ['hɑlə,kɔst, 'ho:-, 'hɔ-] *n* : holocausto *m*
hologram ['ho:lə,græm, 'hɑ-] *n* : holograma *m*
holster ['ho:lstər] *n* : pistolera *f*
holy ['ho:li] *adj* **-lier; -est** : santo, sagrado
Holy Ghost → Holy Spirit
Holy Spirit *n* the Holy Spirit : el Espíritu Santo
homage ['ɑmɪdʒ, 'hɑ-] *n* : homenaje *m*
home ['ho:m] *n* **1** : casa *f*, hogar *m*, domicilio *m* ⟨to feel at home : sentirse en casa⟩ **2** INSTITUTION : residencia *f*, asilo *m*
homecoming ['ho:m,kʌmɪŋ] *n* : regreso *m* (a casa)
homegrown ['ho:m'gro:n] *adj* **1** : de cosecha propia **2** LOCAL : local
homeland ['ho:m,lænd] *n* : patria *f*, tierra *f* natal, terruño *m*
homeless ['ho:mləs] *adj* : sin hogar, sin techo
homely ['ho:mli] *adj* **-lier; -est** **1** DOMESTIC : casero, hogareño **2** UGLY : feo, poco atractivo
homemade ['ho:m'meɪd] *adj* : casero, hecho en casa
homemaker ['ho:m,meɪkər] *n* : ama *f* de casa, persona *f* que se ocupa de la casa
home plate *n* : base *f* del bateador
home run *n* : jonrón *m*
homesick ['ho:m,sɪk] *adj* : nostálgico ⟨to be homesick : echar de menos a la familia⟩
homesickness ['ho:m,sɪknəs] *n* : nostalgia *f*, morriña *f*
homespun ['ho:m,spʌn] *adj* : simple, sencillo
homestead ['ho:m,stɛd] *n* : estancia *f*, hacienda *f*
homeward[1] ['ho:mwərd] *or* **homewards** [-wərdz] *adv* : de vuelta a casa, hacia casa
homeward[2] *adj* : de vuelta, de regreso
homework ['ho:m,wərk] *n* : tarea *f*, deberes *mpl Spain*, asignación *f PRi*

homey ['ho:mi] *adj* **homier; -est** : hogareño
homicidal [,hɑmə'saɪdəl, ,ho:-] *adj* : homicida
homicide ['hɑmə,saɪd, 'ho:-] *n* : homicidio *m*
hominy ['hɑməni] *n* : maíz *m* descascarillado
homogeneity [,ho:mədʒə'ni:əti, -'neɪ-] *n, pl* **-ties** : homogeneidad *f*
homogeneous [,ho:mə'dʒi:niəs, -njəs] *adj* : homogéneo — **homogeneously** *adv*
homogenize [ho:'mɑdʒə,naɪz, hə-] *vt* **-nized; -nizing** : homogeneizar
homograph ['hɑmə,græf, 'ho:-] *n* : homógrafo *m*
homologous [ho:'mɑləgəs, hə-] *adj* : homólogo
homonym ['hɑmə,nɪm, 'ho:-] *n* : homónimo *m*
homophone ['hɑmə,fo:n, 'ho:-] *n* : homófono *m*
homosexual[1] [,ho:mə'sɛkʃuəl] *adj* : homosexual
homosexual[2] *n* : homosexual *mf*
homosexuality [,ho:mə,sɛkʃu'æləti] *n* : homosexualidad *f*
honcho ['hɑn,tʃo:] *n* : pez *m* gordo ⟨the head honcho : el jefe⟩
Honduran [hɑn'dʊrən, -'djʊr-] *n* : hondureño *m*, -ña *f* — **Honduran** *adj*
hone ['ho:n] *vt* **honed; honing** : afilar
honest ['ɑnəst] *adj* : honesto, honrado — **honestly** *adv*
honesty ['ɑnəsti] *n, pl* **-ties** : honestidad *f*, honradez *f*
honey ['hʌni] *n, pl* **-eys** : miel *f*
honeybee ['hʌni,bi:] *n* : abeja *f*
honeycomb ['hʌni,ko:m] *n* : panal *m*
honeymoon[1] ['hʌni,mu:n] *vi* : pasar la luna de miel
honeymoon[2] *n* : luna *f* de miel
honeysuckle ['hʌni,sʌkəl] *n* : madreselva *f*
honk[1] ['hɑŋk, 'hɔŋk] *vi* **1** : graznar (dícese del ganso) **2** : tocar la bocina (dícese de un vehículo), pitar
honk[2] *n* : graznido *m* (del ganso), bocinazo *m* (de un vehículo)
honor[1] ['ɑnər] *vt* **1** RESPECT : honrar **2** : cumplir con ⟨to honor one's word : cumplir con su palabra⟩ **3** : aceptar (un cheque, etc.)
honor[2] *n* **1** : honor *m* ⟨in honor of : en honor de⟩ **2 honors** *npl* AWARDS : honores *mpl*, condecoraciones *fpl* **3** Your Honor : Su Señoría
honorable ['ɑnərəbəl] *adj* : honorable, honroso — **honorably** [-bli] *adv*
honorary ['ɑnə,rɛri] *adj* : honorario
hood ['hʊd] *n* **1** : capucha *f* **2** : capó *m*, bonete *m Car* (de un automóvil)
hooded ['hʊdəd] *adj* : encapuchado
hoodlum ['hʊdləm, 'hu:d-] *n* THUG : maleante *mf*, matón *m*
hoodwink ['hʊd,wɪŋk] *vt* : engañar

hoof ['hʊf, 'hu:f] *n, pl* **hooves** ['hʊvz, 'hu:vz] *or* **hoofs** : pezuña *f*, casco *m*

hoofed ['hʊft, 'hu:ft] *adj* : ungulado

hook¹ ['hʊk] *vt* : enganchar — *vi* : abrocharse, engancharse

hook² *n* : gancho *m*, percha *f*

hooked ['hʊkt] *adj* **1** : en forma de gancho **2 to be hooked on** : estar enganchado a

hooker ['hʊkər] *n* : prostituta *f*, fulana *f fam*

hookworm ['hʊk,wərm] *n* : anquilostoma *m*

hooligan ['hu:lɪgən] *n* : gamberro *m*, -rra *f*

hoop ['hu:p] *n* : aro *m*

hooray [hʊ'reɪ] → **hurrah**

hoot¹ ['hu:t] *vi* **1** SHOUT : gritar ⟨to hoot with laughter : morirse de risa, reírse a carcajadas⟩ **2** : ulular (dícese de un búho), tocar la bocina (dícese de un vehículo), silbar (dícese de un tren o un barco)

hoot² *n* **1** : ululato *m* (de un búho), silbido *m* (de un tren), bocinazo *m* (de un vehículo) **2** GUFFAW : carcajada *f*, risotada *f* **3 I don't give a hoot** : me vale un comino, me importa un pito

hop¹ ['hɑp] *vi* **hopped; hopping** : brincar, saltar

hop² *n* **1** LEAP : salto *m*, brinco *m* **2** FLIGHT : vuelo *m* corto **3** : lúpulo *m* (planta)

hope¹ ['ho:p] *v* **hoped; hoping** *vi* : esperar — *vt* : esperar que ⟨we hope she comes : esperamos que venga⟩ ⟨I hope not : espero que no⟩

hope² *n* : esperanza *f*

hopeful ['ho:pfəl] *adj* : esperanzado — **hopefully** *adv*

hopeless ['ho:pləs] *adj* **1** DESPAIRING : desesperado **2** IMPOSSIBLE : imposible ⟨a hopeless case : un caso perdido⟩

hopelessly ['ho:pləsli] *adv* **1** : sin esperanzas, desesperadamente **2** COMPLETELY : totalmente, completamente **3** IMPOSSIBLY : imposiblemente

hopelessness ['ho:pləsnəs] *n* : desesperanza *f*

hopper ['hɑpər] *n* : tolva *f*

hopscotch ['hɑp,skɑtʃ] *n* : tejo *m*

horde ['hord] *n* : horda *f*, multitud *f*

horizon [hə'raɪzən] *n* : horizonte *m*

horizontal [,horə'zɑntəl] *adj* : horizontal — **horizontally** *adv*

hormone ['hɔr,mo:n] *n* : hormona *f* — **hormonal** [hɔr'mo:nəl] *adj*

horn ['hɔrn] *n* **1** : cuerno *m* (de un toro, una vaca, etc.) **2** : cuerno *m*, trompa *f* (instrumento musical) **3** : bocina *f*, claxon *m* (de un vehículo)

horned ['hɔrnd, 'hɔrnəd] *adj* : cornudo, astado, con cuernos

hornet ['hɔrnət] *n* : avispón *m*

horny ['hɔrni] *adj* **hornier; -est 1** CALLOUS : calloso **2** LUSTFUL *fam* : caliente *fam*

horoscope ['hɔrə,sko:p] *n* : horóscopo *m*

horrendous [hɔ'rɛndəs] *adj* : horrendo, horroroso, atroz

horrible ['hɔrəbəl] *adj* : horrible, espantoso, horroroso — **horribly** [-bli] *adv*

horrid ['hɔrɪd] *adj* : horroroso, horrible — **horridly** *adv*

horrific [hɔ'rɪfɪk] *adj* : terrorífico, horroroso

horrify ['hɔrə,faɪ] *vt* **-fied; -fying** : horrorizar

horrifying ['hɔrə,faɪɪŋ] *adj* : horripilante, horrorozo

horror ['hɔrər] *n* : horror *m*

hors d'oeuvre [ɔr'dərv] *n, pl* **hors d'oeuvres** [-'dərvz] : entremés *m*

horse ['hɔrs] *n* : caballo *m*

horseback ['hɔrs,bæk] *n* **on ~** : a caballo

horse chestnut *n* : castaña *f* de Indias

horsefly ['hɔrs,flaɪ] *n, pl* **-flies** : tábano *m*

horsehair ['hɔrs,hær] *n* : crin *f*

horseman ['hɔrsmən] *n, pl* **-men** [-mən, -,mɛn] : jinete *m*, caballista *m*

horsemanship ['hɔrsmən,ʃɪp] *n* : equitación *f*

horseplay ['hɔrs,pleɪ] *n* : payasadas *fpl*

horsepower ['hɔrs,pauər] *n* : caballo *m* de fuerza

horseradish ['hɔrs,rædɪʃ] *n* : rábano *m* picante

horseshoe ['hɔrs,ʃu:] *n* : herradura *f*

horsewhip ['hɔrs,hwɪp] *vt* **-whipped; -whipping** : azotar, darle fuetazos (a alguien)

horsewoman ['hɔrs,wʊmən] *n, pl* **-women** [-,wɪmən] : amazona *f*, jinete *f*, caballista *f*

horsey *or* **horsy** ['hɔrsi] *adj* **horsier; -est** : relacionado a los caballos, caballar

horticultural [,hɔrtə'kʌltʃərəl] *adj* : hortícola

horticulture ['hɔrtə,kʌltʃər] *n* : horticultura *f*

hose¹ ['ho:z] *vt* **hosed; hosing** : regar o lavar con manguera

hose² *n* **1** *pl* **hose** SOCKS : calcetines *mpl*, medias *fpl* **2** *pl* **hose** STOCKINGS : medias *fpl* **3** *pl* **hoses** : manguera *f*, manga *f*

hosiery ['ho:ʒəri, 'ho:ʒə-] *n* : calcetería *f*, medias *fpl*

hospice ['hɑspəs] *n* : hospicio *m*

hospitable [hɑ'spɪtəbəl, 'hɑs,pɪ-] *adj* : hospitalario — **hospitably** [-bli] *adv*

hospital ['hɑs,pɪtəl] *n* : hospital *m*

hospitality [,hɑspə'tæləti] *n, pl* **-ties** : hospitalidad *f*

hospitalization [,hɑs,pɪtələ'zeɪʃən] *n* : hospitalización *f*

hospitalize ['hɑs,pɪtəl,aɪz] *vt* **-ized; -izing** : hospitalizar

host¹ ['ho:st] *vt* : presentar (un programa de televisión, etc.)

host² *n* **1** : anfitrión *m*, -triona *f* (en la casa, a un evento); presentador *m*, -dora *f* (de un programa de televisión, etc.) **2** *or* **host organism** : huésped *m*

3 TROOPS : huestes *fpl* **4** MULTITUDE : multitud *f* ⟨for a host of reasons : por muchas razones⟩ **5** EUCHARIST : hostia *f*, Eucaristía *f*

hostage ['hɑstɪdʒ] *n* : rehén *m*

hostel ['hɑstəl] *n* : albergue *m* juvenil

hostess ['ho:stɪs] *n* : anfitriona *f* (en la casa), presentadora *f* (de un programa)

hostile ['hɑstəl, -ˌtaɪl] *adj* : hostil — **hostilely** *adv*

hostility [hɑs'tɪləʈi] *n, pl* **-ties** : hostilidad *f*

hot ['hɑt] *adj* **hotter; hottest 1** : caliente, cálido, caluroso ⟨hot water : agua caliente⟩ ⟨a hot climate : un clima cálido⟩ ⟨a hot day : un día caluroso⟩ **2** ARDENT, FIERY : ardiente, acalorado ⟨to have a hot temper : tener mal genio⟩ **3** SPICY : picante **4** FRESH : reciente, nuevo ⟨hot news : noticias de última hora⟩ **5** EAGER : ávido **6** STOLEN : robado

hot air *n* : palabrería *f*

hotbed ['hɑtˌbɛd] *n* **1** : semillero *m* (de plantas) **2** : hervidero *m*, semillero *m* (de crimen, etc.)

hot dog *n* : perro *m* caliente

hotel [ho:'tɛl] *n* : hotel *m*

hothead ['hɑtˌhɛd] *n* : exaltado *m*, -da *f*

hotheaded ['hɑt'hɛdəd] *adj* : exaltado

hothouse ['hɑtˌhaʊs] *n* : invernadero *m*

hot plate *n* : placa *f* (de cocina)

hot rod *n* : coche *m* con motor modificado

hot water *n* **to get into hot water** : meterse en un lío

hound¹ ['haʊnd] *vt* : acosar, perseguir

hound² *n* : perro *m* (de caza)

hour ['aʊər] *n* : hora *f*

hourglass ['aʊərˌglæs] *n* : reloj *m* de arena

hourly ['aʊərli] *adv & adj* : cada hora, por hora

house¹ ['haʊz] *vt* **housed; housing** : albergar, alojar, hospedar

house² ['haʊs] *n, pl* **houses** ['haʊzəz, -səz] **1** HOME : casa *f* **2** : cámara *f* (del gobierno) **3** BUSINESS : casa *f*, empresa *f*

houseboat ['haʊsˌbo:t] *n* : casa *f* flotante

housebroken ['haʊsˌbro:kən] *adj* : enseñado

housefly ['haʊsˌflaɪ] *n, pl* **-flies** : mosca *f* común

household¹ ['haʊsˌho:ld] *adj* **1** DOMESTIC : doméstico, de la casa **2** FAMILIAR : conocido por todos

household² *n* : casa *f*, familia *f*

householder ['haʊsˌho:ldər] *n* : dueño *m*, -ña *f* de casa

housekeeper ['haʊsˌki:pər] *n* : ama *f* de llaves

housekeeping ['haʊsˌki:pɪŋ] *n* : gobierno *m* de la casa, quehaceres *mpl* domésticos

housemaid ['haʊsˌmeɪd] *n* : criada *f*, mucama *f*, muchacha *f*, sirvienta *f*

housewarming ['haʊsˌwɔrmɪŋ] *n* : fiesta *f* de estreno de una casa

housewife ['haʊsˌwaɪf] *n, pl* **-wives** : ama *f* de casa

housework ['haʊsˌwərk] *n* : faenas *fpl* domésticas, quehaceres *mpl* domésticos

housing ['haʊzɪŋ] *n* **1** HOUSES : vivienda *f* **2** COVERING : caja *f* protectora

hove → **heave**

hovel ['hʌvəl, 'hɑ-] *n* : casucha *f*, tugurio *m*

hover ['hʌvər, 'hɑ-] *vi* **1** : cernerse, sostenerse en el aire **2 to hover about** : rondar

how ['haʊ] *adv* **1** : cómo ⟨how are you? : ¿cómo estás?⟩ ⟨I don't know how to fix it : no se cómo arreglarlo⟩ **2** : qué ⟨how beautiful! : ¡qué bonito!⟩ **3** : cuánto ⟨how old are you? : ¿cuántos años tienes?⟩ **4 how about...? :** ¿qué te parece...?

however¹ [haʊ'ɛvər] *adv* **1** : por mucho que, por más que ⟨however hot it is : por mucho calor que haga⟩ **2** NEVERTHELESS : sin embargo, no obstante

however² *conj* : comoquiera que, de cualquier manera que

howl¹ ['haʊl] *vi* : aullar

howl² *n* : aullido *m*, alarido *m*

hub ['hʌb] *n* **1** CENTER : centro *m* **2** : cubo *m* (de una rueda)

hubbub ['hʌˌbʌb] *n* : algarabía *f*, alboroto *m*, jaleo *m*

hubcap ['hʌbˌkæp] *n* : tapacubos *m*

huckster ['hʌkstər] *n* : buhonero *m*, -ra *f*; vendedor *m*, -dora *f* ambulante

huddle¹ ['hʌdəl] *vi* **-dled; -dling 1** : apiñarse, amontonarse **2 to huddle together** : acurrucarse

huddle² *n* : grupo *m* (cerrado) ⟨to go into a huddle : conferenciar en secreto⟩

hue ['hju:] *n* : color *m*, tono *m*

huff ['hʌf] *n* : enojo *m*, enfado *m* ⟨to be in a huff : estar enojado⟩

huffy ['hʌfi] *adj* **huffier; -est** : enojado, enfadado

hug¹ ['hʌg] *vt* **hugged; hugging 1** EMBRACE : abrazar **2** : ir pegado a ⟨the road hugs the river : el camino está pegado al río⟩

hug² *n* : abrazo *m*

huge ['hju:dʒ] *adj* **huger; hugest** : inmenso, enorme — **hugely** *adv*

hulk ['hʌlk] *n* **1** : persona *f* fornida **2** : casco *m* (barco), armatoste *m* (edificio, etc.)

hulking ['hʌlkɪŋ] *adj* : grandote *fam*, pesado

hull¹ ['hʌl] *vt* : pelar

hull² *n* **1** HUSK : cáscara *f* **2** : casco *m* (de un barco, un avión, etc.)

hullabaloo ['hʌləbəˌlu:] *n, pl* **-loos** : alboroto *m*, jaleo *m*

hum¹ ['hʌm] *v* **hummed; humming** *vi* **1** BUZZ : zumbar **2** : estar muy activo, moverse ⟨to hum with activity : bullir de actividad⟩ — *vt* : tararear (una melodía)

hum² *n* : zumbido *m*, murmullo *m*
human¹ ['hju:mən, 'ju:-] *adj* : humano
— **humanly** *adv*
human² *n* : ser *m* humano
humane [hju:'meɪn, ju:-] *adj* : humano,
humanitario — **humanely** *adv*
humanism ['hju:mə,nɪzəm, 'ju:-] *n* : humanismo *m*
humanist¹ ['hju:mənɪst, 'ju:-] *n* : humanista *mf*
humanist² *or* **humanistic** [,hju:mə-
'nɪstɪk, ,ju:-] *adj* : humanístico
humanitarian¹ [hju:,mænə'triən, ju:-]
adj : humanitario
humanitarian² *n* : humanitario *m*, -ria *f*
humanity [hju:'mænəti, ju:-] *n, pl* **-ties**
: humanidad *f*
humankind ['hju:mən'kaɪnd, 'ju:-] *n*
: género *m* humano
humble¹ ['hʌmbəl] *vt* **-bled; -bling** 1
: humillar 2 **to humble oneself** : humillarse
humble² *adj* **-bler; -blest** : humilde,
modesto — **humbly** ['hʌmbli] *adv*
humbug ['hʌm,bʌg] *n* 1 FRAUD : charlatán *m*, -tana *f*; farsante *mf* 2 NON-
SENSE : patrañas *fpl*, tonterías *fpl*
humdrum ['hʌm,drʌm] *adj* : monótono,
rutinario
humid ['hju:məd, 'ju:-] *adj* : húmedo
humidifier [hju:'mɪdə,faɪər, ju:-] *n* : humidificador *m*
humidify [hju:'mɪdə,faɪ, ju:-] *vt* **-fied;
-fying** : humidificar
humidity [hju:'mɪdəti, ju:-] *n, pl* **-ties**
: humedad *f*
humiliate [hju:'mɪli,eɪt, ju:-] *vt* **-ated;
-ating** : humillar
humiliating [hju:'mɪli,eɪtɪŋ, ju:-] *adj*
: humillante
humiliation [hju:,mɪli'eɪʃən, ju:-] *n* : humillación *f*
humility [hju:'mɪləti, ju:-] *n* : humildad
f
hummingbird ['hʌmɪŋ,bərd] *n* : colibrí
m, picaflor *m*
hummock ['hʌmək] *n* : montículo *m*
humor¹ ['hju:mər, 'ju:-] *vt* : seguir el humor a, complacer
humor² *n* : humor *m*
humorist ['hju:mərɪst, 'ju:-] *n* : humorista *mf*
humorless ['hju:mərləs, 'ju:-] *adj* : sin
sentido del humor ⟨a humorless smile
: una sonrisa forzada⟩
humorous ['hju:mərəs, 'ju:-] *adj* : humorístico, cómico — **humorously** *adv*
hump ['hʌmp] *n* : joroba *f*, giba *f*
humpback ['hʌmp,bæk] *n* 1 HUMP
: joroba *f*, giba *f* 2 HUNCHBACK
: jorobado *m*, -da *f*; giboso *m*, -sa *f*
humpbacked ['hʌmp,bækt] *adj*
: jorobado, giboso
humus ['hju:məs, 'ju:-] *n* : humus *m*
hunch¹ ['hʌntʃ] *vt* : encorvar — *vi or* **to
hunch up** : encorvarse
hunch² *n* PREMONITION : presentimiento *m*

hunchback ['hʌntʃ,bæk] *n* 1 HUMP
: joroba *f*, giba *f* 2 HUMPBACK : jorobado *m*, -da *f*; giboso *m*, -sa *f*
hunchbacked ['hʌntʃ,bækt] *adj* : jorobado, giboso
hundred¹ ['hʌndrəd] *adj* : cien, ciento
hundred² *n, pl* **-dreds** *or* **-dred** : ciento
m
hundredth¹ ['hʌndrədθ] *adj* : centésimo
hundredth² *n* 1 : centésimo *m*, -ma *f* (en
una serie) 2 : centésimo *m*, centésima
parte *f*
hung → **hang**
Hungarian [hʌŋ'gæriən] *n* 1 : húngaro
m, -ra *f* 2 : húngaro *m* (idioma) — **Hungarian** *adj*
hunger¹ ['hʌŋgər] *vi* 1 : tener hambre
2 **to hunger for** : ansiar, anhelar
hunger² *n* : hambre *m*
hungrily ['hʌŋgrəli] *adv* : ávidamente
hungry ['hʌŋgri] *adj* **-grier; -est** 1
: hambriento 2 **to be hungry** : tener
hambre
hunk ['hʌŋk] *n* : trozo *m*, pedazo *m*
hunt¹ ['hʌnt] *vt* 1 PURSUE : cazar 2 **to
hunt for** : buscar
hunt² *n* 1 PURSUIT : caza *f*, cacería *f* 2
SEARCH : búsqueda *f*, busca *f*
hunter ['hʌntər] *n* : cazador *m*, -dora *f*
hunting ['hʌntɪŋ] *n* : caza *f* ⟨to go hunting : ir de caza⟩
hurdle¹ ['hərdəl] *vt* **-dled; -dling** : saltar,
salvar (un obstáculo)
hurdle² *n* : valla *f* (en deportes), obstáculo *m*
hurl ['hərl] *vt* : arrojar, tirar, lanzar
hurrah [hʊ'rɑ, -'rɔ] *interj* : ¡hurra!
hurricane ['hərə,keɪn] *n* : huracán *m*
hurried ['hərid] *adj* : apresurado, precipitado
hurriedly ['hərədli] *adv* : apresuradamente, de prisa
hurry¹ ['həri] *v* **-ried; -rying** *vi* : apurarse,
darse prisa, apresurarse — *vt* : apurar,
darle prisa (a alguien)
hurry² *n* : prisa *f*, apuro *f*
hurt¹ ['hərt] *v* **hurt; hurting** *vt* 1 INJURE
: hacer daño a, herir, lastimar ⟨to hurt
oneself : hacerse daño⟩ 2 DISTRESS,
OFFEND : hacer sufrir, ofender, herir
— *vi* : doler ⟨my foot hurts : me duele
el pie⟩
hurt² *n* 1 INJURY : herida *f* 2 DISTRESS,
PAIN : dolor *m*, pena *f*
hurtful ['hərtfəl] *adj* : hiriente, doloroso
hurtle ['hərtəl] *vi* **-tled; -tling** : lanzarse,
precipitarse
husband¹ ['hʌzbənd] *vt* : economizar,
bien administrar
husband² *n* : esposo *m*, marido *m*
husbandry ['hʌzbəndri] *n* 1 MANAGE-
MENT, THRIFT : economía *f*, buena administración *f* 2 AGRICULTURE : agricultura *f* ⟨animal husbandry : cría de
animales⟩
hush¹ ['hʌʃ] *vt* 1 SILENCE : hacer callar,
acallar 2 CALM : calmar, apaciguar
hush² *n* : silencio *m*

hush–hush [ˈhʌʃˌhʌʃ, ˌhʌʃˈhʌʃ] *adj*
: muy secreto, confidencial
husk[1] [ˈhʌsk] *vt* : descascarar
husk[2] *n* : cáscara *f*
huskily [ˈhʌskəli] *adv* : con voz ronca
husky[1] [ˈhʌski] *adj* **-kier; -est 1** HOARSE
: ronco **2** BURLY : fornido
husky[2] *n, pl* **-kies** : perro *m*, -rra *f* esquimal
hustle[1] [ˈhəsəl] *v* **-tled; -tling** *vt* : darle prisa (a alguien), apurar ⟨they hustled me in : me hicieron entrar a empujones⟩ — *vi* : apurarse, ajetrearse
hustle[2] *n* BUSTLE : ajetreo *m*
hut [ˈhʌt] *n* : cabaña *f*, choza *f*, barraca *f*
hutch [ˈhʌtʃ] *n* **1** CUPBOARD : alacena *f* **2 rabbit hutch** : conejera *f*
hyacinth [ˈhaɪəˌsɪnθ] *n* : jacinto *m*
hybrid[1] [ˈhaɪbrɪd] *adj* : híbrido
hybrid[2] *n* : híbrido *m*
hydrant [ˈhaɪdrənt] *n* : boca *f* de riego, hidrante *m CA, Col* ⟨fire hydrant : boca de incendios⟩
hydraulic [haɪˈdrɔlɪk] *adj* : hidráulico — **hydraulically** *adv*
hydrocarbon [ˌhaɪdroˈkarbən] *n* : hidrocarburo *m*
hydrochloric acid [ˌhaɪdroˈklorɪk] *n* : ácido *m* clorhídrico
hydroelectric [ˌhaɪdroɪˈlɛktrɪk] *adj* : hidroeléctrico
hydrogen [ˈhaɪdrədʒən] *n* : hidrógeno *m*
hydrogen bomb *n* : bomba *f* de hidrógeno
hydrogen peroxide *n* : agua *f* oxigenada, peróxido *m* de hidrógeno
hydrophobia [ˌhaɪdrəˈfoːbiə] *n* : hidrofobia *f*, rabia *f*
hydroplane [ˈhaɪdrəˌpleɪn] *n* : hidroplano *m*
hyena [haɪˈiːnə] *n* : hiena *f*
hygiene [ˈhaɪˌdʒiːn] *n* : higiene *f*
hygienic [haɪˈdʒɛnɪk, -ˈdʒiː-; ˌhaɪˈdʒiˈnɪk] *adj* : higiénico — **hygienically** [-nɪkli] *adv*
hygienist [haɪˈdʒiːnɪst, -ˈdʒɛ-; ˈhaɪˌdʒiː-] *n* : higienista *mf*
hygrometer [haɪˈgramətər] *n* : higrómetro *m*
hymn [ˈhɪm] *n* : himno *m*

hymnal [ˈhɪmnəl] *n* : himnario *m*
hype [ˈhaɪp] *n* : bombo *m* publicitario
hyperactive [ˌhaɪpərˈæktɪv] *adj* : hiperactivo
hyperactivity [ˌhaɪpərˌækˈtɪvəti] *n, pl* **-ties** : hiperactividad *f*
hyperbole [haɪˈpərbəli] *n* : hipérbole *f*
hyperbolic [ˌhaɪpərˈbalɪk] *adj* : hiperbólico
hypercritical [ˌhaɪpərˈkrɪtəkəl] *adj* : hipercrítico
hypersensitive [ˌhaɪpərˌsɛntsəˈtɪ-vəti] *n* : hipersensibilidad *f*
hypertension [ˈhaɪpərˌtɛntʃən] *n* : hipertensión *f*
hyphen [ˈhaɪfən] *n* : guión *m*
hyphenate [ˈhaɪfənˌeɪt] *vt* **-ated; -ating** : escribir con guión
hypnosis [hɪpˈnoːsɪs] *n, pl* **-noses** [-ˌsiːz] : hipnosis *f*
hypnotic [hɪpˈnatɪk] *adj* : hipnótico, hipnotizador
hypnotism [ˈhɪpnəˌtɪzəm] *n* : hipnotismo *m*
hypnotize [ˈhɪpnəˌtaɪz] *vt* **-tized; -tizing** : hipnotizar
hypochondria [ˌhaɪpəˈkandriə] *n* : hipocondría *f*
hypochondriac [ˌhaɪpəˈkandriˌæk] *n* : hipocondríaco *m*, -ca *f*
hypocrisy [hɪpˈakrəsi] *n, pl* **-sies** : hipocresía *f*
hypocrite [ˈhɪpəˌkrɪt] *n* : hipócrita *mf*
hypocritical [ˌhɪpəˈkrɪtɪkəl] *adj* : hipócrita
hypodermic[1] [ˌhaɪpəˈdərmɪk] *adj* : hipodérmico
hypodermic[2] *n* : aguja *f* hipodérmica
hypotenuse [haɪˈpatənˌuːs, -ˌuːz, -ˌjuːs, -ˌjuːz] *n* : hipotenusa *f*
hypothesis [haɪˈpaθəsɪs] *n, pl* **-eses** [-ˌsiːz] : hipótesis *f*
hypothetical [ˌhaɪpəˈθɛtɪkəl] *adj* : hipotético — **hypothetically** [-tɪkli] *adv*
hysteria [hɪsˈtɛriə, -tɪr-] *n* : histeria *f*, histerismo *m*
hysterical [hɪsˈtɛrɪkəl] *adj* : histérico — **hysterically** [-ɪkli] *adv*
hysterics [hɪsˈtɛrɪks] *n* : histeria *f*, histerismo *m*

I

i [ˈaɪ] *n, pl* **i's** *or* **is** [ˈaɪz] : novena letra del alfabeto inglés
I [ˈaɪ] *pron* : yo
Iberian [aɪˈbɪriən] *adj* : ibérico
ibis [ˈaɪbəs] *n, pl* **ibis** *or* **ibises** : ibis *f*
ice[1] [ˈaɪs] *v* **iced; icing** *vt* **1** FREEZE : congelar, helar **2** CHILL : enfriar **3 to ice a cake** : escarchar un pastel — *vi* : helarse, congelarse
ice[2] *n* **1** : hielo *m* **2** SHERBET : sorbete *m*, nieve *f Cuba, Mex, PRi*

iceberg [ˈaɪsˌbərg] *n* : iceberg *m*
icebox [ˈaɪsˌbaks] → **refrigerator**
icebreaker [ˈaɪsˌbreɪkər] *n* : rompehielos *m*
ice cap *n* : casquete *m* glaciar
ice–cold [ˈaɪsˈkoːld] *adj* : helado
ice cream *n* : helado *m*, mantecado *m PRi*
Icelander [ˈaɪsˌlændər, -lən-] *n* : islandés *m*, -desa *f*
Icelandic[1] [aɪsˈlændɪk] *adj* : islandés

Icelandic² n : islandés m (idioma)
ice–skate ['aɪsˌskeɪt] vi **-skated; -skating** : patinar
ice skater n : patinador m, -dora f
ichthyology [ˌɪkthi'ɑləʤi] n : ictiología f
icicle ['aɪˌsɪkəl] n : carámbano m
icily ['aɪsəli] adv : fríamente, con frialdad ⟨he stared at me icily : me fijó la mirada con mucha frialdad⟩
icing ['aɪsɪŋ] n : glaseado m, betún m Mex
icon ['aɪˌkɑn, -kən] n : icono m
iconoclasm [aɪ'kɑnəˌklæzəm] n : iconoclasia f
iconoclast [aɪ'kɑnəˌklæst] n : iconoclasta mf
icy ['aɪsi] adj **icier; -est** 1 : cubierto de hielo ⟨an icy road : una carretera cubierta de hielo⟩ 2 FREEZING : helado, gélido, glacial 3 ALOOF : frío, distante
id ['ɪd] n : id m
I'd ['aɪd] (contraction of **I should** or **I would**) → **should, would**
idea [aɪ'di:ə] n : idea f
ideal¹ [aɪ'di:əl] adj : ideal
ideal² n : ideal m
idealism [aɪ'di:əˌlɪzəm] n : idealismo m
idealist [aɪ'di:əlɪst] n : idealista mf
idealistic [aɪˌdi:ə'lɪstɪk] adj : idealista
idealistically [aɪˌdi:ə'lɪstɪkli] adv : con idealismo
idealization [aɪˌdi:ələ'zeɪʃən] n : idealización f
idealize [aɪ'di:əˌlaɪz] vt **-ized; -izing** : idealizar
ideally [aɪ'di:əli] adv : perfectamente
identical [aɪ'dɛntɪkəl] adj : idéntico — **identically** [-tɪkli] adv
identifiable [aɪˌdɛntə'faɪəbəl] adj : identificable
identification [aɪˌdɛntəfə'keɪʃən] n 1 : identificación f 2 **identification card** : carnet m, cédula f de identidad, identificación f
identify [aɪ'dɛntəˌfaɪ] v **-fied; -fying** vt : identificar — vi **to identify with** : identificarse con
identity [aɪ'dɛntəti] n, pl **-ties** : identidad f
ideological [ˌaɪdiə'lɑʤɪkəl, ˌɪ-] adj : ideológico — **ideologically** [-ʤɪkli] adv
ideology [ˌaɪdi'ɑləʤi, ˌɪ-] n, pl **-gies** : ideología f
idiocy ['ɪdiəsi] n, pl **-cies** 1 : idiotez f 2 NONSENSE : estupidez f, tontería f
idiom ['ɪdiəm] n 1 LANGUAGE : lenguaje m 2 EXPRESSION : modismo m, expresión f idiomática
idiomatic [ˌɪdiə'mætɪk] adj : idiomático
idiosyncrasy [ˌɪdio'sɪŋkrəsi] n, pl **-sies** : idiosincrasia f
idiosyncratic [ˌɪdiosɪn'krætɪk] adj : idiosincrásico — **idiosyncratically** [-tɪkli] adv
idiot ['ɪdiət] n 1 : idiota mf (en medicina) 2 FOOL : idiota mf; tonto m, -ta f; imbécil mf fam

idiotic [ˌɪdi'ɑtɪk] adj : estúpido, idiota
idiotically [ˌɪdi'ɑtɪkli] adv : estúpidamente
idle¹ ['aɪdəl] v **idled; idling** vi 1 LOAF : holgazanear, flojear, haraganear 2 : andar al ralentí (dícese de un automóvil), marchar en vacío (dícese de una máquina) — vt : dejar sin trabajo
idle² adj **idler; idlest** 1 VAIN : frívolo, vano, infundado ⟨idle curiosity : pura curiosidad⟩ 2 INACTIVE : inactivo, parado, desocupado 3 LAZY : holgazán, haragán, perezoso
idleness ['aɪdəlnəs] n 1 INACTIVITY : inactividad f, ociosidad f 2 LAZINESS : holgazanería f, flojera f, pereza f
idler ['aɪdələr] n : haragán m, -gana f; holgazán m, -zana f
idly ['aɪdəli] adv : ociosamente
idol ['aɪdəl] n : ídolo m
idolater or **idolator** [aɪ'dɑlətər] n : idólatra mf
idolatrous [aɪ'dɑlətrəs] adj : idólatra
idolatry [aɪ'dɑlətri] n, pl **-tries** : idolatría f
idolize ['aɪdəˌlaɪz] vt **-ized; -izing** : idolatrar
idyll ['aɪdəl] n : idilio m
idyllic [aɪ'dɪlɪk] adj : idílico
if ['ɪf] conj 1 : si ⟨I would do it if I could : lo haría si pudiera⟩ ⟨if so : si es así⟩ ⟨as if : como si⟩ ⟨if I were you : yo que tú⟩ 2 WHETHER : si ⟨I don't know if they're ready : no sé si están listos⟩ 3 THOUGH : aunque, si bien ⟨it's pretty, if somewhat old-fashioned : es lindo aunque algo anticuado⟩
igloo ['ɪˌglu:] n, pl **-loos** : iglú m
ignite [ɪg'naɪt] v **-nited; -niting** vt : prenderle fuego a, encender — vi : prender, encenderse
ignition [ɪg'nɪʃən] n 1 IGNITING : ignición f, encendido m 2 or **ignition switch** : encendido m, arranque m ⟨to turn on the ignition : arrancar el motor⟩
ignoble [ɪg'no:bəl] adj : innoble — **ignobly** adv
ignominious [ˌɪgnə'mɪniəs] adj : ignominioso, deshonroso — **ignominiously** adv
ignominy ['ɪgnəˌmɪni] n, pl **-nies** : ignominia f
ignoramus [ˌɪgnə'reɪməs] n : ignorante mf; bestia mf; bruto m, -ta f
ignorance ['ɪgnərənts] n : ignorancia f
ignorant ['ɪgnərənt] adj 1 : ignorante 2 **to be ignorant of** : no ser consciente de, desconocer, ignorar
ignorantly ['ɪgnərəntli] adv : ignorantemente, con ignorancia
ignore [ɪg'nor] vt **-nored; -noring** : ignorar, hacer caso omiso de, no hacer caso de
iguana [ɪ'gwɑnə] n : iguana f, garrobo f CA
ilk ['ɪlk] n : tipo m, clase f, índole f
ill¹ ['ɪl] adv worse ['wərs]; **worst** ['wərst] : mal ⟨to speak ill of : hablar mal de⟩

<he can ill afford to fail : mal puede permitirse el lujo de fracasar>
ill² *adj* **worse; worst 1** SICK : enfermo **2** BAD : malo <ill luck : mala suerte>
ill³ *n* **1** EVIL : mal *m* **2** MISFORTUNE : mal *m*, desgracia *f* **3** AILMENT : enfermedad *f*
I'll ['aɪl] (*contraction of* **I shall** *or* **I will**) → **shall, will**
illegal [ɪl'li:gəl] *adj* : ilegal — **illegally** *adv*
illegality [ˌɪli'gæləti] *n* : ilegalidad *f*
illegibility [ɪlˌlɛdʒə'bɪləti] *n, pl* **-ties** : ilegibilidad *f*
illegible [ɪl'lɛdʒəbəl] *adj* : ilegible — **illegibly** [-bli] *adv*
illegitimacy [ˌɪlɪ'dʒɪtəməsi] *n* : ilegitimidad *f*
illegitimate [ˌɪlɪ'dʒɪtəmət] *adj* **1** BASTARD : ilegítimo, bastardo **2** UNLAWFUL : ilegítimo, ilegal — **illegitimately** *adv*
ill–fated ['ɪl'feɪtəd] *adj* : malhadado, infortunado, desventurado
illicit [ɪl'lɪsət] *adj* : ilícito — **illicitly** *adv*
illiteracy [ɪl'lɪtərəsi] *n, pl* **-cies** : analfabetismo *m*
illiterate¹ [ɪl'lɪtərət] *adj* : analfabeto
illiterate² *n* : analfabeto *m*, -ta *f*
ill–mannered [ˌɪl'manərd] *adj* : descortés, maleducado
ill–natured [ˌɪl'neɪtʃərd] *adj* : desagradable, de mal genio
ill–naturedly [ˌɪl'neɪtʃərdli] *adv* : desagradablemente
illness ['ɪlnəs] *n* : enfermedad *f*
illogical [ɪl'ladʒɪkəl] *adj* : ilógico — **illogically** [-kli] *adv*
ill–tempered [ˌɪl'tempərd] → **ill–natured**
ill–treat [ˌɪl'tri:t] *vt* : maltratar
ill–treatment [ˌɪl'tri:tmənt] *n* : maltrato *m*
illuminate [ɪ'lu:məˌneɪt] *vt* **-nated; -nating 1** : iluminar, alumbrar **2** ELUCIDATE : esclarecer, elucidar
illumination [ɪˌlu:mə'neɪʃən] *n* **1** LIGHTING : iluminación *f*, luz *f* **2** ELUCIDATION : esclarecimiento *m*, elucidación *f*
ill–use ['ɪl'ju:z] → **ill–treat**
illusion [ɪ'lu:ʒən] *n* : ilusión *f*
illusory [ɪ'lu:səri, -zəri] *adj* : engañoso, ilusorio
illustrate ['ɪləsˌtreɪt] *v* **-trated; -trating** : ilustrar
illustration [ˌɪlə'streɪʃən] *n* **1** PICTURE : ilustración *f* **2** EXAMPLE : ejemplo *m*, ilustración *f*
illustrative [ɪ'lʌstrətɪv, 'ɪləˌstreɪtɪv] *adj* : ilustrativo — **illustratively** *adv*
illustrator ['ɪləˌstreɪtər] *n* : ilustrador *m*, -dora *f*; dibujante *mf*
illustrious [ɪ'lʌstriəs] *adj* : ilustre, eminente, glorioso
illustriousness [ɪ'lʌstriəsnəs] *n* : eminencia *f*, prestigio *m*
ill will *n* : animosidad *f*, malquerencia *f*, mala voluntad *f*

I'm ['aɪm] (*contraction of* **I am**) → **be**
image¹ ['ɪmɪdʒ] *vt* **-aged; -aging** : imaginar, crear una imagen de
image² *n* : imagen *f*
imagery ['ɪmɪdʒri] *n, pl* **-eries 1** IMAGES : imágenes *fpl* **2** : imaginería *f* (en el arte)
imaginable [ɪ'mædʒənəbəl] *adj* : imaginable — **imaginably** [-bli] *adv*
imaginary [ɪ'mædʒəˌnɛri] *adj* : imaginario
imagination [ɪˌmædʒə'neɪʃən] *n* : imaginación *f*
imaginative [ɪ'mædʒənətɪv, -əˌneɪtɪv] *adj* : imaginativo — **imaginatively** *adv*
imagine [ɪ'mædʒən] *vt* **-ined; -ining** : imaginar(se)
imbalance [ɪm'bælənts] *n* : desajuste *m*, desbalance *m*, desequilibrio *m*
imbecile¹ ['ɪmbəsəl, -ˌsɪl] *or* **imbecilic** [ˌɪmbə'sɪlɪk] *adj* : imbécil, estúpido
imbecile² *n* **1** : imbécil *mf* (en medicina) **2** FOOL : idiota *mf*; imbécil *mf fam*; estúpido *m*, -da *f*
imbecility [ˌɪmbə'sɪləti] *n, pl* **-ties** : imbecilidad *f*
imbibe [ɪm'baɪb] *v* **-bibed; -bibing** *vt* **1** DRINK : beber **2** ABSORB : absorber, embeber — *vi* : beber
imbue [ɪm'bju:] *vt* **-bued; -buing** : imbuir
imitate ['ɪməˌteɪt] *vt* **-tated; -tating** : imitar, remedar
imitation¹ [ˌɪmə'teɪʃən] *adj* : de imitación, artificial
imitation² *n* : imitación *f*
imitative ['ɪməˌteɪtɪv] *adj* : imitativo, imitador, poco original
imitator ['ɪməˌteɪtər] *n* : imitador *m*, -dora *f*
immaculate [ɪ'mækjələt] *adj* **1** PURE : inmaculado, puro **2** FLAWLESS : impecable, intachable — **immaculately** *adv*
immaterial [ˌɪmə'tɪriəl] *adj* **1** INCORPOREAL : incorpóreo **2** UNIMPORTANT : irrelevante, sin importancia
immature [ˌɪmə'tʃur, -'tjur, -'tur] *adj* : inmaduro, verde (dícese de la fruta)
immaturity [ˌɪmə'tʃurəti, -'tjur-, -'tur-] *n, pl* **-ties** : inmadurez *f*, falta *f* de madurez
immeasurable [ɪ'mɛʒərəbəl] *adj* : inconmensurable, incalculable — **immeasurably** *adv*
immediacy [ɪ'mi:diəsi] *n* : inmediatez *f*
immediate [ɪ'mi:diət] *adj* **1** INSTANT : inmediato, instantáneo <immediate relief : alivio instantáneo> **2** DIRECT : inmediato, directo <the immediate cause of death : la causa directa de la muerte> **3** URGENT : urgente, apremiante **4** CLOSE : cercano, próximo, inmediato <her immediate family : sus familiares más cercanos> <in the immediate vicinity : en los alrededores, en las inmediaciones>
immediately [ɪ'mi:diətli] *adv* : inmediatamente, enseguida

immemorial [ˌɪmə'moriəl] *adj* : in-memorial

immense [ɪ'mɛnts] *adj* : inmenso, enorme — **immensely** *adv*

immensity [ɪ'mɛntsəṭi] *n, pl* **-ties** : inmensidad *f*

immerse [ɪ'mərs] *vt* **-mersed; -mersing** 1 SUBMERGE : sumergir 2 **to immerse oneself in** : enfrascarse en

immersion [ɪ'mərʒən] *n* 1 : inmersión *f* (en un líquido) 2 : enfrascamiento *m* (en una actividad)

immigrant ['ɪmɪgrənt] *n* : inmigrante *mf*

immigrate ['ɪməˌgreɪt] *vi* **-grated; -grating** : inmigrar

immigration [ˌɪmə'greɪʃən] *n* : inmigración *f*

imminence ['ɪmənənts] *n* : inminencia *f*

imminent ['ɪmənənt] *adj* : inminente — **imminently** *adv*

immobile [ɪm'o:bəl] *adj* 1 FIXED, IMMOVABLE : inmovible, fijo 2 MOTIONLESS : inmóvil

immobility [ˌɪmo'bɪləṭi] *n, pl* **-ties** : inmovilidad *f*

immobilize [ɪ'mo:bəˌlaɪz] *vt* **-lized; -lizing** : inmovilizar, paralizar

immoderate [ɪ'madərət] *adj* : inmoderado, desmesurado, desmedido, excesivo — **immoderately** *adv*

immodest [ɪ'madəst] *adj* 1 INDECENT : inmodesto, indecente, impúdico 2 CONCEITED : inmodesto, presuntuoso, engreído — **immodestly** *adv*

immodesty [ɪ'madəsti] *n* : inmodestia *f*

immoral [ɪ'mɔrəl] *adj* : inmoral

immorality [ˌɪmɔ'ræləṭi, ˌɪmə-] *n, pl* **-ties** : inmoralidad *f*

immorally [ɪ'mɔrəli] *adv* : de manera inmoral

immortal¹ [ɪ'mɔrtəl] *adj* : inmortal

immortal² *n* : inmortal *mf*

immortality [ˌɪˌmɔr'tæləṭi] *n* : inmortalidad *f*

immortalize [ɪ'mɔrtəlˌaɪz] *vt* **-ized; -izing** : inmortalizar

immovable [ɪ'mu:vəbəl] *adj* 1 FIXED : fijo, inmovible 2 UNYIELDING : inflexible

immune [ɪ'mju:n] *adj* 1 : inmune ⟨immune to smallpox : inmune a la viruela⟩ 2 EXEMPT : exento, inmune

immune system *n* : sistema *m* inmunológico

immunity [ɪ'mju:nəṭi] *n, pl* **-ties** 1 : inmunidad *f* 2 EXEMPTION : exención *f*

immunization [ˌɪmjʊnə'zeɪʃən] *n* : inmunización *f*

immunize ['ɪmjʊˌnaɪz] *vt* **-nized; -nizing** : inmunizar

immunology [ˌɪmjʊ'nalədʒi] *n* : inmunología *f*

immutable [ɪ'mju:ṭəbəl] *adj* : inmutable

imp ['ɪmp] *n* RASCAL : diablillo *m*; pillo *m*, -lla *f*

impact¹ [ɪm'pækt] *vt* 1 STRIKE : chocar con, impactar 2 AFFECT : afectar, impactar, impresionar — *vi* 1 STRIKE : hacer impacto, golpear 2 **to impact on** : tener un impacto sobre

impact² ['ɪmˌpækt] *n* 1 COLLISION : impacto *m*, choque *m*, colisión *f* 2 EFFECT : efecto *m*, impacto *m*, consecuencias *fpl*

impacted [ɪm'pæktəd] *adj* : impactado, incrustado (dícese de los dientes)

impair [ɪm'pær] *vt* : perjudicar, dañar, afectar

impairment [ɪm'pærmənt] *n* : perjuicio *m*, daño *m*

impala [ɪm'palə, -'pæ-] *n, pl* **impalas** or **impala** : impala *m*

impale [ɪm'peɪl] *vt* **-paled; -paling** : empalar

impanel [ɪm'pænəl] *vt* **-eled** or **-elled; eling** or **-elling** : elegir (un jurado)

impart [ɪm'part] *vt* 1 CONVEY : impartir, dar, conferir 2 DISCLOSE : revelar, divulgar

impartial [ɪm'parʃəl] *adj* : imparcial — **impartially** *adv*

impartiality [ɪmˌparʃi'æləṭi] *n, pl* **-ties** : imparcialidad *f*

impassable [ɪm'pæsəbəl] *adj* : infranqueable, intransitable — **impassably** [-bli] *adv*

impasse ['ɪmˌpæs] *n* 1 DEADLOCK : impasse *m*, punto *m* muerto 2 DEAD END : callejón *m* sin salida

impassioned [ɪm'pæʃənd] *adj* : apasionado, vehemente

impassive [ɪm'pæsɪv] *adj* : impasible, indiferente

impassively [ɪm'pæsɪvli] *adv* : impasiblemente, sin emoción

impatience [ɪm'peɪʃənts] *n* : impaciencia *f*

impatient [ɪm'peɪʃənt] *adj* : impaciente — **impatiently** *adv*

impeach [ɪm'pi:tʃ] *vt* : destituir (a un funcionario) de su cargo

impeachment [ɪm'pi:tʃmənt] *n* 1 ACCUSATION : acusación *f* 2 DISMISSAL : destitución *f*

impeccable [ɪm'pɛkəbəl] *adj* : impecable — **impeccably** [-bli] *adv*

impecunious [ˌɪmpɪ'kju:niəs] *adj* : falto de dinero

impede [ɪm'pi:d] *vt* **-peded; -peding** : impedir, dificultar, obstaculizar

impediment [ɪm'pɛdəmənt] *n* 1 HINDRANCE : impedimento *m*, obstáculo *m* 2 **speech impediment** : defecto *m* del habla

impel [ɪm'pɛl] *vt* **-pelled; -pelling** : impeler

impend [ɪm'pɛnd] *vi* : ser inminente

impenetrable [ɪm'pɛnətrəbəl] *adj* 1 : impenetrable ⟨an impenetrable forest : una selva impenetrable⟩ 2 INSCRUTABLE : incomprensible, inescrutable, impenetrable — **impenetrably** [-bli] *adv*

impenitent [ɪm'pɛnətənt] *adj* : impenitente

imperative[1] [ɪm'pɛrətɪv] *adj* **1** AUTHOR-
ITATIVE : imperativo, imperioso **2**
NECESSARY : imprescindible — **im-
peratively** *adv*
imperative[2] *n* : imperativo *m*
imperceptible [,ɪmpər'sɛptəbəl] *adj* : imperceptible — **imperceptibly** [-bli] *adv*
imperfect [ɪm'pərfɪkt] *adj* : imperfecto,
defectuoso — **imperfectly** *adv*
imperfection [ɪm,pər'fkʃən] *n* : imperfección *f*, defecto *m*
imperial [ɪm'pɪriəl] *adj* **1** : imperial **2**
SOVEREIGN : soberano **3** IMPERIOUS
: imperioso, señorial
imperialism [ɪm'pɪriə,lɪzəm] *n* : imperialismo *m*
imperialist[1] [ɪm'pɪriəlɪst] *adj* : imperialista
imperialist[2] *n* : imperialista *mf*
imperialistic [ɪm,pɪri:ə'lɪstɪk] *adj* : imperialista
imperil [ɪm'pɛrəl] *vt* **-iled** *or* **-illed; -iling**
or **-illing** : poner en peligro
imperious [ɪm'pɪriəs] *adj* : imperioso —
imperiously *adv*
imperishable [ɪm'pɛrɪʃəbəl] *adj* : imperecedero
impermanent [ɪm'pərmənənt] *adj*
: pasajero, inestable, efímero — **im-
permanently** *adv*
impermeable [ɪm'pərmiəbəl] *adj* : impermeable
impersonal [ɪm'pərsənəl] *adj* : impersonal — **impersonally** *adv*
impersonate [ɪm'pərsən,eɪt] *vt* **-ated;
-ating** : hacerse pasar por, imitar
impersonation [ɪm,pərsən'eɪʃən] *n* : imitación *f*
impersonator [ɪm'pərsən,eɪtər] *n* : imitador *m*, -dora *f*
impertinence [ɪm'pərtənənts] *n* : impertinencia *f*
impertinent [ɪm'pərtənənt] *adj* **1** IR-
RELEVANT : impertinente, irrelevante
2 INSOLENT : impertinente, insolente
impertinently [ɪm'pərtənəntli] *adv* : con
impertinencia, impertinentemente
imperturbable [,ɪmpər'tərbəbəl] *adj*
: imperturbable
impervious [ɪm'pərviəs] *adj* **1** IMPENE-
TRABLE : impermeable **2** INSENSITIVE
: insensible ⟨impervious to criticism
: insensible a la crítica⟩
impetuosity [ɪm,pɛtʃu'asəti] *n, pl* **-ties**
: impetuosidad *f*
impetuous [ɪm'pɛtʃuəs] *adj* : impetuoso,
impulsivo
impetuously [ɪm'pɛtʃuəsli] *adv* : de manera impulsiva, impetuosamente
impetus ['ɪmpətəs] *n* : ímpetu *m*, impulso *m*
impiety [ɪm'paɪəti] *n, pl* **-ties** : impiedad
f
impinge [ɪm'pɪndʒ] *vi* **-pinged; -pinging
1 to impinge on** AFFECT : afectar a, incidir en **2 to impinge on** VIOLATE : violar, vulnerar
impious ['ɪmpiəs, ɪm'paɪəs] *adj* : impío,
irreverente

impish ['ɪmpɪʃ] *adj* MISCHIEVOUS : pícaro, travieso
impishly ['ɪmpɪʃli] *adv* : con picardía
implacable [ɪm'plækəbəl] *adj* : implacable — **implacably** [-bli] *adv*
implant[1] [ɪm'plænt] *vt* **1** INCULCATE, IN-
STILL : inculcar, implantar **2** INSERT
: implantar, insertar
implant[2] ['ɪm,plænt] *n* : implante *m* (de
pelo), injerto *m* (de piel)
implantation [,ɪm,plæn'teɪʃən] *n* : implantación *f*
implausibility [ɪm,plɔzə'bɪləti] *n, pl* **-ties**
: inverosimilitud *f*
implausible [ɪm'plɔzəbəl] *adj* : inverosímil, poco convincente
implement[1] ['ɪmplə,mnt] *vt* : poner en
práctica, implementar
implement[2] ['ɪmpləmənt] *n* : utensilio *m*,
instrumento *m*, implemento *m*
implementation [,ɪmpləmən'teɪʃən] *n*
: implementación *f*, ejecución *f*, cumplimiento *m*
implicate ['ɪmplə,keɪt] *vt* **-cated; -cating**
: implicar, involucrar
implication [,ɪmplə'keɪʃən] *n* **1** CONSE-
QUENCE : implicación *f*, consecuencia
f **2** INFERENCE : insinuación *f*, inferencia *f*
implicit [ɪm'plɪsət] *adj* **1** IMPLIED : implícito, tácito **2** ABSOLUTE : absoluto,
completo ⟨implicit faith : fe ciega⟩ —
implicitly *adv*
implied [ɪm'plaɪd] *adj* : implícito, tácito
implode [ɪm'plo:d] *vi* **-ploded; -ploding**
: implosionar
implore [ɪm'plor] *vt* **-plored; -ploring**
: implorar, suplicar
implosion [ɪm'plo:ʒən] *n* : implosión *f*
imply [ɪm'plaɪ] *vt* **-plied; -plying 1** SUG-
GEST : insinuar, dar a entender **2** IN-
VOLVE : implicar, suponer ⟨rights imply obligations : los derechos implican
unas obligaciones⟩
impolite [,ɪmpə'laɪt] *adj* : descortés,
maleducado
impoliteness [,ɪmpə'laɪtnəs] *n* : descortesía *f*, falta *f* de educación
impolitic [ɪm'palə,tɪk] *adj* : imprudente,
poco político
imponderable[1] [ɪm'pandərəbəl] *adj*
: imponderable
imponderable[2] *n* : imponderable *m*
import[1] [ɪm'port] *vt* **1** SIGNIFY : significar **2** : importar ⟨to import foreign
cars : importar autos extranjeros⟩
import[2] ['ɪm,port] *n* **1** SIGNIFICANCE
: importancia *f*, significación *f* **2** → **importation**
importance [ɪm'portənts] *n* : importancia *f*
important [ɪm'portənt] *adj* : importante
importantly [ɪm'portəntli] *adv* **1** : con
importancia **2 more importantly** : lo
que es más importante
importation [,ɪm,pɔr'teɪʃən] *n* : importación *f*
importer [ɪm'portər] *n* : importador *m*,
-dora *f*

importunate [ɪm'pɔrtʃənət] *adj* : importuno, insistente

importune [ˌɪmpər'tu:n, -'tju:n; ɪm'pɔrtʃən] *vt* **-tuned; -tuning** : importunar, implorar

impose [ɪm'po:z] *v* **-posed; -posing** *vt* : imponer ⟨to impose a tax : imponer un impuesto⟩ — *vi* **to impose on** : abusar de, molestar ⟨to impose on her kindness : abusar de su bondad⟩

imposing [ɪm'po:zɪŋ] *adj* : imponente, impresionante

imposition [ˌɪmpə'zɪʃən] *n* : imposición *f*

impossibility [ɪmˌpasə'bɪləti] *n, pl* **-ties** : imposibilidad *f*

impossible [ɪm'pasəbəl] *adj* **1** : imposible ⟨an impossible task : una tarea imposible⟩ ⟨to make life impossible for : hacerle la vida imposible a⟩ **2** UNACCEPTABLE : inaceptable

impossibly [ɪm'pasəbli] *adv* : imposiblemente, increíblemente

impostor *or* **imposter** [ɪm'pastər] *n* : impostor *m*, -tora *f*

impotence ['ɪmpətənts] *n* : impotencia *f*

impotency ['ɪmpətəntsi] → **impotence**

impotent ['ɪmpətənt] *adj* : impotente

impound [ɪm'paʊnd] *vt* : incautar, embargar, confiscar

impoverish [ɪm'pavərɪʃ] *vt* : empobrecer

impoverishment [ɪm'pavərɪʃmənt] *n* : empobrecimiento *m*

impracticable [ɪm'præktɪkəbəl] *adj* : impracticable

impractical [ɪm'præktɪkəl] *adj* : poco práctico

imprecise [ˌɪmprɪ'saɪs] *adj* : impreciso

imprecisely [ˌɪmprɪ'saɪsli] *adv* : con imprecisión

impreciseness [ˌɪmprɪ'saɪsnəs] → **imprecision**

imprecision [ˌɪmprɪ'sɪʒən] *n* : imprecisión *f*, falta de precisión *f*

impregnable [ɪm'pregnəbəl] *adj* : inexpugnable, impenetrable, inconquistable

impregnate [ɪm'preg,neɪt] *vt* **-nated; -nating 1** FERTILIZE : fecundar **2** PERMEATE, SATURATE : impregnar, empapar, saturar

impresario [ˌɪmprə'sari,o, -'sær-] *n, pl* **-rios** : empresario *m*, -ria *f*

impress [ɪm'pres] *vt* **1** IMPRINT : imprimir, estampar **2** : impresionar, causar impresión a ⟨I was not impressed : no me hizo buena impresión⟩ **3 to impress (something) on someone** : recalcarle (algo) a alguien — *vi* : impresionar, hacer una impresión

impression [ɪm'preʃən] *n* **1** IMPRINT : marca *f*, huella *f*, molde *m* (de los dientes) **2** EFFECT : impresión *f*, efecto *m*, impacto *m* **3** PRINTING : impresión *f* **4** NOTION : impresión *f*, noción *f*

impressionable [ɪm'preʃənəbəl] *adj* : impresionable

impressionism [ɪm'preʃəˌnɪzəm] *n* : impresionismo *m*

impressionist [ɪm'preʃənɪst] *n* : impresionista *mf* — **impressionist** *adj*

impressive [ɪm'presɪv] *adj* : impresionante — **impressively** *adv*

impressiveness [ɪm'presɪvnəs] *n* : calidad de ser impresionante

imprint¹ [ɪm'prɪnt, 'ɪmˌ-] *vt* : imprimir, estampar

imprint² ['ɪmˌprɪnt] *n* : marca *f*, huella *f*

imprison [ɪm'prɪzən] *vt* **1** JAIL : encarcelar, aprisionar **2** CONFINE : recluir, encerrar

imprisonment [ɪm'prɪzənmənt] *n* : encarcelamiento *m*

improbability [ɪmˌprabə'bɪləti] *n, pl* **-ties** : improbabilidad *f*, inverosimilitud *f*

improbable [ɪm'prabəbəl] *adj* : improbable, inverosímil

impromptu¹ [ɪm'prampˌtu:, -ˌtju:] *adv* : sin preparación, espontáneamente

impromptu² *adj* : espontáneo, improvisado

impromptu³ *n* : improvisación *f*

improper [ɪm'prapər] *adj* **1** INCORRECT : incorrecto, impropio **2** INDECOROUS : indecoroso

improperly [ɪm'praprli] *adv* : incorrectamente, indebidamente

impropriety [ˌɪmprə'praɪəti] *n, pl* **-eties 1** INDECOROUSNESS : indecoro *m*, falta *f* de decoro **2** ERROR : impropiedad *f*, incorrección *f*

improve [ɪm'pru:v] *v* **-proved; -proving** : mejorar

improvement [ɪm'pru:vmənt] *n* : mejoramiento *m*, mejora *f*

improvidence [ɪm'pravədənts] *n* : imprevisión *f*

improvisation [ɪmˌpravə'zeɪʃən, ˌɪmprəvə-] *n* : improvisación *f*

improvise ['ɪmprəˌvaɪz] *v* **-vised; -vising** : improvisar

imprudence [ɪm'pru:dənts] *n* : imprudencia *f*, indiscreción *f*

imprudent [ɪm'pru:dənt] *adj* : imprudente, indiscreto

impudence ['ɪmpjədənts] *n* : insolencia *f*, descaro *m*

impudent ['ɪmpjədənt] *adj* : insolente, descarado — **impudently** *adv*

impugn [ɪm'pju:n] *vt* : impugnar

impulse ['ɪmˌpʌls] *n* **1** : impulso *m* **2 on impulse** : sin reflexionar

impulsive [ɪm'pʌlsɪv] *adj* : impulsivo — **impulsively** *adv*

impulsiveness [ɪm'pʌlsɪvnəs] *n* : impulsividad *f*

impunity [ɪm'pju:nəti] *n* **1** : impunidad *f* **2 with impunity** : impunemente

impure [ɪm'pjʊr] *adj* **1** : impuro ⟨impure thoughts : pensamientos impuros⟩ **2** CONTAMINATED : con impurezas, impuro

impurity [ɪm'pjʊrəti] *n, pl* **-ties** : impureza *f*

impute • incalculable

impute [ɪm'pju:t] *vt* **-puted; -puting** AT-
TRIBUTE : imputar, atribuir

in¹ ['ɪn] *adv* **1** INSIDE : dentro, adentro
⟨let's go in : vamos adentro⟩ **2** HAR-
VESTED : recogido ⟨the crops are in : las
cosechas ya están recogidas⟩ **3 to be
in** : estar ⟨is Linda in? : ¿está Linda?⟩
4 to be in : estar en poder ⟨the De-
mocrats are in : los demócratas están
en el poder⟩ **5 to be in for** : ser objeto de, estar a punto de ⟨they're in for
a treat : los van a agasajar⟩ ⟨he's in for
a surprise : se va a llevar una sorpre-
sa⟩ **6 to be in on** : participar en, tomar
parte en

in² *adj* **1** INSIDE : interior ⟨the in part
: la parte interior⟩ **2** FASHIONABLE : de
moda

in³ *prep* **1** (*indicating location or position*) ⟨in the lake : en el lago⟩ ⟨a pain
in the leg : un dolor en la pierna⟩ ⟨in
the sun : al sol⟩ ⟨in the rain : bajo la
lluvia⟩ ⟨the best restaurant in Buenos
Aires : el mejor restaurante de Buenos
Aires⟩ **2** INTO : en, a ⟨he broke it in
pieces : lo rompió en pedazos⟩ ⟨she
went in the house : se metió a la casa⟩
3 DURING : por, durante ⟨in the afternoon : por la tarde⟩ **4** WITHIN : dentro de ⟨I'll be back in a week : vuelvo
dentro de una semana⟩ **5** (*indicating
manner*) : en, con, de ⟨in Spanish : en
español⟩ ⟨written in pencil : escrito
con lápiz⟩ ⟨in this way : de esta man-
era⟩ **6** (*indicating states or circumstances*) ⟨to be in luck : tener suerte⟩
⟨to be in love : estar enamorado⟩ ⟨to
be in a hurry : tener prisa⟩ **7** (*indicating purpose*) : en ⟨in reply : en respuesta, como réplica⟩

in⁴ *n* **ins and outs** : pormenores *mpl*

inability [ˌɪnə'bɪləti] *n, pl* **-ties** : incapacidad *f*

inaccessibility [ˌɪnɪkˌsɛsə'bɪləti] *n, pl*
-ties : inaccesibilidad *f*

inaccessible [ˌɪnɪk'sɛsəbəl] *adj* : inaccesible

inaccuracy [ɪn'ækjərəsi] *n, pl* **-cies 1**
: inexactitud *f* **2** MISTAKE : error *m*

inaccurate [ɪn'ækjərət] *n* : inexacto,
erróneo, incorrecto

inaccurately [ɪn'ækjərətli] *adv* : incorrectamente, con inexactitud

inaction [ɪn'ækʃən] *n* : inactividad *f*, inacción *f*

inactive [ɪn'æktɪv] *adj* : inactivo

inactivity [ˌɪnˌæk'tɪvəti] *n, pl* **-ties** : inactividad *f*, ociosidad *f*

inadequacy [ɪn'ædɪkwəsi] *n, pl* **-cies 1**
INSUFFICIENCY : insuficiencia *f* **2** IN-
COMPETENCE : ineptitud *f*, incompe-
tencia *f*

inadequate [ɪn'ædɪkwət] *adj* **1** INSUF-
FICIENT : insuficiente, inadecuado **2**
INCOMPETENT : inepto, incompetente

inadmissible [ˌɪnæd'mɪsəbəl] *adj* : inadmisible

inadvertent [ˌɪnəd'vərtənt] *adj* : inadvertido, involuntario — **inadvertently**
adv

inadvisable [ˌɪnæd'vaɪzəbəl] *adj* : desaconsejable

inalienable [ɪn'eɪljənəbəl, -'eɪliənə-] *adj*
: inalienable

inane [ɪ'neɪn] *adj* **inaner; -est** : estúpido, idiota, necio

inanimate [ɪn'ænəmət] *adj* : inanimado,
exánime

inanity [ɪ'nænəti] *n, pl* **-ties 1** STUPIDI-
TY : estupidez *f* **2** NONSENSE : idiotez
f, disparate *m*

inapplicable [ɪn'æplɪkəbəl, ˌɪnə-'plɪkə-
bəl] *adj* IRRELEVANT : inaplicable, irrelevante

inappreciable [ˌɪnə'pri:ʃəbəl] *adj* : inapreciable, imperceptible

inappropriate [ˌɪnə'pro:priət] *adj* : inapropiado, inadecuado, impropio

inappropriateness [ˌɪnə'pro:priətnəs] *n*
: lo inapropiado, impropiedad *f*

inapt [ɪn'æpt] *adj* **1** UNSUITABLE : inadecuado, inapropiado **2** INEPT : inepto

inarticulate [ˌɪnɑr'tɪkjələt] *adj* : inarticu-
ulado, incapaz de expresarse

inarticulately [ˌɪnɑr'tɪkjələtli] *adv* : inarticuladamente

inasmuch as [ˌɪnæz'mʌtʃæz] *conj* : ya
que, dado que, puesto que

inattention [ˌɪnə'tentʃən] *n* : falta *f* de
atención, distracción *f*

inattentive [ˌɪnə'tentɪv] *adj* : distraído,
despistado

inattentively [ˌɪnə'tentɪvli] *adv* : distraídamente, sin prestar atención

inaudible [ɪn'ɔdəbəl] *adj* : inaudible

inaudibly [ɪn'ɔdəbli] *adv* : de forma inaudible

inaugural¹ [ɪ'nɔgjərəl, -gərəl] *adj* : inaugural, de investidura

inaugural² *n* **1** *or* **inaugural address**
: discurso *m* de investidura **2** INAU-
GURATION : investidura *f* (de una persona)

inaugurate [ɪ'nɔgjəˌreɪt, -gə-] *vt* **-rated;
-rating 1** BEGIN : inaugurar **2** INDUCT
: investir ⟨to inaugurate the president
: investir al presidente⟩

inauguration [ɪˌnɔgjə'reɪʃən, -gə-] *n* **1**
: inauguración *f* (de un edificio, un sistema, etc.) **2** : investidura *f* (de una persona)

inauspicious [ˌɪnɔ'spɪʃəs] *adj* : desfavorable, poco propicio

inborn ['ɪnˌbɔrn] *adj* **1** CONGENITAL, IN-
NATE : innato, congénito **2** HEREDI-
TARY : hereditario

inbred ['ɪnˌbrɛd] *adj* **1** : engendrado por
endogamia **2** INNATE : innato

inbreed ['ɪnˌbri:d] *vt* **-bred; -breeding**
: engendrar por endogamia

inbreeding ['ɪnˌbri:dɪŋ] *n* : endogamia *f*

Inca ['ɪŋkə] *n* : inca *mf*

incalculable [ɪn'kælkjələbəl] *adj* : incalculable — **incalculably** [-bli] *adv*

incandescence [ˌɪnkən'dɛsənts] *n* : incandescencia *f*

incandescent [ˌɪnkən'dɛsənt] *adj* **1** : incandescente **2** BRILLIANT : brillante

incantation [ˌɪnˌkæn'teɪʃən] *n* : conjuro *m*, ensalmo *m*

incapable [ɪn'keɪpəbəl] *adj* : incapaz

incapacitate [ˌɪnkə'pæsəˌteɪt] *vt* **-tated; -tating** : incapacitar

incapacity [ˌɪnkə'pæsəti] *n, pl* **-ties** : incapacidad *f*

incarcerate [ɪn'kɑrsəˌreɪt] *vt* **-ated; -ating** : encarcelar

incarceration [ɪnˌkɑrsə'reɪʃən] *n* : encarcelamiento *m*, encarcelación *f*

incarnate[1] [ɪn'kɑrˌneɪt] *vt* **-nated; -nating** : encarnar

incarnate[2] [ɪn'kɑrnət, -ˌneɪt] *adj* : encarnado

incarnation [ˌɪnˌkɑr'neɪʃən] *n* : encarnación *f*

incendiary[1] [ɪn'sɛndiˌri] *adj* : incendiario

incendiary[2] *n, pl* **-aries** : incendiario *m*, -ria *f*; pirómano *m*, -na *f*

incense[1] [ɪn'sɛnts] *vt* **-censed; -censing** : indignar, enfadar, enfurecer

incense[2] ['ɪnˌsɛnts] *n* : incienso *m*

incentive [ɪn'sɛntɪv] *n* : incentivo *m*, aliciente *m*, motivación *f*, acicate *m*

inception [ɪn'sɛpʃən] *n* : comienzo *m*, principio *m*

incessant [ɪn'sɛsənt] *adj* : incesante, continuo — **incessantly** *adv*

incest ['ɪnˌsɛst] *n* : incesto *m*

incestuous [ɪn'sɛstʃuəs] *adj* : incestuoso

inch[1] ['ɪntʃ] *v* : avanzar poco a poco

inch[2] *n* **1** : pulgada *f* **2 every inch** : absoluto, seguro ⟨every inch a winner : un seguro ganador⟩ **3 within an inch of** : a punto de

incidence ['ɪntsədənts] *n* **1** FREQUENCY : frecuencia *f*, índice *m* ⟨a high incidence of crime : un alto índice de crímenes⟩ **2 angle of incidence** : ángulo *m* de incidencia

incident[1] ['ɪntsədənt] *adj* : incidente

incident[2] *n* : incidente *m*, incidencia *f*, episodio *m* (en una obra de ficción)

incidental[1] [ˌɪntsə'dɛntəl] *adj* **1** SECONDARY : incidental, secundario **2** ACCIDENTAL : casual, fortuito

incidental[2] *n* **1** : algo incidental **2 incidentals** *npl* : imprevistos *mpl*

incidentally [ˌɪntsə'dɛntəli, -'dɛntli] *adv* **1** BY CHANCE : incidentalmente, casualmente **2** BY THE WAY : a propósito, por cierto

incinerate [ɪn'sɪnəˌreɪt] *vt* **-ated; -ating** : incinerar

incinerator [ɪn'sɪnəˌreɪtər] *n* : incinerador *m*

incipient [ɪn'sɪpiənt] *adj* : incipiente, naciente

incise [ɪn'saɪz] *vt* **-cised; -cising 1** ENGRAVE : grabar, cincelar, inscribir **2** : hacer una incisión en

incision [ɪn'sɪʒən] *n* : incisión *f*

incisive [ɪn'saɪsɪv] *adj* : incisivo, penetrante

incisively [ɪn'saɪsɪvli] *adv* : con agudeza

incisor [ɪn'saɪzər] *n* : incisivo *m*

incite [ɪn'saɪt] *vt* **-cited; -citing** : incitar, instigar

incitement [ɪn'saɪtmənt] *n* : incitación *f*

inclemency [ɪn'klɛməntsi] *n, pl* **-cies** : inclemencia *f*

inclement [ɪn'klɛmənt] *adj* : inclemente, tormentoso

inclination [ˌɪnklə'neɪʃən] *n* **1** PROPENSITY : inclinación *f*, tendencia *f* **2** DESIRE : deseo *m*, ganas *fpl* **3** BOW : inclinación *f*

incline[1] [ɪn'klaɪn] *v* **-clined; -clining** *vi* **1** SLOPE : inclinarse **2** TEND : inclinarse, tender ⟨he is inclined to be late : tiende a llegar tarde⟩ — *vt* **1** LOWER : inclinar, bajar ⟨to incline one's head : bajar la cabeza⟩ **2** SLANT : inclinar **3** PREDISPOSE : predisponer

incline[2] ['ɪnˌklaɪn] *n* : inclinación *f*, pendiente *f*

inclined [ɪn'klaɪnd] *adj* **1** SLOPING : inclinado **2** PRONE : prono, dispuesto, dado

inclose, inclosure → **enclose, enclosure**

include [ɪn'kluːd] *vt* **-cluded; -cluding** : incluir, comprender

inclusion [ɪn'kluːʒən] *n* : inclusión *f*

inclusive [ɪn'kluːsɪv] *adj* : inclusivo

incognito [ˌɪnˌkɑg'niːˌto, ɪn'kɑgnə-ˌtoː] *adv & adj* : de incógnito

incoherence [ˌɪnko'hɪrənts, -'hɛr-] *n* : incoherencia *f*

incoherent [ˌɪnko'hɪrənt, -'hɛr-] *adj* : incoherente — **incoherently** *adv*

incombustible [ˌɪnkəm'bʌstəbəl] *adj* : incombustible

income ['ɪnˌkʌm] *n* : ingresos *mpl*, entradas *fpl*

income tax *n* : impuesto *m* sobre la renta

incoming ['ɪnˌkʌmɪŋ] *adj* **1** ARRIVING : que se recibe (dícese del correo), que llega (dícese de las personas), ascendente (dícese de la marea) **2** NEW : nuevo, entrante ⟨the incoming president : el nuevo presidente⟩ ⟨the incoming year : el año entrante⟩

incommunicado [ˌɪnkəˌmjuːnə'kado] *adj* : incomunicado

incomparable [ɪn'kɑmpərəbəl] *adj* : incomparable, sin igual

incompatible [ˌɪnkəm'pætəbəl] *adj* : incompatible

incompetence [ɪn'kɑmpətənts] *n* : incompetencia *f*, impericia *f*, ineptitud *f*

incompetent [ɪn'kɑmpətənt] *adj* : incompetente, inepto, incapaz

incomplete [ˌɪnkəm'pliːt] *adj* : incompleto — **incompletely** *adv*

incomprehensible [ˌɪnˌkɑmpri'hɛnt-səbəl] *adj* : incomprensible

inconceivable [ˌɪnkən'siːvəbəl] *adj* **1** INCOMPREHENSIBLE : incomprensible **2** UNBELIEVABLE : inconcebible, increíble

inconceivably [ˌɪnkən'si:vəbli] *adv* : inconcebiblemente, increíblemente

inconclusive [ˌɪnkən'klu:sɪv] *adj* : inconcluyente, no decisivo

incongruity [ˌɪnkən'gru:əṭi, -ˌkɑn-] *n, pl* **-ties** : incongruencia *f*

incongruous [ɪn'kɑŋgruəs] *adj* : incongruente, inapropiado, fuera de lugar

incongruously [ɪn'kɑŋgruəsli] *adv* : de manera incongruente, inapropiadamente

inconsequential [ˌɪnˌkɑnsə'kwɛntʃəl] *adj* : intrascendente, de poco importancia

inconsiderable [ˌɪnkən'sɪdərəbəl] *adj* : insignificante

inconsiderate [ˌɪnkən'sɪdərət] *adj* : desconsiderado, sin consideración — **inconsiderately** *adv*

inconsistency [ˌɪnkən'sɪstəntsi] *n, pl* **-cies** : inconsecuencia *f*, inconsistencia *f*

inconsistent [ˌɪnkən'sɪstənt] *adj* : inconsecuente, inconsistente

inconsolable [ˌɪnkən'so:ləbəl] *adj* : inconsolable — **inconsolably** [-bli] *adv*

inconspicuous [ˌɪnkən'spɪkjuəs] *adj* : discreto, no conspicuo, que no llama la atención

inconspicuously [ˌɪnkən'spɪkjuəsli] *adv* : discretamente, sin llamar la atención

incontestable [ˌɪnkən'tɛstəbəl] *adj* : incontestable, indiscutible — **incontestably** [-bli] *adv*

incontinence [ɪn'kɑntənənts] *n* : incontinencia *f*

incontinent [ɪn'kɑntənənt] *adj* : incontinente

inconvenience¹ [ˌɪnkən'vi:njənts] *vt* **-nienced; -niencing** : importunar, incomodar, molestar

inconvenience² *n* : incomodidad *f*, molestia *f*

inconvenient [ˌɪnkən'vi:njənt] *adj* : inconveniente, importuno, incómodo — **inconveniently** *adv*

incorporate [ɪn'kɔrpəˌreɪt] *vt* **-rated; -rating 1** INCLUDE : incorporar, incluir **2** : incorporar, constituir en sociedad (dícese de un negocio)

incorporation [ɪnˌkɔrpə'reɪʃən] *n* : incorporación *f*

incorporeal [ˌɪnˌkɔr'pɔriəl] *adj* : incorpóreo

incorrect [ˌɪnkə'rɛkt] *adj* **1** INACCURATE : incorrecto **2** WRONG : equivocado, erróneo **3** IMPROPER : impropio — **incorrectly** *adv*

incorrigible [ɪn'kɔrədʒəbəl] *adj* : incorregible

incorruptible [ˌɪnkə'rʌptəbəl] *adj* : incorruptible

increase¹ [ɪn'kri:s, 'ɪnˌkri:s] *v* **-creased; -creasing** *vi* GROW : aumentar, crecer, subir (dícese de los precios) — *vt* AUGMENT : aumentar, acrecentar

increase² ['ɪnˌkri:s, ɪn'kri:s] *n* : aumento *m*, incremento *m*, subida *f* (de precios)

increasing [ɪn'kri:sɪŋ, 'ɪnˌkri:sɪŋ] *adj* : creciente

increasingly [ɪn'kri:sɪŋli] *adv* : cada vez más

incredible [ɪn'krɛdəbəl] *adj* : increíble — **incredibly** [-bli] *adv*

incredulity [ˌɪnkrɪ'du:ləṭi, -'dju:-] *n* : incredulidad *f*

incredulous [ɪn'krɛdʒələs] *adj* : incrédulo, escéptico

incredulously [ɪn'krɛdʒələslí] *adv* : con incredulidad

increment ['ɪŋkrəmənt, 'ɪn-] *n* : incremento *m*, aumento *m*

incremental [ˌɪŋkrə'mɛntəl, ˌɪn-] *adj* : de incremento

incriminate [ɪn'krɪməˌneɪt] *vt* **-nated; -nating** : incriminar

incrimination [ɪnˌkrɪmə'neɪʃən] *n* : incriminación *f*

incriminatory [ɪn'krɪmənəˌtori] *adj* : incriminatorio

incubate ['ɪŋkjuˌbeɪt, 'ɪn-] *v* **-bated; -bating** *vt* : incubar, empollar — *vi* : incubar(se), empollar

incubation [ˌɪŋkju'beɪʃən, ˌɪn-] *n* : incubación *f*

incubator ['ɪŋkjuˌbeɪṭər, 'ɪn-] *n* : incubadora *f*

inculcate [ɪn'kʌlˌkeɪt, 'ɪnˌkʌl-] *vt* **-cated; -cating** : inculcar

incumbency [ɪn'kʌmbəntsi] *n, pl* **-cies 1** OBLIGATION : incumbencia *f* **2** : mandato *m* (en la política)

incumbent¹ [ɪn'kʌmbənt] *adj* : obligatorio

incumbent² *n* : titular *mf*

incur [ɪn'kər] *vt* **incurred; incurring** : provocar (al enojo), incurrir en (gastos, obligaciones)

incurable [ɪn'kjurəbəl] *adj* : incurable, sin remedio

incursion [ɪn'kərʒən] *n* : incursión *f*

indebted [ɪn'dɛṭəd] *adj* **1** : endeudado **2 to be indebted to** : estar en deuda con, estarle agradecido a

indebtedness [ɪn'dɛṭədnəs] *n* : endeudamiento *m*

indecency [ɪn'di:səntsi] *n, pl* **-cies** : indecencia *f*

indecent [ɪn'di:sənt] *adj* : indecente — **indecently** *adv*

indecipherable [ˌɪndɪ'saɪfərəbəl] *adj* : indescifrable

indecision [ˌɪndɪ'sɪʒən] *n* : indecisión *f*, irresolución *f*

indecisive [ˌɪndɪ'saɪsɪv] *adj* **1** INCONCLUSIVE : indeciso, que no es decisivo **2** IRRESOLUTE : indeciso, irresoluto, vacilante **3** INDEFINITE : indefinido — **indecisively** *adv*

indecorous [ɪn'dɛkərəs, ˌɪndɪ'korəs] *adj* : indecoroso — **indecorously** *adv*

indecorousness [ɪn'dɛkərəsnəs, ˌɪndɪ'korəs-] *n* : indecoro *m*

indeed [ɪn'di:d] *adv* **1** TRULY : verdaderamente, de veras **2** (*used as intensifier*) ⟨thank you very much indeed

: muchísimas gracias⟩ **3** OF COURSE : claro, por supuesto

indefatigable [ˌɪndɪˈfætɪɡəbəl] *adj* : incansable, infatigable — **indefatigably** [-bli] *adv*

indefensible [ˌɪndɪˈfɛntsəbəl] *adj* **1** VULNERABLE : indefendible, vulnerable **2** INEXCUSABLE : inexcusable

indefinable [ˌɪndɪˈfaɪnəbəl] *adj* : indefinible

indefinite [ɪnˈdɛfənət] *adj* **1** : indefinido, indeterminado ⟨indefinite pronouns : pronombres indefinidos⟩ **2** VAGUE : vago, impreciso

indefinitely [ɪnˈdɛfənətli] *adv* : indefinidamente, por un tiempo indefinido

indelible [ɪnˈdɛləbəl] *adj* : indeleble, imborrable — **indelibly** [-bli] *adv*

indelicacy [ɪnˈdɛləkəsi] *n* : falta *f* de delicadeza

indelicate [ɪnˈdɛlɪkət] *adj* **1** IMPROPER : indelicado, indecoroso **2** TACTLESS : indiscreto, falto de tacto

indemnify [ɪnˈdɛmnəˌfaɪ] *vt* **-fied; -fying 1** INSURE : asegurar **2** COMPENSATE : indemnizar, compensar

indemnity [ɪnˈdɛmnəti] *n, pl* **-ties 1** INSURANCE : indemnidad *f* **2** COMPENSATION : indemnización *f*

indent [ɪnˈdɛnt] *vt* : sangrar (un párrafo)

indentation [ˌɪnˌdɛnˈteɪʃən] *n* **1** NOTCH : muesca *f*, mella *f* **2** INDENTING : sangría *f* (de un párrafo)

indenture¹ [ɪnˈdɛntʃər] *vt* **-tured; -turing** : ligar por contrato

indenture² *n* : contrato de aprendizaje

independence [ˌɪndəˈpɛndənts] *n* : independencia *f*

Independence Day *n* : día *m* de la Independencia (4 de julio en los EE.UU.)

independent¹ [ˌɪndəˈpɛndənt] *adj* : independiente — **independently** *adv*

independent² *n* : independiente *mf*

indescribable [ˌɪndɪˈskraɪbəbəl] *adj* : indescriptible, incalificable — **indescribably** [-bli] *adv*

indestructibility [ˌɪndɪˌstrʌktəˈbɪləti] *n* : indestructibilidad *f*

indestructible [ˌɪndɪˈstrʌktəbəl] *adj* : indestructible

indeterminate [ˌɪndɪˈtərmənət] *adj* **1** VAGUE : vago, impreciso, indeterminado **2** INDEFINITE : indeterminado, indefinido

index¹ [ˈɪnˌdɛks] *vt* **1** : ponerle un índice a (un libro o una revista) **2** : incluir en un índice ⟨all proper names are indexed : todos los nombres propios están incluidos en el índice⟩ **3** INDICATE : indicar, señalar **4** REGULATE : indexar, indiciar ⟨to index prices : indiciar los precios⟩

index² *n, pl* **-dexes** *or* **-dices** [ˈɪndəˌsiːz] **1** : índice *m* (de un libro, de precios) **2** INDICATION : indicio *m*, índice *m*, señal *f* ⟨an index of her character : una señal de su carácter⟩

index finger *n* FOREFINGER : dedo *m* índice

Indian [ˈɪndiən] *n* **1** : indio *m*, -dia *f* **2** → American Indian — **Indian** *adj*

indicate [ˈɪndəˌkeɪt] *vt* **-cated; -cating 1** POINT OUT : indicar, señalar **2** SHOW, SUGGEST : ser indicio de, ser señal de **3** EXPRESS : expresar, señalar **4** REGISTER : marcar, poner (una medida, etc.)

indication [ˌɪndəˈkeɪʃən] *n* : indicio *m*, señal *f*

indicative [ɪnˈdɪkətɪv] *adj* : indicativo

indicator [ˈɪndəˌkeɪtər] *n* : indicador *m*

indict [ɪnˈdaɪt] *vt* : acusar, procesar (por un crimen)

indictment [ɪnˈdaɪtmənt] *n* : acusación *f*

indifference [ɪnˈdɪfrənts, -ˈdɪfə-] *n* : indiferencia *f*

indifferent [ɪnˈdɪfrənt, -ˈdɪfə-] *adj* **1** UNCONCERNED : indiferente **2** MEDIOCRE : mediocre

indifferently [ɪnˈdɪfrəntli, -ˈdɪfə-] *adv* **1** : con indiferencia, indiferentemente **2** SO-SO : de modo regular, más o menos

indigence [ˈɪndɪdʒənts] *n* : indigencia *f*

indigenous [ɪnˈdɪdʒənəs] *adj* : indígena, nativo

indigent [ˈɪndɪdʒənt] *adj* : indigente, pobre

indigestible [ˌɪndaɪˈdʒɛstəbəl, -dɪ-] *adj* : difícil de digerir

indigestion [ˌɪndaɪˈdʒɛstʃən, -dɪ-] *n* : indigestión *f*, empacho *m*

indignant [ɪnˈdɪɡnənt] *adj* : indignado

indignantly [ɪnˈdɪɡnəntli] *adv* : con indignación

indignation [ˌɪndɪɡˈneɪʃən] *n* : indignación *f*

indignity [ɪnˈdɪɡnəti] *n, pl* **-ties** : indignidad *f*

indigo [ˈɪndɪˌɡoː] *n, pl* **-gos** *or* **-goes** : añil *m*, índigo *m*

indirect [ˌɪndəˈrɛkt, -daɪ-] *adj* : indirecto — **indirectly** *adv*

indiscernible [ˌɪndɪˈsərnəbəl, -ˈzər-] *adj* : imperceptible

indiscreet [ˌɪndɪˈskriːt] *adj* : indiscreto, imprudente — **indiscreetly** *adv*

indiscretion [ˌɪndɪˈskrɛʃən] *n* : indiscreción *f*, imprudencia *f*

indiscriminate [ˌɪndɪˈskrɪmənət] *adj* : indiscriminado

indiscriminately [ˌɪndɪˈskrɪmənətli] *adv* : sin discriminación, sin discernimiento

indispensable [ˌɪndɪˈspɛntsəbəl] *adj* : indispensable, necesario, imprescindible — **indispensably** [-bli] *adv*

indisposed [ˌɪndɪˈspoːzd] *adj* **1** ILL : indispuesto, enfermo **2** AVERSE, DISINCLINED : opuesto, reacio ⟨to be indisposed toward working : no tener ganas de trabajar⟩

indisputable [ˌɪndɪˈspjuːtəbəl, ɪnˈdɪspjuːtə-] *adj* : indiscutible, incuestionable, incontestable — **indisputably** [-bli] *adv*

indistinct [ˌɪndɪˈstɪŋkt] *adj* : indistinto — **indistinctly** *adv*

indistinctness [ˌɪndɪˈstɪŋktnəs] *n* : falta *f* de claridad

indistinguishable [ˌɪndɪˈstɪŋgwɪʃəbəl] *adj* : indistinguible

individual¹ [ˌɪndəˈvɪdʒuəl] *adj* **1** PERSONAL : individual, personal ⟨individual traits : características personales⟩ **2** SEPARATE : individual, separado **3** PARTICULAR : particular, propio

individual² *n* : individuo *m*

individualism [ˌɪndəˈvɪdʒəwəˌlɪzəm] *n* : individualismo *m*

individualist [ˌɪndəˈvɪdʒuəlɪst] *n* : individualista *mf*

individuality [ˌɪndəˌvɪdʒuˈæləti] *n, pl* **-ties** : individualidad *f*

individually [ˌɪndəˈvɪdʒuəli, -dʒəli] *adv* : individualmente

indivisible [ˌɪndɪˈvɪzəbəl] *adj* : indivisible

indoctrinate [ɪnˈdɑktrəˌneɪt] *vt* **-nated; -nating 1** TEACH : enseñar, instruir **2** PROPAGANDIZE : adoctrinar

indoctrination [ɪnˌdɑktrəˈneɪʃən] *n* : adoctrinamiento *m*

indolence [ˈɪndələnts] *n* : indolencia *f*

indolent [ˈɪndələnt] *adj* : indolente

indomitable [ɪnˈdɑmətəbəl] *adj* : invencible, indomable, indómito — **indomitably** [-bli] *adv*

Indonesian [ˌɪndoˈniːʒən, -ʃən] *n* : indonesio *m*, -sia *f* — **Indonesian** *adj*

indoor [ˈɪnˈdor] *adj* : interior (dícese de las plantas), para estar en casa (dícese de la ropa), cubierto (dícese de las piscinas, etc.), bajo techo (dícese de los deportes)

indoors [ˈɪnˈdorz] *adv* : adentro, dentro

indubitable [ɪnˈduːbətəbəl, -ˈdjuː-] *adj* : indudable, incuestionable, indiscutible

indubitably [ɪnˈduːbətəbli, -ˈdjuː-] *adv* : indudablemente

induce [ɪnˈduːs, -ˈdjuːs] *vt* **-duced; -ducing 1** PERSUADE : persuadir, inducir **2** CAUSE : inducir, provocar ⟨to induce labor : provocar un parto⟩

inducement [ɪnˈduːsmənt, -ˈdjuːs-] *n* **1** INCENTIVE : incentivo *m*, aliciente *m* **2** : inducción *f*, provocación *f* (de un parto)

induct [ɪnˈdʌkt] *vt* **1** INSTALL : instalar, investir **2** ADMIT : admitir (como miembro) **3** CONSCRIPT : reclutar (al servicio militar)

inductee [ˌɪnˌdʌkˈtiː] *n* : recluta *mf*, conscripto *m*, -ta *f*

induction [ɪnˈdʌkʃən] *n* **1** INTRODUCTION : iniciación *f*, introducción *f* **2** : inducción *f* (en la lógica o la electricidad)

inductive [ɪnˈdʌktɪv] *adj* : inductivo

indulge [ɪnˈdʌldʒ] *v* **-dulged; -dulging** *vt* **1** GRATIFY : gratificar, satisfacer **2** SPOIL : consentir, mimar — *vi* **to indulge in** : permitirse

indulgence [ɪnˈdʌldʒənts] *n* **1** SATISFYING : satisfacción *f*, gratificación *f* **2** HUMORING : complacencia *f*, indulgencia *f* **3** SPOILING : consentimiento *m* **4** : indulgencia *f* (en la religión)

indulgent [ɪnˈdʌldʒənt] *adj* : indulgente, consentido — **indulgently** *adv*

industrial [ɪnˈdʌstriəl] *adj* : industrial — **industrially** *adv*

industrialist [ɪnˈdʌstriəlɪst] *n* : industrial *mf*

industrialization [ɪnˌdʌstriələˈzeɪ-ʃən] *n* : industrialización *f*

industrialize [ɪnˈdʌstriəˌlaɪz] *vt* **-ized; -izing** : industrializar

industrious [ɪnˈdʌstriəs] *adj* : diligente, industrioso, trabajador

industriously [ɪnˈdʌstriəsli] *adv* : con diligencia, con aplicación

industriousness [ɪnˈdʌstriəsnəs] *n* : diligencia *f*, aplicación *f*

industry [ˈɪndəstri] *n, pl* **-tries 1** DILIGENCE : diligencia *f*, aplicación *f* **2** : industria *f* ⟨the steel industry : la industria siderúrgica⟩

inebriated [ɪˈniːbriˌeɪtəd] *adj* : ebrio, embriagado

inebriation [ɪˌniːbriˈeɪʃən] *n* : ebriedad *f*, embriaguez *f*

ineffable [ɪnˈɛfəbəl] *adj* : inefable — **ineffably** [-bli] *adv*

ineffective [ˌɪnɪˈfɛktɪv] *adj* **1** INEFFECTUAL : ineficaz, inútil **2** INCAPABLE : incompetente, ineficiente, incapaz

ineffectively [ˌɪnɪˈfɛktɪvli] *adv* : ineficazmente, infructuosamente

ineffectual [ˌɪnɪˈfɛktʃuəl] *adj* : inútil, ineficaz — **ineffectually** *adv*

inefficiency [ˌɪnɪˈfɪʃəntsi] *n, pl* **-cies** : ineficiencia *f*, ineficacia *f*

inefficient [ˌɪnɪˈfɪʃənt] *adj* **1** : ineficiente, ineficaz **2** INCAPABLE, INCOMPETENT : incompetente, incapaz — **inefficiently** *adv*

inelegance [ɪnˈɛləgənts] *n* : inelegancia *f*

inelegant [ɪnˈɛləgənt] *adj* : inelegante, poco elegante

ineligibility [ɪnˌɛlədʒəˈbɪləti] *n* : inelegibilidad *f*

ineligible [ɪnˈɛlədʒəbəl] *adj* : inelegible

inept [ɪˈɛnpt] *adj* : inepto ⟨inept at : incapaz para⟩

ineptitude [ɪˈɛnptəˌtuːd, -ˌtjuːd] *n* : ineptitud *f*, incompetencia *f*, incapacidad *f*

inequality [ˌɪnɪˈkwɑləti] *n, pl* **-ties** : desigualdad *f*

inert [ɪˈnərt] *adj* **1** INACTIVE : inerte, inactivo **2** SLUGGISH : lento

inertia [ɪˈnərʃə] *n* : inercia *f*

inescapable [ˌɪnɪˈskeɪpəbəl] *adj* : inevitable, ineludible — **inescapably** [-bli] *adv*

inessential [ˌɪnɪˈsɛntʃəl] *adj* : que no es esencial, innecesario

inestimable [ɪnˈɛstəməbəl] *adj* : inestimable, inapreciable

inevitability [ɪnˌɛvət̬əˈbɪlət̬i] *n*, *pl* **-ties** : inevitabilidad *f*

inevitable [ɪnˈɛvət̬əbəl] *adj* : inevitable — **inevitably** [-bli] *adv*

inexact [ˌɪnɪgˈzækt] *adj* : inexacto

inexactly [ˌɪnɪgˈzæktli] *adv* : sin exactitud

inexcusable [ˌɪnɪkˈskjuːzəbəl] *adj* : inexcusable, imperdonable — **inexcusably** [-bli] *adv*

inexhaustible [ˌɪnɪgˈzɔstəbəl] *adj* **1** INDEFATIGABLE : infatigable, incansable **2** ENDLESS : inagotable — **inexhaustibly** [-bli] *adv*

inexorable [ɪnˈɛksərəbəl] *adj* : inexorable — **inexorably** [-bli] *adv*

inexpensive [ˌɪnɪkˈspɛntsɪv] *adj* : barato, económico

inexperience [ˌɪnɪkˈspɪriənts] *n* : inexperiencia *f*

inexperienced [ˌɪnɪkˈspɪriəntst] *adj* : inexperto, novato

inexplicable [ˌɪnɪkˈsplɪkəbəl] *adj* : inexplicable — **inexplicably** [-bli] *adv*

inexpressible [ˌɪnɪkˈsprɛsəbəl] *adj* : inexpresable, inefable

inextricable [ˌɪnɪkˈstrɪkəbəl, ɪˈnɛk-ˌstrɪ-] *adj* : inextricable — **inextricably** [-bli] *adv*

infallibility [ɪnˌfæləˈbɪlət̬i] *n* : infalibilidad *f*

infallible [ɪnˈfæləbəl] *adj* : infalible — **infallibly** [-bli] *adv*

infamous [ˈɪnfəməs] *adj* : infame — **infamously** *adv*

infamy [ˈɪnfəmi] *n*, *pl* **-mies** : infamia *f*

infancy [ˈɪnfəntsi] *n*, *pl* **-cies** : infancia *f*

infant [ˈɪnfənt] *n* : bebé *m*; niño *m*, -ña *f*

infantile [ˈɪnfənˌtaɪl, -təl, -ˌtiːl] *adj* : infantil, pueril

infantile paralysis → **poliomyelitis**

infantry [ˈɪnfəntri] *n*, *pl* **-tries** : infantería *f*

infatuated [ɪnˈfætʃuˌeɪt̬əd] *adj* **to be infatuated with** : estar encaprichado con

infatuation [ɪnˌfætʃuˈeɪʃən] *n* : encaprichamiento *m*, enamoramiento *m*

infect [ɪnˈfɛkt] *vt* : infectar, contagiar

infection [ɪnˈfɛkʃən] *n* : infección *f*, contagio *m*

infectious [ɪnˈfɛkʃəs] *adj* : infeccioso, contagioso

infer [ɪnˈfər] *vt* **inferred; inferring 1** DEDUCE : deducir, inferir **2** SURMISE : concluir, suponer, tener entendido **3** IMPLY : sugerir, insinuar

inference [ˈɪnfərənts] *n* : deducción *f*, inferencia *f*, conclusión *f*

inferior¹ [ɪnˈfɪriər] *adj* : inferior, malo

inferior² *n* : inferior *mf*

inferiority [ɪnˌfɪriˈɔrət̬i] *n*, *pl* **-ties** : inferioridad *f* ⟨inferiority complex : complejo de inferioridad⟩

infernal [ɪnˈfərnəl] *adj* **1** : infernal ⟨infernal fires : fuegos infernales⟩ **2** DIABOLICAL : infernal, diabólico **3** DAMNABLE : maldito, condenado

inferno [ɪnˈfərˌnoː] *n*, *pl* **-nos** : infierno *m*

infertile [ɪnˈfərt̬əl, -ˌtaɪl] *adj* : estéril, infecundo

infertility [ˌɪnfərˈtɪlət̬i] *n* : esterilidad *f*, infecundidad *f*

infest [ɪnˈfɛst] *vt* : infestar, plagar

infestation [ˌɪnˌfɛsˈteɪʃən] *n* : infestación *f*, plaga *f*

infidel [ˈɪnfədəl, -ˌdɛl] *n* : infiel *mf*

infidelity [ˌɪnfəˈdɛlət̬i, -faɪ-] *n*, *pl* **-ties 1** UNFAITHFULNESS : infidelidad *f* **2** DISLOYALTY : deslealtad *f*

infield [ˈɪnˌfiːld] *n* : cuadro *m*, diamante *m*

infiltrate [ɪnˈfɪlˌtreɪt, ˈɪnfɪl-] *v* **-trated; -trating** *vt* : infiltrar — *vi* : infiltrarse

infiltration [ˌɪnfɪlˈtreɪʃən] *n* : infiltración *f*

infinite [ˈɪnfənət] *adj* **1** LIMITLESS : infinito, sin límites **2** VAST : infinito, vasto, extenso

infinitely [ˈɪnfənətli] *adv* : infinitamente

infinitesimal [ˌɪnˌfɪnəˈtɛsəməl] *adj* : infinitésimo, infinitesimal — **infinitesimally** *adv*

infinitive [ɪnˈfɪnət̬ɪv] *n* : infinitivo *m*

infinity [ɪnˈfɪnət̬i] *n*, *pl* **-ties 1** : infinito *m* (en matemáticas, etc.) **2** : infinidad *f* ⟨an infinity of stars : una infinidad de estrellas⟩

infirm [ɪnˈfərm] *adj* **1** FEEBLE : enfermizo, endeble **2** INSECURE : inseguro

infirmary [ɪnˈfərməri] *n*, *pl* **-ries** : enfermería *f*, hospital *m*

infirmity [ɪnˈfərmət̬i] *n*, *pl* **-ties 1** FRAILTY : debilidad *f*, endeblez *f* **2** AILMENT : enfermedad *f*, dolencia *f* ⟨the infirmities of age : los achaques de la vejez⟩

inflame [ɪnˈfleɪm] *v* **-flamed; -flaming** *vt* **1** KINDLE : inflamar, encender **2** : inflamar (una herida) **3** STIR UP : encender, provocar, inflamar — *vi* : inflamarse

inflammable [ɪnˈflæməbəl] *adj* **1** FLAMMABLE : inflamable **2** IRASCIBLE : irascible, explosivo

inflammation [ˌɪnfləˈmeɪʃən] *n* : inflamación *f*

inflammatory [ɪnˈflæməˌtori] *adj* : inflamatorio, incendiario

inflatable [ɪnˈfleɪt̬əbəl] *adj* : inflable

inflate [ɪnˈfleɪt] *vt* **-flated; -flating** : inflar, hinchar

inflation [ɪnˈfleɪʃən] *n* : inflación *f*

inflationary [ɪnˈfleɪʃəˌnɛri] *adj* : inflacionario, inflacionista

inflect [ɪnˈflɛkt] *vt* **1** CONJUGATE, DECLINE : conjugar, declinar **2** MODULATE : modular (la voz)

inflection [ɪnˈflɛkʃən] *n* : inflexión *f*

inflexibility [ɪnˌflɛksəˈbɪlət̬i] *n*, *pl* **-ties** : inflexibilidad *f*

inflexible [ɪnˈflɛksəbəl] *adj* : inflexible

inflict [ɪnˈflɪkt] *vt* **1** : infligir, causar, imponer **2 to inflict oneself on** : imponer uno su presencia (a alguien)

infliction [ɪnˈflɪkʃən] *n* : imposición *f*

influence¹ ['ɪn,flu:ənts, ɪn'flu:ənts] *vt*
-enced; -encing : influenciar, influir
en
influence² *n* **1** : influencia *f*, influjo *m*
⟨to exert influence over : ejercer influencia sobre⟩ ⟨the influence of gravity : el influjo de la gravedad⟩ **2 under
the influence** : bajo la influencia del
alcohol, embriagado
influential [,ɪnflu'entʃəl] *adj* : influyente
influenza [,ɪnflu'enzə] *n* : gripe *f*, influenza *f*, gripa *f Col, Mex*
influx ['ɪn,flʌks] *n* : afluencia *f* (de gente),
entrada *f* (de mercancías), llegada *f* (de
ideas)
inform [ɪn'fɔrm] *vt* : informar, notificar,
avisar — *vi* **to inform on** : delatar, denunciar
informal [ɪn'fɔrməl] *adj* **1** UNCEREMO-
NIOUS : sin ceremonia, sin etiqueta **2**
CASUAL : informal, familiar (dícese del
lenguaje) **3** UNOFFICIAL : extraoficial
informality [,ɪnfɔr'mæləti, -fər-] *n, pl*
-ties : informalidad *f*, familiaridad *f*,
falta *f* de ceremonia
informally [ɪn'fɔrməli] *adv* : sin ceremonias, de manera informal, informalmente
informant [ɪn'fɔrmənt] *n* : informante
mf; informador *m*, -dora *f*
information [,ɪnfər'meɪʃən] *n* : información *f*
informative [ɪn'fɔrmətɪv] *adj* : informativo, instructivo
informer [ɪn'fɔrmər] *n* : informante *mf*;
informador *m*, -dora *f*
infraction [ɪn'frækʃən] *n* : infracción *f*,
violación *f*, transgresión *f*
infrared [,ɪnfrə'rɛd] *adj* : infrarrojo
infrastructure ['ɪnfrə,strʌktʃər] *n* : infraestructura *f*
infrequent [ɪn'fri:kwənt] *adj* : infrecuente, raro
infrequently [ɪn'fri:kwəntli] *adv* : raramente, con poca frecuencia
infringe [ɪn'frɪndʒ] *v* **-fringed; -fringing**
vt : infringir, violar — *vi* **to infringe on**
: abusar de, violar
infringement [ɪn'frɪndʒmənt] *n* **1** VIO-
LATION : violación *f* (de la ley), incumplimiento *m* (de un contrato) **2**
ENCROACHMENT : usurpación *f* (de
derechos, etc.)
infuriate [ɪn'fjʊri,eɪt] *vt* **-ated; -ating**
: enfurecer, poner furioso
infuriating [ɪn'fjʊri,eɪtɪŋ] *adj* : indignante, exasperante
infuse [ɪn'fju:z] *vt* **-fused; -fusing 1** IN-
STILL : infundir **2** STEEP : hacer una
infusión de
infusion [ɪn'fju:ʒən] *n* : infusión *f*
ingenious [ɪn'dʒi:njəs] *adj* : ingenioso —
ingeniously *adv*
ingenue *or* **ingénue** ['ændʒə,nu:, 'æn-;
'ænʒə-, 'ɑ-] *n* : ingenua *f*
ingenuity [,ɪndʒə'nu:əti, -'nju:-] *n, pl*
-ities : ingenio

ingenuous [ɪn'dʒɛnjʊəs] *adj* **1** FRANK
: cándido, franco **2** NAIVE : ingenuo
— **ingenuously** *adv*
ingenuousness [ɪn'dʒɛnjʊəsnəs] *n* **1**
FRANKNESS : candidez *f*, candor *m* **2**
NAÏVETÉ : ingenuidad *f*
ingest [ɪn'dʒɛst] *vt* : ingerir
ingestion [ɪn'dʒɛstʃən] *n* : ingestión *f*
inglorious [ɪn'glɔriəs] *adj* : deshonroso,
ignominioso
ingot ['ɪŋgət] *n* : lingote *m*
ingrained [ɪn'greɪnd] *adj* : arraigado
ingrate ['ɪn,greɪt] *n* : ingrato *m*, -ta *f*
ingratiate [ɪn'greɪʃi,eɪt] *vt* **-ated; -ating**
: conseguir la benevolencia de ⟨to ingratiate oneself with someone : congraciarse con alguien⟩
ingratiating [ɪn'greɪʃi,eɪtɪŋ] *adj* : halagador, zalamero, obsequioso
ingratitude [ɪn'grætʃə,tu:d, -,tju:d] *n* : ingratitud *f*
ingredient [ɪn'gri:diənt] *n* : ingrediente
m, componente *m*
ingrown ['ɪn,gro:n] *adj* **1** : crecido hacia adentro **2 ingrown toenail** : uña *f*
encarnada
inhabit [ɪn'hæbət] *vt* : vivir en, habitar,
ocupar
inhabitable [ɪn'hæbətəbəl] *adj* : habitable
inhabitant [ɪn'hæbətənt] *n* : habitante
mf
inhalant [ɪn'heɪlənt] *n* : inhalante *m*
inhalation [,ɪnhə'leɪʃən, ,ɪnə-] *n* : inhalación *f*
inhale [ɪn'heɪl] *v* **-haled; -haling** *vt* : inhalar, aspirar — *vi* : inspirar
inhaler [ɪn'heɪlər] *n* : inhalador *m*
inhere [ɪn'hɪr] *vi* **-hered; -hering** : ser inherente
inherent [ɪn'hɪrənt, -'hɛr-] *adj* : inherente, intrínseco — **inherently** *adv*
inherit [ɪn'hɛrət] *vt* : heredar
inheritance [ɪn'hɛrətənts] *n* : herencia *f*
inheritor [ɪn'hɛrətər] *n* : heredero *m*, -da
f
inhibit [ɪn'hɪbət] *vt* IMPEDE : inhibir, impedir
inhibition [,ɪnhə'bɪʃən, ,ɪnə-] *n* : inhibición *f*, cohibición *f*
inhuman [ɪn'hju:mən, -'ju:-] *adj* : inhumano, cruel — **inhumanly** *adv*
inhumane [,ɪnhju'meɪn, -ju-] *adj* INHU-
MAN : inhumano, cruel
inhumanity [,ɪnhju'mænəti, -ju-] *n, pl*
-ties : inhumanidad *f*, crueldad *f*
inimical [ɪ'nɪmɪkəl] *adj* **1** UNFAVORABLE
: adverso, desfavorable **2** HOSTILE
: hostil — **inimically** *adv*
inimitable [ɪ'nɪmətəbəl] *adj* : inimitable
iniquitous [ɪ'nɪkwətəs] *adj* : inicuo, malvado
iniquity [ɪ'nɪkwəti] *n, pl* **-ties** : iniquidad
f
initial¹ [ɪ'nɪʃəl] *vt* **-tialed** *or* **-tialled; -tial-
ing** *or* **-tialling** : poner las iniciales a,
firmar con las iniciales
initial² *adj* : inicial, primero — **initially**
adv

initial³ *n* : inicial *f*
initiate¹ [ɪ'nɪʃi,eɪt] *vt* **-ated; -ating 1** BE-GIN : comenzar, iniciar **2** INDUCT : instruir **3** INTRODUCE : introducir, instruir
initiate² [ɪ'nɪʃiət] *n* : iniciado *m*, -da *f*
initiation [ɪ,nɪʃi'eɪʃən] *n* : iniciación *f*
initiative [ɪ'nɪʃətɪv] *n* : iniciativa *f*
initiatory [ɪ'nɪʃiə,tori] *adj* **1** INTRODUC-TORY : introductorio **2** : de iniciación ⟨initiatory rites : ritos de iniciación⟩
inject [ɪn'ʤɛkt] *vt* : inyectar
injection [ɪn'ʤɛkʃən] *n* : inyección *f*
injudicious [,ɪnʤu'dɪʃəs] *adj* : imprudente, indiscreto, poco juicioso
injunction [ɪn'ʤʌŋkʃən] *n* **1** ORDER : orden *f*, mandato *m* **2** COURT ORDER : mandamiento *m* judicial
injure ['ɪnʤər] *vt* **-jured; -juring 1** WOUND : herir, lesionar **2** HURT : lastimar, dañar, herir **3 to injure oneself** : hacerse daño
injurious [ɪn'ʤuriəs] *adj* : perjudicial ⟨injurious to one's health : perjudicial a la salud⟩
injury ['ɪnʤəri] *n*, *pl* **-ries 1** WRONG : mal *m*, injusticia *f* **2** DAMAGE, HARM : herida *f*, daño *m*, perjuicio *m*
injustice [ɪn'ʤʌstəs] *n* : injusticia *f*
ink¹ ['ɪŋk] *vt* : entintar
ink² *n* : tinta *f*
inkling ['ɪŋklɪŋ] *n* : presentimiento *m*, indicio *m*, sospecha *f*
inkwell ['ɪŋk,wɛl] *n* : tintero *m*
inky ['ɪŋki] *adj* **1** : manchado de tinta **2** BLACK : negro, impenetrable ⟨inky darkness : negra oscuridad⟩
inland¹ ['ɪn,lænd, -lənd] *adv* : hacia el interior, tierra adentro
inland² *adj* : interior
inland³ *n* : interior *m*
in-law ['ɪn,lɔ] *n* **1** : pariente *m* político **2 in-laws** *npl* : suegros *mpl*
inlay¹ [ɪn'leɪ, 'ɪn,leɪ] *vt* **-laid** [-'leɪd, -,leɪd]; **-laying** : incrustar, taracear
inlay² ['ɪn,leɪ] *n* **1** : incrustación *f* **2** : empaste *m* (de un diente)
inlet ['ɪn,lɛt, -lət] *n* : cala *f*, ensenada *f*
inmate ['ɪn,meɪt] *n* : paciente *mf* (en un hospital); preso *m*, -sa *f* (en una prisión); interno *m*, -na *f* (en un asilo)
in memoriam [,ɪnmə'moriəm] *prep* : en memoria de
inmost ['ɪn,mo:st] → **innermost**
inn ['ɪn] *n* **1** : posada *f*, hostería *f*, fonda *f* **2** TAVERN : taberna *f*
innards ['ɪnərdz] *npl* : entrañas *fpl*, tripas *fpl fam*
innate [ɪ'neɪt] *adj* **1** INBORN : innato **2** INHERENT : inherente
inner ['ɪnər] *adj* : interior, interno
innermost ['ɪnər,mo:st] *adj* : más íntimo, más profundo
innersole ['ɪnər'so:l] → **insole**
inning ['ɪnɪŋ] *n* : entrada *f*
innkeeper ['ɪn,ki:pər] *n* : posadero *m*, -ra *f*
innocence ['ɪnəsənts] *n* : inocencia *f*

innocent¹ ['ɪnəsənt] *adj* : inocente — **innocently** *adv*
innocent² *n* : inocente *mf*
innocuous [ɪ'nɑkjəwəs] *adj* **1** HARM-LESS : inocuo **2** INOFFENSIVE : inofensivo
innovate ['ɪnə,veɪt] *vi* **-vated; -vating** : innovar
innovation [,ɪnə'veɪʃən] *n* : innovación *f*, novedad *f*
innovative ['ɪnə,veɪṭɪv] *adj* : innovador
innovator ['ɪnə,veɪṭər] *n* : innovador *m*, -dora *f*
innuendo [,ɪnju'ɛndo] *n*, *pl* **-dos** or **-does** : insinuación *f*, indirecta *f*
innumerable [ɪ'nu:mərəbəl, -'nju:-] *adj* : innumerable
inoculate [ɪ'nɑkjə,leɪt] *vt* **-lated; -lating** : inocular
inoculation [ɪ,nɑkjə'leɪʃən] *n* : inoculación *f*
inoffensive [,ɪnə'fɛntsɪv] *adj* : inofensivo
inoperable [ɪn'ɑpərəbəl] *adj* : inoperable
inoperative [ɪn'ɑpərəṭɪv, -,reɪ-] *adj* : inoperante
inopportune [ɪn,ɑpər'tu:n, -'tju:n] *adj* : inoportuno — **inopportunely** *adv*
inordinate [ɪn'ɔrdənət] *adj* : excesivo, inmoderado, desmesurado — **inordinately** *adv*
inorganic [,ɪn,ɔr'gænɪk] *adj* : inorgánico
inpatient ['ɪn,peɪʃənt] *n* : paciente *mf* hospitalizado
input¹ ['ɪn,pʊt] *vt* **inputted** or **input; inputting** : entrar (datos, información)
input² *n* **1** CONTRIBUTION : aportación *f*, contribución *f* **2** ENTRY : entrada *f* (de datos) **3** ADVICE, OPINION : consejos *mpl*, opinión *f*
inquest ['ɪn,kwɛst] *n* INQUIRY, INVESTI-GATION : investigación *f*, averiguación *f*, pesquisa *f* (judicial)
inquire [ɪn'kwaɪr] *v* **-quired; -quiring** *vt* : preguntar, informarse de, inquirir ⟨he inquired how to get in : preguntó como entrar⟩ — *vi* **1** ASK : preguntar, informarse ⟨to inquire about : informarse sobre⟩ ⟨to inquire after (someone) : preguntar por (alguien)⟩ **2 to inquire into** INVESTIGATE : investigar, inquirir sobre
inquiringly [ɪn'kwaɪrɪŋli] *adv* : inquisitivamente
inquiry ['ɪn,kwaɪri, ɪn'kwaɪri; 'ɪnkwəri, 'ɪŋ-] *n*, *pl* **-ries 1** QUESTION : pregunta *f* ⟨to make inquiries about : pedir información sobre⟩ **2** INVESTIGATION : investigación *f*, inquisición *f*, pesquisa *f*
inquisition [,ɪnkwə'zɪʃən, ,ɪŋ-] *n* **1** : inquisición *f*, interrogatorio *m*, investigación *f* **2 the Inquisition** : la Inquisición *f*
inquisitive [ɪn'kwɪzəṭɪv] *adj* : inquisidor, inquisitivo, curioso — **inquisitively** *adv*

inquisitiveness [ɪn'kwɪzətɪvnəs] *n* : curiosidad *f*
inquisitor [ɪn'kwɪzətər] *n* : inquisidor *m*, -dora *f*; interrogador *m*, -dora *f*
inroad ['ɪn₁roːd] *n* **1** ENCROACHMENT, INVASION : invasión *f*, incursión *f* **2 to make inroads into** : ocupar parte de (un tiempo), agotar parte de (ahorros, recursos), invadir (un territorio)
insane [ɪn'seɪn] *adj* **1** MAD : loco, demente ⟨to go insane : volverse loco⟩ **2** ABSURD : absurdo, insensato ⟨an insane scheme : un proyecto insensato⟩
insanely [ɪn'seɪnli] *adv* : como un loco ⟨insanely suspicious : loco de recelo⟩
insanity [ɪn'sænəti] *n, pl* **-ties 1** MADNESS : locura *f* **2** FOLLY : locura *f*, insensatez *f*
insatiable [ɪn'seɪʃəbəl] *adj* : insaciable
— **insatiably** [-bli] *adv*
inscribe [ɪn'skraɪb] *vt* **-scribed; -scribing 1** ENGRAVE : inscribir, grabar **2** ENROLL : inscribir **3** DEDICATE : dedicar (un libro)
inscription [ɪn'skrɪpʃən] *n* : inscripción *f* (en un monumento), dedicación *f* (en un libro), leyenda *f* (de una ilustración, etc.)
inscrutable [ɪn'skruːt̬əbəl] *adj* : inescrutable, misterioso — **inscrutably** [-bli] *adv*
inseam ['ɪn₁siːm] *n* : entrepierna *f*
insect ['ɪn₁sɛkt] *n* : insecto *m*
insecticidal [ɪn₁sɛktə'saɪdəl] *adj* : insecticida
insecticide [ɪn'sɛktə₁saɪd] *n* : insecticida *m*
insecure [₁ɪnsɪ'kjʊr] *adj* : inseguro, poco seguro — **insecurely** *adv*
insecurely [₁ɪnsɪ'kjʊrli] *adv* : inseguramente
insecurity [₁ɪnsɪ'kjʊrəti] *n, pl* **-ties** : inseguridad *f*
inseminate [ɪn'sɛmə₁neɪt] *vt* **-nated; -nating** : inseminar
insemination [ɪn₁sɛmə'neɪʃən] *n* : inseminación *f*
insensibility [ɪn₁sɛntsə'bɪləti] *n, pl* **-ties** : insensibilidad *f*
insensible [ɪn'sɛntsəbəl] *adj* **1** UNCONSCIOUS : inconsciente, sin conocimiento **2** NUMB : insensible, entumecido **3** UNAWARE : inconsciente
insensitive [ɪn'sɛntsət̬ɪv] *adj* : insensible
insensitivity [ɪn₁sɛntsə'tɪvəti] *n, pl* **-ties** : insensibilidad *f*
inseparable [ɪn'sɛpərəbəl] *adj* : inseparable
insert¹ [ɪn'sərt] *vt* **1** : insertar, introducir, poner, meter ⟨insert your key in the lock : mete tu llave en la cerradura⟩ **2** INTERPOLATE : interpolar, intercalar
insert² ['ɪn₁sərt] *n* : inserción *f*, hoja *f* insertada (en una revista, etc.)
insertion [ɪn'sərʃən] *n* : inserción *f*
inset ['ɪn₁sɛt] *n* : página *f* intercalada (en un libro), entredós *m* (de encaje en la ropa)

inshore¹ ['ɪn'ʃor] *adv* : hacia la costa
inshore² *adj* : cercano a la costa, costero ⟨inshore fishing : pesca costera⟩
inside¹ [ɪn'saɪd, 'ɪn₁saɪd] *adv* : adentro, dentro ⟨to run inside : correr para adentro⟩ ⟨inside and out : por dentro y por fuera⟩
inside² *adj* **1** : interior, de adentro, de dentro ⟨the inside lane : el carril interior⟩ **2** : confidencial ⟨inside information : información confidencial⟩
inside³ *n* **1** : interior *m*, parte *f* de adentro **2 insides** *npl* BELLY, GUTS : tripas *fpl fam* **3 inside out** : al revés
inside⁴ *prep* **1** INTO : al interior de **2** WITHIN : dentro de **3** (*referring to time*) : en menos de ⟨inside an hour : en menos de una hora⟩
inside of *prep* INSIDE : dentro de
insider [ɪn'saɪdər] *n* : persona *f* enterada
insidious [ɪn'sɪdiəs] *adj* : insidioso — **insidiously** *adv*
insidiousness [ɪn'sɪdiəsnəs] *n* : insidia *f*
insight ['ɪn₁saɪt] *n* : perspicacia *f*, penetración *f*
insightful [ɪn'saɪtfəl] *adj* : perspicaz
insignia [ɪn'sɪgniə] *or* **insigne** [-₁ni:] *n, pl* **-nia** *or* **-nias** : insignia *f*, enseña *f*
insignificance [₁ɪnsɪg'nɪfɪkənts] *n* : insignificancia *f*
insignificant [₁ɪnsɪg'nɪfɪkənt] *adj* : insignificante
insincere [₁ɪnsɪn'sɪr] *adj* : insincero, poco sincero
insincerely [₁ɪnsɪn'sɪrli] *adv* : con poca sinceridad
insincerity [₁ɪnsɪn'sɛrəti, -'sɪr-] *n, pl* **-ties** : insinceridad *f*
insinuate [ɪn'sɪnjʊ₁eɪt] *vt* **-ated; -ating** : insinuar
insinuation [ɪn₁sɪnjʊ'eɪʃən] *n* : insinuación *f*
insipid [ɪn'sɪpəd] *adj* : insípido
insist [ɪn'sɪst] *v* : insistir
insistence [ɪn'sɪstənts] *n* : insistencia *f*
insistent [ɪn'sɪstənt] *adj* : insistente — **insistently** *adv*
insofar as [₁ɪnso'faræz] *conj* : en la medida en que, en tanto que, en cuanto a
insole ['ɪn₁soːl] *n* : plantilla *f*
insolence ['ɪntsələnts] *n* : insolencia *f*
insolent ['ɪntsələnt] *adj* : insolente
insolubility [ɪn₁saljʊ'bɪləti] *n* : insolubilidad *f*
insoluble [ɪn'saljʊbəl] *adj* : insoluble
insolvency [ɪn'salvəntsi] *n, pl* **-cies** : insolvencia *f*
insolvent [ɪn'salvənt] *adj* : insolvente
insomnia [ɪn'samniə] *n* : insomnio *m*
insomuch as [₁ɪnso'mʌtʃæz] → **inasmuch as**
insomuch that *conj* SO : así que, de manera que
inspect [ɪn'spɛkt] *vt* : inspeccionar, examinar, revisar
inspection [ɪn'spɛkʃən] *n* : inspección *f*, examen *m*, revisión *f*, revista *f* (de tropas)

inspector [ɪn'spɛktər] *n* : inspector *m*, -tora *f*

inspiration [ˌɪntspə'reɪʃən] *n* : inspiración *f*

inspirational [ˌɪntspə'reɪʃənəl] *adj* : inspirador

inspire [ɪn'spaɪr] *v* **-spired; -spiring** *vt* 1 INHALE : inhalar, aspirar 2 STIMULATE : estimular, animar, inspirar 3 INSTILL : inspirar, infundir — *vi* : inspirar

instability [ˌɪntstə'bɪləti] *n, pl* **-ties** : inestabilidad *f*

install [ɪn'stɔl] *vt* **-stalled; -stalling** 1 : instalar ⟨to install the new president : instalar el presidente nuevo⟩ ⟨to install a fan : montar un abanico⟩ 2 **to install oneself** : instalarse

installation [ˌɪntstə'leɪʃən] *n* : instalación *f*

installment [ɪn'stɔlmənt] *n* 1 : plazo *m*, cuota *f* ⟨to pay in four installments : pagar a cuatro plazos⟩ 2 : entrega *f* (de una publicación o telenovela) 3 INSTALLATION : instalación *f*

instance ['ɪntstənts] *n* 1 INSTIGATION : instancia *f* 2 EXAMPLE : ejemplo *m* ⟨for instance : por ejemplo⟩ 3 OCCASION : instancia *f*, caso *m*, ocasión *f* ⟨he prefers, in this instance, to remain anonymous : en este caso prefiere quedarse anónimo⟩

instant[1] ['ɪntstənt] *adj* 1 IMMEDIATE : inmediato, instantáneo ⟨an instant reply : una respuesta inmediata⟩ 2 : instantáneo ⟨instant coffee : café instantáneo⟩

instant[2] *n* : momento *m*, instante *m*

instantaneous [ˌɪntstən'teɪniəs] *adj* : instantáneo

instantaneously [ˌɪntstən'teɪniəsli] *adv* : instantáneamente, al instante

instantly ['ɪntstəntli] *adv* : al instante, instantáneamente

instead [ɪn'stɛd] *adv* 1 : en cambio, en lugar de eso, en su lugar ⟨Dad was going, but Mom went instead : papá iba a ir, pero mamá fue en su lugar⟩ 2 RATHER : al contrario

instead of *prep* : en vez de, en lugar de

instep ['ɪnˌstɛp] *n* : empeine *m*

instigate ['ɪntstəˌgeɪt] *vt* **-gated; -gating** INCITE, PROVOKE : instigar, incitar, provocar, fomentar

instigation [ˌɪntstə'geɪʃən] *n* : instancia *f*, incitación *f*

instigator ['ɪntstəˌgeɪtər] *n* : instigador *m*, -dora *f*; incitador *m*, -dora *f*

instill [ɪn'stɪl] *vt* **-stilled; -stilling** : inculcar, infundir

instinct ['ɪnˌstɪŋkt] *n* 1 TALENT : instinto *m*, don *m* ⟨an instinct for the right word : un don para escoger la palabra apropiada⟩ 2 : instinto *m* ⟨maternal instincts : instintos maternales⟩

instinctive [ɪn'stɪŋktɪv] *adj* : instintivo

instinctively [ɪn'stɪŋktɪvli] *adv* : instintivamente, por instinto

instinctual [ɪn'stɪŋktʃuəl] *adj* : instintivo

institute[1] ['ɪntstəˌtuːt, -ˌtjuːt] *vt* **-tuted; -tuting** 1 ESTABLISH : establecer, instituir, fundar 2 INITIATE : iniciar, empezar, entablar

institute[2] *n* : instituto *m*

institution [ˌɪntstə'tuːʃən, -'tjuː-] *n* 1 ESTABLISHING : institución *f*, establecimiento *m* 2 CUSTOM : institución *f*, tradición *f* ⟨the institution of marriage : la institución del matrimonio⟩ 3 ORGANIZATION : institución *f*, organismo *m* 4 ASYLUM : asilo *m*

institutional [ˌɪntstə'tuːʃənəl, -'tjuː-] *adj* : institucional

institutionalize [ˌɪntstə'tuːʃənəˌlaɪz, -'tjuː-] *vt* **-ized; -izing** 1 : institucionalizar ⟨institutionalized values : valores institucionalizados⟩ 2 : internar ⟨institutionalized orphans : huérfanos internados⟩

instruct [ɪn'strʌkt] *vt* 1 TEACH, TRAIN : instruir, adiestrar, enseñar 2 COMMAND : mandar, ordenar, dar instrucciones a

instruction [ɪn'strʌkʃən] *n* 1 TEACHING : instrucción *f*, enseñanza *f* 2 COMMAND : orden *f*, instrucción *f* 3 **instructions** *npl* DIRECTIONS : instrucciones *fpl*, modo *m* de empleo

instructional [ɪn'strʌkʃənəl] *adj* : instructivo, educativo

instructive [ɪn'strʌktɪv] *adj* : instructivo

instructor [ɪn'strʌktər] *n* : instructor *m*, -tora *f*

instrument ['ɪntstrəmənt] *n* : instrumento *m*

instrumental [ˌɪntstrə'mɛntəl] *adj* : instrumental

instrumentalist [ˌɪntstrə'mɛntəlɪst] *n* : instrumentista *mf*

insubordinate [ˌɪnsə'bɔrdənət] *adj* : insubordinado

insubordination [ˌɪnsəˌbɔrdən'eɪʃən] *n* : insubordinación *f*

insubstantial [ˌɪnsəb'stæntʃəl] *adj* : insustancial, poco nutritivo (dícese de una comida), poco sólido (dícese de una estructura o un argumento)

insufferable [ɪn'sʌfərəbəl] *adj* UNBEARABLE : insufrible, intolerable, inaguantable, insoportable — **insufferably** [-bli] *adv*

insufficiency [ˌɪnsə'fɪʃəntsi] *n, pl* **-cies** : insuficiencia *f*

insufficient [ˌɪnsə'fɪʃənt] *adj* : insuficiente — **insufficiently** *adv*

insular ['ɪntsʊlər, -sjʊ-] *adj* 1 : isleño (dícese de la gente), insular (dícese del clima) ⟨insular residents : residentes de la isla⟩ 2 NARROW-MINDED : de miras estrechas

insularity [ˌɪntsʊ'lærəti, -sjʊ-] *n* : insularidad *f*

insulate ['ɪntsəˌleɪt] *vt* **-lated; -lating** : aislar

insulation [ˌɪntsə'leɪʃən] *n* : aislamiento *m*

insulator ['ɪntsəˌleɪtər] *n* : aislador *m* (pieza), aislante *m* (material)

insulin ['ɪntsələn] *n* : insulina *f*
insult¹ [ɪn'sʌlt] *vt* : insultar, ofender, injuriar
insult² ['ɪnˌsʌlt] *n* : insulto *m*, injuria *f*, agravio *m*
insulting [ɪn'sʌltɪŋ] *adj* : ofensivo, injurioso, insultante
insultingly [ɪn'sʌltɪŋli] *adv* : ofensivamente, de manera insultante
insuperable [ɪn'suːpərəbəl] *adj* : insuperable — **insuperably** [-bli] *adv*
insurable [ɪn'ʃʊrəbəl] *adj* : asegurable
insurance [ɪn'ʃʊrənts, 'ɪnˌʃʊr-] *n* : seguro *m* ⟨life insurance : seguro de vida⟩ ⟨insurance company : compañía de seguros⟩
insure [ɪn'ʃʊr] *vt* **-sured; -suring 1** UNDERWRITE : asegurar **2** ENSURE : asegurar, garantizar
insured [ɪn'ʃʊrd] *n* : asegurado *m*, -da *f*
insurer [ɪn'ʃʊrər] *n* : asegurador *m*, -dora *f*
insurgent¹ [ɪn'sərdʒənt] *adj* : insurgente
insurgent² *n* : insurgente *mf*
insurmountable [ˌɪnsər'maʊntəbəl] *adj* : insuperable, insalvable — **insurmountably** [-bli] *adv*
insurrection [ˌɪnsə'rɛkʃən] *n* : insurrección *f*, levantamiento *m*, alzamiento *m*
intact [ɪn'tækt] *adj* : intacto
intake ['ɪnˌteɪk] *n* **1** OPENING : entrada *f*, toma *f* ⟨fuel intake : toma de combustible⟩ **2** : entrada *f* (de agua o aire), consumo *m* (de sustancias nutritivas) **3 intake of breath** : inhalación *f*
intangible [ɪn'tændʒəbəl] *adj* : intangible, impalpable — **intangibly** [-bli] *adv*
integer ['ɪntɪdʒər] *n* : entero *m*
integral ['ɪntɪɡrəl] *adj* : integral, esencial
integrate ['ɪntəˌɡreɪt] *v* **-grated; -grating** *vt* **1** UNITE : integrar, unir **2** DESEGREGATE : eliminar la segregación de — *vi* : integrarse
integration [ˌɪntə'ɡreɪʃən] *n* : integración *f*
integrity [ɪn'tɛɡrəti] *n* : integridad *f*
intellect ['ɪntəlˌɛkt] *n* : intelecto *m*, inteligencia *f*, capacidad *f* intelectual
intellectual¹ [ˌɪntə'lɛktʃʊəl] *adj* : intelectual — **intellectually** *adv*
intellectual² *n* : intelectual *mf*
intellectualism [ˌɪntə'lɛktʃʊəˌlɪzəm] *n* : intelectualismo *m*
intelligence [ɪn'tɛlədʒənts] *n* **1** : inteligencia *f* **2** INFORMATION, NEWS : inteligencia *f*, información *f*, noticias *fpl*
intelligent [ɪn'tɛlədʒənt] *adj* : inteligente — **intelligently** *adv*
intelligentsia [ɪnˌtɛlə'dʒɛntsiə, -'ɡɛn-] *ns & pl* : intelectualidad *f*
intelligibility [ɪnˌtɛlədʒə'bɪləti] *n* : inteligibilidad *f*
intelligible [ɪn'tɛlədʒəbəl] *adj* : inteligible, comprensible — **intelligibly** [-bli] *adv*
intemperance [ɪn'tɛmpərənts] *n* : inmoderación *f*, intemperancia *f*

intemperate [ɪn'tɛmpərət] *adj* : excesivo, inmoderado, desmedido
intend [ɪn'tɛnd] *vt* **1** MEAN : querer decir ⟨that's not what I intended : eso no es lo que quería decir⟩ **2** PLAN : tener planeado, proyectar, proponerse ⟨I intend to finish by Thursday : me propongo acabar para el jueves⟩
intended [ɪn'tɛndəd] *adj* **1** PLANNED : previsto, proyectado **2** INTENTIONAL : intencional, deliberado
intense [ɪn'tɛnts] *adj* **1** EXTREME : intenso, extremo ⟨intense pain : dolor intenso⟩ **2** : profundo, intenso ⟨to my intense relief : para mi alivio profundo⟩ ⟨intense enthusiasm : entusiasmo ardiente⟩
intensely [ɪn'tɛntsli] *adv* : sumamente, profundamente, intensamente
intensification [ɪnˌtɛntsəfə'keɪʃən] *n* : intensificación *f*
intensify [ɪn'tɛntsəˌfaɪ] *v* **-fied; -fying** *vt* **1** STRENGTHEN : intensificar, redoblar ⟨to intensify one's efforts : redoblar uno sus esfuerzos⟩ **2** SHARPEN : intensificar, agudizar (dolor, ansiedad) — *vi* : intensificarse, hacerse más intenso
intensity [ɪn'tɛntsəti] *n, pl* **-ties** : intensidad *f*
intensive [ɪn'tɛntsɪv] *adj* : intensivo — **intensively** *adv*
intent¹ [ɪn'tɛnt] *adj* **1** FIXED : concentrado, fijo ⟨an intent stare : una mirada fija⟩ **2 intent on** *or* **intent upon** : resuelto a, atento a
intent² *n* **1** PURPOSE : intención *f*, propósito *m* **2 for all intents and purposes** : a todos los efectos, prácticamente
intention [ɪn'tɛntʃən] *n* : intención *f*, propósito *m*
intentional [ɪn'tɛntʃənəl] *adj* : intencional, deliberado
intentionally [ɪn'tɛntʃənəli] *adv* : a propósito, adrede
intently [ɪn'tɛntli] *adv* : atentamente, fijamente
inter [ɪn'tər] *vt* **-terred; -terring** : enterrar, inhumar
interact [ˌɪntər'ækt] *vi* : interactuar, actuar recíprocamente, relacionarse
interaction [ˌɪntər'ækʃən] *n* : interacción *f*, interrelación *f*
interactive [ˌɪntər'æktɪv] *adj* : interactivo
interbreed [ˌɪntər'briːd] *v* **-bred** [-'brɛd]; **-breeding** *vt* : cruzar — *vi* : cruzarse
intercalate [ɪn'tərkəˌleɪt] *vt* **-lated; -lating** : intercalar
intercede [ˌɪntər'siːd] *vi* **-ceded; -ceding** : interceder
intercept [ˌɪntər'sɛpt] *vt* : interceptar
interception [ˌɪntər'sɛpʃən] *n* : intercepción *f*
intercession [ˌɪntər'sɛʃən] *n* : intercesión *f*

interchange¹ [ˌɪntər'ʧeɪnʤ] *vt* **-changed; -changing** : intercambiar
interchange² ['ɪntər.ʧeɪnʤ] *n* **1** EXCHANGE : intercambio *m*, cambio *m* **2** JUNCTION : empalme *m*, enlace *m* de carreteras
interchangeable [ˌɪntər'ʧeɪnʤəbəl] *adj* : intercambiable
intercity ['ɪntər'sɪti] *adj* : interurbano
intercollegiate [ˌɪntərkə'li:ʤət, -ʤiət] *adj* : interuniversitario
interconnect [ˌɪntərkə'nɛkt] *vt* **1** : conectar, interconectar (en tecnología) **2** RELATE : interrelacionar — *vi* **1** : conectar **2** : interrelacionarse
intercontinental [ˌɪntər.kɑntən'nɛtəl] *adj* : intercontinental
intercourse ['ɪntər.kors] *n* **1** RELATIONS : relaciones *fpl*, trato *m* **2** COPULATION : acto *m* sexual, relaciones *fpl* sexuales, coito *m*
interdenominational [ˌɪntərdɪˌnɑmə'neɪʃənəl] *adj* : interconfesional
interdepartmental [ˌɪntərdɪˌpɑrt'mɛntəl, -ˌdi:-] *adj* : interdepartamental
interdependence [ˌɪntərdɪ'pɛndənts] *n* : interdependencia *f*
interdependent [ˌɪntərdɪ'pɛndənt] *adj* : interdependiente
interdict [ˌɪntər'dɪkt] *vt* **1** PROHIBIT : prohibir **2** : cortar (las líneas de comunicación o provisión del enemigo)
interest¹ ['ɪntrəst, -tə.rɛst] *vt* : interesar
interest² *n* **1** SHARE, STAKE : interés *m*, participación *f* **2** BENEFIT : provecho *m*, beneficio *m*, interés *m* ⟨in the public interest : en el interés público⟩ **3** CHARGE : interés *m*, cargo *m* ⟨compound interest : interés compuesto⟩ **4** CURIOSITY : interés *m*, curiosidad *f* **5** COLOR : color *m*, interés *m* ⟨places of local interest : lugares de color local⟩ **6** HOBBY : afición *f*
interesting ['ɪntrəstɪŋ, -tə.rɛstɪŋ] *adj* : interesante — **interestingly** *adv*
interface ['ɪntər.feɪs] *n* **1** : punto *m* de contacto ⟨oil-water interface : punto de contacto entre el agua y el aceite⟩ **2** : interfaz *f* (de una computadora), interfase *f*
interfere [ˌɪntər'fɪr] *vi* **-fered; -fering** **1** INTERPOSE : interponerse, hacer interferencia ⟨to interfere with a play : obstruir una jugada⟩ **2** MEDDLE : entrometerse, interferir, intervenir **3 to interfere with** DISRUPT : afectar (una actividad), interferir (la radiotransmisión) **4 to interfere with** TOUCH : tocar ⟨someone interfered with my papers : alguien tocó mis papeles⟩
interference [ˌɪntər'fɪrənts] *n* : interferencia *f*, intromisión *f*
intergalactic [ˌɪntərgə'læktɪk] *adj* : intergaláctico
intergovernmental [ˌɪntər.gʌvər-'mɛntəl, -vərn-] *adj* : intergubernamental
interim¹ ['ɪntərəm] *adj* : interino, provisional

interim² *n* **1** : interín *m*, intervalo *m* **2 in the interim** : en el interín, mientras tanto
interior¹ [ɪn'tɪriər] *adj* : interior
interior² *n* : interior *m*
interject [ˌɪntər'ʤɛkt] *vt* : interponer, agregar
interjection [ˌɪntər'ʤɛkʃən] *n* **1** : interjección *f* (en lingüística) **2** EXCLAMATION : exclamación *f* **3** INTERPOSITION, INTERRUPTION : interposición *f*, interrupción *f*
interlace [ˌɪntər'leɪs] *vt* **-laced; -lacing** **1** INTERWEAVE : entrelazar **2** INTERSPERSE : intercalar
interlock [ˌɪntər'lɑk] *vt* **1** UNITE : trabar, unir **2** ENGAGE, MESH : engranar — *vi* : entrelazarse, trabarse
interloper [ˌɪntər'lo:pər] *n* **1** INTRUDER : intruso *m*, -sa *f* **2** MEDDLER : entrometido *m*, -da *f*
interlude ['ɪntər.lu:d] *n* **1** INTERVAL : intervalo *m*, intermedio *m* (en el teatro) **2** : interludio *m* (en música)
intermarriage [ˌɪntər'mærɪʤ] *n* **1** : matrimonio *m* mixto (entre miembros de distintas razas o religiones) **2** : matrimonio *m* entre miembros del mismo grupo
intermarry [ˌɪntər'mæri] *vi* **-married; -marrying** **1** : casarse (con miembros de otros grupos) **2** : casarse entre sí (con miembros del mismo grupo)
intermediary¹ [ˌɪntər'mi:di.ɛri] *adj* : intermediario
intermediary² *n, pl* **-aries** : intermediario *m*, -ria *f*
intermediate¹ [ˌɪntər'mi:diət] *adj* : intermedio
intermediate² *n* GO-BETWEEN : intermediario *m*, -ria *f*; mediador *m*, -dora *f*
interment [ɪn'tərmənt] *n* : entierro *m*
interminable [ɪn'tərmənəbəl] *adj* : interminable, constante — **interminably** [-bli] *adv*
intermingle [ˌɪntər'mɪŋgəl] *vt* **-mingled; -mingling** : entremezclar, mezclar — *vi* : entremezclarse
intermission [ˌɪntər'mɪʃən] *n* : intermisión *f*, intervalo *m*, intermedio *m*
intermittent [ˌɪntər'mɪtənt] *adj* : intermitente — **intermittently** *adv*
intermix [ˌɪntər'mɪks] *vt* : entremezclar
intern¹ ['ɪn.tərn, ɪn'tərn] *vt* : confinar (durante la guerra) — *vi* : servir de interno, hacer las prácticas
intern² ['ɪn.tərn] *n* : interno *m*, -na *f*
internal [ɪn'tərnəl] *adj* : interno, interior ⟨internal bleeding : hemorragia interna⟩ ⟨internal affairs : asuntos interiores, asuntos domésticos⟩ — **internally** *adv*
international [ˌɪntər'næʃənəl] *adj* : internacional — **internationally** *adv*
internationalize [ˌɪntər'næʃənə.laɪz] *vt* **-ized; -izing** : internacionalizar
internee [ˌɪn.tər'ni:] *n* : interno *m*, -na *f*
Internet ['ɪntər.nɛt] *n* : Internet *mf*

internist [ˈɪnˌtərnɪst] *n* : internista *mf*

interpersonal [ˌɪntərˈpərsənəl] *adj* : interpersonal

interplay [ˈɪntərˌpleɪ] *n* : interacción *f*, juego *m*

interpolate [ɪnˈtərpəˌleɪt] *vt* **-lated;** **-lating** : interpolar

interpose [ˌɪntərˈpoːz] *v* **-posed; -posing** *vt* : interponer, interrumpir con — *vi* : interponerse

interposition [ˌɪntərpəˈzɪʃən] *n* : interposición *f*

interpret [ɪnˈtərprət] *vt* : interpretar

interpretation [ɪnˌtərprəˈteɪʃən] *n* : interpretación *f*

interpretative [ɪnˈtərprəˌteɪɾɪv] *adj* : interpretativo

interpreter [ɪnˈtərprəɾər] *n* : intérprete *mf*

interpretive [ɪnˈtərprəɾɪv] *adj* : interpretativo

interracial [ˌɪntərˈreɪʃəl] *adj* : interracial

interrelate [ˌɪntəriˈleɪt] *v* **-related;** **-relating** : interrelacionar

interrelationship [ˌɪntəriˈleɪʃənˌʃɪp] *n* : interrelación *f*

interrogate [ɪnˈtɛrəˌgeɪt] *vt* **-gated;** **-gating** : interrogar, someter a un interrogatorio

interrogation [ɪnˌtɛrəˈgeɪʃən] *n* : interrogación *f*

interrogative[1] [ˌɪntəˈrɑgəɾɪv] *adj* : interrogativo

interrogative[2] *n* : interrogativo *m*

interrogator [ɪnˈtɛrəˌgeɪɾər] *n* : interrogador *m*, -dora *f*

interrogatory [ˌɪntəˈrɑgəˌtɔri] *adj* → **interrogative**[1]

interrupt [ˌɪntəˈrʌpt] *v* : interrumpir

interruption [ˌɪntəˈrʌpʃən] *n* : interrupción *f*

intersect [ˌɪntərˈsɛkt] *vt* : cruzar, cortar — *vi* : cruzarse (dícese de los caminos), intersectarse (dícese de las líneas o figuras), cortarse

intersection [ˌɪntərˈsɛkʃən] *n* : intersección *f*, cruce *m*

intersperse [ˌɪntərˈspərs] *vt* **-spersed;** **-spersing** : intercalar, entremezclar

interstate [ˌɪntərˈsteɪt] *adj* : interestatal

interstellar [ˌɪntərˈstelər] *adj* : interestelar

interstice [ɪnˈtərstəs] *n, pl* **-stices** [-stəˌsiːz, -stəsəz] : intersticio *m*

intertwine [ˌɪntərˈtwaɪn] *vi* **-twined;** **-twining** : entrelazarse

interval [ˈɪntərvəl] *n* : intervalo *m*

intervene [ˌɪntərˈviːn] *vi* **-vened;** **-vening** **1** ELAPSE : transcurrir, pasar ⟨the intervening years : los años intermediarios⟩ **2** INTERCEDE : intervenir, interceder, mediar

intervention [ˌɪntərˈvɛnʃən] *n* : intervención *f*

interview[1] [ˈɪntərˌvjuː] *vt* : entrevistar — *vi* : hacer entrevistas

interview[2] *n* : entrevista *f*

interviewer [ˈɪntərˌvjuːər] *n* : entrevistador *m*, -dora *f*

interweave [ˌɪntərˈwiːv] *v* **-wove** [-ˈwoːv]; **-woven** [-ˈwoːvən]; **-weaving** *vt* : entretejer, entrelazar — *vi* INTERTWINE : entrelazarse, entretejerse

interwoven [ˌɪntərˈwoːvən] *adj* : entretejido

intestate [ɪnˈtɛsˌteɪt, -tət] *adj* : intestado

intestinal [ɪnˈtɛstənəl] *adj* : intestinal

intestine [ɪnˈtɛstən] *n* **1** : intestino *m* **2 small intestine** : intestino *m* delgado **3 large intestine** : intestino *m* grueso

intimacy [ˈɪntəməsi] *n, pl* **-cies** **1** CLOSENESS : intimidad *f* **2** FAMILIARITY : familiaridad *f*

intimate[1] [ˈɪntəˌmeɪt] *vt* **-mated; -mating** : insinuar, dar a entender

intimate[2] [ˈɪntəmət] *adj* **1** CLOSE : íntimo, de confianza ⟨intimate friends : amigos íntimos⟩ **2** PRIVATE : íntimo, privado ⟨intimate clubs : clubes íntimos⟩ **3** INNERMOST, SECRET : íntimo, secreto ⟨intimate fantasies : fantasías secretas⟩

intimate[3] *n* : amigo *m* íntimo, amiga *f* íntima

intimidate [ɪnˈtɪməˌdeɪt] *vt* **-dated; -dating** : intimidar

intimidation [ɪnˌtɪməˈdeɪʃən] *n* : intimidación *f*

into [ˈɪnˌtuː] *prep* **1** (*indicating motion*) : en, a, contra, dentro de ⟨she got into bed : se metió en la cama⟩ ⟨to get into a plane : subir a un avión⟩ ⟨he crashed into the wall : chocó contra la pared⟩ ⟨looking into the sun : mirando al sol⟩ **2** (*indicating state or condition*) : a, en ⟨to burst into tears : echarse a llorar⟩ ⟨the water turned into ice : el agua se convirtió en hielo⟩ ⟨to translate into English : traducir al inglés⟩ **3** (*indicating time*) ⟨far into the night : hasta bien entrada la noche⟩ ⟨he's well into his eighties : tiene los ochenta bien cumplidos⟩ **4** (*in mathematics*) ⟨3 into 12 is 4 : 12 dividido por 3 es 4⟩

intolerable [ɪnˈtɑlərəbəl] *adj* : intolerable — **intolerably** [-bli] *adv*

intolerance [ɪnˈtɑlərənts] *n* : intolerancia *f*

intolerant [ɪnˈtɑlərənt] *adj* : intolerante

intonation [ˌɪntoˈneɪʃən] *n* : entonación *f*

intone [ɪnˈtoːn] *vt* **-toned; -toning** : entonar

intoxicant [ɪnˈtɑksɪkənt] *n* : bebida *f* alcohólica

intoxicate [ɪnˈtɑksəˌkeɪt] *vt* **-cated; -cating** : emborrachar, embriagar

intoxicated [ɪnˈtɑksəˌkeɪɾəd] *adj* : borracho, embriagado

intoxicating [ɪnˈtɑksəˌkeɪɾɪŋ] *adj* : embriagador

intoxication [ɪnˌtɑksəˈkeɪʃən] *n* : embriaguez *f*

intractable [ɪnˈtræktəbəl] *adj* : obstinado, intratable

intramural [ˌɪntrəˈmjʊrəl] *adj* : interno, dentro de la universidad

intransigence [ɪn'trænts̬ədʒənts, -'trænz-] *n* : intransigencia *f*

intransigent [ɪn'trænts̬ədʒənt, -'trænzə-] *adj* : intransigente

intransitive [ɪn'trænts̬ət̬ɪv, -'trænzə-] *adj* : intransitivo

intravenous [ˌɪntrə'viːnəs] *adj* : intravenoso — **intravenously** *adv*

intrepid [ɪn'trɛpəd] *adj* : intrépido

intricacy ['ɪntrɪkəsi] *n, pl* -**cies** : complejidad *f*, lo intrincado

intricate ['ɪntrɪkət] *adj* : intrincado, complicado — **intricately** *adv*

intrigue[1] [ɪn'triːg] *v* -**trigued; -triguing** : intrigar

intrigue[2] ['ɪnˌtriːg, ɪn'triːg] *n* : intriga *f*

intriguing [ɪn'triːgɪŋ] *adj* : intrigante, fascinante

intrinsic [ɪn'trɪnzɪk, -'trɪnts̬ɪk] *adj* : intrínseco, esencial — **intrinsically** [-zɪkli, -sɪ-] *adv*

introduce [ˌɪntrə'duːs, -'djuːs] *vt* -**duced; -ducing 1** : presentar ⟨let me introduce my father : permítame presentar a mi padre⟩ **2** : introducir (algo nuevo), lanzar (un producto), presentar (una ley), proponer (una idea o un tema)

introduction [ˌɪntrə'dʌkʃən] *n* : introducción *f*, presentación *f*

introductory [ˌɪntrə'dʌktəri] *adj* : introductorio, preliminar, de introducción

introspection [ˌɪntrə'spɛkʃən] *n* : introspección *f*

introspective [ˌɪntrə'spɛktɪv] *adj* : introspectivo — **introspectively** *adv*

introvert ['ɪntrəˌvərt] *n* : introvertido *m*, -da *f*

introverted ['ɪntrəˌvərt̬əd] *adj* : introvertido

intrude [ɪn'truːd] *v* -**truded; -truding** *vi* **1** INTERFERE : inmiscuirse, entrometerse **2** DISTURB, INTERRUPT : molestar, estorbar, interrumpir — *vt* : introducir por fuerza

intruder [ɪn'truːdər] *n* : intruso *m*, -sa *f*

intrusion [ɪn'truːʒən] *n* : intrusión *f*

intrusive [ɪn'truːsɪv] *adj* : intruso

intuit [ɪn'tuːɪt, -'tjuː-] *vt* : intuir

intuition [ˌɪntu'ɪʃən, -tju-] *n* : intuición *f*

intuitive [ɪn'tuːət̬ɪv, -'tjuː-] *adj* : intuitivo — **intuitively** *adv*

inundate ['ɪnənˌdeɪt] *vt* -**dated; -dating** : inundar

inundation [ˌɪnən'deɪʃən] *n* : inundación *f*

inure [ɪ'nʊr, -'njʊr] *vt* -**ured; -uring** : acostumbrar, habituar

invade [ɪn'veɪd] *vt* -**vaded; -vading** : invadir

invader [ɪn'veɪdər] *n* : invasor *m*, -sora *f*

invalid[1] [ɪn'væləd] *adj* : inválido, nulo

invalid[2] ['ɪnvələd] *adj* : inválido, discapacitado

invalid[3] ['ɪnvələd] *n* : inválido *m*, -da *f*

invalidate [ɪn'væləˌdeɪt] *vt* -**dated; -dating** : invalidar

invalidity [ˌɪnvə'lɪdət̬i] *n, pl* -**ties** : invalidez *f*, falta de validez *f*

invaluable [ɪn'væljəbəl, -'væljʊə-] *adj* : invalorable, inestimable, inapreciable

invariable [ɪn'væriəbəl] *adj* : invariable, constante — **invariably** [-bli] *adv*

invasion [ɪn'veɪʒən] *n* : invasión *f*

invasive [ɪn'veɪsɪv] *adj* : invasivo

invective [ɪn'vɛktɪv] *n* : invectiva *f*, improperio *m*, vituperio *m*

inveigh [ɪn'veɪ] *vi* **to inveigh against** : arremeter contra, lanzar invectivas contra

inveigle [ɪn'veɪgəl, -'viː-] *vt* -**gled; -gling** : engatusar, embaucar, persuadir con engaños

invent [ɪn'vɛnt] *vt* : inventar

invention [ɪn'vɛntʃən] *n* : invención *f*, invento *m*

inventive [ɪn'vɛntɪv] *adj* : inventivo

inventiveness [ɪn'vɛntɪvnəs] *n* : ingenio *m*, inventiva *f*

inventor [ɪn'vɛntər] *n* : inventor *m*, -tora *f*

inventory[1] ['ɪnvənˌtɔri] *vt* -**ried; -rying** : inventariar

inventory[2] *n, pl* -**ries 1** LIST : inventario *m* **2** STOCK : existencias *fpl*

inverse[1] [ɪn'vərs, 'ɪnˌvərs] *adj* : inverso — **inversely** *adv*

inverse[2] *n* : inverso *m*

inversion [ɪn'vərʒən] *n* : inversión *f*

invert [ɪn'vərt] *vt* : invertir

invertebrate[1] [ɪn'vərt̬əbrət, -ˌbreɪt] *adj* : invertebrado

invertebrate[2] *n* : invertebrado *m*

invest [ɪn'vɛst] *vt* **1** AUTHORIZE : investir, autorizar **2** CONFER : conferir **3** : invertir, dedicar ⟨he invested his savings in stocks : invirtió sus ahorros en acciones⟩ ⟨to invest one's time : dedicar uno su tiempo⟩

investigate [ɪn'vɛstəˌgeɪt] *v* -**gated; -gating** : investigar

investigation [ɪnˌvɛstə'geɪʃən] *n* : investigación *f*, estudio *m*

investigative [ɪn'vɛstəˌgeɪt̬ɪv] *adj* : investigador

investigator [ɪn'vɛstəˌgeɪt̬ər] *n* : investigador *m*, -dora *f*

investiture [ɪn'vɛstəˌtʃʊr, -tʃər] *n* : investidura *f*

investment [ɪn'vɛstmənt] *n* : inversión *f*

investor [ɪn'vɛstər] *n* : inversor *m*, -sora *f*; inversionista *mf*

inveterate [ɪn'vɛt̬ərət] *adj* **1** DEEP-SEATED : inveterado, enraizado **2** HABITUAL : empedernido, incorregible

invidious [ɪn'vɪdiəs] *adj* **1** OBNOXIOUS : repugnante, odioso **2** UNJUST : injusto — **invidiously** *adv*

invigorate [ɪn'vɪgəˌreɪt] *vt* -**rated; -rating** : vigorizar, animar

invigorating [ɪn'vɪgəˌreɪt̬ɪŋ] *adj* : vigorizante, estimulante

invigoration [ɪnˌvɪgə'reɪʃən] *n* : animación *f*

invincibility [ɪnˌvɪnts̬ə'bɪlət̬i] *n* : invencibilidad *f*

invincible [ɪn'vɪntsəbəl] *adj* : invencible — **invincibly** [-bli] *adv*
inviolable [ɪn'vaɪələbəl] *adj* : inviolable
inviolate [ɪn'vaɪələt] *adj* : inviolado, puro
invisibility [ɪn,vɪzə'bɪləti] *n* : invisibilidad *f*
invisible [ɪn'vɪzəbəl] *adj* : invisible — **invisibly** [-bli] *adv*
invitation [,ɪnvə'teɪʃən] *n* : invitación *f*
invite [ɪn'vaɪt] *vt* **-vited; -viting 1** ATTRACT : atraer, tentar ⟨a book that invites interest : un libro que atrae el interés⟩ **2** PROVOKE : provocar, buscar ⟨to invite trouble : buscarse problemas⟩ **3** ASK : invitar ⟨we invited them for dinner : los invitamos acenar⟩ **4** SOLICIT : solicitar, buscar (preguntas, comentarios, etc.)
inviting [ɪn'vaɪtɪŋ] *adj* : atractivo, atrayente
invocation [,ɪnvə'keɪʃən] *n* : invocación *f*
invoice[1] ['ɪn,vɔɪs] *vt* **-voiced; -voicing** : facturar
invoice[2] *n* : factura *f*
invoke [ɪn'vo:k] *vt* **-voked; -voking 1** : invocar, apelar a ⟨she invoked our aid : apeló a nuestra ayuda⟩ **2** CITE : invocar, citar ⟨to invoke a precedent : invocar un precedente⟩ **3** CONJURE UP : hacer aparecer, invocar
involuntary [ɪn'valən,teri] *adj* : involuntario — **involuntarily** [ɪn-,valən'trəli] *adv*
involve [ɪn'valv] *vt* **-volved; -volving 1** ENGAGE : ocupar (con una tarea, etc.) **2** IMPLICATE : involucrar, enredar, implicar ⟨to be involved in a crime : estar involucrado en un crimen⟩ **3** CONCERN : concernir, afectar **4** CONNECT : conectar, relacionar **5** ENTAIL, INCLUDE : suponer, incluir, consistir en ⟨what does the job involve? : ¿en qué consiste el trabajo?⟩ **6 to be involved with someone** : tener una relación (amorosa) con alguien
involved [ɪn'valvd] *adj* **1** COMPLEX, INTRICATE : complicado, complejo **2** CONCERNED : interesado, afectado
involvement [ɪn'valvmənt] *n* **1** PARTICIPATION : participación *f*, complicidad *f* **2** RELATIONSHIP : relación *f*
invulnerable [ɪn'vʌlnərəbəl] *adj* : invulnerable
inward[1] ['ɪnwərd] *or* **inwards** [-wərdz] *adv* : hacia adentro, hacia el interior
inward[2] *adj* INSIDE : interior, interno
inwardly ['ɪnwərdli] *adv* **1** MENTALLY, SPIRITUALLY : por dentro **2** INTERNALLY : internamente, interiormente **3** PRIVATELY : para sus adentros, para sí
iodide ['aɪə,daɪd] *n* : yoduro *m*
iodine ['aɪə,daɪn, -dən] *n* : yodo *m*, tintura *f* de yodo
iodize ['aɪə,daɪz] *vt* **-dized; -dizing** : yodar

ion ['aɪən, 'aɪ,ɑn] *n* : ion *m*
ionic [aɪ'ɑnɪk] *adj* : iónico
ionize ['aɪə,naɪz] *v* **ionized; ionizing** : ionizar
ionosphere [aɪ'ɑnə,sfɪr] *n* : ionosfera *f*
iota [aɪ'o:tə] *n* : pizca *f*, ápice *m*
IOU [,aɪ,o'ju:] *n* : pagaré *m*, vale *m*
IPA [,aɪ,pi:'eɪ] *n* International Phonetic Alphabet : AFI *m*
IQ [,aɪ'kju:] *n* (intelligence quotient) : CI *m*, coeficiente *m* intelectual
Iranian [ɪ'reɪniən, -'ræ-, -'rɑ-; aɪ'-] *n* : iraní *mf* — **Iranian** *adj*
Iraqi [ɪ'rɑki:] *n* : iraquí *mf* — **Iraqi** *adj*
irascibility [ɪ,ræsə'bɪləti] *n* : irascibilidad *f*
irascible [ɪ'ræsəbəl] *adj* : irascible
irate [aɪ'reɪt] *adj* : furioso, airado, iracundo — **irately** *adv*
ire ['aɪr] *n* : ira *f*, cólera *f*
iridescence [,ɪrə'dɛsənts] *n* : iridiscencia *f*
iridescent [,ɪrə'dɛsənt] *adj* : iridiscente
iridium [ɪ'rɪdiəm] *n* : iridio *m*
iris ['aɪrəs] *n, pl* **irises** *or* **irides** ['aɪrə-,di:z, 'ɪr-] **1** : iris *m* (del ojo) **2** : lirio *m* (planta)
Irish[1] ['aɪrɪʃ] *adj* : irlandés
Irish[2] **1** : irlandés *m* (idioma) **2 the Irish** *npl* : los irlandeses
Irishman ['aɪrɪʃmən] *n, pl* **-men** : irlandés *m*
Irishwoman ['aɪrɪʃ,wʊmən] *n, pl* **-women** : irlandesa *f*
irk ['ərk] *vt* : fastidiar, irritar, preocupar
irksome ['ərksəm] *adj* : irritante, fastidioso — **irksomely** *adv*
iron[1] ['aɪərn] *v* : planchar
iron[2] *n* **1** : hierro *m*, fierro *m* ⟨a will of iron : una voluntad de hierro, una voluntad férrea⟩ **2** : plancha *f* (para planchar la ropa)
ironclad ['aɪərn'klæd] *adj* **1** : acorazado, blindado **2** STRICT : riguroso, estricto
ironic [aɪ'rɑnɪk] *or* **ironical** [-nɪkəl] *adj* : irónico — **ironically** [-kli] *adv*
ironing ['aɪərnɪŋ] *n* **1** PRESSING : planchada *f* **2** : ropa *f* para planchar
ironing board *n* : tabla *f* (de planchar)
ironwork ['aɪərn,wərk] *n* **1** : obra *f* de hierro **2 ironworks** *npl* : fundición *f*
ironworker ['aɪərn,wərkər] *n* : fundidor *m*, -dora *f*
irony ['aɪrəni] *n, pl* **-nies** : ironía *f*
irradiate [ɪ'reɪdi,eɪt] *vt* **-ated; -ating** : irradiar, radiar
irradiation [ɪ,reɪdi'eɪʃən] *n* : irradiación *f*, radiación *f*
irrational [ɪ'ræʃənəl] *adj* : irracional — **irrationally** *adv*
irrationality [ɪ,ræʃə'næləti] *n, pl* **-ties** : irracionalidad *f*
irreconcilable [ɪ,rɛkən'saɪləbəl] *adj* : irreconciliable
irrecoverable [,ɪrɪ'kʌvərəbəl] *adj* : irrecuperable — **irrecoverably** [-bli] *adv*

irredeemable [ˌɪrɪˈdiːməbəl] *adj* **1** : irredimible (dícese de un bono) **2** HOPELESS : irremediable, irreparable

irreducible [ˌɪrɪˈduːsəbəl, -ˈdjuː-] *adj* : irreducible — **irreducibly** [-bli] *adv*

irrefutable [ˌɪrɪˈfjuːt̬əbəl, ɪrˈrɛfjə-] *adj* : irrefutable

irregular[1] [ɪˈrɛgjələr] *adj* : irregular — **irregularly** *adv*

irregular[2] *n* **1** : soldado *m* irregular **2 irregulars** *npl* : artículos *mpl* defectuosos

irregularity [ɪˌrɛgjəˈlærət̬i] *n, pl* **-ties** : irregularidad *f*

irrelevance [ɪˈrɛləvənts] *n* : irrelevancia *f*

irrelevant [ɪˈrɛləvənt] *adj* : irrelevante

irreligious [ˌɪrɪˈlɪdʒəs] *adj* : irreligioso

irreparable [ɪˈrɛpərəbəl] *adj* : irreparable

irreplaceable [ˌɪrɪˈpleɪsəbəl] *adj* : irreemplazable, insustituible

irrepressible [ˌɪrɪˈprɛsəbəl] *adj* : incontenible, incontrolable

irreproachable [ɪrɪˈproːtʃəbəl] *adj* : irreprochable, intachable

irresistible [ˌɪrɪˈzɪst̬əbəl] *adj* : irresistible — **irresistibly** [-bli] *adv*

irresolute [ɪˈrɛzəˌluːt] *adj* : irresoluto, indeciso

irresolutely [ɪˈrɛzəˌluːtli, -ˌrzəˈluːt-] *adv* : de manera indecisa

irresolution [ɪˌrɛzəˈluːʃən] *n* : irresolución *f*

irrespective of [ˌɪrɪˈspɛktɪvəv] *prep* : sin tomar en consideración, sin tener en cuenta

irresponsibility [ˌɪrɪˌspantsəˈbɪlət̬i] *n, pl* **-ties** : irresponsabilidad *f*, falta *f* de responsabilidad

irresponsible [ˌɪrɪˈspantsəbəl] *adj* : irresponsable — **irresponsibly** [-bli] *adv*

irretrievable [ˌɪrɪˈtriːvəbəl] *adj* IRRECOVERABLE : irrecuperable

irreverence [ɪˈrɛvərənts] *n* : irreverencia *f*, falta *f* de respeto

irreverent [ɪˈrɛvərənt] *adj* : irreverente, irrespetuoso

irreversible [ˌɪrɪˈvərsəbəl] *adj* : irreversible

irrevocable [ɪˈrɛvəkəbəl] *adj* : irrevocable — **irrevocably** [-bli] *adv*

irrigate [ˈɪrəˌgeɪt] *vt* **-gated; -gating** : irrigar, regar

irrigation [ˌɪrəˈgeɪʃən] *n* : irrigación *f*, riego *m*

irritability [ˌɪrət̬əˈbɪlət̬i] *n, pl* **-ties** : irritabilidad *f*

irritable [ˈɪrət̬əbəl] *adj* : irritable, colérico

irritably [ˈɪrət̬əbli] *adv* : con irritación

irritant[1] [ˈɪrət̬ənt] *adj* : irritante

irritant[2] *n* : agente *m* irritante

irritate [ˈɪrəˌteɪt] *vt* **-tated; -tating 1** ANNOY : irritar, molestar **2** : irritar (en medicina)

irritating [ˈɪrəˌteɪt̬ɪŋ] *adj* : irritante

irritatingly [ˈɪrəˌteɪt̬ɪŋli] *adv* : de modo irritante, fastidiosamente

irritation [ˌɪrəˈteɪʃən] *n* : irritación *f*

is → **be**

Islam [ɪsˈlɑm, ɪz-, -ˈlæm; ˈɪsˌlɑm, ˈɪz-, -ˌlæm] *n* : el Islam

Islamic [ɪsˈlɑmɪk, ɪz-, -ˈlæ-] *adj* : islámico

island [ˈaɪlənd] *n* : isla *f*

islander [ˈaɪləndər] *n* : isleño *m*, -ña *f*

isle [ˈaɪl] *n* : isla *f*, islote *m*

islet [ˈaɪlət] *n* : islote *m*

isolate [ˈaɪsəˌleɪt] *vt* **-lated; -lating** : aislar

isolated [ˈaɪsəˌleɪt̬əd] *adj* : aislado, solo

isolation [ˌaɪsəˈleɪʃən] *n* : aislamiento *m*

isometric [ˌaɪsəˈmɛtrɪk] *adj* : isométrico

isometrics [ˌaɪsəˈmɛtrɪks] *ns & pl* : isometría *f*

isosceles [aɪˈsɑsəˌliːz] *adj* : isósceles

isotope [ˈaɪsəˌtoːp] *n* : isótopo *m*

Israeli [ɪzˈreɪli] *n* : israelí *mf* — **Israeli** *adj*

issue[1] [ˈɪˌʃuː] *v* **-sued; -suing** *vi* **1** EMERGE : emerger, salir, fluir **2** DESCEND : descender (dícese de los padres o antepasados específicos) **3** EMANATE, RESULT : emanar, surgir, resultar — *vt* **1** EMIT : emitir **2** DISTRIBUTE : emitir, distribuir ⟨to issue a new stamp : emitir un sello nuevo⟩ **3** PUBLISH : publicar

issue[2] *n* **1** EMERGENCE, FLOW : emergencia *f*, flujo *m* **2** PROGENY : descendencia *f*, progenie *f* **3** OUTCOME, RESULT : desenlace *m*, resultado *m*, consecuencia *f* **4** MATTER, QUESTION : asunto *m*, cuestión *f* **5** PUBLICATION : publicación *f*, distribución *f*, emisión *f* **6** : número *m* (de un periódico o una revista)

isthmus [ˈɪsməs] *n* : istmo *m*

it [ˈɪt] *pron* **1** (*as subject; generally omitted*) : él, ella, ello ⟨it's a big building : es un edificio grande⟩ ⟨who was it? : ¿quién era?⟩ **2** (*as indirect object*) : le ⟨I'll give it some water : voy a darle agua⟩ **3** (*as direct object*) : lo, la ⟨give it to me : dámelo⟩ **4** (*as object of a preposition; generally omitted*) : él, ella, ello ⟨behind it : detrás, detrás de él⟩ **5** (*in impersonal constructions*) ⟨it's raining : está lloviendo⟩ ⟨it's 8 o'clock : son las ocho⟩ **6** (*as the implied subject or object of a verb*) ⟨it is necessary to study : es necesario estudiar⟩ ⟨to give it all one's got : dar lo mejor de sí⟩

Italian [ɪˈtæliən, aɪ-] *n* **1** : italiano *m*, -na *f* **2** : italiano *m* (idioma) — **Italian** *adj*

italic[1] [ɪˈtælɪk, aɪ-] *adj* : en cursiva, en bastardilla

italic[2] *n* : cursiva *f*, bastardilla *f*

italicize [ɪˈtæləˌsaɪz, aɪ-] *vt* **-cized; -cizing** : poner en cursiva

itch[1] [ˈɪtʃ] *vi* **1** : picar ⟨her arm itched : le pica el brazo⟩ **2** : morirse ⟨they were itching to go outside : se morían por salir⟩ — *vt* : dar picazón, hacer picar

itch² *n* **1** ITCHING : picazón *f*, picor *m*, comezón *f* **2** RASH : sarpullido *m*, erupción *f* **3** DESIRE : ansia *f*, deseo *m*

itchy ['ɪtʃi] *adj* **itchier; -est** : que pica, que da comezón

it'd ['ɪt̮əd] (*contraction of* **it had** *or* **it would**) → **have, would**

item ['aɪt̮əm] *n* **1** OBJECT : artículo *m*, pieza *f* ⟨item of clothing : prenda de vestir⟩ **2** : punto *m* (en una agenda), número *m* (en el teatro), ítem *m* (en un documento) **3 news item** : noticia *f*

itemize ['aɪt̮ə,maɪz] *vt* **-ized; -izing** : detallar, enumerar, listar

itinerant [aɪ'tɪnərənt] *adj* : itinerante, ambulante

itinerary [aɪ'tɪnə,rɛri] *n, pl* **-aries** : itinerario *m*

it'll ['ɪt̮əl] (*contraction of* **it shall** *or* **it will**) → **shall, will**

its ['ɪts] *adj* : su, sus ⟨its kennel : su perrera⟩ ⟨a city and its inhabitants : una ciudad y sus habitantes⟩

it's ['ɪts] (*contraction of* **it is** *or* **it has**) → **be, have**

itself [ɪt'sɛlf] *pron* **1** (*used reflexively*) : se ⟨the cat gave itself a bath : el gato se bañó⟩ **2** (*used for emphasis*) : (él) mismo, (ella) misma, sí (mismo), solo ⟨he is courtesy itself : es la misma cortesía⟩ ⟨in and of itself : por sí mismo⟩ ⟨it opened by itself : se abrió solo⟩

IUD [,aɪ,ju:'di:] *n* :intrauterine *d*evice : DIU *m*, dispositivo *m* intrauterino

I've ['aɪv] (*contraction of* **I have**) → **have**

ivory ['aɪvəri] *n, pl* **-ries** **1** : marfil *m* **2** : color *m* de marfil

ivy ['aɪvi] *n, pl* **ivies** **1** : hiedra *f*, yedra *f* **2** → **poison ivy**

J

j ['dʒeɪ] *n, pl* **j's** *or* **js** ['dʒeɪz] : décima letra del alfabeto inglés

jab¹ ['dʒæb] *v* **jabbed; jabbing** *vt* **1** PUNCTURE : clavar, pinchar **2** POKE : dar, golpear (con la punta de algo) ⟨he jabbed me in the ribs : me dio un codazo en las costillas⟩ — *vi* **to jab at** : dar, golpear

jab² *n* **1** PRICK : pinchazo *m* **2** POKE : golpe *m* abrupto

jabber¹ ['dʒæbər] *v* : farfullar

jabber² *n* : galimatías *m*, farfulla *f*

jack¹ ['dʒæk] *vt* **to jack up 1** : levantar (con un gato) **2** INCREASE : subir, aumentar

jack² *n* **1** : gato *m*, cric *m* ⟨hydraulic jack : gato hidráulico⟩ **2** FLAG : pabellón *m* **3** SOCKET : enchufe *m* hembra **4** : jota *f*, valet *m* ⟨jack of hearts : jota de corazones⟩ **5 jacks** *npl* : cantillos *mpl*

jackal ['dʒækəl] *n* : chacal *m*

jackass ['dʒæk,æs] *n* : asno *m*, burro *m*

jacket ['dʒækət] *n* **1** : chaqueta *f* **2** COVER : sobrecubierta *f* (de un libro), carátula *f* (de un disco)

jackhammer ['dʒæk,hæmər] *n* : martillo *m* neumático

jack–in–the–box ['dʒækɪnðə,baks] *n* : caja *f* de sorpresa

jackknife¹ ['dʒæk,naɪf] *vi* **-knifed; -knifing** : doblarse como una navaja, plegarse

jackknife² *n* : navaja *f*

jack–of–all–trades *n* : persona *f* que sabe un poco de todo, persona *f* de muchos oficios

jack–o'–lantern ['dʒækə,læntərn] *n* : linterna *f* hecha de una calabaza

jackpot ['dʒæk,pat] *n* **1** : primer premio *m*, gordo *m* **2 to hit the jackpot** : sacarse la lotería, sacarse el gordo

jackrabbit ['dʒæk,ræbət] *n* : liebre *f* grande de Norteamérica

jade ['dʒeɪd] *n* : jade *m*

jaded ['dʒeɪdəd] *adj* **1** TIRED : agotado **2** BORED : hastiado

jagged ['dʒægəd] *adj* : dentado, mellado

jaguar ['dʒæg,war, 'dʒægjʊ,war] *n* : jaguar *m*

jai alai ['haɪ,laɪ] *n* : jai alai *m*, pelota *f* vasca

jail¹ ['dʒeɪl] *vt* : encarcelar

jail² *n* : cárcel *f*

jailbreak ['dʒeɪl,breɪk] *n* : fuga *f*, huida *f* (de la cárcel)

jailer *or* **jailor** ['dʒeɪlər] *n* : carcelero *m*, -ra *f*

jalapeño [,halə'peɪnjo, ,hæ-, -'pi:no] *n* : jalapeño *m*

jalopy [dʒə'lapi] *n, pl* **-lopies** : cacharro *m fam*, carro *m* destartalado

jalousie ['dʒæləsi] *n* : celosía *f*

jam¹ ['dʒæm] *v* **jammed; jamming** *vt* **1** CRAM : apiñar, embutir **2** BLOCK : atascar, atorar **3 to jam on the brakes** : frenar en seco — *vi* STICK : atascarse, atrancarse

jam² *n* **1** *or* **traffic jam** : atasco *m*, embotellamiento *m* (de tráfico) **2** PREDICAMENT : lío *m*, aprieto *m*, apuro *m* **3** : mermelada *f* ⟨strawberry jam : mermelada de fresa⟩

Jamaican [dʒə'meɪkən] *n* : jamaiquino *m*, -na *f*; jamaicano *m*, -na *f* — **Jamaican** *adj*

jamb ['dʒæm] *n* : jamba *f*

jamboree [,dʒæmbə'ri:] *n* : fiesta *f* grande

jangle¹ ['dʒæŋgəl] *v* **-gled; -gling** *vi* : hacer un ruido metálico — *vt* **1** : hacer sonar **2 to jangle one's nerves** : irritar, crispar

jangle² *n* : ruido *m* metálico

janitor ['dʒænət̮ər] *n* : portero *m*, -ra *f*; conserje *mf*

January ['dʒænju,ɛri] *n* : enero *m*

Japanese [,dʒæpə'ni:z, -'ni:s] *n* **1**

: japonés *m*, -nesa *f* **2** : japonés *m* (idioma) — **Japanese** *adj*

jar¹ ['dʒɑr] *v* **jarred; jarring** *vi* **1** GRATE : chirriar **2** CLASH : desentonar **3** SHAKE : sacudirse **4 to jar on** : crispar, enervar — *vt* JOLT : sacudir

jar² *n* **1** GRATING : chirrido *m* **2** JOLT : vibración *f*, sacudida *f* **3** : tarro *m*, bote *m*, pote *m* ⟨a jar of honey : un tarro de miel⟩

jargon ['dʒɑrgən] *n* : jerga *f*

jasmine ['dʒæzmən] *n* : jazmín *m*

jasper ['dʒæspər] *n* : jaspe *m*

jaundice ['dʒɔndɪs] *n* : ictericia *f*

jaundiced ['dʒɔndɪst] *adj* **1** : ictérico **2** EMBITTERED, RESENTFUL : amargado, resentido, negativo ⟨with a jaundiced eye : con una actitud de cinismo⟩

jaunt ['dʒɔnt] *n* : excursión *f*, paseo *m*

jauntily ['dʒɔntəli] *adv* : animadamente

jauntiness ['dʒɔntinəs] *n* : animación *f*, vivacidad *f*

jaunty ['dʒɔnti] *adj* **-tier; -est** **1** SPRIGHTLY : animado, alegre **2** RAKISH : desenvuelto, desenfadado

Javanese [ˌdʒævə'niːz, ˌdʒɑ-, -'niːs] *n* **1** : javanés *m* (idioma) **2** : javanés *m*, -nesa *f* — **Javanese** *adj*

javelin ['dʒævələn] *n* : jabalina *f*

jaw¹ ['dʒɔ] *vi* GAB : cotorrear *fam*, parlotear *fam*

jaw² *n* **1** : mandíbula *f*, quijada *f* **2** : mordaza *f* (de una herramienta) **3 the jaws of death** : las garras *f* de la muerte

jawbone ['dʒɔˌboːn] *n* : mandíbula *f*

jay ['dʒeɪ] *n* : arrendajo *m*, chara *f Mex*, azulejo *m Mex*

jaybird ['dʒeɪˌbərd] *n* → **jay**

jaywalk ['dʒeɪˌwɔk] *vi* : cruzar la calle sin prudencia

jaywalker ['dʒeɪˌwɔkər] *n* : peatón *m* imprudente

jazz¹ ['dʒæz] *vt* **to jazz up** : animar, alegrar

jazz² *n* : jazz *m*

jazzy ['dʒæzi] *adj* **jazzier; -est** **1** : con ritmo de jazz **2** FLASHY, SHOWY : llamativo, ostentoso

jealous ['dʒɛləs] *adj* : celoso, envidioso — **jealously** *adv*

jealousy ['dʒɛləsi] *n* : celos *mpl*, envidia *f*

jeans ['dʒiːnz] *npl* : jeans *mpl*, vaqueros *mpl*

jeep ['dʒiːp] *n* : jeep *m*

jeer¹ ['dʒɪr] *vi* **1** BOO : abuchear **2** SCOFF : mofarse, burlarse — *vt* RIDICULE : mofarse de, burlarse de

jeer² *n* **1** : abucheo *m* **2** TAUNT : mofa *f*, burla *f*

Jehovah [dʒɪ'hoːvə] *n* : Jehová *m*

jell ['dʒɛl] *vi* **1** SET : gelificarse, cuajar **2** FORM : cuajar, formarse (una idea, etc.)

jelly¹ ['dʒɛli] *v* **jellied; jellying** *vi* **1** JELL : gelificarse, cuajar **2** : hacer jalea — *vt* : gelificar

jelly² *n, pl* **-lies** **1** : jalea *f* **2** GELATIN : gelatina *f*

jellyfish ['dʒɛliˌfɪʃ] *n* : medusa *f*

jeopardize ['dʒɛpərˌdaɪz] *vt* **-dized; -dizing** : arriesgar, poner en peligro

jeopardy ['dʒɛpərdi] *n* : peligro *m*, riesgo *m*

jerk¹ ['dʒərk] *vt* **1** JOLT : sacudir **2** TUG, YANK : darle un tirón a — *vi* JOLT : dar sacudidas ⟨the train jerked along : el tren iba moviéndose a sacudidas⟩

jerk² *n* **1** TUG : tirón *m*, jalón *m* **2** JOLT : sacudida *f* brusca **3** FOOL : estúpido *m*, -da *f*; idiota *mf*

jerkin ['dʒərkən] *n* : chaqueta *f* sin mangas, chaleco *m*

jerky ['dʒərki] *adj* **jerkier; -est** **1** : espasmódico (dícese de los movimientos) **2** CHOPPY : inconexo (dícese de la prosa) — **jerkily** [-kəli] *adv*

jerry-built ['dʒɛriˌbɪlt] *adj* : mal construido, chapucero

jersey ['dʒərzi] *n, pl* **-seys** : jersey *m*

jest¹ ['dʒɛst] *vi* : bromear

jest² *n* : broma *f*, chiste *m*

jester ['dʒɛstər] *n* : bufón *m*, -fona *f*

Jesuit ['dʒɛzuət] *n* : jesuita *m* — **Jesuit** *adj*

Jesus ['dʒiːzəs, -zəz] *n* **1** : Jesús *m* **2 Jesus Christ** : Jesucristo *m* **3 Jesus (Christ)!** *fam* : ¡por Dios!

jet¹ ['dʒɛt] *v* **jetted; jetting** *vt* SPOUT : arrojar a chorros — *vi* **1** GUSH : salir a chorros, chorrear **2** FLY : viajar en avión, volar

jet² *n* **1** STREAM : chorro *m* **2** *or* **jet airplane** : avión *m* a reacción, reactor *m* **3** : azabache *m* (mineral) **4 jet engine** : reactor *m*, motor *m* a reacción **5 jet lag** : desajuste *m* de horario (debido a un vuelo largo)

jet-propelled *adj* : a reacción

jetsam ['dʒɛtsəm] *n* **flotsam and jetsam** : restos *mpl*, desechos *mpl*

jettison ['dʒɛtəsən] *vt* **1** : echar al mar **2** DISCARD : desechar, deshacerse de

jetty ['dʒɛti] *n, pl* **-ties** **1** PIER, WHARF : desembarcadero *m*, muelle *m* **2** BREAKWATER : malecón *m*, rompeolas *m*

Jew ['dʒuː] *n* : judío *m*, -día *f*

jewel ['dʒuːəl] *n* **1** : joya *f*, alhaja *f* **2** GEM : piedra *f* preciosa, gema *f* **3** : rubí *m* (de un reloj) **4** TREASURE : joya *f*, tesoro *m*

jeweler *or* **jeweller** ['dʒuːələr] *n* : joyero *m*, -ra *f*

jewelry ['dʒuːəlri] *n* : joyas *fpl*, alhajas *fpl*

Jewish ['dʒuːɪʃ] *adj* : judío

jib ['dʒɪb] *n* : foque *m* (de un barco)

jibe ['dʒaɪb] *vi* **jibed; jibing** AGREE : concordar

jiffy ['dʒɪfi] *n, pl* **-fies** : santiamén *m*, segundo *m*, momento *m*

jig¹ ['dʒɪg] *v* **jigged; jigging** : bailar la giga

jig² *n* **1** : giga *f* **2 the jig is up** : se acabó la fiesta

jigger ['dʒɪgər] *n* : medida de 1 a 2 onzas (para licores)

jiggle¹ ['ʤɪgəl] v **-gled; -gling** vt : agitar o sacudir ligeramente — vi : agitarse, vibrar
jiggle² n : sacudida f, vibración f
jigsaw ['ʤɪg,sɔ] n **1** : sierra f de vaivén **2 jigsaw puzzle** : rompecabezas m
jilt ['ʤɪlt] vt : dejar plantado, dar calabazas a
jimmy¹ ['ʤɪmi] vt **-mied; -mying** : forzar con una palanqueta
jimmy² n, pl **-mies** : palanqueta f
jingle¹ ['ʤɪŋgəl] v **-gled; -gling** vi : tintinear — vt : hacer sonar
jingle² n **1** TINKLE : tintineo m, retintín m **2** : canción f rimada
jingoism ['ʤɪŋgo,ɪzəm] n : jingoísmo m, patriotería f
jingoistic [,ʤɪŋgo'ɪstɪk] or **jingoist** ['ʤɪŋgoɪst] adj : jingoísta, patriotero
jinx¹ ['ʤɪŋks] vt : traer mala suerte a, salar CoRi, Mex
jinx² n **1** : cenizo m, -za f **2 to put a jinx on** : echarle el mal de ojo a
jitters ['ʤɪtərz] npl : nervios mpl ⟨he got the jitters : se puso nervioso⟩
jittery ['ʤɪtəri] adj : nervioso
job ['ʤab] n **1** : trabajo m ⟨he did odd jobs for her : le hizo algunos trabajos⟩ **2** CHORE, TASK : tarea f, quehacer m **3** EMPLOYMENT : trabajo m, empleo m, puesto m
jobber ['ʤabər] n MIDDLEMAN : intermediario m, -ria f
jock ['ʤak] n : deportista mf, atleta mf
jockey¹ ['ʤaki] v **-eyed; -eying** vt **1** MANIPULATE : manipular **2** MANEUVER : maniobrar — vi **to jockey for position** : maniobrar para conseguir algo
jockey² n, pl **-eys** : jockey mf
jocose [ʤo'kos] adj : jocoso
jocular ['ʤakjʊlər] adj : jocoso — **jocularly** adv
jocularity [,ʤakjʊ'lærəti] n : jocosidad f
jodhpurs ['ʤadpərz] npl : pantalones mpl de montar
jog¹ ['ʤag] v **jogged; jogging** vt **1** NUDGE : dar, empujar, codear **2 to jog one's memory** : refrescar la memoria — vi **1** RUN : correr despacio, trotar, hacer footing (como ejercicio) **2** TRUDGE : andar a trote corto
jog² n **1** PUSH, SHAKE : empujoncito m, sacudida f leve **2** TROT : trote m corto, footing m (en deportes) **3** TWIST : recodo m, vuelta f, curva f
jogger ['ʤagər] n : persona f que hace footing
join ['ʤɔɪn] vt **1** CONNECT, LINK : unir, juntar ⟨to join in marriage : unir en matrimonio⟩ **2** ADJOIN : lindar con, colindar con **3** MEET : reunirse con, encontrarse con ⟨we joined them for lunch : nos reunimos con ellos para almorzar⟩ **4** : hacerse socio de (una organización), afiliarse a (un partido), entrar en (una empresa) — vi **1** UNITE : unirse **2** MERGE : empalmar (dícese de las carreteras), confluir (dícese de

los ríos) **3 to join up** : hacerse socio, enrolarse
joiner ['ʤɔɪnər] n **1** CARPENTER : carpintero m, -ra f **2** : persona f que se une a varios grupos
joint¹ ['ʤɔɪnt] adj : conjunto, colectivo, mutuo ⟨a joint effort : un esfuerzo conjunto⟩ — **jointly** adv
joint² n **1** : articulación f, coyuntura f ⟨out of joint : dislocado⟩ **2** ROAST : asado m **3** JUNCTURE : juntura f, unión f **4** DIVE : antro m, tasca f
joist ['ʤɔɪst] n : viga f
joke¹ ['ʤok] vi **joked; joking** : bromear
joke² n **1** STORY : chiste m **2** PRANK : broma f
joker ['ʤokər] n **1** PRANKSTER : bromista mf **2** : comodín m (en los naipes)
jokingly ['ʤo:kɪŋli] adv : en broma
jollity ['ʤaləti] n, pl **-ties** MERRIMENT : alegría f, regocijo m
jolly ['ʤali] adj **-lier; -est** : alegre, jovial
jolt¹ ['ʤo:lt] vi JERK : dar tumbos, dar sacudidas — vt : sacudir
jolt² n **1** JERK : sacudida f brusca **2** SHOCK : golpe m (emocional)
jonquil ['ʤankwɪl] n : junquillo m
Jordanian [ʤɔr'deɪniən] n : jordano m, -na f — **Jordanian** adj
josh ['ʤaʃ] vt TEASE : tomarle el pelo a (alguien) — vi JOKE : bromear
jostle ['ʤasəl] v **-tled; -tling** vi **1** SHOVE : empujar, dar empellones **2** CONTEND : competir — vt **1** SHOVE : empujar **2 to jostle one's way** : abrirse paso a empellones
jot¹ ['ʤat] vt **jotted; jotting** : anotar, apuntar ⟨jot it down : apúntalo⟩
jot² n BIT : ápice m, jota f, pizca f
jounce¹ ['ʤæʊnts] v **jounced; jouncing** vt JOLT : sacudir — vi : dar tumbos, dar sacudidas
jounce² n JOLT : sacudida f, tumbo m
journal ['ʤərnəl] n **1** DIARY : diario m **2** PERIODICAL : revista f, publicación f periódica **3** NEWSPAPER : periódico m, diario m
journalism ['ʤərnəl,ɪzəm] n : periodismo m
journalist ['ʤərnəlɪst] n : periodista mf
journalistic [,ʤərnəl'ɪstɪk] adj : periodístico
journey¹ ['ʤərni] vi **-neyed; -neying** : viajar
journey² n, pl **-neys** : viaje m
journeyman ['ʤərnimən] n, pl **-men** [-mən, -,mn] : oficial m
joust¹ ['ʤæʊst] vi : justar
joust² n : justa f
jovial ['ʤo:viəl] adj : jovial — **jovially** adv
joviality [,ʤo:vi'æləti] n : jovialidad f
jowl ['ʤæʊl] n **1** JAW : mandíbula f **2** CHEEK : mejilla f, cachete m
joy ['ʤɔɪ] n **1** HAPPINESS : gozo m, alegría f, felicidad f **2** DELIGHT : placer m, deleite m ⟨the child is a real joy : el niño es un verdadero placer⟩

joyful ['dʒɔɪfəl] *adj* : gozoso, alegre, feliz — **joyfully** *adv*
joyless ['dʒɔɪləs] *adj* : sin alegría, triste
joyous ['dʒɔɪəs] *adj* : alegre, feliz, eufórico — **joyously** *adv*
joyousness ['dʒɔɪəsnəs] *n* : alegría *f*, felicidad *f*, euforia *f*
joyride ['dʒɔɪˌraɪd] *n* : paseo *m* temerario e irresponsable (en coche)
joystick ['dʒɔɪˌstɪk] *n* : joystick *m*
jubilant ['dʒuːbələnt] *adj* : jubiloso, alborozado — **jubilantly** *adv*
jubilation [ˌdʒuːbəˈleɪʃən] *n* : júbilo *m*
jubilee ['dʒuːbəˌliː] *n* **1** : quincuagésimo aniversario *m* **2** CELEBRATION : celebración *f*, festejos *mpl*
Judaic [dʒʊˈdeɪɪk] *adj* : judaico
Judaism ['dʒuːdəˌɪzəm, 'dʒuːdi-, 'dʒuːˌdeɪ-] *n* : judaísmo *m*
judge[1] ['dʒʌdʒ] *vt* **judged; judging 1** ASSESS : evaluar, juzgar **2** DEEM : juzgar, considerar **3** TRY : juzgar (ante el tribunal) **4 judging by** : a juzgar por
judge[2] *n* **1** : juez *mf*, jueza *f* **2 to be a good judge of** : saber juzgar a, entender mucho de
judgment *or* **judgement** ['dʒʌdʒmənt] *n* **1** RULING : fallo *m*, sentencia *f* **2** OPINION : opinión *f* **3** DISCERNMENT : juicio *m*, discernimiento *m*
judgmental [ˌdʒʌdʒˈmntəl] *adj* : crítico — **judgmentally** *adv*
judicature ['dʒuːdɪkəˌtʃʊr] *n* : judicatura *f*
judicial [dʒʊˈdɪʃəl] *adj* : judicial — **judicially** *adv*
judiciary[1] [dʒʊˈdɪʃiˌri, -ˈdɪʃəri] *adj* : judicial
judiciary[2] *n* **1** JUDICATURE : judicatura *f* **2** : poder *m* judicial
judicious [dʒʊˈdɪʃəs] *adj* SOUND, WISE : juicioso, sensato — **judiciously** *adv*
judo ['dʒuːˌdoː] *n* : judo *m*
jug ['dʒʌg] *n* **1** : jarra *f*, jarro *m*, cántaro *m* **2** JAIL : cárcel *f*, chirona *f fam*
juggernaut ['dʒʌgərˌnɔt] *n* : gigante *m*, fuerza *f* irresistible ⟨a political juggernaut : un gigante político⟩
juggle ['dʒʌgəl] *v* **-gled; -gling** *vt* **1** : hacer juegos malabares con **2** MANIPULATE : manipular, jugar con — *vi* : hacer juegos malabares
juggler ['dʒʌgələr] *n* : malabarista *mf*
jugular ['dʒʌgjulər] *adj* : yugular ⟨jugular vein : vena yugular⟩
juice ['dʒuːs] *n* **1** : jugo *m* (de carne, de frutas) *m*, zumo *m* (de frutas) **2** ELECTRICITY : electricidad *f*, luz *f*
juicer ['dʒuːsər] *n* : exprimidor *m*
juiciness ['dʒuːsinəs] *n* : jugosidad *f*
juicy ['dʒuːsi] *adj* **juicier; -est 1** SUCCULENT : jugoso, suculento **2** PROFITABLE : jugoso, lucrativo **3** RACY : picante
jukebox ['dʒuːkˌbɑks] *n* : rocola *f*, máquina *f* de discos
julep ['dʒuːləp] *n* : bebida *f* hecha con whisky americano y menta

July [dʒʊˈlaɪ] *n* : julio *m*
jumble[1] ['dʒʌmbəl] *vt* **-bled; -bling** : mezclar, revolver
jumble[2] *n* : revoltijo *m*, fárrago *m*, embrollo *m*
jumbo[1] ['dʒʌmˌboː] *adj* : gigante, enorme, de tamaño extra grande
jumbo[2] *n*, *pl* **-bos** : coloso *m*, cosa *f* de tamaño extra grande
jump[1] ['dʒʌmp] *vi* **1** LEAP : saltar, brincar **2** START : levantarse de un salto, sobresaltarse **3** MOVE, SHIFT : moverse, pasar ⟨to jump from job to job : pasar de un empleo a otro⟩ **4** INCREASE, RISE : dar un salto, aumentarse de golpe, subir bruscamente **5** BUSTLE : animarse, ajetrearse **6 to jump to conclusions** : sacar conclusiones precipitadas — *vt* **1** : saltar ⟨to jump a fence : saltar una valla⟩ **2** SKIP : saltarse **3** ATTACK : atacar, asaltar **4 to jump the gun** : precipitarse
jump[2] *n* **1** LEAP : salto *m* **2** START : sobresalto *m*, respingo *m* **3** INCREASE : subida *f* brusca, aumento *m* **4** ADVANTAGE : ventaja *f* ⟨we got the jump on them : les llevamos la ventaja⟩
jumper ['dʒʌmpər] *n* **1** : saltador *m*, -dora *f* (en deportes) **2** : jumper *m*, vestido *m* sin mangas
jumpy ['dʒʌmpi] *adj* **jumpier; -est** : asustadizo, nervioso
junction ['dʒʌŋkʃən] *n* **1** JOINING : unión *f* **2** : cruce *m* (de calles), empalme *m* (de un ferrocarril), confluencia *f* (de ríos)
juncture ['dʒʌŋktʃər] *n* **1** UNION : juntura *f*, unión *f* **2** MOMENT, POINT : coyuntura *f* ⟨at this juncture : en esta coyuntura, en este momento⟩
June ['dʒuːn] *n* : junio *m*
jungle ['dʒʌŋgəl] *n* : jungla *f*, selva *f*
junior[1] ['dʒuːnjər] *adj* **1** YOUNGER : más joven ⟨John Smith, Junior : John Smith, hijo⟩ **2** SUBORDINATE : subordinado, subalterno
junior[2] *n* **1** : persona *f* de menor edad ⟨she's my junior : es menor que yo⟩ **2** SUBORDINATE : subalterno *m*, -na *f*; subordinado *m*, -da *f* **3** : estudiante *mf* de penúltimo año
juniper ['dʒuːnəpər] *n* : enebro *m*
junk[1] ['dʒʌŋk] *vt* : echar a la basura
junk[2] *n* **1** RUBBISH : desechos *mpl*, desperdicios *mpl* **2** STUFF : trastos *mpl fam*, cachivaches *mpl fam* **3 piece of junk** : cacharro *m*, porquería *f*
junket ['dʒʌŋkət] *n* : viaje *m* (pagado con dinero público)
junta ['hʊntə, 'dʒʌn-, 'hʌn-] *n* : junta *f* militar
Jupiter ['dʒuːpətər] *n* : Júpiter *m*
jurisdiction [ˌdʒʊrəsˈdɪkʃən] *n* : jurisdicción *f*
jurisprudence [ˌdʒʊrəsˈpruːdənts] *n* : jurisprudencia *f*
jurist ['dʒʊrɪst] *n* : jurista *mf*; magistrado *m*, -da *f*

juror ['dʒʊrər] n : jurado m, -da f
jury ['dʒʊri] n, pl **-ries** : jurado m
just¹ ['dʒʌst] adv **1** EXACTLY : justo, precisamente, exactamente **2** POSSIBLY : posiblemente ⟨it just might work : tal vez resulte⟩ **3** BARELY : justo, apenas ⟨just in time : justo a tiempo⟩ **4** ONLY : sólo, solamente, nada más ⟨just us : sólo nosotros⟩ **5** QUITE : muy, simplemente ⟨it's just horrible! : ¡qué horrible!⟩ **6 to have just (done something)** : acabar de (hacer algo) ⟨he just called : acaba de llamar⟩
just² adj : justo — **justly** adv
justice ['dʒʌstɪs] n **1** : justicia f **2** JUDGE : juez mf, jueza f

justification [ˌdʒʌstəfə'keɪʃən] n : justificación f
justify ['dʒʌstə,faɪ] vt **-fied; -fying** : justificar — **justifiable** [ˌdʒʌstə-'faɪəbəl] adj
jut ['dʒʌt] vi **jutted; jutting** : sobresalir
jute ['dʒuːt] n : yute m
juvenile¹ ['dʒuːvə,naɪl, -vənəl] adj **1** : juvenil ⟨juvenile delinquent : delincuente juvenil⟩ ⟨juvenile court : tribunal de menores⟩ **2** CHILDISH : infantil
juvenile² n : menor mf
juxtapose ['dʒʌkstə,poːz] vt **-posed; -posing** : yuxtaponer
juxtaposition [ˌdʒʌkstəpə'zɪʃən] n : yuxtaposición f

K

k ['keɪ] n, pl **k's** or **ks** ['keɪz] : undécima letra del alfabeto inglés
kaiser ['kaɪzər] n : káiser m
kale ['keɪl] n : col f rizada
kaleidoscope [kə'laɪdə,skoːp] n : calidoscopio m
kamikaze [ˌkɑmi'kɑzi] n : kamikaze m — **kamikaze** adj
kangaroo [ˌkæŋgə'ruː] n, pl **-roos** : canguro m
kaolin ['keɪələn] n : caolín m
karaoke [ˌkæri'oːki] n : karaoke m
karat ['kærət] n : quilate m
karate [kə'rɑṭi] n : karate m
katydid ['keɪṭi,dɪd] n : saltamontes m
kayak ['kaɪ,æk] n : kayac m, kayak m
keel¹ ['kiːl] vi **to keel over** : volcar (dícese de un barco), desplomarse (dícese de una persona)
keel² n : quilla f
keen ['kiːn] adj **1** SHARP : afilado, filoso ⟨a keen blade : una hoja afilada⟩ **2** PENETRATING : cortante, penetrante ⟨a keen wind : un viento cortante⟩ **3** ENTHUSIASTIC : entusiasta **4** ACUTE : agudo, fino ⟨keen hearing : oído fino⟩ ⟨keen intelligence : inteligencia aguda⟩
keenly ['kiːnli] adv **1** ENTHUSIASTICALLY : con entusiasmo **2** INTENSELY : vivamente, profundamente ⟨keenly aware of : muy consciente de⟩
keenness ['kiːnnəs] n **1** SHARPNESS : lo afilado, lo filoso **2** ENTHUSIASM : entusiasmo m **3** ACUTENESS : agudeza f
keep¹ ['kiːp] v **kept** ['kɛpt]; **keeping** vt **1** : cumplir (la palabra a uno), acudir a (una cita) **2** OBSERVE : observar (una fiesta) **3** GUARD : guardar, cuidar **4** CONTINUE : mantener ⟨to keep silence : mantener silencio⟩ **5** SUPPORT : mantener (una familia) **6** RAISE : criar (animales) **7** : llevar, escribir (un diario, etc.) **8** RETAIN : guardar, conservar, quedarse con **9** STORE : guardar **10** DETAIN : hacer quedar, detener **11** PRESERVE : guardar ⟨to keep a secret : guardar un secreto⟩ — vi **1** : conser-

varse (dícese de los alimentos) **2** CONTINUE : seguir, no dejar ⟨he keeps on pestering us : no deja de molestarnos⟩ **3 to keep from** : abstenerse de ⟨I couldn't keep from laughing : no podía contener la risa⟩
keep² n **1** TOWER : torreón m (de un castillo), torre f del homenaje **2** SUSTENANCE : manutención f, sustento m **3 for keeps** : para siempre
keeper ['kiːpər] n **1** : guarda mf (en un zoológico); conservador m, -dora f (en un museo) **2** GAMEKEEPER : guardabosque mf
keeping ['kiːpɪŋ] n **1** CONFORMITY : conformidad f, acuerdo m ⟨in keeping with : de acuerdo con⟩ **2** CARE : cuidado m ⟨in the keeping of : al cuidado de⟩
keepsake ['kiːp,seɪk] n : recuerdo m
keep up vt CONTINUE, MAINTAIN : mantener, seguir con — vi **1** : mantenerse al corriente ⟨he kept up with the news : se mantenía al tanto de las noticias⟩ **2** CONTINUE : continuar **3 to keep up with someone** : mantener contacto con alguien
keg ['kɛg] n : barril m
kelp ['kɛlp] n : alga f marina
ken ['kɛn] n **1** SIGHT : vista f, alcance m de la vista **2** UNDERSTANDING : comprensión f, alcance m del conocimiento ⟨it's beyond his ken : no lo puede entender⟩
kennel ['kɛnəl] n : caseta f para perros, perrera f
Kenyan ['kɛnjən, 'kiːn-] n : keniano m, -na f — **Kenyan** adj
kept → keep
kerchief ['kərtʃəf, -ˌtʃiːf] n : pañuelo m
kernel ['kərnəl] n **1** : almendra f (de semillas y nueces) **2** : grano m (de cereales) **3** CORE : meollo m ⟨a kernel of truth : un fondo de verdad⟩
kerosene or **kerosine** ['kɛrə,siːn, ˌkɛrə'-] n : queroseno m, kerosén m, kerosene m

ketchup ['kɛtʃəp, 'kæ-] *n* : salsa *f* catsup
kettle ['kɛtəl] *n* **1** : hervidor *m*, pava *f* *Arg, Bol, Chile* **2** → teakettle
kettledrum ['kɛtəl,drʌm] *n* : timbal *m*
key[1] ['kiː] *vt* **1** ATTUNE : adaptar, adecuar **2 to key up** : poner nervioso, inquietar
key[2] *adj* : clave, fundamental
key[3] *n* **1** : llave *f* **2** SOLUTION : clave *f*, soluciones *fpl* **3** : tecla *f* (de un piano o una máquina) **4** : tono *m*, tonalidad *f* (en la música) **5** ISLET, REEF : cayo *m*, islote *m*
· **keyboard** ['kiː,bord] *n* : teclado *m*
keyhole ['kiː,hoːl] *n* : bocallave *f*, ojo *m* (de una cerradura)
keynote[1] ['kiː,noːt] *vt* -noted; -noting **1** : establecer la tónica de (en música) **2** : pronunciar el discurso principal de
keynote[2] *n* **1** : tónica *f* (en música) **2** : idea *f* fundamental
keystone ['kiː,stoːn] *n* : clave *f*, dovela *f*
keystroke ['kiː,stroːk] *n* : pulsación *f* (de tecla)
khaki ['kæki, 'kɑ-] *n* : caqui *m*
khan ['kɑn, 'kæn] *n* : kan *m*
kibbutz [kə'bʊts, -'buːts] *n, pl* -butzim [-,bʊt'siːm, -,buːt-] : kibutz *m*
kibitz ['kɪbɪts] *vi* : dar consejos molestos
kibitzer ['kɪbɪtsər, kɪ'bɪt-] *n* : persona *f* que da consejos molestos
kick[1] ['kɪk] *vi* **1** : dar patadas (dícese de una persona), cocear (dícese de un animal) **2** PROTEST : patalear, protestar **3** RECOIL : dar un culatazo (dícese de un arma de fuego) — *vt* : patear, darle una patada (a alguien)
kick[2] *n* **1** : patada *f*, puntapié *m*, coz *f* (de un animal) **2** RECOIL : culatazo *m* (de un arma de fuego) **3** : fuerza *f* ⟨a drink with a kick : una bebida fuerte⟩
kicker ['kɪkər] *n* : pateador *m*, -dora *f* (en deportes)
kickoff ['kɪk,ɔf] *n* : saque *m* (inicial)
kick off *vi* **1** : hacer el saque inicial (en deportes) **2** BEGIN : empezar — *vt* : empezar
kid[1] ['kɪd] *v* kidded; kidding *vt* **1** FOOL : engañar **2** TEASE : tomarle el pelo (a alguien) — *vi* JOKE : bromear ⟨I'm only kidding : lo digo en broma⟩
kid[2] *n* **1** : chivo *m*, -va *f*; cabrito *m*, -ta *f* **2** CHILD : chico *m*, -ca *f*; niño *m*, -ña *f*
kidder ['kɪdər] *n* : bromista *mf*
kiddingly ['kɪdɪŋli] *adv* : en broma
kidnap ['kɪd,næp] *vt* -napped *or* -naped [-,næpt]; -napping *or* -naping [-,næpɪŋ] : secuestrar, raptar
kidnapper *or* **kidnaper** ['kɪd,næpər] *n* : secuestrador *m*, -dora *f*; raptor *m*, -tora *f*
kidnapping ['kɪd,næpɪŋ] *n* : secuestro *m*
kidney ['kɪdni] *n, pl* -neys : riñón *m*
kidney bean *n* : frijol *m*
kill[1] ['kɪl] *vt* **1** : matar **2** END : acabar con, poner fin a **3 to kill time** : matar el tiempo

kill[2] *n* **1** KILLING : matanza *f* **2** PREY : presa *f*
killer ['kɪlər] *n* : asesino *m*, -na *f*
killjoy ['kɪl,dʒɔɪ] *n* : aguafiestas *mf*
kiln ['kɪl, 'kɪln] *n* : horno *m*
kilo ['kiː,loː] *n, pl* -los : kilo *m*
kilobyte ['kɪlə,baɪt] *n* : kilobyte *m*
kilocycle ['kɪlə,saɪkəl] *n* : kilociclo *m*
kilogram ['kɪlə,græm, 'kiː-] *n* : kilogramo *m*
kilohertz ['kɪlə,hərts] *n* : kilohertzio *m*
kilometer [kɪ'lɑmətər, 'kɪlə,miː-] *n* : kilómetro *m*
kilowatt ['kɪlə,wɑt] *n* : kilovatio *m*
kilt ['kɪlt] *n* : falda *f* escocesa
kilter ['kɪltər] *n* **1** ORDER : buen estado *m* **2 out of kilter** : descompuesto, estropeado
kimono [kə'moːno, -nə] *n, pl* -nos : kimono *m*, quimono *m*
kin ['kɪn] *n* : familiares *mpl*, parientes *mpl*
kind[1] ['kaɪnd] *adj* : amable, bondadoso, benévolo
kind[2] *n* **1** ESSENCE : esencia *f* ⟨a difference in degree, not in kind : una diferencia cuantitativa y no cualitativa⟩ **2** CATEGORY : especie *f*, género *m* **3** TYPE : clase *f*, tipo *m*, índole *f*
kindergarten ['kɪndər,gɑrtən, -dən] *n* : kinder *m*, kindergarten *m*, jardín *m* de infantes, jardín *m* de niños *Mex*
kindhearted [,kaɪnd'hɑrtəd] *adj* : bondadoso, de buen corazón
kindle ['kɪndəl] *v* -dled; -dling *vt* **1** IGNITE : encender **2** AROUSE : despertar, suscitar — *vi* : encenderse
kindliness ['kaɪndlinəs] *n* : bondad *f*
kindling ['kɪndlɪŋ, 'kɪndlən] *n* : astillas *fpl*, leña *f*
kindly[1] ['kaɪndli] *adv* **1** AMIABLY : amablemente, bondadosamente **2** COURTEOUSLY : cortésmente, con cortesía ⟨we kindly ask you not smoke : les rogamos que no fumen⟩ **3** PLEASE : por favor **4 to take kindly to** : aceptar de buena gana
kindly[2] *adj* -lier; -est : bondadoso, amable
kindness ['kaɪndnəs] *n* : bondad *f*
kind of *adv* SOMEWHAT : un tanto, algo
kindred[1] ['kɪndrəd] *adj* SIMILAR : similar, afín ⟨kindred spirits : almas gemelas⟩
kindred[2] *n* **1** FAMILY : familia *f*, parentela *f* **2** → kin
kinfolk ['kɪn,foːk] *or* **kinfolks** [-,foːks] *npl* → kin
king ['kɪŋ] *n* : rey *m*
kingdom ['kɪŋdəm] *n* : reino *m*
kingfisher ['kɪŋ,fɪʃər] *n* : martín *m* pescador
kingly ['kɪŋli] *adj* -lier; -est : regio, real
king-size ['kɪŋ,saɪz] *or* **king-sized** [-,saɪzd] *adj* : de tamaño muy grande, extra largo (dícese de cigarrillos)
kink ['kɪŋk] *n* **1** : rizo *m* (en el pelo), vuelta *f* (en una cuerda) **2** CRAMP

: calambre *m* ⟨to have a kink in the neck : tener tortícolis⟩
kinky ['kɪŋki] *adj* **-kier; -est** : rizado (dícese del pelo), enroscado (dícese de una cuerda)
kinship ['kɪn,ʃɪp] *n* : parentesco *m*
kinsman ['kɪnzmən] *n, pl* **-men** [-mən, -,mɛn] : familiar *m*, pariente *m*
kinswoman ['kɪnz,wʊmən] *n, pl* **-women** [-,wɪmən] : familiar *f*, pariente *f*
kiosk ['ki:,ask] *n* : quiosco *m*
kipper ['kɪpər] *n* : arenque *m* ahumado
kiss¹ ['kɪs] *vt* : besar — *vi* : besarse
kiss² *n* : beso *m*
kit ['kɪt] *n* **1** SET : juego *m*, kit *m* **2** CASE : estuche *m*, caja *f* **3 first–aid kit** : botiquín *m* **4 tool kit** : caja *f* de herramientas **5 travel kit** : neceser *m*
kitchen ['kɪtʃən] *n* : cocina *f*
kite ['kaɪt] *n* **1** : milano *m* (ave) **2** : cometa *f*, papalote *m Mex* ⟨to fly a kite : hacer volar una cometa⟩
kith ['kɪθ] *n* : amigos *mpl* ⟨kith and kin : amigos y parientes⟩
kitten ['kɪtən] *n* : gatito *m*, -ta *f*
kitty ['kɪti] *n, pl* **-ties 1** FUND, POOL : bote *m*, fondo *m* común **2** CAT : gato *m*, gatito *m*
kitty–corner ['kɪti,kɔrnər] *or* **kitty–cornered** [-nərd] → **catercorner**
kiwi ['ki:,wi:] *n* : kiwi *m*
kleptomania [,klɛptə'meɪniə] *n* : cleptomanía *f*
kleptomaniac [,klɛptə'meɪni,æk] *n* : cleptómano *m*, -na *f*
knack ['næk] *n* : maña *f*, facilidad *f*
knapsack ['næp,sæk] *n* : mochila *f*, morral *m*
knave ['neɪv] *n* : bellaco *m*, pícaro *m*
knead ['ni:d] *vt* **1** : amasar, sobar **2** MASSAGE : masajear
knee ['ni:] *n* : rodilla *f*
kneecap ['ni:,kæp] *n* : rótula *f*
kneel ['ni:l] *vi* **knelt** ['nɛlt] *or* **kneeled** ['ni:ld]; **kneeling** : arrodillarse, ponerse de rodillas
knell ['nɛl] *n* : doble *m*, toque *m* ⟨death knell : toque de difuntos⟩
knew → **know**
knickers ['nɪkərz] *npl* : pantalones *mpl* bombachos de media pierna
knickknack ['nɪk,næk] *n* : chuchería *f*, baratija *f*
knife¹ ['naɪf] *vt* **knifed** ['naɪft]; **knifing** : acuchillar, apuñalar
knife² *n, pl* **knives** ['naɪvz] : cuchillo *m*
knight¹ ['naɪt] *vt* : conceder el título de *Sir* a
knight² *n* **1** : caballero *m* ⟨knight errant : caballero andante⟩ **2** : caballo *m* (en ajedrez) **3** : uno que tiene el título de *Sir*
knighthood ['naɪt,hʊd] *n* **1** : caballería *f* **2** : título *m* de *Sir*
knightly ['naɪtli] *adj* : caballeresco
knit¹ ['nɪt] *v* **knit** *or* **knitted** ['nɪtəd]; **knitting** *vt* **1** UNITE : unir, enlazar **2** : tejer ⟨to knit a sweater : tejer un suéter⟩ **3**

to knit one's brows : fruncir el ceño — *vi* **1** : tejer **2** : soldarse (dícese de los huesos)
knit² *n* : prenda *f* tejida
knitter ['nɪtər] *n* : tejedor *m*, -dora *f*
knob ['nɑb] *n* **1** LUMP : bulto *m*, protuberancia *f* **2** HANDLE : perilla *f*, tirador *m*, botón *m*
knobbed ['nɑbd] *adj* **1** KNOTTY : nudoso **2** : que tiene perilla o botón
knobby ['nɑbi] *adj* **knobbier; -est 1** KNOTTY : nudoso **2 knobby knees** : rodillas *fpl* huesudas
knock¹ ['nɑk] *vt* **1** HIT, RAP : golpear, golpetear **2** : hacer chocar ⟨they knocked heads : se dieron en la cabeza⟩ **3** CRITICIZE : criticar — *vi* **1** RAP : dar un golpe, llamar (a la puerta) **2** COLLIDE : darse, chocar
knock² *n* : golpe *m*, llamada *f* (a la puerta), golpeteo *m* (de un motor)
knock down *vt* : derribar, echar al suelo
knocker ['nɑkər] *n* : aldaba *f*, llamador *m*
knock–kneed ['nɑk'ni:d] *adj* : patizambo
knockout ['nɑk,aʊt] *n* : nocaut *m*, knockout *m* (en deportes)
knock out *vt* : dejar sin sentido, poner fuera de combate (en el boxeo)
knoll ['no:l] *n* : loma *f*, otero *m*, montículo *m*
knot¹ ['nɑt] *v* **knotted; knotting** *vt* : anudar — *vi* : anudarse
knot² *n* **1** : nudo *m* (en cordel o madera), nódulo *m* (en los músculos) **2** CLUSTER : grupo *m* **3** : nudo *m* (unidad de velocidad)
knotty ['nɑti] *adj* **-tier; -est 1** GNARLED : nudoso **2** COMPLEX : espinoso, enredado, complejo
know ['no:] *v* **knew** ['nu:, 'nju:]; **known** ['no:n]; **knowing** *vt* **1** : saber ⟨he knows the answer : sabe la respuesta⟩ **2** : conocer (a una persona, un lugar) ⟨do you know Julia? : ¿conoces a Julia?⟩ **3** RECOGNIZE : reconocer **4** DISCERN, DISTINGUISH : distinguir, discernir **5 to know how to** : saber ⟨I don't know how to dance : no sé bailar⟩ — *vi* : saber
knowable ['no:əbəl] *adj* : conocible
knowing ['no:ɪŋ] *adj* **1** KNOWLEDGEABLE : informado ⟨a knowing look : una mirada de complicidad⟩ **2** ASTUTE : astuto **3** DELIBERATE : deliberado, intencional
knowingly ['no:ɪŋli] *adv* **1** : con complicidad ⟨she smiled knowingly : sonrió con una mirada de complicidad⟩ **2** DELIBERATELY : a sabiendas, adrede, a propósito
know–it–all ['no:ɪt,ɔl] *n* : sabelotodo *mf fam*
knowledge ['nɑlɪdʒ] *n* **1** AWARENESS : conocimiento *m* **2** LEARNING : conocimientos *mpl*, saber *m*
knowledgeable ['nɑlɪdʒəbəl] *adj* : informado, entendido, enterado

known ['noːn] *adj* : conocido, familiar
knuckle ['nʌkəl] *n* : nudillo *m*
koala [koˈwɑlə] *n* : koala *m*
kohlrabi [ˌkoːlˈrɑbi, -ˈræ-] *n, pl* **-bies** : colinabo *m*
Koran [kəˈrɑn, -ˈræn] *n* **the Koran** : el Corán
Korean [kəˈriːən] *n* **1** : coreano *m*, -na *f* **2** : coreano *m* (idioma) — **Korean** *adj*
kosher ['koːʃər] *adj* : aprobado por la ley judía

kowtow [ˌkaʊˈtaʊ, ˈkaʊˌtaʊ] *vi* **to kowtow to** : humillarse ante, doblegarse ante
krypton ['krɪpˌtɑn] *n* : criptón *m*
kudos ['kjuːˌdɑs, 'kuː-, -ˌdoːz] *n* : fama *f*, renombre *m*
kumquat ['kʌmˌkwɑt] *n* : naranjita *f* china
Kurd ['kʊrd, 'kərd] *n* : kurdo *m*, -da *f*
Kurdish ['kʊrdɪʃ, 'kər-] *adj* : kurdo
Kuwaiti [kʊˈweɪti] *n* : kuwaití *mf* — **Kuwaiti** *adj*

L

l ['ɛl] *n, pl* **l's** *or* **ls** ['lz] : duodécima letra del alfabeto inglés
lab ['læb] → **laboratory**
label[1] ['leɪbəl] *vt* **-beled** *or* **-belled; -beling** *or* **-belling** **1** : etiquetar, poner etiqueta a **2** BRAND, CATEGORIZE : calificar, tildar, tachar ⟨they labeled him as a fraud : lo calificaron de farsante⟩
label[2] *n* **1** : etiqueta *f*, rótulo *m* **2** DESCRIPTION : calificación *f*, descripción *f* **3** BRAND : marca *f*
labial ['leɪbiəl] *adj* : labial
labor[1] ['leɪbər] *vi* **1** WORK : trabajar **2** STRUGGLE : avanzar penosamente (dícese de una persona), funcionar con dificultad (dícese de un motor) **3 to labor under a delusion** : hacerse ilusiones, tener una falsa impresión — *vt* BELABOR : insistir en, extenderse sobre
labor[2] *n* **1** EFFORT, WORK : trabajo *m*, esfuerzos *mpl* **2** : parto *m* ⟨to be in labor : estar de parto⟩ **3** TASK : tarea *f*, labor *m* **4** WORKERS : mano *f* de obra
laboratory ['læbrəˌtori, ləˈbɔrə-] *n, pl* **-ries** : laboratorio *m*
Labor Day *n* : Día *m* del Trabajo
laborer ['leɪbərər] *n* : peón *m*; trabajador *m*, -dora *f*
laborious [ləˈboriəs] *adj* : laborioso, difícil
laboriously [ləˈboriəsli] *adv* : laboriosamente, trabajosamente
labor union → **union**
labyrinth ['læbəˌrɪnθ] *n* : laberinto *m*
lace[1] ['leɪs] *vt* **laced; lacing** **1** TIE : acordonar, atar los cordones de **2** : adornar de encaje ⟨I laced the dress in white : adorné el vestido de encaje blanco⟩ **3** SPIKE : echar licor a
lace[2] *n* **1** : encaje *m* **2** SHOELACE : cordón *m* (de zapatos), agujeta *f Mex*
lacerate ['læsəˌreɪt] *vt* **-ated; -ating** : lacerar
laceration [ˌlæsəˈreɪʃən] *n* : laceración *f*
lack[1] ['læk] *vt* : carecer de, no tener ⟨she lacks patience : carece de paciencia⟩ — *vi* : faltar ⟨they lack for nothing : no les falta nada⟩
lack[2] *n* : falta *f*, carencia *f*
lackadaisical [ˌlækəˈdeɪzɪkəl] *adj*

: apático, indiferente, lánguido — **lackadaisically** [-kli] *adv*
lackey ['læki] *n, pl* **-eys** **1** FOOTMAN : lacayo *m* **2** TOADY : adulador *m*, -dora *f*
lackluster ['lækˌlʌstər] *adj* **1** DULL : sin brillo, apagado, deslustrado **2** MEDIOCRE : deslucido, mediocre
laconic [ləˈkɑnɪk] *adj* : lacónico — **laconically** [-nɪkli] *adv*
lacquer[1] ['lækər] *vt* : laquear, pintar con laca
lacquer[2] *n* : laca *f*
lacrosse [ləˈkrɔs] *n* : lacrosse *f*
lactic acid ['læktɪk] *n* : ácido *m* láctico
lacuna [ləˈkuːnə, -ˈkjuː-] *n, pl* **-nae** [-ˌniː, -ˌnaɪ] *or* **-nas** : laguna *f*
lacy ['leɪsi] *adj* **lacier; -est** : de encaje, como de encaje
lad ['læd] *n* : muchacho *m*, niño *m*
ladder ['lædər] *n* : escalera *f*
laden ['leɪdən] *adj* : cargado
ladle[1] ['leɪdəl] *vt* **-dled; -dling** : servir con cucharón
ladle[2] *n* : cucharón *m*, cazo *m*
lady ['leɪdi] *n, pl* **-dies** **1** : señora *f*, dama *f* **2** WOMAN : mujer *f*
ladybird ['leɪdiˌbərd] → **ladybug**
ladybug ['leɪdiˌbʌg] *n* : mariquita *f*
lag[1] ['læg] *vi* **lagged; lagging** : quedarse atrás, retrasarse, rezagarse
lag[2] *n* **1** DELAY : retraso *m*, demora *f* **2** INTERVAL : lapso *m*, intervalo *m*
lager ['lɑgər] *n* : cerveza *f* rubia
laggard[1] ['lægərd] *adj* : retardado, retrasado
laggard[2] *n* : rezagado *m*, -da *f*
lagoon [ləˈguːn] *n* : laguna *f*
laid → **lay**[1]
laid-back ['leɪdˈbæk] *adj* : tranquilo, relajado
lain *pp* → **lie**[1]
lair ['lær] *n* : guarida *f*, madriguera *f*
laissez-faire [ˌlɛˌseɪˈfær, ˌleɪˌzeɪ-] *n* : liberalismo *m* económico
laity ['leɪəti] *n* **the laity** : los laicos, el laicado
lake ['leɪk] *n* : lago *m*
lama ['lɑmə] *n* : lama *m*
lamb ['læm] *n* **1** : cordero *m*, borrego *m* (animal) **2** : carne *f* de cordero

lambaste [læm'beɪst] *or* **lambast** [-'bæst] *vt* **-basted; -basting 1** BEAT, THRASH : golpear, azotar, darle una paliza (a alguien) **2** CENSURE : arremeter contra, censurar

lame[1] ['leɪm] *vt* **lamed; laming** : lisiar, hacer cojo

lame[2] *adj* **lamer; lamest 1** : cojo, renco, rengo **2** WEAK : pobre, débil, poco convincente ⟨a lame excuse : una excusa débil⟩

lamé [la'meɪ, læ-] *n* : lamé *m*

lame duck *n* : persona *f* sin poder ⟨a lame-duck President : un presidente saliente⟩

lamely ['leɪmli] *adv* : sin convicción

lameness ['leɪmnəs] *n* **1** : cojera *f*, renquera *f* **2** : falta *f* de convicción, debilidad *f*, pobreza *f* ⟨the lameness of her response : la pobreza de su respuesta⟩

lament[1] [lə'mɛnt] *vt* **1** MOURN : llorar, llorar por **2** DEPLORE : lamentar, deplorar — *vi* : llorar

lament[2] *n* : lamento *m*

lamentable ['læməntəbəl, lə'mɛntə-] *adj* : lamentable, deplorable — **lamentably** [-bli] *adv*

lamentation [,læmən'teɪʃən] *n* : lamentación *f*, lamento *m*

laminate[1] ['læmə,neɪt] *vt* **-nated; -nating** : laminar

laminate[2] ['læmənət] *n* : laminado *m*

laminated ['læmə,neɪtəd] *adj* : laminado

lamp ['læmp] *n* : lámpara *f*

lampoon[1] [læm'puːn] *vt* : satirizar

lampoon[2] *n* : sátira *f*

lamprey ['læmpri] *n, pl* **-preys** : lamprea *f*

lance[1] ['læn*t*s] *vt* **lanced; lancing** : abrir con lanceta, sajar

lance[2] *n* : lanza *f*

lance corporal *n* : cabo *m* interino, soldado *m* de primera clase

lancet ['læn*t*sət] *n* : lanceta *f*

land[1] ['lænd] *vt* **1** : desembarcar (pasajeros de un barco), hacer aterrizar (un avión) **2** CATCH : pescar, sacar (un pez) del agua **3** GAIN, SECURE : conseguir, ganar ⟨to land a job : conseguir empleo⟩ **4** DELIVER : dar, asestar ⟨he landed a punch : asestó un puñetazo⟩ — *vi* **1** : aterrizar, tomar tierra, atracar ⟨the plane just landed : el avión acaba de aterrizar⟩ ⟨the ship landed an hour ago : el barco atracó hace una hora⟩ **2** ALIGHT : posarse, aterrizar ⟨to land on one's feet : caer de pie⟩

land[2] *n* **1** GROUND : tierra *f* ⟨dry land : tierra firme⟩ **2** TERRAIN : terreno *m* **3** NATION : país *m*, nación *f* **4** DOMAIN : mundo *m*, dominio *m* ⟨the land of dreams : el mundo de los sueños⟩

landfill ['lænd,fɪl] *n* : vertedero *m* (de basuras)

landing ['lændɪŋ] *n* **1** : aterrizaje *m* (de aviones), desembarco *m* (de barcos) **2** : descansillo *m* (de una escalera)

landing field *n* : campo *m* de aterrizaje

landing strip → **airstrip**

landlady ['lænd,leɪdi] *n, pl* **-dies** : casera *f*, dueña *f*, arrendadora *f*

landless ['lændləs] *adj* : sin tierra

landlocked ['lænd,lɑkt] *adj* : sin salida al mar

landlord ['lænd,lɔrd] *n* : dueño *m*; casero *m*, arrendador *m*

landlubber ['lænd,lʌbər] *n* : marinero *m* de agua dulce

landmark ['lænd,mɑrk] *n* **1** : señal *f* (geográfica), punto *m* de referencia **2** MILESTONE : hito *m* ⟨a landmark in our history : un hito en nuestra historia⟩ **3** MONUMENT : monumento *m* histórico

landowner ['lænd,oːnər] *n* : hacendado *m*, -da *f*; terrateniente *mf*

landscape[1] ['lænd,skeɪp] *vt* **-scaped; -scaping** : ajardinar

landscape[2] *n* : paisaje *m*

landslide ['lænd,slaɪd] *n* **1** : desprendimiento *m* de tierras, derrumbe *m* **2** **landslide victory** : victoria *f* arrolladora

landward ['lændwərd] *adv* : en dirección de la tierra, hacia tierra

lane ['leɪn] *n* **1** PATH, WAY : camino *m*, sendero *m* **2** : carril *m* (de una carretera)

language ['læŋgwɪdʒ] *n* **1** : idioma *m*, lengua *f* ⟨the English language : el idioma inglés⟩ **2** : lenguaje *m* ⟨body language : lenguaje corporal⟩

languid ['læŋgwɪd] *adj* : lánguido — **languidly** *adv*

languish ['læŋgwɪʃ] *vi* **1** WEAKEN : languidecer, debilitarse **2** PINE : consumirse, suspirar (por) ⟨to languish for love : suspirar por el amor⟩ ⟨he languished in prison : estuvo pudriéndose en la cárcel⟩

languor ['læŋgər] *n* : languidez *f*

languorous ['læŋgərəs] *adj* : lánguido — **languorously** *adv*

lank ['læŋk] *adj* **1** THIN : delgado, larguirucho *fam* **2** LIMP : lacio

lanky ['læŋki] *adj* **lankier; -est** : delgado, larguirucho *fam*

lanolin ['lænəlɪn] *n* : lanolina *f*

lantern ['læntərn] *n* : linterna *f*, farol *m*

Laotian [leɪ'oːʃən, 'lauʃən] *n* : laosiano *m*, -na *f* — **Laotian** *adj*

lap[1] ['læp] *v* **lapped; lapping** *vt* **1** FOLD : plegar, doblar **2** WRAP : envolver **3** : lamer, besar ⟨waves were lapping the shore : las olas lamían la orilla⟩ **4 to lap up** : beber a lengüetadas (como un gato) — *vi* OVERLAP : traslaparse

lap[2] *n* **1** : falda *f*, regazo *m* (del cuerpo) **2** OVERLAP : traslapo *m* **3** : vuelta *f* (en deportes) **4** STAGE : etapa *f* (de un viaje)

lapdog ['læp,dɔg] *n* : perro *m* faldero

lapel [lə'pɛl] *n* : solapa *f*

lapp ['læp] *n* : lapón *m*, -pona *f* — **Lapp** *adj*

lapse[1] ['læps] *vi* **lapsed; lapsing 1** FALL, SLIP : caer ⟨to lapse into bad habits : caer en malos hábitos⟩ ⟨to lapse into unconsciousness : perder el conocimiento ⟨to lapse into silence : quedarse callado⟩ **2** FADE : decaer, desvanecerse ⟨her dedication lapsed : su dedicación se desvaneció⟩ **3** CEASE : cancelarse, perderse **4** ELAPSE : transcurrir, pasar **5** EXPIRE : caducar

lapse² *n* **1** SLIP : lapsus *m*, desliz *m*, falla *f* ⟨a lapse of memory : una falla de memoria⟩ **2** INTERVAL : lapso *m*, intervalo *m*, período *m* **3** EXPIRATION : caducidad *f*

laptop¹ [ˈlæpˌtɑp] *adj* : portátil, laptop

laptop² *n* : laptop *m*

larboard [ˈlɑrbərd] *n* : babor *m*

larcenous [ˈlɑrsənəs] *adj* : de robo

larceny [ˈlɑrsəni] *n, pl* **-nies** : robo *m*, hurto *m*

larch [ˈlɑrtʃ] *n* : alerce *f*

lard [ˈlɑrd] *n* : manteca *f* de cerdo

larder [ˈlɑrdər] *n* : despensa *f*, alacena *f*

large [ˈlɑrdʒ] *adj* **larger; largest 1** BIG : grande **2** COMPREHENSIVE : amplio, extenso **3 by and large** : por lo general

largely [ˈlɑrdʒli] *adv* : en gran parte, en su mayoría

largeness [ˈlɑrdʒnəs] *n* : lo grande

largesse *or* **largess** [lɑrˈʒɛs, -ˈdʒɛs] *n* : generosidad *f*, largueza *f*

lariat [ˈlæriət] *n* : lazo *m*

lark [ˈlɑrk] *n* **1** FUN : diversión *f* ⟨what a lark! : ¡qué divertido!⟩ **2** : alondra *f* (pájaro)

larva [ˈlɑrvə] *n, pl* **-vae** [-ˌviː, -ˌvaɪ] : larva *f* — **larval** [-vəl] *adj*

laryngitis [ˌlærənˈdʒaɪtəs] *n* : laringitis *f*

larynx [ˈlærɪŋks] *n, pl* **-rynges** [ləˈrɪnˌdʒiːz] *or* **-ynxes** [ˈlærɪŋksəz] : laringe *f*

lasagna [ləˈzɑnjə] *n* : lasaña *f*

lascivious [ləˈsɪviəs] *adj* : lascivo

lasciviousness [ləˈsɪviəsnəs] *n* : lascivia *f*, lujuria *f*

laser [ˈleɪzər] *n* : láser *m*

laser disc *n* : disco *m* láser

lash¹ [ˈlæʃ] *vt* **1** WHIP : azotar **2** BIND : atar, amarrar

lash² *n* **1** WHIP : látigo *m* **2** STROKE : latigazo *m* **3** EYELASH : pestaña *f*

lass [ˈlæs] *or* **lassie** [ˈlæsi] *n* : muchacha *f*, chica *f*

lassitude [ˈlæsəˌtuːd, -ˌtjuːd] *n* : lasitud *f*

lasso¹ [ˈlæˌsoː, læˈsuː] *vt* : lazar

lasso² *n, pl* **-sos** *or* **-soes** : lazo *m*, reata *f Mex*

last¹ [ˈlæst] *vi* **1** CONTINUE : durar ⟨how long will it last? : ¿cuánto durará?⟩ **2** ENDURE : aguantar, durar **3** SURVIVE : durar, sobrevivir **4** SUFFICE : durar, bastar — *vt* **1** : durar ⟨it will last a lifetime : durará toda la vida⟩ **2 to last out** : aguantar

last² *adv* **1** : en último lugar, al último ⟨we came in last : llegamos en último lugar⟩ **2** : por última vez, la última vez ⟨I saw him last in Bogota : lo vi por última vez en Bogotá⟩ **3** FINALLY : por último, en conclusión

last³ *adj* **1** FINAL : último, final **2** PREVIOUS : pasado ⟨last year : el año pasado⟩

last⁴ *n* **1** : el último, la última, lo último ⟨at last : por fin, al fin, finalmente⟩ **2** : horma *f* (de zapatero)

lasting [ˈlæstɪŋ] *adj* : perdurable, duradero, estable

lastly [ˈlæstli] *adv* : por último, finalmente

latch¹ [ˈlætʃ] *vt* : cerrar con picaporte

latch² *n* : picaporte *m*, pestillo *m*, pasador *m*

late¹ [ˈleɪt] *adv* **later; latest 1** : tarde ⟨to arrive late : llegar tarde⟩ ⟨to sleep late : dormir hasta tarde⟩ **2** : a última hora, a finales ⟨late in the month : a finales del mes⟩ **3** RECENTLY : recién, últimamente ⟨as late as last year : todavía en el año pasado⟩

late² *adj* **later; latest 1** TARDY : tardío, de retraso ⟨to be late : llegar tarde⟩ **2** : avanzado ⟨because of the late hour : a causa de la hora avanzada⟩ **3** DECEASED : difunto, fallecido **4** RECENT : reciente, último ⟨our late quarrel : nuestra última pelea⟩

latecomer [ˈleɪtˌkʌmər] *n* : rezagado *m*, -da *f*

lately [ˈleɪtli] *adv* : recientemente, últimamente

lateness [ˈleɪtnəs] *n* **1** DELAY : retraso *m*, atraso *m*, tardanza *f* **2** : lo avanzado (de la hora)

latent [ˈleɪtənt] *adj* : latente — **latently** *adv*

lateral [ˈlætərəl] *adj* : lateral — **laterally** *adv*

latex [ˈleɪˌtɛks] *n, pl* **-tices** [ˈleɪtəˌsiːz, ˈlætə-] *or* **-texes** : látex *m*

lath [ˈlæθ, ˈlæð] *n, pl* **laths** *or* **lath** : listón *m*

lathe [ˈleɪð] *n* : torno *m*

lather¹ [ˈlæðər] *vt* : enjabonar — *vi* : espumar, hacer espuma

lather² *n* **1** : espuma *f* (de jabón) **2** : sudor *m* (de caballo) **3 to get into a lather** : ponerse histérico

Latin¹ *adj* : latino

Latin² *n* **1** : latín *m* (idioma) **2** → **Latin American**

Latin–American [ˈlætənəˈmrikən] *adj* : latinoamericano

Latin American *n* : latinoamericano *m*, -na *f*

latitude [ˈlætəˌtuːd, -ˌtjuːd] *n* : latitud *f*

latrine [ləˈtriːn] *n* : letrina *f*

latte [ˈlɑˌteɪ] *n* : café *m* con leche

latter¹ [ˈlætər] *adj* **1** SECOND : segundo **2** LAST : último

latter² *pron* **the latter** : éste, ésta, éstos *pl*, éstas *pl*

lattice [ˈlætəs] *n* : enrejado *m*, celosía *f*

Latvian [ˈlætviən] *n* : letón *m*, -tona *f* — **Latvian** *adj*

laud¹ [ˈlɔd] *vt* : alabar, loar

laud² *n* : alabanza *f*, loa *f*

laudable ['lɔdəbəl] *adj* : loable — **laud-ably** [-bli] *adv*

laugh[1] ['læf] *vi* : reír, reírse

laugh[2] *n* **1** LAUGHTER : risa *f* **2** JOKE : chiste *m*, broma *f* ⟨he did it for a laugh : lo hizo en broma, lo hizo para divertirse⟩

laughable ['læfəbəl] *adj* : risible, de risa

laughingstock ['læfɪŋ,stɑk] *n* : hazmerreír *m*

laughter ['læftər] *n* : risa *f*, risas *fpl*

launch[1] ['lɔntʃ] *vt* **1** HURL : lanzar **2** : botar (un barco) **3** START : iniciar, empezar

launch[2] *n* **1** : lancha *f* (bote) **2** LAUNCHING : lanzamiento *m*

launder ['lɔndər] *vt* **1** : lavar y planchar (ropa) **2** : blanquear, lavar (dinero)

launderer ['lɔndərər] *n* : lavandero *m*, -ra *f*

laundress ['lɔndrəs] *n* : lavandera *f*

laundry ['lɔndri] *n, pl* **laundries** **1** : ropa *f* sucia, ropa *f* para lavar ⟨to do the laundry : lavar la ropa⟩ **2** : lavandería *f* (servicio de lavar)

laureate ['lɔriət] *n* : laureado *m*, -da *f* ⟨poet laureate : poeta laureado⟩

laurel ['lɔrəl] *n* **1** : laurel *m* (planta) **2** **laurels** *npl* : laureles *mpl* ⟨to rest on one's laurels : dormirse uno en sus laureles⟩

lava ['lɑvə, 'læ-] *n* : lava *f*

lavatory ['lævə,tori] *n, pl* **-ries** : baño *m*, cuarto *m* de baño

lavender ['lævəndər] *n* : lavanda *f*, espliego *m*

lavish[1] ['lævɪʃ] *vt* : prodigar (a), colmar (de)

lavish[2] *adj* **1** EXTRAVAGANT : pródigo, generoso, derrochador **2** ABUNDANT : abundante **3** LUXURIOUS : lujoso, espléndido

lavishly ['lævɪʃli] *adv* : con generosidad, espléndidamente ⟨to live lavishly : vivir a lo grande⟩

lavishness ['lævɪʃnəs] *n* : generosidad *f*, esplendidez *f*

law ['lɔ] *n* **1** : ley *f* ⟨to break the law : violar la ley⟩ **2** : derecho *m* ⟨criminal law : derecho criminal⟩ **3** : abogacía *f* ⟨to practice law : ejercer la abogacía⟩

law–abiding ['lɔə,baɪdɪŋ] *adj* : observante de la ley

lawbreaker ['lɔ,breɪkər] *n* : infractor *m*, -tora *f* de la ley

lawful ['lɔfəl] *adj* : legal, legítimo, lícito — **lawfully** *adv*

lawgiver ['lɔ,gɪvər] *n* : legislador *m*, -dora *f*

lawless ['lɔləs] *adj* : anárquico, ingobernable — **lawlessly** *adv*

lawlessness ['lɔləsnəs] *n* : anarquía *f*, desorden *m*

lawmaker ['lɔ,meɪkər] *n* : legislador *m*, -dora *f*

lawman ['lɔmən] *n, pl* **-men** [-mən, -,mɛn] : agente *m* del orden

lawn ['lɔn] *n* : césped *m*, pasto *m*

lawn mower *n* : cortadora *f* de césped

lawsuit ['lɔ,su:t] *n* : pleito *m*, litigio *m*, demanda *f*

lawyer ['lɔɪər, 'lɔjər] *n* : abogado *m*, -da *f*

lax ['læks] *adj* : laxo, relajado — **laxly** *adv*

laxative ['læksətɪv] *n* : laxante *m*

laxity ['læksəti] *n* : relajación *f*, descuido *m*, falta *f* de rigor

lay[1] ['leɪ] *vt* **laid** ['leɪd]; **laying** **1** PLACE, PUT : poner, colocar ⟨she laid it on the table : lo puso en la mesa⟩ ⟨to lay eggs : poner huevos⟩ **2** : hacer ⟨to lay a bet : hacer una apuesta⟩ **3** IMPOSE : imponer ⟨to lay a tax : imponer un impuesto⟩ ⟨to lay the blame on : echarle la culpa a⟩ **4 to lay out** PRESENT : presentar, exponer ⟨he laid out his plan : presentó su proyecto⟩ **5 to lay out** DESIGN : diseñar (el trazado de)

lay[2] → **lie**[1]

lay[3] *adj* SECULAR : laico, lego

lay[4] *n* **1** : disposición *f*, configuración *f* ⟨the lay of the land : la configuración del terreno⟩ **2** BALLAD : romance *m*, balada *f*

layer ['leɪər] *n* **1** : capa *f* (de pintura, etc.), estrato *m* (de roca) **2** : gallina *f* ponedora

layman ['leɪmən] *n, pl* **-men** [-mən, -,mɛn] : laico *m*, lego *m*

layoff ['leɪ,ɔf] *n* : despido *m*

lay off *vt* : despedir

layout ['leɪ,aʊt] *n* : disposición *f*, distribución *f* (de una casa, etc.), trazado *m* (de una ciudad)

lay up *vt* **1** STORE : guardar, almacenar **2 to be laid up** : estar enfermo, tener que guardar cama

laywoman ['leɪ,wʊmən] *n, pl* **-women** [-,wɪmən] : laica *f*, lega *f*

laziness ['leɪzinəs] *n* : pereza *f*, flojera *f*

lazy ['leɪzi] *adj* **-zier; -est** : perezoso, holgazán — **lazily** ['leɪzəli] *adv*

leach ['li:tʃ] *vt* : filtrar

lead[1] ['li:d] *vt* **led** ['lɛd]; **leading** **1** GUIDE : conducir, llevar, guiar **2** DIRECT : dirigir **3** HEAD : encabezar, ir al frente de **4 to lead to** : resultar en, llevar a ⟨it only leads to trouble : sólo resulta en problemas⟩

lead[2] *n* : delantera *f*, primer lugar *m* ⟨to take the lead : tomar la delantera⟩

lead[3] ['lɛd] *n* **1** : plomo *m* (metal) **2** : mina *f* (de lápiz) **3 lead poisoning** : saturnismo *m*

leaden ['lɛdən] *adj* **1** : plomizo ⟨a leaden sky : un cielo plomizo⟩ **2** HEAVY : pesado

leader ['li:dər] *n* : jefe *m*, -fa *f*; líder *mf*; dirigente *mf*; gobernante *mf*

leadership ['li:dər,ʃɪp] *n* : mando *m*, dirección *f*

leaf[1] ['li:f] *vi* **1** : echar hojas (dícese de un árbol) **2 to leaf through** : hojear (un libro)

leaf[2] *n, pl* **leaves** ['li:vz] **1** : hoja *f* (de plantas o libros) **2 to turn over a new leaf** : hacer borrón y cuenta nueva

leafless ['li:fləs] *adj* : sin hojas, pelado

leaflet ['li:flət] *n* : folleto *m*

leafy ['li:fi] *adj* **leafier; -est** : frondoso

league[1] ['li:g] *v* **leagued; leaguing** *vt* : aliar, unir — *vi* : aliarse, unirse

league[2] *n* **1** : legua *f* (medida de distancia) **2** ASSOCIATION : alianza *f*, sociedad *f*, liga *f*

leak[1] ['li:k] *vt* **1** : perder, dejar escapar (un líquido o un gas) **2** : filtrar (información) — *vi* **1** : gotear, escaparse, fugarse (dícese de un líquido o un gas) **2** : hacer agua (dícese de un bote) **3** : filtrarse, divulgarse (dícese de información)

leak[2] *n* **1** HOLE : agujero *m* (en recipientes), gotera *f* (en un tejado) **2** ESCAPE : fuga *f*, escape *m* **3** : filtración *f* (de información)

leakage ['li:kɪʤ] *n* : escape *m*, fuga *f*

leaky ['li:ki] *adj* **leakier; -est** : agujereado (dícese de un recipiente), que hace agua (dícese de un bote), con goteras (dícese de un tejado)

lean[1] ['li:n] *vi* **1** BEND : inclinarse, ladearse **2** RECLINE : reclinarse **3** RELY : apoyarse (en), depender (de) **4** INCLINE, TEND : inclinarse, tender — *vt* : apoyar

lean[2] *adj* **1** THIN : delgado, flaco **2** : sin grasa, magro (dícese de la carne)

leanness ['li:nnəs] *n* : delgadez *f*

lean–to ['li:n,tu:] *n* : cobertizo *m*

leap[1] ['li:p] *vi* **leaped** ['li:pt, 'lɛpt] *or* **leapt; leaping** : saltar, brincar

leap[2] *n* : salto *m*, brinco *m*

leap year *n* : año *m* bisiesto

learn ['lərn] *vt* **1** : aprender ⟨to learn to sing : aprender a cantar⟩ **2** MEMORIZE : aprender de memoria **3** DISCOVER : saber, enterarse de — *vi* **1** : aprender ⟨to learn from experience : aprender por experiencia⟩ **2** FIND OUT : enterarse, saber

learned ['lərnəd] *adj* : erudito

learner ['lərnər] *n* : principiante *mf*, estudiante *mf*

learning ['lərnɪŋ] *n* : erudición *f*, saber *m*

lease[1] ['li:s] *vt* **leased; leasing** : arrendar

lease[2] *n* : contrato *m* de arrendamiento

leash[1] ['li:ʃ] *vt* : atraillar (un animal)

leash[2] *n* : traílla *f*

least[1] ['li:st] *adv* : menos ⟨when least expected : cuando menos se espera⟩

least[2] *adj* (*superlative of* **little**) : menor, más mínimo

least[3] *n* **1** : lo menos ⟨at least : por lo menos⟩ **2 to say the least** : por no decir más

leather ['lɛðər] *n* : cuero *m*

leathery ['lɛðəri] *adj* : curtido (dícese de la piel), correoso (dícese de la carne)

leave[1] ['li:v] *v* **left** ['lɛft]; **leaving** *vt* **1** BEQUEATH : dejar, legar **2** DEPART : dejar, salir(se) de **3** ABANDON : abandonar, dejar **4** FORGET : dejar, olvidarse de ⟨I left the books at the library : dejé los libros en la biblioteca⟩ **5 to be left** : quedar ⟨it's all I have left : es todo lo que me queda⟩ **6 to be left over** : sobrar **7 to leave out** : omitir, excluir — *vi* : irse, salir, partir, marcharse ⟨she left yesterday morning : se fue ayer por la mañana⟩

leave[2] *n* **1** PERMISSION : permiso *m* ⟨by your leave : con su permiso⟩ **2** *or* **leave of absence** : permiso *m*, licencia *f* ⟨maternity leave : licencia por maternidad⟩ **3 to take one's leave** : despedirse

leaven ['lɛvən] *n* : levadura *f*

leaves → **leaf**[2]

leaving ['li:vɪŋ] *n* **1** : salida *f*, partida *f* **2 leavings** *npl* : restos *mpl*, sobras *fpl*

Lebanese [,lɛbə'ni:z, -'ni:s] *n* : libanés *m*, -nesa *f* — **Lebanese** *adj*

lecherous ['lɛtʃərəs] *adj* : lascivo, libidinoso — **lecherously** *adv*

lechery ['lɛtʃəri] *n* : lascivia *f*, lujuria *f*

lecture[1] ['lɛktʃər] *v* **-tured; -turing** *vi* : dar clase, dictar clase, dar una conferencia — *vt* SCOLD : sermonear, echar una reprimenda a, regañar

lecture[2] *n* **1** : conferencia *f* **2** REPRIMAND : reprimenda *f*

lecturer ['lɛktʃərər] *n* **1** SPEAKER : conferenciante *mf* **2** TEACHER : profesor *m*, -sora *f*

led → **lead**[1]

ledge ['lɛʤ] *n* : repisa *f* (de una pared), antepecho *m* (de una ventana), saliente *m* (de una montaña)

ledger ['lɛʤər] *n* : libro *m* mayor, libro *m* de contabilidad

lee[1] ['li:] *adj* : de sotavento

lee[2] *n* : sotavento *m*

leech ['li:tʃ] *n* : sanguijuela *f*

leek ['li:k] *n* : puerro *m*

leer[1] ['lɪr] *vi* : mirar con lascivia

leer[2] *n* : mirada *f* lasciva

leery ['lɪri] *adj* : receloso

lees ['li:z] *npl* : posos *mpl*, heces *fpl*

leeward[1] ['li:wərd, 'lu:ərd] *adj* : de sotavento

leeward[2] *n* : sotavento *m*

leeway ['li:,weɪ] *n* : libertad *f*, margen *m*

left[1] ['lɛft] *adv* : hacia la izquierda

left[2] → **leave**[1]

left[3] *adj* : izquierdo

left[4] *n* : izquierda *f* ⟨on the left : a la izquierda⟩

left–hand ['lɛft'hænd] *adj* **1** : de la izquierda **2** → **left–handed**

left–handed ['lɛft'hændəd] *adj* **1** : zurdo (dícese de una persona) **2** : con doble sentido ⟨a left-handed compliment : un cumplido a medias⟩

leftist ['lɛftɪst] *n* : izquierdista *mf* — **leftist** *adj*

leftover ['lɛft,o:vər] *adj* : sobrante, que sobra

leftovers [ˈlɛftˌoːvərz] *npl* : restos *mpl*, sobras *fpl*

left wing *n* **the left wing** : la izquierda

left–winger [ˈlɛftˈwɪŋər] *n* : izquierdista *mf*

leg [ˈlɛg] *n* **1** : pierna *f* (de una persona, de carne, de ropa), pata *f* (de un animal, de muebles) **2** STAGE : etapa *f* (de un viaje), vuelta *f* (de una carrera)

legacy [ˈlɛgəsi] *n, pl* **-cies** : legado *m*, herencia *f*

legal [ˈliːgəl] *adj* **1** : legal, jurídico ⟨legal advisor : asesor jurídico⟩ ⟨the legal profession : la abogacía⟩ **2** LAWFUL : legítimo, legal

legalistic [ˌliːgəˈlɪstɪk] *adj* : legalista

legality [liˈgæləti] *n, pl* **-ties** : legalidad *f*

legalize [ˈliːgəˌlaɪz] *vt* **-ized; -izing** : legalizar

legally [ˈliːgəli] *adv* : legalmente

legate [ˈlɛgət] *n* : legado *m*

legation [lɪˈgeɪʃən] *n* : legación *f*

legend [ˈlɛdʒənd] *n* **1** STORY : leyenda *f* **2** INSCRIPTION : leyenda *f*, inscripción *f* **3** : signos *mpl* convencionales (en un mapa)

legendary [ˈlɛdʒənˌdɛri] *adj* : legendario

legerdemain [ˌlɛdʒərdəˈmeɪn] → **sleight of hand**

leggings [ˈlɛgɪŋz, ˈlɛgənz] *npl* : mallas *fpl*

legibility [ˌlɛdʒəˈbɪləti] *n* : legibilidad *f*

legible [ˈlɛdʒəbəl] *adj* : legible

legibly [ˈlɛdʒəbli] *adv* : de manera legible

legion [ˈliːdʒən] *n* : legión *f*

legionnaire [ˌliːdʒəˈnær] *n* : legionario *m*, -ria *f*

legislate [ˈlɛdʒəsˌleɪt] *vi* **-lated; -lating** : legislar

legislation [ˌlɛdʒəsˈleɪʃən] *n* : legislación *f*

legislative [ˈlɛdʒəsˌleɪtɪv] *adj* : legislativo, legislador

legislator [ˈlɛdʒəsˌleɪtər] *n* : legislador *m*, -dora *f*

legislature [ˈlɛdʒəsˌleɪtʃər] *n* : asamblea *f* legislativa

legitimacy [lɪˈdʒɪtəməsi] *n* : legitimidad *f*

legitimate [lɪˈdʒɪtəmət] *adj* **1** VALID : legítimo, válido, justificado **2** LAWFUL : legítimo, legal

legitimately [lɪˈdʒɪtəmətli] *adv* : legítimamente

legitimize [lɪˈdʒɪtəˌmaɪz] *vt* **-mized; -mizing** : legitimar, hacer legítimo

legume [ˈlɛˌgjuːm, lɪˈgjuːm] *n* : legumbre *f*

leisure [ˈliːʒər, ˈlɛ-] *n* **1** : ocio *m*, tiempo *m* libre ⟨a life of leisure : una vida de ocio⟩ **2 to take one's leisure** : reposar **3 at your leisure** : cuando te venga bien, cuando tengas tiempo

leisurely [ˈliːʒərli, ˈlɛ-] *adj & adv* : lento, sin prisas

lemming [ˈlɛmɪŋ] *n* : lemming *m*

lemon [ˈlɛmən] *n* : limón *m*

lemonade [ˌlɛməˈneɪd] *n* : limonada *f*

lemony [ˈlɛməni] *adj* : a limón

lend [ˈlɛnd] *vt* **lent** [ˈlɛnt]; **lending 1** : prestar ⟨to lend money : prestar dinero⟩ **2** GIVE : dar ⟨it lends force to his criticism : da fuerza a su crítica⟩ **3 to lend oneself to** : prestarse a

length [ˈlɛŋkθ] *n* **1** : longitud *f*, largo *m* ⟨10 feet in length : 10 pies de largo⟩ **2** DURATION : duración *f* **3** : trozo *m* (de madera), corte *m* (de tela) **4 to go to any lengths** : hacer todo lo posible **5 at ~** : extensamente ⟨to speak at length : hablar largo y tendido⟩

lengthen [ˈlɛŋkθən] *vt* **1** : alargar ⟨can they lengthen the dress? : ¿se puede alargar el vestido?⟩ **2** EXTEND, PROLONG : prolongar, extender — *vi* : alargarse, crecer ⟨the days are lengthening : los días están creciendo⟩

lengthways [ˈlɛŋkθˌweɪz] → **lengthwise**

lengthwise [ˈlɛŋkθˌwaɪz] *adv* : a lo largo, longitudinalmente

lengthy [ˈlɛŋkθi] *adj* **lengthier; -est 1** OVERLONG : largo y pesado **2** EXTENDED : prolongado, largo

leniency [ˈliːniənsi] *n, pl* **-cies** : lenidad *f*, indulgencia *f*

lenient [ˈliːniənt] *adj* : indulgente, poco severo

leniently [ˈliːniəntli] *adv* : con lenidad, con indulgencia

lens [ˈlɛnz] *n* **1** : cristalino *m* (del ojo) **2** : lente *mf* (de un instrumento o una cámara) **3** → **contact lens**

lent → **lend**

Lent [ˈlɛnt] *n* : Cuaresma *f*

lentil [ˈlɛntəl] *n* : lenteja *f*

Leo [ˈliːoː] *n* : Leo *mf*

leopard [ˈlɛpərd] *n* : leopardo *m*

leotard [ˈliːəˌtɑrd] *n* : leotardo *m*, malla *f*

leper [ˈlɛpər] *n* : leproso *m*, -sa *f*

leprechaun [ˈlɛprəˌkɑn] *n* : duende *m* (irlandés)

leprosy [ˈlɛprəsi] *n* : lepra *f* — **leprous** [ˈlɛprəs] *adj*

lesbian¹ [ˈlɛzbiən] *adj* : lesbiano

lesbian² *n* : lesbiana *f*

lesbianism [ˈlɛzbiəˌnɪzəm] *n* : lesbianismo *m*

lesion [ˈliːʒən] *n* : lesión *f*

less¹ [ˈlɛs] *adv* (*comparative of* **little¹**) : menos ⟨the less you know, the better : cuanto menos sepas, mejor⟩ ⟨less and less : cada vez menos⟩

less² *adj* (*comparative of* **little²**) : menos ⟨less than three : menos de tres⟩ ⟨less money : menos dinero⟩ ⟨nothing less than perfection : nada menos que la perfección⟩

less³ *pron* : menos ⟨I'm earning less : estoy ganando menos⟩

less⁴ *prep* : menos ⟨one month less two days : un mes menos dos días⟩

lessee [lɛˈsiː] *n* : arrendatario *m*, -ria *f*

lessen [ˈlɛsən] *vt* : disminuir, reducir — *vi* : disminuir, reducirse

lesser ['lɛsər] *adj* : menor ⟨to a lesser degree : en menor grado⟩
lesson ['lɛsən] *n* **1** CLASS : clase *f*, curso *m* **2** : lección *f* ⟨the lessons of history : las lecciones de la historia⟩
lessor ['lɛˌsɔr, l'sɔr] *n* : arrendador *m*, -dora *f*
lest ['lɛst] *conj* : para (que) no ⟨lest we forget : para que no olvidemos⟩
let ['lɛt] *vt* **let**; **letting 1** ALLOW : dejar, permitir ⟨let me see it : déjame verlo⟩ **2** MAKE : hacer ⟨let me know : házmelo saber, avísame⟩ ⟨let them wait : que esperen, haz que esperen⟩ **3** RENT : alquilar **4** (*used in the first person plural imperative*) ⟨let's go! : ¡vamos!, ¡vámonos!⟩ ⟨let us pray : oremos⟩ **5 to let down** DISAPPOINT : fallar **6 to let off** FORGIVE : perdonar **7 to let out** REVEAL : revelar **8 to let up** ABATE : amainar, disminuir ⟨the pace never lets up : el ritmo nunca disminuye⟩
letdown *n* : chasco *m*, decepción *f*
lethal ['li:θəl] *adj* : letal — **lethally** *adv*
lethargic [lɪ'θɑrdʒɪk] *adj* : letárgico
lethargy ['lɛθərdʒi] *n* : letargo *m*
let on *vi* **1** ADMIT : reconocer ⟨don't let on! : ¡no digas nada!⟩ **2** PRETEND : fingir
let's ['lɛts] (*contraction of* **let us**) → **let**
letter[1] ['lɛtər] *vt* : marcar con letras, inscribir letras en
letter[2] *n* **1** : letra *f* (del alfabeto) **2** : carta *f* ⟨a letter to my mother : una carta a mi madre⟩ **3 letters** *npl* ARTS : letras *fpl* **4 to the letter** : al pie de la letra
lettering ['lɛtərɪŋ] *n* : letra *f*
lettuce ['lɛtəs] *n* : lechuga *f*
leukemia [lu:'ki:miə] *n* : leucemia *f*
levee ['lɛvi] *n* : dique *m*
level[1] ['lɛvəl] *vt* **-eled** *or* **-elled**; **-eling** *or* **-elling 1** FLATTEN : nivelar, aplanar **2** AIM : apuntar (una pistola), dirigir (una acusación) **3** RAZE : rasar, arrasar
level[2] *adj* **1** EVEN : llano, plano, parejo **2** CALM : tranquilo ⟨to keep a level head : no perder la cabeza⟩
level[3] *n* : nivel *m*
leveler ['lɛvələr] *n* : nivelador *m*, -dora *f*
levelheaded ['lɛvəl'hɛdəd] *adj* : sensato, equilibrado
levelly ['lɛvəli] *adv* CALMLY : con ecuanimidad *f*, con calma
levelness ['lɛvəlnəs] *n* : uniformidad *f*
lever ['lɛvər, 'li:-] *n* : palanca *f*
leverage ['lɛvərɪdʒ, 'li:-] *n* **1** : apalancamiento *m* (en física) **2** INFLUENCE : influencia *f*, palanca *f fam*
leviathan [lɪ'vaɪəθən] *n* : leviatán *m*, gigante *m*
levity ['lɛvəti] *n* : ligereza *f*, frivolidad *f*
levy[1] ['lɛvi] *vt* **levied**; **levying 1** IMPOSE : imponer, exigir, gravar (un impuesto) **2** COLLECT : recaudar (un impuesto)
levy[2] *n, pl* **levies** : impuesto *m*, gravamen *m*
lewd ['lu:d] *adj* : lascivo — **lewdly** *adv*
lewdness ['lu:dnəs] *n* : lascivia *f*

lexical ['lɛksikəl] *adj* : léxico
lexicographer [ˌlɛksə'kɑgrəfər] *n* : lexicógrafo *m*, -fa *f*
lexicographical [ˌlɛksəko'græfɪkəl] *or* **lexicographic** [-'græfɪk] *adj* : lexicográfico
lexicography [ˌlɛksə'kɑgrəfi] *n* : lexicografía *f*
lexicon ['lɛksɪˌkɑn] *n, pl* **-ica** [-kə] *or* **-icons** : léxico *m*, lexicón *m*
liability [ˌlaɪə'bɪləti] *n, pl* **-ties 1** RESPONSIBILITY : responsabilidad *f* **2** SUSCEPTIBILITY : propensión *f* **3** DRAWBACK : desventaja *f* **4 liabilities** *npl* DEBTS : deudas *fpl*, pasivo *m*
liable ['laɪəbəl] *adj* **1** RESPONSIBLE : responsable **2** SUSCEPTIBLE : propenso **3** PROBABLE : probable ⟨it's liable to happen : es probable que suceda⟩
liaison ['li:əˌzɑn, li'eɪ-] *n* **1** CONNECTION : enlace *m*, relación *f* **2** AFFAIR : amorío *m*, aventura *f*
liar ['laɪər] *n* : mentiroso *m*, -sa *f*; embustero *m*, -ra *f*
libel[1] ['laɪbəl] *vt* **-beled** *or* **-belled**; **-beling** *or* **-belling** : difamar, calumniar
libel[2] *n* : difamación *f*, calumnia *f*
libeler ['laɪbələr] *n* : difamador *m*, -dora *f*; calumniador *m*, -dora *f*; libelista *mf*
libelous *or* **libellous** ['laɪbələs] *adj* : difamatorio, calumnioso, injurioso
liberal[1] ['lɪbrəl, 'lɪbərəl] *adj* **1** TOLERANT : liberal, tolerante **2** GENEROUS : generoso **3** ABUNDANT : abundante **4 liberal arts** : humanidades *fpl*, artes *fpl* liberales
liberal[2] *n* : liberal *mf*
liberalism ['lɪbrəˌlɪzəm, 'lɪbərə-] *n* : liberalismo *m*
liberality [ˌlɪbə'ræləti] *n, pl* **-ties** : liberalidad *f*, generosidad *f*
liberalize ['lɪbrəˌlaɪz, 'lɪbərə-] *vt* **-ized**; **-izing** : liberalizar
liberally ['lɪbrəli, 'lɪbərə-] *adv* **1** GENEROUSLY : generosamente **2** ABUNDANTLY : abundantemente **3** FREELY : libremente
liberate ['lɪbəˌreɪt] *vt* **-ated**; **-ating** : liberar, libertar
liberation [ˌlɪbə'reɪʃən] *n* : liberación *f*
liberator ['lɪbəˌreɪtər] *n* : libertador *m*, -dora *f*
Liberian [laɪ'bɪriən] *n* : liberiano *m*, -na *f* — **Liberian** *adj*
libertine ['lɪbərˌti:n] *n* : libertino *m*, -na *f*
liberty ['lɪbərti] *n, pl* **-ties 1** : libertad *f* **2 to take the liberty of** : tomarse la libertad de **3 to take liberties with** : tomarse confianzas con, tomarse libertades con
libido [lə'bi:do:, -'baɪ-] *n, pl* **-dos** : libido *f* — **libidinous** [lə'bɪdənəs] *adj*
Libra ['li:brə] *n* : Libra *mf*
librarian [laɪ'brɛriən] *n* : bibliotecario *m*, -ria *f*
library ['laɪˌbrɛri] *n, pl* **-braries** : biblioteca *f*

librettist [lɪ'brɛʇɪst] *n* : libretista *mf*
libretto [lɪ'brɛʇo] *n, pl* **-tos** *or* **-ti** [-ʇi:] : libreto *m*
Libyan ['lɪbiən] *n* : libio *m*, **-bia** *f* — **Libyan** *adj*
lice → **louse**
license¹ ['laɪsənʦ] *vt* **licensed; licensing** : licenciar, autorizar, dar permiso a
license² *or* **licence** *n* **1** PERMISSION : licencia *f*, permiso *m* **2** PERMIT : licencia *f*, carnet *m Spain* ⟨driver's license : licencia de conducir⟩ **3** FREEDOM : libertad *f* **4** LICENTIOUSNESS : libertinaje *m*
licentious [laɪ'sɛnʧəs] *adj* : licencioso, disoluto — **licentiously** *adv*
licentiousness [laɪ'sɛnʧəsnəs] *n* : libertinaje *m*
lichen ['laɪkən] *n* : liquen *m*
licit ['lɪsət] *adj* : lícito
lick¹ ['lɪk] *vt* **1** : lamer **2** BEAT : darle una paliza (a alguien)
lick² *n* **1** : lamida *f*, lengüetada *f* ⟨a lick of paint : una mano de pintura⟩ **2** BIT : pizca *f*, ápice *m* **3 a lick and a promise** : una lavada a la carrera
licorice ['lɪkərɪʃ, -rəs] *n* : regaliz *m*, dulce *m* de regaliz
lid ['lɪd] *n* **1** COVER : tapa *f* **2** EYELID : párpado *m*
lie¹ ['laɪ] *vi* **lay** ['leɪ]; **lain** ['leɪn]; **lying** ['laɪɪŋ] **1** : acostarse, echarse ⟨I lay down : me acosté⟩ **2** : estar, estar situado, encontrarse ⟨the book lay on the table : el libro estaba en la mesa⟩ ⟨the city lies to the south : la ciudad se encuentra al sur⟩ **3** CONSIST : consistir **4 to lie in** : residir en ⟨the power lies in the people : el poder reside en el pueblo⟩
lie² *vi* **lied; lying** ['laɪɪŋ] : mentir
lie³ *n* **1** UNTRUTH : mentira *f* ⟨to tell lies : decir mentiras⟩ **2** POSITION : posición *f*
liege ['li:ʤ] *n* : señor *m* feudal
lien ['li:n, 'li:ən] *n* : derecho *m* de retención
lieutenant [lu:'tɛnənt] *n* : teniente *mf*
lieutenant colonel *n* : teniente *mf* coronel
lieutenant commander *n* : capitán *m*, -tana *f* de corbeta
lieutenant general *n* : teniente *mf* general
life ['laɪf] *n, pl* **lives** ['laɪvz] **1** : vida *f* ⟨plant life : la vida vegetal⟩ **2** EXISTENCE : vida *f*, existencia *f* **3** BIOGRAPHY : biografía *f*, vida *f* **4** DURATION : duración *f*, vida *f* **5** LIVELINESS : vivacidad *f*, animación *f*
lifeblood ['laɪf,blʌd] *n* : parte *f* vital, sustento *m*
lifeboat ['laɪf,bo:t] *n* : bote *m* salvavidas
lifeguard ['laɪf,gɑrd] *n* : socorrista *mf*, salvavidas *mf*
lifeless ['laɪfləs] *adj* : sin vida, muerto
lifelike ['laɪf,laɪk] *adj* : que parece vivo, natural, verosímil

lifelong ['laɪf'lɔŋ] *adj* : de toda la vida ⟨a lifelong friend : un amigo de toda la vida⟩
life preserver *n* : salvavidas *m*
lifesaver ['laɪf,seɪvər] *n* **1** : salvación *f* **2** → **lifeguard**
lifesaving ['laɪf,seɪvɪŋ] *n* : socorrismo *m*
lifestyle ['laɪf,staɪl] *n* : estilo *m* de vida
lifetime ['laɪf,taɪm] *n* : vida *f*, curso *m* de la vida
lift¹ ['lɪft] *vt* **1** RAISE : levantar, alzar, subir **2** END : levantar ⟨to lift a ban : levantar una prohibición⟩ — *vi* **1** RISE : levantarse, alzarse **2** CLEAR UP : despejar ⟨the fog lifted : se disipó la niebla⟩
lift² *n* **1** LIFTING : levantamiento *m*, alzamiento *m* **2** BOOST : impulso *m*, estímulo *m* **3 to give someone a lift** : llevar en coche a alguien
liftoff ['lɪft,ɔf] *n* : despegue *m*
ligament ['lɪgəmənt] *n* : ligamento *m*
ligature ['lɪgə,ʧur, -ʧər] *n* : ligadura *f*
light¹ ['laɪt] *v* lit ['lɪt] *or* **lighted; lighting** *vt* **1** ILLUMINATE : iluminar, alumbrar **2** IGNITE : encender, prenderle fuego a — *vi* : encenderse, prender
light² *vi* **lighted** *or* **lit** ['lɪt]; **lighting** **1** LAND, SETTLE : posarse **2** DISMOUNT : bajarse, apearse
light³ ['laɪt] *adv* **1** LIGHTLY : suavemente, ligeramente **2 to travel light** : viajar con poco equipaje
light⁴ *adj* **1** LIGHTWEIGHT : ligero, liviano, poco pesado **2** EASY : fácil, ligero, liviano ⟨light reading : lectura fácil⟩ ⟨light work : trabajo liviano⟩ **3** GENTLE, MILD : fino, suave, leve ⟨a light breeze : una brisa suave⟩ ⟨a light rain : una lluvia fina⟩ **4** FRIVOLOUS : de poca importancia, superficial **5** BRIGHT : bien iluminado, claro **6** PALE : claro (dícese de los colores), rubio (dícese del pelo)
light⁵ *n* **1** ILLUMINATION : luz *f* **2** DAYLIGHT : luz *f* del día **3** DAWN : amanecer *m*, madrugada *f* **4** LAMP : lámpara *f* ⟨to turn on off the light : apagar la luz⟩ **5** ASPECT : aspecto *m* ⟨in a new light : con otros ojos⟩ ⟨in the light of : en vista de, a la luz de⟩ **6** MATCH : fósforo *m*, cerillo *m* **7 to bring to light** : sacar a (la) luz
lightbulb ['laɪt,bʌlb] *n* : bombilla *f*, foco *m*, bombillo *m CA, Col, Ven*
lighten ['laɪtən] *vt* **1** ILLUMINATE : iluminar, dar más luz a **2** : aclararse (el pelo) **3** : aligerar (una carga, etc.) **4** RELIEVE : aliviar **5** GLADDEN : alegrar ⟨it lightened his heart : alegró su corazón⟩
lighter ['laɪtər] *n* : encendedor *m*
lighthearted ['laɪt'hɑrtəd] *adj* : alegre, despreocupado, desenfadado — **lightheartedly** *adv*
lightheartedness ['laɪt'hɑrtədnəs] *n* : desenfado *m*, alegría *f*
lighthouse ['laɪt,haʊs] *n* : faro *m*

lighting ['laɪṭɪŋ] *n* : iluminación *f*

lightly ['laɪtli] *adv* **1** GENTLY : suavemente **2** SLIGHTLY : ligeramente **3** FRIVOLOUSLY : a la ligera **4 to let off lightly** : tratar con indulgencia

lightness ['laɪtnəs] *n* **1** BRIGHTNESS : luminosidad *f*, claridad *f* **2** GENTLENESS : ligereza *f*, suavidad *f*, delicadeza *f* **3** : ligereza *f*, liviandad *f* (de peso)

lightning ['laɪtnɪŋ] *n* : relámpago *m*, rayo *m*

lightning bug → **firefly**

lightproof ['laɪt,pru:f] *adj* : impenetrable por la luz, opaco

lightweight ['laɪt'weɪt] *adj* : ligero, liviano, de poco peso

light-year ['laɪt,jɪr] *n* : año *m* luz

lignite ['lɪg,naɪt] *n* : lignito *m*

likable *or* **likeable** ['laɪkəbəl] *adj* : simpático, agradable

like¹ ['laɪk] *v* **liked; liking** *vt* **1** : agradar, gustarle (algo a uno) ⟨he likes rice : le gusta el arroz⟩ ⟨she doesn't like flowers : a ella no le gustan las flores⟩ ⟨I like you : me caes bien⟩ **2** WANT : querer, desear ⟨I'd like a hamburger : quiero una hamburguesa⟩ ⟨he would like more help : le gustaría tener más ayuda⟩ — *vi* : querer ⟨do as you like : haz lo que quieras⟩

like² *adj* : parecido, semejante, similar

like³ *n* **1** PREFERENCE : preferencia *f*, gusto *m* **2 the like** : cosa *f* parecida, cosas *fpl* por el estilo ⟨I've never seen the like : nunca he visto cosa parecida⟩

like⁴ *conj* **1** AS IF : como si ⟨they looked at me like I was crazy : se me quedaron mirando como si estuviera loca⟩ **2** AS : como, igual que ⟨she doesn't love you like I do : ella no te quiere como yo⟩

like⁵ *prep* **1** : como, parecido a ⟨she acts like my mother : se comporta como mi madre⟩ ⟨he looks like me : se parece a mí⟩ **2** : propio de, típico de ⟨that's just like her : eso es muy típico de ella⟩ **3** : como ⟨animals like cows : animales como vacas⟩ **4 like this, like that** : así ⟨do it like that : hazlo así⟩

likelihood ['laɪkli,hʊd] *n* : probabilidad *f* ⟨in all likelihood : con toda probabilidad⟩

likely¹ ['laɪkli] *adv* : probablemente ⟨most likely he's sick : lo más probable es que esté enfermo⟩ ⟨they're likely to come : es probable que vengan⟩

likely² *adj* **-lier; -est 1** PROBABLE : probable ⟨to be likely to : ser muy probable que⟩ **2** SUITABLE : apropiado, adecuado **3** BELIEVABLE : verosímil, creíble **4** PROMISING : prometedor

liken ['laɪkən] *vt* : comparar

likeness ['laɪknəs] *n* **1** SIMILARITY : semejanza *f*, parecido *m* **2** PORTRAIT : retrato *m*

likewise ['laɪk,waɪz] *adv* **1** SIMILARLY : de la misma manera, asimismo **2** ALSO : también, además, asimismo

liking ['laɪkɪŋ] *n* **1** FONDNESS : afición *f* (por una cosa), simpatía *f* (por una persona) **2** TASTE : gusto *m* ⟨is it to your liking? : ¿te gusta?⟩

lilac ['laɪlək, -,læk, -,lɑk] *n* : lila *f*

lilt ['lɪlt] *n* : cadencia *f*, ritmo *m* alegre

lily ['lɪli] *n, pl* **lilies 1** : lirio *m*, azucena *f* **2 lily of the valley** : lirio *m* de los valles, muguete *m*

lima bean ['laɪmə] *n* : frijol *m* de media luna

limb ['lɪm] *n* **1** APPENDAGE : miembro *m*, extremidad *f* **2** BRANCH : rama *f*

limber¹ ['lɪmbər] *vi or* **to limber up** : calentarse, prepararse

limber² *adj* : ágil (dícese de las personas), flexible (dícese de los objetos)

limbo ['lɪm,bo:] *n, pl* **-bos 1** : limbo *m* (en la religión) **2** OBLIVION : olvido *m* ⟨the project is in limbo : el proyecto ha caído en el olvido⟩

lime ['laɪm] *n* **1** : cal *f* (óxido) **2** : lima *f* (fruta), limón *m* verde *Mex*

limelight ['laɪm,laɪt] *n* **to be in the limelight** : ser el centro de atención, estar en el candelero

limerick ['lɪmərɪk] *n* : poema *m* jocoso de cinco versos

limestone ['laɪm,sto:n] *n* : piedra *f* caliza, caliza *f*

limit¹ ['lɪmət] *vt* : limitar, restringir

limit² *n* **1** MAXIMUM : límite *m*, máximo *m* ⟨speed limit : límite de velocidad⟩ **2 limits** *npl* : límites *mpl*, confines *mpl* ⟨city limits : límites de la ciudad⟩ **3 that's the limit!** : ¡eso es el colmo!

limitation [,lɪmə'teɪʃən] *n* : limitación *f*, restricción *f*

limited ['lɪmətəd] *adj* : limitado, restringido

limitless ['lɪmətləs] *adj* : ilimitado, sin límites

limousine ['lɪmə,zi:n, ,lɪmə'-] *n* : limusina *f*

limp¹ ['lɪmp] *vi* : cojear

limp² *adj* **1** FLACCID : fláccido **2** LANK : lacio (dícese del pelo) **3** WEAK : débil ⟨to feel limp : sentirse desfallecer, sentirse sin fuerzas⟩

limp³ *n* : cojera *f*

limpid ['lɪmpəd] *adj* : límpido, claro

limply ['lɪmpli] *adv* : sin fuerzas

limpness ['lɪmpnəs] *n* : flaccidez *f*, debilidad *f*

linden ['lɪndən] *n* : tilo *m*

line¹ ['laɪn] *v* **lined; lining** *vt* **1** : forrar, cubrir ⟨to line a dress : forrar un vestido⟩ ⟨to line the walls : cubrir las paredes⟩ **2** MARK : rayar, trazar líneas en **3** BORDER : bordear **4** ALIGN : alinear — *vi* **to line up** : ponerse en fila, hacer cola

line² *n* **1** CORD, ROPE : cuerda *f* **2** WIRE : cable *m* ⟨power line : cable eléctrico⟩ **3** : línea *f* (de teléfono) **4** ROW : fila *f*, hilera *f* **5** NOTE : nota *f*, líneas *fpl* ⟨drop me a line : mándame unas líneas⟩ **6** COURSE : línea *f* ⟨line of inquiry : línea de investigación⟩ **7** AGREEMENT : conformidad *f* ⟨to be in line with : ser conforme a⟩ ⟨to fall into line : estar de acuerdo⟩ **8** OCCUPATION : ocupación *f*, rama *f*, especialidad *f* **9** LIMIT : línea *f*, límite *m* ⟨dividing line : línea divisoria⟩ ⟨to draw the line : fijar límites⟩ **10** SERVICE : línea *f* ⟨bus line : línea de autobuses⟩ **11** MARK : línea *f*, arruga *f* (de la cara)

lineage ['lɪniidʒ] *n* : linaje *m*, abolengo *m*

lineal ['lɪniəl] *adj* : en línea directa

lineaments ['lɪniəmənts] *npl* : facciones *fpl* (de la cara), rasgos *mpl*

linear ['lɪniər] *adj* : lineal

linen ['lɪnən] *n* : lino *m*

liner ['laɪnər] *n* **1** LINING : forro *m* **2** SHIP : buque *m*, transatlántico *m*

lineup ['laɪnˌəp] *n* **1** : fila *f* de sospechosos **2** : formación *f* (en deportes) **3** ALIGNMENT : alineación *f*

linger ['lɪŋgər] *vi* **1** TARRY : quedarse, entretenerse, rezagarse **2** PERSIST : persistir, sobrevivir

lingerie [ˌlɑndʒəˈreɪ, ˌlænʒəˈriː] *n* : ropa *f* íntima femenina, lencería *f*

lingo ['lɪŋgo] *n*, *pl* **-goes 1** LANGUAGE : idioma *m* **2** JARGON : jerga *f*

linguist ['lɪŋgwɪst] *n* : lingüista *mf*

linguistic [lɪŋˈgwɪstɪk] *adj* : lingüístico

linguistics [lɪŋˈgwɪstɪks] *n* : lingüística *f*

liniment ['lɪnəmənt] *n* : linimento *m*

lining ['laɪnɪŋ] *n* : forro *m*

link¹ ['lɪŋk] *vt* : unir, enlazar, conectar — *vi* **to link up** : unirse, conectar

link² *n* **1** : eslabón *m* (de una cadena) **2** BOND : conexión *f*, lazo *m*, vínculo *m*

linkage ['lɪŋkɪdʒ] *n* : conexión *f*, unión *f*, enlace *m*

linoleum [ləˈnoːliəm] *n* : linóleo *m*

linseed oil ['lɪnˌsiːd] *n* : aceite *m* de linaza

lint ['lɪnt] *n* : pelusa *f*

lintel ['lɪntəl] *n* : dintel *m*

lion ['laɪən] *n* : león *m*

lioness ['laɪənɪs] *n* : leona *f*

lionize ['laɪəˌnaɪz] *vt* **-ized; -izing** : tratar a una persona como muy importante

lip ['lɪp] *n* **1** : labio *m* **2** EDGE, RIM : pico *m* (de una jarra), borde *m* (de una taza)

lipreading ['lɪpˌriːdɪŋ] *n* : lectura *f* de los labios

lipstick ['lɪpˌstɪk] *n* : lápiz *m* de labios, barra *f* de labios

liquefy ['lɪkwəˌfaɪ] *v* **-fied; -fying** *vt* : licuar — *vi* : licuarse

liqueur [lɪˈkʊr, -ˈkər, -ˈkjʊr] *n* : licor *m*

liquid¹ ['lɪkwəd] *adj* : líquido

liquid² *n* : líquido *m*

liquidate ['lɪkwəˌdeɪt] *vt* **-dated; -dating** : liquidar

liquidation [ˌlɪkwəˈdeɪʃən] *n* : liquidación *f*

liquidity [lɪkˈwɪdəti] *n* : liquidez *f*

liquor ['lɪkər] *n* : alcohol *m*, bebidas *fpl* alcohólicas, licor *m*

lisp¹ ['lɪsp] *vi* : cecear

lisp² *n* : ceceo *m*

lissome ['lɪsəm] *adj* **1** FLEXIBLE : flexible **2** LITHE : ágil y grácil

list¹ ['lɪst] *vt* **1** ENUMERATE : hacer una lista de, enumerar **2** INCLUDE : poner en una lista, incluir — *vi* : escorar (dícese de un barco)

list² *n* **1** ENUMERATION : lista *f* **2** SLANT : escora *f*, inclinación *f*

listen ['lɪsən] *vi* **1** : escuchar, oír **2 to listen to** HEED : prestar atención a, hacer caso de, escuchar **3 to listen to** reason : atender a razones

listener ['lɪsənər] *n* : oyente *mf*, persona *f* que sabe escuchar

listless ['lɪstləs] *adj* : lánguido, apático — **listlessly** *adv*

listlessness ['lɪstləsnəs] *n* : apatía *f*, languidez *f*, desgana *f*

lit ['lɪt] → **light**

litany ['lɪtəni] *n*, *pl* **-nies** : letanía *f*

liter ['liːtər] *n* : litro *m*

literacy ['lɪtərəsi] *n* : alfabetismo *m*

literal ['lɪtərəl] *adj* : literal — **literally** *adv*

literary ['lɪtəˌrri] *adj* : literario

literate ['lɪtərət] *adj* : alfabetizado

literature ['lɪtərəˌtʃʊr, -ˈfər] *n* : literatura *f*

lithe ['laɪð, 'laɪθ] *adj* : ágil y grácil

lithesome ['laɪðsəm, 'laɪθ-] → **lissome**

lithium ['lɪθiəm] *n* : litio *m*

lithograph ['lɪθəˌgræf] *n* : litografía *f*

lithographer [lɪˈθɑgrəfər, 'lɪθəˌgræfər] *n* : litógrafo *m*, -fa *f*

lithography [lɪˈθɑgrəfi] *n* : litografía *f*

lithosphere ['lɪθəˌsfɪr] *n* : litosfera *f*

Lithuanian [ˌlɪθəˈweɪniən] *n* **1** : lituano *m* (idioma) **2** : lituano *m*, -na *f* — **Lithuanian** *adj*

litigant ['lɪtɪgənt] *n* : litigante *mf*

litigate ['lɪtəˌgeɪt] *vi* **-gated; -gating** : litigar

litigation [ˌlɪtəˈgeɪʃən] *n* : litigio *m*

litmus paper ['lɪtməs] *n* : papel *m* de tornasol

litter¹ ['lɪtər] *vt* : tirar basura en, ensuciar — *vi* : tirar basura

litter² *n* **1** : camada *f*, cría *f* ⟨a litter of kittens : una cría de gatitos⟩ **2** STRETCHER : camilla *f* **3** RUBBISH : basura *f* **4** : arena *f* higiénica (para gatos)

little¹ ['lɪtəl] *adv* **less** ['lɛs]; **least** ['liːst] **1** : poco ⟨she sings very little : canta muy poco⟩ **2 little did I know that . . .** : no tenía la menor idea de que . . . **3 as little as possible** : lo menos posible

little² *adj* **littler** *or* **less** ['lɛs] *or* **lesser** ['lɛsər]; **littlest** *or* **least** ['liːst] **1** SMALL : pequeño **2** : poco ⟨they speak little Spanish : hablan poco español⟩ ⟨little by little : poco a poco⟩ **3** TRIVIAL : sin importancia, trivial

little³ *n* **1** : poco *m* ⟨little has changed : poco ha cambiado⟩ **2 a little** : un poco, algo ⟨it's a little surprising : es algo sorprendente⟩

Little Dipper → **dipper**

liturgical [ləˈtərdʒɪkəl] *adj* : litúrgico — **liturgically** [-kli] *adv*

liturgy ['lɪtərdʒi] *n, pl* **-gies** : liturgia *f*
livable ['lɪvəbəl] *adj* : habitable
live[1] ['lɪv] *vi* **lived; living 1** EXIST : vivir ⟨as long as I live : mientras viva⟩ ⟨to live from day to day : vivir al día⟩ **2** : llevar una vida, vivir ⟨he lived simply : llevó una vida sencilla⟩ **3** SUBSIST : mantenerse, vivir **4** RESIDE : vivir, residir
live[2] ['laɪv] *adj* **1** LIVING : vivo **2** BURNING : encendido ⟨a live coal : una brasa⟩ **3** : con corriente ⟨live wires : cables con corriente⟩ **4** : cargado, sin estallar ⟨a live bomb : una bomba sin estallar⟩ **5** CURRENT : de actualidad ⟨a live issue : un asunto de actualidad⟩ **6** : en vivo, en directo ⟨a live interview : una entrevista en vivo⟩
livelihood ['laɪvli‚hʊd] *n* : sustento *m*, vida *f*, medio *m* de vida
liveliness ['laɪvlinəs] *n* : animación *f*, vivacidad *f*
livelong ['lɪv'lɔŋ] *adj* : entero, completo
lively ['laɪvli] *adj* **-lier; -est** : animado, vivaz, vivo, enérgico
liven ['laɪvən] *vt* : animar — *vi* : animarse
liver ['lɪvər] *n* : hígado *m*
livery ['lɪvəri] *n, pl* **-eries** : librea *f*
lives → **life**
livestock ['laɪv‚stɑk] *n* : ganado *m*
live wire *n* : persona *f* vivaz y muy activa
livid ['lɪvəd] *adj* **1** BLACK-AND-BLUE : amoratado **2** PALE : lívido **3** ENRAGED : furioso
living[1] ['lɪvɪŋ] *adj* : vivo
living[2] *n* **to make a living** : ganarse la vida
living room *n* : living *m*, sala *f* de estar
lizard ['lɪzərd] *n* : lagarto *m*
llama ['lɑmə, 'jɑ-] *n* : llama *f*
load[1] ['lo:d] *vt* : cargar, embarcar
load[2] *n* **1** CARGO : carga *f* **2** WEIGHT : peso *m* **3** BURDEN : carga *f*, peso *m* **4 loads** *npl* : montón *m*, pila *f*, cantidad *f* ⟨loads of work : un montón de trabajo⟩
loaf[1] ['lo:f] *vi* : holgazanear, flojear, haraganear
loaf[2] *n, pl* **loaves** ['lo:vz] **1** : pan *m*, pan *m* de molde, barra *f* de pan **2 meat loaf** : pan *m* de carne
loafer ['lo:fər] *n* : holgazán *m*, -zana *f*; haragán *m*, -gana *f*; vago *m*, -ga *f*
loam ['lo:m] *n* : marga *f*, suelo *m*
loan[1] ['lo:n] *vt* : prestar
loan[2] *n* : préstamo *m*, empréstito *m* (del banco)
loath ['lo:θ, 'lo:ð] *adj* : poco dispuesto ⟨I am loath to say it : me resisto a decirlo⟩
loathe ['lo:ð] *vt* **loathed; loathing** : odiar, aborrecer
loathing ['lo:ðɪŋ] *n* : aversión *f*, odio *m*, aborrecimiento *m*
loathsome ['lo:θsəm, 'lo:ð-] *adj* : odioso, repugnante
lob[1] ['lɑb] *vt* **lobbed; lobbing** : hacerle un globo (a otro jugador)

lob[2] *n* : globo *m* (en deportes)
lobby[1] ['lɑbi] *v* **-bied; -bying** *vt* : presionar, ejercer presión sobre — *vi* **to lobby for** : presionar para (lograr algo)
lobby[2] *n, pl* **-bies 1** FOYER : vestíbulo *m* **2** LOBBYISTS : grupo *m* de presión, lobby *m*
lobbyist ['lɑbiɪst] *n* : miembro *m* de un lobby
lobe ['lo:b] *n* : lóbulo *m*
lobed ['lo:bd] *adj* : lobulado
lobotomy [lə'bɑtəmi, lo-] *n, pl* **-mies** : lobotomía *f*
lobster ['lɑbstər] *n* : langosta *f*
local[1] ['lo:kəl] *adj* : local
local[2] *n* **1** : anestesia *f* local **2 the locals** : los vecinos del lugar, los habitantes
locale [lo'kæl] *n* : lugar *m*, escenario *m*
locality [lo'kæləti] *n, pl* **-ties** : localidad *f*
localize ['lo:kə‚laɪz] *vt* **-ized; -izing** : localizar
locally ['lo:kəli] *adv* : en la localidad, en la zona
locate ['lo:‚keɪt, lo'keɪt] *v* **-cated; -cating** *vt* **1** POSITION : situar, ubicar **2** FIND : localizar, ubicar — *vi* SETTLE : establecerse
location [lo'keɪʃən] *n* **1** POSITION : posición *f*, emplazamiento *m*, ubicación *f* **2** PLACE : lugar *m*, sitio *m*
lock[1] ['lɑk] *vt* **1** FASTEN : cerrar **2** CONFINE : encerrar ⟨they locked me in the room : me encerraron en la sala⟩ **3** IMMOBILIZE : bloquear (una rueda) — *vi* **1** : cerrarse (dícese de una puerta) **2** : trabarse, bloquearse (dícese de una rueda)
lock[2] *n* **1** : mechón *m* (de pelo) **2** FASTENER : cerradura *f*, cerrojo *m*, chapa *f* **3** : esclusa *f* (de un canal)
locker ['lɑkər] *n* : armario *m*, cajón *m* con llave, lócker *m*
locket ['lɑkət] *n* : medallón *m*, guardapelo *m*, relicario *m*
lockjaw ['lɑk‚dʒɔ] *n* : tétano *m*
lockout ['lɑk‚aʊt] *n* : cierre *m* patronal, lockout *m*
locksmith ['lɑk‚smɪθ] *n* : cerrajero *m*, -ra *f*
lockup ['lɑk‚ʌp] *n* JAIL : cárcel *f*
locomotion [‚lo:kə'mo:ʃən] *n* : locomoción *f*
locomotive[1] [‚lo:kə'mo:tɪv] *adj* : locomotor
locomotive[2] *n* : locomotora *f*
locust ['lo:kəst] *n* **1** : langosta *f*, chapulín *m* CA, Mex **2** CICADA : cigarra *f*, chicharra *f* **3** : acacia *f* blanca (árbol)
locution [lo'kju:ʃən] *n* : locución *f*
lode ['lo:d] *n* : veta *f*, vena *f*, filón *m*
lodestar ['lo:d‚stɑr] *n* : estrella *f* polar
lodestone ['lo:d‚sto:n] *n* : piedra *f* imán
lodge[1] ['lɑdʒ] *v* **lodged; lodging** *vt* **1** HOUSE : hospedar, alojar **2** FILE : presentar ⟨to lodge a complaint : presentar una demanda⟩ — *vi* **1** : posarse, meterse ⟨the bullet lodged in the door

: la bala se incrustó en la puerta⟩ 2
STAY : hospedarse, alojarse

lodge² *n* **1** : pabellón *m*, casa *f* de campo ⟨hunting lodge : refugio de caza⟩ **2** : madriguera *f* (de un castor) **3** : logia *f* ⟨Masonic lodge : logia masónica⟩

lodger ['lɑdʒər] *n* : inquilino *m*, -na *f*; huésped *m*, -peda *f*

lodging ['lɑdʒɪŋ] *n* **1** : alojamiento *m* **2 lodgings** *npl* ROOMS : habitaciones *fpl*

loft ['lɔft] *n* **1** ATTIC : desván *m*, buhardilla *f* **2** : loft *m* (en un depósito comercial) **3** HAYLOFT : pajar *m* **4** : galería *f* ⟨choir loft : galería del coro⟩

loftily ['lɔftəli] *adv* : altaneramente, con altivez

loftiness ['lɔftinəs] *n* **1** NOBILITY : nobleza *f* **2** ARROGANCE : altanería *f*, arrogancia *f* **3** HEIGHT : altura *f*, elevación *f*

lofty ['lɔfti] *adj* **loftier; -est 1** NOBLE : noble, elevado **2** HAUGHTY : altivo, arrogante, altanero **3** HIGH : majestuoso, elevado

log¹ ['lɔg, 'lɑg] *vi* **logged; logging 1** : talar (árboles) **2** RECORD : registrar, anotar **3 to log on** : entrar (al sistema) **4 to log off** : salir (del sistema)

log² *n* **1** : tronco *m*, leño *m* **2** RECORD : diario *m*

logarithm ['lɔgə,rɪðəm, 'lɑ-] *n* : logaritmo *m*

logger ['lɔgər, 'lɑ-] *n* : leñador *m*, -dora *f*

loggerhead ['lɔgər,hd, 'lɑ-] *n* **1** : tortuga *f* boba **2 to be at loggerheads** : estar en pugna, estar en desacuerdo

logic ['lɑdʒɪk] *n* : lógica *f* — **logical** ['lɑdʒɪkəl] *adj* — **logically** [-kli] *adv*

logistic [lə'dʒɪstɪk, lo-] *adj* : logístico

logistics [lə'dʒɪstɪks, lo-] *ns & pl* : logística *f*

logo ['lo:,go:] *n, pl* **logos** [-,go:z] : logotipo *m*

loin ['lɔɪn] *n* **1** : lomo *m* ⟨pork loin : lomo de cerdo⟩ **2 loins** *npl* : lomos *mpl* ⟨to gird one's loins : prepararse para la lucha⟩

loiter ['lɔɪtər] *vi* : vagar, perder el tiempo

loll ['lɑl] *vi* **1** SLOUCH : repantigarse **2** IDLE : holgazanear, hacer el vago

lollipop *or* **lollypop** ['lɑli,pɑp] *n* : dulce *m* en palito, chupete *m* *Chile, Peru*, paleta *f CA, Mex*

lone ['lo:n] *adj* **1** SOLITARY : solitario **2** ONLY : único

loneliness ['lo:nlinəs] *n* : soledad *f*

lonely ['lo:nli] *adj* **-lier; -est 1** SOLITARY : solitario, aislado **2** LONESOME : solo ⟨to feel lonely : sentirse muy solo⟩

loner ['lo:nər] *n* : solitario *m*, -ria *f*; recluso *m*, -sa *f*

lonesome ['lo:nsəm] *adj* : solo, solitario

long¹ ['lɔŋ] *vi* **1 to long for** : añorar, desear, anhelar **2 to long to** : anhelar, estar deseando ⟨they longed to see her : estaban deseando verla, tenían muchas ganas de verla⟩

long² *adv* **1** : mucho, mucho tiempo ⟨it didn't take long : no llevó mucho tiempo⟩ ⟨will it last long? : ¿va a durar mucho?⟩ **2 all day long** : todo el día **3 as long as** *or* **so long as** : mientras, con tal que **4 long before** : mucho antes **5 so long!** : ¡hasta luego!, ¡adiós!

long³ *adj* **longer** ['lɔŋgər]; **longest** ['lɔŋgəst] **1** (*indicating length*)) : largo ⟨the dress is too long : el vestido es demasiado largo⟩ ⟨a long way from : bastante lejos de⟩ ⟨in the long run : a la larga⟩ **2** (*indicating time*)) : largo, prolongado ⟨a long illness : una enfermedad prolongada⟩ ⟨a long walk : un paseo largo⟩ ⟨at long last : por fin⟩ **3 to be long on** : estar cargado de

long⁴ *n* **1 before long** : dentro de poco **2 the long and the short** : lo esencial, lo fundamental

longevity [lɑn'dʒɛvəti] *n* : longevidad *f*

longhand ['lɔŋ,hænd] *n* : escritura *f* a mano, escritura *f* cursiva

longhorn ['lɔŋ,hɔrn] *n* : longhorn *mf*

longing [lɔŋɪŋ] *n* : vivo deseo *m*, ansia *f*, anhelo *m*

longingly [lɔŋɪŋlli] *adv* : ansiosamente, con ansia

longitude ['lɑndʒə,tu:d, -,tju:d] *n* : longitud *f*

longitudinal [,lɑndʒə'tu:dənəl, -'tju:-] *adj* : longitudinal — **longitudinally** *adv*

long–lived ['lɔŋ'lɪvd, -'laɪvd] *adj* : longevo

longshoreman ['lɔŋ'ʃormən] *n, pl* **-men** [-mən, -,mɛn] : estibador *m*, -dora *f*

long–standing ['lɔŋ'stændɪŋ] *adj* : de larga data

long–suffering ['lɔŋ'sʌfərɪŋ] *adj* : paciente, sufrido

look¹ ['lʊk] *vi* **1** GLANCE : mirar ⟨to look out the window : mirar por la ventana⟩ **2** INVESTIGATE : buscar, mirar ⟨look in the closet : busca en el closet⟩ ⟨look before you leap : mira lo que haces⟩ **3** SEEM : parecer ⟨he looks happy : parece estar contento⟩ ⟨I look like my mother : me parezco a mi madre⟩ **4 to look after** : cuidar, cuidar de **5 to look for** EXPECT : esperar **6 to look for** SEEK : buscar — *vt* : mirar

look² *n* **1** GLANCE : mirada *f* **2** EXPRESSION : cara *f* ⟨a look of disapproval : una cara de desaprobación⟩ **3** ASPECT : aspecto *m*, apariencia *f*, aire *m* **4 looks** *npl* : belleza *f*

lookout ['lʊk,aʊt] *n* **1** : centinela *mf*, vigía *mf* **2 to be on the lookout for** : estar al acecho de, andar a la caza de

loom¹ ['lu:m] *vi* **1** : aparecer, surgir ⟨the city loomed up in the distance : la ciudad surgió en la distancia⟩ **2** IMPEND : amenazar, ser inminente **3 to loom large** : cobrar mucha importancia

loom² *n* : telar *m*

loon ['lu:n] *n* : somorgujo *m*, somormujo *m*

loony *or* **looney** ['lu:ni] *adj* **-nier; -est** : loco, chiflado *fam*

loop¹ ['lu:p] *vt* **1** : hacer lazadas con **2 to loop around** : pasar alrededor de — *vi* **1** : rizar el rizo (dícese de un avión) **2** : serpentear (dícese de una carretera)

loop² *n* **1** : lazada *f* (en hilo o cuerda) **2** BEND : curva *f* **3** CIRCUIT : circuito *m* cerrado **4** : rizo *m* (en la aviación) ⟨to loop the loop : rizar el rizo⟩

loophole ['lu:p,ho:l] *n* : escapatoria *f*, pretexto *m*

loose¹ ['lu:s] *vt* **loosed; loosing 1** RELEASE : poner en libertad, soltar **2** UNTIE : deshacer, desatar **3** DISCHARGE, UNLEASH : descargar, desatar

loose² → **loosely**

loose³ *adj* **looser; -est 1** INSECURE : flojo, suelto, poco seguro ⟨a loose tooth : un diente flojo⟩ **2** ROOMY : suelto, holgado ⟨loose clothing : ropa holgada⟩ **3** OPEN : suelto, abierto ⟨loose soil : suelo suelto⟩ ⟨a loose weave : una tejida abierta⟩ **4** FREE : suelto ⟨to break loose : soltarse⟩ **5** SLACK : flojo, flexible **6** APPROXIMATE : libre, aproximado ⟨a loose translation : una traducción aproximada⟩

loosely ['lu:sli] *adv* **1** : sin apretar **2** ROUGHLY : aproximadamente, más o menos

loosen ['lu:sən] *vt* : aflojar

loose–leaf ['lu:s'li:f] *adj* : de hojas sueltas

looseness ['lu:snəs] *n* **1** : aflojamiento *m*, holgura *f* (de ropa) **2** IMPRECISION : imprecisión *f*

loot¹ ['lu:t] *vt* : saquear, robar

loot² *n* : botín *m*

looter ['lu:t̬ər] *n* : saqueador *m*, -dora *f*

lop ['lɑp] *vt* **lopped; lopping** : cortar, podar

lope¹ ['lo:p] *vi* **loped; loping** : correr a paso largo

lope² *n* : paso *m* largo

lopsided ['lɑp,saɪdəd] *adj* **1** CROOKED : torcido, chueco, ladeado **2** ASYMETRICAL : asimétrico

loquacious [lo'kweɪʃəs] *adj* : locuaz

lord ['lɔrd] *n* **1** : señor *m*, noble *m* **2** : lord *m* (en la Gran Bretaña) **3 the Lord** : el Señor **4 good Lord!** : ¡Dios mío!

lordly ['lɔrdli] *adj* **-lier; -est** HAUGHTY : arrogante, altanero

lordship ['lɔrd,ʃɪp] *n* : señoría *f*

Lord's Supper *n* : Eucaristía *f*

lore ['lor] *n* : saber *m* popular, tradición *f*

lose ['lu:z] *v* **lost** ['lɔst]; **losing** ['lu:-zɪŋ] *vt* **1** : perder ⟨I lost my umbrella : perdí mi paraguas⟩ ⟨to lose blood : perder sangre⟩ ⟨to lose one's voice : quedarse fónico⟩ ⟨to have nothing to lose : no tener nada que perder⟩ ⟨to lose no time : no perder tiempo⟩ ⟨to lose weight : perder peso, adelgazar⟩ ⟨to lose one's temper : perder los estribos, enojarse, enfadarse⟩ ⟨to lose sight of : perder de vista⟩ **2** : costar, hacer perder ⟨the errors lost him his job : los errores le

costaron su empleo⟩ **3** : atrasar ⟨my watch loses 5 minutes a day : mi reloj atrasa 5 minutos por día⟩ **4 to lose oneself** : perderse, ensimismarse — *vi* **1** : perder ⟨we lost to the other team : perdimos contra el otro equipo⟩ **2** : atrasarse ⟨the clock loses time : el reloj se atrasa⟩

loser ['lu:zər] *n* : perdedor *m*, -dora *f*

loss ['lɔs] *n* **1** LOSING : pérdida *f* ⟨loss of memory : pérdida de memoria⟩ ⟨to sell at a loss : vender con pérdida⟩ ⟨to be at a loss to : no saber como⟩ **2** DEFEAT : derrota *f*, juego *m* perdido **3 losses** *npl* DEATHS : muertos *mpl*

lost ['lɔst] *adj* **1** : perdido ⟨a lost cause : una causa perdida⟩ ⟨lost in thought : absorto⟩ **2 to get lost** : perderse **3 to make up for lost time** : recuperar el tiempo perdido

lot ['lɑt] *n* **1** DRAWING : sorteo *m* ⟨by lot : por sorteo⟩ **2** SHARE : parte *f*, porción *f* **3** FATE : suerte *f* **4** LAND, PLOT : terreno *m*, solar *m*, lote *m*, parcela *f* ⟨parking lot : estacionamiento⟩ **5 a lot of** *or* **lots of** : mucho, un montón de, bastante ⟨lots of books : un montón de libros, muchos libros⟩ ⟨a lot of people : mucha gente⟩

loth ['lo:θ, 'lo:ð] → **loath**

lotion ['lo:ʃən] *n* : loción *f*

lottery ['lɑt̬əri] *n*, *pl* **-teries** : lotería *f*

lotus ['lo:t̬əs] *n* : loto *m*

loud¹ ['laʊd] *adv* : alto, fuerte ⟨out loud : en voz alta⟩

loud² *adj* **1** : alto, fuerte ⟨a loud voice : una voz alta⟩ **2** NOISY : ruidoso ⟨a loud party : una fiesta ruidosa⟩ **3** FLASHY : llamativo, chillón

loudly ['laʊdli] *adv* : alto, fuerte, en voz alta

loudness ['laʊdnəs] *n* : volumen *m*, fuerza *f* (del ruido)

loudspeaker ['laʊd,spi:kər] *n* : altavoz *m*, altoparlante *m*

lounge¹ ['laʊndʒ] *vi* **lounged; lounging** : holgazanear, gandulear

lounge² *n* : salón *m*, sala *f* de estar

louse ['laʊs] *n*, *pl* **lice** ['laɪs] : piojo *m*

lousy ['laʊzi] *adj* **lousier; -est 1** : piojoso, lleno de piojos **2** BAD : pésimo, muy malo

lout ['laʊt] *n* : bruto *m*, patán *m*

louver *or* **louvre** ['lu:vər] *n* : persiana *f*, listón *m* de persiana

lovable ['lʌvəbəl] *adj* : adorable, amoroso, encantador

love¹ ['lʌv] *v* **loved; loving** *vt* **1** : querer, amar ⟨I love you : te quiero⟩ **2** ENJOY : encantarle a alguien, ser (muy) aficionado a, gustarle mucho a uno (algo) ⟨she loves flowers : le encantan las flores⟩ ⟨he loves golf : es muy aficionado al golf⟩ ⟨I'd love to go with you : me gustaría mucho acompañarte⟩ — *vi* : querer, amar

love² *n* **1** : amor *m*, cariño *m* ⟨to be in love with : estar enamorado de⟩ ⟨to fall

in love with : enamorarse de⟩ **2** EN-
THUSIASM, INTEREST : amor *m*, afición
m, gusto *m* ⟨love of music : afición a
la música⟩ **3** BELOVED : amor *m*; amado *m*, -da *f*; enamorado *m*, -da *f*
loveless [ˈlʌvləs] *adj* : sin amor
loveliness [ˈlʌvlinəs] *n* : belleza *f*, hermosura *f*
lovelorn [ˈlʌvˌlɔrn] *adj* : herido de amor,
perdidamente enamorado
lovely [ˈlʌvli] *adj* **-lier; -est** : hermoso,
bello, lindo, precioso
lover [ˈlʌvər] *n* : amante *mf* (de personas); aficionado *m*, -da *f* (a alguna actividad)
loving [ˈlʌvɪŋ] *adj* : amoroso, cariñoso
lovingly [ˈlʌvɪŋli] *adv* : cariñosamente
low¹ [ˈloː] *vi* : mugir
low² *adv* : bajo, profundo ⟨to aim low
: apuntar bajo⟩ ⟨to lie low : mantenerse escondido⟩ ⟨to turn the lights
down low : bajar las luces⟩
low³ *adj* **lower** [ˈloːər]; **-est 1** : bajo ⟨a
low building : un edificio bajo⟩ ⟨a low
bow : una profunda reverencia⟩ **2**
SOFT : bajo, suave ⟨in a low voice : en
voz baja⟩ **3** SHALLOW : bajo, poco profundo **4** HUMBLE : humilde, modesto
5 DEPRESSED : deprimido, bajo de
moral **6** INFERIOR : bajo, inferior **7**
UNFAVORABLE : mal ⟨to have a low
opinion of him : tener un mal concepto de él⟩ **8 to be low on** : tener poco
de, estar escaso de
low⁴ *n* **1** : punto *m* bajo ⟨to reach an all-
time low : estar más bajo que nunca⟩
2 *or* **low gear** : primera velocidad *f* **3**
: mugido *m* (de una vaca)
lowbrow [ˈloːˌbrɑʊ] *n* : persona *f* inculta
lower¹ [ˈloːər] *vt* **1** DROP : bajar ⟨to lower one's voice : bajar la voz⟩ **2** : arriar, bajar ⟨to lower the flag : arriar la
bandera⟩ **3** REDUCE : reducir, bajar **4
to lower oneself** : rebajarse
lower² [ˈloːər] *adj* : inferior, más bajo, de
abajo
lowland [ˈloːlənd, -ˌlænd] *n* : tierras *fpl*
bajas
lowly [ˈloːli] *adj* **-lier; -est** : humilde,
modesto
loyal [ˈlɔɪəl] *adj* : leal, fiel — **loyally** *adv*
loyalist [ˈlɔɪəlɪst] *n* : partidario *m*, -ria *f*
del régimen
loyalty [ˈlɔɪəlti] *n*, *pl* **-ties** : lealtad *f*, fidelidad *f*
lozenge [ˈlɑzəndʒ] *n* : pastilla *f*
LSD [ˌɛlˌɛsˈdiː] *n* : LSD *m*
lubricant [ˈluːbrɪkənt] *n* : lubricante *m*
lubricate [ˈluːbrɪˌkeɪt] *vt* **-cated; -cating**
: lubricar — **lubrication** [ˌluːbrɪ
ˈkeɪʃən] *n*
lucid [ˈluːsəd] *adj* : lúcido, claro — **lu-
cidly** *adv*
lucidity [luːˈsɪdəti] *n* : lucidez *f*
luck [ˈlʌk] *n* **1** : suerte *f* **2 to have bad
luck** : tener mala suerte **3 good luck!**
: ¡(buena) suerte!
luckily [ˈlʌkəli] *adv* : afortunadamente,
por suerte

luckless [ˈlʌkləs] *adj* : desafortunado
lucky [ˈlʌki] *adj* **luckier; -est 1** : afortunado, que tiene suerte ⟨a lucky
woman : una mujer afortunada⟩ **2**
FORTUITOUS : fortuito, de suerte **3** OP-
PORTUNE : oportuno **4** : de (la) suerte
⟨lucky number : número de la suerte⟩
lucrative [ˈluːkrətɪv] *adj* : lucrativo,
provechoso — **lucratively** *adv*
ludicrous [ˈluːdəkrəs] *adj* : ridículo, absurdo — **ludicrously** *adv*
ludicrousness [ˈluːdəkrəsnəs] *n* : ridiculez *f*, absurdo *m*
lug [ˈlʌg] *vt* **lugged; lugging** : arrastrar,
transportar con dificultad
luggage [ˈlʌgɪdʒ] *n* : equipaje *m*
lugubrious [luˈguːbriəs] *adj* : lúgubre —
lugubriously *adv*
lukewarm [ˈluːkˈwɔrm] *adj* **1** TEPID
: tibio **2** HALFHEARTED : poco entusiasta
lull¹ [ˈlʌl] *vt* **1** CALM, SOOTHE : calmar,
sosegar **2 to lull to sleep** : arrullar,
adormecer
lull² *n* : calma *f*, pausa *f*
lullaby [ˈlʌləˌbaɪ] *n*, *pl* **-bies** : canción *f*
de cuna, arrullo *m*, nana *f*
lumber¹ [ˈlʌmbər] *vt* : aserrar (madera)
— *vi* : moverse pesadamente
lumber² *n* : madera *f*
lumberjack [ˈlʌmbərˌdʒæk] *n* : leñador
m, -dora *f*
lumberyard [ˈlʌmbərˌjɑrd] *n* : almacén
m de maderas
luminary [ˈluːməˌnɛri] *n*, *pl* **-naries**
: lumbrera *f*, luminaria *f*
luminescence [ˌluːməˈnɛsənts] *n* : luminiscencia *f* — **luminescent** [-ˈnɛs-
ənt] *adj*
luminosity [ˌluːməˈnɑsəti] *n*, *pl* **-ties**
: luminosidad *f*
luminous [ˈluːmənəs] *adj* : luminoso —
luminously *adv*
lump¹ [ˈlʌmp] *vt* *or* **to lump together**
: juntar, agrupar, amontonar — *vi*
CLUMP : agruparse, aglutinarse
lump² *n* **1** GLOB : grumo *m* **2** PIECE
: pedazo *m*, trozo *m*, terrón *m* ⟨a lump
of coal : un trozo de carbón⟩ ⟨a lump
of sugar : un terrón de azúcar⟩ **3**
SWELLING : bulto *m*, hinchazón *f*,
protuberancia *f* **4 to have a lump in
one's throat** : tener un nudo en la garganta
lumpy [ˈlʌmpi] *adj* **lumpier; -est 1**
: lleno de grumos (dícese de una salsa)
2 UNEVEN : desigual, disparejo
lunacy [ˈluːnəsi] *n*, *pl* **-cies** : locura *f*
lunar [ˈluːnər] *adj* : lunar
lunatic¹ [ˈluːnəˌtɪk] *adj* : lunático, loco
lunatic² *n* : loco *m*, -ca *f*
lunch¹ [ˈlʌntʃ] *vi* : almorzar, comer
lunch² *n* : almuerzo *m*, comida *f*, lonche
m
luncheon [ˈlʌntʃən] *n* **1** : comida *f*, almuerzo *m* **2 luncheon meat** : fiambres
fpl

lung [ˈlʌŋ] *n* : pulmón *m*

lunge¹ [ˈlʌndʒ] *vi* **lunged; lunging 1** THRUST : atacar (en la esgrima) **2 to lunge forward** : arremeter, lanzarse

lunge² *n* **1** : arremetida *f*, embestida *f* **2** : estocada *f* (en la esgrima)

lurch¹ [ˈlərtʃ] *vi* **1** PITCH : cabecear, dar bandazos, dar sacudidas **2** STAGGER : tambalearse

lurch² *n* **1** : sacudida *f*, bandazo *m* (de un vehículo) **2** : tambaleo *m* (de una persona)

lure¹ [ˈlʊr] *vt* **lured; luring** : atraer

lure² *n* **1** ATTRACTION : atractivo *m* **2** ENTICEMENT : señuelo *m*, aliciente *m* **3** BAIT : cebo *m* artificial (en la pesca)

lurid [ˈlʊrəd] *adj* **1** GRUESOME : espeluznante, horripilante **2** SENSATIONAL : sensacionalista, chocante **3** GAUDY : chillón

lurk [ˈlərk] *vi* : estar al acecho

luscious [ˈlʌʃəs] *adj* **1** DELICIOUS : delicioso, exquisito **2** SEDUCTIVE : seductor, cautivador

lush [ˈlʌʃ] *adj* **1** LUXURIANT : exuberante, lozano **2** LUXURIOUS : suntuoso, lujoso

lust¹ [ˈlʌst] *vi* **to lust after** : desear (a una persona), codiciar (riquezas, etc.)

lust² *n* **1** LASCIVIOUSNESS : lujuria *f*, lascivia *f* **2** CRAVING : deseo *m*, ansia *f*, anhelo *m*

luster *or* **lustre** [ˈlʌstər] *n* **1** GLOSS,

SHEEN : lustre *m*, brillo *m* **2** SPLENDOR : lustre *m*, esplendor *m*

lusterless [ˈlʌstərləs] *adj* : deslustrado, sin brillo

lustful [ˈlʌstfəl] *adj* : lujurioso, lascivo, lleno de deseo

lustrous [ˈlʌstrəs] *adj* : brillante, brilloso, lustroso

lusty [ˈlʌsti] *adj* **lustier; -est** : fuerte, robusto, vigoroso — **lustily** [ˈlʌstəli] *adv*

lute [ˈluːt] *n* : laúd *m*

luxuriant [ˌlʌgˈʒʊriənt, ˌlʌkˈʃʊr-] *adj* **1** : exuberante, lozano (dícese de las plantas) **2** : abundante y hermoso (dícese del pelo) — **luxuriantly** *adv*

luxuriate [ˌlʌgˈʒʊriˌeɪt, ˌlʌkˈʃʊr-] *vi* **-ated; -ating 1** : disfrutar **2 to luxuriate in** : deleitarse con

luxurious [ˌlʌgˈʒʊriəs, ˌlʌkˈʃʊr-] *adj* : lujoso, suntuoso — **luxuriously** *adv*

luxury [ˈlʌkʃəri, ˈlʌgʒə-] *n, pl* **-ries** : lujo *m*

lye [ˈlaɪ] *n* : lejía *f*

lying → **lie¹, lie²**

lymph [ˈlɪmpf] *n* : linfa *f*

lymphatic [lɪmˈfætɪk] *adj* : linfático

lynch [ˈlɪntʃ] *vt* : linchar

lynx [ˈlɪŋks] *n, pl* **lynx** *or* **lynxes** : lince *m*

lyre [ˈlaɪr] *n* : lira *f*

lyric¹ [ˈlɪrɪk] *adj* : lírico

lyric² *n* **1** : poema *m* lírico **2 lyrics** *npl* : letra *f* (de una canción)

lyrical [ˈlɪrɪkəl] *adj* : lírico, elocuente

M

m [ˈɛm] *n, pl* **m's** *or* **ms** [ˈɛmz] : decimotercera letra del alfabeto inglés

ma'am [ˈmæm] → **madam**

macabre [məˈkɑb, -ˈkɑbər, -ˈkɑbrə] *adj* : macabro

macadam [məˈkædəm] *n* : macadán *m*

macaroni [ˌmækəˈroːni] *n* : macarrones *mpl*

macaroon [ˌmækəˈruːn] *n* : macarrón *m*, mostachón *m*

macaw [məˈkɔ] *n* : guacamayo *m*

mace [ˈmeɪs] *n* **1** : maza *f* (arma o símbolo) **2** : macis *f* (especia)

machete [məˈʃɛti] *n* : machete *m*

machination [ˌmækəˈneɪʃən, ˌmæʃə-] *n* : maquinación *f*, intriga *f*

machine¹ [məˈʃiːn] *vt* **-chined; -chining** : trabajar a máquina

machine² *n* **1** : máquina *f* ⟨machine shop : taller de máquinas⟩ ⟨machine language : lenguaje de la máquina⟩ **2** : aparato *m*, maquinaria *f* (en política)

machine gun *n* : ametralladora *f*

machinery [məˈʃiːnəri] *n, pl* **-eries 1** : maquinaria *f* **2** WORKS : mecanismo *m*

machinist [məˈʃiːnɪst] *n* : maquinista *mf*

machismo [mɑˈtʃiːzmoː] *n* : machismo *m*, masculinidad *f*

macho [ˈmɑtʃoː] *adj* : machote, macho

mackerel [ˈmækərəl] *n, pl* **-el** *or* **-els** : caballa *f*

mackinaw [ˈmækəˌnɔ] *n* : chaqueta *f* escocesa de lana

mad [ˈmæd] *adj* **madder; maddest 1** INSANE : loco, demente **2** RABID : rabioso **3** FOOLISH : tonto, insensato **4** ANGRY : enojado, furioso **5** CRAZY : loco ⟨I'm mad about you : estoy loco por ti⟩

Madagascan [ˌmædəˈgæskən] *n* : malgache *mf* — **Madagascan** *adj*

madam [ˈmædəm] *n, pl* **mesdames** [meɪˈdɑm, -ˈdæm] : señora *f*

madcap¹ [ˈmædˌkæp] *adj* ZANY : alocado, disparatado

madcap² *n* : alocado *m*, -da *f*

madden [ˈmædən] *vt* : enloquecer, enfurecer

maddening [ˈmædənɪŋ] *adj* : enloquecedor, exasperante ⟨I find it maddening : me saca de quicio⟩

made → **make¹**

madhouse [ˈmædˌhaʊs] *n* : manicomio *m* ⟨the office was a madhouse : la oficina parecía una casa de locos⟩

madly [ˈmædli] *adv* : como un loco, locamente

madman [ˈmædˌmæn, -mən] *n, pl* **-men** [-mən, -ˌmɛn] : loco *m*, demente *m*
madness [ˈmædnəs] *n* : locura *f*, demencia *f*
madwoman [ˈmædˌwʊmən] *n, pl* **-women** [-ˌwɪmən] : loca *f*, demente *f*
maelstrom [ˈmeɪlstrəm] *n* : remolino *m*, vorágine *f*
maestro [ˈmaɪˌstroː] *n, pl* **-stros** *or* **-stri** [-ˌstriː] : maestro *m*
Mafia [ˈmɑfiə] *n* : Mafia *f*
magazine [ˈmæɡəˌziːn] *n* **1** STOREHOUSE : almacén *m*, polvorín *m* (de explosivos) **2** PERIODICAL : revista *f* **3** : cargador *m* (de un arma de fuego)
magenta [məˈdʒɛntə] *n* : magenta *f*, color *m* magenta
maggot [ˈmæɡət] *n* : gusano *m*
magic[1] [ˈmædʒɪk] *or* **magical** [ˈmædʒɪkəl] *adj* : mágico
magic[2] *n* : magia *f*
magically [ˈmædʒɪkli] *adv* : mágicamente ⟨they magically appeared : aparecieron como por arte de magia⟩
magician [məˈdʒɪʃən] *n* **1** SORCERER : mago *m*, -ga *f* **2** CONJURER : prestidigitador *m*, -dora *f*; mago *m*, -ga *f*
magistrate [ˈmædʒəˌstreɪt] *n* : magistrado *m*, -da *f*
magma [ˈmæɡmə] *n* : magma *m*
magnanimity [ˌmæɡnəˈnɪməti] *n, pl* **-ties** : magnanimidad *f*
magnanimous [mæɡˈnænəməs] *adj* : magnánimo, generoso — **magnanimously** *adv*
magnate [ˈmæɡˌneɪt, -nət] *n* : magnate *mf*
magnesium [mæɡˈniːziəm, -ʒəm] *n* : magnesio *m*
magnet [ˈmæɡnət] *n* : imán *m*
magnetic [mæɡˈnɛtɪk] *adj* : magnético — **magnetically** [-tɪkli] *adv*
magnetic field *n* : campo *m* magnético
magnetism [ˈmæɡnəˌtɪzəm] *n* : magnetismo *m*
magnetize [ˈmæɡnəˌtaɪz] *vt* **-tized; -tizing 1** : magnetizar, imantar **2** ATTRACT : magnetizar, atraer
magnification [ˌmæɡnəfəˈkeɪʃən] *n* : aumento *m*, ampliación *f*
magnificence [mæɡˈnɪfəsənts] *n* : magnificencia *f*
magnificent [mæɡˈnɪfəsənt] *adj* : magnífico — **magnificently** *adv*
magnify [ˈmæɡnəˌfaɪ] *vt* **-fied; -fying 1** ENLARGE : ampliar **2** EXAGGERATE : magnificar, exagerar
magnifying glass *n* : lupa *f*
magnitude [ˈmæɡnəˌtuːd, -ˌtjuːd] *n* **1** GREATNESS : magnitud *f*, grandeza *f* **2** QUANTITY : cantidad *f* **3** IMPORTANCE : magnitud *f*, envergadura *f*
magnolia [mæɡˈnoːljə] *n* : magnolia *f* (flor), magnolio *m* (árbol)
magpie [ˈmæɡˌpaɪ] *n* : urraca *f*
mahogany [məˈhɑɡəni] *n, pl* **-nies** : caoba *f*

maid [ˈmeɪd] *n* **1** MAIDEN : doncella *f* **2** *or* **maidservant** [ˈmeɪdˌsərvənt] : sirvienta *f*, muchacha *f*, mucama *f*, criada *f*
maiden[1] [ˈmeɪdən] *adj* **1** UNMARRIED : soltera **2** FIRST : primero ⟨maiden voyage : primera travesía⟩
maiden[2] *n* : doncella *f*
maidenhood [ˈmeɪdənˌhʊd] *n* : doncellez *f*
maiden name *n* : nombre *m* de soltera
mail[1] [ˈmeɪl] *vt* : enviar por correo, echar al correo
mail[2] *n* **1** : correo *m* ⟨airmail : correo aéreo⟩ **2** : malla *f* ⟨coat of mail : cota de malla⟩
mailbox [ˈmeɪlˌbɑks] *n* : buzón *m*
mailman [ˈmeɪlˌmæn, -mən] *n, pl* **-men** [-mən, -ˌmɛn] : cartero *m*
maim [ˈmeɪm] *vt* : mutilar, desfigurar, lisiar
main[1] [ˈmeɪn] *adj* : principal, central ⟨the main office : la oficina central⟩
main[2] *n* **1** HIGH SEAS : alta mar *f* **2** : tubería *f* principal (de agua o gas), cable *m* principal (de un circuito) **3 with might and main** : con todas sus fuerzas
mainframe [ˈmeɪnˌfreɪm] *n* : mainframe *m*, computadora *f* central
mainland [ˈmeɪnˌlænd, -lənd] *n* : continente *m*
mainly [ˈmeɪnli] *adv* **1** PRINCIPALLY : principalmente, en primer lugar **2** MOSTLY : principalmente, en la mayor parte
mainstay [ˈmeɪnˌsteɪ] *n* : pilar *m*, sostén *m* principal
mainstream[1] [ˈmeɪnˌstriːm] *adj* : dominante, corriente, convencional
mainstream[2] *n* : corriente *f* principal
maintain [meɪnˈteɪn] *vt* **1** SERVICE : dar mantenimiento a (una máquina) **2** PRESERVE : mantener, conservar ⟨to maintain silence : guardar silencio⟩ **3** SUPPORT : mantener, sostener **4** ASSERT : mantener, sostener, afirmar
maintenance [ˈmeɪntənənts] *n* : mantenimiento *m*
maize [ˈmeɪz] *n* : maíz *m*
majestic [məˈdʒɛstɪk] *adj* : majestuoso — **majestically** [-tɪkli] *adv*
majesty [ˈmædʒəsti] *n, pl* **-ties 1** : majestad *f* ⟨Your Majesty : su Majestad⟩ **2** SPLENDOR : majestuosidad *f*, esplendor *m*
major[1] [ˈmeɪdʒər] *vi* **-jored; -joring** : especializarse
major[2] *adj* **1** GREATER : mayor **2** NOTEWORTHY : mayor, notable **3** SERIOUS : grave **4** : mayor (en la música)
major[3] *n* **1** : mayor *mf*, comandante *mf* (en las fuerzas armadas) **2** : especialidad *f* (universitaria)
Majorcan [mɑˈdʒɔrkən, mə-, -ˈjɔr-] *n* : mallorquín *m*, -quina *f* — **Majorcan** *adj*
major general *n* : general *mf* de división

majority [mə'dʒorəti̞] *n, pl* **-ties** **1** ADULTHOOD : mayoría *f* de edad **2** : mayoría *f*, mayor parte *f* ⟨the vast majority : la inmensa mayoría⟩

make[1] ['meɪk] *v* **made** ['meɪd;]; **making** *vt* **1** CREATE : hacer ⟨to make noise : hacer ruido⟩ **2** FASHION, MANUFACTURE : hacer, fabricar ⟨she made a dress : hizo un vestido⟩ **3** DEVISE, FORM : desarrollar, elaborar, formar **4** CONSTITUTE : hacer, constituir ⟨made of stone : hecho de piedra⟩ **5** PREPARE : hacer, preparar **6** RENDER : hacer, poner ⟨it makes him nervous : lo pone nervioso⟩ ⟨to make someone happy : hacer feliz a alguien⟩ ⟨it made me sad : me dio pena⟩ **7** PERFORM : hacer ⟨to make a gesture : hacer un gesto⟩ **8** COMPEL : hacer, forzar, obligar **9** EARN : ganar ⟨to make a living : ganarse la vida⟩ — *vi* **1** HEAD : ir, dirigirse ⟨we made for home : nos fuimos a casa⟩ **2 to make do** : arreglárselas **3 to make good** REPAY : pagar **4 to make good** SUCCEED : tener éxito

make[2] *n* BRAND : marca *f*

make–believe[1] [ˌmeɪkbə'li:v] *adj* : imaginario

make–believe[2] *n* : fantasía *f*, invención *f* ⟨a world of make-believe : un mundo de ensueño⟩

make out *vt* **1** WRITE : hacer (un cheque) **2** DISCERN : distinguir, divisar **3** UNDERSTAND : comprender, entender — *vi* : arreglárselas ⟨how did you make out? : ¿qué tal te fue?⟩

maker ['meɪkər] *n* : fabricante *mf*

makeshift ['meɪkˌʃɪft] *adj* : provisional, improvisado

makeup ['meɪkˌʌp] *n* **1** COMPOSITION : composición *f* **2** CHARACTER : carácter *m*, temperamento *m* **3** COSMETICS : maquillaje *m*

make up *vt* **1** INVENT : inventar **2** : recuperar ⟨she made up the time : recuperó las horas perdidas⟩ — *vi* RECONCILE : hacer las paces, reconciliarse

making ['meɪkɪŋ] *n* **1** : creación *f*, producción *f* ⟨in the making : en ciernes⟩ **2 to have the makings of** : tener madera de (dícese de personas), tener los ingredientes para

maladjusted [ˌmælə'dʒʌstəd] *adj* : inadaptado

malady ['mælədi] *n, pl* **-dies** : dolencia *f*, enfermedad *f*, mal *m*

malaise [mə'leɪz, mæ-] *n* : malestar *m*

malapropism ['mæləˌprɑˌpɪzəm] *n* : uso *m* incorrecto y cómico de una palabra

malaria [mə'lɛriə] *n* : malaria *f*, paludismo *m*

malarkey [mə'lɑrki] *n* : tonterías *fpl*, estupideces *fpl*

Malawian [mə'lɑwiən] *n* : malauiano *m*, -na *f* — **Malawian** *adj*

Malay [mə'leɪ, 'meɪˌleɪ] *n* **1** *or* **Malayan** [mə'leɪən, meɪ-; 'meɪˌleɪən] : malayo *m*, -ya *f* **2** : malayo *m* (idioma) — **Malay** *or* **Malayan** *adj*

Malaysian [mə'leɪʒən, -ʃən] *n* : malasio *m*, -sia *f*; malaisio *m*, -sia *f* — **Malaysian** *adj*

male[1] ['meɪl] *adj* **1** : macho **2** MASCULINE : masculino

male[2] *n* : macho *m* (de animales o plantas), varón *m* (de personas)

malefactor ['mæləˌfæktər] *n* : malhechor *m*, -chora *f*

maleness ['meɪlnəs] *n* : masculinidad *f*

malevolence [mə'lɛvələnts] *n* : malevolencia *f*

malevolent [mə'lɛvələnt] *adj* : malévolo

malformation [ˌmælfɔr'meɪʃən] *n* : malformación *f*

malformed [mæl'fɔrmd] *adj* : mal formado, deforme

malfunction[1] [mæl'fʌŋkʃən] *vi* : funcionar mal

malfunction[2] *n* : mal funcionamiento *m*

malice ['mæləs] *n* **1** : malicia *f*, malevolencia *f* **2 with malice aforethought** : con premeditación

malicious [mə'lɪʃəs] *adj* : malicioso, malévolo — **maliciously** *adv*

malign[1] [mə'laɪn] *vt* : calumniar, difamar

malign[2] *adj* : maligno

malignancy [mə'lɪgnəntsi] *n, pl* **-cies** : malignidad *f*

malignant [mə'lɪgnənt] *adj* : maligno

malinger [mə'lɪŋgər] *vi* : fingirse enfermo

malingerer [mə'lɪŋgərər] *n* : uno que se finge enfermo

mall ['mɔl] *n* **1** PROMENADE : alameda *f*, paseo *m* (arbolado) **2** : centro *m* comercial ⟨shopping mall : galería comercial⟩

mallard ['mælərd] *n, pl* **-lard** *or* **-lards** : pato *m* real, ánade *mf* real

malleable ['mæliəbəl] *adj* : maleable

mallet ['mælət] *n* : mazo *m*

malnourished [mæl'nərɪʃt] *adj* : desnutrido, malnutrido

malnutrition [ˌmælnu'trɪʃən, -nju-] *n* : desnutrición *f*, malnutrición *f*

malodorous [mæl'o:dərəs] *adj* : maloliente

malpractice [ˌmæl'præktəs] *n* : mala práctica *f*, negligencia *f*

malt ['mɔlt] *n* : malta *f*

maltreat [mæl'tri:t] *vt* : maltratar

mama *or* **mamma** ['mɑmə] *n* : mamá *f*

mammal ['mæməl] *n* : mamífero *m*

mammalian [mə'meɪliən, mæ-] *adj* : mamífero

mammary ['mæməri] *adj* **1** : mamario **2 mammary gland** : glándula mamaria

mammogram ['mæməˌgræm] *n* : mamografía *f*

mammoth[1] ['mæməθ] *adj* : colosal, gigantesco

mammoth[2] *n* : mamut *m*

man[1] ['mæn] *vt* **manned; manning** : tripular (un barco o avión), encargarse de (un servicio)

man² *n, pl* **men** ['mɛn] **1** PERSON : hombre *m*, persona *f* **2** MALE : hombre *m* **3** MANKIND : humanidad *f*

manacles ['mænɪkəlz] *npl* HANDCUFFS : esposas *fpl*

manage ['mænɪdʒ] *v* **-aged; -aging** *vt* **1** HANDLE : controlar, manejar **2** DIRECT : administrar, dirigir **3** CONTRIVE : lograr, ingeniárselas para — *vi* COPE : arreglárselas

manageable ['mænɪdʒəbəl] *adj* : manejable

management ['mænɪdʒmənt] *n* **1** DIRECTION : administración *f*, gestión *f*, dirección *f* **2** HANDLING : manejo *m* **3** MANAGERS : dirección *f*, gerencia *f*

manager ['mænɪdʒər] *n* : director *m*, -tora *f*; gerente *mf*; administrador *m*, -dora *f*

managerial [,mænə'dʒɪriəl] *adj* : directivo, gerencial

mandarin ['mændərən] *n* **1** : mandarín *m* **2** *or* **mandarin orange** : mandarina *f*

mandate ['mæn,deɪt] *n* : mandato *m*

mandatory ['mændə,tori] *adj* : obligatorio

mandible ['mændəbəl] *n* : mandíbula *f*

mandolin [,mændə'lɪn, 'mændələn] *n* : mandolina *f*

mane ['meɪn] *n* : crin *f* (de un caballo), melena *f* (de un león o una persona)

maneuver¹ [mə'nu:vər, -'nju:-] *vt* **1** PLACE, POSITION : maniobrar, posicionar, colocar **2** MANIPULATE : manipular, maniobrar — *vi* : maniobrar

maneuver² *n* : maniobra *f*

manfully ['mænfəli] *adj* : valientemente

manganese ['mæŋgə,ni:z, -,ni:s] *n* : manganeso *m*

mange ['meɪndʒ] *n* : sarna *f*

manger ['meɪndʒər] *n* : pesebre *m*

mangle ['mæŋgəl] *vt* **-gled; -gling 1** CRUSH, DESTROY : aplastar, despedazar, destrozar **2** MUTILATE : mutilar ⟨to mangle a text : mutilar un texto⟩

mango ['mæŋ,goː] *n, pl* **-goes** : mango *m*

mangrove ['mæŋ,groːv, 'mæŋ-] *n* : mangle *m*

mangy ['meɪndʒi] *adj* **mangier; -est 1** : sarnoso **2** SHABBY : gastado

manhandle ['mæn,hændəl] *vt* **-dled; -dling** : maltratar, tratar con poco cuidado

manhole ['mæn,hoːl] *n* : boca *f* de alcantarilla

manhood ['mæn,hʊd] *n* **1** : madurez *f* (de un hombre) **2** COURAGE, MANLINESS : hombría *f*, valor *m* **3** MEN : hombres *mpl*

manhunt ['mæn,hʌnt] *n* : búsqueda *f* (de un criminal)

mania ['meɪniə, -njə] *n* : manía *f*

maniac ['meɪni,æk] *n* : maníaco *m*, -ca *f*; maniático *m*, -ca *f*

maniacal [mə'naɪəkəl] *adj* : maníaco, maniaco

manicure¹ ['mænə,kjʊr] *vt* **-cured; -curing 1** : hacer la manicura a **2** TRIM : recortar

manicure² *n* : manicura *f*

manicurist ['mænə,kjʊrɪst] *n* : manicuro *m*, -ra *f*

manifest¹ ['mænə,fɛst] *vt* : manifestar

manifest² *adj* : manifiesto, patente — **manifestly** *adv*

manifestation [,mænəfə'steɪʃən] *n* : manifestación *f*

manifesto [,mænə'fɛs,to:] *n, pl* **-tos** *or* **-toes** : manifiesto *m*

manifold¹ ['mænə,fo:ld] *adj* : diverso, variado

manifold² *n* : colector *m* (de escape)

manipulate [mə'nɪpjə,leɪt] *vt* **-lated; -lating** : manipular

manipulation [mə,nɪpjə'leɪʃən] *n* : manipulación *f*

manipulative [mə'nɪpjə,leɪtɪv, -lətɪv] *adj* : manipulador

mankind ['mæn'kaɪnd, ,kaɪnd] *n* : género *m* humano, humanidad *f*

manliness ['mænlinəs] *n* : hombría *f*, masculinidad *f*

manly ['mænli] *adj* **-lier; -est** : varonil, viril

man-made ['mæn'meɪd] *adj* : artificial ⟨man-made fabrics : telas sintéticas⟩

manna ['mænə] *n* : maná *m*

mannequin ['mænɪkən] *n* **1** DUMMY : maniquí *m* **2** MODEL : modelo *mf*

manner ['mænər] *n* **1** KIND, SORT : tipo *m*, clase *f* **2** WAY : manera *f*, modo *m* **3** STYLE : estilo *m* (artístico) **4 manners** *npl* CUSTOMS : costumbres *fpl* ⟨Victorian manners : costumbres victorianas⟩ **5 manners** *npl* ETIQUETTE : modales *mpl*, educación *f*, etiqueta *f* ⟨good manners : buenos modales⟩

mannered ['mænərd] *adj* **1** AFFECTED, ARTIFICIAL : amanerado, afectado **2** **well-mannered** : educado, cortés **3** → **ill-mannered**

mannerism ['mænə,rɪzəm] *n* : peculiaridad *f*, gesto *m* particular

mannerly ['mænərli] *adj* : cortés, bien educado

mannish ['mænɪʃ] *adj* : masculino, hombruno

man-of-war [,mænə'wɔr, -əv'wɔr] *n, pl* **men-of-war** [,mɛn-] WARSHIP : buque *m* de guerra

manor ['mænər] *n* **1** : casa *f* solariega, casa *f* señorial **2** ESTATE : señorío *m*

manpower ['mæn,paʊər] *n* : personal *m*, mano *f* de obra

mansion ['mænʃən] *n* : mansión *f*

manslaughter ['mæn,slɔtər] *n* : homicidio *m* sin premeditación

mantel ['mæntəl] *n* : repisa *f* de chimenea

mantelpiece ['mæntəl,pi:s] → **mantel**

mantis ['mæntəs] *n, pl* **-tises** *or* **-tes** ['mæn,ti:z] : mantis *f* religiosa

mantle ['mæntəl] *n* : manto *m*

manual¹ ['mænjʊəl] *adj* : manual — **manually** *adv*

manual² *n* : manual *m*

manufacture¹ [ˌmænjə'fæktʃər] *vt* **-tured; -turing** : fabricar, manufacturar, confeccionar (ropa), elaborar (comestibles)

manufacture² *n* : manufactura *f*, fabricación *f*, confección *f* (de ropa), elaboración *f* (de comestibles)

manufacturer [ˌmænjə'fæktʃərər] *n* : fabricante *m*; manufacturero *m*, -ra *f*

manure [mə'nʊr, -'njʊr] *n* : estiércol *m*

manuscript ['mænjəˌskrɪpt] *n* : manuscrito *m*

many¹ ['meni] *adj* **more** ['mor]; **most** ['moːst] : muchos

many² *pron* : muchos *pl*, -chas *pl*

map¹ ['mæp] *vt* **mapped; mapping 1** : trazar el mapa de **2** PLAN : planear, proyectar ⟨to map out a program : planear un programa⟩

map² *n* : mapa *m*

maple ['meɪpəl] *n* : arce *m*

mar ['mɑr] *vt* **marred; marring 1** SPOIL : estropear, echar a perder **2** DEFACE : desfigurar

maraschino [ˌmærə'skiːnoː, -'ʃiː-] *n*, *pl* **-nos** : cereza *f* al marrasquino

marathon ['mærəˌθɑn] *n* **1** RACE : maratón *m* **2** CONTEST : competencia *f* de resistencia

maraud [mə'rɔd] *vi* : merodear

marauder [mə'rɔdər] *n* : merodeador *m*, -dora *f*

marble ['mɑrbəl] *n* **1** : mármol *m* **2** : canica *f* ⟨to play marbles : jugar a las canicas⟩

march¹ ['mɑrtʃ] *vi* **1** : marchar, desfilar ⟨they marched past the grandstand : desfilaron ante la tribuna⟩ **2** : caminar con resolución ⟨she marched right up to him : se le acercó sin vacilación⟩

march² *n* **1** MARCHING : marcha *f* **2** PASSAGE : paso *m* (del tiempo) **3** PROGRESS : avance *m*, progreso *m* **4** : marcha *f* (en música)

March ['mɑrtʃ] *n* : marzo *m*

marchioness ['mɑrʃənɪs] *n* : marquesa *f*

Mardi Gras ['mɑrdiˌgrɑ] *n* : martes *m* de Carnaval

mare ['mær] *n* : yegua *f*

margarine ['mɑrdʒərən] *n* : margarina *f*

margin ['mɑrdʒən] *n* : margen *m*

marginal ['mɑrdʒənəl] *adj* **1** : marginal **2** MINIMAL : mínimo — **marginally** *adv*

marigold ['mærəˌgoːld] *n* : maravilla *f*, caléndula *f*

marijuana [ˌmærə'hwɑnə] *n* : marihuana *f*

marina [mə'riːnə] *n* : puerto *m* deportivo

marinade [ˌmærə'nɑd] *n* : adobo *m*, marinada *f*

marinate ['mærəˌneɪt] *vt* **-nated; -nating** : marinar

marine¹ [mə'riːn] *adj* **1** : marino ⟨marine life : vida marina⟩ **2** NAUTICAL : náutico, marítimo **3** : de la infantería de marina

marine² *n* : soldado *m* de marina

mariner ['mærɪnər] *n* : marinero *m*, marino *m*

marionette [ˌmæriə'nɛt] *n* : marioneta *f*, títere *m*

marital ['mærətəl] *adj* **1** : matrimonial **2 marital status** : estado *m* civil

maritime ['mærəˌtaɪm] *adj* : marítimo

marjoram ['mɑrdʒərəm] *n* : mejorana *f*

mark¹ ['mɑrk] *vt* **1** : marcar **2** CHARACTERIZE : caracterizar **3** SIGNAL : señalar **4** NOTICE : prestar atención a, hacer caso de **5 to mark off** : demarcar, delimitar

mark² *n* **1** TARGET : blanco *m* **2** : marca *f*, señal *f* ⟨put a mark where you left off : pon una señal donde terminaste⟩ **3** INDICATION : señal *f*, indicio *m* **4** GRADE : nota *f* **5** IMPRINT : huella *f*, marca *f* **6** BLEMISH : marca *f*, imperfección *f*

marked ['mɑrkt] *adj* : marcado, notable — **markedly** ['mɑrkədli] *adv*

marker ['mɑrkər] *n* : marcador *m*

market¹ ['mɑrkət] *vt* : poner en venta, comercializar

market² *n* **1** MARKETPLACE : mercado *m* ⟨the open market : el mercado libre⟩ **2** DEMAND : demanda *f*, mercado *m* **3** STORE : tienda *f* **4** → **stock market**

marketable ['mɑrkətəbəl] *adj* : vendible

marketing ['mɑrkətɪŋ] *n* : mercadotecnia *f*, mercadeo *m*

marketplace ['mɑrkətˌpleɪs] *n* : mercado *m*

marksman ['mɑrksmən] *n*, *pl* **-men** [-mən, -ˌmɛn] : tirador *m*

marksmanship ['mɑrksmənˌʃɪp] *n* : puntería *f*

marlin ['mɑrlɪn] *n* : marlín *m*

marmalade ['mɑrməˌleɪd] *n* : mermelada *f*

marmoset ['mɑrməˌsɛt] *n* : tití *m*

marmot ['mɑrmət] *n* : marmota *f*

maroon¹ [mə'ruːn] *vt* : abandonar, aislar

maroon² *n* : rojo *m* oscuro, granate *m*

marquee [mɑr'kiː] *n* : marquesina *f*

marquess ['mɑrkwɪs] *or* **marquis** ['mɑrkwɪs, mɑr'kiː] *n*, *pl* **-quesses** *or* **-quises** [-'kiːz, -'kiːzəz] *or* **-quis** [-'kiː, -'kiːz] : marqués *m*

marquise [mɑr'kiːz] → **marchioness**

marriage ['mærɪdʒ] *n* **1** : matrimonio *m* **2** WEDDING : casamiento *m*, boda *f*

marriageable ['mærɪdʒəbəl] *adj* **of marriageable age** : de edad de casarse

married ['mærid] *adj* **1** : casado **2 to get married** : casarse

marrow ['mæroː] *n* : médula *f*, tuétano *m*

marry ['mæri] *vt* **-ried; -rying 1** : casar ⟨the priest married them : el cura los casó⟩ **2** : casarse con ⟨she married John : se casó con John⟩

Mars ['mɑrz] *n* : Marte *m*
marsh ['mɑrʃ] *n* 1 : pantano *m* 2 **salt marsh** : marisma *f*
marshal[1] ['mɑrʃəl] *vt* -shaled *or* -shalled; -shaling *or* -shalling 1 : poner en orden, reunir 2 USHER : conducir
marshal[2] *n* 1 : maestro *m* de ceremonias 2 : mariscal *m* (en el ejército); jefe *m*, -fa *f* (de la policía, de los bomberos, etc.)
marshmallow ['mɑrʃˌmɛlo:, -ˌmælo:] *n* : malvavisco *m*
marshy ['mɑrʃi] *adj* **marshier; -est** : pantanoso
marsupial [mɑrˈsu:piəl] *n* : marsupial *m*
mart ['mɑrt] *n* MARKET : mercado *m*
marten ['mɑrtən] *n, pl* -ten *or* -tens : marta *f*
martial ['mɑrʃəl] *adj* : marcial
martin ['mɑrtən] *n* 1 SWALLOW : golondrina *f* 2 SWIFT : vencejo *m*
martyr[1] ['mɑrtər] *vt* : martirizar
martyr[2] *n* : mártir *mf*
martyrdom ['mɑrtərdəm] *n* : martirio *m*
marvel[1] ['mɑrvəl] *vi* -veled *or* -velled; -veling *or* -velling : maravillarse
marvel[2] *n* : maravilla *f*
marvelous ['mɑrvələs] *or* **marvellous** *adj* : maravilloso — **marvelously** *adv*
Marxism ['mɑrkˌsɪzəm] *n* : marxismo *m*
Marxist[1] ['mɑrksɪst] *adj* : marxista
Marxist[2] *n* : marxista *mf*
mascara [mæsˈkærə] *n* : rímel *m*, rimel *m*
mascot ['mæsˌkɑt, -kət] *n* : mascota *f*
masculine ['mæskjələn] *adj* : masculino
masculinity [ˌmæskjəˈlɪnəti] *n* : masculinidad *f*
mash[1] ['mæʃ] *vt* 1 : hacer puré de (papas, etc.) 2 CRUSH : aplastar, majar
mash[2] *n* 1 FEED : afrecho *m* 2 : malta *f* (para hacer bebidas alcohólicas) 3 PASTE, PULP : papilla *f*, pasta *f*
mask[1] ['mæsk] *vt* 1 CONCEAL, DISGUISE : enmascarar, ocultar 2 COVER : cubrir, tapar
mask[2] *n* : máscara *f*, careta *f*, mascarilla *f* (de un cirujano o dentista)
masochism ['mæsəˌkɪzəm, 'mæzə-] *n* : masoquismo *m*
masochist ['mæsəˌkɪst, 'mæzə-] *n* : masoquista *mf*
masochistic [ˌmæsəˈkɪstɪk, ˌmæzə-] *adj* : masoquista
mason ['meɪsən] *n* 1 BRICKLAYER : albañil *mf* 2 *or* **stonemason** ['stoːnˌ-] : mampostero *m*, cantero *m*
masonry ['meɪsənri] *n, pl* -ries 1 BRICKLAYING : albañería *f* 2 *or* **stonemasonry** ['stoːnˌ-] : mampostería *f*
masquerade[1] [ˌmæskəˈreɪd] *vi* -aded; -ading 1 : disfrazarse (de), hacerse pasar (por) 2 : asistir a una mascarada
masquerade[2] *n* 1 : mascarada *f*, baile *m* de disfraces 2 FACADE : farsa *f*, fachada *f*
mass[1] ['mæs] *vi* : concentrarse, juntarse en masa — *vt* : concentrar

mass[2] *n* 1 : masa *f* ⟨atomic mass : masa atómica⟩ 2 BULK : mole *f*, volumen *m* 3 MULTITUDE : cantidad *f*, montón *m* (de cosas), multitud *f* (de gente) 4 **the masses** : las masas, el pueblo, el populacho
Mass ['mæs] *n* : misa *f*
massacre[1] ['mæsɪkər] *vt* -cred; -cring : masacrar
massacre[2] *n* : masacre *f*
massage[1] [məˈsɑʒ, -ˈsɑdʒ] *vt* -saged; -saging : masajear
massage[2] *n* : masaje *m*
masseur [mæˈsər] *n* : masajista *m*
masseuse [mæˈsøz, -ˈsu:z] *n* : masajista *f*
massive ['mæsɪv] *adj* 1 BULKY : voluminoso, macizo 2 HUGE : masivo, enorme — **massively** *adv*
mast ['mæst] *n* : mástil *m*, palo *m*
master[1] ['mæstər] *vt* 1 SUBDUE : dominar 2 : llegar a dominar ⟨she mastered French : llegó a dominar el francés⟩
master[2] *n* 1 TEACHER : maestro *m*, profesor *m* 2 EXPERT : experto *m*, -ta *f*; maestro *m*, -tra *f* 3 : amo *m* (de animales o esclavos), señor *m* (de la casa) 4 **master's degree** : maestría *f*
masterful ['mæstərfəl] *adj* 1 IMPERIOUS : autoritario, imperioso, dominante 2 SKILLFUL : magistral — **masterfully** *adv*
masterly ['mæstərli] *adj* : magistral
mastermind ['mæstərˌmaɪnd] *n* : cerebro *m*, artífice *mf*
masterpiece ['mæstərˌpi:s] *n* : obra *f* maestra
masterwork ['mæstərˌwərk] → **masterpiece**
mastery ['mæstəri] *n* 1 DOMINION : dominio *m*, autoridad *f* 2 SUPERIORITY : superioridad *f* 3 EXPERTISE : maestría *f*
masticate ['mæstəˌkeɪt] *v* -cated; -cating : masticar
mastiff ['mæstɪf] *n* : mastín *m*
mastodon ['mæstəˌdɑn] *n* : mastodonte *m*
masturbate ['mæstərˌbeɪt] *v* -bated; -bating *vi* : masturbarse — *vt* : masturbar
masturbation [ˌmæstərˈbeɪʃən] *n* : masturbación *f*
mat[1] ['mæt] *v* matted; matting *vt* TANGLE : enmarañar — *vi* : enmarañarse
mat[2] *n* 1 : estera *f* 2 TANGLE : maraña *f* 3 PAD : colchoneta *f* (de gimnasia) 4 *or* **matt** *or* **matte** ['mæt] FRAME : marco *m* (de cartón)
mat[3] → **matte**
matador ['mætəˌdɔr] *n* : matador *m*
match[1] ['mætʃ] *vt* 1 PIT : enfrentar, oponer 2 EQUAL, FIT : igualar, corresponder a, coincidir con 3 : combinar con, hacer juego con ⟨her shoes match her dress : sus zapatos hacen juego con su vestido⟩ — *vi* 1 CORRESPOND : concordar, coincidir 2 : hacer juego ⟨with a tie to match : con una corbata que hace juego⟩

match² *n* **1** EQUAL : igual *mf* ⟨he's no match for her : no puede competir con ella⟩ **2** FIGHT, GAME : partido *m*, combate *m* (en boxeo) **3** MARRIAGE : matrimonio *m*, casamiento *m* **4** : fósforo *m*, cerilla *f*, cerillo *m* *in various countries*⟩ ⟨he lit a match : encendió un fósforo⟩ **5 to be a good match** : hacer buena pareja (dícese de las personas), hacer juego (dícese de la ropa)

matchless [ˈmætʃləs] *adj* : sin igual, sin par

matchmaker [ˈmætʃˌmeɪkər] *n* : casamentero *m*, -ra *f*

mate¹ [ˈmeɪt] *v* **mated; mating** *vi* **1** FIT : encajar **2** PAIR : emparejarse **3** (*relating to animals*) : aparearse, copular — *vt* : aparear, acoplar (animales)

mate² *n* **1** COMPANION : compañero *m*, -ra *f*; camarada *mf* **2** : macho *m*, hembra *f* (de animales) **3** : oficial *mf* (de un barco) ⟨first mate : primer oficial⟩ **4** : compañero *m*, -ra *f*; pareja *f* (de un zapato, etc.)

material¹ [məˈtɪriəl] *adj* **1** PHYSICAL : material, físico ⟨the material world : el mundo material⟩ ⟨material needs : necesidades materiales⟩ **2** IMPORTANT : importante, esencial **3 material evidence** : prueba *f* sustancial

material² *n* **1** : material *m* **2** CLOTH : tejido *m*, tela *f*

materialism [məˈtɪriəˌlɪzəm] *n* : materialismo *m*

materialist [məˈtɪriəlɪst] *n* : materialista *mf*

materialistic [məˌtɪriəˈlɪstɪk] *adj* : materialista

materialize [məˈtɪriəˌlaɪz] *v* **-ized; -izing** *vt* : materializar, hacer aparecer — *vi* : materializarse, aparecer

maternal [məˈtərnəl] *adj* MOTHERLY : maternal — **maternally** *adv*

maternity¹ [məˈtərnəti] *adj* : de maternidad ⟨maternity clothes : ropa de futura mamá⟩ ⟨maternity leave : licencia por maternidad⟩

maternity² *n, pl* **-ties** : maternidad *f*

math [ˈmæθ] → **mathematics**

mathematical [ˌmæθəˈmætɪkəl] *adj* : matemático — **mathematically** *adv*

mathematician [ˌmæθəməˈtɪʃən] *n* : matemático *m*, -ca *f*

mathematics [ˌmæθəˈmætɪks] *ns & pl* : matemáticas *fpl*, matemática *f*

matinee *or* **matinée** [ˌmætənˈeɪ] *n* : matiné *f*

matriarch [ˈmeɪtriˌɑrk] *n* : matriarca *f*

matriarchy [ˈmeɪtriˌɑrki] *n, pl* **-chies** : matriarcado *m*

matriculate [məˈtrɪkjəˌleɪt] *v* **-lated; -lating** *vt* : matricular — *vi* : matricularse

matriculation [məˌtrɪkjəˈleɪʃən] *n* : matrícula *f*, matriculación *f*

matrimony [ˈmætrəˌmoːni] *n* : matrimonio *m* — **matrimonial** [ˌmætrəˈmoːniəl] *adj*

matrix [ˈmeɪtrɪks] *n, pl* **-trices** [ˈmeɪtrəˌsiːz, ˈmæ-] *or* **-trixes** [ˈmeɪtrɪksəz] : matriz *f*

matron [ˈmeɪtrən] *n* : matrona *f*

matronly [ˈmeɪtrənli] *adj* : de matrona, matronal

matte [ˈmæt] *adj* : mate, de acabado mate

matter¹ [ˈmætər] *vi* : importar ⟨it doesn't matter : no importa⟩

matter² *n* **1** QUESTION : asunto *m*, cuestión *f* ⟨a matter of taste : una cuestión de gusto⟩ **2** SUBSTANCE : materia *f*, sustancia *f* **3 matters** *npl* CIRCUMSTANCES : situación *f*, cosas *fpl* ⟨to make matters worse : para colmo de males⟩ **4 to be the matter** : pasar ⟨what's the matter? : ¿qué pasa?⟩ **5 as a matter of fact** : en efecto, en realidad **6 for that matter** : de hecho **7 no matter how much** : por mucho que

matter-of-fact [ˈmætərəvˈfækt] *adj* : práctico, realista

mattress [ˈmætrəs] *n* : colchón *m*

mature¹ [məˈtʊr, -ˈtjʊr, -ˈtʃʊr] *vi* **-tured; -turing 1** : madurar **2** : vencer ⟨when does the loan mature? : ¿cuándo vence el préstamo?⟩

mature² *adj* **-turer; -est 1** : maduro **2** DUE : vencido

maturity [məˈtʊrəti, -ˈtjʊr-, -ˈtʃʊr-] *n* : madurez *f*

maudlin [ˈmɔdlɪn] *adj* : sensiblero

maul¹ [ˈmɔl] *vt* **1** BEAT : golpear, pegar **2** MANGLE : mutilar **3** MANHANDLE : maltratar

maul² *n* MALLET : mazo *m*

Mauritanian [ˌmɔrəˈteɪniən] *n* : mauritano *m*, -na *f* — **Mauritanian** *adj*

mausoleum [ˌmɔsəˈliːəm, ˌmɔzə-] *n, pl* **-leums** *or* **-lea** [-ˈliːə] : mausoleo *m*

mauve [ˈmoːv, ˈmoʊv] *n* : malva *m*

maven *or* **mavin** [ˈmeɪvən] *n* EXPERT : experto *m*, -ta *f*

maverick [ˈmævrɪk, ˈmævə-] *n* **1** : ternero *m* sin marcar **2** NONCONFORMIST : inconformista *mf*, disidente *mf*

mawkish [ˈmɔkɪʃ] *adj* : sensiblero

maxim [ˈmæksəm] *n* : máxima *f*

maximize [ˈmæksəˌmaɪz] *vt* **-mized; -mizing** : maximizar, llevar al máximo

maximum¹ [ˈmæksəməm] *adj* : máximo

maximum² *n, pl* **-ma** [ˈmæksəmə] *or* **-mums** : máximo *m*

may [ˈmeɪ] *v aux, past* **might** [ˈmaɪt] *present s & pl* **may 1** (*expressing permission*) : poder ⟨you may go : puedes ir⟩ **2** (*expressing possibility or probability*) : poder ⟨you may be right : puede que tengas razón⟩ ⟨it may happen occasionally : puede pasar de vez en cuando⟩ **3** (*expressing desires, intentions, or contingencies*) ⟨may the best man win : que gane el mejor⟩ ⟨I laugh that I may not weep : me río para no llorar⟩ ⟨come what may : pase lo que pase⟩

May [ˈmeɪ] *n* : mayo *m*

Maya ['maɪə] *or* **Mayan** ['maɪən] *n* : maya *mf* — **Maya** *or* **Mayan** *adj*
maybe ['meɪbi] *adv* PERHAPS : quizás, tal vez
mayfly ['meɪˌflaɪ] *n, pl* **-flies** : efímera *f*
mayhem ['meɪˌhɛm, 'meɪəm] *n* 1 MUTILATION : mutilación *f* 2 DEVASTATION : estragos *mpl*
mayonnaise ['meɪəˌneɪz] *n* : mayonesa *f*
mayor ['meɪər, 'mɛr] *n* : alcalde *m*, -desa *f*
mayoral ['meɪərəl, 'mɛrəl] *adj* : de alcalde
maze ['meɪz] *n* : laberinto *m*
me ['mi:] *pron* 1 : me ⟨she called me : me llamó⟩ ⟨give it to me : dámelo⟩ 2 (*after a preposition*) : mí ⟨for me : para mí⟩ ⟨with me : conmigo⟩ 3 (*after conjunctions and verbs*) : yo ⟨it's me : soy yo⟩ ⟨as big as me : tan grande como yo⟩ 4 (*emphatic use*) : yo ⟨me, too! : ¡yo también!⟩ ⟨who, me? : ¿quién, yo?⟩
meadow ['mɛdo:] *n* : prado *m*, pradera *f*
meadowland ['mɛdoˌlænd] *n* : pradera *f*
meadowlark ['mɛdoˌlɑrk] *n* : pájaro *m* cantor con el pecho amarillo
meager *or* **meagre** ['mi:gər] *adj* 1 THIN : magro, flaco 2 POOR, SCANTY : exiguo, escaso, pobre
meagerly ['mi:gərli] *adv* : pobremente
meagerness ['mi:gərnəs] *n* : escasez *f*, pobreza *f*
meal ['mi:l] *n* 1 : comida *f* ⟨a hearty meal : una comida sustanciosa⟩ 2 : harina *f* (de maíz, etc.)
mealtime ['mi:lˌtaɪm] *n* : hora *f* de comer
mean[1] ['mi:n] *vt* **meant** ['mɛnt]; **meaning** 1 INTEND : querer, pensar, tener la intención de ⟨I didn't mean to do it : lo hice sin querer⟩ ⟨what do you mean to do? : ¿qué piensas hacer?⟩ 2 SIGNIFY : querer decir, significar ⟨what does that mean? : ¿qué quiere decir eso?⟩ 3 : importar ⟨health means everything : lo que más importa es la salud⟩
mean[2] *adj* 1 HUMBLE : humilde 2 NEGLIGIBLE : despreciable ⟨it's no mean feat : no es poca cosa⟩ 3 STINGY : mezquino, tacaño 4 CRUEL : malo, cruel ⟨to be mean to someone : tratar mal a alguien⟩ 5 AVERAGE, MEDIAN : medio
mean[3] *n* 1 MIDPOINT : término *m* medio 2 AVERAGE : promedio *m*, media *f* aritmética 3 **means** *npl* WAY : medio *m*, manera *f*, vía *f* 4 **means** *npl* RESOURCES : medios *mpl*, recursos *mpl* 5 **by all means** : por supuesto, cómo no 6 **by means of** : por medio de 7 **by no means** : de ninguna manera, de ningún modo
meander [mi'ændər] *vi* **-dered; -dering** 1 WIND : serpentear 2 WANDER : vagar, andar sin rumbo fijo
meaning ['mi:nɪŋ] *n* 1 : significado *m*, sentido *m* ⟨double meaning : doble sen-

tido⟩ 2 INTENT : intención *f*, propósito *m*
meaningful ['mi:nɪŋfəl] *adj* : significativo — **meaningfully** *adv*
meaningless ['mi:nɪŋləs] *adj* : sin sentido
meanness ['mi:nnəs] *n* 1 CRUELTY : crueldad *f*, mezquindad *f* 2 STINGINESS : tacañería *f*
meantime[1] ['mi:nˌtaɪm] *adv* → **meanwhile**[1]
meantime[2] *n* 1 : interín *m* 2 **in the meantime** : entretanto, mientras tanto
meanwhile[1] ['mi:nˌhwaɪl] *adv* : entretanto, mientras tanto
meanwhile[2] *n* → **meantime**[2]
measles ['mi:zəlz] *ns & pl* : sarampión *m*
measly ['mi:zli] *adj* **-slier; -est** : miserable, mezquino
measurable ['mɛʒərəbəl, 'meɪ-] *adj* : mensurable — **measurably** [-bli] *adv*
measure[1] ['mɛʒər, 'meɪ-] *v* **-sured; -suring** : medir ⟨he measured the table : midió la mesa⟩ ⟨it measures 15 feet tall : mide 15 pies de altura⟩
measure[2] *n* 1 AMOUNT : medida *f*, cantidad *f* ⟨in large measure : en gran medida⟩ ⟨a full measure : una cantidad exacta⟩ ⟨a measure of proficiency : una cierta competencia⟩ ⟨for good measure : de ñapa, por añadidura⟩ 2 DIMENSIONS, SIZE : medida *f*, tamaño *m* 3 RULER : regla *f* ⟨tape measure : cinta métrica⟩ 4 MEASUREMENT : medida *f* ⟨cubic measure : medida de capacidad⟩ 5 MEASURING : medición *f* 6 **measures** *npl* : medidas *fpl* ⟨security measures : medidas de seguridad⟩
measureless ['mɛʒərləs, 'meɪ-] *adj* : inmensurable
measurement ['mɛʒərmənt, 'meɪ-] *n* 1 MEASURING : medición *f* 2 DIMENSION : medida *f*
measure up *vi* **to measure up to** : estar a la altura de
meat ['mi:t] *n* 1 FOOD : comida *f* 2 : carne *f* ⟨meat and fish : carne y pescado⟩ 3 SUBSTANCE : sustancia *f*, esencia *f* ⟨the meat of the story : la sustancia del cuento⟩
meatball ['mi:tˌbɔl] *n* : albóndiga *f*
meaty ['mi:ṭi] *adj* **meatier; -est** : con mucha carne, carnoso
mechanic [mɪ'kænɪk] *n* : mecánico *m*, -ca *f*
mechanical [mɪ'kænɪkəl] *adj* : mecánico — **mechanically** *adv*
mechanics [mɪ'kænɪks] *ns & pl* 1 : mecánica *f* ⟨fluid mechanics : la mecánica de fluidos⟩ 2 MECHANISMS : mecanismos *mpl*, aspectos *mpl* prácticos
mechanism ['mɛkəˌnɪzəm] *n* : mecanismo *m*
mechanization [ˌmɛkənə'zeɪʃən] *n* : mecanización *f*

mechanize ['mɛkə,naɪz] *vt* **-nized; -nizing** : mecanizar
medal ['mɛdəl] *n* : medalla *f*, condecoración *f*
medalist ['mɛdəlɪst] *or* **medallist** *n* : medallista *mf*
medallion [mə'dæljən] *n* : medallón *m*
meddle ['mɛdəl] *vi* **-dled; -dling** : meterse, entrometerse
meddler ['mɛdələr] *n* : entrometido *m*, -da *f*
meddlesome ['mɛdəlsəm] *adj* : entrometido
media ['miːdiə] *npl* : medios *mpl* de comunicación
median[1] ['miːdiən] *adj* : medio
median[2] *n* : valor *m* medio
mediate ['miːdi,eɪt] *vi* **-ated; -ating** : mediar
mediation [,miːdi'eɪʃən] *n* : mediación *f*
mediator ['miːdi,eɪtər] *n* : mediador *m*, -dora *f*
medical ['mɛdɪkəl] *adj* : médico
medicate ['mɛdə,keɪt] *vt* **-cated; -cating** : medicar ⟨medicated powder : polvos medicinales⟩
medication [,mɛdə'keɪʃən] *n* **1** TREATMENT : tratamiento *m*, medicación *f* **2** MEDICINE : medicamento *m* ⟨to be on medication : estar medicado⟩
medicinal [mə'dɪsənəl] *adj* : medicinal
medicine ['mɛdəsən] *n* **1** MEDICATION : medicina *f*, medicamento *m* **2** : medicina *f* ⟨he's studying medicine : estudia medicina⟩
medicine man *n* : hechicero *m*
medieval *or* **mediaeval** [mɪ'diːvəl, ,miː-, ,m-, -di'iːvəl] *adj* : medieval
mediocre [,miːdi'oːkər] *adj* : mediocre
mediocrity [,miːdi'ɑkrəti] *n*, *pl* **-ties** : mediocridad *f*
meditate ['mɛdə,teɪt] *vi* **-tated; -tating** : meditar
meditation [,mɛdə'teɪʃən] *n* : meditación *f*
meditative ['mɛdə,teɪtɪv] *adj* : meditabundo
medium[1] ['miːdiəm] *adj* : mediano ⟨of medium height : de estatura mediana, de estatura regular⟩
medium[2] *n*, *pl* **-diums** *or* **-dia** ['miːdiə] **1** MEAN : punto *m* medio, término *m* medio ⟨happy medium : justo medio⟩ **2** MEANS : medio *m* **3** SUBSTANCE : medio *m*, sustancia *f* ⟨a viscous medium : un medio viscoso⟩ **4** : medio *m* de comunicación **5** : medio *m* (artístico)
medley ['mɛdli] *n*, *pl* **-leys** : popurrí *m* (de canciones)
meek ['miːk] *adj* **1** LONG-SUFFERING : paciente, sufrido **2** SUBMISSIVE : sumiso, dócil, manso
meekly ['miːkli] *adv* : dócilmente
meekness ['miːknəs] *n* : mansedumbre *f*, docilidad *f*
meet[1] ['miːt] *v* **met** ['mɛt]; **meeting** *vt* **1** ENCOUNTER : encontrarse con **2** JOIN

: unirse con **3** CONFRONT : enfrentarse a **4** SATISFY : satisfacer, cumplir con ⟨to meet costs : pagar los gastos⟩ **5** : conocer ⟨I met his sister : conocí a su hermana⟩ — *vi* ASSEMBLE : reunirse, congregarse
meet[2] *n* : encuentro *m*
meeting ['miːtɪŋ] *n* **1** : reunión *f* ⟨to open the meeting : abrir la sesión⟩ **2** ENCOUNTER : encuentro *m* **3** : entrevista *f* (formal)
meetinghouse ['miːtɪŋ,haʊs] *n* : iglesia *f* (de ciertas confesiones protestantes)
megabyte ['mɛgə,baɪt] *n* : megabyte *m*
megahertz ['mɛgə,hərts, -,hrts] *n* : megahercio *m*
megaphone ['mɛgə,foːn] *n* : megáfono *m*
melancholy[1] ['mɛlən,kɑli] *adj* : melancólico, triste, sombrío
melancholy[2] *n*, *pl* **-cholies** : melancolía *f*
melanoma [,mɛlə'noːmə] *n*, *pl* **-mas** : melanoma *m*
meld ['mɛld] *vt* : fusionar, unir — *vi* : fusionarse, unirse
melee ['meɪ,leɪ, meɪ'leɪ] *n* BRAWL : reyerta *f*, riña *f*, pelea *f*
meliorate ['miːljə,reɪt, 'miːliə-] → **ameliorate**
mellow[1] ['mɛloː] *vt* : suavizar, endulzar — *vi* : suavizarse, endulzarse
mellow[2] *adj* **1** RIPE : maduro **2** MILD : apacible ⟨a mellow character : un carácter apacible⟩ ⟨mellow wines : vinos añejos⟩ **3** : suave, dulce ⟨mellow colors : colores suaves⟩ ⟨mellow tones : tonos dulces⟩
mellowness ['mɛlonəs] *n* : suavidad *f*, dulzura *f*
melodic [mə'lɑdɪk] *adj* : melódico — **melodically** [-dɪkli] *adv*
melodious [mə'loːdiəs] *adj* : melodioso — **melodiously** *adv*
melodiousness [mə'loːdiəsnəs] *n* : calidad *f* de melódico
melodrama ['mɛlə,drɑmə, -,dræ-] *n* : melodrama *m*
melodramatic [,mɛlədrə'mætɪk] *adj* : melodramático — **melodramatically** [-tɪkli] *adv*
melody ['mɛlədi] *n*, *pl* **-dies** : melodía *f*, tonada *f*
melon ['mɛlən] *n* : melón *m*
melt ['mɛlt] *vt* **1** : derretir, disolver **2** SOFTEN : ablandar ⟨it melted his heart : ablandó su corazón⟩ — *vi* **1** : derretirse, disolverse **2** SOFTEN : ablandarse **3** DISAPPEAR : desvanecerse, esfumarse ⟨the clouds melted away : las nubes se desvanecieron⟩
melting point *n* : punto *m* de fusión
member ['mɛmbər] *n* **1** LIMB : miembro *m* **2** : miembro *m* (de un grupo); socio *m*, -cia *f* (de un club) **3** PART : miembro *m*, parte *f*
membership ['mɛmbər,ʃɪp] *n* **1** : membresía *f* ⟨application for membership

: solicitud de entrada⟩ 2 MEMBERS : membresía f, miembros mpl, socios mpl

membrane ['mɛm,breɪn] n : membrana f — **membranous** ['mɛmbrə-nəs] adj

memento [mɪ'mɛn,to:] n, pl **-tos** or **-toes** : recuerdo m

memo ['mɛmo:] n, pl **memos** : memorándum m

memoirs ['mɛm,wɑrz] npl : memorias fpl, autobiografía f

memorabilia [,mɛmərə'bɪliə, -'bɪljə] npl 1 : objetos mpl de interés histórico 2 MEMENTOS : recuerdos mpl

memorable ['mɛmərəbəl] adj : memorable, notable — **memorably** [-bli] adv

memorandum [,mɛmə'rændəm] n, pl **-dums** or **-da** [-də] : memorándum m

memorial[1] [mə'moriəl] adj : conmemorativo

memorial[2] n : monumento m conmemorativo

Memorial Day n : el último lunes de mayo (observado en Estados Unidos como día feriado para conmemorar a los caídos en guerra)

memorialize [mə'moriə,laɪz] vt **-ized; -izing** COMMEMORATE : conmemorar

memorization [,mɛmərə'zeɪʃən] n : memorización f

memorize ['mɛmə,raɪz] vt **-rized; -rizing** : memorizar, aprender de memoria

memory ['mɛmri, 'mɛmə-] n, pl **-ries** 1 : memoria f ⟨he has a good memory : tiene buena memoria⟩ 2 RECOLLECTION : recuerdo m 3 COMMEMORATION : memoria f, conmemoración f

men → **man**[2]

menace[1] ['mɛnəs] vt **-aced; -acing** 1 THREATEN : amenazar 2 ENDANGER : poner en peligro

menace[2] n : amenaza f

menacing ['mɛnəsɪŋ] adj : amenazador, amenazante

menagerie [mə'nædʒəri, -'næʒəri] n : colección f de animales salvajes

mend[1] ['mɛnd] vt 1 CORRECT : enmendar, corregir ⟨to mend one's ways : enmendarse⟩ 2 REPAIR : remendar, arreglar, reparar — vi HEAL : curarse

mend[2] n : remiendo m

mendicant ['mɛndɪkənt] n BEGGAR : mendigo m, -ga f

menhaden [mɛn'heɪdən, mən-] ns & pl : pez m de la misma familia que los arenques

menial[1] ['mi:niəl] adj : servil, bajo

menial[2] n : sirviente m, -ta f

meningitis [,mɛnən'dʒaɪtəs] n, pl **-gitides** [-'dʒɪtə,di:z] : meningitis f

menopause ['mɛnə,pɔz] n : menopausia f

menorah [mə'norə] n : candelabro m (usado en los oficios religiosos judíos)

menstrual ['mɛnstruəl] adj : menstrual

menstruate ['mɛnstru,eɪt] vi **-ated; -ating** : menstruar

menstruation [,mɛnstru'eɪʃən] n : menstruación f

mental ['mɛntəl] adj : mental ⟨mental hospital : hospital psiquiátrico⟩ — **mentally** adv

mentality [mɛn'tæləti] n, pl **-ties** : mentalidad f

menthol ['mɛn,θɔl, -,θo:l] n : mentol m

mentholated [,mɛn'θə,leɪtəd] adj : mentolado

mention[1] ['mɛntʃən] vt : mencionar, mentar, referirse a ⟨don't mention it! : ¡de nada!, ¡no hay de qué!⟩

mention[2] n : mención f

mentor ['mɛn,tor, 'mɛntər] n : mentor m

menu ['mɛn,ju:] n 1 : menú m, carta f (en un restaurante) 2 : menú m (de computadoras)

meow[1] [mi:'aʊ] vi : maullar

meow[2] n : maullido m, miau m

mercantile ['mərkən,ti:l, -,taɪl] adj : mercantil

mercenary[1] ['mərsəne,ri] adj : mercenario

mercenary[2] n, pl **-naries** : mercenario m, -ria f

merchandise ['mərtʃən,daɪz, -,daɪs] n : mercancía f, mercadería f

merchandiser ['mərtʃən,daɪzər] n : comerciante mf; vendedor m, -dora f

merchant ['mərtʃənt] n : comerciante mf

merchant marine n : marina f mercante

merciful ['mərsɪfəl] adj : misericordioso, clemente

mercifully ['mərsɪfli] adv 1 : con misericordia, con compasión 2 FORTUNATELY : afortunadamente

merciless ['mərsɪləs] adj : despiadado — **mercilessly** adv

mercurial [,mər'kjʊriəl] adj TEMPERAMENTAL : temperamental, volátil

mercury ['mərkjəri] n, pl **-ries** : mercurio m

Mercury n : Mercurio m

mercy ['mərsi] n, pl **-cies** 1 CLEMENCY : misericordia f, clemencia f 2 BLESSING : bendición f

mere ['mɪr] adj, superlative **merest** : mero, simple

merely ['mɪrli] adv : solamente, simplemente

merge ['mərdʒ] v **merged; merging** vi : unirse, fusionarse (dícese de las compañías), confluir (dícese de los ríos, las calles, etc.) — vt : unir, fusionar, combinar

merger ['mərdʒər] n : unión f, fusión f

meridian [mə'rɪdiən] n : meridiano m

meringue [mə'ræŋ] n : merengue m

merino [mə'ri:no] n, pl **-nos** 1 : merino m, -na f 2 or **merino wool** : lana f merino

merit[1] ['mɛrət] vt : merecer, ser digno de

merit[2] n : mérito m, valor m

meritorious [,mɛrə'toriəs] adj : meritorio

mermaid ['mər,meɪd] n : sirena f

merriment ['mɛrɪmənt] n : alegría f, júbilo m, regocijo m

merry ['mɛri] *adj* **-rier; -est** : alegre —
merrily ['mɛrəli] *adv*
merry–go–round ['mɛrigo,raʊnd] *n*
: carrusel *m*, tiovivo *m*
merrymaker ['mɛri,meɪkər] *n* : juerguista *mf*
merrymaking ['mɛri,meɪkɪŋ] *n* : juerga
f
mesa ['meɪsə] *n* : mesa *f*
mesdames → **madam, Mrs.**
mesh[1] ['mɛʃ] *vi* **1** ENGAGE : engranar
(dícese de las piezas mecánicas) **2** TAN-
GLE : enredarse **3** COORDINATE : coordinarse, combinar
mesh[2] *n* **1** : malla *f* ⟨wire mesh : malla
metálica⟩ **2** NETWORK : red *f* **3** MESH-
ING : engranaje *m* ⟨in mesh : engrana-
do⟩
mesmerize ['mɛzmə,raɪz] *vt* **-ized;
-izing 1** HYPNOTIZE : hipnotizar **2**
FASCINATE : cautivar, embelesar, fascinar
mess[1] ['mɛs] *vt* **1** SOIL : ensuciar **2 to
mess up** DISARRANGE : desordenar,
desarreglar **3 to mess up** BUNGLE
: echar a perder — *vi* **1** PUTTER : entretenerse **2** INTERFERE : meterse, entrometerse ⟨don't mess with me : no te
metas conmigo⟩
mess[2] *n* **1** : rancho *m* (para soldados,
etc.) **2** DISORDER : desorden *m* ⟨your
room is a mess : tienes el cuarto hecho
un desastre⟩ **3** CONFUSION, TURMOIL
: confusión *f*, embrollo *m*, lío *m fam*
message ['mɛsɪdʒ] *n* : mensaje *m*, recado *m*
messenger ['mɛsəndʒər] *n* : mensajero
m, -ra *f*
Messiah [mə'saɪə] *n* : Mesías *m*
Messrs. → **Mr.**
messy ['mɛsi] *adj* **messier; -est** UNTIDY
: desordenado, sucio
met → **meet**
metabolic [,mɛtə'bɑlɪk] *adj* : metabólico
metabolism [mə'tæbə,lɪzəm] *n* : metabolismo *m*
metabolize [mə'tæbə,laɪz] *vt* **-lized;
-lizing** : metabolizar
metal ['mɛtəl] *n* : metal *m*
metallic [mə'tælɪk] *adj* : metálico
metallurgical [,mɛtəl'ərdʒɪkəl] *adj* : metalúrgico
metallurgy ['mɛtəl,ərdʒi] *n* : metalurgia
f
metalwork ['mɛtəl,wərk] *n* : objeto *m* de
metal
metalworking ['mɛtəl,wərkɪŋ] *n* : metalistería *f*
metamorphosis [,mɛtə'mɔrfəsɪs] *n, pl*
-phoses [-,si:z] : metamorfosis *f*
metaphor ['mɛtə,fɔr, -fər] *n* : metáfora
f
metaphoric [,mɛtə'fɔrɪk] *or* **metaphorical** [-ɪkəl] *adj* : metafórico
metaphysical [,mɛtə'fɪzəkəl] *adj*
: metafísico
metaphysics [,mɛtə'fɪzɪks] *n* : metafísica *f*

mete ['mi:t] *vt* **meted; meting** ALLOT
: repartir, distribuir ⟨to mete out punishment : imponer castigos⟩
meteor ['mi:tiər, -ti:,ɔr] *n* : meteoro *m*
meteoric [,mi:ti'ɔrɪk] *adj* : meteórico
meteorite ['mi:tiə,raɪt] *n* : meteorito *m*
meteorologic [,mi:ti,ɔrə'lɑdʒɪk] *or* **meteorological** [-'lɑdʒɪkəl] *adj* : meteorológico
meteorologist [,mi:tiə'rɑlədʒɪst] *n* : meteorólogo *m*, -ga *f*
meteorology [,mi:tiə'rɑlədʒi] *n* : meteorología *f*
meter ['mi:tər] *n* **1** : metro *m* ⟨it measures 2 meters : mide 2 metros⟩ **2** : contador *m*, medidor *m* (de electricidad,
etc.) ⟨parking meter : parquímetro⟩ **3**
: metro *m* (en literatura o música)
methane ['mɛ,θeɪn] *n* : metano *m*
method ['mɛθəd] *n* : método *m*
methodical [mə'θɑdɪkəl] *adj* : metódico
— **methodically** *adv*
Methodist ['mɛθədɪst] *n* : metodista *mf*
— **Methodist** *adj*
methodology [,mɛθə'dɑlədʒi] *n, pl* **-gies**
: metodología *f*
meticulous [mə'tɪkjələs] *adj* : meticuloso — **meticulously** *adv*
meticulousness [mə'tɪkjələsnəs] *n*
: meticulosidad *f*
metric ['mɛtrɪk] *or* **metrical** [-trɪkəl] *adj*
: métrico
metric system *n* : sistema *m* métrico
metronome ['mɛtrə,no:m] *n*
: metrónomo *m*
metropolis [mə'trɑpələs] *n* : metrópoli
f, metrópolis *f*
metropolitan [,mɛtrə'pɑlətən] *adj* : metropolitano
mettle ['mɛtəl] *n* : temple *m*, valor *m* ⟨on
one's mettle : dispuesto a mostrar su
valía⟩
Mexican ['mɛksɪkən] *n* : mexicano *m*,
-na *f* — **Mexican** *adj*
mezzanine ['mɛzə,ni:n, ,mɛzə'ni:n] *n* **1**
: entrepiso *m*, entresuelo *m* **2** : primer
piso *m* (de un teatro)
miasma [maɪ'æzmə] *n* : miasma *m*
mica ['maɪkə] *n* : mica *f*
mice → **mouse**
micro ['maɪkro] *adj* : muy pequeño, microscópico
microbe ['maɪ,kro:b] *n* : microbio *m*
microbiology [,maɪkrobaɪ'alədʒi] *n* : microbiología *f*
microchip ['maɪkro,tʃɪp] *n* : microchip
m
microcomputer ['maɪkrokəm,pju:tər] *n*
: microcomputadora *f*
microcosm ['maɪkro,kɑzəm] *n* : micro-
cosmo *m*
microfilm ['maɪkro,fɪlm] *n* : microfilm
m
micrometer [maɪ'krɑmətər] *n* : micrómetro *m*
micron ['maɪ,krɑn] *n* : micrón *m*
microorganism [,maɪkro'ɔrgə,nɪzəm] *n*
: microorganismo *m*, microbio *m*

microphone [ˈmaɪkrəˌfoːn] *n* : micrófono *m*

microprocessor [ˈmaɪkroˌprɑˌssər] *n* : microprocesador *m*

microscope [ˈmaɪkrəˌskoːp] *n* : microscopio *m*

microscopic [ˌmaɪkrəˈskɑpɪk] *adj* : microscópico

microscopy [maɪˈkrɑskəpi] *n* : microscopía *f*

microwave [ˈmaɪkrəˌweɪv] *n* **1** : microonda *f* **2** *or* **microwave oven** : microondas *m*

mid [ˈmɪd] *adj* : medio ⟨mid morning : a media mañana⟩ ⟨in mid-August : a mediados de agosto⟩ ⟨in mid ocean : en alta mar⟩

midair [ˈmɪdˈær] *n* **in** ~ : en el aire ⟨to catch in midair : agarrar al vuelo⟩

midday [ˈmɪdˈdeɪ] *n* NOON : mediodía *m*

middle[1] [ˈmɪdəl] *adj* **1** CENTRAL : medio, del medio, de en medio **2** INTERMEDIATE : intermedio, mediano ⟨middle age : la mediana edad⟩

middle[2] *n* **1** CENTER : medio *m*, centro *m* ⟨fold it down the middle : dóblalo por la mitad⟩ **2 in the middle of** : en medio de (un espacio), a mitad de (una actividad) ⟨in the middle of the month : a mediados del mes⟩

Middle Ages *npl* : Edad *f* Media

middle class *n* : clase *f* media

middleman [ˈmɪdəlˌmæn] *n, pl* **-men** [-mən, -ˌmɛn] : intermediario *m*, -ria *f*

middling [ˈmɪdlɪŋ, -lən] *adj* **1** MEDIUM, MIDDLE : mediano **2** MEDIOCRE : mediocre, regular

midfielder [ˈmɪdˌfiːldər] *n* : mediocampista *mf*

midge [ˈmɪdʒ] *n* : mosca *f* pequeña

midget [ˈmɪdʒət] *n* **1** : enano *m*, -na *f* (persona) **2** : cosa *f* diminuta

midland [ˈmɪdlənd, -ˌlænd] *n* : región *f* central (de un país)

midnight [ˈmɪdˌnaɪt] *n* : medianoche *f*

midpoint [ˈmɪdˌpɔɪnt] *n* : punto *m* medio, término *m* medio

midriff [ˈmɪdˌrɪf] *n* : diafragma *m*

midshipman [ˈmɪdˌʃɪpmən, ˌmɪdˈʃɪp-] *n, pl* **-men** [-mən, -ˌmɛn] : guardiamarina *m*

midst[1] [ˈmɪdst] *n* : medio *m* ⟨in our midst : entre nosotros⟩ ⟨in the midst of : en medio de⟩

midst[2] *prep* : entre

midstream [ˈmɪdˈstriːm, -ˌstriːm] *n* : medio *m* de la corriente ⟨in the midstream of his career : en medio de su carrera⟩

midsummer [ˈmɪdˈsʌmər, -ˌsʌ-] *n* : pleno verano *m*

midtown [ˈmɪdˌtaʊn] *n* : centro *m* (de una ciudad)

midway [ˈmɪdˌweɪ] *adv* HALFWAY : a mitad de camino

midweek [ˈmɪdˌwiːk] *n* : medio *m* de la semana ⟨in midweek : a media semana⟩

midwife [ˈmɪdˌwaɪf] *n, pl* **-wives** [-ˌwaɪvz] : partera *f*, comadrona *f*

midwinter [ˈmɪdˈwɪntər, -ˌwin-] *n* : pleno invierno *m*

midyear [ˈmɪdˌjɪr] *n* : medio *m* del año ⟨at midyear : a mediados del año⟩

mien [ˈmiːn] *n* : aspecto *m*, porte *m*, semblante *m*

miff [ˈmɪf] *vt* : ofender

might[1] [ˈmaɪt] (*used to express permission or possibility or as a polite alternative to* may) → **may** ⟨it might be true : podría ser verdad⟩ ⟨might I speak with Sarah? : ¿se puede hablar con Sarah?⟩

might[2] *n* : fuerza *f*, poder *m*

mightily [ˈmaɪtəli] *adv* : con mucha fuerza, poderosamente

mighty[1] [ˈmaɪti] *adv* VERY : muy ⟨mighty good : muy bueno, buenísimo⟩

mighty[2] *adj* **mightier; -est 1** POWERFUL : poderoso, potente **2** GREAT : grande, imponente

migraine [ˈmaɪˌgreɪn] *n* : jaqueca *f*, migraña *f*

migrant [ˈmaɪgrənt] *n* : trabajador *m*, -dora *f* ambulante

migrate [ˈmaɪˌgreɪt] *vi* **-grated; -grating** : emigrar

migration [maɪˈgreɪʃən] *n* : migración *f*

migratory [ˈmaɪgrəˌtori] *adj* : migratorio

mild [ˈmaɪld] *adj* **1** GENTLE : apacible, suave ⟨a mild disposition : un temperamento suave⟩ **2** LIGHT : leve, ligero ⟨a mild punishment : un castigo leve, un castigo poco severo⟩ **3** TEMPERATE : templado (dícese del clima) — **mildly** *adv*

mildew[1] [ˈmɪlˌduː, -ˌdjuː] *vi* : enmohecerse

mildew[2] *n* : moho *m*

mildness [ˈmaɪldnəs] *n* : apacibilidad *f*, suavidad *f*

mile [ˈmaɪl] *n* : milla *f*

mileage [ˈmaɪlɪdʒ] *n* **1** ALLOWANCE : viáticos *mpl* (pagados por milla recorrida) **2** : distancia *f* recorrida (en millas), kilometraje *m*

milestone [ˈmaɪlˌstoːn] *n* LANDMARK : hito *m*, jalón *m* ⟨a milestone in his life : un hito en su vida⟩

milieu [miːˈljuː, -ˈjə] *n, pl* **-lieus** *or* **-lieux** [-ˈjuːz, -ˈjə] SURROUNDINGS : entorno *m*, medio *m*, ambiente *m*

militant[1] [ˈmɪlətənt] *adj* : militante, combativo

militant[2] *n* : militante *mf*

militarism [ˈmɪlətəˌrɪzəm] *n* : militarismo *m*

militaristic [ˌmɪlətəˈrɪstɪk] *adj* : militarista

military[1] [ˈmɪləˌteri] *adj* : militar

military[2] *n* **the military** : las fuerzas armadas

militia [məˈlɪʃə] *n* : milicia *f*

milk[1] [ˈmɪlk] *vt* **1** : ordeñar (una vaca, etc.) **2** EXPLOIT : explotar

milk² *n* : leche *f*

milkman ['mɪlk͵mæn, -mən] *n, pl* **-men** [-mən, -͵mɛn] : lechero *m*

milk shake *n* : batido *m*, licuado *m*

milkweed ['mɪlk͵wi:d] *n* : algodoncillo *m*

milky ['mɪlki] *adj* **milkier; -est** : lechoso

Milky Way *n* : Vía *f* Láctea

mill¹ ['mɪl] *vt* : moler (granos), fresar (metales), acordonar (monedas) — *vi* **to mill about** : arremolinarse

mill² *n* **1** : molino *m* (para moler granos) **2** FACTORY : fábrica *f* ⟨textile mill : fábrica textil⟩ **3** GRINDER : molinillo *m*

millennium [mə'lɛniəm] *n, pl* **-nia** [-niə] *or* **-niums** : milenio *m*

miller ['mɪlər] *n* : molinero *m*, -ra *f*

millet ['mɪlət] *n* : mijo *m*

milligram ['mɪlə͵græm] *n* : miligramo *m*

milliliter ['mɪlə͵li:tər] *n* : mililitro *m*

millimeter ['mɪlə͵mi:tər] *n* : milímetro *m*

milliner ['mɪlənər] *n* : sombrerero *m*, -ra *f* (de señoras)

millinery ['mɪlə͵nɛri] *n* : sombreros *mpl* de señora

million¹ ['mɪljən] *adj* **a million** : un millón de

million² *n, pl* **millions** *or* **million** : millón *m*

millionaire [͵mɪljə'nær, 'mɪljə͵nær] *n* : millonario *m*, -ria *f*

millionth¹ ['mɪljənθ] *adj* : millonésimo

millionth² *n* : millonésimo *m*

millipede ['mɪlə͵pi:d] *n* : milpiés *m*

millstone ['mɪl͵sto:n] *n* : rueda *f* de molino, muela *f*

mime¹ ['maɪm] *v* **mimed; miming** *vt* MIMIC : imitar, remedar — *vi* PANTOMIME : hacer la mímica

mime² *n* **1** : mimo *mf* **2** PANTOMIME : pantomima *f*

mimeograph ['mɪmiə͵græf] *n* : mimeógrafo *m*

mimic¹ ['mɪmɪk] *vt* **-icked; -icking** : imitar, remedar

mimic² *n* : imitador *m*, -dora *f*

mimicry ['mɪmɪkri] *n, pl* **-ries** : mímica *f*, imitación *f*

minaret [͵mɪnə'rɛt] *n* : alminar *m*, minarete *m*

mince ['mɪnts] *v* **minced; mincing** *vt* **1** CHOP : picar, moler (carne) **2 not to mince one's words** : no tener uno pelos en la lengua — *vi* : caminar de manera afectada

mincemeat ['mɪnts͵mi:t] *n* : mezcla *f* de fruta picada, sebo, y especias

mind¹ ['maɪnd] *vt* **1** TEND : cuidar, atender ⟨mind the children : cuida a los niños⟩ **2** OBEY : obedecer **3** : preocuparse por, sentirse molestado por ⟨I don't mind his jokes : sus bromas no me molestan⟩ **4** : tener cuidado con ⟨mind the ladder! : ¡cuidado con la escalera!⟩ — *vi* **1** OBEY : obedecer **2** CARE : importarle a uno ⟨I don't mind : no me importa, me es igual⟩

mind² *n* **1** MEMORY : memoria *f*, recuerdo *m* ⟨keep it in mind : téngalo en cuenta⟩ **2** : mente *f* ⟨the mind and the body : la mente y el cuerpo⟩ **3** INTENTION : intención *f*, propósito *m* ⟨to have a mind to do something : tener intención de hacer algo⟩ **4** : razón *f* ⟨he's out of his mind : está loco⟩ **5** OPINION : opinión *f* ⟨to change one's mind : cambiar de opinión⟩ **6** INTELLECT : capacidad *f* intelectual

minded ['maɪndəd] *adj* **1** (*used in combination*) ⟨narrow-minded : de mentalidad cerrada⟩ ⟨health-minded : preocupado por la salud⟩ **2** INCLINED : inclinado

mindful ['maɪndfəl] *adj* AWARE : consciente — **mindfully** *adv*

mindless ['maɪndləs] *adj* **1** SENSELESS : estúpido, sin sentido ⟨mindless violence : violencia sin sentido⟩ **2** HEEDLESS : inconsciente

mindlessly ['maɪndləsli] *adv* **1** SENSELESSLY : sin sentido **2** HEEDLESSLY : inconscientemente

mine¹ ['maɪn] *vt* **mined; mining 1** : extraer (oro, etc.) **2** : minar (con artefactos explosivos)

mine² *n* : mina *f* ⟨gold mine : mina de oro⟩

mine³ *pron* : mío, mía ⟨that one's mine : ése es el mío⟩ ⟨some friends of mine : unos amigos míos⟩

minefield ['maɪn͵fi:ld] *n* : campo *m* de minas

miner ['maɪnər] *n* : minero *m*, -ra *f*

mineral ['mɪnərəl] *n* : mineral *m* — **mineral** *adj*

mineralogy [͵mɪnə'rɑlədʒi, -'ræ-] *n* : mineralogía *f*

mingle ['mɪŋɡəl] *v* **-gled; -gling** *vt* MIX : mezclar — *vi* **1** MIX : mezclarse **2** CIRCULATE : circular

miniature¹ ['mɪniə͵tʃur, 'mɪni͵tʃur, -tʃər] *adj* : en miniatura, diminuto

miniature² *n* : miniatura *f*

minibus ['mɪni͵bʌs] *n* : microbús *m*, pesera *f Mex*

minicomputer ['mɪnikəm͵pju:tər] *n* : minicomputadora *f*

minimal ['mɪnəməl] *adj* : mínimo

minimally ['mɪnəməli] *adv* : en grado mínimo

minimize ['mɪnə͵maɪz] *vt* **-mized; -mizing** : minimizar

minimum¹ ['mɪnəməm] *adj* : mínimo

minimum² *n, pl* **-ma** ['mɪnəmə] *or* **-mums** : mínimo *m*

miniseries ['mɪni͵sɪri:z] *n* : miniserie *f*

miniskirt ['mɪni͵skərt] *n* : minifalda *f*

minister¹ ['mɪnəstər] *vi* **to minister to** : cuidar (de), atender a

minister² *n* **1** : pastor *m*, -tora *f* (de una iglesia) **2** : ministro *m*, -tra *f* (en política)

ministerial [͵mɪnə'stɪriəl] *adj* : ministerial

ministry ['mɪnəstri] *n, pl* **-tries 1** : ministerio *m* (en política) **2** : sacerdocio *m* (en el catolicismo), clerecía *f* (en el protestantismo)

minivan ['mɪni͵væn] *n* : minivan *f*
mink ['mɪŋk] *n, pl* **mink** *or* **minks** : visón *m*
minnow ['mɪno:] *n, pl* **-nows** : pececillo *m* de agua dulce
minor¹ ['maɪnər] *adj* : menor
minor² *n* **1** : menor *mf* (de edad) **2** : asignatura *f* secundaria (de estudios)
minority [mə'nɔrəti, maɪ-] *n, pl* **-ties** : minoría *f*
minstrel ['mɪntstrəl] *n* : juglar *m*, trovador *m* (en el medioevo)
mint¹ ['mɪnt] *vt* : acuñar
mint² *adj* : sin usar ⟨in mint condition : como nuevo⟩
mint³ *n* **1** : menta *f* ⟨mint tea : té de menta⟩ **2** : pastilla *f* de menta **3** : casa *f* de la moneda ⟨the U.S. Mint : la casa de la moneda de los EE.UU.⟩ **4** FORTUNE : dineral *m*, fortuna *f*
minuet [͵mɪnjʊ'ɛt] *n* : minué *m*
minus¹ ['maɪnəs] *n* **1** : cantidad *f* negativa **2 minus sign** : signo *m* de menos
minus² *prep* **1** : menos ⟨four minus two : cuatro menos dos⟩ **2** WITHOUT : sin ⟨minus his hat : sin su sombrero⟩
minuscule *or* **miniscule** ['mɪnəs͵kju:l, mɪ'nʌs-] *adj* : minúsculo
minute¹ [maɪ'nu:t, mɪ-, -'nju:t] *adj* **-nuter; -est 1** TINY : diminuto, minúsculo **2** DETAILED : minucioso
minute² ['mɪnət] *n* **1** : minuto *m* ⟨ten minutes late : diez minutos de retraso⟩ **2** MOMENT : momento *m* **3 minutes** *npl* : actas *fpl* (de una reunión)
minutely [maɪ'nu:tli, mɪ-, -'nju:t-] *adv* : minuciosamente
miracle ['mɪrɪkəl] *n* : milagro *m*
miraculous [mə'rækjələs] *adj* : milagroso — **miraculously** *adv*
mirage [mɪ'rɑʒ, *chiefly Brit* 'mɪr͵ɑʒ] *n* : espejismo *m*
mire¹ ['maɪr] *vi* **mired; miring** : atascarse
mire² *n* **1** MUD : barro *m*, lodo *m* **2** : atolladero *m* ⟨stuck in a mire of debt : agobiado por la deuda⟩
mirror¹ ['mɪrər] *vt* : reflejar
mirror² *n* : espejo *m*
mirth ['mərθ] *n* : alegría *f*, regocijo *m*
mirthful ['mərθfəl] *adj* : alegre, regocijado
misadventure [͵mɪsəd'vɛntʃər] *n* : malaventura *f*, desventura *f*
misanthrope ['mɪsən͵θro:p] *n* : misántropo *m*, -pa *f*
misanthropic [͵mɪsən'θrɑpɪk] *adj* : misantrópico
misanthropy [mɪ'sænθrəpi] *n* : misantropía *f*
misapprehend [͵mɪs͵æprə'hɛnd] *vt* : entender mal
misapprehension [͵mɪs͵æprə'hɛntʃən] *n* : malentendido *m*
misappropriate [͵mɪsə'pro:pri͵eɪt] *vt* **-ated; -ating** : malversar
misbegotten [͵mɪsbi'gɑtən] *adj* **1** ILLEGITIMATE : ilegítimo **2** : mal concebido ⟨misbegotten laws : leyes mal concebidas⟩

misbehave [͵mɪsbi'heɪv] *vi* **-haved; -having** : portarse mal
misbehavior [͵mɪsbi'heɪvjər] *n* : mala conducta *f*
miscalculate [mɪs'kælkjə͵leɪt] *v* **-lated; -lating** : calcular mal
miscalculation [mɪs͵kælkjə'leɪʃən] *n* : error *m* de cálculo, mal cálculo *m*
miscarriage [͵mɪs'kærɪʤ, 'mɪs͵kærɪʤ] *n* **1** : aborto *m* **2** FAILURE : fracaso *m*, malogro *m* ⟨a miscarriage of justice : una injusticia, un error judicial⟩
miscarry [͵mɪs'kæri, 'mɪs͵kæri] *vi* **-ried; -rying 1** ABORT : abortar **2** FAIL : malograrse, fracasar
miscellaneous [͵mɪsə'leɪniəs] *adj* : misceláneo
miscellany ['mɪsə͵leɪni] *n, pl* **-nies** : miscelánea *f*
mischance [mɪs'tʃænts] *n* : desgracia *f*, infortunio *m*, mala suerte *f*
mischief ['mɪstʃəf] *n* : diabluras *fpl*, travesuras *fpl*
mischievous ['mɪstʃəvəs] *adj* : travieso, pícaro
mischievously ['mɪstʃəvəsli] *adv* : de manera traviesa
misconception [͵mɪskən'sɛpʃən] *n* : concepto *m* erróneo, idea *f* falsa
misconduct [mɪs'kɑndəkt] *n* : mala conducta *f*
misconstrue [͵mɪskən'stru:] *vt* **-strued; -struing** : malinterpretar
misdeed [mɪs'di:d] *n* : fechoría *f*
misdemeanor [͵mɪsdɪ'mi:nər] *n* : delito *m* menor
miser ['maɪzər] *n* : avaro *m*, -ra *f*; tacaño *m*, -ña *f*
miserable ['mɪzərəbəl] *adj* **1** UNHAPPY : triste, desdichado **2** WRETCHED : miserable, desgraciado ⟨a miserable hut : una choza miserable⟩ **3** UNPLEASANT : desagradable, malo ⟨miserable weather : tiempo malísimo⟩ **4** CONTEMPTIBLE : despreciable, mísero ⟨for a miserable $10 : por unos míseros diez dólares⟩
miserably ['mɪzərəbli] *adv* **1** SADLY : tristemente **2** WRETCHEDLY : miserablemente, lamentablemente **3** UNFORTUNATELY : desgraciadamente
miserly ['maɪzərli] *adj* : avaro, tacaño
misery ['mɪzəri] *n, pl* **-eries** : miseria *f*, sufrimiento *m*
misfire [mɪs'faɪr] *vi* **-fired; -firing** : fallar
misfit ['mɪs͵fɪt] *n* : inadaptado *m*, -da *f*
misfortune [mɪs'fɔrtʃən] *n* : desgracia *f*, desventura *f*, infortunio *m*
misgiving [mɪs'gɪvɪŋ] *n* : duda *f*, recelo *m*
misguided [mɪs'gaɪdəd] *adj* : desacertado, equivocado, mal informado
mishap ['mɪs͵hæp] *n* : contratiempo *m*, percance *m*, accidente *m*
misinform [͵mɪsɪn'fɔrm] *vt* : informar mal
misinterpret [͵mɪsɪn'tərprət] *vt* : malinterpretar

misinterpretation [ˌmɪsɪnˌtərprəˈteɪ-ʃən] *n* : mala interpretación *f*, malentendido *m*

misjudge [mɪsˈdʒʌdʒ] *vt* **-judged; -judging** : juzgar mal

mislay [mɪsˈleɪ] *vt* **-laid** [-leɪd]; **-laying** : extraviar, perder

mislead [mɪsˈliːd] *vt* **-led** [-ˈlɛd]; **-leading** : engañar

misleading [mɪsˈliːdɪŋ] *adj* : engañoso

mismanage [mɪsˈmænɪdʒ] *vt* **-aged; -aging** : administrar mal

mismanagement [mɪsˈmænɪdʒmənt] *n* : mala administración *f*

misnomer [mɪsˈnoːmər] *n* : nombre *m* inapropiado

misogynist [mɪˈsɑdʒənɪst] *n* : misógino *m*

misogyny [məˈsɑdʒəni] *n* : misoginia *f*

misplace [mɪsˈpleɪs] *vt* **-placed; -placing** : extraviar, perder

misprint [ˈmɪsˌprɪnt, mɪsˈ-] *n* : errata *f*, error *m* de imprenta

mispronounce [ˌmɪsprəˈnaʊnts] *vt* **-nounced; -nouncing** : pronunciar mal

mispronunciation [ˌmɪsprəˌnʌntsiˈeɪʃən] *n* : pronunciación *f* incorrecta

misquote [mɪsˈkwoːt] *vt* **-quoted; -quoting** : citar incorrectamente

misread [mɪsˈriːd] *vt* **-read; -reading** 1 : leer mal ⟨she misread the sentence : leyó mal la frase⟩ 2 MISUNDERSTAND : malinterpretar ⟨they misread his intention : malinterpretaron su intención⟩

misrepresent [ˌmɪsˌrprɪˈzɛnt] *vt* : distorsionar, falsear, tergiversar

misrule[1] [mɪsˈruːl] *vt* **-ruled; -ruling** : gobernar mal

misrule[2] *n* : mal gobierno *m*

miss[1] [ˈmɪs] *vt* 1 : errar, faltar ⟨to miss the target : no dar en el blanco⟩ 2 : no encontrar, perder ⟨they missed each other : no se encontraron⟩ ⟨I missed the plane : perdí el avión⟩ 3 : echar de menos, extrañar ⟨we miss him a lot : lo echamos mucho de menos⟩ 4 OVERLOOK : pasar por alto, perder (una oportunidad, etc.) 5 AVOID : evitar ⟨they just missed hitting the tree : por muy poco chocan contra el árbol⟩ 6 OMIT : saltarse ⟨he missed breakfast : se saltó el desayuno⟩

miss[2] *n* 1 : fallo *m* (de un tiro, etc.) 2 FAILURE : fracaso *m* 3 : señorita *f* ⟨Miss Jones called us : nos llamó la señorita Jones⟩ ⟨excuse me, miss : perdone, señorita⟩

missal [ˈmɪsəl] *n* : misal *m*

misshapen [mɪˈʃeɪpən] *adj* : deforme

missile [ˈmɪsəl] *n* 1 : misil *m* ⟨guided missile : misil guiado⟩ 2 PROJECTILE : proyectil *m*

missing [ˈmɪsɪŋ] *adj* 1 ABSENT : ausente ⟨who's missing? : ¿quién falta?⟩ 2 LOST : perdido, desaparecido ⟨missing persons : los desaparecidos⟩

mission [ˈmɪʃən] *n* 1 : misión *f* (mandada por una iglesia) 2 DELEGATION : misión *f*, delegación *f*, embajada *f* 3 TASK : misión *f*

missionary[1] [ˈmɪʃəˌnɛri] *adj* : misionero

missionary[2] *n*, *pl* **-aries** : misionero *m*, -ra *f*

missive [ˈmɪsɪv] *n* : misiva *f*

misspell [mɪsˈspɛl] *vt* : escribir mal

misspelling [mɪsˈspɛlɪŋ] *n* : falta *f* de ortografía

misstep [ˈmɪsˌstɛp] *n* : traspié *m*, tropezón *m*

mist [ˈmɪst] *n* 1 HAZE : neblina *f*, niebla *f* 2 SPRAY : rocío *m*

mistake[1] [mɪˈsteɪk] *vt* **-took** [-ˈstʊk]; **-taken** [-ˈsteɪkən]; **-taking** 1 MISINTERPRET : malinterpretar 2 CONFUSE : confundir ⟨he mistook her for Clara : la confundió con Clara⟩

mistake[2] *n* 1 MISUNDERSTANDING : malentendido *m*, confusión *f* 2 ERROR : error *m* ⟨I made a mistake : me equivoqué, cometí un error⟩

mistaken [mɪˈsteɪkən] *adj* WRONG : equivocado — **mistakenly** *adv*

mister [ˈmɪstər] *n* : señor *m* ⟨watch out, mister : cuidado, señor⟩

mistiness [ˈmɪstinəs] *n* : nebulosidad *f*

mistletoe [ˈmɪsəlˌtoː] *n* : muérdago *m*

mistreat [mɪsˈtriːt] *vt* : maltratar

mistreatment [mɪsˈtriːtmənt] *n* : maltrato *m*, abuso *m*

mistress [ˈmɪstrəs] *n* 1 : dueña *f*, señora *f* (de una casa) 2 LOVER : amante *f*

mistrust[1] [mɪsˈtrʌst] *vt* : desconfiar de

mistrust[2] *n* : desconfianza *f*

mistrustful [mɪsˈtrʌstfəl] *adj* : desconfiado

misty [ˈmɪsti] *adj* **mistier; -est** 1 : nebinoso, nebuloso 2 TEARFUL : lloroso

misunderstand [ˌmɪsˌʌndərˈstænd] *vt* **-stood** [-ˈstʊd]; **-standing** 1 : entender mal 2 MISINTERPRET : malinterpretar ⟨don't misunderstand me : no me malinterpretes⟩

misunderstanding [ˌmɪsˌʌndərˈstændɪŋ] *n* 1 MISINTERPRETATION : malentendido *m* 2 DISAGREEMENT, QUARREL : disputa *f*, discusión *f*

misuse[1] [mɪsˈjuːz] *vt* **-used; -using** 1 : emplear mal 2 ABUSE, MISTREAT : abusar de, maltratar

misuse[2] [mɪsˈjuːs] *n* 1 : mal empleo *m*, mal uso *m* 2 WASTE : derroche *m*, despilfarro *m* 3 ABUSE : abuso *m*

mite [ˈmaɪt] *n* 1 : ácaro *m* 2 BIT : poco *m* ⟨a mite tired : un poquito cansado⟩

miter *or* **mitre** [ˈmaɪtər] *n* 1 : mitra *f* (de un obispo) 2 *or* **miter joint** : inglete *m*

mitigate [ˈmɪtəˌgeɪt] *vt* **-gated; -gating** : mitigar, aliviar

mitigation [ˌmɪtəˈgeɪʃən] *n* : mitigación *f*, alivio *m*

mitosis [maɪˈtoːsɪs] *n*, *pl* **-toses** [-ˌsiːz] : mitosis *f*

mitt [ˈmɪt] *n* : manopla *f*, guante *m* (de béisbol)

mitten ['mɪtən] *n* : manopla *f*, mitón *m*
mix¹ ['mɪks] *vt* **1** COMBINE : mezclar **2** STIR : remover, revolver **3 to mix up** CONFUSE : confundir — *vi* : mezclarse
mix² *n* : mezcla *f*
mixer ['mɪksər] *n* **1** : batidora *f* (de la cocina) **2 cement mixer** : hormigonera *f*
mixture ['mɪkstʃər] *n* : mezcla *f*
mix-up ['mɪks,ʌp] *n* CONFUSION : confusión *f*, lío *m fam*
mnemonic [nɪ'mɑnɪk] *adj* : mnemónico
moan¹ ['mo:n] *vi* : gemir
moan² *n* : gemido *m*
moat ['mo:t] *n* : foso *m*
mob¹ ['mɑb] *vt* **mobbed; mobbing 1** ATTACK : atacar en masa **2** HOUND : acosar, rodear
mob² *n* **1** THRONG : multitud *f*, turba *f*, muchedumbre *f* **2** GANG : pandilla *f*
mobile¹ ['mo:bəl, -,bi:l, -,baɪl] *adj* : móvil ⟨mobile home : caravana, casa rodante⟩
mobile² ['mo:,bi:l] *n* : móvil *m*
mobility [mo'bɪləti] *n* : movilidad *f*
mobilize ['mo:bə,laɪz] *vt* **-lized; -lizing** : movilizar
moccasin ['mɑkəsən] *n* **1** : mocasín *m* **2** *or* **water moccasin** : serpiente *f* venenosa de Norteamérica
mocha ['mo:kə] *n* **1** : mezcla *f* de café y chocolate **2** : color *m* chocolate
mock¹ ['mɑk, 'mɔk] *vt* **1** RIDICULE : burlarse de, mofarse de **2** MIMIC : imitar, remedar (de manera burlona)
mock² *adj* **1** SIMULATED : simulado **2** PHONY : falso
mockery ['mɑkəri, 'mɔ-] *n, pl* **-eries 1** JEER, TAUNT : burla *f*, mofa *f* ⟨to make a mockery of : burlarse de⟩ **2** FAKE : imitación *f* (burlona)
mockingbird ['mɑkɪŋ,bərd, 'mɔ-] *n* : sinsonte *m*
mode ['mo:d] *n* **1** FORM : modo *m*, forma *f* **2** MANNER : modo *m*, manera *f*, estilo *m* **3** FASHION : moda *f*
model¹ ['mɑdəl] *v* **-eled** *or* **-elled; -eling** *or* **-elling** *vt* SHAPE : modelar — *vi* : trabajar de modelo
model² *adj* **1** EXEMPLARY : modelo, ejemplar ⟨a model student : un estudiante modelo⟩ **2** MINIATURE : en miniatura
model³ *n* **1** PATTERN : modelo *m* **2** MINIATURE : modelo *m*, miniatura *f* **3** EXAMPLE : modelo *m*, ejemplo *m* **4** MANNEQUIN : modelo *mf* **5** DESIGN : modelo *m* ⟨the '97 model : el modelo '97⟩
modem ['mo:dəm, -,dɛm] *n* : módem *m*
moderate¹ ['mɑdə,reɪt] *v* **-ated; -ating** *vt* : moderar, temperar — *vi* **1** CALM : moderarse, calmarse **2** : fungir como moderador (en un debate, etc.)
moderate² ['mɑdərət] *adj* : moderado
moderate³ ['mɑdərət] *n* : moderado *m*, -da *f*

moderately ['mɑdərətli] *adv* **1** : con moderación **2** FAIRLY : medianamente
moderation [,mɑdə'reɪʃən] *n* : moderación *f*
moderator ['mɑdə,reɪtər] *n* : moderador *m*, -dora *f*
modern ['mɑdərn] *adj* : moderno
modernism ['mɑdər,nɪzəm] *n* : modernismo *m*
modernist ['mɑdərnɪst] *n* : modernista *mf* — **modernist** *adj*
modernity [mə'dərnəti] *n* : modernidad *f*
modernization [,mɑdərnə'zeɪʃən] *n* : modernización *f*
modernize ['mɑdər,naɪz] *v* **-ized; -izing** *vt* : modernizar — *vi* : modernizarse
modest ['mɑdəst] *adj* **1** HUMBLE : modesto **2** DEMURE : recatado, pudoroso **3** MODERATE : modesto, moderado — **modestly** *adv*
modesty ['mɑdəsti] *n* : modestia *f*
modicum ['mɑdɪkəm] *n* : mínimo *m*, pizca *f*
modification [,mɑdəfə'keɪʃən] *n* : modificación *f*
modifier ['mɑdə,faɪər] *n* : modificante *m*, modificador *m*
modify ['mɑdə,faɪ] *vt* **-fied; -fying** : modificar, calificar (en gramática)
modish ['mo:dɪʃ] *adj* STYLISH : a la moda, de moda
modular ['mɑdʒələr] *adj* : modular
modulate ['mɑdʒə,leɪt] *vt* **-lated; -lating** : modular
modulation [,mɑdʒə'leɪʃən] *n* : modulación *f*
module ['mɑ,dʒu:l] *n* : módulo *m*
mogul ['mo:gəl] *n* : magnate *mf*, potentado *m*, -da *f*
mohair ['mo:,hær] *n* : mohair *m*
moist ['mɔɪst] *adj* : húmedo
moisten ['mɔɪsən] *vt* : humedecer
moistness ['mɔɪstnəs] *n* : humedad *f*
moisture ['mɔɪstʃər] *n* : humedad *f*
moisturize ['mɔɪstʃə,raɪz] *vt* **-ized; -izing** : humedecer (el aire), humectar (la piel)
moisturizer ['mɔɪtʃə,raɪzər] *n* : crema *f* hidratante, crema *f* humectante
molar ['mo:lər] *n* : muela *f*, molar *m*
molasses [mə'læsəz] *n* : melaza *f*
mold¹ ['mo:ld] *vt* : moldear, formar (carácter, etc.) — *vi* : enmohecerse ⟨the bread will mold : el pan se enmohecerá⟩
mold² *n* **1** *or* **leaf mold** : mantillo *m* **2** FORM : molde *m* ⟨to break the mold : romper el molde⟩ **3** FUNGUS : moho *m*
molder ['mo:ldər] *vi* CRUMBLE : desmoronarse
molding ['mo:ldɪŋ] *n* : moldura *f* (en arquitectura)
moldy ['mo:ldi] *adj* **moldier; -est** : mohoso
mole ['mo:l] *n* **1** : lunar *m* (en la piel) **2** : topo *m* (animal)

molecule ['malɪˌkjuːl] *n* : molécula *f* —
molecular [mə'lɛkjələr] *adj*
molehill ['moːlˌhɪl] *n* : topera *f*
molest [mə'lɛst] *vt* **1** ANNOY, DISTURB
: molestar **2** : abusar (sexualmente)
mollify ['maləˌfaɪ] *vt* **-fied; -fying**
: apaciguar, aplacar
mollusk *or* **mollusc** ['maləsk] *n* : molusco *m*
mollycoddle ['maliˌkadəl] *vt* **-dled;
-dling** PAMPER : consentir, mimar
molt ['moːlt] *vi* : mudar, hacer la muda
molten ['moːltən] *adj* : fundido
mom ['mam, 'mʌm] *n* : mamá *f*
moment ['moːmənt] *n* **1** INSTANT : momento *m* ⟨one moment, please : un momento, por favor⟩ **2** TIME : momento
m ⟨at the moment : de momento, ac-
tualmente⟩ ⟨from that moment : desde entonces⟩ **3** IMPORTANCE : importancia *f* ⟨of great moment : de gran
importancia⟩
momentarily [ˌmoːmən'tɛrəli] *adv* **1**
: momentáneamente **2** SOON : dentro
de poco, pronto
momentary ['moːmənˌtɛri] *adj* : momentáneo
momentous [mo'mɛntəs] *adj* : de suma
importancia, fatídico
momentum [mo'mɛntəm] *n, pl* **-ta** [-tə]
or **-tums 1** : momento *m* (en física) **2**
IMPETUS : ímpetu *m*, impulso *m*
mommy ['mami, 'mʌ-] *n* : mami *f*
monarch ['maˌnark, -nərk] *n* : monarca
mf
monarchism ['maˌnarˌkɪzəm, -nər-] *n*
: monarquismo *m*
monarchist ['maˌnarkɪst, -nər-] *n*
: monárquico *m*, -ca *f*
monarchy ['maˌnarki, -nər-] *n, pl* **-chies**
: monarquía *f*
monastery ['manəˌstɛri] *n, pl* **-teries**
: monasterio *m*
monastic [mə'næstɪk] *adj* : monástico
— **monastically** [-tɪkli] *adv*
Monday ['mʌnˌdeɪ, -di] *n* : lunes *m*
monetary ['manəˌtɛri, 'mʌnə-] *adj*
: monetario
money ['mʌni] *n, pl* **-eys** *or* **-ies** ['mʌniz]
: dinero *m*, plata *f*
moneyed ['mʌnid] *adj* : adinerado
moneylender ['mʌniˌlɛndər] *n* : prestamista *mf*
money order *n* : giro *m* postal
Mongol ['maŋgəl, -ˌgoːl] → **Mongolian**
Mongolian [man'goːliən, maŋ-] *n* : mongol *m*, -gola *f* — **Mongolian** *adj*
mongoose ['manˌguːs, 'maŋ-] *n, pl*
-gooses : mangosta *f*
mongrel ['maŋgrəl, 'mʌŋ-] *n* **1** : perro
m mestizo, perro *m* corriente *Mex* **2**
HYBRID : híbrido *m*
monitor¹ ['manətər] *vt* : controlar, monitorear
monitor² *n* **1** : ayudante *mf* (en una escuela) **2** : monitor *m* (de una computadora, etc.)
monk ['mʌŋk] *n* : monje *m*

monkey¹ ['mʌŋki] *vi* **-keyed; -keying 1
to monkey around** : hacer payasadas,
payasear **2 to monkey with** : juguetear
con
monkey² *n, pl* **-keys** : mono *m*, -na *f*
monkeyshines ['mʌŋkiˌʃaɪnz] *npl*
PRANKS : picardías *fpl*, travesuras *fpl*
monkey wrench *n* : llave *f* inglesa
monocle ['manɪkəl] *n* : monóculo *m*
monogamous [mə'nagəməs] *adj*
: monógamo
monogamy [mə'nagəmi] *n* : monogamia *f*
monogram¹ ['manəˌgræm] *vt*
-grammed; -gramming : marcar con
monograma ⟨monogrammed towels
: toallas con monograma⟩
monogram² *n* : monograma *m*
monograph ['manəˌgræf] *n* : monografía *f*
monolingual [ˌmanə'lɪŋgwəl] *adj* : monolingüe
monolith ['manəˌlɪθ] *n* : monolito *m*
monolithic [ˌmanə'lɪθɪk] *adj* : monolítico
monologue ['manəˌlɔg] *n* : monólogo *m*
monoplane ['manəˌpleɪn] *n* : mono-
plano *m*
monopolize [mə'napəˌlaɪz] *vt* **-lized;
-lizing** : monopolizar
monopoly [mə'napəli] *n, pl* **-lies** : monopolio *m*
monosyllabic [ˌmanosə'læbɪk] *adj*
: monosilábico
monosyllable ['manoˌsɪləbəl] *n* : monosílabo *m*
monotheism ['manoθiːˌɪzəm] *n* : monoteísmo *m*
monotheistic [ˌmanoθiːˈɪstɪk] *adj* : mo-
noteísta
monotone ['manəˌtoːn] *n* : voz *f* monó-
tona
monotonous [mə'natənəs] *adj* : monótono — **monotonously** *adv*
monotony [mə'natəni] *n* : monotonía *f*,
uniformidad *f*
monoxide [mə'nakˌsaɪd] *n* : monóxido
m
monsoon [man'suːn] *n* : monzón *m*
monster ['mantstər] *n* : monstruo *m*
monstrosity [man'strasəti] *n, pl* **-ties**
: monstruosidad *f*
monstrous ['mantstrəs] *adj* : monstruoso — **monstrously** *adv*
montage [man'taʒ] *n* : montaje *m*
month ['mʌnθ] *n* : mes *m*
monthly¹ ['mʌnθli] *adv* : mensualmente
monthly² *adj* : mensual
monthly³ *n, pl* **-lies** : publicación *f* mensual
monument ['manjəmənt] *n* : monumento *m*
monumental [ˌmanjə'mɛntəl] *adj* : monumental — **monumentally** *adv*
moo¹ ['muː] *vi* : mugir
moo² *n* : mugido *m*
mood ['muːd] *n* : humor *m* ⟨to be in a
good mood : estar de buen humor⟩ ⟨to

be in the mood for : tener ganas de⟩
⟨to be in no mood for : no estar para⟩
moodiness ['muːdinəs] *n* **1** SADNESS
: melancolía *f*, tristeza *f* **2** : cambios
mpl de humor, carácter *m* temperamental
moody ['muːdi] *adj* **moodier; -est 1**
GLOOMY : melancólico, deprimido **2**
TEMPERAMENTAL : temperamental, de
humor variable
moon ['muːn] *n* : luna *f*
moonbeam ['muːnˌbiːm] *n* : rayo *m* de
luna
moonlight¹ ['muːnˌlaɪt] *vi* : estar pluriempleado
moonlight² *n* : claro *m* de luna, luz *f* de
la luna
moonlit ['muːnˌlɪt] *adj* : iluminado por
la luna ⟨a moonlit night : una noche
de luna⟩
moonshine ['muːnˌʃaɪn] *n* **1** MOONLIGHT : luz *f* de la luna **2** NONSENSE
: disparates *mpl*, tonterías *fpl* **3**
: whisky *m* destilado ilegalmente
moor¹ ['mʊr, 'mɔr] *vt* : amarrar
moor² *n* : brezal *m*, páramo *m*
Moor ['mʊr] *n* : moro *m*, -ra *f*
mooring ['mʊrɪŋ, 'mɔr-] *n* DOCK : atracadero *m*
Moorish ['mʊrɪʃ] *adj* : moro
moose ['muːs] *ns & pl* : alce *m* (norteamericano)
moot ['muːt] *adj* DEBATABLE : discutible
mop¹ ['mɑp] *vt* **mopped; mopping** : trapear
mop² *n* : trapeador *m*
mope ['moːp] *vi* **moped; moping** : andar deprimido, quedar abatido
moped ['moːˌpɛd] *n* : ciclomotor *m*
moraine [mə'reɪn] *n* : morena *f*
moral¹ ['mɔrəl] *adj* : moral ⟨moral judgment : juicio moral⟩ ⟨moral support
: apoyo moral⟩ — **morally** *adv*
moral² *n* **1** : moraleja *f* (de un cuento,
etc.) **2 morals** *npl* : moral *f*, moralidad
f
morale [mə'ræl] *n* : moral *f*
moralist ['mɔrəlɪst] *n* : moralista *mf*
moralistic [ˌmɔrə'lɪstɪk] *adj* : moralista
morality [mə'ræləti] *n, pl* **-ties** : moralidad *f*
morass [mə'ræs] *n* **1** SWAMP : ciénaga
f, pantano *m* **2** CONFUSION, MESS : lío
m fam, embrollo *m*
moratorium [ˌmɔrə'toriəm] *n, pl* **-riums**
or **-ria** [-iə] : moratoria *f*
moray ['mɔrˌeɪ, mə'reɪ] *n* : morena *f*
morbid ['mɔrbɪd] *adj* **1** : mórbido, morboso (en medicina) **2** GRUESOME
: morboso, horripilante
morbidity [mɔr'bɪdəti] *n, pl* **-ties** : morbosidad *f*
more¹ ['mor] *adv* : más ⟨what more can
I say? : ¿qué más puedo decir?⟩ ⟨more
important : más importante⟩ ⟨once
more : una vez más⟩
more² *adj* : más ⟨nothing more than that
: nada más que eso⟩ ⟨more work : más
trabajo⟩

more³ *n* : más *m* ⟨the more you eat, the
more you want : cuanto más comes,
tanto más quieres⟩
more⁴ *pron* : más ⟨more were found : se
encontraron más⟩
moreover [mor'oːvər] *adv* : además
mores ['mɔrˌeɪz, -iːz] *npl* CUSTOMS : costumbres *fpl*, tradiciones *fpl*
morgue ['mɔrg] *n* : morgue *f*
moribund ['mɔrəˌbʌnd] *adj* : moribundo
Mormon ['mɔrmən] *n* : mormón *m*,
-mona *f* — **Mormon** *adj*
morn ['mɔrn] → **morning**
morning ['mɔrnɪŋ] *n* : mañana *f* ⟨good
morning! : ¡buenos días!⟩
Moroccan [mə'rɑkən] *n* : marroquí *mf*
— **Moroccan** *adj*
moron ['mɔrˌɑn] *n* **1** : retrasado *m*, -da
f mental **2** DUNCE : estúpido *m*, -da *f*;
tonto *m*, -ta *f*
morose [mə'roːs] *adj* : hosco, sombrío
— **morosely** *adv*
moroseness [mə'roːsnəs] *n* : malhumor
m
morphine ['mɔrˌfiːn] *n* : morfina *f*
morphology [mɔr'fɑlədʒi] *n, pl* **-gies**
: morfología *f*
morrow ['mɑroː] *n* : día *m* siguiente
Morse code ['mɔrs] *n* : código *m* morse
morsel ['mɔrsəl] *n* **1** BITE : bocado *m* **2**
FRAGMENT : pedazo *m*
mortal¹ ['mɔrtəl] *adj* : mortal ⟨mortal
blow : golpe mortal⟩ ⟨mortal fear
: miedo mortal⟩ — **mortally** *adv*
mortal² *n* : mortal *mf*
mortality [mɔr'tæləti] *n* : mortalidad *f*
mortar ['mɔrtər] *n* **1** : mortero *m*, molcajete *m Mex* ⟨mortar and pestle
: mortero y maja⟩ **2** : mortero *m* ⟨mortar shell : granada de mortero⟩ **3** CEMENT : mortero *m*, argamasa *f*
mortgage¹ ['mɔrgɪdʒ] *vt* **-gaged;
-gaging** : hipotecar
mortgage² *n* : hipoteca *f*
mortification [ˌmɔrtəfə'keɪʃən] *n* **1**
: mortificación *f* **2** HUMILIATION : humillación *f*, vergüenza *f*
mortify ['mɔrtəˌfaɪ] *vt* **-fied; -fying 1**
: mortificar (en religión) **2** HUMILIATE
: humillar, avergonzar
mortuary ['mɔrtʃəˌweri] *n, pl* **-aries** FUNERAL HOME : funeraria *f*
mosaic [mo'zeɪɪk] *n* : mosaico *m*
Moslem ['mɑzləm] → **Muslim**
mosque ['mɑsk] *n* : mezquita *f*
mosquito [mə'skiːˌto] *n, pl* **-toes** : mosquito *m*, zancudo *m*
moss ['mɔs] *n* : musgo *m*
mossy ['mɔsi] *adj* **-ier; -est** : musgoso
most¹ ['moːst] *adv* : más ⟨the most interesting book : el libro más interesante⟩
most² *adj* **1** : la mayoría de, la mayor
parte de ⟨most people : la mayoría de
la gente⟩ **2** GREATEST : más (dícese de
los números), mayor (dícese de las cantidades) ⟨the most ability : la mayor capacidad⟩

most[3] *n* : más *m*, máximo *m* ⟨the most I can do : lo más que puedo hacer⟩ ⟨three weeks at the most : tres semanas como máximo⟩

most[4] *pron* : la mayoría, la mayor parte ⟨most will go : la mayoría irá⟩

mostly ['mo:stli] *adv* MAINLY : en su mayor parte, principalmente

mote ['mo:t] *n* SPECK : mota *f*

motel [mo'tɛl] *n* : motel *m*

moth ['mɔθ] *n* : palomilla *f*, polilla *f*

mother[1] ['mʌðər] *vt* **1** BEAR : dar a luz a **2** PROTECT : cuidar de, proteger

mother[2] *n* : madre *f*

motherhood ['mʌðər,hʊd] *n* : maternidad *f*

mother–in–law ['mʌðərɪn,lɔ] *n, pl* **mothers–in–law** : suegra *f*

motherland ['mʌðər,lænd] *n* : patria *f*

motherly ['mʌðərli] *adj* : maternal

mother–of–pearl [,mʌðərəv'pərl] *n* : nácar *m*, madreperla *f*

motif [mo'ti:f] *n* : motivo *m*

motion[1] ['mo:ʃən] *vt* : hacerle señas (a alguien) ⟨she motioned us to come in : nos hizo señas para que entráramos⟩

motion[2] *n* **1** MOVEMENT : movimiento *m* ⟨to set in motion : poner en marcha⟩ **2** PROPOSAL : moción *f* ⟨to second a motion : apoyar una moción⟩

motionless ['mo:ʃənləs] *adj* : inmóvil, quieto

motion picture *n* MOVIE : película *f*

motivate ['mo:tə,veɪt] *vt* **-vated; -vating** : motivar, mover, inducir

motivation [,mo:tə'veɪʃən] *n* : motivación *f*

motive[1] ['mo:tɪv] *adj* : motor ⟨motive power : fuerza motriz⟩

motive[2] *n* : motivo *m*, móvil *m*

motley ['mɑtli] *adj* : abigarrado, variopinto

motor[1] ['mo:tər] *vi* : viajar en coche

motor[2] *n* : motor *m*

motorbike ['mo:tər,baɪk] *n* : motocicleta *f* (pequeña), moto *f*

motorboat ['mo:tər,bo:t] *n* : bote *m* a motor, lancha *f* motora

motorcar ['mo:tər,kɑr] *n* : automóvil *m*

motorcycle ['mo:tər,saɪkəl] *n* : motocicleta *f*

motorcyclist ['mo:tər,saɪkəlɪst] *n* : motociclista *mf*

motorist ['mo:tərɪst] *n* : automovilista *mf*, motorista *mf*

mottle ['mɑtəl] *vt* **-tled; -tling** : manchar, motear ⟨mottled skin : piel manchada⟩ ⟨a mottled surface : una superficie moteada⟩

motto ['mɑto:] *n, pl* **-toes** : lema *m*

mould ['mo:ld] → **mold**

mound ['maʊnd] *n* **1** PILE : montón *m* **2** KNOLL : montículo *m* **3** burial mound : túmulo *m*

mount[1] ['maʊnt] *vt* **1** : montar a (un caballo), montar en (una bicicleta), subir a **2** : montar (artillería, etc.) — *vi* INCREASE : aumentar

mount[2] *n* **1** SUPPORT : soporte *m* **2** HORSE : caballería *f*, montura *f* **3** MOUNTAIN : monte *m*, montaña *f*

mountain ['maʊntən] *n* : montaña *f*

mountaineer [,maʊntən'ɪr] *n* : alpinista *mf*; montañero *m*, -ra *f*

mountaineering [,maʊntən'ɪrɪŋ] *n* : alpinismo *m*

mountainous ['maʊntənəs] *adj* : montañoso

mountaintop ['maʊntən,tɑp] *n* : cima *f*, cumbre *f*

mourn ['morn] *vt* : llorar (por), lamentar ⟨to mourn the death of : llorar la muerte de⟩ — *vi* : llorar, estar de luto

mourner ['mornər] *n* : doliente *mf*

mournful ['mornfəl] *adj* **1** SORROWFUL : lloroso, plañidero, triste **2** GLOOMY : deprimente, entristecedor — **mournfully** *adv*

mourning ['mornɪŋ] *n* : duelo *m*, luto *m*

mouse ['maʊs] *n, pl* **mice** ['maɪs] **1** : ratón *m*, -tona *f* **2** : ratón *m* (de una computadora)

mousetrap ['maʊs,træp] *n* : ratonera *f*

mousse ['mu:s] *n* : mousse *mf*

moustache ['mʌ,stæʃ, mə'stæʃ] → **mustache**

mouth[1] ['maʊð] *vt* **1** : decir con poca sinceridad, repetir sin comprensión **2** : articular en silencio ⟨she mouthed the words : formó las palabras con los labios⟩

mouth[2] ['maʊθ] *n* : boca *f* (de una persona o un animal), entrada *f* (de un túnel), desembocadura *f* (de un río)

mouthful ['maʊθ,fʊl] *n* : bocado *m* (de comida), bocanada *f* (de líquido o humo)

mouthpiece ['maʊθ,pi:s] *n* : boquilla *f* (de un instrumento musical)

mouthwash ['maʊθ,wɔʃ, -,wɑʃ] *n* : enjuague *m* bucal

movable ['mu:vəbəl] *or* **moveable** *adj* : movible, móvil

move[1] ['mu:v] *v* **moved; moving** *vi* **1** GO : ir **2** RELOCATE : mudarse, trasladarse **3** STIR : moverse ⟨don't move! : ¡no te muevas!⟩ **4** ACT : actuar — *vt* **1** : mover ⟨move it over there : ponlo allí⟩ ⟨he kept moving his feet : no dejaba de mover los pies⟩ **2** INDUCE, PERSUADE : inducir, persuadir, mover **3** TOUCH : conmover ⟨it moved him to tears : lo hizo llorar⟩ **4** PROPOSE : proponer

move[2] *n* **1** MOVEMENT : movimiento *m* **2** RELOCATION : mudanza *f* (de casa), traslado *m* **3** STEP : paso *m* ⟨a good move : un paso acertado⟩

movement ['mu:vmənt] *n* : movimiento *m*

mover ['mu:vər] *n* : persona *f* que hace mudanzas

movie ['mu:vi] *n* **1** : película *f* **2 movies** *npl* : cine *m*

moving ['mu:vɪŋ] *adj* **1** : en movimiento ⟨a moving target : un blanco móvil⟩

2 TOUCHING : conmovedor, emocionante

mow¹ ['moː] *vt* **mowed; mowed** *or* **mown** ['moːn]; **mowing** : cortar (la hierba)

mow² ['maʊ] *n* : pajar *m*

mower ['moːər] → **lawn mower**

Mr. ['mɪstər] *n, pl* **Messrs.** ['mɛsərz] : señor *m*

Mrs. ['mɪsəz, -səs, *esp South* 'mɪzəz, -zəs] *n, pl* **Mesdames** [meɪ'dɑm, -'dæm] : señora *f*

Ms. ['mɪz] *n* : señora *f*, señorita *f*

much¹ ['mʌtʃ] *adv* **more** ['mor]; **most** ['moːst] : mucho ⟨I'm much happier : estoy mucho más contenta⟩ ⟨she talks as much as I do : habla tanto como yo⟩

much² *adj* **more; most** : mucho ⟨it has much validity : tiene mucha validez⟩ ⟨too much time : demasiado tiempo⟩

much³ *pron* : mucho, -cha ⟨I don't need much : no necesito mucho⟩

mucilage ['mjuːsəlɪdʒ] *n* : mucílago *m*

muck ['mʌk] *n* **1** MANURE : estiércol *m* **2** DIRT, FILTH : mugre *f*, suciedad *f* **3** MIRE, MUD : barro *m*, fango *m*, lodo *m*

mucous ['mjuːkəs] *adj* : mucoso ⟨mucous membrane : membrana mucosa⟩

mucus ['mjuːkəs] *n* : mucosidad *f*

mud ['mʌd] *n* : barro *m*, fango *m*, lodo *m*

muddle¹ ['mʌdəl] *v* **-dled; -dling** *vt* **1** CONFUSE : confundir **2** BUNGLE : echar a perder, malograr — *vi* : andar confundido ⟨to muddle through : arreglárselas⟩

muddle² *n* : confusión *f*, embrollo *m*, lío *m*

muddleheaded [,mʌdəl'hɛdəd, 'mʌdəl,-] *adj* CONFUSED : confuso, despistado

muddy¹ ['mʌdi] *vt* **-died; -dying** : llenar de barro

muddy² *adj* **-dier; -est** : barroso, fangoso, lodoso, enlodado ⟨you're all muddy : estás cubierto de barro⟩

muff¹ ['mʌf] *vt* BUNGLE : echar a perder, fallar (un tiro, etc.)

muff² *n* : manguito *m*

muffin ['mʌfən] *n* : magdalena *f*, mantecada *f Mex*

muffle ['mʌfəl] *vt* **-fled; -fling 1** ENVELOP : cubrir, tapar **2** DEADEN : amortiguar (un sonido)

muffler ['mʌflər] *n* **1** SCARF : bufanda *f* **2** : silenciador *m*, mofle *m CA, Mex* (de un automóvil)

mug¹ ['mʌg] *v* **mugged; mugging** *vi* : posar (con afectación), hacer muecas ⟨mugging for the camera : haciendo muecas para la cámara⟩ — *vt* ASSAULT : asaltar, atracar

mug² *n* CUP : tazón *m*

mugger ['mʌgər] *n* : atracador *m*, -dora *f*

mugginess ['mʌginəs] *n* : bochorno *m*

muggy ['mʌgi] *adj* **-gier; -est** : bochornoso

mulatto [mʊ'lɑto, -'læ-] *n, pl* **-toes** *or* **-tos** : mulato *m*, -ta *f*

mulberry ['mʌl,bɛri] *n, pl* **-ries** : morera *f* (árbol), mora *f* (fruta)

mulch¹ ['mʌltʃ] *vt* : cubrir con pajote

mulch² *n* : pajote *m*

mule ['mjuːl] *n* **1** : mula *f* **2** : obstinado *m*, -da *f*; terco *m*, -ca *f*

mulish ['mjuːlɪʃ] *adj* : obstinado, terco

mull ['mʌl] *vt* **to mull over** : reflexionar sobre

mullet ['mʌlət] *n, pl* **-let** *or* **-lets** : mújol *m*, múgil *m*

multicolored [,mʌlti'kʌlərd, ,mʌltaɪ-] *adj* : multicolor, abigarrado

multicultural [,mʌlti'kʌltʃərəl] *adj* : multicultural

multifaceted [,mʌlti'fæsəṭəd, ,mʌltaɪ-] *adj* : multifacético

multifamily [,mʌlti'fæmli, ,mʌltaɪ-] *adj* : multifamiliar

multifarious [,mʌltə'færiəs] *adj* DIVERSE : diverso, variado

multilateral [,mʌlti'læṭərəl, ,mʌltaɪ-] *adj* : multilateral

multimedia [,mʌlti'miːdiə, ,mʌltaɪ-] *adj* : multimedia

multimillionaire [,mʌlti,mɪljə'nær, ,mʌltaɪ-, -'mɪljə,nær] *adj* : multimillonario

multinational [,mʌlti'næʃənəl, ,mʌltaɪ-] *adj* : multinacional

multiple¹ ['mʌltəpəl] *adj* : múltiple

multiple² *n* : múltiplo *m*

multiple sclerosis [sklə'roːsɪs] *n* : esclerosis *f* múltiple

multiplication [,mʌltəplə'keɪʃən] *n* : multiplicación *f*

multiplicity [,mʌltə'plɪsəti] *n, pl* **-ties** : multiplicidad *f*

multiplier ['mʌltə,plaɪər] *n* : multiplicador *m* (en matemáticas)

multiply ['mʌltə,plaɪ] *v* **-plied; -plying** *vt* : multiplicar — *vi* : multiplicarse

multipurpose [,mʌlti'pərpəs, ,mʌltaɪ-] *adj* : multiuso

multitude ['mʌltə,tuːd, -,tjuːd] *n* **1** CROWD : multitud *f*, muchedumbre *f* **2** HOST : multitud *f*, gran cantidad *f* ⟨a multitude of ideas : numerosas ideas⟩

multivitamin [,mʌlti'vaɪṭəmən, ,mʌltaɪ-] *adj* : multivitamínico

mum¹ ['mʌm] *adj* SILENT : callado

mum² *n* → **chrysanthemum**

mumble¹ ['mʌmbəl] *v* **-bled; -bling** *vt* : mascullar, musitar — *vi* : mascullar, hablar entre dientes, murmurar

mumble² *n* **to speak in a mumble** : hablar entre dientes

mummy ['mʌmi] *n, pl* **-mies** : momia *f*

mumps ['mʌmps] *ns & pl* : paperas *fpl*

munch ['mʌntʃ] *v* : mascar, masticar

mundane [,mʌn'deɪn, 'mʌn,-] *adj* **1** EARTHLY, WORLDLY : mundano, terrenal **2** COMMONPLACE : rutinario, ordinario

municipal [mjʊ'nɪsəpəl] *adj* : municipal

municipality [mjʊ,nɪsə'pæləṭi] *n, pl* **-ties** : municipio *m*

munitions [mjʊ'nɪʃənz] *npl* : municiones *fpl*

mural[1] [ˈmjʊrəl] *adj* : mural

mural[2] [ˈmjʊrəlɪst] *n* : mural *m*

murder[1] [ˈmərdər] *vt* : asesinar, matar — *vi* : matar

murder[2] *n* : asesinato *m*, homicidio *m*

murderer [ˈmərdərər] *n* : asesino *m*, -na *f*; homicida *mf*

murderess [ˈmərdərɪs, -dəˌrɛs, -dərəs] *n* : asesina *f*, homicida *f*

murderous [ˈmərdərəs] *adj* : asesino, homicida

murk [ˈmərk] *n* DARKNESS : oscuridad *f*, tinieblas *fpl*

murkiness [ˈmərkinəs] *n* : oscuridad *f*, tenebrosidad *f*

murky [ˈmərki] *adj* **-kier; -est** : oscuro, tenebroso

murmur[1] [ˈmərmər] *vi* **1** DRONE : murmurar **2** GRUMBLE : refunfuñar, regañar, rezongar — *vt* MUMBLE : murmurar

murmur[2] *n* **1** COMPLAINT : queja *f* **2** DRONE : murmullo *m*, rumor *m*

muscle[1] [ˈmʌsəl] *vi* **-cled; -cling** : meterse ⟨to muscle in on : meterse por la fuerza en, entrometerse en⟩

muscle[2] *n* **1** : músculo *m* **2** STRENGTH : fuerza *f*

muscular [ˈmʌskjələr] *adj* **1** : muscular ⟨muscular tissue : tejido muscular⟩ **2** BRAWNY : musculoso

muscular dystrophy *n* : distrofia *f* muscular

musculature [ˈmʌskjələˌtʃʊr, -tʃər] *n* : musculatura *f*

muse[1] [ˈmjuːz] *vi* **mused; musing** PONDER, REFLECT : cavilar, meditar, reflexionar

muse[2] *n* : musa *f*

museum [mjʊˈziːəm] *n* : museo *m*

mush [ˈmʌʃ] *n* **1** : gachas *fpl* (de maíz) **2** SENTIMENTALITY : sensiblería *f*

mushroom[1] [ˈmʌʃˌruːm, -ˌrʊm] *vi* GROW, MULTIPLY : crecer rápidamente, multiplicarse

mushroom[2] *n* : hongo *m*, champiñón *m*, seta *f*

mushy [ˈmʌʃi] *adj* **mushier; -est 1** SOFT : blando **2** MAWKISH : sensiblero

music [ˈmjuːzɪk] *n* : música *f*

musical[1] [ˈmjuːzɪkəl] *adj* : musical, de música — **musically** *adv*

musical[2] *n* : comedia *f* musical

music box *n* : cajita *f* de música

musician [mjʊˈzɪʃən] *n* : músico *m*, -ca *f*

musk [ˈmʌsk] *n* : almizcle *m*

musket [ˈmʌskət] *n* : mosquete *m*

musketeer [ˌmʌskəˈtɪr] *n* : mosquetero *m*

muskrat [ˈmʌskˌræt] *n, pl* **-rat** *or* **-rats** : rata *f* almizclera

Muslim[1] [ˈmʌzləm, ˈmʊs-, ˈmʊz-] *adj* : musulmán

Muslim[2] *n* : musulmán *m*, -mana *f*

muslin [ˈmʌzlən] *n* : muselina *f*

muss[1] [ˈmʌs] *vt* : desordenar, despeinar (el pelo)

muss[2] *n* : desorden *m*

mussel [ˈmʌsəl] *n* : mejillón *m*

must[1] [ˈmʌst] *v aux* **1** (*expressing obligation or necessity*) : deber, tener que ⟨you must stop : debes parar⟩ ⟨we must obey : tenemos que obedecer⟩ **2** (*expressing probability*) : deber (de), haber de ⟨you must be tired : debes de estar cansado⟩ ⟨it must be late : ha de ser tarde⟩

must[2] *n* : necesidad *f* ⟨exercise is a must : el ejercicio es imprescindible⟩

mustache [ˈmʌˌstæʃ, mʌˈstæʃ] *n* : bigote *m*, bigotes *mpl*

mustang [ˈmʌˌstæŋ] *n* : mustang *m*

mustard [ˈmʌstərd] *n* : mostaza *f*

muster[1] [ˈmʌstər] *vt* **1** ASSEMBLE : reunir **2 to muster up** : armarse de, cobrar (valor, fuerzas, etc.)

muster[2] *n* **1** INSPECTION : revista *f* (de tropas) ⟨it didn't pass muster : no resistió un examen minucioso⟩ **2** COLLECTION : colección *f*

mustiness [ˈmʌstinəs] *n* : lo mohoso

musty [ˈmʌsti] *adj* **mustier; -est** : mohoso, que huele a moho, que huele a encerrado

mutant[1] [ˈmjuːtənt] *adj* : mutante

mutant[2] *n* : mutante *m*

mutate [ˈmjuːˌteɪt] *vi* **-tated; -tating 1** : mutar (genéticamente) **2** CHANGE : transformarse

mutation [mjuːˈteɪʃən] *n* : mutación *f* (genética)

mute[1] [ˈmjuːt] *vt* **muted; muting** MUFFLE : amortiguar, ponerle sordina a (un instrumento musical)

mute[2] *adj* **muter; mutest** : mudo — **mutely** *adv*

mute[3] *n* **1** : mudo *m*, -da *f* (persona) **2** : sordina *f* (para un instrumento musical)

mutilate [ˈmjuːtəˌleɪt] *vt* **-lated; -lating** : mutilar

mutilation [ˌmjuːtəˈleɪʃən] *n* : mutilación *f*

mutineer [ˌmjuːtənˈɪr] *n* : amotinado *m*, -da *f*

mutinous [ˈmjuːtənəs] *adj* : amotinado

mutiny[1] [ˈmjuːtəni] *vi* **-nied; -nying** : amotinarse

mutiny[2] *n, pl* **-nies** : amotinamiento *m*, motín *m*

mutt [ˈmʌt] *n* MONGREL : perro *m* mestizo, perro *m* corriente *Mex*

mutter [ˈmʌtər] *vi* **1** MUMBLE : mascullar, hablar entre dientes, murmurar **2** GRUMBLE : refunfuñar, regañar, rezongar

mutton [ˈmʌtən] *n* : carne *f* de carnero

mutual [ˈmjuːtʃʊəl] *adj* **1** : mutuo ⟨mutual respect : respeto mutuo⟩ **2** COMMON : común ⟨a mutual friend : un amigo común⟩

mutually [ˈmjuːtʃʊəli, -tʃəli] *adv* **1** : mutuamente ⟨mutually beneficial : mutuamente beneficioso⟩ **2** JOINTLY : conjuntamente

muzzle¹ ['mʌzəl] *vt* -zled; -zling : ponerle un bozal a (un animal), amordazar
muzzle² *n* **1** SNOUT : hocico *m* **2** : bozal *m* (para un perro, etc.) **3** : boca *f* (de un arma de fuego)
my¹ ['maɪ] *adj* : mi ⟨my parents : mis padres⟩
my² *interj* : ¡caramba!, ¡Dios mío!
myopia [maɪ'o:piə] *n* : miopía *f*
myopic [maɪ'o:pɪk, -'ɑ-] *adj* : miope
myriad¹ ['mɪriəd] *adj* INNUMERABLE : innumerable
myriad² *n* : miríada *f*
myrrh ['mər] *n* : mirra *f*
myrtle ['mərt̬əl] *n* : mirto *m*, arrayán *m*
myself [maɪ'sɛlf] *pron* **1** (*used reflexively*) : me ⟨I washed myself : me lavé⟩ **2** (*used for emphasis*) : yo mismo, yo misma ⟨I did it myself : lo hice yo mismo⟩
mysterious [mɪ'stɪriəs] *adj* : misterioso — **mysteriously** *adv*

mysteriousness [mɪ'stɪriəsnəs] *n* : lo misterioso
mystery ['mɪstəri] *n, pl* -teries : misterio *m*
mystic¹ ['mɪstɪk] *adj* : místico
mystic² *n* : místico *m*, -ca *f*
mystical ['mɪstɪkəl] *adj* : místico — **mystically** *adv*
mysticism ['mɪstə,sɪzəm] *n* : misticismo *m*
mystify ['mɪstə,faɪ] *vt* -fied; -fying : dejar perplejo, confundir
mystique [mɪ'sti:k] *n* : aura *f* de misterio
myth ['mɪθ] *n* : mito *m*
mythic ['mɪθɪk] *adj* : mítico
mythical ['mɪθɪkəl] *adj* : mítico
mythological [,mɪθə'lɑdʒɪkəl] *adj* : mitológico
mythology [mɪ'θɑlədʒi] *n, pl* -gies : mitología *f*

N

n ['ɛn] *n, pl* **n's** *or* **ns** ['ɛnz] : decimocuarta letra del alfabeto inglés
nab ['næb] *vt* **nabbed; nabbing** : prender, pillar *fam*, pescar *fam*
nadir ['neɪdər, 'neɪ,dɪr] *n* : nadir *m*, punto *m* más bajo
nag¹ ['næg] *v* **nagged; nagging** *vi* **1** COMPLAIN : quejarse, rezongar **2 to nag at** HASSLE : molestar, darle (la) lata (a alguien) — *vt* **1** PESTER : molestar, fastidiar **2** SCOLD : regañar, estarle encima a *fam*
nag² *n* **1** GRUMBLER : gruñón *m*, -ñona *f* **2** HORSE : jamelgo *m*
naiad ['neɪəd, 'naɪ-, -,æd] *n, pl* **-iads** *or* **-iades** [-ə,di:z] : náyade *f*
nail¹ ['neɪl] *vt* : clavar, sujetar con clavos
nail² *n* **1** FINGERNAIL : uña *f* ⟨nail file : lima (de uñas)⟩ ⟨nail polish : laca de uñas⟩ **2** : clavo *m* ⟨to hit the nail on the head : dar en el clavo⟩
naive *or* **naïve** [nɑ'i:v] *adj* **-iver; -est 1** INGENUOUS : ingenuo, cándido **2** GULLIBLE : crédulo
naively [nɑ'i:vli] *adv* : ingenuamente
naiveté [,nɑ,i:və'teɪ, nɑ'i:və,-] *n* : ingenuidad *f*
naked ['neɪkəd] *adj* **1** UNCLOTHED : desnudo **2** UNCOVERED : desenvainado (dícese de una espada), pelado (dícese de los árboles), expuesto al aire (dícese de una llama) **3** OBVIOUS, PLAIN : manifiesto, puro, desnudo ⟨the naked truth : la pura verdad⟩ **4 to the naked eye** : a simple vista
nakedly ['neɪkədli] *adv* : manifiestamente
nakedness ['neɪkədnəs] *n* : desnudez *f*
name¹ ['neɪm] *vt* **named; naming 1** CALL : llamar, bautizar, ponerle nombre a **2** MENTION : mentar, mencionar, dar el nombre de ⟨they have named a

suspect : han dado el nombre de un sospechoso⟩ **3** APPOINT : nombrar **4 to name a price** : fijar un precio
name² *adj* **1** KNOWN : de nombre ⟨name brand : marca conocida⟩ **2** PROMINENT : de renombre, de prestigio
name³ *n* **1** : nombre *m* ⟨what is your name? : ¿cómo se llama?⟩ **2** SURNAME : apellido *m* **3** EPITHET : epíteto *m* ⟨to call somebody names : llamar a alguien de todo⟩ **4** REPUTATION : fama *f*, reputación *f* ⟨to make a name for oneself : darse a conocer, hacerse famoso⟩
nameless ['neɪmləs] *adj* **1** ANONYMOUS : anónimo **2** INDESCRIBABLE : indecible, indescriptible
namelessly ['neɪmləsli] *adv* : anónimamente
namely ['neɪmli] *adv* : a saber
namesake ['neɪm,seɪk] *n* : tocayo *m*, -ya *f*; homónimo *m*, -ma *f*
Namibian [nə'mɪbiən] *n* : namibio *m*, -bia *f* — **Namibian** *adj*
nanny ['næni] *n, pl* **nannies** : niñera *f*; nana *f CA, Col, Mex, Ven*
nap¹ ['næp] *vi* **napped; napping 1** : dormir, dormir la siesta **2 to be caught napping** : estar desprevenido
nap² *n* **1** SLEEP : siesta *f* ⟨to take a nap : echarse una siesta⟩ **2** FUZZ, PILE : pelo *m*, pelusa *f* (de telas)
nape ['neɪp, 'næp] *n* : nuca *f*, cerviz *f*, cogote *m*
naphtha ['næfθə] *n* : nafta *f*
napkin ['næpkən] *n* : servilleta *f*
narcissism ['nɑrsə,sɪzəm] *n* : narcisismo *m*
narcissist ['nɑrsəsɪst] *n* : narcisista *mf*
narcissistic [,nɑrsə'sɪstɪk] *adj* : narcisista
narcissus [nɑr'sɪsəs] *n, pl* **-cissus** *or*

-cissuses *or* **-cissi** [-'sɪ,saɪ, -,si:] : narciso *m*

narcotic[1] [nɑr'kɑtɪk] *adj* : narcótico

narcotic[2] *n* : narcótico *m*, estupefaciente *m*

narrate ['nær,eɪt] *vt* **-rated; -rating** : narrar, relatar

narration [næ'reɪʃən] *n* : narración *f*

narrative[1] ['nærətɪv] *adj* : narrativo

narrative[2] *n* : narración *f*, narrativa *f*, relato *m*

narrator ['nær,eɪtər] *n* : narrador *m*, -dora *f*

narrow[1] ['nær,oː] *vi* : estrecharse, angostarse ⟨the river narrowed : el río se estrechó⟩ — *vt* **1** : estrechar, angostar **2** LIMIT : restringir, limitar ⟨to narrow the search : limitar la búsqueda⟩

narrow[2] *adj* **1** : estrecho, angosto **2** LIMITED : estricto, limitado ⟨in the narrowest sense of the word : en el sentido más estricto de la palabra⟩ **3 to have a narrow escape** : escapar por un pelo

narrowly ['næroli] *adv* **1** BARELY : por poco **2** CLOSELY : de cerca

narrow-minded [,næro'maɪndəd] *adj* : de miras estrechas

narrowness ['næronəs] *n* : estrechez *f*

narrows ['næro:z] *npl* STRAIT : estrecho *m*

narwhal ['nɑr,hwɑl, 'nɑrwəl] *n* : narval *m*

nasal ['neɪzəl] *adj* : nasal, gangoso ⟨a nasal voice : una voz gangosa⟩

nasally ['neɪzəli] *adv* **1** : por la nariz **2** : con voz gangosa

nastily ['næstəli] *adv* : con maldad, cruelmente

nastiness ['næstinəs] *n* : porquería *f*

nasturtium [nə'stərʃəm, næ-] *n* : capuchina *f*

nasty ['næsti] *adj* **-tier; -est 1** FILTHY : sucio, mugriento **2** OBSCENE : obsceno **3** MEAN, SPITEFUL : malo, malicioso **4** UNPLEASANT : desagradable, feo **5** REPUGNANT : asqueroso, repugnante ⟨a nasty smell : un olor asqueroso⟩

natal ['neɪtəl] *adj* : natal

nation ['neɪʃən] *n* : nación *f*

national[1] ['næʃənəl] *adj* : nacional

national[2] *n* : ciudadano *m*, -na *f*; nacional *mf*

nationalism ['næʃənə,lɪzəm] *n* : nacionalismo *m*

nationalist[1] ['næʃənəlɪst] *adj* : nacionalista

nationalist[2] *n* : nacionalista *mf*

nationalistic [,næʃənə'lɪstɪk] *adj* : nacionalista

nationality [,næʃə'næləti] *n, pl* **-ties** : nacionalidad *f*

nationalization [,næʃənələ'zeɪʃən] *n* : nacionalización *f*

nationalize ['næʃənə,laɪz] *vt* **-ized; -izing** : nacionalizar

nationally ['næʃənəli] *adv* : a escala nacional, a nivel nacional

nationwide ['neɪʃən'waɪd] *adj* : en toda la nación, por todo el país

native[1] ['neɪtɪv] *adj* **1** INNATE : innato **2** : natal ⟨her native city : su ciudad natal⟩ **3** INDIGENOUS : indígena, autóctono

native[2] *n* **1** ABORIGINE : nativo *m*, -va *f*; indígena *mf* **2** : natural *m* ⟨he's a native of Mexico : es natural de México⟩

Native American → **American Indian**

nativity [nə'tɪvəti, neɪ-] *n, pl* **-ties 1** BIRTH : navidad *f* **2 the Nativity** : la Natividad, la Navidad

natty ['næti] *adj* **-tier; -est** : elegante, garboso

natural[1] ['nætʃərəl] *adj* **1** : natural, de la naturaleza ⟨natural woodlands : bosques naturales⟩ ⟨natural childbirth : parto natural⟩ **2** INNATE : innato, natural **3** UNAFFECTED : natural, sin afectación **4** LIFELIKE : natural, vivo

natural[2] *n* **to be a natural** : tener un talento innato (para algo)

natural gas *n* : gas *m* natural

natural history *n* : historia *f* natural

naturalism ['nætʃərə,lɪzəm] *n* : naturalismo *m*

naturalist ['nætʃərəlɪst] *n* : naturalista *mf* — **naturalist** *adj*

naturalistic [,nætʃərə'lɪstɪk] *adj* : naturalista

naturalization [,nætʃərələ'zeɪʃən] *n* : naturalización *f*

naturalize ['nætʃərə,laɪz] *vt* **-ized; -izing** : naturalizar

naturally ['nætʃərəli] *adv* **1** INHERENTLY : naturalmente, intrínsecamente **2** UNAFFECTEDLY : de manera natural **3** OF COURSE : por supuesto, naturalmente

naturalness ['nætʃərəlnəs] *n* : naturalidad *f*

natural science *n* : ciencias *fpl* naturales

nature ['neɪtʃər] *n* **1** : naturaleza *f* ⟨the laws of nature : las leyes de la naturaleza⟩ **2** KIND, SORT : índole *f*, clase *f* ⟨things of this nature : cosas de esta índole⟩ **3** DISPOSITION : carácter *m*, natural *m*, naturaleza *f* ⟨it is his nature to be friendly : es de natural simpático⟩ ⟨human nature : la naturaleza humana⟩

naught ['nɔt] *n* **1** : nada *f* ⟨to come to naught : reducirse a nada, fracasar⟩ **2** ZERO : cero *m*

naughtily ['nɔtəli] *adv* : traviesamente, con malicia

naughtiness ['nɔtinəs] *n* : mala conducta *f*, travesuras *fpl*, malicia *f*

naughty ['nɔti] *adj* **-tier; -est 1** MISCHIEVOUS : travieso, pícaro **2** RISQUÉ : picante, subido de tono

nausea ['nɔzia, 'nɔʃə] *n* **1** SICKNESS : náuseas *fpl* **2** DISGUST : asco *m*

nauseate ['nɔzi,eɪt, -ʒi-, -si-, -ʃi-] *vt* **-ated; -ating 1** SICKEN : darle náuseas (a alguien) **2** DISGUST : asquear, darle asco (a alguien)

nauseating *adj* : nauseabundo, repugnante

nauseatingly ['nɔzi,eɪtɪŋli, -ʒi-, -si-, -ʃi-] *adv* : hasta el punto de dar asco ⟨nauseatingly sweet : tan dulce que da asco⟩

nauseous ['nɔʃəs, -ziəs] *adj* **1** SICK : mareado, con náuseas **2** SICKENING : nauseabundo

nautical ['nɔtɪkəl] *adj* : náutico

nautilus ['nɔtələs] *n, pl* **-luses** *or* **-li** [-,laɪ, -,liː] : nautilo *m*

Navajo ['nævə,hoː, 'nɑ-] *n* : navajo *m*, -ja *f* — **Navajo** *adj*

naval ['neɪvəl] *adj* : naval

nave ['neɪv] *n* : nave *f*

navel ['neɪvəl] *n* : ombligo *m*

navigability [,nævɪgə'bɪləti] *n* : navegabilidad *f*

navigable ['nævɪgəbəl] *adj* : navegable

navigate ['nævə,geɪt] *v* **-gated; -gating** *vi* : navegar — *vt* **1** STEER : gobernar (un barco), pilotar (un avión) **2** : navegar por (un río, etc.)

navigation [,nævə'geɪʃən] *n* : navegación *f*

navigator ['nævə,geɪtər] *n* : navegante *mf*

navy ['neɪvi] *n, pl* **-vies 1** FLEET : flota *f* **2** : marina *f* de guerra, armada *f* ⟨the United States Navy : la armada de los Estados Unidos⟩ **3** *or* **navy blue** : azul *m* marino

nay[1] ['neɪ] *adv* : no

nay[2] *n* : no *m*, voto *m* en contra

Nazi ['nɑtsi, 'næt-] *n* : nazi *mf*

Nazism ['nɑt,sɪzəm, 'næt-] *or* **Naziism** ['nɑtsi,ɪzəm, 'næt-] *n* : nazismo *m*

Neanderthal man [ni'ændər,θɔl, -,tɔl] *n* : hombre *m* de Neanderthal

near[1] ['nɪr] *vt* **1** : acercarse a ⟨the ship is nearing port : el barco se está acercando al puerto⟩ **2** : estar a punto de ⟨she is nearing graduation : está a punto de graduarse⟩

near[2] *adv* CLOSE : cerca ⟨my family lives quite near : mi familia vive muy cerca⟩ **2** NEARLY : casi ⟨I came near to finishing : casi terminé⟩

near[3] *adj* **1** CLOSE : cercano, próximo **2** SIMILAR : parecido, semejante

near[4] *prep* : cerca de

nearby[1] [nɪr'baɪ, 'nɪr,baɪ] *adv* : cerca

nearby[2] *adj* : cercano

nearly ['nɪrli] *adv* **1** ALMOST : casi ⟨nearly asleep : casi dormido⟩ **2 not nearly** : ni con mucho, ni mucho menos ⟨it was not nearly so bad as I had expected : no fue ni con mucho tan malo como esperaba⟩

nearness ['nɪrnəs] *n* : proximidad *f*

nearsighted ['nɪr,saɪtəd] *adj* : miope, corto de vista

nearsightedly ['nɪr,saɪtədli] *adv* : con miopía

nearsightedness ['nɪr,saɪtədnəs] *n* : miopía *f*

neat ['niːt] *adj* **1** CLEAN, ORDERLY : ordenado, pulcro, limpio **2** UNDILUTED : solo, sin diluir **3** SIMPLE, TASTEFUL : sencillo y de buen gusto **4** CLEVER : hábil, ingenioso ⟨a neat trick : un truco ingenioso⟩

neatly ['niːtli] *adv* **1** TIDILY : ordenadamente **2** CLEVERLY : ingeniosamente

neatness ['niːtnəs] *n* : pulcritud *f*, limpieza *f*, orden *m*

nebula ['nɛbjʊlə] *n, pl* **-lae** [-,liː, -,laɪ] : nebulosa *f*

nebulous ['nɛbjʊləs] *adj* : nebuloso, vago

necessarily [,nɛsə'sɛrəli] *adv* : necesariamente, forzosamente

necessary[1] ['nɛsə,seri] *adj* **1** INEVITABLE : inevitable **2** COMPULSORY : necesario, obligatorio **3** ESSENTIAL : imprescindible, preciso, necesario

necessary[2] *n, pl* **-saries** : lo esencial, lo necesario

necessitate [nɪ'sɛsə,teɪt] *vt* **-tated; -tating** : necesitar, requerir

necessity [nɪ'sɛsəti] *n, pl* **-ties 1** NEED : necesidad *f* **2** REQUIREMENT : requisito *m* indispensable **3** POVERTY : indigencia *f*, necesidad *f* **4** INEVITABILITY : inevitabilidad *f*

neck[1] ['nɛk] *vi* : besuquearse

neck[2] *n* **1** : cuello *m* (de una persona), pescuezo *m* (de un animal) **2** COLLAR : cuello *m* **3** : cuello *m* (de una botella), mástil *m* (de una guitarra)

neckerchief ['nɛkərtʃəf, -,tʃiːf] *n, pl* **-chiefs** [-tʃəfs, -,tʃiːfs] : pañuelo *m* (para el cuello), mascada *f Mex*

necklace ['nɛkləs] *n* : collar *m*

neckline ['nɛk,laɪn] *n* : escote *m*

necktie ['nɛk,taɪ] *n* : corbata *f*

nectar ['nɛktər] *n* : néctar *m*

nectarine [,nɛktə'riːn] *n* : nectarina *f*

née *or* **nee** ['neɪ] *adj* : de soltera ⟨Mrs. Smith, née Whitman : la señora Smith, de soltera Whitman⟩

need[1] ['niːd] *vt* **1** : necesitar ⟨I need your help : necesito su ayuda⟩ ⟨I need money : me falta dinero⟩ **2** REQUIRE : requerir, exigir ⟨that job needs patience : ese trabajo exige paciencia⟩ **3 to need to** : tener que ⟨he needs to study : tiene que estudiar⟩ ⟨they need to be scolded : hay que reprenderlos⟩ — *v aux* **1** MUST : tener que, deber ⟨need you shout? : ¿tienes que gritar?⟩ **2 to be needed** : hacer falta ⟨you needn't worry : no hace falta que te preocupes, no hay por qué preocuparse⟩

need[2] *n* **1** NECESSITY : necesidad *f* ⟨in case of need : en caso de necesidad⟩ **2** LACK : falta *f* ⟨the need for better training : la falta de mejor capacitación⟩ ⟨to be in need : necesitar⟩ **3** POVERTY : necesidad *f*, indigencia *f* **4 needs** *npl* : requisitos *mpl*, carencias *fpl*

needful ['niːdfəl] *adj* : necesario

needle[1] ['niːdəl] *vt* **-dled; -dling** : pinchar

needle[2] *n* **1** : aguja *f* ⟨to thread a needle : enhebrar una aguja⟩ ⟨knitting needle : aguja de tejer⟩ **2** POINTER : aguja *f*, indicador *m*

needlepoint ['niːdəlˌpɔint] *n* **1** LACE : encaje *m* de mano **2** EMBROIDERY : bordado *m* en cañamazo

needless ['niːdləs] *adj* : innecesario

needlessly ['niːdləsli] *adv* : sin ninguna necesidad, innecesariamente

needlework ['niːdəlˌwərk] *n* : bordado *m*

needn't ['niːdənt] (*contraction of* **need not**) → **need**

needy¹ ['niːdi] *adj* **needier; -est** : necesitado

needy² *n* **the needy** : los necesitados *mpl*

nefarious [nɪ'færiəs] *adj* : nefario, nefando, infame

negate [nɪ'geɪt] *vt* **-gated; -gating 1** DENY : negar **2** NULLIFY : invalidar, anular

negation [nɪ'geɪʃən] *n* : negación *f*

negative¹ ['nɛgətɪv] *adj* : negativo

negative² *n* **1** : negación *f* (en lingüística) **2** : negativa *f* ⟨to answer in the negative : contestar con una negativa⟩ **3** : término *m* negativo (en matemáticas) **4** : negativo *m*, imagen *f* en negativo (en fotografía)

negatively ['nɛgətɪvli] *adv* : negativamente

neglect¹ [nɪ'glɛkt] *vt* **1** : desatender, descuidar ⟨to neglect one's health : descuidar la salud⟩ **2** : no cumplir con, faltar a ⟨to neglect one's obligations : faltar uno a sus obligaciones⟩ ⟨he neglected to tell me : omitió decírmelo⟩

neglect² *n* **1** : negligencia *f*, descuido *m*, incumplimiento *m* ⟨through neglect : por negligencia⟩ ⟨neglect of duty : incumplimiento del deber⟩ **2 in a state of neglect** : abandonado, descuidado

neglectful [nɪ'glɛktfəl] *adj* : descuidado

negligee [ˌnɛglə'ʒeɪ] *n* : negligé *m*

negligence ['nɛglɪʤənts] *n* : descuido *m*, negligencia *f*

negligent ['nɛglɪʤənt] *adj* : negligente, descuidado — **negligently** *adv*

negligible ['nɛglɪʤəbəl] *adj* : insignificante, despreciable

negotiable [nɪ'goːʃəbəl, -ʃiə-] *adj* : negociable

negotiate [nɪ'goːʃiˌeɪt] *v* **-ated; -ating** *vi* : negociar — *vt* **1** : negociar, gestionar ⟨to negotiate a treaty : negociar un trato⟩ **2** : salvar, franquear ⟨they negotiated the obstacles : salvaron los obstáculos⟩ ⟨to negotiate a turn : tomar una curva⟩

negotiation [nɪˌgoːʃi'eɪʃən, -si'eɪ-] *n* : negociación *f*

negotiator [nɪ'goːʃiˌeɪtər, -siˌeɪ-] *n* : negociador *m*, -dora *f*

Negro ['niːˌgroː] *n, pl* **-groes** : negro *m*, -gra *f*

neigh¹ ['neɪ] *vi* : relinchar

neigh² *n* : relincho *m*

neighbor¹ ['neɪbər] *vt* : ser vecino de, estar junto a ⟨her house neighbors mine : su casa está junto a la mía⟩ — *vi* : estar cercano, lindar, colindar ⟨her land neighbors on mine : sus tierras lindan con las mías⟩

neighbor² *n* **1** : vecino *m*, -na *f* **2 love thy neighbor** : ama a tu prójimo

neighborhood ['neɪbərˌhʊd] *n* **1** : barrio *m*, vecindad *f*, vecindario *m* **2 in the neighborhood of** : alrededor de, cerca de

neighborly ['neɪbərli] *adv* : amable, de buena vecindad

neither¹ ['niːðər, 'naɪ-] *adj* : ninguno (de los dos)

neither² *conj* **1** : ni ⟨neither asleep nor awake : ni dormido ni despierto⟩ **2** NOR : ni (tampoco) ⟨I'm not asleep— neither am I : no estoy dormido—ni yo tampoco⟩

neither³ *pron* : ninguno

nemesis ['nɛməsɪs] *n, pl* **-eses** [-ˌsiːz] **1** RIVAL : rival *mf* **2** RETRIBUTION : justo castigo *m*

Neoclassical [ˌniːoː'klæsɪkəl] *adj* : neoclásico

neologism [ni'αləˌʤɪzəm] *n* : neologismo *m*

neon¹ ['niːˌαn] *adj* : de neón ⟨neon sign : letrero de neón⟩

neon² *n* : neón *m*

neophyte ['niːəˌfaɪt] *n* : neófito *m*, -ta *f*

Nepali [nə'pɔli, -'pα-, -'pæ-] *n* : nepalés *m*, -lesa *f* — **Nepali** *adj*

nephew ['nɛˌfjuː, *chiefly British* 'nɛˌvjuː] *n* : sobrino *m*

nepotism ['nɛpəˌtɪzəm] *n* : nepotismo *m*

Neptune ['nɛpˌtuːn, -ˌtjuːn] *n* : Neptuno *m*

nerd ['nərd] *n* : ganso *m*, -sa *f*

nerve ['nərv] *n* **1** : nervio *m* **2** COURAGE : coraje *m*, valor *m*, fuerza *f* de la voluntad ⟨to lose one's nerve : perder el valor⟩ **3** AUDACITY, GALL : atrevimiento *m*, descaro *m* ⟨of all the nerve! : ¡qué descaro!⟩ **4 nerves** *npl* : nervios *mpl* ⟨a fit of nerves : un ataque de nervios⟩

nervous ['nərvəs] *adj* **1** : nervioso ⟨the nervous system : el sistema nervioso⟩ **2** EXCITABLE : nervioso, excitable ⟨to get nervous : excitarse, ponerse nervioso⟩ **3** FEARFUL : miedoso, temeroso

nervously ['nərvəsli] *adv* : nerviosamente

nervousness ['nərvəsnəs] *n* : nerviosismo *m*, nerviosidad *f*, ansiedad *f*

nervy ['nərvi] *adj* **nervier; -est 1** COURAGEOUS : valiente **2** IMPUDENT : atrevido, descarado, fresco *fam* **3** NERVOUS : nervioso

nest¹ ['nɛst] *vi* : anidar

nest² *n* **1** : nido *m* (de un ave), avispero *m* (de una avispa), madriguera *f* (de un animal) **2** REFUGE : nido *m*, refugio *m* **3** SET : juego *m* ⟨a nest of tables : un juego de mesitas⟩

nestle ['nɛsəl] *vi* **-tled; -tling** : acurrucarse, arrimarse cómodamente

net[1] ['nɛt] *vt* **netted; netting 1** CATCH : pescar, atrapar con una red **2** CLEAR : ganar neto ⟨they netted $5000 : ganaron $5000 netos⟩ **3** YIELD : producir neto

net[2] *adj* : neto ⟨net weight : peso neto⟩ ⟨net gain : ganancia neta⟩

net[3] *n* : red *f*, malla *f*

nether ['nɛðər] *adj* **1** : inferior, más bajo **2 the nether regions** : el infierno

nettle[1] ['nɛt̬əl] *vt* **-tled; -tling** : irritar, provocar, molestar

nettle[2] *n* : ortiga *f*

network ['nɛt̬ˌwərk] *n* **1** SYSTEM : red *f* **2** CHAIN : cadena *f* ⟨a network of supermarkets : una cadena de supermercados⟩

neural ['nʊrəl, 'njʊr-] *adj* : neural

neuralgia [nʊ'rældʒə, njʊ-] *n* : neuralgia *f*

neuritis [nʊ'raɪt̬əs, njʊ-] *n, pl* **-ritides** [-'rɪt̬əˌdiːz] *or* **-ritises** : neuritis *f*

neurological [ˌnʊrə'lɑdʒɪkəl, ˌnjʊr-] *or* **neurologic** [ˌnʊrə'lɑdʒɪk, ˌnjʊr-] *adj* : neurológico

neurologist [nʊ'rɑlədʒɪst, njʊ-] *n* : neurólogo *m*, -ga *f*

neurology [nʊ'rɑlədʒi, njʊ-] *n* : neurología *f*

neurosis [nʊ'roːsɪs, njʊ-] *n, pl* **-roses** [-ˌsiːz] : neurosis *f*

neurotic[1] [nʊ'rɑt̬ɪk, njʊ-] *adj* : neurótico

neurotic[2] *n* : neurótico *m*, -ca *f*

neuter[1] ['nuːt̬ər, 'njuː-] *vt* : castrar

neuter[2] *adj* : neutro

neutral[1] ['nuːtrəl, 'njuː-] *adj* **1** IMPARTIAL : neutral, imparcial ⟨to remain neutral : permanecer neutral⟩ **2** : neutro ⟨a neutral color : un color neutro⟩ **3** : neutro (en la química o la electricidad)

neutral[2] *n* : punto *m* muerto (de un automóvil)

neutrality [nuː'trælət̬i, njuː-] *n* : neutralidad *f*

neutralization [ˌnuːtrələ'zeɪʃən, ˌnjuː-] *n* : neutralización *f*

neutralize ['nuːtrəˌlaɪz, 'njuː-] *vt* **-ized; -izing** : neutralizar

neutron ['nuːˌtrɑn, 'njuː-] *n* : neutrón *m*

never ['nɛvər] *adv* **1** : nunca, jamás ⟨he never studies : nunca estudia⟩ **2 never again** : nunca más, nunca jamás **3 never mind** : no importa

nevermore [ˌnɛvər'mor] *adv* : nunca más

nevertheless [ˌnɛvərðə'lɛs] *adv* : sin embargo, no obstante

new ['nuː, 'njuː] *adj* **1** : nuevo ⟨a new dress : un vestido nuevo⟩ **2** RECENT : nuevo, reciente ⟨what's new? : ¿qué hay de nuevo?⟩ ⟨a new arrival : un recién llegado⟩ **3** DIFFERENT : nuevo, distinto ⟨this problem is new : este problema es distinto⟩ ⟨new ideas : ideas nuevas⟩ **4 like new** : como nuevo

newborn ['nuːˌbɔrn, 'njuː-] *adj* : recién nacido

newcomer ['nuːˌkʌmər, 'njuː-] *n* : recién llegado *m*, recién llegada *f*

newfangled ['nuː'fæŋɡəld, 'njuː-] *adj* : novedoso

newfound ['nuː'faʊnd, 'njuː-] *adj* : recién descubierto

newly ['nuːli, 'njuː-] *adv* : recién, recientemente

newlywed ['nuːliˌwɛd, 'njuː-] *n* : recién casado *m*, -da *f*

new moon *n* : luna *f* nueva

newness ['nuːnəs, 'njuː-] *n* : novedad *f*

news ['nuːz, 'njuːz] *n* : noticias *fpl*

newscast ['nuːzˌkæst, 'njuːz-] *n* : noticiero *m*, informativo *m*

newscaster ['nuːzˌkæstər, 'njuːz-] *n* : presentador *m*, -dora *f*; locutor *m*, -tora *f*

newsletter ['nuːzˌlɛt̬ər, 'njuːz-] *n* : boletín *m* informativo

newsman ['nuːzmən, 'njuːz-, -ˌmæn] *n, pl* **-men** [-mən, -ˌmɛn] : periodista *m*, reportero *m*

newspaper ['nuːzˌpeɪpər, 'njuːz-] *n* : periódico *m*, diario *m*

newspaperman ['nuːzˌpeɪpərˌmæn, 'njuːz-] *n, pl* **-men** [-mən, -ˌmɛn] **1** REPORTER : periodista *m*, reportero *m* **2** : dueño *m* de un periódico

newsprint ['nuːzˌprɪnt, 'njuːz-] *n* : papel *m* de prensa

newsstand ['nuːzˌstænd, 'njuːz-] *n* : quiosco *m*, puesto *m* de periódicos

newswoman ['nuːzˌwʊmən, 'njuːz-] *n, pl* **-women** [-ˌwɪmən] : periodista *f*, reportera *f*

newsworthy ['nuːzˌwərði, 'njuːz-] *adj* : de interés periodístico

newsy ['nuːzi, 'njuː-] *adj* **newsier; -est** : lleno de noticias

newt ['nuːt, 'njuːt] *n* : tritón *m*

New Testament *n* : Nuevo Testamento *m*

New Year *n* : Año *m* Nuevo

New Year's Day *n* : día *m* del Año Nuevo

New Yorker [nuː'jɔrkər, njuː-] *n* : neoyorquino *m*, -na *f*

New Zealander [nuː'ziːləndər, njuː-] *n* : neozelandés *m*, -desa *f*

next[1] ['nɛkst] *adv* **1** AFTERWARD : después, luego ⟨what will you do next? : ¿qué harás después?⟩ **2** NOW : después, ahora, entonces ⟨next I will sing a song : ahora voy a cantar una canción⟩ **3** : la próxima vez ⟨when next we meet : la próxima vez que nos encontremos⟩

next[2] *adj* **1** ADJACENT : contiguo, de al lado **2** COMING : que viene, próximo ⟨next Friday : el viernes que viene⟩ **3** FOLLOWING : siguiente ⟨the next year : el año siguiente⟩

next–door ['nɛkst'dor] *adj* : de al lado

next to[1] *adv* ALMOST : casi, prácticamente ⟨next to impossible : casi imposible⟩

next to² *prep* : junto a, al lado de
nexus ['nɛksəs] *n* : nexo *m*
nib ['nɪb] *n* : plumilla *f*
nibble¹ ['nɪbəl] *v* **-bled; -bling** *vt* : pellizcar, mordisquear, picar — *vi* : picar
nibble² *n* : mordisco *m*
Nicaraguan [ˌnɪkəˈrɑgwən] *n* : nicaragüense *mf* — **Nicaraguan** *adj*
nice ['naɪs] *adj* **nicer; nicest 1** REFINED : pulido, refinado **2** SUBTLE : fino, sutil **3** PLEASING : agradable, bueno, lindo ⟨nice weather : buen tiempo⟩ **4** RESPECTABLE : bueno, decente **5 nice and** : bien, muy ⟨nice and hot : bien caliente⟩ ⟨nice and slow : despacito⟩
nicely ['naɪsli] *adv* **1** KINDLY : amablemente **2** POLITELY : con buenos modales **3** ATTRACTIVELY : de buen gusto
niceness ['naɪsnəs] *n* : simpatía *f*, amabilidad *f*
nicety ['naɪsəti] *n, pl* **-ties 1** DETAIL, SUBTLETY : sutileza *f*, detalle *m* **2 niceties** *npl* : lujos *mpl*, detalles *mpl*
niche ['nɪtʃ] *n* **1** RECESS : nicho *m*, hornacina *f* **2** : nicho *m*, hueco *m* ⟨to make a niche for oneself : hacerse un hueco, encontrarse una buena posición⟩
nick¹ ['nɪk] *vt* : cortar, hacer una muesca en
nick² *n* **1** CUT : corte *m*, muesca *f* **2 in the nick of time** : en el momento crítico, justo a tiempo
nickel ['nɪkəl] *n* **1** : níquel *m* **2** : moneda *f* de cinco centavos
nickname¹ ['nɪkˌneɪm] *vt* **-named; -naming** : apodar
nickname² *n* : apodo *m*, mote *m*, sobrenombre *m*
nicotine ['nɪkəˌtiːn] *n* : nicotina *f*
niece ['niːs] *n* : sobrina *f*
Nigerian [naɪˈdʒɪriən] *n* : nigeriano *m*, -na *f* — **Nigerian** *adj*
niggardly ['nɪgərdli] *adj* : mezquino, tacaño
niggling ['nɪgəlɪŋ] *adj* **1** PETTY : insignificante **2** PERSISTENT : constante, persistente ⟨a niggling doubt : una duda constante⟩
nigh¹ ['naɪ] *adv* **1** NEARLY : casi **2 to draw nigh** : acercarse, avecinarse
nigh² *adj* : cercano, próximo
night¹ ['naɪt] *adj* : nocturno, de la noche ⟨the night sky : el cielo nocturno⟩ ⟨night shift : turno de la noche⟩
night² *n* **1** EVENING : noche *f* ⟨at night : de noche⟩ ⟨last night : anoche⟩ ⟨tomorrow night : mañana por la noche⟩ **2** DARKNESS : noche *f*, oscuridad *f* ⟨night fell : cayó la noche⟩
nightclothes ['naɪtˌkloːðz, -ˌkloːz] *npl* : ropa *f* de dormir
nightclub ['naɪtˌklʌb] *n* : cabaret *m*, club *m* nocturno
night crawler ['naɪtˌkrɔlər] *n* EARTHWORM : lombriz *f* (de tierra)
nightfall ['naɪtˌfɔl] *n* : anochecer *m*
nightgown ['naɪtˌgaʊn] *n* : camisón *m* (de noche)

nightingale ['naɪtən̩ˌgeɪl, 'naɪtɪŋ-] *n* : ruiseñor *m*
nightly¹ ['naɪtli] *adv* : cada noche, todas las noches
nightly² *adj* : de todas las noches
nightmare ['naɪtˌmær] *n* : pesadilla *f*
nightmarish ['naɪtˌmærɪʃ] *adj* : de pesadilla
night owl *n* : noctámbulo *m*, -la *f*
nightshade ['naɪtˌʃeɪd] *n* : hierba *f* mora
nightshirt ['naɪtˌʃərt] *n* : camisa *f* de dormir
nightstick ['naɪtˌstɪk] *n* : porra *f*
nighttime ['naɪtˌtaɪm] *n* : noche *f*
nihilism ['naɪəˌlɪzəm] *n* : nihilismo *m*
nil ['nɪl] *n* : nada *f*, cero *m*
nimble ['nɪmbəl] *adj* **-bler; -blest 1** AGILE : ágil **2** CLEVER : hábil, ingenioso
nimbleness ['nɪmbəlnəs] *n* : agilidad *f*
nimbly ['nɪmbli] *adv* : con agilidad, ágilmente
nincompoop ['nɪnkəmˌpuːp, 'nɪŋ-] *n* FOOL : tonto *m*, -ta *f*; bobo *m*, -ba *f*
nine¹ ['naɪn] *adj* **1** : nueve **2 nine times out of ten** : casi siempre
nine² *n* : nueve *m*
nine hundred¹ *adj* : novecientos
nine hundred² *n* : novecientos *m*
ninepins ['naɪnˌpɪnz] *n* : bolos *mpl*
nineteen¹ [naɪnˈtiːn] *adj* : diecinueve
nineteen² *n* : diecinueve *m*
nineteenth¹ [naɪnˈtiːnθ] *adj* : decimonoveno, decimonono ⟨the nineteenth century : el siglo diecinueve⟩
nineteenth² *n* **1** : decimonoveno *m*, -na *f*; decimonono *m*, -na *f* (en una serie) **2** : diecinueveavo *m*, diecinueveava parte *f*
ninetieth¹ ['naɪntiəθ] *adj* : nonagésimo
ninetieth² *n* **1** : nonagésimo *m*, -ma *f* (en una serie) **2** : noventavo *m*, noventava parte *f*
ninety¹ ['naɪnti] *adj* : noventa
ninety² *n, pl* **-ties** : noventa *m*
ninth¹ ['naɪnθ] *adj* : noveno
ninth² *n* **1** : noveno *m*, -na *f* (en una serie) **2** : noveno *m*, novena parte *f*
ninny ['nɪni] *n, pl* **ninnies** FOOL : tonto *m*, -ta *f*; bobo *m*, -ba *f*
nip¹ ['nɪp] *vt* **nipped; nipping 1** PINCH : pellizcar **2** BITE : morder, mordisquear **3 to nip in the bud** : cortar de raíz
nip² *n* **1** TANG : sabor *m* fuerte **2** PINCH : pellizco *m* **3** NIBBLE : mordisco *m* **4** SWALLOW : trago *m*, traguito *m* **5 there's a nip in the air** : hace fresco
nipple ['nɪpəl] *n* : pezón *m* (de una mujer), tetilla *f* (de un hombre)
nippy ['nɪpi] *adj* **-pier; -est 1** SHARP : fuerte, picante **2** CHILLY : frío ⟨it's nippy today : hoy hace frío⟩
nit ['nɪt] *n* : liendre *f*
nitrate ['naɪˌtreɪt] *n* : nitrato *m*
nitric acid ['naɪtrɪk] *n* : ácido *m* nítrico
nitrite ['naɪˌtraɪt] *n* : nitrito *m*
nitrogen ['naɪtrədʒən] *n* : nitrógeno *m*
nitroglycerin *or* **nitroglycerine** [ˌnaɪtroˈglɪsərən] *n* : nitroglicerina *f*

nitwit ['nɪt,wɪt] *n* : zonzo *m*, -za *f*; bobo *m*, -ba *f*
no¹ ['no:] *adv* : no ⟨are you leaving?— no : ¿te vas?—no⟩ ⟨no less than : no menos de⟩ ⟨to say no : decir que no⟩ ⟨like it or no : quieras o no quieras⟩
no² *adj* **1** : ninguno ⟨it's no trouble : no es ningún problema⟩ ⟨she has no money : no tiene dinero⟩ **2** (*indicating a small amount*) ⟨we'll be there in no time : llegamos dentro de poco, no tardamos nada⟩ **3** (*expressing a negation*) ⟨he's no liar : no es mentiroso⟩
no³ *n*, *pl* **noes** *or* **nos** ['no:z] **1** DENIAL : no *m* ⟨I won't take no for an answer : no aceptaré un no por respuesta⟩ **2** : vota *f* en contra ⟨the noes have it : se ha rechazado la moción⟩
nobility [no'bɪləti] *n* : nobleza *f*
noble¹ ['no:bəl] *adj* **-bler; -blest 1** IL-LUSTRIOUS : noble, glorioso **2** ARIS-TOCRATIC : noble **3** STATELY : majestuoso, magnífico **4** LOFTY : noble, elevado ⟨noble sentiments : sentimientos elevados⟩
noble² *n* : noble *mf*, aristócrata *mf*
nobleman ['no:bəlmən] *n*, *pl* **-men** [-mən, -,mɛn] : noble *m*, aristócrata *m*
nobleness ['no:bəlnəs] *n* : nobleza *f*
noblewoman ['no:bəl,wumən] *n*, *pl* **-women** [-,wɪmən] : noble *f*, aristócrata *f*
nobly ['no:bli] *adv* : noblemente
nobody¹ ['no:bədi, -,badi] *n*, *pl* **-bodies** : don nadie *m* ⟨he's a mere nobody : es un don nadie⟩
nobody² *pron* : nadie
nocturnal [nak'tərnəl] *adj* : nocturno
nocturne ['nak,tərn] *n* : nocturno *m*
nod¹ ['nad] *v* **nodded; nodding** *vi* **1** : saludar con la cabeza, asentir con la cabeza **2 to nod off** : dormirse, quedarse dormido — *vt* : inclinar (la cabeza) ⟨to nod one's head in agreement : asentir con la cabeza⟩
nod² *n* : saludo *m* con la cabeza, señal *m* con la cabeza, señal *m* de asentimiento
node ['no:d] *n* : nudo *m* (de una planta)
nodule ['na,ʤu:l] *n* : nódulo *m*
noel [no'ɛl] *n* **1** CAROL : villancico *m* de Navidad **2 Noel** CHRISTMAS : Navidad *f*
noes → **no³**
noise¹ ['nɔɪz] *vt* **noised; noising** : rumorear, publicar
noise² *n* : ruido *m*
noiseless ['nɔɪzləs] *adj* : silencioso, sin ruido
noiselessly ['nɔɪzləsli] *adv* : silenciosamente
noisemaker ['nɔɪz,meɪkər] *n* : matraca *f*
noisiness ['nɔɪzinəs] *n* : ruido *m*
noisome ['nɔɪsəm] *adj* : maloliente, fétido
noisy ['nɔɪzi] *adj* **noisier; -est** : ruidoso — **noisily** ['nɔɪzəli] *adv*
nomad¹ ['no:,mæd] → **nomadic**

nomad² *n* : nómada *mf*
nomadic [no'mædɪk] *adj* : nómada
nomenclature ['no:mən,kleɪʧər] *n* : nomenclatura *f*
nominal ['namənəl] *adj* **1** : nominal ⟨the nominal head of his party : el jefe nominal de su partido⟩ **2** TRIFLING : insignificante
nominally ['namənəli] *adv* : sólo de nombre, nominalmente
nominate ['namə,neɪt] *vt* **-nated; -nating 1** PROPOSE : proponer (como candidato), nominar **2** APPOINT : nombrar
nomination [,namə'neɪʃən] *n* **1** PRO-POSAL : propuesta *f*, postulación *f* **2** APPOINTMENT : nombramiento *m*
nominative¹ ['namənətɪv] *adj* : nominativo
nominative² *n* *or* **nominative case** : nominativo *m*
nominee [,namə'ni:] *n* : candidato *m*, -ta *f*
nonaddictive [,nanə'dɪktɪv] *adj* : que no crea dependencia
nonalcoholic [,nan,ælkə'hɔlɪk] *adj* : sin alcohol, no alcohólico
nonaligned [,nanə'laɪnd] *adj* : no alineado
nonbeliever [,nanbə'li:vər] *n* : no creyente *mf*
nonbreakable [,nan'breɪkəbəl] *adj* : irrompible
nonce ['nants] *n* **for the nonce** : por el momento
nonchalance [,nanʃə'lants] *n* : indiferencia *f*, despreocupación *f*
nonchalant [,nanʃə'lant] *adj* : indiferente, despreocupado, impasible
nonchalantly [,nanʃə'lantli] *adv* : con aire despreocupado, con indiferencia
noncombatant [,nankəm'bætənt, -'kambə-] *n* : no combatiente *mf*
noncommissioned officer [,nankə-'mɪʃənd] *n* : suboficial *mf*
noncommittal [,nankə'mɪtəl] *adj* : evasivo, que no se compromete
nonconductor [,nankən'dʌktər] *n* : aislante *m*
nonconformist [,nankən'fɔrmɪst] *n* : inconformista *mf*, inconforme *mf*
nonconformity [,nankən'fɔrməti] *n* : inconformidad *f*, no conformidad *f*
noncontagious [,nankən'teɪʤəs] *adj* : no contagioso
nondenominational [,nandɪ,namə-'neɪʃənəl] *adj* : no sectario
nondescript [,nandɪ'skrɪpt] *adj* : anodino, soso
nondiscriminatory [,nandɪ'skrɪmənə-,tori] *adj* : no discriminatorio
nondrinker [,nan'drɪŋkər] *n* : abstemio *m*, -mia *f*
none¹ ['nʌn] *adv* : de ninguna manera, de ningún modo, nada ⟨he was none too happy : no se sintió nada contento⟩ ⟨I'm none the worse for it : no estoy peor por ello⟩ ⟨none too soon : a buena hora⟩

none² *pron* : ninguno, ninguna
nonentity [ˌnɑn'entəti] *n, pl* **-ties** : persona *f* insignificante, nulidad *f*
nonessential [ˌnɑnɪ'sentʃəl] *adj* : secundario, no esencial
nonessentials [ˌnɑnɪ'sentʃəlz] *npl* : cosas *fpl* secundarias, cosas *fpl* accesorias
nonetheless [ˌnʌnðə'les] *adv* : sin embargo, no obstante
nonexistence [ˌnɑnɪg'zɪstənts] *n* : inexistencia *f*
nonexistent [ˌnɑnɪg'zɪstənt] *adj* : inexistente
nonfat [ˌnɑn'fæt] *adj* : sin grasa
nonfattening [ˌnɑn'fætənɪŋ] *adj* : que no engorda
nonfiction [ˌnɑn'fɪkʃən] *n* : no ficción *f*
nonflammable [ˌnɑn'flæməbəl] *adj* : no inflamable
nonintervention [ˌnɑnˌɪntər'ventʃən] *n* : no intervención *f*
nonmalignant [ˌnɑnmə'lɪgnənt] *adj* : no maligno, benigno
nonnegotiable [ˌnɑnnɪ'goːʃəbəl, -ʃiə-] *adj* : no negociable
nonpareil¹ [ˌnɑnpə'rel] *adj* : sin parangón, sin par
nonpareil² *n* : persona *f* sin igual, cosa *f* sin par
nonpartisan [ˌnɑn'pɑrtəzən, -sən] *adj* : imparcial
nonpaying [ˌnɑn'peɪɪŋ] *adj* : que no paga
nonpayment [ˌnɑn'peɪmənt] *n* : impago *m*, falta *f* de pago
nonperson [ˌnɑn'pərsən] *n* : persona *f* sin derechos
nonplus [ˌnɑn'plʌs] *vt* **-plussed; -plussing** : confundir, desconcertar, dejar perplejo
nonprescription [ˌnɑnprɪ'skrɪpʃən] *adj* : disponible sin receta del médico
nonproductive [ˌnɑnprə'dʌktɪv] *adj* : improductivo
nonprofit [ˌnɑn'prɑfət] *adj* : sin fines lucrativos
nonproliferation [ˌnɑnprəˌlɪfə'reɪʃən] *adj* : no proliferación
nonresident [ˌnɑn'rezədənt, -ˌdent] *n* : no residente *mf*
nonscheduled [ˌnɑn'skeˌdʒuːld] *adj* : no programado, no regular
nonsectarian [ˌnɑnˌsek'tæriən] *adj* : no sectario
nonsense ['nɑnˌsents, 'nɑntsənts] *n* : tonterías *fpl*, disparates *mpl*
nonsensical [nɑn'sentsɪkəl] *adj* ABSURD : absurdo, disparatado — **nonsensically** [-kli] *adv*
nonsmoker [ˌnɑn'smoːkər] *n* : no fumador *m*, -dora *f*; persona *f* que no fuma
nonstandard [ˌnɑn'stændərd] *adj* : no regular, no estándar
nonstick [ˌnɑn'stɪk] *adj* : antiadherente
nonstop¹ [ˌnɑn'stɑp] *adv* : sin parar ⟨he talked nonstop : habló sin parar⟩
nonstop² *adj* : directo, sin escalas ⟨nonstop flight : vuelo directo⟩

nonsupport [ˌnɑnsə'pɔrt] *n* : falta *f* de manutención
nontaxable [ˌnɑn'tæksəbəl] *adj* : exento de impuestos
nontoxic [ˌnɑn'tɑksɪk] *adj* : no tóxico
nonviolence [ˌnɑn'vaɪlənts, -'vaɪə-] *n* : no violencia *f*
nonviolent [ˌnɑn'vaɪlənt, -'vaɪə-] *adj* : pacífico, no violento
noodle ['nuːdəl] *n* : fideo *m*, tallarín *m*
nook ['nʊk] *n* : rincón *m*, recoveco *m*, escondrijo *m* ⟨in every nook and cranny : en todos los rincones⟩
noon ['nuːn] *n* : mediodía *m*
noonday ['nuːnˌdeɪ] *n* : mediodía *m* ⟨the noonday sun : el sol de mediodía⟩
no one *pron* NOBODY : nadie
noontime ['nuːnˌtaɪm] *n* : mediodía *m*
noose ['nuːs] *n* **1** LASSO : lazo *m* **2 hangman's noose** : dogal *m*, soga *f*
nor ['nɔr] *conj* : ni ⟨neither good nor bad : ni bueno ni malo⟩ ⟨nor I! : ¡ni yo tampoco!⟩
Nordic ['nɔrdɪk] *adj* : nórdico
norm ['nɔrm] *n* **1** STANDARD : norma *f*, modelo *m* **2** CUSTOM, RULE : regla *f* general, lo normal
normal ['nɔrməl] *adj* : normal — **normally** *adv*
normalcy ['nɔrməlsi] *n* : normalidad *f*
normality [nɔr'mæləti] *n* : normalidad *f*
normalize ['nɔrməˌlaɪz] *vt* : normalizar
Norse ['nɔrs] *adj* : nórdico
north¹ ['nɔrθ] *adv* : al norte
north² *adj* : norte, del norte ⟨the north coast : la costa del norte⟩
north³ *n* **1** : norte *m* **2 the North** : el Norte *m*
North American *n* : norteamericano *m*, -na *f* — **North American** *adj*
northbound ['nɔrθˌbaʊnd] *adv* : con rumbo al norte
northeast¹ [nɔrθ'iːst] *adv* : hacia el nordeste
northeast² *adj* : nordeste, del nordeste
northeast³ *n* : nordeste *m*, noreste *m*
northeasterly¹ [nɔrθ'iːstərli] *adv* : hacia el nordeste
northeasterly² *adj* : nordeste, del nordeste
northeastern [nɔrθ'iːstərn] *adj* : nordeste, del nordeste
northerly¹ ['nɔrðərli] *adv* : hacia el norte
northerly² *adj* : del norte ⟨a northerly wind : un viento del norte⟩
northern ['nɔrðərn] *adj* : norte, norteño, septentrional
Northerner ['nɔrðərnər] *n* : norteño *m*, -ña *f*
northern lights → **aurora borealis**
North Pole : Polo *m* Norte
North Star *n* : estrella *f* polar
northward ['nɔrθwərd] *adv & adj* : hacia el norte
northwest¹ [nɔrθ'west] *adv* : hacia el noroeste
northwest² *adj* : del noroeste
northwest³ *n* : noroeste *m*

northwesterly[1] [nɔrθ'wɛstərli] *adv* : hacia el noroeste

northwesterly[2] *adj* : del noroeste

northwestern [nɔrθ'wɛstərn] *adj* : noroeste, del noroeste

Norwegian [nɔr'wiːdʒən] *n* **1** : noruego *m*, -ga *f* **2** : noruego *m* (idioma) — **Norwegian** *adj*

nose[1] ['noːz] *v* **nosed; nosing** *vt* **1** SMELL : olfatear **2** : empujar con el hocico ⟨the dog nosed open the bag : el perro abrió el saco con el hocico⟩ **3** EDGE, MOVE : mover poco a poco — *vi* **1** PRY : entrometerse, meter las narices **2** EDGE : avanzar poco a poco

nose[2] *n* **1** : nariz *f* (de una persona), hocico *m* (de un animal) ⟨to blow one's nose : sonarse las narices⟩ **2** SMELL : olfato *m*, sentido *m* del olfato **3** FRONT : parte *f* delantera, nariz *f* (de un avión), proa *f* (de un barco) **4 to follow one's nose** : dejarse guiar por el instinto

nosebleed ['noːz,bliːd] *n* : hemorragia *f* nasal

nosedive ['noːz,daɪv] *n* **1** : descenso *m* en picada (de un avión) **2** : caída *f* súbita (de precios, etc.)

nose–dive ['noːz,daɪv] *vi* : descender en picada, caer en picada

nostalgia [nɑ'stældʒə, nə-] *n* : nostalgia *f*

nostalgic [nɑ'stældʒɪk, nə-] *adj* : nostálgico

nostril ['nɑstrəl] *n* : ventana *f* de la nariz

nostrum ['nɑstrəm] *n* : panacea *f*

nosy *or* **nosey** ['noːzi] *adj* **nosier; -est** : entrometido

not ['nɑt] *adv* **1** (*used to form a negative*) : no ⟨she is not tired : no está cansada⟩ ⟨not to say something would be wrong : no decir nada sería injusto⟩ **2** (*used to replace a negative clause*) : no ⟨are we going or not? : ¿vamos a ir o no?⟩ ⟨of course not! : ¡claro que no!⟩

notable[1] ['noːtəbəl] *adj* **1** NOTEWORTHY : notable, de notar **2** DISTINGUISHED, PROMINENT : distinguido, destacado

notable[2] *n* : persona *f* importante, personaje *m*

notably ['noːtəbli] *adv* : notablemente, particularmente

notarize ['noːtə,raɪz] *vt* **-rized; -rizing** : autenticar, autorizar

notary public ['noːtəri] *n, pl* **-ries public** *or* **-ry publics** : notario *m*, -ria *f*; escribano *m*, -na *f*

notation [noː'teɪʃən] *n* **1** NOTE : anotación *f*, nota *f* **2** : notación *f* ⟨musical notation : notación musical⟩

notch[1] ['nɑtʃ] *vt* : hacer una muesca en, cortar

notch[2] *n* : muesca *f*, corte *m*

note[1] ['noːt] *vt* **noted; noting 1** NOTICE : notar, observar, tomar nota de **2** RECORD : anotar, apuntar

note[2] *n* **1** : nota *f* (musical) **2** COMMENT : nota *f*, comentario *m* **3** LETTER : nota *f*, cartita *f* **4** PROMINENCE : prestigio *m* ⟨a musician of note : un músico destacado⟩ **5** ATTENTION : atención *f* ⟨to take note of : prestar atención a⟩

notebook ['noːt,bʊk] *n* **1** : libreta *f*, cuaderno *m* **2** : notebook *m* (computadora)

noted ['noːtəd] *adj* EMINENT : renombrado, eminente, celebrado

noteworthy ['noːt,wərði] *adj* : notable, de notar, de interés

nothing[1] ['nʌθɪŋ] *adv* **1** : de ninguna manera ⟨nothing daunted, we carried on : sin amilanarnos, seguimos adelante⟩ **2 nothing like** : no . . . en nada ⟨he's nothing like his brother : no se parece en nada a su hermano⟩

nothing[2] *n* **1** NOTHINGNESS : nada *f* **2** ZERO : cero *m* **3** : persona *f* de poca importancia, cero *m* **4** TRIFLE : nimiedad *f*

nothing[3] *pron* : nada ⟨there's nothing better : no hay nada mejor⟩ ⟨nothing else : nada más⟩ ⟨nothing but : solamente⟩ ⟨they mean nothing to me : ellos me son indiferentes⟩

nothingness ['nʌθɪŋnəs] *n* **1** VOID : vacío *m*, nada *f* **2** NONEXISTENCE : inexistencia *f* **3** TRIFLE : nimiedad *f*

notice[1] ['noːtɪs] *vt* **-ticed; -ticing** : notar, observar, advertir, darse cuenta de

notice[2] *n* **1** NOTIFICATION : aviso *m*, notificación *f* **2** ATTENTION : atención *f* ⟨to take notice of : prestar atención a⟩

noticeable ['noːtɪsəbəl] *adj* : evidente, perceptible — **noticeably** [-bli] *adv*

notification [,noːtəfə'keɪʃən] *n* : notificación *f*, aviso *m*

notify ['noːtə,faɪ] *vt* **-fied; -fying** : notificar, avisar

notion ['noːʃən] *n* **1** IDEA : idea *f*, noción *f* **2** WHIM : capricho *m*, antojo *m* **3 notions** *npl* : artículos *mpl* de mercería

notoriety [,noːtə'raɪəti] *n* : mala fama *f*, notoriedad *f*

notorious [noː'toːriəs] *adj* : de mala fama, célebre, bien conocido

notwithstanding[1] [,nɑtwɪθ'stændɪŋ, -wɪð-] *adv* NEVERTHELESS : no obstante, sin embargo

notwithstanding[2] *conj* : a pesar de que

notwithstanding[3] *prep* : a pesar de, no obstante

nougat ['nuːgət] *n* : turrón *m*

nought ['nɔt, 'nɑt] → **naught**

noun ['naʊn] *n* : nombre *m*, sustantivo *m*

nourish ['nərɪʃ] *vt* **1** FEED : alimentar, nutrir, sustentar **2** FOSTER : fomentar, alentar

nourishing ['nərɪʃɪŋ] *adj* : alimenticio, nutritivo

nourishment ['nərɪʃmənt] *n* : nutrición *f*, alimento *m*, sustento *m*

novel[1] ['nɑvəl] *adj* : original, novedoso

novel² *n* : novela *f*
novelist ['nɑvəlɪst] *n* : novelista *mf*
novelty ['nɑvəlt̬i] *n, pl* **-ties 1** : novedad
  f **2 novelties** *npl* TRINKETS : baratijas
  fpl, chucherías *fpl*
November [noˈvɛmbər] *n* : noviembre *m*
novice ['nɑvɪs] *n* : novato *m*, -ta *f*; principiante *mf*; novicio *m*, -cia *f*
now¹ ['naʊ] *adv* **1** PRESENTLY : ahora,
  ya, actualmente ⟨from now on : de ahora en adelante⟩ ⟨long before now : ya
  hace tiempo⟩ ⟨now and then : de vez
  en cuando⟩ **2** IMMEDIATELY : ahora
  (mismo), inmediatamente ⟨do it right
  now! : ¡hazlo ahora mismo!⟩ **3** THEN
  : ya, entonces ⟨now they were ready
  : ya estaban listos⟩ **4** (*used to introduce
  a statement, a question, a command, or
  a transition*) ⟨now hear this! : ¡presten
  atención!⟩ ⟨now what do you think of
  that? : ¿qué piensas de eso?⟩
now² *n* (*indicating the present time*) ⟨un-
  til now : hasta ahora⟩ ⟨by now : ya⟩
  ⟨ten years from now : dentro de 10
  años⟩
now³ *conj* **now that** : ahora que, ya que
nowadays ['naʊəˌdeɪz] *adv* : hoy en día,
  actualmente, en la actualidad
nowhere¹ ['noːˌʍɛr] *adv* **1** : en ninguna parte, a ningún lado ⟨nowhere to be
  found : en ninguna parte, por ningún
  lado⟩ ⟨you're going nowhere : no estás
  yendo a ningún lado, no estás yendo a
  ninguna parte⟩ **2 nowhere near** : ni
  con mucho, nada cerca ⟨it's nowhere
  near here : no está nada cerca de aquí⟩
nowhere² *n* **1** : ninguna parte *f* **2 out
  of nowhere** : de la nada
noxious ['nɑkʃəs] *adj* : nocivo, dañino,
  tóxico
nozzle ['nɑzəl] *n* : boca *f*
nuance ['nuːˌɑnts, 'njuː-] *n* : matiz *m*
nub ['nʌb] *n* **1** KNOB, LUMP : protuberancia *f*, nudo *m* **2** GIST : quid *m*, meollo *m*
nuclear ['nuːkliər, 'njuː-] *adj* : nuclear
nucleus ['nuːkliəs, 'njuː-] *n, pl* **-clei**
  [-kliˌaɪ] : núcleo *m*
nude¹ ['nuːd, 'njuːd] *adj* **nuder; nudest**
  : desnudo
nude² *n* : desnudo *m*
nudge¹ ['nʌdʒ] *vt* **nudged; nudging**
  : darle con el codo (a alguien)
nudge² *n* : toque *m* que se da con el codo
nudism ['nuːˌdɪzəm, 'njuː-] *n* : nudismo
  m
nudist ['nuːdɪst, 'njuː-] *n* : nudista *mf*
nudity ['nuːdət̬i, 'njuː-] *n* : desnudez *f*
nugget ['nʌgət] *n* : pepita *f*
nuisance ['nuːsənts, 'njuː-] *n* **1** BOTHER
  : fastidio *m*, molestia *f*, lata *f* **2** PEST
  : pesado *m*, -da *f fam*
null ['nʌl] *adj* : nulo ⟨null and void : nulo
  y sin efecto⟩
nullify ['nʌləˌfaɪ] *vt* **-fied; -fying** : invalidar, anular
nullity ['nələt̬i] *n, pl* **-ties** : nulidad *f*
numb¹ ['nʌm] *vt* : entumecer, adormecer

numb² *adj* : entumecido, dormido
  ⟨numb with fear : paralizado de miedo⟩
number¹ ['nʌmbər] *vt* **1** COUNT, IN-
  CLUDE : contar, incluir **2** : numerar
  ⟨number the pages : numera las pági-
  nas⟩ **3** TOTAL : ascender a, sumar
number² *n* **1** : número *m* ⟨in round
  numbers : en números redondos⟩
  ⟨telephone number : número de telé-
  fono⟩ **2 a number of** : varios, unos
  pocos, unos cuantos
numberless ['nʌmbərləs] *adj* : innumerable, sin número
numbness ['nʌmnəs] *n* : entumecimiento *m*
numeral ['nuːmərəl, 'njuː-] *n* : número
  m ⟨Roman numeral : número romano⟩
numerator ['nuːməˌreɪt̬ər, 'njuː-] *n* : numerador *m*
numeric [nʊˈmɛrɪk, njʊ-] *adj* : numérico
numerical [nʊˈmɛrɪkəl, njʊ-] *adj* : numérico — **numerically** [-kli] *adv*
numerous ['nuːmərəs, 'njuː-] *adj* : numeroso
numismatics [ˌnuːməzˈmæt̬ɪks, ˌnjuː-] *n*
  : numismática *f*
numskull ['nʌmˌskʌl] *n* : tonto *m*, -ta *f*;
  mentecato *m*, -ta *f*; zoquete *m fam*
nun ['nʌn] *n* : monja *f*
nuptial ['nʌpʃəl] *adj* : nupcial
nuptials ['nʌpʃəlz] *npl* WEDDING : nupcias *fpl*, boda *f*
nurse¹ ['nərs] *vt* **nursed; nursing 1**
  SUCKLE : amamantar **2** : cuidar (de),
  atender ⟨to nurse the sick : cuidar a los
  enfermos⟩ ⟨to nurse a cold : curarse
  de un resfriado⟩
nurse² *n* **1** : enfermero *m*, -ra *f* **2** →
  nursemaid
nursemaid ['nərsˌmeɪd] *n* : niñera *f*
nursery ['nərsəri] *n, pl* **-eries 1** *or* **day
  nursery** : guardería *f* **2** : vivero *m* (de
  plantas)
nursing home *n* : hogar *m* de ancianos,
  clínica *f* de reposo
nurture¹ ['nərtʃər] *vt* **-tured; -turing 1**
  FEED, NOURISH : nutrir, alimentar **2**
  EDUCATE : criar, educar **3** FOSTER : alimentar, fomentar
nurture² *n* **1** UPBRINGING : crianza *f*,
  educación *f* **2** FOOD : alimento *m*
nut ['nʌt] *n* **1** : nuez *f* **2** : tuerca *f* ⟨nuts
  and bolts : tuercas y tornillos⟩ **3** LU-
  NATIC : loco *m*, -ca *f*; chiflado *m*, -da *f
  fam* **4** ENTHUSIAST : fanático *m*, -ca *f*;
  entusiasta *mf*
nutcracker ['nʌtˌkrækər] *n* : cascanueces *m*
nuthatch ['nʌtˌhætʃ] *n* : trepador *m*
nutmeg ['nʌtˌmɛg] *n* : nuez *f* moscada
nutrient ['nuːtriənt, 'njuː-] *n* : nutriente
  m, alimento *m* nutritivo
nutriment ['nuːtrəmənt, 'njuː-] *n* : nutrimento *m*
nutrition [nʊˈtrɪʃən, njʊ-] *n* : nutrición *f*
nutritional [nʊˈtrɪʃənəl, njʊ-] *adj* : alimenticio
nutritious [nʊˈtrɪʃəs, njʊ-] *adj* : nutritivo, alimenticio

nuts ['nʌts] *adj* **1** FANATICAL : fanático **2** CRAZY : loco, chiflado *fam*
nutshell ['nʌtˌʃɛl] *n* **1** : cáscara *f* de nuez **2 in a nutshell** : en pocas palabras
nutty ['nʌt̬i] *adj* **-tier; -tiest** : loco, chiflado *fam*

nuzzle ['nʌzəl] *v* **-zled; -zling** *vi* NESTLE : acurrucarse, arrimarse — *vt* : acariciar con el hocico
nylon ['naɪˌlɑn] *n* **1** : nilón *m* **2 nylons** *npl* : medias *fpl* de nilón
nymph ['nɪmpf] *n* : ninfa *f*

O

o ['oː] *n, pl* **o's** *or* **os** ['oːz] **1** : decimoquinta letra del alfabeto inglés **2** ZERO : cero *m*
O ['oː] → **oh**
oaf ['oːf] *n* : zoquete *m*; bruto *m*, -ta *f*
oafish ['oːfɪʃ] *adj* : torpe, lerdo
oak ['oːk] *n, pl* **oaks** *or* **oak** : roble *m*
oaken ['oːkən] *adj* : de roble
oar ['or] *n* : remo *m*
oarlock ['orˌlɑk] *n* : tolete *m*, escálamo *m*
oasis [oˈeɪsɪs] *n, pl* **oases** [-ˌsiːz] : oasis *m*
oat ['oːt] *n* : avena *f*
oath ['oːθ] *n, pl* **oaths** ['oːðz, 'oːθs] **1** : juramento *m* ⟨to take an oath : prestar juramento⟩ **2** SWEARWORD : mala palabra *f*, palabrota *f*
oatmeal ['oːtˌmiːl] *n* : avena *f* ⟨instant oatmeal : avena instantánea⟩
obdurate ['ɑbdʊrət, -djʊ-] *adj* : inflexible, firme, obstinado
obedience [oˈbiːdiənts] *n* : obediencia *f*
obedient [oˈbiːdiənt] *adj* : obediente —
obediently *adv*
obelisk ['ɑbəˌlɪsk] *n* : obelisco *m*
obese [oˈbiːs] *adj* : obeso
obesity [oˈbiːsət̬i] *n* : obesidad *f*
obey [oˈbeɪ] *v* **obeyed; obeying** : obedecer ⟨to obey the law : cumplir la ley⟩
obfuscate ['ɑbfəˌskeɪt] *vt* **-cated; -cating** : ofuscar, confundir
obituary [oˈbɪtʃuˌɛri] *n, pl* **-aries** : obituario *m*, necrología *f*
object[1] ['ɑbdʒɛkt] *vt* : objetar — *vi* : oponerse, poner reparos, hacer objeciones
object[2] ['ɑbdʒɪkt] *n* **1** : objeto *m* **2** OBJECTIVE, PURPOSE : objetivo *m*, propósito *m* **3** : complemento *m* (en gramática)
objection [əbˈdʒɛkʃən] *n* : objeción *f*
objectionable [əbˈdʒɛkʃənəbəl] *adj* : ofensivo, indeseable — **objectionably** [-bli] *adv*
objective[1] [əbˈdʒɛktɪv] *adj* **1** IMPARTIAL : objetivo, imparcial **2** : de complemento, directo (en gramática)
objective[2] *n* **1** : objetivo *m* **2** *or* **objective case** : acusativo *m*
objectively [əbˈdʒɛktɪvli] *adv* : objetivamente
objectivity [ˌɑbˌdʒɛkˈtɪvət̬i] *n, pl* **-ties** : objetividad *f*
obligate ['ɑbləˌgeɪt] *vt* **-gated; -gating** : obligar
obligation [ˌɑbləˈgeɪʃən] *n* : obligación *f*

obligatory [əˈblɪgəˌtori] *adj* : obligatorio
oblige [əˈblaɪdʒ] *vt* **obliged; obliging** **1** COMPEL : obligar **2** : hacerle un favor (a alguien), complacer ⟨to oblige a friend : hacerle un favor a un amigo⟩ **3 to be much obliged** : estar muy agradecido
obliging [əˈblaɪdʒɪŋ] *adj* : servicial, complaciente — **obligingly** *adv*
oblique [oˈbliːk] *adj* **1** SLANTING : oblicuo **2** INDIRECT : indirecto — **obliquely** *adv*
obliterate [əˈblɪt̬əˌreɪt] *vt* **-ated; -ating** **1** ERASE : obliterar, borrar **2** DESTROY : destruir, eliminar
obliteration [əˌblɪt̬əˈreɪʃən] *n* : obliteración *f*
oblivion [əˈblɪviən] *n* : olvido *m*
oblivious [əˈblɪviəs] *adj* : inconsciente — **obliviously** *adv*
oblong[1] ['ɑˌblɔŋ] *adj* : oblongo
oblong[2] *n* : figura *f* oblonga, rectángulo *m*
obnoxious [ɑbˈnɑkʃəs, əb-] *adj* : repugnante, odioso — **obnoxiously** *adv*
oboe ['oːˌboː] *n* : oboe *m*
oboist ['oˌboɪst] *n* : oboe *mf*
obscene [ɑbˈsiːn, əb-] *adj* : obsceno, indecente — **obscenely** *adv*
obscenity [ɑbˈsɛnət̬i, əb-] *n, pl* **-ties** : obscenidad *f*
obscure[1] [ɑbˈskjʊr, əb-] *vt* **-scured; -scuring** **1** CLOUD, DIM : oscurecer, nublar **2** HIDE : ocultar
obscure[2] *adj* **1** DIM : oscuro **2** REMOTE, SECLUDED : recóndito **3** VAGUE : oscuro, confuso, vago **4** UNKNOWN : desconocido ⟨an obscure poet : un poeta desconocido⟩ — **obscurely** *adv*
obscurity [ɑbˈskjʊrət̬i, əb-] *n, pl* **-ties** : oscuridad *f*
obsequious [əbˈsiːkwiəs] *adj* : servil, excesivamente atento
observable [əbˈzərvəbəl] *adj* : observable, perceptible
observance [əbˈzərvənts] *n* **1** FULFILLMENT : observancia *f*, cumplimiento *m* **2** PRACTICE : práctica *f*
observant [əbˈzərvənt] *adj* : observador
observation [ˌɑbsərˈveɪʃən, -zər-] *n* : observación *f*
observatory [əbˈzərvəˌtori] *n, pl* **-ries** : observatorio *m*
observe [əbˈzərv] *v* **-served; -serving** *vt* **1** OBEY : observar, obedecer **2** CELEBRATE : celebrar, guardar (una práctica religiosa) **3** WATCH : observar, mi-

rar **4** REMARK : observar, comentar —
vi LOOK : mirar
observer [ab'zərvər] *n* : observador *m*,
-dora *f*
obsess [əb'sɛs] *vt* : obsesionar
obsession [ab'sɛʃən, əb-] *n* : obsesión *f*
obsessive [ab'sɛsɪv, əb-] *adj* : obsesivo
— **obsessively** *adv*
obsolescence [ˌabsə'lɛsənts] *n* : obsolescencia *f*
obsolescent [ˌabsə'lɛsənt] *adj* : obsolescente ⟨to become obsolescent : caer
en desuso⟩
obsolete [ˌabsə'li:t, 'absəˌ-] *adj* : obsoleto, anticuado
obstacle ['abstɪkəl] *n* : obstáculo *m*, impedimento *m*
obstetric [əb'stɛtrɪk] *or* **obstetrical**
[-trɪkəl] *adj* : obstétrico
obstetrician [ˌabstə'trɪʃən] *n* : obstetra
mf; tocólogo *m*, -ga *f*
obstetrics [əb'stɛtrɪks] *ns & pl* : obstetricia *f*, tocología *f*
obstinacy ['abstənəsi] *n, pl* -**cies** : obstinación *f*, terquedad *f*
obstinate ['abstənət] *adj* : obstinado,
terco — **obstinately** *adv*
obstreperous [əb'strɛpərəs] *adj* **1**
CLAMOROUS : ruidoso, clamoroso **2**
UNRULY : rebelde, indisciplinado
obstruct [əb'strʌkt] *vt* : obstruir, bloquear
obstruction [əb'strʌkʃən] *n* : obstrucción *f*, bloqueo *m*
obstructive [əb'strʌktɪv] *adj* : obstructor
obtain [əb'teɪn] *vt* : obtener, conseguir
— *vi* PREVAIL : imperar, prevalecer
obtainable [əb'teɪnəbəl] *adj* : obtenible,
asequible
obtrude [əb'tru:d] *v* -**truded; -truding** *vt*
1 EXTRUDE : expulsar **2** IMPOSE : imponer — *vi* INTRUDE : inmiscuirse, entrometerse
obtrusive [əb'tru:sɪv] *adj* **1** IMPERTI-
NENT, MEDDLESOME : impertinente,
entrometido **2** PROTRUDING : prominente
obtuse [ab'tu:s, əb-, -'tju:s] *adj* : obtuso, torpe
obtuse angle *n* : ángulo obtuso
obviate ['abviˌeɪt] *vt* -**ated; -ating** : obviar, evitar
obvious ['abviəs] *adj* : obvio, evidente,
manifiesto
obviously ['abviəsli] *adv* **1** CLEARLY
: obviamente, evidentemente **2** OF
COURSE : claro, por supuesto
occasion¹ [ə'keɪʒən] *vt* : ocasionar,
causar
occasion² *n* **1** OPPORTUNITY : oportunidad *f*, ocasión *f* **2** CAUSE : motivo *m*,
razón *f* **3** INSTANCE : ocasión *f* **4**
EVENT : ocasión *f*, acontecimiento *m*
5 on ~ : de vez en cuando, ocasionalmente
occasional [ə'keɪʒənəl] *adj* : ocasional
occasionally [ə'keɪʒənəli] *adv* : de vez
en cuando, ocasionalmente

occidental [ˌaksə'dɛntəl] *adj* : oeste, del
oeste, occidental
occult¹ [ə'kʌlt, 'aˌkʌlt] *adj* **1** HIDDEN,
SECRET : oculto, secreto **2** ARCANE
: arcano, esotérico
occult² *n* **the occult** : las ciencias ocul-
tas
occupancy ['akjəpəntsi] *n, pl* -**cies**
: ocupación *f*, habitación *f*
occupant ['akjəpənt] *n* : ocupante *mf*
occupation [ˌakjə'peɪʃən] *n* : ocupación
f, profesión *f*, oficio *m*
occupational [ˌakjə'peɪʃənəl] *adj* : ocupacional
occupy ['akjəˌpaɪ] *vt* -**pied; -pying** : ocupar
occur [ə'kər] *vi* **occurred; occurring 1**
EXIST : encontrarse, existir **2** HAPPEN
: ocurrir, acontecer, suceder, tener lugar **3** : ocurrirse ⟨it occurred to him
that . . . : se le ocurrió que . . . ⟩
occurrence [ə'kərənts] *n* : acontecimiento *m*, suceso *m*, ocurrencia *f*
ocean ['o:ʃən] *n* : océano *m*
oceanic [ˌo:ʃi'ænɪk] *adj* : oceánico
oceanography [ˌo:ʃə'nagrəfi] *n*
: oceanografía *f*
ocelot ['asəˌlat, 'o:-] *n* : ocelote *m*
ocher *or* **ochre** ['o:kər] *n* : ocre *m*
o'clock [ə'klak] *adv* (*used in telling time*)
⟨it's ten o'clock : son las diez⟩ ⟨at six
o'clock : a las seis⟩
octagon ['aktəˌgan] *n* : octágono *m*
octagonal [ak'tægənəl] *adj* : octagonal
octave ['aktɪv] *n* : octava *f*
October [ak'to:bər] *n* : octubre *m*
octopus ['aktəˌpus, -pəs] *n, pl* -**puses** *or*
-**pi** [-ˌpaɪ] : pulpo *m*
ocular ['akjələr] *adj* : ocular
oculist ['akjəlɪst] *n* **1** OPHTHALMOLO-
GIST : oftalmólogo *m*, -ga *f*; oculista *mf*
2 OPTOMETRIST : optometrista *mf*
odd ['ad] *adj* **1** : sin pareja, suelto ⟨an
odd sock : un calcetín sin pareja⟩ **2**
UNEVEN : impar ⟨odd numbers
: números impares⟩ **3** : y pico, y tantos ⟨forty odd years ago : hace cuarenta
y pico años⟩ **4** : alguno, uno que otro
⟨odd jobs : algunos trabajos⟩ **5**
STRANGE : extraño, raro
oddball ['adˌbɔl] *n* : excéntrico *m*, -ca *f*;
persona *f* rara
oddity ['adəti] *n, pl* -**ties** : rareza *f*, cosa
f rara
oddly ['adli] *adv* : de manera extraña
oddness ['adnəs] *n* : rareza *f*, excentricidad *f*
odds ['adz] *npl* **1** CHANCES : probabili-
dades *fpl* **2** : puntos *mpl* de ventaja (de
una apuesta) **3 to be at odds** : estar en
desacuerdo
odds and ends *npl* : costillas *fpl*, cosas
fpl sueltas, cachivaches *mpl*
ode ['o:d] *n* : oda *f*
odious ['o:diəs] *adj* : odioso — **odious-
ly** *adv*
odor ['o:dər] *n* : olor *m*
odorless ['o:dərləs] *adj* : inodoro, sin
olor

odorous ['oːdərəs] *adj* : oloroso
odyssey ['ɑdəsi] *n, pl* **-seys** : odisea *f*
o'er ['or] → **over**
of ['ʌv, 'əv] *prep* **1** FROM : de ⟨a man of the city : un hombre de la ciudad⟩ **2** (*indicating character or background*) : de ⟨a woman of great ability : una mujer de gran capacidad⟩ **3** (*indicating cause*) : de ⟨he died of the flu : murió de la gripe⟩ **4** BY : de ⟨the works of Shakespeare : las obras de Shakespeare⟩ **5** (*indicating contents, material, or quantity*) : de ⟨a house of wood : una casa de madera⟩ ⟨a glass of water : un vaso de agua⟩ **6** (*indicating belonging or connection*) : de ⟨the front of the house : el frente de la casa⟩ **7** ABOUT : sobre, de ⟨tales of the West : los cuentos del Oeste⟩ **8** (*indicating a particular example*) : de ⟨the city of Caracas : la ciudad de Caracas⟩ **9** FOR : por, a ⟨love of country : amor por la patria⟩ **10** (*indicating time or date*) ⟨five minutes of ten : las diez menos cinco⟩ ⟨the eighth of April : el ocho de abril⟩
off¹ ['ɔf] *adv* **1** (*indicating change of position or state*) ⟨to march off : marcharse⟩ ⟨he dozed off : se puso a dormir⟩ **2** (*indicating distance in space or time*) ⟨some miles off : a varias millas⟩ ⟨the holiday is three weeks off : faltan tres semanas para la fiesta⟩ **3** (*indicating removal*) ⟨the knob came off : se le cayó el pomo⟩ **4** (*indicating termination*) ⟨shut the television off : apaga la televisión⟩ **5** (*indicating suspension of work*) ⟨to take a day off : tomarse un día de descanso⟩ **6 off and on** : de vez en cuando
off² *adj* **1** FARTHER : más remoto, distante ⟨the off side of the building : el lado distante del edificio⟩ **2** STARTED : empezado ⟨to be off on a spree : irse de juerga⟩ **3** OUT : apagado ⟨the light is off : la luz está apagada⟩ **4** CANCELED : cancelado, suspendido **5** INCORRECT : erróneo, incorrecto **6** REMOTE : remoto, lejano ⟨an off chance : una posibilidad remota⟩ **7** FREE : libre ⟨I'm off today : hoy estoy libre⟩ **8 to be well off** : vivir con desahogo, tener bastante dinero
off³ *prep* **1** (*indicating physical separation*) : de ⟨she took it off the table : lo tomó de la mesa⟩ ⟨a shop off the main street : una tienda al lado de la calle principal⟩ **2** : a la costa de, a expensas de ⟨he lives off his sister : vive a expensas de su hermana⟩ **3** (*indicating the suspension of an activity*) ⟨to be off duty : estar libre⟩ ⟨he's off liquor : ha dejado el alcohol⟩ **4** BELOW : por debajo de ⟨he's off his game : está por debajo de su juego normal⟩
offal ['ɔfəl] *n* **1** RUBBISH, WASTE : desechos *mpl*, desperdicios *mpl* **2** VISCERA : vísceras *fpl*, asaduras *fpl*

offend [ə'fɛnd] *vt* **1** VIOLATE : violar, atentar contra **2** HURT : ofender ⟨to be easily offended : ser muy susceptible⟩
offender [ə'fɛndər] *n* : delincuente *mf*; infractor *m*, -tora *f*
offense *or* **offence** [ə'fɛnts, 'ɔ,fɛnts] *n* **1** INSULT : ofensa *f*, injuria *f*, agravio *m* ⟨to take offense : ofenderse⟩ **2** ASSAULT : ataque *m* **3** : ofensiva *f* (en deportes) **4** CRIME, INFRACTION : infracción *f*, delito *m*
offensive¹ [ə'fɛntsɪv, 'ɔ,fɛnt-] *adj* : ofensivo — **offensively** *adv*
offensive² *n* : ofensiva *f*
offer¹ ['ɔfər] *vt* **1** : ofrecer ⟨they offered him the job : le ofrecieron el puesto⟩ **2** PROPOSE : proponer, sugerir **3** SHOW : ofrecer, mostrar ⟨to offer resistance : ofrecer resistencia⟩
offer² *n* : oferta *f*, ofrecimiento *m*, propuesta *f*
offering ['ɔfərɪŋ] *n* : ofrenda *f*
offhand¹ ['ɔf'hænd] *adv* : sin preparación, sin pensarlo
offhand² *adj* **1** IMPROMPTU : improvisado **2** ABRUPT : brusco
office ['ɔfəs] *n* **1** : cargo *m* ⟨to run for office : presentarse como candidato⟩ **2** : oficina *f*, despacho *m*, gabinete *m* (en la casa) ⟨office hours : horas de oficina⟩
officeholder ['ɔfəs,hoːldər] *n* : titular *mf*
officer ['ɔfəsər] *n* **1** *or* **police officer** : policía *mf*, agente *mf* de policía **2** OFFICIAL : oficial *mf*; funcionario *m*, -ria *f*; director *m*, -tora *f* (en una empresa) **3** COMMISSIONED OFFICER : oficial *mf*
official¹ [ə'fɪʃəl] *adj* : oficial — **officially** *adv*
official² *n* : funcionario *m*, -ria *f*; oficial *mf*
officiate [ə'fɪʃi,eɪt] *v* **-ated; -ating** *vi* **1** : arbitrar (en deportes) **2 to officiate at** : oficiar, celebrar — *vt* : arbitrar
officious [ə'fɪʃəs] *adj* : oficioso
offing ['ɔfɪŋ] *n* **in the offing** : en perspectiva
offset ['ɔf,sɛt] *vt* **-set; -setting** : compensar
offshoot ['ɔf,ʃuːt] *n* **1** OUTGROWTH : producto *m*, resultado *m* **2** BRANCH, SHOOT : retoño *m*, rama *f*, vástago *m* (de una planta)
offshore¹ ['ɔf'ʃor] *adv* : a una distancia de la costa
offshore² *adj* **1** : de (la) tierra ⟨an offshore wind : un viento que sopla de tierra⟩ **2** : (de) costa afuera, cercano a la costa ⟨an offshore island : una isla costera⟩
offspring ['ɔf,sprɪŋ] *ns & pl* **1** YOUNG : crías *fpl* (de los animales) **2** PROGENY : prole *f*, progenie *f*
off-white ['ɔf'hwaɪt] *adj* : blancuzco
often ['ɔfən, 'ɔftən] *adv* : muchas veces, a menudo, seguido

oftentimes ['ɔfən,taɪmz, 'ɔftən-] *or* **ofttimes** ['ɔft,taɪmz] → **often**

ogle ['o:gəl] *vt* **ogled; ogling** : comerse con los ojos, quedarse mirando a

ogre ['o:gər] *n* : ogro *m*

oh ['o:] *interj* : ¡oh!, ¡ah!, ¡ay! ⟨oh, of course : ah, por supuesto⟩ ⟨oh no! : ¡ay no!⟩ ⟨oh really? : ¿de veras?⟩

ohm ['o:m] *n* : ohm *m*, ohmio *m*

oil[1] ['ɔɪl] *vt* : lubricar, engrasar, aceitar

oil[2] *n* **1** : aceite *m* **2** PETROLEUM : petróleo *m* **3** *or* **oil painting** : óleo *m*, pintura *f* al óleo **4** *or* **oil paint(s)** : óleo *m*

oilcloth ['ɔɪl,klɔθ] *n* : hule *m*

oiliness ['ɔɪlinəs] *n* : lo aceitoso

oilskin ['ɔɪl,skɪn] *n* **1** : hule *m* **2 oilskins** *npl* : impermeable *m*

oily ['ɔɪli] *adj* **oilier; -est** : aceitoso, grasiento, grasoso ⟨oily fingers : dedos grasientos⟩

ointment ['ɔɪntmənt] *n* : ungüento *m*, pomada *f*

OK[1] [,o:'keɪ] *vt* **OK'd** *or* **okayed** [,o:'keɪd]; **OK'ing** *or* **okaying** APPROVE, AUTHORIZE : dar el visto bueno a, autorizar, aprobar

OK[2] *or* **okay** [,o:'keɪ] *adv* **1** WELL : bien **2** YES : sí, por supuesto

OK[3] *adj* : bien ⟨he's OK : está bien⟩ ⟨it's OK with me : estoy de acuerdo⟩

OK[4] *n* : autorización *f*, visto *m* bueno

okra ['o:krə, *South also* -kri] *n* : quingombó *m*

old[1] ['o:ld] *adj* **1** ANCIENT : antiguo ⟨old civilizations : civilizaciones antiguas⟩ **2** FAMILIAR : viejo ⟨old friends : viejos amigos⟩ ⟨the same old story : el mismo cuento⟩ **3** *(indicating a certain age)* ⟨he's ten years old : tiene diez años (de edad)⟩ **4** AGED : viejo, anciano ⟨an old woman : una anciana⟩ **5** FORMER : antiguo ⟨her old neighborhood : su antiguo barrio⟩ **6** WORN-OUT : viejo, gastado

old[2] *n* **1 the old** : los viejos, los ancianos **2 in the days of old** : antaño, en los tiempos antiguos

olden ['o:ldən] *adj* : de antaño, de antigüedad

old–fashioned ['o:ld'fæʃənd] *adj* : anticuado, pasado de moda

old maid *n* **1** SPINSTER : soltera *f* **2** FUSSBUDGET : maniático *m*, -ca *f*; melindroso *m*, -sa *f*

Old Testament *n* : Antiguo Testamento *m*

old–time ['o:ld'taɪm] *adj* : antiguo

old–timer ['o:ld'taɪmər] *n* **1** VETERAN : veterano *m*, -na *f* **2** *or* **oldster** : anciano *m*, -na *f*

old–world ['o:ld'wərld] *adj* : pintoresco (de antaño)

oleander ['o:li,ændər] *n* : adelfa *f*

oleomargarine [,o:lio'mardʒərən] → **margarine**

olfactory [ɑl'fæktəri, ol-] *adj* : olfativo

oligarchy ['ɑlə,gɑrki, 'o:lə-] *n, pl* **-chies** : oligarquía *f*

olive ['ɑlɪv, -ləv] *n* **1** : aceituna *f*, oliva *f* (fruta) **2** : olivo *m* (árbol) **3** *or* **olive green** : color *m* aceituna, verde *m* oliva

Olmec ['ɑl,mɛk, 'o:l-] *n* : olmeca *mf* — **Olmec** *adj*

Olympic [ə'lɪmpɪk, o-] *adj* : olímpico

Olympic Games *npl* : Juegos *mpl* Olímpicos

Olympics [ə'lɪmpɪks, o-] *npl* : olimpiadas *fpl*

Omani [o'mɑni, -'mæ-] *n* : omaní *mf* — **Omani** *adj*

ombudsman ['ɑm,bʊdzmən, ɑm-'bʊdz-] *n, pl* **-men** [-mən, -,mɛn] : ombudsman *m*

omelet *or* **omelette** ['ɑmlət, 'ɑmə-] *n* : omelette *mf*, tortilla *f* (de huevo)

omen ['o:mən] *n* : presagio *m*, augurio *m*, agüero *m*

ominous ['ɑmənəs] *adj* : ominoso, agorero, de mal agüero

ominously ['ɑmənəsli] *adv* : de manera amenazadora

omission [o'mɪʃən] *n* : omisión *f*

omit [o'mɪt] *vt* **omitted; omitting 1** LEAVE OUT : omitir, excluir **2** NEGLECT : omitir ⟨they omitted to tell us : omitieron decírnoslo⟩

omnipotence [ɑm'nɪpətənts] *n* : omnipotencia *f* — **omnipotent** [ɑm-'nɪpətənt] *adj*

omnipresent [,ɑmnɪ'prɛzənt] *adj* : omnipresente

omniscient [ɑm'nɪʃənt] *adj* : omnisciente

omnivorous [ɑm'nɪvərəs] *adj* **1** : omnívoro **2** AVID : ávido, voraz

on[1] ['ɑn, 'ɔn] *adv* **1** *(indicating contact with a surface)* ⟨put the top on : pon la tapa⟩ ⟨he has a hat on : lleva un sombrero puesto⟩ **2** *(indicating forward movement)* ⟨from that moment on : a partir de ese momento⟩ ⟨farther on : más adelante⟩ **3** *(indicating operation or an operating position)* ⟨turn the light on : prende la luz⟩

on[2] *adj* **1** *(being in operation)* ⟨the radio is on : el radio está prendido⟩ **2** *(taking place)* ⟨the game is on : el juego ha comenzado⟩ **3 to be on to** : estar enterado de

on[3] *prep* **1** *(indicating position)* : en, sobre, encima de ⟨on the table : en (sobre, encima de) la mesa⟩ ⟨shadows on the wall : sombras en la pared⟩ ⟨on horseback : a caballo⟩ **2** AT, TO : a ⟨on the right : a la derecha⟩ **3** ABOARD, IN : en, a ⟨on the plane : en el avión⟩ ⟨he got on the train : subió al tren⟩ **4** *(indicating time)* ⟨she worked on Saturdays : trabajaba los sábados⟩ ⟨every hour on the hour : a la hora en punto⟩ **5** *(indicating means or agency)* : por ⟨he cut himself on a tin can : se cortó con una lata⟩ ⟨to talk on the telephone : hablar por teléfono⟩ **6** *(indicating a state or process)* : en ⟨on fire : en llamas⟩ ⟨on the increase : en aumento⟩ **7** (*indicating connection or membership*) : en ⟨on a committee : en una comisión⟩ **8** (*indicating an activity*) ⟨on vacation : de vacaciones⟩ ⟨on a diet : a dieta⟩ **9** ABOUT, CONCERNING : sobre ⟨a book on insects : un libro sobre insectos⟩ ⟨reflect on that : reflexiona sobre eso⟩

once¹ [ˈwʌnts] *adv* **1** : una vez ⟨once a month : una vez al mes⟩ ⟨once and for all : de una vez por todas⟩ **2** EVER : alguna vez **3** FORMERLY : antes, anteriormente

once² *adj* FORMER : antiguo

once³ *n* **1** : una vez **2** at ~ SIMULTANEOUSLY : al mismo tiempo, simultáneamente **3** at ~ IMMEDIATELY : inmediatamente, en seguida

once⁴ *conj* : una vez que, tan pronto como

once–over [ˌwʌntsˈoːvər, ˈwʌntsˌ-] *n* **to give someone the once–over** : echarle un vistazo a alguien

oncoming [ˈɑnˌkʌmɪŋ, ˈɔn-] *adj* : que viene

one¹ [ˈwʌn] *adj* **1** (*being a single unit*) : un, una ⟨he only wants one apple : sólo quiere una manzana⟩ **2** (*being a particular one*) : un, una ⟨he arrived early one morning : llegó temprano una mañana⟩ **3** (*being the same*) : mismo, misma ⟨they're all members of one team : todos son miembros del mismo equipo⟩ ⟨one and the same thing : la misma cosa⟩ **4** SOME : alguno, alguna; un, una ⟨I'll see you again one day : algún día te veré otra vez⟩ ⟨at one time or another : en una u otra ocasión⟩

one² *n* **1** : uno *m* (número) **2** (*indicating the first of a set or series*) ⟨from day one : desde el primer momento⟩ **3** (*indicating a single person or thing*) ⟨the one (girl) on the right : la de la derecha⟩ ⟨he has the one but needs the other : tiene uno pero necesita el otro⟩

one³ *pron* **1** : uno, una ⟨one of his friends : una de sus amigas⟩ ⟨one never knows : uno nunca sabe, nunca se sabe⟩ ⟨to cut one's finger : cortarse el dedo⟩ **2 one and all** : todos, todo el mundo **3 one another** : el uno al otro, se ⟨they loved one another : se amaban⟩ **4 that one** : aquél, aquella **5 which one?** : ¿cuál?

one–on–one [ˌwʌnɑnˈwʌn, -ɑn-] *adj* : uno a uno — **one–on–one** *adv*

onerous [ˈɑnərəs, ˈoːnə-] *adj* : oneroso, gravoso

oneself [ˌwʌnˈsɛlf] *pron* **1** (*used reflexively or for emphasis*) : se, sí mismo, uno mismo ⟨to control oneself : controlarse⟩ ⟨to talk to oneself : hablarse a sí mismo⟩ ⟨to do it oneself : hacérselo uno mismo⟩

one–sided [ˈwʌnˈsaɪdəd] *adj* **1** : de un solo lado **2** LOPSIDED : asimétrico **3** BIASED : parcial, tendencioso **4** UNILATERAL : unilateral

onetime [ˈwʌnˈtaɪm] *adj* FORMER : antiguo

one–way [ˈwʌnˈweɪ] *adj* **1** : de sentido único, de una sola dirección ⟨a one-way street : una calle de sentido único⟩ **2** : de ida, sencillo ⟨a one-way ticket : un boleto de ida⟩

ongoing [ˈɑnˌgoːɪŋ] *adj* **1** CONTINUING : en curso, corriente **2** DEVELOPING : en desarrollo

onion [ˈʌnjən] *n* : cebolla *f*

online [ˈɔnˈlaɪn, ˈɑn-] *adj* : en línea

onlooker [ˈɔnˌlʊkər, ˈɑn-] *n* : espectador *m*, -dora *f*, circunstante *mf*

only¹ [ˈoːnli] *adv* **1** MERELY : sólo, solamente, nomás ⟨for only two dollars : por tan sólo dos dólares⟩ ⟨only once : sólo una vez, no más de una vez⟩ ⟨I only did it to help : lo hice por ayudar nomás⟩ **2** SOLELY : únicamente, sólo, solamente ⟨only he knows it : solamente él lo sabe⟩ **3** (*indicating a result*) ⟨it will only cause him problems : no hará más que crearle problemas⟩ **4 if only** : ojalá, por lo menos ⟨if only it were true! : ¡ojalá sea cierto!⟩ ⟨if he could only dance : si por lo menos pudiera bailar⟩

only² *adj* : único ⟨an only child : un hijo único⟩ ⟨the only chance : la única oportunidad⟩

only³ *conj* BUT : pero ⟨I would go, only I'm sick : iría, pero estoy enfermo⟩

onset [ˈɑnˌsɛt] *n* : comienzo *m*, llegada *f*

onslaught [ˈɑnˌslɔt, ˈɔn-] *n* : arremetida *f*, embestida *f*, embate *m*

onto [ˈɑnˌtuː, ˈɔn-] *prep* : sobre

onus [ˈoːnəs] *n* : responsabilidad *f*, carga *f*

onward¹ [ˈɑnwərd, ˈɔn-] *or* **onwards** *adv* FORWARD : adelante, hacia adelante

onward² *adj* : hacia adelante

onyx [ˈɑnɪks] *n* : ónix *m*

ooze¹ [ˈuːz] *v* **oozed; oozing** *vi* : rezumar — *vt* **1** : rezumar **2** EXUDE : irradiar, rebosar ⟨to ooze confidence : irradiar confianza⟩

ooze² *n* SLIME : cieno *m*, limo *m*

opacity [oˈpæsəti] *n, pl* **-ties** : opacidad *f*

opal [ˈoːpəl] *n* : ópalo *m*

opaque [oˈpeɪk] *adj* **1** : opaco **2** UNCLEAR : poco claro

open¹ [ˈoːpən] *vt* **1** : abrir ⟨open the door : abre la puerta⟩ **2** UNCOVER : destapar **3** UNFOLD : desplegar, abrir **4** CLEAR : abrir (un camino, etc.) **5** INAUGURATE : abrir (una tienda), inaugurar (una exposición, etc.) **6** INITIATE : iniciar, entablar, abrir ⟨to open the meeting : abrir la sesión⟩ ⟨to open a discussion : entablar un debate⟩ — *vi* **1** : abrirse **2** BEGIN : empezar, comenzar

open² *adj* **1** : abierto ⟨an open window : una ventana abierta⟩ **2** FRANK : abierto, franco, directo **3** UNCOV-

ERED : descubierto, abierto **4** EX-TENDED : extendido, abierto ⟨with open arms : con los brazos abiertos⟩ **5** UNRESTRICTED : libre, abierto **6** UN-DECIDED : pendiente, por decidir, sin resolver ⟨an open question : una cuestión pendiente⟩ **7** AVAILABLE : vacante, libre ⟨the job is open : el puesto está vacante⟩

open³ *n* **in the open 1** OUTDOORS : al aire libre **2** KNOWN : conocido, sacado a la luz

open–air ['o:pən'ær] *adj* OUTDOOR : al aire libre

open–and–shut ['o:pənənd'ʃʌt] *adj* : claro, evidente ⟨an open-and-shut case : un caso muy claro⟩

opener ['o:pənər] *n* : destapador *m*, abrelatas *m*, abridor *m*

openhanded [,o:pən'hændəd] *adj* : generoso, liberal

openhearted [,o:pən'hɑrtəd] *adj* **1** FRANK : franco, sincero **2** : generoso, de gran corazón

opening ['o:pənɪŋ] *n* **1** BEGINNING : comienzo *m*, principio *m*, apertura *f* **2** APERTURE : abertura *f*, brecha *f*, claro *m* (en el bosque) **3** OPPORTUNITY : oportunidad *f*

openly ['o:pənli] *adv* **1** FRANKLY : abiertamente, francamente **2** PUBLICLY : públicamente, declaradamente

openness ['o:pənnəs] *n* : franqueza *f*

opera ['ɑprə, 'ɑpərə] *n* **1** : ópera *f* **2** → opus

opera glasses *npl* : gemelos *mpl* de teatro

operate ['ɑpə,reɪt] *v* -**ated**; -**ating** *vi* **1** ACT, FUNCTION : operar, funcionar, actuar **2 to operate on (someone)** : operar a (alguien) — *vt* **1** WORK : operar, manejar, hacer funcionar (una máquina) **2** MANAGE : manejar, administrar (un negocio)

operatic [,ɑpə'rætɪk] *adj* : operístico

operation [,ɑpə'reɪʃən] *n* **1** FUNCTION-ING : funcionamiento *m* **2** USE : uso *m*, manejo *m* (de máquinas) **3** SURGERY : operación *f*, intervención *f* quirúrgica

operational [,ɑpə'reɪʃənəl] *adj* : operacional, de operación

operative ['ɑpərətɪv, -,reɪ-] *adj* **1** OPER-ATING : vigente, en vigor **2** WORKING : operativo **3** SURGICAL : quirúrgico

operator ['ɑpə,reɪtər] *n* : operador *m*, -dora *f*

operetta [,ɑpə'rɛtə] *n* : opereta *f*

ophthalmologist [,ɑf,θæl'mɑlʤɪst, -θəl'mɑ-] *n* : oftalmólogo *m*, -ga *f*

ophthalmology [,ɑf,θæl'mɑlʤi, -θəl'mɑ-] *n* : oftalmología *f*

opiate ['o:piət, -pi,eɪt] *n* : opiato *m*

opinion [ə'pɪnjən] *n* : opinión *f*

opinionated [ə'pɪnjə,neɪtəd] *adj* : testarudo, dogmático

opium ['o:piəm] *n* : opio *m*

opossum [ə'pɑsəm] *n* : zarigüeya *f*, oposum *m*

opponent [ə'po:nənt] *n* : oponente *mf*; opositor *m*, -tora *f*; contrincante *mf* (en deportes)

opportune [,ɑpər'tu:n, -'tju:n] *adj* : oportuno — **opportunely** *adv*

opportunist [,ɑpər'tu:nɪst, -'tju:-] *n* : oportunista *mf*

opportunistic [,ɑpərtu'nɪstɪk, -tju-] *adj* : oportunista *mf*

opportunity [,ɑpər'tu:nəṭi, -'tju:-] *n, pl* -**ties** : oportunidad *f*, ocasión *f*, chance *m*, posibilidades *fpl*

oppose [ə'po:z] *vt* -**posed**; -**posing 1** : ir en contra de, oponerse a ⟨good opposes evil : el bien se opone al mal⟩ **2** COM-BAT : luchar contra, combatir, resistir

opposite¹ ['ɑpəzət] *adv* : enfrente

opposite² *adj* **1** FACING : de enfrente ⟨the opposite side : el lado de enfrente⟩ **2** CONTRARY : opuesto, contrario ⟨in opposite directions : en direcciones contrarias⟩ ⟨the opposite sex : el sexo opuesto, el otro sexo⟩

opposite³ *n* : lo contrario, lo opuesto

opposite⁴ *prep* : enfrente de, frente a

opposition [,ɑpə'zɪʃən] *n* **1** : oposición *f*, resistencia *f* **2 in opposition to** AGAINST : en contra de

oppress [ə'prɛs] *vt* **1** PERSECUTE : oprimir, perseguir **2** BURDEN : oprimir, agobiar

oppression [ə'prɛʃən] *n* : opresión *f*

oppressive [ə'prɛsɪv] *adj* **1** HARSH : opresivo, severo **2** STIFLING : agobiante, sofocante ⟨oppressive heat : calor sofocante⟩

oppressor [ə'prɛsər] *n* : opresor *m*, -sora *f*

opprobrium [ə'pro:briəm] *n* : oprobio *m*

opt ['ɑpt] *vi* : optar

optic ['ɑptɪk] *or* **optical** [-tɪkəl] *adj* : óptico

optical disk *n* : disco *m* óptico

optician [ɑp'tɪʃən] *n* : óptico *m*, -ca *f*

optics ['ɑptɪks] *npl* : óptica *f*

optimal ['ɑptəməl] *adj* : óptimo

optimism ['ɑptə,mɪzəm] *n* : optimismo *m*

optimist ['ɑptəmɪst] *n* : optimista *mf*

optimistic [,ɑptə'mɪstɪk] *adj* : optimista

optimistically [,ɑptə'mɪstɪkli] *adv* : con optimismo, positivamente

optimum¹ ['ɑptəməm] *adj* → **optimal**

optimum² *n, pl* -**ma** ['ɑptəmə] : lo óptimo, lo ideal

option ['ɑpʃən] *n* : opción *f* ⟨she has no option : no tiene más remedio⟩

optional ['ɑpʃənəl] *adj* : facultativo, optativo

optometrist [ɑp'tɑmətrɪst] *n* : optometrista *mf*

optometry [ɑp'tɑmətri] *n* : optometría *f*

opulence ['ɑpjələn/s] *n* : opulencia *f*

opulent ['ɑpjələnt] *adj* : opulento

opus ['o:pəs] *n, pl* **opera** ['o:pərə, 'ɑpə-] : opus *m*, obra *f* (de música)

or ['ɔr] *conj* **1** (*indicating an alternative*) : o (**u** *before words beginning with* o *or* ho) ⟨coffee or tea : café o té⟩ ⟨one day or another : un día u otro⟩ 2 (*follow-ing a negative*) : ni ⟨he didn't have his keys or his wallet : no llevaba ni sus llaves ni su billetera⟩

oracle ['ɔrəkəl] *n* : oráculo *m*

oral ['ɔrəl] *adj* : oral — **orally** *adv*

orange ['ɔrɪndʒ] *n* **1** : naranja *f*, china *f* PRi (fruto) **2** : naranja *m* (color), color *m* de china PRi

orangeade [ˌɔrɪndʒ'eɪd] *n* : naranjada *f*

orangutan [ə'ræŋəˌtæŋ, -'ræŋgə-, -ˌtæn] *n* : orangután *m*

oration [ə'reɪʃən] *n* : oración *f*, discurso *m*

orator ['ɔrətər] *n* : orador *m*, -dora *f*

oratorio [ˌɔrə'toriˌoː] *n*, *pl* **-rios** : oratorio *m*

oratory ['ɔrəˌtori] *n*, *pl* **-ries** : oratoria *f*

orb ['ɔrb] *n* : orbe *m*

orbit[1] ['ɔrbət] *vt* **1** CIRCLE : girar alrededor de, orbitar **2** : poner en órbita (un satélite, etc.) — *vi* : orbitar

orbit[2] *n* : órbita *f*

orbital ['ɔrbətəl] *adj* : orbital

orchard ['ɔrtʃərd] *n* : huerto *m*

orchestra ['ɔrkəstrə] *n* : orquesta *f*

orchestral [ɔr'kɛstrəl] *adj* : orquestal

orchestrate ['ɔrkəˌstreɪt] *vt* **-trated; -trating 1** : orquestar, instrumentar (en música) **2** ORGANIZE : arreglar, organizar

orchestration [ˌɔrkə'streɪʃən] *n* : orquestación *f*

orchid ['ɔrkɪd] *n* : orquídea *f*

ordain [ɔr'deɪn] *vt* **1** : ordenar (en religión) **2** DECREE : decretar, ordenar

ordeal [ɔr'diːl, 'ɔrˌdiːl] *n* : prueba *f* dura, experiencia *f* terrible

order[1] ['ɔrdər] *vt* **1** ORGANIZE : arreglar, ordenar, poner en orden **2** COMMAND : ordenar, mandar **3** REQUEST : pedir, encargar ⟨to order a meal : pedir algo de comer⟩ — *vi* : hacer un pedido

order[2] *n* **1** : orden *f* ⟨a religious order : una orden religiosa⟩ **2** COMMAND : orden *f*, mandato *m* ⟨to give an order : dar una orden⟩ **3** REQUEST : orden *f*, pedido *m* ⟨purchase order : orden de compra⟩ **4** ARRANGEMENT : orden *m* ⟨in chronological order : por orden cronológico⟩ **5** DISCIPLINE : orden *m* ⟨law and order : el orden público⟩ **6 in order to** : para **7 out of order** : descompuesto, averiado **8 orders** *npl* or **holy orders** : órdenes *fpl* sagradas

orderliness ['ɔrdərlinəs] *n* : orden *m*

orderly[1] ['ɔrdərli] *adj* **1** METHODICAL : ordenado, metódico **2** PEACEFUL : pacífico, disciplinado

orderly[2] *n*, *pl* **-lies 1** : ordenanza *m* (en el ejército) **2** : camillero *m* (en un hospital)

ordinal ['ɔrdənəl] *n* or **ordinal number** : ordinal *m*, número *m* ordinal

ordinance ['ɔrdənənts] *n* : ordenanza *f*, reglamento *m*

ordinarily [ˌɔrdən'ɛrəli] *adv* : ordinariamente, por lo general

ordinary ['ɔrdənˌɛri] *adj* **1** NORMAL, USUAL : normal, usual **2** AVERAGE : común y corriente, normal **3** MEDIOCRE : mediocre, ordinario

ordination [ˌɔrdən'eɪʃən] *n* : ordenación *f*

ordnance ['ɔrdnənts] *n* : artillería *f*

ore ['or] *n* : mineral *m* (metalífero), mena *f*

oregano [ə'rɛgəˌnoː] *n* : orégano *m*

organ ['ɔrgən] *n* **1** : órgano *m* (instrumento) **2** : órgano *m* (del cuerpo) **3** PERIODICAL : publicación *f* periódica, órgano *m*

organic [ɔr'gænɪk] *adj* : orgánico — **organically** *adv*

organism ['ɔrgəˌnɪzəm] *n* : organismo *m*

organist ['ɔrgənɪst] *n* : organista *mf*

organization [ˌɔrgənə'zeɪʃən] *n* **1** ORGANIZING : organización *f* **2** BODY : organización *f*, organismo *m*

organizational [ˌɔrgənə'zeɪʃənəl] *adj* : organizativo

organize ['ɔrgəˌnaɪz] *vt* **-nized; -nizing** : organizar, arreglar, poner en orden

organizer ['ɔrgəˌnaɪzər] *n* : organizador *m*, -dora *f*

orgasm ['ɔrˌgæzəm] *n* : orgasmo *m*

orgy ['ɔrdʒi] *n*, *pl* **-gies** : orgía *f*

orient ['oriˌɛnt] *vt* : orientar

Orient *n* **the Orient** : el Oriente

oriental [ˌori'ɛntəl] *adj* : del Oriente, oriental

Oriental *n* : oriental *mf*

orientation [ˌoriən'teɪʃən] *n* : orientación *f*

orifice ['ɔrəfəs] *n* : orificio *m*

origin ['ɔrədʒən] *n* **1** ANCESTRY : origen *m*, ascendencia *f* **2** SOURCE : origen *m*, raíz *f*, fuente *f*

original[1] [ə'rɪdʒənəl] *adj* : original

original[2] *n* : original *m*

originality [əˌrɪdʒə'næləti] *n* : originalidad *f*

originally [ə'rɪdʒənəli] *adv* **1** AT FIRST : al principio, originariamente **2** CREATIVELY : originalmente, con originalidad

originate [ə'rɪdʒəˌneɪt] *v* **-nated; -nating** *vt* : originar, iniciar, crear — *vi* **1** BEGIN : originarse, empezar **2** COME : provenir, proceder, derivarse

originator [ə'rɪdʒəˌneɪtər] *n* : creador *m*, -dora *f*; inventor *m*, -tora *f*

oriole ['oriˌoːl, -iəl] *n* : oropéndola *f*

ornament[1] ['ɔrnəmənt] *vt* : adornar, decorar, ornamentar

ornament[2] *n* : ornamento *m*, adorno *m*, decoración *f*

ornamental [ˌɔrnə'mɛntəl] *adj* : ornamental, de adorno, decorativo

ornamentation [ˌɔrnəmən'teɪʃən, -mɛn-] *n* : ornamentación *f*

ornate [ɔr'neɪt] *adj* : elaborado, recargado

ornery ['ɔrnəri, 'ɑrnəri] *adj* **ornerier; -est** : de mal genio, malhumorado

ornithologist [ˌɔrnə'θɑlədʒɪst] *n* : ornitólogo *m*, -ga *f*

ornithology [ˌɔrnəˈθɑlədʒi] *n, pl* **-gies** : ornitología *f*

orphan¹ [ˈɔrfən] *vt* : dejar huérfano

orphan² *n* : huérfano *m*, -na *f*

orphanage [ˈɔrfənɪdʒ] *n* : orfelinato *m*, orfanato *m*

orthodontics [ˌɔrθəˈdɑntɪks] *n* : ortodoncia *f*

orthodontist [ˌɔrθəˈdɑntɪst] *n* : ortodoncista *mf*

orthodox [ˈɔrθəˌdɑks] *adj* : ortodoxo

orthodoxy [ˈɔrθəˌdɑksi] *n, pl* **-doxies** : ortodoxia *f*

orthographic [ˌɔrθəˈgræfɪk] *adj* : ortográfico

orthography [ɔrˈθɑgrəfi] *n, pl* **-phies** SPELLING : ortografía *f*

orthopedic [ˌɔrθəˈpiːdɪk] *adj* : ortopédico

orthopedics [ˌɔrθəˈpiːdɪks] *ns & pl* : ortopedia *f*

orthopedist [ˌɔrθəˈpiːdɪst] *n* : ortopedista *mf*

oscillate [ˈɑsəˌleɪt] *vi* **-lated; -lating** : oscilar

oscillation [ˌɑsəˈleɪʃən] *n* : oscilación *f*

osmosis [ɑzˈmoːsɪs, ɑs-] *n* : ósmosis *f*, osmosis *f*

osprey [ˈɑspri, -ˌpreɪ] *n* : pigargo *m*

ostensible [ɑˈstɛntsəbəl] *adj* APPARENT : aparente, ostensible — **ostensibly** [-bli] *adv*

ostentation [ˌɑstənˈteɪʃən] *n* : ostentación *f*, boato *m*

ostentatious [ˌɑstənˈteɪʃəs] *adj* : ostentoso — **ostentatiously** *adv*

osteopath [ˈɑstiəˌpæθ] *n* : osteópata *f*

osteopathy [ˌɑstiˈɑpəθi] *n* : osteopatía *f*

osteoporosis [ˌɑstiopəˈroːsɪs] *n, pl* **-roses** [-ˌsiːz] : osteoporosis *f*

ostracism [ˈɑstrəˌsɪzəm] *n* : ostracismo *m*

ostracize [ˈɑstrəˌsaɪz] *vt* **-cized; -cizing** : condenar al ostracismo, marginar, aislar

ostrich [ˈɑstrɪtʃ, ˈɔs-] *n* : avestruz *m*

other¹ [ˈʌðər] *adv* **other than** : aparte de, fuera de

other² *adj* : otro ⟨the other boys : los otros muchachos⟩ ⟨smarter than other people : más inteligente que los demás⟩ ⟨on the other hand : por otra parte, por otro lado⟩ ⟨every other day : cada dos días⟩

other³ *pron* : otro, otra ⟨one in front of the other : uno tras otro⟩ ⟨myself and three others : yo y tres otros, yo y tres más⟩ ⟨somewhere or other : en alguna parte⟩

otherwise¹ [ˈʌðərˌwaɪz] *adv* **1** DIFFERENTLY : de otro modo, de manera distinta ⟨he could not act otherwise : no pudo actuar de manera distinta⟩ **2** : eso aparte, por lo demás ⟨I'm dizzy, but otherwise I'm fine : estoy mareado pero, por lo demás, estoy bien⟩ **3** OR ELSE : de lo contrario, si no ⟨do what I tell you, otherwise you'll be sorry : haz

lo que te digo, de lo contrario, te arrepentirás⟩

otherwise² *adj* : diferente, distinto ⟨the facts are otherwise : la realidad es diferente⟩

otter [ˈɑtər] *n* : nutria *f*

Ottoman [ˈɑtəmən] *n* **1** : otomano *m*, -na *f* **2** : otomana *f* (mueble) — **Ottoman** *adj*

ouch [ˈaʊtʃ] *interj* : ¡ay!, ¡huy!

ought [ˈɔt] *v aux* : deber ⟨you ought to take care of yourself : deberías cuidarte⟩

oughtn't [ˈɔtənt] (*contraction of* **ought not**) → **ought**

ounce [ˈaʊnts] *n* : onza *f*

our [ˈɑr, ˈaʊr] *adj* : nuestro

ours [ˈaʊrz, ˈɑrz] *pron* : nuestro, nuestra ⟨a cousin of ours : un primo nuestro⟩

ourselves [ɑrˈsɛlvz, aʊr-] *pron* **1** (*used reflexively*) : nos, nosotros ⟨we amused ourselves : nos divertimos⟩ ⟨we were always thinking of ourselves : siempre pensábamos en nosotros⟩ **2** (*used for emphasis*) : nosotros mismos, nosotras mismas ⟨we did it ourselves : lo hicimos nosotros mismos⟩

oust [ˈaʊst] *vt* : desbancar, expulsar

ouster [ˈaʊstər] *n* : expulsión *f* (de un país, etc.), destitución *f* (de un puesto)

out¹ [ˈaʊt] *vi* : revelarse, hacerse conocido

out² *adv* **1** (*indicating direction or movement*) : para afuera ⟨she opened the door and looked out : abrió la puerta y miró para afuera⟩ **2** (*indicating a location away from home or work*) : fuera, afuera ⟨to eat out : comer afuera⟩ **3** (*indicating loss of control or possession*) ⟨they let the secret out : sacaron el secreto a la luz⟩ **4** (*indicating completion or discontinuance*) ⟨his money ran out : se le acabó el dinero⟩ ⟨to turn out the light : apagar la luz⟩ **5** OUTSIDE : fuera, afuera ⟨out in the garden : afuera en el jardín⟩ **6** ALOUD : en voz alta, en alto ⟨to cry out : gritar⟩

out³ *adj* **1** EXTERNAL : externo, exterior **2** OUTLYING : alejado, distante ⟨the out islands : las islas distantes⟩ **3** ABSENT : ausente **4** UNFASHIONABLE : fuera de moda **5** EXTINGUISHED : apagado

out⁴ *prep* **1** (*used to indicate an outward movement*) : por ⟨I looked out the window : miré por la ventana⟩ ⟨she ran out the door : corrió por la puerta⟩ **2** → **out of**

out–and–out [ˈaʊtənˈaʊt] *adj* UTTER : redomado, absoluto

outboard motor [ˈaʊtˌbord] *n* : motor *m* fuera de borde

outbound [ˈaʊtˌbaʊnd] *adj* : que sale, de salida

outbreak [ˈaʊtˌbreɪk] *n* : brote *m* (de una enfermedad), comienzo *m* (de guerra), ola *f* (de violencia), erupción *f* (de granos)

outbuilding ['aʊt,bɪldɪŋ] *n* : edificio *m* anexo

outburst ['aʊt,bərst] *n* : arranque *m*, arrebato *m*

outcast ['aʊt,kæst] *n* : marginado *m*, -da *f*; paria *mf*

outcome ['aʊt,kʌm] *n* : resultado *m*, desenlace *m*, consecuencia *f*

outcrop ['aʊt,krɑp] *n* : afloramiento *m*

outcry ['aʊt,kraɪ] *n, pl* **-cries** : clamor *m*, protesta *f*

outdated [,aʊt'deɪt̬əd] *adj* : anticuado, fuera de moda

outdistance [,aʊt'dɪstənts] *vt* **-tanced; -tancing** : aventajar, dejar atrás

outdo [,aʊt'du:] *vt* **-did** [-'dɪd]; **-done** [-'dʌn]; **-doing; -does** [-'dʌz] : superar

outdoor ['aʊt'dor] *adj* : al aire libre ⟨outdoor sports : deportes al aire libre⟩ ⟨outdoor clothing : ropa de calle⟩

outdoors¹ ['aʊt'dorz] *adv* : afuera, al aire libre

outdoors² *n* : aire *m* libre

outer ['aʊt̬ər] *adj* **1** : exterior, externo **2 outer space** : espacio *m* exterior

outermost ['aʊt̬ər,mo:st] *adj* : más remoto, más exterior, extremo

outfield ['aʊt,fi:ld] *n* **the outfield** : los jardines

outfielder ['aʊt,fi:ldər] *n* : jardinero *m*, -ra *f*

outfit¹ ['aʊt,fɪt] *vt* **-fitted; -fitting** EQUIP : equipar

outfit² *n* **1** EQUIPMENT : equipo *m* **2** COSTUME, ENSEMBLE : traje *m*, conjunto *m* **3** GROUP : conjunto *m*

outgo ['aʊt,go:] *n, pl* **outgoes** : gasto *m*

outgoing ['aʊt,go:ɪŋ] *adj* **1** OUTBOUND : que sale **2** DEPARTING : saliente ⟨an outgoing president : un presidente saliente⟩ **3** EXTROVERTED : extrovertido, expansivo

outgrow [,aʊt'gro:] *vt* **-grew** [-'gru:]; **-grown** [-'gro:n]; **-growing 1** : crecer más que ⟨that tree outgrew all the others : ese árbol creció más que todos los otros⟩ **2 to outgrow one's clothes** : quedarle pequeña la ropa a uno

outgrowth ['aʊt,gro:θ] *n* **1** OFFSHOOT : brote *m*, vástago *m* (de una planta) **2** CONSEQUENCE : consecuencia *f*, producto *m*, resultado *m*

outing ['aʊt̬ɪŋ] *n* : excursión *f*

outlandish [aʊt'lændɪʃ] *adj* : descabellado, muy extraño

outlast [,aʊt'læst] *vt* : durar más que

outlaw¹ ['aʊt,lɔ] *vt* : hacerse ilegal, declarar fuera de la ley, prohibir

outlaw² *n* : bandido *m*, -da *f*; bandolero *m*, -ra *f*; forajido *m*, -da *f*

outlay ['aʊt,leɪ] *n* : gasto *m*, desembolso *m*

outlet ['aʊt,lɛt, -lət] *n* **1** EXIT : salida *f*, escape *m* ⟨electrical outlet : toma de corriente⟩ **2** RELIEF : desahogo *m* **3** MARKET : mercado *m*, salida *f*

outline¹ ['aʊt,laɪn] *vt* **-lined; -lining 1** SKETCH : diseñar, esbozar, bosquejar **2** DEFINE, EXPLAIN : perfilar, delinear, explicar ⟨she outlined our responsibilities : delineó nuestras responsabilidades⟩

outline² *n* **1** PROFILE : perfil *m*, silueta *f*, contorno *m* **2** SKETCH : bosquejo *m*, boceto *m* **3** SUMMARY : esquema *m*, resumen *m*, sinopsis *m* ⟨an outline of world history : un esquema de la historia mundial⟩

outlive [,aʊt'lɪv] *vt* **-lived; -living** : sobrevivir a

outlook ['aʊt,lʊk] *n* **1** VIEW : vista *f*, panorama *f* **2** POINT OF VIEW : punto *m* de vista **3** PROSPECTS : perspectivas *fpl*

outlying ['aʊt,laɪɪŋ] *adj* : alejado, distante, remoto ⟨the outlying areas : las afueras⟩

outmoded [,aʊt'mo:dəd] *adj* : pasado de moda, anticuado

outnumber [,aʊt'nʌmbər] *vt* : superar en número a, ser más numeroso de

out of *prep* **1** (*indicating direction or movement from within*) : de, por ⟨we ran out of the house : salimos corriendo de la casa⟩ ⟨to look out of the window : mirar por la ventana⟩ **2** (*being beyond the limits of*) ⟨out of control : fuera de control⟩ ⟨to be out of sight : desaparecer de vista⟩ **3** OF : de ⟨one out of four : uno de cada cuatro⟩ **4** (*indicating absence or loss*) : sin ⟨out of money : sin dinero⟩ ⟨we're out of matches : nos hemos quedado sin fósforos⟩ **5** BECAUSE OF : por ⟨out of curiosity : por curiosidad⟩ **6** FROM : de ⟨made out of plastic : hecho de plástico⟩

out-of-date [,aʊtəv'deɪt] *adj* : anticuado, obsoleto, pasado de moda

out-of-door [,aʊtəv'dor] *or* **out-of-doors** [-'dorz] → **outdoor**

out-of-doors *n* → **outdoors²**

outpatient ['aʊt,peɪʃənt] *n* : paciente *m* externo, paciente *f* externa

outpost ['aʊt,po:st] *n* : puesto *m* avanzado

output¹ ['aʊt,pʊt] *vt* **-putted** *or* **-put; -putting** : producir

output² *n* : producción *f* (de una fábrica), rendimiento *m* (de una máquina), productividad *f* (de una persona)

outrage¹ ['aʊt,reɪdʒ] *vt* **-raged; -raging 1** INSULT : ultrajar, injuriar **2** INFURIATE : indignar, enfurecer

outrage² *n* **1** ATROCITY : atropello *m*, atrocidad *f*, atentado *m* **2** SCANDAL : escándalo *m* **3** ANGER : ira *f*, furia *f*

outrageous [,aʊt'reɪdʒəs] *adj* **1** SCANDALOUS : escandaloso, ofensivo, atroz **2** UNCONVENTIONAL : poco convencional, extravagante **3** EXORBITANT : exorbitante, excesivo (dícese de los precios, etc.)

outright¹ [,aʊt'raɪt] *adv* **1** COMPLETELY : por completo, totalmente ⟨to sell outright : vender por completo⟩ ⟨he refused it outright : lo rechazó rotunda-

mente⟩ **2** DIRECTLY : directamente, sin
reserva **3** INSTANTLY : al instante, en
el acto
outright² [ˈaʊtˌraɪt] *adj* **1** COMPLETE
: completo, absoluto, categórico ⟨an
outright lie : una mentira absoluta⟩ **2**
: sin reservas ⟨an outright gift : un regalo sin reservas⟩
outset [ˈaʊtˌsɛt] *n* : comienzo *m*, principio *m*
outshine [ˌaʊtˈʃaɪn] *vt* **-shone** [-ˈʃoːn,
-ˈʃɑn] *or* **-shined; -shining** : eclipsar
outside¹ [ˌaʊtˈsaɪd, ˈaʊtˌ-] *adv* : fuera,
afuera
outside² *adj* **1** : exterior, externo ⟨the
outside edge : el borde exterior⟩ ⟨out-
side influences : influencias externas⟩
2 REMOTE : remoto ⟨an outside chance
: una posibilidad remota⟩
outside³ *n* **1** EXTERIOR : parte *f* de
afuera, exterior *m* **2** MOST : máximo
m ⟨three weeks at the outside : tres semanas como máximo⟩ **3 from the outside** : desde afuera, desde fuera
outside⁴ *prep* : fuera de, afuera de ⟨out-
side my window : fuera de mi ventana⟩
⟨outside regular hours : fuera del horario normal⟩ ⟨outside the law : afuera
de la ley⟩
outside of *prep* **1** → **outside⁴** **2** → **besides²**
outsider [ˌaʊtˈsaɪdər] *n* : forastero *m*, -ra
f
outskirts [ˈaʊtˌskərts] *npl* : afueras *fpl*,
alrededores *mpl*
outsmart [ˌaʊtˈsmɑrt] → **outwit**
outspoken [ˌaʊtˈspoːkən] *adj* : franco,
directo
outstanding [ˌaʊtˈstændɪŋ] *adj* **1** UN-
PAID : pendiente **2** NOTABLE : destacado, notable, excepcional, sobresaliente
outstandingly [ˌaʊtˈstændɪŋli] *adv* : excepcionalmente
outstretched [ˌaʊtˈstrɛtʃt] *adj* : extendido
outstrip [ˌaʊtˈstrɪp] *vt* **-stripped** *or* **-strip**
[-ˈstrɪpt]; **-stripping** **1** : aventajar, dejar atrás ⟨he outstripped the other runners : aventajó a los otros corredores⟩
2 SURPASS : aventajar, sobrepasar
outward¹ [ˈaʊtwərd] *or* **outwards**
[-wərdz] *adv* : hacia afuera, hacia el exterior
outward² *adj* **1** : hacia afuera ⟨an outward flow : un flujo hacia afuera⟩ **2**
: externo ⟨outward beauty : belleza ex-
terna⟩
outwardly [ˈaʊtwərdli] *adv* **1** EXTER-
NALLY : exteriormente **2** APPARENTLY
: aparentemente ⟨outwardly friendly
: aparentemente simpático⟩
outwit [ˌaʊtˈwɪt] *vt* **-witted; -witting** : ser
más listo que
ova → **ovum**
oval¹ [ˈoːvəl] *adj* : ovalado, oval
oval² *n* : óvalo *m*
ovarian [oˈværiən] *adj* : ovárico

ovary [ˈoːvəri] *n, pl* **-ries** : ovario *m*
ovation [oˈveɪʃən] *n* : ovación *f*
oven [ˈʌvən] *n* : horno *m*
over¹ [ˈoːvər] *adv* **1** (*indicating movement across*) ⟨he flew over to London
: voló a Londres⟩ ⟨come on over! : ¡ven
acá!⟩ **2** (*indicating an additional
amount*) ⟨the show ran 10 minutes over
: el espectáculo terminó 10 minutos de
tarde⟩ **3** ABOVE, OVERHEAD : por encima **4** AGAIN : otra vez, de nuevo ⟨over
and over : una y otra vez⟩ ⟨to start over
: volver a empezar⟩ **5 all over** EVERY-
WHERE : por todas partes **6 to fall over**
: caerse **7 to turn over** : poner boca
abajo, voltear
over² *adj* **1** HIGHER, UPPER : superior
2 REMAINING : sobrante, que sobra **3**
ENDED : terminado, acabado ⟨the
work is over : el trabajo está termina-
do⟩
over³ *prep* **1** ABOVE : encima de, arriba
de, sobre ⟨over the fireplace : encima
de la chimenea⟩ ⟨the hawk flew over
the hills : el halcón voló sobre los ce-
rros⟩ **2** : más de ⟨over $50 : más de
$50⟩ **3** ALONG : por, sobre ⟨to glide
over the ice : deslizarse sobre el hielo⟩
4 (*indicating motion through a place or
thing*) ⟨they showed me over the house
: me mostraron la casa⟩ **5** ACROSS : por
encima de, sobre ⟨he jumped over the
ditch : saltó por encima de la zanja⟩ **6**
UPON : sobre ⟨a cape over my shoulders : una capa sobre los hombros⟩ **7**
ON : por ⟨to speak over the telephone
: hablar por teléfono⟩ **8** DURING : en,
durante ⟨over the past 25 years : durante los últimos 25 años⟩ **9** BECAUSE
OF : por ⟨they fought over the money
: se pelearon por el dinero⟩
overabundance [ˌoːvərəˈbʌndənts] *n*
: superabundancia *f*
overabundant [ˌoːvərəˈbʌndənt] *adj*
: superabundante
overactive [ˌoːvərˈæktɪv] *adj* : hiperactivo
overall [ˌoːvərˈɔl] *adj* : total, global, de
conjunto
overalls [ˈoːvərˌɔlz] *npl* : overol *m*
overawe [ˌoːvərˈɔ] *vt* **-awed; -awing** : intimidar, impresionar
overbearing [ˌoːvərˈbærɪŋ] *adj* : dominante, imperioso, prepotente
overblown [ˌoːvərˈbloːn] *adj* **1** INFLAT-
ED : inflado, exagerado **2** BOMBASTIC
: grandilocuente, rimbombante
overboard [ˈoːvərˌbord] *adv* : por la borda, al agua
overburden [ˌoːvərˈbərdən] *vt* : sobrecargar, agobiar
overcast [ˈoːvərˌkæst] *adj* CLOUDY
: nublado
overcharge [ˌoːvərˈtʃɑrdʒ] *vt* **-charged;
-charging** : cobrarle de más (a alguien)
overcoat [ˈoːvərˌkoːt] *n* : abrigo *m*
overcome [ˌoːvərˈkʌm] *v* **-came**
[-ˈkeɪm]; **-come; -coming** *vt* **1** CON-

QUER : vencer, derrotar, superar **2**
OVERWHELM : abrumar, agobiar — *vi*
: vencer
overconfidence [ˌoːvərˈkɑnfədənts] *n*
: exceso *m* de confianza
overconfident [ˌoːvərˈkɑnfədənt] *adj*
: demasiado confiado
overcook [ˌoːvərˈkʊk] *vt* : recocer, cocer
demasiado
overcrowded [ˌoːvərˈkraʊdəd] *adj* **1**
PACKED : abarrotado, atestado de
gente **2** OVERPOPULATED : superpoblado
overdo [ˌoːvərˈduː] *vt* **-did** [-ˈdɪd]; **-done**
[-ˈdʌn]; **-doing; -does** [-ˈdʌz] **1** : hacer demasiado **2** EXAGGERATE : exagerar **3** OVERCOOK : recocer
overdose [ˈoːvərˌdoːs] *n* : sobredosis *f*
overdraft [ˈoːvərˌdræft] *n* : sobregiro *m*,
descubierto *m*
overdraw [ˌoːvərˈdrɔ] *vt* **-drew** [-ˈdruː];
-drawn [-ˈdrɔn]; **-drawing 1** : sobregirar ⟨my account is overdrawn : tengo
la cuenta en descubierto⟩ **2** EXAG-
GERATE : exagerar
overdue [ˌoːvərˈduː] *adj* **1** UNPAID : vencido y sin pagar **2** TARDY : de retraso,
tardío
overeat [ˌoːvərˈiːt] *vi* **-ate** [-ˈeɪt]; **-eaten**
[-ˈiːtən]; **-eating** : comer demasiado
overelaborate [ˌoːvərɪˈlæbərət] *adj* : recargado
overestimate [ˌoːvərˈestəˌmeɪt] *vt*
-mated; -mating : sobreestimar
overexcited [ˌoːvərɪkˈsaɪtəd] *adj* : sobreexcitado
overexpose [ˌoːvərɪkˈspoːz] *vt* **-posed;
-posing** : sobreexponer
overfeed [ˌoːvərˈfiːd] *vt* **-fed** [-ˈfɛd];
-feeding : sobrealimentar
overflow¹ [ˌoːvərˈfloː] *vt* **1** : desbordar **2**
INUNDATE : inundar — *vi* : desbor-
darse, rebosar
overflow² [ˈoːvərˌfloː] *n* **1** : derrame *m*,
desbordamiento *m* (de un río) **2** SUR-
PLUS : exceso *m*, excedente *m*
overfly [ˌoːvərˈflaɪ] *vt* **-flew** [-ˈfluː];
-flown [-ˈfloːn]; **-flying** : sobrevolar
overgrown [ˌoːvərˈgroːn] *adj* **1** : cubierto ⟨overgrown with weeds : cubierto de malas hierbas⟩ **2** : demasiado grande
overhand¹ [ˈoːvərˌhænd] *adv* : por encima de la cabeza
overhand² *adj* : por lo alto (tirada)
overhang¹ [ˌoːvərˈhæŋ] *v* **-hung** [-ˈhʌŋ];
-hanging *vt* **1** : sobresalir por encima
de **2** THREATEN : amenazar — *vi* : sobresalir
overhang² [ˈoːvərˌhæŋ] *n* : saliente *mf*
overhaul [ˌoːvərˈhɔl] *vt* **1** : revisar ⟨to
overhaul an engine : revisar un motor⟩
2 OVERTAKE : adelantar
overhead¹ [ˌoːvərˈhɛd] *adv* : por encima,
arriba, por lo alto
overhead² [ˈoːvərˌhɛd] *adj* : de arriba
overhead³ [ˈoːvərˌhɛd] *n* : gastos *mpl*
generales

overhear [ˌoːvərˈhɪr] *vt* **-heard; -hearing**
: oír por casualidad
overheat [ˌoːvərˈhiːt] *vt* : recalentar, sobrecalentar, calentar demasiado
overjoyed [ˌoːvərˈdʒɔɪd] *adj* : rebosante
de alegría
overkill [ˈoːvərˌkɪl] *n* : exceso *m*, excedente *m*
overland¹ [ˈoːvərˌlænd, -lənd] *adv* : por
tierra
overland² *adj* : terrestre, por tierra
overlap¹ [ˌoːvərˈlæp] *v* **-lapped; -lapping**
vt : traslapar — *vi* : traslaparse, solaparse
overlap² [ˈoːvərˌlæp] *n* : traslapo *m*
overlay¹ [ˌoːvərˈleɪ] *vt* **-laid** [-ˈleɪd];
-laying : recubrir, revestir
overlay² [ˈoːvərˌleɪ] *n* : revestimiento *m*
overload [ˌoːvərˈloːd] *vt* : sobrecargar
overlong [ˌoːvərˈlɔŋ] *adj* : excesivamente largo, largo y pesado
overlook [ˌoːvərˈlʊk] *vt* **1** INSPECT : inspeccionar, revisar **2** : tener vista a, dar
a ⟨a house overlooking the valley : una
casa que tiene vista al valle⟩ **3** MISS
: pasar por alto **4** EXCUSE : dejar pasar,
disculpar
overly [ˈoːvərli] *adv* : demasiado
overnight¹ [ˌoːvərˈnaɪt] *adv* **1** : por la
noche, durante la noche **2** : de la noche
a la mañana ⟨we can't do it overnight
: no podemos hacerlo de la noche a la
mañana⟩
overnight² [ˈoːvərˌnaɪt] *adj* **1** : de noche
⟨an overnight stay : una estancia de
una noche⟩ ⟨an overnight bag : una
bolsa de viaje⟩ **2** SUDDEN : repentino
overpass [ˈoːvərˌpæs] *n* : paso *m* elevado, paso *m* a desnivel *Mex*
overpopulated [ˌoːvərˈpɑpjəˌleɪtəd] *adj*
: sobrepoblado
overpower [ˌoːvərˈpaʊər] *vt* **1** CON-
QUER, SUBDUE : vencer, superar **2**
OVERWHELM : abrumar, agobiar
⟨overpowered by the heat : sofocado
por el calor⟩
overpraise [ˌoːvərˈpreɪz] *vt* **-praised;
-praising** : adular
overrate [ˌoːvərˈreɪt] *vt* **-rated; -rating**
: sobrevalorar, sobrevaluar
override [ˌoːvərˈraɪd] *vt* **-rode** [-ˈroːd];
-ridden [-ˈrɪdən]; **-riding 1** : predominar sobre, contar más que ⟨hunger
overrode our manners : el hambre pre-
dominó sobre los modales⟩ **2** ANNUL
: anular, invalidar ⟨to override a veto
: anular un veto⟩
overrule [ˌoːvərˈruːl] *vt* **-ruled; -ruling**
: anular (una decisión), desautorizar
(una persona), denegar (un pedido)
overrun [ˌoːvərˈrʌn] *v* **-ran** [-ˈræn];
-running *vt* **1** INVADE : invadir **2** IN-
FEST : infestar, plagar **3** EXCEED : exceder, rebasar — *vi* : rebasar el tiempo previsto
overseas¹ [ˌoːvərˈsiːz] *adv* : en el extranjero ⟨to travel overseas : viajar al
extranjero⟩

overseas² ['oːvərˌsiːz] *adj* : extranjero, exterior

oversee [ˌoːvər'siː] *vt* **-saw** [-'sɔ]; **-seen** [-'siːn]; **-seeing** SUPERVISE : supervisar

overseer ['oːvərˌsiːər] *n* : supervisor *m*, -sora *f*; capataz *mf*

overshadow [ˌoːvər'ʃæˌdoː] *vt* **1** DARKEN : oscurecer, ensombrecer **2** ECLIPSE, OUTSHINE : eclipsar

overshoe ['oːvərˌʃuː] *n* : chanclo *m*

overshoot [ˌoːvər'ʃuːt] *vt* **-shot** [-'ʃɑt]; **-shooting** : pasarse de ⟨to overshoot the mark : pasarse de la raya⟩

oversight ['oːvərˌsaɪt] *n* : descuido *m*, inadvertencia *f*

oversleep [ˌoːvər'sliːp] *vi* **-slept** [-'slɛpt]; **-sleeping** : no despertarse a tiempo, quedarse dormido

overspread [ˌoːvər'sprɛd] *vt* **-spread; -spreading** : extenderse sobre

overstaffed [ˌoːvər'stæft] *adj* : con exceso de personal

overstate [ˌoːvər'steɪt] *vt* **-stated; -stating** EXAGGERATE : exagerar

overstatement [ˌoːvər'steɪtmənt] *n* : exageración *f*

overstep [ˌoːvər'stɛp] *vt* **-stepped; -stepping** EXCEED : sobrepasar, traspasar, exceder

overt [oː'vərt, 'oːˌvərt] *adj* : evidente, manifiesto, patente

overtake [ˌoːvər'teɪk] *vt* **-took** [-'tʊk]; **-taken** [-'teɪkən]; **-taking** : pasar, adelantar, rebasar *Mex*

overthrow¹ [ˌoːvər'θroː] *vt* **-threw** [-'θruː]; **-thrown** [-'θroːn]; **-throwing 1** OVERTURN : dar la vuelta a, volcar **2** DEFEAT, TOPPLE : derrocar, derribar, deponer

overthrow² ['oːvərˌθroː] *n* : derrocamiento *m*, caída *f*

overtime ['oːvərˌtaɪm] *n* **1** : horas *fpl* extras (de trabajo) **2** : prórroga *f* (en deportes)

overtly [oː'vərtli, 'oːˌvərt-] *adv* OPENLY : abiertamente

overtone ['oːvərˌtoːn] *n* **1** : armónico *m* (en música) **2** HINT, SUGGESTION : tinte *m*, insinuación *f*

overture ['oːvərˌtʃʊr, -tʃər] *n* **1** PROPOSAL : propuesta *f* **2** : obertura *f* (en música)

overturn [ˌoːvər'tərn] *vt* **1** UPSET : dar la vuelta a, volcar **2** NULLIFY : anular, invalidar — *vi* TURN OVER : volcar, dar un vuelco

overuse [ˌoːvər'juːz] *vt* **-used; -using** : abusar de

overview ['oːvərˌvjuː] *n* : resumen *m*, visión *f* general

overweening [ˌoːvər'wiːnɪŋ] *adj* **1** ARROGANT : arrogante, soberbio **2** IMMODERATE : desmesurado

overweight [ˌoːvər'weɪt] *adj* : demasiado gordo, demasiado pesado

overwhelm [ˌoːvər'hwɛlm] *vt* **1** CRUSH, DEFEAT : aplastar, arrollar **2** SUBMERGE : inundar, sumergir **3** OVERPOWER : abrumar, agobiar ⟨overwhelmed by remorse : abrumado de remordimiento⟩

overwhelming [ˌoːvər'hwɛlmɪŋ] *adj* **1** CRUSHING : abrumador, apabullante **2** SWEEPING : arrollador, aplastante ⟨an overwhelming majority : una mayoría aplastante⟩

overwork [ˌoːvər'wərk] *vt* **1** : hacer trabajar demasiado **2** OVERUSE : abusar de — *vi* : trabajar demasiado

overwrought [ˌoːvər'rɔt] *adj* : alterado, sobreexcitado

ovoid ['oːˌvɔɪd] *or* **ovoidal** [oː'vɔɪdəl] *adj* : ovoide

ovulate ['ɑvjəˌleɪt, 'oː-] *vi* **-lated; -lating** : ovular

ovulation [ˌɑvjə'leɪʃən, ˌoː-] *n* : ovulación *f*

ovum ['oːvəm] *n, pl* **ova** [-və] : óvulo *m*

owe ['oː] *vt* **owed; owing** : deber ⟨you owe me $10 : me debes $10⟩ ⟨he owes his wealth to his father : le debe su riqueza a su padre⟩

owing to *prep* : debido a

owl ['aʊl] *n* : búho *m*, lechuza *f*, tecolote *m Mex*

own¹ ['oːn] *vt* **1** POSSESS : poseer, tener, ser dueño de **2** ADMIT : reconocer, admitir — *vi* **to own up** : reconocer (algo), admitir (algo)

own² *adj* : propio, personal, particular ⟨his own car : su propio coche⟩

own³ *pron* **my; (your, his/her, our, their); own** : el mío, la mía; el tuyo, la tuya; el suyo, la suya; el nuestro, la nuestra ⟨to each his own : cada uno a lo suyo⟩ ⟨money of my own : mi propio dinero⟩ ⟨to be on one's own : estar solo⟩

owner ['oːnər] *n* : dueño *m*, -ña *f*; propietario *m*, -ria *f*

ownership ['oːnərˌʃɪp] *n* : propiedad *f*

ox ['ɑks] *n, pl* **oxen** ['ɑksən] : buey *m*

oxidation [ˌɑksə'deɪʃən] *n* : oxidación *f*

oxide ['ɑkˌsaɪd] *n* : óxido *m*

oxidize ['ɑksəˌdaɪz] *vt* **-dized; -dizing** : oxidar

oxygen ['ɑksɪdʒən] *n* : oxígeno *m*

oyster ['ɔɪstər] *n* : ostra *f*, ostión *m Mex*

ozone ['oːˌzoːn] *n* : ozono *m*

P

p ['pi:] *n, pl* **p's** *or* **ps** ['pi:z] : decimo-sexta letra del alfabeto inglés

pace[1] ['peɪs] *v* **paced; pacing** *vi* : caminar, ir y venir — *vt* **1** : caminar por ⟨she paced the floor : caminaba de un lado a otro del cuarto⟩ **2 to pace a runner** : marcarle el ritmo a un corredor

pace[2] *n* **1** STEP : paso *m* **2** RATE : paso *m*, ritmo *m* ⟨to set the pace : marcar el paso, marcar la pauta⟩

pacemaker ['peɪs,meɪkər] *n* : marcapasos *m*

pacific [pə'sɪfɪk] *adj* : pacífico

pacifier ['pæsə,faɪər] *n* : chupete *m*, chupón *m*, mamila *f Mex*

pacifism ['pæsə,fɪzəm] *n* : pacifismo *m*

pacifist ['pæsəfɪst] *n* : pacifista *mf*

pacify ['pæsə,faɪ] *vt* **-fied; -fying 1** SOOTHE : apaciguar, pacificar **2** : pacificar (un país, una región, etc.)

pack[1] ['pæk] *vt* **1** PACKAGE : empaquetar, embalar, envasar **2** : empacar, meter (en una maleta) ⟨to pack one's bag : hacer la maleta⟩ **3** FILL : llenar, abarrotar ⟨a packed theater : un teatro abarrotado⟩ **4 to pack off** SEND : mandar — *vi* : empacar, hacer las maletas

pack[2] *n* **1** BUNDLE : bulto *m*, fardo *m* **2** BACKPACK : mochila *f* **3** PACKAGE : paquete *m*, cajetilla *f* (de cigarrillos, etc.) **4** : manada *f* (de lobos, etc.), jauría *f* (de perros) ⟨a pack of thieves : una pandilla de ladrones⟩

package[1] ['pækɪdʒ] *vt* **-aged; -aging** : empaquetar, embalar

package[2] *n* : paquete *m*, bulto *m*

packaging ['pækɪdʒɪŋ] *n* **1** : embalaje *m* **2** WRAPPING : envoltorio *m*

packer ['pækər] *n* : empacador *m*, -dora *f*

packet ['pækət] *n* : paquete *m*

packing ['pækɪŋ] *n* : embalaje *m*

pact ['pækt] *n* : pacto *m*, acuerdo *m*

pad[1] ['pæd] *vt* **padded; padding 1** FILL, STUFF : rellenar, acolchar (una silla, una pared) **2** : meter paja en, rellenar ⟨to pad a speech : rellenar un discurso⟩

pad[2] *n* **1** CUSHION : almohadilla *f* ⟨a shoulder pad : una hombrera⟩ **2** TABLET : bloc *m* (de papel) **3** *or* **lily pad** : hoja *f* grande (de un nenúfar) **4 ink pad** : tampón *m* **5 launching pad** : plataforma *f* (de lanzamiento)

padding ['pædɪŋ] *n* **1** FILLING : relleno *m* **2** : paja *f* (en un discurso, etc.)

paddle[1] ['pædəl] *v* **-dled; -dling** *vt* **1** : hacer avanzar (una canoa) con canalete **2** HIT : azotar, darle nalgadas a (con una pala o paleta) — *vi* **1** : remar (en una canoa) **2** SPLASH : chapotear, mojarse los pies

paddle[2] *n* **1** : canalete *m*, zagual *m* (de una canoa, etc.) **2** : pala *f*, paleta *f* (en deportes)

paddock ['pædək] *n* **1** PASTURE : potrero *m* **2** : paddock *m*, cercado *m* (en un hipódromo)

paddy ['pædi] *n, pl* **-dies** : arrozal *m*

padlock[1] ['pæd,lɑk] *vt* : cerrar con candado

padlock[2] *n* : candado *m*

pagan[1] ['peɪgən] *adj* : pagano

pagan[2] *n* : pagano *m*, -na *f*

paganism ['peɪgən,ɪzəm] *n* : paganismo *m*

page[1] ['peɪdʒ] *vt* **paged; paging** : llamar por altavoz

page[2] *n* **1** BELLHOP : botones *m* **2** : página *f* (de un libro, etc.)

pageant ['pædʒənt] *n* **1** SPECTACLE : espectáculo *m* **2** PROCESSION : desfile *m*

pageantry ['pædʒəntri] *n* : pompa *f*, fausto *m*

pager ['peɪdʒər] *n* BEEPER : buscapersonas *m*

pagoda [pə'goːdə] *n* : pagoda *f*

paid → **pay**

pail ['peɪl] *n* : balde *m*, cubo *m*, cubeta *f Mex*

pailful ['peɪl,fʊl] *n* : balde *m*, cubo *m*, cubeta *f Mex*

pain[1] ['peɪn] *vt* : doler

pain[2] *n* **1** PENALTY : pena *f* ⟨under pain of death : so pena de muerte⟩ **2** SUFFERING : dolor *m*, malestar *m*, pena *f* (mental) **3 pains** *npl* EFFORT : esmero *m*, esfuerzo *m* ⟨to take pains : esmerarse⟩

painful ['peɪnfəl] *adj* : doloroso — **painfully** *adv*

painkiller ['peɪn,kɪlər] *n* : analgésico *m*

painless ['peɪnləs] *adj* : indoloro, sin dolor

painlessly ['peɪnləsli] *adv* : sin dolor

painstaking ['peɪn,steɪkɪŋ] *adj* : esmerado, cuidadoso, meticuloso — **painstakingly** *adv*

paint[1] ['peɪnt] *v* : pintar

paint[2] *n* : pintura *f*

paintbrush ['peɪnt,brʌʃ] *n* : pincel *m* (de un artista), brocha *f* (para pintar casas, etc.)

painter ['peɪntər] *n* : pintor *m*, -tora *f*

painting ['peɪntɪŋ] *n* : pintura *f*

pair[1] ['pær] *vt* : emparejar, poner en parejas — *vi* : emparejarse

pair[2] *n* : par *m* (de objetos), pareja *f* (de personas o animales) ⟨a pair of scissors : unas tijeras⟩

pajamas [pə'dʒɑməz, -'dʒæ-] *npl* : pijama *m*, piyama *mf*

Pakistani [,pæki'stæni, ,pɑki'stɑni] *n* : paquistaní *mf* — **Pakistani** *adj*

pal ['pæl] *n* : amigo *m*, -ga *f*; compinche *mf fam*; chamo *m*, -ma *f Ven fam*; cuate *m*, -ta *f Mex*

palace ['pæləs] *n* : palacio *m*

palatable ['pælətəbəl] *adj* : sabroso

palate ['pælət] *n* **1** : paladar *m* (de la boca) **2** TASTE : paladar *m*, gusto *m*

palatial [pə'leɪʃəl] *adj* : suntuoso, espléndido

palaver [pə'lævər, -'lɑ-] *n* : palabrería *f*

pale¹ ['peɪl] *v* **paled; paling** *vi* : palidecer — *vt* : hacer pálido

pale² *adj* **paler; palest 1** : pálido ⟨to turn pale : palidecer, ponerse pálido⟩ **2** : claro (dícese de los colores)

paleness ['peɪlnəs] *n* : palidez *f*

paleontologist [ˌpeɪliˌɑn'tɑlədʒɪst] *n* : paleontólogo *m*, -ga *f*

paleontology [ˌpeɪliˌɑn'tɑlədʒi] *n* : paleontología *f*

Palestinian [ˌpælə'stɪniən] *n* : palestino *m*, -na *f* — **Palestinian** *adj*

palette ['pælət] *n* : paleta *f* (para mezclar pigmentos)

palisade [ˌpælə'seɪd] *n* **1** FENCE : empalizada *f*, estacada *f* **2** CLIFFS : acantilado *m*

pall¹ ['pɔl] *vi* : perder su sabor, dejar de gustar

pall² *n* **1** : paño *m* mortuorio (sobre un ataúd) **2** COVER : cortina *f* (de humo, etc.) **3 to cast a pall over** : ensombrecer

pallbearer ['pɔlˌbɛrər] *n* : portador *m*, -dora *f* del féretro

pallet ['pælət] *n* **1** BED : camastro *m* **2** PLATFORM : plataforma *f* de carga

palliative ['pæliˌeɪtɪv, 'pæljətɪv] *adj* : paliativo

pallid ['pæləd] *adj* : pálido

pallor ['pælər] *n* : palidez *f*

palm¹ ['pɑm, 'pɑlm] *vt* **1** CONCEAL : escamotear (un naipe, etc.) **2 to palm off** : encajar, endilgar *fam* ⟨he palmed it off on me : me lo endilgó⟩

palm² *n* **1** *or* **palm tree** : palmera *f* **2** : palma *f* (de la mano)

Palm Sunday *n* : Domingo *m* de Ramos

palomino [ˌpælə'miːˌnoː] *n*, *pl* **-nos** : caballo *m* de color dorado

palpable ['pælpəbəl] *adj* : palpable — **palpably** [-bli] *adv*

palpitate ['pælpəˌteɪt] *vi* **-tated; -tating** : palpitar

palpitation [ˌpælpə'teɪʃən] *n* : palpitación *f*

palsy ['pɔlzi] *n*, *pl* **-sies 1** : parálisis *f* **2** → **cerebral palsy**

paltry ['pɔltri] *adj* **-trier; -est** : mísero, mezquino, insignificante ⟨a paltry excuse : una mala excusa⟩

pampas ['pæmpəz, 'pɑmpəs] *npl* : pampa *f*

pamper ['pæmpər] *vt* : mimar, consentir, chiquear *Mex*

pamphlet ['pæmpflət] *n* : panfleto *m*, folleto *m*

pan¹ ['pæn] *vt* **panned; panning** CRITICIZE : poner por los suelos — *vi* **to pan for gold** : cribar el oro con batea, lavar oro

pan² *n* **1** : cacerola *f*, cazuela *f* **2 frying pan** : sartén *mf*, freidera *f Mex*

panacea [ˌpænə'siːə] *n* : panacea *f*

Panamanian [ˌpænə'meɪniən] *n* : panameño *m*, -ña *f* — **Panamanian** *adj*

pancake ['pænˌkeɪk] *n* : panqueque *m*

pancreas ['pæŋkriəs, 'pæn-] *n* : páncreas *m*

panda ['pændə] *n* : panda *mf*

pandemonium [ˌpændə'moːniəm] *n* : pandemonio *m*, pandemónium *m*

pander ['pændər] *vi* **to pander to** : satisfacer, complacer (a alguien) ⟨to pander to popular taste : satisfacer el gusto popular⟩

pane ['peɪn] *n* : cristal *m*, vidrio *m*

panel¹ ['pænəl] *vt* **-eled** *or* **-elled; -eling** *or* **-elling** : adornar con paneles

panel² *n* **1** : lista *f* de nombres (de un jurado, etc.) **2** GROUP : panel *m*, grupo *m* ⟨discussion panel : panel de discusión⟩ **3** : panel *m* (de una pared, etc.) **4 instrument panel** : tablero *m* de instrumentos

paneling ['pænəlɪŋ] *n* : paneles *mpl*

pang ['pæŋ] *n* : puntada *f*, punzada *f*

panic¹ ['pænɪk] *v* **-icked; -icking** *vt* : llenar de pánico — *vi* : ser presa de pánico

panic² *n* : pánico *m*

panicky ['pænɪki] *adj* : presa de pánico

panorama [ˌpænə'ræmə, -'rɑ-] *n* : panorama *m*

panoramic [ˌpænə'ræmɪk, -'rɑ-] *adj* : panorámico

pansy ['pænzi] *n*, *pl* **-sies** : pensamiento *m*

pant¹ ['pænt] *vi* : jadear, resoplar

pant² *n* : jadeo *m*, resoplo *m*

pantaloons [ˌpæntə'luːnz] → **pants**

pantheon ['pænˌθiˌɑn, -ən] *n* : panteón *m*

panther ['pænθər] *n* : pantera *f*

panties ['pæntiz] *npl* : calzones *mpl*; pantaletas *fpl Mex*, *Ven*; bragas *fpl Spain*

pantomime¹ ['pæntəˌmaɪm] *v* **-mimed; -miming** *vt* : representar mediante la pantomima — *vi* : hacer la mímica

pantomime² *n* : pantomima *f*

pantry ['pæntri] *n*, *pl* **-tries** : despensa *f*

pants ['pænts] *npl* **1** TROUSERS : pantalón *m*, pantalones *mpl* **2** → **panties**

panty hose ['pænti] *ns & pl* : medias *fpl*, panties *mfpl*, pantimedias *fpl Mex*

pap ['pæp] *n* : papilla *f* (para bebés, etc.)

papa ['pɑpə] *n* : papá *m*

papal ['peɪpəl] *adj* : papal

papaya [pə'paɪə] *n* : papaya *f* (fruta)

paper¹ ['peɪpər] *vt* WALLPAPER : empapelar

paper² *adj* : de papel

paper³ *n* **1** : papel *m* ⟨a piece of paper : un papel⟩ **2** DOCUMENT : papel *m*, documento *m* **3** NEWSPAPER : periódico *m*, diario *m*

paperback ['peɪpərˌbæk] *n* : libro *m* en rústica

paper clip *n* : clip *m*, sujetapapeles *m*

paperweight ['peɪpərˌweɪt] *n* : pisapapeles *m*

paperwork ['peɪpər,wərk] *n* : papeleo *m*
papery ['peɪpəri] *adj* : parecido al papel
papier–mâché [,peɪpərmə'ʃeɪ, ,pæ-,pjeɪmæ'ʃeɪ] *n* : papel *m* maché
papoose [pæ'puːs, pə-] *n* : niño *m*, -ña *f* de los indios norteamericanos
paprika [pə'priːkə, pæ-] *n* : pimentón *m*, paprika *f*
papyrus [pə'paɪrəs] *n, pl* **-ruses** *or* **-ri** [-ri, -,raɪ] : papiro *m*
par ['par] *n* **1** VALUE : valor *m* (nominal), par *f* ⟨below par : debajo de la par⟩ **2** EQUALITY : igualdad *f* ⟨to be on a par with : estar al mismo nivel que⟩ **3** : par *m* (en golf)
parable ['pærəbəl] *n* : parábola *f*
parabola [pə'ræbələ] *n* : parábola *f* (en matemáticas)
parachute¹ ['pærə,ʃuːt] *vi* **-chuted; -chuting** : lanzarse en paracaídas
parachute² *n* : paracaídas *m*
parachutist ['pærə,ʃuːtɪst] *n* : paracaidista *mf*
parade¹ [pə'reɪd] *vi* **-raded; -rading 1** MARCH : desfilar **2** SHOW OFF : pavonearse, lucirse
parade² *n* **1** PROCESSION : desfile *m* **2** DISPLAY : alarde *m*
paradigm ['pærə,daɪm] *n* : paradigma *m*
paradise ['pærə,daɪs, -,daɪz] *n* : paraíso *m*
paradox ['pærə,dɑks] *n* : paradoja *f*
paradoxical [,pærə'dɑksɪkəl] *adj* : paradójico — **paradoxically** *adv*
paraffin ['pærəfən] *n* : parafina *f*
paragon ['pærə,gɑn, -gən] *n* : dechado *m*
paragraph¹ ['pærə,græf] *vt* : dividir en párrafos
paragraph² *n* : párrafo *m*, acápite *m*
Paraguayan [,pærə'gwaɪən, -'gweɪ-] *n* : paraguayo *m*, -ya *f* — **Paraguayan** *adj*
parakeet ['pærə,kiːt] *n* : periquito *m*
paralegal [,pærə'liːgəl] *n* : asistente *mf* de abogado
parallel¹ ['pærə,lɛl, -ləl] *vt* **1** MATCH, RESEMBLE : ser paralelo a, ser análogo a, corresponder con **2** : extenderse en línea paralela con ⟨the road parallels the river : el camino se extiende a lo largo del río⟩
parallel² *adj* : paralelo
parallel³ *n* **1** : línea *f* paralela, superficie *f* paralela **2** : paralelo *m* (en geografía) **3** SIMILARITY : paralelismo *m*, semejanza *f*
parallelogram [,pærə'lɛlə,græm] *n* : paralelogramo *m*
paralysis [pə'ræləsɪs] *n, pl* **-yses** [-,siːz] : parálisis *f*
paralyze ['pærə,laɪz] *vt* **-lyzed; -lyzing** : paralizar
parameter [pə'ræmətər] *n* : parámetro *m*
paramount ['pærə,maʊnt] *adj* : supremo ⟨of paramount importance : de suma importancia⟩
paranoia [,pærə'nɔɪə] *n* : paranoia *f*

paranoid ['pærə,nɔɪd] *adj* : paranoico
parapet ['pærəpət, -,pɛt] *n* : parapeto *m*
paraphernalia [,pærəfə'neɪljə, -fər-] *ns & pl* : parafernalia *f*
paraphrase¹ ['pærə,freɪz] *vt* **-phrased; -phrasing** : parafrasear
paraphrase² *n* : paráfrasis *f*
paraplegic¹ [,pærə'pliːdʒɪk] *adj* : parapléjico
paraplegic² *n* : parapléjico *m*, -ca *f*
parasite ['pærə,saɪt] *n* : parásito *m*
parasitic [,pærə'sɪtɪk] *adj* : parasitario
parasol ['pærə,sɔl] *n* : sombrilla *f*, quitasol *m*, parasol *m*
paratrooper ['pærə,truːpər] *n* : paracaidista *mf* (militar)
parboil ['par,bɔɪl] *vt* : sancochar, cocer a medias
parcel¹ ['parsəl] *vt* **-celed** *or* **-celled; -celing** *or* **-celling** *or* **to parcel out** : repartir, parcelar (tierras)
parcel² *n* **1** LOT : parcela *f*, lote *m* **2** PACKAGE : paquete *m*, bulto *m*
parch ['partʃ] *vt* : resecar
parchment ['partʃmənt] *n* : pergamino *m*
pardon¹ ['pardən] *vt* **1** FORGIVE : perdonar, disculpar ⟨pardon me! : ¡perdone!, ¡disculpe la molestia!⟩ **2** REPRIEVE : indultar (a un delincuente)
pardon² *n* **1** FORGIVENESS : perdón *m* **2** REPRIEVE : indulto *m*
pardonable ['pardənəbəl] *adj* : perdonable, disculpable
pare ['pær] *vt* **pared; paring 1** PEEL : pelar **2** TRIM : recortar **3** REDUCE : reducir ⟨he pared it (down) to 50 pages : lo redujo a 50 páginas⟩
parent ['pærənt] *n* **1** : madre *f*, padre *m* **2 parents** *npl* : padres *mpl*
parentage ['pærəntɪdʒ] *n* : linaje *m*, abolengo *m*, origen *m*
parental [pə'rɛntəl] *adj* : de los padres
parenthesis [pə'rɛnθəsɪs] *n, pl* **-theses** [-,siːz] : paréntesis *m*
parenthetic [,pærən'θɛtɪk] *or* **parenthetical** [-tɪkəl] *adj* : parentético — **parenthetically** [-tɪkli] *adv*
parenthood ['pærənt,hʊd] *n* : paternidad *f*
parfait [par'feɪ] *n* : postre *m* elaborado con frutas y helado
pariah [pə'raɪə] *n* : paria *mf*
parish ['pærɪʃ] *n* : parroquia *f*
parishioner [pə'rɪʃənər] *n* : feligrés *m*, -gresa *f*
parity ['pærəti] *n, pl* **-ties** : paridad *f*
park¹ ['park] *vt* : estacionar, parquear, aparcar *Spain* — *vi* : estacionarse, parquearse, aparcar *Spain*
park² *n* : parque *m*
parka ['parkə] *n* : parka *f*
parking ['parkɪŋ] *n* : estacionamiento *m*, aparcamiento *m* *Spain*
parkway ['park,weɪ] *n* : carretera *f* ajardinada, bulevar *m*
parley¹ ['parli] *vi* : parlamentar, negociar

parley² *n, pl* **-leys** : negociación *f*, parlamento *m*

parliament [ˈpɑrləmənt, ˈpɑrljə-] *n* : parlamento *m*

parliamentary [ˌpɑrləˈmɛntəri, ˌpɑrljə-] *adj* : parlamentario

parlor [ˈpɑrlər] *n* **1** : sala *f*, salón *m* (en una casa) **2** : salón *m* ⟨beauty parlor : salón de belleza⟩ **3 funeral parlor** : funeraria *f*

parochial [pəˈroːkiəl] *adj* **1** : parroquial **2** PROVINCIAL : pueblerino, de miras estrechas

parody¹ [ˈpærədi] *vt* **-died; -dying** : parodiar

parody² *n, pl* **-dies** : parodia *f*

parole [pəˈroːl] *n* : libertad *f* condicional

paroxysm [ˈpærəkˌsɪzəm, pəˈrɑk-] *n* : paroxismo *m*

parquet [ˈpɑrˌkeɪ, pɑrˈkeɪ] *n* : parquet *m*, parqué *m*

parrakeet → **parakeet**

parrot [ˈpærət] *n* : loro *m*, papagayo *m*

parry¹ [ˈpæri] *v* **-ried; -rying** *vi* : parar un golpe — *vt* EVADE : esquivar (una pregunta, etc.)

parry² *n, pl* **-ries** : parada *f*

parsimonious [ˌpɑrsəˈmoːniəs] *adj* : tacaño, mezquino

parsley [ˈpɑrsli] *n* : perejil *m*

parsnip [ˈpɑrsnɪp] *n* : chirivía *f*

parson [ˈpɑrsən] *n* : pastor *m*, -tora *f*; clérigo *m*

parsonage [ˈpɑrsənɪdʒ] *n* : rectoría *f*, casa *f* del párroco

part¹ [ˈpɑrt] *vi* **1** SEPARATE : separarse, despedirse ⟨we should part as friends : debemos separarnos amistosamente⟩ **2** OPEN : abrirse ⟨the curtains parted : las cortinas se abrieron⟩ **3 to part with** : deshacerse de — *vt* **1** SEPARATE : separar **2 to part one's hair** : hacerse la raya, peinarse con raya

part² *n* **1** SECTION, SEGMENT : parte *f*, sección *f* **2** PIECE : pieza *f* (de una máquina, etc.) **3** ROLE : papel *m* **4** : raya *f* (del pelo)

partake [pɑrˈteɪk, pər-] *vi* **-took** [-ˈtʊk]; **-taken** [-ˈteɪkən]; **-taking 1 to partake of** CONSUME : comer, beber, tomar **2 to partake in** : participar en (una actividad, etc.)

partial [ˈpɑrʃəl] *adj* **1** BIASED : parcial, tendencioso **2** INCOMPLETE : parcial, incompleto **3 to be partial to** : ser aficionado a

partiality [ˌpɑrʃiˈæləti] *n, pl* **-ties** : parcialidad *f*

partially [ˈpɑrʃəli] *adv* : parcialmente

participant [pərˈtɪsəpənt, pɑr-] *n* : participante *mf*

participate [pərˈtɪsəˌpeɪt, pɑr-] *vi* **-pated; -pating** : participar

participation [pərˌtɪsəˈpeɪʃən, pɑr-] *n* : participación *f*

participle [ˈpɑrtəˌsɪpəl] *n* : participio *m*

particle [ˈpɑrtɪkəl] *n* : partícula *f*

particular¹ [pərˈtɪkjələr] *adj* **1** SPECIFIC : particular, en particular ⟨this partic-ular person : esta persona en particular⟩ **2** SPECIAL : particular, especial ⟨with particular emphasis : con un énfasis especial⟩ **3** FUSSY : exigente, maniático ⟨to be very particular : ser muy especial⟩ ⟨I'm not particular : me da igual⟩

particular² *n* **1** DETAIL : detalle *m*, sentido *m* **2 in particular** : en particular, en especial

particularly [pərˈtɪkjələrli] *adv* **1** ESPECIALLY : particularmente, especialmente **2** SPECIFICALLY : específicamente, en especial

partisan [ˈpɑrtəzən, -sən] *n* **1** ADHERENT : partidario *m*, -ria *f* **2** GUERRILLA : partisano *m*, -na *f*; guerrillero *m*, -ra *f*

partition¹ [pərˈtɪʃən, pɑr-] *vt* : dividir ⟨to partition off (a room) : dividir (una habitación) con un tabique⟩

partition² *n* **1** DISTRIBUTION : partición *f*, división *f*, reparto *m* **2** DIVIDER : tabique *m*, mampara *f*, biombo *m*

partly [ˈpɑrtli] *adv* : en parte, parcialmente

partner [ˈpɑrtnər] *n* **1** COMPANION : compañero *m*, -ra *f* **2** : pareja *f* (en un juego, etc.) ⟨dancing partner : pareja de baile⟩ **3** SPOUSE : cónyuge *mf* **4** *or* **business partner** : socio *m*, -cia *f*; asociado *m*, -da *f*

partnership [ˈpɑrtnərˌʃɪp] *n* **1** ASSOCIATION : asociación *f*, compañerismo *m* **2** : sociedad *f* (de negociantes) ⟨to form a partnership : asociarse⟩

part of speech : categoría *f* gramatical

partridge [ˈpɑrtrɪdʒ] *n, pl* **-tridge** *or* **-tridges** : perdiz *f*

party [ˈpɑrti] *n, pl* **-ties 1** : partido *m* (político) **2** PARTICIPANT : parte *f*, participante *mf* **3** GROUP : grupo *m* (de personas) **4** GATHERING : fiesta *f* ⟨to throw a party : dar una fiesta⟩

parvenu [ˈpɑrvəˌnuː, -ˌnjuː] *n* : advenedizo *m*, -za *f*

pass¹ [ˈpæs] *vi* **1** : pasar, cruzarse ⟨a car passed by : pasó un coche⟩ ⟨we passed in the hallway : nos cruzamos en el pasillo⟩ **2** CEASE : pasarse ⟨the pain passed : se pasó el dolor⟩ **3** ELAPSE : pasar, transcurrir **4** PROCEED : pasar ⟨let me pass : déjame pasar⟩ **5** HAPPEN : pasar, ocurrir **6** : pasar, aprobar (en un examen) **7** RULE : fallar ⟨the jury passed on the case : el jurado falló en el caso⟩ **8** *or* **to pass down** : pasar ⟨the throne passed to his son : el trono pasó a su hijo⟩ **9 to let pass** OVERLOOK : pasar por alto **10 to pass as** : pasar por **11 to pass away** *or* **to pass on** DIE : fallecer, morir — *vt* **1** : pasar por ⟨they passed the house : pasaron por la casa⟩ **2** OVERTAKE : pasar, adelantar **3** SPEND : pasar (tiempo) **4** HAND : pasar ⟨pass me the salt : pásame la sal⟩ **5** : aprobar (un examen, una ley)

pass² *n* **1** CROSSING, GAP : paso *m*, desfiladero *m*, puerto *m* ⟨mountain pass : puerto de montaña⟩ **2** PERMIT : pase *m*, permiso *m* **3** : pase *m* (en deportes) **4** SITUATION : situación *f* ⟨things have come to a pretty pass! : ¡hasta dónde hemos llegado!⟩

passable ['pæsəbəl] *adj* **1** ADEQUATE : adecuado, pasable **2** : transitable (dícese de un camino, etc.)

passably ['pæsəbli] *adv* : pasablemente

passage ['pæsɪʤ] *n* **1** PASSING : paso *m* ⟨the passage of time : el paso del tiempo⟩ **2** PASSAGEWAY : pasillo *m* (dentro de un edificio), pasaje *m* (entre edificios) **3** VOYAGE : travesía *f* (por el mar), viaje *m* ⟨to grant safe passage : dar un salvoconducto⟩ **4** SECTION : pasaje *m* (en música o literatura)

passageway ['pæsɪʤˌweɪ] *n* : pasillo *m*, pasadizo *m*, corredor *m*

passbook ['pæsˌbʊk] *n* BANKBOOK : libreta *f* de ahorros

passé [pæ'seɪ] *adj* : pasado de moda

passenger ['pæsənʤər] *n* : pasajero *m*, -ra *f*

passerby [ˌpæsər'baɪ, 'pæsərˌ-] *n, pl* **passersby** : transeúnte *mf*

passing ['pæsɪŋ] *n* DEATH : fallecimiento *m*

passion ['pæʃən] *n* : pasión *f*, ardor *m*

passionate ['pæʃənət] *adj* **1** IRASCIBLE : irascible, iracundo **2** ARDENT : apasionado, ardiente, ferviente, fogoso

passionately ['pæʃənətli] *adv* : apasionadamente, fervientemente, con pasión

passive¹ ['pæsɪv] *adj* : pasivo — **passively** *adv*

passive² *n* : voz *f* pasiva (en gramática)

passivity [pæ'sɪvəti] *n* : pasividad *f*

Passover ['pæsˌoːvər] *n* : Pascua *f* (en el judaísmo)

passport ['pæsˌport] *n* : pasaporte *m*

password ['pæsˌwərd] *n* : contraseña *f*

past¹ ['pæst] *adv* : por delante ⟨he drove past : pasamos en coche⟩

past² *adj* **1** AGO : hace ⟨10 years past : hace 10 años⟩ **2** LAST : último ⟨the past few months : los últimos meses⟩ **3** BYGONE : pasado ⟨in past times : en tiempos pasados⟩ **4** : pasado (en gramática)

past³ *n* : pasado *m*

past⁴ *prep* **1** BY : por, por delante de ⟨he ran past the house : pasó por la casa corriendo⟩ **2** BEYOND : más allá de ⟨just past the corner : un poco más allá de la esquina⟩ ⟨we went past the exit : pasamos la salida⟩ **3** AFTER : después de ⟨past noon : después del mediodía⟩ ⟨half past two : las dos y media⟩

pasta ['pɑstə, 'pæs-] *n* : pasta *f*

paste¹ ['peɪst] *vt* **pasted; pasting** : pegar (con engrudo)

paste² *n* **1** : pasta *f* ⟨tomato paste : pasta de tomate⟩ **2** : engrudo *m* (para pegar)

pasteboard ['peɪstˌbord] *n* : cartón *m*, cartulina *f*

pastel [pæ'stɛl] *n* : pastel *m* — **pastel** *adj*

pasteurization [ˌpæsʧərə'zeɪʃən, ˌpæstjə-] *n* : pasteurización *f*

pasteurize ['pæsʧəˌraɪz, 'pæstjə-] *vt* **-ized; -izing** : pasteurizar

pastime ['pæsˌtaɪm] *n* : pasatiempo *m*

pastor ['pæstər] *n* : pastor *m*, -tora *f*

pastoral ['pæstərəl] *adj* : pastoral

past participle *n* : participio *m* pasado

pastry ['peɪstri] *n, pl* **-ries** **1** DOUGH : pasta *f*, masa *f* **2** **pastries** *npl* : pasteles *mpl*

pasture¹ ['pæsʧər] *v* **-tured; -turing** *vi* GRAZE : pacer, pastar — *vt* : apacentar, pastar

pasture² *n* : pastizal *m*, potrero *m*, pasto *m*

pasty ['peɪsti] *adj* **pastier; -est** **1** : pastoso (en consistencia) **2** PALLID : pálido

pat¹ ['pæt] *vt* **patted; patting** : dar palmaditas a, tocar

pat² *adv* : de memoria ⟨to have down pat : saberse de memoria⟩

pat³ *adj* **1** APT : apto, apropiado **2** GLIB : fácil **3** UNYIELDING : firme ⟨to stand pat : mantenerse firme⟩

pat⁴ *n* **1** TAP : golpecito *m*, palmadita *f* ⟨a pat on the back : una palmadita en la espalda⟩ **2** CARESS : caricia *f* **3** : porción *f* ⟨a pat of butter : una porción de mantequilla⟩

patch¹ ['pæʧ] *vt* **1** MEND, REPAIR : remendar, parchar, ponerle un parche a **2 to patch together** IMPROVISE : confeccionar, improvisar **3 to patch up** : arreglar ⟨they patched things up : hicieron las paces⟩

patch² *n* **1** : parche *m*, remiendo *m* (para la ropa) ⟨eye patch : parche para el ojo⟩ **2** PIECE : mancha *f*, trozo *m* ⟨a patch of sky : un trozo de cielo⟩ **3** PLOT : parcela *f*, terreno *m* ⟨cabbage patch : parcela de repollos⟩

patchwork ['pæʧˌwərk] *n* : labor *f* de retazos

patchy ['pæʧi] *adj* **patchier; -est** **1** IRREGULAR : irregular, desigual **2** INCOMPLETE : parcial, incompleto

patent¹ ['pætənt] *vt* : patentar

patent² ['pætənt, 'peɪt-] *adj* **1** OBVIOUS : patente, evidente **2** ['pæt-] PATENTED : patentado

patent³ ['pætənt] *n* : patente *f*

patently ['pætəntli] *adv* : patentemente, evidentemente

paternal [pə'tərnəl] *adj* **1** FATHERLY : paternal **2** : paterno ⟨paternal grandfather : abuelo paterno⟩

paternity [pə'tərnəti] *n* : paternidad *f*

path ['pæθ, 'pɑθ] *n* **1** TRACK, TRAIL : camino *m*, sendero *m*, senda *f* **2** COURSE, ROUTE : recorrido *m*, trayecto *m*, trayectoria *f*

pathetic [pə'θɛtɪk] *adj* : patético — **pathetically** [-tɪkli] *adv*

pathological [ˌpæθə'lɑʤɪkəl] *adj* : patológico

pathologist [pə'θalədʒɪst] *n* : patólogo *m*, -ga *f*

pathology [pə'θalədʒi] *n, pl* **-gies** : patología *f*

pathos ['peɪˌθɑs, 'pæ-, -ˌθɔs] *n* : patetismo *m*

pathway ['pæθˌweɪ] *n* : camino *m*, sendero *m*, senda *f*, vereda *f*

patience ['peɪʃənts] *n* : paciencia *f*

patient¹ ['peɪʃənt] *adj* : paciente — **patiently** *adv*

patient² *n* : paciente *mf*

patio ['pætiˌoː] *n, pl* **-tios** : patio *m*

patriarch ['peɪtriˌɑrk] *n* : patriarca *m*

patriarchy ['peɪtriˌɑrki] *n, pl* **-chies** : patriarcado *m*

patrimony ['pætrəˌmoːni] *n, pl* **-nies** : patrimonio *m*

patriot ['peɪtriət] *n* : patriota *mf*

patriotic [ˌpeɪtri'ɑtɪk] *adj* : patriótico — **patriotically** *adv*

patriotism ['peɪtriəˌtɪzəm] *n* : patriotismo *m*

patrol¹ [pə'troːl] *v* **-trolled; -trolling** : patrullar

patrol² *n* : patrulla *f*

patrolman [pə'troːlmən] *n, pl* **-men** [-mən, -ˌmɛn] : policía *mf*, guardia *mf*

patron ['peɪtrən] *n* **1** SPONSOR : patrocinador *m*, -dora *f* **2** CUSTOMER : cliente *m*, -ta *f* **3** *or* **patron saint** : patrono *m*, -na *f*

patronage ['peɪtrənɪdʒ, 'pæ-] *n* **1** SPONSORSHIP : patrocinio *m* **2** CLIENTELE : clientela *f* **3** : influencia *f* (política)

patronize ['peɪtrəˌnaɪz, 'pæ-] *vt* **-ized; -izing** **1** SPONSOR : patrocinar **2** : ser cliente de (un negocio) **3** : tratar con condescendencia

patter¹ ['pætər] *vi* **1** TAP : golpetear, tamborilear (dícese de la lluvia) **2 to patter about** : corretear (con pasos ligeros)

patter² *n* **1** TAPPING : golpeteo *m*, tamborileo *m* (de la lluvia), correteo *m* (de pies) **2** CHATTER : palabrería *f*, parloteo *m fam*

pattern¹ ['pætərn] *vt* **1** BASE : basar (en un modelo) **2 to pattern after** : hacer imitación de

pattern² *n* **1** MODEL : modelo *m*, patrón *m* (de costura) **2** DESIGN : diseño *m*, dibujo *m*, estampado *m* (de tela) **3** NORM, STANDARD : pauta *f*, norma *f*, patrón *m*

patty ['pæti] *n, pl* **-ties** : porción *f* de carne picada (u otro alimento) en forma de ruedita ⟨a hamburger patty : una hamburguesa⟩

paucity ['pɔsəti] *n* : escasez *f*

paunch ['pɔntʃ] *n* : panza *f*, barriga *f*

pauper ['pɔpər] *n* : pobre *mf*, indigente *mf*

pause¹ ['pɔz] *vi* **paused; pausing** : hacer una pausa, pararse (brevemente)

pause² *n* : pausa *f*

pave ['peɪv] *vt* **paved; paving** : pavimentar ⟨to pave with stones : empedrar⟩

pavement ['peɪvmənt] *n* : pavimento *m*, empedrado *m*

pavilion [pə'vɪljən] *n* : pabellón *m*

paving ['peɪvɪŋ] → **pavement**

paw¹ ['pɔ] *vt* : tocar, manosear, sobar

paw² *n* : pata *f*, garra *f*, zarpa *f*

pawn¹ ['pɔn] *vt* : empeñar, prendar

pawn² *n* **1** PLEDGE, SECURITY : prenda *f* **2** PAWNING : empeño *m* **3** : peón *m* (en ajedrez)

pawnbroker ['pɔnˌbroːkər] *n* : prestamista *mf*

pawnshop ['pɔnˌʃɑp] *n* : casa *f* de empeños, monte *m* de piedad

pay¹ ['peɪ] *v* **paid** ['peɪd]; **paying** *vt* **1** : pagar (una cuenta, a un empleado, etc.) **2 to pay attention** : poner atención, prestar atención, hacer caso **3 to pay back** : pagar, devolver ⟨she paid them back : les devolvió el dinero⟩ ⟨I'll pay you back for what you did! : ¡me las pagarás!⟩ **4 to pay off** SETTLE : saldar, cancelar (una deuda, etc.) **5 to pay one's respects** : presentar uno sus respetos **6 to pay a visit** : hacer una visita — *vi* : valer la pena ⟨crime doesn't pay : no hay crimen sin castigo⟩

pay² *n* : paga *f*

payable ['peɪəbəl] *adj* DUE : pagadero

paycheck ['peɪˌtʃɛk] *n* : sueldo *m*, cheque *m* del sueldo

payee [peɪ'iː] *n* : beneficiario *m*, -ria *f* (de un cheque, etc.)

payment ['peɪmənt] *n* **1** : pago *m* **2** INSTALLMENT : plazo *m*, cuota *f* **3** REWARD : recompensa *f*

payoff ['peɪˌɔf] *n* **1** REWARD : recompensa *f* **2** PROFIT : ganancia *f* **3** BRIBE : soborno *m*

payroll ['peɪˌroːl] *n* : nómina *f*

PC [ˌpiː'siː] *n, pl* **PCs** *or* **PC's** : PC *mf*, computadora *f* personal

pea ['piː] *n* : chícharo *m*, guisante *m*, arveja *f*

peace ['piːs] *n* **1** : paz *f* ⟨peace treaty : tratado de paz⟩ ⟨peace and tranquility : paz y tranquilidad⟩ **2** ORDER : orden *m* (público)

peaceable ['piːsəbəl] *adj* : pacífico — **peaceably** [-bli] *adv*

peaceful ['piːsfəl] *adj* **1** PEACEABLE : pacífico **2** CALM, QUIET : tranquilo, sosegado — **peacefully** *adv*

peacemaker ['piːsˌmeɪkər] *n* : conciliador *m*, -dora *f*; mediador *m*, -dora *f*

peach ['piːtʃ] *n* : durazno *m*, melocotón *m*

peacock ['piːˌkɑk] *n* : pavo *m* real

peak¹ ['piːk] *vi* : alcanzar su nivel máximo

peak² *adj* : máximo

peak³ *n* **1** POINT : punta *f* **2** CREST, SUMMIT : cima *f*, cumbre *f* **3** APEX : cúspide *f*, apogeo *m*, nivel *m* máximo

peaked ['piːkəd] *adj* SICKLY : pálido

peal¹ ['piːl] *vi* : repicar

peal² *n* : repique *m*, tañido *m* (de campanada) ⟨peals of laughter : carcajadas⟩

peanut ['pi:ˌnʌt] *n* : maní *m*, cacahuate *m Mex*, cacahuete *m Spain*

pear ['pær] *n* : pera *f*

pearl ['pərl] *n* : perla *f*

pearly ['pərli] *adj* **pearlier; -est** : nacarado

peasant ['pɛzənt] *n* : campesino *m*, -na *f*

peat ['pi:t] *n* : turba *f*

pebble ['pɛbəl] *n* : guijarro *m*, piedrecita *f*, piedrita *f*

pecan [pɪ'kɑn, -'kæn, 'pi:ˌkæn] *n* : pacana *f*, nuez *f Mex*

peccadillo [ˌpɛkə'dɪlo] *n, pl* **-loes** *or* **-los** : pecadillo *m*

peccary ['pɛkəri] *n, pl* **-ries** : pécari *m*, pecarí *m*

peck¹ ['pɛk] *vt* : picar, picotear

peck² *n* **1** : medida *f* de áridos equivalente a 8.810 litros **2** : picotazo *m* (de un pájaro) ⟨a peck on the cheek : un besito en la mejilla⟩

pectoral ['pɛktərəl] *adj* : pectoral

peculiar [pɪ'kju:ljər] *adj* **1** DISTINCTIVE : propio, peculiar, característico ⟨peculiar to this area : propio de esta zona⟩ **2** STRANGE : extraño, raro — **peculiarly** *adv*

peculiarity [pɪˌkju:li'ærəti, -ˌkju:li'ær-] *n, pl* **-ties** **1** DISTINCTIVENESS : peculiaridad *f* **2** ODDITY, QUIRK : rareza *f*, idiosincrasia *f*, excentricidad *f*

pecuniary [pɪ'kju:niˌɛri] *adj* : pecuniario

pedagogical [ˌpɛdə'gɑdʒɪkəl, -'go:-] *adj* : pedagógico

pedagogy ['pɛdəˌgo:dʒi, -ˌgɑ-] *n* : pedagogía *f*

pedal¹ ['pɛdəl] *v* **-aled** *or* **-alled; -aling** *or* **-alling** *vi* : pedalear — *vt* : darle a los pedales de

pedal² *n* : pedal *m*

pedant ['pɛdənt] *n* : pedante *mf*

pedantic [pɪ'dæntɪk] *adj* : pedante

pedantry ['pɛdəntri] *n, pl* **-ries** : pedantería *f*

peddle ['pɛdəl] *vt* **-dled; -dling** : vender (en las calles)

peddler ['pɛdlər] *n* : vendedor *m*, -dora *f* ambulante; mercachifle *m*

pedestal ['pɛdəstəl] *n* : pedestal *m*

pedestrian¹ [pə'dɛstriən] *adj* **1** COMMONPLACE : pedestre, ordinario **2** : de peatón, peatonal ⟨pedestrian crossing : paso de peatones⟩

pedestrian² *n* : peatón *m*, -tona *f*

pediatric [ˌpi:di'ætrɪk] *adj* : pediátrico

pediatrician [ˌpi:diə'trɪʃən] *n* : pediatra *mf*

pediatrics [ˌpi:di'ætrɪks] *ns & pl* : pediatría *f*

pedigree ['pɛdəˌgri:] *n* **1** FAMILY TREE : árbol *m* genealógico **2** LINEAGE : pedigrí *m* (de un animal), linaje *m* (de una persona)

peek¹ ['pi:k] *vi* **1** PEEP : espiar, mirar furtivamente **2** GLANCE : echar un vistazo

peek² *n* **1** : miradita *f* (furtiva) **2** GLANCE : vistazo *m*, ojeada *f*

peel¹ ['pi:l] *vt* **1** : pelar (fruta, etc.) **2** *or* **to peel away** : quitar — *vi* : pelarse (dícese de la piel), desconcharse (dícese de la pintura)

peel² *n* : cáscara *f*

peep¹ ['pi:p] *vi* **1** PEEK : espiar, mirar furtivamente **2** CHEEP : piar **3 to peep out** SHOW : asomarse

peep² *n* **1** CHEEP : pío *m* (de un pajarito) **2** GLANCE : vistazo *m*, ojeada *f*

peer¹ ['pɪr] *vi* : mirar detenidamente, mirar con atención

peer² *n* **1** EQUAL : par *m*, igual *mf* **2** NOBLE : noble *mf*

peerage ['pɪrɪdʒ] *n* : nobleza *f*

peerless ['pɪrləs] *adj* : sin par, incomparable

peeve¹ ['pi:v] *vt* **peeved; peeving** : fastidiar, irritar, molestar

peeve² *n* : queja *f*

peevish ['pi:vɪʃ] *adj* : quejoso, fastidioso — **peevishly** *adv*

peevishness ['pi:vɪʃnəs] *n* : irritabilidad *f*

peg¹ ['pɛg] *vt* **pegged; pegging** **1** PLUG : tapar (con una clavija) **2** FASTEN, FIX : sujetar (con estaquillas) **3 to peg out** MARK : marcar (con estaquillas)

peg² *n* : estaquilla *f* (para clavar), clavija *f* (para tapar)

pejorative [pɪ'dʒɔrətɪv] *adj* : peyorativo — **pejoratively** *adv*

pelican ['pɛlɪkən] *n* : pelícano *m*

pellagra [pə'lægrə, -'leɪ-] *n* : pelagra *f*

pellet ['pɛlət] *n* **1** BALL : bolita *f* ⟨food pellet : bolita de comida⟩ **2** SHOT : perdigón *m*

pell-mell ['pɛl'mɛl] *adv* : desordenadamente, atropelladamente

pelt¹ ['pɛlt] *vt* **1** THROW : lanzar, tirar (algo a alguien) **2 to pelt with stones** : apedrear — *vi* BEAT : golpear con fuerza ⟨the rain was pelting down : llovía a cántaros⟩

pelt² *n* : piel *f*, pellejo *m*

pelvic ['pɛlvɪk] *adj* : pélvico

pelvis ['pɛlvɪs] *n, pl* **-vises** *or* **-ves** ['pɛlˌvi:z] : pelvis *f*

pen¹ ['pɛn] *vt* **penned; penning** **1** *or* **pen in** : encerrar (animales) **2** WRITE : escribir

pen² *n* **1** CORRAL : corral *m*, redil *m* (para ovejas) **2** : pluma *f* ⟨fountain pen : pluma fuente⟩ ⟨ballpoint pen : bolígrafo⟩

penal ['pi:nəl] *adj* : penal

penalize ['pi:nəlˌaɪz, 'pɛn-] *vt* **-ized; -izing** : penalizar, sancionar, penar

penalty ['pɛnəlti] *n, pl* **-ties** **1** PUNISHMENT : pena *f*, castigo *m* **2** DISADVANTAGE : desventaja *f*, castigo *m*, penalty *m* (en deportes) **3** FINE : multa *f*

penance ['pɛnənts] *n* : penitencia *f*

pence → penny

penchant ['pɛntʃənt] *n* : inclinación *f*, afición *f*

pencil¹ ['pɛntsəl] *vt* **-ciled** *or* **-cilled; -cil-ing** *or* **-cilling** : escribir con lápiz, dibujar con lápiz
pencil² *n* : lápiz *m*
pendant ['pɛndənt] *n* : colgante *m*
pending¹ ['pɛndɪŋ] *adj* : pendiente
pending² *prep* **1** DURING : durante **2** AWAITING : en espera de
pendulum ['pɛndʒələm, -djʊləm] *n* : péndulo *m*
penetrate ['pɛnə,treɪt] *vt* **-trated; -trating** : penetrar
penetrating ['pɛnə,treɪtɪŋ] *adj* : penetrante, cortante
penetration [,pɛnə'treɪʃən] *n* : penetración *f*
penguin ['pɛŋgwɪn, 'pɛn-] *n* : pingüino *m*
penicillin [,pɛnə'sɪlən] *n* : penicilina *f*
peninsula [pə'nɪntsələ, -'nɪntʃʊlə] *n* : península *f*
penis ['pi:nəs] *n, pl* **-nes** [-,ni:z] *or* **-nis-es** : pene *m*
penitence ['pɛnətənts] *n* : arrepentimiento *m*, penitencia *f*
penitent¹ ['pɛnətənt] *adj* : arrepentido, penitente
penitent² *n* : penitente *mf*
penitentiary [,pɛnə'tɛntʃəri] *n, pl* **-ries** : penitenciaría *f*, prisión *m*, presidio *m*
penmanship ['pɛnmən,ʃɪp] *n* : escritura *f*, caligrafía *f*
pen name *n* : seudónimo *m*
pennant ['pɛnənt] *n* : gallardete *m* (de un barco), banderín *m*
penniless ['pɛniləs] *adj* : sin un centavo
penny ['pɛni] *n, pl* **-nies** *or* **pence** ['pɛnts] **1** : penique *m* (del Reino Unido) **2** *pl* **-nies** CENT : centavo *m* (de los Estados Unidos)
pension¹ ['pɛntʃən] *vt or* **to pension off** : jubilar
pension² *n* : pensión *m*, jubilación *f*
pensive ['pɛntsɪv] *adj* : pensativo, meditabundo — **pensively** *adv*
pent ['pɛnt] *adj* : encerrado ⟨pent-up feelings : emociones reprimidas⟩
pentagon ['pɛntə,gɑn] *n* : pentágono *m*
pentagonal [pɛn'tægənəl] *adj* : pentagonal
penthouse ['pɛnt,haʊs] *n* : ático *m*, penthouse *m*
penultimate [pɪ'nʌltəmət] *adj* : penúltimo
penury ['pɛnjəri] *n* : penuria *f*, miseria *f*
peon ['pi:,ɑn, -ən] *n, pl* **-ons** *or* **-ones** [per'o:ni:z] : peón *m*
peony ['pi:əni] *n, pl* **-nies** : peonía *f*
people¹ ['pi:pəl] *vt* **-pled; -pling** : poblar
people² *ns & pl* **1** : people *npl* : gente *f*, personas *fpl* ⟨people like him : él le cae bien a la gente⟩ ⟨many people : mucha gente, muchas personas⟩ **2** *pl* **peoples** : pueblo *m* ⟨the Cuban people : el pueblo cubano⟩
pep¹ ['pɛp] *vt* **pepped; pepping** *or* **to pep up** : animar
pep² *n* : energía *f*, vigor *m*

pepper¹ ['pɛpər] *vt* **1** : añadir pimienta a **2** RIDDLE : acribillar (a balazos) **3** SPRINKLE : salpicar ⟨peppered with quotations : salpicado de citas⟩
pepper² *n* **1** : pimienta *f* (condimento) **2** : pimiento *m*, pimentón *m* (fruta) **3** → chili
peppermint ['pɛpər,mɪnt] *n* : menta *f*
peppery ['pɛpəri] *adj* : picante
peppy ['pɛpi] *adj* **peppier; -est** : lleno de energía, vivaz
peptic ['pɛptɪk] *adj* **peptic ulcer** : úlcera *f* estomacal
per ['pər] *prep* **1** : por ⟨miles per hour : millas por hora⟩ **2** ACCORDING TO : según ⟨per his specifications : según sus especificaciones⟩
per annum [pər'ænəm] *adv* : al año, por año
percale [,pər'keɪl, 'pər-,; ,pər'kæl] *n* : percal *m*
per capita [pər'kæpɪtə] *adv & adj* : per cápita
perceive [pər'si:v] *vt* **-ceived; -ceiving 1** REALIZE : percatarse de, concientizarse de, darse cuenta de **2** NOTE : percibir, notar
percent¹ [pər'sɛnt] *adv* : por ciento
percent² *n, pl* **-cent** *or* **-cents 1** : por ciento ⟨10 percent of the population : el 10 por ciento de la población⟩ **2** → percentage
percentage [pər'sɛntɪdʒ] *n* : porcentaje *m*
perceptible [pər'sɛptəbəl] *adj* : perceptible — **perceptibly** [-bli] *adv*
perception [pər'sɛpʃən] *n* **1** : percepción *f* ⟨color perception : la percepción de los colores⟩ **2** INSIGHT : perspicacia *f* **3** IDEA : idea *f*, imagen *f*
perceptive [pər'sɛptɪv] *adj* : perspicaz
perceptively [pər'sɛptɪvli] *adv* : con perspicacia
perch¹ ['pərtʃ] *vi* **1** ROOST : posarse **2** SIT : sentarse (en un sitio elevado) — *vt* PLACE : posar, colocar
perch² *n* **1** ROOST : percha *f* (para los pájaros) **2** *pl* **perch** *or* **perches** : perca *f* (pez)
percolate ['pərkə,leɪt] *vi* **-lated; -lating** : colarse, filtrarse ⟨percolated coffee : café filtrado⟩
percolator ['pərkə,leɪtər] *n* : cafetera *f* de filtro
percussion [pər'kʌʃən] *n* **1** STRIKING : percusión *f* **2** *or* **percussion instruments** : instrumentos *mpl* de percusión
peremptory [pə'rɛmptəri] *adj* : perentorio
perennial¹ [pə'rɛniəl] *adj* **1** : perenne, vivaz ⟨perennial flowers : flores perennes⟩ **2** RECURRENT : perenne, continuo ⟨a perennial problem : un problema eterno⟩
perennial² *n* : planta *f* perenne, planta *f* vivaz
perfect¹ [pər'fɛkt] *vt* : perfeccionar

perfect² ['pərfɪkt] *adj* : perfecto — **perfectly** *adv*
perfection [pər'fɛkʃən] *n* : perfección *f*
perfectionist [pər'fɛkʃənɪst] *n* : perfeccionista *mf*
perfidious [pər'fɪdiəs] *adj* : pérfido
perforate ['pərfə,reɪt] *vt* -**rated**; -**rating** : perforar
perforation [,pərfə'reɪʃən] *n* : perforación *f*
perform [pər'fɔrm] *vt* **1** CARRY OUT : realizar, hacer, desempeñar **2** PRESENT : representar, dar (una obra teatral, etc.) — *vi* : actuar (en una obra teatral), cantar (en una ópera, etc.), tocar (en un concierto, etc.), bailar (en un ballet, etc.)
performance [pər'fɔrmənts] *n* **1** EXECUTION : ejecución *f*, realización *f*, desempeño *m*, rendimiento *m* **2** INTERPRETATION : interpretación *f* ⟨his performance of Hamlet : su interpretación de Hamlet⟩ **3** PRESENTATION : representación *f* (de una obra teatral), función *f*
performer [pər'fɔrmər] *n* : artista *mf*; actor *m*, -triz *f*; intérprete *mf* (de música)
perfume¹ [pər'fju:m, 'pər,-] *vt* -**fumed**; -**fuming** : perfumar
perfume² ['pər,fju:m, pər'-] *n* : perfume *m*
perfunctory [pər'fʌŋktəri] *adj* : mecánico, superficial, somero
perhaps [pər'hæps] *adv* : tal vez, quizá, quizás
peril ['pɛrəl] *n* : peligro *m*
perilous ['pɛrələs] *adj* : peligroso — **perilously** *adv*
perimeter [pə'rɪmətər] *n* : perímetro *m*
period ['pɪriəd] *n* **1** : punto *m* (en puntuación) **2** : período *m* ⟨a two-hour period : un período de dos horas⟩ **3** STAGE : época *f* (histórica), fase *f*, etapa *f*
periodic [,pɪri'ɑdɪk] *or* **periodical** [-dɪkəl] *adj* : periódico — **periodically** [-dɪkli] *adv*
periodical [,pɪri'ɑdɪkəl] *n* : publicación *f* periódica, revista *f*
peripheral [pə'rɪfərəl] *adj* : periférico
periphery [pə'rɪfəri] *n*, *pl* -**eries** : periferia *f*
periscope ['pɛrə,sko:p] *n* : periscopio *m*
perish ['pɛrɪʃ] *vi* DIE : perecer, morirse
perishable¹ ['pɛrɪʃəbəl] *adj* : perecedero
perishable² *n* : producto *m* perecedero
perjure ['pərdʒər] *vt* -**jured**; -**juring** (*used in law*) **to perjure oneself** : perjurar, perjurarse
perjury ['pərdʒəri] *n* : perjurio *m*
perk¹ ['pərk] *vt* **1** : levantar (las orejas, etc.) **2** *or* **to perk up** FRESHEN : arreglar — *vi* **to perk up** : animarse, reanimarse
perk² *n* : extra *m*
perky ['pərki] *adj* **perkier**; -**est** : animado, alegre, lleno de vida
permanence ['pərmənənts] *n* : permanencia *f*

permanent¹ ['pərmənənt] *adj* : permanente — **permanently** *adv*
permanent² *n* : permanente *f*
permeability [,pərmiə'bɪləti] *n* : permeabilidad *f*
permeable ['pərmiəbəl] *adj* : permeable
permeate ['pərmi,eɪt] *v* -**ated**; -**ating** *vt* **1** PENETRATE : penetrar, impregnar **2** PERVADE : penetrar, difundirse por — *vi* : penetrar
permissible [pər'mɪsəbəl] *adj* : permisible, lícito
permission [pər'mɪʃən] *n* : permiso *m*
permissive [pər'mɪsɪv] *adj* : permisivo
permit¹ [pər'mɪt] *vt* -**mitted**; -**mitting** : permitir, dejar ⟨weather permitting : si el tiempo lo permite⟩
permit² ['pər,mɪt, pər'-] *n* : permiso *m*, licencia *f*
pernicious [pər'nɪʃəs] *adj* : pernicioso
peroxide [pə'rɑk,saɪd] *n* **1** : peróxido *m* **2** → **hydrogen peroxide**
perpendicular¹ [,pərpən'dɪkjələr] *adj* **1** VERTICAL : vertical **2** : perpendicular ⟨perpendicular lines : líneas perpendiculares⟩ — **perpendicularly** *adv*
perpendicular² *n* : perpendicular *f*
perpetrate ['pərpə,treɪt] *vt* -**trated**; -**trating** : perpetrar, cometer (un delito)
perpetrator ['pərpə,treɪtər] *n* : autor *m*, -tora *f* (de un delito)
perpetual [pər'pɛtʃuəl] *adj* **1** EVERLASTING : perpetuo, eterno **2** CONTINUAL : perpetuo, continuo, constante
perpetually [pər'pɛtʃuəli, -tʃəli] *adv* : para siempre, eternamente
perpetuate [pər'pɛtʃu,eɪt] *vt* -**ated**; -**ating** : perpetuar
perpetuity [,pərpə'tu:əti, -'tju:-] *n*, *pl* -**ties** : perpetuidad *f*
perplex [pər'plɛks] *vt* : dejar perplejo, confundir
perplexed [pər'plɛkst] *adj* : perplejo
perplexity [pər'plɛksəti] *n*, *pl* -**ties** : perplejidad *f*, confusión *f*
persecute ['pərsɪ,kju:t] *vt* -**cuted**; -**cuting** : perseguir
persecution [,pərsɪ'kju:ʃən] *n* : persecución *f*
perseverance [,pərsə'vɪrənts] *n* : perseverancia *f*
persevere [,pərsə'vɪr] *vi* -**vered**; -**vering** : perseverar
Persian ['pərʒən] *n* **1** : persa *mf* **2** : persa *m* (idioma) — **Persian** *adj*
persist [pər'sɪst] *vi* : persistir
persistence [pər'sɪstənts] *n* **1** CONTINUATION : persistencia *f* **2** TENACITY : perseverancia *f*, tenacidad *f*
persistent [pər'sɪstənt] *adj* : persistente — **persistently** *adv*
person ['pərsən] *n* **1** HUMAN, INDIVIDUAL : persona *f*, individuo *m*, ser *m* humano **2** : persona *f* (en gramática) **3** **in person** : en persona
personable ['pərsənəbəl] *adj* : agradable

personage [ˈpərsənɪʤ] *n* : personaje *m*
personal [ˈpərsənəl] *adj* **1** OWN, PRIVATE : personal, particular, privado ⟨for personal reasons : por razones personales⟩ **2** : en persona ⟨to make a personal appearance : presentarse en persona, hacerse acto de presencia⟩ **3** : íntimo, personal ⟨personal hygiene : higiene personal⟩ **4** INDISCREET, PRYING : indiscreto, personal
personal computer *n* : computadora *f* personal, ordenador *m* personal *Spain*
personal digital assistant *n* : asistente *m* personal digital
personality [ˌpərsənˈælət̬i] *n*, *pl* **-ties 1** DISPOSITION : personalidad *f*, temperamento *m* **2** CELEBRITY : personalidad *f*, personaje *m*, celebridad *f*
personalize [ˈpərsənəˌlaɪz] *vt* **-ized; -izing** : personalizar
personally [ˈpərsənəli] *adv* **1** : personalmente, en persona ⟨I'll do it personally : lo haré personalmente⟩ **2** : como persona ⟨personally she's very amiable : como persona es muy amable⟩ **3** : personalmente ⟨personally, I don't believe it : yo, personalmente, no me lo creo⟩
personification [pərˌsɑnəfəˈkeɪʃən] *n* : personificación *f*
personify [pərˈsɑnəˌfaɪ] *vt* **-fied; -fying** : personificar
personnel [ˌpərsənˈɛl] *n* : personal *m*
perspective [pərˈspɛktɪv] *n* : perspectiva *f*
perspicacious [ˌpərspəˈkeɪʃəs] *adj* : perspicaz
perspiration [ˌpərspəˈreɪʃən] *n* : transpiración *f*, sudor *m*
perspire [pərˈspaɪr] *vi* **-spired; -spiring** : transpirar, sudar
persuade [pərˈsweɪd] *vt* **-suaded; -suading** : persuadir, convencer
persuasion [pərˈsweɪʒən] *n* : persuasión *f*
persuasive [pərˈsweɪsɪv, -zɪv] *adj* : persuasivo — **persuasively** *adv*
persuasiveness [pərˈsweɪsɪvnəs, -zɪv-] *n* : persuasión *f*
pert [ˈpərt] *adj* **1** SAUCY : descarado, impertinente **2** JAUNTY : alegre, animado ⟨a pert little hat : un sombrero coqueto⟩
pertain [pərˈteɪn] *vi* **1** BELONG : pertenecer (a) **2** RELATE : estar relacionado (con)
pertinence [ˈpərtənənts] *n* : pertinencia *f*
pertinent [ˈpərtənənt] *adj* : pertinente
perturb [pərˈtərb] *vt* : perturbar
perusal [pəˈruːzəl] *n* : lectura *f* cuidadosa
peruse [pəˈruːz] *vt* **-rused; -rusing 1** READ : leer con cuidado **2** SCAN : recorrer con la vista ⟨he perused the newspaper : echó un vistazo al periódico⟩

Peruvian [pəˈruːviən] *n* : peruano *m*, -na *f* — **Peruvian** *adj*
pervade [pərˈveɪd] *vt* **-vaded; -vading** : penetrar, difundirse por
pervasive [pərˈveɪsɪv, -zɪv] *adj* : penetrante
perverse [pərˈvərs] *adj* **1** CORRUPT : perverso, corrompido **2** STUBBORN : obstinado, porfiado, terco (sin razón) — **perversely** *adv*
perversion [pərˈvərʒən] *n* : perversión *f*
perversity [pərˈvərsət̬i] *n*, *pl* **-ties 1** CORRUPTION : corrupción *f* **2** STUBBORNNESS : obstinación *f*, terquedad *f*
pervert[1] [pərˈvərt] *vt* **1** DISTORT : pervertir, distorsionar **2** CORRUPT : pervertir, corromper
pervert[2] [ˈpərˌvərt] *n* : pervertido *m*, -da *f*
pesky [ˈpɛski] *adj* : molestoso, molesto
peso [ˈpeɪˌsoː] *n*, *pl* **-sos** : peso *m*
pessimism [ˈpɛsəˌmɪzəm] *n* : pesimismo *m*
pessimist [ˈpɛsəmɪst] *n* : pesimista *mf*
pessimistic [ˌpɛsəˈmɪstɪk] *adj* : pesimista
pest [ˈpɛst] *n* **1** NUISANCE : peste *f*; latoso *m*, -sa *f fam* ⟨to be a pest : dar (la) lata⟩ **2** : insecto *m* nocivo, animal *m* nocivo ⟨the squirrels were pests : las ardillas eran una plaga⟩
pester [ˈpɛstər] *vt* **-tered; -tering** : molestar, fastidiar
pesticide [ˈpɛstəˌsaɪd] *n* : pesticida *m*
pestilence [ˈpɛstələnts] *n* : pestilencia *f*, peste *f*
pestle [ˈpɛsəl, ˈpɛstəl] *n* : mano *f* de mortero, mazo *m*, maja *f*
pet[1] [ˈpɛt] *vt* **petted; petting** : acariciar
pet[2] *n* **1** : animal *m* doméstico **2** FAVORITE : favorito *m*, -ta *f*
petal [ˈpɛt̬əl] *n* : pétalo *m*
petite [pəˈtiːt] *adj* : pequeña, menuda, chiquita
petition[1] [pəˈtɪʃən] *vt* : peticionar
petition[2] *n* : petición *f*
petitioner [pəˈtɪʃənər] *n* : peticionario *m*, -ria *f*
petrify [ˈpɛtrəˌfaɪ] *vt* **-fied; -fying** : petrificar
petroleum [pəˈtroːliəm] *n* : petróleo *m*
petticoat [ˈpɛt̬iˌkoːt] *n* : enagua *f*, fondo *m Mex*
pettiness [ˈpɛt̬inəs] *n* **1** INSIGNIFICANCE : insignificancia *f* **2** MEANNESS : mezquindad *f*
petty [ˈpɛt̬i] *adj* **-tier; -est 1** MINOR : menor ⟨petty cash : dinero para gastos menores⟩ **2** INSIGNIFICANT : insignificante, trivial, nimio **3** MEAN : mezquino
petty officer *n* : suboficial *mf*
petulance [ˈpɛtʃələnts] *n* : irritabilidad *f*, mal genio *m*
petulant [ˈpɛtʃələnt] *adj* : irritable, de mal genio
petunia [pɪˈtuːnjə, -ˈtjuː-] *n* : petunia *f*
pew [ˈpjuː] *n* : banco *m* (de iglesia)

pewter ['pju:tər] *n* : peltre *m*
pH [ˌpi:'eɪtʃ] *n* : pH *m*
phallic ['fælɪk] *adj* : fálico
phallus ['fæləs] *n, pl* **-li** ['fæˌlaɪ] *or* **-luses** : falo *m*
phantasy ['fæntəsi] → **fantasy**
phantom ['fæntəm] *n* : fantasma *m*
pharaoh ['fɛrˌo:, 'feɪˌro:] *n* : faraón *m*
pharmaceutical [ˌfɑrmə'su:tɪkəl] *adj* : farmacéutico
pharmacist ['fɑrməsɪst] *n* : farmacéutico *m*, -ca *f*
pharmacology [ˌfɑrmə'kɑləʤi] *n* : farmacología *f*
pharmacy ['fɑrməsi] *n, pl* **-cies** : farmacia *f*
pharynx ['færɪŋks] *n, pl* **pharynges** [fə'rɪnˌʤi:z] : faringe *f*
phase[1] ['feɪz] *vt* **phased; phasing 1** SYNCHRONIZE : sincronizar, poner en fase **2** STAGGER : escalonar **3 to phase in** : introducir progresivamente **4 to phase out** : retirar progresivamente, dejar de producir
phase[2] *n* **1** : fase *f* (de la luna, etc.) **2** STAGE : fase *f*, etapa *f*
pheasant ['fɛzənt] *n, pl* **-ant** *or* **-ants** : faisán *m*
phenomenal [fɪ'nɑmənəl] *adj* : extraordinario, excepcional
phenomenon [fɪ'nɑməˌnɑn, -nən] *n, pl* **-na** [-nə] *or* **-nons 1** : fenómeno *m* **2** *pl* **-nons** PRODIGY : fenómeno *m*, prodigio *m*
philanthropic [ˌfɪlən'θrɑpɪk] *adj* : filantrópico
philanthropist [fə'læntθrəpɪst] *n* : filántropo *m*, -pa *f*
philanthropy [fə'læntθrəpi] *n, pl* **-pies** : filantropía *f*
philately [fə'lætəli] *n* : filatelia *f*
philodendron [ˌfɪlə'dɛndrən] *n, pl* **-drons** *or* **-dra** [-drə] : arácea *f*
philosopher [fə'lɑsəfər] *n* : filósofo *m*, -fa *f*
philosophic [ˌfɪlə'sɑfɪk] *or* **philosophical** [-fɪkəl] *adj* : filosófico — **philosophically** [-kli] *adv*
philosophize [fə'lɑsəˌfaɪz] *vi* **-phized; -phizing** : filosofar
philosophy [fə'lɑsəfi] *n, pl* **-phies** : filosofía *f*
phlebitis [flɪ'baɪtəs] *n* : flebitis *f*
phlegm ['flɛm] *n* : flema *f*
phlox ['flɑks] *n, pl* **phlox** *or* **phloxes** : polemonio *m*
phobia ['fo:biə] *n* : fobia *f*
phoenix ['fi:nɪks] *n* : fénix *m*
phone[1] ['fo:n] *v* → **telephone**[1]
phone[2] *n* → **telephone**[2]
phoneme ['fo:ˌni:m] *n* : fonema *m*
phonetic [fə'nɛtɪk] *adj* : fonético
phonetics [fə'nɛtɪks] *n* : fonética *f*
phonics ['fɑnɪks] *n* : método *m* fonético de aprender a leer
phonograph ['fo:nəˌgræf] *n* : fonógrafo *m*, tocadiscos *m*
phony[1] *or* **phoney** ['fo:ni] *adj* **-nier; -est** : falso

phony[2] *or* **phoney** *n, pl* **-nies** : farsante *mf*; charlatán *m*, -tana *f*
phosphate ['fɑsˌfeɪt] *n* : fosfato *m*
phosphorescence [ˌfɑsfə'rɛsənts] *n* : fosforescencia *f*
phosphorescent [ˌfɑsfə'rɛsənt] *adj* : fosforescente — **phosphorescently** *adv*
phosphorus ['fɑsfərəs] *n* : fósforo *m*
photo ['fo:ˌto:] *n, pl* **-tos** : foto *f*
photocopier ['fo:ˌto:ˌkɑpiər] *n* : fotocopiadora *f*
photocopy[1] ['fo:ˌto:ˌkɑpi] *vt* **-copied; -copying** : fotocopiar
photocopy[2] *n, pl* **-copies** : fotocopia *f*
photoelectric [ˌfo:ˌtoɪ'lɛktrɪk] *adj* : fotoeléctrico
photogenic [ˌfo:ˌtə'ʤenɪk] *adj* : fotogénico
photograph[1] ['fo:ˌtəˌgræf] *vt* : fotografiar
photograph[2] *n* : fotografía *f*, foto *f* ⟨to take a photograph of : tomarle una fotografía a, tomar una fotografía de⟩
photographer [fə'tɑgrəfər] *n* : fotógrafo *m*, -fa *f*
photographic [ˌfo:ˌtə'græfɪk] *adj* : fotográfico — **photographically** [-fɪkli] *adv*
photography [fə'tɑgrəfi] *n* : fotografía *f*
photosynthesis [ˌfo:ˌto:'sɪntθəsɪs] *n* : fotosíntesis *f*
photosynthetic [ˌfo:ˌto:sɪn'θɛtɪk] *adj* : fotosintético, de fotosíntesis
phrase[1] ['freɪz] *vt* **phrased; phrasing** : expresar
phrase[2] *n* : frase *f*, locución *f* ⟨to coin a phrase : para decirlo así⟩
phylum ['faɪləm] *n, pl* **-la** [-lə] : phylum *m*
physical[1] ['fɪzɪkəl] *adj* **1** : físico ⟨physical laws : leyes físicas⟩ **2** MATERIAL : material, físico **3** BODILY : físico, corpóreo — **physically** [-kli] *adv*
physical[2] *n* CHECKUP : chequeo *m*, reconocimiento *m* médico
physician [fə'zɪʃən] *n* : médico *m*, -ca *f*
physicist ['fɪzəsɪst] *n* : físico *m*, -ca *f*
physics ['fɪzɪks] *ns & pl* : física *f*
physiognomy [ˌfɪzi'agnəmi] *n, pl* **-mies** : fisonomía *f*
physiological ['fɪziə'lɑʤɪkəl] *or* **physiologic** [-ʤɪk] *adj* : fisiológico
physiologist [ˌfɪzi'aləʤɪst] *n* : fisiólogo *m*, -ga *f*
physiology [ˌfɪzi'aləʤi] *n* : fisiología *f*
physique [fə'zi:k] *n* : físico *m*
pi ['paɪ] *n, pl* **pis** ['paɪz] : pi *f*
pianist [pi'ænɪst, 'pi:ənɪst] *n* : pianista *mf*
piano [pi'æno:] *n, pl* **-anos** : piano *m*
piazza [pi'æzə, -'atsə] *n, pl* **-zas** *or* **-ze** [-'atˌseɪ] : plaza *f*
picaresque [ˌpɪkə'rɛsk, ˌpi:-] *adj* : picaresco
picayune [ˌpɪki'ju:n] *adj* : trivial, nimio, insignificante
piccolo ['pɪkəˌlo:] *n, pl* **-los** : flautín *m*
pick[1] ['pɪk] *vt* **1** : picar, labrar (con un pico) ⟨he picked the hard soil : picó la

tierra dura⟩ **2** : quitar, sacar (poco a poco) ⟨to pick meat off the bones : quitar pedazos de carne de los huesos⟩ **3** : recoger, arrancar (frutas, flores, etc.) **4** SELECT : escoger, elegir **5** PROVOKE : provocar ⟨to pick a quarrel : buscar pleito, buscar pelea⟩ **6 to pick a lock** : forzar una cerradura **7 to pick someone's pocket** : robarle algo del bolsillo de alguien ⟨someone picked my pocket! : ¡me robaron la cartera del bolsillo!⟩ — *vi* **1** NIBBLE : picar, picotear **2 to pick and choose** : ser exigente **3 to pick at** : tocar, rascarse (una herida, etc.) **4 to pick on** TEASE : mofarse de, atormentar

pick² *n* **1** CHOICE : selección *f* **2** BEST : lo mejor ⟨the pick of the crop : la crema y nata⟩ **3** → **pickax**

pickax ['pɪk,æks] *n* : pico *m*, zapapico *m*, piqueta *f*

pickerel ['pɪkərəl] *n, pl* **-el** *or* **-els** : lucio *m* pequeño

picket¹ ['pɪkət] *v* : piquetear

picket² *n* **1** STAKE : estaca *f* **2** STRIKER : huelguista *mf*, integrante *mf* de un piquete

pickle¹ ['pɪkəl] *vt* **-led; -ling** : encurtir, escabechar

pickle² *n* **1** BRINE : escabeche *m* **2** GHERKIN : pepinillo *m* (encurtido) **3** JAM, TROUBLE : lío *m*, apuro *m*

pickpocket ['pɪk,pɑkət] *n* : carterista *mf*

pickup ['pɪk,əp] *n* **1** IMPROVEMENT : mejora *f* **2** *or* **pickup truck** : camioneta *f*

pick up *vt* **1** LIFT : levantar **2** TIDY : arreglar, ordenar — *vi* IMPROVE : mejorar

picnic¹ ['pɪk,nɪk] *vi* **-nicked; -nicking** : ir de picnic

picnic² *n* : picnic *m*

pictorial [pɪk'toriəl] *adj* : pictórico

picture¹ ['pɪktʃər] *vt* **-tured; -turing 1** DEPICT : representar **2** IMAGINE : imaginarse ⟨can you picture it? : ¿te lo puedes imaginar?⟩

picture² *n* **1** : cuadro *m* (pintado o dibujado), ilustración *f*, fotografía *f* **2** DESCRIPTION : descripción *f* **3** IMAGE : imagen *f* ⟨he's the picture of his father : es la viva imagen de su padre⟩ **4** MOVIE : película *f*

picturesque [,pɪktʃə'rɛsk] *adj* : pintoresco

pie ['paɪ] *n* : pastel *m* (con fruta o carne), empanada *f* (con carne)

piebald ['paɪ,bɔld] *adj* : picazo, pío

piece¹ ['pi:s] *vt* **pieced; piecing 1** PATCH : parchar, arreglar **2 to piece together** : construir pieza por pieza

piece² *n* **1** FRAGMENT : trozo *m*, pedazo *m* **2** COMPONENT : pieza *f* ⟨a three-piece suit : un traje de tres piezas⟩ **3** UNIT : pieza *f* ⟨a piece of fruit : una (pieza de) fruta⟩ **4** WORK : obra *f*, pieza *f* (de música, etc.) **5** (*in board games*) : ficha *f*, pieza *f*, figura *f* (en ajedrez)

piecemeal¹ ['pi:s,mi:l] *adv* : poco a poco, por partes

piecemeal² *adj* : hecho poco a poco, poco sistemático

pied ['paɪd] *adj* : pío

pier ['pɪr] *n* **1** : pila *f* (de un puente) **2** WHARF : muelle *m*, atracadero *m*, embarcadero *m* **3** PILLAR : pilar *m*

pierce ['pɪrs] *vt* **pierced; piercing 1** PENETRATE : atravesar, traspasar, penetrar (en) ⟨the bullet pierced his leg : la bala le atravesó la pierna⟩ ⟨to pierce one's heart : traspasarle el corazón a uno⟩ **2** PERFORATE : perforar, agujerear (las orejas, etc.) **3 to pierce the silence** : desgarrar el silencio

piety ['paɪəţi] *n, pl* **-eties** : piedad *f*

pig ['pɪg] *n* **1** HOG, SWINE : cerdo *m*, -da *f*; puerco *m*, -ca *f* **2** SLOB : persona *f* desaliñada; cerdo *m*, -da *f* **3** GLUTTON : glotón *m*, -tona *f* **4** *or* **pig iron** : lingote *m* de hierro

pigeon ['pɪdʒən] *n* : paloma *f*

pigeonhole ['pɪdʒən,ho:l] *n* : casilla *f*

pigeon—toed ['pɪdʒən,to:d] *adj* : patituerto

piggish ['pɪgɪʃ] *adj* **1** GREEDY : glotón **2** DIRTY : cochino, sucio

piggyback ['pɪgi,bæk] *adv & adj* : a cuestas

pigheaded ['pɪg,hɛdəd] *adj* : terco, obstinado

piglet ['pɪglət] *n* : cochinillo *m*; lechón *m*, -chona *f*

pigment ['pɪgmənt] *n* : pigmento *m*

pigmentation [,pɪgmən'teɪʃən] *n* : pigmentación *f*

pigmy → **pygmy**

pigpen ['pɪg,pɛn] *n* : chiquero *m*, pocilga *f*

pigsty ['pɪg,staɪ] → **pigpen**

pigtail ['pɪg,teɪl] *n* : coleta *f*, trenza *f*

pike ['paɪk] *n, pl* **pike** *or* **pikes 1** : lucio *m* (pez) **2** LANCE : pica *f* **3** → **turnpike**

pile¹ ['paɪl] *v* **piled; piling** *vt* : amontonar, apilar — *vi* **to pile up** : amontonarse, acumularse

pile² *n* **1** STAKE : pilote *m* **2** HEAP : montón *m*, pila *f* **3** NAP : pelo *m* (de telas)

piles ['paɪlz] *npl* HEMORRHOIDS : hemorroides *fpl*, almorranas *fpl*

pilfer ['pɪlfər] *vt* : robar (cosas pequeñas), ratear

pilgrim ['pɪlgrəm] *n* : peregrino *m*, -na *f*

pilgrimage ['pɪlgrəmɪdʒ] *n* : peregrinación *f*

pill ['pɪl] *n* : pastilla *f*, píldora *f*

pillage¹ ['pɪlɪdʒ] *vt* **-laged; -laging** : saquear

pillage² *n* : saqueo *m*

pillar ['pɪlər] *n* : pilar *m*, columna *f*

pillory ['pɪləri] *n, pl* **-ries** : picota *f*

pillow ['pɪ,lo:] *n* : almohada *f*

pillowcase ['pɪ,lo:,keɪs] *n* : funda *f*

pilot¹ ['paɪlət] *vt* : pilotar, pilotear

pilot² *n* : piloto *mf*

pilot light *n* : piloto *m*

pimento [pə'mɛn,to:] → **pimiento**

pimiento [pə'mɛn,to:, -'mjɛn-] *n, pl* **-tos** : pimiento *m* morrón

pimp ['pɪmp] *n* : proxeneta *m*

pimple ['pɪmpəl] *n* : grano *m*

pimply ['pɪmpəli] *adj* **-plier; -est** : cubierto de granos

pin¹ ['pɪn] *vt* **pinned; pinning 1** FASTEN : prender, sujetar (con alfileres) **2** HOLD, IMMOBILIZE : inmovilizar, sujetar **3 to pin one's hopes on** : poner sus esperanzas en

pin² *n* **1** : alfiler *m* ⟨safety pin : alfiler de gancho⟩ ⟨a bobby pin : una horquilla⟩ **2** BROOCH : alfiler *m*, broche *m*, prendedor *m* **3** *or* **bowling pin** : bolo *m*

pinafore ['pɪnə,for] *n* : delantal *m*

pincer ['pɪntsər] *n* **1** CLAW : pinza *f* (de una langosta, etc.) **2 pincers** *npl* : pinzas *fpl*, tenazas *fpl*, tenaza *f*

pinch¹ ['pɪntʃ] *vt* **1** : pellizcar ⟨she pinched my cheek : me pellizcó el cachete⟩ **2** STEAL : robar — *vi* : apretar ⟨my shoes pinch : me aprietan los zapatos⟩

pinch² *n* **1** EMERGENCY : emergencia *f* ⟨in a pinch : en caso necesario⟩ **2** PAIN : dolor *m*, tormento *m* **3** SQUEEZE : pellizco *m* (con los dedos) **4** BIT : pizca *f*, pellizco *m* ⟨a pinch of cinnamon : una pizca de canela⟩

pinch hitter *n* **1** SUBSTITUTE : sustituto *m*, -ta *f* **2** : bateador *m* emergente (en beisbol)

pincushion ['pɪn,kuʃən] *n* : acerico *m*, alfiletero *m*

pine¹ ['paɪn] *vi* **pined; pining 1 to pine away** : languidecer, consumirse **2 to pine for** : añorar, suspirar por

pine² *n* **1** : pino *m* (árbol) **2** : madera *f* de pino

pineapple ['paɪn,æpəl] *n* : piña *f*, ananá *m*, ananás *m*

ping–pong ['pɪŋ,paŋ, -,pɔŋ] *n* : ping-pong *m*

pinion¹ ['pɪnjən] *vt* : sujetar los brazos de, inmovilizar

pinion² *n* : piñón *m*

pink¹ ['pɪŋk] *adj* : rosa, rosado

pink² *n* **1** : clavelito *m* (flor) **2** : rosa *m*, rosado *m* (color) **3 to be in the pink** : estar en plena forma, rebosar de salud

pinkeye ['pɪŋk,aɪ] *n* : conjuntivitis *f* aguda

pinkish ['pɪŋkɪʃ] *adj* : rosáceo

pinnacle ['pɪnɪkəl] *n* **1** : pináculo *m* (de un edificio) **2** PEAK : cima *f*, cumbre *f* (de una montaña) **3** ACME : pináculo *m*, cúspide *f*, apogeo *m*

pinpoint ['pɪn,pɔɪnt] *vt* : precisar, localizar con precisión

pint ['paɪnt] *n* : pinta *f*

pinto ['pɪn,to:] *n, pl* **pintos** : caballo *m* pinto

pinworm ['pɪn,wərm] *n* : oxiuro *m*

pioneer¹ [,paɪə'nɪr] *vt* : promover, iniciar, introducir

pioneer² *n* : pionero *m*, -ra *f*

pious ['paɪəs] *adj* **1** DEVOUT : piadoso, devoto **2** SANCTIMONIOUS : beato

piously ['paɪəsli] *adv* **1** DEVOUTLY : piadosamente **2** SANCTIMONIOUSLY : santurronamente

pipe¹ ['paɪp] *v* **piped; piping** *vi* : hablar en voz chillona — *vt* **1** PLAY : tocar (el caramillo o la flauta) **2** : conducir por tuberías ⟨to pipe water : transportar el agua por tubería⟩

pipe² *n* **1** : caramillo *m* (instrumento musical) **2** BAGPIPE : gaita *f* **3** : tubo *m*, caño *m* ⟨gas pipes : tubería de gas⟩ **4** : pipa *f* (para fumar)

pipeline ['paɪp,laɪn] *n* **1** : conducto *m*, oleoducto *m* (para petróleo), gasoducto *m* (para gas) **2** CONDUIT : vía *f* (de información, etc.)

piper ['paɪpər] *n* : músico *m*, -ca *f* que toca el caramillo o la gaita

piping ['paɪpɪŋ] *n* **1** : música *f* del caramillo o de la gaita **2** TRIM : cordoncillo *m*, ribete *m* con cordón

piquant ['pi:kənt, 'pɪkwənt] *adj* **1** SPICY : picante **2** INTRIGUING : intrigante, estimulante

pique¹ ['pi:k] *vt* **piqued; piquing 1** IRRITATE : picar, irritar **2** AROUSE : despertar (la curiosidad, etc.)

pique² *n* : pique *m*, resentimiento *m*

piracy ['paɪrəsi] *n, pl* **-cies** : piratería *f*

piranha [pə'ranə, -'ranjə, -'rænjə] *n* : piraña *f*

pirate¹ ['paɪrət] *n* : pirata *mf*

pirate² *vt* **-rated; -rating** : piratear (software, etc.)

pirouette [,pɪrə'wɛt] *n* : pirueta *f*

pis → pi

Pisces ['paɪ,si:z, 'pɪ-; 'pɪs,keɪs] *n* : Piscis *mf*

pistachio [pə'stæʃi,o:, -'sta-] *n, pl* **-chios** : pistacho *m*

pistil ['pɪstəl] *n* : pistilo *m*

pistol ['pɪstəl] *n* : pistola *f*

piston ['pɪstən] *n* : pistón *m*, émbolo *m*

pit¹ ['pɪt] *v* **pitted; pitting** *vt* **1** : marcar de hoyos, picar (una superficie) **2** : deshuesar (una fruta) **3 to pit against** : enfrentar a, oponer a — *vi* : quedar marcado

pit² *n* **1** HOLE : fosa *f*, hoyo *m* ⟨a bottomless pit : un pozo sin fondo⟩ **2** MINE : mina *f* **3** : foso *m* ⟨orchestra pit : foso orquestal⟩ **4** POCKMARK : marca *f* (en la cara), cicatriz *f* de viruela **5** STONE : hueso *m*, pepa *f* (de una fruta) **6 pit of the stomach** : boca *f* del estómago

pitch¹ ['pɪtʃ] *vt* **1** SET UP : montar, armar (una tienda) **2** THROW : lanzar, arrojar **3** ADJUST, SET : dar el tono de (un discurso, un instrumento musical) — *vi* **1** *or* **pitch forward** FALL : caerse **2** LURCH : cabecear (dícese de un barco o un avión), dar bandazos

pitch² *n* **1** LURCHING : cabezada *f*, cabeceo *m* (de un barco o un avión) **2** SLOPE : (grado de) inclinación *f*, pendiente *f* **3** : tono *m* (en música) ⟨per-

fect pitch : oído absoluto⟩ **4** THROW
: lanzamiento *m* **5** DEGREE : grado *m*,
nivel *m*, punto *m* ⟨the excitement
reached a high pitch : la excitación
llegó a un punto culminante⟩ **6** *or*
sales pitch : presentación *f* (de un
vendedor) **7** TAR : pez *f*, brea *f*
pitcher [ˈpɪtʃər] *n* **1** JUG : jarra *f*, jarro
m, cántaro *m*, pichel *m* **2** : lanzador *m*,
-dora *f* (en béisbol, etc.)
pitchfork [ˈpɪtʃˌfɔrk] *n* : horquilla *f*, horca *f*
piteous [ˈpɪtiəs] *adj* : lastimoso, lastimero — **piteously** *adv*
pitfall [ˈpɪtˌfɔl] *n* : peligro *m* (poco obvio), dificultad *f*
pith [ˈpɪθ] *n* **1** : médula *f* (de una planta) **2** CORE : meollo *m*, entraña *f*
pithy [ˈpɪθi] *adj* **pithier; -est** : conciso y
sustancioso ⟨pithy comments : co-
mentarios sucintos⟩
pitiable [ˈpɪtiəbəl] → **pitiful**
pitiful [ˈpɪtɪfəl] *adj* **1** LAMENTABLE : lastimero, lastimoso, lamentable **2** CON-
TEMPTIBLE : despreciable, lamentable
— **pitifully** [-fli] *adv*
pitiless [ˈpɪtɪləs] *adj* : despiadado — **piti-
lessly** *adv*
pittance [ˈpɪtənts] *n* : miseria *f*
pituitary [pəˈtuːəˌteri, -ˈtjuː-] *adj* : pituitario
pity[1] [ˈpɪti] *vt* **pitied; pitying** : compadecer, compadecerse de
pity[2] *n*, *pl* **pities 1** COMPASSION : compasión *f*, piedad *f* **2** SHAME : lástima *f*,
pena *f* ⟨what a pity! : ¡qué lástima!⟩
pivot[1] [ˈpɪvət] *vi* **1** : girar sobre un eje **2
to pivot on** : girar sobre, depender de
pivot[2] *n* : pivote *m*
pivotal [ˈpɪvətəl] *adj* : fundamental, central
pixie *or* **pixy** [ˈpɪksi] *n*, *pl* **pixies** : elfo
m, hada *f*
pizza [ˈpiːtsə] *n* : pizza *f*
pizzazz *or* **pizazz** [pəˈzæz] *n* **1** GLAMOR
: encanto *m* **2** VITALITY : animación *f*,
vitalidad *f*
placard [ˈplækərd, -ˌkɑrd] *n* POSTER
: cartel *m*, póster *m*, afiche *m*
placate [ˈpleɪˌkeɪt, ˈplæ-] *vt* **-cated;
-cating** : aplacar, apaciguar
place[1] [ˈpleɪs] *vt* **placed; placing 1** PUT,
SET : poner, colocar **2** SITUATE : situar, ubicar, emplazar ⟨to be well placed
: estar bien situado⟩ ⟨to place in a job
: colocar en un trabajo⟩ **3** IDENTIFY,
RECALL : identificar, ubicar, recordar
⟨I can't place him : no lo ubico⟩ **4 to
place an order** : hacer un pedido
place[2] *n* **1** SPACE : sitio *m*, lugar *m*
⟨there's no place to sit : no hay sitio
para sentarse⟩ **2** LOCATION, SPOT : lugar *m*, sitio *m*, parte *f* ⟨place of work
: lugar de trabajo⟩ ⟨our summer place
: nuestra casa de verano⟩ ⟨all over the
place : por todas partes⟩ **3** RANK : lugar *m*, puesto *m* ⟨he took first place
: ganó el primer lugar⟩ **4** POSITION : lugar *m* ⟨everything in its place : todo en

su debido lugar⟩ ⟨to feel out of place
: sentirse fuera de lugar⟩ **5** SEAT
: asiento *m*, cubierto *m* (a la mesa) **6**
JOB : puesto *m* **7** ROLE : papel *m*, lugar *m* ⟨to change places : cambiarse los
papeles⟩ **8 to take place** : tener lugar
9 to take the place of : sustituir a
placebo [pləˈsiːˌboː] *n*, *pl* **-bos** : placebo
m
placement [ˈpleɪsmənt] *n* : colocación *f*
placenta [pləˈsɛntə] *n*, *pl* **-tas** *or* **-tae** [-ti,
-ˌtaɪ] : placenta *f*
placid [ˈplæsəd] *adj* : plácido, tranquilo
— **placidly** *adv*
plagiarism [ˈpleɪdʒəˌrɪzəm] *n* : plagio *m*
plagiarist [ˈpleɪdʒərɪst] *n* : plagiario *m*,
-ria *f*
plagiarize [ˈpleɪdʒəˌraɪz] *vt* **-rized;
-rizing** : plagiar
plague[1] [ˈpleɪɡ] *vt* **plagued; plaguing 1**
AFFLICT : plagar, afligir **2** HARASS
: acosar, atormentar
plague[2] *n* **1** : plaga *f* (de insectos, etc.)
2 : peste *f* (en medicina)
plaid[1] [ˈplæd] *adj* : escocés, de cuadros
⟨a plaid skirt : una falda escocesa⟩
plaid[2] *n* TARTAN : tela *f* escocesa, tartán
m
plain[1] [ˈpleɪn] *adj* **1** SIMPLE, UN-
ADORNED : liso, sencillo, sin adornos
2 CLEAR : claro ⟨in plain language : en
palabras claras⟩ **3** FRANK : franco,
puro ⟨the plain truth : la pura verdad⟩
4 HOMELY : ordinario, poco atractivo
5 in plain sight : a la vista de todos
plain[2] *n* : llanura *f*, llano *m*, planicie *f*
plainly [ˈpleɪnli] *adv* **1** CLEARLY : claramente **2** FRANKLY : francamente, con
franqueza **3** SIMPLY : sencillamente
plaintiff [ˈpleɪntɪf] *n* : demandante *mf*
plaintive [ˈpleɪntɪv] *adj* MOURNFUL : lastimero, plañidero
plait[1] [ˈpleɪt, ˈplæt] *vt* **1** PLEAT : plisar **2**
BRAID : trenzar
plait[2] *n* **1** PLEAT : pliegue *m* **2** BRAID
: trenza *f*
plan[1] [ˈplæn] *v* **planned; planning** *vt* **1**
: planear, proyectar, planificar ⟨to plan
a trip : planear un viaje⟩ ⟨to plan a city
: planificar una ciudad⟩ **2** INTEND
: tener planeado, proyectar — *vi* : hacer planes
plan[2] *n* **1** DIAGRAM : plano *m*, esquema
m **2** SCHEME : plan *m*, proyecto *m*, programa *m* ⟨to draw up a plan : elaborar
un proyecto⟩
plane[1] [ˈpleɪn] *vt* **planed; planing** : cepillar (madera)
plane[2] *adj* : plano
plane[3] *n* **1** : plano *m* (en matemáticas,
etc.) **2** LEVEL : nivel *m* **3** : cepillo *m*
(de carpintero) **4** → **airplane**
planet [ˈplænət] *n* : planeta *f*
planetarium [ˌplænəˈteriəm] *n*, *pl* **-iums**
or **-ia** [-iə] : planetario *m*
planetary [ˈplænəˌteri] *adj* : planetario
plank [ˈplæŋk] *n* **1** BOARD : tablón *m*,
tabla *f* **2** : artículo *m*, punto *m* (de una
plataforma política)

plankton ['plæŋktən] *n* : plancton *m*

plant¹ ['plænt] *vt* **1** : plantar, sembrar (semillas) ⟨planted with flowers : plantado de flores⟩ **2** PLACE : plantar, colocar ⟨to plant an idea : inculcar una idea⟩

plant² *n* **1** : planta *f* ⟨leafy plants : plantas frondosas⟩ **2** FACTORY : planta *f*, fábrica *f* ⟨hydroelectric plant : planta hidroeléctrica⟩ **3** MACHINERY : maquinaria *f*, equipo *m*

plantain ['plæntən] *n* **1** : llantén *m* (mala hierba) **2** : plátano *m*, plátano *m* macho *Mex* (fruta)

plantation [plæn'teɪʃən] *n* : plantación *f*, hacienda *f* ⟨a coffee plantation : un cafetal⟩

planter ['plæntər] *n* **1** : hacendado *m*, -da *f* (de una hacienda) **2** FLOWERPOT : tiesto *m*, maceta *f*

plaque ['plæk] *n* **1** TABLET : placa *f* **2** : placa *f* (dental)

plasma ['plæzmə] *n* : plasma *m*

plaster¹ ['plæstər] *vt* **1** : enyesar, revocar (con yeso) **2** COVER : cubrir, llenar ⟨a wall plastered with notices : una pared cubierta de avisos⟩

plaster² *n* **1** : yeso *m*, revoque *m* (para paredes, etc.) **2** : escayola *f*, yeso *m* (en medicina) **3** **plaster of Paris** ['pærɪs] : yeso *m* mate

plaster cast *n* : vaciado *m* de yeso

plasterer ['plæstərər] *n* : revocador *m*, -dora *f*

plastic¹ ['plæstɪk] *adj* **1** : de plástico **2** PLIABLE : plástico, flexible **3** **plastic surgery** : cirugía *f* plástica

plastic² *n* : plástico *m*

plasticity [plæ'stɪsəti] *n*, *pl* **-ties** : plasticidad *f*

plate¹ ['pleɪt] *vt* **plated; plating** : chapar (en metal)

plate² *n* **1** PLAQUE, SHEET : placa *f* ⟨a steel plate : una placa de acero⟩ **2** UTENSILS : vajilla *f* (de metal) ⟨silver plate : vajilla de plata⟩ **3** DISH : plato *m* **4** DENTURES : dentadura *f* postiza **5** ILLUSTRATION : lámina *f* (en un libro) **6** **license plate** : matrícula *f*, placa *f* de matrícula

plateau [plæ'toː] *n*, *pl* **-teaus** *or* **-teaux** [-'toːz] : meseta *f*

platform ['plæt,fɔrm] *n* **1** STAGE : plataforma *f*, estrado *m*, tribuna *f* **2** : andén *m* (de una estación de ferrocarril) **3** **political platform** : plataforma *f* política, programa *m* electoral

plating ['pleɪtɪŋ] *n* **1** : enchapado *m* **2** **silver plating** : plateado *m*

platinum ['plætənəm] *n* : platino *m*

platitude ['plætə,tuːd, -,tjuːd] *n* : lugar *m* común, perogrullada *f*

platonic [plə'tɑnɪk] *adj* : platónico

platoon [plə'tuːn] *n* : sección *f* (en el ejército)

platter ['plætər] *n* : fuente *f*

platypus ['plætɪpəs, -,pʊs] *n*, *pl* **platypuses** *or* **platypi** [-,paɪ, -,piː] : ornitorrinco *m*

plausibility [,plɔzə'bɪləti] *n*, *pl* **-ties** : credibilidad *f*, verosimilitud *f*

plausible ['plɔzəbəl] *adj* : creíble, convincente, verosímil — **plausibly** [-bli] *adv*

play¹ ['pleɪ] *vi* **1** : jugar ⟨to play with a doll : jugar con una muñeca⟩ ⟨to play with an idea : darle vueltas a una idea⟩ **2** FIDDLE, TOY : jugar, juguetear ⟨don't play with your food : no juegues con la comida⟩ **3** : tocar ⟨to play in a band : tocar en un grupo⟩ **4** : actuar (en una obra de teatro) — *vt* **1** : jugar (un deporte, etc.), jugar a (un juego), jugar contra (un contrincante) **2** : tocar (música o un instrumento) **3** PERFORM : interpretar, hacer el papel de (un carácter), representar (una obra de teatro) ⟨she plays the lead : hace el papel principal⟩ **4** **to play back** : poner (una grabación) **5** **to play down** : minimizar **6** **to play up** : resaltar

play² *n* **1** GAME, RECREATION : juego *m* ⟨children at play : niños jugando⟩ ⟨a play on words : un juego de palabras⟩ **2** ACTION : juego *m* ⟨the ball is in play : la pelota está en juego⟩ ⟨to bring into play : poner en juego⟩ **3** DRAMA : obra *f* de teatro, pieza *f* (de teatro) **4** MOVEMENT : juego *m* (de la luz, una brisa, etc.) **5** SLACK : juego *m* ⟨there's not enough play in the wheel : la rueda no da lo suficiente⟩

playacting ['pleɪ,æktɪŋ] *n* : actuación *f*, teatro *m*

player ['pleɪər] *n* **1** : jugador *m*, -dora *f* (en un juego) **2** ACTOR : actor *m*, actriz *f* **3** MUSICIAN : músico *m*, -ca *f*

playful ['pleɪfəl] *adj* **1** FROLICSOME : juguetón **2** JOCULAR : jocoso — **playfully** *adv*

playfulness ['pleɪfəlnəs] *n* : lo juguetón, jocosidad *f*, alegría *f*

playground ['pleɪ,graʊnd] *n* : patio *m* de recreo, jardín *m* para jugar

playhouse ['pleɪ,haʊs] *n* **1** THEATER : teatro *m* **2** : casita *f* de juguete

playing card *n* : naipe *m*, carta *f*

playmate ['pleɪ,meɪt] *n* : compañero *m*, -ra *f* de juego

play-off ['pleɪ,ɔf] *n* : desempate *m*

playpen ['pleɪ,pɛn] *n* : corral *m* (para niños)

plaything ['pleɪ,θɪŋ] *n* : juguete *m*

playwright ['pleɪ,raɪt] *n* : dramaturgo *m*, -ga *f*

plaza ['plæzə, 'plɑ-] *n* **1** SQUARE : plaza *f* **2** **shopping plaza** MALL : centro *m* comercial

plea ['pliː] *n* **1** : acto *m* de declararse ⟨he entered a plea of guilty : se declaró culpable⟩ **2** APPEAL : ruego *m*, súplica *f*

plead ['pliːd] *v* **pleaded** *or* **pled** ['plɛd]; **pleading** *vi* **1** : declararse (culpable o inocente) **2** **to plead for** : suplicar, implorar — *vt* **1** : alegar, pretextar ⟨he pleaded illness : pretextó la enfermedad⟩ **2** **to plead a case** : defender un caso

pleasant [ˈplɛzənt] *adj* : agradable, grato, bueno — **pleasantly** *adv*
pleasantness [ˈplɛzəntnəs] *n* : lo agradable, amenidad *f*
pleasantries [ˈplɛzəntriz] *npl* : cumplidos *mpl*, cortesías *fpl* ⟨to exchange pleasantries : intercambiar cumplidos⟩
please¹ [ˈpliːz] *v* **pleased; pleasing** *vt* **1** GRATIFY : complacer ⟨please yourself! : ¡cómo quieras!⟩ **2** SATISFY : contentar, satisfacer — *vi* **1** SATISFY : complacer, agradar ⟨anxious to please : deseoso de complacer⟩ **2** LIKE : querer ⟨do as you please : haz lo que quieras, haz lo que te parezca⟩
please² *adv* : por favor
pleased [ˈpliːzd] *adj* : contento, satisfecho, alegre
pleasing [ˈpliːzɪŋ] *adj* : agradable — **pleasingly** *adv*
pleasurable [ˈplɛʒərəbəl] *adj* PLEASANT : agradable
pleasure [ˈplɛʒər] *n* **1** WISH : deseo *m*, voluntad *f* ⟨at your pleasure : cuando guste⟩ **2** ENJOYMENT : placer *m*, disfrute *m*, goce *m* ⟨with pleasure : con mucho gusto⟩ **3** : placer *m*, gusto *m* ⟨it's a pleasure to be here : me da gusto estar aquí⟩ ⟨the pleasures of reading : los placeres de leer⟩
pleat¹ [ˈpliːt] *vt* : plisar
pleat² *n* : pliegue *m*
plebeian [plɪˈbiən] *adj* : ordinario, plebeyo
pledge¹ [ˈplɛdʒ] *vt* **pledged; pledging 1** PAWN : empeñar, prendar **2** PROMISE : prometer, jurar
pledge² *n* **1** SECURITY : garantía *f*, prenda *f* **2** PROMISE : promesa *f*
plenteous [ˈplɛntiəs] *adj* : copioso, abundante
plentiful [ˈplɛntɪfəl] *adj* : abundante — **plentifully** [-fli] *adv*
plenty [ˈplɛnti] *n* : abundancia *f* ⟨plenty of time : tiempo de sobra⟩ ⟨plenty of visitors : muchos visitantes⟩
plethora [ˈplɛθərə] *n* : plétora *f*
pleurisy [ˈplʊrəsi] *n* : pleuresía *f*
pliable [ˈplaɪəbəl] *adj* : flexible, maleable
pliant [ˈplaɪənt] → **pliable**
pliers [ˈplaɪərz] *npl* : alicates *mpl*, pinzas *fpl*
plight [ˈplaɪt] *n* : situación *f* difícil, apuro *m*
plod [ˈplɑd] *vi* **plodded; plodding 1** TRUDGE : caminar pesadamente y lentamente **2** DRUDGE : trabajar laboriosamente
plot¹ [ˈplɑt] *v* **plotted; plotting** *vt* **1** DEVISE : tramar **2 to plot out** : trazar, determinar (una posición, etc.) — *vi* CONSPIRE : conspirar
plot² *n* **1** LOT : terreno *m*, parcela *f*, lote *m* **2** STORY : argumento *m* (en el teatro), trama *f* (en un libro, etc.) **3** CONSPIRACY, INTRIGUE : complot *m*, intriga *f*
plotter [ˈplɑtər] *n* : conspirador *m*, -dora *f*; intrigante *mf*

plow¹ *or* **plough** [ˈplaʊ] *vt* **1** : arar (la tierra) **2 to plow the seas** : surcar los mares
plow² *or* **plough** *n* **1** : arado *m* **2** → **snowplow**
plowshare [ˈplaʊˌʃɛr] *n* : reja *f* del arado
ploy [ˈplɔɪ] *n* : estratagema *f*, maniobra *f*
pluck¹ [ˈplʌk] *vt* **1** PICK : arrancar **2** : desplumar (un pollo, etc.) — *vi* **to pluck at** : tirar de
pluck² *n* **1** TUG : tirón *m* **2** COURAGE, SPIRIT : valor *m*, ánimo *m*
plucky [ˈplʌki] *adj* **pluckier; -est** : valiente, animoso
plug¹ [ˈplʌɡ] *vt* **plugged; plugging 1** BLOCK : tapar **2** PROMOTE : hacerle publicidad a, promocionar **3 to plug in** : enchufar
plug² *n* **1** STOPPER : tapón *m* **2** : enchufe *m* (eléctrico) **3** ADVERTISEMENT : publicidad *f*, propaganda *f*
plum [ˈplʌm] *n* **1** : ciruela *f* (fruta) **2** : color *m* ciruela **3** PRIZE : premio *m*, algo muy atractivo
plumage [ˈpluːmɪdʒ] *n* : plumaje *m*
plumb¹ [ˈplʌm] *vt* **1** : aplomar ⟨to plumb a wall : aplomar una pared⟩ **2** SOUND : sondear, sondar
plumb² *adv* **1** VERTICALLY : a plomo, verticalmente **2** EXACTLY : justo, exactamente **3** COMPLETELY : completamente, absolutamente ⟨plumb crazy : loco de remate⟩
plumb³ *adj* : a plomo
plumb⁴ *n or* **plumb line** : plomada *f*
plumber [ˈplʌmər] *n* : plomero *m*, -ra *f*; fontanero *m*, -ra *f*
plumbing [ˈplʌmɪŋ] *n* **1** : plomería *f*, fontanería *f* (trabajo del plomero) **2** PIPES : cañería *f*, tubería *f*
plume [ˈpluːm] *n* **1** FEATHER : pluma *f* **2** TUFT : penacho *m* (en un sombrero, etc.)
plumed [ˈpluːmd] *adj* : con plumas ⟨white-plumed birds : aves de plumaje blanco⟩
plummet [ˈplʌmət] *vi* : caer en picada, desplomarse
plump¹ [ˈplʌmp] *vi or* **to plump down** : dejarse caer (pesadamente)
plump² *adv* **1** STRAIGHT : a plomo **2** DIRECTLY : directamente, sin rodeos ⟨he ran plump into the door : dio de cara con la puerta⟩
plump³ *adj* : llenito *fam*, regordete *fam*, rechoncho *fam*
plumpness [ˈplʌmpnəs] *n* : gordura *f*
plunder¹ [ˈplʌndər] *vi* : saquear, robar
plunder² *n* : botín *m*
plunderer [ˈplʌndərər] *n* : saqueador *m*, -dora *f*
plunge¹ [ˈplʌndʒ] *v* **plunged; plunging** *vt* **1** IMMERSE : sumergir **2** THRUST : hundir, clavar — *vi* **1** DIVE : zambullirse (en el agua) **2** : meterse precipitadamente o violentamente ⟨they plunged into war : se enfrascaron en

una guerra⟩ ⟨he plunged into depression : cayó en la depresión⟩ 3 DESCEND : descender en picada ⟨the road plunges dizzily : la calle desciende vertiginosamente⟩

plunge² *n* 1 DIVE : zambullida *f* 2 DROP : descenso *m* abrupto ⟨the plunge in prices : el desplome de los precios⟩

plural¹ ['plʊrəl] *adj* : plural

plural² *n* : plural *m*

plurality [plʊ'ræləṭi] *n*, *pl* -ties : pluralidad *f*

pluralize ['plʊrə,laɪz] *vt* -ized; -izing : pluralizar

plus¹ ['plʌs] *adj* 1 POSITIVE : positivo ⟨a plus factor : un factor positivo⟩ 2 (*indicating a quantity in addition*) ⟨a grade of C plus : una calificación entre C y B⟩ ⟨a salary of $30,000 plus : un sueldo de más de $30,000⟩

plus² *n* 1 *or* **plus sign** : más *m*, signo *m* de más 2 ADVANTAGE : ventaja *f*

plus³ *prep* : más (en matemáticas)

plus⁴ *conj* AND : y

plush¹ ['plʌʃ] *adj* 1 : afelpado 2 LUXURIOUS : lujoso

plush² *n* : felpa *f*, peluche *m*

plushy ['plʌʃi] *adj* **plushier; -est** : lujoso

Pluto ['plu:ṭo:] *n* : Plutón *m*

plutocracy [plu:'tɑkrəsi] *n*, *pl* -cies : plutocracia *f*

plutonium [plu:'to:niəm] *n* : plutonio *m*

ply¹ ['plaɪ] *v* **plied; plying** *vt* 1 USE, WIELD : manejar ⟨to ply an ax : manejar un hacha⟩ 2 PRACTICE : ejercer ⟨to ply a trade : ejercer un oficio⟩ 3 **to ply with questions** : acosar con preguntas

ply² *n*, *pl* **plies** 1 LAYER : chapa *f* (de madera), capa *f* (de papel) 2 STRAND : cabo *m* (de hilo, etc.)

plywood ['plaɪ,wʊd] *n* : contrachapado *m*

pneumatic [nʊ'mæṭɪk, njʊ-] *adj* : neumático

pneumonia [nʊ'mo:njə, njʊ-] *n* : pulmonía *f*, neumonía *f*

poach ['po:tʃ] *vt* 1 : cocer a fuego lento ⟨to poach an egg : escalfar un huevo⟩ 2 **to poach game** : cazar ilegalmente — *vi* : cazar ilegalmente

poacher ['po:tʃər] *n* : cazador *m* furtivo, cazadora *f* furtiva

pock ['pɑk] *n* 1 PUSTULE : pústula *f* 2 → pockmark

pocket¹ ['pɑkət] *vt* 1 : meterse en el bolsillo ⟨he pocketed the pen : se metió la pluma en el bolsillo⟩ 2 STEAL : embolsarse

pocket² *n* 1 : bolsillo *m*, bolsa *f* *Mex* ⟨a coat pocket : el bolsillo de un abrigo⟩ ⟨air pockets : bolsas de aire⟩ 2 CENTER : foco *m*, centro *m* ⟨a pocket of resistance : un foco de resistencia⟩

pocketbook ['pɑkət,bʊk] *n* 1 PURSE : cartera *f*, bolso *m*, bolsa *f* *Mex* 2 MEANS : recursos *mpl*

pocketknife ['pɑkət,naɪf] *n*, *pl* -knives : navaja *f*

pocket–size ['pɑkət'saɪz] *adj* : de bolsillo

pockmark ['pɑk,mɑrk] *n* : cicatriz *f* de viruela, viruela *f*

pod ['pɑd] *n* : vaina *f* ⟨pea pod : vaina de guisantes⟩

podiatrist [pə'daɪətrɪst, po-] *n* : podólogo *m*, -ga *f*

podiatry [pə'daɪətri, po-] *n* : podología *f*, podiatría *f*

podium ['po:diəm] *n*, *pl* -diums *or* -dia [-diə] : podio *m*, estrado *m*, tarima *f*

poem ['po:əm] *n* : poema *m*, poesía *f*

poet ['po:ət] *n* : poeta *mf*

poetic [po'ɛṭɪk] *or* **poetical** [-ṭɪkəl] *adj* : poético

poetry ['po:ətri] *n* : poesía *f*

pogrom ['po:grəm, pə'grɑm, 'pɑgrəm] *n* : pogrom *m*

poignancy ['pɔɪnjəntsi] *n*, *pl* -cies : lo conmovedor

poignant ['pɔɪnjənt] *adj* 1 PAINFUL : penoso, doloroso ⟨poignant grief : profundo dolor⟩ 2 TOUCHING : conmovedor, emocionante

poinsettia [pɔɪn'sɛṭiə, -'sɛṭə] *n* : flor *f* de Nochebuena

point¹ ['pɔɪnt] *vt* 1 SHARPEN : afilar (la punta de) 2 INDICATE : señalar, indicar ⟨to point the way : señalar el camino⟩ 3 AIM : apuntar 4 **to point out** : señalar, indicar — *vi* 1 **to point at** : señalar (con el dedo) 2 **to point to** INDICATE : señalar, indicar

point² *n* 1 ITEM : punto *m* ⟨the main points : los puntos principales⟩ 2 QUALITY : cualidad *f* ⟨her good points : sus buenas cualidades⟩ ⟨it's not his strong point : no es su (punto) fuerte⟩ 3 (*indicating a chief idea or meaning*) ⟨it's beside the point : no viene al caso⟩ ⟨to get to the point : ir al grano⟩ ⟨to stick to the point : no salirse del tema⟩ 4 PURPOSE : fin *m*, propósito *m* ⟨there's no point to it : no vale la pena, no sirve para nada⟩ 5 PLACE : punto *m*, lugar *m* ⟨points of interest : puntos interesantes⟩ 6 : punto *m* (en una escala) ⟨boiling point : punto de ebullición⟩ 7 MOMENT : momento *m*, coyuntura *f* ⟨at this point : en este momento⟩ 8 TIP : punta *f* 9 HEADLAND : punta *f*, cabo *m* 10 PERIOD : punto *m* (marca de puntuación) 11 UNIT : punto *m* ⟨he scored 15 points : ganó 15 puntos⟩ ⟨shares fell 10 points : las acciones bajaron 10 enteros⟩ 12 **compass points** : puntos *mpl* cardinales 13 **decimal point** : punto *m* decimal, coma *f*

point–blank¹ ['pɔɪnt'blæŋk] *adv* 1 : a quemarropa ⟨to shoot point-blank : disparar a quemarropa⟩ 2 BLUNTLY, DIRECTLY : a bocajarro, sin rodeos, francamente

point–blank² *adj* 1 : a quemarropa ⟨point-blank shots : disparos a quemarropa⟩ 2 BLUNT, DIRECT : directo, franco

pointed ['pɔɪntəd] *adj* **1** POINTY : puntiagudo **2** PERTINENT : atinado **3** CONSPICUOUS : marcado, manifiesto
pointedly ['pɔɪntədli] *adv* : intencionadamente, directamente
pointer ['pɔɪntər] *n* **1** STICK : puntero *m* (para maestros, etc.) **2** INDICATOR, NEEDLE : indicador *m*, aguja *f* **3** : perro *m* de muestra **4** HINT, TIP : consejo *m*
pointless ['pɔɪntləs] *adj* : inútil, ocioso, vano ⟨it's pointless to continue : no tiene sentido continuar⟩
point of view *n* : perspectiva *f*, punto *m* de vista
pointy ['pɔɪnti] *adj* : puntiagudo
poise¹ ['pɔɪz] *vt* **poised; poising** BALANCE : equilibrar, balancear
poise² *n* : aplomo *m*, compostura *f*
poison¹ ['pɔɪzən] *vt* **1** : envenenar, intoxicar **2** CORRUPT : corromper
poison² *n* : veneno *m*
poison ivy *n* : hiedra *f* venenosa
poisonous ['pɔɪzənəs] *adj* : venenoso, tóxico, ponzoñoso
poke¹ ['po:k] *v* **poked; poking** *vt* **1** JAB : golpear (con la punta de algo), dar ⟨he poked me with his finger : me dio con el dedo⟩ **2** THRUST : introducir, asomar ⟨I poked my head out the window : asomé la cabeza por la ventana⟩ — *vi* **1 to poke around** RUMMAGE : hurgar **2 to poke along** DAWDLE : demorarse, entretenerse
poke² *n* : golpe *m* abrupto (con la punta de algo)
poker ['po:kər] *n* **1** : atizador *m* (para el fuego) **2** : póker *m*, poker *m* (juego de naipes)
polar ['po:lər] *adj* : polar
polar bear *n* : oso *m* blanco
Polaris [po'lærɪs, -'lɑr-] → **North Star**
polarize ['po:lə,raɪz] *vt* **-ized; -izing** : polarizar
pole ['po:l] *n* **1** : palo *m*, poste *m*, vara *f* ⟨telephone pole : poste de teléfonos⟩ **2** : polo *m* ⟨the South Pole : el Polo Sur⟩ **3** : polo *m* (eléctrico o magnético)
Pole ['po:l] *n* : polaco *m*, -ca *f*
polecat ['po:l,kæt] *n, pl* **polecats** or **polecat** **1** : turón *m* (de Europa) **2** SKUNK : mofeta *f*, zorrillo *m*
polemical [pə'lɛmɪkəl] *adj* : polémico
polemics [pə'lɛmɪks] *ns & pl* : polémica *f*
polestar ['po:l,stɑr] → **North Star**
police¹ [pə'li:s] *vt* **-liced; -licing** : mantener el orden en ⟨to police the streets : patrullar las calles⟩
police² *ns & pl* **1** : policía *f* (organización) **2** POLICE OFFICERS : policías *mfpl*
policeman [pə'li:smən] *n, pl* **-men** [-mən, -,mɛn] : policía *m*
police officer *n* : policía *mf*, agente *mf* de policía

policewoman [pə'li:s,wʊmən] *n, pl* **-women** [-,wɪmən] : policía *f*, mujer *f* policía
policy ['pɑləsi] *n, pl* **-cies** **1** : política *f* ⟨foreign policy : política exterior⟩ **2** or **insurance policy** : póliza *f* de seguros, seguro *m*
polio¹ ['po:li,o:] *adj* : de polio ⟨polio vaccine : vacuna contra la polio⟩
polio² *n* → **poliomyelitis**
poliomyelitis [,po:li,o:,maɪə'laɪţəs] *n* : poliomielitis *f*, polio *f*
polish¹ ['pɑlɪʃ] *vt* **1** : pulir, lustrar, sacar brillo a ⟨to polish one's nails : pintarse las uñas⟩ **2** REFINE : pulir, perfeccionar
polish² *n* **1** LUSTER : brillo *m*, lustre *m* **2** REFINEMENT : refinamiento *m* **3** : betún *m* (para zapatos), cera *f* (para suelos y muebles), esmalte *m* (para las uñas)
Polish¹ ['po:lɪʃ] *adj* : polaco
Polish² *n* : polaco *m* (idioma)
polite [pə'laɪt] *adj* **-liter; -est** : cortés, correcto, educado
politely [pə'laɪtli] *adv* : cortésmente, correctamente, con buenos modales
politeness [pə'laɪtnəs] *n* : cortesía *f*
politic ['pɑlə,tɪk] *adj* : diplomático, prudente
political [pə'lɪţɪkəl] *adj* : político — **politically** [-ţɪkli] *adv*
politician [,pɑlə'tɪʃən] *n* : político *m*, -ca *f*
politics ['pɑlə,tɪks] *ns & pl* : política *f*
polka ['po:lkə, 'po:kə] *n* : polka *f*
polka dot ['po:kə,dɑt] *n* : lunar *m* (en un diseño)
poll¹ ['po:l] *vt* **1** : obtener (votos) ⟨she polled over 1000 votes : obtuvo más de 1000 votos⟩ **2** CANVASS : encuestar, sondear — *vi* : obtener votos
poll² *n* **1** SURVEY : encuesta *f*, sondeo *m* **2 polls** *npl* : urnas *fpl* ⟨to go to the polls : acudir a las urnas, ir a votar⟩
pollen ['pɑlən] *n* : polen *m*
pollinate ['pɑlə,neɪt] *vt* **-nated; -nating** : polinizar
pollination [,pɑlə'neɪʃən] *n* : polinización *f*
pollster ['po:lstər] *n* : encuestador *m*, -dora *f*
pollutant [pə'lu:tənt] *n* : contaminante *m*
pollute [pə'lu:t] *vt* **-luted; -luting** : contaminar
pollution [pə'lu:ʃən] *n* : contaminación *f*
pollywog or **polliwog** ['pɑli,wɔg] *n* TADPOLE : renacuajo *m*
polo ['po:,lo:] *n* : polo *m*
poltergeist ['po:ltər,gaɪst] *n* : poltergeist *m*, fantasma *m* travieso
polyester ['pɑli,ɛstər, ,pɑli'-] *n* : poliéster *m*
polygamous [pə'lɪgəməs] *adj* : polígamo
polygamy [pə'lɪgəmi] *n* : poligamia *f*
polygon ['pɑli,gɑn] *n* : polígono *m*

polymer ['pɑləmər] *n* : polímero *m*

Polynesian [ˌpɑləˈniːʒən, -ʃən] *n* : polinesio *m*, -sia *f* — **Polynesian** *adj*

polyunsaturated [ˌpɑliˌʌnˈsætʃə-ˌreɪtəd] *adj* : poliinsaturado

pomegranate ['pɑməˌgrænət, 'pɑm-ˌgrænət] *n* : granada *f* (fruta)

pommel¹ ['pʌməl] *vt* → **pummel**

pommel² ['pʌməl, 'pɑ-] *n* 1 : pomo *m* (de una espada) 2 : perilla *f* (de una silla de montar)

pomp ['pɑmp] *n* 1 SPLENDOR : pompa *f*, esplendor *m* 2 OSTENTATION : boato *m*, ostentación *f*

pom–pom ['pɑmˌpɑm] *n* : borla *f*, pompón *m*

pomposity [pɑmˈpɑsəti] *n, pl* **-ties** : pomposidad *f*

pompous ['pɑmpəs] *adj* : pomposo — **pompously** *adv*

poncho ['pɑnˌtʃoː] *n, pl* **-chos** : poncho *m*

pond ['pɑnd] *n* : charca *f* (natural), estanque *m* (artificial)

ponder ['pɑndər] *vt* : reflexionar, considerar — *vi* **to ponder over** : reflexionar sobre, sopesar

ponderous ['pɑndərəs] *adj* : pesado

pontiff ['pɑntɪf] *n* POPE : pontífice *m*

pontificate [pɑnˈtɪfəˌkeɪt] *vi* **-cated; -cating** : pontificar

pontoon [pɑnˈtuːn] *n* : pontón *m*

pony ['poːni] *n, pl* **-nies** : poni *m*, poney *m*, jaca *f*

ponytail ['poːniˌteɪl] *n* : cola *f* de caballo, coleta *f*

poodle ['puːdəl] *n* : caniche *m*

pool¹ ['puːl] *vt* : mancomunar, hacer un fondo común de

pool² *n* 1 : charca *f* ⟨a swimming pool : una piscina⟩ 2 PUDDLE : charco *m* 3 RESERVE, SUPPLY : fondo *m* común (de recursos), reserva *f* 4 : billar *m* (juego)

poor ['pʊr, 'por] *adj* 1 : pobre ⟨poor people : los pobres⟩ 2 SCANTY : pobre, escaso ⟨poor attendance : baja asistencia⟩ 3 UNFORTUNATE : pobre ⟨poor thing! : ¡pobrecito!⟩ 4 BAD : malo ⟨to be in poor health : estar mal de salud⟩

poorly ['pʊrli, 'por-] *adv* : mal

pop¹ ['pɑp] *v* **popped; popping** *vi* 1 BURST : reventarse, estallar 2 : ir, venir, o aparecer abruptamente ⟨he popped into the house : se metió en la casa⟩ ⟨a menu pops up : aparece un menú⟩ 3 **to pop out** PROTRUDE : salirse, saltarse ⟨my eyes popped out of my head : se me saltaban los ojos⟩ — *vt* 1 BURST : reventar 2 : hacer o meter abruptamente ⟨he popped it into his mouth : se lo metió en la boca⟩

pop² *adj* : popular ⟨pop music : música popular⟩

pop³ *n* 1 : estallido *m* pequeño (de un globo, etc.) 2 SODA : refresco *m*, gaseosa *f*

popcorn ['pɑpˌkɔrn] *n* : palomitas *fpl* (de maíz)

pope ['poːp] *n* : papa *m* ⟨Pope John : el Papa Juan⟩

poplar ['pɑplər] *n* : álamo *m*

poplin ['pɑplɪn] *n* : popelín *m*, popelina *f*

poppy ['pɑpi] *n, pl* **-pies** : amapola *f*

populace ['pɑpjələs] *n* 1 MASSES : pueblo *m* 2 POPULATION : población *f*

popular ['pɑpjələr] *adj* 1 : popular ⟨the popular vote : el voto popular⟩ 2 COMMON : generalizado, común ⟨popular beliefs : creencias generalizadas⟩ 3 : popular, de gran popularidad ⟨a popular singer : un cantante popular⟩

popularity [ˌpɑpjəˈlærəti] *n* : popularidad *f*

popularize ['pɑpjələˌraɪz] *vt* **-ized; -izing** : popularizar

popularly ['pɑpjələrli] *adv* : popularmente, vulgarmente

populate ['pɑpjəˌleɪt] *vt* **-lated; -lating** : poblar

population [ˌpɑpjəˈleɪʃən] *n* : población *f*

populist ['pɑpjəlɪst] *n* : populista *mf* — **populist** *adj*

populous ['pɑpjələs] *adj* : populoso

porcelain ['porsələn] *n* : porcelana *f*

porch ['portʃ] *n* : porche *m*

porcupine ['pɔrkjəˌpaɪn] *n* : puerco *m* espín

pore¹ ['por] *vi* **pored; poring** 1 GAZE : mirar (con atención) 2 **to pore over** : leer detenidamente, estudiar

pore² *n* : poro *m*

pork ['pork] *n* : carne *f* de cerdo, carne *f* de puerco

pornographic [ˌpɔrnəˈgræfɪk] *adj* : pornográfico

pornography [pɔrˈnɑgrəfi] *n* : pornografía *f*

porous ['porəs] *adj* : poroso

porpoise ['porpəs] *n* 1 : marsopa *f* 2 DOLPHIN : delfín *m*

porridge ['porɪdʒ] *n* : sopa *f* espesa de harina, gachas *fpl*

port¹ ['port] *adj* : de babor ⟨on the port side : a babor⟩

port² *n* 1 HARBOR : puerto *m* 2 ORIFICE : orificio *m* (de una válvula, etc.) 3 : puerto *m* (de una computadora) 4 PORTHOLE : portilla *f* 5 *or* **port side** : babor *m* (de un barco) 6 : oporto *m* (vino)

portable ['portəbəl] *adj* : portátil

portal ['portəl] *n* : portal *m*

portend [porˈtɛnd] *vt* : presagiar, augurar

portent ['porˌtɛnt] *n* : presagio *m*, augurio *m*

portentous [porˈtɛntəs] *adj* : profético, que presagia

porter ['portər] *n* : maletero *m*, mozo *m* (de estación)

portfolio [portˈfoːliˌo] *n, pl* **-lios** 1 FOLDER : cartera *f* (para llevar papeles), carpeta *f* 2 : cartera *f* (diplomática) **3** investment **portfolio** : cartera de inversiones

porthole ['pɔrt,hoːl] *n* : portilla *f* (de un barco), ventanilla *f* (de un avión)

portico ['pɔrtɪ,koː] *n*, *pl* **-coes** *or* **-cos** : pórtico *m*

portion¹ ['pɔrʃən] *vt* DISTRIBUTE : repartir

portion² *n* PART, SHARE : porción *f*, parte *f*

portly ['pɔrtli] *adj* **-lier; -est** : corpulento

portrait ['pɔrtrət, -,treɪt] *n* : retrato *m*

portray [pɔr'treɪ] *vt* **1** DEPICT : representar, retratar **2** DESCRIBE : describir **3** PLAY : interpretar (un personaje)

portrayal [pɔr'treɪəl] *n* **1** REPRESENTATION : representación *f* **2** PORTRAIT : retrato *m*

Portuguese [,pɔrtʃəˈgiːz, -ˈgiːs] *n* **1** : portugués *m*, **-guesa** *f* (persona) **2** : portugués *m* (idioma) — **Portuguese** *adj*

pose¹ ['poːz] *v* **posed; posing** *vt* PRESENT : plantear (una pregunta, etc.), representar (una amenaza) — *vi* **1** : posar (para una foto, etc.) **2 to pose as** : hacerse pasar por

pose² *n* **1** : pose *f* ⟨to strike a pose : asumir una pose⟩ **2** PRETENSE : pose *f*, afectación *f*

posh ['pɑʃ] *adj* : elegante, de lujo

position¹ [pəˈzɪʃən] *vt* : colocar, situar, ubicar

position² *n* **1** APPROACH, STANCE : posición *f*, postura *f*, planteamiento *m* **2** LOCATION : posición *f*, ubicación *f* **3** STATUS : posición *f* (en una jerarquía) **4** JOB : puesto *m*

positive ['pɑzətɪv] *adj* **1** DEFINITE : incuestionable, inequívoco ⟨positive evidence : pruebas irrefutables⟩ **2** CONFIDENT : seguro **3** : positivo (en gramática, matemáticas, y física) **4** AFFIRMATIVE : positivo, afirmativo ⟨a positive response : una respuesta positiva⟩

positively ['pɑzətɪvli] *adv* **1** FAVORABLY : favorablemente **2** OPTIMISTICALLY : positivamente **3** DEFINITELY : definitivamente, en forma concluyente **4** (*used for emphasis*) : realmente, verdaderamente ⟨it's positively awful! : ¡es verdaderamente malo!⟩

possess [pəˈzɛs] *vt* **1** HAVE, OWN : poseer, tener **2** SEIZE : apoderarse de ⟨he was possessed by fear : el miedo se apoderó de él⟩

possession [pəˈzɛʃən] *n* **1** POSSESSING : posesión *f* **2** : posesión *f* (por un demonio, etc.) **3 possessions** *npl* PROPERTY : bienes *mpl*, propiedad *f*

possessive¹ [pəˈzɛsɪv] *adj* **1** : posesivo (en gramática) **2** JEALOUS : posesivo, celoso

possessive² *n* *or* **possessive case** : posesivo *m*

possessor [pəˈzɛsər] *n* : poseedor *m*, **-dora** *f*

possibility [,pɑsəˈbɪləti] *n*, *pl* **-ties** : posibilidad *f*

possible ['pɑsəbəl] *adj* : posible

possibly ['pɑsəbli] *adv* **1** CONCEIVABLY : posiblemente ⟨it can't possibly be true! : ¡no puede ser!⟩ **2** PERHAPS : quizás, posiblemente

possum ['pɑsəm] → **opossum**

post¹ ['poːst] *vt* **1** MAIL : echar al correo, mandar por correo **2** ANNOUNCE : anunciar ⟨they've posted the grades : han anunciado las notas⟩ **3** AFFIX : fijar, poner (noticias, etc.) **4** STATION : apostar **5 to keep (someone) posted** : tener al corriente (a alguien)

post² *n* **1** POLE : poste *m*, palo *m* **2** STATION : puesto *m* **3** CAMP : puesto *m* (militar) **4** JOB, POSITION : puesto *m*, empleo *m*, cargo *m*

postage ['poːstɪdʒ] *n* : franqueo *m*

postal ['poːstəl] *adj* : postal

postcard ['poːst,kɑrd] *n* : postal *f*, tarjeta *f* postal

poster ['poːstər] *n* : póster *m*, cartel *m*, afiche *m*

posterior¹ [pɑˈstɪriər, po-] *adj* : posterior

posterior² *n* BUTTOCKS : trasero *m*, nalgas *fpl*, asentaderas *fpl*

posterity [pɑˈstɛrəti] *n* : posteridad *f*

postgraduate¹ [,poːstˈgrædʒuət] *adj* : de postgrado

postgraduate² *n* : postgraduado *m*, **-da** *f*

posthaste ['poːstˈheɪst] *adv* : a toda prisa

posthumous ['pɑstʃəməs] *adj* : póstumo — **posthumously** *adv*

postman ['poːstmən, -,mæn] → **mailman**

postmark¹ ['poːst,mɑrk] *vt* : matasellar

postmark² *n* : matasellos *m*

postmaster ['poːst,mæstər] *n* : administrador *m*, **-dora** *f* de correos

postmodern [,poːstˈmɑdərn] *adj* : posmoderno

postmortem [,poːstˈmɔrtəm] *n* : autopsia *f*

postnatal [,poːstˈneɪtəl] *adj* : postnatal ⟨postnatal depression : depresión posparto⟩

post office *n* : correo *m*, oficina *f* de correos

postoperative [,poːstˈɑpərətɪv, -,reɪ-] *adj* : posoperatorio

postpaid [poːstˈpeɪd] *adv* : con franqueo pagado

postpone [,poːstˈpoːn] *vt* **-poned; -poning** : postergar, aplazar, posponer

postponement [,poːstˈpoːnmənt] *n* : postergación *f*, aplazamiento *m*

postscript ['poːst,skrɪpt] *n* : postdata *f*, posdata *f*

postulate ['pɑstʃə,leɪt] *vt* **-lated; -lating** : postular

posture¹ ['pɑstʃər] *vi* **-tured; -turing** : posar, asumir una pose

posture² *n* : postura *f*

postwar [,poːstˈwɔr] *adj* : de (la) posguerra

posy ['po:zi] *n, pl* **-sies** **1** FLOWER : flor *f* **2** BOUQUET : ramo *m*, ramillete *m*

pot¹ ['pɑt] *vt* **potted; potting** : plantar (en una maceta)

pot² *n* **1** : olla *f* (de cocina) **2 pots and pans** : cacharros *mpl*

potable ['po:ʈəbəl] *adj* : potable

potash ['pɑt,æʃ] *n* : potasa *f*

potassium [pə'tæsiəm] *n* : potasio *m*

potato [pə'teɪʈo] *n, pl* **-toes** : papa *f*, patata *f Spain*

potato chips *npl* : papas *fpl* fritas (de bolsa)

potbellied ['pɑt,bɛlid] *adj* : panzón, barrigón *fam*

potbelly ['pɑt,bɛli] *n* : panza *f*, barriga *f*

potency ['po:ʈəntsi] *n, pl* **-cies** **1** POWER : fuerza *f*, potencia *f* **2** EFFECTIVENESS : eficacia *f*

potent ['po:ʈənt] *adj* **1** POWERFUL : potente, poderoso **2** EFFECTIVE : eficaz ⟨a potent medicine : una medicina bien fuerte⟩

potential¹ [pə'tɛntʃəl] *adj* : potencial, posible

potential² *n* **1** : potencial *m* ⟨growth potential : potencial de crecimiento⟩ ⟨a child with potential : un niño que promete⟩ **2** : potencial *m* (eléctrico) — **potentially** *adv*

potful ['pɑt,fʊl] *n* : contenido *m* de una olla ⟨a potful of water : una olla de agua⟩

pothole ['pɑt,ho:l] *n* : bache *m*

potion ['po:ʃən] *n* : brebaje *m*, poción *f*

potluck ['pɑt,lʌk] *n* **to take potluck** : tomar lo que haya

potpourri [,po:pʊ'ri:] *n* : popurrí *m*

potshot ['pɑt,ʃɑt] *n* **1** : tiro *m* al azar ⟨to take potshots at : disparar al azar a⟩ **2** CRITICISM : crítica *f* (hecha al azar)

potter ['pɑʈər] *n* : alfarero *m*, -ra *f*

pottery ['pɑʈəri] *n, pl* **-teries** : cerámica *f*

pouch ['paʊtʃ] *n* **1** BAG : bolsa *f* pequeña **2** : bolsa *f* (de un animal)

poultice ['po:lʈəs] *n* : emplasto *m*, cataplasma *f*

poultry ['po:ltri] *n* : aves *fpl* de corral

pounce ['paʊnts] *vi* **pounced; pouncing** : abalanzarse

pound¹ ['paʊnd] *vt* **1** CRUSH : machacar, machucar, majar **2** BEAT : golpear, machacar ⟨she pounded the lessons into them : les machacaba las lecciones⟩ ⟨he pounded home his point : les hizo entender su razonamiento⟩ — *vi* **1** BEAT : palpitar (dícese del corazón) **2** RESOUND : retumbar, resonar **3** : andar con paso pesado ⟨we pounded through the mud : caminamos pesadamente por el barro⟩

pound² *n* **1** : libra *f* (unidad de peso) **2** : libra *f* (unidad monetaria) **3 dog pound** : perrera *f*

pour ['por] *vt* **1** : echar, verter, servir (bebidas) ⟨pour it into a pot : viértalo en una olla⟩ **2** : proveer con abundancia ⟨they poured money into it : le invirtieron mucho dinero⟩ **3 to pour out** : dar salida a ⟨he poured out his feelings to her : se desahogó con ella⟩ — *vi* **1** FLOW : manar, fluir, salir ⟨blood was pouring from the wound : la sangre le salía de la herida⟩ **2 it's pouring (outside)** : está lloviendo a cántaros

pout¹ ['paʊt] *vi* : hacer pucheros

pout² *n* : puchero *m*

poverty ['pɑvərʈi] *n* : pobreza *f*, indigencia *f*

powder¹ ['paʊdər] *vt* **1** : empolvar ⟨to powder one's face : empolvarse la cara⟩ **2** PULVERIZE : pulverizar

powder² *n* : polvo *m*, polvos *mpl*

powdery ['paʊdəri] *adj* : polvoriento, como polvo

power¹ ['paʊər] *vt* : impulsar, propulsar

power² *n* **1** AUTHORITY : poder *m*, autoridad *f* ⟨executive powers : poderes ejecutivos⟩ **2** ABILITY : capacidad *f*, poder *m* **3** : potencia *f* (política) ⟨foreign powers : potencias extranjeras⟩ **4** STRENGTH : fuerza *f* **5** : potencia *f* (en física y matemáticas)

powerful ['paʊərfəl] *adj* : poderoso, potente — **powerfully** *adv*

powerhouse ['paʊər,haʊs] *n* : persona *f* dinámica

powerless ['paʊərləs] *adj* : impotente

power plant *n* : central *f* eléctrica

powwow ['paʊ,waʊ] *n* : conferencia *f*

pox ['pɑks] *n, pl* **pox** *or* **poxes** **1** CHICKEN POX : varicela *f* **2** SYPHILIS : sífilis *f*

practicable ['præktɪkəbəl] *adj* : practicable, viable, factible

practical ['præktɪkəl] *adj* : práctico

practicality [,præktɪ'kæləʈi] *n, pl* **-ties** : factibilidad *f*, viabilidad *f*

practical joke *n* : broma *f* (pesada)

practically ['præktɪkli] *adv* **1** : de manera práctica **2** ALMOST : casi, prácticamente

practice¹ *or* **practise** ['præktəs] *vt* **-ticed** *or* **-tised; -ticing** *or* **-tising** **1** : practicar ⟨he practiced his German on us : practicó el alemán con nosotros⟩ ⟨to practice politeness : practicar la cortesía⟩ **2** : ejercer ⟨to practice medicine : ejercer la medicina⟩

practice² *n* **1** USE : práctica *f* ⟨to put into practice : poner en práctica⟩ **2** CUSTOM : costumbre *f* ⟨it's a common practice here : por aquí se acostumbra hacerlo⟩ **3** TRAINING : práctica *f* **4** : ejercicio *m* (de una profesión)

practitioner [præk'tɪʃənər] *n* **1** : profesional *mf* **2 general practitioner** : médico *m*, -ca *f*

pragmatic [præg'mæʈɪk] *adj* : pragmático — **pragmatically** *adv*

pragmatism ['prægmə,tɪzəm] *n* : pragmatismo

prairie ['prɛri] *n* : pradera *f*, llanura *f*

praise[1] ['preɪz] *vt* **praised; praising**
: elogiar, alabar ⟨to praise God : alabar
a Dios⟩
praise[2] *n* : elogio *m*, alabanza *f*
praiseworthy ['preɪz,wərði] *adj* : digno
de alabanza, loable
prance[1] ['præn*t*s] *vi* **pranced; prancing**
1 : hacer cabriolas, cabriolar ⟨a prancing horse : un caballo haciendo cabri-
olas⟩ **2** SWAGGER : pavonearse
prance[2] *n* : cabriola *f*
prank ['præŋk] *n* : broma *f*, travesura *f*
prankster ['præŋkstər] *n* : bromista *mf*
prattle[1] ['prætəl] *vt* **-tled; -tling** : parlotear *fam*, cotorrear *fam*, balbucear
(como un niño)
prattle[2] *n* : parloteo *m fam*, cotorreo *m*
fam, cháchara *f fam*
prawn ['prɔn] *n* : langostino *m*, camarón
m, gamba *f*
pray ['preɪ] *vt* ENTREAT : rogar, suplicar
— *vi* : rezar
prayer ['prɛr] *n* **1** : plegaria *f*, oración *f*
⟨to say one's prayers : orar, rezar⟩ ⟨the
Lord's Prayer : el Padrenuestro⟩ **2**
PRAYING : rezo *m*, oración *f* ⟨to kneel
in prayer : arrodillarse para rezar⟩
praying mantis → **mantis**
preach ['priːtʃ] *vi* : predicar — *vt* ADVO-
CATE : abogar por ⟨to preach cooperation : promover la cooperación⟩
preacher ['priːtʃər] *n* **1** : predicador *m*,
-dora *f* **2** MINISTER : pastor *m*, -tora *f*
preamble ['priː,æmbəl] *n* : preámbulo *m*
prearrange [,priːə'reɪndʒ] *vt* **-ranged;
-ranging** : arreglar de antemano
precarious [pri'kæriəs] *adj* : precario —
precariously *adv*
precariousness [pri'kæriəsnəs] *n* : precariedad *f*
precaution [pri'kɔʃən] *n* : precaución *f*
precautionary [pri'kɔʃə,nɛri] *adj* : preventivo, cautelar, precautorio
precede [pri'siːd] *v* **-ceded; -ceding**
: preceder a
precedence ['prɛsədən*t*s, prɪ'siːdən*t*s] *n*
: precedencia *f*
precedent ['prɛsədənt] *n* : precedente *m*
precept ['priː,sɛpt] *n* : precepto *m*
precinct ['priː,sɪŋkt] *n* **1** DISTRICT : distrito *m* (policial, electoral, etc.) **2**
precincts *npl* PREMISES : recinto *m*,
predio *m*, límites *mpl* (de una ciudad)
precious ['prɛʃəs] *adj* **1** : precioso ⟨pre-
cious gems : piedras preciosas⟩ **2** DEAR
: querido **3** AFFECTED : afectado
precipice ['prɛsəpəs] *n* : precipicio *m*
precipitate [pri'sɪpə,teɪt] *v* **-tated;
-tating** *vt* **1** HASTEN, PROVOKE : precipitar, provocar **2** HURL : arrojar **3**
: precipitar (en química) — *vi* : precipitarse (en química), condensarse (en
meteorología)
precipitation [pri,sɪpə'teɪʃən] *n* **1** HASTE
: precipitación *f*, prisa *f* **2** : precipita-
ciones *fpl* (en meteorología)
precipitous [pri'sɪpətəs] *adj* **1** HASTY,
RASH : precipitado **2** STEEP : escarpa-

do, empinado ⟨a precipitous drop : una
caída vertiginosa⟩
précis [preɪ'siː] *n, pl* **précis** [-'siːz] : resumen *m*
precise [pri'saɪs] *adj* **1** DEFINITE : preciso, explícito **2** EXACT : exacto, preciso ⟨precise calculations : cálculos
precisos⟩ — **precisely** *adv*
preciseness [pri'saɪsnəs] *n* : precisión *f*,
exactitud *f*
precision [pri'sɪʒən] *n* : precisión *f*
preclude [pri'kluːd] *vt* **-cluded; -cluding**
: evitar, impedir, excluir (una posibilidad, etc.)
precocious [pri'koːʃəs] *adj* : precoz —
precociously *adv*
precocity [pri'kɑsəti] *n* : precocidad *f*
preconceive [,priːkən'siːv] *vt* **-ceived;
-ceiving** : preconcebir
preconception [,priːkən'spʃən] *n* : idea
f preconcebida
precondition [,priːkən'dɪʃən] *n* : precondición *f*, condición *f* previa
precook [,priː'kʊk] *vt* : precocinar
precursor [pri'kərsər] *n* : precursor *m*,
-sora *f*
predator ['prɛdətər] *n* : depredador *m*,
-dora *f*
predatory ['prɛdə,tori] *adj* : depredador
predecessor ['prɛdə,sɛsər, 'priː-] *n* : antecesor *m*, -sora *f*; predecesor *m*, -sora
f
predestination [pri,dɛstə'neɪʃən]   *n*
: predestinación *f*
predestine [pri'dɛstən] *vt* **-tined; -tining**
: predestinar
predetermine [,priːdɪ'tərmən]   *vt*
-mined; -mining : predeterminar
predicament [pri'dɪkəmənt] *n* : apuro
m, aprieto *m*
predicate[1] ['prɛdə,keɪt] *vt* **-cated; -cat-
ing 1** AFFIRM : afirmar, aseverar **2 to
be predicated on** : estar basado en
predicate[2] ['prɛdɪkət] *n* : predicado *m*
predict [pri'dɪkt] *vt* : pronosticar, predecir
predictable [pri'dɪktəbəl] *adj* : previsible — **predictably** [-bli] *adv*
prediction [pri'dɪkʃən] *n* : pronóstico *m*,
predicción *f*
predilection [,prɛdəl'ɛkʃən, ,priː-]   *n*
: predilección *f*
predispose [,priːdɪ'spoːz] *vt* **-posed;
-posing** : predisponer
predisposition [,priː,dɪspə'zɪʃən] *n* : predisposición *f*
predominance [pri'dɑmənən*t*s] *n* : predominio *m*
predominant [pri'dɑmənənt] *adj* : predominante — **predominantly** *adv*
predominate [pri'dɑmə,neɪt] *vi* **-nated;
-nating 1** : predominar (en cantidad)
2 PREVAIL : prevalecer
preeminence [pri'ɛmənən*t*s] *n* : preeminencia *f*
preeminent [pri'ɛmənənt] *adj* : preeminente
preeminently [pri'ɛmənəntli] *adv* : especialmente

preempt [pri'ɛmpt] *vt* **1** APPROPRIATE : apoderarse de, apropiarse de **2** : reemplazar (un programa de televisión, etc.) **3** FORESTALL : adelantarse a (un ataque, etc.)

preen ['pri:n] *vt* : arreglarse (el pelo, las plumas, etc.)

prefabricated [ˌpri:'fæbrəˌkeɪtəd] *adj* : prefabricado

preface ['prɛfəs] *n* : prefacio *m*, prólogo *m*

prefatory ['prɛfəˌtori] *adj* : preliminar

prefer [pri'fər] *vt* **-ferred; -ferring 1** : preferir ⟨I prefer coffee : prefiero café⟩ **2 to prefer charges against** : presentar cargos contra

preferable ['prɛfərəbəl] *adj* : preferible

preferably ['prɛfərəbli] *adv* : preferentemente, de preferencia

preference ['prɛfrənts, 'prɛfər-] *n* : preferencia *f*, gusto *m*

preferential [ˌprɛfə'rɛntʃəl] *adj* : preferencial, preferente

prefigure [pri'fɪɡjər] *vt* **-ured; -uring** FORESHADOW : prefigurar, anunciar

prefix ['pri:ˌfɪks] *n* : prefijo *m*

pregnancy ['prɛɡnəntsi] *n, pl* **-cies** : embarazo *m*, preñez *f*

pregnant ['prɛɡnənt] *adj* **1** : embarazada (dícese de una mujer), preñada (dícese de un animal) **2** MEANINGFUL : significativo

preheat [ˌpri:'hi:t] *vt* : precalentar

prehensile [pri'hɛntsəl, -'hɛnˌsaɪl] *adj* : prensil

prehistoric [ˌpri:his'tɔrɪk] *or* **prehistorical** [-ɪkəl] *adj* : prehistórico

prejudge [ˌpri:'dʒʌdʒ] *vt* **-judged; -judging** : prejuzgar

prejudice¹ ['prɛdʒədəs] *vt* **-diced; -dicing 1** DAMAGE : perjudicar **2** BIAS : predisponer, influir en

prejudice² *n* **1** DAMAGE : perjuicio *m* (en derecho) **2** BIAS : prejuicio *m*

prelate ['prɛlət] *n* : prelado *m*

preliminary¹ [pri'lɪməˌnɛri] *adj* : preliminar

preliminary² *n, pl* **-naries 1** : preámbulo *m*, preludio *m* **2 preliminaries** *npl* : preliminares *mpl*

prelude ['prɛˌlu:d, 'prɛlˌju:d; 'preɪˌlu:d, 'pri:-] *n* : preludio *m*

premarital [ˌpri:'mærətəl] *adj* : prematrimonial

premature [ˌpri:mə'tʊr, -'tjʊr, -'tʃʊr] *adj* : prematuro — **prematurely** *adv*

premeditate [pri'mɛdəˌteɪt] *vt* **-tated; -tating** : premeditar

premeditation [priˌmɛdə'teɪʃən] *n* : premeditación *f*

premenstrual [pri'mɛntstruəl] *adj* : premenstrual

premier¹ [pri'mɪr, -'mjɪr; 'pri:miər] *adj* : principal

premier² *n* PRIME MINISTER : primer ministro *m*, primera ministra *f*

premiere¹ [pri'mjɛr, -'mɪr] *vt* **-miered; -miering** : estrenar

premiere² *n* : estreno *m*

premise ['prɛmɪs] *n* **1** : premisa *f* ⟨the premise of his arguments : la premisa de sus argumentos⟩ **2 premises** *npl* : recinto *m*, local *m*

premium ['pri:miəm] *n* **1** BONUS : prima *f* **2** SURCHARGE : recargo *m* ⟨to sell at a premium : vender (algo) muy caro⟩ **3 insurance premium** : prima *f* (de seguros) **4 to set a premium on** : darle un gran valor (a algo)

premonition [ˌpri:mə'nɪʃən, ˌprɛmə-] *n* : presentimiento *m*, premonición *f*

prenatal [ˌpri:'neɪtəl] *adj* : prenatal

preoccupation [priˌɑkjə'peɪʃən] *n* : preocupación *f*

preoccupied [pri'ɑkjəˌpaɪd] *adj* : abstraído, ensimismado, preocupado

preoccupy [pri'ɑkjəˌpaɪ] *vt* **-pied; -pying** : preocupar

preparation [ˌprɛpə'reɪʃən] *n* **1** PREPARING : preparación *f* **2** MIXTURE : preparado *m* ⟨a preparation for burns : un preparado para quemaduras⟩ **3 preparations** *npl* ARRANGEMENTS : preparativos *mpl*

preparatory [pri'pærəˌtori] *adj* : preparatorio

prepare [pri'pær] *v* **-pared; -paring** *vt* : preparar — *vi* : prepararse

prepay [ˌpri:'peɪ] *vt* **-paid; -paying** : pagar por adelantado

preponderance [pri'pɑndərənts] *n* : preponderancia *f*

preponderant [pri'pɑndərənt] *adj* : preponderante — **preponderantly** *adv*

preposition [ˌprɛpə'zɪʃən] *n* : preposición *f*

prepositional [ˌprɛpə'zɪʃənəl] *adj* : preposicional

prepossessing [ˌpri:pə'zɛsɪŋ] *adj* : atractivo, agradable

preposterous [pri'pɑstərəs] *adj* : absurdo, ridículo

prerequisite¹ [pri'rɛkwəzət] *adj* : necesario, esencial

prerequisite² *n* : condición *f* necesario, requisito *m* previo

prerogative [pri'rɑɡətɪv] *n* : prerrogativa *f*

presage ['prɛsɪdʒ, pri'seɪdʒ] *vt* **-saged; -saging** : presagiar

preschool ['pri:ˌsku:l] *adj* : preescolar ⟨preschool students : estudiantes de preescolar⟩

prescribe [pri'skraɪb] *vt* **-scribed; -scribing 1** ORDAIN : prescribir, ordenar **2** : recetar (medicinas, etc.)

prescription [pri'skrɪpʃən] *n* : receta *f*

presence ['prɛzənts] *n* : presencia *f*

present¹ [pri'zɛnt] *vt* **1** INTRODUCE : presentar ⟨to present oneself : presentarse⟩ **2** : presentar (una obra de teatro, etc.) **3** GIVE : entregar (un regalo, etc.), regalar, obsequiar **4** SHOW : presentar, ofrecer ⟨it presents a lovely view : ofrece una vista muy linda⟩

present² ['prɛzənt] *adj* **1** : actual ⟨present conditions : condiciones actuales⟩

2 : presente ⟨all the students were present : todos los estudiantes estaban presentes⟩

present³ ['prɛzənt] *n* **1** GIFT : regalo *m*, obsequio *m* **2** : presente *m* ⟨at present : en este momento⟩ **3** *or* **present tense** : presente *m*

presentable [pri'zɛntəbəl] *adj* : presentable

presentation [ˌpri:ˌzɛn'teɪʃən, ˌprɛzən-] *n* : presentación *f* ⟨presentation ceremony : ceremonia de entrega⟩

presentiment [pri'zɛntəmənt] *n* : presentimiento *m*, premonición *f*

presently ['prɛzəntli] *adv* **1** SOON : pronto, dentro de poco **2** NOW : actualmente, ahora

present participle *n* : participio *m* presente, participio *m* activo

preservation [ˌprɛzər'veɪʃən] *n* : conservación *f*, preservación *f*

preservative [pri'zərvətɪv] *n* : conservante *m*

preserve¹ [pri'zərv] *vt* **-served; -serving 1** PROTECT : proteger, preservar **2** : conservar (los alimentos, etc.) **3** MAINTAIN : conservar, mantener

preserve² *n* **1** *or* **preserves** *npl* : conserva *f* ⟨peach preserves : duraznos en conserva⟩ **2** : coto *m* ⟨game preserve : coto de caza⟩

preside [pri'zaɪd] *vi* **-sided; -siding 1 to preside over** : presidir ⟨he presided over the meeting : presidió la reunión⟩ **2 to preside over** : supervisar ⟨she presides over the department : dirige el departamento⟩

presidency ['prɛzədəntsi] *n, pl* **-cies** : presidencia *f*

president ['prɛzədənt] *n* : presidente *m*, -ta *f*

presidential [ˌprɛzə'dɛntʃəl] *adj* : presidencial

press¹ ['prɛs] *vt* **1** PUSH : apretar **2** SQUEEZE : apretar, prensar (frutas, flores, etc.) **3** IRON : planchar (ropa) **4** URGE : instar, apremiar ⟨he pressed me to come : insistió en que viniera⟩ — *vi* **1** PUSH : apretar ⟨press hard : aprieta con fuerza⟩ **2** CROWD : apiñarse **3** : abrirse paso ⟨I pressed through the crowd : me abrí paso entre el gentío⟩ **4** URGE : presionar

press² *n* **1** CROWD : multitud *f* **2** : imprenta *f*, prensa *f* ⟨to go to press : entrar en prensa⟩ **3** URGENCY : urgencia *f*, prisa *f* **4** PRINTER, PUBLISHER : imprenta *f*, editorial *f* **5 the press** : la prensa ⟨freedom of the press : libertad de prensa⟩

pressing ['prɛsɪŋ] *adj* URGENT : urgente

pressure¹ ['prɛʃər] *vt* **-sured; -suring** : presionar, apremiar

pressure² *n* **1** : presión *f* ⟨to be under pressure : estar bajo presión⟩ **2** → **blood pressure**

pressurize ['prɛʃəˌraɪz] *vt* **-ized; -izing** : presurizar

prestige [prɛ'sti:ʒ, -'sti:dʒ] *n* : prestigio *m*

prestigious [prɛ'stɪdʒəs] *adj* : prestigioso

presto ['prɛsˌto:] *adv* : de pronto

presumably [pri'zu:məbli] *adv* : es de suponer, supuestamente ⟨presumably, he's guilty : supone que es culpable⟩

presume [pri'zu:m] *vt* **-sumed; -suming 1** ASSUME, SUPPOSE : suponer, asumir, presumir **2 to presume to** : atreverse a, osar

presumption [pri'zʌmpʃən] *n* **1** AUDACITY : atrevimiento *m*, osadía *f* **2** ASSUMPTION : presunción *f*, suposición *f*

presumptuous [pri'zʌmptʃuəs] *adj* : descarado, atrevido

presuppose [ˌpri:sə'po:z] *vt* **-posed; -posing** : presuponer

pretend [pri'tɛnd] *vt* **1** CLAIM : pretender **2** FEIGN : fingir, simular — *vi* : fingir

pretender [pri'tɛndər] *n* : pretendiente *mf* (al trono, etc.)

pretense *or* **pretence** ['pri:ˌtɛnts, pri'tɛnts] *n* **1** CLAIM : afirmación *f* (falsa), pretensión *f* **2** FEIGNING : fingimiento *m*, simulación *f* ⟨to make a pretense of doing something : fingir hacer algo⟩ ⟨a pretense of order : una apariencia de orden⟩ **3** PRETEXT : pretexto *m* ⟨under false pretenses : con pretextos falsos, de manera fraudulenta⟩

pretension [pri'tɛnʃən] *n* **1** CLAIM : pretensión *f*, afirmación *f* **2** ASPIRATION : aspiración *f*, ambición *f* **3** PRETENTIOUSNESS : pretensiones *fpl*, presunción *f*

pretentious [pri'tɛntʃəs] *adj* : pretencioso

pretentiousness [pri'tɛntʃəsnəs] *n* : presunción *f*, pretensiones *fpl*

pretext ['pri:ˌtɛkst] *n* : pretexto *m*, excusa *f*

prettily ['prɪtəli] *adv* : atractivamente

prettiness ['prɪtinəs] *n* : lindeza *f*

pretty¹ ['prɪti] *adv* : bastante, bien ⟨it's pretty obvious : está bien claro⟩ ⟨it's pretty much the same : es más o menos igual⟩

pretty² *adj* **-tier; -est** : bonito, lindo, guapo ⟨a pretty girl : una muchacha guapa⟩ ⟨what a pretty dress! : ¡qué vestido más lindo!⟩

pretzel ['prɛtsəl] *n* : galleta *f* salada (en forma de nudo)

prevail [pri'veɪl] *vi* **1** TRIUMPH : prevalecer **2** PREDOMINATE : predominar **3 to prevail upon** : persuadir, convencer ⟨I prevailed upon her to sing : la convencí para que cantara⟩

prevailing [pri'veɪlɪŋ] *adj* : imperante, prevaleciente

prevalence ['prɛvələnts] *n* : preponderancia *f*, predominio *m*

prevalent ['prɛvələnt] *adj* **1** COMMON : común y corriente, general **2** WIDESPREAD : extendido

prevaricate [pri'værə,keɪt] *vi* **-cated;**
-cating LIE : mentir
prevarication [pri,værə'keɪʃən] *n* : mentira *f*
prevent [pri'vɛnt] *vt* **1** AVOID : prevenir,
evitar ⟨steps to prevent war : medidas
para evitar la guerra⟩ **2** HINDER : impedir
preventable [pri'vɛntəbəl] *adj* : evitable
preventative [pri'vɛntətɪv] → **preventive**
prevention [pri'vɛntʃən] *n* : prevención
f
preventive [pri'vɛntɪv] *adj* : preventivo
preview ['pri:,vju] *n* : preestreno *m*
previous ['pri:viəs] *adj* : previo, anteri-
or ⟨previous knowledge : conocimien-
tos previos⟩ ⟨the previous day : el día
anterior⟩ ⟨in the previous year : en el
año pasado⟩
previously ['pri:viəsli] *adv* : antes
prewar [,pri:'wɔr] *adj* : de antes de la
guerra
prey ['preɪ] *n, pl* **preys** : presa *f*
prey on *vt* **1** : cazar, alimentarse de ⟨it
preys on fish : se alimenta de peces⟩
to prey on one's mind : hacer presa en
alguien, atormentar a alguien
price¹ ['praɪs] *vt* **priced; pricing** : poner
un precio a
price² *n* : precio *m* ⟨peace at any price
: la paz a toda costa⟩
priceless ['praɪsləs] *adj* : inestimable, inapreciable
pricey ['praɪsi] *adj* : caro
prick¹ ['prɪk] *vt* **1** : pinchar **2 to prick
up one's ears** : levantar las orejas —
vi : pinchar
prick² *n* **1** STAB : pinchazo *m* ⟨a prick
of conscience : un remordimiento⟩ **2**
→ **pricker**
pricker ['prɪkər] *n* THORN : espina *f*
prickle¹ ['prɪkəl] *vi* **-led; -ling** : sentir un
cosquilleo, tener un hormigueo
prickle² *n* **1** : espina *f* (de una planta) **2**
TINGLE : cosquilleo *m*, hormigueo *m*
prickly ['prɪkəli] *adj* **1** THORNY : espinoso **2** : que pica ⟨a prickly sensation : un hormigueo⟩
prickly pear *n* : tuna *f*
pride¹ ['praɪd] *vt* **prided; priding** : estar
orgulloso de ⟨to pride oneself on : preciarse de, enorgullecerse de⟩
pride² *n* : orgullo *m*
priest ['pri:st] *n* : sacerdote *m*, cura *m*
priestess ['pri:stɪs] *n* : sacerdotisa *f*
priesthood ['pri:st,hʊd] *n* : sacerdocio *m*
priestly ['pri:stli] *adj* : sacerdotal
prig ['prɪg] *n* : mojigato *m*, -ta *f*; gazmoño *m*, -ña *f*
prim ['prɪm] *adj* **primmer; primmest 1**
PRISSY : remilgado **2** PRUDISH : mojigato, gazmoño
primarily [praɪ'mɛrəli] *adv* : principalmente, fundamentalmente
primary¹ ['praɪ,mɛri, 'praɪməri] *adj* **1**
FIRST : primario **2** PRINCIPAL : principal **3** BASIC : fundamental

primary² *n, pl* **-ries** : elección *f* primaria
primary color *n* : color *m* primario
primary school → **elementary school**
primate *n* **1** ['praɪ,meɪt, -mət] : primado *m* (obispo) **2** [-,meɪt] : primate *m*
(animal)
prime¹ ['praɪm] *vt* **primed; priming 1**
: cebar ⟨to prime a pump : cebar una
bomba⟩ **2** PREPARE : preparar (una
superficie para pintar) **3** COACH
: preparar (a un testigo, etc.)
prime² *adj* **1** CHIEF, MAIN : principal,
primero **2** EXCELLENT : de primera
(categoría), excelente
prime³ *n* **the prime of one's life** : la flor
de la vida
prime minister *n* : primer ministro *m*,
primera ministra *f*
primer¹ ['prɪmər] *n* **1** READER : cartilla
f **2** MANUAL : manual *m*
primer² ['praɪmər] *n* **1** : cebo *m* (para
explosivos) **2** : base *f* (de pintura)
prime time *n* : horas *fpl* de mayor audiencia
primeval [praɪ'mi:vəl] *adj* : primitivo,
primigenio
primitive ['prɪmətɪv] *adj* : primitivo
primly ['prɪmli] *adv* : mojigatamente
primness ['prɪmnəs] *n* : mojigatería *f*,
gazmoñería *f*
primordial [praɪ'mɔrdiəl] *adj* : primordial, fundamental
primp ['prɪmp] *vi* : arreglarse, acicalarse
primrose ['prɪm,ro:z] *n* : primavera *f*,
prímula *f*
prince ['prɪnts] *n* : príncipe *m*
princely ['prɪntsli] *adj* : principesco
princess ['prɪntsəs, 'prɪn,sɛs] *n* : princesa *f*
principal¹ ['prɪntsəpəl] *adj* : principal —
principally *adv*
principal² *n* **1** PROTAGONIST : protagonista *mf* **2** : director *m*, -tora *f* (de una
escuela) **3** CAPITAL : principal *m*, capital *m* (en finanzas)
principality [,prɪntsə'pæləti] *n, pl* **-ties**
: principado *m*
principle ['prɪntsəpəl] *n* : principio *m*
print¹ ['prɪnt] *vt* : imprimir (libros, etc.)
— *vi* : escribir con letra de molde
print² *n* **1** IMPRESSION : marca *f*, huella
f, impresión *f* **2** : texto *m* impreso ⟨to
be out of print : estar agotado⟩ **3** LET-
TERING : letra *f* **4** ENGRAVING : grabado *m* **5** : copia *f* (en fotografía) **6** : estampado *m* (de tela)
printer ['prɪntər] *n* **1** : impresor *m*, -sora
f (persona) **2** : impresora *f* (máquina)
printing ['prɪntɪŋ] *n* **1** : impresión *f*
(acto) ⟨the third printing : la tercera
tirada⟩ **2** : imprenta *f* (profesión) **3**
LETTERING : letras *fpl* de molde
printing press *n* : prensa *f*
print out *vt* : imprimir (de una computadora)
printout ['prɪnt,aʊt] *n* : copia *f* impresa
(de una computadora)
prior ['praɪər] *adj* **1** : previo **2 prior to**
: antes de

priority [praɪ'ɔrəţi] *n, pl* **-ties** : prioridad *f*

priory ['praɪəri] *n, pl* **-ries** : priorato *m*

prism ['prɪzəm] *n* : prisma *m*

prison ['prɪzən] *n* : prisión *f*, cárcel *f*

prisoner ['prɪzənər] *n* : preso *m*, -sa *f*; recluso *m*, -sa *f* ⟨prisoner of war : prisionero de guerra⟩

prissy ['prɪsi] *adj* **-sier; -est** : remilgado, melindroso

pristine ['prɪs,tiːn, prɪs'-] *adj* : puro, prístino

privacy ['praɪvəsi] *n, pl* **-cies** : privacidad *f*

private[1] ['praɪvət] *adj* **1** PERSONAL : privado, particular ⟨private property : propiedad privada⟩ **2** INDEPENDENT : privado, independiente ⟨private studies : estudios privados⟩ **3** SECRET : secreto **4** SECLUDED : aislado, privado — **privately** *adv*

private[2] *n* : soldado *m* raso

privateer [,praɪvə'tɪr] *n* : corsario *m*

privation [praɪ'veɪʃən] *n* : privación *f*

privilege ['prɪvlɪdʒ, 'prɪvə-] *n* : privilegio *m*

privileged ['prɪvlɪdʒd, 'prɪvə-] *adj* : privilegiado

privy[1] ['prɪvi] *adj* **to be privy to** : estar enterado de

privy[2] *n, pl* **privies** : excusado *m*, retrete *m* (exterior)

prize[1] ['praɪz] *vt* **prized; prizing** : valorar, apreciar

prize[2] *adj* **1** : premiado ⟨a prize stallion : un semental premiado⟩ **2** OUTSTANDING : de primera, excepcional

prize[3] *n* **1** AWARD : premio *m* ⟨third prize : el tercer premio⟩ **2** : joya *f*, tesoro *m* ⟨he's a real prize : es un tesoro⟩

prizefighter ['praɪz,faɪţər] *n* : boxeador *m*, -dora *f* profesional

prizewinning ['praɪz,wɪnɪŋ] *adj* : premiado

pro[1] ['proː] *adv* : a favor

pro[2] *adj* → **professional**[1]

pro[3] *n* **1** : pro *m* ⟨the pros and cons : los pros y los contras⟩ **2** → **professional**[2]

probability [,prɑbə'bɪləţi] *n, pl* **-ties** : probabilidad *f*

probable ['prɑbəbəl] *adj* : probable — **probably** [-bli] *adv*

probate[1] ['proː,beɪt] *vt* **-bated; -bating** : autenticar (un testamento)

probate[2] *n* : autenticación *f* (de un testamento)

probation [proː'beɪʃən] *n* **1** : período *m* de prueba (para un empleado, etc.) **2** : libertad *f* condicional (para un preso)

probationary [proː'beɪʃə,neri] *adj* : de prueba

probe[1] ['proːb] *vt* **probed; probing** **1** : sondar (en medicina y tecnología) **2** INVESTIGATE : investigar, sondear

probe[2] *n* **1** : sonda *f* (en medicina, etc.) ⟨space probe : sonda espacial⟩ **2** INVESTIGATION : investigación *f*, sondeo *m*

probity ['proːbəţi] *n* : probidad *f*

problem[1] ['prɑbləm] *adj* : difícil

problem[2] *n* : problema *m*

problematic [,prɑblə'mæţɪk] *or* **problematical** [-ţɪkəl] *adj* : problemático

proboscis [prə'bɑsɪs] *n, pl* **-cises** *also* **-cides** [-sə,diːz] : probóscide *f*

procedural [prə'siːdʒərəl] *adj* : de procedimiento

procedure [prə'siːdʒər] *n* : procedimiento *m* ⟨administrative procedures : trámites administrativos⟩

proceed [proː'siːd] *vi* **1** : proceder ⟨to proceed to do something : proceder a hacer algo⟩ **2** CONTINUE : continuar, proseguir ⟨he proceeded to the next phase : pasó a la segunda fase⟩ **3** ADVANCE : avanzar ⟨as the conference proceeded : mientras seguía avanzando la conferencia⟩ ⟨the road proceeds south : la calle sigue hacia el sur⟩

proceeding [proː'siːdɪŋ] *n* **1** PROCEDURE : procedimiento *m* **2 proceedings** *npl* EVENTS : acontecimientos *mpl* **3 proceedings** *npl* MINUTES : actas *fpl* (de una reunión, etc.)

proceeds ['proː,siːdz] *npl* : ganancias *fpl*

process[1] ['prɑ,sɛs, 'proː-] *vt* : procesar, tratar

process[2] *n, pl* **-cesses** ['prɑ,sɛsəz, 'proː-, -səsəz, -sə,siːz] **1** : proceso *m* ⟨the process of elimination : el proceso de eliminación⟩ **2** METHOD : proceso *m*, método *m* ⟨manufacturing processes : procesos industriales⟩ **3** : acción *f* judicial ⟨due process of law : el debido proceso (de la ley)⟩ **4** SUMMONS : citación *f* **5** PROJECTION : protuberancia *f* (anatómica) **6 in the process of** : en vías de ⟨in the process of repair : en reparaciones⟩

procession [prə'sɛʃən] *n* : procesión *f*, desfile *m* ⟨a funeral procession : un cortejo fúnebre⟩

processional [prə'sɛʃənəl] *n* : himno *m* para una procesión

processor ['prɑ,sɛsər, 'proː-, -səsər] *n* **1** : procesador *m* (de una computadora) **2 food processor** : procesador *m* de alimentos

proclaim [proː'kleɪm] *vt* : proclamar

proclamation [,prɑklə'meɪʃən] *n* : proclamación *f*

proclivity [proː'klɪvəţi] *n, pl* **-ties** : proclividad *f*

procrastinate [prə'kræstə,neɪt] *vi* **-nated; -nating** : demorar, aplazar las responsabilidades

procrastination [prə,kræstə'neɪʃən] *n* : aplazamiento *m*, demora *f*, dilación *f*

procreate ['proː,kri,eɪt] *vi* **-ated; -ating** : procrear

procreation [,proː,kri'eɪʃən] *n* : procreación *f*

proctor[1] ['prɑktər] *vt* : supervisar (un examen)

proctor[2] *n* : supervisor *m*, -sora *f* (de un examen)

procure [prə'kjʊr] vt -cured; -curing 1
OBTAIN : procurar, obtener 2 BRING
ABOUT : provocar, lograr, conseguir
procurement [prə'kjʊrmənt] n : obtención f
prod¹ ['prɑd] vt prodded; prodding 1
JAB, POKE : pinchar, golpear (con la
punta de algo) 2 GOAD : incitar, estimular
prod² n 1 JAB, POKE : golpe m (con la
punta de algo), pinchazo m 2 STIMU-
LUS : estímulo m 3 cattle prod : picana
f, aguijón m
prodigal¹ ['prɑdɪgəl] adj SPENDTHRIFT
: pródigo, despilfarrador, derrochador
prodigal² n : pródigo m, -ga f; derrochador m, -dora f
prodigious [prə'dɪdʒəs] adj 1 MAR-
VELOUS : prodigioso, maravilloso 2
HUGE : enorme, vasto ⟨prodigious
sums : muchísimo dinero⟩ — prodi-
giously adv
prodigy ['prɑdədʒi] n, pl -gies : prodigio
m ⟨child prodigy : niño prodigio⟩
produce¹ [prə'du:s, -'dju:s] vt -duced;
-ducing 1 EXHIBIT : presentar,
mostrar 2 YIELD : producir 3 CAUSE
: producir, causar 4 CREATE : producir
⟨to produce a poem : escribir un poe-
ma⟩ 5 : poner en escena (una obra de
teatro), producir (una película)
produce² ['prɑ,du:s, 'pro:-, -,dju:s] n
: productos mpl agrícolas
producer [prə'du:sər, -'dju:-] n : productor m, -tora f
product ['prɑ,dʌkt] n : producto m
production [prə'dʌkʃən] n : producción
f
productive [prə'dʌktɪv] adj : productivo
productivity [,pro:,dʌk'tɪvəṭi, ,prɑ-] n
: productividad f
profane¹ [pro'feɪn] vt -faned; -faning
: profanar
profane² adj 1 SECULAR : profano 2 IR-
REVERENT : irreverente, impío
profanity [pro'fænəṭi] n, pl -ties 1 IR-
REVERENCE : irreverencia f, impiedad
f 2 : blasfemias fpl, obscenidades fpl
⟨don't use profanity : no digas blas-
femias⟩
profess [prə'fɛs] vt 1 DECLARE : declarar, manifestar 2 CLAIM : pretender
3 : profesar (una religión, etc.)
professedly [prə'fɛsədli] adv 1 OPENLY
: declaradamente 2 ALLEGEDLY
: supuestamente
profession [prə'fɛʃən] n : profesión f
professional¹ [prə'fɛʃənəl] adj : profesional — professionally adv
professional² n : profesional mf
professionalism [prə'fɛʃənə,lɪzəm] n
: profesionalismo m
professor [prə'fɛsər] n : profesor m (universitario), profesora f (universitaria);
catedrático m, -ca f
proffer ['prɑfər] vt -fered; -fering : ofrecer, dar

proficiency [prə'fɪʃəntsi] n : competencia f, capacidad f
proficient [prə'fɪʃənt] adj : competente,
experto — proficiently adv
profile ['pro:,faɪl] n : perfil m ⟨a portrait
in profile : un retrato de perfil⟩ ⟨to
keep a low profile : no llamar la atención, hacerse pasar desapercibido⟩
profit¹ ['prɑfət] vi : sacar provecho (de),
beneficiarse (de)
profit² n 1 ADVANTAGE : provecho m,
partido m, beneficio m 2 GAIN : beneficio m, utilidad f, ganancia f ⟨to make
a profit : sacar beneficios⟩
profitable ['prɑfəṭəbəl] adj : rentable, lucrativo — profitably [-bli] adv
profitless ['prɑfətləs] adj : infructuoso,
inútil
profligate ['prɑflɪgət, -,geɪt] adj 1 DIS-
SOLUTE : disoluto, licencioso 2 SPEND-
THRIFT : despilfarrador, derrochador,
pródigo
profound [prə'faʊnd] adj : profundo
profoundly [prə'faʊndli] adv : profundamente, en profundidad
profundity [prə'fʌndəṭi] n, pl -ties : profundidad f
profuse [prə'fju:s] adj 1 COPIOUS : profuso, copioso 2 LAVISH : pródigo —
profusely adv
profusion [prə'fju:ʒən] n : abundancia f,
profusión f
progenitor [pro'dʒɛnəṭər] n : progenitor
m, -tora f
progeny ['prɑdʒəni] n, pl -nies : progenie f
progesterone [pro'dʒɛstə,ro:n] n : progesterona f
prognosis [prɑg'no:sɪs] n, pl -noses
[-,si:z] : pronóstico m (médico)
program¹ ['pro:,græm, -grəm] vt
-grammed or -gramed; -gramming or
-graming : programar
program² n : programa m
programmable ['pro:,græməbəl] adj
: programable
programmer ['pro:,græmər] n : programador m, -dora f
programming ['pro:,græmɪŋ] n : programación f
progress¹ [prə'grɛs] vi 1 PROCEED
: progresar, adelantar 2 IMPROVE
: mejorar
progress² ['prɑgrəs, -,grɛs] n 1 AD-
VANCE : progreso m, adelanto m,
avance m ⟨to make progress : hacer
progresos⟩ 2 BETTERMENT : mejora f,
mejoramiento m
progression [prə'grɛʃən] n 1 ADVANCE
: avance m 2 SEQUENCE : desarrollo
m (de eventos)
progressive [prə'grɛsɪv] adj 1 : progresista ⟨a progressive society : una sociedad progresista⟩ 2 : progresivo ⟨a
progressive disease : una enfermedad
progresiva⟩ 3 or Progressive : progresista (en política) 4 : progresivo (en
gramática)

progressively [prə'grɛsɪvli] *adv* : progresivamente, poco a poco
prohibit [pro'hɪbət] *vt* : prohibir
prohibition [ˌpro:ə'bɪʃən, ˌpro:hə-] *n* : prohibición *f*
prohibitive [pro'hɪbətɪv] *adj* : prohibitivo
project[1] [prə'dʒɛkt] *vt* **1** PLAN : proyectar, planear **2** : proyectar (imágenes, misiles, etc.) — *vi* PROTRUDE : sobresalir, salir
project[2] ['prɑˌdʒɛkt, -dʒɪkt] *n* : proyecto *m*, trabajo *m* (de un estudiante) ⟨research project : proyecto de investigación⟩
projectile [prə'dʒɛktəl, -ˌtaɪl] *n* : proyectil *m*
projection [prə'dʒɛkʃən] *n* **1** PLAN : plan *m*, proyección *f* **2** : proyección *f* (de imágenes, misiles, etc.) **3** PROTRUSION : saliente *m*
projector [prə'dʒɛktər] *n* : proyector *m*
proletarian[1] [ˌpro:lə'tɛriən] *adj* : proletario
proletarian[2] *n* : proletario *m*, -ria *f*
proletariat [ˌpro:lə'tɛriət] *n* : proletariado *m*
proliferate [prə'lɪfəˌreɪt] *vi* -ated; -ating : proliferar
proliferation [prəˌlɪfə'reɪʃən] *n* : proliferación *f*
prolific [prə'lɪfɪk] *adj* : prolífico
prologue ['pro:ˌlɔg] *n* : prólogo *m*
prolong [prə'lɔŋ] *vt* : prolongar
prolongation [ˌpro:ˌlɔŋ'geɪʃən] *n* : prolongación *f*
prom ['prɑm] *n* : baile *m* formal (de un colegio)
promenade[1] [ˌprɑmə'neɪd, -'nɑd] *vi* -naded; -nading : pasear, pasearse, dar un paseo
promenade[2] *n* : paseo *m*
prominence ['prɑmənənts] *n* **1** PROJECTION : prominencia *f* **2** EMINENCE : eminencia *f*, prestigio *m*
prominent ['prɑmənənt] *adj* **1** OUTSTANDING : prominente, destacado **2** PROJECTING : prominente, saliente
prominently ['prɑmənəntli] *adv* : destacadamente, prominentemente
promiscuity [ˌprɑmɪs'kju:əti] *n, pl* -ties : promiscuidad *f*
promiscuous [prə'mɪskjʊəs] *adj* : promiscuo — **promiscuously** *adv*
promise[1] ['prɑməs] *v* -ised; -ising : prometer
promise[2] *n* **1** : promesa *f* ⟨he kept his promise : cumplió su promesa⟩ **2 to show promise** : prometer
promising ['prɑməsɪŋ] *adj* : prometedor
promissory ['prɑməˌsori] *adj* : que promete ⟨a promissory note : un pagaré⟩
promontory ['prɑmənˌtori] *n, pl* -ries : promontorio *m*
promote [prə'mo:t] *vt* -moted; -moting **1** : ascender (a un alumno o a un empleado) **2** ADVERTISE : promocionar,

hacerle publicidad a **3** FURTHER : promover, fomentar
promoter [prə'mo:tər] *n* : promotor *m*, -tora *f*; empresario *m*, -ria *f* (en deportes)
promotion [prə'mo:ʃən] *n* **1** : ascenso *m* (de un alumno o un empleado) **2** FURTHERING : promoción *f*, fomento *m* **3** ADVERTISING : publicidad *f*, propaganda *f*
promotional [prə'mo:ʃənəl] *adj* : promocional
prompt[1] ['prɑmpt] *vt* **1** INDUCE : provocar (una cosa), inducir (a una persona) ⟨curiosity prompted me to ask you : la curiosidad me indujo a preguntarle⟩ **2** : apuntar (a un actor, etc.)
prompt[2] *adj* : pronto, rápido ⟨prompt payment : pago puntual⟩
prompter ['prɑmptər] *n* : apuntador *m*, -dora *f* (en teatro)
promptly ['prɑmptli] *adv* : inmediatamente, rápidamente
promptness ['prɑmptnəs] *n* : prontitud *f*, rapidez *f*
promulgate ['prɑməlˌgeɪt] *vt* -gated; -gating : promulgar
prone ['pro:n] *adj* **1** LIABLE : propenso, proclive ⟨accident-prone : propenso a los accidentes⟩ **2** : boca abajo, decúbito prono ⟨in a prone position : en decúbito prono⟩
prong ['prɔŋ] *n* : punta *f*, diente *m*
pronoun ['pro:ˌnaʊn] *n* : pronombre *m*
pronounce [prə'naʊnts] *vt* -nounced; -nouncing **1** : pronunciar ⟨how do you pronounce your name? : ¿cómo se pronuncia su nombre?⟩ **2** DECLARE : declarar **3 to pronounce sentence** : dictar sentencia, pronunciar un fallo
pronounced [prə'naʊntst] *adj* MARKED : pronunciado, marcado
pronouncement [prə'naʊntsmənt] *n* : declaración *f*
pronunciation [prəˌnʌntsi'eɪʃən] *n* : pronunciación *f*
proof[1] ['pru:f] *adj* : a prueba ⟨proof against tampering : a prueba de manipulación⟩
proof[2] *n* : prueba *f*
proofread ['pru:fˌri:d] *v* -read; -reading *vt* : corregir — *vi* : corregir pruebas
proofreader ['pru:fˌri:dər] *n* : corrector *m*, -tora *f* (de pruebas)
prop[1] ['prɑp] *vt* **propped; propping 1 to prop against** : apoyar contra **2 to prop up** SUPPORT : apoyar, apuntalar, sostener **3 to prop up** SUSTAIN : alentar (a alguien), darle ánimo (a alguien)
prop[2] *n* **1** SUPPORT : puntal *m*, apoyo *m*, soporte *m* **2** : accesorio *m* (en teatro)
propaganda [ˌprɑpə'gændə, ˌpro:-] *n* : propaganda *f*
propagandize [ˌprɑpə'gænˌdaɪz, ˌpro:-] *v* -dized; -dizing *vt* : someter a propaganda — *vi* : hacer propaganda

propagate ['prɑpə‚geɪt] v **-gated; -gating** vi : propagarse — vt : propagar
propagation [‚prɑpə'geɪʃən] n : propagación f
propane ['pro:‚peɪn] n : propano m
propel [prə'pɛl] vt **-pelled; -pelling** : impulsar, propulsar, impeler
propellant or **propellent** [prə'pɛlənt] n : propulsor m
propeller [prə'pɛlər] n : hélice f
propensity [prə'pɛntsəti] n, pl **-ties** : propensión f, tendencia f, inclinación f
proper ['prɑpər] adj **1** RIGHT, SUITABLE : apropiado, adecuado **2** : propio, mismo ⟨the city proper : la propia ciudad⟩ **3** CORRECT : correcto **4** GENTEEL : fino, refinado, cortés **5** OWN, SPECIAL : propio ⟨proper name : nombre propio⟩ — **properly** adv
property ['prɑpərti] n, pl **-ties 1** CHARACTERISTIC : característica f, propiedad f **2** POSSESSIONS : propiedad f **3** BUILDING : inmueble m **4** LAND, LOT : terreno m, lote m, parcela f **5** PROP : accesorio m (en teatro)
prophecy ['prɑfəsi] n, pl **-cies** : profecía f, vaticinio m
prophesy ['prɑfə‚saɪ] v **-sied; -sying** vt **1** FORETELL : profetizar (como profeta) **2** PREDICT : profetizar, predecir, vaticinar — vi : hacer profecías
prophet ['prɑfət] n : profeta m, profetisa f
prophetic [prə'fɛtɪk] or **prophetical** [-tɪkəl] adj : profético — **prophetically** [-tɪkli] adv
propitiate [pro'pɪʃi‚eɪt] vt **-ated; -ating** : propiciar
propitious [prə'pɪʃəs] adj : propicio
proponent [prə'po:nənt] n : defensor m, -sora f; partidario m, -ria f
proportion¹ [prə'porʃən] vt : proporcionar ⟨well-proportioned : de buenas proporciones⟩
proportion² n **1** RATIO : proporción f **2** SYMMETRY : proporción f, simetría f ⟨out of proportion : desproporcionado⟩ **3** SHARE : parte f **4 proportions** npl SIZE : dimensiones fpl
proportional [prə'porʃənəl] adj : proporcional — **proportionally** adv
proportionate [prə'porʃənət] adj : proporcional — **proportionately** adv
proposal [prə'po:zəl] n **1** PROPOSITION : propuesta f, proposición f ⟨marriage proposal : propuesta de matrimonio⟩ **2** PLAN : proyecto m, propuesta f
propose [prə'po:z] v **-posed; -posing** vi : proponer matrimonio — vt **1** INTEND : pensar, proponerse **2** SUGGEST : proponer
proposition [‚prɑpə'zɪʃən] n **1** PROPOSAL : proposición f, propuesta f **2** STATEMENT : proposición f
propound [prə'paʊnd] vt : proponer, exponer
proprietary [prə'praɪə‚tɛri] adj : propietario, patentado

proprietor [prə'praɪətər] n : propietario m, -ria f
propriety [prə'praɪəti] n, pl **-eties 1** DECORUM : decencia f, decoro m **2 proprieties** npl CONVENTIONS : convenciones fpl, cánones mpl sociales
propulsion [prə'pʌlʃən] n : propulsión f
prosaic [pro'zeɪɪk] adj : prosaico
proscribe [pro'skraɪb] vt **-scribing** : proscribir
prose ['pro:z] n : prosa f
prosecute ['prɑsɪ‚kju:t] vt **-cuted; -cuting 1** CARRY OUT : llevar a cabo **2** : procesar, enjuiciar ⟨prosecuted for fraud : procesado por fraude⟩
prosecution [‚prɑsɪ'kju:ʃən] n **1** : procesamiento m ⟨the prosecution of forgers : el procesamiento de falsificadores⟩ **2** PROSECUTORS : acusación f ⟨witness for the prosecution : testigo de cargo⟩
prosecutor ['prɑsɪ‚kju:tər] n : acusador m, -dora f; fiscal mf
prospect¹ ['prɑ‚spɛkt] vi : prospectar (el terreno) ⟨to prospect for gold : buscar oro⟩
prospect² n **1** VISTA : vista f, panorama m **2** POSSIBILITY : posibilidad f **3** OUTLOOK : perspectiva f **4** : posible cliente m, -ta f ⟨a salesman looking for prospects : un vendedor buscando nuevos clientes⟩
prospective [prə'spɛktɪv, 'prɑ‚spɛk-] adj **1** EXPECTANT : futuro ⟨prospective mother : futura madre⟩ **2** POTENTIAL : potencial, posible ⟨prospective employee : posible empleado⟩
prospector ['prɑ‚spɛktər, prə'spɛk-] n : prospector m, -tora f; explorador m, -dora f
prospectus [prə'spɛktəs] n : prospecto m
prosper ['prɑspər] vi : prosperar
prosperity [prɑ'spɛrəti] n : prosperidad f
prosperous ['prɑspərəs] adj : próspero
prostate ['prɑ‚steɪt] n : próstata f
prosthesis [prɑs'θi:sɪs, 'prɑsθə-] n, pl **-theses** [-‚si:z] : prótesis f
prostitute¹ ['prɑstə‚tu:t, -‚tju:t] vt **-tuted; -tuting 1** : prostituir **2 to prostitute oneself** : prostituirse
prostitute² n : prostituto m, -ta f
prostitution [‚prɑstə'tu:ʃən, -'tju:-] n : prostitución f
prostrate¹ ['prɑ‚streɪt] vt **-trated; -trating 1** : postrar **2 to prostrate oneself** : postrarse
prostrate² adj : postrado
prostration [prɑ'streɪʃən] n : postración f
protagonist [pro'tægənɪst] n : protagonista mf
protect [prə'tɛkt] vt : proteger
protection [prə'tɛkʃən] n : protección f
protective [prə'tɛktɪv] adj : protector
protector [prə'tɛktər] n **1** : protector m, -tora f (persona) **2** GUARD : protector m (aparato)

protectorate [prə'tɛktərət] *n* : protectorado *m*

protégé ['pro:ʈə,ʒeɪ] *n* : protegido *m*, -da *f*

protein ['pro:,ti:n] *n* : proteína *f*

protest¹ [pro'tɛst] *vt* **1** ASSERT : afirmar, declarar **2** : protestar ⟨they protested the decision : protestaron (por) la decisión⟩ — *vi* **to protest against** : protestar contra

protest² ['pro:,tɛst] *n* **1** DEMONSTRATION : manifestación *f* (de protesta) ⟨a public protest : una manifestación pública⟩ **2** COMPLAINT : queja *f*, protesta *f*

Protestant ['praʈəstənt] *n* : protestante *mf*

Protestantism ['praʈəstən,tɪzəm] *n* : protestantismo *m*

protocol ['pro:ʈə,kɔl] *n* : protocolo *m*

proton ['pro:,tan] *n* : protón *m*

protoplasm ['pro:ʈə,plæzəm] *n* : protoplasma *m*

prototype ['pro:ʈə,taɪp] *n* : prototipo *m*

protozoan [,pro:ʈə'zo:ən] *n* : protozoario *m*, protozoo *m*

protract [pro'trækt] *vt* : prolongar

protractor [pro'træktər] *n* : transportador *m* (instrumento)

protrude [pro'tru:d] *vi* -**truded**; -**truding** : salir, sobresalir

protrusion [pro'tru:ʒən] *n* : protuberancia *f*, saliente *m*

protuberance [pro'tu:bərənts, -'tju:-] *n* : protuberancia *f*

proud ['praʊd] *adj* **1** HAUGHTY : altanero, orgulloso, arrogante **2** : orgulloso ⟨she was proud of her work : estaba orgullosa de su trabajo⟩ ⟨too proud to beg : demasiado orgulloso para rogar⟩ **3** GLORIOUS : glorioso — **proudly** *adv*

prove ['pru:v] *v* **proved**; **proved** *or* **proven** ['pru:vən]; **proving** *vt* **1** TEST : probar **2** DEMONSTRATE : probar, demostrar — *vi* : resultar ⟨it proved effective : resultó efectivo⟩

Provençal [,pro:van'sal, ,pravən-] *n* **1** : provenzal *mf* **2** : provenzal *m* (idioma) — **Provençal** *adj*

proverb ['pra,vərb] *n* : proverbio *m*, refrán *m*

proverbial [prə'vərbiəl] *adj* : proverbial

provide [prə'vaɪd] *v* -**vided**; -**viding** *vt* **1** STIPULATE : estipular **2 to provide with** : proveer de, proporcionar — *vi* **1** : proveer ⟨the Lord will provide : el Señor proveerá⟩ **2 to provide for** SUPPORT : mantener **3 to provide for** ANTICIPATE : hacer previsiones para, prever

provided [prə'vaɪdəd] *or* **provided that** *conj* : con tal (de) que, siempre que

providence ['pravədənts] *n* **1** PRUDENCE : previsión *f*, prudencia *f* **2** *or* **Providence** : providencia *f* ⟨divine providence : la Divina Providencia⟩ **3 Providence** GOD : Providencia *f*

provident ['pravədənt] *adj* **1** PRUDENT : previsor, prudente **2** FRUGAL : frugal, ahorrativo

providential [,pravə'dɛntʃəl] *adj* : providencial

provider [prə'vaɪdər] *n* **1** PURVEYOR : proveedor *m*, -dora *f* **2** BREADWINNER : sostén *m* (económico)

providing that → **provided**

province ['pravɪnts] *n* **1** : provincia *f* (de un país) ⟨to live in the provinces : vivir en las provincias⟩ **2** FIELD, SPHERE : campo *m*, competencia *f* ⟨it's not in my province : no es de mi competencia⟩

provincial [prə'vɪntʃəl] *adj* **1** : provincial ⟨provincial government : gobierno provincial⟩ **2** : provinciano, pueblerino ⟨a provincial mentality : una mentalidad provinciana⟩

provision¹ [prə'vɪʒən] *vt* : aprovisionar, abastecer

provision² *n* **1** PROVIDING : provisión *f*, suministro *m* **2** STIPULATION : condición *f*, salvedad *f*, estipulación *f* **3 provisions** *npl* : despensa *f*, víveres *mpl*, provisiones *fpl*

provisional [prə'vɪʒənəl] *adj* : provisional, provisorio — **provisionally** *adv*

proviso [prə'vaɪ,zo:] *n*, *pl* -**sos** *or* -**soes** : condición *f*, salvedad *f*, estipulación *f*

provocation [,pravə'keɪʃən] *n* : provocación *f*

provocative [prə'vakəʈɪv] *adj* : provocador, provocativo ⟨a provocative article : un artículo que hace pensar⟩

provoke [prə'vo:k] *vt* -**voked**; -**voking** : provocar

prow ['praʊ] *n* : proa *f*

prowess ['praʊəs] *n* **1** VALOR : valor *m*, valentía *f* **2** SKILL : habilidad *f*, destreza *f*

prowl ['praʊl] *vi* : merodear, rondar — *vt* : rondar por

prowler ['praʊlər] *n* : merodeador *m*, -dora *f*

proximity [prak'sɪməʈi] *n* : proximidad *f*

proxy ['praksi] *n*, *pl* **proxies 1** : poder *m* (de actuar en nombre de alguien) ⟨by proxy : por poder⟩ **2** AGENT : apoderado *m*, -da *f*; representante *mf*

prude ['pru:d] *n* : mojigato *m*, -ta *f*; gazmoño *m*, -ña *f*

prudence ['pru:dənts] *n* **1** SHREWDNESS : prudencia *f*, sagacidad *f* **2** CAUTION : prudencia *f*, cautela *f* **3** THRIFTINESS : frugalidad *f*

prudent ['pru:dənt] *adj* **1** SHREWD : prudente, sagaz **2** CAUTIOUS, FARSIGHTED : prudente, previsor, precavido **3** THRIFTY : frugal, ahorrativo — **prudently** *adv*

prudery ['pru:dəri] *n*, *pl* -**eries** : mojigatería *f*, gazmoñería *f*

prudish ['pru:dɪʃ] *adj* : mojigato, gazmoño

prune[1] ['pru:n] *vt* **pruned; pruning** : podar (arbustos, etc.), acortar (un texto), recortar (gastos, etc.)
prune[2] *n* : ciruela *f* pasa
prurient ['prʊriənt] *adj* : lascivo
pry ['praɪ] *v* **pried; prying** *vi* : curiosear, huronear ⟨to pry into other people's business : meterse uno en lo que no le importa⟩ — *vt or* **to pry open** : abrir (con una palanca), apalancar
psalm ['sɑm, 'sɑlm] *n* : salmo *m*
pseudonym ['su:də,nɪm] *n* : seudónimo *m*
psoriasis [sə'raɪəsɪs] *n* : soriasis *f*, psoriasis *f*
psyche ['saɪki] *n* : psique *f*, psiquis *f*
psychedelic[1] [,saɪkə'dɛlɪk] *adj* : psicodélico
psychedelic[2] *n* : droga *f* psicodélica
psychiatric [,saɪki'ætrɪk] *adj* : psiquiátrico, siquiátrico
psychiatrist [sə'kaɪətrɪst, saɪ-] *n* : psiquiatra *mf*, siquiatra *mf*
psychiatry [sə'kaɪətri, saɪ-] *n* : psiquiatría *f*, siquiatría *f*
psychic[1] ['saɪkɪk] *adj* **1** : psíquico, síquico (en psicología) **2** CLAIRVOYANT : clarividente
psychic[2] *n* : vidente *mf*, clarividente *mf*
psychoanalysis [,saɪkoə'næləsɪs] *n, pl* **-yses** : psicoanálisis *m*, sicoanálisis *m*
psychoanalyst [,saɪko'ænəlɪst] *n* : psicoanalista *mf*, sicoanalista *mf*
psychoanalytic [,saɪko,ænəl'ɪtɪk] *adj* : psicoanalítico, sicoanalítico
psychoanalyze [,saɪko'ænəl,aɪz] *vt* **-lyzed; -lyzing** : psicoanalizar, sicoanalizar
psychological [,saɪkə'lɑdʒɪkəl] *adj* : psicológico, sicológico — **psychologically** *adv*
psychologist [saɪ'kɑlədʒɪst] *n* : psicólogo *m*, -ga *f*; sicólogo *m*, -ga *f*
psychology [saɪ'kɑlədʒi] *n, pl* **-gies** : psicología *f*, sicología *f*
psychopath ['saɪkə,pæθ] *n* : psicópata *mf*, sicópata *mf*
psychopathic [,saɪkə'pæθɪk] *adj* : psicopático, sicopático
psychosis [saɪ'ko:sɪs] *n, pl* **-choses** [-'ko:,si:z] : psicosis *f*, sicosis *f*
psychosomatic [,saɪkəsə'mætɪk] *adj* : psicosomático, sicosomático
psychotherapist [,saɪko'θerəpɪst] *n* : psicoterapeuta *mf*, sicoterapeuta *mf*
psychotherapy [,saɪko'θerəpi] *n, pl* **-pies** : psicoterapia *f*, sicoterapia *f*
psychotic[1] [saɪ'kɑtɪk] *adj* : psicótico, sicótico
psychotic[2] *n* : psicótico *m*, -ca *f*; sicótico *m*, -ca *f*
puberty ['pju:bərti] *n* : pubertad *f*
pubic ['pju:bɪk] *adj* : pubiano, púbico
public[1] ['pʌblɪk] *adj* : público — **publicly** *adv*
public[2] *n* : público *m*
publication [,pʌblə'keɪʃən] *n* : publicación *f*

publicist ['pʌbləsɪst] *n* : publicista *mf*
publicity [pə'blɪsəti] *n* : publicidad *f*
publicize ['pʌblə,saɪz] *vt* **-cized; -cizing** : publicitar
public school *n* : escuela *f* pública
publish ['pʌblɪʃ] *vt* : publicar
publisher ['pʌblɪʃər] *n* : casa *f* editorial (compañía); editor *m*, -tora *f* (persona)
publishing ['pʌblɪʃɪŋ] *n* : industria *f* editorial
pucker[1] ['pʌkər] *vt* : fruncir, arrugar — *vi* : arrugarse
pucker[2] *n* : arruga *f*, frunce *m*, fruncido *m*
pudding ['pʊdɪŋ] *n* : budín *m*, pudín *m*
puddle ['pʌdəl] *n* : charco *m*
pudgy ['pʌdʒi] *adj* **pudgier; -est** : regordete *fam*, rechoncho *fam*, gordinflón *fam*
puerile ['pjʊrəl] *adj* : pueril
Puerto Rican[1] [,pwɛrtə'ri:kən, ,portə-] *adj* : puertorriqueño
Puerto Rican[2] *n* : puertorriqueño *m*, -ña *f*
puff[1] ['pʌf] *vi* **1** BLOW : soplar **2** PANT : resoplar, jadear **3** **to puff up** SWELL : hincharse — *vt* **1** BLOW : soplar ⟨to puff smoke : echar humo⟩ **2** INFLATE : inflar, hinchar ⟨to puff out one's cheeks : inflar las mejillas⟩
puff[2] *n* **1** GUST : soplo *m*, ráfaga *f*, bocanada *f* (de humo) **2** DRAW : chupada *f* (a un cigarrillo) **3** SWELLING : hinchazón *f* **4** **cream puff** : pastelito *m* de crema **5** **powder puff** : borla *f*
puffy ['pʌfi] *adj* **puffier; -est 1** SWOLLEN : hinchado, inflado **2** SPONGY : esponjoso, suave
pug ['pʌg] *n* **1** : doguillo *m* (perro) **2** *or* **pug nose** : nariz *f* achatada
pugnacious [,pʌg'neɪʃəs] *adj* : pugnaz, agresivo
puke ['pju:k] *vi* **puked; puking** : vomitar, devolver
pull[1] ['pʊl, 'pʌl] *vt* **1** DRAW, TUG : tirar de, jalar **2** EXTRACT : sacar, extraer ⟨to pull teeth : sacar muelas⟩ ⟨to pull a gun on : amenazar a (alguien) con pistola⟩ **3** TEAR : desgarrarse (un músculo, etc.) **4** **to pull down** : bajar, echar abajo, derribar (un edificio) **5** **to pull in** ATTRACT : atraer (una muchedumbre, etc.) ⟨to pull in votes : conseguir votos⟩ **6** **to pull off** REMOVE : sacar, quitar **7** **to pull oneself together** : calmarse, tranquilizarse **8** **to pull up** RAISE : levantar, subir — *vi* **1** DRAW, TUG : tirar, jalar **2** (*indicating movement in a specific direction*) ⟨they pulled in front of us : se nos metieron delante⟩ ⟨to pull to a stop : pararse⟩ **3** **to pull through** RECOVER : recobrarse, reponerse **4** **to pull together** COOPERATE : trabajar juntos, cooperar
pull[2] *n* **1** TUG : tirón *m*, jalón *m* ⟨he gave it a pull : le dio un tirón⟩ **2** ATTRACTION : atracción *f*, fuerza *f* ⟨the pull of gravity : la fuerza de la gravedad⟩ **3**

INFLUENCE : influencia *f* **4** HANDLE : tirador *m* (de un cajón, etc.) **5 bell pull** : cuerda *f*
pullet ['pʊlət] *n* : polla *f*, gallina *f* (joven)
pulley ['pʊli] *n*, *pl* **-leys** : polea *f*
pullover ['pʊl₁o:vər] *n* : suéter *m*
pulmonary ['pʊlmə₁nɛri, 'pʌl-] *adj* : pulmonar
pulp ['pʌlp] *n* **1** : pulpa *f* (de una fruta, etc.) **2** MASH : papilla *f*, pasta *f* ⟨wood pulp : pasta de papel, pulpa de papel⟩ ⟨to beat to a pulp : hacer papilla (a alguien)⟩ **3** : pulpa *f* (de los dientes)
pulpit ['pʊl₁pɪt] *n* : púlpito *m*
pulsate ['pʌl₁seɪt] *vi* **-sated; -sating 1** BEAT : latir, palpitar **2** VIBRATE : vibrar
pulsation [₁pʌl'seɪʃən] *n* : pulsación *f*
pulse ['pʌls] *n* : pulso *m*
pulverize ['pʌlvə₁raɪz] *vt* **-ized; -izing** : pulverizar
puma ['pu:mə, 'pju:-] *n* : puma *m*; león *m*, leona *f* (in various countries)
pumice ['pʌməs] *n* : piedra *f* pómez
pummel ['pʌməl] *vt* **-meled; -meling** : aporrear, apalear
pump¹ ['pʌmp] *vt* **1** : bombear ⟨to pump water : bombear agua⟩ ⟨to pump (up) a tire : inflar una llanta⟩ **2** : mover (una manivela, un pedal, etc.) de arriba abajo ⟨to pump someone's hand : darle un fuerte apretón de manos (a alguien)⟩ **3 to pump out** : sacar, vaciar (con una bomba)
pump² *n* **1** : bomba *f* ⟨water pump : bomba de agua⟩ **2** SHOE : zapato *m* de tacón
pumpernickel ['pʌmpər₁nɪkəl] *n* : pan *m* negro de centeno
pumpkin ['pʌmpkɪn, 'pʌŋkən] *n* : calabaza *f*, zapallo *m Arg, Chile, Peru, Uru*
pun¹ ['pʌn] *vi* **punned; punning** : hacer juegos de palabras
pun² *n* : juego *m* de palabras, albur *m Mex*
punch¹ ['pʌntʃ] *vt* **1** HIT : darle un puñetazo (a alguien), golpear ⟨she punched him in the nose : le dio un puñetazo en la nariz⟩ **2** PERFORATE : perforar (papel, etc.), picar (un boleto)
punch² *n* **1** : perforadora *f* ⟨paper punch : perforadora de papel⟩ **2** BLOW : golpe *m*, puñetazo *m* **3** : ponche *m* ⟨fruit punch : ponche de frutas⟩
punctilious [pəŋk'tɪliəs] *adj* : puntilloso
punctual ['pʌŋktʃuəl] *adj* : puntual
punctuality [₁pʌŋktʃu'æləti] *n* : puntualidad *f*
punctually ['pʌŋktʃuəli] *adv* : puntualmente, a tiempo
punctuate ['pʌŋktʃu₁eɪt] *vt* **-ated; -ating** : puntuar
punctuation [₁pʌŋktʃu'eɪʃən] *n* : puntuación *f*
puncture¹ ['pʌŋktʃər] *vt* **-tured; -turing** : pinchar, punzar, perforar, ponchar *Mex*
puncture² *n* : pinchazo *m*, ponchadura *f Mex*

pundit ['pʌndɪt] *n* : experto *m*, -ta *f*
pungency ['pʌndʒəntsi] *n* : acritud *f*, acrimonia *f*
pungent ['pʌndʒənt] *adj* : acre
punish ['pʌnɪʃ] *vt* : castigar
punishable ['pʌnɪʃəbəl] *adj* : punible
punishment ['pʌnɪʃmənt] *n* : castigo *m*
punitive ['pju:nətɪv] *adj* : punitivo
punt¹ ['pʌnt] *vt* : impulsar (un barco) con una pértiga — *vi* : despejar (en deportes)
punt² *n* **1** : batea *f* (barco) **2** : patada *f* de despeje (en deportes)
puny ['pju:ni] *adj* **-nier; -est** : enclenque, endeble
pup ['pʌp] *n* : cachorro *m*, -rra *f* (de un perro); cría *f* (de otros animales)
pupa ['pju:pə] *n*, *pl* **-pae** [-pi, -₁paɪ] *or* **-pas** : crisálida *f*, pupa *f*
pupil ['pju:pəl] *n* **1** : alumno *m*, -na *f* (de colegio) **2** : pupila *f* (del ojo)
puppet ['pʌpət] *n* : títere *m*, marioneta *f*
puppy ['pʌpi] *n*, *pl* **-pies** : cachorro *m*, -rra *f*
purchase¹ ['pərtʃəs] *vt* **-chased; -chasing** : comprar
purchase² *n* **1** PURCHASING : compra *f*, adquisición *f* **2** : compra *f* ⟨last-minute purchases : compras de última hora⟩ **3** GRIP : agarre *m*, asidero *m* ⟨she got a firm purchase on the wheel : se agarró bien del volante⟩
purchase order *n* : orden *f* de compra
pure ['pjʊr] *adj* **purer; purest** : puro
puree¹ [pju'reɪ, -'ri:] *vt* **-reed; -reeing** : hacer un puré con
puree² *n* : puré *m*
purely ['pjʊrli] *adv* **1** WHOLLY : puramente, completamente ⟨purely by chance : por pura casualidad⟩ **2** SIMPLY : sencillamente, meramente
purgative ['pərgətɪv] *n* : purgante *m*
purgatory ['pərgə₁tori] *n*, *pl* **-ries** : purgatorio *m*
purge¹ ['pərdʒ] *vt* **purged; purging** : purgar
purge² *n* : purga *f*
purification [₁pjʊrəfə'keɪʃən] *n* : purificación *f*
purify ['pjʊrə₁faɪ] *vt* **-fied; -fying** : purificar
puritan ['pjʊrətən] *n* : puritano *m*, -na *f* — **puritan** *adj*
puritanical [₁pjʊrə'tænɪkəl] *adj* : puritano
purity ['pjʊrəti] *n* : pureza *f*
purl¹ ['pərl] *v* : tejer al revés, tejer del revés
purl² *n* : punto *m* del revés
purloin [pər'lɔɪn, 'pər₁lɔɪn] *vt* : hurtar, robar
purple ['pərpəl] *n* : morado *m*, color *m* púrpura
purport [pər'port] *vt* : pretender ⟨to purport to be : pretender ser⟩
purpose ['pərpəs] *n* **1** INTENTION : propósito *m*, intención *f* ⟨on purpose

: a propósito, adrede⟩ **2** FUNCTION : función *f* **3** RESOLUTION : resolución *f*, determinación *f*

purposeful [ˈpərpəsfəl] *adj* : determinado, decidido, resuelto

purposefully [ˈpərpəsfəli] *adv* : decididamente, resueltamente

purposely [ˈpərpəsli] *adv* : intencionadamente, a propósito, adrede

purr¹ [ˈpər] *vi* : ronronear

purr² *n* : ronroneo *m*

purse¹ [ˈpərs] *vt* **pursed; pursing** : fruncir ⟨to purse one's lips : fruncir la boca⟩

purse² *n* **1** HANDBAG : cartera *f*, bolso *m*, bolsa *f Mex* ⟨a change purse : un monedero⟩ **2** FUNDS : fondos *mpl* **3** PRIZE : premio *m*

pursue [pərˈsuː] *vt* **-sued; -suing 1** CHASE : perseguir **2** SEEK : buscar, tratar de encontrar ⟨to pursue pleasure : buscar el placer⟩ **3** FOLLOW : seguir ⟨the road pursues a northerly course : el camino sigue hacia el norte⟩ **4** : dedicarse a ⟨to pursue a hobby : dedicarse a un pasatiempo⟩

pursuer [pərˈsuːər] *n* : perseguidor *m*, -dora *f*

pursuit [pərˈsuːt] *n* **1** CHASE : persecución *f* **2** SEARCH : búsqueda *f*, busca *f* **3** ACTIVITY : actividad *f*, pasatiempo *m*

purveyor [pərˈveɪər] *n* : proveedor *m*, -dora *f*

pus [ˈpʌs] *n* : pus *m*

push¹ [ˈpʊʃ] *vt* **1** SHOVE : empujar **2** PRESS : apretar, pulsar ⟨push that button : aprieta ese botón⟩ **3** PRESSURE, URGE : presionar **4 to push around** BULLY : intimidar, mangonear — *vi* **1** SHOVE : empujar **2** INSIST : insistir, presionar **3 to push off** LEAVE : marcharse, irse, largarse *fam* **4 to push on** PROCEED : seguir

push² *n* **1** SHOVE : empujón *m* **2** DRIVE : empuje *m*, energía *f*, dinamismo *m* **3** EFFORT : esfuerzo *m*

push–button [ˈpʊʃˈbʌtən] *adj* : de botones

pushcart [ˈpʊʃˌkart] *n* : carretilla *f* de mano

pushy [ˈpʊʃi] *adj* **pushier; -est** : mandón, prepotente

pussy [ˈpʊsi] *n, pl* **pussies** : gatito *m*, -ta *f*; minino *m*, -na *f*

pussy willow *n* : sauce *m* blanco

pustule [ˈpʌsˌtʃuːl] *n* : pústula *f*

put [ˈpʊt] *v* **put; putting** *vt* **1** PLACE : poner, colocar ⟨put it on the table : ponlo en la mesa⟩ **2** INSERT : meter **3** (*indicating causation of a state or feeling*) : poner ⟨it put her in a good mood : la puso de buen humor⟩ ⟨to put into effect : poner en práctica⟩ **4** IMPOSE : imponer ⟨they put a tax on it : lo gravaron con un impuesto⟩ **5** SUBJECT : someter, poner ⟨to put to the test : poner a prueba⟩ ⟨to put to death : ejecutar⟩ **6** EXPRESS : expresar, decir ⟨he put it

simply : lo dijo sencillamente⟩ **7** APPLY : aplicar ⟨to put one's mind to something : proponerse hacer algo⟩ **8** SET : poner ⟨I put him to work : lo puse a trabajar⟩ **9** ATTACH : dar ⟨to put a high value on : dar gran valor a⟩ **10** PRESENT : presentar, exponer ⟨to put a question to someone : hacer una pregunta a alguien⟩ — *vi* **1 to put to sea** : hacerse a la mar **2 to put up with** : aguantar, soportar

put away *vt* **1** KEEP : guardar **2** *or* **to put aside** : dejar a un lado

put by *vt* SAVE : ahorrar

put down *vt* **1** SUPPRESS : aplastar, suprimir **2** ATTRIBUTE : atribuir ⟨she put it down to luck : lo atribuyó a la suerte⟩

put in *vi* : presentarse ⟨I've put in for the position : me presenté para el puesto⟩ — *vt* DEVOTE : dedicar (unas horas, etc.)

put off *vt* DEFER : aplazar, posponer

put on *vt* **1** ASSUME : afectar, adoptar **2** PRODUCE : presentar (una obra de teatro, etc.) **3** WEAR : ponerse

put out *vt* INCONVENIENCE : importunar, incomodar

putrefy [ˈpjuːtrəˌfaɪ] *v* **-fied; -fying** *vt* : pudrir — *vi* : pudrirse

putrid [ˈpjuːtrɪd] *adj* : putrefacto, pútrido

putter [ˈpʌtər] *vi or* **to putter around** : entretenerse

putty¹ [ˈpʌti] *vt* **-tied; -tying** : poner masilla en

putty² *n, pl* **-ties** : masilla *f*

put up *vt* **1** LODGE : alojar **2** CONTRIBUTE : contribuir, pagar

puzzle¹ [ˈpʌzəl] *vt* **-zled; -zling 1** CONFUSE : confundir, dejar perplejo **2** **to puzzle out** : dar vueltas a, tratar de resolver

puzzle² *n* **1** : rompecabezas *m* ⟨a crossword puzzle : un crucigrama⟩ **2** MYSTERY : misterio *m*, enigma *m*

puzzlement [ˈpʌzəlmənt] *n* : desconcierto *m*, perplejidad *f*

pygmy¹ [ˈpɪgmi] *adj* : enano, pigmeo

pygmy² *n, pl* **-mies 1** DWARF : enano *m*, -na *f* **2 Pygmy** : pigmeo *m*, -mea *f*

pylon [ˈpaɪˌlan, -lən] *n* **1** : torre *f* de conducta eléctrica **2** : pilón *m* (de un puente)

pyramid [ˈpɪrəˌmɪd] *n* : pirámide *f*

pyre [ˈpaɪr] *n* : pira *f*

pyromania [ˌpaɪroˈmeɪniə] *n* : piromanía *f*

pyromaniac [ˌpaɪroˈmeɪniˌæk] *n* : pirómano *m*, -na *f*

pyrotechnics [ˌpaɪrəˈtɛknɪks] *npl* **1** FIREWORKS : fuegos *mpl* artificiales **2** DISPLAY, SHOW : espectáculo *m*, muestra *f* de virtuosismo ⟨computer pyrotechnics : efectos especiales hechos por computadora⟩

python [ˈpaɪθɑn, -θən] *n* : pitón *f*, serpiente *f* pitón

Q

q ['kjuː] *n, pl* q's *or* qs ['kjuːz] : deci-moséptima letra del alfabeto inglés

quack¹ ['kwæk] *vi* : graznar

quack² *n* 1 : graznido *m* (de pato) 2 CHARLATAN : curandero *m*, -ra *f*; matasanos *m fam*

quadrangle ['kwɑ,dræŋgəl] *n* 1 COURTYARD : patio *m* interior 2 → quadrilateral

quadrant ['kwɑdrənt] *n* : cuadrante *m*

quadrilateral [,kwɑdrə'læṭərəl] *n* : cuadrilátero *m*

quadruped ['kwɑdrə,pɛd] *n* : cuadrúpedo *m*

quadruple [kwɑ'druːpəl, -'drʌ-; 'kwɑdrə-] *v* -pled; -pling *vt* : cuadruplicar — *vi* : cuadruplicarse

quadruplet [kwɑ'druːplət, -'drʌ-; 'kwɑdrə-] *n* : cuatrillizo *m*, -za *f*

quagmire ['kwæg,maɪr, 'kwɑg-] *n* 1 : lodazal *m*, barrizal *m* 2 PREDICAMENT : atolladero *m*

quail¹ ['kweɪl] *vi* : encogerse, acobardarse

quail² *n, pl* quail *or* quails : codorniz *f*

quaint ['kweɪnt] *adj* 1 ODD : extraño, curioso 2 PICTURESQUE : pintoresco — quaintly *adv*

quaintness ['kweɪntnəs] *n* : rareza *f*, lo curioso

quake¹ ['kweɪk] *vi* quaked; quaking : temblar

quake² *n* : temblor *m*, terremoto *m*

qualification [,kwɑləfə'keɪʃən] *n* 1 LIMITATION, RESERVATION : reserva *f*, limitación *f* ⟨without qualification : sin reservas⟩ 2 REQUIREMENT : requisito *m* 3 qualifications *npl* ABILITY : aptitud *f*, capacidad *f*

qualified ['kwɑlə,faɪd] *adj* : competente, capacitado

qualifier ['kwɑlə,faɪər] *n* 1 : clasificado *m*, -da *f* (en deportes) 2 : calificativo *m* (en gramática)

qualify ['kwɑlə,faɪ] *v* -fied; -fying *vt* 1 : matizar ⟨to qualify a statement : matizar una declaración⟩ 2 MODIFY : calificar (en gramática) 3 : habilitar ⟨the certificate qualified her to teach : el certificado la habilitó para enseñar⟩ — *vi* 1 : obtener el título, recibirse ⟨to qualify as an engineer : recibirse de ingeniero⟩ 2 : clasificarse (en deportes)

quality ['kwɑləṭi] *n, pl* -ties 1 NATURE : carácter *m* 2 ATTRIBUTE : cualidad *f* 3 GRADE : calidad *f* ⟨of good quality : de buena calidad⟩

qualm ['kwɑm, 'kwɑlm, 'kwɔm] *n* 1 MISGIVING : duda *f*, aprensión *f* 2 RESERVATION, SCRUPLE : escrúpulo *m*, reparo *m*

quandary ['kwɑndri] *n, pl* -ries : dilema *m*

quantitative ['kwɑntə,teɪṭɪv] *adj* : cuantitativo

quantity ['kwɑntəṭi] *n, pl* -ties : cantidad *f*

quantum¹ ['kwɑntəm] *n* : cuanto *m* (en física)

quantum² *adj* : cuántico

quantum theory ['kwɑntəm] *n* : teoría *f* cuántica

quarantine¹ ['kwɔrən,tiːn] *vt* -tined; -tining : poner en cuarentena

quarantine² *n* : cuarentena *f*

quarrel¹ ['kwɔrəl] *vi* -reled *or* -relled; -reling *or* -relling : pelearse, reñir, discutir

quarrel² *n* : pelea *f*, riña *f*, disputa *f*

quarrelsome ['kwɔrəlsəm] *adj* : pendenciero, discutidor

quarry¹ ['kwɔri] *vt* quarried; quarrying 1 EXTRACT : extraer, sacar ⟨to quarry marble : extraer mármol⟩ 2 EXCAVATE : excavar ⟨to quarry a hill : excavar un cerro⟩

quarry² *n, pl* quarries 1 PREY : presa *f* 2 *or* stone quarry : cantera *f*

quart ['kwɔrt] *n* : cuarto *m* de galón

quarter¹ ['kwɔrṭər] *vt* 1 : dividir en cuatro partes 2 LODGE : alojar, acuartelar (tropas)

quarter² *n* 1 : cuarto *m*, cuarta parte *f* ⟨a foot and a quarter : un pie y cuarto⟩ ⟨a quarter after three : las tres y cuarto⟩ 2 : moneda *f* de 25 centavos, cuarto *m* de dólar 3 DISTRICT : barrio *m* ⟨business quarter : barrio comercial⟩ 4 PLACE : parte *f* ⟨from all quarters : de todas partes⟩ ⟨at close quarters : de muy cerca⟩ 5 MERCY : clemencia *f*, cuartel *m* ⟨to give no quarter : no dar cuartel⟩ 6 quarters *npl* LODGING : alojamiento *m*, cuartel *m* (militar)

quarterback ['kwɔrṭər,bæk] *n* : mariscal *m* de campo

quarterly¹ ['kwɔrṭərli] *adv* : cada tres meses, trimestralmente

quarterly² *adj* : trimestral

quarterly³ *n, pl* -lies : publicación *f* trimestral

quartermaster ['kwɔrṭər,mæstər] *n* : intendente *mf*

quartet [kwɔr'tɛt] *n* : cuarteto *m*

quartz ['kwɔrts] *n* : cuarzo *m*

quash ['kwɑʃ, 'kwɔʃ] *vt* 1 ANNUL : anular 2 QUELL : sofocar, aplastar

quaver¹ ['kweɪvər] *vi* 1 SHAKE : temblar ⟨her voice was quavering : le temblaba la voz⟩ 2 TRILL : trinar

quaver² *n* : temblor *m* (de la voz)

quay ['kiː, 'keɪ, 'kweɪ] *n* : muelle *m*

queasiness ['kwiːzinəs] *n* : mareo *m*, náusea *f*

queasy ['kwiːzi] *adj* -sier; -est : mareado

queen ['kwiːn] *n* : reina *f*

queenly ['kwiːnli] *adj* -lier; -est : de reina, regio

queer ['kwɪr] *adj* : extraño, raro, curioso — queerly *adv*

quell ['kwl] *vt* : aplastar, sofocar

quench ['kwɛntʃ] *vt* **1** EXTINGUISH : apagar, sofocar **2** SATISFY : saciar, satisfacer (la sed)

querulous ['kwɛrələs, 'kwɛrjələs, 'kwɪr-] *adj* : quejumbroso, quejoso — **querulously** *adv*

query¹ ['kwɪri, 'kwɛr-] *vt* -ried; -rying **1** ASK : preguntar, interrogar ⟨we queried the professor : preguntamos al profesor⟩ **2** QUESTION : cuestionar, poner en duda ⟨to query a matter : cuestionar un asunto⟩

query² *n, pl* -ries **1** QUESTION : pregunta *f* **2** DOUBT : duda *f*

quest¹ ['kwɛst] *v* : buscar

quest² *n* : búsqueda *f*

question¹ ['kwɛstʃən] *vt* **1** ASK : preguntar **2** DOUBT : poner en duda, cuestionar **3** INTERROGATE : interrogar — *vi* INQUIRE : inquirir, preguntar

question² *n* **1** QUERY : pregunta *f* **2** ISSUE : asunto *m*, problema *f*, cuestión *f* **3** POSSIBILITY : posibilidad *f* ⟨it's out of the question : es indiscutible⟩ **4** DOUBT : duda *f* ⟨to call into question : poner en duda⟩

questionable ['kwɛstʃənəbəl] *adj* : dudoso, discutible, cuestionable ⟨questionable results : resultados discutibles⟩ ⟨questionable motives : motivos sospechosos⟩

questioner ['kwɛstʃənər] *n* : interrogador *m*, -dora *f*

question mark *n* : signo *m* de interrogación

questionnaire [ˌkwɛstʃə'nær] *n* : cuestionario *m*

queue¹ ['kju:] *vi* queued; queuing *or* queueing : hacer cola

queue² *n* **1** PIGTAIL : coleta *f*, trenza *f* **2** LINE : cola *f*, fila *f*

quibble¹ ['kwɪbəl] *vi* -bled; -bling : quejarse por nimiedades, andar con sutilezas

quibble² *n* : objeción *f* de poca monta, queja *f* insignificante

quick¹ ['kwɪk] *adv* : rápidamente

quick² *adj* **1** RAPID : rápido **2** ALERT, CLEVER : listo, vivo, agudo **3 a quick temper** : un genio vivo

quick³ *n* **1** FLESH : carne *f* viva **2 to cut someone to the quick** : herir a alguien en lo más vivo

quicken ['kwɪkən] *vt* **1** REVIVE : resucitar **2** AROUSE : estimular, despertar **3** HASTEN : acelerar ⟨she quickened her pace : aceleró el paso⟩

quickly ['kwɪkli] *adv* : rápidamente, rápido, de prisa

quickness ['kwɪknəs] *n* : rapidez *f*

quicksand ['kwɪkˌsænd] *n* : arena *f* movediza

quicksilver ['kwɪkˌsɪlvər] *n* : mercurio *m*, azogue *m*

quick-tempered ['kwɪk'tɛmpərd] *adj* : irascible, de genio vivo

quick-witted ['kwɪk'wɪtəd] *adj* : agudo

quiet¹ ['kwaɪət] *vt* **1** SILENCE : hacer callar, acallar **2** CALM : calmar, tranquilizar — *vi* **to quiet down** : calmarse, tranquilizarse

quiet² *adv* : silenciosamente ⟨a quiet-running engine : un motor silencioso⟩

quiet³ *adj* **1** CALM : tranquilo, calmoso **2** MILD : sosegado, suave ⟨a quiet disposition : un temperamento sosegado⟩ **3** SILENT : silencioso **4** UNOBTRUSIVE : discreto **5** SECLUDED : aislado ⟨a quiet nook : un rincón aislado⟩ — **quietly** *adv*

quiet⁴ *n* **1** CALM : calma *f*, tranquilidad *f* **2** SILENCE : silencio *m*

quietness ['kwaɪətnəs] *n* : suavidad *f*, tranquilidad *f*, quietud *f*

quietude ['kwaɪəˌtuːd, -ˌtjuːd] *n* : quietud *f*, reposo *m*

quill ['kwɪl] *n* **1** SPINE : púa *f* (de un puerco espín) **2** : pluma *f* (para escribir)

quilt¹ ['kwɪlt] *vt* : acolchar

quilt² *n* : colcha *f*, edredón *m*

quince ['kwɪnts] *n* : membrillo *m*

quinine ['kwaɪˌnaɪn] *n* : quinina *f*

quintessence [kwɪn'tɛsənts] *n* : quintaesencia *f*

quintet [kwɪn'tɛt] *n* : quinteto *m*

quintuple [kwɪn'tuːpəl, -'tjuː-, -'tʌ-; 'kwɪntə-] *adj* : quíntuplo

quintuplet [kwɪn'tʌplət, -'tu:-, -'tjuː-; 'kwɪntə-] *n* : quintillizo *m*, -za *f*

quip¹ ['kwɪp] *vi* quipped; quipping : bromear

quip² *n* : ocurrencia *f*, salida *f*

quirk ['kwərk] *n* : peculiaridad *f*, rareza *f* ⟨a quirk of fate : un capricho del destino⟩

quirky ['kwərki] *adj* -kier; -est : peculiar, raro

quit ['kwɪt] *v* quit; quitting *vt* : dejar, abandonar ⟨to quit smoking : dejar de fumar⟩ — *vi* **1** STOP : parar **2** RESIGN : dimitir, renunciar

quite ['kwaɪt] *adv* **1** COMPLETELY : completamente, totalmente **2** RATHER : bastante ⟨quite near : bastante cerca⟩

quits ['kwɪts] *adj* **to call it quits** : quedar en paz

quitter ['kwɪtər] *n* : derrotista *mf*

quiver¹ ['kwɪvər] *vi* : temblar, estremecerse, vibrar

quiver² *n* **1** : carcaj *m*, aljaba *f* (para flechas) **2** TREMBLING : temblor *m*, estremecimiento *m*

quixotic [kwɪk'sɑtɪk] *adj* : quijotesco

quiz¹ ['kwɪz] *vt* quizzed; quizzing : interrogar, hacer una prueba a (en el colegio)

quiz² *n, pl* quizzes : examen *m* corto, prueba *f*

quizzical ['kwɪzɪkəl] *adj* **1** TEASING : burlón **2** CURIOUS : curioso, interrogativo

quorum ['kworəm] *n* : quórum *m*

quota ['kwo:ṭə] *n* : cuota *f*, cupo *m*
quotable ['kwo:ṭəbəl] *adj* : citable
quotation [kwo'teɪʃən] *n* **1** CITATION : cita *f* **2** ESTIMATE : presupuesto *m*, estimación *f* **3** PRICE : cotización *f*
quotation marks *npl* : comillas *fpl*

quote¹ ['kwo:t] *vt* **quoted; quoting 1** CITE : citar **2** VALUE : cotizar (en finanzas)
quote² *n* **1** → quotation **2** quotes *npl* → quotation marks
quotient ['kwo:ʃənt] *n* : cociente *m*

R

r ['ɑr] *n, pl* **r's** *or* **rs** ['ɑrz] : decimoctava letra del alfabeto inglés
rabbi ['ræˌbaɪ] *n* : rabino *m*, -na *f*
rabbit ['ræbət] *n, pl* **-bit** *or* **-bits** : conejo *m*, -ja *f*
rabble ['ræbəl] *n* **1** MASSES : populacho *m* **2** RIFFRAFF : chusma *f*, gentuza *f*
rabid ['ræbɪd] *adj* **1** : rabioso, afectado con la rabia **2** FURIOUS : furioso **3** FANATIC : fanático
rabies ['reɪbi:z] *ns & pl* : rabia *f*
raccoon [ræ'ku:n] *n, pl* **-coon** *or* **-coons** : mapache *m*
race¹ ['reɪs] *vi* **raced; racing 1** : correr, competir (en una carrera) **2** RUSH : ir a toda prisa, ir corriendo
race² *n* **1** CURRENT : corriente *f* (de agua) **2** : carrera *f* ⟨dog race : carrera de perros⟩ ⟨the presidential race : la carrera presidential⟩ **3** : raza *f* ⟨the black race : la raza negra⟩ ⟨the human race : el género humano⟩
racecourse ['reɪsˌkors] *n* : pista *f* (de carreras)
racehorse ['reɪsˌhors] *n* : caballo *m* de carreras
racer ['reɪsər] *n* : corredor *m*, -dora *f*
racetrack ['reɪsˌtræk] *n* : pista *f* (de carreras)
racial ['reɪʃəl] *adj* : racial — **racially** *adv*
racism ['reɪˌsɪzəm] *n* : racismo *m*
racist ['reɪsɪst] *n* : racista *mf*
rack¹ ['ræk] *vt* **1** : atormentar ⟨racked with pain : atormentado por el dolor⟩ **2 to rack one's brains** : devanarse los sesos
rack² *n* **1** SHELF, STAND : estante *m* ⟨a luggage rack : un portaequipajes⟩ ⟨a coatrack : un perchero, una percha⟩ **2** : potro *m* (instrumento de la tortura)
racket ['rækət] *n* **1** : raqueta *f* (en deportes) **2** DIN : estruendo *m*, bulla *f*, jaleo *m fam* **3** SWINDLE : estafa *f*, timo *m fam*
racketeer [ˌrækə'tɪr] *n* : estafador *m*, -dora *f*
raconteur [ˌræˌkɑn'tər] *n* : anecdotista *mf*
racy ['reɪsi] *adj* **racier; -est** : subido de tono, picante
radar ['reɪˌdɑr] *n* : radar *m*
radial ['reɪdiəl] *adj* : radial
radiance ['reɪdiənts] *n* : resplandor *m*
radiant ['reɪdiənt] *adj* : radiante — **radiantly** *adv*
radiate ['reɪdiˌeɪt] *v* **-ated; -ating** *vt* : irradiar, emitir ⟨to radiate heat : irradi-

ar el calor⟩ ⟨to radiate happiness : rebosar de alegría⟩ — *vi* **1** : irradiar **2** SPREAD : salir, extenderse ⟨to radiate (out) from the center : salir del centro⟩
radiation [ˌreɪdi'eɪʃən] *n* : radiación *f*
radiator ['reɪdiˌeɪtər] *n* : radiador *m*
radical¹ ['rædɪkəl] *adj* : radical — **radically** [-kli] *adv*
radical² *n* : radical *mf*
radicalism ['rædɪkəˌlɪzəm] *n* : radicalismo *m*
radii → **radius**
radio¹ ['reɪdiˌo:] *v* : llamar por radio, transmitir por radio
radio² *n, pl* **-dios** : radio *m* (aparato), radio *f* (emisora, radiodifusión)
radioactive ['reɪdio'æktɪv] *adj* : radiactivo, radioactivo
radioactivity [ˌreɪdioˌæk'tɪvəti] *n, pl* **-ties** : radiactividad *f*, radioactividad *f*
radiologist [ˌreɪdi'ɑləʤɪst] *n* : radiólogo *m*, -ga *f*
radiology [ˌreɪdi'ɑləʤi] *n* : radiología *f*
radish ['rædɪʃ] *n* : rábano *m*
radium ['reɪdiəm] *n* : radio *m*
radius ['reɪdiəs] *n, pl* **radii** [-diˌaɪ] : radio *m*
radon ['reɪˌdɑn] *n* : radón *m*
raffle¹ ['ræfəl] *vt* **-fled; -fling** : rifar, sortear
raffle² *n* : rifa *f*, sorteo *m*
raft ['ræft] *n* **1** : balsa *f* ⟨rubber rafts : balsas de goma⟩ **2** LOT, SLEW : montón *m* ⟨a raft of documents : un montón de documentos⟩
rafter ['ræftər] *n* : par *m*, viga *f*
rag ['ræg] *n* **1** CLOTH : trapo *m* **2 rags** *npl* TATTERS : harapos *mpl*, andrajos *mpl*
ragamuffin ['rægəˌmʌfən] *n* : pilluelo *m*, -la *f*
rage¹ ['reɪʤ] *vi* **raged; raging 1** : estar furioso, rabiar ⟨to fly into a rage : enfurecerse⟩ **2** : bramar, hacer estragos ⟨the wind was raging : el viento bramaba⟩ ⟨flu raged through the school : la gripe hizo estragos por el colegio⟩
rage² *n* **1** ANGER : furia *f*, ira *f*, cólera *f* **2** FAD : moda *f*, furor *m*
ragged ['rægəd] *adj* **1** UNEVEN : irregular, desigual **2** TORN : hecho jirones **3** TATTERED : andrajoso, harapiento
ragout [ræ'gu:] *n* : ragú *m*, estofado *m*
ragtime ['rægˌtaɪm] *n* : ragtime *m*
ragweed ['rægˌwi:d] *n* : ambrosía *f*
raid¹ ['reɪd] *vt* **1** : invadir, hacer una incursión en ⟨raided by enemy troops

: invadido por tropas enemigas⟩ **2**
: asaltar, atracar ⟨the gang raided the
warehouse : la pandilla asaltó el al-
macén⟩ **3** : allanar, hacer una redada
en ⟨police raided the house : la policía
allanó la vivienda⟩

raid² *n* **1** : invasión *f* (militar) **2** : asalto
m (por delincuentes) **3** : redada *f*, allanamiento *m* (por la policía)

raider [ˈreɪdər] *n* **1** ATTACKER : asaltante
mf; invasor *m*, -sora *f* **2 corporate
raider** : tiburón *m*

rail¹ [ˈreɪl] *vi* **1 to rail against** REVILE
: denostar contra **2 to rail at** SCOLD
: regañar, reprender

rail² *n* **1** BAR : barra *f*, barrera *f* **2**
HANDRAIL : pasamanos *m*, barandilla
f **3** TRACK : riel *m* (para ferrocarriles)
4 RAILROAD : ferrocarril *m*

railing [ˈreɪlɪŋ] *n* **1** : baranda *f* (de un
balcón, etc.) **2** RAILS : verja *f*

raillery [ˈreɪləri] *n, pl* **-leries** : bromas *fpl*

railroad [ˈreɪlˌroːd] *n* : ferrocarril *m*

railway [ˈreɪlˌweɪ] → **railroad**

raiment [ˈreɪmənt] *n* : vestiduras *fpl*

rain¹ [ˈreɪn] *vi* **1** : llover ⟨it's raining : está
lloviendo⟩ **2 to rain down** SHOWER
: llover ⟨insults rained down on him : le
llovieron los insultos⟩

rain² *n* : lluvia *f*

rainbow [ˈreɪnˌboː] *n* : arco *m* iris

raincoat [ˈreɪnˌkoːt] *n* : impermeable *m*

raindrop [ˈreɪnˌdrɑp] *n* : gota *f* de lluvia

rainfall [ˈreɪnˌfɔl] *n* : lluvia *f*, precipitación *f*

rainstorm [ˈreɪnˌstɔrm] *n* : temporal *m*
(de lluvia)

rainwater [ˈreɪnˌwɔtər] *n* : agua *f* de lluvia

rainy [ˈreɪni] *adj* **rainier; -est** : lluvioso

raise¹ [ˈreɪz] *vt* **raised; raising 1** LIFT
: levantar, subir, alzar ⟨to raise one's
spirits : levantarle el ánimo a alguien⟩
2 ERECT : levantar, erigir **3** COLLECT
: recaudar ⟨to raise money : recaudar
dinero⟩ **4** REAR : criar ⟨to raise one's
children : criar uno a sus niños⟩ **5**
GROW : cultivar **6** INCREASE : aumentar, subir **7** PROMOTE : ascender **8**
PROVOKE : provocar ⟨it raised a laugh
: provocó una risa⟩ **9** BRING UP : sacar
(temas, objeciones, etc.)

raise² *n* : aumento *m*

raisin [ˈreɪzən] *n* : pasa *f*

raja *or* **rajah** [ˈrɑdʒə, -ˌdʒɑ, -ˌʒɑ] *n* : rajá
m

rake¹ [ˈreɪk] *v* **raked; raking** *vt* **1** : rastrillar ⟨to rake leaves : rastrillar las ho-
jas⟩ **2** SWEEP : barrer ⟨raked with gunfire : barrido con metralla⟩ — *vi* **to rake
through** : revolver, hurgar en

rake² *n* **1** : rastrillo *m* **2** LIBERTINE : libertino *m*, -na *f*; calavera *m*

rakish [ˈreɪkɪʃ] *adj* **1** JAUNTY : desenvuelto, desenfadado **2** DISSOLUTE
: libertino, disoluto

rally¹ [ˈræli] *v* **-lied; -lying** *vi* **1** MEET,
UNITE : reunirse, congregarse **2** RE-

COVER : recuperarse — *vt* **1** ASSEMBLE
: reunir (tropas, etc.) **2** RECOVER : recobrar (la fuerza, el ánimo, etc.)

rally² *n, pl* **-lies** : reunión *f*, mitin *m*, manifestación *f*

ram¹ [ˈræm] *v* **rammed; ramming** *vt* **1**
DRIVE : hincar, clavar ⟨he rammed it
into the ground : lo hincó en la tierra⟩
2 SMASH : estrellar, embestir — *vi* COL-
LIDE : chocar (contra), estrellarse

ram² *n* **1** : carnero *m* (animal) **2 battering ram** : ariete *m*

RAM [ˈræm] *n* : RAM *f*

ramble¹ [ˈræmbəl] *vi* **-bled; -bling 1**
WANDER : pasear, deambular **2 to ram-
ble on** : divagar, perder el hilo **3**
SPREAD : trepar (dícese de una planta)

ramble² *n* : paseo *m*, excursión *f*

rambler [ˈræmblər] *n* **1** WALKER : excursionista *mf* **2** ROSE : rosa *f* trepadora

rambunctious [ræmˈbʌŋkʃəs] *adj* UN-
RULY : alborotado

ramification [ˌræməfəˈkeɪʃən] *n* : ramificación *f*

ramify [ˈræməˌfaɪ] *vi* **-fied; -fying** : ramificarse

ramp [ˈræmp] *n* : rampa *f*

rampage¹ [ˈræmˌpeɪdʒ, ræmˈpeɪdʒ] *vi*
-paged; -paging : andar arrasando
todo, correr destrozando

rampage² [ˈræmˌpeɪdʒ] *n* : alboroto *m*,
frenesí *m* (de violencia)

rampant [ˈræmpənt] *adj* : desenfrenado

rampart [ˈræmˌpɑrt] *n* : terraplén *m*, muralla *f*

ramrod [ˈræmˌrɑd] *n* : baqueta *f*

ramshackle [ˈræmˌʃækəl] *adj* : destartalado

ran → **run**

ranch [ˈræntʃ] *n* **1** : hacienda *f*, rancho
m, finca *f* ganadera **2** FARM : granja *f*
⟨fruit ranch : granja de frutas⟩

rancher [ˈræntʃər] *n* : estanciero *m*, -ra
f; ranchero *m*, -ra *f*

rancid [ˈræntsɪd] *adj* : rancio

rancor [ˈræŋkər] *n* : rencor *m*

random [ˈrændəm] *adj* **1** : fortuito,
aleatorio **2 at ~** : al azar — **randomly** *adv*

rang → **ring**

range¹ [ˈreɪndʒ] *v* **ranged; ranging** *vt*
ARRANGE : alinear, ordenar, arreglar
— *vi* **1** ROAM : deambular ⟨to range
through the town : deambular por el
pueblo⟩ **2** EXTEND : extenderse ⟨the
results range widely : los resultados se
extienden mucho⟩ **3** VARY : variar
⟨discounts range from 20% to 40% : los
descuentos varían entre 20% y 40%⟩

range² *n* **1** ROW : fila *f*, hilera *f* ⟨a mountain range : una cordillera⟩ **2** GRASS-
LAND : pradera *f*, pampa *f* **3** STOVE
: cocina *f* **4** VARIETY : variedad *f*, gama
f **5** SPHERE : ámbito *m*, esfera *f*, campo *m* **6** REACH : registro *m* (de la voz),
alcance *m* (de un arma de fuego) **7
shooting range** : campo *m* de tiro

ranger ['reɪndʒər] *n or* **forest ranger**
: guardabosque *mf*
rangy ['reɪndʒi] *adj* **rangier; -est** : alto y
delgado
rank¹ ['ræŋk] *vt* **1** RANGE : alinear, ordenar, poner en fila **2** CLASSIFY : clasificar — *vi* **1 to rank above** : ser superior a **2 to rank among** : encontrarse
entre, figurar entre
rank² *adj* **1** LUXURIANT : lozano, exuberante (dícese de una planta) **2**
SMELLY : fétido, maloliente **3** OUT-
RIGHT : completo, absoluto ⟨a rank injustice : una injusticia manifiesta⟩
rank³ *n* **1** LINE, ROW : fila *f* ⟨to close
ranks : cerrar filas⟩ **2** GRADE, POSI-
TION : grado *m*, rango *m* (militar) ⟨to
pull rank : abusar de su autoridad⟩ **3**
CLASS : categoría *f*, clase *f* **4 ranks** *npl*
: soldados *mpl* rasos
rank and file *n* **1** RANKS : soldados *mpl*
rasos **2** : bases *fpl* (de un partido, etc.)
rankle ['ræŋkəl] *v* **-kled; -kling** *vi* : doler — *vt* : irritar, herir
ransack ['ræn,sæk] *vt* : revolver, desvalijar, registrar de arriba abajo
ransom¹ ['ræntsəm] *vt* : rescatar, pagar
un rescate por
ransom² *n* : rescate *m*
rant ['rænt] *vi or* **to rant and rave**
: despotricar, desvariar
rap¹ ['ræp] *v* **rapped; rapping** *vt* **1**
KNOCK : golpetear, dar un golpe en **2**
CRITICIZE : criticar — *vi* **1** CHAT : charlar, cotorrear *fam* **2** KNOCK : dar un
golpe
rap² *n* **1** BLOW, KNOCK : golpe *m*,
golpecito *m* **2** CHAT : charla *f* **3** *or* **rap
music** : rap *m* **4 to take the rap** : pagar el pato *fam*
rapacious [rə'peɪʃəs] *adj* **1** GREEDY
: avaricioso, codicioso **2** PREDATORY
: rapaz, de rapiña **3** RAVENOUS : voraz
rape¹ ['reɪp] *vt* **raped; raping** : violar
rape² *n* **1** : colza *f* (planta) **2** : violación
f (de una persona)
rapid ['ræpɪd] *adj* : rápido — **rapidly** *adv*
rapidity [rə'pɪdəti] *n* : rapidez *f*
rapids ['ræpɪdz] *npl* : rápidos *mpl*
rapier ['reɪpiər] *n* : estoque *m*
rapist ['reɪpɪst] *n* : violador *m*, -dora *f*
rapper ['ræpər] *n* : cantante *mf* de rap;
rapero *m*, -ra *f*
rapport [ræ'por] *n* : relación *f* armo-
niosa, entendimiento *m*
rapt ['ræpt] *adj* : absorto, embelesado
rapture ['ræptʃər] *n* : éxtasis *m*
rapturous ['ræptʃərəs] *adj* : extasiado,
embelesado
rare ['rær] *adj* **rarer; rarest 1** RAREFIED
: enrarecido **2** FINE : excelente, excepcional ⟨a rare talent : un talento ex-
cepcional⟩ **3** UNCOMMON : raro, poco
común **4** : poco cocido (dícese de la
carne)
rarefy ['rærə,faɪ] *vt* **-fied; -fying** : rari-
ficar, enrarecer

rarely ['rærli] *adv* SELDOM : pocas veces,
rara vez
raring ['ræ:rən, -ɪŋ] *adj* : lleno de entusiasmo, con muchas ganas
rarity ['rærəti] *n, pl* **-ties** : rareza *f*
rascal ['ræskəl] *n* : pillo *m*, -lla *f*; pícaro
m, -ra *f*
rash¹ ['ræʃ] *adj* : imprudente, precipitado — **rashly** *adv*
rash² *n* : sarpullido *m*, erupción *f*
rashness ['ræʃnəs] *n* : precipitación *f*,
impetuosidad *f*
rasp¹ ['ræsp] *vt* **1** SCRAPE : raspar, es-
cofinar **2 to rasp out** : decir en voz
áspera
rasp² *n* : escofina *f*
raspberry ['ræz,bɛri] *n, pl* **-ries** : frambuesa *f*
rat ['ræt] *n* : rata *f*
ratchet ['rætʃət] *n* : trinquete *m*
rate¹ ['reɪt] *vt* **rated; rating 1** CONSID-
ER, REGARD : considerar, estimar **2**
DESERVE : merecer
rate² *n* **1** PACE, SPEED : velocidad *f*, ritmo *m* ⟨at this rate : a este paso⟩ **2**
: índice *m*, tasa *f* ⟨birth rate : índice de
natalidad⟩ ⟨interest rate : tasa de in-
terés⟩ **3** CHARGE, PRICE : precio *m*,
tarifa *f*
rather ['ræðər, 'rʌ-, 'rɑ-] *adv* **1** (*indicating preference*) ⟨she would rather stay
in the house : preferiría quedarse en
casa⟩ ⟨I'd rather not : mejor que no⟩
2 (*indicating preciseness*) ⟨my father, or
rather my stepfather : mi padre, o
mejor dicho mi padrastro⟩ **3** INSTEAD
: sino que, más que, al contrario ⟨I'm
not pleased; rather I'm disappointed
: no estoy satisfecho, sino desilusiona-
do⟩ **4** SOMEWHAT : algo, un tanto
⟨rather strange : un poco extraño⟩ **5**
QUITE : bastante ⟨rather difficult : bastante difícil⟩
ratification [,rætəfə'keɪʃən] *n* : ratificación *f*
ratify ['rætə,faɪ] *vt* **-fied; -fying** : ratificar
rating ['reɪtɪŋ] *n* **1** STANDING : clasificación *f*, posición *f* **2 ratings** *npl*
: índice *m* de audiencia
ratio ['reɪʃio] *n, pl* **-tios** : proporción *f*,
relación *f*
ration¹ ['ræʃən, 'reɪʃən] *vt* : racionar
ration² *n* **1** : ración *f* **2 rations** *npl* PRO-
VISIONS : víveres *mpl*
rational ['ræʃənəl] *adj* : racional, razonable, lógico — **rationally** *adv*
rationale [,ræʃə'næl] *n* **1** EXPLANATION
: explicación *f* **2** BASIS : base *f*, razones
fpl
rationality [,ræʃə'næləti] *n, pl* **-ties**
: racionalidad *f*
rationalization [,ræʃənələ'zeɪʃən] *n*
: racionalización *f*
rationalize ['ræʃənə,laɪz] *vt* **-ized; -izing**
: racionalizar
rattle¹ ['rætəl] *v* **-tled; -tling** *vi* **1** CLAT-
TER : traquetear, hacer ruido **2 to rat-
tle on** CHATTER : parlotear *fam* — *vt*

1 : hacer sonar, agitar ⟨the wind rattled the door : el viento sacudió la puerta⟩ **2** DISCONCERT, WORRY : desconcertar, poner nervioso **3 to rattle off** : despachar, recitar, decir de corrido
rattle² *n* **1** CLATTER : traqueteo *m*, ruido *m* **2** *or* **baby's rattle** : sonajero *m* **3** : cascabel *m* (de una culebra)
rattler ['rætələr] → **rattlesnake**
rattlesnake ['rætəl,sneɪk] *n* : serpiente *f* de cascabel
ratty ['ræti] *adj* **rattier; -est** : raído, andrajoso
raucous ['rɔkəs] *adj* **1** HOARSE : ronco **2** BOISTEROUS : escandaloso, bullicioso — **raucously** *adv*
ravage¹ ['rævɪdʒ] *vt* **-aged; -aging** : devastar, arrasar, hacer estragos
ravage² *n* : destrozo *m*, destrucción *f* ⟨the ravages of war : los estragos de la guerra⟩
rave ['reɪv] *vi* **raved; raving 1** : delirar, desvariar ⟨to rave like a maniac : desvariar como un loco⟩ **2 to rave about** : hablar con entusiasmo sobre, entusiasmarse por
ravel ['rævəl] *v* **-eled** *or* **-elled; -eling** *or* **-elling** *vt* UNRAVEL : desenredar, desenmarañar — *vi* FRAY : deshilacharse
raven ['reɪvən] *n* : cuervo *m*
ravenous ['rævənəs] *adj* : hambriento, voraz — **ravenously** *adv*
ravine [rə'viːn] *n* : barranco *m*, quebrada *f*
ravish ['rævɪʃ] *vt* **1** PLUNDER : saquear **2** ENCHANT : embelesar, cautivar, encantar
raw ['rɔ] *adj* **rawer; rawest 1** UNCOOKED : crudo **2** UNTREATED : sin tratar, sin refinar, puro ⟨raw data : datos en bruto⟩ ⟨raw materials : materias primas⟩ **3** INEXPERIENCED : novato, inexperto **4** OPEN : abierto, en carne viva ⟨a raw sore : una llaga abierta⟩ **5** : frío y húmedo ⟨a raw day : un día crudo⟩ **6** UNFAIR : injusto ⟨a raw deal : un trato injusto, una injusticia⟩
rawhide ['rɔ,haɪd] *n* : cuero *m* sin curtir
ray ['reɪ] *n* **1** : rayo *m* (de la luz, etc.) ⟨a ray of hope : un resquicio de esperanza⟩ **2** : raya *f* (pez)
rayon ['reɪ,ɑn] *n* : rayón *m*
raze ['reɪz] *vt* **razed; razing** : arrasar, demoler
razor ['reɪzər] *n* **1** *or* **straight razor** : navaja *f* (de afeitar) **2** *or* **safety razor** : maquinilla *f* de afeitar, rastrillo *m Mex* **3** SHAVER : afeitadora *f*, rasuradora *f*
reach¹ ['riːtʃ] *vt* **1** EXTEND : extender, alargar ⟨to reach out one's hand : extender la mano⟩ **2** : alcanzar ⟨I couldn't reach the apple : no pude alcanzar la manzana⟩ **3** : llegar a, llegar hasta ⟨the shadow reached the wall : la sombra llegó hasta la pared⟩ **4** CONTACT : contactar, ponerse en contacto con — *vi* **1** *or* **to reach out** : extender la mano **2** STRETCH : extenderse **3 to**

reach for : tratar de agarrar
reach² *n* : alcance *m*, extensión *f*
react [ri'ækt] *vi* : reaccionar
reaction [ri'ækʃən] *n* : reacción *f*
reactionary¹ [ri'ækʃə,nɛri] *adj* : reaccionario
reactionary² *n, pl* **-ries** : reaccionario *m*, -ria *f*
reactor [ri'æktər] *n* : reactor *m* ⟨nuclear reactor : reactor nuclear⟩
read¹ ['riːd] *v* **read** ['rɛd]; **reading** *vt* **1** : leer ⟨to read a story : leer un cuento⟩ **2** INTERPRET : interpretar ⟨it can be read two ways : se puede interpretar de dos maneras⟩ **3** : decir, poner ⟨the sign read "No smoking" : el letrero decía "No Fumar"⟩ **4** : marcar ⟨the thermometer reads 70° : el termómetro marca 70°⟩ — *vi* **1** : leer ⟨he can read : sabe leer⟩ **2** SAY : decir ⟨the list reads as follows : la lista dice lo siguiente⟩
read² *n* **to be a good read** : ser una lectura amena
readable ['riːdəbəl] *adj* : legible — **readably** [-bli] *adv*
reader ['riːdər] *n* : lector *m*, -tora *f*
readily ['rɛdəli] *adv* **1** WILLINGLY : de buena gana, con gusto **2** EASILY : fácilmente, con facilidad
readiness ['rɛdinəs] *n* **1** WILLINGNESS : buena disposición *f* **2 to be in readiness** : estar preparado
reading ['riːdɪŋ] *n* : lectura *f*
readjust [,riːə'dʒʌst] *vt* : reajustar — *vi* : volverse a adaptar
readjustment [,riːə'dʒʌstmənt] *n* : reajuste *m*
ready¹ ['rɛdi] *vt* **readied; readying** : preparar
ready² *adj* **readier; -est 1** PREPARED : listo, preparado **2** WILLING : dispuesto **3** : a punto de ⟨ready to cry : a punto de llorar⟩ **4** AVAILABLE : disponible ⟨ready cash : efectivo⟩ **5** QUICK : vivo, agudo ⟨a ready wit : un ingenio agudo⟩
ready—made ['rɛdi'meɪd] *adj* : preparado, confeccionado
reaffirm [,riːə'fərm] *vt* : reafirmar
real¹ ['riːl] *adv* VERY : muy ⟨we had a real good time : lo pasamos muy bien⟩
real² *adj* **1** : inmobiliario ⟨real property : bien inmueble, bien raíz⟩ **2** GENUINE : auténtico, genuino **3** ACTUAL, TRUE : real, verdadero ⟨a real friend : un verdadero amigo⟩ **4 for real** SERIOUSLY : de veras, de verdad
real estate *n* : propiedad *f* inmobiliaria, bienes *mpl* raíces
realign [,riːə'laɪn] *vt* : realinear
realignment [,riːə'laɪnmənt] *n* : realineamiento *m*
realism ['riːə,lɪzəm] *n* : realismo *m*
realist ['riːəlɪst] *n* : realista *mf*
realistic [,riːə'lɪstɪk] *adj* : realista
realistically [,riːə'lɪstɪkli] *adv* : de manera realista

reality [ri'æləti] *n, pl* **-ties** : realidad *f*
realizable [ˌri:ə'laɪzəbəl] *adj* : realizable, alcanzable
realization [ˌri:ələ'zeɪʃən] *n* : realización *f*
realize ['ri:əˌlaɪz] *vt* **-ized; -izing 1** ACCOMPLISH : realizar, llevar a cabo **2** GAIN : obtener, realizar, sacar ⟨to realize a profit : realizar beneficios⟩ **3** UNDERSTAND : darse cuenta de, saber
really ['rɪli, 'ri:-] *adv* **1** ACTUALLY : de verdad, en realidad **2** TRULY : verdaderamente, realmente **3** FRANKLY : francamente, en serio
realm ['rɛlm] *n* **1** KINGDOM : reino *m* **2** SPHERE : esfera *f*, campo *m*
ream[1] ['ri:m] *vt* : escariar
ream[2] *n* **1** : resma *f* (de papel) **2 reams** *npl* LOADS : montones *mpl*
reap ['ri:p] *v* : cosechar
reaper ['ri:pər] *n* **1** : cosechador *m*, -dora *f* (persona) **2** : cosechadora *f* (máquina)
reappear [ˌri:ə'pɪr] *vi* : reaparecer
reappearance [ˌri:ə'pɪrənts] *n* : reaparición *f*
rear[1] ['rɪr] *vt* **1** LIFT, RAISE : levantar **2** BREED, BRING UP : criar — *vi or* **to rear up** : encabritarse
rear[2] *adj* : trasero, posterior, de atrás
rear[3] *n* **1** BACK : parte *f* de atrás ⟨to bring up the rear : cerrar la marcha⟩ **2** *or* **rear end** : trasero *m*
rear admiral *n* : contraalmirante *mf*
rearrange [ˌri:ə'reɪndʒ] *vt* **-ranged; -ranging** : colocar de otra manera, volver a arreglar, reorganizar
rearview mirror ['rɪrˌvju:-] *n* : retrovisor *m*
reason[1] ['ri:zən] *vt* THINK : pensar — *vi* : razonar ⟨I can't reason with her : no puedo razonar con ella⟩
reason[2] *n* **1** CAUSE, GROUND : razón *f*, motivo *m* ⟨the reason for his trip : el motivo de su viaje⟩ ⟨for this reason : por esta razón, por lo cual⟩ ⟨the reason why : la razón por la cual, el porqué⟩ **2** SENSE : razón *f* ⟨to lose one's reason : perder los sesos⟩ ⟨to listen to reason : avenirse a razones⟩
reasonable ['ri:zənəbəl] *adj* **1** SENSIBLE : razonable **2** INEXPENSIVE : barato, económico
reasonably ['ri:zənəbli] *adv* **1** SENSIBLY : razonablemente **2** FAIRLY : bastante
reasoning ['ri:zənɪŋ] *n* : razonamiento *m*, raciocinio *m*, argumentos *mpl*
reassess [ˌri:ə'sɛs] *vt* : revaluar, reconsiderar
reassurance [ˌri:ə'ʃurənts] *n* : consuelo *m*, palabras *fpl* alentadoras
reassure [ˌri:ə'ʃur] *vt* **-sured; -suring** : tranquilizar
reassuring [ˌri:ə'ʃurɪŋ] *adj* : tranquilizador
reawaken [ˌri:ə'weɪkən] *vt* : volver a despertar, reavivar
rebate ['ri:ˌbeɪt] *n* : reembolso *m*, devolución *f*

rebel[1] [rɪ'bɛl] *vi* **-belled; -belling** : rebelarse, sublevarse
rebel[2] ['rɛbəl] *adj* : rebelde
rebel[3] ['rɛbəl] *n* : rebelde *mf*
rebellion [rɪ'bɛljən] *n* : rebelión *f*
rebellious [rɪ'bɛljəs] *adj* : rebelde
rebelliousness [rɪ'bɛljəsnəs] *n* : rebeldía *f*
rebirth [ˌri:'bərθ] *n* : renacimiento *m*
reboot [ri'bu:t] *vt* : reiniciar (una computadora)
reborn [ri:'bɔrn] *adj* **to be reborn** : renacer
rebound[1] ['ri:ˌbaund, ˌri:'baund] *vi* : rebotar
rebound[2] ['ri:ˌbaund] *n* : rebote *m*
rebuff[1] [rɪ'bʌf] *vt* : desairar, rechazar
rebuff[2] *n* : desaire *m*, rechazo *m*
rebuild [ˌri:'bɪld] *vt* **-built** [-'bɪlt]**; -building** : reconstruir
rebuke[1] [ri'bju:k] *vt* **-buked; -buking** : reprender, regañar
rebuke[2] *n* : reprimenda *f*, reproche *m*
rebut [ri'bʌt] *vt* **-butted; -butting** : rebatir, refutar
rebuttal [ri'bʌtəl] *n* : refutación *f*
recalcitrant [ri'kælsətrənt] *adj* : recalcitrante
recall[1] [ri'kɔl] *vt* **1** : llamar, retirar ⟨recalled to active duty : llamado al servicio activo⟩ **2** REMEMBER : recordar, acordarse de **3** REVOKE : revocar
recall[2] [ri'kɔl, 'ri:ˌkɔl] *n* **1** : retirada *f* (de personas o mercancías) **2** MEMORY : memoria *f* ⟨to have total recall : poder recordar todo⟩
recant [ri'kænt] *vt* : retractarse de — *vi* : retractarse, renegar
recapitulate [ˌri:kə'pɪtʃəˌleɪt] *v* **-lated; -lating** : resumir, recapitular
recapture [ˌri:'kæptʃər] *vt* **-tured; -turing 1** REGAIN : volver a tomar, reconquistar **2** RELIVE : revivir (la juventud, etc.)
recast [ri:'kæst] *vt* **-cast; -casting 1** : refundir (metales) **2** REWRITE : refundir, modificar
recede [ri'si:d] *vi* **-ceded; -ceding 1** WITHDRAW : retirarse, retroceder **2** FADE : desvanecerse, alejarse **3** SLANT : inclinarse **4 to have a receding hairline** : tener entradas
receipt [ri'si:t] *n* **1** : recibo *m* **2 receipts** *npl* : ingresos *mpl*, entradas *fpl*
receivable [ri'si:vəbəl] *adj* **accounts receivable** : cuentas por cobrar
receive [ri'si:v] *vt* **-ceived; -ceiving 1** GET : recibir ⟨to receive a letter : recibir una carta⟩ ⟨to receive a blow : recibir un golpe⟩ **2** WELCOME : acoger, recibir ⟨to receive guests : tener invitados⟩ **3** : recibir, captar (señales de radio)
receiver [ri'si:vər] *n* **1** : receptor *m*, -tora *f* (en futbol americano) **2** : receptor *m* (de radio o televisión) **3 telephone receiver** : auricular *m*
recent ['ri:sənt] *adj* : reciente — **recently** *adv*

receptacle [ri'sɛptɪkəl] *n* : receptáculo *m*, recipiente *m*
reception [ri'sɛpʃən] *n* : recepción *f*
receptionist [ri'sɛpʃənɪst] *n* : recepcionista *mf*
receptive [ri'sɛptɪv] *adj* : receptivo
receptivity [ˌriːˌsɛp'tɪvəti] *n* : receptividad *f*
recess¹ ['riːˌsɛs, rɪ'sɛs] *vt* **1** : poner en un hueco ⟨recessed lighting : iluminación empotrada⟩ **2** ADJOURN : suspender, levantar
recess² *n* **1** ALCOVE : hueco *m*, nicho *m* **2** BREAK : receso *m*, descanso *m*, recreo *m* (en el colegio)
recession [ri'sɛʃən] *n* : recesión *f*, depresión *f* económica
recessive [ri'sɛsɪv] *adj* : recesivo
recharge [ˌriː'tʃɑrdʒ] *vt* **-charged; -charging** : recargar
rechargeable [ˌriː'tʃɑrdʒəbəl] *adj* : recargable
recipe ['rɛsəˌpiː] *n* : receta *f*
recipient [ri'sɪpiənt] *n* : recipiente *mf*
reciprocal [ri'sɪprəkəl] *adj* : recíproco
reciprocate [ri'sɪprəˌkeɪt] *vi* **-cated; -cating** : reciprocar
reciprocity [ˌrɛsə'prɑsəti] *n, pl* **-ties** : reciprocidad *f*
recital [ri'saɪtəl] *n* **1** PERFORMANCE : recital *m* **2** ENUMERATION : relato *m*, enumeración *f*
recitation [ˌrɛsə'teɪʃən] *n* : recitación *f*
recite [ri'saɪt] *vt* **-cited; -citing 1** : recitar (un poema, etc.) **2** RECOUNT : narrar, relatar, enumerar
reckless ['rɛkləs] *adj* : imprudente, temerario — **recklessly** *adv*
recklessness ['rɛkləsnəs] *n* : imprudencia *f*, temeridad *f*
reckon ['rɛkən] *vt* **1** CALCULATE : calcular, contar **2** CONSIDER : considerar
reckoning ['rɛkənɪŋ] *n* **1** CALCULATION : cálculo *m* **2** SETTLEMENT : ajuste *m* de cuentas ⟨day of reckoning : día del juicio final⟩
reclaim [ri'kleɪm] *vt* **1** : ganar, sanear ⟨to reclaim marshy land : sanear las tierras pantanosas⟩ **2** RECOVER : recobrar, reciclar ⟨to reclaim old tires : reciclar llantas desechadas⟩ **3** REGAIN : reclamar, recuperar ⟨to reclaim one's rights : reclamar uno sus derechos⟩
recline [ri'klaɪn] *vi* **-clined; -clining 1** LEAN : reclinarse **2** REPOSE : recostarse
recluse ['rɛˌkluːs, ri'kluːs] *n* : solitario *m*, -ria *f*
recognition [ˌrɛkɪg'nɪʃən] *n* : reconocimiento *m*
recognizable ['rɛkəgˌnaɪzəbəl] *adj* : reconocible
recognize ['rɛkɪgˌnaɪz] *vt* **-nized; -nizing** : reconocer
recoil¹ [ri'kɔɪl] *vi* : retroceder, dar un culatazo

recoil² ['riːˌkɔɪl, ri'-] *n* : retroceso *m*, culatazo *m*
recollect [ˌrɛkə'lɛkt] *v* : recordar
recollection [ˌrɛkə'lɛkʃən] *n* : recuerdo *m*
recommend [ˌrɛkə'mɛnd] *vt* **1** : recomendar ⟨she recommended the medicine : recomendó la medicina⟩ **2** ADVISE, COUNSEL : aconsejar, recomendar
recommendation [ˌrɛkəmən'deɪʃən] *n* : recomendación *f*
recompense¹ ['rɛkəmˌpɛnts] *vt* **-pensed; -pensing** : indemnizar, recompensar
recompense² *n* : indemnización *f*, compensación *f*
reconcile ['rɛkənˌsaɪl] *v* **-ciled; -ciling** *vt* **1** : reconciliar (personas), conciliar (ideas, etc.) **2** to reconcile oneself to : resignarse a — *vi* MAKE UP : reconciliarse, hacer las paces
reconciliation [ˌrɛkənˌsɪli'eɪʃən] *n* : reconciliación *f* (con personas), conciliación *f* (con ideas, etc.)
recondite ['rɛkənˌdaɪt, ri'kɑn-] *adj* : recóndito, abstruso
recondition [ˌriːkən'dɪʃən] *vt* : reacondicionar
reconnaissance [ri'kɑnəzənts, -sənts] *n* : reconocimiento *m*
reconnoiter *or* **reconnoitre** [ˌriːkə'nɔɪtər, ˌrɛkə-] *v* **-tered** *or* **-tred; -tering** *or* **-tring** *vt* : reconocer — *vi* : hacer un reconocimiento
reconsider [ˌriːkən'sɪdər] *vt* : reconsiderar, repensar
reconsideration [ˌriːkənˌsɪdə'reɪʃən] *n* : reconsideración *f*
reconstruct [ˌriːkən'strʌkt] *vt* : reconstruir
reconstruction [ˌriːkən'strʌkʃən] *n* : reconstrucción *f*
record¹ [ri'kɔrd] *vt* **1** WRITE DOWN : anotar, apuntar **2** REGISTER : registrar, hacer constar **3** INDICATE : marcar (una temperatura, etc.) **4** TAPE : grabar
record² ['rɛkərd] *n* **1** DOCUMENT : registro *m*, documento *m* oficial **2** HISTORY : historial *m* ⟨a good academic record : un buen historial académico⟩ ⟨criminal record : antecedentes penales⟩ **3** : récord *m* ⟨the world record : el récord mundial⟩ **4** : disco *m* (de música, etc.) ⟨to make a record : grabar un disco⟩
recorder [ri'kɔrdər] *n* **1** : flauta *f* dulce (instrumento de viento) **2** **tape recorder** : grabadora *f*
recording [ri'kɔrdɪŋ] *n* : grabación *f*
recount¹ [ri'kaʊnt] *vt* **1** NARRATE : narrar, relatar **2** : volver a contar (votos, etc.)
recount² ['riːˌkaʊnt, ˌri'-] *n* : recuento *m*
recoup [ri'kuːp] *vt* : recuperar, recobrar
recourse ['riːˌkors, ri'-] *n* : recurso *m* ⟨to have recourse to : recurrir a⟩
recover [ri'kʌvər] *vt* REGAIN : recobrar — *vi* RECUPERATE : recuperarse

recovery [ri'kʌvəri] *n, pl* **-eries** : recuperación *f*
re–create [ˌri:kri'eɪt] *vt* **-ated; -ating** : recrear
recreation [ˌrɛkri'eɪʃən] *n* : recreo *m*, esparcimiento *m*, diversión *f*
recreational [ˌrɛkri'eɪʃənəl] *adj* : recreativo, de recreo
recrimination [rɪˌkrɪmə'neɪʃən] *n* : recriminación *f*
recruit[1] [ri'kru:t] *vt* : reclutar
recruit[2] *n* : recluta *mf*
recruitment [ri'kru:tmənt] *n* : reclutamiento *m*, alistamiento *m*
rectal ['rɛktəl] *adj* : rectal
rectangle ['rɛkˌtæŋɡəl] *n* : rectángulo *m*
rectangular [rɛk'tæŋɡjələr] *adj* : rectangular
rectify ['rɛktəˌfaɪ] *vt* **-fied; -fying** : rectificar
rectitude ['rɛktəˌtu:d, -ˌtju:d] *n* : rectitud *f*
rector ['rɛktər] *n* : rector *m*, -tora *f*
rectory ['rɛktəri] *n, pl* **-ries** : rectoría *f*
rectum ['rɛktəm] *n, pl* **-tums** *or* **-ta** [-tə] : recto *m*
recuperate [ri'ku:pəˌreɪt, -'kju:-] *v* **-ated; -ating** *vt* : recuperar — *vi* : recuperarse, restablecerse
recuperation [riˌku:pə'reɪʃən, -ˌkju:-] *n* : recuperación *f*
recur [ri'kər] *vi* **-curred; -curring** : volver a ocurrir, volver a producirse, repetirse
recurrence [ri'kərənts] *n* : repetición *f*, reaparición *f*
recurrent [ri'kərənt] *adj* : recurrente, que se repite
recyclable [ri'saɪkələbəl] *adj* : reciclable
recycle [ri'saɪkəl] *vt* **-cled; -cling** : reciclar
recycling [ri'saɪkəlɪŋ] *n* : reciclaje *m*
red[1] ['rɛd] *adj* **1** : rojo, colorado ⟨to be red in the face : ponerse colorado⟩ ⟨to have red hair : ser pelirrojo⟩ **2** COMMUNIST : rojo, comunista
red[2] *n* **1** : rojo *m*, colorado *m* **2 Red** COMMUNIST : comunista *mf*
red blood cell *n* : glóbulo *m* rojo
red–blooded ['rɛd'blʌdəd] *adj* : vigoroso
redcap ['rɛdˌkæp] → **porter**
redden ['rɛdən] *vt* : enrojecer — *vi* BLUSH : enrojecerse, ruborizarse
reddish ['rɛdɪʃ] *adj* : rojizo
redecorate [ˌri:'dɛkəˌreɪt] *vt* **-rated; -rating** : renovar, pintar de nuevo
redeem [ri'di:m] *vt* **1** RESCUE, SAVE : rescatar, salvar **2** : desempeñar ⟨she redeemed it from the pawnshop : lo desempeñó de la casa de empeños⟩ **3** : redimir (en religión) **4** : canjear, vender ⟨to redeem coupons : canjear cupones⟩
redeemer [ri'di:mər] *n* : redentor *m*, -tora *f*
redefine [ˌri:di'faɪn] *vt* : redefinir
redemption [ri'dɛmpʃən] *n* : redención *f*

redesign [ˌri:di'zaɪn] *vt* : rediseñar
red–handed ['rɛd'hændəd] *adj* : con las manos en la masa
redhead ['rɛdˌhɛd] *n* : pelirrojo *m*, -ja *f*
red–hot ['rɛd'hɑt] *adj* **1** : al rojo vivo, candente **2** CURRENT : de candente actualidad **3** POPULAR : de gran popularidad
rediscover [ˌri:di'skʌvər] *vt* : redescubrir
redistribute [ˌri:di'strɪˌbju:t] *vt* **-uted; -uting** : redistribuir
red–letter ['rɛd'lɛtər] *adj* **red–letter day** : día *m* memorable
redness ['rɛdnəs] *n* : rojez *f*
redo [ˌri:'du:] *vt* **-did** [-dɪd]; **-done** [-'dʌn]; **-doing** **1** : hacer de nuevo **2** → **redecorate**
redolence ['rɛdələnts] *n* : fragancia *f*
redolent ['rɛdələnt] *adj* **1** FRAGRANT : fragante, oloroso **2** SUGGESTIVE : evocador
redouble [ri'dʌbəl] *vt* **-bled; -bling** : redoblar, intensificar (esfuerzos, etc.)
redoubtable [ri'daʊtəbəl] *adj* : temible
redress [ri'drɛs] *vt* : reparar, remediar, enmendar
red snapper *n* : pargo *m*, huachinango *m Mex*
red tape *n* : papeleo *m*
reduce [ri'du:s, -'dju:s] *v* **-duced; -ducing** *vt* **1** LESSEN : reducir, disminuir, rebajar (precios) **2** DEMOTE : bajar de categoría, degradar **3 to be reduced to** : verse rebajado a, verse forzado a **4 to reduce someone to tears** : hacer llorar a alguien — *vi* SLIM : adelgazar
reduction [ri'dʌkʃən] *n* : reducción *f*, rebaja *f*
redundancy [ri'dʌndəntsi] *n, pl* **-cies 1** : superfluidad *f* **2** REPETITION : redundancia *f*
redundant [ri'dʌndənt] *adj* : superfluo, redundante
redwood ['rɛdˌwʊd] *n* : secoya *f*
reed ['ri:d] *n* **1** : caña *f*, carrizo *m*, junco *m* **2** : lengüeta *f* (para instrumentos de viento)
reef ['ri:f] *n* : arrecife *m*, escollo *m*
reek[1] ['ri:k] *vi* : apestar
reek[2] *n* : hedor *m*
reel[1] ['ri:l] *vt* **1 to reel in** : enrollar, sacar (un pez) del agua **2 to reel off** : recitar de un tirón — *vi* **1** SPIN, WHIRL : girar, dar vueltas **2** STAGGER : tambalearse
reel[2] *n* **1** : carrete *m* (de pescar etc.), rollo *m* (de fotos) **2** : baile *m* escocés **3** STAGGER : tambaleo *m*
reelect [ˌri:ɪ'lɛkt] *vt* : reelegir
reenact [ˌri:ɪ'nækt] *vt* : representar de nuevo, reconstruir
reenter [ˌri:'ɛntər] *vt* : volver a entrar
reestablish [ˌri:ɪ'stæblɪʃ] *vt* : restablecer
reevaluate [ˌri:i'væljuˌeɪt] *vt* **-ated; -ating** : revaluar
reevaluation [ˌri:iˌvælju'eɪʃən] *n* : revaluación *f*

reexamine [ˌriːɪg'zæmən, -g-] vt **-ined;
-ining** : volver a examinar, reexaminar
refer [ri'fər] v **-ferred; -ferring** vt DIRECT,
SEND : remitir, enviar ⟨to refer a pa-
tient to a specialist : enviar a un paciente a un especialista⟩ — vi **to refer
to** MENTION : referirse a, aludir a
referee[1] [ˌrɛfə'riː] v **-eed; -eeing** : arbitrar
referee[2] n : árbitro m, -tra f; réferi mf
reference ['rɛfrənts, 'rɛfə-] n **1** ALLU-
SION : referencia f, alusión f ⟨to make
reference to : hacer referencia a⟩ **2**
CONSULTATION : consulta f ⟨for future
reference : para futuras consultas⟩ **3**
or **reference book** : libro m de consulta
4 TESTIMONIAL : informe m, referencia f, recomendación f
referendum [ˌrɛfə'rɛndəm] n, pl **-da** [-də]
or **-dums** : referéndum m
refill[1] [ˌriː'fɪl] vt : rellenar
refill[2] ['riːˌfɪl] n : recambio m
refinance [ˌriːfaɪˌnænts] vt **-nanced;
-nancing** : refinanciar
refine [ri'faɪn] vt **-fined; -fining 1** : refinar (azúcar, petróleo, etc.) **2** PERFECT
: perfeccionar, pulir
refined [ri'faɪnd] adj **1** : refinado (dícese
del azúcar, etc.) **2** CULTURED : culto,
educado, refinado
refinement [ri'faɪnmənt] n : refinamiento m, fineza f, finura f
refinery [ri'faɪnəri] n, pl **-eries** : refinería f
reflect [ri'flɛkt] vt **1** : reflejar ⟨to reflect
light : reflejar la luz⟩ ⟨happiness is reflected in her face : la felicidad se refleja en su cara⟩ **2 to reflect that** : pensar que, considerar que — vi **1 to
reflect on** : reflexionar sobre **2 to reflect badly on** : desacreditar, perjudicar
reflection [ri'flɛkʃən] n **1** : reflexión f,
reflejo m (de la luz, de imágenes, etc.)
2 THOUGHT : reflexión f, meditación f
reflective [ri'flɛktɪv] adj **1** THOUGHT-
FUL : reflexivo, pensativo **2** : reflectante (en física)
reflector [ri'flɛktər] n : reflector m
reflex ['riːˌflɛks] n : reflejo m
reflexive [ri'flɛksɪv] adj : reflexivo ⟨a reflexive verb : un verbo reflexivo⟩
reform[1] [ri'fɔrm] vt : reformar — vi : reformarse
reform[2] n : reforma f
reformation [ˌrɛfər'meɪʃən] n : reforma
f ⟨the Reformation : la Reforma⟩
reformatory [ri'fɔrməˌtori] n, pl **-ries**
: reformatorio m
reformer [ri'fɔrmər] n : reformador m,
-dora f
refract [ri'frækt] vt : refractar — vi : refractarse
refraction [ri'frækʃən] n : refracción f
refractory [ri'fræktəri] adj OBSTINATE
: refractario, obstinado
refrain[1] [ri'freɪn] vi **to refrain from** : abstenerse de

refrain[2] n : estribillo m (en música)
refresh [ri'frɛʃ] vt : refrescar ⟨to refresh
one's memory : refrescarle la memoria
a uno⟩
refreshing [ri'frɛʃɪŋ] adj : refrescante ⟨a
refreshing sleep : un sueño reparador⟩
refreshment [ri'frɛʃmənt] n **1** : refresco m **2 refreshments** npl : refrigerio
m
refrigerate [ri'frɪdʒəˌreɪt] vt **-ated; -ating**
: refrigerar
refrigeration [riˌfrɪdʒə'reɪʃən] n : refrigeración f
refrigerator [ri'frɪdʒəˌreɪtər] n : refrigerador m, -dora f, nevera f
refuel [riː'fjuːəl] v **-eled** or **-elled; -eling**
or **-elling** vi : repostar — vt : llenar de
combustible
refuge ['rɛˌfjuːdʒ] n : refugio m
refugee [ˌrɛfjʊ'dʒiː] n : refugiado m, -da
f
refund[1] [ri'fʌnd, 'riːˌfʌnd] vt : reembolsar, devolver
refund[2] ['riːˌfʌnd] n : reembolso m, devolución f
refundable [ri'fʌndəbəl] adj : reembolsable
refurbish [ri'fərbɪʃ] vt : renovar, restaurar
refusal [ri'fjuːzəl] n : negativa f, rechazo m, denegación f (de una petición)
refuse[1] [ri'fjuːz] vt **-fused; -fusing 1** RE-
JECT : rechazar, rehusar **2** DENY : negar, rehusar, denegar ⟨to refuse permission : negar el permiso⟩ **3 to refuse
to** : negarse a
refuse[2] ['rɛˌfjuːs, -ˌfjuːz] n : basura f,
desechos mpl, desperdicios mpl
refutation [ˌrɛfjʊ'teɪʃən] n : refutación f
refute [ri'fjuːt] vt **-futed; -futing 1** DENY
: desmentir, negar **2** DISPROVE : refutar, rebatir
regain [riː'geɪn] vt **1** RECOVER : recuperar, recobrar **2** REACH : alcanzar ⟨to
regain the shore : llegar a la tierra⟩
regal ['riːgəl] adj : real, regio
regale [ri'geɪl] vt **-galed; -galing 1** EN-
TERTAIN : agasajar, entretener **2**
AMUSE, DELIGHT : deleitar, divertir
regalia [ri'geɪljə] npl : ropaje m,
vestiduras fpl, adornos mpl
regard[1] [ri'gɑrd] vt **1** OBSERVE : observar, mirar **2** HEED : tener en cuenta,
hacer caso de **3** CONSIDER : considerar **4** RESPECT : respetar ⟨highly regarded : muy estimado⟩ **5 as regards**
: en cuanto a, en lo que se refiere a
regard[2] n **1** CONSIDERATION : consideración f **2** ESTEEM : respeto m, estima f **3** PARTICULAR : aspecto m, sentido m ⟨in this regard : en este sentido⟩
4 regards npl : saludos mpl, recuerdos
mpl **5 with regard to** : con relación a,
con respecto a
regarding [ri'gɑrdɪŋ] prep : con respecto a, en cuanto a
regardless [ri'gɑrdləs] adv : a pesar de
todo

regardless of *prep* : a pesar de, sin tener en cuenta ⟨regardless of our mistakes : a pesar de nuestros errores⟩ ⟨regardless of age : sin tener en cuenta la edad⟩
regenerate [ri'dʒɛnə,reɪt] *v* **-ated; -ating** *vt* : regenerar — *vi* : regenerarse
regeneration [ri,dʒɛnə'reɪʃən] *n* : regeneración *f*
regent ['ri:dʒənt] *n* **1** RULER : regente *mf* **2** : miembro *m* de la junta directiva (de una universidad, etc.)
regime [reɪ'ʒi:m, rɪ-] *n* : régimen *m*
regimen ['rɛdʒəmən] *n* : régimen *m*
regiment[1] ['rɛdʒə,mɛnt] *vt* : reglamentar
regiment[2] ['rɛdʒəmənt] *n* : regimiento *m*
region ['ri:dʒən] *n* **1** : región *f* **2 in the region of** : alrededor de
regional ['ri:dʒənəl] *adj* : regional — **regionally** *adv*
register[1] ['rɛdʒəstər] *vt* **1** RECORD : registrar, inscribir **2** INDICATE : marcar (temperatura, medidas, etc.) **3** REVEAL : manifestar, acusar ⟨to register surprise : acusar sorpresa⟩ **4** : certificar (correo) — *vi* ENROLL : inscribirse, matricularse
register[2] *n* : registro *m*
registrar ['rɛdʒə,strar] *n* : registrador *m*, -dora *f* oficial
registration [,rɛdʒə'streɪʃən] *n* **1** REGISTERING : inscripción *f*, matriculación *f*, registro *m* **2** *or* **registration number** : matrícula *f*, número *m* de matrícula
registry ['rɛdʒəstri] *n, pl* **-tries** : registro *m*
regress [ri'grɛs] *vi* : retroceder
regression [ri'grɛʃən] *n* : retroceso *m*, regresión *f*
regressive [ri'grɛsɪv] *adj* : regresivo
regret[1] [ri'grɛt] *vt* **-gretted; -gretting** : arrepentirse de, lamentar ⟨he regrets nothing : no se arrepiente de nada⟩ ⟨I regret to tell you : lamento decirle⟩
regret[2] *n* **1** REMORSE : arrepentimiento *m*, remordimientos *mpl* **2** SADNESS : pesar *m*, dolor *m* **3** **regrets** *npl* : excusas *fpl* ⟨to send one's regrets : excusarse⟩
regretful [ri'grɛtfəl] *adj* : arrepentido, pesaroso
regretfully [ri'grɛtfəli] *adv* : con pesar
regrettable [ri'grɛtəbəl] *adj* : lamentable — **regrettably** [-bli] *adv*
regular[1] ['rɛgjələr] *adj* **1** NORMAL : regular, normal, usual **2** STEADY : uniforme, regular ⟨a regular pace : un paso regular⟩ **3** CUSTOMARY, HABITUAL : habitual, de costumbre
regular[2] *n* : cliente *mf* habitual
regularity [,rɛgjə'lærəti] *n, pl* **-ties** : regularidad *f*
regularly ['rɛgjələrli] *adv* : regularmente, con regularidad
regulate ['rɛgjə,leɪt] *vt* **-lated; -lating** : regular
regulation [,rɛgjə'leɪʃən] *n* **1** REGULATING : regulación *f* **2** RULE : regla *f*,

reglamento *m*, norma *f* ⟨safety regulations : reglas de seguridad⟩
regulator ['rɛgjə,leɪtər] *n* **1** : regulador *m* (mecanismo) **2** : persona *f* que regula
regulatory ['rɛgjələ,tori] *adj* : regulador
regurgitate [ri'gərdʒə,teɪt] *v* **-tated; -tating** : regurgitar, vomitar
rehabilitate [,ri:hə'bɪlə,teɪt, ,ri:ə-] *vt* **-tated; -tating** : rehabilitar
rehabilitation [,ri:hə,bɪlə'teɪʃən, ,ri:ə-] *n* : rehabilitación *f*
rehearsal [ri'hərsəl] *n* : ensayo *m*
rehearse [ri'hərs] *v* **-hearsed; -hearsing** : ensayar
reheat [,ri:'hi:t] *vt* : recalentar
reign[1] ['reɪn] *vi* **1** RULE : reinar **2** PREVAIL : reinar, predominar ⟨the reigning champion : el actual campeón⟩
reign[2] *n* : reinado *m*
reimburse [,ri:əm'bərs] *vt* **-bursed; -bursing** : reembolsar
reimbursement [,ri:əm'bərsmənt] *n* : reembolso *m*
rein[1] ['reɪn] *vt* : refrenar (un caballo)
rein[2] *n* **1** : rienda *f* ⟨to give free rein to : dar rienda suelta a⟩ **2** CHECK : control *m* ⟨to keep a tight rein on : llevar un estricto control de⟩
reincarnation [,ri:ɪn,kar'neɪʃən] *n* : reencarnación *f*
reindeer ['reɪn,dɪr] *n* : reno *m*
reinforce [,ri:ən'fors] *vt* **-forced; -forcing** : reforzar
reinforcement [,ri:ən'forsmənt] *n* : refuerzo *m*
reinstate [,ri:ən'steɪt] *vt* **-stated; -stating** **1** : reintegrar, restituir (una persona) **2** RESTORE : restablecer (un servicio, etc.)
reinstatement [,ri:ən'steɪtmənt] *n* : reintegración *f*, restitución *f*, restablecimiento *m*
reiterate [ri'ɪtə,reɪt] *vt* **-ated; -ating** : reiterar, repetir
reiteration [ri,ɪtə'reɪʃən] *n* : reiteración *f*, repetición *f*
reject[1] [ri'dʒɛkt] *vt* : rechazar
reject[2] ['ri:,dʒɛkt] *n* : desecho *m* (cosa), persona *f* rechazada
rejection [ri'dʒɛkʃən] *n* : rechazo *m*
rejoice [ri'dʒɔɪs] *vi* **-joiced; -joicing** : alegrarse, regocijarse
rejoin [,ri:'dʒɔɪn] *vt* **1** : reincorporarse a, reintegrarse a ⟨he rejoined the firm : se reincorporó a la firma⟩ **2** [ri'-] REPLY, RETORT : replicar
rejoinder [ri'dʒɔɪndər] *n* : réplica *f*
rejuvenate [ri'dʒu:və,neɪt] *vt* **-nated; -nating** : rejuvenecer
rejuvenation [ri,dʒu:və'neɪʃən] *n* : rejuvenecimiento *m*
rekindle [,ri:'kɪndəl] *vt* **-dled; -dling** : reavivar
relapse[1] [ri'læps] *vi* **-lapsed; -lapsing** : recaer, volver a caer
relapse[2] ['ri:,læps, ri'læps] *n* : recaída *f*

relate [ri'leɪt] v **-lated; -lating** vt 1 TELL
: relatar, contar 2 ASSOCIATE : relacionar, asociar ⟨to relate crime to
poverty : relacionar la delincuencia a
la pobreza⟩ — vi 1 CONNECT : conectar, estar relacionado (con) 2 INTER-
ACT : relacionarse (con), llevarse bien
(con) 3 **to relate to** UNDERSTAND
: identificarse con, simpatizar con
related [ri'leɪtəd] adj : emparentado ⟨to
be related to : ser pariente de⟩
relation [ri'leɪʃən] n 1 NARRATION : relato m, narración f 2 RELATIVE : pariente mf, familiar mf 3 RELATIONSHIP
: relación f ⟨in relation to : en relación
con, con relación a⟩ 4 **relations** npl
: relaciones fpl ⟨public relations : relaciones públicas⟩
relationship [ri'leɪʃən,ʃɪp] n 1 CON-
NECTION : relación f 2 KINSHIP : parentesco m
relative[1] ['rɛlətɪv] adj : relativo — **relatively** adv
relative[2] n : pariente mf, familiar mf
relativism ['rɛlətɪ,vɪzəm] n : relativismo
m
relativity [,rɛlə'tɪvəti] n, pl **-ties** : relatividad f
relax [ri'læks] vt : relajar, aflojar — vi
: relajarse
relaxation [,ri:,læk'seɪʃən] n 1 RELAX-
ING : relajación f, aflojamiento m 2 DI-
VERSION : esparcimiento m, distracción f
relaxing [ri'læksɪŋ] adj : relajante
relay[1] ['ri:,leɪ, ri'leɪ] vt **-layed; -laying**
: transmitir
relay[2] ['ri:,leɪ] n 1 : relevo m 2 or **relay
race** : carrera de relevos
release[1] [ri'li:s] vt **-leased; -leasing** 1
FREE : liberar, poner en libertad 2
LOOSEN : soltar, aflojar ⟨to release the
brake : soltar el freno⟩ 3 RELINQUISH
: renunciar a, ceder 4 ISSUE : publicar
(un libro), estrenar (una película),
sacar (un disco)
release[2] n 1 LIBERATION : liberación f,
puesta f en libertad 2 RELINQUISH-
MENT : cesión f (de propiedad, etc.) 3
ISSUE : estreno m (de una película),
puesta f en venta (de un disco), publicación f (de un libro) 4 ESCAPE : escape m, fuga f (de un gas)
relegate ['rɛlə,geɪt] vt **-gated; -gating**
: relegar
relent [ri'lɛnt] vi : ablandarse, ceder
relentless [ri'lɛntləs] adj : implacable,
sin tregua
relentlessly [ri'lɛntləsli] adv : implacablemente
relevance ['rɛləvənts] n : pertinencia f,
relación f
relevant ['rɛləvənt] adj : pertinente —
relevantly adv
reliability [ri,laɪə'brɪləti] n, pl **-ties** 1 : fiabilidad f, seguridad f (de una cosa) 2
: formalidad f, seriedad f (de una persona)

reliable [ri'laɪəbəl] adj : confiable, fiable,
fidedigno, seguro
reliably [ri'laɪəbli] adv : sin fallar ⟨to be
reliably informed : saber (algo) de
fuentes fidedignas⟩
reliance [ri'laɪənts] n 1 DEPENDENCE
: dependencia f 2 CONFIDENCE : confianza f
reliant [ri'laɪənt] adj : dependiente
relic ['rɛlɪk] n 1 : reliquia f 2 VESTIGE
: vestigio m
relief [ri'li:f] n 1 : alivio m, desahogo m
⟨relief from pain : alivio del dolor⟩ 2
AID, WELFARE : ayuda f (benéfica),
asistencia f social 3 : relieve m (en la
escultura) ⟨relief map : mapa en re-
lieve⟩ 4 REPLACEMENT : relevo m
relieve [ri'li:v] vt **-lieved; -lieving** 1 AL-
LEVIATE : aliviar, mitigar ⟨to feel re-
lieved : sentirse aliviado⟩ 2 FREE : liberar, eximir ⟨to relieve someone of
responsibility for : eximir a alguien de
la responsabilidad de⟩ 3 REPLACE : relevar (a un centinela, etc.) 4 BREAK
: romper ⟨to relieve the monotony
: romper la monotonía⟩
religion [ri'lɪdʒən] n : religión f
religious [ri'lɪdʒəs] adj : religioso — **religiously** adv
relinquish [ri'lɪŋkwɪʃ, -'lɪn-] vt 1 GIVE
UP : renunciar a, abandonar 2 RE-
LEASE : soltar
relish[1] ['rɛlɪʃ] vt : saborear (comida), disfrutar con (una idea, una perspectiva,
etc.)
relish[2] n 1 ENJOYMENT : gusto m,
deleite m 2 : salsa f (condimento)
relive [,ri:'lɪv] vt **-lived; -living** : revivir
relocate [,ri:'lo:,keɪt, ,ri:lo'keɪt] v
-cated; -cating vt : reubicar, trasladar
— vi : trasladarse
relocation [,ri:lo'keɪʃən] n : reubicación
f, traslado m
reluctance [ri'lʌktənts] n : renuencia f,
reticencia f, desgana f
reluctant [ri'lʌktənt] adj : renuente, reacio, reticente
reluctantly [ri'lʌktəntli] adv : a regañadientes
rely [ri'laɪ] vi **-lied; -lying** 1 DEPEND : depender (de), contar (con) 2 TRUST
: confiar (en)
remain [ri'meɪn] vi 1 : quedar ⟨very little remains : queda muy poco⟩ ⟨the remaining 10 minutes : los 10 minutos
que quedan⟩ 2 STAY : quedarse, permanecer 3 CONTINUE : continuar,
seguir ⟨to remain the same : continuar
siendo igual⟩ 4 **to remain to** : quedar
por ⟨to remain to be done : quedar por
hacer⟩ ⟨it remains to be seen : está por
ver⟩
remainder [ri'meɪndər] n : resto m, remanente m
remains [ri'meɪnz] npl : restos mpl ⟨mor-
tal remains : restos mortales⟩
remake[1] [ri:'meɪk] vt **-made; -making** 1
TRANSFORM : rehacer 2 : hacer una
nueva versión de (una película, etc.)

remake² ['riː͵meɪk] *n* : nueva versión *f*

remark¹ [rɪ'mɑrk] *vt* **1** NOTICE : observar **2** SAY : comentar, observar — *vi* **to remark on** : hacer observaciones sobre

remark² *n* : comentario *m*, observación *f*

remarkable [rɪ'mɑrkəbəl] *adj* : extraordinario, notable — **remarkably** [-bli] *adv*

rematch ['riː͵mætʃ] *n* : revancha *f*

remedial [rɪ'miːdiəl] *adj* : correctivo ⟨remedial classes : clases para alumnos atrasados⟩

remedy¹ ['rɛmədi] *vt* **-died; -dying** : remediar

remedy² *n, pl* **-dies** : remedio *m*, medicamento *m*

remember [rɪ'mɛmbər] *vt* **1** RECOLLECT : acordarse de, recordar **2** : no olvidar ⟨remember my words : no olvides mis palabras⟩ ⟨to remember to : acordarse de⟩ **3** : dar saludos, dar recuerdos ⟨remember me to her : dale saludos de mi parte⟩ **4** COMMEMORATE : recordar, conmemorar

remembrance [rɪ'mɛmbrənts] *n* **1** RECOLLECTION : recuerdo *m* ⟨in remembrance of : en conmemoración de⟩ **2** MEMENTO : recuerdo *m*

remind [rɪ'maɪnd] *vt* : recordar ⟨remind me to do it : recuérdame que lo haga⟩ ⟨she reminds me of Clara : me recuerda de Clara⟩

reminder [rɪ'maɪndər] *n* : recuerdo *m*

reminisce [͵rɛmə'nɪs] *vi* **-nisced; -niscing** : rememorar los viejos tiempos

reminiscence [͵rɛmə'nɪsənts] *n* : recuerdo *m*, reminiscencia *f*

reminiscent [͵rɛmə'nɪsənt] *adj* **1** NOSTALGIC : reminiscente, nostálgico **2** SUGGESTIVE : evocador, que recuerda — **reminiscently** *adv*

remiss [rɪ'mɪs] *adj* : negligente, descuidado, remiso

remission [rɪ'mɪʃən] *n* : remisión *f*

remit [rɪ'mɪt] *vt* **-mitted; -mitting** **1** PARDON : perdonar **2** SEND : remitir, enviar (dinero)

remittance [rɪ'mɪtənts] *n* : remesa *f*

remnant ['rɛmnənt] *n* : restos *mpl*, vestigio *m*

remodel [rɪ'mɑdəl] *vt* **-eled** *or* **-elled; -eling** *or* **-elling** : remodelar, reformar

remonstrate [rɪ'mɑn͵streɪt] *vi* **-strated; -strating** : protestar ⟨to remonstrate with someone : quejarse a alguien⟩

remorse [rɪ'mɔrs] *n* : remordimiento *m*

remorseful [rɪ'mɔrsfəl] *adj* : arrepentido, lleno de remordimiento

remorseless [rɪ'mɔrsləs] *adj* **1** PITILESS : despiadado **2** RELENTLESS : implacable

remote [rɪ'moːt] *adj* **-moter; -est** **1** FAR-OFF : lejano, remoto ⟨remote countries : países remotos⟩ ⟨in the remote past : en el pasado lejano⟩ **2** SECLUDED : recóndito **3** : a distancia, remoto ⟨remote control : control remoto⟩ **4** SLIGHT : remoto **5** ALOOF : distante

remotely [rɪ'moːtli] *adv* **1** SLIGHTLY : remotamente **2** DISTANTLY : en un lugar remoto, muy lejos

remoteness [rɪ'moːtnəs] *n* : lejanía *f*

removable [rɪ'muːvəbəl] *adj* : removible

removal [rɪ'muːvəl] *n* : separación *f*, extracción *f*, supresión *f* (en algo escrito), eliminación *f* (de problemas, etc.)

remove [rɪ'muːv] *vt* **-moved; -moving** **1** : quitar, quitarse ⟨remove the lid : quite la tapa⟩ ⟨to remove one's hat : quitarse el sombrero⟩ **2** EXTRACT : sacar, extraer ⟨to remove the contents of : sacar el contenido de⟩ **3** ELIMINATE : eliminar, disipar

remunerate [rɪ'mjuːnə͵reɪt] *vt* **-ated; -ating** : remunerar

remuneration [rɪ͵mjuːnə'reɪʃən] *n* : remuneración *f*

remunerative [rɪ'mjuːnərət̬ɪv, -͵reɪ-] *adj* : remunerativo

renaissance [͵rɛnə'sɑnts, -'zɑnts; 'rɛnə-͵-] *n* : renacimiento *m* ⟨the Renaissance : el Renacimiento⟩

renal ['riːnəl] *adj* : renal

rename [͵riː'neɪm] *vt* **-named; -naming** : ponerle un nombre nuevo a

rend ['rɛnd] *vt* **rent** ['rɛnt]; **rending** : desgarrar

render ['rɛndər] *vt* **1** : derretir ⟨to render lard : derretir la manteca⟩ **2** GIVE : prestar, dar ⟨to render aid : prestar ayuda⟩ **3** MAKE : hacer, volver, dejar ⟨it rendered him helpless : lo dejó incapacitado⟩ **4** TRANSLATE : traducir, verter ⟨to render into English : traducir al inglés⟩

rendezvous ['rɑndɪ͵vuː, -deɪ-] *ns & pl* : encuentro *m*, cita *f*

rendition [rɛn'dɪʃən] *n* : interpretación *f*

renegade ['rɛnɪ͵geɪd] *n* : renegado *m*, -da *f*

renege [rɪ'nɪg, -'nɛg] *vi* **-neged; -neging** : no cumplir con (una promesa, etc.)

renew [rɪ'nuː, -'njuː] *vt* **1** REVIVE : renovar, reavivar ⟨to renew the sentiments of youth : renovar los sentimientos de la juventud⟩ **2** RESUME : reanudar **3** EXTEND : renovar ⟨to renew a subscription : renovar una suscripción⟩

renewable [rɪ'nuːəbəl, -'njuː-] *adj* : renovable

renewal [rɪ'nuːəl, -'njuː-] *n* : renovación *f*

renounce [rɪ'naʊnts] *vt* **-nounced; -nouncing** : renunciar a

renovate ['rɛnə͵veɪt] *vt* **-vated; -vating** : restaurar, renovar

renovation [͵rɛnə'veɪʃən] *n* : restauración *f*, renovación *f*

renown [rɪ'naʊn] *n* : renombre *m*, fama *f*, celebridad *f*

renowned [rɪ'naʊnd] *adj* : renombrado, célebre, famoso

rent¹ ['rɛnt] *vt* : rentar, alquilar

rent² *n* **1** : renta *f*, alquiler *m* ⟨for rent : se alquila⟩ **2** RIP : rasgadura *f*

rental¹ ['rɛntəl] *adj* RENT : de alquiler

rental² *n* : alquiler *m*

renter ['rɛntər] *n* : arrendatario *m*, -ria *f*

renunciation [ri,nʌntsi'eɪʃən] *n* : renuncia *f*

reopen [,ri:'o:pən] *vt* : volver a abrir

reorganization [,ri:,ɔrgənə'zeɪʃən] *n* : reorganización *f*

reorganize [,ri:'ɔrgən,aɪz] *vt* **-nized; -nizing** : reorganizar

repair¹ [ri'pær] *vt* : reparar, arreglar, refaccionar

repair² *n* **1** : reparación *f*, arreglo *m* **2** CONDITION : estado *m* ⟨in bad repair : en mal estado⟩

reparation [,rɛpə'reɪʃən] *n* **1** AMENDS : reparación *f* **2 reparations** *npl* COMPENSATION : indemnización *f*

repartee [,rɛpər'ti:, -,pɑr-, -'teɪ] *n* : intercambio *m* de réplicas ingeniosas

repast [ri'pæst, 'ri:,pæst] *n* : comida *f*

repatriate [ri'peɪtri,eɪt] *vt* **-ated; -ating** : repatriar

repay [ri'peɪ] *vt* **-paid; -paying** : pagar, devolver, reembolsar

repeal¹ [ri'pi:l] *vt* : abrogar, revocar

repeal² *n* : abrogación *f*, revocación *f*

repeat¹ [ri'pi:t] *vt* : repetir

repeat² *n* : repetición *f*

repeatedly [ri'pi:ṭədli] *adv* : repetidamente, repetidas veces

repel [ri'pɛl] *vt* **-pelled; -pelling 1** REPULSE : repeler (un enemigo, etc.) **2** RESIST : repeler **3** REJECT : rechazar, repeler **4** DISGUST : repugnar, darle asco (a alguien)

repellent *or* **repellant** [ri'pɛlənt] *n* : repelente *m*

repent [ri'pɛnt] *vi* : arrepentirse

repentance [ri'pɛntənts] *n* : arrepentimiento *m*

repentant [ri'pɛntənt] *adj* : arrepentido

repercussion [,ri:pər'kʌʃən, ,rɛpər-] *n* : repercusión *f*

repertoire ['rɛpər,twɑr] *n* : repertorio *m*

repertory ['rɛpər,tori] *n*, *pl* **-ries** : repertorio *m*

repetition [,rɛpə'tɪʃən] *n* : repetición *f*

repetitious [,rɛpə'tɪʃəs] *adj* : repetitivo, reiterativo — **repetitiously** *adv*

repetitive [ri'pɛtəṭɪv] *adj* : repetitivo, reiterativo

replace [ri'pleɪs] *vt* **-placed; -placing 1** : volver a poner ⟨replace it in the drawer : vuelve a ponerlo en el cajón⟩ **2** SUBSTITUTE : reemplazar, sustituir **3** : reponer ⟨to replace the worn carpet : reponer la alfombra raída⟩

replaceable [ri'pleɪsəbəl] *adj* : reemplazable

replacement [ri'pleɪsmənt] *n* **1** SUBSTITUTION : reemplazo *m*, sustitución *f* **2** SUBSTITUTE : sustituto *m*, -ta *f*; suplente *mf* (persona) **3 replacement part** : repuesto *m*, pieza *f* de recambio

replenish [ri'plɛnɪʃ] *vt* : rellenar, llenar de nuevo

replenishment [ri'plɛnɪʃmənt] *n* : reabastecimiento *m*

replete [ri'pli:t] *adj* : repleto, lleno

replica ['rɛplɪkə] *n* : réplica *f*, reproducción *f*

replicate ['rɛplə,keɪt] *v* **-cated; -cating** *vt* : duplicar, repetir — *vi* : duplicarse

replication [,rɛplə'keɪʃən] *n* **1** REPRODUCTION : reproducción *f* **2** REPETITION : repetición *f* **3** : replicación *f* (celular)

reply¹ [ri'plaɪ] *vi* **-plied; -plying** : contestar, responder

reply² *n*, *pl* **-plies** : respuesta *f*, contestación *f*

report¹ [ri'port] *vt* **1** ANNOUNCE : relatar, anunciar **2** : dar parte de, informar de, reportar ⟨he reported an accident : dio parte de un accidente⟩ ⟨to report a crime : denunciar un delito⟩ **3** : informar acerca de (en un periódico, la televisión, etc.) — *vi* **1** : hacer un informe, informar **2 to report for duty** : presentarse, reportarse

report² *n* **1** RUMOR : rumor *m* **2** REPUTATION : reputación *f* ⟨people of evil report : personas de mala fama⟩ **3** ACCOUNT : informe *m*, reportaje *m* (en un periódico, etc.) **4** BANG : estallido *m* (de un arma de fuego)

report card *n* : boletín *m* de calificaciones, boletín *m* de notas

reportedly [ri'portədli] *adv* : según se dice, según se informa

reporter [ri'portər] *n* : periodista *mf*; reportero *m*, -ra *f*

repose¹ [ri'po:z] *vi* **-posed; -posing** : reposar, descansar

repose² *n* **1** : reposo *m*, descanso *m* **2** CALM : calma *f*, tranquilidad *f*

repository [ri'pɑzə,tori] *n*, *pl* **-ries** : depósito *m*

repossess [,ri:pə'zɛs] *vt* : recuperar, recobrar la posesión de

reprehensible [,rɛpri'hɛntsəbəl] *adj* : reprensible — **reprehensibly** *adv*

represent [,rɛpri'zɛnt] *vt* **1** SYMBOLIZE : representar ⟨the flag represents our country : la bandera representa a nuestro país⟩ **2** : representar, ser un representante de ⟨an attorney who represents his client : un abogado que representa su cliente⟩ **3** PORTRAY : presentar ⟨he represents himself as a friend : se presenta como amigo⟩

representation [,rɛprɪzɛn'teɪʃən, -zən-] *n* : representación *f*

representative¹ [,rɛprɪ'zɛntəṭɪv] *adj* : representativo

representative² *n* **1** : representante *mf* **2** : diputado *m*, -da *f* (en la política)

repress [ri'prɛs] *vt* : reprimir

repression [ri'prɛʃən] *n* : represión *f*

repressive [ri'prɛsɪv] *adj* : represivo

reprieve¹ [ri'pri:v] *vt* **-prieved; -prieving** : indultar

reprieve² *n* : indulto *m*

reprimand¹ ['rɛprə,mænd] *vt* : reprender

reprimand² *n* : reprimenda *f*
reprint¹ [ri'prɪnt] *vt* : reimprimir
reprint² ['riː,prɪnt, ri'prɪnt] *n* : reedición *f*
reprisal [ri'praɪzəl] *n* : represalia *f*
reproach¹ [ri'proːtʃ] *vt* : reprochar
reproach² *n* **1** DISGRACE : deshonra *f* **2** REBUKE : reproche *m*, recriminación *f*
reproachful [ri'proːtʃfəl] *adj* : de reproche
reproduce [,riːprə'duːs, -'djuːs] *v* **-duced; -ducing** *vt* : reproducir — *vi* BREED : reproducirse
reproduction [,riːprə'dʌkʃən] *n* : reproducción *f*
reproductive [,riːprə'dʌktɪv] *adj* : reproductor
reproof [ri'pruːf] *n* : reprobación *f*, reprimenda *f*, reproche *m*
reprove [ri'pruːv] *vt* **-proved; -proving** : reprender, censurar
reptile ['rɛp,taɪl] *n* : reptil *m*
republic [ri'pʌblɪk] *n* : república *f*
republican¹ [ri'pʌblɪkən] *adj* : republicano
republican² *n* : republicano *m*, -na *f*
repudiate [ri'pjuːdi,eɪt] *vt* **-ated; -ating** **1** REJECT : rechazar **2** DISOWN : repudiar, renegar de
repudiation [ri,pjuːdi'eɪʃən] *n* : rechazo *m*, repudio *m*
repugnance [ri'pʌgnənts] *n* : repugnancia *f*
repugnant [ri'pʌgnənt] *adj* : repugnante, asqueroso
repulse¹ [ri'pʌls] *vt* **-pulsed; -pulsing** **1** REPEL : repeler **2** REBUFF : desairar, rechazar
repulse² *n* : rechazo *m*
repulsive [ri'pʌlsɪv] *adj* : repulsivo, repugnante, asqueroso — **repulsively** *adv*
reputable ['rɛpjətəbəl] *adj* : acreditado, de buena reputación
reputation [,rɛpjə'teɪʃən] *n* : reputación *f*, fama *f*
repute [ri'pjuːt] *n* : reputación *f*, fama *f*
reputed [ri'pjuːtəd] *adj* : reputado, supuesto ⟨she's reputed to be the best : tiene fama de ser la mejor⟩
reputedly [ri'pjuːtədli] *adv* : supuestamente, según se dice
request¹ [ri'kwɛst] *vt* : pedir, solicitar, rogar ⟨to request assistance : solicitar asistencia, pedir ayuda⟩ ⟨I requested him to do it : le pedí que lo hiciera⟩
request² *n* : petición *f*, solicitud *f*, pedido *m*
requiem ['rɛkwiəm, 'reɪ-] *n* : réquiem *m*
require [ri'kwaɪr] *vt* **-quired; -quiring** **1** CALL FOR, DEMAND : requerir, exigir ⟨if required : si se requiere⟩ ⟨to require that something be done : exigir que algo se haga⟩ **2** NEED : necesitar, requerir
requirement [ri'kwaɪrmənt] *n* **1** NECESSITY : necesidad *f* **2** DEMAND : requisito *m*, demanda *f*

requisite¹ ['rɛkwəzɪt] *adj* : esencial, necesario
requisite² *n* : requisito *m*, necesidad *f*
requisition¹ [,rɛkwə'zɪʃən] *vt* : requisar
requisition² *n* : requisición *f*, requisa *f*
reread [,riː'riːd] *vt* **-read; -reading** : releer
reroute [,riː'ruːt, -'raʊt] *vt* **-routed; -routing** : desviar
rerun¹ [riː'rʌn] *vt* **-ran; -run; -running** : reponer (un programa televisivo)
rerun² ['riː,rʌn] *n* **1** : reposición *f* (de un programa televisivo) **2** REPEAT : repetición *f*
resale ['riː,seɪl, ,riː'seɪl] *n* : reventa *f* ⟨resale price : precio de venta⟩
rescind [ri'sɪnd] *vt* **1** CANCEL : rescindir, cancelar **2** REPEAL : abrogar, revocar
rescue¹ ['rɛs,kjuː] *vt* **-cued; -cuing** : rescatar, salvar
rescue² *n* : rescate *m*
rescuer ['rɛskjuər] *n* : salvador *m*, -dora *f*
research¹ [ri'sərtʃ, 'riː,sərtʃ] *v* : investigar
research² *n* : investigación *f*
researcher [ri'sərtʃər, 'riː,-] *n* : investigador *m*, -dora *f*
resemblance [ri'zɛmblənts] *n* : semejanza *f*, parecido *m*
resemble [ri'zɛmbəl] *vt* **-sembled; -sembling** : parecerse a, asemejarse a
resent [ri'zɛnt] *vt* : resentirse de, ofenderse por
resentful [ri'zɛntfəl] *adj* : resentido, rencoroso — **resentfully** *adv*
resentment [ri'zɛntmənt] *n* : resentimiento *m*
reservation [,rɛzər'veɪʃən] *n* **1** : reservación *f*, reserva *f* ⟨to make a reservation : hacer una reservación⟩ **2** DOUBT, MISGIVING : reserva *f*, duda *f* ⟨without reservations : sin reservas⟩ **3** : reserva *f* (de indios americanos)
reserve¹ [ri'zərv] *vt* **-served; -serving** : reservar
reserve² *n* **1** STOCK : reserva *f* ⟨to keep in reserve : guardar en reserva⟩ **2** RESTRAINT : reserva *f*, moderación *f* **3** **reserves** *npl* : reservas *fpl* (militares)
reserved [ri'zərvd] *adj* : reservado
reservoir ['rɛzər,vwɑr, -,vwɔr, -,vɔr] *n* : embalse *m*
reset [,riː'sɛt] *vt* **-set; -setting** : reajustar, poner en hora (un reloj), reiniciar (una computadora)
reside [ri'zaɪd] *vi* **-sided; -siding** **1** DWELL : residir **2** LIE : radicar, residir ⟨the power resides in the presidency : el poder radica en la presidencia⟩
residence ['rɛzədənts] *n* : residencia *f*
resident¹ ['rɛzədənt] *adj* : residente
resident² *n* : residente *mf*
residential [,rɛzə'dɛntʃəl] *adj* : residencial
residual [ri'zɪdʒuəl] *adj* : residual
residue ['rɛzə,duː, -,djuː] *n* : residuo *m*, resto *m*

resign [ri'zaɪn] *vt* **1** QUIT : dimitir, renunciar **2 to resign oneself** : aguantarse, resignarse

resignation [ˌrɛzɪg'neɪʃən] *n* : resignación *f*

resignedly [ri'zaɪnədli] *adv* : con resignación

resilience [ri'zɪljənts] *n* **1** : capacidad *f* de recuperación, adaptabilidad *f* **2** ELASTICITY : elasticidad *f*

resiliency [ri'zɪljəntsi] → **resilience**

resilient [ri'zɪljənt] *adj* **1** STRONG : resistente, fuerte **2** ELASTIC : elástico

resin ['rɛzən] *n* : resina *f*

resist [ri'zɪst] *vt* **1** WITHSTAND : resistir ⟨to resist heat : resistir el calor⟩ **2** OPPOSE : oponerse a

resistance [ri'zɪstənts] *n* : resistencia *f*

resistant [ri'zɪstənt] *adj* : resistente

resolute ['rɛzəˌluːt] *adj* : firme, resuelto, decidido

resolutely ['rɛzəˌluːtli, ˌrzə'-] *adv* : resueltamente, firmemente

resolution [ˌrɛzə'luːʃən] *n* **1** SOLUTION : solución *f* **2** RESOLVE : resolución *f*, determinación *f* **3** DECISION : propósito *m*, decisión *f* ⟨New Year's resolutions : propósitos para el Año Nuevo⟩ **4** MOTION, PROPOSAL : moción *f*, resolución *f* (legislativa)

resolve¹ [ri'zɑlv] *vt* **-solved; -solving 1** SOLVE : resolver, solucionar **2** DECIDE : resolver ⟨she resolved to get more sleep : resolvió dormir más⟩

resolve² *n* : resolución *f*, determinación *f*

resonance ['rɛzənənts] *n* : resonancia *f*

resonant ['rɛzənənt] *adj* : resonante, retumbante

resort¹ [ri'zɔrt] *vi* **to resort to** : recurrir ⟨to resort to force : recurrir a la fuerza⟩

resort² *n* **1** RECOURSE : recurso *m* ⟨as a last resort : como último recurso⟩ **2** HANGOUT : lugar *m* popular, lugar *m* muy frecuentado **3** : lugar *m* de vacaciones ⟨tourist resort : centro turístico⟩

resound [ri'zaʊnd] *vi* : retumbar, resonar

resounding [ri'zaʊndɪŋ] *adj* **1** RESONANT : retumbante, resonante **2** ABSOLUTE, CATEGORICAL : rotundo, tremendo ⟨a resounding success : un éxito rotundo⟩

resource ['riːˌsors, ri'sors] *n* **1** RESOURCEFULNESS : ingenio *m*, recursos *mpl* **2 resources** *npl* : recursos *mpl* ⟨natural resources : recursos naturales⟩ **3 resources** *npl* MEANS : recursos *mpl*, medios *mpl*, fondos *mpl*

resourceful [ri'sorsfəl, -'zors-] *adj* : ingenioso

resourcefulness [ri'sorsfəlnəs, -'zors-] *n* : ingenio *m*, recursos *mpl*, inventiva *f*

respect¹ [ri'spɛkt] *vt* : respetar, estimar

respect² *n* **1** REFERENCE : relación *f*, respeto *m* ⟨with respect to : en lo que respecta a⟩ **2** ESTEEM : respeto *m*, es-

tima *f* **3** DETAIL, PARTICULAR : detalle *m*, sentido *m*, respeto *m* ⟨in some respects : en algunos sentidos⟩ **4 respects** *npl* : respetos *mpl* ⟨to pay one's respects : presentar uno susrespetos⟩

respectability [riˌspɛktə'bɪləti] *n* : respetabilidad *f*

respectable [ri'spɛktəbəl] *adj* **1** PROPER : respetable, decente **2** CONSIDERABLE : considerable, respetable ⟨a respectable amount : una cantidad respetable⟩ — **respectably** [-bli] *adv*

respectful [ri'spɛktfəl] *adj* : respetuoso — **respectfully** *adv*

respectfulness [ri'spɛktfəlnəs] *n* : respetuosidad *f*

respective [ri'spɛktɪv] *adj* : respectivo ⟨their respective homes : sus casas respectivas⟩ — **respectively** *adv*

respiration [ˌrɛspə'reɪʃən] *n* : respiración *f*

respirator ['rɛspəˌreɪtər] *n* : respirador *m*

respiratory ['rɛspərəˌtori, ri'spaɪrə-] *adj* : respiratorio

respite ['rɛspɪt, ri'spaɪt] *n* : respiro *m*, tregua *f*

resplendent [ri'splɛndənt] *adj* : resplandeciente — **resplendently** *adv*

respond [ri'spɑnd] *vi* **1** ANSWER : contestar, responder **2** REACT : responder, reaccionar ⟨to respond to treatment : responder al tratamiento⟩

response [ri'spɑnts] *n* : respuesta *f*

responsibility [riˌspɑntsə'bɪləti] *n, pl* **-ties** : responsabilidad *f*

responsible [ri'spɑntsəbəl] *adj* : responsable — **responsibly** [-bli] *adv*

responsive [ri'spɑntsɪv] *adj* **1** ANSWERING : que responde **2** SENSITIVE : sensible, receptivo

responsiveness [ri'spɑntsɪvnəs] *n* : receptividad *f*, sensibilidad *f*

rest¹ ['rɛst] *vi* **1** REPOSE : reposar, descansar **2** RELAX : quedarse tranquilo **3** STOP : pararse, detenerse **4** DEPEND : basarse (en), descansar (sobre), depender (de) ⟨the decision rests with her : la decisión pesa sobre ella⟩ **5 to rest on** : apoyarse en, descansar sobre ⟨to rest on one's arm : apoyarse en el brazo⟩ — *vt* **1** RELAX : descansar **2** SUPPORT : apoyar **3 to rest one's eyes on** : fijar la mirada en

rest² *n* **1** RELAXATION, REPOSE : reposo *m*, descanso *m* **2** SUPPORT : soporte *m*, apoyo *m* **3** : silencio *m* (en música) **4** REMAINDER : resto *m* **5 to come to rest** : pararse

restart [ri'stɑrt] *vt* **1** : volver a empezar **2** RESUME : reanudar **3** : volver a arrancar (un motor), reiniciar (una computadora) — *vi* **1** : reanudarse **2** : volver a arrancar

restatement [ˌriː'steɪtmənt] *n* : repetición *f*

restaurant ['rɛstəˌrɑnt, -rənt] *n* : restaurante *m*

restful ['rɛstfəl] *adj* **1** RELAXING : relajante **2** PEACEFUL : tranquilo, sosegado
restitution [ˌrɛstə'tu:ʃən, -'tju:-] *n* : restitución *f*
restive ['rɛstɪv] *adj* : inquieto, nervioso
restless ['rɛstləs] *adj* **1** FIDGETY : inquieto, agitado **2** IMPATIENT : impaciente **3** SLEEPLESS : desvelado ⟨a restless night : una noche en blanco⟩
restlessly ['rɛstləsli] *adv* : nerviosamente
restlessness ['rɛstləsnəs] *n* : inquietud *f*, agitación *f*
restoration [ˌrɛstə'reɪʃən] *n* : restauración *f*, restablecimiento *m*
restore [ri'stor] *vt* **-stored; -storing 1** RETURN : volver **2** REESTABLISH : restablecer **3** REPAIR : restaurar
restrain [ri'streɪn] *vt* **1** : refrenar, contener **2 to restrain oneself** : contenerse
restrained [ri'streɪnd] *adj* : comedido, templado, contenido
restraint [ri'streɪnt] *n* **1** RESTRICTION : restricción *f*, limitación *f*, control *m* **2** CONFINEMENT : encierro *m* **3** RESERVE : reserva *f*, control *m* de sí mismo
restrict [ri'strɪkt] *vt* : restringir, limitar, constreñir
restricted [ri'strɪktəd] *adj* **1** LIMITED : limitado, restringido **2** CLASSIFIED : secreto, confidencial
restriction [ri'strɪkʃən] *n* : restricción *f*
restrictive [ri'strɪktɪv] *adj* : restrictivo — **restrictively** *adv*
rest room *n* : servicios *mpl*, baño *m*
restructure [ri'strʌktʃər] *vt* **-tured; -turing** : reestructurar
result[1] [ri'zʌlt] *vi* : resultar ⟨to result in : resultar en, tener por resultado⟩
result[2] *n* : resultado *m*, consecuencia *f* ⟨as a result of : como consecuencia de⟩
resultant [ri'zʌltənt] *adj* : resultante
resume [ri'zu:m] *v* **-sumed; -suming** *vt* : reanudar — *vi* : reanudarse
résumé *or* **resume** *or* **resumé** ['rɛzə-ˌmeɪ, ˌrɛzə'-] *n* **1** SUMMARY : resumen *m* **2** CURRICULUM VITAE : currículum *m*, currículo *m*
resumption [ri'zʌmpʃən] *n* : reanudación *f*
resurface [ˌri:'sərfəs] *v* **-faced; -facing** *vt* : pavimentar (una carretera) de nuevo — *vi* : volver a salir en la superficie
resurgence [ri'sərdʒənts] *n* : resurgimiento *m*
resurrect [ˌrɛzə'rɛkt] *vt* : resucitar, desempolvar
resurrection [ˌrɛzə'rɛkʃən] *n* : resurrección *f*
resuscitate [ri'sʌsəˌteɪt] *vt* **-tated; -tating** : resucitar, revivir
resuscitation [riˌsʌsə'teɪʃən] *n* : reanimación *f*, resucitación *f*
retail[1] ['ri:ˌteɪl] *vt* : vender al por menor, vender al detalle

retail[2] *adv* : al por menor, al detalle
retail[3] *adj* : detallista, minorista
retail[4] *n* : venta *f* al detalle, venta *f* al por menor
retailer ['ri:ˌteɪlər] *n* : detallista *mf*, minorista *mf*
retain [ri'teɪn] *vt* : retener, conservar, guardar
retainer [ri'teɪnər] *n* **1** SERVANT : criado *m*, -da *f* **2** ADVANCE : anticipo *m*
retaliate [ri'tæliˌeɪt] *vi* **-ated; -ating** : responder, contraatacar, tomar represalias
retaliation [riˌtæli'eɪʃən] *n* : represalia *f*, retaliación *f*
retard [ri'tɑrd] *vt* : retardar, retrasar
retardation [ˌri:ˌtɑr'deɪʃən] *n* **1** : retardación *f* **2** *or* **mental retardation** : retraso *m* mental
retarded [ri'tɑrdəd] *adj* : retrasado
retch ['rɛtʃ] *vi* : hacer arcadas
retention [ri'tɛntʃən] *n* : retención *f*
retentive [ri'tɛntɪv] *adj* : retentivo
rethink [ri:'θɪŋk] *vt* **-thought; -thinking** : reconsiderar, repensar
reticence ['rɛṭəsənts] *n* : reticencia *f*
reticent ['rɛṭəsənt] *adj* : reticente
retina ['rɛṭənə] *n, pl* **-nas** *or* **-nae** [-ˌni, -ˌnaɪ] : retina *f*
retinue ['rɛṭənˌu:, -ˌju:] *n* : séquito *m*, comitiva *f*, cortejo *m*
retire [ri'taɪr] *vi* **-tired; -tiring 1** RETREAT, WITHDRAW : retirarse, retraerse **2** : retirarse, jubilarse (de su trabajo) **3** : acostarse, irse a dormir
retiree [riˌtaɪ'ri:] *n* : jubilado *m*, -da *f*
retirement [ri'taɪrmənt] *n* : jubilación *f*
retiring [ri'taɪrɪŋ] *adj* SHY : retraído
retort[1] [ri'tort] *vt* : replicar
retort[2] *n* : réplica *f*
retrace [ˌri:'treɪs] *vt* **-traced; -tracing** : volver sobre, desandar ⟨to retrace one's steps : volver uno sobre sus pasos⟩
retract [ri'trækt] *vt* **1** TAKE BACK, WITHDRAW : retirar, retractarse de **2** : retraer (las garras) — *vi* : retractarse
retractable [ri'træktəbəl] *adj* : retractable
retrain [ˌri:'treɪn] *vt* : reciclar, reconvertir
retreat[1] [ri'tri:t] *vi* : retirarse
retreat[2] *n* **1** WITHDRAWAL : retirada *f*, repliegue *m*, retiro *m* ⟨to beat a retreat : batirse en retirada⟩ **2** REFUGE : retiro *m*, refugio *m*
retrench [ri'trɛntʃ] *vt* : reducir (gastos) — *vi* : economizar
retribution [ˌrɛtrə'bju:ʃən] *n* PUNISHMENT : castigo *m*, pena *f* merecida
retrieval [ri'tri:vəl] *n* : recuperación *f* ⟨beyond retrieval : irrecuperable⟩ ⟨data retrieval : recuperación de datos⟩
retrieve [ri'tri:v] *vt* **-trieved; -trieving 1** : cobrar ⟨to retrieve game : cobrar la caza⟩ **2** RECOVER : recuperar
retriever [ri'tri:vər] *n* : perro *m* cobrador

retroactive [ˌrɛtroˈæktɪv] *adj* : retroactivo — **retroactively** *adv*

retrograde [ˈrɛtrəˌgreɪd] *adj* : retrógrado

retrospect [ˈrɛtrəˌspɛkt] *n* **in retrospect** : mirando hacia atrás, retrospectivamente

retrospective [ˌrɛtrəˈspɛktɪv] *adj* : retrospectivo

return¹ [rɪˈtərn] *vi* **1** : volver, regresar ⟨to return home : regresar a casa⟩ **2** REAPPEAR : reaparecer, resurgir **3** ANSWER : responder — *vt* **1** REPLACE, RESTORE : devolver, volver (a poner), restituir ⟨to return something to its place : volver a poner algo en su lugar⟩ **2** YIELD : producir, redituar, rendir **3** REPAY : pagar, devolver ⟨to return a compliment : devolver un cumplido⟩

return² *adj* : de vuelta

return³ *n* **1** RETURNING : regreso *m*, vuelta *f*, retorno *m* **2** *or* **tax return** : declaración *f* de impuestos **3** YIELD : rédito *m*, rendimiento *m*, ganancia *f* **4 returns** *npl* DATA, RESULTS : resultados *mpl*, datos *mpl*

reunion [riˈjuːnjən] *n* : reunión *f*, reencuentro *m*

reunite [ˌriːjʊˈnaɪt] *v* **-nited; -niting** *vt* : (volver a) reunir — *vi* : (volver a) reunirse

reusable [riˈjuːzəbəl] *adj* : reutilizable

reuse [riˈjuːz] *vt* **-used; -using** : reutilizar, usar de nuevo

revamp [ˌriˈvæmp] *vt* : renovar

reveal [rɪˈviːl] *vt* **1** DIVULGE : revelar, divulgar ⟨to reveal a secret : revelar un secreto⟩ **2** SHOW : manifestar, mostrar, dejar ver

revealing [rɪˈviːlɪŋ] *adj* : revelador

reveille [ˈrɛvəli] *n* : toque *m* de diana

revel¹ [ˈrɛvəl] *vi* **-eled** *or* **-elled; -eling** *or* **-elling** **1** CAROUSE : ir de juerga **2 to revel in** : deleitarse en

revel² *n* : juerga *f*, parranda *f fam*

revelation [ˌrɛvəˈleɪʃən] *n* : revelación *f*

reveler *or* **reveller** [ˈrɛvələr] *n* : juerguista *mf*

revelry [ˈrɛvəlri] *n*, *pl* **-ries** : juerga *f*, parranda *f fam*, jarana *f fam*

revenge¹ [rɪˈvɛndʒ] *vt* **-venged; -venging** : vengar ⟨to revenge oneself on : vengarse de⟩

revenge² *n* : venganza *f*

revenue [ˈrɛvəˌnuː, -ˌnjuː] *n* : ingresos *mpl*, rentas *fpl*

reverberate [rɪˈvərbəˌreɪt] *vi* **-ated; -ating** : reverberar

reverberation [rɪˌvərbəˈreɪʃən] *n* : reverberación *f*

revere [rɪˈvɪr] *vt* **-vered; -vering** : reverenciar, venerar

reverence [ˈrɛvərənts] *n* : reverencia *f*, veneración *f*

reverend [ˈrɛvərənd] *adj* : reverendo ⟨the Reverend John Chapin : el reverendo John Chapin⟩

reverent [ˈrɛvərənt] *adj* : reverente — **reverently** *adv*

reverie [ˈrɛvəri] *n*, *pl* **-eries** : ensueño *m*

reversal [rɪˈvərsəl] *n* **1** INVERSION : inversión *f* (del orden normal) **2** CHANGE : cambio *m* total **3** SETBACK : revés *m*, contratiempo *m*

reverse¹ [rɪˈvərs] *v* **-versed; -versing** *vt* **1** INVERT : invertir **2** CHANGE : cambiar totalmente **3** ANNUL : anular, revocar — *vi* : dar marcha atrás

reverse² *adj* **1** : inverso ⟨in reverse order : en orden inverso⟩ ⟨the reverse side : el reverso⟩ **2** OPPOSITE : contrario, opuesto

reverse³ *n* **1** OPPOSITE : lo contrario, lo opuesto **2** SETBACK : revés *m*, contratiempo *m* **3** BACK : reverso *m*, dorso *m*, revés *m* **4** *or* **reverse gear** : marcha *f* atrás, reversa *f Col, Mex*

reversible [rɪˈvərsəbəl] *adj* : reversible

reversion [rɪˈvərʒən] *n* : reversión *f*, vuelta *f*

revert [rɪˈvərt] *vi* : revertir

review¹ [rɪˈvjuː] *vt* **1** REEXAMINE : volver a examinar, repasar (una lección) **2** CRITICIZE : reseñar, hacer una crítica de **3** EXAMINE : examinar, analizar ⟨to review one's life : examinar su vida⟩ **4 to review the troops** : pasar revista a las tropas

review² *n* **1** INSPECTION : revista *f* (de tropas) **2** ANALYSIS, OVERVIEW : resumen *m*, análisis *m* ⟨a review of current affairs : un análisis de las actualidades⟩ **3** CRITICISM : reseña *f*, crítica *f* (de un libro, etc.) **4** : repaso *m* (para un examen) **5** REVUE : revista *f* (musical)

reviewer [rɪˈvjuːər] *n* : crítico *m*, -ca *f*

revile [rɪˈvaɪl] *vt* **-viled; -viling** : injuriar, denostar

revise [rɪˈvaɪz] *vt* **-vised; -vising** : revisar, corregir, refundir ⟨to revise a dictionary : corregir un diccionario⟩

revision [rɪˈvɪʒən] *n* : revisión *f*

revival [rɪˈvaɪvəl] *n* **1** : renacimiento *m* (de ideas, etc.), restablecimiento *m* (de costumbres, etc.), reactivación *f* (de la economía) **2** : reanimación *f*, resucitación *f* (en medicina) **3** *or* **revival meeting** : asamblea *f* evangelista

revive [rɪˈvaɪv] *v* **-vived; -viving** *vt* **1** REAWAKEN : reavivar, reanimar, reactivar (la economía), resucitar (a un paciente) **2** REESTABLISH : restablecer — *vi* **1** : renacer, reanimarse, reactivarse **2** COME TO : recobrar el sentido, volver en sí

revoke [rɪˈvoːk] *vt* **-voked; -voking** : revocar

revolt¹ [rɪˈvoːlt] *vi* **1** REBEL : rebelarse, sublevarse **2 to revolt at** : sentir repugnancia por — *vt* DISGUST : darle asco (a alguien), repugnar

revolt² *n* REBELLION : rebelión *f*, revuelta *f*, sublevación *f*

revolting [rɪˈvoːltɪŋ] *adj* : asqueroso, repugnante

revolution [ˌrɛvə'lu:ʃən] *n* : revolución *f*
revolutionary[1] [ˌrɛvə'lu:ʃənɛˌri] *adj* : revolucionario
revolutionary[2] *n, pl* **-aries** : revolucionario *m*, -ria *f*
revolutionize [ˌrɛvə'lu:ʃənˌaɪz] *vt* **-ized; -izing** : cambiar radicalmente, revolucionar
revolve [ri'valv] *v* **-volved; -volving** *vt* ROTATE : hacer girar — *vi* **1** ROTATE : girar ⟨to revolve around : girar alrededor de⟩ **2 to revolve in one's mind** : darle vueltas en la cabeza a alguien
revolver [ri'valvər] *n* : revólver *m*
revue [ri'vju:] *n* : revista *f* (musical)
revulsion [ri'vʌlʃən] *n* : repugnancia *f*
reward[1] [ri'wɔrd] *vt* : recompensar, premiar
reward[2] *n* : recompensa *f*
rewrite [ˌri:'raɪt] *vt* **-wrote; -written; -writing** : escribir de nuevo, volver a escribir
rhapsody ['ræpsədi] *n, pl* **-dies 1** : elogio *m* excesivo ⟨to go into rhapsodies over : extasiarse por⟩ **2** : rapsodia *f* (en música)
rhetoric ['rɛtərɪk] *n* : retórica *f*
rhetorical [rɪ'tɔrɪkəl] *adj* : retórico
rheumatic [ru'mætɪk] *adj* : reumático
rheumatism ['ru:məˌtɪzəm, 'ru-] *n* : reumatismo *m*
rhinestone ['raɪnˌsto:n] *n* : diamante *m* de imitación
rhino ['raɪˌno:] *n, pl* **rhino** *or* **rhinos** → **rhinoceros**
rhinoceros [raɪ'nɑsərəs] *n, pl* **-eroses** *or* **-eros** *or* **-eri** [-ˌraɪ] : rinoceronte *m*
rhododendron [ˌro:də'dɛndrən] *n* : rododendro *m*
rhombus ['rɑmbəs] *n, pl* **-buses** *or* **-bi** [-ˌbaɪ, -bi] : rombo *m*
rhubarb ['ru:ˌbɑrb] *n* : ruibarbo *m*
rhyme[1] ['raɪm] *vi* **rhymed; rhyming** : rimar
rhyme[2] *n* **1** : rima *f* **2** VERSE : verso *m* (en rima)
rhythm ['rɪðəm] *n* : ritmo *m*
rhythmic ['rɪðmɪk] *or* **rhythmical** [-mɪkəl] *adj* : rítmico — **rhythmically** [-mɪkli] *adv*
rib[1] ['rɪb] *vt* **ribbed; ribbing 1** : hacer en canalé ⟨a ribbed sweater : un suéter en canalé⟩ **2** TEASE : tomarle el pelo (a alguien)
rib[2] *n* **1** : costilla *f* (de una persona o un animal) **2** : nervio *m* (de una bóveda o una hoja), varilla *f* (de un paraguas), canalé *m* (de una prenda tejida)
ribald ['rɪbəld] *adj* : escabroso, procaz
ribbon ['rɪbən] *n* **1** : cinta *f* **2 to tear to ribbons** : hacer jirones
rice ['raɪs] *n* : arroz *m*
rich ['rɪtʃ] *adj* **1** WEALTHY : rico **2** SUMPTUOUS : suntuoso, lujoso **3** : pesado ⟨rich foods : comida pesada⟩ **4** ABUNDANT : abundante **5** : vivo, intenso ⟨rich colors : colores vivos⟩ **6** FERTILE : fértil, rico

riches ['rɪtʃəz] *npl* : riquezas *fpl*
richly ['rɪtʃli] *adv* **1** SUMPTUOUSLY : suntuosamente, ricamente **2** ABUNDANTLY : abundantemente **3 richly deserved** : bien merecido
richness ['rɪtʃnəs] *n* : riqueza *f*
rickets ['rɪkəts] *n* : raquitismo *m*
rickety ['rɪkəti] *adj* : desvencijado, destartalado
ricksha *or* **rickshaw** ['rɪkˌʃɔ] *n* : cochecillo *m* tirado por un hombre
ricochet[1] ['rɪkəˌʃeɪ] *vi* **-cheted** [-ˌʃeɪd] *or* **-chetted** [-ˌʃɛtəd]; **-cheting** [-ˌʃeɪɪŋ] *or* **-chetting** [-ˌʃɛtɪŋ] : rebotar
ricochet[2] *n* : rebote *m*
rid ['rɪd] *vt* **rid; ridding 1** FREE : librar ⟨to rid the city of thieves : librar la ciudad de ladrones⟩ **2 to rid oneself of** : desembarazarse de
riddance ['rɪdənts] *n* : libramiento *m* ⟨good riddance! : ¡adiós y buen viaje!, ¡vete con viento fresco!⟩
riddle[1] ['rɪdəl] *vt* **-dled; -dling** : acribillar ⟨riddled with bullets : acribillado a balazos⟩ ⟨riddled with errors : lleno de errores⟩
riddle[2] *n* : acertijo *m*, adivinanza *f*
ride[1] ['raɪd] *v* **rode** ['ro:d]; **ridden** ['rɪdən]; **riding** *vt* **1** : montar, ir, andar ⟨to ride a horse : montar a caballo⟩ ⟨to ride a bicycle : montar en bicicleta, andar en bicicleta⟩ ⟨to ride the bus : ir en autobús⟩ **2** TRAVERSE : recorrer ⟨he rode 5 miles : recorrió 5 millas⟩ **3** TEASE : burlarse de, ridiculizar **4** CARRY : llevar **5** WEATHER : capear ⟨they rode out the storm : capearon el temporal⟩ **6 to ride the waves** : surcar los mares — *vi* **1** : montar a caballo, cabalgar **2** TRAVEL : ir, viajar (en coche, en bicicleta, etc.) **3** RUN : andar, marchar ⟨the car rides well : el coche anda bien⟩ **4 to ride at anchor** : estar fondeado **5 to let things ride** : dejar pasar las cosas
ride[2] *n* **1** : paseo *m*, vuelta *f* (en coche, en bicicleta, a caballo) ⟨to go for a ride : dar una vuelta⟩ ⟨to give someone a ride : llevar en coche a alguien⟩ **2** : aparato *m* (en un parque de diversiones)
rider ['raɪdər] *n* **1** : jinete *mf* ⟨the rider fell off his horse : el jinete se cayó de su caballo⟩ **2** CYCLIST : ciclista *mf* **3** MOTORCYCLIST : motociclista *mf* **4** CLAUSE : cláusula *f* añadida
ridge ['rɪdʒ] *n* **1** CHAIN : cadena *f* (de montañas o cerros) **2** : caballete *m* (de un techo), cresta *f* (de una ola o una montaña), cordoncillo *m* (de telas)
ridicule[1] ['rɪdəˌkju:l] *vt* **-culed; -culing** : burlarse de, mofarse de, ridiculizar
ridicule[2] *n* : burlas *fpl*
ridiculous [rə'dɪkjələs] *adj* : ridículo, absurdo
ridiculously [rə'dɪkjələsli] *adv* : de forma ridícula
rife ['raɪf] *adj* : abundante, común ⟨to be rife with : estar plagado de⟩

riffraff ['rɪf,ræf] *n* : chusma *f*, gentuza *f*
rifle[1] ['raɪfəl] *v* **-fled; -fling** *vt* RANSACK : desvalijar, saquear — *vi* **to rifle through** : revolver
rifle[2] *n* : rifle *m*, fusil *m*
rift ['rɪft] *n* **1** FISSURE : grieta *f*, fisura *f* **2** BREAK : ruptura *f* (entre personas), división *f* (dentro de un grupo)
rig[1] ['rɪg] *vt* **rigged; rigging 1** : aparejar (un barco) **2** EQUIP : equipar **3** FIX : amañar (una elección, etc.) **4 to rig up** CONSTRUCT : construir, erigir **5 to rig oneself out as** : vestirse de
rig[2] *n* **1** : aparejo *m* (de un barco) **2** *or* **oil rig** : torre *f* de perforación, plataforma *f* petrolífera
rigging ['rɪgɪŋ, -gən] *n* : jarcia *f*, aparejo *m*
right[1] ['raɪt] *vt* **1** FIX, RESTORE : reparar ⟨to right the economy : reparar la economía⟩ **2** STRAIGHTEN : enderezar
right[2] *adv* **1** : bien ⟨to live right : vivir bien⟩ **2** PRECISELY : precisamente, justo ⟨right in the middle : justo en medio⟩ **3** DIRECTLY, STRAIGHT : derecho, directamente ⟨he went right home : fue derecho a casa⟩ **4** IMMEDIATELY : inmediatamente ⟨right after lunch : inmediatamente después del almuerzo⟩ **5** COMPLETELY : completamente ⟨he felt right at home : se sintió completamente cómodo⟩ **6** : a la derecha ⟨to look left and right : mirar a la izquierda y a la derecha⟩
right[3] *adj* **1** UPRIGHT : bueno, honrado ⟨right conduct : conducta honrada⟩ **2** CORRECT : correcto ⟨the right answer : la respuesta correcta⟩ **3** APPROPRIATE : apropiado, adecuado, debido ⟨the right man for the job : el hombre perfecto para el trabajo⟩ **4** STRAIGHT : recto ⟨a right line : una línea recta⟩ **5** : derecho ⟨the right hand : la mano derecha⟩ **6** SOUND : bien ⟨he's not in his right mind : no está bien de la cabeza⟩
right[4] *n* **1** GOOD : bien *m* ⟨to do right : hacer el bien⟩ **2** : derecha *f* ⟨on the right : a la derecha⟩ **3** *or* **right hand** : mano *f* derecha **4** ENTITLEMENT : derecho *m* ⟨the right to vote : el derecho a votar⟩ ⟨women's rights : los derechos de la mujer⟩ **5 the Right** : la derecha (en la política)
right angle *n* : ángulo *m* recto
right–angled ['raɪt'æŋgəld] *or* **right-angle** [-gəl] *adj* **1** : en ángulo recto **2 right–angled triangle** : triángulo *m* rectángulo
righteous ['raɪtʃəs] *adj* : recto, honrado — **righteously** *adv*
righteousness ['raɪtʃəsnəs] *n* : rectitud *f*, honradez *f*
rightful ['raɪtfəl] *adj* **1** JUST : justo **2** LAWFUL : legítimo — **rightfully** *adv*
right–hand ['raɪt'hænd] *adj* **1** : situado a la derecha **2** RIGHT-HANDED : para

la mano derecha, con la mano derecha **3 right–hand man** : brazo *m* derecho
right–handed ['raɪt'hændəd] *adj* **1** : diestro ⟨a right-handed pitcher : un lanzador diestro⟩ **2** : para la mano derecha, con la mano derecha **3** CLOCKWISE : en la dirección de las manecillas del reloj
rightly ['raɪtli] *adv* **1** JUSTLY : justamente, con razón **2** PROPERLY : debidamente, apropiadamente **3** CORRECTLY : correctamente
right–of–way ['raɪtə'weɪ, -əv-] *n, pl* **rights–of–way 1** : preferencia (del tráfico) **2** ACCESS : derecho *m* de paso
rightward ['raɪtwərd] *adj* : a la derecha, hacia la derecha
right–wing ['raɪt'wɪŋ] *adj* : derechista
right wing *n* **the right wing** : la derecha
right–winger ['raɪt'wɪŋər] *n* : derechista *mf*
rigid ['rɪdʒɪd] *adj* : rígido — **rigidly** *adv*
rigidity [rɪ'dʒɪdəți] *n, pl* **-ties** : rigidez *f*
rigmarole ['rɪgmə,roːl, 'rɪgə-] *n* **1** NONSENSE : galimatías *m*, disparates *mpl* **2** PROCEDURES : trámites *mpl*
rigor ['rɪgər] *n* : rigor *m*
rigor mortis [,rɪgər'mɔrtəs] *n* : rigidez *f* cadavérica
rigorous ['rɪgərəs] *adj* : riguroso — **rigorously** *adv*
rile ['raɪl] *vt* **riled; riling** : irritar
rill ['rɪl] *n* : riachuelo *m*
rim ['rɪm] *n* **1** EDGE : borde *m* **2** : llanta *f*, rin *m Col, Mex* (de una rueda) **3** FRAME : montura *f* (de anteojos)
rime ['raɪm] *n* : escarcha *f*
rind ['raɪnd] *n* : corteza *f*
ring[1] ['rɪŋ] *v* **rang** ['ræŋ]; **rung** ['rʌŋ]; **ringing** *vi* **1** : sonar ⟨the doorbell rang : el timbre sonó⟩ ⟨to ring for : llamar⟩ **2** RESOUND : resonar **3** SEEM : parecer ⟨to ring true : parecer cierto⟩ — *vt* **1** : tocar, hacer sonar (un timbre, una alarma, etc.) **2** SURROUND : cercar, rodear
ring[2] *n* **1** : anillo *m*, sortija *f* ⟨wedding ring : anillo de matrimonio⟩ **2** BAND : aro *m*, anillo *m* ⟨piston ring : aro de émbolo⟩ **3** CIRCLE : círculo *m* **4** ARENA : arena *f*, ruedo *m* ⟨a boxing ring : un cuadrilátero, un ring⟩ **5** GANG : banda *f* (de ladrones, etc.) **6** SOUND : timbre *m*, sonido *m* **7** CALL : llamada *f* (por teléfono)
ringer ['rɪŋər] *n* **to be a dead ringer for** : ser un vivo retrato de
ringleader ['rɪŋ,liːdər] *n* : cabecilla *mf*
ringlet ['rɪŋlət] *n* : sortija *f*, rizo *m*
ringworm ['rɪŋ,wərm] *n* : tiña *f*
rink ['rɪŋk] *n* : pista *f* ⟨skating rink : pista de patinaje⟩
rinse[1] ['rɪnts] *vt* **rinsed; rinsing** : enjuagar ⟨to rinse out one's mouth : enjuagarse la boca⟩
rinse[2] *n* : enjuague *m*
riot[1] ['raɪət] *vi* : amotinarse
riot[2] *n* : motín *m*, tumulto *m*, alboroto *m*

rioter ['raɪəṭər] *n* : alborotador *m*, -dora *f*

riotous ['raɪəṭəs] *adj* **1** UNRULY, WILD : desenfrenado, alborotado **2** ABUNDANT : abundante

rip[1] ['rɪp] *v* **ripped; ripping** *vt* : rasgar, arrancar, desgarrar — *vi* : rasgarse, desgarrarse

rip[2] *n* : rasgón *m*, desgarrón *m*

ripe ['raɪp] *adj* **riper; ripest 1** MATURE : maduro ⟨ripe fruit : fruta madura⟩ **2** READY : listo, preparado

ripen ['raɪpən] *v* : madurar

ripeness ['raɪpnəs] *n* : madurez *f*

rip-off ['rɪp,ɔf] *n* **1** THEFT : robo *m* **2** SWINDLE : estafa *f*, timo *m fam*

rip off *vt* **1** : rasgar, arrancar, desgarrar **2** SWINDLE *fam* : estafar, tifar

ripple[1] ['rɪpəl] *v* **-pled; -pling** *vi* : rizarse, ondear, ondular — *vt* : rizar

ripple[2] *n* : onda *f*, ondulación *f*

rise[1] ['raɪz] *vi* **rose** ['ro:z]; **risen** ['rɪz-ən]; **rising 1** GET UP : levantarse ⟨to rise to one's feet : ponerse de pie⟩ **2** : elevarse, alzarse ⟨the mountains rose to the west : las montañas se elevaron al oeste⟩ **3** : salir (dícese del sol y de la luna) **4** : subir (dícese de las aguas, del humo, etc.) ⟨the river rose : las aguas subieron de nivel⟩ **5** INCREASE : aumentar, subir **6** ORIGINATE : nacer, proceder **7 to rise in rank** : ascender **8 to rise up** REBEL : sublevarse, rebelarse

rise[2] *n* **1** ASCENT : ascensión *f*, subida *f* **2** ORIGIN : origen *m* **3** ELEVATION : elevación *f* **4** INCREASE : subida *f*, aumento *m*, alzamiento *m* **5** SLOPE : pendiente *f*, cuesta *f*

riser ['raɪzər] *n* **1** : contrahuella *f* (de una escalera) **2 early riser** : madrugador *m*, -dora *f* **3 late riser** : dormilón *m*, -lona *f*

risk[1] ['rɪsk] *vt* : arriesgar

risk[2] *n* : riesgo *m*, peligro *m* ⟨at risk : en peligro⟩ ⟨at your own risk : por su cuenta y riesgo⟩

risky ['rɪski] *adj* **riskier; -est** : arriesgado, peligroso, riesgoso

risqué [rɪ'skeɪ] *adj* : escabroso, picante, subido de tono

rite ['raɪt] *n* : rito *m*

ritual[1] ['rɪtʃʊəl] *adj* : ritual — **ritually** *adv*

ritual[2] *n* : ritual *m*

rival[1] ['raɪvəl] *vt* **-valed** *or* **-valled; -valing** *or* **-valling** : rivalizar con, competir con

rival[2] *adj* : competidor, rival

rival[3] *n* : rival *mf*; competidor *m*, -dora *f*

rivalry ['raɪvəlri] *n, pl* **-ries** : rivalidad *f*, competencia *f*

river ['rɪvər] *n* : río *m*

riverbank ['rɪvər,bæŋk] *n* : ribera *f*, orilla *f*

riverbed ['rɪvər,bed] *n* : cauce *m*, lecho *m*

riverside ['rɪvər,saɪd] *n* : ribera *f*, orilla *f*

rivet[1] ['rɪvət] *vt* **1** : remachar **2** FIX : fijar (los ojos, etc.) **3** FASCINATE : fascinar, cautivar

rivet[2] *n* : remache *m*

rivulet ['rɪvjələt] *n* : arroyo *m*, riachuelo *m* ⟨rivulets of sweat : gotas de sudor⟩

roach ['ro:tʃ] → **cockroach**

road ['ro:d] *n* **1** : carretera *f*, calle *f*, camino *m* **2** PATH : camino *m*, sendero *m*, vía *f* ⟨on the road to a solution : en vías de una solución⟩

roadblock ['ro:d,blɑk] *n* : control *m*

roadrunner ['ro:d,rʌnər] *n* : correcaminos *m*

roadside ['ro:d,saɪd] *n* : borde *m* de la carretera

roadway ['ro:d,weɪ] *n* : carretera *f*, calzada *f*

roam ['ro:m] *vi* : vagar, deambular, errar — *vt* : vagar por

roan[1] ['ro:n] *adj* : ruano

roan[2] *n* : caballo *m* ruano

roar[1] ['ror] *vi* : rugir, bramar ⟨to roar with laughter : reírse a carcajadas⟩ — *vt* : decir a gritos

roar[2] *n* **1** : rugido *m*, bramido *m* (de un animal) **2** DIN : clamor *m* (de gente), fragor *m* (del trueno), estruendo *m* (del tráfico, etc.)

roast[1] ['ro:st] *vt* : asar (carne, papas), tostar (café, nueces) — *vi* : asarse

roast[2] *adj* **1** : asado ⟨roast chicken : pollo asado⟩ **2 roast beef** : rosbif *m*

roast[3] *n* : asado *m*

rob ['rɑb] *v* **robbed; robbing** *vt* **1** STEAL : robar **2** DEPRIVE : privar, quitar — *vi* : robar

robber ['rɑbər] *n* : ladrón *m*, -drona *f*

robbery ['rɑbəri] *n, pl* **-beries** : robo *m*

robe[1] ['ro:b] *vt* **robed; robing** : vestirse

robe[2] *n* **1** : toga *f* (de magistrados, etc.), sotana *f* (de eclesiásticos) ⟨robe of office : traje de ceremonias⟩ **2** BATHROBE : bata *f*

robin ['rɑbən] *n* : petirrojo *m*

robot ['ro:,bɑt, -bət] *n* : robot *m*

robotic [ro'bɑtɪk] *adj* : robótico, robotizado

robotics [ro'bɑtɪks] *ns & pl* : robótica *f*

robust [ro'bʌst, 'ro:,bʌst] *adj* : robusto, fuerte — **robustly** *adv*

rock[1] ['rɑk] *vt* **1** : acunar (a un niño), mecer (una cuna) **2** SHAKE : sacudir — *vi* SWAY : mecerse, balancearse

rock[2] *adj* : de rock

rock[3] *n* **1** ROCKING : balanceo *m* **2** *or* **rock music** : rock *m*, música *f* rock **3** : roca *f* (substancia) **4** STONE : piedra *f*

rock and roll *n* : rock and roll *m*

rocker ['rɑkər] *n* **1** : balancín *m* **2** *or* **rocking chair** : mecedora *f*, balancín *m* **3 to be off one's rocker** : estar chiflado, estar loco

rocket[1] ['rɑkət] *vi* : dispararse, subir rápidamente

rocket[2] *n* : cohete *m*

rocking horse *n* : caballito *m* (de balancín)
rock salt *n* : sal *f* gema
rocky ['raki] *adj* **rockier; -est 1** : rocoso, pedregoso **2** UNSTEADY : inestable
rod ['rɑd] *n* **1** BAR : barra *f*, varilla *f*, vara *f* (de madera) ⟨a fishing rod : una caña (de pescar)⟩ **2** : medida *f* de longitud equivalente a 5.03 metros (5 yardas)
rode → **ride**[1]
rodent ['ro:dənt] *n* : roedor *m*
rodeo ['ro:di,o:, ro'dei,o:] *n, pl* **-deos** : rodeo *m*
roe ['ro:] *n* : hueva *f*
rogue ['ro:g] *n* SCOUNDREL : pícaro *m*, -ra *f*; pillo *m*, -lla *f*
roguish ['ro:gɪʃ] *adj* : pícaro, travieso
role ['ro:l] *n* : papel *m*, función *f*, rol *m*
roll[1] ['ro:l] *vt* **1** : hacer rodar ⟨to roll the ball : hacer rodar la pelota⟩ ⟨to roll one's eyes : poner los ojos en blanco⟩ **2** : liar (un cigarrillo) **3** *or* **to roll up** : enrollar ⟨to roll (oneself) up into a ball : hacerse una bola⟩ **4** FLATTEN : estirar (masa), laminar (metales), pasar el rodillo por (el césped) **5 to roll up one's sleeves** : arremangarse — *vi* **1** : rodar ⟨the ball kept on rolling : la pelota siguió rodando⟩ **2** SWAY : balancearse ⟨the ship rolled in the waves : el barco se balanceó en las olas⟩ **3** REVERBERATE, SOUND : tronar (dícese del trueno), redoblar (dícese de un tambor) **4 to roll along** PROCEED : ponerse en marcha **5 to roll around** : revolcarse **6 to roll by** : pasar **7 to roll over** : dar una vuelta
roll[2] *n* **1** LIST : lista *f* ⟨to call the roll : pasar lista⟩ ⟨to have on the roll : tener inscrito⟩ **2** *or* **bread roll** : panecito *m*, bolillo *m* Mex **3** : rollo *m* (de papel, de tela, etc.) ⟨a roll of film : un carrete⟩ ⟨a roll of bills : un fajo⟩ **4** : redoble *m* (de tambores), retumbo *m* (del trueno, etc.) **5** ROLLING, SWAYING : balanceo *m*
roller ['ro:lər] *n* **1** : rodillo *m* **2** CURLER : rulo *m*
roller coaster ['ro:lər,ko:stər] *n* : montaña *f* rusa
roller–skate ['ro:lər,skeɪt] *vi* **-skated; -skating** : patinar (sobre ruedas)
roller skate *n* : patín *m* (de ruedas)
rollicking ['ralɪkɪŋ] *adj* : animado, alegre
rolling pin *n* : rodillo *m*
Roman[1] ['ro:mən] *adj* : romano
Roman[2] *n* : romano *m*, -na *f*
Roman Catholic *n* : católico *m*, -ca *f* — **Roman Catholic** *adj*
Roman Catholicism *n* : catolicismo *m*
romance[1] [ro'mænts, 'ro:,mænts] *vi* **-manced; -mancing** FANTASIZE : fantasear
romance[2] *n* **1** : romance *m*, novela *f* de caballerías **2** : novela *f* de amor, novela *f* romántica **3** AFFAIR : romance *m*, amorío *m*

Romanian [ro'meɪniən, ro-] *n* **1** : rumano *m*, -na *f* **2** : rumano *m* (idioma) — **Romanian** *adj*
Roman numeral *n* : número *m* romano
romantic [ro'mæntɪk] *adj* : romántico — **romantically** [-tɪkli] *adv*
romp[1] ['ramp] *vi* FROLIC : retozar, juguetear
romp[2] *n* : retozo *m*
roof[1] ['ru:f, 'rʊf] *vt* : techar
roof[2] *n, pl* **roofs** ['ru:fs, 'rʊfs; 'ru:vz, 'rʊvz] **1** : techo *m*, tejado *m*, techado *m* **2 roof of the mouth** : paladar *m*
roofing ['ru:fɪŋ, 'rʊfɪŋ] *n* : techumbre *f*
rooftop ['ru:f,tap, 'rʊf-] *n* ROOF : tejado *m*
rook[1] ['rʊk] *vt* CHEAT : defraudar, estafar, timar
rook[2] *n* **1** : grajo *m* (ave) **2** : torre *f* (en ajedrez)
rookie ['rʊki] *n* : novato *m*, -ta *f*
room[1] ['ru:m, 'rʊm] *vi* LODGE : alojarse, hospedarse
room[2] *n* **1** SPACE : espacio *m*, sitio *m*, lugar *m* ⟨to make room for : hacer lugar⟩ **2** : cuarto *m*, habitación *f* (en una casa), sala *f* (para reuniones, etc.) **3** BEDROOM : dormitorio *m*, habitación *f*, pieza *f* **4** (*indicating possibility or opportunity*) ⟨room for improvement : posibilidad de mejorar⟩ ⟨there's no room for error : no hay lugar para errores⟩
roomer ['ru:mər, 'rʊmər] *n* : inquilino *m*, -na *f*
rooming house *n* : pensión *f*
roommate ['ru:m,meɪt, 'rʊm-] *n* : compañero *m*, -ra *f* de cuarto
roomy ['ru:mi, 'rʊmi] *adj* **roomier; -est 1** SPACIOUS : espacioso, amplio **2** LOOSE : suelto, holgado ⟨a roomy blouse : una blusa holgada⟩
roost[1] ['ru:st] *vi* : posarse, dormir (en una percha)
roost[2] *n* : percha *f*
rooster ['ru:stər, 'rʊs-] *n* : gallo *m*
root[1] ['ru:t, 'rʊt] *vi* **1** : arraigar ⟨the plant rooted easily : la planta arraigó con facilidad⟩ ⟨deeply rooted traditions : tradiciones profundamente arraigadas⟩ **2** : hozar (dícese de los cerdos) ⟨to root around in : hurgar en⟩ **3 to root for** : apoyar a, alentar — *vt* **to root out** *or* **to root up** : desarraigar (plantas), extirpar (problemas, etc.)
root[2] *n* **1** : raíz *f* (de una planta) **2** ORIGIN : origen *m*, raíz *f* **3** CORE : centro *m*, núcleo *m* ⟨to get to the root of the matter : ir al centro del asunto⟩
rootless ['ru:tləs, 'rʊt-] *adj* : desarraigado
rope[1] ['ro:p] *vt* **roped; roping 1** TIE : amarrar, atar **2** LASSO : lazar **3 to rope off** : acordonar
rope[2] *n* : soga *f*, cuerda *f*
rosary ['ro:zəri] *n, pl* **-ries** : rosario *m*
rose[1] → **rise**[1]
rose[2] ['ro:z] *adj* : rosa, color de rosa

rose³ *n* **1** : rosal *m* (planta), rosa *f* (flor) **2** : rosa *m* (color)

rosebush ['ro:z₁buʃ] *n* : rosal *m*

rosemary ['ro:z₁mɛri] *n, pl* **-maries** : romero *m*

rosette [ro'zɛt] *n* : escarapela *f* (hecho de cintas), roseta *f* (en arquitectura)

Rosh Hashanah [ˌrɑʃhɑ'ʃɑnə, ˌro:ʃ-] *n* : el Año Nuevo judío

rosin ['rɑzən] *n* : colofonia *f*

roster ['rɑstər] *n* : lista *f*

rostrum ['rɑstrəm] *n, pl* **-trums** *or* **-tra** [-trə] : tribuna *f*, estrado *m*

rosy ['ro:zi] *adj* **rosier; -est 1** : sonrosado, de color rosa **2** PROMISING : prometedor, halagüeño

rot¹ ['rɑt] *v* **rotted; rotting** *vi* : pudrirse, descomponerse — *vt* : pudrir, descomponer

rot² *n* : putrefacción *f*, descomposición *f*, podredumbre *f*

rotary¹ ['ro:təri] *adj* : rotativo, rotatorio

rotary² *n, pl* **-ries 1** : máquina *f* rotativa **2** TRAFFIC CIRCLE : rotonda *f*, glorieta *f*

rotate ['ro:ˌteɪt] *v* **-tated; -tating** *vi* REVOLVE : girar, rotar — *vt* **1** TURN : hacer girar, darle vueltas a **2** ALTERNATE : alternar

rotation [ro'teɪʃən] *n* : rotación *f*

rote ['ro:t] *n* **to learn by rote** : aprender de memoria

rotor ['ro:tər] *n* : rotor *m*

rotten ['rɑtən] *adj* **1** PUTRID : podrido, putrefacto **2** CORRUPT : corrompido **3** BAD : malo ⟨a rotten day : un día malísimo⟩

rottenness ['rɑtənnəs] *n* : podredumbre *f*

rotund [ro'tʌnd] *adj* **1** ROUNDED : redondeado **2** PLUMP : regordete *fam*, llenito *fam*

rouge ['ru:ʒ, 'ru:ʤ] *n* : colorete *m*

rough¹ ['rʌf] *vt* **1** ROUGHEN : poner áspero **2 to rough out** SKETCH : esbozar, bosquejar **3 to rough up** BEAT : darle una paliza (a alguien) **4 to rough it** : vivir sin comodidades

rough² *adj* **1** COARSE : áspero, basto **2** UNEVEN : desigual, escabroso, accidentado (dícese del terreno) **3** : agitado (dícese del mar), tempestuoso (dícese del tiempo), violento (dícese del viento) **4** VIOLENT : violento, brutal ⟨a rough neighborhood : un barrio peligroso⟩ **5** DIFFICULT : duro, difícil **6** CRUDE : rudo, tosco, burdo ⟨a rough cottage : una casita tosca⟩ ⟨a rough draft : un borrador⟩ ⟨a rough sketch : un bosquejo⟩ **7** APPROXIMATE : aproximado ⟨a rough idea : una idea aproximada⟩

rough³ *n* **1 the rough** : el rough (en golf) **2 in the rough** : en borrador

roughage ['rʌfɪʤ] *n* : fibra *f*

roughen ['rʌfən] *vt* : poner áspero — *vi* : ponerse áspero

roughly ['rʌfli] *adv* **1** : bruscamente ⟨to treat roughly : maltratar⟩ **2** CRUDELY : burdamente **3** APPROXIMATELY : aproximadamente, más o menos

roughneck ['rʌfˌnɛk] *n* : matón *m*

roughness ['rʌfnəs] *n* : rudeza *f*, aspereza *f*

roulette [ru:'lɛt] *n* : ruleta *f*

round¹ ['raʊnd] *vt* **1** : redondear ⟨she rounded the edges : redondeó los bordes⟩ **2** TURN : doblar ⟨to round the corner : dar la vuelta a la esquina⟩ **3 to round off** : redondear (un número) **4 to round off** *or* **to round out** COMPLETE : rematar, terminar **5 to round up** GATHER : reunir

round² *adv* → **around¹**

round³ *adj* **1** : redondo ⟨a round table : una mesa redonda⟩ ⟨in round numbers : en números redondos⟩ ⟨round shoulders : espaldas cargadas⟩ **2 round trip** : viaje *m* de ida y vuelta

round⁴ *n* **1** CIRCLE : círculo *m* **2** SERIES : serie *f*, sucesión *f* ⟨a round of talks : una ronda de negociaciones⟩ ⟨the daily round : la rutina cotidiana⟩ **3** : asalto *m* (en boxeo), recorrido *m* (en golf), vuelta *f* (en varios juegos) **4** : salva *f* (de aplausos) **5 round of drinks** : ronda *f* **6 round of ammunition** : disparo *m*, cartucho *m* **7 rounds** *npl* : recorridos *mpl* (de un cartero), rondas *fpl* (de un vigilante), visitas *fpl* (de un médico) ⟨to make the rounds : hacer visitas⟩

round⁵ *prep* → **around²**

roundabout ['raʊndəˌbaʊt] *adj* : indirecto ⟨to speak in a roundabout way : hablar con rodeos⟩

roundly ['raʊndli] *adv* **1** THOROUGHLY : completamente **2** BLUNTLY : francamente, rotundamente **3** VIGOROUSLY : con vigor

roundness ['raʊndnəs] *n* : redondez *f*

roundup ['raʊndˌʌp] *n* **1** : rodeo *m* (de animales), redada *f* (de delincuentes, etc.) **2** SUMMARY : resumen *m*

round up *vt* **1** : rodear (ganado), reunir (personas) **2** SUMMARIZE : hacer un resumen de

roundworm ['raʊndˌwərm] *n* : lombriz *f* intestinal

rouse ['raʊz] *vt* **roused; rousing 1** AWAKE : despertar **2** EXCITE : excitar ⟨it roused him to fury : lo enfureció⟩

rout¹ ['raʊt] *vt* **1** DEFEAT : derrotar, aplastar **2 to rout out** : hacer salir

rout² *n* **1** DISPERSAL : desbandada *f*, dispersión *f* **2** DEFEAT : derrota *f* aplastante

route¹ ['ru:t, 'raʊt] *vt* **routed; routing** : dirigir, enviar, encaminar

route² *n* : camino *m*, ruta *f*, recorrido *m*

routine¹ [ru:'ti:n] *adj* : rutinario — **routinely** *adv*

routine² *n* : rutina *f*

rove ['ro:v] *v* **roved; roving** *vi* : vagar, errar — *vt* : errar por

rover ['ro:vər] *n* : vagabundo *m*, -da *f*

row[1] ['ro:] *vt* **1** : avanzar a remo ⟨to row a boat : remar⟩ **2** : llevar a remo ⟨he rowed me to shore : me llevó hasta la orilla⟩ — *vi* : remar

row[2] ['raʊ] *n* **1** : paseo *m* en barca ⟨to go for a row : salir a remar⟩ **2** LINE, RANK : fila *f*, hilera *f* **3** SERIES : serie *f* ⟨three days in a row : tres días seguidos⟩ **4** RACKET : estruendo *m*, bulla *f* **5** QUARREL : pelea *f*, riña *f*

rowboat ['ro:,bo:t] *n* : bote *m* de remos

rowdiness ['raʊdinəs] *n* : bulla *f*

rowdy[1] ['raʊdi] *adj* **-dier; -est** : escandaloso, alborotador

rowdy[2] *n, pl* **-dies** : alborotador *m*, -dora *f*

rower ['ro:ər] *n* : remero *m*, -ra *f*

royal[1] ['rɔɪəl] *adj* : real — **royally** *adv*

royal[2] *n* : persona de linaje real, miembro de la familia real

royalty ['rɔɪəlti] *n, pl* **-ties** **1** : realeza *f* (posición) **2** : miembros *mpl* de la familia real **3 royalties** *npl* : derechos *mpl* de autor

rub[1] ['rʌb] *v* **rubbed; rubbing** *vt* **1** : frotar, restregar ⟨to rub one's hands together : frotarse las manos⟩ **2** MASSAGE : friccionar, masajear **3** CHAFE : rozar **4** POLISH : frotar, pulir **5** SCRUB : fregar **6 to rub elbows with** : codearse con **7 to rub someone the wrong way** : sacar de quicio a alguien, caerle mal a alguien — *vi* **to rub against** : rozar

rub[2] *n* **1** RUBBING : frotamiento *m*, fricción *f* **2** DIFFICULTY : problema *m*

rubber ['rʌbər] *n* **1** : goma *f*, caucho *m*, hule *m* Mex **2 rubbers** *npl* OVERSHOES : chanclos *mpl*

rubber band *n* : goma *f* (elástica), gomita *f*

rubber–stamp ['rʌbər'stæmp] *vt* **1** APPROVE : aprobar, autorizar **2** STAMP : sellar

rubber stamp *n* : sello *m* (de goma)

rubbery ['rʌbəri] *adj* : gomoso

rubbish ['rʌbɪʃ] *n* : basura *f*, desechos *mpl*, desperdicios *mpl*

rubble ['rʌbəl] *n* : escombros *mpl*, ripio *m*

ruble ['ru:bəl] *n* : rublo *m*

ruby ['ru:bi] *n, pl* **-bies** **1** : rubí *m* (gema) **2** : color *m* de rubí

rudder ['rʌdər] *n* : timón *m*

ruddy ['rʌdi] *adj* **-dier; -est** : rubicundo (dícese de la cara, etc.), rojizo (dícese del cielo)

rude ['ru:d] *adj* **ruder; rudest** **1** CRUDE : tosco, rústico **2** IMPOLITE : grosero, descortés, maleducado **3** ABRUPT : brusco ⟨a rude awakening : una sorpresa desagradable⟩

rudely ['ru:dli] *adv* : groseramente

rudeness ['ru:dnəs] *n* **1** IMPOLITENESS : grosería *f*, descortesía *f*, falta *f* de educación **2** ROUGHNESS : tosquedad *f* **3** SUDDENNESS : brusquedad *f*

rudiment ['ru:dəmənt] *n* : rudimento *m*, noción *f* básica ⟨the rudiments of Spanish : los rudimentos del español⟩

rudimentary [,ru:də'mɛntəri] *adj* : rudimentario, básico

rue ['ru:] *vt* **rued; ruing** : lamentar, arrepentirse de

rueful ['ru:fəl] *adj* **1** PITIFUL : lastimoso **2** REGRETFUL : arrepentido, pesaroso

ruffian ['rʌfiən] *n* : matón *m*

ruffle[1] ['rʌfəl] *vt* **-fled; -fling** **1** AGITATE : agitar, rizar (agua) **2** RUMPLE : arrugar (ropa), despeinar (pelo) **3** ERECT : erizar (plumas) **4** VEX : alterar, irritar, perturbar **5** : fruncir volantes en (tela)

ruffle[2] *n* FLOUNCE : volante *m*

ruffly ['rʌfəli] *adj* : con volantes

rug ['rʌg] *n* : alfombra *f*, tapete *m*

rugged ['rʌgəd] *adj* **1** ROUGH, UNEVEN : accidentado, escabroso ⟨rugged mountains : montañas accidentadas⟩ **2** HARSH : duro, severo **3** ROBUST, STURDY : robusto, fuerte

ruin[1] ['ru:ən] *vt* **1** DESTROY : destruir, arruinar **2** BANKRUPT : arruinar, hacer quebrar

ruin[2] *n* **1** : ruina *f* ⟨to fall into ruin : caer en ruinas⟩ **2** : ruina *f*, perdición *f* ⟨to be the ruin of : ser la perdición de⟩ **3 ruins** *npl* : ruinas *fpl*, restos *mpl* ⟨the ruins of the ancient temple : las ruinas del templo antiguo⟩

ruinous ['ru:ənəs] *adj* : ruinoso

rule[1] ['ru:l] *v* **ruled; ruling** *vt* **1** CONTROL, GOVERN : gobernar (un país), controlar (las emociones) **2** DECIDE : decidir, fallar ⟨the judge ruled that . . . : el juez falló que . . . ⟩ **3** DRAW : trazar con una regla — *vi* **1** GOVERN : gobernar, reinar **2** PREVAIL : prevalecer, imperar **3 to rule against** : fallar en contra de

rule[2] *n* **1** REGULATION : regla *f*, norma *f* **2** CUSTOM, HABIT : regla *f* general ⟨as a rule : por lo general⟩ **3** GOVERNMENT : gobierno *m*, dominio *m* **4** RULER : regla *f* (para medir)

ruler ['ru:lər] *n* **1** LEADER, SOVEREIGN : gobernante *mf*; soberano *m*, -na *f* **2** : regla *f* (para medir)

ruling ['ru:lɪŋ] *n* : resolución *f*, fallo *m*

rum ['rʌm] *n* : ron *m*

Rumanian [rʊ'meɪniən] → **Romanian**

rumble[1] ['rʌmbəl] *vi* **-bled; -bling** : retumbar, hacer ruidos (dícese del estómago)

rumble[2] *n* : estruendo *m*, ruido *m* sordo, retumbo *m*

ruminant[1] ['ru:mənənt] *adj* : rumiante

ruminant[2] *n* : rumiante *m*

ruminate ['ru:mə,neɪt] *vi* **-nated; -nating** **1** : rumiar (en zoología) **2** REFLECT : reflexionar, rumiar

rummage ['rʌmɪdʒ] *v* **-maged; -maging** *vi* : hurgar — *vt* RANSACK : revolver ⟨they rummaged the attic : revolvieron el ático⟩

rummy ['rʌmi] *n* : rummy *m* (juego de naipes)
rumor¹ ['ruːmər] *vt* : rumorear ⟨it is rumored that . . . : se rumorea que . . ., se dice que . . .⟩
rumor² *n* : rumor *m*
rump ['rʌmp] *n* **1** : ancas *fpl*, grupa *f* (de un animal) **2** : cadera *f* ⟨rump steak : filete de cadera⟩
rumple ['rʌmpəl] *vt* **-pled; -pling** : arrugar (ropa, etc.), despeinar (pelo)
rumpus ['rʌmpəs] *n* : lío *m*, jaleo *m fam*
run¹ ['rʌn] *v* **ran** ['ræn]; **run; running** *vi* **1** : correr ⟨she ran to catch the bus : corrió para alcanzar el autobús⟩ ⟨run and fetch the doctor : corre a buscar al médico⟩ **2** : circular, correr ⟨the train runs between Detroit and Chicago : el tren circula entre Detroit y Chicago⟩ ⟨to run on time : ser puntual⟩ **3** FUNCTION : funcionar, ir ⟨the engine runs on gasoline : el motor funciona con gasolina⟩ ⟨to run smoothly : ir bien⟩ **4** FLOW : correr, ir **5** LAST : durar ⟨the movie runs for two hours : la película dura dos horas⟩ ⟨the contract runs for three years : el contrato es válido por tres años⟩ **6** : desteñir, despintar (dícese de los colores) **7** EXTEND : correr, extenderse **8 to run for office** : postularse, presentarse — *vt* **1** : correr ⟨to run 10 miles : correr 10 millas⟩ ⟨to run errands : hacer los mandados⟩ ⟨to run out of town : hacer salir del pueblo⟩ **2** PASS : pasar **3** DRIVE : llevar en coche **4** OPERATE : hacer funcionar (un motor, etc.) **5** : echar ⟨to run water : echar agua⟩ **6** MANAGE : dirigir, llevar (un negocio, etc.) **7** EXTEND : tender (un cable, etc.) **8 to run a risk** : correr un riesgo
run² *n* **1** : carrera *f* ⟨at a run : a la carrera, corriendo⟩ ⟨to go for a run : ir a correr⟩ **2** TRIP : vuelta *f*, paseo *m* (en coche), viaje *m* (en avión) **3** SERIES : serie *f* ⟨a run of disappointments : una serie de desilusiones⟩ ⟨in the long run : a la larga⟩ ⟨in the short run : a corto plazo⟩ **4** DEMAND : gran demanda *f* ⟨a run on the banks : una corrida bancaria⟩ **5** (*used for theatrical productions and films*) ⟨to have a long run : mantenerse mucho tiempo en la cartelera⟩ **6** TYPE : tipo *m* ⟨the average run of students : el tipo más común de estudiante⟩ **7** : carrera *f* (en béisbol) **8** : carrera *f* (en una media) **9 to have the run of** : tener libre acceso de (una casa, etc.) **10 ski run** : pista *f* (de esquí)
runaway¹ ['rʌnə,weɪ] *adj* **1** FUGITIVE : fugitivo **2** UNCONTROLLABLE : incontrolable, fuera de control ⟨runaway inflation : inflación desenfrenada⟩ ⟨a runaway success : un éxito aplastante⟩
runaway² *n* : fugitivo *m*, -va *f*
rundown ['rʌn,daʊn] *n* SUMMARY : resumen *m*

run–down ['rʌn'daʊn] *adj* **1** DILAPIDATED : ruinoso, destartalado **2** SICKLY, TIRED : cansado, débil
rung¹ *pp* → **ring¹**
rung² ['rʌn] *n* : peldaño *m*, escalón *m*
run–in ['rʌn,ɪn] *n* : disputa *f*, altercado *m*
runner ['rʌnər] *n* **1** RACER : corredor *m*, -dora *f* **2** MESSENGER : mensajero *m*, -ra *f* **3** TRACK : riel *m* (de un cajón, etc.) **4** : patín *m* (de un trineo), cuchilla *f* (de un patín) **5** : estolón *m* (planta)
runner–up [,rʌnər'ʌp] *n, pl* **runners–up** : subcampeón *m*, -peona *f*
running ['rʌnɪŋ] *adj* **1** FLOWING : corriente ⟨running water : agua corriente⟩ **2** CONTINUOUS : continuo ⟨a running battle : una lucha continua⟩ **3** CONSECUTIVE : seguido ⟨six days running : por seis días seguidos⟩
runny ['rʌni] *adj* **-nier; -est 1** WATERY : caldoso **2 to have a runny nose** : moquear
run over *vt* : atropellar — *vi* OVERFLOW : rebosar
runt ['rʌnt] *n* : animal *m* pequeño ⟨the runt of the litter : el más pequeño de la camada⟩
runway ['rʌn,weɪ] *n* : pista *f* de aterrizaje
rupee [ru'piː, 'ru-ˌ] *n* : rupia *f*
rupture¹ ['rʌptʃər] *v* **-tured; -turing** *vt* **1** BREAK, BURST : romper, reventar **2** : causar una hernia en — *vi* : reventarse
rupture² *n* **1** BREAK : ruptura *f* **2** HERNIA : hernia *f*
rural ['rʊrəl] *adj* : rural, campestre
ruse ['ruːs, 'ruːz] *n* : treta *f*, ardid *m*, estratagema *f*
rush¹ ['rʌʃ] *vi* : correr, ir de prisa ⟨to rush around : correr de un lado a otro⟩ ⟨to rush off : irse corriendo⟩ — *vt* **1** HURRY : apresurar, apurar **2** ATTACK : abalanzarse sobre, asaltar
rush² *adj* : urgente
rush³ *n* **1** HASTE : prisa *f*, apuro *m* **2** SURGE : ráfaga *f* (de aire), torrente *m* (de aguas), avalancha *f* (de gente) **3** DEMAND : demanda *f* ⟨a rush on sugar : una gran demanda para el azúcar⟩ **4** : carga *f* (en futbol americano) **5** : junco *m* (planta)
russet ['rʌsət] *n* : color *m* rojizo
Russian ['rʌʃən] *n* **1** : ruso *m*, -sa *f* **2** : ruso *m* (idioma) — **Russian** *adj*
rust¹ ['rʌst] *vi* : oxidarse — *vt* : oxidar
rust² *n* **1** : herrumbre *f*, orín *m*, óxido *m* (en los metales) **2** : roya *f* (en las plantas)
rustic¹ ['rʌstɪk] *adj* : rústico, campestre — **rustically** [-tɪkli] *adv*
rustic² *n* : rústico *m*, -ca *f*; campesino *m*, -na *f*
rustle¹ ['rʌsəl] *v* **-tled; -tling** *vt* **1** : hacer susurrar, hacer crujir ⟨to rustle a newspaper : hacer crujir un periódico⟩ **2** STEAL : robar (ganado) — *vi* : susurrar, crujir

rustle[2] *n* : murmullo *m*, susurro *m*, crujido *m*

rustler ['rʌsələr] *n* : ladrón *m*, -drona *f* de ganado

rusty ['rʌsti] *adj* **rustier; -est** : oxidado, herrumbroso

rut ['rʌt] *n* **1** GROOVE, TRACK : rodada *f*, surco *m* **2 to be in a rut** : ser esclavo de la rutina

ruthless ['ru:θləs] *adj* : despiadado, cruel — **ruthlessly** *adv*

ruthlessness ['ru:θləsnəs] *n* : crueldad *f*, falta *f* de piedad

Rwandan [rʊ'ɑndən] *n* : ruandés *m*, -desa *f* — **Rwandan** *adj*

rye ['raɪ] *n* **1** : centeno *m* **2** *or* **rye whiskey** : whisky *m* de centeno

S

s ['ɛs] *n, pl* **s's** *or* **ss** ['ɛsəz] : decimonovena letra del alfabeto inglés

Sabbath ['sæbəθ] *n* **1** : sábado *m* (en el judaísmo) **2** : domingo *m* (en el cristianismo)

saber ['seɪbər] *n* : sable *m*

sable ['seɪbəl] *n* **1** BLACK : negro *m* **2** : marta *f* cebellina (animal)

sabotage[1] ['sæbə,tɑʒ] *vt* **-taged; -taging** : sabotear

sabotage[2] *n* : sabotaje *m*

sac ['sæk] *n* : saco *m* (anatómico)

saccharin ['sækərən] *n* : sacarina *f*

saccharine ['sækərən, -,ri:n, -,raɪn] *adj* : meloso, empalagoso

sachet [sæ'ʃeɪ] *n* : bolsita *f* (perfumada)

sack[1] ['sæk] *vt* **1** FIRE : echar (del trabajo), despedir **2** PLUNDER : saquear

sack[2] *n* BAG : saco *m*

sacrament ['sækrəmənt] *n* : sacramento *m*

sacramental [,sækrə'mɛntəl] *adj* : sacramental

sacred ['seɪkrəd] *adj* **1** RELIGIOUS : sagrado, sacro ⟨sacred texts : textos sagrados⟩ **2** HOLY : sagrado **3 sacred to** : consagrado a

sacrifice[1] ['sækrə,faɪs] *vt* **-ficed; -ficing 1** : sacrificar **2 to sacrifice oneself** : sacrificarse

sacrifice[2] *n* : sacrificio *m*

sacrilege ['sækrəlɪdʒ] *n* : sacrilegio *m*

sacrilegious [,sækrə'lɪdʒəs, -'li:-] *adj* : sacrílego

sacrosanct ['sækro,sæŋkt] *adj* : sacrosanto

sad ['sæd] *adj* **sadder; saddest** : triste — **sadly** *adv*

sadden ['sædən] *vt* : entristecer

saddle[1] ['sædəl] *vt* **-dled; -dling** : ensillar

saddle[2] *n* : silla *f* (de montar)

sadism ['seɪ,dɪzəm, 'sæ-] *n* : sadismo *m*

sadist ['seɪdɪst, 'sæ-] *n* : sádico *m*, -ca *f*

sadistic [sə'dɪstɪk] *adj* : sádico — **sadistically** [-tɪkli] *adv*

sadness ['sædnəs] *n* : tristeza *f*

safari [sə'fɑri, -'fær-] *n* : safari *m*

safe[1] ['seɪf] *adj* **safer; safest 1** UNHARMED : ileso ⟨safe and sound : sano y salvo⟩ **2** SECURE : seguro **3 to be on the safe side** : para mayor seguridad **4 to play it safe** : ir a la segura

safe[2] *n* : caja *f* fuerte

safeguard[1] ['seɪf,gɑrd] *vt* : salvaguardar, proteger

safeguard[2] *n* : salvaguarda *f*, protección *f*

safekeeping ['seɪf'ki:pɪŋ] *n* : custodia *f*, protección *f* ⟨to put into safekeeping : poner en buen recaudo⟩

safely ['seɪfli] *adv* **1** UNHARMED : sin incidentes, sin novedades ⟨they landed safely : aterrizaron sin novedades⟩ **2** SECURELY : con toda seguridad, sin peligro

safety ['seɪfti] *n, pl* **-ties** : seguridad *f*

safety belt *n* : cinturón *m* de seguridad

safety pin *n* : alfiler *m* de gancho, alfiler *m* de seguridad, imperdible *m* *Spain*

saffron ['sæfrən] *n* : azafrán *m*

sag[1] ['sæg] *vi* **sagged; sagging 1** DROOP, SINK : combarse, hundirse, inclinarse **2** : colgar, caer ⟨his jowls sagged : le colgaban las mejillas⟩ **3** FLAG : flaquear, decaer ⟨his spirits sagged : se le flaqueó el ánimo⟩

sag[2] *n* : combadura *f*

saga ['sɑgə, 'sæ-] *n* : saga *f*

sagacious [sə'geɪʃəs] *adj* : sagaz

sage[1] ['seɪdʒ] *adj* **sager; -est** : sabio — **sagely** *adv*

sage[2] *n* **1** : sabio *m*, -bia *f* **2** : salvia *f* (planta)

sagebrush ['seɪdʒ,brʌʃ] *n* : artemisa *f*

Sagittarius [,sædʒə'tɛriəs] *n* : Sagitario *mf*

said → say

sail[1] ['seɪl] *vi* **1** : navegar (en un barco) **2** : ir fácilmente ⟨we sailed right in : entramos sin ningún problema⟩ — *vt* **1** : gobernar (un barco) **2 to sail the seas** : cruzar los mares

sail[2] *n* **1** : vela *f* (de un barco) **2** : viaje *m* en velero ⟨to go for a sail : salir a navegar⟩

sailboat ['seɪl,bo:t] *n* : velero *m*, barco *m* de vela

sailfish ['seɪl,fɪʃ] *n* : pez *m* vela

sailor ['seɪlər] *n* : marinero *m*

saint ['seɪnt, *before a name* ,seɪnt *or* sənt] *n* : santo *m*, -ta *f* ⟨Saint Francis : San Francisco⟩ ⟨Saint Rose : Santa Rosa⟩

saintliness ['seɪntlinəs] *n* : santidad *f*

saintly ['seɪntli] *adj* **saintlier; -est** : santo

sake ['seɪk] *n* **1** BENEFIT : bien *m* ⟨for the children's sake : por el bien de los niños⟩ 2 (*indicating an end or a purpose*) ⟨art for art's sake : el arte por el arte⟩ ⟨let's say, for argument's sake, that he's wrong : pongamos que está equivocado⟩ 3 **for goodness' sake!** : ¡por (el amor de) Dios!

salable *or* **saleable** ['seɪləbəl] *adj* : vendible

salacious [sə'leɪʃəs] *adj* : salaz — **salaciously** *adv*

salad ['sæləd] *n* : ensalada *f*

salamander ['sælə,mændər] *n* : salamandra *f*

salami [sə'lɑmi] *n* : salami *m*

salary ['sæləri] *n, pl* **-ries** : sueldo *m*

sale ['seɪl] *n* 1 SELLING : venta *f* 2 : liquidación *f*, rebajas *fpl* ⟨on sale : de rebaja⟩ 3 **sales** *npl* : ventas *fpl* ⟨to work in sales : trabajar en ventas⟩

salesman ['seɪlzmən] *n, pl* **-men** [-mən, -,mɛn] 1 : vendedor *m*, dependiente *m* (en una tienda) 2 **traveling salesman** : viajante *m*, representante *m*

salesperson ['seɪlz,pərsən] *n* : vendedor *m*, -dora *f*; dependiente *m*, -ta *f* (en una tienda)

saleswoman ['seɪlz,wumən] *n, pl* **-women** [-,wɪmən] 1 : vendedora *f*, dependienta *f* (en una tienda) 2 **traveling saleswoman** : viajante *f*, representante *f*

salient ['seɪljənt] *adj* : saliente, sobresaliente

saline ['seɪ,liːn, -,laɪn] *adj* : salino

saliva [sə'laɪvə] *n* : saliva *f*

salivary ['sælə,vɛri] *adj* : salival ⟨salivary gland : glándula salival⟩

salivate ['sælə,veɪt] *vi* **-vated; -vating** : salivar

sallow ['sælo:] *adj* : amarillento, cetrino

sally[1] ['sæli] *vi* **-lied; -lying** SET OUT : salir, hacer una salida

sally[2] *n, pl* **-lies** 1 : salida *f* (militar), misión *f* 2 QUIP : salida *f*, ocurrencia *f*

salmon ['sæmən] *ns & pl* 1 : salmón *m* (pez) 2 : color *m* salmón

salon [sə'lɑn, 'sæ,lɑn, sæ'lɔ̃] *n* : salón *m* ⟨beauty salon : salón de belleza⟩

saloon [sə'luːn] *n* 1 HALL : salón *m* (en un barco) 2 BARROOM : bar *m*

salsa ['sɔlsə, 'sɑl-] *n* : salsa *f* mexicana, salsa *f* picante

salt[1] ['sɔlt] *vt* : salar, echarle sal a

salt[2] *adj* : salado

salt[3] *n* : sal *f*

saltwater ['sɔlt,wɔtər, -,wɑ-] *adj* : de agua salada

salty ['sɔlti] *adj* **saltier; -est** : salado

salubrious [sə'luːbriəs] *adj* : salubre

salutary ['sæljə,tɛri] *adj* : saludable, salubre

salutation [,sæljə'teɪʃən] *n* : saludo *m*, salutación *f*

salute[1] [sə'luːt] *v* **-luted; -luting** *vt* 1 : saludar (con gestos o ceremonias) 2 ACCLAIM : reconocer, aclamar — *vi* : hacer un saludo

salute[2] *n* 1 : saludo *m* (gesto), salva *f* (de cañonazos) 2 TRIBUTE : reconocimiento *m*, homenaje *m*

Salvadoran [,sælvə'dorən] → **El Salvadoran**

salvage[1] ['sælvɪdʒ] *vt* **-vaged; -vaging** : salvar, rescatar

salvage[2] *n* 1 SALVAGING : salvamento *m*, rescate *m* 2 : objetos *mpl* salvados

salvation [sæl'veɪʃən] *n* : salvación *f*

salve[1] ['sæv, 'sav] *vt* **salved; salving** : calmar, apaciguar ⟨to salve one's conscience : aliviarse la conciencia⟩

salve[2] *n* : ungüento *m*

salvo ['sæl,vo:] *n, pl* **-vos** *or* **-voes** : salva *f*

same[1] ['seɪm] *adj* : mismo, igual ⟨the results are the same : los resultados son iguales⟩ ⟨he said the same thing as you : dijo lo mismo que tú⟩

same[2] *pron* : mismo ⟨it's all the same to me : me da lo mismo⟩ ⟨the same to you! : ¡igualmente!⟩

sameness ['seɪmnəs] *n* 1 SIMILARITY : identidad *f*, semejanza *f* 2 MONOTONY : monotonía *f*

sample[1] ['sæmpəl] *vt* **-pled; -pling** : probar

sample[2] *n* : muestra *f*, prueba *f*

sampler ['sæmplər] *n* 1 : dechado *m* (de bordado) 2 COLLECTION : colección *f* 3 ASSORTMENT : surtido *m*

sanatorium [,sænə'toriəm] *n, pl* **-riums** *or* **-ria** [-iə] : sanatorio *m*

sanctify ['sæŋktə,faɪ] *vt* **-fied; -fying** : santificar

sanctimonious [,sæŋktə'moːniəs] *adj* : beato, santurrón

sanction[1] ['sæŋkʃən] *vt* : sancionar, aprobar

sanction[2] *n* 1 AUTHORIZATION : sanción *f*, autorización *f* 2 **sanctions** *npl* : sanciones *fpl* ⟨to impose sanctions on : imponer sanciones a⟩

sanctity ['sæŋktəti] *n, pl* **-ties** : santidad *f*

sanctuary ['sæŋktʃu,ɛri] *n, pl* **-aries** 1 : presbiterio *m* (en una iglesia) 2 REFUGE : refugio *m*, asilo *m*

sand[1] ['sænd] *vt* : lijar (madera)

sand[2] *n* : arena *f*

sandal ['sændəl] *n* : sandalia *f*

sandbank ['sænd,bæŋk] *n* : banco *m* de arena

sandpaper *n* : papel *m* de lija

sandpiper ['sænd,paɪpər] *n* : andarríos *m*

sandstone ['sænd,stoːn] *n* : arenisca *f*

sandstorm ['sænd,stɔrm] *n* : tormenta *f* de arena

sandwich[1] ['sænd,wɪtʃ] *vt* : intercalar, encajonar, meter (entre dos cosas)

sandwich[2] *n* : sandwich *m*, emparedado *m*, bocadillo *m* *Spain*

sandy ['sændi] *adj* **sandier; -est** : arenoso

sane ['seɪn] *adj* **saner; sanest** 1 : cuerdo 2 SENSIBLE : sensato, razonable

sang → **sing**
sanguine ['sæŋgwən] *adj* **1** RUDDY
: sanguíneo, rubicundo **2** HOPEFUL
: optimista
sanitarium [ˌsænə'tɛriəm] *n, pl* **-iums** *or*
-ia [-iə] → **sanatorium**
sanitary ['sænəteri] *adj* **1** : sanitario
⟨sanitary measures : medidas sanitarias⟩ **2** HYGIENIC : higiénico **3 sanitary napkin** : compresa *f*, paño *m*
higiénico
sanitation [ˌsænə'teɪʃən] *n* : sanidad *f*
sanitize ['sænəˌtaɪz] *vt* **-tized; -tizing 1**
: desinfectar **2** EXPURGATE : expurgar
sanity ['sænəti] *n* : cordura *f*, razón *f* ⟨to
lose one's sanity : perder el juicio⟩
sank → **sink**
Santa Claus ['sæntəˌklɔz] *n* : Papá Noel,
San Nicolás
sap¹ ['sæp] *vt* **sapped; sapping 1** UNDERMINE : socavar **2** WEAKEN : minar, debilitar
sap² *n* **1** : savia *f* (de una planta) **2** SUCKER : inocentón *m*, -tona *f*
sapling ['sæplɪŋ] *n* : árbol *m* joven
sapphire ['sæˌfaɪr] *n* : zafiro *m*
sarcasm ['sɑrˌkæzəm] *n* : sarcasmo *m*
sarcastic [sɑr'kæstɪk] *adj* : sarcástico —
sarcastically [-tɪkli] *adv*
sarcophagus [sɑr'kɑfəgəs] *n, pl* **-gi**
[-ˌgaɪ, -ˌdʒaɪ] : sarcófago *m*
sardine [sɑr'diːn] *n* : sardina *f*
sardonic [sɑr'dɑnɪk] *adj* : sardónico —
sardonically [-nɪkli] *adv*
sarsaparilla [ˌsæspə'rɪlə, ˌsɑrs-] *n*
: zarzaparrilla *f*
sash ['sæʃ] *n* **1** : faja *f* (de un vestido),
fajín *m* (de un uniforme) **2** *pl* **sash**
: marco *m* (de una ventana)
sassafras ['sæsəˌfræs] *n* : sasafrás *m*
sassy ['sæsi] *adj* **sassier; -est** → **saucy**
sat → **sit**
Satan ['seɪtən] *n* : Satanás *m*, Satán *m*
satanic [sə'tænɪk, seɪ-] *adj* : satánico —
satanically [-nɪkli] *adv*
satchel ['sætʃəl] *n* : cartera *f*, saco *m*
sate ['seɪt] *vt* **sated; sating** : saciar
satellite ['sætəˌlaɪt] *n* : satélite *m* ⟨spy
satellite : satélite espía⟩
satiate ['seɪʃiˌeɪt] *vt* **-ated; -ating** : saciar,
hartar
satin ['sætən] *n* : raso *m*, satín *m*, satén
m
satire ['sæˌtaɪr] *n* : sátira *f*
satiric [sə'tɪrɪk] *or* **satirical** [-ɪkəl] *adj*
: satírico
satirize ['sætəˌraɪz] *vt* **-rized; -rizing**
: satirizar
satisfaction [ˌsætəs'fækʃən] *n* : satisfacción *f*
satisfactory [ˌsætəs'fæktəri] *adj* : satisfactorio, bueno — **satisfactorily** [-rəli]
adv
satisfy ['sætəsˌfaɪ] *v* **-fied; -fying** *vt* **1**
PLEASE : satisfacer, contentar **2** CONVINCE : convencer **3** FULFILL : satisfacer, cumplir con, llenar **4** SETTLE
: pagar, saldar (una cuenta) — *vi* SUFFICE : bastar

saturate ['sætʃəˌreɪt] *vt* **-rated; -rating 1**
SOAK : empapar **2** FILL : saturar
saturation [ˌsætʃə'reɪʃən] *n* : saturación
f
Saturday ['sætərˌdeɪ, -di] *n* : sábado *m*
Saturn ['sætərn] *n* : Saturno *m*
satyr ['seɪtər, 'sæ-] *n* : sátiro *m*
sauce ['sɔs] *n* : salsa *f*
saucepan ['sɔsˌpæn] *n* : cacerola *f*, cazo
m, cazuela *f*
saucer ['sɔsər] *n* : platillo *m*
sauciness ['sɔsinəs] *n* : descaro *m*, frescura *f*
saucy ['sɔsi] *adj* **saucier; -est** IMPUDENT : descarado, fresco *fam* — **saucily** *adv*
Saudi ['saʊdi, 'sɔ-] → **Saudi Arabian**
Saudi Arabian *n* : saudita *mf*, saudí *mf*
— **Saudi Arabian** *adj*
sauna ['sɔnə, 'saʊnə] *n* : sauna *mf*
saunter ['sɔntər, 'sɑn-] *vi* : pasear,
pasearse
sausage ['sɔsɪdʒ] *n* : salchicha *f*, embutido *m*
sauté [sɔ'teɪ, so:-] *vt* **-téed** *or* **-téd; -téing**
: saltear, sofreír
savage¹ ['sævɪdʒ] *adj* : salvaje, feroz —
savagely *adv*
savage² *n* : salvaje *mf*
savagery ['sævɪdʒri, -dʒəri] *n, pl* **-ries 1**
FEROCITY : ferocidad *f* **2** WILDNESS
: salvajismo *m*
savanna [sə'vænə] *n* : sabana *f*
save¹ ['seɪv] *vt* **saved; saving 1** RESCUE
: salvar, rescatar **2** PRESERVE : preservar, conservar **3** KEEP : guardar, ahorrar (dinero), almacenar (alimentos) **4**
: guardar (en informática)
save² *prep* EXCEPT : salvo, excepto,
menos
savior ['seɪvjər] *n* **1** : salvador *m*, -dora
f **2 the Savior** : el Salvador *m*
savor¹ ['seɪvər] *vt* : saborear
savor² *n* : sabor *m*
savory ['seɪvəri] *adj* : sabroso
saw¹ → **see**
saw² ['sɔ] *vt* **sawed; sawed** *or* **sawn**
['sɔn]; **sawing** : serrar, cortar (con sierra)
saw³ *n* : sierra *f*
sawdust ['sɔˌdʌst] *n* : aserrín *m*, serrín
m
sawhorse ['sɔˌhɔrs] *n* : caballete *m*, burro *m* (en carpintería)
sawmill ['sɔˌmɪl] *n* : aserradero *m*
saxophone ['sæksəˌfoːn] *n* : saxofón *m*
say¹ ['seɪ] *v* **said** ['sɛd]; **saying; says**
['sɛz] *vt* **1** EXPRESS, UTTER : decir, expresar ⟨to say no : decir que no⟩ ⟨that
goes without saying : ni que decir
tiene⟩ ⟨no sooner said than done : dicho y hecho⟩ ⟨to say again : repetir⟩
⟨to say one's prayers : rezar⟩ **2** INDICATE : marcar, poner ⟨my watch says
three o'clock : mi reloj marca las tres⟩
⟨what does the sign say? : ¿qué pone
el letrero?⟩ **3** ALLEGE : decir ⟨it's said
that she's pretty : se dice que es bonita⟩ — *vi* : decir

say² *n, pl* **says** ['seɪz] : voz *f*, opinión *f* ⟨to have no say : no tener ni voz ni voto⟩ ⟨to have one's say : dar uno su opinión⟩

saying ['seɪɪŋ] *n* : dicho *m*, refrán *m*

scab ['skæb] *n* **1** : costra *f*, postilla *f* (en una herida) **2** STRIKEBREAKER : rompehuelgas *mf*, esquirol *mf*

scabbard ['skæbərd] *n* : vaina *f* (de una espada), funda *f* (de un puñal, etc.)

scabby ['skæbi] *adj* **scabbier; -est** : lleno de costras

scaffold ['skæfəld, -ˌfoːld] *n* **1** *or* **scaffolding** : andamio *m* (para obreros, etc.) **2** : patíbulo *m*, cadalso *m* (para ejecuciones)

scald ['skɔld] *vt* **1** BURN : escaldar **2** HEAT : calentar (hasta el punto de ebullición)

scale¹ ['skeɪl] *v* **scaled; scaling** *vt* **1** : escamar (un pescado) **2** CLIMB : escalar (un muro, etc.) **3 to scale down** : reducir — *vi* WEIGH : pesar ⟨he scaled in at 200 pounds : pesó 200 libras⟩

scale² *n* **1** *or* **scales** : balanza *f*, báscula *f* (para pesar) **2** : escama *f* (de un pez, etc.) **3** EXTENT : escala *f*, proporción *f* ⟨wage scale : escala salarial⟩ **4** : escala *f* (en música, en cartografía, etc.) ⟨to draw to scale : dibujar a escala⟩

scallion ['skæljən] *n* : cebollino *m*, cebolleta *f*

scallop ['skɑləp, 'skæ-] *n* **1** : vieira *f* (molusco) **2** : festón *m* (decoración)

scalp¹ ['skælp] *vt* : arrancar la cabellera a

scalp² *n* : cuero *m* cabelludo

scalpel ['skælpəl] *n* : bisturí *m*, escalpelo *m*

scaly ['skeɪli] *adj* **scalier; -est** : escamoso

scam ['skæm] *n* : estafa *f*, timo *m fam*, chanchullo *m fam*

scamp ['skæmp] *n* : bribón *m*, -bona *f*; granuja *mf*; travieso *m*, -sa *f*

scamper ['skæmpər] *vi* : corretear

scan¹ ['skæn] *vt* **scanned; scanning 1** : escandir (versos) **2** SCRUTINIZE : escudriñar, escrutar ⟨to scan the horizon : escudriñar el horizonte⟩ **3** PERUSE : echarle un vistazo a (un periódico, etc.) **4** EXPLORE : explorar (con radar), hacer un escáner de (en ecografía) **5** : escanear (una imagen)

scan² *n* **1** : ecografía *f*, examen *m* ultrasónico (en medicina) **2** : imagen *f* escaneada (en una computadora)

scandal ['skændəl] *n* **1** DISGRACE, OUTRAGE : escándalo *m* **2** GOSSIP : habladurías *fpl*, chismes *mpl*

scandalize ['skændəlˌaɪz] *vt* **-ized; -izing** : escandalizar

scandalous ['skændələs] *adj* : de escándalo

Scandinavian¹ [ˌskændəˈneɪviən] *adj* : escandinavo

Scandinavian² *n* : escandinavo *m*, -va *f*

scanner ['skænər] *n* : escáner *m*, scanner *m*

scant ['skænt] *adj* : escaso

scanty ['skænti] *adj* **scantier; -est** : exiguo, escaso ⟨a scanty meal : una comida insuficiente⟩ — **scantily** [-təli] *adv*

scapegoat ['skeɪpˌgoːt] *n* : chivo *m* expiatorio, cabeza *f* de turco

scapula ['skæpjələ] *n, pl* **-lae** [-ˌliː, -ˌlaɪ] *or* **-las** → **shoulder blade**

scar¹ ['skɑr] *v* **scarred; scarring** *vt* : dejar una cicatriz en — *vi* : cicatrizar

scar² *n* : cicatriz *f*, marca *f*

scarab ['skærəb] *n* : escarabajo *m*

scarce ['skers] *adj* **scarcer; -est** : escaso

scarcely ['skersli] *adv* **1** BARELY : apenas **2** : ni mucho menos, ni nada que se le parezca ⟨he's scarcely an expert : ciertamente no es experto⟩

scarcity ['skersəti] *n, pl* **-ties** : escasez *f*

scare¹ ['sker] *vt* **scared; scaring** : asustar, espantar

scare² *n* **1** FRIGHT : susto *m*, sobresalto *m* **2** ALARM : pánico *m*

scarecrow ['skerˌkroː] *n* : espantapájaros *m*, espantajo *m*

scarf ['skɑrf] *n, pl* **scarves** ['skɑrvz] *or* **scarfs 1** MUFFLER : bufanda *f* **2** KERCHIEF : pañuelo *m*

scarlet ['skɑrlət] *n* : escarlata *f* — **scarlet** *adj*

scarlet fever *n* : escarlatina *f*

scary ['skeri] *adj* **scarier; -est** : espantoso, pavoroso

scathing ['skeɪðɪŋ] *adj* : mordaz, cáustico

scatter ['skætər] *vt* : esparcir, desparramar — *vi* DISPERSE : dispersarse

scavenge ['skævəndʒ] *v* **-venged; -venging** *vt* : rescatar (de la basura), pepenar *CA, Mex* — *vi* : rebuscar, hurgar en la basura ⟨to scavenge for food : andar buscando comida⟩

scavenger ['skævəndʒər] *n* **1** : persona *f* que rebusca en las basuras; pepenador *m*, -dora *f CA, Mex* **2** : carroñero *m*, -ra *f* (animal)

scenario [səˈnæriˌoː, -ˈnɑr-] *n, pl* **-ios 1** PLOT : argumento *m* (en teatro), guión *m* (en cine) **2** SITUATION : situación *f* hipotética ⟨in the worst-case scenario : en el peor de los casos⟩

scene ['siːn] *n* **1** : escena *f* (en una obra de teatro) **2** SCENERY : decorado *m* (en el teatro) **3** VIEW : escena *f* **4** LOCALE : escenario *m* **5** COMMOTION, FUSS : escándalo *m*, escena *f* ⟨to make a scene : armar un escándalo⟩

scenery ['siːnəri] *n, pl* **-eries 1** : decorado *m* (en el teatro) **2** LANDSCAPE : paisaje *m*

scenic ['siːnɪk] *adj* : pintoresco

scent¹ ['sent] *vt* **1** SMELL : oler, olfatear **2** PERFUME : perfumar **3** SENSE : sentir, percibir

scent² *n* **1** ODOR : olor *m*, aroma *m* **2** : olfato *m* ⟨a dog with a keen scent : un

perro con un buen olfato⟩ **3** PERFUME
: perfume *m*
scented ['sɛntəd] *adj* : perfumado
scepter ['sɛptər] *n* : cetro *m*
sceptic ['skɛptɪk] → **skeptic**
schedule[1] ['skɛˌd͡ʒuːl, -d͡ʒəl, *esp Brit*
'ʃɛdˌjuːl] *vt* **-uled; -uling** : planear, programar
schedule[2] *n* **1** PLAN : programa *m*, plan
m ⟨on schedule : según lo previsto⟩
⟨behind schedule : atrasado, con re-
traso⟩ **2** TIMETABLE : horario *m*
scheme[1] ['skiːm] *vi* **schemed; schem-
ing** : intrigar, conspirar
scheme[2] *n* **1** PLAN : plan *m*, proyecto
m **2** PLOT, TRICK : intriga *f*, ardid *m* **3**
FRAMEWORK : esquema *f* ⟨a color
scheme : una combinación de colores⟩
schemer ['skiːmər] *n* : intrigante *mf*
schism ['sɪzəm, 'skɪ-] *n* : cisma *m*
schizophrenia [ˌskɪtsəˈfriːniə, ˌskɪzə-,
-ˈfrɛ-] *n* : esquizofrenia *f*
schizophrenic [ˌskɪtsəˈfrɛnɪk, ˌskɪzə-] *n*
: esquizofrénico *m*, -ca *f* — **schizophrenic** *adj*
scholar ['skɑlər] *n* **1** STUDENT : escolar
mf; alumno *m*, -na *f* **2** EXPERT : especialista *mf*
scholarly ['skɑlərli] *adj* : erudito
scholarship ['skɑlərˌʃɪp] *n* **1** LEARNING
: erudición *f* **2** GRANT : beca *f*
scholastic [skəˈlæstɪk] *adj* : académico
school[1] ['skuːl] *vt* : instruir, enseñar
school[2] *n* **1** : escuela *f*, colegio *m* (institución) **2** : estudiantes *mfpl* y pro-
fesores *mpl* (de una escuela) **3** : escuela
f (en pintura, etc.) ⟨the Flemish school
: la escuela flamenca⟩ **4 school of fish**
: banco *m*, cardumen *m*
schoolboy ['skuːlˌbɔɪ] *n* : escolar *m*,
colegial *m*
schoolgirl ['skuːlˌgərl] *n* : escolar *f*, cole-
giala *f*
schoolhouse ['skuːlˌhaʊs] *n* : escuela *f*
schoolmate ['skuːlˌmeɪt] *n* : compañero
m, -ra *f* de escuela
schoolroom ['skuːlˌruːm, -ˌrʊm] →
classroom
schoolteacher ['skuːlˌtiːt͡ʃər] *n* : maestro
m, -tra *f*; profesor *m*, -sora *f*
schoolwork ['skuːlˌwərk] *n* : trabajo *m*
escolar
schooner ['skuːnər] *n* : goleta *f*
science ['saɪənts] *n* : ciencia *f*
science fiction *n* : ciencia ficción *f*
scientific [ˌsaɪənˈtɪfɪk] *adj* : científico —
scientifically [-fɪkli] *adv*
scientist ['saɪəntɪst] *n* : científico *m*, -ca
f
scintillating ['sɪntəˌleɪtɪŋ] *adj* : chispeante, brillante
scissors ['sɪzərz] *npl* : tijeras *fpl*
sclerosis [skləˈroːsəs] *n, pl* **-roses** : esclerosis *f*
scoff ['skɑf] *vi* **to scoff at** : burlarse de,
mofarse de
scold ['skoːld] *vt* : regañar, reprender,
reñir

scoop[1] ['skuːp] *vt* **1** : sacar (con pala o
cucharón) **2 to scoop out** HOLLOW
: vaciar, ahuecar
scoop[2] *n* : pala *f* (para harina, etc.),
cucharón *m* (para helado, etc.)
scoot ['skuːt] *vi* : ir rápidamente ⟨she
scooted around the corner : volvió la
esquina a toda prisa⟩
scooter ['skuːt̬ər] *n* : patineta *f*,
monopatín *m*, patinete *m*
scope ['skoːp] *n* **1** RANGE : alcance *m*,
ámbito *m*, extensión *f* **2** OPPORTUNI-
TY : posibilidades *fpl*, libertad *f*
scorch ['skɔrt͡ʃ] *vt* : chamuscar, quemar
score[1] ['skor] *v* **scored; scoring** *vt* **1**
RECORD : anotar **2** MARK, SCRATCH
: marcar, rayar **3** : marcar, meter (en
deportes) **4** GAIN : ganar, apuntarse **5**
GRADE : calificar (exámenes, etc.) **6**
: instrumentar, orquestar (música) —
vi **1** : marcar (en deportes) **2** : obtener una puntuación (en un examen)
score[2] *n, pl* **scores** **1** *or pl* **score** TWEN-
TY : veintena *f* **2** LINE, SCRATCH : línea
f, marca *f* **3** : resultado *m* (en deportes)
⟨what's the score? : ¿cómo va el marcador?⟩ **4** GRADE, POINTS : calificación *f* (en un examen), puntuación *f*
(en un concurso) **5** ACCOUNT : cuenta *f* ⟨to settle a score : ajustar una cuen-
ta⟩ ⟨on that score : a ese respecto⟩ **6**
: partitura *f* (musical)
scorn[1] ['skɔrn] *vt* : despreciar, menospreciar, desdeñar
scorn[2] *n* : desprecio *m*, menosprecio *m*,
desdén *m*
scornful ['skɔrnfəl] *adj* : desdeñoso, despreciativo — **scornfully** *adv*
Scorpio ['skɔrpiˌoː] *n* : Escorpio *mf*, Escorpión *mf*
scorpion ['skɔrpiən] *n* : alacrán *m*, escorpión *m*
Scot ['skɑt] *n* : escocés *m*, -cesa *f*
Scotch[1] ['skɑt͡ʃ] *adj* → **Scottish**[1]
Scotch[2] *npl* **the Scotch** : los escoceses
scot–free ['skɑt'friː] *adj* **to get off
scot–free** : salir impune, quedar sin
castigo
Scots ['skɑts] *n* : escocés *m* (idioma)
Scottish[1] ['skɑt̬ɪʃ] *adj* : escocés
Scottish[2] *n* → **Scots**
scoundrel ['skaʊndrəl] *n* : sinvergüenza
mf; bellaco *m*, -ca *f*
scour ['skaʊər] *vt* **1** EXAMINE, SEARCH
: registrar (un área), revisar (documentos, etc.) **2** SCRUB : fregar, restregar
scourge[1] ['skərd͡ʒ] *vt* **scourged; scourg-
ing** : azotar
scourge[2] *n* : azote *m*
scout[1] ['skaʊt] *vi* **1** RECONNOITER : reconocer **2 to scout around for** : explorar en busca de
scout[2] *n* **1** : explorador *m*, -dora *f* **2** *or*
talent scout : cazatalentos *mf*
scow ['skaʊ] *n* : barcaza *f*, gabarra *f*
scowl[1] ['skaʊl] *vi* : fruncir el ceño
scowl[2] *n* : ceño *m* fruncido

scram ['skræm] *vi* **scrammed; scramming** : largarse

scramble¹ ['skræmbəl] *v* **-bled; -bling** *vi* **1** : trepar, gatear (con torpeza) ⟨he scrambled over the fence : se trepó a la cerca con dificultad⟩ **2** STRUGGLE : pelearse (por) ⟨they scrambled for seats : se pelearon por los asientos⟩ — *vt* **1** JUMBLE : mezclar **2 to scramble eggs** : hacer huevos revueltos

scramble² *n* : rebatiña *f*, pelea *f*

scrap¹ ['skræp] *v* **scrapped; scrapping** *vt* DISCARD : desechar — *vi* FIGHT : pelearse

scrap² *n* **1** FRAGMENT : pedazo *m*, trozo *m* **2** FIGHT : pelea *f* **3** *or* **scrap metal** : chatarra *f* **4 scraps** *npl* LEFTOVERS : restos *mpl*, sobras *fpl*

scrapbook ['skræp,bʊk] *n* : álbum *m* de recortes

scrape¹ ['skreɪp] *v* **scraped; scraping** *vt* **1** GRAZE, SCRATCH : rozar, rascar ⟨to scrape one's knee : rasparse la rodilla⟩ **2** CLEAN : raspar ⟨to scrape carrots : raspar zanahorias⟩ **3 to scrape off** : raspar (pintura, etc.) **4 to scrape up** *or* **to scrape together** : juntar, reunir poco a poco — *vi* **1** RUB : rozar **2 to scrape by** : arreglárselas, ir tirando

scrape² *n* **1** SCRAPING : raspadura *f* **2** SCRATCH : rasguño *m* **3** PREDICAMENT : apuro *m*, aprieto *m*

scratch¹ ['skrætʃ] *vt* **1** : arañar, rasguñar ⟨to scratch an itch : rascarse⟩ **2** MARK : rayar, marcar **3 to scratch out** : tachar

scratch² *n* **1** : rasguño *m*, arañazo *m* (en la piel), rayón *m* (en un mueble, etc.) **2** : sonido *m* rasposo ⟨I heard a scratch at the door : oí como que raspaban a la puerta⟩

scratchy ['skrætʃi] *adj* **scratchier; -est** : áspero, que pica ⟨a scratchy sweater : un suéter que pica⟩

scrawl¹ ['skrɔl] *v* : garabatear

scrawl² *n* : garabato *m*

scrawny ['skrɔni] *adj* **scrawnier; -est** : flaco, escuálido

scream¹ ['skriːm] *vi* : chillar, gritar

scream² *n* : chillido *m*, grito *m*

screech¹ ['skriːtʃ] *vi* : chillar (dícese de las personas o de los animales), chirriar (dícese de los frenos, etc.)

screech² *n* **1** : chillido *m*, grito *m* (de una persona o un animal) **2** : chirrido *m* (de frenos, etc.)

screen¹ ['skriːn] *vt* **1** SHIELD : proteger **2** CONCEAL : tapar, ocultar **3** EXAMINE : someter a una revisión, hacerle un chequeo (a un paciente) **4** SIEVE : cribar

screen² *n* **1** PARTITION : biombo *m*, pantalla *f* **2** SIEVE : criba *f* **3** : pantalla *f* (de un televisor, una computadora, etc.) **4** MOVIES : cine *m* **5** *or* **window screen** : ventana *f* de tela metálica

screenplay ['skriːn,pleɪ] *n* SCRIPT : guión *m*

screw¹ ['skruː] *vt* : atornillar — *vi* **1 to screw in** : atornillarse **2 to screw up** *fam* : meter la pata

screw² *n* **1** : tornillo *m* (para fijar algo) **2** TWIST : vuelta *f* **3** PROPELLER : hélice *f*

screwdriver ['skruː,draɪvər] *n* : destornillador *m*, desarmador *m* *Mex*

scribble¹ ['skrɪbəl] *v* **-bled; -bling** : garabatear

scribble² *n* : garabato *m*

scribe ['skraɪb] *n* : escriba *m*

scrimmage ['skrɪmɪdʒ] *n* : escaramuza *f*

scrimp ['skrɪmp] *vi* **1 to scrimp on** : escatimar **2 to scrimp and save** : hacer economías

script ['skrɪpt] *n* **1** HANDWRITING : letra *f*, escritura *f* **2** : guión *m* (de una película, etc.)

scriptural ['skrɪptʃərəl] *adj* : bíblico

scripture ['skrɪptʃər] *n* **1** : escritos *mpl* sagrados (de una religión) **2 the Scriptures** *npl* : las Sagradas Escrituras

scriptwriter ['skrɪpt,raɪtər] *n* : guionista *mf*, libretista *mf*

scroll ['skroːl] *n* **1** : rollo *m* (de pergamino, etc.) **2** : voluta *f* (adorno en arquitectura)

scrotum ['skroːtəm] *n, pl* **scrota** [-tə] *or* **scrotums** : escroto *m*

scrounge ['skraʊndʒ] *v* **scrounged; scrounging** *vt* **1** BUM : gorrear *fam*, sablear *fam* (dinero) **2 to scrounge around for** : buscar, andar a la busca de — *vi* **to scrounge off someone** : vivir a costa de alguien

scrub¹ ['skrʌb] *vt* **scrubbed; scrubbing** : restregar, fregar

scrub² *n* **1** THICKET, UNDERBRUSH : maleza *f*, matorral *m*, matorrales *mpl* **2** SCRUBBING : fregado *m*, restregadura *f*

scrubby ['skrʌbi] *adj* **-bier; -est 1** STUNTED : achaparrado **2** : cubierto de maleza

scruff ['skrʌf] *n* **by the scruff of the neck** : por el cogote, por el pescuezo

scrumptious ['skrʌmpʃəs] *adj* : delicioso, muy rico

scruple ['skruːpəl] *n* : escrúpulo *m*

scrupulous ['skruːpjələs] *adj* : escrupuloso — **scrupulously** *adv*

scrutinize ['skruːtən,aɪz] *vt* **-nized; -nizing** : escrutar, escudriñar

scrutiny ['skruːtəni] *n, pl* **-nies** : escrutinio *m*, inspección *f*

scuba ['skuːbə] *n* **1** *or* **scuba gear** : equipo *m* de submarinismo **2 scuba diver** : submarinista *mf* **3 scuba diving** : submarinismo *m*

scuff ['skʌf] *vt* : rayar, raspar ⟨to scuff one's feet : arrastrar los pies⟩

scuffle¹ ['skʌfəl] *vi* **-fled; -fling 1** TUSSLE : pelearse **2** SHUFFLE : caminar arrastrando los pies

scuffle² *n* **1** TUSSLE : refriega *f*, pelea *f* **2** SHUFFLE : arrastre *m* de los pies

scull¹ ['skʌl] *vi* : remar (con espadilla)

scull[2] *n* OAR : espadilla *f*
sculpt ['skʌlpt] *v* : esculpir
sculptor ['skʌlptər] *n* : escultor *m*, -tora *f*
sculptural ['skʌlptʃərəl] *adj* : escultórico
sculpture[1] ['skʌlptʃər] *vt* **-tured; -turing** : esculpir
sculpture[2] *n* : escultura *f*
scum ['skʌm] *n* **1** FROTH : espuma *f*, nata *f* **2** : verdín *m* (encima de un líquido)
scurrilous ['skərələs] *adj* : difamatorio, calumnioso, injurioso
scurry ['skəri] *vi* **-ried; -rying** : corretear
scurvy ['skəri] *n* : escorbuto *m*
scuttle[1] ['skʌtəl] *v* **-tled; -tling** *vt* : hundir (un barco) — *vi* SCAMPER : corretear
scuttle[2] *n* : cubo *m* (para carbón)
scythe ['saɪð] *n* : guadaña *f*
sea[1] ['si:] *adj* : del mar
sea[2] *n* **1** : mar *mf* ⟨the Black Sea : el Mar Negro⟩ ⟨on the high seas : en alta mar⟩ ⟨heavy seas : mar gruesa, mar agitada⟩ **2** MASS : mar *m*, multitud *f* ⟨a sea of faces : un mar de rostros⟩
seabird ['si:,bərd] *n* : ave *f* marina
seaboard ['si:,bord] *n* : litoral *m*
seacoast ['si:,ko:st] *n* : costa *f*, litoral *m*
seafarer ['si:,færər] *n* : marinero *m*
seafaring[1] ['si:,færɪŋ] *adj* : marinero
seafaring[2] *n* : navegación *f*
seafood ['si:,fu:d] *n* : mariscos *mpl*
seagull ['si:,gʌl] *n* : gaviota *f*
sea horse ['si:,hɔrs] *n* : hipocampo *m*, caballito *m* de mar
seal[1] ['si:l] *vt* **1** CLOSE : sellar, cerrar ⟨to seal a letter : cerrar una carta⟩ ⟨to seal an agreement : sellar un acuerdo⟩ **2 to seal up** : tapar, rellenar (una grieta, etc.)
seal[2] *n* **1** : foca *f* (animal) **2** : sello *m* ⟨seal of approval : sello de aprobación⟩ **3** CLOSURE : cierre *m*, precinto *m*
sea level *n* : nivel *m* del mar
sea lion *n* : león *m* marino
sealskin ['si:l,skɪn] *n* : piel *f* de foca
seam[1] ['si:m] *vt* **1** STITCH : unir con costuras **2** MARK : marcar
seam[2] *n* **1** STITCHING : costura *f* **2** LODE, VEIN : veta *f*, filón *m*
seaman ['si:mən] *n, pl* **-men** [-mən, -,mɛn] **1** SAILOR : marinero *m* **2** : marino *m* (en la armada)
seamless ['si:mləs] *adj* **1** : sin costuras, de una pieza **2** : perfecto ⟨a seamless transition : una transición fluida⟩
seamstress ['si:mpstrəs] *n* : costurera *f*
seamy ['si:mi] *adj* **seamier; -est** : sórdido
séance ['seɪ,ɑnts] *n* : sesión *f* de espiritismo
seaplane ['si:,pleɪn] *n* : hidroavión *m*
seaport ['si:,port] *n* : puerto *m* marítimo
sear ['sɪr] *vt* **1** PARCH, WITHER : secar, resecar **2** SCORCH : chamuscar, quemar

search[1] ['sərtʃ] *vt* : registrar (un edificio, un área), cachear (a una persona), buscar en — *vi* **to search for** : buscar
search[2] *n* : búsqueda *f*, registro *m* (de un edificio, etc.), cacheo *m* (de una persona)
searchlight ['sərtʃ,laɪt] *n* : reflector *m*
seashell ['si:,ʃɛl] *n* : concha *f* (marina)
seashore ['si:,ʃor] *n* : orilla *f* del mar
seasick ['si:,sɪk] *adj* : mareado ⟨to get seasick : marearse⟩
seasickness ['si:,sɪknəs] *n* : mareo *m*
seaside → **seacoast**
season[1] ['si:zən] *vt* **1** FLAVOR, SPICE : sazonar, condimentar **2** CURE : curar, secar ⟨seasoned wood : madera seca⟩ ⟨a seasoned veteran : un veterano avezado⟩
season[2] *n* **1** : estación *f* (del año) **2** : temporada *f* (en deportes, etc.) ⟨baseball season : temporada de beisbol⟩
seasonable ['si:zənəbəl] *adj* **1** : propio de la estación (dícese del tiempo, de las temperaturas, etc.) **2** TIMELY : oportuno
seasonal ['si:zənəl] *adj* : estacional — **seasonally** *adv*
seasoning ['si:zənɪŋ] *n* : condimento *m*, sazón *f*
seat[1] ['si:t] *vt* **1** SIT : sentar ⟨please be seated : siéntense, por favor⟩ **2** HOLD : tener cabida para ⟨the stadium seats 40,000 : el estadio tiene 40,000 asientos⟩
seat[2] *n* **1** : asiento *m*, plaza *f* (en un vehículo) ⟨take a seat : tome asiento⟩ **2** BOTTOM : fondillos *mpl* (de la ropa), trasero *m* (del cuerpo) **3** : sede *f* (de un gobierno, etc.)
seat belt *n* : cinturón *m* de seguridad
sea urchin *n* : erizo *m* de mar
seawall ['si:,wɑl] *n* : rompeolas *m*, dique *m* marítimo
seawater ['si:,wɔtər, -,wɑ-] *n* : agua *f* de mar
seaweed ['si:,wi:d] *n* : alga *f* marina
seaworthy ['si:,wərði] *adj* : en condiciones de navegar
secede [sɪ'si:d] *vi* **-ceded; -ceding** : separarse (de una nación, etc.)
seclude [sɪ'klu:d] *vt* **-cluded; -cluding** : aislar
seclusion [sɪ'klu:ʒən] *n* : aislamiento *m*
second[1] ['sɛkənd] *vt* : secundar, apoyar (una moción)
second[2] *or* **secondly** ['sɛkəndli] *adv* : en segundo lugar
second[3] *adj* : segundo
second[4] *n* **1** : segundo *m*, -da *f* (en una serie) **2** : segundo *m*, ayudante *m* (en deportes) **3** MOMENT : segundo *m*, momento *m*
secondary ['sɛkən,dri] *adj* : secundario
secondhand ['sɛkənd'hænd] *adj* : de segunda mano
second lieutenant *n* : alférez *mf*, subteniente *mf*
second–rate ['sɛkənd'reɪt] *adj* : mediocre, de segunda categoría

secrecy ['si:krəsi] *n, pl* **-cies** : secreto *m*
secret[1] ['si:krət] *adj* : secreto — **secretly** *adv*
secret[2] *n* : secreto *m*
secretarial [ˌsɛkrə'triəl] *adj* : de secretario, de oficina
secretariat [ˌsɛkrə'triət] *n* : secretaría *f*,
secretariado *m*
secretary ['sɛkrəˌtri] *n, pl* **-taries** 1 : secretario *m*, -ria *f* (en una oficina, etc.) 2
: ministro *m*, -tra *f*; secretario *m*, -ria *f*
⟨Secretary of State : Secretario de
Estado⟩
secrete [si'kri:t] *vt* **-creted; -creting** 1
: secretar, segregar (en fisiología) 2
HIDE : ocultar
secretion [si'kri:ʃən] *n* : secreción *f*
secretive ['si:krətɪv, si'kri:tɪv] *adj*
: reservado, callado, secreto
sect ['sɛkt] *n* : secta *f*
sectarian [sɛk'triən] *adj* : sectario
section ['sɛkʃən] *n* : sección *f*, parte *f* (de
un mueble, etc.), sector *m* (de la
población), barrio *m* (de una ciudad)
sectional ['sɛkʃənəl] *adj* 1 : en sección,
en corte ⟨a sectional diagram : un gráfico en corte⟩ 2 FACTIONAL : de grupo,
entre facciones 3 : modular ⟨section-
al furniture : muebles modulares⟩
sector ['sɛktər] *n* : sector *m*
secular ['sɛkjələr] *adj* 1 : secular, laico
⟨secular life : la vida secular⟩ 2 : seglar
(dícese de los sacerdotes, etc.)
secure[1] [si'kjur] *vt* **-cured; -curing** 1
FASTEN : asegurar (una puerta, etc.),
sujetar 2 GET : conseguir
secure[2] *adj* **-curer; -est** : seguro — **securely** *adv*
security [si'kjurəti] *n, pl* **-ties** 1 SAFETY
: seguridad *f* 2 GUARANTEE : garantía
f 3 **securities** *npl* : valores *mpl*
sedan [si'dæn] *n* 1 *or* **sedan chair** : silla *f* de manos 2 : sedán *m* (automóvil)
sedate[1] [si'deɪt] *vt* **-dated; -dating**
: sedar
sedate[2] *adj* : sosegado — **sedately** *adv*
sedation [si'deɪʃən] *n* : sedación *f*
sedative[1] ['sɛdətɪv] *adj* : sedante
sedative[2] *n* : sedante *m*, calmante *m*
sedentary ['sɛdənˌteri] *adj* : sedentario
sedge ['sɛdʒ] *n* : juncia *f*
sediment ['sɛdəmənt] *n* : sedimento *m*
(geológico), poso *m* (en un líquido)
sedimentary [ˌsɛdə'mɛntəri] *adj* : sedimentario
sedition [si'dɪʃən] *n* : sedición *f*
seditious [si'dɪʃəs] *adj* : sedicioso
seduce [si'du:s, -'dju:s] *vt* **-duced; -duc-
ing** : seducir
seduction [si'dʌkʃən] *n* : seducción *f*
seductive [si'dʌktɪv] *adj* : seductor, seductivo
see[1] ['si:] *v* **saw** ['sɔ]; **seen** ['si:n]; **seeing** *vt* 1 : ver ⟨I saw a dog : vi un per-
ro⟩ ⟨see you later! : ¡hasta luego!⟩ 2
EXPERIENCE : ver, conocer 3 UNDER-
STAND : ver, entender 4 ENSURE : asegurarse ⟨see that it's correct : asegúrese

de que sea correcto⟩ 5 ACCOMPANY
: acompañar 6 **to see off** : despedir,
despedirse de — *vi* 1 : ver ⟨seeing is
believing : ver para creer⟩ 2 UNDER-
STAND : entender, ver ⟨now I see! : ¡ya
entiendo!⟩ 3 CONSIDER : ver ⟨let's see
: vamos a ver⟩ 4 **to see to** : ocuparse
de
see[2] *n* : sede *f* ⟨the Holy See : la Santa
Sede⟩
seed[1] ['si:d] *vt* 1 SOW : sembrar 2 : despepitar, quitarle las semillas a
seed[2] *n, pl* **seed** *or* **seeds** 1 : semilla *f*,
pepita *f* (de una fruta) 2 SOURCE : ger-
men *m*, semilla *f*
seedless ['si:dləs] *adj* : sin semillas
seedling ['si:dlɪŋ] *n* : plantón *m*
seedpod ['si:dˌpad] → **pod**
seedy ['si:di] *adj* **seedier; -est** 1 : lleno
de semillas 2 SHABBY : raído (dícese
de la ropa) 3 RUN-DOWN : ruinoso
(dícese de los edificios, etc.), sórdido
seek ['si:k] *v* **sought** ['sɔt]; **seeking** *vt* 1
: buscar ⟨to seek an answer : buscar
una solución⟩ 2 REQUEST : solicitar,
pedir 3 **to seek to** : tratar de, intentar
de — *vi* SEARCH : buscar
seem ['si:m] *vi* : parecer
seeming ['si:mɪŋ] *adj* : aparente, ostensible
seemingly ['si:mɪŋli] *adv* : aparentemente, según parece
seemly ['si:mli] *adj* **seemlier; -est**
: apropiado, decoroso
seep ['si:p] *vi* : filtrarse
seer ['si:ər] *n* : vidente *mf*, clarividente
mf
seesaw[1] ['si:ˌsɔ] *vi* 1 : jugar en un
subibaja 2 VACILLATE : vacilar, oscilar
seesaw[2] *n* : balancín *m*, subibaja *m*
seethe ['si:ð] *vi* **seethed; seething** 1
: bullir, hervir 2 **to seethe with anger**
: rabiar, estar furioso
segment ['sɛgmənt] *n* : segmento *m*
segmented ['sɛgˌmɛntəd, sɛg'mɛn-] *adj*
: segmentado
segregate ['sɛgrɪˌgeɪt] *vt* **-gated; -gating**
: segregar
segregation [ˌsɛgrɪ'geɪʃən] *n* : segregación *f*
seismic ['saɪzmɪk, 'saɪs-] *adj* : sísmico
seize ['si:z] *v* **seized; seizing** *vt* 1 CAP-
TURE : capturar, tomar, apoderarse de
2 ARREST : detener 3 CLUTCH, GRAB
: agarrar, coger, aprovechar (una oportunidad) 4 **to be seized with** : estar so-
brecogido por — *vi or* **to seize up**
: agarrotarse
seizure ['si:ʒər] *n* 1 CAPTURE : toma *f*,
captura *f* 2 ARREST : detención *f* 3
: ataque *m* ⟨an epileptic seizure : un
ataque epiléptico⟩
seldom ['sɛldəm] *adv* : pocas veces, rara
vez, casi nunca
select[1] [sə'lɛkt] *vt* : escoger, elegir, seleccionar (a un candidato, etc.)
select[2] *adj* : selecto
selection [sə'lɛkʃən] *n* : selección *f*, elección *f*

selective [sə'lɛktɪv] *adj* : selectivo
selenium [sə'li:niəm] *n* : selenio *m*
self ['sɛlf] *n, pl* **selves** ['sɛlvz] **1** : ser *m*, persona *f* ⟨the self : el yo⟩ ⟨with his whole self : con todo su ser⟩ ⟨her own self : su propia persona⟩ **2** SIDE : lado (de la personalidad) ⟨his better self : su lado bueno⟩
self–addressed [ˌsɛlfə'drst] *adj* : con la dirección del remitente ⟨include a self-addressed envelope : incluya un sobre con su nombre y dirección⟩
self–appointed [ˌsɛlfə'pɔɪntəd] *adj* : autoproclamado, autonombrado
self–assurance [ˌsɛlfə'ʃurənts] *n* : seguridad *f* en sí mismo
self–assured [ˌsɛlfə'ʃurd] *adj* : seguro de sí mismo
self–centered [ˌsɛlf'sɛntərd] *adj* : egocéntrico
self–confidence [ˌsɛlf'kɑnfədənts] *n* : confianza *f* en sí mismo
self–confident [ˌsɛlf'kɑnfədənt] *adj* : seguro de sí mismo
self–conscious [ˌsɛlf'kɑntʃəs] *adj* : cohibido, tímido
self–consciously [ˌsɛlf'kɑntʃəsli] *adv* : de manera cohibida
self–consciousness [ˌsɛlf'kɑntʃəsnəs] *n* : vergüenza *f*, timidez *f*
self–contained [ˌsɛlfkən'teɪnd] *adj* **1** INDEPENDENT : independiente **2** RESERVED : reservado
self–control [ˌsɛlfkən'tro:l] *n* : autocontrol *m*, control *m* de sí mismo
self–defense [ˌsɛlfdɪ'fɛnts] *n* : defensa *f* propia, defensa *f* personal ⟨to act in self-defense : actuar en defensa propia⟩ ⟨self-defense class : clase de defensa personal⟩
self–denial [ˌsɛlfdɪ'naɪəl] *n* : abnegación *f*
self–destructive [ˌsɛlfdɪ'strʌktɪv] *adj* : autodestructivo
self–determination [ˌsɛlfdɪˌtərmə'neɪʃən] *n* : autodeterminación *f*
self–discipline [ˌsɛlf'dɪsəplən] *n* : autodisciplina *f*
self–employed [ˌsɛlfɪm'plɔɪd] *adj* : que trabaja por cuenta propia, autónomo
self–esteem [ˌsɛlfɪ'sti:m] *n* : autoestima *f*, amor *m* propio
self–evident [ˌsɛlf'ɛvədənt] *adj* : evidente, manifiesto
self–explanatory [ˌsɛlfɪk'splænəˌtori] *adj* : fácil de entender, evidente
self–expression [ˌsɛlfɪk'sprʃən] *n* : expresión *f* personal
self–government [ˌsɛlf'gʌvərmənt, -vərn-] *n* : autogobierno *m*
self–help [ˌsɛlf'hɛlp] *n* : autoayuda *f*
self–important [ˌsɛlfɪm'pɔrtənt] *adj* **1** VAIN : vanidoso, presumido **2** ARROGANT : arrogante
self–indulgent [ˌsɛlfɪn'dʌldʒənt] *adj* : que se permite excesos
self–inflicted [ˌsɛlfɪn'flɪktəd] *adj* : autoinfligido

self–interest [ˌsɛlf'ɪntrəst, -təˌrst] *n* : interés *m* personal
selfish ['sɛlfɪʃ] *adj* : egoísta
selfishly ['sɛlfɪʃli] *adv* : de manera egoísta
selfishness ['sɛlfɪʃnəs] *n* : egoísmo *m*
selfless ['sɛlfləs] *adj* UNSELFISH : desinteresado
self–made [ˌsɛlf'meɪd] *adj* : próspero gracias a sus propios esfuerzos
self–pity [ˌsɛlf'pɪt̬i] *n, pl* **-ties** : autocompasión *f*
self–portrait [ˌsɛlf'pɔrtrət] *n* : autorretrato *m*
self–propelled [ˌsɛlfpro'pɛld] *adj* : autopropulsado
self–reliance [ˌsɛlfri'laɪənts] *n* : independencia *f*, autosuficiencia *f*
self–respect [ˌsɛlfri'spɛkt] *n* : autoestima *f*, amor *m* propio
self–restraint [ˌsɛlfri'streɪnt] *n* : autocontrol *m*, moderación *f*
self–righteous [ˌsɛlf'raɪtʃəs] *adj* : santurrón, moralista
self–sacrifice [ˌsɛlf'sækrəˌfaɪs] *n* : abnegación *f*
selfsame ['sɛlfˌseɪm] *adj* : mismo
self–service [ˌsɛlf'sərvɪs] *adj* **1** : de autoservicio **2 self-service restaurant** : autoservicio *m*
self–sufficiency [ˌsɛlfsə'fɪʃəntsi] *n* : autosuficiencia *f*
self–sufficient [ˌsɛlfsə'fɪʃənt] *adj* : autosuficiente
self–taught [ˌsɛlf'tɔt] *adj* : autodidacta
sell ['sɛl] *v* **sold** ['so:ld]; **selling** *vt* : vender — *vi* : venderse
seller ['sɛlər] *n* : vendedor *m*, -dora *f*
selves → **self**
semantic [sɪ'mæntɪk] *adj* : semántico
semantics [sɪ'mæntɪks] *ns & pl* : semántica *f*
semaphore ['sɛməˌfor] *n* : semáforo *m*
semblance ['sɛmblənts] *n* : apariencia *f*
semen ['si:mən] *n* : semen *m*
semester [sə'mɛstər] *n* : semestre *m*
semicolon ['sɛmiˌko:lən, 'sɛˌmaɪ-] *n* : punto y coma *m*
semiconductor ['sɛmikənˌdʌktər, 'sɛˌmaɪ-] *n* : semiconductor *m*
semifinal ['sɛmiˌfaɪnəl, 'sɛˌmaɪ-] *n* : semifinal *f*
seminar ['sɛməˌnar] *n* : seminario *m*
seminary ['sɛməˌnɛri] *n, pl* **-naries** : seminario *m*
Semitic [sə'mɪt̬ɪk] *adj* : semita
senate ['sɛnət] *n* : senado *m*
senator ['sɛnət̬ər] *n* : senador *m*, -dora *f*
send ['sɛnd] *vt* **sent** ['sɛnt]; **sending 1** : mandar, enviar ⟨to send a letter : mandar una carta⟩ ⟨to send word : avisar, mandar decir⟩ **2** PROPEL : mandar, lanzar ⟨he sent it into left field : lo mandó al jardín izquierdo⟩ ⟨to send up dust : alzar polvo⟩ **3 to send into a rage** : poner furioso
sender ['sɛndər] *n* : remitente *mf* (de una carta, etc.)

Senegalese [ˌsɛnəgəˈliːz, -ˈliːs] n : senegalés m, -lesa f — **Senegalese** adj
senile [ˈsiːˌnaɪl] adj : senil
senility [sɪˈnɪləti] n : senilidad f
senior[1] [ˈsiːnjər] adj **1** ELDER : mayor ⟨John Doe, Senior : John Doe, padre⟩ **2** : superior (en rango), más antiguo (en años de servicio) ⟨a senior official : un alto oficial⟩
senior[2] n **1** : superior m (en rango) **2 to be someone's senior** : ser mayor que alguien ⟨she's two years my senior : me lleva dos años⟩
senior citizen n : persona f de la tercera edad
seniority [ˌsiːˈnjɔrəti] n : antigüedad f (en años de servicio)
sensation [sɛnˈseɪʃən] n : sensación f
sensational [sɛnˈseɪʃənəl] adj : que causa sensación ⟨sensational stories : historias sensacionalistas⟩
sense[1] [ˈsɛnts] vt **sensed; sensing** : sentir ⟨he sensed danger : se dio cuenta del peligro⟩
sense[2] n **1** MEANING : sentido m, significado m **2** : sentido m ⟨the sense of smell : el sentido del olfato⟩ **3 to make sense** : tener sentido
senseless [ˈsɛntsləs] adj **1** MEANINGLESS : sin sentido, sin razón **2** UNCONSCIOUS : inconsciente
senselessly [ˈsɛntsləsli] adv : sin sentido
sensibility [ˌsɛntsəˈbɪləti] n, pl **-ties** : sensibilidad f
sensible [ˈsɛntsəbəl] adj **1** PERCEPTIBLE : sensible, perceptible **2** AWARE : consciente **3** REASONABLE : sensato ⟨a sensible man : un hombre sensato⟩ ⟨sensible shoes : zapatos prácticos⟩ — **sensibly** [-bli] adv
sensibleness [ˈsɛntsəbəlnəs] n : sensatez f, solidez f
sensitive [ˈsɛntsəṭɪv] adj **1** : sensible, delicado ⟨sensitive skin : piel sensible⟩ **2** IMPRESSIONABLE : sensible, impresionable **3** TOUCHY : susceptible
sensitiveness [ˈsɛntsəṭɪvnəs] → **sensitivity**
sensitivity [ˌsɛntsəˈtɪvəti] n, pl **-ties** : sensibilidad f
sensitize [ˈsɛntsəˌtaɪz] vt **-tized; -tizing** : sensibilizar
sensor [ˈsɛnˌsɔr, ˈsɛntsər] n : sensor m
sensory [ˈsɛntsəri] adj : sensorial
sensual [ˈsɛnʃuəl] adj : sensual — **sensually** adv
sensuality [ˌsɛntʃəˈwæləti] n, pl **-ties** : sensualidad f
sensuous [ˈsɛnʃuəs] adj : sensual
sent → **send**
sentence[1] [ˈsɛntənts, -ənz] vt **-tenced; -tencing** : sentenciar
sentence[2] n **1** JUDGMENT : sentencia f **2** : oración f, frase f (en gramática)
sentiment [ˈsɛntəmənt] n **1** BELIEF : opinión f **2** FEELING : sentimiento m **3** → **sentimentality**

sentimental [ˌsɛntəˈmɛntəl] adj : sentimental
sentimentality [ˌsɛntəˌmɛnˈtæləti] n, pl **-ties** : sentimentalismo m, sensiblería f
sentinel [ˈsɛntənəl] n : centinela mf, guardia mf
sentry [ˈsɛntri] n, pl **-tries** : centinela mf
sepal [ˈsiːpəl, ˈsɛ-] n : sépalo m
separable [ˈsɛpərəbəl] adj : separable
separate[1] [ˈsɛpəˌreɪt] v **-rated; -rating** vt **1** DETACH, SEVER : separar **2** DISTINGUISH : diferenciar, distinguir — vi PART : separarse
separate[2] [ˈsɛprət, ˈsɛpə-] adj **1** INDIVIDUAL : separado, aparte ⟨a separate state : un estado separado⟩ ⟨in a separate envelope : en un sobre aparte⟩ **2** DISTINCT : distinto
separately [ˈsɛprətli, ˈsɛpə-] adv : por separado, separadamente, aparte
separation [ˌsɛpəˈreɪʃən] n : separación f
sepia [ˈsiːpiə] n : color m sepia
September [sɛpˈtɛmbər] n : septiembre m, setiembre m
septic [ˈsɛptɪk] adj : séptico ⟨septic tank : fosa séptica⟩
sepulchre [ˈsɛpəlkər] n : sepulcro m
sequel [ˈsiːkwəl] n **1** CONSEQUENCE : secuela f, consecuencia f **2** : continuación f (de una película, etc.)
sequence [ˈsiːkwənts] n **1** SERIES : serie f, sucesión f, secuencia f (matemática o musical) **2** ORDER : orden m
sequester [sɪˈkwɛstər] vt : aislar
sequin [ˈsiːkwən] n : lentejuela f
sequoia [sɪˈkwɔɪə] n : secoya f, secuoya f
sera → **serum**
Serb [ˈsərb] or **Serbian** [ˈsərbiən] n **1** : serbio m, -bia f **2** : serbio m (idioma) — **Serb** or **Serbian** adj
Serbo–Croatian [ˌsərbokroˈeɪʃən] n : serbocroata m (idioma) — **Serbo–Croatian** adj
serenade[1] [ˌsɛrəˈneɪd] vt **-naded; -nading** : darle una serenata (a alguien)
serenade[2] n : serenata f
serene [səˈriːn] adj : sereno — **serenely** adv
serenity [səˈrɛnəti] n : serenidad f
serf [ˈsərf] n : siervo m, -va f
serge [ˈsərdʒ] n : sarga f
sergeant [ˈsɑrdʒənt] n : sargento mf
serial[1] [ˈsɪriəl] adj : seriado
serial[2] n : serie f, serial m (de radio o televisión), publicación f por entregas
serially [ˈsɪriəli] adv : en serie
series [ˈsɪrˌiːz] n, pl **series** : serie f, sucesión f
serious [ˈsɪriəs] adj **1** SOBER : serio **2** DEDICATED, EARNEST : serio, dedicado ⟨to be serious about something : tomar algo en serio⟩ **3** GRAVE : serio, grave ⟨serious problems : problemas graves⟩
seriously [ˈsɪriəsli] adv **1** EARNESTLY : seriamente, con seriedad, en serio **2** SEVERELY : gravemente

seriousness ['sɪriəsnəs] *n* : seriedad *f*, gravedad *f*

sermon ['sərmən] *n* : sermón *m*

serpent ['sərpənt] *n* : serpiente *f*

serrated [sə'reɪt̬əd, 'sɛr₁eɪt̬əd] *adj* : dentado, serrado

serum ['sɪrəm] *n, pl* **serums** *or* **sera** ['sɪrə] : suero *m*

servant ['sərvənt] *n* : criado *m*, -da *f*; sirviente *m*, -ta *f*

serve ['sərv] *v* **served; serving** *vi* **1** : servir ⟨to serve in the navy : servir en la armada⟩ ⟨to serve on a jury : ser miembro de un jurado⟩ **2** DO, FUNCTION : servir ⟨to serve as : servir de, servir como⟩ **3** : sacar (en deportes) — *vt* **1** : servir ⟨to serve God : servir a Dios⟩ **2** HELP : servir ⟨it serves no purpose : no sirve para nada⟩ **3** : servir (comida o bebida) ⟨dinner is served : la cena está servida⟩ **4** SUPPLY : abastecer **5** CARRY OUT : cumplir, hacer ⟨to serve time : servir una pena⟩ **6 to serve a summons** : entregar una citación

server ['sərvər] *n* **1** : camarero *m*, -ra *f*; mesero *m*, -ra *f* (en un restaurante) **2** *or* **serving dish** : fuente *f* (para servir comida) **3** : servidor *m* (en informática)

service¹ ['sərvəs] *vt* **-viced; -vicing 1** MAINTAIN : darle mantenimiento a (una máquina), revisar **2** REPAIR : arreglar, reparar

service² *n* **1** HELP, USE : servicio *m* ⟨to do someone a service : hacerle un servicio a alguien⟩ ⟨at your service : a sus órdenes⟩ ⟨to be out of service : no funcionar⟩ **2** CEREMONY : oficio *m* (religioso) **3** DEPARTMENT, SYSTEM : servicio *m* ⟨social services : servicios sociales⟩ ⟨train service : servicio de trenes⟩ **4** SET : juego *m*, servicio *m* ⟨tea service : juego de té⟩ **5** MAINTENANCE : mantenimiento *m*, revisión *f*, servicio *m* **6** : saque *m* (en deportes) **7 armed services** : fuerzas *fpl* armadas

serviceable ['sərvəsəbəl] *adj* **1** USEFUL : útil **2** DURABLE : duradero

serviceman ['sərvəs₁mæn, -mən] *n, pl* **-men** [-mən, -₁mɛn] : militar *m*

service station → **gas station**

servicewoman ['sərvəs₁wʊmən] *n, pl* **-women** [-₁wɪmən] : militar *f*

servile ['sərvəl, -₁vaɪl] *adj* : servil

serving ['sərvɪŋ] *n* HELPING : porción *f*, ración *f*

servitude ['sərvə₁tuːd, -₁tjuːd] *n* : servidumbre *f*

sesame ['sɛsəmi] *n* : ajonjolí *m*, sésamo *m*

session ['sɛʃən] *n* : sesión *f*

set¹ ['sɛt] *v* **set; setting** *vt* **1** SEAT : sentar **2** *or* **set down** PLACE : poner, colocar **3** ARRANGE : fijar, establecer ⟨to set the date : poner la fecha⟩ ⟨he set the agenda : estableció la agenda⟩ **4** ADJUST : poner (un reloj, etc.) **5** (*indicating the causing of a certain condition*) ⟨to set fire to : prenderle fuego a⟩ ⟨she

set it free : lo soltó⟩ **6** MAKE, START : poner, hacer ⟨I set them working : los puse a trabajar⟩ — *vi* **1** SOLIDIFY : fraguar (dícese del cemento, etc.), cuajar (dícese de la gelatina, etc.) **2** : ponerse (dícese del sol o de la luna)

set² *adj* **1** ESTABLISHED, FIXED : fijo, establecido **2** RIGID : inflexible ⟨to be set in one's ways : tener costumbres muy arraigadas⟩ **3** READY : listo, preparado

set³ *n* **1** COLLECTION : juego *m* ⟨a set of dishes : un juego de platos, una vajilla⟩ ⟨a tool set : una caja de herramientas⟩ **2** *or* **stage set** : decorado *m* (en el teatro), plató *m* (en el cine) **3** APPARATUS : aparato *m* ⟨a television set : un televisor⟩ **4** : conjunto *m* (en matemáticas)

setback ['sɛt₁bæk] *n* : revés *m*, contratiempo *m*

set in *vi* BEGIN : comenzar, empezar

set off *vt* **1** PROVOKE : provocar **2** EXPLODE : hacer estallar (una bomba, etc.) — *vi or* **to set forth** : salir

set out *vi* : salir (de viaje) — *vt* INTEND : proponerse

settee [sɛ'tiː] *n* : sofá *m*

setter ['sɛt̬ər] *n* : setter *mf* ⟨Irish setter : setter irlandés⟩

setting ['sɛt̬ɪŋ] *n* **1** : posición *f*, ajuste *m* (de un control) **2** : engaste *m*, montura *f* (de una gema) **3** SCENE : escenario *m* (de una novela, etc.) **4** SURROUNDINGS : ambiente *m*, entorno *m*, marco *m*

settle ['sɛt̬əl] *v* **settled; settling** *vi* **1** ALIGHT, LAND : posarse (dícese de las aves), depositarse (dícese del polvo) **2** SINK : asentarse (dícese de los edificios) ⟨he settled into the chair : se arrellanó en la silla⟩ **3** : instalarse (en una casa), establecerse (en una ciudad o región) **4 to settle down** : calmarse, tranquilizarse ⟨settle down! : ¡tranquilízate!, ¡cálmate!⟩ **5 to settle down** : sentar cabeza, hacerse sensato ⟨to marry and settle down : casarse y sentar cabeza⟩ — *vt* **1** ARRANGE, DECIDE : fijar, decidir, acordar (planes, etc.) **2** RESOLVE : resolver, solucionar ⟨to settle an argument : resolver una discusión⟩ **3** PAY : pagar ⟨to settle an account : saldar una cuenta⟩ **4** CALM : calmar (los nervios), asentar (el estómago) **5** COLONIZE : colonizar **6 to settle oneself** : acomodarse, hacerse cómodo

settlement ['sɛt̬əlmənt] *n* **1** PAYMENT : pago *m*, liquidación *f* **2** COLONY : asentamiento *m* **3** RESOLUTION : acuerdo *m*

settler ['sɛt̬ələr] *n* : poblador *m*, -dora *f*; colono *m*, -na *f*

setup ['sɛt̬₁ʌp] *n* **1** ASSEMBLY : montaje *m*, ensamblaje *m* **2** ARRANGEMENT : disposición *f* **3** PREPARATION : preparación *f* **4** TRAP, TRICK : encerrona *f*

set up *vt* **1** ASSEMBLE : montar, armar **2** ERECT : levantar, erigir **3** ESTABLISH : establecer, fundar, montar (un negocio) **4** CAUSE : armar ⟨they set up a clamor : armaron un alboroto⟩

seven[1] [ˈsɛvən] *adj* : siete

seven[2] *n* : siete *m*

seven hundred[1] *adj* : setecientos

seven hundred[2] *n* : setecientos *m*

seventeen[1] [ˌsɛvənˈtiːn] *adj* : diecisiete

seventeen[2] *n* : diecisiete *m*

seventeenth[1] [ˌsɛvənˈtiːnθ] *adj* : decimoséptimo

seventeenth[2] *n* **1** : decimoséptimo *m*, -ma *f* (en una serie) **2** : diecisieteavo *m*, diecisieteava parte *f*

seventh[1] [ˈsɛvənθ] *adj* : séptimo

seventh[2] *n* **1** : séptimo *m*, -ma *f* (en una serie) **2** : séptimo *m*, séptima parte *f*

seventieth[1] [ˈsɛvəntiəθ] *adj* : septuagésimo

seventieth[2] *n* **1** : septuagésimo *m*, -ma *f* (en una serie) **2** : setentavo *m*, setentava parte *f*, septuagésima parte *f*

seventy[1] [ˈsɛvənṭi] *adj* : setenta

seventy[2] *n, pl* **-ties** : setenta *m*

sever [ˈsɛvər] *vt* **-ered; -ering** : cortar, romper

several[1] [ˈsɛvrəl, ˈsɛvə-] *adj* **1** DISTINCT : distinto **2** SOME : varios ⟨several weeks : varias semanas⟩

several[2] *pron* : varios, varias

severance [ˈsɛvrənts, ˈsɛvə-] *n* **1** : ruptura *f* (de relaciones, etc.) **2 severance pay** : indemnización *f* (por despido)

severe [səˈvɪr] *adj* **severer; -est 1** STRICT : severo **2** AUSTERE : sobrio, austero **3** SERIOUS : grave ⟨a severe wound : una herida grave⟩ ⟨severe aches : dolores fuertes⟩ **4** DIFFICULT : duro, difícil — **severely** *adv*

severity [səˈvrəṭi] *n* **1** HARSHNESS : severidad *f* **2** AUSTERITY : sobriedad *f*, austeridad *f* **3** SERIOUSNESS : gravedad *f* (de una herida, etc.)

sew [ˈsoː] *v* **sewed; sewn** [ˈsoːn] *or* **sewed; sewing** : coser

sewage [ˈsuːɪdʒ] *n* : aguas *fpl* negras, aguas *fpl* residuales

sewer[1] [ˈsoːər] *n* : uno que cose

sewer[2] [ˈsuːər] *n* : alcantarilla *f*, cloaca *f*

sewing [ˈsoːɪŋ] *n* : costura *f*

sex [ˈsɛks] *n* **1** : sexo *m* ⟨the opposite sex : el sexo opuesto⟩ **2** COPULATION : relaciones *fpl* sexuales

sexism [ˈsɛkˌsɪzəm] *n* : sexismo *m*

sexist[1] [ˈsɛksɪst] *adj* : sexista

sexist[2] *n* : sexista *mf*

sextant [ˈsɛkstənt] *n* : sextante *m*

sextet [sɛkˈstɛt] *n* : sexteto *m*

sexton [ˈsɛkstən] *n* : sacristán *m*

sexual [ˈsɛkʃuəl] *adj* : sexual — **sexually** *adv*

sexuality [ˌsɛkʃuˈæləṭi] *n* : sexualidad *f*

sexy [ˈsɛksi] *adj* **sexier; -est** : sexy

shabbily [ˈʃæbəli] *adv* **1** : pobremente ⟨shabbily dressed : pobremente vestido⟩ **2** UNFAIRLY : mal, injustamente

shabbiness [ˈʃæbinəs] *n* **1** : lo gastado (de ropa, etc.) **2** : lo mal vestido (de personas) **3** UNFAIRNESS : injusticia *f*

shabby [ˈʃæbi] *adj* **shabbier; -est 1** : gastado (dícese de la ropa, etc.) **2** : mal vestido (dícese de las personas) **3** UNFAIR : malo, injusto ⟨shabby treatment : mal trato⟩

shack [ˈʃæk] *n* : choza *f*, rancho *m*

shackle[1] [ˈʃækəl] *vt* **-led; -ling** : ponerle grilletes (a alguien)

shackle[2] *n* : grillete *m*

shad [ˈʃæd] *n* : sábalo *m*

shade[1] [ˈʃeɪd] *v* **shaded; shading** *vt* **1** SHELTER : proteger (del sol o de la luz) **2** *or* **to shade in** : matizar los colores de — *vi* : convertirse gradualmente ⟨his irritation shaded into rage : su irritación iba convirtiéndose en furia⟩

shade[2] *n* **1** : sombra *f* ⟨to give shade : dar sombra⟩ **2** : tono *m* (de un color) **3** NUANCE : matiz *m* **4** : pantalla *f* (de una lámpara), persiana *f* (de una ventana)

shadow[1] [ˈʃædoː] *vt* **1** DARKEN : ensombrecer **2** TRAIL : seguir de cerca, seguirle la pista (a alguien)

shadow[2] *n* **1** : sombra *f* **2** DARKNESS : oscuridad *f* **3** TRACE : sombra *f*, atisbo *m*, indicio *m* ⟨without a shadow of a doubt : sin sombra de duda, sin lugar a dudas⟩ **4 to cast a shadow over** : ensombrecer

shadowy [ˈʃædowi] *adj* **1** INDISTINCT : vago, indistinto **2** DARK : oscuro

shady [ˈʃeɪdi] *adj* **shadier; -est 1** : sombreado (dícese de un lugar), que da sombra (dícese de un árbol) **2** DISREPUTABLE : sospechoso (dícese de una persona), turbio (dícese de un negocio, etc.)

shaft [ˈʃæft] *n* **1** : asta *f* (de una lanza), astil *m* (de una flecha), mango *m* (de una herramienta) **2** *or* **mine shaft** : pozo *m*

shaggy [ˈʃægi] *adj* **shaggier; -est 1** HAIRY : peludo ⟨a shaggy dog : un perro peludo⟩ **2** UNKEMPT : enmarañado, despeinado (dícese del pelo, de las barbas, etc.)

shake[1] [ˈʃeɪk] *v* **shook** [ˈʃʊk]; **shaken** [ˈʃeɪkən]; **shaking** *vt* **1** : sacudir, agitar, hacer temblar ⟨he shook his head : negó con la cabeza⟩ **2** WEAKEN : debilitar, hacer flaquear ⟨it shook her faith : debilitó su confianza⟩ **3** UPSET : afectar, alterar **4 to shake hands with someone** : darle la mano a alguien, estrecharle la mano a alguien — *vi* : temblar, sacudirse

shake[2] *n* : sacudida *f*, apretón *m* (de manos)

shaker [ˈʃeɪkər] *n* **1 salt shaker** : salero *m* **2 pepper shaker** : pimentero *m* **3 cocktail shaker** : coctelera *f*

shake-up [ˈʃeɪkˌʌp] *n* : reorganización *f*

shakily [ˈʃeɪkəli] *adv* : temblorosamente

shaky ['ʃeɪki] *adj* **shakier; -est 1** SHAKING : tembloroso **2** UNSTABLE : poco firme, inestable **3** PRECARIOUS : precario, incierto **4** QUESTIONABLE : dudoso, cuestionable ⟨shaky arguments : argumentos discutibles⟩

shale ['ʃeɪl] *n* : esquisto *m*

shall ['ʃæl] *v aux, past* **should** ['ʃʊd] *present s & pl* **shall 1** (*used to express a command*) ⟨you shall do as I say : harás lo que te digo⟩ **2** (*used to express futurity*) ⟨we shall see : ya veremos⟩ ⟨when shall we expect you? : ¿cuándo te podemos esperar?⟩ **3** (*used to express determination*) ⟨you shall have the money : tendrás el dinero⟩ **4** (*used to express a condition*) ⟨if he should die : si muriera⟩ ⟨if they should call, tell me : si llaman, dímelo⟩ **5** (*used to express obligation*) ⟨he should have said it : debería haberlo dicho⟩ **6** (*used to express probability*) ⟨they should arrive soon : deben (de) llegar pronto⟩ ⟨why should he lie? : ¿porqué ha de mentir?⟩

shallow ['ʃæloː] *adj* **1** : poco profundo (dícese del agua, etc.) **2** SUPERFICIAL : superficial

shallows ['ʃæloːz] *npl* : bajío *m*, bajos *mpl*

sham¹ ['ʃæm] *v* **shammed; shamming** : fingir

sham² *adj* : falso, fingido

sham³ *n* **1** FAKE, PRETENSE : farsa *f*, simulación *f*, imitación *f* **2** FAKER : impostor *m*, -tora *f*; farsante *mf*

shamble ['ʃæmbəl] *vi* **-bled; -bling** : caminar arrastrando los pies

shambles ['ʃæmbəlz] *ns & pl* : caos *m*, desorden *m*, confusión *f*

shame¹ ['ʃeɪm] *vt* **shamed; shaming 1** : avergonzar ⟨he was shamed by their words : sus palabras le dieron vergüenza⟩ **2** DISGRACE : deshonrar

shame² *n* **1** : vergüenza *f* ⟨to have no shame : no tener vergüenza⟩ **2** DISGRACE : vergüenza *f*, deshonra *f* **3** PITY : lástima *f*, pena *f* ⟨what a shame! : ¡qué pena!⟩

shamefaced ['ʃeɪm,feɪst] *adj* : avergonzado

shameful ['ʃeɪmfəl] *adj* : vergonzoso — **shamefully** *adv*

shameless ['ʃeɪmləs] *adj* : descarado, desvergonzado — **shamelessly** *adv*

shampoo¹ [ʃæm'puː] *vt* : lavar (el pelo)

shampoo² *n, pl* **-poos** : champú *m*

shamrock ['ʃæm,rɑk] *n* : trébol *m*

shank ['ʃæŋk] *n* : parte *f* baja de la pierna

shan't ['ʃænt] (*contraction of* **shall not**) → **shall**

shanty ['ʃænti] *n, pl* **-ties** : choza *f*, rancho *m*

shape¹ ['ʃeɪp] *v* **shaped; shaping** *vt* **1** : dar forma a, modelar (arcilla, etc.), tallar (madera, piedra), formar (carácter) ⟨to be shaped like : tener forma de⟩ **2** DETERMINE : decidir, determi-

nar — *vi or* **to shape up** : tomar forma

shape² *n* **1** : forma *f*, figura *f* ⟨in the shape of a circle : en forma de círculo⟩ **2** CONDITION : estado *m*, condiciones *fpl*, forma *f* (física) ⟨to get in shape : ponerse en forma⟩

shapeless ['ʃeɪpləs] *adj* : informe

shapely ['ʃeɪpli] *adj* **shapelier; -est** : curvilíneo, bien proporcionado

shard ['ʃɑrd] *n* : fragmento *m*, casco *m* (de cerámica, etc.)

share¹ ['ʃɛr] *v* **shared; sharing** *vt* **1** APPORTION : dividir, repartir **2** : compartir ⟨they share a room : comparten una habitación⟩ — *vi* : compartir

share² *n* **1** PORTION : parte *f*, porción *f* ⟨one's fair share : lo que le corresponde a uno⟩ **2** : acción *f* (en una compañía) ⟨to hold shares : tener acciones⟩

sharecropper ['ʃɛr,krɑpər] *n* : aparcero *m*, -ra *f*

shareholder ['ʃɛr,hoːldər] *n* : accionista *mf*

shark ['ʃɑrk] *n* : tiburón *m*

sharp¹ ['ʃɑrp] *adv* : en punto ⟨at two o'clock sharp : a las dos en punto⟩

sharp² *adj* **1** : afilado, filoso ⟨a sharp knife : un cuchillo afilado⟩ **2** PENETRATING : cortante, fuerte **3** CLEVER : agudo, listo, perspicaz **4** ACUTE : agudo ⟨sharp eyesight : vista aguda⟩ **5** HARSH, SEVERE : duro, severo, agudo ⟨a sharp rebuke : una reprimenda mordaz⟩ **6** STRONG : fuerte ⟨sharp cheese : queso fuerte⟩ **7** ABRUPT : brusco, repentino **8** DISTINCT : nítido, definido ⟨a sharp image : una imagen bien definida⟩ **9** ANGULAR : anguloso (dícese de la cara) **10** : sostenido (en música)

sharp³ *n* : sostenido *m* (en música)

sharpen ['ʃɑrpən] *vt* : afilar, aguzar ⟨to sharpen a pencil : sacarle punta a un lápiz⟩ ⟨to sharpen one's wits : aguzar el ingenio⟩

sharpener ['ʃɑrpənər] *n* : afilador *m* (para cuchillos, etc.), sacapuntas *m* (para lápices)

sharply ['ʃɑrpli] *adv* **1** ABRUPTLY : bruscamente **2** DISTINCTLY : claramente, marcadamente

sharpness ['ʃɑrpnəs] *n* **1** : lo afilado (de un cuchillo, etc.) **2** ACUTENESS : agudeza *f* (de los sentidos o de la mente) **3** INTENSITY : intensidad *f*, agudeza *f* (de dolores, etc.) **4** HARSHNESS : dureza *f*, severidad *f* **5** ABRUPTNESS : brusquedad *f* **6** CLARITY : nitidez *f*

sharpshooter ['ʃɑrp,ʃuːtər] *n* : tirador *m*, -dora *f* de primera

shatter ['ʃætər] *vt* **1** : hacer añicos ⟨to shatter the silence : romper el silencio⟩ **2 to be shattered by** : quedar destrozado por — *vi* : hacerse añicos, romperse en pedazos

shave¹ ['ʃeɪv] *v* **shaved; shaved** *or* **shaven** ['ʃeɪvən]; **shaving** *vt* **1** : afeitar, rasurar ⟨she shaved her legs : se rasuró las piernas⟩ ⟨they shaved (off) his beard : le afeitaron la barba⟩ **2** SLICE : cortar (en pedazos finos) — *vi* : afeitarse, rasurarse

shave² *n* : afeitada *f*, rasurada *f*

shaver ['ʃeɪvər] *n* : afeitadora *f*, máquina *f* de afeitar, rasuradora *f*

shawl ['ʃɔl] *n* : chal *m*, mantón *m*, rebozo *m*

she ['ʃi:] *pron* : ella

sheaf ['ʃi:f] *n*, *pl* **sheaves** ['ʃi:vz] : gavilla *f* (de cereales), haz *m* (de flechas), fajo *m* (de papeles)

shear ['ʃɪr] *vt* **sheared; sheared** *or* **shorn** ['ʃɔrn]; **shearing** **1** : esquilar, trasquilar ⟨to shear sheep : trasquilar ovejas⟩ **2** CUT : cortar (el pelo, etc.)

shears ['ʃɪrz] *npl* : tijeras *fpl* (grandes)

sheath ['ʃi:θ] *n*, *pl* **sheaths** ['ʃi:ðz, 'ʃi:θs] : funda *f*, vaina *f*

sheathe ['ʃi:ð] *vt* **sheathed; sheathing** : envainar, enfundar

shed¹ ['ʃɛd] *vt* **shed; shedding** **1** : derramar (sangre o lágrimas) **2** EMIT : emitir (luz) ⟨to shed light on : aclarar⟩ **3** DISCARD : mudar (la piel, etc.) ⟨to shed one's clothes : quitarse uno la ropa⟩

shed² *n* : cobertizo *m*

she'd ['ʃi:d] (*contraction of* **she had** *or* **she would**) → **have, would**

sheen ['ʃi:n] *n* : brillo *m*, lustre *m*

sheep ['ʃi:p] *ns & pl* : oveja *f*

sheepfold ['ʃi:p,fo:ld] *n* : redil *m*

sheepish ['ʃi:pɪʃ] *adj* : avergonzado

sheepskin ['ʃi:p,skɪn] *n* : piel *f* de oveja, piel *f* de borrego

sheer¹ ['ʃɪr] *adv* **1** COMPLETELY : completamente, totalmente **2** VERTICALLY : verticalmente

sheer² *adj* **1** TRANSPARENT : vaporoso, transparente **2** ABSOLUTE, UTTER : puro ⟨by sheer luck : por pura suerte⟩ **3** STEEP : escarpado, vertical

sheet ['ʃi:t] *n* **1** *or* **bedsheet** ['bɛd-,ʃi:t] : sábana *f* **2** : hoja *f* (de papel) **3** : capa *f* (de hielo, etc.) **4** : lámina *f*, placa *f* (de vidrio, metal, etc.), plancha *f* (de metal, madera, etc.) ⟨baking sheet : placa de horno⟩

sheikh *or* **sheik** ['ʃi:k, 'ʃeɪk] *n* : jeque *m*

shelf ['ʃɛlf] *n*, *pl* **shelves** ['ʃɛlvz] **1** : estante *m*, anaquel *m* (en una pared) **2** : banco *m*, arrecife *m* (en geología) ⟨continental shelf : plataforma continental⟩

shell¹ ['ʃɛl] *vt* **1** : desvainar (chícharos), pelar (nueces, etc.) **2** BOMBARD : bombardear

shell² *n* **1** SEASHELL : concha *f* **2** : cáscara *f* (de huevos, nueces, etc.), vaina *f* (de chícharos, etc.), caparazón *m* (de crustáceos, tortugas, etc.) **3** : cartucho *m*, casquillo *m* ⟨a .45 caliber shell : un cartucho calibre .45⟩ **4** *or* **racing shell** : bote *m* (para hacer regatas de remos)

she'll ['ʃi:l, 'ʃɪl] (*contraction of* **she shall** *or* **she will**) → **shall, will**

shellac¹ [ʃə'læk] *vt* **-lacked; -lacking** **1** : laquear (madera, etc.) **2** DEFEAT : darle una paliza (a alguien), derrotar

shellac² *n* : laca *f*

shellfish ['ʃɛl,fɪʃ] *n* : marisco *m*

shelter¹ ['ʃɛltər] *vt* **1** PROTECT : proteger, abrigar **2** HARBOR : dar refugio a, albergar

shelter² *n* : refugio *m*, abrigo *m* ⟨to take shelter : refugiarse⟩

shelve ['ʃɛlv] *vt* **shelved; shelving** **1** : poner en estantes **2** DEFER : dar carpetazo a

shenanigans [ʃə'nænɪgənz] *npl* **1** TRICKERY : artimañas *fpl* **2** MISCHIEF : travesuras *fpl*

shepherd¹ ['ʃɛpərd] *vt* **1** : cuidar (ovejas, etc.) **2** GUIDE : conducir, guiar

shepherd² *n* : pastor *m*

shepherdess ['ʃɛpərdəs] *n* : pastora *f*

sherbet ['ʃərbət] *or* **sherbert** [-bərt] *n* : sorbete *m*, nieve *f* Cuba, Mex, PRi

sheriff ['ʃɛrɪf] *n* : sheriff *mf*

sherry ['ʃɛri] *n*, *pl* **-ries** : jerez *m*

she's ['ʃi:z] (*contraction of* **she is** *or* **she has**) → **be, have**

shield¹ ['ʃi:ld] *vt* **1** PROTECT : proteger **2** CONCEAL : ocultar ⟨to shield one's eyes : taparse los ojos⟩

shield² *n* **1** : escudo *m* (armadura) **2** PROTECTION : protección *f*, blindaje *m* (de un cable)

shier, shiest → **shy**

shift¹ ['ʃɪft] *vt* **1** CHANGE : cambiar ⟨to shift gears : cambiar de velocidad⟩ **2** MOVE : mover **3** TRANSFER : transferir ⟨to shift the blame : echarle la culpa (a otro)⟩ — *vi* **1** CHANGE : cambiar **2** MOVE : moverse **3** **to shift for oneself** : arreglárselas solo

shift² *n* **1** CHANGE, TRANSFER : cambio *m* ⟨a shift in priorities : un cambio de prioridades⟩ **2** : turno *m* ⟨night shift : turno de noche⟩ **3** DRESS : vestido *m* (suelto) **4** → **gearshift**

shiftless ['ʃɪftləs] *adj* : perezoso, vago, holgazán

shifty ['ʃɪfti] *adj* **shiftier; -est** : taimado, artero ⟨a shifty look : una mirada huidiza⟩

shilling ['ʃɪlɪŋ] *n* : chelín *m*

shimmer ['ʃɪmər] *vi* GLIMMER : brillar con luz trémula

shin¹ ['ʃɪn] *vi* **shinned; shinning** : trepar, subir ⟨she shinned up the pole : subió al poste⟩

shin² *n* : espinilla *f*, canilla *f*

shine¹ ['ʃaɪn] *v* **shone** ['ʃo:n] *or* **shined**; **shining** *vi* **1** : brillar, relucir ⟨the stars were shining : las estrellas brillaban⟩ **2** EXCEL : brillar, lucirse — *vt* **1** : alumbrar ⟨he shined the flashlight at it : lo alumbró con la linterna⟩ **2** POLISH : sacarle brillo a, lustrar

shine² *n* : brillo *m*, lustre *m*

shingle¹ ['ʃɪŋgəl] *vt* **-gled; -gling** : techar

shingle² *n* : tablilla *f* (para techar)

shingles [ˈʃɪŋɡəlz] *npl* : herpes *m*

shinny [ˈʃɪni] *vi* -**nied**; -**nying** → **shin¹**

shiny [ˈʃaɪni] *adj* **shinier**; -**est** : brillante

ship¹ [ˈʃɪp] *vt* **shipped**; **shipping** 1 LOAD : embarcar (en un barco) 2 SEND : transportar (en barco), enviar ⟨to ship by air : enviar por avión⟩

ship² *n* 1 : barco *m*, buque *m* 2 → **spaceship**

shipboard [ˈʃɪpˌbord] *n* **on** ~ : a bordo

shipbuilder [ˈʃɪpˌbɪldər] *n* : constructor *m*, -tora *f* naval

shipment [ˈʃɪpmənt] *n* 1 SHIPPING : transporte *m*, embarque *m* 2 : envío *m*, remesa *f* ⟨a shipment of medicine : un envío de medicina⟩

shipping [ˈʃɪpɪŋ] *n* 1 SHIPS : barcos *mpl*, embarcaciones *fpl* 2 TRANSPORTATION : transporte *m* (de mercancías)

shipshape [ˈʃɪpˌʃeɪp] *adj* : ordenado

shipwreck¹ [ˈʃɪpˌrɛk] *vt* **to be shipwrecked** : naufragar

shipwreck² *n* : naufragio *m*

shipyard [ˈʃɪpˌjard] *n* : astillero *m*

shirk [ˈʃərk] *vt* : eludir, rehuir ⟨to shirk one's responsibilities : esquivar uno sus responsabilidades⟩

shirt [ˈʃərt] *n* : camisa *f*

shiver¹ [ˈʃɪvər] *vi* 1 : tiritar (de frío) 2 TREMBLE : estremecerse, temblar

shiver² *n* : escalofrío *m*, estremecimiento *m*

shoal [ˈʃoːl] *n* : banco *m*, bajío *m*

shock¹ [ˈʃak] *vt* 1 UPSET : conmover, conmocionar 2 STARTLE : asustar, sobresaltar 3 SCANDALIZE : escandalizar 4 : darle una descarga eléctrica a

shock² *n* 1 COLLISION, JOLT : choque *m*, sacudida *f* 2 UPSET : conmoción *f*, golpe *m* emocional 3 : shock *m* (en medicina) 4 *or* **electric shock** : descarga *f* eléctrica 5 SHEAVES : gavillas *fpl* 6 **shock of hair** : mata *f* de pelo

shock absorber *n* : amortiguador *m*

shocking [ˈʃakɪŋ] *adj* 1 : chocante 2 **shocking pink** : rosa *m* estridente

shoddy [ˈʃadi] *adj* **shoddier**; -**est** : de mala calidad ⟨a shoddy piece of work : un trabajo chapucero⟩

shoe¹ [ˈʃuː] *vt* **shod** [ˈʃad]; **shoeing** : herrar (un caballo)

shoe² *n* 1 : zapato *m* ⟨the shoe industry : la industria del calzado⟩ 2 HORSESHOE : herradura *f* 3 **brake shoe** : zapata *f*

shoelace [ˈʃuːˌleɪs] *n* : cordón *m* (de zapatos)

shoemaker [ˈʃuːˌmeɪkər] *n* : zapatero *m*, -ra *f*

shone → **shine**

shook → **shake**

shoot¹ [ˈʃuːt] *v* **shot** [ˈʃat]; **shooting** *vt* 1 : disparar, tirar ⟨to shoot a bullet : tirar una bala⟩ 2 : pegarle un tiro a, darle un balazo a ⟨he shot her : le pegó un tiro⟩ ⟨they shot and killed him : lo mataron a balazos⟩ 3 THROW : lanzar (una pelota, etc.), echar (una mirada) 4 PHOTOGRAPH : fotografiar 5 FILM : filmar — *vi* 1 : disparar (con un arma de fuego) 2 DART : ir rápidamente ⟨it shot past : pasó como una bala⟩

shoot² *n* : brote *m*, retoño *m*, vástago *m*

shooting star *n* : estrella *f* fugaz

shop¹ [ˈʃap] *vi* **shopped**; **shopping** : hacer compras ⟨to go shopping : ir de compras⟩

shop² *n* 1 WORKSHOP : taller *m* 2 STORE : tienda *f*

shopkeeper [ˈʃapˌkiːpər] *n* : tendero *m*, -ra *f*

shoplift [ˈʃapˌlɪft] *vi* : hurtar mercancía (de una tienda) — *vt* : hurtar (de una tienda)

shoplifter [ˈʃapˌlɪftər] *n* : ladrón *m*, -drona *f* (que roba en una tienda)

shopper [ˈʃapər] *n* : comprador *m*, -dora *f*

shore¹ [ˈʃor] *vt* **shored**; **shoring** : apuntalar ⟨they shored up the wall : apuntalaron la pared⟩

shore² *n* 1 : orilla *f* (del mar, etc.) 2 PROP : puntal *m*

shoreline [ˈʃorˌlaɪn] *n* : orilla *f*

shorn → **shear**

short¹ [ˈʃort] *adv* 1 ABRUPTLY : repentinamente, súbitamente ⟨the car stopped short : el carro se paró en seco⟩ 2 **to fall short** : no alcanzar, quedarse corto

short² *adj* 1 : corto (de medida), bajo (de estatura) 2 BRIEF : corto ⟨short and sweet : corto y bueno⟩ ⟨a short time ago : hace poco⟩ 3 CURT : brusco, cortante, seco 4 : corto (de tiempo, de dinero) ⟨I'm one dollar short : me falta un dólar⟩

short³ *n* 1 **shorts** *npl* : shorts *mpl*, pantalones *mpl* cortos 2 → **short circuit**

shortage [ˈʃortɪdʒ] *n* : falta *f*, escasez *f*, carencia *f*

shortcake [ˈʃortˌkeɪk] *n* : tarta *f* de fruta

shortchange [ˈʃortˈʃeɪndʒ] *vt* -**changed**; -**changing** : darle mal el cambio (a alguien)

short circuit *n* : cortocircuito *m*, corto *m* (eléctrico)

shortcoming [ˈʃortˌkʌmɪŋ] *n* : defecto *m*

shortcut [ˈʃortˌkʌt] *n* 1 : atajo *m* ⟨to take a shortcut : cortar camino⟩ 2 : alternativa *f* fácil, método *m* rápido

shorten [ˈʃortən] *vt* : acortar — *vi* : acortarse

shorthand [ˈʃortˌhænd] *n* : taquigrafía *f*

short-lived [ˈʃortˈlɪvd, -ˈlaɪvd] *adj* : efímero

shortly [ˈʃortli] *adv* 1 BRIEFLY : brevemente ⟨to put it shortly : para decirlo en pocas palabras⟩ 2 SOON : dentro de poco

shortness [ˈʃortnəs] *n* 1 : lo corto ⟨shortness of stature : estatura baja⟩ 2 BREVITY : brevedad *f* 3 CURTNESS : brusquedad *f* 4 SHORTAGE : falta *f*, escasez *f*, carencia *f*

shortsighted [ˈʃɔrtˌsaɪtəd] → **nearsighted**
shot [ˈʃɑt] *n* **1** : disparo *m*, tiro *m* ⟨to
fire a shot : disparar⟩ **2** PELLETS
: perdigones *mpl* **3** : tiro *m* (en deportes) **4** ATTEMPT : intento *m*, tentativa *f* ⟨to have a shot at : hacer un intento por⟩ **5** RANGE : alcance *m* ⟨a
long shot : una posibilidad remota⟩ **6**
PHOTOGRAPH : foto *f* **7** INJECTION : inyección *f* **8** : trago *m* (de licor)
shotgun [ˈʃɑtˌgʌn] *n* : escopeta *f*
should → **shall**
shoulder[1] [ˈʃoːldər] *vt* **1** JOSTLE : empujar (con el hombro) **2** : ponerse al
hombro (una mochila, etc.) **3** : cargar
con (la responsabilidad, etc.)
shoulder[2] *n* **1** : hombro *m* ⟨to shrug
one's shoulders : encoger los hom-
bros⟩ **2** : arcén *m* (de una carretera)
shoulder blade *n* : omóplato *m*, omoplato *m*, escápula *f*
shouldn't [ˈʃʊdənt] (*contraction of*
should not) → **shall**
shout[1] [ˈʃaʊt] *v* : gritar, vocear
shout[2] *n* : grito *m*
shove[1] [ˈʃʌv] *v* **shoved; shoving** : empujar bruscamente
shove[2] *n* : empujón *m*, empellón *m*
shovel[1] [ˈʃʌvəl] *vt* -**veled** *or* -**velled**;
-**veling** *or* -**velling** **1** : mover con (una)
pala ⟨they shoveled the dirt out : sac-
aron la tierra con palas⟩ **2** DIG : cavar
(con una pala)
shovel[2] *n* : pala *f*
show[1] [ˈʃoː] *v* **showed; shown** [ˈʃoːn] *or*
showed; showing *vt* **1** DISPLAY
: mostrar, enseñar **2** REVEAL
: demostrar, manifestar, revelar ⟨he
showed himself to be a coward : se rev-
eló como cobarde⟩ **3** TEACH : enseñar
4 PROVE : demostrar, probar **5** CON-
DUCT, DIRECT : llevar, acompañar ⟨to
show someone the way : indicarle el
camino a alguien⟩ **6** : proyectar (una
película), dar (un programa de televisión) — *vi* **1** : notarse, verse ⟨the
stain doesn't show : la mancha no se
ve⟩ **2** APPEAR : aparecer, dejarse ver
show[2] *n* **1** : demostración *f* ⟨a show of
force : una demostración de fuerza⟩ **2**
EXHIBITION : exposición *f*, exhibición
f ⟨flower show : exposición de flores⟩
⟨to be on show : estar expuesto⟩ **3** : espectáculo *m* (teatral), programa *m* (de
televisión, etc.) ⟨to go to a show : ir al
teatro⟩
showcase [ˈʃoːˌkeɪs] *n* : vitrina *f*
showdown [ˈʃoːˌdaʊn] *n* : confrontación
f (decisiva)
shower[1] [ˈʃaʊər] *vt* **1** SPRAY : regar, mojar **2** HEAP : colmar ⟨they showered
him with gifts : lo colmaron de regalos, le llovieron los regalos⟩ — *vi* **1**
BATHE : ducharse, darse una ducha **2**
RAIN : llover
shower[2] *n* **1** : chaparrón *m*, chubasco
m ⟨a chance of showers : una posibil-

idad de chaparrones⟩ **2** : ducha *f* ⟨to
take a shower : ducharse⟩ **3** PARTY : fiesta *f* ⟨a bridal shower : una despedida de soltera⟩
show off *vt* : hacer alarde de, ostentar
— *vi* : lucirse
show up *vi* APPEAR : aparecer — *vt*
EXPOSE : revelar
showy [ˈʃoːi] *adj* **showier; -est** : llamativo, ostentoso — **showily** *adv*
shrank → **shrink**
shrapnel [ˈʃræpnəl] *ns & pl* : metralla *f*
shred[1] [ˈʃrɛd] *vt* **shredded; shredding**
: hacer trizas, desmenuzar (con las
manos), triturar (con una máquina) ⟨to
shred vegetables : cortar verduras en
tiras⟩
shred[2] *n* **1** STRIP : tira *f*, jirón *m* (de tela)
2 BIT : pizca *f* ⟨not a shred of evidence
: ni la mínima prueba⟩
shrew [ˈʃruː] *n* **1** : musaraña *f* (animal)
2 : mujer *f* regañona, arpía *f*
shrewd [ˈʃruːd] *adj* : astuto, inteligente,
sagaz — **shrewdly** *adv*
shrewdness [ˈʃruːdnəs] *n* : astucia *f*
shriek[1] [ˈʃriːk] *vi* : chillar, gritar
shriek[2] *n* : chillido *m*, alarido *m*, grito
m
shrill [ˈʃrɪl] *adj* : agudo, estridente
shrilly [ˈʃrɪli] *adv* : agudamente
shrimp [ˈʃrɪmp] *n* : camarón *m*, langostino *m*
shrine [ˈʃraɪn] *n* **1** TOMB : sepulcro *m*
(de un santo) **2** SANCTUARY : lugar *m*
sagrado, santuario *m*
shrink [ˈʃrɪŋk] *vi* **shrank** [ˈʃræŋk] *or*
shrunk [ˈʃrʌŋk]; **shrunk** *or* **shrunken**
[ˈʃrʌŋkən]; **shrinking** **1** RECOIL : retroceder ⟨he shrank back : se echó para
atrás⟩ **2** : encogerse (dícese de la ropa)
shrinkage [ˈʃrɪŋkɪdʒ] *n* : encogimiento
m (de ropa, etc.), contracción *f*, reducción *f*
shrivel [ˈʃrɪvəl] *vi* -**veled** *or* -**velled**;
-**veling** *or* -**velling** : arrugarse, marchitarse
shroud[1] [ˈʃraʊd] *vt* : envolver
shroud[2] *n* **1** : sudario *m*, mortaja *f* **2**
VEIL : velo *m* ⟨wrapped in a shroud of
mystery : envuelto en un aura de miste-
rio⟩
shrub [ˈʃrʌb] *n* : arbusto *m*, mata *f*
shrubbery [ˈʃrʌbəri] *n, pl* -**beries** : arbustos *mpl*, matas *fpl*
shrug [ˈʃrʌg] *vi* **shrugged; shrugging**
: encoger de hombros
shrunk → **shrink**
shuck[1] [ˈʃʌk] *vt* : pelar (mazorcas, etc.),
abrir (almejas, etc.)
shuck[2] *n* **1** HUSK : cascarilla *f*, cáscara
f (de una nuez, etc.), hojas *fpl* (de una
mazorca) **2** SHELL : concha *f* (de una
almeja, etc.)
shudder[1] [ˈʃʌdər] *vi* : estremecerse
shudder[2] *n* : estremecimiento *m*,
escalofrío *m*
shuffle[1] [ˈʃʌfəl] *v* -**fled; -fling** *vt* MIX
: mezclar, revolver, barajar (naipes) —
vi : caminar arrastrando los pies

shuffle² *n* **1** : acto *m* de revolver ⟨each player gets a shuffle : a cada jugador le toca barajar⟩ **2** JUMBLE : revoltijo *m* **3** : arrastramiento *m* de los pies

shun [¹ʃʌn] *vi* **shunned; shunning** : evitar, esquivar, eludir

shunt [¹ʃʌnt] *vt* : desviar, cambiar de vía (un tren)

shut [¹ʃʌt] *v* **shut; shutting** *vt* **1** CLOSE : cerrar ⟨shut the lid : tápalo⟩ **2 to shut out** EXCLUDE : excluir, dejar fuera a (personas), no dejar que entre (luz, ruido, etc.) **3 to shut up** CONFINE : encerrar — *vi* : cerrarse ⟨the factory shut down : la fábrica cerró suspuertas⟩

shut–in [¹ʃʌt₁ɪn] *n* : inválido *m*, -da *f* (que no puede salir de casa)

shutter [¹ʃʌt̬ər] *n* **1** : contraventana *f*, postigo *m* (de una ventana o puerta) **2** : obturador *m* (de una cámara)

shuttle¹ [¹ʃʌt̬əl] *v* **-tled; -tling** *vt* : transportar ⟨she shuttled him back and forth : lo llevaba de acá para allá⟩ — *vi* : ir y venir

shuttle² *n* **1** : lanzadera *f* (para tejer) **2** : vehículo *m* que hace recorridos cortos **3** → **space shuttle**

shuttlecock [¹ʃʌt̬əl₁kɑk] *n* : volante *m*

shut up *vi* : callarse ⟨shut up! : ¡cállate (la boca)!⟩

shy¹ [¹ʃaɪ] *vi* **shied; shying** : retroceder, asustarse

shy² *adj* **shier** *or* **shyer** [¹ʃaɪər]; **shiest** *or* **shyest** [¹ʃaɪəst] **1** TIMID : tímido **2** WARY : cauteloso ⟨he's not shy about asking : no vacila en preguntar⟩ **3** SHORT : corto (de dinero, etc.) ⟨I'm two dollars shy : me faltan dos dólares⟩

shyly [¹ʃaɪli] *adv* : tímidamente

shyness [¹ʃaɪnəs] *n* : timidez *f*

Siamese¹ [₁saɪə¹miːz, -¹miːs-] *adj* : siamés ⟨Siamese twins : hermanos siameses⟩

Siamese² *n* **1** : siamés *m*, -mesa *f* **2** : siamés *m* (idioma) **3** *or* **Siamese cat** : gato *m* siamés

sibling [¹sɪblɪŋ] *n* : hermano *m*, hermana *f*

Sicilian [sə¹sɪljən] *n* : siciliano *m*, -na *f* — **Sicilian** *adj*

sick [¹sɪk] *adj* **1** : enfermo **2** NAUSEOUS : mareado, con náuseas ⟨to get sick : vomitar⟩ **3** : para uso de enfermos ⟨sick day : día de permiso (por enfermedad)⟩

sickbed [¹sɪk₁bɛd] *n* : lecho *m* de enfermo

sicken [¹sɪkən] *vt* **1** : poner enfermo **2** REVOLT : darle asco (a alguien) — *vi* : enfermar(se), caer enfermo

sickening [¹sɪkənɪŋ] *adj* : asqueroso, repugnante, nauseabundo

sickle [¹sɪkəl] *n* : hoz *f*

sickly [¹sɪkli] *adj* **sicklier; -est 1** : enfermizo **2** → **sickening**

sickness [¹sɪknəs] *n* **1** : enfermedad *f* **2** NAUSEA : náuseas *fpl*

side [¹saɪd] *n* **1** : lado *m*, costado *m* (de una persona), ijada *f* (de un animal) **2** : lado *m*, cara *f* (de una moneda, etc.) **3** : lado *m*, parte *f* ⟨he's on my side : está de mi parte⟩ ⟨to take sides : tomar partido⟩

sideboard [¹saɪd₁bord] *n* : aparador *m*

sideburns [¹saɪd₁bərnz] *npl* : patillas *fpl*

sided [¹saɪdəd] *adj* : que tiene lados ⟨one-sided : de un lado⟩

side effect *n* : efecto *m* secundario

sideline [¹saɪd₁laɪn] *n* **1** : línea *f* de banda (en deportes) **2** : actividad *f* suplementaria (en negocios) **3 to be on the sidelines** : estar al margen

sidelong [¹saɪd₁lɔŋ] *adj* : de reojo, de soslayo

sideshow [¹saɪd₁ʃoː] *n* : espectáculo *m* secundario, atracción *f* secundaria

sidestep [¹saɪd₁stɛp] *v* **-stepped; -stepping** *vi* : dar un paso hacia un lado — *vt* AVOID : esquivar, eludir

sidetrack [¹saɪd₁træk] *vt* : desviar (una conversación, etc.), distraer (a una persona)

sidewalk [¹saɪd₁wɔk] *n* : acera *f*, vereda *f*, andén *m* CA, Col, banqueta *f* Mex

sideways¹ [¹saɪd₁weɪz] *adv* **1** : hacia un lado ⟨it leaned sideways : se inclinaba hacia un lado⟩ **2** : de lado, de costado ⟨lie sideways : acuéstese de costado⟩

sideways² *adj* : hacia un lado ⟨a sideways glance : una mirada de reojo⟩

siding [¹saɪdɪŋ] *n* **1** : apartadero *m* (para trenes) **2** : revestimiento *m* exterior (de un edificio)

sidle [¹saɪdəl] *vi* **-dled; -dling** : moverse furtivamente

siege [¹siːʤ, ¹siːʒ] *n* : sitio *m* ⟨to be under siege : estar sitiado⟩

siesta [si¹ɛstə] *n* : siesta *f*

sieve [¹sɪv] *n* : tamiz *m*, cedazo *m*, criba *f* (en mineralogía)

sift [¹sɪft] *vt* **1** : tamizar, cerner ⟨sift the flour : tamice la harina⟩ **2** *or* **to sift through** : examinar cuidadosamente, pasar por el tamiz

sifter [¹sɪftər] *n* : tamiz *m*, cedazo *m*

sigh¹ [¹saɪ] *vi* : suspirar

sigh² *n* : suspiro *m*

sight¹ [¹saɪt] *vt* : ver (a una persona), divisar (la tierra, un barco)

sight² *n* **1** : vista *f* (facultad) ⟨out of sight : fuera de vista⟩ **2** : algo visto ⟨it's a familiar sight : se ve con frecuencia⟩ ⟨she's a sight for sore eyes : da gusto verla⟩ **3** : lugar *m* de interés (para turistas, etc.) **4** : mira *f* (de un rifle, etc.) **5** GLIMPSE : mirada *f* breve ⟨I caught sight of her : la divisé, alcancé a verla⟩

sighting [¹saɪtɪŋ] *n* : avistamiento *m*

sightless [¹saɪtləs] *adj* : invidente, ciego

sightseer [¹saɪt₁siːər] *n* : turista *mf*

sign¹ [¹saɪn] *vt* **1** : firmar ⟨to sign a check : firmar un cheque⟩ **2** *or* **to sign on** HIRE : contratar (a un empleado), fichar (a un jugador) — *vi* **1** : hacer una seña ⟨she signed for him to stop : le hizo una seña para que se parara⟩ **2** : comunicarse por señas

sign² *n* **1** SYMBOL : símbolo *m*, signo *m* ⟨minus sign : signo de menos⟩ **2** GESTURE : seña *f*, señal *f*, gesto *m* **3** : letrero *m*, cartel *m* ⟨neon sign : letrero de neón⟩ **4** TRACE : señal *f*, indicio *m*

signal¹ [ˈsɪgnəl] *vt* **-naled** *or* **-nalled; -naling** *or* **-nalling 1** : hacerle señas (a alguien) ⟨she signaled me to leave : me hizo señas para que saliera⟩ **2** INDICATE : señalar, indicar — *vi* : hacer señas, comunicar por señas

signal² *adj* NOTABLE : señalado, notable

signal³ *n* : señal *f*

signature [ˈsɪgnəˌtʃʊr] *n* : firma *f*

signet [ˈsɪgnət] *n* : sello *m*

significance [sɪgˈnɪfɪkənts] *n* **1** MEANING : significado *m* **2** IMPORTANCE : importancia *f*

significant [sɪgˈnɪfɪkənt] *adj* **1** IMPORTANT : importante **2** MEANINGFUL : significativo — **significantly** *adv*

signify [ˈsɪgnəˌfaɪ] *vt* **-fied; -fying 1** : indicar ⟨he signified his desire for more : haciendo señas indicó que quería más⟩ **2** MEAN : significar

sign language *n* : lenguaje *m* por señas

signpost [ˈsaɪnˌpoːst] *n* : poste *m* indicador

silence¹ [ˈsaɪlənts] *vt* **-lenced; -lencing** : silenciar, acallar

silence² *n* : silencio *m*

silent [ˈsaɪlənt] *adj* **1** : callado ⟨to remain silent : quedarse callado, guardar silencio⟩ **2** QUIET, STILL : silencioso **3** MUTE : mudo ⟨a silent letter : una letra muda⟩

silently [ˈsaɪləntli] *adv* : silenciosamente, calladamente

silhouette¹ [ˌsɪləˈwɛt] *vt* **-etted; -etting** : destacar la silueta de ⟨it was silhouetted against the sky : se perfilaba contra el cielo⟩

silhouette² *n* : silueta *f*

silica [ˈsɪlɪkə] *n* : sílice *f*

silicon [ˈsɪlɪkən, -ˌkɑn] *n* : silicio *m*

silk [ˈsɪlk] *n* : seda *f*

silken [ˈsɪlkən] *adj* **1** : de seda ⟨a silken veil : un velo de seda⟩ **2** SILKY : sedoso ⟨silken hair : cabellos sedosos⟩

silkworm [ˈsɪlkˌwərm] *n* : gusano *m* de seda

silky [ˈsɪlki] *adj* **silkier; -est** : sedoso

sill [ˈsɪl] *n* : alféizar *m* (de una ventana), umbral *m* (de una puerta)

silliness [ˈsɪlinəs] *n* : tontería *f*, estupidez *f*

silly [ˈsɪli] *adj* **sillier; -est** : tonto, estúpido, ridículo

silo [ˈsaɪˌloː] *n*, *pl* **silos** : silo *m*

silt [ˈsɪlt] *n* : cieno *m*

silver¹ [ˈsɪlvər] *adj* **1** : de plata ⟨a silver spoon : una cuchara de plata⟩ **2** → **silvery**

silver² *n* **1** : plata *f* **2** COINS : monedas *fpl* **3** → **silverware 4** : color *m* plata

silverware [ˈsɪlvərˌwær] *n* **1** : artículos *mpl* de plata, platería *f* **2** FLATWARE : cubertería *f*

silvery [ˈsɪlvəri] *adj* : plateado

similar [ˈsɪmələr] *adj* : similar, parecido, semejante

similarity [ˌsɪməˈlærəti] *n*, *pl* **-ties** : semejanza *f*, parecido *m*

similarly [ˈsɪmələrli] *adv* : de manera similar

simile [ˈsɪməˌli:] *n* : símil *m*

simmer [ˈsɪmər] *v* : hervir a fuego lento

simper¹ [ˈsɪmpər] *vi* : sonreír como un tonto

simper² *n* : sonrisa *f* tonta

simple [ˈsɪmpəl] *adj* **simpler; -plest 1** INNOCENT : inocente **2** PLAIN : sencillo, simple **3** EASY : simple, sencillo, fácil **4** STRAIGHTFORWARD : puro, simple ⟨the simple truth : la pura verdad⟩ **5** NAIVE : ingenuo, simple

simpleton [ˈsɪmpəltən] *n* : bobo *m*, -ba *f*; tonto *m*, -ta *f*

simplicity [sɪmˈplɪsəti] *n* : simplicidad *f*, sencillez *f*

simplification [ˌsɪmpləfəˈkeɪʃən] *n* : simplificación *f*

simplify [ˈsɪmpləˌfaɪ] *vt* **-fied; -fying** : simplificar

simply [ˈsɪmpli] *adv* **1** PLAINLY : sencillamente **2** SOLELY : simplemente, sólo **3** REALLY : absolutamente

simulate [ˈsɪmjəˌleɪt] *vt* **-lated; -lating** : simular

simulation [ˌsɪmjəˈleɪʃən] *n* : simulación *f*

simultaneous [ˌsaɪməlˈteɪniəs] *adj* : simultáneo — **simultaneously** *adv*

sin¹ [ˈsɪn] *vi* **sinned; sinning** : pecar

sin² *n* : pecado *m*

since¹ [ˈsɪnts] *adv* **1** : desde entonces ⟨they've been friends ever since : desde entonces han sido amigos⟩ ⟨she's since become mayor : más tarde se hizo alcalde⟩ **2** AGO : hace ⟨he's long since dead : murió hace mucho⟩

since² *conj* **1** : desde que ⟨since he was born : desde que nació⟩ **2** INASMUCH AS : ya que, puesto que, dado que

since³ *prep* : desde

sincere [sɪnˈsɪr] *adj* **-cerer; -est** : sincero — **sincerely** *adv*

sincerity [sɪnˈsɛrəti] *n* : sinceridad *f*

sinew [ˈsɪnˌjuː, ˈsɪˌnuː] *n* **1** TENDON : tendón *m*, nervio *m* (en la carne) **2** POWER : fuerza *f*

sinewy [ˈsɪnjui, ˈsɪnui] *adj* **1** STRINGY : fibroso **2** STRONG, WIRY : fuerte, nervudo

sinful [ˈsɪnfəl] *adj* : pecador (dícese de las personas), pecaminoso

sing [ˈsɪŋ] *v* **sang** [ˈsæŋ] *or* **sung** [ˈsʌŋ]; **sung; singing** : cantar

singe [ˈsɪndʒ] *vt* **singed; singeing** : chamuscar, quemar

singer [ˈsɪŋər] *n* : cantante *mf*

single¹ [ˈsɪŋgəl] *vt* **-gled; -gling** *or* **to single out 1** SELECT : escoger **2** DISTINGUISH : señalar

single² *adj* **1** UNMARRIED : soltero **2** SOLE : solo ⟨a single survivor : un solo

sobreviviente⟩ ⟨every single one : cada uno, todos⟩
single³ *n* **1** : soltero *m*, -ra *f* ⟨for married couples and singles : para los matrimonios y los solteros⟩ **2** *or* **single room** : habitación *f* individual **3** DOLLAR : billete *m* de un dólar
single–handed ['sɪŋgəl'hændəd] *adj* : sin ayuda, solo
singly ['sɪŋgli] *adv* : individualmente, uno por uno
singular¹ ['sɪŋgjələr] *adj* **1** : singular (en gramática) **2** OUTSTANDING : singular, sobresaliente **3** STRANGE : singular, extraño
singular² *n* : singular *m*
singularity [ˌsɪŋgjə'lærəṭi] *n*, *pl* **-ties** : singularidad *f*
singularly ['sɪŋgjələrli] *adv* : singularmente
sinister ['sɪnəstər] *adj* : siniestro
sink¹ ['sɪŋk] *v* **sank** ['sæŋk] *or* **sunk** ['sʌŋk]; **sunk; sinking** *vi* **1** : hundirse (dícese de un barco) **2** DROP, FALL : descender, caer ⟨to sink into a chair : dejarse caer en una silla⟩ ⟨her heart sank : se le cayó el alma a los pies⟩ **3** DECREASE : bajar — *vt* **1** : hundir (un barco, etc.) **2** EXCAVATE : excavar (un pozo para minar), perforar (un pozo de agua) **3** PLUNGE, STICK : clavar, hincar **4** INVEST : invertir (fondos)
sink² *n* **1 kitchen sink** : fregadero *m*, lavaplatos *m Chile, Col, Mex* **2 bathroom sink** : lavabo *m*, lavamanos *m*
sinner ['sɪnər] *n* : pecador *m*, -dora *f*
sinuous ['sɪnjuəs] *adj* : sinuoso — **sinuously** *adv*
sinus ['saɪnəs] *n* : seno *m*
sip¹ ['sɪp] *v* **sipped; sipping** *vt* : sorber — *vi* : beber a sorbos
sip² *n* : sorbo *m*
siphon¹ ['saɪfən] *vt* : sacar con sifón
siphon² *n* : sifón *m*
sir ['sər] *n* **1** (*in titles*) : sir *m* **2** (*as a form of address*) : señor *m* ⟨Dear Sir : Muy señor mío⟩ ⟨yes sir! : ¡sí, señor!⟩
sire¹ ['saɪr] *vt* **sired; siring** : engendrar, ser el padre de
sire² *n* : padre *m*
siren ['saɪrən] *n* : sirena *f*
sirloin ['sər,lɔɪn] *n* : solomillo *m*
sirup → **syrup**
sisal ['saɪsəl, -zəl] *n* : sisal *m*
sissy ['sɪsi] *n*, *pl* **-sies** : mariquita *f fam*
sister ['sɪstər] *n* **1** : hermana *f* **2 Sister** : hermana *f*, Sor *f* ⟨Sister Mary : Sor María⟩
sisterhood ['sɪstər,hʊd] *n* **1** : condición *f* de ser hermana **2** : sociedad *f* de mujeres
sister–in–law ['sɪstərɪn,lɔ] *n*, *pl* **sisters–in–law** : cuñada *f*
sisterly ['sɪstərli] *adj* : de hermana
sit ['sɪt] *v* **sat** ['sæt]; **sitting** *vi* **1** : sentarse, estar sentado ⟨he sat down : se sentó⟩ **2** ROOST : posarse **3** : sesionar ⟨the legislature is sitting : la legislatu-

ra está en sesión⟩ **4** POSE : posar (para un retrato) **5** LIE, REST : estar (ubicado) ⟨the house sits on a hill : la casa está en una colina⟩ — *vt* SEAT : sentar, colocar ⟨I sat him on the sofa : lo senté en el sofá⟩
sitcom ['sɪt,kɑm] → **situation comedy**
site ['saɪt] *n* **1** PLACE : sitio *m*, lugar *m* **2** LOCATION : emplazamiento *m*, ubicación *f*
sitter ['sɪtər] → **baby–sitter**
sitting room → **living room**
situated ['sɪtʃu,eɪṭəd] *adj* LOCATED : ubicado, situado
situation [ˌsɪtʃu'eɪʃən] *n* **1** LOCATION : situación *f*, ubicación *f*, emplazamiento *m* **2** CIRCUMSTANCES : situación *f* **3** JOB : empleo *m*
situation comedy *n* : comedia *f* de situación
six¹ ['sɪks] *adj* : seis
six² *n* : seis *m*
six–gun ['sɪks,gʌn] *n* : revólver *m* (con seis cámaras)
six hundred¹ *adj* : seiscientos
six hundred² *n* : seiscientos *m*
six–shooter ['sɪks,ʃuːtər] → **six–gun**
sixteen¹ [sɪks'tiːn] *adj* : dieciséis
sixteen² *n* : dieciséis *m*
sixteenth¹ [sɪks'tiːnθ] *adj* : decimosexto
sixteenth² *n* **1** : decimosexto *m*, -ta *f* (en una serie) **2** : dieciseisavo *m*, dieciseisava parte *f*
sixth¹ ['sɪksθ, 'sɪkst] *adj* : sexto
sixth² *n* **1** : sexto *m*, -ta *f* (en una serie) **2** : sexto *m*, sexta parte *f*
sixtieth¹ ['sɪkstiəθ] *adj* : sexagésimo
sixtieth² *n* **1** : sexagésimo *m*, -ma *f* (en una serie) **2** : sesentavo *m*, sesentava parte *f*
sixty¹ ['sɪksti] *adj* : sesenta
sixty² *n*, *pl* **-ties** : sesenta *m*
sizable *or* **sizeable** ['saɪzəbəl] *adj* : considerable
size¹ ['saɪz] *vt* **sized; sizing 1** : clasificar según el tamaño **2 to size up** : evaluar, apreciar
size² *n* **1** DIMENSIONS : tamaño *m*, talla *f* (de ropa), número *m* (de zapatos) **2** MAGNITUDE : magnitud *f*
sizzle ['sɪzəl] *vi* **-zled; -zling** : chisporrotear
skate¹ ['skeɪt] *vi* **skated; skating** : patinar
skate² *n* **1** : patín *m* ⟨roller skate : patín de ruedas⟩ **2** : raya *f* (pez)
skateboard ['skeɪt,bord] *n* : monopatín *m*
skater ['skeɪtər] *n* : patinador *m*, -dora *f*
skein ['skeɪn] *n* : madeja *f*
skeletal ['skləṭəl] *adj* **1** : óseo (en anatomía) **2** EMACIATED : esquelético
skeleton ['skɛləṭən] *n* **1** : esqueleto *m* (anatómico) **2** FRAMEWORK : armazón *mf*
skeptic ['skɛptɪk] *n* : escéptico *m*, -ca *f*
skeptical ['skɛptɪkəl] *adj* : escéptico
skepticism ['skɛptə,sɪzəm] *n* : escepticismo *m*

sketch[1] ['skɛtʃ] *vt* : bosquejar — *vi* : hacer bosquejos
sketch[2] *n* **1** DRAWING, OUTLINE : esbozo *m*, bosquejo *m* **2** ESSAY : ensayo *m*
sketchy ['skɛtʃi] *adj* **sketchier; -est** : incompleto, poco detallado
skewer[1] ['skju:ər] *vt* : ensartar (carne, etc.)
skewer[2] *n* : brocheta *f*, broqueta *f*
ski[1] ['ski:] *vi* **skied; skiing** : esquiar
ski[2] *n, pl* **skis** : esquí *m*
skid[1] ['skɪd] *vi* **skidded; skidding** : derrapar, patinar
skid[2] *n* : derrape *m*, patinazo *m*
skier ['ski:ər] *n* : esquiador *m*, -dora *f*
skiff ['skɪf] *n* : esquife *m*
skill ['skɪl] *n* **1** DEXTERITY : habilidad *f*, destreza *f* **2** CAPABILITY : capacidad *f*, arte *m*, técnica *f* ⟨organizational skills : la capacidad para organizar⟩
skilled ['skɪld] *adj* : hábil, experto
skillet ['skɪlət] *n* : sartén *mf*
skillful ['skɪlfəl] *adj* : hábil, diestro
skillfully ['skɪlfəli] *adv* : con habilidad, con destreza
skim[1] ['skɪm] *vt* **skimmed; skimming 1** *or* **to skim off** : espumar, descremar (leche) **2** : echarle un vistazo a (un libro, etc.), pasar rozando (una superficie)
skim[2] *adj* : descremado ⟨skim milk : leche descremada⟩
skimp ['skɪmp] *vi* **to skimp on** : escatimar
skimpy ['skɪmpi] *adj* **skimpier; -est** : exiguo, escaso, raquítico
skin[1] ['skɪn] *vt* **skinned; skinning** : despellejar, desollar
skin[2] *n* **1** : piel *f*, cutis *m* (de la cara) ⟨dark skin : piel morena⟩ **2** RIND : piel *f*
skin diving *n* : buceo *m*, submarinismo *m*
skinflint ['skɪn,flɪnt] *n* : tacaño *m*, -ña *f*
skinned ['skɪnd] *adj* : de piel ⟨tough-skinned : de piel dura⟩
skinny ['skɪni] *adj* **skinnier; -est** : flaco
skip[1] ['skɪp] *v* **skipped; skipping** *vi* : ir dando brincos — *vt* : saltarse
skip[2] *n* : brinco *m*, salto *m*
skipper ['skɪpər] *n* : capitán *m*, -tana *f*
skirmish[1] ['skərmɪʃ] *vi* : escaramuzar
skirmish[2] *n* : escaramuza *f*, refriega *f*
skirt[1] ['skərt] *vt* **1** BORDER : bordear **2** EVADE : evadir, esquivar
skirt[2] *n* : falda *f*, pollera *f*
skit ['skɪt] *n* : sketch *m* (teatral)
skittish ['skɪtɪʃ] *adj* : asustadizo, nervioso
skulk ['skʌlk] *vi* : merodear
skull ['skʌl] *n* **1** : cráneo *m*, calavera *f* **2 skull and crossbones** : calavera *f* (bandera pirata)
skunk ['skʌŋk] *n* : zorrillo *m*, mofeta *f*
sky ['skaɪ] *n, pl* **skies** : cielo *m*
skylark ['skaɪ,lɑrk] *n* : alondra *f*
skylight ['skaɪ,laɪt] *n* : claraboya *f*, tragaluz *m*

skyline ['skaɪ,laɪn] *n* : horizonte *m*
skyrocket ['skaɪ,rɑkət] *vi* : dispararse
skyscraper ['skaɪ,skreɪpər] *n* : rascacielos *m*
slab ['slæb] *n* : losa *f* (de piedra), tabla *f* (de madera), pedazo *m* grueso (de pan, etc.)
slack[1] ['slæk] *adj* **1** CARELESS : descuidado, negligente **2** LOOSE : flojo **3** SLOW : de poco movimiento
slack[2] *n* **1** : parte *f* floja ⟨to take up the slack : tensar (una cuerda, etc.)⟩ **2 slacks** *npl* : pantalones *mpl*
slacken ['slækən] *vt* : aflojar — *vi* : aflojarse
slacker ['slækər] *n* : vago *m*, -ga *f*; holgazán *m*, -zana *f*
slag ['slæg] *n* : escoria *f*
slain → **slay**
slake ['sleɪk] *vt* **slaked; slaking** : saciar (la sed), satisfacer (la curiosidad)
slam[1] ['slæm] *v* **slammed; slamming** *vt* **1** : cerrar de golpe ⟨he slammed the door : dio un portazo⟩ **2** : tirar o dejar caer de golpe ⟨he slammed down the book : dejó caer el libro de un golpe⟩ — *vi* **1** : cerrarse de golpe **2 to slam into** : chocar contra
slam[2] *n* : golpe *m*, portazo *m* (de una puerta)
slander[1] ['slændər] *vt* : calumniar, difamar
slander[2] *n* : calumnia *f*, difamación *f*
slanderous ['slændərəs] *adj* : difamatorio, calumnioso
slang ['slæŋ] *n* : argot *m*, jerga *f*
slant[1] ['slænt] *vi* : inclinarse, ladearse — *vt* **1** SLOPE : inclinar **2** ANGLE : sesgar, orientar, dirigir ⟨a story slanted towards youth : un artículo dirigido a los jóvenes⟩
slant[2] *n* **1** INCLINE : inclinación *f* **2** PERSPECTIVE : perspectiva *f*, enfoque *m*
slap[1] ['slæp] *vt* **slapped; slapping** : bofetear, cachetear, dar una palmada (en la espalda, etc.)
slap[2] *n* : bofetada *f*, cachetada *f*, palmada *f*
slash[1] ['slæʃ] *vt* **1** GASH : cortar, hacer un tajo en **2** REDUCE : reducir, rebajar (precios)
slash[2] *n* : tajo *m*, corte *m*
slat ['slæt] *n* : tablilla *f*, listón *m*
slate ['sleɪt] *n* **1** : pizarra *f* ⟨a slate roof : un techo de pizarra⟩ **2** : lista *f* de candidatos (políticos)
slaughter[1] ['slɔtər] *vt* **1** BUTCHER : matar (animales) **2** MASSACRE : masacrar (personas)
slaughter[2] *n* **1** : matanza *f* (de animales) **2** MASSACRE : masacre *f*, carnicería *f*
slaughterhouse ['slɔtər,haʊs] *n* : matadero *m*
Slav ['slɑv, 'slæv] *n* : eslavo *m*, -va *f*
slave[1] ['sleɪv] *vi* **slaved; slaving** : trabajar como un burro
slave[2] *n* : esclavo *m*, -va *f*
slaver ['slævər, 'sleɪ-] *vi* : babear

slavery ['sleɪvəri] *n* : esclavitud *f*

Slavic ['slɑvɪk, 'slæ-] *adj* : eslavo

slavish ['sleɪvɪʃ] *adj* **1** SERVILE : servil **2** IMITATIVE : poco original

slay ['sleɪ] *vt* **slew** ['sluː]; **slain** ['sleɪn]; **slaying** : asesinar, matar

slayer ['sleɪər] *n* : asesino *m*, -na *f*

sleazy ['sliːzi] *adj* **sleazier; -est 1** SHODDY : chapucero, de mala calidad **2** DILAPIDATED : ruinoso **3** DISREPUTABLE : de mala fama

sled[1] ['slɛd] *v* **sledded; sledding** *vi* : ir en trineo — *vt* : transportar en trineo

sled[2] *n* : trineo *m*

sledge ['slɛdʒ] *n* **1** : trineo *m* (grande) **2** → **sledgehammer**

sledgehammer ['slɛdʒˌhæmər] *n* : almádena *f*, combo *m Chile, Peru*

sleek[1] ['sliːk] *vt* SLICK : alisar

sleek[2] *adj* : liso y brillante

sleep[1] ['sliːp] *vi* **slept** ['slɛpt]; **sleeping** : dormir

sleep[2] *n* **1** : sueño *m* **2 to go to sleep** : dormirse

sleeper ['sliːpər] *n* **1** : durmiente *mf* ⟨to be a light sleeper : tener el sueño ligero⟩ **2** *or* **sleeping car** : coche *m* cama, coche *m* dormitorio

sleepily ['sliːpəli] *adv* : de manera somnolienta

sleepiness ['sliːpinəs] *n* : somnolencia *f*

sleepless ['sliːpləs] *adj* : sin dormir, desvelado ⟨to have a sleepless night : pasar la noche en blanco⟩

sleepwalker ['sliːpˌwɔkər] *n* : sonámbulo *m*, -la *f*

sleepy ['sliːpi] *adj* **sleepier; -est 1** DROWSY : somnoliento, soñoliento ⟨to be sleepy : tener sueño⟩ **2** LETHARGIC : aletargado, letárgico

sleet[1] ['sliːt] *vi* **to be sleeting** : caer aguanieve

sleet[2] *n* : aguanieve *f*

sleeve ['sliːv] *n* : manga *f* (de una camisa, etc.)

sleeveless ['sliːvləs] *adj* : sin mangas

sleigh[1] ['sleɪ] *vi* : ir en trineo

sleigh[2] *n* : trineo *m* (tirado por caballos)

sleight of hand [ˌslaɪtəvˈhænd] : prestidigitación *f*, juegos *mpl* de manos

slender ['slɛndər] *adj* **1** SLIM : esbelto, delgado **2** SCANTY : exiguo, escaso ⟨a slender hope : una esperanza lejana⟩

sleuth ['sluːθ] *n* : detective *mf*; sabueso *m*, -sa *f*

slew → **slay**

slice[1] ['slaɪs] *vt* **sliced; slicing** : cortar

slice[2] *n* : rebanada *f*, tajada *f*, lonja *f* (de carne, etc.), rodaja *f* (de una verdura, fruta, etc.), trozo *m* (de pastel, etc.)

slick[1] ['slɪk] *vt* : alisar

slick[2] *adj* **1** SLIPPERY : resbaladizo, resbaloso **2** CRAFTY : astuto, taimado

slicker ['slɪkər] *n* : impermeable *m*

slide[1] ['slaɪd] *v* **slid** ['slɪd]; **sliding** ['slaɪdɪŋ] *vi* **1** SLIP : resbalar **2** GLIDE : deslizarse **3** DECLINE : bajar ⟨to let

things slide : dejar pasar las cosas⟩ — *vt* : correr, deslizar

slide[2] *n* **1** SLIDING : deslizamiento *m* **2** SLIP : resbalón *m* **3** : tobogán *m* (para niños) **4** TRANSPARENCY : diapositiva *f* (fotográfica) **5** DECLINE : descenso *m*

slier, sliest → **sly**

slight[1] ['slaɪt] *vt* : desairar, despreciar

slight[2] *adj* **1** SLENDER : esbelto, delgado **2** FLIMSY : endeble **3** TRIFLING : leve, insignificante ⟨a slight pain : un leve dolor⟩ **4** SMALL : pequeño, ligero ⟨not in the slightest : en absoluto⟩

slight[3] *n* SNUB : desaire *m*

slightly ['slaɪtli] *adv* : ligeramente, un poco

slim[1] ['slɪm] *v* **slimmed; slimming** : adelgazar

slim[2] *adj* **slimmer; slimmest 1** SLENDER : esbelto, delgado **2** SCANTY : exiguo, escaso

slime ['slaɪm] *n* **1** : baba *f* (secretada por un animal) **2** MUD, SILT : fango *m*, cieno *m*

slimy ['slaɪmi] *adj* **slimier; -est** : viscoso

sling[1] ['slɪŋ] *vt* **slung** ['slʌŋ]; **slinging 1** THROW : lanzar, tirar **2** HANG : colgar

sling[2] *n* **1** : honda *f* (arma) **2** : cabestrillo *m* ⟨my arm is in a sling : llevo el brazo en cabestrillo⟩

slingshot ['slɪŋˌʃɑt] *n* : tiragomas *m*, resortera *f Mex*

slink ['slɪŋk] *vi* **slunk** ['slʌŋk]; **slinking** : caminar furtivamente

slip[1] ['slɪp] *v* **slipped; slipping** *vi* **1** STEAL : ir sigilosamente ⟨to slip away : escabullirse⟩ ⟨to slip out the door : escaparse por la puerta⟩ **2** SLIDE : resbalarse, deslizarse **3** LAPSE : caer ⟨to slip into error : equivocarse⟩ **4 to let slip** : dejar escapar **5 to slip into** PUT ON : ponerse — *vt* **1** PUT : meter, poner **2** PASS : pasar ⟨she slipped me a note : me pasó una nota⟩ **3 to slip one's mind** : olvidársele a uno

slip[2] *n* **1** PIER : atracadero *m* **2** MISHAP : percance *m*, contratiempo *m* **3** MISTAKE : error *m*, desliz *m* ⟨a slip of the tongue : un lapsus⟩ **4** PETTICOAT : enagua *f* **5** : injerto *m*, esqueje *m* (de una planta) **6 slip of paper** : papelito *m*

slipper ['slɪpər] *n* : zapatilla *f*, pantufla *f*

slipperiness ['slɪpərinəs] *n* **1** : lo resbaloso, lo resbaladizo **2** TRICKINESS : astucia *f*

slippery ['slɪpəri] *adj* **slipperier; -est 1** : resbaloso, resbaladizo ⟨a slippery road : un camino resbaloso⟩ **2** TRICKY : artero, astuto, taimado **3** ELUSIVE : huidizo, escurridizo

slipshod ['slɪpˌʃɑd] *adj* : descuidado, chapucero

slip up *vi* : equivocarse

slit[1] ['slɪt] *vt* **slit; slitting** : cortar, abrir por lo largo

slit² *n* **1** OPENING : abertura *f*, rendija *f* **2** CUT : corte *m*, raja *f*, tajo *m*

slither ['slɪðər] *vi* : deslizarse

sliver ['slɪvər] *n* : astilla *f*

slob ['slɑb] *n* : persona *f* desaliñada ⟨what a slob! : ¡qué cerdo!⟩

slobber¹ ['slɑbər] *vi* : babear

slobber² *n* : baba *f*

slogan ['slo:gən] *n* : lema *m*, eslogan *m*

sloop ['slu:p] *n* : balandra *f*

slop¹ ['slɑp] *v* **slopped; slopping** *vt* : derramar — *vi* : derramarse

slop² *n* : bazofia *f*

slope¹ ['slo:p] *vi* **sloped; sloping** : inclinarse ⟨the road slopes upward : el camino sube (en pendiente)⟩

slope² *n* : inclinación *f*, pendiente *f*, declive *m*

sloppy ['slɑpi] *adj* **sloppier; -est 1** MUDDY, SLUSHY : lodoso, fangoso **2** UNTIDY : descuidado (en el trabajo, etc.), desaliñado (de aspecto)

slot ['slɑt] *n* : ranura *f*

sloth ['slo:θ, 'slɔ:θ] *n* **1** LAZINESS : pereza *f* **2** : perezoso *m* (animal)

slouch¹ ['slaʊtʃ] *vi* : andar con los hombros caídos, repantigarse (en un sillón)

slouch² *n* **1** SLUMPING : mala postura *f* **2** BUNGLER, IDLER : haragán *m*, -gana *f*; inepto *m*, -ta *f* ⟨to be no slouch : no quedarse atrás⟩

slough¹ ['slʌf] *vt* : mudar de (piel)

slough² ['slu:, 'slaʊ] *n* SWAMP : ciénaga *f*

Slovak ['slo:,vɑk, -,væk] *or* **Slovakian** [slo:'vɑkiən, -'væ-] *n* : eslovaco *m*, -ca *f* — **Slovak** *or* **Slovakian** *adj*

Slovene ['slo:,vi:n] *or* **Slovenian** [slo:-'vi:niən] *n* : esloveno *m*, -na *f* — **Slovene** *or* **Slovenian** *adj*

slovenly ['slavənli, 'slʌv-] *adj* : descuidado (en el trabajo, etc.), desaliñado (de aspecto)

slow¹ ['slo:] *vt* : retrasar, reducir la marcha de — *vi* : ir más despacio

slow² *adv* : despacio, lentamente

slow³ *adj* **1** : lento ⟨a slow process : un proceso lento⟩ **2** : atrasado ⟨my watch is slow : mi reloj está atrasado, mi reloj se atrasa⟩ **3** SLUGGISH : lento, poco activo **4** STUPID : lento, torpe, corto de alcances

slowly ['slo:li] *adv* : lentamente, despacio

slowness ['slo:nəs] *n* : lentitud *f*, torpeza *f*

sludge ['slʌdʒ] *n* : aguas *fpl* negras, aguas *fpl* residuales

slug¹ ['slʌg] *vt* **slugged; slugging** : pegarle un porrazo (a alguien)

slug² *n* **1** : babosa *f* (molusco) **2** BULLET : bala *f* **3** TOKEN : ficha *f* **4** BLOW : porrazo *m*, puñetazo *m*

sluggish ['slʌgɪʃ] *adj* : aletargado, lento

sluice¹ ['slu:s] *vt* **sluiced; sluicing** : lavar en agua corriente

sluice² *n* : canal *m*

slum ['slʌm] *n* : barriada *f*, barrio *m* bajo

slumber¹ ['slʌmbər] *vi* : dormir

slumber² *n* : sueño *m*

slump¹ ['slʌmp] *vi* **1** DECLINE, DROP : disminuir, bajar **2** SLOUCH : encorvarse, dejarse caer (en una silla, etc.)

slump² *n* : bajón *m*, declive *m* (económico)

slung → **sling**

slunk → **slink**

slur¹ ['slər] *vt* **slurred; slurring** : ligar (notas musicales), tragarse (las palabras)

slur² *n* **1** : ligado *m* (en música), mala pronunciación *f* (de las palabras) **2** ASPERSION : calumnia *f*, difamación *f*

slurp¹ ['slərp] *vi* : beber o comer haciendo ruido — *vt* : sorber ruidosamente

slurp² *n* : sorbo *m* (ruidoso)

slush ['slʌʃ] *n* : nieve *f* medio derretida

slut ['slʌt] *n* PROSTITUTE : ramera *f*, fulana *f*

sly ['slaɪ] *adj* **slier** ['slaɪər]; **sliest** ['slaɪəst] **1** CUNNING : astuto, taimado **2** UNDERHANDED : soplado — **slyly** *adv*

slyness ['slaɪnəs] *n* : astucia *f*

smack¹ ['smæk] *vi* **to smack of** : oler a, saber a — *vt* **1** KISS : besar, plantarle un beso (a alguien) **2** SLAP : pegarle una bofetada (a alguien) **3** **to smack one's lips** : relamerse

smack² *adv* : justo, exactamente ⟨smack in the face : en plena cara⟩

smack³ *n* **1** TASTE, TRACE : sabor *m*, indicio *m* **2** : chasquido *m* (de los labios) **3** SLAP : bofetada *f* **4** KISS : beso *m*

small ['smɔl] *adj* **1** : pequeño, chico ⟨a small house : una casa pequeña⟩ ⟨small change : monedas de poco valor⟩ **2** TRIVIAL : pequeño, insignificante

smallness ['smɔlnəs] *n* : pequeñez *f*

smallpox ['smɔl,pɑks] *n* : viruela *f*

smart¹ ['smɑrt] *vi* **1** STING : escocer, picar, arder **2** HURT : dolerse, resentirse ⟨to smart under a rejection : dolerse ante un rechazo⟩

smart² *adj* **1** BRIGHT : listo, vivo, inteligente **2** STYLISH : elegante — **smartly** *adv*

smart³ *n* **1** PAIN : escozor *m*, dolor *m* **2** **smarts** *npl* : inteligencia *f*

smartness ['smɑrtnəs] *n* **1** INTELLIGENCE : inteligencia *f* **2** ELEGANCE : elegancia *f*

smash¹ ['smæʃ] *vt* **1** BREAK : romper, quebrar, hacer pedazos **2** WRECK : destrozar, arruinar **3** CRASH : estrellar, chocar — *vi* **1** SHATTER : hacerse pedazos, hacerse añicos **2** COLLIDE, CRASH : estrellarse, chocar

smash² *n* **1** BLOW : golpe *m* **2** COLLISION : choque *m* **3** BANG, CRASH : estrépito *m*

smattering ['smætərɪŋ] *n* **1** : nociones *fpl* ⟨she has a smattering of programming : tiene nociones de programación⟩ **2** : un poco, unos cuantos ⟨a smattering of spectators : unos cuantos espectadores⟩

smear¹ ['smɪr] *vt* **1** DAUB : embadurnar, untar (mantequilla, etc.) **2** SMUDGE : emborronar **3** SLANDER : calumniar, difamar

smear² *n* **1** SMUDGE : mancha *f* **2** SLANDER : calumnia *f*

smell¹ ['smɛl] *v* **smelled** *or* **smelt** ['smɛlt]; **smelling** *vt* : oler, olfatear ⟨to smell danger : olfatear el peligro⟩ — *vi* : oler ⟨to smell good : oler bien⟩

smell² *n* **1** : olfato *m*, sentido *m* del olfato **2** ODOR : olor *m*

smelly ['smɛli] *adj* **smellier; -est** : maloliente

smelt¹ ['smɛlt] *vt* : fundir

smelt² *n, pl* **smelts** *or* **smelt** : eperlano *m* (pez)

smile¹ ['smaɪl] *vi* **smiled; smiling** : sonreír

smile² *n* : sonrisa *f*

smirk¹ ['smərk] *vi* : sonreír con suficiencia

smirk² *n* : sonrisa *f* satisfecha

smite ['smaɪt] *vt* **smote** ['smo:t]; **smitten** ['smɪtən] *or* **smote; smiting 1** STRIKE : golpear **2** AFFLICT : afligir

smith ['smɪθ] *n* : herrero *m*, -ra *f*

smithy ['smɪθi] *n, pl* **smithies** : herrería *f*

smock ['smɑk] *n* : bata *f*, blusón *m*

smog ['smɑg, 'smɔg] *n* : smog *m*

smoke¹ ['smo:k] *v* **smoked; smoking** *vi* **1** : echar humo, humear ⟨a smoking chimney : una chimenea que echa humo⟩ **2** : fumar ⟨I don't smoke : no fumo⟩ — *vt* : ahumar (carne, etc.)

smoke² *n* : humo *m*

smoke detector [dɪ'tɛktər] *n* : detector *m* de humo

smoker ['smo:kər] *n* : fumador *m*, -dora *f*

smokestack ['smo:kˌstæk] *n* : chimenea *f*

smoky ['smo:ki] *adj* **smokier; -est 1** SMOKING : humeante **2** : a humo ⟨a smoky flavor : un sabor a humo⟩ **3** : lleno de humo ⟨a smoky room : un cuarto lleno de humo⟩

smolder ['smo:ldər] *vi* **1** : arder sin llama **2** : arder (en el corazón) ⟨his anger smoldered : su rabia ardía⟩

smooth¹ ['smu:ð] *vt* : alisar

smooth² *adj* **1** : liso (dícese de una superficie) ⟨smooth skin : piel lisa⟩ **2** : suave (dícese de un movimiento) ⟨a smooth landing : un aterrizaje suave⟩ **3** : sin grumos ⟨a smooth sauce : una salsa sin grumos⟩ **4** : fluido ⟨smooth writing : escritura fluida⟩

smoothly ['smu:ðli] *adv* **1** GENTLY, SOFTLY : suavemente **2** EASILY : con facilidad, sin problemas

smoothness ['smu:ðnəs] *n* : suavidad *f*

smother ['smʌðər] *vt* **1** SUFFOCATE : ahogar, sofocar **2** COVER : cubrir **3** SUPPRESS : contener — *vi* : asfixiarse

smudge¹ ['smʌʤ] *v* **smudged; smudging** *vt* : emborronar — *vi* : correrse

smudge² *n* : mancha *f*, borrón *m*

smug ['smʌg] *adj* **smugger; smuggest** : suficiente, pagado de sí mismo

smuggle ['smʌgəl] *vt* **-gled; -gling** : contrabandear, pasar de contrabando

smuggler ['smʌgələr] *n* : contrabandista *mf*

smugly ['smʌgli] *adv* : con suficiencia

smut ['smʌt] *n* **1** SOOT : tizne *m*, hollín *m* **2** FUNGUS : tizón *m* **3** OBSCENITY : obscenidad *f*, inmundicia *f*

smutty ['smʌti] *adj* **smuttier; -est 1** SOOTY : tiznado **2** OBSCENE : obsceno, indecente

snack ['snæk] *n* : refrigerio *m*, bocado *m*, tentempié *m fam* ⟨an afternoon snack : una merienda⟩

snag¹ ['snæg] *v* **snagged; snagging** *vt* : enganchar — *vi* : engancharse

snag² *n* : problema *m*, inconveniente *m*

snail ['sneɪl] *n* : caracol *m*

snake ['sneɪk] *n* : culebra *f*, serpiente *f*

snakebite ['sneɪkˌbaɪt] *n* : mordedura *f* de serpiente

snap¹ ['snæp] *v* **snapped; snapping** *vi* **1** : intentar morder (dícese de un perro, etc.), picar (dícese de un pez) **2** : hablar con severidad ⟨he snapped at me! : ¡me gritó!⟩ **3** BREAK : romperse, quebrarse (haciendo un chasquido) — *vt* **1** BREAK : partir (en dos), quebrar **2** : hacer (algo) de un golpe ⟨to snap open : abrir de golpe⟩ **3** RETORT : decir bruscamente **4** CLICK : chasquear ⟨to snap one's fingers : chasquear los dedos⟩

snap² *n* **1** CLICK, CRACK : chasquido *m* **2** FASTENER : broche *m* **3** CINCH : cosa *f* fácil ⟨it's a snap : es facilísimo⟩

snapdragon ['snæpˌdrægən] *n* : dragón *m* (flor)

snapper ['snæpər] → **red snapper**

snappy ['snæpi] *adj* **snappier; -est 1** FAST : rápido ⟨make it snappy! : ¡date prisa!⟩ **2** LIVELY : vivaz **3** CHILLY : frío **4** STYLISH : elegante

snapshot ['snæpˌʃɑt] *n* : instantánea *f*

snare¹ ['snær] *vt* **snared; snaring** : atrapar

snare² *n* : trampa *f*, red *f*

snare drum *n* : tambor *m* con bordón

snarl¹ ['snɑrl] *vi* **1** TANGLE : enmarañar, enredar **2** GROWL : gruñir

snarl² *n* **1** TANGLE : enredo *m*, maraña *f* **2** GROWL : gruñido *m*

snatch¹ ['snæʧ] *vt* : arrebatar

snatch² *n* : fragmento *m*

sneak¹ ['sni:k] *vi* : ir a hurtadillas — *vt* : hacer furtivamente ⟨to sneak a look : mirar con disimulo⟩ ⟨he sneaked a smoke : fumó un cigarrillo a escondidas⟩

sneak² *n* : soplón *m*, -plona *f*

sneakers ['sni:kərz] *npl* : tenis *mpl*, zapatillas *fpl*

sneaky ['sni:ki] *adj* **sneakier; -est** : solapado

sneer[1] ['snɪr] *vi* : sonreír con desprecio
sneer[2] *n* : sonrisa *f* de desprecio
sneeze[1] ['sni:z] *vi* **sneezed; sneezing** : estornudar
sneeze[2] *n* : estornudo *m*
snicker[1] ['snɪkər] *vi* : reírse disimuladamente
snicker[2] *n* : risita *f*
snide ['snaɪd] *adj* : sarcástico
sniff[1] ['snɪf] *vi* **1** SMELL : oler, husmear (dícese de los animales) **2 to sniff at** : despreciar, desdeñar — *vt* **1** SMELL : oler **2 to sniff out** : olerse, husmear
sniff[2] *n* **1** SNIFFING : aspiración *f* por la nariz **2** SMELL : olor *m*
sniffle ['snɪfəl] *vi* **-fled; -fling** : respirar con la nariz congestionada
sniffles ['snɪfəlz] *npl* : resfriado *m*
snip[1] ['snɪp] *vt* **snipped; snipping** : cortar (con tijeras)
snip[2] *n* : tijeretada *f*, recorte *m*
snipe[1] ['snaɪp] *vi* **sniped; sniping** : disparar
snipe[2] *n, pl* **snipes** *or* **snipe** : agachadiza *f*
sniper ['snaɪpər] *n* : francotirador *m*, -dora *f*
snippet ['snɪpət] *n* : fragmento *m* (de un texto, etc.)
snivel ['snɪvəl] *vi* **-veled** *or* **-velled; -veling** *or* **-velling 1** → **snuffle 2** WHINE : lloriquear
snob ['snɑb] *n* : esnob *mf*, snob *mf*
snobbery ['snɑbəri] *n, pl* **-beries** : esnobismo *m*
snobbish ['snɑbɪʃ] *adj* : esnob, snob
snobbishness ['snɑbɪʃnəs] *n* : esnobismo *m*
snoop[1] ['snu:p] *vi* : husmear, curiosear
snoop[2] *n* : fisgón *m*, -gona *f*
snooze[1] ['snu:z] *vi* **snoozed; snoozing** : dormitar
snooze[2] *n* : siestecita *f*, siestita *f*
snore[1] ['snor] *vi* **snored; snoring** : roncar
snore[2] *n* : ronquido *m*
snort[1] ['snɔrt] *vi* : bufar, resoplar
snort[2] *n* : bufido *m*, resoplo *m*
snout ['snaʊt] *n* : hocico *m*, morro *m*
snow[1] ['sno:] *vi* **1** : nevar ⟨I'm snowed in : estoy aislado por la nieve⟩ **2 to be snowed under** : estar inundado
snow[2] *n* : nieve *f*
snowball ['sno:ˌbɔl] *n* : bola *f* de nieve
snowdrift ['sno:ˌdrɪft] *n* : ventisquero *m*
snowfall ['sno:ˌfɔl] *n* : nevada *f*
snowplow ['sno:ˌplaʊ] *n* : quitanieves *m*
snowshoe ['sno:ˌʃu:] *n* : raqueta *f* (para nieve)
snowstorm ['sno:ˌstɔrm] *n* : tormenta *f* de nieve, ventisca *f*
snowy ['sno:i] *adj* **snowier; -est** : nevoso ⟨a snowy road : un camino nevado⟩
snub[1] ['snʌb] *vt* **snubbed; snubbing** : desairar
snub[2] *n* : desaire *m*
snub–nosed ['snʌbˌno:zd] *adj* : de nariz respingada

snuff[1] ['snʌf] *vt* **1** : apagar (una vela) **2** : sorber (algo) por la nariz
snuff[2] *n* : rapé *m*
snuffle ['snʌfəl] *vi* **-fled; -fling** : respirar con la nariz congestionada
snug ['snʌg] *adj* **snugger; snuggest 1** COMFORTABLE : cómodo **2** TIGHT : ajustado, ceñido ⟨snug pants : pantalones ajustados⟩
snuggle ['snʌgəl] *vi* **-gled; -gling** : acurrucarse ⟨to snuggle up to someone : arrimársele a alguien⟩
snugly ['snʌgli] *adv* **1** COMFORTABLY : cómodamente **2** : de manera ajustada ⟨the shirt fits snugly : la camisa queda ajustada⟩
so[1] ['so:] *adv* **1** (*referring to something indicated or suggested*) ⟨do you think so? : ¿tú crees?⟩ ⟨so it would seem : eso parece⟩ ⟨I told her so : se lo dije⟩ ⟨he's ready, or so he says : según dice, está listo⟩ ⟨it so happened that . . . : resultó que . . .⟩ ⟨do it like so : hazlo así⟩ ⟨so be it : así sea⟩ **2** ALSO : también ⟨so do I : yo también⟩ **3** THUS : así, de esta manera **4** : tan ⟨he'd never been so happy : nunca había estado tan contento⟩ **5** CONSEQUENTLY : por lo tanto
so[2] *conj* **1** THEREFORE : así que **2** *or* **so that** : para que, así que, de manera que **3 so what?** : ¿y qué?
soak[1] ['so:k] *vi* : estar en remojo — *vt* **1** : poner en remojo **2 to soak up** ABSORB : absorber
soak[2] *n* : remojo *m*
soap[1] ['so:p] *vt* : enjabonar
soap[2] *n* : jabón *m*
soapsuds ['so:pˌsʌdz] → **suds**
soapy ['so:pi] *adj* **soapier; -est** : jabonoso ⟨a soapy taste : un gusto a jabón⟩ ⟨a soapy texture : una textura de jabón⟩
soar ['sor] *vi* **1** FLY : volar **2** RISE : remontar el vuelo (dícese de las aves) ⟨her hopes soared : su esperanza renació⟩ ⟨prices are soaring : los precios están subiendo vertiginosamente⟩
sob[1] ['sɑb] *vi* **sobbed; sobbing** : sollozar
sob[2] *n* : sollozo *m*
sober ['so:bər] *adj* **1** : sobrio ⟨he's not sober enough to drive : está demasiado borracho para manejar⟩ **2** SERIOUS : serio
soberly ['so:bərli] *adv* **1** : sobriamente **2** SERIOUSLY : seriamente
sobriety [sə'braɪəti, so-] *n* **1** : sobriedad *f* ⟨sobriety test : prueba de alcoholemia⟩ **2** SERIOUSNESS : seriedad *f*
so-called ['so:'kɔld] *adj* : supuesto, presunto ⟨the so-called experts : los expertos, así llamados⟩
soccer ['sɑkər] *n* : futbol *m*, fútbol *m*
sociable ['so:ʃəbəl] *adj* : sociable
social[1] ['so:ʃəl] *adj* : social — **socially** *adv*
social[2] *n* : reunión *f* social

socialism ['so:ʃə‚lɪzəm] *n* : socialismo *m*
socialist¹ ['so:ʃəlɪst] *adj* : socialista
socialist² *n* : socialista *mf*
socialize ['so:ʃə‚laɪz] *v* **-ized; -izing** *vt* **1**
NATIONALIZE : nacionalizar **2** : socializar (en psicología) — *vi* : alternar, circular ⟨to socialize with friends : alternar con amigos⟩
social work *n* : asistencia *f* social
society [sə'saɪəṭi] *n, pl* **-eties 1** COMPANIONSHIP : compañía *f* **2** : sociedad *f* ⟨a democratic society : una sociedad democrática⟩ ⟨high society : alta sociedad⟩ **3** ASSOCIATION : sociedad *f*, asociación *f*
socioeconomic [‚so:sio‚i:kə'namɪk, -‚ɛkə-] *adj* : socioeconómico
sociology [‚so:si'alədʒi] *n* : sociología *f*
sociological [‚so:siə'ladʒɪkəl] *adj* : sociológico
sociologist [‚so:si'alədʒɪst] *n* : sociólogo *m*, -ga *f*
sock¹ ['sak] *vt* : pegar, golpear, darle un puñetazo a
sock² *n* **1** *pl* **socks** *or* **sox** ['saks] : calcetín *m*, media *f* ⟨shoes and socks : zapatos y calcetines⟩ **2** *pl* **socks** ['saks] PUNCH : puñetazo *m*
socket ['sakət] *n* **1** *or* **electric socket** : enchufe *m*, toma *f* de corriente **2** : glena *f* (de una articulación) ⟨shoulder socket : glena del hombro⟩ **3 eye socket** : órbita *f*, cuenca *f*
sod¹ ['sad] *vt* **sodded; sodding** : cubrir de césped
sod² *n* TURF : césped *m*, tepe *m*
soda ['so:də] *n* **1** *or* **soda water** : soda *f* **2** *or* **soda pop** : gaseosa *f*, refresco *m* **3** *or* **ice–cream soda** : refresco *m* con helado
sodden ['sadən] *adj* SOGGY : empapado
sodium ['so:diəm] *n* : sodio *m*
sodium bicarbonate *n* : bicarbonato *m* de soda
sodium chloride → **salt**
sofa ['so:fə] *n* : sofá *m*
soft ['sɔft] *adj* **1** : blando ⟨a soft pillow : una almohada blanda⟩ **2** SMOOTH : suave (dícese de las texturas, de los sonidos, etc.) **3** NONALCOHOLIC : no alcohólico ⟨a soft drink : un refresco⟩
softball ['sɔft‚bɔl] *n* : softbol *m*
soften ['sɔfən] *vt* : ablandar (algo sólido), suavizar (la piel, un golpe, etc.), amortiguar (un impacto) — *vi* : ablandarse, suavizarse
softly ['sɔftli] *adv* : suavemente ⟨she spoke softly : habló en voz baja⟩
softness ['sɔftnəs] *n* **1** : blandura *f*, lo blando (de una almohada, de la mantequilla, etc.) **2** SMOOTHNESS : suavidad *f*
software ['sɔft‚wær] *n* : software *m*
soggy ['sagi] *adj* **soggier; -est** : empapado
soil¹ ['sɔɪl] *vt* : ensuciar — *vi* : ensuciarse

soil² *n* **1** DIRTINESS : suciedad *f* **2** DIRT, EARTH : suelo *m*, tierra *f* **3** COUNTRY : patria *f* ⟨her native soil : su tierra natal⟩
sojourn¹ ['so:‚dʒərn, so:'dʒərn] *vi* : pasar una temporada
sojourn² *n* : estadía *f*, estancia *f*, permanencia *f*
solace ['saləs] *n* : consuelo *m*
solar ['so:lər] *adj* : solar ⟨the solar system : el sistema solar⟩
sold → **sell**
solder¹ ['sadər, 'sɔ-] *vt* : soldar
solder² *n* : soldadura *f*
soldier¹ ['so:ldʒər] *vi* : servir como soldado
soldier² *n* : soldado *mf*
sole¹ ['so:l] *adj* : único
sole² *n* **1** : suela *f* (de un zapato) **2** : lenguado *m* (pez)
solely ['so:li] *adv* : únicamente, sólo
solemn ['saləm] *adj* : solemne, serio —
solemnly *adv*
solemnity [sə'lɛmnəṭi] *n, pl* **-ties** : solemnidad *f*
solicit [sə'lɪsət] *vt* : solicitar
solicitous [sə'lɪsəṭəs] *adj* : solícito
solicitude [sə'lɪsə‚tu:d, -‚tju:d] *n* : solicitud *f*
solid¹ ['saləd] *adj* **1** : macizo ⟨a solid rubber ball : una bola maciza de caucho⟩ **2** CUBIC : tridimensional **3** COMPACT : compacto, denso **4** STURDY : sólido **5** CONTINUOUS : seguido, continuo ⟨two solid hours : dos horas seguidas⟩ ⟨a solid line : una línea continua⟩ **6** UNANIMOUS : unánime **7** DEPENDABLE : serio, fiable **8** PURE : macizo, puro ⟨solid gold : oro macizo⟩
solid² *n* : sólido *m*
solidarity [‚salə'dærəṭi] *n* : solidaridad *f*
solidify [sə'lɪdə‚faɪ] *v* **-fied; -fying** *vt* : solidificar — *vi* : solidificarse
solidity [sə'lɪdəṭi] *n, pl* **-ties** : solidez *f*
solidly ['salədli] *adv* **1** : sólidamente **2** UNANIMOUSLY : unánimemente
soliloquy [sə'lɪləkwi] *n, pl* **-quies** : soliloquio *m*
solitaire ['salə‚ter] *n* : solitario *m*
solitary ['salə‚teri] *adj* **1** ALONE : solitario **2** SECLUDED : apartado, retirado **3** SINGLE : solo
solitude ['salə‚tu:d, -‚tju:d] *n* : soledad *f*
solo¹ ['so:‚lo:] *vi* : volar en solitario (dícese de un piloto)
solo² *adv & adj* : en solitario, a solas
solo³ *n, pl* **solos** : solo *m*
soloist ['so:loɪst] *n* : solista *mf*
solstice ['salstɪs] *n* : solsticio *m*
soluble ['saljəbəl] *adj* : soluble
solution [sə'lu:ʃən] *n* : solución *f*
solve ['salv] *vt* **solved; solving** : resolver, solucionar
solvency ['salvəntsi] *n* : solvencia *f*
solvent ['salvənt] *n* : solvente *m*
Somali ['so:mali, sə-] *n* : somalí *mf* —
Somali *adj*
somber ['sambər] *adj* **1** DARK : sombrío, oscuro ⟨somber colors : colores

oscuros〉 **2** GRAVE : sombrío, serio **3** MELANCHOLY : sombrío, lúgubre

sombrero [səm'brɛrˌoː] *n, pl* **-ros** : sombrero *m* (mexicano)

some¹ ['sʌm] *adj* **1** : un, algún 〈some lady stopped me : una mujer me detuvo〉 〈some distant galaxy : alguna galaxia lejana〉 **2** : algo de, un poco de 〈he drank some water : tomó (un poco de) agua〉 **3** : unos 〈do you want some apples? : ¿quieres unas manzanas?〉 〈some years ago : hace varios años〉

some² *pron* **1** : algunos 〈some went, others stayed : algunos se fueron, otros se quedaron〉 **2** : un poco, algo 〈there's some left : queda un poco〉 〈I have gum; do you want some? : tengo chicle, ¿quieres?〉

somebody ['sʌmbədi, -ˌbɑdi] *pron* : alguien

someday ['sʌmˌdeɪ] *adv* : algún día

somehow ['sʌmˌhaʊ] *adv* **1** : de alguna manera, de algún modo 〈I'll do it somehow : lo haré de alguna manera〉 **2** : por alguna razón 〈somehow I don't trust her : por alguna razón no me fío de ella〉

someone ['sʌmˌwʌn] *pron* : alguien

someplace ['sʌmˌpleɪs] → **somewhere**

somersault¹ ['sʌmərˌsɔlt] *vi* : dar volteretas, dar un salto mortal

somersault² *n* : voltereta *f*, salto *m* mortal

something ['sʌmθɪŋ] *pron* : algo 〈I want something else : quiero otra cosa〉 〈she's writing a novel or something : está escribiendo una novela o no sé qué〉

sometime ['sʌmˌtaɪm] *adv* : algún día, en algún momento 〈sometime next month : durante el mes que viene〉

sometimes ['sʌmˌtaɪmz] *adv* : a veces, algunas veces, de vez en cuando

somewhat ['sʌmˌhwʌt, -ˌhwʌt] *adv* : algo, un tanto

somewhere ['sʌmˌhwɛr] *adv* **1** (*indicating location*) : en algún lugar 〈it must be somewhere else : estará en otra parte〉 **2** (*indicating destination*) : a algún lugar

son ['sʌn] *n* : hijo *m*

sonar ['soːˌnɑr] *n* : sonar *m*

sonata [sə'nɑtə] *n* : sonata *f*

song ['sɔŋ] *n* : canción *f*, canto *m* (de un pájaro)

songbird ['sɔŋˌbərd] *n* : pájaro *m* cantor

songwriter ['sɔŋˌraɪtər] *n* : compositor *m*, -tora *f*

sonic ['sɑnɪk] *adj* **1** : sónico **2** **sonic boom** : estampido *m* sónico

son–in–law ['sʌnɪnˌlɔ] *n, pl* **sons–in–law** : yerno *m*, hijo *m* político

sonnet ['sɑnət] *n* : soneto *m*

sonorous ['sɑnərəs, sə'norəs] *adj* : sonoro

soon ['suːn] *adv* **1** : pronto, dentro de poco 〈he'll arrive soon : llegará pron-

to〉 **2** QUICKLY : pronto 〈as soon as possible : lo más pronto posible〉 〈the sooner the better : cuanto antes mejor〉 **3** : de buena gana 〈I'd sooner walk : prefiero caminar〉

soot ['sʊt, 'suːt, 'sʌt] *n* : hollín *m*, tizne *m*

soothe ['suːð] *vt* **soothed; soothing 1** CALM : calmar, tranquilizar **2** RELIEVE : aliviar

soothsayer ['suːθˌseɪər] *n* : adivino *m*, -na *f*

sooty ['sʊti, 'suː-, 'sʌ-] *adj* **sootier; -est** : cubierto de hollín, tiznado

sop¹ ['sɑp] *vt* **sopped; sopping 1** DIP : mojar **2** SOAK : empapar **3 to sop up** : rebañar, absorber

sop² *n* **1** CONCESSION : concesión *f* **2** BRIBE : soborno *m*

sophisticated [sə'fɪstəˌkeɪtəd] *adj* **1** COMPLEX : complejo **2** WORLDLY-WISE : sofisticado

sophistication [səˌfɪstə'keɪʃən] *n* **1** COMPLEXITY : complejidad *f* **2** URBANITY : sofisticación *f*

sophomore ['sɑfˌmor, 'sɑfəˌmor] *n* : estudiante *mf* de segundo año

soporific [ˌsɑpə'rɪfɪk, ˌsoː-] *adj* : soporífero

soprano [sə'præˌnoː] *n, pl* **-nos** : soprano *mf*

sorcerer ['sɔrsərər] *n* : hechicero *m*, brujo *m*, mago *m*

sorceress ['sɔrsərəs] *n* : hechicera *f*, bruja *f*, maga *f*

sorcery ['sɔrsəri] *n* : hechicería *f*, brujería *f*

sordid ['sɔrdɪd] *adj* : sórdido

sore¹ ['sor] *adj* **sorer; sorest 1** PAINFUL : dolorido, doloroso 〈I have a sore throat : me duele la garganta〉 **2** ACUTE, SEVERE : extremo, grande 〈in sore straits : en grandes apuros〉 **3** ANGRY : enojado, enfadado

sore² *n* : llaga *f*

sorely ['sorli] *adv* : muchísimo 〈it was sorely needed : se necesitaba urgentemente〉 〈she was sorely missed : la echaban mucho de menos〉

soreness ['sornəs] *n* : dolor *m*

sorghum ['sɔrgəm] *n* : sorgo *m*

sorority [sə'rɔrəti] *n, pl* **-ties** : hermandad *f* (de estudiantes femeninas)

sorrel ['sɔrəl] *n* **1** : alazán *m* (color o animal) **2** : acedera *f* (hierba)

sorrow ['sɑrˌoː] *n* : pesar *m*, dolor *m*, pena *f*

sorrowful ['sɑrəfəl] *adj* : triste, afligido, apenado

sorrowfully ['sɑrəfəli] *adv* : con tristeza

sorry ['sɑri] *adj* **sorrier; -est 1** PITIFUL : lastimero, lastimoso **2 to be sorry** : sentir, lamentar 〈I'm sorry : lo siento〉 **3 to feel sorry for** : compadecer 〈I feel sorry for him : me da pena〉

sort¹ ['sɔrt] *vt* **1** : dividir en grupos **2** CLASSIFY : clasificar **3 to sort out** ORGANIZE : poner en orden **4 to sort out** RESOLVE : resolver

sort² *n* **1** KIND : tipo *m*, clase *f* ⟨a sort of writer : una especie de escritor⟩ **2** NATURE : índole *f* **3 out of sorts** : de mal humor

sortie ['sɔrt̬i, sɔr'ti:] *n* : salida *f*

SOS [ˌɛsˌoː'ɛs] *n* : SOS *m*

so-so ['soː'soː] *adj & adv* : así así, de modo regular

soufflé [suː'fleɪ] *n* : suflé *m*

sought → **seek**

soul ['soːl] *n* **1** SPIRIT : alma *f* **2** ESSENCE : esencia *f* **3** PERSON : persona *f*, alma *f*

soulful ['soːlfəl] *adj* : conmovedor, lleno de emoción

sound¹ ['saʊnd] *vt* **1** : sondar (en navegación) **2** *or* **to sound out** PROBE : sondear **3** : hacer sonar, tocar (una trompeta, etc.) — *vi* **1** : sonar ⟨the alarm sounded : la alarma sonó⟩ **2** SEEM : parecer

sound² *adj* **1** HEALTHY : sano ⟨safe and sound : sano y salvo⟩ ⟨of sound mind and body : en pleno uso de sus facultades⟩ **2** FIRM, SOLID : sólido **3** SENSIBLE : lógico, sensato **4** DEEP : profundo ⟨a sound sleep : un sueño profundo⟩

sound³ *n* **1** : sonido *m* ⟨the speed of sound : la velocidad del sonido⟩ **2** NOISE : sonido *m*, ruido *m* ⟨I heard a sound : oí un sonido⟩ **3** CHANNEL : brazo *m* de mar, canal *m* (ancho)

soundless ['saʊndləs] *adj* : sordo

soundlessly ['saʊndləsli] *adv* : silenciosamente

soundly ['saʊndli] *adv* **1** SOLIDLY : sólidamente **2** SENSIBLY : lógicamente, sensatamente **3** DEEPLY : profundamente ⟨sleeping soundly : durmiendo profundamente⟩

soundness ['saʊndnəs] *n* **1** SOLIDITY : solidez *f* **2** SENSIBLENESS : sensatez *f*, solidez *f*

soundproof ['saʊndˌpruːf] *adj* : insonorizado

soundtrack ['saʊndˌtræk] *n* : banda *f* sonora

sound wave *n* : onda *f* sonora

soup ['suːp] *n* : sopa *f*

sour¹ ['saʊər] *vi* : agriarse, cortarse (dícese de la leche) — *vt* : agriar, cortar (leche)

sour² *adj* **1** ACID : agrio, ácido (dícese de la fruta, etc.), cortado (dícese de la leche) **2** DISAGREEABLE : desagradable, agrio

source ['sors] *n* : fuente *f*, origen *m*, nacimiento *m* (de un río)

sourness ['saʊərnəs] *n* : acidez *f*

south¹ ['saʊθ] *adv* : al sur, hacia el sur ⟨the window looks south : la ventana mira al sur⟩ ⟨she continued south : continuó hacia el sur⟩

south² *adj* : sur, del sur ⟨the south entrance : la entrada sur⟩ ⟨South America : Sudamérica, América del Sur⟩

south³ *n* : sur *m*

South African *n* : sudafricano *m*, -na *f*

— South African *adj*

South American¹ *adj* : sudamericano, suramericano

South American² *n* : sudamericano *m*, -na *f*; suramericano *m*, -na *f*

southbound ['saʊθˌbaʊnd] *adj* : con rumbo al sur

southeast¹ [saʊ'θiːst] *adj* : sureste, sudeste, del sureste

southeast² *n* : sureste *m*, sudeste *m*

southeasterly [saʊ'θiːstərli] *adv & adj* **1** : del sureste (dícese del viento) **2** : hacia el sureste

southeastern [saʊ'θiːstərn] *adj* → **southeast¹**

southerly ['sʌðərli] *adv & adj* : del sur

southern ['sʌðərn] *adj* : sur, sureño, meridional, austral ⟨a southern city : una ciudad del sur del país, una ciudad meridional⟩ ⟨the southern side : el lado sur⟩

Southerner ['sʌðərnər] *n* : sureño *m*, -ña *f*

South Pole : Polo *m* Sur

southward ['saʊθwərd] *or* **southwards** [-wərdz] *adv & adj* : hacia el sur

southwest¹ [saʊθ'wɛst, *as a nautical term often* saʊ'wɛst] *adj* : suroeste, sudoeste, del suroeste

southwest² *n* : suroeste *m*, sudoeste *m*

southwesterly [saʊθ'wɛstərli] *adv & adj* **1** : del suroeste (dícese del viento) **2** : hacia el suroeste

southwestern [saʊθ'wɛstərn] *adj* → **southwest¹**

souvenir [ˌsuːvə'nɪr, 'suːvəˌ-] *n* : recuerdo *m*, souvenir *m*

sovereign¹ ['savərən] *adj* : soberano

sovereign² *n* **1** : soberano *m*, -na *f* (monarca) **2** : soberano *m* (moneda)

sovereignty ['savərənt̬i] *n*, *pl* **-ties** : soberanía *f*

Soviet ['soːviˌɛt, 'sa-, -viət] *adj* : soviético

sow¹ ['soː] *vt* **sowed; sown** ['soːn] *or* **sowed; sowing** **1** PLANT : sembrar **2** SCATTER : esparcir

sow² ['saʊ] *n* : cerda *f*

sox → **sock**

soy ['sɔɪ] *n* : soya *f*, soja *f*

soybean ['sɔɪˌbiːn] *n* : soya *f*, soja *f*

spa ['spa] *n* : balneario *m*

space¹ ['speɪs] *vt* **spaced; spacing** : espaciar

space² *n* **1** PERIOD : espacio *m*, lapso *m*, período *m* **2** ROOM : espacio *m*, sitio *m*, lugar *m* ⟨is there space for me? : ¿hay sitio para mí?⟩ **3** : espacio *m* ⟨blank space : espacio en blanco⟩ **4** : espacio *m* (en física) **5** PLACE : plaza *f*, sitio *m* ⟨to reserve space : reservar plazas⟩ ⟨parking space : sitio para estacionarse⟩

spacecraft ['speɪsˌkræft] *n* : nave *f* espacial

spaceflight ['speɪsˌflaɪt] *n* : vuelo *m* espacial

spaceman ['speɪsmən, -ˌmæn] *n, pl* **-men** [-mən, -ˌmɛn] : astronauta *m*, cosmonauta *m*

spaceship ['speɪsˌʃɪp] *n* : nave *f* espacial

space shuttle *n* : transbordador *m* espacial

space suit *n* : traje *m* espacial

spacious ['speɪʃəs] *adj* : espacioso, amplio

spade[1] ['speɪd] *v* **spaded; spading** : palear — *vi* : usar una pala

spade[2] *n* **1** SHOVEL : pala *f* **2** : pica *f* (naipe)

spaghetti [spə'gɛt̬i] *n* : espagueti *m*, espaguetis *mpl*, spaghetti *mpl*

spam ['spæm] *n* : spam *m*, correo *m* electrónico no solicitado

span[1] ['spæn] *vt* **spanned; spanning** : abarcar (un período de tiempo), extenderse sobre (un espacio)

span[2] *n* **1** : lapso *m*, espacio *m* (de tiempo) ⟨life span : duración de la vida⟩ **2** : luz *f* (entre dos soportes)

spangle ['spæŋɡəl] *n* : lentejuela *f*

Spaniard ['spænjərd] *n* : español *m*, -ñola *f*

spaniel ['spænjəl] *n* : spaniel *m*

Spanish[1] ['spænɪʃ] *adj* : español

Spanish[2] *n* **1** : español *m* (idioma) **2 the Spanish** *npl* : los españoles

spank ['spæŋk] *vt* : darle nalgadas (a alguien)

spar[1] ['spɑr] *vi* **sparred; sparring** : entrenarse (en boxeo)

spar[2] *n* : palo *m*, verga *f* (de un barco)

spare[1] ['spær] *vt* **spared; sparing 1** : perdonar ⟨to spare someone's life : perdonarle la vida a alguien⟩ **2** SAVE : ahorrar, evitar ⟨I'll spare you the trouble : le evitaré la molestia⟩ **3** : prescindir de ⟨I can't spare her : no puedo prescindir de ella⟩ ⟨can you spare a dollar? : ¿me das un dólar?⟩ **4** STINT : escatimar ⟨they spared no expense : no repararon en gastos⟩ **5 to spare** : de sobra

spare[2] *adj* **1** : de repuesto, de recambio ⟨spare tire : llanta de repuesto⟩ **2** EXCESS : de más, de sobra ⟨spare time : tiempo libre⟩ **3** LEAN : delgado

spare[3] *n or* **spare part** : repuesto *m*, recambio *m*

sparing ['spærɪŋ] *adj* : parco, económico — **sparingly** *adv*

spark[1] ['spɑrk] *vi* : chispear, echar chispas — *vt* PROVOKE : despertar, provocar ⟨to spark interest : despertar interés⟩

spark[2] *n* **1** : chispa *f* ⟨to throw off sparks : echar chispas⟩ **2** GLIMMER, TRACE : destello *m*, pizca *f*

sparkle[1] ['spɑrkəl] *vi* **-kled; -kling 1** FLASH, SHINE : destellar, centellear, brillar **2** : estar muy animado (dícese de una conversación, etc.)

sparkle[2] *n* : destello *m*, centelleo *m*

sparkler ['spɑrklər] *n* : luz *f* de bengala

spark plug *n* : bujía *f*

sparrow ['spæro:] *n* : gorrión *m*

sparse ['spɑrs] *adj* **sparser; -est** : escaso — **sparsely** *adv*

spasm ['spæzəm] *n* **1** : espasmo *m* (muscular) **2** BURST, FIT : arrebato *m*

spasmodic [spæz'mɑdɪk] *adj* **1** : espasmódico **2** SPORADIC : irregular, esporádico — **spasmodically** [-dɪkli] *adv*

spastic ['spæstɪk] *adj* : espástico

spat[1] → **spit**[1]

spat[2] ['spæt] *n* : discusión *f*, disputa *f*, pelea *f*

spatial ['speɪʃəl] *adj* : espacial

spatter[1] ['spæt̬ər] *v* : salpicar

spatter[2] *n* : salpicadura *f*

spatula ['spæt̬ələ] *n* : espátula *f*, paleta *f* (para servir)

spawn[1] ['spɔn] *vi* : desovar, frezar — *vt* GENERATE : generar, producir

spawn[2] *n* : hueva *f*, freza *f*

spay ['speɪ] *vt* : esterilizar (una perra, etc.)

speak ['spi:k] *v* **spoke** ['spo:k]; **spoken** ['spo:kən]; **speaking** *vi* **1** TALK : hablar ⟨to speak to someone : hablar con alguien⟩ ⟨who's speaking? : ¿de parte de quien?⟩ ⟨so to speak : por así decirlo⟩ **2 to speak out** : hablar claramente **3 to speak out against** : denunciar **4 to speak up** : hablar en voz alta **5 to speak up for** : defender — *vt* **1** SAY : decir ⟨she spoke her mind : habló con franqueza⟩ **2** : hablar (un idioma)

speaker ['spi:kər] *n* **1** : hablante *mf* ⟨a native speaker : un hablante nativo⟩ **2** : orador *m*, -dora *f* ⟨the keynote speaker : el orador principal⟩ **3** LOUDSPEAKER : altavoz *m*, altoparlante *m*

spear[1] ['spɪr] *vt* : atravesar con una lanza

spear[2] *n* : lanza *f*

spearhead[1] ['spɪrˌhɛd] *vt* : encabezar

spearhead[2] *n* : punta *f* de lanza

spearmint ['spɪrmɪnt] *n* : menta *f* verde

special ['spɛʃəl] *adj* : especial ⟨nothing special : nada en especial, nada en particular⟩ — **specially** *adv*

specialist ['spɛʃəlɪst] *n* : especialista *mf*

specialization [ˌspɛʃələ'zeɪʃən] *n* : especialización *f*

specialize ['spɛʃəˌlaɪz] *vi* **-ized; -izing** : especializarse

specialty ['spɛʃəlti] *n, pl* **-ties** : especialidad *f*

species ['spi:ˌʃi:z, -ˌsi:z] *ns & pl* : especie *f*

specific [spɪ'sɪfɪk] *adj* : específico, determinado — **specifically** [-fɪkli] *adv*

specification [ˌspɛsəfə'keɪʃən] *n* : especificación *f*

specify ['spɛsəˌfaɪ] *vt* **-fied; -fying** : especificar

specimen ['spɛsəmən] *n* **1** SAMPLE : espécimen *m*, muestra *f* **2** EXAMPLE : espécimen *m*, ejemplar *m*

speck ['spɛk] *n* **1** SPOT : manchita *f* **2** BIT, TRACE : mota *f*, pizca *f*, ápice *m*

speckled ['spɛkəld] *adj* : moteado

spectacle ['spɛktɪkəl] *n* **1** : espectáculo *m* **2 spectacles** *npl* GLASSES : lentes *fpl*, gafas *fpl*, anteojos *mpl*, espejuelos *mpl*

spectacular [spɛk'tækjələr] *adj* : espectacular

spectator ['spɛk,teɪṭər] *n* : espectador *m*, -dora *f*

specter *or* **spectre** ['spɛktər] *n* : espectro *m*, fantasma *m*

spectrum ['spɛktrəm] *n*, *pl* **spectra** [-trə] *or* **spectrums** **1** : espectro *m* (de colores, etc.) **2** RANGE : gama *f*, abanico *m*

speculate ['spɛkjə,leɪt] *vi* -lated; -lating **1** : especular (en finanzas) **2** WONDER : preguntarse, hacer conjeturas

speculation [,spɛkjə'leɪʃən] *n* : especulación *f*

speculative ['spɛkjə,leɪṭɪv] *adj* : especulativo

speculator ['spɛkjə,leɪṭər] *n* : especulador *m*, -dora *f*

speech ['spiːtʃ] *n* **1** : habla *f*, modo *m* de hablar, expresión *f* **2** ADDRESS : discurso *m*

speechless ['spiːtʃləs] *adj* : enmudecido, estupefacto

speed[1] ['spiːd] *v* **sped** ['spɛd] *or* **speeded; speeding** *vi* **1** : ir a toda velocidad, correr a toda prisa ⟨he speed off : se fue a toda velocidad⟩ **2** : conducir a exceso de velocidad ⟨a ticket for speeding : una multa por exceso de velocidad⟩ — *vt* **to speed up** : acelerar

speed[2] *n* **1** SWIFTNESS : rapidez *f* **2** VELOCITY : velocidad *f*

speedboat ['spiːd,boːt] *n* : lancha *f* motora

speed bump *n* : badén *m*

speed limit *n* : velocidad *f* máxima, límite *m* de velocidad

speedometer [spɪ'dɑməṭər] *n* : velocímetro *m*

speedup ['spiːd,ʌp] *n* : aceleración *f*

speedy ['spiːdi] *adj* **speedier; -est** : rápido — **speedily** [-dəli] *adv*

spell[1] ['spɛl] *vt* **1** : escribir, deletrear (verbalmente) ⟨how do you spell it? : ¿cómo se escribe?, ¿cómo se deletrea?⟩ **2** MEAN : significar ⟨that could spell trouble : eso puede significar problemas⟩ **3** RELIEVE : relevar

spell[2] *n* **1** TURN : turno *m* **2** PERIOD, TIME : período *m* (de tiempo) **3** ENCHANTMENT : encanto *m*, hechizo *m*, maleficio *m*

spellbound ['spɛl,baʊnd] *adj* : embelesado

speller ['spɛlər] *n* : persona *f* que escribe ⟨she's a good speller : tiene buena ortografía⟩

spelling ['spɛlɪŋ] *n* : ortografía *f*

spend ['spɛnd] *vt* **spent** ['spɛnt]; **spending** **1** : gastar (dinero, etc.) **2** PASS : pasar (el tiempo) ⟨to spend time on : dedicar tiempo a⟩

spendthrift ['spɛnd,θrɪft] *n* : derrochador *m*, -dora *f*; despilfarrador *m*, -dora *f*

sperm ['spərm] *n*, *pl* **sperm** *or* **sperms** : esperma *mf*

spew ['spjuː] *vi* : salir a chorros — *vt* : vomitar, arrojar (lava, etc.)

sphere ['sfɪr] *n* : esfera *f*

spherical ['sfɪrɪkəl, 'sfɛr-] *adj* : esférico

spice[1] ['spaɪs] *vt* **spiced; spicing** **1** SEASON : condimentar, sazonar **2** *or* **to spice up** : salpimentar, hacer más interesante

spice[2] *n* **1** : especia *f* **2** FLAVOR, INTEREST : sabor *m* ⟨the spice of life : la sal de la vida⟩

spick–and–span ['spɪkənd'spæn] *adj* : limpio y ordenado

spicy ['spaɪsi] *adj* **spicier; -est** **1** SPICED : condimentado, sazonado **2** HOT : picante **3** RACY : picante

spider ['spaɪdər] *n* : araña *f*

spigot ['spɪgət, -kət] *n* : llave *f*, grifo *m*, canilla *Arg, Uru*

spike[1] ['spaɪk] *vt* **spiked; spiking** **1** FASTEN : clavar (con clavos grandes) **2** PIERCE : atravesar **3** : añadir alcohol a ⟨he spiked her drink with rum : le puso ron a la bebida⟩

spike[2] *n* **1** : clavo *m* grande **2** CLEAT : clavo *m* **3** : remache *m* (en voleibol) **4** PEAK : pico *m*

spill[1] ['spɪl] *vt* **1** SHED : derramar, verter ⟨to spill blood : derrame sangre⟩ **2** DIVULGE : revelar, divulgar — *vi* : derramarse

spill[2] *n* **1** SPILLING : derrame *m*, vertido *m* ⟨oil spill : derrame de petróleo⟩ **2** FALL : caída *f*

spin[1] ['spɪn] *v* **spun** ['spʌn]; **spinning** *vi* **1** : hilar **2** TURN : girar **3** REEL : dar vueltas ⟨my head is spinning : la cabeza me está dando vueltas⟩ — *vt* **1** : hilar (hilo, etc.) **2** : tejer ⟨to spin a web : tejer una telaraña⟩ **3** TWIRL : hacer girar

spin[2] *n* : vuelta *f*, giro *m* ⟨to go for a spin : dar una vuelta (en coche)⟩

spinach ['spɪnɪtʃ] *n* : espinacas *fpl*, espinaca *f*

spinal column ['spaɪnəl] *n* BACKBONE : columna *f* vertebral

spinal cord *n* : médula *f* espinal

spindle ['spɪndəl] *n* **1** : huso *m* (para hilar) **2** : eje *m* (de un mecanismo)

spindly ['spɪndli] *adj* : larguirucho *fam*, largo y débil (dícese de una planta)

spine ['spaɪn] *n* **1** BACKBONE : columna *f* vertebral, espina *f* dorsal **2** QUILL : púa *f* (de un animal) **3** THORN : espina *f* **4** : lomo *m* (de un libro)

spineless ['spaɪnləs] *adj* **1** : sin púas, sin espinas **2** INVERTEBRATE : invertebrado **3** WEAK : débil (de carácter)

spinet ['spɪnət] *n* : espineta *f*

spinster ['spɪnstər] *n* : soltera *f*

spiny ['spaɪni] *adj* **spinier; -est** : con púas (dícese de los animales), espinoso (dícese de las plantas)

spiral[1] ['spaɪrəl] *vi* **-raled** *or* **-ralled**; **-raling** *or* **-ralling** : ir en espiral
spiral[2] *adj* : espiral, en espiral ⟨a spiral staircase : una escalera de caracol⟩
spiral[3] *n* : espiral *f*
spire ['spaɪr] *n* : aguja *f*
spirit[1] ['spɪrət] *vt* **to spirit away** : hacer desaparecer
spirit[2] *n* 1 : espíritu *m* ⟨body and spirit : cuerpo y espíritu⟩ 2 GHOST : espíritu *m*, fantasma *m* 3 MOOD : espíritu *m*, humor *m* ⟨in the spirit of friendship : en el espíritu de amistad⟩ ⟨to be in good spirits : estar de buen humor⟩ 4 ENTHUSIASM, VIVACITY : espíritu *m*, ánimo *m*, brío *m* 5 **spirits** *npl* : licores *mpl*
spirited ['spɪrətəd] *adj* : animado, energético
spiritless ['spɪrətləs] *adj* : desanimado
spiritual[1] ['spɪrɪtʃuəl, -tʃəl] *adj* : espiritual — **spiritually** *adv*
spiritual[2] *n* : espiritual *m* (canción)
spiritualism ['spɪrɪtʃuə,lɪzəm, -tʃə-] *n* : espiritismo *m*
spirituality [,spɪrɪtʃu'æləti] *n*, *pl* **-ties** : espiritualidad *f*
spit[1] ['spɪt] *v* **spit** *or* **spat** ['spæt]; **spitting** : escupir
spit[2] *n* 1 SALIVA : saliva *f* 2 ROTISSERIE : asador *m* 3 POINT : lengua *f* (de tierra)
spite[1] ['spaɪt] *vt* **spited**; **spiting** : fastidiar, molestar
spite[2] *n* 1 : despecho *m*, rencor *m* 2 **in spite of** : a pesar de (que), pese a (que)
spiteful ['spaɪtfəl] *adj* : malicioso, rencoroso
spitting image *n* **to be the spitting image of** : ser el vivo retrato de
spittle ['spɪtəl] *n* : saliva *f*
splash[1] ['splæʃ] *vt* : salpicar — *vi* 1 : salpicar 2 **to splash around** : chapotear
splash[2] *n* 1 SPLASHING : salpicadura *f* 2 SQUIRT : chorrito *m* 3 SPOT : mancha *f*
splatter ['splætər] → **spatter**
splay ['spleɪ] *vt* : extender (hacia afuera) ⟨to splay one's fingers : abrir los dedos⟩ — *vi* : extenderse (hacia afuera)
spleen ['spli:n] *n* 1 : bazo *m* (órgano) 2 ANGER, SPITE : ira *f*, rencor *m*
splendid ['splɛndəd] *adj* : espléndido — **splendidly** *adv*
splendor ['splɛndər] *n* : esplendor *m*
splice[1] ['splaɪs] *vt* **spliced**; **splicing** : empalmar, unir
splice[2] *n* : empalme *m*, unión *f*
splint ['splɪnt] *n* : tablilla *f*
splinter[1] ['splɪntər] *vt* : astillar — *vi* : astillarse
splinter[2] *n* : astilla *f*
split[1] ['splɪt] *v* **split**; **splitting** *vt* 1 CLEAVE : partir, hender ⟨to split wood : partir madera⟩ 2 BURST : romper, rajar ⟨to split open : abrir⟩ 3 DIVIDE, SHARE : dividir, repartir — *vi* 1 : par-

tirse (dícese de la madera, etc.) 2 BURST, CRACK : romperse, rajarse 3 *or* **to split up** : dividirse
split[2] *n* 1 CRACK : rajadura *f* 2 TEAR : rotura *f* 3 DIVISION : división *f*, escisión *f*
splurge[1] ['splərdʒ] *v* **splurged**; **splurging** *vt* : derrochar — *vi* : derrochar dinero
splurge[2] *n* : derroche *m*
spoil[1] ['spɔɪl] *vt* 1 PILLAGE : saquear 2 RUIN : estropear, arruinar 3 PAMPER : consentir, mimar — *vi* : estropearse, echarse a perder
spoil[2] *n* PLUNDER : botín *m*
spoke[1] → **speak**
spoke[2] ['spo:k] *n* : rayo *m* (de una rueda)
spoken → **speak**
spokesman ['spo:ksmən] *n*, *pl* **-men** [-mən, -,mɛn] : portavoz *mf*; vocero *m*, -ra *f*
spokeswoman ['spo:ks,wumən] *n*, *pl* **-women** [-,wɪmən] : portavoz *f*, vocera *f*
sponge[1] ['spʌndʒ] *vt* **sponged**; **sponging** : limpiar con una esponja
sponge[2] *n* : esponja *f*
spongy ['spʌndʒi] *adj* **spongier**; **-est** : esponjoso
sponsor[1] ['spɑntsər] *vt* : patrocinar, auspiciar, apadrinar (a una persona)
sponsor[2] *n* : patrocinador *m*, -dora *f*; padrino *m*, madrina *f*
sponsorship ['spɑntsər,ʃɪp] *n* : patrocinio *m*, apadrinamiento *m*
spontaneity [,spɑntə'ni:əti, -'neɪ-] *n* : espontaneidad *f*
spontaneous [spɑn'teɪniəs] *adj* : espontáneo — **spontaneously** *adv*
spoof ['spu:f] *n* : burla *f*, parodia *f*
spook[1] ['spu:k] *vt* : asustar
spook[2] *n* : fantasma *m*, espíritu *m*, espectro *m*
spooky ['spu:ki] *adj* **spookier**; **-est** : que da miedo, espeluznante
spool ['spu:l] *n* : carrete *m*
spoon[1] ['spu:n] *vt* : comer, servir, o echar con cuchara
spoon[2] *n* : cuchara *f*
spoonful ['spu:n,fʊl] *n* : cucharada *f* ⟨by the spoonful : a cucharadas⟩
spoor ['spʊr, 'spor] *n* : rastro *m*, pista *f*
sporadic [spə'rædɪk] *adj* : esporádico — **sporadically** [-dɪkli] *adv*
spore ['spor] *n* : espora *f*
sport[1] ['sport] *vi* FROLIC : retozar, juguetear — *vt* SHOW OFF : lucir, ostentar
sport[2] *n* 1 : deporte *m* ⟨outdoor sports : deportes al aire libre⟩ 2 JEST : broma *f* 3 **to be a good sport** : tener espíritu deportivo
sporting ['sportɪŋ] *adj* : deportivo ⟨a sporting chance : buenas posibilidades⟩
sportsman ['sportsmən] *n*, *pl* **-men** [-mən, -,mɛn] : deportista *m*

sportsmanship ['sportsmən,ʃɪp] *n* : espíritu *m* deportivo, deportividad *f* *Spain*

sportswoman ['sports,wʊmən] *n, pl* **-women** [-,wɪmən] : deportista *f*

sporty ['sporʈi] *adj* **sportier; -est** : deportivo

spot¹ ['spɑt] *v* **spotted; spotting** *vt* 1 STAIN : manchar 2 RECOGNIZE, SEE : ver, reconocer ⟨to spot an error : descubrir un error⟩ — *vi* : mancharse

spot² *adj* : hecho al azar ⟨a spot check : un vistazo, un control aleatorio⟩

spot³ *n* 1 STAIN : mancha *f* 2 DOT : punto *m* 3 PIMPLE : grano *m* ⟨to break out in spots : salirle granos a alguien⟩ 4 PREDICAMENT : apuro *m*, aprieto *m*, lío *m* ⟨in a tight spot : en apuros⟩ 5 PLACE : lugar *m*, sitio *m* ⟨to be on the spot : estar en el lugar⟩

spotless ['spɑtləs] *adj* : impecable, inmaculado — **spotlessly** *adv*

spotlight¹ ['spɑt,laɪt] *vt* **-lighted** *or* **-lit** [-,lɪt]; **-lighting** 1 LIGHT : iluminar (con un reflector) 2 HIGHLIGHT : destacar, poner en relieve

spotlight² *n* 1 : reflector *m*, foco *m* 2 **to be in the spotlight** : ser el centro de atención

spotty ['spɑʈi] *adj* **spottier; -est** : irregular, desigual

spouse ['spaʊs] *n* : cónyuge *mf*

spout¹ ['spaʊt] *vt* 1 : lanzar chorros de 2 DECLAIM : declamar — *vi* : salir a chorros

spout² *n* 1 : pico *m* (de una jarra, etc.) 2 STREAM : chorro *m*

sprain¹ ['spreɪn] *vt* : sufrir un esguince en

sprain² *n* : esguince *m*, torcedura *f*

sprawl¹ ['sprɔl] *vi* 1 LIE : tumbarse, echarse, despatarrarse 2 EXTEND : extenderse

sprawl² *n* 1 : postura *f* despatarrada 2 SPREAD : extensión *f*, expansión *f*

spray¹ ['spreɪ] *vt* : rociar (una superficie), pulverizar (un líquido)

spray² *n* 1 BOUQUET : ramillete *m* 2 MIST : rocío *m* 3 ATOMIZER : atomizador *m*, pulverizador *m*

spray gun *n* : pistola *f*

spread¹ ['sprɛd] *v* **spread; spreading** *vt* 1 *or* **to spread out** : desplegar, extender 2 SCATTER, STREW : esparcir 3 SMEAR : untar (mantequilla, etc.) 4 DISSEMINATE : difundir, sembrar, propagar — *vi* 1 : difundirse, correr, propagarse 2 EXTEND : extenderse

spread² *n* 1 EXTENSION : extensión *f*, difusión *f* (de noticias, etc.), propagación *f* (de enfermedades, etc.) 2 : colcha *f* (para una cama), mantel *m* (para una mesa) 3 PASTE : pasta *f* ⟨cheese spread : pasta de queso⟩

spreadsheet ['sprɛd,ʃiːt] *n* : hoja *f* de cálculo

spree ['spri] *n* 1 : acción *f* desenfrenada ⟨to go on a shopping spree : com-

prar como loco⟩ 2 BINGE : parranda *f*, juerga *f* ⟨on a spree : de parranda, de juerga⟩

sprig ['sprɪg] *n* : ramita *f*, ramito *m*

sprightly ['spraɪtli] *adj* **sprightlier; -est** : vivo, animado ⟨with a sprightly step : con paso ligero⟩

spring¹ ['sprɪŋ] *v* **sprang** ['spræŋ] *or* **sprung** ['sprʌŋ]; **sprung; springing** *vi* 1 LEAP : saltar 2 : mover rápidamente ⟨the lid sprang shut : la tapa se cerró de un golpe⟩ ⟨he sprang to his feet : se paró de un salto⟩ 3 **to spring up** : brotar (dícese de las plantas), surgir 4 **to spring from** : surgir de — *vt* 1 RELEASE : soltar (de repente) ⟨to spring the news on someone : sorprender a alguien con las noticias⟩ ⟨to spring a trap : hacer saltar una trampa⟩ 2 ACTIVATE : accionar (un mecanismo) 3 **to spring a leak** : hacer agua

spring² *n* 1 SOURCE : fuente *f*, origen *m* 2 : manantial *m*, fuente *f* ⟨hot spring : fuente termal⟩ 3 : primavera *f* ⟨spring and summer : la primavera y el verano⟩ 4 : resorte *m*, muelle *m* (de metal, etc.) 5 LEAP : salto *m*, brinco *m* 6 RESILIENCE : elasticidad *f*

springboard ['sprɪŋ,bord] *n* : trampolín *m*

springtime ['sprɪŋ,taɪm] *n* : primavera *f*

springy ['sprɪŋi] *adj* **springier; -est** 1 RESILIENT : elástico 2 LIVELY : enérgico

sprinkle¹ ['sprɪŋkəl] *vt* **-kled; -kling** : rociar (con agua), espolvorear (con azúcar, etc.), salpicar

sprinkle² *n* : llovizna *f*

sprinkler ['sprɪŋkələr] *n* : rociador *m*, aspersor *m*

sprint¹ ['sprɪnt] *vi* : echar la carrera, esprintar (en deportes)

sprint² *n* : esprint *m* (en deportes)

sprinter ['sprɪntər] *n* : esprínter *mf*

sprite ['spraɪt] *n* : hada *f*, elfo *m*

sprocket ['sprɑkət] *n* : diente *m* (de una rueda dentada)

sprout¹ ['spraʊt] *vi* : brotar

sprout² *n* : brote *m*, retoño *m*, vástago *m*

spruce¹ ['spruːs] *v* **spruced; sprucing** *vt* : arreglar — *vi* *or* **to spruce up** : arreglarse, acicalarse

spruce² *adj* **sprucer; sprucest** : pulcro, arreglado

spruce³ *n* : picea *f* (árbol)

spry ['spraɪ] *adj* **sprier** *or* **spryer** ['spraɪər]; **spriest** *or* **spryest** ['spraɪəst] : ágil, activo

spun → spin

spunk ['spʌŋk] *n* : valor *m*, coraje *m*, agallas *fpl fam*

spunky ['spʌŋki] *adj* **spunkier; -est** : animoso, corajudo

spur¹ ['spər] *vt* **spurred; spurring** *or* **to spur on** : espolear (un caballo), motivar (a una persona, etc.)

spur² *n* **1** : espuela *f*, acicate *m* **2** STIM-ULUS : acicate *m* **3** : espolón *m* (de aves gallináceas)

spurious ['spjʊriəs] *adj* : espurio

spurn ['spərn] *vt* : desdeñar, rechazar

spurt¹ ['spərt] *vt* SQUIRT : lanzar un cho-rro de — *vi* SPOUT : salir a chorros

spurt² *n* **1** : actividad *f* repentina ⟨a spurt of energy : una explosión de en-ergía⟩ ⟨to do in spurts : hacer por rachas⟩ **2** JET : chorro *m* (de agua, etc.)

sputter¹ ['spʌtər] *vi* **1** JABBER : farfullar **2** : chisporrotear (dícese de la grasa, etc.), petardear (dícese de un motor)

sputter² *n* **1** JABBER : farfulla *f* **2** : chis-porroteo *m* (de grasa, etc.), petardeo *m* (de un motor)

spy¹ ['spaɪ] *v* **spied**; **spying** *vt* SEE : ver, divisar — *vi* : espiar ⟨to spy on some-one : espiar a alguien⟩

spy² *n* : espía *mf*

squab ['skwɑb] *n, pl* **squabs** *or* **squab** : pichón *m*

squabble¹ ['skwɑbəl] *vi* **-bled**; **-bling** : reñir, pelearse, discutir

squabble² *n* : riña *f*, pelea *f*, discusión *f*

squad ['skwɑd] *n* : pelotón *m* (militar), brigada *f* (de policías), cuadrilla *f* (de obreros, etc.)

squadron ['skwɑdrən] *n* : escuadrón *m* (de militares), escuadrilla *f* (de aviones), escuadra *f* (de naves)

squalid ['skwɑlɪd] *adj* : miserable

squall ['skwɔl] *n* **1** : aguacero *m* tor-mentoso, chubasco *m* tormentoso **2** snow squall : tormenta *f* de nieve

squalor ['skwɑlər] *n* : miseria *f*

squander ['skwɑndər] *vt* : derrochar (dinero, etc.), desaprovechar (una oportunidad, etc.), desperdiciar (talen-tos, energías, etc.)

square¹ ['skwær] *vt* **squared**; **squaring** **1** : cuadrar **2** : elevar al cuadrado (en matemáticas) **3** CONFORM : conciliar (con), ajustar (con) **4** SETTLE : saldar (una cuenta) ⟨I squared it with him : lo arreglé con él⟩

square² *adj* **squarer**; **-est 1** : cuadrado ⟨a square house : una casa cuadrada⟩ **2** RIGHT-ANGLED : a escuadra, en án-gulo recto **3** : cuadrado (en matemáti-cas) ⟨a square mile : una milla cuadra-da⟩ **4** HONEST : justo ⟨a square deal : un buen acuerdo⟩ ⟨fair and square : en buena lid⟩

square³ *n* **1** : escuadra *f* (instrumento) **2** : cuadrado *m*, cuadro *m* ⟨to fold into squares : plegar en cuadrados⟩ **3** : plaza *f* (de una ciudad) **4** : cuadrado *m* (en matemáticas)

squarely ['skwærli] *adv* **1** EXACTLY : ex-actamente, directamente, justo **2** HON-ESTLY : honradamente, justamente

square root *n* : raíz *f* cuadrada

squash¹ ['skwɑʃ, 'skwɔʃ] *vt* **1** CRUSH : aplastar **2** SUPPRESS : acallar (protes-tas), sofocar (una rebelión)

squash² *n* **1** *pl* **squashes** *or* **squash** : calabaza *f* (vegetal) **2** *or* **squash rac-quets** : squash *m* (deporte)

squat¹ ['skwɑt] *vi* **squatted**; **squatting 1** CROUCH : agacharse, ponerse en cu-clillas **2** : ocupar un lugar sin derecho

squat² *adj* **squatter**; **squattest** : bajo y ancho, rechoncho *fam* (dícese de una persona)

squat³ *n* **1** : posición *f* en cuclillas **2** : ocupación *f* ilegal (de un lugar)

squaw ['skwɔ] *n* : india *f* (norteameri-cana)

squawk¹ ['skwɔk] *vi* : graznar (dícese de las aves), chillar

squawk² *n* : graznido *m* (de un ave), chillido *m*

squeak¹ ['skwik] *vi* : chillar (dícese de un animal), chirriar (dícese de un ob-jeto)

squeak² *n* : chillido *m*, chirrido *m*

squeaky ['skwiki] *adj* **squeakier**; **-est** : chirriante ⟨a squeaky voice : una voz chillona⟩

squeal¹ ['skwil] *vi* **1** : chillar (dícese de las personas o los animales), chirriar (dícese de los frenos, etc.) **2** PROTEST : quejarse

squeal² *n* **1** : chillido *m* (de una persona o un animal) **2** SCREECH : chirrido *m* (de frenos, etc.)

squeamish ['skwimɪʃ] *adj* : impresion-able, sensible ⟨he's squeamish about cockroaches : las cucarachas le dan asco⟩

squeeze¹ ['skwiz] *vt* **squeezed**; **squeezing 1** PRESS : apretar, exprim-ir (naranjas, etc.) **2** EXTRACT : extraer (jugo, etc.)

squeeze² *n* : apretón *m*

squelch ['skwɛltʃ] *vt* : aplastar (una re-belión, etc.)

squid ['skwɪd] *n, pl* **squid** *or* **squids** : calamar *m*

squint¹ ['skwɪnt] *vi* : mirar con los ojos entornados

squint² *adj or* **squint–eyed** ['skwɪnt,aɪd] : bizco

squint³ *n* : ojos *mpl* bizcos, bizquera *f*

squire ['skwaɪr] *n* : hacendado *m*, -da *f*; terrateniente *mf*

squirm ['skwərm] *vi* : retorcerse

squirrel ['skwərəl] *n* : ardilla *f*

squirt¹ ['skwərt] *vt* : lanzar un chorro de — *vi* SPURT : salir a chorros

squirt² *n* : chorrito *m*

stab¹ ['stæb] *vt* **stabbed**; **stabbing 1** KNIFE : acuchillar, apuñalar **2** STICK : clavar (con una aguja, etc.), golpear (con el dedo, etc.)

stab² *n* **1** : puñalada *f*, cuchillada *f* **2** JAB : pinchazo *m* (con una aguja, etc.), golpe *m* (con un dedo, etc.) **3 to take a stab at** : intentar

stability [stə'bɪləti] *n, pl* **-ties** : estabili-dad *f*

stabilize ['steɪbə,laɪz] *v* **-lized**; **-lizing** *vt* : estabilizar — *vi* : estabilizarse

stable[1] ['steɪbəl] vt **-bled; -bling** : poner (ganado) en un establo, poner (caballos) en una caballeriza

stable[2] adj **-bler; -blest** 1 FIXED, STEADY : fijo, sólido, estable 2 LASTING : estable, perdurable ⟨a stable government : un gobierno estable⟩ 3 : estacionario (en medicina), equilibrado (en psicología)

stable[3] n : establo m (para ganado), caballeriza f o cuadra f (para caballos)

staccato [stə'kɑt̬o:] adj : staccato

stack[1] ['stæk] vt 1 PILE : amontonar, apilar 2 COVER : cubrir, llenar ⟨he stacked the table with books : cubrió la mesa de libros⟩

stack[2] n 1 PILE : montón m, pila f 2 SMOKESTACK : chimenea f

stadium ['steɪdiəm] n, pl **-dia** [-diə] or **-diums** : estadio m

staff[1] ['stæf] vt : proveer de personal

staff[2] n, pl **staffs** ['stæfs, stævz] or **staves** ['stævz, 'steɪvz] 1 : bastón m (de mando), báculo m (de obispo) 2 pl **staffs** PERSONNEL : personal m 3 or **stave** : pentagrama m (en música)

stag[1] ['stæg] adv : solo, sin pareja ⟨to go stag : ir solo⟩

stag[2] adj : sólo para hombres

stag[3] n, pl **stags** or **stag** : ciervo m, venado m

stage[1] ['steɪʤ] vt **staged; staging** : poner en escena (una obra de teatro)

stage[2] n 1 PLATFORM : estrado m, tablado m, escenario m (de un teatro) 2 PHASE, STEP : fase f, etapa f ⟨stage of development : fase de desarrollo⟩ ⟨in stages : por etapas⟩ 3 **the stage** : el teatro m

stagecoach ['steɪʤ,ko:tʃ] n : diligencia f

stagger[1] ['stægər] vi TOTTER : tambalearse — vt 1 ALTERNATE : alternar, escalonar (turnos de trabajo) 2 : hacer tambalear ⟨to be staggered by : quedarse estupefacto por⟩

stagger[2] n : tambaleo m

staggering ['stægərɪŋ] adj : asombroso

stagnant ['stægnənt] adj : estancado

stagnate ['stæg,neɪt] vi **-nated; -nating** : estancarse

staid ['steɪd] adj : serio, sobrio

stain[1] ['steɪn] vt 1 DISCOLOR : manchar 2 DYE : teñir (madera, etc.) 3 SULLY : manchar, empañar

stain[2] n 1 SPOT : mancha f 2 DYE : tinte m, tintura f 3 BLEMISH : mancha f, mácula f

stainless ['steɪnləs] adj : sin mancha ⟨stainless steel : acero inoxidable⟩

stair ['stær] n 1 STEP : escalón m, peldaño m 2 **stairs** npl : escalera f, escaleras fpl

staircase ['stær,keɪs] n : escalera f, escaleras fpl

stairway ['stær,weɪ] n : escalera f, escaleras fpl

stake[1] ['steɪk] vt **staked; staking** 1 : estacar, marcar con estacas (una propiedad) 2 BET : jugarse, apostar 3 **to stake a claim to** : reclamar, reivindicar

stake[2] n 1 POST : estaca f 2 BET : apuesta f ⟨to be at stake : estar en juego⟩ 3 INTEREST, SHARE : interés m, participación f

stalactite [stə'læk,taɪt] n : estalactita f

stalagmite [stə'læg,maɪt] n : estalagmita f

stale ['steɪl] adj **staler; stalest** : viejo ⟨stale bread : pan duro⟩ ⟨stale news : viejas noticias⟩

stalemate ['steɪl,meɪt] n : punto m muerto, impasse m

stalk[1] ['stɔk] vt : acechar — vi : caminar rígidamente (por orgullo, ira, etc.)

stalk[2] n : tallo m (de una planta)

stall[1] ['stɔl] vt 1 : parar (un motor) 2 DELAY : entretener (a una persona), demorar — vi 1 : pararse (dícese de un motor) 2 DELAY : demorar, andar con rodeos

stall[2] n 1 : compartimiento m (de un establo) 2 : puesto m (en un mercado, etc.)

stallion ['stæljən] n : caballo m semental

stalwart ['stɔlwərt] adj 1 STRONG : fuerte ⟨a stalwart supporter : un firme partidario⟩ 2 BRAVE : valiente, valeroso

stamen ['steɪmən] n : estambre m

stamina ['stæmənə] n : resistencia f

stammer[1] ['stæmər] vi : tartamudear, titubear

stammer[2] n : tartamudeo m, titubeo m

stamp[1] ['stæmp] vt 1 : pisotear (con los pies) ⟨to stamp one's feet : patear, dar una patada⟩ 2 IMPRESS, IMPRINT : sellar (una factura, etc.), acuñar (monedas) 3 : franquear, ponerle estampillas a (correo)

stamp[2] n 1 : sello m (para documentos, etc.) 2 DIE : cuño m (para monedas) 3 or **postage stamp** : sello m, estampilla f, timbre m CA, Mex

stampede[1] [stæm'pi:d] vi **-peded; -peding** : salir en estampida

stampede[2] n : estampida f

stance ['stænts] n : postura f

stanch ['stɔntʃ, 'stæntʃ] vt : detener, estancar (un líquido)

stand[1] ['stænd] v **stood** ['stʊd]; **standing** vi 1 : estar de pie, estar parado ⟨I was standing on the corner : estaba parada en la esquina⟩ 2 or **to stand up** : levantarse, pararse, ponerse de pie 3 (indicating a specified position or location) ⟨they stand third in the country : ocupan el tercer lugar en el país⟩ ⟨the machines are standing idle : las máquinas están paradas⟩ 4 (referring to an opinion) ⟨how does he stand on the matter? : ¿cuál es su postura respecto al asunto?⟩ 5 BE : estar ⟨the house stands on a hill : la casa está en una colina⟩ 6 CONTINUE : seguir ⟨the order still stands : el mandato sigue vigente⟩ — *vt* **1** PLACE, SET : poner, colocar ⟨he stood them in a row : los colocó en hilera⟩ **2** TOLERATE : aguantar, soportar ⟨he can't stand her : no la puede tragar⟩ **3 to stand firm** : mantenerse firme **4 to stand guard** : hacer la guardia

stand² *n* **1** RESISTANCE : resistencia *f* ⟨to make a stand against : resistir a⟩ **2** BOOTH, STALL : stand *m*, puesto *m*, kiosko *m* (para vender periódicos, etc) **3** BASE : pie *m*, base *f* **4** : grupo *m* (de árboles, etc.) **5** POSITION : posición *f*, postura *f* **6 stands** *npl* GRANDSTAND : tribuna *f*

standard¹ ['stændərd] *adj* **1** ESTABLISHED : estándar, oficial ⟨standard measures : medidas oficiales⟩ ⟨standard English : el inglés estándar⟩ **2** NORMAL : normal, estándar, común **3** CLASSIC : estándar, clásico ⟨a standard work : una obra clásica⟩

standard² *n* **1** BANNER : estandarte *m* **2** CRITERION : criterio *m* **3** RULE : estándar *m*, norma *f*, regla *f* **4** LEVEL : nivel *m* ⟨standard of living : nivel de vida⟩ **5** SUPPORT : poste *m*, soporte *m*

standardization [ˌstændərdə'zeɪʃən] *n* : estandarización *f*

standardize ['stændər,daɪz] *vt* **-ized; -izing** : estandarizar

standard time *n* : hora *f* oficial

stand by *vt* : atenerse a, cumplir con (una promesa, etc.) — *vi* **1** : mantenerse aparte ⟨to stand by and do nothing : mirar sin hacer nada⟩ **2** : estar preparado, estar listo (para un anuncio, un ataque, etc.)

stand for *vt* **1** REPRESENT : significar **2** PERMIT, TOLERATE : permitir, tolerar

standing ['stændɪŋ] *n* **1** POSITION, RANK : posición *f* **2** DURATION : duración *f*

stand out *vi* **1** : destacar(se) ⟨she stands out from the rest : se destaca entre los otros⟩ **2 to stand out against** RESIST : oponerse a

standpoint ['stænd,pɔɪnt] *n* : punto *m* de vista

standstill ['stænd,stɪl] *n* **1** STOP : detención *f*, paro *m* ⟨to come to a standstill : pararse⟩ **2** DEADLOCK : punto *m* muerto, impasse *m*

stand up *vt* : dejar plantado ⟨he stood me up again : otra vez me dejó plantado⟩ — *vi* **1** ENDURE : durar, resistir **2 to stand up for** : defender **3 to stand up to** : hacerle frente (a alguien)

stank → stink

stanza ['stænzə] *n* : estrofa *f*

staple¹ ['steɪpəl] *vt* **-pled; -pling** : engrapar, grapar

staple² *adj* : principal, básico ⟨a staple food : un alimento básico⟩

staple³ *n* **1** : producto *m* principal **2** : grapa *f* (para engrapar papeles)

stapler ['steɪplər] *n* : engrapadora *f*, grapadora *f*

star¹ ['stɑr] *v* **starred; starring** *vt* **1** : marcar con una estrella o un aster-

isco **2** FEATURE : estar protagonizado por — *vi* : tener el papel principal ⟨to star in : protagonizar⟩

star² *n* : estrella *f*

starboard ['stɑrbərd] *n* : estribor *m*

starch¹ ['stɑrtʃ] *vt* : almidonar

starch² *n* : almidón *m*, fécula *f* (comida)

starchy ['stɑrtʃi] *adj* **starchier; -est** : lleno de almidón ⟨a starchy diet : una dieta feculenta⟩

stardom ['stɑrdəm] *n* : estrellato *m*

stare¹ ['stær] *vi* **stared; staring** : mirar fijamente

stare² *n* : mirada *f* fija

starfish ['stɑr,fɪʃ] *n* : estrella *f* de mar

stark¹ ['stɑrk] *adv* : completamente ⟨stark raving mad : loco de remate⟩ ⟨stark naked : completamente desnudo⟩

stark² *adj* **1** ABSOLUTE : absoluto **2** BARREN, DESOLATE : desolado, desierto **3** BARE : desnudo **4** HARSH : severo, duro

starlight ['stɑr,laɪt] *n* : luz *f* de las estrellas

starling ['stɑrlɪŋ] *n* : estornino *m*

starry ['stɑri] *adj* **starrier; -est** : estrellado

start¹ ['stɑrt] *vi* **1** JUMP : levantarse de un salto, sobresaltarse, dar un respingo **2** BEGIN : empezar, comenzar **3** SET OUT : salir (de viaje, etc.) **4** : arrancar (dícese de un motor) — *vt* **1** BEGIN : empezar, comenzar, iniciar **2** CAUSE : provocar, causar **3** ESTABLISH : fundar, montar, establecer ⟨to start a business : montar un negocio⟩ **4** : arrancar, poner en marcha, encender ⟨to start the car : arrancar el motor⟩

start² *n* **1** JUMP : sobresalto *m*, respingo *m* **2** BEGINNING : principio *m*, comienzo *m* ⟨to get an early start : salir temprano⟩

starter ['stɑrtər] *n* **1** : participante *mf* (en una carrera, etc.); jugador *m* titular, jugadora *f* titular (en beisbol, etc.) **2** APPETIZER : entremés *m*, aperitivo *m* **3** *or* **starter motor** : motor *m* de arranque

startle ['stɑrtəl] *vt* **-tled; -tling** : asustar, sobresaltar

start–up ['stɑrt'ʌp] *adj* : de puesta en marcha

starvation [stɑr'veɪʃən] *n* : inanición *f*, hambre *f*

starve ['stɑrv] *v* **starved; starving** *vi* : morirse de hambre — *vt* : privar de comida

stash ['stæʃ] *vt* : esconder, guardar (en un lugar secreto)

stat ['stæt] **→ statistic**

state¹ ['steɪt] *vt* **stated; stating** **1** REPORT : puntualizar, exponer (los hechos, etc.) ⟨state your name : diga su nombre⟩ **2** ESTABLISH, FIX : establecer, fijar

state² *n* **1** CONDITION : estado *m*, condición *f* ⟨a liquid state : un estado líquido⟩ ⟨state of mind : estado de ánimo⟩

⟨in a bad state : en malas condiciones⟩
2 NATION : estado *m*, nación *f* **3** : estado *m* (dentro de un país) ⟨the States : los Estados Unidos⟩
stateliness ['steɪtlinəs] *n* : majestuosidad *f*
stately ['steɪtli] *adj* **statelier; -est** : majestuoso
statement ['steɪtmənt] *n* **1** DECLARATION : declaración *f*, afirmación *f* **2** *or* **bank statement** : estado *m* de cuenta
stateroom ['steɪt,ru:m, -,rʊm] *n* : camarote *m*
statesman ['steɪtsmən] *n, pl* **-men** [-mən, -,mɛn] : estadista *mf*
static¹ ['stætɪk] *adj* : estático
static² *n* : estática *f*, interferencia *f*
station¹ ['steɪʃən] *vt* : apostar, estacionar
station² *n* **1** : estación *f* (de trenes, etc.) **2** RANK, STANDING : condición *f* (social) **3** : canal *m* (de televisión), estación *f* o emisora *f* (de radio) **4 police station** : comisaría *f* **5 fire station** : estación *f* de bomberos, cuartel *m* de bomberos
stationary ['steɪʃə,nɛri] *adj* **1** IMMOBILE : estacionario, inmovible **2** UNCHANGING : inmutable, inalterable
stationery ['steɪʃə,nɛri] *n* : papel *m* y sobres *mpl* (para correspondencia)
station wagon *n* : camioneta *f* ranchera, camioneta *f* guayín *Mex*
statistic [stə'tɪstɪk] *n* : estadística *f* ⟨according to statistics : según las estadísticas⟩
statistical [stə'tɪstɪkəl] *adj* : estadístico
statistician [,stætə'stɪʃən] *n* : estadístico *m*, -ca *f*
statue ['stæ,tʃu:] *n* : estatua *f*
statuesque [,stætʃu'ɛsk] *adj* : escultural
statuette [,stætʃu'ɛt] *n* : estatuilla *f*
stature ['stætʃər] *n* **1** HEIGHT : estatura *f*, talla *f* **2** PRESTIGE : talla *f*, prestigio *m*
status ['steɪtəs, 'stæ-] *n* : condición *f*, situación *f*, estatus *m* (social) ⟨marital status : estado civil⟩
statute ['stæ,tʃu:t] *n* : ley *f*, estatuto *m*
staunch ['stɔntʃ] *adj* : acérrimo, incondicional, leal ⟨a staunch supporter : un partidario incondicional⟩ — **staunchly** *adv*
stave¹ ['steɪv] *vt* **staved** *or* **stove** ['sto:v]; **staving 1 to stave in** : romper **2 to stave off** : evitar (un ataque), prevenir (un problema)
stave² *n* : duela *f* (de un barril)
staves → **staff**
stay¹ ['steɪ] *vi* **1** REMAIN : quedarse, permanecer ⟨to stay in : quedarse en casa⟩ ⟨he stayed in the city : permaneció en la ciudad⟩ **2** CONTINUE : seguir, quedarse ⟨it stayed cloudy : siguió nublado⟩ ⟨to stay awake : mantenerse despierto⟩ **3** LODGE : hospedarse, alojarse (en un hotel, etc.) — *vt* **1** HALT : detener, suspender (una ejecución, etc.) **2 to stay the course** : aguantar hasta el final

stay² *n* **1** SOJOURN : estadía *f*, estancia *f*, permanencia *f* **2** SUSPENSION : suspensión *f* (de una sentencia) **3** SUPPORT : soporte *m*
stead ['stɛd] *n* **1** : lugar *m* ⟨she went in his stead : fue en su lugar⟩ **2 to stand (someone) in good stead** : ser muy útil a, servir de mucho a
steadfast ['stɛd,fæst] *adj* : firme, resuelto ⟨a steadfast friend : un fiel amigo⟩ ⟨a steadfast refusal : una negativa categórica⟩
steadily ['stɛdəli] *adv* **1** CONSTANTLY : continuamente, sin parar **2** FIRMLY : con firmeza **3** FIXEDLY : fijamente
steady¹ ['stɛdi] *vt* **steadied; steadying** *vt* : sujetar ⟨she steadied herself : recobró el equilibrio⟩ — *vi* : estabilizarse
steady² *adj* **steadier; -est 1** FIRM, SURE : seguro, firme ⟨to have a steady hand : tener buen pulso⟩ **2** FIXED, REGULAR : fijo ⟨a steady income : ingresos fijos⟩ **3** CALM : tranquilo, ecuánime ⟨she has steady nerves : es imperturbable⟩ **4** DEPENDABLE : responsable, fiable **5** CONSTANT : constante
steak ['steɪk] *n* : bistec *m*, filete *m*, churrasco *m*, bife *m Arg, Chile, Uru*
steal ['sti:l] *v* **stole** ['sto:l]; **stolen** ['sto:lən]; **stealing** *vt* : robar, hurtar — *vi* **1** : robar, hurtar **2** : ir sigilosamente ⟨to steal away : escabullirse⟩
stealth ['stɛlθ] *n* : sigilo *m*
stealthily ['stɛlθəli] *adv* : furtivamente
stealthy ['stɛlθi] *adj* **stealthier; -est** : furtivo, sigiloso
steam¹ ['sti:m] *vi* : echar vapor ⟨to steam away : moverse echando vapor⟩ — *vt* **1** : cocer al vapor (en cocina) **2 to steam open** : abrir con vapor
steam² *n* **1** : vapor *m* **2 to let off steam** : desahogarse
steamboat ['sti:m,bo:t] → **steamship**
steam engine *n* : motor *m* de vapor
steamroller ['sti:m,ro:lər] *n* : apisonadora *f*
steamship ['sti:m,ʃɪp] *n* : vapor *m*, barco *m* de vapor
steamy ['sti:mi] *adj* **steamier; -est 1** : lleno de vapor **2** EROTIC : erótico ⟨a steamy romance : un tórrido romance⟩
steed ['sti:d] *n* : corcel *m*
steel¹ ['sti:l] *vt* **to steel oneself** : armarse de valor
steel² *adj* : de acero
steel³ *n* : acero *m*
steely ['sti:li] *adj* **steelier; -est** : como acero ⟨a steely gaze : una mirada fría⟩ ⟨steely determination : determinación férrea⟩
steep¹ ['sti:p] *vt* : remojar, dejar (té, etc.) en infusión
steep² *adj* **1** : empinado, escarpado ⟨a steep cliff : un precipicio escarpado⟩ **2** CONSIDERABLE : considerable, marcado **3** EXCESSIVE : excesivo ⟨steep prices : precios muy altos⟩
steeple ['sti:pəl] *n* : aguja *f*, campanario *m*

steeplechase ['sti:pəl,tʃeɪs] *n* : carrera *f* de obstáculos

steeply ['sti:pli] *adv* : abruptamente

steer[1] ['stɪr] *vt* **1** : conducir (un coche), gobernar (un barco) **2** GUIDE : dirigir, guiar

steer[2] *n* : buey *m*

steering wheel *n* : volante *m*

stein ['staɪn] *n* : jarra *f* (para cerveza)

stellar ['stɛlər] *adj* : estelar

stem[1] ['stɛm] *v* **stemmed; stemming** *vt* : detener, contener, parar ⟨to stem the tide : detener el curso⟩ — *vi* **to stem from** : provenir de, ser el resultado de

stem[2] *n* : tallo *m* (de una planta)

stench ['stɛntʃ] *n* : hedor *m*, mal olor *m*

stencil[1] ['stɛntsəl] *vt* **-ciled** *or* **-cilled; -ciling** *or* **-cilling** : marcar utilizando una plantilla

stencil[2] *n* : plantilla *f* (para marcar)

stenographer [stə'nɑgrəfər] *n* : taquígrafo *m*, -fa *f*

stenographic [,stɛnə'græfɪk] *adj* : taquigráfico

stenography [stə'nɑgrəfi] *n* : taquigrafía *f*

step[1] ['stɛp] *vi* **stepped; stepping 1** : dar un paso ⟨step this way, please : pase por aquí, por favor⟩ ⟨he stepped outside : salió⟩ **2 to step on** : pisar

step[2] *n* **1** : paso *m* ⟨step by step : paso por paso⟩ **2** STAIR : escalón *m*, peldaño *m* **3** RUNG : escalón *m*, travesaño *m* **4** MEASURE, MOVE : medida *f*, paso *m* ⟨to take steps : tomar medidas⟩ **5** STRIDE : paso *m* ⟨with a quick step : con paso rápido⟩

stepbrother ['stɛp,brʌðər] *n* : hermanastro *m*

stepdaughter ['stɛp,dɔtər] *n* : hijastra *f*

stepfather ['stɛp,fɑðər, -,fa-] *n* : padrastro *m*

stepladder ['stɛp,lædər] *n* : escalera *f* de tijera

stepmother ['stɛp,mʌðər] *n* : madrastra *f*

steppe ['stɛp] *n* : estepa *f*

stepping–stone ['stɛpɪŋ,sto:n] *n* : pasadera *f* (en un río, etc.), trampolín *m* (al éxito)

stepsister ['stɛp,sɪstər] *n* : hermanastra *f*

stepson ['stɛp,sʌn] *n* : hijastro *m*

step up *vt* INCREASE : aumentar

stereo[1] ['stɛri,o:, 'stɪr-] *adj* : estéreo

stereo[2] *n*, *pl* **stereos** : estéreo *m*

stereophonic [,stɛrio'fɑnɪk, ,stɪr-] *adj* : estereofónico

stereotype[1] ['stɛrio,taɪp, 'stɪr-] *vt* **-typed; -typing** : estereotipar

stereotype[2] *n* : estereotipo *m*

sterile ['stɛrəl] *adj* : estéril

sterility [stə'rɪləti] *n* : esterilidad *f*

sterilization [,stɛrələ'zeɪʃən] *n* : esterilización *f*

sterilize ['stɛrə,laɪz] *vt* **-ized; -izing** : esterilizar

sterling ['stərlɪŋ] *adj* **1** : de ley ⟨sterling silver : plata de ley⟩ **2** EXCELLENT : excelente

stern[1] ['stərn] *adj* : severo, adusto — **sternly** *adv*

stern[2] *n* : popa *f*

sternness ['stərnnəs] *n* : severidad *f*

sternum ['stərnəm] *n*, *pl* **sternums** *or* **sterna** [-nə] : esternón *m*

stethoscope ['stɛθə,sko:p] *n* : estetoscopio *m*

stevedore ['sti:və,dor] *n* : estibador *m*, -dora *f*

stew[1] ['stu:, 'stju:] *vt* : estofar, guisar — *vi* **1** : cocer (dícese de la carne, etc.) **2** FRET : preocuparse

stew[2] *n* **1** : estofado *m*, guiso *m* **2 to be in a stew** : estar agitado

steward ['stu:ərd, 'stju:-] *n* **1** MANAGER : administrador *m* **2** : auxiliar *m* de vuelo (en un avión), camarero *m* (en un barco)

stewardess ['stu:ərdəs, 'stju:-] *n* **1** MANAGER : administradora *f* **2** : camarera *f* (en un barco) **3** : auxiliar *f* de vuelo, azafata *f*, aeromoza *f* (en un avión)

stick[1] ['stɪk] *v* **stuck** ['stʌk]; **sticking** *vt* **1** STAB : clavar **2** ATTACH : pegar **3** PUT : poner **4 to stick out** : sacar (la lengua, etc.), extender (la mano) — *vi* **1** ADHERE : pegarse, adherirse **2** JAM : atascarse **3 to stick around** : quedarse **4 to stick out** PROJECT : sobresalir (de una superficie), asomar (por detrás o debajo de algo) **5 to stick to** : no abandonar ⟨stick to your guns : manténgase firme⟩ **6 to stick up** : estar parado (dícese del pelo, etc.), sobresalir (de una superficie) **7 to stick with** : serle fiel a (una persona), seguir con (una cosa) ⟨I'll stick with what I know : prefiero lo conocido⟩

stick[2] *n* **1** BRANCH, TWIG : ramita *f* **2** : palo *m*, vara *f* ⟨a walking stick : un bastón⟩

sticker ['stɪkər] *n* : etiqueta *f* adhesiva

stickler ['stɪklər] *n* : persona *f* exigente ⟨to be a stickler for : insistir mucho en⟩

sticky ['stɪki] *adj* **stickier; -est 1** ADHESIVE : pegajoso, adhesivo **2** MUGGY : bochornoso **3** DIFFICULT : difícil

stiff ['stɪf] *adj* **1** RIGID : rígido, tieso ⟨a stiff dough : una masa firme⟩ **2** : agarrotado, entumecido ⟨stiff muscles : músculos entumecidos⟩ **3** STILTED : acartonado, poco natural **4** STRONG : fuerte (dícese del viento, etc.) **5** DIFFICULT, SEVERE : severo, difícil, duro

stiffen ['stɪfən] *vt* **1** STRENGTHEN : fortalecer, reforzar (tela, etc.) **2** : hacer más duro (un castigo, etc.) — *vi* **1** HARDEN : endurecerse **2** : entumecerse (dícese de los músculos)

stiffly ['stɪfli] *adv* **1** RIGIDLY : rígidamente **2** COLDLY : con frialdad

stiffness ['stɪfnəs] *n* **1** RIGIDITY : rigidez *f* **2** COLDNESS : frialdad *f* **3** SEVERITY : severidad *f*

stifle ['staɪfəl] *vt* **-fled; -fling** SMOTHER, SUPPRESS : sofocar, reprimir, contener ⟨to stifle a yawn : reprimir un bostezo⟩

stigma ['stɪgmə] *n, pl* **stigmata** [stɪg'matə, 'stɪgmətə] *or* **stigmas** : estigma *m*

stigmatize ['stɪgmə,taɪz] *vt* **-tized; -tizing** : estigmatizar

stile ['staɪl] *n* : escalones *mpl* para cruzar un cerco

stiletto [stə'lɛ,to:] *n, pl* **-tos** *or* **-toes** : estilete *m*

still¹ ['stɪl] *vt* CALM : pacificar, apaciguar — *vi* : pacificarse, apaciguarse

still² *adv* **1** QUIETLY : quieto ⟨sit still! : ¡quédate quieto!⟩ **2** : de todos modos, aún, todavía ⟨she still lives there : aún vive allí⟩ ⟨it's still the same : sigue siendo lo mismo⟩ **3** IN ANY CASE : de todos modos, aún así ⟨he still has doubts : aún así le quedan dudas⟩ ⟨I still prefer that you stay : de todos modos prefiero que te quedes⟩

still³ *adj* **1** MOTIONLESS : quieto, inmóvil **2** SILENT : callado

still⁴ *n* **1** SILENCE : quietud *f*, calma *f* **2** : alambique *m* (para destilar alcohol)

stillborn ['stɪl,bɔrn] *adj* : nacido muerto

stillness ['stɪlnəs] *n* : calma *f*, silencio *m*

stilt ['stɪlt] *n* : zanco *m*

stilted ['stɪltəd] *adj* : afectado, poco natural

stimulant ['stɪmjələnt] *n* : estimulante *m* — **stimulant** *adj*

stimulate ['stɪmjə,leɪt] *vt* **-lated; -lating** : estimular

stimulation [,stɪmjə'leɪʃən] *n* **1** STIMULATING : estimulación *f* **2** STIMULUS : estímulo *m*

stimulus ['stɪmjələs] *n, pl* **-li** [-,laɪ] **1** : estímulo *m* **2** INCENTIVE : acicate *m*

sting¹ ['stɪŋ] *v* **stung** ['stʌŋ]; **stinging** *vt* **1** : picar ⟨a bee stung him : le picó una abeja⟩ **2** HURT : hacer escocer (físicamente), herir (emocionalmente) — *vi* **1** : picar (dícese de las abejas, etc.) **2** SMART : escocer, arder

sting² *n* : picadura *f* (herida), escozor *m* (sensación)

stinger ['stɪŋər] *n* : aguijón *m* (de una abeja, etc.)

stinginess ['stɪndʒinəs] *n* : tacañería *f*

stingy ['stɪndʒi] *adj* **stingier; -est 1** MISERLY : tacaño, avaro **2** PALTRY : mezquino, mísero

stink¹ ['stɪŋk] *vi* **stank** ['stæŋk] *or* **stunk** ['stʌŋk]; **stunk; stinking** : apestar, oler mal

stink² *n* : hedor *m*, mal olor *m*, peste *f*

stint¹ ['stɪnt] *vt* : escatimar ⟨to stint oneself of : privarse de⟩ — *vi* **to stint on** : escatimar

stint² *n* : período *m*

stipend ['staɪ,pɛnd, -pənd] *n* : estipendio *m*

stipulate ['stɪpjə,leɪt] *vt* **-lated; -lating** : estipular

stipulation [,stɪpjə'leɪʃən] *n* : estipulación *f*

stir¹ ['stər] *v* **stirred; stirring** *vt* **1** AGITATE : mover, agitar **2** MIX : revolver, remover **3** INCITE : incitar, impulsar, motivar **4** *or* **to stir up** AROUSE : despertar (memorias, etc.), provocar (ira, etc.) — *vi* : moverse, agitarse

stir² *n* **1** MOTION : movimiento *m* **2** COMMOTION : revuelo *m*

stirrup ['stərəp, 'stɪr-] *n* : estribo *m*

stitch¹ ['stɪtʃ] *vt* : coser, bordar (para decorar) — *vi* : coser

stitch² *n* **1** : puntada *f* **2** TWINGE : punzada *f*, puntada *f*

stock¹ ['stak] *vt* : surtir, abastecer, vender — *vi* **to stock up** : abastecerse

stock² *n* **1** SUPPLY : reserva *f*, existencias *fpl* (en comercio) ⟨to be out of stock : estar agotadas las existencias⟩ **2** SECURITIES : acciones *fpl*, valores *mpl* **3** LIVESTOCK : ganado *m* **4** ANCESTRY : linaje *m*, estirpe *f* **5** BROTH : caldo *m* **6 to take stock** : evaluar

stockade [sta'keɪd] *n* : estacada *f*

stockbroker ['stak,bro:kər] *n* : corredor *m*, -dora *f* de bolsa

stockholder ['stak,ho:ldər] *n* : accionista *mf*

stocking ['stakɪŋ] *n* : media *f* ⟨a pair of stockings : unas medias⟩

stock market *n* : bolsa *f*

stockpile¹ ['stak,paɪl] *vt* **-piled; -piling** : acumular, almacenar

stockpile² *n* : reservas *fpl*

stocky ['staki] *adj* **stockier; -est** : robusto, fornido

stockyard ['stak,jard] *n* : corral *m*

stodgy ['stadʒi] *adj* **stodgier; -est 1** DULL : aburrido, pesado **2** OLD-FASHIONED : anticuado

stoic¹ ['sto:ɪk] *or* **stoical** [-ɪkəl] *adj* : estoico — **stoically** [-ɪkli] *adv*

stoic² *n* : estoico *m*, -ca *f*

stoicism ['sto:ə,sɪzəm] *n* : estoicismo *m*

stoke ['sto:k] *vt* **stoked; stoking** : atizar (un fuego), echarle carbón a (un horno)

stole¹ → **steal**

stole² ['sto:l] *n* : estola *f*

stolen → **steal**

stolid ['stalɪd] *adj* : impasible, imperturbable — **stolidly** *adv*

stomach¹ ['stʌmɪk] *vt* : aguantar, soportar

stomach² *n* **1** : estómago *m* **2** BELLY : vientre *m*, barriga *f*, panza *f* **3** DESIRE : ganas *fpl* ⟨he had no stomach for a fight : no quería pelea⟩

stomachache ['stʌmɪk,eɪk] *n* : dolor *m* de estómago

stomp ['stamp, 'stɔmp] *vt* : pisotear — *vi* : pisar fuerte

stone¹ ['sto:n] *vt* **stoned; stoning** : apedrear, lapidar

stone² *n* **1** : piedra *f* **2** PIT : hueso *m*, pepa *f* (de una fruta)

Stone Age *n* : Edad *f* de Piedra

stony ['stoːni] *adj* **stonier; -est 1** ROCKY : pedregoso **2** UNFEELING : insensible, frío ⟨a stony stare : una mirada glacial⟩

stood → **stand**

stool ['stuːl] *n* **1** SEAT : taburete *m*, banco *m* **2** FOOTSTOOL : escabel *m* **3** FECES : deposición *f* de heces

stoop¹ ['stuːp] *vi* **1** CROUCH : agacharse **2 to stoop to** : rebajarse a

stoop² *n* **1** : espaldas *fpl* encorvadas ⟨to have a stoop : ser encorvado⟩ **2** : entrada *f* (de una casa)

stop¹ ['stɑp] *v* **stopped; stopping** *vt* **1** PLUG : tapar **2** PREVENT : impedir, evitar ⟨she stopped me from leaving : me impidió que saliera⟩ **3** HALT : parar, detener **4** CEASE : dejar de ⟨he stopped talking : dejó de hablar⟩ — *vi* **1** HALT : detenerse, parar **2** CEASE : cesar, terminar ⟨the rain won't stop : no deja de llover⟩ **3** STAY : quedarse ⟨she stopped with friends : se quedó en casa de unos amigos⟩ **4 to stop by** : visitar

stop² *n* **1** STOPPER : tapón *m* **2** HALT : parada *f*, alto *m* ⟨to come to a stop : pararse, detenerse⟩ ⟨to put a stop to : poner fin a⟩ **3** : parada *f* ⟨bus stop : parada de autobús⟩

stopgap ['stɑp,gæp] *n* : arreglo *m* provisorio

stoplight ['stɑp,laɪt] *n* : semáforo *m*

stoppage ['stɑpɪʤ] *n* : acto *m* de parar ⟨a work stoppage : un paro⟩

stopper ['stɑpər] *n* : tapón *m*

storage ['storɪʤ] *n* : almacenamiento *m*, almacenaje *m*

storage battery *n* : acumulador *m*

store¹ ['stor] *vt* **stored; storing** : guardar, almacenar

store² *n* **1** RESERVE, SUPPLY : reserva *f* **2** SHOP : tienda *f* ⟨grocery store : tienda de comestibles⟩

storehouse ['stor,haʊs] *n* : almacén *m*, depósito *m*

storekeeper ['stor,kiːpər] *n* : tendero *m*, -ra *f*

storeroom ['stor,ruːm, -,rʊm] *n* : almacén *m*, depósito *m*

stork ['stork] *n* : cigüeña *f*

storm¹ ['storm] *vi* **1** : llover o nevar tormentosamente **2** RAGE : ponerse furioso, vociferar **3 to storm out** : salir echando pestes — *vt* ATTACK : asaltar

storm² *n* **1** : tormenta *f*, tempestad *f* **2** UPROAR : alboroto *m*, revuelo *m*, escándalo *m* ⟨a storm of abuse : un torrente de abusos⟩

stormy ['stormi] *adj* **stormier; -est** : tormentoso

story ['stori] *n, pl* **stories 1** NARRATIVE : cuento *m*, relato *m* **2** ACCOUNT : historia *f*, relato *m* **3** : piso *m*, planta *f* (de un edificio) ⟨first story : planta baja⟩

stout ['staʊt] *adj* **1** FIRM, RESOLUTE : firme, resuelto **2** STURDY : fuerte, robusto, sólido **3** FAT : corpulento, gordo

stove¹ ['stoːv] *n* : cocina *f* (para cocinar), estufa *f* (para calentar)

stove² → **stave¹**

stow ['stoː] *vt* **1** STORE : poner, meter, guardar **2** LOAD : cargar — *vi* **to stow away** : viajar de polizón

stowaway ['stoːə,weɪ] *n* : polizón *m*

straddle ['strædəl] *vt* **-dled; -dling** : sentarse a horcajadas sobre

straggle ['strægəl] *vi* **-gled; -gling** : rezagarse, quedarse atrás

straggler ['strægələr] *n* : rezagado *m*, -da *f*

straight¹ ['streɪt] *adv* **1** : derecho, directamente ⟨go straight, then turn right : sigue derecho, luego gira a la derecha⟩ **2** HONESTLY : honestamente ⟨to go straight : enmendarse⟩ **3** CLEARLY : con claridad **4** FRANKLY : francamente, con franqueza

straight² *adj* **1** : recto (dícese de las líneas, etc.), derecho (dícese de algo vertical), lacio (dícese del pelo) **2** HONEST, JUST : honesto, justo **3** NEAT, ORDERLY : arreglado, ordenado

straighten ['streɪtən] *vt* **1** : enderezar, poner derecho **2 to straighten up** : arreglar, ordenar ⟨he straightened up the house : arregló la casa⟩

straightforward [streɪt'forwərd] *adj* **1** FRANK : franco, sincero **2** CLEAR, PRECISE : puro, simple, claro

straightway ['streɪt'weɪ, -,weɪ] *adv* : inmediatamente

strain¹ ['streɪn] *vt* **1** EXERT : forzar (la vista, la voz) ⟨to strain oneself : hacer un gran esfuerzo⟩ **2** FILTER : colar, filtrar **3** INJURE : lastimarse, hacerse daño en ⟨to strain a muscle : sufrir un esguince⟩

strain² *n* **1** LINEAGE : linaje *m*, abolengo *m* **2** STREAK, TRACE : veta *f* **3** VARIETY : tipo *m*, variedad *f* **4** STRESS : tensión *f*, presión *f* **5** SPRAIN : esguince *m*, torcedura *f* (del tobillo, etc.) **6 strains** *npl* TUNE : melodía *f*, acordes *mpl*, compases *fpl*

strainer ['streɪnər] *n* : colador *m*

strait ['streɪt] *n* **1** : estrecho *m* **2 straits** *npl* DISTRESS : aprietos *mpl*, apuros *mpl* ⟨in dire straits : en serios aprietos⟩

straitened ['streɪtənd] *adj* **in straitened circumstances** : en apuros económicos

strand¹ ['strænd] *vt* **1** : varar **2 to be left stranded** : quedar(se) varado, quedar colgado ⟨they left me stranded : me dejaron abandonado⟩

strand² *n* **1** : hebra *f* (de hilo, etc.) ⟨a strand of hair : un pelo⟩ **2** BEACH : playa *f*

strange ['streɪnʤ] *adj* **stranger; -est 1** QUEER, UNUSUAL : extraño, raro **2** UNFAMILIAR : desconocido, nuevo

strangely ['streɪnʤli] *adv* ODDLY : de manera extraña ⟨to behave strangely : portarse de una manera rara⟩ ⟨strangely, he didn't call : curiosamente, no llamó⟩

strangeness ['streɪndʒnəs] *n* **1** ODD-NESS : rareza *f* **2** UNFAMILIARITY : lo desconocido

stranger ['streɪndʒər] *n* : desconocido *m*, -da *f*; extraño *m*, -ña *f*

strangle ['stræŋgəl] *vt* **-gled; -gling** : estrangular

strangler ['stræŋglər] *n* : estrangulador *m*, -dora *f*

strap[1] ['stræp] *vt* **strapped; strapping 1** FASTEN : sujetar con una correa **2** FLOG : azotar (con una correa)

strap[2] *n* **1** : correa *f* **2 shoulder strap** : tirante *m*

strapless ['stræpləs] *n* : sin tirantes

strapping ['stræpɪŋ] *adj* : robusto, fornido

stratagem ['strætədʒəm, -ˌdʒɛm] *n* : estratagema *f*, artimaña *f*

strategic [strə'tiːdʒɪk] *adj* : estratégico

strategist ['strætədʒɪst] *n* : estratega *mf*

strategy ['strætədʒi] *n, pl* **-gies** : estrategia *f*

stratified ['strætəˌfaɪd] *adj* : estratificado

stratosphere ['strætəˌsfɪr] *n* : estratosfera *f*

stratospheric [ˌstrætə'sfɪrɪk, -'sfɛr-] *adj* : estratosférico

stratum ['streɪtəm, 'stræ-] *n, pl* **strata** [-ţə] : estrato *m*, capa *f*

straw *n* **1** : paja *f* ⟨the last straw : el colmo⟩ **2** *or* **drinking straw** : pajita *f*, popote *m Mex*

strawberry ['strɔˌbɛri] *n, pl* **-ries** : fresa *f*

stray[1] ['streɪ] *vi* **1** WANDER : alejarse, extraviarse ⟨the cattle strayed away : el ganado se descarrió⟩ **2** DIGRESS : desviarse, divagar

stray[2] *adj* : perdido, callejero (dícese de un perro o un gato), descarriado (dícese del ganado)

stray[3] *n* : animal *m* perdido, animal *m* callejero

streak[1] ['striːk] *vt* : hacer rayas en ⟨blue streaked with grey : azul veteado con gris⟩ — *vi* : ir como una flecha

streak[2] *n* **1** : raya *f*, veta *f* (en mármol, queso, etc.), mechón *m* (en el pelo) **2** : rayo *m* (de luz) **3** TRACE : veta *f* **4** : racha *f* ⟨a streak of luck : una racha de suerte⟩

stream[1] ['striːm] *vi* : correr, salir a chorros ⟨tears streamed from his eyes : las lágrimas brotaban de sus ojos⟩ — *vt* : derramar, dejar correr ⟨to stream blood : derramar sangre⟩

stream[2] *n* **1** BROOK : arroyo *m*, riachuelo *m* **2** RIVER : río *m* **3** FLOW : corriente *f*, chorro *m*

streamer ['striːmər] *n* **1** PENNANT : banderín *m* **2** RIBBON : serpentina *f* (de papel), cinta *f* (de tela)

streamlined ['striːmˌlaɪnd] *adj* **1** : aerodinámico (dícese de los automóviles, etc.) **2** EFFICIENT : eficiente, racionalizado

street ['striːt] *n* : calle *f*

streetcar ['striːtˌkɑr] *n* : tranvía *m*

strength ['strɛŋkθ] *n* **1** POWER : fuerza *f*, resistencia *f*, dureza *f* **3** INTENSITY : intensidad *f* (de emociones, etc.), lo fuerte (de un sabor, etc.) **4** : punto *m* fuerte ⟨strengths and weaknesses : virtudes y defectos⟩ **5** NUMBER : número *m*, complemento *m* ⟨in full strength : en gran número⟩

strengthen ['strɛŋkθən] *vt* **1** : fortalecer (los músculos, el espíritu, etc.) **2** REINFORCE : reforzar **3** INTENSIFY : intensificar, redoblar (esfuerzos, etc.) — *vi* **1** : fortalecerse, hacerse más fuerte **2** INTENSIFY : intensificarse

strenuous ['strɛnjuəs] *adj* **1** VIGOROUS : vigoroso, enérgico **2** ARDUOUS : duro, riguroso

strenuously ['strɛnjuəsli] *adv* : vigorosamente, duro

stress[1] ['strɛs] *vt* **1** : someter a tensión (física) **2** EMPHASIZE : enfatizar, recalcar **3 to stress out** : estresar

stress[2] *n* **1** : tensión *f* (en un material) **2** EMPHASIS : énfasis *m*, acento *m* (en lingüística) **3** TENSION : tensión *f* (nerviosa), estrés *m*

stressful ['strɛsfəl] *adj* : estresante

stretch[1] ['strɛtʃ] *vt* **1** EXTEND : estirar, extender, desplegar (alas) **2 to stretch the truth** : forzar la verdad, exagerar — *vi* : estirarse

stretch[2] *n* **1** STRETCHING : extensión *f*, estiramiento *m* (de músculos) **2** ELASTICITY : elasticidad *f* **3** EXPANSE : tramo *m*, trecho *m* ⟨the home stretch : la recta final⟩ **4** PERIOD : período *m* (de tiempo)

stretcher ['strɛtʃər] *n* : camilla *f*

strew ['struː] *vt* **strewed; strewed** *or* **strewn** ['struːn]; **strewing 1** SCATTER : esparcir (semillas, etc.), desparramar (papeles, etc.) **2 to strew with** : cubrir de

stricken ['strɪkən] *adj* **stricken with** : aquejado de (una enfermedad), afligido por (tristeza, etc.)

strict ['strɪkt] *adj* : estricto — **strictly** *adv*

strictness ['strɪktnəs] *n* : severidad *f*, lo estricto

stricture ['strɪktʃər] *n* : crítica *f*, censura *f*

stride[1] ['straɪd] *vi* **strode** ['stroːd]; **stridden** ['strɪdən]; **striding** : ir dando trancos, ir dando zancadas

stride[2] *n* : tranco *m*, zancada *f*

strident ['straɪdənt] *adj* : estridente

strife ['straɪf] *n* : conflictos *mpl*, disensión *f*

strike[1] ['straɪk] *v* **struck** ['strʌk]; **striking** *vt* **1** HIT : golpear (a una persona) ⟨to strike a blow : pegar un golpe⟩ **2** DELETE : suprimir, tachar **3** COIN, MINT : acuñar (monedas) **4** : dar (la hora) **5** AFFLICT : sobrevenir ⟨he was stricken with a fever : le sobrevino una fiebre⟩ **6** IMPRESS : impresionar, parecer ⟨her voice struck me : su voz me impresionó⟩ ⟨it struck him as funny : le pareció chistoso⟩ **7** : encender (un fósforo) **8** FIND : descubrir (oro, petróleo) **9** ADOPT : adoptar (una pose, etc.) — *vi* **1** HIT : golpear ⟨to strike against : chocar contra⟩ **2** ATTACK : atacar **3** : declararse en huelga

strike² *n* **1** BLOW : golpe *m* **2** : huelga *f*, paro *m* ⟨to be on strike : estar en huelga⟩ **3** ATTACK : ataque *m*

strikebreaker ['straɪkˌbreɪkər] *n* : rompehuelgas *mf*, esquirol *mf*

strike out *vi* **1** HEAD : salir (para) **2** : ser ponchado (en béisbol) ⟨the batter struck out : poncharon al bateador⟩

striker ['straɪkər] *n* : huelguista *mf*

strike up *vt* START : entablar, empezar

striking ['straɪkɪŋ] *adj* : notable, sorprendente, llamativo ⟨a striking beauty : una belleza imponente⟩ — **strikingly** *adv*

string¹ ['strɪŋ] *vt* **strung** ['strʌŋ]; **stringing** **1** THREAD : ensartar ⟨to string beads : ensartar cuentas⟩ **2** HANG : colgar (con un cordel)

string² *n* **1** : cordel *m*, cuerda *f* **2** SERIES : serie *f*, sarta *f* (de insultos, etc.) **3 strings** *npl* : cuerdas *fpl* (en música)

string bean *n* : judía *f*, ejote *m Mex*

stringent ['strɪndʒənt] *adj* : estricto, severo

stringy ['strɪŋi] *adj* **stringier; -est** : fibroso

strip¹ ['strɪp] *v* **stripped; stripping** *vt* : quitar (ropa, pintura, etc.), desnudar, despojar — *vi* UNDRESS : desnudarse

strip² *n* : tira *f* ⟨a strip of land : una faja⟩

stripe¹ ['straɪp] *vt* **striped** ['straɪpt]; **striping** : marcar con rayas o listas

stripe² *n* **1** : raya *f*, lista *f* **2** BAND : franja *f*

striped ['straɪpt, 'straɪpəd] *adj* : a rayas, de rayas, rayado, listado

strive ['straɪv] *vi* **strove** ['stroːv]; **striven** ['strɪvən] *or* **strived; striving** **1** **to strive for** : luchar por lograr **2 to strive to** : esforzarse por

strobe ['stroːb] *or* **strobe light** *n* : luz *f* estroboscópica

strode → **stride**

stroke¹ ['stroːk] *vt* **stroked; stroking** : acariciar

stroke² *n* : golpe *m* ⟨a stroke of luck : un golpe de suerte⟩

stroll¹ ['stroːl] *vi* : pasear, pasearse, dar un paseo

stroll² *n* : paseo *m*

stroller ['stroːlər] *n* : cochecito *m* (para niños)

strong ['strɔŋ] *adj* **1** : fuerte **2** HEALTHY : sano **3** ZEALOUS : ferviente

stronghold ['strɔŋˌhoːld] *n* : fortaleza *f*, fuerte *m*, bastión *m* ⟨a cultural stronghold : un baluarte de la cultura⟩

strongly ['strɔŋli] *adv* **1** POWERFULLY : fuerte, con fuerza **2** STURDILY

: fuertemente, sólidamente **3** INTENSELY : intensamente, profundamente **4** WHOLEHEARTEDLY : totalmente

struck → **strike¹**

structural ['strʌktʃərəl] *adj* : estructural

structure¹ ['strʌktʃər] *vt* **-tured; -turing** : estructurar

structure² *n* **1** BUILDING : construcción *f* **2** ARRANGEMENT, FRAMEWORK : estructura *f*

struggle¹ ['strʌgəl] *vi* **-gled; -gling** **1** CONTEND : forcejear (físicamente), luchar, contender **2** : hacer con dificultad ⟨she struggled forward : avanzó con dificultad⟩

struggle² *n* : lucha *f*, pelea *f* (física)

strum ['strʌm] *vt* **strummed; strumming** : rasguear

strung → **string¹**

strut¹ ['strʌt] *vi* **strutted; strutting** : pavonearse

strut² *n* **1** : pavoneo *m* ⟨he walked with a strut : se pavoneaba⟩ **2** : puntal *m* (en construcción, etc.)

strychnine ['strɪkˌnaɪn, -nən, -ˌniːn] *n* : estricnina *f*

stub¹ ['stʌb] *vt* **stubbed; stubbing** **1 to stub one's toe** : darse en el dedo (del pie) **2 to stub out** : apagarse

stub² *n* : colilla *f* (de un cigarrillo), cabo *m* (de un lápiz, etc.), talón *m* (de un cheque)

stubble ['stʌbəl] *n* **1** : rastrojo *m* (de plantas) **2** BEARD : barba *f*

stubborn ['stʌbərn] *adj* **1** OBSTINATE : terco, obstinado, empecinado **2** PERSISTENT : pertinaz, persistente — **stubbornly** *adv*

stubbornness ['stʌbərnnəs] *n* **1** OBSTINACY : terquedad *f*, obstinación *f* **2** PERSISTENCE : persistencia *f*

stubby ['stʌbi] *adj* **stubbier; -est** : corto y grueso ⟨stubby fingers : dedos regordetes⟩

stucco ['stʌkoː] *n, pl* **stuccos** *or* **stuccoes** : estuco *m*

stuck → **stick¹**

stuck–up ['stʌkˈʌp] *adj* : engreído, creído *fam*

stud¹ ['stʌd] *vt* **studded; studding** : tachonar, salpicar

stud² *n* **1** *or* **stud horse** : semental *m* **2** : montante *m* (en construcción) **3** HOBNAIL : tachuela *f*, tachón *m*

student ['stuːdənt, 'stjuː-] *n* : estudiante *mf*; alumno *m*, -na *f* (de un colegio)

studied ['stʌdid] *adj* : intencionado, premeditado

studio ['stuːdiˌoː, 'stjuː-] *n, pl* **studios** : estudio *m*

studious ['stuːdiəs, 'stjuː-] *adj* : estudioso — **studiously** *adv*

study¹ ['stʌdi] *v* **studied; studying** **1** : estudiar **2** EXAMINE : examinar, estudiar

study² *n, pl* **studies** **1** STUDYING : estudio *m* **2** OFFICE : estudio *m*, gabinete *m* (en una casa) **3** RESEARCH : investigación *f*, estudio *m*

stuff¹ ['stʌf] *vt* : rellenar, llenar, atiborrar ⟨a stuffed toy : un juguete de peluche⟩

stuff² *n* **1** POSSESSIONS : cosas *fpl* **2** ESSENCE : esencia *f* **3** SUBSTANCE : cosa *f*, cosas *fpl* ⟨some sticky stuff : una cosa pegajosa⟩ ⟨she knows her stuff : es experta⟩

stuffing ['stʌfɪŋ] *n* : relleno *m*

stuffy ['stʌfi] *adj* **stuffier; -est 1** CLOSE : viciado, cargado ⟨a stuffy room : una sala mal ventilada⟩ ⟨stuffy weather : tiempo bochornoso⟩ **2** : tapado (dícese de la nariz) **3** STODGY : pesado, aburrido

stumble¹ ['stʌmbəl] *vi* **-bled; -bling 1** TRIP : tropezar, dar un traspié **2** FLOUNDER : quedarse sin saber qué hacer o decir **3 to stumble across** *or* **to stumble upon** : dar con, tropezar con

stumble² *n* : tropezón *m*, traspié *m*

stump¹ ['stʌmp] *vt* : dejar perplejo ⟨to be stumped : no tener respuesta⟩

stump² *n* **1** : muñón *m* (de un brazo o una pierna) **2** *or* **tree stump** : cepa *f*, tocón *m* **3** STUB : cabo *m*

stun ['stʌn] *vt* **stunned; stunning 1** : aturdir (con un golpe) **2** ASTONISH, SHOCK : dejar estupefacto, dejar atónito, aturdir

stung → **sting¹**

stunk → **stink¹**

stunning ['stʌnɪŋ] *adj* **1** ASTONISHING : asombroso, pasmoso, increíble **2** STRIKING : imponente, impresionante (dícese de la belleza)

stunt¹ ['stʌnt] *vt* : atrofiar

stunt² *n* : proeza *f* (acrobática)

stupefy ['stu:pə,faɪ, 'stju:-] *vt* **-fied; -fying 1** : aturdir, atontar (con drogas, etc.) **2** AMAZE : dejar estupefacto, dejar atónito

stupendous [stʊ'pɛndəs, stju-] *adj* **1** MARVELOUS : estupendo, maravilloso **2** TREMENDOUS : tremendo — **stupendously** *adv*

stupid ['stu:pəd, 'stju:-] *adj* **1** IDIOTIC, SILLY : tonto, bobo, estúpido **2** DULL, OBTUSE : lento, torpe, lerdo

stupidity [stʊ'pɪdəti, stju-] *n* : tontería *f*, estupidez *f*

stupidly ['stu:pədli, 'stju:-] *adv* **1** IDIOTICALLY : estúpidamente, tontamente **2** DENSELY : torpemente

stupor ['stu:pər, 'stju:-] *n* : estupor *m*

sturdily ['stərdəli] *adv* : sólidamente

sturdiness ['stərdinəs] *n* : solidez *f* (de muebles, etc.), robustez *f* (de una persona)

sturdy ['stərdi] *adj* **sturdier; -est** : fuerte, robusto, sólido

sturgeon ['stərdʒən] *n* : esturión *m*

stutter¹ ['stʌtər] *vi* : tartamudear

stutter² *n* STAMMER : tartamudeo *m*

sty ['staɪ] *n* **1** *pl* **sties** PIGPEN : chiquero *m*, pocilga *f* **2** *pl* **sties** *or* **styes** : orzuelo *m* (en el ojo)

style¹ ['staɪl] *vt* **styled; styling 1** NAME : llamar **2** : peinar (pelo), diseñar (vestidos, etc.) ⟨carefully styled prose : prosa escrita con gran esmero⟩

style² *n* **1** : estilo *m* ⟨that's just his style : él es así⟩ ⟨to live in style : vivir a lo grande⟩ **2** FASHION : moda *f*

stylish ['staɪlɪʃ] *adj* : de moda, elegante, chic

stylishly ['staɪlɪʃli] *adv* : con estilo

stylishness ['staɪlɪʃnəs] *n* : estilo *m*

stylist ['staɪlɪst] *n* : estilista *mf*

stylize ['staɪˌlaɪz, 'staɪə-] *vt* : estilizar

stylus ['staɪləs] *n*, *pl* **styli** ['staɪˌlaɪ] **1** PEN : estilo *m* **2** NEEDLE : aguja *f* (de un tocadiscos)

stymie ['staɪmi] *vt* **-mied; -mieing** : obstaculizar

suave ['swɑv] *adj* : fino, urbano

sub¹ ['sʌb] *vi* **subbed; subbing** → **substitute¹**

sub² *n* **1** → **substitute²** **2** → **submarine**

subcommittee ['sʌbkəˌmɪti] *n* : subcomité *m*

subconscious¹ [səb'kɑntʃəs] *adj* : subconsciente — **subconsciously** *adv*

subconscious² *n* : subconsciente *m*

subcontract [ˌsʌb'kɑnˌtrækt] *vt* : subcontratar

subculture ['sʌbˌkʌltʃər] *n* : subcultura *f*

subdivide [ˌsʌbdə'vaɪd, 'sʌbdəˌvaɪd] *vt* **-vided; -viding** : subdividir

subdivision ['sʌbdəˌvɪʒən] *n* : subdivisión *f*

subdue [səb'du:, -'dju:] *vt* **-dued; -duing 1** OVERCOME : sojuzgar (a un enemigo), vencer, superar **2** CONTROL : dominar **3** SOFTEN : suavizar, atenuar (luz, etc.), moderar (lenguaje)

subgroup ['sʌbˌgru:p] *n* : subgrupo *m*

subhead ['sʌbˌhɛd] *or* **subheading** [-ˌhɛdɪŋ] *n* : subtítulo *m*

subject¹ [səb'dʒɛkt] *vt* **1** CONTROL, DOMINATE : controlar, dominar **2** : someter ⟨they subjected him to pressure : lo sometieron a presiones⟩

subject² ['sʌbdʒɪkt] *adj* **1** : subyugado, sometido ⟨a subject nation : una nación subyugada⟩ **2** PRONE : propenso ⟨subject to colds : sujeto a resfriarse⟩ **3 subject to** : sujeto a ⟨subject to congressional approval : sujeto a la aprobación del congreso⟩

subject³ ['sʌbdʒɪkt] *n* **1** : súbdito *m*, -ta *f* (de un gobierno) **2** TOPIC : tema *m* **3** : sujeto *m* (en gramática)

subjection [səb'dʒɛkʃən] *n* : sometimiento *m*

subjective [səb'dʒɛktɪv] *adj* : subjetivo — **subjectively** *adv*

subjectivity [ˌsʌbˌdʒɛk'tɪvəti] *n* : subjetividad *f*

subjugate ['sʌbdʒɪˌgeɪt] *vt* **-gated; -gating** : subyugar, someter, sojuzgar

subjunctive [səbˈdʒʌŋktɪv] *n* : subjuntivo *m* — **subjunctive** *adj*
sublet [ˈsʌbˌlɛt] *vt* **-let; -letting** : subarrendar
sublime [səˈblaɪm] *adj* : sublime
sublimely [səˈblaɪmli] *adv* **1** : de manera sublime **2** UTTERLY : absolutamente, completamente
submarine¹ [ˈsʌbməˌriːn, ˌsʌbməˈ-] *adj* : submarino
submarine² *n* : submarino *m*
submerge [səbˈmərdʒ] *v* **-merged; -merging** *vt* : sumergir — *vi* : sumergirse
submission [səbˈmɪʃən] *n* **1** YIELDING : sumisión *f* **2** PRESENTATION : presentación *f*
submissive [səbˈmɪsɪv] *adj* : sumiso, dócil
submit [səbˈmɪt] *v* **-mitted; -mitting** *vi* YIELD : rendirse ⟨to submit to : someterse a⟩ — *vt* PRESENT : presentar
subnormal [ˌsʌbˈnɔrməl] *adj* : por debajo de lo normal
subordinate¹ [səˈbɔrdənˌeɪt] *vt* **-nated; -nating** : subordinar
subordinate² [səˈbɔrdənət] *adj* : subordinado ⟨a subordinate clause : una oración subordinada⟩
subordinate³ *n* : subordinado *m*, -da *f*; subalterno *m*, -na *f*
subordination [səˌbɔrdənˈeɪʃən] *n* : subordinación *f*
subpoena¹ [səˈpiːnə] *vt* **-naed; -naing** : citar
subpoena² *n* : citación *f*, citatorio *m*
subscribe [səbˈskraɪb] *vi* **-scribed; -scribing 1** : suscribirse (a una revista, etc.) **2 to subscribe to** : suscribir (una opinión, etc.), estar de acuerdo con
subscriber [səbˈskraɪbər] *n* : suscriptor *m*, -tora *f* (de una revista, etc.); abonado *m*, -da *f* (de un servicio)
subscription [səbˈskrɪpʃən] *n* : suscripción *f*
subsequent [ˈsʌbsɪkwənt, -səˌkwɛnt] *adj* : subsiguiente ⟨subsequent to : posterior a⟩
subsequently [ˈsʌbˌsɪkwɛntli, -kwənt-] *adv* : posteriormente
subservient [səbˈsərviənt] *adj* : servil
subside [səbˈsaɪd] *vi* **-sided; -siding 1** SINK : hundirse, descender **2** ABATE : calmarse (dícese de las emociones), amainar (dícese del viento, etc.)
subsidiary¹ [səbˈsɪdiˌɛri] *adj* : secundario
subsidiary² *n, pl* **-ries** : filial *f*, subsidiaria *f*
subsidize [ˈsʌbsəˌdaɪz] *vt* **-dized; -dizing** : subvencionar, subsidiar
subsidy [ˈsʌbsədi] *n, pl* **-dies** : subvención *f*, subsidio *m*
subsist [səbˈsɪst] *vi* : subsistir, mantenerse, vivir
subsistence [səbˈsɪstənts] *n* : subsistencia *f*

substance [ˈsʌbstənts] *n* **1** ESSENCE : sustancia *f*, esencia *f* **2** : sustancia *f* ⟨a toxic substance : una sustancia tóxica⟩ **3** WEALTH : riqueza *f* ⟨a woman of substance : una mujer acaudalada⟩
substandard [ˌsʌbˈstændərd] *adj* : inferior, deficiente
substantial [səbˈstænʧəl] *adj* **1** ABUNDANT : sustancioso ⟨a substantial meal : una comida sustanciosa⟩ **2** CONSIDERABLE : considerable, apreciable **3** SOLID, STURDY : sólido
substantially [səbˈstænʧəli] *adv* : considerablemente
substantiate [səbˈstænʧiˌeɪt] *vt* **-ated; -ating** : confirmar, probar, justificar
substitute¹ [ˈsʌbstəˌtuːt, -ˌtjuːt] *v* **-tuted; -tuting** *vt* : sustituir — *vi* **to substitute for** : sustituir
substitute² *n* **1** : sustituto *m*, -ta *f*; suplente *mf* (persona) **2** : sucedáneo *m* ⟨sugar substitute : sucedáneo de azúcar⟩
substitute teacher *n* : profesor *m*, -sora *f* suplente
substitution [ˌsʌbstəˈtuːʃən, -ˈtjuː-] *n* : sustitución *f*
subterfuge [ˈsʌbtərˌfjuːdʒ] *n* : subterfugio *m*
subterranean [ˌsʌbtəˈreɪniən] *adj* : subterráneo
subtitle [ˈsʌbˌtaɪtəl] *n* : subtítulo *m*
subtle [ˈsʌtəl] *adj* **-tler; -tlest 1** DELICATE, ELUSIVE : sutil, delicado **2** CLEVER : sutil, ingenioso
subtlety [ˈsʌtəlti] *n, pl* **-ties** : sutileza *f*
subtly [ˈsʌtəli] *adv* : sutilmente
subtotal [ˈsʌbˌtoːtəl] *n* : subtotal *m*
subtract [səbˈtrækt] *vt* : restar, sustraer
subtraction [səbˈtrækʃən] *n* : resta *f*, sustracción *f*
suburb [ˈsʌˌbərb] *n* : municipio *m* periférico, suburbio *m*
suburban [səˈbərbən] *adj* : de las afueras (de una ciudad), suburbano
subversion [səbˈvərʒən] *n* : subversión *f*
subversive [səbˈvərsɪv] *adj* : subversivo
subway [ˈsʌbˌweɪ] *n* : metro *m*, subterráneo *m Arg, Uru*
succeed [səkˈsiːd] *vt* FOLLOW : suceder a — *vi* : tener éxito (dícese de las personas), dar resultado (dícese de los planes, etc.) ⟨she succeeded in finishing : logró terminar⟩
success [səkˈsɛs] *n* : éxito *m*
successful [səkˈsɛsfəl] *adj* : exitoso, logrado — **successfully** *adv*
succession [səkˈsɛʃən] *n* : sucesión *f* ⟨in sucesión : sucesivamente⟩
successive [səkˈsɛsɪv] *adj* : sucesivo, consecutivo — **successively** *adv*
successor [səkˈsɛsər] *n* : sucesor *m*, -sora *f*
succinct [səkˈsɪŋkt, səˈsɪŋkt] *adj* : sucinto — **succinctly** *adv*
succor¹ [ˈsʌkər] *vt* : socorrer
succor² *n* : socorro *m*

succotash ['sʌkəˌtæʃ] *n* : guiso *m* de maíz y frijoles

succulent¹ ['sʌkjələnt] *adj* : suculento, jugoso

succulent² *n* : suculenta *f* (planta)

succumb [sə'kʌm] *vi* : sucumbir

such¹ ['sʌtʃ] *adv* **1** SO : tan ⟨such tall buildings : edificios tan grandes⟩ **2** VERY : muy ⟨he's not in such good shape : anda un poco mal⟩ **3 such that** : de tal manera que

such² *adj* : tal ⟨there's no such thing : no existe tal cosa⟩ ⟨in such cases : en tales casos⟩ ⟨animals such as cows and sheep : animales como vacas y ovejas⟩

such³ *pron* **1** : tal ⟨such was the result : tal fue el resultado⟩ ⟨he's a child, and acts as such : es un niño, y se porta como tal⟩ **2** : algo o alguien semejante ⟨books, papers and such : libros, papeles y cosas por el estilo⟩

suck ['sʌk] *vi* **1** : chupar (por la boca), aspirar (dícese de las máquinas) **2** SUCKLE : mamar — *vt* : sorber (bebidas), chupar (dulces, etc.)

sucker ['sʌkər] *n* **1** : ventosa *f* (de un insecto, etc.) **2** : chupón *m* (de una planta) **3** → **lollipop 4** FOOL : tonto *m*, -ta *f*; idiota *mf*

suckle ['sʌkəl] *v* **-led; -ling** *vt* : amamantar — *vi* : mamar

suckling ['sʌklɪŋ] *n* : lactante *mf*

sucrose ['suːˌkroːs, -ˌkroːz] *n* : sacarosa *f*

suction ['sʌkʃən] *n* : succión *f*

Sudanese [ˌsuːdən'iːz, -'iːs] *n* : sudanés *m*, -nesa *f* — **Sudanese** *adj*

sudden ['sʌdən] *adj* **1** : repentino, súbito ⟨all of a sudden : de pronto, de repente⟩ **2** UNEXPECTED : inesperado, improviso **3** ABRUPT, HASTY : precipitado, brusco

suddenly ['sʌdənli] *adv* **1** : de repente, de pronto **2** ABRUPTLY : bruscamente

suddenness ['sʌdənnəs] *n* **1** : lo repentino **2** ABRUPTNESS : brusquedad *f* **3** HASTINESS : lo precipitado

suds ['sʌdz] *npl* : espuma *f* (de jabón)

sue ['suː] *v* **sued; suing** *vt* : demandar — *vi* **to sue for** : demandar por (daños, etc.)

suede ['sweɪd] *n* : ante *m*, gamuza *f*

suet ['suːət] *n* : sebo *m*

suffer ['sʌfər] *vi* : sufrir — *vt* **1** : sufrir, padecer (dolores, etc.) **2** PERMIT : permitir, dejar

sufferer ['sʌfərər] *n* : persona que padece (una enfermedad, etc.)

suffering ['sʌfərɪŋ] *n* : sufrimiento *m*

suffice [sə'faɪs] *vi* **-ficed; -ficing** : ser suficiente, bastar

sufficient [sə'fɪʃənt] *adj* : suficiente

sufficiently [sə'fɪʃəntli] *adv* : (lo) suficientemente, bastante

suffix ['sʌˌfɪks] *n* : sufijo *m*

suffocate ['sʌfəˌkeɪt] *v* **-cated; -cating** *vt* : asfixiar, ahogar — *vi* : asfixiarse, ahogarse

suffocation [ˌsʌfə'keɪʃən] *n* : asfixia *f*, ahogo *m*

suffrage ['sʌfrɪdʒ] *n* : sufragio *m*, derecho *m* al voto

suffuse [sə'fjuːz] *vt* **-fused; -fusing** : impregnar (de olores, etc.), bañar (de luz), teñir (de colores), llenar (de emociones)

sugar¹ ['ʃʊgər] *vt* : azucarar

sugar² *n* : azúcar *mf*

sugarcane ['ʃʊgərˌkeɪn] *n* : caña *f* de azúcar

sugary ['ʃʊgəri] *adj* **1** : azucarado ⟨sugary desserts : postres azucarados⟩ **2** SACCHARINE : empalagoso

suggest [səg'dʒɛst, sə-] *vt* **1** PROPOSE : sugerir **2** IMPLY : indicar, dar a entender

suggestible [səg'dʒɛstəbəl, sə-] *adj* : influenciable

suggestion [səg'dʒɛstʃən, sə-] *n* **1** PROPOSAL : sugerencia *f* **2** INDICATION : indicio *m* **3** INSINUATION : insinuación *f*

suggestive [səg'dʒɛstɪv, sə-] *adj* : insinuante — **suggestively** *adv*

suicidal [ˌsuːə'saɪdəl] *adj* : suicida

suicide ['suːəˌsaɪd] *n* **1** : suicidio *m* (acto) **2** : suicida *mf* (persona)

suit¹ ['suːt] *vt* **1** ADAPT : adaptar **2** BEFIT : convenir a, ser apropiado a **3** BECOME : favorecer, quedarle bien (a alguien) ⟨the dress suits you : el vestido te queda bien⟩ **4** PLEASE : agradecer, satisfacer, convenirle bien (a alguien) ⟨does Friday suit you? : ¿le conviene el viernes?⟩ ⟨suit yourself! : ¡como quieras!⟩

suit² *n* **1** LAWSUIT : pleito *m*, litigio *m* **2** : traje *m* (ropa) **3** : palo *m* (de naipes)

suitability [ˌsuːtə'bɪləti] *n* : idoneidad *f*, lo apropiado

suitable ['suːtəbəl] *adj* : apropiado, idóneo — **suitably** [-bli] *adv*

suitcase ['suːtˌkeɪs] *n* : maleta *f*, valija *f*, petaca *f* *Mex*

suite ['swiːt, *for 2 also* 'suːt] *n* **1** : suite *f* (de habitaciones) **2** SET : juego *m* (de muebles)

suitor ['suːtər] *n* : pretendiente *m*

sulfur ['sʌlfər] *n* : azufre *m*

sulfuric acid [ˌsʌl'fjʊrɪk] *adj* : ácido *m* sulfúrico

sulfurous [ˌsʌl'fjʊrəs, 'sʌlfərəs, 'sʌlfjə-] *adj* : sulfuroso

sulk¹ ['sʌlk] *vi* : estar de mal humor, enfurruñarse *fam*

sulk² *n* : mal humor *m*

sulky ['sʌlki] *adj* **sulkier; -est** : malhumorado, taimado *Chile*

sullen ['sʌlən] *adj* **1** MOROSE : hosco, taciturno **2** DREARY : sombrío, deprimente

sullenly ['sʌlənli] *adv* **1** MOROSELY : hoscamente **2** GLOOMILY : sombríamente

sully ['sʌli] *vt* **sullied; sullying** : manchar, empañar

sultan ['sʌltən] *n* : sultán *m*
sultry ['sʌltri] *adj* **sultrier; -est 1** : bochornoso ⟨sultry weather : tiempo sofocante, tiempo bochornoso⟩ **2** SENSUAL : sensual, seductor
sum¹ ['sʌm] *vt* **summed; summing 1** : sumar (números) **2 → sum up**
sum² *n* **1** AMOUNT : suma *f*, cantidad *f* **2** TOTAL : suma *f*, total *f* **3** : suma *f*, adición *f* (en matemáticas)
sumac ['ʃuːˌmæk, 'suː-] *n* : zumaque *m*
summarize ['sʌməˌraɪz] *v* **-rized; -rizing** : resumir, compendiar
summary¹ ['sʌməri] *adj* **1** CONCISE : breve, conciso **2** IMMEDIATE : inmediato ⟨a summary dismissal : un despido inmediato⟩
summary² *n, pl* **-ries** : resumen *m*, compendio *m*
summer ['sʌmər] *n* : verano *m*
summery ['sʌməri] *adj* : veraniego
summit ['sʌmət] *n* **1** : cumbre *f*, cima *f* (de una montaña) **2** *or* **summit conference** : cumbre *f*
summon ['sʌmən] *vt* **1** CALL : convocar (una reunión, etc.), llamar (a una persona) **2** : citar (en derecho) **3 to summon up** : armarse de (valor, etc.) ⟨to summon up one's strength : reunir fuerzas⟩
summons ['sʌmənz] *n, pl* **summonses 1** SUBPOENA : citación *f*, citatorio *m* *Mex* **2** CALL : llamada *f*, llamamiento *m*
sumptuous ['sʌmptʃuəs] *adj* : suntuoso
sum up *vt* **1** SUMMARIZE : resumir **2** EVALUATE : evaluar — *vi* : recapitular
sun¹ ['sʌn] *vt* **sunned; sunning 1** : poner al sol **2 to sun oneself** : asolearse, tomar el sol
sun² *n* **1** : sol *m* **2** SUNSHINE : luz *f* del sol
sunbeam ['sʌnˌbiːm] *n* : rayo *m* de sol
sunblock ['sʌnˌblɑk] *n* : filtro *m* solar
sunburn¹ ['sʌnˌbərn] *vi* **-burned [-ˌbərnd] *or* -burnt [-ˌbərnt]; -burning** : quemarse por el sol
sunburn² ['sʌnˌbərn] *n* : quemadura *f* de sol
sundae ['sʌndi] *n* : sundae *m*
Sunday ['sʌnˌdeɪ, -di] *n* : domingo *m*
sundial ['sʌnˌdaɪl] *n* : reloj *m* de sol
sundown ['sʌnˌdaʊn] **→ sunset**
sundries ['sʌndriz] *npl* : artículos *mpl* diversos
sundry ['sʌndri] *adj* : varios, diversos
sunflower ['sʌnˌflaʊər] *n* : girasol *m*, mirasol *m*
sung → sing
sunglasses ['sʌnˌglæsəz] *npl* : gafas *fpl* de sol, lentes *mpl* de sol
sunk → sink¹
sunken ['sʌŋkən] *adj* : hundido
sunlight ['sʌnˌlaɪt] *n* : sol *m*, luz *f* del sol
sunny ['sʌni] *adj* **sunnier; -est** : soleado
sunrise ['sʌnˌraɪz] *n* : salida *f* del sol
sunscreen ['sʌnˌskriːn] *n* : filtro *m* solar

sunset ['sʌnˌsɛt] *n* : puesta *f* del sol
sunshine ['sʌnˌʃaɪn] *n* : sol *m*, luz *f* del sol
sunspot ['sʌnˌspɑt] *n* : mancha *f* solar
sunstroke ['sʌnˌstroːk] *n* : insolación *f*
suntan ['sʌnˌtæn] *n* : bronceado *m*
sup ['sʌp] *vi* **supped; supping** : cenar
super ['suːpər] *adj* : súper ⟨super! : ¡fantástico!⟩
superabundance [ˌsuːpərəˈbʌndənts] *n* : superabundancia *f*
superb [suˈpərb] *adj* : magnífico, espléndido — **superbly** *adv*
supercilious [ˌsuːpərˈsɪliəs] *adj* : altivo, altanero, desdeñoso
supercomputer ['suːpərkəmˌpjuːˌtər] *n* : supercomputadora *f*
superficial [ˌsuːpərˈfɪʃəl] *adj* : superficial — **superficially** *adv*
superfluous [suˈpərfluəs] *adj* : superfluo
superhighway ['suːpərˌhaɪˌweɪ, ˌsuː-pər'-] *n* : autopista *f*
superhuman [ˌsuːpərˈhjuːmən] *adj* **1** SUPERNATURAL : sobrenatural **2** HERCULEAN : sobrehumano
superimpose [ˌsuːpərɪmˈpoːz] *vt* **-posed; -posing** : superponer, sobreponer
superintend [ˌsuːpərɪnˈtɛnd] *vt* : supervisar
superintendent [ˌsuːpərɪnˈtɛndənt] *n* : portero *m*, -ra *f* (de un edificio); director *m*, -tora *f* (de una escuela, etc.); superintendente *mf* (de policía)
superior¹ [suˈpɪriər] *adj* **1** BETTER : superior **2** HAUGHTY : altivo, altanero
superior² *n* : superior *m*
superiority [suˌpɪriˈɔrəti] *n, pl* **-ties** : superioridad *f*
superlative¹ [suˈpərlətɪv] *adj* **1** : superlativo (en gramática) **2** SUPREME : supremo **3** EXCELLENT : excelente, excepcional
superlative² *n* : superlativo *m*
supermarket ['suːpərˌmɑrkət] *n* : supermercado *m*
supernatural [ˌsuːpərˈnætʃərəl] *adj* : sobrenatural
supernaturally [ˌsuːpərˈnætʃərəli] *adv* : de manera sobrenatural
superpower ['suːpərˌpaʊər] *n* : superpotencia *f*
supersede [ˌsuːpərˈsiːd] *vt* **-seded; -seding** : suplantar, reemplazar, sustituir
supersonic [ˌsuːpərˈsɑnɪk] *adj* : supersónico
superstar ['suːpərˌstɑr] *n* : superestrella *f*
superstition [ˌsuːpərˈstɪʃən] *n* : superstición *f*
superstitious [ˌsuːpərˈstɪʃəs] *adj* : supersticioso
superstructure ['suːpərˌstrʌktʃər] *n* : superestructura *f*
supervise ['suːpərˌvaɪz] *vt* **-vised; -vising** : supervisar, dirigir
supervision [ˌsuːpərˈvɪʒən] *n* : supervisión *f*, dirección *f*

supervisor ['su:pər,vaɪzər] *n* : supervisor *m*, -sora *f*
supervisory [,su:pər'vaɪzəri] *adj* : de supervisor
supine [sʊ'paɪn] *adj* 1 : en decúbito supino, en decúbito dorsal 2 ABJECT, INDIFFERENT : indiferente, apático
supper ['sʌpər] *n* : cena *f*, comida *f*
supplant [sə'plænt] *vt* : suplantar
supple ['sʌpəl] *adj* -pler; -plest : flexible
supplement[1] ['sʌplə,mɛnt] *vt* : complementar, completar
supplement[2] ['sʌpləmənt] *n* 1 : complemento *m* ⟨dietary supplement : complemento alimenticio⟩ 2 : suplemento *m* (de un libro o periódico)
supplementary [,sʌplə'mɛntəri] *adj* : suplementario
supplicate ['sʌplə,keɪt] *v* -cated; -cating *vi* : rezar — *vt* : suplicar
supplier [sə'plaɪər] *n* : proveedor *m*, -dora *f*; abastecedor *m*, -dora *f*
supply[1] [sə'plaɪ] *vt* -plied; -plying : suministrar, proveer de, proporcionar
supply[2] *n*, *pl* -plies 1 PROVISION : provisión *f*, suministro *m* ⟨supply and demand : la oferta y la demanda⟩ 2 STOCK : reserva *f*, existencias *fpl* (de un negocio) 3 supplies *npl* PROVISIONS : provisiones *fpl*, víveres *mpl*, despensa *f*
support[1] [sə'port] *vt* 1 BACK : apoyar, respaldar 2 MAINTAIN : mantener, sostener, sustentar 3 PROP UP : sostener, apoyar, apuntalar, soportar
support[2] *n* 1 : apoyo *m* (moral), ayuda *f* (económica) 2 PROP : soporte *m*, apoyo *m*
supporter [sə'portər] *n* : partidario *m*, -ria *f*
supportive [sə'portɪv] *adj* : que apoya ⟨his family is very supportive : su familia lo apoya mucho⟩
suppose [sə'po:z] *vt* -posed; -posing 1 ASSUME : suponer, imaginarse 2 BELIEVE : suponer, creer 3 to be supposed to : tener que, deber
supposed [sə'po:zd, -'po:zəd] *adj* : supuesto — **supposedly** [sə'po:zədli] *adv*
supposition [,sʌpə'zɪʃən] *n* : suposición *f*
suppository [sə'pɑzə,tori] *n*, *pl* -ries : supositorio *m*
suppress [sə'prɛs] *vt* 1 SUBDUE : sofocar, suprimir, reprimir (una rebelión, etc.) 2 : suprimir, ocultar (información) 3 REPRESS : reprimir, contener ⟨to suppress a yawn : reprimir un bostezo⟩
suppression [sə'prɛʃən] *n* 1 SUBDUING : represión *f* 2 : supresión *f* (de información) 3 REPRESSION : represión *f*, inhibición *f*
supremacy [sʊ'prɛməsi] *n*, *pl* -cies : supremacía *f*
supreme [sʊ'pri:m] *adj* : supremo

Supreme Being *n* : Ser *m* Supremo
supremely [sʊ'pri:mli] *adv* : totalmente, sumamente
surcharge ['sər,tʃɑrdʒ] *n* : recargo *m*
sure[1] ['ʃʊr] *adv* 1 ALL RIGHT : por supuesto, claro 2 (*used as an intensifier*) ⟨it sure is hot! : ¡hace tanto calor!⟩ ⟨she sure is pretty! : ¡qué linda es!⟩
sure[2] *adj* surer; -est : seguro ⟨to be sure about something : estar seguro de algo⟩ ⟨a sure sign : una clara señal⟩ ⟨for sure : seguro, con seguridad⟩
surely ['ʃʊrli] *adv* 1 CERTAINLY : seguramente 2 (*used as an intensifier*) ⟨you surely don't mean that! : ¡no me digas que estás hablando en serio!⟩
sureness ['ʃʊrnəs] *n* : certeza *f*, seguridad *f*
surety ['ʃʊrəti] *n*, *pl* -ties : fianza *f*, garantía *f*
surf ['sərf] *n* 1 WAVES : oleaje *m* 2 FOAM : espuma *f*
surface[1] ['sərfəs] *v* -faced; -facing *vi* : salir a la superficie — *vt* : revestir (una carretera)
surface[2] *n* 1 : superficie *f* 2 on the surface : en apariencia
surfboard ['sərf,bord] *n* : tabla *f* de surf, tabla *f* de surfing
surfeit ['sərfət] *n* : exceso *m*
surfer ['sərfər] *n* : surfista *mf*
surfing ['sərfɪŋ] *n* : surf *m*, surfing *m*
surge[1] ['sərdʒ] *vi* surged; surging 1 : hincharse (dícese del mar), levantarse (dícese de las olas) 2 SWARM : salir en tropel (dícese de la gente, etc.)
surge[2] *n* 1 : oleaje *m* (del mar), oleada *f* (de gente) 2 FLUSH : arranque *m*, arrebato *m* (de ira, etc.) 3 INCREASE : aumento *m* (súbito)
surgeon ['sərdʒən] *n* : cirujano *m*, -na *f*
surgery ['sərdʒəri] *n*, *pl* -geries : cirugía *f*
surgical ['sərdʒɪkəl] *adj* : quirúrgico — **surgically** [-kli] *adv*
surly ['sərli] *adj* surlier; -est : hosco, arisco
surmise[1] [sər'maɪz] *vt* -mised; -mising : conjeturar, suponer, concluir
surmise[2] *n* : conjetura *f*
surmount [sər'maʊnt] *vt* 1 OVERCOME : superar, vencer, salvar 2 CLIMB : escalar 3 CAP, TOP : coronar
surname ['sər,neɪm] *n* : apellido *m*
surpass [sər'pæs] *vt* : superar, exceder, rebasar, sobrepasar
surplus ['sər,plʌs] *n* : excedente *m*, sobrante *m*, superávit *m* (de dinero)
surprise[1] [sə'praɪz, sər-] *vt* -prised; -prising : sorprender
surprise[2] *n* : sorpresa *f* ⟨to take by surprise : sorprender⟩
surprising [sə'praɪzɪŋ, sər-] *adj* : sorprendente — **surprisingly** *adv*
surrender[1] [sə'rɛndər] *vt* 1 : entregar, rendir 2 to surrender oneself : entregarse — *vi* : rendirse
surrender[2] *n* : rendición *m* (de una ciudad, etc.), entrega *f* (de posesiones)

surreptitious [ˌsərəpˈtɪʃəs] *adj* : subrepticio — **surreptitiously** *adv*

surrogate [ˈsərəgət, -ˌgeɪt] *n* : sustituto *m*

surround [səˈraʊnd] *vt* : rodear

surroundings [səˈraʊndɪŋz] *npl* : ambiente *m*, entorno *m*

surveillance [sərˈveɪlənts, -ˈveɪljənts, -ˈveɪənts] *n* : vigilancia *f*

survey¹ [sərˈveɪ] *vt* **-veyed; -veying 1** : medir (un terreno) **2** EXAMINE : inspeccionar, examinar, revisar **3** POLL : hacer una encuesta de, sondear

survey² [ˈsərˌveɪ] *n, pl* **-veys 1** INSPECTION : inspección *f*, revisión *f* **2** : medición *f* (de un terreno) **3** POLL : encuesta *f*, sondeo *m*

surveyor [sərˈveɪər] *n* : agrimensor *m*, -sora *f*

survival [sərˈvaɪvəl] *n* : supervivencia *f*, sobrevivencia *f*

survive [sərˈvaɪv] *v* **-vived; -viving** *vi* : sobrevivir — *vt* OUTLIVE : sobrevivir a

survivor [sərˈvaɪvər] *n* : superviviente *mf*, sobreviviente *mf*

susceptibility [səˌsɛptəˈbɪləti] *n, pl* **-ties** : vulnerabilidad *f*, propensión *f* (a enfermedades, etc.)

susceptible [səˈsɛptəbəl] *adj* **1** VULNERABLE : vulnerable, sensible ⟨susceptible to flattery : sensible a halagos⟩ **2** PRONE : propenso ⟨susceptible to colds : propenso a resfriarse⟩

suspect¹ [səˈspɛkt] *vt* **1** DISTRUST : dudar de **2** : sospechar (algo), sospechar de (una persona) **3** IMAGINE, THINK : imaginarse, creer

suspect² [ˈsʌsˌpɛkt, səˈspɛkt] *adj* : sospechoso, dudoso, cuestionable

suspect³ [ˈsʌsˌpɛkt] *n* : sospechoso *m*, -sa *f*

suspend [səˈspɛnd] *vt* : suspender

suspenders [səˈspɛndərz] *npl* : tirantes *mpl*

suspense [səˈspɛnts] *n* : incertidumbre *f*, suspenso *m* (en una película, etc.)

suspenseful [səˈspɛntsfəl] *adj* : de suspenso

suspension [səˈspɛnʧən] *n* : suspensión *f*

suspicion [səˈspɪʃən] *n* **1** : sospecha *f* **2** TRACE : pizca *f*, atisbo *m*

suspicious [səˈspɪʃəs] *adj* **1** QUESTIONABLE : sospechoso, dudoso **2** DISTRUSTFUL : suspicaz, desconfiado

suspiciously [səˈspɪʃəsli] *adv* : de modo sospechoso, con recelo

sustain [səˈsteɪn] *vt* **1** NOURISH : sustentar **2** PROLONG : sostener **3** SUFFER : sufrir **4** SUPPORT, UPHOLD : apoyar, respaldar, sostener

sustainable [səˈsteɪnəbəl] *adj* : sostenible

sustenance [ˈsʌstənənts] *n* **1** NOURISHMENT : sustento *m* **2** SUPPORT : sostén *m*

svelte [ˈsfɛlt] *adj* : esbelto

swab¹ [ˈswɑb] *vt* **swabbed; swabbing 1** CLEAN : lavar, limpiar **2** : aplicar a (con hisopo)

swab² *n or* **cotton swab** : hisopo *m* (para aplicar medicinas, etc.)

swaddle [ˈswɑdəl] *vt* **-dled; -dling** [ˈswɑdəlɪŋ] : envolver (en pañales)

swagger¹ [ˈswægər] *vi* : pavonearse

swagger² *n* : pavoneo *m*

swallow¹ [ˈswɑloː] *vt* **1** : tragar (comida, etc.) **2** ENGULF : tragarse, envolver **3** REPRESS : tragarse (insultos, etc.) — *vi* : tragar

swallow² *n* **1** : golondrina *f* (pájaro) **2** GULP : trago *m*

swam → **swim¹**

swamp¹ [ˈswɑmp] *vt* : inundar

swamp² *n* : pantano *m*, ciénaga *f*

swampy [ˈswɑmpi] *adj* **swampier; -est** : pantanoso, cenagoso

swan [ˈswɑn] *n* : cisne *f*

swap¹ [ˈswɑp] *vt* **swapped; swapping** : cambiar, intercambiar ⟨to swap places : cambiarse de sitio⟩

swap² *n* : cambio *m*, intercambio *m*

swarm¹ [ˈswɔrm] *vi* : enjambrar

swarm² *n* : enjambre *m*

swarthy [ˈswɔrði, -θi] *adj* **swarthier; -est** : moreno

swashbuckling [ˈswɑʃˌbʌklɪŋ] *adj* : de aventurero

swat¹ [ˈswɑt] *vt* **swatted; swatting** : aplastar (un insecto), darle una palmada (a alguien)

swat² *n* : palmada *f* (con la mano), golpe *m* (con un objeto)

swatch [ˈswɑʧ] *n* : muestra *f*

swath [ˈswɑθ, ˈswɔθ] *or* **swathe** [ˈswɑð, ˈswɔð, ˈsweɪð] *n* : franja *f* (de grano segado)

swathe [ˈswɑð, ˈswɔð, ˈsweɪð] *vt* **swathed; swathing** : envolver

swatter [ˈswɑtər] → **flyswatter**

sway¹ [ˈsweɪ] *vi* : balancearse, mecerse — *vt* INFLUENCE : influir en, convencer

sway² *n* **1** SWINGING : balanceo *m* **2** INFLUENCE : influjo *m*

swear [ˈswær] *v* **swore** [ˈswor]; **sworn** [ˈsworn]; **swearing** *vi* **1** VOW : jurar **2** CURSE : decir palabrotas — *vt* : jurar

swearword [ˈswærˌwərd] *n* : mala palabra *f*, palabrota *f*

sweat¹ [ˈswɛt] *vi* **sweat** *or* **sweated; sweating 1** PERSPIRE : sudar, transpirar **2** OOZE : rezumar **3** to sweat over : sudar la gota gorda por

sweat² *n* : sudor *m*, transpiración *f*

sweater [ˈswɛtər] *n* : suéter *m*

sweatshirt [ˈswɛtˌʃərt] *n* : sudadera *f*

sweaty [ˈswɛti] *adj* **sweatier; -est** : sudoroso, sudado, transpirado

Swede [ˈswiːd] *n* : sueco *m*, -ca *f*

Swedish¹ [ˈswiːdɪʃ] *adj* : sueco

Swedish² *n* **1** : sueco *m* (idioma) **2 the Swedish** *npl* : los suecos

sweep¹ [ˈswiːp] *v* **swept** [ˈswɛpt]; **sweeping** *vt* **1** : barrer (el suelo, etc.), limpiar (suciedad, etc.) ⟨he swept the books aside : apartó los libros de un manotazo⟩ **2** *or* **to sweep through** : extenderse por (dícese del fuego, etc.), azotar (dícese de una tormenta) — *vi* **1** : barrer, limpiar **2** : extenderse (en una curva), describir una curva ⟨the sun swept across the sky : el sol describía una curva en el cielo⟩

sweep² *n* **1** : barrido *m*, barrida *f* (con una escoba) **2** : movimiento *m* circular **3** SCOPE : alcance *m*

sweeper ['swi:pər] *n* : barrendero *m*, -ra *f*

sweeping ['swi:pɪŋ] *adj* **1** WIDE : amplio (dícese de un movimiento) **2** EXTENSIVE : extenso, radical **3** INDISCRIMINATE : indiscriminado, demasiado general **4** OVERWHELMING : arrollador, aplastante

sweepstakes ['swi:p,steɪks] *ns & pl* **1** : carrera *f* (en que el ganador se lleva el premio entero) **2** LOTTERY : lotería *f*

sweet¹ ['swi:t] *adj* **1** : dulce ⟨sweet desserts : postres dulces⟩ **2** FRESH : fresco **3** : sin sal (dícese de la mantequilla, etc.) **4** PLEASANT : dulce, agradable **5** DEAR : querido

sweet² *n* : dulce *m*

sweeten ['swi:tən] *vt* : endulzar

sweetener ['swi:tənər] *n* : endulzante *m*

sweetheart ['swi:t,hɑrt] *n* : novio *m*, -via *f* ⟨thanks, sweetheart : gracias, cariño⟩

sweetly ['swi:tli] *adv* : dulcemente

sweetness ['swi:tnəs] *n* : dulzura *f*

sweet potato *n* : batata *f*, boniato *m*

swell¹ ['swɛl] *vi* **swelled**; **swelled** *or* **swollen** ['swo:lən, 'swɑl-]; **swelling 1** *or* **to swell up** : hincharse ⟨her ankle swelled : se le hinchó el tobillo⟩ **2** *or* **to swell out** : inflarse, hincharse (dícese de las velas, etc.) **3** INCREASE : aumentar, crecer

swell² *n* **1** : oleaje *m* (del mar) **2** → **swelling**

swelling ['swɛlɪŋ] *n* : hinchazón *f*

swelter ['swɛltər] *vi* : sofocarse de calor

swept → **sweep¹**

swerve¹ ['swərv] *vi* **swerved**; **swerving** : virar bruscamente

swerve² *n* : viraje *m* brusco

swift¹ ['swɪft] *adj* **1** FAST : rápido, veloz **2** SUDDEN : repentino, súbito — **swiftly** *adv*

swift² *n* : vencejo *m* (pájaro)

swiftness ['swɪftnəs] *n* : rapidez *f*, velocidad *f*

swig¹ ['swɪg] *vi* **swigged**; **swigging** : tomar a tragos, beber a tragos

swig² *n* : trago *m*

swill¹ ['swɪl] *vt* : chupar, beber a tragos grandes

swill² *n* **1** SLOP : bazofia *f* **2** GARBAGE : basura *f*

swim¹ ['swɪm] *vi* **swam** ['swæm]; **swum** ['swʌm]; **swimming 1** : nadar **2** FLOAT : flotar **3** REEL : dar vueltas ⟨his head was swimming : la cabeza le daba vueltas⟩

swim² *n* : baño *m*, chapuzón *m* ⟨to go for a swim : ir a nadar⟩

swimmer ['swɪmər] *n* : nadador *m*, -dora *f*

swindle¹ ['swɪndəl] *vt* **-dled**; **-dling** : estafar, timar

swindle² *n* : estafa *f*, timo *m fam*

swindler ['swɪndələr] *n* : estafador *m*, -dora *f*; timador *m*, -dora *f*

swine ['swaɪn] *ns & pl* : cerdo *m*, -da *f*

swing¹ ['swɪŋ] *v* **swung** ['swʌŋ]; **swinging 1** : describir una curva con ⟨he swung the ax at the tree : le dio al árbol con el hacha⟩ **2** : balancear (los brazos, etc.), hacer oscilar **3** SUSPEND : colgar — *vi* **1** SWAY : balancearse (dícese de los brazos, etc.), oscilar (dícese de un objeto), columpiarse, mecerse (en un columpio) **2** SWIVEL : girar (en un pivote) ⟨the door swung shut : la puerta se cerró⟩ **3** CHANGE : virar, cambiar (dícese de las opiniones, etc.)

swing² *n* **1** SWINGING : vaivén *m*, balanceo *m* **2** CHANGE, SHIFT : viraje *m*, movimiento *m* **3** : columpio *m* (para niños) **4 to take a swing at someone** : intentar pegarle a alguien

swipe¹ ['swaɪp] *vt* **swiped**; **swiping 1** STRIKE : dar, pegar (con un movimiento amplio) **2** WIPE : limpiar **3** STEAL : birlar *fam*, robar

swipe² *n* BLOW : golpe *m*

swirl¹ ['swərl] *vi* : arremolinarse

swirl² *n* **1** EDDY : remolino *m* **2** SPIRAL : espiral *f*

swish¹ ['swɪʃ] *vt* : mover (produciendo un sonido) ⟨she swished her skirt : movía la falda⟩ — *vi* : moverse (produciendo un sonido) ⟨the cars swished by : se oían pasar los coches⟩

swish² *n* : silbido *m* (de un látigo, etc.), susurro *m* (de agua), crujido *m* (de ropa, etc.)

Swiss ['swɪs] *n* : suizo *m*, -za *f* — **Swiss** *adj*

swiss chard *n* : acelga *f*

switch¹ ['swɪtʃ] *vt* **1** LASH, WHIP : azotar **2** CHANGE : cambiar de **3** EXCHANGE : intercambiar **4 to switch on** : encender, prender **5 to switch off** : apagar — *vi* **1** : moverse de un lado al otro **2** CHANGE : cambiar **3** SWAP : intercambiarse

switch² *n* **1** WHIP : vara *f* **2** CHANGE, SHIFT : cambio *m* **3** : interruptor *m*, llave *f* (de la luz, etc.)

switchboard ['swɪtʃ,bord] *n* : conmutador *m*, centralita *f*

swivel¹ ['swɪvəl] *vi* **-veled** *or* **-velled**; **-veling** *or* **-velling** : girar (sobre un pivote)

swivel² *n* : base *f* giratoria

swollen *pp* → **swell¹**

swoon¹ ['swu:n] *vi* : desvanecerse, desmayarse

swoon² *n* : desvanecimiento *m*, desmayo *m*

swoop[1] ['swu:p] *vi* : abatirse (dícese de las aves), descender en picada (dícese de un avión)

swoop[2] *n* : descenso *m* en picada

sword ['sɔrd] *n* : espada *f*

swordfish ['sɔrd,fɪʃ] *n* : pez *m* espada

swore, sworn → **swear**

swum *pp* → **swim**[1]

swung → **swing**[1]

sycamore ['sɪkə,mor] *n* : sicomoro *m*

sycophant ['sɪkəfənt, -,fænt] *n* : adulador *m*, -dora *f*

syllabic [sə'læbɪk] *adj* : silábico

syllable ['sɪləbəl] *n* : sílaba *f*

syllabus ['sɪləbəs] *n*, *pl* **-bi** [-,baɪ] *or* **-bus-es** : programa *m* (de estudios)

symbol ['sɪmbəl] *n* : símbolo *m*

symbolic [sɪm'balɪk] *adj* : simbólico — **symbolically** [-kli] *adv*

symbolism ['sɪmbə,lɪzəm] *n* : simbolismo *m*

symbolize ['sɪmbə,laɪz] *vt* **-ized; -izing** : simbolizar

symmetrical [sə'mɛtrɪkəl] *or* **symmetric** [-trɪk] *adj* : simétrico — **symmetrically** [-trɪkli] *adv*

symmetry ['sɪmətri] *n*, *pl* **-tries** : simetría *f*

sympathetic [,sɪmpə'θɛʈɪk] *adj* **1** PLEASING : agradable **2** RECEPTIVE : receptivo, favorable **3** COMPASSIONATE, UNDERSTANDING : comprensivo, compasivo

sympathetically [,sɪmpə'θɛʈɪkli] *adv* : con compasión, con comprensión

sympathize ['sɪmpə,θaɪz] *vi* **-thized; -thizing** : compadecer ⟨I sympathize with you : te compadezco⟩

sympathy ['sɪmpəθi] *n*, *pl* **-thies 1** COMPASSION : compasión *f* **2** UNDERSTANDING : comprensión *f* **3** AGREEMENT : solidaridad *f* ⟨in sympathy with : de acuerdo con⟩ **4** CONDOLENCES : pésame *m*, condolencias *fpl*

symphonic [sɪm'fanɪk] *adj* : sinfónico

symphony ['sɪmpfəni] *n*, *pl* **-nies** : sinfonía *f*

symposium [sɪm'po:ziəm] *n*, *pl* **-sia** [-ziə] *or* **-siums** : simposio *m*

symptom ['sɪmptəm] *n* : síntoma *m*

symptomatic [,sɪmptə'mæʈɪk] *adj* : sintomático

synagogue ['sɪnə,gag, -,gɔg] *n* : sinagoga *f*

sync ['sɪŋk] *n* : sincronización *f* ⟨in sync : sincronizado⟩

synchronize ['sɪŋkrə,naɪz, 'sɪn-] *v* **-nized; -nizing** *vi* : estar sincronizado — *vt* : sincronizar

syncopate ['sɪŋkə,peɪt, 'sɪn-] *vt* **-pated; -pating** : sincopar

syncopation [,sɪŋkə'peɪʃən, ,sɪn-] *n* : síncopa *f*

syndicate[1] ['sɪndə,keɪt] *vi* **-cated; -cating** : formar una asociación

syndicate[2] ['sɪndɪkət] *n* : asociación *f*, agrupación *f*

syndrome ['sɪn,dro:m] *n* : síndrome *m*

synonym ['sɪnə,nɪm] *n* : sinónimo *m*

synonymous [sə'nanəməs] *adj* : sinónimo

synopsis [sə'napsɪs] *n*, *pl* **-opses** [-,si:z] : sinopsis *f*

syntactic [sɪn'tæktɪk] *adj* : sintáctico

syntax ['sɪn,tæks] *n* : sintaxis *f*

synthesis ['sɪnθəsɪs] *n*, *pl* **-theses** [-,si:z] : síntesis *f*

synthesize ['sɪnθə,saɪz] *vt* **-sized; -sizing** : sintetizar

synthetic[1] [sɪn'θʈɪk] *adj* : sintético, artificial — **synthetically** [-ʈɪkli] *adv*

synthetic[2] *n* : producto *m* sintético

syphilis ['sɪfələs] *n* : sífilis *f*

Syrian ['sɪriən] *n* : sirio *m*, -ria *f* — **Syrian** *adj*

syringe [sə'rɪndʒ, 'sɪrɪndʒ] *n* : jeringa *f*, jeringuilla *f*

syrup ['sərəp, 'sɪrəp] *n* : jarabe *m*, almíbar *m* (de azúcar y agua)

system ['sɪstəm] *n* **1** METHOD : sistema *m*, método *m* **2** APPARATUS : sistema *m*, instalación *f*, aparato *m* ⟨electrical system : instalación eléctrica⟩ ⟨digestive system : aparato digestivo⟩ **3** BODY : organismo *m*, cuerpo *m* ⟨diseases that affect the whole system : enfermedades que afectan el organismo entero⟩ **4** NETWORK : red *f*

systematic [,sɪstə'mæʈɪk] *adj* : sistemático — **systematically** [-ʈɪkli] *adv*

systematize ['sɪstəmə,taɪz] *vt* **-tized; -tizing** : sistematizar

systemic [sɪs'tɛmɪk] *adj* : sistémico

T

t ['ti:] *n*, *pl* **t's** *or* **ts** ['ti:z] : vigésima letra del alfabeto inglés

tab ['tæb] *n* **1** FLAP, TAG : lengüeta *f* (de un sobre, una caja, etc.), etiqueta *f* (de ropa) **2** → **tabulator 3** BILL, CHECK : cuenta *f* **4** to keep tabs on : tener bajo vigilancia

tabby ['tæbi] *n*, *pl* **-bies 1** *or* **tabby cat** : gato *m* atigrado **2** : gata *f*

tabernacle ['tæbər,nækəl] *n* : tabernáculo *m*

table ['teɪbəl] *n* **1** : mesa *f* ⟨a table for two : una mesa para dos⟩ **2** LIST : tabla *f* ⟨multiplication table : tabla de multiplicar⟩ **3** table of contents : índice *m* de materias

tableau ['tæ'blo:, 'tæ,-] *n*, *pl* **-leaux** [-'blo:z, -,blo:z] : retablo *m*, cuadro *m* vivo (en teatro)

tablecloth ['teɪbəl,klɔθ] *n* : mantel *m*

tablespoon ['teɪbəl,spu:n] *n* **1** : cuchara *f* (de mesa) **2** → **tablespoonful**

tablespoonful ['teɪbəl‚spuːn‚fʊl] *n* : cucharada *f*

tablet ['tæblət] *n* **1** PLAQUE : placa *f* **2** PAD : bloc *m* (de papel) **3** PILL : tableta *f*, pastilla *f*, píldora *f* ⟨an aspirin tablet : una tableta de aspirina⟩

table tennis *n* : tenis *m* de mesa

tableware ['teɪbəl‚wær] *n* : vajillas *fpl*, cubiertos *mpl* (de mesa)

tabloid ['tæ‚blɔɪd] *n* : tabloide *m*

taboo[1] [tə'buː, tæ-] *adj* : tabú

taboo[2] *n* : tabú *m*

tabular ['tæbjələr] *adj* : tabular

tabulate ['tæbjə‚leɪt] *vt* **-lated; -lating** : tabular

tabulator ['tæbjə‚leɪtər] *n* : tabulador *m*

tacit ['tæsɪt] *adj* : tácito, implícito — **tacitly** *adv*

taciturn ['tæsɪ‚tərn] *adj* : taciturno

tack[1] ['tæk] *vt* **1** : sujetar con tachuelas **2 to tack on** ADD : añadir, agregar

tack[2] *n* **1** : tachuela *f* **2** COURSE : rumbo *m* ⟨to change tack : cambiar de rumbo⟩

tackle[1] ['tækəl] *vt* **-led; -ling 1** : taclear (en futbol americano) **2** CONFRONT : abordar, enfrentar, emprender (un problema, un trabajo, etc.)

tackle[2] *n* **1** EQUIPMENT, GEAR : equipo *m*, aparejo *m* **2** : aparejo *m* (de un buque) **3** : tacleada *f* (en futbol americano)

tacky ['tæki] *adj* **tackier; -est 1** STICKY : pegajoso **2** CHEAP, GAUDY : de mal gusto, naco *Mex*

tact ['tækt] *n* : tacto *m*, delicadeza *f*, discreción *f*

tactful ['tæktfəl] *adj* : discreto, diplomático, de mucho tacto

tactfully ['tæktfəli] *adv* : discretamente, con mucho tacto

tactic ['tæktɪk] *n* : táctica *f*

tactical ['tæktɪkəl] *adj* : táctico, estratégico

tactics ['tæktɪks] *ns & pl* : táctica *f*, estrategia *f*

tactile ['tæktəl, -‚taɪl] *adj* : táctil

tactless ['tæktləs] *adj* : indiscreto, poco delicado

tactlessly ['tæktləsli] *adv* : rudamente, sin tacto

tadpole ['tæd‚poːl] *n* : renacuajo *m*

taffeta ['tæfətə] *n* : tafetán *m*, tafeta *f* *Arg, Mex, Uru*

taffy ['tæfi] *n, pl* **-fies** : caramelo *m* de melaza, chicloso *m Mex*

tag[1] ['tæg] *v* **tagged; tagging** *vt* **1** LABEL : etiquetar **2** TAIL : seguir de cerca **3** TOUCH : tocar (en varios juegos) — *vi* **to tag along** : pegarse, acompañar

tag[2] *n* **1** LABEL : etiqueta *f* **2** SAYING : dicho *m*, refrán *m*

tail[1] ['teɪl] *vt* FOLLOW : seguir de cerca, pegarse

tail[2] *n* **1** : cola *f*, rabo *m* (de un animal) **2** : cola *f*, parte *f* posterior ⟨a comet's tail : la cola de un cometa⟩ **3 tails** *npl* : cruz *f* (de una moneda) ⟨heads or tails : cara o cruz⟩

tailed ['teɪld] *adj* : que tiene cola

tailgate[1] ['teɪl‚geɪt] *vi* **-gated; -gating** : seguir a un vehículo demasiado de cerca

tailgate[2] *n* : puerta *f* trasera (de un vehículo)

taillight ['teɪl‚laɪt] *n* : luz *f* trasera (de un vehículo), calavera *f Mex*

tailor[1] ['teɪlər] *vt* **1** : confeccionar o alterar (ropa) **2** ADAPT : adaptar, ajustar

tailor[2] *n* : sastre *m*, -tra *f*

tailpipe ['teɪl‚paɪp] *n* : tubo *m* de escape

tailspin ['teɪl‚spɪn] *n* : barrena *f*

taint[1] ['teɪnt] *vt* : contaminar, corromper

taint[2] *n* : corrupción *f*, impureza *f*

take[1] ['teɪk] *v* **took** ['tʊk]; **taken** ['teɪkən]; **taking** *vt* **1** CAPTURE : capturar, apresar **2** GRASP : tomar, agarrar ⟨to take the bull by the horns : tomar al toro por los cuernos⟩ **3** CATCH : tomar, agarrar ⟨taken by surprise : tomado por sorpresa⟩ **4** CAPTIVATE : encantar, fascinar **5** INGEST : tomar, ingerir ⟨take two pills : tome dos píldoras⟩ **6** REMOVE : sacar, extraer ⟨take an orange : saca una naranja⟩ **7** : tomar, coger (un tren, un autobús, etc.) **8** NEED, REQUIRE : tomar, requerir ⟨these things take time : estas cosas toman tiempo⟩ **9** BRING, CARRY : llevar, sacar, cargar ⟨take them with you : llévalos contigo⟩ ⟨take the trash out : saca la basura⟩ **10** BEAR, ENDURE : soportar, aguantar (dolores, etc.) **11** ACCEPT : aceptar (un cheque, etc.), seguir (consejos), asumir (la responsabilidad) **12** SUPPOSE : suponer ⟨I take it that . . . : supongo que . . . ⟩ **13** (*indicating an action or an undertaking*) ⟨to take a walk : dar un paseo⟩ ⟨to take a class : tomar una clase⟩ **14 to take place** HAPPEN : tener lugar, suceder, ocurrir — *vi* : agarrar (dícese de un tinte), prender (dícese de una vacuna)

take[2] *n* **1** PROCEEDS : recaudación *f*, ingresos *mpl*, ganancias *fpl* **2** : toma *f* (de un rodaje o una grabación)

take back *vt* : retirar (palabras, etc.)

take in *vt* **1** : tomarle a, achicar (un vestido, etc.) **2** INCLUDE : incluir, abarcar **3** ATTEND : ir a ⟨to take in a movie : ir al cine⟩ **4** GRASP, UNDERSTAND : captar, entender **5** DECEIVE : engañar

takeoff ['teɪk‚ɔf] *n* **1** PARODY : parodia *f* **2** : despegue *m* (de un avión o cohete)

take off *vt* REMOVE : quitar ⟨take off your hat : quítate el sombrero⟩ — *vi* **1** : despegar (dícese de un avión o un cohete) **2** LEAVE : irse, partir

take on *vt* **1** TACKLE : abordar, emprender (problemas, etc.) **2** ACCEPT : aceptar, encargarse de, asumir (una responsabilidad) **3** CONTRACT : contratar (trabajadores) **4** ASSUME : adoptar, asumir, adquirir ⟨the neighborhood took on a dingy look : el barrio asumió una apariencia deprimente⟩

takeover ['teɪkˌoːvər] *n* : toma *f* (de poder o de control), adquisición *f* (de una empresa por otra)

take over *vt* : tomar el poder de, tomar las riendas de — *vi* : asumir el mando

taker ['teɪkər] *n* : persona *f* interesada ⟨available to all takers : disponible a cuantos estén interesados⟩

take up *vt* **1** LIFT : levantar **2** SHORTEN : acortar (una falda, etc.) **3** BEGIN : empezar, dedicarse a (un pasatiempo, etc.) **4** OCCUPY : ocupar, llevar (tiempo, espacio) **5** PURSUE : volver a (una cuestión, un asunto) **6** CONTINUE : seguir con

talc ['tælk] *n* : talco *m*

talcum powder ['tælkəm] *n* : talco *m*, polvos *mpl* de talco

tale ['teɪl] *n* **1** ANECDOTE, STORY : cuento *m*, relato *m*, anécdota *f* **2** FALSEHOOD : cuento *m*, mentira *f*

talent ['tælənt] *n* : talento *m*, don *m*

talented ['tæləntəd] *adj* : talentoso

talisman ['tælɪsmən, -lɪz-] *n*, *pl* **-mans** : talismán *m*

talk¹ ['tɔk] *vi* **1** : hablar ⟨he talks for hours : se pasa horas hablando⟩ **2** CHAT : charlar, platicar — *vt* **1** SPEAK : hablar ⟨to talk French : hablar francés⟩ ⟨to talk business : hablar de negocios⟩ **2** PERSUADE : influenciar, convencer ⟨she talked me out of it : me convenció que no lo hiciera⟩ **3 to talk over** DISCUSS : hablar de, discutir

talk² *n* **1** CONVERSATION : charla *f*, plática *f*, conversación *f* **2** GOSSIP, RUMOR : chisme *m*, rumores *mpl*

talkative ['tɔkətɪv] *adj* : locuaz, parlanchín, charlatán

talker ['tɔkər] *n* : conversador *m*, -dora *f*; hablador *m*, -dora *f*

talk show *n* : programa *m* de entrevistas

tall ['tɔl] *adj* : alto ⟨how tall is he? : ¿cuánto mide?⟩

tallness ['tɔlnəs] *n* HEIGHT : estatura *f* (de una persona), altura *f* (de un objeto)

tallow ['tæloː] *n* : sebo *m*

tally¹ ['tæli] *v* **-lied; -lying** *vt* RECKON : contar, hacer una cuenta de — *vi* MATCH : concordar, corresponder, cuadrar

tally² *n*, *pl* **-lies** : cuenta *f* ⟨to keep a tally : llevar la cuenta⟩

talon ['tælən] *n* : garra *f* (de un ave de rapiña)

tambourine [ˌtæmbəˈriːn] *n* : pandero *m*, pandereta *f*

tame¹ ['teɪm] *vt* **tamed; taming** : domar, amansar, domesticar

tame² *adj* **tamer; -est 1** DOMESTICATED : domesticado, manso **2** DOCILE : manso, dócil **3** DULL : aburrido, soso

tamely ['teɪmli] *adv* : mansamente, dócilmente

tamer ['teɪmər] *n* : domador *m*, -dora *f*

tamp ['tæmp] *vt* : apisonar

tamper ['tæmpər] *vi* **to tamper with** : adulterar (una sustancia), forzar (un sello, una cerradura), falsear (documentos), manipular (una máquina)

tampon ['tæmˌpɑn] *n* : tampón *m*

tan¹ ['tæn] *v* **tanned; tanning** *vt* **1** : curtir (pieles) **2** : broncear — *vi* : broncearse

tan² *n* **1** SUNTAN : bronceado *m* ⟨to get a tan : broncearse⟩ **2** : color *m* canela, color *m* café con leche

tandem¹ ['tændəm] *adv or* **in tandem** : en tándem

tandem² *n* : tándem *m* (bicicleta)

tang ['tæŋ] *n* : sabor *m* fuerte

tangent ['tændʒənt] *n* : tangente *f* ⟨to go off on a tangent : irse por la tangente⟩

tangerine ['tændʒəˌriːn, ˌtændʒə'-] *n* : mandarina *f*

tangible ['tændʒəbəl] *adj* : tangible, palpable — **tangibly** [-bli] *adv*

tangle¹ ['tæŋgəl] *v* **-gled; -gling** *vt* : enredar, enmarañar — *vi* : enredarse

tangle² *n* : enredo *m*, maraña *f*

tango¹ ['tæŋˌgoː] *vi* : bailar el tango

tango² *n*, *pl* **-gos** : tango *m*

tangy ['tæŋi] *adj* **tangier; -est** : que tiene un sabor fuerte

tank ['tæŋk] *n* : tanque *m*, depósito *m* ⟨fuel tank : depósito de combustibles⟩

tankard ['tæŋkərd] *n* : jarra *f*

tanker ['tæŋkər] *n* : buque *m* cisterna, camión *m* cisterna, avión *m* cisterna ⟨an oil tanker : un petrolero⟩

tanner ['tænər] *n* : curtidor *m*, -dora *f*

tannery ['tænəri] *n*, *pl* **-neries** : curtiduría *f*, tenería *f*

tannin ['tænən] *n* : tanino *m*

tantalize ['tæntəˌlaɪz] *vt* **-lized; -lizing** : tentar, atormentar (con algo inasequible)

tantalizing ['tæntəˌlaɪzɪŋ] *adj* : tentador, seductor

tantamount ['tæntəˌmaʊnt] *adj* : equivalente

tantrum ['tæntrəm] *n* : rabieta *f*, berrinche *m* ⟨to throw a tantrum : hacer un berrinche⟩

tap¹ ['tæp] *vt* **tapped; tapping 1** : ponerle una espita a, sacar líquido de (un barril, un tanque, etc.) **2** : intervenir (una línea telefónica) **3** PAT, TOUCH : tocar, golpear ligeramente ⟨he tapped me on the shoulder : me tocó en el hombro⟩

tap² *n* **1** FAUCET : llave *f*, grifo *m* ⟨beer on tap : cerveza de barril⟩ **2** : extracción *f* (de líquido) ⟨a spinal tap : una punción lumbar⟩ **3** PAT, TOUCH : golpecito *m*, toque *m*

tape¹ ['teɪp] *vt* **taped; taping 1** : sujetar o arreglar con cinta adhesiva **2** RECORD : grabar

tape² *n* **1** : cinta *f* (adhesiva, magnética, etc.) **2** → **tape measure**

tape measure *n* : cinta *f* métrica

taper¹ ['teɪpər] *vi* **1** : estrecharse gradualmente ⟨its tail tapers towards the tip : su cola va estrechándose hacia la punta⟩ **2** *or* **to taper off** : disminuir gradualmente

taper² *n* **1** CANDLE : vela *f* larga y delgada **2** TAPERING : estrechamiento *m* gradual

tapestry ['tæpəstri] *n, pl* **-tries** : tapiz *m*

tapeworm ['teɪpˌwərm] *n* : solitaria *f*, tenia *f*

tapioca [ˌtæpi'o:kə] *n* : tapioca *f*

tar¹ ['tɑr] *vt* **tarred; tarring** : alquitranar

tar² *n* : alquitrán *m*, brea *f*, chapopote *m* *Mex*

tarantula [tə'ræntʃələ, -'ræntələ] *n* : tarántula *f*

tardiness ['tɑrdinəs] *n* : tardanza *f*, retraso *m*

tardy ['tɑrdi] *adj* **-dier; -est** LATE : tardío, de retraso

target¹ ['tɑrgət] *vt* : fijar como objetivo, dirigir, destinar

target² *n* **1** : blanco *m* ⟨target practice : tiro al blanco⟩ **2** GOAL, OBJECTIVE : meta *f*, objetivo *m*

tariff ['tærɪf] *n* DUTY : tarifa *f*, arancel *m*

tarnish¹ ['tɑrnɪʃ] *vt* **1** DULL : deslustrar **2** SULLY : empañar, manchar (una reputación, etc.) — *vi* : deslustrarse

tarnish² *n* : deslustre *m*

tarpaulin [tɑr'pɔlən, 'tɑrpə-] *n* : lona *f* (impermeable)

tarragon ['tærəˌgɑn, -gən] *n* : estragón *m*

tarry¹ ['tæri] *vi* **-ried; -rying** : demorarse, entretenerse

tarry² ['tɑri] *adj* **1** : parecido al alquitrán **2** : cubierto de alquitrán

tart¹ ['tɑrt] *adj* **1** SOUR : ácido, agrio **2** CAUSTIC : mordaz, acrimonioso — **tartly** *adv*

tart² *n* : tartaleta *f*

tartan ['tɑrtən] *n* : tartán *m*

tartar ['tɑrtər] *n* **1** : tártaro *m* ⟨tartar sauce : salsa tártara⟩ **2** : sarro *m* (dental)

tartness ['tɑrtnəs] *n* **1** SOURNESS : acidez *f* **2** ACRIMONY, SHARPNESS : mordacidad *f*, acrimonia *f*, acritud *f*

task ['tæsk] *n* : tarea *f*, trabajo *m*

taskmaster ['tæskˌmæstər] *n* **to be a hard taskmaster** : ser exigente, ser muy estricto

tassel ['tæsəl] *n* : borla *f*

taste¹ ['teɪst] *v* **tasted; tasting** *vt* : probar (alimentos), degustar, catar (vinos) ⟨taste this soup : prueba esta sopa⟩ — *vi* : saber ⟨this tastes good : esto sabe bueno⟩

taste² *n* **1** SAMPLE : prueba *f*, bocado *m* (de comida), trago *m* (de bebidas) **2** FLAVOR : gusto *m*, sabor *m* **3** : gusto *m* ⟨she has good taste : tiene buen gusto⟩ ⟨in bad taste : de mal gusto⟩

taste bud *n* : papila *f* gustativa

tasteful ['teɪstfəl] *adj* : de buen gusto

tastefully ['teɪstfəli] *adv* : con buen gusto

tasteless ['teɪstləs] *adj* **1** FLAVORLESS : sin sabor, soso, insípido **2** : de mal gusto ⟨a tasteless joke : un chiste de mal gusto⟩

taster ['teɪstər] *n* : degustador *m*, -dora *f*; catador *m*, -dora *f* (de vinos)

tastiness ['teɪstinəs] *n* : lo sabroso

tasty ['teɪsti] *adj* **tastier; -est** : sabroso, gustoso

tatter ['tætər] *n* **1** SHRED : tira *f*, jirón *m* (de tela) **2 tatters** *npl* : andrajos *mpl*, harapos *mpl* ⟨to be in tatters : estar por los suelos⟩

tattered ['tætərd] *adj* : andrajoso, en jirones

tattle ['tætəl] *vi* **-tled; -tling 1** CHATTER : parlotear *fam*, cotorrear *fam* **2 to tattle on someone** : acusar a alguien

tattletale ['tætəlˌteɪl] *n* : soplón *m*, -plona *f fam*

tattoo¹ [tæ'tu:] *vt* : tatuar

tattoo² *n* : tatuaje *m* ⟨to get a tattoo : tatuarse⟩

taught → **teach**

taunt¹ ['tɔnt] *vt* MOCK : mofarse de, burlarse de

taunt² *n* : mofa *f*, burla *f*

Taurus ['tɔrəs] *n* : Tauro *mf*

taut ['tɔt] *adj* : tirante, tenso — **tautly** *adv*

tautness ['tɔtnəs] *n* : tirantez *f*, tensión *f*

tavern ['tævərn] *n* : taberna *f*

tawdry ['tɔdri] *adj* **-drier; -est** : chabacano, vulgar

tawny ['tɔni] *adj* **-nier; -est** : leonado

tax¹ ['tæks] *vt* **1** : gravar, cobrar un impuesto sobre **2** CHARGE : acusar ⟨they taxed him with neglect : fue acusado de incumplimiento⟩ **3 to tax someone's strength** : ponerle a prueba las fuerzas (a alguien)

tax² *n* **1** : impuesto *m*, tributo *m* **2** BURDEN : carga *f*

taxable ['tæksəbəl] *adj* : sujeto a un impuesto

taxation [tæk'seɪʃən] *n* : impuestos *mpl*

tax–exempt ['tæksɪg'zɛmpt, -ɛg-] *adj* : libre de impuestos

taxi¹ ['tæksi] *vi* **taxied; taxiing** *or* **taxying; taxis** *or* **taxies 1** : ir en taxi **2** : rodar sobre la pista de aterrizaje (dícese de un avión)

taxi² *n, pl* **taxis** : taxi *m*, libre *m Mex*

taxicab ['tæksiˌkæb] *n* → **taxi²**

taxidermist ['tæksəˌdərmɪst] *n* : taxidermista *mf*

taxidermy ['tæksəˌdərmi] *n* : taxidermia *f*

taxpayer ['tæksˌpeɪər] *n* : contribuyente *mf*, causante *mf Mex*

TB [ˌti:'bi:] → **tuberculosis**

tea ['ti:] *n* **1** : té *m* (planta y bebida) **2** : merienda *f*, té *m* (comida)

teach ['ti:tʃ] *v* **taught** ['tɔt]; **teaching** *vt* : enseñar, dar clases de ⟨she teaches math : da clases de matemáticas⟩ ⟨she taught me everything I know : me enseñó todo lo que sé⟩ — *vi* : enseñar, dar clases

teacher ['ti:ʧər] *n* : maestro *m*, -tra *f* (de enseñanza primaria); profesor *m*, -sora *f* (de enseñanza secundaria)

teaching ['ti:ʧɪŋ] *n* : enseñanza *f*

teacup ['ti:ˌkʌp] *n* : taza *f* para té

teak ['ti:k] *n* : teca *f*

teakettle ['ti:ˌktəl] *n* : tetera *f*

teal ['ti:l] *n, pl* **teal** *or* **teals** : cerceta *f* (pato)

team¹ ['ti:m] *vi or* **to team up 1** : formar un equipo (en deportes) **2** COLLABORATE : asociarse, juntarse, unirse

team² *adj* : de equipo

team³ *n* **1** : tiro *m* (de caballos), yunta *f* (de bueyes o mulas) **2** : equipo *m* (en deportes, etc.)

teammate ['ti:mˌmeɪt] *n* : compañero *m*, -ra *f* de equipo

teamster ['ti:mstər] *n* : camionero *m*, -ra *f*

teamwork ['ti:mˌwərk] *n* : trabajo *m* en equipo, cooperación *f*

teapot ['ti:ˌpɑt] *n* : tetera *f*

tear¹ ['tær] *v* **tore** ['tor]; **torn** ['torn]; **tearing** *vt* **1** RIP : desgarrar, romper, rasgar (tela) ⟨to tear to pieces : hacer pedazos⟩ **2** *or* **to tear apart** DIVIDE : dividir **3** REMOVE : arrancar ⟨torn from his family : arrancado de su familia⟩ **4 to tear down** : derribar — *vi* **1** RIP : desgarrarse, romperse **2** RUSH : ir a gran velocidad ⟨she went tearing down the street : se fue como rayo por la calle⟩

tear² *n* : desgarradura *f*, rotura *f*, desgarro *m* (muscular)

tear³ ['tɪr] *n* : lágrima *f*

teardrop ['tɪrˌdrɑp] *n* → **tear³**

tearful ['tɪrfəl] *adj* : lloroso, triste — **tearfully** *adv*

tease¹ ['ti:z] *vt* **teased; teasing 1** MOCK : burlarse de, mofarse de **2** ANNOY : irritar, fastidiar

tease² *n* **1** TEASING : burla *f*, mofa *f* **2** : bromista *mf*; guasón *m*, -sona *f*

teaspoon ['ti:ˌspu:n] *n* **1** : cucharita *f* **2** → **teaspoonful**

teaspoonful ['ti:ˌspu:nˌfʊl] *n, pl* **-spoonfuls** [-ˌfʊlz] *or* **-spoonsful** [-ˌspu:nzˌfʊl] : cucharadita *f*

teat ['ti:t] *n* : tetilla *f*

technical ['tɛknɪkəl] *adj* : técnico — **technically** [-kli] *adv*

technicality [ˌtɛknə'kæləti] *n, pl* **-ties** : detalle *m* técnico

technician [tɛk'nɪʃən] *n* : técnico *m*, -ca *f*

technique [tɛk'ni:k] *n* : técnica *f*

technological [ˌtɛknə'lɑʤɪkəl] *adj* : tecnológico

technology [tɛk'nɑləʤi] *n, pl* **-gies** : tecnología *f*

teddy bear ['tɛdi] *n* : oso *m* de peluche

tedious ['ti:diəs] *adj* : aburrido, pesado, monótono — **tediously** *adv*

tediousness ['ti:diəsnəs] *n* : lo aburrido, lo pesado

tedium ['ti:diəm] *n* : tedio *m*, pesadez *f*

tee ['ti:] *n* : tee *mf*

teem ['ti:m] *vi* **to teem with** : estar repleto de, estar lleno de

teenage ['ti:nˌeɪʤ] *or* **teenaged** [-eɪʤd] *adj* : adolescente, de adolescencia

teenager ['ti:nˌeɪʤər] *n* : adolescente *mf*

teens ['ti:nz] *npl* : adolescencia *f*

teepee → **tepee**

teeter¹ ['ti:tər] *vi* : balancearse, tambalearse

teeter² *n or* **teeter–totter** ['ti:tər-ˌtɑtər] → **seesaw**

teeth → **tooth**

teethe ['ti:ð] *vi* **teethed; teething** : formársele a uno los dientes ⟨the baby's teething : le están saliendo los dientes al niño⟩

telecast¹ ['tɛləˌkæst] *vt* **-cast; -casting** : televisar, transmitir por televisión

telecast² *n* : transmisión *f* por televisión

telecommunication [ˌtɛləkəˌmju:nə'keɪʃən] *n* : telecomunicación *f*

telegram ['tɛləˌgræm] *n* : telegrama *m*

telegraph¹ ['tɛləˌgræf] *v* : telegrafiar

telegraph² *n* : telégrafo *m*

telepathic [ˌtɛlə'pæθɪk] *adj* : telepático — **telepathically** [-θɪkli] *adv*

telepathy [tə'lɛpəθi] *n* : telepatía *f*

telephone¹ ['tɛləˌfo:n] *v* **-phoned; -phoning** *vt* : llamar por teléfono a, telefonear — *vi* : telefonear

telephone² *n* : teléfono *m*

telescope¹ ['tɛləˌsko:p] *vi* **-scoped; -scoping** : plegarse (como un telescopio)

telescope² *n* : telescopio *m*

telescopic [ˌtɛlə'skɑpɪk] *adj* : telescópico

televise ['tɛləˌvaɪz] *vt* **-vised; -vising** : televisar

television ['tɛləˌvɪʒən] *n* : televisión *f*

tell ['tɛl] *v* **told** ['to:ld]; **telling** *vt* **1** COUNT : contar, enumerar ⟨all told : en total⟩ **2** INSTRUCT : decir ⟨he told me how to fix it : me dijo cómo arreglarlo⟩ ⟨they told her to wait : le dijeron que esperara⟩ **3** RELATE : contar, relatar, narrar ⟨to tell a story : contar una historia⟩ **4** DIVULGE, REVEAL : revelar, divulgar ⟨he told me everything about her : me contó todo acerca de ella⟩ **5** DISCERN : discernir, notar ⟨I can't tell the difference : no noto la diferencia⟩ — *vi* **1** SAY : decir ⟨I won't tell : no voy a decírselo a nadie⟩ **2** KNOW : saber ⟨you never can tell : nunca se sabe⟩ **3** SHOW : notarse, hacerse sentir ⟨the strain is beginning to tell : la tensión se empieza a notar⟩

teller ['tɛlər] *n* **1** NARRATOR : narrador *m*, -dora *f* **2** *or* **bank teller** : cajero *m*, -ra *f*

temerity [tə'mɛrəti] *n, pl* **-ties** : temeridad *f*

temp ['tɛmp] *n* : empleado *m*, -da *f* temporal

temper¹ ['tɛmpər] *vt* **1** MODERATE : moderar, temperar **2** ANNEAL : templar (acero, etc.)

temper² *n* **1** DISPOSITION : carácter *m*, genio *m* **2** HARDNESS : temple *m*, dureza *f* (de un metal) **3** COMPOSURE : calma *f*, serenidad *f* ⟨to lose one's temper : perder los estribos⟩ **4** RAGE : furia *f* ⟨to fly into a temper : ponerse furioso⟩

temperament ['tɛmpərmənt, -prə-, -pərə-] *n* : temperamento *m*

temperamental [ˌtɛmpər'mɛntəl, -prə-, -pərə-] *adj* : temperamental

temperance ['tɛmprənʦ] *n* : templanza *f*, temperancia *f*

temperate ['tɛmpərət] *adj* : templado (dícese del clima, etc.), moderado

temperature ['tɛmpər‚ʧur, -prə-, -pərə-, -ʧər] *n* **1** : temperatura *f* **2** FEVER : calentura *f*, fiebre *f*

tempest ['tɛmpəst] *n* : tempestad *f*

tempestuous [tɛm'pɛsʧuəs] *adj* : tempestuoso

temple ['tɛmpəl] *n* **1** : templo *m* (en religión) **2** : sien *f* (en anatomía)

tempo ['tɛm‚po:] *n*, *pl* **-pi** [-‚pi:] *or* **-pos** : ritmo *m*, tempo *m* (en música)

temporal ['tɛmpərəl] *adj* : temporal

temporarily [ˌtɛmpə'rɛrəli] *adv* : temporalmente, provisionalmente

temporary ['tɛmpə‚rɛri] *adj* : temporal, provisional, provisorio

tempt ['tɛmpt] *vt* : tentar

temptation [tɛmp'teɪʃən] *n* : tentación *f*

tempter ['tɛmptər] *n* : tentador *m*

temptress ['tɛmptrəs] *n* : tentadora *f*

ten¹ ['tɛn] *adj* : diez

ten² *n* **1** : diez *m* (número) **2** : decena *f* ⟨tens of thousands : decenas de millares⟩

tenable ['tɛnəbəl] *adj* : sostenible, defendible

tenacious [tə'neɪʃəs] *adj* : tenaz

tenacity [tə'næsəti] *n* : tenacidad *f*

tenancy ['tɛnənʦi] *n*, *pl* **-cies** : tenencia *f*, inquilinato *m* (de un inmueble)

tenant ['tɛnənt] *n* : inquilino *m*, -na *f*; arrendatario *m*, -ria *f*

tend ['tɛnd] *vt* : atender, cuidar (de), ocuparse de — *vi* : tender ⟨it tends to benefit the consumer : tiende a beneficiar al consumidor⟩

tendency ['tɛnənʦi] *n*, *pl* **-cies** : tendencia *f*, proclividad *f*, inclinación *f*

tender¹ ['tɛndər] *vt* : entregar, presentar ⟨I tendered my resignation : presenté mi renuncia⟩

tender² *adj* **1** : tierno, blando ⟨tender steak : bistec tierno⟩ **2** AFFECTIONATE, LOVING : tierno, cariñoso, afectuoso **3** DELICATE : tierno, sensible, delicado

tender³ *n* **1** OFFER : propuesta *f*, oferta *f* (en negocios) **2** legal tender : moneda *f* de curso legal

tenderize ['tɛndə‚raɪz] *vt* **-ized; -izing** : ablandar (carnes)

tenderloin ['tɛndr‚lɔɪn] *n* : lomo *f* (de res o de puerco)

tenderly ['tɛndərli] *adv* : tiernamente, con ternura

tenderness ['tɛndərnəs] *n* : ternura *f*

tendon ['tɛndən] *n* : tendón *m*

tendril ['tɛndrɪl] *n* : zarcillo *m*

tenement ['tɛnəmənt] *n* : casa *f* de vecindad

tenet ['tɛnət] *n* : principio *m*

tennis ['tɛnəs] *n* : tenis *m*

tenor ['tɛnər] *n* **1** PURPORT : tenor *m*, significado *m* **2** : tenor *m* (en música)

tenpins ['tɛn‚pɪnz] *npl* : bolos *mpl*, boliche *m*

tense¹ ['tɛnʦ] *v* **tensed; tensing** *vt* : tensar — *vi* : tensarse, ponerse tenso

tense² *adj* **tenser; tensest** **1** TAUT : tenso, tirante **2** NERVOUS : tenso, nervioso

tense³ *n* : tiempo *m* (de un verbo)

tensely ['tɛnʦli] *adv* : tensamente

tenseness ['tɛnʦnəs] → **tension**

tension ['tɛnʃən] *n* **1** TAUTNESS : tensión *f*, tirantez *f* **2** STRESS : tensión *f*, nerviosismo *m*, estrés *m*

tent ['tɛnt] *n* : tienda *f* de campaña

tentacle ['tɛntɪkəl] *n* : tentáculo *m*

tentative ['tɛntətɪv] *adj* **1** HESITANT : indeciso, vacilante **2** PROVISIONAL : sujeto a cambios, provisional

tentatively ['tɛntətɪvli] *adv* : provisionalmente

tenth¹ ['tɛnθ] *adj* : décimo

tenth² *n* **1** : décimo *m*, -ma *f* (en una serie) **2** : décimo *m*, décima parte *f*

tenuous ['tɛnjuəs] *adj* : tenue, débil ⟨tenuous reasons : razones poco convincentes⟩

tenuously ['tɛnjuəsli] *adv* : tenuemente, ligeramente

tenure ['tɛnjər] *n* : tenencia *f* (de un cargo o una propiedad), titularidad *f* (de un puesto académico)

tepee ['ti:‚pi:] *n* : tipi *m*

tepid ['tɛpɪd] *adj* : tibio

tequila [tə'ki:lə] *n* : tequila *m*

term¹ ['tərm] *vt* : calificar de, llamar, nombrar

term² *n* **1** PERIOD : término *m*, plazo *m*, período *m* **2** : término *m* (en matemáticas) **3** WORD : término *m*, vocablo *m* ⟨legal terms : términos legales⟩ **4** **terms** *npl* CONDITIONS : términos *mpl*, condiciones *fpl* **5** **terms** *npl* RELATIONS : relaciones *fpl* ⟨to be on good terms with : tener buenas relaciones con⟩ **6** **in terms of** : con respecto a, en cuanto a

terminal¹ ['tərmənəl] *adj* : terminal

terminal² *n* **1** : terminal *m*, polo *m* (en electricidad) **2** : terminal *m* (de una computadora) **3** STATION : terminal *f*, estación *f* (de transporte público)

terminate ['tərmə‚neɪt] *v* **-nated; -nating** *vi* : terminar(se), concluirse — *vt* : terminar, poner fin a

termination [ˌtərmə'neɪʃən] *n* : cese *m*, terminación *f*

terminology [ˌtərmə'nɑlədʒi] *n*, *pl* **-gies** : terminología *f*

terminus ['tərmənəs] *n*, *pl* **-ni** [-‚naɪ] *or* **-nuses** **1** END : término *m*, fin *m* **2** : terminal *f* (de transporte público)

termite ['tər͵maɪt] *n* : termita *f*

tern ['tərn] *n* : golondrina *f* de mar

terrace[1] ['tɛrəs] *vt* **-raced; -racing** : formar en terrazas, disponer en bancales

terrace[2] *n* **1** PATIO : terraza *f*, patio *m* **2** : terraplén *m*, terraza *f*, bancal *m* (en agricultura)

terra-cotta [͵tɛrə'kɑtə] *n* : terracota *f*

terrain [tə'reɪn] *n* : terreno *m*

terrapin ['tɛrəpɪn] *n* : galápago *m* norteamericano

terrarium [tə'ræriəm] *n, pl* **-ia** [-iə] *or* **-iums** : terrario *m*

terrestrial [tə'rɛstriəl] *adj* : terrestre

terrible ['tɛrəbəl] *adj* : atroz, horrible, terrible

terribly ['tɛrəbli] *adv* **1** BADLY : muy mal **2** EXTREMELY : terriblemente, extremadamente

terrier ['tɛriər] *n* : terrier *mf*

terrific [tə'rɪfɪk] *adj* **1** FRIGHTFUL : aterrador **2** EXTRAORDINARY : extraordinario, excepcional **3** EXCELLENT : excelente, estupendo

terrify ['tɛrə͵faɪ] *vt* **-fied; -fying** : aterrorizar, aterrar, espantar

terrifying ['tɛrə͵faɪɪŋ] *adj* : espantoso, aterrador

territory ['tɛrə͵tori] *n, pl* **-ries** : territorio *m* — **territorial** [͵tɛrə'toriəl] *adj*

terror ['tɛrər] *n* : terror *m*

terrorism ['tɛrər͵ɪzəm] *n* : terrorismo *m*

terrorist[1] ['tɛrərɪst] *adj* : terrorista

terrorist[2] *n* : terrorista *mf*

terrorize ['tɛrər͵aɪz] *vt* **-ized; -izing** : aterrorizar

terry ['tɛri] *n, pl* **-ries** *or* **terry cloth** : (tela de) toalla *f*

terse ['tərs] *adj* **terser; tersest** : lacónico, conciso, seco — **tersely** *adv*

tertiary ['tər͵ʃi͵ɛri] *adj* : terciario

test[1] ['tɛst] *vt* : examinar, evaluar — *vi* : hacer pruebas

test[2] *n* : prueba *f*, examen *m*, test *m* ⟨to put to the test : poner a prueba⟩

testament ['tɛstəmənt] *n* **1** WILL : testamento *m* **2** : Testamento *m* (en la Biblia) ⟨the Old Testament : el Antiguo Testamento⟩

testicle ['tɛstɪkəl] *n* : testículo *m*

testify ['tɛstə͵faɪ] *v* **-fied; -fying** *vi* : testificar, atestar, testimoniar — *vt* : testificar

testimonial [͵tɛstə'mo:niəl] *n* **1** REFERENCE : recomendación *f* **2** TRIBUTE : homenaje *m*, tributo *m*

testimony ['tɛstə͵mo:ni] *n, pl* **-nies** : testimonio *m*, declaración *f*

test tube *n* : probeta *f*, tubo *m* de ensayo

testy ['tɛsti] *adj* **-tier; -est** : irritable

tetanus ['tɛtənəs] *n* : tétano *m*, tétanos *m*

tête-à-tête [͵tɛtə'tɛt, ͵teɪtə'teɪt] *n* : conversación *f* en privado

tether[1] ['tɛðər] *vt* : atar (con una cuerda), amarrar

tether[2] *n* : atadura *f*, cadena *f*, correa *f*

text ['tɛkst] *n* **1** : texto *m* **2** TOPIC : tema *m* **3** → **textbook**

textbook ['tɛkst͵bʊk] *n* : libro *m* de texto

textile ['tɛk͵staɪl, 'tɛkstəl] *n* : textil *m*, tela *f* ⟨the textile industry : la industria textil⟩

textual ['tɛkstʃʊəl] *adj* : textual

texture ['tɛkstʃər] *n* : textura *f*

Thai ['taɪ] *n* **1** : tailandés *m*, -desa *f* **2** : tailandés *m* (idioma) — **Thai** *adj*

than[1] ['ðæn] *conj* : que, de ⟨it's worth more than that : vale más que eso⟩ ⟨more than you think : más de lo que piensas⟩

than[2] *prep* : que, de ⟨you're better than he is : eres mejor que él⟩ ⟨more than once : más de una vez⟩

thank ['θæŋk] *vt* : agradecer, darle (las) gracias (a alguien) ⟨thank you! : ¡gracias!⟩ ⟨I thanked her for the present : le di las gracias por el regalo⟩ ⟨I thank you for your help : le agradezco su ayuda⟩

thankful ['θæŋkfəl] *adj* : agradecido

thankfully ['θæŋkfəli] *adv* **1** GRATEFULLY : con agradecimiento **2** FORTUNATELY : afortunadamente, por suerte ⟨thankfully, it's over : se acabó, gracias a Dios⟩

thankfulness ['θæŋkfəlnəs] *n* : agradecimiento *m*, gratitud *f*

thankless ['θæŋkləs] *adj* : ingrato ⟨a thankless task : un trabajo ingrato⟩

thanks ['θæŋks] *npl* **1** : agradecimiento *m* **2 thanks!** : ¡gracias!

Thanksgiving [θæŋks'gɪvɪŋ, 'θæŋks͵-] *n* : el día de Acción de Gracias (fiesta estadounidense)

that[1] ['ðæt] *adv* (*in negative constructions*) : tan ⟨it's not that expensive : no es tan caro⟩ ⟨not that much : no tanto⟩

that[2] *adj, pl* **those** : ese, esa, aquel, aquella ⟨do you see those children? : ¿ves a aquellos niños?⟩

that[3] *conj & pron* : que ⟨he said that he was afraid : dijo que tenía miedo⟩ ⟨the book that he wrote : el libro que escribió⟩

that[4] *pron, pl* **those** ['ðo:z] **1** : ése, ésa, eso ⟨that's my father : ése es mi padre⟩ ⟨those are the ones he likes : ésos son los que le gustan⟩ ⟨what's that? : ¿qué es eso?⟩ **2** (*referring to more distant objects or time*) : aquél, aquélla, aquello ⟨those are maples and these are elms : aquéllos son arces y éstos son olmos⟩ ⟨that came to an end : aquello se acabó⟩

thatch[1] ['θætʃ] *vt* : cubrir o techar con paja

thatch[2] *n* : paja *f* (usada para techos)

thaw[1] ['θɔ] *vt* : descongelar — *vi* : derretirse (dícese de la nieve), descongelarse (dícese de los alimentos)

thaw[2] *n* : deshielo *m*

the[1] [ðə, *before vowel sounds usu* ði:] *adv*
1 (*used to indicate comparison*) ⟨the
sooner the better : cuanto más pronto,
mejor⟩ ⟨she likes this one the best : éste
es el que más le gusta⟩ **2** (*used as a conjunction*) : cuanto ⟨the more I learn,
the less I understand : cuanto más
aprendo, menos entiendo⟩

the[2] *art* : el, la, los, las ⟨the gloves : los
guantes⟩ ⟨the suitcase : la maleta⟩
⟨forty cookies to the box : cuarenta
galletas por caja⟩

theater *or* **theatre** [ˈθiːəṭər] *n* **1** : teatro
m (edificio) **2** DRAMA : teatro *m*, drama *m*

theatrical [θiˈætrɪkəl] *adj* : teatral,
dramático

thee [ˈðiː] *pron* : te, ti

theft [ˈθɛft] *n* : robo *m*, hurto *m*

their [ˈðɛr] *adj* : su ⟨their friends : sus
amigos⟩

theirs [ˈðɛrz] *pron* : (el) suyo, (la) suya,
(los) suyos, (las) suyas ⟨they came for
theirs : vinieron por el suyo⟩ ⟨theirs is
bigger : la suya es más grande, la de ellos es más grande⟩ ⟨a brother of theirs
: un hermano suyo, un hermano de
ellos⟩

them [ˈðɛm] *pron* **1** (*as a direct object*)
: los (*Spain sometimes* les), las ⟨I know
them : los conozco⟩ **2** (*as indirect object*) : les, se ⟨I sent them a letter : les
mandé una carta⟩ ⟨give it to them
: dáselo (a ellos)⟩ **3** (*as object of a preposition*) : ellos, ellas ⟨go with them : ve
con ellos⟩ **4** (*for emphasis*) : ellos,
ellas ⟨I wasn't expecting them : no los
esperaba a ellos⟩

thematic [θiˈmæṭɪk] *adj* : temático

theme [ˈθiːm] *n* **1** SUBJECT, TOPIC : tema
m **2** COMPOSITION : composición *f*, trabajo *m* (escrito) **3** : tema *m* (en música)

themselves [ðəmˈsɛlvz, ðɛm-] *pron* **1**
(*as a reflexive*) : se, sí ⟨they enjoyed
themselves : se divirtieron⟩ ⟨they divided it among themselves : lo
repartieron entre sí, se lo repartieron⟩
2 (*for emphasis*) : ellos mismos, ellas
mismas ⟨they built it themselves : ellas
mismas lo construyeron⟩

then[1] [ˈðɛn] *adv* **1** : entonces, en ese
tiempo ⟨I was sixteen then : tenía entonces dieciséis años⟩ ⟨since then : desde entonces⟩ **2** NEXT : después, luego
⟨we'll go to Toronto, then to Winnipeg
: iremos a Toronto, y luego a Winnipeg⟩
3 BESIDES : además, aparte ⟨then
there's the tax : y aparte está el impuesto⟩ **4** : entonces, en ese caso ⟨if
you like music, then you should attend
: si te gusta la música, entonces deberías asistir⟩

then[2] *adj* : entonces ⟨the then governor
of Georgia : el entonces gobernador de
Georgia⟩

thence [ˈðɛnts, ˈθɛnts] *adv* : de ahí, de ahí
en adelante

theologian [ˌθiːəˈloːdʒən] *n* : teólogo *m*,
-ga *f*

theological [ˌθiːəˈlɑdʒɪkəl] *adj* : teológico

theology [θiˈɑlədʒi] *n, pl* **-gies** : teología *f*

theorem [ˈθiːərəm, ˈθɪrəm] *n* : teorema *m*

theoretical [ˌθiːəˈrɛṭɪkəl] *adj* : teórico —
theoretically *adv*

theorist [ˈθiːərɪst] *n* : teórico *m*, -ca *f*

theorize [ˈθiːəˌraɪz] *vi* **-rized; -rizing**
: teorizar

theory [ˈθiːəri, ˈθɪri] *n, pl* **-ries** : teoría *f*

therapeutic [ˌθɛrəˈpjuːṭɪk] *adj* : terapéutico — **therapeutically** *adv*

therapist [ˈθɛrəpɪst] *n* : terapeuta *mf*

therapy [ˈθɛrəpi] *n, pl* **-pies** : terapia *f*

there[1] [ˈðɛr] *adv* **1** : ahí, allí, allá ⟨stand
over there : párate ahí⟩ ⟨over there
: por allí, por allá⟩ ⟨who's there?
: ¿quién es?⟩ **2** : ahí, en esto, en eso
⟨there is where we disagree : en eso es
donde no estamos de acuerdo⟩

there[2] *pron* **1** (*introducing a sentence or
clause*) ⟨there comes a time to decide
: llega un momento en que tiene uno
que decidir⟩ **2 there is, there are** : hay
⟨there are many children here : aquí
hay muchos niños⟩ ⟨there's a good hotel downtown : hay un buen hotel en
el centro⟩

thereabouts [ˌðærəˈbaʊts, ˈðærəˌ-] *or*
thereabout [-ˈbaʊt, -ˌbaʊt] *adv or*
thereabouts : por ahí, más o menos ⟨at
five o'clock or thereabouts : por ahí de
las cinco⟩

thereafter [ðærˈæftər] *adv* : después
⟨shortly thereafter : poco después⟩

thereby [ðærˈbaɪ, ˈðærˌbaɪ] *adv* : de tal
modo, de ese manera, así

therefore [ˈðærˌfor] *adv* : por lo tanto,
por consiguiente

therein [ðærˈɪn] *adv* **1** : allí adentro, ahí
adentro ⟨the contents therein : lo que
allí se contiene⟩ **2** : allí, en ese aspecto ⟨therein lies the problem : allí está
el problema⟩

thereof [ðærˈʌv, -ˈɑv] *adv* : de eso, de
esto

thereupon [ˈðærəˌpɑn, -ˌpɔn; ˌðærəˈpɑn,
-ˈpɔn] *adv* : acto seguido, inmediatamente (después)

therewith [ðærˈwɪð, -ˈwɪθ] *adv* : con eso,
con ello

thermal [ˈθərməl] *adj* **1** : térmico (en física) **2** HOT : termal

thermodynamics [ˌθərmodaɪˈnæmɪks]
ns & pl : termodinámica *f*

thermometer [θərˈmɑməṭər] *n* : termómetro *m*

thermos [ˈθərməs] *n* : termo *m*

thermostat [ˈθərməˌstæt] *n* : termostato *m*

thesaurus [θɪˈsɔrəs] *n, pl* **-sauri** [-ˈsɔrˌaɪ]
or **-sauruses** [-ˈsɔrəsəz] : diccionario *m*
de sinónimos

these → **this**

thesis ['θi:sɪs] *n, pl* **theses** ['θi:ˌsi:z] : tesis *f*

they ['ðeɪ] *pron* : ellos, ellas ⟨they are here : están aquí⟩ ⟨they don't know : ellos no saben⟩

they'd ['ðeɪd] (*contraction of* they had *or* they would) → have, would

they'll ['ðeɪl, 'ðɛl] (*contraction of* they shall *or* they will) → shall, will

they're ['ðɛr] (*contraction of* they are) → be

they've ['ðeɪv] (*contraction of* they have) → have

thiamine ['θaɪəmɪn, -ˌmi:n] *n* : tiamina *f*

thick¹ ['θɪk] *adj* **1** : grueso ⟨a thick plank : una tabla gruesa⟩ **2** : espeso, denso ⟨thick syrup : jarabe espeso⟩ — **thickly** *adv*

thick² *n* **1 in the thick of** : en medio de ⟨in the thick of the battle : en lo más reñido de la batalla⟩ **2 through thick and thin** : a las duras y a las maduras

thicken ['θɪkən] *vt* : espesar (un líquido) — *vi* : espesarse

thickener ['θɪkənər] *n* : espesante *m*

thicket ['θɪkət] *n* : matorral *m*, maleza *f*, espesura *f*

thickness ['θɪknəs] *n* : grosor *m*, grueso *m*, espesor *m*

thickset ['θɪk'sɛt] *adj* STOCKY : robusto, fornido

thick–skinned ['θɪk'skɪnd] *adj* : poco sensible, que no se ofende fácilmente

thief ['θi:f] *n, pl* **thieves** ['θi:vz] : ladrón *m*, -drona *f*

thieve ['θi:v] *v* **thieved; thieving** : hurtar, robar

thievery ['θi:vəri] *n* : hurto *m*, robo *m*, latrocinio *m*

thigh ['θaɪ] *n* : muslo *m*

thighbone ['θaɪˌbo:n] *n* : fémur *m*

thimble ['θɪmbəl] *n* : dedal *m*

thin¹ ['θɪn] *v* **thinned; thinning** *vt* : hacer menos denso, diluir, aguar (un líquido), enrarecer (un gas) — *vi* : diluirse, aguarse (dícese de un líquido), enrarecerse (dícese de un gas)

thin² *adj* **thinner; -est 1** LEAN, SLIM : delgado, esbelto, flaco **2** SPARSE : ralo, escaso ⟨a thin beard : una barba rala⟩ **3** WATERY : claro, aguado, diluido **4** FINE : delgado, fino ⟨thin slices : rebanadas finas⟩

thing ['θɪŋ] *n* **1** AFFAIR, MATTER : cosa *f*, asunto *m* ⟨don't talk about those things : no hables de esas cosas⟩ ⟨how are things? : ¿cómo van las cosas?⟩ **2** ACT, EVENT : cosa *f*, suceso *m*, evento *m* ⟨the flood was a terrible thing : la inundación fue una cosa terrible⟩ **3** OBJECT : cosa *f*, objeto *m* ⟨don't forget your things : no olvides tus cosas⟩

think ['θɪŋk] *v* **thought** ['θɔt]; **thinking** *vt* **1** : pensar ⟨I thought to return early : pensaba regresar temprano⟩ **2** BELIEVE : pensar, creer, opinar **3** PONDER : pensar, reflexionar **4** CONCEIVE : ocurrirse, concebir ⟨we've thought up a plan : se nos ha ocurrido un plan⟩ —

vi **1** REASON : pensar, razonar **2** CONSIDER : pensar, considerar ⟨think of your family first : primero piensa en tu familia⟩

thinker ['θɪŋkər] *n* : pensador *m*, -dora *f*

thinly ['θɪnli] *adv* **1** LIGHTLY : ligeramente **2** SPARSELY : escasamente ⟨thinly populated : poco populado⟩ **3** BARELY : apenas

thinness ['θɪnnəs] *n* : delgadez *f*

thin–skinned ['θɪn'skɪnd] *adj* : susceptible, muy sensible

third¹ ['θərd] *or* **thirdly** [-li] *adv* : en tercer lugar ⟨she came in third : llegó en tercer lugar⟩

third² *adj* : tercero ⟨the third day : el tercer día⟩

third³ *n* **1** : tercero *m*, -ra *f* (en una serie) **2** : tercero *m*, tercera parte *f*

third world *n* **the Third World** : el Tercer Mundo *m*

thirst¹ ['θərst] *vi* **1** : tener sed **2 to thirst for** DESIRE : tener sed de, estar sediento de

thirst² *n* : sed *f*

thirsty ['θərsti] *adj* **thirstier; -est** : sediento, que tiene sed ⟨I'm thirsty : tengo sed⟩

thirteen¹ [ˌθər'ti:n] *adj* : trece

thirteen² *n* : trece *m*

thirteenth¹ [ˌθər'ti:nθ] *adj* : décimo tercero

thirteenth² *n* **1** : decimotercero *m*, -ra *f* (en una serie) **2** : treceavo *m*, treceava parte *f*

thirtieth¹ ['θərtiəθ] *adj* : trigésimo

thirtieth² *n* **1** : trigésimo *m*, -ma *f* (en una serie) **2** : treintavo *m*, treintava parte *f*

thirty¹ ['θərti] *adj* : treinta

thirty² *n, pl* **thirties** : treinta *m*

this¹ ['ðɪs] *adv* : así, a tal punto ⟨this big : así de grande⟩

this² *adj, pl* **these** ['ði:z] : este ⟨these things : estas cosas⟩ ⟨read this book : lee este libro⟩

this³ *pron, pl* **these** : esto ⟨what's this? : ¿qué es esto?⟩ ⟨this wasn't here yesterday : esto no estaba aquí ayer⟩

thistle ['θɪsəl] *n* : cardo *m*

thong ['θɔŋ] *n* **1** STRAP : correa *f*, tira *f* **2** FLIP-FLOP : chancla *f*, chancleta *f*

thorax ['θor,æks] *n, pl* **-raxes** *or* **-races** ['θorəˌsi:z] : tórax *m*

thorn ['θorn] *n* : espina *f*

thorny ['θorni] *adj* **thornier; -est** : espinoso

thorough ['θəro:] *adj* **1** CONSCIENTIOUS : concienzudo, meticuloso **2** COMPLETE : absoluto, completo — **thoroughly** *adv*

thoroughbred ['θəroˌbrɛd] *adj* : de pura sangre (dícese de un caballo)

Thoroughbred *n or* **Thoroughbred horse** : pura sangre *mf*

thoroughfare ['θoroˌfær] *n* : vía *f* pública, carretera *f*

thoroughness ['θəronəs] *n* : esmero *m*, meticulosidad *f*

those → that
thou ['ðaʊ] *pron* : tú
though¹ ['ðo:] *adv* 1 HOWEVER, NEV-
ERTHELESS : sin embargo, no obstante
2 as ~ : como si ⟨as though nothing
had happened : como si nada hubiera
pasado⟩
though² *conj* : aunque, a pesar de
⟨though it was raining, we went out
: salimos a pesar de la lluvia⟩
thought¹ → think
thought² ['θɔt] *n* 1 THINKING : pensamiento *m*, ideas *fpl* ⟨Western thought
: el pensamiento occidental⟩ 2 COGI-
TATION : pensamiento *m*, reflexión *f*,
raciocinio *m* 3 IDEA : idea *f*, ocurrencia *f* ⟨it was just a thought : fue sólo
una idea⟩
thoughtful ['θɔtfəl] *adj* 1 PENSIVE : pensativo, meditabundo 2 CONSIDERATE
: considerado, atento, cortés —
thoughtfully *adv*
thoughtfulness ['θɔtfəlnəs] *n* : consideración *f*, atención *f*, cortesía *f*
thoughtless ['θɔtləs] *adj* 1 CARELESS
: descuidado, negligente 2 INCONSID-
ERATE : desconsiderado — thought-
lessly *adv*
thousand¹ ['θaʊzənd] *adj* : mil
thousand² *n*, *pl* -sands *or* -sand : mil *m*
thousandth¹ ['θaʊzənθ] *adj* : milésimo
thousandth² *n* 1 : milésimo *m*, -ma *f* (en
una serie) 2 : milésimo *m*, milésima
parte *f*
thrash ['θræʃ] *vt* 1 → thresh 2 BEAT
: golpear, azotar, darle una paliza (a alguien) 3 FLAIL : sacudir, agitar bruscamente
thread¹ ['θrɛd] *vt* 1 : enhilar, enhebrar
(una aguja) 2 STRING : ensartar (cuentas en un hilo) 3 to thread one's way
: abrirse paso
thread² *n* 1 : hilo *m*, hebra *f* ⟨needle and
thread : aguja e hilo⟩ ⟨the thread of an
argument : el hilo de un debate⟩ 2
: rosca *f*, filete *m* (de un tornillo)
threadbare ['θrɛd'bær] *adj* 1 SHABBY,
WORN : raído, gastado 2 TRITE : trillado, tópico, manido
threat ['θrɛt] *n* : amenaza *f*
threaten ['θrɛtən] *v* : amenazar
threatening ['θrɛtənɪŋ] *adj* : amenazador — threateningly *adv*
three¹ ['θri:] *adj* : tres
three² *n* : tres *m*
3-D ['θri:'di:] *adj* → three–dimensional
three–dimensional ['θri:də'mɛntʃənəl]
adj : tridimensional
threefold ['θri:,fo:ld] *adj* TRIPLE : triple
three hundred¹ *adj* : trescientos
three hundred² *n* : trescientos *m*
threescore ['θri:'skor] *adj* SIXTY : sesenta
thresh ['θrɛʃ] *vt* : trillar (grano)
thresher ['θrɛʃər] *n* : trilladora *f*
threshold ['θrɛʃ,ho:ld, -,o:ld] *n* : umbral
m
threw → throw¹

thrice ['θraɪs] *adv* : tres veces
thrift ['θrɪft] *n* : economía *f*, frugalidad *f*
thriftless ['θrɪftləs] *adj* : despilfarrador,
manirroto
thrifty ['θrɪfti] *adj* thriftier; -est
: económico, frugal — thriftily
['θrɪftəli] *adv*
thrill¹ ['θrɪl] *vt* : emocionar — *vi* to thrill
to : dejarse conmover por, estreme-
cerse con
thrill² *n* : emoción *f*
thriller ['θrɪlər] *n* 1 : evento *m* emocionante 2 : obra *f* de suspenso
thrilling ['θrɪlɪŋ] *adj* : emocionante, excitante
thrive ['θraɪv] *vi* throve ['θro:v] *or*
thrived; thriven ['θrɪvən] 1 FLOURISH
: florecer, crecer abundantemente 2
PROSPER : prosperar
throat ['θro:t] *n* : garganta *f*
throaty ['θro:ti] *adj* throatier; -est : ronco (dícese de la voz)
throb¹ ['θrɑb] *vi* throbbed; throbbing
: palpitar, latir (dícese del corazón), vibrar (dícese de un motor, etc.)
throb² *n* : palpitación *f*, latido *m*, vibración *f*
throe ['θro:] *n* 1 PAIN, SPASM : espasmo
m, dolor *m* ⟨the throes of childbirth
: los dolores de parto⟩ 2 throes *npl*
: lucha *f* larga y ardua ⟨in the throes of
: en el medio de⟩
throne ['θro:n] *n* : trono *m*
throng¹ ['θrɔŋ] *vt* CROWD : atestar, atiborrar, llenar — *vi* : aglomerarse,
amontonarse
throng² *n* : muchedumbre *f*, gentío *m*,
multitud *f*
throttle¹ ['θrɑtəl] *vt* -tled; -tling 1
STRANGLE : estrangular, ahogar 2 to
throttle down : desacelerar (un motor)
throttle² *n* 1 : válvula *f* reguladora 2 at
full throttle : a toda máquina
through¹ ['θru:] *adv* 1 : a través, de un
lado a otro ⟨let them through : déjen-
los pasar⟩ 2 : de principio a fin ⟨she
read the book through : leyó el libro
de principio a fin⟩ 3 COMPLETELY
: completamente ⟨soaked through
: completamente empapado⟩
through² *adj* 1 DIRECT : directo ⟨a
through train : un tren directo⟩ 2 FIN-
ISHED : terminado, acabado ⟨we're
through : hemos terminado⟩
through³ *prep* 1 : a través de, por
⟨through the door : por la puerta⟩ ⟨a
road through the woods : un camino
que atraviesa el bosque⟩ 2 BETWEEN
: entre ⟨a path through the trees : un
sendero entre los árboles⟩ 3 BECAUSE
OF : a causa de, como consecuencia de
4 (*in expressions of time*) ⟨through the
night : durante la noche⟩ ⟨to go
through an experience : pasar por una
experiencia⟩ 5 : a, hasta ⟨from Monday through Friday : de lunes a
viernes⟩

throughout[1] [θru:ˈaʊt] *adv* **1** EVERY-
WHERE : por todas partes **2** THROUGH
: desde el principio hasta el fin de (algo)
throughout[2] *prep* **1** : en todas partes de,
a través de ⟨throughout the United
States : en todo Estados Unidos⟩ **2** : de
principio a fin de, durante ⟨through-
out the winter : durante todo el in-
vierno⟩
throve → **thrive**
throw[1] [ˈθro:] *vt* **threw** [ˈθru:]; **thrown**
[ˈθro:n]; **throwing** **1** TOSS : tirar, lanzar, echar, arrojar, aventar *Col, Mex*
⟨to throw a ball : tirar una pelota⟩ **2**
UNSEAT : desmontar (a un jinete) **3**
CAST : proyectar ⟨it threw a long shadow : proyectó una sombra larga⟩ **4 to
throw a party** : dar una fiesta **5 to
throw into confusion** : desconcertar **6
to throw out** DISCARD : botar, tirar (en
la basura)
throw[2] *n* TOSS : tiro *m*, tirada *f*, lanzamiento *m*, lance *m* (de dados)
thrower [ˈθro:ər] *n* : lanzador *m*, -dora *f*
throw up *v* VOMIT : vomitar, devolver
thrush [ˈθrʌʃ] *n* : tordo *m*, zorzal *m*
thrust[1] [ˈθrʌst] *vt* **thrust; thrusting** **1**
SHOVE : empujar bruscamente **2**
PLUNGE, STAB : apuñalar, clavar ⟨he
thrust a dagger into her heart : la
apuñaló en el corazón⟩ **3 to thrust
one's way** : abrirse paso **4 to thrust
upon** : imponer a
thrust[2] *n* **1** PUSH, SHOVE : empujón *m*,
empellón *m* **2** LUNGE : estocada *f* (en
esgrima) **3** IMPETUS : ímpetu *m*, impulso *m*, propulsión *f* (de un motor)
thud[1] [ˈθʌd] *vi* **thudded; thudding** : producir un ruido sordo
thud[2] *n* : ruido *m* sordo (que produce
un objeto al caer)
thug [ˈθʌg] *n* : matón *m*
thumb[1] [ˈθʌm] *vt* : hojear (con el pulgar)
thumb[2] *n* : pulgar *m*, dedo *m* pulgar
thumbnail [ˈθʌm,neɪl] *n* : uña *f* del pulgar
thumbtack [ˈθʌm,tæk] *n* : tachuela *f*,
chinche *f*
thump[1] [ˈθʌmp] *vt* POUND : golpear,
aporrear — *vi* : latir con vehemencia
(dícese del corazón)
thump[2] *n* THUD : ruido *m* sordo
thunder[1] [ˈθʌndər] *vi* **1** : tronar ⟨it
rained and thundered all night : llovió
y tronó durante la noche⟩ **2** BOOM : retumbar, bramar, resonar — *vt* ROAR,
SHOUT : decir a gritos, vociferar
thunder[2] *n* : truenos *mpl*
thunderbolt [ˈθʌndər,bo:lt] *n* : rayo *m*
thunderclap [ˈθʌndər,klæp] *n* : trueno
m
thunderous [ˈθʌndərəs] *adj* : atronador,
ensordecedor, estruendoso
thundershower [ˈθʌndər,ʃaʊər] *n* : lluvia *f* con truenos y relámpagos
thunderstorm [ˈθʌndər,stɔrm] *n* : tormenta *f* con truenos y relámpagos
thunderstruck [ˈθʌndər,strʌk] *adj*
: atónito

Thursday [ˈθərz,deɪ, -di] *n* : jueves *m*
thus [ˈðʌs] *adv* **1** : así, de esta manera **2**
SO : hasta (cierto punto) ⟨the weath-
er's been nice thus far : hasta ahora ha
hecho buen tiempo⟩ **3** HENCE : por
consiguiente, por lo tanto
thwart [ˈθwɔrt] *vt* : frustrar
thy [ˈðaɪ] *adj* : tu
thyme [ˈtaɪm, ˈθaɪm] *n* : tomillo *m*
thyroid [ˈθaɪ,rɔɪd] *n or* **thyroid gland**
: tiroides *mf*, glándula *f* tiroidea
thyself [ðaɪˈsɛlf] *pron* : ti, ti mismo
tiara [tiˈærə, -ˈɑr-] *n* : diadema *f*
Tibetan [təˈbɛtən] *n* **1** : tibetano *m*, -na
f **2** : tibetano *m* (idioma) — **Tibetan**
adj
tibia [ˈtɪbiə] *n, pl* -**iae** [-bi,i:] : tibia *f*
tic [ˈtɪk] *n* : tic *m*
tick[1] [ˈtɪk] *vi* **1** : hacer tictac **2** OPER-
ATE, RUN : operar, andar (dícese de un
mecanismo) ⟨what makes him tick?
: ¿qué es lo que lo mueve?⟩ — *vt or* **to
tick off** CHECK : marcar
tick[2] *n* **1** : tictac *m* (de un reloj) **2** CHECK
: marca *f* **3** : garrapata *f* (insecto)
ticket[1] [ˈtɪkət] *vt* LABEL : etiquetar
ticket[2] *n* **1** : boleto *m*, entrada *f* (de un
espectáculo), pasaje *m* (de avión, tren,
etc.) **2** SLATE : lista *f* de candidatos
tickle[1] [ˈtɪkəl] *v* -**led; -ling** *vt* **1** AMUSE
: divertir, hacerle gracia (a alguien) **2**
: hacerle cosquillas (a alguien) ⟨don't
tickle me! : ¡no me hagas cosquillas!⟩
— *vi* : picar
tickle[2] *n* : cosquilleo *m*, cosquillas *fpl*,
picor *m* (en la garganta)
ticklish [ˈtɪkəlɪʃ] *adj* **1** : cosquilloso
(dícese de una persona) **2** DELICATE,
TRICKY : delicado, peliagudo
tidal [ˈtaɪdəl] *adj* : de marea, relativo a
la marea
tidal wave *n* : maremoto *m*
tidbit [ˈtɪd,bɪt] *n* **1** BITE, SNACK : bocado *m*, golosina *f* **2** : dato *m* o noticia *f*
interesante ⟨useful tidbits of information : informaciones útiles⟩
tide[1] [ˈtaɪd] *vt* **tided; tiding** *or* **to tide over**
: proveer lo necesario para aguantar
una dificultad ⟨this money will tide you
over until you find work : este dinero
te mantendrá hasta que encuentres em-
pleo⟩
tide[2] *n* **1** : marea *f* **2** CURRENT : corriente *f* (de eventos, opiniones, etc.)
tidily [ˈtaɪdəli] *adv* : ordenadamente
tidiness [ˈtaɪdinəs] *n* : aseo *m*, limpieza
f, orden *m*
tidings [ˈtaɪdɪŋz] *npl* : nuevas *fpl*
tidy[1] [ˈtaɪdi] *vt* -**died; -dying** : asear,
limpiar, poner en orden
tidy[2] *adj* -**dier; -est** **1** CLEAN, NEAT
: limpio, aseado, en orden **2** SUBSTAN-
TIAL : grande, considerable ⟨a tidy sum
: una suma considerable⟩
tie[1] [ˈtaɪ] *v* **tied; tying** *or* **tieing** *vt* **1** : atar,
amarrar ⟨to tie a knot : atar un nudo⟩
⟨to tie one's shoelaces : atarse los cor-
dones⟩ **2** BIND, UNITE : ligar, atar **3**
: empatar ⟨they tied the score : em-

pataron el marcador⟩ — *vi* : empatar
⟨the two teams were tied : los dos
equipos empataron⟩
tie² *n* **1** : ligadura *f*, cuerda *f*, cordón *m*
(para atar algo) **2** BOND, LINK : atadu-
ra *f*, ligadura *f*, vínculo *m*, lazo *m* ⟨fam-
ily ties : lazos familiares⟩ **3** *or* **railroad
tie** : traviesa *f* **4** DRAW : empate *m* (en
deportes) **5** NECKTIE : corbata *f*
tier ['tɪr] *n* : hilera *f*, escalón *m*
tiff ['tɪf] *n* : disgusto *m*, disputa *f*
tiger ['taɪɡər] *n* : tigre *m*
tight¹ ['taɪt] *adv* TIGHTLY : bien, fuerte
⟨shut it tight : ciérralo bien⟩
tight² *adj* **1** : bien cerrado, hermético ⟨a
tight seal : un cierre hermético⟩ **2**
STRICT : estricto, severo **3** TAUT
: tirante, tenso **4** SNUG : apretado, ajustado, ceñido ⟨a tight dress : un vestido
ceñido⟩ **5** DIFFICULT : difícil ⟨to be in
a tight spot : estar en un aprieto⟩ **6**
STINGY : apretado, avaro, agarrado
fam **7** CLOSE : reñido ⟨a tight game
: un juego reñido⟩ **8** SCARCE : escaso
⟨money is tight : escasea el dinero⟩
tighten ['taɪtən] *vt* : tensar (una cuerda,
etc.), apretar (un nudo, un tornillo,
etc.), apretarse (el cinturón), reforzar
(las reglas)
tightly ['taɪtli] *adv* : bien, fuerte
tightness ['taɪtnəs] *n* : lo apretado, lo
tenso, tensión *f*
tightrope ['taɪt,ro:p] *n* : cuerda *f* floja
tights ['taɪts] *npl* : leotardo *m*, malla *f*
tightwad ['taɪt,wɑd] *n* : avaro *m*, -ra *f*;
tacaño *m*, -ña *f*
tigress ['taɪɡrəs] *n* : tigresa *f*
tile¹ ['taɪl] *vt* **tiled; tiling** : embaldosar
(un piso), revestir de azulejos (una
pared), tejar (un techo)
tile² *n* **1** *or* **floor tile** : losa *f*, baldosa *f*,
mosaico *m Mex* (de un piso) **2** : azule-
jo *m* (de una pared) **3** : teja *f* (de un
techo)
till¹ ['tɪl] *vt* : cultivar, labrar
till² *n* : caja *f*, caja *f* registradora
till³ *prep & conj* → **until**
tiller ['tɪlər] *n* **1** : cultivador *m*, -dora *f*
(de la tierra) **2** : caña *f* del timón (de
un barco)
tilt¹ ['tɪlt] *vt* : ladear, inclinar — *vi*
: ladearse, inclinarse
tilt² *n* **1** SLANT : inclinación *f* **2** **at full
tilt** : a toda velocidad
timber ['tɪmbər] *n* **1** : madera *f* (para
construcción) **2** BEAM : viga *f*
timberland ['tɪmbər,lænd] *n* : bosque *m*
maderero
timbre ['tæmbər, 'tɪm-] *n* : timbre *m*
time¹ ['taɪm] *vt* **timed; timing 1** SCHED-
ULE : fijar la hora de, calcular el momento oportuno para **2** CLOCK
: cronometrar, medir el tiempo de (una
competencia, etc.)
time² *n* **1** : tiempo *m* ⟨the passing of time
: el paso del tiempo⟩ ⟨she doesn't have
time : no tiene tiempo⟩ **2** MOMENT
: tiempo *m*, momento *m* ⟨this is not the
time to bring it up : no es el momento

de sacar el tema⟩ **3** : vez *f* ⟨she called
you three times : te llamó tres veces⟩
⟨three times greater : tres veces may-
or⟩ **4** AGE : tiempo *m*, era *f* ⟨in your
grandparents' time : en el tiempo de tus
abuelos⟩ **5** TEMPO : tiempo *m*, ritmo
m (en música) **6** : hora *f* ⟨what time is
it? : ¿qué hora es?⟩ ⟨it's time for dinner : es hora de comer⟩ ⟨at the usual
time : a la hora acostumbrada⟩ ⟨to
keep time : ir a la hora⟩ ⟨to lose time
: atrasar⟩ **7** EXPERIENCE : rato *m*, experiencia *f* ⟨we had a nice time together
: pasamos juntos un rato agradable⟩
⟨to have a rough time : pasarlo mal⟩
⟨have a good time! : ¡que se diviertan!⟩
8 at times SOMETIMES : a veces **9 for
the time being** : por el momento, de
momento **10 from time to time** OCCA-
SIONALLY : de vez en cuando **11 in
time** PUNCTUALLY : a tiempo **12 in
time** EVENTUALLY : con el tiempo **13
time after time** : una y otra vez
timekeeper ['taɪm,ki:pər] *n* : cronometrador *m*, -dora *f*
timeless ['taɪmləs] *adj* : eterno
timely ['taɪmli] *adj* **-lier; -est** : oportuno
timepiece ['taɪm,pi:s] *n* : reloj *m*
timer ['taɪmər] *n* : temporizador *m*,
cronómetro *m*
times ['taɪmz] *prep* : por ⟨3 times 4 is 12
: 3 por 4 son 12⟩
timetable ['taɪm,teɪbəl] *n* : horario *m*
timid ['tɪmɪd] *adj* : tímido — **timidly** *adv*
timidity [tə'mɪdəti] *n* : timidez *f*
timorous ['tɪmərəs] *adj* : timorato,
miedoso
timpani ['tɪmpəni] *npl* : timbales *mpl*
tin ['tɪn] *n* **1** : estaño *m*, hojalata *f* (metal) **2** CAN : lata *f*, bote *m*, envase *m*
tincture ['tɪŋktʃər] *n* : tintura *f*
tinder ['tɪndər] *n* : yesca *f*
tine ['taɪn] *n* : diente *m* (de un tenedor,
etc.)
tinfoil ['tɪn,fɔɪl] *n* : papel *m* (de) aluminio
tinge¹ ['tɪndʒ] *vt* **tinged; tingeing** *or*
tinging ['tɪndʒɪŋ] TINT : matizar, teñir
ligeramente
tinge² *n* **1** TINT : matiz *m*, tinte *m* sutil
2 TOUCH : dejo *m*, sensación *f* ligera
tingle¹ ['tɪŋɡəl] *vi* **-gled; -gling** : sentir
(un) hormigueo, sentir (un) cosquilleo
tingle² *n* : hormigueo *m*, cosquilleo *m*
tinker ['tɪŋkər] *vi* **to tinker with** : arreglar
con pequeños ajustes, toquetear (con
intento de arreglar)
tinkle¹ ['tɪŋkəl] *vi* **-kled; -kling** : tintinear
tinkle² *n* : tintineo *m*
tinsel ['tɪntsəl] *n* : oropel *m*
tint¹ ['tɪnt] *vt* : teñir, colorear
tint² *n* : tinte *m*
tiny ['taɪni] *adj* **-nier; -est** : diminuto,
minúsculo
tip¹ ['tɪp] *v* **tipped; tipping** *vt* **1** *or* **to tip
over** : volcar, voltear, hacer caer **2** TILT
: ladear, inclinar ⟨to tip one's hat
: saludar con el sombrero⟩ **3** TAP : to-

car, golpear ligeramente **4** : darle una propina (a un mesero, etc.) ⟨I tipped him $5 : le di $5 de propina⟩ **5** : adornar o cubrir la punta de ⟨wings tipped in red : alas que tienen las puntas rojas⟩ **6 to tip off** : dar información a — *vi* TILT : ladearse, inclinarse

tip² *n* **1** END, POINT : punta *f*, extremo *m* ⟨on the tip of one's tongue : en la punta de la lengua⟩ **2** GRATUITY : propina *f* **3** ADVICE, INFORMATION : consejo *m*, información *f* (confidencial)

tip–off [ˈtɪpˌɔf] *n* **1** SIGN : indicación *f*, señal *f* **2** TIP : información *f* (confidencial)

tipple [ˈtɪpəl] *vi* **-pled; -pling** : tomarse unas copas

tipsy [ˈtɪpsi] *adj* **-sier; -est** : achispado

tiptoe¹ [ˈtɪpˌtoː] *vi* **-toed; -toeing** : caminar de puntillas

tiptoe² *adv* : de puntillas

tiptoe³ *n* : punta *f* del pie

tip–top¹ [ˈtɪpˈtɑp, -ˌtɑp] *adj* EXCELLENT : excelente

tip–top² *n* SUMMIT : cumbre *f*, cima *f*

tirade [ˈtaɪˌreɪd] *n* : diatriba *f*

tire¹ [ˈtaɪr] *v* **tired; tiring** *vt* : cansar, agotar, fatigar — *vi* : cansarse

tire² *n* : llanta *f*, neumático *m*, goma *f*

tired [ˈtaɪrd] *adj* : cansado, agotado, fatigado ⟨to get tired : cansarse⟩

tireless [ˈtaɪrləs] *adj* : incansable, infatigable — **tirelessly** *adv*

tiresome [ˈtaɪrsəm] *adj* : fastidioso, pesado, tedioso — **tiresomely** *adv*

tissue [ˈtɪˌʃuː] *n* **1** : pañuelo *m* de papel **2** : tejido *m* ⟨lung tissue : tejido pulmonar⟩

titanic [taɪˈtænɪk, tə-] *adj* GIGANTIC : titánico, gigantesco

titanium [taɪˈteɪniəm, tə-] *n* : titanio *m*

titillate [ˈtɪtəlˌeɪt] *vt* **-lated; -lating** : excitar, estimular placenteramente

title¹ [ˈtaɪtəl] *vt* **-tled; -tling** : titular, intitular

title² *n* : título *m*

titter¹ [ˈtɪtər] *vi* GIGGLE : reírse tontamente

titter² *n* : risita *f*, risa *f* tonta

tizzy [ˈtɪzi] *n, pl* **tizzies** : estado *m* agitado o nervioso ⟨I'm all in a tizzy : estoy todo alterado⟩

TNT [ˌtiːˌɛnˈtiː] *n* : TNT *m*

to¹ [ˈtuː] *adv* **1** : a un estado consciente ⟨to come to : volver en sí⟩ **2 to and fro** : de aquí para allá, de un lado para otro

to² *prep* **1** (*indicating a place*) : a ⟨to go to the doctor : ir al médico⟩ ⟨I'm going to John's : voy a la casa de John⟩ **2** TOWARD : a, hacia ⟨two miles to the south : dos millas hacia el sur⟩ **3** ON : en, sobre ⟨apply salve to the wound : póngale ungüento a la herida⟩ **4** UP TO : hasta, a ⟨to a degree : hasta cierto grado⟩ ⟨from head to toe : de pies a cabeza⟩ **5** (*in expressions of time*) ⟨it's quarter to seven : son las siete menos

cuarto⟩ **6** UNTIL : a, hasta ⟨from May to December : de mayo a diciembre⟩ **7** (*indicating belonging or possession*) : de, a ⟨the key to the lock : la llave del candado⟩ **8** (*indicating response*) : a ⟨dancing to the rhythm : bailando al compás⟩ **9** (*indicating comparison or proportion*) : a ⟨it's similar to mine : es parecido al mío⟩ ⟨they won 4 to 2 : ganaron 4 a 2⟩ **10** (*indicating agreement or conformity*) : a, de acuerdo con ⟨made to order : hecho a la orden⟩ ⟨to my knowledge : a mi saber⟩ **11** (*indicating inclusion*) : en cada, por ⟨twenty to the box : veinte por caja⟩ **12** (*used to form the infinitive*) ⟨to understand : entender⟩ ⟨to go away : irse⟩

toad [ˈtoːd] *n* : sapo *m*

toadstool [ˈtoːdˌstuːl] *n* : hongo *m* (no comestible)

toady [ˈtoːdi] *n, pl* **toadies** : adulador *m*, -dora *f*

toast¹ [ˈtoːst] *vt* **1** : tostar (pan) **2** : brindar por ⟨to toast the victors : brindar por los vencedores⟩ **3** WARM : calentar ⟨to toast oneself : calentarse⟩

toast² *n* **1** : pan *m* tostado, tostadas *fpl* **2** : brindis *m* ⟨to propose a toast : proponer un brindis⟩

toaster [ˈtoːstər] *n* : tostador *m*

tobacco [təˈbækoː] *n, pl* **-cos** : tabaco *m*

toboggan¹ [təˈbɑgən] *vi* : deslizarse en tobogán

toboggan² *n* : tobogán *m*

today¹ [təˈdeɪ] *adv* **1** : hoy ⟨she arrives today : hoy llega⟩ **2** NOWADAYS : hoy en día

today² *n* : hoy *m* ⟨today is a holiday : hoy es día de fiesta⟩

toddle [ˈtɑdəl] *vi* **-dled; -dling** : hacer pininos, hacer pinitos

toddler [ˈtɑdələr] *n* : niño *m* pequeño, niña *f* pequeña (que comienza a caminar)

to–do [təˈduː] *n, pl* **to–dos** [-ˈduːz] FUSS : lío *m*, alboroto *m*

toe [ˈtoː] *n* : dedo *m* del pie

toenail [ˈtoːˌneɪl] *n* : uña *f* del pie

toffee *or* **toffy** [ˈtɔfi, ˈtɑ-] *n, pl* **toffees** *or* **toffies** : caramelo *m* elaborado con azúcar y mantequilla

toga [ˈtoːgə] *n* : toga *f*

together [təˈgɛðər] *adv* : juntamente, juntos (el uno con el otro) ⟨Susan and Sarah work together : Susan y Sarah trabajan juntas⟩ **2 ~ with** : junto con

togetherness [təˈgɛðərnəs] *n* : unión *f*, compañerismo *m*

togs [ˈtɑgz, ˈtɔgz] *npl* : ropa *f*

toil¹ [ˈtɔɪl] *vi* : trabajar arduamente

toil² *n* : trabajo *m* arduo

toilet [ˈtɔɪlət] *n* **1** : arreglo *m* personal **2** BATHROOM : (cuarto de) baño *m*, servicios *mpl* (públicos), sanitario *m* Col, Mex, Ven **3** : inodoro *m* ⟨to flush the toilet : jalar la cadena⟩

toilet paper *n* : papel *m* higiénico

toiletries [ˈtɔɪlətriz] *npl* : artículos *mpl* de tocador

token ['to:kən] *n* **1** PROOF, SIGN : prueba *f*, muestra *f*, señal *m* **2** SYMBOL : símbolo *m* **3** SOUVENIR : recuerdo *m* **4** : ficha *f* (para transporte público, etc.)
told → **tell**
tolerable ['talərəbəl] *adj* : tolerable — **tolerably** [-bli] *adv*
tolerance ['talərənts] *n* : tolerancia *f*
tolerant ['talərənt] *adj* : tolerante — **tolerantly** *adv*
tolerate ['talə,reɪt] *vt* -**ated; -ating 1** ACCEPT : tolerar, aceptar **2** BEAR, ENDURE : tolerar, aguantar, soportar
toleration [,talə'reɪʃən] *n* : tolerancia *f*
toll[1] ['to:l] *vt* : tañer, sonar (una campana) — *vi* : sonar, doblar (dícese de las campanas)
toll[2] *n* **1** : peaje *m* (de una carretera, un puente, etc.) **2** CASUALTIES : pérdida *f*, número *m* de víctimas **3** TOLLING : tañido *m* (de campanas)
tollbooth ['to:l,bu:θ] *n* : caseta *f* de peaje
tollgate ['to:l,geɪt] *n* : barrera *f* de peaje
tomahawk ['tamə,hɔk] *n* : hacha *f* de guerra (de los indígenas norteamericanos)
tomato [tə'meɪt̬o, -'ma-] *n, pl* -**toes** : tomate *m*
tomb ['tu:m] *n* : sepulcro *m*, tumba *f*
tomboy ['tam,bɔɪ] *n* : marimacho *mf*; niña *f* que se porta como muchacho
tombstone ['tu:m,sto:n] *n* : lápida *f*
tomcat ['tam,kæt] *n* : gato *m* (macho)
tome ['to:m] *n* : tomo *m*
tomorrow[1] [tə'maro] *adv* : mañana
tomorrow[2] *n* : mañana *m*
tom–tom ['tam,tam] *n* : tam-tam *m*
ton ['tən] *n* : tonelada *f*
tone[1] ['to:n] *vt* **toned; toning 1** *or* to **tone down** : atenuar, suavizar, moderar **2** *or* to **tone up** STRENGTHEN : tonificar, vigorizar
tone[2] *n* : tono *m* ⟨in a friendly tone : en tono amistoso⟩ ⟨a greyish tone : un tono grisáceo⟩
tongs ['taŋz, 'tɔŋz] *npl* : tenazas *fpl*
tongue ['tʌŋ] *n* **1** : lengua *f* **2** LANGUAGE : lengua *f*, idioma *m*
tongue–tied ['tʌŋ,taɪd] *adj* **to get tongue–tied** : trabársele la lengua a uno
tonic[1] ['tanɪk] *adj* : tónico
tonic[2] *n* **1** : tónico *m* **2** *or* **tonic water** : tónica *f*
tonight[1] [tə'naɪt] *adv* : esta noche
tonight[2] *n* : esta noche *f*
tonsil ['tantsəl] *n* : amígdala *f*, angina *f* Mex
tonsillitis [,tantsə'laɪt̬əs] *n* : amigdalitis *f*, anginas *fpl* Mex
too ['tu:] *adv* **1** ALSO : también **2** EXCESSIVELY : demasiado ⟨it's too hot in here : aquí hace demasiado calor⟩
took → **take**[1]
tool[1] ['tu:l] *vt* **1** : fabricar, confeccionar (con herramientas) **2** EQUIP : instalar maquinaria en (una fábrica)

tool[2] *n* : herramienta *f*
toolbox ['tu:l,baks] *n* : caja *f* de herramientas
toot[1] ['tu:t] *vt* : sonar (un claxon o un pito)
toot[2] *n* : pitido *m*, bocinazo *m* (de un claxon)
tooth ['tu:θ] *n, pl* **teeth** ['ti:θ] : diente *m*
toothache ['tu:θ,eɪk] *n* : dolor *m* de muelas
toothbrush ['tu:θ,brʌʃ] *n* : cepillo *m* de dientes
toothless ['tu:θləs] *adj* : desdentado
toothpaste ['tu:θ,peɪst] *n* : pasta *f* de dientes, crema *f* dental, dentífrico *m*
toothpick ['tu:θ,pɪk] *n* : palillo *m* (de dientes), mondadientes *m*
top[1] ['tap] *vt* **topped; topping 1** COVER : cubrir, coronar **2** SURPASS : sobrepasar, superar **3** CLEAR : pasar por encima de
top[2] *adj* : superior ⟨the top shelf : la repisa superior⟩ ⟨one of the top lawyers : uno de los mejores abogados⟩
top[3] *n* **1** : parte *f* superior, cumbre *f*, cima *f* (de un monte, etc.) ⟨to climb to the top : subir a la cumbre⟩ **2** COVER : tapa *f*, cubierta *f* **3** : trompo *m* (juguete) **4 on top of** : encima de
topaz ['to:,pæz] *n* : topacio *m*
topcoat ['tap,ko:t] *n* : sobretodo *m*, abrigo *m*
topic ['tapɪk] *n* : tema *m*, tópico *m*
topical ['tapɪkəl] *adj* : de interés actual
topmost ['tap,mo:st] *adj* : más alto
top–notch ['tap'natʃ] *adj* : de lo mejor, de primera categoría
topographic [,tapə'græfɪk] *or* **topographical** [-fɪkəl] *adj* : topográfico
topography [tə'pagrəfi] *n, pl* -**phies** : topografía *f*
topple ['tapəl] *v* -**pled; -pling** *vi* : caerse, venirse abajo — *vt* : volcar, derrocar (un gobierno, etc.)
topsoil ['tap,sɔɪl] *n* : capa *f* superior del suelo
topsy–turvy [,tapsi'tərvi] *adv* & *adj* : patas arriba, al revés
torch ['tɔrtʃ] *n* : antorcha *f*
tore → **tear**[1]
torment[1] [tɔr'mɛnt, 'tɔr,-] *vt* : atormentar, torturar, martirizar
torment[2] ['tɔr,mɛnt] *n* : tormento *m*, suplicio *m*, martirio *m*
tormentor [tɔr'mɛntər] *n* : atormentador *m*, -dora *f*
torn *pp* → **tear**[1]
tornado [tɔr'neɪdo] *n, pl* -**does** *or* -**dos** : tornado *m*
torpedo[1] [tɔr'pi:do] *vt* : torpedear
torpedo[2] *n, pl* -**does** : torpedo *m*
torpid ['tɔrpɪd] *adj* **1** SLUGGISH : aletargado **2** APATHETIC : apático
torpor ['tɔrpər] *n* : letargo *m*, apatía *f*
torrent ['tɔrənt] *n* : torrente *m*
torrential [tə'rɛntʃəl, tɔ-] *adj* : torrencial
torrid ['tɔrɪd] *adj* : tórrido
torso ['tɔr,so:] *n, pl* -**sos** *or* -**si** [-,si:] : torso *m*

tortilla [tɔr'tiːjə] *n* : tortilla *f* (de maíz)
tortoise ['tɔrtəs] *n* : tortuga *f* (terrestre)
tortoiseshell ['tɔrtəs,ʃɛl] *n* : carey *m*, concha *f*
tortuous ['tɔrtʃʊəs] *adj* : tortuoso
torture[1] ['tɔrtʃər] *vt* **-tured; -turing** : torturar, atormentar
torture[2] *n* : tortura *f*, tormento *m* ⟨it was sheer torture! : ¡fue un verdadero suplicio!⟩
torturer ['tɔrtʃərər] *n* : torturador *m*, -dora *f*
toss[1] ['tɔs, 'tɑs] *vt* **1** AGITATE, SHAKE : sacudir, agitar, mezclar (una ensalada) **2** THROW : tirar, echar, lanzar — *vi* : sacudirse, moverse agitadamente ⟨to toss and turn : dar vueltas⟩
toss[2] *n* THROW : lanzamiento *m*, tiro *m*, tirada *f*, lance *m* (de dados, etc.)
toss–up ['tɔs,ʌp] *n* : posibilidad *f* igual ⟨it's a toss-up : quizá sí, quizá no⟩
tot ['tɑt] *n* : pequeño *m*, -ña *f*
total[1] ['toːtəl] *vt* **-taled** *or* **-talled; -taling** *or* **-talling 1** *or* **to total up** ADD : sumar, totalizar **2** AMOUNT TO : ascender a, llegar a
total[2] *adj* : total, completo, absoluto — **totally** *adv*
total[3] *n* : total *m*
totalitarian [toː,tælə'tɛriən] *adj* : totalitario
totalitarianism [toː,tælə'tɛriə,nizəm] *n* : totalitarismo *m*
totality [toː'tæləti] *n, pl* **-ties** : totalidad *f*
tote ['toːt] *vt* **toted; toting** : cargar, llevar
totem ['toːtəm] *n* : tótem *m*
totter ['tɑtər] *vi* : tambalearse
touch[1] ['tʌtʃ] *vt* **1** FEEL, HANDLE : tocar, tentar **2** AFFECT, MOVE : conmover, afectar, tocar ⟨his gesture touched our hearts : su gesto nos tocó el corazón⟩ — *vi* : tocarse
touch[2] *n* **1** : tacto *m* (sentido) **2** DETAIL : toque *m*, detalle *m* ⟨a touch of color : un toque de color⟩ **3** BIT : pizca *f*, gota *f*, poco *m* **4** ABILITY : habilidad *f* ⟨to lose one's touch : perder la habilidad⟩ **5** CONTACT : contacto *m*, comunicación *f* ⟨to keep in touch : mantenerse en contacto⟩
touchdown ['tʌtʃ,daʊn] *n* : touchdown *m* (en futbol americano)
touching ['tʌtʃɪŋ] *adj* MOVING : conmovedor
touchstone ['tʌtʃ,stoːn] *n* : piedra *f* de toque
touch up *vt* : retocar
touchy ['tʌtʃi] *adj* **touchier; -est 1** : sensible, susceptible (dícese de una persona) **2** : delicado ⟨a touchy subject : un tema delicado⟩
tough[1] ['tʌf] *adj* **1** STRONG : fuerte, resistente (dícese de materiales) **2** LEATHERY : correoso ⟨a tough steak : un bistec duro⟩ **3** HARDY : fuerte, robusto (dícese de una persona) **4** STRICT

: severo, exigente **5** DIFFICULT : difícil **6** STUBBORN : terco, obstinado
tough[2] *n* : matón *m*, persona *f* ruda y brusca
toughen ['tʌfən] *vt* : fortalecer, endurecer — *vi* : endurecerse, hacerse más fuerte
toughness ['tʌfnəs] *n* : dureza *f*
toupee [tuː'peɪ] *n* : peluquín *m*, bisoñé *m*
tour[1] ['tʊr] *vi* : tomar una excursión, viajar — *vt* : recorrer, hacer una gira por
tour[2] *n* **1** : gira *f*, tour *m*, excursión *f* **2**
tour of duty : período *m* de servicio
tourism ['tʊr,izəm] *n* : turismo *m*
tourist ['tʊrɪst, 'tər-] *n* : turista *mf*
tournament ['tʊrnəmənt, 'tər-] *n* : torneo *m*
tourniquet ['tərnɪkət, 'tʊr-] *n* : torniquete *m*
tousle ['taʊzəl] *vt* **-sled; -sling** : desarreglar, despeinar (el cabello)
tout ['taʊt] *vt* : promocionar, elogiar (con exageración)
tow[1] ['toː] *vt* : remolcar
tow[2] *n* : remolque *m*
toward ['tord, tə'word] *or* **towards** ['tordz, tə'wordz] *prep* **1** (indicating direction) : hacia, rumbo a ⟨heading toward town : dirigiéndose rumbo al pueblo⟩ ⟨efforts towards peace : esfuerzos hacia la paz⟩ **2** (indicating time) : alrededor de ⟨toward midnight : alrededor de la medianoche⟩ **3** REGARDING : hacia, con respecto a ⟨his attitude toward life : su actitud hacia la vida⟩ **4** FOR : para, como pago parcial de (una compra o deuda)
towel ['taʊəl] *n* : toalla *f*
tower[1] ['taʊər] *vi* **to tower over** : descollar sobre, elevarse sobre, dominar
tower[2] *n* : torre *f*
towering ['taʊərɪŋ] *adj* : altísimo, imponente
town ['taʊn] *n* : pueblo *m*, ciudad *f* (pequeña)
township ['taʊn,ʃɪp] *n* : municipio *m*
tow truck ['toː,trʌk] *n* : grúa *f*
toxic ['tɑksɪk] *adj* : tóxico
toxicity [tɑk'sɪsəti] *n, pl* **-ties** : toxicidad *f*
toxin ['tɑksɪn] *n* : toxina *f*
toy[1] ['tɔɪ] *vi* : juguetear, jugar
toy[2] *adj* : de juguete ⟨a toy rifle : un rifle de juguete⟩
toy[3] *n* : juguete *m*
trace[1] ['treɪs] *vt* **traced; tracing 1** : calcar (un dibujo, etc.) **2** OUTLINE : delinear, trazar (planes, etc.) **3** TRACK : describir (un curso, una historia) **4** FIND : localizar, ubicar
trace[2] *n* **1** SIGN, TRACK : huella *f*, rastro *m*, indicio *m*, vestigio *m* ⟨he disappeared without a trace : desapareció sin dejar rastro⟩ **2** BIT, HINT : pizca *f*, ápice *m*, dejo *m*
trachea ['treɪkiə] *n, pl* **-cheae** [-ki,iː] : tráquea *f*

tracing paper *n* : papel *m* de calcar

track¹ ['træk] *vt* **1** TRAIL : seguir la pista de, rastrear **2** : dejar huellas de ⟨he tracked mud all over : dejó huellas de lodo por todas partes⟩

track² *n* **1** : rastro *m*, huella *f* (de animales), pista *f* (de personas) **2** PATH : pista *f*, sendero *m*, camino *m* **3** *or* **railroad track** : vía *f* (férrea) **4** → **racetrack** **5** : oruga *f* (de un tanque, etc.) **6** : pista *f* (deporte) **7 to keep track of** : llevar la cuenta de

track–and–field ['trækənd'fiːld] *adj* : de pista y campo

tract ['trækt] *n* **1** AREA : terreno *m*, extensión *f*, área *f* **2** : tracto *m* ⟨digestive tract : tracto digestivo⟩ **3** PAMPHLET : panfleto *m*, folleto *m*

traction ['trækʃən] *n* : tracción *f*

tractor ['træktər] *n* **1** : tractor *m* (vehículo agrícola) **2** TRUCK : camión *m* (con remolque)

trade¹ ['treɪd] *v* **traded; trading** *vi* : comerciar, negociar — *vt* EXCHANGE : intercambiar, canjear

trade² *n* **1** OCCUPATION : oficio *m*, profesión *f*, ocupación *f* ⟨a carpenter by trade : carpintero de oficio⟩ **2** COMMERCE : comercio *m*, industria *f* ⟨free trade : libre comercio⟩ ⟨the book trade : la industria del libro⟩ **3** EXCHANGE : intercambio *m*, canje *m*

trade–in ['treɪd,ɪn] *n* : artículo *m* que se canjea por otro

trademark ['treɪd,mɑrk] *n* **1** : marca *f* registrada **2** CHARACTERISTIC : sello *m* característico (de un grupo, una persona, etc.)

trader ['treɪdər] *n* : negociante *mf*, tratante *mf*, comerciante *mf*

tradesman ['treɪdzmən] *n, pl* **-men** [-mən, -,mɛn] **1** CRAFTSMAN : artesano *m*, -na *f* **2** SHOPKEEPER : tendero *m*, -ra *f*; comerciante *mf*

trade wind *n* : viento *m* alisio

tradition [trə'dɪʃən] *n* : tradición *f*

traditional [trə'dɪʃənəl] *adj* : tradicional — **traditionally** *adv*

traffic¹ ['træfɪk] *vi* **trafficked; trafficking** : traficar (con)

traffic² *n* **1** COMMERCE : tráfico *m*, comercio *m* ⟨the drug traffic : el narcotráfico⟩ **2** : tráfico *m*, tránsito *m*, circulación *f* (de vehículos, etc.)

traffic circle *n* : rotonda *f*, glorieta *f*

trafficker ['træfɪkər] *n* : traficante *mf*

traffic light *n* : semáforo *m*, luz *f* (de tránsito)

tragedy ['trædʒədi] *n, pl* **-dies** : tragedia *f*

tragic ['trædʒɪk] *adj* : trágico — **tragically** *adv*

trail¹ ['treɪl] *vi* **1** DRAG : arrastrarse **2** LAG : quedarse atrás, retrasarse **3 to trail away** *or* **to trail off** : disminuir, menguar, desvanecerse — *vt* **1** DRAG : arrastrar **2** PURSUE : perseguir, seguir la pista de

trail² *n* **1** TRACK : rastro *m*, huella *f*, pista *f* ⟨a trail of blood : un rastro de sangre⟩ **2** : cola *f*, estela *f* (de un meteoro) **3** PATH : sendero *m*, camino *m*, vereda *f*

trailer ['treɪlər] *n* **1** : remolque *m*, tráiler *m* (de un camión) **2** : caravana *f* (vivienda ambulante)

train¹ ['treɪn] *vt* **1** : adiestrar, entrenar (atletas), capacitar (trabajadores), amaestrar (animales) **2** POINT : apuntar (un arma, etc.) — *vi* : entrenar(se) (físicamente), prepararse (profesionalmente) ⟨she's training at the gym : se está entrenando en el gimnasio⟩

train² *n* **1** : cola *f* (de un vestido) **2** RETINUE : cortejo *m*, séquito *m* **3** SERIES : serie *f* (de eventos) **4** : tren *m* ⟨passenger train : tren de pasajeros⟩

trainee [treɪ'niː] *n* : aprendiz *m*, -diza *f*

trainer ['treɪnər] *n* : entrenador *m*, -dora *f*

training ['treɪnɪŋ] *n* : adiestramiento *m*, entrenamiento *m* (físico), capacitación *f* (de trabajadores)

traipse ['treɪps] *vi* **traipsed; traipsing** : andar de un lado para otro, vagar

trait ['treɪt] *n* : rasgo *m*, característica *f*

traitor ['treɪtər] *n* : traidor *m*, -dora *f*

traitorous ['treɪtərəs] *adj* : traidor

trajectory [trə'dʒɛktəri] *n, pl* **-ries** : trayectoria *f*

tramp¹ ['træmp] *vi* : caminar (a paso pesado) — *vt* : deambular por, vagar por ⟨to tramp the streets : vagar por las calles⟩

tramp² *n* **1** VAGRANT : vagabundo *m*, -da *f* **2** HIKE : caminata *f*

trample ['træmpəl] *vt* **-pled; -pling** : pisotear, hollar

trampoline [,træmpə'liːn, 'træmpə,-] *n* : trampolín *m*, cama *f* elástica

trance ['trænts] *n* : trance *m*

tranquil ['træŋkwəl] *adj* : calmo, tranquilo, sereno — **tranquilly** *adv*

tranquilize ['træŋkwə,laɪz] *vt* **-ized; -izing** : tranquilizar

tranquilizer ['træŋkwə,laɪzər] *n* : tranquilizante *m*

tranquillity *or* **tranquility** [træŋ'kwɪləti] *n* : sosiego *m*, tranquilidad *f*

transact [træn'zækt] *vt* : negociar, gestionar, hacer (negocios)

transaction [træn'zækʃən] *n* **1** : transacción *f*, negocio *m*, operación *f* **2 transactions** *npl* RECORDS : actas *fpl*

transatlantic [,trænts ət'læntɪk, ,trænz-] *adj* : transatlántico

transcend [træn'sɛnd] *vt* : trascender, sobrepasar

transcendent [træn'sɛndənt] *adj* : trascendente — **transcendence** [træn'sɛndənts] *n*

transcendental [,trænt,sɛn'dɛntəl, -sən-] *adj* : trascendental ⟨transcendental meditation : meditación trascendental⟩

transcribe [træn'skraɪb] *vt* **-scribed; -scribing** : transcribir

transcript ['træn͵skrɪpt] *n* : copia *f* oficial

transcription [træn'skrɪpʃən] *n* : transcripción *f*

transfer¹ [træn*ts*'fər, 'træn*ts*͵fər] *v* **-ferred; -ferring** *vt* **1** : trasladar (a una persona), transferir (fondos) **2** : transferir, traspasar, ceder (propiedad) **3** PRINT : imprimir (un diseño) — *vi* **1** MOVE : trasladarse, cambiarse **2** CHANGE : transbordar, cambiar (de un transporte a otro) ⟨he transfers at E Street : hace un transborde a la calle E⟩

transfer² ['træn*ts*͵fər] *n* **1** TRANSFERRING : transferencia *f* (de fondos, de propiedad, etc.), traslado *m* (de una persona) **2** DECAL : calcomanía *f* **3** : boleto *m* (para cambiar de un avión, etc., a otro)

transferable [træn*ts*'fərəbəl] *adj* : transferible

transference [træn*ts*'fərənts] *n* : transferencia *f*

transfigure [træn*ts*'fɪgjər] *vt* **-ured; -uring** : transfigurar, transformar

transfix [træn*ts*'fɪks] *vt* **1** PIERCE : traspasar, atravesar **2** IMMOBILIZE : paralizar

transform [træn*ts*'fɔrm] *vt* : transformar

transformation [͵træn*ts*fər'meɪʃən] *n* : transformación *f*

transformer [træn*ts*'fɔrmər] *n* : transformador *m*

transfusion [træn*ts*'fju:ʒən] *n* : transfusión *f*

transgress [træn*ts*'grɛs, trænz-] *vt* : transgredir, infringir

transgression [træn*ts*'grɛʃən, trænz-] *n* : transgresión *f*

transient¹ ['træntʃənt, 'trænsiənt] *adj* : pasajero, transitorio — **transiently** *adv*

transient² *n* : transeúnte *mf*

transistor [træn'zɪstər, -'sɪs-] *n* : transistor *m*

transit ['træn*ts*ɪt, 'trænzɪt] *n* **1** PASSAGE : pasaje *m*, tránsito *m* ⟨in transit : en tránsito⟩ **2** TRANSPORTATION : transporte *m* (público) **3** : teodolito *m* (instrumento topográfico)

transition [træn'sɪʃən, -'zɪʃ-] *n* : transición *f*

transitional [træn'sɪʃənəl, -'zɪʃ-] *adj* : de transición

transitive ['træn*ts*ətɪv, 'trænzə-] *adj* : transitivo

transitory ['træn*ts*ə͵tori, 'trænzə-] *adj* : transitorio

translate [træn*ts*'leɪt, trænz-; 'træn*ts*͵-, 'trænz͵-] *vt* **-lated; -lating** : traducir

translation [træn*ts*'leɪʃən, trænz-] *n* : traducción *f*

translator [træn*ts*'leɪtər, trænz-; 'træn*ts*͵-, 'trænz͵-] *n* : traductor *m*, -tora *f*

translucent [træn*ts*'lu:sənt, trænz-] *adj* : translúcido

transmission [træn*ts*'mɪʃən, trænz-] *n* : transmisión *f*

transmit [træn*ts*'mɪt, trænz-] *vt* **-mitted; -mitting** : transmitir

transmitter [træn*ts*'mɪtər, trænz-; 'træn*ts*͵-, 'trænz͵-] *n* : transmisor *m*, emisor *m*

transom ['træn*ts*əm] *n* : montante *m* (de una puerta), travesaño *m* (de una ventana)

transparency [træn*ts*'pærəntsi] *n, pl* **-cies** : transparencia *f*

transparent [træn*ts*'pærənt] *adj* **1** : transparente, traslúcido ⟨a transparent fabric : una tela transparente⟩ **2** OBVIOUS : transparente, obvio, claro — **transparently** *adv*

transpiration [͵træn*ts*pə'reɪʃən] *n* : transpiración *f*

transpire [træn*ts*'paɪr] *vi* **-spired; -spiring 1** : transpirar (en biología y botánica) **2** TURN OUT : resultar **3** HAPPEN : suceder, ocurrir, tener lugar

transplant¹ [træn*ts*'plænt] *vt* : trasplantar

transplant² ['træn*ts*͵plænt] *n* : trasplante *m*

transport¹ [træn*ts*'port, 'træn*ts*͵-] *vt* **1** CARRY : transportar, acarrear **2** ENRAPTURE : transportar, extasiar

transport² ['træn*ts*͵port] *n* **1** TRANSPORTATION : transporte *m*, transportación *f* **2** RAPTURE : éxtasis *m* **3** *or* **transport ship** : buque *m* de transporte (de personal militar)

transportation [͵træn*ts*pər'teɪʃən] *n* : transporte *m*, transportación *f*

transpose [træn*ts*'po:z] *vt* **-posed; -posing** : trasponer, trasladar, transportar (una composición musical)

transverse [træn*ts*'vərs, trænz-] *adj* : transversal, transverso, oblicuo — **transversely** *adv*

trap¹ ['træp] *vt* **trapped; trapping** : atrapar, apresar (en una trampa)

trap² *n* : trampa *f* ⟨to set a trap : tender una trampa⟩

trapdoor ['træp'dor] *n* : trampilla *f*, escotillón *m*

trapeze [træ'pi:z] *n* : trapecio *m*

trapezoid ['træpə͵zɔɪd] *n* : trapezoide *m*, trapecio *m*

trapper ['træpər] *n* : trampero *m*, -ra *f*; cazador *m*, -dora *f* (que usa trampas)

trappings ['træpɪŋz] *npl* **1** : arreos *mpl*, jaeces *mpl* (de un caballo) **2** ADORNMENTS : adornos *mpl*, pompa *f*

trash ['træʃ] *n* : basura *f*

trashy ['træʃi] *adj* : de pacotilla

trauma ['trɔmə, 'traʊ-] *n* : trauma *m*

traumatic [trə'mætɪk, trɔ-, traʊ-] *adj* : traumático

travel¹ ['trævəl] *vi* **-eled** *or* **-elled; -eling** *or* **-elling 1** JOURNEY : viajar **2** GO, MOVE : desplazarse, moverse, ir ⟨the waves travel at uniform speed : las ondas se desplazan a una velocidad uniforme⟩

travel² *n or* **travels** *npl* : viajes *mpl*

traveler *or* **traveller** ['trævələr] *n* : viajero *m*, -ra *f*

traverse [trə'vərs, træ'vərs, 'trævərs] *vt* **-versed; -versing** CROSS : atravesar, extenderse a través de, cruzar

travesty ['trævəsti] *n, pl* **-ties** : parodia *f*

trawl¹ ['trɔl] *vi* : pescar con red de arrastre, rastrear

trawl² *n or* **trawl net** : red *f* de arrastre

trawler ['trɔlər] *n* : barco *m* de pesca (utilizado para rastrear)

tray ['treɪ] *n* : bandeja *f*, charola *f Bol, Mex, Peru*

treacherous ['trɛtʃərəs] *adj* **1** TRAITOROUS : traicionero, traidor **2** DANGEROUS : peligroso

treacherously ['trɛtʃərəsli] *adv* : a traición

treachery ['trɛtʃəri] *n, pl* **-eries** : traición *f*

tread¹ ['trɛd] *v* **trod** ['trɑd]; **trodden** ['trɑdən] *or* **trod; treading** *vt* TRAMPLE : pisotear, hollar — *vi* **1** WALK : caminar, andar **2 to tread on** : pisar

tread² *n* **1** STEP : paso *m*, andar *m* **2** : banda *f* de rodadura (de un neumático, etc.) **3** : escalón *m* (de una escalera)

treadle ['trɛdəl] *n* : pedal *m* (de una máquina)

treadmill ['trɛd,mɪl] *n* **1** : rueda *f* de andar **2** ROUTINE : rutina *f*

treason ['tri:zən] *n* : traición *f* (a la patria, etc.)

treasure¹ ['trɛʒər, 'trɛɪ-] *vt* **-sured; -suring** : apreciar, valorar

treasure² *n* : tesoro *m*

treasurer ['trɛʒərər, 'trɛɪ-] *n* : tesorero *m*, -ra *f*

treasury ['trɛʒəri, 'trɛɪ-] *n, pl* **-suries** : tesorería *f*, tesoro *m*

treat¹ ['tri:t] *vt* **1** DEAL WITH : tratar (un asunto) ⟨the article treats of poverty : el artículo trata de la pobreza⟩ **2** HANDLE : tratar (a una persona), manejar (un objeto) ⟨to treat something as a joke : tomar(se) algo a broma⟩ **3** INVITE : invitar, convidar ⟨he treated me to a meal : me invitó a comer⟩ **4** : tratar, atender (en medicina) **5** PROCESS : tratar ⟨to treat sewage : tratar las aguas negras⟩

treat² *n* : gusto *m*, placer *m* ⟨it was a treat to see you : fue un placer verte⟩ ⟨it's my treat : yo invito⟩

treatise ['tri:tɪs] *n* : tratado *m*, estudio *m*

treatment ['tri:tmənt] *n* : trato *m*, tratamiento *m* (médico)

treaty ['tri:ti] *n, pl* **-ties** : tratado *m*, convenio *m*

treble¹ ['trɛbəl] *vt* **-bled; -bling** : triplicar

treble² *adj* **1** → **triple 2** : de tiple, soprano (en música) **3 treble clef** : clave *f* de sol

treble³ *n* : tiple *m*, parte *f* de soprano

tree ['tri:] *n* : árbol *m*

treeless ['tri:ləs] *adj* : carente de árboles

trek¹ ['trɛk] *vi* **trekked; trekking** : hacer un viaje largo y difícil

trek² *n* : viaje *m* largo y difícil

trellis ['trɛlɪs] *n* : enrejado *m*, espaldera *f*, celosía *f*

tremble ['trɛmbəl] *vi* **-bled; -bling** : temblar

tremendous [trɪ'mɛndəs] *adj* : tremendo — **tremendously** *adv*

tremor ['trɛmər] *n* : temblor *m*

tremulous ['trɛmjələs] *adj* : trémulo, tembloroso

trench ['trɛntʃ] *n* **1** DITCH : zanja *f* **2** : trinchera *f* (militar)

trenchant ['trɛntʃənt] *adj* : cortante, mordaz

trend¹ ['trɛnd] *vi* : tender, inclinarse

trend² *n* **1** TENDENCY : tendencia *f* **2** FASHION : moda *f*

trendy ['trɛndi] *adj* **trendier; -est** : de moda

trepidation [,trɛpə'deɪʃən] *n* : inquietud *f*, ansiedad *f*

trespass¹ ['trɛspəs, -,pæs] *vi* **1** SIN : pecar, transgredir **2** : entrar ilegalmente (en propiedad ajena)

trespass² *n* **1** SIN : pecado *m*, transgresión *f* ⟨forgive us our trespasses : perdónanos nuestras deudas⟩ **2** : entrada *f* ilegal (en propiedad ajena)

tress ['trɛs] *n* : mechón *m*

trestle ['trɛsəl] *n* **1** : caballete *m* (armazón) **2** *or* **trestle bridge** : puente *m* de caballete

triad ['traɪˌæd] *n* : tríada *f*

trial¹ ['traɪəl] *adj* : de prueba ⟨trial period : período de prueba⟩

trial² *n* **1** : juicio *m*, proceso *m* ⟨to stand trial : ser sometido a juicio⟩ **2** AFFLICTION : aflicción *f*, tribulación *f* **3** TEST : prueba *f*, ensayo *m*

triangle ['traɪˌæŋgəl] *n* : triángulo *m*

triangular [traɪ'æŋgjələr] *adj* : triangular

tribal ['traɪbəl] *adj* : tribal

tribe ['traɪb] *n* : tribu *f*

tribesman ['traɪbzmən] *n, pl* **-men** [-mən, -,mɛn] : miembro *m* de una tribu

tribulation [,trɪbjə'leɪʃən] *n* : tribulación *f*

tribunal [traɪ'bju:nəl, trɪ-] *n* : tribunal *m*, corte *f*

tributary ['trɪbjəˌtɛri] *n, pl* **-taries** : afluente *m*

tribute ['trɪbˌju:t] *n* : tributo *m*

trick¹ ['trɪk] *vt* : engañar, embaucar

trick² *n* **1** RUSE : trampa *f*, treta *f*, artimaña *f* **2** PRANK : broma *f* ⟨we played a trick on her : le gastamos una broma⟩ **3** : truco *m* ⟨magic tricks : trucos de magia⟩ ⟨the trick is to wait five minutes : el truco está en esperar cinco minutos⟩ **4** MANNERISM : peculiaridad *f*, manía *f* **5** : baza *f* (en juegos de naipes)

trickery ['trɪkəri] *n* : engaños *mpl*, trampas *fpl*

trickle¹ ['trɪkəl] *vi* **-led; -ling** : gotear, chorrear

trickle² *n* : goteo *m*, hilo *m*
trickster ['trɪkstər] *n* : estafador *m*, -dora *f*; embaucador *m*, -dora *f*
tricky ['trɪki] *adj* **trickier; -est** **1** SLY : astuto, taimado **2** DIFFICULT : delicado, peliagudo, difícil
tricycle ['traɪsəkəl, -ˌsɪkəl] *n* : triciclo *m*
trident ['traɪdənt] *n* : tridente *m*
triennial ['traɪ'ɛniəl] *adj* : trienal
trifle¹ ['traɪfəl] *vi* **-fled; -fling** : jugar, juguetear
trifle² *n* : nimiedad *f*, insignificancia *f*
trifling ['traɪflɪŋ] *adj* : trivial, insignificante
trigger¹ ['trɪgər] *vt* : causar, provocar
trigger² *n* : gatillo *m*
trigonometry [ˌtrɪgə'namətri] *n* : trigonometría *f*
trill¹ ['trɪl] *vi* QUAVER : trinar, gorjear — *vt* : vibrar ⟨to trill the *r* : vibrar la *r*⟩
trill² *n* **1** QUAVER : trino *m*, gorjeo *m* **2** : vibración *f* (en fonética)
trillion ['trɪljən] *n* : billón *m*
trilogy ['trɪlədʒi] *n*, *pl* **-gies** : trilogía *f*
trim¹ ['trɪm] *vt* **trimmed; trimming** **1** DECORATE : adornar, decorar **2** CUT : recortar **3** REDUCE : recortar, reducir ⟨to trim the excess : recortar el exceso⟩
trim² *adj* **trimmer; trimmest** **1** SLIM : esbelto **2** NEAT : limpio y arreglado, bien cuidado
trim³ *n* **1** CONDITION : condición *f*, estado *m* ⟨to keep in trim : mantenerse en buena forma⟩ **2** CUT : recorte *m* **3** TRIMMING : adornos *mpl*
trimming ['trɪmɪŋ] *n* : adornos *mpl*, accesorios *mpl*
Trinity ['trɪnəti] *n* : Trinidad *f*
trinket ['trɪŋkət] *n* : chuchería *f*, baratija *f*
trio ['tri:ˌo:] *n*, *pl* **trios** : trío *m*
trip¹ ['trɪp] *v* **tripped; tripping** *vi* **1** : caminar (a paso ligero) **2** STUMBLE : tropezar **3** to trip up ERR : equivocarse, cometer un error — *vt* **1** : hacerle una zancadilla (a alguien) ⟨you tripped me on purpose! : ¡me hiciste la zancadilla a propósito!⟩ **2** ACTIVATE : activar (un mecanismo) **3** to trip up : hacer equivocar (a alguien)
trip² *n* **1** JOURNEY : viaje *m* ⟨to take a trip : hacer un viaje⟩ **2** STUMBLE : tropiezo *m*, traspié *m*
tripartite [traɪ'parˌtaɪt] *adj* : tripartito
tripe ['traɪp] *n* **1** : mondongo *m*, callos *mpl*, pancita *f* Mex **2** TRASH : porquería *f*
triple¹ ['trɪpəl] *vt* **-pled; -pling** : triplicar
triple² *adj* : triple
triple³ *n* : triple *m*
triplet ['trɪplət] *n* **1** : terceto *m* (en poesía, música, etc.) **2** : trillizo *m*, -za *f* (persona)
triplicate ['trɪplɪkət] *n* : triplicado *m*
tripod ['traɪˌpad] *n* : trípode *m*
trite ['traɪt] *adj* **triter; tritest** : trillado, tópico, manido

triumph¹ ['traɪəmpf] *vi* : triunfar
triumph² *n* : triunfo *m*
triumphal [traɪ'ʌmpfəl] *adj* : triunfal
triumphant [traɪ'ʌmpfənt] *adj* : triunfante, triunfal — **triumphantly** *adv*
trivia ['trɪviə] *ns & pl* : trivialidades *fpl*, nimiedades *fpl*
trivial ['trɪviəl] *adj* : trivial, intrascendente, insignificante
triviality [ˌtrɪvi'æləti] *n*, *pl* **-ties** : trivialidad *f*
trod, trodden → tread¹
troll ['tro:l] *n* : duende *m* o gigante *m* de cuentos folklóricos
trolley ['trali] *n*, *pl* **-leys** : tranvía *m*
trombone [tram'bo:n] *n* : trombón *m*
trombonist [tram'bo:nɪst] *n* : trombón *m*
troop¹ ['tru:p] *vi* : desfilar, ir en tropel
troop² *n* **1** : escuadrón *m* (de caballería) **2** GROUP : grupo *m*, banda *f* (de personas) **3 troops** *npl* SOLDIERS : tropas *fpl*, soldados *mpl*
trooper ['tru:pər] *n* **1** : soldado *m* (de caballería) **2** : policía *m* montado **3** : policía *m* (estatal)
trophy ['tro:fi] *n*, *pl* **-phies** : trofeo *m*
tropic¹ ['trapɪk] *or* **tropical** [-pɪkəl] *adj* : tropical
tropic² *n* **1** : trópico *m* ⟨tropic of Cancer : trópico de Cáncer⟩ **2 the tropics** : el trópico
trot¹ ['trat] *vi* **trotted; trotting** : trotar
trot² *n* : trote *m*
trouble¹ ['trʌbəl] *v* **-bled; -bling** *vt* **1** DISTURB, WORRY : molestar, perturbar, inquietar **2** AFFLICT : afligir, afectar — *vi* : molestarse, hacer un esfuerzo ⟨they didn't trouble to come : no se molestaron en venir⟩
trouble² *n* **1** PROBLEMS : problemas *mpl*, dificultades *fpl* ⟨to be in trouble : estar en un aprieto⟩ ⟨heart trouble : problemas de corazón⟩ **2** EFFORT : molestia *f*, esfuerzo *m* ⟨to take the trouble : tomarse la molestia⟩ ⟨it's not worth the trouble : no vale la pena⟩
troublemaker ['trʌbəlˌmeɪkər] *n* : agitador *m*, -dora *f*; alborotador *m*, -dora *f*
troublesome ['trʌbəlsəm] *adj* : problemático, dificultoso — **troublesomely** *adv*
trough ['trɔf] *n*, *pl* **troughs** ['trɔfs, 'trɔvz] **1** : comedero *m*, bebedero *m* (de animales) **2** CHANNEL, HOLLOW : depresión *f* (en el suelo), seno *m* (de olas)
trounce ['traʊnts] *vt* **trounced; trouncing** **1** THRASH : apalear, darle una paliza (a alguien) **2** DEFEAT : derrotar contundentemente
troupe ['tru:p] *n* : troupe *f*
trousers ['traʊzərz] *npl* : pantalón *m*, pantalones *mpl*
trout ['traʊt] *n*, *pl* **trout** : trucha *f*
trowel ['traʊəl] *n* **1** : llana *f*, paleta *f* (de albañil) **2** : desplantador *m* (de jardinero)
truant ['tru:ənt] *n* : alumno *m*, -na *f* que falta a clase sin permiso

truce ['tru:s] *n* : tregua *f*, armisticio *m*

truck¹ ['trʌk] *vt* : transportar en camión

truck² *n* 1 : camión *m* (vehículo automóvil), carro *m* (manual) 2 DEALINGS : tratos *mpl* ⟨to have no truck with : no tener nada que ver con⟩

trucker ['trʌkər] *n* : camionero *m*, -ra *f*

truculent ['trʌkjələnt] *adj* : agresivo, beligerante

trudge ['trʌʤ] *vi* trudged; trudging : caminar a paso pesado

true¹ ['tru:] *vt* trued; trueing : aplomar (algo vertical), nivelar (algo horizontal), centrar (una rueda)

true² *adv* 1 TRUTHFULLY : lealmente, sinceramente 2 ACCURATELY : exactamente, certeramente

true³ *adj* truer; truest 1 LOYAL : fiel, leal 2 : cierto, verdadero, verídico ⟨it's true : es cierto, es la verdad⟩ ⟨a true story : una historia verídica⟩ 3 GENUINE : auténtico, genuino — truly *adv*

true–blue ['tru:'blu:] *adj* LOYAL : leal, fiel

truffle ['trʌfəl] *n* : trufa *f*

truism ['tru:,ɪzəm] *n* : perogrullada *f*, verdad *f* obvia

trump¹ ['trʌmp] *vt* : matar (en juegos de naipes)

trump² *n* : triunfo *m* (en juegos de naipes)

trumped–up ['trʌmpt'ʌp] *adj* : inventado, fabricado ⟨trumped-up charges : falsas acusaciones⟩

trumpet¹ ['trʌmpət] *vi* 1 : sonar una trompeta 2 : berrear, bramar (dícese de un animal) — *vt* : proclamar a los cuatro vientos

trumpet² *n* : trompeta *f*

trumpeter ['trʌmpəʈər] *n* : trompetista *mf*

truncate ['trʌŋ,keɪt, 'trʌn-] *vt* -cated; -cating : truncar

trundle ['trʌndəl] *v* -dled; -dling *vi* : rodar lentamente — *vt* : hacer rodar, empujar lentamente

trunk ['trʌŋk] *n* 1 : tronco *m* (de un árbol o del cuerpo) 2 : trompa *f* (de un elefante) 3 CHEST : baúl *m* 4 : maletero *m*, cajuela *f* Mex (de un auto) 5 trunks *npl* : traje *m* de baño (de caballero)

truss¹ ['trʌs] *vt* : atar (con fuerza)

truss² *n* 1 FRAMEWORK : armazón *m* (de una estructura) 2 : braguero *m* (en medicina)

trust¹ ['trʌst] *vi* : confiar, esperar ⟨to trust in God : confiar en Dios⟩ — *vt* 1 ENTRUST : confiar, encomendar 2 : confiar en, tenerle confianza a ⟨I trust you : te tengo confianza⟩

trust² *n* 1 CONFIDENCE : confianza *f* 2 HOPE : esperanza *f*, fe *f* 3 CREDIT : crédito *m* ⟨to sell on trust : fiar⟩ 4 : fideicomiso *m* ⟨to hold in trust : guardar en fideicomiso⟩ 5 : trust *m* (consorcio empresarial) 6 CUSTODY : responsabilidad *f*, custodia *f*

trustee [,trʌs'ti:] *n* : fideicomisario *m*, -ria *f*; fiduciario *m*, -ria *f*

trustful ['trʌstfəl] *adj* : confiado — trustfully *adv*

trustworthiness ['trəst,wərðinəs] *n* : integridad *f*, honradez *f*

trustworthy ['trəst,wərði] *adj* : digno de confianza, confiable

trusty ['trəsti] *adj* trustier; -est : fiel, confiable

truth ['tru:θ] *n*, *pl* truths ['tru:ðz, 'tru:θs] : verdad *f*

truthful ['tru:θfəl] *adj* : sincero, veraz — truthfully *adv*

truthfulness ['tru:θfəlnəs] *n* : sinceridad *f*, veracidad *f*

try¹ ['traɪ] *v* tried; trying *vt* 1 : enjuiciar, juzgar, procesar ⟨he was tried for murder : fue procesado por homicidio⟩ 2 : probar ⟨did you try the salad? : ¿probaste la ensalada?⟩ 3 TEST : tentar, poner a prueba ⟨to try one's patience : tentarle la paciencia a uno⟩ 4 ATTEMPT : tratar (de), intentar 5 or to try on : probarse (ropa) — *vi* : tratar, intentar

try² *n*, *pl* tries : intento *m*, tentativa *f*

tryout ['traɪ,aʊt] *n* : prueba *f*

tsar ['zɑr, 'tsɑr, 'sɑr] → czar

T-shirt ['ti:,ʃərt] *n* : camiseta *f*

tub ['tʌb] *n* 1 CASK : cuba *f*, barril *m*, tonel *m* 2 CONTAINER : envase *m* (de plástico, etc.) ⟨a tub of margarine : un envase de margarina⟩ 3 BATHTUB : tina *f* (de baño), bañera *f*

tuba ['tu:bə, 'tju:-] *n* : tuba *f*

tube ['tu:b, 'tju:b] *n* 1 PIPE : tubo *m* 2 : tubo *m* (de dentífrico, etc.) 3 or inner tube : cámara *f* 4 : tubo *m* (de un aparato electrónico) 5 : trompa *f* (en anatomía)

tubeless ['tu:bləs, 'tju:b-] *adj* : sin cámara (dícese de una llanta)

tuber ['tu:bər, 'tju:-] *n* : tubérculo *m*

tubercular [tʊ'bərkjələr, tju-] → tuberculous

tuberculosis [tʊ,bərkjə'lo:sɪs, tju-] *n*, *pl* -loses [-,si:z] : tuberculosis *f*

tuberculous [tʊ'bərkjələs, tju-] *adj* : tuberculoso

tuberous ['tu:bərəs, 'tju:-] *adj* : tuberoso

tubing ['tu:bɪŋ, 'tju:-] *n* : tubería *f*

tubular ['tu:bjələr, 'tju:-] *adj* : tubular

tuck¹ ['tʌk] *vt* 1 PLACE, PUT : meter, colocar ⟨tuck in your shirt : métete la camisa⟩ 2 : guardar, esconder ⟨to tuck away one's money : guardar uno bien su dinero⟩ 3 COVER : arropar (a un niño en la cama)

tuck² *n* : pliegue *m*, alforza *f*

Tuesday ['tu:z,deɪ, 'tju:z-, -di] *n* : martes *m*

tuft ['tʌft] *n* : penacho *m* (de plumas), copete *m* (de pelo)

tug¹ ['tʌg] *v* tugged; tugging *vi* : tirar, jalar, dar un tirón — *vt* : jalar, arrastrar, remolcar (con un barco)

tug² *n* 1 : tirón *m*, jalón *m* 2 → tugboat

tugboat ['tʌg,bo:t] *n* : remolcador *m*

tug–of–war [ˌtʌgə'wɔr] n, pl **tugs–of–war** : tira y afloja m

tuition [tu'ɪʃən] n or **tuition fees** : tasas fpl de matrícula, colegiatura f Mex

tulip ['tu:lɪp, 'tju:-] n : tulipán m

tumble¹ ['tʌmbəl] v -**bled**; -**bling** vi 1 : dar volteretas (en acrobacia) **2** FALL : caerse, venirse abajo — vt 1 TOPPLE : volcar **2** TOSS : hacer girar

tumble² n : voltereta f, caída f

tumbler ['tʌmblər] n 1 ACROBAT : acróbata mf, saltimbanqui mf **2** GLASS : vaso m (de mesa) **3** : clavija f (de una cerradura)

tummy ['tʌmi] n, pl -**mies** BELLY : panza f, vientre m

tumor ['tu:mər, 'tju:-] n : tumor m

tumult ['tu:ˌmʌlt, 'tju:-] n : tumulto m, alboroto m

tumultuous [tʊ'mʌltʃuəs, tju:-] adj : tumultuoso

tuna ['tu:nə, 'tju:-] n, pl -**na** or -**nas** : atún m

tundra ['tʌndrə] n : tundra f

tune¹ ['tu:n, 'tju:n] v **tuned**; **tuning** vt 1 ADJUST : ajustar, hacer más preciso, afinar (un motor) **2** : afinar (un instrumento musical) **3** : sintonizar (un radio o televisor) — vi **to tune in** : sintonizar (con una emisora)

tune² n 1 MELODY : tonada f, canción f, melodía f **2 in tune** : afinado (dícese de un instrumento o de la voz), sintonizado, en sintonía

tuneful ['tu:nfəl, 'tju:n-] adj : armonioso, melódico

tuner ['tu:nər, 'tju:-] n : afinador m, -dora f (de instrumentos); sintonizador m (de un radio o un televisor)

tungsten ['tʌŋkstən] n : tungsteno m

tunic ['tu:nɪk, 'tju:-] n : túnica f

tuning fork n : diapasón m

Tunisian [tu:'niːʒən, tju:'nɪziən] n : tunecino m, -na f — **Tunisian** adj

tunnel¹ ['tʌnəl] vi -**neled** or -**nelled**; -**neling** or -**nelling** : hacer un túnel

tunnel² n : túnel m

turban ['tərbən] n : turbante m

turbid ['tərbɪd] adj : turbio

turbine ['tərbən, -ˌbaɪn] n : turbina f

turboprop ['tərbo:ˌprɑp] n : turbopropulsor m (motor), avión m turbopropulsado

turbulence ['tərbjələnts] n : turbulencia f

turbulent ['tərbjələnt] adj : turbulento — **turbulently** adv

tureen [tə'ri:n, tju-] n : sopera f

turf ['tərf] n SOD : tepe m

turgid ['tərdʒɪd] adj 1 SWOLLEN : turgente **2** : ampuloso, hinchado ⟨turgid style : estilo ampuloso⟩

Turk ['tərk] n : turco m, -ca f

turkey ['tərki] n, pl -**keys** : pavo m

Turkish¹ ['tərkɪʃ] adj : turco

Turkish² n : turco m (idioma)

turmoil ['tərˌmɔɪl] n : agitación f, desorden m, confusión f

turn¹ ['tərn] vt 1 : girar, voltear, volver ⟨to turn one's head : voltear la cabeza⟩ ⟨she turned her chair toward the fire : giró su asiento hacia la hoguera⟩ **2** ROTATE : darle vuelta a, hacer girar ⟨turn the handle : dale vuelta a la manivela⟩ **3** SPRAIN, WRENCH : dislocar, torcer **4** UPSET : revolver (el estómago) **5** TRANSFORM : convertir ⟨to turn water into wine : convertir el agua en vino⟩ **6** SHAPE : tornear (en carpintería) — vi 1 ROTATE : girar, dar vueltas **2** : girar, doblar, dar una vuelta ⟨turn left : doble a la izquierda⟩ ⟨to turn around : dar la media vuelta⟩ **3** BECOME : hacerse, volverse, ponerse **4** SOUR : agriarse, cortarse (dícese de la leche) **5 to turn to** : recurrir a ⟨they have no one to turn to : no tienen quien les ayude⟩

turn² n 1 : vuelta f, giro m ⟨a sudden turn : una vuelta repentina⟩ **2** CHANGE : cambio m **3** CURVE : curva f (en un camino) **4** : turno m ⟨they're awaiting their turn : están esperando su turno⟩ ⟨whose turn is it? : ¿a quién le toca?⟩

turnaround ['tərnəˌraʊnd] n PROCESSING : procesamiento m

turncoat ['tərnˌko:t] n : traidor m, -dora f

turn down vt 1 REFUSE : rehusar, rechazar ⟨they turned down our invitation : rehusaron nuestra invitación⟩ **2** LOWER : bajar (el volumen)

turn in vt : entregar ⟨to turn in one's work : entregar uno su trabajo⟩ ⟨they turned in the suspect : entregaron al sospechoso⟩ — vi : acostarse, irse a la cama

turnip ['tərnəp] n : nabo m

turn off vt : apagar (la luz, la radio, etc.)

turn on vt : prender (la luz, etc.), encender (un motor, etc.)

turnout ['tərnˌaʊt] n : concurrencia f

turn out vt 1 EVICT, EXPEL : expulsar, echar, desalojar **2** PRODUCE : producir **3** → **turn off** — vi 1 : concurrir, presentarse ⟨many turned out to vote : muchos concurrieron a votar⟩ **2** PROVE, RESULT : resultar

turnover ['tərnˌo:vər] n 1 : empanada f (salada o dulce) **2** : volumen m (de ventas) **3** : rotación f (de personal) ⟨a high turnover : un alto nivel de rotación⟩

turn over vt 1 TRANSFER : entregar, transferir (un cargo o una responsabilidad) **2** : voltear, darle vuelta a ⟨turn the cassette over : voltea el cassette⟩

turnpike ['tərnˌpaɪk] n : carretera f de peaje

turnstile ['tərnˌstaɪl] n : torniquete m (de acceso)

turntable ['tərnˌteɪbəl] n : tornamesa mf

turn up vi 1 APPEAR : aparecer, presentarse **2** HAPPEN : ocurrir, suceder (inesperadamente) — vt : subir (el volumen)

turpentine ['tərpənˌtaɪn] n : aguarrás m, trementina f

turquoise ['tər,kɔɪz, -,kwɔɪz] *n* : turquesa *f*
turret ['tərət] *n* **1** TOWER : torre *f* pequeña **2** : torreta *f* (de un tanque, un avión, etc.)
turtle ['tərṭəl] *n* : tortuga *f* (marina)
turtledove ['tərṭəl,dʌv] *n* : tórtola *f*
turtleneck ['tərṭəl,nɛk] *n* : cuello *m* de tortuga, cuello *m* alto
tusk ['tʌsk] *n* : colmillo *m*
tussle[1] ['tʌsəl] *vi* **-sled; -sling** SCUFFLE : pelearse, reñir
tussle[2] *n* : riña *f*, pelea *f*
tutor[1] ['tu:ṭər, 'tju:-] *vt* : darle clases particulares (a alguien)
tutor[2] *n* : tutor *m*, -tora *f*; maestro *m*, -tra *f* (particular)
tuxedo [,tək'si:,do:] *n, pl* **-dos** *or* **-does** : esmoquin *m*, smoking *m*
TV [,ti:'vi:, 'ti:,vi:] → **television**
twain ['tweɪn] *n* : dos *m*
twang[1] ['twæŋ] *vt* : pulsar la cuerda de (una guitarra) — *vi* : hablar en tono nasal
twang[2] *n* **1** : tañido *m* (de una cuerda de guitarra) **2** : tono *m* nasal (de voz)
tweak[1] ['twi:k] *vt* : pellizcar
tweak[2] *n* : pellizco *m*
tweed ['twi:d] *n* : tweed *m*
tweet[1] ['twi:t] *vi* : piar
tweet[2] *n* : gorjeo *m*, pío *m*
tweezers ['twi:zərz] *npl* : pinzas *fpl*
twelfth[1] ['twɛlfθ] *adj* : duodécimo
twelfth[2] *n* **1** : duodécimo *m*, -ma *f* (en una serie) **2** : doceavo *m*, doceava parte *f*
twelve[1] ['twɛlv] *adj* : doce
twelve[2] *n* : doce *m*
twentieth[1] ['twʌntiəθ, 'twɛn-] *adj* : vigésimo
twentieth[2] *n* **1** : vigésimo *m*, -ma *f* (en una serie) **2** : veinteavo *m*, veinteava parte *f*
twenty[1] ['twʌnti, 'twɛn-] *adj* : veinte
twenty[2] *n, pl* **-ties** : veinte *m*
twice ['twaɪs] *adv* : dos veces ⟨twice a day : dos veces al día⟩ ⟨it costs twice as much : cuesta el doble⟩
twig ['twɪg] *n* : ramita *f*
twilight ['twaɪ,laɪt] *n* : crepúsculo *m*
twill ['twɪl] *n* : sarga *f*, tela *f* cruzada
twin[1] ['twɪn] *adj* : gemelo, mellizo
twin[2] *n* : gemelo *m*, -la *f*; mellizo *m*, -za *f*
twine[1] ['twaɪn] *v* **twined; twining** *vt* : entrelazar, entrecruzar — *vi* : enroscarse (alrededor de algo)
twine[2] *n* : cordel *m*, cuerda *f*, mecate *m* CA, Mex, Ven
twinge[1] ['twɪndʒ] *vi* **twinged; twinging** *or* **twingeing** : sentir punzadas
twinge[2] *n* : punzada *f*, dolor *m* agudo
twinkle[1] ['twɪŋkəl] *vi* **-kled; -kling 1** : centellear, titilar (dícese de las estrellas o de la luz) **2** : chispear, brillar (dícese de los ojos)
twinkle[2] *n* : centelleo *m* (de las estrellas), brillo *m* (de los ojos)
twirl[1] ['twərl] *vt* : girar, darle vueltas a — *vi* : girar, dar vueltas (rápidamente)

twirl[2] *n* : giro *m*, vuelta *f*
twist[1] ['twɪst] *vt* : torcer, retorcer ⟨he twisted my arm : me torció el brazo⟩ — *vi* : retorcerse, enroscarse, serpentear (dícese de un río, un camino, etc.)
twist[2] *n* **1** BEND : vuelta *f*, recodo *m* (en el camino, el río, etc.) **2** TURN : giro *m* ⟨give it a twist : hazlo girar⟩ **3** SPIRAL : espiral *f* ⟨a twist of lemon : una rodajita de limón⟩ **4** : giro *m* inesperado (de eventos, etc.)
twisted ['twɪstəd] *adj* : retorcido ⟨a twisted mind : una mente retorcida⟩
twister ['twɪstər] **1** → **tornado 2** → **waterspout**
twitch[1] ['twɪtʃ] *vi* : moverse nerviosamente, contraerse espasmódicamente (dícese de un músculo)
twitch[2] *n* : espasmo *m*, sacudida *f* ⟨a nervous twitch : un tic nervioso⟩
twitter[1] ['twɪṭər] *vi* CHIRP : gorjear, cantar (dícese de los pájaros)
twitter[2] *n* : gorjeo *m*
two[1] ['tu:] *adj* : dos
two[2] *n, pl* **twos** : dos *m*
twofold[1] ['tu:'fo:ld] *adv* : al doble
twofold[2] ['tu:,fo:ld] *adj* : doble
two hundred[1] *adj* : doscientos
two hundred[2] *n* : doscientos *m*
twosome ['tu:səm] *n* COUPLE : pareja *f*
tycoon [taɪ'ku:n] *n* : magnate *mf*
tying → **tie**[1]
type[1] ['taɪp] *v* **typed; typing** *vt* **1** TYPEWRITE : escribir a máquina, pasar (un texto) a máquina **2** CATEGORIZE : categorizar, identificar — *vi* : escribir a máquina
type[2] *n* **1** KIND : tipo *m*, clase *f*, categoría *f* **2** *or* **printing type** : tipo *m*
typeface ['taɪp,feɪs] *n* : tipo *m* de imprenta
typewrite ['taɪp,raɪt] *v* **-wrote; -written** : escribir a máquina
typewriter ['taɪp,raɪṭər] *n* : máquina *f* de escribir
typhoid[1] ['taɪ,fɔɪd, taɪ'-] *adj* : relativo al tifus o a la tifoidea
typhoid[2] *n or* **typhoid fever** : tifoidea *f*
typhoon [taɪ'fu:n] *n* : tifón *m*
typhus ['taɪfəs] *n* : tifus *m*, tifo *m*
typical ['tɪpɪkəl] *adj* : típico, característico — **typically** *adv*
typify ['tɪpə,faɪ] *vt* **-fied; -fying** : ser típico o representativo (un grupo, una clase, etc.)
typist ['taɪpɪst] *n* : mecanógrafo *m*, -fa *f*
typographic [,taɪpə'græfɪk] *or* **typographical** [-fɪkəl] *adj* : tipográfico — **typographically** [-fɪkli] *adv*
typography [taɪ'pɑgrəfi] *n* : tipografía *f*
tyrannical [tə'rænɪkəl, taɪ-] *adj* : tiránico — **tyrannically** [-nɪkli] *adv*
tyrannize ['tɪrə,naɪz] *vt* **-nized; -nizing** : tiranizar
tyranny ['tɪrəni] *n, pl* **-nies** : tiranía *f*
tyrant ['taɪrənt] *n* : tirano *m*, -na *f*
tzar ['zɑr, 'tsɑr, 'sɑr] → **czar**

U

u ['juː] *n, pl* **u's** *or* **us** ['juːz] : vigésima primera letra del alfabeto inglés

ubiquitous [juːˈbɪkwətəs] *adj* : ubicuo, omnipresente

udder ['ʌdər] *n* : ubre *f*

UFO [juːˌɛfˈoː, ˈjuːˌfoː] *n, pl* **UFO's** *or* **UFOs** (*unidentified flying object*) : ovni *m*, OVNI *m*

Ugandan [juːˈgændən, -ˈgɑn-; uːˈgɑn-] *n* : ugandés *m*, -desa *f* — **Ugandan** *adj*

ugliness ['ʌglinəs] *n* : fealdad *f*

ugly ['ʌgli] *adj* **uglier; -est 1** UNATTRACTIVE : feo **2** DISAGREEABLE : desagradable, feo ⟨ugly weather : tiempo feo⟩ ⟨to have an ugly temper : tener mal genio⟩

Ukrainian [juːˈkreɪniən, -ˈkraɪ-] *n* **1** : ucraniano *m*, -na *f* **2** : ucraniano *m* (idioma) — **Ukrainian** *adj*

ukulele [ˌjuːkəˈleɪli] *n* : ukelele *m*

ulcer ['ʌlsər] *n* : úlcera *f* (interna), llaga *f* (externa)

ulcerate ['ʌlsəˌreɪt] *vi* **-ated; -ating** : ulcerarse

ulceration [ˌʌlsəˈreɪʃən] *n* **1** : ulceración *f* **2** ULCER : úlcera *f*, llaga *f*

ulcerous ['ʌlsərəs] *adj* : ulceroso

ulna ['ʌlnə] *n* : cúbito *m*

ulterior [ˌʌlˈtɪriər] *adj* : oculto ⟨ulterior motive : motivo oculto, segunda intención⟩

ultimate ['ʌltəmət] *adj* **1** FINAL : último, final **2** SUPREME : supremo, máximo **3** FUNDAMENTAL : fundamental, esencial

ultimately ['ʌltəmətli] *adv* **1** FINALLY : por último, finalmente **2** EVENTUALLY : a la larga, con el tiempo

ultimatum [ˌʌltəˈmeɪtəm, -ˈmɑ-] *n, pl* **-tums** *or* **-ta** [-ṭə] : ultimátum *m*

ultrasound ['ʌltrəˌsaʊnd] *n* **1** : ultrasonido *m* **2** : ecografía *f* (técnica o imagen)

ultraviolet [ˌʌltrəˈvaɪələt] *adj* : ultravioleta

umbilical cord [ˌʌmˈbɪlɪkəl] *n* : cordón *m* umbilical

umbrage ['ʌmbrɪdʒ] *n* **to take umbrage at** : ofenderse por

umbrella [ˌʌmˈbrɛlə] *n* **1** : paraguas *m* **2 beach umbrella** : sombrilla *f*

umpire¹ ['ʌmˌpaɪr] *v* **-pired; -piring** : arbitrar

umpire² *n* : árbitro *m*, -tra *f*

umpteenth [ˌʌmpˈtiːnθ] *adj* : enésimo

unable [ˌʌnˈeɪbəl] *adj* : incapaz ⟨to be unable to : no poder⟩

unabridged [ˌʌnəˈbrɪdʒd] *adj* : íntegro

unacceptable [ˌʌnɪkˈsɛptəbəl] *adj* : inaceptable

unaccompanied [ˌʌnəˈkʌmpənid] *adj* : solo, sin acompañamiento (en música)

unaccountable [ˌʌnəˈkaʊntəbəl] *adj* : inexplicable, incomprensible — **unaccountably** [-bli] *adv*

unaccustomed [ˌʌnəˈkʌstəmd] *adj* **1** UNUSUAL : desacostumbrado, inusual **2** UNUSED : inhabituado ⟨unaccustomed to noise : inhabituado al ruido⟩

unacquainted [ˌʌnəˈkweɪntəd] *adj* **to be unacquainted with** : desconocer, ignorar

unadorned [ˌʌnəˈdɔrnd] *adj* : sin adornos, puro y simple

unadulterated [ˌʌnəˈdʌltəˌreɪtəd] *adj* **1** PURE : puro ⟨unadulterated food : comida pura⟩ **2** ABSOLUTE : completo, absoluto

unaffected [ˌʌnəˈfɛktəd] *adj* **1** : no afectado, indiferente **2** NATURAL : sin afectación, natural

unaffectedly [ˌʌnəˈfɛktədli] *adv* : de manera natural

unafraid [ˌʌnəˈfreɪd] *adj* : sin miedo

unaided [ˌʌnˈeɪdəd] *adj* : sin ayuda, solo

unambiguous [ˌʌnæmˈbɪgjuəs] *adj* : inequívoco

unanimity [ˌjuːnəˈnɪməṭi] *n* : unanimidad *f*

unanimous [juˈnænəməs] *adj* : unánime — **unanimously** *adv*

unannounced [ˌʌnəˈnaʊnst] *adj* : sin dar aviso

unanswered [ˌʌnˈæntsərd] *adj* : sin contestar

unappealing [ˌʌnəˈpiːlɪŋ] *adj* : desagradable

unappetizing [ˌʌnˈæpəˌtaɪzɪŋ] *adj* : poco apetitoso, poco apetecible

unarmed [ˌʌnˈɑrmd] *adj* : sin armas, desarmado

unassisted [ˌʌnəˈsɪstəd] *adj* : sin ayuda

unassuming [ˌʌnəˈsuːmɪŋ] *adj* : modesto, sin pretensiones

unattached [ˌʌnəˈtætʃt] *adj* **1** LOOSE : suelto **2** INDEPENDENT : independiente **3** : solo (ni casado ni prometido)

unattractive [ˌʌnəˈtræktɪv] *adj* : poco atractivo

unauthorized [ˌʌnˈɔθəˌraɪzd] *adj* : sin autorización, no autorizado

unavailable [ˌʌnəˈveɪləbəl] *adj* : no disponible

unavoidable [ˌʌnəˈvɔɪdəbəl] *adj* : inevitable, ineludible

unaware¹ [ˌʌnəˈwær] *adv* → **unawares**

unaware² *adj* : inconsciente

unawares [ˌʌnəˈwærz] *adv* **1** : por sorpresa ⟨to catch someone unawares : agarrar a alguien desprevenido⟩ **2** UNINTENTIONALLY : inconscientemente, inadvertidamente

unbalanced [ˌʌnˈbæləntst] *adj* : desequilibrado

unbearable [ˌʌnˈbærəbəl] *adj* : insoportable, inaguantable — **unbearably** [-bli] *adv*

unbecoming [ˌʌnbɪˈkʌmɪŋ] *adj* **1** UNSEEMLY : impropio, indecoroso **2** UNFLATTERING : poco favorecedor unbelievable [ˌʌnbə'liːvəbəl] adj : increíble — unbelievably [-bli] adv

unbend [ˌʌn'bɛnd] vi -bent [-'bɛnt]; -bending RELAX : relajarse

unbending [ˌʌn'bɛndɪŋ] adj : inflexible

unbiased [ˌʌn'baɪəst] adj : imparcial, objetivo

unbind [ˌʌn'baɪnd] vt -bound [-'baʊnd]; -binding 1 UNFASTEN, UNTIE : desatar, desamarrar 2 RELEASE : liberar

unbolt [ˌʌn'boːlt] vt : abrir el cerrojo de, descorrer el pestillo de

unborn [ˌʌn'bɔrn] adj : aún no nacido, que va a nacer

unbosom [ˌʌn'buzəm, -'buː-] vt : revelar, divulgar

unbreakable [ˌʌn'breɪkəbəl] adj : irrompible

unbridled [ˌʌn'braɪdəld] adj : desenfrenado

unbroken [ˌʌn'broːkən] adj 1 INTACT : intacto, sano 2 CONTINUOUS : continuo, ininterrumpido

unbuckle [ˌʌn'bʌkəl] vt -led; -ling : desabrochar

unburden [ˌʌn'bərdən] vt 1 UNLOAD : descargar 2 to unburden oneself : desahogarse

unbutton [ˌʌn'bʌtən] vt : desabrochar, desabotonar

uncalled–for [ˌʌn'kɔld,fɔr] adj : inapropiado, innecesario

uncanny [ən'kæni] adj -nier; -est 1 STRANGE : extraño 2 EXTRAORDINARY : raro, extraordinario — uncannily [-'kænəli] adv

unceasing [ˌʌn'siːsɪŋ] adj : incesante, continuo — unceasingly adv

unceremonious [ˌʌn,sɛrə'moːniəs] adj 1 INFORMAL : sin ceremonia, sin pompa 2 ABRUPT : abrupto, brusco — unceremoniously adv

uncertain [ˌʌn'sərtən] adj 1 INDEFINITE : indeterminado 2 UNSURE : incierto, dudoso 3 CHANGEABLE : inestable, variable ⟨uncertain weather : tiempo inestable⟩ 4 HESITANT : indeciso 5 VAGUE : poco claro

uncertainly [ˌʌn'sərtənli] adv : dudosamente, con desconfianza

uncertainty [ˌʌn'sərtənti] n, pl -ties : duda f, incertidumbre f

unchangeable [ˌʌn'tʃeɪndʒəbəl] adj : inalterable, inmutable

unchanged [ˌʌn'tʃeɪndʒd] adj : sin cambiar

unchanging [ˌʌn'tʃeɪndʒɪŋ] adj : inalterable, inmutable, firme

uncharacteristic [ˌʌn,kærɪktə'rɪstɪk] adj : inusual, desacostumbrado

uncharged [ˌʌn'tʃɑrdʒd] adj : sin carga (eléctrica)

uncivilized [ˌʌn'sɪvə,laɪzd] adj 1 BARBAROUS : incivilizado, bárbaro 2 WILD : salvaje

uncle ['ʌŋkəl] n : tío m

unclean [ˌʌn'kliːn] adj 1 IMPURE : impuro 2 DIRTY : sucio

unclear [ˌʌn'klɪr] adj : confuso, borroso, poco claro

Uncle Sam ['sæm] n : el Tío Sam

unclog [ˌʌn'klɑg] vt -clogged; -clogging : desatascar, destapar

unclothed [ˌʌn'kloːð] adj : desnudo

uncomfortable [ˌʌn'kʌmpfərtəbəl] adj 1 : incómodo (dícese de una silla, etc.) 2 UNEASY : inquieto, incómodo

uncommitted [ˌʌnkə'mɪtəd] adj : sin compromisos

uncommon [ˌʌn'kamən] adj 1 UNUSUAL : raro, poco común 2 REMARKABLE : excepcional, extraordinario

uncommonly [ˌʌn'kamənli] adv : extraordinariamente

uncompromising [ˌʌn'kamprə,maɪzɪŋ] adj : inflexible, intransigente

unconcerned [ˌʌnkən'sərnd] adj : indiferente — unconcernedly [-'sərnəd-li] adv

unconditional [ˌʌnkən'dɪʃənəl] adj : incondicional — unconditionally adv

unconscious[1] [ˌʌn'kantʃəs] adj : inconsciente — unconsciously adv

unconscious[2] n : inconsciente m

unconsciousness [ˌʌn'kantʃəsnəs] n : inconsciencia f

unconstitutional [ˌʌn,kantstə'tuːʃənəl, -'tjuː-] adj : inconstitucional

uncontrollable [ˌʌnkən'troːləbəl] adj : incontrolable, incontenible — uncontrollably [-bli] adv

uncontrolled [ˌʌnkən'troːld] adj : incontrolado

unconventional [ˌʌnkən'vɛntʃənəl] adj : poco convencional

unconvincing [ˌʌnkən'vɪntsɪŋ] adj : poco convincente

uncouth [ˌʌn'kuːθ] adj CRUDE, ROUGH : grosero, rudo

uncover [ˌʌn'kʌvər] vt 1 : destapar (un objeto), dejar al descubierto 2 EXPOSE, REVEAL : descubrir, revelar, exponer

uncultivated [ˌʌn'kʌltə,veɪtəd] adj : inculto

uncurl [ˌʌn'kərl] vt UNROLL : desenrollar — vi : desenrollarse, desrizarse (dícese del pelo)

uncut [ˌʌn'kʌt] adj 1 : sin cortar ⟨uncut grass : hierba sin cortar⟩ 2 : sin tallar, en bruto ⟨an uncut diamond : un diamante en bruto⟩ 3 UNABRIDGED : completo, íntegro

undaunted [ˌʌn'dɔntəd] adj : impávido

undecided [ˌʌndi'saɪdəd] adj 1 IRRESOLUTE : indeciso, irresoluto 2 UNRESOLVED : pendiente, no resuelto

undefeated [ˌʌndi'fiːtəd] adj : invicto

undeniable [ˌʌndi'naɪəbəl] adj : innegable — undeniably [-bli] adv

under[1] ['ʌndər] adv 1 LESS : menos ⟨$10 or under : $10 o menos⟩ 2 UNDERWATER : debajo del agua 3 : bajo los efectos de la anestesia

under[2] adj 1 LOWER : (más) bajo, inferior 2 SUBORDINATE : inferior 3 : insuficiente ⟨an under dose of medicine : una dosis insuficiente de medicina⟩

under³ *prep* **1** BELOW, BENEATH : debajo de, abajo de ⟨under the table : abajo de la mesa⟩ ⟨we walked under the arch : pasamos por debajo del arco⟩ ⟨under the sun : bajo el sol⟩ **2** : menos de ⟨in under 20 minutes : en menos de 20 minutos⟩ **3** (*indicating rank or authority*) : bajo ⟨under the command of : bajo las órdenes de⟩ **4** SUBJECT TO : bajo ⟨under suspicion : bajo sospecha⟩ ⟨under the circumstances : dadas las circunstancias⟩ **5** ACCORDING TO : según, de acuerdo con, conforme a ⟨under the present laws : según las leyes actuales⟩

underage [ˌʌndərˈeɪʤ] *adj* : menor de edad

underbrush [ˈʌndərˌbrəʃ] *n* : maleza *f*

underclothes [ˈʌndərˌkloːz, -ˌkloːðz] → **underwear**

underclothing [ˈʌndərˌkloːðɪŋ] → **underwear**

undercover [ˌʌndərˈkʌvər] *adj* : secreto, clandestino

undercurrent [ˈʌndərˌkərənt] *n* **1** : corriente *f* submarina **2** UNDERTONE : corriente *f* oculta, trasfondo *m*

undercut [ˌʌndərˈkʌt] *vt* -**cut**; -**cutting** : vender más barato que

underdeveloped [ˌʌndərdɪˈvɛləpt] *adj* : subdesarrollado, atrasado

underdog [ˈʌndərˌdɔg] *n* : persona *f* que tiene menos posibilidades

underdone [ˌʌndərˈdʌn] *adj* RARE : poco cocido

underestimate [ˌʌndərˈɛstəˌmeɪt] *vt* -**mated**; -**mating** : subestimar, menospreciar

underexposed [ˌʌndərɪkˈspoːzd] *adj* : subexpuesto (en fotografía)

underfoot [ˌʌndərˈfʊt] *adv* **1** : bajo los pies ⟨to trample underfoot : pisotear⟩ **2 to be underfoot** : estorbar ⟨they're always underfoot : están siempre estorbando⟩

undergarment [ˈʌndərˌgɑrmənt] *n* : prenda *f* íntima

undergo [ˌʌndərˈgoː] *vt* -**went** [-ˈwɛnt]; -**gone** [-ˈgɔn]; -**going** : sufrir, experimentar ⟨to undergo an operation : someterse a una intervención quirúrgica⟩

undergraduate [ˌʌndərˈgræʤuət] *n* : estudiante *m* universitario, estudiante *f* universitaria

underground¹ [ˌʌndərˈgraʊnd] *adv* **1** : bajo tierra **2** SECRETLY : clandestinamente, en secreto ⟨to go underground : pasar a la clandestinidad⟩

underground² [ˈʌndərˌgraʊnd] *adj* **1** SUBTERRANEAN : subterráneo **2** SECRET : secreto, clandestino

underground³ [ˈʌndərˌgraʊnd] *n* : movimiento *m* o grupo *m* clandestino

undergrowth [ˈʌndərˌgroːθ] *n* : maleza *f*, broza *f*

underhand¹ [ˈʌndərˌhænd] *adv* **1** SECRETLY : de manera clandestina **2** *or*

underhanded : sin levantar el brazo por encima del hombro (en deportes)

underhand² *adj* **1** SLY : solapado **2** : por debajo del hombro (en deportes)

underhanded [ˌʌndərˈhændəd] *adj* **1** SLY : solapado **2** SHADY : turbio, poco limpio

underline [ˈʌndərˌlaɪn] *vt* -**lined**; -**lining** **1** : subrayar **2** EMPHASIZE : subrayar, acentuar, hacer hincapié en

underlying [ˌʌndərˈlaɪɪŋ] *adj* **1** : subyacente ⟨the underlying rock : la roca subyacente⟩ **2** FUNDAMENTAL : fundamental, esencial

undermine [ˌʌndərˈmaɪn] *vt* -**mined**; -**mining** **1** : socavar (una estructura, etc.) **2** SAP, WEAKEN : minar, debilitar

underneath¹ [ˌʌndərˈniːθ] *adv* : debajo, abajo ⟨the part underneath : la parte de abajo⟩

underneath² *prep* : debajo de, abajo de

undernourished [ˌʌndərˈnərɪʃt] *adj* : desnutrido

underpants [ˈʌndərˌpænts] *npl* : calzoncillos *mpl*, calzones *mpl*

underpass [ˈʌndərˌpæs] *n* : paso *m* a desnivel

underprivileged [ˌʌndərˈprɪvlɪʤd] *adj* : desfavorecido

underrate [ˌʌndərˈreɪt] *vt* -**rated**; -**rating** : subestimar, menospreciar

underscore [ˈʌndərˌskor] *vt* -**scored**; -**scoring** → **underline**

undersea¹ [ˌʌndərˈsiː] *or* **underseas** [-ˈsiːz] *adv* : bajo la superficie del mar

undersea² *adj* : submarino

undersecretary [ˌʌndərˈsɛkrəˌtɛri] *n, pl* -**ries** : subsecretario *m*, -ria *f*

undersell [ˌʌndərˈsɛl] *vt* -**sold**; -**selling** : vender más barato que

undershirt [ˈʌndərˌʃərt] *n* : camiseta *f*

undershorts [ˈʌndərˌʃɔrts] *npl* : calzoncillos *mpl*

underside [ˈʌndərˌsaɪd, ˌʌndərˈsaɪd] *n* : parte *f* de abajo

undersized [ˌʌndərˈsaɪzd] *adj* : más pequeño de lo normal

understand [ˌʌndərˈstænd] *v* -**stood** [-ˈstʊd]; -**standing** *vt* **1** COMPREHEND : comprender, entender ⟨I don't understand it : no lo entiendo⟩ ⟨that's understood : eso se comprende⟩ ⟨to make oneself understood : hacerse entender⟩ **2** BELIEVE : entender ⟨to give someone to understand : dar a alguien a entender⟩ **3** INFER : tener entendido ⟨I understand that she's leaving : tengo entendido que se va⟩ — *vi* : comprender, entender

understandable [ˌʌndərˈstændəbəl] *adj* : comprensible

understanding¹ [ˌʌndərˈstændɪŋ] *adj* : comprensivo, compasivo

understanding² *n* **1** GRASP : comprensión *f*, entendimiento *m* **2** SYMPATHY : comprensión *f* (mutua) **3** INTERPRETATION : interpretación *f* ⟨it's my understanding that ... : tengo la impresión de que ..., tengo entendido que . . . ⟩ **4** AGREEMENT : acuerdo *m*, arreglo *m*

understate [ˌʌndərˈsteɪt] *vt* **-stated; -stating** : minimizar, subestimar

understatement [ˌʌndərˈsteɪtmənt] *n* : atenuación *f* ⟨that's an understatement : decir sólo eso es quedarse corto⟩

understudy [ˈʌndərˌstʌdi] *n, pl* **-dies** : sobresaliente *mf*, suplente *mf* (en el teatro)

undertake [ˌʌndərˈteɪk] *vt* **-took** [-ˈtʊk]; **-taken** [-ˈteɪkən]; **-taking 1** : emprender (una tarea), asumir (una responsabilidad) **2** PROMISE : comprometerse (a hacer algo)

undertaker [ˈʌndərˌteɪkər] *n* : director *m*, -tora *f* de funeraria

undertaking [ˈʌndərˌteɪkɪŋ, ˌʌndərˈ-] *n* **1** ENTERPRISE, TASK : empresa *f*, tarea *f* **2** PLEDGE : promesa *f*, garantía *f*

undertone [ˈʌndərˌtoːn] *n* **1** : voz *f* baja ⟨to speak in an undertone : hablar en voz baja⟩ **2** HINT, UNDERCURRENT : trasfondo *m*, matiz *m*

undertow [ˈʌndərˌtoː] *n* : resaca *f*

undervalue [ˌʌndərˈvæljuː] *vt* **-ued; -uing** : menospreciar, subestimar

underwater¹ [ˌʌndərˈwɔt̬ər, -ˈwɑ-] *adv* : debajo (del agua)

underwater² *adj* : submarino

under way [ˌʌndərˈweɪ] *adv* : en marcha, en camino ⟨to get under way : ponerse en marcha⟩

underwear [ˈʌndərˌwær] *n* : ropa *f* interior, ropa *f* íntima

underworld [ˈʌndərˌwərld] *n* **1** HELL : infierno *m* **2 the underworld** CRIMINALS : la hampa, los bajos fondos

underwrite [ˈʌndərˌraɪt, ˌʌndərˈ-] *vt* **-wrote** [-ˌroːt, -ˈroːt]; **-written** [-ˌrɪt̬ən, -ˈrɪt̬ən]; **-writing 1** INSURE : asegurar **2** FINANCE : financiar **3** BACK, ENDORSE : suscribir, respaldar

underwriter [ˈʌndərˌraɪt̬ər, ˌʌndərˈ-] *n* INSURER : asegurador *m*, -dora *f*

undeserving [ˌʌndiˈzərvɪŋ] *adj* : indigno

undesirable¹ [ˌʌndiˈzaɪrəbəl] *adj* : indeseable

undesirable² *n* : indeseable *mf*

undeveloped [ˌʌndiˈvɛləpt] *adj* : sin desarrollar, sin revelar (dícese de una película)

undies [ˈʌndiːz] → **underwear**

undignified [ʌnˈdɪgnəfaɪd] *adj* : indecoroso

undiluted [ˌʌndaɪˈluːt̬əd, -də-] *adj* : sin diluir, concentrado

undiscovered [ˌʌndɪˈskʌvərd] *adj* : no descubierto

undisputed [ˌʌndɪˈspjuːt̬əd] *adj* : indiscutible

undisturbed [ˌʌndɪˈstərbd] *adj* : tranquilo (dícese de una persona), sin tocar (dícese de un objeto)

undivided [ˌʌndɪˈvaɪdəd] *adj* : íntegro, completo

undo [ˌʌnˈduː] *vt* **-did** [-ˈdɪd]; **-done** [-ˈdʌn]; **-doing 1** UNFASTEN : desabrochar, desatar, abrir **2** ANNUL : anular **3** REVERSE : deshacer, reparar (daños, etc.) **4** RUIN : arruinar, destruir

undoing [ˌʌnˈduːɪŋ] *n* : ruina *f*, perdición *f*

undoubted [ˌʌnˈdaʊt̬əd] *adj* : cierto, indudable — **undoubtedly** *adv*

undress [ˌʌnˈdrɛs] *vt* : desvestir, desabrigar, desnudar — *vi* : desvestirse, desnudarse

undrinkable [ˌʌnˈdrɪŋkəbəl] *adj* : no potable

undue [ˌʌnˈduː, -ˈdjuː] *adj* : excesivo, indebido — **unduly** *adv*

undulate [ˈʌndʒəˌleɪt] *vi* **-lated; -lating** : ondular

undulation [ˌʌndʒəˈleɪʃən] *n* : ondulación *f*

undying [ˌʌnˈdaɪɪŋ] *adj* : perpetuo, imperecedero

unearth [ˌʌnˈərθ] *vt* **1** EXHUME : desenterrar, exhumar **2** DISCOVER : descubrir

unearthly [ˌʌnˈərθli] *adj* **-lier; -est** : sobrenatural, de otro mundo

uneasily [ˌʌnˈiːzəli] *adv* : inquietamente, con inquietud

uneasiness [ˌʌnˈiːzinəs] *n* : inquietud *f*

uneasy [ˌʌnˈiːzi] *adj* **-easier; -est 1** AWKWARD : incómodo **2** WORRIED : preocupado, inquieto **3** RESTLESS : inquieto, agitado

uneducated [ˌʌnˈɛdʒəˌkeɪt̬əd] *adj* : inculto, sin educación

unemployed [ˌʌnɪmˈplɔɪd] *adj* : desempleado

unemployment [ˌʌnɪmˈplɔɪmənt] *n* : desempleo *m*

unending [ˌʌnˈɛndɪŋ] *adj* : sin fin, interminable

unendurable [ˌʌnɪnˈdʊrəbəl, -ɛn-, -ˈdjʊr-] *adj* : insoportable, intolerable

unequal [ˌʌnˈiːkwəl] *adj* **1** : desigual **2** INADEQUATE : incapaz, incompetente ⟨to be unequal to a task : no estar a la altura de una tarea⟩

unequaled *or* **unequalled** [ˌʌnˈiːkwəld] *adj* : sin igual

unequivocal [ˌʌnɪˈkwɪvəkəl] *adj* : inequívoco, claro — **unequivocally** *adv*

unerring [ˌʌnˈɛrɪŋ, -ˈər-] *adj* : infalible

unethical [ˌʌnˈɛθɪkəl] *adj* : poco ético

uneven [ˌʌnˈiːvən] *adj* **1** ODD : impar (dícese de un número) **2** : desigual, desnivelado (dícese de una superficie) ⟨uneven terrain : terreno accidentado⟩ **3** IRREGULAR : irregular, poco uniforme **4** UNEQUAL : desigual

unevenly [ˌʌnˈiːvənli] *adv* : desigualmente, irregularmente

uneventful [ˌʌnɪˈvɛntfəl] *adj* : sin incidentes, tranquilo

unexpected [ˌʌnɪkˈspɛkt̬əd] *adj* : imprevisto, inesperado — **unexpectedly** *adv*

unfailing [ˌʌnˈfeɪlɪŋ] *adj* **1** CONSTANT : constante **2** INEXHAUSTIBLE : inagotable **3** SURE : a toda prueba, indefectible

unfair [ˌʌn'fær] *adj* : injusto — **unfairly** *adv*

unfairness [ˌʌn'færnəs] *n* : injusticia *f*

unfaithful [ˌʌn'feɪθfəl] *adj* : desleal, infiel — **unfaithfully** *adv*

unfaithfulness [ˌʌn'feɪθfəlnəs] *n* : infidelidad *f*, deslealtad *f*

unfamiliar [ˌʌnfə'mɪljər] *adj* **1** STRANGE : desconocido, extraño ⟨an unfamiliar place : un lugar nuevo⟩ **2 to be unfamiliar with** : no estar familiarizado con, desconocer

unfamiliarity [ˌʌnfəˌmɪli'ærəti] *n* : falta *f* de familiaridad

unfashionable [ˌʌn'fæʃənəbəl] *adj* : fuera de moda

unfasten [ˌʌn'fæsən] *vt* : desabrochar, desatar (una cuerda, etc.), abrir (una puerta)

unfavorable [ˌʌn'feɪvərəbəl] *adj* : desfavorable, mal — **unfavorably** [-bli] *adv*

unfeeling [ˌʌn'fiːlɪŋ] *adj* : insensible — **unfeelingly** *adv*

unfinished [ˌʌn'fɪnɪʃd] *adj* : inacabado, incompleto

unfit [ˌʌn'fɪt] *adj* **1** UNSUITABLE : inadecuado, impropio **2** UNSUITED : no apto, incapaz **3** : incapacitado (físicamente) ⟨to be unfit : no estar en forma⟩

unflappable [ˌʌn'flæpəbəl] *adj* : imperturbable

unflattering [ˌʌn'flæʈərɪŋ] *adj* : poco favorecedor

unfold [ˌʌn'foːld] *vt* **1** EXPAND : desplegar, desdoblar, extender ⟨to unfold a map : desplegar un mapa⟩ **2** DISCLOSE, REVEAL : revelar, exponer (un plan, etc.) — *vi* **1** DEVELOP : desarrollarse, desenvolverse ⟨the story unfolded : el cuento se desarrollaba⟩ **2** EXPAND : extenderse, desplegarse

unforeseeable [ˌʌnfor'siːəbəl] *adj* : imprevisible

unforeseen [ˌʌnfor'siːn] *adj* : imprevisto

unforgettable [ˌʌnfər'gɛʈəbəl] *adj* : inolvidable, memorable — **unforgettably** [-bli] *adv*

unforgivable [ˌʌnfər'gɪvəbəl] *adj* : imperdonable

unfortunate[1] [ˌʌn'fɔrʧənət] *adj* **1** UNLUCKY : desgraciado, infortunado, desafortunado ⟨how unfortunate! : ¡qué mala suerte!⟩ **2** INAPPROPRIATE : inoportuno ⟨an unfortunate comment : un comentario poco feliz⟩

unfortunate[2] *n* : desgraciado *m*, -da *f*

unfortunately [ˌʌn'fɔrʧənətli] *adv* : desafortunadamente

unfounded [ˌʌn'faʊndəd] *adj* : infundado

unfreeze [ˌʌn'friːz] *v* **-froze** [-'froːz]; **-frozen** [-'froːzən]; **-freezing** *vt* : descongelar — *vi* : descongelarse

unfriendliness [ˌʌn'frɛndlinəs] *n* : hostilidad *f*, antipatía *f*

unfriendly [ˌʌn'frɛndli] *adj* **-lier; -est** : poco amistoso, hostil

unfurl [ˌʌn'fərl] *vt* : desplegar, desdoblar — *vi* : desplegarse

unfurnished [ˌʌn'fərnɪʃt] *adj* : desamueblado

ungainly [ˌʌn'geɪnli] *adj* : desgarbado

ungodly [ˌʌn'gɑdli, -'gɑd-] *adj* **1** IMPIOUS : impío **2** OUTRAGEOUS : atroz, terrible ⟨at an ungodly hour : a una hora intempestiva⟩

ungrateful [ˌʌn'greɪtfəl] *adj* : desagradecido, ingrato — **ungratefully** *adv*

ungratefulness [ˌʌn'greɪtfəlnəs] *n* : ingratitud *f*

unhappily [ˌʌn'hæpəli] *adv* **1** SADLY : tristemente **2** UNFORTUNATELY : desafortunadamente, lamentablemente

unhappiness [ˌʌn'hæpinəs] *n* : infelicidad *f*, tristeza *f*, desdicha *f*

unhappy [ˌʌn'hæpi] *adj* **-pier; -est** **1** UNFORTUNATE : desafortunado, desventurado **2** MISERABLE, SAD : infeliz, triste, desdichado **3** INOPPORTUNE : inoportuno, poco feliz

unharmed [ˌʌn'hɑrmd] *adj* : salvo, ileso

unhealthy [ˌʌn'hɛlθi] *adj* **-thier; -est** **1** UNWHOLESOME : insalubre, malsano, nocivo a la salud ⟨an unhealthy climate : un clima insalubre⟩ **2** SICKLY : de mala salud, enfermizo

unheard-of [ˌʌn'hərdəv] *adj* : sin precedente, inaudito, insólito

unhinge [ˌʌn'hɪndʒ] *vt* **-hinged; -hinging** **1** : desquiciar (una puerta, etc.) **2** DISRUPT, UNSETTLE : trastornar, perturbar

unholy [ˌʌn'hoːli] *adj* **-lier; -est** **1** : profano, impío **2** UNGODLY : atroz, terrible

unhook [ˌʌn'hʊk] *vt* **1** : desenganchar, descolgar (de algo) **2** UNDO : desabrochar

unhurt [ˌʌn'hərt] *adj* : ileso

unicorn ['juːnəˌkɔrn] *n* : unicornio *m*

unidentified [ˌʌnaɪ'dɛntəˌfaɪd] *adj* : no identificado ⟨unidentified flying object : objeto volador no identificado⟩

unification [ˌjuːnəfə'keɪʃən] *n* : unificación *f*

uniform[1] ['juːnəˌfɔrm] *adj* : uniforme, homogéneo, constante

uniform[2] *n* : uniforme *m*

uniformed ['juːnəˌfɔrmd] *adj* : uniformado

uniformity [ˌjuːnə'fɔrməti] *n, pl* **-ties** : uniformidad *f*

unify ['juːnəˌfaɪ] *vt* **-fied; -fying** : unificar, unir

unilateral [ˌjuːnə'læʈərəl] *adj* : unilateral — **unilaterally** *adv*

unimaginable [ˌʌnɪ'mædʒənəbəl] *adj* : inimaginable, inconcebible

unimportant [ˌʌnɪm'pɔrtənt] *adj* : intrascendente, insignificante, sin importancia

uninhabited [ˌʌnɪn'hæbəʈəd] *adj* : deshabitado, desierto, despoblado

uninhibited [ˌʌnɪn'hɪbəṭəd] *adj* : desenfadado, desinhibido, sin reservas

uninjured [ˌʌn'ɪnʤərd] *adj* : ileso

unintelligent [ˌʌnɪn'tɛləʤənt] *adj* : poco inteligente

unintelligible [ˌʌnɪn'tɛləʤəbəl] *adj* : ininteligible, incomprensible

unintentional [ˌʌnɪn'tɛnʧənəl] *adj* : no deliberado, involuntario

unintentionally [ˌʌnɪn'tɛnʧənəli] *adv* : involuntariamente, sin querer

uninterested [ˌʌn'ɪntəˌrɛstəd, -trəstəd] *adj* : indiferente

uninteresting [ˌʌn'ɪntəˌrɛstɪŋ, -trəstɪŋ] *adj* : poco interesante, sin interés

uninterrupted [ˌʌnˌɪntə'rʌptəd] *adj* : ininterrumpido, continuo

union ['ju:njən] *n* **1** : unión *f* **2** *or* **labor union** : sindicato *m*, gremio *m*

unionize ['ju:njəˌnaɪz] *v* **-ized; -izing** *vt* : sindicalizar, sindicar — *vi* : sindicalizarse

unique [juˈni:k] *adj* **1** SOLE : único, solo **2** UNUSUAL : extraordinario

uniquely [juˈni:kli] *adv* **1** EXCLUSIVELY : exclusivamente **2** EXCEPTIONALLY : excepcionalmente

unison ['ju:nəsən, -zən] *n* **1** : unísono *m* (en música) **2** CONCORD : acuerdo *m*, armonía *f*, concordia *f* **3 in ~** SIMULTANEOUSLY : simultáneamente, al unísono

unit ['ju:nɪt] *n* **1** : unidad *f* **2** : módulo *m* (de un mobiliario)

unitary ['ju:nəˌteri] *adj* : unitario

unite [juˈnaɪt] *v* **united; uniting** *vt* : unir, juntar, combinar — *vi* : unirse, juntarse

unity ['ju:nəti] *n, pl* **-ties 1** UNION : unidad *f*, unión *f* **2** HARMONY : armonía *f*, acuerdo *m*

universal [ˌju:nə'vərsəl] *adj* **1** GENERAL : general, universal ⟨a universal rule : una regla universal⟩ **2** WORLDWIDE : universal, mundial — **universally** *adv*

universe ['ju:nəˌvərs] *n* : universo *m*

university [ˌju:nə'vərsəti] *n, pl* **-ties** : universidad *f*

unjust [ˌʌn'ʤʌst] *adj* : injusto — **unjustly** *adv*

unjustifiable [ˌʌnˌʤʌstə'faɪəbəl] *adj* : injustificable

unjustified [ˌʌn'ʤʌstəˌfaɪd] *adj* : injustificado

unkempt [ˌʌn'kɛmpt] *adj* : descuidado, desaliñado, despeinado (dícese del pelo)

unkind [ˌʌn'kaɪnd] *adj* : poco amable, cruel — **unkindly** *adv*

unkindness [ˌʌn'kaɪndnəs] *n* : crueldad *f*, falta *f* de amabilidad

unknowing [ˌʌn'no:ɪŋ] *adj* : inconsciente, ignorante — **unknowingly** *adv*

unknown [ˌʌn'no:n] *adj* : desconocido

unlawful [ˌʌn'lɔfəl] *adj* : ilícito, ilegal — **unlawfully** *adv*

unleash [ˌʌn'li:ʃ] *vt* : soltar, desatar

unless [ən'lɛs] *conj* : a menos que, salvo que, a no ser que

unlike[1] [ˌʌn'laɪk] *adj* **1** DIFFERENT : diferente, distinto **2** UNEQUAL : desigual

unlike[2] *prep* **1** : diferente de, distinto de ⟨unlike the others : distinto a los demás⟩ **2** : a diferencia de ⟨unlike her sister, she is shy : a diferencia de su hermana, es tímida⟩

unlikelihood [ˌʌn'laɪkliˌhʊd] *n* : improbabilidad *f*

unlikely [ˌʌn'laɪkli] *adj* **-lier; -est 1** IMPROBABLE : improbable, poco probable **2** UNPROMISING : poco prometedor

unlimited [ˌʌn'lɪməṭəd] *adj* : ilimitado

unload [ˌʌn'lo:d] *vt* **1** REMOVE : descargar, desembarcar (mercancías o pasajeros) **2** : descargar (un avión, un camión, etc.) **3** DUMP : deshacerse de — *vi* : descargar (dícese de un avión, un camión, etc.)

unlock [ˌʌn'lɑk] *vt* **1** : abrir (con llave) **2** DISCLOSE, REVEAL : revelar

unluckily [ˌʌn'lʌkəli] *adv* : desgraciadamente

unlucky [ˌʌn'lʌki] *adj* **-luckier; -est 1** : de mala suerte, desgraciado, desafortunado ⟨an unlucky year : un año de mala suerte⟩ **2** INAUSPICIOUS : desfavorable, poco propicio **3** REGRETTABLE : lamentable

unmanageable [ˌʌn'mænɪʤəbəl] *adj* : difícil de controlar, poco manejable, ingobernable

unmarried [ˌʌn'mærid] *adj* : soltero

unmask [ˌʌn'mæsk] *vt* EXPOSE : desenmascarar

unmerciful [ˌʌn'mərsɪfəl] *adj* MERCILESS : despiadado — **unmercifully** *adv*

unmistakable [ˌʌnmɪ'steɪkəbəl] *adj* : evidente, inconfundible, obvio — **unmistakably** [-bli] *adv*

unmoved [ˌʌn'mu:vd] *adj* : impasible ⟨to be unmoved by : permanecer impasible ante⟩

unnatural [ˌʌn'næʧərəl] *adj* **1** ABNORMAL, UNUSUAL : anormal, poco natural, poco normal **2** AFFECTED : afectado, forzado ⟨an unnatural smile : una sonrisa forzada⟩ **3** PERVERSE : perverso, antinatural

unnecessary [ˌʌn'nɛsəˌseri] *adj* : innecesario — **unnecessarily** [-ˌnɛsə'serəli] *adv*

unnerve [ˌʌn'nərv] *vt* **-nerved; -nerving** : turbar, desconcertar, poner nervioso

unnoticed [ˌʌn'no:ṭəst] *adj* : inadvertido ⟨to go unnoticed : pasar inadvertido⟩

unobstructed [ˌʌnəb'strʌktəd] *adj* : libre, despejado

unobtainable [ˌʌnəb'teɪnəbəl] *adj* : inasequible

unobtrusive [ˌʌnəb'stru:sɪv] *adj* : discreto

unoccupied [ˌʌn'ɑkjəˌpaɪd] *adj* **1** IDLE : desempleado, desocupado **2** EMPTY : desocupado, libre, deshabitado

unofficial [ˌʌnə'fɪʃəl] *adj* : extraoficial, oficioso, no oficial

unorganized [ˌʌn'ɔrgəˌnaɪzd] *adj* : desorganizado

unorthodox [ˌʌn'ɔrθəˌdɑks] *adj* : poco ortodoxo, poco convencional

unpack [ˌʌn'pæk] *vt* : desempacar — *vi* : desempacar, deshacer las maletas

unpaid [ˌʌn'peɪd] *adj* : no remunerado, no retribuido ⟨an unpaid bill : una cuenta pendiente⟩

unparalleled [ˌʌn'pærəˌlɛld] *adj* : sin igual

unpatriotic [ˌʌnˌpeɪtri'ɑtɪk] *adj* : antipatriótico

unpleasant [ˌʌn'plɛzənt] *adj* : desagradable — **unpleasantly** *adv*

unplug [ˌʌn'plʌg] *vt* **-plugged; -plugging 1** UNCLOG : destapar, desatascar **2** DISCONNECT : desconectar, desenchufar

unpopular [ˌʌn'pɑpjələr] *adj* : impopular, poco popular

unpopularity [ˌʌnˌpɑpjə'lærəti] *n* : impopularidad *f*

unprecedented [ˌʌn'prɛsəˌdɛntəd] *adj* : sin precedentes, inaudito, nuevo

unpredictable [ˌʌnpri'dɪktəbəl] *adj* : impredecible

unprejudiced [ˌʌn'prɛdʒədəst] *adj* : imparcial, objetivo

unprepared [ˌʌnpri'pærd] *adj* : no preparado ⟨an unprepared speech : un discurso improvisado⟩

unpretentious [ˌʌnpri'tɛntʃəs] *adj* : modesto, sin pretensiones

unprincipled [ˌʌn'prɪntsəpəld] *adj* : sin principios, carente de escrúpulos

unproductive [ˌʌnprə'dʌktɪv] *adj* : improductivo

unprofitable [ˌʌn'prɑfətəbəl] *adj* : no rentable, poco provechoso

unpromising [ˌʌn'prɑməsɪŋ] *adj* : poco prometedor

unprotected [ˌʌnprə'tɛktəd] *adj* : sin protección, desprotegido

unprovoked [ˌʌnprə'voːkt] *adj* : no provocado

unpublished [ˌʌn'pʌblɪʃt] *adj* : inédito

unpunished [ˌʌn'pʌnɪʃt] *adj* : impune ⟨to go unpunished : escapar sin castigo⟩

unqualified [ˌʌn'kwɑləˌfaɪd] *adj* **1** : no calificado, sin título **2** COMPLETE : completo, absoluto ⟨an unqualified denial : una negación incondicional⟩

unquestionable [ˌʌn'kwɛstʃənəbəl] *adj* : incuestionable, indudable, indiscutible — **unquestionably** [-bli] *adv*

unquestioning [ˌʌn'kwɛstʃənɪŋ] *adj* : incondicional, absoluto, ciego

unravel [ˌʌn'rævəl] *v* **-eled** *or* **-elled; -eling** *or* **-elling** *vt* **1** DISENTANGLE : desenmarañar, desenredar **2** SOLVE : aclarar, desenmarañar, desentrañar — *vi* : deshacerse

unreal [ˌʌn'riːl] *adj* : irreal

unrealistic [ˌʌnˌriːə'lɪstɪk] *adj* : poco realista

unreasonable [ˌʌn'riːzənəbəl] *adj* **1** IRRATIONAL : poco razonable, irrazonable, irracional **2** EXCESSIVE : excesivo ⟨unreasonable prices : precios excesivos⟩

unreasonably [ˌʌn'riːzənəbli] *adv* **1** IRRATIONALLY : irracionalmente, de manera irrazonable **2** EXCESSIVELY : excesivamente

unrefined [ˌʌnri'faɪnd] *adj* **1** : no refinado, sin refinar (dícese del azúcar, de la harina, etc.) **2** : poco refinado, inculto (dícese de una persona)

unrelated [ˌʌnri'leɪtəd] *adj* : no relacionado, inconexo

unrelenting [ˌʌnri'lɛntɪŋ] *adj* **1** STERN : severo, inexorable **2** CONSTANT, RELENTLESS : constante, implacable

unreliable [ˌʌnri'laɪəbəl] *adj* : que no es de fiar, de poca confianza, inestable (dícese del tiempo)

unrepentant [ˌʌnri'pɛntənt] *adj* : impenitente

unresolved [ˌʌnri'zɑlvd] *adj* : pendiente, no resuelto

unrest [ˌʌn'rɛst] *n* : inquietud *f*, malestar *m* ⟨political unrest : disturbios políticos⟩

unrestrained [ˌʌnri'streɪnd] *adj* : desenfrenado, incontrolado

unrestricted [ˌʌnri'strɪktəd] *adj* : sin restricción ⟨unrestricted access : libre acceso⟩

unrewarding [ˌʌnri'wɔrdɪŋ] *adj* THANKLESS : ingrato

unripe [ˌʌn'raɪp] *adj* : inmaduro, verde

unrivaled *or* **unrivalled** [ˌʌn'raɪvəld] *adj* : incomparable

unroll [ˌʌn'roːl] *vt* : desenrollar — *vi* : desenrollarse

unruffled [ˌʌn'rʌfəld] *adj* **1** SERENE : sereno, tranquilo **2** SMOOTH : tranquilo, liso ⟨unruffled waters : aguas tranquilas⟩

unruliness [ˌʌn'ruːlinəs] *n* : indisciplina *f*

unruly [ˌʌn'ruːli] *adj* : indisciplinado, díscolo, rebelde

unsafe [ˌʌn'seɪf] *adj* : inseguro

unsaid [ˌʌn'sɛd] *adj* : sin decir ⟨to leave unsaid : quedar por decir⟩

unsanitary [ˌʌn'sænəˌteri] *adj* : antihigiénico

unsatisfactory [ˌʌnˌsætəs'fæktəri] *adj* : insatisfactorio

unsatisfied [ˌʌn'sætəsˌfaɪd] *adj* : insatisfecho

unscathed [ˌʌn'skeɪðd] *adj* UNHARMED : ileso

unscheduled [ˌʌn'skɛˌdʒuːld] *adj* : no programado, imprevisto

unscientific [ˌʌnˌsaɪən'tɪfɪk] *adj* : poco científico

unscrupulous [ˌʌn'skruːpjələs] *adj* : inescrupuloso, sin escrúpulos — **unscrupulously** *adv*

unseal [ˌʌn'siːl] *vt* : abrir, quitarle el sello a

unseasonable [ˌʌn'siːzənəbəl] *adj* **1** : extemporáneo ⟨unseasonable rain

: lluvia extemporánea⟩ 2 UNTIMELY : extemporáneo, inoportuno

unseemly [ˌʌn'siːmli] *adj* -lier; -est 1 INDECOROUS : indecoroso 2 INAPPROPRIATE : impropio, inapropiado

unseen [ˌʌn'siːn] *adj* 1 UNNOTICED : inadvertido 2 INVISIBLE : oculto, invisible

unselfish [ˌʌn'sɛlfɪʃ] *adj* : generoso, desinteresado — **unselfishly** *adv*

unselfishness [ˌʌn'sɛlfɪʃnəs] *n* : generosidad *f*, desinterés *m*

unsettle [ˌʌn'sɛtəl] *vt* -tled; -tling DISTURB : trastornar, alterar, perturbar

unsettled [ˌʌn'sɛtəld] *adj* 1 CHANGEABLE : inestable, variable ⟨unsettled weather : tiempo inestable⟩ 2 DISTURBED : agitado, inquieto ⟨unsettled waters : aguas agitadas⟩ 3 UNDECIDED : pendiente (dícese de un asunto), indeciso (dícese de una persona) 4 UNPAID : sin saldar, pendiente 5 UNINHABITED : despoblado, no colonizado

unshaped [ˌʌn'ʃeɪpt] *adj* : sin forma, informe

unsightly [ˌʌn'saɪtli] *adj* UGLY : feo, de aspecto malo

unskilled [ˌʌn'skɪld] *adj* : no calificado

unskillful [ˌʌn'skɪlfəl] *adj* : inexperto, poco hábil

unsnap [ˌʌn'snæp] *vt* -snapped; -snapping : desabrochar

unsociable *adj* : poco sociable

unsolved [ˌʌn'sɑlvd] *adj* : no resuelto, sin resolver

unsophisticated [ˌʌnsə'fɪstəˌkeɪtəd] *adj* 1 NAIVE, UNWORLDLY : ingenuo, de poco mundo 2 SIMPLE : simple, poco sofisticado, rudimentario

unsound [ˌʌn'saʊnd] *adj* 1 UNHEALTHY : enfermizo, de mala salud 2 : poco sólido, defectuoso (dícese de una estructura, etc.) 3 INVALID : inválido, erróneo 4 **of unsound mind** : mentalmente incapacitado

unspeakable [ˌʌn'spiːkəbəl] *adj* 1 INDESCRIBABLE : indecible, inexpresable, incalificable 2 HEINOUS : atroz, nefando, abominable — **unspeakably** [-bli] *adv*

unspecified [ˌʌn'spɛsəˌfaɪd] *adj* : indeterminado, sin especificar

unspoiled [ˌʌn'spɔɪld] *adj* 1 : conservado, sin estropear (dícese de un lugar) 2 : que no está mimado (dícese de un niño)

unstable [ˌʌn'steɪbəl] *adj* 1 CHANGEABLE : variable, inestable, cambiable ⟨an unstable pulse : un pulso irregular⟩ 2 UNSTEADY : inestable, poco sólido (dícese de una estructura)

unsteadily [ˌʌn'stɛdəli] *adv* : de modo inestable

unsteadiness [ˌʌn'stɛdinəs] *n* : inestabilidad *f*, inseguridad *f*

unsteady [ˌʌn'stɛdi] *adj* 1 UNSTABLE : inestable, variable 2 SHAKY : tembloroso

unstoppable [ˌʌn'stɑpəbəl] *adj* : irrefrenable, incontenible

unsubstantiated [ˌʌnsəb'stænʧiˌeɪtəd] *adj* : no corroborado, no demostrado

unsuccessful [ˌʌnsək'sɛsfəl] *adj* : fracasado, infructuoso

unsuitable [ˌʌn'suːtəbəl] *adj* : inadecuado, impropio, inapropiado ⟨an unsuitable time : una hora inconveniente⟩

unsuited [ˌʌn'suːtəd] *adj* : inadecuado, inepto

unsung [ˌʌn'sʌŋ] *adj* : olvidado

unsure [ˌʌn'ʃʊr] *adj* : incierto, dudoso

unsurpassed [ˌʌnsər'pæst] *adj* : sin par, sin igual

unsuspecting [ˌʌnsə'spɛktɪŋ] *adj* : desprevenido, desapercibido, confiado

unsympathetic [ˌʌnˌsɪmpə'θɛtɪk] *adj* : poco comprensivo, indiferente

untangle [ˌʌn'teɪŋgəl] *vt* -gled; -gling : desenmarañar, desenredar

unthinkable [ˌʌn'θɪŋkəbəl] *adj* : inconcebible, impensable

unthinking [ˌʌn'θɪŋkɪŋ] *adj* : irreflexivo, inconsciente — **unthinkingly** *adv*

untidy [ˌʌn'taɪdi] *adj* 1 SLOVENLY : desaliñado 2 DISORDERLY : desordenado, desarreglado

untie [ˌʌn'taɪ] *vt* -tied; -tying *or* -tieing : desatar, deshacer

until¹ [ˌʌn'tɪl] *prep* : hasta ⟨until now : hasta ahora⟩

until² *conj* : hasta que ⟨until they left : hasta que salieron⟩ ⟨don't answer until you're sure : no contestes hasta que (no) estés seguro⟩

untimely [ˌʌn'taɪmli] *adj* 1 PREMATURE : prematuro ⟨an untimely death : una muerte prematura⟩ 2 INOPPORTUNE : inoportuno, intempestivo

untold [ˌʌn'toːld] *adj* 1 : nunca dicho ⟨the untold secret : el secreto sin contar⟩ 2 INCALCULABLE : incalculable, indecible

untouched [ˌʌn'tʌʧt] *adj* 1 INTACT : intacto, sin tocar, sin probar (dícese de la comida) 2 UNAFFECTED : insensible, indiferente

untoward [ˌʌn'tɔrd, -'toːərd, -tə-'wɔrd] *adj* 1 : indecoroso, impropio (dícese del comportamiento) 2 ADVERSE, UNFORTUNATE : desafortunado, adverso ⟨untoward effects : efectos perjudiciales⟩ 3 UNSEEMLY : indecoroso

untrained [ˌʌn'treɪnd] *adj* : inexperto, no capacitado

untreated [ˌʌn'triːtəd] *adj* : no tratado (dícese de una enfermedad, etc.), sin tratar (dícese de un material)

untroubled [ˌʌn'trʌbəld] *adj* : tranquilo ⟨to be untroubled by : no estar afectado por⟩

untrue [ˌʌn'truː] *adj* 1 UNFAITHFUL : infiel 2 FALSE : falso

untrustworthy [ˌʌn'trʌstˌwərði] *adj* : de poca confianza (dícese de una persona), no fidedigno (dícese de la información)

untruth [ˌʌn'truːθ, 'ʌnˌ-] *n* : mentira *f*, falsedad *f*

untruthful [ˌʌn'truːθfəl] *adj* : mentiroso, falso

unusable [ˌʌn'juːzəbəl] *adj* : inútil, inservible

unused [ˌʌn'juːzd, *in sense 1 usually* -'juːst] *adj* **1** UNACCUSTOMED : inhabituado **2** NEW : nuevo **3** IDLE : no utilizado (dícese de la tierra) **4** REMAINING : restante ⟨the unused portion : la porción restante⟩

unusual [ˌʌn'juːʒʊəl] *adj* : inusual, poco común, raro

unusually [ˌʌn'juːʒʊəli, -'juːʒəli] *adv* : excepcionalmente, extraordinariamente, fuera de lo común

unwanted [ˌʌn'wɑntəd] *adj* : superfluo, de sobre

unwarranted [ˌʌn'wɔrəntəd] *adj* : injustificado

unwary [ˌʌn'wæri] *adj* : incauto

unwavering [ˌʌn'weɪvərɪŋ] *adj* : firme, inquebrantable ⟨an unwavering gaze : una mirada fija⟩

unwelcome [ˌʌn'wɛlkəm] *adj* : importuno, molesto

unwell [ˌʌn'wɛl] *adj* : enfermo, mal

unwholesome [ˌʌn'hoːlsəm] *adj* **1** UNHEALTHY : malsano, insalubre **2** PERNICIOUS : pernicioso **3** LOATHSOME : repugnante, muy desagradable

unwieldy [ˌʌn'wiːldi] *adj* CUMBERSOME : difícil de manejar, torpe y pesado

unwilling [ˌʌn'wɪlɪŋ] *adj* : poco dispuesto ⟨to be unwilling to : no estar dispuesto a⟩

unwillingly [ˌʌn'wɪlɪŋli] *adv* : a regañadientes, de mala gana

unwind [ˌʌn'waɪnd] *v* **-wound** [-'waʊnd]; **-winding** *vt* UNROLL : desenrollar — *vi* **1** : desenrollarse **2** RELAX : relajar

unwise [ˌʌn'waɪz] *adj* : imprudente, desacertado, poco aconsejable

unwisely [ˌʌn'waɪzli] *adv* : imprudentemente

unwitting [ˌʌn'wɪtɪŋ] *adj* **1** UNAWARE : inconsciente **2** INADVERTENT : involuntario, inadvertido ⟨an unwitting mistake : un error inadvertido⟩ — **unwittingly** *adv*

unworthiness [ˌʌn'wərðinəs] *n* : falta *f* de valía

unworthy [ˌʌn'wərði] *adj* **1** UNDESERVING : indigno ⟨to be unworthy of : no ser digno de⟩ **2** UNMERITED : inmerecido

unwrap [ˌʌn'ræp] *vt* **-wrapped; -wrapping** : desenvolver, deshacer

unwritten [ˌʌn'rɪtən] *adj* : no escrito

unyielding [ˌʌn'jiːldɪŋ] *adj* : firme, inflexible, rígido

unzip [ˌʌn'zɪp] *vt* **-zipped; -zipping** : abrir el cierre de

up¹ ['ʌp] *v* **upped** ['ʌpt]; **upping; ups** *vt* INCREASE : aumentar, subir ⟨they upped the prices : aumentaron los precios⟩ — *vi* **to up and** : agarrar y *fam* ⟨she up and left : agarró y se fue⟩

up² *adv* **1** ABOVE : arriba, en lo alto ⟨up in the mountains : arriba en las montañas⟩ **2** UPWARDS : hacia arriba ⟨push it up : empújalo hacia arriba⟩ ⟨the sun came up : el sol salió⟩ ⟨prices went up : los precios subieron⟩ **3** (*indicating an upright position or waking state*) ⟨to sit up : ponerse derecho⟩ ⟨they got up late : se levantaron tarde⟩ ⟨I stayed up all night : pasé toda la noche sin dormir⟩ **4** (*indicating volume or intensity*) ⟨to speak up : hablar más fuerte⟩ **5** (*indicating a northerly direction*) ⟨the climate up north : el clima del norte⟩ ⟨I'm going up to Canada : voy para Canadá⟩ **6** (*indicating the appearance or existence of something*) ⟨the book turned up : el libro apareció⟩ **7** (*indicating consideration*) ⟨she brought the matter up : mencionó el asunto⟩ **8** COMPLETELY : completamente ⟨eat it up : cómetelo todo⟩ **9** : en pedazos ⟨he tore it up : lo rompió en pedazos⟩ **10** (*indicating a stopping*) ⟨the car pulled up to the curb : el carro paró al borde de la acera⟩ **11** (*indicating an even score*) ⟨the game was 10 up : empataron a 10⟩

up³ *adj* **1** (*risen above the horizon*) ⟨the sun is up : ha salido el sol⟩ **2** (*being above a normal or former level*) ⟨prices are up : los precios han aumentado⟩ ⟨the river is up : las aguas están altas⟩ **3** : despierto, levantado ⟨up all night : despierto toda la noche⟩ **4** BUILT : construido ⟨the house is up : la casa está construida⟩ **5** OPEN : abierto ⟨the windows are up : las ventanas están abiertas⟩ **6** (*moving or going upward*) ⟨the up staircase : la escalera para subir⟩ **7** ABREAST : enterado, al día, al corriente ⟨to be up on the news : estar al corriente de las noticias⟩ **8** PREPARED : preparado ⟨we were up for the test : estuvimos preparados para el examen⟩ **9** FINISHED : terminado, acabado ⟨time is up : se ha terminado el tiempo permitido⟩ **10 to be up** : pasar ⟨what's up? : ¿qué pasa?⟩

up⁴ *prep* **1** (*to, toward, or at a higher point of*) ⟨he went up the stairs : subió la escalera⟩ **2** (*to or toward the source of*) ⟨to go up the river : ir río arriba⟩ **3** ALONG : a lo largo, por ⟨up the coast : a lo largo de la costa⟩ ⟨just up the way : un poco más adelante⟩ ⟨up and down the city : por toda la ciudad⟩

upbraid [ˌʌp'breɪd] *vt* : reprender, regañar

upbringing ['ʌpˌbrɪŋɪŋ] *n* : crianza *f*, educación *f*

upcoming [ˌʌp'kʌmɪŋ] *adj* : próximo

update¹ [ˌʌp'deɪt] *vt* **-dated; -dating** : poner al día, poner al corriente, actualizar

update² ['ʌpˌdeɪt] *n* : actualización *f*, puesta *f* al día

upend [ˌʌp'ɛnd] *vt* **1** : poner vertical **2** OVERTURN : volcar

upgrade¹ [ˈʌpˌgreɪd, ˌʌpˈ-] *vt* **-graded; -grading 1** PROMOTE : ascender **2** IMPROVE : mejorar

upgrade² [ˈʌpˌgreɪd] *n* **1** SLOPE : cuesta *f*, pendiente *f* **2** RISE : aumento *m* de categoría (de un puesto), ascenso *m* (de un empleado) **3** IMPROVEMENT : mejoramiento *m*

upheaval [ˌʌpˈhiːvəl] *n* **1** : levantamiento *m* (en geología) **2** DISTURBANCE, UPSET : trastorno *m*, agitación *f*, conmoción *f*

uphill¹ [ˌʌpˈhɪl] *adv* : cuesta arriba

uphill² [ˈʌpˌhɪl] *adj* **1** ASCENDING : en subida **2** DIFFICULT : difícil, arduo

uphold [ˌʌpˈhoːld] *vt* **-held; -holding 1** SUPPORT : sostener, apoyar, mantener **2** RAISE : levantar **3** CONFIRM : confirmar (una decisión judicial)

upholster [ˌʌpˈhoːlstər] *vt* : tapizar

upholsterer [ˌʌpˈhoːlstərər] *n* : tapicero *m*, -ra *f*

upholstery [ˌʌpˈhoːlstəri] *n, pl* **-steries** : tapicería *f*

upkeep [ˈʌpˌkiːp] *n* : mantenimiento *m*

upland [ˈʌplənd, -ˌlænd] *n* : altiplanicie *f*, altiplano *m*

uplift¹ [ˌʌpˈlɪft] *vt* **1** RAISE : elevar, levantar **2** ELEVATE : elevar, animar (el espíritu, la mente, etc.)

uplift² [ˈʌpˌlɪft] *n* : elevación *f*

upon [əˈpɔn, əˈpɑn] *prep* : en, sobre ⟨upon the desk : sobre el escritorio⟩ ⟨upon leaving : al salir⟩ ⟨questions upon questions : pregunta tras pregunta⟩

upper¹ [ˈʌpər] *adj* **1** HIGHER : superior ⟨the upper classes : las clases altas⟩ **2** : alto (en geografía) ⟨the upper Mississippi : el alto Mississippi⟩

upper² *n* : parte *f* superior (del calzado, etc.)

uppercase [ˌʌpərˈkeɪs] *adj* : mayúsculo

upper hand *n* : ventaja *f*, dominio *m*

uppermost [ˈʌpərˌmoːst] *adj* : más alto ⟨it was uppermost in his mind : era lo que más le preocupaba⟩

upright¹ [ˈʌpˌraɪt] *adj* **1** VERTICAL : vertical **2** ERECT : erguido, derecho **3** JUST : recto, honesto, justo

upright² *n* : montante *m*, poste *m*, soporte *m*

uprising [ˈʌpˌraɪzɪŋ] *n* : insurrección *f*, revuelta *f*, alzamiento *m*

uproar [ˈʌpˌror] *n* COMMOTION : alboroto *m*, jaleo *m*, escándalo *m*

uproarious [ˌʌpˈroriəs] *adj* **1** CLAMOROUS : estrepitoso, clamoroso **2** HILARIOUS : muy divertido, hilarante — **uproariously** *adv*

uproot [ˌʌpˈruːt, -ˈrʊt] *vt* : desarraigar

upset¹ [ˌʌpˈsɛt] *vt* **-set; -setting 1** OVERTURN : volcar **2** SPILL : derramar **3** DISTURB : perturbar, disgustar, inquietar, alterar **4** SICKEN : sentar mal a ⟨it upsets my stomach : me sienta mal al estómago⟩ **5** DISRUPT : trastornar, desbaratar (planes, etc.) **6** DEFEAT : derrotar (en deportes)

upset² *adj* **1** DISPLEASED, DISTRESSED : disgustado, alterado **2 to have an upset stomach** : estar mal del estómago, estar descompuesto (de estómago)

upset³ [ˈʌpˌsɛt] *n* **1** OVERTURNING : vuelco *m* **2** DISRUPTION : trastorno *m* (de planes, etc.) **3** DEFEAT : derrota *f* (en deportes)

upshot [ˈʌpˌʃɑt] *n* : resultado *m* final

upside–down [ˌʌpˌsaɪdˈdaʊn] *adj* : al revés

upside down [ˌʌpˌsaɪdˈdaʊn] *adv* **1** : al revés **2** : en confusión, en desorden

upstairs¹ [ˌʌpˈstærz] *adv* : arriba, en el piso superior

upstairs² [ˈʌpˌstærz, ˌʌpˈ-] *adj* : de arriba

upstairs³ [ˈʌpˌstærz, ˌʌpˈ-] *ns & pl* : piso *m* de arriba, planta *f* de arriba

upstanding [ˌʌpˈstændɪŋ, ˈʌpˌ-] *adj* HONEST, UPRIGHT : honesto, íntegro, recto

upstart [ˈʌpˌstɑrt] *n* : advenedizo *m*, -za *f*

upswing [ˈʌpˌswɪŋ] *n* : alza *f*, mejora *f* notable ⟨to be on the upswing : estar mejorándose⟩

uptight [ˌʌpˈtaɪt] *adj* : tenso, nervioso

up to *prep* **1** : hasta ⟨up to a year : hasta un año⟩ ⟨in mud up to my ankles : en barro hasta los tobillos⟩ **2 to be up to** : estar a la altura de ⟨I'm not up to going : no estoy en condiciones de ir⟩ **3 to be up to** : depender de ⟨it's up to the director : depende del director⟩

up–to–date [ˌʌptəˈdeɪt] *adj* **1** CURRENT : corriente, al día ⟨to keep up-to-date : mantenerse al corriente⟩ **2** MODERN : moderno

uptown [ˈʌpˈtaʊn] *adv* : hacia la parte alta de la ciudad, hacia el distrito residencial

upturn [ˈʌpˌtərn] *n* : mejora *f*, auge *m* (económico)

upward¹ [ˈʌpwərd] *or* **upwards** [-wərdz] *adv* **1** : hacia arriba **2 ～ of** : más de

upward² *adj* : ascendente, hacia arriba

upwind [ˌʌpˈwɪnd] *adv & adj* : contra el viento

uranium [jʊˈreɪniəm] *n* : uranio *m*

Uranus [jʊˈreɪnəs, ˈjʊrənəs] *n* : Urano *m*

urban [ˈərbən] *adj* : urbano

urbane [ˌərˈbeɪn] *adj* : urbano, cortés

urchin [ˈərtʃən] *n* **1** SCAMP : granuja *mf*; pillo *m*, -lla *f* **2 sea urchin** : erizo *m* de mar

Urdu [ˈʊrduː, ˈər-] *n* : urdu *m*

urethra [jʊˈriːθrə] *n, pl* **-thras** *or* **-thrae** [-ˌθriː] : uretra *f*

urge¹ [ˈərdʒ] *vt* **urged; urging 1** PRESS : instar, apremiar, insistir ⟨we urged him to come : insistimos en que viniera⟩ **2** ADVOCATE : recomendar, abogar por **3 to urge on** : animar, alentar

urge² *n* : impulso *m*, ganas *fpl*, compulsión *f*

urgency [ˈərdʒəntsi] *n, pl* **-cies** : urgencia *f*

urgent ['ərdʒənt] *adj* **1** PRESSING : urgente, apremiante **2** INSISTENT : insistente **3 to be urgent** : urgir

urgently ['ərdʒəntli] *adv* : urgentemente

urinal ['jʊrənəl, *esp Brit* jʊ'raɪnəl] *n* : orinal *m* (recipiente), urinario *m* (lugar)

urinary ['jʊrə,nɛri] *adj* : urinario

urinate ['jʊrə,neɪt] *vi* **-nated; -nating** : orinar

urination [,jʊrə'neɪʃən] *n* : orinación *f*

urine ['jʊrən] *n* : orina *f*

urn ['ərn] *n* **1** VASE : urna *f* **2** : recipiente *m* (para servir café, etc.)

Uruguayan [,ʊrə'gwaɪən, ,jʊr-, -'gweɪ-] *n* : uruguayo *m*, -ya *f* — **Uruguayan** *adj*

us ['ʌs] *pron* **1** (*as direct object*) : nos ⟨they were visiting us : nos visitaban⟩ **2** (*as indirect object*) : nos ⟨he gave us a present : nos dio un regalo⟩ **3** (*as object of preposition*) : nosotros, nosotras ⟨stay with us : quédese con nosotros⟩ ⟨both of us : nosotros dos⟩ **4** (*for emphasis*) : nosotros ⟨it's us! : ¡somos nosotros!⟩

usable ['ju:zəbəl] *adj* : utilizable

usage ['ju:sɪdʒ, -zɪdʒ] *n* **1** HABIT : costumbre *f*, hábito *m* **2** USE : uso *m*

use¹ ['ju:z] *v* **used** ['ju:zd, *in phrase "used to" usually* 'ju:stu:]; **using** *vt* **1** EMPLOY : emplear, usar **2** CONSUME : consumir, tomar (drogas, etc.) **3** UTILIZE : usar, utilizar ⟨to use tact : usar tacto⟩ ⟨he used his friends to get ahead : usó a sus amigos para mejorar su posición⟩ **4** TREAT : tratar ⟨they used the horse cruelly : maltrataron al caballo⟩ **5 to use up** : agotar, consumir, gastar — *vi* (*used in the past with* **to** *to indicate a former fact or state*) : soler, acostumbrar ⟨winters used to be colder : los inviernos solían ser más fríos, los inviernos eran más fríos⟩ ⟨she used to dance : acostumbraba bailar⟩

use² ['ju:s] *n* **1** APPLICATION, EMPLOYMENT : uso *m*, empleo *m*, utilización *f* ⟨out of use : en desuso⟩ ⟨ready for use : listo para usar⟩ ⟨to be in use : usarse, estar funcionando⟩ ⟨to make use of : servirse de, aprovechar⟩ **2** USEFULNESS : utilidad *f* ⟨to be of no use : no servir (para nada)⟩ ⟨it's no use! : ¡es inútil!⟩ **3 to have the use of** : poder usar, tener acceso a **4 to have no use for** : no necesitar ⟨she has no use for po-

etry : a ella no le gusta la poesía⟩

used ['ju:zd] *adj* **1** SECONDHAND : usado, de segunda mano ⟨used cars : coches usados⟩ **2** ACCUSTOMED : acostumbrado ⟨used to the heat : acostumbrado al calor⟩

useful ['ju:sfəl] *adj* : útil, práctico — **usefully** *adv*

usefulness ['ju:sfəlnəs] *n* : utilidad *f*

useless ['ju:sləs] *adj* : inútil — **uselessly** *adv*

uselessness ['ju:sləsnəs] *n* : inutilidad *f*

user ['ju:zər] *n* : usuario *m*, -ria *f*

usher¹ ['ʌʃər] *vt* **1** ESCORT : acompañar, conducir **2 to usher in** : hacer pasar (a alguien) ⟨to usher in a new era : anunciar una nueva época⟩

usher² *n* : acomodador *m*, -dora *f*

usherette [,ʌʃə'rɛt] *n* : acomodadora *f*

usual ['ju:ʒəl] *adj* **1** NORMAL : usual, normal **2** CUSTOMARY : acostumbrado, habitual, de costumbre **3** ORDINARY : ordinario, típico

usually ['ju:ʒʊəli, 'ju:ʒəli] *adv* : usualmente, normalmente

usurp [jʊ'sərp, -'zərp] *vt* : usurpar

usurper [jʊ'sərpər, -'zər-] *n* : usurpador *m*, -dora *f*

utensil [jʊ'tɛntsəl] *n* **1** : utensilio *m* (de cocina) **2** IMPLEMENT : implemento *m*, útil *m* (de labranza, etc.)

uterine ['ju:tə,raɪn, -rən] *adj* : uterino

uterus ['ju:tərəs] *n, pl* **uteri** [-,raɪ] : útero *m*, matriz *f*

utilitarian [ju:,tɪlə'tɛriən] *adj* : utilitario

utility [ju:'tɪləti] *n, pl* **-ties 1** USEFULNESS : utilidad *f* **2 public utility** : empresa *f* de servicio público

utilization [,ju:tələ'zeɪʃən] *n* : utilización *f*

utilize ['ju:tə,laɪz] *vt* **-lized; -lizing** : utilizar, hacer uso de

utmost¹ ['ʌt,mo:st] *adj* **1** FARTHEST : extremo, más lejano **2** GREATEST : sumo, mayor ⟨of the utmost importance : de suma importancia⟩

utmost² *n* : lo más posible ⟨to the utmost : al máximo⟩

utopia [jʊ'to:piə] *n* : utopía *f*

utopian [jʊ'to:piən] *adj* : utópico

utter¹ ['ʌtər] *vt* : decir, articular, pronunciar (palabras)

utter² *adj* : absoluto — **utterly** *adv*

utterance ['ʌtərənts] *n* : declaración *f*, articulación *f*

V

v ['vi:] *n, pl* **v's** *or* **vs** ['vi:z] : vigésima segunda letra del alfabeto inglés

vacancy ['veɪkəntsi] *n, pl* **-cies 1** EMPTINESS : vacío *m*, vacuidad *f* **2** : vacante *f*, puesto *m* vacante ⟨to fill a vacancy

: ocupar un puesto⟩ **3** : habitación *f* libre (en un hotel) ⟨no vacancies : completo⟩

vacant ['veɪkənt] *adj* **1** EMPTY : libre, desocupado (dícese de los edificios,

etc.) **2** : vacante (dícese de los puestos) **3** BLANK : vacío, ausente ⟨a vacant stare : una mirada ausente⟩
vacate ['veɪˌkeɪt] *vt* **-cated; -cating** : desalojar, desocupar
vacation¹ [veɪ'keɪʃən, və-] *vi* : pasar las vacaciones, vacacionar *Mex*
vacation² *n* : vacaciones *fpl* ⟨to be on vacation : estar de vacaciones⟩
vacationer [veɪ'keɪʃənər, və-] *n* : turista *mf*, veraneante *mf*, vacacionista *mf CA, Mex*
vaccinate ['væksəˌneɪt] *vt* **-nated; -nating** : vacunar
vaccination [ˌvæksə'neɪʃən] *n* : vacunación *f*
vaccine [væk'siːn, 'vækˌ-] *n* : vacuna *f*
vacillate ['væsəˌleɪt] *vi* **-lated; -lating 1** HESITATE : vacilar **2** SWAY : oscilar
vacillation [ˌvæsə'leɪʃən] *n* : indecisión *f*, vacilación *f*
vacuous ['vækjuəs] *adj* **1** EMPTY : vacío **2** INANE : vacuo, necio, estúpido
vacuum¹ ['væˌkjuːm, -kjəm] *vt* : limpiar con aspiradora, pasar la aspiradora por
vacuum² *n, pl* **vacuums** *or* **vacua** ['vækjuə] : vacío *m*
vacuum cleaner *n* : aspiradora *f*
vagabond¹ ['vægəˌband] *adj* : vagabundo
vagabond² *n* : vagabundo *m*, -da *f*
vagary ['veɪgəri, və'geri] *n, pl* **-ries** : capricho *m*
vagina [və'dʒaɪnə] *n, pl* **-nae** [-ˌniː, -ˌnaɪ] *or* **-nas** : vagina *f*
vagrancy ['veɪgrəntsi] *n, pl* **-cies** : vagancia *f*
vagrant¹ ['veɪgrənt] *adj* : vagabundo
vagrant² *n* : vagabundo *m*, -da *f*
vague ['veɪg] *adj* **vaguer; -est 1** IMPRECISE : vago, impreciso ⟨a vague feeling : una sensación indefinida⟩ ⟨I haven't the vaguest idea : no tengo la más remota idea⟩ **2** UNCLEAR : borroso, poco claro ⟨a vague outline : un perfil indistinto⟩ **3** ABSENTMINDED : distraído
vaguely ['veɪgli] *adv* : vagamente, de manera imprecisa
vagueness ['veɪgnəs] *n* : vaguedad *f*, imprecisión *f*
vain ['veɪn] *adj* **1** WORTHLESS : vano **2** FUTILE : vano, inútil ⟨in vain : en vano⟩ **3** CONCEITED : vanidoso, presumido
vainly ['veɪnli] *adv* : en vano, vanamente, inútilmente
valance ['vælənts, 'veɪ-] *n* **1** FLOUNCE : volante *m* (de una cama, etc.) **2** : galería *f* de cortina (sobre una ventana)
vale ['veɪl] *n* : valle *m*
valedictorian [ˌvælədɪk'toriən] *n* : estudiante *mf* que pronuncia el discurso de despedida en ceremonia de graduación
valedictory [ˌvælə'dɪktəri] *adj* : de despedida
valentine ['vælənˌtaɪn] *n* : tarjeta *f* que se manda el Día de los Enamorados (el 14 de febrero)

Valentine's Day *n* : Día *m* de los Enamorados
valet ['væˌleɪ, væ'leɪ, 'vælət] *n* : ayuda *m* de cámara
valiant ['væljənt] *adj* : valiente, valeroso
valiantly ['væljəntli] *adv* : con valor, valientemente
valid ['væləd] *adj* : válido
validate ['væləˌdeɪt] *vt* **-dated; -dating** : validar, dar validez a
validity [və'lɪdəti, væ-] *n* : validez *f*
valise [və'liːs] *n* : maleta *f* (de mano)
valley ['væli] *n, pl* **-leys** : valle *m*
valor ['vælər] *n* : valor *m*, valentía *f*
valorous ['vælərəs] *adj* : valeroso, valiente
valuable¹ ['væljuəbəl, 'væljəbəl] *adj* **1** EXPENSIVE : valioso, de valor **2** WORTHWHILE : valioso, apreciable
valuable² *n* : objeto *m* de valor
valuation [ˌvælju'eɪʃən] *n* **1** APPRAISAL : valoración *f*, tasación *f* **2** VALUE : valuación *f*
value¹ ['vælˌjuː] *vt* **-ued; -uing 1** APPRAISE : valorar, avaluar, tasar **2** APPRECIATE : valorar, apreciar
value² *n* **1** : valor *m* ⟨of little value : de poco valor⟩ ⟨to be a good value : estar bien de precio, tener buen precio⟩ ⟨at face value : en su sentido literal⟩ **2 values** *npl* : valores *mpl* (morales), principios *mpl*
valueless ['væljuːləs] *adj* : sin valor
valve ['vælv] *n* : válvula *f*
vampire ['væmˌpaɪr] *n* **1** : vampiro *m* **2** *or* **vampire bat** : vampiro *m*
van¹ ['væn] → **vanguard**
van² *n* : furgoneta *f*, camioneta *f*
vanadium [və'neɪdiəm] *n* : vanadio *m*
vandal ['vændəl] *n* : vándalo *m*
vandalism ['vændəˌlɪzəm] *n* : vandalismo *m*
vandalize ['vændəˌlaɪz] *vt* : destrozar, destruir, estropear
vane ['veɪn] *n or* **weather vane** : veleta *f*
vanguard ['vænˌgard] *n* : vanguardia *f*
vanilla [və'nɪlə, -'nɛ-] *n* : vainilla *f*
vanish ['vænɪʃ] *vi* : desaparecer, disiparse, desvanecerse
vanity ['vænəti] *n, pl* **-ties 1** : vanidad *f* **2** *or* **vanity table** : tocador *m*
vanquish ['væŋkwɪʃ, 'væn-] *vt* : vencer, conquistar
vantage point ['væntɪdʒ] *n* : posición *f* ventajosa
vapid ['væpəd, 'veɪ-] *adj* : insípido, insulso
vapor ['veɪpər] *n* : vapor *m*
vaporize ['veɪpəˌraɪz] *v* **-rized; -rizing** *vt* : vaporizar — *vi* : vaporizarse, evaporarse
vaporizer ['veɪpəˌraɪzər] *n* : vaporizador *m*
variability [ˌvɛriə'bɪləti] *n, pl* **-ties** : variabilidad *f*
variable¹ ['vɛriəbəl] *adj* : variable ⟨variable cloudiness : nubosidad variable⟩

variable² *n* : variable *f*, factor *m*
variance ['vɛriənts] *n* **1** DISCREPANCY : varianza *f*, discrepancia *f* **2** DISAGREEMENT : desacuerdo *m* ⟨at variance with : en desacuerdo con⟩
variant¹ ['vɛriənt] *adj* : variante, divergente
variant² *n* : variante *f*
variation [ˌvɛri'eiʃən] *n* : variación *f*, diferencias *fpl*
varicose ['værəˌkoːs] *adj* : varicoso
varicose veins *npl* : varices *fpl*, várices *fpl*
varied ['vɛrid] *adj* : variado, dispar, diferente
variegated ['vɛriəˌgeitd] *adj* : abigarrado, multicolor
variety [və'raiəti] *n, pl* **-ties 1** DIVERSITY : diversidad *f*, variedad *f* **2** ASSORTMENT : surtido *m* ⟨for a variety of reasons : por diversas razones⟩ **3** SORT : clase *f* **4** BREED : variedad *f* (de plantas)
various ['vɛriəs] *adj* : varios, diversos
varnish¹ ['vɑrnɪʃ] *vt* : barnizar
varnish² *n* : barniz *f*
varsity ['vɑrsəti] *n, pl* **-ties** : equipo *m* universitario
vary ['vɛri] *v* **varied; varying** *vt* : variar, diversificar — *vi* **1** CHANGE : variar, cambiar **2** DEVIATE : desviarse
vascular ['væskjələr] *adj* : vascular
vase ['veis, 'veiz, 'vɑz] *n* : jarrón *m*, florero *m*
vassal ['væsəl] *n* : vasallo *m*, -lla *f*
vast ['væst] *adj* : inmenso, enorme, vasto
vastly ['væstli] *adv* : enormemente
vastness ['væstnəs] *n* : vastedad *f*, inmensidad *f*
vat ['væt] *n* : cuba *f*, tina *f*
vaudeville ['vɔdvəl, -ˌvɪl; 'vɔdəˌvɪl] *n* : vodevil *m*
vault¹ ['vɔlt] *vi* LEAP : saltar
vault² *n* **1** JUMP : salto *m* ⟨pole vault : salto de pértiga, salto con garrocha⟩ **2** DOME : bóveda *f* **3** : bodega *f* (para vino), bóveda *f* de seguridad (de un banco) **4** CRYPT : cripta *f*
vaulted ['vɔltəd] *adj* : abovedado
vaunted ['vɔntəd] *adj* : cacareado, alardeado ⟨a much vaunted wine : un vino muy alardeado⟩
VCR [ˌviːˌsiː'ɑr] *n* : video *m*, videocasetera *f*
veal ['viːl] *n* : ternera *f*, carne *f* de ternera
veer ['vɪr] *vi* : virar (dícese de un barco), girar (dícese de un coche), torcer (dícese de un camino)
vegetable¹ ['vɛʤtəbəl, 'vɛʤətə-] *adj* : vegetal
vegetable² *n* **1** : vegetal *m* ⟨the vegetable kingdom : el reino vegetal⟩ **2** : verdura *f*, hortaliza *f* (para comer)
vegetarian [ˌvɛʤə'tɛriən] *n* : vegetariano *mf*
vegetarianism [ˌvɛʤə'tɛriəˌnɪzəm] *n* : vegetarianismo *m*

vegetate ['vɛʤəˌteit] *vi* **-tated; -tating** : vegetar
vegetation [ˌvɛʤə'teiʃən] *n* : vegetación *f*
vegetative ['vɛʤəˌteitɪv] *adj* : vegetativo
vehemence ['viːəmənts] *n* : intensidad *f*, vehemencia *f*
vehement ['viːəmənt] *adj* : intenso, vehemente
vehemently ['viːəməntli] *adv* : vehementemente, con vehemencia
vehicle ['viːəkəl, 'viːˌhɪkəl] *n* **1** *or* **motor vehicle** : vehículo *m* **2** MEDIUM : vehículo *m*, medio *m*
vehicular [vi'hɪkjələr, və-] *adj* : vehicular ⟨vehicular homicide : muerte por atropello⟩
veil¹ ['veil] *vt* **1** CONCEAL : velar, disimular **2** : cubrir con un velo ⟨to veil one's face : cubrirse con un velo⟩
veil² *n* : velo *m* ⟨bridal veil : velo de novia⟩
vein ['vein] *n* **1** : vena *f* (en anatomía, botánica, etc.) **2** LODE : veta *f*, vena *f*, filón *m* **3** STYLE : vena *f* ⟨in a humorous vein : en vena humorística⟩
veined ['veind] *adj* : veteado (dícese del queso, de los minerales, etc.)
velocity [və'lɑsəti] *n, pl* **-ties** : velocidad *f*
velour [və'lʊr] *or* **velours** [-'lʊrz] *n* : velour *m*
velvet¹ ['vɛlvət] *adj* **1** : de terciopelo **2** → **velvety**
velvet² *n* : terciopelo *m*
velvety ['vɛlvəti] *adj* : aterciopelado
venal ['viːnəl] *adj* : venal, sobornable
vend ['vɛnd] *vt* : vender
vendetta [vɛn'dɛtə] *n* : vendetta *f*
vendor ['vɛndər] *n* : vendedor *m*, -dora *f*; puestero *m*, -ra *f*
veneer¹ [və'nɪr] *vt* : enchapar, chapar
veneer² *n* **1** : enchapado *m*, chapa *f* **2** APPEARANCE : apariencia *f*, barniz *m* ⟨a veneer of culture : un barniz de cultura⟩
venerable ['vɛnərəbəl] *adj* : venerable
venerate ['vɛnəˌreit] *vt* **-ated; -ating** : venerar
veneration [ˌvɛnə'reiʃən] *n* : veneración *f*
venereal disease [və'nɪriəl] *n* : enfermedad *f* venérea
venetian blind [və'niːʃən] *n* : persiana *f* veneciana
Venezuelan [ˌvɛnə'zweilən, -zu'ei-] *n* : venezolano *m*, -na *f* — **Venezuelan** *adj*
vengeance ['vɛnʤənts] *n* : venganza *f* ⟨to take vengeance on : vengarse de⟩
vengeful ['vɛnʤfəl] *adj* : vengativo
venial ['viːniəl] *adj* : venial ⟨a venial sin : un pecado venial⟩
venison ['vɛnəsən, -zən] *n* : venado *m*, carne *f* de venado
venom ['vɛnəm] *n* **1** : veneno *m* **2** MALICE : veneno *m*, malevolencia *f*

venomous [ˈvɛnəməs] *adj* : venenoso
vent[1] [ˈvɛnt] *vt* : desahogar, dar salida a ⟨to vent one's feelings : desahogarse⟩
vent[2] *n* **1** OPENING : abertura *f* (de escape), orificio *m* **2** *or* **air vent** : respiradero *m*, rejilla *f* de ventilación **3** OUTLET : desahogo *m* ⟨to give vent to one's anger : desahogar la ira⟩
ventilate [ˈvɛntəlˌeɪt] *vt* **-lated; -lating** : ventilar
ventilation [ˌvɛntəlˈeɪʃən] *n* : ventilación *f*
ventilator [ˈvɛntəlˌeɪtər] *n* : ventilador *m*
ventricle [ˈvɛntrɪkəl] *n* : ventrículo *m*
ventriloquism [vɛnˈtrɪləˌkwɪzəm] *n* : ventriloquia *f*
ventriloquist [vɛnˈtrɪləˌkwɪst] *n* : ventrílocuo *m*, -cua *f*
venture[1] [ˈvɛntʃər] *v* **-tured; -turing** *vt* **1** RISK : arriesgar **2** OFFER : aventurar ⟨to venture an opinion : aventurar una opinión⟩ — *vi* : arriesgarse, atreverse, aventurarse
venture[2] *n* **1** UNDERTAKING : empresa *f* **2** GAMBLE, RISK : aventura *f*, riesgo *m*
venturesome [ˈvɛntʃərsəm] *adj* **1** ADVENTUROUS : audaz, atrevido **2** RISKY : arriesgado
venue [ˈvɛnˌjuː] *n* **1** PLACE : lugar *m* **2** : jurisdicción *f* (en derecho)
Venus [ˈviːnəs] *n* : Venus *m*
veracity [vəˈræsəti] *n, pl* **-ties** : veracidad *f*
veranda *or* **verandah** [vəˈrændə] *n* : terraza *f*, veranda *f*
verb [ˈvərb] *n* : verbo *m*
verbal [ˈvərbəl] *adj* : verbal
verbalize [ˈvərbəˌlaɪz] *vt* **-ized; -izing** : expresar con palabras, verbalizar
verbally [ˈvərbəli] *adv* : verbalmente, de palabra
verbatim[1] [vərˈbeɪtəm] *adv* : palabra por palabra, textualmente
verbatim[2] *adj* : literal, textual
verbose [vərˈboːs] *adj* : verboso, prolijo
verdant [ˈvərdənt] *adj* : verde, verdeante
verdict [ˈvərdɪkt] *n* **1** : veredicto *m* (de un jurado) **2** JUDGMENT, OPINION : juicio *m*, opinión *f*
verge[1] [ˈvərdʒ] *vi* **verged; verging** : estar al borde, rayar ⟨it verges on madness : raya en la locura⟩
verge[2] *n* **1** EDGE : borde *m* **2** **to be on the verge of** : estar a pique de, estar al borde de, estar a punto de
verification [ˌvɛrəfəˈkeɪʃən] *n* : verificación *f*
verify [ˈvɛrəˌfaɪ] *vt* **-fied; -fying** : verificar, comprobar, confirmar
veritable [ˈvɛrətəbəl] *adj* : verdadero — **veritably** *adv*
vermicelli [ˌvərməˈtʃɛli, -ˈsɛli] *n* : fideos *mpl* finos
vermin [ˈvərmən] *ns & pl* : alimañas *fpl*, bichos *mpl*, sabandijas *fpl*
vermouth [vərˈmuːth] *n* : vermut *m*
vernacular[1] [vərˈnækjələr] *adj* : vernáculo

vernacular[2] *n* : lengua *f* vernácula
versatile [ˈvərsətəl] *adj* : versátil
versatility [ˌvərsəˈtɪləti] *n* : versatilidad *f*
verse [ˈvərs] *n* **1** LINE, STANZA : verso *m*, estrofa *f* **2** POETRY : poesía *f* **3** : versículo *m* (en la Biblia)
versed [ˈvərst] *adj* : versado ⟨to be well versed in : ser muy versado en⟩
version [ˈvərʒən] *n* : versión *f*
versus [ˈvərsəs] *prep* : versus
vertebra [ˈvərtəbrə] *n, pl* **-brae** [-ˌbreɪ, -ˌbriː] *or* **-bras** : vértebra *f*
vertebrate[1] [ˈvərtəbrət, -ˌbreɪt] *adj* : vertebrado
vertebrate[2] *n* : vertebrado *m*
vertex [ˈvərˌtɛks] *n, pl* **vertices** [ˈvərtəˌsiːz] **1** : vértice *m* (en matemáticas y anatomía) **2** SUMMIT, TOP : ápice *m*, cumbre *f*, cima *f*
vertical[1] [ˈvərtɪkəl] *adj* : vertical — **vertically** *adv*
vertical[2] *n* : vertical *f*
vertigo [ˈvərtɪˌgoː] *n, pl* **-goes** *or* **-gos** : vértigo *m*
verve [ˈvərv] *n* : brío *m*
very[1] [ˈvɛri] *adv* **1** EXTREMELY : muy, sumamente ⟨very few : muy pocos⟩ ⟨I am very sorry : lo siento mucho⟩ **2** (*used for emphasis*) ⟨at the very least : por lo menos, como mínimo⟩ ⟨the very same dress : el mismo vestido⟩
very[2] *adj* **verier; -est** **1** EXACT, PRECISE : mismo, exacto ⟨at that very moment : en ese mismo momento⟩ ⟨it's the very thing : es justo lo que hacía falta⟩ **2** BARE, MERE : solo, mero ⟨the very thought of it : sólo pensarlo⟩ **3** EXTREME : extremo, de todo ⟨at the very top : arriba de todo⟩
vesicle [ˈvɛsɪkəl] *n* : vesícula *f*
vespers [ˈvɛspərz] *npl* : vísperas *fpl*
vessel [ˈvɛsəl] *n* **1** CONTAINER : vasija *f*, recipiente *m* **2** BOAT, CRAFT : nave *f*, barco *m*, buque *m* **3** : vaso *m* ⟨blood vessel : vaso sanguíneo⟩
vest[1] [ˈvɛst] *vt* **1** CONFER : conferir ⟨to vest authority in : conferirle la autoridad a⟩ **2** CLOTHE : vestir
vest[2] *n* **1** : chaleco *m* **2** UNDERSHIRT : camiseta *f*
vestibule [ˈvɛstəˌbjuːl] *n* : vestíbulo *m*
vestige [ˈvɛstɪdʒ] *n* : vestigio *m*, rastro *m*
vestment [ˈvɛstmənt] *n* : vestidura *f*
vestry [ˈvɛstri] *n, pl* **-tries** : sacristía *f*
vet [ˈvɛt] *n* **1** → **veterinarian** **2** → **veteran**[2]
veteran[1] [ˈvɛtərən, ˈvɛtrən] *adj* : veterano
veteran[2] *n* : veterano *m*, -na *f*
Veterans Day *n* : día *m* del Armisticio (celebrado el 11 de noviembre en los Estados Unidos)
veterinarian [ˌvɛtərəˈnɛriən, ˌvɛtəˈnɛr-] *n* : veterinario *m*, -ria *f*
veterinary [ˈvɛtərəˌnɛri] *adj* : veterinario
veto[1] [ˈviːˌtoː] *vt* **1** FORBID : prohibir **2** : vetar ⟨to veto a bill : vetar un proyecto de ley⟩

veto² *n, pl* **-toes** 1 : veto *m* ⟨the power of veto : el derecho de veto⟩ 2 BAN : veto *m*, prohibición *f*
vex ['vɛks] *vt* : contrariar, molestar, irritar
vexation [vɛk'seɪʃən] *n* : contrariedad *f*, irritación *f*
via ['vaɪə, 'viːə] *prep* : por, vía
viability [ˌvaɪə'bɪləti] *n* : viabilidad *f*
viable ['vaɪəbəl] *adj* : viable
viaduct ['vaɪəˌdʌkt] *n* : viaducto *m*
vial ['vaɪəl] *n* : frasco *m*
vibrant ['vaɪbrənt] *adj* 1 LIVELY : vibrante, animado, dinámico 2 BRIGHT : fuerte, vivo (dícese de los colores)
vibrate ['vaɪˌbreɪt] *vi* **-brated; -brating** 1 OSCILLATE : vibrar, oscilar 2 THRILL : bullir ⟨to vibrate with excitement : bullir de emoción⟩
vibration [vaɪ'breɪʃən] *n* : vibración *f*
vicar ['vɪkər] *n* : vicario *m*, -ria *f*
vicarious [vaɪ'kæriːəs, vɪ-] *adj* : indirecto — **vicariously** *adv*
vice ['vaɪs] *n* : vicio *m*
vice admiral *n* : vicealmirante *mf*
vice president *n* : vicepresidente *m*, -ta *f*
viceroy ['vaɪsˌrɔɪ] *n* : virrey *m*, -rreina *f*
vice versa [ˌvaɪsɪ'vərsə, ˌvaɪs'vər-] *adv* : viceversa
vicinity [və'sɪnəti] *n, pl* **-ties** 1 NEIGHBORHOOD : vecindad *f*, inmediaciones *fpl* 2 NEARNESS : proximidad *f*
vicious ['vɪʃəs] *adj* 1 DEPRAVED : depravado, malo 2 SAVAGE : malo, fiero, salvaje ⟨a vicious dog : un perro feroz⟩ 3 MALICIOUS : malicioso
viciously ['vɪʃəsli] *adv* : con saña, brutalmente
viciousness ['vɪʃəsnəs] *n* : brutalidad *f*, ferocidad *f* (de un animal), malevolencia *f* (de un comentario, etc.)
vicissitudes [və'sɪsəˌtuːdz, vaɪ-, -ˌtjuːdz] *npl* : vicisitudes *fpl*
victim ['vɪktəm] *n* : víctima *f*
victimize ['vɪktəˌmaɪz] *vt* **-mized; -mizing** : tomar como víctima, perseguir, victimizar *Arg, Mex*
victor ['vɪktər] *n* : vencedor *m*, -dora *f*
Victorian [vɪk'toːriən] *adj* : victoriano
victorious [vɪk'toːriəs] *adj* : victorioso — **victoriously** *adv*
victory ['vɪktəri] *n, pl* **-ries** : victoria *f*, triunfo *m*
victuals ['vɪtəlz] *npl* : víveres *mpl*, provisiones *fpl*
video¹ ['vɪdiˌoː] *adj* : de video ⟨video recording : grabación de video⟩
video² *n* 1 : video *m* (medio o grabación) 2 → **videotape²**
video camera *n* : videocámara *f*
videocassette [ˌvɪdiokə'sɛt] *n* : videocasete *m*, videocassette *m*
videocassette recorder → **VCR**
video game *n* : videojuego *m*, juego *m* de video
videotape¹ ['vɪdioˌteɪp] *vt* **-taped; -taping** : grabar en video, videograbar

videotape² *n* : videocinta *f*
vie ['vaɪ] *vi* **vied; vying** ['vaɪɪŋ] : competir, rivalizar
Vietnamese [viˌɛtnə'miːz, -'miːs] *n* 1 : vietnamita *mf* 2 : vietnamita *m* (idioma) — **Vietnamese** *adj*
view¹ ['vjuː] *vt* 1 OBSERVE : mirar, ver, observar 2 CONSIDER : considerar, contemplar
view² *n* 1 SIGHT : vista *f* ⟨to come into view : aparecer⟩ 2 ATTITUDE, OPINION : opinión *f*, parecer *m*, actitud *f* ⟨in my view : en mi opinión⟩ 3 SCENE : vista *f*, panorama *f* 4 INTENTION : idea *f*, vista *f* ⟨with a view to : con vistas a, con la idea de⟩ 5 in view of : dado que, en vista de (que)
viewer ['vjuːər] *n or* **television viewer** : telespectador *m*, -dora *f*; televidente *mf*
viewpoint ['vjuːˌpɔɪnt] *n* : punto *m* de vista
vigil ['vɪdʒəl] *n* 1 : vigilia *f*, vela *f* 2 to keep vigil : velar
vigilance ['vɪdʒələnts] *n* : vigilancia *f*
vigilant ['vɪdʒələnt] *adj* : vigilante
vigilante [ˌvɪdʒə'lænˌtiː] *n* : integrante *mf* de un comité de vigilancia (que actúa como policía)
vigilantly ['vɪdʒələntli] *adv* : con vigilancia
vigor ['vɪgər] *n* : vigor *m*, energía *f*, fuerza *f*
vigorous ['vɪgərəs] *adj* : vigoroso, enérgico — **vigorously** *adv*
Viking ['vaɪkɪŋ] *n* : vikingo *m*, -ga *f*
vile ['vaɪl] *adj* **viler; vilest** 1 WICKED : vil, infame 2 REVOLTING : asqueroso, repugnante 3 TERRIBLE : horrible, atroz ⟨vile weather : tiempo horrible⟩ ⟨to be in a vile mood : estar de un humor de perros⟩
vilify ['vɪləˌfaɪ] *vt* **-fied; -fying** : vilipendiar, denigrar, difamar
villa ['vɪlə] *n* : casa *f* de campo, quinta *f*
village ['vɪlɪdʒ] *n* : pueblo *m* (grande), aldea *f* (pequeña)
villager ['vɪlɪdʒər] *n* : vecino *m*, -na *f* (de un pueblo); aldeano *m*, -na *f* (de una aldea)
villain ['vɪlən] *n* : villano *m*, -na *f*; malo *m*, -la *f* (en ficción, películas, etc.)
villainess ['vɪlənɪs, -nəs] *n* : villana *f*
villainous ['vɪlənəs] *adj* : infame, malvado
villainy ['vɪləni] *n, pl* **-lainies** : vileza *f*, maldad *f*
vim ['vɪm] *n* : brío *m*, vigor *m*, energía *f*
vindicate ['vɪndəˌkeɪt] *vt* **-cated; -cating** 1 EXONERATE : vindicar, disculpar 2 JUSTIFY : justificar
vindication [ˌvɪndə'keɪʃən] *n* : vindicación *f*, justificación *f*
vindictive [vɪn'dɪktɪv] *adj* : vengativo
vine ['vaɪn] *n* 1 GRAPEVINE : vid *f*, parra *f* 2 : planta *f* trepadora, enredadera *f*
vinegar ['vɪnɪgər] *n* : vinagre *m*

vinegary [ˈvɪnɪɡəri] *adj* : avinagrado
vineyard [ˈvɪnjərd] *n* : viña *f*, viñedo *m*
vintage[1] [ˈvɪntɪʤ] *adj* **1** : añejo (dícese de un vino) **2** CLASSIC : clásico, de época
vintage[2] *n* **1** : cosecha *f* ⟨the 1947 vintage : la cosecha de 1947⟩ **2** ERA : época *f*, era *f* ⟨slang of recent vintage : argot de la época reciente⟩
vinyl [ˈvaɪnəl] *n* : vinilo
viola [viˈoːlə] *n* : viola *f*
violate [ˈvaɪəˌleɪt] *vt* **-lated; -lating 1** BREAK : infringir, violar, quebrantar ⟨to violate the rules : violar las reglas⟩ **2** RAPE : violar **3** DESECRATE : profanar
violation [ˌvaɪəˈleɪʃən] *n* **1** : violación *f*, infracción *f* (de una ley) **2** DESECRATION : profanación *f*
violence [ˈvaɪlənts, ˈvaɪə-] *n* : violencia *f*
violent [ˈvaɪlənt, ˈvaɪə-] *adj* : violento
violently [ˈvaɪləntli, ˈvaɪə-] *adv* : violentamente, con violencia
violet [ˈvaɪlət, ˈvaɪə-] *n* : violeta *f*
violin [ˌvaɪəˈlɪn] *n* : violín *m*
violinist [ˌvaɪəˈlɪnɪst] *n* : violinista *mf*
violoncello [ˌvaɪələnˈʧeloː, ˌviˌ-] → **cello**
VIP [ˌviːˌaɪˈpiː] *n, pl* **VIPs** [-ˈpiːz] : VIP *mf*, persona *f* de categoría
viper [ˈvaɪpər] *n* : víbora *f*
viral [ˈvaɪrəl] *adj* : viral, vírico ⟨viral pneumonia : pulmonía viral⟩
virgin[1] [ˈvərʤən] *adj* **1** CHASTE : virginal ⟨the virgin birth : el alumbramiento virginal⟩ **2** : virgen, intacto ⟨a virgin forest : una selva virgen⟩ ⟨virgin wool : lana virgen⟩
virgin[2] *n* : virgen *mf*
virginity [vərˈʤɪnəti] *n* : virginidad *f*
Virgo [ˈvərˌɡoː, ˈvɪr-] *n* : Virgo *mf*
virile [ˈvɪrəl, -ˌaɪl] *adj* : viril, varonil
virility [vəˈrɪləti] *n* : virilidad *f*
virtual [ˈvərʧuəl] *adj* : virtual ⟨a virtual dictator : un virtual dictador⟩ ⟨virtual reality : realidad virtual⟩
virtually [ˈvərʧuəli, ˈvərʧəli] *adv* : en realidad, de hecho, casi
virtue [ˈvərˌʧuː] *n* **1** : virtud *f* **2 by virtue of** : en virtud de, debido a
virtuosity [ˌvərʧuˈɑsəti] *n, pl* **-ties** : virtuosismo *m*
virtuoso [ˌvərʧuˈoːsoː, -zoː] *n, pl* **-sos** *or* **-si** [-ˌsiː, -ˌziː] : virtuoso *m*, -sa *f*
virtuous [ˈvərʧuəs] *adj* : virtuoso, bueno — **virtuously** *adv*
virulence [ˈvɪrələnts, ˈvɪrjə-] *n* : virulencia *f*
virulent [ˈvɪrələnt, ˈvɪrjə-] *adj* : virulento
virus [ˈvaɪrəs] *n* : virus *m*
visa [ˈviːzə, -sə] *n* : visa *f*
vis-à-vis [ˌviːzəˈviː, -sə-] *prep* : con relación a, con respecto a
viscera [ˈvɪsərə] *npl* : vísceras *fpl*
visceral [ˈvɪsərəl] *adj* : visceral
viscosity [vɪsˈkɑsəti] *n, pl* **-ties** : viscosidad *f*
viscount [ˈvaɪˌkaʊnt] *n* : vizconde *m*

viscountess [ˈvaɪˌkæʊntɪs] *n* : vizcondesa *f*
viscous [ˈvɪskəs] *adj* : viscoso
vise [ˈvaɪs] *n* : torno *m* de banco, tornillo *m* de banco
visibility [ˌvɪzəˈbɪləti] *n, pl* **-ties** : visibilidad *f*
visible [ˈvɪzəbəl] *adj* **1** : visible ⟨the visible stars : las estrellas visibles⟩ **2** OBVIOUS : evidente, patente
visibly [ˈvɪzəbli] *adv* : visiblemente
vision [ˈvɪʒən] *n* **1** EYESIGHT : vista *f*, visión *f* **2** APPARITION : visión *f*, aparición *f* **3** FORESIGHT : visión *f* (del futuro), previsión *f* **4** IMAGE : imagen *f* ⟨she had visions of a disaster : se imaginaba un desastre⟩
visionary[1] [ˈvɪʒəˌnɛri] *adj* **1** FARSIGHTED : visionario, con visión de futuro **2** UTOPIAN : utópico, poco realista
visionary[2] *n, pl* **-ries** : visionario *m*, -ria *f*
visit[1] [ˈvɪzət] *vt* **1** : visitar, ir a ver **2** AFFLICT : azotar, afligir ⟨visited by troubles : afligido con problemas⟩ — *vi* : hacer (una) visita
visit[2] *n* : visita *f*
visitor [ˈvɪzətər] *n* : visitante *mf* (a una ciudad, etc.), visita *f* (a una casa)
visor [ˈvaɪzər] *n* : visera *f*
vista [ˈvɪstə] *n* : vista *f*
visual [ˈvɪʒuəl] *adj* : visual ⟨the visual arts : las artes visuales⟩ — **visually** *adv*
visualize [ˈvɪʒuəˌlaɪz] *vt* **-ized; -izing** : visualizar, imaginarse, hacerse una idea de — **visualization** [ˌvɪʒəwələˈzeɪʃən] *n*
vital [ˈvaɪtəl] *adj* **1** : vital ⟨vital organs : órganos vitales⟩ **2** CRUCIAL : esencial, crucial, decisivo ⟨of vital importance : de suma importancia⟩ **3** LIVELY : enérgico, lleno de vida, vital
vitality [vaɪˈtæləti] *n, pl* **-ties** : vitalidad *f*, energía *f*
vitally [ˈvaɪtəli] *adv* : sumamente
vital statistics *npl* : estadísticas *fpl* demográficas
vitamin [ˈvaɪtəmən] *n* : vitamina *f* ⟨vitamin deficiency : carencia vitamínica⟩
vitreous [ˈvɪtriəs] *adj* : vítreo
vitriolic [ˌvɪtriˈɑlɪk] *adj* : mordaz, virulento
vituperation [vaɪˌtuːpəˈreɪʃən, -ˌtjuː-] *n* : vituperio *m*
vivacious [vəˈveɪʃəs, vaɪ-] *adj* : vivaz, animado, lleno de vida
vivaciously [vəˈveɪʃəsli, vaɪ-] *adv* : con vivacidad, animadamente
vivacity [vəˈvæsəti, vaɪ-] *n* : vivacidad *f*
vivid [ˈvɪvəd] *adj* **1** LIVELY : lleno de vitalidad **2** BRILLIANT : vivo, intenso ⟨vivid colors : colores vivos⟩ **3** INTENSE, SHARP : vívido, gráfico ⟨a vivid dream : un sueño vívido⟩
vividly [ˈvɪvədli] *adv* **1** BRIGHTLY : con colores vivos **2** SHARPLY : vívidamente
vividness [ˈvɪvədnəs] *n* **1** BRIGHTNESS : intensidad *f*, viveza *f* **2** SHARPNESS : lo gráfico, nitidez *f*

vivisection [ˌvɪvə'sɛkʃən, 'vɪvə-] *n*
: vivisección *f*
vixen ['vɪksən] *n* : zorra *f*, raposa *f*
vocabulary [vo:'kæbjə,lɛri] *n, pl* **-laries**
1 : vocabulario *m* 2 LEXICON : léxico
m
vocal ['vo:kəl] *adj* 1 : vocal 2 LOUD,
OUTSPOKEN : ruidoso, muy franco
vocal cords *npl* : cuerdas *fpl* vocales
vocalist ['vo:kəlɪst] *n* : cantante *mf*, vocalista *mf*
vocalize ['vo:kəl,aɪz] *vt* **-ized; -izing** : vocalizar
vocation [vo'keɪʃən] *n* : vocación *f* ⟨to
have a vocation for : tener vocación
de⟩
vocational [vo'keɪʃənəl] *adj* : profesional ⟨vocational guidance : orientación
profesional⟩
vociferous [vo'sɪfərəs] *adj* : ruidoso, vociferante
vodka ['vɑdkə] *n* : vodka *m*
vogue ['vo:g] *n* : moda *f*, boga *f* ⟨to
be in vogue : estar de moda, estar en
boga⟩
voice[1] ['vɔɪs] *vt* **voiced; voicing** : expresar
voice[2] *n* 1 : voz *f* ⟨in a low voice : en
voz baja⟩ ⟨to lose one's voice
: quedarse sin voz⟩ ⟨the voice of the
people : la voz del pueblo⟩ 2 **to make
one's voice heard** : hacerse oír
voice box → **larynx**
voiced ['vɔɪst] *adj* : sonoro
voice mail *n* : correo *m* de voz
void[1] ['vɔɪd] *vt* : anular, invalidar ⟨to
void a contract : anular un contrato⟩
void[2] *adj* 1 EMPTY : vacío, desprovisto
⟨void of content : desprovisto de con-
tenido⟩ 2 INVALID : inválido, nulo
void[3] *n* : vacío *m*
volatile ['vɑlətəl] *adj* : volátil, inestable
volatility [ˌvɑlə'tɪləti] *n* : volatilidad *f*, inestabilidad *f*
volcanic [vɑl'kænɪk] *adj* : volcánico
volcano [vɑl'keɪ,no:] *n, pl* **-noes** *or* **-nos**
: volcán *m*
vole ['vo:l] *n* : campañol *m*
volition [vo'lɪʃən] *n* : volición *f*, voluntad *f* ⟨of one's own volition : por voluntad propia⟩
volley ['vɑli] *n, pl* **-leys** 1 : descarga *f*
(de tiros) 2 : torrente *m*, lluvia *f* (de insultos, etc.) 3 : salva *f* (de aplausos) 4
: volea *f* (en deportes)
volleyball ['vɑli,bɔl] *n* : voleibol *m*
volt ['vo:lt] *n* : voltio *m*
voltage ['vo:ltɪdʒ] *n* : voltaje *m*
volubility [ˌvɑljə'bɪləti] *n* : locuacidad *f*
voluble ['vɑljəbəl] *adj* : locuaz
volume ['vɑljəm, -,ju:m] *n* 1 BOOK : volumen *m*, tomo *m* 2 SPACE : capacidad
f, volumen *m* (en física) 3 AMOUNT

: cantidad *f*, volumen *m* 4 LOUDNESS
: volumen *m*
voluminous [və'lu:mənəs] *adj* : voluminoso
voluntary ['vɑlən,tɛri] *adj* : voluntario
— **voluntarily** [ˌvɑlən'tɛrəli] *adv*
volunteer[1] [ˌvɑlən'tɪr] *vt* : ofrecer, dar
⟨to volunteer one's assistance : ofrecer
la ayuda⟩ — *vi* : ofrecerse, alistarse
como voluntario
volunteer[2] *n* : voluntario *m*, -ria *f*
voluptuous [və'lʌptʃuəs] *adj* : voluptuoso
vomit[1] ['vɑmət] *v* : vomitar
vomit[2] *n* : vómito *m*
voodoo ['vu:,du:] *n, pl* **voodoos** : vudú
m
voracious [vɔ'reɪʃəs, və-] *adj* : voraz
voraciously [vɔ'reɪʃəsli, və-] *adv* : vo-
razmente, con voracidad
vortex ['vɔr,tɛks] *n, pl* **vortices** ['vɔrtə-
,si:z] : vórtice *m*
vote[1] ['vo:t] *vi* **voted; voting** : votar ⟨to
vote Democratic : votar por los
demócratas⟩
vote[2] *n* 1 : voto *m* 2 SUFFRAGE : sufragio *m*, derecho *m* al voto
voter ['vo:tər] *n* : votante *mf*
voting ['vo:tɪŋ] *n* : votación *f*
vouch ['vaʊtʃ] *vi* **to vouch for** : garantizar (algo), responder de (algo), responder por (alguien)
voucher ['vaʊtʃər] *n* 1 RECEIPT : comprobante *m* 2 : vale *m* ⟨travel voucher : vale de viajar⟩
vow[1] [vaʊ] *vt* : jurar, prometer, hacer
voto de
vow[2] *n* : promesa *f*, voto *m* (en la religión) ⟨a vow of poverty : un voto de
pobreza⟩
vowel ['vaʊəl] *n* : vocal *m*
voyage[1] ['vɔɪɪdʒ] *vi* **-aged; -aging** : viajar
voyage[2] *n* : viaje *m*
voyager ['vɔɪɪdʒər] *n* : viajero *m*, -ra *f*
vulcanize ['vʌlkə,naɪz] *vt* **-nized; -nizing**
: vulcanizar
vulgar ['vʌlɡər] *adj* 1 COMMON, PLE-
BIAN : ordinario, populachero, del vulgo 2 COARSE, CRUDE : grosero, de mal
gusto, majadero *Mex* 3 INDECENT : indecente, colorado (dícese de un chiste,
etc.)
vulgarity [ˌvʌl'ɡærəti] *n, pl* **-ties**
: grosería *f*, vulgaridad *f*
vulgarly ['vʌlɡərli] *adv* : vulgarmente,
groseramente
vulnerability [ˌvʌlnərə'bɪləti] *n, pl* **-ties**
: vulnerabilidad *f*
vulnerable ['vʌlnərəbəl] *adj* : vulnerable
vulture ['vʌltʃər] *n* : buitre *m*, zopilote *m*
CA, Mex
vying → **vie**

W

w ['dʌbəl,ju:] *n, pl* **w's** *or* **ws** [-,ju:z] : vigésima tercera letra del alfabeto inglés

wad¹ ['wɑd] *vt* **wadded; wadding 1** : hacer un taco con, formar en una masa **2** STUFF : rellenar

wad² *n* : taco *m* (de papel), bola *f* (de algodón, etc.), fajo *m* (de billetes)

waddle¹ ['wɑdəl] *vi* **-dled; -dling** : andar como un pato

waddle² *n* : andar *m* de pato

wade ['weɪd] *v* **waded; wading** *vi* **1** : caminar por el agua **2 to wade through** : leer (algo) con dificultad — *vt or* **to wade across** : vadear

wading bird *n* : zancuda *f*, ave *f* zancuda

wafer ['weɪfər] *n* : barquillo *m*, galleta *f* de barquillo

waffle ['wɑfəl] *n* **1** : wafle *m* **2 waffle iron** : waflera *f*

waft ['wɑft, 'wæft] *vt* : llevar por el aire — *vi* : flotar

wag¹ ['wæg] *v* **wagged; wagging** *vt* : menear — *vi* : menearse, moverse

wag² *n* **1** : meneo *m* (de la cola) **2** JOKER, WIT : bromista *mf*

wage¹ ['weɪdʒ] *vt* **waged; waging** : hacer, librar ⟨to wage war : hacer la guerra⟩

wage² *n or* **wages** *npl* : sueldo *m*, salario *m* ⟨minimum wage : salario mínimo⟩

wager¹ ['weɪdʒər] *v* : apostar

wager² *n* : apuesta *f*

waggish ['wægɪʃ] *adj* : burlón, bromista (dícese de una persona), chistoso (dícese de un comentario)

waggle ['wægəl] *vt* **-gled; -gling** : menear, mover (de un lado a otro)

wagon ['wægən] *n* **1** : carro *m* (tirado por caballos) **2** CART : carrito *m* **3** → **station wagon**

waif ['weɪf] *n* : niño *m* abandonado, animal *m* sin hogar

wail¹ ['weɪl] *vi* : gemir, lamentarse

wail² *n* : gemido *m*, lamento *m*

wainscot ['weɪnskət, -,skɑt, -,sko:t] *or* **wainscoting** [-skətɪŋ, -,skɑ-, -,sko:-] *n* : boiserie *f*, revestimiento de paneles de madera

waist ['weɪst] *n* : cintura *f* (del cuerpo humano), talle *m* (de ropa)

waistline ['weɪst,laɪn] *n* → **waist**

wait¹ ['weɪt] *vi* : esperar ⟨to wait for something : esperar algo⟩ ⟨wait and see! : ¡espera y verás!⟩ ⟨I can't wait : me muero de ganas⟩ — *vt* **1** AWAIT : esperar **2** DELAY : retrasar ⟨don't wait lunch : no retrase el almuerzo⟩ **3** SERVE : servir, atender ⟨to wait tables : servir (a la mesa)⟩

wait² *n* **1** : espera *f* **2 to lie in wait** : estar al acecho

waiter ['weɪtər] *n* : mesero *m*, camarero *m*, mozo *m* *Arg, Chile, Col, Peru*

waiting room *n* : sala *f* de espera

waitress ['weɪtrəs] *n* : mesera *f*, camarera *f*, moza *f* *Arg, Chile, Col, Peru*

waive ['weɪv] *vt* **waived; waiving** : renunciar a ⟨to waive one's rights : renunciar a sus derechos⟩ ⟨to waive the rules : no aplicar las reglas⟩

waiver ['weɪvər] *n* : renuncia *f*

wake¹ ['weɪk] *v* **woke** ['wo:k]; **woken** ['wo:kən] *or* **waked; waking** *vi or* **to wake up** : despertar(se) ⟨he woke at noon : se despertó al mediodía⟩ ⟨wake up! : ¡despiértate!⟩ — *vt* : despertar

wake² *n* **1** VIGIL : velatorio *m*, velorio *m* (de un difunto) **2** TRAIL : estela *f* (de un barco, un huracán, etc.) **3** AFTERMATH : consecuencias *fpl* ⟨in the wake of : tras, como consecuencia de⟩

wakeful ['weɪkfəl] *adj* **1** SLEEPLESS : desvelado **2** VIGILANT : alerta, vigilante

waken ['weɪkən] → **awake**

walk¹ ['wɔk] *vi* **1** : caminar, andar, pasear ⟨you're walking too fast : estás caminando demasiado rápido⟩ ⟨to walk around the city : pasearse por la ciudad⟩ **2** : ir andando, ir a pie ⟨we had to walk home : tuvimos que ir a casa a pie⟩ **3** : darle base por bolas (a un bateador) — *vt* **1** : recorrer, caminar ⟨she walked two miles : caminó dos millas⟩ **2** ACCOMPANY : acompañar **3** : sacar a pasear (a un perro)

walk² *n* **1** : paseo *m*, caminata *f* ⟨to go for a walk : ir a caminar, dar un paseo⟩ **2** PATH : camino *m* **3** GAIT : andar *m* **4** : marcha *f* (en beisbol) **5 walk of life** : esfera *f*, condición *f*

walker ['wɔkər] *n* **1** : paseante *mf* **2** HIKER : excursionista *mf* **3** : andador *m* (aparato)

walking stick *n* : bastón *m*

walkout ['wɔk,aʊt] *n* STRIKE : huelga *f*

walk out *vi* **1** STRIKE : declararse en huelga **2** LEAVE : salir, irse **3 to walk out on** : abandonar, dejar

walkway ['wɔk,weɪ] *n* **1** SIDEWALK : acera *f* **2** PATH : sendero *m* **3** PASSAGEWAY : pasadizo *m*

wall¹ ['wɔl] *vt* **1 to wall in** : cercar con una pared o un muro, tapiar, amurallar **2 to wall off** : separar con una pared o un muro **3 to wall up** : tapiar, condenar (una ventana, etc.)

wall² *n* **1** : muro *m* (exterior) ⟨the walls of the city : las murallas de la ciudad⟩ **2** : pared *f* (interior) **3** BARRIER : barrera *f* ⟨a wall of mountains : una barrera de montañas⟩ **4** : pared *f* (en anatomía)

wallaby ['wɑləbi] *n, pl* **-bies** : ualabí *m*

walled ['wɔld] *adj* : amurallado

wallet ['wɑlət] *n* : billetera *f*, cartera *f*

wallflower ['wɔl,flaʊər] *n* **1** : alhelí *m* (flor) **2 to be a wallflower** : comer pavo

wallop¹ ['wɑləp] *vt* **1** TROUNCE : darle una paliza (a alguien) **2** SOCK : pegar fuerte

wallop² *n* : golpe *m* fuerte, golpazo *m*

wallow¹ ['wɑˌloː] *vi* **1** : revolcarse ⟨to wallow in the mud : revolcarse en el lodo⟩ **2** DELIGHT : deleitarse ⟨to wallow in luxury : nadar en lujos⟩

wallow² *n* : revolcadero *m* (para animales)

wallpaper¹ ['wɔlˌpeɪpər] *vt* : empapelar

wallpaper² *n* : papel *m* pintado

walnut ['wɔlˌnʌt] *n* **1** : nuez *f* (fruta) **2** : nogal *m* (árbol y madera)

walrus ['wɔlrəs, 'wɑl-] *n*, *pl* **-rus** *or* **-ruses** : morsa *f*

waltz¹ ['wɔlts] *vi* **1** : valsar, bailar el vals **2** BREEZE : pasar con ligereza ⟨to waltz in : entrar tan campante⟩

waltz² *n* : vals *m*

wan ['wɑn] *adj* **wanner; -est 1** PALLID : pálido **2** DIM : tenue ⟨wan light : luz tenue⟩ **3** LANGUID : lánguido ⟨a wan smile : una sonrisa lánguida⟩ — **wanly** *adv*

wand ['wɑnd] *n* : varita *f* (mágica)

wander ['wɑndər] *vi* **1** RAMBLE : deambular, vagar, vagabundear **2** STRAY : alejarse, desviarse, divagar ⟨she let her mind wander : dejó vagar la imaginación⟩ — *vt* : recorrer ⟨to wander the streets : vagar por las calles⟩

wanderer ['wɑndərər] *n* : vagabundo *m*, -da *f*; viajero *m*, -ra *f*

wanderlust ['wɑndərˌlʌst] *n* : pasión *f* por viajar

wane¹ ['weɪn] *vi* **waned; waning 1** : menguar (dícese de la luna) **2** DECLINE : disminuir, decaer, menguar

wane² *n* **on the wane** : decayendo, en decadencia

wangle ['wæŋgəl] *vt* **-gled; -gling** FINAGLE : arreglárselas para conseguir

wannabe ['wɑnəˌbiː] *n* : aspirante *mf* (a algo); imitador *m*, -dora *f* (de alguien)

want¹ ['wɑnt, 'wɔnt] *vt* **1** LACK : faltar **2** REQUIRE : requerir, necesitar **3** DESIRE : querer, desear

want² *n* **1** LACK : falta *f* **2** DESTITUTION : indigencia *f*, miseria *f* **3** DESIRE, NEED : deseo *m*, necesidad *f*

wanting ['wɑntɪŋ, 'wɔn-] *adj* **1** ABSENT : ausente **2** DEFICIENT : deficiente ⟨he's wanting in common sense : le falta sentido común⟩

wanton ['wɑntən, 'wɔn-] *adj* **1** LEWD, LUSTFUL : lascivo, lujurioso, licencioso **2** INHUMANE, MERCILESS : despiadado ⟨wanton cruelty : crueldad despiadada⟩

wapiti ['wɑpəti] *n*, *pl* **-ti** *or* **-tis** : uapití *m*

war¹ ['wɔr] *vi* **warred; warring** : combatir, batallar, hacer la guerra

war² *n* : guerra *f* ⟨to go to war : entrar en guerra⟩

warble¹ ['wɔrbəl] *vi* **-bled; -bling** : gorjear, trinar

warble² *n* : trino *m*, gorjeo *m*

warbler ['wɔrblər] *n* : pájaro *m* gorjeador, curruca *f*

ward¹ ['wɔrd] *vt* **to ward off** : desviar, protegerse contra

ward² *n* **1** : sala *f* (de un hospital, etc.) ⟨maternity ward : sala de maternidad⟩ **2** : distrito *m* electoral o administrativo (de una ciudad) **3** : pupilo *m*, -la *f* (de un tutor, etc.)

warden ['wɔrdən] *n* **1** KEEPER : guarda *mf*; guardián *m*, -diana *f* ⟨game warden : guardabosque⟩ **2** *or* **prison warden** : alcaide *m*

wardrobe ['wɔrdˌroːb] *n* **1** CLOSET : armario *m* **2** CLOTHES : vestuario *m*, guardarropa *f*

ware ['wær] *n* **1** POTTERY : cerámica *f* **2 wares** *npl* GOODS : mercancía *f*, mercadería *f*

warehouse ['wærˌhaʊs] *n* : depósito *m*, almacén *m*, bodega *f* *Chile, Col, Mex*

warfare ['wɔrˌfær] *n* **1** WAR : guerra *f* **2** STRUGGLE : lucha *f* ⟨the warfare against drugs : la lucha contra las drogas⟩

warhead ['wɔrˌhɛd] *n* : ojiva *f*, cabeza *f* (de un misil)

warily ['wærəli] *adv* : cautelosamente, con cautela

wariness ['wærinəs] *n* : cautela *f*

warlike ['wærˌlaɪk] *adj* : belicoso, guerrero

warm¹ ['wɔrm] *vt* **1** HEAT : calentar, recalentar **2 to warm one's heart** : reconfortar a uno, alegrar el corazón **3 to warm up** : calentar (los músculos, un automóvil, etc.) — *vi* **1** : calentarse **2 to warm to** : tomarle simpatía (a alguien), entusiasmarse con (algo)

warm² *adj* **1** LUKEWARM : tibio, templado **2** : caliente, cálido, caluroso ⟨a warm wind : un viento cálido⟩ ⟨a warm day : un día caluroso, un día de calor⟩ ⟨warm hands : manos calientes⟩ **3** : caliente, que abriga ⟨warm clothes : ropa de abrigo⟩ ⟨I feel warm : tengo calor⟩ **4** CARING, CORDIAL : cariñoso, cordial **5** : cálido (dícese de colores) **6** FRESH : fresco, reciente ⟨a warm trail : un rastro reciente⟩ **7** (*used for riddles*) : caliente

warm–blooded ['wɔrm'blʌdəd] *adj* : de sangre caliente

warmhearted ['wɔrm'hɑrtəd] *adj* : cariñoso

warmly ['wɔrmli] *adv* **1** AFFECTIONATELY : calurosamente, afectuosamente **2 to dress warmly** : abrigarse

warmonger ['wɔrˌmɑŋgər, -ˌmʌŋ-] *n* : belicista *mf*

warmth ['wɔrmpθ] *n* **1** : calor *m* **2** AFFECTION : cariño *m*, afecto *m* **3** ENTHUSIASM : ardor *m*, entusiasmo *m*

warm–up ['wɔrmˌʌp] *n* : calentamiento *m*

warn ['wɔrn] *vt* **1** CAUTION : advertir, alertar **2** INFORM : avisar, informar

warning ['wɔrnɪŋ] *n* **1** ADVICE : advertencia *f*, aviso *m* **2** ALERT : alerta *f*, alarma *f*

warp¹ ['wɔrp] *vt* **1** : alabear, combar **2** PERVERT : pervertir, deformar — *vi* : pandearse, alabearse, combarse

warp² *n* **1** : urdimbre *f* ⟨the warp and the weft : la urdimbre y la trama⟩ **2** : alabeo *m* (en la madera, etc.)

warrant¹ ['wɔrənt] *vt* **1** ASSURE : asegurar, garantizar **2** GUARANTEE : garantizar **3** JUSTIFY, MERIT : justificar, merecer

warrant² *n* **1** AUTHORIZATION : autorización *f*, permiso *m* ⟨an arrest warrant : una orden de detención⟩ **2** JUSTIFICATION : justificación *f*

warranty ['wɔrənti, ˌwɔrən'ti:] *n, pl* **-ties** : garantía *f*

warren ['wɔrən] *n* : madriguera *f* (de conejos)

warrior ['wɔriər] *n* : guerrero *m*, -ra *f*

warship ['wɔrˌʃɪp] *n* : buque *m* de guerra

wart ['wɔrt] *n* : verruga *f*

wartime ['wɔrˌtaɪm] *n* : tiempo *m* de guerra

wary ['wæri] *adj* **warier; -est** : cauteloso, receloso ⟨to be wary of : desconfiar de⟩

was → **be**

wash¹ ['wɔʃ, 'wɑʃ] *vt* **1** CLEAN : lavar(se), limpiar, fregar ⟨to wash the dishes : lavar los platos⟩ ⟨to wash one's hands : lavarse las manos⟩ **2** DRENCH : mojar **3** LAP : bañar ⟨waves were washing the shore : las olas bañaban la orilla⟩ **4** CARRY, DRAG : arrastrar **5 to wash away** : llevarse (un puente, etc.) — *vi* **1** : lavarse (dícese de una persona o la ropa) ⟨the dress washes well : el vestido se lava bien⟩ **2 to wash against** *or* **to wash over** : bañar

wash² *n* **1** : lavado *m* ⟨to give something a wash : lavar algo⟩ **2** LAUNDRY : artículos *mpl* para lavar, ropa *f* sucia **3** : estela *f* (de un barco)

washable ['wɔʃəbəl, 'wɑ-] *adj* : lavable

washboard ['wɔʃˌbord, 'wɑʃ-] *n* : tabla *f* de lavar

washbowl ['wɔʃˌboːl, 'wɑʃ-] *n* : lavabo *m*, lavamanos *m*

washcloth ['wɔʃˌklɔθ, 'wɑʃ-] *n* : toallita *f* (para lavarse)

washed–out ['wɔʃt'aʊt, 'wɑʃt-] *adj* **1** : desvaído (dícese de colores) **2** EXHAUSTED : agotado, desanimado

washed–up ['wɔʃt'ʌp, 'wɑʃt-] *adj* : acabado (dícese de una persona), fracasado (dícese de un negocio, etc.)

washer ['wɔʃər, 'wɑ-] *n* **1** → **washing machine 2** : arandela *f* (de una llave, etc.)

washing ['wɔʃɪŋ, 'wɑ-] *n* WASH : ropa *f* para lavar

washing machine *n* : máquina *f* de lavar, lavadora *f*

washout ['wɔʃˌaʊt, 'wɑʃ-] *n* **1** : erosión *f* (de la tierra) **2** FAILURE : fracaso *m* ⟨she's a washout : es un desastre⟩

washroom ['wɔʃˌruːm, 'wɑʃ-, -ˌrʊm] *n* : servicios *mpl* (públicos), baño *m*, sanitario *m* *Col, Mex, Ven*

wasn't ['wʌzənt] (*contraction of* **was not**) → **be**

wasp ['wɑsp] *n* : avispa *f*

waspish ['wɑspɪʃ] *adj* **1** IRRITABLE : irritable, irascible **2** CAUSTIC : cáustico, mordaz

waste¹ ['weɪst] *v* **wasted; wasting** *vt* **1** DEVASTATE : arrasar, arruinar, devastar **2** SQUANDER : desperdiciar, despilfarrar, malgastar ⟨to waste time : perder tiempo⟩ — *vi or* **to waste away** : consumirse, chuparse

waste² *adj* **1** BARREN : yermo, baldío **2** DISCARDED : de desecho **3** EXCESS : sobrante

waste³ *n* **1** → **wasteland 2** MISUSE : derroche *m*, desperdicio *m*, despilfarro *m* ⟨a waste of time : una pérdida de tiempo⟩ **3** RUBBISH : basura *f*, desechos *mpl*, desperdicios *mpl* **4** EXCREMENT : excremento *m*

wastebasket ['weɪstˌbæskət] *n* : cesto *m* (de basura), papelera *f*, zafacón *m* *Car*

wasteful ['weɪstfəl] *adj* : despilfarrador, derrochador, pródigo

wastefulness ['weɪstfəlnəs] *n* : derroche *m*, despilfarro *m*

wasteland ['weɪstˌlænd, -lənd] *n* : baldío *m*, yermo *m*, desierto *m*

watch¹ ['wɑtʃ] *vi* **1** *or* **to keep watch** : velar **2** OBSERVE : mirar, ver, observar **3 to watch for** AWAIT : esperar, quedar a la espera de **4 to watch out** : tener cuidado ⟨watch out! : ¡ten cuidado!, ¡ojo!⟩ — *vt* **1** OBSERVE : mirar, observar **2** *or* **to watch over** : vigilar, cuidar **3** : tener cuidado de ⟨watch what you do : ten cuidado con lo que haces⟩

watch² *n* **1** : guardia *f* ⟨to be on watch : estar de guardia⟩ **2** SURVEILLANCE : vigilancia *f* **3** LOOKOUT : guardia *mf*, centinela *f*, vigía *mf* **4** TIMEPIECE : reloj *m*

watchdog ['wɑtʃˌdɔg] *n* : perro *m* guardián

watcher ['wɑtʃər] *n* : observador *m*, -dora *f*

watchful ['wɑtʃfəl] *adj* : alerta, vigilante, atento

watchfulness ['wɑtʃfəlnəs] *n* : vigilancia *f*

watchman ['wɑtʃmən] *n, pl* **-men** [-mən, -ˌmɛn] : vigilante *m*, guarda *m*

watchword ['wɑtʃˌwərd] *n* **1** PASSWORD : contraseña *f* **2** SLOGAN : lema *m*, eslogan *m*

water¹ ['wɔtər, 'wɑ-] *vt* **1** : regar (el jardín, etc.) **2 to water down** DILUTE : diluir, aguar — *vi* : lagrimear (dícese de los ojos), hacérsele agua la boca a uno ⟨my mouth is watering : se me hace agua la boca⟩

water² *n* : agua *f*

water buffalo *n* : búfalo *m* de agua

watercolor ['wɔtərˌkʌlər, 'wɑ-] *n* : acuarela *f*

watercourse ['wɔtərˌkors, 'wɑ-] *n* : curso *m* de agua

watercress ['wɔtərˌkrɛs, 'wɑ-] *n* : berro *m*

waterfall ['wɔtər,fɔl, 'wɑ-] *n* : cascada *f*, salto *m* de agua, catarata *f*
waterfowl ['wɔtər,faʊl, 'wɑ-] *n* : ave *f* acuática
waterfront ['wɔtər,frʌnt, 'wɑ-] *n* **1** : tierra *f* que bordea un río, un lago, o un mar **2** WHARF : muelle *m*
water lily *n* : nenúfar *m*
waterlogged ['wɔtər,lɔgd, 'wɑtər-,lɑgd] *adj* : lleno de agua, empapado, inundado (dícese del suelo)
watermark ['wɔtər,mɑrk, 'wɑ-] *n* **1** : marca *f* del nivel de agua **2** : filigrana *f* (en el papel)
watermelon ['wɔtər,mɛlən, 'wɑ-] *n* : sandía *f*
water moccasin → **moccasin**
waterpower ['wɔtər,paʊər, 'wɑ-] *n* : energía *f* hidráulica
waterproof¹ ['wɔtər,pruːf, 'wɑ-] *vt* : hacer impermeable, impermeabilizar
waterproof² *adj* : impermeable, a prueba de agua
watershed ['wɔtər,ʃɛd, 'wɑ-] *n* **1** : línea *f* divisoria de aguas **2** BASIN : cuenca *f* (de un río)
waterskiing ['wɔtər,skiːɪŋ, 'wɑ-] *n* : esquí *m* acuático
waterspout ['wɔtər,spaʊt, 'wɑ-] *n* WHIRLWIND : tromba *f* marina
watertight ['wɔtər,taɪt, 'wɑ-] *adj* **1** : hermético **2** IRREFUTABLE : irrebatible, irrefutable ⟨a watertight contract : un contrato sin lagunas⟩
waterway ['wɔtər,weɪ, 'wɑ-] *n* : vía *f* navegable
waterworks ['wɔtər,wərks, 'wɑ-] *npl* : central *f* de abastecimiento de agua
watery ['wɔtəri, 'wɑ-] *adj* **1** : acuoso, como agua **2** : aguado, diluido ⟨watery soup : sopa aguada⟩ **3** : lloroso ⟨watery eyes : ojos llorosos⟩ **4** WASHED-OUT : desvaído (dícese de colores)
watt ['wɑt] *n* : vatio *m*
wattage ['wɑtɪdʒ] *n* : vataje *m*
wattle ['wɑtəl] *n* : carúncula *f* (de un ave, etc.)
wave¹ ['weɪv] *v* **waved; waving** *vi* **1** : saludar con la mano, hacer señas con la mano ⟨she waved at him : lo saludó con la mano⟩ **2** FLUTTER, SHAKE : ondear, agitarse **3** UNDULATE : ondular — *vt* **1** SHAKE : agitar **2** BRANDISH : blandir **3** CURL : ondular, marcar (el pelo) **4** SIGNAL : hacerle señas a (con la mano) ⟨he waved farewell : se despidió con la mano⟩
wave² *n* **1** : ola *f* (de agua) **2** CURL : onda *f* (en el pelo) **3** : onda *f* (en física) **4** SURGE : oleada *f* ⟨a wave of enthusiasm : una oleada de entusiasmo⟩ **5** GESTURE : señal *f* con la mano, saludo *m* con la mano
wavelength ['weɪv,lɛŋkθ] *n* : longitud *f* de onda
waver ['weɪvər] *vi* **1** VACILLATE : vacilar, fluctuar **2** FLICKER : parpadear, titilar, oscilar **3** FALTER : flaquear, tambalearse

wavy ['weɪvi] *adj* **wavier; -est** : ondulado
wax¹ ['wæks] *vi* **1** : crecer (dícese de la luna) **2** BECOME : volverse, ponerse ⟨to wax indignant : indignarse⟩ — *vt* : encerar
wax² *n* **1** BEESWAX : cera *f* de abejas **2** : cera *f* ⟨floor wax : cera para el piso⟩ **3** *or* **earwax** ['ɪr,wæks] : cerilla *f*, cerumen *m*
waxen ['wæksən] *adj* : de cera
waxy ['wæksi] *adj* **waxier; -est** : ceroso
way ['weɪ] *n* **1** PATH, ROAD : camino *m*, vía *f* **2** ROUTE : camino *m*, ruta *f* ⟨to go the wrong way : equivocarse de camino⟩ ⟨I'm on my way : estoy de camino⟩ **3** : línea *f* de conducta, camino *m* ⟨he chose the easy way : optó por el camino fácil⟩ **4** MANNER, MEANS : manera *f*, modo *m*, forma *f* ⟨in the same way : del mismo modo, igualmente⟩ ⟨there are no two ways about it : no cabe la menor duda⟩ ⟨no way! : ¡de ninguna manera!⟩ **5** (*indicating a wish*) ⟨have it your way : como tú quieras⟩ ⟨to get one's own way : salirse uno con la suya⟩ **6** STATE : estado *m* ⟨things are in a bad way : las cosas marchan mal⟩ **7** RESPECT : aspecto *m*, sentido *m* **8** CUSTOM : costumbre *f* ⟨to mend one's ways : dejar las malas costumbres⟩ **9** PASSAGE : camino *m* ⟨to get in the way : meterse en el camino⟩ **10** DISTANCE : distancia *f* ⟨to come a long way : hacer grandes progresos⟩ **11** DIRECTION : dirección *f* ⟨come this way : venga por aquí⟩ ⟨which way did he go? : ¿por dónde fue?⟩ **12 by the way** : a propósito, por cierto **13 by way of** VIA : vía, pasando por **14 out of the way** REMOTE : remoto, recóndito **15** → **under way**
wayfarer ['weɪ,færər] *n* : caminante *mf*
waylay ['weɪ,leɪ] *vt* **-laid** [-,leɪd]; **-laying** ACCOST : abordar
wayside ['weɪ,saɪd] *n* : borde *m* del camino
wayward ['weɪwərd] *adj* **1** UNRULY : díscolo, rebelde **2** UNTOWARD : adverso
we ['wiː] *pron* : nosotros, nosotras
weak ['wiːk] *adj* **1** FEEBLE : débil, endeble **2** : flojo, pobre ⟨a weak excuse : una excusa poco convincente⟩ **3** DILUTED : aguado, diluido ⟨weak tea : té poco cargado⟩ **4** FAINT : tenue (dícese de los colores, las luces, los sonidos, etc.)
weaken ['wiːkən] *vt* : debilitar — *vi* : debilitarse, flaquear
weakling ['wiːklɪŋ] *n* : alfeñique *m fam*; debilucho *m*, -cha *f*
weakly¹ ['wiːkli] *adv* : débilmente
weakly² *adj* **weaklier; -est** : débil, enclenque
weakness ['wiːknəs] *n* **1** FEEBLENESS : debilidad *f* **2** FAULT, FLAW : flaqueza *f*, punto *m* débil

wealth [ˈwɛlθ] *n* **1** RICHES : riqueza *f* **2** PROFUSION : abundancia *f*, profusión *f*

wealthy [ˈwɛlθi] *adj* **wealthier; -est** : rico, acaudalado, adinerado

wean [ˈwiːn] *vt* **1** : destetar (a los niños o las crías) **2 to wean someone away from** : quitarle a alguien la costumbre de

weapon [ˈwɛpən] *n* : arma *f*

weaponless [ˈwɛpənləs] *adj* : desarmado

weaponry [ˈwɛpənri] *n* : armamento *m*

wear¹ [ˈwær] *v* **wore** [ˈwor]; **worn** [ˈworn]; **wearing** *vt* **1** : llevar (ropa, un reloj, etc.), calzar (zapatos) ⟨to wear a happy smile : sonreír alegremente⟩ **2** *or* **to wear away** : desgastar, erosionar (rocas, etc.) **3 to wear out** : gastar ⟨he wore out his shoes : gastó sus zapatos⟩ **4 to wear out** EXHAUST : agotar, fatigar ⟨to wear oneself out : agotarse⟩ — *vi* **1** LAST : durar **2 to wear off** DIMINISH : disminuir **3 to wear out** : gastarse

wear² *n* **1** USE : uso *m* ⟨for everyday wear : para todos los días⟩ **2** CLOTHING : ropa *f* ⟨children's wear : ropa de niños⟩ **3** DETERIORATION : desgaste *m* ⟨to be the worse for wear : estar deteriorado⟩

wearable [ˈwærəbəl] *adj* : que puede ponerse (dícese de una prenda)

wear and tear *n* : desgaste *m*

weariness [ˈwɪrinəs] *n* : fatiga *f*, cansancio *m*

wearisome [ˈwɪrisəm] *adj* : aburrido, pesado, cansado

weary¹ [ˈwɪri] *v* **-ried; -rying** *vt* **1** TIRE : cansar, fatigar **2** BORE : hastiar, aburrir — *vi* : cansarse

weary² *adj* **-rier; -est 1** TIRED : cansado **2** FED UP : harto **3** BORED : aburrido

weasel [ˈwiːzəl] *n* : comadreja *f*

weather¹ [ˈwɛðər] *vt* **1** WEAR : erosionar, desgastar **2** ENDURE : aguantar, sobrellevar, capear ⟨to weather the storm : capear el temporal⟩

weather² *n* : tiempo *m*

weather–beaten [ˈwɛðərˌbiːtən] *adj* : curtido

weatherman [ˈwɛðərˌmæn] *n, pl* **-men** [-mən, -ˌmɛn] METEOROLOGIST : meteorólogo *m*, -ga *f*

weatherproof [ˈwɛðərˌpruːf] *adj* : que resiste a la intemperie, impermeable

weather vane → **vane**

weave¹ [ˈwiːv] *v* **wove** [ˈwoːv] *or* **weaved; woven** [ˈwoːvən] *or* **weaved; weaving** *vt* **1** : tejer (tela) **2** INTERLACE : entretejer, entrelazar **3 to weave one's way through** : abrirse camino por — *vi* **1** : tejer **2** WIND : serpentear, zigzaguear

weave² *n* : tejido *m*, trama *f*

weaver [ˈwiːvər] *n* : tejedor *m*, -dora *f*

web¹ [ˈwɛb] *vt* **webbed; webbing** : cubrir o proveer con una red

web² *n* **1** COBWEB, SPIDERWEB : telaraña *f*, tela *f* de araña **2** ENTANGLEMENT, SNARE : red *f*, enredo *m* ⟨a web of intrigue : una red de intriga⟩ **3** : membrana *f* interdigital (de aves) **4** NETWORK : red *f* ⟨a web of highways : una red de carreteras⟩ **5 the Web** : la web

webbed [ˈwɛbd] *adj* : palmeado ⟨webbed feet : patas palmeadas⟩

Web site *n* : sitio *m* web

wed [ˈwɛd] *vt* **wedded; wedding 1** MARRY : casarse con **2** UNITE : ligar, unir

we'd [ˈwiːd] (*contraction of* **we had, we should,** *or* **we would**) → **have, should, would**

wedding [ˈwɛdɪŋ] *n* : boda *f*, casamiento *m*

wedge¹ [ˈwɛdʒ] *vt* **wedged; wedging 1** : apretar (con una cuña) ⟨to wedge open : mantener abierto con una cuña⟩ **2** CRAM : meter, embutir

wedge² *n* **1** : cuña *f* **2** PIECE : porción *f*, trozo *m*

wedlock [ˈwɛdˌlɑk] → **marriage**

Wednesday [ˈwɛnzˌdeɪ, -di] *n* : miércoles *m*

wee [ˈwiː] *adj* : pequeño, minúsculo ⟨in the wee hours : a las altas horas⟩

weed¹ [ˈwiːd] *vt* **1** : desherbar, desyerbar **2 to weed out** : eliminar, quitar

weed² *n* : mala hierba *f*

weedy [ˈwiːdi] *adj* **weedier; -est 1** : cubierto de malas hierbas **2** LANKY, SKINNY : flaco, larguirucho *fam*

week [ˈwiːk] *n* : semana *f*

weekday [ˈwiːkˌdeɪ] *n* : día *m* laborable

weekend [ˈwiːkˌɛnd] *n* : fin *m* de semana

weekly¹ [ˈwiːkli] *adv* : semanalmente

weekly² *adj* : semanal

weekly³ *n, pl* **-lies** : semanario *m*

weep [ˈwiːp] *v* **wept** [ˈwɛpt]; **weeping** : llorar

weeping willow *n* : sauce *m* llorón

weepy [ˈwiːpi] *adj* **weepier; -est** : lloroso, triste

weevil [ˈwiːvəl] *n* : gorgojo *m*

weft [ˈwɛft] *n* : trama *f*

weigh [ˈweɪ] *vt* **1** : pesar **2** CONSIDER : considerar, sopesar **3 to weigh anchor** : levar anclas **4 to weigh down** : sobrecargar (con una carga), abrumar (con preocupaciones, etc.) — *vi* **1** : pesar ⟨it weighs 10 pounds : pesa 10 libras⟩ **2** COUNT : tener importancia, contar **3 to weigh on one's mind** : preocuparle a uno

weight¹ [ˈweɪt] *vt* **1** : poner peso en, sujetar con un peso **2** BURDEN : cargar, oprimir

weight² *n* **1** HEAVINESS : peso *m* ⟨to lose weight : bajar de peso, adelgazar⟩ **2** : peso *m* ⟨weights and measures : pesos y medidas⟩ **3** : pesa *f* ⟨to lift weights : levantar pesas⟩ **4** BURDEN : peso *m*, carga *f* ⟨to take a weight off one's mind : quitarle un peso de encima a uno⟩ **5**

IMPORTANCE : peso *m* **6** INFLUENCE : influencia *f*, autoridad *f* ⟨to throw one's weight around : hacer sentir su influencia⟩

weighty ['weɪʈi] *adj* **weightier; -est 1** HEAVY : pesado **2** IMPORTANT : importante, de peso

weird ['wɪrd] *adj* **1** MYSTERIOUS : misterioso **2** STRANGE : extraño, raro — **weirdly** *adv*

welcome[1] ['wɛlkəm] *vt* **-comed; -coming** : darle la bienvenida a, recibir

welcome[2] *adj* : bienvenido ⟨to make someone welcome : acoger bien a alguien⟩ ⟨you're welcome! : ¡de nada!, ¡no hay de qué!⟩

welcome[3] *n* : bienvenida *f*, recibimiento *m*, acogida *f*

weld[1] ['wɛld] *v* : soldar

weld[2] *n* : soldadura *f*

welder ['wɛld,fær] *n* : soldador *m*, -dora *f*

welfare ['wɛl,fær] *n* **1** WELL-BEING : bienestar *m* **2** : asistencia *f* social

well[1] ['wɛl] *vi or* **to well up** : brotar, manar

well[2] *adv* **better** ['bɛʈər]; **best** ['bɛst] **1** RIGHTLY : bien, correctamente **2** SATISFACTORILY : bien ⟨to turn out well : resultar bien, salir bien⟩ **3** COMPLETELY : completamente ⟨well-hidden : completamente escondido⟩ **4** INTIMATELY : bien ⟨I knew him well : lo conocía bien⟩ **5** CONSIDERABLY, FAR : muy, bastante ⟨well ahead : muy adelante⟩ ⟨well before the deadline : bastante antes de la fecha⟩ **6 as well** ALSO : también **7** → **as well as**

well[3] *adj* **1** SATISFACTORY : bien ⟨all is well : todo está bien⟩ **2** DESIRABLE : conveniente ⟨it would be well if you left : sería conveniente que te fueras⟩ **3** HEALTHY : bien, sano

well[4] *n* **1** : pozo *m* (de agua, petróleo, gas, etc.), aljibe *m* (de agua) **2** SOURCE : fuente *f* ⟨a well of information : una fuente de información⟩ **3** *or* **stairwell** : caja *f*, hueco *m* (de la escalera)

well[5] *interj* **1** (*used to introduce a remark*) : bueno **2** (*used to express surprise*) : ¡vaya!

we'll ['wiːl, wɪl] (*contraction of* **we shall** *or* **we will**) → **shall, will**

well–balanced ['wɛl'bælənst] *adj* : equilibrado

well–being ['wɛl'biːɪŋ] *n* : bienestar *m*

well–bred ['wɛl'brɛd] *adj* : fino, bien educado

well–defined [ˌwɛldi'faɪnd] *adj* : bien definido

well–done ['wɛl'dʌn] *adj* **1** : bien hecho ⟨well-done! : ¡bravo!⟩ **2** : bien cocido

well–known ['wɛl'noːn] *adj* : famoso, bien conocido

well–meaning ['wɛl'miːnɪŋ] *adj* : bienintencionado, que tiene buenas intenciones

well–nigh ['wɛl'naɪ] *adv* : casi ⟨well-nigh impossible : casi imposible⟩

well–off ['wɛl'ɔf] → **well–to–do**

well–rounded ['wɛl'raʊndəd] *adj* : completo, equilibrado

well–to–do [ˌwɛltə'duː] *adj* : próspero, adinerado, rico

Welsh ['wɛlʃ] *n* **1** : galés *m*, galesa *f* **2** : galés *m* (idioma) — **Welsh** *adj*

welt ['wɛlt] *n* **1** : vira *f* (de un zapato) **2** WHEAL : verdugón *m*

welter ['wɛltər] *n* : fárrago *m*, revoltijo *m* ⟨a welter of data : un fárrago de datos⟩

wend ['wɛnd] *vi* **to wend one's way** : ponerse en camino, encaminar sus pasos

went → **go**[1]

wept → **weep**

were → **be**

we're ['wɪr, 'wər, 'wiːər] (*contraction of* **we are**) → **be**

werewolf ['wɪr,wʊlf, 'wɛr-, 'wər-, -,wʌlf] *n, pl* **-wolves** [-,wʊlvz, -,wʌlvz] : hombre *m* lobo

west[1] ['wɛst] *adv* : al oeste

west[2] *adj* : oeste, del oeste, occidental ⟨west winds : vientos del oeste⟩

west[3] *n* **1** : oeste *m* **2 the West** : el Oeste, el Occidente

westerly ['wɛstərli] *adv & adj* : del oeste

western ['wɛstərn] *adj* **1** : Occidental, del Oeste **2** : occidental, oeste

Westerner ['wɛstərnər] *n* : habitante *mf* del oeste

West Indian *n* : antillano *m*, -na *f* — **West Indian** *adj*

westward ['wɛstwərd] *adv & adj* : hacia el oeste

wet[1] ['wɛt] *vt* **wet** *or* **wetted; wetting** : mojar, humedecer

wet[2] *adj* **wetter; wettest 1** : mojado, húmedo ⟨wet clothes : ropa mojada⟩ **2** RAINY : lluvioso **3 wet paint** : pintura *f* fresca

wet[3] *n* **1** MOISTURE : humedad *f* **2** RAIN : lluvia *f*

we've ['wiːv] (*contraction of* **we have**) → **have**

whack[1] ['hwæk] *vt* : golpear (fuertemente), aporrear

whack[2] *n* **1** : golpe *m* fuerte, porrazo *m* **2** ATTEMPT : intento *m*, tentativa *f*

whale[1] ['hweɪl] *vi* **whaled; whaling** : cazar ballenas

whale[2] *n, pl* **whales** *or* **whale** : ballena *f*

whaleboat ['hweɪl,boːt] *n* : ballenero *m*

whalebone ['hweɪl,boːn] *n* : barba *f* de ballena

whaler ['hweɪlər] *n* **1** : ballenero *m*, -ra *f* **2** → **whaleboat**

wharf ['hwɔrf] *n, pl* **wharves** ['hwɔrvz] : muelle *m*, embarcadero *m*

what[1] ['hwɑt, 'hwʌt] *adv* **1** HOW : cómo, cuánto ⟨what he suffered! : ¡cómo sufría!⟩ **2 what with** : entre ⟨what with one thing and another : entre una cosa y otra⟩

what[2] *adj* **1** (*used in questions*) : qué ⟨what more do you want? : ¿qué más quieres?⟩ ⟨what color is it? : ¿de qué

color es?⟩ **2** (*used in exclamations*)
: qué ⟨what an idea! : ¡qué idea!⟩ **3**
ANY, WHATEVER : cualquier ⟨give what
help you can : da cualquier contribución que puedas⟩
what³ *pron* **1** (*used in direct questions*)
: qué ⟨what happened? : ¿qué pasó?⟩
⟨what does it cost? : ¿cuánto cuesta?⟩
2 (*used in indirect statements*) : lo que,
que ⟨I don't know what to do : no sé
que hacer⟩ ⟨do what I tell you : haz lo
que te digo⟩ **3 what for** WHY : porqué
4 what if : y si ⟨what if he knows? : ¿y
si lo sabe?⟩
whatever¹ [hwɑt'ɛvər, ˌhwʌt-] *adj* **1** ANY
: cualquier, cualquier ... que ⟨what-
ever way you prefer : de cualquier
manera que prefiera, como prefiera⟩ **2**
(*in negative constructions*) ⟨there's no
chance whatever : no hay ninguna posi-
bilidad⟩ ⟨nothing whatever : nada en
absoluto⟩
whatever² *pron* **1** ANYTHING : (todo) lo
que ⟨I'll do whatever I want : haré lo
que quiera⟩ **2** (*no matter what*) ⟨what-
ever it may be : sea lo que sea⟩ **3** WHAT
: qué ⟨whatever do you mean? : ¿qué
quieres decir?⟩
whatsoever¹ [ˌhwɑtso'ɛvər, ˌhwʌt-] *adj*
→ **whatever¹**
whatsoever² *pron* → **whatever²**
wheal ['hwi:l] *n* : verdugón *m*
wheat ['hwi:t] *n* : trigo *m*
wheaten ['hwi:tən] *adj* : de trigo
wheedle ['hwi:dəl] *vt* **-dled; -dling** CA-
JOLE : engatusar ⟨to wheedle some-
thing out of someone : sonsacarle algo
a alguien⟩
wheel¹ ['hwi:l] *vt* : empujar (una bicicleta, etc.), mover (algo sobre ruedas)
— *vi* **1** ROTATE : girar, rotar **2 to wheel
around** TURN : darse la vuelta
wheel² *n* **1** : rueda *f* **2** *or* **steering wheel**
: volante *m* (de automóviles, etc.),
timón *m* (de barcos o aviones) **3
wheels** *npl* : maquinaria *f*, fuerza *f* im-
pulsora ⟨the wheels of government : la
maquinaria del gobierno⟩
wheelbarrow ['hwi:lˌbærˌo:] *n* : carretilla *f*
wheelchair ['hwi:lˌʧær] *n* : silla *f* de
ruedas
wheeze¹ ['hwi:z] *vi* **wheezed; wheezing**
: resollar, respirar con dificultad
wheeze² *n* : resuello *m*
whelk ['hwɛlk] *n* : buccino *m*
whelp¹ ['hwɛlp] *vi* : parir
whelp² *n* : cachorro *m*, -rra *f*
when¹ ['hwɛn] *adv* : cuándo ⟨when will
you return? : ¿cuándo volverás?⟩ ⟨he
asked me when I would be home : me
preguntó cuándo estaría en casa⟩
when² *conj* **1** (*referring to a particular
time*) : cuando, en que ⟨when you are
ready : cuando estés listo⟩ ⟨the days
when I clean the house : los días en que
limpio la casa⟩ **2** IF : cuando, si ⟨how
can I go when I have no money?⟩

: ¿cómo voy a ir si no tengo dinero?⟩
3 ALTHOUGH : cuando ⟨you said it was
big when actually it's small : dijiste que
era grande cuando en realidad es pe-
queño⟩
when³ *pron* : cuándo ⟨since when are
you the boss? : ¿desde cuándo eres el
jefe?⟩
whence ['hwɛnts] *adv* : de donde
whenever¹ [hwɛn'vər] *adv* **1** : cuando
sea ⟨tomorrow or whenever : mañana
o cuando sea⟩ **2** (*in questions*) : cuándo
whenever² *conj* **1** : siempre que, cada
vez que ⟨whenever I go, I'm disappointed : siempre que voy, quedo de-
silusionado⟩ **2** WHEN : cuando ⟨when-
ever you like : cuando quieras⟩
where¹ ['hwɛr] *adv* : dónde, adónde
⟨where is he? : ¿dónde está?⟩ ⟨where
did they go? : ¿adónde fueron?⟩
where² *conj* : donde, adonde ⟨she knows
where the house is : sabe donde está la
casa⟩ ⟨she goes where she likes : va
adonde quiera⟩
where³ *pron* : donde ⟨Chicago is where
I live : Chicago es donde vivo⟩
whereabouts¹ ['hwɛrəˌbaʊts] *adv*
: dónde, por dónde ⟨whereabouts is the
house? : ¿dónde está la casa?⟩
whereabouts² *ns & pl* : paradero *m*
whereas [hwɛr'æz] *conj* **1** : consideran-
do que (usado en documentos legales)
2 : mientras que ⟨I like the white one
whereas she prefers the black : me gusta el blanco mientras que ella prefiere
el negro⟩
whereby [hwɛr'baɪ] *adv* : por lo cual
wherefore ['hwɛrˌfor] *adv* : por qué
wherein [hwɛr'ɪn] *adv* : en el cual, en el
que
whereof [hwɛr'ʌv, -'ɑv] *conj* : de lo cual
whereupon ['hwɛrəˌpɑn, -ˌpɔn] *conj*
: con lo cual, después de lo cual
wherever¹ [hwɛr'ɛvər] *adv* **1** WHERE
: dónde, adónde **2** : en cualquier parte
⟨or wherever : o donde sea⟩
wherever² *conj* : dondequiera que,
donde sea ⟨wherever you go : dondequiera que vayas⟩
wherewithal ['hwɛrwɪˌðɔl, -ˌθɔl] *n*
: medios *mpl*, recursos *mpl*
whet ['hwɛt] *vt* **whetted; whetting 1**
SHARPEN : afilar **2** STIMULATE : estimular ⟨to whet the appetite : estimular el apetito⟩
whether ['hwɛðər] *conj* **1** : si ⟨I don't
know whether it is finished : no sé si
está acabado⟩ ⟨we doubt whether he'll
show up : dudamos que aparezca⟩ **2**
(*used in comparisons*) ⟨whether I like
it or not : tanto si quiero como si no⟩
⟨whether he comes or he doesn't : venga o no⟩
whetstone ['hwɛtˌsto:n] *n* : piedra *f* de
afilar
whey ['hweɪ] *n* : suero *m* (de la leche)
which¹ ['hwɪʧ] *adj* : qué, cuál ⟨which tie
do you prefer? : ¿cuál corbata pre-

fieres?⟩ ⟨which ones? : ¿cuáles?⟩ ⟨tell me which house is yours : dime qué casa es la tuya⟩

which² *pron* **1** : cuál ⟨which is the right answer? : ¿cuál es la respuesta correcta?⟩ **2** : que, el (la) cual ⟨the cup which broke : la taza que se quebró⟩ ⟨the house, which is made of brick : la casa, la cual es de ladrillo⟩

whichever¹ [hwɪtʃˈɛvər] *adj* : el (la) que, cualquiera que ⟨whichever book you like : cualquier libro que te guste⟩

whichever² *pron* : el (la) que, cualquiera que ⟨take whichever you want : toma el que quieras⟩ ⟨whichever I choose : cualquiera que elija⟩

whiff¹ [ˈhwɪf] *v* PUFF : soplar

whiff² *n* **1** PUFF : soplo *m*, ráfaga *f* **2** SNIFF : olor *m* **3** HINT : dejo *m*, pizca *f*

while¹ [ˈhwaɪl] *vt* **whiled; whiling** : pasar ⟨to while away the time : matar el tiempo⟩

while² *n* **1** TIME : rato *m*, tiempo *m* ⟨after a while : después de un rato⟩ ⟨in a while : dentro de poco⟩ **2 to be worth one's while** : valer la pena

while³ *conj* **1** : mientras ⟨whistle while you work : silba mientras trabajas⟩ **2** WHEREAS : mientras que **3** ALTHOUGH : aunque ⟨while it's very good, it's not perfect : aunque es muy bueno, no es perfecto⟩

whim [ˈhwɪm] *n* : capricho *m*, antojo *m*

whimper¹ [ˈhwɪmpər] *vi* : lloriquear, gimotear

whimper² *n* : quejido *m*

whimsical [ˈhwɪmzɪkəl] *adj* **1** CAPRICIOUS : caprichoso, fantasioso **2** ERRATIC : errático — **whimsically** *adv*

whine¹ [ˈhwaɪn] *vi* **whined; whining** **1** : lloriquear, gimotear, gemir **2** COMPLAIN : quejarse

whine² *n* : quejido *m*, gemido *m*

whinny¹ [ˈhwɪni] *vi* **-nied; -nying** : relinchar

whinny² *n, pl* **-nies** : relincho *m*

whip¹ [ˈhwɪp] *v* **whipped; whipping** *vt* **1** SNATCH : sacar (rápidamente), arrebatar ⟨she whipped the cloth off the table : arrebató el mantel de la mesa⟩ **2** LASH : azotar **3** DEFEAT : vencer, derrotar **4** INCITE : incitar, despertar ⟨to whip up enthusiasm : despertar el entusiasmo⟩ **5** BEAT : batir (huevos, crema, etc.) — *vi* FLAP : agitarse

whip² *n* **1** : látigo *m*, azote *m*, fusta *f* (de jinete) **2** : miembro *m* de un cuerpo legislativo encargado de disciplina

whiplash [ˈhwɪpˌlæʃ] *n or* **whiplash injury** : traumatismo *m* cervical

whippet [ˈhwɪpət] *n* : galgo *m* pequeño, galgo *m* inglés

whir¹ [ˈhwər] *vi* **whirred; whirring** : zumbar

whir² *n* : zumbido *m*

whirl¹ [ˈhwərl] *vi* **1** SPIN : dar vueltas, girar ⟨my head is whirling : la cabeza me

está dando vueltas⟩ **2 to whirl about** : arremolinarse, moverse rápidamente

whirl² *n* **1** SPIN : giro *m*, vuelta *f*, remolino *m* (dícese del polvo, etc.) **2** BUSTLE : bullicio *m*, torbellino *m* (de actividad, etc.) **3 to give it a whirl** : intentar hacer, probar

whirlpool [ˈhwərlˌpuːl] *n* : vorágine *f*, remolino *m*

whirlwind [ˈhwərlˌwɪnd] *n* : remolino *m*, torbellino *m*, tromba *f*

whisk¹ [ˈhwɪsk] *vt* **1** : llevar ⟨she whisked the children off to bed : llevó a los niños a la cama⟩ **2** : batir ⟨to whisk eggs : batir huevos⟩ **3 to whisk away** *or* **to whisk off** : sacudir

whisk² *n* **1** WHISKING : sacudida *f* (movimiento) **2** : batidor *m* (para batir huevos, etc.)

whisk broom *n* : escobilla *f*

whisker [ˈhwɪskər] *n* **1** : pelo *m* (de la barba o el bigote) **2 whiskers** *npl* : bigotes *mpl* (de animales)

whiskey *or* **whisky** [ˈhwɪski] *n, pl* **-keys** *or* **-kies** : whisky *m*

whisper¹ [ˈhwɪspər] *vi* : cuchichear, susurrar — *vt* : decir en voz baja, susurrar

whisper² *n* **1** WHISPERING : susurro *m*, cuchicheo *m* **2** RUMOR : rumor *m* **3** TRACE : dejo *m*, pizca *f*

whistle¹ [ˈhwɪsəl] *v* **-tled; -tling** *vi* : silbar, chiflar, pitar (dícese de un tren, etc.) — *vt* : silbar ⟨to whistle a tune : silbar una melodía⟩

whistle² *n* **1** WHISTLING : chiflido *m*, silbido *m* **2** : silbato *m*, pito *m* (instrumento)

whit [ˈhwɪt] *n* BIT : ápice *m*, pizca *f*

white¹ [ˈhwaɪt] *adj* **whiter; -est** : blanco

white² *n* **1** : blanco *m* (color) **2** : clara *f* (de huevos) **3** *or* **white person** : blanco *m*, -ca *f*

white blood cell *n* : glóbulo *m* blanco

whitecaps [ˈhwaɪtˌkæps] *npl* : cabrillas *fpl*

white–collar [ˈhwaɪtˈkɑlər] *adj* **1** : de oficina **2 white–collar worker** : oficinista *mf*

whitefish [ˈhwaɪtˌfɪʃ] *n* : pescado *m* blanco

whiten [ˈhwaɪtən] *vt* : blanquear — *vi* : ponerse blanco

whiteness [ˈhwaɪtnəs] *n* : blancura *f*

white–tailed deer [ˈhwaɪtˈteɪld] *n* : ciervo *f* de Virginia

whitewash¹ [ˈhwaɪtˌwɔʃ] *vt* **1** : enjalbegar, blanquear ⟨to whitewash a fence : enjalbegar una valla⟩ **2** CONCEAL : encubrir (un escándalo, etc.)

whitewash² *n* **1** : jalbegue *m*, lechada *f* **2** COVER-UP : encubrimiento *m*

whither [ˈhwɪðər] *adv* : adónde

whiting [ˈhwaɪtɪŋ] *n* : merluza *f*, pescadilla *f* (pez)

whitish [ˈhwaɪtɪʃ] *adj* : blancuzco

whittle [ˈhwɪtəl] *vt* **-tled; -tling** **1** : tallar (madera) **2 to whittle down** : reducir, recortar ⟨to whittle down expenses : reducir los gastos⟩

whiz¹ *or* **whizz** [ˈʰwɪz] *vi* **whizzed; whizzing 1** BUZZ : zumbar **2 to whiz by** : pasar muy rápido, pasar volando

whiz² *or* **whizz** *n, pl* **whizzes 1** BUZZ : zumbido *m* **2 to be a whiz** : ser un prodigio, ser muy hábil

who [ˈhuː] *pron* **1** (*used in direct and indirect questions*) : quién ⟨who is that? : ¿quién es ése?⟩ ⟨who did it? : ¿quién lo hizo?⟩ ⟨we know who they are : sabemos quiénes son⟩ **2** (*used in relative clauses*) : que, quien ⟨the lady who lives there : la señora que vive allí⟩ ⟨for those who wait : para los que esperan, para quienes esperan⟩

whodunit [huːˈdʌnɪt] *n* : novela *f* policíaca

whoever [huːˈɛvər] *pron* **1** : quienquiera que, quien ⟨whoever did it : quienquiera que lo hizo⟩ ⟨give it to whoever you want : dalo a quien quieras⟩ **2** (*used in questions*) : quién ⟨whoever could that be? : ¿quién podría ser?⟩

whole¹ [ˈhoːl] *adj* **1** UNHURT : ileso **2** INTACT : intacto, sano **3** ENTIRE : entero, íntegro ⟨the whole island : toda la isla⟩ ⟨whole milk : leche entera⟩ **4 a whole lot** : muchísimo

whole² *n* **1** : todo *m* **2 as a whole** : en conjunto **3 on the whole** : en general

wholehearted [ˈhoːlˈhɑrtəd] *adj* : sin reservas, incondicional

whole number *n* : entero *m*

wholesale¹ [ˈhoːlˌseɪl] *v* **-saled; -saling** *vt* : vender al por mayor — *vi* : venderse al por mayor

wholesale² *adv* : al por mayor

wholesale³ *adj* **1** : al por mayor ⟨wholesale grocer : tendero al por mayor⟩ **2** TOTAL : total, absoluto ⟨wholesale slaughter : matanza sistemática⟩

wholesale⁴ *n* : mayoreo *m*

wholesaler [ˈhoːlˌseɪlər] *n* : mayorista *mf*

wholesome [ˈhoːlsəm] *adj* **1** : sano ⟨wholesome advice : consejo sano⟩ **2** HEALTHY : sano, saludable

whole wheat *adj* : de trigo integral

wholly [ˈhoːli] *adv* **1** COMPLETELY : completamente **2** SOLELY : exclusivamente, únicamente

whom [ˈhuːm] *pron* **1** (*used in direct questions*) : a quién ⟨whom did you choose? : ¿a quién elegiste?⟩ **2** (*used in indirect questions*) : de quién, con quién, en quién ⟨I don't know whom to consult : no sé con quién consultar⟩ **3** (*used in relative clauses*) : que, a quien ⟨the lawyer whom I recommended to you : el abogado que te recomendé⟩

whomever [huːmˈɛvər] *pron* WHOEVER : quienquiera, quien ⟨marry whomever you please : cásate con quien quieras⟩

whoop¹ [ˈʰwuːp, ˈʰwʊp] *vi* : gritar, chillar

whoop² *n* : grito *m*

whooping cough *n* : tos *f* ferina

whopper [ˈʰwɑpər] *n* **1** : cosa *f* enorme **2** LIE : mentira *f* colosal

whopping [ˈʰwɑpɪŋ] *adj* : enorme

whore [ˈhor] *n* : puta *f*, ramera *f*

whorl [ˈʰworl, ˈʰwərl] *n* : espiral *f*, espira *f* (de una concha), línea *f* (de una huella digital)

whose¹ [ˈhuːz] *adj* **1** (*used in questions*) : de quién ⟨whose truck is that? : ¿de quién es ese camión?⟩ **2** (*used in relative clauses*) : cuyo ⟨the person whose work is finished : la persona cuyo trabajo está terminado⟩

whose² *pron* : de quién ⟨tell me whose it was : dime de quién era⟩

why¹ [ˈʰwaɪ] *adv* : por qué ⟨why did you do it? : ¿por qué lo hizo?⟩

why² *n, pl* **whys** REASON : porqué *m*, razón *f*

why³ *conj* : por qué ⟨I know why he left : yo sé por qué salió⟩ ⟨there's no reason why it should exist : no hay razón para que exista⟩

why⁴ *interj* (*used to express surprise*) : ¡vaya!, ¡mira!

wick [ˈwɪk] *n* : mecha *f*

wicked [ˈwɪkəd] *adj* **1** EVIL : malo, malvado **2** MISCHIEVOUS : travieso, pícaro ⟨a wicked grin : una sonrisa traviesa⟩ **3** TERRIBLE : terrible, horrible ⟨a wicked storm : una tormenta horrible⟩

wickedly [ˈwɪkədli] *adv* : con maldad

wickedness [ˈwɪkədnəs] *n* : maldad *f*

wicker¹ [ˈwɪkər] *adj* : de mimbre

wicker² *n* **1** : mimbre *m* **2** → **wickerwork**

wickerwork [ˈwɪkərˌwərk] *n* : artículos *mpl* de mimbre

wicket [ˈwɪkət] *n* **1** WINDOW : ventanilla *f* **2** *or* **wicket gate** : postigo *m* **3** : aro *m* (en croquet), palos *mpl* (en críquet)

wide¹ [ˈwaɪd] *adv* **wider; widest 1** WIDELY : por todas partes ⟨to travel far and wide : viajar por todas partes⟩ **2** COMPLETELY : completamente, totalmente ⟨wide open : abierto de par en par⟩ **3 wide apart** : muy separados

wide² *adj* **wider; widest 1** VAST : vasto, extensivo ⟨a wide area : una área extensiva⟩ **2** : ancho ⟨three meters wide : tres metros de ancho⟩ **3** BROAD : ancho, amplio **4** *or* **wide-open** : muy abierto **5 wide of the mark** : desviado, lejos del blanco

wide-awake [ˈwaɪdəˈweɪk] *adj* : (completamente) despierto

wide-eyed [ˈwaɪdˈaɪd] *adj* **1** : con los ojos muy abiertos **2** NAIVE : inocente, ingenuo

widely [ˈwaɪdli] *adv* : extensivamente, por todas partes

widen [ˈwaɪdən] *vt* : ampliar, ensanchar — *vi* : ampliarse, ensancharse

widespread [ˈwaɪdˈsprɛd] *adj* : extendido, extenso, difuso

widow¹ [ˈwɪˌdoː] *vt* : dejar viuda ⟨to be widowed : enviudar⟩

widow² *n* : viuda *f*

widower ['wɪdowər] *n* : viudo *m*
width ['wɪdθ] *n* : ancho *m*, anchura *f*
wield ['wi:ld] *vt* **1** USE : usar, manejar ⟨to wield a broom : usar una escoba⟩ **2** EXERCISE : ejercer ⟨to wield influence : influir⟩
wiener ['wi:nər] → **frankfurter**
wife ['waɪf] *n, pl* **wives** ['waɪvz] : esposa *f*, mujer *f*
wifely ['waɪfli] *adj* : de esposa, conyugal
wig ['wɪg] *n* : peluca *f*
wiggle[1] ['wɪgəl] *v* **-gled; -gling** *vt* : menear, contonear ⟨to wiggle one's hips : contonearse⟩ — *vi* : menearse
wiggle[2] *n* : meneo *m*, contoneo *m*
wiggly ['wɪgəli] *adj* **-glier; -est** **1** : que se menea **2** WAVY : ondulado
wigwag ['wɪg,wæg] *vi* **-wagged; -wagging** : comunicar por señales
wigwam ['wɪg,wɑm] *n* : wigwam *m*
wild[1] ['waɪld] *adv* **1** → **wildly** **2 to run wild** : descontrolarse
wild[2] *adj* **1** : salvaje, silvestre, cimarrón ⟨wild horses : caballos salvajes⟩ ⟨wild rice : arroz silvestre⟩ **2** DESOLATE : yermo, agreste **3** UNRULY : desenfrenado **4** CRAZY : loco, fantástico ⟨wild ideas : ideas locas⟩ **5** BARBAROUS : salvaje, bárbaro **6** ERRATIC : errático ⟨a wild throw : un tiro errático⟩
wild[3] *n* → **wilderness**
wild card *n* **1** : factor *m* desconocido **2** : comodín *m* (carta o símbolo)
wildcat ['waɪld,kæt] *n* **1** : gato *m* montés **2** BOBCAT : lince *m* rojo
wilderness ['wɪldərnəs] *n* : yermo *m*, desierto *m*
wildfire ['waɪld,faɪr] *n* **1** : fuego *m* descontrolado **2 to spread like wildfire** : propagarse como un reguero de pólvora
wildflower ['waɪld,flaʊər] *n* : flor *f* silvestre
wildfowl ['waɪld,faʊl] *n* : ave *f* de caza
wildlife ['waɪld,laɪf] *n* : fauna *f*
wildly ['waɪldli] *adv* **1** FRANTICALLY : frenéticamente, como un loco **2** EXTREMELY : extremadamente ⟨wildly happy : loco de felicidad⟩
wile[1] ['waɪl] *vt* **wiled; wiling** LURE : atraer
wile[2] *n* : ardid *m*, artimaña *f*
will[1] ['wɪl] *v, past* **would** ['wʊd]; *pres sing & pl* **will** *vt* WISH : querer ⟨do what you will : haz lo que quieras⟩ — *v aux* **1** *(expressing willingness)* ⟨no one would take the job : nadie aceptaría el trabajo⟩ ⟨I won't do it : no lo haré⟩ **2** *(expressing habitual action)* ⟨he will get angry over nothing : se pone furioso por cualquier cosa⟩ **3** *(forming the future tense)* ⟨tomorrow we will go shopping : mañana iremos de compras⟩ **4** *(expressing capacity)* ⟨the couch will hold three people : en el sofá cabrán tres personas⟩ **5** *(expressing determination)* ⟨I will go despite them : iré a pesar de

ellos⟩ **6** *(expressing probability)* ⟨that will be the mailman : eso ha de ser el cartero⟩ **7** *(expressing inevitability)* ⟨accidents will happen : los accidentes ocurrirán⟩ **8** *(expressing a command)* ⟨you will do as I say : harás lo que digo⟩
will[2] *vt* **1** ORDAIN : disponer, decretar ⟨if God wills it : si Dios lo dispone, si Dios quiere⟩ **2** : lograr a fuerza de voluntad ⟨they were willing him to succeed : estaban deseando que tuviera éxito⟩ **3** BEQUEATH : legar
will[3] *n* **1** DESIRE : deseo *m*, voluntad *f* **2** VOLITION : voluntad *f* ⟨free will : libre albedrío⟩ **3** WILLPOWER : voluntad *f*, fuerza *f* de voluntad ⟨a will of iron : una voluntad férrea⟩ **4** : testamento *m* ⟨to make a will : hacer testamento⟩
willful *or* **wilful** ['wɪlfəl] *adj* **1** OBSTINATE : obstinado, terco **2** INTENTIONAL : intencionado, deliberado — **willfully** *adv*
willing ['wɪlɪŋ] *adj* **1** INCLINED, READY : listo, dispuesto **2** OBLIGING : servicial, complaciente
willingly ['wɪlɪŋli] *adv* : con gusto
willingness ['wɪlɪŋnəs] *n* : buena voluntad *f*
willow ['wɪ,lo:] *n* : sauce *m*
willowy ['wɪlowi] *adj* : esbelto
willpower ['wɪl,paʊər] *n* : voluntad *f*, fuerza *f* de voluntad
wilt ['wɪlt] *vi* **1** : marchitarse (dícese de las flores) **2** LANGUISH : debilitarse, languidecer
wily ['waɪli] *adj* **wilier; -est** : artero, astuto
wimp ['wɪmp] *n* **1** COWARD : gallina *f*, cobarde *mf* **2** WEAKLING : debilucho *m*, -cha *f*; alfeñique *m*
win[1] ['wɪn] *v* **won** ['wʌn]; **winning** *vi* : ganar — *vt* **1** : ganar, conseguir **2 to win over** : ganarse a **3 to win someone's heart** : conquistar a alguien
win[2] *n* : triunfo *m*, victoria *f*
wince[1] ['wɪnts] *vi* **winced; wincing** : estremecerse, hacer una mueca de dolor
wince[2] *n* : mueca *f* de dolor
winch ['wɪntʃ] *n* : torno *m*
wind[1] ['wɪnd] *vt* : dejar sin aliento ⟨to be winded : quedarse sin aliento⟩
wind[2] ['waɪnd] *v* **wound** ['waʊnd]; **winding** *vi* MEANDER : serpentear — *vt* **1** COIL, ROLL : envolver, enrollar **2** TURN : hacer girar ⟨to wind a clock : darle cuerda a un reloj⟩
wind[3] ['wɪnd] *n* **1** : viento *m* ⟨against the wind : contra el viento⟩ **2** BREATH : aliento *m* **3** FLATULENCE : flatulencia *f*, ventosidad *f* **4 to get wind of** : enterarse de
wind[4] ['waɪnd] *n* **1** TURN : vuelta *f* **2** BEND : recodo *m*, curva *f*
windbreak ['wɪnd,breɪk] *n* : barrera *f* contra el viento, abrigadero *m*
windfall ['wɪnd,fɔl] *n* **1** : fruta *f* caída **2** : beneficio *m* imprevisto
wind instrument *n* : instrumento *m* de viento

windlass ['wɪndləs] *n* : cabrestante *m*
windmill ['wɪnd,mɪl] *n* : molino *m* de viento
window ['wɪn,do:] *n* **1** : ventana *f* (de un edificio o una computadora), ventanilla *f* (de un vehículo o avión), vitrina *f* (de una tienda) **2** → **windowpane**
windowpane ['wɪn,do:,peɪn] *n* : vidrio *m*
window–shop ['wɪndo,ʃɑp] *vi* **-shopped; -shopping** : mirar las vitrinas
windpipe ['wɪnd,paɪp] *n* : tráquea *f*
windshield ['wɪnd,ʃi:ld] *n* **1** : parabrisas *m* **2 windshield wiper** : limpiaparabrisas *m*
windup ['waɪnd,ʌp] *n* : conclusión *f*
wind up *vt* END : terminar, concluir — *vi* : terminar, acabar
windward¹ ['wɪndwərd] *adj* : de barlovento
windward² *n* : barlovento *m*
windy ['wɪndi] *adj* **windier; -est 1** : ventoso ⟨it's windy : hace viento⟩ **2** VERBOSE : verboso, prolijo
wine¹ ['waɪn] *v* **wined; wining** *vi* : beber vino — *vt* **to wine and dine** : agasajar
wine² *n* : vino *m*
wing¹ ['wɪŋ] *vi* FLY : volar
wing² *n* **1** : ala *f* (de un ave, un avión, o un edificio) **2** FACTION : ala *f* ⟨the right wing of the party : el ala derecha del partido⟩ **3 wings** *npl* : bastidores *mpl* (de un teatro) **4 on the wing** : al vuelo, volando **5 under one's wing** : bajo el cargo de uno
winged ['wɪŋd, 'wɪŋəd] *adj* : alado
wink¹ ['wɪŋk] *vi* **1** : guiñar el ojo **2** BLINK : pestañear, parpadear **3** FLICKER : parpadear, titilar
wink² *n* **1** : guiño *m* (del ojo) **2** NAP : siesta *f* ⟨not to sleep a wink : no pegar el ojo⟩
winner ['wɪnər] *n* : ganador *m*, -dora *f*
winning ['wɪnɪŋ] *adj* **1** VICTORIOUS : ganador **2** CHARMING : encantador
winnings ['wɪnɪŋz] *npl* : ganancias *fpl*
winnow ['wɪ,no:] *vt* : aventar (el grano, etc.)
winsome ['wɪnsəm] *adj* CHARMING : encantador
winter¹ ['wɪntər] *adj* : invernal, de invierno
winter² *n* : invierno *m*
wintergreen ['wɪntər,gri:n] *n* : gaulteria *f*
wintertime ['wɪntər,taɪm] *n* : invierno *m*
wintry ['wɪntri] *adj* **wintrier; -est 1** WINTER : invernal, de invierno **2** COLD : frío ⟨she gave us a wintry greeting : nos saludó fríamente⟩
wipe¹ ['waɪp] *vt* **wiped; wiping 1** : limpiar, pasarle un trapo a ⟨to wipe one's feet : limpiarse los pies⟩ **2 to wipe away** : enjugar (lágrimas), borrar (una memoria) **3 to wipe out** ANNIHILATE : aniquilar, destruir
wipe² *n* : pasada *f* (con un trapo, etc.)

wire¹ ['waɪr] *vt* **wired; wiring 1** : instalar el cableado en (una casa, etc.) **2** BIND : atar con alambre **3** TELEGRAPH : telegrafiar, mandarle un telegrama (a alguien)
wire² *n* **1** : alambre *m* ⟨barbed wire : alambre de púas⟩ **2** : cable *m* (eléctrico o telefónico) **3** CABLEGRAM, TELEGRAM : telegrama *m*, cable *m*
wireless ['waɪrləs] *adj* : inalámbrico
wiretapping ['waɪr,tæpɪŋ] *n* : intervención *f* electrónica
wiring ['waɪrɪŋ] *n* : cableado *m*
wiry ['waɪri] *adj* **wirier; -est 1** : hirsuto, tieso (dícese del pelo) **2** : esbelto y musculoso (dícese del cuerpo)
wisdom ['wɪzdəm] *n* **1** KNOWLEDGE : sabiduría *f* **2** JUDGMENT, SENSE : sensatez *f*
wisdom tooth *n* : muela *f* de juicio
wise¹ ['waɪz] *adj* **wiser; wisest 1** LEARNED : sabio **2** SENSIBLE : sabio, sensato, prudente **3** KNOWLEDGEABLE : entendido, enterado ⟨they're wise to his tricks : conocen muy bien sus mañas⟩
wise² *n* : manera *f*, modo *m* ⟨in no wise : de ninguna manera⟩
wisecrack ['waɪz,kræk] *n* : broma *f*, chiste *m*
wisely ['waɪzli] *adv* : sabiamente, sensatamente
wish¹ ['wɪʃ] *vt* **1** WANT : desear, querer **2 to wish (something) for** : desear ⟨they wished me well : me desearon lo mejor⟩ — *vi* **1** : pedir (como deseo) **2** : querer ⟨as you wish : como quieras⟩
wish² *n* **1** : deseo *m* ⟨to grant a wish : conceder un deseo⟩ **2 wishes** *npl* : saludos *mpl*, recuerdos *mpl* ⟨to send best wishes : mandar muchos recuerdos⟩
wishbone ['wɪʃ,bo:n] *n* : espoleta *f*
wishful ['wɪʃfəl] *adj* **1** HOPEFUL : deseoso, lleno de esperanza **2 wishful thinking** : ilusiones *fpl*
wishy–washy ['wɪʃi,wɔʃi, -,wɑʃi] *adj* : insípido, soso
wisp ['wɪsp] *n* **1** BUNCH : manojo *m* (de paja) **2** STRAND : mechón *m* (de pelo) **3** : voluta *f* (de humo)
wispy ['wɪspi] *adj* **wispier; -est** : tenue, ralo (dícese del pelo)
wisteria [wɪs'tɪriə] *n* : glicinia *f*
wistful ['wɪstfəl] *adj* : añorante, anhelante, melancólico — **wistfully** *adv*
wistfulness ['wɪstfəlnəs] *n* : añoranza *f*, melancolía *f*
wit ['wɪt] *n* **1** INTELLIGENCE : inteligencia *f* **2** CLEVERNESS : ingenio *m*, gracia *f*, agudeza *f* **3** HUMOR : humorismo *m* **4** JOKER : chistoso *m*, -sa *f* **5 wits** *npl* : razón *f*, buen juicio *m* ⟨scared out of one's wits : muerto de miedo⟩ ⟨to be at one's wit's end : estar desesperado⟩
witch ['wɪtʃ] *n* : bruja *f*
witchcraft ['wɪtʃ,kræft] *n* : brujería *f*, hechicería *f*

witch doctor *n* : hechicero *m*, -ra *f*
witchery [ˈwɪtʃəri] *n*, *pl* **-eries** 1 → **witch-craft** 2 CHARM : encanto *m*
witch–hunt [ˈwɪtʃˌhʌnt] *n* : caza *f* de brujas
with [ˈwɪð, ˈwɪθ] *prep* 1 : con ⟨I'm going with you : voy contigo⟩ ⟨coffee with milk : café con leche⟩ 2 AGAINST : con ⟨to argue with someone : discutir con alguien⟩ 3 (*used in descriptions*) : con, de ⟨the girl with red hair : la muchacha de pelo rojo⟩ 4 (*indicating manner, means, or cause*) : con ⟨to cut with a knife : cortar con un cuchillo⟩ ⟨fix it with tape : arréglalo con cinta⟩ ⟨with luck : consuerte⟩ 5 DESPITE : a pesar de, aún con ⟨with all his work, the business failed : a pesar de su trabajo, el negocio fracasó⟩ 6 REGARDING : con respecto a, con ⟨the trouble with your plan : el problema con su plan⟩ 7 AC-CORDING TO : según ⟨it varies with the season : varía según la estación⟩ 8 (*indicating support or understanding*) : con ⟨I'm with you all the way : estoy contigo hasta el fin⟩
withdraw [wɪðˈdrɔ, wɪθ-] *v* **-drew** [-ˈdruː]; **-drawn** [-ˈdrɔn]; **-drawing** *vt* 1 REMOVE : retirar, apartar, sacar (dinero) 2 RE-TRACT : retractarse de — *vi* : retirarse, recluirse (de la sociedad)
withdrawal [wɪðˈdrɔəl, wɪθ-] *n* 1 : retirada *f*, retiro *m* (de fondos, etc.), retraimiento *m* (social) 2 RETRACTION : retractación *f* 3 **withdrawal symptoms** : síndrome *m* de abstinencia
withdrawn [wɪðˈdrɔn, wɪθ-] *adj* : retraído, reservado, introvertido
wither [ˈwɪðər] *vt* : marchitar, agostar — *vi* 1 WILT : marchitarse 2 WEAKEN : decaer, debilitarse
withhold [wɪθˈhoːld, wɪð-] *vt* **-held** [-ˈhld]; **-holding** : retener (fondos), aplazar (una decisión), negar (permiso, etc.)
within¹ [wɪðˈɪn, wɪθ-] *adv* : dentro
within² *prep* 1 : dentro de ⟨within the limits : dentro de los límites⟩ 2 (*in expressions of distance*) : a menos de ⟨within 10 miles of the ocean : a menos de 10 millas del mar⟩ 3 (*in expressions of time*) : dentro de ⟨within an hour : dentro de una hora⟩ ⟨within a month of her birthday : a poco menos de un mes de su cumpleaños⟩
without¹ [wɪðˈaʊt, wɪθ-] *adv* 1 OUTSIDE : fuera 2 **to do without** : pasar sin algo
without² *prep* 1 OUTSIDE : fuera de 2 : sin ⟨without fear : sin temor⟩ ⟨he left without his briefcase : se fue sin su portafolios⟩
withstand [wɪθˈstænd, wɪð-] *vt* **-stood** [-ˈstʊd]; **-standing** 1 BEAR : aguantar, soportar 2 RESIST : resistir, resistirse a
witless [ˈwɪtləs] *adj* : estúpido, tonto
witness¹ [ˈwɪtnəs] *n* 1 SEE : presenciar, ver, ser testigo de 2 : atestiguar (una firma, etc.) — *vi* TESTIFY : atestiguar, testimoniar

witness² *n* 1 TESTIMONY : testimonio *m* ⟨to bear witness : atestiguar, testimoniar⟩ 2 : testigo *mf* ⟨witness for the prosecution : testigo de cargo⟩
witticism [ˈwɪtəˌsɪzəm] *n* : agudeza *f*, ocurrencia *f*
witty [ˈwɪti] *adj* **-tier; -est** : ingenioso, ocurrente, gracioso
wives → **wife**
wizard [ˈwɪzərd] *n* 1 SORCERER : mago *m*, brujo *m*, hechicero *m* 2 : genio *m* ⟨a math wizard : un genio en matemáticas⟩
wizened [ˈwɪzənd, ˈwiː-] *adj* : arrugado, marchito
wobble¹ [ˈwɑbəl] *vi* **-bled; -bling** : bambolearse, tambalearse, temblar (dícese de la voz)
wobble² *n* : tambaleo *m*, bamboleo *m*
wobbly [ˈwɑbəli] *adj* : bamboleante, tambaleante, inestable
woe [ˈwoː] *n* 1 GRIEF, MISFORTUNE : desgracia *f*, infortunio *m*, aflicción *f* 2 **woes** *npl* TROUBLES : penas *fpl*, males *mpl*
woeful [ˈwoːfəl] *adj* 1 SORROWFUL : afligido, apenado, triste 2 UNFORTU-NATE : desgraciado, infortunado 3 DE-PLORABLE : lamentable
woke, woken → **wake¹**
wolf¹ [ˈwʊlf] *vt or* **to wolf down** : engullir
wolf² *n*, *pl* **wolves** [ˈwʊlvz] : lobo *m*, -ba *f*
wolfram [ˈwʊlfrəm] → **tungsten**
wolverine [ˌwʊlvəˈriːn] *n* : glotón *m* (animal)
woman [ˈwʊmən] *n*, *pl* **women** [ˈwɪmən] : mujer *f*
womanhood [ˈwʊmənˌhʊd] *n* 1 : condición *f* de mujer 2 WOMEN : mujeres *fpl*
womanly [ˈwʊmənli] *adj* : femenino
womb [ˈwuːm] *n* : útero *m*, matriz *f*
won → **win**
wonder¹ [ˈwʌndər] *vi* 1 SPECULATE : preguntarse, pensar ⟨to wonder about : preguntarse por⟩ 2 MARVEL : asombrarse, maravillarse — *vt* : preguntarse ⟨I wonder if they're coming : me pregunto si vendrán⟩
wonder² *n* 1 MARVEL : maravilla *f*, milagro *m* ⟨to work wonders : hacer maravillas⟩ 2 AMAZEMENT : asombro *m*
wonderful [ˈwʌndərfəl] *adj* : maravilloso, estupendo
wonderfully [ˈwʌndərfəli] *adv* : maravillosamente, de maravilla
wonderland [ˈwʌndərˌlænd, -lənd] *n* : país *m* de las maravillas
wonderment [ˈwʌndərmənt] *n* : asombro *m*
wondrous [ˈwʌndrəs] → **wonderful**
wont¹ [ˈwɔnt, ˈwoːnt, ˈwɑnt] *adj* : acostumbrado, habituado
wont² *n* : hábito *m*, costumbre *f*
won't [ˈwoːnt] (*contraction of* **will not**) → **will¹**
woo [ˈwuː] *vt* 1 COURT : cortejar 2 : buscar el apoyo de (clientes, votantes, etc.)

wood[1] ['wʊd] *adj* : de madera
wood[2] *n* 1 *or* **woods** *npl* FOREST : bosque *m* 2 : madera *f* (materia) 3 FIREWOOD : leña *f*
woodchuck ['wʊd̩ʧʌk] *n* : marmota *f* de América
woodcut ['wʊd̩kʌt] *n* 1 : plancha *f* de madera (para imprimir imágenes) 2 : grabado *m* en madera
woodcutter ['wʊd̩kʌt̬ər] *n* : leñador *m*, -dora *f*
wooded ['wʊdəd] *adj* : arbolado, boscoso
wooden ['wʊdən] *adj* 1 : de madera ⟨a wooden cross : una cruz de madera⟩ 2 STIFF : rígido, inexpresivo (dícese del estilo, de la cara, etc.)
woodland ['wʊdlənd, -ˌlænd] *n* : bosque *m*
woodpecker ['wʊd̩pɛkər] *n* : pájaro *m* carpintero
woodshed ['wʊd̩ʃɛd] *n* : leñera *f*
woodsman ['wʊdzmən] *n* → **woodcutter**
woodwind ['wʊd̩wɪnd] *n* : instrumento *m* de viento de madera
woodworking ['wʊd̩wərkɪŋ] *n* : carpintería *f*
woody ['wʊdi] *adj* **woodier; -est** 1 → **wooded** 2 : leñoso ⟨woody plants : plantas leñosas⟩ 3 : leñoso (dícese de la textura), a madera (dícese del aroma, etc.)
woof ['wʊf] → **weft**
wool ['wʊl] *n* : lana *f*
woolen[1] *or* **woollen** ['wʊlən] *adj* : de lana
woolen[2] *or* **woollen** *n* 1 : lana *f* (tela) 2 **woolens** *npl* : prendas *fpl* de lana
woolly ['wʊli] *adj* **-lier; -est** 1 : lanudo 2 CONFUSED : confuso, vago
woozy ['wu:zi] *adj* **-zier; -est** : mareado
word[1] ['wərd] *vt* : expresar, formular, redactar
word[2] *n* 1 : palabra *f*, vocablo *m*, voz *f* ⟨word for word : palabra por palabra⟩ ⟨in one's own words : en sus propias palabras⟩ ⟨words fail me : me quedo sin habla⟩ 2 REMARK : palabra *f* ⟨by word of mouth : de palabra⟩ ⟨to have a word with : hablar (dos palabras) con⟩ 3 COMMAND : orden *f* ⟨to give the word : dar la orden⟩ ⟨just say the word : no tienes que decirlo⟩ 4 MESSAGE, NEWS : noticias *fpl* ⟨is there any word from her? : ¿hay noticias de ella?⟩ ⟨to send word : mandar un recado⟩ 5 PROMISE : palabra *f* ⟨to keep one's word : cumplir uno su palabra⟩ 6 **words** *npl* QUARREL : palabra *f*, riña *f* ⟨to have words with : tener unas palabras con, reñir con⟩ 7 **words** *npl* TEXT : letra *f* (de una canción, etc.)
wordiness ['wərdinəs] *n* : verbosidad *f*
wording ['wərdɪŋ] *n* : redacción *f*, lenguaje *m* (de un documento)
word processing *n* : procesamiento *m* de textos
word processor *n* : procesador *m* de textos

wordy ['wərdi] *adj* **wordier; -est** : verboso, prolijo
wore → **wear**[1]
work[1] ['wərk] *v* **worked** ['wərkt] *or* **wrought** ['rɔt]; **working** *vt* 1 OPERATE : trabajar, operar ⟨to work a machine : operar una máquina⟩ 2 : lograr, conseguir (algo) con esfuerzo ⟨to work one's way up : lograr subir por sus propios esfuerzos⟩ 3 EFFECT : efectuar, llevar a cabo, obrar (milagros) 4 MAKE, SHAPE : elaborar, fabricar, formar ⟨a beautifully wrought vase : un florero bellamente elaborado⟩ 5 **to work up** : estimular, excitar ⟨don't get worked up : no te agites⟩ — *vi* 1 LABOR : trabajar ⟨to work full-time : trabajar a tiempo completo⟩ 2 FUNCTION : funcionar, servir
work[2] *adj* : laboral
work[3] *n* 1 LABOR : trabajo *m*, labor *f* 2 EMPLOYMENT : trabajo *m*, empleo *m* 3 TASK : tarea *f*, faena *f* 4 DEED : obra *f*, labor *f* ⟨works of charity : obras de caridad⟩ 5 : obra *f* (de arte o literatura) 6 → **workmanship** 7 **works** *npl* FACTORY : fábrica *f* 8 **works** *npl* MECHANISM : mecanismo *m*
workable ['wərkəbəl] *adj* 1 : explotable (dícese de una mina, etc.) 2 FEASIBLE : factible, realizable
workaday ['wərkə̩deɪ] *adj* : ordinario, banal
workbench ['wərk̩bɛnʧ] *n* : mesa *f* de trabajo
workday ['wərk̩deɪ] *n* 1 : jornada *f* laboral 2 WEEKDAY : día *m* hábil, día *m* laborable
worker ['wərkər] *n* : trabajador *m*, -dora *f*; obrero *m*, -ra *f*
working ['wərkɪŋ] *adj* 1 : que trabaja ⟨working mothers : madres que trabajan⟩ ⟨the working class : la clase obrera⟩ 2 : de trabajo ⟨working hours : horas de trabajo⟩ 3 FUNCTIONING : que funciona, operativo 4 SUFFICIENT : suficiente ⟨a working majority : una mayoría suficiente⟩ ⟨working knowledge : conocimientos básicos⟩
workingman ['wərkɪŋ̩mæn] *n*, *pl* **-men** [-mən, -ˌmɛn] : obrero *m*
workman ['wərkmən] *n*, *pl* **-men** [-mən, -ˌmɛn] 1 → **workingman** 2 ARTISAN : artesano *m*
workmanlike ['wərkmən̩laɪk] *adj* : bien hecho, competente
workmanship ['wərkmən̩ʃɪp] *n* 1 WORK : ejecución *f*, trabajo *m* 2 CRAFTSMANSHIP : artesanía *f*, destreza *f*
workout ['wərk̩aʊt] *n* : ejercicios *mpl* físicos, entrenamiento *m*
work out *vt* 1 DEVELOP, PLAN : idear, planear, desarrollar 2 RESOLVE : solucionar, resolver ⟨to work out the answer : calcular la solución⟩ — *vi* 1 TURN OUT : resultar 2 SUCCEED : lograr, dar resultado, salir bien 3 EXERCISE : hacer ejercicio

workroom [ˈwərkˌruːm, -ˌrʊm] *n* : taller *m*

workshop [ˈwərkˌʃɑp] *n* : taller *m* ⟨ceramics workshop : taller de cerámica⟩

workstation [ˈwərkˌsteɪʃən] *n* : estación *f* de trabajo (en informática)

world¹ [ˈwərld] *adj* : mundial, del mundo ⟨world championship : campeonato mundial⟩

world² *n* : mundo *m* ⟨around the world : alrededor del mundo⟩ ⟨a world of possibilities : un mundo de posibilidades⟩ ⟨to think the world of someone : tener a alguien en alta estima⟩ ⟨to be worlds apart : no tener nada que ver (uno con otro)⟩

worldly [ˈwərldli] *adj* **1** : mundano ⟨wordly goods : bienes materiales⟩ **2** SOPHISTICATED : sofisticado, de mundo

worldwide¹ [ˈwərldˈwaɪd] *adv* : mundialmente, en todo el mundo

worldwide² *adj* : global, mundial

World Wide Web *n* : World Wide Web *f*

worm¹ [ˈwərm] *vi* CRAWL : arrastrarse, deslizarse (como gusano) — *vt* **1** : desparasitar (un animal) **2 to worm one's way into** : introducirse en ⟨he wormed his way into her confidence : se ganó su confianza⟩ **3 to worm something out of someone** : sonsacarle algo a alguien

worm² *n* **1** : gusano *m*, lombriz *f* **2 worms** *npl* : lombrices *fpl* (parásitos)

wormy [ˈwərmi] *adj* **wormier; -est** : infestado de gusanos

worn *pp* → **wear¹**

worn–out [ˈwornˈaʊt] *adj* **1** USED : gastado, desgastado **2** TIRED : agotado

worried [ˈwərid] *adj* : inquieto, preocupado

worrier [ˈwəriər] *n* : persona *f* que se preocupa mucho

worrisome [ˈwərisəm] *adj* **1** DISTURBING : preocupante, inquietante **2** : que se preocupa mucho (dícese de una persona)

worry¹ [ˈwəri] *v* **-ried; -rying** *vt* : preocupar, inquietar — *vi* : preocuparse, inquietarse, angustiarse

worry² *n, pl* **-ries** : preocupación *f*, inquietud *f*, angustia *f*

worse¹ [ˈwərs] *adv* (*comparative of* **bad** *or of* **ill**) : peor

worse² *adj* (*comparative of* **bad** *or of* **ill**) : peor ⟨from bad to worse : de mal en peor⟩ ⟨to get worse : empeorar⟩ ⟨to feel worse : sentirse peor⟩

worse³ *n* : estado *m* peor ⟨to take a turn for the worse : ponerse peor⟩ ⟨so much the worse : tanto peor⟩

worsen [ˈwərsən] *vt* : empeorar — *vi* : empeorar(se)

worship¹ [ˈwərʃəp] *v* **-shiped** *or* **-shipped; -shiping** *or* **-shipping** *vt* : adorar, venerar ⟨to worship God : adorar a Dios⟩ — *vi* : practicar una religión

worship² *n* : adoración *f*, culto *m*

worshiper *or* **worshipper** [ˈwərʃəpər] *n* : devoto *m*, -ta *f*; adorador *m*, -dora *f*

worst¹ [ˈwərst] *vt* DEFEAT : derrotar

worst² *adv* (*superlative of* **ill** *or of* **bad** *or* **badly**) : peor ⟨the worst dressed of all : el peor vestido de todos⟩

worst³ *adj* (*superlative of* **bad** *or of* **ill**) : peor ⟨the worst movie : la peor película⟩

worst⁴ *n* **the worst** : lo peor, el (la) peor ⟨the worst is over : ya ha pasado lo peor⟩

worsted [ˈwʊstəd, ˈwərstəd] *n* : estambre *m*

worth¹ [ˈwərθ] *n* **1** : valor *m* (monetario) ⟨ten dollars' worth of gas : diez dólares de gasolina⟩ **2** MERIT : valor *m*, mérito *m*, valía *f* ⟨an employee of great worth : un empleado de gran valía⟩

worth² *prep* **to be worth** : valer ⟨her holdings are worth a fortune : sus propiedades valen una fortuna⟩ ⟨it's not worth it : no vale la pena⟩

worthiness [ˈwərðinəs] *n* : mérito *m*

worthless [ˈwərθləs] *adj* **1** : sin valor ⟨worthless trinkets : chucherías sin valor⟩ **2** USELESS : inútil

worthwhile [wərθˈhwaɪl] *adj* : que vale la pena

worthy [ˈwərði] *adj* **-thier; -est 1** : digno ⟨worthy of promotion : digno de un ascenso⟩ **2** COMMENDABLE : meritorio, encomiable

would [ˈwʊd] *past of* **will 1** (*expressing preference*) ⟨I would rather go alone than with her : preferiría ir sola que con ella⟩ **2** (*expressing intent*) ⟨those who would ban certain books : aquellos que prohibirían ciertos libros⟩ **3** (*expressing habitual action*) ⟨he would often take his kids to the park : solía llevar a sus hijos al parque⟩ **4** (*expressing contingency*) ⟨I would go if I had the money : iría yo si tuviera el dinero⟩ **5** (*expressing probability*) ⟨she would have won if she hadn't tripped : habría ganado si no hubiera tropezado⟩ **6** (*expressing a request*) ⟨would you kindly help me with this? : ¿tendría la bondad de ayudarme con esto?⟩

would–be [ˈwʊdˈbiː] *adj* : potencial ⟨a would-be celebrity : un aspirante a celebridad⟩

wouldn't [ˈwʊdənt] (*contraction of* **would not**) → **would**

wound¹ [ˈwuːnd] *vt* : herir

wound² *n* : herida *f*

wound³ [ˈwaʊnd] → **wind²**

wove, woven → **weave¹**

wow [ˈwaʊ] *interj* : ¡guau!, ¡híjole! *Mex*, ¡hala! *Spain*

wrangle¹ [ˈræŋgəl] *vi* **-gled; -gling** : discutir, reñir ⟨to wrangle over : discutir por⟩

wrangle² *n* : riña *f*, disputa *f*

wrap¹ [ˈræp] *v* **wrapped; wrapping** *vt* **1** COVER : envolver, cubrir ⟨to wrap a package : envolver un paquete⟩

⟨wrapped in mystery : envuelto en misterio⟩ **2** ENCIRCLE : rodear, ceñir ⟨to wrap one's arms around someone : estrechar a alguien⟩ **3 to wrap up** FINISH : darle fin a (algo) — *vi* **1** COIL : envolverse, enroscarse **2 to wrap up** DRESS : abrigarse ⟨wrap up warmly : abrígate bien⟩

wrap² *n* **1** WRAPPER : envoltura *f* **2** : prenda *f* que envuelve (como un chal, una bata, etc.)

wrapper ['ræpər] *n* : envoltura *f*, envoltorio *m*

wrapping ['ræpɪŋ] *n* : envoltura *f*, envoltorio *m*

wrath ['ræθ] *n* : ira *f*, cólera *f*

wrathful ['ræθfəl] *adj* : iracundo

wreak ['ri:k] *vt* : infligir, causar ⟨to wreak havoc : crear caos, causar estragos⟩

wreath ['ri:θ] *n, pl* **wreaths** ['ri:ðz, 'ri:θs] : corona *f* (de flores, etc.)

wreathe ['ri:ð] *vt* **wreathed; wreathing 1** ADORN : coronar (de flores, etc.) **2** ENVELOP : envolver ⟨wreathed in mist : envuelto en niebla⟩

wreck¹ ['rɛk] *vt* : destruir, arruinar, estrellar (un automóvil), naufragar (un barco)

wreck² *n* **1** WRECKAGE : restos *mpl* (de un buque naufragado, un avión siniestrado, etc.) **2** RUIN : ruina *f*, desastre *m* ⟨this place is a wreck! : ¡este lugar está hecho un desastre!⟩ ⟨to be a nervous wreck : tener los nervios destrozados⟩

wreckage ['rɛkɪdʒ] *n* : restos *mpl* (de un buque naufragado, un avión siniestrado, etc.), ruinas *fpl* (de un edificio)

wrecker ['rɛkər] *n* **1** TOW TRUCK : grúa *f* **2** : desguazador *m* (de autos, barcos, etc.), demoledor *m* (de edificios)

wren ['rɛn] *n* : chochín *m*

wrench¹ ['rɛntʃ] *vt* **1** PULL : arrancar (de un tirón) **2** SPRAIN, TWIST : torcerse (un tobillo, un músculo, etc.)

wrench² *n* **1** TUG : tirón *m*, jalón *m* **2** SPRAIN : torcedura *f* **3** *or* **monkey wrench** : llave *f* inglesa

wrest ['rɛst] *vt* : arrancar

wrestle¹ ['rɛsəl] *v* **-tled; -tling** *vi* **1** : luchar, practicar la lucha (en deportes) **2** STRUGGLE : luchar ⟨to wrestle with a dilemma : lidiar con un dilema⟩ — *vt* : luchar contra

wrestle² *n* STRUGGLE : lucha *f*

wrestler ['rɛsələr] *n* : luchador *m*, -dora *f*

wrestling ['rɛsəlɪŋ] *n* : lucha *f*

wretch ['rɛtʃ] *n* : infeliz *mf*; desgraciado *m*, -da *f*

wretched ['rɛtʃəd] *adj* **1** MISERABLE, UNHAPPY : desdichado, afligido ⟨I feel wretched : me siento muy mal⟩ **2** UNFORTUNATE : miserable, desgraciado, lastimoso ⟨wretched weather : tiempo espantoso⟩ **3** INFERIOR : inferior, malo

wretchedly ['rɛtʃədli] *adv* : miserablemente, lamentablemente

wriggle ['rɪgəl] *vi* **-gled; -gling** : retorcerse, menearse

wring ['rɪŋ] *vt* **wrung** ['rʌŋ]; **wringing 1** *or* **to wring out** : escurrir, exprimir (el lavado) **2** EXTRACT : arrancar, sacar (por la fuerza) **3** TWIST : torcer, retorcer **4 to wring someone's heart** : partirle el corazón a alguien

wringer ['rɪŋər] *n* : escurridor *m*

wrinkle¹ ['rɪŋkəl] *v* **-kled; -kling** *vt* : arrugar — *vi* : arrugarse

wrinkle² *n* : arruga *f*

wrinkly ['rɪŋkəli] *adj* **wrinklier; -est** : arrugado

wrist ['rɪst] *n* **1** : muñeca *f* (en anatomía) **2** *or* **wristband** ['rɪst-ˌbænd] CUFF : puño *m*

writ ['rɪt] *n* : orden *f* (judicial)

write ['raɪt] *v* **wrote** ['ro:t]; **written** ['rɪtən]; **writing** : escribir

write down *vt* : apuntar, anotar

write off *vt* CANCEL : cancelar

writer ['raɪtər] *n* : escritor *m*, -tora *f*

writhe ['raɪð] *vi* **writhed; writhing** : retorcerse

writing ['raɪtɪŋ] *n* **1** : escritura *f* **2** HANDWRITING : letra *f* **3 writings** *npl* WORKS : escritos *mpl*, obra *f*

wrong¹ ['rɔŋ] *vt* **wronged; wronging** : ofender, ser injusto con

wrong² *adv* : mal, incorrectamente

wrong³ *adj* **wronger** ['rɔŋər]; **wrongest** ['rɔŋəst] **1** EVIL, SINFUL : malo, injusto, inmoral **2** IMPROPER, UNSUITABLE : inadecuado, inapropiado, malo **3** INCORRECT : incorrecto, erróneo, malo ⟨a wrong answer : una mala respuesta⟩ **4 to be wrong** : equivocarse, estar equivocado

wrong⁴ *n* **1** INJUSTICE : injusticia *f*, mal *m* **2** OFFENSE : ofensa *f*, agravio *m* (en derecho) **3 to be in the wrong** : haber hecho mal, estar equivocado

wrongdoer ['rɔŋˌdu:ər] *n* : malhechor *m*, -chora *f*

wrongdoing ['rɔŋˌdu:ɪŋ] *n* : fechoría *f*, maldad *f*

wrongful ['rɔŋfəl] *adj* **1** UNJUST : injusto **2** UNLAWFUL : ilegal

wrongly ['rɔŋli] *adv* **1** : injustamente **2** INCORRECTLY : erróneamente, incorrectamente

wrote → write

wrought ['rɔt] *adj* **1** SHAPED : formado, forjado ⟨wrought iron : hierro forjado⟩ **2** *or* **wrought up** : agitado, excitado

wrung → wring

wry ['raɪ] *adj* **wrier** ['raɪər]; **wriest** ['raɪəst] **1** TWISTED : torcido ⟨a wry neck : un cuello torcido⟩ **2** : irónico, sardónico (dícese del humor)

X

x¹ *n, pl* **x's** *or* **xs** [ˈɛksəz] **1** : vigésima cuarta letra del alfabeto inglés **2** : incógnita *f* (en matemáticas)

x² [ˈks] *vt* **x–ed** [ˈɛkst]; **x–ing** *or* **x'ing** [ˈɛksiŋ] DELETE : tachar

xenon [ˈziːˌnɑn, ˈzɛ-] *n* : xenón *m*

xenophobia [ˌzɛnəˈfoːbiə, ˌziː-] *n* : xenofobia *f*

Xmas [ˈkrɪsməs] *n* : Navidad *f*

x–ray [ˈɛksˌreɪ] *vt* : radiografiar

X ray [ˈɛksˌreɪ] *n* **1** : rayo *m* X **2** *or* **X–ray photograph** : radiografía *f*

xylophone [ˈzaɪləˌfoːn] *n* : xilófono *m*

Y

y [ˈwaɪ] *n, pl* **y's** *or* **ys** [ˈwaɪz] : vigésima quinta letra del alfabeto inglés

yacht¹ [ˈjɑt] *vi* : navegar (a vela), ir en yate ⟨to go yachting : irse a navegar⟩

yacht² *n* : yate *m*

yak [ˈjæk] *n* : yac *m*

yam [ˈjæm] *n* **1** : ñame *m* **2** SWEET POTATO : batata *f*, boniato *m*

yank¹ [ˈjæŋk] *vt* : tirar de, jalar, darle un tirón a

yank² *n* : tirón *m*

Yankee [ˈjæŋki] *n* : yanqui *mf*

yap¹ [ˈjæp] *vi* **yapped; yapping 1** BARK, YELP : ladrar, gañir **2** CHATTER : cotorrear *fam*, parlotear *fam*

yap² *n* : ladrido *m*, gañido *m*

yard [ˈjɑrd] *n* **1** : yarda *f* (medida) **2** SPAR : verga *f* (de un barco) **3** COURTYARD : patio *m* **4** : jardín *m* (de una casa) **5** : depósito *m* (de mercancías, etc.)

yardage [ˈjɑrdɪdʒ] *n* : medida *f* en yardas

yardarm [ˈjɑrdˌɑrm] *n* : penol *m*

yardstick [ˈjɑrdˌstɪk] *n* **1** : vara *f* **2** CRITERION : criterio *m*, norma *f*

yarn [ˈjɑrn] *n* **1** : hilado *m* **2** TALE : historia *f*, cuento *m* ⟨to spin a yarn : inventar una historia⟩

yawl [ˈjɔl] *n* : yola *f*

yawn¹ [ˈjɔn] *vi* **1** : bostezar **2** OPEN : abrirse

yawn² *n* : bostezo *m*

ye [ˈjiː] *pron* : vosotros, vosotras

yea¹ [ˈjeɪ] *adv* YES : sí

yea² *n* : voto *m* a favor

year [ˈjɪr] *n* **1** : año *m* ⟨last year : el año pasado⟩ ⟨he's ten years old : tiene diez años⟩ **2** : curso *m*, año *m* (escolar) **3 years** *npl* AGES : siglos *mpl*, años *mpl* ⟨I haven't seen them in years : hace siglos que no los veo⟩

yearbook [ˈjɪrˌbʊk] *n* : anuario *m*

yearling [ˈjɪrlɪŋ, ˈjərlən] *n* : animal *m* menor de dos año

yearly¹ [ˈjɪrli] *adv* : cada año, anualmente

yearly² *adj* : anual

yearn [ˈjərn] *vi* : anhelar, ansiar

yearning [ˈjərnɪŋ] *n* : anhelo *m*

yeast [ˈjiːst] *n* : levadura *f*

yell¹ [ˈjɛl] *vi* : gritar, chillar — *vt* : gritar

yell² *n* : grito *m*, alarido *m* ⟨to let out a yell : dar un grito⟩

yellow¹ [ˈjɛlo] *vi* : ponerse amarillo, volverse amarillo

yellow² *adj* **1** : amarillo **2** COWARDLY : cobarde

yellow³ *n* : amarillo *m*

yellow fever *n* : fiebre *f* amarilla

yellowish [ˈjɛloɪʃ] *adj* : amarillento

yellow jacket *n* : avispa *f* (con rayas amarillas)

yelp¹ [ˈjɛlp] *vi* : dar un gañido (dícese de un animal), dar un grito (dícese de una persona)

yelp² *n* : gañido *m* (de un animal), grito *m* (de una persona)

yen [ˈjɛn] *n* **1** DESIRE : deseo *m*, ganas *fpl* **2** : yen *m* (moneda japonesa)

yeoman [ˈjoːmən] *n, pl* **-men** [-mən, -mɛn] : suboficial *mf* de marina

yes¹ [ˈjɛs] *adv* : sí ⟨to say yes : decir que sí⟩

yes² *n* : sí *m*

yesterday¹ [ˈjɛstərˌdeɪ, -di] *adv* : ayer

yesterday² *n* **1** : ayer *m* **2 the day before yesterday** : anteayer

yet¹ [ˈjɛt] *adv* **1** BESIDES, EVEN : aún ⟨yet more problems : más problemas aún⟩ ⟨yet again : otra vez⟩ **2** SO FAR : aún, todavía ⟨not yet : todavía no⟩ ⟨as yet : hasta ahora, todavía⟩ **3** : ya ⟨has he come yet? : ¿ya ha venido?⟩ **4** EVENTUALLY : todavía, algún día **5** NEVERTHELESS : sin embargo

yet² *conj* : pero

yew [ˈjuː] *n* : tejo *m*

yield¹ [ˈjiːld] *vt* **1** SURRENDER : ceder ⟨to yield the right of way : ceder el paso⟩ **2** PRODUCE : producir, dar, rendir (en finanzas) — *vi* **1** GIVE : ceder ⟨to yield under pressure : ceder por la presión⟩ **2** GIVE IN, SURRENDER : ceder, rendirse, entregarse

yield² *n* : rendimiento *m*, rédito *m* (en finanzas)

yin and yang [ˈjɪnændˈjæn, -ˈjɑŋ] *n* : yin *m* y yang *f*

yodel¹ [ˈjoːdəl] *vi* **-deled** *or* **-delled; -deling** *or* **-delling** : cantar al estilo tirolés

yodel² *n* : canción *f* al estilo tirolés

yoga [ˈjoːgə] *n* : yoga *m*

yogurt [ˈjoːgərt] *n* : yogur *m*, yogurt *m*

yoke¹ [ˈjoːk] *vt* **yoked; yoking** : uncir (animales)

yoke² *n* **1** : yugo *m* (para uncir animales)

⟨the yoke of oppression : el yugo de la opresión⟩ **2** TEAM : yunta *f* (de bueyes) **3** : canesú *m* (de ropa)

yokel [ˈjoːkəl] *n* : palurdo *m*, -da *f*

yolk [ˈjoːk] *n* : yema *f* (de un huevo)

Yom Kippur [ˌjoːmkɪˈpʊr, ˌjɑm-, -ˈkɪpər] *n* : el Día *m* del Perdón, Yom Kippur

yon [ˈjɑn] → **yonder**

yonder[1] [ˈjɑndər] *adv* : allá ⟨over yonder : allá lejos⟩

yonder[2] *adj* : aquel ⟨yonder hill : aquella colina⟩

yore [ˈjoːr] *n* **in days of yore** : antaño

you [ˈjuː] *pron* **1** (*used as subject — familiar*) : tú; vos (*in some Latin American countries*); ustedes *pl*; vosotros, vosotras *pl Spain* **2** (*used as subject — formal*) : usted, ustedes *pl* **3** (*used as indirect object — familiar*) : te, les *pl* (se *before lo, la, los, las*), os *pl Spain* ⟨he told it to you : te lo contó⟩ ⟨I gave them to (all of them) you : se los di⟩ **4** (*used as indirect object — formal*) : lo (*Spain sometimes* le), la; los (*Spain sometimes* les), las *pl* **5** (*used after a preposition — familiar*) : ti; vos (*in some Latin American countries*); ustedes *pl*; vosotros, vosotras *pl Spain* **6** (*used after a preposition — formal*) : usted, ustedes *pl* **7** (*used as an impersonal subject*) ⟨you never know : nunca se sabe⟩ ⟨you have to be aware : hay que ser consciente⟩ ⟨you mustn't do that : eso no se hace⟩ **8 with you** (*familiar*) : contigo; con ustedes *pl*; con vosotros, con vosotras *pl Spain* **9 with you** (*formal*) : con usted, con ustedes *pl*

you'd [ˈjuːd, ˈjʊd] (*contraction of* **you had** *or* **you would**) → **have, would**

you'll [ˈjuːl, ˈjʊl] (*contraction of* **you shall** *or* **you will**) → **shall, will**

young[1] [ˈjʌŋ] *adj* **younger** [ˈjʌŋɡər]; **youngest** [-ɡəst] **1** : joven, pequeño, menor ⟨young people : los jóvenes⟩ ⟨my younger brother : mi hermano menor⟩ ⟨she is the youngest : es la más pequeña⟩ **2** FRESH, NEW : tierno (dícese de las verduras), joven (dícese del vino) **3** YOUTHFUL : joven, juvenil

young[2] *npl* : jóvenes *mfpl* (de los humanos), crías *fpl* (de los animales)

youngster [ˈjʌŋkstər] *n* **1** YOUTH : joven *mf* **2** CHILD : chico *m*, -ca *f*; niño *m*, -ña *f*

your [ˈjʊr, ˈjoːr, jər] *adj* **1** (*familiar singular*) : tu ⟨your cat : tu gato⟩ ⟨your

books : tus libros⟩ ⟨wash your hands : lávate las manos⟩ **2** (*familiar plural*) : su, vuestro *Spain* ⟨your car : su coche, el coche de ustedes⟩ **3** (*formal*) : su ⟨your houses : sus casas⟩ **4** (*impersonal*) : el, la, los, las ⟨on your left : a la izquierda⟩

you're [ˈjʊr, ˈjoːr, ˈjər, ˈjuːər] (*contraction of* **you are**) → **be**

yours [ˈjʊrz, ˈjoːrz] *pron* **1** (*belonging to one person — familiar*) : (el) tuyo, (la) tuya, (los) tuyos, (las) tuyas ⟨these are mine; yours are there : ésas son mías; las tuyas están allí⟩ ⟨is this one yours? : ¿éste es tuyo?⟩ **2** (*belonging to more than one person — familiar*) : (el) suyo, (la) suya, (los) suyos, (las) suyas; (el) vuestro, (la) vuestra, (los) vuestros, (las) vuestras *Spain* ⟨our house and yours : nuestra casa y la suya⟩ **3** (*formal*) : (el) suyo, (la) suya, (los) suyos, (las) suyas

yourself [jərˈsɛlf] *pron, pl* **yourselves** [-ˈslvz] **1** (*used reflexively — familiar*) : te, se *pl*, os *pl Spain* ⟨wash yourself : lávate⟩ ⟨you dressed yourselves : se vistieron, os vestisteis⟩ **2** (*used reflexively — formal*) : se ⟨did you hurt yourself? : ¿se hizo daño?⟩ ⟨you've gotten yourselves dirty : se ensuciaron⟩ **3** (*used for emphasis*) : tú mismo, tú misma; usted mismo, usted misma; ustedes mismas *pl*; vosotros mismos, vosotras mismas *pl Spain* ⟨you did it yourselves? : ¿lo hicieron ustedes mismos?, ¿lo hicieron por sí solos?⟩

youth [ˈjuːθ] *n, pl* **youths** [ˈjuːðz, ˈjuːθs] **1** : juventud *f* ⟨in her youth : en su juventud⟩ **2** BOY : joven *m* **3** : jóvenes *mfpl*, juventud *f* ⟨the youth of our city : los jóvenes de nuestra ciudad⟩

youthful [ˈjuːθfəl] *adj* **1** : de juventud **2** YOUNG : joven **3** JUVENILE : juvenil

youthfulness [ˈjuːθfəlnəs] *n* : juventud *f*

you've [ˈjuːv] (*contraction of* **you have**) → **have**

yowl[1] [ˈjæʊl] *vi* : aullar

yowl[2] *n* : aullido *m*

yo-yo [ˈjoːˌjoː] *n, pl* **-yos** : yoyo *m*, yoyó *m*

yucca [ˈjʌkə] *n* : yuca *f*

Yugoslavian [ˌjuːɡoˈslɑviən] *n* : yugoslavo *m*, -va *f* — **Yugoslavian** *adj*

yule [ˈjuːl] *n* CHRISTMAS : Navidad *f*

yuletide [ˈjuːlˌtaɪd] *n* : Navidades *fpl*

yuppie [ˈjʌpi] *n* : yuppy *mf*

Z

z ['zi:] *n, pl* **z's** *or* **zs** : vigésima sexta letra del alfabeto inglés

Zambian ['zæmbiən] *n* : zambiano *m*, **-na** *f* — **Zambian** *adj*

zany¹ ['zeɪni] *adj* **-nier; -est** : alocado, disparatado

zany² *n, pl* **-nies** : bufón *m*, **-fona** *f*

zap¹ ['zæp] *vt* **zapped; zapping 1** ELIMINATE : eliminar **2** : enviar o transportar rápidamente — *vi* : ir rápidamente

zap² *n* **1** ZEST : sabor *m*, sazón *f* **2** BLAST : golpe *m* fuerte

zap³ *interj* : ¡zas!

zeal ['zi:l] *n* : fervor *m*, celo *m*, entusiasmo *m*

zealot ['zɛlət] *n* : fanático *m*, **-ca** *f*

zealous ['zɛləs] *adj* : celoso — **zealously** *adv*

zebra ['zi:brə] *n* : cebra *f*

zenith ['zi:nəθ] *n* **1** : cenit *m* (en astronomía) **2** PEAK : apogeo *m*, cenit *m* ⟨at the zenith of his career : en el apogeo de su carrera⟩

zephyr ['zɛfər] *n* : céfiro *m*

zeppelin ['zɛplən, -pəlɪn] *n* : zepelín *m*

zero¹ ['zi:ro, 'zɪro] *vi* **to zero in on** : apuntar hacia, centrarse en (un problema, etc.)

zero² *adj* : cero, nulo ⟨zero degrees : cero grados⟩ ⟨zero opportunities : oportunidades nulas⟩

zero³ *n, pl* **-ros** : cero *m* ⟨below zero : bajo cero⟩

zest ['zɛst] *n* **1** GUSTO : entusiasmo *m*, brío *m* **2** FLAVOR : sabor *m*, sazón *f*

zestful ['zɛstfəl] *adj* : brioso

zigzag¹ ['zɪg,zæg] *vi* **-zagged; -zagging** : zigzaguear

zigzag² *adv & adj* : en zigzag

zigzag³ *n* : zigzag *m*

Zimbabwean [zɪm'bɑbwiən, -bweɪ-] *n* : zimbabuense *mf* — **Zimbabwean** *adj*

zinc ['zɪŋk] *n* : cinc *m*, zinc *m*

zing ['zɪŋ] *n* **1** HISS, HUM : zumbido *m*, silbido *m* **2** ENERGY : brío *m*

zinnia ['zɪniə, 'zi:-, -njə] *n* : zinnia *f*

Zionism ['zaɪə,nɪzəm] *n* : sionismo *m*

Zionist ['zaɪənɪst] *n* : sionista *mf*

zip¹ ['zɪp] *v* **zipped; zipping** *vt or* **to zip up** : cerrar el cierre de — *vi* **1** SPEED : pasarse volando ⟨the day zipped by : el día se pasó volando⟩ **2** HISS, HUM : silbar, zumbar

zip² *n* **1** ZING : zumbido *m*, silbido *m* **2** ENERGY : brío *m*

zip code *n* : código *m* postal

zipper ['zɪpər] *n* : cierre *m*, cremallera *f*, zíper *m CA, Mex*

zippy ['zɪpi] *adj* **-pier; -est** : brioso

zircon ['zər,kɑn] *n* : circón *m*, zircón *m*

zirconium [,zər'ko:niəm] *n* : circonio *m*

zither ['zɪðər, -θər] *n* : cítara *f*

zodiac ['zo:di,æk] *n* : zodíaco *m*

zombie ['zɑmbi] *n* : zombi *mf*, zombie *mf*

zone¹ ['zo:n] *vt* **zoned; zoning 1** : dividir en zonas **2** DESIGNATE : declarar ⟨to zone for business : declarar como zona comercial⟩

zone² *n* : zona *f*

zoo ['zu:] *n, pl* **zoos** : zoológico *m*, zoo *m*

zoological [,zo:ə'lɑʤɪkəl, ,zu:ə-] *adj* : zoológico

zoologist [zo'ɑləʤɪst, zu:-] *n* : zoólogo *m*, **-ga** *f*

zoology [zo'ɑləʤi, zu:-] *n* : zoología *f*

zoom¹ ['zu:m] *vi* **1** : zumbar, ir volando ⟨to zoom past : pasar volando⟩ **2** CLIMB : elevarse ⟨the plane zoomed up : el avión se elevó⟩

zoom² *n* **1** : zumbido *m* ⟨the zoom of an engine : el zumbido de un motor⟩ **2** : subida *f* vertical (de un avión, etc.) **3** *or* **zoom lens** : zoom *m*

zucchini [zu'ki:ni] *n, pl* **-ni** *or* **-nis** : calabacín *m*, calabacita *f Mex*

Zulu ['zu:lu:] *n* **1** : zulú *mf* **2** : zulú *m* (idioma) — **Zulu** *adj*

zygote ['zaɪ,go:t] *n* : zigoto *m*, cigoto *m*

100 Important English Idioms
100 Frases idiomáticas
importantes en inglés

ace
(to have) an ace in the hole → *(tener) un as bajo la manga*
: a powerful and often secret advantage or strategy that can be used if needed ⟨*his popularity among elderly voters gives him an ace in the hole for the coming election*⟩
(to come/be) within an ace of → *(estar) a un paso de (lograr o sufrir algo)*
: (to be) very close to experiencing something either positive or negative ⟨*they came within an ace of winning the championship*⟩

alley
to be right up one's alley → *ser lo mío/tuyo (etc.)*
: to fit one's interest or strengths ⟨*I love books, so volunteering at the library is right up my alley*⟩

ant
(to have/get) ants in one's pants → *(estar) impaciente/inquieto*
: (to experience) a strong feeling of excitement and impatience ⟨*the children got ants in their pants waiting for the show to begin*⟩

apart
to come apart at the seams → *venirse abajo*
: to fail, break apart, or be in very bad condition ⟨*this house is coming apart at the seams*⟩

apple
the apple of one's eye → *la niña de los ojos de alguien*
: a person or thing that one cherishes ⟨*his daughter is the apple of his eye*⟩

arm
(to cost) an arm and a leg → *(costar) un ojo de la cara*
: (to be) a very large amount of money ⟨*it's a reliable car, and it doesn't cost an arm and a leg*⟩

ax
(to have) an ax to grind → *(tener) intereses personales (en algo)*
: (to have) a hidden and often selfish purpose for doing something ⟨*she claims she has no ax to grind in criticizing the proposal*⟩

ball
to drop the ball → *fallar*
: to make a mistake especially by not doing something important ⟨*I think the mayor dropped the ball by not hiring more police officers*⟩
to start the ball rolling → *poner (algo) en marcha*
: to begin an activity or process ⟨*she tried to get the ball rolling by asking him a few questions*⟩

ball game
a whole new ball game → *se viró la tortilla*
: a situation or activity that has changed ⟨*dealing with the economy is a whole new ball game now*⟩

bar
to raise/lower the bar → *subir/bajar el nivel de lo exigido*
: to change a standard used to judge success ⟨*the police department raised the bar for hiring future officers*⟩

bark
to bark up the wrong tree → *errar, equivocarse*
: to try to do something in a way that will not be successful ⟨*she claims

researchers are barking up the wrong tree by focusing on conventional treatments⟩

beans
to spill the beans → *descubrir el pastel*
: to reveal secret information ⟨*the party is a surprise, so don't spill the beans*⟩

belt
to tighten one's belt → *apretarse el cinturón/la correa, ahorrar*
: to make changes in order to save money ⟨*companies are tightening their belts during the recession*⟩

birds
to be birds of a feather → *ser tal para cual*
: to be of the same kind or nature ⟨*those two guys are birds of a feather*⟩

bite
to bite off more than one can chew → *tratar de abarcar demasiado*
: to take on more responsibility than one can handle ⟨*I really bit off more than I could chew when I took on this project*⟩

boat
to miss the boat → *perder el tren*
: to fail to make use of an opportunity ⟨*if I don't act now I could miss the boat on this investment*⟩
to rock the boat → *hacer olas*
: to cause trouble by changing or trying to change a situation that others are comfortable with ⟨*the system isn't perfect, but nobody wants to rock the boat*⟩

bone
to have a bone to pick (with someone) → *tener que ajustar cuentas (con alguien)*
: to have something to argue or complain about (with someone) ⟨*I have a bone to pick with you about your barking dog*⟩

burn
to burn a hole in one's pocket → *darle ganas (a alguien) de gastar dinero*
: to cause an eagerness to spend money one has ⟨*he just got his tax refund, and it's burning a hole in his pocket*⟩
to burn the midnight oil → *quemarse las pestañas/cejas*
: to work or study until very late at night ⟨*the students have been burning the midnight oil preparing for exams*⟩

bush
to beat around the bush → *andarse con rodeos*
: to avoid saying something by talking about other things ⟨*stop beating around the bush and tell me why you're here*⟩

candle
to not hold a candle to (someone or something) → *no llegar ni a la suela del zapato (a alguien), no poder comparar con (algo)*
: to not be on the same level as or as good as (something or someone) ⟨*this new movie doesn't hold a candle to the original*⟩

castles
to build castles in the air → *construir castillos en el aire*
: to focus on a dream, plan, or idea that has little chance of success ⟨*he's just building castles in the air if he thinks he can open a restaurant without any money*⟩

chew
to chew the fat → *charlar, platicar*
: to talk together in a friendly or casual way ⟨*they would sit for hours and chew the fat*⟩

chicken
to count one's chickens before they hatch → *vender la piel del oso antes de cazarlo*
: to plan for something desired before knowing it will definitely happen ⟨*don't*

count your chickens before they hatch—we don't know yet if she will accept our offer⟩

chop
to bust one's chops → *molestar a alguien a modo de chiste*
: to tease or criticize in a playful way ⟨*my boss likes to bust my chops when I don't look sharp*⟩

class
to be in a class by oneself → *ser único/raro*
: to be very different from others in a good or bad way ⟨*there have been a lot of corporate scandals, but this one is in a class by itself*⟩

cleaner
to take (someone) to the cleaner's → *dejar limpio/pelado (a alguien), dejar sin dinero (a alguien)*
: to get all or most of someone's money or possessions often in an unfair way ⟨*his former business partner took him to the cleaners, leaving him with all the bills*⟩

color
to show one's true colors → *revelarse como (cierto tipo de persona)*
: to reveal one's real nature or character ⟨*he seemed nice at first, but he showed his true colors during the crisis*⟩

contention
(to be a) bone of contention → *(ser la) nota discordante, (ser la) manzana de la discordia*
: (to be) something that causes anger and disagreement ⟨*the tariffs have been a bone of contention between the two nations*⟩

corner
to back/paint oneself into a corner → *meterse en camisa de once varas, meterse en un lío*
: to put oneself into a difficult position ⟨*the candidate backed/painted himself into a corner by proposing a tax increase*⟩

cry
to cry wolf → *dar la voz de alarma (sin causa)*
: make people think there is danger when there is really none ⟨*news organizations have been warned not to cry wolf*⟩

dark
to keep (someone) in the dark → *ocultarle algo (a alguien)*
: to keep (someone) in a state of not knowing about something ⟨*the public was kept in the dark about the agreement*⟩

drummer
to march to the beat of a different drummer → *ser poco convencional*
: to think, live, or behave in an unusual way ⟨*his strange behavior was no surprise—he had always marched to the beat of a different drummer*⟩

duck
to take to something like a duck (takes) to water → *tener un talento innato para algo*
: to learn something very quickly or easily ⟨*she took to dancing like a duck (takes) to water*⟩

ear
to play it by ear → *improvisar, hacer algo sobre la marcha*
: to do something without special preparation; improvise ⟨*I don't know how they'll react to our proposal, so we'll just have to play it by ear*⟩

eight ball
to be behind the eight ball → *estar en un apuro*
: to be in a bad position ⟨*the loss of this contract puts the company behind the eight ball*⟩

envelope
to push the envelope → *trascender los límites*
: to go beyond the usual or normal limits by doing something especially

new or risky ⟨*the director was pushing the envelope with his experimental new films*⟩

eye
  to see eye to eye → *estar de acuerdo (con alguien)*
  : to have the same opinion; agree ⟨*they don't see eye to eye on the issue of taxes*⟩

fence
  to sit on the fence → *nadar entre dos aguas*
  : to be unable to decide about something ⟨*he tried to persuade those still sitting on the fence to vote in his favor*⟩

fiddle
  to play second fiddle → *ser plato de segunda mesa*
  : to be relegated to a less important position or status than someone or something else ⟨*the new player had to play second fiddle to the star of the team*⟩

fish
  to feel like/be a fish out of water → *sentirse/estar como gallina en corral ajeno*
  : to be a person who is in a place or situation that seems unnatural or uncomfortable ⟨*he's a small-town boy who feels like a fish out of water here in the big city*⟩

foot
  to put one's foot in one's mouth → *meter la pata*
  : to say something that causes unintended embarrassment or hurt feelings ⟨*I really put my foot in my mouth when I asked her about her job. I didn't know she'd just been fired*⟩

gold
  to go for the gold → *picar alto, aspirar a mucho*
  : to put forth maximum effort to seek top success, prize, or honors ⟨*no holding back! I'm going for the gold*⟩

grease
  to grease the palm of (someone) → *untarle la mano (a alguien), sobornar (a alguien)*
  : to give (someone) money for doing something illegal or dishonest for you ⟨*they had to grease the palms of a few officials to get the building permits they needed*⟩

heaven
  to be a match made in heaven → *hacer buena pareja*
  : to be a match/marriage that is very good and successful ⟨*their happy marriage was a match made in heaven*⟩

high note
  on a high note → *con una nota positiva*
  : in a pleasant or enjoyable way ⟨*our vacation ended on a high note when we got to meet the ambassador*⟩

horn
  to blow one's own horn → *darse bombo*
  : to talk about oneself or one's achievements especially proudly ⟨*we've had a very successful year, and I think we have a right to blow our own horn*⟩
  to get on the horn → *llamar por teléfono*
  : to contact someone by telephone ⟨*he got on the horn to the police*⟩

ice
  to break the ice → *romper el hielo*
  : to say or do something that helps people relax and begin talking ⟨*he opened the meeting with a joke to break the ice*⟩

insult
  to add insult to injury → *por si fuera poco*
  : to do or say something that makes a bad situation worse ⟨*most people were forced to work longer hours each week, and to add insult to injury, the company decided not to give pay raises*⟩

jury

the jury is still out on (something) → *(algo) todavía no es seguro*
: something has not yet been decided or has not yet become clear ⟨*the jury is still out on whether the new restaurant will succeed*⟩

kill

to kill two birds with one stone → *matar dos pájaros de un tiro*
: to achieve two things by doing a single action ⟨*we can kill two birds with one stone by dropping off the mail when we go the grocery store*⟩

knife

to (go) under the knife → *operarse*
: to have a medical operation ⟨*I'm going under the knife to have my appendix removed tomorrow*⟩

knot

to tie the knot → *casarse*
: to get married ⟨*when are you two going to tie the knot?*⟩

lead balloon

to go over like a lead balloon → *caerle/sentarle muy mal (a alguien)*
: to fail completely ⟨*he told a joke about his mother-in-law and it went over like a lead balloon*⟩

leg

to pull someone's leg → *tomarle el pelo (a alguien)*
: to playfully make someone believe something that is not true ⟨*I panicked when he said the test was tomorrow, but then I realized he was just pulling my leg*⟩

lid

to keep a lid on (something) → *mantener (algo) oculto/tapado*
: to prevent (something) from being widely known ⟨*she tried to keep a lid on news of the company's financial situation*⟩

limelight

to be in the limelight → *estar en el candelero*
: to be experiencing public attention or notice ⟨*when his new book caused an unexpected controversy, he was in the limelight once again*⟩

line

to line one's pockets → *embolsarse dinero, meter la mano en la caja/lata*
: to take or get a lot of money by doing something illegal or dishonest ⟨*corrupt officials have been lining their pockets at the public's expense*⟩

luck

to be down on one's luck → *estar pasando (por) una mala racha*
: to be suffering through a difficult time ⟨*she asked for a handout because she's been down on her luck lately*⟩

lunch

to be out to lunch → *estar desconectado de la realidad, no estar en sus cabales*
: to be unaware of what is really happening because of confusion or mental instability ⟨*I could not understand his rambling; I think that guy's out to lunch*⟩

marble

to lose one's marbles → *perder la chaveta*
: to become insane ⟨*when he started ranting about how the government was out to get him, I thought he'd lost his marbles*⟩

memory

to take a stroll/trip/walk (etc.) down memory lane → *rememorar viejos tiempos*
: to think or talk about pleasant things from the past ⟨*we took a stroll down memory lane, talking about our time at school together*⟩

move

to move heaven and earth → *mover cielo y tierra*
: to do everything possible to accomplish something ⟨*he vowed that he would move heaven and earth to finish the project on schedule*⟩

music
>   **to be music to one's ears** → *sonarle a música celestial (a alguien), ser música celestial (para alguien)*
>   : to be something that one is happy to hear ⟨*when she said she'd marry me, that was music to my ears*⟩

nose
>   **to pay through the nose** → *pagar un dineral*
>   : to pay a very high price ⟨*I found the perfect dress, but I paid through the nose for it*⟩

nowhere
>   **in the middle of nowhere** → *quién sabe dónde*
>   : very far from other people or houses ⟨*I had to walk three miles after my car broke down in the middle of nowhere*⟩

p's and q's
>   **to mind your p's and q's** → *tener cuidado con lo que se hace*
>   : to be careful about behaving in a polite or proper way ⟨*we knew to mind our p's and q's around our aunt*⟩

page
>   **to borrow/take a page from someone's book** → *seguir el ejemplo de alguien*
>   : to do the same thing that someone else has done ⟨*you may want to borrow/take a page from his book and study harder for your finals*⟩

pop
>   **to pop the question** → *proponerle matrimonio a alguien*
>   : to propose marriage to someone ⟨*she got tired of waiting for him to pop the question*⟩

preach
>   **to preach to the choir** → *tratar de convencer a los que ya están convencidos*
>   : to speak for or against something to people who already agree with your opinions ⟨*his speeches to supporters won't win him any more votes, for he's just preaching to the choir*⟩

pull
>   **to pull a fast one (on someone)** → *jugarle una mala pasada (a alguien)*
>   : to deceive or trick (someone) ⟨*someone might try to pull a fast one on you, so be careful*⟩

raise
>   **to raise the dead** → *resucitar a los muertos*
>   : to cause a dead person to rise from the grave ⟨*that noise is loud enough to raise the dead*⟩

river
>   **to send someone up the river** → *encarcelar a alguien*
>   : to send someone to prison ⟨*they sent him up the river for 10 years*⟩
>   **to sell someone down the river** → *traicionar a alguien*
>   : to betray someone ⟨*I can't believe my best friend would sell me down the river*⟩

rope
>   **to learn/know the ropes** → *aprender/saber como se hacen las cosas*
>   : to become/be familiar with the special way things are done in a particular place or activity ⟨*it will take a few weeks for new employees to learn the ropes*⟩

rub
>   **to rub elbows (with someone)** → *codearse (con alguien)*
>   : to meet and talk (with someone) in a friendly, informal way ⟨*the awards dinner gave me the opportunity to rub elbows with some of today's greatest American poets*⟩

ruffle
>   **to ruffle a few feathers** → *hacer enojar a la gente*
>   : to upset or offend one or more persons ⟨*his critical remarks ruffled a few feathers of board members*⟩

100 Important English Idioms

sack
> **to hit the sack** → *irse a la cama*
> : to go to bed for the night ⟨*I'm tired, so I'm going to hit the sack*⟩

saddle
> **to be back in the saddle** → *recuperar el control*
> : to be once again in control ⟨*after a few setbacks, he's back in the saddle*⟩

screw
> **to have a screw loose** → *faltarle un tornillo (a alguien), tener un tornillo suelto*
> : to be crazy ⟨*you've got to have a screw loose to think that's a good idea*⟩

seventh heaven
> **to be in seventh heaven** → *estar en el séptimo cielo*
> : to be in a state of extreme happiness and joy ⟨*when I told her she was about to become a grandma, she was in seventh heaven*⟩

shoes
> **to fill someone's shoes** → *ocupar el puesto de alguien*
> : to do what someone else does with the same level of quality or success ⟨*I don't think anyone will be able to fill her shoes after she retires*⟩
> **to put oneself in someone's shoes** → *ponerse en el pellejo de alguien*
> : to imagine oneself in another person's situation ⟨*when considering how much to donate to the homeless, try to put yourself in their shoes*⟩

shoot
> **to shoot from the hip** → *hablar sin detenerse a pensar*
> : to act or speak quickly without thinking about the possible results ⟨*I haven't thought up a formal plan, so I'm shooting from the hip with this suggestion*⟩

socks
> **to knock/blow someone's socks off** → *impresionar/deslumbrar a alguien*
> : to affect or impress one in a very strong and favorable way ⟨*here's a song that will knock your socks off*⟩

stab
> **to stab (someone) in the back** → *darle una puñalada por la espalda (a alguien)*
> : to betray someone's trust ⟨*he's the kind of person who gets you to trust him then stabs you in the back*⟩

stop
> **to pull out all the stops** → *dar el do de pecho, tirar/echar la casa por la ventana*
> : to do everything possible to achieve success ⟨*when he throws a party, he really pulls out all the stops*⟩

straw
> **to clutch/grasp at straws** → *agarrarse a/de cualquier esperanza*
> : to try to solve a problem by doing things that probably will not help ⟨*economists were grasping at straws to end the global financial crisis*⟩

think
> **to have another think coming** → *estar muy equivocado*
> : to be wrong or mistaken ⟨*if he thinks he can fool me, he has another think coming*⟩

thunder
> **to steal someone's thunder** → *adelantársele a alguien (al anunciar o revelar algo)*
> : to prevent someone from enjoying rightful success or attention by doing or saying whatever that person was planning to do or say ⟨*I didn't mean to steal your thunder, but I just had to tell your mom about your promotion*⟩

torch
> **to carry a torch** → *seguir enamorado de alguien (sin ser correspondido)*
> : to continue to have romantic feelings for someone who does not return the feelings ⟨*is she still carrying a torch for him after all this time?*⟩

wart
> **warts and all** → *con todos sus defectos*
> : despite someone's or something's flaws ⟨*he was often selfish and thoughtless, but she loved him, warts and all*⟩

wash

to wash one's hands of (someone or something) → *lavarse las manos de (alguien o algo)*

: to refuse to be involved with (something or someone) anymore ⟨*I've tried to help them, but they won't listen to me, so I'm washing my hands of the whole mess*⟩

wear

to wear the pants → *llevar los pantalones, mandar*

: to be the one to make the important decisions for a group ⟨*you'd better ask her permission because she wears the pants in the family*⟩

wet

to get one's feet wet → *iniciarse en algo, dar sus primeros pasos en algo*

: to begin a new job or activity with relatively simple tasks to become more familiar with it ⟨*the new office assistant got her feet wet by doing some simple filing tasks*⟩

wringer

to put (someone) through the wringer → *hacerle sudar la gota gorda a alguien, agotar a alguien*

: to put someone through a series of very difficult or unpleasant experiences ⟨*they were put through the wringer by the insurance investigator*⟩

Abreviaturas comunes
en español
Common Spanish Abbreviations

SPANISH ABBREVIATION AND EXPANSION		ENGLISH EQUIVALENT	
abr.	abril	Apr.	April
a/c	a cargo de	c/o	care of
A.C., a.C.	antes de Cristo	BC	before Christ
a. de J.C.	antes de Jesucristo	BC	before Christ
ago.	agosto	Aug.	August
a.m.	ante meridiem (de la mañana)	a.m., AM	ante meridiem (before noon)
Apdo., Aptdo.	apartado (de correos)	—	P.O. box
A.T.	Antiguo Testamento	O.T.	Old Testament
av., avda.	avenida	ave.	avenue
ayte.	ayudante	asst.	assistant
blvar., br.	bulevar	blvd.	boulevard
c/, C/	calle	st.	street
C	centígrado, Celsius	C	centigrade, Celsius
C.	compañía	Co.	company
CA	corriente alterna	AC	alternating current
cap.	capítulo	ch., chap.	chapter
c.c.	centímetros cúbicos	cc, cu. cm.	cubic centimeters
CC	corriente continua	DC	direct current
cg.	centígramo	cg	centigram
CI	coeficiente intelectual *o* de inteligencia	IQ	intelligence quotient
Cía.	compañía	Co.	company
cm.	centímetro	cm	centimeter
col.	columna	col.	column
C.P.	código postal	—	zip code
c/u	cada uno, cada una	ea.	each
d.C.	después de Cristo	AD	anno Domini (in the year of our Lord)
dcha.	derecha	—	right
d. de J.C.	después de Jesucristo	AD	anno Domini (in the year of our lord)
dep., dpto.	departamento	dept.	department
DF, D.F.	Distrito Federal	—	Federal District
dic.	diciembre	Dec.	December
do.	domingo	Sun.	Sunday
Dr.; Dra.	doctor; doctora	Dr.	doctor
E, E.	Este, este	E	East, east
edif.	edificio	bldg.	building
EEUU, EE.UU.	Estados Unidos	US, U.S.	United States
ej.	por ejemplo	e.g.	for example
ene.	enero	Jan.	January
etc.	etcétera	etc.	et cetera
f	femenino	f	female
F	Fahrenheit	F	Fahrenheit
feb.	febrero	Feb.	February
g., gr.	gramo	g., gm, gr.	gram
gob.	gobierno	govt.	government
h.	hora	hr.	hour
Hnos.	hermanos	Bros.	brothers
izq.	izquierda	l.	left

juev.	jueves	**Thurs.**	Thursday
jul.	julio	**Jul.**	July
jun.	junio	**Jun.**	June
kg.	kilogramo	**kg**	kilogram
km.	kilómetro	**km**	kilometer
l.	litro	**l, lit.**	liter
lun.	lunes	**Mon.**	Monday
m	masculino	**m**	male, masculine
m	metro	**m**	meter
mar.	marzo	**Mar.**	March
mart.	martes	**Tues.**	Tuesday
Méx.	mexicano, México	**Mex.**	Mexican, Mexico
mg.	miligramo	**mg**	milligram
miérc.	miércoles	**Wednes.**	Wednesday
min	minuto	**min.**	minute
ml.	mililitro	**ml**	mililiter
mm.	milímetro	**mm**	millimeter
N, N.	Norte, norte	**N, no.**	North, north
n.°	número	**no.**	number
NE	nordeste	**NE**	northeast
NN.UU.	Naciones Unidas	**UN**	United Nations
NO	noroeste	**NW**	northwest
nov.	noviembre	**Nov.**	November
N.T.	Nuevo Testamento	**N.T.**	New Testament
NU	Naciones Unidas	**UN**	United Nations
núm.	número	**num.**	number
NY	Nueva York, New York	**NY**	New York
O, O.	Oeste, oeste	**W**	West, west
oct.	octubre	**Oct.**	October
p., pág.	página	**p., pg.**	page
P	(talla) pequeña	**S**	small
págs.	páginas	**pp.**	pages
RCP	reanimación cardiopulmonar, resucitación cardiopulmonar	**CPR**	cardiopulmonary resuscitation
P.D.	postdata	**P.S.**	postscript
p. ej.	por ejemplo	**e.g.**	for example
p.m.	post meridiem (de la tarde)	**p.m., PM**	post meridiem (afternoon)
p°	paseo	**Ave.**	avenue
PR	Puerto Rico	**PR**	Puerto Rico
ptas., pts.	pesetas	—	—
pto.	punto	**pt.**	point
r.p.m.	revoluciones por minuto	**rpm.**	revolutions per minute
s.	siglo	**c., cent.**	century
S, S.	Sur, sur	**S, so.**	South, south
S., Sto., Sta.	san, santo, santa	**St.**	saint
S.A.	sociedad anónima	**Inc.**	incorporated (company)
sáb.	sábado	**Sat.**	Saturday
SE	sudeste, sureste	**SE**	southeast
seg.	segundo, segundos	**sec.**	second, seconds
sep., sept.	septiembre	**Sept.**	September
S.L.	sociedad limitada	**Ltd.**	limited (corporation)
SO	sudoeste, suroeste	**SW**	southwest
Sr.	Sénior	**Sr.**	Senior
tb.	también	—	also
tel., Tel.	teléfono	**tel.**	telephone
v	versus	**v., vs.**	versus
v.g., v.gr.	verbigracia	**e.g.**	for example
vier., viern.	viernes	**Fri.**	Friday
vol.	volumen	**vol.**	volume

Common English Abbreviations
Abreviaturas comunes en inglés

LA ABREVIATURA INGLÉS Y LA AMPLIACIÓN		EL EQUIVALENTE ESPAÑOL	
AAA	American Automobile Association	—	—
AC	alternating current	CA	corriente alterna
AD	anno Domini (in the year of our Lord)	d.C., d. de J.C.	después de Cristo, después de Jesucristo
AK, Alas.	Alaska	—	Alaska
AL, Ala.	Alabama	—	Alabama
a.m., AM	ante meridiem (before noon)	a.m.	ante meridiem (de la mañana)
Am., Amer.	America, American	—	América, americano
amt.	amount	—	cantidad
ans.	answer	—	respuesta
Apr.	April	abr.	abril
AR, Ark.	Arkansas	—	Arkansas
asst.	assistant	ayte.	ayudante
atty.	attorney	—	abogado, -da
Aug.	August	ago.	agosto
ave.	avenue	av., avda.; pº	avenida; paseo
AZ, Ariz.	Arizona	—	Arizona
BC	before Christ	a.C., A.C., a. de J.C.	antes de Cristo, antes de Jesucristo
BCE	before the Christian Era, before the Common Era	—	antes de la era cristiana, antes de la era común
bet.	between	—	entre
bldg.	building	edif.	edificio
blvd.	boulevard	blvar., br.	bulevar
Br., Brit.	Britain, British	—	Gran Bretaña, británico
Bro(s).	brother(s)	Hno(s).	hermano(s)
c, cm	centimeter	cm.	centímetro
c., cent.	century	s.	siglo
C	Celsius, centigrade	C	Celsius, centígrado
CA, Cal., Calif.	California	—	California
Can., Canad.	Canada, Canadian	—	Canadá, canadiense
cap.	capital (place)	—	capital
cap.	capital (letter)	—	mayúscula
cc, cu. cm	cubic centimeters	c.c.	centímetros cúbicos
CEO	chief executive officer	—	presidente, -ta (de una corporación)
ch., chap.	chapter	cap.	capítulo
Co.	company	C., Cía.	compañía
CO, Colo.	Colorado	—	Colorado
c/o	care of	a/c	a cargo de
COD	cash on delivery, collect on delivery	—	(pago) contra reembolso
col.	column	col.	columna
corp.	corporation	—	corporación
CPR	cardiopulmonary resuscitation	RCP	reanimación cardiopulmonar, resucitación cardiopulmonar
CT, Conn.	Connecticut	—	Connecticut

D.A.	district attorney	—	fiscal (del distrito)
DC	direct current	CC	corriente continua
DC	District of Columbia	—	—
DE, Del.	Delaware	—	Delaware
Dec.	December	dic.	diciembre
dept.	department	dep., dpto.	departamento
doz.	dozen	—	docena
Dr.	doctor	Dr., Dra.	doctor, doctora
E	East, east	E, E.	Este, este
ea.	each	c/u	cada uno, cada una
e.g.	for example	v.g., v.gr.	verbigracia
EMT	emergency medical technician	—	técnico, -ca en urgencias médicas
Eng.	England, English	—	Inglaterra, inglés
esp.	especially	—	especialmente
etc.	et cetera	etc.	etcétera
f	female	f	femenino
F	Fahrenheit	F	Fahrenheit
Feb.	February	feb.	febrero
fem.	feminine	—	femenino
FL, Fla.	Florida	—	Florida
Fri.	Friday	vier., viern.	viernes
ft.	feet, foot	—	pie(s)
g, gm	gram	g., gr.	gramo
Ga., GA	Georgia	—	Georgia
gal.	gallon	—	galón
govt.	government	gob.	gobierno
gr.	gram	g., gr.	gramo
HI	Hawaii	—	Hawai, Hawaii
hr.	hour	h.	hora
ht.	height	—	altura
IA, Ia.	Iowa	—	Iowa
ID	Idaho	—	Idaho
IL, Ill.	Illinois	—	Illinois
in.	inch	—	pulgada
IN, Ind.	Indiana	—	Indiana
Inc.	incorporated (company)	S.A.	sociedad anónima
Jan.	January	ene.	enero
Jul.	July	jul.	julio
Jun.	June	jun.	junio
Jr.	Junior	Jr.	Júnior
kg	kilogram	kg.	kilogramo
km	kilometer	km.	kilómetro
KS, Kan., Kans.	Kansas	—	Kansas
KY, Ky.	Kentucky	—	Kentucky
l	liter	l.	litro
l.	left	izq.	izquierda
L	large	G	(talla) grande
LA, La.	Louisiana	—	Luisiana, Louisiana
lb.	pound	—	libra
Ltd.	limited (corporation)	S.L.	sociedad limitada
m	male, masculine	m	masculino
m	meter	m	metro
M	medium	M	(talla) mediana
MA, Mass.	Massachusetts	—	Massachusetts
Mar.	March	mar.	marzo
masc.	masculine	—	masculino
MD, Md.	Maryland	—	Maryland
M.D.	Doctor of Medicine	—	doctor de medicina
ME, Me.	Maine	—	Maine
Mex.	Mexican, Mexico	Méx.	mexicano, México
mg	milligram	mg.	miligramo
mi.	mile	—	milla
MI, Mich.	Michigan	—	Michigan
min.	minute	min	minuto

ml	mililiter	ml.	mililitro
mm	millimeter	mm.	milímetro
MN, Minn.	Minnesota	—	Minnesota
mo.	month	—	mes
MO, Mo.	Missouri	—	Missouri
Mon.	Monday	lun.	lunes
mpg	miles per gallon	—	millas por galón
mph	miles per hour	—	millas por hora
MS, Miss.	Mississippi	—	Mississippi, Misisipí
mt., mtn.	mount, mountain	—	monte, montaña
MT, Mont.	Montana	—	Montana
N	North, north	N	Norte, norte
NC	North Carolina	—	Carolina del Norte, North Carolina
ND, N. Dak.	North Dakota	—	Dakota del Norte, North Dakota
NE	northeast	NE	nordeste
NE, Neb., Nebr.	Nebraska	—	Nebraska
NH	New Hampshire	—	New Hampshire
NJ	New Jersey	—	Nueva Jersey, New Jersey
NM., N. Mex.	New Mexico	—	Nuevo México, New Mexico
no.	north	N	norte
no.	number	n.º	número
Nov.	November	nov.	noviembre
N.T.	New Testament	N.T.	Nuevo Testamento
NV, Nev.	Nevada	—	Nevada
NW	northwest	NO	noroeste
NY	New York	NY	Nueva York, New York
Oct.	October	oct.	octubre
OH, O	Ohio	—	Ohio
OK, Okla.	Oklahoma	—	Oklahoma
OR, Ore., Oreg.	Oregon	—	Oregon
O.T.	Old Testament	A.T.	Antiguo Testamento
oz.	ounce, ounces	—	onza, onzas
p.	page	p.	página
PA, Pa., Penn.	Pennsylvania	—	Pennsylvania, Pensilvania
PD	police department	—	departamento de policía
pg.	page	pág.	página
pkg.	package	—	paquete
p.m., PM	post meridiem (afternoon)	p.m.	post meridiem (de la tarde)
P.O.	post office	—	oficina de correos, correo
pp.	pages	págs.	páginas
PR	Puerto Rico	PR	Puerto Rico
pres.	president	—	presidente, -ta
P.S.	postscript	P.D.	postdata
P.S.	public school	—	escuela pública
pt.	point	pto.	punto
PTA	Parent-Teacher Association	—	—
PTO	Parent-Teacher Organization	—	—
q, qt.	quart	—	cuarto de galón
r., rt.	right	dcha.	derecha
rd.	road	c/, C/	calle
recd.	received	—	recibido
RI	Rhode Island	—	Rhode Island
rpm	revolutions per minute	r.p.m.	revoluciones por minuto

rte.	route	—	ruta
S	small	P	(talla) pequeña
S	South, south	S	Sur, sur
Sat.	Saturday	sáb.	sábado
SC	South Carolina	—	Carolina del Sur, South Carolina
SD, S. Dak.	South Dakota	—	Dakota del Sur, South Dakota
SE	southeast	SE	sudeste, sureste
sec.	second, seconds	seg.	segundo, segundos
Sept.	September	sep., sept.	septiembre
so.	south	S	sur
sq.	square	—	cuadrado
Sr.	Senior	Sr.	Sénior
st.	street	c/, C/	calle
St.	saint	S., Sto., Sta.	santo, santa
Sun.	Sunday	dom.	domingo
SW	southwest	SO	sudoeste, suroeste
t., tsp.	teaspoon	—	cucharadita
T, tb., tbsp.	tablespoon	—	cucharada (grande)
tel.	telephone	tel., Tel.	teléfono
Thu., Thur., Thurs.	Thursday	juev.	jueves
TM	trademark	—	marca (de un producto)
TN, Tenn.	Tennessee	—	Tennessee
Tue., Tues.	Tuesday	mart.	martes
TX, Tex.	Texas	—	Texas
UN	United Nations	NU, NN.UU.	Naciones Unidas
US	United States	EEUU, EE.UU.	Estados Unidos
USA	United States of America	EEUU, EE.UU.	Estados Unidos de América
usu.	usually	—	usualmente
UT	Utah	—	Utah
v., vs.	versus	v	versus
VA, Va.	Virginia	—	Virginia
vol.	volume	vol.	volumen
VP	vice president	—	vicepresidente, -ta
VT, Vt.	Vermont	—	Vermont
W	West, west	O	Oeste, oeste
WA, Wash.	Washington (state)	—	Washington
Wed.	Wednesday	miérc.	miércoles
WI, Wis., Wisc.	Wisconsin	—	Wisconsin
wt.	weight	—	peso
WV, W. Va.	West Virginia	—	Virginia del Oeste, West Virginia
WY, Wyo.	Wyoming	—	Wyoming
yd.	yard	—	yarda
yr.	year	—	año

Nations of the World
Naciones del mundo

Africa/África

ENGLISH/INGLÉS	SPANISH/ESPAÑOL
Algeria	Argelia
Angola	Angola
Benin	Benin
Botswana	Botswana, Botsuana
Burkina Faso	Burkina Faso
Burundi	Burundi
Cameroon	Camerún
Cape Verde	Cabo Verde
Central African Republic	República Centroafricana
Chad	Chad
Comoros	Comores, Comoras
Congo, Democratic Republic of	Congo, República Democrática del
Congo, Republic of the	Congo, República del
Djibouti	Yibuti, Djibouti
Egypt	Egipto
Equatorial Guinea	Guinea Ecuatorial
Eritrea	Eritrea
Ethiopia	Etiopía
Gabon	Gabón
Gambia	Gambia
Ghana	Ghana
Guinea	Guinea
Guinea-Bissau	Guinea-Bissau
Ivory Coast	Costa de Marfil
Kenya	Kenya, Kenia
Lesotho	Lesotho, Lesoto
Liberia	Liberia
Libya	Libia
Madagascar	Madagascar
Malawi	Malawi, Malaui
Mali	Malí
Mauritania	Mauritania
Mauritius	Mauricio
Morocco	Marruecos
Mozambique	Mozambique
Namibia	Namibia
Niger	Níger
Nigeria	Nigeria
Rwanda	Ruanda, Rwanda
São Tomé and Príncipe	Santo Tomé y Príncipe
Senegal	Senegal
Seychelles	Seychelles
Sierra Leone	Sierra Leona
Somalia	Somalia
South Africa, Republic of	Sudáfrica, República de
Sudan	Sudán
Swaziland	Suazilandia, Swazilandia
Tanzania	Tanzanía, Tanzania
Togo	Togo
Tunisia	Túnez
Uganda	Uganda
Zambia	Zambia
Zimbabwe	Zimbabwe, Zimbabue

Antarctica/Antártida

No independent countries
No tiene países independientes

Asia/Asia

ENGLISH/INGLÉS	SPANISH/ESPAÑOL
Afghanistan	Afganistán
Armenia	Armenia
Azerbaijan	Azerbaiyán, Azerbaiján
Bahrain	Bahrein
Bangladesh	Bangladesh
Bhutan	Bután, Bhután
Brunei	Brunei
Cambodia	Camboya
China	China
Cyprus	Chipre
East Timor	Timor Oriental
Georgia	Georgia
India	India
Indonesia	Indonesia
Iran	Irán
Iraq	Iraq, Irak
Israel	Israel
Japan	Japón
Jordan	Jordania
Kazakhstan	Kazajistán, Kazajstán
Korea, North	Corea del Norte
Korea, South	Corea del Sur
Kuwait	Kuwait
Kyrgyzstan	Kirguizistán, Kirguistán
Laos	Laos
Lebanon	Líbano
Malaysia	Malasia
Maldives	Maldivas
Mongolia	Mongolia
Myanmar	Myanmar
Nepal	Nepal
Oman	Omán
Pakistan	Pakistán, Paquistán
Philippines	Filipinas
Qatar	Qatar
Saudi Arabia	Arabia Saudita, Arabia Saudí
Singapore	Singapur
Sri Lanka	Sri Lanka
Syria	Siria
Taiwan	Taiwán, Taiwan
Tajikistan	Tayikistán
Thailand	Tailandia
Turkey	Turquía
Turkmenistan	Turkmenistán
United Arab Emirates	Emiratos Árabes Unidos
Uzbekistan	Uzbekistán
Vietnam	Vietnam
Yemen	Yemen

Europe/Europa

ENGLISH/INGLÉS	SPANISH/ESPAÑOL
Albania	Albania
Andorra	Andorra
Austria	Austria
Belarus	Bielorrusia, Belarús
Belgium	Bélgica
Bosnia and Herzegovina	Bosnia-Herzegovina

ENGLISH/INGLÉS	SPANISH/ESPAÑOL
Bulgaria	Bulgaria
Croatia	Croacia
Czech Republic	República Checa
Denmark	Dinamarca
Estonia	Estonia
Finland	Finlandia
France	Francia
Germany	Alemania
Greece	Grecia
Hungary	Hungría
Iceland	Islandia
Ireland	Irlanda
Italy	Italia
Kosovo	Kosovo
Latvia	Letonia
Liechtenstein	Liechtenstein
Lithuania	Lituania
Luxembourg	Luxemburgo
Macedonia	Macedonia
Malta	Malta
Moldova	Moldova
Monaco	Mónaco
Montenegro	Montenegro
Netherlands	Países Bajos
Norway	Noruega
Poland	Polonia
Portugal	Portugal
Romania	Rumania, Rumanía
Russia	Rusia
San Marino	San Marino
Serbia	Serbia
Slovakia	Eslovaquia
Slovenia	Eslovenia
Spain	España
Sweden	Suecia
Switzerland	Suiza
Ukraine	Ucrania
United Kingdom	Reino Unido
Vatican City	Ciudad del Vaticano

North America/Norteamérica

Antigua and Barbuda	Antigua y Barbuda
Bahamas	Bahamas
Barbados	Barbados
Belize	Belice
Canada	Canadá
Costa Rica	Costa Rica
Cuba	Cuba
Dominica	Dominica
Dominican Republic	República Dominicana
El Salvador	El Salvador
Grenada	Granada
Guatemala	Guatemala
Haiti	Haití
Honduras	Honduras
Jamaica	Jamaica
Mexico	México, Méjico
Nicaragua	Nicaragua
Panama	Panamá
Saint Kitts and Nevis	Saint Kitts y Nevis, San Cristóbal y Nieves
Saint Lucia	Santa Lucía
Saint Vincent and the Grenadines	San Vicente y las Granadinas

ENGLISH/INGLÉS   **SPANISH/ESPAÑOL**

Trinidad and Tobago   Trinidad y Tobago
United States of America   Estados Unidos de América

Oceania/Oceanía

Australia   Australia
Fiji   Fiji, Fiyi
Kiribati   Kiribati
Marshall Islands   Islas Marshall
Micronesia, Federated States of   Micronesia, Estados Federados de
Nauru   Nauru
New Zealand   Nueva Zelanda, Nueva Zelandia
Palau   Palaos
Papua New Guinea   Papúa Nueva Guinea, Papua Nueva
                                         Guinea
Samoa   Samoa
Solomon Islands   Islas Salomón
Tonga   Tonga
Tuvalu   Tuvalu
Vanuatu   Vanuatu

South America/Sudamérica

Argentina   Argentina
Bolivia   Bolivia
Brazil   Brasil
Chile   Chile
Colombia   Colombia
Ecuador   Ecuador
Guyana   Guyana
Paraguay   Paraguay
Peru   Perú
Suriname   Surinam
Uruguay   Uruguay
Venezuela   Venezuela

Metric System: Conversions
Sistema métrico: conversiones

Length

unit	number of meters	approximate U.S. equivalents	
millimeter	0.001	0.039	inch
centimeter	0.01	0.39	inch
meter	1	39.37	inches
kilometer	1,000	0.62	mile

Longitud

unidad	número de metros	equivalentes aproximados de los EE.UU.	
milímetro	0.001	0.039	pulgada
centímetro	0.01	0.39	pulgada
metro	1	39.37	pulgadas
kilómetro	1,000	0.62	milla

Area

unit	number of square meters	approximate U.S. equivalents	
square centimeter	0.0001	0.16	square inch
square meter	1	10.76	square feet
hectare	10,000	2.47	acres
square kilometer	1,000,000	0.39	square mile

Superficie

unidad	número de metros cuadrados	equivalentes aproximados de los EE.UU.	
centímetro cuadrado	0.0001	0.16	pulgada cuadrada
metro cuadrado	1	10.76	pies cuadrados
hectárea	10,000	2.47	acres
kilómetro cuadrado	1,000,000	0.39	milla cuadrada

Volume

unit	number of cubic meters	approximate U.S. equivalents	
cubic centimeter	0.000001	0.061	cubic inch
cubic meter	1	1.31	cubic yards

Volumen

unidad	número de metros cúbicos	equivalentes aproximados de los EE.UU	
centímetro cúbico	0.000001	0.061	pulgada cúbica
metro cúbico	1	1.31	yardas cúbicas

Capacity

unidad	number of liters	approximate U.S. equivalents		
		CUBIC	DRY	LIQUID
liter	1	61.02 cubic inches	0.91 quart	1.06 quarts

Capacidad

unidad	número de litros	equivalentes aproximados de los EE.UU.		
		CÚBICO	SECO	LÍQUIDO
litro	1	61.02 pulgadas cúbicas	0.91 cuarto	1.06 cuartos

Mass and Weight

unit	number of grams	approximate U.S. equivalents	
milligram	0.001	0.015	grain
centigram	0.01	0.15	grain
gram	1	0.035	ounce
kilogram	1,000	2.20	pounds
metric ton	1,000,000	1.10	short tons

Masa y peso

unidad	número de gramos	equivalentes aproximados de los EE.UU.	
miligramo	0.001	0.015	grano
centigramo	0.01	0.15	grano
gramo	1	0.035	onza
kilogramo	1.000	2.20	libras
tonelada métrica	1,000,000	1.10	toneladas cortas